THE

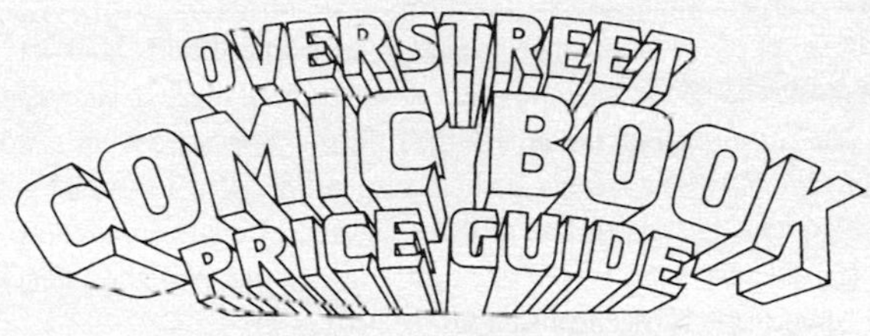

24th Edition

BOOKS FROM 1900 - PRESENT INCLUDED

CATALOGUE & EVALUATION GUIDE - ILLUSTRATED

By
Robert M. Overstreet

SPECIAL CONTRIBUTORS TO THIS EDITION

Dr. John Townsend, Gary M. Carter, Pat Calhoun, Joe Mannarino, Jerry Weist, Tom Inge, and Walter Wang

SPECIAL ADVISORS TO THIS EDITION

Bruce Hamilton • Hugh O'Kennon • Ron Pussell • Gary M. Carter
Walter Wang • John Snyder • Terry Stroud • Dan Malan • Michael Naiman
Steve Geppi • Gary Colabuono • James Payette • Sean Linkenback
Harry Matetsky • Jerry Weist • John Verzyl • Mark Wilson
Joe Mannarino • Gary Guzzo • Robert Hall • Joe Dungan

The Confident Collector ™

AVON BOOKS NEW YORK

Serious Comic Book Collectors, Don't Miss

THE OVERSTREET COMIC BOOK GRADING GUIDE

By Robert M. Overstreet and Gary M. Carter

A Confident Collector Title from Avon Books

Important Notice. All of the information, including valuations, in this book has been compiled from the most reliable sources, and every effort has been made to eliminate errors and questionable data. Nevertheless, the possibility of error always exists in a work of such immense scope. The publisher will not be held responsible for losses which may occur in the purchase, sale, or other transaction of items because of information contained herein. Readers who feel they have discovered errors are invited to *write* and inform us, so the errors may be corrected in subsequent editions.

Cover concept by Heide Balaban, Marvel Comics.
Cover Illustration by Bob Wiacek (inker), Mike Parobeck (penciller) & Sean Tiffany (colorist).

THE OVERSTREET COMIC BOOK PRICE GUIDE (24th Edition) is an original publication of Avon Books. This edition has never before appeared in book form.

AVON BOOKS
A division of
The Hearst Corporation
1350 Avenue of the Americas
New York, New York 10019

Published by arrangement with Overstreet Publications, Inc.
Library of Congress Catalog Card Number: 91-92480
ISBN:0-380-77854-8

First Avon Books Trade Printing: May 1994
AVON TRADEMARK REG. U.S. PAT. OFF. AND IN OTHER COUNTRIES, MARCA REGISTRADA, HECHO EN U.S.A.

Printed in the U.S.A.
10 9 8 7 6 5 4 3 2 1

TABLE OF CONTENTS

INTRODUCTION.....A-9

ABOUT THIS BOOK
How To Use This Book.....A-9
Comic Book Values Listed.....A-9
How Comic Books Are Listed.....A-9
What Comic Books Are Listed.....A-10
Policy of Listing New Comic Books.....A-10

GRADING COMIC BOOKS
Grading Comic Books.....A-10
Get The Tools.....A-10
How To Grade.....A-11
Grading Definitions.....A-11
Restored Comics.....A-12
Scarcity of Comic Books Related to Grade.....A-16

COLLECTING COMIC BOOKS
Know The Buzz Words.....A-16
How to Start Collecting.....A-22
Collecting In The 1990s.....A-24
Collecting Back Issues.....A-26

PRESERVATION & STORAGE
Proper Handling of Comic Books.....A-26
Storage Of Comic Books.....A-28

BUYING & SELLING
How To Sell Your Comics.....A-28
Where to Buy and Sell.....A-30
Comic Book Conventions.....A-30
Where To Advertise.....A-34

PUBLISHERS DATA
Cover Bar Codes.....A-36
Marvel Reprints.....A-36
Comic Book Publishers Codes.....A-36
Timely/Marvel/Atlas Comics Publishers Codes.....A-36

COMIC BOOK ARTISTS
Comic Book Artists listed.....A-38
Artist's First Work.....A-38

QUICK REFERENCE LISTS
1st Appearance.....A-40
1st Appearance: Villain.....A-68
1st Appearance: Group.....A-72
1st Appearance: Villain Group.....A-74
1st Cross-overs.....A-76
1st Superpets.....A-76
1st Of A Publisher.....A-76
1st Prototype.....A-78

THE COMIC BOOK MARKET
Key Comics Sold in 1993.....A-78
Market At A Glance.....A-80
Annual Report.....A-82
Market Watch 1993.....A-89
Sotheby's Market Report.....A-93
Christie's Market Report.....A-95
Pacific Comic Exchange Market Report.....A-96

TOP BOOKS LISTED
Investor's Data.....A-98
Top Golden Age Books.....A-98
Top Silver Age Books.....A-102
Top Modern Age Books.....A-106
Top Crime Comics.....A-106
Top Hanna-Barbera Comics.....A-108
Top Horror Comics.....A-112
Top Science Fiction Comics.....A-116
Top Sports Comics.....A-122
Top War Comics.....A-122
Top Western Comics.....A-126

COMIC BOOK HISTORY
History of Comic Books.....A-129
Overstreet's Comic Book Hall Of Fame.....A-129
Historic Firsts.....A-134
Development of the American Comic Book (A Chronology) by M. Thomas Inge.....A-136

FOREIGN COMIC BOOKS
Collecting Foreign Comics and American Reprints.....A-142
Canadian Reprints.....A-142

COMIC BOOK FANDOM
History of Comics Fandom.....A-144

NEWSPAPER COMICS
Collecting Newspaper Strips.....A-145

COMIC BOOK ORIGINAL ART
Collecting Original Art.....A-145

FEATURE ARTICLES
Three Uncanny Decades Of X-Men! by John Townsend, Ph.D.....A-146
Living On Borrowed Time! by Pat S. Calhoun & Gary M. Carter.....A-157

CLASSICS COMICS
Explaining the Classic Series by Dan Malan See Classic Comics

ADVERTISING
Advertising Information.....173
Comic and Nostalgia Shops (Directory).....A-165
Advertisers Index.....A-174
First Ad Section begins.....A-176
Second Ad Section begins.....A-477

ACKNOWLEDGEMENTS

Larry Bigman (Frazetta-Williamson data); Glenn Bray (Kurtzman data); Dan Malan & Charles Heffelfinger (Classic Comics data); Gary M. Carter (DC data)); J. B. Clifford Jr. (E. C. data); Gary Coddington (Superman data); Wilt Conine (Fawcett data); Dr. S. M. Davidson (Cupples & Leon data); Al Dellinges (Kubert data); Kevin Hancer (Tarzan data); Charles Heffelfinger and Jim Ivey (March of Comics listing;); R. C. Holland and Ron Pussell (Seduction and Parade of Pleasure data); Grant Irwin (Quality data); Richard Kravitz (Kelly data); Phil Levine (giveaway data); Fred Nardelli (Frazetta data); Michelle Nolan (love comics); Mike Nolan (MLJ, Timely, Nedor data); George Olshevsky (Timely data); Don Rosa (Late 1940s to 1950s data); Richard Olson (LOA & R. F. Outcault data); Scott Pell ('50s data); Greg Robertson (National data); Mark Arnold (Harvey data); Frank Scigliano (Little Lulu data); Gene Seger (Buck Rogers data); Rick Sloane (Archie data); David R. Smith, Archivist, Walt Disney Productions (Disney data); Don and Maggie Thompson (Four Color listing); Mike Tiefenbacher & Jerry Sinkovec (Atlas and National data); Raymond True (Classic Comics data); Jim Vadeboncoeur Jr. (Williamson and Atlas data); Kim Weston (Disney and Barks data); Cat Yronwode (Spirit data); Andrew Zerbe and Gary Behymer (M. E. data).

My appreciation must also be extended to John Snyder, Steve Geppi, Gary M. Carter, Bruce Hamilton, Don Maris, and especially to Hugh and Louise O'Kennon for their support and help. Special acknowledgement is also given to Ron Pussell, Michelle Nolan, Garth Wood, Terry Stroud, John Newberry, Tony Starks, Dan Kurdilla, Stephen Baer and Dave Puckett for submitting corrective data; to Dr. Richard Olson for grading information; to Dan Malan for revamping the Classics section; to Terry Stroud, Ron Pussell, Hugh O'Kennon, Dave Smith, Rod Dyke, James Payette, John Snyder, Gary M. Carter, Joe Dungan, Sean Linkenback, Stephen Fishler, Jerry Weist, Walter Wang, Steve Geppi, Harley Yee, Joe Mannarino, Bruce Hamilton, John Verzyl, Gary Colabuono, Dave Anderson (OK) and Dave Anderson (VA.)-pricing; to Tom Inge for his "Chronology of the American Comic Book;" to Pat Calhoun and Gary M. Carter for their entertaining articles; to Bill Spicer and Zetta DeVoe (Western Publishing Co.) for their contribution of data; and especially to Bill for his kind permission to reprint portions of his and Jerry Bails' America's Four Color Pastime; and to Bill Howard for his marketing advice.

Special Credit is due our new assistant research editor, Todd Hoffer for his late nights entering data, his concern and advice of layout and content, and his management of the Overstreet booth at the major conventions last year.

My appreciation is also given to Mike Renegar, Jeff Overstreet, Tony Overstreet and the rest of our excellent staff for editing, proofing and processing of data published in this edition.

I will always be indebted to Jerry Bails, Landon Chesney, Bruce Hamilton and Larry Bigman who were an early inspiration to the creation of this book.

Finally, a very big "thank you" is due my wife Caroline Overstreet and my editor Gary M. Carter for their inspiration, advice and hard work in getting this reference work to the printer on time. A special thanks is also due everyone that placed ads in this edition.

Acknowledgement is also due to the following people who have so generously contributed much needed data for this edition:

Stephen Baer
Tim Barnes
John M. Benson
John Binder, MD
Hugh Browning
Gary S. Carlson
Paul Castiglia
Monte Cohen
Craig Delich
Joe Desris
Don Duddridge
Alan Dulfon
Allen Ellis
Bob Ford
Ray E. Funk
David Gerstein
Terry Harms
Tom Hayes
P.T. Healy
D. Jandso
Chris Khalaf
Milford King
Patrick Kochanek, MD
Kelby Leow
Jim Koo
Richard Kolkman
Dan Kurdilla
Joey Marchese
Hugh O'Kennon
Lynn Potter
Thomas L. Potter, Jr.
Michael Rhode
Patrick Shaughnessi
Steve Sibra
William Tighe
Jimmy Watkins
Creg Westphal

Special thanks to **Gary Guzzo** at Marvel Comics for his continuing support of and dedication to the quality and accuracy of the Overstreet Comic Book Price Guide.

INTRODUCTION

Congratulations! We at Overstreet welcome you to the hobby of comic books. This book is the most comprehensive reference work available on comics. It is also respected and used by serious dealers and collectors everywhere. The Overstreet price is the accepted price around the world, and we have not earned this priviledge easily. Through hard work, deligence and constant contact with the market for decades, Overstreet has become the most trusted name in comics.

HOW TO USE THIS BOOK

This volume is an accurate, detailed alphabetical list of comic books and their retail values. Comic books are listed by title, regardless of company. Prices listed are shown in good, fine and near mint condition with many key books priced in an additional very fine grade. Comic books that fall inbetween the grades listed can be priced simply with the following procedure: Very good is half way between good and fine; very fine is half way between fine and near mint. The older true mint books usually bring a premium over the near mint price. Books in fair bring 50 to 70% of the good price. Some books only show a very fine price as the highest grade. The author has not been able to determine if these particular books exist in better than very fine condition, thus the omission of a near mint price. Most comic books are listed in groups. i.e., 11-20, 21-30, 31-50, etc. The prices listed opposite these groupings represent the value of all issues in that group. More detailed information is given for individual comic books for your information. If you are looking for a particular character, consult the first appearance indexes which will help you locate the correct title and issue. This book also contains hundreds of ads covering all aspects of this hobby. Whether you are buying or selling, the advertising sections can be of trememdous benefit to you.

COMIC BOOK VALUES LISTED

All values listed in this book are in U.S. currency and are retail prices based on (but not limited to) reports from our extensive network of experienced advisors which include convention sales, mail order, auctions, unpublished personal sales and stores. Overstreet, with several decades of market experience, has developed a unique and comprehensive system for gathering, documenting, averaging and pricing data on comic books. The end result is a true fair market value for your use. We have earned the reputation for our cautious, conservative approach to pricing comic books. You, the collector can be assured that the prices listed in this volume are the most accurate and useful in print.

IMPORTANT NOTE: This book is not a dealer's price list, although some dealers may base their prices on the values listed. The true value of any comic book is what you are willing to pay. Prices listed herein are an indication of what collectors (not dealers) would probably pay. For one reason or another, these collectors might want certain books badly, or else need specific issues to complete their runs and so are willing to pay more.

DEALERS POSITION: Dealers are not in a position to pay the full prices listed, but work on a percentage depending largely on the amount of investment required and the quality of material offered. Usually they will pay from 20 to 70 percent of the list price depending on how long it will take them to sell the collection after making the investment; the higher the demand and better the condition, the more the percentage. Most dealers are faced with expenses such as advertising, travel, telephone and mailing, rent, employee salaries, plus convention costs. These costs all go in before the books are sold. The high demand books usually sell right away but there are many other titles that are difficult to sell due to low demand. Sometimes a dealer will have cost tied up in this type of matrial for several years before finally moving it. Remember, his position is that of handling, demand and overhead. Most dealers are victims of these economics.

HOW COMIC BOOKS ARE LISTED

Comic books are listed alphabetically by title. All titles are listed as if they are one word, ignoring spaces, hyphens and apostrophes. The true title of a comic book can be found listed with the publishers information or indicia usually found at the bottom of the inside front cover. Usually, the official title are those words that are listed in all caps. Titles that appear on the front cover can vary with the offical title listed inside.

Comic book titles, sequence of issues, dates of first and last issues, publishing companies, origin and special issues are listed when known. Prominent and collectable artists are also pointed out (usually in foot notes). Page counts will always include covers.

Most comic books began with a #1, but occassionally many titles began with an odd number. There is a reason for this. Publishers had to register new titles with the post office for 2nd class permits. The registration fee was expensive. To avoid this expense, many publishers would continue the numbering of new titles from old defunct titles. For instance, *Weird Science* #12 (1st issue) was continued from the defunct *Saddle Romances* #11 (the last issue). In doing this, the publishers hoped to avoid having to register new titles. However, the post office would soon discover the new title and force the publisher to pay the registration fee as well as to list the correct number. For instance, the previous title mentioned began with #12 (1st issue). Then #13 through 15 were published. The next issue became #5 after the Post Office correction. Now the sequence of published issues (see the listings) is #12-15,5-on. This created a problem in early fandom for the collector, because the numbers 12-15 in this title were duplicated.

WHAT COMIC BOOKS ARE LISTED: The Guide will be listing primarily American comic books due to space limitation. Most newsstand comic books will be listed. Some variations of the regular comic book format are listed. These basically include those pre-1933 comic strip reprint books with varying size usually with cardboard covers, but sometimes with hardback. As forerunners of the modern comic book format, they deserve to be listed despite their obvious differences in presentation. Other books that will be listed are giveaway comics but only those that contain known characters, work by known collectible artists, or those of special interest.

POLICY OF LISTING NEW COMIC BOOKS; The current market has experienced an explosion of publishers with hundreds of new titles appearing in black and white and color. Many of these comics are listed in this book, but not all due to space limitation. We will attempt to list complete information only on those titles that show some collector interest. The selection of titles to include is constantly being monitored by our board of advisors who work on our monthly magazine. Of course a much better coverage of recent books will be made in the monthly throughout the year. Please do not contact us to list your new comic *books. Listings are determined by the marketplace. However,* we are interested in receiving review copies of all new comic books published.

Grading

owl card

ONE Card

GRADING COMIC BOOKS

GET THE TOOLS

For complete, detailed information on grading and restoration, consult the *Overstreet Comic Book Grading Guide*. Copies are available through all normal distribution channels or can be ordered direct from the publisher by sending $12 plus $2.00 postage and handling.

The Overstreet Comic Book Grading Card, known as the **ONE** and **OWL Card** is also available. This card has two functions. The **ONE Card** (Overstreet's Numerical Equivalent) is used to convert grading condition terms to the New numerical grading system. The **OWL Card** (Overstreet's Whiteness Level) is used for grading the whiteness of paper. The color scale on the **OWL Card** is simply placed over the interior comic book paper. The paper color is matched with the color on the card to get the **OWL** number. The **ONE/OWL Card** will be available through all normal distribution channels or may be ordered direct from the publisher by sending $1.30 per card, post paid.

HOW TO GRADE

Before a comic book's true value can be assessed, its condition or state of preservation must be determined. In all comic books, the better the condition, the more desirable and valuable the book. Comic books in **MINT** condition will bring several times the price of the same book in **POOR** condition. Therefore it is very important to be able to properly grade your books. Comics should be graded from the inside out, so the following comic book areas should be examined before assigning a final grade.

Check inside pages, inside spine and covers and outside spine and covers for any tears, markings, brittleness, tape, soiling, chunks out or other defects that would affect the grade. After all the above steps have been taken, then the reader can begin to consider an overall grade for his or her book. The grading of a comic book is done by simply looking at the book and describing its condition, which may range from absolutely perfect newsstand condition (MINT) to extremely worn, dirty, and torn (POOR.)

Numerous variables influence the evaluation of a comic book's condition and all must be considered in the final evaluation. As grading is the most subjective aspect of determining a comic's value, it is very important that the grader be careful and not allow wishful thinking to influence what the eyes see. It is also very important to realize that older comics in MINT condition are extremely scarce and are rarely advertised for sale; most of the higher grade comics advertised range from VERY FINE to NEAR MINT.

GRADING DEFINITIONS

Note: This edition uses both the traditional grade abbreviations and the ONE number throughout the listings. The Overstreet Numerical Equivalent (ONE spread range is given with each grade.)

MINT (MT) (ONE 100-98): Near perfect in every way. Only the most subtle bindery or printing defects are allowed. Cover is flat with no surface wear. Cover inks are bright with high reflectivity and minimal fading. Corners are cut square and sharp. Staples are generally centered, clean with no rust. Cover is generally well centered and firmly secured to interior pages. Paper is supple and fresh. Spine is tight and flat.

NEAR MINT (NM) (ONE 97-90): Nearly perfect with only minor imperfections such as tiny corner creases or staple stress lines, a few color flecks, bindery tears, tiny impact creases or a combination of the above where the overall eye appeal is less than Mint. Only the most subtle binding and/or printing defects allowed. Cover is flat with no surface wear. Cover inks are bright with high reflectivity and minimum of fading. Corners are cut square and sharp with ever so slight blunting permitted. Staples are generally centered, clean with no rust. Cover is well centered and firmly secured to interior pages. Paper is supple and like new. Spine is tight and flat.

VERY FINE (VF) (ONE 89-75): An excellent copy with outstanding eye-appeal. Sharp, bright and clean with supple pages. Cover is relatively flat with minimal surface wear beginning to show. Cover inks are generally bright with moderate to high reflectivity. Slight wear beginning to show including some minute wear at corners. Staples may show some discoloration. Spine may have a few transverse stress lines but is relatively flat. A light inch crease is acceptible. Pages and covers can be yellowish/tannish (at the least but not brown and will usually be off-white to white).

FINE (FN) (ONE 74-55): An exceptional, above-average copy that shows minor wear, but is still relatively flat and clean with no major creasing or other serious defects. Eye appeal is somewhat reduced because of noticeable surface wear and the accumulation of smaller defects, especially on the spine and edges. A Fine condition comic book appears to have been read many times and has been handled with moderate care. Compared to a VF, cover inks are beginning to show a significant reduction in reflectivity but is still highly collectible and desirable.

VERY GOOD (VG) (ONE 54-35): The average used comic book. A comic in this grade shows moderate wear, can have a reading or center crease or a rolled spine, but has not accumulated enough total defects to reduce eye appeal to the point where it is not a desirable copy. Some discoloration, fading and even minor soiling is allowed. No chunks can be missing but a small piece can be out at the corner or edge. Store stamps, name stamps, arrival dates, initials, etc. have no effect on this grade. Cover and interior pages can have minor tears and folds and the centerfold may be loose or detached. One or both staples might be loose, but cover is not completely detached. Common bindery and printing defects do not affect grade. Pages and inside covers may be brown but not brittle. Tape should never be used for comic book repair, however many VG condition comics have minor tape repair.

GOOD (GD) (ONE 34-15): A copy in this grade has all pages and covers, although there may be small pieces missing. Books in this grade are commonly creased, scuffed, abraded and soiled, but completely readable. Often paper quality is low but not brittle. Cover reflectivity is low and in some cases completely absent. Most collectors consider this the lowest collectible grade because comic books in lesser condition are usually incomplete and/or brittle. This grade can have a large accumulation of defects but still maintains its basic structural integrity.

FAIR (FR) (ONE 14-5): A copy in this grade has all pages and most of the covers, although there may be up to 1/3 of the front cover missing or all of the back cover, but not both. A comic in this grade is soiled, ragged and unattractive. Creases and folds are prevalent and paper quality may be very low. The centerfold may be missing if it does not affect a story. Spine may be completely split its entire length. Staples may be gone, and/or cover completely detached. Corners are commonly severely rounded or absent. Coupons may be cut from front cover and/or back cover and/or interior pages. These books are mostly readable although soiling, staining, tears, markings or chunks missing may interfere with reading the complete story. Very often paper quality is low and may even be brittle around the edges but not in the central portion of the pages.

POOR (PR) (ONE 4-1): Most comic books in this grade have been sufficiently degraded to where there is no longer any collector value. Copies in this grade typically have: Pages and/or more than approximately 1/3 of the front cover missing. They may have extremely severe stains, mildew or heavy cover abrasion to the point where cover inks are indistinct/absent. They may have been defaced with paints, varnishes, glues, oil, indelible markers or dyes. Other defects often include severe rips, tears, folding and creasing. Another common defect in this grade is moderate to severe brittleness, often to the point where the comic book literally "falls apart" when examined.

DUST JACKETS: Many of the early strip reprint comics were printed in hardback with dust jackets. Books with dust jackets are worth more. The value can increase from 20 to 50 percent depending on the rarity of book. Usually, the earlier the book, the greater the percentage. Unless noted, prices listed are without dust jackets. The condition of the dust jacket should be graded independently of the book itself.

RESTORED COMICS:

Our board of advisors suggests that **professionally restored comic books** are an accepted component of the comic book market; but only if the following criteria is met: 1–Must be professional work. 2–Complete disclosure of the extent and type of restoration. 3–Both parties are informed. 4–Priced accordingly depending on availability and demand. **Note:** A professionally restored book, reasonably priced, while not worth as much as the same book unrestored, will increase in value at the same rate. However, if you pay the unrestored price for a restored book, you would be paying a premium, which of course may not be a good investment.

Initial indications on sales and auction results suggest the following. Unrestored keys in Fine or better condition may prove in the future to be better investments, as their availability decreases, and should not be restored to an apparent higher grade. Restoration should be concentrated on books in less than Fine condition. **Warning:** Before getting restoration done, seek advise from a professional and avoid doing it yourself.

Many rare and expensive books are being repaired and restored by professionals and amateurs alike. If the book is expensive, there is a strong likelihood that some type of repair, cleaning or restoration has been done. In most cases, after restoration, these books are not actually higher grades, but are altered lower grade books. Note: Expert restoration is always preferable to amateur work and is sometimes very difficult to spot and can be easily missed when grading. In some cases, the work done is so good that it is impossible to spot. Depending upon the extent and type of restoration and the

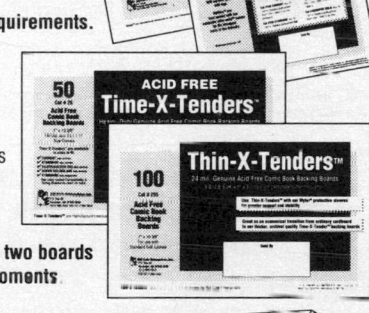

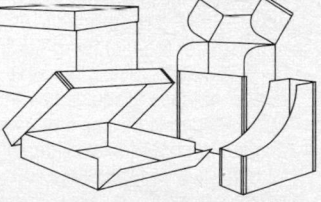

cases, the work done is so good that it is impossible to spot. Depending upon the extent and type of restoration and the quality of what was done, you will have to decide whether the value has increased or decreased. In many cases we have observed in the market that the value has been increased on certain books that were originally in low grade before restoration where the appearance and structural integrity was greatly improved afterwards. Restoration on higher grade copies may or may not affect value depending on what is done. Of course, when a comic book is graded, everything must be taken into account in the final grade given.

To the novice grading will appear difficult at first; but, as experience is gained accuracy will improve. Whenever in doubt (after using *the Overstreet Comic Book Grading Guide*), consult with a reputable dealer or experienced collector in your area. The following grading guide is given to aid the collector.

SCARCITY OF COMIC BOOKS RELATED TO GRADE

1900-1933 Comics: Most of these books are bound with thick cardboard covers and are very rare to non-existent in fine or better condition. Due to their extreme age, paper browning is very common. Brittleness could be a problem.

1933-1940 Comics: There are many issues from this period that are very scarce in any condition, especially from the early to mid-1930s. Surviving copies of any particular issue range from a handful to several hundred. Near Mint to Mint copies are virtually non-existent with known examples of any particular issue limited to five or less copies. Most surviving copies are in FVF or less condition. Brittleness or browning of paper is fairly common and could be a problem.

1941-1952 Comics: Surviving comic books would number from less than 100 to several thousand copies of each issue. Near Mint to Mint copies are a little more common but are still relatively scarce with only a dozen or so copies in this grade existing of any particular issue. Exceptions would be recent warehouse finds of most Dell comics (6-100 copies, but usually 30 or less), and Harvey comics (1950s-1970s) surfacing. Due to low paper quality of the late 1940s and 1950s, many comics from this period are rare in Near Mint to Mint condition. Most remaining copies are VF or less. Browning of paper could be a problem.

1953-1959 Comics: As comic book sales continued to drop during the 1950s, production values were lowered resulting in cheaply printed comics. For this reason, high grade copies are extremely rare. Many Atlas and Marvel comics have chipping along the trimmed edges (Marvel chipping) which reduces even more the number of surviving high grade copies.

1960-1970 Comics: Early 60s comics are rare in Near Mint to Mint condition. Most copies of early 60s Marvels and DCs grade no higher than VF. Many early keys in NM or M exist in numbers less than 10-20 of each. Mid to late 60s books in high grade are more common due to the hoarding of comics that began in the mid-60s.

1970-Present: Comics of today are common in high grade. VF to NM is the standard rather than the exception.

When you consider how few Golden and Silver Age books exist compared to the current market, you will begin to appreciate the true rarity of these early books. In many cases less than 5-10 copies exist of a particular issue in Near Mint to Mint condition, while most of the 1930s books do not exist in this grade at all.

KNOW THE BUZZ WORDS

Many of the following terms and abbreviations are used in the comic book market and are explained here: (Note: Consult the *Overstreet Comic Book Grading Guide* for a more detailed list of terms).

a-Story art; **a(i)**-Story art inks; **a(p)**-Story art pencils; **a(r)**-Story art reprint.

Adult material–Contains story and/or art for mature readers. Re: sex, violence, strong language.

Adzine-A magazine primarily devoted to the advertising of comic books and collectibles as its first publishing priority as opposed to written articles.

Annual-A book that is published yearly.

Arrival date-Markings on a comic book cover (usually in pencil) made by either the newsstand dealer or the distributor. These markings denote the date the book was placed on the newsstand. Usually the arrival date is one to two months prior to the cover date.

Ashcan-A publisher's inhouse facsimile of a proposed new title. Most ashcans have black & white covers

KNOW THE BUZZ WORDS (Cont'd)

Other ashcans are totally black and white.

B&W-Black and white art.

Baxter paper–A high quality, white, heavy paper used in the printing of some comics.

Bi-monthly-Published every two months.

Bi-weekly-Published every two weeks.

Bondage cover-Usually denotes a female in bondage.

Brittleness-The final stage of paper deterioration.

c-Cover art; **c(i)**-Cover inks; **c(p)**-Cover pencils; **c(r)**-Cover reprint.

Bronze Age–(1.) Non-specific term not in general acceptance by collectors which denotes comics published from approximately 1970 through 1980, (2) Term which describes the "Age" of comic books after the Silver Age.

Browning –Paper aging between tanning and brittleness.

Cameo-When a character appears briefly in one or two panels.

CCA-Comics Code Authority.

CCA seal-An emblem that was placed on the cover of all CCA approved comics beginning in April-May, 1955

Center Crease– (see Subscription Crease)

Centerfold-The two folded pages in the center of a comic at the terminal end of the staples.

CFO–Abbreviation for "Centerfold out."

Chromium cover–A special Chromium foil used on covers

Church, Edgar collection-A large high grade comic book collection discovered by Mile High Comics in Colorado (over 22,000 books).

Classic Cover–A cover considered by collectors to be highly desirable.

Cleaning–A process in which dirt and dust is removed.

Color Touch–A restoration process by which colored ink is used to hide color flecks, flakes and larger areas.

Colorist-Artist that applies color to the black and white pen and ink art.

Comic book dealer–(1). A seller of comic books. (2.) One who makes a living buying and selling comic books.

Comic book repair-When a tear, loose staple or centerfold has been mended without changing or adding to the original finish of the book. Repair may involve tape, glue or nylon gossamer and is easily detected. It is considered a defect.

Comic book restoration-Any attempt, whether professional or amateur, to enhance the appearance of a comic book. These procedures may include any or all of the following techniques: Recoloring, adding missing paper, stain, ink, dirt, tape removal, whitening, pressing out wrinkles, staple replacement, trimming, re-glossing, etc. Note: Unprofessional work can lower the value of a book. In all cases, a restored book can never be worth the same as an unrestored book in the same condition.

Comics Code Authority-In 1954 the major publishers joined together and formed a committee who set up guide lines for acceptable comic contents. It was their task to approve the contents of comics before publication.

Complete Run–All issues of a given title.

Con-A Convention or public gathering of fans.

Condition–The state of preservation of a comic book.

Cosmic Aeroplane-Refers to a large collection discovered by Cosmic Aeroplane Books.

Costumed Hero–A costumed crime fighter with "developed" powers instead of "super" powers.

Coupon Cut–Comic book missing a coupon.

Cover Loose–Cover is detached from staple.

Cover Trimmed–Cover has been reduced in size through trimming.

Crease–A paper fold that occurs in comic books from misuse

Crossover–When one character appears briefly in another characters story.

Deacidification–The process of reducing acid in paper.

Debut-The first time that a character appears anywhere.

Defect–Any fault or flaw that detracts from perfection.

Denver Collection–A collection of early '40s high grade #1s bought at auction in Pennsylvania by a Denver, Colorado dealer.

Die-cut cover–When areas of a cover are cut away for special effect.

Distributor painted stripes–Color brushed or sprayed on the edges of comic book stacks as special coding by distributors (not a defect).

Double–A duplicate copy.

Double cover-An error in the binding process which results in two or more covers being bound to a single book. Multiple covers are not considered a defect.

Drug propaganda story-Where comic makes an editorial stand about drug abuse.

Drug use story-Shows the actual use of drugs: shooting, taking a trip, harmful effects, etc.

Dust Shadow–Usually an edge of a comic exposed to the gathering of dust creating a dark strip.

Edgar Church–See "Mile High."

Embossed cover–When a pattern is pressed into the cover creating a raised area.

Eye Appeal–A term used to describe the overall appeal of a comic's apparent condition.

Fanzine-An amateur fan publication.

File Copy-A high grade comic originating from the publisher's file. Not all file copies are in pristine condi-

Your First Line of Defense

Comics worth collecting are worth protecting. Count on Comic Defense System® ProBags®, Backer Boards, and Storage Boxes for Maximum Collection Protection™ at a minimum cost per comic.

Bag 'em™

Secure the perimeters of all your comics with super-clear virgin polypropylene **ProBags**.

Board 'em™

Reinforce your defenses with all-white **Backer Boards**, safeguarding your comics from accidental bends and folds.

Box 'em™

Maintain your stronghold with double-wall corrugated cardboard **Storage Boxes** — easy to assemble and transport.

Command the full line of quality Comic Defense System products — your first, best line of defense for comics of any size, age and condition!

Look for the symbol of Maximum Collection Protection™ at a comic shop near you.

KNOW THE BUZZ WORDS (Cont'd)

tion. Note: An arrival date on the cover of a comic does not indicate that it is a file copy.

First app.-Same as debut.

Flashback-When a previous story is being recalled.

Foil cover–A thin metallic foil that is hot stamped on comic covers.

Four color-A printing process in which all primary colors plus black are used. Also refers to the Four Color series published by Dell.

Foxing-Tiny orange-brown spots on the cover or pages of a comic book caused by mold growth.

G. A.-Golden Age period.

Gatefold cover–A double cover folded in itself.

Genre–Categories of comic book subject matter grouped as to type.

Giveaway–Type of comic book used as a premium.

Golden Age (G.A.)-The period beginning with Action #1 (June, 1938) and ending with World War II in 1945.

Headlight-Protruding breasts.

Hologram cover–True 3-D holograms are prepared and affixed to comic book covers and cards for special effect.

Hot stamping–The process of pressing foil, prism paper and inks on cover stock.

i-Art inks.

Indicia-Publishers title, issue number, date, copyright and general information statement usually located on the inside front cover, facing page or inside back cover.

Infinity cover-Shows a scene that repeats itself to infinity.

Inker-Artist that does the inking.

Intro-Same as debut.

JLA-Justice League of America.

JLI-Justice League International.

JSA-Justice Society of America.

Key Issue–An important issue in a run

Lamont Larson-Refers to a large high grade collection of comics. Many of the books have Lamont or Larson written on the cover.

Linticular covers–(aka flicker covers)–Images that move when viewed at different angles specially prepared and affixed to the cover.

Logo-The title of a strip or comic book as it appears on the cover or title page.

LSH-Legion of Super-Heroes.

Marvel chipping-A defect that occurred during the trimming process of 1950s & 1960s Marvels which produced a ragged edge around the comic cover. Usually takes the form of a tiny chip or chips along the right hand edge of the cover.

Mile High-Refers to a large NM-Mint collection of comics originating from Denver, Colorado (Edgar Church collection).

Modern Age–Period from 1980 to the present.

Mylar™—An inert, very hard, space-age plastic used to make high quality protective bags and sleeves used for comic book storage. Mylar ™ is a trademark of the DuPont Co.

nd-No date.

nn-No number.

N. Y. Legis. Comm.-New York Legislative Committee to Study the Publication of Comics (1951).

One-shot-When only one issue is published of a title, or when a series is published where each issue is a different title (i.e. Four Color Comics).

Origin-When the story of the character's creation is given.

Over guide-When a comic book is priced at a value over Overstreet guide list.

p-Art pencils.

Painted cover–Cover taken from an actual painting instead of a line drawing.

Paper cover–Comic book cover made from the same newsprint as interior pages (self cover). These books are extremely rare in high grade.

Pedigree-A book from a famous collection, e.g. Allentown, Larson, Church/Mile High, Denver, San Francisco, Cosmic Aeroplane, White Mountain, etc. Note: Beware of non-pedigree collections being promoted as pedigree books. Only out-standing high grade collections similar to those listed qualify.

Penciler-Artist that does the pencils.

Photo cover–Made from a photograph instead of a line drawing or painting.

POG–(passion orange guava)-A game that originated in Hawaii which uses small paper milk caps or discs.

POP-Parade of Pleasure, book about the censorship of comics.

Post-Code-Comic books published with the CCA seal.

Post-Golden Age-Comic books published between 1945 and 1950.

Post-Silver Age-Comic books published from 1969 to present.

Poughkeepsie-Refers to a large collection of Dell Comics' "file copies" believed to have originated from the warehouse of Western Publishing in Poughkeepsie, N.Y.

Pre-Code-Comic books published before the CCA seal.

Pre-Golden Age-Comic books published prior to Action #1 (June, 1938).

Pre-Hero–A term that describes the issues in a run prior to a super hero entering the run.

Pre-Silver Age-Comic books published between 1950 and Showcase #4 (1956).

KNOW THE BUZZ WORDS (Cont'd)

Printing defect-A defect caused by the printing process. Examples would include paper wrinkling, miscut edges, mis-folded spine, untrimmed pages, off-registered color, off-centered trimming, mis-folded and mis-bound pages. It should be noted that these are defects that lower the grade of the book.

Prism cover–Special reflective foil material with 3-dimensional repeated designs. Used for special effect.

Provenance-When the owner of a book is known and is stated for the purpose of authenticating and documenting the history of the book. Example: A book from the Stan Lee or Forrest Ackerman collection would be an example of a value-adding provenance.

Quarterly-Published every three months (four times a year).

R or r-Reprint.

Rare-10 to 20 copies estimated to exist.

Rat Chew–Damage caused by gnawing rates or mice.

Reprint comics-Comic books that contain newspaper strip reprints.

Restoration–The fine art of repairing a comic book to look as close as possible to its original condition.

Rice paper-A thin, transparent paper commonly used by restorers to repair tears and replace small pieces on covers and pages of comic books.

Rolled Spine–A spine condition caused by folding back pages while reading.

S. A.-Silver Age.

Saddle Stitch–The staple binding of comic books.

S&K-Joe Simon and Jack Kirby (artists).

Scarce-20 to 100 copies estimated to exist.

Silver Age-Officially begins with Showcase #4 in 1956 and ends in 1969.

Silver proof-A black & white actual size print on thick glossy paper given to the colorist to indicate colors to the engraver.

SOTI-Seduction of the Innocent, book about the censorship of comics. Refer to listing in this guide.

Spine-The area representing the folded and stapled part of a comic book.

Spine roll-A defect caused by improper storage which results in uneven pages and the shifting or bowing of the spine.

Splash panel-A large panel that usually appears at the front of a comic story.

Squarebound-A comic book glue-bound with a square spined cover.

Store Stamp–Store name stamped in ink on cover.

Stress lines-Light, tiny wrinkles occuring along the spine, projecting from the staples or appearing any where on the covers of a comic book.

Subscription crease-A center crease caused by the folding of comic books for mailing to subscribers. This is considered a defect.

Sun Shadow–See dust shadow.

Super-hero–A costumed hero crime fighter with powers beyond those of mortal man.

Super-villain–A costumed criminal with powers beyond those of mortal man.

Swipe–A panel, sequence, or story obviously borrowed from previously published material.

3-D comic-Comic art that is drawn and printed in two-color layers, producing a true 3-D effect when viewed through special glasses.

3-D Effect comic-Comic art that is drawn to appear 3-D, but isn't.

Title Page–The first page showing the title of a story.

Under guide-When a comic book is priced at a value less than Overstreet guide list.

Very rare-1 to 10 copies estimated to exist.

Warehouse copy-Originating from a publisher's warehouse; similar to file copy.

X-over-When one character crosses over into another's strip.

Zine-See Fanzine.

HOW TO START COLLECTING

New comic books are available in many different kinds of stores: Grocery stores, drug stores, Wal-Mart, K-Mart, book stores, comic book stores and card and comics specialty shops are a few examples. Local flea markets and of coruse, comic book conventions in your area are excellent sources for new and old comic books.

Most collectors begin by buying new issues in mint condition directly off the newsstand or from their local comic store. (Subscription copies are available from several mail-order services as well.) Each week new comics appear on the stands that are destined to become true collectors items. The trick is to locate a store that carries a complete line of comics. In several localities this may be difficult. Most collectors frequent several magazine stands in order not to miss something they want. Even then, it pays to keep in close contact with collectors in other areas. Sooner or later, nearly every collector has to rely upon a friend in Fandom or a dealer to obtain for him an item that is unavailable locally (see ads in this book).

Every month we send something special to every good customer

When you pay all your monthly invoices on time, and your checks all clear when presented, you'll get some very special correspondence from Capital City — a rebate check! We call it our *Cash Back Bonus*™ and it's worth 1-7% of the previous month's total purchases, including all reorders and supplies, based on the net volume of your monthly order.

The bigger the better

As the size of your order increases, so does your bonus, which can mean hundreds, even thousands, of dollars back just for paying on time. And *Cash Back* is a value to every customer, because you'll get at least 1% back on any size order.

Delivering the Capital Advantage™

When you deliver for us, we deliver for you. Get complete details on the *Cash Back Bonus* in Capital City's *Orderpak*® or call us today at

608/223-2000!

Capital™

Before you buy any comic to add to your collection, you should carefully inspect its condition. Unlike stamps and coins, defective comics are generally not highly prized. The cover should be properly cut and printed. Remember that every blemish or sign of wear depreciates the beauty and value of your comics.

The serious collector usually buys extra copies of popular titles. He may trade these multiples for items unavailable locally (for example, foreign comics), or he may store the multiples for resale at some future date. Such speculation is, of course, a gamble. Selecting the right investment books is tricky business that requires special knowledge. With experience, the beginner will improve his buying skills. Remember, if you play the new comics market, be prepared to buy and sell fast as values rise and fall rapidly.

COLLECTING IN THE 1990S

Comic Book collecting has become more fun and exciting than ever before. The stands are filled with a broad selection of every type of comic book imaginable; but look closely. There is something new about today's comic book. The inside pages are printed on slick paper that makes the colors jump. The covers are beautiful, exciting and dazzling. Most comic book companies, especially Marvel, DC, Image, Valiant, Defiant and Malibu are placing these eye-catching specialty covers on their comic books.

Yes, the face of today's newsstand has really changed with more pizzazz and glitter than ever-before. Gimmicks to encourage point of purchase sales abound. Take your pick. Holograms, prism, foil, embossed, die-cut, 3-D, posters, cards, talking covers, scratch and sniff, you name it. Check out that die-cut *Sabretooth* cover by Marvel, or that *X-Factor* #92 with the *Havok* hologram on the cover, or that black bagged *Superman* #75 (death issue), or even that multicolor foil *WildCats* Trilogy cover by Image.

Polybagged comics–It is the official policy of Overstreet Publications to grade comics regardless of whether they are still sealed in their polybag or not. Sealed comics in bags are not always in mint condition and could even be damaged. The value should not suffer as long as the bag (opened) and all of its original manufactured contents are preserved and kept together.

Collecting on a budget –Collectors check out their local newsstand or comic specialty store for the latest arrivals. Hundreds of brand new comic books are displayed each week for the collector–Much more than anyone can afford to purchase. Due to this, today's reader must be careful and budget his money wisely in choosing what to buy.

Trading Cards–Very popular today are the trading cards which are being offered by most publishers. Much like the baseball card market, comic cards are now offered by more and more outlets. In fact, many baseball card collectors and dealers are now collecting comic books. Because of this, today's comic book market is growing and changing faster than ever before. The card sets and rare issues are a very popular, and an interesting alternative to comic book collecting.

Pogs–More varied types of special giveaways are now being included in and with comic books, magazines, food products, etc. to boost sales. One of the most unique is the milk cap or pog phenomenon. Pogs (Passion Orange Guava) originated in Hawaii, and are connected to a popular game. They come as singles or in sets with holograms, die-cut, embossed, prism, etc. just as the comic cards. Pogs are now popular in California, Japan and Canada, and are spreading eastward. DC, SkyBox, Marvel, Image, Eclipse and others are currently producing product for this market.

Collecting artists–Many collectors enjoy favorite artists and follow their work from issue to issue, title to title, company to company. In recent years, some artists have achieved stardom status. Autograph signings occur at all major comic conventions as well as special promotions with local stores. Fans line up by the hundreds at such events to meet these super stars. Some of the

local stores. Fans line up by the hundreds at such events to meet these super stars. Some of the current top artists of new comics are: Todd McFarlane, Rob Liefeld, Jae Lee, Jim Lee, Joe Quesada, Whilce Portacio, Franchesco, Sam Kieth, Marc Silvestri, Dale Keown and Mark Bagley. Original artwork from these artists have been bringing record prices at auctions and from dealers lists.

Collecting by companies–Some collectors become loyal to a particular company, and only collect their titles. It is another way to specialize and collect in a market that expands faster than your pocket book.

Collecting number ones–For decades, comic enthusiasts have always collected number ones. It is yet another way to control spending and build a very interesting collection for the future. Number ones have everything going for them. Some introduce new characters. Other issues are sometimes underprinted, creating a rarity factor. A number one collection crosses many subjects, as well as companies, and makes an intriguing display.

Pricing on computer discs–Overstreet prices and general listings are now available on computer discs. These discs are updated every month with the latest listings and prices. Check your local computer stores and comic shops for copies. Also, check ads in all the trade publications.

COLLECTING BACK ISSUES

A back issue is any comic currently not available on the stands. Collectors of current titles often want to find the earlier issues in order to complete the run. Thus a back issue collector is born. Comic books have been published and collected for over 90 years. However, the earliest known comic book dealers didn't appear until the late 1930s. But today, there are hundreds of dealers that sell old comic books (See ads in this book).

Locating back issues–The first place to begin of course, is with your collector friends who may have unwanted back issues or duplicates for sale. Look in the yellow pages to see if you have a comic book store available. If you do, they would know of other collectors in your area. Advertising in local papers could get good results. Go to regional markets and look for comic book dealers. There are many trade publications in the hobby that would put you in touch with out-of-town dealers. *The Overstreet Comic Book Monthly, The Overstreet Quarterly* and of course, this *annual guide* have ads buying and selling old comic books. Some dealers publish regular price lists of old comic books for sale. Get on their mailing list.

Putting a quality collection of old comics together takes a lot of time, effort and money. Many old comics are not easy to find. Persistence and luck play a big part in acquiring needed issues. Most quality collections are put together over a long period of time by placing mail orders with dealers and other collectors.

Comics of early vintage are extremely expensive if they are purchased through a regular dealer or collector. Unless you have unlimited funds to invest in your hobby, you will find it necessary to restrict your collecting in certain ways. However you define your collection, you should be careful to set your goals well within affordable limits.

PROPER HANDLING OF COMIC BOOKS

Comic books are fragile and easy to damage. Most dealers and collectors hesitate to let anyone personally handle their rare comics. It is common courtesy to ask permission before handling another person's comic book. Most dealers would prefer to remove the comic from its bag and show it to the customer themselves. In this way, if the book is damaged, it would be the dealer's responsibility–not the customer's. Remember, the slightest crease or chip could render an otherwise Mint book to Near Mint or even Very Fine.

comic book. The following steps are provided to aid the novice in the proper handling of comic books: 1. Remove the comic from its protective sleeve or bag very carefully. 2. Gently lay the comic (unopened) in the palm of your hand so that it will stay relatively flat and secure. 3. You can now leaf through the book by carefully rolling or flipping the pages with the thumb and forefinger of your other hand. Caution: Be sure the book always remains relatively flat or slightly rolled. Avoid creating stress points on the covers with your fingers and be particularly cautious in bending covers back too far on Mint books. 4. After examining the book, carefully insert it back into the bag or protective sleeve. Watch corners and edges for folds or tears as you replace the book.

STORAGE OF COMIC BOOKS

Proper storage is the most important factor in prolonging the life of your comic books. Exposure to oxygen and atmospheric pollutants as well as heat coupled with high humidity is believed to be the primary cause of aging and yellowing. Improper storage can accelerate the aging process.

The importance of storage is proven when looking at the condition of books from large collections that have surfaced over the past few years. In some cases, an entire collection has brown or yellowed pages approaching brittleness. Collections of this type were probably stored in too much heat or moisture, or exposed to atmospheric pollution (sulfur dioxide or light). On the other hand, other collections of considerable age (30 to 50 years) have emerged with creamy white, supple pages and little sign of aging. Thus we learn that proper storage is imperative to insure the long life of our comic book collections.

Store books in a dark, cool place with relative humidity of 40-75 % and a temperature as cool as possible. Avoid excessive heat. Air conditioning is recommended. Do not use regular cardboard boxes, since most contain harmful acids. Use acid-free boxes instead. Seal books in Mylar or other suitable wrappings or bags and store them in the proper containers or cabinets, to protect them from heat, excessive dampness, ultraviolet light (use tungsten filament lights), polluted air, and dust.

Many collectors seal their books in plastic bags and store them in a cool dark room in cabinets or on shelving. Plastic bags should be changed every two to three years, since most contain harmful acids. Cedar chest storage is recommended, but the ideal method of storage is to stack your comics (preferably in Mylar bags) vertically in acid-free boxes. The boxes can be arranged on shelving for easy access. Storage boxes, plastic bags, backing boards, Mylar bags, archival supplies, etc. are available from dealers. (See ads in this edition).

Some research has been done on deacidifying comic book paper, but no easy or inexpensive, clear-cut method is available to the average collector. In fact, it has not been proven whether deacidification is even necessary. The best and longest-lasting procedure involves soaking the paper in solutions or spraying each page with specially prepared solutions. These procedures should be left to experts. Covers of comics pose a special problem in deacidifying due to their varied composition of papers used.

HOW TO SELL YOUR COMICS

If you have a collection of comics for sale, large or small, the following steps should be taken. (1) Make a detailed list of the books for sale, being careful to grade them accurately, showing any noticeable defects; i.e., torn or missing pages, centerfolds, etc. (2) Decide whether to sell or trade wholesale to a dealer all in one lump or to go through the long laborious process of advertising and selling piece by piece to collectors. Both have their advantages and disadvantages.

In selling to dealers, you will get the best price by letting everything go at once-the good with

the bad–all for one price. Simply select names either from ads in this book or from some of the adzines. Send them your list and ask for bids. The bids received will vary depending on the demand, rarity and condition of the books you have. The more in demand, and better the condition, the higher the bids will be.

On the other hand, you could become a "dealer" and sell the books yourself. Order a copy of one or more of the adzines. Take note how most dealers lay out their ads. Type up your ad copy, carefully pricing each book (using the Guide as a reference). Send finished ad copy with payment to adzine editor to be run. You will find that certain books will sell at once while others will not sell at all. The ad will probably have to be retyped, remaining books repriced, and run again. Price books according to how fast you want them to move. If you try to get top dollar, expect a much longer period of time. Otherwise, the better deal you give the collector, the faster they will move. Remember, in being your own dealer, you will have overhead expenses in postage, mailing supplies and advertising cost. Some books might even be returned for refund due to misgrading, etc.

In selling all at once to a dealer, you get instant cash, immediate profit, and eliminate the long process of running several ads to dispose of the books; but if you have patience, and a small amount of business sense, you could realize more profit selling them directly to collectors yourself.

WHERE TO BUY AND SELL

Throughout this book you will find the advertisements of many reputable dealers who sell back-issue comics magazines. If you are an inexperienced collector, be sure to compare prices before you buy. When a dealer is selected (ask for references), send him a small order (under $100) first to check out his grading accuracy, promptness in delivery, guarantees of condition advertised, and whether he will accept returns when dissatisfied. Never send large sums of cash through the mail. Send money orders or checks for your personal protection. Beware of bargains, as the items advertised sometimes do not exist, but are only a fraud to get your money.

The Price Guide is indebted to everyone who placed ads in this volume, whose support has helped in curbing printing costs. Your mentioning this book when dealing with the advertisers would be greatly appreciated.

COMIC BOOK CONVENTIONS

The first comic book conventions, or cons were originally conceived as the comic-book counterpart to science-fiction fandom conventions. There were many attempts to form successful national cons prior to the time of the first one that materialized, but they were all stillborn. It is interesting that after only three relatively organized years of existence, the first comic con was held. Of course, its magnitude was nowhere near as large as most established cons held today.

What is a comic con? As might be expected, there are comic books to be found at these gatherings. Dealers, collectors, fans, publishers, distributors, manufacturors, whatever they call themselves can be found trading, selling, and buying the adventures of their favorite characters for hours on end. Additionally most cons have guests of honor, usually professionals in the field of comic art, either writers, artists, or editors. The committees put together panels for the con attendees where the assem-

Recent photo of one of the mega comic book conventions (San Diego).

©DC

©MCG

Buying
Golden Age
Silver Age

©MCG

©DC

I offer the following to all customers:

BUYING:

- Top Prices Paid
- Immediate Cash
- Will travel to view large collections
- Experience

©DC

©FH

SELLING:

- Accurate Grading
- Reasonable Prices
- Dependable Service
- Large Selection
- Experience

©CEN

©DC

Send For Latest List

HARLEY YEE

P.O. Box 19578
Detroit, MI 48219-0578

(313) 533-2731

©DC

©MCG

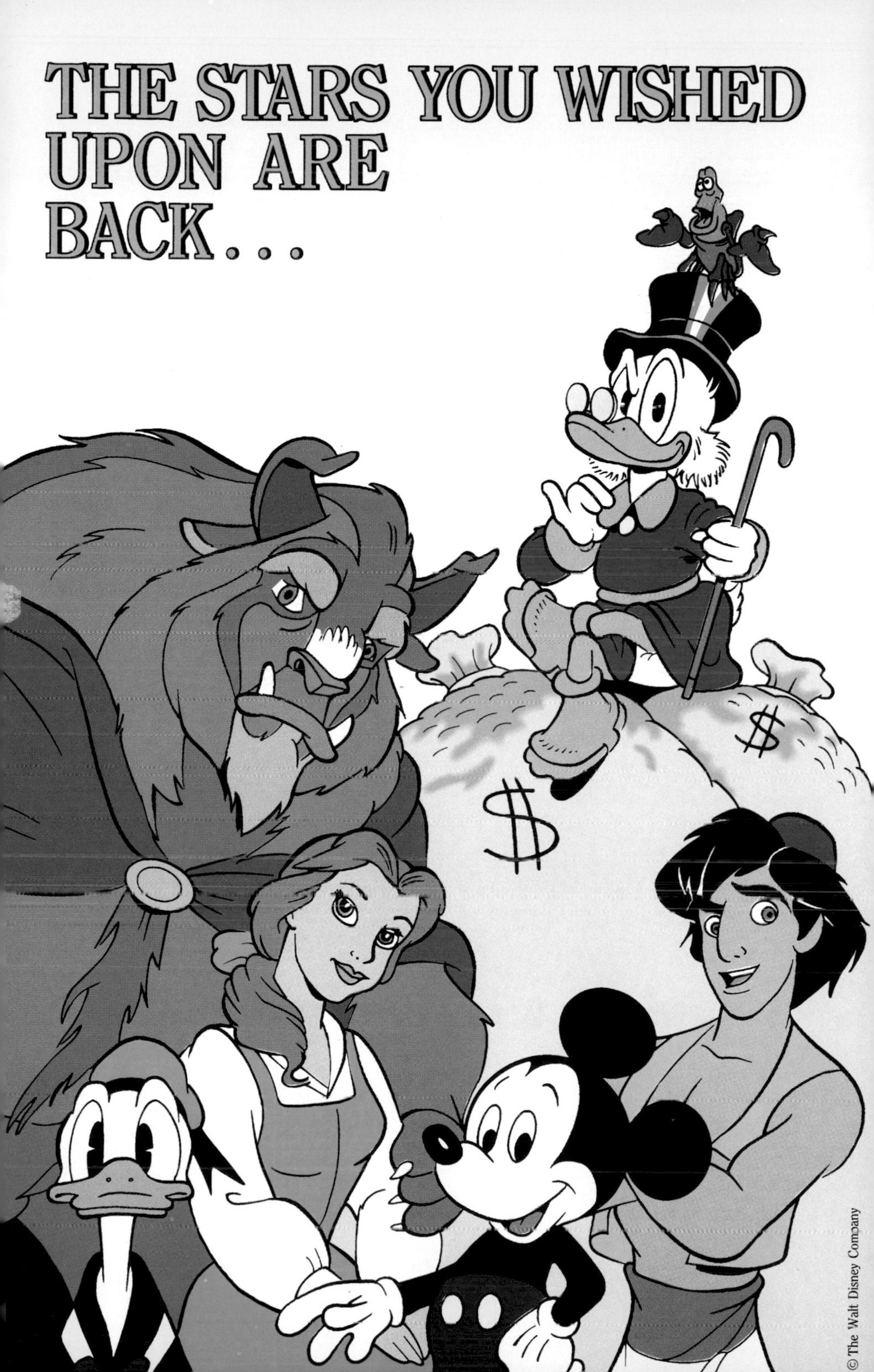
THE STARS YOU WISHED UPON ARE BACK...
$
$
© The Walt Disney Company

New Adventures from **Marvel** *in* **1994**!

The Adventures Continue from ***Gladstone*** *in* ***1994****!*

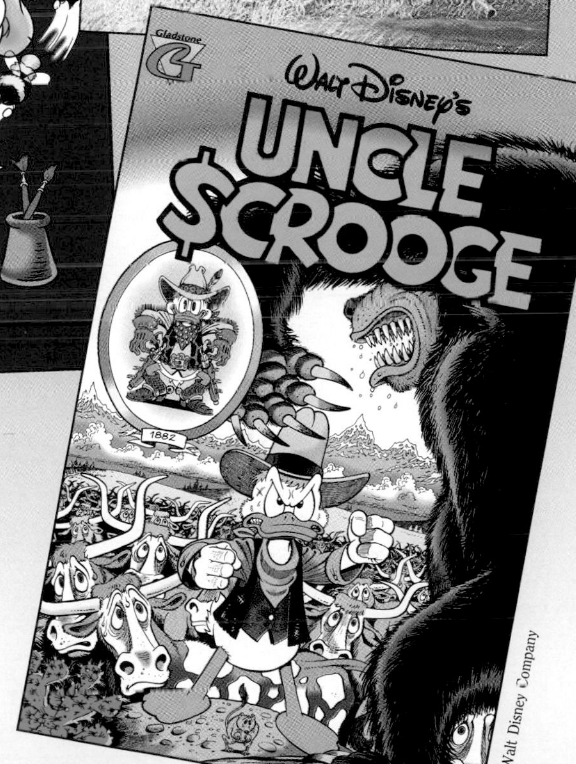

Gladstone
Walt Disney's
DONALD DUCK
ADVENTUR

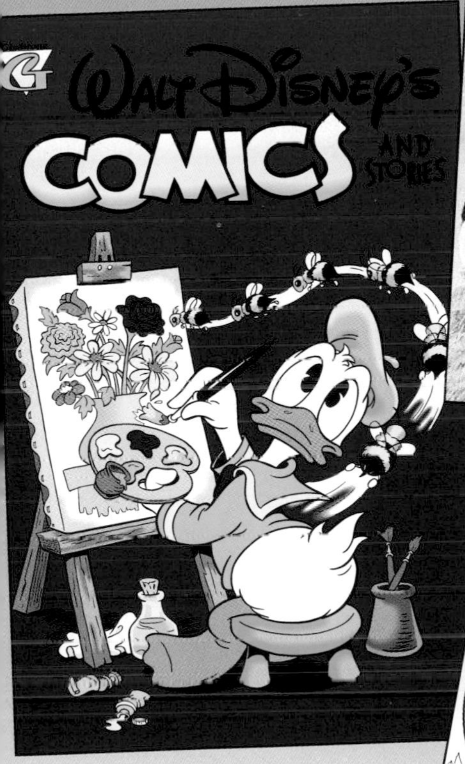

Gladstone
Walt Disney's
UNCLE
$CROOGE
1882

MARVEL® COMICS
APPROVED BY THE COMICS CODE AUTHORITY
Disney's
Beauty and the Beast

Gladstone
Walt Disney's
DONALD AND MICKEY

Gladstone
Walt Disney's
DONALD DUCK

Gladstone
Walt Disney's
UNCLE $CROOGE ADVENTURES

New Adventures from **Marvel** *in* **1994**!

The Adventures Continue from ***Gladstone*** *in* ***1994***!

bled pros talk about certain areas of comics, most of the time fielding questions from the assembled audience. At cons one can usually find displays of various and sundry things, usually toys, thousands of comic books, original art, and more. There can be the showing of movies or videos; Of course there is always the chance to get together with friends at cons and just talk about comics; one also has a good opportunity to make new friends who have similar interests and with whom one can correspond after the con.

It is difficult to describe accurately what goes on at a con. The best way to find out is to go to one and see for yourself.

You never know who you will meet at a comic book convention! © MEG

The largest cons are San Diego (August), Philadelphia (October), Chicago (July), New York (February), Atlanta (July) and Dallas (June). For accurate dates and addresses, consult ads in this edition as well as some of the adzines. Please remember when writing for convention information it is common courtesy to include a self addressed, stamped envelope for reply.

WHERE TO ADVERTISE

There are three great places to advertise:

☆ *Overstreet's Annual 1994-95 Comic Book Price Guide.*

☆ *Overstreet's Comic Book Monthly*

☆ *Overstreet's Gold & Silver Quarterly*

THE OVERSTREET ANNUAL

REACHES MORE SERIOUS COLLETORS THAN ANY OTHER PUBLICATION!

SOLD AT BOOK STORES EVERY-WHERE!

The Overstreet Annual, Monthly and Quarterly reach More serious collectors than any other publication.

Reasonable rates are available. Write: **Overstreet**, P. O. Box 2610, Cleveland, TN 37320-2610, (615) 472-4135. Subscription rate for monthly: $24.95 (10 iss. mailed 3rd class)(10 issue priority $64.95).

Published annually.

Rates are available for *Full, Half, Quarter, Eighth, & Classified.*

YOU CAN ALSO LIST YOUR STORE AT REASONABLE RATES.

IF YOU WANT TO REACH THOUSANDS OF SERIOUS COLLECTORS, WE HAVE SPECIAL ADVERTISING RATES AVAILABLE JUST FOR YOU!

THREE GREAT WAYS TO ADVERTISE!!

ANNUAL • QUARTERLY • MONTHLY

Keeps you informed about the hottest New Comics
FULL COLOR • PRICE GUIDE • MORE!!

OVERSTREET COMIC BOOK QUARTERLY

Updates the Annual prices 4 times a year.Dozens of articles and graphics

Reach Thousands of serious readers!!

Advertise in all of our publications. Ask us about an advertising package tailor made just for you!!

IT'S SMART TO ADVERTISE WITH OVERSTREET

We have been reaching thousands of buying customers for a quarter of a century!!

COVER BAR CODES FOR NEW COMIC BOOKS

Newsstand

Direct Sale

Todays comic books are cover coded for the direct sales (comic shop, newsstand, and foreign markets). They are all first printings, with the special coding being the only difference. The comics sold to the comic shops have to be coded differently, as they are sold on a no-return basis while newsstand comics are not. The Price Guide has not detected any price difference between these versions. Currently, the difference is easily detected by looking at the front cover bar code (a box located at the lower left). The bar code used to be filled in for newsstand sales and left blank or contains a character for comic shop sales. Now, as you can see above, the direct sale edition is clearly marked and both versions contain the bar code.

MARVEL REPRINTS: In recent years Marvel has reprinted some of their comics. There has been confusion in identifying the reprints from the originals. However, in 99 percent of the cases, the reprints have listed "reprint," or "2nd printing," etc. in the indicia, along with a later copyright date in some cases. Some Marvel 2nd printings will have a gold logo. The only known exceptions are a few of the movie books such as *Star Wars*, the *Marvel Treasury Editions,* and tie-in books such as *G.I. Joe.* These books were reprinted and not identified as reprints. The *Star Wars* reprints have a large diamond with no date and a blank UPC symbol on the cover. The other reprints had some cover variation such as a date missing, different colors, etc. Beginning in mid-1990, all Marvel 2nd printings have a gold logo.

Gold Key and other comics were also sold with a Whitman label. There are collectors who prefer the regular labels to Whitman, although the Price Guide does not differentiate in the price. Beginning in 1980, all comics produced by Western carried the Whitman label.

COMIC BOOK PUBLISHERS CODES– The following abbreviations are used with the cover reproductions throughout the book for copyright credit purposes. The companies they represent are listed here:

AC -(Americomics)
ACE-Ace Periodicals
ACG-American Comics Group
AJAX-Ajax-Farrell
AP-Archie Publications
ATLAS-Atlas Comics (see below)
AVON-Avon Periodicals
BP-Better Publications
C & L-Cupples & Leon
CC-Charlton Comics
CEN-Centaur Publications
CCG-Columbia Comics Group
CG-Catechetical Guild
CHES-Harry 'A' Chesler
CLDS-Classic Det. Stories
CM-Comics Magazine
DC-DC Comics, Inc.
DEF-Defiant Comics
DELL-Dell Publishing Co.
DH-Dark Horse
DMP-David McKay Publishing
DS-D. S. Publishing Co.
EAS-Eastern Color Printing Co.
EC-E. C. Comics
ECL-Eclipse Comics
ENWIL-Enwil Associates
EP-Elliott Publications
ERB-Edgar Rice Burroughs
FAW-Fawcett Publications
FC-First Comics
FF-Famous Funnies
FH-Fiction House Magazines
FOX-Fox Features Syndicate
GIL-Gilberton
GK-Gold Key
GP-Great Publications
HARV-Harvey Publications
H-B-Hanna-Barbera
HILL-Hillman Periodicals
HOKE-Holyoke Publishing Co.
IM-Image Comics
KING-King Features Syndicate
LEV-Lev Gleason Publications
MAL-Malibu Comics
ME-Magazine Enterprises
MEG-Marvel Ent. Group
MLJ-MLJ Magazines
MS-Mirage Studios
NOVP-Novelty Press
PG-Premier Group
PINE-Pines
PMI-Parents' Magazine Institute
PRIZE-Prize Publications
QUA-Quality Comics Group
REAL-Realistic Comics
RH-Rural Home
S & S-Street and Smith Publishers
SKY-Skywald Publications
STAR-Star Publications
STD-Standard Comics
STJ-St. John Publishing Co.
SUPR-Superior Comics
TC-Tower Comics
TM-Trojan Magazines
TOBY-Toby Press
TOPS-Tops Comics
UFS-United Features Syndicate
VAL-Valiant
VITL-Vital Publications
WDC-The Walt Disney Company
WEST-Western Publishing Co.
WHIT-Whitman Publishing Co.
WHW-William H. Wise
WMG-William M. Gaines (E. C.)
WP-Warren Publishing Co.
YM-Youthful Magazines
Z-D-Ziff-Davis Publishing Co.

TIMELY/MARVEL/ATLAS COMICS. "A Marvel Magazine" and "Marvel Group" was the symbol used between December 1946 and May 1947 (not used on all titles/issues during period). The Timely Comics symbol was used between July 1942 and September 1942 (not on all titles/issues during period). The round "Marvel Comic" symbol was used between February 1949 and June 1950. Early comics code symbol (star and bar) was used between April 1952 and February 1955. The Atlas globe symbol was used between December 1951 and September 1957. The M over C symbol (beginning of Marvel Comics) was used between July 1961 until the price increased to 12 cents on February 1962.

MARVEL/TIMELY/ATLAS Publishers' Abbreviation Codes:

ACI-Animirth Comics, Inc.
AMI-Atlas Magazines, Inc.
ANC-Atlas News Co., Inc.
BPC-Bard Publishing Corp.
BFP-Broadcast Features Pubs.
CBS-Crime Bureau Stories
CIDS-Classic Detective Stories
CCC-Comic Combine Corp.
CDS-Current Detective Stories
CFI-Crime Files, Inc.
CmPI-Comedy Publications, Inc.
CmPS-Complete Photo Story
CnPC-Cornell Publishing Corp.
CPC-Chipiden Publishing Corp.
CPI-Crime Publications, Inc.
CPS-Canam Publishing Sales Corp.
CSI-Classics Syndicate, Inc.
DCI-Daring Comics, Inc.
EPC-Euclid Publishing Co.
EPI-Emgee Publications, Inc.
FCI-Fantasy Comics, Inc.
FPI-Foto Parade, Inc.
GPI-Gem Publishing, Inc.
HPC-Hercules Publishing Corp.
IPS-Interstate Publishing Corp.
JPI-Jaygee Publications, Inc.
LBI-Lion Books, Inc.
LCC-Leading Comic Corp.
LMC-Leading Magazine Corp.
MALE-Male Publishing Corp.
MAP-Miss America Publishing Corp.
MCI-Marvel Comics, Inc.
MgPC-Margood Publishing Corp.
MjMC-Marjean Magazine Corp.
MMC-Mutual Magazine Corp.
MPC-Medalion Publishing Corp.
MPI-Manvis Publications, Inc.
NPI-Newsstand Publications, Inc.
NPP-Non-Pareil Publishing Corp.
OCI-Official Comics, Inc.
OMC-Official Magazine Corp.
OPI-Olympia Publications, Inc.
PPI-Postal Publications, Inc.
PrPI-Prime Publications, Inc.
RCM-Red Circle Magazines, Inc.
SAI-Sports Actions, Inc.
SePI-Select Publications, Inc.
SnPC-Snap Publishing Co.
SPC-Select Publishing Co.
SPI-Sphere Publications, Inc.
TCI-Timely Comics, Inc.
TP-Timely Publications
20 CC-20th Century Comics Corp.
USA-U.S.A. Publications, Inc.
VPI-Vista Publications, Inc.
WFP-Western Fiction Publishing
WPI-Warwick Publications, Inc.
YAI-Young Allies, Inc.
ZPC-Zenith Publishing Co., Inc.

COMIC BOOK ARTISTS

Many of the popular artists are pointed out in the listings. When more than one artist worked on a story, their names are separated by a (/). The first name did the pencil drawings and the second the inks. When two or more artists work on a story, only the most prominent will be noted in some cases. We wish all good artists could be listed, but due to space limitation, only the most popular can. The following list of artists are considered to be either the most collected in the comic field or are historically significant and should be pointed out. Artists designated below with an (*) indicate that only their most noted work will be listed. The rest will eventually have all their work shown as the information becomes avbailable. This list could change from year to year as new artists come into prominence.

Adams, Arthur
Adams, Neal
*Aparo, Jim
*Austin, Terry
Bagley, Mark
Baker, Matt
Barks, Carl
Beck, C. C.
*Brunner, Frank
*Buscema, John
Byrne, John
Capullo, Greg
*Check, Sid
Cole, Jack
Cole, L. B.
Craig, Johnny
Crandall, Reed
Davis, Jack
Disbrow, Jayson
*Ditko, Steve
Eisner, Will
*Elder, Bill
Evans, George
Everett, Bill
Feldstein, Al
Fine, Lou
Foster, Harold
Fox, Matt
Frazetta, Frank
*Giffen, Keith
Golden, Michael
Gottfredson, Floyd
*Guardineer, Fred
Gustavson, Paul
*Heath, Russ
Howard, Wayne
Ingels, Graham
Jones, Jeff
Kamen, Jack
Kane, Bob
*Kane, Gil
Kelly, Walt
Kieth, Sam
Kinstler, E. R.
Kirby, Jack
Krenkel, Roy
Krigstein, Bernie
*Kubert, Joe
Kurtzman, Harvey
Lapham, Dave
Larsen, Erik
Lee, Jae
Lee, Jim
Manning, Russ
McFarlane, Todd
McWilliams, Al
Meskin, Mort
Miller, Frank
Moreira, Ruben
*Morisi, Pete
*Newton, Don
Nostrand, Howard
Orlando, Joe
Pakula, Mac
*Palais, Rudy
*Perez, George
Portacio, Whilce
Powell, Bob
Quesada, Joe
Raboy, Mac
Raymond, Alex
Ravielli, Louis
*Redondo, Nestor
Rogers, Marshall
Schomburg, Alex
Sears, Bart
Siegel & Shuster
Silvestri, Marc
Simon & Kirby (S&K)
*Simonson, Walt
Smith, Barry
Smith, Paul
Stanley, John
*Starlin, Jim
Steranko, Jim
Stevens, Dave
Thibert, Art
Torres, Angelo
Toth, Alex
Tuska, George
Ward, Bill
Williamson, Al
Woggon, Bill
Wolverton, Basil
Wood, Wallace
Wrightson, Bernie

COMIC BOOK ARTISTS & THEIR FIRST WORK

Adams, Neal -(1 pg.) Archie's Jokebook Mag. #41, 9/59
Adams, Neal -(1st on Batman, cvr only) Detective Comics #370, 12/67
Adams, Neal -(1st Warren art) Creepy #14
Barks, Carl - (art only) Donald Duck Four Color #9, 8/42; (scripts only) Large Feature Comic #7, ?/42
Broderick, Pat - (cover & art) Planet of Vampires #1, 2/75
Brunner, Frank - (fan club sketch) Creepy #10, 1965
Buckler, Rich - Flash Gordon #10, 11/67
Burnley, Jack - (cover & art) New York World's Fair nn, '40
Buscema, John -(1st at Marvel) Strange Tales #150, 11/66
Byrne, John - Nightmare #20, 8/74; (1st at DC) Untold Legend of the Batman #1, 7/80; (1st at Marvel) Giant-Size Dracula #5, 6/75
Capullo, Greg - (1st on X-Force) X-Force Annual #1, '92
Cole, Jack - (1 pg.) Star Comics #11, 4/38
Crandall, Reed - Hit Comics #10, 4/41
Davis, Jack - (cartoon) Tip Top Comics #32, 12/38
Ditko, Steve - (1st publ.) Black Magic V4#3, 11-12/53 (1st drawn story), Fantastic Fears #5, 1-2/54
Ellison, Harlan -(1st pro story) Weird Science-Fantasy #24, 6/54
Everett, Bill - Amazing Mystery Funnies V1#2, 9/38
Fine, Lou - (1st cvr) Wonder Comics #2, 6/39; Jumbo Comics #4,12/38
Frazetta, Frank - Tally-Ho Comics nn, 12/44
Giffen, Keith -(1 pg.) Deadly Hands of Kung-Fu #17, 11/75 (1st story) Deadly Hands of Kung-Fu #22, 4?/76; (tied w/Deadly Hands) Amazing Adventures #35, 3/76
Golden, Michael - Marvel Classics Comics #28, '77
Grell, Mike - Adventure Comics #435, 9-10/74
Ingels, Graham (art at E.C.) - Saddle Justice #4, Sum '48
Kaluta, Michael - Teen Confessions #59, 12/69
Kelly, Walt - New Comics #1, 12/35
Keown, Dale - Nth Man the Ultimate Ninja #8 (1st at Marvel, 1/90; Samurai #13 ?/87; (1st on Hulk) Incredible Hulk #367, 3/90
Kieth, Sam - Primer #5 11?/83
Kirby, Jack - Jumbo Comics #1, 9/38; (1st signed work)
Kubert, Adam/Andy/Joe art team - Sgt. Rock #422, 7/88
Kurtzman, Harvey - Tip Top Comics #36, 4/39; (1st at

COMIC BOOK ARTISTS (Cont'd)
E.C.) Lucky Fights It Through nn, 1949
Larsen, Erik - Megaton #1, 11/83
Lee, Jae - Marvel Comics Presents #85, 91;
Lee, Jim - (1st at Marvel) Alpha Flight #51, 10/87; (1st on X-Men) X-Men #248?,?/89
(art on Punisher) - Punisher War Journal #1 11/88
Liefeld, Rob -(1st at DC) Warlord #131 9/88; (1st at Marvel) X-Factor #40 4?/89; (1st full story) Megaton #8, 8/87; (inside front cover only) Megaton #5, 6/86; (art on New Mutants) - New Mutants Annual #5 '89
Lim, Ron (art on Silver Surfer) - Silver Surfer Annual #1, '88
Mayer, Sheldon - New Comics #1, 12/35
McFarlane, Todd - Coyote #11, ?/85; (1st full story) All Star Squadron #47, 7/85; (1st on Hulk) Incredible Hulk #330, 4/87
Medina, Angel -(pin-up only) Megaton #3, 2/86
Miller, Frank -(1st on Batman) DC Special Series #21, Spr '80; (1st on Daredevil) Spectacular Spider-Man #27 2/79
Newton, Don - Many Ghosts of Dr. Graves #45, 5/74
Perez, George -(1st at DC) Flash #289, 9/80; (2 pgs.) Astonishing Tales #25, 8/74
Portacio, Whilce -(1st on X-Men) X-Men #201, 1/86
Quesada, Joe -(1st on X-Factor) X-Factor Annual #7, '92
Raboy, Mac -(1st cover for Fawcett) Master Comics #21 12/41
Romita, John - (1st at Marvel) - Daredevil #12, 1/66
Shuster, Joe -(cover) New Adventure Comics #16, 6/37
Siegel & Shuster - New Fun Comics #6, 10/35
Simon & Kirby - Blue Bolt #3, 8/40
Simonson, Walter - Magnus, Robot Fighter #10, 5/65
Smith, Barry - X-Men #53, 2/69
Smith, Paul -(1 pg. pin-up) King Conan #7, 9/81; (1st full story) Marvel Fanfare #1, 3/82
Steranko, Jim - Spyman #1 Sep '66; (1st at Marvel) Strange Tales #151, 12/66
Swan, Curt - Dick Cole #1, 12-1/48-49
Thomas, Roy -(scripts) Son of Vulcan #50, 1/66
Torres, Angelo - Crime Mysteries #13, 5/54
Weiss, Alan -(illo) Blue Beetle #5, 3-4/65
Williamson, Al -(1st at E.C.) Tales From the Crypt #31, 9/52; (text illos) Famous Funnies #169, 8/48
Wood, Wally (art at E.C.) - Saddle Romances #10, 1-2/50
Wrightson, Bernie - House of Mystery #179, 4/68; (1st at Marvel) Chamber of Darkness #7, 10/70; (1st cover) Web of Horror #3, 4/70;(fan club sketch) Creepy #9
Zeck, Mike -(illos) Barney and Betty Rubble #11, 2/75

QUICK REFERENCE LISTS

The following lists were compiled to give our readers more detailed information about their favorite comic books. We invite your criticism, comments, and suggestions for omitted entries.

1ST APPEARANCE

A-Man the Amazing Man - Amazing-Man Comics #5, 9/39
Adam Strange - Showcase #17, 11-12/58
Adult Legion - Superman #147, 8/61
Agent Liberty - Superman #60 (2nd Series), 10/91
Air Man - (Hawkman imitator) Keen Detective Funnies #23, 8/40
Air Wave - Detective Comics #60, 2/42
Air Wave II - Green Lantern #100, 1/78
Airboy - Air Fighters Comics V1#2, 11/42
Airwave I - Detective Comics #60, 2/42
Alex Summers - (becomes Havok) X-Men #54, 3/69
Alfred - Batman #16 4-5/43; (1st skinny Alfred) Detective Comics #83, 1/44
Alice Cooper - Marvel Premiere #50, 10/79
Alicia Masters - Fantastic Four #8, 11/62
Aliens - Aliens #1 May '88; Magnus, Robot Fighter #1, 2/63
Alley Oop - Funnies #1, 10/36
Alpha Flight - X-Men #120, 4/78
Amazing Man - All Star Squadron #23, 7/83
American Ace - (1st newsstand app.) Marvel Mystery Comics #2, 12/39
American Crusader - Thrilling Comics #19, 8/41
American Eagle - Marvel Two-In-One Annual #6 1981; (1st published app.) Motion Picture Funnies Weekly #1, 1939
Ancient One - Strange Tales #110, 7/63
Andy Panda - Crackajack Funnies #39, 9/41
Angel - Marvel Comics #1, 10-11/39.
Angel (now Archangel) - X-Men #1, 9/63
Angel & the Ape - Showcase #77, 9/68
Animal Man - (in costume) Strange Adventures #190, 7/66; (no costume) Strange Adventures #180 9/65; (re-intro) Wonder Woman #267, 5/80
Ant-Man - (costume) Tales to Astonish #35, 9/62 (new) Marvel Premiere #47, 4/79; (no costume) Tales to Astonish #27, 1/62; (re-intro) Avengers #46, 11/67
Anthro - Showcase #74, 5/68
Apache Kid - Two Gun Western #5, 11/50
Ape, The - Startling Comics #21, 5/43
Aqua-Girl - Aquaman #33, 5-6/67
Aquababy - Aquaman #23, 9-10/65
Aquaboy - Superboy #171
Aquagirl - (try out, not same as other) Adventure Comics #266, 11/59
Aquagirl - Aquaman #33, 5-6/67
Aqualad - Adventure Comics #269, 2/60
Aquarian (Wundarr) - Adventure Into Fear #17, '73
Aquaman - More Fun Comics #73, 11/41;
Arak - Warlord #48, 8/81
Archangel - (cameo) (formerly Angel) X-Factor #23 12/87; (full app.) X-Factor #24, 1/88
Archie Andrews - Pep Comics #22, 12/41
Arion - Warlord #55
Arrow - Funny Pages V2#10, 9/38
Arthur Stacy - Amazing Spider-Man #93, 2/71
Asbestos Lady - Captain America Comics #63, 7/47
Astro Boy - Astro Boy #1, 8/65
Atom - All-American Comics #19, 10/40; (S.A.) Showcase #34, 9-10/61
Atoman - Atoman #1, 2/46
Atomaster - Comic Books #1, 1950
Atomic Mouse - Atomic Mouse #1, 3/53
Atomic Rabbit - Atomic Rabbit #1, 8/55
Atomic Thunderbolt - Atomic Thunderbolt #1, 2/46
Aunt May - Amazing Fantasy #15, 8-9/62; prototype, Strange Tales #92, 6/62
Aurora - X-Men #120
Avenger - Shadow Comics #2, 4/40
Azrael - (cameo) Tales of the Teen Titans #52, 4/85; (full app.) Tales of the Teen Titans #53, 5/85
Baby Huey - Casper, the Friendly Ghost #1, 9/49; (1st Harvey app.) Harvey Comics Hits #60, 9/52
Badger - Badger #1, 12/83
Balbo, the Boy Magician - Master Comics #32, 11/42
Bamm Bamm - (Flintstones) Flintstones #16, 1/64
Barker - National Comics #42, 5/44
Barney Bear - Our Gang Comics #1, 9-10/42
Baron Strucker - Sgt. Fury #5, 1/64
Bat Lash - Showcase #76, 8/68
Bat-Girl - Batman #139, 4/61; (new)-Detective #359, 1/67
Batgirl - Detective Comics #359, 1/67
Batman - Detective Comics #27 5/39; (new look w/new costume) Detective Comics #327, 5/64
Batman, Jr. - World's Finest Comics #215, 10/72
Batmite - Detective Comics #267, 5/59
Batwoman - Detective Comics #233, 7/56; (1st modern app. G.A. Batwoman) Brave and the Bold #182, 1/82; (new) Detective Comics #624, 12/90 (re-intro) Batman Family #10, 3-4/77
Beagle Boys - Walt Disney's Comics and Stories #134, 11/51
Beast - X-Men #1, 9/63; (new) (1st in mutated form) Amazing Adventures #11, 3/72
Beast Boy - (becomes Changeling) Doom

1ST APPEARANCE (Cont'd)
Patrol #99, 11/65
Belit - Giant-Size Conan #1, 9/74
Bennett Brant - Amazing Spider-Man #11, 4/64
Bernie the Brain - Sugar & Spike #72 ? '/68
Berserkers, The - X-Men/Alpha Flight #1, 12/85
Betty - Pep Comics #22, 12/41
Betty Brant - Amazing Spider-Man #4, 9/63
Bill Barnes - (Air Ace) Shadow Comics #1, 3/40
Binary - (formerly Ms. Marvel) X-Men #164, 12/82
Birdman, The - Weird Comics #1, 4/40
Bishop - (cameo) X-Men #282, 11/91; (full app.) X-Men #283, 12/91
Bizarro Jimmy Olsen - Adventure Comics #287, 8/61
Bizarro Lana Lang - Adventure Comics #292, 1/62
Bizarro Lois Lane - Action Comics #255, 8/59
Bizarro Lucy Lane - Adventure Comics #292, 1/62
Bizarro Marilyn Monroe - Adventure Comics #294 3/62
Bizarro Perry White - Adventure Comics #287, 8/61
Bizarro President Kennedy - Adventure Comics #294, 3/62
Black Bolt - (1st full app.) Fantastic Four #46, 1/66 (cameo) (from Inhumans) Fantastic Four #45, 12/65
Black Canary - Flash Comics #86, 8/47; (silver age)-Justice League of America #74; (1st modern app.) Detective Comics #554 ,9/85; (1st solo story) Flash Comics #92, 2/48
Black Cat - Pocket Comics #1, 8/41
Black Cobra - Captain Flight Comics #8 ? '46
Black Condor - Crack Comics #1, 5/40
Black Dwarf - Spotlight Comics #1, 11/44
Black Flame - Starslayer #20, 9/84; Action Comics #304, 9/63
Black Fury - Fantastic Comics #18, 5/41
Black Goliath - Black Goliath #1, 2/76
BlackHawk - Military Comics #1, 8/41
Black Hood - Top-Notch Comics #9, 10/40; (S.A.) Adventures of the Fly #7, 7/60
Black Jack - Zip Comics #20, 11/41
Black Knight - Black Knight #1, 5/55
Black Knight - Tales to Astonish #52, 2/64
Black Knight II - Avengers #48, 1/68
Black Lightning - Black Lightning #1, 4/77
Black Marvel - Mystic Comics #5, 3/41
Black Orchid - Adventure Comics #428, 6-7/73; (new)-Black Orchid #1, 12/88
Black Owl - Prize Comics #2, 4/40
Black Panther - Stars & Stripes #3, 7/41
Black Panther - Fantastic Four #52, 7/66
Black Phantom - Tim Holt #25, 9/51
Black Pirate - Sensation Comics #1, 1/42
Black Rider - All Western Winners #2, Win '48-49
Black Spider - Super-Mystery Comics V1#3, 10/40
Black Terror - Exciting Comics #9, 5/41
Black Widow - Mystic Comics #4, 7-8/40
Black Widow - Tales of Suspense #52, 4/64
Blackie the Hawk - Blackhawk #75, 4/'54
Blackie the Hawk - (re-intro) Blackhawk #108, 1/57
Blade the Vampire Slayer - Tomb of Dracula #10 ?/73?
Blok - (Legion) Superboy #253, 7/79
Blonde Phantom - All-Select Comics #11 Fall '46; (re-intro) Sensational She-Hulk #4, 8/89
Blondie - Ace Comics #1, 4/37
Bloodshot - (cameo) Eternal Warrior #4,11/92; (1st full app.) Rai #0, 11/92
Bloodstone - Marvel Presents #1, 10/75
Blue Beetle - (G.A.) Mystery Men Comics #1, 8/39 (Charlton)-Blue Beetle #18, 2/55; (Ted Kord) Captain Atom #83, 11/66; (1st DC app.) Crisis on Infinite Earths #1, 4/85
Blue Blade - USA Comics #5 Sum '42
Blue Blaze - Mystic Comics #1, 3/40
Blue Bolt - Blue Bolt #1, 6/40
Blue Circle - Blue Circle Comics #1, 6/44
Blue Devil - Fury of Firestorm #24, 6/84
Blue Streak - Crash Comics #1, 5/'40
Bo Bunny - Funny Stuff #70, 1-2?/53
Bobby Benson - Bobby Benson's B-Bar-B Riders #1, 5-6/50
Boboes - Marvel Mystery Comics #32, 6/42
Bomba - Bomba, the Jungle Boy #1, 9-10/67
Bombshell - Boy Comics #3, 4/42
Booster Gold - Booster Gold #1, 2/86
Bouncer - Bouncer nn 1944
Bouncing Boy - (Legion) Action Comics #276, 5/61
Boy Commandos - Detective Comics #64, 6/42
Bozo the Robot - Smash Comics #1, 8/39
Braniac 5 - Action Comics #276, 5/61
Brick Bradford - King Comics #1, 4/36
Broncho Bill - Tip Top Comics #1, 4/36
Brother Power - Brother Power, the Geek #1, 9-10/68, (re-intro) Saga of Swamp Thing Annual #5, 1989
Buck Rogers - (in comics) Famous Funnies #3, 9/34
Buckskin - Super Mystery V2#1, 4/41
Bucky - Captain America Comics #1, 3/41 (silver age)-Avengers #4, 3/64; (Captain America's sidekick)
Bugs Bunny - Looney Tunes & Merrie Melodies #1, 1941
Bullet - Amazing Mystery Funnies V3#1, 1/40
Bulletboy - Master Comics #48, 3/44
Bulletman - Nickel Comics #1, 5/40
Bumblebee - Teen Titans (1st series) #48, 1977
Buzzy - All Funny Comics #1, Win '43-44
Buzzy the Crow - Harvey Comics Hits #60, 9/52
B'Wanna Beast - Showcase #66
Cable - (1st full app.) New Mutants #87 3/90; (cameo) New Mutants #86, 2/90
Cain - (House of Mystery host) House of Mystery #176, 10/67
Calico Kid - (becomes Ghost Rider) Tim Holt #6, 5/49
Camilla - Jungle Comics #1, 1/40
Candy - Police Comics #37, 12/44
Captain & the Kids - Famous Comics Cartoon Books #1200, 1934; Tip Top Comics #1, 4/36
Captain Action - Captain Action & Action Boy nn, 1967
Captain Aero - Captain Aero Comics V1#7, 12/41
Captain America - Captain America Comics #1, 3/41 ; (silver age)-Strange Tales #114, 11/63 (Acrobat disquised as); Avengers #4, 3/64; (fomerly Super Patriot) Captain America #333, 9/87; (new) Captain America #181, 1/75 (new) (formerly Nomad) Captain America #183, 3/75.
Captain Atom - (1st DC app.) Crisis on Infinite Earths #6, 9/85; (new) Captain Atom #84, 1/67(new) Captain Atom #1, 3/87; (S.A.) Space Adventures #33, 3/60
Captain Battle - Silver Streak Comics #10, 5/41
Captain Britain - Captain Britain #1, 3/87; (1st U.S. app.) Marvel Team-Up #65, 1/78
Captain Comet - Strange Adventures #9, 6/51; (re-intro) Secret Society of Super-Villains #2, 7-8/76
Captain Commando - Pep Comics #30, 8/42
Captain Courageous - Banner Comics #3, 9/41
Captain Daring - Buccaneers #19, 1/50; Daring Mystery Comics #7, 4/41
Captain Desmo - Adventure Comics #32, 11/38
Captain Easy - Funnies #1, 10/36; Famous Comics Cartoon Books #1202, 1934
Captain Fearless - Silver Streak Comics #1,12/39
Captain Fight - Fight Comics #16, 12/41
Captain Flag - Blue Ribbon Comics #16, 9/41
Captain Flash - Captain Flash #1, 11/54
Captain Freedom - Speed Comics #13, 5/41
Captain Future - Man of Tomorrow - Startling Comics #1, 6/40
Captain George Stacy - Amazing Spider-Man #56, 1/68
Captain Marvel (Shazam) - Whiz Comics #1, 2/40; (M.F.Enterprises) Captain Marvel #1, 4/66 (modern) Shazam: the New Beginning #1, 4/87; (new) Legends #1, 11/86; (re-intro) Shazam! #1, 2/73
Captain Marvel (female) - Amazing Spider-Man Annual #16, '82
Captain Marvel of the Kree - Marvel Super-Heroes #12, 12/67
Captain Marvel, Jr. - Whiz Comics #25, 12/41
Captain Midnight - Funnies #57, 7/41
Captain Savage - Mystery Men Comics #4, 11/39
Captain Storm - Captain Storm #1, 5-6/64
Captain Strong - Action Comics #421, 3/73
Captain Terror - U.S.A. #2, 11/41
Captain Terry Thunder - Jungle Comics #1, 1/40
Captain Thunder - Flash Comics (Fawcett) #1, 1/40
Captain Thunder - Superman #276, ? '74
Captain Triumph - Crack Comics #27, 1/43
Captain Universe - Micronauts #8, 8/79
Captain Victory - Our Flag Comics #1, 8/41
Captain Wizard - Red Band Comics #3, ? '45
Captain Wonder - Kid Komics #1, 2/43
Captain Yank - Big Shot Comics #29, 11/42
Casper the Friendly Ghost - (1st Harvey app.) Harvey Comics Hits #60, 9/52; Casper #1, 9/49
Cat -Cat, The #1, 11/72
Cat Girl - Adventures of the Fly #9, 11/60
Catman - Crash Comics #5, 11/40
Cave Carson - Brave and the Bold #31, 8-9/60

1ST APPEARANCE (Cont'd)

Cerebus - Cerebus the Aardvark #1, 12/77
Challenger - Mystic Comics #6, 10/41
Chameleon - Target Comics V1#6, 7/40
Chameleon Boy - (Legion) Action Comics #267, 8/60
Champ - Champion Comics #2, 12/39
Changeling - (formerly Beast Boy) New Teen Titans #1, 11/80; (X-Men) X-Men #35, 8/67
Charlie Chan - Feature Comics #23, 8/39
Charlie-27 - Marvel Super Heroes #18, 1/69
Checkmate - Action Comics #598, 3/88
Chemical King - (Legion) Adventure Comics #371, 8/68
Chlorophyll Kid - (Legion) Adventure Comics #306, 2/63
Chop Chop - (Blackhawk's sidekick) Military Comics #3, 10/41
Chuck - (Black Fury's aide) Fantastic Comics #18, 5/41
Cisco Kid - Cisco Kid Comics #1, Win '44
Claw the Unconquered - Claw the Unconquered #1, 5-6/75
Clea - Strange Tales #126, 11/64
Cletus Kasady - (1st full app.) Amazing Spider-Man #345, 3/91; (cameo; becomes Carnage) Amazing Spider-Man #344, 2/91
Clip Carson - More Fun Comics #68, 6/41
Cloak - (Spy Master) Big Shot Comics #1, 5/'40
Cloak & Dagger - Spec. Spider-Man #64, 3/82
Clock - Crack Comics #1, 5/40
Clock - Funny Pages V1#6, 11/36
Clown - Super-Mystery Comics V1#5, 12/40
Clown - Spitfire Comics #1, 8/41
Cobra Kid - (Black Cobra's sidekick) Captain Flight Comics #8 ? '46
Colossal Boy - (Legion) Action Comics #267, 8/60
Colossus - Tales of Suspense #14, 2/61; Giant-Size X-Men #1 Sum '75
Combat Kelly - Combat Kelly #1, 11/51; (new) Combat Kelly #1, 6/72
Comet - Pep Comics #1, 1/40; (re-intro) Comet #1, 10/83; (S.A.) Advent. of the Fly #30, 10/64
Commando Yank - Wow Comics #6, 7/15/42
Commissioner Gordon - Detective Comics #27, 5/39
Conan, the Barbarian - (1st in comics) Conan, the Barbarian #1, 10/70
Concrete - Dark Horse Presents #1, 7/86
Congo Bill - More Fun Comics #56, 6/40
Congorilla - Action Comics #248, 1/59
Conqueror, The - Victory Comics #1, 8/41
Cookie - Topsy-Turvy #1, 4/45
Corporal Collins - Blue Ribbon Comics #2, 12/39
Cosmic Boy - (Legion) Advent. Comics #247 4/58
Cosmo Cat - All Top Comics #1, 1945
Cosmo Mann - Bang-Up Comics #1, 12/41
Cosmo, the Phantom of Disguise - Detective Comics #1, 3/37
Cotton Carver - Adventure Comics #50, 5/40
Cougar - The Cougar #1, 4/75
Creeper - Showcase #73, 3-4/67
Crimebuster - Boy Comics #3, 4/42
Crimson Avenger - Detective Comics #20, 10/38
Crusader - Aquaman #56, 3-4/71; (formerly old Marvel Boy) Fantastic Four #164, 11/75
Crypt Keeper - Crime Patrol #15, 12-1/49-50
Crystal - Fantastic Four #45, 12/65
Cyborg - (New Teen Titans) DC Comics Presents #26, 10/80
Cyclone - Whirlwind Comics #1, 6/40
Cyclops - X-Men #1, 9/63
Cyclotronic Man - Black Lightning #4, 7/77
D-Man - Captain America #328, 4/86
Daffy Duck - Looney Tunes & Merrie Melodies #1, 1941
Daimon Hellstrom - (1st full app.) Ghost Rider #2, 10/73; (cameo) (Son of Satan) Ghost Rider #1, 9/73
Daisy Duck - (back cover only) Large Feature Comic #16, 6/41
Dale Daring - Adventure Comics #32, 11/38
Dan Hastings - Star Comics #1, 2/37
Danny Chase - New Teen Titans Annual #3, 1987
Daredevil - Silver Streak Comics #6, 9/40 (blue & yellow costume)
Daredevil - Daredevil #1, 4/64
Darkhawk - Darkhawk #1, 3/91
Darklon the Mystic - Eerie #79, 11/76
Dart & sidekick Ace - Weird Comics #5, 8/40
David - (Samson's aide) Fantastic Comics #10, 9/40
Dawnstar - (Legion) Superboy #226, 4/77
Dazzler - X-Men #130, 2/80
Deadman - Strange Adventures #205, 10/67
Deadpool - New Mutants #98, 2/91
Death - Sandman #8, 1990
Death's Head - (new) (1 pg. strip on back-c) Dragon's Claws #3, 9/88; (new) (1st full app.) Dragon's Claws #5, 11?/88
Deathlok the Demolisher - Astonishing Tales #25, 8/74
Deathstroke the Terminator - New Teen Titans #2, 12/80 (1st solo story - New Titans #70, 10/90
Demon - Demon #1, 8-9/72
Dennis the Menace - Dennis the Menace #1, 8/53
Deputy Dawg - New Terrytoons #1, 6-8/60
Destroyer, The - USA Comics #6, 12/42
Destroyer - Invaders #16, 5/77; Mystic Comics #6, 10/41
Destroyer Duck - Destroyer Duck #1, 1982
Destructor - The Destructor #1, 2/75
Dev-Em, the Knave from Krypton - Adventure Comics #287, 8/61
Devil-Slayer - Marvel Spotlight #33, 4/77
Dial "H" for Hero - (Robby Reed) House of Mystery #156, 11-12/65
Dick Cole - Blue Bolt #1, 6/40
Dick Tracy - (1st comic book app.) Popular Comics #1, 2/36
Dixie Dugan - Feature Funnies #1, 10/37
Doc Samson - Incredible Hulk #141, 7/71
Doc Savage - (1st in comics) Shadow Comics #1, 3/40; (pulp-1st app.)- 3/33
Doc Strong - Blue Ribbon Comics #4, 6/40
Doctor Fate - (female) Doctor Fate #25, 2/91
Doctor Midnight - (new) Infinity, Inc. #21,12/85
Doctor Solar - Doctor Solar #1, 10/62; (1st in costume) Doctor Solar #5 ? '63
Doctor Strange - Strange Tales #110, 7/63
Dodo & the Frog - Funny Stuff #18, 2/47
Doiby Dickles - (Green Lantern's sidekick) All-American Comics #27, 6/41
Doll Man - Feature Comics #27, 12/39
Dolphin - (of Forgotten Heroes) Showcase #79, 12/68
Dominic Fortune - Marvel Preview #2, 1975; (1st color app.) Marvel Premiere #56, 10/80; (new) Iron Man #213, 12/86
Domino - New Mutants #98, 2/91
Donald Duck - The Wise Little Hen, 1934
Don Winslow - Popular Comics #1, 2/36
Doodles Duck - Dodo & the Frog #80, 9-10/54
Dotty & Ditto - Top-Notch Comics #33, 2/43
Dr. Fate - More Fun Comics #55, 5/40; (silver age)-Justice League of America #21
Dr. Hypno - Amazing-Man Comics #14, 7/40
Dr. Mid-Nite - (1st story app.) All-American Comics #25, 4/41; (text only) All-American Comics #24, 3/41;
Dr. Mystic - (Superman prototype) Comics Magazine #1, 5/36
Dr. Neff, Ghost Breaker - Red Dragon Comics #3, 5/48
Dr. Occult - New Fun Comics #6, 10/35; (1st in color &1st DC app.)-More Fun Comics #14, 10/36
Dr. Spektor - Mystery Comics Digest #5, ? '72?
Dr. Strange - Thrilling Comics #1, 2/40
Dr. Strange - Strange Tales #110, 7/63
Dr. Who - Marvel Premiere #57, 12/80
Dracula - Tomb of Dracula #1, 4/72; Dracula #2, 11/66
Dragon - (1st full app.) Megaton #3, 2/86; (cameo)(later Savage Dragon) Megaton #2, 10/85
Drax the Destroyer - Iron Man #55, 2/73
Dreadstar - Epic Illustrated #15, 12/82
Dream Girl - (Legion) Advent. Comics #317, 2/64
Duo Damsel - (Legion)(formerly Triplicate Girl) Adventure Comics #341, 2/66
Duplicate Boy - Adventure Comics #324
Dusty - (Shield's sidekick) Pep Comics #11, 1/41
Dynamic Man - Mystic Comics #1, 3/40
Dynamite Thor - Blue Beetle #6, 3-4/41
Dynamo - Thunder Agents #1, 11/65; (Electro #1 only) Science Comics #1, 2/40
Dynamo, The Eagle - Weird Comics #8, 11/40
Eagle - Science Comics #1, 2/40
Ebony - Police Comics #12, 10/42
Echo The - All-New Comics #1, 1/43
Eclipso - House of Secrets #61, 7-8/63
Eddie Brock - (becomes Venom) Amazing Spider-Man #298, 3/88
Egbert - Egbert #1 Spr '46
El Diablo - All Star Western #2, 10-11/70
Elasti-Girl - My Greatest Adventure #80, 6/63
Elastic Lad - (Jimmy Olsen) Superman's Pal Jimmy Olsen #31 ?/62
Electro, the Marvel of the Age - Marvel Mystery Comics #4, 2/40
Elektra - Daredevil #168, ? /81?
Element Girl - Metamorpho #10, 1-2/67
Element Lad - (Legion) Adventure Comics #307, 4/63
Elfquest - Fantasy Quarterly #1, Spr '78
Ella Cinders - Famous Comics Cartoon Books #1203, 1934; Tip Top Comics #1, 4/36

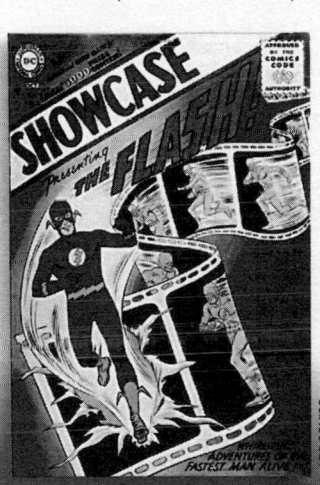

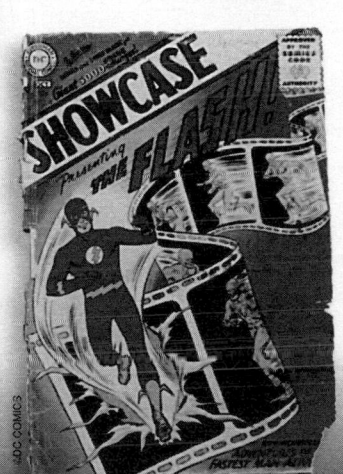

1ST APPEARANCE (Cont'd)

Ellery Queen - (1st app. in comics) Crackajack Funnies #23, 5/40
Elmer Fudd - Looney Tunes & Merrie Melodies #1, 1941
Elongated Man - Flash #112, 4-5/60
E-Man - E-Man #1, 10/73
Enchantress - Journey Into Mystery #103, 4/64
Enemy Ace - Our Army at War #151, 2/65
Erg - (becomes Wildfire) Superboy #198 ? '73?
Eternal Warrior - (cameo) Solar #10, 6/92; (full app.) Solar #11, 7/92
Evangeline - Primer #6, 2/84
Everyman - Captain America #267, 3/82
Face - (Tony Trent) Big Shot Comics #1, 5/40
Faceless Creature - Strange Adv. #124, 1/61
Falcon - Pep Comics #1, 1/40
Falcon - Captain America #117, 9/69; Daring Mystery Comics #5, 6/40
Fantomah, Mystery Woman - Jungle Comics #1, 1/40
Fatman - Fatman the Human Flying Saucer #1, 4/67
Fearless Flint, the Flint Man - Famous Funnies #89, 12/42
Feral - (of X-Force) New Mutants #99, 3/91
Ferret - Man of War #2, 1/42
Ferret, Mystery Detective - Marvel Mystery Comics #4, 2/40
Ferris - (becomes Star Sapphire) Showcase #22, 9-10/59
Ferro Lad - (Legion) Adventure Comics #346, 7/66
Fiery Mask - Daring Mystery Comics #1, 1/40
Fighting American - Fighting American #1, 4-5/54
Fighting Yank - Startling Comics #10, 9/41
Fin - Daring Mystery Comics #7, 4/41
Fin Fang Foom - Strange Tales #89, 10/61
Fire - Super Friends #25
Fireball - Pep Comics #12, 2/41; (S.A.) Mighty Crusaders #4, 5?/66
Firebrand - Police Comics #1, 8/41
Firefist - Blue Beetle #1, 6/86
Firefly - Top-Notch Comics #8 ,9/40
Firehair - Rangers Comics #21, 2/45
Firehawk - Fury of Firestorm #17, 10/83
Fire Lad - Adventure Comics #306, 2/63
Firelord - Thor #225, 7/74
FireStar - X-Men #193, 4/85
Firestorm - Firestorm, the Nuclear Man #1, 3/78; (new) Firestorm, the Nuclear Man Annual #5,10/87
Flag, The - Our Flag Comics #2, 10/41
Flame, The - Wonderworld Comics #3, 7/39
Flamebird - (Jimmy Olsen as) Superman #158 12/62 (new) Secret Origins Annual #3, 1989
Flaming Carrot - Visions #1, 1979
Flash - Flash Comics #1 1/40; (G.A.) (1st app. in S.A.) Flash #123, 9/61
Flash - Showcase #4, 9-10/56
Flash Gordon - King Comics #1, 4/36
Flash Lightning - (becomes Lash Lightning) Sure-Fire Comics #1, 6/40
Flash Rabbit - All Top Comics #1, 1945
Flexo the Rubber Man - Mystic Comics #1, 3/40
Flintstones - Dell Giant #48, 7/61
Fly - Double Life of Private Strong #1, 6/59
Fly Girl - (1st in costume) Adventures of the Fly #14, 9?/61; (w/o costume) Adventures of the Fly #13, 7?/61
Fly-Man, The - Spitfire Comics #1, 8/41
Forbush Man - Not Brand Echh #5, 12/67
Forge - (X-Force) X-Men #184, 8/84
Fox - Blue Ribbon Comics #4, 6/40; (New) Black Hood #11, 11/92
Frankenstein - Prize Comics #7, 12/40; Frankenstein #2, 9/66
Frankenstein's monster - (cameo) Silver Surfer #7, 8/69
Freckles & His Friends - Famous Comics Cartoon Books #1204, 1934
Fred Bender - (becomes Dr. Eclipse) Solar #14, 10/92
Freezum - Blue Bolt V2#5, 10/41
Fritzi Ritz - Tip Top Comics #1, 4/36
Fu Manchu - (1st in Detective) Detective Comics #17, 7/38; 1st cvr. Det. #1, 3/37
G. I. Robot - Weird War Tales #101, 7/81
Gambit - (cameo) X-Men Annual #14, 1990; (full app.) X-Men #266, 8/90
Gandy Goose - Terry-Toons Comics #1, 10/42
Gangbuster - Adventures of Superman #434, 11/87
Gargoyle - Defenders #94, 4/80
Gary Concord - (Ultra Man) All-American Comics #8, 11/39
Genius Jones - All Funny Comics #1, Win '43-44
Gentleman Ghost - Atom & Hawkman #43, 6-7/69
Ghost Breaker - Star Spangled Comics #122, 11/51
Ghost Patrol - Flash Comics #29, 5/42
Ghost Patrol - Wings #66, 2/46
Ghost Rider - (formerly Calico Kid) Tim Holt #11 ?/49
Ghost Rider - (western) Ghost Rider #1, 2/67; (Johnny Blaze) Marvel Spotlight #5, 8/72; (new-Daniel Ketch) Ghost Rider V2#1, 5/90
Giant-Man - (formerly Ant-Man) Tales to Astonish #49, 11/63
Gideon - New Mutants #98, 2/91
Gladstone Gander - Walt Disney's Comics and Stories #88, 1/48
Glory Grant - Amazing Spider-Man #140, 1/75
Gnort - Justice League International #10
God Of Thunder, The - Weird Comics #1, 4/40
Godiva - New Teen Titans Annual #3, 11/87
Golden Arrow - Whiz Comics #1, 2/40
Golden Dragon - Adventure Comics #32, 11/38
Golden Girl - Golden Lad #5, 6/46
Golden Gladiator - Brave and the Bold #1, 8-9/55
Golden Gorilla - Action Comics #224, 1/57
Golden Lad - Golden Lad #1, 7/45
Golem - Strange Tales #174, 2/74
Goliath - (formerly Giant-Man) Avengers #28, 5/66 (formerly Hawkeye) Avengers #63, 4/69
Grandma Duck - Donald and Mickey Merry Christmas nn, 1945
Gray Ghost - Sensation Comics #1, 1/42
Great Gazoo - (Flintstones) Flintstones #34
Green Arrow - More Fun Comics #73, 11/41
Green Falcon - Blue Ribbon Comics #4, 6/40
Green Flame - Super Friends #42, 3/81
Green Fury - (formerly Green Flame) Infinity, Inc. #32, 11/86
Green Hornet - (1st in comics) Green Hornet Comics #1, 12/40; (silver age) Green Hornet #1, 2/67
Green Lama - Prize Comics #7, 12/40
Green Lantern - All-American Comics #16, 7/40; (S.A.) Showcase #22, 9-10/59
Green Mask - Mystery Men Comics #1, 8/39
Green Turtle - Blazing Comics #1, 6/44
Grendel - Primer #2, 2/83
Grey Mask - Suspense Comics #1, 12/43
Grimjack - Starslayer #10, 11/83
Grim Reaper, The - Wonder Comics #1, 5/44
Groo the Wanderer - Destroyer Duck #1, 1982
Gruesomes - (Flintstones) Flintstones #24
Guardian - Star Spangled Comics #7, 4/42; (formerly Vindicator) Alpha Flight #2, 9/83
Guardian Angel - (formerly Hop Harrigan) All-American Comics #25, 4/41
Guardsman I - Iron Man #43, 11?/71?
Guardsman II - Iron Man #96, 3/77
Gunner & Sarge - All-American Men of War #67 ? '58?; Our Fighting Forces #45, 5/59
Guy Gardner - (later a Green Lantern) Green Lantern #59, 3/68; (1st app. as a Green Lantern) Green Lantern #116, 5/79
Gwen Stacy - Amazing Spider-Man #31, 12/65
Gyro Gearloose - Walt Disney's Comics and Stories #140, 5/52
Halo - Blue Beetle #24, 8/43
Hangman - Pep Comics #17, 7/41
Hangman - (re-intro) Comet #6, 12/91; (S.A.) Fly Man #33, 9/65
Happy Houlihans - Blackstone, the Magician Detective #1, Fall '47
Harada - Solar #3, 11/91
Harbinger - Harbinger #1, 1/92
Harlequin (Joker's Daughter)- Teen Titans #48, '77
Harry Osborn - (later becomes Gr. Goblin II) Amazing Spider-Man #31, 12/65
Harvey Bullock - Batman #361, 7/83
Havok - (no costume) X-Men #56, 5/69; (with costume) X-Men #58, 7/69
Hawk & Dove - Showcase #75, 7-8/67
Hawkeye - Tales of Suspense #57, 9/64; (formerly Goliath) Avengers #98, 4/72
Hawkgirl - (formerly Shiera Sanders) All Star Comics #5, 6-7/41; (silver age)- Brave & the Bold #34, 2-3/61
Hawkman - Flash Comics #1, 1/40; (S.A.) Brave and the Bold #34, 2-3/61; (mod ern)-Hawkworld: Book #1, 1989
Heap - Air Fighters Comics V1#3, 12/42
Heckle & Jeckle - Terry-Toons Comics #50, 11/46
Hedy Devine - Hedy Devine Comics #22, 8/47
Hedy Wolfe - Miss America Magazine #2, 11/44
Heimdall - Journey Into Mystery #85, 10/62
Hellblazer - (John Constantine) Saga of SwampThing #37, 6/85
Hellcat - Avengers #144, 2/76
Her - (formerly Paragon) Marvel Two-In-One #61, 3/80
Herbie - Forbidden Worlds #73 ? '59?
Hercules - Blue Ribbon Comics #4, 6/40; Incredible Hulk #3, 9/62; Hit Comics #1, 7/40, Mystic Comics #3, 6/40

We'll pay
TOP DOLLAR
for your
collection!

1ST APPEARANCE (Cont'd)

Herman & Catnip - Harvey Comics Hits #60, 9/52

High Evolutionary - Thor #134, 11/66

Him - (Warlock) (cameo) Fantastic Four #67, 10/67 (Warlock) (full app.) Thor #165, 6/69

Hocus & Pocus - Action Comics #83, 4/45

Hooded Horseman - Blazing West #14, 11-12/'50

Hooded Wasp - Shadow Comics #7, 11/40

Hop Harrigan - All-American Comics #1, 4/39

Hoppy the Marvel Bunny - Fawcett's Funny Animals #1, 12/42

Hourman - Adventure Comics #48, 3/40; (1st app. in S.A.) Justice League of America #21, 8/63

Hourman - (new) Infinity, Inc. #21,12/85

Howard the Duck - Fear #19, 12/73

Hulk - (green skin) Incredible Hulk #2, 7/62; (grey skin) Incredible Hulk #1, 5/62; (new) Incredible Hulk #377, 1/91; (re-intro with grey skin) Incredible Hulk #324, 10/86

Hulk 2099 - 2099 Unlimited #1, 9/93

Human Target - Action Comics #419, 1/73

Human Top - Red Raven Comics #1, 8/40; Tough Kid Squad #1, 3/42

Human Torch - Marvel Comics #1, 10-11/39; (Johnny Storm) Fantastic Four #1, 11/61; (re-intro G.A.) Avengers West Coast #50, 9?/89

Humphrey - Joe Palooka #15, 12/47

Hunchback, The - Wow Comics #2, Spr, 1941

Huntress - (G.A.) Sensation Comics #68, 8/47; (1st S.A. app. of G.A. Huntress) Brave and the Bold #62, 10-11/65; (modern) All Star Comics #69, 11-12/77

Hurricane - Captain America Comics #1, 3/41

Hydroman - Heroic Comics #1, 8/40

Hyper, the Phenomenal - Hyper Mystery Comics #1, 5/40

Ibis the Invincible - Whiz Comics #1, 2/40

Ice - Super Friends #9

Ice Cream Soldier - Our Army at War #85, 8/59

Iceman - X-Men #1, 9/63

Imp - Captain America Comics #12, 3/42

Impossible Man - Fantastic Four #11, 2/63; (re-intro) Fantastic Four #176, 11/76

Impossible Woman - Marvel Two-In-One #60, 2/80

Inferno - (S.A.) Mighty Crusaders #4, 5?/66

Inferno, the Flame Breather - Zip Comics #10, 1/41

Insect Queen - (Lana Lang) (Legion) Superboy #124, 10/65

Invisible Girl - (Sue Storm) Fantastic-4 #1, 11/61

Invisible Kid - (Legion) Action Comics #267, 8/60 (new) Legion of Super-Heroes Annual #1, 1982

Invisible Scarlett O'Neil - Famous Funnies #81, 4/42

Iron Fist - Marvel Premiere #15, 5/74; (re-intro, cameo) Namor, the Sub-Mariner #8, 11/90; (re-intro, full app.) Namor, the Sub-Mariner #10 1/91

Iron Major - Our Army at War #158, 9/65

Iron Man - (new armor) Tales of Suspense #40, 4/63(new) Iron Man #231, 6/88; (new) (Jim Rhodes) Iron Man; (Tony Starks) Tales of Suspense #39, 3/63

Iron Wolf - Weird Worlds #8, 11-12/'73

Isis - Shazam! #25 ? '76

Jack Monroe - (1st full app.) Captain America #154 10/72; (cameo) Captain America #153, 9/72

Jack of Hearts - Deadly Hands of Kung-Fu #22, 4?/76; (1st solo book) Marvel Premiere #44, 10/78

Jack Q. Frost - Unearthly Spectaculars #1, 10/65

Jack Woods - Adventure Comics #39, 1/39

Jaguar - Adventures of the Jaguar #1, 9/61

Jarella (Hulk's love)- The Incred. Hulk #140, 6/71

Jason Bard - (becomes Robin) Detective Comics #392, 10/69

Jason Todd - Batman #357, 3/83; (1st in Robin costume) Batman #366, 12/83

Jean DeWolf - Marvel Team Up #48, 8/76

Jester - Smash Comics #22, 5/41

Jigsaw - Jigsaw #1, 9/66

Jiminy Cricket - Mickey Mouse Mag. V5#3, 12/39

Jimmy "Minuteman" Martin - Adventure Comics #53, 8/40

Jimmy Martin as Hourman's aide - Adventure Comics #71, 2/42

Jimmy Olsen - Action Comics #6,11/38; (new) Man of Steel #2, 10/86

Jo-Jo, Congo King - Jo-Jo Comics #7, 7/47

Joe Palooka - Joe Palooka nn, 1933; (1st in comic book format) Feature Funnies #1, 10/37

Joe Robertson - Amazing Spider-Man #52, 9/67

John Carter of Mars - Funnies #30, 4/39

John Carter, Warlord of Mars - Weird Worlds #1, 8-9/72

John Connor - Terminator #12 ?/89

John Constantine - (Hellblazer) Saga of Swamp Thing #37, 6/85

John Force - (Magic Agent) Magic Agent #1, 1-2/62

John Jameson - Amazing Spider-Man #1, 3/63

John Law - Smash Comics #3, 10/39

John Stewart - (later a Green Lantern) Green Lantern #87, 12-1/71-72

Jonah Hex - All Star Western #10, 2-3/72

Johnny Blaze - (re-intro) Ghost Rider V2#10, 2/91 (Ghost Rider) Marvel Spotlight #5, 8/72

Johnny Cloud - All-American Men of War #82 '6?

Johnny Dynamite - Dynamite #3, 9/53

Johnny Peril - Comic Cavalcade #15, 6-7/46

Johnny Quick - More Fun Comics #71, 9/41

Johnny Thunder - All-American Comics #100, 8/48, Flash Comics #1, 1/40; (1st S.A. app.) Flash #137, 1963

Jon Linton - Amazing Myst. Funnies V2#11, 11/39

Jonah Hex - All Star Western #10, 2-3/72

J'onn J'onzz (See Martian Manhunter)

Jonni Thunder - (Thunderbolt) Jonni Thunder #1, 2/85

Jonny Double - Showcase #78, 11/68

Jordan Brothers - Green Lantern #9, 11-12/61

Jose Delgado - (becomes Gangbuster) Adventures of Superman #432, 9/87

Jubilee - X-Men #244, 2?/89

Judomaster - Special War Series V4#4, 11/65; (1st DC app.) Crisis on Infinite Earths #6, 9/85

Jughead Jones - Pep Comics #22, 12/41

Julie Madison - Detective Comics #31, 9/39

Jungle Jim - Ace Comics #1, 4/37

Junior Woodchucks - Walt Disney's Comics and Stories #125, 2/51

Kaanga, Lord of the Jungle - Jungle Comics #1, 1/40

Kamandi - Kamandi, the Last Boy on Earth #1, 10-11/72

Karate Kid - (Legion) Adventure Comics #346, 7/66

Karma - (New Mutants) Marvel Team-Up #100, 12/80

Katy Keene - Wilbur Comics #5, Sum '45

Kazar the Great - Marvel Comics #1, 10-11/39; (silver age)-X-men #10, 3/65

Ken Shannon - Police Comics #103, 12/50

Kid Eternity - Hit Comics #25, 12/42

Kid Flash - (later becomes Flash) Flash #110, 12-1/'59-60

Killer Frost I - Firestorm, the Nuclear Man #3, 6-7/78

King Kull - Creatures on the Loose #10, 3/71

Kit - (Black Cat's sidekick) Black Cat Comics #28, 4/51

Kitty Pryde - (Ariel) (X-Men) X-Men #129, 1/80

Kobra - Kobra #1, 2-3/76

Kole - (New Teen Titan) New Teen Titans #8, 5?/85

Kong the Untamed - Kong the Untamed #1, 6-7/75

Kraven - (War of the Worlds) Amazing Adventures #18, 5/73

Krazy Kat - Ace Comics #1, 4/37

Krypto - Adventure Comics #210, 3/55

Kryptonite (Blue) - Superman #128, 4/59

Kryptonite (Gold) - Superman #140, 4/60

Kryptonite (Red) - Adventure #299, 8/62

Kryptonite Kid - Superboy #83 ?/'60

Lady Blackhawk - Blackhawk #133, 2/58

Lady Luck - Spirit nn, 6/2/40

Lana Lang - (becomes Insect Queen) Superboy #10, 9-10/50

Lance Hale - Silver Streak Comics #3, 3/40

Lance O'Casey - Whiz Comics #1, 2/40

Lancer - Super-Mystery Comics V3#3, 1/43

Lash Lightning - (formerly Flash Lightning) Lightning Comics V2#2, 8/41

Lassie - Adventures of Lassie nn ?/49

Lemonade Kid - Bobby Benson's B-Bar-B Riders #15, 6/50

Leopard Girl - Jungle Action #1, 10/54

Li'l Abner - Tip Top Comics #1, 4/36

Li'l Jinx - Pep Comics #62, 7/47

Liberator - Exciting Comics #15, 12/41

Liberty Belle - Star Spangled #20, 5/43

Light Lass - (formerly Lightning Lass) Adventure Comics #317, 2/64

Lightning - Thunder Agents #4, 4/66

Lightning - (cover only) Jumbo Comics #14, 4/40 (1st story app.) Jumbo Comics #15, 5/40

Lightning Boy - (Legion) Adven. Comics #247 4/58

Lightning Girl - Lightning Comics V3#1, 6/42

Lightning Lad - (formerly Lightning Boy) Adventure Comics #267, 12/59

Lightning Lass - (Legion) Adventure Comics #308, 5/63

Lilith - Vampire Tales #6 ?/74; (Dracula's daughter) Giant-Size Chillers #1, 6/74;

1ST APPEARANCE (Cont'd)

(re-intro) New Teen Titans #2, 9/84; (Teen Titans) Teen Titans #25, 1-2/70

Little Audrey - Little Audrey #1, 4/48

Little Dot - Sad Sack Comics #1, 9/49

Little Dynamite - Boy Comics #6, 10/42

Little Lotta - Little Dot #1, 9/53

Little Lulu - Marge's Little Lulu 4-Color #74, 6/45 (as text illo) King Comics #46, 2/40

Little Max - Joe Palooka #27, 12/48

Little Orphan Annie - Popular Comics #1, 2/36

Little Wise Guys - Daredevil Comics #13, 10/42

Living Mummy - Supernatural Thrillers #5, 8/73

Liz Allen - Amazing Spider-Man #4, 9/63

Lobo - (1st full story) Omega Men #10, 1/84 - (1st solo story, back-up) Omega Men #37, 4/86; (cameo) Omega Men #3, 6/83

Lockheed - X-Men #166, 2/83

Lois Lane - Action Comics #1, 6/38; (new) Man of Steel #2, 10/86

Lois Lane as Superwoman - Action Comics #60, 5/43

Lone Warrior - Banner Comics #3, 9/41

Longshot - Longshot #1, 9/85

Lori Lemaris the Mermaid - Superman #129, 5/59

Lt. Marvels - Whiz Comics #21, 9/41

Lucy Lane - Superman's Pal Jimmy Olsen #36 ?/62

Luke Cage - (Hero for Hire) Hero For Hire #1, 6/72

Lynx & sidekick Blackie - Mystery Men Comics #13, 8/40

Mad Hatter - Mad Hatter #1, 1-2/46

Madame Satan - Pep Comics #16, 6/41

Madame Web - Amazing Spider-Man #210, 11/80

Madelyne Pryor - (of X-Men) Avengers Annual #10, 1981

Madrox - Giant-Size Fantastic Four #4, 2/75

Mage - (re-intro) Grendel #16, 1/88

Magic Morro - Super Comics #21, 2/40

Magician from Mars - Amazing-Man Comics #7, 11/39

Magicman - Forbidden Worlds #125

Magma - New Mutants #10, 12/83

Magno the Magnetic Man & Davey - Super-Mystery Comics V1#1, 7/40

Magnus, Robot Fighter - Magnus, Robot Fighter #1, 2/63

Major Mynah - Atom #37, 6-7/68

Man Bat - Detective #400, 6/70

Man in Black - Front Page Comic Book #1, 1945

Man of War - Man of War #1, 11/41

Manowar - Target Comics #1, 2/40

Man-Thing - Savage Tales #1, 5/71; (1st full story) Fear #15, 8/73

Mandrake the Magician - King Comics #1, 4/36

Manhunter - Police Comics #8, 3/42; (1st in new costume) Detective Comics #437, 10-11/73; (Paul Kirk) Adventure Comics #58, 1/41; (new)-Adventure Comics #73, 4/42

Mantis - Avengers #112, 6/73

Margie - Comedy Comics #34, Fall '46

Mark Merlin - House of Secrets #23, 8/59

Marshal Law - Marshal Law #1, 10/87

Martan, the Marvel Man - Popular Comics #46, 12/39

Martian Manhunter - (J'onn J'onzz) Justice League of America #228, 7/84

Marvel Boy - (1st & only app.) Daring Mystery Comics #6, 9/40Detective Comics #225, 11/55; (re-intro)

Marvel Girl - (becomes Phoenix) X-Men #1, 9/63

Marvel Man - (later Quasar) Captain America #217, 1/78

Mary Jane & Sniffles - Looney Tunes & Merrie Melodies #1, 1941

Mary Jane Watson - (1st mention) Amazing Spider-Man #15, 8/64; (cameo, face not shown) Amazing Spider-Man #25, 6/65; (cameo, face shown) Amazing Spider-Man #42, 11/66; (cameo, not shown) Amazing Spider-Man #38, 7/66; (re-intro) Amazing Spider-Man #243, 8/83

Mary Marvel - Captain Marvel Adv. #18, 12/42

Mask, The - Exciting Comics #1, 4/40

Mask, The - Suspense Comics #2, 1944

Masked Marvel - Keen Detective Funnies V2#7, 7/39

Masked Raider - Marvel Comics #1, 10-11/39

Master Key - Scoop Comics #1,11/41

Master Man - Master Comics #1, 3/40

Master of Kung-Fu - (Shang-Chi) Special Marvel Edition #15, 12/73

Matter Eater Lad -(**Legion**) Adventure Comics #303, 12/62

Maximillian O'Leary - (Sargon's aide) All-American Comics #70, 1-2/46

Maya - Atom #1, 6-7/62

Megaton - Megaton #1, 11/83

Menthor - Thunder Agents #1, 11/65

Mento - (non-member) Doom Patrol #91, 11/64

Mentor - Iron Man #55, 2/73

Mera - Aquaman #11, 9-10/63

Merboy - Wonder Woman #107

Mercury - (Silver Streak's sidekick) Silver Streak Comics #11, 6/41

Mercury Man - Space Adventures #44 ?/61?

Metal Men - Showcase #37, 3-4/62

Metallo - (Jor-El's robot) Superboy #49, 6/56

Metamorpho - Brave and the Bold #57, 12-1/64-65

Mickey Finn - (1st comic book app.) Feature Funnies #1, 10/37

Mickey Mouse - Mickey Mouse Book nn, '30

Midnight - Smash Comics #18, 1/41

Mighty Girl - Adventure Comics #453, 9-10/77

Mighty Mouse - Terry-Toons Comics #38, 11/45

Mighty Samson - Mighty Samson #1, 7/64

Millie the Model - Gay Comics #1, 3/44

Milton Berle - Uncle Milty #1, 12/50

Minnie Mouse - Mickey Mouse Book nn 1930

Minute Man - Master Comics #11, 2/41

Minuteman - (re-intro) Shazam! #31, 9-10/77

Miss Arrowette - World's Finest #113, 4/60

Miss America - (modern) Giant-Size Avengers #1, 8/74

Miss Masque - Exciting Comics #51, 9/46; America's Best Comics #23, 9/47

Miss Patriot - Marvel Mystery Comics #50, 12/43

Miss Victory - Captain Fearless Comics #1, 8/41

Mister Miracle - Mister Miracle #1, 3-4/71

Mister X - (on cover only) Vortex #2

Moby Duck - Donald Duck #112

Mockingbird - Marvel Team-Up #95, 7/80

Modred the Mystic - Marvel Chillers #1, 10/75

Molly O'Day - Molly O'Day #1, 2/45

Mon-El - (Legion) Superboy #89, 6/61

Monarch Starstalker - Marvel Premiere #32, 10/76

Moon Girl - Happy Houlihans #1, Fall, '47 Moon Girl and the Prince #1, Fall, '47

Moon Knight - Werewolf by Night #32, 8/75; (1st solo book) Marvel Spotlight #28, 6/76

Moondragon - Iron Man #54, 1/73; (re-intro) Warlock and the Infinity Watch #2, 3/92

Morbius - Amaz. Spider-Man #101, 10/71

Morgan Edge - (cameo) Superman's Pal Jimmy Olsen #133, 10/70

Morlock 2001 - Morlock 2001 #1, 2/75

Moth Man - Mystery Men Comics #9, 4/40

Mr. America - (formerly Tex Thompson) Action Comics #33, 2/41

Mr. Fantastic - (Reed Richards) Fantastic Four #1, 11/61

Mr. Justice - Blue Ribbon Comics #9, 2/41

Mr. Miracle - Captain Fearless Comics #1, 8/41

Mr. Monster - Super Duper Comics #3, 5-6/47, (new) Vanguard Illustrated #7, 5/84

Mr. Mystic - Spirit nn, 6/2/40

Mr. Satan - Zip Comics #1, 2/40

Mr. Scarlet - Wow Comics #1, Wint, '40-'41

Mr. Tawny - Captain Marvel #79, 12/47; (Silver Age) Shazam! #2, 4/73

Mr. Terrific - Sensation Comics #1, 1/42; (1st app. in S.A.) Justice League of America #37, 8?/65

Ms. Marvel - (becomes Binary) Ms. Marvel #1, 1/77

Ms. Victory - Femforce Special #1, Fall '84; (new) Femforce #25

Mutt & Jeff- (1st in comic book format) Funnies #1, 10/36

Mutt & Jeff - Mutt & Jeff #1, 1910

Mystery Men of Mars - All-American Comics #1, 4/39

Nam - Savage Tales #1, 11/85

Namora - Marvel Mystery Comics #82, 5/47

Ned Leeds - (later becomes Hobgoblin) Amazing Spider-Man #18, 11/64

Negative Man - My Greatest Adventure #80, 6/63

Neil the Horse - Charlton Bullseye #2, 8?/81

Nemesis - Adventures into the Unknown #154 ?/66?

Nemesis Kid - (Legion) Adv. Comics #346, 7/66

Neon the Unknown - Hit Comics #1, 7/40

Neuman, Alfred E. - (cover only, fake ad) Mad #21, 3/55

Nevada Jones - Zip Comics #1, 2/40

New Gods - New Gods #1, 2-3/71

Nick Fury - (formerly Sgt. Fury) Strange Tales #135, 8/65

Night Hawk - All-New Comics #1, 1/43

Nightcrawler - Giant-Size X-Men #1, Sum '75

Nightgirl - Adventure Comics #306, 11/63

Nighthawk - Avengers #71, 12/69

Nightmare - (Casper's horse) Casper, the Friendly Ghost #19, 4/54

Nightmaster - Showcase #82, 5/69

'EARANCE (Cont'd)

...de - Amazing-Man Comics #24, ... Captain Atom #82, 9/66; (1st DC ... Crisis on Infinite Earths #6, 9/85

...hrasher - Thor #412

...ving - (Dick Grayson) Tales of the ...n Titans #44, 7/84; (Superman as) ...perman #158, 12/62; (Van-Zee) ...uperman Family #183, 5-6/77

...a - (later Namorita in New Warriors) Sub-Mariner #50

...omad - (formerly Steve Rogers) Captain America #180, 12/74

Noman - Thunder Agents #1, 11/65

Norman Osborn - (Green Goblin I) Amazing Spider-Man #37, 6/66

Nova - Nova #1, 9/76

Nth Man - Marvel Comics Presents #25 ?/89

Nukla - Nukla #1, 10-12/65

Nutsy Squirrel - Funny Folks #1, 4-5/46

Nyoka, the Jungle Girl - Master Comics #50, 5/44

Ocean Master - Aquaman #25, 1-2/66

Odin - (1st full app.) Journey Into Myst. #86, 11/62; (cameo) Journey Into Mystery #85,10/62

Omac - Omac #1, 9-10/74

Omega - Omega the Unknown #1, 3/76

Oracle, The - Startling Comics #20, 2/43

Orion - (New Gods) New Gods #1, 2-3/71; (of New Gods) (1st new costume) First Issue Special #13, 4/76

Oswald the Rabbit - New Fun Comics #1, 2/35

Outlaw Kid - Outlaw Kid #1, 9/54

Owl - Crackajack Funnies #25, 7/40

Pantha - (New Titan) New Titans #74, 3/91

Paragon - (becomes Her) Incredible Hulk Annual #6, 1977

Pat Parker - (in costume) Speed Comics #15, 11/41 (no costume) Speed Comics #13, 5/41

Pat, Patsy & Pete - Looney Tunes & Merrie Melodies #1, 1941

Patchwork Man - (cameo) Swamp Thing #2, 12-1/72-73; (full app.) Swamp Thing #3, 2-3/73

Patriot - Marvel Mystery Comics #21, 7/41; (modern age) Marvel Premiere #29, 4/76

Patsy Walker - Miss America Magazine #2, 11/44

Peacemaker - Fightin' Five V2#40 ?/66; (1st DC app.) Crisis on Infinite Earths #6, 9/85

Pebbles - (Flintstones) Flintstones #11, 6/63

Perry White - Superman #7, 11-12/40

Pete Ross - (Legion) Superboy #86, 1/61; (tryout only) Superboy #77, 9?/59

Peter Parker's parents - Amazing Spider-Man Special #5, 11/68; (re-intro) Amazing Spider-Man #365, 8/92

Peter Porkchops - Leading Comics #23, 2-3/47

Phantasmo, Master of the World - Funnies #45, 7/40

Phantom - Ace Comics #11, 2/38

Phantom Eagle - (S.A.) Marvel Super-Heroes #16, 9/68; (G.A.) Wow Comics #6, 7/42

Phantom Falcon - Wings #68, 4/46

Phantom Girl - (Legion) Action Comics #276, 5/61

Phantom Lady - Police Comics #1, 8/41

Phantom Lady - Phantom Lady #13, 8/47

Phantom of the Fair - Amazing Mystery Funnies V2#7, 7/39

Phantom Rider - Star Comics #16, 12/38

Phantom Stranger - Phantom Stranger #1, 5-6/69

Phoenix - (formerly Marvel Girl) X-Men #101, 10/76

Phoenix II - (Rachel) X-Men #141, 1/81

Pinocchio - (cameo) Mickey Mouse Mag.V5#2, 11/39; (full app.) Mickey Mouse Mag.V5#3, 12/39

Pip the Troll - Strange Tales #179, 4/75

Plastic Man - Police Comics #1, 8/41; (S.A. tryout) House of Mystery #160, 7/66; (S.A.) Plastic Man #1, 11-12/66

Pluto - Thor #127, 4/66

Pogo - Animal Comics #1, 12-1/41-42

Polar Boy -Adventure #306, 11/63

Polaris - (X-Men) X-Men #44, 5/68

Popsicle Pete - All-American Comics #6, 9/39

Porky Pig - Looney Tunes & Merrie Melodies #1, '41

Pow Wow Smith - Detective Comics #151, 9/49

Power Girl - All Star Comics #58, 1-2/76

Power Man - (Rip Regan) Fight Comics #3, 3/40

Power Nelson the Future Man - Prize Comics #1, 3/40

Powerhouse Pepper - Joker Comics #1, 4/42

Predator - Predator #1, 6/89

Presto Kid - Red Mask #51, 9/55

Prince Ra-Man - (formerly Mark Merlin) House of Secrets #73, 7-8/65

Prince Valiant - Ace Comics #26, 5/39

Princess Pantha - Thrilling Comics #56, 10/46

Princess Projectra - (Legion) Adventure Comics #346, 7/66

Professor Supermind & Son - Popular Comics #60, 2/41

Professor Warren - Amaz. Spider-Man #31, 12/65

Professor X - X-Men #1, 9/63

Psylocke - New Mutants Annual #2, 10/86

Punisher - Amaz. Spider-Man #129, 2/74

Punisher 2099 - Punisher War Journal #50, 1/93

Pureheart the Powerful - Archie as Pureheart the Powerful #1, 9/66

Purple Mask - Daring Mystery Comics #3, 4/40

Pyroman - America's Best Comics #3, 11/42; Startling Comics #18, 12/42

Quantum Queen - Adventure Comics #375, 12/68

Quasar - (formerly Marvel Man) Incredible Hulk #234, 4/79; (re-intro) Avengers #302, 4/89

Question - Captain Atom #83, 11/66; (1st DC app.) Crisis on Infinite Earths #6, 9/85

Quicksilver - National Comics #5, 11/40; X-Men #4, 3/64

Quislet - (Legion) Legion of Super-Heroes #14, 9/85

Quisp - Aquaman #1, 1-2/62

Rachel - (Pheonix II) X-Men #141, 1/81

Radar - Captain Marvel Adventures #35, 5/44; Master Comics #50, 5/44

Rage - Avengers #326, 11/90

Ragman - Ragman #1, 8-9/76

Rags Rabbit - Nutty Comics #5 ?/46

Rai - Magnus Robot Fighter #5, 10/91; (new) Rai #0, 11/92

Rainbow Boy - Heroic Comics #14, 9/42

Randy Robertson - Amazing Spider-Man #67 12/68

Ravage 2099 - Marvel Comics Presents #117, '92

Raven, The - Sure-Fire Comics #1, 6/40

Raven - Thunder Agents #8, 9?/66; (New Teen Titans) DC Comics Presents #26, 10/80

Rawhide Kid - Rawhide Kid #1, 3/55

Ray - Smash Comics #14, 9/40

Ray O'Light - All-New Comics #1, 1/43

Red Bee - Hit Comics #1, 7/40

Red Blazer - Pocket Comics #1, 8/41; All-New Comics #6, 1/44

Red Demon - Black Cat Comics #4, 2-3/47

Red Dragon - (1st story app.) Red Dragon Comics #6, 3/43; (text app. only) Red Dragon Comics #5, 1/43

Red Guardian - Avengers #43, 8/67; (new) Defenders #3, 5/76

Red Hawk - Blazing Comics #1, 6/44

Red Hawk - Straight Arrow #2, 4-5/50

Red Mask - Best Comics #1, 11/39

Red Raven - Red Raven Comics #1, 8/40; (1st modern app. G.A. Red Raven) X-Men #44, 5/69

Red Rocket - Captain Flight Comics #5, 11/44

Red Rube - Zip Comics #39, 8/43

Red Ryder - (1st app. in comics, strip-r) Crackajack Funnies #9, 3/39

Red Sonja - (1st full app.) Conan, the Barbarian #24, 3/73; (cameo) Conan #23, 2/73

Red Tornado - (formerly Ma Hunkle) All-American Comics #20, 11/40; (S.A.) Justice League of America #64, 8/68

Red White & Blue - All-American Comics #1, 4/39

Red Wolf - Avengers #80, 9/70; (1st solo book) Marvel Spotlight #1, 11/71

Reflecto - (Legion) Legion of Super-Heroes #277, 7/81

Rex Dexter of Mars - Mystery Men Comics #1, 8/39

Rex King - Supersnipe #6, 10/42

Rex The Wonder Dog - Rex the W. Dog #1, 1-2/52

Richie Rich - LIttle Dot #1, 9/53

Richy the Amazing Boy - Blue Ribbon Comics #1, 11/39

Rip Hunter - Showcase #20, 5-6/59

Robby Reed - (Dial "H" for Hero) House of Mystery #156, 11-12/65

Robin - (1st app. in S.A.) Justice League of America #55 ?/67; (Batman's sidekick) Detective Comics #38, 4/40; (Carrie Kelly) Batman: The Dark Knight #2, 4/86; (Jason Todd) Batman #368, 2/84; (Carrie Kelly)-The Dark Knight Returns #2, 4/86; (Timothy Drake) Batman 442 '(1st); #457 (official)-12/90

Robin Hood - (DC) Brave and the Bold #5 4-4/56

Robocop - Robocop #1, 10/87

Robotman - Star Spangled Comics #7, 4/42, (new) Showcase #94 Aug-Sept '77; (S.A.) My Greatest Adventure #80, 6/63

Rocket Girl - Hello Pal Comics #1, 1/43

Rocket Man - Hello Pal Comics #1, 1/43

Rocketeer - (cameo) Starslayer #1, 2/82; (full app.) Starslayer #2, 4/82

Rocketgirl - Scoop Comics #1, 11/41

Rocketman - Scoop Comics #1, 11/41

Rocky X of the Rocketeers - Boy Comics #80

1ST APPEARANCE (Cont'd)

Rogue - (of X-Men) Avengers Annual #10, 1981(see X-Men #158)

Roh Kar, the Man Hunter from Mars - Batman #78, 8-9/53

Rom - Rom #1, 12/79

Rond Vidar - (Universo's son, Legion) Adventure Comics #349, 10/66

Rose And The Thorn - Superman's Girlfriend Lois Lane #105, 1968

Roy Raymond - Detective Comics #153, 11/49

Roy the Super Boy - Top-Notch Comics #8, 9/40

Rudolph the Red Nosed Reindeer - Rudolph the Red Nosed Reindeer nn, 1939

Ruff and Reddy - Four Color #937, 9/58

Rulah, Jungle Goddess - Zoot #7, 6/47

Rusty & His Pals - Adventure Comics #32, 11/38

Sabre - Eclipse Graphic Album Series #1, 10/78

Sabrina the Teen-age Witch - Archie's Madhouse #22, 10/62

Sad Sack - True Comics #55,12/46

Saint, The - Silver Streak Comics #18, 2/42

Samson - Fantastic Comics #1, 12/39

Sandman - (1st published app.) New York World's Fair nn, 1939; (1st app. in S.A.) Justice League of America #46, 8/66; (1st conceived story) Adventure Comics #40, 7/39; (modern) Sandman (2nd Series) #1, 1/09

Sandy the Golden Boy - Adventure Comics #69, 12/41

Sarge Steel - Sarge Steel #1, 12/64

Sargon The Sorcerer - All American Comics #26, 5/41

Sasquatch - X-Men #120,

Satana - Vampire Tales #2 ?/73

Saturn Girl - Adventure Comics #247, 4/58

Scalphunter - Weird Western Tales #39, 3-4/77

Scarlet Avenger - Zip Comics #1, 2/40

Scarlet Witch - X Men #4, 3/64

Scorpion - Scorpion #1, 2/75

Scribbly - The Funnies #2, 11/36

Sensor Girl - (Legion) Legion of Super-Heroes #14, 9/85

Sergeant Spook - Blue Bolt #1, 6/40

Sgt. Bilko - Sgt. Bilko #1, 5-6/57

Sgt. Fury - (becomes Nick Fury of Shield) Sgt. Fury #1, 5/63

Sgt. Rock - Our Army at War #81, 4/59

Sgt. Rock by Kubert - Our Army at War #83, 6/59

Shade the Changing Man - Shade #1, 6-7/77

Shadow - (1st in comics) Shadow Comics #1, 3/40.(DC)-The Shadow #1, 10-11/73

Shadowcat - X-Men #129

Shadow Lass - (Legion) Adventure Comics #365, 2/68

Shadow, Jr. - Shadow Comics V6#9,12/46

Shadowhawk - Youngblood #2, 6/92

Shadowman - Shadowman #1, 5/92; (cameo) X-O Manowar #4, 5/92

Shang-Chi - (Master of Kung-Fu) Special Marvel Edition #15, 12/73

Shanna, the She-Devil - Shanna, the She-Devil #1, 12/72

Shakira - Warlord #32

Sharon Carter - Tales of Suspense #76 (formerly Agent 13), 1966

Shatterstar - (cameo, of X-Force) New Mutants Annual #6, 1990

Shazam (Captain Marvel) - Shazam #1, 2/73

She-Bat - Detective Comics #424, 6?/72

She-Hulk - Savage She-Hulk #1, 2/80

Sheena - Jumbo Comics #1, 9/38

Sherlock Holmes - Classic Comics #33, 1/47

Shield - Pep Comics #1, 1/40; (S.A.) Adventures of the Fly #8, 9/60

Shiera Sanders - (later becomes Hawkgirl) Flash Comics #1, 1/40

Shining Knight - Adventure Comics #66, 9/41

Shock Gibson - Speed Comics #1, 10/39

Shrinking Violet - (Legion) Action Comics #276, 5/61

Sif - Journey Into Mystery #102, 3/64

Silent Knight - Brave and the Bold #1, 8-9/55

Silly Seal - Krazy Komics #1, 7/42

Silver Fox - Blue Ribbon Comics #2, 12/39

Silver Knight - Wonder Comics #18, 6/48

Silver Sable - Amazing Spider-Man #265, 6/85

Silver Streak - Silver Streak Comics #3, 13/40

Silver Surfer - Fantastic Four #48, 3/66

Siryn - (of X-Force) Spider-Woman #37, 4/81

Skippy - Skippy's Own Book Of Comics, 1934

Skull the Slayer - Skull, the Slayer #1, 8/75

Sky Wizard - Miracle Comics #1, 2/40

Skyman - Big Shot Comics #1, 5/40; (formerly Star Spangled Kid) Infinity, Inc. #31, 10/86

Skywolf - Air Fighters Comics V1#2, 11/42

Slam Bradley - Detective Comics #1, 3/37

Sleepwalker - Sleepwalker #1, 6/91

Snapper Carr - Brave and the Bold #28, 2-3/60

Snow White & the Seven Dwarfs - Mickey Mouse Magazine V3#3, 12/37

Socko Strong - Adventure Comics #40, 7/39

Solomon Kane - (1st color app.) Marvel Premiere #33, 12/76

Son Of Satan (Daimon Hellstrom) - Ghost Rider #1, 9/73 (cameo); (full app.) Ghost Rider#2 10/73

Son of Vulcan - Mysteries of Unexplored Worlds #46, 5/65

Space Ace - Manhunt! #1, 10/47

Space Cabbie - Mystery In Space #21, 8-9/54

Space Museum - Strange Adventures #104, 5/59

Space Ranger - Showcase #15, 7-8/58

Sparkler, The - Super Spy #1, 10/40

Sparkman - Sparkler Comics #1, 7/41

Sparky - (Blue Beetle's sidekick) Blue Beetle #14, 9/42; (Red Blazer's sidekick) All-New Comics #6, 1/44

Sparky Watts - Big Shot Comics #14, 6/41

Spawn - Spawn #1, 5/92

Spectre - (1st full app. in costume) More Fun Comics #54, 4/40; (in costume splash panel) More Fun Comics #52, 2/40; (S.A.) Showcase #60, 1-2/66; (in costume in one panel ad) More Fun Comics #51, 1/40

Speed Centaur - Amazing Mystery Funnies V2#8, 8/39

Speed Saunders - Detective Comics #1, 3/37

Speed Spaulding - Famous Funnies #72, 7/40

Speedball - Amazing Spider-Man Annual #22, '88

Speedboy - (Fighting American's sidekick) Fighting American #1, 4-5/54

Speedy - (Green Arrow's sidekick) More Fun Comics #73, 11/41

Spencer Smythe - Amazing Spider-Man #25, 6/65

Spider-Man - Amazing Fantasy #15, 89/62; (cosmic) Spectacular Spider-Man #158, 12/89

Spider-Man (black costume) -Amazing Spider-Man #252, 5/84

Spider-Man 2099 - Amazing Spider-Man #365, 8/92

Spider-Woman - Marvel Spotlight #32, 2/77; (new) Marvel Super Heroes Secret Wars #7, 11/84

Spirit - Spirit nn, 6/40; (1st comic book app.) Police Comics #11, 9/42

Spooky - Casper, the Friendly Ghost #10, 6/53

Spy Smasher - Whiz Comics #1, 2/40

Stalker - Stalker #1, 6-7/75

Stanley & His Monster - Fox and the Crow #95, 12-1?/65-66

Starboy - (Legion) Adventure Comics #282, 3/61

Starfire - (Teen Titans) Teen Titans #18, 11-12/68; (new) (New Teen Titans) DC Comics Presents #26, 10/80

Starfox - Iron Man #55, 2/73

Starhawk - (1st full app.) Defenders #28, 10/75; (cameo) Defenders #27, 9/75; (re-intro) Guardians of the Galaxy #22, 3/92

Star-Lord - Marvel Preview #4, 11/75

Starman - Adventure Comics #61 4/41; (1st app. in S.A.) Justice League of America #29, 8/64; (new) First Issue Special #12, 3/76

Star Sapphire - All-Flash #32,,12-1/47-48; (formerly Ferris) Green Lantern #16, 10/62; (re-intro, 1st full app.) Green Lantern #191, 8/85; (re-intro, cameo) Green Lantern #191, 8/85

Starslayer - Starslayer #1, 2/82

Star Spangled Kid - Action Comics #40, 9/41

Stars and Stripes - Stars and Stripes Comics #4, 9/41

Star Spangled Kid - Star Spangled Comics #1, 10/41

Steel Fist - Blue Circle Comics #1, 6/44

Steel Sterling - Zip Comics #1, 2/40; (silver age) Fly Man #39, 9/66

Steel the Indestructable Man -Steel #1 3/78, (re-intro) All Star Squadron #8, 4/82

Steve Conrad Adventurer - Adventure Comics #47, 2/40

Stone Boy - Adventure C omics #306, 2/63

Storm - Giant-Size X-Men #1, Sum '75

Stormy Foster, the Great Defender - Hit Comics #18, 12/41

Straight Arrow - Straight Arrow #1, 2-3/50

Stranger - X-Men #11, 5/65

Stratosphere Jim - Crackajack Funnies #18, 12/39

Stripesy - Action Comics #40, 9/41

Strongman - Crash Comics #1, 5/40

Stuff - (Vigilante sidekick) Action Comics #45, 2/42

Stumbo the Giant - Hot Stuff, the Little Devil #2, 12/57

Stuntman - Stuntman #1, 4-5/46

WORLD'S FINEST COMICS & COLLECTIBLES

"The Right Choice"

• Dedicated to customer service since 1985 •

© DC Comics, Inc.

© DC Comics

- **Selling your comics?**
- Do you want the best price?
- Do you want fast service?
- **Then contact us!**

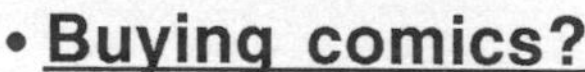

- **Buying comics?**
  - Do you want:

    Accurate grading?
    Competitive pricing?
    Great selection?
- **Then contact us!**

© DC Comics, Inc.

© DC Comics

Take a few minutes and read the next eleven pages. Find out why you should do business with us. Find out why we are fast becoming the number one mail order company in the world!

© DC Comics, Inc.

© DC Comics

Phone - (206) 274-9163

FAX - (206) 274-2270

Address:
World's Finest Comics
P.O. Box 340
Castle Rock, WA. 98611

GOLDENAGE COMIC BOOKS

WANTED

• WE ARE SEEKING QUALITY GOLDENAGE COMIC BOOKS AND WILL PAY MORE THAN ANYONE ELSE FOR WHAT WE WANT.

• DO YOU HAVE ANY OF THE BOOKS PICTURED HERE OR ANY OTHER IMPORTANT COMIC BOOKS?

• IF YOU DO, THEN GIVE US A CALL. WE WILL GIVE YOU THE BEST PRICE!

WORLD'S FINEST COMICS & COLLECTIBLES

"The Right Choice"

© DC Comics

(800) 225-4189
OR
(206) 274-9163
FAX
(206) 274-2270

© DC Comics

© DC Comics

© DC Comics

© DC Comics

SILVERAGE COMIC BOOKS

WANTED

<u>1954 through 1964</u>

• WE ARE ALSO SEEKING QUALITY SILVERAGE COMIC BOOKS AND WILL PAY MORE THAN ANYONE ELSE FOR WHAT WE WANT.

• WE ARE LOOKING FOR <u>ALL</u> OF THE BOOKS SHOWN HERE PLUS LITERALLY <u>THOUSANDS</u> OF OTHER SILVERAGE BOOKS IN HIGH GRADE.

WORLD'S FINEST COMICS & COLLECTIBLES

"The Right Choice"

© Marvel

• IMMEDIATE CASH
• HIGHEST PRICES PAID

(800) 225-4189
OR
(206) 274-9163
FAX
(206) 274-2270

© DC Comics

© Marvel

© DC Comics

© Marvel

BUYING

1920 through 1964 Wanted

Paying up to 100% of

© DC Comics, Inc.

• We are the World's largest mail order comic book dealer, specializing in comic books dated from 1920 through 1964.

Being a mail order company we are not dependent on any one local economy to support our business. Our customer base consists of the entire United States, as well as Canada,

Europe, Australia, Japan, and other countries.

Our large customer base allows us to buy at much higher prices than any other dealer.

<u>* WE PAY MORE BECAUSE WE CAN SELL MORE *</u>

© Marvel

• We offer immediate immediate payment.

How fast? For books and collections shipped to us we can send payment to you within 24 hours!

If we travel to you for large valuable collections, payment is made immediately.

• If you ship your books to us **WE** pay the cost!

Please call before you ship. This allows us to give you complete and thorough shipping instructions. You can <u>expect</u> a reply the same day we receive your package.

© Marvel Comics

• <u>You are under NO risk or obligation at any time</u>. If you do not except our offer we will return your books at our expense within 24 hours.

WORLD'S FINEST COMICS & COLLECTIBLES

"The Right Choice"

• Dedicated to customer service since 1985 •

BUYING CARTOON POSTERS

ORIGINALS ONLY

- **Highest Prices Paid**
- **Immediate Payment**
- **Free Appraisal**

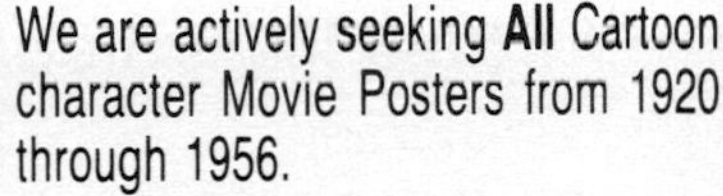

We are actively seeking **All** Cartoon character Movie Posters from 1920 through 1956.

Including:

All Disney Full Feature Cartoons & Shorts
All Fleisher Cartoons
All Super hero Cartoons & Serials
All Warner Brothers Cartoons
All MGM, Universal & Columbia Cartoons

If you have a Cartoon Poster—**We'll buy it!** Lobby Cards too!

Give us a call today at (206) 274-9163 or write:

WORLD'S FINEST COMICS & COLLECTIBLES

P.O. Box 340

Castle Rock, WA 98611

Phone: (206) 274-9163 or FAX (206) 274-2270

Have any Old Movie Posters with Real People? We buy those too

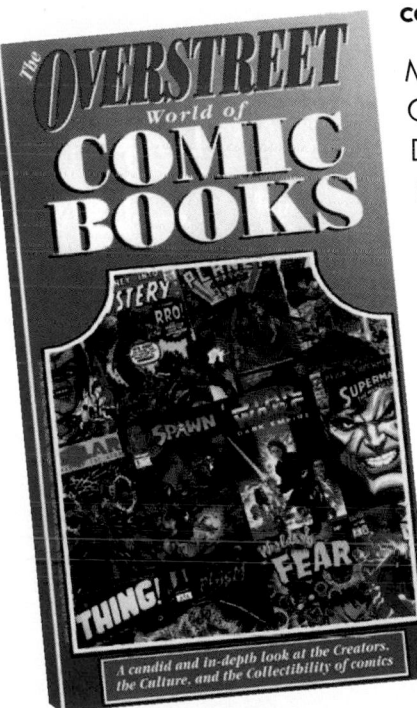

Action Comics #692, 1993, © DC

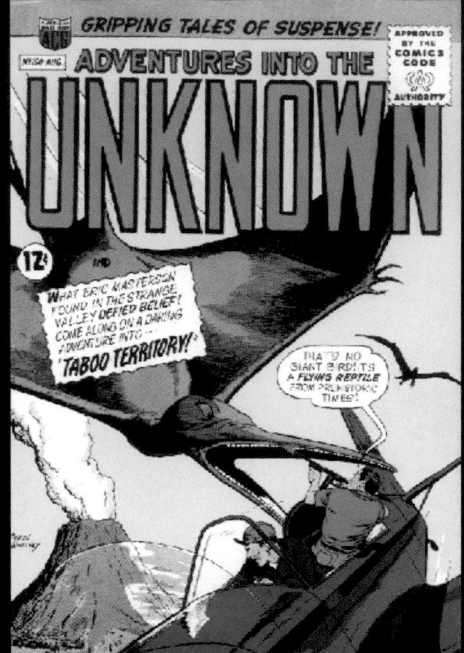

Adventures into the Unknown #150, 1964, © Best Syndicated

All American Men of War #82, 1960, © DC

Amazing Adult Fantasy #9, 1962, © MEG

Aquaman #1, 1962, © DC

Archie's Christmas Stocking #4, 1957, © Archie

Atom-Age Combat #5, 1952, © St. Paul

Batman #126, 1959, © DC

The Beverly Hillbillies #5, 1964, © Filmways

Blackhawk #71, 1953, © DC

Bone #1, 1993, © Jeff Smith

Captain Atom V2 #87, 1967, © Charlton

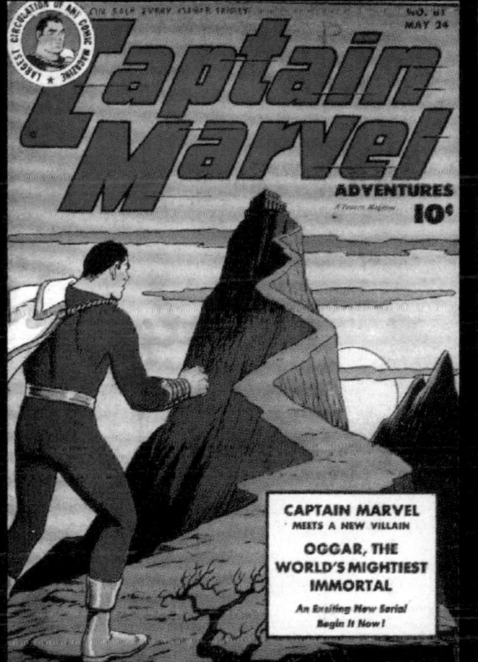

Captain Marvel #61, 1946, © Fawcett

Classic Comics #21, 1944, © Gilberton

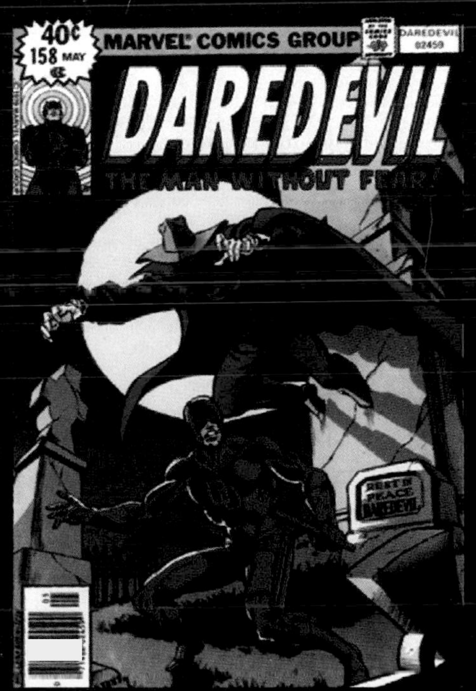

Daredevil #158, 1979, © MEG

Daring Mystery Comics #4, 1940, © MEG

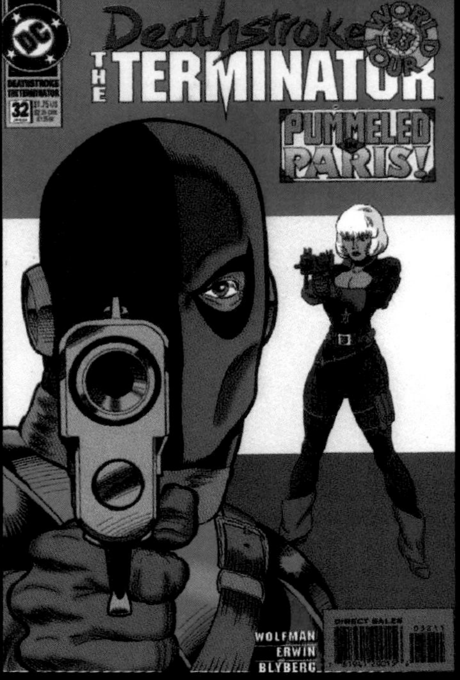

Deathstroke the Terminator #32, 1994, © DC

Detective Comics #400, 1970, © DC

Famous Funnies #14, 1935, © EAS

Fantastic Giants #24, 1966, © Charlton

Feature Comics #100, 1946, © Quality

Flash #129, 1962, © DC

Forbidden Worlds #86, © 1960, © ACG

Forever People #1, 1971, © DC

We just love
to buy and sell
comic memorabilia.

RED RYDER
RODE MATIC
Radio Decoder

"An Idea Whose Time Has Come...Again!"

The GREAT AMERICAN RING CLUB Inc. is proud to announce the rebirth of the character premium ring! We have been and will be offering to the discerning collector; LIMITED EDITION, PRECIOUS METAL, TRUE PREMIUM, and CHARACTER related rings. All of our rings are of the FINEST QUALITY available on the market today. It is our goal to not only create the most desirable collectibles available... our rings are true PREMIUMS, INVESTMENT QUALITY, SOUGHT AFTER, and PRIZED by their owners just as their ancestors of the Golden Age are today. Watch for our advertisements, or write us for further information.

SPECIAL OFFER!

FOR OVERSTREET READERS ONLY
ORDER YOUR EXCLUSIVE
SHADOW™ RING TODAY!

(NO PHOTO AVAILABLE AT TIME OF PRINTING)

The Shadow™

Send Order To: G.A.R.C. INC. P.O. Box 300546 Fern Park, FL. 32730

Yes! Please enter my order for ___ exclusive Shadow™ ring(s). I have enclosed payment of $49.95 plus $3.75 S&H and my state's sales tax for each ring ordered. I am paying my order by ☐ Check ☐ Money Order ☐ Credit Card; Bill My VISA / MC (CIRCLE ONE)

VISA/MC NUMBER ______ EXP. DATE ______

SIGNATURE ______

NAME ______ RING SIZE ______

ADDRESS ______

CITY/STATE/ZIP ______

NUMBER OF RINGS ORDERED ______

AMOUNT ENCLOSED ______

Please allow 8-12 weeks for delivery. All orders subject to acceptance. Offer expires May 31, 1995, or while supplies last.

Rings pictured are working models and prototypes. Actual rings offered may vary. Pictured are the original, vintage Lone Ranger NAVY©LRInc., Superman Gum©D.C. Comics, and Frank Buck Premium Rings. Surrounded L to R by G.I. JOE TM &© Hasbro Inc, Predator TM &©20th Century Fox, G.A.R.C. Inc., Zorro TM &©Zorro Prod., and FEMFORCE TM &©AC COMICS.

1ST APPEARANCE (Cont'd)

Stuntman Stetson - Feature Comics #140, 11/49

Sub-Mariner - (1st newsstand app.) Marvel Comics #1, 10-11/39; (1st pub lished app.) Motion Pic.Funnies Weekly #1, 1939; (silver age)-Fantastic Four #4, 5/62(new) Namor, the Sub-Mariner #26, 5/92

Sub-Zero Man - Blue Bolt #1, 6/40

SunBoy - (Legion) Action Comics #276, 5/61

Sunfire - (X-Men) X-Men #64, 1/70

Super American - Fight Comics #15, 10/41

Superbaby - Superboy #8, 5-6/50

Superboy - More Fun Comics #101, 1-2/45

Super Cat - Animal Crackers #1, 1946

Super Duck - Jolly Jingles #10, Sum '43; (re-intro) Laugh #24 ?/90

Supergirl - Action Comics #252, 5/59; (re-intro) Action Comics #674, 2/92; (tryout only) Superboy #5, 11-12/49

Super Goof - Phantom Blot #2 ?/65

Super Mouse - Coo Coo Comics #1, 10/42

Super Patriot - Nick Fury Agent of Shield #13, 6?/69; (new) Captain America #323, 11/86

Super Rabbit - Comedy Comics #14, 3/43

Super Richie - Richie Rich Millions #68, 11/4

Superichie - Superichie #5, 10/76

Superkatt - Giggle #9, 6/44

Superman - Action Comics #1, 6/38

Superman, Jr. - World's Finest Comics #215, 10/72

Supersnipe - Shadow Comics V2#3, 3/42

Superwoman - DC Comics Presents Annual #2, 7/83

Supreme - Youngblood #3, 10/92

Swamp Thing - House of Secrets #92, 6-7/71

Swift Deer - (J. Thunder's sidekick) All-American Western #113, 4-5/50

Sword - Captain Courageous Comics #6, 3/42; Super-Mystery Comics V3#3, 1/43

T-Man - Police Comics #103, 12/50

Tailspin Tommy - Tailspin Tommy Story & Picture Book #266, 1931; (1st in comic book format) Funnies #1, 10/36

Tank Killer - G. I. Combat #67, 12?/58

Tarantula - All-Star Comics #1, 10/41

Target - Target Comics V1#10, 11/40

Targitt - (in costume) Targit #2, 6/75; (no costume) Targitt #1, 3/75

Tarzan - Tarzan Book #1, 1929; (1st comic book app.) Tip Top Comics #1, 4/36

Teenage Mutant Ninja Turtles - Teenage Mutant Ninja Turatles #1, 1984

Tellus - (Legion) Legion of Super-Heroes #14, 9/85

Terminator - Rust #12, 8/88

Terra - (New Teen Titan) New Teen Titans #26, 12/82

Terra-Man - Superman #249, 12/71

Terry & The Pirates - Popular Comics #1, 2/36

Tessie the Typist - Joker Comics #2, 6/42

Tex Thompson - (becomes Mr. America) Action Comics #1, 6/38

Thing - (Ben Grimm) Fantastic Four #1, 11/61

Thongor - Creatures On The Loose #22, 1973

Thor - (Beta Ray Bill) Thor #337, 11/83; (Dargo) Thor #384, 10/87; (Donald Blake) Journey Into Mystery #83, 8/62; (Eric Masterson) Thor #433, 6/91

Thorndike (becomes Hourman's aide) Adventure Comics #74, 5/42

Three Lt. Marvels -Whiz #21, 9/41 (re-intro) Shazam! #30, 7-8/77

Three-D Man - Marvel Premiere #35, 4/77

Thunderbird - Giant-Size X-Men #1, Sum '75

Thunderbolt - Power Man #41, 10/76; (1st DC app.) Crisis on Infinite Earths #6, 9/85; (Jonni Thunder) Jonni Thunder #1, 2/85; (Peter Cannon) Thunderbolt #1, 1/66

Thunderbunny - Charlton Bullseye #6 12?/81

Thunderstrike - (Eric Masterson) Thor #459, 2/93

Tick - Tick #1, 6/88

Tiger Girl - Fight Comics #32, 6/44

Tigra - Startling Comics #45, 5/47

Tigra - (formerly The Cat) Giant-Size Creatures #1, 5/75

Tim - (Black Terror's sidekick) Exciting Comics #9, 5/41

Timber Wolf - (Legion) Adventure Comics #327, 12/64

Timothy Drake - Batman #436, 8/89; (1st in Robin costume) Batman #442, 1990

Timothy the Ghost - Zoo Funnies #1, 7/53

TNT & Dan the Dyna-Mite - World's Finest Comics #5, Spr '42

Todd Hunter - Adventure Comics #32, 11/38

Tom & Jerry - Our Gang Comics #1, 9-10/42

Tom Brent - Adventure Comics #32, 11/38

Tom Mix -The Comics #1, 3/37

Tomahawk - Star Spangled Comics #69, 6/47

Tommy the Amazing Kid - Amazing-Man Comics #23, 8/41

Tommy Tomorrow - Real Fact Comics #6, 1-2/47

Tony Trent - (The Face) Big Shot Comics #1, 5/40

Tor - One Million Years Ago #1, 9/53

Torchy - Doll Man Quarterly #8, Spr '46

Toro - (Human Torch's sidekick) Human Torch #2(#1), Fall '40; (modern) Sub-Mariner #14, 6/69

Torpedo - (new) Daredevil #126, 9/75

Tragg - Mystery Comics Digest #3 ?/72

Trail Colt - Manhunt! #8, 5/48

Triplicate Girl - (Legion) Action Comics #276, 5/61

Tubby - King Comics #46, 2/40; Marge's Little Lulu Four Color #74, ? '45

Tuk the Cave Boy - Captain America Comics #1, 3/41

Turbo - New Warriors #28, 10/92

Turok - Turok Four Color #596, 12/54; (re-intro in Valiant Universe) Magnus Robot Fighter #12, 5/92

Two Gun Kid - Two Gun Kid #1, 3/48

Ty-Gor, Son of the Tiger - Blue Ribbon Comics #4, 6/40

Tygra - Startling Comics #45, 5/47

Tyroc - (Legion) Superboy #216

U.S. Agent - Captain America #354, 6/89

Ultra Boy - (Legion) Superboy #98, 7/62

Ultra Man - (Gary Concord) All-American Comics #8, 11/9

Uncle Ben - Amazing Fantasy #15, 8-9/62

Uncle Marvel - Captain Marvel Adv. #43, 2/45, Wow Comics #18, 10/43

Uncle Sam - National Comics #1, 7/40

Uncle Scrooge - Donald Duck 4-Color #178, 12/47

Underdog - Underdog #1, 7/70

Union Jack I - Invaders #7, 7/76

Union Jack II - Invaders #20, 9/77

Union Jack III - Captain America #254, 2/81

Unknown Soldier - Star Spangled War Stories #151, 6-7/70

Untouchables - Four Color 1237, 10-12/61

Usagi Yojimbo - Albedo #1, 4/85

U.S. Jones - Wonderworld #28, 8/41

Val - Strange Tales #159, 8/67

V-Man - Big-3 #7, 1/42; V...-Comics #1, 1/42

Valkyrie - Air Fighters Comics V2#2,11/43

Vampirella - Vampirella #1, 9/69

Vanessa - (Kingpin's wife) Amazing Spider-Man #83, 4/70

Vanguard - New Teen Titans Annual #1, 1985; Iron Man #109, 4/78; Megaton #1, 11/83

Vault Keeper - War Against Crime #10, 12-1/49-50

Veiled Avenger - Spotlight Comics #1, 11/44

Venus - Venus #1, 8/48

Veronica Lodge - Pep Comics #26, 4/42

Vicki Vale - Batman #45, 2-3/48

Victoria Bentley - Strange Tales #114, 11/63

Victory Boys - USA Comics #5, Sum '42

Vigilante - Action Comics #42, 11/41; (female) (1st full app.) Deathstroke: the Terminator #10, 5/92; (female) (cameo) Deathstroke: the Terminator #9, 4/92; (modern, in costume) New Teen Titans Annual #2, 1985; (modern not in costume) New Teen Titans #23, 9/82; (S.A.) Justice League of America #78, 5?/70

Viking Prince - Brave and the Bold #1, 8-9/55

Vindicator - (formerly Weapon Alpha) (becomes Guardian) X-Men #120, 4/79

Vision - (G.A.) Marvel Mystery Comics #13, 11/40; (S.A.) Avengers #57, 10/68

Vixen - Action Comics #521, 7/81

Voice, The - Popular Comics #51, 5/40

Voltage, Man of Lightning - Fat & Slat #1, Sum '47

Vulcan - Super-Mystery Comics V1#1, 7/40

Wagon Train - Four Color #895, 3/58

Wambi, Jungle Boy - Jungle Comics #1, 1/40

Warlock - (Him) (cameo) Fantastic Four #67, 10/67 (Him) (full app.) Thor #165, 6/69; New Mutants #18, 8/84; (re-intro) Silver Surfer #46, 2/91

Warlord - First Issue Special #8, 11/75

Warpath - (with costume) X-Men #193, 5/85; (without costume) New Mutants #16, 6/84

Wash Tubbs - Famous Comics Cartoon Books #1202, 1934

Wasp, The - Speed Comics #12, 3/41

Wasp - Tales to Astonish #44, 6/63

Wasplet - (Hooded Wasp's sidekick) Shadow Comics #7, 11/40

Watcher - Fantastic Four #13, 4/63

Waverider - Armageddon 2001 #1, 5/91

Weapon Alpha - (becomes Vindicator) X-Men #109, 2/78

Web - Zip Comics #27, 7/42; (S.A.) Fly Man #36, 3/66

Wendigo - Incredible Hulk #162, 4/73

Wendy the Good Little Witch - Casper, the Friendly Ghost #20, ?/54

HIGH QUALITY COMICS
Presents:
• OVER 200,000 COMICS FOR COLLECTORS
• THOUSANDS OF HOT SILVER AGE COMICS IN HIGH TO MEDIUM GRADES
• A HUGE INVENTORY OF RECENT ('75-'90) COMICS
• BUYING - SELLING - TRADING ! !
• SEND $ 1.00 FOR OUR GIANT CATALOG
• SEND YOUR WANT LIST W/S.A.S.E. FOR REPLIES
• BUYING COLLECTIONS - LARGE & SMALL OLD & NEW
PAYING TOP PRICES ! ! ! !
WRITE OR CALL:
(619) 723-7269
HIGH QUALITY COMICS
1106 2nd St.
SUITE 110
ENCINITAS, CA
92024

1ST APPEARANCE (Cont'd)

Werewolf - Werewolf #1, 12/66
Werewolf by Night - Marvel Spotlight #2, 1?/72
Whirlybats - Detective Comics #257, 7/58
White Rider & Super Horse - Blue Bolt #1, 6/40
White Streak - Target Comics V1#1, 2/40
White Tiger - Deadly Hands of Kung-Fu #19, 1?/76
White Witch - (Legion) Adventure Comics #351, 12/66
Whizzer, The - USA Comics #1, 8/41 (modern) Giant-Size Avengers #1, 8/74
Whizzer McGee - (Phantasmo's sidekick) Funnies #45, 7/40
Wiggles the Wonderworm - Taffy Comics #1, 3/45
Wilbur - Zip Comics #18, 9/41
Wild Bill Elliott - Four Color #278, 5/50
Wildcat - Sensation Comics #1, 1/42; (S.A.) Brave and the Bold #62, 10-11/65
Wildfire - (formerly Erg) Superboy #201, '74
Will O' the Wisp - Amazing Spider-Man #167, 4/77
Willie - Gay Comics #1, 3/44
Winky, Blinky & Noddy - All-Flash #5, Sum '42
Witch Hazel - Marge's Little Lulu #39, 9/51
Witness - Mystic Comics #7, 12/40
Wizard - Top-Notch Comics #1, 12/39; (S.A.) Fly Man #33, 9/65
Wizard - Strange Tales #102, 11/62
Wolverine - (1st full app.) Incre. Hulk #181, 11/74; (cameo) Incredible Hulk #180, 10/74
Wonder Boy - Blue Bolt #1, 6/40; National Comics #1, 7/40
Wonder Boy - Bomber Comics #1, 3/44
Wonder Duck - Wonder Duck #1, 9/49
Wonder Girl - Wonder Woman #107, 7/61; (new) (Teen Titan) Brave and the Bold #60, 6-7/65
Wonder Man - Startling Comics #1, 6/40
Wonderman - Wonder Comics #9, 1945
Wonder Man - Avengers #9, 10/64; Wonder Comics #1, 5/39; (re-intro) Avengers #151, 9/76
Wonder Tot - Wonder Woman #122
Wonder Woman - All Star Comics #8, 12-1/41-42; (Orana) Wonder Woman #250, 12/78
Wonder Woman Family - Wonder Woman #124, 12/62
Wonderman - (Brad Spencer) Mystery Comics #1, 1944
Wong - Strange Tales #110, 7/63
Woodgod - Marvel Premiere #31, 8/76
Woody Woodpecker - Funnies #64, 5/42
Woozy Winks - Police Comics #13, 11/42
X-O Manowar - X-O Manowar #1, 2/92
X-Terminators - X-Terminators #1, 10/88
Yank and Doodle - Prize Comics #13, 8/41
Yankee Doodle Jones - Yankee Comics #1, 9/41
Yarko the Great, Master Magician - Wonder Comics #2, 6/39
Yellow Claw - Yellow Claw #1, 10/56
Yellowjacket - Yellowjacket #1, 9/44
Yellowjacket - Avengers #59, 12/68; (formerly Goliath) Avengers #63, 4/69
Zanzibar - Mystery Men Comics #1, 8/39
Zardi, the Eternal Man - Amazing-Man Comics #11, 4/40
Zatanna - Hawkman #4, 10-11/64
Zatara - Action Comics #1, 6/38
Zebra - All-New Comics #7, 3/44; Pocket Comics #1, 8/41
Zegra, Jungle Empress - Zegra #2, 10/48
Ziggy Pig - Krazy Komics #1, 7/42
Zombie - Menace #5, 7/53
Zorro - Zorro Four Color #228, 5/49
Yogi Bear - Four Color #1067, 12-2/59-60
Yosemite Sam - Yosemite Sam #1, 12/70

1ST APPEARANCE: VILLAIN

Abomination - Tales to Astonish #90, 4/67
Abra Kadabra - Flash #128, 2?/62
Absorbing Man - Journey Into Mystery #114, 3/65
Amazo The Android - Brave & The Bold #30, 6-7/60
Angle Man - Wonder Woman #70, 11/54
Annihilus - Fantastic Four Annual #6, 11/68
Apocalypse - (cameo) X-Factor #5, 6/86; (full app.) X-Factor #6, 7/86
Arcade - Marvel Team-Up #66, 2/78
Atomic Skull - Superman #323, 5/78
Attuma - Fantastic Four #33, 12/64
Bane - Batman: Vengeance of Bane Special #1, '92
Banshee - X-Men #28, 1/67
Baron Blood - Invaders #7, 7/76
Baron Mordo - Strange Tales #111, 8/63
Baron Strucker - Sgt. Fury #5, 1963
Baron Zemo - Captain America #276
Batmite - Detective #267, 5/59
Batroc - Tales of Suspense #76, 4/66
Beetle - Strange Tales #123, 8/64
Bengal - Daredevil #258, 9/88
Beyonder - Marvel Two-In-One #63, 1986
Big Man - Amazing Spider-Man #10, 3/64
Bizarro - Superboy #68, 10-11/56
Bizarro Batman - World's Finest Comics #156
Bizarro Flash - Superman's Girlfriend Lois Lane #74, 5/67
Bizarro Krypto - Superboy #82, ?/60
Bizarro Lana Lang - Adventure Comics #292, 1/62
Bizarro Lucy Lane -Adventure Comics #292, 1/62
Bizarro Lex Luthor - Adventure Comics #293, 2/62
Bizarro Lois Lane - Action Comics #255, 8/59
Bizarro Mxyzptlk - Adventure Comics #286, 7/61
Bizarro Supergirl - Superman #140, 10/60
Bizarro Titano - Adventure Comics #295, 4/62
Black Cat - Amazing Spider-Man #194, 7/79
Black Mask - Batman #386, 8/85
Blackout - Ghost Rider #2, 6/90
Black Racer - New Gods #3, 6-7/71
Black Spider - Detective Comics #463
Blastarr - Fantastic Four #62, 5/67
Blizzard - Iron Man #86, ?/76?
Blob - X-Men #3, 1/64
Blockbuster - Detective Comics #345, 11/65
Boomerang - Tales to Astonish #81, 7/66
Brain Storm - Justice League/America #32, 12/64
Brain Wave - All Star Comics #15, 2-3/43
Brainiac - Action Comics #242, 7/58; (modern)-Advs. of Superman #438, 2/88
Brainwasher - (Kingpin) Amazing Spider-Man #59, 4/68
Brother Blood - New Teen Titans #21, 7/82
Brother Voodoo - Strange Tales #169, 9/73
Bullet - Daredevil #250, 12/88
Bullseye - Nick Fury Agent of Shield #15, 11/69
Calypso - Amazing Spider-Man #209, 10/80
Captain Boomerang - Flash #117, 12/60
Captain Cold - Showcase #8, 5-6/57
Captain Fear - Adventure Comics #425, 12-1/72-73
Captain Nazi - Master Comics #21, 12/41
Cardinal - New Warriors #28, 10/92
Carnage - (1st full app.) Amazing Spider-Man #361, 4/92; (cameo) Amazing Spider-Man #360, 3/92
Carrion - Spect. Spider-Man #25, 12/78
Cat-Man - Detective Comics #311, 1/63
Catwoman - (1st in costume) Batman #3, Fall '40; (1st time called Catwoman) Batman #2, Sum '40; (modern, Selina Kyle) Batman #404, 2/87;(new costume w/o cat-head mask) Batman #35, 5-6/46; (new) Detective Comics #624, 12/90 (S.A.) Superman's Girlfriend Lois Lane #70, 11/66; (The Cat) Batman #1, Spr '40
Cavalier - Detective Comics #81, 11/43
Chameleon - Amazing Spider-Man #1, 3/63
Changeling - X-Men #35, 8/67
Cheetah - Wonder Woman #6, Fall '43; (new) (cameo) Wonder Woman #274, 12/80; (new) (full app.) Wonder Woman #275, 1/81
Chronos - Atom #3, 10-11/62
Chunk - Flash #9, 2/88
Claw - Silver Streak Comics #1, 12/39
Clayface I - (Basil Karlo) Detective Comics #40, 6/ 40
Clayface II - (Matt Hagen) Detective Comics #298, 12/61
Clayface III - (Preston Payne) Detective Comics #478, 7-8/78
Clock King - World's Finest Comics #111, 8/60
Clown - Flash #270, 2/79
Cobra (see Human Cobra)
Colonel Computron - Flash #304, 12/81
Composite Superman - World's Finest #142
Computo - Adventure Comics #340, 1/66
Constrictor - Incredible Hulk #212, 6/77
Copperhead - Daredevil #124, 6?/75
Crime Master - Amazing Spider-Man #26,

1ST APPEARANCE VILLAIN (Cont'd)
7/65

Crimson Dynamo - (Anton Vanko) Tales of Suspense #46, 10/63

Crimson Dynamo II - (Boris Turgenov) Tales of Suspense #52, 4/64

Crimson Dynamo III - (Alex Nevsky) Iron Man #21, 3/78

Crimson Dynamo IV - (Yuri Petrovich) Champions #8, 10/76

Crimson Dynamo V - (Dimitri Bukharin) Iron Man #109, 4/78

Cyclone - Amazing Spider-Man #143, 4/75

Dark Phoenix - X-Men #134

Darkseid - (1st full app.) Forever People #1, 2-3/71; (cameo) Superman's Pal Jimmy Olsen #134, 12/70

Deadshot - Batman #59, 6-7/50; (1st mod ern app.) Detective Comics #474, 11-12/77

Death's Head - Daredevil #56, 9/69

Deathstalker - (formerly Death's Head) Daredevil #114, 7?/74

Demogoblin - Web of Spider-Man #86, 3/92

Despero - Justice League of America #1, 10-11/60

Destroyer - Journey Into Mystery #118, 7/65

Diablo - Fantastic Four #30, 9/64

Doctor Destiny - Justice League of America #5, 6-7/61

Doctor Doom - Fantastic Four #5, 6/62

Doctor Light I - Justice League of America#12, 6/62

Doctor Light II - Crisis on Infinite Earths #4, 6/85

Doctor Octopus - Amazing Spider-Man #3, 6/63

Doctor Polaris - Green Lantern #21, 6/63

Doctor Regulus - Adventure Comics #348, 9/66

Doom 2099 - Marvel Comics Presents #118, '92

Doomsday - (cameo) Superman: The Man of Steel #17, 11/92; (full app.) Superman: The Man of Steel #18, 12/'92

Dormammu - Strange Tales #126, 11/64

Dr. Death - (modern) Batman #345, 3/82

Dr. Doom - Fantastic Four #5, 6/62

Dr. Double X - Detective Comics #261,11/58

Dr Light - Justice League of America #12, '62

Dr. Octopus - Amazing Spider-Man #3, 5/63

Dr. Phosphorous - Detective Comics #469,

Dr. Psycho - Wonder Woman #5, 6-7/43

Dr. Spectro - Captain Atom #78, 12/65; (new) Captain Atom #6, 8/87; (1st DC app.) Crisis on Infinite Earths #9, 12/85

Dragon Man - Fantastic Four #35 ,2/65

Drax the Destroyer - (re-intro) (cameo) Silver Surfer #35, 3/90; (re-intro) (full app.) Silver Surfer #37, 5/90

Dreadknight - Iron Man #101, 8/77

Dragon Man - Fantastic Four #35, 2/65

Dummy - (Vigilante villain) Leading Comics #1, Win '41-42

Electro - Amazing Spider-Man #9, 2/64

Enchantress - Journey Into Mystery #103, 4/64

Enchantress - Strange Adventures #187

Enforcer - Ghost Rider #22, ?/77

Evil Star - Green Lantern #37, 7/65

Exterminator - (becomes Death-Stalker) Daredevil #39, 4/68

Fatal Five - Adventure Comics #352, 1/67

Fatman - Batman #113, 2/58

Felix Faust - Justice League of America #10, 3/62

Fiddler - All-Flash #32, 12-1/47-48

Fin Fang Foom - Strange Tales #89, 10/61

Firelord - Thor #225

Foolkiller - (1st) Man-Thing #3, 3/74

Foolkiller II - (Greg Salinger) (cameo) Omega the Unknown #8, 5/77; (Greg Salinger) (full app.) Omega the Unknown #9, 7/77

Galactus - Fantastic Four #48, 3/66

Gambler - Green Lantern #12, Sum '44

Gamora - Strange Tales #180, 6/75; (re-intro) Silver Surfer #46, 2/91

Gentleman Ghost - (modern) Batman #310, 4/79

Gibbon - Amazing Spider-Man #110, 7/72

Gladiator - Daredevil #18, 7/66

Golden Glider - Flash #250 ,6/77

Gorgon - Fantastic Four #44,11/65

Gorilla Grodd, the Super G'orilla - Flash #106, 4-5/'59

Green Goblin I - (Norman Osborn) Amazing Spider-Man #14, 7/64

Green Goblin II - (Harry Osborn) Amazing Spider-Man #136, 9/74

Grey Gargoyle - Journey Into Mystery #107, 8/64

Grim Reaper - Avengers #52, 5/68

Grizzly - Amazing Spider-Man #139, 12/74

Hammerhead - Amazing Spider-Man #113, 10/72

Harlequin - All-American Comics #89, 9/47

Hate Monger - Fantastic Four #21, 12/63

Havok - X-Men #56 (not in costume); 58(in costume)

Heat Wave - Flash #140, 6/63

Hector Hammond - Green Lantern #5, 3-4/61

Hela - Journey Into Mystery #102, 3/64

High Evolutionary - Thor #134, 11/66

Hobgoblin - (new) (Macendale) Spectacular Spider-Man #147, 2/89

Hobgoblin I - (Ned Leeds) Amazing Spider-Man #238, 3/83

Hobgoblin II - (Macendale/Jack O'Lantern) Amazing Spider-Man #289, 6/87

Hugo Strange - (1st modern app.) Detective Comics #470, 3-4/77

Human Cobra - Journey Into Mystery #98, 11/63

Human Top - (Whirlwind) Tales to Astonish #50, 12/63

Humbug - Web of Spider-Man #19, 10/86

Hydro Man - Amazing Spider-Man #212, 12/81

Hyena - Firestorm #4, 8-9/78

Icicle - All-American Comics #90,10/47

Insect Queen (Lana Lang) - Superboy #124, 10/65

Iron Jaw - Boy Comics #3, 4/42

Jack O'Lantern - (Macendale) Machine Man #19, 2/81 (new) Captain America #396, 1/92

Jackal - Amazing Spider-Man #129, 2/74

Jester - Daredevil #42 ,7/68

Jigsaw - Amazing Spider-Man #188, 1/79

Joker - Batman #1, Spr '40

Joker's Daughter - Batman Family #6, 7-8/76

Juggernaut - X-Men #12, 7/65

Kang - Avengers #8, 9/64

Kanjar Ro - Justice League of America #3, 2-3/61

Key, The - Justice League of America #41, 12/65

Killer Croc - Batman #357, 3/83

Killer Shark - Blackhawk #50, 3/52

Kingpin - Amazing Spider-Man #50, 7/67

Klaw - Fantastic Four #53, 8/66

Kraven the Hunter - Amazing Spider-Man #15, 8/64

Kurgo - Fantastic Four #7, 10/62

Leader - Tales to Astonish #62, 12/64

Legion of Super Villains - Superman #147, 8/61

Lex Luthor - (bald) Superman #10, 5-6/41; (new) Man of Steel #4, 12/86; (red hair) Action Comics #23, 5/40; (silver age)-Adventure comics #271, 4/60

Lightmaster - Spectacular Spider-Man #3, 2/77

Living Monolith - X-Men #56

Lizard - Amazing Spider-Man #6, 11/63

Loki - Journey Into Mystery #85, 10/62

Looter - Amazing Spider-Man #36, 5/66

Lord Shilling - (Tomahawk foe) Tomahawk #28, 11/54

Lunatik - (1st full app.) Defenders #56, 2/78; (cameo) Defenders #53, 11/77

Mad Hatter - Batman #49, 10-11/48; Detective Comics #230, 4/56

Mad Thinker - Fantastic Four #15, 6/63

Madame Medusa - Fantastic Four #36, 3/65

Maelstrom - Marvel Two-In-One #71, 1/81

Magneto - X-Men #1, 9/63

Magpie - (new) Man of Steel #3, 11/86

Magus - Strange Tales #178, 2/75; (re-intro) Warlock and the Infinity Watch #7, 8/92

Malevolence - (Mephisto's daughter) Guardians of the Galaxy #7, 12/90

Man-Ape - Avengers #62

Man-Bat - Detective Comics #400, 6/70

Man-Wolf - Amazing Spider-Man #124, 9/73

Mandarin - Tales of Suspense #50, 2/64

Manhunters - 1st Issue Special #5, 8/75

Mephisto - Silver Surfer #3, 12/68

Metallo (Jor-El's robot) - (new) Superman #310, 4/77; (new) Superman #1, 1/87; (re-intro) Action Comics #252, 5/59; (re-intro, 3rd app.) Adventure Comics #276, 9/60; Superboy #49, 6/56 (1st app.)

Microwave Man - Action Comics #487, 9/78

Mime - Batman #412, 10/87

Mimic - X-Men #19, 4/66

Mirror Master - Flash #105, 2-3/59

Mist - Adventure Comics #67, 10/41

Mister Element - Showcase #13, 3-4/58

Mister Sinister - X-Men #221

Modok - Tales of Suspense #94, 10/67

Modred the Mystic - (re-intro) Darkhold #3, 12/92

Mole Man- Fantastic Four #1, 11/61

Molecule Man - Fantastic Four #20, 11/63

Molten Man - Amazing Spider-Man #28, 9/65

Morbius the Living Vampire - Amazing Spider-Man #101, 10/71

Mordru - Adventure Comics #369, 6/68

Mortan - (Adam Strange foe) Mystery In Space #62

Mr. Atom - Captain Marvel Adventures #78, 11/47

Mr. Baffle - Detective Comics #63, 5/42

Mr. Hyde - Journey Into Mystery #99,12/63

Mr. Mind - Captain Marvel Adventures #22,

1ST APPEARANCE VILLAIN (Cont'd)

3/43; (re-intro) Shazam! #2, 4/73
Mr. Mxyzptlk - Superman #131, 8/59; (new) Superman #11, 11/87; Superman #30, 10/44
Mr. Tawny - Captain Marvel Adventures #79, 12/47
Multi-Man - Challengers of the Unknown #14, 12-1/59-60
Mysterio - Amazing Spider-Man #13, 6/64
Nightmare - Strange Tales #110, 7/63
Nightshade - Captain America #164, 8/73
Nitro - Captain Marvel #34, 9/74
Ocean Master - Aquaman #29
Outsider - Detective Comics #334, 12/64
Owl - Daredevil #3, 8/64
Paladin - Daredevil #150, 2/78
Parasite - Action Comics #340, 9/66; Fury of Fire-storm #58, 1987
Penguin - Detective Comics #58, 12/41; (S.A.) Batman #155, 4/63
Pied Piper - Flash #106, 4-5/59
Pieface - Green Lantern #2, 9-10/60
Plant-Master - Atom #1, 6-7/62
Plunderer - Daredevil #12, 1/66
Poison Ivy - Batman #181, ?/66
Porcupine - Tales To Astonish #48, 10/63
Prankster - Action Comics #51, 8/42
Princess Python - Amazing Spider-Man #22, 3/65
Professor Amos Fortune - Justice League of America #6, 8-9/61
Professor Zoom - Flash #139 ?/63
Prowler - Amazing Spider-Man #78, 11/69
Psycho Pirate - All Star Comics #23, Win '44-45
Psycho-Man - Fantastic Four Annual #5, 11/67
Puma - Amazing Spider-Man #256, 9/84
Punisher - Amazing Spider-Man #129, 2/74
Puppet Master - Batman #3, Fall '40; Fantastic Four #8, 11/62
Rainbow Raider - Flash #286, 6/80
Rama-Tut - Fantastic Four #19, 10/63
Rampage - Superman #7, 7/87
Rancor - (1st full app.) Guardians of the Galaxy #9, 2/91; (cameo) (descendant of Wolverine) Guardians of the Galaxy #8, 1/91
Ras Al Ghul - Batman #232, 7/71
Reaper - Batman #237, 12/71
Red Ghost - Fantastic Four #13, 4/63
Red Skull - Captain America Comics #1, 3/41; (S.A.) Tales of Suspense #65, 5/65
Rhino - Amazing Spider-Man #41, 10/66
Riddler - Detective Comics #140, 10/48; (S.A.) Batman #171, 5/65
Ringmaster - Incredible Hulk #3, 9/62
Rose - Amazing Spider-Man #253, 6/84
Rose and the Thorn - Flash Comics #89, 11/47; (new) Superman's Girlfriend Lois Lane #105
Saber-Tooth - Flash #291, 11/80
Sabretooth - Iron Fist #14, 8/77
Sandman - Amazing Spider-Man #4, 9/63
Sandstorm - Web of Spider-Man #107, 12/93
Sargon - (re-intro) Flash #186, 8?/69
Sargon the Sorcerer - (1st story app.) All-American Comics #26, 5/41; (text only) All-American Comics #24, 3/41
Sauron - X-Men #60
Scarecrow - Tales of Suspense #51, 3/64; World's Finest Comics #3, Fall '41; Dead of Night #11, 8/75; (S.A.) Batman #189 ? '67?
Schemer - Amazing Spider-Man #83, 4/70
Scorpion - Amazing Spider-Man #20, 1/65
Serpent Crown - Sub-Mariner #9, 1/69
Sha-Shan - Amazing Spider-Man #108, 5/72
Shade - (modern) Flash #298, 6/81
Shadow Thief - Brave and the Bold #36, 6-7/61
Shaper - Incredible Hulk #155, 9/72
Shark - Amazing-Man Comics #6, 10/39; Green Lantern #24, 10/63
Shocker - Amazing Spider-Man #46, 3/67
Shotgun - Daredevil #272, 9?/89
Shroud - Super-Villain Team-Up #5, 4/76
Signalman - Batman #112, 12/57; (S.A.) Detective Comics #466
Silvermane - Amazing Spider-Man #73, 6/69
Silver Samurai - Daredevil #111, 6/74
Sinestro - Green Lantern #7, 7-8/61
Sivana - Whiz Comics #1, 2/40
Sivana, Jr. - Captain Marvel Adventures #52, 1/46
Sky Pirate - Green Lantern #27, 8-9/47
Solarr - Captain America #160, 4/73
Solo - Web of Spider-Man #19, 10/86
Solomon Grundy - All-American Comics #61, 11/44, (S.A.) Showcase #55, 3-4/65
Sonar - Green Lantern #14, 7/62
Sorcerer - Alpha Flight #71, 5/89
Speed McGee - Flash #5, 10/87
Spirit of Vengeance - (futuristic Ghost Rider) Guardians of the Galaxy #13, 6/91
Spyder - New Mutants #68, 10/88
Star Thief - Warlock #14, 10/76
Stilt-Man - Daredevil #8, 6/65
Sting Ray - Sub-Mariner #19, 11/69
Stranger - X-Men #11, 5/65
Sub-Mariner - (S.A) Fantastic Four #4, 5/62
Sunburst - New Adventures of Superboy #45, 9/83
Super Skrull - Fantastic Four #18, 9/63
Supremo - Superboy #132, ?/66
Swordsman - Avengers #19, 8/65
Tantrum - Night Thrasher: Four Control #2, 11/92
Tarantula - Amazing Spider-Man #134, 7/74
Taskmaster - Avengers #119, 1/80
Tattooed Man - Green Lantern #23, 9?/63
Terra-Man - Superman #249, 4/72
Terrax - Fantastic Four #211, 10/79
Terrible Tinkerer - Amazing Spider-Man #2, 5/63
Thanos - Iron Man #55, 2/73; (re-intro) (cameo) Silver Surfer #34, 2/90; (re-intro) (full app.) Silver Surfer #35, 3/90
Thinker - All-Flash #12, Fall '43
Thundra - Fantastic Four #129, 12/72
Tiger Shark - (new) Namor, the Sub-Mariner #35 2/93; (S.A.) Sub-Mariner #5, 9/68
Time Trapper - Adventure Comics #321, 6/64
Titanium Man - Tales of Suspense #69, 9/65
Titano - Superman #127, 2/59
Toad - X-Men #4, 3/64
Tombstone - Web of Spider-Man #36, 3/88; (full app.) Spectacular Spider-Man #138, 5/88
Top - Flash #122, 6-7?/61
Torpedo - Daredevil #126, 8?/75
Toyman - Action Comics #64, 9/43; (new) Superman #13, 1/88; (S.A.) Action Comics #432, 2/74
Trapster - Strange Tales #104, 1/63
Trauma - Incredible Hulk #394, 6/92
Trickster - Flash #113, 6-7/60
Turtle - Showcase #4, 9-10/56
Tweedledum & Tweedledee - Detective Comics #74, 4/43
Two-Face - Detective Comics #66, 8/42; (S.A) Batman #234, 9/71
Typhoid Mary - Daredevil #254, 5/88
Ulik - Thor #137
Ultron - Avengers #54
Ulthoon - (Adam Strange foe) Mystery In Space #61
Umar - Strange Tales #150, 11/66
Unicorn - Tales of Suspense #56, 8/64
Universo - Adventure Comics #349, 10/66
Unus the Untouchable - X-Men #8, 11/64
U. S. Jones - Wonderworld Comics #28, 8/41
Vandall Savage - Green Lantern #10 ,Win '43; (S.A.) Flash #137, ?/63
Vanisher - X-Men #2, 11/63
Venom - (1st full app.) Amazing Spider-Man #300, 5/88; (cameo w/costume) Amazing Spider-Man #298 (cameo, no costume), #299, 4/88
Vindicator - X-Men #109, 5/78
Viper - Captain America #110, 2/69
Vulture - Amazing Spider-Man #2, 5/63
Warpath - X-Men #193, 5/85
Watcher - Fantastic Four #13, 4/63
Weapon Omega - Alpha Flight #102, 11/81
Weather Wizard - Flash #110, 12-1/59-60
Whirlwind - (Human Top) Tales to Astonish #50, 12/63
White Queen - X-Men #132, 4/80
Wizard - Strange Tales #102, 11/62
Zemo - Avengers #6, 7/64
Zzzax - Incredible Hulk #166, 8/73

1ST APPEARANCE: GROUP

Adult Legion - Superman #147, 8/61
All Star Squadron - Justice League of America #193, 8/81
All Winners Squad - All Winners Comics #19, Fall, 1946
Alpha Flight - (cameo) X-Men #120, 4/79; (full app.) X Men #121, 5/79
Atari Force - New Teen Titans #27, 1/83
Atomic Knights - Strange Adventures #117, 6/60
Avengers - Avengers #1, 9/63
Avengers new line up - Avengers #16, 5/65; Avengers #150, 8/76; Avengers #181, 3/79; Avengers #211, 9/81
Avengers West Coast - West Coast Avengers #1, 9/84
Big-3 - (Blue Beetle/Flame/Samson)-Big-3 #1, Fall, 1940
Bizarro Legionnaires - Adventure Comics #329, 2/65
Boy Commandos - Detective Comics

1ST APPEARANCE Group (Cont'd) #64,6/42
Brainiac 5 - Action Comics #276, 5/61
Challengers of the Unknown - Showcase #6, 1-2/57
Champions - Champions #1, 10/75
Creature Commandos - Weird War Tales #93, 11/80
Damage Control - Marvel Comics Presents #19, 5/89
Darkstars - Dark Stars #1, 10/92
Defenders - Marvel Feature #1, 12/71; (new) Defenders #125, 11/83; (prelude) Sub-Mariner #34, 2/71
Doom Patrol - My Greatest Adventure #80, 6/63; (new) Showcase #94, 8-9/77
Easy Company - Our Army At War #81, 4/59
Elementals, The - Justice Machine Annual #1, 1/84
Eternals - Eternals #1, 7/76
Excalibur - Excalibur Special Edition nn, 1987
Explorers - Boy Explorers #1, 5-6/46
Fab 4 - Super Heroes #1, 1/67
Fantastic Four - Fantastic Four #1, 11/61; (1st in costumes) Fantastic Four #3, 3/62; (new team) Fantastic Four #306, 9/87
Federal Men - New Comics #2, 1/36
Femforce - Femforce Special #1, Fall, 1984
Fightin' Five - Fightin' Five V2#28, 7/64
Forever People - Forever People #1, 2-3/71
Freedom Fighters - Justice League of America #107, 1975
Frightful Four - Fantastic Four #36, 10/64
Future X-Men - X-Men #141, 1/81
Ghost Patrol - Flash Comics #29, 5/42
Girl Commandos - Speed Comics #13, 4/41
Great Lakes Avengers - West Coast Avengers #46, 7/89
Green Lantern Corp. - Green Lantern #130
Guardians of the Galaxy - Marvel Super-Heroes #18, 1/69; (1st solo book) Marvel Presents #3, 2/76
Guardians of the Universe - Green Lantern #1, 7-8/60
H.A.R.D. Corps - Harbinger #10, 10/92
Inferior Five - Showcase #62, 5-6/66
Infinity, Inc. - All Star Squadron #25, 9/83
Inhumans - Fantastic Four #45, 12/65
Injustice Society Of The World - All Star Comics #37, 10-11/47
Intergalactic Vigilante Squadron - Adventure Comics #237, 6/57
International Sea Devils - Sea Devils #22, 3-4/66
Invaders - Avengers #71, 12/69; (re-intro) Namor, the Sub-Mariner #12, 3/91
Justice League Europe - Justice League International #24, 2/89; (new) Justice League Spectacular #1, 1992
Justice League International - (new) Justice League Spectacular #1, 1992
Justice League of America - Brave and the Bold #28, 2-3/60; Legends #6, 4/87; (new team) Justice League of America Annual #2, 1984
Justice Society of America - All Star Comics #3, Win, '40-'41; (1st S.A. cameo) Flash #137, ?/63
Kiss - (1st full app.) Howard the Duck #13, 6/77; (cameo) Howard the Duck #12, 3/77
Knights of the Galaxy - Mystery In Space #1, 4-5/51
Legion of Monsters - (Ghost Rider, Man-Thing, Morbius, Werewolf) Marvel Premiere #28, 1975
Legion of Substitute Heroes - Adventure Comics #306, 3/63
Legion of Super Heroes - Adventure Comics #247, 4/58
Legion Of Super Pets - Adventure Comics #293, 2/62
Liberators - Avengers #83, 12/70
Liberty Legion - Marvel Premiere #29, 1975
Losers - (Storm/Gunner/Sarge/J. Cloud) G. I. Combat #138,10-11/69
Lt. Marvels - Whiz Comics #21, 9/41
Marvel Family - Captain Marvel Adventures #18, 12/42
Masters Of Evil - Avengers #6, 2/64
Masters of the Universe - New Teen Titans #25, 11/82
Mercenaries - G.I. Combat #244, 1982
Metal Men - Showcase #37, 3-4/62
Mighty Crusaders - Mighty Crusaders #1, 11/65
New Gods - New Gods #1, 2-3/71
New Mutants - Marvel Graphic Novel #4, 1982
New Teen Titans - DC Comics Presents #26, 10/80
New Warriors - (cameo) Thor #411, 12/89; (full app.) Thor #412, 12/89
Newsboy Legion - Star Spangled Comics #7, 4/42; (re-intro) Superman's Pal Jimmy Olsen #133, 10/70
Next Men - Dark Horse Presents #54, 9/91
Night Force - New Teen Titans #21, 7/82
Omega Men - Green Lantern #141, 6/81
Our Gang - Our Gang Comics #1, 9-10/42
Outsiders - Brave and the Bold #200, 7/83
Planeteers - Real Fact Comics #16, 9-10/48
Power Elite - Starman #4, Win, '88
Power Pack - Power Pack #1, 8/84
Sea Devils - Showcase #27, 7-8/60
Secret Six - Secret Six #1, 4-5/68; (re-intro) Action Comics #601, 6/88
Sentinels - X-Men #14,11/65
Seven Soldiers of Victory - Leading Comics #1, Wint,'41-'42
Shadowmaster - Punisher #24 ?/89
S.H.I.E.L.D. - Nick Fury Agent of Shield #1, 6/68
Stargazers - Vanguard Ill. #2, 12/83
Starjammers - (cameo) X-Men #104, 4/77; (full app.) X-Men #107, 10/77
Star Rovers - Mystery In Space #66, 1961
Stargrazers - Vanguard Illustrated #2, 12/83
Suicide Squad - Brave and the Bol #25, 8-9/59; (new) Legends #3, 1/87
Super Friends - Super Friends #1, 11/76
Team America - Captain America #269, 5/82
Team Titans - (Teen Titans) New Titans Annual #7, 1991
Teenage Mutant Ninja Turtles - Gobbledygook #1, 1984
Teen Titans - Brave and the Bold #54, 6-7/64; (re-intro.) DC Super Stars #1, 3/76
Terrific Three - (Jaguar, Mr. Justice, Steel Sterling) Mighty Crusaders #5, 9/66
Three Mouseketeers - Funny Stuff #1, Sum '44
Thunder Agents - Thunder Agents #1, 11/65
Tiger Squadron - Blue Beetle #20, 4/43
Toxic Crusaders - Toxic Crusaders #1, 5/92
Tough Kid Squad - Tough Kid Squad #1, 3/42
Transformers - Transformers #1, 9/84
Tribe - WILDC.A.T.S.: Covert Action Teams #4, 3/93
Ultra-Men - (Fox, Web, Capt. Flag) Mighty Crusaders #5, 9/66
Wanderers - Adventure Comics #375, 12/68
Warlords - West Coast Avengers - West Coast Avengers #1, 9/84
Wildcats - WILDC.A.T.S.: Covert Action Teams #1, 8/92
X-Factor - Avengers #263, 1/86; (new team) X-Factor #71, 10/91
X-Force - (cameo) New Mutants #100, 4/91
X-Men - X-Men #1, 9/63; X-Men #1, 10/91; (new team) X-Men #253, 1989; (new team) X-Men #281, 10/91; (new) Giant-Size X-Men #1, Sum, '75
X-Terminators - X-Terminators #1, 10/88
Young Allies - Young Allies #1, Sum '41
Youngblood - (1 pg. ad) Megaton #8, 8/87; (2pgs.) Megaton Ex;plosion nn, 1987

1ST APPEARANCE: VILLAIN GROUP

Blue Trinity - Flash #7, 12/87
Brotherhood of Evil - (new) New Teen Titans #15, 1/82
Brotherhood of Evil Mutants - X-Men #4, 3/64; (new) X-Men #141, 1/81
Citadel - Green Lantern #136, 1/81
Enforcers - Amazing Spider-Man #10, 3/64
Fearsome Five - New Teen Titans #3, 1/81

1ST APP. Villain Group (Cont'd)

Frightful Four - (Sandman/Wizard/P.P. Pete) Fantastic Four #36, 3/65

Injustice Society - All Star Comics #37, 10-11/47

Krypton Foes - Superman #65, 7-8/50

Legion of Super-Villains - Superman #147, 8/61

Masters of Evil - Avengers #6, 7/64; (new) Avengers #54, 7/68

Phantom Zone Villains (Dr. Zadu & Emdine) - Superboy #100, 10/62

Royal Flush Gang - Justice League of America #43 ?/66; (new) Justice League of America #203, 6/82

Secret Society of Super-Villains - **Secret Society of super Villians** #1, 5-6/76

Sinister Six - Amazing Spider-Man Annual #1, 1964

Skrulls - Fantastic Four #2, 1/62

Toad Men - Incredible Hulk #2, 7/62

1ST CROSS-OVERS

Ant-Man - Fantastic Four #16, 7/63

Avengers - Fantastic Four #25, 4/64

Conan - Savage Tales #1, 5/71

Daredevil - Amazing Spider-Man #16, 9/64

Doctor Strange - Fantastic Four #27, 6/64

Fantastic Four - Amazing Spider-Man 3/63

Hulk - Fantastic Four #12, 3/63

G.A. Green Lantern x-over in S.A. - Showcase #55, 3-4/65

Iceman - Strange Tales #120, 5/64

Iron Man x-over outside Avengers - Tales to Astonish #82, 8/66

Nick Fury x-over - (as agent of Shield) Tales of Suspense #92, 8/67

S.A. Captain America x-over - Sgt. Fury #13, 12/64

Sgt. Fury - Fantastic Four #21, 12/63

Silver Surfer x-over - (cameo) Tales to Astonish #92, 6/67; (full app.) Tales to Astonish #93, 7/67

Spider-Man - Strange Tales Annual #2, 7/63

Sub-Mariner - (outside Fantastic Four) Avengers #3, 1/64

Thing - Strange Tales #116, 1/64

Thor - Strange Tales #123, 8/64

X-Men - Tales of Suspense #49, 1/64

1ST SUPERPETS

Bat-Hound - Batman #92, 6/55

Captain Carrot - New Teen Titans #16, 2/82

Comet - (Superhorse) Adventure Comics #293, 2/62

Cosmo - (Challengers Spacepet) Challengsers of the Unknown #18, 9-10/60

Krypto the Super Dog - Adventure Comics #210, 3/55

Legion of Super Pets - Adventure Comics #293, 2/62

Rang-A-Tang the Wonder Dog - Blue Ribbon Comics #1, 11/39

Streak the Wonder Dog - Green Lantern #30, 2-3/48

Streaky the Super Cat - Action Comics #261, 2/60

Supermonkey - Superboy #76, 8?/59

Wolf - (Boy Commandos mascot) Boy Commandos #34, 7-8/49

1ST OF A PUBLISHER

Ace Magazines - Sure-Fire #1, 6/40

American Comics Group - Giggle #1 & Ha Ha #1, 10/43

Atlas Comics - All Winners #11, Wint. '43/44

Avon Comics - Molly O'Day #1, 2/45

Better Publications (Standard) - Best Comics #1, 11/39

Bilbara Publishing Co. - Cyclone #1, 6/40

Brookwood Publications - Speed Comics #1, 10/39

Carlton Publishing Co. - Zoom Comics #1, 12/45

Catechetical Guild - Topix #1, 11/42

Centaur Publications - Funny Pages V2#6, 3/38; Funny Picture Stories V2#6, 3/38; Star Comics #10, 3/38; Star Ranger V2#10, 3/38

Charlton Comics - Zoo Funnies #1, 11/45

Columbia Comics Group - Big Shot #1, 5/40

Comico - Primer #1, 10/82

Comics Magazine - Comics Magazine #1, 5/36

Dark Horse - Dark Horse Presents #1, 7/86

David McKay Publ. - King Comics #1, 4/36

DC Comics - New Fun Comics #1, 2/35

Defiant Comics - Warriors Of Plasm #1, 8/93

Dell Publishing Co. - Popular Comics #1, 2/36

Eastern Color - Funnies On Parade nn, 1933

Elliot Publications - Double Comics, 1940

Fawcett Publications - Whiz Comics #2 (#1), 2/40

Fiction House - Jumbo Comics #1, 9/38

Flying Cadet - Flying Cadet #1, 1/43

Fox Features Syndicate - Wonder Comics #1, 5/39

Funnies, Inc. - Motion Picture Funnies Weekly #1, 1939

Gilberton Publ. - Classic Comics #1, 10/41

Globe Syndicate- Circus Comics #1, 6/38

Great Publications - Great Comics #1, 11/41

Harry 'A' Chesler - Star Comics #1, 2/37

Harvey Comics - Pocket Comics #1, 8/41

Hawley Publications - Captain Easy nn, 1939

Hillman Periodicals - Miracle Comics #1, 2/40

Holyoke (Continental) - Crash Comics #1, 5/40

Hugo Gernsback - Superworld #1, 4/40

Hyper Publications - Hyper Mystery #1, 5/40

Image Comics - Youngblood #1, 4/92

K.K. Publications - Mickey Mouse Magazine #1, Sum, 1935

Lev Gleason - Silver Streak #1, 12/39

Mirage Studios - Gobbledygook #1, no mo. '84

MLJ Magazines - Blue Ribbon Comics #1, 11/39

Nita Publications - Whirlwind Comics #1, 6/40

Novelty Publications - Target Comics #1, 6/40

Parents' Magazine Institute - True Comics #1, 4/41

Prize Publications - Prize Comics #1, 3/40

Progressive Publishers - Feature Comics #21, 6/39

Quality Comics Group - Feature Comics #21, 6/39

Ralston-Purina Co. - Tom Mix #1, 9/40

Standard Comics (Better Publ.) - Best Comics #1, 11/39

Street and Smith Publications - Shadow Comics #1, 3/40

Sun Publications - Colossus Comics #1, 3/40

Timely Comics - Marvey Mystery #1, 11/39

United Features Syndicate - Tip Top Comics #1, 4/36

Valiant Comics - (hero)-Magnus Robot Fighter, 5/91

Warren all comics magazine - Creepy #1 no mo. '64

Whitman Publishing Co. - Mammoth Comics #1, 1937

Will Eisner - Spirit #1, 6/2/40

William H. Wise - Columbia Comics #1, 1943

1ST PROTOTYPE

Ancient One - Strange Tales #92, 1/62
Ant-Man - Strange Tales #73, 2/60; Strange Tales #78, 11/60
Aunt May - Strange Tales #97, 6/62
Doctor Doom - Tales of Suspense #31, 7/62
Doctor Strange - Journey Into Mystery #78, 3/62; Strange Tales #79, 12/60; Tales of Suspense #32, 8/62
Electro - Tales To Astonish #15, 1/61
Giant-Man - Strange Tales #70, 8/59
Hulk - Journey Into Mystery #62, 11/60; Journey Into Mystery #66, 3/61
Human Torch - Strange Tales #76, 8/60
Iron Man - Strange Tales #75, 6/60; Tales of Suspense #9, 5/60; Tales of Suspense #16, 4/61
Kamandi - Alarming Tales #1, 9/57
Lava Men - Tales of Suspense #7, 1/60
Magneto - Strange Tales #84, 5/61
Mr. Hyde - Journey Into Mystery #79, 4/62
Professor X - Amazing Adult Fantasy #14, 7/62; Strange Tales #69, 6/59
Quicksilver - Strange Tales #67, 2/59
Red Tornado - House Of Mystery #155, 9-10/65
Sandman - Journey Into Mystery #70, 7/61
Savage Dragon - Marvel Comics Presnets #50, 1990
Spider-Man - Journey Into Mystery #73, 10/61
Stone Men - Tales of Suspense #28, 4/62; Tales to Astonish #5, 9/59; Tales to Astonish #16, 2/61
Superman - (Dr. Mystic) Comics Magazine #1, 5/36; More Fun Comics #14, 10/36; New Book of Comics #2, Spr/38
Toad Men - Tales to Astonish #7, 1/60
Uncle Ben - Strange Tales #97, 6/62
Watcher - Tales of Suspense #35, 11/62

Some of today's popular super hero characters were developed from or after earlier forms or prototypes. These prototype characters sometimes were introduced to test new ideas and concepts which later developed into full fledged super heros, or old material sometimes would inspire new characters. The above is a list of all known prototypes. The Marvel/Atlas issues have been verified by Stan Lee, Steve Ditko and Jack Kirby.

KEY COMICS SOLD IN 1993

The following list of books sold were reported to Overstreet during the year and represent only a small portion of the total amount of important books that sell.

GOLD (Reported sales)

Action Comics #1-VG45 - $20,000
Adventure #40-FN70 - $5000, VG50 - $5500
Adventure #61-VF(R)82 - $2600
All American #16-GD33 - $5000
All American #19-GD36 - $1400
All American #61-FN68 - $900
All Flash #1-VF82(R) - $3250; FN74 - 1800
All Star Comics #3-VG45 - $11,500
Batman #1-VG45 - $5500, FR12 - $3500, GD18 - $5000
Blue Beetle #1-VF88(Larson) - $1800
Captain America #1-GVG - $4400, VG45 - $6300, VG45(R) - $4200
Captain America #2-VF78 - $3700
Colossus #1-VF87 - $1500
Comic Cavalcade #1-FN68 - $1700
Dective Comics #27-FN68 - $81,000 & LATER FOR $101,000, G31 - $20,000 (+ 2 low grade Superman #1s), G30 - $25,750
Detective Comics #33-FN(r)/74 - $5500; #33FN(R)62 - $4000
Detective Picture Stories #1-FN62 - $2000
Famous Funnies Series 1-VG45 - $7,500
Flash #104-VF(R) - $1730
Human Torch #1-VF89 - $12,000
Kid Komics #1-VF82 - $1000
Mad #1-VF82 - $2100
Marvel Comics #1-VF86 - $40,000
Master Comics #1-NM96 - $5,600
More Fun #54-VF89(R) - $2000
More Fun #55-VF89(R) - $3600
New Book Of Comics #1-NM92- $7500, FN68 - $4485
New Comics #1-NM94 - $10,000
New Fun Comics #2-FR14 - $2500
Pep Comics #22-VG50 - $1500
Shield Wizard #1-NM - $2200
Silver Streak #1-VF86 - $4800, VF87 - $6500
Sub-Mariner #1-VF86 - $3,800
Superboy #1-FN70 - $1500
Superman #1-FN65 - $22,000, VF(R) - $18,000, FN(R) - $10,350, GD34(R) - $6000, GD(trimmed) - $4,000, no cover, brittle -$700
Tales Of Terror Annual #1-FN65 - $1350
Wonder Woman #1-FN74 - $3900
World's Best #1-VG50 - $1400
Young Allies #1 (San Francisco) - $3800; VG50 - $1100, GD32 - $1400, GD32 - $700
Zip Comics #1-VF - $1100

SILVER (Reported sales)

Amazing Fantasy #15-VF82 - $39,100, VF - $16,100, VG50 - $2200, FN70 - $3800, VG37 - $1700, GD23 - $1500, FR14 - $900
Amazing Spider-Man #1-VF85 - $19,000, VF80 - $6700, VF(cleaned) - $6,800, FN65 - $2800, VG48 - $2000, VG45 - $1700, FR12 - $850
Amazing Spider-Man #14-VF75 - $700
Avengers #1-VF80 - $1200, FN68 - $575, VG46 - $375
Brave and the Bold #34-VF88 - $1200
Captain America #100-VF89 - $240
Fantastic Four #1-VF86–$27,600, NM96 - $19,000, VF85(color touch) - $7,500
Flash #105-FN74 - $1800
Green Lantern #1-VG50 - $375
Incredible Hulk #1-VF82 - $7130, FN68 - $1500, FN70 - $2200

Silver (Reported Sales) (Cont'd)

Iron Man #1-VF89 - $240, VF80 - $190
Journey Into Mystery #83-VF86 - $2300, VF(R) - $1800, VG50 - $735
Showcase #4-VF82(R) - $9000, VG50 - $5060
Silver Surfer #1-VF80 - $250, FN70 - $186
Silver Surfer #4-VF89 - $275
Star Trek #1-VF82 - $325
Strange Tales #101-VF82 - $400
Tales Of Suspense #39-VF75 - $1600, FN68 - $950, VG45 $560, GD34 - $450
X-Men #1-FN56 - $760, VG48 - $450, VG42 - $400

PEDIGREE BOOKS SOLD

Allentown (AT), Bethlehem (BH), Mile High (MH), San Francisco (SF), White Mountain (WM)

Adventure Comics #64 (MH) - $3500
Amazing Fantasy #15 (WM) - $39,100
Amaz. Myst. Funnies V2/12 (MH) - $3500
Batman #9 (AT) - $2,000
Boy Commandos #13 (MH) $450
Captain America #29 (MH) - $3000
Detective Comics #38(AT) - $25,000
Detective Comics #102 (MH) - $3000
Detective Comics #111 (MH) - $1550
Fantastic Four #1 (WM) - $27,600
Green Hornet #20 (MH) - $700
Green Lantern #12 (MH) - $2875
Lois Lane #1 (BH) - $4830
Lone Ranger #2 (MH) - $650
Shield Wizard #1(Denver) - $2500
Wonder Woman #45 (MH) - $890

MARKET AT A GLANCE

The following is a quick reference list of selected books from the Gold and Silver Age showing last years price, this years price and the rate of change.

GOLDEN AGE

Title	1994 price	% change	1993 price
Action Comics #1	$90,000	20%	$75,000
Adventure Comics #40	16,000	14%	14,000
All-American Comics #16	37,000	16%	32,000
All-American Comics #25	4,200	20%	3,500
All Flash #1	5,800	16%	5,000
All-Star Comics #3	20,000	14%	17,500
All Winners #1	5,000	25%	4,000
Batman #1	36,000	7%	33,500
Big Book Of Fun #1	9,750	30%	7,500
Captain America Comics #1	36,000	20%	30,000
Daredevil #1	4,000	25%	3,200
Detective Comics #1	36,000	20%	30,000
Detective Comics #27	92,000	8%	85,000
Detective Comics #33	18,000	6%	17,000
Donald Duck 4-Color #4	6,000	20%	5,000
Flash Comics #1	23,000	15%	20,000
Funnies On Parade	7,200	20%	6,000
Green Lantern #1	13,000	30%	10,000
Jumbo Comics #1	12,000	60%	7,500
King Comics #1	6,200	18%	5,250
Marvel Comics #1	75,000	19%	65,000
Marvel Mystery Comics #9	6,500	18%	5,500
More Fun Comics #14	9,000	20%	7,500
More Fun Comics #52	28,000	12%	25,000
New Book Of Comics #1	9,400	92%	4,900
New Comics #1	10,750	54%	7,000
New Fun Comics #6	10,900	82%	6,000
N.Y. World's Fair 1939	11,000	29%	8,500
Silver Streak Comics #1	4,800	20%	4,000
Silver Streak Comics #6	4,200	24%	3,400
Superman #1	70,000	8%	65,000
Tip Top Comics #1	3,500	17%	3,000
Whiz #1	42,000	0	42,000
Wonder Woman #1	6,500	18%	5,250
Young Allies #1	4,000	25%	3,200

SILVER AGE

Title	1994 price	% change	1993 price
Amazing Fantasy #15	20,000	186%	7,000
Amazing Spider-Man #1	13,500	99%	6,800
Atom Ant #1	150	200%	75
Avengers #1	1,675	34%	1,250
Brave & The Bold #28	3,070	18%	2,600
Brave & The Bold #29	1,750	75%	1,000
Brave & The Bold #34	1,250	56%	800
Challengers Of The Unknown #1	1,250	42%	950
Dell Giant #48 (Flintstones #1)	225	40%	160
Detective Comics #225	3,500	40%	2,500
Fantastic Four #1	12,000	67%	7,200
Flash #105	2,750	38%	2,000
Green Lantern #1	1,600	14%	1,400

FREE CATALOG!

The Motor City Comics catalog contains thousands of golden age and silver age comic books.

We offer accurate grading, competitive pricing, a complete wantlist service, 8 years experience and a complete return policy.

Your satisfaction is guaranteed.

CALL OR WRITE TODAY FOR A *FREE* COPY !

MOTOR CITY COMICS

19785 W. 12 MILE RD.
SUITE 231
SOUTHFIELD, MI 48076
PHONE: (810)350-2633
FAX: (810)354-3181

PLEASE NOTE: THIS CATALOG CONTAINS COMICS FROM 1935-1970 ONLY.

All titles and characters are trademarks of DC Comics © 1993, all rights reserved

TM

DC COMICS RETAILER IN INDIANAPOLIS, INDIANA

TM

- New Comics Weeks Early-Every Title Published • Baseball Cards, Sets, Supplies
- 250,000 Back Issues-Old & New, Middle Aged Too • Imported Toys & Models
- We Pay Premium For Old Comics: 1938-65
- New Comics Same Day Released
- Role Playing Games • T-Shirts

INFORMATION HOTLINE 257-1450

NORTH	SOUTH	SOUTH	EAST	WEST
In Broad Ripple Village 6265 N. Carrollton Ave. **Thurs. thru Sun.**	In Southport Center Next To Wal-Mart 7311 U.S. 31 South **Open 7 Days**	At Madison Ave. & Thompson Rd. 5002 S. Madison Ave. **Thurs. thru Sun.**	Northwest of Washington Square 982 N. Mitthoeffer Rd. **Open 7 Days**	In 38th St. Plaza Southeast of Target 3837 N. High School Rd. **Open 7 Days**
253-8882	**889-8899**	**787-3773**	**898-5010**	**293-4386**

Market At A Glance (Cont'd)

Title	1994 price	% change	1993 price
Incredible Hulk #1	7,100	78%	4,000
Jimmy Olsen #1	1,700	42%	1,200
Jonny Quest #1	225	28%	175
Justice League Of America #1	2,200	26%	1.750
Lois Lane #1	1,200	33%	900
Showcase #4	18,000	91%	9,400
Showcase #6	2,150	43%	1,500
Showcase #8	7,500	97%	3,800
Showcase #9	3,100	121%	1,400
Showcase #14	3,000	88%	1,600
Showcase #22	3,300	39%	2,250
Secret Squirrel #1	60	71%	35
Tales Of Suspense #1	950	46%	650
Tales Of Suspense #39	2,550	28%	2,000
Tales Of The Unexpected #40	600	41%	425
Tales To Astonish #1	900	50%	600
Tales To Astonish #27	2,300	53%	1,500
X-Men #1	3,000	40%	2,150

Golden Age books remained very scarce in high grade. Golden Age sales were very good with most all titles selling in all grades. However, the story for 1993 was the explosive prices paid for high grade Silver Age Keys. The $40,000 Amazing Fantasy sale At Sotheby's fueled the flames. Low grade Marvels from the mid 1960s up were hard to sell at guide list prices. 1993 saw a glut of new product on the market which impacted store owners, publishers, distributors and investors. The Golden Age market is poised ready to explode in 1994 in the wake of the 1993 Silver Age advance.

ANNUAL REPORT

by Bob Overstreet

The comic marketplace once again posted substantial price gains despite the slow national economic recovery. Led by the tremendous surge in the silver age area, overall prices showed significant upward movement. Strong bullish sentiment continued throughout the comic marketplace!

SILVER AGE: Sales and demand for high grade keys is phenomenal. Record prices were realized, especially after the announced $39,100 sale for a high grade *Amazing Fantasy* #15 at Sotheby's in 1993. Early *Showcase* and *Spiderman* in high grade are the hottest, followed closely by early high grade *Fantastic Four* and *Incredible Hulk*. A *Spider-Man* #1 VF87 sold for $19,000; a NM *Fantastic Four* #1 sold for $19,000 and an *Amazing Fantasy* #15VF86 sold for $19,000. As fast moving as the high grade sales are, sales are equally as slow in the lower grades of less than Fine, especially in the 1965-on material. This prompted us to again change the spreads between good and mint condition. You will note many adjustments of the good prices throughout this book. With this edition, we have also listed four prices for all the keys to show more accurately the increased spreads for these books in high grade. A large high grade silver age collection called the Bethlehem collection sold from one dealer to another late in the year for $180,000. The *Showcase* #4 (VF89) from this collection, sold for $30,000 cash.

© MEG

HOTTEST BOOK OF 1993!!
First Spider-Man brings
a staggering $39,100!!!

The auction houses continued to offer comic book and related items for sale (see their detailed market report following this report).

GOLDEN AGE: Sales were brisk at slightly above guide levels for most items. Late in the year, dealers began getting more and more offers to buy high grade silver age collections due to the record price levels they have reached. These collectors are interested in buying high grade golden age books, pre-code horror, pre-code Atlas and other investment books in their place. Consequently, supplies of this material just do not exist for this shift in demand. These and other strong indicators in the market suggest that all mainline Timely and DC books are again posed for explosive demand which could result in another round of price increases. If this happens as predicted, the rest of the golden age market will follow with appropriate increases as well. At the San Diego Con in 1993, high grade copies of Timely and Dcs were just not available at guide price levels.

Two years ago, baseball card dealers and others began looking for new investment areas due to the slump in their markets. The much publicized booming comic book market became very attractive as an alternative to their drooping markets. As a result these new arrivals into our market began speculating in the recent comics, much as they did in the card market over the past 10 years. With thousands of new buyers now entering the marketplace, prices on recent speculator comics soared. As prices shot up, more and more speculators were attracted to the market causing prices to rise even more. Due to this, 1993 saw a tremendous glut of new product available to the consumer. As is the case with previous speculative markets, the time comes to sell. Many speculators began unloading their hoards of new comic books bought over the past two years. Due to this, the values of these titles began to fall rapidly. By year's end, many of the new stores began to close.

Overstreet experienced an exciting year of change. Our Bi-monthly magazine became a monthly, we moved to a new address, a new quarterly was born and a video was produced. Our staff enjoyed meeting everyone at our booths at the major comic book conventions and look forward to seeing you again this year. Look for several more new products coming from Overstreet again this year.

The **Overstreet Comic Book Grading Guide** and the **ONE/OWL** Comic Book Grading Card remained current as updated versions will not be published for several years. It is our hope that these new tools for grading will make the job easier for the novice as well as the seasoned collector/dealer.

1930s book brings $10,000!

© DC

The San Diego Comic Con was larger than ever. There was a lot of commotion around our booth there with the video cameras running and all the interviews going on. We enjoyed seeing our old friends as well as making new acquaintences. Many dealers reported to us "best sales ever" since this con opened in 1970.

The Philadelphia Comic Fest convention in October became the largest comic convention ever with over 30,000 people attending. The trade show was slow, but the comic-con was bustling with activity. Our booth was mobbed every day and we enjoyed seeing and talking to everyone there. Again dealers there reported excellent sales of gold and silver age books. A *New Comics* #1NM sold for $10,000.

1920s Titles–Rare, especially in fine or better condition. Sales data recorded are usually from lower grade copies.

1930s Titles–Most titles and issues were very scarce with few collections turning up. Demand still far outweighs supply. DC titles were the most requested. *More Fun, Adventure,* early *Detective* were still very, very hot. *Detective Picture Stories* #1-FN62 sold for $2000. A *Famous Funnics* Series 1-VG45 fetched $7,500; a *Future Comics* #1FN74 sold for $600, a *King Comics* #1-VG45 sold for $1950, a *New Book Of Comics* #1-NM92 sold for $7500; another FN70 brought $4485. A *New Fun* #2-FR14 sold for $2500. a *New Comics* #1-NM94 for $10,000. a *Popular Comics* #1-GD48 for $675. and a *Skippy's Own Book of Comics* VG45 for $875.

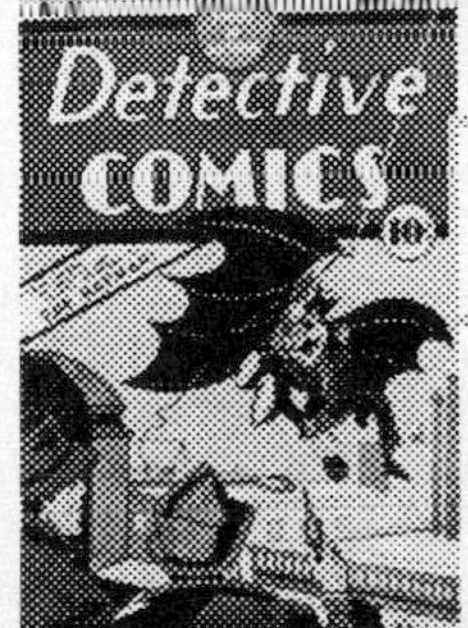

© DC

First Batman sells for $81,000!!

1940s Titles-Superhero titles were the most popular, With DC and Timely leading the pact. Gleason and MLJ titles showed increased demand along with Warner Brothers and Disney funny animal books in high grade. Late '40s titles remained scarce, all publishers.

DC-Sales were again very strong for many titles in all grades. High grade copies of most titles were very scarce and sold at above guide list whenever copies turned up. High interest should continue through 1994. Among the hottest titles were early *Actions* #1-15, 100-140, *Adventures* with Simon and Kirby covers and key issues, *Flash, More Fun* (very scarce run), *Star Spangled, Sensation, Green Lantern, All-American, All Star, Superman* #1-20 and *Wonder*

Woman. The ashcan of *All-Star Comics* #1 sold for a record price of $15,000.00. A few sales are: *Action Comics* #1-VG45–$20,000, 23-VG48–$400, *Adventure Comics* #32-VF82–$1500, 40-FN69–$5000, VG50–$5500, 44-VG49–$950, 50-FN62–$450, 61-VF(R)82–$2600, *All American* #16-GD33–$5000, 19-GD36–$1400, 61-FN68–$900, *All Flash* #1-VF(R)–$3250, FN74–$1800, *All Star* #3-VG45–$11,500, 25-FN68–$475, 33-VF80–$950, *Batman* #1-FR11–$3500, GD18$5000, 1-VG45–$5500, 9VF(R)–$1075, 18-VF82–$700, *Comic Cavalcade* #1-FN68–$1700, *Detective Comics* #27-FN68–$81,000, & resold for $101,000, GD30–$25,750, 33-FN(R)74–$5500, 38-FN(R)62--$4000, 59-VF86–$1100, *Flash Comics* #2-GD28–$630, *Green Lantern* #14-VF86–$650, *More Fun* #55-VF(R)89–$3600, 63-FN55–$650, 101-GD25–$625, *Superboy* #1-FN69–$1500, *Superman* #1-FN65–$22,000, FN(R)–$10,350, GD(R)34–$6000, 100-FR10–$88, Wonder Woman #1-FN74–$3900. *World's Best* #1-VG50–$1400. *World's Finest* #7-FN62–$375.

© MEG

First Marvel Comic in VF takes $40,000!

TIMELY-*Captain America* and related titles showed increased demand, selling at above guide list prices all year long. All other Timely titles, in every grade, also enjoyed excellent sales as well. Alex Schomburg cover issues also sold very well. Some reported sales: *All Select* #1-VG45–$750, *All Winners* V2#1VF80–$500, *Captain America* #1-VG45–$6300, VG(R)45–$4200, GD29–$4400, 2-VF78–$3700, 5-FN62–$950, 8-VG42–$600, 15-FN74–$625, 28-VF70–$850, 30-FN68–$365, 62-NM94–$700, *Complete Comics* #2-NM94–$600, *Human Torch* #1-VF89–$12,000, 2-FN65–$1000, 5-VF(R)–$1075, 5-FN71–$900, *Kid Komics* #1-VF82–$1000, *Marvel Mystery* #1-VF86–$40,000, 4-VG45–$495, 8-FN60–$1000, 17-NM94–$1200, *Sub-Mariner* #33-VF70 (Bethlehem)–$550,, *Young Allies* #1-NM94(San Francisco)– $3800, VG48–$1100, GD32–$700, 4-FN68–$600.

FAWCETT-Captain Marvel and related titles showed good sales as well as *Captain Midnight, Nickel, Bulletman, Spy Smasher, Marvey Family*, etc., *Master, Mary Marvel* and *Wow* enjoyed average sales. Mac Raboy cover issues remained popular, while most western titles had slow to average sales. All Sports titles were very hot. and scarce. Reported Sales: *Captain Marvel Adventures* #4-VG48–$308, 7-FN65–$210, 13-FN68–$228, 17-FN69–$211, 18-VG49–$220, 25-VF85–$275, 50-NM94–$135, 75-FN68–$57, *Master Comics* #1-NM94–$5,600, *Special Edition Comics* #1-GD30–$950, *Spy Smasher* #8-FN69–$235, *Whiz Comics* #8-FN65–$386.

CENTAUR- A very scarce company to collect. Sales are average for the few copies that entered the market. Reported sales: *Amazing Mystery Funnies* V2#12(MH)–$3500, 21(MH)–$2000, *Green Giant Comics* #1-GD17–$950. *Keen Detective Funnies* #9-GD25–$65, V2#7VG53–$500, VG46–$450, *Masked Marvel* #3-VG48–$240.

FOX-Excellent demand for *Mysterymen, Blue Beetle, Wonderworld, Fantastic,* etc. whenever copies surfaced for sale. Lou Fine cover issues are still very popular. Later 40s good girl art books like *Jo-Jo, Rulah, Woman Outlaws, Zoot, All Top, Blue Beetle, Crimes By Women,* etc. enjoyed brisk sales. Documented sales: *Blue Beetle* #1-VF(Larson)88–$1800, *Jo-Jo* #8-FN65–$81, *Junior* #12-VG48–$95, *Meet Corliss Archer* #1-FN68–$155, *Weird Comics* #1-VF80–$700, *Zoot* #10-FN68–$136, 13-VF86–$133. 16-VG48–$49

CLASSICS-High demand for early originals (#1-43) in top condition and early CC reprints. There was slow growth in later originals and reprints, but demand remained high for giveaways, giants, gift boxes, etc. Reported sale of U.S. CC: #1(0)VFN $3100.00

FICTION HOUSE-*Planet* continued to be a very solid title receiving the most attention. Early issues of *Jumbo* were impossible to find. Other titles such as *Jungle, Rangers, Wings, Fight* sold well at and above guide price levels. Good girl artwork of this line continued to be very popular with collectors, with books selling at or above current guide levels in all conditions. Pickup in demand for all offbeat titles. Reported sales: *Jumbo Comics* #1VF88–$11,000, 97-VF86–$100, *Jungle Comics* #94-VF82–$60, 98-FN65–$85, *Ka'a'nga* #1-VG45–$65, *Planet Comics* #3-FN65–$650, 22-VG45–$168, 43-FN65–$175, 45-FN70–$240, 49-FN68–$175, 2-VG45–$90, *Sheena* #8-FN65–$75.

Mile High set of Hit #1-24 picked up at $40,000 in 1993!!

QUALITY & MLJ/ARCHIE- Good solid sales for Quality's. *Blue Ribbon, Plastic Man, National, Military, Blackhawk, Hit, Dollman,* etc. MLJ's *Top Notch, Zip* and *Pep* showed strong sales. Archie's early (#1-10) *Archie* titles and Annuals, *Giant Series* #1-28, *Archie's Mechanics, Jughead's Fantasy, Archie's Madhouse,* etc. enjoyed increased demand during the year. Reported sales: *Archie's Joke Book* #1-VG49–$114, *Blackhawk* #10-FN69–$300, *Hit Comics* run(Mile High) #1-24–$40,000, *Jackpot Comics* #1-FN65–$600, 9-FN68–$211, *Pep Comics* #22-VG50–$1500, *Plastic Man* #2-VG49–$219, 7GD25–$40, 20(MH)–$850, *Police Comics* #19-NM94–$575, *Shield Wizard* #1-NM94–$2200, *Top-Notch* #9-VF82 - $1400, *Uncle Sam* #1-VG50–$315, *Zip Comics* # 1VF82 $1100.

GLEASON-Very strong sales for early issues of *Daredevil, Silver Streak* and *Boy.* Late 40s crime titles were strong. Reported sales: *Daredevil Comics* #26-VF86–$135, *Silver Streak* #1-VF88–$6500, VF86–$4800, 15-NM94 (Larson)–$550.

© Hanna-Barbera

Hanna-Barbera on the move!!

HARVEY-*Green Hornet* stayed popular with good sales while *Dick Tracy* showed no growth again this year. A *Green Hornet* #20(MH) sold for $700.

DISNEY-Duck one shots and *Dell Giants* in high grade were scarce and in high demand. Most titles enjoyed good sales, especially for high grade copies. Many books in the $4-$8 range were very popular Lower grades of later issues of *Walt Disney's Comics & Stories* were available and slow. Uncle Scrooge continued to show strong sales. Reported sales: *Dell Giant* #47-NM96–$115, *Donald Duck Beach Party* #4-NM96–$80, 4-Color #108-FN65–$300, 159-FN68–$240, 178-FN69–$295, 275-FN69–$115, *Ludwig Von Drake* #1-FN65–$10, *Uncle Scrooge* #17-FN68–$43, 27-FN69–37, *Walt Disney's C&S* #45-VG45–$56, 47-GD25–$28, 57-FN68–$93.

FUNNY ANIMAL- After many years of dormancy, 1993 saw two funny animal books rise to prominence, which were *Bone* and *Ren & Stimpy.* All DC titles were popular, esp. *Racoon Kids, Do Do & The Frog, Fox and the Crow, Funny Stuff, Nutsy Squirrel & Real Screen.* The Warner Bros., Jay Ward and Hanna Barbera character books all sold extremely well at above guide price levels. *Beep Beep the Road Runner, Tasmanian Devil* and *Speedy Gonzales* were on many want lists. *Hanna Barbera Super TV Heroes* were very hot, along with most other TV character books such as *Jetsons,*

Secret Squirrel, Jonny Quest, Bob Clampett's Beany & Cecil, Atom Ant, Augie Doggie, Peter Potamus and *Flintstones*. to name a few. Dell, ACG, *Felix The Cat* and Timely titles remained popular. There is still a solid Pogo following, but at current price levels.

First Issue in VF sells for record price!!

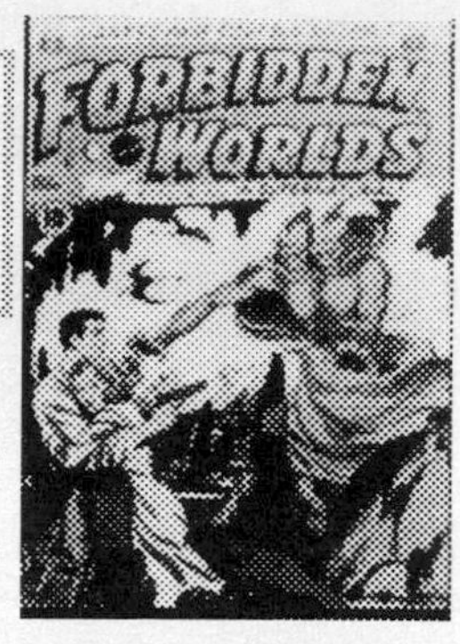

© ACG

WAR COMICS-All DC war titles were very hot: *All-American Men of War, Star Spangled War Stories, G. I. Combat, Our Army At War* are the top titles. All Dinosaur cover issues are in very high demand. The first Sgt. Rock (Our Army At War #81) has become the very first $1000 War comic. Sgt. Rock's Prize Battle Tales #1 is another popular book. The war books with a science fiction theme have received renewed interest. *Atomic War, Atomic Attack, Attack* (1st series), *Commander Battle and Atomic Sub* are all hot titles. However the early 40s war comics and the Atlas 50s war books are still generally slow.

SCIENCE FICTION-Almost every pre-code comic, irregardless of publisher is being collected. DC again has the most collected titles followed by Atlas, EC, ACG and Charlton. *DC's Mystery In Space, Strange Adventures, My Greatest Adventures* #6-up and *Tales Of The Unexpected a*re in high demand and are the top titles. *Tales Of The Unexpected* #40, 43 and *Showcase* 15, *Mystery In Space* 53 and *Showcase* 17 and 19 became very high demand books during the year. In fact all DC titles sold very well in all grades. The Atlas titles of this genre are also hot with *Space Action, Speed Carter Spaceman, Journey Into Unknown Worlds #36-38, Space Squadron, Space Worlds, Spaceman* and company leading the pact. Charlton's *Space Adventures* as well as E.C.'s *Weird Science* and *Weird Fantasy* were showing renewed collector's interest. The early *Super World Comics*, not to mention the run of *Planet Comics* are also fan favorites. Pedigree White Mountain copies were selling for as high as 4-5 times guide list. One of the hottest titles of this genre continued to be *Star Trek*. A *Star Trek* #1VF82 sold for $325. Reported sales: *Earth Man On Venus* #1-GD25–$75, *Forbidden Worlds* #1-VF82–$450, *Mystery In Space* #2-GD29–$138, 12-VG45–$66, 16-GD25–$29, 18-VG45–$54, 26-VG45–$54, 26-VG45–$42, 84-VF86–$35, 98-NM94–$18, *Robotmen of the Lost Planet* #1-GD29–$95, *Rocket To The Moon* #1-VF82–$375, *Strange Adventures* #10-VG45–$92, *Strange Worlds* #1-VG45–$100.

NEDOR-All Schomburg cover issues enjoyed hot sales at above guide list prices with *Black Terror, Fighting Yank, Startling, America's Best*, etc. at the top of the list. A *Black Terror* #1-VG36 sold for $200.

© MEG

MISCELLANEOUS-Interest is primarily for keys and first issues of superhero titles. Increased demand for odd titles such as *Topix, Oral Robert's True Stories, Catholic Comics* and other Religious one-shots. Reported sales: *Atomic Comics* #1(Green)-VF86–$650, Big Shot #1-FN65–$400, *Captain Atom* #1(1950)-VF82–$100, *Colossus Comics* #1-VF82–$1500, *Jingle Jangle* #4-VF82–$75, *Madhatter* #1-NM94–$350,

NEWSPAPER REPRINT-Average sales, esp. *Super Comics, Popular Comics, Famous Funnies, Big Shot, Joe Palooka, etc.*

Record price for Atlas sci/fi comic in NM $1200!!

1950s TITLES-The hottest publishers are Atlas, DC, Charlton, ACG and EC. followed by Avon and Dell.

ATLAS-Many new prototype issues have been discovered from this company! See list in this edition. All horror and science fiction titles were very popular and remained scarce in high grade. Pedigre copies, i.e. White Mountain, Magic Lightning, etc. sold very well at multiples of guide list. The titles that launched the silver age heros, such as *Strange Tales, Journey Into Mystery, Tales of Suspense, Tales to Astonish*, etc. were sizzling hot and couldn't meet demand. Many issues with special artists were popular. *Journey Into Unknown Worlds, Riot, Marvel Tales, Mystery Tales, Mystic*, etc. were popular titles. Hottest were the 1950s super hero: *Captain America, Men's Adventures, Sub-Mariner, Human Torch & Young Men.* The crime, war and offbeat titles also sold well. Definitely the hot publisher of the year in pre-code collecting. Reported sales: *Journey Into U. Worlds* #36-NM94-$1200. *Strange Worlds* #1-VG50–$120. *Tales of Suspense* #1-VF86–$1350.

TV/MOVIE TITLES-Most movie titles were meeting current demand with average sales. but there was Solid demand for most TV titles. *The Addams Family, Astro Boy, Avengers* (T.V.), *Dark Shadows, Jetsons, Munsters, Space Ghost, Secret Squirrel, Star Trek,* were very hot. Most other TV titles enjoyed good sales, especially whenever Dell or Gold Key file copies were offered. Gold Key is on the move and is definitely worth watching in the coming years.

High interest in HBO's Tales From the Crypt keeps E.C. comics popular!

WESTERNS-Atlas titles were in highest demand. All other titles including Dells, Fawcetts, DCs, etc. were slow to average in sales with the photo cover issues in highest demand. The T.V. western books enjoyed moderate demand. *Bonanza, Wanted: Dead or Alive, Big Valley, GunSmoke, Rawhide, The Rifleman, Sugarfoot, Wagon Train, Maverick, Wild Wild West*, etc. are a few of the popular titles. Reported sales: *Roy Rogers* 4-Color #38FN65–$525.

EC-Average sales overall, but *Mad* comics and mags were very hot. especially the magazine issues #24-75. The Kurtzman war titles showed a slight pickup after his death. The popular HBO *Tales From the Crypt* is still keeping high interest in the horror mags at current price levels, and the science fiction titles remained popular. A *Mad* #1 in VF82 sold for $2100. The Gaines EC file copy sets again all sold at auction for multiples of guide list. Reported sales: *Crime Patrol* #16-GD30–$137, *Haunt Of Fear* #2-FN65–$265, 9-FN65–$107, *Mad* #5-VG50–$201, *Tales Of Terror Annual* #1-FN65–$1350, #3-VF86–$750, *Two-Fisted Annual* #2-VG45–$94, *Vault Of Horror* #12-GD–$350.

GIANTS-Record sales for most Dell issues in high grade. Picked up interest for early Marvel, DC and Charlton issues. Average sales in lower grade if strictly graded and priced accordingly. Reported sales: *Tom & Jerry Winter Carnival* #1-FN65–$101, *Tom & Jerry Summer Fun* #3-NM94–$75.

3-D COMICS-Average sales were again reported.

ROMANCE COMICS-Average sales overall. DC, Atlas and ACG titles are popular with increased demand for Simon & Kirby titles such as *Young Romance* and *Young Love*. A *Forbidden Love* #1-FN68 sold for $248.

ERB COMICS-The first 30 *Tarzan* issues had moderate sales, including the Four Color books, but the rest of the run remained slow.

HUMOR COMICS-The DC titles sold very well, especially *Adventures of Bob Hope, Sergeant Bilko, Adventures of Ozzie & Harriet, Jackie Gleason, Jerry Lewis* and *Scribbly.* Other hot titles were *Abbott & Costello, Crazy Man Crazy (Magazine), Dennis The Menace, Riot, Get Lost (and other Mad immitators), Little Dot, Little Lotta, Millie The Model (especially the annuals), Little Lulu, Hot Stuff, Powerhouse Pepper, Richie Rich #1-10 (high grade), Sad Sack (later issues) and Spooky.* All ACG titles remained in high demand.

GOOD-GIRL-ART COMICS-Good sales overall, with strong demand for the main titles from Fox (*Phantom Lady, Blue Beetle, Zoot, Junior, Zegra, Rulah, Jo-Jo, All Top*, etc.), Fiction House (*Sheena, Jungle, Jumbo*, late *Wings* and *Rangers*, etc.) and Atlas (*Patsy and Hedy, etc.*),.as well as many Archie titles (*Katy Keene, Betty & Veronica, Jughead, Archie*, etc.).

1950s DC-Very hot! *Rex the Wonder Dog, Congo Bill, New Adventures of Charlie Chan, Phantom Stranger*, etc. Romance titles such as *Secret Hearts, Young Love* and *Young Romances* sold very well. All Horror, science fiction and war titles again were heavily purchased books with the higher grade issues selling for above current guide levels. Still the most popular single company collected from this period.

HORROR AND CRIME COMICS-1993 saw increased demand for these genres which were very hot. Atlas, DC, ACG, Charlton, and EC were the leading companies. The pre-code issues were the most sought. ACG's *Out Of The Night, Adventures Into The Unknown*, etc. were very hot. Reported Sales: *Chamber Of Chills* #1-VF86–$100, *Eerie* #3-VG45–$60, *Mister Mystery* #1-FN68–$125, 2-VF85–$135,

SPORT COMICS-Not that many titles and issues to collect. All are popular and sell very well.

ART COMICS-This past year, the top artist list was dominated by four names: Todd McFarlane, Jim Lee, Joe Quesada and Rob Liefeld. In the older books, Ditko and Kirby reign supreme, but the artist of the year is Alex Schomburg. Anything, absolutely anything with a Schomburg cover sells instantly. Other collected artists are Everett, Russ Heath,

Wolverton and especially Joe Maneely whose excellent Atlas covers have become very popular. Classic L.B. Cole covers (*Suspense* #8 and 11, *Criminals on the Run* V4#7, *Mask Comics* #1, etc. showed increased collectors interest.

ORIGINAL ART-See the following Christie's and Sotheby's auction report. Congratulations to Avon Books and Jerry Weist for his new paperback price guide on original art available through all normal distribution channels.

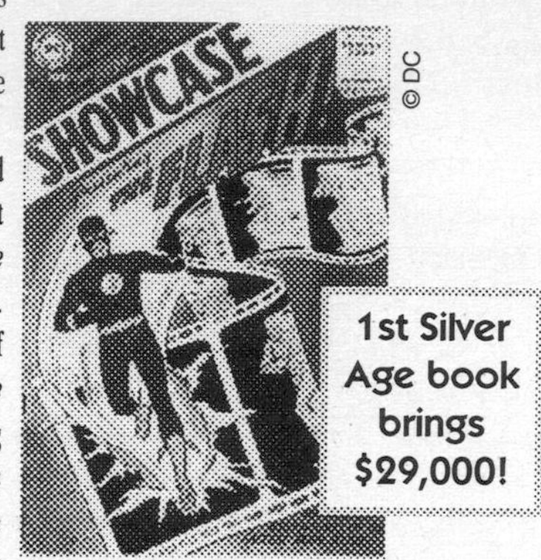

1st Silver Age book brings $29,000!

SILVER AGE DC-HOT FLASH !! A Showcase #4 in NM92 sold privately for $29,000 cash. *Showcase* is a hot title and the first 38 issues in VF or better are on everyone's want list. *Showcase* #25 and *Wonder Woman* #105 are also in very high demand. This is still the hottest area of collecting with VF-MT copies of most books fetching 150% of guide overall. *Brave and the Bold* #29 (the 2nd JLA) had increased interest. However, long run anthology titles, like *World's Finest*, *Adventure* and *Action* sell good in high grade, but are slow in low grade. Titles like *Strange Adventures, Mystery In Space, Tales of the Unexpected, My Greatest Adventure, House Of Mystery, House Of Secrets, Challengers of the Unknown*, etc. are collected in all grades. Current hot titles include *Adventure* Legion issues, *Brave and the Bold, Showcase, Flash, Rip Hunter, Lois Lane* #1-20, *Jimmy Olsen* #1-35, war comics with Sgt. Rock, Gunner & Sarge, Enemy Ace and Dinosaurs. Later titles such as Jonah Hex and Spectre are also very popular. Kirby's *Demon, Forever People,* and *Mister Miracle* are showing renewed interest as well. Reported sales: A near complete run of *My Greatest Adventure* #6-48, all in VF with white pages sold for 3.5 times guide list. Reported sales: *Action Comics* #242-VG45–$225, $267-VG45–$106, *Adventure Comics* #267-VG45–$166, *Atom* #2-VF82–$155, *Brave and the Bold* #34-VF88–$1200, *Challengers* #3-GD25–$56, 6-GD25–$46, *Detective Comics* #296-FN68–$37, *Flash* #105-FN74–$1800, *Forever People* #1-VF82–$23, *Green Lantern* #1-VG50–$375, 31-VF82–$47, *Joker* #1-VF82–$25, 3-VF82–$11, *Justice League* #1-GD30–$325, Lois Lane #1(Bethlehem)–$4830, *Showcase* #2-GD29–$125 ,4-FN(R)–$9000, VG49–$5060, 8-VF82–$3105, 23-VG50–$322, 27-FN65–$220, *Strange Adventures* #205-FN65–$24, *Superman Annual* #3-FN65–$63,.

SILVER AGE MARVEL-High Grade, High Grade, High Grade! 1993 saw the fastest expansion ever for high grade keys of this companies titles. Sotheby's sold a VF *Amazing Fantasy* 15 (White Mountain copy) for an unbelieavable $39,100! The news of this sale sent the comics market reeling. Two other recorded sales of high grade unrestored copies for $25,000+ each followed. Since that time there have been several unconfirmed reports of other copies selling in the high teens. A *Fantastic Four* #1VF sold for $27,600. There is still a high demand for all mainstream titles in VF-MT condition, especially the key #1s and other issues. However, The demand changes drastically as the grade drops. Low grade copies of particularly post 1965 issues became fairly common and hard to sell. Consequently, the availability of these books in low grade is forcing the spread between good and near mint to higher levels.

The hammer drops!!! Fantastic Four #1 VF brings record price at auction–$27,600!!

All Marvel annuals and Giant size issues enjoyed increased demand. There was demand for Amaz. Spider-Man #3 with the speculation that Dr. Octopus will be the villain in the upcoming movie. Pre-super hero issues were very hot. The later reprints of these stories like *Beware* and *Creatures On The Loose* became in high demand. Other popular titles were: *Amazing Spider-Man, Fantastic Four, Incredible Hulk* #1-6(especially #6, the all Ditko edition), *Sgt. Fury*

#1 & 13, *Fantastic Four Annual* #1, *Silver Surfer* (1st series), *Strange Tales* #110, *Annual* #1, *Tales of Suspense* #39, *X-Men* #1-20 *and Journey Into Mystery* #83, *Tales To Astonish* #27 & 35, *Tales Of Suspense* #39, *Iron Man* #1, *Captain America* #100. There continued to be a short supply of all early keys in high grade which continued to drive the prices up.

Reported sales: *Amazing Fantasy* #15-VF85–$39,100, VF82–$16,100, FN68–$3800, VG50–$2200, VG45–$1600, VG37–$1700, GD25–$1500, FR14–$900, *Amazing Spider-Man* #1-VF86–$19,000, VF80–$6700, VF(cleaned)–$6,800, FN65–$2800, VG48–$2000, VG45–$1700, FR12–$850, 3-NM94–$1475, 14-VF75–$700, 17-NM94–$515, 23-FN69–$168, *Avengers* 1-VF80–$1200, FN69–$775, FN68–$575, VG46–$375, 4-NM94(reprint)–$66, Annual #1-VF82–$33, *Captain America* #100-VF80–$200, VF89–$240, *Captain Marvel* #1-FN65–$41, 33-NM94–$30, *Conan* #3-60-VF(set)–$650, *Daredevil* #1-FN65–$540, VG48–$400, VG45–$320, GD34–$200, FR12–$132, 2-VF82–$260, *Fantastic Four* #1-NM94–$19,000, NM94–$19,000, VF86–$7,500(color touch) GD48–$1512, FR12–$450, 1(reprint)NM94–$102, 3 VG49–$350, 4-VG46–$400, 5-VG50–$500, 9FN65–$225, 48-VF86–$700, 48FN69–$310, *Incredible Hulk* #1-VF82–$7130, FN68–$2200, 2VG45–$336, 5-VF82–$880, GD25–$450, 102VG45–$42, *Iron Man* #1VF89–$240, VF80–$190, *Journey Into Mystery* #83-VF86–$2300, VF(R)–$1800, VG49–$735, *Man-Thing* #1-NM94–$18, *Marvel Premiere* #28-VF86–$12, *Marvel Spotlight* 11-NM–$48, Sgt. Fury #2-VF82–$140, 4-FN68–$56, *Silver Surfer* #1-VF80 $250, FN68–$186, 4-VF89–$275, 4-VF82–$240, *Strange Tales* #101-VF82–$400, 103-FN68–$100, 109-FN68–$62 110-FN68–$375, *Tales Of Suspense* #39-VF75–$1600, FN68–$950, VG45–$560, GD34–$450, 45-NM94–$300, 49-VF86–$180, *Tales To Astonish* #27-GD32–$240, *X-Men* #1FN56–$760, VG48–$450, VG42–$400, GD25–$200. 2-VG49–$280.

Green Skin in VF sells for record price of $7130!!

SILVER AGE DELL/GOLD KEY-This company's titles should seriously be examined for future investment potential. Most 60s issues are scarce in grade since the majority of the market at that time was buying and collecting Marvels and DCs. The late year drop in prices for the Valiant titles should not affect the value of these books. *Green Hornet, Tales From The Tomb, Doc Savage*, all T.V. titles, especially *Star Trek* are highly collected.

SILVER AGE CHARLTON-Moderate sales on *Capt. Atom, Flash Gordon, Phantom, Thunderbolt, Space Adventures*, etc. The market is beginning to look at these books which are now over 20 years old. All T.V. titles and especially the funny T.V. titles became hot, such as *Jetsons, Flintstones*, etc.

SILVER AGE ACG-There is continued demand for 1960s super hero issues of *Adventures Into The Unknown* and *Forbidden Worlds. Herbie* issues are also very hot.

WARREN MAGAZINES-*Creepy, Eerie* and especially *Vampirella* began selling very well during the year.

MISCELLANEOUS-*Barbie & Ken, Captain Flash, Space Western, Win A Prize* are a few hot titles. A *Barbie & Ken* #1VF82 sold for $160, a *Beatles* #1VF82 brought $350 and a *Turok* #18VF86 fetched $80.

MARKET WATCH: 1993

1993 was the year of the roller coaster ride in the comic book industry. The year began with much of the momentum created in the fourth quarter of 1992 by the death of Superman. The huge, unanticipated demand for all the Doomsday issues, especially *Superman* #75, the issue in which Superman actually died, drove the prices on these issues to dizzying heights within hours of the release of the books. The media attention received by Superman's death also brought in the general public in numbers never seen before. At the same time, the comic book market was viewed as a fertile market for the speculators from the over saturated sports card market in some of the early issues of Valiant and other smaller publishers. The feeding frenzy was on. The prices on back issues, as well as "key" new releases increased every month in all the price guides. The investment potential was touted by too many so called investment counselors. First appearances, death issues, new costumes, origin issues, and other rationalizations of importance drove prices in an upward spiral that seemed too easy not to cash in on.

Image Comics, the new upstart publisher with the fan favorite artists was still very much off schedule. This artificial shortage of Image titles made it easy for speculators to buy up multiple copies of the three or four releases that did come out each month. The relatively small print runs of early "pre-Unity" Valiant's made them easy targets for market manipulation by a few speculators. The influx of new money from the sports card speculators bought up large amounts of the normal supply of comics in the secondary market, creating shortages of certain issues and their weekly price increases. But as always is the case, when the music stopped, many speculators were left without a chair.

The market peaked in April 1993, ironically, with the return of Superman. Everyone was so sure that the Reign of the Supermen, the storyline bringing back Superman, would duplicate the Doomsday phenomenon, in which he was killed. Everyone was wrong. The simultaneous release of four issues, each in two versions, each heralding one would be replacement for the Man of Steel was more than the market could bear. Not only did the books not go up in price, but the unsold copies were soon trading not only below cover price, but below cost. This coupled with the 1.6 million copies of Turok #1 produced bills that many retailers could not afford.

But the market still had many excellent projects and sales were still very strong, although not up to the expectations of many get rich quick speculators. While Superman was coming back with sales far above the levels before his death, Batman was having his own set of problems that were driving his sales upward too. The Knightfall storyline which reached its climax with Batman's back being broken by the villain Bane, and a new champion, Azrael, taking up the cape and cowl of the Dark Knight. This storyline, like the Reign of the Supermen was released on a weekly schedule at a $1.25 cover price and attracted many new readers into the market. The inexpensive cover price, the intriguing storyline, the top notch rendering, the weekly installment and the headliner character, all added up to a project that helped overcome much of the damage done by the speculators and the over ordering.

Potentially, the biggest pay day for the retailers, and a project that could have balanced the losses incurred from the Reign of the Supermen over ordering was Deathmate. Deathmate was the joint venture of Image and Valiant, the two hottest companies of 1992. Deathmate was a coming together of the two universes for six issues. Two from Valiant, two from Image, and a shared Prologue and Epilogue. The orders were very impressive and the product was eagerly anticipated. The product did not live up to the expectations of the orders. The entire project was late as the Prologue was delayed due to the failure of Image to produce their input on schedule. The Valiant issues were released more or less on time but the Image issues were dreadfully late. The eagerness subsided, the expectation faded. The orders were reduced, the project did not deliver its promise.

Malibu–The Best Marketing Program of the Year!!

Hard Case #2 © Malibu

The most underestimated project of 1993 was the launch of the Ultraverse from Malibu Comics. From its inception, Image Comics was an imprint that was distributed by Malibu. Early in 1993, Image Comics broke away from Malibu and went off on their own. Immediately, Malibu accelerated the timetable on the already planned launch of their own Superhero universe, the Ultraverse. The kick off event was the Ultraverse conference held in Southern California in February 1993. There, the distributors, key retailers, and the media were introduced to the creators of the Ultraverse and given sneak peaks of the characters, the promotions and other plans for the launch of the Ultraverse. While the conference was very impressive, there was much skepticism whether Malibu could pull it off in a very crowded Superhero market in the Summer of 1993. Malibu made believers of the skeptics. Launching in June of 1993, with three titles, *Prime, Hardcase* and *Strangers* with by far the best marketing program of the year, Malibu quickly became the bright spot of the Summer. The key to their success was of course the quality of the basic product. The Ultraverse was created as a writer driven universe. This conscious effort to make the storyline the most important feature of each book paid off handsomely. Excellent artwork was the second most important consideration. Close to on time delivery was an important acknowledgment of the changing marketplace and the concerns of the retailer. The basics were in place but it was the extras that made the difference. A national television advertising campaign, a simultaneous release of a card set from Skybox, a coupon redemption program, full hologram cover limited editions of the launch issues, store point of purchase displays, a print to initial orders only policy to avoid a glut of product on the market, and other marketing programs and decisions kept the Ultraverse issues in demand, with stable prices while many other titles from other publishers were being offered at below cover price and even below cost at conventions as the speculators bailed out and the retailers tried to recover their cash flow.

Dark Horse's *Comics Greatest World* (Arcadia #2) © DH

Also launching a Superhero universe during 1993 was Dark Horse. While their success fell short of Malibu's Ultraverse, Dark Horse had a very successful launch of Comics Greatest World. To mitigate the competition for the consumer dollar in an overcrowded market, Dark Horse came up with a clever marketing concept. For sixteen weeks over the Summer, they would release one sixteen page comic a week, each with a retail price of $1. While this strategy did allow readers to sample Comics Greatest World each week, the sixteen weeks proved to be too long an introductory period. Immediately following the sixteen week launch, Comics Greatest World did not produce enough releases to hold the interest of many of the readers. Retrospectively, Comics Greatest World may prove to be the tortoise who wins the race, but at least for now, it is running a distant second.

The much heralded return of Jim Shooter to the comic book world also occurred in the Summer of 1993 with the launch of Shooter's Defiant Comics universe. With fresh venture capital money, and full control of the company Shooter set out to "just produce great comics". The first six months of the Defiant universe proved to be a little rocky. Their launch title, *Plasm* was immediately in legal dispute as Marvel forced them to change the name to *Warriors of Plasm* and even attempted to prevent their use of the characters and concepts, claiming a copyright violation. While the courts sided with Defiant, the drain of energy and other resources took its toll. Even before the launch of *Plasm* #1, the title had more than its share of controversy. The actual launch of the title was actually two months prior to the #1 issue via a Plasm #0 card set issued by The River Group. When the card packs were opened, a complete set assembled and put into the pages of a Plasm #0 binder, the first tale of the Defiant universe was revealed. But the binders were severely allocated and the price in the secondary market quickly escalated to acceptable levels before a second printing was announced and brought to market. There was also an unannounced comic book version of Plasm #0 that was bound into a distributor catalog, much to the surprise and chagrin of other distributors, many retailers and many consumers. In spite of the problems, Plasm and Warriors of Plasm were well ordered and well received by the market. Defiant's second title, Dark Dominion, also had its share of problems. Two artistic team changes, a month's delay in issue #1, an issue #0 card set that released the same week as issue #2 instead of a month prior to issue #1 and a much weaker comic book market added up to many unsold copies in retailer inventories. After a somewhat controversial launch with more than its share of problems, Defiant remains defiant and promises to carry on.

Hit from Topps–*Jurassic Park !!* (#3 shown)

© Universal

Other publishers who attempted to break into the superhero arena in 1993 were Continuity, Harris and Topps. Continuity had a moderately successful launch with their Deathwatch 2000 crossover storyline but they quickly fell victim to the late shipping which has always plagued the company. Harris Publications, a mass market magazine publisher attempted to break into the comic book field with *Vampirella*, which was very successful. Their further attempts were well received until they too became victims of late shipping, forcing them to cancel many issues and re-solicit. After a very successful launch with the licensed comic book adaptation of Bram Stoker's Dracula, and an even more successful follow up with the licensed comic book adaptation of Jurassic Park, Topps entered the superhero arena via the Jack Kirby Kirbyverse. This material did not catch the attention or interest of the reader/collectors and the project quickly died.

A critical step taken by many publishers to insure the continued growth of the comic book industry was the broadening of the genres offered in comic book form. While the main genre is superheroes, we saw many successful licensed movie and television adaptations. To name a few, *Ren and Stimpy* from Marvel, *Aliens, Robocop, Predator, Star Wars,* and *Indiana Jones* from Dark Horse, *Star Trek* and *Star Trek: The Next Generation* from DC, *Mr. T* and *Married With Children* from Now, and *Star Trek: Deep Space Nine* and *Street Fighter* from Malibu. There were major attempts by both DC's Vertigo and Marvel's Razorline and the Clive Barker titles to reach out to an older audience who are not interested in superheroes but will read well written, graphically illustrated stories. Similar attempts to reach the younger audience were made by DC and Marvel through their comic book/ animated television shows *Batman* and *X-Men* respectively.

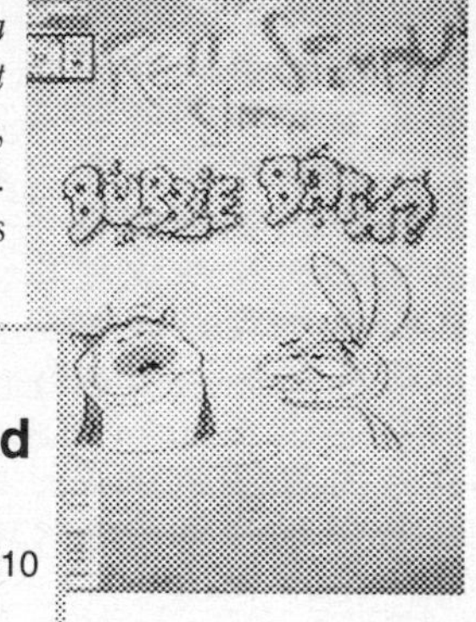

Genres broadened in 1993

(Ren & Stimpy #10 © Nickelodeon)

In an attempt to stand out on the comic rack, many publishers employed gimmick covers. Some of the gimmicks, or sales enhancements as the publishers call them included foil covers, die cut covers, glow in the dark covers, chromium covers, holographic covers, and hologram covers. While these gimmicks were accepted and even embraced in the beginning, their overuse quickly caused them to fall out of favor with the consumer and retailer. Other sales incentives, especially variant editions were offered by publishers to retailers in an effort to get them to increase their orders on certain titles. The success of these marketing strategies, while short term benefiting the individual publisher, long term added to the glut of product in the marketplace.

How the excess product in the marketplace was handled proved to be a major factor in extending the difficulties the marketplace experienced. The excess product caused by the speculators and retailers over ordering, the successful efforts by the publishers through the use of sales incentives to get retailers to order more, and the closing down of many retailers who were unable to pay their bills left enormous amounts of unsold product in the marketplace at the publisher, distributor and retailer level. Too much of this product was offered at close out prices and eventually found its way to market at very cheap prices. Although the number of issues was only a few hundred, the number of copies was several million. At any convention during the second half of 1993, thousands upon thousands of comic books were available at deep discount from cover price, sometimes as much as 90% off cover price. Thus the confidence of the collector was severely tested when they saw comic books they had paid two or three dollars for being offered for as little as 25¢. This general loss of confidence is one of the major obstacles that must be overcome before the comic book market can enjoy further growth. A positive side of the inventory dumping is that much of the inventory found its way into the mass market through pre-packs that wound up in Wal-Mart, CVS drug stores, and K-Mart. The Blockbuster chain of video stores began experimental programs carrying comic books. Starlog launched a franchise comic book-science fiction retail store concept and Walden Books continued studying expansion of the comic book sections of their book stores.

What will 1994 bring to the comic book marketplace? Some very exciting projects that should herald a turnaround for the market include the wedding of two members of the X-Men, Jean Grey and Scott Summers, a two part Batman Spawn crossover project between Image Comics and DC Comics, the Jump on Now/Ultraverse Origins television commercial campaign from Malibu Comics encouraging viewers to get involved with the Ultraverse, the first story is done entirely in Valiant Vision, and the launch of the Bravura line of creator owned characters from Malibu Comics. With the painful lessons of over ordering and speculation fresh in their minds, consumers, retailers and distributors should have a happy and healthy 1994.

With helpful assistance from Steve Geppi, Hugh O'Kennon, Ron Pussell, Sean Linkenback, Dan Malan, John Snyder, Terry Stroud, Gary Colabuono, Jerry Jacobs, Walter Wang, James Payette, Jerry Weist, Stephen Fishler, Bruce Hamilton, John Verzyl, Gary M. Carter, Mark Wilson and Joe Mannarino.

SOTHEBY'S 3RD COMIC AUCTION, SPRING, 1993 (The Day Silver Turned Into Gold) (by Jerry Weist & Roger Hill)

The 3rd annual Sotheby's Comic Books and Comic Art Auction, held in New York City on June 26, 1993, proved to be the most successful auction of its kind held to date. It was our first weekend Saturday auction after moving to the new annual Spring time-frame. How could an auction that failed to sell the "payout" copy of *Marvel Comics* #1, *Action Comics* #1, *Detective Comics* #27 and *Superman* #1 be regarded as highly successful? Read on.

To begin with, overall figures were the best yet in the business. The low end total (total low estimates for all 582 lots in the auction) were just shy of 1.4 million dollars; the total sale, with the buyer's premium, was just short of 1.35 million dollars, resulting in the first comic book auction to nearly realize its low end.

The unsold percentage, or "B.I. rate" (bought-in by the auction house) improved to 24%. If one were to eliminate the high estimates of the big Golden Age books, the Frazetta painting and the contemporary Superman artwork, all of which went unsold, this auction would easily have realized its high end estimate. That could have been achieved, when coupled with the white-hot bidding that surged, went out of control, and turned 1950's artwork and comics, and Silver Age artwork and comics into "Blue Chip" investments of the moment, or the gold standard for our market.

As is usually the case with all auctions, many of the prices realized for each year's auction, are dependent upon the quality of material offered for sale. Sotheby's took a calculated risk in presenting a triple tier of Silver Age comics: The "White Mountain" Marvels–representing the top tier–followed by fairly strong Marvel runs in FN condition, followed by very complete hero and pre-hero Marvel runs with tanning paper.

Amazing Fantasy #15 (white Mountain copy) brings unbelievable price of **$39,100!!**

Here is a sampling of some of the prices realized: The much revered "White Mountain" copy of *Amazing Fantasy* #15 established a new world record high for a Silver Age comic when it sold for $39,100 (over five times guide), followed by the second highest price ever paid for the "White Mountain" copy of *Fantastic Four* #1, selling at $27,600 (nearly four times guide). A near complete run of FF #1-38, in FN sold for $5,175; near complete set of *Spider-Man* #1-70, in FN sold for $7,188, near complete run of *X-Men* #1-54 in FN sold for $1,955; near complete set of *Strange Tales* #67-118 in VG brought $978 and a near complete lot of *Journey Into Mystery* #50-108, ranging from GD to FN, sold for $978 as well.

DC Comics sold briskly also. One of the finest condition copies of *Showcase* #8 sold for $3,105. Other strong sales included: *Showcase* #15-19 in FN condition - $1,840; *Showcase* lot of #22-24 and near complete run of *Green Lantern* #1-50 in VF - $3,105, and a lot of *Sensation Mystery* #113-116 and *Phantom Stranger* #2-6, ranging from GD to FN - $1,380.

Original art collectors were in abundance at the sale, and on the phone, and following the trend we have been witnessing for the past five years, Marvel and DC Silver Age art continued to set record prices. The biggest surprise to most of us was the last minute inclusion (not pictured or listed in the catalog) of John Romita's cover art to *Spider-Man* #40, which realized the incredible sale price of $18,975 - the highest price ever paid for any Silver Age cover. Romita's splash page from *Spider-Man* #39 sold for a hefty $5,750, and a Ditko page from *Spider-Man* #6 sold for $3,105. Jack Kirby artwork, as always, did quite well with the *Thor* #141 alternate cover art fetching $4,255; and unused penciled *Captain America* cover - $1,725, and the covers for *Captain America* #108 and #212 selling for $2,415 and $2,070 respectively.

The Silver Age art popularity carried over to DC as well, with record prices being realized on many fine examples in the auction, including: cover to *Flash* #120 by Carmine Infantino - $10,350, two-page JSA pin-up by Murphy Anderson - $9,200, splash page to *JLA* #1 by Mike Sekowsky - $8,050, splash page to *Brave and Bold* #36 (Hawkman) by Joe Kubert - $7,763, cover to *Hawkman* #4 by Murphy Anderson - $5,175, cover to *Adventure Comics* #302 by Curt Swan - $4,888, and the Neal Adams cover to *Superman* #233 - $4,888. Almost all Silver Age art in the auction did very well, with most pieces selling well over the high estimates.

We think it very likely in years to come that our offering of EC artwork and comics in this 3rd auction will be regarded as a major milestone. For the first time at auction, collectors were treated to rare complete sets of EC pre-trend runs, all of which sold, followed by record prices being set on select runs of complete New-Trend titles. Also, for the first time ever, EC Pre-Trend art was on hand, including the very first *Crypt of Terror* story by Al Feldstein from *Crime Patrol* #15 and #16 each sold for $4,025, followed by Jack Davis' "Foul Play" horror story from *Haunt of Hear* #19 selling at $6,038. Al Williamson's "Mad Journey" from *Weird Fantasy* #14 did well at $10, 350, with Wally Wood's "You Rocket" from *Incredible Science-Fiction* #31 pulling down $3,450 and Al Feldstein's painted cover re-creation to *Weird Fantasy* #16 selling for $5,463.

E.C. art brings top prices!!

Although our Golden Age offering was admittedly weak in certain areas, and several "big ticket" books didn't sell, others did, including a copy of *Double Action Comics* #2 in VG for $3,163, *Superman* #2, 3, 4, and 6 in GD sold as a group for $2,070, *Sensation* #1 in FN sold at $1,955 and *Whiz* #1 in VG sold for $7,763. On the other hand, Golden Age comic art seemed to have a sustained following with enthusiastic bidding pushing the cover art to *Motion Picture Funnies Weekly* #1 up to $20,700, followed by the cover to #2 going for $3,738, #3 went at $1,840 and #4 finishing at $2,588. An early Joe Shuster unpublished *Superman* page sold for $3,738, an L. B. Cole cover recreation to *Mask Comics* #2 went for $978, and the cover to *Jungle Comics* #46 by Raphael Astarita from 1943, sold for $3,450.

Original newspaper strip art performed consistently well with the following results: The original *Krazy Kat* watercolor specialty illustration by George Herriman that adorned the front cover of our catalog sold for a healthy $10,350; and early Thimble Theatre Sunday page by Segar went for $6,900; two *Flash Gordon* Sunday pages with Jungle Jim toppers by Alex Raymond sold for $9,775 each; the beautifully hand-colored Burne Hogarth *Tarzan* Sunday page from 1950 went for $14,950 and a 1946 *Prince Valiant* Sunday page by Hal Foster brought $9,775. The highest price paid for a single piece of art in this auction was the beautiful full color *Uncle Scrooge* painting titled "Hands off my Playthings" by Carl Barks, which sold for $112,500.

Barks duck painting sells for whopping $112,500!!

In regards to contemporary comic art this auction brought forth further evidence that the market place will bear only so much in relation to quality vs. price vs. current sales results. The twelve covers for the popular *Watchmen* series, scripted by Alan Moore, with artwork by David Gibbons sold for $17,250 - $2,500 below its low end estimate. This is still a very healthy price for contemporary comic cover art when you figure the ratio to each cover was $1,437.50. The artwork from *Superman* #78 and *Adventures of Superman* #500 by Dan Jurgens and Brett Breeding could not realize bidding for less than half of the low end estimate. Lot #154, featuring twenty seven interior pages of art by Jurgens and Breeding, with an estimate of $40,000 to $45,000 failed to sell at $17,500. This art failed to sell for $648 per page when estimated at $1,666 per page on the high estimate. The message is clear that collectors are not blinded by sales in the hundreds of thousands of dollars, and will not buy artwork at greatly inflated prices. It definitely tells us something when our attending bidding audience breaks into a thunderous applause following the non-sale of several lots of contemporary artwork.

However, there were other positive results and sales on other contemporary lots such as a Dan Jurgens and Walt Simonson cover for *Superman* #69 that was reasonably estimated at $750 to $1,000, and wound up selling over the high end at a price of $1,150. A John Byrne and Walt Simonson *World of Krypton* #4 cover was estimated at $400 to $600, and sold for $920, followed by a two page title splash from *Web of Spiderman* #6 by Todd McFarlane, estimated at $700 to $900, and pulling in a sale price of $2,185, and last but not least, the original cover art to *Wolverine* #27 by Jim Lee that was estimated at $500 to $700 and sold for $1,610.

Sotheby's has come to regard the A.C.G. (Committee for Authenticity, Certification and Grading) as a crucial part of each years auction. We are very lucky indeed to have the expertise of so many professional and experienced long-time collectors and dealers who each year engage in a combined process of grading, evaluating and checking each comic lot for restoration. Their combined efforts and hard work provides an unbiased opinion of every book sold in auction, and allows so many collectors and buyers the opportunity to bid with confidence. This past year a near perfect blend and balance was attained with Gary Carter as Chair-person, and a staff including Susan Cicconi, Hans Curtis, Joe Dungan, Bruce Edwards, John Hauser, Roger Hill, Pat Kohanek, Michael Naiman, James Payette and Joe Vereneault working together. We believe that in years to come many collectors will cherish great memories of each years best purchase from a Sotheby's auction, while the consultant will cherish memories of being honored by working with such a talented group of comic enthusiasts.

And what does the future hold for the auctions? We think the best is yet to come. Rumors are already running rampant through the marketplace. The grapevine of Fandom is buzzing with excitement and anticipation about what is being called the "best ever" auction yet. We can only wonder what the outcome will be when the origin artwork by Joe Shuster, executed in 1935 for the most important comic character of all time, Superman, is brought to the auction block. What prices will be realized for complete collections of *Action Comics* #1-500, *Superman* #1-300, *Adventure Comics* #103-500, *Lois Lane* #1 up, *Jimmy Olsen* #1 up, *World's Finest* #1 up and *Superboy* #1 up? What will *Detective Comics* #27 (unrestored) in VG, with 8. Owl paper, bring with an estimate of $25,000 to $30,000, and a similar copy from the same collection, of *Action Comics* #1, with very limited restoration by Susan Cicconi, at a much lower estimate?

What will happen when twenty-one classic Silver Age Marvel comic cover recreations by Jack Kirby, Dick Ayers and John Romita Sr. - though a special arrangement in cooperation between Marvel Comics, Sotheby's and the artists - come onto the auction block? These cover recreations will include *Amazing Fantasy* #15, *Spider-Man* #1, *Fantastic Four* #1 and #5, *Journey Into Mystery* #83, *Avengers* #1, *Hulk* #3, *Strange Tales* #101, *Tales to Astonish* #27, *Spider-Man* #39, 50, 54 and 100, among others. The sale of these important cover recreations promises to be one of the biggest highlights of the auction.

As a result of increasing demand, what will happen when Sotheby's presents a wide selection of Gold Key and Dell comics in mint condition? Through an exclusive arrangement with Western Publishing, we will be offering near complete "file copy" mint condition runs for such titles as: *Twilight Zone, Flintstones, The Jetsons, Boris Karloff, Dark Shadows* and a host of others. What will the Western "file copies" for *Mickey Mouse Magazine* sell for? What will the Murphy Anderson file copies of *Captain America* #1-14, followed by a near complete run, sell for? What will happen in the aftermath of the "White Mountain" Marvels, when other high-grade Marvel and DC runs are brought into the market place? Will the original cover artwork for *Hulk* #102, *Sub-Mariner* and *Iron Man* #1, *Mystery in Space* #73, and *Superman* #170 and other Silver Age artwork continue to spiral?

All these questions and more will be answered by a single day of bidding at what many collectors are already calling the "auction event of the decade." Stay tuned!

CHRISTIE'S COMIC COLLECTIBLES SALE, HELD OCT. 30, 1993 By Joe Mannarino

This sale was again highlighted by record prices.Frank Frazetta's "A Princess of Mars" oil, sold for $90,500 a record at auction for a Frazetta. Jack Kirby - The original art to a Marvel poster featuring Galactus and The Silver Surfer sold for $10,925, a record at auction for the artist. J. Allen St. John - Original cover art from the Amazing Stories pulp magazine dated March 1944, sold for $25,300, a record price at auction for a pulp cover.

The auction was well attended with numerous phone and left bids. Frazetta again did very well, aside from the aforementioned "A Princess Of Mars", the "Mothman", oil on canvas board, sold for $68,500, A watercolor from the upcoming "Pillow Book" sold for $10,580 and two pencil illustrations also sold.

Without question the hottest group of material was Silver Age original comic art, Kirby and Ditko in particular. Twenty-seven of twenty-nine lots of Kirby art exceeded estimates, i.e. pin-up of Captain America from *Avengers* #10 $9,200 the splash (pg. 1) of *Fantastic Four* #21 est. $1,500-2,500 realized $6,555, pg. 22 of FF #5 realized $5,175, pg. 9 of Thor #126 - $3,680, pg. 5 *Avengers* #2 $2,990, pg. 11 FF #7 - $3,220, pg. 7 *Hulk* #5 - $2,300. Ditko featured pg.

12 *Spider-Man* #12 - $2,990, pg. 22 *Hulk* #6 $2,530 and pg. 13 *Spider-Man* #36 $2,530. Impressively prices were consistent across all titles including pre-hero.

In comic books the William Gaines file copies, were again a big hit. *Vault of Horror* #13-40 offered with *War Against Crime* #10 & #11 sold for $12,650, *Weird Science* #1-22 sold for $11,500. High grade Silver Age remains very strong, a VF *Amazing Fantasy* #15 sold for $16,100, a VF *Hulk* #1 with exceptional page quality sold for $7,130, the Kubert file copy of *Showcase* #4 in VG+ condition sold for $5,060, the Bethlehem copy of *Lois Lane* #1 sold for $4,830 (over four times guide) and #2, 3 & 4 sold for $1,600 as a lot. runs of Silver Age Marvels sold for well above estimate. Silver Age DC's also sold well with lots of *Showcase, Mystery In Space, Strange Adventures* and *Brave and The Bold* all selling. In Golden Age *Superman* #1, restored FN, realized $10,350 and *New Book Of Comics* #1, FN+ realized $4,485.

Gaine's EC vault is opened. Left to right: Bob Overstreet, Bill Gaines, Russ Cochran.

Record Prices for EC comics!

Art in general did extremely well, other examples include: Cover *Vault Of Horror* #12 $5,700, Murphy Anderson, *Hawkman* #8 cover $5,750, and three rare Joe Maneely covers estimated $600-800 each realized, $3,900, $2,185, and $1,985 respectively. Comic strip art was highlighted by a Gottfredson Mickey Mouse Sunday $9,200, and a 1949 Hal Foster, Prince Valiant Sunday $9,200.

The auction was propitious in that it continued to introduce new collectors to the field as well as continuing to validate the current strong interest in comic related collectibles. The gallery was standing room only and nearly 75% of the items sold were purchased by newcomers to the field. Of equal significance, the majority of the items went to collectors as opposed to prospective investors. The Comic Collectibles sale was the biggest dollar sale of the year for the Christie's East Collectible Department.

Pacific Comic Exchange, Inc. Sales (By Robert J. Roter)

Pacific Comic Exchange, Inc. ("PCE") specializes exclusively in vintage comic books and operates in the same manner as a real estate brokerage house. Prices are negotiable between buyer and seller and all sales are documented through the Monthly Listing Report.

1993 saw a record increase in trading at PCE. Many new price levels were achieved on individual book sales. The pattern was consistent throughout the year - key books in high grade sold quickly on the network with active bidding beginning as soon as they were listed on the Exchange. In some cases, books were sold within hours of being listed.

Sample sales for 1993 (prices include the 10% buyers commission) are listed below. All books are reported in the Comic Grading Service of America ("CGSA") grading scale with the Page Quality (PQ) rating: **Action Comics** #1 (slight restoration) VG/FN 30 (5.5) $24,200; **Adventure Comics** #36, Mile High Copy, NM 88 (3.0) $1,980; **All Select Comics** #1, Carson City Copy, NM 85 (3.3) $3,300; **All Star Comics** #38, Pennsylvania Copy, NM/MT 90 (2.0) $1,375; **All Top Comics** #8, Mile High Copy, NM 88 (1.0) $1,925; **Amazing Spider-Man** #1 VF 60 (3.5) $4,620; **Avengers** #1 NM 80 (4.0) $1,980; **Batman** #1 GD 10 (8.0) $4,730; **Brave & The Bold** #28 VF 68 (4.5) $3,960; **Captain America Comics** #1 VG/FN 30 (4.5) $7,040; **Detective Comics** #38 GD/VG (6.0) $2,310; **Famous Funnies Carnival of Comics** 1933 VF/NM 70 (4.0)

$3,850; **Fantastic Four** #1 VF/NM 70 (4.0) $9,900, **Fantastic Four** #1 VF/NM 70 (3.5) $11,000; **Flash** #105 VF 60 (4.0) $2,520; **Flash Comics** #1 (Trimmed with Moderate Restoration) VG 20 (4.5) $2,750; **Green Lantern** #1 (GA) VF 65 (4.5) $11,000, **Green Lantern** #2 (GA) VF/NM 70 (3.5) $2,560; **House Of Mystery** #1 NM 75 (3.5) $1,650; **Human Torch** #2 FN 45 (5.0) $2,145; **Journey Into Mystery** #83 VF 60 (3.3) $2,475; **MAD** #1 White Mountain Copy NM 75 (2.0) $2,200, **MAD** #5 Gaines File Copy MT 94 (1.0) $2,200; **Marvel Comics** #1 (extensively restores) GD/VG 15 (7.5) $8,800, **Marvel Comics** #1 Carson City Copy VF 60 (3.5) $55,000; **Phantom Lady** #17 FN 45 (5.0) $1,210; **Real Fact Comics** #5 NM 80 (2.0) $1,430; **Showcase** #8 FN/VF 50 (3.5) $3,410; **Strange Tales** #110 NM 75 (3.5) $1,540; **Superboy** #1 FN/VF 50 (4.5) $1,595; **Tales Of Suspense** #39 NM 80 (3.5) $4,400; **Tales To Astonish** #27 NM 80 (3.5) $6,050; **Turok Son Of Stone** #1, File Copy NM 80 (3.5) $1,500; **USA** #1 FN/VF 50 (5.5) $2,035; **Wonder Woman** #5, Mile High Copy NM/MT 90 (0.0) $2,090; **X-Men** #1 NM 75 (3.5) $3,300; **Young Allies Comics** #1 VF 65 (4.0) $2,420.

In summary, low and mid grade non-key books tended to bring 80% to 100% of Overstreet Guide value. High grade material generally brought above guide prices, whereas keys in high grade would bring multiples of guide.

One area that performed poorly was restored Silver Age. Buyers consistently shied away from books that were altered. In contrast, scarce Golden Age material would still sell if the restoration was minor or priced accordingly.

INVESTOR'S DATA

The following tables denote the rate of appreciation of the top Golden Age books and the top Silver Age books, as well as selected genres over the past year and the past five years (1989-1994). The retail value for a NM copy of each book in 1994 is compared to its value in 1993 and 1989. The rate of return for 1994 over 1993, and 1994 over 1989 are given. The place in rank is given for each comic by year, with its corresponding NM value. These tables can be very useful in forecasting trends in the marketplace. For instance, the investor might want to know which book is yielding the best dividend from one year to the next, or one might just be interested in seeing how the popularity of books changes from year to year. For instance, *All-American* #16 was in 8th place in 1993 and has increased to 6th place in 1994. *Amazing Fantasy* #15 increased from 3rd to 1st place from 1993 to 1994.

The following tables are meant as a guide to the investor. However, it should be pointed out that trends may change at anytime and that some books can meet market resistance with a slowdown in price increases, while others can develop into real comers from a presently dormant state. In the long run, if the investor sticks to the books that are appreciating steadily each year, he shouldn't go very far wrong.

The Silver Age titles exploded in 1993, especially early issues of Marvels and DCs in high grade. Golden & Silver Age titles are continuing to appreciate faster than economic inflationary values during the same period.

TOP GOLDEN AGE BOOKS

1994 OVER 1993 AND 1989 GUIDE VALUES

Issue No.	1994 Rank	1994 NM Price	1993 Rank	1993 NM Price	$ Incr.	% Incr.	Change In Rank
Detective Comics #27	1	$92,000	1	$85,000	$7,000	8%	0
Action Comics #1	2	$90,000	2	$75,000	$15,000	20%	0
Marvel Comics #1	3	$75,000	4	$63,000	$12,000	19%	1
Superman #1	4	$70,000	3	$65,000	$5,000	8%	-1
Whiz Comics #2 (#1)	5	$42,000	5	$42,000	$0	0%	0
All American Comics #16	6	$37,000	8	$32,000	$5,000	16%	2
Batman #1	7	$36,000	7	$33,500	$2,500	8%	0
Detective Comics #1	8	$36,000	9	$30,000	$6,000	20%	1
Captain America Comics #1	9	$36,000	6	$30,000	$6,000	20%	1
New Fun Comics #1	10	$29,200	11	$23,800	$5,400	23%	1
More Fun Comics #52	11	$28,000	10	$25,000	$3,000	12%	-1
Flash Comics #1	12	$23,000	12	$20,000	$3,000	15%	0
All Star Comics #3	13	$20,000	13	$17,500	$2,500	14%	0
Detective Comics #33	14	$18,000	15	$17,000	$1,000	6%	1
Detective Comics #38	15	$18,000	16	$16,000	$2,000	13%	1
More Fun Comics #53	16	$17,500	17	$15,500	$2,000	13%	1
Captain Marvel Adventures #1	17	$17,000	14	$17,000	$0	0%	-3
Adventure Comics #40	18	$16,000	18	$14,000	$2,000	14%	0
Famous Funnies-Series 1 #1	19	$14,000	19	$12,000	$2,000	17%	0
Green Lantern #1	20	$13,000	24	$10,000	$3,000	30%	4

BONZAI COMICS
WE SPECIALIZE IN THE
RARE, OBSCURE, HARD TO FIND
UNDERGROUNDS·GOLD AND SILVER AGE
WE HAVE IN STOCK HIGH GRADE COPIES OF
SUPERMAN #1 · CAPT. AMERICA #1 · AMAZING FANTASY #15
RUNS OF SPIDERMAN #1-100 —— FANTASTIC FOUR #1-100
CALL IN YER WANTS
212·502·3991★BUYING & SELLING

TOP GOLDEN AGE BOOKS (cont'd) Issue No.	1994 Rank	1994 NM Price	1993 Rank	1993 NM Price	$ Increase	% Increase	Change In Rank
New Fun Comics #2	21	$12,500	20	$11,250	$1,250	11%	-1
Detective Comics #29	22	$12,500	21	$11,000	$1,500	14%	-1
Detective Comics #31	23	$12,500	22	$11,000	$1,500	14%	-1
Jumbo Comics #1	24	$12,000	37	$7,500	$4,500	60%	13
Century Of Comics nn	25	$11,900	23	$10,500	$1,400	13%	-2
New York World's Fair 1939	26	$11,000	28	$8,500	$2,500	29%	2
New Fun Comics #6	27	$10,900	50	$6,000	$4,900	82%	23
New Comics #1	28	$10,750	41	$7,000	$3,750	54%	13
Amazing Man #5	29	$10,500	25	$9,500	$1,000	11%	-4
Famous Funnies-No. 1 #1	30	$10,000	26	$9,000	$1,000	11%	-4
Big Book Of Fun Comics #1	31	$9,750	34	$7,500	$2,250	30%	3
Marvel Mystery Comics #2	32	$9,500	27	$8,500	$1,000	12%	-5
Human Torch #2 (#1)	33	$9,500	32	$7,800	$1,700	22%	-1
Detective Comics #2	34	$9,430	35	$7,500	$1,930	26%	1
New Book Of Comics #1	35	$9,400	78	$4,900	$4,500	92%	43
Comic Magazine #1	36	$9,000	29	$8,250	$750	9%	-7
Mickey Mouse Magazine #1	37	$9,000	30	$8,000	$1,000	13%	-7
Wow Comics #1	38	$9,000	31	$8,000	$1,000	13%	-7
More Fun Comics #14	39	$9,000	38	$7,500	$1,500	20%	-1
Adventure Comics #48	40	$8,500	33	$7,500	$1,000	13%	-7
Daring Mystery #1	41	$8,000	40	$7,000	$1,000	14%	-1
All Star Comics #1	42	$7,800	39	$7,000	$800	11%	-3
Double Action #2	43	$7,500	36	$7,500	$0	0%	-7
Four Color Ser. 1 (Mickey Mouse) #16	44	$7,500	43	$6,665	$835	13%	-1
All Star Comics #8	45	$7,500	44	$6,500	$1,000	15%	-1
Detective Comics #3	46	$7,400	47	$6,000	$1,400	23%	1
Funnies On Parade nn	47	$7,200	48	$6,000	$1,200	20%	1
Sub-Mariner Comics #1	48	$7,200	52	$6,000	$1,200	20%	4
Walt Disney's Comics & Stories #1	49	$7,000	42	$6,700	$300	4%	-7
Marvel Mystery Comics #5	50	$7,000	45	$6,500	$500	8%	-5
More Fun Comics #55	51	$7,000	49	$6,000	$1,000	17%	-2
World's Best #1	52	$7,000	53	$6,000	$1,000	17%	1
New Fun Comics #3	53	$6,750	62	$5,250	$1,500	29%	9
New Fun Comics #4	54	$6,750	63	$5,250	$1,500	29%	9
New Fun Comics #5	55	$6,750	64	$5,250	$1,500	29%	9
Red Raven #1	56	$6,500	51	$6,000	$500	8%	-5
Big All-American #1	57	$6,500	56	$5,500	$1,000	18%	-1
Marvel Mystery Comics #9	58	$6,500	57	$5,500	$1,000	18%	-1
Mystic Comics #1	59	$6,500	58	$5,500	$1,000	18%	-1
Wonder Woman #1	60	$6,500	75	$5,000	$1,500	30%	15
Detective Comics #28	61	$6,300	59	$5,400	$900	17%	-2
Action Comics #2	62	$6,200	54	$5,600	$600	11%	-8
King Comics #1	63	$6,200	61	$5,250	$950	18%	-2
Adventure Comics #61	64	$6,000	46	$6,000	$0	0%	-18
All American Comics #19	65	$6,000	55	$5,500	$500	9%	-10
Famous Funnies-Carnival/Comics nn	66	$6,000	60	$5,300	$700	13%	-6
Sensation Comics #1	67	$6,000	66	$5,200	$800	15%	-1
Four Color Ser. 1 (Donald Duck) #4	68	$6,000	69	$5,000	$1,000	20%	1
New York World's Fair 1940	69	$6,000	72	$5,000	$1,000	20%	3
All American Comics #17	70	$6,000	79	$4,700	$1,300	28%	9
All Flash #1	71	$5,800	67	$5,000	$800	16%	-4
Batman #2	72	$5,700	65	$5,200	$500	10%	-7
Archie Comics #1	73	$5,500	68	$5,000	$500	10%	-5
March Of Comics (Donald Duck) nn(#4)	74	$5,500	70	$5,000	$500	10%	-4
Mickey Mouse Book (Bibo & Lang) 1930	75	$5,500	71	$5,000	$500	10%	-4
Planet Comics #1	76	$5,500	73	$5,000	$500	10%	-3
Special Edition Comics #1	77	$5,500	74	$5,000	$500	10%	-3
New Book Of Comics #2	78	$5,380	122	$2,200	$3,180	145%	44
Feature Book (Dick Tracy) nn(#1)	79	$5,250	76	$4,900	$350	7%	-3
Feature Book (Popeye) nn(#1)	80	$5,250	77	$4,900	$350	7%	-3
Adventure Comics #73	81	$5,200	82	$4,500	$700	16%	1
Action Comics #3	82	$5,000	80	$4,600	$400	9%	-2
Green Giant #1	83	$5,000	81	$4,600	$400	9%	-2
Captain America Comics #2	84	$5,000	83	$4,500	$500	11%	-1
More Fun Comics #73	85	$5,000	84	$4,500	$500	11%	-1
Superman #2	86	$5,000	86	$4,500	$500	11%	0
Four Color (Donald Duck) #9	87	$5,000	89	$4,200	$800	19%	2
All Winners #1	88	$5,000	93	$4,000	$1,000	25%	5
More Fun Comics #54	89	$4,800	87	$4,400	$400	9%	-2
Action Comics #7	90	$4,800	88	$4,200	$600	14%	-2
Wonder Comics #1	91	$4,800	91	$4,200	$600	14%	0

TOP GOLDEN AGE BOOKS (cont'd) Issue No.	1994 Rank	1994 NM Price	1993 Rank	1993 NM Price	$ Increase	% Increase	Change In Rank
Silver Steak #1	92	$4,800	94	$4,000	$800	20%	2
USA Comics #1	93	$4,600	95	$4,000	$600	15%	2
Skippy's Own Book Of Comics nn	94	$4,500	85	$4,500	$0	0%	-9
More Fun Comics #101	95	$4,500	90	$4,200	$300	7%	-5
Adventure Comics #72	96	$4,500	92	$4,000	$500	13%	-4
Action Comics #10	97	$4,400	96	$3,800	$600	16%	-1
Tough Kid Squad #1	98	$4,200	97	$3,800	$400	11%	-1
All American Comics #25	99	$4,200	100	$3,500	$700	20%	1
New Comics #2	100	$4,200	105	$3,450	$750	22%	5
Silver Steak #6	101	$4,200	108	$3,400	$800	24%	7
Batman #3	102	$4,000	98	$3,700	$300	8%	-4
All American Comics #18	103	$4,000	99	$3,500	$500	14%	-4
Comic Cavalcade #1	104	$4,000	101	$3,500	$500	14%	-3
Detective Comics #35	105	$4,000	102	$3,500	$500	14%	-3
Four Color (Donald Duck) #29	106	$4,000	106	$3,400	$600	18%	0
Pep Comics #22	107	$4,000	107	$3,400	$600	18%	0
Daredevil #1	108	$4,000	109	$3,200	$800	25%	1
Young Allies Comics #1	109	$4,000	111	$3,200	$800	25%	2
Military Comics #1	110	$3,900	103	$3,500	$400	11%	-7
Superboy #1	111	$3,800	104	$3,500	$300	9%	-7
Marvel Mystery Comics #3	112	$3,800	110	$3,200	$600	19%	-2
Captain America Comics #3	113	$3,600	115	$3,000	$600	20%	2
More Fun Comics #67	114	$3,500	116	$3,000	$500	17%	2
Pep Comics #1	115	$3,500	117	$3,000	$500	17%	2
Superman #3	116	$3,500	118	$3,000	$500	17%	2
Tip Top Comics #1	117	$3,500	119	$3,000	$500	17%	2
Action Comics #4	118	$3,300	112	$3,000	$300	10%	-6
Action Comics #5	119	$3,300	113	$3,000	$300	10%	-6
Action Comics #6	120	$3,300	114	$3,000	$300	10%	-6
Star Spangled Comics #7	121	$3,300	121	$2,700	$600	22%	0
Master Comics #1	122	$3,200	120	$2,800	$400	14%	-2
Motion Picture Funnies Weekly #1		$8,400		$8,400	$0		

Note: The above chart includes books, (*Motion Picture Funnies Weekly*), and others where the highest grade in the listings is a VF price. A NM price has been estimatedd in each case for the purpose of this chart.

TOP SILVER AGE BOOKS

1994 OVER 1993 AND 1989 GUIDE VALUES

Issue No.	1994 Rank	1994 NM Price	1993 Rank	1993 NM Price	$ Incr.	% Incr.	Change In Rank
Amazing Fantasy #15	1	$20,000	3	$7,000	$13,000	186%	2
Showcase #4	2	$18,000	1	$9,400	$8,600	91%	-1
Amazing Spider-Man #1	3	$13,500	4	$6,800	$6,700	99%	1
Fantastic Four #1	4	$12,000	2	$7,200	$4,800	67%	-2
Showcase #8	5	$7,500	6	$3,800	$3,700	97%	1
Incredible Hulk #1	6	$7,100	5	$4,000	$3,100	78%	-1
Detective Comics #225	7	$3,500	9	$2,500	$1,000	40%	2
Showcase #22	8	$3,300	10	$2,250	$875	47%	2
Showcase #9	9	$3,100	25	$1,400	$1,700	121%	16
Brave And The Bold #28	10	$3,070	8	$2,600	$470	18%	-2
X-Men #1	11	$3,000	12	$2,150	$850	40%	1
Showcase #14	12	$3,000	20	$1,600	$1,400	88%	8
Flash #105(#1)	13	$2,750	14	$2,000	$750	38%	1
Journey Into Mystery #83	14	$2,730	11	$2,200	$530	24%	-3
Adventure Comics #247	15	$2,600	8	$2,600	$0	0%	-7
Tales Of Suspense #39	16	$2,550	14	$2,000	$550	28%	-2
Tales To Astonish #27	17	$2,300	23	$1,500	$800	53%	6
Showcase #13	18	$2,250	20	$1,600	$650	41%	2
Justice League Of America #1	19	$2,200	16	$1,750	$450	26%	-3
Showcase #6	20	$2,150	23	$1,500	$650	43%	3
Adventure Comics #210	21	$2,100	17	$1,650	$450	27%	-4
Amazing Spider-Man #2	22	$2,050	15	$1,800	$250	14%	-7
Fantastic Four #2	23	$2,000	20	$1,600	$400	25%	-3
Showcase #1	24	$1,800	23	$1,500	$200	20%	-1
Fantastic Four #5	25	$1,750	27	$1,250	$500	40%	2
Brave And The Bold #29	26	$1,750	39	$1,000	$750	75%	13
Superman's Pal, Jimmy Olsen #1	27	$1,700	31	$1,200	$500	42%	4
Avengers #1	28	$1,675	27	$1,250	$425	34%	-1
Fantastic Four #4	29	$1,625	31	$1,200	$425	35%	2

TOP SILVER AGE BOOKS (cont'd) ......1994 Issue No. Rank	1994 Nm Price	1993 Rank	1993 NM Price	$ Increase	% Increase	Change In Rank
Incredible Hulk #2 30	$1,600	31	$1,200	$400	33%	1
Green Lantern #1 31	$1,600	25	$1,400	$200	14%	-6
Brave And The Bold #30..........32	$1,450	39	$1,000	$450	45%	7
Showcase #10..........33	$1,450	39	$1,000	$450	45%	6
Brave And The Bold #1..........34	$1,350	31	$1,200	$150	13%	-3
Challengers Of The Unknown #1 35	$1,350	41	$950	$400	42%	6
Fantastic Four #3..........36	$1,325	39	$1,000	$325	33%	3
Incredible Hulk #6 37	$1,300	39	$1,000	$300	30%	2
Brave And The Bold #34..........38	$1,250	51	$800	$450	56%	13
Daredevil #1..........39	$1,225	32	$1,100	$125	11%	-7
Showcase #17..........40	$1,200	41	$950	$250	26%	1
Superman's Girl Friend, Lois Lane #1 41	$1,200	42	$900	$300	33%	1
Amazing Spider-Man #3..........42	$1,175	39	$1,000	$175	18%	-3
Showcase #24..........43	$1,150	51	$800	$350	44%	8
Batman #100..........44	$1,125	39	$1,000	$125	13%	-5
Showcase #7..........45	$1,125	57	$750	$375	50%	12
Showcase #23..........46	$1,100	51	$800	$300	38%	5
Tales To Astonish #35..........47	$1,100	51	$800	$300	38%	4
Showcase #12..........48	$1,075	68	$625	$450	72%	20
Amazing Spider-Man #4..........49	$1,050	51	$800	$250	31%	2
X-Men #2 50	$1,025	51	$800	$225	28%	1
Amazing Spider-Man #14..........51	$1,000	43	$875	$125	14%	-8
Tales Of Suspense #40..........52	$1,000	51	$800	$200	25%	-1
Our Army At War #81..........53	$1,000	52	$775	$225	29%	-1
Showcase #11..........54	$1,000	68	$625	$375	60%	14
Showcase #34..........55	$975	44	$850	$125	15%	-11
Incredible Hulk #3..........56	$975	57	$750	$225	30%	1
Mystery In Space #53..........57	$965	60	$675	$290	43%	3
Superman #100..........58	$950	57	$750	$200	27%	-1
Tales Of Suspense #1..........59	$950	66	$650	$300	46%	7
Showcase #15..........60	$925	66	$650	$275	42%	6
Tales To Astonish #1..........61	$900	75	$600	$300	50%	14
Amazing Spider-Man #5..........62	$850	59	$700	$150	21%	-3
Showcase #19..........63	$850	95	$475	$375	79%	32
Action Comics #252..........64	$800	57	$750	$50	7%	-7
Detecive Comics #233..........65	$800	57	$750	$50	7%	-8
Incredible Hulk #4..........66	$780	75	$600	$180	30%	9
Incredible Hulk #5..........67	$780	75	$600	$180	30%	8
Amazing Spider-Man #6..........68	$750	59	$700	$50	7%	-9
Detecive Comics #226..........69	$750	81	$540	$210	39%	12
My Greatest Adventure #1..........70	$740	79	$575	$165	29%	9
Showcase #18..........71	$720	95	$475	$245	52%	24
Action Comics #242..........72	$700	66	$650	$50	8%	-6
Fantastic Four #6..........73	$700	66	$650	$50	8%	-7
Flash #106..........74	$700	66	$650	$50	8%	-8
Sugar & Spike #1..........75	$700	66	$650	$50	8%	-9
Tales Of The Unexpected #1..........76	$700	80	$550	$150	27%	4
Superman's Pal, Jimmy Olsen #2 77	$675	75	$600	$75	13%	-2
Strange Tales #110..........78	$675	79	$575	$100	17%	1
Amazing Adventures #1..........79	$675	87	$500	$175	35%	8
Flash #123..........80	$650	75	$600	$50	8%	-5
Brave And The Bold #2..........81	$650	98	$450	$200	44%	17
Showcase #5..........82	$630	75	$600	$30	5%	-7
Journey Into Mystery #84..........83	$625	75	$600	$25	4%	-8
Flash #110..........84	$600	79	$575	$25	4%	-5
Showcase #35..........85	$600	95	$475	$125	26%	10
Tales Of The Unexpected #40..........86	$600	101	$425	$175	41%	15
Justice League Of America #2..........87	$590	96	$460	$130	28%	9
Adventure Comics #267..........88	$580	79	$575	$5	1%	-9
Fantastic Four #48..........89	$575	87	$500	$75	15%	-2
Strange Tales #101..........90	$575	87	$500	$75	15%	-3
Showcase #16..........91	$575	103	$375	$200	53%	12
Amazing Spider-Man #9..........92	$550	87	$500	$50	10%	-5
House Of Secrets #1..........93	$550	101	$425	$125	29%	8
Showcase #2..........94	$530	87	$500	$30	6%	-7
Green Lantern #2..........95	$520	87	$500	$20	4%	-8
Fantastic Four #7..........96	$500	95	$475	$25	5%	-1
Fantastic Four #8..........97	$500	95	$475	$25	5%	-2
Fantastic Four #9..........98	$500	95	$475	$25	5%	-3
Fantastic Four #10..........99	$500	95	$475	$25	5%	-4
Showcase #3..........100	$500	95	$475	$25	5%	-5
Showcase #20..........101	$500	98	$450	$50	11%	-3

SAN MATEO COMIC BOOKS, BASEBALL CARDS & ORIGINAL ART

106 S. 'B' St. San Mateo, California 94401 — Open 12-6 p.m. 7 days a week (415) 344-1536 fax(415) 344- 0366

We have one of the finest selections of Original Art around, more than 15,000 Covers, Pages, Splashes. Complete Stories, Daily & Sunday Strips, Cover Paintings, Animation Drawings & Cels etc. **Many Artists**: ADAMS, ADKINS, ALCALA, ANDERSON, ANDRU, APARO, AYERS, BACHALO,BARKS, BINGHAM, BISSETTE, BOLLAND, BORING, BREYFOGLE, BRIGHT, BRODERICK, BROWN, BRUNNER, BUCKLER, BUSCEMA, BYRNE, CHADWICK, CHAYKIN, CIROCCO, COCKRUM, COLAN, COLON, COWAN, CRANDALL, CULLINS, DAVIS, DAY, DELBO, DEMULDER, DE STEFANO, DEZUNIGA, DIILLIN, DITKO, DODSON, DUURSEMA, DRAKE, EASTMAN AND LAIRD, EISNER, EVERETT, FINE, FRADON, FRAZETTA, FRENZ, GARCIA LOPEZ, GIFFEN, GIOLETI, GIORDANO, GLANSMAN, GOLDEN, GRELL,GROSS, GUICE, GULACY, HAMILTON, HANNIGAN, HARRIS, HECK, HEMBECK, HERNANDEZ BROS., HOBERG, HOWELL,HUGHES,INFANTINO, JANSON, JONES, JURGENS, KALUTA, KANE, KAYANAN, KIDA,KIETH, KIRBY, KUBERT, KUPPERBERG, LAROCQUE, LAYTON, LEIALOHA, LEIBER, LIGHTLE, MACFARLANE, MAGUIRE, MANNING, MAYERICK, MCDONNELL, MCMANUS, MESSEMER, MIGNOLA, MILGROM, MILLER, MOLDOFF, MOONEY, MORROW, MUTH, NEBRES, NEWTON, NINO, NOVICK, NOWLAN, O'NEILL, ORDWAY, PEREZ, H.G. PETER, PLOOG, POWELL, PURCELL, RABOY, RANDALL, RAYMOND, ROBBINS, ROGERS, ROMITA, ROSS, ROTH, RUSSELL, SAVIUK, SCHAFFENBERGER, SEKOWSKY, SEVERIN, SHAW, SHELTON, SHOOTER, SIENKIEWICZ, SIM, SIMONSON, SMITH, STARLIN, STATON, STERANKO, SUTTON, SUYDAM, SWAN, THORNE, TOTH, TOTLEBEN, TUSKA, VALLEJO, VEITCH, VESS, VON EDEN, VOSBERG, WAGNER, WARD, WHEELAN, WILLIAMSON, WILLINGHAM, WOCH, WOOD, WRIGHTSON, YEATES, ZECK.
and **Companies**: MARVEL, D.C., VERTIGO, VALIENT, IMAGE, ECLIPSE, FIRST.

Send $3.00, $4.00 for foreign orders (refunded on 1st order) for a giant 100+ page catalog to: San Mateo Comic Art 106 S. 'B' St., San Mateo, California 94401.

ORIGINAL ART SPECIALS—Our pick of 5 pages from Marvel $35.00; 10 pages from Marvel $60.00; 5 D.C. pages $30.00; 10 D.C. pages $50.00; 5 Marvel & D.C. pages $30.00; 1 pencil page by Frank Brunner $10.00; 1 main cell + bonus cells from Herb Trimpe's Crest Team vs. Cavity Creeps commercial $14.00-3 different sets $26.00. 1 pg. X-Factor or New Mutants $30.00; 1 page from G.I. Joe $20.00; 1 Star Trek Daily $20.00; 1 page from Marvel's Secret Wars $20.00; 1 Spiderman Daily $35.00; 1 Spiderman Daily with no Spiderman $15.00; 1 Spiderman page $40.00

MIX & MATCH. . . Nice pages featuring the following characters in costume: Angel, Arak, Barren Earth, Batman, Bluedevil, Capt. America, Capt. Brittain, Clea, Cloud, Conan, Daredevil, Dazler, Defenders, Dr. Doom, Dr. Strange, El Diablo, Falcon, Firehawk, Firestorm, Flash, Gargoyle, Godzilla, He-Man & Masters of the Universe, Iceman, Jonah Hex, Hulk, Indiana Jones, Ironman, Kull, Legion of Superheroes, Leiko Wu, Moon Dragon, Jennifer Morgan, Omega Men, Peter Parker, Powerman, Red Tomado, Robin, Rom, Sgt. Fury, Shakira, Shang Chi, Sheena, SheHulk, Shogun Warriors, Space 1999, Star Trek, Submariner, Sundevils, Superfriends, Superman, Thor, Transformers, V the t.v. series, Valda, Valkyrie, Vigilante, Warlord, Ironfist. Pick as many pages as you want $20.00 2 for $35.00; 5 for $80.00; 10 for $150.00 Add $5.00 ($10 foreign) Postage & Insurance on orders. We are interested in buying large or small collections of original comic book or strip art, plus quality collections of comic books and baseball card sets, stars & unopened boxes.

TOP SILVER AGE BOOKS (cont'd) Issue No.	1994 Rank	1994 Nm Price	1993 Rank	1993 NM Price	$ Increase	% Increase	Change In Rank
Showcase #27	102	$500	101	$425	$75	18%	-1
World's Finest Comics #71	103	$500	102	$400	$100	25%	-1

TOP MODERN AGE BOOKS
(1980 to 1993)

Title	Year Publ.	Publisher	#24Guide Value	% Change	#23 Guide Value
Spider-Man #1 (Platinum cover)	1991	Marvel	$250	-29%	$350
Teenage Mutant Ninja Turtles #1	1984	Mirage	$240	-4%	$250
Gobbledygook #1 (Early TMNT)	1984	Mirage	$220	-0-	$220
Gobbledygook #2	1984	Mirage	$220	-0-	$220
Sandman (Variant) #8 (600 copies)	1989	DC	$160	7%	$150
Harbinger #0 (Advance copy)	1992	Valiant	$120	-20%	$150
Superman #75 (Platinum Ed.)	1993	DC	$100	0	0
Unity #1 (Platinum logo)	1992	Valiant	$75	-46%	$140
Eternal Warrior #1 (Gold foil)	1992	Valiant	$39	-72%	$140
Harbinger #1(1st app. Harbinger)	1992	Valiant	$100	0	$100
Archer & Armstrong #0 (Gold Ed.)	1993	Valiant	$35	-59%	$85
H.A.R.D. Corp #1 (Advance copy)	1992	Valiant	$65	-35%	$100
Justice League (Variant) #3 (Yellow bacground & Superman Logo	1987	DC	$100	-5%	$105
Unity #0 (Red logo)	1992	Valiant	$60	-40%	$100
Unity #0 (Gold logo)	1992	Valiant	$35	0	0
Unity #1 (Gold logo)	1992	Valiant	$65	-35%	$100
Adventures Of Superman #500 (Platinum Edition)	1993	DC	$100	0	0
Magnus Robot Fighter #0 (order via coupons)	1991	Valiant	$60	-40%	$100
Magnus Robot Fighter #12 (1st app.Turok)	1992	Valiant	$45	-10%	$50
Teenage Mutant Ninja Turtles #3 (variant Ed.)	1985	Mirage	$80	-6%	$85
Predator vs Magnus Robot Fighter #1 Dark Horse/ Platinum cover	1992	Valiant	$35	-56%	$80
Flaming Carrot Comics #1 (One shot)	1981	Kikkian	$60	-20%	$75
Solar #10 (1st Warrior & Geomancer)	1992	Valiant	$40	-20%	$50
Teenage Mutant Ninja Turtles #2	1984	Mirage	$70	-7%	$75
Amazing Spider-Man #238 (1st Hobgoblin)	1983	Marvel	$70	17%	$60
Freex #1 (Hologram cover)	1993	Malibu	$40	0	0
Hardcase #1 (Hologram cover)	1993	Malibu	$45	0	0
Mantra #1 (Hologram cover)	1993	Malibu	$40	0	0
Prime #1 (Hologram cover)	1993	Malibu	$40	0	0
RAI #4 (Low print run)	1992	Valiant	$38	27%	$30
Strangers #1 (Hologram cover)	1993	Malibu	$35	0	0
Venom: Lethal Protector #1 (Gold Ed.)	1993	Marvel	$25	0	0

TOP CRIME COMICS
1994 OVER 1993 AND 1989 GUIDE VALUE

Title Issue#	$1994	$1993	% change '93 to '94	$1989	% change '89 to '94
Crime Does Not Pay 22	$850	$750	12%	$525	62%
Crime SuspenStories 15(1)	$725	$675	7%	$420	73%
True Crime 2	$600	$575	4%	$610	-2%
Crime SuspenStories 1	$525	$500	5%	$350	50%
Mr. District Attorney 1	$475	$400	16%	$150	217%
Complete Book of True Crime nn	$450	$425	6%	$315	43%
Crime Does Not Pay 23	$450	$400	11%	$295	53%
Crimes By Women 1	$450	$400	11%	$265	70%
True Crime 3	$420	$400	5%	$390	8%
Crime Does Not Pay 24	$400	$350	13%	$245	63%
Crime Does Not Pay, Best Of, 1944 1944	$400	$350	13%	$190	111%
Gangbusters 1	$375	$325	13%	$180	108%
True Crime 4	$375	$350	7%	$350	7%
International Crime Patrol 6	$350	$350	0%	$210	67%
Monster Crime 1	$350	$330	6%	$245	43%
War Against Crime 1	$350	$350	0%	$260	35%
Killers 1	$330	$320	3%	$315	5%
Killers 2	$325	$320	2%	$315	3%
True Crime V2#1	$320	$290	9%	$252	27%
Crime SuspenStories 2	$315	$300	5%	$210	50%
Crime Does Not Pay, Best Of, 1945 1945	$300	$275	8%	$154	95%
Crime Patrol 7	$300	$280	7%	$195	54%
Crime Reporter 2	$275	$260	5%	$225	22%

TOP CRIME COMICS (Cont'd)

Title Issue#	$1994	$1993	% change '93 to '94	$1989	% change '89 to '94
Crime Smashers 1	$275	$250	9%	$190	45%
Crime Patrol 8	$270	$250	7%	$175	54%
Crime Patrol 9	$270	$250	7%	$175	54%
Crime Patrol 10	$270	$250	7%	$175	54%
Crime Patrol 11	$270	$250	7%	$175	54%
Crime Patrol 12	$270	$250	7%	$175	54%
Crime Patrol 13	$270	$250	7%	$175	54%
Crime Patrol 14	$270	$250	7%	$175	54%
Crime Comics (Giant Comics Ed.) 4	$265	$245	8%	$154	72%
Police Case Book (Giant Comics Ed.) 5	$255	$235	8%	$140	82%
Law Against Crime 1	$245	$220	10%	$170	44%
Crimes By Women 2	$240	$210	13%	$140	71%
Crimes By Women 3	$240	$210	13%	$160	50%
Crimes By Women 6	$240	$215	10%	$140	71%
Suspense 1	$240	$210	13%	$110	118%
Crime Does Not Pay 25	$235	$200	15%	$132	78%
Crime Does Not Pay 26	$235	$200	15%	$132	78%
Crime Does Not Pay 27	$235	$200	15%	$132	78%
Crime Does Not Pay 28	$235	$200	15%	$132	78%
Crime Does Not Pay 29	$235	$200	15%	$132	78%
Crime Does Not Pay 30	$235	$200	15%	$132	78%
Lawbreakers Suspense Stories 11	$230	$200	13%	$154	49%
Crime Does Not Pay, Best Of, 1946 1946	$225	$200	11%	$132	70%
Crime Does Not Pay, Best Of, 1947 1947	$225	$200	11%	$132	70%
Crime Does Not Pay, Best Of, 1948 1948	$225	$200	11%	$132	70%
Law Against Crime 3	$225	$210	7%	$175	29%
Fox Giant (Album Of Crime) nn	$220	$210	5%	$168	31%
Fox Giant (All Famous Crime Stories) nn	$220	$210	5%	$168	31%
Fox Giant (Almanac Of Crime) '48 nn	$220	$210	5%	$168	31%
True Crime 5	$220	$200	9%	$175	26%
Crime SuspenStories 3	$210	$200	5%	$145	45%
Crime SuspenStories 4	$210	$200	5%	$145	45%
Crime SuspenStories 5	$210	$200	5%	$145	45%
Fox Giant (All Great Crime Stories) nn	$210	$200	5%	$168	25%
Fox Giant (Almanac Of Crime) '50 nn	$210	$200	5%	$168	25%
Fox Giant (Journal Of Crime) nn	$210	$200	5%	$154	36%
Fox Giant (Truth About Crime) nn	$210	$200	5%	$154	36%
Fox Giant (Crimes Inc.) nn	$195	$185	5%	$154	27%
Fox Giant (March Of Crime) '48 nn	$195	$185	5%	$154	27%
Fox Giant (March Of Crime) '49 nn	$195	$185	5%	$154	27%
Fox Giant (March Of Crime) '49 nn	$195	$185	5%	$154	27%
Gangsters and Gun Molls 1	$190	$175	8%	$125	52%
Crime Mysteries 1	$180	$165	8%	$125	44%
Crime Smasher 1	$180	$165	8%	$90	100%
Crime Mysteries 4	$165	$150	9%	$125	32%
Crime Reporter 1	$165	$150	9%	$110	50%
Crime SuspenStories 13	$165	$135	18%	$105	57%
Crime SuspenStories 16	$165	$135	18%	$105	57%
Prison Break 1	$165	$150	9%	$120	38%
Real Clue Crime V2#4	$165	$135	18%	$80	106%
Crime SuspenStories 20	$140	$125	11%	$90	56%
Criminals On The Run 7	$140	$120	14%	$84	67%
Crime SuspenStories 11	$120	$115	4%	$75	60%
Crime SuspenStories 12	$120	$115	4%	$75	60%
Crime SuspenStories 14	$120	$115	4%	$75	60%
Crime SuspenStories 15	$120	$115	4%	$75	60%

Note: This chart covers The Crime comics Genre 1942-1955. It should be noted that Detective Picture Stories and Detective Comics are not included in this list even though some historians place them in the crime comics genre. These two titles have been excluded because their value is so high that they would skew the data in the chart.

TOP HANNA-BARBERA COMICS

1994 OVER 1993 AND 1989 GUIDE VALUE

Title Issue	$1994	% change $1993	'93 to '94	%change $1989	'89 to '94
Dell Giant #48	$225	$160	29%	$70	221%
Jonny Quest #1	$225	$175	22%	$40	463%
Dell Giant #31	$180	$130	28%	$70	157%
Dell Giant #41	$180	$130	28%	$55	227%

HEY! LETTERING FOR A BUCK A BALLOON! DETAILS FOR A STAMP!

$24.00 POST-PAID
WHIZBANG
TM
THE COMPUTER FONT FOR COMIC BOOK LETTERING!

TOP HANNA-BARBERA COMICS (cont'd) Title Issue	$1994	$1993	% change '93 to '94	$1989	%change '89 to '94
Dell Giant #44	$180	$130	28%	$60	200%
Jetsons #1	$160	$145	9%	$50	220%
Atom Ant #1	$150	$75	200%	$25	500%
Golden Picture Story Book #1	$100	$90	10%	$28	257%
Golden Picture Story Book #2	$100	$90	10%	$28	257%
Jetsons (March of Comics) #276	$90	$75	17%	$40	125%
Top Cat #1	$90	$80	11%	$18	400%
Jetsons #2	$85	$80	6%	$30	183%
Hanna-Barbera Super TV Heroes #1	$80	$80	0%	$25	220%
Hanna-Barbera Super TV Heroes #2	$75	$55	27%	$18	317%
H.R. Pufnstuf #1	$75	$75	0%	$5	1400%
Ruff and Reddy (Four Color) #937	$75	$50	33%	$21	257%
Augie Doggie #1	$70	$60	14%	$21	233%
Hanna-Barbera Super TV Heroes #3	$70	$45	36%	$15	367%
Hanna-Barbera Super TV Heroes #4	$70	$45	36%	$15	367%
Hanna-Barbera Super TV Heroes #5	$70	$45	36%	$15	367%
Hanna-Barbera Super TV Heroes #6	$70	$45	36%	$15	367%
Hanna-Barbera Super TV Heroes #7	$70	$45	36%	$15	367%
Yogi Bear (Four Color) #1067	$70	$60	14%	$24	192%
Jetsons #3	$65	$60	8%	$20	225%
Jetsons #4	$65	$60	8%	$20	225%
Jetsons #5	$65	$60	8%	$20	225%
Jetsons #6	$65	$60	8%	$20	225%
Jetsons #7	$65	$60	8%	$20	225%
Jetsons #8	$65	$60	8%	$20	225%
Jetsons #9	$65	$60	8%	$20	225%
Jetsons #10	$65	$60	8%	$20	225%
Jetsons (March of Comics) #330	$65	$60	8%	$30	117%
Yogi Bear (Four Color) #1349	$65	$60	8%	$14	364%
Flintstones #2	$60	$55	8%	$24	150%
Flintstones Bigger & Boulder #1	$60	$55	8%	$24	150%
Quick-Draw McGraw (Four Color) #1040	$60	$50	17%	$26	131%
Secret Squirrel #1	$60	$35	71%	$18	233%
Flintstones (March of Comics) #229	$55	$50	9%	$30	83%
Huckleberry Hound (Four Color) #990	$55	$40	37%	$18	206%
Jetsons (March of Comics) #348	$55	$50	9%	$24	129%
Quick-Draw McGraw #12	$55	$45	18%	$28	96%
Quick-Draw McGraw #13	$55	$45	18%	$28	96%
Jetsons (Charlton) #1	$52	$48	8%	$24	117%
Flintstones #11	$50	$45	10%	$18	178%
Flintstones Bigger & Boulder #2	$50	$45	10%	$20	150%
Flintstones with Pebbles & Bamm Bamm #1	$50	$45	10%	$20	150%
Flintstones (March of Comics) #243	$50	$45	10%	$28	79%
Flintstones (March of Comics) #271	$50	$45	10%	$28	79%
Hanna-Barbera Band Wagon #1	$50	$45	10%	$25	100%
Hanna-Barbera Band Wagon #2	$50	$45	10%	$25	100%
Pebbles Flintstone #1	$50	$45	10%	$21	138%
Ruff and Reddy (Four Color) #981	$50	$35	30%	$14	257%
Ruff and Reddy (Four Color) #1038	$50	$35	30%	$14	257%
Secret Squirrel Kite Fun Book #1966	$50	$40	20%	$16	213%
Snagglepuss #1	$50	$40	20%	$16	213%
Snooper and Blabber Detectives #1	$50	$40	20%	$16	213%
Huckleberry Hound #18	$48	$40	17%	$24	100%
Huckleberry Hound #19	$48	$40	17%	$24	100%
Flintstones #3	$45	$38	16%	$16	181%
Flintstones #4	$45	$38	16%	$16	181%
Flintstones #5	$45	$38	16%	$16	181%
Flintstones #6	$45	$38	16%	$16	181%
Flintstones (March of Comics) #289	$45	$40	11%	$21	114%
Flintstones (March of Comics) #299	$45	$40	11%	$21	114%
Huck & Yogi Jamboree #nn	$45	$40	11%	$15	200%
Lippy the Lion and Hardy Har Har #1	$45	$40	11%	$18	150%
Top Cat #2	$45	$40	11%	$12	275%
Yogi Bear (Four Color) #1104	$45	$40	11%	$18	150%
Yogi Bear (Four Color) #1162	$45	$40	11%	$18	150%
Jetsons #11	$44	$40	9%	$16	175%
Jetsons #12	$44	$40	9%	$16	175%
Jetsons #13	$44	$40	9%	$16	175%
Jetsons #14	$44	$40	9%	$16	175%
Jetsons #15	$44	$40	9%	$16	175%
Jetsons #16	$44	$40	9%	$16	175%
Jetsons #17	$44	$40	9%	$16	175%

TOP HORROR COMICS
1994 OVER 1993 AND 1989 GUIDE VALUE

Title Issue#	$1994	$1993	% change '93 to '94	$1989	%change '89 to 94
Vault of Horror 12	$2,500	$2,200	12%	$750	233%
Tales of Terror Annual 1	$2,400	$2,200	8%	$1,400	71%
Strange Tales 1	$1,450	$1,000	31%	$455	219%
Crypt of Terror 17	$1,200	$1,200	0%	$490	145%
Haunt of Fear 15	$1,200	$1,100	8%	$700	71%
Journey into Mystery 1	$1,200	$900	25%	$315	281%
Crime Patrol 15	$1,150	$900	22%	$400	188%
Tales of Terror Annual 2	$1,000	$950	5%	$700	43%
War Against Crime 10	$1,000	$900	10%	$370	170%
Tales of Suspense 1	$950	$650	32%	$250	280%
Tales to Astonish 1	$900	$600	33%	$260	246%
House of Mystery 1	$850	$600	29%	$280	204%
Crime Patrol 16	$800	$650	19%	$330	142%
Crypt of Terror 18	$800	$800	0%	$365	119%
Crypt of Terror 19	$800	$800	0%	$365	119%
Tales of Terror Annual 3	$750	$700	7%	$490	53%
My Greatest Adventure 1	$740	$575	22%	$250	196%
Tales of the Unexpected 1	$700	$550	21%	$210	233%
Amazing Adventures 1	$675	$500	26%	$150	350%
Tales From the Crypt 20	$650	$625	4%	$295	120%
Adventures into the Unknown 1	$625	$540	14%	$265	136%
Forbidden Worlds 1	$600	$525	13%	$350	71%
War Against Crime 11	$600	$550	8%	$320	88%
Vault of Horror 13	$575	$550	4%	$350	64%
Haunt of Fear 16	$550	$550	0%	$365	51%
Haunt of Fear 17	$550	$550	0%	$365	51%
House of Secrets 1	$550	$425	23%	$160	244%
Eerie 1	$525	$425	19%	$245	114%
Tales From the Crypt 21	$525	$500	5%	$245	114%
Vault of Horror 14	$525	$500	5%	$300	75%
Journey into Mystery 2	$500	$400	20%	$160	213%
Strange Tales 2	$500	$400	20%	$210	138%
Marvel Tales 93	$450	$400	11%	$210	114%
Vault of Horror 15	$425	$400	6%	$250	70%
Tales From the Crypt 22	$420	$400	5%	$195	115%
Black Magic 1	$400	$300	25%	$95	321%
Haunt of Fear 4	$400	$400	0%	$280	43%
Strange Tales 4	$400	$325	19%	$170	135%
Tales to Astonish 2	$400	$300	25%	$120	233%
Amazing Adult Fantasy 7	$385	$225	42%	$84	358%
Journey into Mystery 3	$375	$300	20%	$125	200%
Journey into Mystery 4	$375	$300	20%	$125	200%
Mister Mystery 7	$375	$345	8%	$265	42%
Strange Tales 3	$365	$300	18%	$154	137%
Strange Tales 5	$365	$300	18%	$154	137%
My Greatest Adventure 2	$355	$275	23%	$110	223%
House of Mystery 2	$350	$250	29%	$110	218%
Tales From the Crypt 33	$350	$340	3%	$146	140%
Tales of Suspense 2	$350	$250	29%	$100	250%
Tales of Suspense 3	$350	$250	29%	$100	250%
Astonishing 3	$340	$300	12%	$175	94%
Mister Mystery 12	$340	$300	12%	$190	79%
Thing 12	$330	$300	9%	$225	47%
Thing 13	$330	$300	9%	$225	47%
Thing 14	$330	$300	9%	$225	47%
Thing 15	$330	$300	9%	$225	47%
Marvel Tales 94	$325	$290	11%	$175	86%
Tales of Suspense 4	$325	$275	15%	$110	195%
Tales of the Unexpected 2	$325	$275	15%	$90	261%
Amazing Adult Fantasy 8	$315	$185	41%	$70	350%
Forbidden Worlds 3	$315	$275	13%	$160	97%
Tales From the Crypt 23	$315	$300	5%	$146	116%
Tales From the Crypt 24	$315	$300	5%	$146	116%
Tales From the Crypt 25	$315	$300	5%	$146	116%
Venus 13	$315	$275	13%	$175	80%
Venus 14	$315	$275	13%	$175	80%
Venus 15	$315	$275	13%	$175	80%
Venus 16	$315	$275	13%	$175	80%

COMIC MAN

SOME COLLECTORS NEVER SELL a single book from their collection. However, many collectors at some time wish to sell. Some offer their books to the dealer they acquired them from. It is then that many are forced to learn the grim truth about their dealer.

The same copy of action #10 that your dealer regarded so highly when selling it to you (a nice clean F/VF etc.), now says it is a low grade G/VG, has brown pages, hard to sell, etc. When you tell him you bought it from him as a F/VF, he turns red, and may say "I can try to sell it for you." etc. Sound Familiar?

I experienced this many times even with dealers in this guide. Out of these experiences, I transformed into **COMIC MAN**. I vowed to use my experience and resources to assist fellow collectors and treat people with fairness and honesty. I hold several auction/mail bid sales per year. I will travel to view important collections and I answer all correspondence promptly.

Items I am most interested in are:
(However I do buy everything)

- **All copies of Superman and Action #1**
- **All Golden Age Books poor – mint**
- **Silver Age Key Issues**
- **Original comic art especially Chester Gould**
- **Animation cells and drawings especially vintage**
- **Sports and non-sports cards/memorabilia**

SEND LISTS OR CALL
COMIC MAN

In Michigan
26847 Grand River (in Dula Center)
Redford, MI 48240
(313) 532-4744

Chicago Area
4171 Dundee #302
North Brook, IL 68062
(708) 459-1980

Toll Free 800 866-1882

Please call me or write before sending items. In many cases we can come to you. Also write us with your want lists, and to receive our lists/auction catalogs.

TOP HORROR COMICS (Cont'd)

Title Issue#	$1994	$1993	% change '93 to '94	$1989	%change '89 to 94
Venus 17	$315	$275	13%	$175	80%
Venus 18	$315	$275	13%	$175	80%
Venus 19	$315	$275	13%	$175	80%
Marvel Tales 102	$310	$275	11%	$190	63%
Adventures into the Unknown 3	$300	$260	13%	$140	114%
Amazing Adult Fantasy 14	$300	$180	40%	$60	400%
Forbidden Worlds 2	$300	$265	12%	$132	127%
Haunt of Fear 5	$300	$300	0%	$210	43%
Tales to Astonish 5	$300	$200	33%	$75	300%
Thing 1	$300	$250	17%	$150	100%
Thing 9	$300	$260	13%	$180	67%
Vault of Horror 16	$300	$290	3%	$195	54%
Ghost 1	$290	$260	10%	$175	66%
Tales From the Crypt 31	$290	$280	3%	$146	99%
Fantastic Fears 5	$285	$250	12%	$154	85%
Marvel Tales 104	$285	$250	12%	$175	63%
Amazing Adult Fantasy 9	$275	$160	42%	$60	358%
Amazing Adult Fantasy 10	$275	$160	42%	$60	358%
Amazing Adult Fantasy 11	$275	$160	42%	$60	358%
Amazing Adult Fantasy 12	$275	$160	42%	$60	358%
Amazing Adult Fantasy 13	$275	$160	42%	$60	358%
Amazing Adventures 2	$275	$275	0%	$75	267%
Dark Mysteries 1	$275	$250	9%	$175	57%
House of Mystery 3	$275	$200	27%	$90	206%
House of Secrets 2	$275	$190	31%	$84	227%
Tales to Astonish 3	$275	$200	27%	$100	175%
Tales to Astonish 4	$275	$200	27%	$70	293%
Thing 7	$275	$250	9%	$160	72%
Thing 17	$275	$250	9%	$175	57%
Uncanny Tales 1	$275	$240	13%	$120	129%
Adventures into the Unknown 2	$270	$240	11%	$120	125%
Marvel Tales 97	$265	$240	9%	$125	112%
Mystery Tales 1	$265	$210	21%	$100	165%
Strange Suspense Stories 1	$265	$240	9%	$120	121%
Strange Tales 6	$265	$225	15%	$115	130%
Strange Tales 7	$265	$225	15%	$115	130%
Strange Tales 8	$265	$225	15%	$115	130%
Strange Tales 9	$265	$225	15%	$115	130%
Strange Tales 10	$265	$235	11%	$120	121%
Tales From the Crypt 26	$265	$250	6%	$115	130%
Tales From the Crypt 27	$265	$250	6%	$115	130%
Tales From the Crypt 28	$265	$250	6%	$115	130%
Tales From the Crypt 29	$265	$250	6%	$115	130%
Tales From the Crypt 30	$265	$250	6%	$115	130%
Tales of Suspense 9	$260	$160	38%	$65	300%
Forbidden Worlds 5	$250	$225	10%	$132	89%
Journey into Unknown Worlds 14	$250	$225	10%	$136	84%
Journey into Unknown Worlds 15	$250	$225	10%	$136	84%
Strange World of Your Dreams 1	$250	$220	12%	$125	100%
Thing 11	$250	$220	12%	$140	79%
Witchcraft 1	$250	$225	10%	$175	43%
Out of the Night 1	$240	$210	13%	$132	82%
Spellbound 1	$240	$200	17%	$100	140%
Tales of Suspense 7	$240	$160	33%	$65	269%
Astonishing 4	$235	$210	11%	$140	68%
Astonishing 5	$235	$210	11%	$140	68%
Astonishing 6	$235	$210	11%	$140	68%
Eerie 2	$235	$210	11%	$154	53%
Eerie 3	$235	$210	11%	$154	53%
Haunt of Fear 14	$235	$235	0%	$145	62%
Marvel Tales 95	$230	$190	17%	$90	156%
Marvel Tales 96	$230	$190	17%	$90	156%
Marvel Tales 98	$230	$190	17%	$100	130%
Marvel Tales 99	$230	$190	17%	$90	156%
Marvel Tales 100	$230	$190	17%	$100	130%
Marvel Tales 101	$230	$190	17%	$90	156%
Marvel Tales 103	$230	$190	17%	$90	156%
Marvel Tales 105	$230	$190	17%	$90	156%
Tales to Astonish 7	$230	$165	28%	$50	360%
Vault of Horror 17	$230	$220	4%	$146	58%
Vault of Horror 18	$230	$220	4%	$146	58%
Vault of Horror 19	$230	$220	4%	$146	58%

TOP SCIENCE FICTION COMICS
1994 OVER 1993 AND 1989 GUIDE VALUE

Title Issue#	$1994	$1993	% change '93 to '94	$1989	% change '89 to '94
Planet Comics 1	$5,500	$5,000	9%	$2,300	139%
Planet Comics 2	$1,900	$1,700	11%	$1,120	70%
Mystery In Space 1	$1,600	$1,450	9%	$840	90%
Superworld Comics 1	$1,600	$1,200	25%	$700	129%
Strange Adventures 1	$1,500	$1,300	13%	$665	126%
Planet Comics 3	$1,450	$1,300	10%	$945	53%
Planet Comics 15	$1,400	$1,300	7%	$455	208%
Planet Comics 4	$1,250	$1,150	8%	$805	55%
Showcase (Adam Strange) 17	$1,200	$950	21%	$260	362%
Planet Comics 5	$1,150	$1,050	9%	$735	56%
Planet Comics 6	$1,150	$1,050	9%	$735	56%
Fawcett Movie (Man From Planet X, The) 15	$1,050	$1,050	0%	$1,050	0%
Weird Science-Fantasy Annual 1952	$1,000	$900	10%	$725	38%
Planet Comics 7	$925	$840	9%	$615	50%
Planet Comics 8	$925	$840	9%	$615	50%
Planet Comics 9	$925	$840	9%	$615	50%
Planet Comics 10	$925	$840	9%	$615	50%
Planet Comics 11	$925	$840	9%	$615	50%
Planet Comics 12	$925	$840	9%	$615	50%
Showcase (Space Ranger) 15	$925	$650	30%	$100	825%
Showcase (Adam Strange) 19	$850	$475	44%	$155	448%
Strange Adventures 9	$850	$750	12%	$490	73%
Superworld Comics 2	$850	$750	12%	$490	73%
Journey Into Unknown Worlds 36	$725	$650	10%	$210	245%
Planet Comics 13	$725	$675	7%	$455	59%
Planet Comics 14	$725	$675	7%	$455	59%
Weird Science 12	$725	$725	0%	$575	26%
Showcase (Adam Strange) 18	$720	$475	34%	$155	365%
Planet Comics 21	$700	$640	9%	$460	52%
Strange Adventures 2	$700	$600	14%	$315	122%
Superworld Comics 3	$700	$600	14%	$385	82%
Weird Fantasy 13	$700	$700	0%	$560	25%
Planet Comics 16	$685	$625	9%	$420	63%
Planet Comics 17	$685	$625	9%	$420	63%
Planet Comics 18	$685	$625	9%	$420	63%
Planet Comics 19	$685	$625	9%	$420	63%
Planet Comics 20	$685	$625	9%	$420	63%
Planet Comics 22	$685	$625	9%	$420	63%
Planet Comics 23	$625	$575	8%	$420	49%
Planet Comics 24	$625	$575	8%	$420	49%
Planet Comics 25	$625	$575	8%	$420	49%
Planet Comics 26	$625	$575	8%	$420	49%
Mystery In Space 2	$600	$550	8%	$350	71%
Showcase (Space Ranger) 16	$575	$375	35%	$100	475%
Weird Science-Fantasy Annual 1953	$575	$550	4%	$460	25%
Strange Worlds 3	$560	$510	9%	$540	4%
Mystery In Space 3	$500	$450	10%	$280	79%
Planet Comics 27	$500	$460	8%	$330	52%
Planet Comics 28	$500	$460	8%	$330	52%
Planet Comics 29	$500	$460	8%	$330	52%
Planet Comics 30	$500	$460	8%	$330	52%
Showcase (Rip Hunter) 20	$500	$450	10%	$60	733%
Space Detective 1	$500	$475	5%	$435	15%
Motion Pic. Comics (When Worlds Collide) 110	$485	$485	0%	$475	2%
Rocket to the Moon nn	$480	$465	3%	$385	25%
Strange Adventures 3	$450	$375	17%	$195	131%
Strange Adventures 4	$450	$375	17%	$195	131%
Weird Tales Of The Future 2	$450	$425	6%	$335	34%
Weird Tales Of The Future 3	$450	$425	6%	$335	34%
Weird Tales Of The Future 5	$450	$425	6%	$335	34%
Planet Comics 31	$425	$385	9%	$280	52%
Planet Comics 32	$425	$385	9%	$280	52%
Planet Comics 33	$425	$385	9%	$280	52%
Planet Comics 34	$425	$385	9%	$280	52%
Planet Comics 35	$425	$385	9%	$280	52%
Weird Science 13	$410	$410	0%	$315	30%
Mystery In Space 4	$400	$350	13%	$190	111%
Mystery In Space 5	$400	$350	13%	$190	111%

TOP SCIENCE FICTION COMICS (cont'd)

Title Issue#	$1994	$1993	% change '93 to '94	$1989	% change '89 to '94
Strange Adventures 5	$400	$325	19%	$180	122%
Strange Adventures 6	$400	$325	19%	$180	122%
Strange Adventures 7	$400	$325	19%	$180	122%
Strange Adventures 8	$400	$325	19%	$180	122%
Strange Adventures 10	$400	$325	19%	$180	122%
Weird Fantasy 14	$385	$385	0%	$300	28%
Planet Comics 36	$375	$350	7%	$245	53%
Planet Comics 37	$375	$350	7%	$245	53%
Planet Comics 38	$375	$350	7%	$245	53%
Planet Comics 39	$375	$350	7%	$245	53%
Planet Comics 40	$375	$350	7%	$245	53%
Planet Comics 41	$375	$350	7%	$245	53%
Planet Comics 42	$375	$350	7%	$245	53%
Planet Comics 43	$375	$350	7%	$245	53%
Planet Comics 44	$375	$350	7%	$245	53%
Planet Comics 45	$375	$350	7%	$245	53%
Space Patrol 1	$375	$340	9%	$245	53%
Space Patrol's Special Mission nn	$370	$350	5%	$300	23%
Fawcett Movie (Destination Moon) nn	$365	$350	4%	$330	11%
Journey Into Unknown Worlds 37	$365	$325	11%	$160	128%
Star Trek 1	$360	$350	3%	$50	620%
Star Wars (35 cent) 1	$360	$350	3%	$185	95%
Weird Science 14	$360	$360	0%	$285	26%
Weird Science 15	$360	$360	0%	$285	26%
Attack On Planet Mars nn	$350	$345	1%	$300	17%
Mystery In Space 6	$340	$300	12%	$150	127%
Mystery In Space 7	$340	$300	12%	$150	127%
Mystery In Space 8	$340	$300	12%	$150	127%
Mystery In Space 9	$340	$300	12%	$150	127%
Mystery In Space 10	$340	$300	12%	$150	127%
Strange Worlds 1	$340	$320	6%	$265	28%
Atomic War 1	$335	$300	10%	$235	43%
Strange Adventures 117	$330	$300	9%	$55	500%
Journey Into Unknown Worlds 7	$325	$285	12%	$154	111%
Space Busters 1	$325	$300	8%	$210	55%
Weird Fantasy 15	$325	$325	0%	$245	33%
Weird Fantasy 16	$325	$325	0%	$245	33%
Rip Hunter 1	$315	$300	5%	$70	350%
Weird Science-Fantasy 29	$315	$315	0%	$295	7%
Journey Into Unknown Worlds 38	$310	$275	11%	$132	135%
Crusader From Mars 1	$300	$285	5%	$190	58%
Flying Saucers 1	$300	$280	7%	$245	22%
Out Of This World 1	$300	$290	3%	$245	22%
Planet Comics 46	$300	$265	12%	$180	67%
Planet Comics 47	$300	$265	12%	$180	67%
Planet Comics 48	$300	$265	12%	$180	67%
Planet Comics 49	$300	$265	12%	$180	67%
Planet Comics 50	$300	$265	12%	$180	67%
Planet Comics 51	$300	$265	12%	$180	67%
Planet Comics 52	$300	$265	12%	$180	67%
Planet Comics 53	$300	$265	12%	$195	54%
Planet Comics 54	$300	$265	12%	$180	67%
Planet Comics 55	$300	$265	12%	$180	67%
Planet Comics 56	$300	$265	12%	$180	67%
Planet Comics 57	$300	$265	12%	$180	67%
Planet Comics 58	$300	$265	12%	$180	67%
Planet Comics 59	$300	$265	12%	$180	67%
Planet Comics 60	$300	$265	12%	$180	67%
Space Action 1	$300	$270	10%	$160	88%
Space Patrol 2	$300	$280	7%	$210	43%
Strange Worlds 2	$300	$280	7%	$230	30%
Strange Worlds 1	$300	$240	20%	$115	161%
Strange Worlds 4	$290	$270	7%	$225	29%
Flying Saucers nn('52)	$285	$265	7%	$225	27%
Lars Of Mars 10	$285	$260	9%	$180	58%
Space Squadron 1	$285	$260	9%	$125	128%
Rocket Ship X 1	$280	$280	0%	$245	14%
Strange Adventures 11	$280	$250	11%	$140	100%
Strange Adventures 12	$280	$250	11%	$154	82%
Strange Adventures 13	$280	$250	11%	$154	82%
Strange Adventures 14	$280	$250	11%	$140	100%

TOP SCIENCE FICTION COMICS (cont'd)

Title Issue#	$1994	$1993	% change '93 to '94	$1989	% change '89 to '94
Strange Adventures 15	$280	$250	11%	$140	100%
Strange Adventures 16	$280	$250	11%	$100	180%
Strange Adventures 17	$280	$250	11%	$154	82%
Strange Adventures 18	$280	$250	11%	$100	180%
Strange Adventures 19	$280	$250	11%	$100	180%
Strange Adventures 20	$280	$250	11%	$100	180%
Space Detective 2	$275	$240	13%	$210	31%
Spaceman 1	$275	$240	13%	$110	150%
Weird Fantasy 17	$275	$275	0%	$195	41%
Weird Tales Of The Future 1	$275	$250	9%	$170	62%
Space Busters 2	$270	$250	7%	$170	59%
Space Busters 3	$270	$250	7%	$170	59%
Vic Torry & His Flying Saucer nn	$265	$250	6%	$175	51%
Atomic War 2	$250	$225	10%	$160	56%
Atomic War 3	$250	$225	10%	$160	56%
Atomic War 4	$250	$225	10%	$168	49%
Crusader From Mars 2	$250	$225	10%	$154	62%
Weird Fantasy 14	$250	$250	0%	$210	19%
Weird Fantasy 21	$250	$250	0%	$210	19%
Weird Tales Of The Future 4	$250	$235	6%	$160	56%
Weird Tales Of The Future 7	$250	$225	10%	$170	47%
Space Squadron 2	$245	$220	10%	$104	136%
Space Western 40	$245	$210	14%	$154	59%
Lars Of Mars 11	$240	$220	8%	$160	50%
Space Action 2	$240	$210	13%	$132	82%
Space Action 3	$240	$210	13%	$132	82%
Strange Adventures 39	$240	$210	13%	$140	71%
Strange Worlds 5	$240	$220	8%	$190	26%
Journey Into Unknown Worlds 9	$230	$200	13%	$84	174%
Weird Science 5	$230	$230	0%	$175	31%
Weird Science 6	$230	$230	0%	$175	31%
Weird Science 7	$230	$230	0%	$175	31%
Weird Science 8	$230	$230	0%	$175	31%
Weird Science 9	$230	$230	0%	$175	31%
Weird Science 10	$230	$230	0%	$175	31%
Weird Science 19	$230	$230	0%	$175	31%
Weird Science 20	$230	$230	0%	$175	31%
Weird Science 21	$230	$230	0%	$175	31%
Weird Science 22	$230	$230	0%	$175	31%
Mystery In Space 11	$225	$200	11%	$110	105%
Mystery In Space 12	$225	$200	11%	$110	105%
Mystery In Space 13	$225	$200	11%	$110	105%
Mystery In Space 14	$225	$200	11%	$110	105%
Mystery In Space 15	$225	$200	11%	$110	105%
Mystery In Space 19	$225	$200	11%	$110	105%
Strange Adventures 21	$215	$175	19%	$84	156%
Strange Adventures 22	$215	$175	19%	$84	156%
Strange Adventures 23	$215	$175	19%	$84	156%
Strange Adventures 24	$215	$175	19%	$84	156%
Strange Adventures 25	$215	$175	19%	$84	156%
Strange Adventures 26	$215	$175	19%	$84	156%
Strange Adventures 27	$215	$175	19%	$84	156%
Strange Adventures 28	$215	$175	19%	$84	156%
Strange Adventures 29	$215	$175	19%	$84	156%
Strange Adventures 30	$215	$175	19%	$84	156%
Increcible Science Fiction 31	$210	$200	5%	$154	36%
Increcible Science Fiction 32	$210	$200	5%	$154	36%
Space Ace 5	$210	$200	5%	$105	100%
Space Adventures 12	$205	$185	10%	$140	46%
Mystery In Space 16	$200	$175	13%	$100	100%
Mystery In Space 17	$200	$175	13%	$100	100%
Mystery In Space 18	$200	$175	13%	$100	100%
Mystery In Space 20	$200	$175	13%	$100	100%
Mystery In Space 21	$200	$175	13%	$100	100%
Mystery In Space 22	$200	$175	13%	$100	100%
Mystery In Space 23	$200	$175	13%	$100	100%
Mystery In Space 24	$200	$175	13%	$100	100%
Mystery In Space 25	$200	$175	13%	$100	100%
Space Adventures 1	$200	$175	13%	$84	138%
Space Western 42	$200	$170	15%	$125	60%
Weird Fantasy 6	$200	$200	0%	$150	33%
Weird Fantasy 7	$200	$200	0%	$150	33%

TOP SCIENCE FICTION COMICS (cont'd)

Title Issue#	$1994	$1993	% change '93 to '94	$1989	% change '89 to '94
Weird Fantasy 8	$200	$200	0%	$150	33%
Weird Fantasy 9	$200	$200	0%	$150	33%
Weird Fantasy 10	$200	$200	0%	$150	33%

TOP SPORTS COMICS

1994 over 1993 and 1989

Title Issue#	1994 $	1993 $	% change '93 to '94	1989 $	%change '89 to '94
Baseball Heroes nn	$420	$385	8%	$200	110%
Jackie Robinson nn	$400	$375	6%	$175	129%
Baseball Comics 1	$385	$375	3%	$225	71%
Pride Of The Yankees nn	$375	$350	7%	$175	114%
Larry Doby, Baseball Hero nn	$350	$325	7%	$175	100%
Thrilling True Story of the Baseball Giants nn	$350	$325	7%	$160	119%
Yogi Berra nn	$325	$300	8%	$160	103%
Thrilling True Story of the Baseball Yankees nn	$310	$290	6%	$160	94%
Baltimore Colts nn	$300	$275	8%	$170	76%
Joe Louis 1	$300	$275	8%	$140	114%
My Greatest Thrills In Baseball nn	$300	$275	8%	$154	95%
Phil Rizzuto nn	$300	$275	8%	$140	114%
Jackie Robinson 2	$260	$240	8%	$120	117%
Sport Comics 1	$250	$225	10%	$105	138%
Jackie Robinson 3	$220	$200	9%	$100	120%
Jackie Robinson 4	$220	$200	9%	$100	120%
Jackie Robinson 5	$220	$200	9%	$100	120%
Jackie Robinson 6	$220	$200	9%	$100	120%
Joe Louis 2	$200	$180	10%	$110	82%
Baseball Thrills 10	$190	$175	8%	$100	90%
Sport Stars 1	$175	$150	14%	$75	133%
Babe Ruth Sports 1	$160	$130	19%	$70	129%
Sports Action 2	$140	$120	14%	$45	211%
Baseball Thrills 2	$135	$120	11%	$60	125%
Baseball Thrills 3	$135	$120	11%	$60	125%
True Sport Picture Stories 5	$135	$120	11%	$70	93%
All Sports 2	$125	$110	12%	$50	150%

TOP WAR COMICS

1994 over 1993 and 1989

Title Issue#	$1994	$1993	& change '93 to '94	$1989	% change '89 to '94
Our Army At War 81	$1,000	$775	23%	$105	852%
Rangers Comics 1	$800	$700	13%	$505	58%
Our Army At War 1	$700	$600	14%	$225	211%
Sgt. Fury 1	$600	$400	33%	$140	329%
Two-Fisted Tales 18	$525	$500	5%	$430	22%
Star Spangled War 131	$500	$400	20%	$154	225%
Two-Fisted Tales Annual 1	$475	$450	5%	$430	10%
All American Men Of War 127	$450	$400	11%	$135	233%
Our Fighting Forces 1	$450	$400	11%	$168	168%
Two-Fisted Tales 19	$385	$365	5%	$315	22%
Frontline Combat 1	$360	$290	19%	$240	50%
Our Army At War 2	$350	$300	14%	$105	233%
Our Army At War 83	$350	$275	21%	$24	1358%
Rangers Comics 2	$350	$325	7%	$230	52%
Star Spangled War 132	$350	$250	29%	$100	250%
Two-Fisted Tales Annual 2	$350	$335	4%	$315	11%
Atom-Age Combat 1	$335	$175	48%	$120	179%
Atomic War 1	$335	$300	10%	$235	43%
Our Army At War 91	$325	$275	15%	$32	916%
All American Men Of War 128	$315	$275	13%	$85	271%
Rangers Comics 3	$300	$275	8%	$190	58%
Star Spangled War 133	$300	$200	33%	$100	200%
Our Army At War 3	$275	$250	9%	$100	175%
Our Army At War 4	$275	$250	9%	$100	175%
Our Army At War 82	$275	$200	27%	$40	588%
Rangers Comics 4	$275	$250	9%	$167	65%

TOP WAR COMICS (CONT'D) **Title Issue#**	**$1994**	**$1993**	**& change '93 to '94**	**$1989**	**% change '89 to '94**
Rangers Comics 5	$275	$250	9%	$167	65%
Atomic War 2	$250	$225	10%	$160	56%
Atomic War 3	$250	$225	10%	$160	56%
Atomic War 4	$250	$225	10%	$168	49%
G.I. Combat 1	$250	$210	16%	$80	213%
War Comics 1	$240	$220	8%	$154	56%
G.I. Combat 44	$235	$190	19%	$70	236%
Two-Fisted Tales 20	$235	$220	6%	$190	24%
Army and Navy Comics 1	$230	$210	9%	$140	64%
Remember Pearl Harbor nn	$225	$210	7%	$132	70%
Army and Navy Comics 5	$220	$200	9%	$132	67%
Our Fighting Forces 2	$220	$200	9%	$80	175%
Rangers Comics 6	$220	$200	9%	$140	57%
Rangers Comics 7	$220	$200	9%	$140	57%
Rangers Comics 8	$220	$200	9%	$140	57%
Rangers Comics 9	$220	$200	9%	$140	57%
Rangers Comics 10	$220	$200	9%	$140	57%
Frontline Combat 2	$210	$200	5%	$160	31%
Our Army At War 5	$200	$175	13%	$50	300%
Our Army At War 6	$200	$175	13%	$50	300%
Our Army At War 7	$200	$175	13%	$50	300%
Our Army At War 8	$200	$175	13%	$56	257%
Our Army At War 9	$200	$175	13%	$56	257%
Our Army At War 10	$200	$175	13%	$56	257%
Our Army At War 11	$200	$175	13%	$56	257%
Our Army At War 14	$200	$175	13%	$56	257%
Rangers Comics 11	$200	$180	10%	$125	60%
Rangers Comics 12	$200	$180	10%	$125	60%
Rangers Comics 13	$200	$180	10%	$125	60%
Sgt. Fury 2	$200	$175	13%	$45	344%
Star Spangled War 90	$200	$175	13%	$50	300%
Our Fighting Forces 3	$185	$175	5%	$65	185%
Star Spangled War 3	$185	$165	11%	$70	164%
Star Spangled War 4	$185	$165	11%	$70	164%
Star Spangled War 5	$185	$165	11%	$70	164%
Star Spangled War 6	$185	$165	11%	$56	230%
Our Army At War 13	$175	$160	9%	$56	213%
Rangers Comics 21	$175	$160	9%	$105	67%
Two-Fisted Tales 21	$175	$165	6%	$145	21%
Two-Fisted Tales 22	$175	$165	6%	$145	21%
Frontline Combat 3	$155	$150	3%	$120	29%
Our Army At War 12	$150	$125	17%	$40	275%
Our Army At War 15	$150	$125	17%	$40	275%
Our Army At War 16	$150	$125	17%	$40	275%
Our Army At War 17	$150	$125	17%	$40	275%
Our Army At War 18	$150	$125	17%	$40	275%
Our Army At War 19	$150	$125	17%	$40	275%
Our Army At War 20	$150	$125	17%	$40	275%
Rangers Comics 14	$150	$135	10%	$90	67%
Rangers Comics 15	$150	$135	10%	$90	67%
Rangers Comics 16	$150	$135	10%	$90	67%
Rangers Comics 17	$150	$135	10%	$90	67%
Rangers Comics 18	$150	$135	10%	$90	67%
Rangers Comics 19	$150	$135	10%	$90	67%
Rangers Comics 20	$150	$135	10%	$90	67%
Sgt. Fury 13	$150	$110	27%	$10	1400%
Our Army At War 85	$140	$110	21%	$24	483%
Star Spangled War 7	$140	$120	14%	$42	233%
Star Spangled War 8	$140	$120	14%	$42	233%
Star Spangled War 9	$140	$120	14%	$42	233%
Star Spangled War 10	$140	$120	14%	$42	233%
Our Fighting Forces 4	$135	$125	7%	$50	170%
Our Fighting Forces 5	$135	$125	7%	$50	170%
Two-Fisted Tales 23	$135	$125	7%	$105	29%
Two-Fisted Tales 24	$135	$125	7%	$105	29%
Two-Fisted Tales 25	$135	$125	7%	$105	29%
Frontline Combat 4	$130	$125	4%	$100	30%
Fightin' Marines 2	$125	$110	12%	$80	56%
Our Army At War 84	$125	$100	20%	$30	317%
Our Army At War 86	$125	$100	20%	$24	421%
Our Army At War 87	$125	$100	20%	$24	421%
Our Army At War 88	$125	$100	20%	$24	421%

GOLDEN AGE

© DC

SILVER AGE

© Marvel

WANT LIST COMICS

WE FILL WANT LISTS

ATTENTION: INVESTORS AND COLLECTORS

Can't find those missing comic books **yet**? Are these books priced **TOO high** or are they just **IMPOSSIBLE** to find? Have local stores and conventions **not** produced what you want? **(Have you sent us a want list yet?)**

WHAT ARE YOU WAITING FOR?

"The **Batman #1** you sold me was in the **nicest, unrestored condition** I've seen!", **Bob Overstreet, author "The Official Overstreet Comic Book Price Guide".**

"I have **really** been happy with all the books you've sold to me. I only buy **very** high grade unrestored Silver Age books which are extremely tough to find for most dealers. Every book you have sent me has been graded strictly and priced fairly. **You have definitely met up to my high expectations!**" Donald Dame, Portage, MI.

These are just two of the **many** satisfied customers that have bought books from us in the past. Over the years, we have developed a **very strong return customer base** because we **ACCURATELY** price, grade and describe books (in detail) over the phone and through the mail. For a small fee we will even videotape any comic book we have in stock. **Customer references are always available upon request.** If a book is restored, we will tell you **up front** so you won't be **UNpleasantly** surprised or deceived. As each year goes by, we complete more and more of our customers' comic want lists. For example, **in 1993 alone,** we acquired rare Golden Age treasures for our clients like **Detective 27, All-American 16, Action 1, Famous Funnies Series 1, Superman 1, Detective 1, Flash 1, Captain America 1 and Adventure 40.** Yes, we can definitely find rare books - - we do it all the time! **Because of the high demand for Silver Age books,** we have purchased **MULTIPLE** copies of nearly all key issues like Showcase 4, 22, Green Lantern 1, Amazing Fantasy 15, FF1, Hulk 1, Amazing Spiderman 1, 14, Brave and the Bold 28 and Flash 105. **WE SPECIALIZE IN GOLDEN AGE AND SILVER AGE BOOKS (1933-1969),** but we also have some later issues (1970 - 1985).

We don't claim that we can fill every list all the time, but if any company can accomplish this, it **would certainly** be us! We can say this with **much confidence** because we travel to the **majority** of the 50 states and Canada plus attend many of the major comic book conventions (San Diego, Chicago, Dallas, Charlotte, etc.) to uncover books **you would not** have the opportunity to find. When we are not on the road, we spend **MANY** hours on the phone locating books from our **long** list of past and present comic sources we've developed over the **20 years** we have been dealing in comic books. When sending your want list, **please** include an SASE if possible, **your phone number,** and a good time to reach you. We **DON'T** send out catalogs, so **please** ask us for **specific** books and **conditions** desired. We will contact you **when** we find the items you've requested. **Phone calls are also welcomed. WE WILL GLADLY SUGGEST AND PERSONALLY PUT TOGETHER COMIC BOOK INVESTMENT PORTFOLIOS FOR BIG AND SMALL INVESTORS. OUR ADVICE IS ALWAYS FREE!**

SAVE YOURSELF ALL THE HASSLE AND LET US DO THE LOOKING FOR YOU
CALL OR MAIL US YOUR WANT LIST!

YOU HAVE NOTHING TO LOSE AND EVERYTHING ON YOUR WANT LIST TO GAIN!!!

Competitive pricing always. Accurate grading. Friendly, courteous service. **Interest free time payments/layaways possible.** Visa, Mastercard and American Express accepted for total payment **OR** down payment on books. No collect calls. Books shipped within 48 hours of payment.

Our NEW office/warehouse # is:

1-918-299-0440

Call us anytime between 11 am and 11 pm CST

WANT LIST COMICS
BOX 701932
TULSA, OK 74170-1932

*** Advisor to the Overstreet Price Guide ***
References gladly provided!

TOP WESTERN COMICS
1994 OVER 1993 AND 1989 GUIDE VALUE

Title Issue#	$1994	$1993	% change '93 to '94	$1989	% change '89 to '94
Gene Autry 1	$1,900	$1,800	5%	$750	153%
Hopalong Cassidy 1	$1,800	$1,800	0%	$665	171%
Tom Mix 1	$1,200	$1,000	17%	$455	164%
Red Ryder Comics 1	$800	$700	13%	$560	43%
Western Picture Stories 1	$750	$700	7%	$560	34%
Tomahawk 1	$650	$575	12%	$280	132%
Lash LaRue Western 1	$575	$550	4%	$315	83%
Roy Rogers Four Color 38	$575	$500	13%	$315	83%
Gene Autry 2	$525	$500	5%	$310	69%
Cowboy Comics 13	$500	$450	10%	$310	61%
Red Ryder Comics 3	$500	$250	100%	$350	43%
Rocky Lane Western 1	$500	$400	25%	$280	79%
Tom Mix Western 1	$500	$475	5%	$265	89%
Western Picture Stories 2	$500	$450	10%	$350	43%
Lone Ranger Large Feature Comic 7	$450	$450	0%	$350	29%
Sunset Carson 1	$450	$450	0%	$380	18%
Tom Mix 2	$450	$400	11%	$260	73%
John Wayne 1	$435	$400	8%	$260	67%
Two Gun Kid 1	$425	$375	12%	$210	102%
Western Comics 1	$415	$375	10%	$175	137%
Jimmy Wakely 1	$400	$365	9%	$200	100%
Kid Colt Outlaw 1	$400	$350	13%	$190	111%
Lone Ranger Large Feature Comic 3	$400	$400	0%	$280	43%
Lone Ranger 1	$400	$400	0%	$315	27%
Western Picture Stories 3	$400	$375	6%	$280	43%
Western Picture Stories 4	$400	$375	6%	$280	43%
Lone Ranger Feature Book 21	$375	$375	0%	$280	34%
Lone Ranger Feature Book 24	$375	$375	0%	$280	34%
Western Desperado 8	$375	$325	13%	$190	97%
Dale Evans Comics 1	$365	$315	14%	$140	161%
Gene Autry 3	$365	$350	4%	$240	52%
Gene Autry 4	$365	$350	4%	$240	52%
Gene Autry 5	$365	$350	4%	$240	52%
Cowboy Comics 14	$350	$325	7%	$210	67%
Cowboy Western Comics 27	$350	$325	7%	$175	100%
Cowboy Western Comics 30	$350	$325	7%	$175	100%
Gene Autry 11	$350	$350	0%	$225	56%
Hopalong Cassidy 2	$350	$350	0%	$245	43%
Rawhide Kid 1	$350	$300	14%	$110	218%
Roy Rogers 1	$350	$350	0%	$250	40%
Sunset Carson 2	$350	$350	0%	$260	35%
Tex Ritter Western 1	$350	$300	14%	$175	100%
Durango Kid 1	$340	$300	12%	$245	39%
Ghost Rider 1	$330	$300	9%	$230	43%
Gene Autry 12	$325	$325	0%	$225	44%
Rod Cameron Western 1	$325	$290	11%	$175	86%
Tom Mix 3	$325	$300	8%	$225	44%
Tom Mix 4	$325	$300	8%	$225	44%
Tom Mix 5	$325	$300	8%	$225	44%
Tom Mix 6	$325	$300	8%	$225	44%
Tom Mix 7	$325	$300	8%	$225	44%
Tom Mix 8	$325	$300	8%	$225	44%
Tom Mix 9	$325	$300	8%	$225	44%
Gene Autry 6	$315	$300	5%	$205	54%
Gene Autry 7	$315	$300	5%	$205	54%
Gene Autry 8	$315	$300	5%	$205	54%
Gene Autry 9	$315	$300	5%	$205	54%
Gene Autry 10	$315	$300	5%	$205	54%
John Wayne 2	$315	$310	2%	$265	19%
John Wayne 3	$315	$310	2%	$265	19%
John Wayne 4	$315	$310	2%	$265	19%
Tomahawk 2	$315	$275	13%	$160	97%
John Wayne 6	$310	$300	3%	$250	24%
John Wayne 8	$310	$300	3%	$250	24%
Ghost Rider 2	$300	$285	5%	$245	22%
Ghost Rider 3	$300	$285	5%	$245	22%
Ghost Rider 4	$300	$285	5%	$245	22%

TOP WESTERN COMICS (Cont'd) Title Issue#	$1994	$1993	% change '93 to '94	$1989	% change '89 to '94
Ghost Rider 5	$300	$285	5%	$245	22%
Ken Maynard 1	$300	$275	8%	$170	76%
Roy Rogers Four Color 63	$300	$300	0%	$210	43%
Tim Holt 1	$300	$285	5%	$225	33%
Andy Devine Western 1	$275	$250	9%	$140	96%
Gene Autry Four Color 47	$275	$275	0%	$225	22%
Gene Autry 1	$275	$275	0%	$225	22%
Gun Fighter 5	$275	$265	4%	$210	31%
Gun Figher 6	$275	$265	4%	$210	31%
Jimmy Wakely 3	$275	$250	9%	$154	79%
Jimmy Wakely 4	$275	$250	9%	$154	79%
Jimmy Wakely 6	$275	$250	9%	$154	79%
Jimmy Wakely 7	$275	$250	9%	$154	79%
Red Ryder Comics 4	$275	$250	9%	$190	45%
Red Ryder Comics 5	$275	$250	9%	$190	45%
Red Ryder Comics 6	$275	$250	9%	$190	45%
Six Gun Heroes 1	$275	$250	9%	$154	79%
Sunset Carson 3	$275	$275	0%	$180	53%
Sunset Carson 4	$275	$275	0%	$180	53%
Bob Steele Western 1	$265	$225	15%	$125	112%
Tom Mix 10	$265	$250	6%	$170	56%
Tom Mix 11	$265	$250	6%	$170	56%
Tom Mix 12	$265	$250	6%	$170	56%
All American Western 103	$255	$225	12%	$120	113%
Bulls-Eye 1	$250	$225	10%	$150	67%
Jimmy Wakely 2	$250	$225	10%	$140	79%
John Wayne 7	$250	$240	4%	$210	19%
Lash LaRue Western 2	$250	$235	6%	$175	43%
Lone Ranger Four Color 82	$250	$250	0%	$190	32%
Monte Hale Western 29	$250	$225	10%	$140	79%
Smiley Burnette Western 1	$250	$240	4%	$100	150%
Women Outlaws 1	$250	$230	8%	$190	32%
All Star Western 58	$240	$215	10%	$120	100%
Gabby Hayes Western 1	$240	$210	13%	$154	56%
Gene Autry Four Color 57	$240	$240	0%	$180	33%
Saddle Justice 3	$235	$235	0%	$175	34%
Saddle Justice 4	$235	$235	0%	$175	34%
Cisco Kid Comics 1	$225	$200	11%	$140	61%
John Wayne 5	$225	$220	2%	$180	25%
Red Ryder Comics 7	$225	$200	11%	$140	61%
Red Ryder Comics 8	$225	$200	11%	$140	61%
Red Ryder Comics 9	$225	$200	11%	$140	61%
Red Ryder Comics 10	$225	$200	11%	$140	61%
Tom Mix Western 2	$225	$200	11%	$154	46%
Roy Rogers Four Color 86	$215	$215	0%	$160	34%
Roy Rogers Four Color 95	$215	$215	0%	$160	34%
Bob Colt Western 1	$210	$200	5%	$125	68%
Lash LaRue Western 3	$210	$200	5%	$150	40%
Saddle Justice 5	$210	$210	0%	$160	31%
Saddle Justice 6	$210	$210	0%	$160	31%
Saddle Justice 7	$210	$210	0%	$160	31%
Saddle Justice 8	$210	$210	0%	$160	31%
Tim Holt 11	$210	$200	5%	$170	24%
Women Outlaws 2	$210	$190	10%	$160	31%
Jimmy Wakely 5	$200	$175	13%	$105	90%
Jimmy Wakely 8	$200	$175	13%	$105	90%
Jimmy Wakely 9	$200	$175	13%	$105	90%
Jimmy Wakely 10	$200	$175	13%	$105	90%
Jimmy Wakely 11	$200	$175	13%	$105	90%
Jimmy Wakely 12	$200	$175	13%	$105	90%
Jimmy Wakely 13	$200	$175	13%	$105	90%
Jimmy Wakely 14	$200	$175	13%	$105	90%
Jimmy Wakely 15	$200	$175	13%	$105	90%
Jimmy Wakely 18	$200	$175	13%	$105	90%
Kid Colt Outlaw 2	$200	$175	13%	$90	122%
Rocky Lane Western 2	$200	$175	13%	$100	100%
Trail Colt 1	$200	$200	0%	$180	11%
Western Comics 2	$200	$180	10%	$95	111%
Western Thrillers 1	$200	$180	10%	$120	67%

HISTORY OF COMIC BOOKS

The very first comic book was a 1933 giveaway called *Funnies On Parade.* Containing repackaged Sunday comic strips, it set the standard for many comic books to follow until DC comics published *New Fun Comics*, the first comic book to contain original material.

Since that time, thousands of every type of comic book imaginable has been published. For decades, historians, collectors and bibliofiles have tried to identify, list and document all the important, trend-setting comic books. This interesting topic continues to be debated and discussed by experts everywhere. In an attempt to answer these questions, Overstreet would like to nominate the following books to Overstreet's Hall Of Fame. The author invites your critique, comments and ideas concerning the accuracy of this list for future editions. Remember, only the very top books will be considered for inclusion.

THE OVERSTREET COMIC BOOK HALL OF FAME
(1933 - 1993)

PRE GOLDEN AGE
1933 - May, 1938

Funnies on Parade nn, © EAS

Funnies On Parade #nn, 1933, Eastern Color (1st comic book)
Century Of Comics #nn, 1933, Eastern Color (2nd comic book, 1st 100 pgs).
Famous Funnies-Carnival Of Comics nn, 1933, Eastern Color, (3rd comic book)
Famous Funnies-Series 1 1934, Eastern Color, (1st 10 cent comic book)
Famous Funnies-#1, 7/34, Eastern Color (1st newsstand comic book)

New-Fun Comics #1, © DC

New Fun Comics #1, 2/35, DC (1st DC comic book)
Big Book Of Fun Comics #1, Spring/35, DC, (1st annual in comics)
New Fun Comics #6, 10/35, DC (1st Siegel & Shuster work in comics)
More Fun Comics #14, 10/36, DC (1st Superman prototype at DC, 1st in color)

Detective Comics #1, © DC

Detective Comics #1, 3/37, DC (1st issue of title that launched Batman)

GOLDEN AGE
June, 1938 - 1945

Action Comics #1, 6/38, DC (1st Superman)
Funny Pages #V2#10, 9/38, Centaur (1st Arrow, 1st costumed hero

Jumbo Comics #1, © FH

Jumbo Comics #1, 9/38, Fiction House (1st Sheena, 1st Fiction House comic book)
Movie Comics #1, 4/39, DC (1st movie comic)
New York World's Fair #1939, 4/39, DC (1st published Sandman story)

Detective Comics #27, © DC

Detective Comics #27, 5/39, DC (1st Batman)
Wonder Comics #1, 5/39, Fox (1st Wonderman, 1st Superman imitator)
Superman #nn(#1), Summer/39, DC (1st issue, 1st hero to get his own book)
Adventure Comics #40, 7/39, DC (1st conceived Sandman story)

Marvel Comics #1, © MEG

Marvel Comics #1, 10/39, Timely (1st newsstand Sub-Mariner, 1st Human Torch, 1st Marvel comic)
Silver Steak #1, 12/39, Lev Gleason (1st Gleason comic book, 1st Claw)
Flash Comics #1, 1/40, DC

HALL OF FAME (Cont'd)

(1st Flash)
Pep Comics #1, 1/40, MLJ/Archie (1st Shield, 1st Patriotic hero)
Planet Comics #1, 1/40, Fiction House (1st all science fiction comic book)

More Fun Comics #52, © DC

More Fun Comics #52, 2/40, DC (1st Spectre)
Whiz Comics #2 (#1), 2/40, Fawcett (1st Captain Marvel & Spy Smasher, 1st Fawcett comic)
Adventure Comics #48, 3/40, DC (1st Hourman)
More Fun Comics #53, 3/4,0 DC (Part II of 1st Spectre story)
Four Color Ser. 1 (Donald Duck) #4, 3?/40, (1st four color Donald Duck)

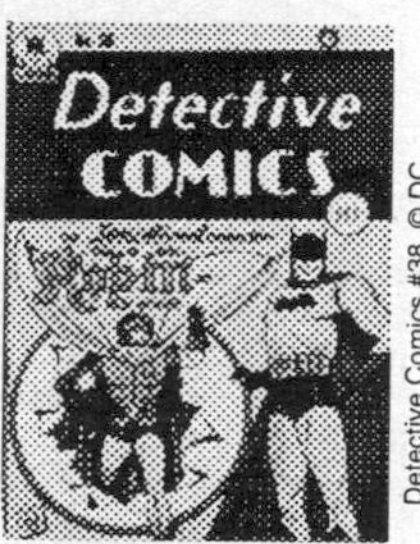

Detective Comics #38, © DC

Detective Comics #38, 4/40, DC (1st Robin)
Batman #1, Spring/40, DC (1st issue of DC's 2nd most important character; 1st Joker story)
More Fun Comics #55, 5/40, DC (1st Dr. Fate)

All American Comics #16, © DC

All American Comics #16, 7/40, DC (1st Green Lantern)
Blue Bolt #3, 7/40, Fox (1st Simon & Kirby story art)

Marvel Mystery Comics #9, 7/40, Timely(1st super hero battle; key battle issue)
Red Raven #1, 8/4, Timely (Early Kirby art)
Special Edition Comics #1, 8/40, Fawcett (1st comic devoted to Captain Marvel)
Silver Steak #6, 9/40, Lev Gleason (1st Daredevil)
Human Torch #2 (#1), Fall/4, Timely (1st issue of early Marvel star)

Walt Disney's C& S #1, © WDC

Walt Disney's Comics & Stories #1, 10/40, Dell, (1st funny animal comic book series)
All American Comics #19, 10/40, DC (1st Atom)

All Star Comics #3, © DC

All Star Comics #3, Winter/40/41, DC (1st super hero group)
Adventure Comics #72, 3/41, DC (1st Simon & Kirby Sandman)
Captain America Comics #1, 3/41, Timely, (1st Captain America)
Captain Marvel Adventures #1, 3/41, Fawcett, (1st issue of Fawcett's top character)
Sub-Mariner Comics #1, Spring/41, Timely, (1st issue of Marvel's important character)

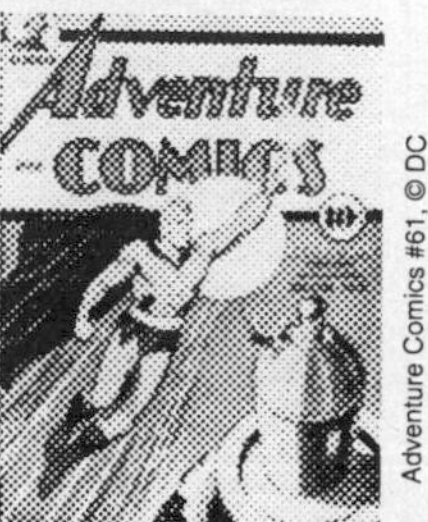

Adventure Comics #61, © DC

Adventure Comics #61, 4/41, DC (1st Starman)
All Flash #1, Summer/41, DC (1st issue of top DC character)
Daredevil #1, 7/41, Lev Gleason (1st issue of top character)
Military Comics #1, 8/41, Quality (1st Blackhawk)
Famous Fuinnies #100, 10/41, Eastern(1st comic book to reach 100)

Green Lantern #1, © DC

Green Lantern #1, Fall/41, DC (1st issue of top DC character)
More Fun Comics #73, 11/41, DC (1st Aquaman)
Pep Comics #22, 12/41, MLJ/Archie (1st Archie)
Four Color Ser. 1 (Mickey Mouse) #16, 1941, (1st comic devoted to Mickey Mouse)
Looney Tunes #1 Fall/41, Dell (1st Bugs Bunny, Porky Pig & Elmer Fudd in comics)

All Star Comics #8, © DC

All Star Comics #8, 12-1/41-42, DC (1st Wonder Woman)
Animal Comics #1, 12/1/41-42, Dell (1st Pogo by Walt Kelly)
Sensation Comics #1, 1/42, DC (1st series to star Wonder Woman)

Crime Does Not Pay #22, © LEV

HALL OF FAME (Cont'd)

Crime Does Not Pay #22, 6/42, Gleason (1st Crime Comic book series)
Wonder Woman #1, Summer/42, (1st issue of top DC character)
Four Color (Donald Duck) #9, 8/42 Dell (1st Barks story/art on Donald Duck)
Archie Comics #1, Winter/42-43, MLJ/ Archie, (1st Teenage comic)
Capt Marvel Adventures #22, 3/43, Fawcett, (Begins Mr. Mind serial)
Plastic Man #1, Summer/43, Quality (1st issue of top Quality character)

Big All-American #1, © DC

Big All-American Comic Book #1, 1944,DC,(1st annual of All American Comics)
More Fun Comics #101, 1-2/45, DC (1st Superboy)
Molly O'Day #1, 2/45, Avon (1st Avon comic)
Terry Toones #38, 11/45, Timely (1st Mighty Mouse)

POST GOLDEN AGE
1946 - 1949

Romantic Picture Novelette #1, 1946, ME, 1st love comic theme (one shot)

All Winners #19, © MEG

All Winners #19, Fall/46, Timely 1st All Winners Squad, 1st Marvel group)
All Winners #21, Winter/46-47, Timely (2nd All Winners Squad)
Eerie #1, 1/47, Avon (1st horror comic)
Young Romance Comics,#1, 9-10/ 47, Prize, (1st romance series)
Four Color (Uncle Scrooge) #178, 12/47, Dell, (1st Uncle Scrooge)
Phantom Lady #17, 4/48, Fox (Classic cover issue-good girl art)

Adventures Into the Unknown #1, © ACG

Adventures Into The Unknown #1, Fall/48,ACG, (1st horror series)
Moon Girl #5, Winter/48, EC (1st E.C. horror story)
Casper #1, 9/49, St John (1st Baby Huey)

Crime Patrol #15, © WMG

Crime Patrol #15, 12-1/ 49-50, EC (1st Crypt Keeper)
War Against Crime #10, 12/1/ 49/50, EC (1st Vault Keeper)

PRE-SILVER AGE
1950 - Aug, 1956

Howdy Doody #1, 1/50, Dell (1st T.V. comic)
Archie Annual #1, 1950, Archie (1st Archie annual)
Crypt Of Terror #17, 4-5/50, EC (1st issue of Crypt Keeper tales, E.C. horror)
Haunt Of Fear #15(#1), 5-6/50, EC (1st Issue of E.C. horror, trend setting)
Weird Fantasy #13 (#1), 5-6/50, EC (1st issue of E.C. science fiction, trend setting)

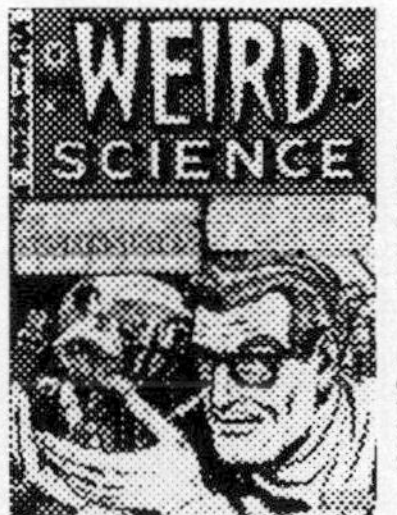

Weird Science #12, © WMG

Weird Science #12 (#1), 5-6/50, EC (1st issue of E.C. science fiction, trend setting)

Strange Tales #1, 6/51, Marvel (1st issue of top Marvel title)

Mad #1, © Warner Bros.

Mad #1, 10-11/52,EC (1st satire comic)
Journey Into Mystery #1, 6/52, Marvel (1st issue of top title)
Little Dot #1, 9/53, Harvey (1st Richie Rich)
World's Finest Comics #71, 7-8/54, DC (1st Superman/Batman team issue)
Superman's Pal, Jimmy Olsen #1, 9-10/54, DC, (1st issue of top DC title)

My Greatest Adventure #1, © DC

My Greatest Adventure #1, 1-2/55, DC (1st issue of top DC fantasy title)
Brave And The Bold #1, 8-9/55, DC (1st issue of top DC showcase title)
Superman #100, 9-10/55, DC (Landmark issue)

Detective Comics #225, © DC

Detecive Comics #225, 11/55, DC (1st Martian Manhunter)
Tales Of The Unexpected #1, 2-3/56, DC, (1st issue of top DC fantasy title)
Showcase #1, 3-/4/56, DC (1st issue of top DC showcase title)
Sugar & Spike #1, 4-5/56, DC

HALL OF FAME (Cont'd)

(1st issue of top title by Sheldon Mayer)

Batman #100, 6/56, DC (Landmark issue)

Detective Comics #233, 7/56, DC (1st Batwoman)

SILVER AGE
Sept, 1956 - 1969

Showcase #4, © DC

House Of Secrets #1, 11-12/56, DC (1st issue of top DC horror title)

Showcase #4, 9-10/56, DC (1st silver age book) (the Flash)

Showcase #6, 1-2/57, DC (1st silver age group) (Challengers)

Showcase #9, 7-8/57, DC (1st Lois Lane book)

Superman's Girl Friend, Lois Lane #1, 3-4/58. DC, (1st issue of top character)

Challengers #1, © DC

Adventure Comics #247, 4/58, DC (1st Legion of Superheroes)

Challengers Of The Unknown #1, 4/5/58, DC, (1st issue of 1st silver age group)

Showcase #15, 7-8/58, DC (1st Space Range)

Showcase #17, 11-12/58, DC (1st Adam Strange)

Tales Of Suspense #1, 1/59, Marvel (1st issue of top fantasy title)

Flash #105, © DC

Tales To Astonish #1, 1/59, Marvel (1st issue of top fantasy title)

Flash #105(#1), 2-3/59, DC (1st issue of top DC title)

Our Army At War #81, 4/59, DC (1st Sgt. Rock)

Action Comics #252, 5/59, DC (1st Supergirl)

Showcase #20, 5-6/59, DC (1st Rip Hunter)

Double Life Of Private Strong #1,

Mystery In Space #53, © DC

6/59, Archie, (1st silver age Shield, 1st Fly)

Mystery In Space #53, 8/59, DC (1st Adam Strange)

Tales Of The Unexpected #40, 8/59, DC(1st Space Ranger in own title)

Adventures of the Fly #1, 8/59, Archie (1st issue of top Archie title)

Showcase #22, 9-10/59, DC (1st silver age Green Lantern)

Brave and the Bold #28, © DC

Flash #110, 12-1/ 59-60, DC (1st Kid Flash)

Brave And The Bold #28, 2-3/60, DC (1st Justice League of America)

Green Lantern #1, 7-8/60, DC (1st issue of top DC character)

Showcase #27, 7-8/60, DC (1st Sea Devils)

Brave And The Bold #31, 8-9/60, DC

Brave and the Bold #34, © DC

(1st Cave Carson)

Justice League Of America #1, 10-11/60, DC, (1st issue of top DC title)

Showcase #30, 1-2/61, DC (1st silver age Aquaman)

Brave And The Bold #34, 2-3/61, DC (1st silver age Hawkman)

Amazing Adventures #1, 6/61, Marvel (1st Dr. Doom, the 1st Marvel-Age superhero)

Showcase #34, © DC

Flash #123, 9/61, DC (1st G.A. Flash in silver age)

Showcase #34, 9-10/61, DC (1st silver age Atom)

Fantastic Four #1, 11/61, Marvel (1st Fantastic Four)

Amazing Adult Fantasy #7, 12/61, Marvel(1st issue of title that leads to Spider-Man)

Tales To Astonish #27, 1/62, Marvel (1st Antman)

Showcase #37, 3-4/62, DC (1st Metal Men)

Incredible Hulk #1, © MEG

Fantastic Four #4, 5/62, Marvel (1st silver age Sub-Mariner)

Incredible Hulk #1, 5/62, Marvel (1st Hulk)

Mystery In Space #75, 5/62, DC (Early JLA cross-over in Adam Strange)

Amazing Fantasy #15, © MEG

HALL OF FAME (Cont'd)

Fantastic Four #5, 7/62, Marvel (1st Dr. Doom)

Journey Into Mystery #83, 8/62, Marvel (1st Thor)

Amazing Fantasy #15, 8-9/62, Marvel (1st Spider-Man)

Tales To Astonish #35, 9/62, Marvel (2nd Antman, 1st in costume)

Strange Tales #101, 10/62, Marvel (1st silver Human Torch solo story)

Tales of Suspense #39, © MEG

Amazing Spider-Man #1, 3/63, Marvel (1st Spider-Man in own title)

Tales Of Suspense #39, 3/63, Marvel (1st Iron Man)

Strange Tales #110, 7/63, Marvel (1st Dr. Strange)

Avengers #1, 9/63, Marvel (1st Avengers)

X-Men #1, 9/63, Marvel (1st X-Men)

Mystery In Space #87, 11/63, DC (1st Hawkman in title)

Avengers #4, 3/64, Marvel (1st silver Captain America)

Daredevil #1, 4/64, Marvel (1st Daredevil)

Fantastic Four #48, © MEG

Amazing Spider-Man #14, 7/64, Marvel (1st Green Goblin)

Fantastic Four #48, 3/66, Marvel (1st Silver Surfer)

Strange Tales #135, 7/65, Marvel (Origin &1st app. Nick Fury)

Strange Adventures #205, 10/67, DC (1st Deadman)

POST SILVER AGE
1970 - 1979

Detective Comics #400, 6/70, DC (1st Man-Bat)

Star Spangled War stories #151, 6/7/70, DC, (1st Unknown Soldier)

Superman's Pal, Jimmy Olsen #133, 10/70, DC, (1st silver age Newsboy

Forever People #1, © DC

Legion)

Forever People #1, 2-3/71, DC (1st Forever People)

New Gods #1, 3/71, DC

Mister Miracle #1, © DC

(1st New Gods)

Mister Miracle #1, 3/71, DC (1st Mister Miracle)

Savage Tales #1, 5/71, Marvel (1st Man-Thing)

House of Secrets #92, 6/71, DC (1st app. Swamp Thing by Bernie Wrightson)

Amazing Spider-Man #101, 10/71, Marvel (1st Morbius the Living Vampire)

Marvel Feature #1 © MEG

Marvel Feature #1, 12/71, Marvel (Origin and 1st app. Defenders)

All Star Western #10 , 2-3/72, DC (1st Jonah Hex)

Tomb of Dracula #1, 4/72, Marvel (1st app. Dracula)

Marvel Spotlight #2, 6/72, Marvel (1st app. Werewolf by Night)

Marvel Spotlight #5, 8/72, Marvel (Origin and 1st app. new Ghost Rider)

Kamandi: The Last Boy on Earth #1, 10/72, DC, (Origin and 1st app. Kamandi)

Iron Man #55, 2/73, Marvel (1st. app. Thanos & Drax the Destroyer)

Iron Man #55, © MEG

Marvel Spotlight #12, 10/73, Marvel (1st. solo Son of Satan)

Marvel Special Edition #15, 12/73 Marvel (1st Master of Kung Fu)

Amazing Spider-Man #129, © MEG

Amazing Spider-Man #129, 2/74, Marvel (1st Punisher)

Astonishing Tales #25, 8/74, Marvel (1st Deathlok)

Incredible Hulk #181, 11/74, Marvel (1st app. of Wolverine) (story)

Giant Size X Men #1, Summer/75, Marvel (1st New X-Men; intro Nightcrawler, Storm, Colossus & Thunderbird)

X-Men #94, © MEG

X-Men #94, 8/75, Marvel (New X-Men team begins)

All Star Comics #58, 1/2/76, DC (1st Power Girl)

Marvel Spotlight #32, 2/77, Marvel (1st Spider-Woman)

Black Lightning #1, 4/77, DC (1st Black Lightning)

Cerebus #1, 12/77, Aardvark-Vanaheim (1st app. Cerebus (B/W))

MODERN AGE
1980 - PRESENT

Savage She Hulk #1, 2/80, Marvel (1st She-Hulk)

HALL OF FAME (Cont'd)

Avengers Annual #10, 1981, Marvel (1st Rogue)

Spectacular Spider-man #64, 3/82, Marvel (1st Cloak & Dagger)

Amazing Spider-Man #238, 3/83, Marvel (1st Hobgoblin)

Amazing Spider-Man #252, 5/84, Marvel (1st Spider-Man in black costume)

Detective Comics #327, 5/84, DC (New Batman) (Silver Age/ Modern)

Teenage M.N.T. #1, © Miirage

Teenage Mutant Ninja Turtles #1, pre 6/84, Mirage, (1st app. Teenage Mutant Ninja Turtles)

Crisis On Infinite Earths #7, 10/85, DC (Supergirldies)

Batman: The Dark Knight #1, 3/86, DC (Batman changes form)

Batman #404, 2/87, DC (1st Modern Catwoman)

Aliens #1, 5/88, Dark Horse (1st app. of Aliens in comics/b&w)

Amazing Spider-Man #300, 5/88, Marvel (1st venom) (full app & story)

Sandman (2nd Series) #1, 1/89, DC (New Sandman) (Modern)

Sandman #8, © DC

Sandman #8, 8/89, DC (1st Death)

Spectacular Spider-Man #158, 12/89, Marvel, (New Spider-Man) (cosmic-powered)

X-Men Annual #14, 1990, Marvel (1st Gambit)

New Mutants #86, 2/90, Marvel (1st Cable) (cameo)

Superman (2nd Series) #50, 12/90, DC (Clark Kent proposes to Lois Lane)

X-Men #1, 10/91, Marvel (Print run of 8,000,000 copies)

Harbinger #1,1/92, Valiant (1st. app. Harbinger)

Youngblood #1, © Liefeld

Youngblood #1, 4/92, Image (1st Image comic)

Batman : Vengeance of Bane #1 1/93 DC (1st app. of Bane) (Knightfall)

Superman (2nd Series) #75, 1/93, DC (Death of Superman) (Huge Media Coverage)

Batman #497, 7/93, DC (Culmination of the Knightfall series)

HISTORIC FIRSTS

(First comic book of a genre, publisher, theme or type, etc.)

Aviation Comic–Wings Comics #1, 9/40

Comic Book Annual–Big Book Of Fun Comics #1, spr, 1936

Comic Book–Funnies On Parade nn, 1933

Comic Book to go into endless reprints–Classic Comics #1, 10/41

Comic Book to kill off a super hero–Pep Comics #17, 7/41 (The Comet)

Comic Book with metallic logo–Silver Streak #1, 12/39

Comic Book with original material–New Fun Comics #1, 2/35

Costumed Hero Battle comic–Marvel Mystery #9, 7/40

Costumed Hero Comic (Strip)–Ace Comics #11, 2/38 (The Phantom)

Costumed Hero Comic (Original material)–Funny Pages V2/10 9/38 (The Arrow)(3 months after Superman)

Costumed Hero sidekick comic – Detective Comics #38, 4/40 (Robin)

Crime–Crime Does Not Pay #22, 6/42

Detective comic–Detective Picture Stories #1, 12/36

Disney Single Character comic book –Donald Duck nn, 1938

Disney Single Character comic book in color–Donald Duck 4-Color #4, 3/40

Educational theme comic–Classic Comics #1, 10/41

5 cent comic–Nickel Comics #1, 1938

15 cent comic–New York World's Fair, 1940

Flying Saucer comic–Spirit Section 9/28/47 (3 months after 1st sighting in Idaho on 6/25/47

Funny Animal Series–Walt Disney's Comic & Stories #1, 10/40

Funny Animal single character comic–Donald Duck nn, 1938

Giveaway comic–Funnies On Parade nn, 1933

Golden Age comic–Action Comics #1, 6/38

1st Golden Age comic book © DC

Heroine Single Theme comic–Sheena, Queen of the Jungle #1, Spr, 1942

Horror comic (one shot)–Eerie Comics #1, 1/47

Horror comic (series)–Adventures Into The Unknown #1, Fall, 1948

Jungle comic–Jumbo Comics #1, 9/38

Large Sized comic–New Fun Comics #1, 2/35

Love comic (One Shot)–Romantic Picture Novelettes #1, 1946 (Mary Worth strip-r)

Love comic (series)–Young Romance Comics #1, 10/47

Magician comic–Super Magic Comics #1, 5/41

Magician comic series–Super Magician Comics #2, 9/41

Marvel Silver Age Annual–Strange Tales Annual #1, 1962

Masked Hero–Funny Pages #6, 11/36 (The Clock)

Movie comic–Movie Comics #1, 4/39

Negro comic–Negro Heroes, Spr, 1947

Newsstand comic–Famous Funnies #1, 7/34

#2 in comics–Famous Funnies #2, 8/34

100 page comic–Century of Comics nn, 1933

100th issue–Famous Funnies #100, 11/43

COMICS BOUGHT AND SOLD

BUYING: 1940's to 1975

- Paying up to 50% of Overstreet prices for comics in Fine or better condition

SELLING: Gold and Silver Age plus back issues

- Marvel, DC, Dell, Gold Key, Classics, EC, ACG, Timely, Fawcett, Fiction House, Disney, Others
- Thousands of titles available
- Satisfaction guaranteed

FOREIGN ORDERS ACCEPTED

PHOENIX ENTERPRISES
RD 1 Box 423
Erin, NY 14838
Tel (607) 796-2547

Satisfied customers since 1978

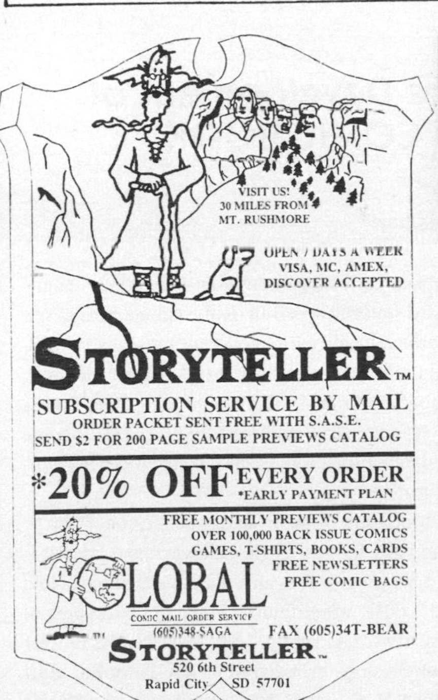

MAN & SUPERMAN

WHY ON EARTH ARE YOU PAYING FULL PRICE TO BUILD YOUR COLLECTION?

When you come to Man & Superman to get what you need, the benefits of your decision come your way as fast as your order.

Choose from an amazing inventory of Golden Age to Current comics, magazines, and pulps.

Purchase new comics for at least 15% off cover price.

We'll also give you the best prices available on other collectibles: videos, T-shirts, cards, posters, and original art.

$1 * Golden Age-Silver Age Catalog * $1 * Silver Age-Current Catalog * $1

If you can't find something, let us. Want lists always accepted. Let Man & Superman work for you!

Plus, a one-time membership fee of just $20 enrolls you in The Infinite, our unique collector's group, making you eligible for: our user-friendly subscription service, additional discounts, tantalizing specials, hot giveaways, free catalogs, the unquestionably unique Infinite Awareness newsletter, and lots of unpredictable, eye-popping surprises.

Make check or money order payable in U.S. funds to Man & Superman.

Man & Superman * 42 Music Sq. W. Suite 293 * Nashville, TN 37203-3234
Call 615 255 5943 for more info.

Don't live wanting * Don't die wondering

HISTORIC FIRSTS (Cont'd)
One Shot Series–Feature Book nn, 1937
Patriotic Hero comic–Pep Comics #1, 1/40 (The Shield)
Prototype comic–The Comics Magazine #1, 5/36 (Superman)
Public Event comic–New York World's Fair 1939
Religious Theme series–Topix Comics #1, 11/42
Reprint comic–Funnies On Parade nn, 1933
Satire comic–Mad #1, 10-11/52
Science Fiction comic–Planet Comics #1, 1/40
Sidekick group comic–Young Allies #1, Sum, 1941
Silver Age Archie comic–Double Life of Private Strong, #1, 6/59
Silver Age comic–Showcase #4, 9-10/56
Silver Age DC Annual–Superman Annual #1, 10/60
Silver Age Marvel Annual–Strange Tales Annual #1, 1962
Silver Age Marvel comic–Fantastic Four #1, 11/61
Single Character comic–Skippy's Own Book Of Comics, 1934
Single original character comic–Superman #1, Sum, 1939
Single Strip Reprint Character comic–Mutt and Jeff #1, Sum, 1939
Single Theme comic–Detective Picture Stories #1, 12/36
Single Theme comic, the first important–Detective Comics #1, 3/37
Single Theme Reprint Strip comic–Mutt and Jeff #1, Sum, 1939
Small-sized comic–Little Giant Comics#1, 7/38
Sports comic–Champion Comics #2, 12/39
Squarebound comic–New Book Of Comics #1, 1937
Squarebound series–World's Best #1, Spr, 1941

Superman #1, © DC

1st single original character comic

Super Hero comic–Action Comics #1, 6/38 (Superman)
Super Hero Team–All Star Comics #3, Wint, 1940-41
Super Heroine comic–All Star Comics #8, 11-12/41
Super Heroine comic series–Sensation Comics #1, 1/42
Superman imitator–Wonder Comics#1, 5/39 (Wonder Man)
Teen-age comic–Pep Comics #22, 12/41
Teen-age comic series–Archie Comics #1, Wint, 1942-43
10 cent comic–Famous Funnies Series 1, 3-5/34
3-D comic–Mighty Mouse 3-D #1, 9/53
T.V. comic–Howdy Doody #1, 1/50
25 cent comic–New York World's Fair, 1939
True Life comic–Sport Comics #1, 10/40
Villain cover (Fu Manchu)–Detective Comics #1, 3/37
Villain Story (Fu Manchu)–Detective Comics #17, 7/38
Villain Cover/story (Original to comics)– Silver Streak #1, 12/39 (The Claw)
War comic–War Comics #1, 5/40
Weekly comic book–The Spirit #1, 6/2/40
Western comic–Western Picture Stories #1, 2/37 & Star Ranger #1, 2/37
Western of one character–The Lone Ranger Comics nn, 1939
Western run of one character (Giveaway)–Tom Mix #1, 9/40
Western newsstand run of one character–Red Ryder Comics #1, 8/41
Western with photo cover–Roy Rogers 4-color #38, 4/44
X-Over comic–Marvel Mystery #9,

A Chronology of the Development of THE AMERICAN COMIC BOOK

By
M. Thomas Inge*

Precursors: The facsimile newspaper strip reprint collections constitute the earliest "comic books." The first of these was a collection of Richard Outcault's **Yellow Kid** from the Hearst New York American in March 1897. Commercial and promotional reprint collections, usually in cardboard covers, appeared through the 1920s and featured such newspaper strips as **Mutt and Jeff, Foxy Grandpa, Buster Brown**, and **Barney Google**. During 1922 a reprint magazine, **Comic Monthly**, appeared with each issue devoted to a separate strip, and from 1929 to 1930 George Delacorte published 36 issues of **The Funnies** in tabloid format with original comic pages in color, becoming the first four-color comic newsstand publication.

1933: The Ledger syndicate published a small broadside of their Sunday comics on 7" by 9" plates. Employees of Eastern Color Printing Company in New York, sales manager Harry I. Wildenberg and salesman Max C. Gaines, saw it and figured that two such plates would fit a tabloid page, which would produce a book about 7-1/2" x 10" when folded. Thus 10,000 copies of **Funnies on Parade**, containing 32 pages of Sunday newspaper reprints, was published for Proctor and Gamble to be given away as premiums. Some of the strips included were: **Joe Palooka, Mutt and Jeff, Hairbreadth Harry**, and **Reg'lar Fellas**. M. C. Gaines was very impressed with this book and convinced Eastern Color that he could sell a lot of them to such big advertisers as Milk-O-Malt, Wheatena, Kinney Shoe Stores, and others to be used as premiums and radio give-aways. So, Eastern Color printed **Famous Funnies: A Carnival of Comics**, and then **Century of Comics**, both as before, containing Sunday newspaper reprints. Mr. Gaines sold these books in quantities of 100,000 to 250,000.

1934: The give-away comics were so successful that Mr. Gaines believed that youngsters would buy comic books for ten cents like the "Big Little Books" coming out at that time. So, early in 1934, Eastern Color ran off 35,000 copies of **Famous Funnies, Series 1**, 64 pages of reprints for Dell Publishing Company to be sold for ten cents in chain stores. Since it sold out promptly on the stands, Eastern Color, in May 1934, issued **Famous Funnies** No. 1 (dated July 1934) which became, with issue No. 2 in July, the first monthly comic magazine. The title continued for over 20 years through 218 issues, reaching a circulation peak of over 400,000 copies a month. At the same time, Mr. Gaines went to the sponsors of Percy Crosby's **Skippy**, who was on the radio, and convinced them to put out a Skippy book, advertise it on the air, and give away a free copy to anyone who bought a tube of Phillip's toothpaste. Thus 500,000 copies of **Skippy's Own Book of Comics** was run off and distributed through drug stores everywhere. This was the first four-color comic book of reprints devoted to a single character.

1935: Major Malcolm Wheeler-Nicholson's National Periodical Publications issued in February a tabloid-sized comic publication called **New Fun**, which became **More Fun** after the sixth issue and converted to the normal comic-book size after issue eight. **More Fun** was the first comic book of a standard size to publish original material and continued publication until 1949. **Mickey Mouse Magazine** began in the summer, to become **Walt Disney's Comics and Stories** in 1940, and combined original material with reprinted newspaper strips in most issues.

1936: In the wake of the success of **Famous Funnies**, other publishers, in conjunction with the major newspaper strip syndicates, inaugurated more reprint comic books: **Popular Comics** (News Tribune, February), **Tip Top Comics** (United Features, April), **King Comics** (King Features, April), and **The Funnies** (new series, NEA, October). Four issues of **Wow Comics**, from David McKay and Henle Publications, appeared, edited by S. M. Iger and including early art by Will Eisner, Bob Kane, and Alex Raymond. The first non-reprint comic book devoted to a single theme was **Detective Picture Stories** issued in December by The Comics Magazine Company.

1937: The second single theme title, **Western Picture Stories**, came in February from The Comics Magazine Company, and the third was **Detective Comics**, an offshoot of **More Fun**, which began in March to be published to the present. The book's initials, "D.C.," have long served to refer to National Periodical Publications, which was purchased from Major Nicholson by Harry Donenfeld late this year.

1938: "DC" copped a lion's share of the comic book market with the publication of **Action Comics** No. 1 in June which contained the first appearance of Superman by writer Jerry Siegel and artist Joe Shuster, a discovery of Max C. Gaines. The "man of steel" inaugurated the "Golden Era" in comic book history. Fiction House, a pulp publisher, entered the comic book field in September with **Jumbo Comics**, featuring Sheena, Queen of the Jungle, and appearing in over-sized format for the first eight issues.

1939: The continued success of "DC" was assured in May with the publication of **Detective Comics** No. 27 containing the first episode of Batman by artist Bob Kane and writer Bill Finger. **Superman Comics** appeared in the summer. Also, during the summer, a black and white premium comic titled **Motion Picture Funnies Weekly** was published to be given away at motion picture theatres. The plan was to issue it weekly and to have continued stories so that the kids would come back week after week not to miss an episode. Four issues were planned but only

McKay and Henle Publications, appeared, edited by S. M. Iger and including early art by Will Eisner, Bob Kane, and Alex Raymond. The first non-reprint comic book devoted to a single theme was **Detective Picture Stories** issued in December by The Comics Magazine Company.

1937: The second single theme title, **Western Picture Stories**, came in February from The Comics Magazine Company, and the third was **Detective Comics**, an offshoot of **More Fun**, which began in March to be published to the present. The book's initials, "D.C.," have long served to refer to National Periodical Publications, which was purchased from Major Nicholson by Harry Donenfeld late this year.

1938: "DC" copped a lion's share of the comic book market with the publication of **Action Comics** No. 1 in June which contained the first appearance of Superman by writer Jerry Siegel and artist Joe Shuster, a discovery of Max C. Gaines. The "man of steel" inaugurated the "Golden Era" in comic book history. Fiction House, a pulp publisher, entered the comic book field in September with **Jumbo Comics**, featuring Sheena, Queen of the Jungle, and appearing in over-sized format for the first eight issues.

1939: The continued success of "DC" was assured in May with the publication of **Detective Comics** No. 27 containing the first episode of Batman by artist Bob Kane and writer Bill Finger. **Superman Comics** appeared in the summer. Also, during the summer, a black and white premium comic titled **Motion Picture Funnies Weekly** was published to be given away at motion picture theatres. The plan was to issue it weekly and to have continued stories so that the kids would come back week after week not to miss an episode. Four issues were planned but only one came out. This book contains the first appearance and origin of the Sub-Mariner by Bill Everett (8 pages) which was later reprinted in **Marvel Comics**. In November, the first issue of **Marvel Comics** came out, featuring the Human Torch by Carl Burgos and the Sub-Mariner reprint with color added.

1940: The April issue of **Detective Comics** No. 38 introduced Robin the Boy Wonder as a sidekick to Batman, thus establishing the "Dynamic Duo" and a major precedent for later costumed heroes who would also have boy companions. **Batman Comics** began in the spring. Over 60 different comic book titles were being issued, including **Whiz Comics** begun in February by Fawcett Publications. A creation of writer Bill Parker and artist C. C. Beck, Whiz's Captain Marvel was the only superhero ever to surpass Superman in comic book sales. Drawing on their own popular pulp magazine heroes, Street and Smith Publications introduced **Shadow Comics** in March and **Doc Savage Comics** in May. A second trend was established with the summer appearance of the first issue of **All Star Comics**, which brought several superheroes together in one story and in its third issue that winter would announce the establishment of the Justice Society of America.

1941: Wonder Woman was introduced in the spring issue of **All Star Comics** No. 8, the creation of psychologist William Moulton Marston and artist Harry Peter. **Captain Marvel Adventures** began this year. By the end of 1941, over 160 titles were being published, including **Captain America** by Jack Kirby and Joe Simon, **Police Comics** with Jack Cole's Plastic Man and later Will Eisner's Spirit, **Military Comics** with Blackhawk by Eisner and Charles Cuidera, **Daredevil Comics** with the original character by Charles Biro, **Air Fighters** with Airboy also by Biro, and **Looney Tunes & Merrie Melodies** with Porky Pig, Bugs Bunny, and Elmer Fudd, reportedly created by Bob Clampett for the Leon Schlesinger Productions animated films and drawn for the comics by Chase Craig. Also, Albert Kanter's Gilberton Company initiated the **Classics Illustrated** series with The Three Musketeers.

1942: Crime Does Not Pay by editor Charles Biro and publisher Lev Gleason, devoted to factual accounts of criminals' lives, began a different trend in realistic crime stories. **Wonder Woman** appeared in the summer. John Goldwater's character Archie, drawn by Bob Montana, first published in **Pep Comics**, was given his own magazine **Archie Comics**, which has remained popular over 40 years. The first issue of **Animal Comics** contained Walt Kelly's "Albert Takes the Cake," featuring the new character of Pogo. In mid-1942, the undated Dell Four Color title, No. 9, **Donald**

Duck Finds Pirate Gold, appeared with art by Carl Barks and Jack Hannah. Barks, also featured in **Walt Disney's Comics and Stories**, remained the most popular delineator of Donald Duck and later introduced his greatest creation, Uncle Scrooge, in **Christmas on Bear Mountain** (Dell Four Color No. 178). The fantasy work of George Carlson appeared in the first issue of **Jingle Jangle Comics**, one of the most imaginative titles for children ever to be published.

1945: The first issue of **Real Screen Comics** introduced the Fox and the Crow by James F. Davis, and John Stanley began drawing the **Little Lulu** comic book based on a popular feature in the **Saturday Evening Post** by Marjorie Henderson Buell from 1935 to 1944. Bill Woggon's Katy Keene appears in issue No. 5 of **Wilbur Comics** to be followed by appearances in **Laugh, Pep, Suzie** and her own comic book in 1950. The popularity of Dick Briefer's satiric version of the Frankenstein monster, originally drawn for **Prize Comics** in 1941, led to the publication of **Frankenstein Comics** by Prize publications.

1950: The son of Max C. Gaines, William M. Gaines, who earlier had inherited his father's firm Educational Comics (later Entertaining Comics), began publication of a series of well-written and masterfully drawn titles which would establish a "New Trend" in comics magazines: **Crypt of Terror** (later **Tales from the Crypt**, April), **The Vault of Horror** (April), **The Haunt of Fear** (May), **Weird Science** (May), **Weird Fantasy** (May), **Crime SuspenStories** (October), and **Two Fisted Tales** (November), the latter stunningly edited by Harvey Kurtzman.

1952: In October "E.C." published the first number of **Mad** under Kurtzman's creative editorship, thus establishing a style of humor which would inspire other publications and powerfully influence the underground comic book movement of the 1960s.

1953: All Fawcett titles featuring Captain Marvel were ceased after many years of litigation in the courts during which National Periodical Publications claimed that the super-hero was an infringement on the copyrighted Superman.

1954: The appearance of Fredric Wertham's book **Seduction of the Innocent** in the spring was the culmination of a continuing war against comic books fought by those who believed they corrupted youth and debased culture. The U. S. Senate Subcommittee on Juvenile Delinquency investigated comic books and in response the major publishers banded together in October to create the Comics Code Authority and adopted, in their own words, "the most stringent code in existence for any communications media." Before the Code took effect, more than 1,000,000,000 issues of comic books were being sold annually.

1955: In an effort to avoid the Code, "E.C." launched a "New Direction" series of titles, such as **Impact, Valor, Aces High, Extra, M.D.**, and **Psychoanalysis**, none of which lasted beyond the year. **Mad** was changed into a larger magazine format with issue No. 24 in July to escape the Comics Code entirely, and "E.C." closed down its line of comic books altogether.

1956: Beginning with the Flash in **Showcase** No. 4, Julius Schwartz began a popular revival of "DC" superheroes which would lead to the "Silver Age" in comic book history.

1957: Atlas reduced the number of titles published by two-thirds, with **Journey into Mystery** and **Strange Tales** surviving, while other publishers did the same or went out of business. Atlas would survive as a part of the Marvel Comics Group.

1960: After several efforts at new satire magazines (**Trump** and **Humbug**), Harvey Kurtzman, no longer with Gaines, issued in August the first number of another abortive effort, **Help!**, where the early work of underground cartoonists Jay Lynch, Skip Williamson, Gilbert Shelton, and Robert Crumb appeared.

1961: Stan Lee edited in November the first **Fantastic Four**, featuring Mr. Fantastic, the Human Torch, the Thing, and the Invisible Girl, and inaugurated an enormously popular line of titles from Marvel Comics featuring a more contemporary style of superhero.

1962: Lee introduced **The Amazing Spider-Man** in August, with art by Steve Ditko, **The Hulk** in May and **Thor** in August, the last two produced by Dick Ayers and Jack Kirby.

1965: James Warren issued **Creepy**, a larger black and white comic book, outside Comics Code's control, which emulated the "E.C." horror comic line. Warren's **Eerie** began in September and **Vampirella** in September 1969.

1968: Robert Crumb's **Zap** No. 1 appeared, the first underground comic book to achieve wide popularity, although the undergrounds had their roots in 1962 with **Adventures of Jesus** by Foolbert Sturgeon (Frank Stack) and 1964 with **God Nose** by Jack Jackson.

1970: Editor Roy Thomas at Marvel begins **Conan the Barbarian** based on fiction by Robert E. Howard with art by Barry Smith, and Neal Adams began to draw for "DC" a series of **Green Lantern/Green Arrow** stories which would deal with relevant social issues such as racism, urban poverty, and drugs.

1972: The Swamp Thing by Berni Wrightson begins in November from "DC."

1973: In February, "DC" revived the original **Captain Marvel** with new art by C. C. Beck and reprints in the first issue of **Shazam** and in October **The Shadow** with scripts by Denny O'Neil and art by Mike Kaluta.

1974: "DC" began publication in the spring of a series of over-sized facsimile reprints of the most valued comic books of the past under the general title of "Famous First Editions," beginning with a reprint of **Action** No. 1 and including afterwards **Detective Comics** No. 27, **Sensation Comics** No. 1, **Whiz Comics** No. 2, **Batman** No. 1, **Wonder Woman** No. 1, **All-Star Comics** No. 3, **Flash Comics** No. 1, and **Superman** No. 1. Mike Friedrich, an independent publisher, released **StarHReach** with work by Jim Starlin, Neal Adams, and Dick Giordano, with ownership of the characters and stories invested in the creators themselves.

1975: In the first collaborative effort between the two major comic book publishers of the previous decade, Marvel and "DC" produced together an over-sized comic book version of MGM's **Marvelous Wizard of Oz** in the fall, and then the following year in an unprecedented cross-over produced **Superman vs. the Amazing Spider-Man**, written by Gerry Conway, drawn by Ross Andru, and inked by Dick Giordano.

1976: Frank Brunner's Howard the Duck, who had appeared earlier in Marvel's **Fear** and **Man-Thing**, was given his own book in January, which because of distribution problems became an overnight collector's item. After decades of litigation, Jerry Siegel and Joe Shuster were given financial recompense and recognition by National Periodical Publications for their creation of Superman, after several friends of the team made a public issue of the case.

1977: Stan Lee's **Spider-Man** was given a second birth, fifteen years after his first, through a highly successful newspaper comic strip, which began syndication on January 3 with art by John Romita. This invasion of the comic strip by comic book characters continued with the appearance on June 6 of Marvel's **Howard the Duck**, with story by Steve Gerber and visuals by Gene Colan. In an unusually successful collaborative effort, Marvel began publication of the comic book adaption of the George Lucas film **Star Wars**, with script by Roy Thomas and art by Howard Chaykin, at least three months before the film was released nationally on May 25. The demand was so great that all six issues of **Star Wars** were reprinted at least seven times, and the installments were reprinted in two volumes of an over-sized Marvel Special Edition and a single paperback volume for the book trade. Dave Sim, with an issue dated December, began self-publication of his **Cerebus the Aardvark**, the success of which would help establish the independent market for non-traditional black-and-white comics.

1978: In an effort to halt declining sales, Warner Communications drastically cut back on the number of "DC" titles and overhauled its distribution process in June. The interest of the visual media in comic book characters reached a new high with the Hulk, Spider-Man, and Doctor Strange, the subjects of television shows; with various projects begun to produce film versions of Flash Gordon, Dick Tracy, Popeye, Conan, The Phantom, and Buck Rogers; and with the movement reaching an outlandish peak of publicity with the release of **Superman** in December. Two signifi-

Jack Kirby. Eclipse Enterprises published Don McGregor and Paul Gulacy's **Sabre**, the first graphic album produced for the direct sales market, and initiated a policy of paying royalties and granting copyrights to comic book creators. Wendy and Richard Pini's **Elfquest**, a self-publishing project begun this year, eventually became so popular that it achieved bookstore distribution. The magazine **Heavy Metal** brought to American attention the avant-garde comic book work of European artists.

1980: Publication of the November premier issue of **The New Teen Titans**, with art by George Perez and story by Marv Wolfman, brought back to widespread popularity a title originally published by "DC" in 1966.

1981: The distributor Pacific Comics began publishing titles for direct sales through comic shops with the inaugural issue of Jack Kirby's **Captain Victory and the Galactic Rangers** and offered royalties to artists and writers on the basis of sales. "DC" would do the same for regular newsstand comics in November (with payments retroactive to July 1981), and Marvel followed suit by the end of the year. The first issue of **Raw**, irregularly published by Art Spiegelman and Francoise Mouly, carried comic book art into new extremes of experimentation and innovation with work by European and American artists. With issue No. 158, Frank Miller began to write and draw Marvel's **Daredevil** and brought a vigorous style of violent action to comic book pages.

1982: The first slick format comic book in regular size appeared, **Marvel Fanfare** No. 1, with a March date. Fantagraphics Books began publication in July of **Love and Rockets** by Mario, Gilbert, and Jaime Hernandez and brought a new ethnic sensibility and sophistication in style and content to comic book narratives for adults.

1983: This year saw more comic book publishers, aside from Marvel and DC, issuing more titles than had existed in the past 40 years, most small independent publishers relying on direct sales, such as Americomics, Capital, Eagle, Eclipse, First, Pacific, and Red Circle, and with Archie, Charlton, and Whitman publishing on a limited scale. Frank Miller's mini-series **Ronin** demonstrated a striking use of sword play and martial arts typical of Japanese comic book art, and Howard Chaykin's stylish but controversial **American Flagg** appeared with an October date on its first issue.

1984: A publishing, media, film, and merchandising phenomenon began with the first issue of **Teenage Mutant Ninja Turtles** from Mirage Studios by Kevin Eastman and Peter Laird.

1985: Ohio State University's Library of Communication and Graphic Arts hosted the first major exhibition devoted to the comic book May 19 through August 2. In what was billed as an irreversible decision, the silver age superheroine Supergirl was killed in the seventh (October) issue of **Crisis on Infinite Earths**, a limited series intended to reorganize and simplify the DC universe on the occasion of the publisher's 50th anniversary.

1986: In recognition of its twenty-fifth anniversary, Marvel began publication of several new ongoing titles comprising Marvel's "New Universe," a self-contained fictional world. DC attracted extensive publicity and media coverage with its revisions of the character of **Superman** by John Byrne and of **Batman** in the **Dark Knight** series by Frank Miller. **Watchmen**, a limited-series graphic novel by Alan Moore and artist Dave Gibbons, began publication with a September issue from DC and Marvel's **The `Nam**, written by Vietnam veteran Doug Murray and penciled by Michael Golden, began with its December issue. DC issued guidelines in December for labelling their titles as either for mature readers or for readers of all ages; in response, many artists and writers publicly objected or threatened to resign.

1987: Art Spiegelman's **Maus: A Survivor's Tale** was nominated for the National Book Critics Circle Award in biography, the first comic book to be so honored. A celebration of Superman's fiftieth Birthday began with the opening of an exhibition on his history at the Smithsonian's Museum of American History in Washington, D.C., in June and a symposium on "The Superhero in America" in October.

1988: Superman's birthday celebration continued with a public party in New York and a CBS

ber 601 for May 24, **Action Comics** became the first modern weekly comic book, which ceased publication after 42 issues with the December 13 number. In August, DC initiated a new policy of allowing creators of new characters to retain ownership of them rather than rely solely on work-for-hire.

1989: The fiftieth anniversary of Batman was marked by the release of the film **Batman**, starring Michael Keaton as Bruce Wayne and Jack Nicholson as the Joker; it grossed more money in the weekend it opened than any other motion picture in film history to that time.

1990: The publication of a new **Classics Illustrated** series began in January from Berkley/First with adaptations of Poe's **The Raven and Other Poems** by Gahan Wilson, Dickens' **Great Expectations** by Rick Geary, Carroll's **Through the Looking Glass** by Kyle Baker, and Melville's **Moby Dick** by Bill Sienkiewicz, with extensive media attention. The adaptation of characters to film continued with the most successful in terms of popularity and box office receipts being **Teenage Mutant Ninja Turtles** and Warren Beatty's **Dick Tracy**. In November, the engagement of Clark Kent and Lois Lane was announced in **Superman** No. 50 which brought public fanfare about the planned marriage.

1991: One of the first modern comic books to appear in the Soviet Union was a Russian version of **Mickey Mouse** published in Moscow on May 16 in a printing of 200,000 copies which were sold out within hours. Issue number one of a new series of Marvel's **X-Men**, with story and art by Chris Claremont and Jim Lee, was published in October in five different editions with a print run of eight million copies, the highest circulation title in the history of the comic book. On December 18, Sotheby's of New York held its first auction of comic book material.

1992: The opening weekend for **Batman Returns** in June was the biggest in film box office history, bringing in over 46 million dollars, exceeding the record set by **Batman** in 1989. In November the death of **Superman** generated considerable media attention. A record number of over 100 publishers of comic books and graphic albums issued titles this year, some of the most prominent being Archie, Caliber, DC, Dark Horse, Disney, Eclipse, Fantagraphics, Gladstone, Harvey, Innovation, Kitchen Sink, Malibu, Marvel, Now, Personality, Revolutionary, Tundra, Viz, and Voyager.

FOREIGN COMIC BOOKS

COLLECTING FOREIGN COMICS AND AMERICAN REPRINTS

One extremely interesting source of comics of early vintage–one which does not necessarily have to be expensive–is the foreign market. Many American strips, from both newspapers and magazines, are reprinted abroad (both in English and in other languages) months and even years after they appear in the states. By working out trade agreements with foreign collectors, one can obtain, for practically the cover price, substantial runs of a number of newspaper strips and reprints of American comic books dating back five, ten, or occasionally even twenty or more years. These reprints are often in black and white, and sometimes the reproduction is poor, but this is not always the case. In any event, this is a source of material that every serious collector should look into.

Once the collector discovers comics published in foreign lands, he often becomes fascinated with the original strips produced in these countries. Many are excellent, and have a broader range of appeal than those of American comic books.

CANADIAN REPRINTS (E.C.s: by J. B. Clifford)

Several E.C. titles were published in Canada by Superior Comics from 1949 to at least 1953. Canadian editions of the following E.C. titles are known: (Pre-Trend) *Saddle Romances, Moon Girl, A Moon A Girl. . .Romance, Modern Love, Saddle Justice*; (New-Trend) *Crypt of Terror, Tales*

From the Crypt, Haunt of Fear, Vault of Horror, Weird Science, Weird Fantasy, Two-Fisted Tales, Frontline Combat, and *Mad. Crime SuspenStories* was also published in Canada under the title *Weird SuspenStories* (Nos. 1-3 known). No reprints of Shock SuspenStories by Superior are known, nor have any "New Direction" reprints ever been reported. No reprints later than January 1954 are known. Canadian reprints sometimes exchanged cover and contents with adjacent numbers (e.g., a *Frontline Combat* 12 with a *Frontline Comba*t No. 11 cover). They are distinguished both in cover and contents. As the interior pages are always reprinted poorly, these comics are of less value (about 1/2) than the U.S. editions; they were printed from asbestos plates made from the original plates. On some reprints, the Superior seal replaces the E.C. seal. Superior publishers took over Dynamic in 1947.

CANADIAN REPRINTS (Dells: by Ronald J. Ard)

Canadian editions of Dell comics, and presumably other lines (Fiction House, Atlas/Marvel, Superior, etc.), began in March-April, 1948 and lasted until February-March, 1951. They were a response to the great Canadian dollar crisis of 1947. Intensive development of the post-war Canadian economy was financed almost entirely by American capital. This massive import or money reached such a level that Canada was in danger of having grossly disproportionate balance of payments which could drive it into technical bankruptcy in the midst of the biggest boom in its history. The Canadian government responded by banning a long list of imports. Almost 500 separate items were involved. Alas, the consumers of approximately 499 of them were politically more formidable than the consumers of comic books.

Dell responded by publishing its titles in Canada, through an arrangement with Wilson Publishing Company of Toronto. This company had not existed for a number of years and it is reasonable to assume that its sole business was the production and distribution of Dell titles in Canada. There is no doubt that they had a captive market. If you check the publication data on the U. S. editions of the period you will see the sentence "Not for sale in Canada." Canada was thus the only area of the Free World in those days technically beyond the reach of the American comic book industry.

We do not know whether French editions existed of the Dell titles put out by Wilson. The English editions were available nationwide. They were priced at 10 cents and were all 36 pages in length, at a time when their American parents were 52 pages. The covers were made of coarser paper, similar to that used in the Dell Four Color series in 1946 and 1947 and were abandoned as the more glossy cover paper became more economical. There was also a time lag of from six to eight weeks between, say, the date an American comic appeared and the date that the Canadian edition appeared.

Many Dell covers had seasonal themes and by the time the Canadian edition came out (two months later) the season was over. Wilson solved this problem by switching covers around so that the appropriate season would be reflected when the books hit the stands. Most Dell titles were published in Canada during this period including the popular Atom Bomb giveaway, *Walt Disney Comics and Stories* and the *Donald Duck* and *Mickey Mouse* Four Color one-shots. The quality of the Duck one-shots is equal to that of their American counterparts and generally bring about 30 percent less.

By 1951 the Korean War had so stimulated Canadian exports that the restrictions on comic book importation, which in any case were an offense against free trade principle, could be lifted without danger of economic collapse. Since this time Dell, as well as other companies, have been shipping direct into Canada.

CANADIAN REPRINTS (DCs: by Doug A. England)

Many DC comics were reprinted in Canada by National Comics Publications Limited and Simcoe Publishing and Distributing Co., both of Toronto, for years 1948-1950 at least. Like the Dells, these issues were

36 pages rather than the 52 pages offered in the U.S. editions, and the inscription "Published in Canada" would appear in place of "A 52 Page Magazine" or "52 Big Pages" appearing on U.S. editions. These issues contained no advertisements and some had no issue numbers.
672-2913.

COMIC BOOK FANDOM

THE HISTORY OF COMICS FANDOM

At this time it is possible to discern two distinct and largely unrelated movements in the history of Comics Fandom. The first of these movements began about 1953 as a response to the then popular, trend setting EC lines of comics. The first true comics fanzines of this movement were short lived. Bob Stewart's EC FAN BULLETIN was a hectographed newsletter that ran two issues about six months apart; and Jimmy Taurasi's FANTASY COMICS, a newsletter devoted to all science-fiction comics of the period, was a monthly that ran for about six months. These were followed by other newsletters, such as Mike May's EC FAN JOURNAL, and George Jennings' EC WORLD PRESS. EC fanzines of a wider and more critical scope appeared somewhat later. Two of the finest were POTRZEBIE, the product of a number of fans, and Ron Parker's HOOHAH. Gauging from the response that POTRZEBIE received from a plug in an EC letter column, Ted White estimated the average age of EC fans to lie in the range of 9 to 13, while many EC fans were in their mid-teens. This fact was taken as discouraging to many of the faneds, who had hoped to reach an older audience. Consequently, many of them gave up their efforts in behalf of Comics Fandom, especially with the demise of the EC groups, and turned their attention to science-fiction fandom with its longer tradition and older membership. While the flourish of fan activity in response to the EC comics was certainly noteworthy, it is fair to say that it never developed into a full-fledged, independent, and self-sustaining movement.

The second comics fan movement began in 1960. It was largely a response to (though it later became a stimulus for) the Second Heroic Age of Comics. Most fan historians date the Second Heroic Age from the appearance of the new FLASH comics magazine (numbered 105 and dated February 1959). The letter departments of Julius Schwartz (editor at National Periodicals), and later those of Stan Lee (Marvel Group) and Bill Harris (Gold Key) were most influential in bringing comics readers into Fandom. Beyond question, it was the reappearance of the costumed hero that sparked the comics fan movement of the sixties. Sparks were lit among some science-fiction fans first, when experienced fan writers, who were part of an established tradition, produced the first in a series of articles on the comics of the forties–ALL IN COLOR FOR A DIME. The series was introduced in XERO No. 1 (September 1960), a general fanzine for science-fiction fandom edited and published by Dick Lupoff.

Meanwhile, outside science-fiction fandom, Jerry Bails and Roy Thomas, two strictly comics fans of long-standing, conceived the first true comics fanzine in response to the Second Heroic Age. The fanzine, ALTER EGO, appeared in March 1961. The first several issues were widely circulated among comics fans, and were to influence profoundly the comics fan movement to follow. Unlike the earlier EC fan movement, this new movement attracted many fans in their twenties and thirties. A number of these older fans had been active collectors for years but had been largely unknown to each other. Joined by scores of new, younger fans, this group formed the nucleus of a new movement that is still growing and shows every indication of being self-sustaining. Although it has borrowed a few of the more appropriate terms coined by science-fiction fans, Comics Fandom of the Sixties was an independent if fledging movement, without, in most cases, the advantages and disadvantages of a longer tradition. What Comics Fandom did derive from science-fiction fandom it did so thanks largely to the fanzines produced by so-called double fans. The most notable of this type is COMIC ART, edited and published by Don and Maggie Thompson.

The ROCKETS BLAST COMIC COLLECTOR, by G.B. Love was the first sucessful adzine in the early 1960s and was instrumental and important in the early development of the comics market. G.B. remembers beginning his fanzine THE ROCKET'S BLAST in late 1961. Only six copies of the first issue was printed and consisted of only 4 pages. Shortly thereafter Mr. Love had a letter published in MYSTERY IN SPACE, telling all about his new fanzine. His circulation began to grow. Buddy Saunders, a well known comic book store owner, designed the first ROCKET'S BLAST logo, and was an artist for this publication for many years thereafter. With issue #29 he took over THE COMICOLLECTOR fanzine from Biljo White and combined it with the ROCKET'S BLAST to from the RBCC. He remembers that the RBCC hit its highest circulation of 2500 around 1971. Many people who wrote, drew or otherwise contributed to the RBCC went on to become well known writers, artists, dealers and store-owners in the comics field.

COLLECTING STRIPS

Collecting newspaper comic strips is somewhat different than collecting magazines, although it can be equally satisfying.

Obviously, most strip collectors begin by clipping strips from their local paper, but many soon branch out to strips carried in out-of-town papers. Naturally this can become more expensive and it is often frustrating, because it is easy to miss editions of out-of-town papers. Consequently, most strip collectors work out trade agreements with collectors in other cities in order to get an uninterrupted supply of the strips they want. This usually necessitates saving local strips to be used for trade purposes only.

Back issues of strips dating back several decades are also available from time to time from dealers. The prices per panel vary greatly depending on the age, condition, and demand for the strip. When the original strips are unavailable, it is sometimes possible to get photostatic copies from collectors, libraries, or newspaper morgues.

COLLECTING ORIGINAL ART

In addition to magazines and strips, some enthusiasts also collect the original art for the comics. These black and white, inked drawings are usually done on illustration paper at about 30 percent up (i.e., 30 percent larger than the original printed panels). Because original art is a one-of-a kind article, it is highly prized and often difficult to obtain.

Interest in original comic art has increased tremendously in the past several years. Many companies now return the originals to the artists who have in turn offered them for sale, usually at cons but sometimes through agents and dealers. As with any other area of collecting, rarity and demand governs value. Although the masters' works bring fine art prices, most art is available at moderate prices. Comic strips are the most popular facet with collectors, followed by comic book art. Once scarce, current and older comic book art has surfaced within the last few years. In 1974 several original painted covers of vintage comic books and coloring books turned up from Dell, Gold Key,

THREE UNCANNY DECADES OF X-MEN!

by John Townsend, Ph.D.

Dateline: Nov. 21, 1992. **Location:** New York City. The set of "Saturday Night Live", NBC's perennial cutting-edge TV comedy show. The program airs a hilarious 7-minute parody on Superman's funeral, who has recently been killed saving the world.

Every comic superhero who's "anyone" is in attendance, paying his or her last respects. Batman, Flash, Green Lantern, and Luthor appear. Even Spider-Man, Hulk, and Reed Richards, the deceased hero's Marvel competitors, give a eulogy. And, down to the Hulk's final Stan Leeism, "Nuff said," the spoof reflects quite a knowledge of the nuances of comics. Viewers are treated to a much more accurate picture of the hobby than mainstream America's usual "Pow-Bam-Zap" mentality... with one exception: Where are the stars of the most successful superhero title of the past 15 years? Where are the mutants? Where are the X-Men?

X-Men #94

Actually, there may be "Storm-like" and "Jean Grey-like" characters in the background of the skit... but the conspicuous absence of the mutant team illustrates the double edge of the X-Men's phenomenal success. They have dominated the 55-year-old comic superhero industry for almost the last quarter of its existence. They have a massive, intensely loyal, and long-term following. (In fact, Spider-Man himself is often advertised as "The Non-Mutant Super-Hero!") But ask the man on the street, "Who's the short X-Man with long claws and an attitude?" He'll likely just scratch his head and keep on walking... never having heard of "Wolverine!"

But the secret mystery of the mutants' success is actually easy to understand. Long ago, they captured the serious fan. Concentrating on the loyalty of the dedicated reader, they gained a soap opera-like following in which the casual reader doesn't "get it"—but the fan does. The one who would rather go without lunch than miss an issue. The one who cares about the personal lives of the characters. This is really their story - and that of their **Uncanny X-Men.**

The X-Men Phenomenon

Here's just a partial listing of X-Men accolades:

***Best-selling family of comic titles in history.** Nine ongoing titles with numerous miniseries, specials and reprints are currently selling 50 million copies annually.

***Two of the top four best-selling issues in comic history.** X-Men II #1 (Oct 1991) sold 8.2 million, the highest first print run in history. X-Force #1 (Aug 1991) sold 3.6 million copies.

***Most popular super-team in comic history.**

***Showcase for Wolverine, the most popular character of the 80's.**

***Best-selling title of the 1980's decade.** An industry standard. For the last ten years, **Uncanny X-Men** has been the benchmark for distribution companies. **The** title to which all other comics' sales are measured.

***One of the "Big Four" most prolific superhero family of titles.** Publishing over 1,000 issues over the past 30 years, the X-Men rank with Superman, Batman and Spider-Man in sheer output.

***Most consecutive issues of a superhero comic by one writer.** Chris Claremont, a primary driving force behind the group, was involved from #94 (Aug 1975) to #279 (Aug 1991). That's 186 issues in 16 years.

***Number one Saturday morning TV program.** Fox's animated "X-Men Adventures" led the pack in the '92 season.

Today, the ten ongoing X-titles consistently appear in the top 100 of Capital and Diamond's monthly sales lists. They are, with abbreviations: **Uncanny (UXM), X-Factor (XFA), Excalibur (EXC), Wolverine (WOL), X-Force (XFO), X-Men Vol. II (XM2), X-Men Adventures (XMA), Cable (CBL), X-Men Unlimited (XMU) and X-Men 2099 (X99).** As if that weren't enough, the mutants also produce a seemingly endless stream of cards, toys, and video games.

What's an X-Man Anyway?

X-Men are by definition, pretty much unique... or at the very least, they possess unique qualities. The X-Men's first unique quality lies in the fact that they are **mutants**, whose genetic structure has been altered by chance or radiation. In comicdom, mutations produce fantastic "parahuman" powers, from super-strength to telepathy. "X" refers to the "ex-tra" gene and its powers. Usually latent in childhood, the powers are activated in adolescence by the "puberty trigger." As in actual science, only a small percentage of mutations are beneficial. Most are lethal.

Technically, mutants are of the species *Homo Superior,* a cousin to "normal" *Homo Sapiens.* It's such a plausible explanation, that I had grown up believing it before I found out that Stan Lee had invented his own species! One day I even called the Los Angeles Library System, looking for the term, and they couldn't find it.

The second X-uniqueness is their **purpose.**

The Uncanny X-Men #120

While most superheroes live to fight evil, the X-Men were founded to achieve the dream of Professor Charles Xavier, world's most powerful mutant telepath. Xavier's dream is that mutants and non-mutants may someday live in peace. For the X-Men, this entails battling both evil mutants as well as "ordinary" villains.

What complicates matters is the rabid anti-mutant sentiment which often forces the teams to revert to basic survival, even going so far as to protect the very individuals who persecute them. The struggle revolving around Xavier's dream is the thread underlying all the X-stories. It's often the "dead ends" (normals) vs. the "genejokes" (mutants).

To achieve his dream, Xavier created *the* haven for teenage mutants... The School for Gifted Youngsters (located at 1407 Graymalkin Lane, Salem Center, Westchester County in upstate New York). Living under cover at Xavier's school, the adolescents played dual roles in which they were both private school students and superheroes-in-training. Those original members were the winged Angel, agile Beast, opti-beamed Cyclops, frigid Iceman, and tele-powered Marvel Girl.

Things have changed. A second team joined as adults, not kids. Replacing the first group, who grew up and left, this new team consisted of the sonic Banshee, organically-steeled Colossus, teleporter Nightcrawler, weather mistress Storm, blazing Sunfire, super strong Thunderbird, and the dangerous Wolverine (Cyclops and Marvel Girl also remained).

Over the years, the "parahuman" roster has increased, adding the power-absorbent Bishop, cyborg Cable, inventor Forge, supercharger Gambit, ability-absorbent Rogue, psionic Psylocke, and the

The X-Family Issues 1983-1993

	UXM	NM	XFA	EXC	WOL	XFO	X-V2	XADV	CBL	XMU	X99
1983	165-176	1-10									
1984	177-188	11-22									
1985	189-200	23-34									
1986	201-212	35-46	1-11								
1987	213-224	47-58	12-23								
1988	225-239	59-70	24-35	1-3	1-2						
1989	240-255	71-84	36-49	4-17	3-19						
1990	256-271	85-96	50-61	18-32	20-34						
1991	272-283	97-100	62-73	33-45	35-49	1-5	1-3				
1992	284-295		74-85	46-59	50-64	6-17	4-15	1-2			
1993	296-307		86-97	60-72	65-76	18-29	16-27	3-14	1-6	1-3	1-3

intangible Shadowcat, to name a few. And not all the X-Men call Xavier "Professor" anymore. He's "Charles" to Jean Grey...and "Charley" to Wolverine.

The number of different X-Men teams has increased as well. With a total of eight X-groups over the decades, there are currently six today.(X-Men Blue and Gold, Excalibur, X-Force, X-Factor and X-Men 2099).

No two teams are alike—especially in their approach to Xavier's dream. For example, teams **Gold, Blue, and Excalibur** function as the "adults." They strive to fight against evil by playing it clean. They attempt to be rational, acting within the law as much as possible. **X-Factor**, however, is more "parental" and authoritarian-based. They work under the U.S. Government, and are often accused of being traitors, or "Uncle A-Tom-ics" (XFA #71, Oct 1991, p.16).

Like the original team, the **New Mutants** were "compliant children" under Xavier's tutelage. Their successors, **X-Force**, are the "rebellious adolescents." They have given up on the dream of peace. Shrugging off the rules, they attempt to forge their own survival, much the same way that their creator, Rob Liefeld, did with the comics industry. These differences add a rich texture to the adventures.

Behind the Scenes: The History of the Title

Pre-history. The concepts for the X-Men can be traced back to the beginning of Marvel in late 1939, when the company was called Timely. Bill Everett created the first "mutant" superhero in the form of an aquatic "superman" with a twist. The character, christened Prince Namor the Sub-Mariner, was actually an anti-hero! Marvel also debuted a wingless hero named Angel by Paul Gustavson.

Other early precursors can be found back in the 50's and early 60's, when the company's name changed from Timely to Atlas. Those wonderful Stan Lee/Jack Kirby/Steve Ditko/Don Heck "pre-hero" monster books provided many X-like prototypes. For example, Professor X's prototype appears in "Man in the Sky" (Amazing Adult Fantasy #14, Jul 1962), and Magneto's namesake ruled the world of metals in Strange Tales #84 (May 1961).

The X-Men Begin. Then in 1963, X-Men #1 hit the stand. Analysis of the history since #1 is an amazing story of developments, innovations, and evolutionary characters. Since 1963, six distinct X-Men "eras" can be identified:

Era #1: The Foundation (X-Men #1-19, Sep '63-Apr '66)

Though the X-Men achieved superstar status in the 80's, they are a Silver Age team. Brainchildren of Stan Lee and Jack Kirby, who fathered the Marvel Universe in the early 60's, they are part of the "Marvel big bang" which produced Spider-Man, the Fantastic Four, the Hulk, and many others.

The explosion, however, was taking its toll on its creators. As Lee tells it, "I was getting tired of making up super-power origins." Kirby also maintains that "At that time, radiation's effects were the topic of discussion." From this emerged an all-encompassing theory of super powers which had no limits: genetic aberrations. You could invent **any** power imaginable—and not have to rack your brain trying to explain how it got there.

Lee took the concept to publisher Martin Goodman with the title, "The Mutants." Thinking kids wouldn't understand the term, Goodman vetoed it. Lee's next effort, "The X-Men", met with success. "After Goodman said yes," Lee recalls, "I thought to myself, 'How come 'X-Men' makes more sense than 'Mutants'?'" But the title seemed intriguing and mysterious—and it stuck.

It should be noted that National Periodical Publications (DC), Marvel's cross-town competition, had a similar idea that same year. Their venture into the realm was called The Doom Patrol, which debuted in My Greatest Adventure #80 (June 1963), 3 months before X-Men #1. Doom Patrol also featured a bunch of misfit superpowered beings led by a wheelchair-bound authoritarian leader. However, the similarities are, in all likelihood, coincidental.

Beyond just creating the team, Lee and Kirby also introduced thematic ideas including Xavier's dream, the mutant persecution theme, and the family concept. All these themes would later be pivotal.

Era #2: The Development (X-Men #20-66, May '66-Mar '70)

With an ever-increasing workload, the torch soon passed to writer Roy Thomas. The academician deepened the team's history with an origin series for each hero in #38-57 (also written by Drake, Fite, and Friedrich), as well as an exciting run with Neal Adams from #56-65. In addition, Barry Windsor-Smith's first comic book art is in #53-55, as well as some stunning Steranko work in #50-51.

The Uncanny X-Men #213

An interesting side note is that #59 (Aug 1969) is Chris Claremont's first work on the X-Men, an uncredited plot assist. A new assistant with Marvel at the time, Claremont suggested to Thomas that the pesky Sentinels attempt to snuff out the sun, incinerating themselves instead.

A surprising piece of X-Trivia for many new collectors, the title never sold that well, right from the start. Many readers considered it a "Fantastic Four Wannabee" group. Also, the team's lifestyle was an obstacle. What sane teenager wanted to "escape" to a comic which showed obedient kids living under the authority of a professor? Finally, there was no "raw strength" character to tear down buildings and generally bat cleanup. It seemed the ongoing publication of the mutants was in trouble.

Era #3: Death of the Mutants (#67-93, Dec '70-Apr '75)

The X-Men "died" with #66 (March 1970), and was canceled for 9 months. Marvel's early expansion now suffered with the shaky comic market of 1969-70, and the softest titles were dropped. There were other fatalities, such as Captain Marvel, Dr. Strange, and Silver Surfer. However, publisher Goodman could still turn a profit with a low-overhead reprint series. The title was revived in reprint form from #67 (Dec 1970) to #93 (Apr 1975). For over four years, X-Men were 5-to-7 year-old recycled adventures. However, the mutants "stayed alive" by guesting in other titles such as Amazing Adventures Vol. II, Incredible Hulk, and Captain America.

Era #4: Phoenix Rising (G.S. #1 to Uncanny #143, Sum '75-Mar '81)

1974 gave the parahumans a new lease on life with two important events: First, then editor-in-chief Roy Thomas assigned the task of creating a "Wolverine" character to writer Len Wein. Wein's careful research produced the enormously popular, adamantium-clawed berserker, who became one of Marvel's superstars.

Second, publisher Stan Lee, president Al Landau, Thomas and production manager John VerPoorten met to create a new international title, with superheroes from around the world. Thomas, a longtime DC "Blackhawks" fan, immediately thought about the X-Men, and assigned the project to Wein and veteran artist Dave Cockrum.

The Uncanny X-Men #266

The Eight Keys

Even with the volumes of X-sagas, there are several "must-reads." The chart below summarizes the eight landmark X-Men runs... those which have best developed and defined the teams.

X-Men Key Issues

1	X-Men #1 (Sep 1963) First app. of original team, Professor and Magneto
2	X-Men #38-57 (Nov 1967 to Jun 1969) Origins of the X-Men series - mutants personas are developed
3	Giant-Size X-Men #1 (Summer 1975) X-Men #94 (Aug 1975) 1st app. of new team
4	X-Men #129-137 (Jan 1980 to Sep 1980) The 'Dark Phoenix' saga. Jean Grey's noble 'suicide' takes the title to #1
5	X-Men #141 (Jan 1981) Uncanny X-Men #142 (Feb 1981) The 'Day of Future Past' series. Mutant persecution theme made real
6	Wolverine #1-4 (Sep 1982 to Dec 1982) This miniseries redefines the character's grim nature. A pivotal point for violent and realistic depictions of comic superheroes everywhere.
7	Uncanny X-Men #200-201 (Dec 1985 to Jan 1986) Professor X leaves. A 5 year storyline begins with Magneto in charge, Jean Grey resurrected. The renaissance of the original team as X-Factor
8	Uncanny X-Men #277-281 (Jun 1991 to Oct 1991) The return of Xavier and the birth of four new teams. The end of the previous storyline - with the beginning of a whole new X-line

The two major talents created the second team, using both existing characters and their own creations. The result was Giant-Size #1 and X-Men #94. However, during this time Wein succeeded Thomas as editor-in-chief. An unmanageable workload forced Wein to give the title to newcomer Chris Claremont, who became involved from #94 on.

The Uncanny X-Men #281

Claremont: the "Puberty Trigger."

Claremont, who is also known as "Mr. X", galvanized the mutants. Activating the latent potentials of a 12-year-old mid-list title, he became the X-Men's own "puberty trigger."

Claremont brought an intensely character-driven writing style to the table, so that the fan was drawn into the mutant's innermost feelings. Claremont phrases it this way: "Passion always comes before logic. You can always paste in logic. But the reader must first care about the characters."

Xavier's dream of peace, and the obstacle of anti-mutant bigotry, became Claremont's primary focus. The X-Men often battled supervillains, evil mutants, and bigots... all at the same time!

Character development and the prejudice theme evolved the "family" theme. Hated and isolated, they stayed together. As do foxhole buddies in wars, they learned to trust each other, depend on each other, and function as a team.

The X-Men perfectly reflected the post-Vietnam/post-Watergate era. Many American youth were disillusioned and disconnected. What better way to capture the adolescent than to provide a place where misunderstood young adults had each other... and adventure, too?

At the same time, Claremont was able to produce stories of immense range, from the "microscopic" (personal and intimate) to the "telescopic" (cosmic and star-spanning). The reader always felt that something of great import was going on.

And the artwork! In these beginning years, Cockrum's dependable style set the tone for a new era of graphic storytelling. John Byrne's powerfully emotional renderings and co-plotting blended perfectly with Claremont's vision.

There were several other important factors behind the success of the new X-Men. For example: the "anything goes", freewheeling nature of the title (as when new member Thunderbird was killed in his second appearance). A graphically hard-hitting and realistic style (a la Wolverine's violence). Strong superheroines like Jean Grey and Storm, garnering a substantial female readership. Supportive editorship (Jim Shooter, Louise Simonson, and Ann Nocenti). The direct sales market in the late 70's, making possible a highly committed fan following. It was a made-for-success formula. Building on these values, Claremont/Cockrum watched the mutants' popularity rise.

DC fans were also intrigued by Cockrum's "self-swipe" in #107 (Oct 1977). When the Shi'ar Imperial Guard debuted, the characters were almost identical to DC's Legion of Super-Heroes. Seems that Cockrum had just come to Marvel from a 2-year art stint with the Legionnaires in Superboy, and did it just for kicks. He recalls, "DC thought it was funny, too. We tried to do a Marvel-DC crossover with both teams, but it didn't work out."

Dynasty, Year One

It was, however, during the Claremont/ Byrne team-up that the X-Men became the #1 title in 1980. The Dark Phoenix saga provided the unprecedented "noble suicide" of major character Jean Grey. Then, scant months later, the Days of Future Past (title borrowed from the now famous 1967 Moody Blues album) series gripped the public with the prospect of a Holocaust-like future, complete with legalized mutant extermination.

It was an incredible time. Readers everywhere took note that this was **the** title. Kids waited en masse in front of their comic shops every Thursday. As Bob Harras, group editor of the X-titles says, "Claremont and Byrne showed us what comics could be."

Era #5: Persecution, Peril, and Passion (#144-279, Apr '81-Aug '91)

After Byrne left (Issue #143), the next decade produced what Claremont calls the "canon", the body of work comprising the mutant mythos. "Mr. X" used top artists like Cockrum, Jim Lee, John Romita Jr., Marc Silvestri, and Barry Windsor-Smith.

The mutants' uncanny success spurred a wealth of spin-offs, most of which still exist: Alpha Flight, Dazzler, Excalibur, New Mutants, Wolverine's solo title, and X-Factor. Claremont believed in teamwork, often co-plotting with artists, and some believe that his best stories seem to be these collaborative efforts. As a writer, Claremont often told intricate, years-long plots which filled the letters pages with complaints from loyal but bewildered fans. His artists helped provide wrap-ups to closed doors for the reader. Appeasing the fans' need for action, Claremont let the mutants fight... anyone and everyone! They battled villains who ravaged the universe, such as mutants Magneto and the Brotherhood of Evil Mutants, and normals like Juggernaut. Some villains ravaged mutantdom like the Marauders which were themselves mutants, and non-mutants like the Sentinels and Magistrates.

X-Men #1

The Uncanny X-Men #282

They also fought each other. Sometimes they were possessed by aliens, and sometimes they were cloned. Sometimes they just got ornery. It's been happening since Beast and Iceman squared off in #1 and it's been a Marvel tradition since Fantastic Four #1.

X-Men fought when they were in love too. Cyclops and Jean Grey struggled for years. Colossus and Kitty dealt with an age gap. The Professor has had at least three girlfriends: Moira MacTaggert, Gabrielle Haller, and the exotic Princess Lilandra. It seems love hurts! Finally, the angst-ridden heroes fought within themselves, filling thought balloons with their own soul struggles. Wolverine battled his killer instincts and Cyclops felt guilty about everything. Rogue ached to be touched, but would damage the "toucher." Readers were smitten.

In 1991, philosophical differences with Marvel caused Claremont to leave the mutants. His last Uncanny was #279 (Aug); his last X-Men scripting was X-Men Vol. II, #3 (Dec). By the time he left, the writer had crafted about 75% of the total stories of the Uncanny title. Claremont and his artists had left behind an enviable standard of excellence in graphic storytelling. That same year, the parahumans

The Uncanny X-Men #300

again made comic history, with the record-shattering X-Force #1 (Aug) and X-Men Vol. II #1 (Oct). The momentum continued.

Era #6: The New Epoch (#280, Sep 1991-Present)

1992 brought about another important X-change. Editor Bob Harras, who had succeeded Ann Nocenti in June 1988, became group editor of the X-family, a position he retains to this day. It is his task to not only edit several mutant titles, but to also supervise the editing of the rest, maintaining the overall cohesiveness of the X-Men universe (see "X-Family Issues" Chart).

X-Men 2099 #1

Among Harras' new titles are X-Men Adventures (#1, Nov 1992), based on the hit TV show. Cable (#1, May 1993) is the third mutant, after Dazzler and Wolverine, with his own ongoing series. X-Men Unlimited (#1, June 1993) further showcases the teams' exploits. The ninth team, "Generation X", led by Banshee, debuts in 1994. X-Men 2099, not part of the Harras group, but the "Future Marvel" group, came out this past year (#1, Oct 1993). In addition, numerous specials and miniseries are constantly being created.

Success has its price. The mutants have a new challenge: the older fan wants character development and intriguing plots. The younger fan likes hot artwork and lots of action. Harras, his assistant editor Lisa Patrick, and the entire X-team are working hard to maintain this tension. And, judging from sales and interest, they are succeeding.

Timeline Charts

With over 1,000 published X-books and over 100 new ones annually, even the longtime fan can get confused by the mutants' stories. The "Timeline" Charts A and B summarize the X-Men's history on the following two pages.

The charts organize the Uncanny title by year and cover date, from 1963-1993. Principal writers and artists are listed for each year (most prolific per year are boldfaced).

Most hero and villain appearances are already listed in the Overstreet Price Guide. The "Developments" section of this chart notes significant non-Guided events within the X-Universe, especially those dealing with mutant persecution.

Conclusion

The mutants' story has changed the comics industry forever. This graphic soap opera has constantly entertained, educated, excited and exasperated fans. And as long as people need well-crafted and drawn tales of the struggle to realize Xavier's dream of

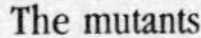

X-MEN TIMELINE PART A: 1963-1980

Year & Issue #s	***Principal*** Writer	Artists	Developments
1963-4 #1-8	**S. Lee**	**Kirby**	**Team #1 (Original) begins** (#1, Sep). Cyclops 1st deputy leader (#7). 1st mutant bigotry, vs. Beast/Iceman (#8).
1965 #9-15	**S. Lee**	**Kirby** Gavin (Roth)	Mutant persecution with Sentinels (#14). 1st use of terms "mutant menace" and slur "mutie" (pp. 6-7).
1966 #16-27	S. Lee **Thomas**	Kirby **Gavin (Roth)**	1st app/org. Mimic (#19): 1st X-man to die (Hulk #161, 3/73).
1967 #28-39	**Thomas**	**Roth** Andru Heck	**Origins of X-Men** series begins (#38). Prof. X absent for 2 years (#33-65).
1968 #40-51	**Thomas** **Friedrich** **Drake**	**Heck** Roth Steranko	**Origins of X-Men** series continues.
1969 #52-63	**Thomas** Drake	Heck Roth **Adams**	**Origins of X-Men** series ends (#57).
1970-4 #64-91	**Thomas** O'Neil	Heck Adams/S. Buscema	**Reprint Era:** X-Men "go underground", after battle vs. Hulk (#66) generates anti-mutant bigotry (Amaz. Adv. II, #12; 5/72).
1975 #92-96	**Wein** **Claremont**	**Cockrum**	**Team #2 begins, Team #1 ends** (Giant-Size #1, X-Men #94).
1976 #97-102	**Claremont**	**Cockrum**	**Cosmic space themes** begins with Lilandra and Shi'ars (#97).
1977 #103-108	**Claremont** Mantlo	**Cockrum** Brown Byrne	Space opera sagas.
1978 #109-116	**Claremont**	**Byrne** Cockrum DeZuniga	Adventures in Antarctica and Savage Land (#112-116).
1979 #117-128	**Claremont**	**Byrne** Austin	**Origins: Xavier's Dream** of peace between mutants and nonmutants (#117, flashback story).
1980 #129-140	**Claremont**	**Byrne** Austin	**Dark Phoenix** saga (#129-137): Jean Grey commits noble "suicide." Storm replaces Cyclops as leader (#138).

X-MEN TIMELINE PART B: 1981-1993

Year & Issue #s	***Principal*** Writer	Artists	Developments
1981 #141-152	**Claremont**	Byrne Anderson **Cockrum**	**Days of Future Past:** Saga of possible future mutant extermination (#141-142). **Mutant Control Act**, 1st app (future).
1982 #153-164	**Claremont**	**Cockrum** Sienkiewicz Anderson	**Team #3 begins**: New Mutants (MGN #4). Kitty erases U.S. Govt. X-Men files (#158). Wolverine miniseries redefines character.
1983 #165-176	**Claremont**	**P. Smith** Simonson Romita, Jr.	**Spinoff titles begin:** New Mutants #1 (Mar). Alpha Flight #1 (Aug).
1984 #177-188	**Claremont**	**Romita, Jr.** Windsor-Smith	**Mutant Control Act** proposed (#181). "Dazzler: the Movie" (MGN #12). Story fuels "mutant menace" fears.
1985 #189-200	**Claremont**	**Romita, Jr.** Windsor-Smith	**Prof. X leaves** for 5 years. Magneto leads X-Men and New Mutants (#200-276).
1986 #201-212	**Claremont**	Leonardi **Romita, Jr.** W-Smith	**Team #4 begins:** X-Factor #1 (2/86). **X-Xover #1:** Mutant Massacre (#210-213; NM #46; XFA #9-11).
1987 #213-224	**Claremont**	Davis Guice **Silvestri**	**Team #5 begins:** Excalibur (Special Ed.). Anti-mutant ad in comic ad section (#223). **Mutant Reg. Act** enacted (#224).
1988 #225-239	**Claremont**	**Silvestri** Leonardi	**X-Xover #2:** Fall of Mutants (#225-7; NM #59-61; XFA #24-26). Team #2 "dies" (#227). Excalibur #1 (Oct). Wolverine #1 (Nov).
1989 #240-255	**Claremont**	**Silvestri** Liefeld J. Lee	Team #2 operates underground from Australia.
1990 #256-271	**Claremont**	**J. Lee** Silvestri Jaaska	**X-Xover #3:** X-tinction Agenda (#270-72; NM #95-97; XFA #60-62). Team #2 "alive", returns to U.S. (#270).
1991 #272-283	**Claremont** Byrne Nicieza	**J. Lee** Adam Kubert Portacio	**Teams #6,7,8 begin, #2,3 end:** X-Force #1 (Aug); Gold & Blue teams (#281). XM Vol II, #1 (Oct).
1992 #284-295	Byrne **Lobdell**	**Portacio** Raney Peterson	**X-Xover #4:** X-Cutioner's Song (#294-7; XFA #84-87; XFO #16-19; XV2 #14-16). X-Men Adventures #1 (Nov).
1993 #296-307	**Lobdell**	**Peterson** **Romita, Jr.**	Cable #1 (May); X-Men Unlimited #1 (June) X-Men 2099 #1 (Oct). **Team #9: Generation X** (ads for 1994)

peace, the X-Men will remain what they have always been: superheroes who are, at heart, very much like us. Congratulations to all the professionals who have been part of the "uncanny" journey!

Thanks to the following - INTERVIEWS: Chris Claremont, Dave Cockrum, Bob Harras, Jack Kirby, Stan Lee, Pamela Rutt, Jim Shooter, Roy Thomas, Don Thompson, and Len Wein. RESEARCH INFORMATION: Jerry Bails, Dave Belmont, Chris Benedict, Gary M. Carter, Keith Contarino, Rob Crane, Christi Flowers, Ernie Gerber, Jeff Grady, Mark Gruenwald, John Hauser, Jason Jackson, Jerry Jacobs, Mike Kadin, Josh Leto, Daniel Martinez, George Olshevsky, Lisa Patrick, Greg Pharis, Matt Powers, Rob Ronin, Steve Saffell, Barry Short, Dave Smith, Robin Snyder, and Marty Stever. RESEARCH ASSISTANCE: Derek Lane. LAYOUT CONSULTATION: Michael Naiman.

X-Men Adventures #2

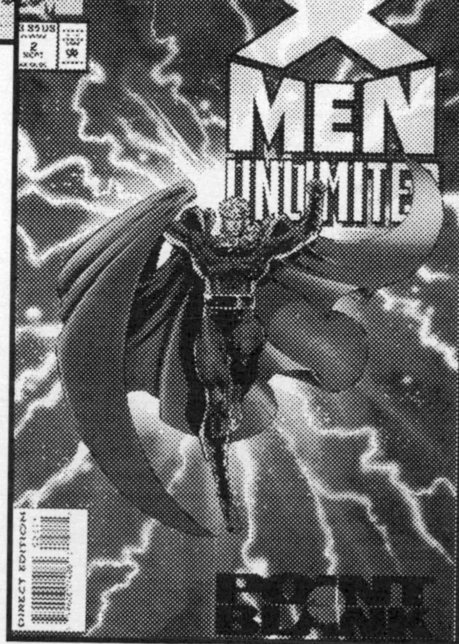

X-Men Unlimited #7

LIVING ON BORROWED TIME!

A Nostalgic Look at the Early years of DC's CHALLENGERS OF THE UNKNOWN!

by Pat S. Calhoun
& Gary M. Carter

The threat of atomic war became a national obsession in the 1950s and many Americans truly believed we were all "living on borrowed time!" It was upon this very theme that Jack Kirby based the concept of his famous DC Silver Age team… The Challengers Of The Unknown!

THE FIRST SILVER AGE TEAM

In their 1957 origin story, four men, each noted achievers in their chosen fields, survive what should have been a fatal plane crash. In the exhilarating aftermath, they decide two things: They will band together and take on "the unknown" as a team -on the theory that the thrill of adventure and discovery could overcome the fear of death… They also decide that after walking away from that plane wreck they are "living on borrowed time" and have little to lose.

This is only the beginning of the full-length novel that introduced the Challengers in DC's **Showcase #6 (Jan-Feb 1957, pictured lower right)**. Created, written, and drawn by the legendary Jack Kirby, the early Challengers Of The Unknown issues have become the focus of intense collector interest and demand.

Comic historians, collectors, and fans so often focus only on Kirby's key role in the creation of silver masterpieces like the Fantastic Four, X-Men, Avengers, Thor, and Ant-Man for Marvel, and often overlook the incredibly important early appearances of the Challengers. So before stumbling into the quicksand of underestimation, consider just a few points about the Challengers first appearance in Showcase #6.

Its the second Silver Age <u>Hero</u> comic, coming right on the heels of Showcase #4 which starred the founder of the Silver Age, the Flash! It's the first Silver Age <u>team</u> comic and features the first <u>all-new</u> Silver Age hero concept. Showcase #6 marks a brilliant start of DC's use of full-length stories, an important factor in DC's Silver Age success formula.

Kirby's Challengers - Ace Morgan; test pilot, Rocky Davis; champion wrestler, Prof Haley; deep sea diver, and Red Ryan; mountain climber, were also featured in Showcase #7, #11, & #12 and Challengers Of The Unknown #1-8. All 12 are extraordinarily entertaining extravaganzas crammed full of exceptionally good concepts. In these superb early issues, the Challs confront ancient mystery, alien menace, and interplanetary technology gone awry.

In fact the Challengers are defined by their adversaries. They have no super powers, but they get the job done… overcoming some pretty awesome antagonists in the process. Kirby, in the tradition of the great pulp writers of his youth, didn't pit the Challs against small scale, penny-ante crooks. Kirby thought on a grand scale, placing the entire planet in some monstrous peril that the "four fugitives from eternity" must overcome… with wit, skill, courage, and teamwork!

"The Secrets of the Sorcerer's Box" featured in the first Showcase "tryout" is the title of the origin

Showcase #6

Showcase #7

effort. The real action starts after the team has already gained some fame. They are summoned by a man who claims to be a descendant of Merlin the magician. He leads them to a huge antique box with four compartments, each one holding (so they are told) a device of great power, forged from long forgotten lore. The Challs agree (for a million bucks) to open these chambers and deal with whatever emerges from them. Thus (with three chapters left in the story) we see how beautifully and cleanly Kirby structures his plots. Each of the remaining chapters allows the Challengers and the readers to confront one of the marvels from this potentially evil "Pandora's box".

Chapter 2, "Dragon Seed", has the Challs coping with a giant living indestructible statue. Chapter 3, "The Freezing Sun", concerns a sentient orb that sucks the heat out of things - especially humans. Chapter 4, "The Whirling Weaver", releases a mechanical spider that spins a gooey web across an entire city. Of course the fourth compartment holds the final plot resolution (which we won't reveal) which ties things up definitely, if a trifle abruptly.

The art in the four Showcase issues is truly incredible, and is perhaps the purest, most unadulterated Kirby of all time. Kirby (with Joe Simon) had worked on hero teams for DC before. During the Golden Age, The Boy Commandos in Detective Comics and numerous issues of their own magazine set a new standard in comics all through the war years. And don't forget the wonderful and vastly under-rated Newsboy Legion in Star Spangled Comics. The strip put a new spin on the "kid team" concept by adding the costumed "Guardian" to the mix. (As an aside, it can be noted that back in the early and mid 1960's, Guardian and the Newsboy Legion were among the authors' favorite strips. Both would eagerly purchase issues when afforded the opportunity to acquire Golden Age books. Pat used his paper route money and Gary and his younger brother, Lane, used what they earned mowing lawns. A copy of Star Spangled #7, originally purchased from the Cherokee Book Shop in 1965 for $35, still resides in the Carter collection today.)

Unlike the Boy Commandos and the Newsboy Legion, The Kirby's Challengers took a very different direction and combined both hero comics and science fiction. For example, "Ultivac is Loose" from **Showcase #7 (Mar-Apr 1957, pictured at left)** is a blockbuster novel that captures this spirit perfectly. With its giant human-shaped computer on the rampage this one really reminds you of pre-hero Marvel's monster mode.

Kirby's treatment of artificial intelligence has real conceptual depth. To contrast with (and play against) the cold, artificial intelligence that is Ultivac, Kirby introduces a humanistic counterpoint in the person of June Robbins, the most important member of the Challs' supporting cast. Besides being an expert on robotics, June is eager for adventure. As she confronts Ultivac, she proves to be the one person that he... er it... will listen to. Because of her essential contribution to vanquishing Ultivac, she is made an honorary member of the team. In succeeding issues, June Robbins is regularly featured, and together they share the thrills and dangers of the unknown.

Ultivac has a spectacular opening. After a superb introductory page, the guys are sitting around trying to drum up their next "challenge". Then a stranger arrives at their door and starts talking in fearful tones about this "calculator" he's built. Suddenly a giant metal hand (attached to a huge robot) comes smashing through the wall, scoops up the stranger, sprouts mechanical wings, and flies away.

This is the start of a solid story, and while it doesn't have the marvelous "three-ring circus" structuring of "The Sorcerer's Box", it nonetheless makes dazzling use of the "full-length story" format. The cliffhanger style chapters perfectly show Kirby's adeptness at extended narrative.

Chapter Two begins ominously as June's own computer calculates the Challs' chances against

Ultivac. After a moment it spouts the ominous prediction "A Challenger Must Die!"

Kirby doesn't let us down in the third chapter either. As was the case in numerous Kirby fantasy triumphs, he uses a plot idea from a beloved sci fi, fantasy, or horror film. In this case it's Ultivac held hostage and on display in Yankee Stadium in a scene right out of King Kong!

In the final chapter, "The Fatal Prediction", Kirby wraps things up with an awesome courtroom climax. June's plea for understanding between human and machine erodes into violence and an intense brush with death for one of the team on borrowed time.

After an eight-month hiatus in which Showcase featured the second Flash and both Lois Lane tryouts, the fearless four return in **Showcase #11 (Nov-Dec 1957)** with their third Kirby bonanza... and it's a book length gem about an alien invasion from inside the earth. It seems these subterranean extra-terrestrials plan to make the planet's mass more to their liking with a series of gigantic explosions. Again the master story teller taps right into a prime vein of 1950's paranoia as the country contemplated the potential Armageddon of nuclear war.

"The Day the Earth Blew Up" is another slam-bang combination of cool concepts and thrill-a-minute storytelling. The last chapter, titled "One Minute to Doom", has the clock ticking as the Challengers battle to stop the literal "end of human existence." It should be noted that this ish reprints the introductory page of Showcase #7, and it's even better the second time around. Four panels "showcase" the Challs doing their vocational thing. Ace is testing emergency ejection seat equipment on the edge of space. Prof is submerged in the depths of the ocean in a bathysphere. Red is scaling Mount Everest, and Rocky is wrestling an alligator.

And speaking of reprints, don't let the hefty price of the four Showcase tryout issues discourage you from reading these great classics. Sprinkled about like so may nuggets in a stream, DC was nice enough to reprise the stories from all of them in various issues of the Challengers title between #64 and #80. The reproductions are pretty faithful to the originals, with a few minor differences. The most interesting is the switching of Red and Rocky's hair color on the cover of Challengers #77 (Dec-Jan 1970-71). On the original cover of Showcase #12, Red's hair is... well... Red and Rocky's is Black the way Kirby intended. This minor annoyance does not, however, detract from the readability of this inexpensive clone.

(Chronology Note: On the stands at the same time as Showcase #11 is World Of Fantasy #9, one of the only two Atlas fantasy titles to survive the Atlas "Implosion." For more information on Pre Hero Marvel and the Atlas line of comics, see the article "Journey Into The Unknown World Of Atlas Fantasy" published in The Overstreet Comic Book Price Guide #22, 1992.)

Showcase #12

The story in **Showcase #12 (Jan-Feb 1958, pictured lower left)** is entitled "Menace of the Ancient Vials" and ends the tryout run with another cornucopia of epic Silver Age wonders. Again centuries-forgotten sorcery is unleashed, this time producing giant people, giant octopi, and fiery dragons. In the last chapter, the villain (while attempting to usurp this dark power) creates ninety-nine clones of himself! In short it's Kirby at the peak of his narrative and rendering skills going to town in a cover to cover masterpiece.

These full-length novels hint at the great Justice League of America adventures that will score such high points for DC starting in 1960. And since it's accepted legend that the JLA inspired Stan Lee and the gang at Marvel to try a new hero team of their own (i.e. the Fantastic Four), one might even hypothesize about the pre-eminent role of the Jack Kirby Challengers in the chain of events which led to the Marvel Universe.

Although not often compared, the Kirby Challengers Of The Unknown actually resemble the

Kirby Fantastic Four in several interesting ways. (1) Each team is comprised of four members. (2) Each contains characters with contrasting personas and abilities. (3) Both teams seem loosely based in the Earth, air, fire, and water allegory. Ace's flying high in the sky contrasts with Prof's diving deep under water, while "Rocky" hints at earth, and "Red" (at least in color) resembles fire.

Likewise the FF has the Torch for fire, Mr. Fantastic's stretchability is almost liquidious, the Thing "looks" like earth, and the Invisible Girl "looks" like air. (3) Like the FF, the Challengers even squabbled occasionally, although never so much as there Marvel counterparts. (4) And, Like the Challs, there's no lack of Sci Fi stuff in the FF... from the cosmic-ray origin and the Skrulls from outer space, to the eventual outrageousness of Galactus and his glitzy lackey, the Silver Surfer. (5) Plus many of the FF's finer moments also came in the form of full-length novels.

Kirby's other work for late fifties DC included some nicely rendered Green Arrow yarns in Adventure, and a handful of "mostly monster" fantasies and covers in House Of Secrets, House Of Mystery, Tales Of The Unexpected, and My Greatest Adventure... four of DC's six wonderful fantasy/sci fi mags. By comparison, these "shorter" offerings seem more like standard DC product, making the Showcase Challengers one of the most distinctive and unique DC offerings from the era.

This "assimilation" into the DC universe also took hold of the Challs once they received their own title. The early Silver Age DC comics were remarkably consistent. Some were better than others, but the form, mood, and intent were similar (and somewhat predictable) throughout all the various mags.

IN THEIR OWN MAG AT LAST

When **Challengers Of The Unknown #1 (Apr-May 1958)** hit the stands in February, it was only the second Showcase feature to receive its own title (Lois Lane was the first by one month). The inaugural issue gave readers a strong suggestion that the "league of death-cheaters" would be a title they'd be seeing a lot more of. And they were right!

Also on the stands at this time: Showcase #13 (the third Flash tryout), and Adventure #247 (the introduction of the Legion of Super Heroes). Things were really starting to happen at DC. The number one issue is also the first time the Challengers starred in two shorter stories. One was a fourteen-pager and the other a ten-pager.

"The Man Who Tampered With Infinity" is a mad scientist who has teleported a couple of beasties from elsewhere, and it's up to the intrepid foursome to capture the alien animals. Of course they also need to stop the scientist and rescue June and themselves... This one's OK, but taking top honors go to the shorter, ten-pager which is both featured on the cover and closes out the book.

Entitled "The Human Pets", this Kirby killer is a "set piece". The Challs are lured into a spaceship and end up on another planet as an alien child's "pets". So the team must try to attract the attentions of the alien kid's parents. But meanwhile the interplanetary foursome must also cope with a few other minor problems... like another captive "pet" who seems to think the humans might be tasty morsels. Even though these plot elements transpire as expected, this tale is "done to an absolute turn," and is deservedly ranked as one of the great early DC Silver Age classics.

Challs #1 also boasts yet another awesome introductory page, again showing the team on borrowed time in the air and under the sea, atop a mountain, and deep in the jungle. This time the four introductory panels have wide yellow borders and a round blurb in the center, almost as if the fearless four were framed in a gun-sight... targeted by the unknown!

Challengers Of The Unknown #2 (Jun-Jul 1958) is another two-tale issue, the first of which features June Robbins as "The Traitorous Challenger". But it turns out that she had a good rea-

Challengers #4

son to thwart the team's attempts to combat a huge atomic-powered creature on a rampage. It seems one of her computers predicted that such a battle would prove fatal to the foursome. Other than firming up June's role as a recurring character, this is not much of a yarn. But the cover story "The Monster Maker" compensates for any disappointment. This is another working of key Challengers Of The Unknown situations in the form of a bad guy who steals a secret weapon. And what a weapon... it's a high-tech process that can actually make a person's thoughts into actual things. It was this that made possible the giant hands attacking the Challs' plane on the cover, coming straight from the crook's imagination.

Fortunately the intrepid team manages to get the weapon to Ace as well, who then begins a "thought duel" with their villainous foe. Ace counters the giant hands, for instance, with a pair of giant handcuffs. This story also calls Ace's mastery of hypnotism into play, a "trick" he'd used on an alien in an earlier story (Showcase #11). The whole thing isn't quite as corny as it sounds. Ace does use some pretty good psychology to turn the tables and literally out-thinks his opponent.

(Chronology Note: On the stands at the same time as Challengers #2 is Action #242, the first appearance of Brainiac.)

Challengers Of The Unknown #3 (Aug-Sep 1958) starts off with "The Secret of the Sorcerer's Mirror", a formula yarn with all the right elements in place. High-tech trouble from the past falls into the hands of unscrupulous souls in the present. This time it's Red's turn to save the day with some timely prestidigitation. In the cover story, "The Invincible Challenger", Rocky develops strange powers after testing a chemical designed to make space flight easier on the human body. Although the situation barely skirts the absurd once again, smooth storytelling and plausible motivations make it all work.

(Chronology Note: On the stands at the same time as Challengers #3 is Showcase #15, The first appearance of Space Ranger.)

THE KIRBY/WOOD COLLABORATION

Challengers Of The Unknown #4 (Oct-Nov 1958, pictured on facing page) is special for two reasons. First, "The Wizard of Time" is a full-length novel, the first one since receiving their own title. And second, this ish marks the first appearance of Wally Wood as inker. Kirby's powerful pencils finished with the slick sheen of Wood's inks makes for an incredible, delectable, and scarce art combination. This time-travel thriller, is set in ancient Greece, ancient Egypt , and the distant future... providing plenty of razzle-dazzle backdrops for this hot drawing team to render. The Challs chase Darius Tiko through the centuries. The villain is hoping to combine ancient scientific secrets with the super science of tomorrow's technology... all in his quest for power. Although the ending is almost literally a deus ex machina, this story is fast-paced and satisfying.

(Chronology Note: On the stands at the same time as Challengers #4 is Superboy #68, the first appearance of the original Bizarro... and Journey Into Mystery resumes publication with Issue #49 after a 16 month absence from the newsstand.)

Challengers Of The Unknown #5 (Dec-Jan 1958-59) is another book-length story, plotted around a mystical meteor fragment that holds the key to super powers and a would-be-tyrant that ends up in possession of it. The tale is superbly structured (marred only by an overly pat ending) and the Kirby/Wood art is triumphant!

(Chronology Note: On the stands at the same time as Challengers #5 is Tales Of Suspense #1 and Tales To Astonish #1, the pre hero Marvel companion titles to Strange Tales and Journey Into Mystery.)

Challengers #6

"Captives of the Space Circus" in **Challengers Of The Unknown #6 (Feb-Mar 1959, pictured above)** is another bravura combination of close-to-absurd concepts and a juvenile "sense of wonder" treatment. The daring quartet is kidnapped and turned into performing animals in an interplanetary circus, complete with birdmen, bouncing-ball aliens, and sea-monsters. Once again the ending puts a real strain on our "suspension of disbelief", but factoring in the elegance of the Kirby/Wood art, it adds up to a moderately memorable yarn.

In "The Sorceress of Forbidden Valley" June's plane crashes on a remote island, and she falls prey to the centuries-old magic of a lost civilization reminiscent of Shangri-La from the classic 1937 film "Lost Horizon". The bones of the plot stick out a bit here too, but it's a satisfying, if somewhat abrupt, ten-pager.

(Chronology Note: On the stands at the same time as Challengers #6 is Flash #105, the famous first issue of the Silver Age Flash in his own title, 2 1/2 years after Showcase #4 introduced the Scarlet Speedster.)

Challengers Of The Unknown #7 (Apr-May 1959, pictured above) starts off with a topsy-turvy version of #6's "Space Circus" theme, but this time the "zoo car" of a "space train" bound for Pluto crash-lands on Earth. "The Beasts From Planet Nine" escape and the fearless four must cope with an assortment of alien animals that are truly classic. The fertile mind of Kirby has devised such oddities as a dinosaur that can roll itself into an armored wheel, a giant fire-breathing bird, and last but not least, a huge jellyfish that can wrap itself around a ship and dissolve the whole thing in moments!

Ace stars in this one. Teamed with Red, he engineers the capture of the dragon-bird, and in the end tackles the dinosaur one-on-one. Once again, the Kirby/Wood collaborative art is superlative. The work is colorfully conceived, masterfully staged, and scrupulously polished to perfection. "Isle of No Return" is similarly pleasing. The plot is the usual stolen scientific secrets stuff, but with the Challengers shrinking to the proportions of Ray Palmer's alter ego, the Atom, in an interesting predecessor to Showcase #34.

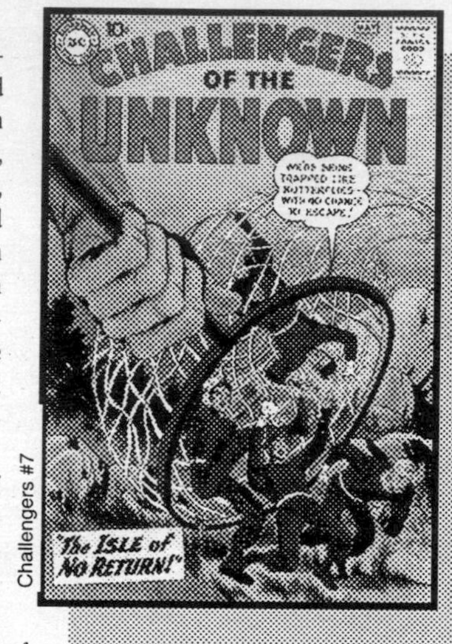

Challengers #7

(Chronology Note: On the stands at the same time as Challengers #7 is Action #252, the origin and first appearance of Supergirl... and Detective #267, which introduced the oddest member of the Batman entourage, Batmite.)

Challengers Of The Unknown #8 (Jun-Jul 1959. pictured on facing page) has a standout cover, with the death-defying foursome enclosed in transparent globes that are being shot into space. The opening yarn, "The Man Who Stole the Future", is yet another take on the hi-tech hijacking theme that puts awesome weaponry into malevolent hands. Amazingly, this seemingly shopworn plot is carried to new heights. It is splendidly choreographed, and fast paced... and most importantly, it is believable. This twelve-pager stands as a shining example of how to breathe freshness into old formulas and is truly the Challs at their best.

The cover story, "Prisoners of Robot Planet", comes off pretty well too. The quartet is transported, via those aforementioned space-spheres, to an alien world, to help quell a revolt by the planet's mechanical work-force. It seems some mysterious form of radiation has triggered this "robot rebellion". The fearless four are contacted by an alien emissary from the troubled world and volunteer to help the aliens regain control over their metal servants. There's always some strain on our "suspension of disbelief" when the Challs go interplanetary, but when the strategies are logical and the skirmishes exciting (as they are here), the results are highly enjoyable.

By issue #8, the faults of the series have been revealed, as well as the virtues, and the issues which follow #8 don't change things much. The long view of history will probably note the failure to create an expanding cast of supporting characters as one of these flaws. A large stable of supporting characters keeps main characters from becoming stale and is a key element of title longevity (just look at Batman). Comic Book History must also credit Kirby with demonstrating the viability of the "team" concept in the Silver Age, thus opening the door for the various super-groups that would flourish in the next decade.

Issue 8 is also noted by comic book historians as the last one to feature the superb style of the Kirby/Wood team on the interior art and the ONLY issue to sport a cover penciled by Kirby and inked by Wood. This special farewell gift from the team marks the end of a remarkable 2 1/2 years of production excellence that would never be seen again in the DC universe. Although future issues would carry on with their strong characters and singular situations, it is safe to say that the intensity of these first twelve issues provided a crucial momentum for the issues that followed.

(Chronology Note: On the stands at same time as Challengers #8 is Showcase #20, the first appearance of Rip Hunter, Time Master.)

CONTINUING WITHOUT KIRBY

Challengers Of The Unknown #9 (Aug-Sep 1959, pictured on following page, lower right) is the first non-Kirby issue. But the Challs flavor is retained - although it does look more like DC product since DC staffers took over the art - much of which looks to be by Bob Brown. "The Men Who Lost Their Memories" is the old cat-and-mouse of super-science in a bad guy's clutches, with June Robbins helping out after the fearless foursome gets zapped into amnesia. "The Plot to Destroy Earth" is an alien invasion yarn wherein three strange and powerful creatures are sent to prepare Earth's destruction. The creatures prove to be unstoppable, but Ace comes up with some sly subterfuge that just might turn things around before Earth gets carved into pieces...

It's worth noting that also dated Aug-Sep 1959 was Brave and The Bold #25 featuring the first appearance of the Suicide Squad - DC's attempt to create another group loosely based on the plot concepts behind the Challengers. The silver DC universe was really starting to fill out, with Adam Strange and Space Ranger having started their series in August, and the first Green Lantern Showcase issue coming up (#22 Sep-Oct 1959).

Challengers #8

(Chronology Note: On the stands at same time as Challengers #9 is Kirby's marvelous, often overlooked, and incredibly creative contribution to the Archie Silver Age hero universe, The Fly #1... and World Of Fantasy #19. WOF 19 is the last issue of the title and actually begins the era of "Marvel Monsters" and features a classic Kirby cover reminiscent of the Cyclops from the 1958 Film "7th Voyage Of Sinbad.")

Challengers Of The Unknown #10 (Oct-Nov 1959, pictured on following page, upper left) is also solid. One could label it standard DC product, but realize that this is National at its sizzling silver peak - one of the most fondly remembered eras in the history of comics. "The Cave-Man Beast" results when a scientist involved in communicating with animals imbibes a formula that turns him into an animal. Once again, while the boys are busy trying to corral this "missing link", June is working behind the scenes and finds the formula's antidote. Rocky and Red trade some pretty intense insults in this one; perhaps June's presence has them feeling like rivals.

"The Four Faces of Doom" is a highly provocative cover, and the yarn inside does its best to live up to it. The daredevil quartet enters a time warp that takes them back to an ancient, yet highly advanced civilization. As it happens the team arrives during a fight when a rebel group is trying to take control of the city. After some mix-ups the borrowed-timers get together with the "good guys" and help suppress the rebel forces. The "time loop" aspects of this one make for a nice epilog.

Challengers Of The Unknown #11 (Dec-Jan 1959-60) ushers us into the new decade with a worthwhile and historically notable entry - the first non-Kirby full-length novel. "The Creatures from the Forbidden World" is another one of those where the Challs help overturn the invasion of

Challengers #10

Challengers #9

an alien planet. This time they get there via a "dimensional portal,"- and there's definitely some self-interest going on - because if the invaders can't be stopped in the alternate universe they plan on coming through the portal themselves and conquering Earth. The plot follows the usual patterns, but this story demonstrates, once again, that when properly polished, these stock situations can still entertain us.

This ish also boasts the only cover done in the "wash" or "grey tone" style that was another DC hallmark.

(Chronology Note: On the stands at the same time as Challengers #11 is Flash #110, the first appearance of Kid Flash.)

THE 1960s AND BEYOND

As the decade turned, the Challengers still held favor with readers for awhile. But in 1961 the intrepid team finally faced a challenge they could not overcome... a challenge that would eventually cause the decline and eventual demise of their title... and ironically, a challenge from the very comic book genius that created them, Jack Kirby. That insurmountable challenge was called the Fantastic Four and the Marvel Age it ushered in.

During the next nine years, Challengers Of The Unknown underwent numerous changes in an attempt to re-excite readers, including new artists... the addition of intra-team conflicts and a more "Marvel-like" combative dialogue... new costumes... even DC's infamous "Go Go Checks".

All these changes were in vain. The original series was eventually discontinued one year later (just after the end of the Silver Age) with issue #77 (Dec-Jan 1970-71). Although two short lived attempts were made to revive the title (issue #78 in Feb 1973, and Issue #81 in Jun-Jul 1977) these attempts never succeeded in recapturing the imagination of comic fans.

Comic book historians still debate the final epitaph for the Challengers of the Unknown. Some speculate that the fans of Rocky, Red, Ace, and Prof simply outgrew the team. Others conjecture that the ever deteriorating art and stories of the middle and late 60s are to blame for the group's downfall. Still others suggest that clones of the pioneering team still survive in cartoon shows like "The Centurions" which successfully recycle the Kirby story telling formula.

Comic book historians do not debate the fact the chronology of the Challengers is a perfect allegory for the Silver Age. The cultural changes which first spawned, sustained, and eventually killed the title also put an end to the entire historic age.

But the historic rhetoric matters little to the army of still loyal fans who have always recognized the incredible artistic and literary genius contained in these DC classics from the late 1950s. These Loyal fans will never forget the first Silver Age team... that challenged the unknown... and lived on borrowed time!

Publishers Note: Noted authority on 1950's and 60's comics and author of numerous articles about the history of comic books, Pat S. Calhoun is a regular columnist for Overstreet's Comic Book Monthly and is a contributor to and Associate Editor of Overstreet's Golden Age/Silver Age Quarterly. Gary M. Carter is founding president of the American Association Of Comic Book Collectors, chairman of the AACBC National Grading Committee, co-author of the Overstreet Comic Book Grading Guide, author of numerous research articles on the history and rarity of comic books, and is a nationally recognized comic book historian. Both Pat and Gary have been avidly reading, collecting, and loving comic books since childhood.

DIRECTORY OF COMIC AND NOSTALGIA SHOPS
(Paid advertising store listings)

You can have your store listed here for very reasonable rates. Send for details and deadline for next year's guide. The following list of stores have paid to be included in this list. We cannot assume any responsibility in your dealings with these shops. This list is provided for your information only. When planning your trips, it would be advisable to make appointments in advance. Remember, To get your shop included in the next edition, **write for rates.** Items stocked by these shops are listed just after the telephone numbers and are coded as follows:

(a) Golden Age Comics
(b) Silver Age Comics
(c) New Comics, magazines
(d) Pulps
(e) Paperbacks
(f) Big Little Books
(g) Magazines (old)
(h) Books (old)
(i) Movie Posters, Lobby Cards
(j) Original Art
(k) Toys (old)
(l) Records (old)
(m) Trading Cards
(n) Underground Comics
(o) Video Tapes
(p) Premiums
(q) Comic Related Posters
(r) Comic Supplies
(s) Role Playing Games
(t) Star Trek Items
(u) Dr. Who Items
(v) Japanimation Items

ALABAMA

All Star Comics & Cards
203B W. Washington St.
Athens, AL 35611
PH: 205-232-9193
(a-c,l,m,p,q,r,t)

At Lary's
501 Quintard Ave.,
Suite 20
Anniston, AL 36201
PH: 205-238-8373
(b,d,e,q,r)

Wizard's Comics
324 N. Comics
Florence, AL 35230
PH: 205-766-6821
(a-c,g-k,m-v)

Sincere Comics
4667 Airport Blvd.
Mobile, AL 36609
(a-c,e,m,o,q-t)

Hellen's Comics
113 Mill St.
Oxford, AL 36205
PH: 205-835-3040
(c,e,g,l,m)

ARIZONA

Greg's Comics
2722 South Alma School
Rd. #8, Mesa, AZ 85210
PH: 602-752-1881
(a-c,g,k,m,r,t)

Ed Kalb (Mail Order Only)
1353 S. Los Alamos
Mesa, AZ 85204 (a-g,i)
(2 stamps for lists)

All About Books & Comics
517 E. Camelback
Phoenix, AZ 85012
PH: 602-277-0757
(a-f,h,m,o,q-v)

All About Books & Comics West
4208 N. Dunlap
Phoenix, AZ 85051
PH: 602-435-0410
(a-f,h,m,o,q-v)

All About Books & Comics III, 13835 N.
Tatum Suite #1
Phoenix, AZ 85032
PH: 602-494-1976
(b,c,m,n,q-t,v)

All About's Discount Outlet
527 E. Camelback
Phoenix, AZ 85012
PH: 602-277-1614
(a-c,e,g,i,m,q,s)

Key Comics
P O Box 3855
Scottsdale, AZ
85271-3855
PH: 602-949-8499 (a-c,j)

The One Book Shop
120-A East University Dr.
Tempe, AZ 85281-3728
PH: 602-967-3551
(c,g,i,m-o,q,r,t-v)

ARKANSAS

Paperbacks Plus
2207 Rogers Ave.
Ft. Smith, AR 72901
PH: 501-785-5642
(b,c,e,g,h,m,q-s)

The Comic Book Store
9307 Treasure Hill
Little Rock, AR 72120
PH: 501-227-9777
(a-c,e,g,m,o,q-v)

Pie-Eyes
8001 Geyer Springs RD.
Southwest Mall
Little Rock, AR 72209,
PH: 501-568-1414
(a-i,k-n,p-t)

TNT Collectors Hut
503 West Hale Ave.
Osceola, AR 72370
PH: 501-563-5760 (c,m,r)

Collector's Edition Comics
3217 John F. Kennedy
Blvd., North Little Rock,
AR 72116
PH: 501-791-4222
(a-c,e,g,m,o,q-v)

CALIFORNIA

Comic Heaven
24 W. Main Street
Alhambra, CA 91801
PH: 818-289-3945
(a-c,g,,j,q,t)

Comic Relief
2138 University Avenue
Berkeley, CA 94704
PH: 415-843-5002
(a-d,f-h,j,n,q,r,v)

Crush Comics
2869 Castro Valley Blvd.
Castro Valley, CA 94546
PH: 510-581-4779
(a-c,g,k,m,q,r,t)

Collectors Ink
932-A W. 8th Ave.
Chico, CA 95926
PH: 916-345-0958
(a-c,e,g,m,o-r,t-v)

Superior Comics
1970 Newport Blvd.
Costa Mesa, CA 92627
PH: 714-631-3933
(a-c,f,g,j,k,m,n,q-s,v)

High-Quality Comics
(Mail Order Only)
1106 2nd St. Suite #110
Encinitas, CA 92024
PH: 619-723-7269
(b,c,g,j,n)

Comic Gallery
322-J W. El Norte Pkwy
Escondido, CA 92026
PH: 619-745-5660
(b,c,m,n,q-t,v)

Geoffrey's Comics
15530 Crenshaw Blvd.
Gardena, CA 90249
PH: 310-538-3198
(a-c,n,o,r,v)

Shooting Star Comics and Games
618 E. Colorado Blvd.
Glendale, CA 91205
PH: 818-502-1535
(b,c,m-o,q-s,v)

Treasures of Youth
1201 C Street
Hayward, CA 94541
PH: 510-888-9675
(a,b,d-m,r,t,v)

Another World
1615 Colorado Blvd.
Los Angeles, CA 90041
PH: 213-257-7757
(a-i,m,n,q,r,t-v)

Cheap Comics
7779 Melrose Ave.
Los Angeles, CA 90046
PH: 213-655-9323
(a-d,g,k,m,n,q,t,v)

Golden Apple Comics
7711 Melrose Avenue
Los Angeles, CA 90046
PH: 213-658-6047
(a-c,e,m-o,q,r,u)

Golden Apple Comics
8934 West Pico Blvd.
Los Angeles, CA 90034
PH: 310-274-2008
(c,m-o,q-s,v)

Pacific Comic Exchange, Inc., P O Box 34849
Los Angeles, CA 90034
PH: 310-836-7234 (PCEI)
(a,b)

Great Wall Of Comics
1639 G Street
Merced, CA 95340
PH: 209-385-3602
(a-c,m,p-r)

Bonanza Books & Comics
Roseburg Square Center
813 W. Roseburg Avenue
Modesto, CA 95350-5058
PH: 209-529-0415
(a-h,j,k,m,o-u)

Ninth Nebula
The Comic Book Store
11517 Burbank Blvd.
North Hollywood, CA
91601, PH: 818-509-2901
(a-c,g-j,m-o,q,r,t-v)

Golden Apple Comics
8962 Reseda Blvd.
Northridge, CA 91324
PH: 818-993-7804
(a-c,e,j-o,q,r,v)

Freedonia Funnyworks
350 S. Tustin Ave.
Orange, CA 92666
PH: 714-639-5830
(a-g,j,k,m-r)

Lee's Comics
3783 El Camino Real
Palo Alto, CA 94306
PH: 415-493-3957
(a-h,j,m-o,r-v)

Comic Dungeon
3485 University Avenue
Riverside, CA 92501
PH: 909-684-8544
(b,c,m,r)

Comic Gallery
9460-G Mira Mesa Blvd.
San Diego, CA 92126
PH: 619-578-9444
(b,c,m,n,q-t,v)

Comic Gallery
4224 Balboa Ave.
San Diego, CA 92117
PH: 619-483-4853
(b,c,m,n,q-t,v)

Comic Relief
1597 Haight Street
San Francisco, CA 94117
PH: 415-552-9010
(a-d,f-h,j,n,q,r,v)

San Diego Comics & Collectibles
6937 El Cajon Blvd.
San Diego, CA 92115
PH: 619-698-1177
(a-c,e,k,m,r,t)

Comics and Da-Kind
1643 Noriega Street
San Francisco, CA 94122
PH: 415-753-9678
(a,b,g,r)

Comics and Da-Kind
1653 Noriega Street
San Francisco, CA 94122
PH: 415-753-9678
(c,m,o,q,r,t,v)

The Comic Shop
2164 E. 14th Street
San Leandro, CA 94577
PH: 510-483-0205
(a-c,g,m,o,q,r)

San Mateo Books, Baseball Cards & Original Art
106 South B St.
San Mateo, CA 94401
PH: 415-344-1536
(a-c,g,j,m,n,q,r)

Lee's Comics
2222 S. El Camino Real
San Mateo, CA 94402
PH: 415-571-1489
(a-h,j,m-o,r-v)

Cool City Comics
1632 Ocean Park
Santa Monica CA 90405
PH: 310-396-7005
(b,c,i,j,k,q,r)

Hi De Ho Comics & Fantasy
525 Santa Monica Blvd.
Santa Monica, CA 90401
PH: 310-394-2820
(a-j,m-o,q-v)

Graphic Illusion Original Art
12440 Moorpark Ave.
#106
Studio City, CA 91607
PH: 818-509-2968
(a-c,j,m)

Hi De Ho Comics & Fantasy
1720 N. Moorpark Rd.
Thousand Oaks, CA
91360m PH: 805-495-
1705 (a-j,m-o,q-v)

Silver City Comics
4671 Torrance Blvd.
Torrance, CA 90503
PH: 310-542-8034
(a-c,g,m,q,r)

Ralph's Comic Corner
2377 E. Main Street
Ventura, CA 93003
PH: 805-653-2732
(a-c,m-o,q-v)

The Second Time Around Bookshop
391 E. Main Street
Ventura, CA 93001
PH: 805-643-3154
(b,c,e,g-i)

COLORADO

Heroes & Dragons #2
Citadel Mall
Colorado Springs, CO
80909, PH: 719-550-9570
(b-e,m,o,q-v)

Heroes & Dragons #1
220 N. Tejon St.
Colorado Springs, CO
80903, PH: 719-635-2516
(a-c,e,m-o,q-v)

CONNECTICUT

Dragons Den
43 Greenwich Ave.
Greenwich, CT 06830
PH: 203-622-1171
(b,c,g,m,q-t,v)

A Timeless Journey
2538 Summer Street
Stamford, CT 06905
PH: 203-353-1720
(a-c,g,j,k,m,o,q,r,t)

DELAWARE

Captain Blue Hen Comics
Baycourt Plaza Rte. 113
Dover, DE 19901
PH: 302-734-3222
(a-c,g,h,k,m-o,q-s,v)

FLORIDA

Comic Source
63 S. Federal Hwy.
Boca Raton, FL 33432
PH: 407-395-7135
(a-c,m,q,r)

Acevedo's Collectables
4761 S. University Dr.
Davie, FL 33325
PH: 305-434-0540
(c,g,m,q,r)

Cliff's Books
209 N. Woodland Blvd.
(17-92),
DeLand, FL 32720
PH: 904-738-9464
(a-c,e,f,h,k-n,q-t)

Family Book Shop
1301 N. Woodland Blvd.
DeLand, FL 32720
PH: 904-736-6501
(b,c,e,h,m,r,s)

Tropic Comics East
5439 N. Federal Highway
Ft. Lauderdale, FL 33308
PH: 305-351-0001
(a-d,j,n,q,r,v)

Tropic Comics South, Inc.
743 N.E. 167th St.
N. Miami Beach, FL 33162
PH: 305-940-8700
(a-d,j,n,r,v)

Bay Hill Used Books & Comics
7657 Turkey Lake Rd.
Orlando, FL 32819
PH: 407-363-0040
(b,c,e,g,m,p,q-t)

Enterprise 1701
2814 Corrine Dr.
Orlando, FL 32803
PH: 407-896-1701
(b,c,e,g,i,m-o,q-v)

Sincere Comics
3300 N. Pace Blvd.
Pensacola, FL 32505
PH: (a-c,e,f,m,o,q-t)

Tropic Comics
313 S. State Rd. 7
Plantation, FL 33317
PH: 305-587-8878
(a-d,j,k,n,q,r,t,v)

Comics "R" Us
537 E. Sample Rd.
Pompano Beach, FL
33064, PH: 305-784-8801
(a-c,g,j,k,m,o,q,r,t)

South Miami Comics
5745 Sunset Drive
South Miami, FL 33143
PH: 1-800-826-3089 (a,b)

Comic & Gaming Exchange
8432 W. Oakland
Pk. Blvd.
Sunrise, FL 33351
PH: 305-742-0777
(b-e,g,k,m-v)

Tropic Comics North, Inc.
1018 21st St. (U.S. 1)
Vero Beach, FL 32960
PH: 407-562-8501
(a-c,j,n,q-s)

GEORGIA

Showcase Collectibles
2880 Holcomb Bridge Rd.
#19, Alpharetta, GA 30202
PH: 404-594-0778
(a-c,g,i,q-s)

Titan Games & Comics VI
2000D Cheshire Bridge
Rd, Atlanta, GA 30324
PH: 404-982-0227
(a-c,g,k,m,o,q-v)

Titan Games & Comics
5436 Riverdale Rd.
College Park, GA 30349
PH: 404-996-9129
(a-d,g,k,m-v)

Comic Company
1058 Mistletoe Rd.
Decatur, GA 30033
PH: 404-248-9846
(a-c,g,m,n,p,r)

Titan Games & Comics IV
2131 Pleasant Hill Rd.
Duluth, GA 30136
PH: 404-497-0202
(a-c,g,k,m,o,q-v)

Titan Games & Comics V
937 North Glynn St. #13
Fayetteville, GA 30214
PH: 404-461-9432
(a-c,g,k,m,o,q-v)

Odin's Cosmic Bookshelf
4760 Hwy. 29 Suite A-1
Lilburn, GA 30247
PH: 404-923-0123
(a-c,e,h,m,q-t,v)

Showcase Collectibles
5920 Roswell Rd.
Sandy Springs, GA
PH: 404-255-5170
(a-c,g,i,o,q-s,v)

Titan Games & Comics III, 2585 Spring Rd.
Smyrna, GA 30080
PH: 404-433-8226
(a-c,g,k,m,o,q-v)

Titan Games & Comics II
3853-C Lawrenceville
Hwy, Tucker, GA 30084
PH: 404-491-8067
(a-c,g,k,m,o,q-v)

HAWAII

Compleat Comics Company
1728 Kaahumanu Ave.
Wailuku, HI 96793
PH: 808-242-5875
(b,c,m-o,q-t)

IDAHO

King's Komix Kastle
1706 N. 18th St.
(By Appointment)
Boise, ID 83702
PH: 208-343-7142
(a-i,m,n,q,r)

King's Komix Kastle II
2560 Leadville (Drop-In)
Mail: 1706 N. 18th
Boise, ID 83702
PH: 208-343-7055
(a-i,m,n,q,r)

New Mythology Comics & Science Fiction
1725 Broadway
Boise, ID 83706
PH: 208-344-6744
(a-c,e,m,n,q-t)

ILLINOIS

Friendly Frank's Distribution
908 Westgate
Addison, IL 60101

Graham Crackers Comics, Ltd.
369 W. Army Trail Rd.
Bloomingdale, IL 60108
PH: 708-894-8810
(c,k,m,q-s,v)

Larry's Comic Book Store
1219 W. Devon Ave.
Chicago, IL 60660
PH: 312-274-1832
(a-c,o,r,u,v)

Larry Laws (Appointment only), 831 Cornelia
Chicago, IL 60657-1734
PH: 312-477-9247
(e,g,h,m,o)

Moondog's
Ford City Shopping Center
7601 S. Cicero Avenue
Chicago, IL 60652
PH: 312-581-6060
(a-c,m,o,q-v)

Moondog's
Lincoln Park
2301 N. Clark Street
Chicago, IL 60614
PH: 312-248-6060
(a-c,m,o,q-v)

Joe Sarno's Comic Kingdom
5941 W. Irving Park Road
Chicago, IL 60634
PH: 312-545-2231
(a-d,j,m,r)

Yesterday's
1143 West Addison St.
Chicago, IL 60613
PH: 312-248-8087
(a,b,d-g,l-n,r,t)

The Paper Escape
205 W. First Street
Dixon, IL 61021
PH: 815-284-7567
(c,e,m,q,s,t)

Graham Crackers Comics, Ltd.
5230 S. Main Street
Downers Grove, IL 60515
PH: 708-852-1810
(c,k,m,o,q-s,v)

GEM Comics
156 N. York Rd.
Elmhurst, IL 60126
PH: 708-833-8787
(b,c,m,q-s)

Moondog's
Downtown Mt. Prospect
139 W. Prospect Avenue
Mt. Prospect, IL 60056
PH: 708-398-6060
(a-c,m,o,q-v)

Moondog's
Randhurst Shopping Ctr.
999 Elmhurst Road
Mt. Prospect, IL 60056
PH: 708-577-8668
(a-c,m,o,q-v)

Graham Crackers Comics, Ltd.
5 E. Chicago Avenue
Naperville, IL 60540
PH: 708-355-4310
(a-c,g,j,k,m-o,q-t,v)

Tomorrow Is Yesterday
5600 N. 2nd Street
Rockford, IL 61111
PH: 815-633-0330
(a-j,m-o,q-v)

Moondog's
Schaumburg Plaza
1455 W. Schaumburg Rd.
Schaumburg, IL 60194
PH: 708-529-6060
(a-c,m,o,q-v)

Graham Crackers Comics, Ltd.
108 E. Main Street
St. Charles, IL 60174
PH: 708-854-0610
(c,k,m,r-s,v)

Unicorn Comics & Cards
216 S. Villa Avenue
Villa Park, IL 60181
PH: 708-279-5777
(a-c,g,h,j,l-n,q-s)

INDIANA

The Book Broker
2127 S. Weinbach Avenue
Evansville, IN 47714
PH: 812-479-5647
(a-c,e,g,h,l-o,q-v)

Comic Carnival
6265 N. Carrollton, Ave.
Indianapolis, IN 46220
PH: 317-253-8882
(a-j,.m-u)

Comic Carnival
7311 U.S. 31 South
Indianapolis, IN 46227
PH: 317-889-8899
(a-j,m-u)

Comic Carnival
5002 S. Madison Ave.
Indianapolis, IN 46227
PH: 317-787-3773
(a-j,m-u)

Comic Carnival
982 N. Mitthoeffer Rd.
Indianapolis, IN 46229
PH: 317-898-5010
(a-j,m-u)

Comic Carnival
3837 N. High School Rd.
Indianapolis, IN 46254
PH: 317-293-4386
(a-j,m-u)

Galactic Greg's
1900 Franklin
Michigan City, IN 46360
PH: 219-879-7119
(a-c,m,n,q-t)

Galactic Greg's
1407 E. Lincoln Way
Valparaiso, IN 46383
PH: 219-464-0119
(a-c,m,n,q-t)

IOWA

Oak Leaf Comics
1926 Valley Park Drive
Cedar Falls, IA 50613
PH: 319-277-1835
(a-c,m,n,q-t)

Oak Leaf Comics
23 5th Street SW
Mason City, IA 50401
PH: 515-424-0333
(a-c,f,i-k,m,o,q-v)

KANSAS

Friendly Frank's Distribution
1401 Fairfax Trafficway
105 B Bldg.
Kansas City, KS 66115
PH: 913-371-0333
(c,e,m-o,q-v)

Kwality Comics
1111 Massachusetts
Lawrence, KS 66044
PH: 913-843-7239
(a-c,e,i,m,q-t,v)

Prairie Dog Comics East
Normandie Center,
6516 E. Central
Wichita, KS 67206
PH: 316-688-5576
(a-n,p-s)

Prairie Dog Comics West
Maple Ridge Mall
7130 W. Maple Suite 240
Wichita, KS 67209
PH: 316-942-3456 (a-v)

KENTUCKY

Pac-Rat's, Inc.
1051 Bryant Way
Bowling Green, KY 42103
PH: 502-782-8092
(a-c,g,l,m,o-t)

Comic Book World
7130 Turfway Road
Florence, KY 41042
PH: 606-371-9562
(a-c,m,o,q-v)

Comic Book World
6905 Shepherdsville Road
Louisville, KY 40219
PH: 502-964-5500
(a-c,m,o,q-v)

The Great Escape
2433 Bardstown Road
Louisville, KY 40205
PH: 502-456-2216
(a-c,e,g,i,l-o,q-v)

LOUISIANA

B. T. & W. D. Giles
P O Box 271
Keithville, LA 71047
PH: 318-925-6654
(a,b,d-f,h)

More Fun Comics
8200 Oak Street
New Orleans, LA 70118
PH: 504-865-1800
(a-c,f,g,m,n,q,r,v)

MAINE

Lippincott Books
624 Hammond Street
Bangor, ME 04401
PH: 207-942-4398
(a,b,d-h,n,p,r,t)

Moonshadow Comics
359 Maine Mall
South Portland, ME 04106
PH: 207-772-4605
(a-c,g,i,m,n,q-u)

Book Barn
US Route 1
Wells, ME 04090
PH: 207-646-4926
(a-c,e,h,j,m,r,t,u)

MARYLAND

Universal Comics
5300 East Drive
Arbutus, MD 21227
PH: 410-242-4578
(b,c,e,k,m,r)

Comic Book Kingdom, Inc.
4307 Harford Road
Baltimore, MD 21214
PH: 410-426-4529
(a-c,f-h,m,q,r)

Big Planet Comics
4908 Fairmont Avenue
Bethesda, MD 20814
PH: 301-654-6856
(c,n,q,r,t)

Alternate Worlds
72 Cranbrook Rd.,
Yorktowne Plaza
Cockeysville, MD 21030
PH: 410-666-3290
(b,c,e,m-o,q-v)

The Closet Of Comics
7315 Baltimore Avenue
College Park, MD 20740
PH: 301-699-0498
(b,c,m-o,r)

Comic Classics
203 E. Main Street
Frostburg, MD 21532
PH: 301-689-1823
(a-c,e,g,m,n,q,r,t)

Comic Classics
365 Main Street
Laurel, MD 20707
PH: 301-490-9811 or 410-792-4744 (a-c,e,g,m-o,q-v)

Zenith Comics & Collectibles, Inc.
18200 Georgia Avenue
Olney, MD 20832
PH: 301-774-1345
(a-c,m,o-t)

Adventure Comics
1055 Rockville Pike
Rockville, MD 20852
PH: 301-251-2888 or 1-800-272-9862 (a-c,q,r)

Barbarian Book Shop
11234 Grandview Avenue
Wheaton, MD 20902
PH: 301-946-4184
(a-c,e,f,h-k,m-o,q-v)

MASSACHUSETTS

New England Comics
170 Harvard Avenue
Allston, MA 02134
PH: 617-783-1848
(a-c,e,m,o,q-v)

New England Comics
168 Harvard Avenue
Boston, MA 02134
PH: 617-783-1848
(a-c,e,m,o,q-v)

New England Comics
1840 Centre Street
Boston, MA 02132
PH: 617-325-1848
(a-c,e,m,o,q-v)

New England Comics
748 Crescent Street
East Crossing Plaza
Brockton, MA 02402
PH: 508-559-5068
(a-c,e,m,o,q-v)

New England Comics
316 Harvard Street
Brookline, MA 02146
PH: 617-566-0115
(a-c,e,m,o,q-v)

New England Comics
12B Eliot Street
Harvard Square
Cambridge, MA 02138
PH: 617-354-5352
(a-c,e,m,o,q-v)

That's Entertainment
387 Main Street
Fitchburg, MA 01420
PH: 508-342-8607 (a-v)

Bop City Comics
Rt. 9 Marshalls Mall
Framingham, MA 01701
PH: 508-872-2317 (a-v)

New England Comics
12A Pleasant Street
Malden, MA 02148
PH: 617-322-2404
(a-c,e,m,o,q-v)

New England Comics
732 Washington Street
Norwood, MA 02062
PH: 617-769-4552
(a-c,e,m,o,q-v)

New England Comics
11 Court Street
Plymouth, MA 02360
PH: 508-746-8797
(a-c,e,m,o,q-v)

Outer Limits Limited
377 Court Street, Rt. 3A
Cordage Park, Bldg. 3
N. Plymouth, MA 02360
PH: 508-747-2550
(b,c,g,m,q,r,t)

New England Comics
1511 Hancock Street
Quincy, MA 02169
PH: 617-770-1848
(a-c,e,m,o,q-v)

Fabulous Fiction Comics and Games
Rt. 131, Fiske Hill Plaza
Sturbridge, MA 01566
PH: 508-347-8088
(a-e,h,o,q-v)

The Outer Limits
463 Moody Street
Waltham, MA 02154
PH: 617-891-0444
(a-k,m-v)

Bookstore & Restaurant, Inc.
Kendrick Ave. Mayo Beach,
Wellfleet, MA 02667
PH: 508-349-3154 (a-i)

New England Comics
1840 Centre Street
West Roxbury, MA 02132
PH: 617-325-1848
(a-c,e,m,o,q-v)

Stan's Toy Chest
8 West Main Street
Westboro, MA 01581
PH: 508-366-5091
(a-c,j-t,v)

Best Comic Shop Of Worcester
244 Park Avenue
Worcester, MA 01609
PH: 508-755-4207 (a-v)

Fabulous Fiction Book Store
984 Main Street.
Worcester, MA 01603
PH: 508-754-8826
(a-e,h,o,q-v)

That's Entertainment
244 Park Avenue
Worcester, MA 01609
PH: 508-755-4207 (a-v)

MICHIGAN

Tom & Terry Comics
508 Lafayette Avenue
Bay City, MI 48708
PH: 517-895-5525
(b,c,e,i,m,o-u)

Curious Comic Shop
210 M. A. C. Avenue
E. Lansing, MI 48823
PH: 517-332-0222
(a-c,m-v)

Curious Book Shop
307 E. Grand River
E. Lansing, MI 48823
PH: 517-332-0112
(d-k,m,p,t,v)

Amazing Book Store, Inc.
3718 Richfield Road
Flint, MI 48506
PH: 313-736-3025 (a-c,r)

Argos Book Shop
1405 Robinson Road SE
Grand Rapids, MI 49806
PH: 616-454-0111
(a-k,m-v)

Tardy's Collectors CornerInc.
2009 Eastern Ave. SE
Grand Rapids, MI 49507
PH: 616-247-7828
(a-c,m,n,q,r)

Friendly Frank's Distribution
26055 Dequindre
Madison Heights, MI
48071, PH: 313-542-2525
(c,e,m-o,q-v)

MINNESOTA

Comic College
Mall of America Campus
352 E. Broadway, Mall of America
Bloomington, MN 55425
PH: 612-858-9298
(c,j,m,n,o,q,r)

John Mlachnik
(Appointment Only)(Want Lists Encouraged)
P O Box 69
Chisholm, MN 55719
PH: 218-254-3763 (a,b)

Collector's Connection
21 East Superior Street
Duluth, MN 55802
PH: 218-722-9551
(b,c,m,r-t)

Collector's Connection
Miller Hill Mall
1600 Miller Trunk Hwy.
#112, Duluth, MN 55811
PH: 218-726-1360
(b,c,m,r-t)

Comic College
Original Campus
3151 Hennepin Ave. S.
Minneapolis, MN 55408
PH: 612-858-9298
(a-h,j,k,m-r)

Comic College
Calhoun Square Campus
3001 Henepin Ave. S.
Minneapolis, MN 55408
PH: 612-823-0115
(c,j,m,n,o,q,r)

Nostalgia Zone
P O Box 6106
Minneapolis, MN 55406
PH: 612-645-5950
(a,b,d-n,p,q,t)

Midway Book & Comic
1579 University Avenue
St. Paul, MN 55104
PH: 612-644-7605
(a-h,n,r)

MISSISSIPPI

Star Store
4212 N. State Street
Jackson, MS 39206
PH: 601-362-8001 (a-t)

MISSOURI

Byrd's Books & Collectibles
HC 1 Box 717
Fairdealing, MO 63939
PH: 314-857-2727
(a-c,e,g-i,l,m,r-t)

E.M. Comics (Joplin Flea Market)
12th & Virginia, Joplin, MO
PH: 316-231-9166
(b,c,m,q,k)

B & R Comix Center
4747 Morganford
Saint Louis, MO 63116

PH: 314-353-4013
(b,c,g,h,n,o,r,t)

Mo's Comics & Stories
4573 Gravois
St. Louis, MO 63116
PH: 314-353-9500
(a-c,f,p,r)

MONTANA

The Book Exchange
2335 Brooks Street
Tremper's Shopping Ctr.
Missoula, MT 59801
PH: 406-728-6342
(c-e,h,q-s)

NEBRASKA

The Dragon's Lair
8316 Blondo Street
Omaha, NE 68134-6339
PH: 402-399-9141

NEVADA

Fandom's Comicworld Outlet
2001 East 2nd Street
Reno, NV
PH: 702-786-6663
(a-c,i,j,k,q,r,v)

Fandom's Comicworld & Gallery
669 N. McCarran
Sparks, NV
PH: 702-358-7977
(a-c,i,j,m,q,r)

NEW HAMPSHIRE

James F. Payette
P O Box 750
Bethlehem, NH 03574
PH: 603-869-2097
(a,b,d-h)

NEW JERSEY

The Hobby Shop
Rt 34 Strathmore Shopping Ctr.
Aberdeen, NJ 07747
PH: 908-583-0505
(a-c,m,r-t)

Comics Plus
Laurel Square, Hwy. 70 & 88, Brick, NJ 08723
PH: 908-206-1070
(a-c,g,h,k,m,q,r)

Time Warp Comics & Games
584 Pompton Avenue
Cedar Grove, NJ 07009
PH: 201-857-9788
(c,e,m-t,v)

Grafik XS
288 Parker Avenue
Clifton, NJ 07011
PH: 201-340-5255
(a-c,e,j,k,m-r,t,v)

Comic Collectibles
P O Box 536
East Brunswick, NJ 08816
PH: 908-238-9023

Star Spangled Comics
353 Rt. 22 (at Green Brook Rd.)
Green Brook, NJ 08812
PH: 908-356-8338
(a-c,j,m,o,q-s,v)

Dreamer's Comics
229-235 Main Street
Main Street Plaza
Hackettstown, NJ 07840
PH: 908-850-5255
(a-c,k,m,o,q,r,v)

Thunder Raod Sportscards & Comics
1637 Rt. 33
3 Seasons Center
Hamilton Square, NJ
08690, PH: 609-587-5353
(a-c,m,r)

The Comic Book Shop
Lakeside Shopping Ctr.
Route 15 South
Lake Hopatcong, NJ
07849, PH: 201-663-4440
(b,c,e,m,q-s)

The Hobby Shop
Route 34 Strathmore Shopping Ctr.
Matawan, NJ 07747
PH: 908-583-0505
(a-c,m,r-t)

Comics Plus
Squire Plaza, 1300 Hwy. 35, Middletown, NJ 07748
PH: 908-706-0102
(a-c,g,h,k,m,q,r)

Montclair Book Center
221 Glenridge Avenue
Montclair, NJ 07042
PH: 201-783-3630
(a-h, m,n,q-u)

Fat Jack's Comicrypt
521 White Horse Pike
Oaklyn, NJ 08107
PH: 609-858-3877
(a-c,g,m,n,q,r,v)

Passaic Book Center
594 Main Avenue
Passaic, NJ 07055
PH: 201-778-6646
(a-i,l-o,q-u).

Philip M. Levine and Sons, Rare & Esoteric Books
P O Box 246 (Appointment Only)
Three Bridges, NJ 08887
PH: 908-788-0532
(a,b,d,n-p)

Mr. Collector
327 Union Blvd.
Totowa, NJ 07512
PH: 201-595-0900
(a-c,m,r)

Thunder Road Sportscards & Comics
1973 N. Olden Avenue
Trenton, NJ 08618
PH: 609-771-1055
(a-c,m,r)

COMIC BOOK STORE LISTINGS (cont'd)

Comics Plus
Ocean Plaza Hwy. 35
& Sunset Ave.
Wanamassa, NJ 07712
PH: 908-922-3308
(a-c,g,h,k,m,q,r)

Comic Museum
790 Woodlane Road
Westampton, NJ 08060
PH: 609-261-0996
(a-c,e,m,n,q,r,u,v)

Jim Hanley's Universe
A&P Shopping Center
Rt. 1 & Ford Ave.
Woodbridge, NJ 08863
PH: 908-417-5744
(a-c,e,g,m-o,q-v)

JHV Associates
(Appointment Only)
P O Box 317
Woodbury Heights, NJ
08097
PH: 609-845-4010 (a,b,d)

NEW MEXICO

Bruce's Comics
2432 Cerrillo Road
Santa Fe, NM 87501
PH: 505-474-0494
(a-c,g,j,n,q,r)

NEW YORK

Earthworld
327 Central Avenue
Albany, NY 12206
PH: 518-465-5495
(a-c,m-o,q-t,v)

Fantaco Enterprises, Inc.
21 Central Avenue
Albany, NY 12210
PH: 518-463-1400
(c,m-o,r,s,v)

Long Island Comics
1575 Sun Rise Highway
Bay Shore, L.I., New York
11706, PH: 516-665-4342
(a-c,g,j,q,t)

Gary Dolgoff Comics
Brooklyn Navy Yard
Building 280, Suite
608/609
PH: 718-596-5719
(Mail order only)

Pinocchio Comic Shop
1814 McDonald Avenue
Brooklyn, NY 11223
PH: 718-645-2573
(b,c,g,m,r)

Twilight Book & Game Emporium, Inc.
8140 Brewerton Road
Cicero, NY 13039
PH: 315-699-6848
(a-c,e,m-v)

Comics For Collectors
60 East Market Street
Corning, NY 14830
PH: 607-936-3994
(a-c,j,m,n,q-v)

Comics For Collectors
211 West Water Street
Elmira, NY 14901
PH: 607-732-2299
(a-c,j,m,n,q-v)

Comics For Collectors
206 North Aurora Street
Ithaca, NY 14850
PH: 607-272-3007
(a-c,j,m,n,q-v)

Best Comics Distribution Center
252-01 Northern Blvd.
Little Neck, NY 11362
PH: 718-279-2099 or 1-
800-966-2099
(a-c,m,n,r,t,v)

Funny Business Comics, Ltd.
660B Amsterdam Ave.
(92nd St.)
New York City, NY 10025
PH: 212-799-9477
(b,e,n,q,r)

Big Apple Comic
2489 Broadway (92/93 St.)
New York, NY 10025
PH: 201-585-2765
(a-d,j,m,n,r)

Jim Hanley's Universe
166 Chambers St.
New York, NY 10007
PH: 212-349-2930
(a-c,e,g,m-o,q-v)

Action Comics
1724 2nd Ave. (btwn 89th
& 90th Sts.)
New York, , NY 10128
PH: 212-534-0096
(a-c,j,k,m,q-t)

Jim Hanley's Universe
126 West 32nd St.
New York, NY 10001
PH: 212-268-7088
(a-c,e,g,m-o,q-v)

Alex's MVP Cards & Comics
256 E. 89th Street
New York, NY 10128
PH: 212-831-2273
(a-c,j,k,m,q,r)

Miller's Mint Ltd.
313 E. Main Street
Patchogue, NY 11772
PH: 516-475-5353
(a,b,g,m,r,t)

Fantastic Planet
24 Oak Street
Plattsburgh, NY 12901
PH: 518-563-2946
(a-c,e,m,q-v)

Flash Point Comics, Cards & Toys,
320 Main Street
Port Jefferson, NY 11777
PH: 516-331-9401
(c,e,k,m,q-u)

Dragons Den
Poughkeepsie Plaza Mall
Rt. 9, Poughkeepsie, NY
12601
PH: 914-471-1401

Iron Vic Comics
1 Raymond Ave.
Poughkeepsie, NY 12603
PH: 914-473-8365
(a-d,g,j,m,n,r)

Empire Comic s
1176 Mt. Hope Ave.
Roches ter, NY 14620
PH: 716-442-0371
(a-c,f,h,k,q-s)

Empire Comics
375 Stone Rd.
Rochester, NY 14616
PH: 716-663-6877
(a-c,h,k,q-s)

Electric City Comics
2801 Guilderland Avenue
Rotterdam, NY 12306
PH: 518-356-1301
(b,c,e,m,n,q,r,t)

Amazing Comics
12 Gillette Avenue
Sayville, NY 11782
PH: 516-567-8069
(a-c,e,j,m,o,q-s)

One If By Cards, Two If By Comics
1107 Central Avenue
Scarsdale, NY 10583
PH: 914-725-2225
(b,c,m,r,s)

Electric City Comics
1704 Van Vranken Ave.
Schenectady, NY 12308
PH: 518-377-1500
(a-c,e,g,j,m,n,q,r,t-v)

Jim Hanley's Universe
350 New Dorp Lane
Staten Island, NY 10306
(a-c,e,g,m-o,q-v)

Twilight Book & Game Emporium, Inc.
1401 N. Salina Street
Syracuse, NY 13208
PH: 315-471-3139
(a-c,e,g,m-v)

Twilight Book & Game Emporium, Inc.
Carousel Center
Syracuse, NY 13290
PH: 315-466-1601
(a-c,e,m,o,q-v)

Aquilonia Comics
412 Fulton Street
Troy, NY 12180
PH: 518-271-1069
(a-c,g,m,n,q,r,t,u)

Ravenswood Inc.
263 Genesee Street
Utica, NY 13501
PH: 315-735-3699
(a-c,g,m,p-u)

Iron Vic Comics II
420 Windsor Hwy
Vail's Gate, NY 12584
PH: 914-565-6525
(a-d,g,j,m,n,r)

Collector's Comics
3247 Sunrise Hwy.
Wantagh, NY 11793
PH: 516-783-8700
(a-c,e,g,m,n,q-s,v)

Dragons Den
2614 Central Park Ave.
Yonkers, NY 10710
PH: 914-793-4630

Dragons Den
Cross County Shopping
Center
Yonkers, NY 10704
(Opening March, 1994)

NORTH CAROLINA

Dragon's Hoard
344 Merrimon Avenue
Asheville, NC 28801
PH: 704-254-3829
(c,e,i,m,o,s-v)

Super Giant Comics
273-A Tunnel Road
Asheville, NC 28805
PH: 704-253-6188
(a-e,g,h,j,l-n,q,r)

Heroes Aren't Hard To Find
Corner Central Ave. & The
Plaza, P.O. Box 9181
Charlotte, NC 28299
PH: 704-375-7462
(a-c,g,j,k,m-o,q,t,v)

Heroes Aren't Hard To Find
(Mail Order & Wholesale)
P.O. Box 9181
Charlotte, NC 28299
PH: 704-376-5766, 800-
321-4370
(a-c,g,j,k,m-o,q-t,v)

Cumberland Coin Exchange
5701 Yadkin Road
P O Box 11112
Fayetteville, NC 28303
PH: 919-864-8256
(c,m,n,r)

Heroes Are Here
208 S. Berkeley Blvd.
Goldsboro, NC 27534
PH: 919-751-3131
(a-c,m,q,r)

Acme Comics
2150 Lawndale Drive
Greensboro, NC 27408
PH: 910-574-2263
(b,c,g,m-r,t,v)

Acme Comics
3808-C High Point Road
Greensboro, NC 27407
PH: 910-855-0217
(a-c,g,k,m-r,t,v)

Parts Unknown, The Comic Book Store
801 Merritt Drive,
The Cottonmill Square
Greensboro, NC 27407
PH: 919-294-0091
(a-c,m,r)

Heroes Are Here, Too
116 E. Fifth St.
Greenville, NC 27834
PH: 919-757-0948
s(a-c,m,q,r)

The Nostalgia Newsstand
919 Dickinsen Avenue
Greenville, NC 27834
PH: 919-758-6909
(b,c,e,n,q,r)

L & W Entertainment
206 Queen Street
Grifton, NC 28530
PH: 919-524-3333
(c,e,i,k,m,o,q,r,t,v)

Tales Resold
3936 Atlantic Avenue
Raleigh, NC 27604
PH: 919-878-8551
(a-c,e,g,h,j,m,q,r,t,u)

Booktrader Comics
121 Country Club Road
Rocky Mount, NC 27804
PH: 919-443-3993 (b,c,e,r)

Comics and Cards Unlimited
506 Waynesville Plaza
Waynesville, NC 28786
PH: 704-456-8787
(a-c,e,h,m,q,r,s)

COMIC BOOK STORE LISTINGS (cont'd)

Heroes Aren't Hard To Find
Silas Creek Shopping Ctr.
3234 Silas Creek Parkway
Winston-Salem, NC 27103
PH: 919-765-4370
(a-c,g,j,k,m-o,q-t,v)

Acme Comics
1100 Silas Creek Pkwy
Parkway Plaza Shopping Ctr.,
Winston Salem, NC 27127
PH: 910-777-0290
(b,c,g,m-r,t,v)

Ray's Comics and Collectibles
Hickory Tree Crossing
Shopping Ctr.,Hwy 150 South
Winston Salem, NC 27127
PH: 910-764-2055
(a-c,e,g-m,q-t)

NORTH DAKOTA

Barry's Collectors Corner
City Center Mall
Grand Forks, ND 58201
PH: 781-772-2518
(a-c,g,k-n,r-t)

OHIO

Dark Star III Books & Comics
1273 N. Fairfield Rd.
Beavercreek, OH 45432
PH: 513-427-3213
(b,c,e,h,m,q-v)

Comic Book World
4016 Harrison Avenue
Cincinnati, OH 45211
PH: 513-661-6300
(a-c,m,o,q-v)

Bookery Fantasy & Comics
35 N. Broad Street
Fairborn, OH 45324
PH: 1-800-953-1408
(a-h,j,k,m-o,q-v)

Bookery Fantasy SA/GA
608 Middle Street
Fairborn, OH 45324
PH: 1-800-953-1408
(a,b,d,e,f,h)

Dark Star II Books & Comics
1410 W. Dorothy Lane
Kettering, OH 45409
PH: 513-293-7307
(b,c,e,h,m,n,q-v)

Rich's Comic Shoppe
2441 N. Verity Parkway
Middletown, OH 45042
PH: 513-424-1095
(a-c,k,m,q,r,t,u)

Funnie Farm Bookstore
328 N. Dixie Drive
Vandalia, OH 45377
PH: 513-898-2794
(a-c,m,q,r,s)

Dark Star Books & Comics
237 Xenia Ave.
Yellow Springs, OH 45387
PH: 513-767-9400
(a-c,e-h,m,n,q-v)

OKLAHOMA

Comic Empire Of Tulsa
3122 S. Mingo
Tulsa, OK 74146
PH: 918-664-5808
(a-c,m,n,q,r)

Starbase 21
2130 S. Sheridan Rd.
Tulsa, OK 74129
PH: 918-838-3388
(a-c,e,g-j,m,o,q-v)

Want List Comics
(Appointment Only)
P O Box 701932
Tulsa, OK 74170-1932
PH: 918-299-0440
(a,b,f,h-k,m)

OREGON

Emerald City Comics
770 E. 13th
Eugene, OR 97401
PH: 503-345-2568
(c,e,m,o,p,r-t)

Emerald City III
2101 Bailey Hill Rd.
Eugene, OR 97405
PH: 503-342-5243
(c,e,m,p,r,s)

Nostalgia Collectibles
527 Willamette
Eugene, OR 97401
PH: 503-484-9202
(a-g,i-n,p,q,r,t)

Beyond Comics
322 E. Main
Medford, OR 97501
PH: 503-779-9543
(b,c,q,r,s)

Armchair Bookstore
3205 SE Milwaukie Ave.
Portland, OR 97202
PH: 503-238-6680
(a,b,d-h,n,o)

Future Deams Comic Art Library, 10508 NE Halsey
Portland, OR 97220
PH: 503-255-5245
(Over 15,000 issues available to read)

Future Dreams Gateway
10506 NE Halsey
Portland, OR 97220
PH: 503-255-5245
(a-e,g-j,m,n,q,r,t)

Future Dreams Burnside
1800 East burnside
Portland, OR 97214-1599
PH: 503-231-8311
(a-e,g-j,m,n,q,r,t)

PENNSYLVANIA

Cap's Comics Cavalcade
1894 Catasauqua Road
Allentown, PA 18103
PH: 610-264-5540
(a-c,e-g,k,m,n,p-v)

Dreamscape Comics
404 West Broad Street
Bethlehem, PA 18018
PH 215-867-1178
(a-c,m,q-s)

Showcase Comice I
874 W. Lancaster Ave.
Bryn Mawr, PA 19010
PH: 610-527-6236
(a-c,g,k,m,n,q-s,v

Time Tunnel Collectibles
1001 Castle Shannon
Blvd., Castle Shannon, PA
15234, PH: 412-531-8833
(a-c,g,j,m,q,r)

Adventures In Comics
3279 West Liberty Avenue
Dormont, PA 15216
PH: 412-531-5644
(a-c,k,m,o,q-v)

Dreamscape Comics
25th Street Shopping
Center, Easton, PA 18042
PH:215-250-9818
(a-c,m,q-s)

New Dimension Comics
435 Lawrence Avenue
Ellwood City, PA 16117
PH: 412-758-2324
(a-c,m,r)

New Dimension Comics
20550 Route 19
Cranberry Township
Evans City, PA 16033
PH: 412-776-0433
(a-c,m,r)

Charlies Collectors Corner
100 D West Second Street
Hummelstown, PA 17036
PH: 717-566-7216
(b,c,m,r)

Captain Blue Hen Comics
1800 Lincoln Hwy. East
Lancaster, PA 17602
PH: 717-397-8011
(a-e,g-i,k,l-o,q-t,v)

Comic Express
Silver Spring Plaza
3545 Marietta Avenue
Lancaster, PA 17601
PH: 717-285-3040
(b,c,e,g,h,m,q,r)

Showcase Comics II
Granite Run Mall, Rte 1
Media, PA 19063
PH: 610-891-9229
(a-c,g,k,m,q-s,t,v)

Duncan Comics, Books, and Accessories
1047 Perry Hwy.
Perrysville, PA 15237
PH: 412-635-0886
(b,c,e,g,h,m,o,q,r)

Fat Jack's Comicrypt I
2006 Sansom Street
Philadelphia, PA 19103
PH: 215-963-0788
(a-c,g,m,n,q,r,v)

Fat Jack's Comicrypt II
7598 Haverford Ave. (rear)
Philadelphia, PA 19151
PH: 215-473-6333
(a-c,g,m,n,q,r,v)

Fat Jack's Comicrypt III
5506 North 5th Street
Philadelphia, PA 19120
PH: 215-924-8210
(a-c,g,m,n,q,r,v)

Showcase Comics III
620 South St.
Philadelphia, PA 19147
PH: 215-625-9613
(a-c,g,k,m,n,r,s,v)

BEM: The Store
622 South Avenue
Pittsburgh, PA 15221
PH: 412-243-2736
(a-e,g-j,l-o,q,r,v)

Eide's Entertainment
1111 Penn Avenue
Pittsburgh, PA 15222
PH: 412-261-0900
(a-r,t-v)

Phantom Of The Attic
214 S. Craig Street
Pittsburgh, PA 15213
PH: 412-621-1210
(b,c,m-o,q-s)

RHODE ISLAND

Fantasy Zone Comics
7610 Post Road
North Kingstown, RI
02852, PH: 401-294-6044
(b,c,m,q,r,t)

Fantasy Zone Comics
1200 Bald Hill Road
Warwick, RI 02886
PH: 401-823-XMen
(b,c,m,o,q,r,t)

SOUTH CAROLINA

Super Giant Comics
3464 Cinema Center
Anderson, SC 29621
PH: 803-225-9024
(a-c,g,j,l-n,q,r,t)

Book Exchange
1219 Savannah Hwy.
Charleston, SC 29407
PH: 803-556-5051
(a-c,e,h,r)

Heroes Aren't Hard To Find
Northbridge Shopping
Center, 1670 Highway 171
Charleston, SC 29407
PH: 803-766-6611
(a-c,g,j,k,m-o,q-t,v)

Heroes Aren't Hard To Find
1415-A Laurens Road
Greenville, SC 29607
PH: 803-235-3488
(a-c,g,j,k,m-o,q-t,v)

Heroes Aren't Hard To Find
Westgate Mall, I-26 & US 29,
Spartanburg, SC 29301
PH: 803-574-1713
(a-c,g,j,k,m-o,q-t,v)

Mizz Comics
2500 Winchester Place
Ste. 103, Essex Square
Spartanburg, SC 29301
PH: 803-576-4990
(a-c,g,j,m,n,q,t)

SOUTH DAKOTA

Storyteller Entertainment
520 6th Street
Rapid City, SD 57701
PH: 605-348-7242
(a-c,e,h,i,m,q-t)

TENNESSEE

Collector's Choice #4
1308 Decatur Pike
Athens, TN 37303
PH: 615-744-9281
(b,c,m,q-s,p)

Choo Choo Comics
3611 Ringgold Rd.
Chattanooga, TN 37412
PH: 615-698-5584
(a-c,k,m,o,r-t,v)

Collector's Choice #3
2260 Gunbarrel Rd.
Chattanooga, TN 37412
PH: 615-855-4128
(b,c,m,q-s,p)

Collector's Choice #1
3405 Keith St.
Cleveland, TN 37312
PH: 615-472-6649
(b,c,m,q,r,s,p)

Comics Universe
1869 Hwy 45 By-Pass
Jackson, TN 38305
PH: 901-664-9131
(a-c,j,m,o,q-s)

Mountain Empire Collectibles #3
1210 North Roan Street
Johnson City, TN 37601
PH: 615-929-8245
(a-c,e,g-i,m,p-t)

Mountain Empire Collectibles #2
1451 East Center Street
Kingsport, TN 37664
PH: 615-245-0364
(a-e,g,h,j,k,m,p-t)

Collector's Choice #2
2104 W. Cumberland Ave.
Knoxville, TN 37916
PH: 615-546-2665
(b,c,m,q-s,p,v)

The Great Escape
111-B Gallatin Road North
Madison, TN 37115
PH: 615-865-8052
(a-c,e-i,k-m,o,q-v)

Comics & Collectibles
4730 Poplar Avenue #2
Memphis, TN 38117
PH: 901-683-7171
(a-c,g,m-o,q-s,v)

Memphis Comics & Records
665 S. Highland
Memphis, TN 38111
PH: 901-452-1312 (a-t)

The Great Escape
1925 Broadway
Nashville, TN 37203
PH: 615-327-0646 (a-v)

Walt's Paperback Books
2604 Franklin Road
Nashville, TN 37204
PH: 615-298-2506
(b,c,e,m,o,r)

TEXAS

Lone Star Comics Books & Games
504 East Abram Street
Arlington, TX 76010
PH: 817-Metro-265-0491
(a-c,e,g,k,m,q-t,v)

Lone Star Comics Books & Games
3415 South Cooper St., #141
Arlington, TX 76015
PH: 817-557-5252
(b,c,g,k,m,q-t,v)

Friendly Frank's Distribution
2959 Ladybird Lane
Dallas, TX 75220
PH: 214-351-3093
(c,e,m-o,q-v)

Lone Star Comics Books & Games
11661 Preston Forest Village, Dallas, TX 75230
PH: 214-373-0934
(a-c,e,k,m,n,q-t,v)

Remember When
2431 Valwood Pkwy.
Dallas, TX 75234
PH: 214-243-3439
(a-c,g,i,j,m,q,t,u)

Lone Star Comics Books & Games
6312 Hulen Bend Blvd.
Ft. Worth, TX 76132
(a-c,e,g,k,m,q-t,v)

B & D Trophy Co.
4404 N. Shepherd
Houston, TX 77018
PH: 713-694-8436 (b,c,r)

Bedrock City Comic Co.
6521 Westheimer
Houston, TX 77057
PH: 713-780-0675
(a-c,f,g,k,m-r,t,v)

Third Planet
2718 Southwest Freeway
Houston, TX 77098
PH: 713-528-1067 (a-v)

Lone Star Comics Books & Games
931 Melbourne
Hurst, TX 76053
PH: 817-595-4375
(a-c,e,g,k,m,q-t,v)

Lone Star Comics Books & Games
2550 N. Beltline Rd.
Irving, TX 75062
PH: 817-659-0317
(a-c,e,g,k,m,q-t,v)

Lone Star Comics Books & Games
3600 Gus Thomasson, Suite 107, Mesquite, TX 75150, PH: 214-681-2040
(b,c,e,k,m,q-t,v)

Lone Star Comics Books & Games
1900 Preston Rd. #345
Plano, TX 75093
PH: 214-985-1953
(a-c,e,g,m,q-t,v)

UTAH

The Bookshelf
2456 Washington Blvd.
Ogden, UT 84401
PH: 801-621-4752
(a-e,g,h,l,m,o,q-t,v)

VERMONT

Comics Outpost
27 Granite Street
Barre, VT 05641
PH: 802-476-4553 or 1-800-564-4553
(a-c,m,q-t)

VIRGINIA

Comic Card Collectorama
(Formerly Capital Comics Center.),
2008 Mt. Vernon Ave.
Alexandria, VA 22301
PH: 703-548-3466
(a-c,f,h,i,m,p,q,r,t,v)

Mountain Empire Collectibles #1
509 State Street
Bristol, VA 24201
PH: 703-466-6337
(a-c,e,g,i,m,p,q-t)

Burke Centre Used Books & Comics
5741 Burke Centre Pkwy
Burke, VA 22015
PH: 703-250-5114
(a-h,m,q-u)

Fantasia Comics & Records
1419 1/2 University Ave.
Charlottesville, VA 22903
PH: 804-971-1029
(b,c,l-n,p-u)

Fantasia Comics
1691 Seminole Trail
Charlottesville, VA 22901
PH: 804-974-7512
(b,c,m,n,p,q-u)

Trilogy Shop #3
3916-A6 Portsmouth Blvd.
Chesapeake, VA 23321
PH: 804-488-6578
(c,m,o,q-s)

Zeno's Books
1112 Sparrow Rd.
Chesapeake, VA 23325
PH: 804-420-2344
(a-j,m,r,t)

Fantasia Comics & Stuff,
Southgate Shopping Center
Culpeper, VA 22701
PH: 703-825-7747
(b,c,m,p,q,r,s)

Hole In The Wall Books
905 West Broad Street
Falls Church, VA 22046
PH: 703-536-2511
(b-e,g,h,l,n,q-v)

Marie's Books And Things, 1701 Princess Anne St., Fredericksburg, VA 22401
PH: 703-373-5196
(a-c,e,h,l,m,r)

Bender's Books & Cards
22 South Mallory Street
Hampton, VA 23663
PH: 804-723-3741
(a-j,m-v)

Franklin Farm Used Books & Comics
13340-B Franklin Farm Rd., Herndon, VA 22071
PH: 703-437-9530
(a-h,m,q-u)

Cosmic Books
10953 Lute Court
Manassas, VA 22110
PH: 703-330-8573
(b-e,g,h,j,l,q-u)

Trilogy Shop #2
700 E. Little Creek Rd.
Norfolk, VA 23518
PH: 804-587-2540
(b,c,m,o,q-v)

Dave's Comics
7019 "F" Three Chopt Rd., Richmond, VA 23226
PH: 804-282-1211
(b,c,m,o,r-t,v)

Nostalgia Plus
1601 Willow Lawn Drive
Richmond, VA 23232
PH: 804-282-5532
(a-c,m,n,q,r,t)

B & D Comic Shop
802 Elm Avenue SW
Roanoke, VA 24016
PH: 703-342-6642
(b,c,e,g,m,o,q-t)

Big Planet Comics
426 Maple Ave. East
Vienna, VA 22180
PH: 703-242-9412
(c,n,q,r,t)

Comics & Things
4406 Holland Road
Virginia Beach, VA 23452
PH: 804-486-5870
(a-e,g-i,k-m,o-v)

Trilogy Shop #1
5773 Princess Anne Rd.
Virginia Beach, VA 23462
PH: 804-490-2205
(a-c,i,k,m,o,q-v)

Trilogy Shop #4
857 S. Lynnhaven Rd.
Virginia Beach, VA 23452
PH: 804-468-0412
(c,m,o,q-s)

Zeno's Books & Comics
359 Independence Blvd.
Virginia Beach, VA 23462
PH: 804-490-1517
(a-j,m,r,t)

WASHINGTON

Everett Comics & Cards
2936 Colby Avenue
Everett, WA 98201
PH: 206-252-8181
(a-c,k,m-o,q-u)

Comics Northwest
514 State Ave. Suite 104
Marysville, WA 98270
PH: 206-659-4003
(b,c,k,m,q-t)

The Comic Character Shop
Old Firehouse Antique Mall
110 Alaskan Way South
Seattle, WA 98104
PH: 206-283-0532
(a,b,f,h-k,q)

Corner Comics
6565 NE 181st Street
Seattle, WA 98155
PH: 206-486-XMEN
(a-c,e,q,r)

Corner Comics II
5226 University Way NE
Seattle, WA 98105
PH: 206-525-9394
(a-c,q,r)

Gemini Book Exchange & Comic Center
9614 16th Avenue SW
Seattle, WA 98106
PH: 206-762-5543
(b,c,e,h,m-o,r,s)

Golden Age Collectables, Ltd.
1501 Pike Place Market
401 Lower Level
Seattle, WA 98101
PH: 205-622-9799
(a-g,i-k,m-o,q-v)

Rocket Comics
8544 Greenwood N.
Seattle, WA 98103
PH: 206-784-7300
(a-c,k,m,q)

Collectors Nook
213 North I Street
Tacoma, WA 98403
PH: 206-272-9828
(b,e,g,h,m,s)

WEST VIRGINIA

Comic World
613 W. Lee Street
Charleston, WV 25302
PH: 304-343-3874
(a-c,m,q,r)

Comic World
1204 4th Avenue
Huntington, WV 25701
PH: 304-522-3923
(a-c,m,q,r)

Triple Play
2002 3rd Avenue
Huntington, WV 25703
PH: 304-522-1700
(a-c,e,g,m,q-s)

Triple Play/Fielders Choice
414 Stratton St.
Logan, WV 25614
PH: 304-752-9315
(a-c,e,g,m,q-s)

Triple Play/All Star
335 4th Avenue
S. Charleston, WV
25303
PH: 304-744-2602
(a-c,e,g,m,q-s)

WISCONSIN

Capital City Comics
1910 Monroe Street
Madison, WI 53711
PH: 608-251-8445
(a-k,m-r,t-v)

20th Century Books
108 King Street
Madison, WI 53703
PH: 608-251-6226
(c,e,h,m,n,r,t-v)

Capital City Comics
2565 North Downer St.
Milwaukee, WI 53210
PH: 414-332-8199
(a-k,m-r,t-v)

John Hauser
(Appointment Only)
P O Box 51673
New Berlin, WI 53151
PH: 414-789-8227
(a,b,e)

The Mill
1405 Hwy. 47 South
P.O. Box 1456
Woodruff, WI 54568-1456, PH: 715-356-5468
(a,b,e-h,k,r)

WYOMING

Storyteller Entertainment
900 Camel Drive
Gillette, WY 82716
PH: 307-682-2855
(b,c,e,i,m,q-t)

CANADA

ALBERTA

Another Dimension
324-10 Street NW
Calgary, Alberta T2N
1V8, PH: 403-283-7078
(a-c,m,q,r,t)

Another Dimension
4625 Varsity Drive NW
Calgary, Alberta T2A
0Z9, PH: 403-288-1802
(b,c,m,q,r,t)

Another Dimension
7610 Elbow Drive SW
Calgary, Alberta T2V
1K2, PH: 403-255-2588
(a-c,m,q,r-t)

Another Dimension
2640-52 Street NE
Calgary, Alberta T1Y
3R6, PH: 403-293-1272
(b,c,m,q-t)

BRITISH COLUMBIA

L. A. Comics & Books
371 Victoria Street
Kamloops, B. C. V2C
2A3, PH: 604-828-1995
(b,c,e,h,l,m,n,r)

Page After Page
1771 Harvey Avenue
Kelowna, B. C. V1Y
6G4, PH: 604-860-6554
(a,c,e,h,q,r)

Ted's Paperback & Comics
269 Leon Avenue
Kelowna, B. C. V1Y 6J1
PH: 604-763-1258
(a,b,c,e,r)

Golden Age Collectables
830 Granville St.
Vancouver, B.C. Can.
V3Z 1K3
PH: 604-683-2819
(a-d,f,i,j,n,o)

MANITOBA

The Collector's Slave
156 Imperial Avenue
Winnipeg, Manitoba
R2M 0K8 PH: 204-237-4428 (b,c,e-g,k-n,p-r,t,u)

ONTARIO

Pendragon Comics
3759 Lakeshore Blvd.
West
Etobicoke, Ontario M8W
1R1, PH: 416-253-6974
(a-c,e,g,k,m,o-t)

Pendragon Comics
1107 Lorne Park Rd.
Lorne Park Plaza Unit
#18, Mississauga,
Ontario L5H 3A1
PH: 416-278-8625
(b,c,e,g,k,m,o-t)

Gambit Games
479 Elgin Street
Ottawa, Ontario K1C
2M5, PH: 613-237-4976
(b,c,f,g,m,n,s,t)

QUEBEC

Heroes Comic Laval
1116 Cure LaBelle
Chomedey Laval,
Quebec H7V 2V5
PH: 514-686-9155
(a-e,m,q-t,v)

Cosmix
931 Decarie
Montreal, Quebec H4L,
3M3, PH: 514-744-9494
(a-c,e,m,o,q-t,v)

Komico Inc.
4210 Decarie
Montreal, Quebec H4A
3K3, PH: 514-489-4009
(b,c,g,o,q,r)

Metropolis Comics and Cards
1418 Pierce Street
Montreal, Quebec H3H ,
PH: 514-989-9587
(a-c,e,m,q,r)

Premiere Issue
27-A D'Auteuil
Quebec City (Vieux-Quebec)
G1R 4B9 PH: 418-692-3985 (a-c,e,i,m,q-u)

UK

Stateside Comics At Birmingham, 1st Floor,
Virgin Megastore, 98
Corporation St.,
Birmingham B4 6SX,
England PH: 021 236
5735

Incognito Comics
14 Starnes Court, Union
Street, Maidstone, Kent,
England, ME14 1EB
PH: 0622-683642
(a-c,m,q,r,t-v)

Stateside Comics At Virgin, Lower Ground
Floor, Virgin Megastore,
14 Oxford St., London
W1N 9FL, England
PH: 071 637 3966

Stateside Comics At Virgin, 1st Floor, Virgin
Marbel Arch, 527-531
Oxford St., London W1,
England
PH: 071 499 8839,

Stateside Comics At Virgin, Lower Ground
Floor, Virgin Megastore,
608 Wheeler Gate,
Nottingham, Notts. NG1
2NB England 06092
414242,

Stateside Comics At Hamleys
4th Floor, Hamleys,
188-196 Regent Street,
London W1 6BT,
England
PH: 071 287 3097

Stateside Comics-Mail Order, 125 East Barnet
Rd. , Barnet, Herts EN4
*RF, England
PH: 081 449 5535

Stateside Comics North London, 125
East Barnet Rd., Barnet,
Herts EN4 8RF,
England. PH: 081 449
2991

Stateside Comics At Virgin, Lower Ground
Floor, Virgin Megastore,
28-32 Union St.,
Glasgow, G1 3QX,
Scotland
PH: 041 221 2915

HOW TO ADVERTISE IN THIS BOOK:

There are three important reasons to advertise in *Overstreet's Comic Book Price Guide Annual.* This book is the most credible source of comic book information. The annual has the lowest ad rates per reader of any publication. But most importantly, when you advertise in the Overstreet annual, you get results. With over 2,000,000 copies in circulation, your ad goes on forever.

RATES: We are planning special and exciting things for our **25th anniversary Annual** in 1995! Get your ads in early. Please inquire about our low rates.

COLOR AD DEADLINE: October 15, 1994 Please reserve space by Oct. 15, 1994 and have film to us by Nov. 15th, 1994 with full payment.. (Advertiser supplies color separations, 133 line screen, right reading, emulsion down, with each negative clearly marked C,M,Y,K.). Inquire about supplying color on computer Apple computer disc.

Premium color positions *(Inquire about availability)*

Inside front cover, Inside back cover, Outside back cover; any 8 pg. color insert, front, back or center of book, 1st and last pages of color sections.

BLACK & WHITE AD DEADLINE: November 15, 1994. Please have camera ready copy to us by the deadline with full payment.

Premium Black & White Position *(inquire about availability)*

Page 1, page 2, page 3, page 4, pages A-13-15, page A-32, A-33, A-64, A-65, first and last pages of ad sections, last page of book or any page opposite a color page.

Image Dimensions

Size:	***Nonbleed***
Full Page	4 3/4" wide x 7-1/2" tall
1/2 Page	4-3/4" wide x 3-3/4" tall
1/4 Page	2-1/4" wide x 3-3/4" tall
1/8 Page	2-1/4" wide x 1-7/8" tall

Full page ads: Image Size=4-3/4" wide x 7-1/2" tall; Trim Size=5-3/8" wide by 8-3/8" tall; Bleed size=5-5/8" wide x 8-5/8" tall.

General Advertising Information

- If copyrighted characters are used, written permission from the copyright holder must accompany all ads.
- All ads must be camera ready (if half tones are used, they should be shot "light" with an 85 or 100 line screen.)
- All ads must be "G" rated – suitable for all ages.
- All quarter page up advertisers receive a complementary copy of the issue which contains their ad.
- All advertisers must supply Overstreet with their street address and telephone number.
- All payments must be in US funds drawn on a US bank.
- Payment must be included with ad copy.

Special Positions

Special (fixed) positions are available at 15% premium over the gross rate and are subject to availability. (Full page ads only).

Changes or Corrections

Changes and/or corrections must be in writing and received by ad deadline. Overstreet may charge advertiser for any alterations to ad copy.

DIRECTORY OF ADVERTISERS (Cl = Classified, c = color)

Ablesoft c
Acme Comics (Peter Koch) 499
Al Capps 496
Alexander, David T. 506,507
All Colour Productions....................A-109
American Comic Book Co. A-180,526
Anderson, David J., D.D.S. A-217,513
At Your Service Subscriptions....................A-228
Avalon Comics A-200,201

Barnes, Tim....................cl
Bear Mountain (J. Nichols)....................A-197
Bedrock City Comic Company....................479
Best Comics Distribution Center A-208
Bonzai Comics A-99
Bookery Fantasy & Comics 508,509

Caldwell, James Thomas A-196
Capital City Comics....................A-204
Capital City Distribution A-19,21,23,192,193,c
Choo Choo Comics....................485
Christians, A....................cl
Christie's....................A-221
Classified Ads 530,531
Cole Enterprises, Bill....................A-13,14,15
Collectors Ink A-203
Collector's Slave, The....................510
Collector's Unlimited....................A-37
Comicbook Hotline, Inc. cl
Comic Book Shop, The....................517
Comic Carnival....................A-81
Comic Conservation Co. (Hinds)....................A-41,218,489
Comic Accessories Plus 488
Comic Empire (Crazy Jerry)....................cl
Comic Heaven....................A-229230,231,232,233
Comic Man A-113
Comic Net 483
Comic Relief....................A-224
Comic Treasures....................A-208,500
Comics And Stories....................A-181,c
Comics Buyers Guide A-77
Comics On Call (Heroes World Dist.)....................A-33
Comics Plus....................510
Comics Unlimited Ltd. A-205,493
Compu-Comic Software Associates....................A-117
Crazy Jerry (Comic Empire)....................cl
Curtis 1000 478

Data Loggers....................cl
DC Comics, Inc. c
Diamond Comic Distributors c
Diamond International Galleries....................c
Dolgoff, Gary A-2,32,532,533,c
Dolnick, Steve A-49
Dragon's Den A-101,212,503
Dream Factory A-103
Dupius, Rick....................cl
Durango Comics....................504

Edgeman....................A-178,179
Eschenberg, Conrad A-69

Fantasy Illustrated....................A-209
Fantasy Masterpieces....................494
Florida Extravaganza '95 (Mike Herz)....................A-119
Ford, Darren....................cl
Four Color Comics A-1,182,183,480,481
Frazer, Samuel....................A-39
Fuchs, Danny cl

Gaudino, Phil....................510,cl
Gem Comics A-81
Geoffrey's Comics....................501
Gerber Publishing A-234
Glenn's Books (Rausch)....................cl
Golden Age Collectibles....................A-3
Golden Apple 523
Gordy's Character Toys & Models....................504
Grafik XS....................A-109
Great American Ring Co., The (M. Herz)....................A-119,c
Green, John F. cl

Haack, James....................A-111,cl
Hake's Americana & Collectibles A-177
Halegua, Richard 515
Hamilton, Bruce 524
Hamilton Comics ....c,cover 4
Hauser, John 497
Hay, Marty....................A-227
Heroes Aren't Hard to Find 495,511
Heroes Convention A-226
Heroes World Distr. (Comics On Call) A-33
Herz, Mike (Great American Ring co.) A-119,c
Hi-De-Ho Comics & Fantasy....................517
High Quality Comics....................A-67
Hinds, Jef (Comic Conservation Lab) A-41,218,489
Horvitz, Tom....................A-121,484
HSI (Stavros Merjos)....................A-65

Image Comics A-206,207
International Comic Book Co. cl
Iron Vic Comics (Peter Koch) 499

J-A-V Comics....................500
J&S Comics A-198,199
Jim Hanley's Universe 514
Jimmy's The Best Records & Comics....................A-196
Jim's TV Collectibles....................504

Kalb, Ed....................A-210,211,cl
Key Comics A-73
Koch, Joseph 519,520,521
Koch, Peter....................499
Kohne, A cl

DIRECTORY OF ADVERTISERS (cont'd)

Komic Krypt 487

L.A. Comic Conventions (B. Schwartz) A-73
La Tremouille, Robert J. cl
Lenore's TV Guide..490
Levine, Philip A. & Sons 491
Levy, H.M. cl
Limited Treasured Editions (Lee Tennant)
....A-222,223,498
Los Angeles Comic Book & Science Fiction
Convention A-73

Magazines S J. Haack) cl
Man & Superman A-135
Mannarino, Joe (Comics & Stories).................A-181,c
Marvel Comics...Cover 4,c
Merjos, Stavros (HSI)..A-65
Metropolis Comics...............A-4,188,189,190,191,477
Micro Color International c
Mint+ Comics Club A-73
Mitchell, Ken...cl
Modules (J. Haack) cl
Monkey House Comics cl
Moondog's Comics...................................A-25,27,29
Montclair Book Center 527
Motor City Comics...........................A-81,216,228,516
Mountain Empire Collectibles....................................cl
Muchin, Richard (Tomorrow's Treas.)....................482
Multi-Book & Periodical A-127

Narcisi, Lisa...cl
Neverwhere Den, The A-123
New England Comics...A-75
Nichols, John (Bear Mountain)..............................A-197
Norvick, Bill...490
Nostalgia Zone, The 517

O'Kennon, Hugh 502
O'Leary's Books..486
1 if by Cards, 2 if by Comics A-219
Overstreet Comic Book Monthly c
Overstreet Grading Guide...518
Overstreet Premium Ring.......................................A-220
Overstreet Products A-213
Overstreet Quarterly c
Overstreet Video A-176,c
Overstreet Where to Advertise...................................A-35
Pacific Comic Exchange A-194,195,214,215
Passaic Book Center..A-71
Payette, James A-184,185,186,187
Phoenix Ent. A-135

Pierce, Ken..A-109
Plant, Bud (comic art) 527

Quasar Comics 527

Rann, Rick..cl
Redbeard's Book Den c
Restoration Lab A-45
Rosenberg, Marnin..A-97
RTS Unlimited, Inc. A-107

San Diego Comic Con..A-17
San Mateo Comics..A-105
Schwartz, Bruce (L.A. Comic Con) A-73
Showcase Collectibles..528
Showcase New England..534
Slobodian, Calvin cl
Sotheby's..A-43
Starbase 21 529
Stateside Comics A-115
Storyteller...A-135
Studio Daedalus (WhizBang) A-109
Styx International c
Sulipa's Comic World, Doug 522
Swing Frame...512

Tennant Enterprises, Lee A-222,223,498
Third Planet Books...A-225
Tomorrow's Treasures (Muchin) 482
Toy Scouts A-51
TRH Gallery A-121,484
Tropic Comics..505
TV Guide Specialists 517

Verb, Hal cl
Vereneault, Joseph H...A-47
Vincent's Collectibles A-79

Wall To Wall Comics & Cards A-228
Want List Comics A-125,202,525
Wanted by Private Collectors 490
Weiss Auctions, Philip 476
Westfield Company, The...c
WhizBang (Studio Daedalus) A-109
Whyte, Donald A A-73
Wilson, David cl
Wonderland Comics & SF 490
Wong, E.K. cl
World's Finest Comics A-54-64

Yaruss, David...cl
Yee, Harley A-31,492,cl

TV FOR COMIC COLLECTORS

New from Overstreet & Threshold Home Video!

Featuring interviews, cameos, and commentary from an all-star lineup:

Murphy Anderson
Carl Barks
Dan Barry
Bill Cole
Peter David
Will Eisner
Harlan Ellison
Danny Fuchs
Bill Gaines
Steve Geppi
Bruce Hamilton
Russ Heath
Roger Hill
Gil Kane
Jack Kirby
Stan Lee
Paul Levitz
Todd McFarlane
Shelly Moldoff
Marty Nodell
Paul Norris
Bob Overstreet
Chris Pedrin
Robert Rogovin
Julius Schwartz
Jim Shooter
Jeff Smith
Dick Sprang
Vincent Sullivan
Jerry Weist

and many, many more!

The Overstreet WORLD OF COMIC BOOKS one hour video is now available direct from Overstreet! Only $19.95 each plus $3.50 postage and handling!

Overstreet Publications, Inc.
PO Box 2610, Cleveland, TN 37320-2610
(615) 472-4135
Allow 4-6 weeks for delivery.

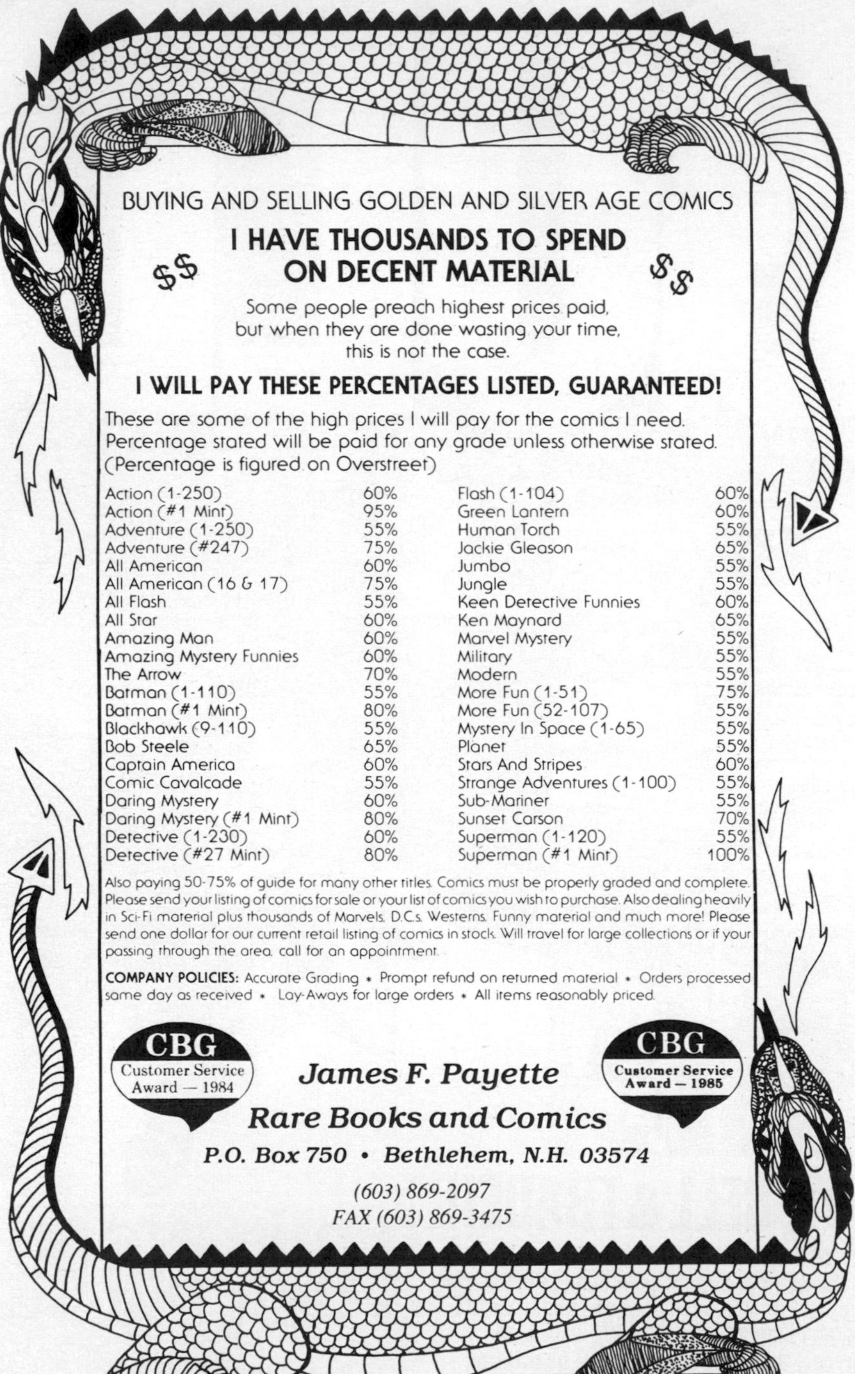

BUYING AND SELLING GOLDEN AND SILVER AGE COMICS
I HAVE THOUSANDS TO SPEND
$$ ON DECENT MATERIAL $$
Some people preach highest prices paid, but when they are done wasting your time, this is not the case.
I WILL PAY THESE PERCENTAGES LISTED, GUARANTEED!
These are some of the high prices I will pay for the comics I need. Percentage stated will be paid for any grade unless otherwise stated. (Percentage is figured on Overstreet)
Action (1-250) 60%
Action (#1 Mint) 95%
Adventure (1-250) 55%
Adventure (#247) 75%
All American 60%
All American (16 & 17) 75%
All Flash 55%
All Star 60%
Amazing Man 60%
Amazing Mystery Funnies 60%
The Arrow 70%
Batman (1-110) 55%
Batman (#1 Mint) 80%
Blackhawk (9-110) 55%
Bob Steele 65%
Captain America 60%
Comic Cavalcade 55%
Daring Mystery 60%
Daring Mystery (#1 Mint) 80%
Detective (1-230) 60%
Detective (#27 Mint) 80%
Flash (1-104) 60%
Green Lantern 60%
Human Torch 55%
Jackie Gleason 65%
Jumbo 55%
Jungle 55%
Keen Detective Funnies 60%
Ken Maynard 65%
Marvel Mystery 55%
Military 55%
Modern 55%
More Fun (1-51) 75%
More Fun (52-107) 55%
Mystery In Space (1-65) 55%
Planet 55%
Stars And Stripes 60%
Strange Adventures (1-100) 55%
Sub-Mariner 55%
Sunset Carson 70%
Superman (1-120) 55%
Superman (#1 Mint) 100%
Also paying 50-75% of guide for many other titles. Comics must be properly graded and complete. Please send your listing of comics for sale or your list of comics you wish to purchase. Also dealing heavily in Sci-Fi material plus thousands of Marvels, D.C.s, Westerns, Funny material and much more! Please send one dollar for our current retail listing of comics in stock. Will travel for large collections or if your passing through the area, call for an appointment.
COMPANY POLICIES: Accurate Grading • Prompt refund on returned material • Orders processed same day as received • Lay-Aways for large orders • All items reasonably priced.
CBG Customer Service Award — 1984
CBG Customer Service Award — 1985
James F. Payette
Rare Books and Comics
P.O. Box 750 • Bethlehem, N.H. 03574
(603) 869-2097
FAX (603) 869-3475

COMIC COLLECTOR/
DEALER
WANTS YOUR COMICS!
Paying up to 100% or more of guide for
many comics of interest.
▼ POINTS TO CONSIDER ▼
1. I have 20 years experience in comic fandom. I have bought many of the major collections over the years and purchased them against competing bidders.
2. Consigning your comics to an auction does not always let you realize your collection's potentail. Many collectors and dealers end up purchasing a large portion of these comics well below market value. Plus the fact that you do not receive your money in a timely manner. Selling to us would assure you of immediate payment.
3. Being a collector/dealer allows me the ability to buy your entire collection and pay you the most for it. We will figure individual demand items at a high percentage and adjust the percentage on lesser items. The end result is maximizing your value.
4. You have nothing to lose by making contact with me. Why miss out on your best offer?
Give us a try! CALL 603-869-2097 TODAY!
James F. Payette
Rare Books & Comics
P.O. Box 750 • Bethlehem, NH 03574
Phone 603-869-2097 • Fax 603-869-3475
PLEASE SEE MY OTHER ADS FOR FURTHER REFERENCE

We are paying 60% of guide for the following:

- Adventure (32-267)
- Adv. of Bob Hope (1-50)
- Adv. of Jerry Lewis (1-50)
- Adv. of Ozzie & Harriet
- All American
- All Flash
- All New
- All Top (8-18)
- Blackhawk (9-110)
- Blue Beetle (47-57)
- Captain America (1st)
- Flash (1st)
- Hit (1-20)
- House of Mystery (1-50)
- House of Secrets (1-25)
- Leading (1-14)
- Legend of Dan'l Boone
- Mary Marvel
- Military
- Movie Comics (D.C.)
- My Greatest Adventure (1-50)
- Mystery Men
- National (1-23)
- New Book of Comics
- Phantom Stranger
- Science (Fox)
- Shadow (Fox)
- Showcase (1-30)
- Speed (1-20)
- Superman (1-125)
- Superman's Pal (1-30)

We are paying 55% of guide for the following:

- Airboy
- Air Fighters
- All Select
- All Star
- All Winners
- Amazing Spiderman (1-20)
- America's Greatest
- Blonde Phamtom
- Brave & the Bold (1-30)
- Brenda Starr (1-12)
- Bulletman
- Captain Marvel
- Captain Marvel Jr.
- Captain Midnight
- Catman
- Challengers of the Unknown (1-10)
- Classics Comics (1st 1-20)
- Comic Cavalcade (1-29)
- Crash
- Daredevil (1st 1-20)
- Daring Mystery
- Dollman
- Fantastic
- Fantastic Four (1-20)
- Frontier Fighters
- Green Hornet (1-20)
- Human Torch
- Ibis
- John Wayne
- JO-JO (7-29)
- Journey into Mystery (1-85)
- Jungle (1-10)
- Kid Komics
- Lash Larue (1-46)
- Marvel Family
- Marvel Mystery
- Master
- Miss Fury
- Modern
- More Fun (52-107)
- Mystery In Space (1-90)
- Mystic (1st)
- Nickel
- Pep (1-40)
- Phamtom Lady
- Planet
- Pogo Possum
- Police (1-20)
- Rangers (1-20)
- Rulah
- Saint
- Sensation
- Shield Wizard
- Silver Streak (1-17)
- Smash
- Spy Smasher
- Star Spangled
- Strange Adventure (1-120)
- Strange Tales (1-100)
- Sub-Mariner (1st)
- Superboy (1-50)
- Tomahawk (1-30)
- Top-Notch
- U.S.A.
- W.D. Comics & Stories (1-40)
- Weird Comics
- Whiz
- World's Finest (1-110)
- Young Allies
- Zip (1-39)
- Zoot (7-16)

We are also paying 50-75% of guide for many other titles. Comics must be properly graded and complete. Please send your listing of comics for sale or your list of comics you wish to purchase. We are also dealing heavily in Sci-Fi material plus thousands of Marvels, D.C.'s Western, Funny Material and Much More! Please Send one dollar for our current retail listing of comics in stock. Will Travel for Large Collections or if you're passing through the area call for an appointment.

JAMES F. PAYETTE
RARE BOOKS AND COMICS
P.O. BOX 750, BETHLEHEM, NH 03574
(603) 869-2097 Fax (603) 869-3475

© DIS

COMIC BOOKS WANTED

NO COLLECTION TOO LARGE OR TOO SMALL

NO ONE PAYS MORE!

IF YOU HAVE COMIC BOOKS TO SELL, CONTACT US!

WE WILL TRAVEL TO VIEW LARGE COLLECTIONS

© MCG

© DC

© DC

METROPOLIS COMICS

7 W. 18TH Street
New York, NY 10011
(212)627-9691 FAX: (212)627-5947
By Appointment Only

© FAW

© FAW

METROPOLIS COMICS

- Accurate Grading • Competitive Pricing
- Large Selection Of Golden & Silver age
- Complete Want List Service
- New Approval Policy (Available to Want List Customers Only)

Will ship all books under $5000 to any want list customer without prepayment.

Payment due within 7 days unless other arrangements are made.
Time payments possible.

© DC

© MCG

METROPOLIS

7 W. 18th Street
New York, NY 10011
(212) 627-9691 FAX: (212) 627-5947
By Appointment Only

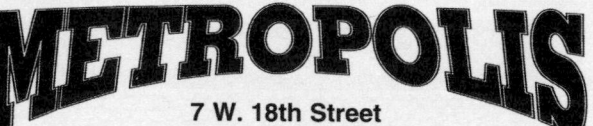

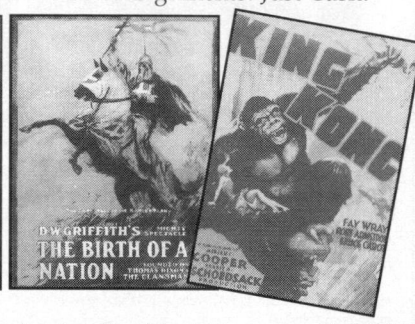

Break Through With Capital City

Capital City is breaking through with a distribution center near you!

Now with 21 locations coast to coast

Capital offers the best quality product at the lowest price. Capital specializes in a variety of comics, games, videos, trading cards, and more!

If you're a retailer interested in increasing your business, it's time to break through to success with Capital City. Explore new opportunities by calling (608) 223-2000. Ask for a national customer service representative, and we'll open an account for you today.

TM

PACIFIC COMIC EXCHANGE, INC.

The Pacific Comic Exchange, Inc. (PCE) is the first computerized *"on-line"* comic book trading company specializing in Golden and Silver Age comics from 1933-1969. All comics listed on *"The Exchange"* have been graded and certified by the Comic Grading Service of America (CGSA), which has developed a new standardized numerical grading system that ensures an unprecedented degree of accuracy and consistency.

CGSA	M	NM/M	NM	VFN/NM	VFN	FN/VFN	FN	VG/FN	VG	G/VG	G	Fr	Pr
	100,99,98,97,96,95,94,93,92,91	90	88,85,80,75	70	65,60,55	50	45,40,35	30	25,20	15	10	6	3
PgQ	0 1 2 2.5	3	3.3 4	5	6	6.5	7	7.5	8	8.5	9	9.5	10

LIQUIDITY

- ❖ **PCE** is an international network of dealers, collectors, and retailers,
- ❖ Providing an excellent selection of Golden and Silver Age comics,
- ❖ Negotiable prices, prompt payment to Sellers.
- ❖ Sellers enjoy the lowest brokerage commissions (8% to 13%) in the industry.

CONFIDENCE AND PROTECTION

- ❖ **CGSA** certified books are guaranteed to be in stated condition.
- ❖ Full disclosure of any restoration, is certified by such respected experts as **Susan Ciccone** of **The Restoration Lab.**
- ❖ All books are uniquely identified and catalogued - Buyers and Sellers are protected from fraudulent substitution or damage.

ACCESS

- ❖ *"The Exchange"* is accessible via phone, computer or mail.
- ❖ Detailed monthly reports (available through subscription) of sales data, updated listings, special market analyses, etc., help Buyers and Sellers make informed decisions.
- ❖ Buyers have access to a large selection of Golden and Silver age comics at negotiable prices.

COMPREHENSIVE ON-LINE SERVICE

- ❖ All statistics available *"on-line"*: prices, market trends, grading, restoration information, etc.
- ❖ "Want Lists" link Sellers with interested Buyers.
- ❖ Buyers and Sellers can utilize extended "after hours" trading.

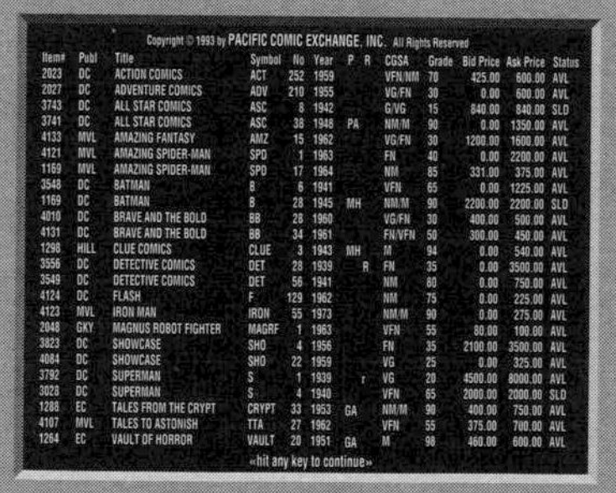
Copyright © 1993 by PACIFIC COMIC EXCHANGE, INC. All Rights Reserved

Item#	Publ	Title	Symbol	No	Year	P	R	CGSA	Grade	Bid Price	Ask Price	Status
2023	DC	ACTION COMICS	ACT	252	1959			VFN/NM	70	425.00	600.00	AVL
2027	DC	ADVENTURE COMICS	ADV	210	1955			VG/FN	30	0.00	600.00	AVL
3743	DC	ALL STAR COMICS	ASC	8	1942			G/VG	15	840.00	840.00	SLD
3741	DC	ALL STAR COMICS	ASC	38	1948	PA		NM/M	90	0.00	1350.00	AVL
4133	MVL	AMAZING FANTASY	AMZ	15	1962			VG/FN	30	1200.00	1600.00	AVL
4121	MVL	AMAZING SPIDER-MAN	SPD	1	1963			FN	40	0.00	2200.00	AVL
1169	MVL	AMAZING SPIDER-MAN	SPD	17	1964			NM	85	331.00	375.00	AVL
3548	DC	BATMAN	B	6	1941			VFN	65	0.00	1225.00	AVL
1169	DC	BATMAN	B	28	1945	MH		NM/M	90	2200.00	2200.00	SLD
4010	DC	BRAVE AND THE BOLD	BB	28	1960			VG/FN	30	400.00	500.00	AVL
4131	DC	BRAVE AND THE BOLD	BB	34	1961			FN/VFN	50	300.00	450.00	AVL
1298	HILL	CLUE COMICS	CLUE	3	1943	MH		M	94	0.00	540.00	AVL
3556	DC	DETECTIVE COMICS	DET	28	1939		R	FN	35	0.00	3500.00	AVL
3549	DC	DETECTIVE COMICS	DET	56	1941			NM	80	0.00	750.00	AVL
4124	DC	FLASH	F	129	1962			NM	75	0.00	225.00	AVL
4123	MVL	IRON MAN	IRON	55	1973			NM/M	90	0.00	275.00	AVL
2048	GKY	MAGNUS ROBOT FIGHTER	MAGRF	1	1963			VFN	55	80.00	100.00	AVL
3823	DC	SHOWCASE	SHO	4	1956			FN	35	2100.00	3500.00	AVL
4084	DC	SHOWCASE	SHO	22	1959			VG	25	0.00	325.00	AVL
3792	DC	SUPERMAN	S	1	1939		r	VG	20	4500.00	8000.00	AVL
3028	DC	SUPERMAN	S	4	1940			VFN	65	2000.00	2000.00	SLD
1288	EC	TALES FROM THE CRYPT	CRYPT	33	1953	GA		NM/M	90	400.00	750.00	AVL
4107	MVL	TALES TO ASTONISH	TTA	27	1962			VFN	55	375.00	700.00	AVL
1264	EC	VAULT OF HORROR	VAULT	20	1951	GA		M	98	460.00	600.00	AVL

«hit any key to continue»

TRADE WITH CONFIDENCE, TRADE WITH PCE

Call or write (include your telephone number) for more information about opening a free trading account, viewing a demonstration of the **PCE** *"on-line"* service, or selling comics on *"The Exchange."*

Meetings and consultations are arranged by appointment only.

Pacific Comic Exchange, Inc.
P.O. Box 34849 ❖ Los Angeles, CA ❖ 90034
Tel: (310) 836-PCEI Fax: (310) 836-7127 Modem: (310) 836-3076

DET27 25$29850 MFC52 15$3575 S1 20$7700 B1 15$5500 BB28 65$2750 SHO4 25$2300 AMZ15 40$2200

THE COMIC GRADING SERVICE OF AMERICA

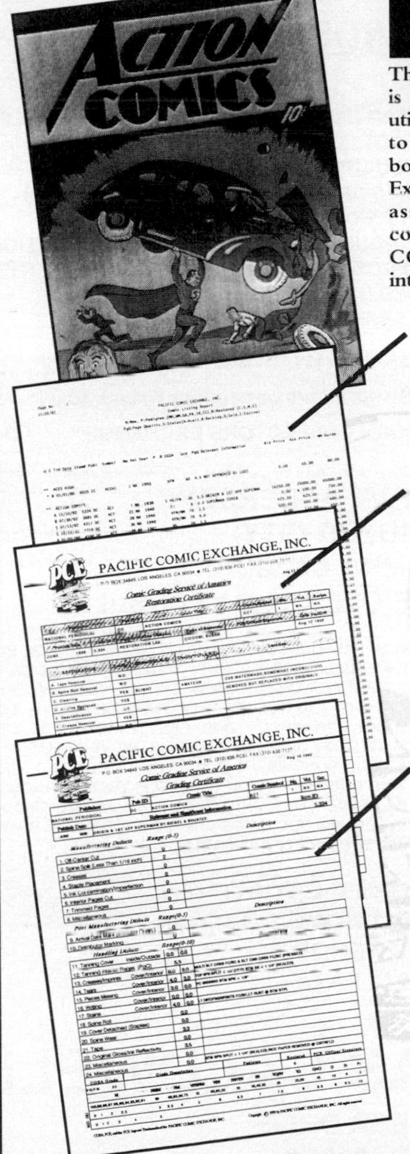

The Comic Grading Service of America (CGSA) is the first professional comic grading service to utilize a revolutionary, scientific grading system to assure accurately and consistently graded books. All books listed on the Pacific Comic Exchange (PCE) are graded in this fashion and assure that your purchase is made with confidence and knowledge. Alternatively, the CGSA will certify your books or act as an intermediary between Buyer and Seller.

THE COMIC LISTING REPORT

❖ Every month **PCE** issues a report (available through subscription) about the comic books available for sale. Each book is listed with a grade (verified by **CGSA**), Bid and Ask prices, and other relevant information.

CGSA RESTORATION CERTIFICATE

❖ The **CGSA** in collaboration with **Susan Ciccone** of **The Restoration Lab**, requires all restored books undergo a complete evaluation before being listed on *"The Exchange."* This certificate records, in depth, any change or modification made to the book. This procedure insures that the buyer is informed of the "true" condition of the restored book and protected against fraud. This information is also available *"on-line"* or upon request to users of *"The Exchange."*

CGSA GRADING CERTIFICATE

❖ **PCE** prides itself for using the first ever 100 point scale grading system (provided by the **CGSA**). Each book is examined on a defect-by-defect basis with a description and numerical value assigned for every defect. These values are used to create an accurate assessment of the books condition.

❖ Each book is evaluated independently by a team of expert graders who use the 100 point system to arrive at a final grade. This ensures Buyer and Seller an objective and accurate final grade.

❖ The **CGSA** system is the "state of the art" in comic book grading. Grading is now a science and no longer an "eye of the beholder" art.

Pacific Comic Exchange, Inc.
P.O. Box 34849 ❖ Los Angeles, CA ❖ 90034
Tel: (310) 836-PCEI Fax: (310) 836-7127 Modem: (310) 836-3076

DET27 25$29850 MFC52 15$3575 S1 20$7700 B1 15$5500 BB28 65$2750 SHO4 25$2300 AMZ15 40$2200

CGSA is a division of the Pacific Comic Exchange, Inc.
CGSA, PCE, and the PCE logo are trademarks of the Pacific Comic Exchange, Inc.

WANTED — BUYING

WE SPECIALIZE IN BUYING ENTIRE COLLECTIONS

PAYING 60% of GUIDE for ALL PRE-1964 ISSUES

PAYING *40%* OF GUIDE FOR ALL 1964–69 ISSUES

ONLY LISTED OVERSTREET PRICES WILL BE USED. BOOKS MUST FULLY QUALIFY FOR NEXT HIGHER GRADE TO RECEIVE THE NEXT HIGHER PRICE.

ALSO BUYING:

Issues from 1970–date of all currently published titles. In VF or Better we pay 100% of Good.

Duplicates will be accepted up to 10% of total shipment.

No need to write first. We will buy all you ship under the above conditions.

Reprints, overgraded and items below fair condition not wanted and returned only at sender's expense plus handling charges.

All buying prices listed here apply to collections when sold intact. We reserve the right to make appropriate changes (either higher or lower) when negotiating on individual or selected issues.

SUPER SALES CATALOG ONLY $2.00

Contains everything from Superheroes to Ducks! Includes Westerns, Independents, Combat, Space, Magazines and much, much more.

MOST COMPLETE LISTING NEXT TO OVERSTREET'S

Covers virtually every issue printed in the last 20-25 years and all available for sale in three different grades. Order your catalog today!

Individual titles of interest sent FREE with SASE.

ALSO AVAILABLE:

Complete inventory lists of Pre-1964 Books in these categories:

- ★ Westerns
- ★ Movies and TV
- ★ Funny Animals, Disney, Archie, etc.
- ★ Superhero, Adventure, etc.

EACH LIST ONLY $1.00 or *ALL 4 LISTS FOR $2.00*

(One list may be requested free when ordering Super Sales Catalog)

COMICS ARE OUR BUSINESS, COMIC CARDS OUR HOBBY

Collectors Ink

932-A W. 8th Ave. ☆ Chico, CA ☆ 95926

(916) 345-0958 ☆ Tues.–Sat. 10–5:30

In association with

THE PENNY RANCH

SERVING THE COLLECTING COMMUNITY SINCE 1967

SHADOWHAWK

NOT JUST
ANOTHER
PUBLISHER,
BUT A
TIGHTLY KNIT
FAMILY!
image™
COMICS OF CHOICE

(ED KALB, Page 2)
1-6 ....2.25

INHUMANS (1975)
1 ....5.50
2,4-11 ....2.50

INVADERS (1975)
6-10 ....2.25
11-41 ....1.75
Annual 1 ....3.50

IRON MAN
78-99,101-117 ....2.50
100 ....7.25
118 ....5.50
119-128 ....2.50
129-149 ....2.00
150,169,170 ....4.00
151-168,171-199 ....1.25
200,225 ....4.00
201-224,232-241 ....1.00
226-231,242,244 ....2.50
243,245-249 ....1.00
250 ....1.75
251-280,282-289 ....1.00
281,290 ....2.50
291-295,up 1.00
Annual 4 ....3.50
5-14 ....1.50

JOHN CARTER WARLORD OF MARS (1977)
1,18 ....3.00
2-17,19-28 ....1.25

JUSTICE (1986)
1-32 75

KITTY PRYDE AND WOLVERINE
1-3 ....1.75
4-6 ....2.75

LONGSHOT (1985)
1,2,6 ....10.00
3-5 ....8.00

MARVEL CLASSICS (1976)
2-36 ....2.00

MARVEL COMICS PRESENTS
1 ....5.00
2-37,42-47 ....1.00
38-41,48-62 ....2.00
63,66-71,83,84 ....1.00
64,65,72-82,85-87 ....2.00
88-131,up 1.00

MARVEL FANFARE
1,2 ....6.00
3,4 ....4.00
5,6,33,42,45,51,54,55 ....2.00
7-32,34-41,43,44,46-50,52, 53,56-60 ....1.25

MARVEL FEATURE (1975, Red Sonja)
1 ....5.00
2-7 (Thorne) 2.00

MARVEL PREMIERE (1972)
6-10 ....3.50
11-14 ....2.50
16-24 ....4.50
26,27,29-49 ....1.25

MARVEL SPOTLIGHT (1971)
12 ....15.00
13,14 ....7.50
15,16,22 ....6.00
17-21,23,24 ....4.50
28,29,32,33 ....5.50

MARVEL SWIMSUIT SPECIAL
1993 ....4.00

MARVEL TEAM UP
16-29 ....4.00
30-45,47-52 ....2.50
46,58,65 ....4.50
53,54,55 ....6.75
56,57,59-61,69 ....2.50
62-64,66-68 ....2.00
70-85,87-90 ....1.50
86,91 ....4.00
92-99 ....1.50
100 ....5.50
101-116,118-149 ....1.25
117 ....7.50
150 ....3.50
Annual 1 ....13.50
2 ....2.50
3-7 ....1.75

MARVEL TWO IN ONE
2,4,7,9 ....4.00
6 ....7.50
8,15,27 ....5.50
10-14 ....2.00
16-26,28-51 ....1.50
52,53,55-68 ....1.25
54 ....7.50
69,80 ....4.00
70-79,81-99 ....1.25
100 ....2.50

MASTER OF KUNG FU (1974)
21-30 ....3.00
31-51 ....2.00
52-99,101-124 ....1.25
100,125 ....3.00

MICRONAUTS (1979)
1,37 ....2.50
1 (10 copies) 17.50
2-36,38-59 ....1.00

MIDNIGHT SONS UNLIMITED
1,2 ....3.50

MOON KNIGHT (1980)
1 ....4.00
2-14,16-34,36-38 ....1.25
15,35 ....2.50

MORBIUS
1 ....2.50
2-13 ....1.25

MS. MARVEL (1977)
1,16 ....4.00
2-15,17-23 ....2.00

NAMOR THE SUB-MARINER
27-31 ....2.75
32-36 ....2.25
37 ....1.75
38-43,up 1.00

NEW MUTANTS (1983)
1 ....0.00
2,16 ....3.50
3-15,17,19,20 ....2.00
18,21 ....4.00
22-74,76-84 ....1.25
75,85,99 ....3.50
86,90,91,95-98 ....6.75
88,89 ....10.75
93,94 ....8.00
100 ....4.50

NEW WARRIORS
1 ....10.50
2 ....6.75
3-5,8,9 ....3.50
6,7 ....2.75
10 10 ....1.25
20-39,up 1.00

NOVA (1976)
1 ....9.00
2 ....4.50
3,5 ....2.50
4,6-25 ....1.75

PETER PARKER THE SPECTACULAR SPIDER-MAN
1 ....35.00
2,6-8 ....12.00
3-5 ....5.50
9,10,17,18 ....4.50
11-16,19-26 ....2.75
27,28 ....10.50
29-55 ....2.50
56,64 ....6.75
57-63,65-68 ....2.25
69,70,75 ....4.00
71-74,76-80,84 ....1.50
81,82 ....5.50
83 ....4.50
85 ....13.50
86-99 ....1.25
100 ....3.50
101-115,117,118 ....1.00
116,119 ....5.00
120-130,134-139 ....1.00
131-133,140-143 ....3.75
144-146,148-157 ....1.00
147 ....8.00
158 ....5.50
159,160,189 ....3.50
161-188,190-199,201-up 1.00
200 ....2.50
Annual 1 ....4.50
2,3,13 ....2.50
4-12 ....1.75

POWER MAN/HERO FOR HIRE & IRON FIST (1972)
10-16,18-20 ....3.00
17 ....5.50
21-31 ....2.00
32-47,51-56 ....1.50
58-65,67-77 ....1.00
79-83,85-124 ....1.00

PUNISHER (1986, mini)
1 ....22.50
2,3 ....10.75
4,5 ....6.75

PUNISHER (1987)
1 ....17.50
2-7 ....5.50
8,9 ....6.75
10 ....12.00
11-15 ....3.50
16-25 ....2.00
26-49,51-74 ....1.00
50,75 ....2.25
76-83,up 1.00
Annual 1 ....6.00
2-5 ....1.75

PUNISHER 2099
1 ....2.00
2-12,up 1.00

PUNISHER WAR JOURNAL
1 ....12.00
2 ....6.00
3-5 ....4.00
6 ....6.75
7,8 ....4.00
9-15 ....2.00
16-57,up 1.25

RAVAGE 2099
1 ....2.00
2-12,up 1.00

RED SONJA (1977)
1 ....4.00
2-15 ....1.50

ROM (1979)
1,17,18 ....3.50
2-16,19-75 ....1.00
Annual 1-4 ....1.25

SABRETOOTH
1 ....2.50

SAVAGE SHE-HULK (1980)
2-25 ....1.25

SECRET DEFENDERS
1 ....2.50
2-5 ....1.50

SECRET WARS I
1 ....2.50
2-7,9-12 ....1.50
8 ....6.00

SECRET WARS II
1-9 ....1.25

SENSATIONAL SHE HULK
1,50 ....2.50
2-49,51-up 1.25

SILVER SURFER (1987)
1 ....7.50
2-14 ....1.50
15 ....6.00
16 ....3.50
17-33 ....1.25
34 ....7.25
35 ....6.00
36-38,46,47,50 ....4.00
39-45,48,49 ....2.75
51-85,up 1.00
Annual 1 ....4.00
2-5 ....1.75
6 ....2.50

SILVER SURFER/ WARLOCK RESURRECTION
1-4 ....2.25

SOLO AVENGERS (1987)
1 ....2.50
2-20 ....1.00

SPIDER-MAN
1 silver 3.50
1 green 3.50
1 silver, bag 30.00
1 green, bag 10.75
2-8,26 ....2.50
9-16 ....2.00
17-25,27-42,up 1.25

SPIDER-MAN 2099
1 ....2.00
2-10,up 1.00

SPIDER-MAN UNLIMITED
1,2 ....3.50

SPIDER WOMAN (1978)
1 ....5.00
2-36,39-49 ....1.25
37,38,50 ....3.00

STAR WARS (1977)
1 ....7.50
2-4 ....3.50
5-10 ....2.50
11-21 ....2.00
22-50 ....1.75
51-83 ....1.50

SUPER VILLAIN TEAM UP (1975)
2 ....3.00
3-17 ....2.50

THING (1983)
1 ....4.00
2-36 ....1.00

THOR
215-224 ....3.00
227-239 ....2.00
240-260 ....1.75
261-299,301-305 ....1.50
300,306 ....3.50
307-336 ....1.50
337 ....6.00
338,374,384,400 ....3.50
339-373,375-383 ....1.00
385-399,401-410 ....1.00
411 ....5.00
412 ....10.00
413-428,431 ....1.00
429,430,432,450 ....2.25
433 ....3.50
434-449,451-466,up 1.00
Annual 5-7 ....4.00
8-17 ....1.75
18 ....2.50

TOMB OF DRACULA (1972)
13,15-17,50 ....3.50
22-49 ....2.25
51-69 ....2.00

2001 A SPACE ODYSSEY (1976)
1-10 ....1.50

VENOM
1-6 ....2.50

VISION AND THE SCARLET WITCH
1-4 (1982) 1.25
1-12 (1985) 1.00

WARLOCK (1975)
11 ....12.00
12-14 ....7.25
15 ....15.00

WARLOCK CHRONICLES
1 ....2.50
2,3 ....2.00

WEB OF SPIDER-MAN
1 ....16.50
2 ....5.50
3-10 ....3.00
11-19 ....2.00
20-28 ....1.50
29 ....12.50
30,48 ....8.00
31,32,38 ....5.50
33-37,39-47,49 ....1.50
50 ....2.75
51-58 ....1.25
59-61,69,90 ....4.00
62-68,70-89,91-99,101-104, up 1.25
100 ....2.50
Annual 1,2 ....3.00
3-8 ....2.25
9 ....2.50

WEREWOLF BY NIGHT (1972)
5-10 ....4.50
11-31,34-36,38-43 ....3.00

WEST COAST AVENGERS (1984, mini)
1-4 ....2.00

WEST COAST AVENGERS (1985)
1 ....4.50
2-46 ....1.00
Annual 1-3 ....1.50

WHAT IF? (1977)
1 ....15.00
2-13 ....3.50
14-16 ....2.75
17,27,28 ....4.50
18-26,29,30,32-47 ....2.00

WOLVERINE (1982)
1 ....16.00
2-4 ....12.50

WOLVERINE (1987)
1 ....17.50
2 ....6.50
3-5 ....5.50
6-9 ....4.00
10 ....15.00
11-17 ....2.75
18-29 ....2.50
30-40,43 ....1.75
41,42 ....4.50
44-49 ....1.50
50 ....3.00
51-71,up 1.25

WOLVERINE SAGA
1-4 ....2.75

X-FACTOR (1986)
1 ....6.00
2-7 ....2.00
8-22 ....1.75
23 ....5.50
24 ....7.50
25,26 ....3.00
27-39,41,50 ....1.25
40,51-53,60 ....4.00
42-49 ....1.00
54-59 ....1.25
61-65 ....3.50
66-68,71 ....2.75
69,70,72-83,87-91,93,up 1.00
84-86 ....1.50
92 ....3.00
Annual 1-7 ....1.75
8 ....2.50

X-FORCE
1 (5 issues with different cards) set 10.75
2,3,5-15,19-24,up 1.25
4,16-18 ....1.50

X-MEN (UNCANNY)
97,99,100,108,109 ....25.00
102,107,110,112,113,115-118,129,139,141 ....12.00
119,122,130,140,142 ....10.00
120,121 ....25.00
123-128,131-138 ....6.75
143,155-161,163,164,166-170,172 ....3.00
144-154,165 ....2.50
162 ....4.50
171 ....6.00
173-183 ....2.50
184,193 ....4.00
185-192,194-199 ....2.25
200,205 ....4.50
201 ....13.50
202-204,206-209 ....2.25
210,211,222 ....7.50
212,213 ....16.00
214-221,223,224 ....1.50
225-227 ....4.00
228-247,249-255 ....1.50
248 ....13.50
256-258 ....6.00
259-265 ....1.50
266,268 ....17.50
267 ....7.50
269-273,275,283 ....4.00
274,276,277,281,282 ....2.25
278-280,284-293,297-299
301-up 1.25
294-296 ....1.50
300 ....3.50
Annual 3 ....10.00
6-8 ....2.25
9,10,14 ....4.00
11-13,15,16 ....1.75
17 ....2.50

X-MEN (1991)
1 (set of all 5 editions) ..10.75
2,3 ....1.50
11-20,up 1.25

X-MEN AND ALPHA FLIGHT (1985)
1,2 ....2.75

X-MEN AND THE MICRONAUTS (1984)
1-4 ....1.25

X-MEN 2099
1 ....1.75

X-MEN UNLIMITED
1 ....3.50

THE BEST IN THE HOBBY!

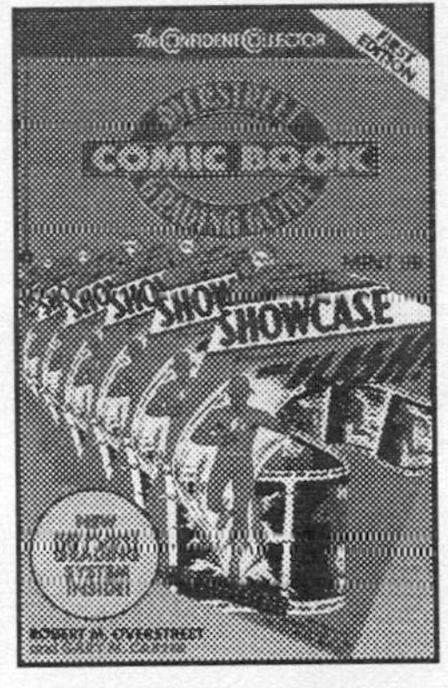

1

OVERSTREET COMIC BOOK GRADING GUIDE (with *FREE* Grading Card). Grading is the key to value!! The Overstreet Comic Book GRADING GUIDE is the only book that teaches you how to grade your comics in simple, easy to understand terms. The 1st edition also introduces the new Overstreet 100 point comic book grading system, contains "defects guide," and features an astonishing color section with examples of rare pedigree copies. This handy book comes with a grading card that helps you identify page whiteness. The Card, a $2.49 value, is included absolutely FREE with each order. The Overstreet Grading Guide is only $12.00 per copy, plus $3.00 Postage & Handling.

OVERSTREET GOLDEN AGE & SILVER AGE QUARTERLY. The ultimate magazine for Golden Age and Silver Age collectors, each giant 176 page issue contains exclusive articles, features, and investment tips... written especially for the ADVANCED comic book collector! Three issues a year contain the only update of Golden Age prices available... and every forth issue of the Overstreet Golden Age & Silver Age Quarterly contains the valuable Overstreet Golden Age and Silver Age YEARLY INVESTMENT GUIDE, with exclusive investor information available only from Overstreet! 3 GIANT issues mailed Priority is only $23.95 postage paid!

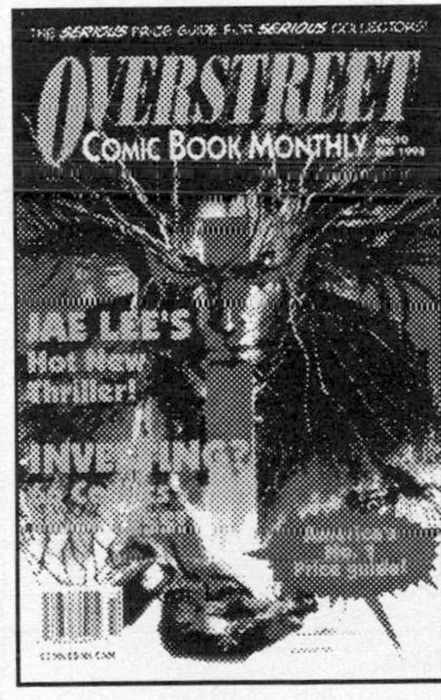

The most exciting magazine in the hobby today... The OVERSTREET COMIC BOOK MONTHLY! Rob Liefeld, Todd McFarlane, Joe Quesada, Jae Lee... are just a few of the names mentioned in the pages of America's leading monthly comic book price guide magazine! Filled with articles, previews, interviews with hot artists, market reports, and the most accurate comic and card price guide in print... the Overstreet Comic Book Monthly... is the hottest comic book collector's magazine on the stands!!! Don't miss a single issue! Subscribe today! A ten issue subscription, mailed 3rd Class, is just $24.95 postage paid! In a hurry? Want to be among the first in the country see what your comics are worth? Get ten big issues of the Overstreet Comic Book Monthly mailed for just $64.95 postage paid!

Available at your local comic shop or direct from Overstreet
Visa & MasterCard Orders by phone: (615) 472-4135
Monday through Friday, 8:30 a.m. til 5:30 p.m., Eastern time!

SELLERS

- ❖ Do you want top dollar for your comics?
- ❖ Do you want an international market for your comics but don't want to pay for advertising?
- ❖ Do you want someone else to take care of qualifying buyers and shipping your books?

PCE IS HERE TO HELP!

Sample Sales for 1993:

© DC

SOLD: Action Comics 1
$24,200

© MEG

SOLD: Marvel Comics 1
$55,000

	CGSA		
Action Comics 1	R VG/FN	30	$24,200
All Select Comics 1 (Carson City)	NM	85	$3,300
Amazing Spider-Man 1	VFN	60	$4,600
Avengers 1	NM	80	$2,000
Batman 1	G	10	$4,750
Captain America Comics 1	VG/FN	30	$7,050
Detective Comics 38	G/VG	15	$2,300
Famous Funnies Carnival Comics	VF/NM	70	$3,850
Fantastic Four 1	VF/NM	70	$9,900
Flash 105	VFN	60	$2,550
Flash Comics 1	R taVG	20	$2,750

	CGSA		
Green Lantern 1 (Golden Age)	VFN	65	$11,000
Incredible Hulk 1	VFN	65	$3,650
Journey Into Mystery 83	VFN	60	$2,500
Mad 5 (Gaines File Copy)	M	94	$2,200
Marvel Comics 1	VFN	60	$55,000
Showcase 8	FN/VFN	50	$3,400
Strange Tales 110	NM	75	$1,550
Tales of Suspense 39	NM	80	$4,400
Tales to Astonish 27	NM	80	$6,050
Turok Son of Stone 1 (File Copy)	NM	80	$1,500
X-Men 1	NM	75	$3,300

R: Restored, t: Trimmed, a: Appearance

SEE WHAT PCE CAN DO FOR YOU

- ❖ You set the Ask Price for your books and can adjust the price at any time.
- ❖ We list your books on our international exchange and take full responsibility for marketing your books.
- ❖ We have buyers prepay for all books and we take care of packaging and shipping.
- ❖ We insure all books while listed on The Exchange.
- ❖ We charge the lowest commissions (8-13%) in the industry.

Pacific Comic Exchange, Inc.

Corporate Office:
337 S.Robertson Blvd, Suite 203, Beverly Hills, CA 90211
Tel: (310) 836-7234 (PCEI)

Shipping Address:
P.O. Box 34849 Los Angeles, CA 90034
Fax: (310) 836-7127

CGSA is a division of the Pacific Comic Exchange, Inc.
CGSA, PCE, and the PCE logo are trademarks of the Pacific Comic Exchange, Inc.

MOTOR CITY COMICS

IS BUYING!

GOLDEN AGE & SILVER AGE

TOP PRICES PAID !!!

WE ARE ALWAYS PAYING 60-200% OF GUIDE FOR ANY PRE-1970 COMICS.

>>>WE WILL TRAVEL ANYWHERE TO VIEW LARGE COLLECTIONS.

ALSO SELLING

WE OFFER >>>ACCURATE GRADING

>>>COMPETITIVE PRICING

>>>LARGE SELECTION OF GOLD AND SILVER AGE

>>>WANT LIST SERVICE

*>>>**FREE** CATALOGS, CALL OR WRITE FOR A COPY.*

MOTOR CITY COMICS

19785 W. 12 MILE RD., SUITE 231

SOUTHFIELD, MI 48076

PHONE: (810)350-2633 FAX: (810)354-3181

COMIC RELIEF
In Berkeley, CA.
We Mail Order Anywhere!
West Coast's Largest Selection of Gold and Silver-Age Collectibles!
Over 7,000 Graphic Novels, Art Books, and Movie/TV Books in Stock!
Computerized Want-list Service!
COMIC RELIEF
2138 University Avenue
Berkeley, CA 94704
(510) 843-5002
Call for new location!
1597 Haight Street
San Francisco, CA 94117
(415) 552-9010
COMIC RELIEF™

THIRD PLANET

Comics • Books • Sci-Fi

2718 SOUTHWEST FREEWAY
HOUSTON, TX 77098
713-528-1067

Houston. March 84.

THIRD PLANET is proud to announce the purchase of it's own building making us one of the worlds largest nostalgia shop with over 7600 square feet of space.

With over 1,000,000 comics, 50,000 45 records, 10,000 movie posters, 800 different models, 1,000's of comic and sci-fi related posters, a complete art gallery of limited edition art prints by some of the greatest artist around (Olivia, Canty, Adams, Smith, etc.) as well as custom framing and matting, giant video tape room with all Japamation tapes in stock, a large selection of the finest sci-fi pewter and porcelain, Dr. Who, Star Trek and Star Wars selections of large proportions and a mail order service available as well as many other fine products very few stores can compare to.

THIRD PLANET also wholesales to full time professional dealers.

So deal with the people who have over 10 years experience in the business and know how to fill your every need. If we do not have it and can not get it for you we will travel to the far reaches of the galaxy to get it anyway.

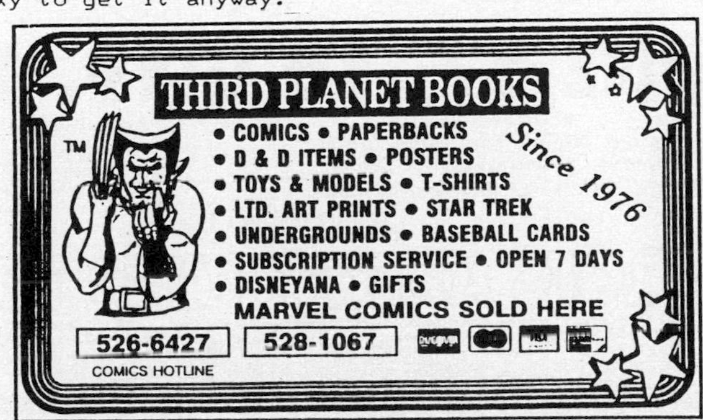

COMING IN JUNE 1994...

THE
NEXT
COMIC

HEAVEN

AUCTION

OVER 5,000 GOLDEN AND SILVER AGE COMIC BOOKS WILL BE OFFERED

Comic Heaven
John and Nanette Verzyl
24 W. Main Street
Alhambra, CA 91801
1-818-289-3945

A BRIEF HISTORICAL NOTE ABOUT "COMIC HEAVEN"

John Verzyl started collecting comic books in 1965, and within ten years, he had amassed thousands of Golden and Silver Age comic books. In 1979, with his wife Nanette, he opened "COMIC HEAVEN", a retail store devoted entirely to the buying and selling of comic books.

Over the years, John Verzyl has come to be recognized as an authority in the field of comic books,. He has served as an advisor to the "Overstreet Price Guide". Thousands of his "mint" comics were photographed for Ernst Gerbers newly-released "Photo-Journal Guide To Comic Books". His tables and displays at the annual San Diego Comic Convention draw customers from all over the country.

The first COMIC HEAVEN AUCTION was held in 1987, and today his Auction Catalogs are mailed out to more then ten thousand interested collectors (and dealers).

Comic Heaven
John and Nanette Verzyl
24 W. Main Street
Alhambra, CA 91801
1-818-289-3945

DIAMOND COMIC DISTRIBUTORS PRESENTS

The Photo-Journal Guide To Comic Books and Marvel Comics

Each of these four, full-color, coffee table-sized reference volumes chronicles and celebrates the history of comics with:
More than 8,000 color photos of classic comic covers!
Detailed chapters on every aspect of comic collecting!
Extensive cataloguing by:
Permanent ID Number • Scarcity Index
Relative Value Index • Issue Dates • Artist

Photo-Journal Guide To Comic Books Vol. 1 & 2
By Ernst Gerber.
Spotlighting thousands of Golden Age comics (from the late '30s to 1965).

Vol 1 (A-J)—HC, 11x14, 425pg, FC
Was $75.00—**Now $47.00 retail!**

Vol 2 (K-Z)—HC, 11x14, 425pg, FC
Was $75.00—**Now $47.00 retail!**

Photo-Journal Guide To Comic Books Vol. 3 & 4
By Ernst Gerber.
Showcasing all **Marvel Comics,** covers, and stories from 1961—the beginning of Marvel's heyday—through the late '70s and into the '80s!

Vol 3—HC, FC
Was $29.95—**Now $24.50 retail!**

Vol 4—HC, FC
Was $29.95—**Now $24.50 retail!**

"The best book ever in the history of comic book collecting!"
Steve Geppi, President,
Diamond Comic Distributors

Now available at a fine comic book specialty shop near you!

Retailers: Order your volumes of **The Photo-Journal Guide To Comic Books** today through the industry's leading source of backlist best-sellers, the **Diamond Star System!**

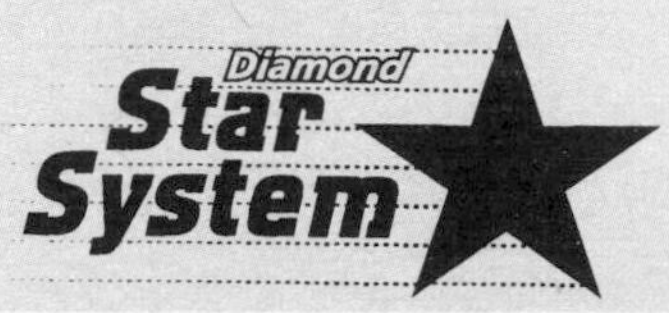

Abbott and Costello #25, © STJ

Aces High #3, © WMG

Action Comics #14, © DC

GD25 FN65 NM94 — GD25 FN65 NM94

The correct title listing for each comic book can be determined by consulting the indicia (publication data) on the beginning interior pages of the comic. The official title is determined by those words of the title in capital letters only, and not by what is on the cover.

Titles are listed in this book as if they were one word, ignoring spaces, hyphens, and apostrophes, to make finding titles easier.

Comic publishers are invited to send us sample copies for possible inclusion in future guides.

Near Mint is the highest value listed in this price guide. True mint books from the 1970s and 1990s do exist, so the Near Mint value listed should be interpreted as a Mint value for those books.

A-1 (See A-One)

ABBIE AN' SLATS (...With Becky No. 1-4) (See Comics On Parade, Fight for Love, Giant Comics Edition 2, Giant Comics Editions #1, Sparkler Comics, Tip Topper, Treasury of Comics, & United Comics)
1940; March, 1948 - No. 4, Aug, 1948 (Reprints)
United Features Syndicate

	GD25	FN65	NM94
Single Series 25 ('40)	24.00	73.00	170.00
Single Series 28	22.00	65.00	150.00
1 (1948)	11.50	35.00	80.00
2-4: 3-r/Sparkler #68-72	5.85	17.50	40.00

ABBOTT AND COSTELLO (...Comics)(See Giant Comics Editions #1 & Treasury of Comics)
Feb, 1948 - No. 40, Sept, 1956 (Mort Drucker art in most issues)
St. John Publishing Co.

	GD25	FN65	NM94
1	34.00	100.00	240.00
2	17.00	50.00	115.00
3-9 (#8, 8/49; #9, 2/50)	10.00	30.00	70.00
10-Son of Sinbad story by Kubert (new)	14.00	43.00	100.00
11,13-20 (#11, 10/50; #13, 8/51; #15, 12/52)	7.50	22.50	45.00
12-Movie issue	10.00	30.00	60.00
21-30: 28-r/#8. 30-Painted-c	5.85	17.50	35.00
31-40: 33,38-Reprints	5.00	15.00	30.00
3-D #1 (11/53)-Infinity-c	26.00	75.00	175.00

ABBOTT AND COSTELLO (TV)
Feb, 1968 - No. 22, Aug, 1971 (Hanna-Barbera)
Charlton Comics

	GD25	FN65	NM94
1	5.00	15.00	35.00
2	2.60	7.50	18.00
3-10	2.00	6.00	14.00
11-22	1.65	4.00	10.00

ABC (See America's Best TV Comics)

ABRAHAM LINCOLN LIFE STORY (See Dell Giants)

ABSENT-MINDED PROFESSOR, THE (See 4-Color Comics No.1199)

ABYSS, THE (Dark Horse)(Value: cover or less)

ACE COMICS
April, 1937 - No. 151, Oct-Nov, 1949
David McKay Publications

	GD25	FN65	NM94
1-Jungle Jim by Alex Raymond, Blondie, Ripley's Believe It Or Not, Krazy Kat begin (1st app. of each)	215.00	645.00	1500.00
2	67.00	200.00	440.00
3-5	47.00	142.00	315.00
6-10	35.00	105.00	230.00
11-The Phantom begins (1st app., 2/38) (in brown costume)	44.00	132.00	290.00
12-20	27.00	80.00	175.00
21-25,27-30	22.00	68.00	150.00
26-Origin/1st app. Prince Valiant (5/39, begins series?)	61.00	182.00	400.00
31-40: 37-Krazy Kat ends	16.00	48.00	105.00
41-60	13.00	40.00	85.00
61-64,66-76-(7/43; last 68 pgs.)	12.00	35.00	75.00
65-(8/42)-Flag-c	12.50	38.00	85.00
77-84 (3/44; all 60 pgs.)	10.00	30.00	65.00
85-99 (52 pgs.)	8.35	25.00	50.00
100 (7/45; last 52 pgs.)	9.75	29.00	58.00
101-134: 128-(11/47)-Brick Bradford begins. 134-Last Prince Valiant (all 36 pgs.)	7.00	21.00	42.00
135-151: 135-(6/48)-Lone Ranger begins	5.85	17.50	35.00

ACE KELLY (See Tops Comics & Tops In Humor)

ACE KING (See Adventures of the Detective)

ACES (Eclipse)(Value: cover or less)

ACES HIGH
Mar-Apr, 1955 - No. 5, Nov-Dec, 1955
E.C. Comics

	GD25	FN65	NM94
1-Not approved by code	13.50	41.00	95.00
2	10.00	30.00	65.00
3-5	9.15	27.50	55.00

NOTE: *All have stories by **Davis, Evans, Krigstein,** and **Wood; Evans** c-1-5.*

ACTION ADVENTURE (War) (Formerly Real Adventure)
V1#2, June, 1955 - No. 4, Oct, 1955
Gillmor Magazines

	GD25	FN65	NM94
V1#2-4	3.00	7.50	15.00

ACTION COMICS (...Weekly #601-642; also see The Comics Magazine #1, More Fun #14-17 & Special Edition)
6/38 - No. 583, 9/86; No. 584, 1/87 - Present
National Periodical Publ./Detective Comics/DC Comics

	GD25	FN65	VF82	NM94
1-Origin & 1st app. Superman by Siegel & Shuster, Marco Polo, Tex Thompson, Pep Morgan, Chuck Dawson & Scoop Scanlon; 1st app. Zatara & Lois Lane; Superman story missing 4 pgs. which were included when reprinted in Superman #1; Clark Kent works for Daily Star; story continued in #2	11,250.00	33,750.00	61,875.00	90,000.00

(Estimated up to 75+ total copies exist, 4 in NM/Mint)
(Issues 1 through 10 are all scarce to rare)

1-Reprint, Oversize 13-1/2"x10." **WARNING:** This comic is an exact reprint of the original except for its size. DC published it in 1974 with a second cover titling it as a Famous First Edition. There have been many reported cases of the outer cover being removed and the interior sold as the original edition. The reprint with the new outer cover removed is practically worthless. See Famous First Edition for value.

	GD25	FN65	NM94
1(1976,1983)-Giveaway; paper cover, 16pgs. in color; reprints complete Superman story from #1 ('38)	2.40	6.00	12.00
1(1987 Nestle Quik giveaway; 1988, 50 cent-c)		.50	1.00
1(1993)-Came w/Reign of Superman packs	.30	.75	1.50
2	935.00	2800.00	6200.00
3 (Scarce)-Superman apps. in costume in only one panel	750.00	2250.00	5000.00
4-6: 6-1st Jimmy Olsen (called office boy)	500.00	1500.00	3300.00
7-Superman cover	700.00	2100.00	4800.00
8,9	435.00	1300.00	2800.00
10-Superman cover	635.00	1900.00	4400.00
11,14: 14-Clip Carson begins, ends #41	235.00	700.00	1500.00
12-Has 1 pg. Batman ad for Det. #27 (5/39)	235.00	700.00	1500.00
13-Superman cover; last Scoop Scanlon	370.00	1100.00	2400.00
15-Superman cover	317.00	950.00	2000.00
16	167.00	500.00	1100.00
17-Superman cover; last Marco Polo	260.00	775.00	1700.00
18-Origin 3 Aces; 1st X-Ray Vision?	167.00	500.00	1100.00
19-Superman covers begin	235.00	700.00	1500.00
20-'S' left off Superman's chest; Clark Kent works at 'Daily Star'	217.00	650.00	1400.00
21,22,24,25: 24-Kent at Daily Planet. 25-Last app. Gargantua T. Potts, Tex Thompson's sidekick	135.00	400.00	850.00

23-1st app. Luthor (w/red hair) & Black Pirate; Black Pirate by Moldoff; 1st

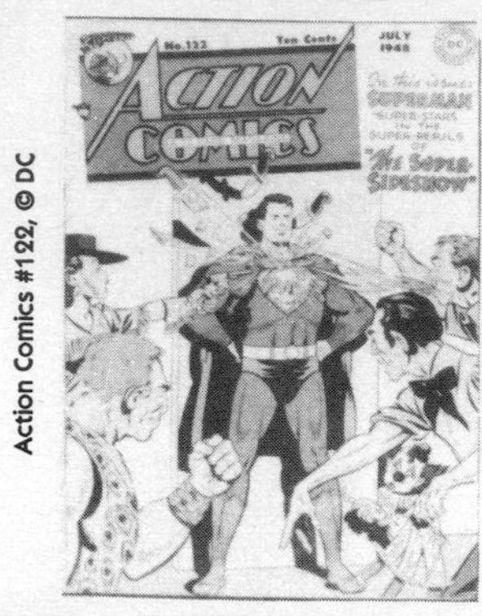

Action Comics #122, © DC

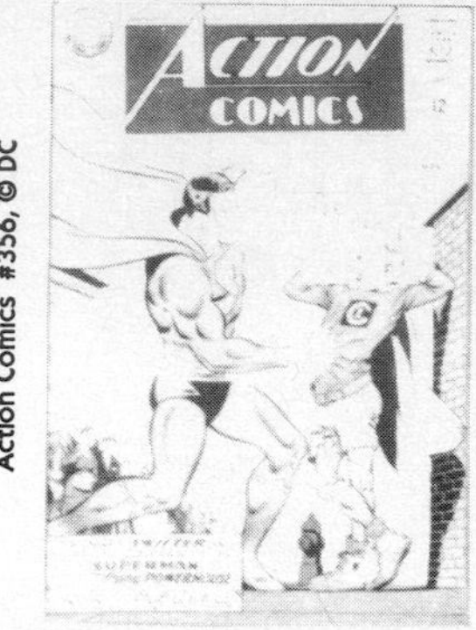

Action Comics #356, © DC

Action Comics #648, © DC

	GD25	FN65	NM94
mention of The Daily Planet (4/40)	200.00	600.00	1750.00
26-30: 29-1st Lois Lane-c (10/40)	108.00	325.00	700.00
31,32: 32-Intro/1st app. Krypto Ray Gun in Superman story by Burnley	83.00	250.00	550.00
33-Origin Mr. America	100.00	300.00	650.00
34-40: 37-Origin Congo Bill. 40-(9/41)-Intro/1st app. Star Spangled Kid & Stripesy	83.00	250.00	550.00
41	75.00	225.00	500.00
42-1st app./origin Vigilante; Bob Daley becomes Fat Man; origin Mr. America's magic flying carpet; The Queen Bee & Luthor app; Black Pirate ends; not in #41	110.00	335.00	725.00
43-46,48-50: 44-Fat Man's i.d. revealed to Mr. America. 45-1st app. Stuff (Vigilante's oriental sidekick)	75.00	225.00	500.00
47-1st Luthor cover in comics (4/42)	93.00	280.00	650.00
51-1st app. The Prankster	75.00	225.00	500.00
52-Fat Man & Mr. America become the Ameri-commandos; origin Vigilante retold	79.00	240.00	525.00
53-60: 56-Last Fat Man. 57-2nd Lois Lane-c in Action (3rd anywhere, 2/43). 59-Kubert Vigilante begins?, ends #70. 60-First app. Lois Lane as Superwoman	54.00	165.00	350.00
61-63,65-70: 63-Last 3 Aces	47.00	140.00	300.00
64-Intro Toyman	57.00	170.00	380.00
71-79: 74-Last Mr. America	44.00	135.00	290.00
80-2nd app. & 1st Mr. Mxyztplk-c (1/45)	70.00	210.00	450.00
81-90: 83-Intro Hocus & Pocus	44.00	135.00	290.00
91-99: 93-X-Mas-c. 99-1st small logo (7/46)	41.00	125.00	270.00
100	92.00	275.00	600.00
101-Nuclear explosion-c	54.00	165.00	365.00
102-120: 105,117-X-Mas-c	39.00	118.00	255.00
121-126,128-140: 135,136,138-Zatara by Kubert	37.00	112.00	250.00
127-Vigilante by Kubert; Tommy Tomorrow begins (12/48, see Real Fact #6)	47.00	145.00	305.00
141-157,159-161: 151-Luthor/Mr. Mxyztplk/Prankster team-up. 156-Lois Lane as Super Woman. 160- Last 52 pgs.	37.00	110.00	250.00
158-Origin Superman retold	67.00	200.00	440.00
162-180: 168,176-Used in **POP**, pg. 90	26.00	79.00	185.00
181-201: 191-Intro. Janu in Congo Bill. 198-Last Vigilante. 201-Last pre-code issue	26.00	79.00	185.00
202-220	23.00	70.00	160.00
221-240: 224-1st Golden Gorilla story	18.00	54.00	125.00
241,243-251: 241-Batman x-over. 248-Congo Bill becomes Congorilla. 251-Last Tommy Tomorrow	14.00	41.00	95.00
242-Origin & 1st app. Brainiac (7/58); 1st mention of Shrunken City of Kandor	100.00	300.00	700.00
252-Origin & 1st app. Supergirl (5/59); re-intro new Metallo (his 2nd app. since Superboy #49)	114.00	343.00	800.00
253-2nd app. Supergirl	25.00	75.00	175.00
254-1st meeting of Bizarro & Superman-c/story	22.00	65.00	150.00
255-1st Bizarro Lois Lane-c/story & both Bizarros leave Earth to make Bizarro World	14.00	43.00	100.00
256-261: 259-Red Kryptonite used. 261-1st X-Kryptonite which gave Streaky his powers; last Congorilla in Action; origin & 1st app. Streaky The Super Cat	10.00	30.00	65.00
262,264-266,268-270	7.00	21.00	50.00
263-Origin Bizarro World	10.00	30.00	70.00
267(8/60)-3rd Legion app; 1st app. Chameleon Boy, Colossal Boy, & Invisible Kid	40.00	120.00	280.00
271-275,277-282: Last 10 cent issue	6.50	19.00	45.00
276(5/61)-6th Legion app; 1st app. Brainiac 5, Phantom Girl, Triplicate Girl, Bouncing Boy, Sun Boy, & Shrinking Violet; Supergirl joins Legion	18.00	54.00	125.00
283(12/61)-Legion of Super-Villains app.	7.00	21.00	50.00
284(1/62)-Mon-el app.	7.00	21.00	50.00
285(2/62)-12th Legion app; Brainiac 5 cameo; Supergirl's existence revealed to world	7.00	21.00	50.00
286(3/62)-Legion of Super Villains app.	3.70	11.00	26.00

	GD25	FN65	NM94
287(4/62)-14th Legion app.(cameo)	3.70	11.00	26.00
288-Mon-el app.; r-origin Supergirl	3.70	11.00	26.00
289(6/62)-16th Legion app.(Adult); Lightning Man & Saturn Woman's marriage 1st revealed	3.70	11.00	26.00
290(7/62)-17th Legion app. (cameo); Phantom Girl app. 290-1st Supergirl emergency squad	3.70	11.00	26.00
291,292,294-299: 291-1st meeting Supergirl & Mr. Mxyzptlk. 292-2nd app. Superhorse (see Adv. #293). 297-Mon-el app; 298-Legion cameo	3.20	8.00	20.00
293-Origin Comet(Superhorse)	7.00	21.00	50.00
300-(5/63)	3.60	10.75	25.00
301-303,305-308,310-320: 306-Brainiac 5, Mon-el app. 307-Saturn Girl app. 314-r-origin Supergirl; J.L.A. x-over. 317-Death of Nor-Kan of Kandor. 319-Shrinking Violet app.	1.85	5.50	13.00
304-Origin & 1st app. Black Flame	2.40	7.25	17.00
309-Legion app.; Batman & Robin-c & cameo	2.15	6.50	15.00
321-333,335-340: 336-Origin Akvar(Flamebird). 340-Origin, 1st app. Parasite	1.65	4.00	10.00
334-Giant G-20; origin Supergirl, Streaky, Superhorse & Legion (all-r)	2.40	7.25	17.00
341-346,348-359: 344-Batman x-over. 350-Batman, Green Arrow & Green Lantern app. in Supergirl back-up story	1.20	3.00	7.00
347,360-Giant Supergirl G-33,G-45; 347-Origin Comet-r plus 3 Bizarro stories. 360-Legion-r; r/origin Supergirl	1.70	5.00	12.00
361-372,374-380: 365-Legion app. 370-New facts about Superman's origin. 376-Last Supergirl in Action. 377-Legion begins	1.00	2.50	6.00
373-Giant Supergirl G-57; Legion-r	1.50	3.75	9.00
381-402: 392-Last Legion in Action. Saturn Girl gets new costume. 393-402-All Superman issues	.80	2.00	5.00
403-413: All 52pg. issues; 411-Origin Eclipso-(r). 413- Metamorpho begins, ends #418	1.00	2.00	5.00
414-424: 419-Intro. Human Target. 421-Intro Capt. Strong; Green Arrow begins. 422,423-Origin Human Target	1.00	2.00	5.00
425-Neal Adams-a(p); The Atom begins	1.20	3.00	7.00
426-436,438,439: 432-1st S.A. app. The Toyman		1.60	4.00
437,443-100 pg. giants	1.00	2.00	5.00
440-1st Grell-a on Green Arrow	1.25	3.00	7.50
441-Grell-a on Green Arrow continues	1.00	2.50	6.00
442,444-499: 454-Last Atom. 458-Last Green Arrow. 484-Earth II Superman & Lois Lane wed. 487,488-(44pgs.). 487-Origin & 1st app. Microwave Man; origin Atom retold		1.20	3.00
500-($1.00, 68 pgs.)-Infinity-c; Superman life story; shows Legion statues in museum		1.20	3.00
501-551,554-582: 511-514-Airwave II solo stories. 513-The Atom begins. 517 Aquaman begins; ends #541. 521-1st app. The Vixen. 532,536-New Teen Titans cameo. 535,536- Omega Men app. 544- (Mando paper, 68 pgs.)-Origins new Luthor & Brainiac; Omega Men cameo. 546-J.L.A., New Teen Titans app. 551-Starfire becomes Red-Star		.70	1.75
552,553-Animal Man-c & app. (2/84 & 3/84)	1.05	2.60	6.25
583-Alan Moore scripts	1.25	3.00	7.50
584-Byrne-a begins; New Teen Titans app.		.70	1.75
585-599: 586-Legends x-over. 596-Millennium x-over. 598-1st app. Checkmate			1.00
600-($2.50, 84 pgs., 5/88)		1.60	4.00
601-642-Weekly issues ($1.50, 52 pgs.): 601-Re-intro The Secret Six. 611-614: Catwoman stories (new costume in #611). 613-618: Nightwing stories			1.50
643-Superman & monthly issues begin again; Perez-c/a/scripts begin; swipes cover to Superman #1			1.50
644-649,651-661,663-666,668-679: 645-1st app. Maxima. 654-Part 3 of Batman storyline. 655-Free extra 8 pgs. 660-Death of Lex Luthor. 661-Begin $1.00-c. 674-Supergirl logo & c/story (reintro). 675-Deathstroke cameo. 679-Last $1.00 issue			1.00
650-($1.50, 52 pgs.)-Lobo cameo (last panel)			1.50
662-Clark Kent reveals i.d. to Lois Lane; story continued in Superman #53		1.40	3.50

Action Comics Annual #2, © DC

Adolescent Radioactive Black Belt Hamsters Massacre the Japanese Invasion #1, © Don Chin

Adventure Comics #75, © DC

GD25 FN65 NM94

667-($1.75, 52 pgs.) .70 1.75
680-682 1.25
683-Doomsday cameo 1.25 3.00 7.50
683-2nd & 3rd printings 1.25
684-Doomsday battle issue 1.30 3.25 8.00
685,686-Funeral for a Friend issues .80 2.00
685-2nd & 3rd printings 1.25
687-($1.95)-Collector's Edition with die-cut-c .80 2.00
687-($1.50)-Newsstand Edition with mini-poster 1.50
688-698 ($1.50): 688-Guy Gardner-c/story 1.50
695-($2.50)-Collector's Edition w/embossed foil-c 1.00 2.50
Annual 1(1987)-Art Adams-c/a(p) 1.00 2.50 6.00
Annual 2(1989, $1.75, 68 pgs.)-Perez-c/a(i) .80 2.00
Annual 3('91, $2.00, 68 pgs.)-Armageddon 2001 .80 2.00
Annual 4('92, $2.50, 68 pgs.)-Eclipso vs. Shazam 1.00 2.50
Annual 5('93, $2.50, 68 pgs.) 1.00 2.50
Theater Giveaway (1947, 32 pgs., 6-1/2 x 8-1/4", nn)- Vigilante story based on Vigilante Columbia serial; no Superman-c or story
64.00 192.00 450.00

NOTE: ***Supergirl's*** *origin in 262, 280, 285, 291, 305, 309.* ***N. Adams*** *c-356, 358, 359, 361-364, 366, 367, 370-374, 377-379i, 398-400, 402, 404-406, 419p, 466, 468, 473i, 485.* ***Austin*** *c/a-682i.* ***Baily*** *a-24, 25.* ***Burnley*** *a-28-33; c-48?, 53-55, 58, 59?, 60-63, 65, 66p, 67p, 70p, 71p, 79p, 82p, 84-86p, 90-92p, 93p?, 94p, 107p, 108p.* ***Byrne*** *a-584-598p, 599i, 600p; c-596-600.* ***Giffen*** *a-560, 563, 565, 577, 579; c-539, 560, 563, 565, 577, 579.* ***Grell*** *a-440-442, 444-446, 450-452, 456-458; c-456.* ***Guardineer*** *a-24, 25; c-8, 11, 12, 14-16, 18, 25.* ***Guice*** *a(p)-670-681, 683-693; c-683, 685, 686, 687(direct), 688-693i.* ***Bob Kane's*** *Clip Carson-14-41.* ***Gil Kane*** *a-443r, 493r, 539-541, 544-546, 551-554, 601-605; c-535p, 540, 541, 544p, 545-549, 551-554.* ***Meskin*** *a-42-121(most).* ***Moldoff*** *a-23-25, 443r.* ***Mooney*** *a-667p.* ***Mortimer*** *c-153, 154, 159-172, 174, 178-181, 184, 186-189, 191-193, 196, 200, 206.* ***Perez*** *a-600i, 643-652p; c-529p, 643-651.* ***Fred Ray*** *c-34, 36-46, 50, 52.* ***Siegel & Shuster*** *a-1-27.* ***Starlin*** *a-509.* ***Leonard Starr*** *a-597i(part),* ***Staton*** *a-525p, 526p, 531p, 535p, 536p.* ***Swan/Moldoff*** *c-281, 286, 287, 293, 298, 334.* ***Thibert*** *c-676, 677p, 678-681, 684.* ***Toth*** *a-406, 407, 413, 431.* ***Tuska*** *a-486p, 550.* ***Williamson*** *a-568i.*

ACTION FORCE (Marvel)(Value: cover or less)

ACTUAL CONFESSIONS (Formerly Love Adventures)
No. 13, October, 1952 - No. 14, December, 1952
Atlas Comics (MPI)
13,14 3.00 7.50 15.00

ACTUAL ROMANCES (Becomes True Secrets #3 on?)
October, 1949 - No. 2, Jan, 1950 (52 pgs.)
Marvel Comics (IPS)
1 6.70 20.00 40.00
2-Photo-c 4.00 11.00 22.00

ADAM AND EVE (Spire Christian)(Value: cover or less)

ADAM STRANGE (DC)(Value: cover or less)(See Green Lantern #132, Mystery In Space #53 & Showcase #17)

ADAM-12 (TV)
Dec, 1973 - No. 10, Feb, 1976 (Photo covers)
Gold Key
1 3.20 8.00 20.00
2-10 1.65 4.00 10.00

ADDAMS FAMILY (TV cartoon)
Oct, 1974 - No. 3, Apr, 1975 (Hanna-Barbera)
Gold Key
1 5.00 15.00 36.00
2,3 3.20 8.00 20.00

ADLAI STEVENSON
December, 1966
Dell Publishing Co.
12-007-612-Life story; photo-c 4.00 11.00 22.00

ADOLESCENT RADIOACTIVE BLACK BELT HAMSTERS (Eclipse)(Value: cover or less)

ADULT TALES OF TERROR ILLUSTRATED (See Terror Illustrated)

ADVANCED DUNGEONS & DRAGONS (DC)(Value: cover or less)

GD25 FN65 NM94

ADVENTURE BOUND (See 4-Color Comics No. 239)

ADVENTURE COMICS (Formerly New Adventure)(...Presents Dial H For Hero #479-490)
No. 32, 11/38 - No. 490, 2/82; No. 491, 9/82 - No. 503, 9/83
National Periodical Publications/DC Comics
32-Anchors Aweigh (ends #52), Barry O'Neil (ends #60, not in #33), Captain Desmo (ends #47), Dale Daring (ends #47), Federal Men (ends #70), The Golden Dragon (ends #36), Rusty & His Pals (ends #52) by Bob Kane, Todd Hunter (ends #38) and Tom Brent (ends #39) begin
171.00 515.00 1200.00
33-38: 37-Cover used on Double Action #2 83.00 225.00 650.00
39(6/39):-Jack Wood begins, ends #42; 1st mention of Marijuana in comics
100.00 300.00 700.00
GD25 FN65 VF82 NM94
40-(Rare, 7/39, on stands 6/10/39)-The Sandman begins by Bert Christman (who died in WWII); believed to be 1st conceived story (see N.Y. World's Fair for 1st published app.); Socko Strong begins, ends #54
1780.00 5335.00 10,680.00 16,000.00
GD25 FN65 NM94
41 257.00 770.00 1800.00
42,44: Sandman-c by Flessel. 44-Opium story 315.00 945.00 2200.00
43,45 171.00 515.00 1200.00
46,47-Sandman covers by Flessel. 47-Steve Conrad Adventurer begins, ends #76 250.00 750.00 1750.00
GD25 FN65 VF82 NM94
48-Intro & 1st app. The Hourman by Bernard Bailey (Hourman c-48,50,52-59)
945.00 2835.00 5670.00 8500.00
(Estimated up to 80 total copies exist, 5 in NM/Mint)
GD25 FN65 NM94
49,50: 50-Cotton Carver by Jack Lehti begins, ends #64
135.00 400.00 900.00
51,60-Sandman-c 170.00 500.00 1100.00
52-59: 53-1st app. Jimmy "Minuteman" Martin & the Minutemen of America in Hourman; ends #78. 58-Paul Kirk Manhunter begins (1st app.), ends #72
116.00 350.00 750.00
GD25 FN65 VF82 NM94
61-1st app. Starman by Jack Burnley (4/41); Starman c-61-72
665.00 2000.00 4000.00 6000.00
(Estimated up to 100+ total copies exist, 7 in NM/Mint)
GD25 FN65 NM94
62-65,67,68,70: 67-Origin & 1st app. The Mist. 70-Last Federal Men
108.00 325.00 700.00
66-Origin/1st app. Shining Knight (9/41) 138.00 410.00 875.00
69-1st app. Sandy the Golden Boy (Sandman's sidekick) by Bob Kane; Sandman dons new costume 128.00 388.00 850.00
71-Jimmy Martin becomes costume aide to the Hourman; 1st app.Hourman's Miracle Ray machine 100.00 300.00 650.00
GD25 FN65 VF82 NM94
72-1st Simon & Kirby Sandman (3/42, 1st DC work)
500.00 1500.00 3000.00 4500.00
(Estimated up to 100+ total copies exist, 8 in NM/Mint)
73-(Scarce)-Origin Manhunter by Simon & Kirby; begin new series; Manhunter-c 580.00 1735.00 3465.00 5200.00
(Estimated up to 100+ total copies exist, 7 in NM/Mint)
GD25 FN65 NM94
74-80: 74-Thorndyke replaces Jimmy, Hourman's assistant; new Manhunter c begin by S&K. 77-Origin Genius Jones; Mist story. 79-Manhunter-c. 80-Last S&K Manhunter & Burnley Starman 130.00 390.00 850.00
81-90: 83-Last Hourman. 84-Mike Gibbs begins, ends #102
83.00 250.00 530.00
91-Last Simon & Kirby Sandman 75.00 225.00 475.00
92-99,101,102: 92-Last Manhunter. 102-Last Starman, Sandman, & Genius Jones; most-S&K-c (Genius Jones cont'd in More Fun #108)
57.00 170.00 375.00
100 92.00 275.00 600.00

Adventure Comics #145, © DC

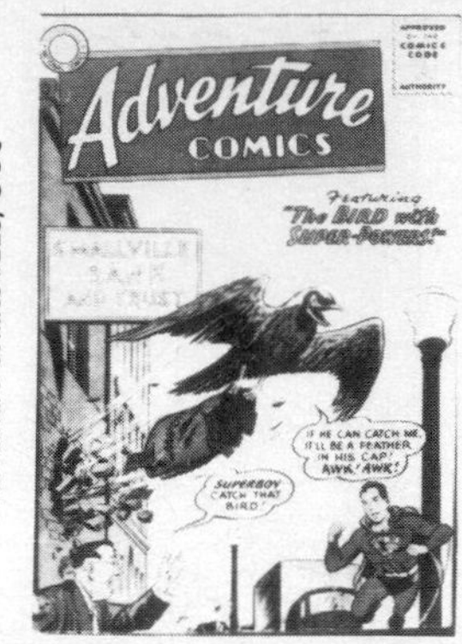

Adventure Comics #925, © DC

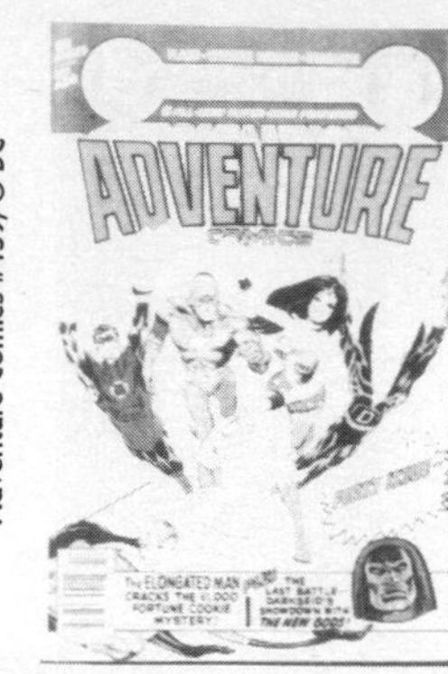

Adventure Comics #459, © DC

GD25 FN65 NM94

103-Aquaman, Green Arrow, Johnny Quick & Superboy all move over from More Fun Comics #107; 8th app. Superboy; Superboy-c begin; 1st small logo (4/46) 217.00 650.00 1500.00
104 72.00 215.00 500.00
105-110 54.00 162.00 350.00
111-120: 113-X-Mas-c 50.00 150.00 340.00
121-126,128-130: 128-1st meeting Superboy & Lois Lane 42.00 125.00 275.00
127-Brief origin Shining Knight retold 44.00 132.00 290.00
131-141,143-149: 132-Shining Knight 1st return to King Arthur time; origin aide Sir Butch 35.00 105.00 230.00
142-Origin Shining Knight & Johnny Quick retold 40.00 120.00 260.00
150,151,153,155,157,159,161,163-All have 6 pg. Shining Knight stories by Frank Frazetta. 159-Origin Johnny Quick 47.00 140.00 300.00
152,154,156,158,160,162,164-169: 166-Last Shining Knight. 168-Last 52 pg. issue 27.00 81.00 190.00
170-180 25.00 75.00 175.00
181-199: 189-B&W and color illo in **POP** 23.00 65.00 160.00
200 (5/54) 43.00 129.00 300.00
201-209: 207-Last Johnny Quick (not in 205). 209-Last Pre-code issue; origin Speedy 29.00 86.00 200.00

GD25 FN65 VF82 NM94

210-1st app. Krypto (Superdog)-c/story (3/55) 175.00 525.00 1313.00 2100.00

GD25 FN65 NM94

211-213,215-220: 220-Krypto app. 23.00 70.00 160.00
214-2nd app. Krypto 36.00 107.00 250.00
221-246: 237-1st Intergalactic Vigilante Squadron (6/57) 19.00 58.00 135.00

GD25 FN65 VF82 NM94

247(4/58)-1st Legion of Super Heroes app.; 1st app. Cosmic Boy, Lightning Boy (later Lightning Lad in #267), & Saturn Girl (origin) 260.00 780.00 1690.00 2600.00

GD25 FN65 NM94

248-252,254,255: 255-Intro. Red Kryptonite in Superboy (used in #252 but w/no effect) 14.00 43.00 100.00
253-1st meeting of Superboy & Robin; Green Arrow by Kirby in #250-255 20.00 60.00 140.00
256-Origin Green Arrow by Kirby 57.00 170.00 400.00
257-259: 258-Green Arrow x-over in Superboy 13.00 40.00 90.00
260-1st Silver-Age origin Aquaman (5/59) 61.00 182.00 425.00
261-266,268,270: 262-Origin Speedy in Green Arrow. 266-(11/59)-Origin & 1st app. Aquagirl (tryout, not same as later character). 270-Congorilla begins, ends #281,283 9.00 28.00 65.00
267(12/59)-2nd Legion of Super Heroes; Lightning Boy now called Lightning Lad; new costumes for Legion 83.00 249.00 580.00
269-Intro. Aqualad (2/60); last Green Arrow (not in #206) 19.00 58.00 135.00
271-Origin Luthor 21.00 62.00 145.00
272-274,277-280: 279-Intro White Kryptonite in Superboy. 280-1st meeting Superboy-Lori Lemaris 7.00 21.00 48.00
275-Origin Superman-Batman team retold (see World's Finest #94) 17.00 51.00 120.00
276-(9/60) Re-intro Metallo (3rd app?); story similar to Superboy #49 7.00 21.00 48.00
281,284,287-289: 281-Last Congorilla. 284-Last Aquaman in Adv. 287,288-Intro Dev-Em, the Knave from Krypton. 287-1st Bizarro Perry White & J. Olsen. 288-Bizarro-c. 289-Legion cameo (statues) 7.00 21.00 48.00
282(3/61)-5th Legion app; intro/origin Star Boy 15.00 45.00 105.00
283-Intro. The Phantom Zone 14.00 43.00 100.00
285-1st Tales of the Bizarro World-c/story (ends #299) in Adv. (see Action #255) 11.00 34.00 80.00
286-1st Bizarro Mxyzptlk; Bizarro-c 10.00 30.00 70.00
290(11/61)-8th Legion app; origin Sunboy in Legion (last 10 cent issue) 14.00 43.00 100.00
291,292,295-298: 292-1st Bizarro Lana Lang & Lucy Lane. 295-1st Bizarro Titano 4.70 14.00 33.00
293(2/62)-13th Legion app; Mon-el & Legion Super Pets (1st app./origin) app. (1st Superhorse). 1st Bizarro Luthor & Kandor 9.00 27.00 63.00
294-1st Bizarro M. Monroe, Pres. Kennedy 9.00 28.00 65.00
299-1st Gold Kryptonite (8/62) 5.50 17.00 40.00
300-Tales of the Legion of Super-Heroes series begins (9/62); Mon-el leaves Phantom Zone (temporarily), joins Legion 39.00 120.00 275.00
301-Origin Bouncing Boy 12.00 35.00 82.00
302-305: 303-1st app. Matter Eater Lad. 304-Death of Lightning Lad in Legion 8.00 24.00 55.00
306-310: 306-Intro. Legion of Substitute Heroes. 307-1st app. Element Lad in Legion. 308-1st app. Lightning Lass in Legion 5.50 17.00 40.00
311-320: 312-Lightning Lad back in Legion. 315-Last new Superboy story; Colossal Boy app. 316-Origins & powers of Legion given. 317-Intro. Dream Girl in Legion; Lightning Lass becomes Light Lass; Hall of Fame series begins. 320-Dev-Em 2nd app. 4.30 13.00 30.00
321-Intro Time Trapper 3.40 10.00 24.00
322-330: 327-Intro/1st app. Lone Wolf in Legion. 329-Intro The Bizarro Legionnaires 3.25 9.50 22.00
331-340: 337-Chlorophyll Kid & Night Girl app. 340-Intro Computo in Legion 2.40 7.25 17.00
341-Triplicate Girl becomes Duo Damsel 1.80 5.50 12.50
342-345,347,350,351: 345-Last Hall of Fame; returns in 356,371. 351-1st app. White Witch 1.60 3.75 9.50
346,348,349: 346-1st app. Karate Kid, Princess Projectra, Ferro Lad, & Nemesis Kid. 348-Origin Sunboy; intro Dr. Regulus in Legion. 349-Intro Universo & Rond Vidar 1.65 4.50 10.50
352,354-360: 355-Insect Queen joins Legion (4/67) 1.30 3.25 8.00
353-Death of Ferro Lad in Legion 2.00 6.00 13.75
361-364,366,368-370: 369-Intro Mordru in Legion 1.10 2.70 6.50
365,367,371,372: 365-Intro Shadow Lass; lists origins & powers of L.S.H. 367-New Legion headquarters. 371-Intro. Chemical King. 372-Timber Wolf & Chemical King join 1.25 3.00 7.50
373,374,376-380: Last Legion in Adventure 1.10 2.70 6.50
375-Intro Quantum Queen & The Wanderers 1.20 3.00 7.00
381-Supergirl begins; 1st full length supergirl story & her 1st solo book (6/69) 1.00 2.50
382-389,391-400: 399-Unpubbed G.A. Black Canary story. 400-New costume for Supergirl .90 2.25
390-Giant Supergirl G-69 1.20 3.00 7.00
401,402,404-410: 409-420-(52 pg. issues) .90 2.25
403-68pg. Giant G-81; Legion-r/#304,305,308,312 1.00 2.50 5.50
411,413: 413-Hawkman by Kubert; G.A. Robotman-r/Det. #178; Zatanna begins, ends #421 1.10
412-Reprints origin/1st app. Animal Man/Strange Adventures #180 1.70 4.25
414-Reprints 2nd Animal Man/Str. Advs. #184 1.20 3.00
415,420-Animal Man reprints from Strange Adventures #190 (origin recap) & #195 1.50
416-Giant DC-100 Pg. Super Spect. #10; GA-r 1.50
417-Morrow Vigilante; Frazetta Shining Knight-r/Adv. #161; origin The Enchantress 1.25
418,419,421-424: Last Supergirl in Adv. 1.00
425-New look, content change to adventure; Toth-a, origin Capt. Fear .65 1.60
426,427,431-458: 426-1st Adventurers Club. 427-Last Vigilante. 431-440-Spectre app. 433-437-Cover title is Weird Adv. Comics. 435-Mike Grell's 1st comic work (9-10/74). 436-Last 20¢ issue. 440-New Spectre origin. 441-452-Aquaman app. 445-447-The Creeper app. 449-451-Martian Manhunter app. 453-458-Superboy app. 453-Intro Mighty Girl. 457,458-Eclipso app. 1.00
428-1st app. Black Canary (c/story, 6-7/73) 1.20 3.00 7.00
429,428-Black Canary-c/stories 1.40 3.50
459,460-New Gods/Darkseid storyline concludes from New Gods #19 (#459 is dated 9-10/78) without missing a month 1.20 3.00
461,462: 461-Justice Society begins; ends 466. 461,462-Death Earth II

Adventure Into Mystery #1, © MCG

Adventures In 3-D #1, © HARV

Adventures Into the Unknown #22, © ACG

	GD25	FN65	NM94

Batman (both $1.00, 68 pgs.) 1.80 4.50

403-400($1.00 size, 68pgs.): 459-Flash (ends #466), Deadman (ends #466), Wonder Woman (ends #464), Green Lantern (ends #460), 460-Aquaman begins; ends 478 1.00

467-Starman by Ditko, Plastic Man begin 1.50

468-490: 469,470-Origin Starman. 478-Last Starman & Plastic Man. 479-Dial 'H' For Hero begins, ends #490 1.00

491-499: 488,489-Deathstroke-c/cameos. 491-100pg. Digest size begins; r/ Legion of Super Heroes/Adv. #247,267; Spectre, Aquaman, Superboy, S&K Sandman, Bl. Canary-r & new Shazam by Newton begin. 493-Challengers of the Unknown begins by Tuska w/brief origin. 492,495,496,499-S&K Sandman-r/Adventure in all; 494-499-Spectre-r/Spectre 1-3, 5-7. 493-495,497-499-G.A. Captain Marvel-r. 498-Plastic Man-r begin; origin Bouncing Boy-r/ #001 1.20

500-All Legion-r (Digest size, 148 pgs.) .65 1.60

501-503-G.A.-r 1.20

NOTE: *Bizarro covers-285, 286, 288, 294, 295, 329. Vigilante app.-420, 426, 427.* ***N. Adams*** *a(r)-495i-498i; c-365-369, 371-373, 375-379, 381-383.* ***Austin*** *a-449i 451i.* ***Bernard Baily*** *c-48, 50, 52-59.* ***Bolland*** *c-475.* ***Durnley*** *c-61-72, 116-120p.* ***Ditko*** *a-467p-478p; c-467p.* ***Craig Flessel*** *c-32, 33, 40, 42, 44, 46, 47, 51, 60.* ***Giffen*** *c-491p-494p, 500p.* ***Grell*** *a-435-437, 440.* ***Guardineer*** *c-34, 35, 45.* ***Kaluta*** *c-425.* ***Bob Kane*** *a-38.* ***G. Kane*** *a-414r, 425; c-496-499, 537.* ***Kirby*** *a-250-256.* ***Kubert*** *a-413.* ***Meskin*** *a-81,127.* ***Moldoff*** *a-494i; c-49.* ***Morrow*** *a-413-415, 417, 422, 502r, 503r.* ***Newton*** *a-459-461, 464-466, 491p, 492p.* ***Orlando*** *a-457p, 458p.* ***Perez*** *c-484-486, 490p.* ***Simon/Kirby*** *c-73-97, 100-102.* ***Starlin*** *c-471.* ***Staton*** *a-445-447i, 456-458p, 459, 460, 461p-465p, 466,467p-478p, 502p(r); c-458, 461(back).* ***Toth*** *a-418, 419, 425, 431, 495p-497p.* ***Tuska*** *a494p.*

ADVENTURE COMICS

No date (early 1940s) Paper cover, 32 pgs.

IGA

Two different issues; Super-Mystery reprints from 1941 17.00 51.00 120.00

ADVENTURE IN DISNEYLAND (Giveaway)

May, 1955 (16 pgs., soft-c) (Dist. by Richfield Oil)

Walt Disney Productions

nn 4.20 12.50 25.00

ADVENTURE INTO FEAR

1951

Superior Publ. Ltd.

1-Exist? 10.00 30.00 60.00

ADVENTURE INTO MYSTERY

May, 1956 - No. 8, July, 1957

Atlas Comics (BFP No. 1/OPI No. 2-8)

1-Powell s/f-a; Forte-a; Everett-c 18.00 54.00 125.00

2-Flying Saucer story 10.00 30.00 65.00

3,6,8: 3,6-Everett-c 8.50 26.00 52.00

4-Williamson-a, 4 pgs; Powell-a 10.00 30.00 65.00

5-Everett-c/a, Orlando-a 8.50 26.00 52.00

7-Torres-a; Everett-c 9.15 27.50 55.00

8-Moriera, Sale, Torres, Woodbridge-a, Severin-c 9.15 27.50 55.00

ADVENTURE IS MY CAREER

1945 (44 pgs.)

U.S. Coast Guard Academy/Street & Smith

nn-Simon, Milt Gross-a 10.00 30.00 70.00

ADVENTURERS, THE (Aircel)(Value: cover or less)

ADVENTURES (No. 2 Spectacular... on cover)

Nov, 1949 - No. 2, Feb, 1950 (No. 1 ...in Romance on cover)

St. John Publishing Co. (Slightly large size)

1(Scarce); Bolle, Starr-a(2) 15.00 45.00 105.00

2(Scarce)-Slave Girl; China Bombshell app.; Bolle, L. Starr-a 25.00 75.00 175.00

ADVENTURES FOR BOYS

December, 1954

Bailey Enterprises

nn-Comics, text, & photos 4.00 10.00 20.00

ADVENTURES IN PARADISE (See 4-Color No. 1301)

ADVENTURES IN ROMANCE (See Adventures)

ADVENTURES IN SCIENCE (See Classics Illustrated Special Issue)

ADVENTURES IN 3-D

Nov, 1953 - No. 2, Jan, 1954

Harvey Publications

1-Nostrand, Powell-a, 2-Powell-a 12.00 36.00 85.00

ADVENTURES INTO DARKNESS (See Seduction of the Innocent 3-D)

No. 5, Aug, 1952 - No. 14, 1954

Better-Standard Publications/Visual Editions

5-Katz-c/a; Toth-a(p) 13.50 41.00 95.00

6-Tuska, Katz-a 9.15 27.50 55.00

7-Katz-c/a 10.00 30.00 60.00

8,9-Toth-a(p) 10.00 30.00 65.00

10,11-Jack Katz-a 8.35 25.00 50.00

12-Toth-a?; lingerie panels 8.35 25.00 50.00

13-Toth-a(p); Cannibalism story cited by T. E. Murphy articles 10.00 30.00 65.00

14 7.50 22.50 45.00

NOTE: ***Fawcette*** *a-13.* ***Moriera*** *a-5.* ***Sekowsky*** *a-10, 11, 13(2).*

ADVENTURES INTO TERROR (Formerly Joker Comics)

No. 43, Nov, 1950 - No. 31, May, 1954

Marvel/Atlas Comics (CDS)

43(#1) 25.00 75.00 175.00

44(#2, 2/51)-Sol Brodsky-c 17.00 52.00 120.00

3(4/51), 4 11.50 34.00 80.00

5-Wolverton-c panel/Mystic #6; Rico-c panel also; Atom Bomb story 13.50 41.00 95.00

6,8: 8-Wolverton text illo r-/Marvel Tales #104 10.00 30.00 70.00

7-Wolverton-a "Where Monsters Dwell", 6 pgs.; Tuska-c; Maneely-c panels 28.00 85.00 200.00

9,10,12-Krigstein-a. 9-Decapitation panels 10.00 30.00 70.00

11,13-20 8.35 25.00 50.00

21-24,26-31 7.50 22.50 45.00

25-Matt Fox-a 10.00 30.00 60.00

NOTE: ***Ayers*** *a-21.* ***Colan*** *a-3, 5, 14, 21, 24, 25, 28, 29, c-27.* ***Colletta*** *a-30.* ***Everett*** *c-13, 21, 25.* ***Fass*** *a-28, 29.* ***Forte*** *a-28.* ***Heath*** *a-43, 44, 4-6, 22, 24, 26; c-43, 9, 11.* ***Lazarus*** *a-7.* ***Maneely*** *a-7(3 pg.), 10, 11, 21., 22 c-15, 29.* ***Don Rico*** *a-4, 5(3 pg.).* ***Sekowsky*** *a-43, 3, 4.* ***Sinnott*** *a-8, 9, 11, 28.* ***Tuska*** *a-14; c-7.*

ADVENTURES INTO THE UNKNOWN

Fall, 1948 - No. 174, Aug, 1967 (No. 1-33: 52 pgs.)

American Comics Group

(1st continuous series horror comic; see Eerie #1)

1-Guardineer-a; adapt. of 'Castle of Otranto' by Horace Walpole 89.00 270.00 625.00

2 39.00 115.00 270.00

3-Feldstein-a (9 pgs) 43.00 130.00 300.00

4,5 22.00 65.00 150.00

6-10 16.50 50.00 115.00

11-16,18-20: 13-Starr-a 12.00 30.00 05.00

17-Story similar to movie 'The Thing' 15.00 45.00 105.00

21-26,28-30 11.00 32.00 75.00

27-Williamson/Krenkel-a (8 pgs.) 17.00 52.00 120.00

31-50: 38-Atom bomb panels 0.15 27.50 55.00

51-(1/54)-(3-D effect-c/story)-Only white cover 19.00 57.00 130.00

52-58: (3-D effect-c/stories with black covers). 52-E.C. swipe/Haunt Of Fear #14 16.00 49.00 115.00

59-3-D effect story only; new logo 11.00 32.00 75.00

60-Woodesque-a by Landau 6.50 19.00 45.00

Adventures Into Weird Worlds #22, © MEG

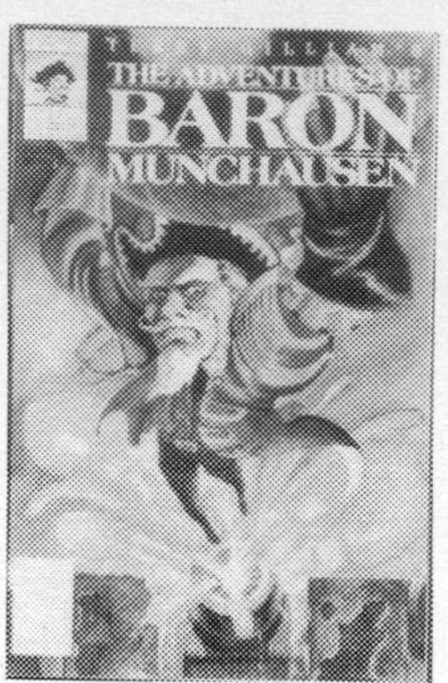

Advs. of Baron Munchausen#1, © Columbia Pictures

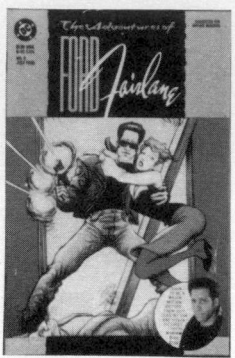

Advs. of Ford Fairlane #3, © 20th Century Fox

GD25 FN65 NM94

61-Last pre-code issue (1-2/55) 5.50 17.00 40.00
62-70 4.00 12.00 28.00
71-90 3.20 8.00 20.00
91,96(#95 on inside),107,116-All contain Williamson-a
4.00 12.00 28.00
92-95,97-99,101-106,108-115,117-127: 109-113,118-Whitney painted-c
2.60 7.50 18.00
100 3.25 9.50 22.00
128-Williamson/Krenkel/Torres-a(r)/Forbidden Worlds #63; last 10 cent issue
2.60 7.50 18.00
129-152 2.15 6.50 15.00
153, 157-Magic Agent app. 1.85 5.50 13.00
154-Nemesis series begins (origin), ends #170 2.35 7.00 16.50
155,156,158-167,169-174 1.75 5.25 12.50
168-Ditko-a(p) 2.50 7.50 17.50

NOTE: *"Spirit of Frankenstein" series in 5, 6, 8-10, 12, 16.* ***Buscema*** *a-100, 106, 108-110, 158r, 165r.* ***Craig*** *a-152, 160.* ***Goode*** *a-45, 47, 60.* ***Landau*** *a-51, 59-63.* ***Lazarus*** *a-48, 51, 52, 56, 58, 79, 87; c-31-56, 58.* ***Reinman*** *a-102, 111, 112, 115-118, 124, 130, 137, 141, 145, 164.* ***Whitney*** *c-12-30, 57, 59-on (most.)* ***Torres/Williamson*** *a-116.*

ADVENTURES INTO WEIRD WORLDS
Jan, 1952 - No. 30, June, 1954
Marvel/Atlas Comics (ACI)

1-Atom bomb panels 25.00 75.00 175.00
2-Sci/fic stories (2); one by Maneely 16.00 48.00 110.00
3-10: 7-Tongue ripped out. 10-Krigstein, Everett-a 10.00 30.00 70.00
11-21: 21-Hitler in Hell story 10.00 30.00 60.00
22-26: 24-Man holds hypo & splits in two 7.50 22.50 45.00
27-Matt Fox end of world story-a; severed head cover
13.00 40.00 110.00
28-Atom bomb story; decapitation panels 10.00 30.00 60.00
29,30 5.00 15.00 35.00

NOTE: ***Ayers*** *a-8, 26.* ***Everett*** *a-4, 5; c-6, 8, 10-13, 18, 19, 22, 24, 25; a-4, 25.* ***Fass*** *a-7.* ***Forte*** *a-21, 24.* ***Al Hartley*** *a-2.* ***Heath*** *a-1, 4, 17, 22; c-7, 9, 20.* ***Maneely*** *a-2, 3, 11, 20, 22, 23, 25; c-1, 3, 22, 25-27, 29.* ***Reinman*** *a-24, 28.* ***Rico*** *a-13.* ***Robinson*** *a-13.* ***Sinnott*** *a-25, 30.* ***Tuska*** *a-1, 2, 12, 15.* ***Whitney*** *a-7.* ***Wildey*** *a-28. Bondage c-22.*

ADVENTURES IN WONDERLAND
April, 1955 - No. 5, Feb, 1956 (Jr. Readers Guild)
Lev Gleason Publications

1-Maurer-a 5.35 16.00 32.00
2-4 4.00 10.00 21.00
5-Christmas issue 4.00 12.00 24.00

ADVENTURES OF ALAN LADD, THE
Oct-Nov, 1949 - No. 9, Feb-Mar, 1951 (All 52 pgs.)
National Periodical Publications

1-Photo-c 65.00 193.00 450.00
2-Photo-c 39.00 118.00 275.00
3-6: Last photo-c 29.00 85.00 200.00
7-9 24.00 70.00 165.00

NOTE: ***Dan Barry*** *a-1.* ***Moreira*** *a-3-7.*

ADVENTURES OF ALICE
1945 (Also see Alice in Wonderland & ...at Monkey Island)
Civil Service Publ./Pentagon Publishing Co.

1 8.50 26.00 52.00
2-Through the Magic Looking Glass 7.00 21.00 42.00

ADVENTURES OF BARON MUNCHAUSEN, THE (Now)(Value: cover or less)

ADVENTURES OF BAYOU BILLY, THE
Sept, 1989 - No. 5, June, 1990 ($1.00, color)
Archie Comics

1-5: Esposito-c/a(i). 5-Kelley Jones-c 1.00

ADVENTURES OF BOB HOPE, THE (Also see True Comics #59)
Feb-Mar, 1950 - No. 109, Feb-Mar, 1968 (#1-10: 52pgs.)
National Periodical Publications

1-Photo-c 100.00 300.00 700.00

GD25 FN65 NM94

2-Photo-c 50.00 150.00 350.00
3,4-Photo-c 32.00 95.00 225.00
5-10 25.00 75.00 175.00
11-20 14.00 43.00 100.00
21-31 (2-3/55; last precode) 10.00 30.00 70.00
32-40 8.00 24.00 55.00
41-50 6.50 19.00 45.00
51-70 4.30 13.00 30.00
71-93,95-105: 95-1st app. Super-Hip & 1st monster issue (11/65)
2.15 6.50 15.00
94-Aquaman cameo 2.60 7.50 18.00
106-109-All monster-c/stories by N. Adams-c/a 4.00 12.00 28.00

NOTE: *Buzzy in #34. Kitty Karr of Hollywood in #15, 17-20, 23, 28. Liz in #26, 109. Miss Beverly Hills of Hollywood in #7, 8, 10, 13, 14. Miss Melody Lane of Broadway in #15. Rusty in #23, 25. Tommy in #24. No 2nd feature in #2-4, 6, 8, 11, 12, 28-108.*

ADVENTURES OF CAPTAIN AMERICA
Sept, 1991 - No. 4, Jan, 1992 ($4.95, color, mini-series, 52 pgs.)
Marvel Comics

1-4: 1-Embossed-c. 2-4-Austin-c/a(i) 1.00 2.00 5.00

ADVENTURES OF CHRISSIE CLAUS, THE (Hero)(Value: cover or less)

ADVENTURES OF DEAN MARTIN AND JERRY LEWIS, THE
(The Adventures of Jerry Lewis #41 on; see Movie Love #12)
July-Aug, 1952 - No. 40, Oct, 1957
National Periodical Publications

1 64.00 193.00 450.00
2 32.00 95.00 225.00
3-10: 3-3 pg origin on how they became a team; I Love Lucy text featurette
14.00 43.00 100.00
11-19: Last precode (2/55) 10.00 30.-0 60.00
20-30 7.50 22.50 45.00
31-40 5.35 16.00 32.00

ADVENTURES OF FELIX THE CAT, THE
May, 1992 -Present ($1.25, color, quarterly)
Harvey Comics

1,2-Messmer-r 1.25

ADVENTURES OF FORD FAIRLANE, THE
May, 1990 - No. 4, Aug, 1990 ($1.50, mini-series, mature readers)
DC Comics

1-4: Movie tie-in; Don Heck inks 1.50

ADVENTURES OF G. I. JOE
1969 (3-1/4x7") (20 & 16 pgs.)
Giveaways

First Series: 1-Danger of the Depths. 2-Perilous Rescue. 3-Secret Mission to Spy Island. 4-Mysterious Explosion. 5-Fantastic Free Fall. 6-Eight Ropes of Danger. 7-Mouth of Doom. 8-Hidden Missile Discovery. 9-Space Walk Mystery. 10-Fight for Survival. 11-The Shark's Surprise. **Second Series:** 2-Flying Space Adventure. 4-White Tiger Hunt. 7-Capture of the Pygmy Gorilla. 12-Secret of the Mummy's Tomb. Third Series: Reprinted surviving titles of First Series. Fourth Series: 13-Adventure Team Headquarters. 14-Search For the Stolen Idol.
each.... .80

ADVENTURES OF HAWKSHAW (See Hawkshaw The Detective)
1917 (9-3/4x13-1/2", 48 pgs., Color & two-tone)
The Saalfield Publishing Co.

nn-By Gus Mager (only 24 pgs. of strips, reverse of each page is blank)
23.00 70.00 160.00

ADVENTURES OF HOMER COBB, THE
September, 1947 (Oversized)
Say/Bart Prod. (Canadian)

1-(Scarce)-Feldstein-a 19.00 58.00 135.00

ADVENTURES OF HOMER GHOST (See Homer The Happy Ghost)
June, 1957 - No. 2, August, 1957
Atlas Comics

V1#1,2 4.00 11.00 22.00

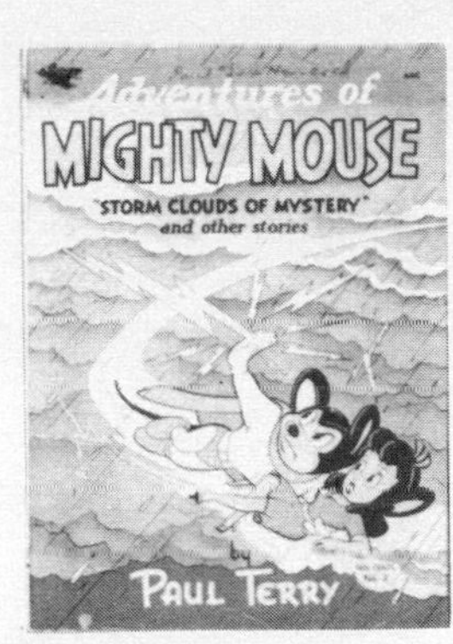

Adventures of Mighty Mouse #3, © Viacom

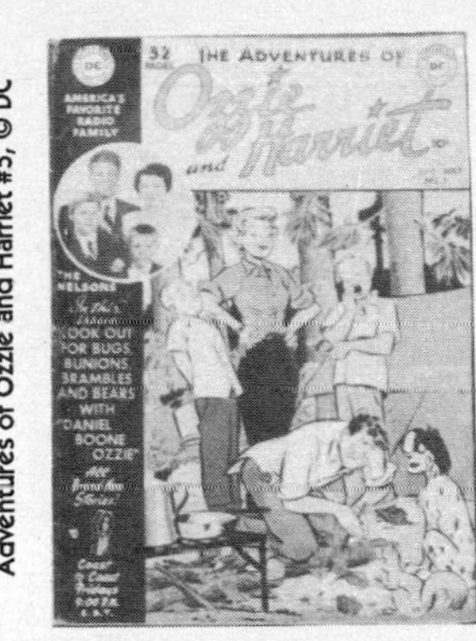

Adventures of Ozzie and Harriet #5, © DC

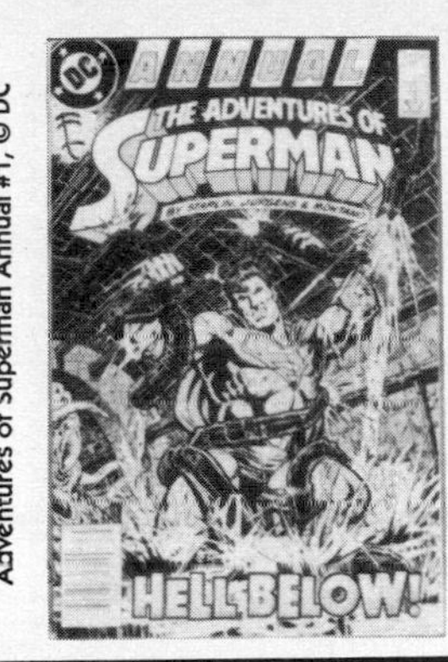

Adventures of Superman Annual #1, © DC

ADVENTURES OF JERRY LEWIS, THE (Advs. of Dean Martin & Jerry Lewis No. 1-40)(See Super DC Giant)
No. 41, Nov, 1957 - No. 124, May-June, 1971
National Periodical Publications

	GD25	FN65	NM94
41-60	4.00	12.00	28.00
61-80: 68,74-Photo-c	3.00	9.00	22.00
81-91,93-96,98-100: 89-Bob Hope app.	1.85	5.50	13.00
92-Superman cameo	2.60	7.50	18.00
97-Batman/Robin/Joker-c/story; Riddler & Penguin app.	3.60	10.75	25.00
101,103,104-Neal Adams-c/a;	3.20	8.00	20.00
102-Beatles app.; Neal Adams c/a	3.40	10.00	24.00
105-Superman x-over	2.00	6.00	14.00
106-111,113-116	1.00	2.50	6.00
112-Flash x-over	2.00	6.00	14.00
117-Wonder Woman x-over	1.30	3.25	8.00
118-124	1.00	2.00	5.00

ADVENTURES OF JO-JOY, THE (See Jo-Joy)

ADVENTURES OF LUTHER ARKWRIGHT, THE (Dark Horse)(Value: cover or less)

ADVENTURES OF MARGARET O'BRIEN, THE
1947 (20 pgs. in color; slick cover; regular size) (Premium)
Bambury Fashions (Clothes)

	GD25	FN65	NM94
In "The Big City"-movie adaptation (scarce)	13.50	41.00	95.00

ADVENTURES OF MIGHTY MOUSE (Mighty Mouse Advs. No. 1)
No. 2, Jan, 1952 - No. 18, May, 1955
St. John Publishing Co.

	GD25	FN65	NM94
2	16.00	48.00	110.00
3-5	10.00	30.00	60.00
6-18	6.70	20.00	40.00

ADVENTURES OF MIGHTY MOUSE (2nd Series)
(Two No. 144's; formerly Paul Terry's Comics; No. 129-137 have nn's)
(Becomes Mighty Mouse No. 161 on)
No. 126, Aug, 1955 - No. 160, Oct, 1963
St. John/Pines/Dell/Gold Key

	GD25	FN65	NM94
126(8/55), 127(10/55), 128(11/55)-St. John	4.00	11.00	22.00
nn(129, 4/56)-144(8/59)-Pines	3.60	9.00	18.00
144(10-12/59)-155(7-9/62) Dell	3.00	7.50	15.00
156(10/62)-160(10/63) Gold Key	3.00	7.50	15.00

NOTE: *Early issues titled "Paul Terry's Adventures of....*

ADVENTURES OF MIGHTY MOUSE (Formerly Mighty Mouse)
No. 166, Mar, 1979 - No. 172, Jan, 1980
Gold Key

	GD25	FN65	NM94
166-172	1.00	2.50	6.00

ADVS. OF MR. FROG & MISS MOUSE (See Dell Junior Treasury No. 4)

ADVENTURES OF OZZIE AND HARRIET, THE (Radio)
Oct-Nov, 1949 - No. 5, June-July, 1950
National Periodical Publications

	GD25	FN65	NM94
1-Photo-c	62.00	185.00	435.00
2	34.00	100.00	235.00
3-5	29.00	85.00	200.00

ADVENTURES OF PATORUZU
Aug, 1946 - Winter, 1946
Green Publishing Co.

	GD25	FN65	NM94
nn's-Contains Animal Crackers reprints	4.00	10.00	20.00

ADVENTURES OF PINKY LEE, THE (TV)
July, 1955 - No. 5, Dec, 1955
Atlas Comics

	GD25	FN65	NM94
1	17.00	52.00	120.00
2-5	10.00	30.00	70.00

ADVENTURES OF PIPSQUEAK, THE (Formerly Pat the Brat)
No. 34, Sept, 1959 - No. 39, July, 1960
Archie Publications (Radio Comics)

	GD25	FN65	NM94
34	4.00	11.00	22.00
35-39	3.00	7.50	15.00

ADVENTURES OF QUAKE & QUISP, THE (See Quaker Oats "Plenty of Glutton")

ADVENTURES OF REX THE WONDER DOG, THE (Rex...No. 1)
Jan-Feb, 1952 - No. 45, May-June, 1959; No. 46, Nov-Dec, 1959
National Periodical Publications

	GD25	FN65	NM94
1-(Scarce)-Toth-c/a	82.00	245.00	575.00
2-(Scarce)-Toth-c/a	39.00	118.00	275.00
3-(Scarce)-Toth-a	32.00	95.00	225.00
4,5	22.00	67.00	155.00
6-10	16.00	48.00	110.00
11-Atom bomb-c/story	17.00	52.00	120.00
12-19: 19-Last precode (1-2/55)	10.00	30.00	60.00
20-46	7.50	22.50	45.00

NOTE: *Infantino, Gil Kane art in 5-19 (most)*

ADVENTURES OF ROBIN HOOD, THE (Formerly Robin Hood)
No. 7, 9/57 - No. 8, 11/57 (Based on Richard Greene TV Show)
Magazine Enterprises (Sussex Publ. Co.)

	GD25	FN65	NM94
7,8-Richard Greene photo-c. 7-Powell-a	10.00	30.00	60.00

ADVENTURES OF ROBIN HOOD, THE
March, 1974 - No. 7, Jan, 1975 (Disney cartoon) (36 pgs.)
Gold Key

	GD25	FN65	NM94
1(90291-403)-Part-r of $1.50 editions	1.00	2.50	5.00
2-7: 1-7 are part-r	.60	1.50	3.00

ADVENTURES OF SLIM AND SPUD, THE
1924 (3-3/4x 9-3/4")(104 pg. B&W strip reprints)
Prairie Farmer Publ. Co.

	GD25	FN65	NM94
nn	13.00	40.00	90.00

ADVENTURES OF STUBBY, SANTA'S SMALLEST REINDEER, THE
nd (early 1940s) 12 pgs.
W. T. Grant Co. (Giveaway)

	GD25	FN65	NM94
nn	4.00	10.00	20.00

ADVENTURES OF SUPERBOY, THE (See Superboy, 2nd series)

ADVENTURES OF SUPERMAN (Formerly Superman)
No. 424, Jan, 1987 - No. 499, Feb, 1993; No. 500, Early June - Present
DC Comics

	GD25	FN65	NM94
424		.80	2.00
425-449: 426-Legends x-over. 432-1st app. Jose Delgado who becomes Gangbuster in #434. 436-Byrne scripts begin. 436,437-Millennium x-over. 438-New Brainiac app. 440-Batman app.		.70	1.75
450-463: 457-Perez plots. 463-Superman/Flash race; cover swipe/Superman #199			1.50
464-Lobo-c & app. (pre-dates Lobo #1)		1.60	4.00
465-479,481-491: 467-Part 2 of Batman story. 473-Hal Jordan, Guy Gardner x-over. 477-Legion app. 491-Last $1.00-c			1.00
480-($1.75, 52 pgs.)		.70	1.75
492-495: 495-Forever People-c/story			1.25
496-Doomsday cameo	1.00	2.50	6.00
496,497-2nd printings			1.25
497-Doomsday battle issue	1.00	2.50	0.00
498,499-Funeral for a Friend; Supergirl app.		1.20	3.00
498-2nd & 3rd printings			1.25
500-($2.95, 68 pgs.)-Collector's Edition w/card		1.20	3.00
500-($2.50, 68 pgs.)-Regular Edition w/different-c		1.00	2.50
500-Platinum Edition			100.00
501-($1.95)-Collector's Edition with die-cut-c		.80	2.00
501-($1.50)-Regular Edition w/mini-poster & diff.-c			1.50
502-510: 502-Supergirl-c/story			1.50

Adventures of the Dover Boys #1, © AP

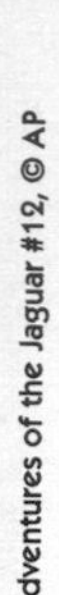

Adventures of the Jaguar #12, © AP

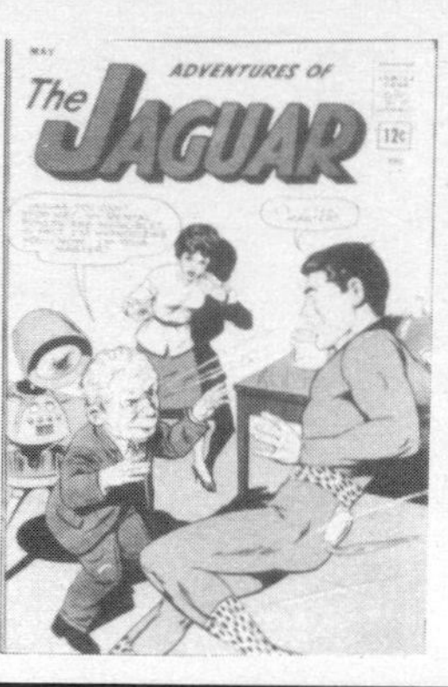

Against Blackshard 3-D #1, © Blackthorne

GD25 FN65 NM94

505-($2.50)-Holo-grafx foil-c Edition 1.00 2.50
Annual 1 (1987, $1.25, 52 pgs.)-Starlin-c 1.40
Annual 2,3 (1990, 1991, $2.00, 68 pgs.): 2-Byrne-c/a(i); Legion '90 (Lobo) app. 3-Armageddon 2001 x-over .80 2.00
Annual 4,5 (1992, 1993, $2.50, 68 pgs.): 4-Guy Gardner/Lobo-c/story; Eclipso storyline; Quesada-c(p). 5-Bloodlines storyline 1.00 2.50

ADVENTURES OF THE BIG BOY (Giveaway)
1956 - Present (East & West editions of early issues)
Timely Comics/Webs Adv. Corp./Illus. Features

	GD25	FN65	NM94
1-Everett-a	45.00	135.00	320.00
2-Everett-a	23.00	70.00	160.00
3-5	8.65	26.00	52.00
6-10: 6-Sci/fic issue	5.35	16.00	32.00
11-20	3.20	8.00	16.00
21-30	1.80	4.50	9.00
31-50		1.80	4.50
51-100		1.00	2.50
101-150			1.20
151-240			.50
241-417: 266-Superman x-over. 417-(1992)			.20
1-50 ('76-'84,Paragon Prod.)			.20
Summer, 1959 issue, large size	3.60	9.00	18.00

ADVENTURES OF THE DETECTIVE
No date (1930's) 36 pgs.; 9-1/2x12"; B&W (paper cover)
Humor Publ. Co.

	GD25	FN65	NM94
nn-Not reprints; Ace King by Martin Nadle	11.00	32.00	75.00
2nd version (printed in red & blue)	11.00	32.00	75.00

ADVENTURES OF THE DOVER BOYS
September, 1950 - No. 2, 1950 (No month given)
Archie Comics (Close-up)

	GD25	FN65	NM94
1,2	6.35	19.00	38.00

ADVENTURES OF THE FLY (The Fly #1-6; Fly Man No. 32-39; See The Double Life of Private Strong & Laugh Comics)
Aug, 1959 - No. 30, Oct, 1964; No. 31, May, 1965
Archie Publications/Radio Comics

	GD25	FN65	NM94
1-Shield app.; origin The Fly; S&K-c/a	50.00	150.00	350.00
2-Williamson, S&K-a	29.00	85.00	200.00
3-Origin retold; Davis, Powell-a	22.00	65.00	150.00
4-Neal Adams-a(p)(1 panel); S&K-c; Powell-a; 2 pg. Shield story	12.00	36.00	85.00
5-10: 7-1st S.A. app. Black Hood (7/60). 8-1st S.A. app. Shield (9/60). 9-Shield app. 9-1st app. Cat Girl. 10-Black Hood app.	8.00	24.00	55.00
11-13,15-20: 13-1st app. Fly Girl w/o costume. 16-Last 10 cent issue. 20-Origin Fly Girl retold	5.00	14.00	32.00
14-Origin & 1st app. Fly Girl in costume	6.50	19.00	45.00
21-30: 23-Jaguar cameo. 27-29-Black Hood 1 pg. strips. 30-Comet x-over (1st S.A. app.) in Fly Girl	3.25	9.50	22.00
31-Black Hood, Shield, Comet app.	3.60	10.75	25.00

NOTE: ***Simon** c-2-4. **Tuska** a-1. Cover title to #31 is Flyman; Advs. of the Fly inside.*

ADVENTURES OF THE JAGUAR, THE (See Blue Ribbon Comics, Laugh Comics & Mighty Crusaders)
Sept, 1961 - No. 15, Nov, 1963
Archie Publications (Radio Comics)

	GD25	FN65	NM94
1-Origin Jaguar (1st app?) by J.Rosenberger	16.00	50.00	115.00
2,3: 3-Last 10 cent issue	8.50	25.00	58.00
4-6-Catgirl app. (#4's-c is same as splash pg.)	5.50	17.00	40.00
7-10	4.00	12.00	28.00
11-15: 13,14-Catgirl, Black Hood app. in both	3.25	9.50	22.00

ADVENTURES OF THE OUTSIDERS, THE (Formerly Batman & The Outsiders; also see The Outsiders)
No. 33, May, 1986 - No. 46, June, 1987
DC Comics

GD25 FN65 NM94

33-46: 39-45-r/Outsiders #1-7 by Aparo 1.00

ADVENTURES OF THE SUPER MARIO BROTHERS
1990 - No. 9?, 1990? ($1.50, color) (Also see Super Mario Brothers)
Valiant

V2#1-9 1.50

ADVENTURES OF THE THING, THE (Also see The Thing)
Apr, 1992 - No. 4, July, 1992, ($1.25, color, mini-series)
Marvel Comics

1-4: 1-r/Marvel Two-In-One #50 by Byrne; Kieth-c. 2-4-r/Marvel Two-In-One #80,51 & 77; 2-Ghost Rider-c/story. 3-Miller-r 1.25

ADVENTURES OF TINKER BELL (See 4-Color No. 982)

ADVENTURES OF TOM SAWYER (See Dell Junior Treasury No. 10)

ADVENTURES OF WILLIE GREEN, THE
1915 (8-1/2X16", 50 cents, B&W, soft-c)
Frank M. Acton Co.

	GD25	FN65	NM94
Book 1-By Harris Brown; strip-r	13.50	41.00	95.00

ADVENTURES OF YOUNG DR. MASTERS, THE
Aug, 1964 - No. 2, Nov, 1964
Archie Comics (Radio Comics)

	GD25	FN65	NM94
1,2	1.00	2.50	6.00

ADVENTURES ON OTHER WORLDS (See Showcase #17 & 18)

ADVENTURES ON THE PLANET OF THE APES
Oct, 1975 - No. 11, Dec, 1976
Marvel Comics Group

	GD25	FN65	NM94
1-Planet of the Apes-r in color; Starlin-c		1.20	3.00
2-5		.90	2.20
6-11		.70	1.80

NOTE: ***Alcala** a-6-11r. **Buckler** c-2p. **Nasser** c-7. **Starlin** c-6. **Tuska** a-1-5r.*

ADVENTURES WITH SANTA CLAUS
No date (early 50's) (24 pgs.; 9-3/4x 6-3/4"; paper cover) (Giveaway)
Promotional Publ. Co. (Murphy's Store)

	GD25	FN65	NM94
nn-Contains 8 pgs. ads	4.00	10.00	21.00
16 page version	4.00	10.00	21.00

AFRICA
1955
Magazine Enterprises

	GD25	FN65	NM94
1(A-1#137)-Cave Girl,Thun'da;Powell-c/a(4)	14.00	43.00	100.00

AFRICAN LION (See 4-Color No. 665)

AFTER DARK
No. 6, May, 1955 - No. 8, Sept, 1955
Sterling Comics

	GD25	FN65	NM94
6-8-Sekowsky-a in all	5.00	15.00	30.00

AGAINST BLACKSHARD 3-D (Sirius)(Value: cover or less)

AGENT LIBERTY SPECIAL
1992 ($2.00, color, 52 pgs.)
DC Comics

	GD25	FN65	NM94
1-From Superman; 1st solo adv.; Guice-c/a(i)		.80	2.00

AGENT THREE-ZERO
Sept, 1993 - Present ($3.95, color, 52 pgs.)
Galaxinovels, Inc.

	GD25	FN65	NM94
1-Polybagged with card & mini-poster		1.60	4.00

AGGIE MACK
Jan, 1948 - No. 8, Aug, 1949
Four Star Comics Corp./Superior Comics Ltd.

	GD25	FN65	NM94
1-Feldstein-a, "Johnny Prep"	13.00	40.00	100.00
2,3-Kamen-c	8.35	25.00	50.00
4-Feldstein "Johnny Prep"; Kamen-c	10.00	30.00	70.00

Air Ace V2#7, © S&S

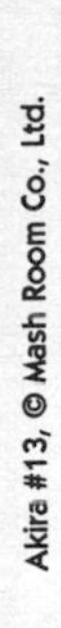
Akira #13, © Mash Room Co., Ltd.

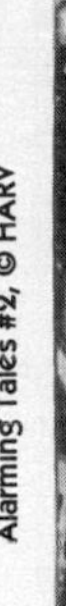
Alarming Tales #2, © HARV

	GD25	FN65	NM94
5-8-Kamen-c/a	9.15	27.50	55.00

AGGIE MACK (See 4-Color Comics No. 1335)

AIN'T IT A GRAND & GLORIOUS FEELING?
1922 (52 pgs.; 9x9-3/4"; stiff cardboard cover)
Whitman Publishing Co.

	GD25	FN65	NM94
nn-1921 daily strip-r; B&W, color-c; Briggs-a	13.50	41.00	95.00

AIR ACE (Formerly Bill Barnes No. 1-12)
V2#1, Jan, 1944 - V3#8(No. 20), Feb-Mar, 1947
Street & Smith Publications

	GD25	FN65	NM94
V2#1	12.00	36.00	85.00
V2#2-12: 7-Powell-a	7.50	22.50	45.00
V3#1-6	5.00	15.00	30.00
V3#7-Powell bondage-c/a; all atomic issue	10.00	30.00	70.00
V3#8 (V5#8 on-c)-Powell-c/a	5.85	17.50	35.00

AIRBOY (Eclipse)(Value: cover or less)

AIRBOY COMICS (Air Fighters Comics No. 1-22)
V2#11, Dec, 1945 - V10#4, May, 1953 (No V3#3)
Hillman Periodicals

	GD25	FN65	NM94
V2#11	40.00	125.00	275.00
12-Valkyrie app.	28.00	85.00	190.00
V3#1,2(no #3)	24.00	72.00	165.00
4-The Heap app. in Skywolf	21.00	63.00	145.00
5-8,10,11: 6-Valkyrie app.	17.00	52.00	120.00
9-Origin The Heap	21.00	63.00	145.00
12-Skywolf & Airboy x-over; Valkyrie app.	22.00	68.00	155.00
V4#1-Iron Lady app.	21.00	63.00	145.00
2,3,12: 2-Rackman begins	12.00	36.00	85.00
4-Simon & Kirby-c	14.00	42.00	95.00
5-11-All S&K-a	18.00	55.00	120.00
V5#1-11: 4-Infantino Heap. 5-Skull-c. 10-Origin The Heap	10.00	30.00	65.00
12-Krigstein-a(p)	12.00	35.00	80.00
V6#1-3,5-12: 6,8-Origin The Heap	10.00	30.00	65.00
4-Origin retold	11.00	32.00	75.00
V7#1-12: 7,8,10-Origin The Heap	10.00	30.00	65.00
V8#1-3,6-12	9.15	27.50	55.00
4-Krigstein-a	10.00	30.00	65.00
5(#100)	10.00	30.00	60.00
V9#1-12: 2-Valkyrie app. 7-One pg. Frazetta ad	8.35	25.00	50.00
V10#1-4	8.35	25.00	50.00

NOTE: ***Barry** a-V2#3, 7. **Bolle** a-V4#12. **McWilliams** a-V3#7, 9. **Powell** a-V7#2, 3, V8#1, 6. **Starr** a-V5#1, 12. **Dick Wood** a-V4#12. Bondage-c V5#8.*

AIR FIGHTERS CLASSICS (Eclipse)(Value: cover or less)

AIR FIGHTERS COMICS (Airboy Comics #23 (V2#11) on)
Nov, 1941; No. 2, Nov, 1942 - V2#10, Fall, 1945
Hillman Periodicals

	GD25	FN65	NM94
V1#1-(Produced by Funnies, Inc.); Black Commander only app.	133.00	400.00	900.00
2(11/42)-(Produced by Quality artists & Biro for Hillman); Origin & 1st app. Airboy & Iron Ace; Black Angel (1st app.), Flying Dutchman & Skywolf (1st app.) begin; Fuje-a; Biro-c/a	217.00	650.00	1450.00
3 Origin/1st app. The Heap; origin Skywolf	108.00	325.00	750.00
4	75.00	225.00	500.00
5,6	57.00	172.00	400.00
7-12	43.00	130.00	300.00
V2#1,3-9: 5-Flag-c; Fuje-a. 7-Valkyrie app.	41.00	122.00	275.00
2-Skywolf by Giunta; Flying Dutchman by Fuje, 1st meeting Valkyrie & Airboy (she worked for the Nazis in beginning); 1st app. Valkyrie (11/43)	52.00	158.00	350.00
10-Origin The Heap & Skywolf	50.00	150.00	325.00

NOTE: ***Fuje** a-V1#2, 5, 7, V2#2, 3, 5, 7-9. **Giunta** a-V2#2, 3, 7, 9.*

AIRFIGHTERS MEET SGT. STRIKE SPECIAL, THE (Eclipse)(Value: cover or less)

AIR FORCES (See American Air Forces)

AIRMAIDENS SPECIAL (Eclipse)(Value: cover or less)

AIR POWER (CBS TV & the U.S. Air Force Presents)
1956 (32pgs, 5-1/4x7-1/4", soft-c)
Prudential Insurance Co. giveaway

	GD25	FN65	NM94
nn-Toth-a? Based on 'You Are There' TV program by Walter Cronkite	8.35	25.00	50.00

AIR RAIDERS (Marvel)(Value: cover or less)

AIR WAR STORIES
Sept-Nov, 1964 - No. 8, Aug, 1966
Dell Publishing Co.

	GD25	FN65	NM94
1-Painted-c; Glanzman-c/a begins	4.00	10.00	20.00
2-8: 2-Painted-c (all painted?)	2.40	6.00	12.00

AKIRA
Sept, 1988 - No. 37? ($3.50-$3.75, color, deluxe, 68 pgs.)
Epic Comics (Marvel)

	GD25	FN65	NM94
1	2.15	6.50	15.00
1,2-2nd printings ('89, $3.95)		1.40	3.50
2	1.50	3.75	9.00
3-5	1.25	3.00	7.50
6-15	1.00	2.50	5.50
16-33: 17-Begin $3.95-c		1.40	3.50
34,35 ($4.95-c)	1.00	2.00	5.00

ALADDIN (Disney Comics)(Value: cover or less)(Also see Dell Junior Treasury No. 2)

ALAN LADD (See The Adventures of ...)

ALARMING ADVENTURES
Oct, 1962 - No. 3, Feb, 1963
Harvey Publications

	GD25	FN65	NM94
1-Crandall/Williamson-a	5.85	17.50	35.00
2,3: 2-Williamson/Crandall-a	4.00	11.00	22.00

NOTE: ***Bailey** a-1, 3. **Crandall** a-1p, 2i. **Powell** a-2(2). **Severin** c-1-3. **Torres** a-2? **Tuska** a-1. **Williamson** a-1i, 2p, 3.*

ALARMING TALES
Sept, 1957 - No. 6, Nov, 1958
Harvey Publications (Western Tales)

	GD25	FN65	NM94
1-Kirby-c/a(4); Kamandi prototype story by Kirby	10.00	30.00	65.00
2-Kirby-a(4)	10.00	30.00	60.00
3,4-Kirby-a. 4-Powell, Wildey-a	6.70	20.00	40.00
5-Kirby/Williamson-a; Wildey-a; Severin-c	7.50	22.50	45.00
6-Williamson-a?; Severin-c	5.00	15.00	35.00

ALBEDO
April, 1985 - No. 14, Spring, 1989 (B&W)
Thoughts And Images

	GD25	FN65	NM94
0-Yellow cover; 50 copies	6.50	19.00	45.00
0-White cover, 450 copies	5.00	15.00	35.00
0-Blue, 1st printing, 500 copies	1.85	5.50	13.00
0-Blue, 2nd printing, 1000 copies	1.30	3.25	8.00
0-3rd printing		.80	2.00
0-4th printing			1.20
1-Dark red; 1st app. Usagi Yojimbo	1.60	3.80	9.75
1-Bright red	1.60	3.80	9.75
2	1.00	2.50	6.00
3-14		.80	2.00

ALBERTO (See The Crusaders)

ALBERT THE ALLIGATOR & POGO POSSUM (See 4-Color Comics #105, 148)

ALBUM OF CRIME (See Fox Giants)

ALBUM OF LOVE (See Fox Giants)

AL CAPP'S DOGPATCH (Also see Mammy Yokum)
No. 71, June, 1949 - No. 4, Dec, 1949
Toby Press

Algie #2 (reprint), © Accepted

Alien Encounters #12, © Eclipse

Alien Nation #1, © 20th Century Fox Films

	GD25	FN65	NM94
71(#1)-Reprints from Tip Top #112-114	22.00	65.00	150.00
2-4: 4-Reprints from Li'l Abner #73	14.00	43.00	100.00

AL CAPP'S SHMOO (Also see Oxydol-Dreft)
July, 1949 - No. 5, April, 1950 (None by Al Capp)
Toby Press

	GD25	FN65	NM94
1	27.00	81.00	190.00
2-5: 3-Sci-fi trip to moon. 4-X-Mas-c; origin/1st app. Super-Shmoo	20.00	60.00	140.00

AL CAPP'S WOLF GAL
1951 - No. 2, 1952
Toby Press

	GD25	FN65	NM94
1,2-Edited-r from Li'l Abner #63,64	27.00	81.00	190.00

ALEXANDER THE GREAT (See 4-Color No. 688)

ALF (TV) (See Star Comics Digest)
Mar, 1988 - No. 50, Feb, 1992 ($1.00, color)
Marvel Comics

	GD25	FN65	NM94
1-49: 22-X-Men parody			1.00
50-($1.75, 52 pgs.)-Final issue; photo-c		.70	1.75
Annual 1-3		.70	1.75
...Comics Digest 1 (1988)-Reprints Alf #1,2			1.50
Holiday Special 1 (1988, $1.75, 68 pgs.)		.70	1.75
Holiday Special 2 (Winter, 1989, $2.00, 68 pgs.)		.80	2.00
Spring Special 1 (Spr/89, $1.75, 68 pgs.)		.70	1.75

ALGIE
Dec, 1953 - No. 3, 1954
Timor Publ. Co.

	GD25	FN65	NM94
1-Teenage	3.60	9.00	18.00
2,3	2.80	7.00	14.00
Accepted Reprint #2(nd)	1.60	4.00	8.00
Super Reprint #15	1.40	3.50	7.00

ALIAS: (Now)(Value: cover or less)

ALICE (New Adventures in Wonderland)
No. 10, 7-8/51 - No. 2, 11-12/51
Ziff-Davis Publ. Co.

	GD25	FN65	NM94
10-Painted-c; Berg-a	14.00	43.00	100.00
11-Dave Berg-a	8.35	25.00	50.00
2-Dave Berg-a	6.70	20.00	40.00

ALICE AT MONKEY ISLAND (See The Adventures of Alice)
No. 3, 1946
Pentagon Publ. Co. (Civil Service)

	GD25	FN65	NM94
3	5.85	17.50	35.00

ALICE IN BLUNDERLAND
1952 (Paper cover, 16 pages in color)
Industrial Services

	GD25	FN65	NM94
nn-Facts about big government waste and inefficiency	12.00	36.00	84.00

ALICE IN WONDERLAND (See Advs. of Alice, 4-Color No. 331,341, Dell Jr. Treasury No. 1, The Dreamery, Movie Comics, Single Series No. 24, Walt Disney Showcase No. 22, and World's Greatest Stories)

ALICE IN WONDERLAND
1965; 1982
Western Printing Company/Whitman Publ. Co.

	GD25	FN65	NM94
Meets Santa Claus(1950s), nd, 16 pgs.	3.60	9.00	18.00
Rexall Giveaway(1965, 16 pgs., 5x7-1/4) Western Printing (TV, Hanna-Barbera)	2.80	7.00	14.00
Wonder Bakery Giveaway(16 pgs, color, nn, nd) (Continental Baking Company, 1969)	2.80	7.00	14.00
1-(Whitman; 1982)-r/4-Color #331			1.20

ALICE IN WONDERLAND MEETS SANTA
nd (16 pgs., 6-5/8x9-11/16", paper cover)
No publisher (Giveaway)

	GD25	FN65	NM94
nn	10.00	30.00	65.00

ALIEN ENCOUNTERS (Eclipse)(Value: cover or less)

ALIEN LEGION (See Epic & Marvel Graphic Novel #25)
April, 1984 - No. 20, Sept, 1987
Epic Comics (Marvel)

	GD25	FN65	NM94
1-$2.00 cover, high quality paper		.80	2.00
2-20			1.50

ALIEN LEGION (2nd series)
Aug, 1987 (indicia) (10/87 on-c) - No. 18, Aug, 1990 ($1.25, color)
Epic Comics (Marvel)

	GD25	FN65	NM94
V2#1-6			1.25
7-18: 7-Begin $1.50 cover			1.50

ALIEN LEGION: BINARY DEEP
1993 ($3.50, color, one-shot, 52 pgs.)
Epic Comics (Marvel)

	GD25	FN65	NM94
nn-With bound-in trading card		1.40	3.50

ALIEN LEGION: JUGGER GRIMROD
Aug, 1992 ($5.95, color, one-shot, 52 pgs.)
Epic Comics (Marvel)

	GD25	FN65	NM94
Book One	1.00	2.50	6.00

ALIEN LEGION: ONE PLANET AT A TIME
May, 1993 - No. 3, July, 1993 ($4.95, color, squarebound, 52 pgs.)
Epic Comics (Marvel)

	GD25	FN65	NM94
Book 1-3: Hoang Nguyen	1.00	2.00	5.00

ALIEN LEGION: ON THE EDGE (The... #2 & 3)
Nov, 1990 - No. 3, Jan, 1991 ($4.50, color, mini-series, 52 pgs.)
Epic Comics (Marvel)

	GD25	FN65	NM94
1-3		1.80	4.50

ALIEN LEGION: TENNANTS OF HELL
1991 - No. 2, 1991 ($4.50, color, squarebound, 52 pgs.)
Epic Comics (Marvel)

	GD25	FN65	NM94
Book 1,2-Stroman-c/a(p)		1.80	4.50

ALIEN NATION
Dec, 1988 ($2.50; 68 pgs.)
DC Comics

	GD25	FN65	NM94
1-Adapts movie; painted-c		1.00	2.50

ALIENS, THE (Captain Johner and...)(Also see Magnus Robot...)
Sept-Dec, 1967; No. 2, May, 1982
Gold Key

	GD25	FN65	NM94
1-Reprints from Magnus #1,3,4,6-10, all by Russ Manning	2.15	6.50	15.00
2-Reprints from Magnus #1 by Manning		1.60	4.00

ALIENS (See Alien: The Illustrated... & Dark Horse Presents #24)
May, 1988 - No. 6, July, 1989 ($1.95, B&W, mini-series)
Dark Horse Comics

	GD25	FN65	NM94
1-Based on movie sequel; 1st app. Aliens	5.00	15.00	35.00
1-2nd printing	1.50	3.75	9.00
1-3rd - 6th printings; 4th w/new inside front-c		.80	2.00
2	3.60	10.75	25.00
2-2nd printing		1.60	4.00
2-3rd printing w/new inside f/c		.80	2.00
3	1.70	5.00	12.00
4	1.30	3.25	8.00
5,6	1.00	2.50	6.00
3-6-2nd printings		.80	2.00
Mini Comic #1 (2/89, 4x6")-Was included with Aliens Portfolio	1.65	4.00	10.00

Alien Worlds #4, © Bruce Jones

All-American Comics #12, © DC

All-American Comics #47, © DC

GD25 FN65 NM94

...Collection 1 ($10.95,)-r/#1-6 plus Dark Horse Presents #24 plus new-a 1.60 4.70 11.00
...Collection 1-2nd printing (1991, $11.95)-Printed on higher quality paper than 1st print; Dorman painted-c 1.70 5.00 12.00
Hardcover ('90, $24.95, B&W)-r/1-6, DHP #24 3.60 10.75 25.00
Platinum Edition (See Dark Horse Presents: Aliens Platinum Edition)

ALIENS
V2#1, Aug, 1989 - No. 4, 1990 ($2.25, color, mini-series)
Dark Horse Comics

V2#1 ($2.25, color)-Adapts sequel 1.70 5.00 12.00
1-2nd printing ($2.25) .90 2.25
2-4 1.00 2.50 6.00

ALIENS: COLONIAL MARINES
Jan, 1993 - No. 12, 1994 ($2.50, color, limited series)
Dark Horse Comics

1-12 1.00 2.50

ALIENS: EARTH WAR
June, 1990 - No. 4, Oct, 1990 ($2.50, color, mini-series)
Dark Horse Comics

1-All have Sam Kieth-a & Bolton painted-c 1.65 4.00 10.00
1-2nd printing 1.00 2.50
2 1.30 3.25 8.00
3,4 1.10 2.70 6.50

ALIENS: GENOCIDE
Nov, 1991 - No. 4, Feb, 1992 ($2.50, color, mini-series)
Dark Horse Comics

1-4: All have Arthur Suydam painted-c 1.00 2.50

ALIENS: HIVE
Feb, 1992 - No. 4, May, 1992 ($2.50, color, mini-series)
Dark Horse Comics

1-4: Kelley Jones-c/a in all 1.00 2.50

ALIENS: LABYRINTH
Sept, 1993 - No. 4, May, 1993 ($2.50, color, mini-series)
Dark Horse Comics

1-4: Painted-c 1.00 2.50

ALIENS: NEWT'S TALE (Dark Horse)(Value: cover or less)

ALIENS/PREDATOR: THE DEADLIEST OF SPECIES
July, 1993 - No. 12, 1995 ($2.50, color, limited series, bi-monthly)
Dark Horse Comics

1-6: Bolton painted-c; Guice-a(p) 1.00 2.50
1-Embossed foil platinum edition 30.00

ALIENS: ROGUE
Apr, 1993 - No. 4, July, 1993 ($2.50, color, mini-series)
Dark Horse Comics

1-4: Painted-c 1.00 2.50

ALIENS: SACRIFICE
May, 1993 ($4.95, color, one-shot, 52 pgs.)
Dark Horse Comics

nn-Peter Milligan scripts; painted-c/a 1.00 2.00 5.00

ALIENS VS. PREDATOR (See Dark Horse Presents #36)
June, 1990 - No. 4, Dec, 1990, ($2.50, color, mini-series)
Dark Horse Comics

1-Painted-c 1.70 5.00 12.00
1-2nd printing 1.00 2.50
0-(7/90, $1.95, B&W)-r/Dark Horse Pres. #34-36 2.15 6.50 15.00
2,3 1.50 3.75 9.00
4-Dave Dorman painted-c 1.00 2.00 5.00

ALIEN TERROR (See 3-D Alien Terror)

GD25 FN65 NM94

ALIEN: THE ILLUSTRATED STORY (Also see Aliens)
1980 ($3.95, color, soft-c, 8X11")
Heavy Metal Books

nn-Movie adaptation; Simonson-a 1.60 4.00

ALIEN 3
June, 1992 - No. 3, July, 1992 ($2.50, color, mini-series)
Dark Horse Comics

1-3: Adapts 3rd movie; Suydam painted-c 1.00 2.50

ALIEN WORLDS (Pacific)(Value: cover or less)(See Eclipse Graphic Album #22)

ALL-AMERICAN COMICS (...Western #103-126, ...Men of War #127 on; also see The Big All-American Comic Book)
April, 1939 - No. 102, Oct, 1948
All-American/National Periodical Publications

1-Hop Harrigan (1st app.), Scribbly by Mayer (1st app.), Toonerville Folks, Ben Webster, Spot Savage, Mutt & Jeff, Red White & Blue (1st app.), Adv. in the Unknown, Tippie, Reg'lar Fellers, Skippy, Bobby Thatcher, Mystery Men of Mars, Daiseybelle, Wiley of West Point begin 357.00 1070.00 2500.00
2-Ripley's Believe It or Not begins, ends #24 110.00 325.00 750.00
3-5: 5-The American Way begins, ends #10 80.00 240.00 550.00
6,7: 6-Last Spot Savage; Popsicle Pete begins, ends #26, 28. 7-Last Bobby Thatcher 67.00 200.00 475.00
8-The Ultra Man begins & 1st-c app. 105.00 310.00 725.00
9,10: 10-X-Mas-c 72.00 215.00 500.00
11-15: 11-Ultra Man-c. 12-Last Toonerville Folks. 15-Last Tippie & Reg'lar Fellars; Ultra Man-c 64.00 193.00 450.00

GD25 FN65 VF82 NM94

16-(Rare)-Origin/1st app. Green Lantern by Sheldon Mayer (c/a)(7/40) & begin series; appears in costume on-c & only one panel inside; created by Martin Nodell. Inspired by Aladdin's Lamp; the suggested alter ego name Alan Ladd, was never capitalized on. It was changed to Alan Scott before Alan Ladd became a major film star (he was in two films before this issue); new logo begins 3,700.00 11,100.00 24,050.00 37,000.00
(Estimated up to 35+ total copies exist, 3 in NM/Mint)

GD25 FN65 NM94

17-(Scarce)-2nd Green Lantern 860.00 2570.00 6000.00
18-N.Y. World's Fair-c/story 585.00 1750.00 4000.00

GD25 FN65 VF82 NM94

19-Origin/1st app. The Atom (10/40); last Ultra Man 860.00 2570.00 4285.00 6000.00
(Estimated up to 80 total copies exist, 5 in NM/Mint)

GD25 FN65 NM94

20-Atom dons costume; Ma Hunkle becomes Red Tornado (1st app.)(1st DC costumed heroine, before Wonder Woman, 11/40); Rescue on Mars begins, ends #25; 1 pg. origin Green Lantern 250.00 750.00 1750.00
21-23: 21-Last Wiley of West Point & Skippy. 23-Last Daiseybelle; 3 Idiots begin, end #82 150.00 450.00 1000.00
24-Sisty & Dinky become the Cyclone Kids; Ben Webster ends. Origin Dr. Mid-Nite & Sargon, The Sorcerer in text with app. 185.00 550.00 1300.00

GD25 FN65 VF82 NM94

25-Origin & 1st story app. Dr. Mid-Nite by Stan Asch; Hop Harrigan becomes Guardian Angel; last Adventure in the Unknown 600.00 1800.00 3000.00 4200.00
(Estimated up to 120 total copies exist, 6 in NM/Mint)

GD25 FN65 NM94

26-Origin/1st story app. Sargon, the Sorcerer 192.00 575.00 1350.00
27: #27-32 are misnumbered in indicia with correct No. appearing on-c. Intro. Doiby Dickles, Green Lantern's sidekick 250.00 750.00 1750.00
28-Hop Harrigan gives up costumed i.d. 100.00 300.00 675.00
29,30 100.00 300.00 675.00
31-40: 35-Doiby learns Green Lantern's i.d. 75.00 225.00 500.00
41-50: 50-Sargon ends 67.00 200.00 440.00
51-60: 59-Scribbly & the Red Tornado ends 57.00 170.00 375.00
61-Origin/1st app. Solomon Grundy (11/44) 230.00 685.00 1600.00

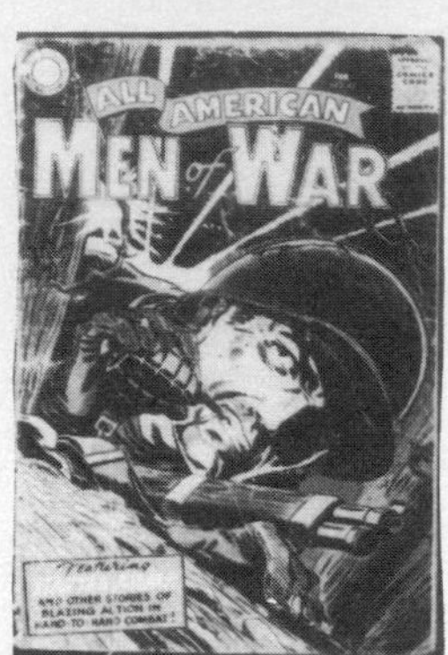

All-American Men of War #42, © DC

All-American Western #119, © DC

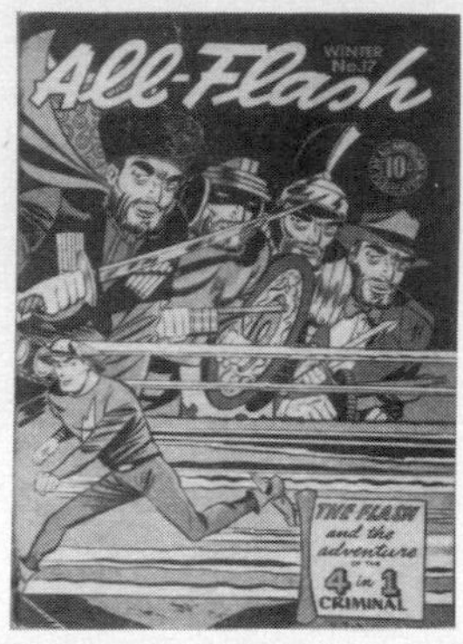

All-Flash #17, © DC

	GD25	FN65	NM94
62-70: 70-Kubert Sargon; intro Sargon's helper, Maximillian O'Leary	48.00	145.00	310.00
71-88,90-99: 71-Last Red White & Blue. 72-Black Pirate begins (not in #74-82); last Atom. 73-Winky, Blinky & Noddy begins, ends #82. 79,83-Mutt & Jeff-c. 90-Origin/1st app. Icicle. 99-Last Hop Harrigan	42.00	125.00	280.00
89-Origin & 1st app. Harlequin	50.00	150.00	350.00
100-1st app. Johnny Thunder by Alex Toth (8/48); western theme begins	83.00	250.00	575.00
101-Last Mutt & Jeff	67.00	200.00	475.00
102-Last Green Lantern, Black Pirate & Dr. Mid-Nite	89.00	270.00	625.00

NOTE: *No Atom in 47, 62-69.* ***Kinstler*** *Black Pirate-89.* ***Stan Aschmeier*** *a (Dr. Mid-Nite) 25-84; c-7.* ***Mayer*** *c-1, 2(part), 6, 10.* ***Moldoff*** *c-16-23.* ***Nodell*** *c-31.* ***Paul Reinman*** *a (Green Lantern)-53-55p, 56-84, 87; (Black Pirate)-83-88, 90; c-52, 55-76, 78, 80, 81, 87.* ***Toth*** *a-88, 92, 96, 98-102; c(p)-92, 96-102. Scribbly by* ***Mayer*** *in #1-59. Ultra Man by* ***Mayer*** *in #8-19.*

ALL-AMERICAN MEN OF WAR (Previously All-American Western)
No. 127, Aug-Sept, 1952 - No. 117, Sept-Oct, 1966
National Periodical Publications

	GD25	FN65	NM94
127 (#1, 1952)	64.00	195.00	450.00
128 (1952)	45.00	135.00	315.00
2(12-1/'52-53)-5	37.00	110.00	260.00
6-10	22.00	66.00	155.00
11-18: Last precode (2/55)	20.00	60.00	140.00
19-28	14.00	43.00	100.00
29,30,32-Wood-a	16.00	48.00	110.00
31,33-40	11.00	34.00	80.00
41-50	9.00	28.00	65.00
51-66	7.00	21.00	50.00
67-1st Gunner & Sarge by Andru & Esposito	12.00	36.00	85.00
68-70	7.00	20.00	47.00
71-80	4.30	13.00	30.00
81,83-88: 88-Last 10 cent issue	3.25	9.50	22.00
82-Johnny Cloud begins, ends #111,114,115	5.50	16.00	38.00
89-100	3.20	8.00	20.00
101-117: 112-Balloon Buster series begins, ends #114,116; 115-Johnny Cloud app.	2.15	6.50	15.00

NOTE: ***Colan*** *a-112.* ***Drucker*** *a-47, 65, 71, 74, 77.* ***Grandenetti*** *c(p)-127, 128, 2-17(most).* ***Heath*** *a-27, 32, 47, 71, 95, 111, 112; c-85, 91, 94-96, 100, 101, 112, others?* ***Kirby*** *a-29.* ***Krigstein*** *a-128('52), 2, 3, 5.* ***Kubert*** *a-29, 36, 38, 41, 43, 47, 49, 50, 52, 53, 55, 56, 60, 63, 65, 69, 71-73, 102, 103, 105, 106, 108, 114; c-41, 77, 102, 103, 105, 106, 108, 114, others? Tank Killer in 69, 71, 76 by* ***Kubert. P. Reinman*** *c-55, 57, 61, 62, 71, 72, 74-76, 80.*

ALL-AMERICAN SPORTS
October, 1967
Charlton Comics

	GD25	FN65	NM94
1	1.80	4.50	9.00

ALL-AMERICAN WESTERN (Formerly All-American Comics; Becomes All-American Men of War)
No. 103, Nov, 1948 - No. 126, June-July, 1952 (103-121: 52 pgs.)
National Periodical Publications

	GD25	FN65	NM94
103-Johnny Thunder & his horse Black Lightning continues by Toth, ends #126; Foley of The Fighting 5th, Minstrel Maverick, & Overland Coach begin; Captain Tootsie by Beck; mentioned in Love and Death	36.00	110.00	255.00
104-Kubert-a	25.00	75.00	175.00
105,107-Kubert-a	21.00	62.00	145.00
106,108-110,112: 112-Kurtzman "Pot-Shot Pete," (1 pg.)	16.00	48.00	110.00
111,114-116-Kubert-a	18.00	54.00	125.00
113-Intro. Swift Deer, J. Thunder's new sidekick (4-5/50); classic Toth-c; Kubert-a	20.00	60.00	140.00
117-126: 121-Kubert-a	13.00	40.00	90.00

NOTE: ***G. Kane*** *c(p)-119, 120, 123.* ***Kubert*** *a-103-105, 107, 111, 112(1 pg.), 113-116, 121.* ***Toth*** *a 103-126; c(p)-103-116, 121, 122, 124-126. Some copies of #125 have #12 on-c.*

ALL COMICS
1945
Chicago Nite Life News

	GD25	FN65	NM94
1	9.15	27.50	55.00

ALLEY OOP (See The Comics, 4-Color #3, The Funnies, Red Ryder and Super Book #9)

ALLEY OOP
No. 10, 1947 - No. 18, Oct, 1949
Standard Comics

	GD25	FN65	NM94
10	17.00	52.00	120.00
11-18: 17,18-Schomburg-c	13.00	40.00	90.00

ALLEY OOP
Nov, 1955 - No. 3, March, 1956 (Newspaper reprints)
Argo Publ.

	GD25	FN65	NM94
1	11.00	32.00	75.00
2,3	9.15	27.50	55.00

ALLEY OOP
12-2/62-63 - No. 2, 9-11/63
Dell Publishing Co.

	GD25	FN65	NM94
1,2	6.70	20.00	40.00

ALL-FAMOUS CRIME (Formerly Law Against Crime #1-3; becomes All-Famous Police Cases #6 on)
No. 4, 2/50 - No. 5, 5/50; No. 8, 5/51 - No. 10, 11/51
Star Publications

	GD25	FN65	NM94
4 (#1-1st series)-Formerly Law-Crime	8.35	25.00	50.00
5 (#2)	5.00	15.00	30.00
8 (#3-2nd series)	7.50	22.50	45.00
9 (#4)-Used in **SOTI**, illo-"The wish to hurt or kill couples in lovers' lanes is a not uncommon perversion;" L.B. Cole-c/a(r)/Law-Crime #3	12.00	36.00	85.00
10 (#5)-Becomes All-Famous Police Cases #6	5.00	15.00	30.00

NOTE: *All have* ***L.B. Cole*** *covers.*

ALL FAMOUS CRIME STORIES (See Fox Giants)

ALL-FAMOUS POLICE CASES (Formerly All Famous Crime #10 [#5])
No. 6, Feb, 1952 - No. 16, Sept, 1954
Star Publications

	GD25	FN65	NM94
6	6.70	20.00	40.00
7,8: 7-Kubert-a. 8-Marijuana story	5.00	15.00	30.00
9-16	4.20	12.50	25.00

NOTE: ***L. B. Cole*** *c-all; a-15, 1pg.* ***Hollingsworth*** *a-15.*

ALL-FLASH (...Quarterly No. 1-5)
Summer, 1941 - No. 32, Dec-Jan, 1947-48
National Periodical Publications/All-American

	GD25	FN65	VF82	NM94
1-Origin The Flash retold by E. E. Hibbard; Hibbard c-1-10,12-14,16,31p	725.00	2175.00	3990.00	5800.00

(Estimated up to 200 total copies exist, 11 in NM/Mint)

	GD25	FN65	NM94
2-Origin recap	157.00	471.00	1100.00
3,4	104.00	315.00	725.00
5-Winky, Blinky & Noddy begins (1st app.), ends #32	80.00	240.00	525.00
6-10	62.00	190.00	425.00
11-13: 12-Origin/1st The Thinker. 13-The King app.	56.00	170.00	375.00
14-Green Lantern cameo	64.00	190.00	445.00
15-20: 18-Mutt & Jeff begins, ends #22	50.00	150.00	340.00
21-31	40.00	120.00	275.00
32-Origin/1st app. The Fiddler; 1st Star Sapphire	63.00	185.00	425.00

NOTE: *Book length stories in 2-13, 16. Bondage c-31, 32.* ***Martin Naydell*** *c-15, 17-28.*

ALL FOR LOVE (Young Love V3#5-on)
Apr-May, 1957 - V3#4, Dec-Jan, 1959-60
Prize Publications

	GD25	FN65	NM94
V1#1	5.35	16.00	32.00
2-6: 5-Orlando-c	3.60	9.00	18.00
V2#1-5(1/59), 5(3/59)	2.40	6.00	12.00

All Great Comics #1, © FOX

All-Negro Comics #1, © All-Negro Comics

All-Picture Comedy Carnival #1, © STJ

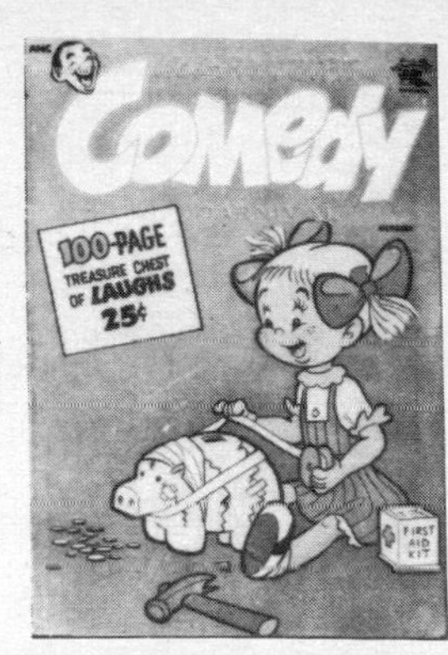

GD25 FN65 NM94

V3#1(5/59), 1(7/59)-4: 2-Powell-a 1.60 4.00 8.00

ALL FUNNY COMICS
Winter, 1943-44 - No. 23, May-June, 1948
Tilsam Publ./National Periodical Publications (Detective)

1-Genius Jones (1st app.), Buzzy (1st app., ends #4), Dover & Clover (see More Fun #93) begin; Bailey-a 38.00 115.00 265.00
2 14.00 43.00 100.00
3-10 10.00 30.00 65.00
11-13,15,18,19-Genius Jones app. 8.35 25.00 50.00
14,17,20-23 6.70 20.00 40.00
16-DC Super Heroes app. 22.00 65.00 150.00

ALL GOOD
Oct, 1949 (260 pgs., 50 cents)
St. John Publishing Co.

(8 St. John comics bound together) 54.00 160.00 375.00
NOTE: *Also see Li'l Audrey Yearbook & Treasury of Comics.*

ALL GOOD COMICS (See Fox Giants)
Spring, 1946 (36 pgs.)
Fox Features Syndicate

1-Joy Family, Dick Transom, Rick Evans, One Round Hogan 11.00 32.00 75.00

ALL GREAT (See Fox Giants)
1946 (36 pgs.)
Fox Feature Syndicate

1-Crazy House, Bertie Benson Boy Detective, Gussie the Gob 10.00 30.00 70.00

ALL GREAT
nd (1945?) (132 pgs.)
William H. Wise & Co.

nn-Capt. Jack Terry, Joan Mason, Girl Reporter, Baron Doomsday; Torture scenes 25.00 75.00 175.00

ALL GREAT COMICS (Formerly Phantom Lady #13? Dagar, Desert Hawk No. 14 on)
No. 14, Oct, 1947 - No. 13, Dec, 1947
Fox Features Syndicate

14-Brenda Starr-r (Scarce) 28.00 82.00 195.00
13-Origin Dagar, Desert Hawk; Brenda Starr (all-r); Kamen-c 23.00 70.00 160.00

ALL-GREAT CONFESSIONS (See Fox Giants)

ALL GREAT CRIME STORIES (See Fox Giants)

ALL GREAT JUNGLE ADVENTURES (See Fox Giants)

ALL HALLOW'S EVE (Innovation)(Value: cover or less)

ALL HERO COMICS
March, 1943 (100 pgs.) (Cardboard cover)
Fawcett Publications

1-Captain Marvel Jr., Capt. Midnight, Golden Arrow, Ibis the Invincible, Spy Smasher, & Lance O'Casey 100.00 300.00 700.00

ALL HUMOR COMICS
Spring, 1946 - No. 17, December, 1949
Quality Comics Group

1 12.00 36.00 85.00
2-Atomic Tot story; Gustavson-a 6.70 20.00 40.00
3-9: 3-Intro Kelly Poole who is cover feature #3 on. 5-1st app. Hickory? 8-Gustavson-a 4.00 11.00 22.00
10-17 3.20 8.00 16.00

ALL LOVE (...Romances No. 26)(Formerly Ernie Comics)
No. 26, May, 1949 - No. 32, May, 1950
Ace Periodicals (Current Books)

26(No. 1)-Ernie, Lily Belle app. 5.35 16.00 32.00

GD25 FN65 NM94

27-L. B. Cole-a 5.85 17.50 35.00
28-32 3.60 9.00 18.00

ALL-NEGRO COMICS
June, 1947 (15 cents)
All-Negro Comics

1 (Rare) 135.00 400.00 900.00
NOTE: *Seldom found in fine or mint condition; many copies have brown pages.*

ALL-NEW COLLECTORS' EDITION (Formerly Limited ...)
Jan, 1978 - Vol. 8, No. C-62, 1979 (No. 54-58: 76 pgs.)
DC Comics, Inc.

C-53-Rudolph the Red-Nosed Reindeer 1.50
C-54-Superman Vs. Wonder Woman .80 2.00
C-55-Superboy & the Legion of Super-Heroes 1.00 2.00 5.00
C-56-Superman Vs. Muhammad Ali: story & wraparound N. Adams-c 1.20 3.00
C-58-Superman Vs. Shazam .80 2.00
C-60-Rudolph's Summer Fun(8/78) .80 2.00
C-61-See Famous First Edition
C-62-Superman the Movie (68 pgs.; 1979)-Photo-c from movie plus photos inside (also see DC Special Series #25) .80 2.00

ALL-NEW COMICS (...Short Story Comics No. 1-3)
Jan, 1943 - No. 14, Nov, 1946; No. 15, Mar-Apr, 1947 (10 x 13-1/2")
Family Comics (Harvey Publications)

1-Steve Case, Crime Rover, Johnny Rebel, Kayo Kane, The Echo, Night Hawk, Ray O'Light, Detective Shane begin; Red Blazer on cover only; Sultan-a (all 1st app.?) 92.00 275.00 650.00
2-Origin Scarlet Phantom by Kubert 42.00 125.00 295.00
3 33.00 100.00 230.00
4,5 30.00 90.00 210.00
6-The Boy Heroes & Red Blazer (text story) begin, end #12; Black Cat app.; intro. Sparky in Red Blazer 33.00 100.00 230.00
7-Kubert, Powell-a; Black Cat & Zebra app. 33.00 100.00 230.00
8,9: 8-Shock Gibson app.; Kubert, Powell-a; Schomburg bondage-c. 9-Black Cat app.; Kubert-a 33.00 100.00 230.00
10-12: 10-The Zebra app. (from Green Hornet Comics); Kubert-a(3). 11-Girl Commandos, Man In Black app. 12-Kubert-a 28.00 85.00 195.00
13-Stuntman by Simon & Kirby; Green Hornet, Joe Palooka, Flying Fool app.; Green Hornet-c 33.00 100.00 235.00
14-The Green Hornet & The Man in Black Called Fate by Powell, Joe Palooka app.; J. Palooka-c by Ham Fisher 28.00 85.00 195.00
15 (Rare)-Small size (5-1/2x8-1/2"; B&W; 32 pgs.). Distributed to mail subscribers only. Black Cat and Joe Palooka app.Estimated value....$200-250
NOTE: *Also see Boy Explorers No. 2, Flash Gordon No. 5, and Stuntman No. 3.* **Powell** *a-11.* **Schomburg** *c-5, 7-11. Captain Red Blazer & Spark on c-5-11 (w/Boy Heroes #12).*

ALL-OUT WAR
Sept-Oct, 1979 - No. 6, Aug, 1980 ($1.00, 68 pgs.)
DC Comics

1-6: 1-The Viking Commando(origin), Force Three(origin), & Black Eagle Squadron begin 1.50
NOTE: **Ayers** *a(p)-1-6.* **Elias** *r-2.* **Evans** *a-1-6.* **Kubert** *c-16.*

ALL PICTURE ADVENTURE MAGAZINE
Oct, 1952 - No. 2, Nov, 1952 (100 pg. Giants, 25 cents, squarebound)
St. John Publishing Co.

1-War comics 17.00 52.00 120.00
2-Horror-crime comics 23.00 70.00 160.00
NOTE: *Above books contain three St. John comics rebound; variations possible.* **Baker** *art known in both.*

ALL PICTURE ALL TRUE LOVE STORY
October, 1952 (100 pages, 25 cents)
St. John Publishing Co.

1-Canteen Kate by Matt Baker 32.00 95.00 220.00

ALL-PICTURE COMEDY CARNIVAL
October, 1952 (100 pages, 25 cents)(Contains 4 rebound comics)

All-Select Comics #7, © MEG

All Star Comics #37, © DC

All-Star Squadron #5, © DC

St. John Publishing Co.

1-Contents can vary; Baker-a 32.00 95.00 220.00

ALL REAL CONFESSION MAGAZINE (See Fox Giants)

ALL ROMANCES (Mr. Risk No. 7 on)
Aug, 1949 - No. 6, June, 1950
A. A. Wyn (Ace Periodicals)

1 6.00 18.00 36.00
2 3.00 7.50 15.00
3-6 2.40 6.00 12.00

ALL-SELECT COMICS (Blonde Phantom No. 12 on)
Fall, 1943 - No. 11, Fall, 1946
Timely Comics (Daring Comics)

1-Capt. America (by Rico #1), Human Torch, Sub-Mariner begin; Black Widow story (4 pgs.) 315.00 945.00 2200.00
2-Red Skull app. 129.00 385.00 900.00
3-The Whizzer begins 85.00 257.00 600.00
4,5-Last Sub-Mariner 64.00 193.00 450.00
6-9: 6-The Destroyer app. 8-No Whizzer 57.00 171.00 400.00
10-The Destroyer & Sub-Mariner app.; last Capt. America & Human Torch issue 57.00 171.00 400.00
11-1st app. Blonde Phantom; Miss America app.; all Blonde Phantom-c by Shores 100.00 300.00 700.00

NOTE: ***Schomburg** c-1-10. **Sekowsky** a-7. #7 & 8 show 1944 in indicia, but should be 1945.*

ALL SPORTS COMICS (Formerly Real Sports Comics; becomes All Time Sports Comics No. 4 on)
No. 2, Dec-Jan, 1948-49; No. 3, Feb-Mar, 1949
Hillman Periodicals

2-Krigstein-a(p), Powell, Starr-a 18.00 55.00 125.00
3-Mort Lawrence-a 14.00 43.00 100.00

ALL STAR COMICS (All Star Western No. 58 on)
Sum, '40 - No. 57, Feb-Mar, '51; No. 58, Jan-Feb, '76 -No. 74, Sept-Oct, '78
National Periodical Publ./All-American/DC Comics

GD25 FN65 VF82 NM94

1-The Flash(#1 by E.E. Hibbard), Hawkman(by Shelly), Hourman(by Bernard Baily), The Sandman(by Craig Flessel), The Spectre(by Baily), Biff Bronson, Red White & Blue(ends #2?) begin; Ultra Man's only app. (#1-3 are quarterly; #4 begins bi-monthly issues) 975.00 2925.00 5365.00 7800.00
(Estimated up to 200+ total copies exist, 6 in NM/Mint)

GD25 FN65 NM94

2-Green Lantern (by Martin Nodell), Johnny Thunder begin 400.00 1200.00 2800.00

GD25 FN65 VF82 NM94

3-Origin & 1st app. The Justice Society of America (Win/40); Dr. Fate & The Atom begin, Red Tornado cameo; reprinted in Famous First Edition 2000.00 6000.00 13,000.00 20,000.00
(Estimated up to 150+ total copies exist, 6 in NM/Mint)

3-Reprint, Oversize 13-1/2"x10." **WARNING:** This comic is an exact reprint of the original except for its size. DC published it in 1974 with a second cover titling it as a Famous First Edition. There have been many reported cases of the outer cover being removed and the interior sold as the original edition. The reprint with the new outer cover removed is practically worthless. See Famous First Edition for value.

GD25 FN65 NM94

4-1st adventure for J.S.A. 383.00 1150.00 2500.00
5-1st app. Shiera Sanders as Hawkgirl (1st costumed super-heroine, 6-7/41) 383.00 1150.00 2500.00
6-Johnny Thunder joins JSA 267.00 800.00 1700.00
7-Batman, Superman, Flash cameo; last Hourman; Doiby Dickles app. 285.00 850.00 1800.00

GD25 FN65 VF82 NM94

8-Origin & 1st app. Wonder Woman (12-1/41-42)(added as 9pgs. making book 76 pgs.; origin cont'd in Sensation #1; see W.W. #1 for more detailed origin); Dr. Fate dons new helmet; Hop Harrigan text stories & Starman begin; Shiera app.; Hop Harrigan JSA guest; Starman & Dr. Midnite become members 940.00 2800.00 5150.00 7500.00
(Estimated up to 150 total copies exist, 6 in NM/Mint)

GD25 FN65 NM94

9,10: 9-JSA's girlfriends cameo; Shiera app. 10-Flash, Green Lantern cameo; Sandman new costume 235.00 700.00 1500.00
11,12: 11-Wonder Woman begins; Spectre cameo; Shiera app. 12- Wonder Woman becomes JSA Secretary 200.00 600.00 1300.00
13-15: Sandman w/Sandy in #14 & 15. 15-Origin & 1st app. Brain Wave; Shiera app. 185.00 550.00 1200.00
16-20: 19-Sandman w/Sandy. 20-Dr. Fate & Sandman cameo 135.00 400.00 900.00
21-23: 21-Spectre & Atom cameo; Dr. Fate by Kubert; Dr. Fate, Sandman end. 22-Last Hop Harrigan; Flag-c. 23-Origin/1st app. Psycho Pirate; last Spectre & Starman 115.00 350.00 800.00
24-Flash & Green Lantern cameo; Mr. Terrific only app.; Wildcat, JSA guest; Kubert Hawkman begins 115.00 350.00 800.00
25-27: 25-Flash & Green Lantern start again. 26-Robot-c. 27-Wildcat, JSA guest (#24-26: only All-American imprint) 110.00 325.00 725.00
28-32 96.00 290.00 630.00
33-Solomon Grundy & Doiby Dickles app; classic Solomon Grundy cover 215.00 650.00 1400.00
34,35-Johnny Thunder cameo in both 88.00 260.00 575.00
36-Batman & Superman JSA guests 200.00 600.00 1400.00
37-Johnny Thunder cameo; origin & 1st app. Injustice Society; last Kubert Hawkman 130.00 325.00 750.00
38-Black Canary begins; JSA Death issue 150.00 375.00 850.00
39,40: 39-Last Johnny Thunder 100.00 250.00 525.00
41-Black Canary joins JSA; Injustice Society app. (2nd app.?) 97.00 242.00 500.00
42-Atom & the Hawkman don new costumes 100.00 250.00 525.00
43-49,51-56: 43-New logo. 55-Sci/Fi story 100.00 250.00 525.00
50-Frazetta art, 3 pgs. 110.00 275.00 550.00
57-Kubert-a, 6 pgs. (Scarce); last app. G.A. Green Lantern, Flash & Dr. Mid-Nite 120.00 300.00 600.00
V12#58-74(1976-78)-Flash, Hawkman, Dr. Mid-Nite, Wildcat, Dr. Fate, Green Lantern, Star Spangled Kid, & Robin app.; intro Power Girl. 58-JSA app. 69-1st modern app. Huntress (see Sensation) .60 1.25

NOTE: *No Atom-27, 36; no Dr. Fate-13; no Flash-8, 9, 11-23; no Green Lantern-8, 9,11-23; Hawkman in 1-57 (only one to app. in all 57 issues); no Johnny Thunder-5, 36; no Wonder Woman-9, 10, 23. Book length stories in 4-9, 11-14, 18-22, 25, 26, 29, 30, 32-36, 42, 43. Johnny Peril in #42-46, 48, 49, 51, 52,54-57. **Baily** a-1-10, 12, 13, 14i, 15-20. **Burnley** Starman-8-13; c-12, 13. **Grell** c-58. **E.E. Hibbard** c-3, 4, 6-10. **Infantino** c-40. **Kubert** Hawkman-24-30, 33-37. **Lampert/Baily/Flessel** c-1, 2. **Moldoff** Hawkman-3-23; c-11. **Mart Naydell** c-25i, 26i, 27-32. **Purcell** c-5. **Simon & Kirby** Sandman 14-17, 19. **Staton** a-66-74p. c-74p. **Toth** a-37(2), 38(2), 40, 41; c-38, 41. **Wood** a-58i-63i, 64, 65; c-63i, 64, 65.*

ALL STAR INDEX, THE (Eclipse)(Value: cover or less)

ALL-STAR SQUADRON (See Justice League of America #193)
Sept, 1981 - No. 67, March, 1987
DC Comics

1-Original Atom, Hawkman, Dr. Mid-Nite, Robotman (origin), Plastic Man, Johnny Quick, Liberty Belle, Shining Knight begin 1.00
2-24: 5-Danette Reilly becomes new Firebrand. 8-Re-intro Steel, the Indestructable Man. 12-Origin G.A. Hawkman retold. 23-Origin/1st app. The Amazing Man. 24-Batman app. 1.00
25-1st app. Infinity, Inc. (9/83) 1.00
26-Origin Infinity, Inc. (2nd app.); Robin app. 1.00
27-46,48,49: 33-Origin Freedom Fighters of Earth-X. 41-Origin Starman 1.00
47-Origin Dr. Fate; McFarlane-a (1st full story)/part-c (7/85) 1.20 3.00
50-Double size; Crisis x-over 1.00
51-67: 51-56-Crisis x-over. 61-Origin Liberty Belle. 62-Origin The Shining Knight. 63-Origin Robotman. 65-Origin Johnny Quick. 66-Origin Tarantula 1.00
Annual 1-3: 1(11/82)-Retells origin of G.A. Atom, Guardian & Wildcat. 2(11/83)-Infinity, Inc. app. 3(9/84) 1.00

NOTE: ***Kubert** c-2, 7-18. JLA app. in 14, 15. JSA app. in 4, 14, 15, 19, 27, 28.*

ALL-STAR STORY OF THE DODGERS, THE

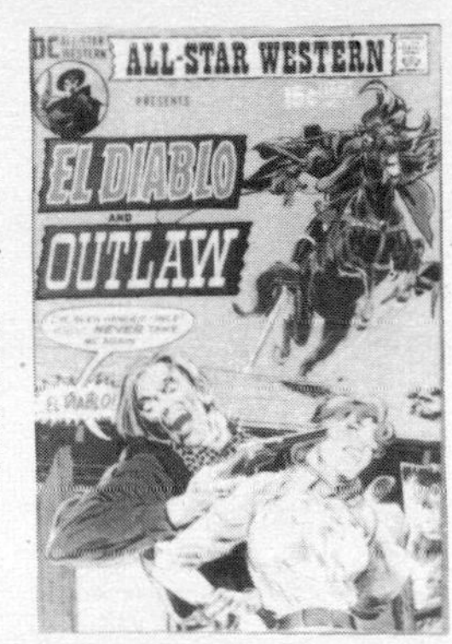

All-Star Western #3, © DC

All Top Comics #6 (1957), © Green Publ.

All-True Crime #40, © MCG

GD25 FN65 NM94

April, 1979 (Full Color) ($1.00)
Stadium Communications

1 — 1.00

ALL STAR WESTERN (Formerly All Star Comics No. 1-57)
No. 58, Apr-May, 1951 - No. 119, June-July, 1961
National Periodical Publications

	GD25	FN65	NM94
58-Trigger Twins (ends #116), Strong Bow, The Roving Ranger & Don Caballero begin	34.00	103.00	240.00
59,60: Last 52 pgs.	16.00	48.00	110.00
61-66: 61-64-Toth-a	13.00	40.00	90.00
67-Johnny Thunder begins; Gil Kane-a	16.00	48.00	110.00
68-81: Last precode (2-3/55)	8.35	25.00	50.00
82-98	7.00	21.00	42.00
99-Frazetta-r/Jimmy Wakely #4	8.35	25.00	50.00
100	7.50	22.50	45.00
101-107,109-116,118,119	5.00	15.00	30.00
108-Origin J. Thunder; J. Thunder logo begins	11.50	34.00	80.00
117-Origin Super Chie	9.15	27.50	55.00

NOTE: ***G. Kane** c(p)-58, 59, 61, 63, 64, 68, 69, 70-95(most), 97-199(most). **Infantino** art in most issues. Madame .44 app.-#117-119.*

ALL-STAR WESTERN (Weird Western Tales No. 12 on)
Aug-Sept, 1970 - No. 11, Apr-May, 1972
National Periodical Publications

	GD25	FN65	NM94
1-Pow-Wow Smith-r; Infantino-a	1.65	4.00	10.00
2-8: 2-Outlaw begins; El Diablo by Morrow begins; has cameos by Williamson, Torres, Gil Kane, Giordano & Phil Seuling. 3-Origin El Diablo. 5-Last Outlaw issue. 6-Billy the Kid begins, ends #8		1.40	3.50
9-Frazetta-a, 3pgs.(r)	1.00	2.00	5.00
10-Jonah Hex begins (1st app., 2-3/72)	8.50	25.50	60.00
11-2nd app. Jonah Hex	3.60	10.75	25.00

NOTE: ***Neal Adams** c-1-5; **Aparo** a-5. **G. Kane** a-3, 4, 6, 8. **Kubert** a-4r, 7-9r. **Morrow** a-2-4, 10, 11. No. 7-11 have 52 pages.*

ALL SURPRISE (Becomes Jeanie #13 on) (Funny animal)
Fall, 1943 - No. 12, Winter, 1946-47
Timely/Marvel (CPC)

	GD25	FN65	NM94
1-Super Rabbit, Gandy & Sourpuss begin	17.00	52.00	120.00
2	8.35	25.00	50.00
3-10,12	5.85	17.50	35.00
11-Kurtzman "Pigtales" art	7.50	22.50	50.00

ALL TEEN (Formerly All Winners; All Winners & Teen Comics No. 21 on)
No. 20, January, 1947
Marvel Comics (WFP)

	GD25	FN65	NM94
20-Georgie, Mitzi, Patsy Walker, Willie app.; Syd Shores-c	5.85	17.50	35.00

ALL THE FUNNY FOLKS
1926 (hardcover, 112 pgs., 11-1/2x3-1/2") (Full color)
World Press Today, Inc.

	GD25	FN65	NM94
nn-Barney Google, Spark Plug, Jiggs & Maggie, Tillie The Toiler, Happy Hooligan, Hans & Fritz, Toots & Casper, etc.	50.00	150.00	350.00

ALL-TIME SPORTS COMICS (Formerly All Sports Comics)
V2No. 4, Apr-May, 1949 - V2No. 7, Oct-Nov, 1949 (All 52 pgs.)
Hillman Periodicals

	GD25	FN65	NM94
V2#4	12.00	36.00	85.00
5-7: 5-(V1#5 inside)-Powell-a. 7-Krigstein-p	10.00	30.00	65.00

ALL TOP
1944 (132 pages)
William H. Wise Co.

	GD25	FN65	NM94
Capt. V, Merciless the Sorceress, Red Robbins, One Round Hogan, Mike the M.P., Snooky, Pussy Katnip app.	20.00	60.00	140.00

ALL TOP COMICS (My Experience No. 19 on)
1945; No. 2, Sum, 1946 - No. 18, Mar, 1949; 1957 - 1959
Fox Features Synd./Green Publ./Norlen Mag.

	GD25	FN65	NM94
1-Cosmo Cat & Flash Rabbit begin (1st app.)	14.00	42.00	100.00
2 (#1-7 are funny animal)	8.35	25.00	50.00
3-7	5.05	17.50	35.00
8-Blue Beetle, Phantom Lady, & Rulah, Jungle Goddess begin (11/47); Kamen-c	92.00	275.00	600.00
9-Kamen-c	55.00	165.00	350.00
10-Kamen bondage-c	58.00	175.00	375.00
11-13,15-17: 15-No Blue Beetle	40.00	120.00	265.00
14-No Blue Beetle; used in **SOTI**, illo- "Corpses of colored people strung up by their wrists"	50.00	150.00	335.00
18-Dagar, Jo-Jo app; no Phantom Lady or Blue Beetle	32.00	95.00	200.00
6(1957-Green Publ.)-Patoruzu the Indian; Cosmo Cat on cover only	2.80	7.00	14.00
6(1958-Literary Ent.)-Muggy Doo; Cosmo Cat on cover only	2.80	7.00	14.00
6(1959-Norlen)-Atomic Mouse; Cosmo Cat on cover only	2.80	7.00	14.00
6(1959)-Little Eva	2.80	7.00	14.00
6(Cornell)-Supermouse on-c	2.80	7.00	14.00

NOTE: *Jo-Jo by **Kamen**-12,18.*

ALL TRUE ALL PICTURE POLICE CASES
Oct, 1952 - No. 2, Nov, 1952 (100 pages)
St. John Publishing Co.

	GD25	FN65	NM94
1-Three rebound St. John crime comics	27.00	80.00	185.00
2-Three comics rebound	22.00	65.00	150.00

NOTE: *Contents may vary.*

ALL-TRUE CRIME (...Cases No. 26-35; formerly Official True Crime Cases)
No. 26, Feb, 1948 - No. 52, Sept, 1952
Marvel/Atlas Comics(OFI No. 26,27/CFI No. 28,29/LCC No. 30-46/LMC No. 47-52)

	GD25	FN65	NM94
26(#1)-Syd Shores-c	12.00	36.00	85.00
27(4/48)-Electric chair-c	10.00	30.00	65.00
28-41,43-48,50-52: 35-37-Photo-c	4.20	12.50	25.00
42,49-Krigstein-a. 49-Used in **POP**, Pg 79	5.85	17.50	35.00

NOTE: ***Robinson** a-47, 50. **Shores** c-26. **Tuska** a-48(3).*

ALL-TRUE DETECTIVE CASES (Kit Carson No. 5 on)
Feb-Mar, 1954 - No. 4, Aug-Sept, 1954
Avon Periodicals

	GD25	FN65	NM94
1	12.00	36.00	85.00
2-Wood-a	11.50	34.00	80.00
3-Kinstler-c	5.85	17.50	35.00
4-Wood(?), Kamen-a	10.00	30.00	70.00
nn(100 pgs.)-7 pg. Kubert-a, Kinstler back-c	24.00	70.00	165.00

ALL TRUE ROMANCE (...Illustrated No. 3)
3/51 - No. 20, 12/54; No. 22, 3/55 - No. 30?, 7/57; No. 3(#31), 9/57
No. 4(#32), 11/57; No. 33, 2/58 - No. 34, 3/58
Artful Publ. #1-3/Harwell(Comic Media) #4-20?/Ajax-Farrell(Excellent Publ.) No. 22 on/Four Star Comic Corp.

	GD25	FN65	NM94
1 (3/51)	10.00	30.00	60.00
2 (10/51; 11/51 on-c)	5.35	16.00	32.00
3(12/51) - #5(5/52)	4.35	13.00	26.00
6-Wood-a, 9 pgs. (exceptional)	12.00	36.00	85.00
7-10	4.00	10.00	20.00
11-13,16-19 (2/54)	3.20	8.00	10.00
14-Marijuana story	3.60	9.00	18.00
20,22: Last precode issue (Ajax, 3/55)	2.60	6.50	13.00
23-27,29,30	2.20	5.50	11.00
28 (9/56)-L. B. Cole, Disbrow-a	4.00	12.00	24.00
3,4,33,34 (Farrell, '57-'58)	1.40	3.50	7.00

ALL WESTERN WINNERS (Formerly All Winners; becomes Western Winners with No. 5; see Two-Gun Kid No. 5)
No. 2, Winter, 1948-49 - No. 4, April, 1949

All Winners Comics #3, © MEG

Alpha Flight #81, © MEG

Amazing Adult Fantasy #7, © MEG

GD25 FN65 NM94

Marvel Comics(CDS)

2-Black Rider (origin & 1st app.) & his horse Satan, Kid Colt & his horse Steel, & Two-Gun Kid & his horse Cyclone begin; Shores c-2-4 38.00 115.00 265.00

3-Anti-Wertham editorial 24.00 70.00 165.00

4-Black Rider i.d. revealed; Heath, Shores-a 24.00 70.00 165.00

ALL WINNERS COMICS (All Teen #20)
Summer, 1941 - No. 19, Fall, 1946; No. 21, Winter, 1946-47 (no No. 20) (No. 21 continued from Young Allies No. 20)
USA No. 1-7/WFP No. 10-19/YAI No. 21

GD25 FN65 VF82 NM94

1-The Angel & Black Marvel only app.; Capt. America by Simon & Kirby, Human Torch & Sub-Mariner begin (#1 was advertised as All Aces) 625.00 1875.00 3440.00 5000.00

GD25 FN65 NM94

2-The Destroyer & The Whizzer begin; Simon & Kirby Captain America &-c 214.00 640.00 1500.00

3 150.00 450.00 1000.00

4-Classic War-c by Al Avison 170.00 510.00 1150.00

5 100.00 300.00 675.00

6-The Black Avenger only app.; no Whizzer story; Hitler, Hirohito & Mussolini-c 112.00 335.00 750.00

7-10 84.00 250.00 565.00

11,13-18: 11-1st Atlas globe on-c (Winter, 1943-44; also see Human Torch #14). 14-16-No Human Torch 56.00 165.00 375.00

12-Red Skull story; last Destroyer; no Whizzer story 60.00 180.00 425.00

19-(Scarce)-1st app. & origin All Winners Squad (Capt. America & Bucky, Human Torch & Toro, Sub-Mariner, Whizzer, & Miss America; r-in Fantasy Masterpieces #10 135.00 410.00 950.00

21-(Scarce)-All Winners Squad; bondage-c 121.00 365.00 850.00

NOTE: ***Everett*** *Sub-Mariner-1, 3, 4;* ***Burgos*** *Torch-1, 3, 4.* ***Schomburg*** *c-1, 7-18.* ***Shores*** *c-19p, 21.*

(2nd Series - August, 1948, Marvel Comics (CDS))
(Becomes All Western Winners with No. 2)

1-The Blonde Phantom, Capt. America, Human Torch, & Sub-Mariner app. 105.00 315.00 735.00

ALL YOUR COMICS (See Fox Giants)
Spring, 1946 (36 pages)
Fox Feature Syndicate (R. W. Voight)

1-Red Robbins, Merciless the Sorceress app. 10.00 30.00 60.00

ALMANAC OF CRIME (See Fox Giants)

AL OF FBI (See Little Al of the FBI)

ALONG THE FIRING LINE WITH ROGER BEAN
1916 (Hardcover, B&W) (6x17") (66 pages)
Chas. B. Jackson

3-by Chic Jackson (1915 daily strips) 13.50 40.00 90.00

ALPHA AND OMEGA (Spire Christian)(Value: cover or less)

ALPHA FLIGHT (See X-Men #120,121 & X-Men/Alpha Flight)
Aug, 1983 - Present (#52-on are direct sale only)
Marvel Comics Group

1-Byrne-a begins (52pgs.)-Wolverine & Nightcrawler cameo 1.00 2.50

2-12: 2-Vindicator becomes Guardian; origin Marrina & Alpha Flight. 3-Concludes origin Alpha Flight. 6-Origin Shaman. 7-Origin Snowbird. 10,11-Origin Sasquatch. 12-(52 pgs.)-Death of Guardian .70 1.75

13-Wolverine app. 1.00 2.50 6.00

14-16,18-28: 16-Wolverine cameo. 20-New headquarters. 25-Return of Guardian. 28-Last Byrne issue 1.25

17-X-Men x-over (70% reprinted from X-Men #109); Wolverine cameo 1.20 3.00

29-32,35-49 1.00

33,34: 33-X-Men (Wolverine) app. 34-Origin Wolverine 1.60 4.00

50-Double size 1.25

51-Jim Lee's 1st work at Marvel (10/87); Wolverine cameo; 1st Lee Wolverine 1.00 2.00 5.00

52,53-Wolverine app.; Lee-a on Wolverine; 53-Lee/Portacio-a 1.20 3.00

54,63,64-No Jim Lee-a 1.00

55-62-Jim Lee-a(p) 1.00 2.50

65-74,76-86: 65-Begin $1.50-c. 71-Intro The Sorcerer (villain). 74-Wolverine, Spider-Man & The Avengers app. 89-Original Guardian returns 1.25

75-Double size ($1.95, 52 pgs.) 1.50

87-90-Wolverine 4 part story w/Jim Lee covers 1.40 3.50

91-99,101-104: 91-Dr. Doom app. 94-F.F. x-over. 99-Galactus, Avengers app. 102-Intro Weapon Omega. 104-Last $1.50-c 1.50

100-($2.00, 52 pgs.)-Avengers & Galactus app. .70 1.75

105,107-119,121-129: 107-X-Factor x-over. 110-112-Infinity War x-overs. 110, 111-Wolverine app. (brief). 111-Thanos cameo 1.50

106-Northstar revelation issue 1.10 2.75

106-2nd printing (direct sale only) 1.25

120-($2.25)-Polybagged w/Superpowers poster .70 1.75

130-($2.25, 52 pgs.) .90 2.25

Annual 1 (9/86, $1.25) 1.25

Annual 2(12/87, $1.25) 1.00

Special V2#1(6/92, $2.50, 52 pgs.)-Wolverine-c/s .90 2.25

NOTE: ***Austin*** *c-1i, 2i, 53i.* ***Byrne*** *c-81, 82.* ***Guice*** *c-85, 91-99.* ***Jim Lee*** *a(p)-51, 53, 55-62, 64; c-53, 87-90.* ***Whilce Portacio*** *a(i)-39-47, 49-54.*

ALPHA FLIGHT SPECIAL
July, 1991 - No. 4, Oct, 1991 ($1.50, color, limited series)
Marvel Comics

1-3: Reprints Alpha Flight #97-99 w/covers 1.50

4 ($2.00, 52 pgs.)-Reprints Alpha Flight #100 .80 2.00

ALPHA WAVE (Darkline)(Value: cover or less)

ALPHONSE & GASTON & LEON
1903 (15x10", Sunday strip reprints in color)
Hearst's New York American & Journal

nn-by Fred Opper 57.00 170.00 400.00

ALTER EGO (First)(Value: cover or less)

ALVIN (TV) (See 4-Color Comics No. 1042)
Oct-Dec, 1962 - No. 28, Oct, 1973
Dell Publishing Co.

12-021-212 (#1) 11.00 32.00 75.00

2 6.70 20.00 40.00

3-10 5.00 15.00 30.00

11-28 4.20 12.50 25.00

Alvin For President (10/64) 3.60 9.00 18.00

...& His Pals in Merry Christmas with Clyde Crashcup & Leonardo 1 (02-120-402)-(12-2/64), reprinted in 1966 (12-023-604) 5.85 17.50 35.00

AMAZING ADULT FANTASY (Formerly Amazing Adventures #1-6; becomes Amazing Fantasy #15)
No. 7, Dec, 1961 - No. 14, July, 1962
Marvel Comics Group (AMI)

7-Ditko-c/a begins, ends #14 32.00 95.00 385.00

8-Last 10 cent issue 26.00 80.00 315.00

9-13: 12-1st app. Mailbag. 13-Anti-communist story 23.00 70.00 275.00

14-Prototype ish. (Professor X) 25.00 75.00 300.00

AMAZING ADVENTURE FUNNIES (Fantoman No. 2 on)
June, 1940 - No. 2, Sept. 1940
Centaur Publications

1-The Fantom of the Fair by Gustavson (r/Amaz. Mystery Funnies V2#7, V2#8), The Arrow, Skyrocket Steele From the Year X by Everett (r/AMF

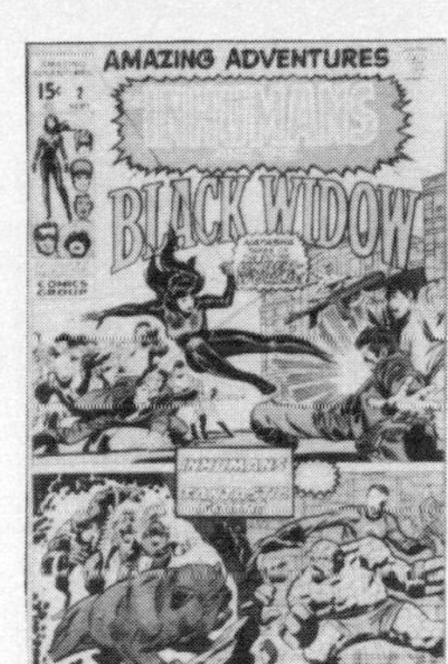

Amazing Adventures #2 (9/70), © MEG

Amazing Detective Cases #12, © MEG

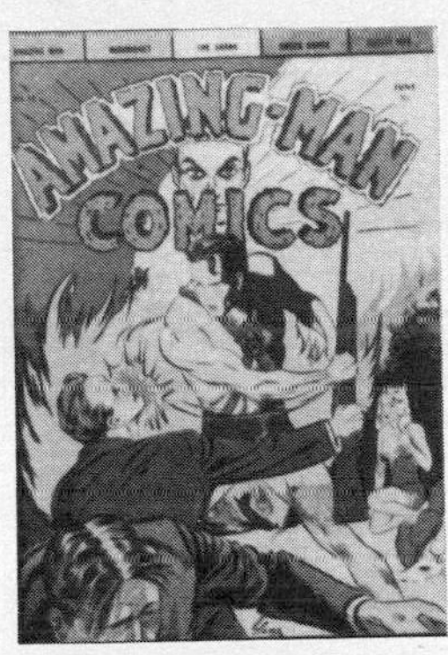

Amazing-Man Comics #13, © CEN

GD25 FN65 NM94

#2); Burgos-a 135.00 400.00 850.00
2-Reprints; Published after Fantoman #2 92.00 275.00 600.00
NOTE: *Burgos a-1(2). Everett a-1(3). Gustavson a-1(5), 2(3). Pinajian a-2.*

AMAZING ADVENTURES (Also see Boy Cowboy & Science Comics)
1950; No. 1, Nov, 1950 - No. 6, Fall, 1952 (Painted covers)
Ziff-Davis Publ. Co.

1950 (no month given) (8-1/2x11) (8 pgs.) Has the front & back cover plus Schomburg story used in Amazing Advs. #1 (Sent to subscribers of Z-D s/f magazines & ordered through mail for 10 cents. Used to test market) Estimated value.... 200.00
1-Wood, Schomburg, Anderson, Whitney-a 40.00 120.00 280.00
2-5: 2,4,5-Anderson-a. 3,5-Starr-a 16.00 48.00 110.00
6-Krigstein-a 20.00 60.00 145.00

AMAZING ADVENTURES (Becomes Amazing Adult Fantasy #7 on)
June, 1961 - No. 6, Nov, 1961
Atlas Comics (AMI)/Marvel Comics No. 3 on

1-Origin Dr. Droom (1st Marvel-Age Superhero) by Kirby; Ditko & Kirby-a in all; Kirby c-1-6 75.00 225.00 675.00
2 31.00 92.00 275.00
3-6: 6-Last Dr. Droom 25.00 75.00 225.00

AMAZING ADVENTURES
Aug, 1970 - No. 39, Nov, 1976
Marvel Comics Group

1-Inhumans by Kirby(p) & Black Widow (1st app. in Tales of Suspense #52) double feature begins 2.15 6.50 15.00
2-4: 2-F.F. brief app. 4-Last Kirby Inhumans 1.00 2.00 5.00
5-8-Neal Adams-a(p); 8-Last Black Widow 1.20 3.00 7.00
9,10: Magneto app. 10-Last Inhumans (origin-r by Kirby) 1.00 2.00 5.00
11-New Beast begins(1st app. in mutated form; origin in flashback); X-Men cameo in flashback (#11-17 are X-Men tie-ins) 1.65 4.00 10.00
12-17: 13-Brotherhood of Evil Mutants x-over from X-Men. 15-X-Men app. 17-Last Beast (origin); X-Men app. 1.20 3.00 7.00
18-War of the Worlds begins (5/73); 1st app. Killraven; Neal Adams-a(p) 1.70 5.00 12.00
19-39: 35-Giffen's first published story (art), along with Deadly Hands of Kung-Fu #22 (3/76) 1.40 3.50
NOTE: *N. Adams c-6-8. Buscema a-1p, 2p. Colan a-3-5p, 26p. Ditko a-24r. Everett a(i)3-5, 7-9. Giffen a-35i, 38p. G. Kane c-11, 25p, 29p. Ploog a-12i. Russell a-27-32, 34-37, 39; c-28, 30-32, 33i, 34, 35, 37, 39i. Starliing a-17. Starlin c-15p, 16, 17, 27. Sutton a-11-15p.*

AMAZING ADVENTURES
December, 1979 - No. 14, January, 1981
Marvel Comics Group

V2#1-Reprints story/X-Men #1 & 38 (origins) 1.60 4.00
2-14: 2-6-Early X-Men-r. 7,8-Origin Iceman 1.20 3.00
NOTE: *Byrne c-6p, 9p. Kirby a-1-14r; c-7, 9. Steranko a-12r. Tuska a-7-9.*

AMAZING ADVENTURES
July, 1988 ($4.95, One-shot, color, squarebound, 80 pgs.)
Marvel Comics

1-Anthology; Austin, Golden-a 1.00 2.00 5.00

AMAZING ADVENTURES OF CAPTAIN CARVEL AND HIS CARVEL CRUSADERS, THE (See Carvel Comics)

AMAZING CHAN & THE CHAN CLAN, THE (TV)
May, 1973 - No. 4, Feb, 1974 (Hanna-Barbera)
Gold Key

1 1.65 4.00 10.00
2-4 1.00 2.50 6.00

AMAZING COMICS (Complete Comics No. 2)
Fall, 1944
Timely Comics (EPC)

1-The Destroyer, The Whizzer, The Young Allies (by Sekowsky), Sergeant Dix; Schomburg-c 100.00 300.00 700.00

GD25 FN65 NM94

AMAZING DETECTIVE CASES (Formerly Suspense No. 2?)
No. 3, Nov, 1950 - No. 14, Sept, 1952
Marvel/Atlas Comics (CCC)

3 12.00 36.00 85.00
4-6 7.50 22.50 45.00
7-10 5.85 17.50 35.00
11,14: 11-(3/52)-change to horror 9.15 27.50 55.00
12-Krigstein-a 9.15 27.50 55.00
13-(Scarce)-Everett-a; electrocution-c/story 11.00 32.00 75.00
NOTE: *Colan a-9. Maneely c-13. Sekowsky a-12. Sinnott a-13. Tuska a-10.*

AMAZING FANTASY (Formerly Amazing Adult Fantasy #7-14)
No. 15, Aug, 1962 (Sept, 1962 shown in indicia)
Marvel Comics Group (AMI)

GD25 FN65 VF82 NM94

15-Origin/1st app. of Spider-Man by Ditko (11 pgs.); 1st app. Aunt May & Uncle Ben; Kirby/Ditko-c 1335.00 4000.00 12,000.00 20,000.00

AMAZING GHOST STORIES (Formerly Nightmare)
No. 14, Oct, 1954 - No. 16, Feb, 1955
St. John Publishing Co.

GD25 FN65 NM94

14-Pit & the Pendulum story by Kinstler; Baker-c 14.00 43.00 100.00
15-r/Weird Thrillers #5; Baker-c, Powell-a 10.00 30.00 70.00
16-Kubert reprints of Weird Thrillers #4; Baker-c; Roussos, Tuska-a; Kinstler-a (1 pg.) 11.00 32.00 75.00

AMAZING HIGH ADVENTURE
8/84; No. 2, 10/85; No. 3, 10/86 - No. 5, 1987 (Baxter No. 3,4)($2.00)
Marvel Comics

1-5 .80 2.00
NOTE: *Bissette a-4. Bolton c/a-4. Severin a-1, 3. P. Smith a-2. Williamson a-2i.*

AMAZING-MAN COMICS (Formerly Motion Picture Funnies Weekly?)
(Also see Stars And Stripes Comics)
No. 5, Sept, 1939 - No. 27, Feb, 1942
Centaur Publications

GD25 FN65 VF82 NM94

5(#1)(Rare)-Origin/1st app. A-Man the Amazing Man by Bill Everett; The Cat-Man by Tarpe Mills (also #8), Mighty Man by Filchock, Minimidget & sidekick Ritty, & The Iron Skull by Burgos begins 1310.00 3940.00 7220.00 10,500.00
(Estimated up to 60 total copies exist, 3 in NM/Mint)

GD25 FN65 NM94

6-Origin The Amazing Man retold; The Shark begins; Ivy Menace by Tarpe Mills app. 267.00 800.00 1750.00
7-Magician From Mars begins; ends #11 158.00 475.00 1000.00
8-Cat-Man dresses as woman 117.00 350.00 750.00
9-Magician From Mars battles the 'Elemental Monster,' swiped into The Spectre in More Fun #54 & 55 117.00 350.00 750.00
10,11: 11-Zardi, the Eternal Man begins; ends #16; Amazing Man dons costume; last Everett issue 100.00 300.00 650.00
12,13 96.00 285.00 625.00
14-Reef Kinkaid, Rocke Wayburn (ends #20), & Dr. Hypno (ends #21) begin; no Zardi or Chuck Hardy 75.00 225.00 500.00
15,17-20: 15-Zardi returns; no Rocke Wayburn. 17-Dr. Hypno returns; no Zardi 58.00 175.00 385.00
16-Mighty Man's powers of super strength & ability to shrink & grow explained; Rocke Wayburn returns; no Dr. Hypno; Al Avison (a character) begins, ends #18 (a tribute to the famed artist) 63.00 185.00 415.00
21-Origin Dash Dartwell (drug-use story); origin & only app. T.N.T. 58.00 175.00 385.00
22-Dash Dartwell, the Human Meteor & The Voice app; last Iron Skull & The Shark; Silver Streak app. 58.00 175.00 385.00
23-Two Amazing Man stories; Intro/origin Tommy the Amazing Kid; The Marksman only app. 63.00 185.00 415.00
24,27: 24-King of Darkness, Nightshade, & Blue Lady begin; end #26; 1st app. Super-Ann 58.00 175.00 385.00
25,26 (Scarce)-Meteor Martin by Wolverton in both; 26-Electric Ray app.

Amazing Mystery Funnies #18, © CEN.

The Amazing Spider-Man #7, © MEG

The Amazing Spider-Man #41, © MEG

GD25 FN65 NM94

85.00 257.00 600.00

NOTE: *Everett a-5-11; c-5-11. Gilman a-14-20. Giunta/Mirando a-7-10. Sam Glanzman a-14-16, 18-21, 23. Louis Glanzman a-6, 9-11, 14-21; c-13-19, 21. Robert Golden a-9. Gustavson a-6; c-22, 23. Lubbers a-14-21. Simon a-10. Frank Thomas a-6, 9-11, 14, 15, 17-21.*

AMAZING MYSTERIES (Formerly Sub-Mariner Comics No. 31)
No. 32, May, 1949 - No. 35, Jan, 1950
Marvel Comics (CCC)

32-The Witness app; 1st Marvel horror comic 43.00 130.00 300.00
33-Horror format 16.00 48.00 110.00
34,35-Change to Crime. 34,35-Photo-c 10.00 30.00 70.00

AMAZING MYSTERY FUNNIES
Aug, 1938 - No. 24, Sept, 1940 (All 52 pgs.)
Centaur Publications

V1#1-Everett-c(1st); Dick Kent Adv. story; Skyrocket Steele in the Year X on cover only 265.00 800.00 1800.00
2-Everett 1st-a (Skyrocket Steele) 125.00 375.00 850.00
3 70.00 210.00 465.00
3(#4, 12/38)-nn on cover, #3 on inside; bondage-c 60.00 175.00 385.00
V2#1-4,6: 2-Drug use story. 3-Air-Sub DX begins by Burgos. 4-Dan Hastings, Hastings, Sand Hog begins (ends #5). 6-Last Skyrocket Steele 54.00 160.00 365.00
5-Classic Everett-c 73.00 215.00 475.00
7 (Scarce)-Intro. The Fantom of the Fair & begins; Everett, Gustavson, Burgos-a 265.00 800.00 1750.00
8-Origin & 1st app. Speed Centaur 105.00 310.00 685.00
9-11: 11-Self portrait and biog. of Everett; Jon Linton begins; early Robot cover (11/39) 60.00 175.00 385.00
12 (Scarce)-1st Space Patrol; Wolverton-a (12/39); new costume Phantom of the Fair 132.00 400.00 900.00
V3#1(#17, 1/40)-Intro. Bullet; Tippy Taylor serial begins, ends #24 (continued in The Arrow #2) 60.00 175.00 385.00
18,20: 18-Fantom of the Fair by Gustavson 54.00 160.00 365.00
19,21-24-Space Patrol by Wolverton in all 80.00 240.00 525.00

NOTE: *Burgos a-V2#3-9. Eisner a-V1#2, 3(2). Everett a-V1#2-4, V2#1, 3-6; c-V1#1-4, V2#3, 5, 18. Filchock a-V2#9. Flessel a-V2#6. Guardineer a-V1#4, V2#4-6; Gustavson a-V2#4, 5, 9-12, V3#1, 18, 19; c-V2#7, 9, 12, V3#1, 21, 22; McWilliams a-V2#9, 10. TarpeMills a-V2#2, 4-6, 9-12, V3#1. Leo Morey(Pulp artist) c-V2#10; text illo-V2#11. FrankThomas a-6-V2/11. Webster a-V2#4.*

AMAZING SAINTS (Logos)(Value: cover or less)

AMAZING SPIDER-MAN, THE (See All Detergent Comics, Amazing Fantasy, America's Best TV Comics, Aurora, Deadly Foes of Spider-Man, Giant-Size Spider-Man, Giant Size Super-Heroes Feat...., Marvel Coll. Item Classics, Marvel Fanfare, Marvel Graphic Novel, Marvel Spec. Ed., Marvel Tales, Marvel Team-Up, Marvel Treasury Ed., Nothing Can Stop the Juggernaut, Official Marvel Index To..., Power Record Comics, Spectacular..., Spider-Man, Spider-Man Digest, Spider-Man Saga, Spider-Man 2099, Spider-Man Vs. Wolverine, Spidey Super Stories, Strange Tales Annual #2, Superman Vs. ..., Try-Out Winner Book, Web of Spider-Man & Within Our Reach)

AMAZING SPIDER-MAN, THE
March, 1963 - Present
Marvel Comics Group

GD25 FN65 VF82 NM94

1-Retells origin by Steve Ditko; 1st Fantastic Four x-over; intro. John Jameson & The Chameleon; Spider-Man's 2nd app.; Kirby-c 900.00 2700.00 8100.00 13,500.00

GD25 FN65 NM94

1-Reprint from the Golden Record Comic set 11.00 32.00 75.00
with record (mid-'60s) 21.00 65.00 150.00
2-1st app. the Vulture & the Terrible Tinkerer 205.00 615.00 2050.00
3-1st full-length story; Human Torch cameo; intro. & 1st app. Doc Octopus; early Dr. Doom & Ant-Man app. (7/63) 131.00 392.00 1175.00
4-Origin & 1st app. The Sandman (see Strange Tales #115 for 2nd app.); Intro. Betty Brant & Liz Allen 117.00 350.00 1050.00
5-Dr. Doom app. 106.00 319.00 850.00
6-1st app. Lizard 94.00 281.00 750.00
7,8,10: 7-Vs. The Vulture; 1st monthly issue. 8-Fantastic Four app. in back-up story by Ditko/Kirby. 10-1st app. Big Man & The Enforcers 71.00 214.00 500.00
9-Origin & 1st app. Electro (2/64) 79.00 236.00 550.00
11,12: 11-1st app. Bennett Brant 39.00 118.00 275.00
13-1st app. Mysterio 54.00 161.00 375.00

GD25 FN65 VF82 NM94

14-(7/64)-1st app. The Green Goblin (c/story)(Norman Osborn); Hulk x-over 100.00 300.00 650.00 1000.00

GD25 FN65 NM94

15-1st app. Kraven the Hunter; 1st mention of Mary Jane Watson (not shown) 47.00 141.00 330.00
16-Spider-Man battles Daredevil (1st x-over 9/64); still in old yellow costume 34.00 101.00 235.00
17-2nd app. Green Goblin (c/story); Human Torch x-over (also in #18 & #21) 57.00 171.00 400.00
18-1st app. Ned Leeds who later becomes Hobgoblin; Fantastic Four back-up story; 3rd app. Sandman 36.00 107.00 250.00
19-Sandman app. 29.00 86.00 200.00
20-Origin & 1st app. The Scorpion 34.00 103.00 240.00
21-2nd app. The Beetle (see Strange Tales) 23.00 70.00 160.00
22-1st app. Princess Python 21.00 62.00 145.00
23-3rd app. The Green Goblin (c/story) 35.00 105.00 245.00
24 19.00 58.00 135.00
25-(6/65)-1st app. Mary Jane Watson (cameo; face not shown); 1st app. Spencer Smythe 24.00 71.00 165.00
26-4th app. The Green Goblin (c/story); 1st app. Crime Master; dies in #27 26.00 79.00 185.00
27-5th app. The Green Goblin (c/story) 24.00 73.00 170.00
28-Origin & 1st app. Molten Man (9/65, scarcer in high grade) 32.00 96.00 225.00
29,30 17.00 51.00 120.00
31-38: 31-1st app. Harry Osborn who later becomes 2nd Green Goblin, Gwen Stacy & Prof. Warren. 34-2nd app. Kraven the Hunter. 36-1st app. Looter. 37-Intro. Norman Osborn. 38-(7/66)-2nd app. Mary Jane Watson (cameo; face not shown); last Ditko issue 14.00 43.00 100.00
39-The Green Goblin-c/story; Green Goblin's i.d. revealed as Norman Osborn; Romita-a begins (8/66; see Daredevil #16 for 1st Romita-a on Spider-Man) 18.00 54.00 125.00
40-1st told origin The Green Goblin (c/story) 29.00 86.00 200.00
41-1st app. Rhino 13.00 40.00 90.00
42-(11/66)-3rd app. Mary Jane Watson (cameo in last 2 panels); 1st time face is shown 12.00 36.00 85.00
43-49: 44,45-2nd & 3rd app. The Lizard. 46-Intro. Shocker. 47-M. J. Watson & Peter Parker 1st date. 47-Green Goblin cameo; Harry & Norman Osborn app. 47,49-3rd & 4th app. Kraven the Hunter 8.00 24.00 55.00
50-1st app. Kingpin (7/67) 35.00 105.00 245.00
51-2nd app. Kingpin 14.00 41.00 95.00
52-60: 52-1st app. Joe Robertson & 3rd app. Kingpin. 56-1st app. Capt. George Stacy. 57,58-Ka-Zar app. 59-1st app. Brainwasher (alias Kingpin); 1st-c app. M. J. Watson. 6.00 19.00 45.00
61-74: 67-1st app. Randy Robertson. 69-Kingpin app. 73-1st app. Silvermane. 74-Last 12 cent issue 5.50 16.00 38.00
75-89,91-93,95,99: 78,79-1st app. The Prowler. 83-1st app. Schemer & Vanessa (Kingpin's wife). 84,85-Kingpin-c/story. 93-1st app. Arthur Stacy 4.30 13.00 30.00
90-Death of Capt. Stacey 5.00 16.00 37.00
94-Origin retold 7.00 21.00 50.00
96-98-Green Goblin app. (97,98-Green Goblin-c); drug books not approved by CCA 9.00 28.00 65.00
100-Anniversary issue (9/71); Green Goblin cameo (2 pgs.) 19.00 58.00 135.00
101-1st app. Morbius the Living Vampire; last 15 cent issue 21.00 64.00 150.00
101-Silver ink 2nd printing (9/92, $1.75) .80 2.00
102-Origin Morbius (25 cents, 52 pgs.) 14.00 43.00 100.00
103-118: 104,111-Kraven the Hunter-c/stories. 108-1st app. Sha-Shan. 109-Dr. Strange-c/story (6/72). 110-1st app. Gibbon. 113-1st app.

The Amazing Spider-Man #252, © MEG

The Amazing Spider-Man #262, © MEG

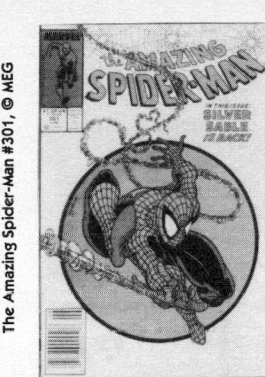

The Amazing Spider-Man #301, © MEG

	GD25	FN65	NM94
Hammerhead	2.60	7.50	18.00
119,120-Spider-Man vs. Hulk (4 & 5/73)	4.30	13.00	30.00
121-Death of Gwen Stacy (6/73) (killed by Green Goblin) (reprinted in Marvel Tales #98 & 192)	11.00	32.00	75.00
122-Death of The Green Goblin (c/story, 7/73) (reprinted in Marvel Tales #99 & 192)	14.00	43.00	100.00
123-128: 124-1st app. Man-Wolf (9/73), origin in #125. 127-1st mention of Harry Osborn becoming Green Goblin	2.60	7.50	18.00
129-1st app. Jackal & The Punisher (2/74)	39.00	110.00	275.00
130-133,138-160: 131-Last 20¢ issue. 139-1st app. Grizzly. 140-1st app. Glory Grant. 143-1st app. Cyclone. 159-Last 25¢ issue	1.70	5.00	12.00
134-Punisher cameo (7/74); 1st app. Tarantula	3.25	9.50	22.00
135-2nd full Punisher app. (8/74)	9.00	28.00	65.00
136-Reappearance of The Green Goblin (Harry Osborn; Norman Osborn's son)	4.30	13.00	30.00
137-Green Goblin-c/story (2nd Harry Osborn)	2.15	6.50	15.00
161-Nightcrawler app. from X-Men; Punisher cameo	1.70	5.00	12.00
162-Punisher, Nightcrawler app.	3.25	9.50	22.00
163-173,181-190: 167-1st app. Will O' The Wisp. 171-Nova app. 181-Origin retold; gives life history of Spidey; Punisher cameo in flashback (1 panel) 182-(7/78)-Peter proposes to Mary Jane for 1st time, but she refuses	1.30	3.25	8.00
174,175-Punisher app.	2.60	7.50	18.00
176-180-Green Goblin app	2.00	6.00	14.00
191-193,195-199,203-208,210-219: 193-Peter & Mary Jane break up. 196-Faked death of Aunt May. 203-2nd app. Dazzler. 209-1st app. Calypso (Kraven's girlfriend). 210-1st app. Madame Web. 212-1st app. Hydro Man; origin Sandman	1.20	3.00	7.00
194-1st app. Black Cat	2.00	6.00	14.00
200-Giant origin issue (1/80)	3.60	10.75	25.00
201,202-Punisher app.	3.25	9.50	22.00
209-Origin & 1st app. Calypso (10/80)	1.50	3.75	9.00
220-237: 225-Foolkiller app. 226,227-Black Cat returns. 236-Tarantula dies. 234-Free 16 pg. insert "Marvel Guide to Collecting Comics." 235-Origin Will-'O-The-Wisp	1.20	3.00	7.00
238-(3/83)-1st app. Hobgoblin (Ned Leeds); came with skin "Tattooz" decal	10.00	30.00	70.00
238-Without tattooz decal	3.60	10.75	25.00
239-2nd app. Hobgoblin & 1st battle w/Spidey	5.50	16.00	38.00
240-243,246-248: 241-Origin The Vulture. 243-Reintro Mary Jane Watson after 4 year absence	1.20	3.00	7.00
244-3rd app. Hobgoblin (cameo only)	1.65	4.00	10.00
245-4th app. Hobgoblin (cameo only), Lefty Donovan gains powers of Hobgoblin & battles Spider-Man	2.15	6.50	15.00
249-251: 3 part Hobgoblin/Spider-Man battle. 249-Retells origin & death of 1st Green Goblin. 251-Last old costume	1.85	5.50	13.00
252-Spider-Man dons new black costume (5/84); ties with Marvel Team-Up #141 & Spectacular Spider-Man #90 for 1st new costume (See Marvel S-H Secret Wars #8)	3.85	11.50	27.00
253-1st app. The Rose	1.30	3.25	8.00
254	1.00	2.50	6.00
255,263,264,266-273,277-280,282,283: 279-Jack O'Lantern-c/story. 282-X-Factor x-over		1.60	4.00
256-1st app. Puma	1.00	2.00	5.00
257-Hobgoblin cameo; 2nd app. Puma; M. J. Watson reveals she knows Spidey's i.d.	1.65	4.00	10.00
258-Hobgoblin app. (minor)	1.70	5.00	12.00
259-Full Hobgoblin app.; Spidey back to old costume; origin Mary Jane Watson	2.50	7.50	17.50
260-Hobgoblin app.	1.65	4.00	10.00
261-Hobgoblin-c/story; painted-c by Vess	1.70	5.00	12.00
262-Spider-Man unmasked; photo-c	1.25	3.00	7.50
265-1st app. Silver Sable (6/85)	2.00	6.00	14.00
265-Silver ink 2nd printing ($1.25)		1.20	3.00
274-Zarathos (The Spirit of Vengeance) app. (3/86)		1.60	4.00
275-($1.25, 52 pgs.)-Hobgoblin-c/story; origin-r by Ditko	1.85	5.50	13.00

	GD25	FN65	NM94
276-Hobgoblin app.	1.65	4.00	10.00
281-Hobgoblin battles Jack O'Lantern	1.70	5.00	12.00
284-Punisher cameo; Gang War story begins; Hobgoblin-c/story	1.65	4.00	10.00
285-Punisher app.; minor Hobgoblin app.	2.65	8.00	18.50
286,287: 286-Hobgoblin-c & app. (minor). 287-Hobgoblin app. (minor)	1.00	2.50	6.00
288-Full Hobgoblin app.; last Gang War	1.50	3.75	9.00
289-(6/87, $1.25, 52 pgs.)-Hobgoblin's i.d. revealed as Ned Leeds; death of Ned Leeds; Macendale (Jack O'Lantern) becomes new Hobgoblin (1st app.)	3.40	10.00	24.00
290-292: 290-Peter proposes to Mary Jane. 292-She accepts; leads into Amazing Spider-Man Annual #21	1.00	2.00	5.00
293,294-Part 2 & 5 of Kraven story from Web of Spider-Man. 294-Death of Kraven	1.50	3.75	9.00
295-297	1.00	2.50	6.00
298-Todd McFarlane-c/a begins (3/88); 1st app. Eddie Brock who becomes Venom; (cameo on last pg.)	5.50	17.00	40.00
299-1st app. Venom with costume (cameo)	3.60	10.75	25.00
300 ($1.50, 52 pgs.; 25th Anniversary)-1st full Venom app.; last black costume (5/88)	9.00	28.00	65.00
301-305: 301 ($1.00 issues begin). 304-1st bi-weekly issue	2.30	6.75	16.00
306-311,313,314: 306-Swipes-c from Action #1. 315-317-Venom app.	1.65	4.70	11.00
312-Hobgoblin battles Green Goblin	3.25	9.50	22.00
315-317-Venom app.	3.20	8.00	20.00
318-323,325: 319-Bi-weekly begins again	1.30	3.25	8.00
324-Sabretooth app.; McFarlane cover only	1.85	5.50	13.00
326,327,329: 327-Cosmic Spidey continues from Spectacular Spider-Man (no McFarlane-c/a)		1.60	4.00
328-Hulk x-over; last McFarlane issue	1.65	4.70	11.00
330,331-Punisher app. 331-Minor Venom app.		1.60	4.00
332,333-Venom-c/story	1.50	3.75	9.00
334-336,338-343: 341-Tarantula app.		1.20	3.00
337-Hobgoblin app.		1.60	4.00
344-1st app. Cletus Kasady (Carnage)	1.00	3.00	9.75
345-1st full app. Cletus Kasady; Venom cameo on last pg.	1.70	5.00	12.00
346,347-Venom app.	1.65	4.00	10.00
348,349,351-359: 348-Avengers x-over. 351,352-Nova of New Warriors app. 353-Darkhawk app.; brief Punisher app. 354-Punisher cameo & Nova, Night Thrasher (New Warriors), Darkhawk & Moon Knight app. 357,358-Punisher, Darkhawk, Moon Knight, Night Thrasher, Nova x-over. 358-3 part gatefold-c; last $1.00-c. 360-Carnage cameo		1.00	2.50
350-($1.50, 52pgs.)-Origin retold; Spidey vs. Dr. Doom; pin-ups		1.20	3.00
360-Carnage cameo	1.35	3.40	8.25
361-Intro Carnage (the Spawn of Venom); begin 3 part story; recap of how Spidey's alien costume became Venom	2.70	8.00	19.00
361-2nd printing ($1.25)		.80	2.00
362,363-Carnage & Venom-c/story	1.60	3.80	9.75
362-2nd printing			1.50
364,366-374,376-388: 364-The Shocker app. (old villain). 366-Peter's parents-c/story. 369-Harry Osborn back-up (Gr. Goblin II). 373-Venom back-up. 374-Venom-c/story. 376-Cardiac app. 378-Maximum Carnage part 3. 381,382-Hulk app.			1.25
365-($3.95, 84 pgs.)-30th anniversary issue w/hologram-c; Spidey/Venom/Carnage pull-out poster; contains 5 pg. preview of Spider-Man 2099 (1st app.); Spidey's origin retold; Lizard app.; reintro Peter's parents in Stan Lee 3 pg. text w/illo (saga continues thru #370)	1.00	2.60	6.25
375-($3.95, 68 pgs.)-Holo-grafx foil-c; vs. Venom story; ties into Venom: Lethal Protector #1	1.00	2.50	5.75
Annual 1 (1964, 72 pgs.)-Origin Spider-Man; 1st app. Sinister Six (Dr. Octopus, Electro, Kraven the Hunter, Mysterio, Sandman, Vulture) (41 pg. story); plus			

The Amazing Spider-Man Annual #16, © MEG

Amazon, The #1, © Comico

The American Air Forces #3, © ME

GD25 FN65 NM94

gallery of Spidey foes 40.00 120.00 360.00
Annual 2 (1965, 25 cents, 72 pgs.)-Reprints from #1,2,5 plus new Doctor Strange story 15.00 45.00 150.00
Special 3 (11/66, 25 cents, 72 pgs.)-Avengers & Hulk x-over; Doctor Octopus-r from #11,12; Romita-a 6.50 19.00 45.00
Special 4 (11/67, 25 cents, 68 pgs.)-Spidey battles Human Torch (new 41 pg. story) 7.00 21.00 50.00
Special 5 (11/68, 25 cents, 68 pgs.)-New 40 pg. Red Skull story; 1st app. Peter Parker's parents; last annual with new-a 8.00 24.00 55.00
Special 6 (11/69, 25 cents, 68 pgs.)-Reprints 41 pg. Sinister Six story from annual #1 plus 2 Kirby/Ditko stories (r) 3.50 8.00 19.50
Special 7 (12/70, 25 cents, 68 pgs.)-All-r(#1,2) 3.50 8.00 19.50
Special 8 (12/71) 3.50 8.00 19.50
King Size 9 ('73)-Reprints Spectacular Spider-Man (mag.) #2; 40 pg. Green Goblin-c/story (re-edited from 58 pgs.) 3.50 8.00 19.50
Annual 10 (1976)-Origin Human Fly(vs. Spidey); new-a begins 1.20 3.00 7.00
Annual 11,12: 11 (1977). 12 (1978)-Spider-Man vs. Hulk-r/#119,120 1.20 3.00 7.00
Annual 13 (1979)-Byrne/Austin-a (new) 1.30 3.25 8.00
Annual 14 (1980)-Miller-c/a(p), 40pgs. 1.30 3.25 8.00
Annual 15 (1981)-Miller-c/a(p); Punisher app. 3.25 9.50 22.00
Annual 16-20: 16 (1982)-Origin/1st app. new Capt. Marvel (female heroine). 17 (1983). 18 (1984). 19 (1985). 20 (1986)-Origin Iron Man of 2020 1.00 2.50 6.00
Annual 21 (1987)-Special wedding issue; newsstand & direct sale versions exist & are worth same 1.30 3.25 8.00
Annual 22 (1988, $1.75, 68 pgs.)-1st app. Speedball; Evolutionary War x-over 1.30 3.25 8.00
Annual 23 (1989, $2.00, 68 pgs.)-Atlantis Attacks; origin Spider-Man retold; She-Hulk app.; Byrne-c; Liefeld-a(p), 23 pgs. 1.00 2.50 6.00
Annual 24 (1990, $2.00, 68 pgs.)-Ant-Man app. 1.40 3.50
Annual 25 (1991, $2.00, 68 pgs.)-3 pg. origin recap; Iron Man app.; 1st Venom solo story; Ditko-a (6 pgs.) 1.65 4.00 10.00
Annual 26 (1992, $2.25, 68 pgs.)-New Warriors-c/story; Venom solo story cont'd in Spectacular Spider-Man Annual #12 1.00 2.50 6.00
Annual 27 (1993, $2.95, 68 pgs.)-Bagged w/card 1.20 3.00
Soul of the Hunter nn (8/92, $5.95, 52 pgs.) 1.00 2.50 6.00
...: Skating on Thin Ice 1(1990, $1.25, Canadian)-McFarlane-c; anti-drug issue 1.00 2.00 5.00
...: Skating on Thin Ice 1 (2/93, $1.50, American) .80 2.00
...: Double Trouble 2 (1990, $1.25, Canadian) 1.20 3.00
...: Double Trouble 2 (2/93, $1.50, American) .80 2.00
...: Hit and Run 3 (1990, $1.25, Canadian)-Ghost Rider-c/story 1.20 3.00
...: Hit and Run 3 (2/93. $1.50, American) .80 2.00
...: Chaos in Calgary 4 (2/93, $1.50, American) .80 2.00
Parallel Lives (1990, $8.95, 68pgs.)-Graphic novel 1.50 3.75 9.00
Aim Toothpaste giveaway(36 pgs., reg. size)-1 pg. origin recap; Green Goblin-c/story 1.00 2.50 6.00
Aim Toothpaste giveaway (16 pgs., reg. size)-Dr. Octopus app. 1.00 2.00 5.00
All Detergent Giveaway (1979, 36 pgs.), nn-Origin-r 1.65 4.00 10.00
Giveaway-Acme & Dingo Children's Boots (1980)-Spider-Woman app. 1.60 4.00
...& Power Pack (1984, nn)(Nat'l Committee for Prevention of Child Abuse (two versions, mail offer & store giveaway)-Mooney-a; Byrne-c 1.00
...& The Hulk (Special Edition)(6/8/80; 20 pgs.); Supplement to Chicago Tribune (giveaway) 1.30 3.25 8.00
...& The Incredible Hulk (1981, 1982; 36 pgs.), Sanger Harris supplement to Dallas Times, Dallas Herald, Denver Post, Kansas City Star, Tulsa World; The Jones Store-giveaway (1983, 16 pgs.) 1.65 4.00 10.00
..., Captain America, The Incredible Hulk, & Spider-Woman (1981) (7-11 Stores giveaway; 36 pgs.) 1.00 2.00 5.00
...: Christmas In Dallas (1983) (Supplement to Dallas Times Herald) giveaway 1.00 2.00 5.00
..., Fire-Star, and Iceman At the Dallas Ballet Nutcracker (1983; supplement to Dallas Times Herald)-Mooney-p 1.00 2.00 5.00
Giveaway-Esquire & Eye Magazines(2/69)-Miniature-Still attached 7.00 21.00 50.00
..., Storm & Powerman (1982; 20 pgs.)(American Cancer Society) giveaway 1.00 2.00 5.00
...Vs. The Hulk (Special Edition; 1979, 20 pgs.)(Supplement to Columbus Dispatch)-Giveaway 1.00 2.00 5.00
...Vs. the Prodigy Giveaway, 16 pgs. in color (1976, 5x6-1/2")-Sex education; (1 million printed; 35-50 cents) 1.20 3.00

NOTE: **Austin** *a(i)-248, 335, 337, Annual 13; c(i)-188, 241, 242, 248, 331, 334, 343, Annual 25i.* *J.* **Buscema** *a(p)-72, 73, 76-81, 84, 85.* **Byrne** *a-189p, 190p, 206p, Annual 3r, 6r, 7r, 13p; c-189p, 268, 296, Annual 12.* **Ditko** *a-1-38, Annual 1, Special 3(r), 2, 24(2); c-1-38.* **Guice** *c/a-Annual 18i.* **Gil Kane** *a(p)-89-105, 120-124, 150, Annual 10, 12i, 24p; c-90p, 96, 98, 99, 101-105p, 129p, 131p, 132p, 137-140p, 143p, 148p, 149p, 151p, 153p, 160p, 161p, Annual 10p, 24.* **Kirby** *a-8.* **McFarlane** *a-298p, 299p, 300-303, 304-323p, 325p, 328; c-298-325, 328.* **Miller** *c-218, 219.* **Mooney** *a-65i, 67-82i, 84-88i, 173i, 178i, 189i, 190i, 192i, 193i, 196-202i, 207i, 211-219i, 221i, 222i, 226i, 227i, 229-233i, Annual 11i, 17i.* **Nasser** *c-228p.* **Nebres** *a-Annual 24i.* **Russell** *c-357i.* **Simonson** *c-222, 337i.* **Starlin** *a-113i, 114i, 187p.*

AMAZING WILLIE MAYS, THE
No date (Sept, 1954)
Famous Funnies Publ.

nn 55.00 165.00 385.00

AMAZING WORLD OF SUPERMAN (See Superman)

AMAZON, THE (Comico)(Value: cover or less)

AMAZON ATTACK 3-D (3-D Zone)(Value: cover or less)

AMBUSH (See 4-Color Comics No. 314)

AMBUSH BUG (Also see Son of...)
June, 1985 - No. 4, Sept, 1985 (75 cents, mini-series)
DC Comics

1-4: Giffen-c/a in all 1.00
...Nothing Special 1 (9/92, $2.50, 68pg.)-Giffen-c/a 1.00 2.50
...Stocking Stuffer (2/86, $1.25)-Giffen-c/a 1.30

AMERICA IN ACTION
1942; Winter, 1945 (36 pages)
Dell(Imp. Publ. Co.)/Mayflower House Publ.

1942-Dell-(68 pages) 12.00 36.00 85.00
1(1945)-Has 3 adaptations from American history; Kiefer, Schrotter & Webb-a 10.00 30.00 60.00

AMERICA MENACED!
1950 (Paper cover)
Vital Publications
nn-Anti-communism estimated value.... 175.00

AMERICAN, THE
July, 1987 - No. 9, 1989 ($1.50-$1.75, B&W)
Dark Horse Comics

1 ($1.50) 1.00 2.00 5.00
2-Begin $1.75-c? 1.40 3.50
3-5 1.00 2.50
6-9 .70 1.75
...Collection ($5.95, B&W)-reprints 1.00 2.50 6.00
...Special 1 (1990, $2.25, B&W) .90 2.25

AMERICAN AIR FORCES, THE (See A-1 Comics)
Sept-Oct, 1944 - No. 4, 1945; No. 5, 1951 - No. 12, 1954
William H. Wise(Flying Cadet Publ. Co./Hasan(No.1)/Life's Romances/ Magazine Ent. No. 5 on)

1-Article by Zack Mosley, creator of Smilin' Jack 8.35 25.00 50.00
2-4 5.35 16.00 32.00

NOTE: *All part comic, part magazine. Art by* **Whitney, Chas. Quinlan, H. C. Kiefer,** *and* **Tony Dipreta.**

5(A-1 45)(Formerly Jet Powers), 6(A-1 54), 7(A-1 58), 8(A-1 65), 9(A-1 67), 10(A-1 74), 11(A-1 79), 12(A-1 91) 4.00 10.50 21.00

American Flagg! #31, © First Comics & Howard Chaykin

America's Best Comics #20, © STD

Amethyst Princess of Gemworld #8, © DC

GD25 FN65 NM94 | GD25 FN65 NM94

NOTE: *Powell c/a-5-12.*

AMERICAN COMICS
1940's
Theatre Giveaways (Liberty Theatre, Grand Rapids, Mich. known)

Many possible combinations. "Golden Age" superhero comics with new cover added and given away at theaters. Following known: Superman #59, Capt. Marvel #20, Capt. Marvel Jr. #5, Action #33, Classics Comics #8, Whiz #39. Value would vary with book and should be 70-80 percent of the original.

AMERICAN FLAGG! (First)(Value: cover or less)

AMERICAN GRAPHICS
No. 1, 1954; No. 2, 1957 (25 cents)
Henry Stewart

	GD25	FN65	NM94
1-The Maid of the Mist, The Last of the Eries (Indian Legends of Niagara) (sold at Niagara Falls)	7.00	21.00	42.00
2-Victory at Niagara & Laura Secord (Heroine of the War of 1812)	4.70	14.00	28.00

AMERICAN INDIAN, THE (See Picture Progress)

AMERICAN LIBRARY
1943 - No. 6, 1944 (68 pages) (15 cents, B&W, text & pictures)
David McKay Publications

	GD25	FN65	NM94
nn (#1)-Thirty Seconds Over Tokyo (movie)	27.00	80.00	185.00
nn (#2)-Guadalcanal Diary; painted-c (only 10¢)	22.00	65.00	130.00
3-6: 3-Look to the Mountain. 4-Case of the Crooked Candle (Perry Mason). 5-Duel in the Sun. 6-Wingate's Raiders	10.00	30.00	65.00

AMERICAN: LOST IN AMERICA, THE (Dark Horse)(Value: cover or less)

AMERICAN TAIL: FIEVEL GOES WEST, AN
Early Jan, 1992 - No. 3, Early Feb, 1992 ($1.00, color, mini-series)
Marvel Comics

	GD25	FN65	NM94
1-Adapts Universal animated movie; Wildman-a			1.00

AMERICA'S BEST COMICS
Feb, 1942; No. 2, Sept, 1942 - No. 31, July, 1949 (New logo with #9)
Nedor/Better/Standard Publications

	GD25	FN65	NM94
1-The Woman in Red, Black Terror, Captain Future, Doc Strange, The Liberator, & Don Davis, Secret Ace begin	92.00	280.00	650.00
2-Origin The American Eagle; The Woman in Red ends	46.00	140.00	325.00
3-Pyroman begins (11/42, 1st app.; also see Startling Comics #18, 12/42)	35.00	105.00	240.00
4	29.00	85.00	200.00
5-Last Capt. Future (not in #4); Lone Eagle app.	25.00	75.00	175.00
6,7: 6-American Crusader app. 7-Hitler, Mussolini & Hirohito-c	22.00	65.00	150.00
8-Last Liberator	18.00	55.00	125.00
9-The Fighting Yank begins; The Ghost app.	20.00	60.00	140.00
10-14: 10-Flag-c. 14-American Eagle ends	17.00	50.00	115.00
15-20	14.00	43.00	100.00
21,22: 21-Infinity-c. 22-Capt. Future app.	13.00	40.00	90.00
23-Miss Masque begins; last Doc Strange	17.00	52.00	120.00
24-Miss Masque bondage-c	15.00	45.00	105.00
25-Last Fighting Yank; Sea Eagle app.	13.00	40.00	90.00
26-31: 26-The Phantom Detective & The Silver Knight app.; Frazetta text illo & some panels in Miss Masque. 27,28-Commando Cubs. 27-Doc Strange. 28-Tuska Black Terror. 29-Last Pyroman	17.00	50.00	110.00

NOTE: *American Eagle not in 3, 8, 9, 13. Fighting Yank not in 10, 12. Liberator not in 2, 6, 7. Pyroman not in 9, 11, 14-16, 23, 25-27.* ***Schomburg (Xela)*** *c-5, 7-31. Bondage c-18, 24.*

AMERICA'S BEST TV COMICS (TV)
1967 (Produced by Marvel Comics) (25 cents, 68 pgs.)
American Broadcasting Company

	GD25	FN65	NM94
1-Spider-Man, Fantastic Four (by Kirby/Ayers), Casper, King Kong, George of the Jungle, Journey to the Center of the Earth stories (promotes new TV cartoon show)	6.00	18.00	42.00

AMERICA'S BIGGEST COMICS BOOK
1944 (196 pages) (One Shot)
William H. Wise

	GD25	FN65	NM94
1-The Grim Reaper, The Silver Knight, Zudo, the Jungle Boy, Commando Cubs, Thunderhoof app.	33.00	100.00	210.00

AMERICA'S FUNNIEST COMICS
1944 - No. 2, 1944 (80 pages) (15 cents)
William H. Wise

	GD25	FN65	NM94
nn(#1), 2	18.00	55.00	125.00

AMERICA'S GREATEST COMICS
May?, 1941 - No. 8, Summer, 1943 (100 pgs.) (Soft cardboard covers)
Fawcett Publications (15 cents)

	GD25	FN65	NM94
1-Bulletman, Spy Smasher, Capt. Marvel, Minute Man & Mr. Scarlet begin; Mac Raboy-c	192.00	575.00	1200.00
2	92.00	275.00	575.00
3	71.00	210.00	465.00
4,5: 4-Commando Yank begins; Golden Arrow, Ibis the Invincible & Spy Smasher cameo in Captain Marvel	56.00	165.00	365.00
6,7: 7-Balbo the Boy Magician app.; Captain Marvel, Bulletman cameo in Mr. Scarlet	42.00	125.00	275.00
8-Capt. Marvel Jr. & Golden Arrow app.; Spy Smasher x-over in Capt. Midnight; no Minute Man or Commando Yank	42.00	125.00	275.00

AMERICA'S SWEETHEART SUNNY (See Sunny, ...)

AMERICA VS. THE JUSTICE SOCIETY
Jan, 1985 - No. 4, Apr, 1985 ($1.00, mini-series)
DC Comics

	GD25	FN65	NM94
1-Double size; Alcala-a(i) in all	.30	.75	1.50
2-4		.50	1.00

AMERICOMICS (Americomics)(Value: cover or less)

AMETHYST
Jan, 1985 - No. 16, Aug, 1986 (75 cents)
DC Comics

	GD25	FN65	NM94
1-16: 8-Fire Jade's i.d. revealed			1.00
Special 1 (10/86, $1.25)			1.25

AMETHYST
Nov, 1987 - No. 4, Feb, 1988 ($1.25, color, mini-series)
DC Comics

	GD25	FN65	NM94
1-4			1.25

AMETHYST, PRINCESS OF GEMWORLD
May, 1983 - No. 12, April, 1984 (12 issue maxi-series)
DC Comics

	GD25	FN65	NM94
1-60 cent cover			1.00
1,2-35 cent-tested in Austin & Kansas City	2.15	6.50	15.00
2-12: Perez-c(p) #6-11			1.00
Annual 1(9/84)			1.25

ANARCHO DICTATOR OF DEATH (See Comics Novel)

ANCHORS ANDREWS (The Saltwater Daffy)
Jan, 1953 - No. 4, July, 1953 (Anchors the Saltwater... No. 4)
St. John Publishing Co.

	GD25	FN65	NM94
1-Canteen Kate by Matt Baker (9 pgs.)	10.00	30.00	70.00
2-4	4.00	10.00	20.00

ANDY & WOODY (See March of Comics No. 40, 55, 76)

ANDY BURNETT (See 4-Color Comics No. 865)

ANDY COMICS (Formerly Scream Comics; becomes Ernie Comics)
No. 20, June, 1948 - No. 21, Aug, 1948
Current Publications (Ace Magazines)

	GD25	FN65	NM94
20,21-Archie-type comic	4.20	12.50	25.00

ANDY DEVINE WESTERN
Dec, 1950 - No. 2, 1951

Angel and the Ape #3 (5/91), © DC

Animal Adventures #3 (reprint), © Accepted

Animal Comics #21, © Dell

Fawcett Publications

	GD25	FN65	NM94
1	39.00	118.00	275.00
2	30.00	90.00	210.00

ANDY GRIFFITH SHOW, THE (See 4-Color No. 1252, 1341)

ANDY HARDY COMICS (See Movie Comics No. 3 by Fiction House)
April, 1952 - No. 6, Sept-Nov, 1954
Dell Publishing Co.

	GD25	FN65	NM94
4-Color 389 (#1)	4.00	10.00	21.00
4-Color 447,480,515,5,6	2.80	7.00	14.00
...& the New Automatic Gas Clothes Dryer (1952, 16 pgs., 5x7-1/4") Bendix Giveaway (soft-c)	4.00	10.00	21.00

ANDY PANDA (Also see Crackajack Funnies #39, The Funnies, New Funnies & Walter Lantz ...)
1943 - No. 56, Nov-Jan, 1961-62 (Walter Lantz)
Dell Publishing Co.

	GD25	FN65	NM94
4-Color 25(#1, 1943)	37.00	110.00	260.00
4-Color 54('44)	23.00	70.00	160.00
4-Color 85('45)	14.00	43.00	100.00
4-Color 130('46),154,198	10.00	30.00	60.00
4-Color 216,240,258,280,297	6.70	20.00	40.00
4-Color 326,345,358	4.00	10.00	20.00
4-Color 383,409	3.20	8.00	16.00
16(11-1/52-53) - 30	1.80	4.50	9.00
31-56	1.40	3.50	7.00

(See March of Comics #5, 22, 79, & Super Book #4, 15, 27.)

ANGEL
Aug, 1954 - No. 16, Nov-Jan, 1958-59
Dell Publishing Co.

	GD25	FN65	NM94
4-Color 576(#1, 8/54)	2.80	7.00	14.00
2(5-7/55) - 16	1.80	4.50	9.00

ANGEL AND THE APE (Meet Angel No. 7) (See Limited Collector's Edition C-34 & Showcase No. 77)
Nov-Dec, 1968 - No. 6, Sept-Oct, 1969
National Periodical Publications

	GD25	FN65	NM94
Showcase #77 (9/68)-1st app. Angel & the Ape	3.00	10.00	32.00
1-(11-12/68)-Not Wood-a	3.00	9.00	20.00
2-6-Wood inks in all	1.70	5.00	12.00

ANGEL AND THE APE (2nd series)
Mar, 1991 - No. 4, June, 1991 ($1.00, color, mini-series)
DC Comics

	GD25	FN65	NM94
1-4			1.00

ANGELIC ANGELINA
1909 (11-1/2x17"; 30 pgs.; 2 colors)
Cupples & Leon Company

	GD25	FN65	NM94
nn-By Munson Paddock	23.00	70.00	160.00

ANGEL LOVE
Aug, 1986 - No. 8, Mar, 1987 (75 cents, mini-series)
DC Comics

	GD25	FN65	NM94
1-8			1.00
Special 1 (1987, $1.25, 52 pgs.)			1.25

ANGEL OF LIGHT, THE (See The Crusaders)

ANIMAL ADVENTURES
Dec, 1953 - No. 3, May?, 1954
Timor Publications/Accepted Publications (reprints)

	GD25	FN65	NM94
1-Funny animal	3.60	9.00	18.00
2,3: 2-Featuring Soopermutt (2/54)	2.00	5.00	10.00
1-3 (reprints, nd)	1.40	3.50	7.00

ANIMAL ANTICS (Movie Town... No. 24 on)
Mar-Apr, 1946 - No. 23, Nov-Dec, 1949 (All 52 pgs.?)
National Periodical Publications

	GD25	FN65	NM94
1-Raccoon Kids begins by Otto Feur; some-c by Grossman; Seaman Sy Wheeler by Kelly in some issues	36.00	108.00	240.00
2	17.00	52.00	120.00
3-10: 10-Post-c/a	11.00	32.00	75.00
11-23: 14,15,18,19-Post-a	7.50	22.50	45.00

ANIMAL COMICS
Dec-Jan, 1941-42 - No. 30, Dec-Jan, 1947-48
Dell Publishing Co.

	GD25	FN65	NM94
1-1st Pogo app. by Walt Kelly (Dan Noonan art in most issues)	91.00	275.00	640.00
2-Uncle Wiggily begins	39.00	118.00	275.00
3,5	27.00	81.00	190.00
4,6,7-No Pogo	16.00	48.00	110.00
8-10	19.00	57.00	130.00
11-15	12.00	36.00	85.00
16-20	9.15	27.50	55.00
21-30: 25-30-"Jigger" by John Stanley	6.70	20.00	40.00

NOTE: ***Dan Noonan*** *a-18-30.* ***Gollub*** *art in most later issues; c-29, 30.* ***Kelly*** *c-7-26.*

ANIMAL CONFIDENTIAL (Dark Horse)(Value: cover or less)

ANIMAL CRACKERS (Also see Adventures of Patoruzu)
1946; No. 31, July, 1950; No. 9, 1959
Green Publ. Co./Norlen/Fox Feat.(Hero Books)

	GD25	FN65	NM94
1-Super Cat begins (1st app.)	10.00	30.00	60.00
2	5.85	17.50	35.00
3-10 (Exist?)	3.00	7.50	15.00
31(Fox)-Formerly My Love Secret	4.20	12.50	25.00
9(1959-Norlen)-Infinity-c	2.00	5.00	10.00
nn, nd ('50s), no publ.; infinity-c	2.00	5.00	10.00

ANIMAL FABLES
July-Aug, 1946 - No. 7, Nov-Dec, 1947
E. C. Comics(Fables Publ. Co.)

	GD25	FN65	NM94
1-Freddy Firefly (clone of Human Torch), Korky Kangaroo, Petey Pig, Danny Demon begin	30.00	90.00	210.00
2-Aesop Fables begin	19.00	58.00	135.00
3-6	16.00	48.00	110.00
7-Origin Moon Girl	49.00	145.00	340.00

ANIMAL FAIR (Fawcett's...)
March, 1946 - No. 11, Feb, 1947
Fawcett Publications

	GD25	FN65	NM94
1	17.00	52.00	120.00
2	10.00	30.00	60.00
3-6	6.70	20.00	40.00
7-11	4.70	14.00	28.00

ANIMAL FUN
1953
Premier Magazines

	GD25	FN65	NM94
1-(3-D)-Ziggy Pig, Silly Seal, Billy & others	28.00	85.00	200.00

ANIMAL MAN (See Action Comics #552, 553, DC Comics presents #77, 78, Secret Origins #39, Strange Adventures #180 & Wonder Woman #267, 268)
Sept, 1988 - Present ($1.25-$1.50, color)
DC Comics

	GD25	FN65	NM94
1-Bolland c-all; Grant Morrison scripts begin	2.30	6.75	16.00
2-Superman cameo	1.65	4.70	11.00
3,4	1.10	2.70	6.50
5-10: 6-Invasion tie-in. 9-Manhunter-c/story		1.80	4.50
11-20: 11-Begin $1.50-c		1.20	3.00
21-26: 24-Arkham Asylum story; Bizarro Superman app. 25-Inferior Five app. 26-Last Morrison scripts; Morrison apps. in story; part photo-c (of Morrison?)		1.20	3.00
27-49,51-55,57-59: 41-Begin $1.75-c, end #59		.80	2.00

Anne Rices The Mummy #1, © Anne O'Brien Rice

Annie Oakley and Tagg #9, © Dell

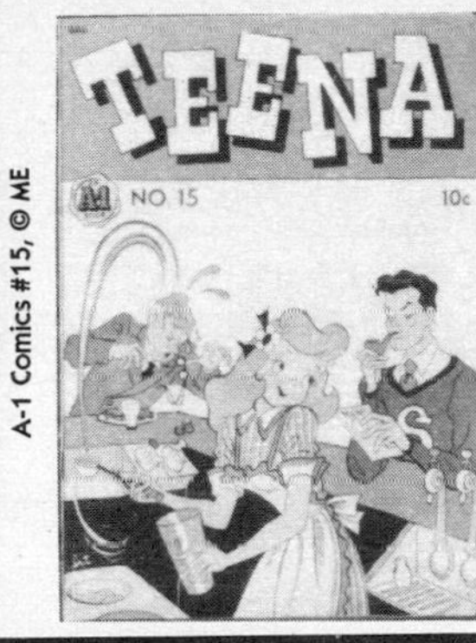

A-1 Comics #15, © ME

GD25 FN65 NM94

50-($2.95, 52 pgs.)-Last issue w/Veitch scripts 1.20 3.00
56-($3.50, 68 pgs.) 1.40 3.50
60-70: 60-Begin $1.95-c .80 2.00
Annual 1 (1993, $3.95, 68 pgs.)-Bolland-c 1.60 4.00

ANIMAL WORLD, THE (See 4-Color Comics No. 713)

ANIMATED COMICS
No date given (Summer, 1947?)
E. C. Comics
1 (Rare) 62.00 186.00 425.00

ANIMATED FUNNY COMIC TUNES (See Funny Tunes)

ANIMATED MOVIE-TUNES (Movie Tunes No. 3)
Fall, 1945 - No. 2, Sum, 1946
Margood Publishing Corp. (Timely)
1,2-Super Rabbit, Ziggy Pig & Silly Seal 12.00 36.00 85.00

ANIMAX
Dec, 1986 - No. 4, June, 1987
Star Comics (Marvel)
1-4: Based on toys 1.00

ANNE RICE'S THE MUMMY OR RAMSES THE DAMNED
Oct, 1990 - No. 12, 1991 ($2.50, color, high quality, mini-series)
Millennium Publications
1-12: Adapts novel; Mooney-p in all 1.00 2.50

ANNETTE (See 4-Color Comics No. 905)

ANNETTE'S LIFE STORY (See 4-Color No. 1100)

ANNIE
Oct, 1982 - No. 2, Nov, 1982 (60 cents)
Marvel Comics Group
1,2-Movie adaptation 1.25
Treasury Edition ($2.00, tabloid size) .80 2.00

ANNIE OAKLEY (See Tessie The Typist #19, Two-Gun Kid & Wild Western)
Spring, 1948 - No. 4, 11/48; No. 5, 6/55 - No. 11, 6/56
Marvel/Atlas Comics(MPI No. 1-4/CDS No. 5 on)
1 (1st Series, 1948)-Hedy Devine app. 28.00 85.00 200.00
2 (7/48, 52 pgs.)-Kurtzman-a, "Hey Look," 1 pg; Intro. Lana; Hedy Devine app; Captain Tootsie by Beck 17.00 52.00 120.00
3,4 14.00 43.00 100.00
5 (2nd Series, 1955)-Reinman-a ; Maneely-c 10.00 30.00 65.00
6-9: 6,8-Woodbridge-a. 9-Williamson-a (4 pgs.) 9.15 27.50 55.00
10,11: 11-Severin-c 7.50 22.50 45.00

ANNIE OAKLEY AND TAGG (TV)
1953 - No. 18, Jan-Mar, 1959; July, 1965 (Photo-c #3 on)
Dell Publishing Co./Gold Key
4-Color 438 (#1) 12.00 36.00 85.00
4-Color 481,575 (#2,3) 8.35 25.00 50.00
4(7-9/55)-10 7.50 22.50 45.00
11-18(1-3/59) 5.85 17.50 35.00
1(7/65-Gold Key)-Photo-c 5.00 15.00 30.00
NOTE: *Manning a-13. Photo back c-4, 9, 11.*

ANOTHER WORLD (See Strange Stories From...)

ANTHRO (See Showcase #74)
July-Aug, 1968 - No. 6, July-Aug, 1969
National Periodical Publications
Showcase #74 (5/68)-1st app. Anthro; Post-c/a 5.00 14.00 45.00
1-(7-8/68)-Howie Post-a in all 4.50 14.00 32.00
2-6: 6-Wood-c/a (inks) 2.40 7.25 17.00

ANTONY AND CLEOPATRA (See Ideal, a Classical Comic)

ANYTHING GOES
Oct, 1986 - No. 6, 1987 ($2.00, mini-series, mature readers)
Fantagraphics Books (#1-5: color & B&W; #6: B&W)
1-Flaming Carrot app. (1st in color?); G. Kane-c 1.20 3.00
2-4,6: 2-Miller-c(p); Alan Moore scripts; early Sam Kieth-a (2 pgs.). 3-Capt. Jack, Cerebus app.; Cerebus-c by N. Adams. 4-Perez-c .80 2.00
5-2nd color Teenage Mutant Ninja Turtles app. 1.20 3.00

A-1
1992 - No. 4, 1993 ($5.95, color, mini-series, mature readers)
Epic Comics (Marvel)
1-4: 3-Bisley-c 1.00 2.50 6.00

A-1 COMICS (A-1 appears on covers No. 1-17 only)(See individual title listings. 1st two issues not numbered.)
1944 - No. 139, Sept-Oct, 1955 (No #2)
Life's Romances Publ.-No. 1/Compix/Magazine Ent.
nn-Kerry Drake, Johnny Devildog, Rocky, Streamer Kelly (slightly large size) 17.00 52.00 120.00
1-Dotty Dripple (1 pg.), Mr. Ex, Bush Berry, Rocky, Lew Loyal (20 pgs.) 9.15 27.50 55.00
3-8,10-Texas Slim & Dirty Dalton, The Corsair, Teddy Rich, Dotty Dripple, Inca Dinca, Tommy Tinker, Little Mexico & Tugboat Tim, The Masquerader & others. 7-Corsair-c/s. 8-Intro. Rodeo Ryan 4.00 11.00 22.00
9-Texas Slim (all) 4.00 11.00 22.00
11-Teena; Ogden Whitney-c 5.85 17.50 35.00
12,15-Teena 5.00 15.00 30.00
13-Guns of Fact & Fiction (1948). Used in **SOTI**, pg. 19; Ingels & Johnny Craig-a 17.00 52.00 120.00
14-Tim Holt Western Adventures #1 (1948) 43.00 130.00 300.00
16-Vacation Comics; The Pixies, Tom Tom, Flying Fredd, & Koko & Kola 3.60 9.00 18.00
17-Tim Holt #2; photo-c; last issue to carry A-1 on cover (9-10/48) 25.00 75.00 175.00
18,20-Jimmy Durante; photo covers 27.00 80.00 190.00
19-Tim Holt #3; photo-c 18.00 55.00 125.00
21-Joan of Arc (1949)-Movie adaptation; Ingrid Bergman photo-covers & interior photos; Whitney-a 18.00 55.00 125.00
22-Dick Powell (1949)-Photo-c 17.00 52.00 120.00
23-Cowboys and Indians #6; Doc Holliday-c/story 5.35 16.00 32.00
24-Trail Colt #1-Frazetta, r-in Manhunt #13; Ingels-c; L. B. Cole-a 29.00 85.00 200.00
25-Fibber McGee & Molly (1949) (Radio) 7.50 22.50 45.00
26-Trail Colt #2-Ingels-c 23.00 70.00 160.00
27-Ghost Rider #1(1950)-Origin Ghost Rider 47.00 141.00 330.00
28-Christmas-(Koko & Kola #6) (1950) 4.00 10.00 20.00
29-Ghost Rider #2-Frazetta-c (1950) 43.00 130.00 300.00
30-Jet Powers #1-Powell-a 22.00 67.00 155.00
31-Ghost Rider #3-Frazetta-c & origin ('51) 43.00 130.00 300.00
32-Jet Powers #2 16.00 48.00 110.00
33-Muggsy Mouse #1('51) 4.70 14.00 28.00
34-Ghost Rider #4-Frazetta-c (1951) 43.00 130.00 300.00
35-Jet Powers #3-Williamson/Evans-a 25.00 75.00 175.00
36-Muggsy Mouse #2; Racist-c 5.85 17.50 35.00
37-Ghost Rider #5-Frazetta-c (1951) 43.00 130.00 300.00
38-Jet Powers #4-Williamson & Wood-a 25.00 75.00 175.00
39-Muggsy Mouse #3 2.80 7.00 14.00
40-Dogface Dooley #1('51) 4.35 13.00 26.00
41-Cowboys 'N' Indians #7 4.00 12.00 24.00
42-Best of the West #1-Powell-a 31.00 95.00 220.00
43-Dogface Dooley #2 3.60 9.00 18.00
44-Ghost Rider #6 17.00 52.00 120.00
45-American Air Forces #5-Powell-c/a 4.00 10.50 21.00
46-Best of the West #2 14.00 43.00 100.00
47-Thun'da, King of the Congo #1-Frazetta-c/a('52) 86.00 260.00 600.00
48-Cowboys 'N' Indians #8 4.00 12.00 24.00
49-Dogface Dooley #3 3.60 9.00 18.00

A-1 Comics #119, © ME

A-1 Comics #123, © ME

Apache Kid #14, © MEG

	GD25	FN65	NM94
50-Danger Is Their Business #11 ('52)-Powell-a	9.15	27.50	55.00
51-Ghost Rider #7 ('52)	17.00	52.00	120.00
52-Best of the West #3	13.00	40.00	90.00
53-Dogface Dooley #4	3.60	9.00	18.00
54-American Air Forces #6(8/52)-Powell-a	4.00	10.50	21.00
55-U.S. Marines #5-Powell-a	4.00	11.00	22.00
56-Thun'da #2-Powell-c/a 1	13.00	40.00	90.00
57-Ghost Rider #8	15.00	45.00	105.00
58-American Air Forces #7-Powell-a	4.00	10.50	21.00
59-Best of the West #4	13.00	40.00	90.00
60-The U.S. Marines #6-Powell-a	4.00	11.00	22.00
61-Space Ace #5(1953)-Guardineer-a	30.00	90.00	210.00
62-Starr Flagg, Undercover Girl #5 (#1)	26.00	77.00	180.00
63-Manhunt #13-Frazetta reprinted from A-1 #24	19.00	58.00	135.00
64-Dogface Dooley #5	3.60	9.00	18.00
65-American Air Forces #8-Powell-a	4.00	10.50	21.00
66-Best of the West #5	13.00	40.00	90.00
67-American Air Forces #9-Powell-a	4.00	10.50	21.00
68-U.S. Marines #7-Powell-a	4.00	11.00	22.00
69-Ghost Rider #9(10/52)	15.00	45.00	105.00
70-Best of the West #6	10.00	30.00	65.00
71-Ghost Rider #10(12/52)-Vs. Frankenstein	15.00	45.00	105.00
72-U.S. Marines #8-Powell-a(3)	4.00	11.00	22.00
73-Thun'da #3-Powell-c/a	10.00	30.00	65.00
74-American Air Forces #10-Powell-a	4.00	10.50	21.00
75-Ghost Rider #11(3/52)	12.00	36.00	85.00
76-Best of the West #7	10.00	30.00	65.00
77-Manhunt #14	13.50	41.00	95.00
78-Thun'da #4-Powell-c/a	10.00	30.00	65.00
79-American Air Forces #11-Powell-a	4.00	10.50	21.00
80-Ghost Rider #12(6/52)-One-eyed Devil-c	12.00	36.00	85.00
81-Best of the West #8	10.00	30.00	65.00
82-Cave Girl #11(1953)-Powell-c/a; origin (#1)	28.00	85.00	195.00
83-Thun'da #5-Powell-c/a	10.00	30.00	60.00
84-Ghost Rider #13(7-8/53)	12.00	36.00	85.00
85-Best of the West #9	10.00	30.00	65.00
86-Thun'da #6-Powell-c/a	10.00	30.00	60.00
87-Best of the West #10(9-10/53)	10.00	30.00	65.00
88-Bobby Benson's B-Bar-B Riders #20	6.70	20.00	40.00
89-Home Run #3-Powell-a; Stan Musial photo-c	16.00	48.00	110.00
90-Red Hawk #11(1953)-Powell-c/a	9.15	27.50	55.00
91-American Air Forces #12-Powell-a	4.00	10.50	21.00
92-Dream Book of Romance #5-Photo-c; Guardineer-a	5.85	17.50	35.00
93-Great Western #8('54)-Origin The Ghost Rider; Powell-a	13.00	41.00	95.00
94-White Indian #11-Frazetta-a(r); Powell-c	16.00	48.00	110.00
95-Muggsy Mouse #4	2.80	7.00	14.00
96-Cave Girl #12, with Thun'da; Powell-c/a	21.00	62.00	145.00
97-Best of the West #11	10.00	30.00	65.00
98-Undercover Girl #6-Powell-c	24.00	70.00	165.00
99-Muggsy Mouse #5	2.80	7.00	14.00
100-Badmen of the West #1-Meskin-a(?)	16.00	48.00	110.00
101-White Indian #12-Frazetta-a(r)	16.00	48.00	110.00
101-Dream Book of Romance #6 (4-6/54); Marlon Brando photo-c; Powell, Bolle, Guardineer-a	11.50	34.00	80.00
103-Best of the West #12-Powell-a	10.00	30.00	65.00
104-White Indian #13-Frazetta-a(r)('54)	16.00	48.00	110.00
105-Great Western #9-Ghost Rider app.; Powell-a, 6 pgs.; Bolle-c	8.35	25.00	50.00
106-Dream Book of Love #1 (6-7/54)-Powell, Bolle-a; Montgomery Clift, Donna Reed photo-c	7.50	22.50	45.00
107-Hot Dog #1	4.70	14.00	28.00
108-Red Fox #15 (1954)-L.B. Cole c/a; Powell-a	10.00	30.00	70.00
109-Dream Book of Romance #7 (7-8/54). Powell-a; movie photo-c	4.70	14.00	28.00

	GD25	FN65	NM94
110-Dream Book of Romance #8 (10/54)-Movie photo-c	4.70	14.00	28.00
111-I'm a Cop #1 ('54); drug mention story; Powell-a	9.15	27.50	55.00
112-Ghost Rider #14 ('54)	12.00	36.00	85.00
113-Great Western #10; Powell-a	8.35	25.00	50.00
114-Dream Book of Love #2-Guardineer, Bolle-a; Peter Lorre, Victor Mature photo-c	5.85	17.50	35.00
115-Hot Dog #3	3.60	9.00	18.00
116-Cave Girl #13-Powell-c/a	21.00	62.00	145.00
117-White Indian #14	8.35	25.00	50.00
118-Undercover Girl #7-Powell-c	24.00	70.00	165.00
119-Straight Arrow's Fury #1 (origin); Fred Meagher-c/a	10.00	30.00	60.00
120-Badmen of the West #2	10.00	30.00	65.00
121-Mysteries of Scotland Yard #1; reprinted from Manhunt (5 stories)	10.00	30.00	70.00
122-Black Phantom #1 (11/54)	24.00	73.00	170.00
123-Dream Book of Love #3 (10-11/54)-Movie photo-c	4.70	14.00	28.00
124-Dream Book of Romance #8 (10-11/54)	4.70	14.00	28.00
125-Cave Girl #14-Powell-c/a	21.00	62.00	145.00
126-I'm a Cop #2-Powell-a	5.00	15.00	30.00
127-Great Western #11('54)-Powell-a	8.35	25.00	50.00
128-I'm a Cop #3-Powell-a	5.00	15.00	30.00
129-The Avenger #1('55)-Powell-c	24.00	72.00	165.00
130-Strongman #1-Powell-a	14.00	43.00	100.00
131-The Avenger #2('55)-Powell-c/a	16.00	48.00	110.00
132-Strongman #2	11.50	34.00	80.00
133-The Avenger #3-Powell-c/a	16.00	48.00	110.00
134-Strongman #3	11.50	34.00	80.00
135-White Indian #15	8.35	25.00	50.00
136-Hot Dog #4	3.60	9.00	18.00
137-Africa #1-Powell-c/a(4)	14.00	43.00	100.00
138-The Avenger #4-Powell-c/a	16.00	48.00	110.00
139-Strongman #4-Powell-a	11.50	34.00	80.00

NOTE: *Bolle a-110. Photo-c-17-22, 89, 92, 101, 106, 109, 110, 114, 123, 124.*

APACHE
1951
Fiction House Magazines

	GD25	FN65	NM94
1-Baker-c	13.00	40.00	90.00
I.W. Reprint No. 1-r/#1 above	2.00	5.00	10.00

APACHE HUNTER
1954 (18 pgs. in color) (promo copy) (saddle stitched)
Creative Pictorials

	GD25	FN65	NM94
nn-Severin, Heath stories	14.00	43.00	100.00

APACHE KID (Formerly Reno Browne; Western Gunfighters #20 on)
(Also see Two-Gun Western & Wild Western)
No. 53, 12/50 - No. 10, 1/52; No. 11, 12/54 - No. 19, 4/56
Marvel/Atlas Comics(MPC No. 53-10/CPS No. 11 on)

	GD25	FN65	NM94
53(#1)-Apache Kid & his horse Nightwind (origin), Red Hawkins by Syd Shores begins	19.00	57.00	130.00
2(2/51)	10.00	30.00	60.00
3-5	6.70	20.00	40.00
6-10 (1951-52)	5.00	15.00	30.00
11-19 (1954-56)	4.00	12.00	24.00

NOTE: ***Heath** c-11, 13. **Maneely** a-53; c-53(#1), 12, 14-16. **Powell** a-14. **Severin** c-17.*

APACHE MASSACRE (See Chief Victorio's...)

APACHE TRAIL
Sept, 1957 - No. 4, June, 1958
Steinway/America's Best

	GD25	FN65	NM94
1	5.85	17.50	35.00
2-4: 2-Tuska-a	4.00	10.00	20.00

Appleseed Book 3, Volume 1, © Masamune Shirow and Seishinsha

Aquaman #1 (1-2/62), © DC

Archer & Armstrong #17, © Voyager Comm.

APPLESEED
Sept, 1988 - Book 4, Vol. 4, Aug, 1991 (B&W, $2.50-$2.75, 52 pgs)
Eclipse Comics

	GD25	FN65	NM94
Book One, Volume 1 ($2.50)	1.65	4.00	10.00
Book One, Volume 2-5: 5-(1/89, $2.75 cover)		1.00	2.50
Book Two, Vol. 1(2/89) -5(7/89): Art Adams-c		1.00	2.50
Book Three, Volume 1(8/89) -4 ($2.75)		1.00	2.50
Book Three, Volume 5 ($3.50)		1.20	3.00
Book Four, Volume 1(1/91) -4 (3.50, 68 pgs.)		1.20	3.00

APPROVED COMICS
March, 1954 - No. 12, Aug, 1954 (All painted-c)
St. John Publishing Co. (Most have no c-price)

	GD25	FN65	NM94
1-The Hawk #5-r	5.85	17.50	35.00
2-Invisible Boy-r(3/54)-Origin; Saunders-c	10.00	30.00	70.00
3-Wild Boy of the Congo #11-r(4/54)	5.85	17.50	35.00
4,5: 4-Kid Cowboy-r. 5-Fly Boy-r	5.85	17.50	35.00
6-Daring Adv.-r(5/54); Krigstein-a(2); Baker-c	8.35	25.00	50.00
7-The Hawk #6-r	5.85	17.50	35.00
8-Crime on the Run (6/54); Powell-a; Saunders-c	5.85	17.50	35.00
9-Western Bandit Trails #3-r, with new-c; Baker-c/a	8.35	25.00	50.00
11-Fightin' Marines #3-r; Canteen Kate app; Baker-c/a	9.00	26.00	52.00
12-North West Mounties #4-r(8/54); new Baker-c	9.15	27.50	55.00

AQUAMAN (See Adventure #260, Brave & the Bold, DC Comics Presents #5, DC Special #28, DC Special Series #1, DC Super Stars #7, Detective, Justice League of America, More Fun #73, Showcase #30-33, Super DC Giant, Super Friends, and World's Finest Comics)

AQUAMAN
Jan-Feb, 1962 - No. 56, Mar-Apr, 1971; No. 57, Aug-Sept, 1977 - No. 63, Aug-Sept, 1978
National Periodical Publications/DC Comics

	GD25	FN65	NM94
Showcase #30 (1-2/61)-Origin S.A. Aquaman	45.00	135.00	450.00
Showcase #31 (3-4/61)-Aquaman	25.00	75.00	250.00
Showcase #32 (5-6/61)-Aquaman	25.00	75.00	250.00
Showcase #33 (7-8/61)-Aquaman	30.00	90.00	300.00
1-(1-2/62)-Intro. Quisp	00.00	00.00	300.00
2	18.00	54.00	125.00
3-5	12.00	36.00	85.00
6-10	9.00	26.00	60.00
11-20: 11-1st app. Mera. 18-Aquaman weds Mera; JLA cameo	6.50	19.00	45.00
21-32,34-40: 23-Birth of Aquababy. 26-Huntress app.(3-4/66). 29-1st app. Ocean Master, Aquaman's step-brother. 30-Batman & Superman-c & cameo	4.30	13.00	30.00
33-1st app. Aqua-Girl (see Adventure #266)	6.50	19.00	45.00
41-47,49	1.70	5.00	12.00
48-Origin reprinted	2.30	6.75	16.00
50-52-Deadman by Neal Adams	3.25	9.50	22.00
53-56('71): 56-1st app. Crusader	1.20	3.00	7.00
57('77)-63: 58-Origin retold		1.80	4.50

NOTE: ***Aparo** a-40-45, 46p, 47-59; c-58-63. **Nick Cardy** c-1-39. **Newton** a-60-63.*

AQUAMAN
Feb, 1986 - No. 4, May, 1986 (Mini-series)
DC Comics

	GD25	FN65	NM94
1-New costume		1.00	4.00
2-4		1.00	2.50
Special 1 ('88, $1.50, 52 pgs.)		.80	2.00

AQUAMAN
June, 1989 - No. 5, Oct, 1989 ($1.00, mini-series)
DC Comics

	GD25	FN65	NM94
1-5: Giffen plots/breakdowns; Swan-p			1.00
Special 1 (Legend of..., $2.00, 1989, 52 pgs.)-Giffen plots/breakdowns; Swan-p		.80	2.00

AQUAMAN
Dec, 1991 - No. 13, Dec, 1992 ($1.00/$1.25, color)
DC Comics

	GD25	FN65	NM94
1-5: 5-Last $1.00-c			1.00
6-13: 9-Sea Devils app.			1.25

AQUAMAN: TIME & TIDE
Dec,1993 - No. 4, March, 1994 ($1.50, color, mini-series)
DC Comics

	GD25	FN65	NM94
1-4: Peter David scripts; origin retold			1.50

AQUANAUTS (See 4-Color No. 1197)

ARABIAN NIGHTS (See Cinema Comics Herald)

ARACHNOPHOBIA
1990 ($5.95, color, 68 pg. graphic novel)
Hollywood Comics (Disney Comics)

	GD25	FN65	NM94
nn-Movie adaptation; Spiegle-a	1.00	2.50	6.00
Comic edition ($2.95, 68 pgs.)		1.20	3.00

ARAK/SON OF THUNDER (See Warlord #48)
Sept, 1981 - No. 50, Nov, 1985
DC Comics

	GD25	FN65	NM94
1-50: 1-Origin; 1st app. Angelica, Princess of White Cathay. 3-Intro Valda, The Iron Maiden. 12-Origin Valda. 20-Origin Angelica. 24-$1.00 size. 50-Double size			1.00
Annual 1(10/84)			1.00

ARCHER & ARMSTRONG
July (June inside), 1992 - Present ($2.50, color)
Valiant

	GD25	FN65	NM94
0-(7/92)-B. Smith-c/a; Reese-i assists	1.65	4.00	10.00
0-(Gold Logo)			35.00
1-(8/92)-Origin & 1st app. Archer; Miller-c; B. Smith/Layton-a		1.60	4.00
2-2nd app. Turok(c/story); Smith/Layton-a; Simonson-c		1.50	3.75
3,4-Smith-c&a(p) & scripts		1.40	3.50
5-7		1.30	3.25
8-($4.50, 52 pgs.)-Combined with Eternal Warrior #8; B. Smith-c/a & scripts; 1st app. Ivar the Time Walker		1.60	4.00
9-22: 10-2nd app. Ivar. 10,11-B. Smith-c		.90	2.25

ARCHIE AND BIG ETHEL (Spire Christian)(Value: cover or less)

ARCHIE & FRIENDS
Dec, 1992 - Present ($1.25, color)
Archie Comics

	GD25	FN65	NM94
1-8			1.25

ARCHIE AND ME (See Archie Giant Series Mag. #578, 591, 603, 616, 626)
Oct, 1964 - No. 161, Feb, 1987
Archie Publications

	GD25	FN65	NM94
1	14.00	43.00	100.00
2	8.35	25.00	50.00
3-5	4.20	12.50	25.00
6-10	2.00	6.00	14.00
11-20	1.20	3.00	7.00
21-30: 26-X-Mas-c		1.80	4.50
31-63: 43-63-(All Giants)		1.00	2.50
64-162-(Regular size)			1.00

ARCHIE AND MR. WEATHERBEE (Spire Christian)(Value: cover or less)

ARCHIE...ARCHIE ANDREWS, WHERE ARE YOU? (...Comics Digest #9, 10; ...Comics Digest Mag. No. 11 on)
Feb, 1977 - Present (Digest size, 160-128 pages)
Archie Publications

	GD25	FN65	NM94
1		1.60	4.00
2,3,5,7-9-N. Adams-a; 8-r-/origin The Fly by S&K. 9-Steel Sterling-r			

Archie Comics #45, © AP

Archie Comics #117, © AP

Archie Comics #133, © AP

GD25 FN65 NM94

1.20 3.00
4,6,10-50 ($1.00-$1.50): 17-Katy Keene story .80 2.00
51-92 1.50

ARCHIE AS PUREHEART THE POWERFUL (Also see Archie Giant Series #142, Jughead as Captain Hero, Life With Archie & Little Archie)
Sept, 1966 - No. 6, Nov, 1967
Archie Publications (Radio Comics)

1-Super hero parody 7.00 21.00 50.00
2 4.00 13.00 30.00
3-6 3.00 9.00 20.00

NOTE: *Evilheart cameos in all. Title: Archie As Pureheart the Powerful #1-3; ...As Capt. Pureheart-#4-6.*

ARCHIE AT RIVERDALE HIGH (See Archie Giant Series Magazine #573, 586, 604 & Riverdale High)
Aug, 1972 - No. 113, Feb, 1987
Archie Publications

1 4.50 14.00 32.00
2 2.00 6.00 14.00
3-5 1.20 3.00 7.00
6-10 1.60 4.00
11-30 .80 2.00
31-114: 96-Anti-smoking issue 1.00

ARCHIE COMICS (Also see Christmas & Archie, Everything's..., Explorers of the Unknown, Jackpot, Little..., Oxydol-Dreft, Pep, Riverdale High, Teenage Mutant Ninja Turtles Adventures & To Riverdale and Back Again)

ARCHIE COMICS (Archie #158 on)(First Teen-age comic)(Radio show 1st aired 6/2/45, by NBC)
Winter, 1942-43 - No. 19, 3-4/46; No. 20, 5-6/46 - Present
MLJ Magazines No. 1-19/Archie Publ.No. 20 on

GD25 FN65 VF82 NM94
1 (Scarce)-Jughead, Veronica app.; 1st app. Mrs. Andrews
550.00 1650.00 3575.00 5500.00
(Estimated up to 50+ total copies exist, 5 in NM/Mint)

GD25 FN65 NM94
2 157.00 471.00 1100.00
3 (60 pgs.) 115.00 343.00 800.00
4,5: 4-Article about Archie radio series 75.00 225.00 525.00
6-10: 6-X-Mas-c. 7-1st definitive love triangle story
54.00 160.00 375.00
11-20: 15,17,18-Dotty & Ditto by Woggon. 16-Woggon-a
35.00 105.00 245.00
21-30: 23-Betty & Veronica by Woggon. 25-Woggon-a. 34-Pre-Dilton try-out (named Dilbert) 25.00 75.00 175.00
31-40 15.00 45.00 105.00
41-50 10.00 30.00 70.00
51-70 (1954): 51,65-70,72-74-Katy Keene app. 6.70 20.00 40.00
71-99: 94-1st Coach Kleets 4.70 14.00 28.00
100 5.85 17.50 35.00
101-130 (1962) 2.80 7.00 14.00
131-160 1.40 3.50 7.00
161-200 1.60 4.00
201-240 .70 1.85
241-282 1.50
283-Cover/story plugs "International Children's Appeal" which was a fraudulent charity, according to TV's 20/20 news program broadcast July 20, 1979
.80 2.10
284-424: 300-Anniversary issue 1.25
Annual 1('50)-116 pgs. (Scarce) 121.00 365.00 850.00
Annual 2('51) 60.00 180.00 425.00
Annual 3('52) 39.00 120.00 275.00
Annual 4,5(1953-54) 29.00 85.00 200.00
Annual 6-10(1955-59) 16.00 48.00 110.00
Annual 11-15(1960-65) 7.50 22.50 45.00
Annual 16-20(1966-70) 2.30 6.75 16.00
Annual 21-26(1971-75) 1.00 2.50 6.00
Annual Digest 27('75)-62('83-'93, $1.50)(...Magazine #35 on)
1.00 2.50
...All-Star Specials(Winter '75, $1.25)-6 remaindered Archie comics rebound in each; titles: "The World of Giant Comics" "Giant Grab Bag of Comics," "Triple Giant Comics," & "Giant Spec. Comics 1.00 2.00 5.00
...And the History of Electronics (5/90)-Radio Shack giveaway
1.00
Mini-Comics (1970-Fairmont Potato Chips Giveaway-Miniature)(8 issues-nn's., 8 pgs. each) 1.65 4.00 10.00
Official Boy Scout Outfitter (1946, 9-1/2x6-1/2, 16 pgs.)-B. R. Baker Co. (Scarce) 39.00 120.00 275.00
Shoe Store giveaway (1948, Feb?) 13.00 40.00 90.00

NOTE: ***Al Fagly** c-17-35. **Bob Montana** c-38, 41-50, 58, Annual 1-4. **Bill Woggon** c-53, 54.*

ARCHIE COMICS DIGEST (...Magazine No. 37-95)
Aug, 1973 - Present (Small size, 160-128 pages)
Archie Publications

1 4.30 13.00 30.00
2 2.30 6.75 16.00
3-5 1.30 3.25 8.00
6-10 1.00 2.00 5.00
11-33: 32,33-The Fly-r by S&K 1.00 2.50
34-126: 36-Katy Keene story 1.50

NOTE: ***Neal Adams** a-1, 2, 4, 5, 19-21, 24, 25, 27, 29, 31, 33. X-mas c-88, 94, 100, 106.*

ARCHIE GETS A JOB (Spire Christian)(Value: cover or less)

ARCHIE GIANT SERIES MAGAZINE
1954 - Present (No No. 36-135, no No. 252-451)(#1 not code approved)
Archie Publications

1-Archie's Christmas Stocking 79.00 235.00 550.00
2-Archie's Christmas Stocking('55) 46.00 140.00 325.00
3-6-Archie's Christmas Stocking('56-'59) 29.00 85.00 200.00
7-10: 7-Katy Keene Holiday Fun(9/60); Bill Woggon-c. 8-Betty & Veronica Summer Fun(10/60). 9-The World of Jughead (12/60). 10-Archie's Christmas Stocking(1/61) 19.00 58.00 135.00
11,13,16,18: 11-Betty & Veronica Spectacular (6/61). 13-Betty & Veronica Summer Fun (10/61). 16-Betty & Veronica Spectacular (6/62). 18-Betty & Veronica Summer Fun (10/62) 17.00 52.00 120.00
12,14,15,17,19,20: 12-Katy Keene Holiday Fun (9/61). 14-The World of Jughead (12/61). 15-Archie's Christmas Stocking (1/62). 17-Archie's Jokes (9/62); Katy Keene app. 19-The World of Jughead (12/62). 20-Archie's Christmas Stocking (1/63) 12.00 36.00 85.00
21,23,26,28: 21-Betty & Veronica Spectacular (6/63). 23-Betty & Veronica Summer Fun (10/63). 26-Betty & Veronica Spectacular (6/64). 28-Betty & Veronica Summer Fun (9/64) 10.00 30.00 65.00
22,24,25,27,29,30: 22-Archie's Jokes (9/63). 24-The World of Jughead (12/63). 25-Archie's Christmas Stocking (1/64). 27-Archie's Jokes (8/64). 29-Around the World with Archie (10/64). 30-The World of Jughead (12/64)
6.70 20.00 40.00
31-35,136-141: 31-Archie's Christmas Stocking (1/65). 32-Betty & Veronica Spectacular (6/65). 33-Archie's Jokes (8/65). 34-Betty & Veronica Summer Fun (9/65). 35-Around the World with Archie (10/65). 136-The World of Jughead (12/65). 137-Archie's Christmas Stocking (1/66). 138-Betty & Veronica Spectacular (6/66). 139-Archie's Jokes (6/66). 140-Betty & Veronica Summer Fun (8/66). 141-Around the World with Archie (9/66)
4.70 14.00 28.00
142-Archie's Super-Hero Special (10/66)-Origin Capt. Pureheart, Capt. Hero, and Evilheart 5.00 15.00 30.00
143-160: 143-The World of Jughead (12/66). 144-Archie's Christmas Stocking (1/67). 145-Betty & Veronica Spectacular (6/67). 146-Archie's Jokes (6/67). 147-Betty & Veronica Summer Fun (8/67) 148-World of Archie (9/67). 149-World of Jughead (10/67). 150-Archie's Christmas Stocking (1/68). 151-World of Archie (2/68). 152-World of Jughead (2/68). 153-Betty & Veronica Spectacular (6/68). 154-Archie Jokes (6/68). 155-Betty & VeronicaSummer Fun (8/68). 156-World of Archie (10/68). 157-World of Jughead (12/68). 158-Archie's Christmas Stocking (1/69). 159-Betty & Veronica Christmas

Archie Giant Series Magazine #587, © AP

Archie Giant Series Magazine #599, © AP

Archie Giant Series Magazine #601, © AP

GD25 FN65 NM94

Spectacular (1/69). 160-World of Archie (2/69) 2.80 7.00 14.00

161-200: 161-World of Jughead (2/69). 162-Betty & Veronica Spectacular (6/69). 163-Archie's Jokes(8/69). 164-Betty & Veronica Summer Fun (9/69). 165-World of Archie (9/69). 166-World of Jughead (9/69). 167-Archie's Christmas Stocking (1/70). 168-Betty & Veronica Christmas Spect. (1/70). 169-Archie's Christmas Love-In (1/70). 170-Jughead's Eat-Out Comic Book Mag. (12/69). 171-World of Archie (2/70). 172-World of Jughead (2/70). 173-Betty & Veronica Spectacular (6/70). 174-Archie's Jokes (8/70). 175-Betty & Veronica Summer Fun (9/70). 176-Li'l Jinx Giant Laugh-Out (8/70). 177-World of Archie (9/70). 178-World of Jughead (9/70). 179-Archie's Christmas Stocking (1/71). 180-Betty & Veronica Christmas Spect. (1/71). 181-Archie's Christmas Love-In (1/71). 182-World of Archie (2/71). 183-World of Jughead (2/71). 184-Betty & Veronica Spectacular (6/71). 185-Li'l Jinx Giant Laugh-Out (6/71). 186-Archie's Jokes (8/71). 187-Betty & Veronica Summer Fun (9/71). 188-World of Archie (9/71). 189-World of Jughead (9/71). 190-Archie's Christmas Stocking (12/71). 191-Betty & Veronica Christmas Spectacular (2/72). 192-Archie's Christmas Love-In (1/72). 193-World of Archie (3/72). 194-World of Jughead (4/72). 195-Li'l Jinx Christmas Bag (1/72). 196-Sabrina's Christmas Magic (1/72). 197-Betty & Veronica Spectacular (6/72). 198-Archie's Jokes (8/72). 199-Betty & Veronica Summer Fun (9/72). 200-World of Archie (10/72) 1.00 2.00 5.00

201-251: 201-Betty & Veronica Spectacular (10/72). 202-World of Jughead (11/72). 203-Archie's Christmas Stocking (12/72). 204-Betty & Veronica Christmas Spectacular (2/73). 205-Archie's Christmas Love-In (1/73). 206-Li'l Jinx Christmas Bag (12/72). 207-Sabrina's Christmas Magic (12/72). 208-World of Archie (3/73). 209-World of Jughead (4/73). 210-Betty & Veronica Spectacular (6/73). 211-Archie's Jokes (8/73). 212-Betty & Veronica Summer Fun (9/73). 213-World of Archie (10/73). 214-Betty & Veronica Spectacular (10/73). 215-World of Jughead (11/73). 216-Archie's Christmas Stocking (12/73). 217-Betty & Veronica Christmas Spectacular (2/74). 218-Archie's Christmas Love-In (1/74). 219-Li'l Jinx Christmas Bag (12/73). 220-Sabrina's Christmas Magic (12/73). 221-Betty & Veronica Spectacular (Advertised as World of Archie) (6/74). 222-Archie's Jokes (advertised as World of Jughead) (8/74). 223-Li'l Jinx (8/74). 224-Betty & Veronica Summer Fun (9/74). 225-World of Archie (9/74). 226-Betty & Veronica Spectacular (10/74). 227-World of Jughead (10/74). 228-Archie's Christmas Stocking (12/74). 229-Betty & Veronica Christmas Spectacular (12/74). 230-Archie's Christmas Love-In (1/75). 231-Sabrina's Christmas Magic (1/75). 232-World of Archie (3/75). 233-World of Jughead (4/75). 234-Betty & Veronica Spectacular (6/75). 235-Archie's Jokes (8/75). 236-Betty & Veronica Summer Fun (9/75). 237-World of Archie (9/75) 238-Betty & Veronica Spectacular (10/75). 239-World of Jughead (10/75). 240-Archie's Christmas Stocking (12/75). 241-Betty & Veronica Christmas Spectacular (12/75). 242-Archie's Christmas Love-In (1/76). 243-Sabrina's Christmas Magic (1/76). 244-World of Archie (3/76). 245-World of Jughead (4/76). 246-Betty & Veronica Spectacular (6/76). 247-Archie's Jokes (8/76). 248-Betty & Veronica Summer Fun (9/76). 249-World of Archie (9/76). 250-Betty & Veronica Spectacular (10/76). 251-World of Jughead each.... 1.20 3.00

452-500: 452-Archie's Christmas Stocking (12/76). 453-Betty & Veronica Christmas Spectacular (12/76). 454-Archie's Christmas Love-In (1/77). 455-Sabrina's Christmas Magic (1/77). 456-World of Archie (3/77). 457-World of Jughead (4/77). 458-Betty & Veronica Spectacular (6/77). 459-Archie's Jokes (8/77)-Shows 8/76 in error. 460-Betty & Veronica Summer Fun (9/77). 461-World of Archie (9/77). 462-Betty & Veronica Spectacular (10/77). 463-World of Jughead (10/77). 464-Archie's Christmas Stocking (12/77). 465-Betty & Veronica Christmas Spectacular (12/77). 466-Archie's Christmas Love-In (1/78). 467-Sabrina's Christmas Magic (1/78). 468-World of Archie (2/78). 469-World of Jughead (2/78). 470-Betty & Veronica Spectacular(6/78). 471-Archie's Jokes (8/78). 472-Betty & Veronica Summer Fun (9/78). 473-World of Archie (9/78). 474-Betty & Veronica Spectacular (10/78). 475-World of Jughead (10/78). 476-Archie's Christmas Stocking (12/78). 477-Betty & Veronica Christmas Spectacular (12/78). 478-Archie's Christmas Love-In (1/79). 479-Sabrina Christmas Magic (1/79). 480-The World of Archie (3/79). 481-World of Jughead (4/79). 482-Betty & Veronica Spectacular (6/79). 483-Archie's Jokes (8/79). 484-Betty & Veronica Summer Fun(9/79). 485-The World of Archie (9/79). 486-Betty & Veronica Spectacular(10/79). 487-The World of Jughead (10/79). 488-Archie's Christmas Stocking (12/79). 489-Betty & Veronica Christmas Spectacular (1/80). 490-Archie's Christmas Love-In (1/80). 491-Sabrina's Christmas Magic (1/80).492-The World of Archie (2/80). 493-The World of Jughead (4/80). 494-Betty & Veronica Spectacular (6/80). 495-Archie's Jokes (8/80). 496-Betty & Veronica Summer Fun (9/80). 497-The World of Archie (9/80). 498-Betty & Veronica Spectacular (10/80). 499-The World of Jughead (10/80). 500-Archie's Christmas Stocking (12/80) each... 1.50

501-550: 501-Betty & Veronica Christmas Spectacular (12/80). 502-Archie's Christmas Love-in (1/81). 503-Sabrina Christmas Magic (1/81). 504-The World of Archie (3/81). 505-The World of Jughead (4/81). 506-Betty & Veronica Spectacular (6/81). 507-Archie's Jokes (8/81). 508-Betty & Veronica Summer Fun (9/81). 509-The World of Archie (9/81) 510-Betty & Veronica Spectacular (9/81). 511-The World of Jughead (10/81). 512-Archie's Christmas Stocking (12/81). 513-Betty & Veronica Christmas Spectacular (12/81). 514-Archie's Christmas Love-in (1/82). 515-Sabrina's Christmas Magic (1/82). 516-The World of Archie (3/82). 517-The World of Jughead (4/82). 518-Betty & Veronica Spectacular (6/82). 519-Archie's Jokes (8/82). 520-Betty & Veronica Summer Fun (9/82). 521-The World of Archie (9/82). 522-Betty & Veronica Spectacular (10/82). 523-The World of Jughead (10/82). 524-Archie's Christmas Stocking (1/83). 525-Betty and Veronica Christmas Spectacular (1/83). 526-Betty and Veronica Spectacular (5/83). 527-Little Archie (8/83). 528-Josie and the Pussycats (8/83). 529-Betty and Veronica Summer Fun (8/83). 530-Betty and Veronica Spectacular (9/83). 531-The World of Jughead (9/83). 532-The World of Archie (10/83). 533-Space Pirates by Frank Bolling (10/83). 534-Little Archie (1/84). 535-Archie's Christmas Stocking (1/84) 536-Betty and Veronica Christmas Spectacular (1/84). 537-Betty and Veronica Spectacular (6/84). 538-Little Archie (8/84). 539-Betty and Veronica Summer Fun (8/84). 540-Josie and the Pussycats (8/84). 541-Betty and Veronica Spectacular (9/84). 542-The World of Jughead (9/84). 543-The World of Archie (10/84). 544-Sabrina the Teen-Age Witch (10/84). 545-Little Archie (12/84). 546-Archie's Christmas Stocking (12/84). 547-Betty and Veronica Christmas Spectacular (12/84). 548-? 549-Little Archie. 550-Betty and Veronica Summer Fun each... 1.25

551-600: 551-Josie and the Pussycats. 552-Betty and Veronica Spectacular. 553-The World of Jughead. 554-The World of Archie. 555-Betty's Diary. 556-Little Archie (1/86). 557-Archie's Christmas Stocking (1/86). 558-Betty & Veronica Christmas Spectacular (1/86). 559-Betty & Veronica Spectacular. 560-Little Archie. 561-Betty & Veronica Summer Fun. 562-Josie and the Pussycats. 563-Betty & Veronica Spectacular. 564-World of Jughead. 565-World of Archie. 566-Little Archie. 567-Archie's Christmas Stocking. 568-Betty & Veronica Christmas Spectacular. 569-Betty & Veronica Spring Spectacular. 570-Little Archie. 571-Josie & the Pussycats. 572-Betty & Veronica Summer Fun. 573-Archie At Riverdale High. 574-World of Archie. 575-Betty & Veronica Spectacular. 576-Pep. 577-World of Jughead. 578-Archie And Me. 579-Archie's Christmas Stocking. 580-Betty and Veronica Christmas Spectacular. 581-Little Archie Christmas Special. 582-Betty & Veronica Spring Spectacular. 583-Little Archie. 584-Josie and the Pussycats. 585-Betty & Veronica Summer Fun. 586-Archie At Riverdale High. 587-The World of Archie (10/88); 1st app. Explorers of the Unknown. 588-Betty & Veronica Spectacular. 589-Pep (10/88). 590-The World of Jughead. 591-Archie & Me. 592-Archie's Christmas Stocking. 593-Betty & Veronica Christmas Spectacular. 594-Little Archie. 595-Betty & Veronica Spring Spectacular. 596-Little Archie. 597-Josie and the Pussycats. 598-Betty & Veronica Summer Fun. 599-The World of Archie (10/89); 2nd app. Explorers of the Unknown. 600-Betty and Veronica Spectacular each.... 1.00

601-630: 601-Pep. 602-The World of Jughead. 603-Archie and Me. 604-Archie at Riverdale High. 605-Archie's Christmas Stocking. 606-Betty and Veronica Christmas Spectacular. 607-Little Archie. 608-Betty and Veronica Spectacular. 609-Little Archie. 610-Josie and the Pussycats. 611-Betty and Veronica Summer Fun. 612-The World of Archie. 613-Betty and Veronica Spectacular. 614-Pep (10/90). 615-Veronica's Summer Special. 616-Archie

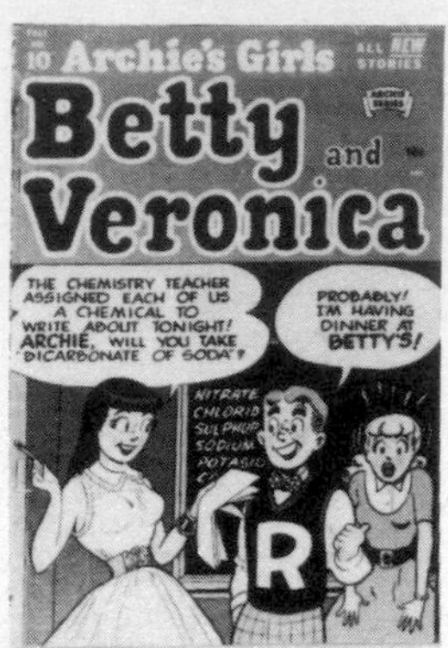

Archie's Girls, Betty & Veronica #10, © AP

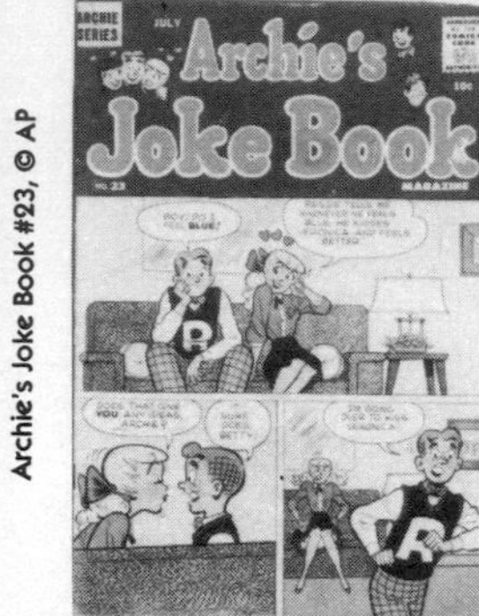

Archie's Joke Book #23, © AP

Archie's Madhouse #36, © AP

	GD25	FN65	NM94

and Me. 617-Archie's Christmas Stocking. 618-Betty & Veronica Christmas Spectacular. 619-Little Archie. 620-Betty and Veronica Spectacular. 621-Betty and Veronica Summer Fun. 622-Josie & the Pussycats; not published. 623-Betty and Veronica Spectacular. 624-Pep Comics. 625-Veronica's Summer Special. 626-Archie and Me. 627-World of Archie. 628-Archie's Pals 'n' Gals Holiday Special. 629-Betty & Veronica Christmas Spectacular. 630-Archie's Christmas Stocking

	GD25	FN65	NM94
each....			1.00

ARCHIE'S ACTIVITY COMICS DIGEST MAGAZINE
1985 - No. 4? (Annual, 128 pgs.; digest size)
Archie Enterprises

	GD25	FN65	NM94
1-4			1.50

ARCHIE'S CAR (Spire Christian)(Value: cover or less)

ARCHIE'S CHRISTMAS LOVE-IN (See Archie Giant Series Mag. No. 169, 181,192, 205, 218, 230, 242, 454, 466, 478, 490, 502, 514)

ARCHIE'S CHRISTMAS STOCKING (See Archie Giant Series Mag. No. 1-6,10, 15, 20, 25, 31, 137, 144, 150, 158, 167, 179, 190, 203, 216, 228, 240, 452, 464, 476, 488, 500, 512, 524, 535, 546, 557, 567, 579, 592, 605, 617, 630)

ARCHIE'S CHRISTMAS STOCKING
1993 ($2.00, color, 52 pgs.)
Archie Comics

	GD25	FN65	NM94
1-Calendar poster bound-in; Dan DeCarlo-c/a		.80	2.00

ARCHIE'S CLEAN SLATE (Spire Christian)(Value: cover or less)

ARCHIE'S DATE BOOK (Spire Christian)(Value: cover or less)

ARCHIE'S DOUBLE DIGEST QUARTERLY MAGAZINE
1981 - Present ($1.95-$2.50, 256pgs.) (A.D.D. Magazine No. 10 on)
Archie Comics

	GD25	FN65	NM94
1-30: 6-Katy Keene story. 29-Pureheart story		1.60	4.00
31-70		1.20	3.00

ARCHIE'S FAMILY ALBUM (Spire Christian)(Value: cover or less)

ARCHIE'S FESTIVAL (Spire Christian)(Value: cover or less)

ARCHIE'S GIRLS, BETTY AND VERONICA (Becomes Betty & Veronica)
1950 - No. 347, April, 1987 (Also see Veronica)
Archie Publications (Close-Up)

	GD25	FN65	NM94
1	100.00	300.00	700.00
2	50.00	150.00	350.00
3-5	29.00	85.00	200.00
6-10: 10-2pg. Katy Keene app.	24.00	72.00	165.00
11-20: 11,13,14,17-19-Katy Keene app. 17-Last pre-code issue (3/55). 20-Debbie's Diary, 2 pgs.	16.00	48.00	110.00
21-30: 27-Katy Keene app.	11.50	34.00	80.00
31-50	10.00	30.00	60.00
51-74	6.70	20.00	40.00
75-Betty & Veronica sell souls to Devil	11.00	32.00	75.00
76-99	4.00	11.00	22.00
100	4.70	14.00	28.00
101-140: 118-Origin Superteen (see Betty & Me #3). 119-Last Superteen story	1.80	4.50	9.00
141-180		1.50	3.75
181-220		.70	1.75
221-347: 300-Anniversary issue			1.20
Annual 1 (1953)	60.00	180.00	425.00
Annual 2(1954)	29.00	85.00	200.00
Annual 3-5 ('55-'57)	22.00	65.00	150.00
Annual 6-8 ('58-'60)	14.00	43.00	100.00

ARCHIE SHOE-STORE GIVEAWAY
1944-49 (12-15 pgs. of games, puzzles, stories like Superman-Tim books, No nos. - came out monthly)
Archie Publications

	GD25	FN65	NM94
(1944-47)-issues	11.50	34.00	80.00
2/48-Peggy Lee photo-c	10.00	30.00	60.00
3/48-Marylee Robb photo-c	9.15	27.50	55.00
4/48-Gloria De Haven photo-c	9.15	27.50	55.00
5/48,6/48,7/48	9.15	27.50	55.00
8/48-Story on Shirley Temple	10.00	30.00	60.00
10/48-Archie as Wolf on cover	10.00	30.00	60.00
5/49-Kathleen Hughes photo-c	6.70	20.00	40.00
7/49	6.70	20.00	40.00
8/49-Archie photo-c from radio show	10.00	30.00	70.00
10/49-Gloria Mann photo-c from radio show	10.00	30.00	60.00
11/49,12/49	6.70	20.00	40.00

ARCHIE'S JOKEBOOK COMICS DIGEST ANNUAL (See Jokebook...)

ARCHIE'S JOKE BOOK MAGAZINE (See Joke Book ...)
1953 - No. 3, Sum, 1954; No. 15, Fall, 1954 - No. 288, 11/82
Archie Publications

	GD25	FN65	NM94
1953-One Shot (#1)	57.00	170.00	400.00
2	32.00	95.00	225.00
3 (no #4-14)	22.00	65.00	150.00
15-20: 15-Formerly Archie's Rival Reggie #14; last pre-code issue (Fall/54). 15-17-Katy Keene app.	16.00	48.00	110.00
21-30	10.00	30.00	70.00
31-40,42,43	6.70	20.00	40.00
41-1st professional comic work by Neal Adams (9/59), 1 pg.	16.00	48.00	110.00
44-47-N. Adams-a in all, 1-2 pgs.	10.00	30.00	60.00
48-Four pgs. N. Adams-a	10.00	30.00	65.00
49-60 (1962)	3.60	9.00	18.00
61-80	2.00	5.00	10.00
81-100		1.80	4.50
101-140		.80	2.00
141-200			1.50
201-288			1.00
Drug Store Giveaway (No. 39 w/new-c)	3.20	8.00	16.00

ARCHIE'S JOKES (See Archie Giant Series Mag. No. 17, 22, 27, 33, 139, 146, 154, 163, 174, 186, 198, 211, 222, 235, 247, 459, 471, 483, 495, 519)

ARCHIE'S LOVE SCENE (Spire Christian)(Value: cover or less)

ARCHIE'S MADHOUSE (Madhouse Ma-ad No. 67 on)
Sept, 1959 - No. 66, Feb, 1969
Archie Publications

	GD25	FN65	NM94
1-Archie begins	24.00	70.00	165.00
2	11.50	34.00	80.00
3-5	9.15	27.50	55.00
6-10	6.35	19.00	38.00
11-17 (Last w/regular characters)	4.35	13.00	26.00
18-21,23-30 (New format): 25-1st app. Captain Sprocket (4/63)	2.00	5.00	10.00
22-1st app. Sabrina, the Teen-age Witch (10/62)	8.35	25.00	50.00
31-40: 34-Bordered-c begin. 35-Beatles cameo	1.00	2.50	5.00
41-66: 43-Mighty Crusaders cameo. 44-Swipes Mad #4 (Super-Duperman) in "Bird Monsters From Outer Space"			1.50
Annual 1 (1962-63)	7.50	22.50	45.00
Annual 2 (1964)	4.00	11.00	22.00
Annual 3 (1965)-Origin Sabrina The Teen-Age Witch	2.40	6.00	12.00
Annual 4-6('66-69)(Becomes Madhouse Ma-ad Annual #7 on)	1.60	4.00	8.00

NOTE: *Cover title to 61-65 is "Madhouse" and to 66 is "Madhouse Ma-ad Jokes."*

ARCHIE'S MECHANICS
Sept, 1954 - No. 3, 1955
Archie Publications

	GD25	FN65	NM94
1-(15 cents; 52 pgs.)	71.00	215.00	500.00
2-(10 cents)-Last pre-code issue	41.00	125.00	290.00
3-(10 cents)	35.00	105.00	250.00

ARCHIE'S ONE WAY (Spire Christian)(Value: cover or less)

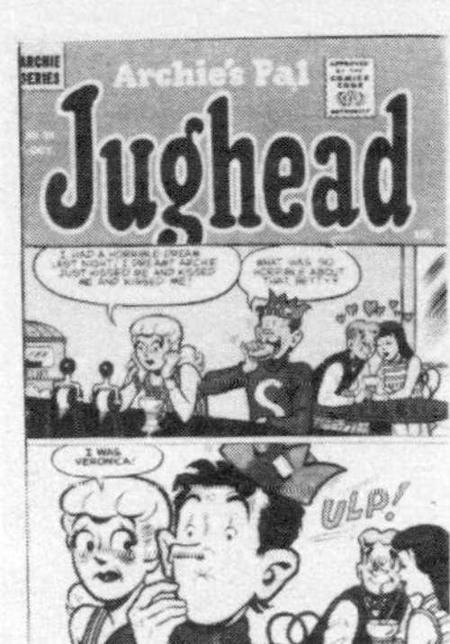

Archie's Pal, Jughead #38, © AP

Area 38 #12, © Kaoru Shintani/Shogakukan, Inc.

Arion, Lord of Atlantis #30, © DC

ARCHIE'S PAL, JUGHEAD (Jughead No. 122 on)
1949 - No. 126, Nov, 1965
Archie Publications

	GD25	FN65	NM94
1 (1949)-1st app. Moose (see Pep #33)	85.00	257.00	600.00
2 (1950)	43.00	130.00	300.00
3-5	27.00	81.00	190.00
6-10: 7-Suzie app.	17.00	50.00	120.00
11-20	13.00	40.00	90.00
21-30: 23-25,28-30-Katy Keene app. 28-Debbie's Diary app.	10.00	30.00	60.00
31-50	5.85	17.50	35.00
51-70	4.00	11.00	22.00
71-100	2.40	6.00	12.00
101-126	1.40	3.50	7.00
Annual 1 (1953, 25¢)	43.00	130.00	300.00
Annual 2 (1954, 25¢)-Last pre-code issue	26.00	80.00	185.00
Annual 3-5 (1955-57, 25¢)	19.00	57.00	130.00
Annual 6-8 (1958-60, 25¢)	12.00	36.00	85.00

ARCHIE'S PAL JUGHEAD COMICS (Formerly Jughead #1-45)
No. 46, June, 1993 - Present ($1.25, color)
Archie Comic Publications

	GD25	FN65	NM94
46-54		.65	1.25

ARCHIE'S PALS 'N' GALS (Also see Archie Giant Series Magazine #628)
1952-53 - No. 6, 1957-58; No. 7, 1958 - No. 231, May, 1992
Archie Publications

	GD25	FN65	NM94
1-(116 pages, 25¢)	54.00	160.00	375.00
2(Annual)('54, 25¢)	29.00	85.00	200.00
3-5(Annual, '55-57, 25¢): 3-Last pre-code issue	20.00	60.00	140.00
6-10('58-'60)	11.00	32.00	75.00
11-20	5.85	17.50	35.00
21-28,30-40	4.00	10.00	20.00
29-Beatles satire	5.00	15.00	30.00
41-60	1.60	4.00	8.00
61-80		1.60	4.00
81-110		.80	2.00
111-231: Later issues $1.00 cover. 197-G. Colan-a			1.00

ARCHIE'S PALS 'N' GALS DOUBLE DIGEST MAGAZINE
Nov, 1992 - Present ($2.50)
Archie Comic Publications

	GD25	FN65	NM94
1-3: 1-Capt. Hero story; Pureheart app. 2-Superduck story; Little Jinx in all		1.00	2.50

ARCHIE'S PARABLES
1973, 1975 (36 pages, 39-49 cents)
Spire Christian Comics (Fleming H. Revell Co.)

	GD25	FN65	NM94
nn-By Al Hartley			1.00

ARCHIE'S R/C RACERS
Sept, 1989 - No. 10, Mar, 1991 (95 cents, $1.00, color)
Archie Comics

	GD25	FN65	NM94
1-10: Radio control cars			1.00

ARCHIE'S RIVAL REGGIE (Reggie & Archie's Joke Book #15 on)
1950 - No. 14, Aug, 1954
Archie Publications

	GD25	FN65	NM94
1-Reggie 1st app. in Jackpot Comics #5	57.00	171.00	400.00
2	28.00	85.00	200.00
3-5	20.00	60.00	140.00
6-10	14.00	43.00	100.00
11-14: Katy Keene in No. 10-14, 1-2pgs.	11.00	32.00	75.00

ARCHIE'S ROLLER COASTER (Spire Christian)(Value: cover or less)

ARCHIE'S SOMETHING ELSE (Spire Christian)(Value: cover or less)

ARCHIE'S SONSHINE (Spire Christian)(Value: cover or less)

ARCHIE'S SPORTS SCENE (Spire Christian)(Value: cover or less)

ARCHIE'S STORY & GAME COMICS DIGEST MAGAZINE
Nov, 1986 - Present (Digest size, $1.25, $1.35, $1.50, 128 pgs.)
Archie Enterprises

	GD25	FN65	NM94
1-30		.80	2.00

ARCHIE'S SUPER HERO SPECIAL (See Archie Giant Series Mag. No. 142)

ARCHIE'S SUPER HERO SPECIAL (...Comics Digest Mag. 2)
Jan, 1979 - No. 2, Aug, 1979 (148 pages, 95 cents)
Archie Publications (Red Circle)

	GD25	FN65	NM94
1-Simon & Kirby r-/Double Life of Pvt. Strong #1,2; Black Hood, The Fly, Jaguar, The Web app.			1.00
2-Contains contents to the never published Black Hood #1; origin Black Hood; N. Adams, Wood, McWilliams, Morrow, S&K-a(r); N. Adams-c. The Shield, The Fly, Jaguar, Hangman, Steel Sterling, The Web, The Fox-r			1.00

ARCHIE'S TV LAUGH-OUT
Dec, 1969 - No. 106, April, 1986
Archie Publications

	GD25	FN65	NM94
1	4.00	12.00	28.00
2	1.65	4.00	10.00
3-5	1.00	2.00	5.00
6-10		.80	2.00
11-20			1.50
21-106			1.00

ARCHIE'S WORLD (Spire Christian)(Value: cover or less)

ARCHIE 3000
May, 1989 - No. 15, May, 1991 (75 & 95 cents, $1.00, color)
Archie Comics

	GD25	FN65	NM94
1-15: 6-X-Mas-c			1.00

ARCOMICS PREMIERE
July, 1993 ($2.95, color)
Arcomics

	GD25	FN65	NM94
1-1st linticular-c on a comic (flicker-c)		1.20	3.00

AREA 88 (Eclipse)(Value: cover or less)

ARENA (Alchemy)(Value: cover or less)

ARIANE AND BLUEBEARD (See Night Music #8)

ARIEL & SEBASTIAN (See Cartoon Tales & The Little Mermaid)

ARION, LORD OF ATLANTIS (Also see Warlord #55)
Nov, 1982 - No. 35, Sept, 1985
DC Comics

	GD25	FN65	NM94
1-35: 1-Story cont'd from Warlord #62			1.00
Special #1 (11/85)			1.00

ARION THE IMMORTAL
July, 1992 - No. 6, Dec, 1992 ($1.50, color, limited series)
DC Comics

	GD25	FN65	NM94
1-6: 4-Gustovich-a(i)			1.50

ARISTOCATS (See Movie Comics & Walt Disney Showcase No. 16)

ARISTOKITTENS, THE (...Meet Jiminy Cricket No. 1)(Disney)
Oct, 1971 - No. 9, Oct, 1975 (No. 6: 52 pages)
Gold Key

	GD25	FN65	NM94
1	2.60	7.50	18.00
2-9	1.50	3.75	9.00

ARIZONA KID, THE (Also see The Comics & Wild Western)
March, 1951 - No. 6, Jan, 1952
Marvel/Atlas Comics(CSI)

	GD25	FN65	NM94
1	13.00	40.00	90.00
2-4: 2-Heath-a(3)	7.50	22.50	45.00
5,6	6.70	20.00	40.00

NOTE: *Heath a-1-3; c-1-3. Maneely c-4-6. Morisi a-4-6. Sinnott a-6.*

Arkham Asylum nn, © DC

Arrowhead #2, © MEG

Astonishing #22, © MEG

GD25 FN65 NM94

ARK, THE (See The Crusaders)

ARKHAM ASYLUM (Also see Animal Man #24, Black Orchid #2 & The Saga of Swamp Thing #52, 53)
1989 ($24.95, hard-c, mature readers, 132 pgs.)
DC Comics

nn-Joker-c/story; Grant Morrison scripts 4.30 13.00 30.00
nn-Soft cover reprint ($14.95) 2.15 6.50 15.00

ARMAGEDDON: ALIEN AGENDA
Nov, 1991 - No. 4, Feb, 1992 ($1.00, color, mini-series)
DC Comics

1-4 1.00

ARMAGEDDON FACTOR, THE (AC)(Value: cover or less)

ARMAGEDDON: INFERNO
Apr, 1992 - No. 4, July, 1992 ($1.00, color, mini-series)
DC Comics

1-4: Many DC heroes app. 3-A. Adams/Austin-a 1.00

ARMAGEDDON 2001
May, 1991 - No. 2, Oct, 1991 ($2.00, squarebound, 68 pgs.)
DC Comics

1-Features many DC heroes; intro Waverider 1.20 3.00
1-2nd & 3rd printings; 3rd has silver ink-c .70 1.75
2 1.00 2.50

ARMOR (Continuity Comics)(Value: cover or less)

ARMY AND NAVY COMICS (Supersnipe No. 6 on)
May, 1941 - No. 5, July, 1942
Street & Smith Publications

1-Cap Fury & Nick Carter 35.00 105.00 230.00
2-Cap Fury & Nick Carter 17.50 52.00 120.00
3,4 12.50 37.50 85.00
5-Supersnipe app.; see Shadow V2#3 for 1st app.; Story of Douglas MacArthur; George Marcoux-c/a 33.00 100.00 220.00

ARMY ATTACK
July, 1964 - No. 4, Feb, 1965; V2#38, July, 1965 - No. 47, Feb, 1967
Charlton Comics

V1#1 3.00 7.50 15.00
2-4(2/65) 1.60 4.00 8.00
V2#38(7/65)-47 (formerly U.S. Air Force #1-37) 1.60 4.00 8.00
NOTE: *Glanzman a-1-3. Montes/Bache a-44.*

ARMY AT WAR (Also see Our Army at War & Cancelled Comic Cavalcade)
Oct-Nov, 1978
DC Comics

1-Kubert-c .80 2.00

ARMY SURPLUS KOMIKZ FEATURING CUTEY BUNNY
1982 - No. 5, 1985 ($1.50, B&W)
Army Surplus Komikz/Eclipse Comics No. 5

1-Cutey Bunny begins .80 2.00
2-5: 5-JLA/X-Men/Batman parody 1.50

ARMY WAR HEROES (Also see Iron Corporal)
Dec, 1963 - No. 38, June, 1970
Charlton Comics

1 3.60 9.00 18.00
2-38: 22-Origin & 1st app. Iron Corporal series by Glanzman. 24-Intro. Archer & Corp. Jack series 1.60 4.00 8.00
Modern Comics Reprint 36 ('78) .80 2.00
NOTE: *Montes/Bache a-1, 16, 17, 21, 23-25, 27-30.*

AROUND THE BLOCK WITH DUNC & LOO (See Dunc and Loo)

AROUND THE WORLD IN 80 DAYS (See Four Color Comics #784 and A Golden Picture Classic)

GD25 FN65 NM94

AROUND THE WORLD UNDER THE SEA (See Movie Classics)

AROUND THE WORLD WITH ARCHIE (See Archie Giant Series Mag. #29, 35, 141)

AROUND THE WORLD WITH HUCKLEBERRY & HIS FRIENDS (See Dell Giant No. 44)

ARRGH! (Satire)
Dec, 1974 - No. 5, Sept, 1975 (25¢)
Marvel Comics Group

1 1.20 3.00
2-5 .70 1.75
NOTE *Alcala a-2; c-3. Everett a-1r, 2r. Maneely a-4r. Sekowsky a-1p. Sutton a-1, 2.*

ARROW, THE (See Funny Pages)
Oct, 1940 - No. 2, Nov, 1940; No. 3, Oct, 1941
Centaur Publications

1-The Arrow begins(r/Funny Pages) 135.00 400.00 900.00
2,3: 2-Tippy Taylor serial continues from Amazing Mystery Funnies #24. 3-Origin Dash Dartwell, the Human Meteor; origin The Rainbow-r; bondage-c 80.00 240.00 525.00
NOTE: *Gustavson a-1, 2; c-3.*

ARROWHEAD (See Black Rider and Wild Western)
April, 1954 - No. 4, Nov, 1954
Atlas Comics (CPS)

1-Arrowhead & his horse Eagle begin 10.00 30.00 60.00
2-4: 4-Forte-a 6.70 20.00 40.00
NOTE: *Heath c-3. Jack Katz a-3. Maneely c-2. Pakula a-2. Sinnott a-1-4; c-1.*

ASSASSINS, INC. (Silverline)(Value: cover or less)

ASTONISHING (Formerly Marvel Boy No. 1, 2)
No. 3, April, 1951 - No. 63, Aug, 1957
Marvel/Atlas Comics(20CC)

3-Marvel Boy continues; 3-5-Marvel Boy-c 49.00 145.00 340.00
4-6-Last Marvel Boy; 4-Stan Lee app. 34.00 100.00 235.00
7-10: 7-Maneely s/f story. 10-Sinnott s/f story 12.00 36.00 85.00
11,12,15,17,20 10.00 30.00 70.00
13,14,16,19-Krigstein-a 11.50 34.00 80.00
18-Jack The Ripper story 12.00 36.00 85.00
21,22,24 9.15 27.50 55.00
23-E.C. swipe-"The Hole In The Wall" from Vault Of Horror #16 10.00 30.00 65.00
25-Crandall-a 9.15 27.50 55.00
26-28 8.35 25.00 50.00
29-Decapitation-c 9.15 27.50 55.00
30-Tentacled eyeball story 11.00 32.00 75.00
31-37-Last pre-code issue 7.50 22.50 45.00
38-43,46,48-52,56,58,59,61 5.85 17.50 35.00
44-Crandall swipe/Weird Fantasy #22 7.50 22.50 45.00
45,47-Krigstein-a 7.50 22.50 45.00
53,54: 53-Crandall, Ditko-a. 54-Torres-a 6.35 19.00 38.00
55-Crandall, Torres-a 7.50 22.50 45.00
57-Williamson/Krenkel-a (4 pgs.) 8.35 25.00 50.00
60-Williamson/Mayo-a (4 pgs.) 8.35 25.00 50.00
62-Torres, Powell-a 5.35 16.00 32.00
63-Last issue; Woodbridge-a 5.35 16.00 32.00
NOTE: *Ayers a-16. Berg a-36, 53, 56. Cameron a-50. Gene Colan a-12, 20, 29, 56. Ditko a-50, 53. Drucker a-41, 62. Everett a-3-6(3), 6, 10, 12, 37, 47, 48, 58; c-3-5, 13,15, 16, 18, 29, 47, 49, 51, 53-55, 57, 59-63. Fass a-11, 34. Forte a-53, 58, 60. Fuje a-11. Heath a-8, 29; c-8, 9, 19, 22, 25, 26. Kirby a-56. Lawrence a-28, 37, 38, 42. Maneely a-7(2); c-7, 31, 33, 34, 56. Moldoff a-33. Morisi a-10, 60. Morrow a-52, 61. Orlando a-47, 58, 61. Pakula a-10. Powell a-43, 44, 48. Ravielli a-28. Reinman a-32, 34, 38. Robinson a-20. J. Romita a-7, 18, 24, 43, 57,61. Roussos a-55. Sale a-28, 38, 59; c-32. Sekowsky a-13. Severin c-46. Shores a-16, 60. Sinnott a-11, 30. Whitney a-13. Ed Win a-20. Canadian reprints exist.*

ASTONISHING TALES (See Ka-Zar)
Aug, 1970 - No. 36, July, 1976 (#1-7: 15 cents; #8: 25 cents)
Marvel Comics Group

1-Ka-Zar (by Kirby(p) #1,2; by B. Smith #3-6) & Dr. Doom (by Wood #1-4; by Tuska #5,6; by Colan #7,8) double feature begins; Kraven the Hunter-

Astonishing Tales #30, © MEG

Atom-Age Combat #4, © STJ

Atomic Attack #5, © YM

	GD25	FN65	NM94
c/story; Nixon cameo	3.20	8.00	20.00
2-Kravon the Hunter-c/story; Kirby, Wood-a	1.65	4.00	10.00
3-6: B. Smith-p; Wood-a-#3,4. 5-Red Skull app.	2.15	6.50	15.00
7,8: 8-(25¢, 52 pgs.)-Last Dr. Doom	1.65	4.00	10.00
9-Lorna-r/Lorna #14		1.20	3.00
10-B. Smith-a(p).	1.10	2.70	6.50
11-Origin Ka-Zar & Zabu	1.00	2.50	5.50
12-Man-Thing by Neal Adams (apps. #13 also)	1.00	2.50	5.50
13-24: 14-Jann of the Jungle-r (1950s).20-Last Ka-Zar. 21-It! the Living Colossus begins, ends #24		.80	2.00
25-1st app. Deathlok the Demolisher; full length stories begin, end #36; Perez's 1st work, 2 pgs. (8/74)	6.50	19.00	45.00
26-28,30: 29-r/origin/1st app. Guardians of the Galaxy from Marvel Super-Heroes #18 plus-c w/4 pgs. omitted; no Deathlok story	2.15	6.50	15.00
29-r/origin/1st app. Guardians of the Galaxy from Marvel Super-Heroes #18 plus-c w/4 pgs. omitted; no Deathlok sty	2.50	7.50	17.50
31-36: 31-Watcher-r/Silver Surfer #3	1.65	4.70	11.00

NOTE: ***Buckler** a-13i, 16p, 25, 26p, 27p, 28, 29p-36p; c-13, 25p, 26-30, 32-35p, 36. **John Buscema** a-9, 12p-14p, 16p; c-4-6p, 12p. **Colan** a-7p, 8p. **Ditko** a-21r. **Everett** a-6i. **G. Kane** a-11p, 15p; c-9, 10p, 11p, 14, 15p, 21p. **McWilliams** a-30i. **Starlin** a-19p; c-16p. **Sutton & Trimpe** a-8. **Tuska** a-5p, 6p, 8p. **Wood** a-1-4. **Wrightson** c-31i.*

ASTRO BOY (TV) (See March of Comics #285 & The Original...)
August, 1965 (12 cents)
Gold Key

	GD25	FN65	NM94
1(10151-508)-1st app. Astro Boy in comics	36.00	107.00	250.00

ASTRO COMICS
1969 - 1979 (Giveaway)
American Airlines (Harvey)

	GD25	FN65	NM94
nn-Harvey's Casper, Spooky, Hot Stuff, Stumbo the Giant, Little Audrey, Little Lotta, & Richie Rich reprints		1.60	4.00

ASYLUM
1993 - Present ($2.50, color)
Millennium Publications

	GD25	FN65	NM94
1-4: 1-Bolton-c/a, Al Williams, Russell-a		1.00	2.50

ATARI FORCE
1982; Jan, 1984 - No. 20, Aug, 1985 (Mando paper)
DC Comics

	GD25	FN65	NM94
1-3 (1982, color, 52 pgs., 5X7")-Given away with Atari games			1.00
1-20: 1-(1/84)-1st app. Tempest, Packrat, Babe, Morphea, & Dart			1.00
Special 1 (4/86)			1.00

NOTE: ***Byrne** c-Special 1i. **Giffen** a-12p, 13i. **Rogers** a-18p, Special 1p.*

A-TEAM, THE (TV)
March, 1984 - No. 3, May, 1984
Marvel Comics Group

	GD25	FN65	NM94
1-3			1.00

ATLANTIS CHRONICLES, THE
Mar, 1990 - No. 7, Sept, 1990 ($2.95, mini-series, 52 pgs.)
DC Comics

	GD25	FN65	NM94
1-7: 7-True origin Aquaman; nudity panels		1.20	3.00

ATLANTIS, THE LOST CONTINENT (See 4-Color No. 1188)

ATLAS (See 1st Issue Special)

ATOM, THE (See Action, All-American #19, Brave & the Bold, D.C. Special Series #1, Detective, Flash Comics #80, Power Of The Atom, Showcase #34, Super Friends, Sword of The Atom & World's Finest)

ATOM, THE (...& the Hawkman No. 39 on)
June-July, 1962 - No. 38, Aug-Sept, 1968
National Periodical Publ.

	GD25	FN65	VF82	NM94
Showcase #34 (9-10/61)-Origin & 1st app. Silver Age Atom by Kane & Anderson	108.00	325.00	650.00	975.00

	GD25	FN65	NM94
Showcase #35 (11-12/61)-2nd app. Atom by Gil Kane; last 10 cent issue	80.00	257.00	600.00
Showcase #36 (1-2/62)-3rd app. Atom by Kane	61.00	182.00	425.00
1-(6-7/62)-Intro Plant-Master; 1st app. Maya	86.00	257.00	600.00
2	32.00	96.00	225.00
3-1st Time Pool story; 1st app. Chronos (origin)	21.00	64.00	150.00
4,5: 4-Snapper Carr x-over	14.00	43.00	100.00
6,8-10: 8-Justice League, Dr. Light app.	11.00	34.00	80.00
7-Hawkman x-over (6-7/63; 1st Atom & Hawkman team-up); 1st app. Hawkman since Brave & the Bold tryouts	26.00	79.00	185.00
11-15: 13-Chronos-c/story	8.00	24.00	55.00
16-20: 19-Zatanna x-over	5.50	17.00	40.00
21-28,30: 28-Chronos-c/story	4.30	13.00	30.00
29-1st solo Golden Age Atom x-over in S.A.	13.00	40.00	90.00
31-35,37,38: 31-Hawkman x-over. 37-Intro. Major Mynah; Hawkman cameo	3.60	10.75	25.00
36-G.A. Atom x-over	4.70	14.00	33.00
Special 1 (1993, $2.50, 68 pgs.)		1.00	2.50

NOTE: ***Anderson** a-1-11i, 13i; c-inks-1-25, 31-35, 37. **Sid Greene** a-8i-38i. **Gil Kane** a-1p-38p; c-1p-28p, 29, 33p, 34. Time Pool stories also in 6, 9,12, 17, 21, 27, 35.*

ATOM AGE (See Classics Illustrated Special Issue)

ATOM-AGE COMBAT
June, 1952 - No. 5, April, 1953; Feb, 1958
St. John Publishing Co.

	GD25	FN65	NM94
1-Buck Vinson in all	29.00	85.00	200.00
2-Flying saucer story	16.00	48.00	110.00
3,5: 3-Mayo-a (6 pgs.). 5-Flying saucer-c/story	12.00	36.00	85.00
4 (Scarce)	15.00	45.00	105.00
1(2/58-St. John)	11.00	32.00	70.00

ATOM-AGE COMBAT
Nov, 1958 - No. 3, March, 1959
Fago Magazines

	GD25	FN65	NM94
1-All have Dick Ayers-c/a	14.00	43.00	100.00
2,3: 2-A-Bomb explosion-c	10.00	30.00	65.00

ATOMAN
Feb, 1946 - No. 2, April, 1946
Spark Publications

	GD25	FN65	NM94
1-Origin & 1st app. Atoman; Robinson/Meskin-a; Kidcrusaders, Wild Bill Hickok, Marvin the Great app.	33.00	100.00	220.00
2-Robinson/Meskin-a; Robinson c-1,2	25.00	75.00	165.00

ATOM & HAWKMAN, THE (Formerly The Atom)
No. 39, Oct-Nov, 1968 - No. 45, Oct-Nov, 1969
National Periodical Publications

	GD25	FN65	NM94
39-45: 43-Last 12 cent issue; 1st app. Gentleman Ghost, origin in #44	3.60	10.75	25.00

NOTE: ***M. Anderson** a-39, 40i, 41i, 43, 44. **Sid Greene** a-40i-45i. **Kubert** a-40p, 41p; c-39-45.*

ATOM ANT (TV)
January, 1966 (Hanna-Barbera, 12¢)
Gold Key

	GD25	FN65	NM94
1(10170-601)	15.00	45.00	150.00

ATOMIC AGE
Nov, 1990 - No. 4, Feb, 1991 ($4.50, mini-series, squarebound, 52 pgs.)
Epic Comics (Marvel)

	GD25	FN65	NM94
1-4: Williamson-a(i)		1.80	4.50

ATOMIC ATTACK (True War Stories; formerly Attack, first series)
No. 5, Jan, 1953 - No. 8, Oct, 1953
Youthful Magazines

	GD25	FN65	NM94
5-Atomic bomb-c	19.00	58.00	135.00
6-8	11.50	34.00	80.00

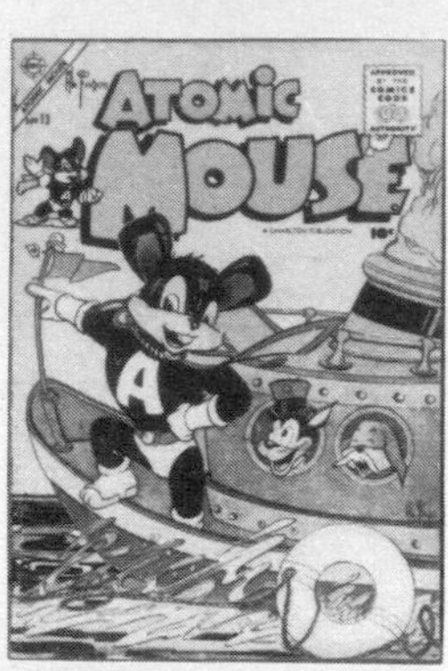

Atomic Mouse #13 ('50s), © CC

Attack #4, © YM

Augie Doggie #1, © Hanna-Barbera

ATOMIC BOMB
1945 (36 pgs.)
Jay Burtis Publications

	GD25	FN65	NM94
1-Airmale & Stampy	27.00	80.00	190.00

ATOMIC BUNNY (Formerly Atomic Rabbit)
No. 12, Aug, 1958 - No. 19, Dec, 1959
Charlton Comics

	GD25	FN65	NM94
12	9.15	27.50	55.00
13-19	5.00	15.00	30.00

ATOMIC COMICS
Jan, 1946 - No. 4, 1946 (Reprints)
Daniels Publications (Canadian)

	GD25	FN65	NM94
1-Rocketman, Yankee Boy, Master Key; bondage-c	14.00	43.00	100.00
2-4 (Exist?)	10.00	30.00	65.00

ATOMIC COMICS
Jan, 1946 - No. 4, July-Aug, 1946 (#1-4 were printed without cover gloss)
Green Publishing Co.

	GD25	FN65	NM94
1-Radio Squad by Siegel & Shuster; Barry O'Neal app.; Fang Gow cover-r/Det. Comics	69.00	205.00	480.00
2-Inspector Dayton; Kid Kane by Matt Baker; Lucky Wings, Congo King, Prop Powers (only app.) begin	35.00	105.00	235.00
3,4: 3-Zero Ghost Detective app.; Baker-a(2) each; 4-Baker-c	22.00	65.00	150.00

ATOMIC KNIGHTS (See Strange Adventures #117)

ATOMIC MOUSE (TV, Movies) (See Blue Bird, Funny Animals, Giant Comics Edition & Wotalife Comics)
3/53 - No. 54, 6/63; No. 1, 12/84; V2#10, 9/85 - No. 13, ?/86
Capitol Stories/Charlton Comics

	GD25	FN65	NM94
1-Origin & 1st app.; Al Fago-c/a in all?	15.00	45.00	105.00
2	8.35	25.00	50.00
3-10: 5-Timmy The Timid Ghost app.; see Zoo Funnies	5.85	17.50	35.00
11-13,16-25	4.00	10.00	20.00
14,15-Hoppy The Marvel Bunny app.	5.00	15.00	30.00
26-(68 pages)	7.00	21.00	42.00
27-40: 36,37-Atom The Cat app.	3.20	8.00	16.00
41-54	1.60	4.00	8.00
1 (1984)			1.00
V2#10 (10/85) -13-Fago-r. #12(1/86)			1.00

ATOMIC RABBIT (Atomic Bunny #12 on; see Giant Comics #3 & Wotalife)
August, 1955 - No. 11, March, 1958
Charlton Comics

	GD25	FN65	NM94
1-Origin & 1st app.; Al Fago-c/a in all?	14.00	43.00	100.00
2	7.50	22.50	45.00
3-10	5.35	16.00	32.00
11-(68 pages)	7.50	22.50	45.00

ATOMIC SPY CASES
Mar-Apr, 1950 (Painted-c)
Avon Periodicals

	GD25	FN65	NM94
1-No Wood-a; A-bomb blast panels; Fass-a	19.00	57.00	130.00

ATOMIC THUNDERBOLT, THE
Feb, 1946 (One shot)
Regor Company

	GD25	FN65	NM94
1-Intro. Atomic Thunderbolt & Mr. Murdo	29.00	85.00	200.00

ATOMIC WAR!
Nov, 1952 - No. 4, April, 1953
Ace Periodicals (Junior Books)

	GD25	FN65	NM94
1-Atomic bomb-c	48.00	145.00	335.00
2,3: 3-Atomic bomb-c	35.00	105.00	250.00
4-Used in **POP**, pg. 96 & illo.	35.00	105.00	250.00

ATOM THE CAT (Formerly Tom Cat; see Giant Comics #3)
No. 9, Oct, 1957 - No. 17, Aug, 1959
Charlton Comics

	GD25	FN65	NM94
9	5.35	16.00	32.00
10,13-17	3.60	9.00	18.00
11,12: 11(64pgs)-Atomic Mouse app. 12(100pgs)	7.00	21.00	42.00

ATTACK
May, 1952 - No. 4, Nov, 1952; No. 5, Jan, 1953 - No. 5, Sept, 1953
Youthful Mag./Trojan No. 5 on

	GD25	FN65	NM94
1-(1st series)-Extreme violence	13.00	40.00	90.00
2,3: 3-Harrison-c/a; bondage, whipping	7.50	22.50	45.00
4-Krenkel-a (7 pgs.); Harrison-a (becomes Atomic Attack #5 on)	8.35	25.00	50.00
5-(#1, Trojan, 2nd series)	6.70	20.00	40.00
6-8 (#2-4), 5	4.70	14.00	28.00

ATTACK
No. 54, 1958 - No. 60, Nov, 1959
Charlton Comics

	GD25	FN65	NM94
54 (100 pages)	5.85	17.50	35.00
55-60	2.00	5.00	10.00

ATTACK!
1962 - No. 15, 3/75; No. 16, 8/79 - No. 48, 10/84
Charlton Comics

	GD25	FN65	NM94
nn(#1)-('62) Special Edition	3.60	9.00	18.00
2('63), 3(Fall, '64)	2.00	5.00	10.00
V4#3(10/66), 4(10/67)-(Formerly Special War Series #2; becomes Attack At Sea V4#5)	1.30	3.25	8.00
1(9/71)		1.80	4.50
2-15(3/75): 4-American Eagle app.		.80	2.00
16(8/79) - 47			1.20
48(10/84)-Wood-r; S&K-c			1.50
Modern Comics 13('78)-r			1.00

ATTACK! (Spire Christian)(Value: cover or less)

ATTACK AT SEA (Formerly Attack!, 1967)
V4#5, October, 1968
Charlton Comics

	GD25	FN65	NM94
V4#5	1.30	3.25	8.00

ATTACK ON PLANET MARS (See Strange Worlds #18)
1951
Avon Periodicals

	GD25	FN65	NM94
nn-Infantino, Fawcette, Kubert & Wood-a; adaptation of Tarrano the Conqueror by Ray Cummings	50.00	150.00	350.00

AUDREY & MELVIN (Formerly Little...)(See Little Audrey & Melvin)
No. 62, September, 1974
Harvey Publications

	GD25	FN65	NM94
62		.80	2.00

AUGIE DOGGIE (TV) (See Hanna-Barbera Band Wagon, Quick-Draw McGraw, Spotlight #2, Top Cat & Whitman Comic Books)
October, 1963 (Hanna-Barbera, 12¢)
Gold Key

	GD25	FN65	NM94
1	10.00	30.00	70.00

AURORA COMIC SCENES INSTRUCTION BOOKLET
1974 (Slick paper, 8 pgs.)(6-1/4x9-3/4")(in full color)
(Included with superhero model kits)
Aurora Plastics Co.

	GD25	FN65	NM94
181-140-Tarzan; Neal Adams-a		1.60	4.00
182-140-Spider-Man. 183-140-Tonto(Gil Kane art). 184-140-Hulk. 185-140-Superman. 186-140-Superboy. 187-140-Batman. 188-140-The Lone Ranger(1974-by Gil Kane). 192-140-Captain America(1975). 193-140-Robin each....		1.20	3.00

Authentic Police Cases #18, © STJ

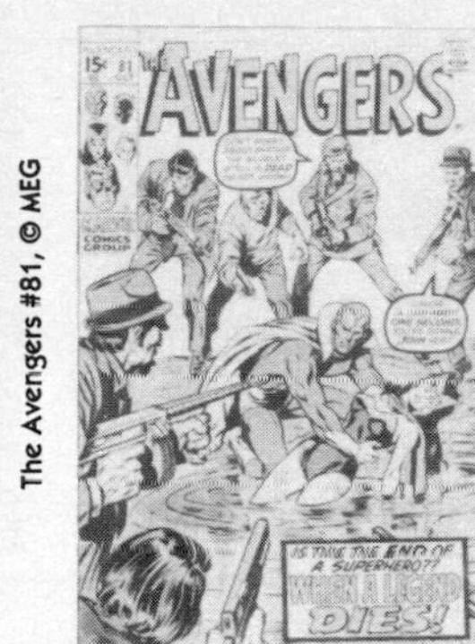

The Avengers #81, © MEG

The Avengers #250, © MEG

AUTHENTIC POLICE CASES
2/48 - No. 6, 11/48; No. 7, 5/50 - No. 38, 3/55
St. John Publishing Co.

	GD25	FN65	NM94
1-Hale the Magician by Tuska begins	17.00	52.00	120.00
2-Lady Satan, Johnny Rebel app.	11.00	32.00	75.00
3-Veiled Avenger app.; blood drainage story plus 2 Lucky Coyne stories; used in **SOTI**, illo. from Red Seal #16	23.00	70.00	160.00
4,5: 4-Masked Black Jack app. 5-Late 1930s Jack Cole-a(r); transvestism story	11.00	32.00	75.00
6-Matt Baker-c; used in **SOTI**, illo-"An invitation to learning", r-in Fugitives From Justice #3; Jack Cole-a; also used by the N.Y. Legis. Comm.	24.00	72.00	165.00
7,8,10-14: 7-Jack Cole-a; Matt Baker art begins #8, ends #?; Vic Flint in #10-14. 11-Baker-a(2)	10.00	30.00	65.00
9-No Vic Flint	8.65	26.00	52.00
15-Drug-c/story; Vic Flint app.; Baker-c	10.00	30.00	65.00
16,18,20,21,23	5.85	17.50	35.00
17,19,22-Baker-c	6.35	19.00	38.00
24-28 (All 100 pages): 26-Transvestism	12.00	36.00	85.00
29,30	4.00	12.00	24.00
31,32,37-Baker-c	4.70	14.00	28.00
33-Transvestism; Baker-c	5.35	16.00	32.00
34-Baker-c	5.35	16.00	32.00
35-Baker-c/a(2)	5.00	15.00	30.00
36-r/#11; Vic Flint strip-r; Baker-c/a(2) unsigned	5.35	16.00	32.00
38-Baker-c/a	5.35	16.00	32.00

NOTE: ***Matt Baker** c-6-16, 17, 19, 22, 27, 29, 31-38; a-13, 16. Bondage c-1, 3.*

AUTUMN ADVENTURES (Walt Disney's)
Autumn, 1990; No. 2, Aut, 1991 ($2.95, color, quarterly, 68 pgs.)
Disney Comics

	GD25	FN65	NM94
1-Donald Duck-r(2) by Barks, Pluto-r, & new-a	.60	1.50	3.00
2-D. Duck-r by Barks; new Super Goof story	.60	1.50	3.00

AVATAR
Feb, 1991 - No. 3, Apr, 1991 ($5.95, color, mini-series, 100 pgs.)
DC Comics

	GD25	FN65	NM94
1-3: Based on TSR's Forgotten Realms	1.20	3.00	0.00

AVENGER, THE (See A-1 Comics)
1955 - No. 4, Aug-Sept, 1955
Magazine Enterprises

	GD25	FN65	NM94
1(A-1 #129)-Origin	24.00	72.00	165.00
2(A-1 #131), 3(A-1 #133), 4(A-1 #138)	16.00	48.00	110.00
IW Reprint #9('64)-Reprints #1 (new cover)	2.80	7.00	14.00

NOTE: ***Powell** a-2-4; c-1-4.*

AVENGERS, THE (See Giant-Size..., Kree/Skrull War Starring..., Marvel Graphic Novel #27, Marvel Super Action, Marvel Super Heroes('66), Marvel Treasury Ed., Marvel Triple Action, Solo Avengers, Tales Of Suspense #49, West Coast Avengers & X-Men Vs....)

AVENGERS, THE (The Mighty Avengers on cover only #63-69)
Sept, 1963 - Present
Marvel Comics Group

	GD25	FN65	VF82	NM94
1-Origin & 1st app. The Avengers (Thor, Iron Man, Hulk, Ant-Man, Wasp); Loki app.	168.00	505.00	1090.00	1675.00

	GD25	FN65	NM94
2-Hulk leaves	64.00	193.00	450.00
3-1st Sub-Mariner x-over (outside the F.F.); Hulk & Sub-Mariner team-up & battle Avengers	40.00	120.00	280.00
4-Revival of Captain America who joins the Avengers; 1st Silver Age app. of Captain America & Bucky (3/64)	95.00	285.00	950.00
4-Reprint from the Golden Record Comic set	8.00	24.00	55.00
With Record (1966)	14.00	43.00	100.00
5-Hulk app.	25.00	75.00	175.00
6-8: 6-Intro. Zemo & his Masters of Evil. 8-Intro Kang	19.00	56.00	130.00
9-Intro Wonder Man who dies in same story.	20.00	60.00	140.00
10-Early Hercules app.	17.00	51.00	120.00
11-Spider-Man-c & x-over (12/64)	20.00	60.00	140.00
12-15: 15-Death of Zemo.	11.00	34.00	80.00
16-New Avengers line-up (Hawkeye, Quicksilver, Scarlet Witch join; Thor, Iron Man, Giant-Man, Wasp leave.)	12.00	36.00	85.00
17-19: 19-Intro. Swordsman; origin Hawkeye	9.00	26.00	60.00
20-22: Wood inks	5.50	17.00	40.00
23-30: 25-Dr. Doom-c/story. 28-Giant-Man becomes Goliath	4.00	12.00	28.00
31-40	3.20	8.00	20.00
41-52,54-56: 43,44-1st app. Red Guardian. 46-Ant-Man returns (re-intro). 47-Magneto-c/story. 48-Origin/1st app. new Black Knight. 52-Black Panther joins; 1st app. The Grim Reaper. 54-1st app. new Masters of Evil	2.15	6.50	15.00
53-X-Men app.	3.00	8.00	19.50
57-1st app. S.A. Vision (10/68)	7.00	21.00	50.00
58-Origin The Vision	5.00	15.00	35.00
59-65: 59-Intro. Yellowjacket. 60-Wasp & Yellowjacket wed. 63-Goliath becomes Yellowjacket; Hawkeye becomes the new Goliath. 65-Last 12 cent issue	2.40	7.25	17.00
66,67: B. Smith-a	2.30	6.75	16.00
68-70	1.65	4.70	11.00
71-1st app. The Invaders (12/69); 1st app. Nighthawk; Black Knight joins	2.60	7.50	18.00
72-82,84-86,88-91: 80-Intro. Red Wolf (9/70). 82-Daredevil app. 88-Written by Harlan Ellison	1.65	4.00	10.00
83-Intro. The Liberators (Wasp, Valkyrie, Scarlet Witch, Medusa & the Black Widow)	1.65	4.00	10.00
87-Origin The Black Panther	3.20	8.00	20.00
92-Last 15 cent issue; Neal Adams-c	1.70	5.00	12.00
93-(52 pgs.)-Neal Adams-c/a	5.50	17.00	40.00
94-96-Neal Adams-c/a	3.85	11.50	27.00
97-G.A. Capt. America, Sub-Mariner, Human Torch, Patriot, Vision, Blazing Skull, Fin, Angel, & new Capt. Marvel x-over	1.70	5.00	12.00
98-Goliath becomes Hawkeye; Smith c/a(i)	3.30	10.00	23.00
99-Smith/Sutton-a	3.30	10.00	23.00
100-(6/72)-Smith-c/a; featuring everyone who was an Avenger	9.00	26.00	60.00
101-106,108,109: 101-Harlan Ellison scripts	1.30	3.25	8.00
107-Starlin-a(p)	1.65	4.70	11.00
110,111-X-Men app.	2.30	6.75	16.00
112-1st app. Mantis	1.65	4.70	11.00
113-120: 116-118-Defenders/Silver Surfer app.	1.15	2.80	6.75
121-124,126-130: 123-Origin Mantis	1.15	2.80	6.75
125-Thanos-c & brief app.	2.20	6.50	15.50
131-140: 136-Ploog-r/Amazing Advs. #12	1.00	2.50	5.50
141-163: 144-Origin & 1st app. Hellcat. 146-25 & 30 cent variants exist. 150-Kirby-a(r); new line-up: Capt. America, Scarlet Witch, Iron Man, Wasp, Yellowjacket, Vision & The Beast. 151-Wonderman returns w/new costume		1.80	4.50
164-166: Byrne-a	1.00	2.50	5.50
167-180: 174-Thanos cameo. 176-Starhawk app.		1.20	3.00
181-191: Byrne-a. 181-New line-up: Capt. America, Scarlet Witch, Iron Man, Wasp, Vision, Beast & The Falcon. 183-Ms. Marvel joins. 185-Origin Quicksilver & Scarlet Witch		1.20	3.00
192-213,215-262: 195-1st Taskmaster. 200-(10/80, 52 pgs.)-Ms. Marvel leaves. 211-New line-up: Capt. America, Iron Man, Tigra, Thor, Wasp & Yellowjacket. 213-Yellowjacket leaves. 215,216-Silver Surfer app. 216-Tigra leaves. 217-Yellowjacket & Wasp return. 221-Hawkeye & She-Hulk join. 227-Capt. Marvel (female) joins; origins of Ant-Man, Wasp, Giant-Man, Goliath, Yellowjacket, & Avengers. 230-Yellowjacket quits. 231-Iron Man leaves. 232-Starfox (Eros) joins. 234-Origin Quicksilver, Scarlet Witch. 236-New logo. 238-Origin Blackout. 240-Spider-Woman revived. 250-($1.00, 52 pgs.)		.80	2.00
214-Ghost Rider-c/story	1.00	2.00	5.00
263-1st app. X-Factor (1/86)(story continues in Fantastic Four #286)	1.00	2.00	5.00

The Avengers Annual #15, © MEG

Avengers West Coast #57, © MEG

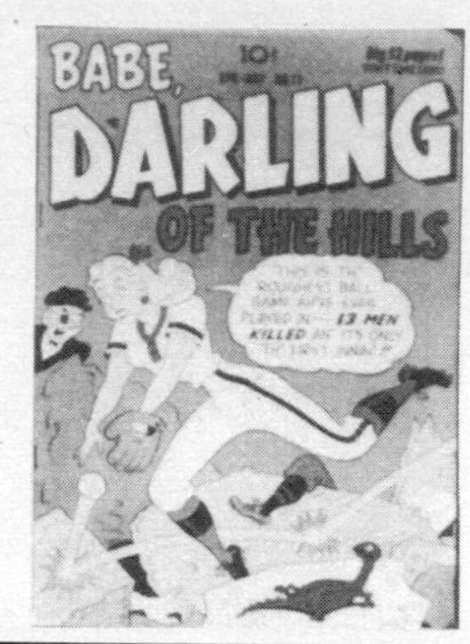

Babe, Darling of the Hills #11, © Prize

GD25 FN65 NM94

264-299: 272-Alpha Flight app. 291-$1.00 issues begin. 297-Black Knight, She-Hulk & Thor resign. 298-Inferno tie-in .80 2.00
300 (2/89, $1.75, 68 pgs.)-Thor joins; Simonson-a 1.20 3.00
301-304,306-325,327,329-343: 302-Re-intro Quasar. 314-318-Spider-Man x-over. 320-324-Alpha Flight app. (320-cameo). 341,342-New Warriors app. 343-Last $1.00-c 1.00
305-Byrne scripts begin .80 2.00
326-1st app. Rage (11/90) 1.30 3.25 8.00
328-Origin Rage 1.20 3.00 7.00
344-346,348,349,351-359,361,362,364,365,367: 365-Contains coupon for Hunt for Magneto contest 1.50
347-($1.75, 56 pgs.) .80 2.00
350-($2.50, 68 pgs.)-Double gatefold-c showing-c to #1; r/#53 w/cover in flip book format; vs. The Starjammers 1.00 2.50
360-($2.95, 52 pgs.)-Embossed all-foil-c; 30th ann. 1.00 2.00 5.00
363-($2.95, 52 pgs.)-All silver foil-c 1.20 3.00
366-($3.95, 68 pgs.)-Embossed all gold foil-c 1.60 4.00
368-Bloodties part 1; Avengers/X-Men x-over 1.50
369-372 1.25
Special 1(9/67, 25 cents, 68 pgs.)-New-a; original & new Avengers team-up 5.00 16.00 38.00
Special 2(9/68, 25 cents, 68 pgs.)-New-a; original vs. new Avengers 2.00 6.00 14.00
Special 3(9/69, 25 cents, 68 pgs.)-r/Avengers #4 plus 3 Capt. America stories by Kirby-a; origin Red Skull 2.30 6.75 16.00
Special 4,5: 4(1/71, 25 cents, 68 pgs.)-Kirby-r/Avengers #5,6. 5(1/72)-Spider-Man x-over 1.00 2.50 6.00
Annual 6(11/76) 1.00 2.00 5.00
Annual 7(11/77)-Starlin-c/a; Warlock dies; Thanos app. 4.30 13.00 30.00
Annual 8(1978)-Dr. Strange, Ms. Marvel app. 1.80 4.50
Annual 9(1979)-Newton-a(p) 1.40 3.50
Annual 10(1981)-Golden-p; X-Men cameo; 1st app. Rogue & Madelyne Pryor 1.30 3.25 8.00
Annual 11-16: 11(1982)-Vs. The Defenders. 12(1983). 13(1984). 14(1985). 15(1986). 16(1987) 1.40 3.50
Annual 17(1988)-Evolutionary War x-over 1.60 4.00
Annual 18(1989, $2.00, 68 pgs.)-Atlantis Attacks 1.20 3.00
Annual 19,20(1990, 1991)(both $2.00, 68 pgs.) 1.00 2.50
Annual 21(1992, $2.25, 68 pgs.) .90 2.25
Annual 22(1993, $2.95, 68 pgs.)-Bagged w/card 1.20 3.00

NOTE: ***Austin*** *c(i)-157, 167, 168, 170-177, 181, 183-188, 198-201, Annual 8.* ***John Buscema*** *a-41-44p, 46p, 47p, 49, 50, 51-62p, 74-77, 79-85, 87-91, 97, 105p, 121p, 124p,125p, 152, 153p, 255-279p, 281-302p; c-41-66, 68-71, 73-91, 97-99, 178, 256-259p, 261-279p, 281-302p.* ***Byrne*** *a-164-166p, 181-191p, 233p, Annual 13, 14p; c-186-190p, 233p, 260, 305p; scripts-305-312.* ***Colan*** *a(p)-63-65, 111, 206-208, 210, 211; c(p)-65, 206-208, 210, 211.* ***Guice*** *a-Annual 12p.* ***Kane*** *c-37p, 159p.* ***Kane/Everett*** *c-97.* ***Kirby*** *a-1-8p, Special 3r, 4r(p); c-1-30, 148, 151-158; layouts-14-16.* ***Miller*** *c-193p.* ***Mooney*** *a-86i, 179p, 180p.* ***Nebres*** *a-178i; c-179i.* ***Newton*** *a-204p, Annual 9p.* ***Perez*** *a(p)-141, 143, 144, 148, 154, 155, 160, 161, 162, 167,168, 170, 171, 194-196, 198-202, Annual 6, 8; c(p)-160-162, 164-166, 170-174, 181,183-185, 191, 192, 194-201, Annual 8.* ***Starlin*** *c-121, 135.* ***Staton*** *a-127-134i.* ***Tuska*** *a-47i,48i, 51i, 53i, 54i, 106p, 107p, 135p, 137-140p, 163p. Guardians of the Galaxy app. in #167, 168, 170, 173, 175, 181.*

AVENGERS, THE (TV)(Also see Steed and Mrs. Peel)
Nov, 1968 ("John Steed & Emma Peel" cover title) (15 cents)
Gold Key

1-Photo-c 24.00 72.00 165.00

AVENGERS SPOTLIGHT (Formerly Solo Avengers #1-20)
No. 21, Aug, 1989 - No. 40, Jan, 1991 (.75-$1.00, color)
Marvel Comics

21 (75 cents)-Byrne-c/a 1.00
22-40 ($1.00): 26-Acts of Vengeance story. 31-34-U.S. Agent series. 36-Heck-i. 37-Mortimer-i. 40-The Black Knight app. 1.00

AVENGERS: THE TERMINATRIX OBJECTIVE
Sept, 1993 - No. 4, Dec, 1993 ($1.25, color)
Marvel Comics

GD25 FN65 NM94

1-($2.50)-Holo-grafx foil-c 1.00 2.50
2-4 1.25

AVENGERS WEST COAST (Formerly West Coast Avengers)
No. 48, Sept, 1989 - No. 102, Jan, 1994 ($1.00-$1.25, color)
Marvel Comics

48,49: Byrne-c/a & scripts continue thru #57 1.10
50-Re-intro original Human Torch 1.50
51-74,76-99,101,102: 54-Cover swipe/F.F. #1. 70-Spider-Woman app. 78-Last $1.00-c. 79-Dr. Strange x-over. 84-Origin Spider-Woman retold; Spider-Man app. (also in #85,86). 87,88-Wolverine-c/story. 101-X-Men x-over 1.25
75-($1.50, 52 pgs.)-Fantastic Four x-over 1.50
100-($3.95, 68 pgs.)-Embossed all red foil-c 1.60 4.00
Annual 8 (1993, $2.95, 68 pgs.)-Bagged w/card 1.20 3.00

AVIATION ADVENTURES AND MODEL BUILDING
No. 16, Dec, 1946 - No. 17, Feb, 1947 (True Aviation Adv...No. 15)
Parents' Magazine Institute

16,17-Half comics and half pictures 5.00 15.00 30.00

AVIATION CADETS
1943
Street & Smith Publications

nn 10.00 30.00 65.00

A-V IN 3-D
Dec, 1984 ($2.00, 28 pgs. w/glasses)
Aardvark-Vanaheim

1-Cerebus, Flaming Carrot, Normalman & Ms. Tree .80 2.00

AWFUL OSCAR (Formerly & becomes Oscar Comics with No. 13)
No. 11, June, 1949 - No. 12, Aug, 1949
Marvel Comics

11,12 5.70 15.00 30.00

AXA (Eclipse)(Value: cover or less)

AXEL PRESSBUTTON (Eclipse)(Value: cover or less)

AZTEC ACE (Eclipse)(Value: cover or less)

BABE (...Darling of the Hills, later issues)(See Big Shot and Sparky Watts)
June-July, 1948 - No. 11, Apr-May, 1950
Prize/Headline/Feature

1-Boody Rogers-a 11.50 34.00 80.00
2-Boody Rogers-a 9.15 27.50 55.00
3-11-All by Boody Rogers 7.00 21.00 42.00

BABE AMAZON OF OZARKS
No. 5, 1948
Standard Comics

5-Exist? 5.00 15.00 30.00

BABE RUTH SPORTS COMICS
April, 1949 - No. 11, Feb, 1951
Harvey Publications

1-Powell-a 23.00 70.00 160.00
2-Powell-a 17.00 52.00 120.00
3-11: Powell-a in most 14.00 43.00 100.00

NOTE: *Baseball c-2-4, 9. Basketball c-1, 6. Football c-5. Yogi Berra c/story-8. Joe DiMaggio c/story-3. Bob Feller c/story-4. Stan Musial c-9.*

BABES IN TOYLAND (See 4-Color No. 1282 & Golden Pix Story Book ST-3)

BABY HUEY
1991 - Present ($1.00/$1.25, color)
Harvey Comics

1-5 1.25

BABY HUEY AND PAPA (See Paramount Animated...)
May, 1962 - No. 33, Jan, 1968 (Also see Casper The Friendly Ghost)
Harvey Publications

Baby Huey, the Baby Giant #1, © Harvey

Bad Company #4, © Fleetway

Baffling Mysteries #15, © ACE

	GD25	FN65	NM94
1	13.00	40.00	90.00
2	5.85	17.50	35.00
3-5	3.60	9.00	18.00
6-10	2.40	6.00	12.00
11-20	1.40	3.50	7.00
21-33	1.20	3.00	6.00

BABY HUEY DUCKLAND
Nov, 1962 - No. 15, Nov, 1966 (25 cent Giants) (All 68 pgs.)
Harvey Publications

	GD25	FN65	NM94
1	9.15	27.50	55.00
2-5	4.00	10.00	20.00
6-15	2.00	5.00	10.00

BABY HUEY, THE BABY GIANT (Also see Big Baby Huey, Casper, Harvey Hits #22, Harvey Comics Hits #60, & Paramount Animated Comics)
9/56 - #97, 10/71; #98, 10/72; #99, 10/80; #100, 10/90 - #102?
Harvey Publications

	GD25	FN65	NM94
1-Infinity-c	28.00	85.00	200.00
2	14.00	43.00	100.00
3-Baby Huey takes anti-pep pills	10.00	30.00	60.00
4,5	7.50	22.50	45.00
6-10	4.00	11.00	22.00
11-20	2.80	7.00	14.00
21-40	2.40	6.00	12.00
41-60	1.60	4.00	8.00
61-79(12/67)	1.20	3.00	6.00
80(12/68) - 95-All 68 pg. Giants	1.60	4.00	8.00
96,97-Both 52 pg. Giants	1.20	3.00	6.00
98-99: Regular size		1.20	3.00
100-102 ($1.00)			1.00

BABY SNOOTS (Also see March of Comics #359, 371, 396, 401, 419, 431, 443, 450, 462, 474, 485)
Aug, 1970 - No. 22, Nov, 1975
Gold Key

	GD25	FN65	NM94
1	1.50	3.75	9.00
2		1.60	4.00
3-22: 22-Titled Snoots, the Forgetful Elefink		.80	2.00

BACHELOR FATHER (TV)
No. 1332, 4-6/62 - No. 2, 1962
Dell Publishing Co.

	GD25	FN65	NM94
4-Color 1332 (#1)	8.35	25.00	50.00
2-Written by Stanley	8.35	25.00	50.00

BACHELOR'S DIARY
1949 (15¢)
Avon Periodicals

	GD25	FN65	NM94
1(Scarce)-King Features panel cartoons & text-r; pin-up, girl wrestling photos; similar to Sideshow	25.00	75.00	175.00

BACK DOWN THE LINE
1991 (Mature adults, 8-1/2 x 11", 52 pgs.)
Eclipse Books

	GD25	FN65	NM94
nn (Soft-c, $8.95)-Bolton-c/a	1.50	3.75	9.00
nn (Limited hard-c, $29.95)			30.00

BACK TO THE FUTURE (TV cartoon)
Nov, 1991 - Present ($1.25, color)
Harvey Comics

	GD25	FN65	NM94
1-4: 1,2-Gil Kane-c; based on animated cartoon			1.25
Special nn (1991, 20 pgs.)-Brunner-c; given away at Universal Studios in Florida			1.00

BACK TO THE FUTURE: FORWARD TO THE FUTURE
Oct, 1992 - No. 3, Feb, 1993 ($1.50, color, mini-series)
Harvey Comics

	GD25	FN65	NM94
1-3			1.50

BAD COMPANY
Aug, 1988 - No. 19?, 1990 ($1.50-$1.75, color, high quality paper)
Quality Comics/Fleetway Quality #15 on

	GD25	FN65	NM94
1-15: 5,6-Guice-c			1.50
16-19: ($1.75-c)		.70	1.75

BADGE OF JUSTICE
No. 22, 1/55 - No. 23, 3/55; 4/55 - No. 4, 10/55
Charlton Comics

	GD25	FN65	NM94
22(1/55)	5.85	17.50	35.00
23(3/55), 1	4.20	12.50	25.00
2-4	3.20	8.00	16.00

BADGER, THE (First)(Value: cover or less)

BADGER GOES BERSERK (First)(Value: cover or less)

BADLANDS (Vortex)(Value: cover or less)

BADLANDS (Dark Horse)(Value: cover or less)

BADMEN OF THE WEST
1951 (Giant - 132 pages)(Painted-c)
Avon Periodicals

	GD25	FN65	NM94
1-Contains rebound copies of Jesse James, King of the Bad Men of Deadwood, Badmen of Tombstone; other combinations possible. Issues with Kubert-a...	24.00	72.00	165.00

BADMEN OF THE WEST! (See A-1 Comics)
1953 - No. 3, 1954
Magazine Enterprises

	GD25	FN65	NM94
1(A-1 100)-Meskin-a?	16.00	48.00	110.00
2(A-1 120), 3: 2-Larsen-a	10.00	30.00	65.00

BADMEN OF TOMBSTONE
1950
Avon Periodicals

	GD25	FN65	NM94
nn	10.00	30.00	65.00

BAFFLING MYSTERIES (Formerly Indian Braves No. 1-4; Heroes of the Wild Frontier No. 26-on)
No. 5, Nov, 1951 - No. 26, Oct, 1955
Periodical House (Ace Magazines)

	GD25	FN65	NM94
5	14.00	43.00	100.00
6-24: 8-Woodish-a by Cameron. 10-E.C. Crypt Keeper swipe on-c. 24-Last pre-code issue	10.00	30.00	60.00
25-Reprints; surrealistic-c	7.50	22.50	45.00
26-Reprints	5.85	17.50	35.00

NOTE: ***Cameron** a-8, 10, 16-18, 20-22. **Colan** a-5, 11, 25r/5. **Sekowsky** a-5, 6, 22. Bondage c-20. Reprints in 18(1), 19(1), 24(3).*

BALBO (See Master Comics #33 & Mighty Midget Comics)

BALDER THE BRAVE
Nov, 1985 - No. 4, 1986 (Mini-series)
Marvel Comics Group

	GD25	FN65	NM94
1-4: Simonson-c/a; character from Thor			1.00

BALLAD OF HALO JONES, THE (Quality)(Value: cover or less)

BALLOONATIKS SUPER HEROES, THE (Best)(Value: cover or less)

BALOO & LITTLE BRITCHES
April, 1968 (Walt Disney)
Gold Key

	GD25	FN65	NM94
1-From the Jungle Book	2.80	7.00	14.00

BALTIMORE COLTS
1950 (Giveaway)
American Visuals Corp.

	GD25	FN65	NM94
nn-Eisner-c	43.00	130.00	300.00

BAMBI (See 4-Color No. 12,30,186, Movie Classics, Movie Comics, and Walt Disney Showcase No. 31)

Barbie #2, © Mattel

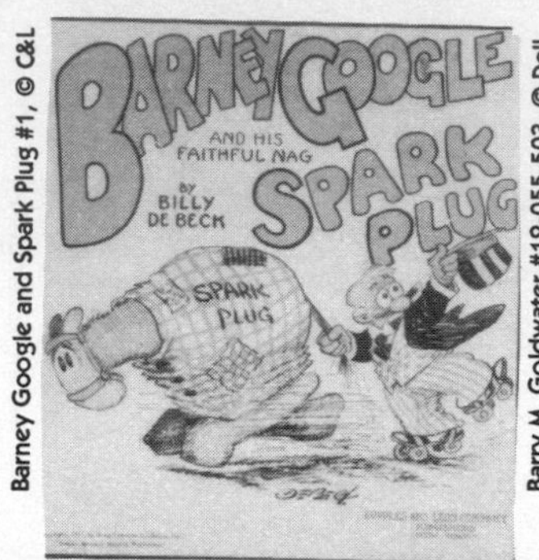

Barney Google and Spark Plug #1, © C&L

Barry M. Goldwater #12-055-503, © Dell

	GD25	FN65	NM94
BAMBI (Disney)			
1941, 1942, 1984			
K. K. Publications (Giveaways)/Whitman Publ. Co.			
1941-Horlick's Malted Milk & various toy stores; text & pictures; most copies mailed out with store stickers on-c	14.00	43.00	100.00
1942-Same as 4-Color #12, but no price (Same as '41 issue?) (Scarce)	22.00	65.00	150.00
1-(Whitman, 1984; 60 cents)-r/4-Color #186		.50	1.00
BAMM BAMM & PEBBLES FLINTSTONE (TV)			
Oct, 1964 (Hanna-Barbera)			
Gold Key			
1	5.00	15.00	35.00
BANANA OIL			
1924 (52 pages)(Black & White)			
MS Publ. Co.			
nn-Milt Gross-a; not reprints	24.00	73.00	170.00
BANANA SPLITS, THE (TV) (See March of Comics No. 364)			
June, 1969 - No. 8, Oct, 1971 (Hanna-Barbera)			
Gold Key			
1-Photo-c	2.30	6.75	16.00
2-8	1.30	3.25	8.00
BAND WAGON (See Hanna-Barbera Band Wagon)			
BANG-UP COMICS			
Dec, 1941 - No. 3, June, 1942			
Progressive Publishers			
1-Cosmo Mann & Lady Fairplay begin; Buzz Balmer by Rick Yager in all (origin #1)	58.00	175.00	375.00
2,3	35.00	105.00	225.00
BANNER COMICS (Becomes Captain Courageous No. 6)			
No. 3, Sept, 1941 - No. 5, Jan, 1942			
Ace Magazines			
3-Captain Courageous (1st app.) & Lone Warrior & Sidekick Dicky begin; Jim Mooney-c	75.00	225.00	475.00
4,5: 4-Flag-c	50.00	150.00	325.00
BARBARIANS, THE			
June, 1975			
Atlas Comics/Seaboard Periodicals			
1-Origin, only app. Andrax; Iron Jaw app.			1.00
BARBIE			
Jan, 1991 - Present ($1.00/$1.25, color)			
Marvel Comics			
1-Polybagged w/Barbie Pink Card; Romita-c		1.60	4.00
2-40: 13-Last $1.00-c			1.25
BARBIE & KEN			
May-July, 1962 - No. 5, Nov-Jan, 1963-64			
Dell Publishing Co.			
01-053-207(#1)-Based on Mattel toy dolls	31.00	92.00	215.00
2-4	22.00	66.00	155.00
5 (Rare)	26.00	80.00	185.00
BARBIE FASHION			
Jan, 1991 - Present ($1.00/$1.25, color)			
Marvel Comics			
1-Polybagged w/doorknob hanger		.80	2.00
2-40: 4-Contains preview to Sweet XVI. 13-Last $1.00-c			1.25
BARKER, THE (Also see National Comics #42)			
Autumn, 1946 - No. 15, Dec, 1949			
Quality Comics Group/Comic Magazine			
1	11.50	34.00	80.00

	GD25	FN65	NM94
2	5.85	17.50	35.00
3-10	4.20	12.50	25.00
11-14	4.00	10.00	20.00
15-Jack Cole-a(p)	4.70	14.00	28.00
NOTE: ***Jack Cole** art in some issues.*			
BARNEY AND BETTY RUBBLE (TV) (Flintstones' Neighbors)			
Jan, 1973 - No. 23, Dec, 1976 (Hanna-Barbera)			
Charlton Comics			
1	3.25	9.50	22.00
2-10	1.65	4.00	10.00
11-23: 11(2/75)-1st Mike Zeck-a (illos)	1.00	2.50	6.00
BARNEY BAXTER (Also see Magic Comics)			
1938 - No. 2, 1956			
David McKay/Dell Publishing Co./Argo			
Feature Books 15(McKay-1938)	24.00	72.00	165.00
4-Color 20(1942)	22.00	65.00	150.00
4,5	11.00	32.00	75.00
1,2(1956-Argo)	5.35	16.00	32.00
BARNEY BEAR ... (Spire Christian)(Value: cover or less)			
BARNEY GOOGLE & SNUFFY SMITH			
1942 - 1943; April, 1964			
Dell Publishing Co./Gold Key			
4-Color 19('42)	35.00	105.00	245.00
4-Color 40('44)	19.00	58.00	135.00
Large Feature Comic 11(1943)	19.00	58.00	135.00
1(10113-404)-Gold Key (4/64)	4.00	10.00	20.00
BARNEY GOOGLE & SNUFFY SMITH			
June, 1951 - No. 4, Feb, 1952 (Reprints)			
Toby Press			
1	10.00	30.00	65.00
2,3	5.85	17.50	35.00
4-Kurtzman-a "Pot Shot Pete," 5 pgs.; reprints John Wayne #5	7.00	21.00	42.00
BARNEY GOOGLE AND SNUFFY SMITH			
March, 1970 - No. 6, Jan, 1971			
Charlton Comics			
1	2.80	7.00	14.00
2-6	1.80	4.50	9.00
BARNEY GOOGLE AND SPARK PLUG (See Comic Monthly & Giant Comic Album)			
1923 - No. 6, 1928 (Daily strip reprints; B&W) (52 pages)			
Cupples & Leon Co.			
1-By Billy DeBeck	27.00	81.00	190.00
2-6	19.00	58.00	135.00
NOTE: *Started in 1918 as newspaper strip; Spark Plug began 1922, 1923.*			
BARNYARD COMICS (Dizzy Duck No. 32 on)			
June, 1944 - No. 31, Sept, 1950; No. 10, 1957			
Nedor/Polo Mag./Standard(Animated Cartoons)			
1(nn, 52 pgs.)	11.50	34.00	80.00
2 (52 pgs.)	6.70	20.00	40.00
3-5	4.70	14.00	28.00
6-12,16	4.00	11.00	22.00
13-15,17,21,23,26,27,29-All contain Frazetta text illos	4.70	14.00	28.00
18-20,22,24,25-All contain Frazetta-a & text illos	10.00	30.00	60.00
28,30,31	2.80	7.00	14.00
10(1957)(Exist?)	1.60	4.00	8.00
BARRY M. GOLDWATER			
March, 1965 (Complete life story)			
Dell Publishing Co.			
12-055-503-Photo-c	4.00	11.00	22.00

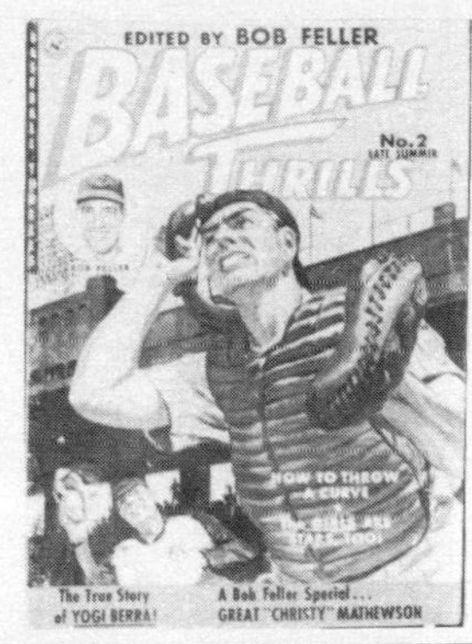

Baseball Thrills #2, © Z-D

Batman #26, © DC

Batman #97, © DC

GD25 FN65 NM94

BARTMAN (Also see Simpson's Comics & Radioactive Man)
1993 - Present ($1.95, color)
Bongo Comics

1-($2.95)-Foil-c; bound-in jumbo Bartman poster 1.20 3.00
2 .80 2.00

BASEBALL COMICS
Spring, 1949 (Reprinted later as a Spirit section)
Will Eisner Productions

1-Will Eisner-c/a 55.00 165.00 385.00

BASEBALL COMICS (Kitchen Sink)(Value: cover or less)

BASEBALL GREATS (Dark Horse)(Value: cover or less)

BASEBALL HEROES
1952 (One Shot)
Fawcett Publications

nn (Scarce)-Babe Ruth photo-c; baseball's Hall of Fame biographies
60.00 180.00 420.00

BASEBALL'S GREATEST HEROES
Dec, 1991 - No. 2, May, 1992 ($1.75, color)
Magnum Comics

1-Mickey Mantle #1; photo-c; Sinnott-a(p) .70 1.75
2-Brooks Robinson #1; photo-c; Sinnott-a(i) .70 1.75

BASEBALL THRILLS
No. 10, Sum, 1951 - No. 3, Sum, 1952 (Saunders painted-c No.1,2)
Ziff-Davis Publ. Co.

10(#1)-Bob Feller story 27.00 81.00 190.00
2-Powell-a(2)(Late Sum, '51)-Babe Ruth story 19.00 58.00 135.00
3-Kinstler-c/a; Joe DiMaggio story 19.00 58.00 135.00

BASEBALL THRILLS 3-D (3-D Zone)(Value: cover or less)

BASICALLY STRANGE (Magazine)
December, 1982 (B&W, $1.95)
John C. Comics (Archie Comics Group)

1-(21,000 printed, all but 1,000 destroyed; pages out of sequence)
.80 2.00
1-Wood, Toth-a; Corben-c. Reprints & new art .80 2.00

BASIC HISTORY OF AMERICA ILLUSTRATED
1976 (B&W) (Soft-c $1.50; Hard-c $4.50)
Pendulum Press

07-1999-America Becomes a World Power 1890-1920. 07-2251-The Industrial Era 1865-1915. 07-226x-Before the Civil War 1830-1860. 07-2278-Americans Move Westward 1800-1850. 07-2286-The Civil War 1850-1876; Redondo-a. 07-2294-The Fight for Freedom 1750-1783. 07-2308-The New World 1500-1750. 07-2316-Problems of the NewNation 1800-1830. 07-2324-Roaring Twenties and the Great Depression 1920-1940. 07-2332-The United States Emerges 1783-1800. 07-2340-America Today 1945-1976. 07-2359-World War II 1940-1945

BASIL (...the Royal Cat)
Jan, 1953 - No. 4, Sept, 1953
St. John Publishing Co.

1-Funny animal 4.00 10.00 20.00
2-4 2.40 6.00 12.00
I.W. Reprint 1 1.00 2.50 5.00

BASIL WOLVERTON'S GATEWAY TO HORROR (Dark Horse)(Value: cover or less)

BASIL WOLVERTON'S PLANET OF TERROR (Dark Horse)(Value: cover or less)

BATGIRL SPECIAL (See Teen Titans #50)
1988 ($1.50, color, one-shot, 52 pgs)
DC Comics

1 1.00 2.50

BAT LASH (See DC Special Series #16, Showcase #76 & Weird Western Tales)
Oct-Nov, 1968 - No. 7, Oct-Nov, 1969 (All 12¢ issues)
National Periodical Publications

GD25 FN65 NM94

Showcase #76 (8/68)-1st app. Bat Lash 3.00 9.00 30.00
1-(10-11/68)-2nd app. Bat Lash 1.85 5.50 13.00
2-7 1.30 3.25 8.00

BATMAN (See Arkham Asylum, Aurora, The Best of DC #2, Blind Justice, The Brave & the Bold, Cosmic Odyssey, DC 100-Page Super Spec. #14,20, DC Special, DC Special Series, Detective, Dynamic Classics, 80-Page Giants, Gotham By Gaslight, Gotham Nights, Greatest Batman Stories Ever Told, Greatest Joker Stories Ever Told, Heroes Against Hunger, The Joker, Justice League of America #250, Justice League Int., Legends of the Dark Knight, Limited Coll. Ed., Man-Bat, Power Record Comics, Real Fact #5, Saga of Ra's Al Ghul, Shadow of the..., Star Spangled, Super Friends, 3-D Batman, Untold Legend of..., Wanted... & World's Finest Comics)

BATMAN
Spring, 1940 - Present (#1-5 were quarterly)
National Periodical Publ./Detective Comics/DC Comics

GD25 FN65 VF82 NM94

1-Origin The Batman retold by Bob Kane; see Detective #33 for 1st origin; 1st app. Joker (2 stories which count as 1st & 2nd app.); 1st app. The Cat (Catwoman)(1st villainess in comics); has Batman story without Robin originally planned for Detective #38. This book was created entirely from the inventory of Det. Comics; 1st Batman/Robin pin-up on back-c
3,600.00 10,000.00 23,400.00 36,000.00
(Estimated up to 250+ total copies exist, 16 in NM/Mint)

1-Reprint, oversize 13-1/2x10". **WARNING**: This comic is an exact duplicate reprint of the original except for its size. DC published it in 1974 with a second cover titling it as a Famous First Edition. There have been many reported cases of the outer cover being removed and the interior sold as the original edition. The reprint with the new outer cover removed is practically worthless. See Famous First Edition for value.

GD25 FN65 NM94

2-3rd app. The Joker; 2nd app. Catwoman (out of costume) in Joker story; 1st time called Catwoman 870.00 2600.00 5700.00
3-3rd app Catwoman (1st in costume & 1st costumed villainess); 1st Puppet Master app. 617.00 1850.00 4000.00
4-5th app. The Joker (see Det. #45 for 4th) 467.00 1400.00 3200.00
5-1st app. of the Batmobile with its bat-head front
350.00 1050.00 2300.00
6-10: 8-Infinity-c. 9-1st Batman x-mas story; Burnley-c. 10-Cat-Woman story (gets new costume) 260.00 775.00 1700.00
11-Classic Joker-c by Ray/Robinson (3rd Joker-c, 6-7/42); Joker & Penguin app. 290.00 875.00 1900.00
12,13,15: 13-Jerry Siegel, creator of Superman appears in a Batman story. 15-New costume Catwoman 210.00 625.00 1400.00
14-2nd Penguin-c; Penguin app. (12-1/42-43) 235.00 700.00 1550.00
16-Intro/origin Alfred (4-5/43); cover is a reverse of #9 cover
470.00 1400.00 3000.00
17-20: 17-Penguin app. 18-Hitler, Hirohito, Mussolini-c. 20-1st Batmobile-c (12-1/43-44) 135.00 400.00 875.00
21,22,24,26,28-30: 21-1st skinny Alfred in Batman (2-3/44). 21,30-Penguin app. 22-1st Alfred solo-c/story (Alfred solo stories in 22-32,36); Catwoman app.; 2nd app. The Cavalier 108.00 325.00 700.00
23-Joker-c/story 167.00 500.00 1100.00
25-Only Joker/Penguin team-up; 1st team-up between two major villains
160.00 475.00 1000.00
27-Burnley Christmas-c; Penguin app. 140.00 410.00 900.00
31,32,34-36,39: 31-Infinity logo-c. 32-Origin Robin retold. 35-Catwoman story (in new costume w/o cat head mask). 36-Penguin app.
80.00 240.00 525.00
33-Christmas-c 96.00 290.00 625.00
37,40,44-Joker-c/stories 108.00 325.00 700.00
38-Penguin-c/story 92.00 275.00 600.00
41,45,46: 41-Penguin app. 45-Christmas-c/story; Catwoman story; Vicki Vale app. (1st app?) 62.00 185.00 415.00
42-2nd Catwoman-c (1st in Batman)(8-9/47); Catwoman story also
78.00 230.00 500.00
43-Penguin-c/story 78.00 230.00 500.00
47-1st detailed origin The Batman (6-7/48); 1st Bat-signal-c this title (see Detective #108) 216.00 650.00 1400.00
48-1000 Secrets of the Batcave; r-in #203; Penguin story
75.00 225.00 500.00
49-Joker-c/story; 1st app. Mad Hatter; Vicki Vale app.

Batman #113, © DC

Batman #200, © DC

Batman #344, © DC

	GD25	FN65	NM94
	108.00	325.00	700.00
50-Two-Face impostor app.	70.00	210.00	465.00
51,54,56,57,59,60: 57-Centerfold is a 1950 calendar. 59-1st app. Deadshot; Batman in the future-c/story	62.00	185.00	415.00
52,55-Joker-c/stories	75.00	225.00	500.00
53-Joker story	67.00	200.00	435.00
58-Penguin-c	67.00	200.00	435.00
61-Origin Batman Plane II	62.00	185.00	415.00
62-Origin Catwoman; Catwoman-c	84.00	250.00	550.00
63,80-Joker stories. 63-Flying saucer story (2-3/51)	54.00	162.00	350.00
64,67,70-72,74-77,79: 72-Last 52 pg. issue. 74-Used in **POP**, Pg. 90. 79-Vicki Vale in "The Bride of Batman"	50.00	150.00	325.00
65,69,84-Catwoman-c/stories. 84-Two-Face app.	54.00	160.00	350.00
66,73-Joker-c/stories. 73-Vicki Vale story	62.00	185.00	415.00
68,81-Two-Face-c/stories	50.00	150.00	325.00
78-(8-9/53)-Roh Kar, The Man Hunter from Mars story-the 1st lawman of Mars to come to Earth (green skinned)	62.00	185.00	415.00
82,83,85-89: 86-Intro Batmarine (Batman's submarine). 89-Last pre-code issue	48.00	142.00	300.00
90,91,93-99: 97-2nd app. Bat-Hound-c/story; Joker app.	34.00	100.00	225.00
92-1st app. Bat-Hound-c/story	44.00	132.00	290.00

	GD25	FN65	VF82	NM94
100 (6/56)	113.00	338.00	731.00	1125.00

	GD25	FN65	NM94
101-104,106-109: 103-3rd Bat-Hound-c/story. 108-Batgirl app.	36.00	107.00	250.00
105-1st Batwoman in Batman (2nd anywhere)	44.00	133.00	310.00
110-Joker story	36.00	107.00	250.00
111-120: 112-1st app. Signalman (super villain). 113-1st app. Fatman	25.00	75.00	175.00
121,122,124-126,128,130: 130-Lex Luthor app.	18.00	54.00	125.00
123-Joker story; Bat-Hound app.	21.00	62.00	145.00
127-Batman vs. Thor the Tunder God-c/story (10/59); Joker story; Superman cameo	21.00	62.00	145.00
129-Origin Robin retold; bondage-c	22.00	66.00	155.00
131-135,137-139,141-143: 131-Intro 2nd Batman & Robin series. 133-1st Bat-Mite in Batman (3rd app. anywhere). 134-Origin The Dummy. 139-Intro 1st Bat-Girl; only app. Signalman as the Blue Bowman. 141-2nd app. old Bat-Girl. 143-Last 10 cent issue	13.00	40.00	90.00
136-Joker-c/story	19.00	56.00	130.00
140,144-Joker stories. 140-Batwoman-c only; Superman cameo	13.00	38.00	88.00
145,148-Joker-c/stories	15.00	45.00	105.00
146,147,149,150	10.00	30.00	70.00
151,153,154,156-158,160-162,164-168,170: 156-Ant-Man/Robin team-up (6/63). 164-New Batmobile (6/64); new look & Mystery Analysts series begins	7.00	21.00	50.00
152-Joker story	7.00	21.00	50.00
155-1st S.A. app. The Penguin (4/63)	30.00	90.00	210.00
159,163-Joker-c/stories	9.00	27.00	63.00
169-Early SA Penguin app. (2nd app?)	12.00	36.00	85.00
171-1st Riddler app.(5/65) since Dec. 1948	43.00	129.00	300.00
172-175,177,178,180,181,183,184: 181-Batman & Robin poster insert; intro. Poison Ivy	5.00	14.00	33.00
176-(80-Pg. Giant G-17); Joker-c/story; Penguin app. in strip-r; Catwoman reprint	6.00	19.00	44.00
179-2nd app. Silver Age Riddler	11.00	32.00	75.00
182,187-(80 Pg. Giants G-24, G-30); Joker-c/stories	5.00	15.00	35.00
185-(80 Pg. Giant G-27)	4.00	13.00	30.00
186-Joker-c/story	3.25	9.50	22.00
188,189,191,192,194-196,199: 189-1st S.A. app. Scarecrow	2.15	6.50	15.00
190-Penguin app.	3.20	8.00	20.00
193-(80-Pg. Giant G-37)	3.20	8.00	20.00
197-4th S.A. Catwoman app. cont'd from Det. #369; 1st new Batgirl app. in Batman (4th anywhere)	6.50	19.00	45.00
198-(80-Pg. Giant G-43); Joker-c/story-r/World's Finest #61; Catwoman-r/ Det. #211; Penguin-r; origin-r/#47	8.00	24.00	55.00
200-(3/68)-Joker cameo; retells origin of Batman & Robin; 1st Neal Adams work this title (cover only)	18.00	54.00	125.00
201-Joker story	3.20	8.00	20.00
202,204-207,209,210	1.65	4.70	11.00
203-(80 Pg. Giant G-49); r/#48, 61, & Det. 185; Batcave Blueprints	2.15	6.50	15.00
208-(80 Pg. Giant G-55); New origin Batman by Gil Kane plus 3 G.A. Batman reprints w/Catwoman, Vicki Vale & Batwoman	2.70	8.00	19.00
211,212,214-217: 212-Last 12 cent issue. 214-Alfred given a new last name-"Pennyworth" (see Detective #96)	1.65	4.70	11.00
213-(80-Pg. Giant G-61); 30th anniversary issue (7-8/69); origin Alfred (r/Batman #16), Joker(r/Det. #168), Clayface; new origin Robin with new facts	4.85	15.00	34.00
218-(80-Pg. Giant G-67)	2.15	6.50	15.00
219-Neal Adams-a	3.20	9.00	21.00
220,221,224-227,229-231	1.65	4.00	10.00
222-Beatles take-off; art lesson by Jack Kirby	3.20	9.00	21.00
223,228,233-(80-Pg. Giants G-73,G-79,G-85)	1.70	5.00	12.00
232,237-N. Adams-a. 232-Intro/1st app. Ras Al Ghul; origin Batman & Robin retold. 237-G.A. Batman-r/Det. #37; 1st app. The Reaper; Wrightson/ Ellison plots	3.85	11.50	27.00
234-1st S.A. app. Two-Face; N. Adams-a; 52 pg. issues begin, end #242	8.00	24.00	55.00
235,236,239-242: 239-XMas-c. 241-Reprint/#5	1.50	3.75	9.00
238-DC-8 100 pg. Super Spec.; G.A. Atom, Sargon (r/Sensation #57), Plastic Man (r/Police #14) stories; Doom Patrol origin-r; Batman, Legion, Aquaman-r; N. Adams wraparound-c	1.60	4.00	9.50
243-245-Neal Adams-a	2.40	7.25	17.00
246-250,252,253: 253-Shadow app.	1.50	3.75	9.00
251-N. Adams-c/a; Joker-c/story	4.85	15.00	34.00
254,256-259,261-All 100 pg. editions; part-r. 258-Joker app.	1.60	4.00	9.50
255-N. Adams-c/a; tells of Bruce Wayne's father who wore bat costume & fought crime (100 pgs.); r/story Batman #22	2.15	6.50	15.00
260-Joker-c/story (100 pgs.)	3.60	10.75	25.00
262-285,287-290,292,293,295-299: 262-(68pgs.). 266-Catwoman back to old costume	1.00	2.50	6.00
286,291,294-Joker-c/stories	1.30	3.25	8.00
300-Double-size	1.30	3.25	8.00
301-320,322-352: 304-(44 pgs.). 310-1st app. The Gentleman Ghost. 311-Batgirl reteams w/Batman. 313,314-Two-Face-c/stories. 316-Robin returns. 322-324-Catwoman (Selina Kyle) app. 322,323-Cat-Man cameos (1st in Batman, 1 panel each). 323-1st meeting Catwoman & Cat-Man. 332-Catwoman's 1st solo. 325-Death of Comm. Gordon. 345-1st app. new Dr. Death. 357,358-1st app. Killer Croc. 361-1st app. Harvey Bullock	1.25	3.00	7.50
321,353,359-Joker-c/stories	1.30	3.25	8.00
354-356,358,360-365,369,370: 358-Killer Croc app.	1.00	2.50	6.00
357-1st app. Jason Todd (3/83); see Det. 524	1.50	3.75	9.00
366-Jason Todd 1st in Robin costume; Joker-c/sy	3.20	9.00	21.00
368-1st new Robin in costume (Jason Todd)	2.30	6.75	16.00
371-399,401-403: 386,387-Intro Black Mask (villain). 401-2nd app. Magpie (see Man of Steel #3 for 1st). 403-Joker cameo		1.20	3.00

NOTE: *Most issues between 397 & 432 were reprinted in 1989 and sold in multi-packs. Some are not identified as reprints but have newer ads copyrighted after cover dates. 2nd and 3rd printings exist.*

	GD25	FN65	NM94
400 ($1.50, 68pgs.)-Dark Knight special; intro by Stephen King; Art Adams/ Austin-a	2.30	6.75	16.00
404-Miller scripts begin (end 407); Year 1; 1st modern app. Catwoman (2/87)	2.00	6.00	14.00
405-407: 407-Year 1 ends (See Det. for Year 2)	1.00	2.00	5.00
408-410: New Origin Jason Todd (Robin)	1.00	2.50	5.50

411-416,421-425: 412-Origin/1st app. Mime. 414-Starlin scripts begin, end

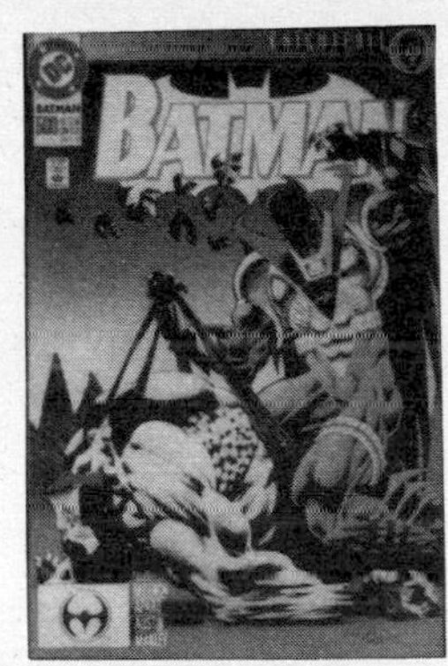

Batman #500 (regular edition), © DC

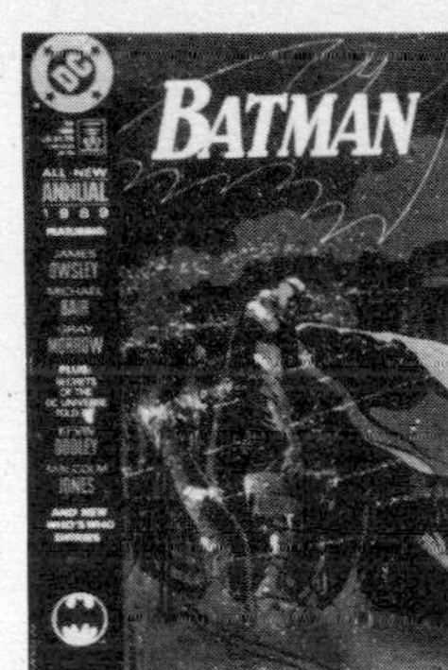

Batman Annual #13, © DC

Batman: Tales of the Demon nn, © DC

	GD25	FN65	NM94
#429. 416-Nightwing-c/story		1.00	2.50
417-420: "Ten Nights of the Beast" storyline	1.65	4.00	10.00
426-($1.50, 52 pgs.)-"A Death In The Family" storyline begins, ends #429	1.20	3.00	7.25
427-"A Death In The Family" part 2	1.00	2.60	6.25
428-Death of Robin (Jason Todd)	1.15	2.75	6.75
429-Joker-c/story; Superman app.	1.00	2.00	5.00
430-432		.80	2.00
433-435-"Many Deaths of the Batman" story by John Byrne-c/scripts		1.00	2.50
436-Year 3 begins (ends #439); origin original Robin retold by Nightwing (Dick Grayson); 1st app. Timothy Drake (8/89)	1.00	2.00	5.00
436-2nd print			1.00
437-439: 437-Origin Robin continued		1.00	2.50
440,441: "A Lonely Place of Dying" Parts 1 & 3			1.00
442-1st app. Timothy Drake in Robin costume	1.00	2.00	5.00
443-456,458,459,462-464: 445-447-Batman goes to Russia. 448,449-"The Penguin Affair" parts 1 & 3. 450,451-Joker-c/stories. 452-454-"Dark Knight Dark City" storyline; Riddler app. 455-Alan Grant scripts begin, ends #466, 470. 464-Last solo Batman story; free 16 pg. preview of Impact Comics line			1.50
457-Timothy Drake officially becomes Robin & dons new costume	1.40	3.50	8.50
457-Direct sale edition (has #000 in indicia)	1.00	2.00	5.00
460,461-Two part Catwoman story		.80	2.00
465-Robin returns to action with Batman			1.50
466-487: 470-War of the Gods x-over. 475,476-The return of Scarface-c/story. 476-Last $1.00-c. 477,478-Photo-c			1.25
488-Cont'd from Batman: Sword of Azrael #4; Azrael-c & app.	1.70	5.00	12.00
489-Bane-c/story; 1st app. Azrael in Bat-costume	1.50	3.75	9.00
490-Riddler-c/story; Azrael & Bane app.	1.25	3.00	7.50
491-Knightfall lead-in; Joker-c/story; Azrael & Bane app.; Kelley Jones-c begin	1.00	2.00	5.00
492-Knightfall part 1; Bane app.	1.65	4.00	10.00
492-Platinum edition (promo copy)			25.00
493-Knightfall part 3	1.20	3.00	7.00
494-Knightfall part 5; Joker-c & app.		1.00	2.50
495-Knightfall part 7; brief Bane & Joker apps.		.80	2.00
496-Knightfall part 9; Joker-c/story; Bane cameo			1.25
497-Knightfall part 11; has B&W outer-c; Bane vs. Batman-c/story	1.65	4.00	10.00
497-2nd printing			1.25
498-Knightfall part 15; Bane & Catwoman-c & app. (see Showcase 93 #7 & 8)		.80	2.00
499-Knightfall part 17; Bane app.		.80	2.00
500-($2.50, 68 pgs.)-Knightfall part 19; Azrael in new Bat-costume; Bane-c/story		1.00	2.50
500-($3.95, 68 pgs.)-Collector's Edition w/die-cut double-c w/foil by Joe Quesada & 2 bound-in post cards		1.60	4.00
501-506: 501-Begin $1.50-c			1.50
Annual 1(8-10/61)-Swan-c	40.00	120.00	400.00
Annual 2	15.00	45.00	150.00
Annual 3(Summer, '62)-Joker-c/story	17.00	51.00	170.00
Annual 4,5	7.00	21.00	70.00
Annual 6,7(7/64, 25 cents, 80 pgs.)	5.00	15.00	50.00
Annual V5#8(1982)-Painted-c		1.60	4.00
Annual 9,10,12: 9(7/85). 10(1986). 12(1988, $1.50)		1.10	2.75
Annual 11(1987, $1.25)-Penguin-c/story; Alan Moore scripts	1.00	2.00	5.00
Annual 13(1989, $1.75, 68 pgs.)-Gives history of Bruce Wayne, Dick Grayson, Jason Todd, Alfred, Comm. Gordon, Barbara Gordon (Batgirl) & Vicki Vale; Morrow-i		.90	2.20
Annual 14('90, $2.00, 68 pgs.)-Origin Two-Face		.80	2.00
Annual 15('91, $2.00, 68 pgs.)-Armageddon 2001 x-over; Joker app.; 2nd printing exists		.80	2.00

	GD25	FN65	NM94
Annual 16('92, $2.50, 68 pgs.)-Joker-c/s; Kieth-c		1.00	2.50
Annual 17('93, $2.50, 68 pgs.)-Azrael in Bat-costume; intro Ballistic		1.00	2.50
Special 1 (4/84)-Golden-c/a	1.00	2.00	5.00
Pizza Hut giveaway(12/77)-exact-r of #122,123; Joker-c/story		1.20	3.00
Prell Shampoo giveaway(1966, 16 pgs.)-"The Joker's Practical Jokes" (6-7/8x3-3/8")	3.60	9.00	18.00

NOTE: ***Art Adams*** *a-400p.* ***Neal Adams*** *c-200, 203, 210, 217, 219-222, 224-227, 229, 230, 232, 234, 236-241, 243-246, 251, 255, Annual 14.* ***Bolland*** *c-445-447.* ***Burnley*** *a-10, 12-18, 20, 25, 27; c-9, 15, 16, 27, 28p, 40p, 42p.* ***Byrne*** *c-401, 433-435, 533-535, Annual 11.* ***Travis Charest*** *c-488-490p.* ***Colan*** *a-340p, 343-345p, 348-351p, 373p, 383p; c-343p, 345p, 350p.* ***J. Cole*** *a-238r.* ***Cowan*** *a-Annual 10p.* ***Golden*** *a-295p, 303p.* ***Alan Grant*** *scripts-455-466, 470, 474-476, 479, 480, Annual 16(part).* ***Grell*** *a-287, 288p, 289p, 290; c-287-290.* ***Infantino/Anderson*** *c-167, 173, 175, 181, 186, 191, 192, 194, 195, 198, 199.* ***Kelley Jones*** *c-491-499, 500(newsstand), 501-505.* ***Kaluta*** *c-242, 2G.* ***Kane/Anderson*** *c-178-180. 48, 253, Annual 12.* ***Bob Kane*** *a-1, 2, 5; c-1-5, 7, 17.* ***G. Kane*** *a-(i)-254, 255, 259, 261, 353i.* ***Kubert*** *a-238r, 400; c-310, 319p, 327, 328, 344.* ***McFarlane*** *c-423.* ***Moldoff*** *c-101-140.* ***Moldoff/Giella*** *a-164-175, 177-181, 183, 184, 186.* ***Moldoff/Greene*** *a-169, 172-174, 177-179, 181, 184.* ***Mooney*** *a-255r.* ***Newton*** *a-305, 306, 328p, 331p, 332p, 337p, 338p, 346p, 352-357p, 360-372p, 374-378p; c-374p, 378p.* ***Nino*** *a-Annual 9.* ***Irv Novick*** *c-201, 202.* ***Perez*** *a-400; c-436-442.* ***Robinson/Roussos*** *a-12, 17, 20, 22, 24, 25, 27, 28, 31, 33, 37.* ***Robinson*** *a-12, 14, 18, 22-32,34, 36, 37, 255r, 260r, 261r; c-6, 8, 10, 12-15, 18, 21, 24, 26, 30, 37, 39.* ***Simonson*** *a-300p, 312p, 321p; c-300p, 312p, 366, 413i.* ***P. Smith*** *a-Annual 9.* ***Dick Sprang*** *c-19, 20, 22, 23, 29, 31-36, 38, 51, 55, 66, 73, 76.* ***Starlin*** *c/a-402.* ***Staton*** *a-334.* ***Wrightson*** *a-265i, 400; c-320r. Catwoman back-ups in 332, 345, 346, 348-351. Joker app. in 1, 2, 4, 5, 7-9, 11-13, 19, 20, 23, 25, 28, 32 & many more. Robin solo back-up stories in 337-339, 341-343.*

BATMAN (Books and trade paperbacks)

	GD25	FN65	NM94
...And Dracula: Red Rain nn(1991, $24.95)-Hard-c; Elseworlds storyline	6.50	19.00	45.00
...And Dracula: Red Rain nn(1992, $9.95)-Soft-c	1.65	4.00	10.00
Arkham Asylum Hard-c ('89, $24.95)	3.60	10.75	25.00
Arkham Asylum trade pb (#14.95)	2.15	6.50	15.00
Birth of the Demon Hard cover (1992, $24.95)	3.60	10.75	25.00
Birth of the Demon Soft cover (1993, $12.95)	1.85	5.50	13.00
Blind Justice nn (1992, $7.50)-r/Det. #598-600	1.25	3.00	7.50
Bride of the Demon Hard cover (1990, $19.95)	3.20	8.00	20.00
Bride of the Demon Soft cover ($12.95)	1.85	5.50	13.00
Death In The Family trade paperback (1988, $3.95)-r/Batman #426-429 by Aparo	1.00	2.00	5.00
Death In The Family: 2nd - 5th printings		1.60	4.00
Digital Justice nn (1990, $24.95, hardcover)-Computer generated art	3.60	10.75	25.00
...Gothic nn (1992, $12.95)-r/Legends of the Dark Knight #6-10	1.85	5.50	13.00
Lonely Place of Dying (1990, $3.95, 132 pgs.)-r/Batman #440-442 & New Titans #60,61; Perez-c		1.60	4.00
...: The Many Deaths of the Batman trade paperback (1992, $3.95, 84 pgs.)-r/Batman #433-435 w/new Byrne-c		1.60	4.00
...: Prey nn (1992, $12.95)-Gulacy/Austin-a	1.85	5.50	13.00
Shaman nn (1993, $12.95)-r/Legends/D.K. #1-5	1.85	5.50	13.00
...: Son of the Demon Hard cover (9/87, $14.95	7.00	21.00	50.00
...: Son of the Demon limited signed & numbered hard-c (1,700)	11.00	32.00	75.00
...: Son of the Demon softcover w/new-c ($8.95)	1.50	3.75	9.00
...: Son of the Demon softcover, 2nd print (1989, $9.95)-4th print	1.65	4.00	10.00
...: Tales of the Demon nn (1991, $17.95, 212 pgs.)-Intro by Sam Hamm; reprints by N. Adams(3) & Golden; contains Saga of Ra's Al Ghul #1	2.60	7.50	18.00
...: Venom trade paperback (1993, $9.95)-r/Legends of the Dark Knight #16-20; embossed-c	1.65	4.00	10.00
Year One Hardcover (1988, $12.95)	1.85	5.50	13.00
Year One trade paperback (1988, $9.95)-r/Batman #404-407 by Miller; introduction by Miller	1.65	4.00	10.00
Year One trade paperback: 2nd & 3rd prints	1.65	4.00	10.00
Year Two trade paperback (1990, $9.95)-r/Det. 575-578 by McFarlane; wraparound-c	1.65	4.00	10.00

Batman: Full Circle nn, © DC

Batman Adventures #13, © DC

Batman: The Cult #2, © DC

GD25 FN65 NM94

BATMAN (One-Shots)
Barman and Other DC Classics 1 (1989, giveaway)-DC Comics/Diamond Comic Distributors; Batman origin-r/Batman #47, Camelot 3000-r by Bolland, Justice League-r('87), New Teen Titans-r by Perez 1.00
...: Catwoman Defiant nn (1992, $4.95, color, one-shot, prestige format)-Milligan scripts; c-interlocks w/Batman: Penguin Triumphant; special foil logo 1.00 2.00 5.00
Full Circle nn (1991, $5.95, stiff-c, 68 pgs.)-Sequel to Batman: Year Two 1.00 2.50 6.00
...Gotham By Gaslight ('89, $3.95) 1.60 4.00
.../Green Arrow: The Poison Arrow nn (1992, $5.95, squarebound, 68 pgs.)-Netzer-c/a 1.00 2.50 6.00
Holy Terror nn (1991, $4.95, 52 pgs.)-Elseworlds 1.00 2.00 5.00
.../Houdini: The Devil's Workshop (1993, $5.95) 1.00 2.50 6.00
...Judge Dredd: Judgement on Gotham nn (1991, $5.95, 68 pgs.)-Grant/Wagner scripts; Simon Bisley-c/a 1.00 2.50 6.00
...Judge Dredd: Judgement on Gotham 2nd print 1.00 2.50 6.00
...: Master of the Future nn (1991, $5.95, 68 pgs.)-Elseworlds storyline; sequel to Gotham By Gaslight; embossed-c 1.00 2.50 6.00
...Movie Special ('89, $2.50, regular) 1.00 2.50
...Movie Special ('89, $4.95, deluxe) 1.00 2.00 5.00
...: Penguin Triumphant nn (1992, $4.95, one-shot)-Staton-a(p); special foil logo 1.00 2.00 5.00
...Returns Movie Special ('92, $3.95) 1.60 4.00
...Returns Movie Prestige ('92, $5.95) 1.00 2.50 6.00
...: Seduction of the Gun nn (1992, $2.50, 68 pgs.) 1.00 2.50
...: The Blue, the Grey, & the Bat nn (1992, $5.95, 68 pgs.)-Weiss/Lopez-a 1.00 2.50 6.00
...: Vengeance of Bane Special 1 (1992, $2.50, 68 pgs.)-Origin & 1st app. Bane (see Batman #491) 3.20 8.00 20.00
...: Vengeance of Bane Special 1-2nd printing 1.00 2.50

BATMAN (Kellogg's Poptarts comics)
1966 (Set of 6) (16 pages)
National Periodical Publications
"The Man in the Iron Mask," "The Penguin's Fowl Play," "The Joker's Happy Victims," "The Catwoman's Catnapping Caper," "The Mad Hatter's Hat Crimes," "The Case of the Batman II" each.... 3.20 8.00 16.00
NOTE: *All above were folded and placed in Poptarts boxes.* ***Infantino*** *art on Catwoman and Joker issues.*

BATMAN ADVENTURES, THE (TV cartoon)
Oct, 1992 - Present (1.25, color)
DC Comics
1-Based on Fox TV cartoon; Penguin-c/s 1.40 3.50
2-6,8-15: 2-Catwoman-c/story. 3-Joker-c/story. 5-Scarecrow .80 2.00
7-Polybagged with Man-Bat trading card 1.25 3.00 7.50
16-18: 16-Begin $1.50-c 1.50

BATMAN AND THE OUTSIDERS (The Adventures of the Outsiders#33 on) (Also see Brave & The Bold #200 & The Outsiders)
Aug, 1983 - No. 32, Apr, 1986 (Mando paper #5 on)
DC Comics
1-32: 1-Batman, Halo, Geo-Force, Katana, Metamorpho & Black Lightning begin. 5-New Teen Titans x-over. 9-Halo begins. 11,12-Origin Katana. 18-More facts about Metamorpho's origin. 28-31-Lookers origin. 32-Team disbands 1.00
Annual 1(9/84)-Miller/Aparo-c; Aparo-i 1.00
Annual 2(9/85)-Metamorpho & Sapphire Stagg wed; Aparo-c 1.00
NOTE: ***Aparo*** *a-1-9, 11, 12p, 16-20; c-1-4, 5i, 6-21.* ***B. Kane*** *a-3r.* ***Layton*** *a-19i, 20i.* ***Lopez*** *a-3p.* ***Perez*** *c-5p.* ***B. Willingham*** *a-14p.*

BATMAN FAMILY, THE
Sept-Oct, 1975 - No. 20, Oct-Nov, 1978 (#1-4, 17-on: 68 pages)
(Combined with Detective Comics with No. 481)
National Periodical Publications/DC Comics

GD25 FN65 NM94

1-Origin Batgirl-Robin team-up (The Dynamite Duo); reprints plus one new story begins; N. Adams-a(r) 1.60 4.00
2-5: 3-Batgirl & Robin learn each's i.d. 1.10 2.75
6,9-Joker's daughter on cover (1st app?) 1.20 3.00
7,8,10,14-16: 10-1st revival Batwoman 1.10 2.75
11-13: Rogers-a(p). 11-New stories begin; Man-Bat begins 1.60 4.00
17-($1.00 size)-Batman, Huntress begin 1.10 2.75
18-20: Huntress by Staton in all. 20-Origin Ragman retold 1.50
NOTE: ***Aparo*** *a-17; c-11-16.* ***Austin*** *a-12i.* ***Chaykin*** *a-14p.* ***Michael Golden*** *a-15-17,18-20p.* ***Grell*** *a-1; c-1.* ***Gil Kane*** *a-2r.* ***Kaluta*** *c-17, 19.* ***Newton*** *a-13.* ***Robinson*** *a-1r, 3i(r), 9r.* ***Russell*** *a-18i, 19i.* ***Starlin*** *a-17; c-18, 20.*

BATMAN GALLERY, THE
1992 ($2.95, color, glossy stock)
DC Comics
1-Reprints covers & art from 1939-1992 1.20 3.00

BATMAN/GRENDEL
1993 - No. 2, 1993 ($4.95, color, mini-series, 52 pgs.)
DC Comics
1-Devil's Riddle; by Matt Wagner 1.00 2.00 5.00
2-Devil's Masque; by Matt Wagner 1.00 2.00 5.00

BATMAN: LEGENDS OF THE DARK KNIGHT (See Legends of the...)

BATMAN MINIATURE (See Batman Kellogg's)

BATMAN RECORD COMIC
1966 (One Shot)
National Periodical Publications
1-With record (still sealed) 16.00 48.00 110.00
Comic only 2.80 7.00 14.00

BATMAN RETURNS: THE OFFICIAL COMIC ADAPTATION OF THE WARNER BROS. MOTION PICTURE
1992
DC Comics
nn-($3.95, regular format)-Adapts movie sequel 1.60 4.00
nn-($5.95, squarebound)-Dorman painted-c 1.00 2.50 6.00

BATMAN: RUN, RIDDLER, RUN
1992 - Book 3, 1992 ($4.95, color, mini-series)
DC Comics
Book 1-3: Mark Badger-a & plot 1.00 2.00 5.00

BATMAN: SHADOW OF THE BAT
June, 1992 - Present ($1.50-$1.75, color)
DC Comics
1-The Last Arkham-c/story begins, ends #4 1.20 3.00
1-(2.50)-Deluxe edition polybagged w/poster, pop-up & book mark 1.00 2.00 5.00
2-7: 7-Last $1.50-c 1.50
8-26: 16-18-Knightfall tie-ins. 19-22-Knightquest tie-ins w/Azrael as Batman. 19,20-Painted-c .70 1.75
Annual 1 (1993, $3.50, 68 pgs.) 1.40 3.50

BATMAN SPECTACULAR (See DC Special Series No. 15)

BATMAN: SWORD OF AZRAEL
Oct, 1992 - No. 4, Jan, 1993 ($1.75, color, mini-series)
DC Comics
1-Wraparound gatefold-c; Quesada-c/a(p) in all; 1st app. Azrael 2.15 6.50 15.00
2-4: 4-Cont'd in Batman #488 1.65 4.00 10.00
Silver Edition 1-4 (1993, $1.95)-Reprints #1-4 .80 2.00
Trade Paperback (1993, $9.95)-Reprints #1-4 1.65 4.00 10.00
Trade Paperback Gold Edition 2.15 6.50 15.00

BATMAN: THE CULT
1988 - No. 4, Nov, 1988 ($3.50, color, deluxe mini-series)

Batman: The Killing Joke #1, © DC

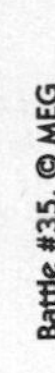
Battle #35, © MEG

Battle Attack #1, © Stanmor Publ.

DC Comics

	GD25	FN65	NM94
1-Wrightson-a/painted-c in all	1.00	2.00	5.00
2-4		1.80	4.00
Trade Paperback ('91, $14.95)-New Wrightson-c	2.15	6.50	15.00

BATMAN: THE DARK KNIGHT
March, 1986 - No. 4, 1986 ($2.95, color, squarebound)
DC Comics

	GD25	FN65	NM94
1-Miller story & c/a(p); set in the future	2.15	6.50	15.00
1-2nd & 3rd printings		1.20	3.00
2-Carrie Kelly becomes Robin (female)	1.25	3.00	7.50
2-2nd & 3rd printings		1.20	3.00
3-Death of Joker; Superman app.	1.00	2.00	5.00
3-2nd printing		1.20	3.00
4-Death of Alfred; Superman app.		1.40	3.50
Hardcover, signed & numbered edition ($40.00)(4000 copies)			150.00
Hardcover, trade edition	4.30	13.00	30.00
Softcover, trade edition (1st printing only)	1.65	4.00	10.00
Softcover, trade edition (2nd thru 8th printings)	1.25	3.00	7.50

NOTE: *The #2 second printings can be identified by matching the grey background colors on the inside front cover and facing page. The inside front cover of the second printing has a dark grey background which does not match the lighter grey of the facing page. On the true 1st printings, the backgrounds are both light grey. All other issues areclearly marked.*

BATMAN: THE KILLING JOKE
1988 ($3.50, color, deluxe, 52 pgs., adults)
DC Comics

	GD25	FN65	NM94
1-Bolland-c/a; Alan Moore scripts	1.50	3.75	9.00
1-2nd thru 8th printings		1.40	3.50

BATMAN: THE OFFICIAL COMIC ADAPTATION OF THE WARNER BROS. MOTION PICTURE
1989 ($2.50, $4.95, 68 pgs.) (Movie adaptation)
DC Comics

	GD25	FN65	NM94
1-Regular format ($2.50)-Ordway-c/a		1.60	4.00
1-Prestige format ($4.95)-Diff.-c, same insides	1.00	2.50	6.00

BATMAN 3-D (Also see 3-D Batman)
1990 ($9.95, w/glasses, 8-1/8x10-3/4")
DC Comics

	GD25	FN65	NM94
nn-Byrne-a/scripts; Riddler, Joker, Penguin & Two-Face app. plus r/1953 3-D Batman; pin-ups by many artists	1.65	4.00	10.00

BATMAN: TWO-FACE STRIKES TWICE
1993 - No. 2, 1993 ($4.95, color, 52 pgs.)
DC Comics

	GD25	FN65	NM94
1,2-Flip book format w/Staton-a (G.A. side)	1.00	2.00	5.00

BATMAN VERSUS PREDATOR
1991 - No. 3, 1992 (Mini-series, color)
DC Comics/Dark Horse Comics

	GD25	FN65	NM94
1 (Prestige format, $4.95)-1 & 3 contain 8 Batman/Predator trading cards; Andy & Adam Kubert-a; Suydam painted-c	1.00	2.50	5.50
1 (Regular format, $1.95)-No trading cards		1.00	2.50
2-(Prestige)-Extra pin-ups inside; Suydam-c	1.00	2.00	5.00
2-(Regular)-Without cards		1.00	2.50
3-(Prestige)-Suydam-c	1.00	2.00	5.00
3 (Regular)-Without cards		1.00	2.50
Trade paperback nn (1992, $5.95, 132pgs.)-r/#1-3 w/new introductions & forward plus new wraparound-c by Gibbons	1.00	2.50	6.00

BATMAN VS. THE INCREDIBLE HULK (See DC Special Series No. 27)

BAT MASTERSON (TV) (Also see Tim Holt #28)
Aug-Oct, 1959; Feb-Apr, 1960 - No. 9, Nov-Jan, 1961-62
Dell Publishing Co.

	GD25	FN65	NM94
4-Color 1013 (#1) (8-10/59)	10.00	30.00	60.00
2-9: Gene Barry photo-c on all	5.85	17.50	35.00

BATS (See Tales Calculated to Drive You Bats)

BATS, CATS & CADILLACS (Now)(Value: cover or less)

BATTLE
March, 1951 - No. 70, June, 1960
Marvel/Atlas Comics(FPI No. 1-62/Male No. 63 on)

	GD25	FN65	NM94
1	11.00	32.00	75.00
2	5.35	16.00	32.00
3-10: 4-1st Buck Pvt. O'Toole. 10-Pakula-a	4.20	12.50	25.00
11-20: 11-Check-a	4.00	10.00	20.00
21,23-Krigstein-a	4.70	14.00	28.00
22,24-36: 32-Tuska-a. 36-Everett-a	3.20	8.00	16.00
37-Kubert-a (Last precode, 2/55)	3.60	9.00	18.00
38-40,42-48	2.80	7.00	14.00
41-Kubert/Moskowitz-a	3.60	9.00	18.00
49-Davis-a	4.00	10.00	20.00
50-54,56-58	2.80	7.00	14.00
55-Williamson-a (5 pgs.)	4.70	14.00	28.00
59-Torres-a	3.20	8.00	16.00
60-62: 60,62-Combat Kelly app. 61-Combat Casey app.	2.80	7.00	14.00
63-66: 63-Ditko-a. 64-66-Kirby-a. 66-Davis-a; has story of Fidel Castro in pre-Communism days (an admiring profile)	4.70	14.00	28.00
67,68: 67-Williamson/Crandall-a (4 pgs.); Kirby, Davis-a. 68-Kirby/Williamson-a (4 pgs.); Kirby/Ditko-a	5.35	16.00	32.00
69,70: 69-Kirby-a. 70-Kirby/Ditko-a	4.35	13.00	26.00

NOTE: ***Andru** a-37. **Berg** a-38, 14, 60-62. **Colan** a-33, 55. **Everett** a-36, 50, 70; c-56, 57. **Heath** a-6, 9, 13, 31, 69; c-6, 9, 12, 26, 35, 37. **Kirby** c-64-69. **Maneely** a-4, 6, 31, 61; c-4, 33, 59, 61. **Orlando** a-47. **Powell** a-53, 55. **Reinman** a-8, 9, 26, 32. **Robinson** a-9, 39. **Romita** a-26. **Severin** a-28, 32-34, 66-69; c-36, 55. **Sinnott** a-33, 37. **Woodbridge** a-52, 55.*

BATTLE ACTION
Feb, 1952 - No. 12, 5/53; No. 13, 11/54 - No. 30, 8/57
Atlas Comics (NPI)

	GD25	FN65	NM94
1-Pakula-a	11.00	32.00	75.00
2	5.35	16.00	32.00
3,4,6,7,9,10: 6-Robinson-c/a. 7-Partial nudity	4.00	11.00	22.00
5-Used in **POP**, pg. 93,94	4.00	10.00	20.00
8-Krigstein-a	4.70	14.00	28.00
11-15 (Last precode, 2/55)	4.00	10.00	20.00
16-26,28,29	2.80	7.00	14.00
27,30-Torres-a	3.60	9.00	18.00

NOTE: *Battle Brady app. 5-7, 10-12. **Berg** a-3. **Check** a-11. **Everett** a-7; c-13, 25. **Heath** a-3, 8; c-3,15, 21. **Maneely** a-1; c-5. **Reinman** a-1. **Robinson** a-6, 7; c-6. **Shores** a-7(2). **Sinnott** a-3. **Woodbridge** a-28, 30.*

BATTLE ATTACK
Oct, 1952 - No. 8, Dec, 1955
Stanmor Publications

	GD25	FN65	NM94
1	5.85	17.50	35.00
2	3.60	9.00	18.00
3-8: 3-Hollingsworth-a	2.40	6.00	12.00

BATTLE BEASTS (Blackthorne)(Value: cover or less)

BATTLE BRADY (Formerly Men in Action No. 1-9; see 3-D Action)
No. 10, Jan, 1953 - No. 14, June, 1953
Atlas Comics (IPC)

	GD25	FN65	NM94
10: 10-12-Syd Shores-c	7.50	22.50	45.00
11-Used in **POP**, pg. 95 plus B&W & color illos	4.20	12.50	25.00
12-14	4.00	10.00	20.00

BATTLE CLASSICS (See Cancelled Comic Cavalcade)
Sept-Oct, 1978 (44 pages)
DC Comics

	GD25	FN65	NM94
1-Kubert-r; new Kubert-c			1.00

BATTLE CRY
1952(May) - No. 20, Sept, 1955
Stanmor Publications

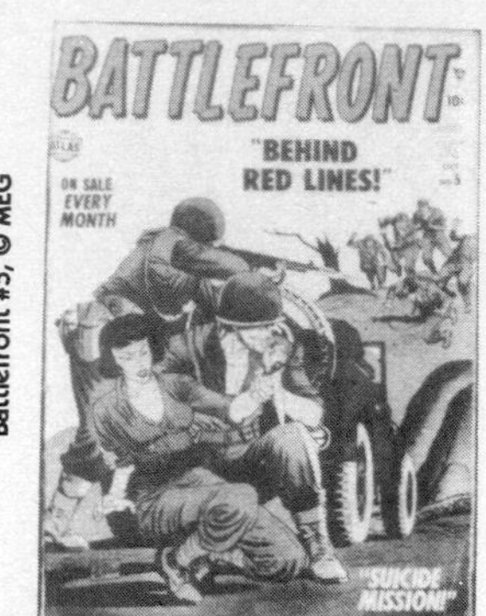

Battlefront #5, © MEG

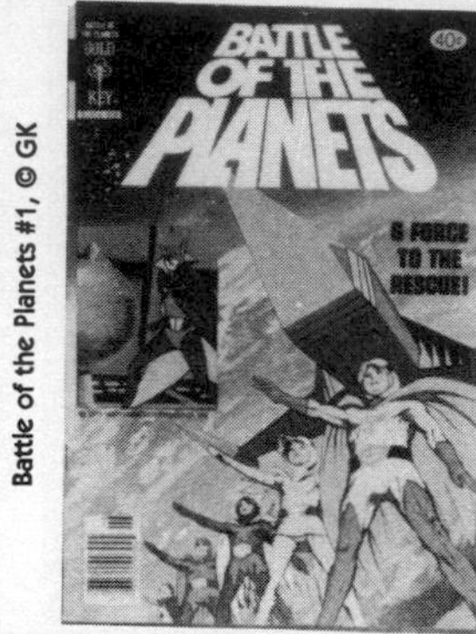

Battle of the Planets #1, © GK

Battletide II #2, © MEG

	GD25	FN65	NM94
1	6.70	20.00	40.00
2	4.00	10.00	20.00
3,5-10: 8-Pvt. Ike begins, ends #13,17	2.40	6.00	12.00
4-Classic E.C. swipe	4.00	10.00	20.00
11-20	1.80	4.50	9.00

NOTE: ***Hollingsworth*** *a-9; c-20.*

BATTLEFIELD (War Adventures on the...)
April, 1952 - No. 11, May, 1953
Atlas Comics (ACI)

	GD25	FN65	NM94
1-Pakula, Reinman-a	10.00	30.00	60.00
2-5: 2-Heath, Maneely, Pakula, Reinman-a	5.00	15.00	30.00
6-11	3.20	8.00	16.00

NOTE: ***Colan*** *a-11.* ***Everett*** *a-8.* ***Heath*** *a-1, 2, 5p; c-2, 8, 9, 11.* ***Ravielli*** *a-11.*

BATTLEFIELD ACTION (Formerly Foreign Intrigues)
No. 16, Nov, 1957 - No. 62, 2-3/66; No. 63, 7/80 - No. 89, 11/84
Charlton Comics

	GD25	FN65	NM94
V2#16	4.00	10.00	20.00
17,20-30	2.00	5.00	10.00
18,19-Check-a (2 stories in #18)	2.40	6.00	12.00
31-62(1966)	1.40	3.50	7.00
63-89(1983-'84)			1.00

NOTE: ***Montes/Bache*** *a-43, 55, 62.* ***Glanzman*** *a-87r.*

BATTLE FIRE
April, 1955 - No. 7, 1955
Aragon Magazine/Stanmor Publications

	GD25	FN65	NM94
1	4.20	12.50	25.00
2	2.80	7.00	14.00
3-7	1.80	4.50	9.00

BATTLE FOR A THREE DIMENSIONAL WORLD (3D Cosmic)(Value: cover or less)

BATTLEFORCE
Nov, 1987 - No. 2?, 1988 ($1.75) (#1: color; #2: B&W)
Blackthorne Publishing

	GD25	FN65	NM94
1,2-Based on game		.70	1.75

BATTLE FOR THE PLANET OF THE APES (See Power Record Comics)

BATTLEFRONT
June, 1952 - No. 48, Aug, 1957
Atlas Comics (PPI)

	GD25	FN65	NM94
1-Heath-c	12.50	37.50	85.00
2-Robinson-a(4)	7.00	21.00	42.00
3-5-Robinson-a(4) in each	5.35	16.00	32.00
6-10: Combat Kelly in No. 6-10	4.70	14.00	28.00
11-22,24-28: 14,16-Battle Brady app. 22-Teddy Roosevelt & His Rough Riders story. 28-Last pre-code (2/55)	3.20	8.00	16.00
23,43-Check-a	4.00	10.00	20.00
29-39,41,44-47	2.80	7.00	14.00
40,42-Williamson-a	4.20	12.50	25.00
48-Crandall-a	4.00	10.00	20.00

NOTE: ***Ayers*** *a-19, 32.* ***Berg*** *a-44.* ***Colan*** *a-21, 22, 32, 33, 40.* ***Drucker*** *a-28, 29.* ***Everett*** *a-44.* ***Heath*** *c-23, 26, 27, 29, 32.* ***Maneely*** *a-22, 23; c-2, 13, 22, 35.* ***Morisi*** *a-42.* ***Morrow*** *a-41.* ***Orlando*** *a-47.* ***Powell*** *a-19, 21, 25, 29, 32, 40, 47.* ***Robinson*** *a-1-4, 5(4); c-4, 5.* ***Robert Sale*** *a-19.* ***Severin*** *a-32; c-40.* ***Woodbridge*** *a-45, 46.*

BATTLEFRONT
No. 5, June, 1952
Standard Comics

	GD25	FN65	NM94
5-Toth-a	10.00	30.00	60.00

BATTLE GROUND
Sept, 1954 - No. 20, Aug, 1957
Atlas Comics (OMC)

	GD25	FN65	NM94
1	10.00	30.00	65.00
2-Jack Katz-a	5.35	16.00	32.00
3,4-Last precode (3/55)	4.00	11.00	22.00
5-8,10	4.00	10.00	20.00
9-Krigstein-a	4.70	14.00	28.00
11,13,18-Williamson-a in each	4.70	14.00	28.00
12,15-17,19,20	3.20	8.00	16.00
14-Kirby-a	4.20	12.50	25.00

NOTE: ***Ayers*** *a-13.* ***Colan*** *a-11, 13.* ***Drucker*** *a-7, 12, 13, 20.* ***Heath*** *c-2, 5, 13.* ***Maneely*** *a-19; c-1, 19.* ***Orlando*** *a-17.* ***Pakula*** *a-11.* ***Severin*** *a-5, 12, 19. c-20.* ***Tuska*** *a-11.*

BATTLE HEROES
Sept, 1966 - No. 2, Nov, 1966 (25 cents)
Stanley Publications

	GD25	FN65	NM94
1,2	1.20	3.00	6.00

BATTLE OF THE BULGE (See Movie Classics)

BATTLE OF THE PLANETS (TV)
6/79 - No. 10, 12/80 (Based on syndicated cartoon by Sandy Frank)
Gold Key/Whitman No. 6 on

	GD25	FN65	NM94
1			1.50
2-10: Mortimer a-1-4,7-10			1.00

BATTLE REPORT
Aug, 1952 - No. 6, June, 1953
Ajax/Farrell Publications

	GD25	FN65	NM94
1	4.70	14.00	28.00
2-6	3.60	9.00	18.00

BATTLE SQUADRON
April, 1955 - No. 5, Dec, 1955
Stanmor Publications

	GD25	FN65	NM94
1	4.00	10.00	20.00
2-5: 3-Iwo Jima & flag-c	2.40	6.00	12.00

BATTLESTAR GALACTICA (TV)(Also see Marvel Comics Super Special #8)
March, 1979 - No. 23, January, 1981
Marvel Comics Group

	GD25	FN65	NM94
1: 1-5 adapt TV episodes		.70	1.75
2-23: 1-3-Partial-r			1.50

NOTE: ***Austin*** *c-9i, 10i.* ***Golden*** *c-18.* ***Simonson*** *a(p)-4, 5, 11-13, 15-20, 22, 23; c(p)-4, 5,11-17, 19, 20, 22, 23.*

BATTLE STORIES (See XMas Comics)
Jan, 1952 - No. 11, Sept, 1953
Fawcett Publications

	GD25	FN65	NM94
1-Evans-a	9.15	27.50	55.00
2	4.70	14.00	28.00
3-11	3.60	9.00	20.00

BATTLE STORIES
1963 - 1964
Super Comics

	GD25	FN65	NM94
Reprints #10-12,15-18: 10-r/U.S Tank Commandos #? 11-r/? 12,17-r/Monty Hall #?; 15-r/American Air Forces #7 by Powell; Bolle-r	.60	1.75	3.00

BATTLETECH (Blackthorne)(Value: cover or less)

BATTLETIDE (Death's Head II & Killpower...)
Dec, 1992 - No. 4, Mar, 1993 ($1.75, color, mini-series)
Marvel Comics UK, Ltd.

	GD25	FN65	NM94
1-4: Wolverine, Psylocke, Dark Angel app.		.70	1.75

BATTLETIDE II (Death's Head II & Killpower...)
Aug, 1993 - No. 4, Nov, 1993 ($1.75, color, mini-series)
Marvel Comics UK, Ltd.

	GD25	FN65	NM94
1-($2.95)-Foil embossed logo		.70	1.75
2-4: 2-Hulk-c/story		.70	1.75

BEACH BLANKET BINGO (See Movie Classics)

BEAGLE BOYS, THE (Walt Disney)(See The Phantom Blot)
11/64; No. 2, 11/65; No. 3, 8/66 - No. 47, 2/79 (See WDC&S #134)
Gold Key

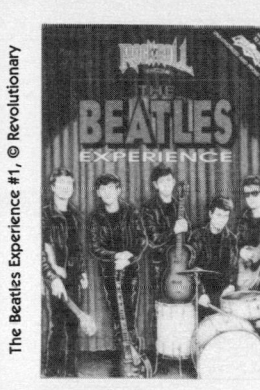

The Beatles Experience #1, © Revolutionary

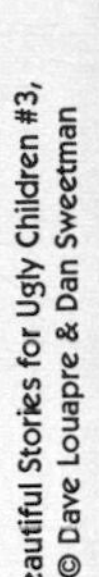

Beautiful Stories for Ugly Children #3, © Dave Louapre & Dan Sweetman

Bedlam! #2, © Eclipse

	GD25	FN65	NM94
1	4.00	11.00	22.00
2-5	2.40	6.00	12.00
6-10	1.60	4.00	8.00
11-20: 11,14,19-r	1.00	2.00	5.00
21-47: 27-r		1.00	2.50

BEAGLE BOYS VERSUS UNCLE SCROOGE
March, 1979 - No. 12, Feb, 1980
Gold Key

	GD25	FN65	NM94
1		1.00	2.50
2-12: 9-r			1.20

BEANBAGS
Winter, 1951 - No. 2, Spring, 1952
Ziff-Davis Publ. Co. (Approved Comics)

	GD25	FN65	NM94
1,2	6.70	20.00	40.00

BEANIE THE MEANIE
1958 - No. 3, May, 1959
Fago Publications

	GD25	FN65	NM94
1-3	3.20	8.00	16.00

BEANY AND CECIL (TV) (Bob Clampett's...)
Jan, 1952 - 1955; July-Sept, 1962 - No. 5, July-Sept, 1963
Dell Publishing Co.

	GD25	FN65	NM94
4-Color 368	22.00	65.00	150.00
4-Color 414,448,477,530,570,635(1/55)	17.00	52.00	120.00
01-057-209 (#1)	16.00	48.00	110.00
2-5	11.50	34.00	80.00

BEAR COUNTRY (Disney) (See 4-Color No. 758)

BEATLES, THE (See Girls' Romances #109, Go-Go, Heart Throbs #101, Herbie #5, Howard the Duck Mag. #4, Laugh #166, Marvel Comics Super Special #4, My LittleMargie #54, Not Brand Echh, Strange Tales #130, Summer Love, Superman's Pal Jimmy Olsen #79, Teen Confessions #37, Tippy's Friends & Tippy Teen)

BEATLES, THE (Life Story)
Sept-Nov, 1964 (35 cents)
Dell Publishing Co.

	GD25	FN65	NM94
1-(Scarce)-Stories with color photo pin ups	43.00	128.00	425.00

BEATLES EXPERIENCE, THE
Mar, 1991 - No. 8, 1991 ($2.50, B&W, limited series)
Revolutionary Comics

	GD25	FN65	NM94
1-8: 1-Gold logo		1.00	2.50

BEATLES YELLOW SUBMARINE (See Movie Comics under Yellow...)

BEAUTIFUL STORIES FOR UGLY CHILDREN
1989 - Present ($2.00-$2.50, B&W, mature readers)
Piranha Press (DC Comics)

	GD25	FN65	NM94
Vol. 1-11 ($2.00)		.80	2.00
12-30 ($2.50)		1.00	2.50

BEAUTY AND THE BEAST, THE
Jan, 1985 - No. 4, Apr, 1985 (Mini-series)
Marvel Comics Group

	GD25	FN65	NM94
1-4: Dazzler & the Beast from X-Men			1.50

BEAUTY AND THE BEAST (Graphic novel)(Also see Cartoon Tales & Disney's New Adventures of...)
1992
Disney Comics

	GD25	FN65	NM94
nn-($4.95, prestige edition)-Adapts animated film	1.00	2.00	5.00
nn-($2.50, newsstand edition)		1.00	2.50

BEAUTY AND THE BEAST: PORTRAIT OF LOVE (TV)
May, 1989 - No. 2, Mar, 1990 ($5.95, 60 pgs., color, squarebound)
First Comics

	GD25	FN65	NM94
1-Based on TV show, Wendy Pini-a/scripts	1.00	2.50	6.00
2-...: Night of Beauty; by Wendy Pini	1.00	2.50	6.00

BEAUTY AND THE BEAST
Sept., 1992 - No. 2, 1992 ($1.50, color, mini-series0
Disney Comics

	GD25	FN65	NM94
1		.80	2.00
2			1.50

BEAVER VALLEY (See 4-Color No. 625)

BEDKNOBS AND BROOMSTICKS (See Walt Disney Showcase No. 6 & 50)

BEDLAM! (Eclipse)(Value: cover or less)

BEDTIME STORY (See Cinema Comics Herald)

BEEP BEEP, THE ROAD RUNNER (TV)(See Daffy & Kite Fun Book)
July, 1958 - No. 14, Aug-Oct, 1962; Oct, 1966 - No. 105, 1983
Dell Publishing Co./Gold Key No. 1 88/Whitman No. 89 on

	GD25	FN65	NM94
4-Color 918 (#1, 7/58)	9.15	27.50	55.00
4-Color 1008,1046 (11-1/59-60)	5.00	15.00	30.00
4(2-4/60)-14(Dell)	4.00	10.00	22.00
1(10/66, Gold Key)	4.35	13.00	26.00
2-5	3.00	7.50	15.00
6-14 (1962)	2.00	5.00	10.00
15-18,20-40	1.40	3.50	7.00
19-With pull-out poster	3.00	7.50	15.00
41-60	.70	1.75	3.50
61-105			1.50

NOTE: *See March of Comics #351, 353, 375, 387, 397, 416, 430, 442, 455. #5, 8-10, 35, 53, 59-62, 68-r; 96-102, 104 are 1/3-r.*

BEETLE BAILEY (See Comics Reading Library, Giant Comic Album & Sarge Snorkel)
#459, 5/53 - #38, 5-7/62; #39, 11/62 - #53, 5/66; #54, 8/66 - #65, 12/67; #67, 2/69 - #119, 11/76; #120, 4/78 - #132, 4/80
Dell Publishing Co./Gold Key #39-53/King #54-66/Charlton #67-119/ Gold Key #120-131/Whitman #132

	GD25	FN65	NM94
4-Color 469 (#1)-By Mort Walker	9.15	27.50	55.00
4-Color 521,552,622	4.70	14.00	28.00
5(2-4/56)-10(5-7/57)	4.00	10.00	20.00
11-20(4-5/59)	2.80	7.00	14.00
21-38(5-7/62)	1.80	4.50	9.00
39-53(5/66)	1.00	2.50	5.00
54-119 (No. 66 publ. overseas only?)	.60	1.50	3.00
120-132		.80	2.00
Bold Detergent Giveaway('69)-same as regular issue (#67) minus price	.60	1.50	3.00
Cerebral Palsy Assn. Giveaway V2#71('69)-V2#73; (#1), 1/70 (Charlton)	.60	1.50	3.00
Red Cross Giveaway, 16pp, 5x7", 1969, paper-c	.60	1.50	3.00

BEETLE BAILEY
Sept, 1992 - Present ($1.25, color)
Harvey Comics

	GD25	FN65	NM94
V2#1-4			1.25
...Giant Size V2#1(10/92),2 (Both $2.25, 68 pgs.)		.90	2.25

BEETLEJUICE (TV)
Oct, 1991 - No. 2? ($1.25, color, quarterly)
Harvey Comics

	GD25	FN65	NM94
1,2			1.25

BEETLEJUICE CRIMEBUSTERS ON THE HAUNT
Sept, 1992 - No. 3, Jan, 1993 ($1.50, color, mini-series)
Harvey Comics

	GD25	FN65	NM94
1-3			1.50

BEE 29, THE BOMBARDIER
Feb, 1945
Neal Publications

	GD25	FN65	NM94
1-(Funny animal)	11.50	34.00	80.00

Beowulf #2, © DC

The Best From Boy's Life #1, © GIL

The Best of the Brave and the Bold #5, © DC

BEHIND PRISON BARS
1952
Realistic Comics (Avon)

	GD25	FN65	NM94
1-Kinstler-c	18.00	54.00	125.00

BEHOLD THE HANDMAID
1954 (Religious) (25 cents with a 20 cent sticker price)
George Pflaum

	GD25	FN65	NM94
nn	3.20	8.00	16.00

BELIEVE IT OR NOT (See Ripley's...)

BEN AND ME (See 4-Color No. 539)

BEN BOWIE AND HIS MOUNTAIN MEN
1952 - No. 17, Nov-Jan, 1958-59
Dell Publishing Co.

	GD25	FN65	NM94
4-Color 443 (#1)	7.50	22.50	45.00
4-Color 513,557,599,626,657	4.00	12.00	24.00
7(5-7/56)-11: 11-Intro/origin Yellow Hair	3.60	9.00	18.00
12-17	2.80	7.00	14.00

BEN CASEY (TV)
June-July, 1962 - No. 10, June-Aug, 1965 (Photo-c)
Dell Publishing Co.

	GD25	FN65	NM94
12-063-207 (#1)	5.00	15.00	30.00
2(10/62)-10: 4-Marijuana & heroin use story	3.60	9.00	18.00

BEN CASEY FILM STORY (TV)
November, 1962 (25 cents) (Photo-c)
Gold Key

	GD25	FN65	NM94
30009-211-All photos	8.35	25.00	50.00

BENEATH THE PLANET OF THE APES (See Movie Comics & Power Record Comics)

BEN FRANKLIN (See Kite Fun Book)

BEN HUR (See 4-Color No. 1052)

BEN ISRAEL (Logos Int.)(Value: cover or less)

BEOWULF (See First Comics Graphic Novel #1)
April-May, 1975 - No. 6, Feb-Mar, 1976
National Periodical Publications

	GD25	FN65	NM94
1			1.50
2-6: 5-Flying saucer-c/story			1.00

BERNI WRIGHTSON, MASTER OF THE MACABRE
July, 1983 - No. 5, Nov, 1984 ($1.50; Baxter paper)
Pacific Comics/Eclipse Comics No. 5

	GD25	FN65	NM94
1-5: Wrightson-c/a(r). 4-Jeff Jones-r (11 pgs.)			1.50

BERRYS, THE (Also see Funny World)
May, 1956
Argo Publ.

	GD25	FN65	NM94
1-Reprints daily & Sunday strips & daily Animal Antics by Ed Nofziger	4.20	12.50	25.00

BEST COMICS
Nov, 1939 - No. 4, Feb, 1940 (Large size, reads sideways)
Better Publications

	GD25	FN65	NM94
1-(Scarce)-Red Mask begins(1st app.) & c/s-all	50.00	150.00	325.00
2-4: 4-Cannibalism story	30.00	92.00	200.00

BEST FROM BOY'S LIFE, THE
Oct, 1957 - No. 5, Oct, 1958 (35 cents)
Gilberton Company

	GD25	FN65	NM94
1-Space Conquerors & Kam of the Ancient Ones begin, end #5	6.70	20.00	40.00
2,3,5	4.00	11.00	22.00
4-L.B. Cole-a	4.20	12.50	25.00

BEST LOVE (Formerly Sub-Mariner Comics No. 32)
No. 33, Aug, 1949 - No. 36, April, 1950 (Photo-c 33-36)
Marvel Comics (MPI)

	GD25	FN65	NM94
33-Kubert-a	7.50	22.50	45.00
34	4.00	10.00	20.00
35,36-Everett-a	5.00	15.00	30.00

BEST OF BUGS BUNNY, THE
Oct, 1966 - No. 2, Oct, 1968
Gold Key

	GD25	FN65	NM94
1,2-Giants	3.15	9.50	25.00

BEST OF DC, THE (Blue Ribbon Digest) (See Limited Coll. Ed. C-52)
Sept-Oct, 1979 - No. 71, Apr, 1986 (100-148 pgs; all reprints)
DC Comics

	GD25	FN65	NM94
1-17,19-34,36-71: 34-Has #497 on-c from Adv. Comics. 60-Plop!; Wood-c(r) & Aragones-r (5/85)			1.00
18-The New Teen Titans		.65	1.60
35-The Year's Best Comics Stories(148 pgs.)			1.20

NOTE: ***N. Adams*** *a-26, 51.* ***Aparo*** *a-9, 14, 26, 30; c-9, 14, 26.* ***Austin*** *a-51i.* ***Buckler*** *a-40p; c-22.* ***Giffen*** *a-50, 52; c-33p.* ***Grell*** *a-33p.* ***Grossman*** *a-37.* ***Heath*** *a-26.* ***Kaluta*** *a-40.* ***G. Kane*** *c-40, 44.* ***Kubert*** *a-21, 26.* ***Layton*** *a-21.* ***S. Mayer*** *c-29, 37, 41, 43, 47; a-28, 29, 37, 41, 43, 47, 58, 65, 68.* ***Moldoff*** *c-64p.* ***Morrow*** *a-40; c-40.* ***W. Mortimer*** *a-39p.* ***Newton*** *a-5, 51.* ***Perez*** *a-24, 50p; c-18, 21, 23.* ***Rogers*** *a-14, 51p.* ***Spiegle*** *a-52.* ***Starlin*** *a-51.* ***Staton*** *a-5, 21.* ***Tuska*** *a-24.* ***Wolverton*** *a-60.* ***Wood*** *a-60, 63; c-60, 63.* ***Wrightson*** *a-60. New art in #14, 18, 24.*

BEST OF DENNIS THE MENACE, THE
Summer, 1959 - No. 5, Spring, 1961 (100 pages)
Hallden/Fawcett Publications

	GD25	FN65	NM94
1-All reprints; Wiseman-a	5.85	17.50	35.00
2-5	4.20	12.50	25.00

BEST OF DONALD DUCK, THE
Nov, 1965 (12 cents, 36 pages)(Says 2nd printing in indicia)
Gold Key

	GD25	FN65	NM94
1-Reprints 4-Color #223 by Barks	5.00	15.00	30.00

BEST OF DONALD DUCK & UNCLE SCROOGE, THE
Nov, 1964 - No. 2, Sept, 1967 (25 cent giant)
Gold Key

	GD25	FN65	NM94
1(30022-411)('64)-Reprints 4-Color #189 & 408 by Carl Barks; cover of F.C. #189 redrawn by Barks	5.00	15.00	35.00
2(30022-709)('67)-Reprints 4-Color #256 & "Seven Cities of Cibola" & U.S. #8 by Barks	4.00	12.00	28.00

BEST OF HORROR AND SCIENCE FICTION COMICS (Webster)(Value: cover or less)

BEST OF MARMADUKE, THE
1960 (A dog)
Charlton Comics

	GD25	FN65	NM94
1-Brad Anderson's strip reprints	3.00	7.50	15.00

BEST OF MS. TREE, THE (Pyramid)(Value: cover or less)

BEST OF THE BRAVE AND THE BOLD, THE (See Super DC Giant)
Oct, 1988 - No. 6, Jan, 1989 ($2.50, color, mini-series)
DC Comics

	GD25	FN65	NM94
1-6: Neal Adams-r in all		1.00	2.50

BEST OF THE WEST (See A-1 Comics)
1951 - No. 12, April-June, 1954
Magazine Enterprises

	GD25	FN65	NM94
1(A-1 42)-Ghost Rider, Durango Kid, Straight Arrow, Bobby Benson begin	31.00	95.00	220.00
2(A-1 46)	14.00	43.00	100.00
3(A-1 52), 4(A-1 59), 5(A-1 66)	13.00	40.00	90.00
6(A-1 70), 7(A-1 76), 8(A-1 81), 9(A-1 85), 10(A-1 87), 11(A-1 97), 12(A-1 103)	10.00	30.00	65.00

NOTE: ***Bolle*** *a-9.* ***Borth*** *a-12.* ***Guardineer*** *a-5, 12.* ***Powell*** *a-1, 12.*

Best Romance #5, © STD

Betty's Diary #1, © AP

Beware #10 (1954), © TM

GD25 FN65 NM94 — GD25 FN65 NM94

BEST OF UNCLE SCROOGE & DONALD DUCK, THE
November, 1966 (25 cents)
Gold Key

1(30030-611)-Reprints part 4-Color #159 & 456 & Uncle Scrooge #6,7 by Carl Barks — 5.85 17.50 35.00

BEST OF WALT DISNEY COMICS, THE
1974 (In color; $1.50; 52 pages) (Walt Disney)
(8-1/2x11" cardboard covers; 32,000 printed of each)
Western Publishing Co.

96170-Reprints 1st two stories less 1 pg. each from 4-Color #62 — 1.30 3.25 8.00
96171-Reprints Mickey Mouse and the Bat Bandit of Inferno Gulch from 1934 (strips) by Gottfredson — 1.30 3.25 8.00
96172-Reprints Uncle Scrooge #386 & two other stories — 1.30 3.25 8.00
96173-Reprints "Ghost of the Grotto" (from 4-Color #159) & "Christmas on Bear Mtn." (from 4-Color #178) — 1.30 3.25 8.00

BEST ROMANCE
No. 5, Feb-Mar, 1952 - No. 7, Aug, 1952
Standard Comics (Visual Editions)

5-Toth-a; photo-c — 8.35 25.00 50.00
6,7-Photo-c — 3.60 9.00 18.00

BEST SELLER COMICS (See Tailspin Tommy)

BEST WESTERN (Formerly Terry Toons? or Miss America Magazine V7#24(#57)?; Western Outlaws & Sheriffs No. 60 on)
No. 58, June, 1949 - No. 59, Aug, 1949
Marvel Comics (IPC)

58,59-Black Rider, Kid Colt, Two-Gun Kid app.; both have Syd Shores-c — 11.50 34.00 80.00

BETTY (See Pep Comics #22 for 1st app.)
Sept, 1992 - Present ($1.25, color)
Archie Comics

1-14 — 1.25

BETTY AND HER STEADY (Going Steady with Betty No. 1)
No. 2, Mar-Apr, 1950
Avon Periodicals

2 — 7.50 22.50 45.00

BETTY AND ME
Aug, 1965 - No. 198?, 1992?
Archie Publications

1 — 10.00 30.00 70.00
2 — 5.85 17.50 35.00
3-5: 3-Origin Superteen. Superteen in new costume #4-7; dons new helmet #5, ends #8 (see Archie's Girls #118) — 4.00 10.00 20.00
6-10 — 2.00 5.00 10.00
11-30 — 1.00 2.00 5.00
31-55 (52 pages #36-55) — 1.00 2.50
56-100 — 1.50
101-198: Later issues $1.00 cover — 1.00

BETTY AND VERONICA (Also see Archie's Girls...)
June, 1987 - Present (75 cents - $1.25)
Archie Enterprises

1-76 — .60 1.25

BETTY & VERONICA ANNUAL DIGEST (...Digest Magazine #2-4, 44 on; ...Comics Digest Mag. #5-43)
November, 1980 - Present ($1.00 - 1.50, digest size)
Archie Publications

1, 2(11/81-Katy Keene story), 3(8/82) - 67('94) — 1.50

BETTY & VERONICA ANNUAL DIGEST (... Magazine #3 on)
Aug?, 1989 - Present ($1.50-$1.75, 128 pgs.)
Archie Comics

1-10: 9-Neon ink logo — .70 1.75

BETTY & VERONICA CHRISTMAS SPECTACULAR (See Archie Giant Series Magazine #159, 168, 180, 191, 204, 217, 229, 241, 453, 465, 477, 489, 501, 513, 525, 536, 547, 558, 568, 580, 593, 606, 618)

BETTY & VERONICA DOUBLE DIGEST MAGAZINE
1987 - Present (Digest size, 256 pgs., $2.25-$2.75)(...Digest #12 on)
Archie Enterprises

1-42: 5,17-Xmas-c. 16-Capt. Hero story — 1.10 2.75

BETTY & VERONICA SPECTACULAR (See Archie Giant Series Mag. #11, 16, 21, 26, 32, 138, 145, 153, 162, 173, 184, 197, 201, 210, 214, 221, 226, 234, 238, 246, 250, 458, 462, 470, 482, 486, 494, 498, 506, 510, 518, 522, 526, 530, 537, 552, 559, 563, 560, 575, 582, 588, 600, 608, 613, 620, 623)

BETTY AND VERONICA SPECTACULAR
Oct, 1992 - Present ($1.25, color)
Archie Comics

1-8: 1-Dan DeCarlo-c/a — 1.25

BETTY & VERONICA SPRING SPECTACULAR (See Archie Giant Series Magazine #569, 582, 595)

BETTY & VERONICA SUMMER FUN (See Archie Giant Series Mag. #8, 13, 18, 23, 28, 34, 140, 147, 155, 164, 175, 187, 199, 212, 224, 236, 248, 460, 484, 496, 508, 520, 529, 539, 550, 561, 572, 585, 598, 611, 621)

BETTY BOOP'S BIG BREAK (First)(Value: cover or less)

BETTY PAGE 3-D COMICS (3-D Zone)(Value: cover or less)

BETTY'S DIARY (See Archie Giant Series Magazine No. 555)
April, 1986 - No. 40, 1991 (75 & 95 cents)
Archie Enterprises

1-40 — 1.00

BEVERLY HILLBILLIES (TV)
4-6/63 - No. 18, 8/67; No. 19, 10/69; No. 20, 10/70; No. 21, Oct, 1971
Dell Publishing Co.

1-Photo-c — 13.00 40.00 90.00
2-Photo-c — 6.00 18.00 42.00
3-9: All have photo covers — 4.30 13.00 30.00
10: No photo cover — 2.30 6.75 16.00
11-21: All have photo covers. 18-Last 12 cent-c — 3.25 9.50 22.00

NOTE: *#1-9, 11-21 are photo covers. #19 reprints cover to #1, but not insides.*

BEWARE (Formerly Fantastic; Chilling Tales No. 13 on)
No. 10, June, 1952 - No. 12, Oct, 1952
Youthful Magazines

10-E.A. Poe's Pit & the Pendulum adaptation by Wildey; Harrison/Bache-a; atom bomb and shrunken head-c — 19.00 57.00 135.00
11-Harrison-a; Ambrose Bierce adapt. — 14.00 43.00 100.00
12-Used in **SOTI**, pg. 388; Harrison-a — 14.00 43.00 100.00

BEWARE
No. 13, 1/53 - No. 16, 7/53; No. 5, 9/53 - No. 15, 5/55
Trojan Magazines/Merit Publ. No. ?

13(#1)-Harrison-a — 17.00 52.00 120.00
14(#2, 3/53)-Krenkel/Harrison-c; dismemberment, severed head panels — 13.00 40.00 90.00
15,16(#3, 5/53; #4, 7/53)-Harrison-a — 10.00 30.00 70.00
5,9,12,13 — 10.00 30.00 70.00
6-Ill. in **SOTI**-"Children are first shocked and then desensitized by all this brutality." Corpse on cover swipe/V.O.H. #26; girl on cover swipe/Advs. Into Darkness #10 — 22.00 65.00 150.00
7,8-Check-a — 11.50 34.00 80.00
10-Frazetta/Check-c; Disbrow, Check-a — 33.00 100.00 230.00
11-Disbrow-a; heart torn out, blood drainage — 13.00 40.00 90.00
14,15: 14-Myron Fass-c. 15-Harrison-a — 10.00 30.00 65.00

NOTE: ***Fass** a-5, 6, 8; c-6, 11, 14. **Forte** a-8. **Hollingsworth** a-15(#3), 16(#4), 9; c-16(#4), 8, 9. **Kiefer** a-16(#4), 5, 6, 10.*

Bewitched #11, © Screen Gems

Bible Tales for Young People #4, © MEG

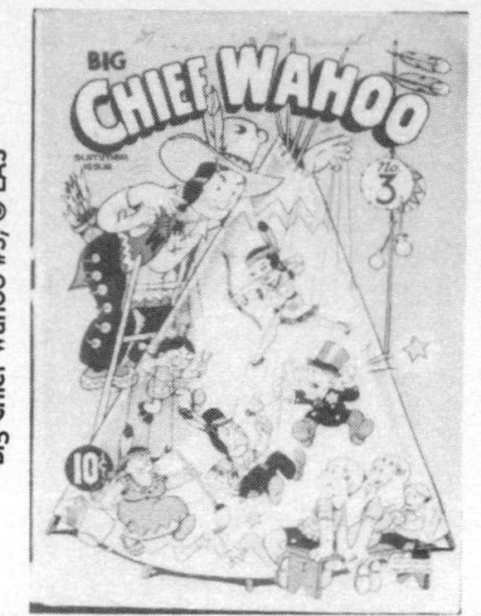

Big Chief Wahoo #3, © EAS

GD25 FN65 NM94 | GD25 FN65 NM94

BEWARE (Becomes Tomb of Darkness No. 9 on)
March, 1973 - No. 8, May, 1974 (All reprints)
Marvel Comics Group

1-Everett-c; Sinnott-r ('54) 1.20 3.00
2-8: 2-Forte, Colan-r. 6-Tuska-a. 7-Torres-r/Mystical Tales #7 1.50

BEWARE TERROR TALES
May, 1952 - No. 8, July, 1953
Fawcett Publications

1-E.C. art swipe/Haunt of Fear #5 & Vault of Horror #26 20.00 60.00 140.00
2 11.50 34.00 80.00
3-8: 8-Tothish-a 10.00 30.00 70.00
NOTE: *Andru a-2. **Bernard Bailey** a-1; c-1-5. **Powell** a-1, 2, 8. **Sekowsky** a-2.*

BEWARE THE CREEPER (See Adventure, Best of the Brave & the Bold, Brave & the Bold, First Issue Special, Flash #318-323, Showcase, and World's Finest #249)
May-June, 1968 - No. 6, March-April, 1969 (All 12¢ issues)
National Periodical Publications

Showcase #73 (3-4/68)-Origin & 1st app. The Creeper; Ditko-c/a 8.00 25.00 75.00
1-(5-6/68)-Ditko-a in all; c-1-5 6.00 19.00 45.00
2-6: 6-G. Kane-c 4.00 13.00 30.00

BEWITCHED (TV)
4-6/65 - No. 11, 10/67; No. 12, 10/68 - No. 13, 1/69; No. 14, 10/69
Dell Publishing Co.

1-Photo-c 11.00 34.00 80.00
2-No photo-c 6.00 17.00 40.00
3-13-All have photo-c 4.00 13.00 30.00
14-No photo-c 3.20 8.00 20.00

BEYOND, THE
Nov, 1950 - No. 30, Jan, 1955
Ace Magazines

1-Bakerish-a(p) 20.00 60.00 140.00
2-Bakerish-a(p) 11.50 34.00 80.00
3-10: 10-Woodish-a by Cameron 8.35 25.00 50.00
11-20: 18-Used in **POP**, pgs. 81,82 6.70 20.00 40.00
21-26,28-30 6.00 18.00 36.00
27-Used in **SOTI**, pg. 111 6.70 20.00 40.00
NOTE: ***Cameron** a-10, 11p, 12p, 15, 16, 21-27, 30; c-20. **Colan** a-6, 13, 17. **Sekowsky** a-2, 3, 5, 7, 11, 14, 27r. No. 1 was to appear as Challenge of the Unknown No. 7.*

BEYOND THE GRAVE
July, 1975 - No. 6, June, 1976; No. 7, Jan, 1983 - No. 17, Oct, 1984
Charlton Comics

1-Ditko-a (6 pgs.); Sutton painted-c 1.60 4.00
2-6: 2-5-Ditko-a; Ditko c-2,3,6 .80 2.00
7-17: ('83-'84) Reprints. 13-Aparo-c(r). 15-Sutton-c 1.25
Modern Comics Reprint 2('78) 1.00

BIBLE TALES FOR YOUNG FOLK (...Young People No. 3-5)
Aug, 1953 - No. 5, Mar, 1954
Atlas Comics (OMC)

1 13.00 40.00 90.00
2-Everett, Krigstein-a 10.00 30.00 70.00
3-5: 4-Robinson-c 8.35 25.00 50.00

BIG (Hit)(Value: cover or less)

BIG ALL-AMERICAN COMIC BOOK, THE (See All-American Comics)
1944 (One Shot) (132 pages) (Early DC Annual)
All-American/National Per.l Publ.

GD25 FN65 VF82 NM94
1-Wonder Woman, Green Lantern, Flash, The Atom, Wildcat, Scribbly, The Whip, Ghost Patrol, Hawkman by Kubert (1st on Hawkman), Hop Harrigan, Johnny Thunder, Little Boy Blue, Mr. Terrific, Mutt & Jeff app.; Sargon on cover only; cover by Kubert/Hibbard/Mayer/others 650.00 1950.00 4225.00 6500.00
(Estimated up to 80+ total copies exist, 6 in NM/Mint)

BIG BABY HUEY (Also see Baby Huey)
Oct, 1991 - Present ($1.00, color, quarterly)
Harvey Comics

GD25 FN65 NM94
1-4 1.00

BIG BOOK OF FUN COMICS (See New Book of Comics)
Spring, 1936 (52pgs., large size)(1st comic book annual & DC annual)
National Periodical Publications

GD25 FN65 VF82
1 (Very rare)-r/New Fun #1-5 1300.00 3250.00 6500.00
(Estimated up to 15 total copies exist, none in NM/Mint)

BIG BOOK ROMANCES
February, 1950(no date given) (148 pages)
Fawcett Publications

GD25 FN65 NM94
1-Contains remaindered Fawcett romance comics - several combinations possible 25.00 75.00 175.00

BIG BOY (See Adventures of the Big Boy)

BIG CHIEF WAHOO
July, 1942 - No. 23, 1945? (Quarterly)
Eastern Color Printing/George Dougherty (distr. by Fawcett)

1-Newspaper-r (on sale 6/15/42) 29.00 85.00 200.00
2-Steve Roper app. 14.00 43.00 100.00
3-5: 4-Chief is holding a Katy Keene comic 11.00 32.00 75.00
6-10: 8-23-Exist? 8.35 25.00 50.00
11-23 5.85 17.50 35.00
NOTE: *Kerry Drake in some issues.*

BIG CIRCUS, THE (See 4-Color No. 1036)

BIG COUNTRY, THE (See 4-Color No. 946)

BIG DADDY ROTH
Oct-Nov, 1964 - No. 4, Apr-May, 1965 (35 cents, magazine)
Millar Publications

1-Toth-a 14.00 43.00 100.00
2-4-Toth-a 10.00 30.00 70.00

BIG HERO ADVENTURES (See Jigsaw)

BIG JIM'S P.A.C.K.
No date (1975) (16 pages)
Mattel, Inc. (Marvel Comics)

nn-Giveaway with Big Jim doll; Buscema/Sinnott-c/a .50

BIG JON & SPARKIE (Radio)(Formerly Sparkie, Radio Pixie)
No. 4, Sept-Oct, 1952 (Painted-c)
Ziff-Davis Publ. Co.

4-Based on children's radio program 11.50 34.00 80.00

BIG LAND, THE (See 4-Color No. 812)

BIG RED (See Movie Comics)

BIG SHOT COMICS
May, 1940 - No. 104, Aug, 1949
Columbia Comics Group

1-Intro. Skyman; The Face (1st app.; Tony Trent), The Cloak (Spy Master), Marvelo, Monarch of Magicians, Joe Palooka, Charlie Chan, Tom Kerry, Dixie Dugan, Rocky Ryan begin; Charlie Chan moves over from Feature Comics #31 (4/40) 115.00 350.00 750.00
2 46.00 132.00 300.00
3-The Cloak called Spy Chief; Skyman-c 40.00 120.00 260.00
4,5 33.00 100.00 220.00
6-10: 8-Christmas-c 29.00 85.00 185.00
11-14: 14-Origin & 1st app. Sparky Watts (6/41) 25.00 75.00 160.00
15-Origin The Cloak 29.00 75.00 185.00
16-20 18.00 55.00 120.00

Big Shot Comics #69, © CCG

Bill & Ted's Bogus Journey #1, © Nelson Films

Bill Boyd Western #13, © FAW

	GD25	FN65	NM94
21-27,29,30: 24-Tojo-c. 29-Intro. Capt. Yank; Bo (a dog) newspaper strip reprints by Frank Beck begin, ends #104. 30-X-Mas-c	14.00	42.00	95.00
28-Hitler, Tojo & Mussolini-c	17.00	50.00	110.00
31,33-40	10.00	30.00	70.00
32-Vic Jordan newspaper strip reprints begin, ends #52; Hitler, Tojo & Mussolini-c	12.50	37.50	80.00
41-50: 42-No Skyman. 43,46-Hitler-c. 50-Origin The Face retold	10.00	30.00	60.00
51-60	7.50	22.50	45.00
61-70: 63 on-Tony Trent, the Face	5.85	17.50	35.00
71-80: 73-The Face cameo. 74-(2/47)-Mickey Finn begins. 74,80-The Face app. in Tony Trent. 78 Last Charlie Chan strip reprints	5.00	15.00	30.00
81-90: 85-Tony Trent marries Babs Walsh. 86-Valentines-c	4.35	13.00	26.00
91-99,101-104: 69-94-Skyman in Outer Space. 96-Xmas-c	4.00	11.00	22.00
100	5.00	15.00	30.00

*NOTE: **Mart Bailey** art on "The Face" No. 1-104. **Guardineer** a-5. Sparky Watts by **Boody Rogers**-No. 14-42, 77-104, (by others No. 43-76). Others than Tony Trent wear "The Face" mask in No. 46-63, 93. Skyman by **Ogden Whitney**-No. 1, 2, 4, 12-37, 49, 70-101. Skyman covers-No. 1, 3, 7-12, 14, 16, 20, 27, 89, 95, 100.*

BIG TEX
June, 1953
Toby Press

	GD25	FN65	NM94
1-Contains (3) John Wayne stories-r with name changed to Big Tex	6.35	19.00	38.00

BIG-3
Fall, 1940 - No. 7, Jan, 1942
Fox Features Syndicate

	GD25	FN65	NM94
1-Blue Beetle, The Flame, & Samson begin	115.00	340.00	750.00
2	50.00	150.00	335.00
3-5	40.00	120.00	265.00
6-Last Samson; bondage-c	33.00	100.00	220.00
7-V-Man app.	33.00	100.00	220.00

BIG TOP COMICS, THE (TV's Great Circus Show)
1951 - No. 2, 1951 (No month)
Toby Press

	GD25	FN65	NM94
1,2	5.00	15.00	30.00

BIG TOWN (Radio/TV) (Also see Movie Comics, 1946)
Jan, 1951 - No. 50, Mar-Apr, 1958 (No. 1-9: 52pgs.)
National Periodical Publications

	GD25	FN65	NM94
1-Dan Barry-a begins	40.00	120.00	280.00
2	19.00	58.00	135.00
3-10	12.00	36.00	85.00
11-20	10.00	30.00	60.00
21-31: Last pre-code (1-2/55)	7.00	21.00	42.00
32-50	5.00	15.00	30.00

BIG VALLEY, THE (TV)
June, 1966 - No. 5, Oct, 1967; No. 6, Oct, 1969
Dell Publishing Co.

	GD25	FN65	NM94
1: Photo-c #1-5	5.00	15.00	30.00
2-6: 6-Reprints #1	3.20	8.00	16.00

BIKER MICE FROM MARS
Nov, 1993 - Present ($1.50, color, based on TV cartoon)
Marvel Comics

	GD25	FN65	NM94
1-6: 1-Intro Vinnie, Modo & Throttle			1.50

BILL & TED'S BOGUS JOURNEY
Sept, 1991 ($2.95, color, squarebound, 84 pgs.)
Marvel Comics

	GD25	FN65	NM94
1-Adapts movie sequel		1.20	3.00

"BILL AND TED'S EXCELLENT ADVENTURE" MOVIE ADAPTATION
1989 (No cover price, color)
DC Comics

	GD25	FN65	NM94
nn-Torres-a			1.00

BILL & TED'S EXCELLENT COMIC BOOK
Dec, 1991 - No. 12, 1992 ($1.00/$1.25, color)
Marvel Comics

	GD25	FN65	NM94
1,2: 2-Last $1.00-c			1.00
3-12			1.25

BILL BARNES COMICS (...America's Air Ace Comics No. 2 on)
(Becomes Air Ace V2#1 on; also see Shadow Comics)
Oct, 1940(No. month given) - No. 12, Oct, 1943
Street & Smith Publications

	GD25	FN65	NM94
1-23 pgs.-comics; Rocket Rooney begins	57.00	170.00	365.00
2-Barnes as The Phantom Flyer app.; Tuska-a	33.00	100.00	220.00
3-5	25.00	75.00	165.00
6-12	21.00	62.00	140.00

BILL BATTLE, THE ONE MAN ARMY (Also see Master Comics No. 133)
Oct, 1952 - No. 4, Apr, 1953 (All photo-c)
Fawcett Publications

	GD25	FN65	NM94
1	5.35	16.00	32.00
2	3.60	9.00	18.00
3,4	2.80	7.00	14.00

BILL BLACK'S FUN COMICS (Americomics)(Value: cover or less)

BILL BOYD WESTERN (Movie star; see Hopalong Cassidy & Western Hero)
Feb, 1950 - No. 23, June, 1952 (1-3,7,11,14-on: 36 pgs.)
Fawcett Publications

	GD25	FN65	NM94
1-Bill Boyd & his horse Midnite begin; photo front/back-c	32.00	95.00	225.00
2-Painted-c	17.00	50.00	115.00
3-Photo-c begin, end #23; last photo back-c	14.00	43.00	100.00
4-6(52pgs.)	11.50	34.00	80.00
7,11(36pgs.)	10.00	30.00	65.00
8-10,12,13(52pgs.)	10.00	30.00	70.00
14-22	10.00	30.00	60.00
23-Last Issue	10.00	30.00	70.00

BILL BUMLIN (See Treasury of Comics No. 3)

BILL ELLIOTT (See Wild Bill Elliott)

BILLI 99 (Dark Horse)(Value: cover or less)

BILL STERN'S SPORTS BOOK
Spring-Summer, 1951 - V2#2, Winter, 1952
Ziff-Davis Publ. Co.(Approved Comics)

	GD25	FN65	NM94
V1#10(1951)	11.50	34.00	80.00
2(Sum'52-reg. size)	10.00	30.00	65.00
V2#2(1952,96 pgs.)-Krigstein, Kinstler-a	11.50	34.00	80.00

BILLY AND BUGGY BEAR (See Animal Fun)
1958; 1964
I.W. Enterprises/Super

	GD25	FN65	NM94
I.W. Reprint #1(early Timely funny animal-r), #7(1958)	.60	1.50	3.00
Super Reprint #10(1964)	.60	1.50	3.00

BILLY BUCKSKIN WESTERN (2-Gun Western No. 4)
Nov, 1955 - No. 3, March, 1956
Atlas Comics (IMC No. 1/MgPC No. 2,3)

	GD25	FN65	NM94
1-Mort Drucker-a; Maneely-c/a	10.00	30.00	65.00
2-Mort Drucker-a	7.00	21.00	42.00
3-Williamson, Drucker-a	7.50	22.50	45.00

BILLY BUNNY (Black Cobra No. 6 on)
Feb-Mar, 1954 - No. 5, Oct-Nov, 1954
Excellent Publications

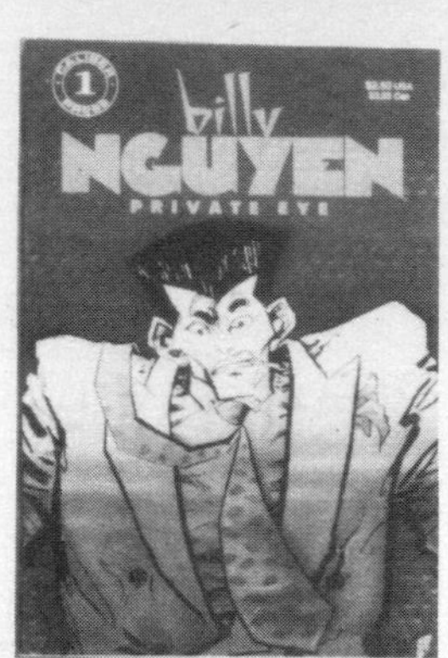

Billy Nguyen Private Eye V2#1, © Hartman/Shaw

Billy The Kid and Oscar #1 © FAW

Black Cat Comics #13, © HARV

	GD25	FN65	NM94
1	4.70	14.00	28.00
2	3.20	8.00	16.00
3-5	2.40	6.00	12.00

BILLY BUNNY'S CHRISTMAS FROLICS
1952 (100 pages, 25 cent giant)
Farrell Publications

	GD25	FN65	NM94
1	10.00	30.00	70.00

BILLY MAKE BELIEVE (See Single Series No. 14)

BILLY NGUYEN, PRIVATE EYE (Caliber Press)(Value: cover or less)

BILLY THE KID (Formerly The Masked Raider; also see Doc Savage Comics & Return of the Outlaw)
No. 9, Nov, 1957 - No. 121, Dec, 1976; No. 122, Sept, 1977 - No. 123, Oct, 1977; No. 124, Feb, 1978 - No. 153, Mar, 1983
Charlton Publ. Co.

	GD25	FN65	NM94
9	6.70	20.00	40.00
10,12,14,17-19	4.20	12.50	25.00
11-(68 pgs., origin, 1st app. The Ghost Train)	5.00	15.00	30.00
13-Williamson/Torres-a	5.35	16.00	32.00
15-Origin; 2pgs. Williamson-a	5.35	16.00	32.00
16-Two pgs. Williamson	5.35	16.00	32.00
20-26-Severin-a(3-4 each)	5.35	16.00	32.00
27-30	3.60	9.00	18.00
31-40	2.40	6.00	12.00
41-60	1.60	4.00	8.00
61-80: 66-Bounty Hunter series begins. Not in #79,82,84-863		1.60	4.00
81-99,101-123: 87-Last Bounty Hunter. 111-Origin The Ghost Train. 117-Gunsmith & Co., The Cheyenne Kid app.		1.20	3.00
100		.80	2.00
124(2/78)-153			1.50
Modern Comics 109 (1977 reprint)			1.20

NOTE: ***Severin** a(r)-121-129, 134; c-23, 25. **Sutton** a-111.*

BILLY THE KID ADVENTURE MAGAZINE
Oct, 1950 - No. 30, 1955
Toby Press

	GD25	FN65	NM94
1-Williamson/Frazetta-a (2 pgs); photo-c	19.00	58.00	135.00
2-Photo-c	6.70	20.00	40.00
3-Williamson/Frazetta "The Claws of Death," 4 pgs. plus Williamson art	21.00	63.00	145.00
4,5,7,8,10: 4,7-Photo-c	4.70	14.00	28.00
6-Frazetta assist on "Nightmare;" photo-c	10.00	30.00	60.00
9-Kurtzman Pot-Shot Pete; photo-c	9.15	27.50	55.00
11,12,15-20: 11-Photo-c	4.00	12.00	24.00
13-Kurtzman-r/John Wayne #12 (Genius)	4.70	14.00	28.00
14-Williamson/Frazetta; r-of #1 (2 pgs.)	6.70	20.00	40.00
21,23-30	3.60	9.00	18.00
22-Williamson/Frazetta-r(1pg.)/#1; photo-c	4.35	13.00	26.00

BILLY THE KID AND OSCAR (Also see Fawcett's Funny Animals)
Winter, 1945 - No. 3, Summer, 1946 (Funny animal)
Fawcett Publications

	GD25	FN65	NM94
1	10.00	30.00	60.00
2,3	5.85	17.50	35.00

BILLY WEST (Bill West No. 9,10)
1949 - No. 9, Feb, 1951; No. 10, Feb, 1952
Standard Comics (Visual Editions)

	GD25	FN65	NM94
1	5.85	17.50	35.00
2	3.60	9.00	18.00
3-10: 7,8-Schomburg-c	2.80	7.00	14.00

NOTE: ***Celardo** a-1-6, 9; c-1-3. **Moreira** a-3. **Roussos** a-2.*

BING CROSBY (See Feature Films)

BINGO (...Comics) (H. C. Blackerby)
1945 (Reprints National material)
Howard Publ.

	GD25	FN65	NM94
1-L. B. Cole opium-c	14.00	43.00	100.00

BINGO, THE MONKEY DOODLE BOY
Aug, 1951; Oct, 1953
St. John Publishing Co.

	GD25	FN65	NM94
1(8/51)-By Eric Peters	4.35	13.00	26.00
1(10/53)	4.00	10.00	20.00

BINKY (Formerly Leave It to...)
No. 72, 4-5/70 - No. 81, 10-11/71; No. 82, Summer/77
National Periodical Publ./DC Comics

	GD25	FN65	NM94
72-81		1.60	4.00
82('77)-(One Shot)		.80	2.00

BINKY'S BUDDIES
Jan-Feb, 1969 - No. 12, Nov-Dec, 1970
National Periodical Publications

	GD25	FN65	NM94
1	1.20	3.00	7.00
2-12		1.60	4.00

BIONIC WOMAN, THE (TV)
October, 1977 - No. 5, June, 1978
Charlton Publications

	GD25	FN65	NM94
1-5			1.25

BIZARRE ADVENTURES (Formerly Marvel Preview)
No. 25, 3/81 - No. 34, 2/83 (#25-33: Magazine-$1.50)
Marvel Comics Group

	GD25	FN65	NM94
25-Lethal Ladies. 26-King Kull			1.25
27-Phoenix, Iceman & Nightcrawler app. 28-The Unlikely Heroes; Elektra by Miller; Neal Adams-a			1.50
29-Horror. 30-Tomorrow. 31-After The Violence Stops; new Hangman story; Miller-a. 32-Gods. 33-Horror; photo-c			1.25
34 ($2.00, Baxter paper, comic size)-Son of Santa; Christmas special; Howard the Duck by Paul Smith			1.50

NOTE: ***Alcala** a-27i. **Austin** a-25i, 28i. **J. Buscema** a-27p, 29, 30p; c-26. **Byrne** a-31 (2 pg.). **Golden** a-25p, 28p. **Perez** a-27p. **Rogers** a-25p. **Simonson** a-29; c-29. **Paul Smith** a-34.*

BLACK AND WHITE (See Large Feature Comic, Series I)

BLACK & WHITE MAGIC (Innovation)(Value: cover or less)

BLACKBEARD'S GHOST (See Movie Comics)

BLACK BEAUTY (See 4-Color No. 440)

BLACK CANARY (See All Star Comics #38, Flash Comics #86 & Justice League of America #75)
Nov, 1991 - No. 4, Feb, 1992 ($1.75, color, mini-series)
DC Comics

	GD25	FN65	NM94
1-4		.70	1.75

BLACK CANARY
Jan, 1993 - No. 12, Dec, 1993 ($1.75, color)
DC Comics

	GD25	FN65	NM94
1-12: 8-The Ray-c/story. 9,10-Huntress-c/story		.70	1.75

BLACK CAT COMICS (...Western #16-19; ...Mystery #30 on)
(See All-New #7,9, The Original Black Cat, Pocket & Speed Comics)
June-July, 1946 - No. 29, June, 1951
Harvey Publications (Home Comics)

	GD25	FN65	NM94
1-Kubert-a; Joe Simon c-1-3	40.00	120.00	260.00
2-Kubert-a	21.00	62.00	130.00
3,4: 4-The Red Demons begin (The Demon #4 & 5)	15.00	45.00	100.00
5,6-The Scarlet Arrow app. in ea. by Powell; S&K-a in both. 6-Origin Red Demon	20.00	60.00	135.00
7-Vagabond Prince by S&K plus 1 more story	20.00	60.00	135.00
8-S&K-a; Kerry Drake begins, ends #13	17.50	52.00	115.00
9-Origin Stuntman (r/Stuntman #1)	21.00	62.00	140.00

10-20: 14,15,17-Mary Worth app. plus Invisible Scarlet O'Neil-#15,20,24

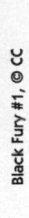

Black Cat Mystery #32, © HARV

Black Fury #1, © CC

Blackhawk #216, © DC

	GD25	FN65	NM94
	12.00	36.00	85.00
21-26	10.00	30.00	70.00
27-Used in **SOTI**, pg. 193; X-Mas-c; 2 pg. John Wayne story	12.00	36.00	85.00
28-Intro. Kit, Black Cat's new sidekick	12.00	36.00	85.00
29-Black Cat bondage-c; Black Cat stories	11.50	34.00	80.00

BLACK CAT MYSTERY (Formerly Black Cat; ...Western Mystery #54; ...Western #55,56; ...Mystery #57; ...Mystic #58-62; Black Cat #63-65)
No. 30, Aug, 1951 - No. 65, April, 1963
Harvey Publications

	GD25	FN65	NM94
30-Black Cat on cover only	11.00	32.00	75.00
31,32,34,37,38,40	8.35	25.00	50.00
33-Used in **POP**, pg. 89; electrocution-c	8.65	26.00	52.00
35-Atomic disaster cover/story	10.00	30.00	65.00
36,39-Used in **SOTI**: #36-Pgs. 270,271; #39-Pgs. 386-388	11.50	34.00	80.00
41-43	8.35	25.00	50.00
44-Eyes, ears, tongue cut out; Nostrand-a	9.15	27.50	55.00
45-Classic "Colorama" by Powell; Nostrand-a	13.00	40.00	90.00
46-49,51-Nostrand-a in all	9.15	27.50	55.00
50-Check-a; Warren Kremer?-c showing a man's face burning away	12.00	36.00	85.00
52,53 (r/#34 & 35)	6.70	20.00	40.00
54-Two Black Cat stories (2/55, last pre-code)	10.00	30.00	60.00
55,56-Black Cat app.	6.70	20.00	40.00
57(7/56)-Kirby-c	5.00	15.00	30.00
58-60-Kirby-a(4). 58,59-Kiurby-c. 60,61-Simon-c	8.35	25.00	50.00
61-Nostrand-a; "Colorama" r/#45	6.70	20.00	40.00
62(3/58)-E.C. story swipe	5.35	16.00	32.00
63-Giant(10/62); Reprints; Black Cat app.; origin Black Kitten	8.00	24.00	48.00
64-Giant(1/63); Reprints; Black Cat app.	8.00	24.00	48.00
65-Giant(4/63); Reprints; Black Cat app.	8.00	24.00	48.00

NOTE: ***Kremer** a-37, 39, 43; c-36, 37, 47. **Meskin** a-51. **Palais** a-30, 31(2), 32(2), 33-35, 37-40. **Powell** a-32-35, 36(2), 40, 41, 43-53, 57. **Simon** c-63-65. **Sparling** a-44. Bondage c-32, 34, 43.*

BLACK COBRA (Bride's Diary No. 4 on) (See Captain Flight #8)
No. 1, 10-11/54, No. 6(No. 2), 12-1/54-55; No. 3, 2-3/55
Ajax/Farrell Publications(Excellent Publ.)

	GD25	FN65	NM94
1-Re-Intro Black Cobra & The Cobra Kid (costumed heroes)	16.00	48.00	110.00
6(#2)-Formerly Billy Bunny	10.00	30.00	65.00
3-(Pre-code)-Torpedoman app.	10.00	30.00	65.00

BLACK CONDOR (Also see Crack Comics & Freedom Fighters)
June, 1992 - No. 12, May, 1993 ($1.25, color)
DC Comics

	GD25	FN65	NM94
1-12: 1-3-Heath-c. 9,10-The Ray guest stars			1.25

BLACK CROSS SPECIAL (Dark Horse)(Value: cover or less)(See Dark Horse Presents)

BLACK DIAMOND (Americomics)(Value: cover or less)

BLACK DIAMOND WESTERN (Formerly Desperado No. 1-8)
No. 9, Mar, 1949 - No. 60, Feb, 1956 (No. 9-28: 52 pgs.)
Lev Gleason Publications

	GD25	FN65	NM94
9-Black Diamond & his horse Reliapon begin; origin Black Diamond	11.50	34.00	80.00
10	6.70	20.00	40.00
11-15	5.00	15.00	30.00
16-28(11/49-11/51)Wolverton's Bing Bang Buster	7.00	21.00	42.00
29-40: 31-One pg. Frazetta anti drug ad	4.00	10.00	20.00
41-50,53-59	3.20	8.00	16.00
51-3-D effect-c/story	9.15	27.50	55.00
52-3-D effect story	8.35	25.00	50.00
60-Last issue	4.00	11.00	22.00

NOTE: ***Biro** c-9-35?. **Fass** a-58, c-54-56, 58. **Guardineer** a-9, 15, 18. **Kida** a-9. **Maurer** a-10. **Ed Moore** a-16. **Morisi** a-55. **Tuska** a-10, 48.*

BLACK DRAGON, THE
May, 1985 - No. 6, Oct, 1985 (Baxter paper; mini-series; adults only)
Epic Comics (Marvel)

	GD25	FN65	NM94
1-Bolton-c/a in all		.80	2.00
2-6			1.00

BLACK FURY (Becomes Wild West No. 58) (See Blue Bird)
May, 1955 - No. 57, Mar-Apr, 1966 (Horse stories)
Charlton Comics Group

	GD25	FN65	NM94
1	4.35	13.00	26.00
2	2.40	6.00	12.00
3-10	1.60	4.00	8.00
11-15,19,20	1.20	3.00	6.00
16-18-Ditko-a	4.20	12.50	25.00
21-30	.90	2.25	4.50
31-57	.70	1.75	3.50

BLACK GOLD
1945? (8 pgs. in color)
Esso Service Station (Giveaway)

	GD25	FN65	NM94
nn-Reprints from True Comics	4.00	11.00	22.00

BLACK GOLIATH
Feb, 1976 - No. 5, Nov, 1976
Marvel Comics Group

	GD25	FN65	NM94
1: 1-3-Tuska-a(p)		1.60	4.00
2-5		.80	2.00

BLACKHAWK (Formerly Uncle Sam #1-8; see Military & Modern Comics)
No. 9, Winter, 1944 - No. 243, 10-11/68; No. 244, 1-2/76 - No. 250, 1-2/77; No. 251, 10/82 - No. 273, 11/84
Comic Magazines(Quality)No. 9-107(12/56); National Periodical Publ. No. 108(1/57)-250; DC Comics No. 251 on

	GD25	FN65	NM94
9 (1944)	200.00	600.00	1400.00
10 (1946)	79.00	235.00	550.00
11-15: 14-Ward-a; 13,14-Fear app.	54.00	160.00	350.00
16-20: 20-Ward Blackhawk	46.00	140.00	300.00
21-30	33.00	100.00	220.00
31-40: 31-Chop Chop by Jack Cole	24.00	122.00	160.00
41-49,51-60	19.00	55.00	125.00
50-1st Killer Shark; origin in text	22.00	65.00	140.00
61-Used in **POP**, pg. 91	17.00	50.00	110.00
62-Used in **POP**, pg. 92 & color illo	17.00	50.00	110.00
63-70,72-80: 65-H-Bomb explosion panel. 66-B&W & color illos **POP**.70-Return of Killer Shark. 75-Intro. Blackie the Hawk	15.00	45.00	100.00
71-Origin retold; flying saucer-c; A-Bomb panels	18.00	55.00	120.00
81-86: Last precode (3/55)	14.00	42.50	95.00
87-92,94-99,101-107	12.00	35.00	75.00
93-Origin in text	12.50	37.50	80.00
100	15.00	45.00	100.00
108-1st DC issue (1/57); re-intro. Blackie, the Hawk, their mascot; not in #115	43.00	129.00	300.00
109-117	13.00	40.00	90.00
118-Frazetta-r/Jimmy Wakely #4 (3 pgs.)	14.00	41.00	95.00
119-130	9.00	28.00	65.00
131-140: 133-Intro. Lady Blackhawk	7.00	21.00	48.00
141-163,165,166: 143-Kurtzman-r/Jimmy Wakely #4. 166-Last 10 cent issue	5.00	15.00	35.00
164-Origin retold	5.00	14.00	32.00
167-180	1.85	5.50	13.00
181-190	1.50	3.75	9.00
191-197,199-202,204-210: 196-Combat Diary series begins. 197-New look for Blackhawks	1.25	3.00	7.50
198-Origin retold	1.60	4.00	9.50
203-Origin Chop Chop (12/64)	1.30	3.25	8.00

211-243(1968): 228-Batman, Green Lantern, Superman, The Flash cameos. 230-Blackhawks become superheroes. 242-Return to old costumes

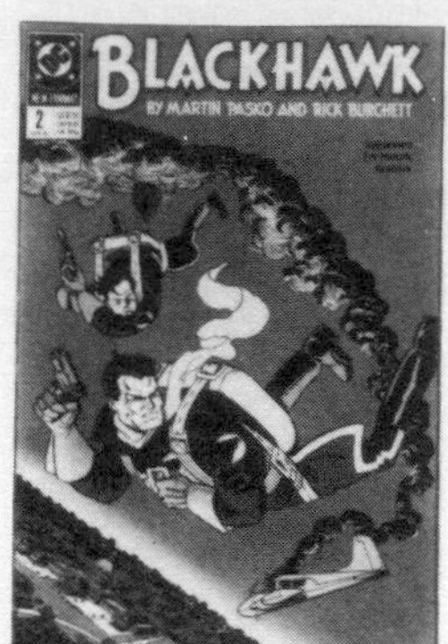

Blackhawk #2(4/89), © DC

Black Knight #3 (8/90), © MEG

Black Lightning #2, © DC

	GD25	FN65	NM94
	1.00	2.00	5.00
244 ('76) -250: 250-Chuck dies		.80	2.00
251-273: 251-Origin retold; Black Knights return. 252-Intro Domino. 253-Part origin Hendrickson. 258-Blackhawk's Island destroyed. 259-Part origin Chop-Chop. 265-273 (75 cent cover price)			1.00

NOTE: **Chaykin** *a-260; c-257-260, 262.* **Crandall** *a-10, 11, 13, 16?, 18-20, 22-26, 30-33, 35p, 36(2), 37, 38?, 39-44, 46-50, 52-58, 60, 63, 64, 66, 67; c-14-20, 22-63(most except #28-33, 36, 37, 39).* **Evans** *a-244, 245,246i, 248-250i.* **G. Kane** *c-263, 264.* **Kubert** *c-244, 245.* **Newton** *a-266p.* **Severin** *a-257.***Spiegle** *a-261-267, 269-273; c-265-272.* **Toth** *a-260p.* **Ward** *a-16-27(Chop Chop, 8pgs. ea.); pencilled stories-No. 17-63(approx.).* **Wildey** *a-268. Chop Chop solo stories in #10-95?*

BLACKHAWK
Mar, 1988 - No. 3, May, 1988 ($2.95, mini-series)
DC Comics

	GD25	FN65	NM94
1-3: Chaykin painted-c/a		1.20	3.00

BLACKHAWK
March, 1989 - No. 16, Aug, 1990 ($1.50, color, mature readers)
DC Comics

	GD25	FN65	NM94
1-6,8-16: 16-Crandall-c swipe			1.50
7-($2.50, 52 pgs.)-Story-r/Military #1		1.00	2.50
Annual 1 (1989, $2.95, 68 pgs.)-Recaps origin of Blackhawk, Lady Blackhawk, and others		1.20	3.00
Special 1 (1992, $3.50, 68 pgs.)-Mature readers		1.40	3.50

BLACKHAWK INDIAN TOMAHAWK WAR, THE
1951 (Also see Fighting Indians of the Wild West)
Avon Periodicals

	GD25	FN65	NM94
nn-Kinstler-c; Kit West story	10.00	30.00	70.00

BLACK HOLE (See Walt Disney Showcase #54)
March, 1980 - No. 4, September, 1980 (Disney movie)
Whitman Publishing Co.

	GD25	FN65	NM94
11295(#1)-Photo-c; Spiegle-a			1.00
2-4-Spiegle-a. 3-McWilliams-a; photo-c			1.00

BLACK HOOD, THE (See Blue Ribbon, Flyman & Mighty Comics)
June, 1983 - No. 3, Oct, 1983 (Printed on Mandell paper)
Red Circle Comics (Archie)

	GD25	FN65	NM94
1-Morrow, McWilliams, Wildey-a; Toth-c			1.50
2,3: MLJ's The Fox by Toth, c/a. 3-Morrow-a			1.00

(Also see Archie's Super-Hero Special Digest #2)

BLACK HOOD
Dec, 1991 - No. 12, Dec, 1992 ($1.00, color)
DC/Impact Comics

	GD25	FN65	NM94
1-12: 11-Intro The Fox. 12-Origin Black Hood			1.00
Annual 1 (1992, $2.50, 68 pgs.)-W/Trading card		1.00	2.50

BLACK HOOD COMICS (Formerly Hangman #2-8; Laugh Comics #20 on; also see Black Swan, Jackpot, Roly Poly & Top-Notch #9)
No. 9, Winter, 1943-44 - No. 19, Summer, 1946 (on radio in 1943)
MLJ Magazines

	GD25	FN65	NM94
9-The Hangman & The Boy Buddies cont'd	54.00	160.00	375.00
10-Hangman & Dusty, the Boy Detective app.	29.00	85.00	200.00
11-Dusty app.; no Hangman	20.00	60.00	140.00
12-18: 14-Kinstler blood-c. 17-Hal Foster swipe from Prince Valiant; 1st issue with "An Archie Magazine" on-c	20.00	60.00	140.00
19-I.D. exposed	25.00	75.00	175.00

NOTE: *Hangman by Fuje in 9, 10.* **Kinstler** *a-15, c-14-16.*

BLACK JACK (Rocky Lane's...; formerly Jim Bowie)
No. 20, Nov, 1957 - No. 30, Nov, 1959
Charlton Comics

	GD25	FN65	NM94
20	5.00	15.00	30.00
21,27,29,30	3.20	8.00	16.00
22-(68 pages)	4.20	12.50	25.00
23-Williamson/Torres-a	5.00	15.00	30.00
24-26,28-Ditko-a	5.85	17.50	35.00

BLACK KNIGHT, THE
May, 1953; 1963
Toby Press

	GD25	FN65	NM94
1-Bondage-c	13.00	40.00	90.00
Super Reprint No. 11 (1963)-Reprints 1953 issue	2.80	7.00	14.00

BLACK KNIGHT, THE (Also see The Avengers #48, Marvel Super Heroes & Tales To Astonish #52)
May, 1955 - No. 5, April, 1956
Atlas Comics (MgPC)

	GD25	FN65	NM94
1-Origin Crusader; Maneely-c/a	60.00	180.00	425.00
2-Maneely-c/a(4)	43.00	130.00	300.00
3-5: 4-Maneely-c/a. 5-Maneely-c, Shores-a	36.00	107.00	250.00

BLACK KNIGHT
June, 1990 - No. 4, Sept, 1990 ($1.50, mini-series)
Marvel Comics

	GD25	FN65	NM94
1-4: 1-Original Black Knight returns			1.50

BLACK LIGHTNING (See Brave & The Bold, Cancelled Comic Cavalcade, DC Comics Presents #16, Detective #490 and World's Finest)
April, 1977 - No. 11, Sept-Oct, 1978
National Periodical Publications/DC Comics

	GD25	FN65	NM94
1		.80	2.00
2-11: 4-Intro Cyclotronic Man. 11-The Ray app.			1.00

NOTE: **Buckler** *c-1-3p, 6-11p. #11 is 44 pgs.*

BLACK MAGIC (...Magazine) (Becomes Cool Cat V8#6 on)
10-11/50 - V4#1, 6-7/53: V4#2, 9-10/53 - V5#3, 11-12/54; V6#1, 9-10/57 - V7#2, 11-12/58: V7#3, 7-8/60 - V8#5, 11-12/61
(V1#1-5, 52pgs.; V1#6-V3#3, 44pgs.)
Crestwood Publ. V1#1-4,V6#1-V7#5/Headline V1#5-V5#3,V7#6-V8#5

	GD25	FN65	NM94
V1#1-S&K-a, 10 pgs.; Meskin-a(2)	57.00	170.00	400.00
2-S&K-a, 17 pgs.; Meskin-a	27.00	81.00	190.00
3-6(8-9/51)-S&K, Roussos, Meskin-a	20.00	60.00	140.00
V2#1(10-11/51),4,5,7(#13),9(#15),12(#18)-S&K-a	14.00	43.00	100.00
2,3,6,8,10,11(#17)	10.00	30.00	70.00
V3#1(#19, 12/52) - 6(#24, 5/53)-S&K-a	11.50	34.00	80.00
V4#1(#25, 6-7/53), 2(#26, 9-10/53)-S&K-a(3-4)	12.00	35.00	85.00
3(#27, 11-12/53)-S&K-a; Ditko-a (1st published-a); also see Captain 3-D & Fantastic Fears #5 (Fantastic Fears #5 was 1st drawn, but not 1st published Ditko-a)	27.00	81.00	190.00
4(#28)-Eyes ripped out/story-S&K, Ditko-a	17.00	52.00	120.00
5(#29, 3-4/54)-S&K, Ditko-a	13.50	41.00	95.00
6(#30, 5-6/54)-S&K, Powell?-a	9.15	27.50	55.00
V5#1(#31, 7-8/54 - 3(#33, 11-12/54)-S&K-a	8.35	25.00	50.00
V6#1(#34, 9-10/57), 2(#35, 11-12/57)	4.70	14.00	28.00
3(1-2/58) - 6(7-8/58)	4.70	14.00	28.00
V7#1(9-10/58) - 3(7-8/60)	4.00	11.00	22.00
4(9-10/60), 5(11-12/60)-Torres-a	4.70	14.00	28.00
6(1-2/61)-Powell-a(2)	4.00	11.00	22.00
V8#1(3-4/61)-Powell-c/a	4.00	11.00	22.00
2(5-6/61)-E.C. story swipe/W.F. #22; Ditko, Powell-a	4.70	14.00	28.00
3(7-8/61)-E.C. story swipe/W.F. #22; Powell-a(2)	4.70	14.00	28.00
4(9-10/61)-Powell-a(5)	4.00	11.00	22.00
5-E.C. story swipe/W.S.F. #28; Powell-a(3)	4.70	14.00	28.00

NOTE: **Bernard Baily** *a-V4#6?, V5#3(2).* **Grandenetti** *a-V2#3, 11.* **Kirby** *c-V1#1-6, V2#1-12, V3#1-6, V4#1, 2, 4-6, V5#1-3.* **McWilliams** *a-V3#2i.* **Meskin** *a-V1#1(2), 2, 3, 4(2), 5(2), 6, V2/1, 2, 3(2), 4(3), 5, 6(2), 7-9, 11, 12i, V3#1(2), 5, 6, V5#1(2), 2.* **Orlando** *a-V6#1, 4, V7#2; c-V6/1-6.* **Powell** *a-V5#1?.* **Roussos** *a-V1#3-5, 6(2), V2#3(2), 4, 5(2), 6, 8, 9, 10(2), 11, 12p, V3#1(2), 2i, 5, V5#2.* **Simon** *a-V2#12, V3#2, V7#5? c-V4#3?, V7#3?, 4, 5?, 6?, V8#1-5.* **Simon & Kirby** *a-V1#1, 2(2), 3-6, V2#1, 4, 5, 7, 9, 12, V3#1-6, V4#1(3), 2(4), 3(2), 4(2), 5, 6, V5#1-3; c-V2#1.* **Leonard Starr** *a-V1#1.* **Tuska** *a-V6#3, 4.* **Woodbridge** *a-V7#4.*

BLACK MAGIC
Oct-Nov, 1973 - No. 9, Apr-May, 1975

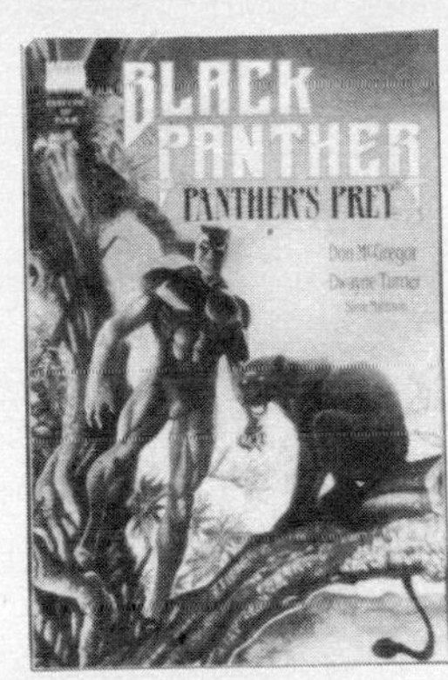

Black Panther: Panther's Prey #1 © MEG

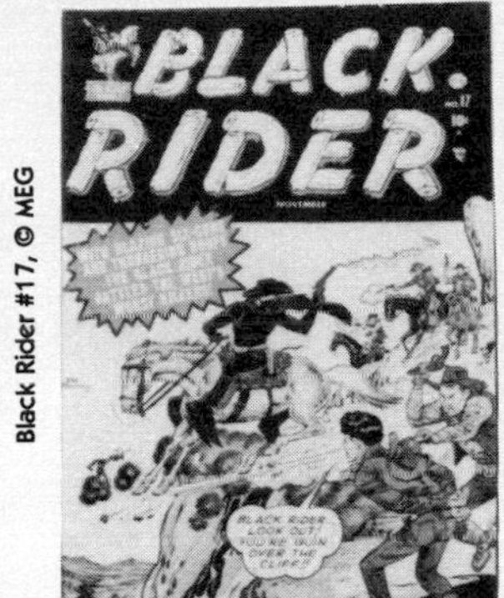

Black Rider #17, © MEG

The Black Terror #26, © STD

GD25 FN65 NM94 GD25 FN65 NM94

National Periodical Publications

1-S&K reprints 1.50
2-9-S&K reprints 1.00

BLACK MAGIC (Eclipse)(Value: cover or less)

BLACKMAIL TERROR (See Harvey Comics Library)

BLACK MASK
1993 - No. 3, 1993 ($4.95, color, mini-series, 52 pgs.)
DC Comics

1-3 1.00 2.00 5.00

BLACK ORCHID (See Adventure Comics #428 & Phantom Stranger)
Holiday, 1988-'89 - No. 3, 1989 ($3.50, mini-series, prestige format)
DC Comics

Book 1,3: Gaiman (Sandman) scripts & McKean-a in all 1.00 2.00 5.00
Book 2-Arkham Asylum story; Batman app. 1.20 3.00 7.00

BLACK ORCHID
Sept, 1993 - Present ($1.95, color)
DC Comics

1-4: Dave McKean-c .90 2.25
1-Platinum Edition 3.20 8.00 20.00
5-8 .80 2.00
Annual 1 (1993, $3.95, 68 pgs.)-Children's Crusade 1.60 4.00

BLACKOUTS (See Broadway Hollywood...)

BLACK PANTHER, THE (Also see Avengers #52, Fantastic Four #52, Jungle Action & Marvel Premiere #51-53)
Jan, 1977 - No. 15, May, 1979
Marvel Comics Group

1 1.00 2.00 5.00
2 1.20 3.00
3-10 1.00 2.50
11-15: 14,15-Avengers x-over .80 2.00

NOTE: *J. Buscema c-15p. Kirby c/a & scripts-1-12. Layton c-13i.*

BLACK PANTHER
July, 1988 - No. 4, Oct, 1988 ($1.25, color)
Marvel Comics Group

1-4 1.25

BLACK PANTHER: PANTHER'S PREY
1991 - No. 4, 1991 ($4.95, squarebound, mini-series, 52 pgs.)
Marvel Comics

1-4 1.00 2.00 5.00

BLACK PHANTOM (See Tim Holt #25, 38)
Nov, 1954 (One shot) (Female outlaw)
Magazine Enterprises

1 (A-1 #122)-The Ghost Rider story plus 3 Black Phantom stories; Headlight-c/a 24.00 73.00 170.00

BLACK PHANTOM
1989 - No. 3, 1990 ($2.50, B&W; #2 color)(Reprints & new-a)
AC Comics

1,2: 1-Ayers-r, Bolle-r/B.P. #1. 2-Redmask-r 1.00 2.50
3 ($2.75, B&W)-B.P., Redmask-r & new-a 1.10 2.75

BLACK PHANTOM, RETURN OF THE (See Wisco)

BLACK RIDER (Formerly Western Winners; Western Tales of Black Rider #28-31; Gunsmoke Western #32 on)(Also see All Western Winners, Best Western, Kid Colt, Outlaw Kid, Rex Hart, Two-Gun Kid, Two-Gun Western, Western Gunfighters, Western Winners, & Wild Western)
No. 8, 3/50 - No. 18, 1/52; No. 19, 11/53 - No. 27, 3/55
Marvel/Atlas Comics(CDS No. 8-17/CPS No. 19 on)

8 (#1)-Black Rider & his horse Satan begin; 36 pgs; Stan Lee photo-c as Black Rider) 29.00 85.00 200.00
9-52 pgs. begin, end #14 14.00 43.00 100.00
10-Origin Black Rider 17.00 52.00 120.00
11-14(Last 52pgs.) 10.00 30.00 70.00
15-19: 19-Two-Gun Kid app. 10.00 30.00 60.00
20-Classic-c; Two-Gun Kid app. 10.00 30.00 70.00
21-26: 21-23-Two-Gun Kid app. 24,25-Arrowhead app. 26-Kid Colt app. 9.15 27.50 55.00
27-Last issue; last precode. Kid Colt app. The Spider (a villain) burns to death 9.15 27.50 55.00

NOTE: *Ayers c-22. **Jack Keller** a-15, 26, 27. **Maneely** a-14; c-16, 17, 25, 27. **Syd Shores** a-19, 21, 22, 23(3), 24(3), 25-27; c-19, 21, 23. **Sinnott** a-24, 25. **Tuska** a-12, 19-21.*

BLACK RIDER RIDES AGAIN!, THE
September, 1957
Atlas Comics (CPS)

1-Kirby-a(3); Powell-a; Severin-c 14.00 43.00 100.00

BLACKSTONE (See Super Magician Comics & Wisco Giveaways)

BLACKSTONE, MASTER MAGICIAN COMICS
Mar-Apr, 1946 - No. 3, July-Aug, 1946
Vital Publications/Street & Smith Publ.

1 16.00 48.00 110.00
2,3 12.00 36.00 85.00

BLACKSTONE, THE MAGICIAN (...Detective on cover only #3 & 4)
No. 2, May, 1948 - No. 4, Sept, 1948 (No #1)(Cont'd from E.C. #1?)
Marvel Comics (CnPC)

2-The Blonde Phantom begins 39.00 120.00 275.00
3,4: 3-Blonde Phantom by Sekowsky 25.00 75.00 175.00

BLACKSTONE, THE MAGICIAN DETECTIVE FIGHTS CRIME
Fall, 1947
E. C. Comics

1-1st app. Happy Houlihans 34.00 103.00 240.00

BLACK SWAN COMICS
1945
MLJ Magazines (Pershing Square Publ. Co.)

1-The Black Hood reprints from Black Hood No. 14; Bill Woggon-a; Suzie app. 13.00 40.00 90.00

BLACK TARANTULA (See Feature Presentations No. 5)

BLACK TERROR (See America's Best Comics & Exciting Comics)
Wint, 1942-43 - No. 27, June, 1949
Better Publications/Standard

1-Black Terror, Crime Crusader begin 104.00 310.00 725.00
2 46.00 138.00 315.00
3 35.00 105.00 250.00
4,5 28.00 82.00 200.00
6-10: 7-The Ghost app. 22.00 65.00 150.00
11-20: 20-The Scarab app. 19.00 57.00 130.00
21-Miss Masque app. 21.00 63.00 145.00
22-Part Frazetta-a on one Black Terror story 21.00 63.00 145.00
23,25-27 18.00 54.00 125.00
24-Frazetta-a (1/4 pg.) 19.00 57.00 130.00

NOTE: ***Schomburg (Xela)** c-2-27; bondage c-2, 17, 24. **Meskin** a-27. **Moreira** a-27. **Robinson/Meskin** a-23, 24(3), 25, 26. **Roussos/Mayo** a-24. **Tuska** a-26, 27.*

BLACK TERROR, THE (Eclipse)(Value: cover or less) (Also see Total Eclipse)

BLACKTHORNE 3-D SERIES (Blackthorne)(Value: cover or less)

BLACK ZEPPELIN (See Gene Day's...)

BLADE RUNNER
Oct, 1982 - No. 2, Nov, 1982 (Movie adaptation)
Marvel Comics Group

1,2-r/Marvel Super Special #22; 1-Williamson-c/a. 2-Williamson-a .75

BLAKE HARPER (See City Surgeon...)

Blasters Special #1, © DC

Blazing Six-Guns #1, © Skywald Comics

Blitzkrieg #3, © DC

BLAST (Satire Magazine)
Feb, 1971 - No. 2, May, 1971
G & D Publications

	GD25	FN65	NM94
1-Wrightson & Kaluta-a	3.00	7.50	15.00
2-Kaluta-a	2.40	6.00	12.00

BLASTERS SPECIAL
1989 ($2.00, one-shot)
DC Comics

	GD25	FN65	NM94
1-Invasion spin-off		.80	2.00

BLAST-OFF (Three Rocketeers)
October, 1965 (12¢)
Harvey Publications (Fun Day Funnies)

	GD25	FN65	NM94
1-Kirby/Williamson-a(2); Williamson/Crandall-a; Williamson/Torres/Krenkel-a; Kirby/Simon-c	3.30	10.00	23.00

BLAZE CARSON (Becomes Rex Hart No. 6 on)(See Kid Colt, Tex Taylor, Wild Western, Wisco)
Sept, 1948 - No. 5, June, 1949
Marvel Comics (USA)

	GD25	FN65	NM94
1: 1,2-Shores-c	16.00	48.00	110.00
2,4,5: 4-Two-Gun Kid app. 5-Tex Taylor app.	11.00	32.00	75.00
3-Used by N.Y. State Legis. Comm. (injury to eye splash); Tex Morgan app.	12.00	36.00	85.00

BLAZE: LEGACY OF BLOOD (See Ghost Rider & Ghost Rider/Blaze)
Dec, 1993 - No. 4, Mar, 1994 ($1.75, color mini-series)
Marvel Comics

	GD25	FN65	NM94
1-4		.70	1.75

BLAZE THE WONDER COLLIE (Formerly Molly Manton's Romances #1?)
No. 2, Oct, 1949 - No. 3, Feb, 1950 (Both have photo covers)
Marvel Comics(SePI)

	GD25	FN65	NM94
2(#1), 3-(Scarce)	14.00	43.00	100.00

BLAZING BATTLE TALES
July, 1975
Seaboard Periodicals (Atlas)

	GD25	FN65	NM94
1-Intro. Sgt. Hawk & the Sky Demon; Severin, McWilliams, Sparling-a; Thorne-c			1.00

BLAZING COMBAT (Magazine)
Oct, 1965 - No. 4, July, 1966 (Black & White, 35 cents)
Warren Publishing Co.

	GD25	FN65	NM94
1-Frazetta painted-c on all	10.00	30.00	65.00
2	3.60	9.00	18.00
3,4: 4-Frazetta half pg. ad	2.40	6.00	12.00
...Anthology (reprints from No. 1-4)	.80	2.00	4.00

NOTE: *Above has art by* ***Colan, Crandall, Evans, Morrow, Orlando, Severin, Torres, Toth, Williamson,*** *and* ***Wood.***

BLAZING COMICS
6/44 - #3, 9/44; #4, 2/45; #5, 3/45; #5(V2#2), 3/55 - #6(V2#3), 1955?
Enwil Associates/Rural Home

	GD25	FN65	NM94
1-The Green Turtle, Red Hawk, Black Buccaneer begin; origin Jun-Gal	31.00	90.00	200.00
2-5: 3-Briefer-a. 5-(V2#2 inside)	18.00	55.00	120.00
5(3/55, V2#2-inside)-Black Buccaneer-c, 6(V2#3-inside, 1955)-Indian/Jap-c	7.50	22.50	45.00

NOTE: *No. 5 & 6 contain remaindered comics rebound and the contents can vary. Cloak & Daggar, Will Rogers, Superman 64, Star Spangled 130, Kaanga known. Value would be half of contents.*

BLAZING SIXGUNS
December, 1952
Avon Periodicals

	GD25	FN65	NM94
1-Kinstler-c/a; Larsen/Alascia-a(2), Tuska?-a; Jesse James, Kit Carson, Wild Bill Hickok app.	10.00	30.00	65.00

BLAZING SIXGUNS
1964
I.W./Super Comics

	GD25	FN65	NM94
I.W. Reprint #1,8,9: 1-r/Wild Bill Hickok #26 & Blazing Sixguns #1 by Avon; Kinstler-c. 8-r/Blazing Western #?; Kinstler-c. 9-r/Blazing Western #1; Ditko-r	1.40	3.50	8.00
Super Reprint #10,11,15,16: 10,11-r/The Rider #2,1. 15-r/Silver Kid Western #?. 16-r/Buffalo Bill #?; Wildey-r; Severin-c. 17(1964)-r/Western True Crime #?	1.40	3.50	7.00
12-Reprints Bullseye #3; S&K-a	3.60	9.00	18.00
18-r/Straight Arrow #? by Powell; Severin-c	1.80	4.50	9.00

BLAZING SIX-GUNS (Also see Sundance Kid)
Feb, 1971 - No. 2, April, 1971 (52 pages)
Skywald Comics

	GD25	FN65	NM94
1-The Red Mask, Sundance Kid begin, Avon's Geronimo reprint by Kinstler; Wyatt Earp app.		1.60	4.00
2-Wild Bill Hickok, Jesse James, Kit Carson-r plus M.E. Red Mask-r		.80	2.00

BLAZING WEST (Also see The Hooded Horseman)
Fall, 1948 - No. 22, Mar-Apr, 1952
American Comics Group(B&I Publ./Michel Publ.)

	GD25	FN65	NM94
1-Origin & 1st app. Injun Jones, Tenderfoot & Buffalo Belle; Texas Tim & Ranger begins, ends #13	12.00	36.00	85.00
2,3	7.50	22.50	45.00
4-Origin & 1st app. Little Lobo; Starr-a	5.35	16.00	32.00
5-10: 5-Starr-a	4.70	14.00	28.00
11-13	4.00	10.00	20.00
14-Origin & 1st app. The Hooded Horseman	7.50	22.50	45.00
15-22: 15,16,18,19-Starr-a	5.00	15.00	30.00

BLAZING WESTERN
Jan, 1954 - No. 5, Sept, 1954
Timor Publications

	GD25	FN65	NM94
1-Ditko-a; Text story by Bruce Hamilton	10.00	30.00	60.00
2-4	4.00	11.00	22.00
5-Disbrow-a	4.70	14.00	28.00

BLESSED PIUS X
No date (32 pages; text, comics) (Paper cover)
Catechetical Guild (Giveaway)

	GD25	FN65	NM94
nn	3.20	8.00	16.00

BLIND JUSTICE (Also see Batman: Blind Justice)
1989 (Giveaway, squarebound)
DC Comics/Diamond Comic Distributors

	GD25	FN65	NM94
nn-Contains Detective #598-600 by Batman movie writer Sam Hamm, w/covers; published same time as originals?		.80	2.00

BLITZKRIEG
Jan-Feb, 1976 - No. 5, Sept-Oct, 1976
National Periodical Publications

	GD25	FN65	NM94
1-Kubert-c on all			1.25
2-5			.75

BLONDE PHANTOM (Formerly All-Select #1-11; Lovers #23 on)(Also see Blackstone, Marvel Mystery, Millie The Model #2, Sub-Mariner Comics #25 & Sun Girl)
No. 12, Winter, 1946-47 - No. 22, March, 1949
Marvel Comics (MPC)

	GD25	FN65	NM94
12-Miss America begins, ends #14	75.00	225.00	500.00
13-Sub-Mariner begins (not in #16)	50.00	150.00	340.00
14,15: 15-Kurtzman's "Hey Look"	42.00	125.00	275.00
16-Captain America with Bucky story by Rico(p), 6 pgs.; Kurtzman's "Hey Look" (1 pg.)	54.00	162.00	365.00
17-22: 22-Anti Wertham editorial	38.00	115.00	250.00

NOTE: ***Shores*** *c-12-18.*

Blondie Comics #13, © KING

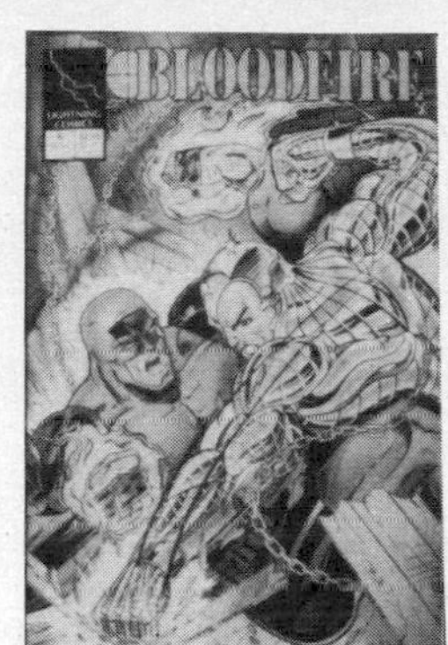

Bloodfire #6, © Joseph A. Zyskowski

Bloodshot #1 © Voyager Communications

GD25 FN65 NM94 GD25 FN65 NM94

BLONDIE (See Ace Comics, Comics Reading Libraries, Dagwood, Daisy & Her Pups, Eat Right to Work..., King & Magic Comics)
1942 - 1946
David McKay Publications
Feature Books 12 (Rare) 50.00 150.00 350.00
Feature Books 27-29,31,34(1940) 11.50 34.00 80.00
Feature Books 36,38,40,42,43,45,47 11.00 32.00 75.00
...1944 (Hard-c, 1938, B&W, 128 pgs.)-1944 daily strip-r 11.00 32.00 75.00

BLONDIE & DAGWOOD FAMILY
Oct, 1963 - No. 4, Dec, 1965 (68 pages)
Harvey Publications (King Features Synd.)
1 3.00 7.50 15.00
2-4 1.80 4.50 0.00

BLONDIE COMICS (...Monthly No. 16-141)
Spring, 1947 - No. 163, Nov, 1965; No. 164, Aug, 1966 - No. 175, Dec, 1967; No. 177, Feb, 1969 - No. 222, Nov, 1976
David McKay #1-15/Harvey #16-163/King #164-175/Charlton #177 on
1 14.00 43.00 100.00
2 8.35 25.00 50.00
3-5 5.85 17.50 35.00
6-10 4.35 13.00 26.00
11-15 3.60 9.00 18.00
16-(3/50; 1st Harvey issue) 4.00 12.00 24.00
17-20 3.20 8.00 16.00
21-30 2.40 6.00 12.00
31-50 1.80 4.50 9.00
51-80 1.60 4.00 8.00
81-124,126-130 1.40 3.50 7.00
125 (80 pgs.) 1.80 4.50 9.00
131-136,138,139 1.20 3.00 6.00
137,140-(80 pages) 1.60 4.00 8.00
141-167(#148,155,157-159,161-163 are 68 pgs.) 1.60 4.00 8.00
168-175,177-222 (no #176) .80 2.00 4.00
Blondie, Dagwood & Daisy 1(100 pgs., 1953) 11.50 34.00 80.00
1950 Giveaway 3.20 8.00 16.00
1962,1964 Giveaway 1.00 2.50 5.00
N. Y. State Dept. of Mental Hygiene Giveaway-('50,'56,'61) Regular size (Diff. issues) 16 pages; no # 1.60 4.00 8.00

BLOOD
Feb, 1988 - No. 4, Apr, 1988 ($3.25, adults)
Epic Comics (Marvel)
1-4 1.30 3.25

BLOOD AND GLORY (Punisher & Captain America)
Oct, 1992 - No. 3, Dec, 1992 ($5.95, color, mini-series)
Marvel Comics
1-3: 1-Embossed wraparound-c 1.00 2.50 6.00

BLOODBATH
Dec, 1993 - No. 2, 1994 ($3.50, color, limited series, 68 pgs.)
DC Comics
1,2: 1-Neon ink-c 1.40 3.50

BLOODFIRE
June, 1993 - Present ($2.95, color)
Lightning Comics
1-($3.50)-Foil-c; 1st app. Bloodfire 1.60 4.00
2-($2.95)-Origin; contracts HIV virus via transfusion 1.20 3.00
3-8: 5-Polybagged w/card & collectors warning on bag 1.20 3.00

BLOOD IS THE HARVEST
1950 (32 pages) (paper cover)
Catechetical Guild
(Scarce)-Anti-communism(13 known copies) 75.00 225.00 540.00
Black & white version (5 known copies), saddle stitched 30.00 90.00 200.00
Untrimmed version (only one known copy), estimated value-$600
NOTE: *In 1979 nine copies of the color version surfaced from the old Guild's files plus the five black & white copies.*

BLOOD IS THE HARVEST (Eclipse)(Value: cover or less)

BLOODLINES: A TALE FROM THE HEART OF AFRICA
1992 ($5.95, color, 52 pgs.)(See Tales From the Heart of Africa)
Epic Comics (Marvel)
1-Story cont'd from Tales From... 1.00 2.50 6.00

BLOOD OF DRACULA
Nov, 1987 - No. 20?, 1990 ($1.75-$1.95, B&W)($2.25 #14,16 on)
Apple Comics
1-13: 6-Begin $1.95-c. 10-Chadwick-c .80 2.00
14,16-20 ($2.25): 14,16-19 Lost Frankenstein pages by Wrightson .90 2.25
15-Contains stereo flexidisc ($3.75) 1.50 3.75

BLOOD OF THE INNOCENT (WaRP)(Value: cover or less)

BLOODSCENT (Comico)(Value: cover or less)

BLOODSEED
Oct, 1993 - No. 2, Nov, 1993 ($1.95, color, mini-series, adults)
Marvel Frontier Comics
1,2: Sharp/Cam Smith-a .80 2.00

BLOODSHOT (See Eternal Warrior #4 & Rai #0)
Feb, 1993 - Present ($2.25/$2.50, color)
Valiant
1-($3.50)-Chromium embossed-c by B. Smith w/poster 1.70 4.25
2-($2.50) 1.00 2.50
3,4: 3-Begin $2.25-c; cont'd in Hard Corps #5. 4-Eternal Warrior-c/story .50 .90 2.25
5,8-16: 5-Rai & Eternal Warrior app. .90 2.25
6-1st app. Ninjak (out of costume) 1.40 3.50
7-1st app. Ninjak in costume 1.00 2.00 5.00
0-($3.50)-Chromium-c by Quesada; origin 1.40 3.50

BLOODSTRIKE
1993 - Present ($1.95, color)
Image Comics
1-4: Liefeld layouts .80 2.00

BLOOD SWORD, THE (Jademan)(Value: cover or less)

BLOOD SWORD DYNASTY (Jademan)(Value: cover or less)

BLOOD SYNDICATE
Apr, 1993 - Present ($1.50, color)
DC Comics (Milestone)
1-($2.95)-Collector's Edition; polybagged with poster, trading card, & acid-free backing board (direct sale only) 1.20 3.00
1-12: 1-Regular Edition ($1.50). 8-Intro Kwai 1.50

BLUE BEETLE, THE (Also see All Top, Big-3, Mystery Men & Weekly Comic Magazine)
Winter, 1939-40 - No. 57, 7/48; No. 58, 4/50 - No. 60, 8/50
Fox Publ. No. 1-11, 31-60; Holyoke No. 12-30
1-Reprints from Mystery Men 1-5; Blue Beetle origin; Yarko the Great-r/from Wonder/Wonderworld 2-5 all by Eisner; Master Magician app.; (Blue Beetle in 4 different costumes) 200.00 600.00 1400.00
2-K-51-r by Powell/Wonderworld 8,9 83.00 215.00 550.00
3-Simon-c 58.00 150.00 400.00
4-Marijuana drug mention story 42.00 125.00 275.00
5-Zanzibar The Magician by Tuska 35.00 105.00 230.00
6-Dynamite Thor begins (1st); origin Blue Beetle 33.00 100.00 220.00
7,8-Dynamo app. in both. 8-Last Thor 30.00 90.00 200.00

Blue Beetle #27, © FOX

Blue Beetle #21(8/55), © DC

Blue Bolt V3#4, © NOVP

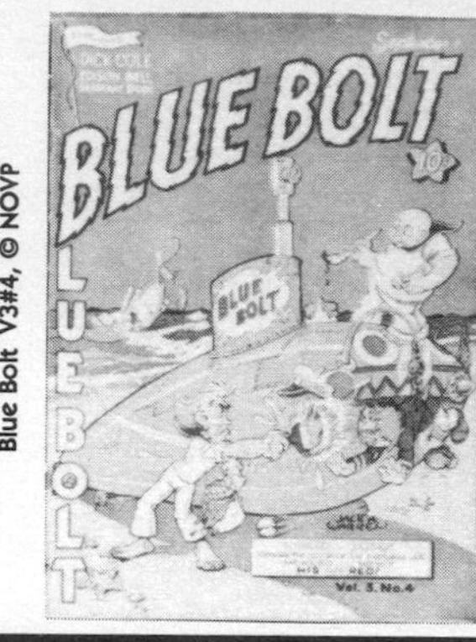

GD25 FN65 NM94

9,10-The Blackbird & The Gorilla app. in both. 10-Bondage/hypo-c
28.00 85.00 190.00
11(2/42)-The Gladiator app. 28.00 85.00 190.00
12(6/42)-The Black Fury app. 28.00 85.00 190.00
13-V-Man begins (1st app.), ends #18; Kubert-a 33.00 100.00 220.00
14,15-Kubert-a in both. 14-Intro. side-kick (c/text only), Sparky (called Spunky #17-19) 32.00 95.00 210.00
16-18: 17-Brodsky-c 25.00 75.00 165.00
19-Kubert-a 27.00 80.00 175.00
20-Origin/1st app. Tiger Squadron; Arabian Nights begin
29.00 85.00 190.00
21-26: 24-Intro. & only app. The Halo. 26-General Patton story & photo
18.00 55.00 120.00
27-Tamaa, Jungle Prince app. 17.00 50.00 110.00
28-30(2/44) 14.00 43.00 100.00
31(6/44), 33-40: "The Threat from Saturn" serial in #34-38
11.00 32.00 75.00
32-Hitler-c 13.00 40.00 90.00
41-45 10.00 30.00 65.00
46-The Puppeteer app. 10.00 30.00 70.00
47-Kamen & Baker-a begin 54.00 160.00 365.00
48-50 42.00 125.00 285.00
51,53 37.00 110.00 250.00
52-Kamen bondage-c 54.00 160.00 375.00
54-Used in **SOTI**. Illo-"Children call these 'headlights' comics"
75.00 225.00 500.00
55,57(7/48)-Last Kamen issue; becomes Western Killers?
35.00 105.00 235.00
56-Used in **SOTI**, pg. 145 35.00 105.00 235.00
58(4/50)-60-No Kamen-a 8.35 25.00 50.00
NOTE: ***Kamen** a-47-51, 53, 55-57; c-47, 49-52. **Powell** a-4(2). Bondage-c 9-12, 46, 52.*

BLUE BEETLE (Formerly The Thing; becomes Mr. Muscles No. 22 on) (See Charlton Bullseye & Space Adventures)
No. 18, Feb, 1955 - No. 21, Aug, 1955
Charlton Comics

18,19-(Pre-1944-r). 19-Bouncer, Rocket Kelly-r 10.00 30.00 70.00
20-Joan Mason by Kamen 12.00 32.00 75.00
21-New material 9.15 27.50 55.00

BLUE BEETLE (Unusual Tales #1-49; Ghostly Tales #55 on)(Also see Captain Atom & Charlton Bullseye)
V2#1, June, 1964 - V2#5, Mar-Apr, 1965; V3#50, July, 1965 - V3#54, Feb-Mar, 1966; #1, June, 1967 - #5, Nov, 1968
Charlton Comics

V2#1-Origin Dan Garrett-Blue Beetle 5.50 17.00 40.00
2-5,V3#50-54: 5-Weiss illo; 1st published-a? 4.30 13.00 30.00
1(1967)-Question series begins by Ditko 9.00 28.00 65.00
2-Origin Ted Kord-Blue Beetle (see Capt. Atom #83 for 1st Ted Kord Blue Beetle); Dan Garrett x-over 4.00 11.00 25.00
3-5 (All Ditko-c/a in #1-5) 3.20 8.00 20.00
1,3(Modern Comics-1977)-Reprints 1.00
NOTE: *#6 only appeared in the fanzine 'The Charlton Portfolio.'*

BLUE BEETLE (Also see Americomics & Crisis On Infinite Earths)
June, 1986 - No. 24, May, 1988
DC Comics

1-Origin retold; intro. Firefist 1.00
2-24: 2-Origin Firefist. 5-7-The Question app. 11-14-New Teen Titans x-over. 18-Begin $1.00-c. 20-Justice League app. 20,21-Millennium tie-ins
1.00

BLUEBERRY (See Lt. Blueberry & Marshal Blueberry)
1989 - No. 5, 1990 ($12.95/$14.95, color, graphic novel)
Epic Comics (Marvel)

1,3,4,5-($12.95)-Moebius-a in all 1.85 5.50 13.00
2-($14.95) 2.15 6.50 15.00

GD25 FN65 NM94

BLUE BIRD COMICS
Late 1940's - 1964 (Giveaway)
Various Shoe Stores/Charlton Comics

nn(1947-50)(36 pgs.)-Several issues; Human Torch, Sub-Mariner app. in some
6.70 20.00 40.00
1959-Li'l Genius, Timmy the Timid Ghost, Wild Bill Hickok (All #1)
1.40 3.50 7.00
1959-(6 titles; all #2) Black Fury #1,4,5, Freddy #4, Li'l Genius, Timmy the Timid Ghost #4, Masked Raider #4, Wild Bill Hickok (Charlton)
1.40 3.50 7.00
1959-(#5) Masked Raider #21 1.40 3.50 7.00
1960-(6 titles)(All #4) Black Fury #8,9, Masked Raider, Freddy #8,9, Timmy the Timid Ghost #9, Li'l Genius #7,9 (Charlt.) 1.40 3.50 7.00
1961,1962-(All #10's) Atomic Mouse #12,13,16, Black Fury #11,12, Freddy, Li'l Genius, Masked Raider, Six Gun Heroes, Texas Rangers in Action, Timmy the Ghost, Wild Bill Hickok, Wyatt Earp #3,11-13,16-18 (Charlton)
1.20 3.00 6.00
1963-Texas Rangers #17 (Charlton) .60 1.75 3.00
1964-Mysteries of Unexplored Worlds #18, Teenage Hotrodders #18, War Heroes #18 (Charlton) 1.00 2.50 5.00
1965-War Heroes #18 .40 1.00 2.00
NOTE: *More than one issue of each character could have been published each year. Numbering is sporadic.*

BLUE BIRD CHILDREN'S MAGAZINE, THE
V1#2, 1957 - No. 10 1958 (16 pages; soft cover; regular size)
Graphic Information Service

V1#2-10: Pat, Pete & Blue Bird app. .80 2.00 4.00

BLUE BOLT
June, 1940 - No. 101 (V10No.2), Sept-Oct, 1949
Funnies, Inc. No. 1/Novelty Press/Premium Group of Comics

V1#1-Origin Blue Bolt by Joe Simon, Sub-Zero Man, White Rider & Super Horse, Dick Cole, Wonder Boy & Sgt. Spook (1st app. of each)
167.00 500.00 1100.00
2-Simon-a 83.00 250.00 550.00
3-1 pg. Space Hawk by Wolverton; S&K-a; 1st S&K super hero (Blue Bolt); same cover date as Red Raven #1 67.00 200.00 450.00
4,5-S&K-a in each; 5-Everett-a begins on Sub-Zero
63.00 185.00 425.00
6,8-10-S&K-a 58.00 175.00 375.00
7-S&K-c/a 59.00 185.00 415.00
11,12: 11-Robot-c 59.00 185.00 415.00
V2#1-Origin Dick Cole & The Twister; Twister x-over in Dick Cole, Sub-Zero, & Blue Bolt; origin Simba Karno who battles Dick Cole thru V2#5 & becomes main supporting character V2#6 on; battle-c 18.00 55.00 125.00
2-Origin The Twister retold in text 14.00 42.00 95.00
3-5: 5-Intro. Freezum 12.00 34.00 80.00
6-Origin Sgt. Spook retold 10.00 30.00 70.00
7-12: 7-Lois Blake becomes Blue Bolt's costume aide; last Twister
9.15 27.50 55.00
V3#1-3 7.00 21.00 42.00
4-12: 4-Blue Bolt abandons costume 5.35 16.00 32.00
V4#1-Hitler, Tojo, Mussolini-c 7.50 22.50 45.00
V4#2-12: 3-Shows V4#3 on-c, V4#4 inside (9-10/43). 5-Infinity-c. 8-Last Sub-Zero 4.70 14.00 28.00
V5#1-8, V6#1-3,5-10, V7#1-12 4.00 10.00 20.00
V6#4-Racist cover 5.00 15.00 30.00
V8#1-6,8-12, V9#1-5,7,8 3.60 9.00 18.00
V8#7,V9#6,9-L. B. Cole-c 4.00 12.00 24.00
V10#1(#100) 4.00 10.00 20.00
V10#2(#101)-Last Dick Cole, Blue Bolt 4.00 10.00 20.00
NOTE: ***Everett** c-V1#4, 11, V2#1, 2. **Gustavson** a-V1#1-12, V2#1-7. **Kiefer** c-V3#1. **Rico** a-V6#10, V7#4. Blue Bolt not in V9#8.*

BLUE BOLT (Becomes Ghostly Weird Stories #120 on; continuation of Novelty Blue Bolt) (...Weird Tales #112-119)
No. 102, Nov-Dec, 1949 - No. 119, May-June, 1953

Blue Bolt Weird Tales #116, © STAR

Blue Ribbon Comics #3 (1/40), © AP

Bobby Benson's B-Bar-B Riders #1, © ME

GD25 FN65 NM94

tar Publications
02-The Chameleon, & Target app. 14.00 43.00 100.00
03,104-The Chameleon app. 104-Last Target 13.00 40.00 90.00
05-Origin Blue Bolt (from #1) retold by Simon; Chameleon & Target app.; opium den story 27.00 81.00 190.00
06-Blue Bolt by S&K begins; Spacehawk reprints from Target by Wolverton begin, ends #110; Sub-Zero begins; ends #109 24.00 70.00 165.00
07-110: 108-Last S&K Blue Bolt reprint. 109-Wolverton-c(r)/inside Spacehawk splash. 110-Target app. 22.00 65.00 155.00
11-Red Rocket & The Mask-r; last Blue Bolt; 1pg. L. B. Cole-a 21.00 63.00 145.00
12-Last Torpedo Man app. 21.00 63.00 145.00
13-Wolverton's Spacehawk-r/Target V3#7 22.00 65.00 155.00
14,116: 116-Jungle Jo-r 21.00 63.00 145.00
15-Sgt. Spook app. 23.00 70.00 160.00
17-Jo-Jo & Blue Bolt-r 21.00 63.00 145.00
18-"White Spirit" by Wood 23.00 70.00 160.00
19-Disbrow/Cole-c; Jungle Jo-r 21.00 63.00 145.00
ccepted Reprint #103(1957?, nd) 5.00 15.00 30.00
OTE: *L. B. Cole c-102-108, 110 on. **Disbrow** a-112(2), 113(3), 114(2), 115(2), 116-118. **ollingsworth** a-117. **Palais** a-112r. Sci/Fi c-105-110. Horror c-111.*

LUE BULLETEER, THE (AC)(Value: cover or less)

LUE CIRCLE COMICS (Also see Roly Poly Comic Book)
une, 1944 - No. 5, Mar, 1945; No. 6, 1950s
nwil Associates/Rural Home
1-The Blue Circle begins (1st app.); origin & 1st app. Steel Fist 13.00 40.00 90.00
2,3: 3-Hitler parody-c 9.15 27.50 55.00
4,5: 5-Last Steel Fist 5.35 17.50 35.00
6-(1950s)-Colossal Features-r 5.35 17.50 35.00

LUE DEVIL (See Fury of Firestorm #24)
une, 1984 - No. 31, Dec, 1986 (75 cents)
C Comics
1-30: 4-Origin Nebiros. 7-Gil Kane-a. 8-Giffen-a. 17-19: Crisis x-over 1.00
31-($1.25, 52 pgs.) 1.25
nnual 1 (11/85) Team ups w/Black Orchid, Creeper, Demon, Madame Xanadu, Man-Bat & Phantom Stranger 1.25

LUE PHANTOM, THE
une-Aug, 1962
ell Publishing Co.
1(01-066-208)-by Fred Fredericks 3.60 9.00 18.00

LUE RIBBON COMICS (...Mystery Comics No. 9-18)
ov, 1939 - No. 22, March, 1942 (1st MLJ series)
LJ Magazines
1-Dan Hastings, Richy the Amazing Boy, Rang-A-Tang the Wonder Dog begin (1st app. of each); Little Nemo app. (not by W. McCay); Jack Cole-a(3) 179.00 535.00 1250.00
2-Bob Phantom, Silver Fox (both in #3), Rang-A-Tang Club & Cpl. Collins begin (1st app. of each); Jack Cole-a 75.00 225.00 500.00
3-J. Cole-a 50.00 150.00 340.00
4-Doc Strong, The Green Falcon, & Hercules begin (1st app. each); origin & 1st app. The Fox & Ty-Gor, Son of the Tiger 54.00 162.00 365.00
5-8: 8-Last Hercules; 6,7-Biro, Meskin-a. 7-Fox app. on-c 37.00 110.00 250.00
9-(Scarce)-Origin & 1st app. Mr. Justice (2/41) 136.00 407.00 950.00
10-13: 12-Last Doc Strong. 13-Inferno, the Flame Breather begins, ends #19; Devil-c 63.00 185.00 415.00
14,15,17,18: 15-Last Green Falcon 54.00 160.00 355.00
16-Origin & 1st app. Captain Flag (9/41) 100.00 300.00 675.00
19-22: 20-Last Ty-Gor. 22-Origin Mr. Justice retold 50.00 150.00 340.00
OTE: *Biro c-3-5; a-2 (Cpl. Collins & Scoop Cody). **S. Cooper** c-9-17. 20-22 contain "Tales from the Witch's Cauldron" (same strip as "Stories of the Black Witch" in Zip Comics). Mr. Justice c-9-18. Captain Flag c-16(w/Mr. Justice), 19-22.*

GD25 FN65 NM94

BLUE RIBBON COMICS (Becomes Teen-Age Diary Secrets #4)
Feb, 1949 - No. 6, Aug, 1949 (See Heckle & Jeckle)
Blue Ribbon (St. John)
1,3-Heckle & Jeckle 5.85 17.50 35.00
2(4/49)-Diary Secrets; Baker-c 9.15 27.50 55.00
4(6/49)-Teen-Age Diary Secrets; Baker c/a(2) 10.00 30.00 60.00
5(8/49)-Teen-Age Diary Secrets; Oversize; photo-c; Baker-a(2)- Continues as Teen-Age Diary Secrets 12.00 36.00 85.00
6-Dinky Duck(8/49) 2.80 7.00 14.00

BLUE-RIBBON COMICS
Nov, 1983 - No. 14, Dec, 1984
Red Circle Prod./Archie Ent. No. 5 on
1-S&K-r/Advs. of the Fly #1,2; Williamson/Torres-r/Fly #2; Ditko-c 1.00
2-14: 3-Origin Steel Sterling. 5-S&K Shield-r. 6,7-The Fox app. 8-Toth centerspread. 8,11-Black Hood. 12-Thunder Agents. 13-Thunder Bunny. 14-Web & Jaguar 1.00
NOTE: ***N. Adams** a(r)-8. **Buckler** a-4i. **Nino** a-2i. **McWilliams** a-8. **Morrow** a-8.*

BLUE STREAK (See Holyoke One-Shot No. 8)

BLYTHE (See 4-Color No. 1072)

B-MAN (See Double-Dare Adventures)

BO (Tom Cat #4 on; also see Big Shot #29 & Dixie Dugan)
June, 1955 - No. 3, Oct, 1955 (a dog)
Charlton Comics Group
1-3-Newspaper reprints by Frank Beck 5.35 16.00 32.00

BOATNIKS, THE (See Walt Disney Showcase No. 1)

BOB & BETTY & SANTA'S WISHING WELL
1941 (12 pages) (Christmas giveaway)
Sears Roebuck & Co.
nn 8.35 25.00 50.00

BOBBY BENSON'S B-BAR-B RIDERS (Radio) (See Best of The West, The Lemonade Kid & Model Fun)
May-June, 1950 - No. 20, May-June, 1953
Magazine Enterprises
1-The Lemonade Kid begins; Powell-a 23.00 70.00 160.00
2 10.00 30.00 70.00
3-5: 4,5-Lemonade Kid-c (#4-Spider-c) 9.15 27.50 55.00
6-8,10 7.50 22.50 45.00
9,11,13-Frazetta-c; Ghost Rider in #13-15 by Ayers-a. 13-Ghost Rider-c 19.00 55.00 130.00
12,17-20: 20-(A-1 #88) 6.70 20.00 40.00
14-Decapitation/Bondage-c & story; horror-c 10.00 30.00 65.00
15-Ghost Rider-c 10.00 30.00 65.00
16-Photo-c 9.15 27.50 55.00
...in the Tunnel of Gold-(1936, 5-1/4x8"; 100 pgs.) Radio giveaway by Hecker-H.O. Company(H.O. Oats); contains 22 color pages of comics, rest in novel form 8.35 25.00 50.00
...And The Lost Herd-same as above 8.35 25.00 50.00
NOTE: ***Ayers** a-13-15, 20. **Powell** a-1-12(4 ea.), 13(3), 14-16(Red Hawk only); c-1-8,1 0, 12. Lemonade Kid in most 1-13.*

BOBBY COMICS
May, 1946
Universal Phoenix Features
1-By S. M. Iger 5.85 17.50 35.00

BOBBY SHELBY COMICS
1949
Shelby Cycle Co./Harvey Publications
nn 3.60 9.00 18.00

BOBBY SHERMAN (TV)
Feb, 1972 - No. 7, Oct, 1972

Bob Colt #8, © FAW

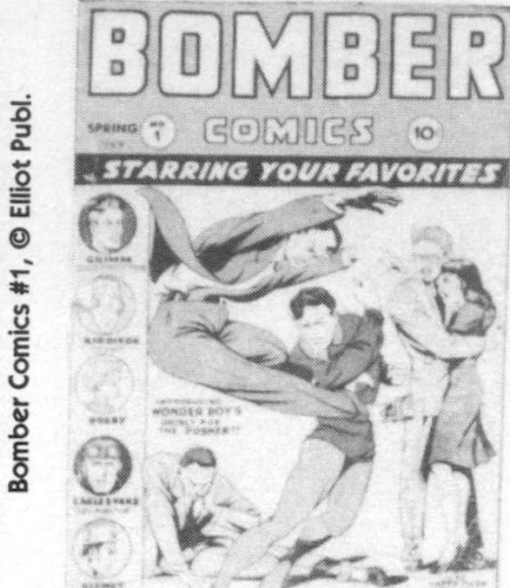

Bomber Comics #1, © Elliot Publ.

Books of Magic #2, © DC

	GD25	FN65	NM94

Charlton Comics

	GD25	FN65	NM94
1-Based on TV show "Getting Together"	3.60	9.00	18.00
2-7: 4-Photo-c	2.00	5.00	10.00

BOBBY THATCHER & TREASURE CAVE
1932 (86 pages; B&W; hardcover; 7x9")
Altemus Co.

	GD25	FN65	NM94
nn-Reprints; Storm-a	8.35	25.00	50.00

BOBBY THATCHER'S ROMANCE
1931 (7x8-3/4")
The Bell Syndicate/Henry Altemus Co.

	GD25	FN65	NM94
nn-By Storm	8.35	25.00	50.00

BOB COLT (Movie star)(See XMas Comics)
Nov, 1950 - No. 10, May, 1952
Fawcett Publications

	GD25	FN65	NM94
1-Bob Colt, his horse Buckskin & sidekick Pablo begin; photo front/back-c begin	30.00	90.00	210.00
2	19.00	58.00	135.00
3-5	17.00	50.00	115.00
6-Flying Saucer story	13.50	41.00	95.00
7-10: 9-Last photo back-c	12.00	36.00	85.00

BOB HOPE (See Adventures of...)

BOB POWELL'S TIMELESS TALES (Eclipse)(Value: cover or less)

BOB SCULLY, TWO-FISTED HICK DETECTIVE
No date (1930's) (36 pages; 9-1/2x12"; B&W; paper cover)
Humor Publ. Co.

	GD25	FN65	NM94
nn-By Howard Dell; not reprints	9.15	27.50	55.00

BOB SON OF BATTLE (See 4-Color No. 729)

BOB STEELE WESTERN (Movie star)
Dec, 1950 - No. 10, June, 1952; 1990
Fawcett Publications/AC Comics

	GD25	FN65	NM94
1-Bob Steele & his horse Bullet begin; photo front/back-c begin	38.00	115.00	265.00
2	19.00	58.00	135.00
3-5: 4-Last photo back-c	16.00	48.00	110.00
6-10: 10-Last photo-c	12.00	36.00	85.00
1 (1990, $2.75, B&W)-Bob Steele & Rocky Lane reprints; photo-c & inside covers	.55	1.60	2.75

BOB SWIFT (Boy Sportsman)
May, 1951 - No. 5, Jan, 1952
Fawcett Publications

	GD25	FN65	NM94
1	5.85	17.50	35.00
2-5: Saunders painted-c #1-5	4.00	10.00	20.00

BOLD ADVENTURES (Pacific)(Value: cover or less)

BOLD STORIES (Also see Candid Tales & It Rhymes With Lust)
Mar, 1950 - July, 1950 (Digest size; 144 pgs.; full color)
Kirby Publishing Co.

	GD25	FN65	NM94
March issue (Very Rare) - Contains "The Ogre of Paris" by Wood	49.00	145.00	340.00
May issue (Very Rare) - Contains "The Cobra's Kiss" by Graham Ingels (21 pgs.)	39.00	120.00	275.00
July issue (Very Rare) - Contains "The Ogre of Paris" by Wood	43.00	130.00	300.00

BOLT AND STAR FORCE SIX (Americomics)(Value: cover or less)

BOMBARDIER (See Bee 29, the Bombardier & Cinema Comics Herald)

BOMBAST
1993 ($2.95, color, one-shot)
Topps Comics

	GD25	FN65	NM94
1-Polybagged w/Kirbychrome trading card		1.20	3.00

BOMBA THE JUNGLE BOY (TV)
Sept-Oct, 1967 - No. 7, Sept-Oct, 1968 (12 cents)
National Periodical Publications

	GD25	FN65	NM94
1-Intro. Bomba; Infantino/Anderson-c	2.15	6.50	15.0
2-7	1.25	3.00	7.5

BOMBER COMICS
March, 1944 - No. 4, Winter, 1944-45
Elliot Publ. Co./Melverne Herald/Farrell/Sunrise Times

	GD25	FN65	NM94
1-Wonder Boy, & Kismet, Man of Fate begin	27.00	82.00	180.0
2-4: 2-4-Have Classics Comics ad to HRN 20	10.00	55.00	120.0

BONANZA (TV)
June-Aug, 1960 - No. 37, Aug, 1970 (All Photo-c)
Dell/Gold Key

	GD25	FN65	NM94
4-Color 1110 (6-8/60)	31.00	95.00	220.0
4-Color 1221,1283, & #01070-207, 01070-210	16.00	48.00	110.0
1(12/62-Gold Key)	16.00	48.00	110.0
2	8.35	25.00	50.0
3-10	4.70	14.00	28.0
11-20	4.00	10.00	20.0
21-37: 29-Reprints	2.80	7.00	14.0

BONE
July, 1991 - Present ($2.95, B&W)
Cartoon Books

	GD25	FN65	NM94
1-Jeff Smith-c/a in all	7.00	21.00	50.0
1-2nd printing	2.15	6.50	15.0
1-3rd thru 5th printings	1.00	2.00	5.0
2-1st printing	2.15	6.50	15.0
2-2nd & 3rd printings	1.00	2.00	5.0
3-1st printing	1.65	4.00	10.0
3-2nd thru 4th printings	1.00	2.00	5.0
4-10		1.60	4.0
11,12		1.20	3.0

BONGO (See Story Hour Series)

BONGO & LUMPJAW (See 4-Color #706,886, & Walt Disney Showcase #3)

BON VOYAGE (See Movie Classics)

BOOK AND RECORD SET (See Power Record Comics)

BOOK OF ALL COMICS
1945 (196 pages)
William H. Wise

	GD25	FN65	NM94
nn-Green Mask, Puppeteer	28.00	85.00	180.0

BOOK OF COMICS, THE
No date (1944) (132 pages) (25 cents)
William H. Wise

	GD25	FN65	NM94
nn-Captain V app.	28.00	85.00	180.0

BOOK OF LOVE (See Fox Giants)

BOOK OF NIGHT, THE (Dark Horse)(Value: cover or less)

BOOK OF THE DEAD
Dec, 1993 - No. 4, Mar, 1994 ($1.75, color, mini-series, 52 pgs.)
Marvel Comics

	GD25	FN65	NM94
1-r/Ploog & Wrightson Frankenstein/Man-Thing. 2-r/Fear #10; Morrow painted cover		.70	1.7

BOOKS OF MAGIC
1990 - No. 4, 1991 ($3.95, color, mini-series, mature readers, 52 pgs.)
DC Comics

	GD25	FN65	NM94
1-Bolton painted-c/a; Phantom Stranger app.	1.65	4.00	10.0
2,3: 2-John Constantine, Dr. Fate, Spectre, Deadman app. 3-Dr. Occult app.; minor Sandman app. (Gaiman scripts all)	1.20	3.00	7.0
4-Early app. of Death (early 1991)	1.30	3.25	8.0

Border Worlds V2#1, © Donald Simpson

A Boy and His 'Bot #1, © Gary Thomas Washington

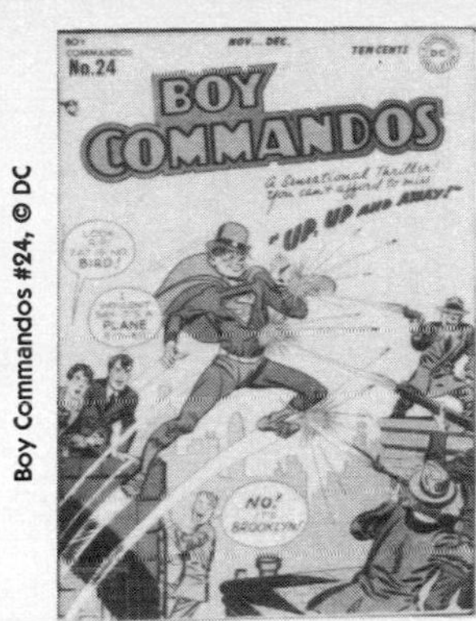

Boy Commandos #24, © DC

GD25 FN65 NM94

BOOSTER GOLD (See Justice League #4)
Feb, 1986 - No. 25, Feb, 1988 (75 cents)
DC Comics
1-25: 4-Rose & Thorn app. 6-Origin. 6,7,23-Superman app. 8,9-LSH app. 22-JLI app. 24,25-Millennium tie-ins 1.00
NOTE: *Austin* c-22i. *Byrne* c-23i.

BOOTS AND HER BUDDIES
No. 5, 9/48 - No. 9, 9/49; 12/55 - No. 3, 1956
Standard Comics/Visual Editions/Argo (NEA Service)

	GD25	FN65	NM94
5-Strip-r	10.00	30.00	70.00
6,8	7.50	22.50	45.00
7-(Scarce)-Spanking panels(3)	9.15	27.50	55.00
9-(Scarce)-Frazetta-a (2 pgs.)	17.00	52.00	120.00
1-3(Argo-1955-56)-Reprints	4.00	10.00	20.00

BOOTS & SADDLES (See 4-Color No. 919, 1029, 1116)

BORDER PATROL
May-June, 1951 - No. 3, Sept-Oct, 1951
P. L. Publishing Co.

	GD25	FN65	NM94
1	7.50	22.50	45.00
2,3	5.00	15.00	30.00

BORDER WORLDS (Kitchen Sink)(Value: cover or less)

BORIS KARLOFF TALES OF MYSTERY (TV) (...Thriller No. 1,2)
No. 3, April, 1963 - No. 97, Feb, 1980
Gold Key

	GD25	FN65	NM94
3-8,10-(Two #5's, 10/63,11/63)	3.20	8.00	16.00
9-Wood-a	4.00	10.00	20.00
11-Williamson-a, Orlando-a, 8 pgs.	4.00	10.00	20.00
12-Torres, McWilliams-a, Orlando-a(2)	2.80	7.00	14.00
13,14,16-20	2.00	5.00	10.00
15-Crandall	2.40	6.00	12.00
21-Jeff Jones-a(3 pgs.) "The Screaming Skull"	2.40	6.00	12.00
22-30: 23-Reprint; photo-c	1.60	4.00	8.00
31-50	1.00	2.00	5.00
51-74: 74-Origin & 1st app. Taurus		1.40	3.50
75-97: 80-86-(52 pages)		.80	2.00
Story Digest 1(7/70-Gold Key)-All text	1.20	3.00	7.00

(See Mystery Comics Digest No. 2, 5, 8, 11, 14, 17, 20, 23, 26)
NOTE: *Bolle* a-51-54, 56, 58, 59. *McWilliams* a-12, 14, 18, 19, 80, 81, 93. *Orlando* a-11-15, 21. Reprints: 78, 81-86, 88, 90, 92, 95, 97.

BORIS KARLOFF THRILLER (TV) (Becomes Boris Karloff Tales...)
Oct, 1962 - No. 2, Jan, 1963 (80 pages)
Gold Key

	GD25	FN65	NM94
1-Photo-c	6.70	20.00	40.00
2	5.00	15.00	30.00

BORIS THE BEAR INSTANT COLOR CLASSICS (Dark Horse)(Value: cover or less)

BORN AGAIN (Spire Christian)(Value: cover or less)

BOUNCER, THE (Formerly Green Mask #9)
1944 - No. 14, Jan, 1945
Fox Features Syndicate

	GD25	FN65	NM94
nn(1944, #10?)	14.00	43.00	100.00
11(#1)(9/44)-Origin; Rocket Kelly, One Round Hogan app.	11.50	34.00	80.00
12-14: 14-Reprints no # issue	10.00	30.00	65.00

BOUNTY GUNS (See 4-Color No. 739)

BOY AND HIS 'BOT, A (Now)(Value: cover or less)

BOY AND THE PIRATES, THE (See 4-Color No. 1117)

BOY COMICS (Captain Battle No. 1 & 2; Boy Illustories No. 43-108)
(Stories by Charles Biro)
No. 3, April, 1942 - No. 119, March, 1956
Lev Gleason Publications (Comic House)

	GD25	FN65	NM94
3(No.1)-Origin Crimebuster, Bombshell & Young Robin Hood; Yankee Longago, Case 1001-1008, Swoop Storm, & Boy Movies begin; 1st app. Iron Jaw	167.00	500.00	1200.00
4-Hitler, Tojo, Mussolini-c	58.00	205.00	475.00
5	47.00	160.00	365.00
6-Origin Iron Jaw; origin & death of Iron Jaw's son; Little Dynamite begins, ends #39	125.00	375.00	875.00
7,9: 7-Flag & Hitler, Tojo, Mussolini-c	46.00	135.00	320.00
8-Death of Iron Jaw	50.00	150.00	350.00
10-Return of Iron Jaw, classic Biro-c	67.00	200.00	470.00
11-14: 11-Classic Iron Jaw-c. 14-Iron Jaw-c	32.00	95.00	225.00
15-Death of Iron Jaw	37.00	110.00	260.00
16,18-20	22.00	65.00	150.00
17-Flag-c	23.00	70.00	160.00
21-26	15.00	45.00	105.00
27-29,31,32-(All 68 pages). 28-Yankee Longago ends. 32-Swoop Storm & Young Robin Hood end	15.00	45.00	105.00
30-(68 pgs.)-Origin Crimebuster retold	20.00	60.00	140.00
33-40: 34-Crimebuster story(2); suicide-c/story	10.00	30.00	70.00
41-50	10.00	30.00	60.00
51-59: 57-Dilly Duncan begins, ends #71	8.35	25.00	50.00
60-Iron Jaw returns	10.00	30.00	60.00
61-Origin Crimebuster & Iron Jaw retold	10.00	30.00	70.00
62-Death of Iron Jaw explained	10.00	30.00	65.00
63-73: 73-Frazetta 1-pg. ad	8.35	25.00	50.00
74-88: 80-1st app. Rocky X of the Rocketeers; becomes "Rocky X" #101; Iron Jaw, Sniffer & the Deadly Dozen begins, ends #118	6.70	20.00	40.00
89-92-The Claw serial app. in all	7.50	22.50	45.00
93-Claw cameo; Rocky X by Sid Check	6.70	20.00	40.00
94-97,99	5.00	15.00	35.00
98-Rocky X by Sid Check	6.70	20.00	40.00
100	6.70	20.00	40.00
101-107,109,111,119: 111-Crimebuster becomes Chuck Chandler. 119-Last Crimebuster	5.35	16.00	32.00
108,110,112-118-Kubert-a	6.70	20.00	40.00

(See Giant Boy Book of Comics)
NOTE: *Boy Movies in 3-5,40,41. Iron Jaw app.-3, 4, 6, 8, 10, 11, 13-15; returns-60-62, 68, 69, 72-79, 81-118.* ***Biro*** *c-all.* ***Briefer*** *a-5, 10, 14, 16-20 among others.* ***Fuje*** *a-55, 18 pgs.* ***Palais*** *a-14, 16, 17, 19, 20 among others.*

BOY COMMANDOS (See Detective #64 & World's Finest Comics #8)
Winter, 1942-43 - No. 36, Nov-Dec, 1949
National Periodical Publications

	GD25	FN65	NM94
1-Origin Liberty Belle; The Sandman & The Newsboy Legion x-over in Boy Commandos; S&K-a, 48 pgs.	270.00	800.00	1900.00
2-Last Liberty Belle; Hitler-c; S&K-a, 46 pgs.	96.00	290.00	675.00
3-S&K-a, 45 pgs.	68.00	205.00	475.00
4,5	43.00	130.00	300.00
6-8,10: 6-S&K-a	29.00	86.00	200.00
9-No S&K-a	20.00	60.00	135.00
11-Infinity-c	20.00	60.00	135.00
12-16,18-20	15.00	45.00	105.00
17-Sci/fi-c/story	17.00	52.00	120.00
21,22,24,25: 22-Judy Canova x-over	12.00	36.00	85.00
23-S&K-c/a(all)	14.00	43.00	100.00
26-Flying Saucer story (3-4/48)-4th of this theme	13.00	40.00	90.00
27,28,30: 30-Cleveland Indians story	12.00	36.00	85.00
29-S&K story (1)	10.50	41.00	95.00
31-35: 32-Dale Evans app. on-c & in story. 34-Intro. Wolf, their mascot	12.00	36.00	85.00
36-Intro The Atomobile c/sci-fi story	14.00	43.00	100.00

NOTE: *Most issues signed by* ***Simon & Kirby*** *are not by them.* ***S&K*** *c-1-9, 13, 14, 17, 21, 23, 30-32.* ***Feller*** *c-30.*

BOY COMMANDOS
Sept-Oct, 1973 - No. 2, Nov-Dec, 1973 (G.A. S&K reprints)
National Periodical Publications

Boy Detective #1, © AVON

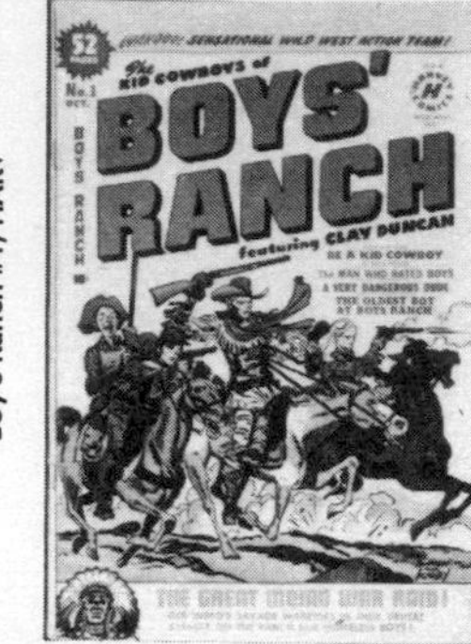

Boy's Ranch #1, HARV

The Brain #1, ME

GD25 FN65 NM94 | GD25 FN65 NM94

1,2: 1-Reprints story from Boy Commandos #1 plus-c & Detective #66 by S&K. 2-Infantino/Orlando-c .40 1.00 2.00

BOY COWBOY (Also see Amazing Adventures & Science Comics)
1950 (8 pgs. in color)
Ziff-Davis Publ. Co.

nn-Sent to subscribers of Ziff-Davis mags. & ordered through mail for 10 cents; used to test market for Kid Cowboy
Estimated value 140.00

BOY DETECTIVE
May-June, 1951 - No. 4, May, 1952
Avon Periodicals

1 11.50 34.00 80.00
2,3: 3-Kinstler-c 7.50 22.50 45.00
4-Kinstler-c/a 10.00 30.00 70.00

BOY EXPLORERS COMICS (Terry and The Pirates No. 3 on)
May-June, 1946 - No. 2, Sept-Oct, 1946
Family Comics (Harvey Publications)

1-Intro The Explorers, Duke of Broadway, Calamity Jane & Danny Dixon... Cadet; S&K-c/a, 24 pgs 52.00 155.00 325.00
2-(Scarce)-Small size (5-1/2x8-1/2"; B&W; 32 pgs.) Distributed to mail subscribers only; S&K-a Estimated value $250.00-$400.00
(Also see All New No. 15, Flash Gordon No. 5, and Stuntman No. 3)

BOY ILLUSTORIES (See Boy Comics)

BOY LOVES GIRL (Boy Meets Girl No. 1-24)
No. 25, July, 1952 - No. 57, June, 1956
Lev Gleason Publications

25(#1) 4.00 12.00 24.00
26,27,29-42: 30-33-Serial, 'Loves of My Life.' 39-Lingerie panels 2.40 6.00 12.00
28-Drug propaganda story 3.20 8.00 16.00
43-Toth-a 4.35 13.00 26.00
44-50: 50-Last pre-code (2/55) 1.80 4.50 9.00
51-57: 57-Ann Brewster-a 1.40 3.50 7.00

BOY MEETS GIRL (Boy Loves Girl No. 25 on)
Feb, 1950 - No. 24, June, 1952 (No. 1-17: 52 pgs.)
Lev Gleason Publications

1-Guardineer-a 4.00 12.00 24.00
2 2.40 6.00 12.00
3-10 1.80 4.50 9.00
11-24 1.60 4.00 8.00
NOTE: ***Briefer*** *a-24.* ***Fuje*** *c-3,7. Painted-c 1-17. Photo-c 19-21, 23.*

BOYS' AND GIRLS' MARCH OF COMICS (See March of Comics)

BOYS' RANCH (Also see Western Tales & Witches' Western Tales)
Oct, 1950 - No. 6, Aug, 1951 (No.1-3, 52 pgs.; No. 4-6, 36 pgs.)
Harvey Publications

1-S&K-c/a(3) 45.00 135.00 315.00
2-S&K-c/a(3) 33.00 100.00 230.00
3-S&K-c/a(2); Meskin-a 29.00 90.00 205.00
4-S&K-c/a, 5 pgs. 24.00 70.00 165.00
5,6-S&K-c, splashes & centerspread only; Meskin-a 14.00 43.00 100.00
Shoe Store Giveaway #5,6 (Identical to regular issues except S&K centerfold replaced with ad) 11.50 34.00 80.00

BOZO (Larry Harmon's Bozo, the World's Most Famous Clown)
1992 ($6.95, color, 68 pgs.)
Innovation Publishing

1-Reprints Four Color #285(#1) 1.20 3.00 7.00

BOZO THE CLOWN (TV) (Bozo No. 7 on)
July, 1950 - No. 4, Oct-Dec, 1963
Dell Publishing Co.

4-Color 285(#1) 14.00 43.00 100.00
2(7-9/51)-7(10-12/52) 10.00 30.00 65.0
4-Color 464,508,551,594(10/54) 10.00 30.00 65.0
1(nn, 5-7/62) - 4(1963) 6.70 20.00 40.0
Giveaway-1961, 16 pgs., 3-1/2x7-1/4", Apsco Products 4.20 12.50 25.0

BOZZ CHRONICLES, THE
Dec, 1985 - No. 6, 1986 (Adults only)(Mini-series)
Epic Comics (Marvel)

1-6 1.5

BRADY BUNCH, THE (TV)(See Kite Fun Book)
Feb, 1970 - No. 2, May, 1970
Dell Publishing Co.

1,2 5.00 15.00 35.0

BRAIN, THE
Sept, 1956 - No. 7, 1958
Sussex Publ. Co./Magazine Enterprises

1-Dan DeCarlo-a in all including reprints 4.70 14.00 28.0
2,3 2.80 7.00 14.0
4-7 1.80 4.50 9.0
I.W. Reprints #1-4,8-10('63),14: 2-Reprints Sussex #2 with new cover added 1.20 3.00 6.0
Super Reprint #17,18(nd) 1.20 3.00 6.0

BRAIN BOY
April-June, 1962 - No. 6, Sept-Nov, 1963 (Painted c-5,6)
Dell Publishing Co.

4-Color 1330(#1)-Gil Kane-a; origin 8.35 25.00 50.0
2(7-9/62),3-6: 4-Origin retold 5.00 15.00 30.0

BRAM STOKER'S DRACULA (Also see Dracula: Vlad the Impaler)
10/92 - No. 4, 1/93 ($2.95, color, mini-series, polybagged, adapts movie)
Topps Comics

1-4 trading cards in all; photo scenes of movie 1.20 3.0
1-2nd printing 1.20 3.0
1-Crimson foil edition (limited to 500) 25.0
2-Bound-in poster; Mignola-c/a in all 1.20 3.0
3,4: 3-Contains coupon to win 1 of 500 crimson foil-c edition of #1. 4-Contains coupon to win 1 of 500 uncut sheets of all 16 trading cards 1.30 3.2
3,4-With coupon missing 1.20 3.0

BRAND ECHH (See Not Brand Echh)

BRAND OF EMPIRE (See 4-Color No. 771)

BRAVADOS, THE (See Wild Western Action)
August, 1971 (52 pages) (One-Shot)
Skywald Publ. Corp.

1-Red Mask, The Durango Kid, Billy Nevada-r .30 .75 1.5

BRAVE AND THE BOLD, THE (See Best Of... & Super DC Giant)
Aug-Sept, 1955 - No. 200, July, 1983
National Periodical Publications/DC Comics

1-Viking Prince by Kubert, Silent Knight, Golden Gladiator begin; part Kubert-c 135.00 405.00 1350.0
2 65.00 195.00 650.0
3,4 37.00 111.00 370.0
5-Robin Hood begins 40.00 120.00 400.0
6-10: 6-Robin Hood by Kubert; Golden Gladiator last app.; Silent Knight; no Viking Prince 25.00 75.00 225.0
11-22,24: 18,21-23-Grey tone-c. 22-Last Silent Knight. 24-Last Viking Prince by Kubert 18.00 55.00 165.0
23-Viking Prince origin by Kubert; 1st B&B single theme issue 23.00 68.00 225.0
25-1st app. Suicide Squad (8-9/59) 22.00 66.00 220.0
26,27-Suicide Squad 26.00 77.00 180.0

The Brave and the Bold #58, © DC

The Brave and the Bold #128, © DC

The Brave and the Bold #134, © DC

GD25 FN65 VF82 NM94

28-(2-3/60)-Justice League intro./1st app.; origin/1st app. Snapper Carr 256.00 768.00 1920.00 3070.00
29-Justice League 175.00 525.00 1138.00 1750.00
30-Justice League 145.00 435.00 943.00 1450.00

GD25 FN65 NM94

31-1st app. Cave Carson (8-9/60); scarce in high grade; 1st try-out series 25.00 75.00 175.00
32-33-Cave Carson 19.00 56.00 130.00

GD25 FN65 VF82 NM94

34-Origin/1st app. Silver-Age Hawkman, Hawkgirl & Byth by Kubert (2-3/61); 1st S.A. Hawkman tryout series 104.00 313.00 781.00 1250.00

GD25 FN65 NM94

35-Hawkman by Kubert (4-5/61)-2nd app. 33.00 100.00 400.00
36-Hawkman by Kubert; origin & 1st app. Shadow Thief (6-7/61)-3rd app. 33.00 98.00 325.00
37-Suicide Squad (2nd tryout series) 19.00 58.00 175.00
38,39-Suicide Squad. 38-Last 10 cent issue 21.00 64.00 150.00
40,41-Cave Carson Inside Earth (2nd try-out series). 40-Kubert-a. 41-Meskin-a 13.00 40.00 90.00
42-Hawkman by Kubert (2nd tryout series) 23.00 68.00 225.00
43-Hawkman by Kubert; more detailed origin 27.00 80.00 265.00
44-Hawkman by Kubert; grey-tone-c 18.00 53.00 175.00
45-49-Strange Sports Stories by Infantino 4.30 13.00 30.00
50-The Green Arrow & Manhunter From Mars (10-11/63); team-ups begin 13.00 40.00 90.00
51-Aquaman & Hawkman (12-1/63-64); pre-dates Hawkman #1 15.00 45.00 150.00
52-3 Battle Stars; Sgt. Rock, Haunted Tank, Johnny Cloud, & Mlle. Marie team-up for 1st time by Kubert (c/a) 10.00 30.00 70.00
53-Atom & The Flash by Toth 5.00 15.00 35.00
54-Kid Flash, Robin & Aqualad; 1st app./origin Teen Titans (6-7/64) 26.00 77.00 180.00
55-Metal Men & The Atom 3.20 8.00 20.00
56-The Flash & Manhunter From Mars 3.20 8.00 20.00
57-Origin & 1st app. Metamorpho (12-1/64-65) 14.00 41.00 95.00
58-Metamorpho by Fradon 6.00 19.00 44.00
59-Batman & Green Lantern; 1st Batman team-up in Brave and the Bold 9.00 28.00 65.00
60-Teen Titans (2nd app.)-1st app. new Wonder Girl (Donna Troy), who joins Titans (6-7/65) 9.00 27.00 63.00
61,62-Origin Starman & Black Canary by Anderson. 62-1st S.A. app. Wildcat (10-11/65); 1st S.A. app. of G.A. Huntress 9.00 26.00 60.00
63-Supergirl & Wonder Woman 2.15 6.50 15.00
64-Batman Versus Eclipso (see H.O.S. #61) 6.50 19.00 45.00
65-Flash & Doom Patrol (4-5/66) 1.65 4.00 10.00
66-Metamorpho & Metal Men (6-7/66) 1.65 4.00 10.00
67-Batman & The Flash by Infantino; Batman team-ups begin, end #200 (8-9/66) 4.00 12.00 28.00
68-Batman/Joker/Riddler/Penguin-c/story; Batman as Bat-Hulk (Hulk parody) 7.00 21.00 49.00
69-Batman & Green Lantern 2.60 7.50 18.00
70-Batman & Hawkman; Craig-a(p) 3.60 9.00 18.00
71-Batman & Green Arrow 3.60 9.00 18.00
72-Spectre & Flash (6-7/67); 4th app. The Spectre; predates Spectre #1 2.40 7.25 17.00
73-Aquaman & The Atom 2.30 6.75 16.00
74-Batman & Metal Men 2.30 6.75 16.00
75-Batman & The Spectre (12-1/67-68); came out between Spectre #1 & #2 2.40 7.25 17.00
76-Batman & Plastic Man (2-3/68); came out between Plastic Man #8 & #9 2.30 6.75 16.00
77-Batman & The Atom 2.30 6.75 16.00
78-Batman, Wonder Woman & Batgirl 2.30 6.75 16.00
79-Batman & Deadman by Neal Adams (8-9/68); early Deadman app. 3.70 11.00 26.00
80-Batman & Creeper (10-11/68); N. Adams-a; early app. The Creeper; came out between Creeper #3 & #4 3.70 11.00 26.00
81-Batman & Flash; N. Adams-a 3.70 11.00 26.00
82-Batman & Aquaman; N. Adams-a; origin Ocean Master retold (2-3/69) 3.70 11.00 26.00
83-Batman & Teen Titans; N. Adams-a (4-5/69) 5.00 15.00 35.00
84-Batman (GA) & Sgt. Rock; N. Adams-a 3.60 10.75 25.00
85-Batman & Green Arrow; 1st new costume for Green Arrow by Neal Adams (8-9/69) 3.60 10.75 25.00
86-Batman & Deadman; N. Adams-a 3.60 10.75 25.00
87-Batman & Wonder Woman 2.40 7.25 17.00
88-Batman & Wildcat 2.40 7.25 17.00
89-Batman & Phantom Stranger (4-5/70); early Phantom Stranger app. (came out between Phantom Stranger #6 & 7 2.40 7.25 17.00
90-Batman & Adam Strange 2.40 7.25 17.00
91-Batman & Black Canary (8-9/70) 2.40 7.25 17.00
92-Batman; intro the Bat Squad 2.40 7.25 17.00
93-Batman-House of Mystery; N. Adams-a 3.30 10.00 23.00
94-Batman-Teen Titans 1.65 4.00 10.00
95-Batman & Plastic Man 1.30 3.25 8.00
96-Batman & Sgt. Rock 1.30 3.25 8.00
97-Batman & Wildcat; 52 pg. issues begin, end #102; reprints origin & 1st app. Deadman from Strange Advs. #205 1.30 3.25 8.00
98-Batman & Phantom Stranger 1.30 3.25 8.00
99-Batman & Flash 1.30 3.25 8.00
100-(2-3/72, 25 cents, 52 pgs.)-Batman-Green Lantern-Green Arrow-Black Canary-Robin; Deadman-r by N. Adams 3.25 9.50 22.00
101-Batman & Metamorpho; Kubert Viking Prince 1.00 2.00 5.00
102-Batman-Teen Titans; N. Adams-a(p) 1.30 3.25 8.00
103-110: Batman team-ups: 103-Metal Men. 104-Deadman. 105-Wonder Woman. 106-Green Arrow. 107-Black Canary. 108-Sgt. Rock. 109-Demon. 110-Wildcat 1.00 2.00 5.00
111-Batman/Joker-c/story 1.65 4.00 10.00
112-117: All 100 pgs.; Batman team-ups: 112-Mr. Miracle. 113-Metal Men; reprints origin/1st Hawkman from Brave and the Bold #34; r/origin Multi-Man/Challengers #14. 114-Aquaman. 115-Atom; r/origin Viking Prince from #23. 116-Spectre. 117-Sgt. Rock; last 100 pg. issue 1.00 2.50 6.00
118-Batman/Wildcat/Joker-c/story 1.65 4.00 10.00
119-128,132-140: Batman team-ups: 119-Man-Bat. 120-Kamandi(68 pgs.). 121-Metal Men. 122-Swamp Thing. 123-Plastic Man/Metamorpho. 124-Sgt. Rock. 125-Flash. 126-Aquaman. 127-Wildcat. 128-Mr. Miracle. 132-Kung-Fu Fighter. 133-Deadman. 134-Green Lantern. 135-Metal Men. 136-Metal Men/Green Arrow. 137-Demon. 138-Mr. Miracle. 139-Hawkman. 140-Wonder Woman 1.20 3.00
129,130-Batman/Green Arrow/Atom parts 1 & 2; Joker & Two Face-c/stories 1.65 4.70 11.00
131-Batman & Wonder Woman vs. Catwoman 1.00 2.50 6.00
141-Batman/Black Canary vs. Joker-c/story 1.65 4.00 10.00
142-190,192-199: Batman team-ups: 142-Aquaman. 143-Creeper; origin Human Target (44 pgs.). 144-Green Arrow; origin Human Target part 2 (44 pgs.). 145-Phantom Stranger. 146-G.A. Batman/Unknown Soldier. 147-Supergirl. 148-Plastic Man; X-Mas-c. 149-Teen Titans. 150-Anniversary issue; Superman. 151-Flash. 152-Atom. 153-Red Tornado. 154-Metamorpho. 155-Green Lantern. 156-Dr. Fate. 157-Batman vs. Kamandi (ties into Kamandi #59). 158-Wonder Woman. 159-Ra's Al Ghul. 160-Supergirl. 161-Adam Strange. 162-G.A. Batman/Sgt. Rock. 163-Black Lightning. 164-Hawkman. 165-Man-Bat. 166-Black Canary; Nemesis (intro) back-up story begins, ends #192; Penguin-c/story. 167-G.A. Batman/Blackhawk; origin Nemesis. 168-Green Arrow. 169-Zatanna. 170-Nemesis. 171-Scalphunter. 172-Firestorm. 173-Guardians of the Universe. 174-Green Lantern. 175-Lois Lane. 176-Swamp Thing. 177-Elongated Man. 178-Creeper. 179-Legion. 180-Spectre. 181-Hawk & Dove. 182-G.A. Robin; G.A. Starman app.; 1st modern app. G.A. Batwoman. 183-Riddler. 184-Huntress. 185-Green Arrow. 186-Hawkman. 187-Metal Men. ,188,189-Rose & the Thorn. 190-Adam Strange. 192-Superboy vs. Mr. I.Q. 193-Nemesis. 194-Flash. 195-I... Vampire. 196-Ragman; origin Ragman retold. 197-Catwoman; Earth II

The Brave and the Bold #190, © DC

Brenda Starr #13 (#1), © SUPR

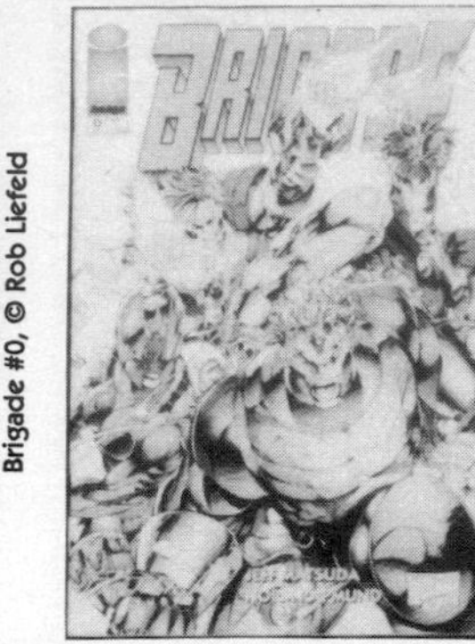
Brigade #0, © Rob Liefeld

GD25 FN65 NM94

Batman & Catwoman marry; 2nd modern app. of G.A. Batwoman. 198-Karate Kid. 199-Batman vs. The Spectre 1.20 3.00
191-Batman/Joker-c/story; Nemesis app. 1.20 3.00 7.00
200-Double-sized (64 pgs.); printed on Mando paper; Earth One & Earth Two Batman app. in separate stories; intro/1st app. Batman & The Outsiders 1.30 3.25 8.00

NOTE: ***Neal Adams*** *a-79-86, 93, 100r, 102; c-75, 76, 79-86, 88-90, 93, 95, 99, 100r.* ***M. Anderson*** *a-115r; c-72i, 96i.* ***Andru/Esposito*** *c-25-27.* ***Aparo*** *a-98, 100-102, 104-125, 126i, 127-136, 138-145, 147, 148i, 149-152, 154, 155, 157-162, 168-170, 173-178, 180-182, 184, 186i-189i, 191i-193i, 195, 196, 200; c-105-109, 111-136, 137i, 138-175, 177, 180-184, 186-200.* ***Austin*** *a-166i.* ***Bernard Baily*** *c-32, 33.* ***Buckler*** *a-185, 186p; c-137, 178p, 185p, 186p.* ***Giordano*** *a-143, 144.* ***Infantino*** *a-67p, 72p, 97r, 98r, 172p, 183p, 190p, 194p; c-45-49, 67p, 69p, 70p, 72p, 96p, 98r.* ***Kaluta*** *c-176.* ***Kane*** *a-115r.* ***Kubert*** *&/or* ***Heath*** *a-1-24; reprints-101, 113, 115, 117.* ***Kubert*** *c-22-24, 34-36, 40, 42-44, 52.* ***Mooney*** *a-114r.* ***Newton*** *a-153p, 156p, 165p.* ***Irv Novick*** *c-1(part), 2-21.* ***Roussos*** *a-114r.* ***Staton*** *148p. 52 pgs.-97, 100; 68 pgs.-120; 100 pgs.-112-117.*

BRAVE AND THE BOLD, THE
Dec, 1991 - No. 6, June, 1992 ($1.75, color, mini-series)
DC Comics

1-6: Green Arrow, The Butcher, The Question in all; Grell scripts in all; Grell c-3,4,6 .70 1.75

BRAVE AND THE BOLD SPECIAL, THE (See DC Special Series No. 8)

BRAVE EAGLE (See 4-Color No. 705, 770, 816, 879, 929)

BRAVE ONE, THE (See 4-Color No. 773)

BREATHTAKER
1990 - No. 4, 1990 ($4.95, prestige format, mature readers, 52 pgs.)
DC Comics

Book 1-4: By Hempel & Wheatley painted-c/a 1.00 2.00 5.00

BREEZE LAWSON, SKY SHERIFF (See Sky Sheriff)

BRENDA LEE STORY, THE
September, 1962
Dell Publishing Co.

01-078-209 10.00 30.00 60.00

BRENDA STARR (Also see All Great)
No. 13, 9/47; No. 14, 3/48; V2#3, 6/48 - V2#12, 12/49
Four Star Comics Corp./Superior Comics Ltd.

V1#13-By Dale Messick 46.00 140.00 325.00
14-Kamen bondage-c 46.00 140.00 325.00
V2#3-Baker-a? 38.00 115.00 265.00
4-Used in **SOTI**, pg. 21; Kamen bondage-c 41.00 125.00 290.00
5-10 34.00 105.00 240.00
11,12 (Scarce) 38.00 115.00 265.00

NOTE: *Newspaper reprints plus original material through #6. All original #7 on.*

BRENDA STARR (...Reporter)(Young Lovers No. 16 on?)
No. 13, June, 1955 - No. 15, Oct, 1955
Charlton Comics

13-15-Newspaper-r 24.00 70.00 165.00

BRENDA STARR REPORTER
October, 1963
Dell Publishing Co.

1 17.00 52.00 120.00

BRER RABBIT (See 4-Color No. 129, 208, 693, Kite Fun Book, Walt Disney Showcase #28 and Wheaties)

BRER RABBIT IN "ICE CREAM FOR THE PARTY"
1955 (16 pages, 5x7-1/4", soft-c) (Walt Disney) (Premium)
American Dairy Association

nn-(Rare) 12.00 36.00 85.00

BRIAN BOLLAND'S BLACK BOOK (Eclipse)(Value: cover or less)

BRICK BRADFORD (Also see Ace Comics & King Comics)
No. 5, July, 1948 - No. 8, July, 1949 (Ritt & Grey reprints)
King Features Syndicate/Standard

GD25 FN65 NM94

5 11.00 32.00 75.00
6-8: 6-Robot-c (by Schomburg?). 7-Schomburg-c. 8-Says #7 inside, #8 on-c 10.00 30.00 60.00

BRIDE'S DIARY (Formerly Black Cobra No. 3)
No. 4, May, 1955 - No. 10, Aug, 1956
Ajax/Farrell Publ.

4 (#1) 4.70 14.00 28.00
5-8 3.20 8.00 16.00
9,10-Disbrow-a 4.70 14.00 28.00

BRIDES IN LOVE (Hollywood Romances & Summer Love No. 46 on)
Aug, 1956 - No. 45, Feb, 1965
Charlton Comics

1 4.20 12.50 25.00
2 2.80 7.00 14.00
3-10 1.80 4.50 9.00
11-20 1.20 3.00 6.00
21-45 .70 1.75 3.50

BRIDES ROMANCES
Nov, 1953 - No. 23, Dec, 1956
Quality Comics Group

1 8.35 25.00 50.00
2 4.00 12.00 24.00
3-10: Last precode (3/55) 3.00 7.50 15.00
11-14,16,17,19-22 2.00 5.00 10.00
15-Baker-a(p); Colan-a 2.40 6.00 12.00
18-Baker-a 3.00 7.50 15.00
23-Baker-c/a 4.00 12.00 24.00

BRIDE'S SECRETS
Apr-May, 1954 - No. 19, May, 1958
Ajax/Farrell(Excellent Publ.)/Four-Star Comic

1 6.70 20.00 40.00
2 4.00 11.00 22.00
3-6: Last precode (3/55) 3.00 7.50 15.00
7-19: 12-Disbrow a. 18-Hollingsworth-a 2.40 6.00 12.00

BRIDE-TO-BE ROMANCES (See True...)

BRIGADE
Aug, 1992 - No. 4, 1992 ($1.95, color, mini-series)
V2#1, May, 1993 - Present ($1.95, color, on-going series)
Image Comics

1-Liefeld part plots/scripts in all, Liefeld-c(p); contains 2 Brigade trading cards 1.20 3.00
1-Gold stamped logo edition 25.00
2-Contains coupon for Image Comics #0 & 2 trading cards .60 4.00
2-With coupon missing .80 2.00
3,4: 3-Contains 2 trading cards .80 2.00
V2#1-Gatefold-c; Liefeld co-plots .80 2.00
2,3: 2-(6/93, V2#1 on inside by mistake) .80 2.00
0-(9/93)-Liefeld scripts; Thibert-c(i) .80 2.00

BRIGAND, THE (See Fawcett Movie Comics No. 18)

BRINGING UP FATHER (See 4-Color #37 & Large Feature Comic #9)

BRINGING UP FATHER
1917 (16-1/2x5-1/2"; cardboard cover; 100 pages; B&W)
Star Co. (King Features)

nn-(Rare) Daily strip reprints by George McManus (no price on-c) 50.00 150.00 350.00

BRINGING UP FATHER
1919 - 1934 (by George McManus)(No. 22 is 9-1/4x9-1/2")
(10x10"; stiff cardboard covers; B&W; daily strip reprints; 52 pgs.)
Cupples & Leon Co.

1 36.00 107.00 250.00

Broadway Hollywood Blackouts #1, © Stanhall

The Brute #1, © Seaboard Periodicals

Buckaroo Banzai #1, © MEG

GD25 FN65 NM94

2-10 18.00 54.00 125.00
11-26 (Scarcer) 27.00 81.00 190.00
The Big Book 1(1926)-Thick book (hardcover); 10-1/4x10-1/4", 142pgs.
40.00 140.00 325.00
The Big Book 2(1929) 38.00 115.00 265.00
NOTE: *The Big Books contain 3 regular issues rebound and probably w/dust jackets.*

BRINGING UP FATHER, THE TROUBLE OF
1921 (9x15") (Sunday reprints in color)
Embee Publ. Co.
nn-(Rare) 46.00 140.00 325.00

BROADWAY HOLLYWOOD BLACKOUTS
Mar-Apr, 1954 - No. 3, July-Aug, 1954
Stanhall
1 8.35 25.00 50.00
2,3 5.35 16.00 32.00

BROADWAY ROMANCES
January, 1950 - No. 5, Sept, 1950
Quality Comics Group
1-Ward-c/a (9 pgs.), Gustavson-a 17.00 52.00 120.00
2-Ward-a (9 pgs.); photo-c 11.00 32.00 75.00
3-5: 4,5-Photo-c 6.35 19.00 38.00

BROKEN ARROW (See 4-Color No. 855,947)

BROKEN CROSS, THE (See The Crusaders)

BRONCHO BILL (See Comics On Parade, Sparkler & Tip Top Comics)
1939 - 1940; No. 5, 1?/48 - No. 16, 8?/50
United Features Syndicate/Standard(Visual Editions) No. 5-on
Single Series 2 ('39) 34.00 105.00 240.00
Single Series 19 ('40)(#2 on cvr) 29.00 85.00 200.00
5 8.35 25.00 50.00
6(4/48)-10(4/49) 4.70 14.00 28.00
11(6/49)-16 4.00 10.00 20.00
NOTE: ***Schomburg** c-6, 7, 9-13, 16.*

BROOKS ROBINSON (See Baseball's Greatest Heroes #2)

BROTHER POWER, THE GEEK (See Saga of Swamp Thing Annual)
Sept-Oct, 1968 - No. 2, Nov-Dec, 1968 (Also see Vertigo Visions)
National Periodical Publications
1-Origin; Simon-c(i?) 3.00 9.00 20.00
2 2.00 6.00 15.00

BROTHERS, HANG IN THERE, THE (Spire Christian)(Value: cover or less)

BROTHERS OF THE SPEAR (Also see Tarzan)
June, 1972 - No. 17, Feb, 1976; No. 18, May, 1982
Gold Key/Whitman No. 18 on
1 2.00 6.00 14.00
2-Painted-c begin, end #17 1.30 3.25 8.00
3-10 1.80 4.50
11-17: 13-17-Spiegle-a .80 2.00
18-Manning-r/#2; Leopard Girl-r 1.00

BROTHERS, THE CULT ESCAPE, THE (Spire Christian)(Value: cover or less)

BROWNIES (See 4-Color No. 192, 244, 293, 337, 365, 398, 436, 482, 522, 605 & New Funnies)

BROWN'S BLUE RIBBON BOOK OF JOKES AND JINGLES (See Buster Brown's...)

BRUCE GENTRY
Jan, 1948 - No. 2, Nov, 1948; No. 3, Jan, 1949 - No. 8, July, 1949
Better/Standard/Four Star Publ./Superior No. 3
1-Ray Bailey strip reprints begin, end #3; E. C. emblem appears as a monogram on stationery in story; negligee panels 26.00 78.00 180.00
2,3 19.00 58.00 135.00
4-8 13.00 40.00 90.00
NOTE: ***Kamenish** a-2-7; c-1-8.*

GD25 FN65 NM94

BRUTE, THE
Feb, 1975 - No. 3, July, 1975
Seaboard Publ. (Atlas)
1-Origin & 1st app; Sekowsky-a(p) 1.50
2,3: 2-Sekowsky-a(p). 3-Weiss-a(p) 1.00

BRUTE FORCE
Aug, 1990 - No. 4, Nov, 1990 ($1.00, color, limited series)
Marvel Comics
1-4: Animal super-heroes 1.00

BUCCANEER
No date (1963)
I. W. Enterprises
I.W. Reprint #1(r-/Quality #20), #8(r-/#23): Crandall-a in each
3.20 8.00 16.00

BUCCANEERS (Formerly Kid Eternity)
No. 19, Jan, 1950 - No. 27, May, 1951 (No. 24-27: 52 pages)
Quality Comics Group
19-Captain Daring, Black Roger, Eric Falcon & Spanish Main begin; Crandall-a 33.00 100.00 230.00
20,23-Crandall-a 23.00 70.00 160.00
21-Crandall-c/a 27.00 81.00 190.00
22-Bondage-c 17.00 52.00 120.00
24-26: 24-Adam Peril, U.S.N. begins. 25-Origin & 1st app. Corsair Queen. 26-last Spanish Main 14.00 43.00 100.00
27-Crandall-c/a 23.00 70.00 160.00
Super Reprint #12 (1964)-Crandall-r/#21 3.20 8.00 16.00

BUCCANEERS, THE (See 4-Color No. 800)

BUCKAROO BANZAI
Dec, 1984 - No. 2, Feb, 1985 (Movie adaptation)
Marvel Comics Group
1,2-r/Marvel Super Special #33 1.00

BUCK DUCK
June, 1953 - No. 4, Dec, 1953
Atlas Comics (ANC)
1-Funny animal stories in all 6.70 20.00 40.00
2-4: 2-Ed Win-a(5) 4.00 11.00 22.00

BUCK JONES (Also see Crackajack Funnies, Famous Feature Stories & Master Comics #7)
No. 299, Oct, 1950 - No. 850, Oct, 1957 (All Painted-c)
Dell Publishing Co.
4-Color 299(#1)-Buck Jones & his horse Silver-B begin; painted back-c begins, ends #5 13.00 40.00 90.00
2(4-6/51) 7.50 22.50 45.00
3-8(10-12/52) 5.85 17.50 35.00
4-Color 460,500,546,589 5.00 15.00 30.00
4-Color 652,733,850 4.00 10.00 20.00

BUCK ROGERS (In the 25th Century)
1933 (36 pages in color) (6x8")
Kelloggs Corn Flakes Giveaway
370A-By Phil Nowlan & Dick Calkins; 1st Buck Rogers radio premium & 1st app. in comics (tells origin) 46.00 140.00 325.00

BUCK ROGERS (Also see Famous Funnies, Pure Oil Comics, Salerno Carnival of Comics, 24 Pages of Comics, & Vicks Comics)
Winter, 1940-41 - No. 6, Sept, 1943
Famous Funnies
1-Sunday strip reprints by Rick Yager; begins with strip #190; Calkins-c
171.00 515.00 1200.00
2 (7/41)-Calkins-c 100.00 300.00 665.00
3 (12/41), 4 (7/42) 83.00 250.00 550.00
5-Story continues with Famous Funnies No. 80; Buck Rogers, Sky Roads

Buck Rogers #1 (TSR), © Dille Family Trust

Buffalo Bill Jr. #11, © Tie-Ups Co.

Bugs Bunny #2 (7/90), © Warner Bros.

GD25 FN65 NM94

75.00 225.00 500.00
6-Reprints of 1939 dailies; contains B.R. story "Crater of Doom" (2 pgs.) by Calkins not-r from Famous Funnies 75.00 225.00 500.00

BUCK ROGERS
No. 100, Jan, 1951 - No. 9, May-June, 1951
Toby Press

100(#7) 20.00 60.00 130.00
101(#8), 9-All Anderson-a('47-'49-r/dailies) 17.00 50.00 115.00

BUCK ROGERS (...in the 25th Century No. 5 on) (TV)
Oct, 1964; No. 2, July, 1979 - No. 16, May, 1982 (No #10)
Gold Key/Whitman No. 7 on

1(10128-410)-Painted c-1-9,11-13; 12 cents 5.00 15.00 30.00
2(8/79)-Movie adaptation 1.20 3.00
3-9,11-16: 3,4-Movie adaptation; 5-New stories 1.50
Giant Movie Edition 11296(64pp, Whitman, $1.50), reprints GK #2-4 minus cover; tabloid size .80 2.00
Giant Movie Edition 02489(Western/Marvel, $1.50), reprints GK #2-4 minus cover .80 2.00
NOTE: *Bolle a-2-4p, Movie Ed.(p). McWilliams a-2-4i, 5-11, Movie Ed.(i).*

BUCK ROGERS (TSR)(Value: cover or less)

BUCK ROGERS ADVENTURE BOOK
1933 (Premium)
Cocomalt

nn-(Rare) 670.00 2000.00 4000.00

BUCKSKIN (Movie) (See 4-Color No. 1011,1107)

BUCKY O'HARE (Continuity)(Value: cover or less)

BUDDIES IN THE U.S. ARMY
Nov, 1952 - No. 2, 1953
Avon Periodicals

1-Lawrence-c 8.35 25.00 50.00
2-Mort Lawrence-c/a 5.85 17.50 35.00

BUDDY TUCKER & HIS FRIENDS (Also see Buster Brown)
1906 (11x17") (In color)
Cupples & Leon Co.

1905 Sunday strip reprints by R. F. Outcault 43.00 130.00 300.00

BUFFALO BEE (See 4-Color No. 957, 1002, 1061)

BUFFALO BILL (Also see Frontier Fighters, Super Western Comics & Western Action Thrillers)
No. 2, Oct, 1950 - No. 9, Dec, 1951
Youthful Magazines

2-Annie Oakley story 7.50 22.50 45.00
3-9: 2-4-Walter Johnson-c/a. 9-Wildey-a 4.20 12.50 25.00

BUFFALO BILL CODY (See Cody of the Pony Express)

BUFFALO BILL, JR. (TV) (See Western Roundup under Dell Giants)
Jan, 1956 - No. 13, Aug-Oct, 1959; 1965 (All photo-c)
Dell Publishing Co./Gold Key

4-Color 673 (#1) 6.70 20.00 40.00
4-Color 742,766,798,828,856(11/57) 4.70 14.00 28.00
7(2-4/58)-13 4.00 10.00 20.00
1(6/65-Gold Key) 2.80 7.00 14.00

BUFFALO BILL PICTURE STORIES
June-July, 1949 - No. 2, Aug-Sept, 1949
Street & Smith Publications

1,2-Wildey, Powell-a in each 8.35 25.00 50.00

BUFFALO BILL'S PICTURE STORIES
1909 (Soft cardboard cover)
Street & Smith Publications

nn 22.00 65.00 150.00

GD25 FN65 NM94

BUGALOOS (TV)
Sept, 1971 - No. 4, Feb, 1972
Charlton Comics

1-4 1.00 2.00 5.00
NOTE: *No. 3(1/72) went on sale late in 1972 (after No. 4) with the 1/73 issues.*

BUGHOUSE (Satire)
Mar-Apr, 1954 - No. 4, Sept-Oct, 1954
Ajax/Farrell (Excellent Publ.)

V1#1 10.00 30.00 70.00
2-4 7.00 21.00 42.00

BUGHOUSE FABLES
1921 (48 pgs.) (4x4-1/2") (10 cents)
Embee Distributing Co. (King Features)

1-Barney Google 18.00 54.00 125.00

BUG MOVIES
1931 (52 pages) (B&W)
Dell Publishing Co.

nn-Not reprints; Stookie Allen-a 14.00 43.00 100.00

BUGS BUNNY (See The Best of..., Camp Comics, Comic Album #2, 6, 10, 14, Dell Giant #28, 32, 46, Dynabrite, Golden Comics Digest #1, 3, 5, 6, 8, 10, 14, 15, 17, 21, 26, 30, 34, 39, 42, 47, Kite Fun Book, Large Feature Comic #8, Looney Tunes and Merry Melodies, March of Comics #44, 59, 75, 83, 97, 115, 132, 149, 160, 179, 188, 201, 220, 231, 245, 259, 273, 287, 301, 315, 329, 343, 363, 367, 380, 392, 403, 415, 428, 440, 452, 464, 476, 487, Porky Pig, Puffed Wheat, Story Hour Series #802, Super Book #14, 26 and Whitman Comic Books)

BUGS BUNNY (See Dell Giants for annuals)
1942 - No. 245, 1983
Dell Publishing Co./Gold Key No. 86-218/Whitman No. 219 on

Large Feature Comic 8(1942)-(Rarely found in fine-mint condition) 80.00 242.00 565.00
4-Color 33 ('43) 52.00 155.00 365.00
4-Color 51 30.00 90.00 210.00
4-Color 88 18.00 54.00 125.00
4-Color 123('46),142,164 12.00 36.00 85.00
4-Color 187,200,217,233 10.00 30.00 70.00
4-Color 250-Used in **SOTI**, pg. 309 10.00 30.00 70.00
4-Color 266,274,281,289,298('50) 10.00 30.00 60.00
4-Color 307,317(#1),327(#2),338,347,355,366,376,393 7.50 22.50 45.00
4-Color 407,420,432 5.35 16.00 32.00
28(12-1/52-53)-30 3.60 9.00 18.00
31-50 2.40 6.00 12.00
51-85(7-9/62) 1.60 4.00 8.00
86(10/62)-88-Bugs Bunny's Showtime-(80 pgs.)(25 cents) 4.50 14.00 35.00
89-100 1.00 2.50 6.00
101-120 1.60 4.00
121-140 1.20 3.00
141-170 1.00 2.50
171-245: 229-Swipe of Barks story/WDC&S #223 1.50
NOTE: *Reprints-100, 102, 104, 123, 143, 144, 147, 167, 173, 175-177, 179-185, 187, 190.*
...Comic-Go-Round 11196-(224 pgs.)($1.95)(Golden Press, 1979) 1.20 3.00
...Winter Fun 1(12/67-Gold Key)-Giant 3.15 9.50 25.00

BUGS BUNNY (Puffed Rice Giveaway)
1949 (32 pages each, 3-1/8x6-7/8")
Quaker Cereals

A1-Traps the Counterfeiters, A2-Aboard Mystery Submarine, A3- Rocket to the Moon, A4-Lion Tamer, A5-Rescues the Beautiful Princess, B1-Buried Treasure, B2-Outwits the Smugglers, B3-Joins the Marines, B4-Meets the Dwarf Ghost, B5-Finds Aladdin's Lamp, C1-Lost in the Frozen North, C2-Secret Agent, C3-Captured by Cannibals, C4-Fights the Man from Mars, C5-And the Haunted Cave
each.... 5.00 15.00 30.00

BUGS BUNNY (3-D)
1953 (Pocket size) (15 titles)

Bullet Crow #2, © Chuck Fiala

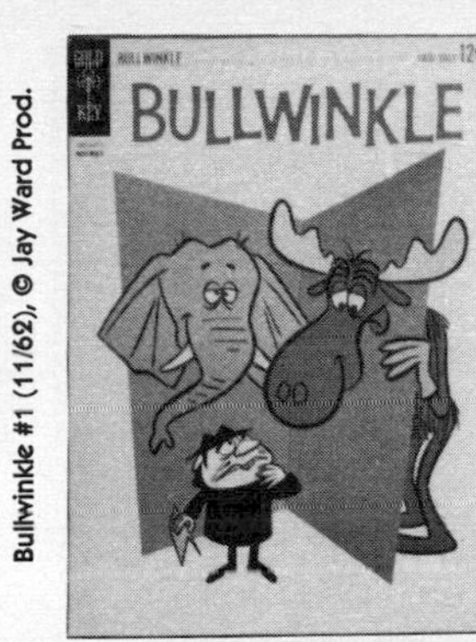

Bullwinkle #1 (11/62), © Jay Ward Prod.

Burke's Law #3 © Four Star

	GD25	FN65	NM94
Cheerios Giveaway			
each....	6.70	20.00	40.00

BUGS BUNNY
June, 1990 - No. 3, Aug, 1990 ($1.00, color, mini-series)
DC Comics

	GD25	FN65	NM94
1-3: Daffy Duck, Elmer Fudd, others app.			1.00

BUGS BUNNY & PORKY PIG
Sept, 1965 (100 pages; paper cover; giant)
Gold Key

	GD25	FN65	NM94
1(30025-509)	5.85	17.50	35.00

BUGS BUNNY'S ALBUM (See 4-Color No. 498,585,647,724)

BUGS BUNNY LIFE STORY ALBUM (See 4-Color No. 838)

BUGS BUNNY MERRY CHRISTMAS (See 4-Color No. 1064)

BULLET CROW, FOWL OF FORTUNE (Eclipse)(Value: cover or less)

BULLETMAN (See Fawcett Miniatures, Master Comics, Mighty Midget Comics, Nickel Comics & XMas Comics)
Sum, 1941 - #12, 2/12/43; #14, Spr, 1946 - #16, Fall, 1946 (No #13)
Fawcett Publications

	GD25	FN65	NM94
1	200.00	600.00	1350.00
2	100.00	300.00	675.00
3	72.00	218.00	475.00
4,5	62.00	188.00	415.00
6-10: 7-Ghost Stories as told by the night watchman of the cemetery begins; Eisnerish-a	54.00	162.00	365.00
11,12,14-16 (nn 13)	46.00	138.00	300.00
Well Known Comics (1942)-Paper-c, glued binding; printed in red (Bestmaid/Samuel Lowe giveaway)	12.50	37.50	85.00

NOTE: ***Mac Raboy** c-1-3, 5, 6, 10. 'Bulletman the Flying Detective' on cover #8 on.*

BULLS-EYE (Cody of The Pony Express No. 8 on)
7-8/54 - No. 5, 3-4/55; No. 6, 6/55; No. 7, 8/55
Mainline No. 1-5/Charlton No. 6,7

	GD25	FN65	NM94
1-S&K-c, 2 pages-a	37.00	110.00	250.00
2-S&K-c/a	32.00	100.00	225.00
3-5-S&K-c/a(2 each)	24.00	72.00	165.00
6-S&K-c/a	18.00	55.00	125.00
7-S&K-c/a(3)	23.00	70.00	160.00
Great Scott Shoe Store giveaway-Reprints #2 with new cover	12.50	37.50	85.00

BULLS-EYE COMICS (Formerly Komik Pages #10; becomes Kayo #12)
No. 11, 1944
Harry 'A' Chesler

	GD25	FN65	NM94
11-Origin K-9, Green Knight's sidekick, Lance; The Green Knight, Lady Satan, Yankee Doodle Jones app.	20.00	60.00	140.00

BULLWHIP GRIFFIN (See Movie Comics)

BULLWINKLE (TV) (...and Rocky No. 20 on; See March of Comics #233 and Rocky & Bullwinkle) (Jay Ward)
3-5/62 - #11, 4/74; #12, 6/76 - #19, 3/78; #20, 4/79 - #25, 2/80
Dell/Gold Key

	GD25	FN65	NM94
4-Color 1270 (3-5/62)	14.00	43.00	100.00
01-090-209 (Dell, 7-9/62)	14.00	43.00	100.00
1(11/62, Gold Key)	11.50	34.00	80.00
2(2/63)	9.00	26.00	60.00
3(4/72)-11(4/74-Gold Key)	4.30	13.00	30.00
12(6/76)-Reprints	1.65	4.00	10.00
13(9/76), 14-New stories	1.70	5.00	12.00
15-25	1.30	3.25	8.00
Mother Moose Nursery Pomes 01-530-207 (5-7/62-Dell)	9.00	28.00	65.00

NOTE: *Reprints: 6, 7, 20-24.*

BULLWINKLE (...& Rocky No. 2 on)(TV)
July, 1970 - No. 7, July, 1971
Charlton Comics

	GD25	FN65	NM94
1	3.60	10.75	25.00
2-7	2.15	6.50	15.00

BULLWINKLE AND ROCKY
Nov, 1987 - No. 9, Mar, 1989
Star Comics/Marvel Comics No. 3 on

	GD25	FN65	NM94
1-9			1.00

BUNNY (Also see Rock Happening)
Dec, 1966 - No. 20, Dec, 1971; No. 21, Nov, 1976
Harvey Publications

	GD25	FN65	NM94
1: 68 pg. Giant	3.00	7.50	15.00
2-18: 68 pg. Giants	2.40	6.00	12.00
19-21: 52 pg. Giants	1.65	4.00	10.00

BURKE'S LAW (TV)
1-3/64; No. 2, 5-7/64; No. 3, 3-5/65 (Gene Barry photo-c, all)
Dell Publishing Co.

	GD25	FN65	NM94
1-Photo-c	4.70	14.00	28.00
2,3-Photo-c	3.60	9.00	18.00

BURNING ROMANCES (See Fox Giants)

BUSTER BEAR
Dec, 1953 - No. 10, June, 1955
Quality Comics Group (Arnold Publ.)

	GD25	FN65	NM94
1-Funny animal	5.00	15.00	30.00
2	3.00	7.50	15.00
3-10	2.40	6.00	12.00
I.W. Reprint #9,10 (Super on inside)	1.20	3.00	6.00

BUSTER BROWN (Also see Brown's Blue Ribbon Book of Jokes and Jingles & Buddy Tucker & His Friends)
1903 - 1916 (11x17" strip reprints in color)
Frederick A. Stokes Co.

	GD25	FN65	VF82
...& His Resolutions (1903) by R. F. Outcault	86.00	257.00	600.00
...Abroad (1904)-86 pgs.; hardback; 8x10-1/4"; B&W; by R. F. Outcault (76 pgs.)	64.00	193.00	450.00
...His Dog Tige & Their Troubles (1904)	64.00	193.00	450.00
...Pranks (1905)	64.00	193.00	450.00
...Antics (1906)-11x17", 66 pgs.	64.00	193.00	450.00
...And Company (1906)-11x17" in color	64.00	193.00	450.00
...Mary Jane & Tige (1906)	64.00	193.00	450.00
...My Resolutions (1906)-68 pgs.; B&W; hardcover; Sunday panel reprints	64.00	193.00	450.00
Collection of Buster Brown Comics (1908)	64.00	193.00	450.00
Buster Brown Up to Date (1910)	64.00	193.00	450.00
...The Fun Maker (1912)	64.00	193.00	450.00
...The Little Rogue (1916)(10x15-3/4," 62 pgs., in color)	54.00	160.00	375.00

NOTE: *Rarely found in fine or mint condition.*

BUSTER BROWN
1904 - 1912 (3x5" to 5x7"; sizes vary)(Advertising premium booklets)
Various Publishers

The Brown Shoe Company, St. Louis, USA
(Color, 5x7", 16 pgs set of five books)

	GD25	FN65	VF82
Brown's Blue Ribbon Book of Jokes and Jingles Book 1 (nn, 1904)-By R. F. Outcault; Buster Brown & Tige, Little Tommy Tucker, Jack & Jill, Little Boy Blue, Dainty Jane; The Yellow Kid app. on back-c (1st comic book premium)	230.00	685.00	1600.00
Buster Brown's Blue Ribbon Book of Jokes and Jingles Book 2 (1905)-Original color art by Outcault	185.00	560.00	1300.00
Buster's Book of Jokes & Jingles Book 3 (1909)-r/Blue Ribbon post cards not signed by R.F. Outcault	185.00	560.00	1300.00

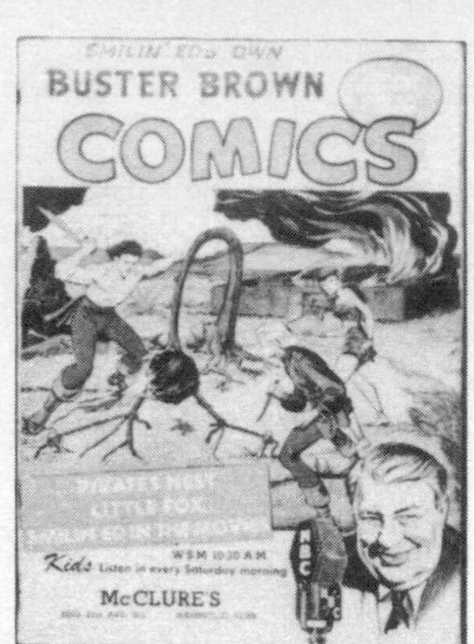

Buster Brown Comics #10, © Buster Brown

Buster Crabbe #1, © FF

The Butcher #2, © DC

GD25 FN65 NM94

Buster's Book of Instructive Jokes and Jingles Book 4 (1910)-Original color art not signed by R.F. Outcault 185.00 560.00 1300.00

...Book of Travels nn (1912, 3x5")-Original color art not signed by Outcault 79.00 235.00 550.00

NOTE: *Estimated 5 to 6 known copies exist of books #1-4.*

The Buster Brown Bread Company

"Buster Brown" Bread Book of Rhymes, The nn (1904, 4x6", 12 pgs.)-Original color art not signed by R.F. Outcault 107.00 320.00 750.00

The Buster Brown Stocking Company

Buster Brown Drawing Book, The nn (nd, 5x6", 20 pgs.)-B&W reproductions of 1903 R.F. Outcault art to trace 54.00 160.00 375.00

Collins Baking Company

Buster Brown Drawing Book nn (1904, 3x5", 12 pgs.)-Original B&W art to trace not signed by R.F. Outcault 54.00 160.00 375.00

C. H. Morton, St. Albans, VT

Merry Antics of Buster Brown, Buddy Tucker & Tige nn (nd, 3-1/2x5-1/2", 16 pgs.)-Original B&W art by R.F. Outcault 54.00 160.00 375.00

Pond's Extract

Buster Brown's Experiences With Pond's Extract nn (1904, 4-1/2x6-3/4", 28 pgs.)-Original color art by R.F. Outcault 93.00 280.00 650.00

Ringen Stove Company

Quick Meal Steel Ranges nn (nd, 3x5", 16 pgs.)-Origiinal B&W art not signed by R.F. Outcault 50.00 150.00 350.00

No Publisher Listed

The Drawiing Book nn (1906, 3-9/16x5", 8 pgs.)-Original B&W art to trace not signed by R.F. Outcault 50.00 150.00 350.00

BUSTER BROWN
1906 - 1917 (11x17" strip reprints in color)
Cupples & Leon Co./N. Y. Herald Co.
(By R. F. Outcault)

	GD25	FN65	VF82
...His Dog Tige & Their Jolly Times (1906, 58 pgs.)	64.00	193.00	450.00
...Latest Frolics (1906, 58 pgs.)	64.00	193.00	450.00
...Amusing Capers (1908, 46 pgs.)	64.00	193.00	450.00
...And His Pets (1909)	64.00	193.00	450.00
...On His Travels (1910)	64.00	193.00	450.00
...Happy Days (1911)	64.00	193.00	450.00
...In Foreign Lands (1912)	57.00	171.00	400.00
...And the Cat (1917)	57.00	171.00	400.00

NOTE: *Rarely found in fine or mint condition.*

BUSTER BROWN COMICS (Radio)(Also see My Dog Tige)
1945 - No. 43, 1959 (No. 5: paper cover)
Brown Shoe Co

	GD25	FN65	NM94
nn, nd (#1)-Covers mention diff. shoe stores	38.00	115.00	265.00
2	14.00	43.00	100.00
3-10	9.15	27.50	55.00
11-20	5.85	17.50	35.00
21-24,26-29	4.20	12.50	25.00
25,33-37,40-43-Crandall-a in all	9.15	27.50	55.00
30-32-"Interplanetary Police Vs. the Space Siren" by Crandall (also in #29 but not by Crandall)	9.15	27.50	55.00
38,39	4.70	14.00	28.00
...Goes to Mars (2/58-Western Printing), slick-c, 20 pgs., reg. size	6.70	20.00	50.00
...In "Buster Makes the Team!" (1959-Custom Comics)	4.70	14.00	32.00
...In The Jet Age ('50s), slick-c, 20 pgs., 5x7-1/4"	8.35	25.00	50.00
...Of the Safety Patrol ('60-Custom Comics)	4.00	10.00	20.00
...Out of This World ('59-Custom Comics)	5.35	16.00	32.00
...Safety Coloring Book ('58, 16 pgs.)-Slick paper	5.00	15.00	30.00

GD25 FN65 NM94

BUSTER BUNNY
Nov, 1949 - No. 16, Oct, 1953
Standard Comics(Animated Cartoons)/Pines

	GD25	FN65	NM94
1-Frazetta 1 pg. text illo.	5.00	15.00	30.00
2	3.00	7.50	15.00
3-16: 15-Racist-c	2.00	5.00	10.00

BUSTER CRABBE (TV)
Nov, 1951 - No. 12, 1953
Famous Funnies Publ.

	GD25	FN65	NM94
1-Frazetta anti-drug ad; text story about Buster Crabbe & Billy the Kid	24.00	70.00	165.00
2-Williamson/Evans-c; text story about Wild Bill Hickok & Pecos Bill	25.00	75.00	175.00
3-Williamson/Evans-c/a	29.00	85.00	200.00
4-Frazetta-c/a, 1pg.; bondage-c	33.00	100.00	230.00
5-Frazetta-c; Williamson/Krenkel/Orlando-a, 11pgs. (per Mr. Williamson)	85.00	255.00	600.00
6-12: 7,9-One pg. Frazetta ad in each	8.35	25.00	50.00

BUSTER CRABBE (The Amazing Adventures of..)
Dec, 1953 - No. 4, June, 1954
Lev Gleason Publications

	GD25	FN65	NM94
1,4: 1-Photo-c. 4-Flash Gordon-c	11.50	34.00	80.00
2,3-Toth-a	14.00	43.00	100.00

BUTCH CASSIDY
June, 1971 - No. 3, Oct, 1971 (52 pages)
Skywald Comics

	GD25	FN65	NM94
1-Red Mask reprint, retitled Maverick; Bolle-a		.80	2.00
2,3: 2-Whip Wilson-r. 3-Dead Canyon Days reprint/Crack Western No. 63; Sundance Kid app.; Crandall-a			1.50

BUTCH CASSIDY (...& the Wild Bunch)
1951
Avon Periodicals

	GD25	FN65	NM94
1-Kinstler-c/a	11.50	34.00	80.00

NOTE: ***Reinman** story; Issue number on inside spine.*

BUTCH CASSIDY (See Fun-In No. 11 & Western Adventure Comics)

BUTCHER, THE (Also see Brave and the Bold, 2nd series)
May, 1990 - No. 5, Sept, 1990 ($1.50, color, mature readers)
DC Comics

	GD25	FN65	NM94
1-5: 1-No indicia inside			1.50

BUZ SAWYER (Sweeney No. 4 on)
June, 1948 - No. 3, 1949
Standard Comics

	GD25	FN65	NM94
1-Roy Crane-a	14.00	43.00	100.00
2-Intro his pal Sweeney	10.00	30.00	60.00
3	8.35	25.00	50.00

BUZ SAWYER'S PAL, ROSCOE SWEENEY (See Sweeney)

BUZZY (See All Funny Comics)
Winter, 1944-45 - No. 75, 1-2/57; No. 76, 10/57; No. 77, 10/58
National Periodical Publications/Detective Comics

	GD25	FN65	NM94
1 (52 pgs. begin)	22.00	65.00	150.00
2	10.00	30.00	70.00
3-5	6.70	20.00	40.00
6-10	5.00	15.00	30.00
11-20	4.20	12.50	25.00
21-30	3.60	9.00	18.00
31,35-38	3.00	7.50	15.00
32-34,39-Last 52 pgs. Scribbly story by Mayer in each (these four stories were done for Scribbly #14 which was delayed for a year)	3.60	9.00	18.00
40-77: 62-Last precode (2/55)	2.80	7.00	14.00

Cage #19, © MEG

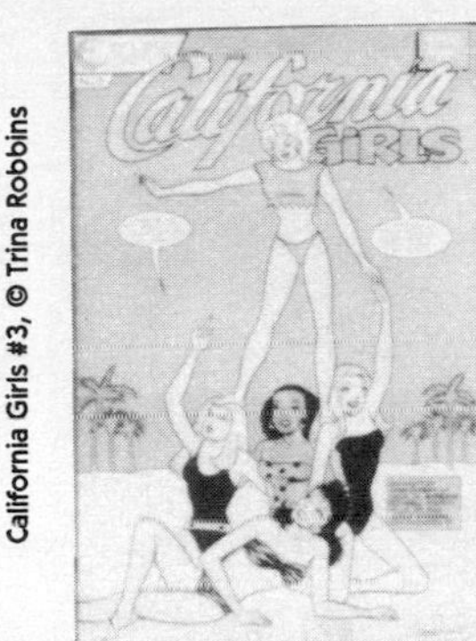
California Girls #3, © Trina Robbins

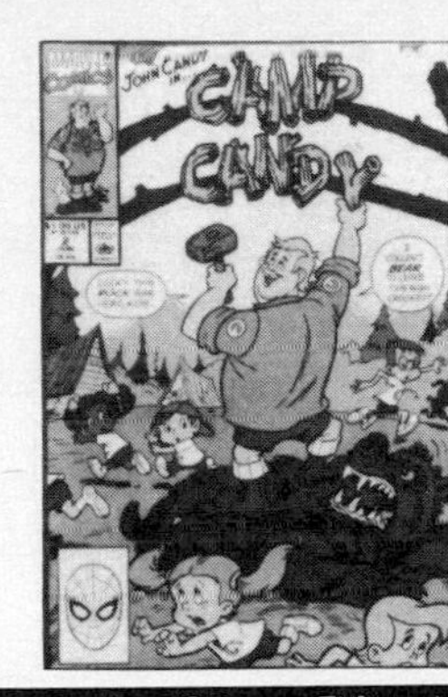
Camp Candy #2, © DIC Animation City/Saban Prod.

GD25 FN65 NM94

BUZZY THE CROW (See Harvey Comics Hits #60, Harvey Hits #18 & Paramount Animated Comics #1)

CABLE (See Ghost Rider &..., & New Mutants #87)
May, 1993 - Present ($2.00, color)
Marvel Comics
1-($3.50, 52 pgs.)-Gold foil-c; Thibert-c/a begins 1.40 3.50
2-10: 3-Extra 16 pg. X-Men/Avengers ann. preview .80 2.00

CABLE - BLOOD AND METAL
Oct, 1992 - No. 2, Nov, 1992 ($2.50, color, mini-series, 52 pgs.)
Marvel Comics
1-Wraparound-c; Cable vs. Stryfe; Romita, Jr.-c/a in both 1.20 3.00
2-Prelude to X-Cutioner's Song x-overs 1.00 2.50

CADET GRAY OF WEST POINT (See Dell Giants)

CADILLACS & DINOSAURS (TV)
Nov, 1990 - No. 6, Apr, 1991 ($2.50, color, limited series, coated paper)
Epic Comics (Marvel)
1-6: r/Xenozoic Tales in color w/new-c 1.00 2.50
...In 3-D #1 (7/92, $3.95, Kitchen Sink)-W/glasses 1.60 4.00

CAGE (Also see Hero for Hire, Power Man & Punisher)
Apr, 1992 - No. 20, Nov, 1993 ($1.25, color)
Marvel Comics
1-($1.50)-Has extra color on-c .80 2.00
2-11,13-20: 3-Punisher-c & minor app. 9-Rhino-c/story; Hulk cameo. 10-Rhino & Hulk-c/story 1.25
12-($1.75, 52 pgs.)-Iron Fist app. .70 1.75

CAGES
1991 - No. 10 ($3.50/$3.95, color, limited series)
Tundra Publ.
1-Dave McKean-c/a in all 1.70 5.00 12.00
2-Misprint exists 1.20 3.00 7.00
3-10: 5-Begin $3.95-c 1.60 4.00

CAIN'S HUNDRED (TV)
May-July, 1962 - No. 2, Sept-Nov, 1962
Dell Publishing Co.
nn(01-094-207) 2.80 7.00 14.00
2 1.80 4.50 9.00

CALIBER PRESENTS
Jan, 1989 - No. 24, 1991 ($1.95-$2.50, B&W, 52 pgs.)
Caliber Press
1-Anthology; 1st app. The Crow; Tim Vigil-c/a 1.70 5.00 12.00
2-Deadworld story; Tim Vigil-a 1.00 2.00 5.00
3-14: 9-Begin $2.50-c 1.20 3.00
15-24 ($3.50, 68 pgs.) 1.40 3.50

CALIFORNIA GIRLS
June, 1987 - No. 8, May, 1988 ($2.00, B&W, 40pgs)
Eclipse Comics
1-8: All contain color paper dolls .80 2.00

CALL FROM CHRIST
1952 (36 pages) (Giveaway)
Catechetical Educational Society
nn 2.00 5.00 10.00

CALLING ALL BOYS (Tex Granger No. 18 on)
Jan, 1946 - No. 17, May, 1948 (Photo c-1-5,7,8)
Parents' Magazine Institute
1 7.50 22.50 45.00
2 4.00 10.00 20.00
3-7,9,11,14-17: 6-Painted-c. 11-Rin Tin Tin photo on-c; Tex Granger begins. 14-J. Edgar Hoover photo on-c. 15-Tex Granger-c begin 2.40 6.00 12.00
8-Milton Caniff story 4.20 12.50 25.00
10-Gary Cooper photo on-c 4.00 12.00 24.00
12-Bob Hope photo on-c 5.85 17.50 35.00
13-Bing Crosby photo on-c 4.70 14.00 28.00

CALLING ALL GIRLS
Sept, 1941 - No. 89, Sept, 1949 (Part magazine, part comic)
Parents' Magazine Institute
1 10.00 30.00 60.00
2-Photo-c 4.70 14.00 28.00
3-Shirley Temple photo-c 5.85 17.50 35.00
4-10: 4,5,7,9-Photo-c. 9-Flag-c 3.20 8.00 16.00
11-20: 11-Photo-c 2.40 6.00 12.00
21-39,41-43(10-11/45)-Last issue with comics 1.80 4.50 9.00
40-Liz Taylor photo-c 5.85 17.50 35.00
44-51(7/46)-Last comic book size issue 1.40 3.50 7.00
52-89 1.20 3.00 6.00
NOTE: *Jack Sparling art in many issues; becomes a girls' magazine "Senior Prom" with #90.*

CALLING ALL KIDS (Also see True Comics)
Dec-Jan, 1945-46 - No. 26, Aug, 1949
Parents' Magazine Institute
1-Funny animal 6.35 19.00 38.00
2 3.60 9.00 18.00
3-10 1.80 4.50 9.00
11-26 1.40 3.50 7.00

CALVIN (See Li'l Kids)

CALVIN & THE COLONEL (TV)
No. 1354, Apr-June, 1962 - No. 2, July-Sept, 1962
Dell Publishing Co.
4-Color 1354(#1) 8.35 25.00 50.00
2 5.85 17.50 35.00

CAMELOT 3000
12/82 - No. 11, 7/84; No. 12, 4/85 (Direct Sale; Mando paper)
DC Comics (Maxi-series)
1-12: 5-Intro Knights of New Camelot 1.00 2.50
NOTE: *Austin a-7i-12i. Bolland a-1-12p; c-1-12.*

CAMERA COMICS
July, 1944 - No. 9, Summer, 1946
U.S. Camera Publishing Corp./ME
nn (7/44) 14.00 43.00 100.00
nn (9/44) 11.50 34.00 80.00
1(10/44)-The Grey Comet 11.50 34.00 80.00
2 10.00 30.00 60.00
3-Nazi WW II-c; photos 8.35 25.00 50.00
4-9: All half photos 7.50 22.50 45.00

CAMP CANDY (TV)
May, 1990 - No. 6, Oct, 1990 ($1.00, color)
Marvel Comics
1-6: Post-c/a(p); featuring John Candy .50 1.00

CAMP COMICS
Feb, 1942 - No. 3, April, 1942 (All have photo-c)
Dell Publishing Co.
1-"Seaman Sy Wheeler" by Kelly, 7 pgs., Bugs Bunny app.; Mark Twain adaptation 39.00 120.00 275.00
2-Kelly-a, 12 pgs.; Bugs Bunny app. 31.00 95.00 220.00
3-(Scarce)-Dave Berg & Walt Kelly-a 39.00 120.00 275.00

CAMP RUNAMUCK (TV)
April, 1966
Dell Publishing Co.
1-Photo-c 3.20 8.00 16.00

Candy #38, © QUA

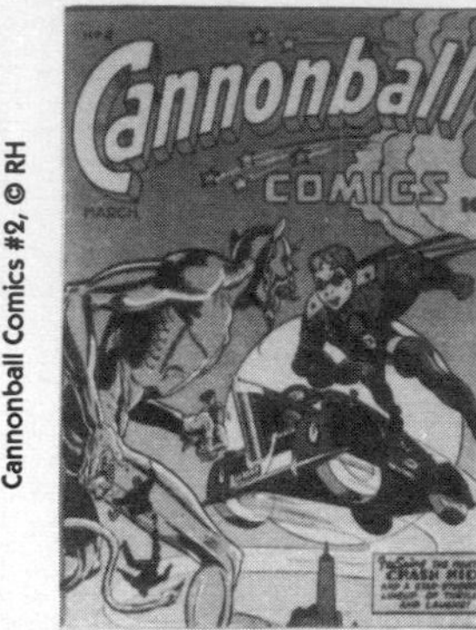

Cannonball Comics #2, © RH

Captain Aero #1, © HOKE

CAMPUS LOVES
Dec, 1949 - No. 5, Aug, 1950
Quality Comics Group (Comic Magazines)

	GD25	FN65	NM94
1-Ward-c/a (9 pgs.)	17.00	51.00	120.00
2-Ward-c/a	12.00	36.00	85.00
3-5: 5-Spanking panels (2)	7.00	21.00	42.00

NOTE: *Gustavson a-1-5. Photo c-3-5.*

CAMPUS ROMANCE (...Romances on cover)
Sept-Oct, 1949 - No. 3, Feb-Mar, 1950
Avon Periodicals/Realistic

	GD25	FN65	NM94
1-Walter Johnson-a; c-/Avon paperback 348	12.00	36.00	85.00
2-Grandenetti-a; c-/Avon paperback 151	10.00	30.00	70.00
3-c-/Avon paperback 201	10.00	30.00	70.00
Realistic reprint	4.70	14.00	28.00

CANADA DRY PREMIUMS (See Swamp Fox, The & Terry & The Pirates)

CANCELLED COMIC CAVALCADE
Summer, 1978 - No. 2, Fall, 1978 (8-1/2x11"; B&W)
(Xeroxed pages on one side only w/blue cover and taped spine)
DC Comics, Inc.

1-(412 pages) Contains xeroxed copies of art for: Black Lightning #12, cover to #13; Claw #13,14; The Deserter #1; Doorway to Nightmare #6; Firestorm #6; The Green Team #2,3.
2-(532 pages) Contains xeroxed copies of art for: Kamandi #60 (including Omac), #61; Prez #5; Shade #9 (including The Odd Man); Showcase #105 (Deadman), 106 (The Creeper); The Vixen #1; and covers to Army t War #2, Bat#tle Classics #3, Demand Classics #1 & 2, Dynamic Classics #3, Mr. Miracle #26, Ragman #6, Weird Mystery #25& 26, & Western Classics #1 & 2. (Rare) (One set sold in 1989 for $1,200.00)

NOTE: *In June, 1978, DC cancelled several of their titles. For copyright purposes, the unpublished original art for these titles was xeroxed, bound in the above books, published and distributed. Only 35 copies were made.*

CANDID TALES (Also see Bold Stories & It Rhymes With Lust)
April, 1950; June, 1950 (Digest size) (144 pages) (Full color)
Kirby Publishing Co.

	GD25	FN65	NM94
nn-(Scarce) Contains Wood female pirate story, 15 pgs., and 14 pgs. in June issue; Powell-a	49.00	145.00	340.00

NOTE: *Another version exists with Dr. Kilmore by Wood; no female pirate story.*

CANDY
Fall, 1944 - No. 3, Spring, 1945
William H. Wise & Co.

	GD25	FN65	NM94
1-Two Scoop Scuttle stories by Wolverton	19.00	58.00	135.00
2,3-Scoop Scuttle by Wolverton, 2-4 pgs.	16.00	48.00	110.00

CANDY (Teen-age)(Also see Police Comics #37)
Autumn, 1947 - No. 64, July, 1956
Quality Comics Group (Comic Magazines)

	GD25	FN65	NM94
1-Gustavson-a	11.00	32.00	75.00
2-Gustavson-a	6.70	20.00	40.00
3-10	4.20	12.50	25.00
11-30	3.20	8.00	16.00
31-63	2.80	7.00	14.00
64-Ward-c(p)?	3.20	8.00	16.00
Super Reprint No. 2,10,12,16,17,18('63-'64)	1.40	3.50	7.00

NOTE: *Jack Cole 1-2 pg. art in many issues.*

CANNONBALL COMICS
Feb, 1945 - No. 2, Mar, 1945
Rural Home Publishing Co.

	GD25	FN65	NM94
1-The Crash Kid, Thunderbrand, The Captive Prince & Crime Crusader begin; skull-c	37.00	110.00	250.00
2-Devil-c	29.00	85.00	200.00

CANTEEN KATE (See All Picture All True Love Story & Fightin' Marines)
June, 1952 - No. 3, Nov, 1952
St. John Publishing Co.

	GD25	FN65	NM94
1-Matt Baker-c/a	27.00	81.00	190.00
2-Matt Baker-c/a	23.00	70.00	160.00
3-(Rare)-Used in **POP**, pg. 75; Baker-c/a	27.00	81.00	190.00

CAP'N CRUNCH COMICS (See Quaker Oats)
1963; 1965 (16 pgs.; miniature giveaways; 2-1/2x6-1/2")
Quaker Oats Co.

	GD25	FN65	NM94
(1963 titles)-"The Picture Pirates," "The Fountain of Youth," "I'm Dreaming of a Wide Isthmus." (1965 titles)-"Bewitched, Betwitched, & Betweaked," "Seadog Meets the Witch Doctor" (another 1965 title suspected)	5.00	15.00	30.00

CAP'N QUICK & A FOOZLE (Eclipse)(Value: cover or less)

CAPTAIN ACTION
Oct-Nov, 1968 - No. 5, June-July, 1969 (Based on Ideal toy)
National Periodical Publications

	GD25	FN65	NM94
1-Origin; Wood-a; Superman-c app.	6.00	19.00	44.00
2,3,5-Kane/Wood-a	3.60	10.75	25.00
4	3.20	8.00	20.00
...& Action Boy('67)-Ideal Toy Co. giveaway (1st app. Captain Action)	6.70	20.00	47.00

CAPTAIN AERO COMICS (Samson No. 1-6; also see Veri Best Sure Fire & Veri Best Sure Shot Comics)
V1#7(#1), Dec, 1941 - V2#4(#10), Jan, 1943; V3#9(#11), Sept, 1943 - V4#3(#17), Oct, 1944; #21, Dec, 1944 - #26, Aug, 1946 (No #18-20)
Holyoke Publishing Co.

	GD25	FN65	NM94
V1#7(#1)-Flag-Man & Solar, Master of Magic, Captain Aero, Cap Stone, Adventurer begin	75.00	225.00	500.00
8(#2)-Pals of Freedom app.	42.00	125.00	275.00
9(#3)-Alias X begins; Pals of Freedom app.	42.00	125.00	275.00
10(#4)-Origin The Gargoyle; Kubert-a	42.00	125.00	275.00
11,12(#5,6)-Kubert-a; Miss Victory in #6	35.00	105.00	225.00
V2#1,2(#7,8): 8-Origin The Red Cross; Miss Victory app.; Brodsky-c(i)	20.00	60.00	135.00
3(#9)-Miss Victory app.	15.00	45.00	100.00
4(#10)-Miss Victory app.	12.00	35.00	80.00
V3#9 - V3#13(#11-15): 11,15-Miss Victory app.	10.00	30.00	60.00
V4#2, V4#3(#16,17)	8.35	25.00	50.00
21-24,26-L. B. Cole covers. 22-Intro/origin Mighty Mite	10.00	32.00	70.00
25-L. B. Cole S/F-c	13.00	40.00	85.00

NOTE: ***L.B. Cole** c-17. **Hollingsworth** a-23. **Infantino** a-23. **Schomburg** c-15, 16*

CAPTAIN AMERICA (See Adventures of..., All-Select, All Winners, Aurora, Avengers #4, Blood and Glory, Captain Britain 16-20, Giant-Size..., The Invaders, Marvel Double Feature, Marvel Fanfare, Marvel Mystery, Marvel Super-Action, Marvel Super Heroes V2#3, Marvel Team-Up, Marvel Treasury Special, Power Record Comics, USA Comics, Young Allies & Young Men)

CAPTAIN AMERICA (Formerly Tales of Suspense #1-99; Captain America and the Falcon #134-223 on cover only)
No. 100, April, 1968 - Present
Marvel Comics Group

	GD25	FN65	NM94
100-Flashback on Cap's revival with Avengers & Sub-Mariner; story continued from Tales of Suspense #99	37.00	113.00	300.00
101	10.00	30.00	80.00
102-108	5.00	15.00	40.00
109-Origin Capt. America	7.00	21.00	55.00
110,111,113-Steranko-c/a. 110-Rick becomes Cap's partner; Hulk x-over; 1st app. Viper. 111-Death of Steve Rogers. 113-Cap's funeral	6.25	19.00	50.00
112-Origin retold	3.00	9.00	24.00
114-116,118-120: 115-Last 12 cent issue	2.50	8.00	20.00
117-1st app. The Falcon (9/69)	3.50	11.00	28.00
121-140: 121-Retells origin. 133-The Falcon becomes Cap's partner; origin Modok. 137,138-Spider-Man x-over. 140-Origin Grey Gargoyle retold	1.60	4.00	9.50

141-153,155-171,176-179: 142-Last 15 cent issue. 143-(52 pgs.). 144-New costume Falcon. 153-1st app. (cameo) Jack Monroe. 155-Origin; redrawn with Falcon added; origin Jack Monroe. 160-1st app. Solarr. 164-1st app.

Captain America #228, © MEG

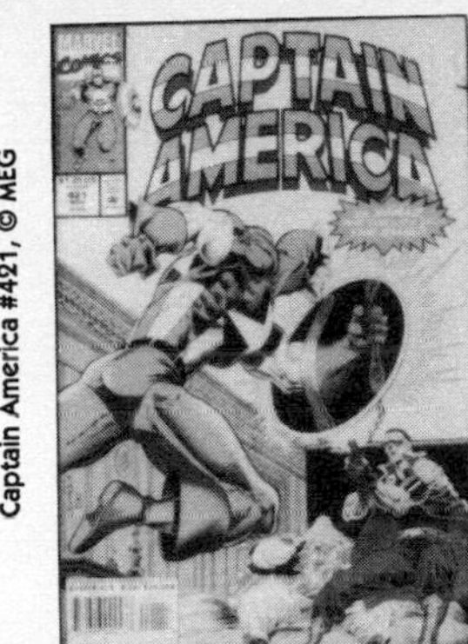

Captain America #421, © MEG

Captain America Comics #18, © MEG

GD25 FN65 NM94

Nightshade. 176-End of Capt. America 1.20 3.00 7.00
154-1st full app. Jack Monroe (Nomad)(10/72) 1.30 3.25 8.00
172-175-X-Men x-over 1.65 4.70 11.00
180-Intro/origin of Nomad (Steve Rogers) 1.20 3.00 7.00
181-Intro/origin new cap. 1.00 2.50 6.00
182,184-200(8/76): 186-True origin The Falcon 1.60 4.00
183-Death of new Cap; Nomad becomes Cap 1.00 2.50 6.00
201-240,242-246: 215-Retells Cap's origin. 216-r/story from Strange Tales #114. 217-1st app. Marvel Man (later Quasar). 229-Marvel Man app. 230-Battles Hulk-c/story cont'd in Hulk #232. 233-Death of Sharon Carter. 234,235-Daredevil x-over; 235(7/79)-Miller pencils. 244,245-Miller-c 1.20 3.00
241-Punisher app.; Miller-c 6.50 19.00 45.00
247-255-Byrne-a. 255-Origin; Miller-c 1.40 3.50
256-281,284,285,289-322,324-326,329-331: 264-Old X-Men cameo in flash-back. 265,266-Nick Fury & Spider-Man app. 267-1st app. Everyman. 269-1st Team America. 281-'50s Bucky returns. 284-Patriot (Jack Mace) app. 285-Death of Patriot. 298-Origin Red Skull .80 2.00
282-Bucky becomes new Nomad (Jack Monroe) 1.65 4.00 10.00
282-Silver Ink 2nd print ($1.75) w/orig. date (6/83) .70 1.75
283-2nd app. Nomad 1.00 2.00 5.00
286-288-Deathlok app. 1.20 3.00
323-1st app. new Super Patriot (see Nick Fury) 1.60 4.00
327-Captain America battles Super Patriot 1.20 3.00
328-Origin & 1st app. D-Man 1.20 3.00
332-Old Cap resigns 1.70 5.00 12.00
333-Intro & origin new Captain (Super Patriot) 1.65 4.00 10.00
334 1.00 2.50 5.50
335-340: 339-Fall of the Mutants tie-in 1.00 2.00 5.00
341-343,345-349 .70 1.70
344-($1.50, 52 pgs.) .90 2.20
350-($1.75, 68 pgs.)-Return of Steve Rogers (original Cap) to original costume 1.80 4.50
351-354: 351-Nick Fury app. 354-1st app. U.S. Agent (6/89, see Avengers West Coast) .70 1.70
355-382,384-396: 373-Bullseye app. 375-Daredevil app. 386-U.S. Agent app. 387-389-Red Skull back-up stories. 396-Last $1.00-c. 396,397-1st app. all new Jack O'Lantern 1.50
383-($2.00, 68 pgs.)-50th anniversary issue; Red Skull story; Jim Lee-c(i) 1.00 2.00 5.00
397-399,401-424: 402-Begin 6 part Man-Wolf story w/Wolverine in #403-407. 405-410-New Jack O'Lantern app. 406-Cable & Shatterstar cameo. 407-Capwolf vs. Cable-c/story. 408-Infinity War x-over; Falcon solo back-up 1.25
400-($2.25, 84 pgs.)-Flip book format w/double gatefold-c; r/Avengers #4 plus-c; contains cover pin-ups 1.40 3.50
425-($2.95, 52 pgs.)-Embossed Foil-c Edition 1.20 3.00
425-($1.75, 52 pgs.)-Regular Edition .70 1.75
Special 1(1/71)-Origin retold 2.15 6.50 15.00
Special 2(1/72)-Colan-r/Not Brand Echh; all-r 1.70 5.00 12.00
Annual 3-7: 3(1976). 4(1977, 52pgs.)-Kirby-c/a(new); Magneto app. 5('81, 52pgs.). 6('82, 52pgs.). 7('83, 52pgs.) 1.00 2.50
Annual 8(9/86)-Wolverine-c/story 6.50 19.00 45.00
Annual 9(1990, $2.00, 68 pgs.)-Nomad back-up 1.00 2.00 5.00
Annual 10('91, $2.00, 68 pgs.)-Origin retold(2 pgs.) .80 2.00
Annual 11(1992, $2.25, 68 pgs.)-Falcon solo story .90 2.25
Annual 12(1993, $2.95, 68 pgs.)-Bagged w/card 1.20 3.00
....The Movie Special nn (5/92, $3.50, 52 pgs.)-Adapts movie; printed on coated stock; The Red Skull app. 1.20 3.00
...& The Campbell Kids (1980, 36pg. giveaway, Campbell's Soup/U.S. Dept. of Energy) .80 2.00
...Fights in the War Against Drugs (1990, no #, giveaway) Distributed to direct sales shops; 2nd printing exists 1.00
...Meets the Asthma Monster (1987, no #, giveaway, Your Physician and Glaxo, Inc.) 1.00
...Vs. Asthma Monster (1990, no #, giveaway, Your Physician & Allen & Hanbury's) 1.00

NOTE: **Austin** *c-225i, 239i, 246i.* **Buscema** *a-115p, 217p; c-136p, 217.* **Byrne** *c-223(part), 238, 239, 247p-254p, 290, 291, 313p; a-247-254p, 255, 313p, 350.* **Colan** *a(p)-116-137, 256, Annual 5; c(p)-116-123, 126, 129.* **Everett** *a-136i, 137i; c-126i.* **Gil Kane** *a-145p; c-147p, 149p, 150p, 170p, 172-174, 180, 181p, 183-190p, 215, 216, 220, 221.* **Kirby** *a(p)-100-109, 112, 193-214, 216, Special 1, 2(layouts), Annual 3, 4; c-100-109, 112, 126p, 193-214.* **Ron Lim** *a(p)-366, 368-378, 380-386; c-366p, 368-378p, 379, 380-393p.* **Miller** *c-241p, 244p, 245p, 255p, Annual 5.* **Mooney** *a-149i.* **Morrow** *a-144.* **Perez** *c-243p, 246p.* **Robbins** *c(p)-183-187, 189-192, 225.* **Roussos** *a-140i, 168i.* **Starlin/Sinnott** *c-162.* **Sutton** *a-244i.* **Tuska** *a-112i, 215p, Special 2.* **Williamson** *a-313i.* **Wood** *a-127i.*

CAPTAIN AMERICA COMICS
Mar, 1941 - No. 75, Jan, 1950; No. 76, 5/54 - No. 78, 9/54
(No. 74 & 75 titled Capt. America's Weird Tales)
Timely/Marvel Comics (TCI 1-20/CmPS 21-68/MjMC 69-75/Atlas Comics (PrPI 76-78)

GD25 FN65 VF82 NM94

1 Origin & 1st app. Captain America & Bucky by S&K; Hurricane, Tuk the Caveboy begin by S&K; 1st app. Red Skull; Hitler-c 3,600.00 10,800.00 23,700.00 36,000.00
(Estimated up to 180 total copies exist, 8 in NM/Mint)

GD25 FN65 NM94

2-S&K Hurricane; Tuk by Avison (Kirby splash); classic Hitler-c 750.00 2250.00 5000.00
3-Red Skull-c & app; Stan Lee's 1st text (1st work for Marvel) 500.00 1500.00 3600.00
4-1st full page panel in comics 350.00 1050.00 2400.00
5 317.00 950.00 2200.00
6-Origin Father Time; Tuk the Caveboy ends 257.00 770.00 1800.00
7-Red Skull app.; classic-c 285.00 857.00 2000.00
8-10-Last S&K issue, (S&K centerfold #6-10) 217.00 650.00 1500.00
11-Last Hurricane, Headline Hunter; Al Avison Captain America begins, ends #20; Avison-c(p) 179.00 535.00 1250.00
12-The Imp begins, ends #16; last Father Time 171.00 515.00 1200.00
13-Origin The Secret Stamp; classic-c 183.00 550.00 1300.00
14,15 171.00 515.00 1200.00
16-Red Skull unmasks Cap 193.00 580.00 1350.00
17-The Fighting Fool only app. 145.00 435.00 1000.00
18,19-Human Torch begins #19 125.00 375.00 825.00
20-Sub-Mariner app.; no H. Torch 125.00 375.00 825.00
21-25: 25-Cap drinks liquid opium 117.00 350.00 800.00
26-30,36: 27-Last Secret Stamp; last 68 pg. issue. 28-60 pg. issues begin. 36-Hitler-c 110.00 325.00 750.00
31-35,38-40: 34-Centerfold poster of Cap 92.00 275.00 625.00
37-Red Skull app. 100.00 300.00 650.00
41-47: 41-Last Jap War-c. 46-German Holocaust-c. 47-Last German War-c 80.00 235.00 525.00
48-58,60 75.00 225.00 500.00
59-Origin retold 150.00 450.00 1000.00
61-Red Skull-c/story 125.00 375.00 825.00
62,64,65: 65-"Hey Look" by Kurtzman 80.00 235.00 525.00
63-Intro/origin Asbestos Lady 83.00 250.00 550.00
66-Bucky is shot; Golden Girl teams up with Captain America & learns his i.d; origin Golden Girl 92.00 275.00 625.00
67-Captain America/Golden Girl team-up; Mxyztplk swipe; last Toro in Human Torch 75.00 225.00 525.00
68,70-Sub-Mariner/Namora, and Captain America/Golden Girl team-up in each. 70-Science fiction-c/story 75.00 225.00 525.00
69,71-73: 69-Human Torch/Sun Girl team-up. 71-Anti Wertham editorial; The Witness, Bucky app. 75.00 225.00 525.00
74-(Scarce)(1949)-Titled "C.A.'s Weird Tales;" Red Skull app. 135.00 407.00 950.00
75(2/50)-Titled "C.A.'s Weird Tales;" no C.A. app.; horror cover/stories 75.00 225.00 525.00
76-78(1954). Human Torch/Toro stories 50.00 150.00 350.00
132-Pg. Issue (B&W-1942)(Canadian)-Has blank inside-c and back-c; contains Marvel Mystery #33 & Capt. America #18 w/cover from Capt. America #22; same contents as Marvel Mystery annual 467.00 1400.00 3200.00
Shoestore Giveaway #77 29.00 85.00 200.00

Captain America Comics #63, © MEG

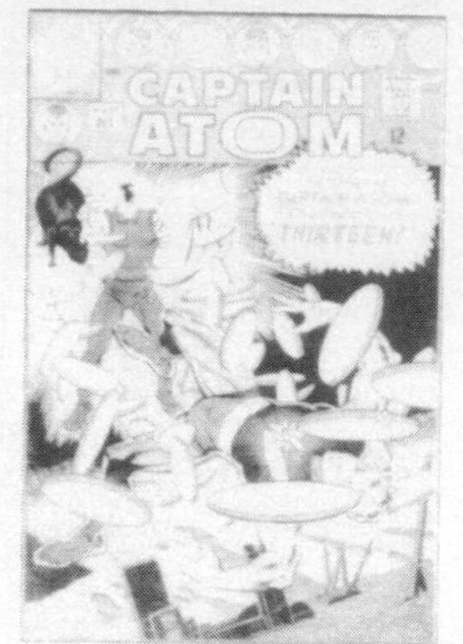

Captain Atom #89 (Charlton), © DC

Captain Canuck #2, © Richard D. Comely

GD25 FN65 NM94

NOTE: *Crandall a-2i, 3i, 9i, 10i.* ***Kirby*** *c-8p.* ***Rico*** *c-69-71.* ***Romita*** *c-77, 78.* ***Schomburg*** *c-3, 4, 26-29, 31, 33, 37-39, 41, 42, 45-54, 58.* ***Sekowsky*** *c-55, 56.* ***Shores*** *c-1, 2, 5-7, 11i, 20-25, 30, 32, 34, 35, 40, 57, 59-67.* ***S&K*** *c-1, 2, 5-7, 9, 10. Bondage c-3, 7, 15, 16, 34, 38.*

CAPTAIN AMERICA SPECIAL EDITION
Feb, 1984 - No. 2, Mar, 1984 ($2.00, Baxter paper)
Marvel Comics Group

1,2-Steranko-c/a(r) .80 2.00

CAPTAIN AND THE KIDS, THE (See Famous Comics Cartoon Books)

CAPTAIN AND THE KIDS, THE (See Comics on Parade, Okay Comics & Sparkler Comics)
1938 -12/39; Sum, 1947 - No. 32, 1955; 4-Color No. 881, Feb, 1958
United Features Syndicate/Dell Publ. Co.

	GD25	FN65	NM94
Single Series 1('38)	59.00	180.00	415.00
Single Series 1(Reprint)(12/39-"Reprint" on-c)	36.00	110.00	250.00
1(Summer, 1947-UFS)	10.00	30.00	60.00
2	5.35	16.00	32.00
3-10	4.00	12.00	24.00
11-20	3.60	9.00	18.00
21-32(1955)	2.80	7.00	14.00
50th Anniversary issue('48)-Contains a 2 page history of the strip, including an account of the famous Supreme Court decision allowing both Pulitzer & Hearst to run the same strip under different names	5.85	17.50	35.00
Special Summer issue, Fall issue (1948)	4.20	12.50	25.00
4-Color 881 (Dell)	3.60	9.00	18.00

CAPTAIN ATOM
1950 - No. 7, 1951 (5x7-1/4") (5 cents, 52 pgs.)
Nationwide Publishers

	GD25	FN65	NM94
1-Sci/fic	19.00	57.00	130.00
2-7	10.00	30.00	65.00
...- Secret of the Columbian Jungle (16 pgs. in color, paper-c, 3-3/4x5-1/8")-Fireside Marshmallow giveaway	3.60	9.00	18.00

CAPTAIN ATOM (Formerly Strange Suspense Stories No. 77)
V2#78, Dec, 1965 - V2#89, Dec, 1967 (Also see Space Adventures)
Charlton Comics

	GD25	FN65	NM94
78-Origin retold; Bache-a (3 pgs.)	8.00	24.00	55.00
79-82: 79-1st app. Dr. Spectro. 82-Intro. Nightshade (9/66)	5.00	15.00	35.00
83-86: Ted Kord Blue Beetle in all. 83-(11/66)-1st app. Ted Kord. 84-1st app. new Captain Atom	4.30	13.00	30.00
87-89-Nightshade by Aparo in all	4.30	13.00	30.00
83-85(Modern Comics-1977)-reprints			1.00

NOTE: ***Aparo*** *a-87-89.* ***Ditko*** *c/a(p) 78-89. #90 only published in fanzine `The Charlton Bullseye' #1, 2.*

CAPTAIN ATOM (Also see Americomics & Crisis On Infinite Earths)
March, 1987 - No. 57, Sept, 1991 (Direct sale only #35 on)
DC Comics

	GD25	FN65	NM94
1-(44 pgs.)-Origin/1st app. with new costume		.80	2.00
2-49: 5-Firestorm x-over. 6-Intro. new Dr. Spectro. 11-Millennium tie-in. 14-Nightshade app. 16-Justice League app. 17-$1.00-c begins; Swamp Thing app. 20-Blue Beetle x-over			1.20
50-($2.00, 52 pgs.)		.80	2.00
51-57: 57-War of the Gods x-over			1.00
Annual 1 (1988, $1.25)-Intro Major Force			1.50
Annual 2 (1988, $1.50)			1.50

CAPTAIN BATTLE (Boy Comics #3 on) (See Silver Streak Comics)
Summer, 1941 - No. 2, Fall, 1941
New Friday Publ./Comic House

	GD25	FN65	NM94
1-Origin Blackout by Rico; Captain Battle begins (1st appeared in Silver Streak #10, 5/41)	75.00	225.00	500.00
2	50.00	150.00	350.00

GD25 FN65 NM94

CAPTAIN BATTLE (2nd Series)
No. 3, Wint, 1942-43 - No. 5, Sum, 1943 (#3: 52pgs., nd)(#5: 68pgs.)
Magazine Press/Picture Scoop No. 5

	GD25	FN65	NM94
3-Origin Silver Streak-r/SS#3; Origin Lance Hale-r/Silver Streak; Simon-a(r)	46.00	135.00	300.00
4,5: 5-Origin Blackout retold	33.00	100.00	225.00

CAPTAIN BATTLE, JR.
Fall, 1943 - No. 2, Winter, 1943-44
Comic House (Lev Gleason)

	GD25	FN65	NM94
1-The Claw vs. The Ghost	63.00	185.00	425.00
2-Wolverton's Scoop Scuttle; Don Rico-c/a; The Green Claw story is reprinted from Silver Streak #6	50.00	150.00	350.00

CAPTAIN BRITAIN (Also see Marvel Team-Up No. 65, 66)
Oct. 13, 1976 - No. 39, July 6, 1977 (Weekly)
Marvel Comics International

	GD25	FN65	NM94
1-Origin; with Capt. Britain's face mask inside	1.00	2.00	5.00
2-Origin, conclusion; Capt. Britain's Boomerang inside		1.45	3.60
3-8: 3,8-Vs. Bank Robbers. 4-7-Vs. Hurricane		.80	2.00
9-15: 9-13-Vs. Dr. Synne. 14,15-Vs. Mastermind		.70	1.80
16-20-With Capt. America; 17 misprinted & color section reprinted in #18		.70	1.80
21-23,25,26-With Capt. America		.70	1.80
24-With C.B.'s Jet Plane inside		1.45	3.60
27,33-35: 27-Origin retold. 33-35-More on origin		.70	1.80
28-32,36-39: 28-32-Vs. Lord Hawk. 36-Star Sceptre. 37-39-Vs. Highwayman & Munipulator			1.50
Annual (1978, Hardback, 64 pgs.)-Reprints #1-7 with pin-ups of Marvel characters	1.30	3.25	8.00
Summer Special (1980, 52 pgs.)-Reprints		.80	2.00

NOTE: *No. 1, 2, & 24 are rarer in mint due to inserts. Distributed in Great Britain only. Nick Fury-r by* ***Steranko*** *in 1-20, 24-31, 35-37. Fantastic Four-r by* ***J. Buscema*** *in all. New* ***Buscema****-a in 24-30. Story from No. 39 continues in Super Spider-Man (British weekly) No. 231-247. Following cancellation of his series, new Captain Britain stories appeared in ``Super Spider-Man" (British weekly) No. 231-247. Captain Britain stories which appear in Super-Spider-Man No 248-253 are reprints of Marvel Team-Up No. 65&66. Capt. Britain strips also appeared in Hulk Comic (weekly) 1, 3-30, 42-55, 57-60, in Marvel Superheroes (monthly) 377-388, in Daredevils (monthly) 1-11, Mighty World of Marvel (monthly) 7-16 & Captain Britain (monthly) 1-present.*

CAPTAIN CANUCK
7/75 - No. 4, 7/77; No. 4, 7-8/79 - No. 14, 3-4/81
Comely Comix (Canada) (All distr. in U. S.)

	GD25	FN65	NM94
1-1st app. Bluefox		1.00	2.50
2-1st app. Dr. Walker, Redcoat & Kebec		.70	1.80
3(5-7/76)-1st app. Heather		.70	1.80
4(1st printing-2/77)-10x14-1/2"; (5.00); B&W; 300 copies serially numbered and signed with one certificate of authenticity	2.15	6.50	15.00
4(2nd printing-7/77)-11x17", B&W; only 15 copies printed; signed by creator Richard Comely, serially #'d and two certificates of authenticity inserted; orange cardboard covers (Very Rare)	4.30	13.00	30.00
4-14: 4(7-8/79)-1st app. Tom Evans & Mr. Gold; origin The Catman. 5-Origin Capt. Canuck's powers; 1st app. Earth Patrol & Chaos Corps. 8-Jonn `The Final Chapter'. 9-1st World Beyond. 11-1st 'Chariots of Fire' story			1.00
Summer Special 1(7-9/80, 95 cents, 64pgs.)			1.00

NOTE: *30,000 copies of No. 2 were destroyed in Winnipeg.*

CAPTAIN CARROT AND HIS AMAZING ZOO CREW
March, 1982 - No. 20, Nov, 1983 (Also see New Teen Titans)
DC Comics

	GD25	FN65	NM94
1-20: 1-Superman app. 3-Re-intro Dodo & The Frog. 9-Re-intro Three Mouseketeers, the Terrific Whatzit. 10,11- Pig Iron reverts back to Peter Porkchops. 20-The Changeling app.			1.00

CAPTAIN CARVEL AND HIS CARVEL CRUSADERS (See Carvel Comics)

CAPTAIN CONFEDERACY
Nov, 1991 - No. 4, Feb, 1992 ($1.95, color)
Epic Comics (Marvel)

Captain Easy #10, © NEA Services

Captain Jet #1, © AJAX

Captain Marvel #1, MEG

GD25 FN65 NM94

1-4: All new stories .80 2.00

CAPTAIN COURAGEOUS COMICS (Banner No. 3-5; see Four Favorites #5)
No. 6, March, 1942
Periodical House (Ace Magazines)

6-Origin & 1st app. The Sword; Lone Warrior, Capt. Courageous app.; Capt. moves to Four Favorites #5 in May 54.00 162.00 350.00

CAPT'N CRUNCH COMICS (See Cap'n...)

CAPTAIN DAVY JONES (See 4-Color No. 598)

CAPTAIN EASY (See The Funnies & Red Ryder #3-32)
1939 - No. 17, Sept, 1949; April, 1956
Hawley/Dell Publ./Standard(Visual Editions)/Argo

nn-Hawley(1939)-Contains reprints from The Funnies & 1938 Sunday strips by Roy Crane 50.00 150.00 350.00
4-Color 24 (1943) 32.00 95.00 225.00
4-Color 111(6/46)-Spanking panels 11.50 34.00 80.00
10(Standard-10/47) 7.50 22.50 45.00
11-17: All contain 1930s & '40s strip-r 5.00 15.00 30.00
Argo 1(4/56)-Reprints 5.00 15.00 30.00
NOTE: *Schomburg c-13, 16.*

CAPTAIN EASY & WASH TUBBS (See Famous Comics Cartoon Books)

CAPTAIN ELECTRON (Brick Computer)(Value: cover or less)

CAPTAIN EO 3-D (Eclipse)(Value: cover or less) (Disney)

CAPTAIN FEARLESS COMICS (Also see Holyoke One-Shot #6, Old Glory Comics & Silver Streak #1)
August, 1941 - No. 2, Sept, 1941
Helnit Publishing Co. (Holyoke Publishing Co.)

1-Origin Mr. Miracle, Alias X, Captain Fearless, Citizen Smith Son of the Unknown Soldier; Miss Victory (1st app.) begins (1st patriotic heroine? before Wonder Woman) 50.00 150.00 340.00
2-Grit Grady, Captain Stone app. 30.00 90.00 200.00

CAPTAIN FLAG (See Blue Ribbon Comics #16)

CAPTAIN FLASH
Nov, 1954 - No. 4, July, 1955
Sterling Comics

1-Origin; Sekowsky-a; Tomboy (female super hero) begins; only pre-code issue 19.00 58.00 135.00
2-4: 4-Flying saucer invasion-c 11.50 34.00 80.00

CAPTAIN FLEET
Fall, 1952
Ziff-Davis Publishing Co.

1-Painted-c 10.00 30.00 65.00

CAPTAIN FLIGHT COMICS
Mar, 1944 - No. 10, Dec, 1945; No. 11, Feb-Mar, 1947
Four Star Publications

nn 15.00 45.00 105.00
2 9.15 27.50 55.00
3,4: 4-Rock Raymond begins, ends #7 8.35 25.00 50.00
5-Bondage, torture-c; Red Rocket begins; the Grenade app. 10.00 30.00 70.00
6,7: 7-L. B. Cole covers begin, end #11 9.15 27.50 55.00
8,9: 8-Yankee Girl begins; intro. Black Cobra & Cobra Kid & begins. 9-Torpedoman app.; last Yankee Girl; Kinstler-a 13.00 40.00 90.00
10-Deep Sea Dawson, Zoom of the Jungle, Rock Raymond, Red Rocket, & Black Cobra app; bondage-c 13.00 40.00 90.00
11-Torpedoman, Blue Flame (Human Torch clone) app.; last Black Cobra, Red Rocket; L. B. Cole-c 13.00 40.00 90.00

CAPTAIN FORTUNE PRESENTS
1955 - 1959 (16 pages; 3-1/4x6-7/8") (Giveaway)
Vital Publications

"Davy Crockett in Episodes of the Creek War," "Davy Crockett at the "Alamo," "In Sherwood Forest Tells Strange Tales of Robin Hood" ('57), "Meets Bolivar the Liberator" ('59), "Tells How Buffalo Bill Fights the Dog Soldiers" ('57), "Young Davy Crockett" 1.80 4.50 9.00

CAPTAIN GALLANT (...of the Foreign Legion) (TV)
(Texas Rangers in Action No. 5 on?)
1955: No. 2, Jan, 1956 - No. 4, Sept, 1956
Charlton Comics

Heinz Foods Premium (#1?)(1955; regular size)-U.S. Pictorial; contains Buster Crabbe photos; Don Heck-a 1.80 4.50 9.00
Non-Heinz version (same as above except pictures of show replaces ads) (#1)-Buster Crabbe photo on-c 8.35 25.00 50.00
2-4: Buster Crabbe in all 6.70 20.00 40.00

CAPTAIN GLORY
April, 1993 ($2.95, color)
Topps Comics

1-Polybagged w/Kirbychrome trading card; Ditko-a & Kirby-c (created by Jack Kirby) 1.20 3.00

CAPTAIN HERO (See Jughead as...)

CAPTAIN HERO COMICS DIGEST MAGAZINE
Sept, 1981
Archie Publications

1-Reprints of Jughead as Super-Guy 1.00

CAPTAIN HOBBY COMICS
Feb, 1948 (Canadian)
Export Publication Ent. Ltd. (Dist. in U.S. by Kable News Co.)

1 4.70 14.00 28.00

CAPT. HOLO IN 3-D (See Blackthorne 3-D Series #65)

CAPTAIN HOOK & PETER PAN (See 4-Color No. 446 and Peter Pan)

CAPTAIN JET (Fantastic Fears No. 7 on)
May, 1952 - No. 5, Jan, 1953
Four Star Publ./Farrell/Comic Media

1-Bakerish-a 10.00 30.00 70.00
2 8.35 25.00 50.00
3-5,6(?) 5.00 15.00 30.00

CAPTAIN JUSTICE
March, 1988 - No. 2, April, 1988
Marvel Comics

1,2-Based on TV series, True Colors 1.25

CAPTAIN KANGAROO (See 4-Color No. 721, 780, 872)

CAPTAIN KIDD (Formerly Dagar; My Secret Story #26 on)(Also see Comic Comics & Fantastic Comics)
No. 24, June, 1949 - No. 25, Aug, 1949
Fox Feature Syndicate

24,25 10.00 30.00 65.00

CAPTAIN MARVEL (See All Hero, All-New Collectors' Ed., America's Greatest, Fawcett Min., Gift, Legends, Limited Collectors' Ed., Marvel Family, Master No. 21, Mighty Midget Comics, Shazam, Special Edition Comics, Whiz, Wisco, and XMas Comics)

CAPTAIN MARVEL (Becomes ...Presents the Terrible 5 No. 5)
April, 1966 - No. 4, Nov, 1966 (25 cent Giants)
M. F. Enterprises

nn-(#1 on pg. 5)-Origin; created by Carl Burgos 2.15 6.50 15.00
2-4: 3-(#3 on page 4)-Fights the Bat 1.30 3.25 8.00

CAPTAIN MARVEL (Marvel's Space-Born Super-Hero! Captain Marvel #1-6; see Giant-Size..., Life Of..., Marvel Graphic Novel #1, Marvel Spotlight V2#1 & Marvel Super-Heroes #12)
May, 1968 - No. 19, Dec, 1969; No. 20, June, 1970 - No. 21, Aug, 1970; No. 22, Sept, 1972 - No. 62, May, 1979
Marvel Comics Group

1 11.00 34.00 90.00

Captain Marvel #34, MEG

Captain Marvel Adventures #42, FAW

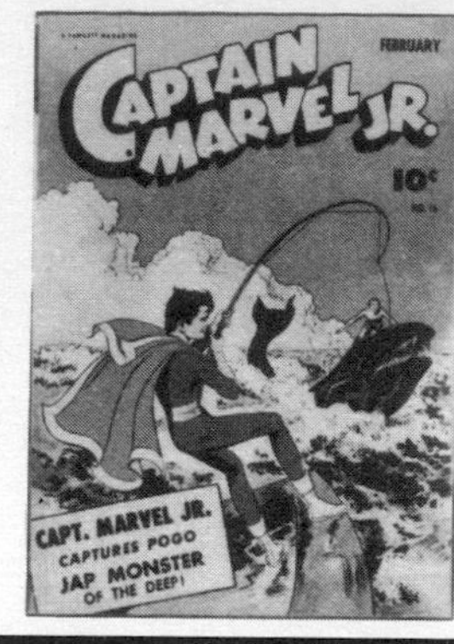

Captain Marvel, Jr. #16, FAW

GD25 FN65 NM94

2 4.00 11.00 28.00
3-5: 4-Captain Marvel battles Sub-Mariner 2.00 7.00 18.00
6-11: 11-Capt. Marvel given great power by Zo the Ruler; Smith/Trimpe-c; Death of Una 2.00 5.00 12.00
12-24: 14-Capt. Marvel vs. Iron Man; last 12 cent issue. 16,17-New costume. 21-Capt. Marvel battles Hulk; last 15¢ issue 1.00 3.00 9.00
25-Starlin-c/a begins; Starlin's 1st Thanos saga begins (3/73), ends #34; Thanos cameo (5 panels) 4.00 11.00 28.00
26-2nd full app. Thanos (see Iron Man #55); 1st Thanos-c 4.00 13.00 35.00
27,28-3rd & 4th app. Thanos. 28-Thanos-c 3.00 9.00 25.00
29,30-Thanos cameos. 29-C.M. gains more powers 1.00 4.00 10.00
31,32: Thanos app. 31-Last 20 cent issue. 32-Thanos-c 2.00 6.00 15.00
33-Thanos-c & app.; Capt. Marvel battles Thanos; 1st origin Thanos 4.00 11.00 30.00
34-1st app. Nitro; C.M. contracts cancer which eventually kills him; last Starlin-c/a & last 20 cent issue 1.00 3.00 7.00
35,37-56,58-62: 39-Origin Watcher. 41,43-Wrightson part inks; #43-c(i). 49-Starlin & Weiss-p assists 1.50
36-Reprints origin/1st app. Capt. Marvel from Marvel Super-Heroes #12; Starlin-a (3 pgs.) 1.00 2.00 5.00
57-Thanos appears in flashback 1.00 3.00 7.00

NOTE: *Alcala a-35. Austin a-46i, 49-53i; c-52i. Buscema a-18p-21p. Colan a(p)-1-4; c(p)-1-4, 8, 9. Heck a-5p-10p, 16p. Gil Kane a-17-21p; c-17-24p, 37p, 53. McWilliams a-40i. #25-34 were reprinted in The Life of Captain Marvel.*

CAPTAIN MARVEL
Nov, 1989 ($1.50, color, one-shot, 52 pgs.)
Marvel Comics

1-Super-hero from Avengers; new powers 1.50

CAPTAIN MARVEL ADVENTURES (See Special Edition Comics for pre #1)
1941 (March) - No. 150, Nov, 1953 (#1 on stands 1/16/41)
Fawcett Publications

GD25 FN65 VF82 NM94

nn(#1)-Captain Marvel & Sivana by Jack Kirby. The cover was printed on unstable paper stock and is rarely found in Fine or Mint condition; blank blank inside-c 1700.00 5100.00 11,050.00 17,000.00
(Estimated up to 140 total copies exist, 3 in NM/Mint)

GD25 FN65 NM94

2-(Advertised as #3, which was counting Special Edition Comics as the real #1); Tuska-a 267.00 800.00 2000.00
3-Metallic silver-c 167.00 500.00 1200.00
4-Three Lt. Marvels app. 117.00 350.00 750.00
5 92.00 275.00 600.00
6-10: 9-1st Otto Binder scripts on Capt. Marvel 67.00 200.00 450.00
11-15: 13-Two-pg. Capt. Marvel pin-up. 15-Comic cards on back-c begin, end #26 54.00 162.00 350.00
16,17: 17-Painted-c 50.00 150.00 330.00
18-Origin & 1st app. Mary Marvel & Marvel Family (12/11/42); painted-c; Mary Marvel by Marcus Swayze 83.00 250.00 550.00
19-Mary Marvel x-over; Christmas-c 46.00 138.00 315.00
20,21-Attached to the cover, each has a miniature comic just like the Mighty Midget Comics #11, except that each has a full color promo ad on the back cover. Most copies were circulated without the miniature comic. These issues with miniatures attached are very rare, and should not be mistaken for copies with the similar Mighty Midget glued in its place. The Mighty Midgets had blank back covers except for a small victory stamp seal. Only the Capt. Marvel and Captain Marvel Jr. No. 11 miniatures have been positively documented as having been affixed tothese covers. Each miniature was only partially glued by its back cover to the Captain Marvel comic making it easy to see if it's the genuine miniature rather than a Mighty Midget.
with comic attached.... 257.00 770.00 1800.00
20,21-Without miniature 42.00 125.00 275.00
22-Mr. Mind serial begins; 1st app. Mr. Mind 62.00 188.00 400.00
23-25 42.00 125.00 275.00
26-30: 26-Flag-c 33.00 100.00 220.00
31-35: 35-Origin Radar 29.00 88.00 200.00
36-40: 37-Mary Marvel x-over 25.00 75.00 165.00
41-46: 42-Christmas-c. 43-Capt. Marvel 1st meets Uncle Marvel (1st app.); Mary Batson cameo. 46-Mr. Mind serial ends 22.00 65.00 145.00
47-50 18.00 55.00 125.00
51-53,55-60: 51-63-Bi-weekly issues. 52-Origin & 1st app. Sivana Jr.; Capt. Marvel Jr. x-over 15.00 45.00 105.00
54-Special oversize 68 pg. issue 17.00 50.00 115.00
61-The Cult of the Curse serial begins 20.00 60.00 135.00
62-66-Serial ends; Mary Marvel x-over in #65. 66-Atomic War-c 15.00 45.00 105.00
67-77,79: 69-Billy Batson's Christmas; Uncle Marvel, Mary Marvel, Capt. Marvel Jr. x-over. 71-Three Lt. Marvels app. 79-Origin Mr. Tawny 14.00 43.00 100.00
78-Origin Mr. Atom 17.00 50.00 115.00
80-Origin Capt. Marvel retold 29.00 88.00 200.00
81-84,86-90: 81,90-Mr. Atom app. 82-Infinity-c. 86-Mr. Tawny app. 13.00 40.00 90.00
85-Freedom Train issue 17.00 50.00 115.00
91-99: 96-Mr. Tawny app. 12.00 36.00 85.00
100-Origin retold 25.00 75.00 175.00
101-115,117-120 12.00 35.00 80.00
116-Flying Saucer issue (1/51) 13.00 40.00 90.00
121-Origin retold 17.00 50.00 115.00
122-137,139-149: 141-Pre-code horror story "The Hideous Head-Hunter." 142-used in **POP**, pgs. 92,96 12.00 35.00 80.00
138-Flying Saucer issue (11/52) 12.00 36.00 85.00
150-(Low distribution) 17.00 50.00 115.00
Bond Bread Giveaways-(24 pgs.; pocket size-7-1/4x3-1/2"; paper cover): "...& the Stolen City" ('48), "The Boy Who Never Heard of Capt. Marvel," "Meets the Weatherman"-(1950)(reprint) each.... 23.00 68.00 150.00
...Well Known Comics (1944; 12 pgs.; 8-1/2x10-1/2")-printed in red & in blue; soft-c; glued binding)-Bestmaid/Samuel Lowe Co. giveaway 16.00 48.00 100.00

NOTE: *Swayze a-12, 14, 15, 18, 19, 40; c-12, 15, 19.*

CAPTAIN MARVEL ADVENTURES
1945 (6x8") (Full color, paper cover)
Fawcett Publications (Wheaties Giveaway)

GD25 FN65 -

nn-"Captain Marvel & the Threads of Life" plus 2 other stories (32 pgs.) 65.00 260.00 -

NOTE: *All copies were taped at each corner to a box of Wheaties and are never found in Fine or Mint condition.*

CAPTAIN MARVEL AND THE GOOD HUMOR MAN (Movie)
1950
Fawcett Publications

GD25 FN65 NM94

nn-Partial photo-c w/Jack Carson & the Captain Marvel Club Boys 30.00 90.00 210.00

CAPTAIN MARVEL AND THE LTS. OF SAFETY
1950 - 1951 (3 issues - no No.'s)
Ebasco Services/Fawcett Publications

"Danger Flies a Kite" ('50), "Danger Takes to Climbing" ('50), "Danger Smashes Street Lights" ('51) 17.00 51.00 120.00

CAPTAIN MARVEL COMIC STORY PAINT BOOK (See Comic Story....)

CAPTAIN MARVEL, JR. (See Fawcett Miniatures, Marvel Family, Master Comics, Mighty Midget Comics, Shazam & Whiz Comics)

CAPTAIN MARVEL, JR.
Nov, 1942 - No. 119, June, 1953 (No #34)
Fawcett Publications

1-Origin Capt. Marvel Jr. retold (Whiz No. 25); Capt. Nazi app. 221.00 665.00 1550.00
2-Vs. Capt. Nazi; origin Capt. Nippon 100.00 300.00 700.00
3,4 63.00 186.00 450.00
5-Vs. Capt. Nazi 58.00 175.00 405.00
6-10: 8-Vs. Capt. Nazi. 9-Flag-c. 10-Hitler-c 47.00 140.00 325.00
11,12,15-Capt. Nazi app. 38.00 115.00 265.00
13,14,16-20: 13-Hitler-c. 14-X-Mas-c. 16-Capt. Marvel & Sivana x-over.

Captain Midnight #29, © The Wander Co.

Captain Planet #1, © TBS Productions

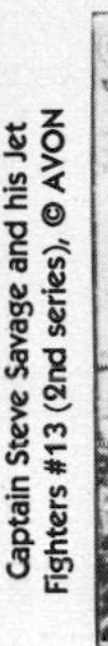
Captain Steve Savage and his Jet Fighters #13 (2nd series), © AVON

GD25 FN65 NM94

19-Capt. Nazi & Capt. Nippon app. 32.00 95.00 225.00
21-30: 25-Flag-c 22.00 65.00 150.00
31-33,36-40: 37-Infinity-c 15.00 45.00 105.00
35-#34 on inside; cover shows origin of Sivana Jr. which is not on inside. Evidently the cover to #35 was printed out of sequence and bound with contents to #34 15.00 45.00 105.00
41-70: 53-Atomic Bomb-c/story 11.00 32.00 75.00
71-99,101-104: 104-Used in **POP**, pg. 89 10.00 30.00 60.00
100 10.00 30.00 65.00
105-114,116-119: 116-Vampira, Queen of Terror app. 119-Electric chair-c 10.00 30.00 60.00
115-Injury to eye-c; Eyeball story w/injury-to-eye panels 11.00 32.00 75.00
...Well Known Comics (1944; 12 pgs.; 8-1/2x10-1/2")(Printed in blue; paper-c, glued binding)-Bestmaid/Samuel Lowe Co. giveaway 13.00 40.00 80.00

NOTE: ***Mac Raboy*** *c-1-10, 12-14, 16, 19, 21, 22, 25, 27, 28, 30-33, 57 among others.*

CAPTAIN MARVEL PRESENTS THE TERRIBLE FIVE
Aug, 1966; V2#5, Sept, 1967 (No #2-4) (25 cents)
M. F. Enterprises

1 2.00 6.00 14.00
V2#5-(Formerly Captain Marvel) 1.30 3.25 8.00

CAPTAIN MARVEL'S FUN BOOK
1944 (1/2" thick) (cardboard covers)
Samuel Lowe Co.

nn-Puzzles, games, magic, etc.; infinity-c 23.00 70.00 160.00

CAPTAIN MARVEL SPECIAL EDITION (See Special Edition)

CAPTAIN MARVEL STORY BOOK
Summer, 1946 - No. 4, Summer?, 1948
Fawcett Publications

1-Half text 42.00 125.00 300.00
2-4 29.00 86.00 195.00

CAPTAIN MARVEL THRILL BOOK (Large-Size)
1941 (Black & White; color cover)
Fawcett Publications

GD25 FN65 VF82

1-Reprints from Whiz #8,10, & Special Edition #1 (Rare) 200.00 600.00 1400.00

NOTE: *Rarely found in Fine or Mint condition.*

CAPTAIN MIDNIGHT (Radio, films, TV) (See The Funnies & Popular Comics) (Becomes Sweethearts No. 68 on)
Sept, 1942 - No. 67, Fall, 1948 (#1-14: 68 pgs.)
Fawcett Publications

GD25 FN65 NM94

1-Origin Captain Midnight; Captain Marvel cameo on cover 157.00 470.00 1100.00
2 79.00 235.00 550.00
3-5 54.00 160.00 375.00
6-10: 9-Raboy-c. 10-Raboy Flag-c 39.00 118.00 275.00
11-20: 11,17,18-Raboy-c 29.00 85.00 200.00
21-30 22.00 65.00 150.00
31-40 16.00 48.00 110.00
41-59,61-67: 54-Sci/fi theme begins? 13.00 40.00 90.00
60-Flying Saucer issue (2/48)-3rd of this theme; see Shadow Comics V7#10 & Boy Commandos #26 17.00 52.00 120.00

CAPTAIN NICE (TV)
Nov, 1967 (One Shot)
Gold Key

1(10211-711)-Photo-c 4.70 14.00 33.00

CAPTAIN N: THE GAME MASTER (TV)
1990 - No. 6? ($1.95, color, thick stock, coated-c)
Valiant Comics

1-6: 4-6-Layton-c .80 2.00

GD25 FN65 NM94

CAPTAIN PARAGON (Americomics)(Value: cover or less)

CAPTAIN PARAGON AND THE SENTINELS OF JUSTICE (AC)(Value: cover or less)

CAPTAIN PLANET AND THE PLANETEERS (TV)
Oct, 1991 - No. 12, Oct, 1992 ($1.00/$1.25, color, based on cartoon series)
Marvel Comics

1-12: 1-N. Adams painted-c. 3-Romita-c 1.25

CAPTAIN POWER AND THE SOLDIERS OF THE FUTURE (TV)(Continuity) (Value: cover or less)

CAPTAIN PUREHEART (See Archie as...)

CAPTAIN ROCKET
November, 1951
P. L. Publ. (Canada)

1 24.00 70.00 165.00

CAPT. SAVAGE AND HIS LEATHERNECK RAIDERS (...And His Battlefield Raiders #9 on)
Jan, 1968 - No. 19, Mar, 1970 (See Sgt. Fury No. 10)
Marvel Comics Group (Animated Timely Features)

1-Sgt. Fury & Howlers cameo 1.65 4.00 10.00
2-10: 2-Origin Hydra. 1-5,7-Ayers/Shores-a 1.00 2.50 6.00
11-19 1.00 2.00 5.00

CAPTAIN SCIENCE (Fantastic No. 8 on)
Nov, 1950 - No. 7, Dec, 1951
Youthful Magazines

1-Wood-a; origin 54.00 160.00 375.00
2 26.00 77.00 180.00
3,6,7; 3,6-Bondage c-swipes/Wings #94,91 23.00 70.00 160.00
4,5-Wood/Orlando-c/a(2) each 50.00 150.00 350.00

NOTE: ***Fass*** *a-4. Bondage c-3, 6, 7.*

CAPTAIN SILVER'S LOG OF SEA HOUND (See Sea Hound)

CAPTAIN SINDBAD (Movie Adaptation) (See Fantastic Voyages of... & Movie Comics)

CAPTAIN STERNN
Sept, 1993 - Present ($4.95, color)
Kitchen Sink Press

1,2-Bernie Wrightson-c/a/scripts 1.00 2.00 5.00

CAPTAIN STEVE SAVAGE (...& His Jet Fighters, No. 2-13)
1950 - No. 8, 1/53; No. 5, 9-10/54 - No. 13, 5-6/56
Avon Periodicals

nn(1st series)-Wood art, 22 pgs. (titled "...Over Korea") 29.00 85.00 200.00
1(4/51)-Reprints nn issue (Canadian) 12.00 36.00 85.00
2-Kamen-a 8.35 25.00 50.00
3-11 (#6, 9-10/54, last precode) 4.70 14.00 28.00
12-Wood-a (6 pgs.) 9.15 27.50 55.00
13-Check, Lawrence-a 5.85 17.50 35.00

NOTE: ***Kinstler*** *c-2-5, 7-9, 11.* ***Lawrence*** *a-8.* ***Ravielli*** *a-5, 9.*

5(9-10/54-2nd series)(Formerly Sensational Police Cases) 5.00 15.00 30.00
6-Reprints nn issue; Wood-a 7.50 22.50 45.00
7-13: 13 reprints cover to #8 (1st series) 3.60 9.00 18.00

CAPTAIN STONE (See Holyoke One-Shot No. 10)

CAPT. STORM (Also see G. I. Combat #138)
May-June, 1964 - No. 18, Mar-Apr, 1967 (Grey tone c-8)
National Periodical Publications

1-Origin 2.60 7.50 18.00
2-18: 3,6,13-Kubert-a. 12-Kubert-c 1.65 4.00 10.00

CAPTAIN 3-D
December, 1953
Harvey Publications

1-Kirby/Ditko-a (Ditko's 2nd work, see Black Magic & Fantastic Fears)

Captain Victory & the Galactic Rangers #1, © Jack Kirby

Car 54 Where Are You? #2, © Eupolis Prod.

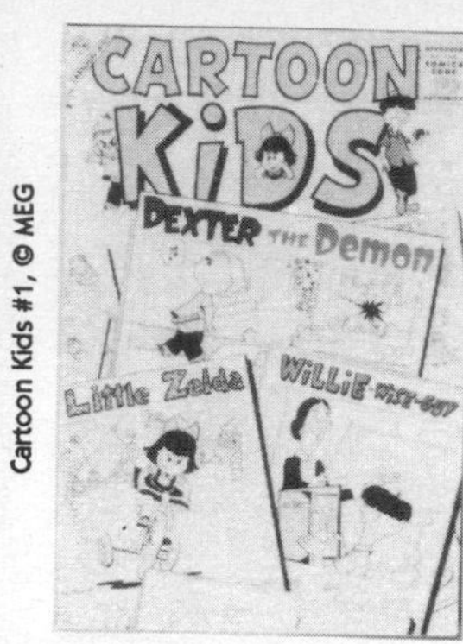

Cartoon Kids #1, © MEG

GD25 FN65 NM94

6.35 19.00 38.00

CAPTAIN THUNDER AND BLUE BOLT (Hero)(Value: cover or less)

CAPTAIN TOOTSIE & THE SECRET LEGION (Advs. of..)(Also see Monte Hale #30, 39 & Real Western Hero)
Oct, 1950 - No. 2, Dec, 1950
Toby Press
1-Not Beck-a; both have sci/fi covers 17.00 52.00 120.00
2-The Rocketeer Patrol app.; not Beck-a 11.00 32.00 75.00

CAPTAIN TRIUMPH (See Crack Comics #27)

CAPTAIN VENTURE & THE LAND BENEATH THE SEA
Oct, 1968 - No. 2, Oct, 1969 (See Space Family Robinson)
Gold Key
1,2: 1-r/Space Family Robinson serial; Spiegle-a in both
4.70 14.00 28.00

CAPTAIN VICTORY AND THE GALACTIC RANGERS (Pacific)(Value: cover or less)

CAPTAIN VIDEO (TV) (See XMas Comics)
Feb, 1951 - No. 6, Dec, 1951 (No. 1,5,6-36pgs.; 2-4, 52pgs.)
Fawcett Publications
1-George Evans-a(2) 54.00 160.00 375.00
2-Used in **SOTI**, pg. 382 41.00 125.00 290.00
3-6-All Evans-a 34.00 100.00 240.00
NOTE: *Minor* ***Williamson*** *assists on most issues. Photo c-1, 5, 6; painted c-2-4.*

CAPTAIN WILLIE SCHULTZ (Also see Fightin' Army)
No. 76, Oct, 1985 - No. 77, Jan, 1986
Charlton Comics
76,77 1.00

CAPTAIN WIZARD COMICS (Also see Meteor & Red Band Comics)
1946
Rural Home
1-Capt. Wizard dons new costume; Impossible Man, Race Wilkins app.
15.00 45.00 105.00

CARAVAN KIDD (Dark Horse)(Value: cover or less)

CARDINAL MINDSZENTY (The Truth Behind the Trial of...)
1949 (24 pages; paper cover, in color)
Catechetical Guild Education Society
nn-Anti-communism 5.85 17.50 35.00
Press Proof-(Very Rare)-(Full color, 7-1/2x11-3/4", untrimmed)
Only two known copies 150.00
Preview Copy (B&W, stapled), 18 pgs.; contains first 13 pgs. of Cardinal Mindszenty and was sent out as an advance promotion.
Only one known copy 150.00 - 200.00
NOTE: *Regular edition also printed in French. There was also a movie released in 1949 called "Guilty of Treason" which is a fact-based account of the trial and imprisonment of Cardinal Mindszenty by the Communist regime in Hungary.*

CARE BEARS (TV, Movie)(See Star Comics Magazine)
Nov, 1985 - No. 20, Jan, 1989 ($1.00 #11 on)
Star Comics/Marvel Comics No. 15 on
1-20: Post-a begins 1.00

CAREER GIRL ROMANCES (Formerly Three Nurses)
June, 1964 - No. 78, Dec, 1973
Charlton Comics
V4#24-31,33-50 .80 2.00 4.00
32-Elvis Presley, Hermans Hermits, Johnny Rivers line drawn-c
6.70 20.00 40.00
51-78 .40 1.00 2.00

CAR 54, WHERE ARE YOU? (TV)
Mar-May, 1962 - No. 7, Sept-Nov, 1963; 1964 - 1965 (All photo-c)
Dell Publishing Co.
4-Color 1257(#1, 3-5/62) 7.50 22.50 45.00

GD25 FN65 NM94

2(6-8/62)-7 3.60 10.75 25.00
2,3(10-12/64), 4(1-3/65)-Reprints #2,3,&4 of 1st series
2.60 7.50 18.00

CARL BARKS LIBRARY OF GYRO GEARLOOSE COMICS AND FILLERS IN COLOR, THE
1992 - Present ($7.95, color, 52 pgs., 8-1/2x11")
Gladstone Publishing
1-6-Carl Barks reprints 1.30 3.25 8.00

CARL BARKS LIBRARY OF WALT DISNEY'S COMICS AND STORIES IN COLOR, THE
No date (1991) - Present ($8.95, color, 60 pgs., 8-1/2x11")
Gladstone Publishing
1-22: 1-Barks Donald Duck-r/WDC&S #31-35. 2-r/#36,38-41. 3-r/#47-51. 4-r/#47-51. 5-r/#52-56. 6-r/#57-61. 7-r/#62-66. 8-r/#67-71. 9-r/#72-76. 10-r/#77-81. 11-r/#82-86. 12-r/#87-91. 13-r/#92-96. All contain one trading card each 1.50 3.75 9.00

CARL BARKS LIBRARY OF WALT DISNEY'S UNCLE SCROOGE COMICS ONE PAGERS IN COLOR
1992 - No. 2, 1992 ($8.95, color, 60 pgs., 8-1/2x11")
Gladstone Publishing
1,2-Carl Barks one page reprints 1.50 3.75 9.00

CARNATION MALTED MILK GIVEAWAYS (See Wisco)

CARNIVAL COMICS (Formerly Kayo #12; becomes Red Seal Comics #14)
1945
Harry 'A' Chesler/Pershing Square Publ. Co.
nn (#13)-Guardineer-a 10.00 30.00 65.00

CARNIVAL OF COMICS
1954 (Giveaway)
Fleet-Air Shoes
nn-Contains a comic bound with new cover; several combinations possible; Charlton's Eh! known 2.00 5.00 10.00

CAROLINE KENNEDY
1961 (One Shot)
Charlton Comics
nn 8.35 25.00 50.00

CAROUSEL COMICS
V1#8, April, 1948
F. E. Howard, Toronto
V1#8 4.20 12.50 25.00

CARTOON KIDS
1957 (no month)
Atlas Comics (CPS)
1-Maneely-c/a; Dexter The Demon, Willie The Wise-Guy, Little Zelda app.
5.00 15.00 30.00

CARTOON TALES (Disney's...)
No date (1992) ($2.95, color, 6-5/8x9-1/2", 52 pgs.)
W.D. Publications (Disney)
nn-Ariel & Sebastian - Serpent Teen 1.20 3.00
nn-Beauty and the Beast - A Tale of Enchantment 1.20 3.00
nn-Darkwing Duck - Just Us Justice Ducks 1.20 3.00
nn-101 Dalmations - Canine Classics 1.20 3.00
nn-Tale Spin - Surprise in the Skies 1.20 3.00
nn-Uncle Scrooge - Blast to the Past 1.20 3.00

CARVEL COMICS (Amazing Advs. of Capt. Carvel)
1975 - No. 5, 1976 (25 cents; #3-5: 35 cents) (#4,5: 3-1/4x5")
Carvel Corp. (Ice Cream)
1-3 1.00
4,5(1976)-Baseball theme 1.00 2.50 6.00

Car Warriors #2, © Steve Jackson Games

Casey-Crime Photographer #1, © MEG

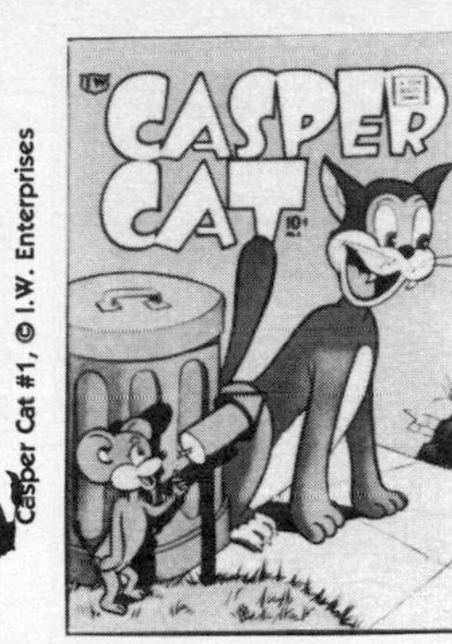

Casper Cat #1, © I.W. Enterprises

CAR WARRIORS
June, 1991 - No. 4, Sept, 1991 ($2.25, color, mini-series)
Epic Comics (Marvel)

	GD25	FN65	NM94
1-4: 1-Says April in indicia		.90	2.25

CASE OF THE SHOPLIFTER'S SHOE (Perry Mason) (See Feature Book No.50)

CASE OF THE WASTED WATER, THE
1972? (Giveaway)
Rheem Water Heating

	GD25	FN65	NM94
nn-Neal Adams-a	4.20	12.50	25.00

CASE OF THE WINKING BUDDHA, THE
1950 (132 pgs.; 25 cents; B&W; 5-1/2x7-5-1/2x8")
St. John Publ. Co.

	GD25	FN65	NM94
nn-Charles Raab-a; reprinted in Authentic Police Cases No. 25	16.00	48.00	110.00

CASEY-CRIME PHOTOGRAPHER (Two-Gun Western No. 5 on)
Aug, 1949 - No. 4, Feb, 1950 (Radio)
Marvel Comics (BFP)

	GD25	FN65	NM94
1-Photo-c; 52 pgs.	10.00	30.00	70.00
2-4: Photo-c	8.35	25.00	50.00

CASEY JONES (See 4-Color No. 915)

CASPER ADVENTURE DIGEST
Oct, 1992 - Present ($1.75, color, digest-size)
Harvey Comics

	GD25	FN65	NM94
V2#1,2-Casper, Richie Rich, Spooky, Wendy		.70	1.75

CASPER AND...
Nov, 1987 - No. 12, June, 1990 (.75-$1.00, all reprints)
Harvey Comics

	GD25	FN65	NM94
1-10: 1-Ghostly Trio. 2-Spooky; begin $1.00-c. 3-Wendy. 4-Nightmare. 5-Ghostly Trio. 6-Spooky. 7-Wendy. 8-Hot Stuff. 9-Baby Huey. 10-Wendy. 11-Ghostly Trio. 12-Spooky			1.00

CASPER AND FRIENDS
Oct, 1991 - No. 5, 1992 ($1.00/$1.25 #5, color)
Harvey Comics

	GD25	FN65	NM94
1-5: Nightmare, Ghostly Trio, Wendy, Spooky			1.25

CASPER AND NIGHTMARE (See Harvey Hits# 37, 45, 52, 56, 59, 62, 65, 68,71, 75)

CASPER AND NIGHTMARE (Nightmare & Casper No. 1-5)
No. 6, 11/64 - No. 44, 10/73; No. 45, 6/74 - No. 46, 8/74 (25 cents)
Harvey Publications

	GD25	FN65	NM94
6: 68 pg. Giants begin, ends #32	4.00	10.00	20.00
7-10	2.00	5.00	10.00
11-20	1.00	2.50	6.00
21-46: 33-37-(52 pg. Giants)		1.60	4.00

NOTE: *Many issues contain reprints.*

CASPER AND SPOOKY (See Harvey Hits No. 20)
Oct, 1972 - No. 7, Oct, 1973
Harvey Publications

	GD25	FN65	NM94
1	1.20	3.00	7.00
2-7		1.40	3.50

CASPER AND THE GHOSTLY TRIO
Nov, 1972 - No. 7, Nov, 1973; No. 8, Aug, 1990 - No. 10, Dec, 1990
Harvey Publications

	GD25	FN65	NM94
1	1.20	3.00	7.00
2-7		1.40	3.50
8-10			1.00

CASPER AND WENDY
Sept, 1972 - No. 8, Nov, 1973
Harvey Publications

	GD25	FN65	NM94
1: 52 pg. Giant	1.20	3.00	7.00
2-8		1.40	3.50

CASPER CAT (See Dopey Duck)
1958; 1963
I. W. Enterprises/Super

	GD25	FN65	NM94
1,7-Reprint, Super No. 14('63)	.70	1.75	3.50

CASPER DIGEST (... Magazine #?; ...Halloween Digest #8, 10)
Oct, 1986 - No. 20? ($1.25-$1.75, digest-size)
Harvey Publications

	GD25	FN65	NM94
1-20: 11-Valentine-c. 18-Halloween-c			1.50

CASPER DIGEST
1991 - Present ($1.75, color, digest-size)
Harvey Comics

	GD25	FN65	NM94
1-11		.70	1.75

CASPER DIGEST STORIES
Feb, 1980 - No. 4, Nov, 1980 (95 cents; 132 pgs.; digest size)
Harvey Publications

	GD25	FN65	NM94
1		1.20	3.00
2-4		.80	2.00

CASPER DIGEST WINNERS
April, 1980 - No. 3, Sept, 1980 (95 cents; 132 pgs.; digest size)
Harvey Publications

	GD25	FN65	NM94
1		.80	2.00
2,3			1.50

CASPER ENCHANTED TALES DIGEST
May, 1992 - No. 2? ($1.75, color, digest-size, 98 pgs.)
Harvey Comics

	GD25	FN65	NM94
1,2-Casper, Spooky, Wendy stories		.70	1.75

CASPER GHOSTLAND
May, 1992 ($1.25, color)
Harvey Comics

	GD25	FN65	NM94
1			1.25

CASPER GIANT SIZE
Oct, 1992 - Present? ($2.25, color, 68 pgs.)
Harvey Comics

	GD25	FN65	NM94
V2#1-Casper, Wendy, Spooky stories		.90	2.25

CASPER HALLOWEEN TRICK OR TREAT
January, 1976 (52 pgs.)
Harvey Publications

	GD25	FN65	NM94
1		1.20	3.00

CASPER IN SPACE (Formerly Casper Spaceship)
No. 6, June, 1973 - No. 8, Oct, 1973
Harvey Publications

	GD25	FN65	NM94
6-8		1.40	3.50

CASPER'S GHOSTLAND
Winter, 1958-59 - No. 97, 12/77; No. 98, 12/79 (25 cents)
Harvey Publications

	GD25	FN65	NM94
1: 68 pgs. begin, ends #61	13.00	40.00	90.00
2	7.50	22.50	45.00
3-10	4.70	14.00	28.00
11-20: 13-X-Mas-c	3.60	9.00	18.00
21-40	2.80	7.00	14.00
41-61: Last 68 pg. issue	1.50	3.75	9.00
62-77: All 52 pgs.	1.00	2.50	5.50
78-98: 94-X-Mas-c		1.60	4.00

NOTE: *Most issues contain reprints.*

CASPER SPACESHIP (Casper in Space No. 6 on)
Aug, 1972 - No. 5, April, 1973
Harvey Publications

Casper the Friendly Ghost #1 (3/91), © Paramount

The Cat #2, © MEG

Catman Comics #13, © HOKE

	GD25	FN65	NM94
1: 52 pg. Giant	1.30	3.25	8.00
2-5		1.40	3.50

CASPER SPECIAL
nd (Dec, 1990) (Giveaway with $1.00 cover)
Target Stores (Harvey)

	GD25	FN65	NM94
Three issues-Given away with Casper video			1.00

CASPER STRANGE GHOST STORIES
October, 1974 - No. 14, Jan, 1977 (All 52 pgs.)
Harvey Publications

	GD25	FN65	NM94
1	1.00	2.50	6.00
2-14		1.00	2.50

CASPER, THE FRIENDLY GHOST (See America's Best TV Comics, Famous TV Funday Funnies, The Friendly Ghost..., Nightmare &..., Richie Rich and..., Tastee-Freez, Treasury of Comics & Wendy the Good Little Witch)

CASPER, THE FRIENDLY GHOST (Becomes Harvey Comics Hits No. 61 (No. 6), and then continued with Harvey issue No. 7)
Sept, 1949 - No. 5, Aug, 1951
St. John Publishing Co.

	GD25	FN65	NM94
1(1949)-Origin & 1st app. Baby Huey & Herman the Mouse (1st time the name Casper app. in any media, even films)	71.00	215.00	500.00
2,3 (2/50 & 8/50)	41.00	125.00	290.00
4,5 (3/51 & 8/51)	32.00	95.00	225.00

CASPER, THE FRIENDLY GHOST (Paramount Picture Star...)
No. 7, Dec, 1952 - No. 70, July, 1958
Harvey Publications (Family Comics)
Note: No. 6 is Harvey Comics Hits No. 61 (10/52)

	GD25	FN65	NM94
7-Baby Huey begins, ends #9	25.00	75.00	175.00
8,9	12.00	36.00	85.00
10-Spooky begins (1st app., 6/53), ends #70?	14.00	43.00	100.00
11-18	8.35	25.00	50.00
19-1st app. Nightmare (4/54)	10.00	30.00	65.00
20-Wendy the Witch begins (1st app., 5/54)	12.00	36.00	85.00
21-30: 24-Infinity-c	6.70	20.00	40.00
31-40	5.00	15.00	30.00
41-50	4.00	12.00	24.00
51-70 (Continues as Friendly Ghost... 8/58)	3.60	9.00	18.00
American Dental Association (Giveaways):			
...'s Dental Health Activity Book-1977		1.20	3.00
...Presents Space Age Dentistry-1972		1.40	3.50
..., His Den, & Their Dentist Fight the Tooth Demons-1974		1.40	3.50

CASPER THE FRIENDLY GHOST (Formerly The Friendly Ghost...)
No. 254, July, 1990 - No. 260, Jan, 1991 ($1.00, color)
Harvey Comics

	GD25	FN65	NM94
254-260			1.00

CASPER THE FRIENDLY GHOST
Mar, 1991 - 8? ($1.00/$1.25, color)
V2#1, Aug, 1992 - Present ($1.95, color, 52 pgs.)
Harvey Comics

	GD25	FN65	NM94
1-8: 1-Casper becomes Mighty Ghost; Spooky & Wendy app. 7-Last $1.00-c. 7,8-Post-a			1.25
V2#1-Cover says "Casper Big Book"; Spooky app.		.80	2.00

CASPER T.V. SHOWTIME
Jan, 1980 - No. 5, Oct, 1980
Harvey Comics

	GD25	FN65	NM94
1		.80	2.00
2-5			1.00

CASSETTE BOOKS
(Classics Illustrated)
1984 (48 pgs, b&w comic with cassette tape)
Cassette Book Co./I.P.S. Publ.

NOTE: *This series was illegal. The artwork was illegally obtained, and the Classics Illustrated copyright owner, Twin Circle Publ. sued to get an injunction to prevent the continued sale of this series. Many C.I. collectors obtained copies before the 1987 injunction, but now they are already scarce. Here again the market is just developing, but sealed mint copies of com ic and tape should be worth at least $25.*
1001 (CI#1-A2)New-PC 1002(CI#3-A2)CI-PC 1003(CI#13-A2)CI-PC
1004(CI#25)CI-LDC 1005(CI#10-A2)New-PC 1006(CI#64)CI-LDC

CASTILIAN (See Movie Classics)

CAT, T.H.E. (TV) (See T.H.E. Cat)

CAT, THE (See Movie Classics)

CAT, THE
Nov, 1972 - No. 4, June, 1973
Marvel Comics Group

	GD25	FN65	NM94
1-Origin & 1st app. The Cat (who later becomes Tigra); Mooney-a(i); Wood-c(i)/a(i)	1.70	5.00	12.00
2,3: 2-Mooney-a(i). 3-Everett inks	1.30	3.25	8.00
4-Starlin/Weiss-a(p)	1.30	3.25	8.00

CAT & MOUSE
Dec, 1988 ($1.75, color w/part B&W)
EF Graphics (Silverline)

	GD25	FN65	NM94
1-1st printing (12/88, 32 pgs.)		.70	1.75
1-2nd printing (5/89, 36 pgs.)		.70	1.75

CAT FROM OUTER SPACE (See Walt Disney Showcase #46)

CATHOLIC COMICS (See Heroes All Catholic...)
June, 1946 - V3No.10, July, 1949
Catholic Publications

	GD25	FN65	NM94
1	14.00	43.00	100.00
2	8.35	25.00	50.00
3-13(7/47)	6.70	20.00	40.00
V2#1-10	4.00	11.00	22.00
V3#1-10: Reprints 10-part Treasure Island serial from Target V2#2-11 (see Key Comics #5)	4.70	14.00	28.00

CATHOLIC PICTORIAL
1947
Catholic Guild

	GD25	FN65	NM94
1-Toth-a(2) (Rare)	24.00	70.00	165.00

CATMAN COMICS (Formerly Crash Comics No. 1-5)
5/41 - No. 17, 1/43; No. 18, 7/43 - No. 22, 12/43; No. 23, 3/44 - No. 26, 11/44; No. 27, 4/45 - No. 30, 12/45; No. 31, 6/46 - No. 32, 8/46
Holyoke Publishing Co./Continental Magazines V2#12, 7/44 on

	GD25	FN65	NM94
1(V1#6)-Origin The Deacon & Sidekick Mickey, Dr. Diamond & Rag-Man; The Black Widow app.; The Catman by Chas. Quinlan & Blaze Baylor begin	100.00	300.00	700.00
2(V1#7)	50.00	150.00	350.00
3(V1#8), 4(V1#9): 3-The Pied Piper begins	37.00	110.00	240.00
5(V2#10)-Origin Kitten; The Hood begins (c-redated), 6,7(V2#11,12)	29.00	86.00	200.00
8(V2#13,3/42)-Origin Little Leaders; Volton by Kubert begins (his 1st comic book work)	42.00	125.00	275.00
9,10(V2#14,15): 10-Origin Blackout retold; Phantom Falcon begins	27.00	82.00	180.00
11(V3#1)-Kubert-a	27.00	82.00	180.00
12(V3#2) - 15, 17, 18(V3#8, 7/43)	21.00	62.00	140.00
16 (V3#5)-Hitler, Tojo, Mussolini, Stalin-c	25.00	75.00	165.00
19 (V2#6)-Hitler, Tojo, Mussolini-c	25.00	75.00	165.00
20(V2#7) - 23(V2#10, 3/44): 20-Hitler-c	21.00	62.00	140.00
nn(V3#13, 5/44)-Rico-a; Schomburg bondage-c	18.00	55.00	120.00
nn(V2#12, 7/44)	18.00	55.00	120.00
nn(V3#1, 9/44)-Origin The Golden Archer; Leatherface app.	18.00	55.00	120.00
nn(V3#2, 11/44)-L. B. Cole-c	25.00	75.00	165.00
27-Origin Kitten retold; L. B. Cole Flag-c	27.00	82.00	180.00

Cat Tales #1, © Malibu Graphics

Catwoman #2 (9/93), © DC

Chain Gang War #2, © John Wagner & David Johnson

	GD25	FN65	NM94
28-Catman learns Kitten's I.D.; Dr. Macabre, Deacon app.; L. B. Cole c/a	29.00	86.00	190.00
29-32-L. B. Cole-c; bondage-#30	25.00	75.00	165.00

NOTE: ***Fuje** a-11, 29(3), 30. **Palais** a-11, 29(2), 30, c-25(7/44). **Rico** a-11(2).*

CAT TALES (3-D)
April, 1989 ($2.95)
Eternity Comics

	GD25	FN65	NM94
1-Felix the Cat-r in 3-D		1.20	3.00

CATWOMAN (Also see Action Comics Weekly #611, Batman #1, Detective Comics, Showcase 93 & Superman's Girlfriend Lois Lane #70, 71)
Feb, 1989 - No. 4, May, 1989 ($1.50, mini-series, mature readers)
DC Comics

	GD25	FN65	NM94
1	1.00	2.50	6.00
2		1.40	3.50
3,4: 3-Batman cameo. 4-Batman app.		1.00	2.50
...: Her Sister's Keeper (1991, $9.95)-r/#1-4	1.65	4.00	10.00

CATWOMAN
Aug, 1993 - Present ($1.50, color)
DC Comics

	GD25	FN65	NM94
1-($1.95)-Embossed-c; Bane app.		.80	2.00
2-8: 3-Bane flashback cameo. 4-Brief Bane app.			1.50

CAUGHT
Aug, 1956 - No. 5, April, 1957
Atlas Comics (VPI)

	GD25	FN65	NM94
1	10.00	30.00	70.00
2,4: 4-Maneely-a (4 pgs.)	5.35	16.00	32.00
3-Maneely, Pakula, Torres-a	5.85	17.50	35.00
5-Crandall, Krigstein-a	7.00	21.00	42.00

NOTE: ***Drucker** a-2. **Heck** a-4. **Severin** c-1, 2, 4, 5. **Shores** a-4.*

CAVALIER COMICS
1945; 1952 (Early DC reprints)
A. W. Nugent Publ. Co.

	GD25	FN65	NM94
2(1945)-Speed Saunders, Fang Gow	11.00	32.00	75.00
2(1952)	5.85	17.50	35.00

CAVE GIRL (Also see Africa)
No. 11, 1953 - No. 14, 1954
Magazine Enterprises

	GD25	FN65	NM94
11(A-1 82)-Origin; all Cave Girl stories	28.00	85.00	195.00
12(A-1 96), 13(A-1 116), 14(A-1 125)-Thunda by Powell in each	21.00	62.00	145.00

NOTE: ***Powell** c/a in all.*

CAVE GIRL
1988 ($2.95, 44 pgs., 16 pgs. of color, rest B&W)
AC Comics

	GD25	FN65	NM94
1-Powell-r/Cave Girl #11; Nyoka photo back-c from movie; Powell/Bill Black-c; Special Limited Edition on-c		1.20	3.00

CAVE KIDS (TV)
Feb, 1963 - No. 16, Mar, 1967 (Hanna-Barbera)
Gold Key

	GD25	FN65	NM94
1	3.20	8.00	20.00
2-5	1.70	5.00	12.00
6-16: 7,12-Pebbles & Bamm Bamm app.	1.50	3.75	9.00

CENTURION OF ANCIENT ROME, THE
1958 (no month listed) (36 pages) (B&W)
Zondervan Publishing House

	GD25	FN65	NM94
(Rare) All by Jay Disbrow Estimated Value....			200.00

CENTURIONS (TV)
June, 1987 - No. 4, Sept, 1987 (75 cents, mini-series)
DC Comics

	GD25	FN65	NM94
1-4			1.00

CENTURY OF COMICS
1933 (100 pages) (Probably the 3rd comic book)
Eastern Color Printing Co.

Bought by Wheatena, Milk-O-Malt, John Wanamaker, Kinney Shoe Stores, & others to be used as premiums and radio giveaways. No publisher listed.

	GD25	FN65	VF82
nn-Mutt & Jeff, Joe Palooka, etc. reprints	1700.00	5100.00	8500.00

(Estimated up to 20 total copies exist, none in NM-Mint)

CEREBUS BI-WEEKLY
Dec. 2, 1988 - No. 26, Nov. 11, 1989 ($1.25, B&W)
Aardvark-Vanaheim

	GD25	FN65	NM94
1-26: Reprints Cerebus #1-26			1.25

CEREBUS: CHURCH & STATE
Feb, 1991 - No. 30, Apr, 1992 ($2.00, B&W, bi-weekly)
Aardvark-Vanaheim

	GD25	FN65	NM94
1-30: r/Cerebus #51-80		.80	2.00

CEREBUS: HIGH SOCIETY
Feb, 1990 - No. 25, 1991 ($1.70, B&W)
Aardvark-Vanaheim

	GD25	FN65	NM94
1-25: r/Cerebus #26-50		.70	1.70

CEREBUS JAM
Apr, 1985
Aardvark-Vanaheim

	GD25	FN65	NM94
1-Eisner, Austin-a		1.20	3.00

CEREBUS THE AARDVARK (See A-V In 3-D, Nucleus, Power Comics)
Dec, 1977 - Present ($1.70-$2.00, B&W)
Aardvark-Vanaheim

	GD25	FN65	NM94
1-1st app. Cerebus; 2000 print run; most copies poorly printed	22.00	65.00	150.00

Note: *There is a counterfeit version known to exist. It can be distinguished from the original in the following ways: inside cover is glossy instead of flat, black background on the front cover is blotted or spotty.*

	GD25	FN65	NM94
2-Dave Sim art in all	7.00	21.00	50.00
3-Origin Red Sophia	5.50	17.00	40.00
4-Origin Elrod the Albino	3.60	10.75	25.00
5,6	3.20	8.00	20.00
7-10	2.15	6.50	15.00
11,12: 11-Origin Capt. Coachroach	2.40	7.25	17.00
13-15: 14-Origin Lord Julius	1.30	3.25	8.00
16-20	1.00	2.00	5.00
21-Scarcer	4.30	13.00	30.00
22-Low distribution; no cover price	1.65	4.70	11.00
23-30: 26-High Society storyline begins	1.00	2.00	5.00
31-Origin Moonroach	1.20	3.00	7.00
32-40		1.60	4.00
41-50,52: 52-Cutey Bunny app.		1.20	3.00
51-Not reprinted; Cutey Bunny app.	1.70	5.00	12.00
53-Intro. Wolveroach (cameo)	1.00	2.00	5.00
54-1st full Wolveroach story	1.20	3.00	7.00
55,56-Wolveroach app.	1.00	2.00	5.00
57-79: 61,62: Flaming Carrot app.		1.00	2.50
80-178: 104-Flaming Carrot app. 112/113-Double issue. 137-Begin $2.25-c		.90	2.25
151-153-2nd printings		.90	2.25

CHAIN GANG WAR
July, 1993 - Present ($1.75, color)
DC Comics

	GD25	FN65	NM94
1-($2.50)-Embossed silver foil-c		1.00	2.50
2-4,6-10: 3-Deathstroke app. 4-Brief Deathstroke app. 6-New Batman cameo		.70	1.75

5-($2.50)-Foil embossed-c; Deathstroke app.; new Batman cameo (Azrael,

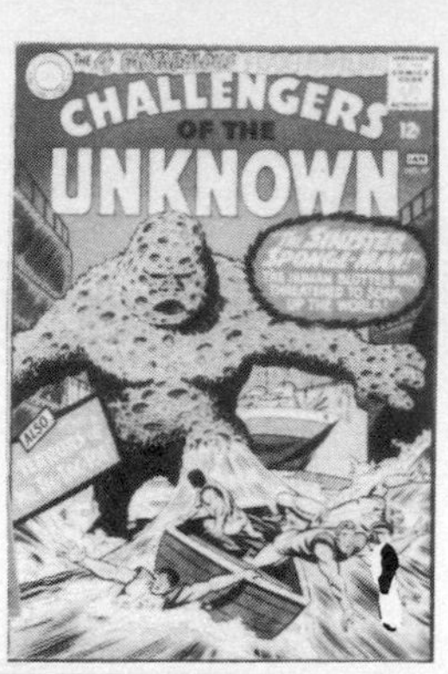

Challengers of the Unknown #47, © DC

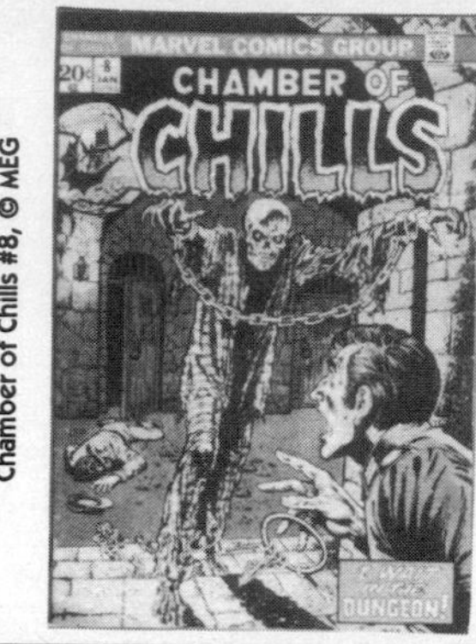

Chamber of Chills #8, © MEG

Champions, The #14, © MEG

GD25 FN65 NM94

1 panel) 1.00 2.50

CHALLENGE OF THE UNKNOWN (Formerly Love Experiences)
No. 6, Sept, 1950 (See Web Of Mystery No. 19)
Ace Magazines

6-"Villa of the Vampire" used in N.Y. Joint Legislative Comm. Publ; Sekowsky-a 12.00 36.00 85.00

CHALLENGER, THE
1945 - No. 4, Oct-Dec, 1946
Interfaith Publications/T.C. Comics

nn; nd; 32 pgs.; Origin the Challenger Club; Anti-Fascist with funny animal filler 19.00 58.00 135.00
2-4-Kubert-a; 4-Fuje-a 16.00 50.00 115.00

CHALLENGERS OF THE UNKNOWN (See Showcase #6, 7, 11, 12, Super DC Giant, and Super Team Family)
4-5/58 - No. 77, 12-1/70-71; No. 78, 2/73 - No. 80, 6-7/73;
No. 81, 6-7/77 - No. 87, 6-7/78
National Per. Publ./DC

GD25 FN65 VF82 NM94
Showcase #6 (1-2/57)-Origin & 1st app. Challengers of the Unknown by Kirby (1st Silver Age super-hero team) (1st original concept S.A. series) 143.00 430.00 1290.00 2150.00

GD25 FN65 NM94
Showcase #7 (3-4/57)-2nd app. by Kirby 94.00 281.00 1125.00
Showcase #11 (11-12/57)-3rd app. by Kirby; 2nd tryout series 100.00 300.00 1000.00
Showcase #12 (1-2/58)-4th app. by Kirby 90.00 269.00 1075.00

GD25 FN65 VF82 NM94
1-(4-5/58)-Kirby/Stein-a(2) 135.00 405.00 880.00 1350.00

GD25 FN65 NM94
2-Kirby/Stein-a(2) 56.00 167.00 500.00
3-Kirby/Stein-a(2) 44.00 133.00 400.00
4-8-Kirby/Wood-a plus c-#8 39.00 117.00 350.00
9,10 19.00 58.00 175.00
11-15: 14-Origin/1st app. Multi-Man (villain) 13.00 38.00 115.00
16-22: 18-Intro. Cosmo, the Challengers Spacepet. 22-Last 10 cent issue 11.00 32.00 95.00
23-30 7.00 21.00 50.00
31-Retells origin of the Challengers 8.00 24.00 55.00
32-40 3.60 10.75 25.00
41-60: 43-New look begins. 48-Doom Patrol app. 49-Intro. Challenger Corps. 51-Sea Devils app. 55-Death of Red Ryan. 60-Red Ryan returns 1.65 4.70 11.00
61-73,75-77: 64,65-Kirby origin-r, parts 1 & 2. 66-New logo. 68-Last 12 cent issue. 69-1st app. Corinna 1.00 2.00 5.00
74-Deadman by Tuska/N. Adams 1.70 5.00 12.00
78-87: 82-Swamp Thing begins 1.20 3.00

NOTE: ***N. Adams** c-67, 68, 70, 72, 74i, 81i. **Buckler** c-83-86p. **Giffen** a-83-87p. **Kirby** a-75-80r; c-75, 77, 78. **Kubert** c-64, 66, 69, 76, 79. **Nasser** c/a-81p, 82p. **Tuska** a-73. **Wood** r-76.*

CHALLENGERS OF THE UNKNOWN
Mar, 1991 - No. 8, Oct, 1991 ($1.75, color, limited series)
DC Comics

1-Bolland-c .80 2.00
2-8: 6-G. Kane-c(p). 7-Steranko-c swipe by Arthur Adams .70 1.75

CHALLENGE TO THE WORLD
1951 (36 pages) (10 cents)
Catechetical Guild

nn 3.20 8.00 16.00

CHAMBER OF CHILLS (...of Clues No. 27 on)
No. 21, June, 1951 - No. 26, Dec, 1954
Harvey Publications/Witches Tales

21 (#1) 17.00 52.00 120.00
22,24 (#2,3) 10.00 30.00 60.00
23 (#4)-Excessive violence; eyes torn out 11.00 32.00 75.00

GD25 FN65 NM94

5(2/52)-Decapitation, acid in face scene 11.00 32.00 75.00
6-Woman melted alive 10.00 30.00 70.00
7-Used in **SOTI**, pg. 389; decapitation/severed head panels 10.00 30.00 60.00
8-10: 8-Decapitation panels 9.15 27.50 55.00
11,12,14 6.70 20.00 40.00
13,15-24-Nostrand-a in all. 13,21-Decapitation panels. 18-Atom bomb panels. 20-Nostrand-c 10.00 30.00 65.00
25,26 5.35 16.00 32.00

NOTE: *About half the issues contain bondage, torture, sadism, perversion, gore, cannabalism, eyes ripped out, acid in face, etc. **Elias** c-4-11, 14-19, 21-26. **Kremer** a-12, 17. **Palais** a-21(1), 23. **Nostrand/Powell** a-13, 15, 16. **Powell** a-21, 23, 24('51), 5-8, 11, 13, 18-21, 23-25. Bondage-c-21, 24('51), 7. 25-r/#5; 26-r/#9.*

CHAMBER OF CHILLS
Nov, 1972 - No. 25, Nov, 1976
Marvel Comics Group

1-Harlan Ellison adaptation 1.20 3.00
2-25 .70 1.75

NOTE: ***Adkins** a-1i, 2i. **Brunner** a-2-4; c-4. **Ditko** r-14, 16, 19, 23, 24. **Everett** a-3i, 11r,21r. **Heath** a-1r. **Gil Kane** c-2p. **Powell** a-13r. **Russell** a-1p, 2p. **Williamson/Mayo** a-13r. **Robert E. Howard** horror story adaptation-2, 3.*

CHAMBER OF CLUES (Formerly Chamber of Chills)
No. 27, Feb, 1955 - No. 28, April, 1955
Harvey Publications

27-Kerry Drake-r/#19; Powell-a; last pre-code 7.50 22.50 45.00
28-Kerry Drake 4.20 12.50 25.00

CHAMBER OF DARKNESS (Monsters on the Prowl #9 on)
Oct, 1969 - No. 8, Dec, 1970
Marvel Comics Group

1-Buscema-a(p) 4.30 13.00 30.00
2-Neal Adams scripts 1.70 5.00 12.00
3-Smith, Buscema-a 1.70 5.00 12.00
4-A Conanesque tryout by Smith (4/70); reprinted in Conan #16; Marie Severin/Everett-c 5.00 15.00 35.00
5,6,8: 5-H.P. Lovecraft adaptation 1.00 2.00 5.00
7-Wrightson-c/a, 7pgs. (his 1st work at Marvel); Wrightson draws himself in 1st & last panels; Kirby/Ditko-r 1.65 4.00 10.00
1-(1/72; 25 cent Special) 1.00 2.50 6.00

NOTE: ***Adkins/Everett** a-8. **Craig** a-5. **Ditko** a-6-8r. **Kirby** a(p)-4, 5, 7r. **Kirby/Everett** c-5. **Severin/Everett** c-6. **Wrightson** c-7, 8.*

CHAMP COMICS (Formerly Champion No. 1-10)
No. 11, Oct, 1940 - No. 29, March, 1944
Worth Publ. Co./Champ Publ./Family Comics(Harvey Publ.)

11-Human Meteor cont'd. 50.00 150.00 325.00
12-20: 14,15-Crandall-c. 18,19-Kirbyish-c. 19-The Wasp app. 20-The Green Ghost app. 39.00 115.00 265.00
21-29: 22-The White Mask app. 23-Flag-c 32.00 95.00 210.00

CHAMPION (See Gene Autry's...)

CHAMPION COMICS (Champ No. 11 on)
No. 2, Dec, 1939 - No. 10, Aug, 1940 (no No.1)
Worth Publ. Co.(Harvey Publications)

2-The Champ, The Blazing Scarab, Neptina, Liberty Lads, Jungleman, Bill Handy, Swingtime Sweetie begin 75.00 225.00 500.00
3-7: 7-The Human Meteor begins? 37.00 110.00 250.00
8-10-Kirbyish-c; bondage #10 42.00 125.00 275.00

CHAMPIONS, THE
October, 1975 - No. 17, Jan, 1978
Marvel Comics Group

1-Origin & 1st app. The Champions (The Angel, Black Widow, Ghost Rider, Hercules, Ice Man); Venus x-over 2.15 6.50 15.00
2-10,16: 2,3-Venus x-over 1.65 4.00 10.00
11-15,17-Byrne-a 1.65 4.70 11.00

NOTE: ***Buckler/Adkins** c-3. **Kane/Adkins** c-1. **Kane/Layton** c-11. **Tuska** a-3p, 4p, 6p. Ghost Rider c-1-4, 7, 8, 10, 14, 16, 17 (4, 10, 14 are more prominent).*

Charlie Chan #3, © PRIZE

Charlie McCarthy #1, © Edgar Bergen

Checkmate #14, © DC

	GD25	FN65	NM94

CHAMPIONS (Eclipse)(Value: cover or less)

CHAMPIONS (Hero)(Value: cover or less)

CHAMPION SPORTS
Oct-Nov, 1973 - No. 3, Feb-Mar, 1974
National Periodical Publications

	GD25	FN65	NM94
1-3			1.50

CHAOS (See The Crusaders)

CHARLIE CHAN (See Big Shot Comics, Columbia Comics, Feature Comics & The New Advs. of...)

CHARLIE CHAN (The Adventures of...) (Zaza The Mystic No. 10 on)
6-7/48 - No. 5, 2-3/49; No.6, 6/55 - No. 9, 3/56
Crestwood(Prize) No. 1-5; Charlton No. 6(6/55) on

	GD25	FN65	NM94
1-S&K-c, 2 pages; Infantino-a	36.00	107.00	300.00
2-S&K-c	22.00	65.00	185.00
3-S&K-c/a	22.00	65.00	185.00
4,5 S&K-c	23.00	70.00	160.00
6(6/55-Charlton)-S&K-c	17.00	52.00	120.00
7-9	10.00	30.00	70.00

CHARLIE CHAN
Oct-Dec, 1965 - No. 2, Mar, 1966
Dell Publishing Co.

	GD25	FN65	NM94
1-Springer-a	4.00	11.00	22.00
2	2.80	7.00	14.00

CHARLIE CHAPLIN
1917 (9x16"; large size; softcover; B&W)
Essanay/M. A. Donohue & Co.

	GD25	FN65	NM94
Series 1, #315-Comic Capers (9-3/4"x15-3/4")-18pp by Segar, Series 1, #316-In the Movies	85.00	260.00	600.00
Series 1, #317-Up in the Air. 318-In the Army	85.00	260.00	600.00
Funny Stunts-(12-1/2x16-3/8") in color	64.00	193.00	450.00

NOTE: *All contain **Segar** -a; pre-Thimble Theatre.*

CHARLIE McCARTHY (See Edgar Bergen Presents...)
No. 171, Nov, 1947 - No. 571, July, 1954 (See True Comics #14)
Dell Publishing Co.

	GD25	FN65	NM94
4-Color 171	16.00	50.00	115.00
4-Color 196-Part photo-c; photo back-c	14.00	43.00	100.00
1(3-5/49)-Part photo-c; photo back-c	14.00	43.00	100.00
2-9(7/52; #5,6-52 pgs.)	6.70	20.00	40.00
4-Color 445,478,527,571	5.00	15.00	30.00

CHARLTON BULLSEYE
1975 - No. 5, 1976 ($1.50, B&W, bi-monthly, magazine format)
CPL/Gang Publications

	GD25	FN65	NM94
1: 1 & 2 are last Capt. Atom by Ditko/Byrne intended for the never published Capt. Atom #90; Nightshade app.; Jeff Jones-a	1.50	3.75	9.00
2-Part 2 Capt. Atom story by Ditko/Byrne	1.50	3.75	9.00
3-Wrong Country by Sanho Kim	1.00	2.50	6.00
4-Doomsday + 1 by John Byrne	1.50	3.75	9.00
5-Doomsday + 1 by Byrne, The Question by Toth; Neal Adams back-c; Toth-c	1.65	4.00	10.00

CHARLTON BULLSEYE
June, 1981 - No. 10, Dec, 1982; Nov, 1986 (Color)
Charlton Publications

	GD25	FN65	NM94
1-Blue Beetle, The Question app.; 1st app. Rocket Rabbit		.80	2.00
2-10: 2-1st app. Neil The Horse; Rocket Rabbit app. 6-Origin & 1st app. Thunderbunny			1.50
Special 1(11/86)(Half In B&W)		1.20	3.00
Special 2-Atomic Mouse app. ('87)		.80	2.00

CHARLTON CLASSICS
April, 1980 - No. 9, Aug, 1981
Charlton Comics

	GD25	FN65	NM94
1		.80	2.00
2-9			1.00

CHARLTON CLASSICS LIBRARY (1776)
V10No.1, March, 1973 (One Shot)
Charlton Comics

	GD25	FN65	NM94
1776 (title) - Adaptation of the film musical "1776"; given away at movie theatres		1.60	4.00

CHARLTON PREMIERE (Formerly Marine War Heroes)
V1#19, July, 1967; V2#1, Sept, 1967 - No. 4, May, 1968
Charlton Comics

	GD25	FN65	NM94
V1#19-Marine War Heroes. V2#1-Trio; intro. Shape. Tyro Team. & Spookman. 2-Children of Doom. 3-Sinistro Boy Fiend; Blue Beetle & Peacemaker x-over. 4-Unlikely Tales; Aparo, Ditko-a	1.00	2.00	5.00

CHARLTON SPORT LIBRARY - PROFESSIONAL FOOTBALL
Winter, 1969-70 (Jan. on cover) (68 pages)
Charlton Comics

	GD25	FN65	NM94
1	1.70	5.00	12.00

CHASING THE BLUES
1912 (52 pages) (7-1/2x10"; B&W; hardcover)
Doubleday Page

	GD25	FN65	NM94
nn-by Rube Goldberg	50.00	150.00	350.00

CHECKMATE (TV)
Oct, 1962 - No. 2, Dec, 1962
Gold Key

	GD25	FN65	NM94
1,2-Photo-c	4.20	12.50	25.00

CHECKMATE (See Action Comics #598)
April, 1988 - No. 33, Jan, 1991 ($1.25)
DC Comics

	GD25	FN65	NM94
1-12			1.25
13-33: $1.50-$2.00, new format			1.50

NOTE: ***Gil Kane** c-2, 4, 7, 8, 10, 11, 15-19.*

CHEERIOS PREMIUMS (Disney)
1947 (32 pages) (Pocket size; 16 titles)
Walt Disney Productions

	GD25	FN65	NM94
Set "W"			
W1-Donald Duck & the Pirates	5.00	15.00	30.00
W2-Bucky Bug & the Cannibal King	3.60	9.00	18.00
W3-Pluto Joins the F.B.I.	3.60	9.00	18.00
W4-Mickey Mouse & the Haunted House	4.35	13.00	26.00
Set "X"			
X1-Donald Duck, Counter Spy	4.00	12.00	24.00
X2-Goofy Lost in the Desert	3.20	8.00	16.00
X3-Br'er Rabbit Outwits Br'er Fox	3.20	8.00	16.00
X4-Mickey Mouse at the Rodeo	4.35	13.00	26.00
Set "Y"			
Y1-Donald Duck's Atom Bomb by Carl Barks	57.00	170.00	400.00
Y2-Br'er Rabbit's Secret	3.20	8.00	16.00
Y3-Dumbo & the Circus Mystery	4.00	12.00	24.00
Y4-Mickey Mouse Meets the Wizard	4.35	13.00	26.00
Set "Z"			
Z1-Donald Duck Pilots a Jet Plane (not by Barks)	4.00	12.00	24.00
Z2-Pluto Turns Sleuth Hound	3.20	8.00	16.00
Z3-The Seven Dwarfs & the Enchanted Mtn.	4.00	12.00	24.00
Z4-Mickey Mouse's Secret Room	4.35	13.00	26.00

CHEERIOS 3-D GIVEAWAYS (Disney)
1954 (Pocket size) (24 titles) (Glasses were cut-outs on boxes)
Walt Disney Productions

	GD25	FN65	NM94
Glasses only....	6.70	20.00	40.00

(Set 1) 1-Donald Duck & Uncle Scrooge, the Firefighters
2-Mickey Mouse & Goofy, Pirate Plunder

Cheval Noir #11, © Dark Horse

Child's Play 2 #1, © Universal City Studios

Chilling Adventures in Sorcery #4, © AP

	GD25	FN65	NM94
3-Donald Duck's Nephews, the Fabulous Inventors			
4-Mickey Mouse, Secret of the Ming Vase			
5-Donald Duck with Huey, Dewey, & Louie; ...the Seafarers (title on 2nd page)			
6-Mickey Mouse, Moaning Mountain			
7-Donald Duck, Apache Gold			
8-Mickey Mouse, Flight to Nowhere (per book)	8.35	25.00	50.00
(Set 2) 1-Donald Duck, Treasure of Timbuktu			
2-Mickey Mouse & Pluto, Operation China			
3-Donald Duck in the Magic Cows			
4-Mickey Mouse & Goofy, Kid Kokonut			
5-Donald Duck, Mystery Ship			
6-Mickey Mouse, Phantom Sheriff			
7-Donald Duck, Circus Adventures			
8-Mickey Mouse, Arctic Explorers (per book)	8.35	25.00	50.00
(Set 3) 1-Donald Duck & Witch Hazel			
2-Mickey Mouse in Darkest Africa			
3-Donald Duck & Uncle Scrooge, Timber Trouble			
4-Mickey Mouse, Rajah's Rescue			
5-Donald Duck in Robot Reporter			
6-Mickey Mouse, Slumbering Sleuth			
7-Donald Duck in the Foreign Legion			
8-Mickey Mouse, Airwalking Wonder (per book)....	8.35	25.00	50.00

CHESTY AND COPTIE
1946 (4 pages) (Giveaway) (Disney)
Los Angeles Community Chest

	GD25	FN65	NM94
nn-(Very Rare) by Floyd Gottfredson	57.00	170.00	400.00

CHESTY AND HIS HELPERS
1943 (12 pgs., Disney giveaway, 5-1/2"x7-1/4")
Los Angeles War Chest

	GD25	FN65	NM94
nn-Chesty & Coptie	64.00	193.00	450.00

CHEVAL NOIR
1989 - Present ($3.50, B&W, 68 pgs.)
Dark Horse Comics

	GD25	FN65	NM94
1-8,10 ($3.50): 6-Moebius poster insert		1.40	3.50
9,11,13,15,17,20,22 ($4.50, 84 pgs.)		1.80	4.50
12,18,19,21,23,25,26 ($3.95): 12-Geary-a; Mignola-c. 26-Moebius-a begins		1.60	4.00
14 ($4.95, 76 pgs.)(7 pgs. color)	1.00	2.00	5.00
16,24 ($3.75): 16-19-Contain trading cards		1.50	3.75
27-46 ($2.95)		1.20	3.00

NOTE: ***Bolland** a-2, 6, 7, 13, 14. **Bolton** a-2, 4; c-4, 20. **Chadwick** c-13. **Dorman** painted c-16. **Geary** a-13, 14. **Kelley Jones** c-27. **Kaluta** a-6; c-6, 18. **Moebius** c-5, 9, 26. **Dave Stevens** c-1, 7. **Sutton** painted c-36.*

CHEYENNE (TV)
No. 734, Oct, 1956 - No. 25, Dec-Jan, 1961-62
Dell Publishing Co.

	GD25	FN65	NM94
4-Color 734(#1)-Clint Walker photo-c	12.00	36.00	85.00
4-Color 772,803: Clint Walker photo-c	7.50	22.50	45.00
4(8-10/57) - 12: 4-9-Clint Walker photo-c. 10-12-Ty Hardin photo-c	5.35	16.00	32.00
13-25 (All Clint Walker photo-c)	4.70	14.00	28.00

CHEYENNE AUTUMN (See Movie Classics)

CHEYENNE KID (Formerly Wild Frontier No. 1-7)
No. 8, July, 1957 - No. 99, Nov, 1973
Charlton Comics

	GD25	FN65	NM94
8 (#1)	5.00	15.00	30.00
9,15-17,19	3.20	8.00	16.00
10-Williamson/Torres-a(3); Ditko-c	6.70	20.00	40.00
11,12-Williamson/Torres-a(2) ea.; 11-(68 pgs.)-Cheyenne Kid meets Geronimo	7.50	22.50	45.00
13-Williamson/Torres-a, 5 pgs.	4.70	14.00	28.00
14,18-Williamson-a, 5 pgs.?	4.70	14.00	28.00
20-22,24,25-Severin c/a(3) each	3.60	9.00	18.00
23,27-29	1.60	4.00	8.00
26,30-Severin-a	2.40	6.00	12.00
31-59	1.00	2.00	5.00
60-99: 66-Wander by Aparo begins, ends #87. Apache Red begins #88, origin in #89		1.40	3.50
Modern Comics Reprint 87,89(1978)			1.00

CHICAGO MAIL ORDER (See C-M-O Comics)

CHIEF, THE (Indian Chief No. 3 on)
No. 290, Aug, 1950 - No. 2, Apr-June, 1951
Dell Publishing Co.

	GD25	FN65	NM94
4-Color 290(#1), 2	5.00	15.00	30.00

CHIEF CRAZY HORSE (See Wild Bill Hickok #21)
1950 (Also see Fighting Indians of the Wild West!)
Avon Periodicals

	GD25	FN65	NM94
nn-Fawcette-c	13.50	41.00	95.00

CHIEF VICTORIO'S APACHE MASSACRE
1951 (Also see Fighting Indians of the Wild West!)
Avon Periodicals

	GD25	FN65	NM94
nn-Williamson/Frazetta-a, 7 pgs.; Larsen-a; Kinstler-c	29.00	85.00	200.00

CHILDREN OF FIRE (Fantagor)(Value: cover or less)

CHILDREN OF THE VOYAGER
Sept, 1993 - No. 4, Dec, 1993 ($1.95, color, mini-series)
Marvel Frontier Comics

	GD25	FN65	NM94
1-($2.95)-Embossed glow-in-the-dark-c		1.00	2.50
2-4			1.50

CHILDREN'S BIG BOOK
1945 (68 pages; stiff covers) (25 cents)
Dorene Publ. Co.

	GD25	FN65	NM94
nn-Comics & fairy tales; David Icove-a	9.15	27.50	55.00

CHILDREN'S CRUSADE, THE
Dec, 1993 - No. 2, Jan, 1994 ($3.95, color, limited series)
DC Comics

	GD25	FN65	NM94
1,2-By Gaiman/Bachalo		1.60	4.00

CHILD'S PLAY: THE SERIES (Innovation)(Value: cover or less)

CHILD'S PLAY 2 THE OFFICIAL MOVIE ADAPTATION (Innovation)(Value: cover or less)

CHILI (Millie's Rival)
5/69 - No. 17, 9/70; No. 18, 8/72 - No. 26, 12/73
Marvel Comics Group

	GD25	FN65	NM94
1	3.20	8.00	20.00
2-5	1.65	4.00	10.00
6-17	1.20	3.00	7.00
18-26	1.00	2.00	5.00
Special 1(12/71)	1.50	3.75	9.00

CHILLER
Nov, 1993 - No. 2, Dec, 1993 ($7.95, color, limited series)
Epic Comics (Marvel)

	GD25	FN65	NM94
1,2	1.30	3.25	8.00

CHILLING ADVENTURES IN SORCERY (...as Told by Sabrina #1, 2)
(Red Circle Sorcery No. 6 on)
9/72 - No. 2, 10/72; No. 3, 10/73 - No. 5, 2/74
Archie Publications (Red Circle Prod.)

	GD25	FN65	NM94
1,2-Sabrina cameo in both	1.00	2.50	6.00
3-Morrow-c/a, all		1.40	3.50
4,5-Morrow-c/a, 5,6 pgs.		1.40	3.50

Chilling Tales #17, © YM

Chip 'N Dale Rescue Rangers #1, © Disney

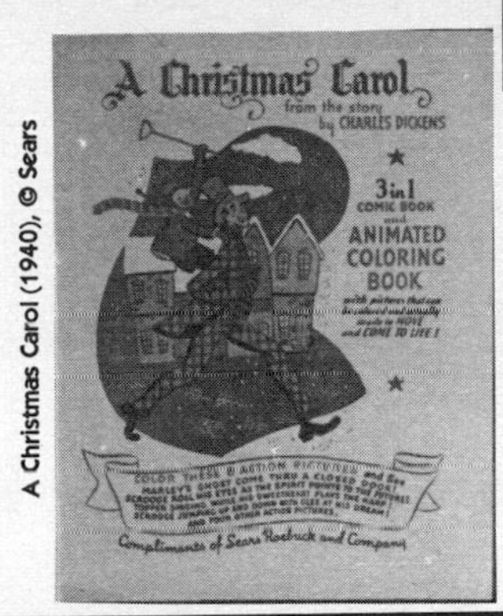

A Christmas Carol (1940), © Sears

CHILLING TALES (Formerly Beware)
No. 13, Dec, 1952 - No. 17, Oct, 1953
Youthful Magazines

	GD25	FN65	NM94
13(No.1)-Harrison-a; Matt Fox-c/a	23.00	70.00	160.00
14-Harrison-a	13.00	40.00	90.00
15-Has #14 on-c; Matt Fox-c; Harrison-a	16.00	48.00	110.00
16-Poe adapt.-`Metzengerstein'; Rudyard Kipling adapt.-'Mark of the Beast,' by Kiefer; bondage-c	12.00	36.00	85.00
17-Matt Fox-c; Sir Walter Scott & Poe adapt	16.00	48.00	110.00

CHILLING TALES OF HORROR (Magazine)
V1#1, 6/69 - V1#7, 12/70; V2#2, 2/71 - V2#5, 10/71 (50¢, B&W, 52 pages)
Stanley Publications

	GD25	FN65	NM94
V1#1	3.20	8.00	20.00
2-7: 7-Cameron-a	1.50	3.75	9.00
V2#2,3,5: 2-Spirit of Frankenstein-r/Adventures into the Unknown #16	1.30	3.25	8.00
V2#4-r/9 pg. Feldstein-a from Adventures into the Unknown #3	1.50	3.75	9.00

NOTE: *Two issues of V2#2 exist, Feb, 1971 and April, 1971.*

CHILLY WILLY (See 4-Color #740, 852, 967, 1017, 1074, 1122, 1177, 1212, 1281)

CHINA BOY (See Wisco)

CHIP 'N' DALE (Walt Disney)(See Walt Disney's C&S #204)
Nov, 1953 - No. 30, June-Aug, 1962; Sept, 1967 - No. 83, 1982
Dell Publishing Co./Gold Key/Whitman No. 65 on

	GD25	FN65	NM94
4-Color 517(#1)	4.70	14.00	28.00
4-Color 581,636	3.00	7.50	15.00
4(12/55-2/56)-10	2.00	5.00	10.00
11-30	1.60	4.00	8.00
1(Gold Key, 1967)-Reprints	2.40	6.00	12.00
2-10	1.00	2.00	5.00
11-20		1.20	3.00
21-83			1.50

NOTE: *All Gold Key/Whitman issues have reprints except No. 32-35, 38-41, 45-47. No. 23-28, 30-42, 45-47, 49 have new covers.*

CHIP 'N DALE RESCUE RANGERS
June, 1990 - No. 19, Dec, 1991 ($1.50, color)
Disney Comics

	GD25	FN65	NM94
1-19: New stories; 1,2-Origin			1.50

CHITTY CHITTY BANG BANG (See Movie Comics)

CHOICE COMICS
Dec, 1941 - No. 3, Feb, 1942
Great Publications

	GD25	FN65	NM94
1-Origin Secret Circle; Atlas the Mighty app.; Zomba, Jungle Fight, Kangaroo Man, & Fire Eater begin	71.00	210.00	475.00
2	46.00	135.00	300.00
3-Double feature; Features movie "The Lost City" (classic cover); continued from Great Comics #3	63.00	185.00	425.00

CHOO CHOO CHARLIE
Dec, 1969
Gold Key

	GD25	FN65	NM94
1-John Stanley-a (scarce)	10.00	30.00	70.00

CHRISTIAN HEROES OF TODAY
1964 (36 pages)
David C. Cook

	GD25	FN65	NM94
nn	.80	2.00	4.00

CHRISTMAS (See A-1 No. 28)

CHRISTMAS ADVENTURE, A (See Classics Comics Giveaways, 12/69)

CHRISTMAS ADVENTURE, THE
1963 (16 pages)
S. Rose (H. L. Green Giveaway)

	GD25	FN65	NM94
nn	1.20	3.00	6.00

CHRISTMAS ALBUM (See March of Comics No. 312)

CHRISTMAS & ARCHIE
Jan, 1975 ($1.00, 68 pages) (10-1/4"x13-1/4")
Archie Comics

	GD25	FN65	NM94
1	1.70	5.00	12.00

CHRISTMAS AT THE ROTUNDA (Titled Ford Rotunda Christmas Book 1957 on) (Regular size)
Given away every Christmas at one location
1954 - 1961
Ford Motor Co. (Western Printing)

	GD25	FN65	NM94
1954-56 issues (nn's)	4.20	12.50	25.00
1957-61 issues (nn's)	4.00	10.00	20.00

CHRISTMAS BELLS (See March of Comics No. 297)

CHRISTMAS CARNIVAL
1952 (100 pages, 25 cents) (One Shot)
Ziff-Davis Publ. Co./St. John Publ. Co. No. 2

	GD25	FN65	NM94
nn	16.00	48.00	110.00
2-Reprints Ziff-Davis issue plus-c	10.00	30.00	70.00

CHRISTMAS CAROL, A (See March of Comics No. 33)

CHRISTMAS CAROL, A
No date (1942-43) (32 pgs.; 8-1/4x10-3/4"; paper cover)
Sears Roebuck & Co. (Giveaway)

	GD25	FN65	NM94
nn-Comics & coloring book	8.35	25.00	50.00

CHRISTMAS CAROL, A
1940s ? (20 pgs.)
Sears Roebuck & Co. (Christmas giveaway)

	GD25	FN65	NM94
nn-Comic book & animated coloring book	6.70	20.00	40.00

CHRISTMAS CAROLS
1959 ? (16 pgs.)
Hot Shoppes Giveaway

	GD25	FN65	NM94
nn	2.40	6.00	12.00

CHRISTMAS COLORING FUN
1964 (20 pgs.; slick cover; B&W inside)
H. Burnside

	GD25	FN65	NM94
nn	1.60	4.00	8.00

CHRISTMAS DREAM, A
1950 (16 pages) (Kinney Shoe Store Giveaway)
Promotional Publishing Co.

	GD25	FN65	NM94
nn	2.40	6.00	12.00

CHRISTMAS DREAM, A
1952? (16 pgs.; paper cover)
J. J. Newberry Co. (Giveaway)

	GD25	FN65	NM94
nn	2.40	6.00	12.00

CHRISTMAS DREAM, A
1952 (16 pgs.; paper cover)
Promotional Publ. Co. (Giveaway)

	GD25	FN65	NM94
nn	2.40	6.00	12.00

CHRISTMAS EVE, A (See March of Comics No. 212)

CHRISTMAS FUN AROUND THE WORLD
No date (early 50's) (16 pages; paper cover)
No publisher

	GD25	FN65	NM94
nn	3.20	8.00	16.00

CHRISTMAS IN DISNEYLAND (See Dell Giants)

CHRISTMAS JOURNEY THROUGH SPACE
1960
Promotional Publishing Co.

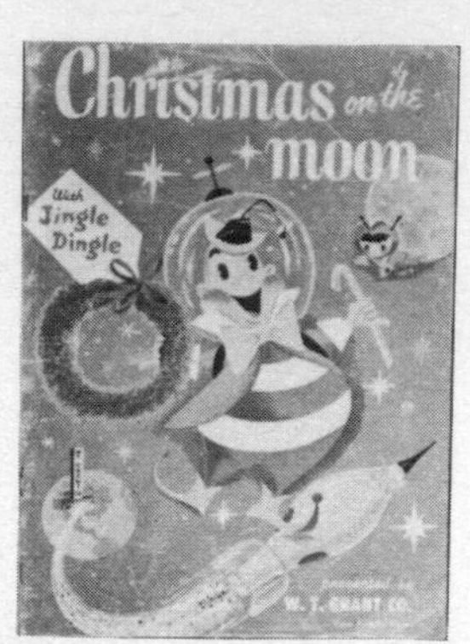

Christmas on the Moon nn, © W.T. Grant

Chromium Man #1, © Triumphant Comics

Cinderella Love #9, © Z-D

GD25 FN65 NM94

nn-Reprints 1954 issue Jolly Christmas Book with new slick cover 4.00 10.00 20.00

CHRISTMAS ON THE MOON
1958 (20 pgs.; slick cover)
W. T. Grant Co. (Giveaway)

nn 4.20 12.50 25.00

CHRISTMAS PARADE (See Dell Giant No. 26, Dell Giants, March of Comics No. 284, Walt Disney Christmas Parade & Walt Disney's...)

CHRISTMAS PARADE (Walt Disney's)
1/63 (no month) - No. 9, 1/72; Wint/88 (#1,5: 80 pgs.; #2-4,7-9: 36 pgs.)
Gold Key

1 (30018-301)-Giant 5.85 17.50 40.00
2-6: 2-r/F.C. #367 by Barks. 3-r/F.C. #178 by Barks. 4-r/F.C. #203 by Barks. 5-r/Christ. Parade #1 (Dell) by Barks; giant. 6-r/Christmas Parade #2 (Dell) by Barks (64 pgs.); giant 5.00 15.00 35.00
7,9: 7-Pull-out poster 3.60 9.00 18.00
8-r/F.C. #367 by Barks; pull-out poster 5.00 15.00 35.00

CHRISTMAS PARTY (See March of Comics No. 256)

CHRISTMAS PLAY BOOK
1946 (16 pgs.; paper cover)
Gould-Stoner Co. (Giveaway)

nn 4.20 12.50 25.00

CHRISTMAS ROUNDUP
1960
Promotional Publishing Co.

nn-Marv Levy-c/a 1.80 4.50 9.00

CHRISTMAS STORIES (See 4-Color No. 959, 1062)

CHRISTMAS STORY (See March of Comics No. 326)

CHRISTMAS STORY BOOK (See Woolworth's Christmas Story Book)

CHRISTMAS STORY CUT-OUT BOOK, THE
No. 393, 1951 (36 pages) (15 cents)
Catechetical Guild

393-Half text & half comics 4.20 12.50 25.00

CHRISTMAS TREASURY, A (See Dell Giants & March of Comics No. 227)

CHRISTMAS USA (Through 300 Years) (Also see Uncle Sam's...)
1956
Promotional Publ. Co. (Giveaway)

nn-Marv Levy-c/a 1.80 4.50 9.00

CHRISTMAS WITH ARCHIE
1973, 1974 (52 pages) (49 cents)
Spire Christian Comics (Fleming H. Revell Co.)

nn .80 2.00

CHRISTMAS WITH MOTHER GOOSE (See 4-Color No. 90, 126, 172, 201, 253)

CHRISTMAS WITH SANTA (See March of Comics No. 92)

CHRISTMAS WITH SNOW WHITE AND THE SEVEN DWARFS
1953 (16 pages, paper cover)
Kobackers Giftstore of Buffalo, N.Y.

nn 4.70 14.00 28.00

CHRISTMAS WITH THE SUPER-HEROES (See Limited Collectors' Edition)
1988; No. 2, 1989 ($2.95)(#2-All new, 68 pgs.)
DC Comics

1-(100 pgs.)-All reprints; N. Adams-r, Byrne-c; Batman, Superman, JLA, LSH Christmas stories; r-Miller's 1st Batman/DC Special Series #21 1.20 3.00
2-Superman by Chadwick, Batman, Wonder Woman, Deadman, Gr. Lantern, Flash app.; Enemy Ace by Byrne 1.20 3.00

GD25 FN65 NM94

CHRISTOPHERS, THE
1951 (36 pages) (Some copies have 15 cent sticker)
Catechetical Guild (Giveaway)

nn-Stalin as Satan in Hell 19.00 57.00 130.00

CHROMA-TICK, THE (Special Edition) (Also see The Tick)
Feb, 1992 - Present ($3.95/$3.50, color, 44 pgs.)
New England Comics Press

1,2-Includes serially numbered trading card set 1.60 4.00
3-8 ($3.50) 1.40 3.50

CHROME (Hot)(Value: cover or less)

CHROMIUM MAN
Aug, 1993 - Present ($2.50, color)
Triumphant Comics

1-1st app. Mr. Death; all serially numbered 1.00 2.50
2-6 1.00 2.50

CHRONICLES OF CORUM, THE (First)(Value: cover or less)

CHUCKLE, THE GIGGLY BOOK OF COMIC ANIMALS
1945 (132 pages) (One Shot)
R. B. Leffingwell Co.

1-Funny animal 16.00 48.00 110.00

CHUCK NORRIS (TV)
Jan, 1987 - No. 3, Sept, 1987
Star Comics (Marvel)

1-3: 1-Ditko-a 1.00

CHUCK WAGON (See Sheriff Bob Dixon's...)

CICERO'S CAT
July-Aug, 1959 - No. 2, Sept-Oct, 1959
Dell Publishing Co.

1,2-Cat from Mutt & Jeff 4.00 11.00 22.00

CIMARRON STRIP (TV)
January, 1968
Dell Publishing Co.

1 4.00 10.00 20.00

CINDER AND ASHE
May, 1988 - No. 4, Aug, 1988 ($1.75, mini-series)
DC Comics

1-4: Mature readers .70 1.75

CINDERELLA (See 4-Color No. 272, 786, & Movie Comics)

CINDERELLA
April, 1982
Whitman Publishing Co.

nn-Reprints 4-Color #272 1.00

CINDERELLA IN "FAIREST OF THE FAIR"
1955 (16 pages, 5x7-1/4", soft-c) (Walt Disney)
American Dairy Association (Premium)

nn 9.15 27.50 55.00

CINDERELLA LOVE
No. 10, 1950; No. 11, 4-5/51; No. 12, 9/51; No. 4, 10-11/51 - No. 11, Fall, 1952; No. 12, 10/53 - No. 15, 8/54; No. 25, 12/54 - No. 29, 10/55 (No #16-24)
Ziff-Davis/St. John Publ. Co. No. 12 on

10(#1)(1st Series, 1950) 8.35 25.00 50.00
11(#2, 4-5/51)-Crandall-a; Saunders painted-c 5.35 16.00 32.00
12(#3, 9/51) 4.00 12.00 24.00
4-8: 4,7-Photo-c 4.00 10.00 20.00
9-Kinstler-a; photo-c 4.70 14.00 28.00
10,11(Fall/'52): 10-Whitney painted-c. 11-Photo-c 4.00 12.00 24.00
12(St. John-10/53)-#14:13-Painted-c.14-Baker-a? 3.60 9.00 18.00
15 (8/54)-Matt Baker-c 4.00 12.00 24.00

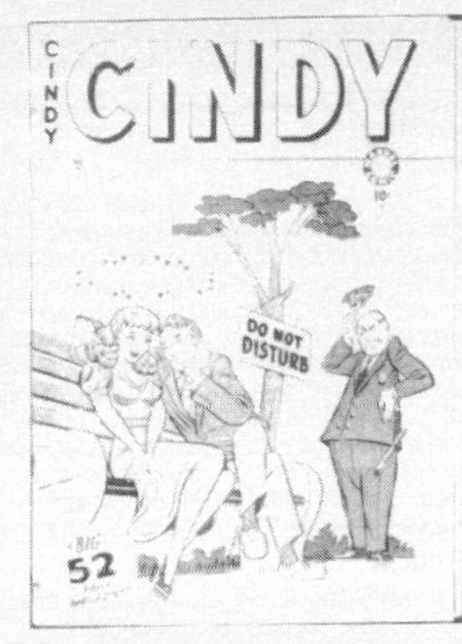

Cindy Comics #38, © MEG

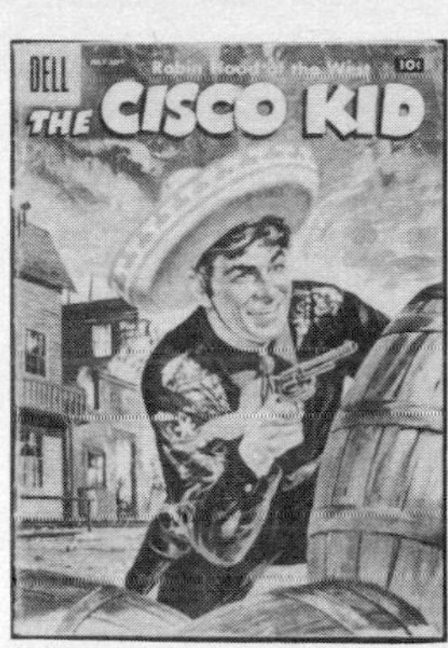

The Cisco Kid #36, © DELL

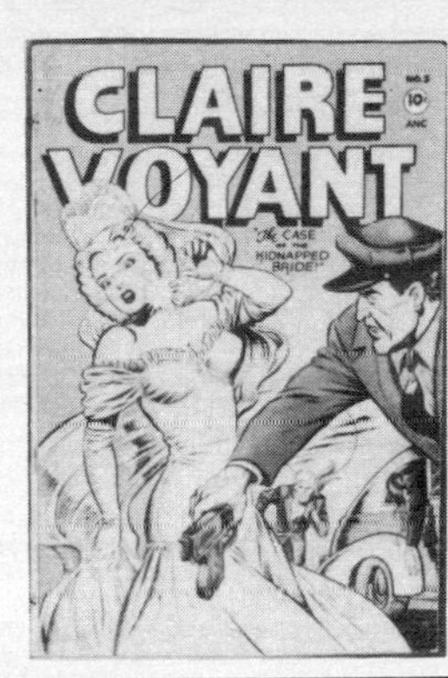

Claire Voyant #3, © STD

	GD25	FN65	NM94
25(2nd Series)(Formerly Romantic Marriage)	3.00	7.50	15.00
26-Baker-c; last precode (2/55)	4.00	12.00	24.00
27,29-Matt Baker-c	4.00	12.00	24.00
28	2.60	6.50	13.00

CINDY COMICS (...Smith No. 39, 40; Crime Can't Win No. 41 on)
(Formerly Krazy Komics)(See Junior Miss & Teen Comics)
No. 27, Fall, 1947 - No. 40, July, 1950
Timely Comics

	GD25	FN65	NM94
27-Kurtzman-a, 3 pgs: Margie, Oscar begin	10.00	30.00	70.00
28-31-Kurtzman-a	7.50	22.50	45.00
32-40: 33-Georgie story; anti-Wertham editorial	5.00	15.00	30.00

NOTE: *Kurtzman's "Hey Look"-#27(3), 29(2), 30(2), 31; "Giggles 'N' Grins"-28.*

CINEMA COMICS HERALD
1941 - 1943 (4-pg. movie "trailers," paper-c, 7-1/2x10-1/2")(Giveaway)
Paramount Pictures/Universal/RKO/20th Century Fox/Republic

	GD25	FN65	NM94
"Mr. Bug Goes to Town"-(1941)	4.20	12.50	25.00
"Bedtime Story"	4.00	11.00	22.00
"Lady For A Night," John Wayne, Joan Blondell (1942)	6.70	20.00	40.00
"Reap The Wild Wind" (1942)	4.00	11.00	22.00
"Thunder Birds" (1942)	4.00	11.00	22.00
"They All Kissed the Bride"	4.00	11.00	22.00
"Arabian Nights," (nd)	4.70	14.00	28.00
"Bombardie" (1943)	4.00	11.00	22.00
"Crash Dive" (1943)-Tyrone Power	4.70	14.00	28.00

NOTE: *The 1941-42 issues contain line art with color photos. 1943 issues are line art.*

CIRCUS (...the Comic Riot)
June, 1938 - No. 3, Aug, 1938
Globe Syndicate

	GD25	FN65	NM94
1-(Scarce)-Spacehawks (2 pgs.), & Disk Eyes by Wolverton (2 pgs.), Pewee Throttle by Cole (2nd comic book work; see Star Comics V1#11), Beau Gus, Ken Craig & The Lords of Crillon, Jack Hinton by Eisner, Van Bragger by Kane	285.00	860.00	2000.00
2,3-(Scarce)-Eisner, Cole, Wolverton, Bob Kane-a in each	157.00	470.00	1100.00

CIRCUS BOY (See 4-Color No. 759, 785, 813 & Movie Classics)

CIRCUS COMICS
1945 - No. 2, June, 1945; Winter, 1948-49
Farm Women's Publishing Co./D. S. Publ.

	GD25	FN65	NM94
1-Funny animal	7.50	22.50	45.00
2	5.00	15.00	30.00
1(1948)-D.S. Publ.; 2 pgs. Frazetta	16.00	48.00	110.00

CIRCUS OF FUN COMICS
1945 - No. 3, Dec, 1947 (A book of games & puzzles)
A. W. Nugent Publishing Co.

	GD25	FN65	NM94
1	9.15	27.50	55.00
2,3	5.85	17.50	35.00

CISCO KID, THE (TV)
July, 1950 - No. 41, Oct-Dec, 1958
Dell Publishing Co.

	GD25	FN65	NM94
4-Color 292(#1)-Cisco Kid, his horse Diablo, & sidekick Pancho & his horse Loco begin; painted-c begin	18.00	54.00	125.00
2(1/51)-5	10.00	30.00	60.00
6-10	8.35	25.00	50.00
11-20	6.70	20.00	40.00
21-36-Last painted-c	5.00	15.00	30.00
37-41: All photo-c	10.00	30.00	60.00

NOTE: ***Buscema** a-40. **Ernest Nordli** painted-c-5-16, 20, 35.*

CISCO KID COMICS
Winter, 1944 - No. 3?, 1945
Bernard Bailey/Swappers Quarterly

	GD25	FN65	NM94
1-Illustrated Stories of the Operas: Faust; Funnyman by Giunta; Cisco Kid (1st app.) & Superbaby begin; Giunta-c	32.00	95.00	225.00
2,3 (Exist?)	24.00	70.00	165.00

CITIZEN SMITH (See Holyoke One-Shot No. 9)

CITY OF THE LIVING DEAD (See Fantastic Tales No. 1)
1952
Avon Periodicals

	GD25	FN65	NM94
nn-Hollingsworth-c/a	24.00	70.00	165.00

CITY SURGEON (Blake Harper...)
August, 1963
Gold Key

	GD25	FN65	NM94
1(10075-308)-Painted-c	2.00	5.00	10.00

CIVIL WAR MUSKET, THE (Kadets of America Handbook)
1960 (36 pages) (Half-size; 25 cents)
Custom Comics, Inc.

	GD25	FN65	NM94
nn	2.80	7.00	14.00

CLAIRE VOYANT (Also see Keen Teens)
1946 - No. 4, 1947 (Sparling strip reprints)
Leader Publ./Standard/Pentagon Publ.

	GD25	FN65	NM94
nn	32.00	95.00	220.00
2,4: 2-Kamen-c. 4-Kamen bondage-c	25.00	75.00	175.00
3-Kamen bridal-c; contents mentioned in Love and Death, a book by Gershom Legman('49) referenced by Dr. Wertham	29.00	85.00	200.00

CLANCY THE COP
1930 - No. 2, 1931 (52 pages; B&W) (not reprints) (10"x10")
Dell Publishing Co. (Soft cover)

	GD25	FN65	NM94
1,2-Vep-a	13.5s0	41.00	95.00

CLASH
1991 - No. 3, 1991 ($4.95, color, mini-series, 52 pgs.)
DC Comics

	GD25	FN65	NM94
Book One - Three: Adam Kubert-c/a	1.00	2.50	5.00

CLASSIC COMICS/ILLUSTRATED - INTRODUCTION
by Dan Malan

Further revisions have been made to help in understanding the **Classics** section. **Classics** reprint editions prior to 1963 had either incorrect dates or no dates listed. Those reprint editions should be identified only by the highest number on the reorder list (HRN). Past price guides listed what were calculated to be approximately correct dates, but many people found it confusing for the price guide to list a date not listed in the comic itself.

We have also attempted to clear up confusion about edition variations, such as color, printer, etc. Such variations will be identified by letters. Editions will now be determined by three categories. Original edition variations will be Edition 1A, 1B, etc. All reprint editions prior to 1963 will be identified by HRN only. All reprint editions from 9/63 on will be identified by the correct date listed in the comic.

We have also included new information on four recent reprintings of **Classics** not previously listed. From 1968-1976 Twin Circle, the Catholic newspaper, serialized over 100 **Classics** titles. That list can be found under non-series items at the end of this section. In 1972 twelve **Classics** were reissued as **Now Age Books Illustrated**. They are listed under **Pendulum Illustrated Classics**. In 1982, 20 **Classics** were reissued, adapted for teaching English as a second language. They are listed under **Regents Illustrated Classics**. Then in 1984, six **Classics** were reissued with cassette tapes. See the listing under **Cassette Books**.

UNDERSTANDING CLASSICS ILLUSTRATED
by Dan Malan

Since **Classics Illustrated** is the most complicated comic book series, with all its reprint editions and variations, with changes in covers and artwork, with a variety of means of identifying editions, and with the most extensive worldwide distribution of any comic-book series; therefore this introductory section is provided to assist you in gaining expertise about this series.

THE HISTORY OF CLASSICS

The **Classics** series was the brain child of Albert L. Kanter, who saw in the new comic-book medium a means of introducing children to the great classics of literature. In October of 1941 his Gilberton Co. began the **Classic Comics** series with **The Three Musketeers**, with 64 pages of storyline. In those early years, the struggling series saw irregular schedules and numerous printers, not to mention variable art quality and liberal story adaptations. With No.13 the page total was reduced to 56 (except for No. 33, originally scheduled to be No. 9), and with No. 15 the coming-next ad on the outside back cover moved inside. In 1945 the Jerry Iger Shop began producing all new CC titles, beginning with No. 23. In 1947 the search for a classier logo resulted in **Classics Illustrated**, beginning with No. 35, The **Last Days of Pompeii**. With No. 45 the page total dropped again to 48, which was to become the standard.

Two new developments in 1951 had a profound effect upon the success of the series. One was the introduction of painted covers, instead of the old line drawn covers, beginning with No. 81, **The Odyssey**. The second was the switch to the major national distributor Curtis. They raised the cover price from 10 to 15 cents, making it the highest priced comic-book, but it did not slow the growth of the series, because they were marketed as books, not comics. Because of this higher quality image, **Classics** flourished during the fifties while other comic series were reeling from outside attacks. They diversified with their new **Juniors**, **Specials**, and **World Around Us** series.

Classics artwork can be divided into three distinct periods. The pre-Iger era (1941-44) was mentioned above for its variable art quality. The Iger era (1945-53) was a major improvement in art quality and adaptations. It came to be dominated by artists Henry Kiefer and Alex Blum, together accounting for some 50 titles. Their styles gave the first real personality to the series. The EC era (1954-62) resulted from the demise of the EC horror series, when many of their artists made the major switch to classical art.

But several factors brought the production of new CI titles to a complete halt in 1962. Gilberton lost its 2nd class mailing permit. External factors like television, cheap paperback books, and Cliff Notes were all eating away at their market. Production halted with No.167, **Faust**, even though many more titles were already in the works. Many of those found their way into foreign series, and are very desirable to collectors. In 1967, **Classics Illustrated** was sold to Patrick Frawley and his Catholic publication, Twin Circle. They issued two new titles in 1969 as part of an attempted revival, but succumbed to major distribution problems in 1971. In 1988, the trio: First Publishing, Berkley Press, and Classics Media Group acquired the use rights for the old CI series art, logo, and name from the Frawley Group. So far they have used only the name in the new series, but do have plans to reprint the old CI.

One of the unique aspects of the **Classics Illustrated** (CI) series was the proliferation of reprint variations. Some titles had as many as 25 editions. Reprinting began in 1943. Some **Classic Comics** (CC) reprints (r) had the logo format revised to a banner logo, and added a motto under the banner. In 1947 CC titles changed to the CI logo, but kept their line drawn covers (LDC). In 1948, Nos. 13, 18, 29 and 41 received second covers (LDC2), replacing covers considered too violent, and reprints of Nos. 13-44 had pages reduced to 48, except for No. 26, which had 48 pages to begin with.

Starting in the mid-1950s, 70 of the 80 LDC titles were reissued with new painted covers (PC). Thirty of them also received new interior artwork (A2). The new artwork was generally higher quality with larger art panels and more faithful but abbreviated storylines. Later on, there were 29 second painted covers (PC2), mostly by Twin Circle. Altogether there were 199 interior art variations (169 (O)s and 30 A2 editions) and 272 different covers (169 (O)s, four LDC2s, 70 new PCs of LDC (O)s, and 29 PC2s). It is mildly astounding to realize that there are nearly 1400 different editions in the U.S. CI series.

FOREIGN CLASSICS ILLUSTRATED

If U.S. **Classics** variations are mildly astounding, the veritable plethora of foreign CI variations will boggle your imagination. While we still anticipate additional discoveries, we presently know about series in 25 languages and 27 countries. There were 250 new CI titles in foreign series, and nearly 400 new foreign covers of U.S. titles. The 1400 U.S. CI editions pale in comparison to the 4000[foreign editions. The very nature of CI lent itself to flourishing as an international series. Worldwide, they published over one billion copies! The first foreign CI series consisted of six Canadian **Classic Comic** reprints in 1946.

Here is a chart showing when CI series first began in each country:

1946: Canada. 1947: Australia. 1948: Brazil/The Netherlands. 1950: Italy. 1951: Greece/Japan/Hong Kong(?)/England/Argentina/Mexico. 1952: West Germany. 1954: Norway. 1955: New Zealand/South Africa. 1956: Denmark/Sweden/Iceland. 1957: Finland/France. 1962: Singapore(?). 1964: India (8 languages). 1971: Ireland (Gaelic). 1973: Belgium(?) /Philippines(?) & Malaysia(?).

Significant among the early series were Brazil and Greece. In 1950, Brazil was the first country to begin doing its own new titles. They issued nearly 80 new CI titles by Brazilian authors. In Greece in 1951 they actually had debates in parliament about the effects of **Classics Illustrated** on Greek culture, leading to the inclusion of 88 new Greek History & Mythology titles in the CI series.

But by far the most important foreign CI development was the joint European series which began in 1956 in 10 countries simultaneously. By 1960, CI had the largest European distribution of any American publication, not just comics! So when all the problems came up with U.S. distribution, they literally moved the CI operation to Europe in 1962, and continued producing new titles in all four CI series. Many of them were adapted and drawn in the U.S., the most famous of which was the British CI #158A. Dr. No, drawn by Norman Nodel. Unfortunately, the British CI series ended in late 1963, which limited the European CI titles available in English to 15. Altogether there were 82 new CI art titles in the joint European series, which ran until 1976.

CLASSICS REFERENCE INFORMATION

The Classics Collector Magazine (formerly **Worldwide Classics Newsletter**) (1987-1993) Dan Malan, Editor/Publisher. This magazine is the nerve center of the classics-collecting hobby, with subscribers in 22 countries. It covers the official CI series (old and new), related classical comic-book series, foreign series, various memorabilia collectibles, and even illustrated books. Features include new discoveries, market analysis, interviews, pictorials, artist info, and classical ads. It is available by subscription directly from the publisher at 7519 Lindbergh Dr., St. Louis, MO 63117, or at local comic specialty shops.

THE COMPLETE GUIDE TO CLASSICS COLLECTIBLES, Volumes One (U.S.) and Two (foreign series) are both now available. Each contains about 800 color photos, plus complete historical, edition, and pricing information, much more than can be covered here. Both are written by Dan Malan, and are available through the same channels as the above TCC.

IDENTIFYING CLASSICS EDITIONS

HRN: This is the highest number on the reorder list. It should be listed in ( ) after the title number. It is crucial to understanding various CI editions.

ORIGINALS (O): This is the all-important First Edition. To determine (O)s,there is one primary rule and two secondary rules (with exceptions):

Rule No. 1: All (O)s and only (O)s have coming-next ads for the next number. **Exceptions**: No. 14(15) (reprint) has an ad on the last inside text page only. No. 14(0) also has a full-page outside back cover ad (also rule 2). Nos.55(75) and 57(75) have coming-next ads. (Rules 2 and 3 apply here). Nos. 168(0) and 169(0) do not have coming-next ads. No.168 was never reprinted; No. 169(0) has HRN (166). No. 169(169) is the only reprint.

Rule No. 2: On nos.1-80, all (O)s and only (O)s list 10c on the front cover. **Exceptions**: Reprint variations of Nos. 37(62), 39(71), and 46(62) list 10c on the front cover. (Rules 1 and 3 apply here.)

Rule No. 3: All (O)s have HRN close to that title No. **Exceptions**: Some reprints also have HRNs close to that title number: a few CC(r)s, 58(62), 60(62), 149(149), 152(149) 153(149), and title nos. in the 160's. (Rules 1 and 2 apply here.)

DATES: Many reprint editions list either an incorrect date or no date. Since Gilberton apparently kept track of CI editions by HRN, they often left the (O) date on reprints. Often, someone with a CI collection for sale will swear that all their copies are originals. That is why we are so detailed in pointing out how to identify original editions. Except for original editions, which should have a coming-next ad, etc., all CI dates prior to 1963 are incorrect! So you want to go by HRN only if it is (165) or below, and go by listed date if it is 1963 or later. There are a few (167) editions with incorrect dates. They could be listed either as (167) or (62/3), which is meant to indicate that they were issued sometime between late 1962 and early 1963.

COVERS: A change from CC to LDC indicates a logo change, not a cover change; while a change from LDC to LDC2, LDC to PC, or from PC to PC2 does indicate a new cover. New PCs can be identified by HRN, and PC2s can be identified by HRN and date. Several covers had color changes, particularly from purple to blue.

Notes: If you see 15 cents in Canada on a front cover, it does not necessarily indicate a Canadian edition. Editions with an HRN between 44 and 75, with 15 cents on the cover are Canadian. Check the publisher's address. An HRN listing two numbers with a / between them indicates that there are two different reorder lists in the front and back covers. Official Twin Circle editions have a full-page back cover ad for their TC magazine, with no CI reorder list. Any CI with just a Twin Circle sticker on the front is not an official TC edition.

TIPS ON LISTING CLASSICS FOR SALE

It may be easy to just list Edition 17, but Classics collectors keep track of CI editions in terms of HRN and/or date, (O) or (r), CC or LDC, PC or PC2, A1 or A2, soft or stiff cover, etc. Try to help them out. For originals, just list (0), unless there are variations such as color (Nos. 10 and 61), printer (Nos. 18-22), HRN (Nos. 95, 108, 160), etc. For reprints, just list HRN if its (165) or below. Above that, list HRN and date. Also, please list type of logo/cover/art for the convenience of buyers. They will appreciate it.

CLASSIC COMICS (Also see Best from Boys Life, Cassette Books, Famous Stories, Fast Fiction, Golden Picture Classics, King Classics, Marvel Classics Comics, Pendulum Illustrated Classics, Picture Parade, Picture Progress, Regents Ill. Classics, Spitfire, Stories by Famous Authors, Superior Stories, and World Around Us.)

CLASSIC COMICS (Classics Illustrated No. 35 on)
10/41 - No. 34, 2/47; No. 35, 3/47 - No. 169, Spring 1969
(Reprint Editions of almost all titles 5/43 - Spring 1971)
(Painted Covers (0)s No. 81 on, and (r)s of most Nos. 1-80)
Elliot Publishing #1-3 (1941-1942)/Gilberton Publications #4-167 (1942-1967)/
Twin Circle Pub. (Frawley) #168-169 (1968-1971)

Abbreviations:
A–Art; C or c–Cover; CC–Classic Comics; CI–Classics Ill.;
Ed–Edition; LDC–Line Drawn Cover; PC–Painted Cover; r–Reprint

1. The Three Musketeers

Ed	HRN	Date	Details	A	C			
1	–	10/41	Date listed-1941; Elliot Pub; 68 pgs.	1	1	457.00	1370.00	3200.00
2	10	–	10¢ price removed on all (r)s; Elliot Pub; CC-r	1	1	26.00	809.00	185.00
3	15	–	Long Isl. Ind. Ed.; CC-r	1	1	19.00	57.00	130.00

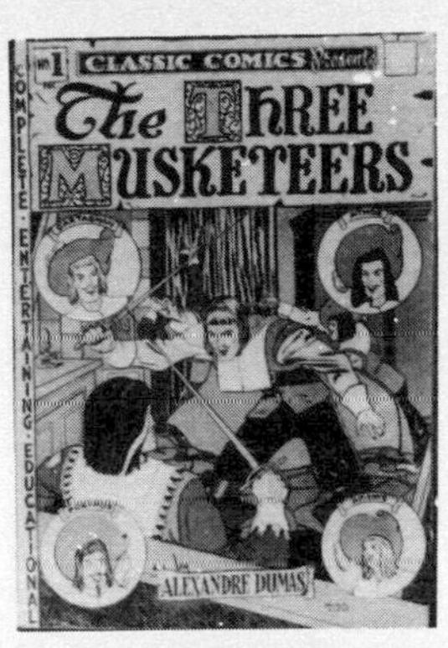

Classic Comics #1 (Orig.), © GIL

Classic Comics #3, © GIL

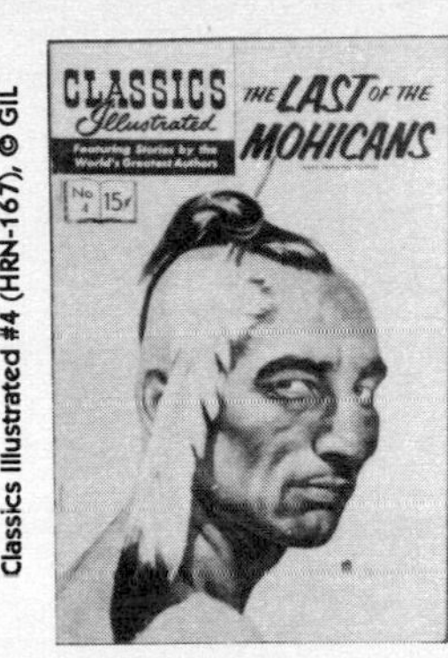

Classics Illustrated #4 (HRN-167), © GIL

Ed	HRN	Date	Details	A	C	GD25	FN65	NM94
4	18/20		Sunrise Times Ed.; CC-r	1	1	15.00	45.00	105.00
5	21	–	Richmond Courior Ed.; CC-r	1	1	13.50	41.00	05.00
6	28	1946	CC-r	1	1	10.00	30.00	70.00
7	36	–	LDC-r	1	1	5.85	17.50	35.00
8	60	–	LDC-r	1	1	4.00	11.00	22.00
9	64	–	LDC-r	1	1	3.60	9.00	18.00
10	78	–	C-price 15¢;LDC-r	1	1	3.20	8.00	16.00
11	93	–	LDC-r	1	1	3.20	8.00	16.00
12	114	–	Last LDC-r	1	1	2.40	6.00	12.00
13	134	–	New-c; old-a; 64 pg. PC-r	1	2	2.40	6.00	12.00
14	143	–	Old-a; PC-r; 64 pg.	1	2	2.00	5.00	10.00
15	150	–	New-a; PC-r; Evans/Crandall-a	2	2	2.40	6.00	12.00
16	149	–	PC-r	2	2	1.25	2.50	5.00
17	167	–	PC-r	2	2	1.25	2.50	5.00
18	167	4/64	PC-r	2	2	1.25	2.50	5.00
19	167	1/65	PC-r	2	2	1.25	2.50	5.00
20	167	3/66	PC-r	2	2	1.25	2.50	5.00
21	166	11/67	PC-r	2	2	1.25	2.50	5.00
22	166	Spr/69	C-price 25¢ ; stiff-c; PC-r	2	2	1.25	2.50	5.00
23	169	Spr/71	PC-r; stiff-c	2	2	1.25	2.50	5.00

2. Ivanhoe

Ed	HRN	Date	Details	A	C	GD25	FN65	NM94
1	(O)	12/41?	Date listed-1941, Elliot Pub; 68 pgs.	1	1	170.00	515.00	1200.00
2	10	–	Price & 'Presents' removed; Elliot Pub; CC-r	1	1	23.00	70.00	160.00
3	15	–	Long Isl. Ind. ed.; CC-r	1	1	17.00	52.00	120.00
4	18/20		Sunrise Times ed.; CC-r	1	1	15.00	45.00	105.00
5	21	–	Richmond Courier ed.; CC-r	1	1	13.50	41.00	95.00
6	28	1946	Last 'Comics'-r	1	1	10.00	30.00	70.00
7	36	–	1st LDC-r	1	1	5.85	17.50	35.00
8	60	–	LDC-r	1	1	4.00	11.00	22.00
9	64	–	LDC-r	1	1	4.00	10.00	20.00
10	78	–	C-price 15¢; LDC-r	1	1	3.20	8.00	16.00
11	89	–	LDC-r	1	1	2.80	7.00	14.00
12	106	–	LDC-r	1	1	2.40	6.00	12.00
13	121	–	Last LDC-r	1	1	2.40	6.00	12.00
14	136	–	New-c&a; PC-r	2	2	2.80	7.00	14.00
15	142	–	PC-r	2	2	1.25	2.50	5.00
16	153	–	PC-r	2	2	1.25	2.50	5.00
17	149	–	PC-r	2	2	1.25	2.50	5.00
18	167	–	PC-r	2	2	1.25	2.50	5.00
19	167	5/64	PC-r	2	2	1.25	2.50	5.00
20	167	1/65	PC-r	2	2	1.25	2.50	5.00
21	167	3/66	PC-r	2	2	1.25	2.50	5.00
22A	166	9/67	PC-r	2	2	1.25	2.50	5.00
22B	166	–	Center ad for Children's Digest & Young Miss; rare; PC-r	2	2	8.35	25.00	50.00
23	166	R/68	C-Price 25¢; PC-r	2	2	1.25	2.50	5.00
24	169	Win/69	Stiff-c	2	2	1.25	2.50	5.00
25	169	Win/71 I	PC-r; stiff-c	2	2	1.25	2.50	5.00

3. The Count of Monte Cristo

Ed	HRN	Date	Details	A	C	GD25	FN65	NM94
1	(O)	3/42	Elliot Pub; 68 pgs.	1	1	121.00	365.00	850.00
2	10	–	Conray Prods; CC-r	1	1	123.00	70.00	160.00
3	15	–	Long Isl. Ind. ed.; CC-r	1	1	17.00	52.00	120.00
4	18/20		Sunrise Times ed.; CC-r	1	1	15.00	45.00	105.00
5	20	–	Sunrise Times ed.; CC-r	1	1	13.50	41.00	95.00
6	21	–	Richmond Courier ed.; CC-r	1	1	13.00	40.00	90.00
7	28	1946	CC-r; new Banner logo	1	1	10.00	30.00	70.00
8	36	–	1st LDC-r	1	1	5.85	17.50	35.00
9	60	–	LDC-r	1	1	4.00	11.00	22.00
10	62	–	LDC-r	1	1	4.35	13.00	26.00
11	71	–	LDC-r	1	1	3.60	9.00	18.00
12	87		C-price 15¢; LDC-r	1	1	3.20	8.00	16.00
13	113	–	LDC-r	1	1	2.40	6.00	12.00
14	135	–	New-c&a; PC-r	2	2	2.40	6.00	12.00
15	143	–	PC-r	2	2	1.25	2.50	5.00
16	153	–	PC-r	2	2	1.25	2.50	5.00
17	161	–	PC-r	2	2	1.25	2.50	5.00
18	167	–	PC-r	2	2	1.25	2.50	5.00
19	167	7/64	PC-r	2	2	1.25	2.50	5.00
20	167	7/65	PC-r	2	2	1.25	2.50	5.00
21	167	7/66	PC-r	2	2	1.25	2.50	5.00
22	166	R/68	C-price 25¢; PC-r	2	2	1.25	2.50	5.00
23	169	–	Win/69 Stiff-c; PC-r	2	2	1.25	2.50	5.00

4. The Last of the Mohicans

Ed	HRN	Date	Details	A	C	GD25	FN65	NM94
1	(O)	8/42?	Date listed-1942; Gilberton #4(0) on; 68 pgs.	1	1	107.00	320.00	750.00
2	12	–	Elliot Pub; CC-r	1	1	22.00	65.00	150.00
3	15	–	Long Isl. Ind. ed.; CC-r	1	1	17.00	52.00	120.00
4	20	–	Long Isl. Ind. ed.; CC-r; banner logo	1	1	15.00	45.00	105.00
5	21	–	Queens Home News ed.; CC-r	1	1	13.50	41.00	95.00
6	28	1946	Last CC-r; new	1	1	10.00	30.00	70.00
7	36	–	1st LDC-r	1	1	5.85	17.50	35.00
8	60	–	LDC-r	1	1	4.00	11.00	22.00
9	64	–	LDC-r	1	1	3.60	9.00	18.00
10	78	–	C-price 15¢; LDC-r	1	1	3.20	8.00	16.00
11	89	–	LDC-r	1	1	2.80	7.00	14.00
12	117	–	Last LDC-r	1	1	2.40	6.00	12.00
13	135	–	New-c; PC-r	1	2	2.40	6.00	12.00
14	141	–	PC-r	1	2	2.00	5.00	10.00
15	150	–	New-a; PC-r; Severin, L.B. Cole-a	2	2	2.40	6.00	12.00
16	161	–	PC-r	2	2	1.25	2.50	5.00
17	167	–	PC-r	2	2	1.25	2.50	5.00
18	167	6/64	PC-r	2	2	1.25	2.50	5.00
19	167	8/65	PC-r	2	2	1.25	2.50	5.00
20	167	8/66	PC-r	2	2	1.25	2.50	5.00
21	166	R/67	C-price 25¢; PC-r	2	2	1.25	2.50	5.00
22	169	Spr/69	Stiff-c; PC-r	2	2	1.25	2.50	5.00

5. Moby Dick

Ed	HRN	Date	Details	A	C	GD25	FN65	NM94
1	(O)	9/42?	Date listed-1942; Gilberton; 68 pgs.	1	1	129.00	385.00	900.00
2	10	–	Conray Prods; Pg. 64 changed from 105 title list to letter from Editor; CC-r	1	1	23.00	70.00	160.00
3	15	–	Long Isl. Ind. ed.;	1	1	17.00	52.00	120.00

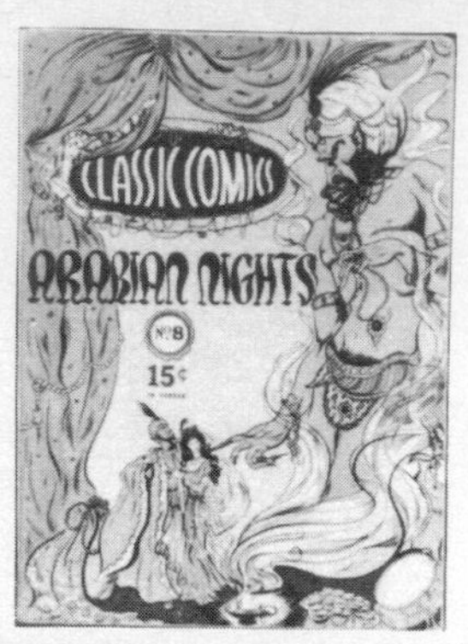

Classic Comics #8 (HRN-20), © GIL

Classics Illustrated #8 (HRN-51), © GIL

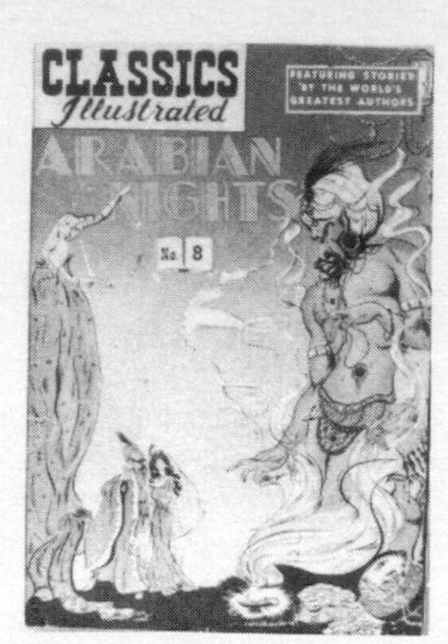

Classics Illustrated #9 (HRN-51), © GIL

Ed	HRN	Date	Details	A	C	GD25	FN65	NM94
			Pg. 64 changed from Letter to the Editor to Ill. poem-Concord Hymn; CC-r					
4	18/20	–	Sunrise Times ed.; CC-r	1	1	16.00	48.00	110.00
5	20	–	Sunrise Times ed.; CC-r	1	1	15.00	45.00	105.00
6	21	–	Sunrise Times ed.; CC-r	1	1	13.50	41.00	95.00
7	28	1946	CC-r; new banner logo	1	1	10.00	30.00	70.00
8	36	–	1st LDC-r	1	1	5.85	17.50	35.00
9	60	–	LDC-r	1	1	4.00	11.00	22.00
10	62	–	LDC-r	1	1	4.35	13.00	26.00
11	71	–	LDC-r	1	1	3.60	9.00	18.00
12	87	–	C-price 15¢; LDC-r	1	1	3.20	8.00	16.00
13	118	–	LDC-r	1	1	2.40	6.00	12.00
14	131	–	New c&a; PC-r	2	2	2.40	6.00	12.00
15	138	–	PC-r	2	2	1.25	2.50	5.00
16	148	–	PC-r	2	2	1.25	2.50	5.00
17	158	–	PC-r	2	2	1.25	2.50	5.00
18	167	–	PC-r	2	2	1.25	2.50	5.00
19	167	6/64	PC-r	2	2	1.25	2.50	5.00
20	167	7/65	PC-r	2	2	1.25	2.50	5.00
21	167	3/66	PC-r	2	2	1.25	2.50	5.00
22	166	9/67	PC-r	2	2	1.25	2.50	5.00
23	166	Win/69	New-c & c-price 25¢; Stiff-c; PC-r	2	3	2.00	5.00	10.00
24	169	Win/71	PC-r	2	3	2.00	5.00	10.00

6. A Tale of Two Cities

Ed	HRN	Date	Details	A	C	GD25	FN65	NM94
1	(O)	10/42	Date listed-1942; 68 pgs. Zeckerberg c/a	1	1	110.00	330.00	775.00
2	14	–	Elliot Pub; CC-r	1	1	20.00	60.00	140.00
3	18	–	Long Isl. Ind. ed.; CC-r	1	1	17.00	50.00	115.00
4	20	–	Sunrise Times ed.; CC-r	1	1	15.00	45.00	105.00
5	28	1946	Last CC-r; new banner logo	1	1	10.00	30.00	70.00
6	51	–	1st LDC-r	1	1	5.35	16.00	32.00
7	64	–	LDC-r	1	1	4.00	10.50	21.00
8	78	–	C-price 15¢; LDC-r	1	1	3.20	8.00	16.00
9	89	–	LDC-r	1	1	2.40	6.00	12.00
10	117	–	LDC-r	1	1	2.40	6.00	12.00
11	132	–	New-c&a; PC-r; Joe Orlando-a	2	2	2.40	6.00	12.00
12	140	–	PC-r	2	2	1.25	2.50	5.00
13	147	–	PC-r	2	2	1.25	2.50	5.00
14	152	–	PC-r; very rare	2	2	11.50	34.00	80.00
15	153	–	PC-r	2	2	1.25	2.50	5.00
16	149	–	PC-r	2	2	1.25	2.50	5.00
17	167	–	PC-r	2	2	1.25	2.50	5.00
18	167	6/64	PC-r	2	2	1.25	2.50	5.00
19	167	8/65	PC-r	2	2	1.25	2.50	5.00
20	166	5/67	PC-r	2	2	1.25	2.50	5.00
21	166	Fall/68	New-c & 25¢; PC-r	2	3	2.00	5.00	10.00
22	169	Sum/70	Stiff-c; PC-r	2	3	2.00	5.00	10.00

7. Robin Hood

Ed	HRN	Date	Details	A	C	GD25	FN65	NM94
1	(O)	12/42	Date listed-1942; first Gift Box ad-bc; 68 pgs.	1	1	85.00	257.00	600.00
2	12	–	Elliot Pub; CC-r	1	1	20.00	60.00	140.00
3	18	–	Long Isl. Ind. ed.; CC-r	1	1	16.00	48.00	110.00
4	20	–	Nassau Bulletin ed.; CC-r	1	1	15.00	45.00	105.00
5	22	–	Queens Cty. Times ed.; CC-r	1	1	13.50	41.00	95.00
6	28	–	CC-r	1	1	10.00	30.00	70.00
7	51	–	LDC-r	1	1	5.35	16.00	32.00
8	64	–	LDC-r	1	1	4.00	10.50	21.00
9	78	–	LDC-r	1	1	3.20	8.00	16.00
10	97	–	LDC-r	1	1	2.80	7.00	14.00
11	106	–	LDC-r	1	1	2.40	6.00	12.00
12	121	–	LDC-r	1	1	2.40	6.00	12.00
13	129	–	New-c; PC-r	1	2	2.40	6.00	12.00
14	136	–	New-a; PC-r	2	2	2.40	6.00	12.00
15	143	–	PC-r	2	2	1.25	2.50	5.00
16	153	–	PC-r	2	2	1.25	2.50	5.00
17	164	–	PC-r	2	2	1.25	2.50	5.00
18	167	–	PC-r	2	2	1.25	2.50	5.00
19	167	6/64	PC-r	2	2	1.50	3.00	6.00
20	167	5/65	PC-r	2	2	1.25	2.50	5.00
21	167	7/66	PC-r	2	2	1.25	2.50	5.00
22	166	12/67	PC-r	2	2	1.50	3.00	6.00
23	169	Sum/69	Stiff-c; c-price 25¢; PC-r	2	2	1.25	2.50	5.00

8. Arabian Nights

Ed	HRN	Date	Details	A	C	GD25	FN65	NM94
1	(O)	2/43	Original; 68 pgs. Lilian Chestney-c/a	1	1	229.00	685.00	1600.00
2	17	–	Long Isl. ed.; pg. 64 changed from Gift Box ad to Letter from British Medical Worker; CC-r	1	1	79.00	235.00	550.00
3	20	–	Nassau Bulletin; Pg. 64 changed from letter to article-Three Men Named Smith; CC-r	1	1	64.00	192.00	450.00
4	28	1946	CC-r; new banner logo	1	1	47.00	140.00	325.00
5	51	–	LDC-r	1	1	25.00	75.00	175.00
6	64	–	LDC-r	1	1	19.00	57.00	130.00
7	78	–	LDC-r	1	1	17.00	51.00	120.00
8	164	–	New-c&a; PC-r	2	2	14.00	43.00	100.00

9. Les Miserables

Ed	HRN	Date	Details	A	C	GD25	FN65	NM94
1A	(O)	3/43	Original; slick paper cover; 68 pgs.	1	1	75.00	225.00	525.00
1B	(O)	3/43	Original; rough, pulp type-c; 68 pgs.	1	1	79.00	235.00	550.00
2	14	–	Elliot Pub; CC-r	1	1	22.00	65.00	150.00
3	18	3/44	Nassau Bul. Pg. 64 changed from Gift Box ad to Bill of Rights article; CC-r	1	1	17.00	52.00	120.00
4	20	–	Richmond Courier ed.; CC-r	1	1	14.00	43.00	100.00
5	28	1946	Gilberton; pgs. 60-64 rearranged/ illos added; CC-r	1	1	11.00	32.00	75.00
6	51	–	LDC-r	1	1	5.85	17.50	35.00
7	71	–	LDC-r	1	1	4.35	13.00	26.00
8	87	–	C-price 15¢; LDC-r	1	1	4.00	10.50	21.00
9	161	–	New-c&a; PC-r	2	2	4.00	12.00	24.00
10	167	9/63	PC-r	2	2	3.20	8.00	16.00

Classic Comics #10 (HRN-14), © GIL

Classic Comics #12 (HRN-20), © GIL

Classic Comics #14 (HRN-21), © GIL

Ed	HRN	Date	Details	A	C	GD25	FN65	NM94
11	167	12/65	PC-r	2	2	3.20	8.00	16.00
12	166	R/1968	New-c & price 25¢; PC-r	2	3	3.60	9.00	18.00

10. Robinson Crusoe (Used in SOTI, pg. 142)

Ed	HRN	Date	Details	A	C	GD25	FN65	NM94
1A	(O)	4/43	Original; Violet-c; 68 pgs; Zuckerberg c/a	1	1	75.00	225.00	525.00
1B	(O)	4/43	Original; blue-grey -c, 68 pgs.	1	1	79.00	235.00	550.00
2A	14	–	Elliot Pub; violet-c; 68 pgs; CC-r	1	1	20.00	60.00	140.00
2B	14	–	Elliot Pub; blue-grey-c; CC-r	1	1	22.00	65.00	150.00
3	18	–	Nassau Bul. Pg. 64 changed from Gift Box ad to Bill of Rights article; CC-r	1	1	16.00	48.00	110.00
4	20	–	Queens Home News ed.; CC-r	1	1	13.50	41.00	95.00
5	28	1946	Gilberton; pg. 64 changes from Bill-Rights to WWII article-One Leg Shot Away; last CC-r	1	1	10.00	30.00	70.00
6	51	–	LDC-r	1	1	5.35	16.00	32.00
7	64	–	LDC-r	1	1	4.00	10.50	21.00
8	78	–	C-price 15¢; LDC-r	1	1	3.20	8.00	16.00
9	97	–	LDC-r	1	1	2.80	7.00	14.00
10	114	–	LDC-r	1	1	2.40	6.00	12.00
11	130	–	New-c; PC-r	1	2	2.40	6.00	12.00
12	140	–	New-a; PC-r	2	2	2.40	6.00	12.00
13	153	–	PC-r	2	2	1.25	2.50	5.00
14	164	–	PC-r	2	2	1.25	2.50	5.00
15	167	–	PC-r	2	2	1.25	2.50	5.00
16	167	7/64	PC-r	2	2	1.25	2.50	5.00
17	167	5/65	PC-r	2	2	1.80	4.50	9.00
18	167	6/66	PC-r	2	2	1.25	2.50	5.00
19	166	Fall/68	C-price 25¢; PC-r	2	2	1.25	2.50	5.00
20	166	R/68	(No Twin Circle ad)	2	2	1.50	3.00	6.00
21	169	Sm/70	Stiff-c; PC-r	2	2	1.50	3.00	6.00

11. Don Quixote

Ed	HRN	Date	Details	A	C	GD25	FN65	NM94
1	10	5/43	First (O) with HRN list; 68 pgs.	1	1	79.00	235.00	550.00
2	18	–	Nassau Bulletin ed.; CC-r	1	1	20.00	60.00	140.00
3	21	–	Queens Home News ed.; CC-r	1	1	16.00	48.00	110.00
4	28	–	CC-r	1	1	10.00	30.00	70.00
5	110	–	New-PC; PC-r	1	2	4.00	10.00	20.00
6	156	–	Pgs. reduced 68 to 52; PC-r	1	2	2.40	6.00	12.00
7	165	–	PC-r	1	2	1.75	3.50	7.00
8	167	1/64	PC-r	1	2	1.75	3.50	7.00
9	167	11/65	PC-r	1	2	1.75	3.50	7.00
10	166	R/1968	New-c & price 25¢; PC-r	1	3	2.80	7.00	14.00

12. Rip Van Winkle and the Headless Horseman

Ed	HRN	Date	Details	A	C	GD25	FN65	NM94
1	11	6/43	Original; 68 pgs.	1	1	79.00	235.00	550.00
2	15	–	Long Isl. Ind. ed.; CC-r	1	1	21.00	62.00	145.00
3	20	–	Long Isl. Ind. ed.;	1	1	16.00	48.00	110.00
4	22	–	Queens Cty. Times ed.; CC-r	1	1	13.50	41.00	95.00
5	28	–	CC-r	1	1	10.00	30.00	70.00
6	60	–	1st LDC-r	1	1	4.70	14.00	28.00
7	62	–	LDC-r	1	1	4.00	11.00	22.00
8	71	–	LDC-r	1	1	3.20	8.00	16.00
9	89	–	C-price 15¢; LDC-r	1	1	2.80	7.00	14.00
10	118	–	LDC-r	1	1	2.40	6.00	12.00
11	132	–	New-c; PC-r	1	2	2.40	6.00	12.00
12	150	–	New-a; PC-r	2	2	2.40	6.00	12.00
13	158	–	PC-r	2	2	1.25	2.50	5.00
14	167	–	PC-r	2	2	1.25	2.50	5.00
15	167	12/63	PC-r	2	2	1.25	2.50	5.00
16	167	4/65	PC-r	2	2	1.50	3.00	6.00
17	167	4/66	PC-r	2	2	1.25	2.50	5.00
18	166	R/1968	New-c&price 25¢; PC-r; stiff-c	2	3	2.00	5.00	10.00
19	169	Sm/70	PC-r; stiff-c	2	3	2.00	5.00	10.00

13. Dr. Jekyll and Mr. Hyde (Used in SOTI, pg. 143)

Ed	HRN	Date	Details	A	C	GD25	FN65	NM94
1	12	8/43	Original 60 pgs.	1	1	100.00	300.00	700.00
2	15	–	Long Isl. Ind. ed.; CC-r	1	1	24.00	73.00	170.00
3	20	–	Long Isl. Ind. ed.; CC-r	1	1	17.00	52.00	120.00
4	28	–	No c-price; CC-r	1	1	14.00	43.00	100.00
5	60	–	New-c; Pgs. reduced from 60 to 52; H.C. Kiefer-c; LDC-r	1	2	4.70	14.00	28.00
6	62	–	LDC-r	1	2	4.00	12.00	24.00
7	71	–	LDC-r	1	2	3.60	9.00	18.00
8	87	–	Date returns (erroneous); LDC-r	1	2	3.20	8.00	16.00
9	112	–	New-c&a; PC-r	2	3	3.20	8.00	16.00
10	153	–	PC-r	2	3	1.25	2.50	5.00
11	161	–	PC-r	2	3	1.25	2.50	5.00
12	167	–	PC-r	2	3	1.25	2.50	5.00
13	167	8/64	PC-r	2	3	1.25	2.50	5.00
14	167	11/65	PC-r	2	3	1.25	2.50	5.00
15	166	R/68	C-price 25¢; PC-r	2	3	1.50	3.00	6.00
16	169	Wn/69	PC-r; stiff-c	2	3	1.25	2.50	5.00

14. Westward Ho!

Ed	HRN	Date	Details	A	C	GD25	FN65	NM94
1	13	9/43	Original; last outside bc coming-next ad; 60 pgs.	1	1	171.00	515.00	1200.00
2	15	–	Long Isl. Ind. ed.; CC-r	1	1	64.00	193.00	450.00
3	21	–	Queens Home News; Pg. 56 changed from coming-next ad to Three Men Named Smith; CC-r	1	1	50.00	150.00	350.00
4	28	1946	Gilberton; Pg. 56 changed again to WWII article-Speaking for America; last CC-r	1	1	40.00	120.00	280.00
5	53	–	Pgs. reduced from 60 to 52; LDC-r	1	1	32.00	95.00	225.00

15. Uncle Tom's Cabin (Used in SOTI, pgs. 102, 103)

Ed	HRN	Date	Details	A	C	GD25	FN65	NM94
1	14	11/43	Original; Outside-bc ad: 2 Gift Boxes; 60 pgs.	1	1	64.00	193.00	450.00
2	15	–	Long Isl. Ind. listed- bottom inside-fc;	1	1	22.00	65.00	150.00

Classics Illustrated #17 (HRN-60), © GIL

Classics Illustrated #18 (HRN-60), © GIL

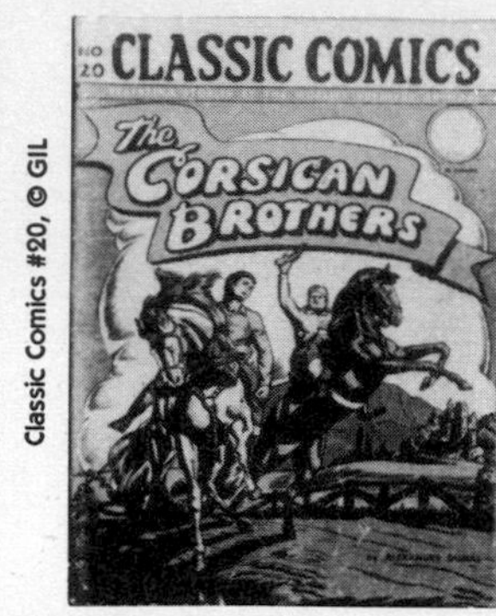

Classic Comics #20, © GIL

Ed	HRN	Date	Details	A	C	GD25	FN65	NM94
			also Gilberton listed bottom-pg. 1; CC-r					
3	21	–	Nassau Bulletin ed.; CC-r	1	1	18.00	54.00	125.00
4	28	–	No c-price; CC-r	1	1	11.00	32.00	75.00
5	53	–	Pgs. reduced 60 to 52; LDC-r	1	1	5.35	16.00	32.00
6	71	–	LDC-r	1	1	4.00	11.00	22.00
7	89	–	C-price 15¢; LDC-r	1	1	4.00	10.00	20.00
8	117	–	New-c/lettering changes; PC-r	1	2	2.40	6.00	12.00
9	128	–	'Picture Progress' promo; PC-r	1	2	1.60	4.00	8.00
10	137	–	PC-r	1	2	1.25	2.50	5.00
11	146	–	PC-r	1	2	1.25	2.50	5.00
12	154	–	PC-r	1	2	1.25	2.50	5.00
13	161	–	PC-r	1	2	1.25	2.50	5.00
14	167	–	PC-r	1	2	1.25	2.50	5.00
15	167	6/64	PC-r	1	2	1.25	2.50	5.00
16	167	5/65	PC-r	1	2	1.25	2.50	5.00
17	166	5/67	PC-r	1	2	1.25	2.50	5.00
18	166	Wn/69	New-stiff-c; PC-r	1	3	2.00	5.00	10.00
19	169	Sm/70	PC-r; stiff-c	1	3	2.00	5.00	10.00

16. Gullivers Travels

Ed	HRN	Date	Details	A	C	GD25	FN65	NM94
1	15	12/43	Original-Lilian Chestney c/a; 60 pgs.	1	1	60.00	182.00	425.00
2	18/20	–	Price deleted; Queens Home News ed; CC-r	1	1	19.00	57.00	130.00
3	22	–	Queens Cty. Times ed.; CC-r	1	1	15.00	45.00	105.00
4	28	–	CC-r	1	1	10.00	30.00	70.00
5	60	–	Pgs. reduced to 48; LDC-r	1	1	4.35	13.00	26.00
6	62	–	LDC-r	1	1	4.00	10.00	20.00
7	78	–	C-price 15¢; LDC-r	1	1	3.20	8.00	16.00
8	89	–	LDC-r	1	1	2.40	6.00	12.00
9	155	–	New-c; PC-r	1	2	2.40	6.00	12.00
10	165	–	PC-r	1	2	1.25	2.50	5.00
11	167	5/64	PC-r	1	2	1.25	2.50	5.00
12	167	11/65	PC-r	1	2	1.25	2.50	5.00
13	166	R/1968	C-price 25¢; PC-r	1	2	1.25	2.50	5.00
14	169	Wn/69	PC-r; stiff-c	1	2	1.25	2.50	5.00

17. The Deerslayer

Ed	HRN	Date	Details	A	C	GD25	FN65	NM94
1	16	1/44	Original; Outside-bc ad: 3 Gift Boxes; 60 pgs.	1	1	57.00	170.00	400.00
2A	18	–	Queens Cty Times (inside-fc); CC-r	1	1	19.00	57.00	130.00
2B	18	–	Gilberton (bottom-pg. 1); CC-r; Scarce	1	1	26.00	78.00	180.00
3	22	–	Queens Cty. Times ed.; CC-r	1	1	15.00	45.00	105.00
4	28	–	CC-r	1	1	10.00	30.00	70.00
5	60	–	Pgs.reduced to 52; LDC-r	1	1	4.35	13.00	26.00
6	64	–	LDC-r	1	1	3.60	9.00	18.00
7	85	–	C-price 15¢; LDC-r	1	1	2.80	7.00	14.00
8	118	–	LDC-r	1	1	2.40	6.00	12.00
9	132	–	LDC-r	1	1	2.40	6.00	12.00
10	167	11/66	Last LDC-r	1	1	2.00	5.00	10.00
11	166	R/1968	New-c & price 25¢; PC-r	1	2	2.40	6.00	12.00
12	169	Spr/71	Stiff-c; letters from parents & educators; PC-r	1	2	2.00	5.00	10.00

18. The Hunchback of Notre Dame

Ed	HRN	Date	Details	A	C	GD25	FN65	NM94
1A	17	3/44	Orig.; Gilberton ed; 60 pgs.	1	1	71.00	215.00	500.00
1B	17	3/44	Orig.; Island Pub. Ed.; 60 pgs.	1	1	64.00	193.00	450.00
2	18/20	–	Queens Home News ed.; CC-r	1	1	20.00	60.00	140.00
3	22	–	Queens Cty. Times ed.; CC-r	1	1	16.00	48.00	110.00
4	28	–	CC-r	1	1	11.50	34.00	80.00
5	60	–	New-c; 8pgs. deleted; Kiefer-c; LDC-r	1	2	4.70	14.00	28.00
6	62	–	LDC-r	1	2	3.60	9.00	18.00
7	78	–	C-price 15¢; LDC-r	1	2	3.20	8.00	16.00
8A	89	–	H.C.Kiefer on bottom right-fc; LDC-r	1	2	2.80	7.00	14.00
8B	89	–	Name omitted; LDC-r	1	2	3.60	9.00	18.00
9	118	–	LDC-r	1	2	2.80	7.00	14.00
10	140	–	New-c; PC-r	1	3	4.00	10.00	20.00
11	146	–	PC-r	1	3	3.20	8.00	16.00
12	158	–	New-c&a; PC-r; Evans/Crandall-a	2	4	2.80	7.00	14.00
13	165	–	PC-r	2	4	1.50	3.00	6.00
14	167	9/63	PC-r	2	4	1.50	3.00	6.00
15	167	10/64	PC-r	2	4	1.50	3.00	6.00
16	167	4/66	PC-r	2	4	1.25	2.50	5.00
17	166	R/1968	New price 25¢; PC-r	2	4	1.25	2.50	5.00
18	169	Sp/70	Stiff-c; PC-r	2	4	1.25	2.50	5.00

19. Huckleberry Finn

Ed	HRN	Date	Details	A	C	GD25	FN65	NM94
1A	18	4/44	Orig.; Gilberton ed.; 60 pgs.	1	1	50.00	150.00	350.00
1B	18	4/44	Orig.; Island Pub.; 60 pgs.	1	1	54.00	160.00	375.00
2	18	–	Nassau Bulletin ed.; fc-price 15¢-Canada; no coming-next ad; CC-r	1	1	20.00	60.00	140.00
3	22	–	Queens City Times ed.; CC-r	1	1	15.00	45.00	105.00
4	28	–	CC-r	1	1	10.00	30.00	70.00
5	60	–	Pgs. reduced to 48; LDC-r	1	1	4.35	13.00	26.00
6	62	–	LDC-r	1	1	4.00	10.00	20.00
7	78	–	LDC-r	1	1	3.20	8.00	16.00
8	89	–	LDC-r	1	1	2.80	7.00	14.00
9	117	–	LDC-r	1	1	2.40	6.00	12.00
10	131	–	New-c&a; PC-r	2	2	2.40	6.00	12.00
11	140	–	PC-r	2	2	1.25	2.50	5.00
12	150	–	PC-r	2	2	1.25	2.50	5.00
13	158	–	PC-r	2	2	1.25	2.50	5.00
14	165	–	PC-r	2	2	1.25	2.50	5.00
15	167	–	PC-r	2	2	1.25	2.50	5.00
16	167	6/64	PC-r	2	2	1.25	2.50	5.00
17	167	6/65	PC-r	2	2	1.25	2.50	5.00
18	167	10/65	PC-r	2	2	1.25	2.50	5.00
19	166	9/67	PC-r	2	2	1.25	2.50	5.00
20	166	Win/69	C-price 25¢; PC-r; stiff-c	2	2	1.25	2.50	5.00

Classics Illustrated #22 (HRN-85), © GIL

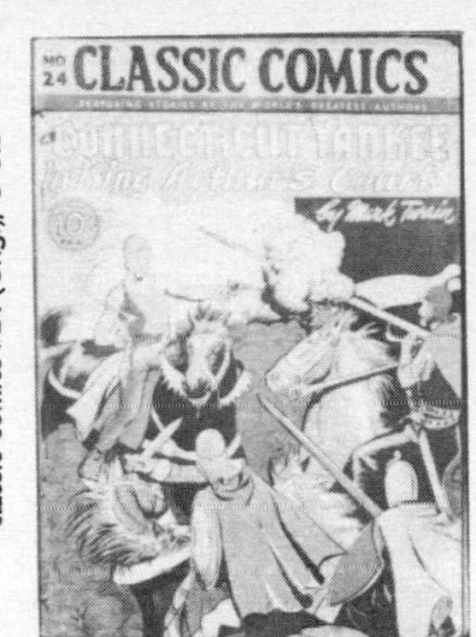

Classic Comics #24 (Orig.), © GIL

Classics Illustrated #26, © GIL

						GD25	FN65	NM94
1	169	Sm/70	PC-r; stiff-c	2	2	1.25	2.50	5.00

0. The Corsican Brothers

d	HRN	Date	Details	A	C	GD25	FN65	NM94
1A	20	6/44	Orig.; Gilberton ed.; bc-ad: 4 Gift Boxes; 60 pgs.	1	1	57.00	170.00	400.00
1B	20	6/44	Orig.; Courier ed.; 60 pgs.	1	1	54.00	160.00	375.00
1C	20	6/44	Orig.; Long Island Ind. ed.; 60 pgs.	1	1	54.00	160.00	375.00
2	22	–	Queens Cty. Times ed.; white logo banner; CC-r	1	1	23.00	70.00	160.00
3	28	–	CC-r	1	1	20.00	60.00	140.00
4	60	–	CI logo; no price; 48 pgs.; LDC-r	1	1	16.00	48.00	110.00
5A	62	–	LDC-r; Classics Ill. logo at top of pgs.	1	1	14.00	43.00	100.00
5B	62	–	w/o logo at top of pg. (scarcer)	1	1	14.00	43.00	100.00
6	78	–	C-price 15¢; LDC-r	1	1	13.00	40.00	90.00
7	97	–	LDC-r	1	1	11.50	34.00	80.00

1. 3 Famous Mysteries ("The Sign of the 4," "The Murders in the Rue Morgue," "The Flayed Hand")

d	HRN	Date	Details	A	C	GD25	FN65	NM94
1A	21	7/44	Orig.; Gilberton ed.; 60 pgs.	1	1	85.00	257.00	600.00
1B	21	7/44	Orig. Island Pub. Co.; 60 pgs.	1	1	89.00	268.00	625.00
1C	21	7/44	Original; Courier Ed.; 60 pgs.	1	1	79.00	235.00	550.00
2	22	–	Nassau Bulletin ed.; CC-r	1	1	31.00	93.00	215.00
3	30	–	CC-r	1	1	24.50	73.00	170.00
4	62	–	LDC-r; 8 pgs. deleted; LDC-r	1	1	19.00	57.00	130.00
5	70	–	LDC-r	1	1	17.00	52.00	120.00
6	85	–	C-price 15¢; LDC-r	1	1	15.00	45.00	105.00
7	114	–	New-c; PC-r	1	2	15.00	45.00	105.00

2. The Pathfinder

d	HRN	Date	Details	A	C	GD25	FN65	NM94
1A	22	10/44	Orig.; No printer listed; ownership statement inside fc lists Gilberton & date; 60 pgs.	1	1	43.00	129.00	300.00
1B	22	10/44	Orig.; Island Pub. ed.; 60 pgs.	1	1	36.00	107.00	250.00
1C	22	10/44	Orig.; Queens Cty Times ed. 60 pgs.	1	1	36.00	107.00	250.00
2	30	–	C-price removed; CC-r	1	1	10.00	30.00	70.00
3	60	–	Pgs. reduced to 52; LDC-r	1	1	4.00	12.00	24.00
4	70	–	LDC-r	1	1	4.00	10.00	20.00
5	85	–	C-price 15¢; LDC-r	1	1	3.20	8.00	16.00
6	118	–	LDC-r	1	1	2.80	7.00	14.00
7	132	–	LDC-r	1	1	2.40	6.00	12.00
8	146	–	LDC-r	1	1	2.40	6.00	12.00
9	167	11/63	New-c; PC-r	1	2	4.00	10.00	20.00
10	167	12/65	PC-r	1	2	2.80	7.00	14.00
11	166	8/67	PC-r	1	2	2.80	7.00	14.00

3. Oliver Twist (1st Classic produced by the Iger Shop)

Ed	HRN	Date	Details	A	C	GD25	FN65	NM94
1	23	7/45	Original; 60 pgs.	1	1	36.00	107.00	250.00
2A	30	–	Printers Union logo on bottom left-fc same as 23(Orig.) (very rare); CC-r	1	1	22.00	65.00	150.00
2B	30	–	Union logo omitted; CC-r	1	1	10.00	30.00	70.00
3	60	–	Pgs. reduced to 48; LDC-r	1	1	4.00	12.00	24.00
4	62	–	LDC-r	1	1	4.00	10.00	20.00
5	71	–	LDC-r	1	1	3.20	8.00	16.00
6	85	–	C-price 15¢; LDC-r	1	1	2.80	7.00	14.00
7	94	–	LDC-r	1	1	2.40	6.00	12.00
8	118	–	LDC-r	1	1	2.40	6.00	12.00
9	136	–	New-PC, old-a; PC-r	1	2	2.40	6.00	12.00
10	150	–	Old-a; PC-r	1	2	1.80	4.50	9.00
11	164	–	Old-a; PC-r	1	2	1.80	4.50	9.00
12	164	–	New-a; PC-r; Evans/Crandall-a	2	2	2.80	7.00	14.00
13	167	–	PC-r	2	2	1.80	4.50	9.00
14	167	8/64	PC-r	2	2	1.25	2.50	5.00
15	167	12/65	PC-r	2	2	1.25	2.50	5.00
16	166	R/1968	New 25¢; PC-r	2	2	1.00	2.00	5.00
17	169	Win/69	Stiff-c; PC-r	2	2	1.25	2.50	5.00

24. A Connecticut Yankee in King Arthur's Court

Ed	HRN	Date	Details	A	C	GD25	FN65	NM94
1	9/45	–	Original	1	1	36.00	107.00	250.00
2	30	–	No price circle; CC-r	1	1	10.00	30.00	70.00
3	60	–	8 pgs. deleted; LDC-r	1	1	4.00	12.00	24.00
4	62	–	LDC-r	1	1	4.00	10.00	20.00
5	71	–	LDC-r	1	1	3.20	8.00	16.00
6	87	–	C-price 15¢; LDC-r	1	1	2.80	7.00	14.00
7	121	–	LDC-r	1	1	2.40	6.00	12.00
8	140	–	New-c&a; PC-r	2	2	2.40	6.00	12.00
9	153	–	PC-r	2	2	1.25	2.50	5.00
10	164	–	PC-r	2	2	1.25	2.50	5.00
11	167	–	PC-r	2	2	1.25	2.50	5.00
12	167	7/64	PC-r	2	2	1.25	2.50	5.00
13	167	6/66	PC-r	2	2	1.25	2.50	5.00
14	166	R/1968	C-price 25¢; PC-r	2	2	1.25	2.50	5.00
15	169	Spr/71	PC-r; stiff-c	2	2	1.25	2.50	5.00

25. Two Years Before the Mast

Ed	HRN	Date	Details	A	C	GD25	FN65	NM94
1	10/45	–	Original; Webb/Heames-a&c	1	1	36.00	107.00	250.00
2	30	–	Price circle blank; CC-r	1	1	11.00	32.00	75.00
3	60	–	8 pgs. deleted; LDC-r	1	1	4.00	12.00	24.00
4	62	–	LDC-r	1	1	4.00	10.50	21.00
5	71	–	LDC-r	1	1	3.20	8.00	16.00
6	85	–	C-price 15¢; LDC-r	1	1	2.80	7.00	14.00
7	114	–	LDC-r	1	1	2.40	6.00	12.00
8	156	–	3 pgs. replaced by fillers; new-c; PC-r	1	2	2.40	6.00	12.00
9	167	12/63	PC-r	1	2	1.25	2.50	5.00
10	167	12/65	PC-r	1	2	1.25	2.50	5.00
11	166	9/67	PC-r	1	2	1.25	2.50	5.00
12	169	Win/69	C-price 25¢; stiff-c PC-r	1	2	1.25	2.50	5.00

26. Frankenstein

Ed	HRN	Date	Details	A	C	GD25	FN65	NM94
1	26	12/45	Orig.; Webb/Brew-	1	1	86.00	257.00	600.00

Classics Illustrated #27, © GIL

Classic Comics #29 (Orig), © GIL

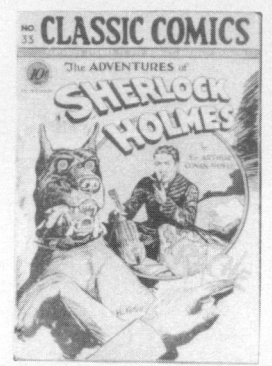

Classic Comics #33 (Orig), © GIL

Ed	HRN	Date	Details	A	C	GD25	FN65	NM94
			ster a&c; 52 pgs.					
2A	30	–	Price circle blank; no indicia; CC-r	1	1	23.00	70.00	160.00
2B	30	–	With indicia; scarce; CC-r	1	1	27.00	80.00	190.00
3	60	–	LDC-r	1	1	6.70	20.00	40.00
4	62	–	LDC-r	1	1	10.00	30.00	60.00
5	71	–	LDC-r	1	1	4.20	12.50	25.00
6A	82	–	C-price 15¢; soft-c LDC-r	1	1	4.00	11.00	22.00
6B	82	–	Stiff-c; LDC-r	1	1	4.70	14.00	28.00
7	117	–	LDC-r	1	1	2.80	7.00	14.00
8	146	–	New Saunders-c; PC-r	1	2	2.80	7.00	14.00
9	152	–	Scarce; PC-r	1	2	4.00	12.00	24.00
10	153	–	PC-r	1	2	1.25	2.50	5.00
11	160	–	PC-r	1	2	1.25	2.50	5.00
12	165	–	PC-r	1	2	1.25	2.50	5.00
13	167	–	PC-r	1	2	1.25	2.50	5.00
14	167	6/64	PC-r	1	2	1.25	2.50	5.00
15	167	6/65	PC-r	1	2	1.25	2.50	5.00
16	167	10/65	PC-r	1	2	1.25	2.50	5.00
17	166	9/67	PC-r	1	2	1.25	2.50	5.00
18	169	Fall/69	C-price 25¢; stiff-c PC-r	1	2	1.25	2.50	5.00
19	169	Spr/71	PC-r; stiff-c	1	2	1.25	2.50	5.00

27. The Adventures of Marco Polo

Ed	HRN	Date	Details	A	C	GD25	FN65	NM94
1	4/46	–	Original	1	1	36.00	107.00	250.00
2	30	–	Last 'Comics' reprint; CC-r	1	1	10.00	30.00	70.00
3	70	–	8 pgs. deleted; no c-price; LDC-r	1	1	4.00	10.50	21.00
4	87	–	C-price 15¢; LDC-r	1	1	3.20	8.00	16.00
5	117	–	LDC-r	1	1	2.40	6.00	12.00
6	154	–	New-c; PC-r	1	2	2.40	6.00	12.00
7	165	–	PC-r	1	2	1.25	2.50	5.00
8	167	4/64	PC-r	1	2	1.25	2.50	5.00
9	167	6/66	PC-r	1	2	1.25	2.50	5.00
10	169	Spr/69	New price 25¢; stiff-c; PC-r	1	2	1.25	2.50	5.00

28. Michael Strogoff

Ed	HRN	Date	Details	A	C	GD25	FN65	NM94
1	6/46	–	Original	1	1	36.00	107.00	250.00
2	51	–	8 pgs. cut; LDC-r	1	1	10.00	30.00	70.00
3	115	–	New-c; PC-r	1	2	3.20	8.00	16.00
4	155	–	PC-r	1	2	1.60	4.00	8.00
5	167	11/63	PC-r	1	2	1.60	4.00	8.00
6	167	7/66	PC-r	1	2	1.60	4.00	8.00
7	169	Sm/69	C-price 25¢; stiff-c PC-r	1	3	2.00	5.00	10.00

29. The Prince and the Pauper

Ed	HRN	Date	Details	A	C	GD25	FN65	NM94
1	7/46	–	Orig.; "Horror"-c	1	1	64.00	193.00	450.00
2	60	–	8 pgs. cut; new-c by Kiefer; LDC-r	1	2	4.35	13.00	26.00
3	62	–	LDC-r	1	2	4.00	11.00	22.00
4	71	–	LDC-r	1	2	3.20	8.00	16.00
5	93	–	LDC-r	1	2	2.80	7.00	14.00
6	114	–	LDC-r	1	2	2.40	6.00	12.00
7	128	–	New-c; PC-r	1	3	2.40	6.00	12.00
8	138	–	PC-r	1	3	1.25	2.50	5.00
9	150	–	PC-r	1	3	1.25	2.50	5.00
10	164	–	PC-r	1	3	1.25	2.50	5.00
11	167	–	PC-r	1	3	1.25	2.50	5.00
12	167	7/64	PC-r	1	3	1.25	2.50	5.00
13	167	11/65	PC-r	1	3	1.25	2.50	5.00
14	166	R/68	C-price 25¢; PC-r	1	3	1.25	2.50	5.00
15	169	Sm/70	PC-r; stiff-c	1	3	1.25	2.50	5.00

30. The Moonstone

Ed	HRN	Date	Details	A	C	GD25	FN65	NM94
1	9/46	–	Original; Rico-c/a	1	1	36.00	107.00	250.00
2	60	–	LDC-r; 8pgs. cut	1	1	5.00	15.00	30.00
3	70	–	LDC-r	1	1	4.00	12.00	24.00
4	155	–	New L.B. Cole-c; PC-r	1	2	5.85	17.50	35.00
5	165	–	PC-r; L.B. Cole-c	1	2	2.80	7.00	14.00
6	167	1/64	PC-r; L.B. Cole-c	1	2	1.60	4.00	8.00
7	167	9/65	PC-r; L.B. Cole-c	1	2	1.50	3.00	6.00
8	166	R/1968	C-price 25¢; PC-r	1	2	1.25	2.50	5.00

31. The Black Arrow

Ed	HRN	Date	Details	A	C	GD25	FN65	NM94
1	10/46	–	Original	1	1	29.00	86.00	200.00
2	51	–	CI logo; LDC-r 8pgs. deleted	1	1	4.70	14.00	28.00
3	64	–	LDC-r	1	1	3.60	9.00	18.00
4	87	–	C-price 15¢; LDC-r	1	1	3.20	8.00	16.00
5	108	–	LDC-r	1	1	2.80	7.00	14.00
6	125	–	LDC-r	1	1	2.40	6.00	12.00
7	131	–	New-c; PC-r	1	2	2.40	6.00	12.00
8	140	–	PC-r	1	2	1.25	2.50	5.00
9	148	–	PC-r	1	2	1.25	2.50	5.00
10	161	–	PC-r	1	2	1.25	2.50	5.00
11	167	–	PC-r	1	2	1.25	2.50	5.00
12	167	7/64	PC-r	1	2	1.25	2.50	5.00
13	167	11/65	PC-r	1	2	1.25	2.50	5.00
14	166	R/1968	C-price 25¢; PC-r	1	2	1.25	2.50	5.00

32. Lorna Doone

Ed	HRN	Date	Details	A	C	GD25	FN65	NM94
1	12/46	–	Original; Matt Baker c&a	1	1	36.00	107.00	250.00
2	53/64	–	8 pgs. deleted; LDC-r	1	1	5.35	16.00	32.00
3	85	–	C-price 15¢; LDC-r; Baker c&a	1	1	4.00	12.00	24.00
4	118	–	LDC-r	1	1	3.20	8.00	16.00
5	138	–	New-c; old-c becomes new title pg.; PC-r	1	2	2.80	7.00	14.00
6	150	–	PC-r	1	2	1.25	2.50	5.00
7	165	–	PC-r	1	2	1.25	2.50	5.00
8	167	1/64	PC-r	1	2	1.25	2.50	5.00
9	167	11/65	PC-r	1	2	1.25	2.50	5.00
10	166	R/1968	New-c; PC-r	1	3	2.40	6.00	12.00

33. The Adventures of Sherlock Holmes

Ed	HRN	Date	Details	A	C	GD25	FN65	NM94
1	33	1/47	Original; Kiefer-c; contains Study in Scarlet & Hound of the Baskervilles; 68 pgs.	1	1	107.00	320.00	750.00
2	53	–	'A Study in Scarlet' (17 pgs.) deleted; LDC-r	1	1	38.00	115.00	265.00
3	71	–	LDC-r	1	1	28.00	86.00	200.00
4A	89	–	C-price 15¢; LDC-r	1	1	23.00	70.00	160.00
4B	89	–	Kiefer's name omitted from-c	1	1	23.00	70.00	160.00

Classics Illustrated #34 (HRN-167), © GIL

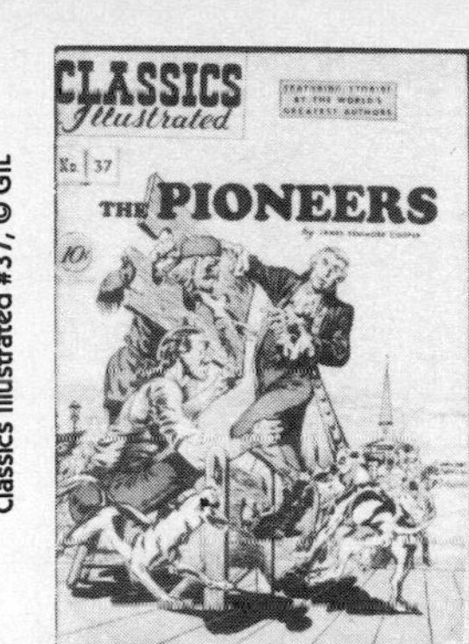

Classics Illustrated #37, © GIL

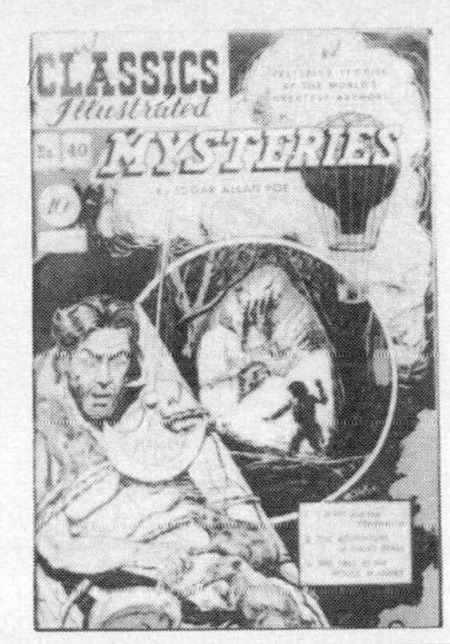

Classics Illustrated #40 (Orig), © GIL

GD25 FN65 NM94 | GD25 FN65 NM94

34. Mysterious Island (Last "Classic Comic")

Ed	HRN	Date	Details	A	C	GD25	FN65	NM94
1	2/47	–	Original; Webb/ Heames c/a	1	1	36.00	107.00	250.00
2	60	–	8 pgs. deleted; LDC-r	1	1	4.00	12.00	24.00
3	62	–	LDC-r	1	1	4.00	10.00	20.00
4	71	–	LDC-r	1	1	4.35	13.00	26.00
5	78	–	C-price 15¢ in circle; LDC-r	1	1	3.20	8.00	16.00
6	92	–	LDC-r	1	1	2.80	7.00	14.00
7	117	–	LDC-r	1	1	2.40	6.00	12.00
8	140	–	New-c; PC-r	1	2	2.40	6.00	12.00
9	156	–	PC-r	1	2	1.25	2.50	5.00
10	167	10/63	PC-r	1	2	1.25	2.50	5.00
11	167	5/64	PC-r	1	2	1.25	2.50	5.00
12	167	6/66	PC-r	1	2	1.25	2.50	5.00
13	166	R/1968	C-price 25¢; PC-r	1	2	1.25	2.50	5.00

35. Last Days of Pompeii (First "Classics Illustrated")

Ed	HRN	Date	Details	A	C	GD25	FN65	NM94
1	–	3/47	Original; LDC; Kiefer-c/a	1	1	36.00	107.00	250.00
2	161	–	New c&a; 15¢; PC-r; Jack Kirby-a	2	2	3.60	9.00	18.00
3	167	1/64	PC-r	2	2	1.60	4.00	8.00
4	167	7/66	PC-r	2	2	1.60	4.00	8.00
5	169	Spr/70	New price 25¢; stiff-c; PC-r	2	2	1.60	4.00	8.00

36. Typee

Ed	HRN	Date	Details	A	C	GD25	FN65	NM94
1	4/47	–	Original	1	1	17.00	52.00	120.00
2	64	–	No c-price; 8 pg. ed.; LDC-r	1	1	4.70	14.00	28.00
3	155	–	New-c; PC-r	1	2	2.40	6.00	12.00
4	167	9/63	PC-r	1	2	1.40	3.50	7.00
5	167	7/65	PC-r	1	2	1.40	3.50	7.00
6	169	Sm/69	C-price 25¢; stiff-c PC-r	1	2	1.50	3.50	7.00

37. The Pioneers

Ed	HRN	Date	Details	A	C	GD25	FN65	NM94
1	37	5/47	Original; Palais-c/a	1	1	16.00	48.00	110.00
2A	62	–	8 pgs. cut; LDC-r; price circle blank	1	1	4.00	11.00	22.00
2B	62	–	10¢; LDC-r;	1	1	10.00	30.00	70.00
3	70	–	LDC-r	1	1	3.20	8.00	16.00
4	92	–	15¢; LDC-r	1	1	2.80	7.00	14.00
5	118	–	LDC-r	1	1	2.40	6.00	12.00
6	131	–	LDC-r	1	1	2.40	6.00	12.00
7	132	–	LDC-r	1	1	2.40	6.00	12.00
8	153	–	LDC-r	1	1	2.00	5.00	10.00
9	167	5/64	LDC-r	1	1	1.60	4.00	8.00
10	167	6/66	LDC-r	1	1	1.60	4.00	8.00
11	166	R/1968	New-c; 25¢; PC-r	1	2	3.20	8.00	16.00

38. Adventures of Cellini

Ed	HRN	Date	Details	A	C	GD25	FN65	NM94
1	6/47	–	Original; Froehlich c/a	1	1	30.00	90.00	210.00
2	164	–	New-c&a; PC-r	2	2	2.80	7.00	14.00
3	167	12/63	PC-r	2	2	1.60	4.00	8.00
4	167	7/66	PC-r	2	2	1.60	4.00	8.00
5	169	Spr/70	Stiff-c; new price 25¢; PC-r	2	2	1.60	4.00	8.00

39. Jane Eyre

Ed	HRN	Date	Details	A	C	GD25	FN65	NM94
1	7/47	–	Original	1	1	23.00	70.00	160.00
2	60	–	No c-price; 8 pgs. cut; LDC-r	1	1	4.35	13.00	26.00
3	62	–	LDC-r	1	1	4.00	10.50	21.00
4	71	–	LDC-r; c-price 10¢	1	1	3.00	9.00	18.00
5	92	–	C-price 15¢; LDC-r	1	1	2.80	7.00	14.00
6	118	–	LDC-r	1	1	2.40	6.00	12.00
7	142	–	New-c; old-a; PC-r	1	2	2.80	7.00	14.00
8	154	–	Old-a; PC-r	1	2	2.40	6.00	12.00
9	165	–	New-a; PC-r	2	2	2.80	7.00	14.00
10	167	12/63	PC-r	2	2	2.80	7.00	14.00
11	167	4/65	PC-r	2	2	2.40	6.00	12.00
12	167	8/66	PC-r	2	2	2.40	6.00	12.00
13	166	R/1968	New-c; PC-r	2	3	4.70	14.00	28.00

40. Mysteries ("The Pit and the Pendulum," "The Advs. of Hans Pfall" & "The Fall of the House of Usher")

Ed	HRN	Date	Details	A	C	GD25	FN65	NM94
1	8/47	–	Original; Kiefer-c/a, Froehlich, Griffiths-a	1	1	64.00	193.00	450.00
2	62	–	LDC-r; 8pgs cut	1	1	23.00	70.00	160.00
3	75	–	LDC-r	1	1	20.00	60.00	140.00
4	92	–	C-price 15¢; LDC-r	1	1	16.00	48.00	110.00

41. Twenty Years After

Ed	HRN	Date	Details	A	C	GD25	FN65	NM94
1	9/47	–	Original; 'horror'-c	1	1	50.00	150.00	350.00
2	62	–	New-c; no c-price 8 pgs. cut; LDC-r; Kiefer-c	1	2	4.35	13.00	26.00
3	78	–	C-price 15¢; LDC-r	1	2	3.60	9.00	18.00
4	156	–	New-c; PC-r	1	3	2.40	6.00	12.00
5	167	12/63	PC-r	1	3	1.20	3.00	6.00
6	167	11/66	PC-r	1	3	1.20	3.00	6.00
7	169	Spr/70	New price 25¢; stiff-c; PC-r	1	3	1.20	2.50	5.00

42. Swiss Family Robinson

Ed	HRN	Date	Details	A	C	GD25	FN65	NM94
1	42	10/47	Orig.; Kiefer-c&a;	1	1	17.00	52.00	120.00
2A	62	–	8 pgs. cut; outside bc: Gift Box ad; LDC-r	1	1	4.00	12.00	24.00
2B	62	–	8 pgs. cut; outside-bc: Reorder list; scarce; LDC-r	1	1	7.50	22.50	45.00
3	75	–	LDC-r	1	1	3.20	8.00	16.00
4	93	–	LDC-r	1	1	2.80	7.00	14.00
5	117	–	LDC-r	1	1	2.40	6.00	12.00
6	131	–	New-c; old-a; PC-r	1	2	2.40	6.00	12.00
7	137	–	Old-a; PC-r	1	2	2.00	5.00	10.00
8	141	–	Old-a; PC-r	1	2	2.00	5.00	10.00
9	152	–	New-a; PC-r	2	2	2.40	6.00	12.00
10	158	–	PC-r	2	2	1.25	2.50	5.00
11	165	–	PC-r	2	2	1.80	4.50	9.00
12	167	12/63	PC-r	2	2	1.50	3.00	6.00
13	167	4/65	PC-r	2	2	1.50	3.00	6.00
14	167	5/66	PC-r	2	2	1.50	3.00	6.00
15	166	11/67	PC-r	2	2	1.25	2.50	5.00
16	169	Spr/69	PC-r; stiff-c	2	2	1.25	2.50	5.00

43. Great Expectations (Used in SOTI, pg. 311)

Ed	HRN	Date	Details	A	C	GD25	FN65	NM94
1	11/47	–	Original; Kiefer-a/c	1	1	79.00	235.00	550.00
2	62	–	No c-price; 8 pgs. cut; LDC-r	1	1	43.00	130.00	300.00

Classics Illustrated #49 (Orig.), © GIL

Classics Illustrated #50 (Orig.), © GIL

Classics Illustrated #51 (Orig.), © GIL

44. Mysteries of Paris (Used in SOTI, pg. 323)

Ed	HRN	Date	Details	A	C	GD25	FN65	NM94
1A	44	12/47	Original; 56 pgs.; Kiefer-c/a	1	1	61.00	182.00	425.00
1B	44	12/47	Orig.; printed on white/heavier paper; (rare)	1	1	64.00	193.00	450.00
2A	62	–	8 pgs. cut; outside-bc: Gift Box ad; LDC-r	1	1	23.00	70.00	160.00
2B	62	–	8 pgs. cut; outside-bc: reorder list; LDC-r	1	1	23.00	70.00	160.00
3	78	–	C-price 15¢; LDC-r	1	1	20.00	60.00	140.00

45. Tom Brown's School Days

Ed	HRN	Date	Details	A	C	GD25	FN65	NM94
1	44	1/48	Original; 1st 48pg. issue	1	1	11.50	34.00	80.00
2	64	–	No c-price; LDC-r	1	1	4.70	14.00	28.00
3	161	–	New-c&a; PC-r	2	2	2.40	6.00	12.00
4	167	2/64	PC-r	2	2	1.60	4.00	8.00
5	167	8/66	PC-r	2	2	1.60	4.00	8.00
6	166	R/1968	C-price 25¢; PC-r	2	2	1.60	4.00	8.00

46. Kidnapped

Ed	HRN	Date	Details	A	C	GD25	FN65	NM94
1	47	4/48	Original; Webb-c/a	1	1	11.00	32.00	75.00
2A	62	–	Price circle blank; LDC-r	1	1	4.00	11.00	22.00
2B	62	–	C-price 10¢; rare; LDC-r	1	1	11.00	32.00	75.00
3	78	–	C-price 15¢; LDC-r	1	1	3.20	8.00	16.00
4	87	–	LDC-r	1	1	2.80	7.00	14.00
5	118	–	LDC-r	1	1	2.40	6.00	12.00
6	131	–	New-c; PC-r	1	2	2.40	6.00	12.00
7	140	–	PC-r	1	2	1.25	2.50	5.00
8	150	–	PC-r	1	2	1.25	2.50	5.00
9	164	–	Reduced pg.width; PC-r	1	2	1.25	2.50	5.00
10	167	–	PC-r	1	2	1.25	2.50	5.00
11	167	3/64	PC-r	1	2	1.25	2.50	5.00
12	167	6/65	PC-r	1	2	1.25	2.50	5.00
13	167	12/65	PC-r	1	2	1.25	2.50	5.00
14	166	9/67	PC-r	1	2	1.25	2.50	5.00
15	166	Win/69	New price 25¢; PC-r; stiff-c	1	2	1.25	2.50	5.00
16	169	Sm/70	PC-r; stiff-c	1	2	1.25	2.50	5.00

47. Twenty Thousand Leagues Under the Sea

Ed	HRN	Date	Details	A	C	GD25	FN65	NM94
1	47	5/48	Orig.; Kiefer-a&c;	1	1	11.00	32.00	75.00
2	64	–	No c-price; LDC-r	1	1	4.00	11.00	22.00
3	78	–	C-price 15¢; LDC-r	1	1	3.20	8.00	16.00
4	94	–	LDC-r	1	1	2.80	7.00	14.00
5	118	–	LDC-r	1	1	2.40	6.00	12.00
6	128	–	New-c; PC-r	1	2	2.40	6.00	10.00
7	133	–	PC-r	1	2	1.80	4.50	9.00
8	140	–	PC-r	1	2	1.25	2.50	5.00
9	148	–	PC-r	1	2	1.25	2.50	5.00
10	156	–	PC-r	1	2	1.25	2.50	5.00
11	165	–	PC-r	1	2	1.25	2.50	5.00
12	167	–	PC-r	1	2	1.25	2.50	5.00
13	167	3/64	PC-r	1	2	1.25	2.50	5.00
14	167	8/65	PC-r	1	2	1.25	2.50	5.00
15	167	10/66	PC-r	1	2	1.25	2.50	5.00
16	166	R/1968	C-price 25¢; new-c PC-r	1	3	2.00	5.00	10.00
17	169	Spr/70	Stiff-c; PC-r	1	3	2.00	5.00	10.00

48. David Copperfield

Ed	HRN	Date	Details	A	C	GD25	FN65	NM94
1	47	6/48	Original; Kiefer-c/a	1	1	11.00	32.00	75.00
2	64	–	Price circle replaced by motif of boy reading; LDC-r	1	1	4.00	11.00	22.00
3	87	–	C-price 15¢; LDC-r	1	1	3.20	8.00	16.00
4	121	–	New-c; PC-r	1	2	2.40	6.00	12.00
5	130	–	PC-r	1	2	1.50	3.00	6.00
6	140	–	PC-r	1	2	1.50	3.00	6.00
7	148	–	PC-r	1	2	1.50	3.00	6.00
8	156	–	PC-r	1	2	1.50	3.00	6.00
9	167	–	PC-r	1	2	1.25	2.50	5.00
10	167	4/64	PC-r	1	2	1.25	2.50	5.00
11	167	6/65	PC-r	1	2	1.25	2.50	5.00
12	166	5/67	PC-r	1	2	1.25	2.50	5.00
13	166	R/67	PC-r; C-price 25¢	1	2	1.80	4.50	9.00
14	166	Spr/69	C-price 25¢; stiff-c PC-r	1	2	1.25	2.50	5.00
15	169	Win/69	Stiff-c; PC-r	1	2	1.25	2.50	5.00

49. Alice in Wonderland

Ed	HRN	Date	Details	A	C	GD25	FN65	NM94
1	47	7/48	Original; 1st Blum a & c	1	1	14.00	43.00	100.00
2	64	–	No c-price; LDC-r	1	1	4.70	14.00	28.00
3A	85	–	C-price 15¢; soft-c LDC-r	1	1	4.00	10.50	21.00
3B	85	–	Stiff-c; LDC-r	1	1	4.00	12.00	24.00
4	155	–	New PC, similar to orig.; PC-r	1	2	4.00	10.50	21.00
5	165	–	PC-r	1	2	3.20	8.00	16.00
6	167	3/64	PC-r	1	2	2.80	7.00	14.00
7	167	6/66	PC-r	1	2	2.80	7.00	14.00
8A	166	Fall/68	New-c; soft-c; 25¢ c-price; PC-r	1	3	4.00	10.00	20.00
8B	166	Fall/68	New-c; stiff-c; 25¢ c-price; PC-r	1	3	5.85	17.50	35.00

50. Adventures of Tom Sawyer (Used in SOTI, pg. 37)

Ed	HRN	Date	Details	A	C	GD25	FN65	NM94
1A	51	8/48	Orig.; Aldo Rubano a&c	1	1	11.50	34.00	80.00
1B	51	9/48	Orig.; Rubano c&a	1	1	11.50	34.00	80.00
1C	51	9/48	Orig.; outside-bc: blue & yellow only; rare	1	1	16.00	48.00	110.00
2	64	–	No c-price; LDC-r	1	1	4.00	10.00	20.00
3	78	–	C-price 15¢; LDC-r	1	1	2.80	7.00	14.00
4	94	–	LDC-r	1	1	2.40	6.00	12.00
5	117	–	LDC-r	1	1	2.00	5.00	10.00
6	132	–	LDC-r	1	1	2.00	5.00	10.00
7	140	–	New-c; PC-r	1	2	2.00	5.00	10.00
8	150	–	PC-r	1	2	1.60	4.00	8.00
9	164	–	New-a; PC-r	2	2	2.00	5.00	10.00
10	167	–	PC-r	2	2	1.25	2.50	5.00
11	167	1/65	PC-r	2	2	1.25	2.50	5.00
12	167	5/66	PC-r	2	2	1.25	2.50	5.00
13	166	12/67	PC-r	2	2	1.25	2.50	5.00
14	169	Fall/69	C-price 25¢; stiff-c; PC-r	2	2	1.25	2.50	5.00
15	169	Win/71	PC-r	2	2	1.25	2.50	5.00

51. The Spy

Ed	HRN	Date	Details	A	C	GD25	FN65	NM94
1A	51	9/48	Original; inside-bc illo: Christmas Carol	1	1	11.00	32.00	75.00

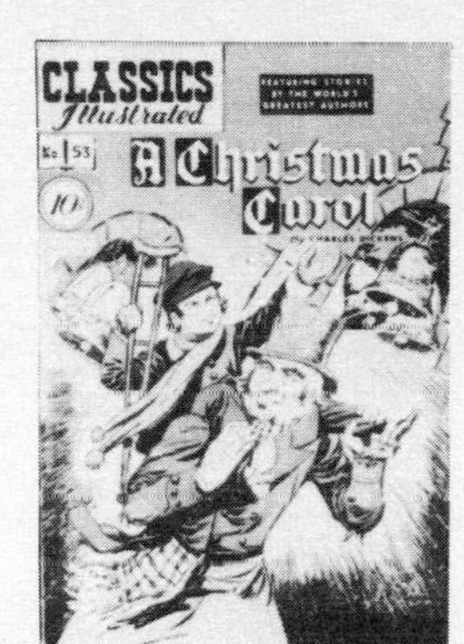

Classics Illustrated #53 (Orig.), © GIL

Classics Illustrated #55 (HRN-167), © GIL

Classics Illustrated #57 (Orig.), © GIL

Ed	HRN	Date	Details	A	C	GD25	FN65	NM94
1B	51	9/48	Original; inside-bc illo: Man in Iron Mask	1	1	11.00	32.00	75.00
1C	51	8/48	Original; outside-bc: full color	1	1	11.00	32.00	75.00
1D	51	8/48	Original; outside-bc: blue & yellow only; scarce	1	1	14.00	43.00	100.00
2	89	–	C-price 15¢; LDC-r	1	1	3.60	9.00	18.00
3	121	–	LDC-r	1	1	2.80	7.00	14.00
4	139	–	New-c; PC-r	1	2	2.40	6.00	12.00
5	156	–	PC-r	1	2	1.25	2.50	5.00
6	167	11/63	PC-r	1	2	1.25	2.50	5.00
7	167	7/66	PC-r	1	2	1.25	2.50	5.00
8A	166	Win/69	C-price 25¢; soft-c; scarce; PC-r	1	2	2.40	6.00	12.00
8B	166	Win/69	C-price 25¢; stiff-c; PC-r	1	2	1.25	2.50	5.00

52. The House of the Seven Gables

Ed	HRN	Date	Details	A	C	GD25	FN65	NM94
1	53	10/48	Orig.; Griffiths a&c	1	1	10.00	30.00	70.00
2	89	–	C-price 15¢; LDC-r	1	1	3.60	9.00	18.00
3	121	–	LDC-r	1	1	2.80	7.00	14.00
4	142	–	New-c&a; PC-r; Woodbridge-a	2	2	2.40	6.00	12.00
5	156	–	PC-r	2	2	1.25	2.50	5.00
6	165	–	PC-r	2	2	1.25	2.50	5.00
7	167	5/64	PC-r	2	2	1.25	2.50	5.00
8	167	3/66	PC-r	2	2	1.25	2.50	5.00
9	166	R/1968	C-price 25¢; PC-r	2	2	1.25	2.50	5.00
10	169	Spr/70	Stiff-c; PC-r	2	2	1.25	2.50	5.00

53. A Christmas Carol

Ed	HRN	Date	Details	A	C	GD25	FN65	NM94
1	53	11/48	Original & only ed; Kiefer-c/a	1	1	11.50	34.00	80.00

54. Man in the Iron Mask

Ed	HRN	Date	Details	A	C	GD25	FN65	NM94
1	55	12/48	Original; Froehlich-a, Kiefer-c	1	1	10.00	30.00	70.00
2	93	–	C-price 15¢; LDC-r	1	1	3.60	9.00	18.00
3A	111	–	(O) logo lettering; scarce; LDC-r	1	1	4.00	12.00	24.00
3B	111	–	New logo as PC; LDC-r	1	1	3.20	8.00	16.00
4	142	–	New-c&a; PC-r	2	2	2.40	6.00	12.00
5	154	–	PC-r	2	2	1.25	2.50	5.00
6	165	–	PC-r	2	2	1.25	2.50	5.00
7	167	5/64	PC-r	2	2	1.25	2.50	5.00
8	167	4/66	PC-r	2	2	1.25	2.50	5.00
9A	166	Win/69	C-price 25¢; soft-c PC-r	2	2	2.80	7.00	14.00
9B	166	Win/69	Stiff-c	2	2	1.25	2.50	5.00

55. Silas Marner (Used in SOTI, pgs. 311, 312)

Ed	HRN	Date	Details	A	C	GD25	FN65	NM94
1	55	1/49	Original-Kiefer-c	1	1	10.00	30.00	70.00
2	75	–	Price circle blank; 'Coming Next' ad; LDC-r	1	1	4.00	11.00	22.00
3	97	–	LDC-r	1	1	2.80	7.00	14.00
4	121	–	New-c; PC-r	1	2	2.40	6.00	12.00
5	130	–	PC-r	1	2	1.25	2.50	5.00
6	140	–	PC-r	1	2	1.25	2.50	5.00
7	154	–	PC-r	1	2	1.25	2.50	5.00
8	165	–	PC-r	1	2	1.25	2.50	5.00
9	167	2/64	PC-r	1	2	1.25	2.50	5.00
10	167	6/65	PC-r	1	2	1.25	2.50	5.00
11	166	5/67	PC-r	1	2	1.25	2.50	5.00
12A	166	Win/69	C-price 25¢; soft-c PC-r	1	2	2.80	7.00	14.00
12B	166	Win/69	C-price 25¢; stiff-c PC-r	1	2	1.25	2.50	5.00

56. The Toilers of the Sea

Ed	HRN	Date	Details	A	C	GD25	FN65	NM94
1	55	2/49	Original; A.M. Froehlich-c/a	1	1	16.00	48.00	110.00
2	165	–	New-c&a; PC-r; Angelo Torres-a	2	2	4.00	10.50	21.00
3	167	3/64	PC-r	2	2	2.80	7.00	14.00
4	167	10/66	PC-r	2	2	2.80	7.00	14.00

57. The Song of Hiawatha

Ed	HRN	Date	Details	A	C	GD25	FN65	NM94
1	55	3/49	Original; Alex Blum a&c	1	1	10.00	30.00	70.00
2	75	–	No c-price; 'Coming Next' ad; LDC-r	1	1	4.00	11.00	22.00
3	94	–	C-price 15¢; LDC-r	1	1	3.20	8.00	16.00
4	118	–	LDC-r	1	1	2.80	7.00	14.00
5	134	–	New-c; PC-r	1	2	2.40	6.00	12.00
6	139	–	PC-r	1	2	1.25	2.50	5.00
7	154	–	PC-r	1	2	1.25	2.50	5.00
8	167	–	Has orig.date; PC-r	1	2	1.25	2.50	5.00
9	167	9/64	PC-r	1	2	1.25	2.50	5.00
10	167	10/65	PC-r	1	2	1.25	2.50	5.00
11	166	F/1968	C-price 25¢; PC-r	1	2	1.25	2.50	5.00

58. The Prairie

Ed	HRN	Date	Details	A	C	GD25	FN65	NM94
1	60	4/49	Original; Palais c/a	1	1	10.00	30.00	70.00
2	62	–	No c-price; no coming-next ad; LDC-r	1	1	5.85	17.50	35.00
3	78	–	C-price 15¢ in dbl. circle; LDC-r	1	1	3.60	9.00	18.00
4	114	–	LDC-r	1	1	2.80	7.00	14.00
5	131	–	LDC-r	1	1	2.40	6.00	12.00
6	132	–	LDC-r	1	1	2.40	6.00	12.00
7	146	–	New-c; PC-r	1	2	2.40	6.00	12.00
8	155	–	PC-r	1	2	1.25	2.50	5.00
9	167	5/64	PC-r	1	2	1.25	2.50	5.00
10	167	4/66	PC-r	1	2	1.25	2.50	5.00
11	169	Sm/69	New price 25¢; stiff-c; PC-r	1	2	1.25	2.50	5.00

59. Wuthering Heights

Ed	HRN	Date	Details	A	C	GD25	FN65	NM94
1	60	5/49	Original; Kiefer-c/a	1	1	10.00	30.00	70.00
2	85	–	C-price 15¢; LDC-r	1	1	4.00	12.00	24.00
3	156	–	New-c; PC-r	1	2	2.40	6.00	12.00
4	167	1/64	PC-r	1	2	1.50	3.00	6.00
5	167	10/66	PC-r	1	2	1.50	3.00	6.00
6	169	Sm/69	C-price 25¢; stiff-c; PC-r	1	2	1.25	2.50	5.00

60. Black Beauty

Ed	HRN	Date	Details	A	C	GD25	FN65	NM94
1	62	6/49	Original; Froehlich-c/a	1	1	10.00	30.00	70.00
2	62	–	No c-price; no coming-next ad; LDC-r (rare)	1	1	10.00	30.00	70.00
3	85	–	C-price 15¢; LDC-r	1	1	4.00	10.00	20.00
4	158	–	New L.B. Cole-	2	2	3.60	9.00	18.00

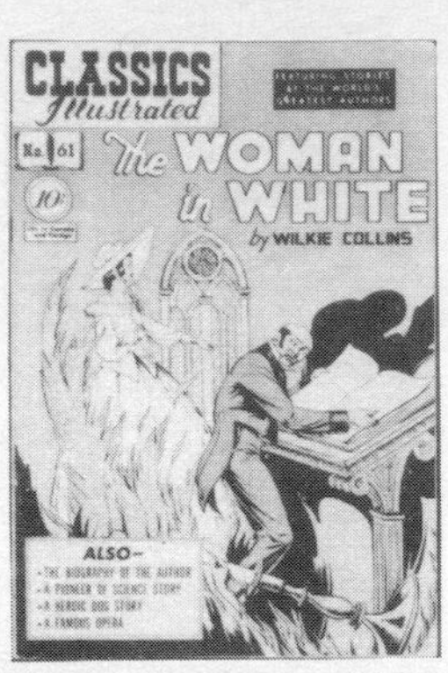

Classics Illustrated #61 (Orig.), © GIL

Classics Illustrated #64 (Orig.), © GIL

Classics Illustrated #66 (Orig.), © GIL

Ed	HRN	Date	Details	A	C	GD25	FN65	NM94
			c/a; PC-r					
5	167	2/64	PC-r	2	2	2.40	6.00	12.00
6	167	3/66	PC-r	2	2	2.40	6.00	12.00
7	166	R/1968	New-c&price, 25¢; PC-r	2	3	5.85	17.50	35.00

61. The Woman in White

Ed	HRN	Date	Details	A	C	GD25	FN65	NM94
1A	62	7/49	Original; Blum-c/a fc-purple; bc: top illos light blue	1	1	10.00	30.00	70.00
1B	62	7/49	Original; Blum-c/a fc-pink; bc: top illos light violet	1	1	10.00	30.00	70.00
2	156	–	New-c; PC-r	1	2	3.20	8.00	16.00
3	167	1/64	PC-r	1	2	2.40	6.00	12.00
4	166	R/1968	C-price 25¢; PC-r	1	2	2.40	6.00	12.00

62. Western Stories ("The Luck of Roaring Camp" and "The Outcasts of Poker Flat")

Ed	HRN	Date	Details	A	C	GD25	FN65	NM94
1	62	8/49	Original; Kiefer-c/a	1	1	10.00	30.00	65.00
2	89	–	C-price 15¢; LDC-r	1	1	4.00	10.00	20.00
3	121	–	LDC-r	1	1	3.20	8.00	16.00
4	137	–	New-c; PC-r	1	2	2.40	6.00	12.00
5	152	–	PC-r	1	2	1.50	3.00	6.00
6	167	10/63	PC-r	1	2	1.50	3.00	6.00
7	167	6/64	PC-r	1	2	1.25	2.50	5.00
8	167	11/66	PC-r	1	2	1.25	2.50	5.00
9	166	R/1968	New-c&price 25¢; PC-r	1	3	2.80	7.00	14.00

63. The Man Without a Country

Ed	HRN	Date	Details	A	C	GD25	FN65	NM94
1	62	9/49	Original; Kiefer-c/a	1	1	10.00	30.00	70.00
2	78	–	C-price 15¢ in double circle; LDC-r	1	1	4.00	11.00	22.00
3	156	–	New-c, old-a; PC-r	1	2	3.20	8.00	16.00
4	165	–	New-a & text pgs.; PC-r; A. Torres-a	2	2	2.40	6.00	12.00
5	167	3/64	PC-r	2	2	1.25	2.50	5.00
6	167	8/66	PC-r	2	2	1.25	2.50	5.00
7	169	Sm/69	New price 25¢; stiff-c; PC-r	2	2	1.25	2.50	5.00

64. Treasure Island

Ed	HRN	Date	Details	A	C	GD25	FN65	NM94
1	62	10/49	Original; Blum-c/a	1	1	10.00	30.00	70.00
2A	82	–	C-price 15¢; soft-c LDC-r	1	1	4.00	10.00	20.00
2B	82	–	Stiff-c; LDC-r	1	1	4.00	11.00	22.00
3	117	–	LDC-r	1	1	3.20	8.00	16.00
4	131	–	New-c; PC-r	1	2	2.40	6.00	12.00
5	138	–	PC-r	1	2	1.25	2.50	5.00
6	146	–	PC-r	1	2	1.25	2.50	5.00
7	158	–	PC-r	1	2	1.25	2.50	5.00
8	165	–	PC-r	1	2	1.25	2.50	5.00
9	167	–	PC-r	1	2	1.25	2.50	5.00
10	167	6/64	PC-r	1	2	1.25	2.50	5.00
11	167	12/65	PC-r	1	2	1.25	2.50	5.00
12A	166	10/67	PC-r	1	2	1.80	4.50	9.00
12B	166	10/67	w/Grit ad stapled in book	1	2	10.00	30.00	60.00
13	169	Spr/69	New price 25¢; stiff-c; PC-r	1	2	1.25	2.50	5.00
14	–	1989	Long John Silver's Seafood Shoppes; $1.95, First/Berkley Publ.; Blum-r	1	2	.40	1.00	2.00

65. Benjamin Franklin

Ed	HRN	Date	Details	A	C	GD25	FN65	NM94
1	64	11/49	Original; Kiefer-c; Iger Shop-a	1	1	10.00	30.00	70.00
2	131	–	New-c; PC-r	1	2	2.80	7.00	14.00
3	154	–	PC-r	1	2	1.25	2.50	5.00
4	167	2/64	PC-r	1	2	1.25	2.50	5.00
5	167	4/66	PC-r	1	2	1.25	2.50	5.00
6	169	Fall/69	New price 25¢; stiff-c; PC-r	1	2	1.25	2.50	5.00

66. The Cloister and the Hearth

Ed	HRN	Date	Details	A	C	GD25	FN65	NM94
1	67	12/49	Original & only ed; Kiefer-a & c	1	1	23.00	70.00	160.00

67. The Scottish Chiefs

Ed	HRN	Date	Details	A	C	GD25	FN65	NM94
1	67	1/50	Original; Blum-a&c	1	1	10.00	30.00	60.00
2	85	–	C-price 15¢; LDC-r	1	1	4.00	10.00	20.00
3	118	–	LDC-r	1	1	3.20	8.00	16.00
4	136	–	New-c; PC-r	1	2	2.40	6.00	12.00
5	154	–	PC-r	1	2	1.60	4.00	8.00
6	167	11/63	PC-r	1	2	1.60	4.00	8.00
7	167	8/65	PC-r	1	2	1.60	4.00	8.00

68. Julius Caesar (Used in SOTI, pgs. 36, 37)

Ed	HRN	Date	Details	A	C	GD25	FN65	NM94
1	70	2/50	Original; Kiefer-c/a	1	1	10.00	30.00	65.00
2	85	–	C-price 15¢; LDC-r	1	1	4.00	10.00	20.00
3	108	–	LDC-r	1	1	3.20	8.00	16.00
4	156	–	New L.B. Cole-c; PC-r	1	2	3.20	8.00	16.00
5	165	–	New-a by Evans, Crandall; PC-r	2	2	3.20	8.00	16.00
6	167	2/64	PC-r	2	2	1.25	2.50	5.00
7	167	10/65	Tarzan books inside cover; PC-r	2	2	1.25	2.50	5.00
8	166	R/1967	PC-r	2	2	1.25	2.50	5.00
9	169	Win/69	PC-r; stiff-c	2	2	1.25	2.50	5.00

69. Around the World in 80 Days

Ed	HRN	Date	Details	A	C	GD25	FN65	NM94
1	70	3/50	Original; Kiefer-c/a	1	1	10.00	30.00	65.00
2	87	–	C-price 15¢; LDC-r	1	1	4.00	10.00	20.00
3	125	–	LDC-r	1	1	3.20	8.00	16.00
4	136	–	New-c; PC-r	1	2	2.40	6.00	12.00
5	146	–	PC-r	1	2	1.25	2.50	5.00
6	152	–	PC-r	1	2	1.25	2.50	5.00
7	164	–	PC-r	1	2	1.25	2.50	5.00
8	167	–	PC-r	1	2	1.25	2.50	5.00
9	167	7/64	PC-r	1	2	1.25	2.50	5.00
10	167	11/65	PC-r	1	2	1.25	2.50	5.00
11	166	7/67	PC-r	1	2	1.25	2.50	5.00
12	169	Spr/69	C-price 25¢; stiff-c; PC-r	1	2	1.25	2.50	5.00

70. The Pilot

Ed	HRN	Date	Details	A	C	GD25	FN65	NM94
1	71	4/50	Original; Blum-c/a	1	1	8.35	25.00	50.00
2	92	–	C-price 15¢; LDC-r	1	1	4.00	10.00	20.00
3	125	–	LDC-r	1	1	3.20	8.00	16.00
4	156	–	New-c; PC-r	1	2	2.40	6.00	12.00
5	167	2/64	PC-r	1	2	1.60	4.00	8.00
6	167	5/66	PC-r	1	2	1.60	4.00	8.00

71. The Man Who Laughs

Ed	HRN	Date	Details	A	C	GD25	FN65	NM94
1	71	5/50	Original; Blum-c/a	1	1	13.00	40.00	90.00

Classics Illustrated #74 (Orig.), © GIL

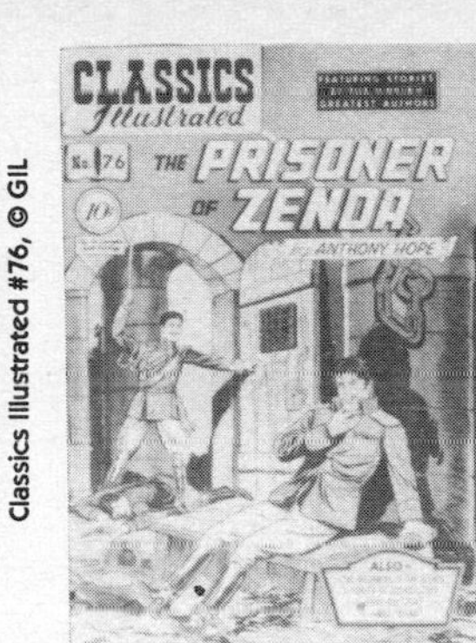
Classics Illustrated #76, © GIL

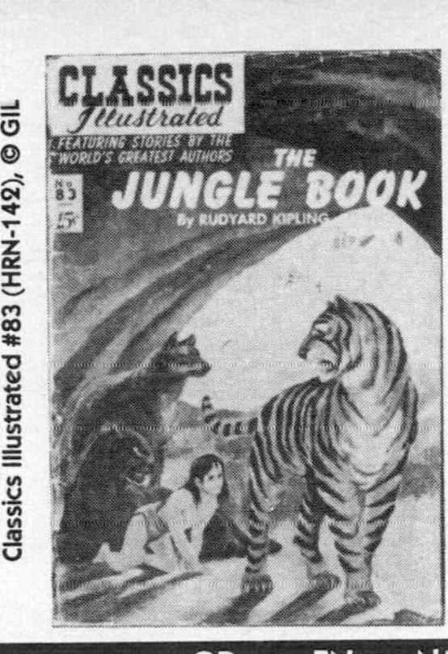
Classics Illustrated #83 (HRN-142), © GIL

Ed	HRN	Date	Details	A	C	GD25	FN65	NM94
2	165	–	New-c&a; PC-r	2	2	8.35	25.00	50.00
3	167	4/64	PC-r	2	2	6.70	20.00	40.00

72. The Oregon Trail

Ed	HRN	Date	Details	A	C	GD25	FN65	NM94
1	7	6/50	Original; Kiefer-c/a	1	1	8.35	25.00	50.00
2	89	–	C-price 15¢; LDC-r	1	1	4.00	10.00	20.00
3	121	–	LDC-r	1	1	3.20	8.00	16.00
4	131	–	New-c; PC-r	1	2	2.40	6.00	12.00
5	140	–	PC-r	1	2	1.50	3.00	6.00
6	150	–	PC-r	1	2	1.25	2.50	5.00
7	164	–	PC-r	1	2	1.25	2.50	5.00
8	167	–	PC-r	1	2	1.25	2.50	5.00
9	167	8/64	PC-r	1	2	1.25	2.50	5.00
10	167	10/65	PC-r	1	2	1.25	2.50	5.00
11	166	R/1968	C-price 25¢; PC-r	1	2	1.25	2.50	5.00

73. The Black Tulip

Ed	HRN	Date	Details	A	C	GD25	FN65	NM94
1	75	7/50	1st & only ed.; Alex Blum c/a	1	1	26.00	77.00	180.00

74. Mr. Midshipman Easy

Ed	HRN	Date	Details	A	C	GD25	FN65	NM94
1	75	8/50	1st & only edition	1	1	26.00	77.00	180.00

75. The Lady of the Lake

Ed	HRN	Date	Details	A	C	GD25	FN65	NM94
1	75	9/50	Original; Kiefer-c/a	1	1	7.50	22.50	45.00
2	85	–	C-price 15¢; LDC-r	1	1	4.00	10.00	20.00
3	118	–	LDC-r	1	1	3.20	8.00	16.00
4	139	–	New-c; PC-r	1	2	2.40	6.00	12.00
5	154	–	PC-r	1	2	1.25	2.50	5.00
6	165	–	PC-r	1	2	1.25	2.50	5.00
7	167	4/64	PC-r	1	2	1.25	2.50	5.00
8	167	5/66	PC-r	1	2	1.25	2.50	5.00
9	169	Spr/69	New price 25¢; stiff-c; PC-r	1	2	1.25	2.50	5.00

76. The Prisoner of Zenda

Ed	HRN	Date	Details	A	C	GD25	FN65	NM94
1	75	10/50	Original; Kiefer-c/a	1	1	7.50	22.50	45.00
2	85	–	C-price 15¢; LDC-r	1	1	4.00	10.00	20.00
3	111	–	LDC-r	1	1	3.20	8.00	16.00
4	128	–	New-c; PC-r	1	2	2.40	6.00	12.00
5	152	–	PC-r	1	2	1.25	2.50	5.00
6	165	–	PC-r	1	2	1.25	2.50	5.00
7	167	4/64	PC-r	1	2	1.25	2.50	5.00
8	167	9/66	PC-r	1	2	1.25	2.50	5.00
9	169	Fall/69	New price 25¢; stiff-c; PC-r	1	2	1.25	2.50	5.00

77. The Iliad

Ed	HRN	Date	Details	A	C	GD25	FN65	NM94
1	78	11/50	Original; Blum-c/a	1	1	7.50	22.50	45.00
2	87	–	C-price 15¢; LDC-r	1	1	4.00	10.00	20.00
3	121	–	LDC-r	1	1	3.20	8.00	16.00
4	139	–	New-c; PC-r	1	2	2.40	6.00	12.00
5	150	–	PC-r	1	2	1.25	2.50	5.00
6	165	–	PC-r	1	2	1.25	2.50	5.00
7	167	10/63	PC-r	1	2	1.25	2.50	5.00
8	167	7/64	PC-r	1	2	1.25	2.50	5.00
9	167	5/66	PC-r	1	2	1.25	2.50	5.00
10	166	R/1968	C-price 25¢; PC-r	1	2	1.25	2.50	5.00

78. Joan of Arc

Ed	HRN	Date	Details	A	C	GD25	FN65	NM94
1	78	12/50	Original; Kiefer-c/a	1	1	7.50	22.50	45.00
2	87	–	C-price 15¢; LDC-r	1	1	4.00	10.00	20.00
3	113	–	LDC-r	1	1	3.20	8.00	16.00
4	128	–	New-c; PC-r	1	2	2.40	6.00	12.00
5	140	–	PC-r	1	2	1.25	2.50	5.00
6	150	–	PC-r	1	2	1.25	2.50	5.00
7	159	–	PC-r	1	2	1.25	2.50	5.00
8	167	–	PC-r	1	2	1.25	2.50	5.00
9	167	12/63	PC-r	1	2	1.25	2.50	5.00
10	167	6/65	PC-r	1	2	1.25	2.50	5.00
11	166	6/67	PC-r	1	2	1.25	2.50	5.00
12	166	Win/69	New-c&price, 25¢; PC-r; stiff-c	1	3	2.40	6.00	12.00

79. Cyrano de Bergerac

Ed	HRN	Date	Details	A	C	GD25	FN65	NM94
1	78	1/51	Orig.; movie promo inside front-c; Blum-a & c	1	1	7.50	22.50	45.00
2	85	–	C-price 15¢; LDC-r	1	1	4.00	10.00	20.00
3	118	–	LDC-r	1	1	3.20	8.00	16.00
4	133	–	New-c; PC-r	1	2	2.80	7.00	14.00
5	150	–	PC-r	1	2	2.00	5.00	10.00
6	167	8/64	PC-r	1	2	2.00	5.00	10.00

80. White Fang (Last line drawn cover)

Ed	HRN	Date	Details	A	C	GD25	FN65	NM94
1	79	2/51	Orig.; Blum-c/a	1	1	7.50	22.50	45.00
2	87	–	C-price 15¢; LDC-r	1	1	4.00	10.00	20.00
3	125	–	LDC-r	1	1	3.20	8.00	16.00
4	132	–	New-c; PC-r	1	2	2.40	6.00	12.00
5	140	–	PC-r	1	2	1.25	2.50	5.00
6	153	–	PC-r	1	2	1.25	2.50	5.00
7	167	–	PC-r	1	2	1.25	2.50	5.00
8	167	9/64	PC-r	1	2	1.25	2.50	5.00
9	167	7/65	PC-r	1	2	1.25	2.50	5.00
10	166	6/67	PC-r	1	2	1.25	2.50	5.00
11	169	Fall/69	New price 25¢; PC-r; stiff-c	1	2	1.25	2.50	5.00

81. The Odyssey (1st painted cover)

Ed	HRN	Date	Details	A	C	GD25	FN65	NM94
1	82	3/51	First 15¢ Original; Blum-c	1	1	5.35	16.00	32.00
2	167	8/64	PC-r	1	1	2.00	5.00	10.00
3	167	10/66	PC-r	1	1	2.00	5.00	10.00
4	169	Spr/69	New, stiff-c; PC-r	1	2	2.40	6.00	12.00

82. The Master of Ballantrae

Ed	HRN	Date	Details	A	C	GD25	FN65	NM94
1	82	4/51	Original; Blum-c	1	1	5.00	15.00	30.00
2	167	8/64	PC-r	1	1	2.40	6.00	12.00
3	166	Fall/68	New, stiff-c; PC-r	1	2	2.40	6.00	12.00

83. The Jungle Book

Ed	HRN	Date	Details	A	C	GD25	FN65	NM94
1	85	5/51	Original; Blum-c Bossert/Blum-a	1	1	5.00	15.00	30.00
2	110	–	PC-r	1	1	1.40	3.50	7.00
3	125	–	PC-r	1	1	1.25	2.50	5.00
4	134	–	PC-r	1	1	1.25	2.50	5.00
5	142	–	PC-r	1	1	1.25	2.50	5.00
6	150	–	PC-r	1	1	1.25	2.50	5.00
7	159	–	PC-r	1	1	1.25	2.50	5.00
8	167	–	PC-r	1	1	1.25	2.50	5.00
9	167	3/65	PC-r	1	1	1.25	2.50	5.00
10	167	11/65	PC-r	1	1	1.25	2.50	5.00
11	167	5/66	PC-r	1	1	1.25	2.50	5.00
12	166	R/1968	New c&a; stiff-c; PC-r	2	2	2.40	6.00	12.00

Classics Illustrated #90, © GIL

Classics Illustrated #94, © GIL

Classics Illustrated #95, © GIL

84. The Gold Bug and Other Stories ("The Gold Bug," "The Tell-Tale Heart," "The Cask of Amontillado")

Ed	HRN	Date	Details	A	C	GD25	FN65	NM94
1	85	6/51	Original; Blum-c/a; Palais, Laverly-a	1	1	11.00	32.00	75.00
2	167	7/64	PC-r	1	1	6.70	20.00	40.00

85. The Sea Wolf

Ed	HRN	Date	Details	A	C	GD25	FN65	NM94
1	85	7/51	Original; Blum-c/a	1	1	4.00	11.00	22.00
2	121	–	PC-r	1	1	1.00	2.00	4.00
3	132	–	PC-r	1	1	1.00	2.00	4.00
4	141	–	PC-r	1	1	1.00	2.00	4.00
5	161	–	PC-r	1	1	1.00	2.00	4.00
6	167	2/64	PC-r	1	1	1.00	2.00	4.00
7	167	11/65	PC-r	1	1	1.00	2.00	4.00
8	169	Fall/69	New price 25¢; stiff-c; PC-r	1	1	1.00	2.00	4.00

86. Under Two Flags

Ed	HRN	Date	Details	A	C	GD25	FN65	NM94
1	87	8/51	Original; first delBourgo-a	1	1	4.00	11.00	22.00
2	117	–	PC-r	1	1	1.00	2.00	4.00
3	139	–	PC-r	1	1	1.00	2.00	4.00
4	158	–	PC-r	1	1	1.00	2.00	4.00
5	167	2/64	PC-r	1	1	1.00	2.00	4.00
6	167	8/66	PC-r	1	1	1.00	2.00	4.00
7	169	Sm/69	New price 25¢; stiff-c; PC-r	1	1	1.00	2.00	4.00

87. A Midsummer Nights Dream

Ed	HRN	Date	Details	A	C	GD25	FN65	NM94
1	87	9/51	Original; Blum c/a	1	1	4.00	11.00	22.00
2	161	–	PC-r	1	1	1.25	2.50	5.00
3	167	4/64	PC-r	1	1	1.00	2.00	4.00
4	167	5/66	PC-r	1	1	1.00	2.00	4.00
5	169	Sm/69	New price 25¢; stiff-c; PC-r	1	1	1.00	2.00	4.00

88. Men of Iron

Ed	HRN	Date	Details	A	C	GD25	FN65	NM94
1	89	10/51	Original	1	1	4.00	12.00	24.00
2	154	–	PC-r	1	1	1.25	2.50	5.00
3	167	1/64	PC-r	1	1	1.25	2.50	5.00
4	166	R/1968	C-price 25¢; PC-r	1	1	1.25	2.50	5.00

89. Crime and Punishment (Cover illo. in POP)

Ed	HRN	Date	Details	A	C	GD25	FN65	NM94
1	89	11/51	Original; Palais-a	1	1	4.00	12.00	24.00
2	152	–	PC-r	1	1	1.00	2.00	4.00
3	167	4/64	PC-r	1	1	1.00	2.00	4.00
4	167	5/66	PC-r	1	1	1.00	2.00	4.00
5	169	Fall/69	New price 25¢ stiff-c; PC-r	1	1	1.00	2.00	4.00

90. Green Mansions

Ed	HRN	Date	Details	A	C	GD25	FN65	NM94
1	89	12/51	Original; Blum-c/a	1	1	4.35	13.00	26.00
2	148	–	New L.B. Cole-c; PC-r	1	2	2.00	5.00	10.00
3	165	–	PC-r	1	2	1.00	2.00	4.00
4	167	4/64	PC-r	1	2	1.00	2.00	4.00
5	167	9/66	PC-r	1	2	1.00	2.00	4.00
6	169	Sm/69	New price 25¢; stiff-c; PC-r	1	2	1.00	2.00	4.00

91. The Call of the Wild

Ed	HRN	Date	Details	A	C	GD25	FN65	NM94
1	92	1/52	Orig.; delBourgo-a	1	1	4.00	11.00	22.00
2	112	–	PC-r	1	1	1.25	2.50	5.00
3	125	–	'Picture Progress' on back-c; PC-r	1	1	1.00	2.00	4.00
4	134	–	PC-r	1	1	1.00	2.00	4.00
5	143	–	PC-r	1	1	1.00	2.00	4.00
6	165	–	PC-r	1	1	1.00	2.00	4.00
7	167	–	PC-r	1	1	1.00	2.00	4.00
8	167	4/65	PC-r	1	1	1.00	2.00	4.00
9	167	3/66	PC-r	1	1	1.00	2.00	4.00
10	166	11/67	PC-r	1	1	1.00	2.00	4.00
11	169	Spr/70	New price 25¢; stiff-c; PC-r	1	1	1.00	2.00	4.00

92. The Courtship of Miles Standish

Ed	HRN	Date	Details	A	C	GD25	FN65	NM94
1	92	2/52	Original; Blum-c/a	1	1	4.00	11.00	22.00
2	165	–	PC-r	1	1	1.00	2.00	4.00
3	167	3/64	PC-r	1	1	1.00	2.00	4.00
4	166	5/67	PC-r	1	1	1.00	2.00	4.00
5	169	Win/69	New price 25¢ stiff-c; PC-r	1	1	1.00	2.00	4.00

93. Pudd'nhead Wilson

Ed	HRN	Date	Details	A	C	GD25	FN65	NM94
1	94	3/52	Orig.; Kiefer-c/a;	1	1	4.35	13.00	26.00
2	165	–	New-c; PC-r	1	2	1.80	4.50	9.00
3	167	3/64	PC-r	1	2	1.40	3.50	7.00
4	166	R/1968	New price 25¢; soft-c; PC-r	1	2	1.40	3.50	7.00

94. David Balfour

Ed	HRN	Date	Details	A	C	GD25	FN65	NM94
1	94	4/52	Original; Palais-a	1	1	4.35	13.00	26.00
2	167	5/64	PC-r	1	1	2.00	5.00	10.00
3	166	R/1968	C-price 25¢; PC-r	1	1	2.00	5.00	10.00

95. All Quiet on the Western Front

Ed	HRN	Date	Details	A	C	GD25	FN65	NM94
1A	96	5/52	Orig.; del Bourgo-a	1	1	9.15	27.50	55.00
1B	99	5/52	Orig.; del Bourgo-a	1	1	8.35	25.00	50.00
2	167	10/64	PC-r	1	1	2.80	7.00	14.00
3	167	11/66	PC-r	1	1	2.80	7.00	14.00

96. Daniel Boone

Ed	HRN	Date	Details	A	C	GD25	FN65	NM94
1	97	6/52	Original; Blum-a	1	1	4.00	11.00	22.00
2	117	–	PC-r	1	1	1.00	2.00	4.00
3	128	–	PC-r	1	1	1.00	2.00	4.00
4	132	–	PC-r	1	1	1.00	2.00	4.00
5	134	–	"Story of Jesus" on back-c; PC-r	1	1	1.00	2.00	4.00
6	158	–	PC-r	1	1	1.00	2.00	4.00
7	167	1/64	PC-r	1	1	1.00	2.00	4.00
8	167	5/65	PC-r	1	1	1.00	2.00	4.00
9	167	11/66	PC-r	1	1	1.00	2.00	4.00
10	166	Win/69	New-c; price 25¢; PC-r; stiff-c	1	2	2.00	5.00	10.00

97. King Solomon's Mines

Ed	HRN	Date	Details	A	C	GD25	FN65	NM94
1	96	7/52	Orig.; Kiefer-a	1	1	4.00	11.00	22.00
2	118	–	PC-r	1	1	1.50	3.50	7.00
3	131	–	PC-r	1	1	1.00	2.00	4.00
4	141	–	PC-r	1	1	1.00	2.00	4.00
5	158	–	PC-r	1	1	1.00	2.00	4.00
6	167	2/64	PC-r	1	1	1.00	2.00	4.00
7	167	9/65	PC-r	1	1	1.00	2.00	4.00
8	169	Sm/69	New price 25¢; stiff-c; PC-r	1	1	1.25	2.50	5.00

Classics Illustrated #99, © GIL

Classics Illustrated #101 (Orig.), © GIL

Classics Illustrated #105 (HRN-167), © GIL

98. The Red Badge of Courage

Ed	HRN	Date	Details	A	C	GD25	FN65	NM94
1	98	8/52	Original	1	1	4.00	11.00	22.00
2	118	–	PC-r	1	1	1.00	2.00	4.00
3	132	–	PC-r	1	1	1.00	2.00	4.00
4	142	–	PC-r	1	1	1.00	2.00	4.00
5	152	–	PC-r	1	1	1.00	2.00	4.00
6	161	–	PC-r	1	1	1.00	2.00	4.00
7	167	–	Has orig.date; PC-r	1	1	1.00	2.00	4.00
8	167	9/64	PC-r	1	1	1.00	2.00	4.00
9	167	10/65	PC-r	1	1	1.00	2.00	4.00
10	166	R/1968	New-c&price 25¢; PC-r; stiff-c	1	2	2.40	6.00	12.00

99. Hamlet (Used in POP, pg. 102)

Ed	HRN	Date	Details	A	C	GD25	FN65	NM94
1	98	9/52	Original; Blum-a	1	1	4.00	12.00	24.00
2	121	–	PC-r	1	1	1.00	2.00	4.00
3	141	–	PC-r	1	1	1.00	2.00	4.00
4	158	–	PC-r	1	1	1.00	2.00	4.00
5	167	–	Has orig.date; PC-r	1	1	1.00	2.00	4.00
6	167	7/65	PC-r	1	1	1.00	2.00	4.00
7	166	4/67	PC-r	1	1	1.00	2.00	4.00
8	169	Spr/69	New-c&price 25¢; PC-r; stiff-c	1	2	2.00	5.00	10.00

100. Mutiny on the Bounty

Ed	HRN	Date	Details	A	C	GD25	FN65	NM94
1	100	10/52	Original	1	1	4.00	11.00	22.00
2	117	–	PC-r	1	1	1.00	2.00	4.00
3	132	–	PC-r	1	1	1.00	2.00	4.00
4	142	–	PC-r	1	1	1.00	2.00	4.00
5	155	–	PC-r	1	1	1.00	2.00	4.00
6	167	–	Has orig. date;PC-r	1	1	1.00	2.00	4.00
7	167	5/64	PC-r	1	1	1.00	2.00	4.00
8	167	3/66	PC-r	1	1	1.00	2.00	4.00
9	169	Spr/70	PC-r; stiff-c	1	1	1.00	2.00	4.00

101. William Tell

Ed	HRN	Date	Details	A	C	GD25	FN65	NM94
1	101	11/52	Original; Kiefer-c delBourgo-a	1	1	4.00	11.00	22.00
2	118	–	PC-r	1	1	1.00	2.00	4.00
3	141	–	PC-r	1	1	1.00	2.00	4.00
4	158	–	PC-r	1	1	1.00	2.00	4.00
5	167	–	Has orig.date; PC-r	1	1	1.00	2.00	4.00
6	167	11/64	PC-r	1	1	1.00	2.00	4.00
7	166	4/67	PC-r	1	1	1.00	2.00	4.00
8	169	Win/69	New price 25¢; stiff-c; PC-r	1	1	1.00	2.00	4.00

102. The White Company

Ed	HRN	Date	Details	A	C	GD25	FN65	NM94
1	101	12/52	Original; Blum-a	1	1	6.70	20.00	40.00
2	165	–	PC-r	1	1	3.60	9.00	18.00
3	167	4/64	PC-r	1	1	3.60	9.00	18.00

103. Men Against the Sea

Ed	HRN	Date	Details	A	C	GD25	FN65	NM94
1	104	1/53	Original; Kiefer-c; Palais-a	1	1	4.35	13.00	26.00
2	114	–	PC-r	1	1	2.80	7.00	14.00
3	131	–	New-c; PC-r	1	2	2.00	5.00	10.00
4	158	–	PC-r	1	2	2.00	5.00	10.00
5	149	–	White reorder list; came after HRN-158; PC-r	1	2	3.60	9.00	18.00
6	167	3/64	PC-r	1	2	1.40	3.50	7.00

104. Bring 'Em Back Alive

Ed	HRN	Date	Details	A	C	GD25	FN65	NM94
1	105	2/53	Original; Kiefer c/a	1	1	4.00	10.50	21.00
2	118	–	PC-r	1	1	1.00	2.00	4.00
3	133	–	PC-r	1	1	1.00	2.00	4.00
4	150	–	PC-r	1	1	1.00	2.00	4.00
5	158	–	PC-r	1	1	1.00	2.00	4.00
6	167	10/63	PC-r	1	1	1.00	2.00	4.00
7	167	9/65	PC-r	1	1	1.00	2.00	4.00
8	169	Win/69	New price 25¢; stiff-c; PC-r	1	1	1.00	2.00	4.00

105. From the Earth to the Moon

Ed	HRN	Date	Details	A	C	GD25	FN65	NM94
1	106	3/53	Original; Blum-a	1	1	4.00	10.50	21.00
2	118	–	PC-r	1	1	1.00	2.00	4.00
3	132	–	PC-r	1	1	1.00	2.00	4.00
4	141	–	PC-r	1	1	1.00	2.00	4.00
5	146	–	PC-r	1	1	1.00	2.00	4.00
6	156	–	PC-r	1	1	1.00	2.00	4.00
7	167	–	Has orig. date; PC-r	1	1	1.00	2.00	4.00
8	167	5/64	PC-r	1	1	1.00	2.00	4.00
9	167	5/65	PC-r	1	1	1.00	2.00	4.00
10A	166	10/67	PC-r	1	1	1.00	2.00	4.00
10B	166	10/67	w/Grit ad stapled in book	1	1	9.35	28.00	56.00
11	169	Sm/69	New price 25¢; stiff-c; PC-r	1	1	1.00	2.00	4.00
12	169	Spr/71	PC-r	1	1	1.00	2.00	4.00

106. Buffalo Bill

Ed	HRN	Date	Details	A	C	GD25	FN65	NM94
1	107	4/53	Orig.; delBourgo-a	1	1	4.00	10.50	21.00
2	118	–	PC-r	1	1	1.00	2.00	4.00
3	132	–	PC-r	1	1	1.00	2.00	4.00
4	142	–	PC-r	1	1	1.00	2.00	4.00
5	161	–	PC-r	1	1	1.00	2.00	4.00
6	167	3/64	PC-r	1	1	1.00	2.00	4.00
7	166	7/67	PC-r	1	1	1.00	2.00	4.00
8	169	Fall/69	PC-r; stiff-c	1	1	1.00	2.00	4.00

107. King of the Khyber Rifles

Ed	HRN	Date	Details	A	C	GD25	FN65	NM94
1	108	5/53	Original	1	1	4.00	11.00	22.00
2	118	–	PC-r	1	1	1.00	2.00	4.00
3	146	–	PC-r	1	1	1.00	2.00	4.00
4	158	–	PC-r	1	1	1.00	2.00	4.00
5	167	–	Has orig.date; PC-r	1	1	1.00	2.00	4.00
6	167	–	PC-r	1	1	1.00	2.00	4.00
7	167	10/66	PC-r	1	1	1.00	2.00	4.00

108. Knights of the Round Table

Ed	HRN	Date	Details	A	C	GD25	FN65	NM94
1A	108	6/53	Original; Blum-a	1	1	4.00	11.00	22.00
1B	109	6/53	Original; scarce	1	1	5.35	16.00	32.00
2	117	–	PC-r	1	1	1.00	2.00	4.00
3	165	–	PC-r	1	1	1.00	2.00	4.00
4	167	4/64	PC-r	1	1	1.00	2.00	4.00
5	166	4/67	PC-r	1	1	1.00	2.00	4.00
6	169	Sm/69	New price 25¢; stiff-c; PC-r	1	1	1.00	2.00	4.00

109. Pitcairn's Island

Ed	HRN	Date	Details	A	C	GD25	FN65	NM94
1	110	7/53	Original; Palais-a	1	1	4.00	12.00	24.00
2	165	–	PC-r	1	1	1.50	3.50	7.00
3	167	3/64	PC-r	1	1	1.50	3.50	7.00
4	166	6/67	PC-r	1	1	1.50	3.50	7.00

Classics Illustrated #111 (HRN-167), © GIL

Classics Illustrated #124 (Orig.), © GIL

Classics Illustrated #130 (HRN-167), © GIL

110. A Study in Scarlet

Ed	HRN	Date	Details	A	C	GD25	FN65	NM94
1	111	8/53	Original	1	1	11.00	32.00	75.00
2	165	–	PC-r	1	1	7.00	21.00	42.00

111. The Talisman

Ed	HRN	Date	Details	A	C	GD25	FN65	NM94
1	112	9/53	Original; last H.C. Kiefer-a	1	1	5.35	16.00	32.00
2	165	–	PC-r	1	1	1.25	2.50	5.00
3	167	5/64	PC-r	1	1	1.25	2.50	5.00
4	166	Fall/68	C-price 25¢; PC-r	1	1	1.25	2.50	5.00

112. Adventures of Kit Carson

Ed	HRN	Date	Details	A	C	GD25	FN65	NM94
1	113	10/53	Original; Palais-a	1	1	5.35	16.00	32.00
2	129	–	PC-r	1	1	1.00	2.00	4.00
3	141	–	PC-r	1	1	1.00	2.00	4.00
4	152	–	PC-r	1	1	1.00	2.00	4.00
5	161	–	PC-r	1	1	1.00	2.00	4.00
6	167	–	PC-r	1	1	1.00	2.00	4.00
7	167	2/65	PC-r	1	1	1.00	2.00	4.00
8	167	5/66	PC-r	1	1	1.00	2.00	4.00
9	166	Win/69	New-c&price 25¢; PC-r; stiff-c	1	2	2.00	5.00	10.00

113. The Forty-Five Guardsmen

Ed	HRN	Date	Details	A	C	GD25	FN65	NM94
1	114	11/53	Orig.; delBourgo-a	1	1	7.50	22.50	45.00
2	166	7/67	PC-r	1	1	4.00	10.50	21.00

114. The Red Rover

Ed	HRN	Date	Details	A	C	GD25	FN65	NM94
1	115	12/53	Original	1	1	7.50	22.50	45.00
2	166	7/67	PC-r	1	1	4.00	10.50	21.00

115. How I Found Livingstone

Ed	HRN	Date	Details	A	C	GD25	FN65	NM94
1	116	1/54	Original	1	1	7.50	22.50	45.00
2	167	1/67	PC-r	1	1	4.00	10.50	21.00

116. The Bottle Imp

Ed	HRN	Date	Details	A	C	GD25	FN65	NM94
1	117	2/54	Orig.; Cameron-a	1	1	7.50	22.50	45.00
2	167	1/67	PC-r	1	1	4.00	10.50	21.00

117. Captains Courageous

Ed	HRN	Date	Details	A	C	GD25	FN65	NM94
1	118	3/54	Orig.; Costanza-a	1	1	6.35	19.00	38.00
2	167	2/67	PC-r	1	1	2.40	6.00	12.00
3	169	Fall/69	New price 25¢; stiff-c; PC-r	1	1	2.00	5.00	10.00

118. Rob Roy

Ed	HRN	Date	Details	A	C	GD25	FN65	NM94
1	119	4/54	Original; Rudy & Walter Palais-a	1	1	7.50	22.50	45.00
2	167	2/67	PC-r	1	1	4.00	10.50	21.00

119. Soldiers of Fortune

Ed	HRN	Date	Details	A	C	GD25	FN65	NM94
1	120	5/54	Original Shaffenberger-a	1	1	7.00	21.00	42.00
2	166	3/67	PC-r	1	1	2.80	7.00	14.00
3	169	Spr/70	New price 25¢; stiff-c; PC-r	1	1	2.00	5.00	10.00

120. The Hurricane

Ed	HRN	Date	Details	A	C	GD25	FN65	NM94
1	121	6/54	Orig.; Cameron-a	1	1	7.50	22.50	45.00
2	166	3/67	PC-r	1	1	4.00	12.00	24.00

121. Wild Bill Hickok

Ed	HRN	Date	Details	A	C	GD25	FN65	NM94
1	122	7/54	Original	1	1	4.00	11.00	22.00
2	132	–	PC-r	1	1	1.00	2.00	4.00
3	141	–	PC-r	1	1	1.00	2.00	4.00
4	154	–	PC-r	1	1	1.00	2.00	4.00
5	167	–	PC-r	1	1	1.00	2.00	4.00
6	167	8/64	PC-r	1	1	1.00	2.00	4.00
7	166	4/67	PC-r	1	1	1.00	2.00	4.00
8	169	Win/69	PC-r; stiff-c	1	1	1.00	2.00	4.00

122. The Mutineers

Ed	HRN	Date	Details	A	C	GD25	FN65	NM94
1	123	9/54	Original	1	1	4.00	11.00	22.00
2	136	–	PC-r	1	1	1.00	2.00	4.00
3	146	–	PC-r	1	1	1.00	2.00	4.00
4	158	–	PC-r	1	1	1.00	2.00	4.00
5	167	11/63	PC-r	1	1	1.00	2.00	4.00
6	167	3/65	PC-r	1	1	1.00	2.00	4.00
7	166	8/67	PC-r	1	1	1.00	2.00	4.00

123. Fang and Claw

Ed	HRN	Date	Details	A	C	GD25	FN65	NM94
1	124	11/54	Original	1	1	4.00	11.00	22.00
2	133	–	PC-r	1	1	1.00	2.00	4.00
3	143	–	PC-r	1	1	1.00	2.00	4.00
4	154	–	PC-r	1	1	1.00	2.00	4.00
5	167	–	Has orig.date; PC-r	1	1	1.00	2.00	4.00
6	167	9/65	PC-r	1	1	1.00	2.00	4.00

124. The War of the Worlds

Ed	HRN	Date	Details	A	C	GD25	FN65	NM94
1	125	1/55	Original; Cameron-c/a	1	1	5.00	15.00	30.00
2	131	–	PC-r	1	1	1.40	3.50	7.00
3	141	–	PC-r	1	1	1.40	3.50	7.00
4	148	–	PC-r	1	1	1.40	3.50	7.00
5	156	–	PC-r	1	1	1.40	3.50	7.00
6	165	–	PC-r	1	1	1.40	3.50	7.00
7	167	–	PC-r	1	1	1.40	3.50	7.00
8	167	11/64	PC-r	1	1	1.40	3.50	7.00
9	167	11/65	PC-r	1	1	1.40	3.50	7.00
10	166	R/1968	C-price 25¢; PC-r	1	1	1.40	3.50	7.00
11	169	Sm/70	PC-r; stiff-c	1	1	1.40	3.50	7.00

125. The Ox Bow Incident

Ed	HRN	Date	Details	A	C	GD25	FN65	NM94
1	3/55	–	Original; Picture Progress replaces reorder list	1	1	4.00	11.00	22.00
2	143	–	PC-r	1	1	1.00	2.00	4.00
3	152	–	PC-r	1	1	1.00	2.00	4.00
4	149	–	PC-r	1	1	1.00	2.00	4.00
5	167	–	PC-r	1	1	1.00	2.00	4.00
6	167	11/64	PC-r	1	1	1.00	2.00	4.00
7	166	4/67	PC-r	1	1	1.00	2.00	4.00
8	169	Win/69	New price 25¢; stiff-c; PC-r	1	1	1.00	2.00	4.00

126. The Downfall

Ed	HRN	Date	Details	A	C	GD25	FN65	NM94
1	5/55	–	Orig.; 'Picture Progress' replaces reorder list; Cameron-c/a	1	1	4.00	11.00	22.00
2	167	8/64	PC-r	1	1	1.60	4.00	8.00
3	166	R/1968	C-price 25¢; PC-r	1	1	1.60	4.00	8.00

Classics Illustrated #133 (HRN-167), © GIL

Classics Illustrated #138, © GIL

Classics Illustrated #140 (HRN-160.), © GIL

127. The King of the Mountains

Ed	HRN	Date	Details	A	C	GD25	FN65	NM94
1	128	7/55	Original	1	1	4.00	11.00	22.00
2	167	6/64	PC-r	1	1	1.60	4.00	8.00
3	166	F/1968	C-price 25¢; PC-r	1	1	1.60	4.00	8.00

128. Macbeth (Used in POP, pg. 102)

Ed	HRN	Date	Details	A	C	GD25	FN65	NM94
1	128	9/55	Orig.; last Blum-a	1	1	4.00	11.00	22.00
2	143	–	PC-r	1	1	1.00	2.00	4.00
3	158	–	PC-r	1	1	1.00	2.00	4.00
4	167	–	PC-r	1	1	1.00	2.00	4.00
5	167	6/64	PC-r	1	1	1.00	2.00	4.00
6	166	4/67	PC-r	1	1	1.00	2.00	4.00
7	166	R/1968	C-Price 25¢; PC-r	1	1	1.00	2.00	4.00
8	169	Spr/70	Stiff-c; PC-r	1	1	1.00	2.00	4.00

129. Davy Crockett

Ed	HRN	Date	Details	A	C	GD25	FN65	NM94
1	129	11/55	Orig.; Cameron-a	1	1	10.00	30.00	60.00
2	167	9/66	PC-r	1	1	5.35	16.00	32.00

130. Caesar's Conquests

Ed	HRN	Date	Details	A	C	GD25	FN65	NM94
1	130	1/56	Original; Orlando-a	1	1	4.00	11.00	22.00
2	142	–	PC-r	1	1	1.00	2.00	4.00
3	152	–	PC-r	1	1	1.00	2.00	4.00
4	149	–	PC-r	1	1	1.00	2.00	4.00
5	167	–	PC-r	1	1	1.00	2.00	4.00
6	167	10/64	PC-r	1	1	1.00	2.00	4.00
7	167	4/66	PC-r	1	1	1.00	2.00	4.00

131. The Covered Wagon

Ed	HRN	Date	Details	A	C	GD25	FN65	NM94
1	131	3/56	Original	1	1	4.00	11.00	22.00
2	143	–	PC-r	1	1	1.00	2.00	4.00
3	152	–	PC-r	1	1	1.00	2.00	4.00
4	158	–	PC-r	1	1	1.00	2.00	4.00
5	167	–	PC-r	1	1	1.00	2.00	4.00
6	167	11/64	PC-r	1	1	1.00	2.00	4.00
7	167	4/66	PC-r	1	1	1.00	2.00	4.00
8	169	Win/69	New price 25¢; stiff-c; PC-r	1	1	1.00	2.00	4.00

132. The Dark Frigate

Ed	HRN	Date	Details	A	C	GD25	FN65	NM94
1	132	5/56	Original	1	1	4.00	11.00	22.00
2	150	–	PC-r	1	1	1.40	3.50	7.00
3	167	1/64	PC-r	1	1	1.40	3.50	7.00
4	166	5/67	PC-r	1	1	1.40	3.50	7.00

133. The Time Machine

Ed	HRN	Date	Details	A	C	GD25	FN65	NM94
1	132	7/56	Orig.; Cameron-a	1	1	5.00	15.00	30.00
2	142	–	PC-r	1	1	1.40	3.50	7.00
3	152	–	PC-r	1	1	1.40	3.50	7.00
4	158	–	PC-r	1	1	1.40	3.50	7.00
5	167	–	PC-r	1	1	1.40	3.50	7.00
6	167	6/64	PC-r	1	1	1.40	3.50	7.00
7	167	3/66	PC-r	1	1	1.40	3.50	7.00
8	166	12/67	PC-r	1	1	1.40	3.50	7.00
9	169	Win/71	New price 25¢; stiff-c; PC-r	1	1	1.40	3.50	7.00

134. Romeo and Juliet

Ed	HRN	Date	Details	A	C	GD25	FN65	NM94
1	134	9/56	Original; Evans-a	1	1	4.00	11.00	22.00
2	161	–	PC-r	1	1	1.00	2.00	4.00
3	167	9/63	PC-r	1	1	1.00	2.00	4.00
4	167	5/65	PC-r	1	1	1.00	2.00	4.00
5	166	6/67	PC-r	1	1	1.00	2.00	4.00
6	166	Win/69	New c&price 25¢; stiff-c; PC-r	1	2	3.60	9.00	18.00

135. Waterloo

Ed	HRN	Date	Details	A	C	GD25	FN65	NM94
1	135	11/56	Orig.; G. Ingels-a	1	1	4.00	11.00	22.00
2	153	–	PC-r	1	1	1.00	2.00	4.00
3	167	–	PC-r	1	1	1.00	2.00	4.00
4	167	9/64	PC-r	1	1	1.00	2.00	4.00
5	166	R/1968	C-prico 25¢; PC-r	1	1	1.00	2.00	4.00

136. Lord Jim

Ed	HRN	Date	Details	A	C	GD25	FN65	NM94
1	136	1/57	Original; Evans-a	1	1	4.00	11.00	22.00
2	165	–	PC-r	1	1	1.00	2.00	4.00
3	167	3/64	PC-r	1	1	1.00	2.00	4.00
4	167	9/66	PC-r	1	1	1.00	2.00	4.00
5	169	Sm/69	New price 25 ¢; stiff-c; PC-r	1	1	1.00	2.00	4.00

137. The Little Savage

Ed	HRN	Date	Details	A	C	GD25	FN65	NM94
1	136	3/57	Original; Evans-a	1	1	4.00	11.00	22.00
2	148	–	PC-r	1	1	1.00	2.00	4.00
3	156	–	PC-r	1	1	1.00	2.00	4.00
4	167	–	PC-r	1	1	1.00	2.00	4.00
5	167	10/64	PC-r	1	1	1.00	2.00	4.00
6	166	8/67	PC-r	1	1	1.00	2.00	4.00
7	169	Spr/70	New price 25¢; stiff-c; PC-r	1	1	1.00	2.00	4.00

138. A Journey to the Center of the Earth

Ed	HRN	Date	Details	A	C	GD25	FN65	NM94
1	136	5/57	Original	1	1	4.70	14.00	28.00
2	146	–	PC-r	1	1	1.25	2.50	5.00
3	156	–	PC-r	1	1	1.25	2.50	5.00
4	158	–	PC-r	1	1	1.25	2.50	5.00
5	167	–	PC-r	1	1	1.25	2.50	5.00
6	167	6/64	PC-r	1	1	1.25	2.50	5.00
7	167	4/66	PC-r	1	1	1.25	2.50	5.00
8	166	R/68	C-price 25¢; PC-r	1	1	1.25	2.50	5.00

139. In the Reign of Terror

Ed	HRN	Date	Details	A	C	GD25	FN65	NM94
1	139	7/57	Original; Evans-a	1	1	4.00	11.00	22.00
2	154	–	PC-r	1	1	1.00	2.00	4.00
3	167	–	Has orig.date; PC-r	1	1	1.00	2.00	4.00
4	167	7/64	PC-r	1	1	1.00	2.00	4.00
5	166	R/1968	C-price 25¢; PC-r	1	1	1.00	2.00	4.00

140. On Jungle Trails

Ed	HRN	Date	Details	A	C	GD25	FN65	NM94
1	140	9/57	Original	1	1	4.00	11.00	22.00
2	150	–	PC-r	1	1	1.00	2.00	4.00
3	160	–	PC-r	1	1	1.00	2.00	4.00
4	167	9/63	PC-r	1	1	1.00	2.00	4.00
5	167	9/65	PC-r	1	1	1.00	2.00	4.00

141. Castle Dangerous

Ed	HRN	Date	Details	A	C	GD25	FN65	NM94
1	141	11/57	Original	1	1	4.00	11.00	22.00
2	152	–	PC-r	1	1	1.25	2.50	5.00
3	167	–	PC-r	1	1	1.25	2.50	5.00
4	166	7/67	PC-r	1	1	1.25	2.50	5.00

142. Abraham Lincoln

Ed	HRN	Date	Details	A	C	GD25	FN65	NM94
1	142	1/58	Original	1	1	4.00	11.00	22.00
2	154	–	PC-r	1	1	1.00	2.00	4.00
3	158	–	PC-r	1	1	1.00	2.00	4.00
4	167	10/63	PC-r	1	1	1.00	2.00	4.00

Classics Illustrated #148, © GIL

Classics Illustrated #149 (Orig?), © GIL

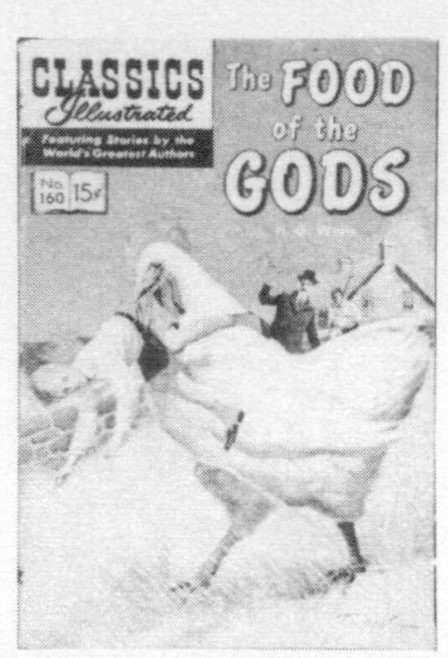

Classics Illustrated #160 (HRN-160), © GIL

Ed	HRN	Date	Details	A	C	GD25	FN65	NM94
5	167	7/65	PC-r	1	1	1.00	2.00	4.00
6	166	11/67	PC-r	1	1	1.00	2.00	4.00
7	169	Fall/69	New price 25¢; stiff-c; PC-r	1	1	1.00	2.00	4.00

143. Kim

Ed	HRN	Date	Details	A	C	GD25	FN65	NM94
1	143	3/58	Original; Orlando-a	1	1	4.00	11.00	22.00
2	165	–	PC-r	1	1	1.00	2.00	4.00
3	167	11/63	PC-r	1	1	1.00	2.00	4.00
4	167	8/65	PC-r	1	1	1.00	2.00	4.00
5	169	Win/69	New price 25¢; stiff-c; PC-r	1	1	1.00	2.00	4.00

144. The First Men in the Moon

Ed	HRN	Date	Details	A	C	GD25	FN65	NM94
1	143	5/58	Original; Woodbridge/Williamson/Torres-a	1	1	4.70	14.00	28.00
2	152	–	(Rare)-PC-r	1	1	5.85	17.50	35.00
3	153	–	PC-r	1	1	1.25	2.50	5.00
4	161	–	PC-r	1	1	1.25	2.50	5.00
5	167	–	PC-r	1	1	1.25	2.50	5.00
6	167	12/65	PC-r	1	1	1.25	2.50	5.00
7	166	Fall/68	New-c&price 25¢; PC-r; stiff-c	1	2	1.80	4.50	9.00
8	169	Win/69	Stiff-c; PC-r	1	2	1.80	4.50	9.00

145. The Crisis

Ed	HRN	Date	Details	A	C	GD25	FN65	NM94
1	143	7/58	Original; Evans-a	1	1	4.00	11.00	22.00
2	156	–	PC-r	1	1	1.00	2.00	4.00
3	167	10/63	PC-r	1	1	1.00	2.00	4.00
4	167	3/65	PC-r	1	1	1.00	2.00	4.00
5	166	R/68	C-price 25¢; PC-r	1	1	1.00	2.00	4.00

146. With Fire and Sword

Ed	HRN	Date	Details	A	C	GD25	FN65	NM94
1	143	9/58	Original; Woodbridge-a	1	1	4.00	11.00	22.00
2	156	–	PC-r	1	1	1.40	3.50	7.00
3	167	11/63	PC-r	1	1	1.40	3.50	7.00
4	167	3/65	PC-r	1	1	1.40	3.50	7.00

147. Ben-Hur

Ed	HRN	Date	Details	A	C	GD25	FN65	NM94
1	147	11/58	Original; Orlando-a	1	1	4.00	11.00	22.00
2	152	–	Scarce; PC-r	1	1	4.00	12.00	24.00
3	153	–	PC-r	1	1	1.00	2.00	4.00
4	158	–	PC-r	1	1	1.00	2.00	4.00
5	167	–	Orig.date; but PC-r	1	1	1.00	2.00	4.00
6	167	2/65	PC-r	1	1	1.00	2.00	4.00
7	167	9/66	PC-r	1	1	1.00	2.00	4.00
8A	166	Fall/68	New-c&price 25¢; PC-r; soft-c	1	2	2.40	6.00	12.00
8B	166	Fall/68	New-c&price 25¢; PC-r; stiff-c; scarce	1	2	4.00	12.00	24.00

148. The Buccaneer

Ed	HRN	Date	Details	A	C	GD25	FN65	NM94
1	148	1/59	Orig.; Evans/Jenny-a; Saunders-c	1	1	4.00	11.00	22.00
2	568	–	Juniors list only PC-r	1	1	1.40	3.50	7.00
3	167	–	PC-r	1	1	1.00	2.00	4.00
4	167	9/65	PC-r	1	1	1.00	2.00	4.00
5	169	Sm/69	New price 25¢; PC-r; stiff-c	1	1	1.00	2.00	4.00

149. Off on a Comet

Ed	HRN	Date	Details	A	C	GD25	FN65	NM94
1	149	3/59	Orig.;G.McCann-a; blue reorder list	1	1	4.00	11.00	22.00
2	155	–	PC-r	1	1	1.00	2.00	4.00
3	149	–	PC-r; white reorder list; no coming-next ad	1	1	1.00	2.00	4.00
4	167	12/63	PC-r	1	1	1.00	2.00	4.00
5	167	2/65	PC-r	1	1	1.00	2.00	4.00
6	167	10/66	PC-r	1	1	1.00	2.00	4.00
7	166	Fall/68	New-c&price 25¢; PC-r	1	2	2.40	6.00	12.00

150. The Virginian

Ed	HRN	Date	Details	A	C	GD25	FN65	NM94
1	150	5/59	Original	1	1	5.00	15.00	30.00
2	164	–	PC-r	1	1	2.40	6.00	12.00
3	167	10/63	PC-r	1	1	2.00	5.00	10.00
4	167	12/65	PC-r	1	1	2.00	5.00	10.00

151. Won By the Sword

Ed	HRN	Date	Details	A	C	GD25	FN65	NM94
1	150	7/59	Original	1	1	5.00	15.00	30.00
2	164	–	PC-r	1	1	2.00	5.00	10.00
3	167	10/63	PC-r	1	1	1.80	4.50	9.00
4	166	7/67	PC-r	1	1	1.80	4.50	9.00

152. Wild Animals I Have Known

Ed	HRN	Date	Details	A	C	GD25	FN65	NM94
1	152	9/59	Orig.; L.B. Cole c/a	1	1	5.00	15.00	30.00
2A	149	–	PC-r; white reorder list; no coming-next ad; IBC: Jr. list #572	1	1	1.25	2.50	5.00
2B	149	–	PC-r; inside-bc: Jr. list to #555	1	1	1.40	3.50	7.00
2C	149	–	PC-r; inside-bc: has World Around Us ad; scarce	1	1	2.80	7.00	14.00
3	167	9/63	PC-r	1	1	1.00	2.00	4.00
4	167	8/65	PC-r	1	1	1.00	2.00	4.00
5	169	Fall/69	New price 25¢; stiff-c; PC-r	1	1	1.00	2.00	4.00

153. The Invisible Man

Ed	HRN	Date	Details	A	C	GD25	FN65	NM94
1	153	11/59	Original	1	1	5.00	15.00	30.00
2A	149	–	PC-r; white reorder list; no coming-next ad; inside-bc: Jr. list to #572	1	1	1.25	2.50	5.00
2B	149	–	PC-r; inside-bc: Jr. list to #555	1	1	1.40	3.50	7.00
3	167	–	PC-r	1	1	1.00	2.00	4.00
4	167	2/65	PC-r	1	1	1.00	2.00	4.00
5	167	9/66	PC-r	1	1	1.00	2.00	4.00
6	166	Win/69	New price 25¢; PC-r; stiff-c	1	1	1.00	2.00	4.00
7	169	Spr/71	Stiff-c; letters spelling 'Invisible Man' are 'solid' not 'invisible;' PC-r	1	1	1.00	2.00	4.00

154. The Conspiracy of Pontiac

Ed	HRN	Date	Details	A	C	GD25	FN65	NM94
1	154	1/60	Original	1	1	5.00	15.00	30.00
2	167	11/63	PC-r	1	1	2.40	6.00	12.00
3	167	7/64	PC-r	1	1	2.40	6.00	12.00
4	166	12/67	PC-r	1	1	2.40	6.00	12.00

Classics Illustrated #163 (Orig.), © GIL

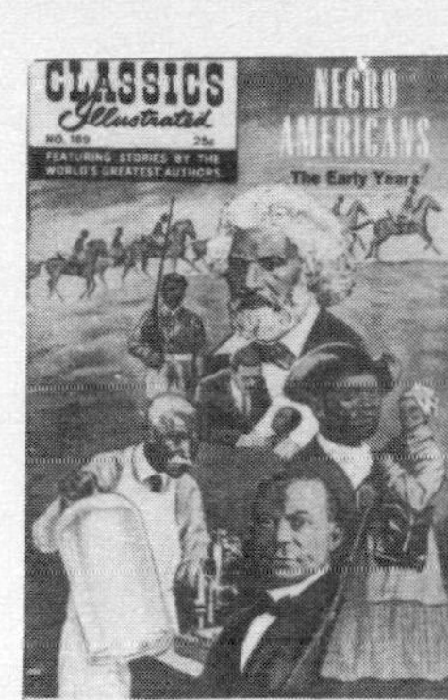
Classics Illustrated #169 (Orig.), © GIL

Classics Giveaways, 12/42 Saks 34th St., © GIL

155. The Lion of the North

Ed	HRN	Date	Details	A	C	GD25	FN65	NM94
1	154	3/60	Original	1	1	4.70	14.00	28.00
2	167	1/64	PC-r	1	1	2.00	5.00	10.00
3	166	R/1967	C-price 25¢; PC-r	1	1	1.80	4.50	9.00

156. The Conquest of Mexico

Ed	HRN	Date	Details	A	C	GD25	FN65	NM94
1	156	5/60	Orig.; Bruno Premiani-c/a	1	1	4.70	14.00	28.00
2	167	1/64	PC-r	1	1	1.40	3.50	7.00
3	166	8/67	PC-r	1	1	1.40	3.50	7.00
4	169	Spr/70	New price 25¢; stiff-c; PC-r	1	1	1.25	2.50	5.00

157. Lives of the Hunted

Ed	HRN	Date	Details	A	C	GD25	FN65	NM94
1	156	7/60	Orig.; L.B. Cole-c	1	1	5.00	15.00	30.00
2	167	2/64	PC-r	1	1	2.40	6.00	12.00
3	166	10/67	PC-r	1	1	2.40	6.00	12.00

158. The Conspirators

Ed	HRN	Date	Details	A	C	GD25	FN65	NM94
1	156	9/60	Original	1	1	5.00	15.00	30.00
2	167	7/64	PC-r	1	1	2.40	6.00	12.00
3	166	10/67	PC-r	1	1	2.40	6.00	12.00

159. The Octopus

Ed	HRN	Date	Details	A	C	GD25	FN65	NM94
1	159	11/60	Orig.; Gray Morrow-a; L.B. Cole-c	1	1	5.00	15.00	30.00
2	167	2/64	PC-r	1	1	2.00	5.00	10.00
3	166	R/1967	C-price 25¢; PC-r	1	1	2.00	5.00	10.00

160. The Food of the Gods

Ed	HRN	Date	Details	A	C	GD25	FN65	NM94
1A	159	1/61	Original	1	1	5.00	15.00	30.00
1B	160	1/61	Original; same, except for HRN	1	1	5.00	15.00	30.00
2	167	1/64	PC-r	1	1	2.00	5.00	10.00
3	166	6/67	PC-r	1	1	2.00	5.00	10.00

161. Cleopatra

Ed	HRN	Date	Details	A	C	GD25	FN65	NM94
1	161	3/61	Original	1	1	5.85	17.50	35.00
2	167	1/64	PC-r	1	1	2.80	7.00	14.00
3	166	8/67	PC-r	1	1	2.80	7.00	14.00

162. Robur the Conqueror

Ed	HRN	Date	Details	A	C	GD25	FN65	NM94
1	162	5/61	Original	1	1	5.00	15.00	30.00
2	167	7/64	PC-r	1	1	2.00	5.00	10.00
3	166	8/67	PC-r	1	1	2.00	5.00	10.00

163. Master of the World

Ed	HRN	Date	Details	A	C	GD25	FN65	NM94
1	163	7/61	Original; Gray Morrow-a	1	1	5.00	15.00	30.00
2	167	1/65	PC-r	1	1	2.00	5.00	10.00
3	166	R/1968	C-price 25¢; PC-r	1	1	2.00	5.00	10.00

164. The Cossack Chief

Ed	HRN	Date	Details	A	C	GD25	FN65	NM94
1	164	(1961)	Orig.; nd(10/61?)	1	1	5.00	15.00	30.00
2	167	4/65	PC-r	1	1	2.00	5.00	10.00
3	166	Fall/68	C-price 25¢; PC-r	1	1	2.00	5.00	10.00

165. The Queen's Necklace

Ed	HRN	Date	Details	A	C	GD25	FN65	NM94
1	164	1/62	Original; Morrow-a	1	1	5.00	15.00	30.00
2	167	4/65	PC-r	1	1	2.00	5.00	10.00
3	166	Fall/68	C-price 25¢; PC-r	1	1	2.00	5.00	10.00

166. Tigers and Traitors

Ed	HRN	Date	Details	A	C	GD25	FN65	NM94
1	165	5/62	Original	1	1	8.00	24.00	48.00
2	167	2/64	PC-r	1	1	3.60	9.00	18.00
3	167	11/66	PC-r	1	1	3.60	9.00	18.00

167. Faust

Ed	HRN	Date	Details	A	C	GD25	FN65	NM94
1	165	8/62	Original	1	1	11.00	32.00	75.00
2	167	2/64	PC-r	1	1	5.35	16.00	32.00
3	166	6/67	PC-r	1	1	5.35	16.00	32.00

168. In Freedom's Cause

Ed	HRN	Date	Details	A	C	GD25	FN65	NM94
1	169	Win/69	Original; Evans/Crandall-a; stiff-c; 25¢; no coming-next ad;	1	1	10.00	30.00	70.00

169. Negro AmericansThe Early Years

Ed	HRN	Date	Details	A	C	GD25	FN65	NM94
1	166	Spr/69	Orig. & last issue; 25¢; Stiff-c; no coming-next ad; other sources indicate publication date of 5/69	1	1	10.00	30.00	70.00
2	169	Spr/69	Stiff-c	1	1	6.70	20.00	40.00

NOTE: Many other titles were prepared or planned but were only issued in British/European series.

CLASSICS GIVEAWAYS (Arranged in chronological order)

12/41–Walter Theatre Enterprises (Huntington, WV) giveaway containing #2 (orig.) w/new generic-c (only 1 known copy) 93.00 280.00 650.00

1942–Double Comics containing CC#1 (orig.) (diff. cover) (not actually a giveaway) (very rare) (also see Double Comics) (only one known copy) 200.00 600.00 1400.00

12/42–Saks 34th St. Giveaway containing CC#7 (orig.) (diff. cover) (very rare; only 6 known copies) 600.00 1800.00 4200.00

2/43–American Comics containing CC#8 (orig.) (Liberty Theatre giveaway) (different cover) (only one known copy) (see American Comics) 129.00 385.00 900.00

12/44–Robin Hood Flour Co. Giveaway - #7-CC(R) (diff. cover) (rare) (edition probably 5 [22]) 257.00 771.00 1800.00

NOTE: How are above editions determined without CC covers? 1942 is dated 1942, and CC#1-first reprint did not come out until 5/43. 12/42 and 2/43 are determined by blue note at bottom of first text page only in original edition. 12/44 is estimated from page width each reprint edition had progressively slightly smaller page width.

1951–Shelter Thru the Ages (C.I. Educational Series) (actually Giveaway by the Ruberoid Co.) (16 pgs.) (contains original artwork by H. C. Kiefer) (there are back cover ad variations)(scarce) 71.00 215.00 500.00

1952–George Daynor Biography Giveaway (CC logo) (partly comic book/pictures/newspaper articles) (story of man who built Palace Depression out of junkyard swamp in NJ) (64 pgs.)(very rare; only 2 known copies, one missing-bc) 785.00 2360.00 5500.00

1953–Westinghouse/Dreams of a Man (C.I. Educational Series) (Westinghouse bio./Westinghouse Co. giveaway) (contains original artwork by H. C. Kiefer) (16 pgs.) (also French/Spanish/Italian versions) (scarce) 79.00 235.00 550.00

NOTE: Reproductions of 1951, 1952, and 1953 exist color photocopy covers and black & white photocopy interior ("W.C.N. Reprint") 2.00 5.00 10.00

1951-53–Coward Shoe Giveaways (all editions very rare); 2 variations of back-c ad exist:

With back-c photo ad: 5 (87), 12 (89), 22 (85), 49 (85), 69 (87), 72 (no HRN), 80 (0), 91 (0), 92 (0), 96 (0), 98 (0), 100 (0), 101 (0), 103-105 (all Os) 36.00 107.00 250.00

With back-c cartoon ad: 106-109 (all 0s), 110 (111), 112 (0) 43.00 130.00 300.00

1956–Ben Franklin 5-10 Store Giveaway (#65-PC with back cover ad)

Classics Illustrated Junior #507, © GIL

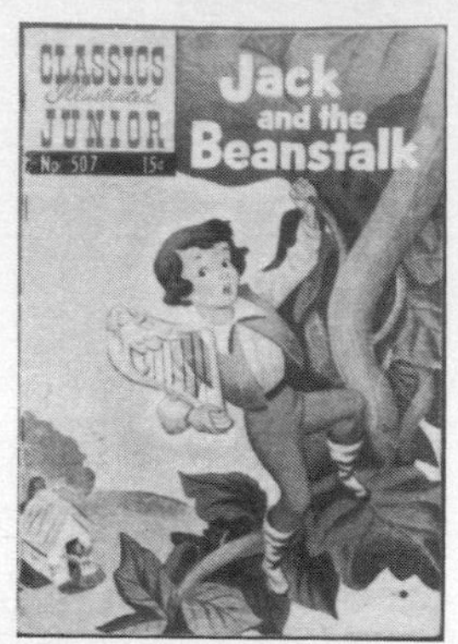

Classics Illustrated Junior #512, © GIL

Classics Illustrated Junior #518, © GIL

	GD25	FN65	NM94
(scarce)	30.00	90.00	210.00
1956–Ben Franklin Insurance Co. Giveaway (#65-PC with diff. back cover ad) (very rare)	71.00	215.00	500.00
11/56–Sealtest Co. Edition - #4 (135) (identical to regular edition except for Sealtest logo printed, not stamped, on front cover) (only two copies known to exist)	36.00	107.00	250.00
1958–Get-Well Giveaway containing #15-CI (new cartoon-type cover) (Pressman Pharmacy) (only one copy known to exist)	36.00	107.00	250.00
1967-68–Twin Circle Giveaway Editions - all HRN 166, with back cover ad for National Catholic Press.			
2(R68), 4(R67), 10(R68), 13(R68)	4.00	12.00	24.00
48(R67), 128(R68), 535(576-R68)	5.00	15.00	30.00
16(R68), 68(R67)	6.70	20.00	40.00
12/69–Christmas Giveaway ("A Christmas Adventure") (reprints Picture Parade #4-1953, new cover) (4 ad variations)			
Stacy's Dept. Store	4.00	10.00	20.00
Anne & Hope Store	7.50	22.50	45.00
Gibson's Dept. Store (rare)	7.50	22.50	45.00
"Merry Christmas" & blank ad space	4.00	10.00	20.00

CLASSICS ILLUSTRATED GIANTS
October, 1949 (One-Shots - "OS")
Gilberton Publications

These Giant Editions, all with new Kiefer front and back covers, were advertised from 10/49 to 2/52. They were 50 cents on the newsstand and 60 cents by mail. They are actually fourclassics in one volume. All the stories are reprints of the Classics Illustrated Series. NOTE: There were also British hardback Adventure & Indian Giants in 1952, with the same covers but different contents: Adventure - 2, 7, 10; Indian - 17, 22, 37, 58. They are also rare.

	GD25	FN65	NM94
"An Illustrated Library of Great Adventure Stories" - reprints of No. 6,7,8,10 (Rare); Kiefer-c	107.00	320.00	750.00
"An Illustrated Library of Exciting Mystery Stories" - reprints of No. 30,21,40, 13 (Rare)	115.00	343.00	800.00
"An Illustrated Library of Great Indian Stories" - reprints of No. 4,17,22,37 (Rare)	100.00	300.00	700.00

INTRODUCTION TO CLASSICS ILLUSTRATED JUNIOR

Collectors of Juniors can be put into one of two categories those who want any copy of each title, and those who want all the originals. Those seeking every original and reprint edition are a limited group, primarily because Juniors have no changes in art or covers to spark interest, and because reprints are so low in value it is difficult to get dealers to look for specific reprint editions. Anyone interested in information about the full scope of Junior editions should write to Jim McLoughlin, 28 Mercury Ave., East Patchogue, NY 11772. He has been doing research in this area for several years.

In recent years it has become apparent that most serious Classics collectors seek Junior originals. Those seeking reprints seek them for low cost. This has made the previous note about the comparative market value of reprints inadequate. Most dealers report difficulty in moving reprints for more than $2-$4 for mint copies. Some may be worth $5-$7, just because of the popularity of the title, such as Snow White, Sleeping Beauty, and Wizard of Oz. Others may be worth $5-$7, because of the scarcity of particular title nos., such as 514, 560, 562, 575 & 576. Three particular reprint editions are worth even more. For the 535-Twin Circle edition, see Giveaways. There are also reprint editions of 501 and 503 which have a full-page bc ad for the very rare Junior record. Those may sell as high as $10-$15 in mint. Original editions of 557 and 558 also have that ad.

There are no reprint editions of 577. The only edition, from 1969, is a 25 cent stiff-cover edition with no ad for the next issue. All other original editions have coming-next ad. But 577, like C.I. #168, was prepared in 1962 but not issued. Copies of 577 can be found in 1963 British/Europ∆104
ean series, which then continued with dozens of additional new Junior titles.

PRICES LISTED BELOW ARE FOR ORIGINAL EDITIONS, WHICH HAVE AN AD FOR THE NEXT ISSUE.

CLASSICS ILLUSTRATED JUNIOR
Oct, 1953 - Spring, 1971
Famous Authors Ltd. (Gilberton Publications)

	GD25	FN65	NM94
501-Snow White & the Seven Dwarfs; Alex Blum-a	9.35	28.00	56.00
502-The Ugly Duckling	5.85	17.50	35.00
503-Cinderella	4.00	10.50	21.00
504-512: 504-The Pied Piper. 505-The Sleeping Beauty. 506-The Three Little Pigs. 507-Jack & the Beanstalk. 508-Goldilocks & the Three Bears. 509-Beauty and the Beast. 510-Little Red Riding Hood. 511-Puss-N Boots. 512-Rumpel Stiltskin	2.80	7.00	14.00
513-Pinocchio	4.00	10.50	21.00
514-The Steadfast Tin Soldier	4.70	14.00	28.00
515-Johnny Appleseed	2.80	7.00	14.00
516-Aladdin and His Lamp	4.00	10.50	21.00
517-519: 517-The Emperor's New Clothes. 518-The Golden Goose. 519-Paul Bunyan	2.80	7.00	14.00
520-Thumbelina	4.00	10.50	21.00
521-King of the Golden River	2.80	7.00	14.00
522-530: 522-The Nightingale. 523-The Gallant Tailor. 524-The Wild Swans. 525-The Little Mermaid. 526-The Frog Prince. 527-The Golden-Haired Giant. 528-The Penny Prince. 529-The Magic Servants. 530-The Golden Bird	2.00	5.00	10.00
531-Rapunzel	2.80	7.00	14.00
532-534: 532-The Dancing Princesses. 533-The Magic Fountain. 534-The Golden Touch	2.00	5.00	10.00
535-The Wizard of Oz	4.70	14.00	28.00
536-538: 536-The Chimney Sweep. 537-The Three Fairies. 538-Silly Hans	2.00	5.00	10.00
539-The Enchanted Fish	4.00	10.50	21.00
540-The Tinder-Box	4.00	10.50	21.00
541-Snow White & Rose Red	2.80	7.00	14.00
542-The Donkey's Tale	2.80	7.00	14.00
543-The House in the Woods	2.00	5.00	10.00
544-The Golden Fleece	4.70	14.00	28.00
545-The Glass Mountain	2.80	7.00	14.00
546-The Elves & the Shoemaker	2.80	7.00	14.00
547-551: 547-The Wishing Table. 548-The Magic Pitcher. 549-Simple Kate. 550-The Singing Donkey. 551-The Queen Bee	2.00	5.00	10.00
552-The Three Little Dwarfs	2.80	7.00	14.00
553-556: 553-King Thrushbeard. 554-The Enchanted Deer. 555-The Three Golden Apples. 556-The Elf Mound	2.00	5.00	10.00
557-Silly Willy	4.00	10.50	21.00
558-The Magic Dish; L.B. Cole-c; soft and stiff-c exist on original	4.00	10.50	21.00
559-The Japanese Lantern; 1 pg. Ingels-a; L.B. Cole-c	4.00	10.50	21.00
560-The Doll Princess; L.B. Cole-c	4.00	10.50	21.00
561-Hans Humdrum; L.B. Cole-c	2.00	5.00	10.00
562-The Enchanted Pony; L.B. Cole-c	4.00	10.50	21.00
563-570: 563-The Wishing Well; L.B. Cole-c. 564-The Salt Mountain; L.B.Cole-c. 565-The Silly Princess; L.B. Cole-c. 566-Clumsy Hans; L.B. Cole-c. 567-The Bearskin Soldier; L.B. Cole-c. 568-The Happy Hedgehog; L.B. Cole-c. 569-The Three Giants. 570-The Pearl Princess	2.00	5.00	10.00
571-574: 571-How Fire Came to the Indians. 572-The Drummer Boy. 573-The Crystal Ball. 574-Brightboots	2.40	6.00	12.00
575-The Fearless Prince	2.80	7.00	14.00
576-The Princess Who Saw Everything	4.00	10.50	21.00
577-The Runaway Dumpling	4.70	14.00	28.00

NOTE: *Prices are for original editions. Last reprint - Spring, 1971.* **Costanza & Shaffenberger** *art in many issues.*

CLASSICS ILLUSTRATED SPECIAL ISSUE
Dec, 1955 - July, 1962 (100 pages) (35 cents)

Classics Illustrated Special Issue #129, © GIL

Clay Cody Gunslinger #1, © PINE

Climax #1, © Gilmore Magazines

GD25 FN65 NM94

Gilberton Co. (Came out semi-annually)
129-The Story of Jesus (titled ...Special Edition) "Jesus on Mountain" cover 5.85 17.50 35.00
"Three Camels" cover (12/58) 8.35 25.00 50.00
"Mountain" cover (no date)-Has checklist on inside b/c to HRN #161 & different testimonial on back-c 4.20 12.50 25.00
"Mountain" cover (1968 re-issue; has white 50 cent circle) 4.00 10.00 20.00
132A-The Story of America (6/56) 4.70 14.00 28.00
135A-The Ten Commandments(12/56) 5.35 16.00 32.00
138A-Adventures in Science(6/57); HRN to 137 4.70 14.00 28.00
138A-(6/57)-2nd version w/HRN to 149 4.00 11.00 22.00
138A-(12/61)-3rd version w/HRN to 149 4.00 10.00 20.00
141A-The Rough Rider (Teddy Roosevelt)(12/57); Evans-a 4.70 14.00 28.00
144A-Blazing the Trails West(6/58)- 73 pages of Crandall/Evans plus Severin-a 4.70 14.00 28.00
147A-Crossing the Rockies(12/58)-Crandall/Evans-a 5.35 16.00 32.00
150A-Royal Canadian Police(6/59)-Ingels, Sid Check-a 5.35 16.00 32.00
153A-Men, Guns & Cattle(12/59)-Evans-a, 26 pgs.; Kinstler-a 5.85 17.50 35.00
156A-The Atomic Age(6/60)-Crandall/Evans, Torres-a 4.70 14.00 28.00
159A-Rockets, Jets and Missiles(12/60)-Evans, Morrow-a 4.70 14.00 28.00
162A-War Between the States(6/61)-Kirby & Crandall/Evans-a; Ingels-a 10.00 30.00 70.00
165A-To the Stars(12/61)-Torres, Crandall/Evans, Kirby-a 4.70 14.00 28.00
166A-World War II('62)-Torres, Crandall/Evans, Kirby-a 5.85 17.50 35.00
167A-Prehistoric World(7/62)-Torres & Crandall/Evans-a; two versions exist (HRN to 165 & HRN to 167) 5.85 17.50 35.00
nn Special Issue-The United Nations (1964; 50 cents; scarce); this is actually part of the European Special Series, which continued on after the U.S. series stopped issuing new titles in 1962. This English edition was prepared specifically for sale at the U.N. It was printed in Norway 29.00 85.00 200.00

NOTE: *There was another U.S. Special Issue prepared in 1962 with artwork by* ***Torres*** *entitled World War I. Unfortunately, it was never issued in any English-language edition. It was issued in 1964 in West Germany, The Netherlands, and some Scandanavian countries, with another edition in 1974 with a new cover.*

CLASSIC PUNISHER (Also see Punisher)
Dec, 1989 ($4.95, B&W, deluxe format, 68 pgs.)
Marvel Comics
1-Reprints Marvel Super Action #1 & Marvel Preview #2 plus new story 1.00 2.00 5.00

CLASSICS ILLUSTRATED
Feb, 1990 - No. 27, July?, 1991 ($3.75-$3.95, color, 52 pgs.)
First Publishing/Berkley Publishing
1-17: 1-Gahan Wilson-c/a. 4-Sienkiewicz painted-c/a. 6-Russell scripts/ layouts. 7-Spiegle-a. 9-Ploog-c/a. 16-Staton-a 1.50 3.75
18-27: 18-Gahan Wilson-c/a; begin $3.95-c. 20-Geary-a. 26-Aesop's Fables (6/91). 26,27-Direct sale only 1.60 4.00

CLASSICS LIBRARY (See King Classics)

CLASSIC STAR WARS (Also see Star Wars)
Aug, 1992 - Present ($2.50, color)
Dark Horse Comics
1-10-Star Wars strip-r by Williamson; Williamson redrew portions of the panels to fit comic book format; Williamson c-1-5,7 1.00 2.50

CLASSIC X-MEN (Becomes X-Men Classic #46 on)
Sept, 1986 - No. 45, Mar, 1990 (#27 on: $1.25)
Marvel Comics Group
1-Begins-r of New X-Men 1.00 2.00 5.00
2-4 1.60 4.00
5-9 1.20 3.00
10-Sabretooth app. 1.60 4.00
11-15 1.00 2.50
16,18-20 .80 2.00
17-Wolverine-c 1.60 4.00
21-25,27-30: 27-r/X-Men #121 .40 1.00 1.75
26-r/X-Men #120; Wolverine-c/app. 1.60 4.00
31-38,40-42,44,45: 35-r/X-Men #129 1.50
39-New Jim Lee back-up story (2nd-a on X-Men) 1.00 2.00 5.00
43-Byrne-c/a(r); $1.75, double-size .80 2.00

NOTE: ***Art Adams*** *c(p)-1-10, 12-16, 18, 19, 25.* ***Austin*** *c-19i.* ***Bolton*** *back up stories in 1-28 at least.* ***Williamson*** *c-12-14i.*

CLAW (See Capt. Battle, Jr. Daredevil Comics & Silver Streak Comics)

CLAW THE UNCONQUERED (See Cancelled Comic Cavalcade)
5-6/75 - No. 9, 9-10/76; No. 10, 4-5/78 - No. 12, 8-9/78
National Periodical Publications/DC Comics
1-1st app. Claw .80 2.00
2,3: 3-Nudity panel 1.50
4-12: 9-Origin 1.20

NOTE: ***Giffen*** *a-8-12p.* ***Kubert*** *c-10-12.* ***Layton*** *a-9i, 12i.*

CLAY CODY, GUNSLINGER
Fall, 1957
Pines Comics
1-Painted-c 4.00 10.00 20.00

CLEAN FUN, STARRING "SHOOGAFOOTS JONES"
1944 (24 pgs.; B&W; oversized covers) (10 cents)
Specialty Book Co.
nn-Humorous situations involving Negroes in the Deep South
White cover issue.... 4.00 10.00 20.00
Dark grey cover issue.... 4.00 11.00 22.00

CLEMENTINA THE FLYING PIG (See Dell Jr. Treasury)

CLEOPATRA (See Ideal, a Classical Comic No. 1)

CLIFF MERRITT SETS THE RECORD STRAIGHT
Giveaway (2 different issues)
Brotherhood of Railroad Trainsmen
...and the Very Candid Candidate by Al Williamson .60 1.50 3.00
...Sets the Record Straight by Al Williamson (2 different-c: one by Williamson, the other by McWilliams) .60 1.50 3.00

CLIFFORD MCBRIDE'S IMMORTAL NAPOLEON & UNCLE ELBY
1932 (12x17"; softcover cartoon book)
The Castle Press
nn-Intro. by Don Herod 10.00 30.00 70.00

CLIMAX!
July, 1955 - No. 2, Sept, 1955
Gillmor Magazines
1,2 (Mystery) 8.35 25.00 50.00

CLINT (Elcipse)(Value: cover or less)

CLINT & MAC (See 4-Color No. 889)

CLIVE BARKER'S BOOK OF THE DAMNED: A HELLRAISER COMPANION
Oct, 1991 - Present ($4.95, color, bi-annual, 52 pgs.)
Epic Comics (Marvel)
Volume 1-4: 1-Simon Bisley-c. 2-(4/92). 3-(11/92)-McKean-a 1.00 2.00 5.00

CLIVE BARKER'S HELLRAISER (Also see Epic, Hellraiser Nightbreed – Jihad, Revelations, Son of Celluloid, Tapping the Vein & Weaveworld)
1989 - No. 20, 1993 ($4.95, color, mature readers, quarterly, 68 pgs.)
Epic Comics (Marvel)

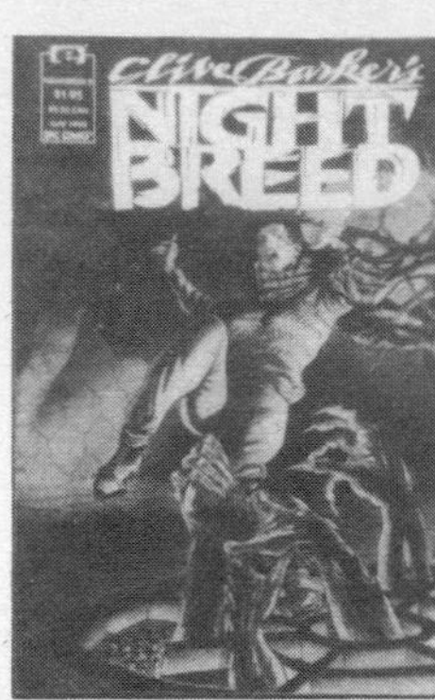

Clive Barker's Nightbreed #2, © Morgan Creek

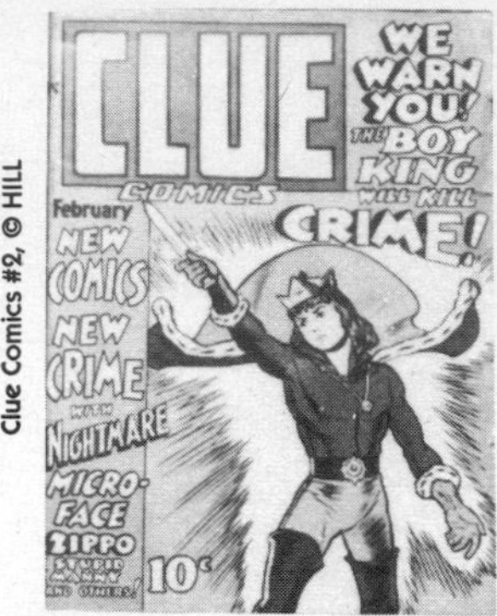

Clue Comics #2, © HILL

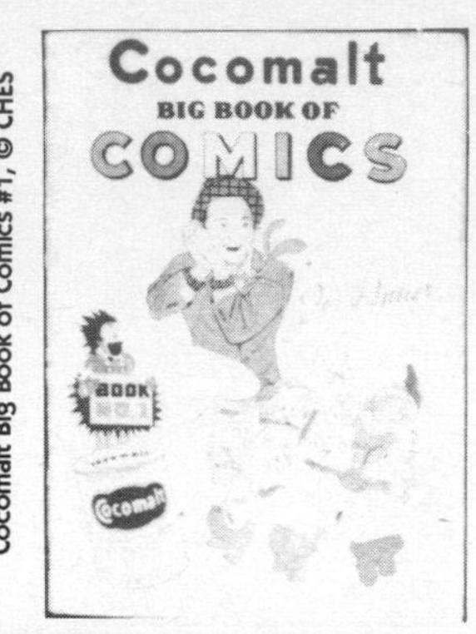

Cocomalt Big Book of Comics #1, © CHES

GD25 FN65 NM94

Book 1-Based on Hellraiser & Hellbound movies; Bolton-c/a; Spiegle & Wrightson-a (graphic album) 1.00 2.00 5.00
Book 2-4,14-20 ($4.95): 20-By Gaiman/McKean 1.00 2.00 5.00
Book 5-9 ($5.95): 7-Bolton-a. 8-Morrow-a 1.00 2.50 6.00
Book 10,11 ($4.50, 52 pgs.): 11-Guice-p. 1.80 4.50
Book 12-Sam Kieth-a 1.00 2.00 5.00
Book 13-20 ($4.95) 1.00 2.00 5.00
Dark Holiday Special ('92, $4.95)-Conrad-a 1.00 2.00 5.00
...Summer Special 1 (1992, $5.95, 68 pgs.) 1.00 2.50 6.00

CLIVE BARKER'S NIGHTBREED (Also see Epic)
Apr, 1990 - No. 24, Feb, 1993 ($1.95/$2.25/$2.50, color, adults)
Epic Comics (Marvel)

1: 1-4-Adapt horror movie 1.20 3.00
2-19-New stories & $2.25-c; Guice-a(p) .90 2.25
20-24: 20-Begin $2.50-c 1.00 2.50

CLIVE BARKER'S THE HARROWERS
Dec, 1993 - Present ($2.50, color)
Epic Comics (Marvel)

1-($2.95)-Glow-in-the-dark-c 1.20 3.00
2-4 1.00 2.50

CLOAK AND DAGGER
Fall, 1952
Ziff-Davis Publishing Co.

1-Saunders painted-c 14.00 43.00 100.00

CLOAK AND DAGGER (Also see Marvel Fanfare)
Oct, 1983 - No. 4, Jan, 1984 (Mini-series)(See Spectacular Spider-Man #64)
Marvel Comics Group

1-4-Austin-c/a(i) in all. 4-Origin 1.50

CLOAK AND DAGGER (Also see Marvel Graphic Novel #34, Mutant Misadventures Of... & Strange Tales, 2nd series)
July, 1985 - No. 11, Jan, 1987
Marvel Comics Group

1 1.50
2-8,10,11 1.00
9-Art Adams-p .80 2.00
...And Power Pack (1990, $7.95, 68 pgs.) 1.30 3.25 8.00

CLONEZONE SPECIAL
1989 ($2.00, B&W)
Dark Horse Comics/First Comics

1-Back-up series from Badger & Nexus .80 2.00

CLOSE ENCOUNTERS (See Marvel Comics Super Special & Marvel Special Edition)

CLOSE SHAVES OF PAULINE PERIL, THE (TV?)
June, 1970 - No. 4, March, 1971 (Jay Ward?)
Gold Key

1 1.65 4.00 10.00
2-4 1.00 2.50 6.00

CLOWN COMICS (No. 1 titled Clown Comic Book)
1945 - No. 3, Wint, 1946
Clown Comics/Home Comics/Harvey Publ.

nn (#1) 5.85 17.50 35.00
2,3 4.00 10.00 22.00

CLUBHOUSE RASCALS (#1 titled ...Presents?)
June, 1956 - No. 2, Oct, 1956 (Also see Three Rascals)
Sussex Publ. Co. (Magazine Enterprises)

1,2: The Brain app. 4.00 10.00 20.00

CLUB "16"
June, 1946 - No. 4, Dec, 1948
Famous Funnies

1-Teen-age humor 7.50 22.50 45.00

GD25 FN65 NM94

2-4 4.20 12.50 25.00

CLUE COMICS (Real Clue Crime V2#4 on)
Jan, 1943 - No. 15(V2#3), May, 1947
Hillman Periodicals

1-Origin The Boy King, Nightmare, Micro-Face, Twilight, & Zippo 63.00 185.00 425.00
2 31.00 92.00 200.00
3-5 22.00 65.00 145.00
6,8,9: 8-Palais-c/a(2) 14.00 43.00 100.00
7-Classic torture-c 20.00 60.00 140.00
10-Origin/1st app. The Gun Master & begin series; content changes to crime 15.00 45.00 105.00
11 10.00 30.00 70.00
12-Origin Rackman; McWilliams-a, Guardineer-a(2) 13.00 40.00 90.00
V2#1-Nightmare new origin; Iron Lady app.; Simon & Kirby-a 20.00 60.00 135.00
V2#2-S&K-a(2)-Bondage/torture-c; man attacks & kills people with electric iron. Infantino-a 20.00 60.00 135.00
V2#3-S&K-a(3) 20.00 60.00 135.00

CLUTCHING HAND, THE
July-Aug, 1954
American Comics Group

1 16.00 48.00 110.00

CLYDE BEATTY COMICS (Also see Crackajack Funnies)
October, 1953 (84 pages)
Commodore Productions & Artists, Inc.

1-Photo front/back-c; movie scenes and comics 19.00 57.00 130.00
...African Jungle Book('56)-Richfield Oil Co. 16 pg. giveaway, soft-c 8.35 25.00 50.00

CLYDE CRASHCUP (TV)
Aug-Oct, 1963 - No. 5, Sept-Nov, 1964
Dell Publishing Co.

1-All written by John Stanley 10.00 30.00 70.00
2-5 8.35 25.00 50.00

C-M-O COMICS
1942 - No. 2, 1942 (68 pages, full color)
Chicago Mail Order Co.(Centaur)

1-Invisible Terror, Super Ann, & Plymo the Rubber Man app. (all Centaur costume heroes) 58.00 175.00 385.00
2-Invisible Terror, Super Ann app. 39.00 116.00 250.00

COBALT BLUE (Innovation)(Value: cover or less)

COCOMALT BIG BOOK OF COMICS
1938 (Regular size; full color; 52 pgs.)
Harry 'A' Chesler (Cocomalt Premium)

1-(Scarce)-Biro-c/a; Little Nemo by Winsor McCay Jr., Dan Hastings; Jack Cole, Guardineer, Gustavson, Bob Wood-a 118.00 355.00 825.00

CODE NAME: ASSASSIN (See 1st Issue Special)

CODENAME: DANGER (Lodestone)(Value: cover or less)

CODENAME: GENETIX
Jan, 1993 - No. 4, May, 1993
Marvel Comics UK

1-4: Wolverine in all .70 1.70

CODENAME SPITFIRE (Formerly Spitfire And The Troubleshooters)
No. 10, July, 1987 - No. 13, Oct, 1987
Marvel Comics Group

10-13: 10-Rogers-c/a 1.00

CODE NAME: TOMAHAWK
Sept, 1986 ($1.75, color, high quality paper)
Fantasy General Comics

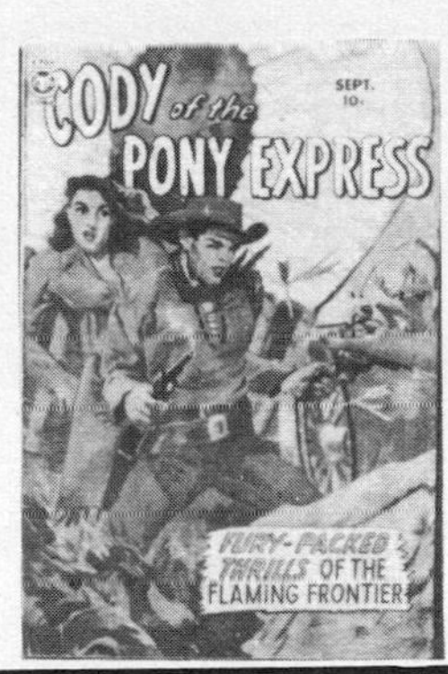

Cody of the Pony Express #1, © FOX

Combat Casey #19, © MEG

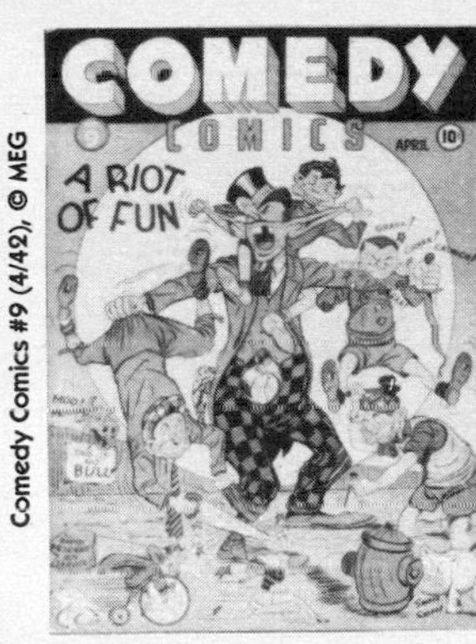

Comedy Comics #9 (4/42), © MEG

GD25 FN65 NM94

1-Sci/fi .70 1.75

CODY OF THE PONY EXPRESS (See Colossal Features Magazine)
Sept, 1950 - No. 3, Jan, 1951 (See Women Outlaws)
Fox Features Syndicate

1-3 (Actually #3-5). 1-Painted-c 8.35 25.00 50.00

CODY OF THE PONY EXPRESS (Buffalo Bill...) (Outlaws of the West #11 on; Formerly Bullseye)
No. 8, Oct, 1955; No. 9, Jan, 1956; No. 10, June, 1956
Charlton Comics

8-Bullseye on splash pg; not S&K-a 4.70 14.00 28.00
9,10: 10-Buffalo Bill app. 4.00 10.00 20.00

CODY STARBUCK (1st app. in Star Reach #1)
July, 1978 (Color, 2nd printing exists)
Star Reach Productions

nn-Howard Chaykin-c/a .80 2.00

CO-ED ROMANCES
November, 1951
P. L. Publishing Co.

1 4.35 13.00 26.00

COLLECTORS ITEM CLASSICS (See Marvel Collectors Item Classics)

COLOSSAL FEATURES MAGAZINE (Formerly I Loved) (See Cody of the Pony Express)
No. 33, May, 1950 - No. 34, July, 1950; No. 3, Sept, 1950
Fox Features Syndicate

33,34-Cody of the Pony Express begins (based on Columbia serial).
33-Painted-c; 34-Photo-c 7.00 21.00 42.00
3-Authentic criminal cases 7.00 21.00 42.00

COLOSSAL SHOW, THE (TV)
October, 1969
Gold Key

1 4.35 13.00 26.00

COLOSSUS COMICS (See Green Giant & Motion Picture Funnies Weekly)
March, 1940
Sun Publications (Funnies, Inc.?)

1-(Scarce)-Tulpa of Tsang(hero); Colossus app. 170.00 515.00 1200.00
NOTE: *Cover by artist that drew Colossus in Green Giant Comics.*

COLOUR OF MAGIC, THE (Terry Pratchett's...)
1991 - No. 4, 1991 ($2.50, color, mini-series)
Innovation Publishing

1-4: Adapts 1st novel of the Discworld series 1.00 2.50

COLT .45 (TV)
No. 924, 8/58 - No. 1058, 11-1/59-60; No. 4, 2-4/60 - No. 9, 5-7/61
Dell Publishing Co.

4-Color 924(#1)-Wayde Preston photo-c on all 10.00 30.00 60.00
4-Color 1004,1058; #4,5,7-9 7.50 22.50 45.00
6-Toth-a 8.35 25.00 50.00

COLUMBIA COMICS
1943
William H. Wise Co.

1-Joe Palooka, Charlie Chan, Capt. Yank, Sparky Watts, Dixie Dugan app.
17.00 52.00 120.00

COLUMBUS
Sept, 1992 ($2.50, B&W, one-shot)
Dark Horse Comics

1-Yeates painted-c 1.00 2.50

COMANCHE (See 4-Color No. 1350)

COMANCHEROS, THE (See 4-Color No. 1300)

GD25 FN65 NM94

COMBAT
June, 1952 - No. 11, April, 1953
Atlas Comics (ANC)

1 10.00 30.00 65.00
2-Heath-c/a 5.00 15.00 30.00
3,5-9,11: 9-Robert Q. Sale-a 4.00 10.00 20.00
4-Krigstein-a 4.70 14.00 28.00
10-B&W and color illos. in **POP** 4.20 12.50 25.00
NOTE: *Combat Casey in 7-11.* ***Heath*** *c-1, 2, 9.* ***Maneely*** *a-1; c-3.* ***Pakula*** *a-1.* ***Reinman*** *a-1.*

COMBAT
Oct-Nov, 1961 - No. 40, Oct, 1973 (No #9)
Dell Publishing Co.

1 5.00 15.00 30.00
2-5: 4-John F. Kennedy c/story (P.T. 109) 3.00 7.50 15.00
6,7,8(4-6/63), 8(7-9/63) 2.40 6.00 12.00
10-27 2.00 5.00 10.00
28-40(reprints #1-14). 30-r/#4 1.40 3.50 7.00
NOTE. ***Glanzman*** *c/a-1-27, 28-40r.*

COMBAT CASEY (Formerly War Combat)
No. 6, Jan, 1953 - No. 34, July, 1957
Atlas Comics (SAI)

6 (Indicia shows 1/52 in error) 7.50 22.50 45.00
7-Spanking panel 5.85 17.50 35.00
8-Used in **POP**, pg. 94 4.00 11.00 22.00
9 3.60 9.00 18.00
10,13-19-Violent art by R. Q. Sale; Battle Brady x-over #10
5.00 15.00 30.00
11,12,20-Last Precode (2/55) 3.60 9.00 18.00
21-34 3.00 7.50 15.00
NOTE: ***Everett*** *a-6.* ***Heath*** *c-10, 17, 19, 30.* ***Maneely*** *c-6, 8.* ***Powell*** *a-29(5), 30(5), 34.* ***Severin*** *c-26, 33.*

COMBAT KELLY
Nov, 1951 - No. 44, Aug, 1957
Atlas Comics (SPI)

1-1st app. Combat Kelly; Heath-a 11.50 34.00 85.00
2 6.70 20.00 40.00
3-10 4.20 12.50 25.00
11-Used in **POP**, pages 94,95 plus color illo. 4.00 11.00 22.00
12-Color illo. in **POP** 4.00 11.00 22.00
13-16 3.00 7.50 15.00
17-Violent art by R. Q. Sale; Combat Casey app. 5.35 16.00 32.00
18-20,22-44: 18-Battle Brady app. 28-Last precode (1/55). 38-Green Berets story (8/56) 3.00 7.50 15.00
21-Transvestism-c 4.00 11.00 22.00
NOTE: ***Berg*** *a-8, 12-14, 16, 17, 19-23, 25, 26, 28, 31-36, 42-44; c-2.* ***Colan*** *a-42.* ***Heath*** *a-4; c-31.* ***Lawrence*** *a-23.* ***Maneely*** *a-4(2), 6, 7(3), 8; c-4, 5, 7, 8, 10, 25.* ***R.Q. Sale*** *a-17, 25.* ***Severin*** *c-41, 42.* ***Whitney*** *a-5.*

COMBAT KELLY (...and the Deadly Dozen)
June, 1972 - No. 9, Oct, 1973
Marvel Comics Group

1-Intro & origin new Combat Kelly; Ayers/Mooney-a; Severin-c (20 cent-c)
1.20 3.00
2-9 1.50

COMBINED OPERATIONS (See The Story of the Commandos)

COMEDY CARNIVAL
no date (1950's) (100 pages)
St. John Publishing Co.

nn-Contains rebound St. John comics 23.00 70.00 160.00

COMEDY COMICS (1st Series) (Formerly Daring Mystery No. 1-8)
(Becomes Margie Comics No. 35 on)
No. 9, April, 1942 - No. 34, Fall, 1946
Timely Comics (TCI 9,10)

9-(Scarce)-The Fin by Everett, Capt. Dash, Citizen V, & The Silver Scorpion app.;

The Comet #1(7/91), © AP

Comic Album #6, © Warner Bros.

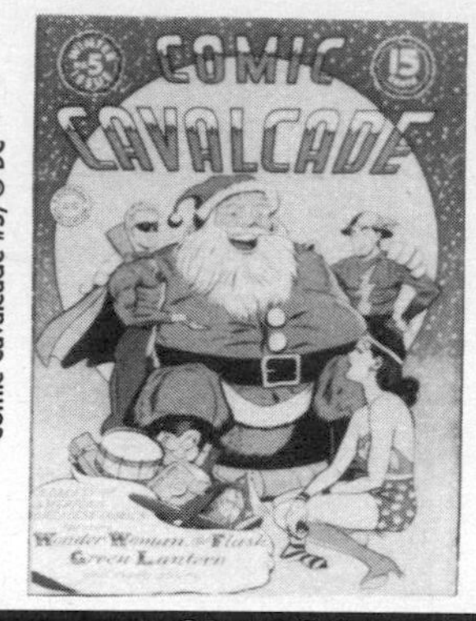

Comic Cavalcade #5, © DC

GD25 FN65 NM94

Wolverton-a; 1st app. Comedy Kid; satire on Hitler & Stalin; The Fin, Citizen V & Silver Scorn cont. from Daring Mystery 133.00 400.00 900.00
10-(Scarce)-Origin The Fourth Musketeer, Victory Boys; Monstro, the Mighty app. 92.00 275.00 625.00
11-Vagabond, Stuporman app. 30.00 90.00 210.00
12,13 10.00 30.00 60.00
14-Origin/1st app. Super Rabbit (3/43) plus-c 31.00 95.00 220.00
15-20 8.35 25.00 50.00
21-32 5.85 17.50 35.00
33-Kurtzman-a (5 pgs.) 8.35 25.00 50.00
34-Intro Margie; Wolverton-a (5 pgs.) 10.00 30.00 75.00

COMEDY COMICS (2nd Series)
May, 1948 - No. 10, Jan, 1950
Marvel Comics (ACI)

1-Hedy, Tessie, Millie begin; Kurtzman's "Hey Look" (he draws himself) 20.00 60.00 140.00
2 8.35 25.00 50.00
3,4-Kurtzman's "Hey Look"(?&3) 10.00 30.00 65.00
5-10 4.35 13.00 26.00

COMET, THE (See The Mighty Crusaders & Pep Comics #1)
Oct, 1983 - No. 2, Dec, 1983
Red Circle Comics (Archie)

1,2: 1-Re-intro & origin The Comet; The American Shield begins. 2-Origin continues 1.00

COMET, THE
July, 1991 - No. 18, Dec, 1992 ($1.00/$1.25, color)
Impact Comics (DC)

1-13: 4-Black Hood app. 6-Re-intro Hangman. 8-Web x-over. 10-Contains Crusaders trading card. 13-Last $1.00-c 1.00
14-18: 14-Origin. Netzer(Nasser) c(p)-11,14-17 1.25
Annual 1 (1992, $2.50; 68 pgs.)-Contains Impact trading card; Shield back-up story 1.00 2.50

COMET MAN, THE
Feb, 1987 - No. 6, July, 1987 (Mini-series)
Marvel Comics Group

1-6 1.00

COMIC ALBUM (Also see Disney Comic Album)
Mar-May, 1958 - No. 18, June-Aug, 1962
Dell Publishing Co.

1-Donald Duck 5.35 16.00 32.00
2-Bugs Bunny 4.00 10.00 20.00
3-Donald Duck 4.70 14.00 28.00
4-6,8-10: 4-Tom & Jerry. 5-Woody Woodpecker. 6,10-Bugs Bunny. 8-Tom & Jerry. 9-Woody Woodpecker 3.20 8.00 16.00
7,11: 7-Popeye (9-11/59). 11-Popeye (9-11/60) 4.00 11.00 22.00
12-14: 12-Tom & Jerry. 13-Woody Woodpecker. 14-Bugs Bunny 2.80 7.00 14.00
15-Popeye 4.00 11.00 22.00
16-Flintstones (12-2/61-62)-3rd app. 6.35 19.00 38.00
17-Space Mouse (3rd app.) 4.00 11.00 22.00
18-Three Stooges; photo-c 7.00 21.00 42.00

COMIC BOOK (Also see Comics From Weatherbird)
1954 (Giveaway)
American Juniors Shoe

Contains a comic rebound with new cover. Several combinations possible. Contents determines price.

COMIC BOOK MAGAZINE
1940 - 1943 (Similar to Spirit Sections)
(7-3/4x10-3/4"; full color; 16-24 pages each)
Chicago Tribune & other newspapers

1940 issues 5.85 17.50 35.00
1941, 1942 issues 4.70 14.00 28.00
1943 issues 4.00 12.00 24.00

NOTE: *Published weekly. Texas Slim, Kit Carson, Spooky, Josie, Nuts & Jolts, Lew Loyal, Brenda Starr, Daniel Boone, Captain Storm, Rocky, Smokey Stover, Tiny Tim, Little Joe, Fu Manchu appear among others. Early issues had photo stories with pictures from the movies; later issues had comic art.*

COMIC BOOKS (Series 1)
1950 (16 pgs.; 5-1/4x8-1/2"; full color; bound at top; paper cover)
Metropolitan Printing Co. (Giveaway)

1-Boots and Saddles; intro The Masked Marshal 4.70 14.00 28.00
1-The Green Jet; Green Lama by Raboy 25.00 75.00 175.00
1-My Pal Dizzy (Teen-age) 2.40 6.00 12.00
1-New World; origin Atomaster (costumed hero) 8.35 25.00 50.00
1-Talullah (Teen-age) 2.40 6.00 12.00

COMIC CAPERS
Fall, 1944 - No. 6, Summer, 1946
Red Circle Mag./Marvel Comics

1-Super Rabbit, The Creeper, Silly Seal, Ziggy Pig, Sharpy Fox begin 14.00 43.00 100.00
2 8.35 25.00 50.00
3-6 5.85 17.50 35.00

COMIC CAVALCADE
Winter, 1942-43 - No. 63, June-July, 1954
(Contents change with No. 30, Dec-Jan, 1948-49 on)
All-American/National Periodical Publications

GD25 FN65 VF82 NM94
1-The Flash, Green Lantern, Wonder Woman, Wildcat, The Black Pirate by Moldoff (also #2), Ghost Patrol, and Red White & Blue begin; Scribbly app., Minute Movie 500.00 1500.00 2750.00 4000.00
(Estimated up to 175 total copies exist, 6 in NM/Mint)

GD25 FN65 NM94
2-Mutt & Jeff begin; last Ghost Patrol & Black Pirate; Minute Movies 147.00 440.00 975.00
3-Hop Harrigan & Sargon, the Sorcerer begin; The King app. 108.00 325.00 700.00
4,5: 4-The Gay Ghost, The King, Scribbly, & Red Tornado app. 5-Christmas-c 94.00 282.00 625.00
6-10: 7-Red Tornado & Black Pirate app.; last Scribbly. 9-Fat & Slat app.; X-mas-c 75.00 225.00 500.00
11,12,14-20: 12-Last Red White & Blue. 15-Johnny Peril begins (1st app., 6-7/46), ends #29. 19-Christmas-c 64.00 192.00 425.00
13-Solomon Grundy app.; X-mas-c 108.00 325.00 715.00
21-23: 23-Harry Lampert-c (Toth swipes) 64.00 192.00 425.00
24-Solomon Grundy x-over in Green Lantern 75.00 225.00 500.00
25-28: 25-Black Canary app.; X-mas-c. 26-28-Johnny Peril app. 28-Last Mutt & Jeff 48.00 145.00 310.00
29-(10-11/48)-Last Flash, Wonder Woman, Green Lantern & Johnny Peril; Wonder Woman invents "Thinking Machine;" 1st computer in comics?; Leave it to Binky story (early app.) 54.00 162.00 365.00
30-(12-1/48-49)-The Fox & the Crow, Dodo & the Frog & Nutsy Squirrel begin 33.00 100.00 225.00
31-35 15.00 45.00 105.00
36-49 10.00 30.00 70.00
50-62(Scarce) 14.00 42.00 95.00
63(Rare) 22.00 68.00 150.00
Giveaway (1944, 8 pgs., paper-c, in color)-One Hundred Years of Co-operation-r/Comic Cavalcade #9 54.00 162.00 350.00
Giveaway (1945, 16 pages, paper-c, in color)-Movie "Tomorrow The World" (Nazi theme); r/Comic Cavalcade #10 79.00 238.00 525.00
Giveaway (c. 1944-45; 8 pgs, paper-c, in color)-The Twain Shall Meet-r/ Comic Cavalcade #8 71.00 212.00 450.00

NOTE: ***Grossman** a-30-63. **E.E. Hibbard** c-(Flash only)-1-4, 7-14, 16-19, 21. **Sheldon Mayer** a(2-3)-40-63. **Moulson** c(G.L.)-7, 15. **Nodell** c(G.L.)-9. **H.G. Peter** c(W. Woman only)-1, 3-21, 24. **Post** a-31, 36. **Purcell** c(G.L.)-2-5, 10. **Reinman** a(Green Lantern)-4-6, 8, 9, 13, 15-21; c(Gr. Lantern)-6, 8, 19. **Toth** a(Green Lantern)-26-28; c-27. Atom app.-22, 23.*

COMIC COMICS
April, 1946 - No. 10, Feb, 1947

Comic Land #1, © Fact and Fiction

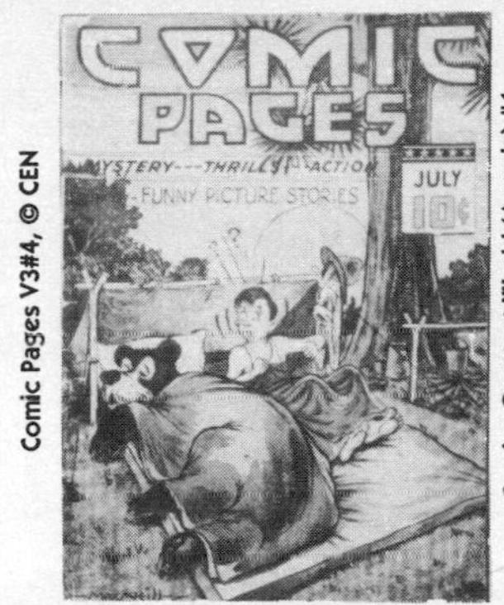

Comic Pages V3#4, © CEN

Comics Greatest World (Arcada) #1, © Dark Horse

GD25 FN65 NM94 | GD25 FN65 NM94

Fawcett Publications

1-Captain Kidd; Nutty Comics #1 in indicia 8.35 25.00 50.00
2-10-Wolverton-a, 4 pgs. each. 5-Captain Kidd app. 10.00 30.00 60.00

COMIC CUTS (Also see The Funnies)
5/19/34 - 7/28/34 (5 cents; 24 pages) (Tabloid size in full color)
(Not reprints; published weekly; created for newsstand sale)
H. L. Baker Co., Inc.

V1#1 - V1#7(6/30/34), V1#8(7/14/34), V1#9(7/28/34)-Idle Jack strips 8.70 26.00 52.00

COMIC LAND
March, 1946
Fact and Fiction Publ.

1-Sandusky & the Senator, Sam Stupor, Sleuth, Marvin the Great, Sir Passer, Phineas Gruff app.; Irv Tirman & Perry Williams art 8.35 25.00 50.00

COMIC MONTHLY
Jan, 1922 - No. 12, Dec, 1922 (32 pgs.)(8x9")(10 cents)
(1st monthly newsstand comic publication) (Reprints 1921 B&W dailies)
Embee Dist. Co.

1-Polly & Her Pals 58.00 175.00 365.00
2-Mike & Ike 12.50 37.50 80.00
3-S'Matter, Pop? 12.50 37.50 80.00
4-Barney Google 25.00 75.00 165.00
5-Tillie the Toiler 17.00 50.00 110.00
6-12: 6-Indoor Sports. 7-Little Jimmy. 8-Toots and Casper. 9,10-Foolish Questions. 11-Barney Google & Spark Plug in the Abadaba Handicap. 12-Polly & Her Pals 11.00 32.00 70.00

COMICO CHRISTMAS SPECIAL (Comico)(Value: cover or less)

COMICO PRIMER (See Primer)

COMIC PAGES (Formerly Funny Picture Stories)
V3#4, July, 1939 - V3#6, Dec, 1939
Centaur Publications

V3#4-Bob Wood-a 46.00 136.00 300.00
5,6: 6-Schwab-c 32.00 95.00 200.00

COMIC PAINTING AND CRAYONING BOOK
1917 (32 pages)(10x13-1/2")(No price on cover)
Saalfield Publ. Co.

nn-Tidy Teddy by F. M. Follett, Clarence the Cop, Mr. & Mrs. Butt-In. Regular comic stories to read or color 15.00 45.00 95.00

COMICS (See All Good)

COMICS, THE
March, 1937 - No. 11, Nov, 1938 (Newspaper strip-r; bi-monthly)
Dell Publishing Co.

1-1st app. Tom Mix in comics; Wash Tubbs, Tom Beatty, Myra North, Arizona Kid, Erik Noble & International Spy w/Doctor Doom begin 100.00 300.00 700.00
2 54.00 160.00 350.00
3-11: 3-Alley Oop begins 46.00 136.00 300.00

COMICS AND STORIES (See Walt Disney's.Comics and Stories)

COMICS CALENDAR, THE (The 1946...)
1946 (116 pgs.; 25 cents)(Stapled at top)
True Comics Press (ordered through the mail)

nn-(Rare) Has a "strip" story for every day of the year in color 32.00 95.00 210.00

COMICS DIGEST (Pocket size)
Winter, 1942-43 (100 pages) (Black & White)
Parents' Magazine Institute

1-Reprints from True Comics (non-fiction World War II stories) 7.50 22.50 45.00

COMIC SELECTIONS (Shoe store giveaway)
1944-46 (Reprints from Calling All Girls, True Comics, True Aviation, & Real Heroes)
Parents' Magazine Press

1 3.60 9.00 18.00
2-5 3.00 7.50 15.00

COMICS EXPRESS (Eclipse)(Value: cover or less)

COMICS FOR KIDS
1945 (no month); No. 2, Sum, 1945 (Funny animal)
London Publishing Co./Timely

1,2-Puffy Pig, Sharpy Fox 9.15 27.50 55.00

COMICS FROM WEATHER BIRD (Also see Comic Book, Edward's Shoes, Free Comics to You & Weather Bird)
1954 - 1957 (Giveaway)
Weather Bird Shoes

Contains a comic bound with new cover. Many combinations possible. Contents would determine price. Some issues do not contain complete comics, but only parts of comics.Value equals 40 to 60 percent of contents.

COMICS GREATEST WORLD
June, 1993 - V4#4, Sept, 1993 ($1.00, color)
Dark Horse Comics

Arcadia 1-4: 1-X: Frank Miller-c. 2-Pit Bulls. 3-Ghost; Dorman-c; Hughes-a. 4-Monster 1.00
1-B&W Press Proof Edition (1500 copies) 20.00
1-Silver-c; distr. retailer bonus w/print & cards 10.00
Retailer's Premium Embossed Silver Foil Logo (r/1-4) 25.00
Golden City 1-4: 1-Rebel; Ordway-c. 2-Mecha; Dave Johnson-c. 3-Titan; Walt Simonson-c. 4-Catalyst; Perez-c 1.00
1-Gold-c; distr. retailer bonus w/print & cards 10.00
Retailer's Premium Embossed Gold Foil Logo (r/1-4) 25.00
Steel Harbor 1-4: 1-Barb Wire; Dorman-c; Gulacy-a(p). 2-The Machine; Mignola-c. 3-Wolfgang; Warner-c. 4-Motorhead 1.00
1-Silver-c; distr. retailer bonus w/print & cards 10.00
Retailer's Premium Embossed Red Foil Logo (r/1-4 25.00
Vortex 1-4: 1-Division 13; Dorman-c. 2-Hero Zero; Art Adams-c. 3-King Tiger; Chadwick-a(p); Darrow-c. 4-Vortex; Miller-c 1.00
1-Gold-c; distr. retailer bonus w/print & cards 10.00
Retailer's Premium Embossed Blue Foil Logo (r/1-4) 25.00

COMICS GREATEST WORLD: OUT OF THE VORTEX
Oct, 1993 - Present ($2.00, color)
Dark Horse Comics

1-4 .80 2.00

COMICS HITS (See Harvey Comics Hits)

COMICS MAGAZINE, THE (...Funny Pages #3)(Funny Pages #6 on)
May, 1936 - No. 5, Sept, 1936 (Paper covers)
Comics Magazine Co.

GD25 FN65 VF82

1-Dr. Mystic, The Occult Detective (1st Superman prototype & 1st super hero) by Siegel & Shuster (1st episode of "The Koth and the Seven;" continues in More Fun #14; originally scheduled for publication at DC). 1 pg. Kelly-a; Sheldon Mayer-a 1000.00 3000.00 6000.00
(Estimated up to 10 total copies exist)

GD25 FN65 NM94

2-Federal Agent (a.k.a. Federal Men) by Siegel & Shuster; 1 pg. Kelly-a 133.00 400.00 900.00
3-5 117.00 350.00 750.00

COMICS NOVEL (Anarcho, Dictator of Death)
1947
Fawcett Publications

1-All Radar 20.00 60.00 140.00

COMICS ON PARADE (No. 30 on are a continuation of Single Series)
April, 1938 - No. 104, Feb, 1955

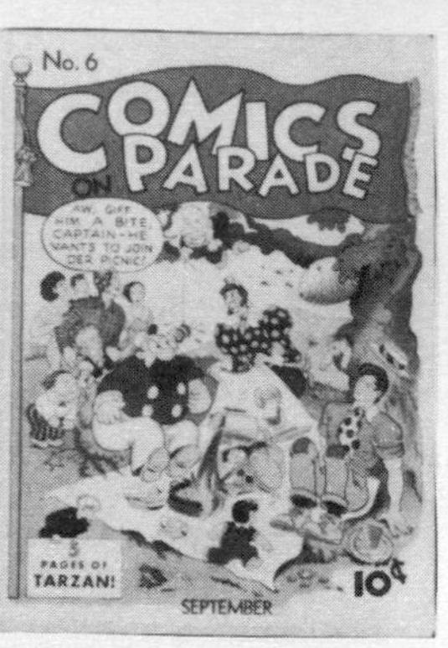

Comics On Parade #6, © UFS

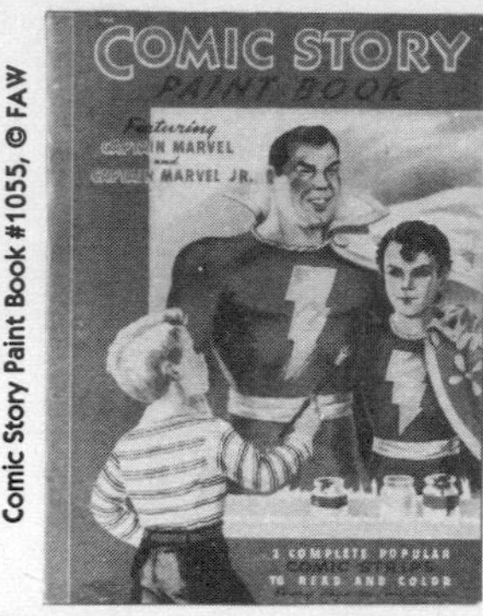

Comic Story Paint Book #1055, © FAW

Commander Battle and the Atomic Sub #2, © ACG

	GD25	FN65	NM94
United Features Syndicate			
1-Tarzan by Foster; Captain & the Kids, Little Mary Mixup, Abbie & Slats, Ella Cinders, Broncho Bill, Li'l Abner begin	183.00	550.00	1300.00
2 (Tarzan & others app. on-c of #1-3,17)	83.00	250.00	550.00
3	67.00	200.00	450.00
4,5	50.00	150.00	335.00
6-10	37.00	110.00	240.00
11-20	30.00	90.00	200.00
21-29: 22-Son of Tarzan begins. 22,24,28-Tailspin Tommy-c. 29-Last Tarzan issue	25.00	75.00	165.00
30-Li'l Abner	17.50	52.00	115.00
31-The Captain & the Kids	12.50	37.50	85.00
32-Nancy & Fritzi Ritz	10.00	30.00	65.00
33-Li'l Abner	15.00	45.00	100.00
34-The Captain & the Kids (10/41)	12.00	35.00	80.00
35-Nancy & Fritzi Ritz	10.00	30.00	65.00
36-Li'l Abner	15.00	45.00	100.00
37-The Captain & the Kids (6/42)	12.00	35.00	80.00
38-Nancy & Fritzi Ritz; infinity-c	10.00	30.00	65.00
39-Li'l Abner	15.00	45.00	100.00
40-The Captain & the Kids (3/43)	12.00	35.00	80.00
41-Nancy & Fritzi Ritz	8.35	25.00	50.00
42-Li'l Abner	15.00	45.00	105.00
43-The Captain & the Kids	12.00	35.00	80.00
44-Nancy & Fritzi Ritz (3/44)	8.35	25.00	50.00
45-Li'l Abner	12.00	35.00	80.00
46-The Captain & the Kids	10.00	30.00	65.00
47-Nancy & Fritzi Ritz	8.35	25.00	50.00
48-Li'l Abner (3/45)	12.00	35.00	80.00
49-The Captain & the Kids	10.00	30.00	65.00
50-Nancy & Fritzi Ritz	8.35	25.00	50.00
51-Li'l Abner	10.00	30.00	65.00
52-The Captain & the Kids (3/46)	7.50	22.50	45.00
53-Nancy & Fritzi Ritz	7.50	22.50	45.00
54-Li'l Abner	10.00	30.00	65.00
55-Nancy & Fritzi Ritz	7.50	22.50	45.00
56-The Captain & the Kids (r/Sparkler)	7.50	22.50	45.00
57-Nancy & Fritzi Ritz	7.50	22.50	45.00
58-Li'l Abner	10.00	30.00	65.00
59-The Captain & the Kids	6.70	20.00	40.00
60-70-Nancy & Fritzi Ritz	6.70	20.00	40.00
71-76-Nancy only	4.70	14.00	28.00
77-99,101-104-Nancy & Sluggo	4.70	14.00	28.00
100-Nancy & Sluggo	5.85	17.50	35.00
Special Issue, 7/46; Summer, 1948 - The Captain & the Kids app.	4.70	14.00	28.00

NOTE: Bound Volume (Very Rare) includes No. 1-12; bound by publisher in pictorial comic boards & distributed at the 1939 World's Fair and through mail order from ads in comic books (also see Tip Top) 208.00 625.00 1400.00
NOTE: *Li'l Abner reprinted from Tip Top.*

COMICS READING LIBRARIES (Educational Series)
1973, 1977, 1979 (36 pages in color) (Giveaways)
King Features (Charlton Publ.)

	GD25	FN65	NM94
R-01-Tiger, Quincy		.80	2.00
R-02-Beetle Bailey, Blondie & Popeye		.80	2.00
R-03-Blondie, Beetle Bailey		.80	2.00
R-04-Tim Tyler's Luck, Felix the Cat	1.65	4.00	10.00
R-05-Quincy, Henry		.80	2.00
R-06-The Phantom, Mandrake	2.30	6.75	16.00
1977 reprint(R-04)	1.00	2.00	5.00
R-07-Popeye, Little King	1.00	2.00	5.00
R-08-Prince Valiant(Foster), Flash Gordon	3.40	10.00	24.00
1977 reprint	1.30	3.25	8.00
R-09-Hagar the Horrible, Boner's Ark		.80	2.00
R-10-Redeye, Tiger		.80	2.00
R-11-Blondie, Hi & Lois		.80	2.00
R-12-Popeye-Swee'pea, Brutus	1.00	2.50	6.00
R-13-Beetle Bailey, Little King		.80	2.00
R-14-Quincy-Hamlet		.80	2.00
R-15-The Phantom, The Genius	2.30	6.75	16.00
R-16-Flash Gordon, Mandrake	3.40	10.00	24.00
1977 reprint	1.30	3.25	8.00
Other 1977 editions....		.50	1.00
1979 editions(68pgs.)		.50	1.00

NOTE: *Above giveaways available with purchase of $45.00 in merchandise. Used as a reading skills aid for small children.*

COMICS REVUE
June, 1947 - No. 5, Jan, 1948
St. John Publ. Co. (United Features Synd.)

	GD25	FN65	NM94
1-Ella Cinders & Blackie	7.50	22.50	45.00
2-Hap Hopper (7/47)	5.00	15.00	30.00
3-Iron Vic (8/47)	4.20	12.50	25.00
4-Ella Cinders (9/47)	5.00	15.00	30.00
5-Gordo No. 1 (1/48)	4.20	12.50	25.00

COMIC STORY PAINT BOOK
1943 (68 pages) (Large size)
Samuel Lowe Co.

	GD25	FN65	NM94
1055-Captain Marvel & a Captain Marvel Jr. story to read & color; 3 panels in color per page (reprints)	45.00	132.00	315.00

COMIX BOOK (B&W Magazine - $1.00)
1974 - No. 5, 1976
Marvel Comics Group/Krupp Comics Works No. 4,5

	GD25	FN65	NM94
1-Underground comic artists; 2 pgs. Wolverton-a	1.00	2.50	6.00
2-Wolverton-a (1 pg.)		1.20	3.00
3-Low distribution (3/75)	1.00	2.00	5.00
4(2/76), 4(5/76), 5		1.20	3.00

NOTE: *Print run No. 1-3: 200-250M; No. 4&5: 10M each.*

COMIX INTERNATIONAL
July, 1974 - No. 5, Spring, 1977 (Full color)
Warren Magazines

	GD25	FN65	NM94
1-Low distribution; all Corben remainders from Warren	3.40	10.00	24.00
2-Wood, Wrightson-r	1.65	4.00	10.00
3-5: 4-Crandall-a	1.00	2.50	6.00

NOTE: *No. 4 had two printings with extra **Corben** story in one. No. 3 may also have a variation. No. 3 has two Jeff Jones reprints from Vampirella.*

COMMANDER BATTLE AND THE ATOMIC SUB
July-Aug, 1954 - No. 7, Aug-Sept, 1955
American Comics Group (Titan Publ. Co.)

	GD25	FN65	NM94
1 (3-D effect)-Moldoff-c	29.00	87.00	205.00
2,4-7: 2-Moldoff-c. 4-(1-2/55)-Last pre-code; Landau-a. 5-3-D effect story (2 pgs.). 6,7-Landau-a	13.00	40.00	90.00
3-H-Bomb-c; Atomic Sub becomes Atomic Spaceship	15.00	45.00	105.00

COMMANDMENTS OF GOD
1954, 1958
Catechetical Guild

	GD25	FN65	NM94
300-Same contents in both editions; diff-c	2.00	5.00	10.00

COMMANDO ADVENTURES
June, 1957 - No. 2, Aug, 1957
Atlas Comics (MMC)

	GD25	FN65	NM94
1,2-Severin-c. 2-Drucker-a?	4.70	14.00	28.00

COMMANDO YANK (See The Mighty Midget Comics & Wow Comics)

COMPLETE BOOK OF COMICS AND FUNNIES
1944 (196 pages) (One Shot) (25 cents)
William H. Wise & Co.

1-Origin Brad Spencer, Wonderman; The Magnet, The Silver Knight by

Complete Book of True Crime nn, © WHW

Conan, the Barbarian #1, © MEG

Conan, the Barbarian #273, © MEG

GD25 FN65 NM94

Kinstler, & Zudo the Jungle Boy app. 30.00 90.00 200.00

COMPLETE BOOK OF TRUE CRIME COMICS
No date (Mid 1940's) (132 pages) (25 cents)
William H. Wise & Co.

nn-Contains Crime Does Not Pay rebound (includes #22) 64.00 193.00 450.00

COMPLETE COMICS (Formerly Amazing Comics No. 1)
No. 2, Winter, 1944-45
Timely Comics (EPC)

2-The Destroyer, The Whizzer, The Young Allies & Sergeant Dix; Schomburg-c 80.00 240.00 550.00

COMPLETE LOVE MAGAZINE (Formerly a pulp with same title)
V26#2, May-June, 1951 - V32#4(#191), Sept, 1956
Ace Periodicals (Periodical House)

V26#2-Painted-c (52 pgs.) 3.00 9.00 18.00
V26#3-6(2/52), V27#1(4/52)-6(1/53) 2.40 6.00 12.00
V28#1(3/53), V28#2(5/53), V29#3(7/53)-6(12/53) 2.00 5.00 10.00
V30#1(2/54), V30#1(#176, 4/54),2,4-6(#181, 1/55) 2.00 5.00 10.00
V30#3(#178)-Rock Hudson photo-c 3.20 8.00 16.00
V31#1(#182, 3/55)-Last precode 1.80 4.50 9.00
V31#2(5/55)-6(#187, 1/56) 1.40 3.50 7.00
V32#1(#188, 3/56)-4(#191, 9/56) 1.40 3.50 7.00
NOTE: *(34 total issues). Photo-c V27#5-on. Painted-c V26#3.*

COMPLETE MYSTERY (True Complete Mystery No. 5 on)
Aug, 1948 - No. 4, Feb, 1949 (Full length stories)
Marvel Comics (PrPl)

1-Seven Dead Men 22.00 65.00 150.00
2-Jigsaw of Doom! 16.00 50.00 115.00
3-Fear in the Night; Burgos-c/a (28 pgs.) 16.00 50.00 115.00
4-A Squealer Dies Fast 16.00 50.00 115.00

COMPLETE ROMANCE
1949
Avon Periodicals

1-(Scarce)-Reprinted as Women to Love 26.00 77.00 180.00

COMPLIMENTARY COMICS
No date (1950's)
Sales Promotion Publ. (Giveaway)

1-Strongman by Powell, 3 stories 5.35 16.00 32.00

CONAN (See Chamber of Darkness #4, Giant-Size..., Handbook of..., King Conan, Marvel Graphic Novel #19, 28, Marvel Treasury Ed., Power Record Comics, Robert E. Howard's..., Savage Sword of Conan, and Savage Tales)

CONAN SAGA, THE
June, 1987 - Present ($2.00-$2.25, B&W magazine)
Marvel Comics

1-Barry Smith-r begin .80 2.00
2-27: 13,15-Boris-c. 22-r/Giant-Size Conan 1,2 .80 2.00
28-86 ($2.25): 31-Red Sonja-r by N. Adams/SSOC #1. 32-Newspaper strip-r begin by Buscema. 33-Smith/Conrad-a. 39-r/Kull #1('71) by Andru/Wood. 44-Swipes-c/Savage Tales #1. 57-Brunner-r/SSOC #30. 66-r/Conan Annual #2 by Buscema. 79-r/Conan #43-45 w/Red Sonja .90 2.25
NOTE: ***J. Buscema*** *r-32-on.* ***Chaykin*** *r-34.* ***Chiodo*** *painted c-63, 65, 66.* ***G. Colan*** *a-47p.* ***Jusko*** *painted c-64.* ***Nino*** *a-37.* ***Ploog*** *a-50.* ***N. Redondo*** *painted c-48, 50, 51, 53, 57, 62.* ***Simonson*** *r-50-54, 56.* ***B. Smith*** *r-51.* ***Starlin*** *c-34.* ***Williamson*** *r-50i.*

CONAN THE BARBARIAN
Oct, 1970 - No. 275, Dec, 1993
Marvel Comics Group

1-Origin/1st app. Conan (in comics) by Barry Smith; Kull app.; #1-9 are 15 cent issues 22.00 67.00 200.00
2 9.00 27.00 80.00
3-(Low distribution in some areas) 17.00 50.00 150.00
4,5 8.00 24.00 55.00
6-9: 8-Hidden panel message, pg. 14 5.00 15.00 35.00
10,11 (25 cent giants): 10-Black Knight-r; Kull story by Severin 6.50 19.00 45.00
12,13: 12-Wrightson-c(i) 3.60 10.75 25.00
14,15-Elric app. 5.50 17.00 40.00
16,19,20: 16-Conan-r/Savage Tales #1 3.25 9.50 22.00
17,18-No Barry Smith-a 1.65 4.00 10.00
21,22: 22-Has reprint from #1 3.20 9.00 21.00
23-1st app. Red Sonja (2/73) 4.15 12.50 29.00
24-1st full Red Sonja story; last Smith-a 3.60 10.75 25.00
25-John Buscema-c/a begins 1.50 3.75 9.00
26-30 1.00 2.00 5.00
31-36,38-40 1.20 3.00
37-Neal Adams-c/a; last 20 cent issue; contains pull-out subscription form 1.00 2.50 6.00
41-57,50,60: 44,45-N. Adams-i(Crusty Bunkers). 45-Adams-c. 40-Origin retold. 59-Origin Belit .80 2.00
58-2nd Belit app. (see Giant-Size Conan #1) 1.20 3.00
61-99: 68-Red Sonja story cont'd from Marvel Feature #7. 84-Intro. Zula. 85-Origin Zula. 87-r/Savage Sword of Conan #3 in color 1.00
100-(52 pg. Giant)-Death of Belit 1.00 2.50
101-114,116-199: 116-r/Power Record Comic PR31 1.00
115-Double size 1.20
200,250 ($1.50): 200-(52 pgs.). 250-(60 pgs.) 1.50
201-249,251,252: 232-Young Conan storyline begins; Conan is born. 244-Return of Zula. 252-Last $1.00-c 1.00
253-274: 262-Adapted from R.E. Howard story 1.25
275-($2.50, 68 pgs.)-Final issue 1.00 2.50
King Size 1(1973, 35 cents)-Smith-r/#2,4; Smith-c 1.30 3.25 8.00
Annual 2(1976, 50 cents)-New full length story 1.40 3.50
Annual 3(1978)-Chaykin/N. Adams-r/SSOC #2 .80 2.00
Annual 4,5: 4(1978)-New full length story. 5(1979)-New full length Buscema story & part-c 1.50
Annual 6(1981)-Kane-c/a 1.50
Annual 7-9: 7(1982)-Based on novel "Conan of the Isles" (new-a). 8(1984). 9(1984) 1.25
Annual 10-12: 10(1986). 11(1986). 12(1987) 1.25
Special Edition 1 (Red Nails) 1.40 3.50
NOTE: ***Arthur Adams*** *c-248, 249.* ***Neal Adams*** *a-116r(i); c-49i.* ***Austin*** *a-125, 126; c-125i, 126i.* ***Brunner*** *c-17i. c-40.* ***Buscema*** *a-25-36p, 38, 39, 41-56p, 58-63p, 65-67p, 68, 70-78p, 84-86p, 88-91p, 93-126p, 136p, 140, 141-144p, 146-158p, 159, 161, 162, 163p, 165-185p, 187-190p, Annual 2(3pgs.). 3-5p, 7p; c(p)-26, 36, 44, 46, 52, 56, 58, 59, 64, 65, 72, 78-80, 83-91, 93-103, 105-126, 136-151, 155-159, 161, 162, 168, 169, 171, 172, 174, 175, 178-185, 188, 189, Annual 4, 5, 7.* ***Chaykin*** *a-79-83.* ***Golden*** *c-152.* ***Kaluta*** *c-167.* ***Gil Kane*** *a-12p, 17p, 18p, 127-130, 131-134p; c-12p, 17p, 18p, 23, 25, 27-32, 34, 35, 38, 39, 41-43, 45-51, 53-55, 57, 60-63, 65-71, 73p, 76p, 127-134.* ***Jim Lee*** *c-242.* ***McFarlane*** *c-241p.* ***Ploog*** *a-57.* ***Russell*** *a-21; c-251i.* ***Simonson*** *c-135. B.* ***Smith*** *a-1-11p, 12, 13-15p, 16, 19-21, 23, 24; c-1-11, 13-16, 19-24p.* ***Starlin*** *a-64.* ***Wood*** *a-47r. Issue Nos. 3-5, 7-9, 11, 16-18, 21, 23, 25, 27-30, 35, 37, 38, 42, 45, 52, 57, 58, 65, 69-71, 73, 79-83, 99, 100, 104, 114, Annual 2 have original Robert E. Howard stories adapted. Issues #32-34 adapted from Norvell Page's novel* ***Flame Winds****.*

CONAN THE BARBARIAN MOVIE SPECIAL
Oct, 1982 - No. 2, Nov, 1982
Marvel Comics Group

1,2-Movie adaptation; Buscema-a 1.00

CONAN THE DESTROYER
Jan, 1985 - No. 2, Mar, 1985 (Movie adaptation)
Marvel Comics Group

1,2-r/Marvel Super Special 1.00

CONAN THE KING (Formerly King Conan)
No. 20, Jan, 1984 - No. 55, Nov, 1989
Marvel Comics Group

20-55: 48-55 ($1.50) 1.50
NOTE: ***Kaluta*** *c-20-23, 24i, 26, 27, 30, 50, 52.* ***Williamson*** *a-37i; c-37i, 38i.*

CONCRETE (Also see Dark Horse Presents & Within Our Reach)
March, 1987 - No. 10, Nov, 1988 ($1.50, B&W)
Dark Horse Comics

1-Paul Chadwick-c/a in all 1.30 3.25 8.00

GD25 FN65 NM94

Concrete Color Special #1, © P. Chadwick

Congo Bill #5, © DC

Contact Comics #1, © Aviation Press

GD25 FN65 NM94

1-2nd print .80 2.00
2 1.00 2.00 5.00
3-Origin 1.20 3.00
4-10 .80 2.00
...Celebrates Earth Day 1990 ($3.50, color, 52 pgs.) 1.40 3.50
...Color Special 1 (2/89, $2.95, 44 pgs.)-r/1st two Conrete apps. from Dark Horse Presents #1,2 plus new-a .20 3.00
Eclectica 1,2 (4/93-5/93), $2.95) 1.20 3.00
...: Land And Sea 1 (2/89, $2.95, B&W)-r/#1,2 .20 3.00
...: A New Life 1 (1989, $2.95, B&W)-r/#3,4 plus new-a (11 pgs.) .20 3.00
...: Odd Jobs 1 (7/90, $3.50)-r/5,6 plus new-a 1.40 3.50

CONCRETE: FRAGILE CREATURE
June, 1991 - No. 4, Feb, 1992 ($2.50, color, mini-series)
Dark Horse Comics
1-4: By Paul Chadwick 1.00 2.50

CONDORMAN (Walt Disney)
Oct, 1981 - No. 3, Jan, 1982
Whitman Publishing
1-3: 1,2-Movie adaptation; photo-c 1.00

CONFESSIONS ILLUSTRATED (Magazine)
Jan-Feb, 1956 - No. 2, Spring, 1956
E. C. Comics
1-Craig, Kamen, Wood, Orlando-a 10.00 30.00 70.00
2-Craig, Crandall, Kamen, Orlando-a 10.00 30.00 60.00

CONFESSIONS OF LOVE
Apr, 1950 - No. 2, July, 1950 (25 cents; 132 pgs. in color)(7-1/4x5-1/4)
Artful Publ.
1-Bakerish-a 19.00 58.00 135.00
2-Art & text; Bakerish-a 11.00 32.00 75.00

CONFESSIONS OF LOVE (Formerly Startling Terror Tales #10; becomes Confessions of Romance No. 7 on)
No. 11, 7/52 - No. 14, 1/53; No. 4, 3/53- No. 6, 8/53
Star Publications
11-13: 12,13-Disbrow-a 6.70 20.00 40.00
14,5,6 4.00 11.00 22.00
4-Disbrow-a 4.70 14.00 28.00
NOTE: *All have* **L. B. Cole** *covers.*

CONFESSIONS OF ROMANCE (Formerly Confessions of Love)
No. 7, Nov, 1953 - No. 11, Nov, 1954
Star Publications
7 5.85 17.50 35.00
8 4.00 11.00 22.00
9-Wood-a 8.35 25.00 50.00
10,11-Disbrow-a 4.70 14.00 28.00
NOTE: *All have* **L. B. Cole** *covers.*

CONFESSIONS OF THE LOVELORN (Formerly Lovelorn)
No. 52, Aug, 1954 - No. 114, June-July, 1960
American Comics Group (Regis Publ./Best Synd. Features)
52 (3-D effect) 14.00 43.00 100.00
53,55 4.00 11.00 22.00
54 (3-D effect) 13.50 41.00 95.00
56-Anti-communist propaganda story, 10 pgs; last pre-code (2/55) 5.00 15.00 30.00
57-90 2.80 7.00 14.00
91-Williamson-a 5.00 15.00 30.00
92-99,101-114 2.00 5.00 10.00
100 2.80 7.00 14.00
NOTE: **Whitney** *a-most issues; c-52, 53. Painted c-106, 107.*

CONFIDENTIAL DIARY (Formerly High School Confidential Diary; Three Nurses No. 18 on)
No. 12, May, 1962 - No. 17, March, 1963
Charlton Comics
12-17 1.00 2.50 5.00

CONGO BILL (See Action Comics & More Fun Comics #56)
Aug-Sept, 1954 - No. 7, Aug-Sept, 1955
National Periodical Publication

	GD25	FN65	VF82
1-(Scarce)	57.00	170.00	400.00
2,7 (Scarce)	50.00	150.00	350.00
3-6 (Scarce), 4-Last pre-code issue	43.00	130.00	300.00

NOTE: *(Rarely found in fine to mint condition.)* **Nick Cardy** *c-1-7.*

CONGORILLA (Also see Actions Comics #224)
Nov, 1992 - No. 4, Feb, 1993 ($1.75, color, mini-series)
DC Comics

	GD25	FN65	NM94
1-4: Brian Bolland c-1,2		.70	1.75

CONNECTICUT YANKEE, A (See King Classics)

CONQUEROR, THE (See 4-Color No. 690)

CONQUEROR COMICS
Winter, 1945
Albrecht Publishing Co.
nn 10.00 30.00 70.00

CONQUEROR OF THE BARREN EARTH
Feb, 1985 - No. 4, May, 1985 (Mini-series)
DC Comics
1-4: Back-up series from Warlord 1.00

CONQUEST
1953 (6 cents)
Store Comics
1-Richard the Lion Hearted, Beowulf, Swamp Fox 4.00 11.00 22.00

CONQUEST
Spring, 1955
Famous Funnies
1-Crandall-a, 1 pg.; contains contents of 1953 issue 3.20 8.00 16.00

CONTACT COMICS
July, 1944 - No. 12, May, 1946
Aviation Press
nn-Black Venus, Flamingo, Golden Eagle, Tommy Tomahawk begin 20.00 60.00 140.00
2-5: 3-Last Flamingo. 3,4-Black Venus by L. B. Cole. 5-The Phantom Flyer app. 14.00 43.00 100.00
6,11-Kurtzman's Black Venus; 11-Last Golden Eagle, last Tommy Tomahawk; Feldstein-a 18.00 55.00 125.00
7-10,12: 12-Sky Rangers, Air Kids, Ace Diamond app. 12.00 36.00 85.00
NOTE: **L. B. Cole** *a-9; c-1-12.* **Giunta** *a-3.* **Hollingsworth** *a-5, 7, 10.* **Palais** *a-11, 12.*

CONTEMPORARY MOTIVATORS
1977 - 1978 (5-3/8x8")(31 pgs., B&W, $1.45)
Pendelum Press
14-3002 The Caine Mutiny; 14-3010 Banner in the Sky; 14-3029 God Is My Co-Pilot;14-3037 Guadalcanal Diary; 14-3045 Hiroshima; 14-3053 Hot Rod; 14-3061 Just Dial a Number; 14-307x Star Wars; 14-3088 The Diary of Anne Frank; 14-3096 Lost Horizon 1.50
NOTE: *Also see Now Age Illustrated. Above may have been distributed the same.*

CONTEST OF CHAMPIONS (See Marvel Super-Hero...)

CONTRACTORS (Eclipse)(Value: cover or less)

COO COO COMICS (... the Bird Brain No. 57 on)
Oct, 1942 - No. 62, April, 1952
Nedor Publ. Co./Standard (Animated Cartoons)
1-Origin/1st app. Super Mouse & begin series (cloned from Superman); the first funny animal super hero series (see Looney Tunes #5 for 1st funny

"Cookie" #1, © ACG

Cosmic Odyssey #3, © DC

Cowboy Action #11, © MEG

GD25 FN65 NM94

animal super hero) 16.00 50.00 115.00
2 9.15 27.50 55.00
3-10 (3/44) 5.00 15.00 30.00
11-33: 33-1 pg. Ingels-a 4.00 11.00 22.00
34-40,43-46,48-Text illos by Frazetta in all. 36-Super Mouse covers begin
5.35 16.00 32.00
41-Frazetta-a(2) 10.00 30.00 70.00
42,47-Frazetta-a & text illos. 7.50 22.50 45.00
49-(8-9/54)-3-D effect-c & 1 stry; Frazetta text illo 6.70 20.00 40.00
50,51-3-D effect-c only. 50-Frazetta text illo 5.85 17.50 35.00
52-62: 56-Last Supermouse? 3.20 8.00 16.00

"COOKIE" (Also see Topsy-Turvy)
April, 1946 - No. 55, Aug-Sept, 1955
Michel Publ./American Comics Group(Regis Publ.)

1-Teen-age humor 12.00 36.00 85.00
2 7.00 21.00 42.00
3-10 5.00 15.00 30.00
11-20 4.00 12.00 24.00
21-23,26,28-30 3.60 9.00 18.00
24,25,27-Starlet O'Hara stories 4.00 10.00 20.00
31-34,37-55 3.20 8.00 16.00
35,36-Starlett O'Hara stories 3.60 9.00 18.00

COOL CAT (Formerly Black Magic)
V8#6, Mar-Apr, 1962 - V9#2, July-Aug, 1962
Prize Publications

V8#6, nn(V9#1, 5-6/62), V9#2 3.60 9.00 18.00

COOL WORLD
Apr, 1992 - No. 4, Sept, 1992 ($1.75, color, mini-series)
DC Comics

1-4: Prequel to animated/live action movie by Ralph Bakshi. 1-Bakshi-c. Bill Wray inks in all .70 1.75
...Movie Adaptation nn ('92, $3.50, 68pg.)-Bakshi-c 1.40 3.50

COPPER CANYON (See Fawcett Movie Comics)

COPS (TV)
Aug, 1988 - No. 15, Aug, 1989 ($1.00, color)
DC Comics

1 ($1.50, 52 pgs.)-Based on Hasbro Toys 1.50
2-15: 14-Orlando-c(p) 1.00

COPS: THE JOB
June, 1992 - No. 4, Sept, 1992 ($1.25, color, mini-series)
Marvel Comics

1-4: All have Jusko scripts & Golden-c 1.25

CORBEN SPECIAL, A (Pacific)(Value: cover or less)

CORKY & WHITE SHADOW (See 4-Color No. 707)

CORLISS ARCHER (See Meet Corliss Archer)

CORMAC MAC ART (Dark Horse)(Value: cover or less)

CORPORAL RUSTY DUGAN (See Holyoke One-Shot #2)

CORPSES OF DR. SACOTTI, THE (See Ideal a Classical Comic)

CORSAIR, THE (See A-1 Comics No. 5, 7, 10)

CORUM: THE BULL AND THE SPEAR (First)(Value: cover or less)

COSMIC BOOK, THE (Ace)(Value: cover or less)

COSMIC BOY (See The Legion of Super-Heroes)
Dec, 1986 - No. 4, Mar, 1987 (Mini-series)
DC Comics

1-4: Legends tie-ins all issues 1.00

COSMIC ODYSSEY
1988 - No. 4, 1988 ($3.50, color, squarebound)
DC Comics

1-4: Superman, Batman, Green Lantern app. 1.40 3.50

COSMO CAT (Becomes Sunny #11 on; also see All Top & Wotalife Comics)
July-Aug, 1946 - No. 10, Oct, 1947; 1957; 1959
Fox Publications/Green Publ. Co./Norlen Mag.

1 12.00 36.00 85.00
2 6.70 20.00 40.00
3-Origin (11-12/46) 7.50 22.50 45.00
4-10 5.00 15.00 30.00
2-4(1957-Green Publ. Co.) 2.80 7.00 14.00
2-4(1959-Norlen Mag.) 1.80 4.50 9.00
I.W. Reprint #1 1.20 3.00 6.00

COSMO THE MERRY MARTIAN
Sept, 1958 - No. 6, Oct, 1959
Archie Publications (Radio Comics)

1-Bob White-a in all 10.00 30.00 65.00
2-6 7.00 21.00 42.00

COTTON WOODS (See 4-Color No. 837)

COUGAR, THE (Cougar No. 2)
April, 1975 - No. 2, July, 1975
Seaboard Periodicals (Atlas)

1,2: 1-Adkins-a(p). 2-Origin; Buckler-c(p) 1.00

COUNTDOWN (See Movie Classics)

COUNT DUCKULA (TV)
Nov, 1988 - No. 15, Jan, 1991 ($1.00, color)
Marvel Comics

1-15: Dangermouse back-ups. 8-Geraldo Rivera photo-c 1.00

COUNT OF MONTE CHRISTO, THE (See 4-Color No. 794)

COURAGE COMICS
1945
J. Edward Slavin

1,2,77 6.70 20.00 40.00

COURTSHIP OF EDDIE'S FATHER (TV)
Jan, 1970 - No. 2, May, 1970
Dell Publishing Co.

1,2-Bill Bixby photo-c 3.20 8.00 20.00

COVERED WAGONS, HO (See 4-Color No. 814)

COWBOY ACTION (Formerly Western Thrillers No. 1-4; Becomes Quick-Trigger Western No. 12 on)
No. 5, March, 1955 - No. 11, March, 1956
Atlas Comics (ACI)

5 7.50 22.50 45.00
6-10: 6-8-Heath-c 5.00 15.00 30.00
11-Williamson-a (4 pgs.); Baker-a 5.85 17.50 35.00

NOTE: ***Ayers*** *a-8.* ***Drucker*** *a-6.* ***Maneely*** *c/a-5, 6.* ***Severin*** *c-10.* ***Shores*** *a-7.*

COWBOY COMICS (...Stories No. 14; formerly Star Ranger)(Star Ranger Funnies No. 15 on)
No. 13, July, 1938 - No. 14, Aug, 1938
Centaur Publishing Co.

13-(Rare)-Ace and Deuce, Lyin Lou, Air Patrol, Aces High, Lee Trent, Trouble Hunters begin 75.00 225.00 500.00
14-Filchock-c 54.00 162.00 350.00

NOTE: ***Guardineer*** *a-13, 14.* ***Gustavson*** *a-13, 14.*

COWBOY IN AFRICA (TV)
March, 1968
Gold Key

1(10219-803)-Chuck Connors photo-c 3.60 10.75 25.00

COWBOY LOVE (Becomes Range Busters?)
7/49 - V2#10, 6/50; No. 11, 1951; No. 28, 2/55 - No. 31, 8/55
Fawcett Publications/Charlton Comics No. 28 on

Cowboys 'n' Injuns #5, © ME

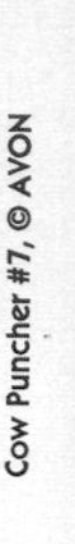
Cow Puncher #7, © AVON

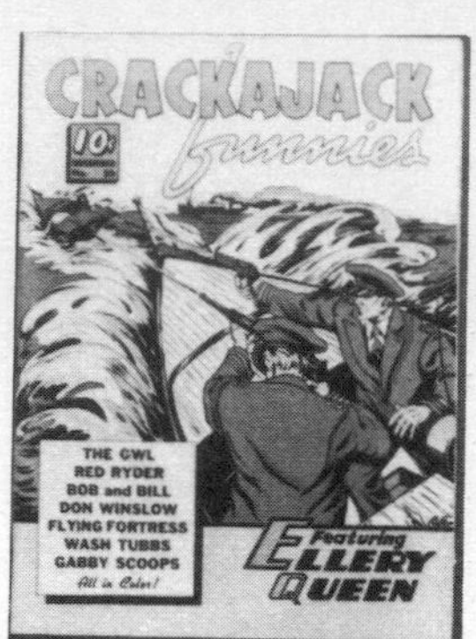

Crackajack Funnies #30, © DELL

	GD25	FN65	NM94
V1#1-Rocky Lane photo back-c	10.00	30.00	70.00
2	4.00	10.00	20.00
V1#3,4,6 (12/49)	3.60	9.00	18.00
5-Bill Boyd photo back-c (11/49)	5.00	15.00	30.00
V2#7-Williamson/Evans-a	6.35	19.00	38.00
V2#8-11	3.20	8.00	16.00
V1#28 (Charlton)-Last precode (2/55) (Formerly Romantic Story?)	3.20	8.00	16.00
V1#29-31 (Charlton; becomes Sweetheart Diary #32 on)	2.80	7.00	14.00

NOTE: ***Powell** a-10. **Marcus Swayze** a-2, 3. Photo c-1-11. No. 1-3, 5-7, 9, 10 are 52 pgs.*

COWBOY ROMANCES (Young Men No. 4 on)
Oct, 1949 - No. 3, Mar, 1950
Marvel Comics (IPC)

	GD25	FN65	NM94
1-Photo-c	13.00	40.00	90.00
2-William Holden, Mona Freeman 'Streets of Laredo' photo-c	10.00	30.00	65.00
3	8.35	25.00	50.00

COWBOYS 'N' INJUNS (...and Indians No. 6 on)
1946 - No. 5, 1947; No. 6, 1949 - No. 8, 1952
Com No. 1-5/Magazine Enterprises No. 6 on

	GD25	FN65	NM94
1	5.85	17.50	35.00
2-5-All funny animal western	4.00	12.00	24.00
6(A-1 23)-Half violent, half funny; Ayers-a	5.85	17.50	35.00
7(A-1 41, 1950), 8(A-1 48)-All funny	4.00	12.00	24.00
I.W. Reprint No. 1,7 (Reprinted in Canada by Superior, No. 7)	1.00	2.50	5.00
Super Reprint #10 (1963)	1.00	2.50	5.00

COWBOY WESTERN COMICS (TV)(Formerly Jack In The Box; Becomes Space Western No. 40-45 & Wild Bill Hickok & Jingles No. 68 on; title: Cowboy Western Heroes No. 47 & 48; Cowboy Western No. 49 on)
No. 17, 7/48 - No. 39, 8/52; No. 46, 10/53; No. 47, 12/53; No. 48, Spr, '54; No. 49, 5-6/54 - No. 67, 3/58 (nn 40-45)
Charlton (Capitol Stories)

	GD25	FN65	NM94
17-Jesse James, Annie Oakley, Wild Bill Hickok begin; Texas Rangers app.	10.00	30.00	70.00
18,19-Orlando-c/a	7.00	21.00	42.00
20-25: 24-Joel McCrea photo-c and adaptation from movie "Three Faces West." 25-Photo-c and adaptation from movie "Northwest Stampede"	5.35	16.00	32.00
26-George Montgomery photo-c and adaptation from movie "Indian Scout;" 1 pg. bio on Will Rogers	8.35	25.00	50.00
27-Sunset Carson photo-c & adapts movie "Sunset Carson Rides Again" plus 1 other Sunset Carson story	50.00	150.00	350.00
28-Sunset Carson line drawn-c; adapts movies "Battling Marshal" & "Fighting Mustangs" starring Sunset Carson	23.00	70.00	160.00
29-Sunset Carson line drawn-c; adapts movies "Rio Grande" with Sunset Carson & "Winchester 73" w/James Stewart plus 5 pg. life history of Sunset Carson featuring Tom Mix	23.00	70.00	160.00
30-Sunset Carson photo-c; adapts movie "Deadline" starring Sunset Carson plus 1 other Sunset Carson story	50.00	150.00	350.00
31-34,38,39,47-50 (no #40-45): 50-Golden Arrow, Rocky Lane & Blackjack (r?) stories	4.35	13.00	26.00
35,36-Sunset Carson-c/stories (2 in each). 35-Inside front-c photo of Sunset Carson plus photo on-c	23.00	70.00	160.00
37-Sunset Carson stories (2)	12.00	36.00	85.00
46-(Formerly Space Western)-Space western story	11.00	32.00	75.00
51-57,59-66: 51-Golden Arrow(r?) & Monte Hale-r renamed Rusty Hall. 53,54-Tom Mix-r. 55-Monte Hale story(r?). 66-Young Eagle story	4.00	10.00	20.00
58-(68 pgs.)-Wild Bill Hickok & Jingles (Guy Madison & Andy Devine) line drawn cover/stories begin, end #67	4.00	12.00	24.00
67-(68 pgs.)-Williamson/Torres-a, 5 pgs.	6.70	20.00	40.00

NOTE: *Many issues trimmed 1" shorter. **Maneely** c/a-67(5). Inside front/back photo c-29.*

COWGIRL ROMANCES (Formerly Jeanie Comics)
No. 28, Jan, 1950 (52 pgs.)
Marvel Comics (CCC)

	GD25	FN65	NM94
28(#1)-Photo-c	13.00	40.00	90.00

COWGIRL ROMANCES
1950 - No. 12, Winter, 1952-53 (No. 1-3: 52 pgs.)
Fiction House Magazines

	GD25	FN65	NM94
1-Kamen-a	19.00	57.00	130.00
2	10.00	30.00	70.00
3-5: 5-12-Whitman-c (most)	10.00	30.00	60.00
6-9,11,12	8.35	25.00	50.00
10-Frazetta?/Williamson-a; Kamen/Baker-a	19.00	57.00	130.00

COW PUNCHER (...Comics)
Jan, 1947; No. 2, Sept, 1947 - No. 7, 1949
Avon Periodicals

	GD25	FN65	NM94
1-Clint Cortland, Texas Ranger, Kit West, Pioneer Queen begin; Kubert-a; Alabam stories begin	24.00	72.00	165.00
2-Kubert, Kamen/Feldstein-a; Kamen-c	20.00	60.00	140.00
3-5,7: 3-Kiefer story	13.00	40.00	90.00
6-Opium drug mention story; bondage, headlight-c; Reinman-a	16.00	48.00	110.00

COWPUNCHER
1953 (nn) (Reprints Avon's No. 2)
Realistic Publications

	GD25	FN65	NM94
nn-Kubert-a	7.50	22.50	45.00

COWSILLS, THE (See Harvey Pop Comics)

COYOTE (Marvel)(Value: cover or less)

CRACKAJACK FUNNIES (Giveaway)
1937 (32 pgs.; full size; soft cover; full color)(Before No. 1?)
Malto-Meal

	GD25	FN65	NM94
nn-Features Dan Dunn, G-Man, Speed Bolton, Freckles, Buck Jones, Clyde Beatty, The Nebbs, Major Hoople, Wash Tubbs	64.00	193.00	450.00

CRACKAJACK FUNNIES
June, 1938 - No. 43, Jan, 1942
Dell Publishing Co.

	GD25	FN65	NM94
1-Dan Dunn, Freckles, Myra North, Wash Tubbs, Apple Mary, The Nebbs, Don Winslow, Tom Mix, Buck Jones (1st app.), Major Hoople, Clyde Beatty, Boots begin	125.00	375.00	850.00
2	58.00	175.00	400.00
3	42.00	125.00	300.00
4,5: 5-Nude woman on cover	33.00	100.00	225.00
6-8,10: 8-Speed Bolton begins (1st app.)	27.00	82.00	185.00
9-(3/39)-Red Ryder strip-r begin by Harman; 1st app. in comics & 1st cover app.	38.00	115.00	265.00
11-14	25.00	75.00	175.00
15-Tarzan text feature begins by Burroughs (9/39); not in #26,35	27.00	82.00	190.00
16-24: 18-Stratosphere Jim begins (1st app., 12/39). 23-Ellery Queen begins plus-c (1st comic book app., 5/40)	18.00	55.00	125.00
25-The Owl begins (1st app., 7/40); in new costume #26 by Frank Thomas (also see Popular Comics #72)	42.00	125.00	300.00
26-30: 28-Part Owl-c	33.00	100.00	230.00
31-Owl covers begin, end #42	29.00	88.00	200.00
32-Origin Owl Girl	37.00	110.00	260.00
33-38: 36-Last Tarzan issue. 37-Cyclone & Midge begin (1st app.)	22.00	65.00	150.00
39-Andy Panda begins (intro/1st app., 9/41)	29.00	86.00	200.00
40-43: 42-Last Owl-c. 43-Terry & the Pirates-r	20.00	60.00	140.00

NOTE: ***McWilliams** art in most issues.*

CRACK COMICS (Crack Western No. 63 on)
May, 1940 - No. 62, Sept, 1949
Quality Comics Group

Crack Comics #32, © QUA

Crash Comics #1, © HOKE

Crazy #1 (2/73), © MEG

	GD25	FN65	NM94
1-Origin & 1st app. The Black Condor by Lou Fine, Madame Fatal, Red Torpedo, Rock Bradden & The Space Legion; The Clock, Alias the Spider (by Gustavson), Wizard Wells, & Ned Brant begin; Powell-a; Note: Madame Fatal is a man dressed as a woman	250.00	750.00	1700.00
2	117.00	350.00	800.00
3	83.00	250.00	550.00
4	75.00	225.00	500.00
5-10: 5-Molly The Model begins. 10-Tor, the Magic Master begins	58.00	175.00	400.00
11-20: 13-1 pg. J. Cole-a. 18-1st app. Spitfire?	50.00	150.00	350.00
21-24-Last Fine Black Condor	40.00	120.00	265.00
25,26: 26-Flag-c	27.00	82.00	185.00
27-(1/43)-Intro & origin Captain Triumph by Alfred Andriola (Kerry Drake artist) & begin series	58.00	175.00	400.00
28-30	23.00	70.00	160.00
31-39: 31-Last Black Condor	13.00	40.00	90.00
40-46	10.00	30.00	65.00
47-57,59,60-Capt. Triumph by Crandall	10.00	30.00	70.00
58,61,62-Last Captain Triumph	9.15	27.50	55.00

NOTE: *Black Condor by* ***Fine****: No. 1, 2, 4-6, 8, 10-24; by* ***Sultan****: No. 3, 7; by* ***Fugitani****: No. 9.* ***Cole*** *a-34.* ***Crandall*** *a-61(unsigned); c-48, 49, 51-61.* ***Guardineer*** *a-17.* ***Gustavson*** *a-1, 17.* ***McWilliams*** *a-15-27. Black Condor c-2, 4, 6, 8, 10, 12, 14, 16, 18, 20-26. Capt. Triumph c-27-62. The Clock c-1, 3, 5, 7, 9, 11, 13, 15, 17, 19.*

CRACKED (Magazine) (Satire) (Also see The 3-D Zone #19)
Feb-Mar, 1958 - Present
Major Magazines

	GD25	FN65	NM94
1-One pg. Williamson-a	11.50	34.00	80.00
2-1st Shut-Ups & Bonus Cut-Outs	5.35	16.00	32.00
3-6	4.00	10.00	20.00
7-10: 7-Reprints 1st 6 covers on-c	3.20	8.00	16.00
11-12, 13(nn,3/60), 14-17, 18(nn,2/61), 19,20	2.80	7.00	14.00
21-27(11/62), 27(No.28, 2/63; mis-#d), 29(5/63)	2.40	6.00	12.00
31-60	1.60	4.00	8.00
61-98,100	1.20	3.00	6.00
99-Alfred E. Neuman on-c	3.60	9.00	18.00
101-200: 234-Don Martin-a begins ($1.75 #? on)	.60	1.50	3.00
201-290	.40	1.00	2.00
Biggest...(Winter, 1977)	1.40	0.50	7.00
Biggest, Greatest...nn('65)	3.60	9.00	18.00
Biggest, Greatest...2('66) - #12('76)	1.80	4.50	9.00
...Blockbuster 1,2('88)	.55	1.60	2.75
...Digest 1(Fall, '86, 148 pgs.) - #5	.40	1.00	2.00
Collectors' Edition 4 ('73; formerly ...Special)	1.40	3.50	7.00
5-70: 23-Ward-a	.60	1.50	3.00
71-84: 83-Elvis, Batman parodies	.70	1.75	3.50
...Party Pack 1,2('88)	.70	1.75	3.50
...Shut-Ups (2/72-'72; Cracked Spec. #3) 1,2	1.20	3.00	6.00
...Special 3('73; formerly Cracked Shut-Ups; ...Collectors' Edition#4 on)	1.20	3.00	6.00
Extra Special...1('76), 2('76)	.60	1.50	3.00
Giant...nn('65)	3.00	7.50	15.00
Giant...2('66)-12('76), nn(9/77)-48('87)	2.00	5.00	10.00
King Sized...1('67)	4.20	12.50	25.00
King Sized...2('68)-11('77)	3.00	7.50	15.00
King Sized...12-22 (Sum/'86)	.40	1.00	2.00
Super...1('68)	4.00	10.50	21.00
Super...2('69)-24('88)	3.00	7.50	15.00
Super...1('87, 100 pgs.)-Severin & Elder-a	.55	1.40	2.75

NOTE: ***Burgos*** *a-1-10.* ***Colan*** *a-257.* ***Davis*** *a-5, 11-17, 24, 40, 80; c-12-14, 16.* ***Elder*** *a-5, 6, 10-13; c-10.* ***Everett*** *a-1-10, 23-25, 61; c-1.* ***Heath*** *a-1-3, 6, 13, 14, 17, 110; c-6.* ***Jaffee*** *a-5, 6.* ***Don Martin*** *c-235, 244, 247, 259, 261, 264.* ***Morrow*** *a-8-10.* ***Reinman*** *a-1-4.* ***Severin*** *c/a-in most all issues.* ***Shores*** *a-3-7.* ***Torres*** *a-7-10.* ***Ward*** *a-22-24, 27, 35, 40, 143, 144, 149, 150, 152, 153, 156.* ***Williamson*** *a-1 (1 pg.).* ***Wolverton*** *a-10 (2 pgs.), Giant nn('65).* ***Wood*** *a-27, 35, 40. Alfred E. Neuman c-177, 200, 202. Batman c-234, 248, 249, 256. Captain America c-256. Christmas c-234, 243. Spider-Man c-260. Star Trek c-127, 169, 207, 228. Star Wars c-145, 146, 148, 149, 152, 155, 173, 174, 199. Superman c-183, 233. #144, 146 have free full-color pre-glued stickers. #145, 147, 155, 163 have free full-color postcards. #123, 137, 154, 157 have free iron-ons.*

CRACK WESTERN (Formerly Crack Comics; Jonesy No. 85 on)
No. 63, Nov, 1949 - No. 84, May, 1953 (36 pgs., 63-68,74-on)
Quality Comics Group

	GD25	FN65	NM94
63(#1)-Two-Gun Lil (origin & 1st app.)(ends #84), Arizona Ames, his horse Thunder (with sidekick Spurs & his horse Calico), Frontier Marshal (ends #70), & Dead Canyon Days (ends #69) begin; Crandall-a	14.00	43.00	100.00
64,65-Crandall-a	11.50	34.00	80.00
66,68-Photo-c. 66-Arizona Ames becomes A. Raines (ends #84)	10.00	30.00	70.00
67-Randolph Scott photo-c; Crandall-a	11.50	34.00	80.00
69(52pgs.)-Crandall-a	10.00	30.00	70.00
70(52pgs.)-The Whip (origin & 1st app.) & his horse Diablo begin (ends #84); Crandall-a	10.00	30.00	70.00
71(52pgs.)-Frontier Marshal becomes Bob Allen F. Marshal (ends #84); Crandall-c/a	11.50	34.00	80.00
72(52pgs.)-Tim Holt photo-c	10.00	30.00	65.00
73(52pgs.)-Photo-c	7.50	22.50	45.00
74-76,78,79,81,83-Crandall-c. 83-Crandall-a(p)	9.15	27.50	55.00
77,80,82	5.85	17.50	35.00
84-Crandall-c/a	10.00	30.00	70.00

NOTE: ***Crandall*** *c-71p, 74-81, 83p(w/****Cuidera****-i).*

CRASH COMICS (Catman Comics No. 6 on)
May, 1940 - No. 5, Nov, 1940
Tem Publishing Co.

	GD25	FN65	NM94
1-The Blue Streak, Strongman (origin), The Perfect Human, Shangra begin (1st app. of each); Kirby-a	146.00	436.00	1000.00
2-Simon & Kirby-a	75.00	225.00	500.00
3,5-Simon & Kirby-a	58.00	175.00	400.00
4-Origin & 1st app. The Catman; S&K-a	96.00	286.00	650.00

NOTE: *Solar Legion by* ***Kirby*** *No. 1-5 (5 pgs. each). Strongman c-1-4. Catman c-5.*

CRASH DIVE (See Cinema Comics Herald)

CRASH RYAN (Also see Dark Horse Presents #44)
Oct, 1984 - No. 4, Jan, 1985 (Baxter paper, limited series)
Epic Comics (Marvel)

	GD25	FN65	NM94
1-4			1.50

CRAZY (Also see This Magazine is Crazy)
Dec, 1953 - No. 7, July, 1954
Atlas Comics (CSI)

	GD25	FN65	NM94
1-Everett-c/a	13.00	40.00	90.00
2	10.00	30.00	70.00
3-7: 4-I Love Lucy satire. 5-Satire on censorship	10.00	30.00	60.00

NOTE: ***Ayers*** *a-5.* ***Berg*** *a-1, 2.* ***Burgos*** *c-5, 6.* ***Drucker*** *a-6.* ***Everett*** *a-1-4.* ***Al Hartley*** *a-4.* ***Heath*** *a-3, 7; c-7.* ***Maneely*** *a-1-7, c-3, 4.* ***Post*** *a-3-6.*

CRAZY (Satire)
Feb, 1973 - No. 3, June, 1973
Marvel Comics Group

	GD25	FN65	NM94
1-3-Not Brand Echh-r. 1-Beatles cameo (r)			1.00

CRAZY MAGAZINE (Satire)
Oct, 1973 - No. 94, Apr, 1983 (40-90 cents, B&W magazine)
(#1, 44pgs; #2-90, reg. issues, 52pgs; #92-95, 68pgs)
Marvel Comics Group

	GD25	FN65	NM94
1-Wolverton(1 pg.), Bode-a; 3 pg. photo story of Neal Adams & Dick Giordano		.80	2.00
2-Kurtzman's "Hey Look" 2 pg. reprint			1.20
3-16: 8-Casper parody. 9-Has 1st 8-c on-c			1.00
17-29,31-36,38-41,43,48,50,51,53,54,56,57,59,60: 20-Superheroes song sheet. 41-Kiss-c. 43-E.C. swipe from Mad #131. 60,92-Star Trek parodies.			1.00
30,37,42,49,52,55,61,64,67,70,73,76,85,88: Super Specials ($1.00, all 84 pgs.). 85-Flintstones. 88-X-Men			1.20
58-Super Special ($1.25); contains free Crazy #1 (2/73) comic reprint			1.25

Crazyman V2#1, © Continuity

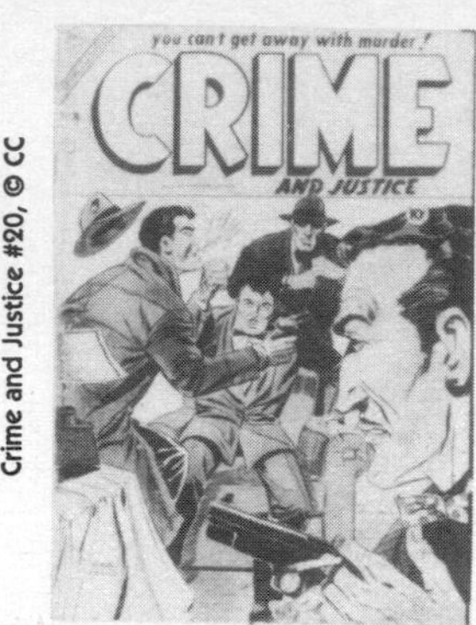

Crime and Justice #20, © CC

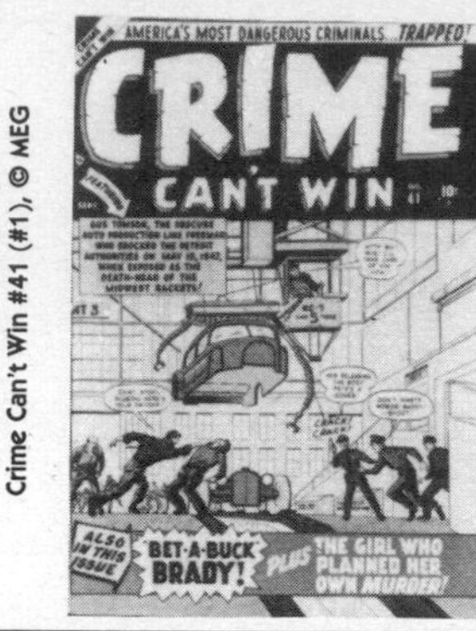

Crime Can't Win #41 (#1), © MEG

GD25 FN65 NM94

62,63,65,66,68,69,71,72,74,75,77,78,80,81,83,84,86,87,89,90: 62-Kiss-c & 2 pg. story. 63-Obnoxio app. 69-Richie Rich. 80-X-Men. 81-Wolverine/Hulk. 87-Obnoxio origin 1.00
79-Super Special ($1.25)-Full color looney labels 1.25
82-Super Special ($1.25); X-Men on-c 1.25
91-94: ($1.25) 91-Super Special; Black Knight by Maneely. 93-E.T.-c, & parody. 94-Avengers parody 1.25
Super Special 1(Summer, 1975, 100 pgs.)-Ploog, Neal Adams-r .65 1.60

NOTE: ***N. Adams*** *a-2, 61r, 94p.* ***Austin*** *a-82i.* ***Buscema*** *a-2, 82.* ***Byrne*** *c-82p.* ***Nick Cardy*** *c-7, 8, 10, 12-16, Super Special 1.* ***Crandall*** *a-76r.* ***Ditko*** *a-68r, 79r, 82r.* ***Drucker*** *a-3.* ***Eisner*** *a-9-16.* ***Kelly Freas*** *c-1-6, 9, 11; a-7.* ***Ploog*** *a-1, 4, 7, 67r, 73r.* ***Rogers*** *a-82.* ***Sparling*** *a-92.* ***Wood*** *a-65r. Howard the Duck in 36, 50, 51, 53, 54, 59, 63, 65, 66, 68, 69, 71, 72, 74, 75, 77. Hulk in 46, c-42, 46, 57, 73. Star Wars in 32, 66; c-37.*

CRAZYMAN
Apr, 1992 - No. 5, 1992 ($2.50, color, high quality paper)
Continuity Comics

1-($3.95, 52 pgs.)-Embossed-c; N. Adams part-i 1.60 4.00
2-5 ($2.50): 2-N. Adams/Bolland-c 1.00 2.50

CRAZYMAN
V2#1, May, 1993 - Present ($2.50, color, high quality paper)
Continuity Comics

V2#1-($2.50)-Entire book is die-cut 1.00 2.50

CRAZY, MAN, CRAZY (Magazine) (Becomes This Magazine is...?)
V2#2, June, 1956 (Formerly From Here to Insanity
Humor Magazines (Charlton)

V2#2-Satire; Wolverton-a, 3 pgs. 9.15 27.50 55.00

CREATURE, THE (See Movie Classics)

CREATURES ON THE LOOSE (Formerly Tower of Shadows No. 1-9)
No. 10, March, 1971 - No. 37, Sept, 1975 (New-a & reprints)(See Kull)
Marvel Comics Group

10-First King Kull story; Wrightson-a; 15 cents 3.60 10.75 25.00
11-37: 16-Origin Warrior of Mars (begins? ends #21). 21,22-Steranko-c. 22-29-Thongor-c/stories. 30-Manwolf begins 1.00 2.50

NOTE: ***Crandall*** *a-13.* ***Ditko*** *r-15, 17, 18, 20, 22, 24, 27, 28.* ***Everett*** *a-16i(new).* ***Matt Fox*** *r-21i.* ***Howard*** *a-26i.* ***Gil Kane*** *a-16p, 17p; c-16, 20, 25, 29, 33p, 35p, 36p.* ***Kirby*** *r-16(2).* ***Morrow*** *a-20, 21.* ***Perez*** *a-33-37; c-34p.* ***Sinnott*** *r-21.* ***Tuska*** *a-31p, 32p.*

CREEPER, THE (See Beware... & 1st Issue Special)

CREEPY (Magazine)(See Warren Presents)
1964 - No. 145, Feb, 1983; No. 146, 1985 (B&W)
Warren Publishing Co./Harris Publ. #146

1-Frazetta-a; Jack Davis-c; 1st Warren all comics mag. 7.00 21.00 50.00
2 3.20 8.00 20.00
3-13: 9-Creepy fan club sketch by Wrightson (1st published-a). 10-Brunner fan club sketch (1st published work) 1.65 4.00 10.00
14-Neal Adams 1st Warren work 2.15 6.50 15.00
15-25 1.40 3.50 8.50
26-40: 32-Harlan Ellison story 1.25 3.00 7.50
41-47,49-54,56-61: 61-Wertham parody 1.00 2.50 6.00
48,55,65-(1973, 1974, 1975 Annuals) 1.25 3.00 7.50
62-64,66-145: 113-All Wrightson-r issue. 139-All Toth-r issue. 144-Giant, $2.25; Frazetta-c 1.00 2.25 6.00
146 ($2.95) 1.30 3.25 8.00
Year Book 1968, 1969 1.30 3.25 8.00
Year Book 1970-Neal Adams, Ditko-a(r) 1.30 3.25 8.00
Annual 1971,1972 1.30 3.25 8.00
1993 Fearbook (1993, $3.95)-Harris Publications 1.00 2.00 5.00

NOTE: *All issues contain many good artists works:* ***Neal Adams, Brunner, Corben, Craig (Taycee), Crandall, Ditko, Evans, Frazetta, Heath, Jeff Jones, Krenkel, McWilliams, Morrow, Nino, Orlando, Ploog, Severin, Torres, Toth, Williamson, Wood, & Wrightson****; covers by* ***Crandall, Davis, Frazetta, Morrow, San Julian, Todd/Bode****; Otto Binder's "Adam Link" stories in No. 2, 4, 6, 8, 9, 12, 13, 15 with* ***Orlando*** *art.* ***Frazetta*** *c-2-7, 9-11, 15-17, 27, 32, 83r, 89r.* ***E.A. Poe*** *adaptations in 66, 69, 70.*

GD25 FN65 NM94

CREEPY THINGS
July, 1975 - No. 6, June, 1976
Charlton Comics

1 1.50
2-6: Ditko-a in 3,5. Sutton c-3,4 1.00
Modern Comics Reprint 2-6(1977) 1.00

CRIME AND JUSTICE (Rookie Cop? No. 27 on)
March, 1951 - No. 26, Sept, 1955
Capitol Stories/Charlton Comics

1 16.00 50.00 115.00
2 5.00 15.00 30.00
3-8,10-13: 6-Negligee panels 4.70 14.00 28.00
9-Classic story "Comics Vs. Crime" 10.00 30.00 70.00
14-Color illos in **POP**; gory story of man who beheads women 7.50 22.50 45.00
15-17,19-26 3.60 9.00 18.00
18-Ditko-a 11.50 34.00 80.00

NOTE: ***Alascia*** *c-20.* ***Ayers*** *a-17.* ***Shuster*** *a-19-21; c-19. Bondage c-11, 12.*

CRIME AND PUNISHMENT (Title inspired by 1935 film)
April, 1948 - No. 74, Aug, 1955
Lev Gleason Publications

1-Mr. Crime app. on-c 14.00 43.00 100.00
2 8.35 25.00 50.00
3-Used in **SOTI**, pg. 112; injury-to-eye panel; Fuje-a 9.15 27.50 55.00
4,5 5.85 17.50 35.00
6-10 5.00 15.00 30.00
11-20 4.20 12.50 25.00
21-30 4.00 10.00 20.00
31-38,40-44,46: 46-One page Frazetta-a 3.20 8.00 16.00
39-Drug mention story "The 5 Dopes" 4.70 14.00 28.00
45-"Hophead Killer" drug story 4.70 14.00 28.00
47-58,60-65,70-74: 58-Used in **POP**, pg. 79 2.80 7.00 14.00
59-Used in **SOTI**, illo-"What comic-book America stands for" 14.00 43.00 100.00
66-Toth-c/a(4); 3-D effect issue (3/54); 1st "Deep Dimension" process 22.00 65.00 150.00
67-"Monkey on His Back"-heroin story; 3-D effect issue 16.00 48.00 110.00
68-3-D effect issue; Toth-c (7/54) 14.00 43.00 100.00
69-"The Hot Rod Gang"-dope crazy kids 5.00 15.00 30.00

NOTE: ***Biro*** *c-most.* ***Everett*** *a-31.* ***Fuje*** *a-3, 4, 12, 13, 17, 18, 20, 26, 27.* ***Guardineer*** *a-2-4, 10, 14, 17, 18, 20, 26-28, 32, 38-44.* ***Kinstler*** *c-69.* ***McWilliams*** *a-41, 48, 49.* ***Tuska*** *a-28, 30, 51, 64, 70.*

CRIME AND PUNISHMENT: MARSHALL LAW TAKES MANHATTAN
1989 ($4.95, color, 52 pgs., direct sale only, mature readers)
Epic Comics (Marvel)

nn-Graphic album featuring Marshall Law 1.00 2.00 5.00

CRIME CAN'T WIN (Formerly Cindy Smith)
No. 41, 9/50 - No. 43, 2/51; No. 4, 4/51 - No. 12, 9/53
Marvel/Atlas Comics (TCI 41/CCC 42,43,4-12)

41(#1) 11.50 34.00 80.00
42(#2) 6.70 20.00 40.00
43(#3)-Horror story 8.35 25.00 50.00
4(4/51),5-12: 10-Possible use in **SOTI**, pg. 161 5.35 16.00 32.00

NOTE: ***Robinson*** *a-9-11.* ***Tuska*** *a-43.*

CRIME CASES COMICS (Formerly Willie Comics)
No. 24, 8/50 - No. 27, 3/51; No. 5, 5/51 - No. 12, 7/52
Marvel/Atlas Comics(CnPC No.24-8/MJMC No.9-12)

24 (#1, 52 pgs.) 8.35 25.00 50.00
25-27(#2-4): 27-Morisi-a 5.85 17.50 35.00
5-12: 11-Robinson-a, 12-Tuska-a 4.70 14.00 28.00

Crime Detective V1#3, © HILL

Crimefighters #1, © MCG

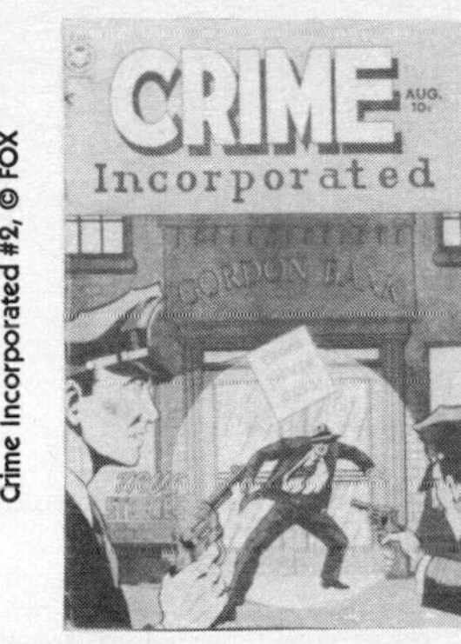

Crime Incorporated #2, © FOX

CRIME CLINIC
No. 10, July-Aug, 1951 - No. 5, Summer, 1952
Ziff-Davis Publishing Co.

	GD25	FN65	NM94
10(#1)-Painted-c; origin Dr. Tom Rogers	13.00	40.00	90.00
11,3-5: 3-Used in **SOTI**, pg. 18. 4,5-Painted-c	10.00	30.00	65.00

NOTE: *Painted covers by* ***Saunders. Starr*** *a-10.*

CRIME DETECTIVE COMICS
Mar-Apr, 1948 - V3#8, May-June, 1953
Hillman Periodicals

	GD25	FN65	NM94
V1#1-The Invisible 6, costumed villains app; Fuje-c	12.00	36.00	85.00
2	5.85	17.50	35.00
3,4,6,7,10-12: 6-McWilliams-a	4.70	14.00	28.00
5-Krigstein-a	5.85	17.50	35.00
8-Kirbyish-a by McCann	4.35	13.00	26.00
9-Used in **SOTI**, pg. 16 & "Caricature of the author in a position comic book publishers wish he were in permanently" illo.	17.00	52.00	120.00
V2#1,4,7-Krigstein-a	5.00	15.00	30.00
2,3,5,6,8-12 (1-2/52)	4.00	10.00	20.00
V3#1-Drug use-c	4.00	10.00	20.00
2-8	3.60	9.00	18.00

NOTE: ***Briefer*** *a-V3#1.* ***Kinstlerish-a*** *by* ***McCann****-V2#7, V3#2.* ***Powell*** *a-11.*

CRIME DETECTOR
Jan, 1954 - No. 5, Sept, 1954
Timor Publications

	GD25	FN65	NM94
1	10.00	30.00	60.00
2	5.00	15.00	30.00
3,4	4.20	12.50	25.00
5-Disbrow-a (classic)	10.00	30.00	70.00

CRIME DOES NOT PAY (Formerly Silver Streak Comics No. 1-21)
No. 22, June, 1942 - No. 147, July, 1955 (1st crime comic)
Comic House/Lev Gleason/Golfing (Title inspired by film)

	GD25	FN65	NM94
22(23 on cover, 22 on indicia)-Origin The War Eagle & only app.; Chip Gardner begins; #22 was rebound in Complete Book of True Crime (Scarce)	125.00	375.00	850.00
23 (Scarce)	67.00	200.00	450.00
24-Intro. & 1st app. Mr. Crime (Scarce)	58.00	175.00	400.00
25-30	34.00	100.00	235.00
31-40	17.50	52.00	120.00
41-Origin & 1st app. Officer Common Sense	13.00	40.00	90.00
42-Electrocution-c	15.00	45.00	105.00
43-46,48-50: 44,45,50 are 68 pg. issues	10.00	30.00	65.00
47-Electric chair-c	15.00	45.00	105.00
51-70: 63,64-Possible use in **SOTI**, pg. 306. 63-Contains Biro & Gleason's self censorship code of 12 listed restrictions (5/48)	8.35	25.00	50.00
71-99: 87-Chip Gardner begins, ends #99	5.85	17.50	35.00
100	6.70	20.00	40.00
101-105,107-110: 102-Chip Gardner app. 105-Used in **POP**, pg. 84	4.20	12.50	25.00
106,114-Frazetta-a, 1 pg.	4.20	12.50	25.00
111-Used in **POP**, pgs. 80 & 81; injury-to-eye story illo	4.20	12.50	25.00
112,113,115-130	3.60	9.00	18.00
131-140	3.00	7.50	15.00
141,142-Last pre-code issue; Kubert-a(1)	4.70	14.00	28.00
143,147-Kubert-a, one story each	4.70	14.00	28.00
144-146	2.80	7.00	14.00
1(Golfing-1945)	3.60	9.00	18.00
The Best of...(1944, 128 pgs.)-Series contains 4 rebound issues	57.00	170.00	400.00
...1945 issue	43.00	130.00	300.00
...1946-48 issues	32.00	95.00	225.00
...1949-50 issues	26.00	78.00	180.00
...1951-53 issues	24.00	70.00	165.00

NOTE: *Many issues contain violent covers and stories. Who Dunnit by* ***Guardineer****-39-42, 44-105, 100-110; Chip Gardner by* ***Bob Fujitani (Fuje)****-88-103.* ***Alderman*** *a-29, 41-44, 49.* ***Dan Barry*** *a-75.* ***Biro*** *c-1-76, 122, 142.* ***Briefer*** *a-29(2), 30, 31, 33, 37, 39.* ***G. Colan*** *a-105.* ***Fuje*** *c-88, 89, 91-94, 96, 98, 99, 102, 103.* ***Guardineer*** *a-57, 71.* ***Kubert*** *c-143.* ***Landau*** *a-118.* ***Maurer*** *a-29, 39, 41, 42.* ***McWilliams*** *a-91, 93, 95, 100-103.* ***Palais*** *a-30, 33, 37, 39, 41-43, 44(2), 46, 49.* ***Powell*** *a-146, 147.* ***Tuska*** *a-48, 50(2), 51, 52, 56, 57(2), 60-64, 66, 67, 71. Painted c-87-102. Bondage c-43, 62, 98.*

CRIME EXPOSED
June, 1948; Dec, 1950 - No. 14, June, 1952
Marvel Comics (PPI)/Marvel Atlas Comics (PrPI)

	GD25	FN65	NM94
1(6/48)	16.00	48.00	110.00
1(12/50)	10.00	30.00	65.00
2	6.70	20.00	40.00
3-11,14: 10-Used in **POP**, pg. 81	5.00	15.00	30.00
12-Krigstein & Robinson-a	5.85	17.50	35.00
13-Used in **POP**, pg. 81; Krigstein-a	6.35	19.00	38.00

NOTE: ***Maneely*** *c-8.* ***Robinson*** *a-11, 12.* ***Tuska*** *a-3, 4.*

CRIMEFIGHTERS
April, 1948 - No. 10, Nov, 1949
Marvel Comics (CmPS 1-3/CCC 4-10)

	GD25	FN65	NM94
1-Some copies are undated & could be reprints	12.00	36.00	85.00
2,3: 3-Morphine addict story	6.70	20.00	40.00
4-10: 6-Anti-Wertham editorial. 9,10-Photo-c	5.85	17.50	35.00

CRIME FIGHTERS (...Always Win)
No. 11, Sept, 1954 - No. 13, Jan, 1955
Atlas Comics (CnPC)

	GD25	FN65	NM94
11,12: 11-Maneely-a	6.70	20.00	40.00
13-Pakula, Reinman, Severin-a	5.85	17.50	35.00

CRIME FIGHTING DETECTIVE (Shock Detective Cases No. 20 on; formerly Criminals on the Run)
No. 11, Apr-May, 1950 - No. 19, June, 1952
Star Publications

	GD25	FN65	NM94
11-L. B. Cole-c/a (2 pgs.)	6.70	20.00	40.00
12,13,15-19: 17-Young King Cole & Dr. Doom app.; L. B. Cole-c on all	5.00	15.00	30.00
14-L. B. Cole-c/a, r/Law-Crime #2	6.35	19.00	38.00

CRIME FILES
No. 5, Sept, 1952 - No. 6, Nov, 1952
Standard Comics

	GD25	FN65	NM94
5-Alex Toth-a; used in **SOTI**, pg. 4 (text)	14.00	43.00	100.00
6-Sekowsky-a	8.35	25.00	50.00

CRIME ILLUSTRATED (Magazine, 25 cents)
Nov-Dec, 1955 - No. 2, Spring, 1956 (Adult Suspense Stories on-c)
E. C. Comics

	GD25	FN65	NM94
1-Ingels & Crandall-a	10.00	30.00	60.00
2-Ingels & Crandall-a	8.35	25.00	50.00

NOTE: ***Craig*** *a-2.* ***Crandall*** *a-1, 2; c-2.* ***Evans*** *a-1.* ***Davis*** *a-2.* ***Ingels*** *a-1, 2.* ***Krigstein/Crandall*** *a-1.* ***Orlando*** *a-1, 2; c-1.*

CRIME INCORPORATED (Formerly Crimes Incorporated)
No. 2, Aug, 1950; No. 3, Aug, 1951
Fox Features Syndicate

	GD25	FN65	NM94
2	12.00	36.00	85.00
3(1951)-Hollingsworth-a	10.00	30.00	65.00

CRIME MACHINE (Magazine)
Feb, 1971 - No. 2, May, 1971 (B&W)
Skywald Publications

	GD25	FN65	NM94
1-Kubert-a(2)(r)(Avon)	2.00	7.50	10.00
2-Torres, Wildey-a; violent-c/a	2.00	6.00	14.00

CRIME MUST LOSE! (Formerly Sports Action?)
No. 4, Oct, 1950 - No. 12, April, 1952
Sports Action (Atlas Comics)

Crime Must Pay the Penalty #5, © ACE

Crime Reporter #3, © STJ

Crime SuspenStories #5, © WMG

4-Ann Brewster-a in all; c-used in N.Y. Legis. Comm. documents
10.00 30.00 60.00
5-12: 9-Robinson-a. 11-Used in **POP**, pg. 89 5.85 17.50 35.00

CRIME MUST PAY THE PENALTY (Formerly Four Favorites; Penalty #47, 48)
No. 33, Feb, 1948; No. 2, June, 1948 - No. 48, Jan, 1956
Ace Magazines (Current Books)

33(#1, 2/48)-Becomes Four Teeners #34? 14.00 43.00 100.00
2(6/48)-Extreme violence; Palais-a? 10.00 30.00 65.00
3-"Frisco Mary" story used in Senate Investigation report, pg. 7
5.85 17.50 35.00
4,8-Transvestism stories 7.50 22.50 45.00
5-7,9,10 4.35 13.00 26.00
11-20 4.00 10.00 20.00
21-32,34-40,42-48 3.60 9.00 18.00
33(7/53)-"Dell Fabry-Junk King"-drug story; mentioned in Love and Death
5.00 15.00 30.00
41-Drug story-"Dealers in White Death" 5.00 15.00 30.00
NOTE: ***Cameron** a-29-31, 34, 35, 39-41. **Colan** a-20, 31. **Kremer** a-3, 37r. **Larsen** a-32. **Palais** a-5?,37.*

CRIME MUST STOP
October, 1952 (52 pgs.)
Hillman Periodicals

V1#1(Scarce)-Similar to Monster Crime; Mort Lawrence, Krigstein-a
35.00 105.00 245.00

CRIME MYSTERIES (Secret Mysteries No. 16 on; combined with Crime Smashers No. 7 on)
May, 1952 - No. 15, Sept, 1954
Ribage Publishing Corp. (Trojan Magazines)

1-Transvestism story 26.00 78.00 180.00
2-Marijuana story (7/52) 16.00 48.00 110.00
3-One pg. Frazetta-a 13.00 40.00 90.00
4-Cover shows girl in bondage having her blood drained; 1 pg. Frazetta-a
24.00 70.00 165.00
5-10 11.00 32.00 75.00
11,12,14 10.00 30.00 65.00
13-(5/54)-Angelo Torres 1st comic work (inks over Check's pencils); Check-a
13.50 41.00 95.00
15-Acid in face-c 16.00 50.00 115.00
NOTE: ***Fass** a-13; c-4, 10. **Hollingsworth** a-10-13, 15; c-2, 12, 13, 15. **Kiefer** a-4. **Woodbridge** a-13? Bondage-c-1, 8, 12.*

CRIME ON THE RUN (See Approved Comics #8)

CRIME ON THE WATERFRONT (Formerly Famous Gangsters)
No. 4, May, 1952 (Painted cover)
Realistic Publications

4 15.00 45.00 105.00

CRIME PATROL (Formerly International #1-5; International Crime Patrol #6; becomes Crypt of Terror #17 on)
No. 7, Summer, 1948 - No. 16, Feb-Mar, 1950
E. C. Comics

7-Intro. Captain Crime 43.00 130.00 300.00
8-14: 12-Ingels-a 39.00 115.00 270.00
15-Intro. of Crypt Keeper (inspired by Witches Tales radio show) & Crypt of Terror (see Tales From the Crypt #33 for origin); used by N.Y. Legis. Comm.-last pg. Feldstein-a 164.00 495.00 1150.00
16-2nd Crypt Keeper app.; Roussos-a 115.00 342.00 800.00
NOTE: ***Craig** c/a in most issues. **Feldstein** a-9-16. **Kiefer** a-8, 10, 11. **Moldoff** a-7.*

CRIME PHOTOGRAPHER (See Casey...)

CRIME REPORTER
Aug, 1948 - No. 3, Dec, 1948 (Shows Oct.)
St. John Publ. Co.

1-Drug club story 24.00 72.00 165.00
2-Used in **SOTI**: illo-"Children told me what the man was going to do with the red-hot poker;" r/Dynamic #17 with editing; Baker-c; Tuska-a
39.00 120.00 275.00
3-Baker-c; Tuska-a 18.00 54.00 125.00

CRIMES BY WOMEN
June, 1948 - No. 15, Aug, 1951; 1954
Fox Features Syndicate

1 64.00 195.00 450.00
2,3: 3-Used in **SOTI**, pg. 234 34.00 105.00 240.00
4,5,7-9,11-15: 8-Used in **POP**. 30.00 90.00 210.00
6-Classic girl fight-c; acid-in-face panel 34.00 105.00 240.00
10-Used in **SOTI**, pg. 72 30.00 90.00 210.00
54(M.S. Publ.-'54)-Reprint; (formerly My Love Secret)
13.00 40.00 90.00

CRIMES INCORPORATED (Formerly My Past)
No. 12, June, 1950 (Crime Incorporated No. 2 on)
Fox Features Syndicate

12 8.00 24.00 48.00

CRIMES INCORPORATED (See Fox Giants)

CRIME SMASHER
Summer, 1948 (One Shot)
Fawcett Publications

1-Formerly Spy Smasher; see Whiz #76 26.00 78.00 180.00

CRIME SMASHERS (Becomes Secret Mysteries No. 16 on)
Oct, 1950 - No. 15, Mar, 1953
Ribage Publishing Corp.(Trojan Magazines)

1-Used in **SOTI**, pg. 19,20, & illo-"A girl raped and murdered;" Sally the Sleuth begins 39.00 120.00 275.00
2-Kubert-c 20.00 60.00 140.00
3,4 14.00 43.00 100.00
5-Wood-a 22.00 65.00 150.00
6,8-11 12.00 36.00 85.00
7-Female heroin junkie story 13.00 40.00 90.00
12-Injury to eye panel; 1 pg. Frazetta-a 13.50 41.00 95.00
13-Used in **POP**, pgs. 79,80; 1 pg. Frazetta-a 11.00 32.00 75.00
14,15 11.00 32.00 75.00
NOTE: ***Hollingsworth** a-14. **Kiefer** a-15. Bondage c-7, 9.*

CRIME SUSPENSTORIES (Formerly Vault of Horror No. 12-14)
No. 15, Oct-Nov, 1950 - No. 27, Feb-Mar, 1955
E. C. Comics

15-Identical to #1 in content; #1 printed on outside front cover. #15 (formerly "The Vault of Horror") printed and blackened out on inside front cover with Vol. 1, No. 1 printed over it. Evidently, several of No. 15 were printed before a decision was made not to drop the Vault of Horror and Haunt of Fear series. The print run was stopped on No. 15 and continued on No. 1. All of No. 15 were changed as described above. 105.00 310.00 725.00
1 75.00 225.00 525.00
2 43.00 130.00 315.00
3-5 30.00 90.00 210.00
6-10 24.00 72.00 165.00
11,12,14,15: 15-The Old Witch guest stars 17.00 52.00 120.00
13,16-Williamson-a 20.00 60.00 140.00
17-Williamson/Frazetta-a (6 pgs.) 23.00 67.00 155.00
18,19: 19-Used in **SOTI**, pg. 235 15.00 45.00 105.00
20-Cover used in **SOTI**, illo-"Cover of a children's comic book"
20.00 60.00 140.00
21,24-27: 24-"Food For Thought" similar to "Cave In" in Amazing Detective Cases #13 (1952) 11.00 32.00 75.00
22,23-Used in Senate investigation on juvenile delinquency. 22-Ax decapitation-c 15.00 45.00 105.00
NOTE: ***Craig** a-1-21; c-1-18, 20-22. **Crandall** a-18-26. **Davis** a-4, 5, 7, 9-12, 20. **Elder** a-17,18. **Evans** a-15, 19, 21, 23, 25, 27; c-23, 24. **Feldstein** c-19. **Ingels** a-1-12, 14, 15, 27. **Kamen** a-2, 4-18, 20-27; c-25-27. **Krigstein** a-22, 24, 25, 27. **Kurtzman** a-1, 3. **Orlando** a-16, 22, 24, 26. **Wood** a-1, 3. Issues No. 11-15 have E. C. "quickie" stories. No. 25 contains the famous "Are You a Red Dupe?" editorial. Ray Bradbury adaptations-15, 17.*

Crisis on Infinite Earths #8, © DC

The Crow #1, © Jim O'Barr

Crying Freeman #1, © Kazuo Koike/Ryoichi Ikegami/Shogakukan, Inc.

CRIME SUSPENSTORIES
Nov, 1992 - Present ($1.50/$2.00, color)
Russ Cochran

	GD25	FN65	NM94
1-3: 1,2-r/Crime SuspenStories #1,2			1.50
4,5 ($2.00)		.80	2.00

CRIMINALS ON THE RUN (Formerly Young King Cole)
(Crime Fighting Detective No. 11 on)
V4#1, Aug-Sept, 1948 - #10, Dec-Jan, 1949-50
Premium Group (Novelty Press)

	GD25	FN65	NM94
V4#1-Young King Cole continues	10.00	30.00	70.00
2-6: 6-Dr. Doom app.	9.15	27.50	55.00
7-Classic "Fish in the Face" c by L. B. Cole	20.00	60.00	140.00
V5#1,2 (#8,9): 9-L. B. Cole-c	9.15	27.50	55.00
10-L. B. Cole-c	9.15	27.50	55.00

NOTE: *Most issues have* **L. B. Cole** *covers.* **McWilliams** *a-V4#6, 7, V5#2; c-V4#5.*

CRIMSON AVENGER, THE (See Detective Comics #20 for 1st app.)
(Also see Leading Comics #1 & World's Best/Finest Comics)
June, 1988 - No. 4, Sept, 1988 ($1.00, color, limited series)
DC Comics

	GD25	FN65	NM94
1-4		.50	1.00

CRISIS ON INFINITE EARTHS (Also see Official...Index)
Apr, 1985 - No. 12, Mar, 1986 (12 issue maxi-series)
DC Comics

	GD25	FN65	NM94
1-1st DC app. Blue Beetle & Detective Karp from Charlton; Perez-c on all		1.60	4.00
2-6: 6-Intro Charlton's Capt. Atom, Nightshade, Question, Judomaster, Peacemaker & Thunderbolt		.80	2.00
7-Double size; death of Supergirl		1.60	4.00
8-Death of Flash	1.00	2.00	5.00
9-11: 9-Intro. Charlton's Ghost. 10-Intro. Charlton's Banshee, Dr. Spectro, Image, Punch & Jewellee		.80	2.00
12-(52 pgs.)-Deaths of Dove, Kole, Lori Lemaris, Sunburst, G.A. Robin & Huntress; Kid Flash becomes new Flash		1.60	4.00

CRITICAL ERROR (Dark Horse)(Value: cover or less)

CRITICAL MASS (See A Shadowline Saga: Critical Mass)

CRITTERS (Also see Usagi Yojimbo Summer Special)
1986 - No. 50, 1990 ($1.70/$2.00, B&W)
Fantagraphics Books

	GD25	FN65	NM94
1-Cutey Bunny, Usagi Yojimbo app.		1.00	2.50
2-11: 3,10,11-Usagi Yojimbo app. 11-Christmas Special (68 pgs.); Usagi Yojimbo		.80	2.00
12-22,24-49: 14,38-Usagi Yojimbo app. 22-Watchmen parody; two diff. covers exist		.70	1.70
23-With Alan Moore Flexi-disc ($3.95)		1.60	4.00
50 ($4.95, 84 pgs.)-Neil the Horse, Capt. Jack, Sam & Max & Usagi Yojimbo app.; Quagmire, Shaw-a	1.00	2.00	5.00
Special 1 (1/88, $2.00)		.80	2.00

CROMWELL STONE (Dark Horse)(Value: cover or less)

CROSLEY'S HOUSE OF FUN (Also see Tee and Vee Crosley...)
1950 (32 pgs.; full color; paper cover)
Crosley Div. AVCO Mfg. Corp. (Giveaway)

	GD25	FN65	NM94
nn-Strips revolve around Crosley appliances	4.00	10.00	20.00

CROSS AND THE SWITCHBLADE, THE (Spire Christian)(Value: cover or less)

CROSSFIRE (Spire Christian)(Value: cover or less)

CROSSFIRE (Eclipse)(Value: cover or less)

CROSSFIRE AND RAINBOW (Eclipse)(Value: cover or less)

CROSSING THE ROCKIES (See Classics Illustrated Special Issue)

CROSSROADS (First)(Value: cover or less)

CROW, THE (Also see Caliber Presents)
Feb, 1989 - No. 4, 1989 ($1.95, B&W, mini-series)
Caliber Press

	GD25	FN65	NM94
1	3.20	8.00	20.00
1-3 2nd printings		.80	2.00
2,4	1.65	4.00	10.00
2-3rd printing		.80	2.00
3-(Scarcer)	2.15	6.50	15.00

CROW, THE (Tundra)(Value: cover or less)

CROWN COMICS
Winter, 1944-45 - No. 19, July, 1949
Golfing/McCombs Publ.

	GD25	FN65	NM94
1-"The Oblong Box" E.A. Poe adaptation	22.00	65.00	150.00
2,3-Baker-a	11.50	34.00	80.00
4-6-Baker-c/a; Voodah app. #4,5	12.00	36.00	85.00
7-Feldstein, Baker, Kamen-a; Baker-c	11.50	34.00	80.00
8-Baker-a; Voodah app.	11.00	32.00	75.00
9-11,13-19: Voodah in #10-19	6.70	20.00	40.00
12-Feldstein?, Starr-a	7.50	22.50	45.00

NOTE: **Bolle** *a-11, 13-16, 18, 19; c-11p, 15.* **Powell** *a-19.* **Starr** *a-11-13; c-11i.*

CRUCIBLE
Feb, 1993 - No. 6, July, 1993 ($1.25, color, mini-series)
DC Comics

	GD25	FN65	NM94
1-(99¢)-Quesada-c(p) & layouts begin			1.00
2-6: 2-Last Quesada-c. 4-Last Quesada layouts			1.25

CRUSADER FROM MARS (See Tops in Adventure)
Jan-Mar, 1952 - No. 2, Fall, 1952
Ziff-Davis Publ. Co.

	GD25	FN65	NM94
1	43.00	130.00	300.00
2-Bondage-c	36.00	107.00	250.00

CRUSADER RABBIT (See 4-Color No. 735,805)

CRUSADERS, THE (Chick)(Value: cover or less)

CRUSADERS (Southern Knights No. 2 on)
1982 (Magazine size, B&W)
Guild Publications

	GD25	FN65	NM94
1-1st app. Southern Knights	1.00	2.00	5.00

CRUSADERS, THE (Also see Black Hood, The Jaguar, The Comet, The Fly, Legend of the Shield, The Mighty... & The Webb)
May, 1992 - No. 8, Dec, 1992 ($1.00/$1.25, color)
Impact Comics (DC Comics)

	GD25	FN65	NM94
1-Contains 3 Impact trading cards			1.25
2-8			1.00

CRY FOR DAWN
1989-Present ($2.25-c, B&W, mature readers)
Cry For Dawn Pub.

	GD25	FN65	NM94
1	3.60	10.75	25.00
1-2nd, 3rd printing		1.20	3.00
2	1.65	4.00	10.00
2-2nd printing		.80	2.00
3	1.10	2.70	6.50
4-9		.90	2.25

CRYING FREEMAN (Viz)(Value: cover or less)

CRYIN' LION COMICS
Fall, 1944 - No. 3, Spring, 1945
William H. Wise Co.

	GD25	FN65	NM94
1 Funny animal	10.00	30.00	70.00
2,3	7.00	21.00	42.00

CRYPT OF SHADOWS
Jan, 1973 - No. 21, Nov, 1975 (#1 & 2 are 20 cents)

Crypt of Terror #19, © WMG

Cyberforce #1, © Marc Silvestri

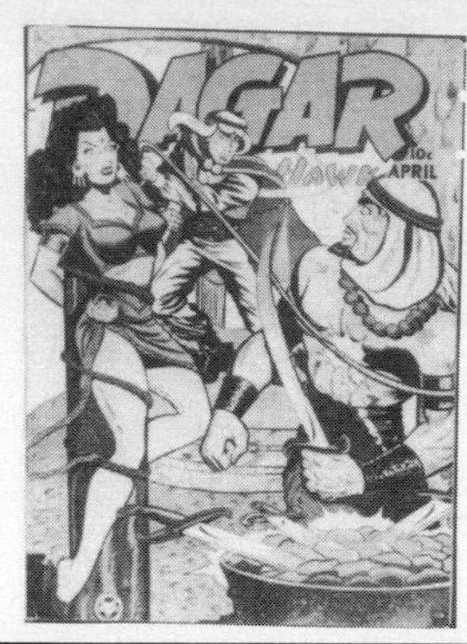

Dagar, Desert Hawk #23, © FOX

GD25 FN65 NM94

Marvel Comics Group

	GD25	FN65	NM94
1-Wolverton-r/Advs. Into Terror #7		1.60	4.00
2-21: 2-Starlin/Everett-c		.80	2.00

NOTE: ***Briefer*** *a-2r.* ***Ditko*** *a-13r, 18-20r.* ***Everett*** *a-6, 14r, c-2i.* ***Heath*** *a-1r.* ***Mort Lawrence*** *a-1r, 8r.* ***Maneely*** *a-2r.* ***Moldoff*** *a-8.* ***Powell*** *a-12r, 14r.*

CRYPT OF TERROR (Formerly Crime Patrol; Tales From the Crypt No. 20 on)
No. 17, Apr-May, 1950 - No. 19, Aug-Sept, 1950
E. C. Comics

	GD25	FN65	NM94
17-1st New Trend to hit stands	171.00	515.00	1200.00
18,19	115.00	342.00	800.00

NOTE: ***Craig*** *c/a-17-19.* ***Feldstein*** *a-17-19.* ***Ingels*** *a-19.* ***Kurtzman*** *a-18.* ***Wood*** *a-18. Canadian reprints known; see Table of Contents.*

CUPID
Dec, 1949 - No. 2, Mar, 1950
Marvel Comics (U.S.A.)

	GD25	FN65	NM94
1-Photo-c	9.15	27.50	55.00
2-Betty Page ('50s pin-up queen) photo-c; Powell-a (see My Love #4)	16.00	48.00	110.00

CURIO
1930's(?) (Tabloid size, 16-20 pages)
Harry 'A' Chesler

	GD25	FN65	NM94
nn	13.00	40.00	90.00

CURLY KAYOE COMICS (Boxing)
1946 - No. 8, 1950; Jan, 1958
United Features Syndicate/Dell Publ. Co.

	GD25	FN65	NM94
1 (1946)-Strip-r (Fritzi Ritz); biography of Sam Leff, Kayoe's artist	10.00	30.00	70.00
2	5.85	17.50	35.00
3-8	4.00	12.00	24.00
United Presents...(Fall, 1948)	4.00	12.00	24.00
4-Color 871 (Dell, 1/58)	4.00	10.00	20.00

CURSE OF THE WEIRD
Dec, 1993 - No. 4, Mar, 1994 ($1.25, color, mini-series)
Marvel Comics

	GD25	FN65	NM94
1-4-Ditko, Heath, Wolverton pre-code horror-r			1.25

CUSTER'S LAST FIGHT
1950
Avon Periodicals

	GD25	FN65	NM94
nn-Partial reprint of Cowpuncher #1	11.50	34.00	80.00

CUTEY BUNNY (See Army Surplus Komikz Featuring...)

CUTIE PIE
May, 1955 - No. 3, Dec, 1955; No. 4, Feb, 1956; No. 5, Aug, 1956
Junior Reader's Guild (Lev Gleason)

	GD25	FN65	NM94
1	4.00	11.00	22.00
2-5: 4-Misdated 2/55	2.80	7.00	14.00

CYBER CRUSH (Fleetway/Quality)(Value: cover or less)

CYBERFORCE
Oct, 1992 - No. 4, 1993; No. 0, Sept, 1993 ($1.95, color, mini-series)
Image Comics

	GD25	FN65	NM94
1-Coupon for Image Comics #0; Silvestri-c/a in all	1.00	2.00	5.00
1-With coupon missing		.80	2.00
2 (3/93), 3,4, 0 (9/93)-By Walt Simonson		.80	2.00

CYBERFORCE
Nov, 1993 - Present ($1.95, color)
Image Comics

	GD25	FN65	NM94
1,2-By Marc Silvestri		.80	2.00

CYBERPUNK (Innovation)(Value: cover or less)

CYBERPUNK: THE SERAPHIM FILES (Innovation)(Value: cover or less)

GD25 FN65 NM94

CYBERRAD
1991 - No. 7, 1992 ($2.00, color)(Direct sale & newsstand-c variations)
V2#1 - Present ($2.00, color)
Continuity Comics

	GD25	FN65	NM94
1-7: 5-Glow-in-the-dark-c by N. Adams (direct sale only). 6-Contains 4 pg. fold-out poster; N. Adams layouts		.80	2.00
V2#1-($2.95, direct sale ed.)-Die-cut-c w/B&W hologram on-c; Neal Adams sketches		1.20	3.00
V2#1-($2.50, newsstand ed.)-Without sketches		1.00	2.50
V2#2-5: 2-N. Adams-c		.80	2.00

CYBER 7 (Eclipse)(Value: cover or less)

CYCLONE COMICS (Also see Whirlwind Comics)
June, 1940 - No. 5, Nov, 1940
Bilbara Publishing Co.

	GD25	FN65	NM94
1-Origin Tornado Tom; Volton begins, Mister Q app. (1st app. of each)	63.00	186.00	425.00
2	33.00	100.00	225.00
3-5: 4,5-Mr. Q app.	27.00	82.00	190.00

CYNTHIA DOYLE, NURSE IN LOVE (Formerly Sweetheart Diary)
No. 66, Oct, 1962 - No. 74, Feb, 1964
Charlton Publications

	GD25	FN65	NM94
66-74	.80	2.00	4.00

DAFFY (Daffy Duck No. 18 on)(See Looney Tunes)
#457, 3/53 - #30, 7-9/62; #31, 10-12/62 - #145, 1983 (No #132,133)
Dell Publishing Co./Gold Key No. 31-127/Whitman No. 128 on

	GD25	FN65	NM94
4-Color 457(#1)-Elmer Fudd x-overs begin	8.35	25.00	50.00
4-Color 536,615('55)	4.20	12.50	25.00
4(1-3/56)-11('57)	3.20	8.00	16.00
12-19(1958-59)	2.40	6.00	12.00
20-40(1960-64)	1.40	3.50	7.00
41-60(1964-68)	.80	2.00	4.00
61-90(1969-74)-Road Runner in most		1.20	3.00
91-131,134-145(1974-83)			1.50
Mini-Comic 1 (1976; 3-1/4x6-1/2")			1.00

NOTE: *Reprint issues-No.41-46, 48, 50, 53-55, 58, 59, 65, 67, 69, 73, 81, 96, 103-108; 136-142, 144, 145(1/3-2/3-r). (See March of Comics No. 277, 288, 303, 313, 331, 347, 357,375, 387, 397, 402, 413, 425, 437, 460).*

DAFFYDILS
1911 (52 pgs.; 6x8"; B&W; hardcover)
Cupples & Leon Co.

	GD25	FN65	NM94
nn-By Tad	17.00	52.00	120.00

DAFFY TUNES COMICS
June, 1947; No. 12, Aug, 1947
Four-Star Publications

	GD25	FN65	NM94
nn	5.85	17.50	35.00
12-Al Fago-c/a	5.00	15.00	30.00

DAGAR, DESERT HAWK (Captain Kidd No. 24 on; formerly All Great)
No. 14, Feb, 1948 - No. 23, Apr, 1949 (No #17,18)
Fox Features Syndicate

	GD25	FN65	NM94
14-Tangi & Safari Cary begin; Edmond Good bondage-c/a	36.00	107.00	250.00
15,16-E. Good-a; 15-Bondage-c	22.00	65.00	150.00
19,20,22: 19-Used in SOTI, pg. 180 (Tangi)	19.00	58.00	135.00
21-'Bombs & Bums Away' panel in 'Flood of Death' story used in **SOTI**	24.00	72.00	165.00
23-Bondage-c	22.00	65.00	150.00

NOTE: *Tangi by* ***Kamen****-14-16, 19, 20; c-20, 21.*

DAGAR THE INVINCIBLE (Tales of Sword & Sorcery...) (Also see Dan Curtis Giveaways & Gold Key Spotlight)
Oct, 1972 - No. 18, Dec, 1976; No. 19, Apr, 1982
Gold Key

	GD25	FN65	NM94
1-Origin; intro. Villains Olstellon & Scor	1.70	5.00	12.00

Dagwood #8, © KING

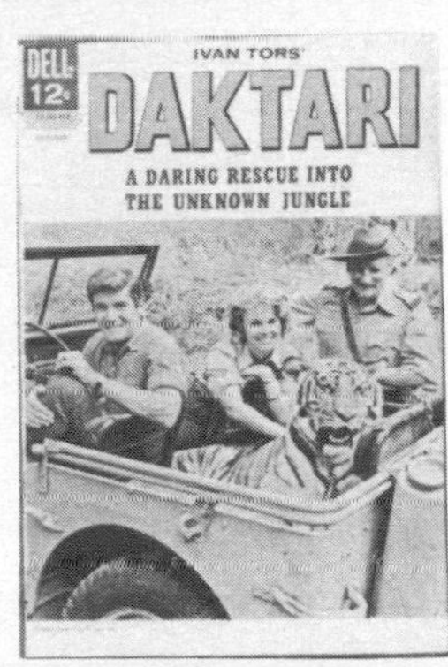

Daktari #3, Ivan Tors Films

Dances with Demons #1, © Marvel Comics UK

GD25 FN65 NM94

2-5: 3-Intro. Graylin, Dagar's woman; Jarn x-over 1.00 2.50 6.00
6-1st Dark Gods story 1.00 2.00 5.00
7-10: 9-Intro. Torgus. 10-1st Three Witches story 1.00 4.00
11-18: 13-Durak & Torgus x-over; story continues in Dr. Spektor #15.
14-Dagar's origin retold. 18-Origin retold 1.00 2.50
19-Origin-r/#18 1.20
NOTE: *Durak app. in 7, 12, 13. Tragg app. in 5, 11.*

DAGWOOD (Chic Young's) (Also see Blondie Comics)
Sept, 1950 - No. 140, Nov, 1965
Harvey Publications

	GD25	FN65	NM94
1	10.00	30.00	60.00
2	5.00	15.00	30.00
3-10	4.00	12.00	24.00
11-30	3.00	7.50	15.00
31-70	1.40	3.50	7.00
71-100	1.20	3.00	6.00
101-128,130,135	1.00	2.50	5.00
129,131-134,136-140-All are 68 pg. issues	1.40	3.50	7.00

NOTE: *Popeye and other one page strips appeared in early issues.*

DAGWOOD SPLITS THE ATOM (Also see Topix V8#4)
1949 (Science comic with King Features characters) (Giveaway)
King Features Syndicate
nn-Half comic, half text; Popeye, Olive Oyl, Henry, Mandrake, Little King, Katzenjammer Kids app. 4.00 12.00 24.00

DAI KAMIKAZE! (Now)(Value: cover or less)

DAISY AND DONALD (See Walt Disney Showcase No. 8)
May, 1973 - No. 59, 1984 (no No. 48)
Gold Key/Whitman No. 42 on

	GD25	FN65	NM94
1-Barks-r/WDC&S #280,308	1.00	2.50	6.00
2-5: 4-Barks-r/WDC&S #224		1.40	3.50
6-10		1.00	2.50
11-20		.80	2.00
21-47,49,50: 32-r/WDC&S #308. 50-r/#3			1.50
51-Barks-r/4-Color #1150		.70	1.75
52-59: 52-r/#2. 55-r/#5			1.20

DAISY & HER PUPS (Blondie's Dogs)
No. 21, 7/51 - No. 27, 7/52; No. 8, 9/52 - No. 25, 7/55
Harvey Publications
21-27 (#1-7): 26,27 have No. 6 & 7 on cover but No. 26 & 27 on inside 1.60 4.00 8.00
8-25: 19-25-Exist? 1.20 3.00 6.00

DAISY COMICS
Dec, 1936 (Small size: 5-1/4x7-1/2")
Eastern Color Printing Co.
nn-Joe Palooka, Buck Rogers (2 pgs. from Famous Funnies No. 18), Napoleon Flying to Fame, Butty & Fally 25.00 75.00 175.00

DAISY DUCK & UNCLE SCROOGE PICNIC TIME (See Dell Giant #33)

DAISY DUCK & UNCLE SCROOGE SHOW BOAT (See Dell Giant #55)

DAISY DUCK'S DIARY (See Dynabrite Comics, Four Color No. 600, 659, 743, 858, 948, 1055, 1150, 1247 & Walt Disney's Comics & Stories #298)

DAISY HANDBOOK
1946; No. 2, 1948 (132 pgs.)(10 cents)(Pocket-size)
Daisy Manufacturing Co.
1-Buck Rogers, Red Ryder; Wolverton-a(2 pgs.) 27.00 80.00 185.00
2-Captain Marvel & Ibis the Invincible, Red Ryder, Boy Commandos & Robotman; Wolverton-a (2 pgs.); contains 8 pg. color catalog 27.00 80.00 185.00

DAISY LOW OF THE GIRL SCOUTS
1954, 1965 (16 pgs.; paper cover)
Girl Scouts of America
1954-Story of Juliette Gordon Low 4.00 10.00 20.00
1965 1.60 4.00 8.00

DAISY MAE (See Oxydol-Dreft)

DAISY'S RED RYDER GUN BOOK
1955 (25 cents, 132 pages)(Pocket-size)
Daisy Manufacturing Co.
nn-Boy Commandos, Red Ryder; 1 pg. Wolverton-a 17.00 52.00 120.00

DAKOTA LIL (See Fawcett Movie Comics)

DAKOTA NORTH
June, 1986 - No. 5, Feb, 1987
Marvel Comics Group
1-5 1.00

DAKTARI (Ivan Tors) (TV)
July, 1967 - No. 3, Oct, 1968; No. 4, Sept, 1969 (All have photo-c)
Dell Publishing Co.

	GD25	FN65	NM94
1	4.00	10.00	20.00
2-4	2.80	7.00	14.00

DALE EVANS COMICS (Also see Queen of the West...)
Sept-Oct, 1948 - No. 24, July-Aug, 1952 (No. 1-19: 52 pgs.)
National Periodical Publications

	GD25	FN65	NM94
1-Dale Evans & her horse Buttermilk begin; Sierra Smith begins by Alex Toth	52.00	155.00	365.00
2-Alex Toth-a	27.00	80.00	185.00
3-11-Alex Toth-a	22.00	65.00	150.00
12-24	11.00	32.00	75.00

NOTE: *Photo-c-1, 2, 4-14.*

DALGODA (Fantagraphics)(Value: cover or less)

DALTON BOYS, THE
1951
Avon Periodicals
1-(No. on spine)-Kinstler-c 10.00 30.00 70.00

DAMAGE CONTROL (See Marvel Comics Presents #19)
5/89 - No. 4, 8/89; V2#1, 12/89 - No. 4, 2/90 ($1.00, color)
V3#1, 6/91 - No. 4, 9/91 ($1.25, all are mini-series)
Marvel Comics
V1#1-3, 4-Wolverine app. V2#1,3 1.00
2,4-Punisher app. .70 1.80
V3#1-4 ($1.25): 1-Spider-Man app. 2-New Warriors app. 3,4-Silver Surfer app. 4-Infinity Guantlet parody 1.00

DANCES WITH DEMONS
Sept, 1993 - No. 4, Dec, 1993 ($1.95, color, mini-series)
Marvel Frontier Comics
1-($2.95)-Foil embossed-c 1.20 3.00
2-4 .80 2.00

DAN CURTIS GIVEAWAYS
1974 (24 pages) (3x6") (in color, all reprints)
Western Publishing Co.
1-Dark Shadows, 2-Star Trek, 3-The Twilight Zone, 4-Ripley's Believe It or Not!, 5-Turok, Son of Stone, 6-Star Trek, 7-The Occult Files of Dr. Spektor, 8-Dagar the Invincible, 9-Grimm's Ghost Stories Set... 3.00 9.00 30.00

DANDEE
1947
Four Star Publications
nn 4.35 13.00 26.00

DAN DUNN (See Crackajack Funnies, Detective Dan, Famous Feature Stories & Red Ryder)

DANDY COMICS (Also see Happy Jack Howard)
Spring, 1947 - No. 7, Spring, 1948
E. C. Comics

	GD25	FN65	NM94
1-Vince Fago-a in all	24.00	72.00	165.00
2	17.00	50.00	115.00

Danger #2, © ME

Dan'l Boone #1, © ME

Daredevil #54, © MEG

	GD25	FN65	NM94
3-7	13.00	40.00	90.00

DANGER
January, 1953 - No. 11, Aug, 1954
Comic Media/Allen Hardy Assoc.

	GD25	FN65	NM94
1-Heck-c/a	10.00	30.00	60.00
2,3,5-7,9-11: 6-``Narcotics" story	4.70	14.00	28.00
4-Marijuana cover/story	6.35	19.00	38.00
8-Bondage/torture/headlights panels	7.50	22.50	45.00

NOTE: ***Morisi*** *a-2, 5, 6(3), 10; c-2. Contains some reprints from Danger & Dynamite.*

DANGER (Jim Bowie No. 15 on; formerly Comic Media title)
No. 12, June, 1955 - No. 14, Oct, 1955
Charlton Comics Group

	GD25	FN65	NM94
12(#1)	5.35	16.00	32.00
13,14: 14-r/#12	4.20	12.50	25.00

DANGER
1964
Super Comics

Super Reprint #10-12 (Black Dwarf; #10-r/Great Comics #1 by Novack. #11-r/Johnny Danger #1. #12-r/Red Seal #?), #15-r/Spy Cases #26. #16-Unpublished Chesler material (Yankee Girl), #17-r/Scoop #8 (Capt. Courage & Enchanted Dagger), #18(nd)-r/Guns Against Gangsters #5 (Gun-Master, Annie Oakley, The Chameleon; L.B. Cole-r)

	GD25	FN65	NM94
	1.20	3.00	6.00

DANGER AND ADVENTURE (Formerly This Magazine Is Haunted; Robin Hood and His Merry Men No. 28 on)
No. 22, Feb, 1955 - No. 27, Feb, 1956
Charlton Comics

	GD25	FN65	NM94
22-Ibis the Invincible, Nyoka app.	7.50	22.50	45.00
23-Nyoka, Lance O'Casey app.	7.50	22.50	45.00
24-27: 24-Mike Danger & Johnny Adventure begin	4.70	14.00	28.00

DANGER IS OUR BUSINESS!
1953(Dec.) - No. 10, June, 1955
Toby Press

	GD25	FN65	NM94
1-Captain Comet by Williamson/Frazetta-a, 6 pgs. (science fiction)	33.00	100.00	230.00
2	7.00	21.00	42.00
3-10	5.35	16.00	32.00
I.W. Reprint #9('64)-Williamson/Frazetta-a r-/#1; Kinstler-c	7.50	22.50	45.00

DANGER IS THEIR BUSINESS (See A-1 Comics No. 50)

DANGER MAN (See 4-Color No. 1231)

DANGER TRAIL (Also see Showcase #50, 51)
July-Aug, 1950 - No. 5, Mar-Apr, 1951 (52 pgs.)
National Periodical Publications

	GD25	FN65	NM94
1-King Farrady begins, ends #4; Toth-a	71.00	215.00	500.00
2-Toth-a	52.00	155.00	365.00
3-Toth-a (rare; considered the rarest early '50s DC comic)	82.00	245.00	575.00
4,5-Toth-a in both. 5-Johnny Peril app.	46.00	140.00	325.00

DANGER TRAIL
Apr, 1993 - No. 4, July, 1993 ($1.50, color, mini-series)
National Periodical Publications

	GD25	FN65	NM94
1-4: Gulacy-c on all			1.50

DANIEL BOONE (See The Exploits of..., Fighting..., 4-Color No. 1163, Frontier Scout..., The Legends of... & March of Comics No. 306)

DAN'L BOONE
Sept, 1955 - No. 8, Sept, 1957
Magazine Enterprises/Sussex Publ. Co. No. 2 on

	GD25	FN65	NM94
1	10.00	30.00	60.00
2	6.35	19.00	38.00
3-8	4.70	14.00	28.00

DANIEL BOONE (TV) (See March of Comics No. 306)
Jan, 1965 - No. 15, Apr, 1969 (All photo-c?)
Gold Key

	GD25	FN65	NM94
1	10.00	30.00	60.00
2-Fess Parker photo-c	5.00	15.00	30.00
3-5: Fess Parker photo-c	3.60	9.00	18.00
6-15: 6,7,10,14-Fess Parker photo-c	2.00	5.00	10.00

DANNY BLAZE (Nature Boy No. 3 on)
Aug, 1955 - No. 2, Oct, 1955
Charlton Comics

	GD25	FN65	NM94
1,2	5.00	15.00	30.00

DANNY DINGLE (See Single Series #17 & Sparkler Comics)

DANNY KAYE'S BAND FUN BOOK
1959
H & A Selmer (Giveaway)

	GD25	FN65	NM94
nn	4.35	13.00	26.00

DANNY THOMAS SHOW, THE (See 4-Color No. 1180,1249)

DARBY O'GILL & THE LITTLE PEOPLE (See 4-Color No. 1024 & Movie Comics)

DARE (Fantagraphics)(Value: cover or less)

DAREDEVIL (...& the Black Widow #92-107 on-c only; see Giant-Size..., Marvel Advs., Marvel Graphic Novel #24, Marvel Super Heroes, '66 & Spider-Man and...)
April, 1964 - Present
Marvel Comics Group

	GD25	FN65	VF82	NM94
1-Origin & 1st app. Daredevil; reprinted in Marvel Super Heroes #1 (1966); death of Battling Murdock; intro Foggy Nelson & Karen Page	136.00	410.00	820.00	1225.00

	GD25	FN65	NM94
2-Fantastic Four cameo; 2nd app. Electro (Spidey villain); Thing guest stars	36.00	107.00	350.00
3-Origin & 1st app. The Owl (villain)	25.00	75.00	250.00
4	24.00	73.00	240.00
5-New Costume; Wood-a begins	15.00	46.00	150.00
6,8-10: 8-Origin/1st app. Stilt-Man	10.00	29.00	95.00
7-Daredevil battles Sub-Mariner & dons new red costume (4/65)	13.00	40.00	130.00
11-15: 12-Romita's 1st work at Marvel; 1st app. Plunderer. 13-Facts about Ka-Zar's origin; Kirby-a	6.00	17.00	55.00
16,17-Spider-Man x-over. 16-1st Romita-a on Spider-Man (5/66)	7.00	21.00	70.00
18-20: 18-Origin & 1st app. Gladiator	4.00	12.00	40.00
21-26,28-30: 24-Ka-Zar app.	3.00	8.00	25.00
27-Spider-Man x-over	3.00	9.00	30.00
31-40: 38-Fantastic Four x-over; cont'd in F.F. #73. 39-1st Exterminator (later becomes Death-Stalker)	2.00	6.00	20.00
41-49: 41-Death Mike Murdock. 42-1st app. Jester. 43-Daredevil battles Captain America; origin partially retold. 45-Statue of Liberty photo-c	2.00	6.00	15.00
50-52-B. Smith-a.	2.00	6.00	18.00
53-Origin retold; last 12 cent issue	3.20	8.00	20.00
54-56,58-60: 54-Spider-Man cameo. 56-1st app. Death's Head (9/69); story cont'd in #57 (not same as new Death's Head)	1.50	3.75	9.00
57-Reveals i.d. to Karen Page; Death's Head app.	1.65	4.00	10.00
61-99: 62-1st app. Nighthawk. 81-Oversize issue; Black Widow begins	1.30	3.25	8.00
100-Origin retold	3.20	8.00	20.00
101-104,106,108-113,115-120: 113-1st app. Deathstalker (cameo)	1.00	2.50	6.00
105-Origin Moondragon by Starlin (12/73); Thanos cameo in flashback (early app.)	1.70	5.00	12.00
107-Starlin-c	1.20	3.00	7.00
114-1st full app. Deathstalker	1.30	3.25	8.00

121-130,133-137: 124-1st app. Copperhead; Black Widow leaves. 126-1st

Daredevil #151, © MEG

Daredevil #293, © MEG

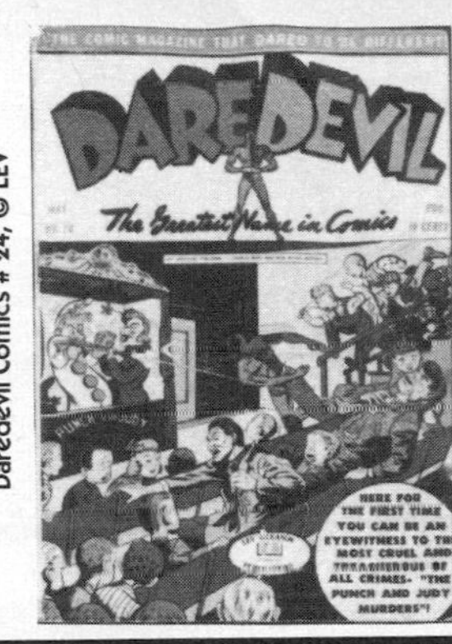

Daredevil Comics # 24, © LEV

	GD25	FN65	NM94
new Torpedo		1.40	3.50
131-Origin/1st app. new Bullseye (see Nick Fury #15)	3.20	8.00	20.00
132-Bullseye app.	1.00	2.00	5.00
138-Ghost Rider-c/story; Death's Head is reincarnated; Byrne-a	1.65	4.70	11.00
139-157: 142-Nova cameo. 146-Bullseye app. 148-30 & 35 cent issues exist. 150-1st app. Paladin. 151-Reveals i.d. to Heather Glenn. 155-Black Widow returns. 156-1960s Daredevil app.		1.40	3.50
158-Frank Miller art begins (5/79); origin/death of Deathstalker (see Captain America #235 & Spectacular Spider-Man #27	5.00	15.00	35.00
159	2.30	6.75	16.00
160,161	1.20	3.00	7.00
162-Ditko-a, no Miller-a		1.00	2.50
163,164: 163-Hulk cameo. 164-Origin retold	1.00	2.50	6.00
165-167,170	1.00	2.00	5.00
168-Origin/1st app. Elektra	2.60	7.50	18.00
169-Elektra app.	1.20	3.00	7.00
171-175: 174,175-Elektra app.		1.60	4.00
176-180-Elektra app. 179-Anti-smoking issue mentioned in the Congressional Record		1.20	3.00
181-Double size; death of Elektra; Punisher cameo out of costume	1.20	3.00	7.00
182-184-Punisher app. by Miller (drug issues)	1.65	4.00	10.00
185-191: 187-New Black Widow. 189-Death of Stick. 190-(52 pgs.)-Elektra returns, part origin. 191-Last Miller Daredevil		.80	2.00
192-195,197-210: 197,200-Bullseye app. 208-Harlan Ellison scripts			1.50
196-Wolverine app.	1.70	5.00	12.00
211-225: 219-Miller scripts			1.00
226-Frank Miller plots begin			1.50
227-Miller scripts begin		1.20	3.00
228-233-Last Miller scripts		.80	2.00
234-237,239,240,242-247			1.00
238-Mutant Massacre; Sabretooth app.	1.00	2.50	6.00
241-Todd McFarlane-a(p)		1.20	3.00
248,249-Wolverine app.	1.00	2.50	6.00
250,251,253,258: 250-1st app. Bullet. 258-Intro The Bengal (a villain)			1.00
252-(52 pgs.); Fall of the Mutants		1.20	3.00
254-Origin & 1st app. Typhoid Mary (5/88)	2.00	6.00	14.00
255-2nd app. Typhoid Mary	1.00	2.50	6.00
256-3rd app. Typhoid Mary	1.00	2.00	5.00
257-Punisher app. (x-over w/Punisher #10)	2.60	7.50	18.00
259,260-Typhoid Mary app. 260-Double size		1.20	3.00
261-291,294,296-299: 272-Intro Shotgun (villain). 282-Silver Surfer app. (cameo in #281). 283-Capt. America app. 297-Typhoid Mary app.; Kingpin storyline begins. 299-Last $1.00-c			1.00
292,293-Punisher app.		.80	2.00
295-Ghost Rider app.		1.00	2.50
300-($2.00, 52 pgs.)-Kingpin story ends		1.20	3.00
301-318,324,326: 305,306-Spider-Man-c/story. 309-Punisher-c/story; Terror app. 310-Calypso-c/story; Infinity War x-over			1.25
319-Prologue to "Fall From Grace" with Elektra	2.15	6.50	15.00
319-2nd printing w/black-c			1.25
320- "Fall From Grace", chapter 1	1.65	4.00	10.00
321- "Fall From Grace" regular ed.; chapter 2; new costume; Venom app.		1.40	3.50
321-($2.00)-Glow-in-the-dark ed.	1.25	3.00	7.50
322- "Fall From Grace" part 3; Eddie Brock app.	1.00	2.00	5.00
323- "Fall From Grace" part 4		.80	2.00
325-($2.50, 52 pgs.)- "Fall From Grace" ends; contains bound-in poster		1.00	2.50
Special 1(9/67, 25 cents, 68 pgs.)-new art	3.60	10.75	25.00
Special 2,3: 2(2/71, 25 cents, 52 pgs.)-Entire book has Powell/Wood-r; Wood-c. 3(1/72)-reprints	1.65	4.00	10.00

	GD25	FN65	NM94
Annual 4(10/76)	1.00	2.00	5.00
Annual 4(#5)('89, $2.00, 68 pgs.)-Atlantis Attacks		1.00	2.50
Annual 6(1990, $2.00, 68 pgs.)-Sutton-a		.80	2.00
Annual 7(1991, $2.00, 68 pgs.)-Guice-a (7 pgs.)		.80	2.00
Annual 8(1992, $2.25, 68 pgs.)-Deathlok-c/story		.90	2.25
Annual 9(1993, $2.95, 68 pgs.)-Polybagged w/card		1.20	3.00

NOTE: ***Art Adams*** *c-238p, 239.* ***Austin*** *a-191i; c-151i, 200i.* ***John Buscema*** *a-136, 137p, 234p, 235p; c-86p, 136i, 137p, 142, 219.* ***Byrne*** *c-200p, 201, 203, 223.* ***Colan*** *a(p)-20-49, 53-82, 84-98, 100, 110, 112, 124, 153, 154, 156, 157, Spec. 1p; c(p)-20-42, 44-49, 53-60, 71, 92, 98, 138, 153, 154, 156, 157, Annual 1.* ***Craig*** *a-50i, 52i.* ***Ditko*** *a-162, 234p, 235p, 264p; c-162.* ***Everett*** *c/a-1; inks-21, 83.* ***Gil Kane*** *a-141p, 146-148p, 151p; c(p)-85, 90, 91, 93, 94, 115, 116, 119, 120, 125-128, 133, 139, 147, 152.* ***Kirby*** *c-2-4, 5p, 12p, 13p, 43, 136p.* ***Layton*** *c-202.* ***Miller*** *scripts-168-182, 183(part), 184-191, 219, 227-233; a-158-161p, 163-184p, 191p; c-158-161p, 163-184p, 185-189, 190p, 191.* ***Orlando*** *a-2-4p.* ***Powell*** *a-9p, 11p, Special 1r, 2r.* ***Simonson*** *c-199, 236p.* ***B. Smith*** *a-83p, 236p; c-51p, 52p.* ***Starlin*** *a-105p.* ***Steranko*** *c-44i.* ***Tuska*** *a-39i, 145p.* ***Williamson*** *a(i)-237, 239, 240, 243, 248-257, 259-282, 283(part), 284, 285, 287, 288(part), 289(part), 293-301; c(i)-237, 243, 244, 248-257, 259-263, 265-278, 280-289, Annual 8.* ***Wood*** *a-5-8i, 10, 11i, Spec. 2i; c-5i, 8-11, 104i.*

DAREDEVIL AND THE PUNISHER (Child's Play trade paperback)
1988 ($4.95, color, squarebound, one-shot)
Marvel Comics

	GD25	FN65	NM94
1-r/Daredevil #182-184 by Miller	1.30	3.25	8.00
1-2nd & 3rd printings	1.00	2.00	5.00

DAREDEVIL COMICS (See Silver Streak Comics)
July, 1941 - No. 134, Sept, 1956 (Charles Biro stories)
Lev Gleason Publications (Funnies, Inc. No. 1)

	GD25	FN65	VF82	NM94
1-No. 1 titled "Daredevil Battles Hitler;" The Silver Streak, Lance Hale, Cloud Curtis, Dickey Dean, Pirate Prince team up w/Daredevil and battle Hitler; Daredevil battles the Claw; Origin of Hitler feature story. Hitler photo app. on-c	500.00	1500.00	2750.00	4000.00

(Estimated up to 215 total copies exist, 12 in NM/Mint)

	GD25	FN65	NM94
2-London, Pat Patriot (by Reed Crandall), Nightro, Real American No. 1, Dickie Dean, Pirate Prince, & Times Square begin; intro. & only app. The Pioneer, Champion of America	200.00	600.00	1400.00
3-Origin of 13	117.00	350.00	800.00
4	100.00	300.00	700.00
5-Intro. Sniffer & Jinx; Ghost vs. Claw begins by Bob Wood, ends #20	92.00	275.00	600.00
6-(#7 in indicia)	78.00	232.00	525.00
7-10: 8-Nightro ends	64.00	192.00	425.00
11-London, Pat Patriot end; bondage/torture-c	58.00	175.00	400.00
12-Origin of The Claw; Scoop Scuttle by Wolverton begins (2-4 pgs.), ends #22, not in #21	92.00	275.00	625.00
13-Intro. of Little Wise Guys (10/42)	92.00	275.00	625.00
14	46.00	138.00	300.00
15-Death of Meatball	67.00	200.00	450.00
16,17	42.00	125.00	275.00
18-New origin of Daredevil (not same as Silver Streak #6)	88.00	262.00	600.00
19,20	35.00	105.00	245.00
21-Reprints cover of Silver Streak #6 (on inside) plus intro. of The Claw from Silver Streak #1	58.00	175.00	395.00
22-30: 27-Bondage/torture-c	23.00	68.00	155.00
31-Death of The Claw	50.00	150.00	350.00
32-37,39,40: 35-Two Daredevil stories begin, end #68 (35-40 are 64 pgs.)	17.00	52.00	120.00
38-Origin Daredevil retold from #18	29.00	86.00	200.00
41-50: 42-Intro. Kilroy in Daredevil	13.00	40.00	90.00
51-69-Last Daredevil issue (12/50)	10.00	30.00	70.00
70-Little Wise Guys take over book; McWilliams-a; Hot Rock Flanagan begins, ends #80	9.15	27.50	55.00
71-79,81: 79-Daredevil returns	7.00	21.00	42.00
80-Daredevil x-over	7.50	22.50	45.00
82,90-One page Frazetta ad in both	7.00	21.00	42.00
83-89,91-99,101-134	5.85	17.50	35.00

Daring Comics #11, © MEG

Dark Angel #13, © MEG

Darkhawk #31, © MEG

100 7.00 21.00 42.00
NOTE: ***Wolverton's*** *Scoop Scuttle-12-20, 22.* ***Biro*** *c/a-all?.* ***Bolle*** *a-125.* ***Maurer*** *a-75.* ***McWilliams*** *a-73, 75, 79, 80.*

DAREDEVIL THE MAN WITHOUT FEAR
Oct, 1993 - No. 5, Feb, 1994 ($2.95, color, limited series)
Marvel Comics

1-5: Foil etched-c; by Miller/Romita, Jr./Williamson 1.60 4.00

DARE THE IMPOSSIBLE (Fleetway/Quality)(Value: cover or less)

DARING ADVENTURES (Also see Approved Comics)
Nov, 1953 (3-D)
St. John Publishing Co.

1 (3-D)-Reprints lead story from Son of Sinbad #1 by Kubert
27.00 80.00 185.00

DARING ADVENTURES
1963 - 1964
I.W. Enterprises/Super Comics

I.W. Reprint #9-r/Blue Bolt #115; Disbrow-a(3) 4.20 12.50 25.00
Super Reprint #10,11('63)-r/Dynamic #24,16; 11-Marijuana story; Yankee Boy app. 2.40 6.00 12.00
Super Reprint #12('64)-Phantom Lady from Fox(r/#14 only? w/splash page omitted) 10.00 30.00 70.00
Super Reprint #15('64)-r/Hooded Menace #1 7.00 21.00 42.00
Super Reprint #16('64)-r/Dynamic #12 2.40 6.00 12.00
Super Reprint #17('64)-r/Green Lama #3 by Raboy
4.00 11.00 22.00
Super Reprint #18-Origin Atlas from unpublished Atlas Comics #1
3.00 7.50 15.00

DARING COMICS (Formerly Daring Mystery) (Jeanie No. 13 on)
No. 9, Fall, 1944 - No. 12, Fall, 1945
Timely Comics (HPC)

9-Human Torch & Sub-Mariner begin 57.00 170.00 375.00
10-The Angel only app. 50.00 150.00 340.00
11,12-The Destroyer app. 50.00 150.00 340.00
NOTE: ***Schomburg*** *c-9-11.* ***Sekowsky*** *c-12?*

DARING CONFESSIONS (Formerly Youthful Hearts)
No. 4, 11/52 - No. 7, 5/53; No. 8, 10/53
Youthful Magazines

4-Doug Wildey-a 7.50 22.50 45.00
5-8: 6,8-Wildey-a 5.35 16.00 32.00

DARING LOVE (Radiant Love No. 2 on)
Sept-Oct, 1953
Gilmor Magazines

1 5.85 17.50 35.00

DARING LOVE (Formerly Youthful Romances)
No. 15, 12/52; No. 16, 2/53-c, 4/53-Indicia; No. 17-4/53-c & indicia
Ribage/Pix

15 6.35 19.00 38.00
16,17: 17-Photo-c 5.00 15.00 30.00
NOTE: ***Colletta*** *a-15.* ***Wildey*** *a-17.*

DARING LOVE STORIES (See Fox Giants)

DARING MYSTERY COMICS (Comedy Comics No. 9 on; title changed to Daring Comics with No. 9)
1/40 - No. 5, 6/40; No. 6, 9/40; No. 7, 4/41 - No. 8, 1/42
Timely Comics (TPI 1-6/TCI 7,8) GD25 FN65 VF82 NM94

1-Origin The Fiery Mask (1st app.) by Joe Simon; Monako, Prince of Magic (1st app.), John Steele, Soldier of Fortune (1st app.), Doc Doyle (1st app.) begin; Flash Foster & Barney Mullen, Sea Rover only app; bondage-c
1000.00 3000.00 5500.00 8000.00
(Estimated up to 60 total copies exist, 5 in NM/Mint)
GD25 FN65 NM94
2-(Rare)-Origin The Phantom Bullet (1st & only app.); The Laughing Mask & Mr. E only app.; Trojak the Tiger Man begins, ends #6; Zephyr Jones & K-4 & His Sky Devils app., also #4 400.00 1200.00 2800.00
3-The Phantom Reporter, Dale of FBI, Breeze Barton, Captain Strong & Marvex the Super-Robot only app.; The Purple Mask begins
267.00 800.00 1800.00
4-Last Purple Mask; Whirlwind Carter begins; Dan Gorman, G-Man app.
167.00 500.00 1150.00
5-The Falcon begins (1st app.); The Fiery Mask, Little Hercules app. by Sagendorf in the Segar style; bondage-c 167.00 500.00 1150.00
6-Origin & only app. Marvel Boy by S&K; Flying Flame, Dynaman, & Stupor-man only app.; The Fiery Mask by S&K; S&K-c 208.00 625.00 1450.00
7-Origin The Blue Diamond, Captain Daring by S&K, The Fin by Everett, The Challenger, The Silver Scorn & The Thunderer by Burgos; Mr. Millions app
192.00 575.00 1350.00
8-Origin Citizen V; Last Fin, Silver Scorn, Capt. Daring by Borth, Blue Diamond & The Thunderer; S&K-c; Rudy the Robot only app.; Citizen V, Fin & Silver Scorn continue in Comedy #9 158.00 475.00 1050.00
NOTE: ***Schomburg*** *c-1-4, 7.* ***Simon*** *a-2, 3, 5.*

DARING NEW ADVENTURES OF SUPERGIRL, THE
Nov, 1982 - No. 13, Nov, 1983 (Supergirl No. 14-on)
DC Comics

1-Origin retold; Lois Lane back-ups in #2-12 1.50
2-13: 8,9-Doom Patrol app. 13-New costume; flag-c 1.00
NOTE: ***Buckler*** *c-1p, 2p.* ***Giffen*** *c-3p, 4p.* ***Gil Kane*** *c-6, ,8, 9, 11-13.*

DARK ANGEL (Formerly Hell's Angel)
No. 6, Dec, 1992 - Present ($1.75, color)
Marvel Comics UK, Ltd.

6-15: 6-Excalibur-c/story. 8-Psylocke app. .90 1.75

DARK CRYSTAL, THE
April, 1983 - No. 2, May, 1983
Marvel Comics Group

1,2-Movie adaptation, part 1&2 .50 1.00

DARK DOMINION
Oct, 1993 - Present ($2.50, color)
Defiant Comics

1-4 1.00 2.50

DARKER IMAGE
Mar, 1993 - No. 4, 1993 ($1.95, color)
Image Comics

1,2: 1-1st app. The Maxx by Sam Kieth, Bloodwulf by Rob Liefeld & Deathblow by Jim Lee & begins; bagged w/card 1.00 2.50
1-B&W interior pgs. w/silver foil logo 10.00

DARKEWOOD (Aircel)(Value: cover or less)

DARK GUARD
Oct, 1993 - Present ($1.75, color)
Marvel Comics UK

1-($2.95)-Foil stamped-c 1.20 3.00
2-5 .70 1.75

DARKHAWK
Mar, 1991 - Present ($1.00,/$1.25 color)
Marvel Comics

1-Origin/1st app. Darkhawk; Hobgoblin cameo 2.15 6.50 15.00
2-Spider-Man & Hobgoblin app. 1.65 4.00 10.00
3-Spider-Man & Hobgoblin app. 1.40 3.50 8.50
4 1.10 2.70 6.50
5 1.00 2.50 6.00
6-Capt. America & Daredevil x-over 1.00 2.00 5.00
7,8 1.60 4.00
9-Punisher app. 1.00 2.50 6.00
10-12: 11-Last $1.00-c. 11,12-Tombstone app. 1.00 2.50
13,14-Venom-c/story 1.00 2.00 5.00
15-24,26-38: 19-Spider-Man & Brotherhood of Evil Mutants-c/story. 20-

Darkhold #13, © MEG

Dark Horse Presents #50, © Dark Horse

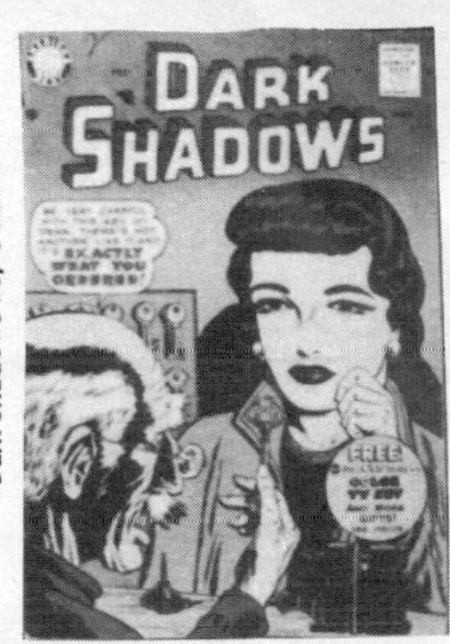

Dark Shadows #3, © AJAX

GD25 FN65 NM94

Spider-Man app. 22-Ghost Rider-c/story. 23-Origin begins, ends #25 1.25
25-($2.95, 52 pgs.)-Red holo-grafx foil-c w/double gatefold poster; origin of Darkhawk armor revealed 1.20 3.00
Annual 1 (1992, $2.25, 68 pgs.)-Vs. Iron Man 1.20 3.00
Annual 2 (1993, $2.95, 68 pgs.)-Polybagged w/card 1.20 3.00

DARKHOLD: PAGES FROM THE BOOK OF SINS
Oct, 1992 - No. 16, Jan, 1994 ($1.75, color) (See Midnight Sons Unlimited)
Marvel Comics
1-($2.75, 52 pgs.)-Polybagged w/poster by Andy & Adam Kubert; part 4 of Rise of the Midnight Sons storyline 1.10 2.75
2-10,12-16: 3-Reintro Modred the Mystic (see Marvel Chillers #1). 5-Punisher & Ghost Rider app. .70 1.75
11-($2.25)-Outer-c is a Darkhold envelope made of black parchment w/gold ink .90 2.25

DARK HORSE CLASSICS
1992 ($3.95, B&W, 52 pgs.)
Dark Horse Comics
nn's: The Last of the Mohicans. 20,000 Leagues Under the Sea 1.60 4.00

DARK HORSE COMICS
Aug, 1992 - Present ($2.50, color)
Dark Horse Comics
1-Dorman double gategold painted-c; Predator, Robocop, Timecop & Renegade stories begin 1.50 3.00
2-6,11-18: 2-Mignola-c. 3-Begin 3 part Aliens story; Aliens-c. 4-Predator-c. 6-Begin 4 part Robocop story. 12-Begin 2 part Aliens & 3 part Predator stories .50 1.25 2.50
7-Begin Star Wars: Tales of the Jedi 1.20 3.00
8-1st app. X and begins 1.00 2.00 5.00
9,10: 9-Star Wars ends. 10-X ends 1.20 3.00

DARK HORSE PRESENTS
July, 1986 - Present ($1.50/$1.75/$1.95/$2.25, B&W)
Dark Horse Comics
1-1st app. Concrete by Paul Chadwick 1.65 4.00 10.00
1-2nd printing (1988, $1.50) 1.00 2.50
1-Silver ink 3rd printing (1992, $2.25)-Says 2nd printing inside .90 2.25
2-Concrete app. 1.20 3.00 7.00
3-Concrete app. 1.00 2.00 5.00
4,5-Concrete app. 1.60 4.00
6-10: 6,8,10-Concrete app. 1.20 3.00
11-19,21-23: 12,14,16,18,22-Concrete app. .80 2.00
20-($2.95, 68 pgs.)-Concrete & Flaming Carrot 1.20 3.00
24-Origin Aliens (11/88); Mr. Monster app. 3.60 10.75 25.00
25-31,33: 28-($2.95, 52 pgs.)-Concrete app. 33-($2.25, 44 pgs.) 1.20 3.00
32-($3.50, 68 pgs.)-Annual; Concrete, American 1.60 4.00
34-Aliens-c/story 1.20 3.00 7.00
35-Predator-c/story; begin $1.95-c 1.20 3.00 7.00
36-1st Aliens Vs. Predator story; painted-c 1.65 4.00 10.00
36-Same as above, but line drawn-c 1.30 3.25 8.00
37-39,41,44,45,47-50: 38-Concrete. 44-Crash Ryan. 48-50-Contain 2 trading cards. 50-S/F story by Perez .80 2.00
40-($2.95, 52 pgs.)-1st Argosy story 1.20 3.00
42,43-Aliens-c/stories 1.00 2.00 5.00
46-Prequel to new Predator II mini-series 1.60 4.00
51-53-Sin City by Frank Miller, parts 2-4; 51,53-Miller-c 1.00 2.50
54-The Next Men begins(1st app.) by Byrne(9/91) 1.30 3.25 8.00
55-2nd app. The Next Men; parts 5 & 6 of Sin City by Miller; Homocide by Morrow in both. 54-Morrow-c; begin $2.25-c. 55-Miller-c 1.60 4.00
56-($3.95, 68 pg. annual)-2 part prologue to Aliens: Genocide; part 7 of Sin City by Miller; Next Men by Byrne 1.60 4.00
57-($3.50, 52 pgs.)-Part 8 of Sin City by Miller; Next Men by Byrne; Byrne & Miller-c; Alien Fire story; swipes cover to Daredevil #1 1.40 3.50
58-66,68-82: 58,59-Part 9,10 Sin City by Miller; Alien Fire stories. 60,61-Part 11,12 Sin City by Miller. 62-Last Sin City (entire book by Miller, c/a; 52pgs.). 64-Dr. Giggles begins (1st app.), ends #66; Boris the Bear story. 66-New Concrete story by Chadwick .90 2.25
67-($3.95, 68 pgs.)-Begin 3 part prelude to Predator: Race War mini-series; Oscar Wilde adapt. by Russell 1.60 4.00
... Fifth Anniversary Special nn (4/91, $9.95)-Part 1 of Sin City by Frank Miller (c/a); Aliens, Aliens vs. Predator, Concrete, Roachmill, Give Me Liberty & The American stories 1.65 4.00 10.00
Aliens Platinum Edition (1992)-r/DHP #24,43,43,56 & Special 3.60 10.75 25.00

NOTE: ***Geary*** *a-59, 60.* ***Miller*** *a-Special, 51-53, 55-62; c-59-62.* ***Moebius*** *a-63; c-63, 70.*

DARK KNIGHT (See Batman: The Dark Knight Returns & Legends of the...)

DARKLON THE MYSTIC (Pacific)(Value: cover or less)

DARKMAN
Sept, 1990; Oct, 1990 - No. 3, Nov, 1990 ($1.50, color, movie adapt.)
Marvel Comics
1 (9/90, $2.25, B&W mag., 68 pgs.) .90 2.25
1-3: Reprints B&W magazine 1.50

DARKMAN
V2#1, Apr, 1993 -No. 6, Sept, 1993 ($2.95, color, limited series)
Marvel Comics
V2#1 ($3.95, 52 pgs.) 1.60 4.00
2-6 1.20 3.00

DARK MANSION OF FORBIDDEN LOVE, THE (Becomes Forbidden Tales of Dark Mansion No. 5 on)
Sept-Oct, 1971 - No. 4, Mar-Apr, 1972
National Periodical Publications
1 1.65 4.70 11.00
2-4: 2-Adams-c. 3-Jeff Jones-c 1.00 2.50 6.00

DARK MYSTERIES
June-July, 1951 - No. 25?, 1955
"Master"-"Merit" Publications
1-Wood-c/a (8 pgs.) 39.00 120.00 275.00
2-Wood/Harrison-c/a (8 pgs.) 30.00 90.00 210.00
3-9: 7-Dismemberment, hypo blood drainage stories 13.00 40.00 90.00
10-Cannibalism story 13.50 41.00 95.00
11-13,15-18: 11-Severed head panels. 13-Dismemberment-c/story. 17-The Old Gravedigger host 10.00 30.00 70.00
14-Several E.C. Craig swipes 11.00 32.00 75.00
19-Injury-to-eye panel; E.C. swipe 13.00 40.00 90.00
20-Female bondage, blood drainage story 11.50 34.00 80.00
21,22-Last pre-code issue, mis-dated 3/54 instead of 3/55 8.35 25.00 50.00
23-25 (#25-Exist?) 6.70 20.00 40.00

NOTE: ***Cameron*** *a-1, 2.* ***Myron Fass*** *c/a-21.* ***Harrison*** *a-3, 7; c-3.* ***Hollingsworth*** *a-7-17, 20, 21, 23.* ***Wildey*** *a-5. Woodish art by* ***Fleishman****-9; c-10. Bondage c-10, 18, 19.*

DARK SHADOWS
October, 1957 - No. 3, May, 1958
Steinway Comic Publications (Ajax)(America's Best)
1 9.15 27.50 55.00
2,3 6.70 20.00 40.00

DARK SHADOWS (TV) (See Dan Curtis Giveaways)
March, 1969 - No. 35, Feb, 1976 (Photo-c: 1-7)
Gold Key
1(30039-903)-With pull-out poster (25 cents) 24.00 71.00 165.00
1-With poster missing 9.00 26.00 60.00
2 8.00 24.00 55.00
3-With pull-out poster 12.00 36.00 85.00
3-With poster missing 6.50 19.00 45.00

Darkstars, The #11, © DC

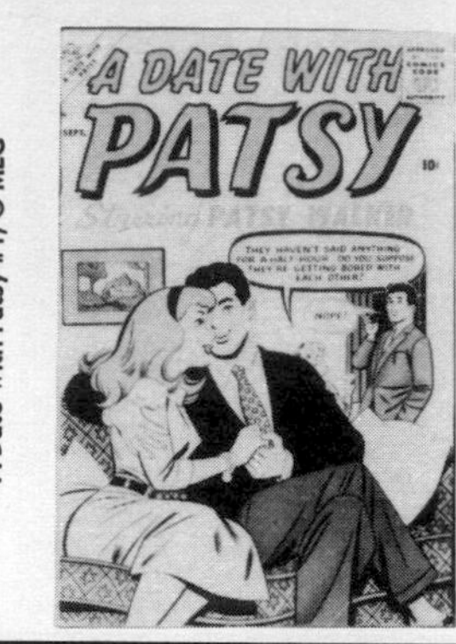

A Date With Patsy #1, © MEG

The Dazzler #42, © MEG

	GD25	FN65	NM94
4-7: Last photo-c	8.00	24.00	55.00
8-10	5.50	17.00	40.00
11-20	4.30	13.00	30.00
21-35: 30-Last painted-c	3.20	8.00	20.00
Story Digest 1 (6/70)-Photo-c	5.50	17.00	40.00

DARK SHADOWS (TV) (See Nightmare on Elm Street)
June, 1992 - No. 4, Spring, 1993 ($2.50, color, mini-series, coated stock)
Innovation Publications

	GD25	FN65	NM94
1-Based on '91 NBC TV mini-series; painted-c		1.20	3.00
2-4		1.00	2.50

DARKSTARS, THE
Oct, 1992 - Present ($1.75, color)
DC Comics

	GD25	FN65	NM94
1-1st app. The Darkstars		1.20	3.00
2-18: 5-Hawkman & Hawkwoman app.		.70	1.75

NOTE: ***Travis Charest** a(p)-4-on; c-2p, 3p. **Stroman** a-1-3; c-1.*

DARKWING DUCK (TV cartoon) (Also see Cartoon Tales)
Nov, 1991 - No. 4, Feb, 1992 ($1.50, color, limited series)
Disney Comics

	GD25	FN65	NM94
1-4: Adapts hour-long premiere TV episode			1.50

DARLING LOVE
Oct-Nov, 1949 - No. 11, 1952 (no month) (52 pgs.)
Close Up/Archie Publ. (A Darling Magazine)

	GD25	FN65	NM94
1-Photo-c	8.35	25.00	50.00
2	4.70	14.00	28.00
3-8,10,11: 5,6-photo-c	4.00	12.00	24.00
9-Krigstein-a	5.00	15.00	30.00

DARLING ROMANCE
Sept-Oct, 1949 - No. 7, 1951 (All photo-c)
Close Up (MLJ Publications)

	GD25	FN65	NM94
1-(52 pgs.)-Betty Page photo-c?	9.15	27.50	55.00
2	5.00	15.00	30.00
3-7	4.35	13.00	26.00

DASTARDLY & MUTTLEY (See Fun-In No. 1-4, 6 and Kite Fun Book)

DATE WITH DANGER
No. 5, Dec, 1952 - No. 6, Feb, 1953
Standard Comics

	GD25	FN65	NM94
5,6	4.70	14.00	28.00

DATE WITH DEBBI (Also see Debbi's Dates)
Jan-Feb, 1969 - No. 17, Sept-Oct, 1971; No. 18, Oct-Nov, 1972
National Periodical Publications

	GD25	FN65	NM94
1	2.40	6.00	12.00
2-5	1.40	3.50	7.00
6-18	1.00	2.50	5.00

DATE WITH JUDY, A (Radio/TV, and 1948 movie)
Oct-Nov, 1947 - No. 79, Oct-Nov, 1960 (No. 1-25: 52 pgs.)
National Periodical Publications

	GD25	FN65	NM94
1-Teenage	19.00	58.00	135.00
2	10.00	30.00	60.00
3-10	7.50	22.50	45.00
11-20	4.70	14.00	28.00
21-40	4.00	11.00	22.00
41-45: 45-Last pre-code (2-3/55)	3.60	9.00	18.00
46-79: 79-Drucker-c/a	2.80	7.00	14.00

DATE WITH MILLIE, A (Life With Millie No. 8 on)
Oct, 1956 - No. 7, Aug, 1957; Oct, 1959 - No. 7, Oct, 1960
Atlas/Marvel Comics (MPC)

	GD25	FN65	NM94
1(10/56)-(1st Series)-Dan DeCarlo-a in #1-7	14.00	43.00	100.00
2	8.35	25.00	50.00
3-7	5.85	17.50	35.00
1(10/59)-(2nd Series)	9.15	27.50	55.00
2-7	5.00	15.00	30.00

DATE WITH PATSY, A (Also see Patsy Walker)
September, 1957
Atlas Comics

	GD25	FN65	NM94
1-Starring Patsy Walker	6.70	20.00	40.00

DAVID AND GOLIATH (See 4-Color No. 1205)

DAVID CASSIDY (TV?)(See Swing With Scooter #33)
Feb, 1972 - No. 14, Sept, 1973
Charlton Comics

	GD25	FN65	NM94
1	1.70	5.00	12.00
2-14: 5,7,9,14-Photo-c	1.30	3.25	8.00

DAVID LADD'S LIFE STORY (See Movie Classics)

DAVY CROCKETT (See Dell Giants, Fightin..., Frontier Fighters, It's Game Time, Power Record Comics, Western Tales & Wild Frontier)

DAVY CROCKETT
1951
Avon Periodicals

	GD25	FN65	NM94
nn-Tuska?, Reinman-a; Fawcette-c	11.00	32.00	75.00

DAVY CROCKETT (...King of the Wild Frontier No. 1,2)(TV)
5/55 - No. 671, 12/55; No. 1, 12/63; No. 2, 11/69 (Walt Disney)
Dell Publishing Co./Gold Key

	GD25	FN65	NM94
4-Color 631(#1)-Fess Parker photo-c	10.00	30.00	60.00
4-Color 639-Photo-c	6.70	20.00	40.00
4-Color 664,671(Marsh-a)-Photo-c	7.50	22.50	45.00
1(12/63-Gold Key)-Fess Parker photo-c; reprints	5.00	15.00	30.00
2(11/69)-Fess Parker photo-c; reprints	3.60	9.00	18.00
...Christmas Book (no date, 16pgs, paper-c)-Sears giveaway	4.20	12.50	25.00
...In the Raid at Piney Creek (1955, 16pgs, 5x7-1/4")-American Motors giveaway; slick, photo-c	5.85	17.50	35.00
...Safety Trails (1955, 16pgs, 3-1/4x7")-Cities Service giveaway	5.85	17.50	35.00

DAVY CROCKETT (...Frontier Fighter #1,2; Kid Montana #9 on)
Aug, 1955 - No. 8, Jan, 1957
Charlton Comics

	GD25	FN65	NM94
1	5.85	17.50	35.00
2	4.00	10.00	20.00
3-8	3.00	7.50	15.00
Hunting With...('55, 16 pgs.)-Ben Franklin Store giveaway (Publ.-S. Rose)	4.00	10.00	20.00

DAYS OF THE MOB (See In the Days of the Mob)

DAYTONA SPECIAL (Vortex)(Value: cover or less)

DAZEY'S DIARY
June-Aug, 1962
Dell Publishing Co.

	GD25	FN65	NM94
01-174-208: Bill Woggon-c/a	4.00	10.00	20.00

DAZZLER, THE (Also see Marvel Graphic Novel & X-Men #130)
March, 1981 - No. 42, Mar, 1986
Marvel Comics Group

	GD25	FN65	NM94
1,2-X-Men app.		.80	2.00
3-37,39-42: 10,11-Galactus app. 21-Double size; photo-c. 42-The Beast app.			1.00
38-Wolverine-c/app.; X-Men app.	1.00	2.50	6.00

NOTE: *No. 1 distributed only through comic shops. **Alcala** a-1i, 2i. **Chadwick** a-38-42p; c(p)-39, 41, 42. **Guice** a-38i, 42i; c-38, 40.*

DC CHALLENGE
Nov, 1985 - No. 12, Oct, 1986 ($1.25, 12 issue maxi-series)
DC Comics

DC Comics Presents #31, © DC

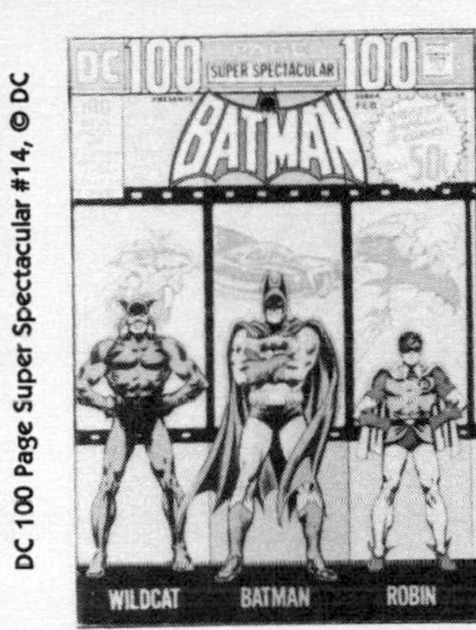

DC 100 Page Super Spectacular #14, © DC

DC Special Series #21, © DC

GD25 FN65 NM94

1-11: 1-Colan-a. 4-Gil Kane-c/a 1.25
12-($2.00)-Perez/Austin-c .80 2.00
NOTE: *Batman app. in 1-4, 6-12. Joker app. in 7.* ***Giffen*** *c/a-11.* ***Swan/Austin*** *c-10.*

DC COMICS PRESENTS
July-Aug, 1978 - No. 97, Sept, 1986 (Superman team-ups in all)
DC Comics

1-12,14-25: 2-Superman/Flash race. 19-Batgirl .50 1.00
13-Legion of Super Heroes (also in #43 & 80) .80 2.00
26-(10/80)-Green Lantern; intro Cyborg, Starfire, Raven (1st app. New Teen Titans in 16 pg. preview); Starlin-c/a; Sargon the Sorcerer back-up 1.20 3.00 7.00
27-40,42-71,73-76,79-84,86-97: 31,58-Robin. 35-Man-Bat. 42,47-Sandman. 52-Doom Patrol. 82-Adam Strange. 83-Batman & Outsiders. 86-88-Crisis x-over. 88-Creeper .50 1.00
41-Superman/Joker-c/story 1.00 2.50
72-Joker/Phantom Stranger-c/story 1.00 2.50
77,78-Animal Man app. (77-cover app. also) 1.20 3.00
85-Swamp Thing; Alan Moore scripts 1.20 3.00
Annual 1-4: 1(9/82)-G.A. Superman. 2(7/83) Intro/origin Superwoman. 3(9/84)-Shazam. 4(10/85)-Superwoman 1.20
NOTE: ***Adkins*** *a-2, 54; c-2.* ***Gil Kane*** *a-28, 35, Annual 3; c-48p, 56, 58, 60, 62, 64, 68, Annual 2, 3.* ***Kirby*** *c/a-84.* ***Kubert*** *c/a-66.* ***Morrow*** *c/a-65.* ***Newton*** *c/a-54p.* ***Orlando*** *c-53i.* ***Perez*** *a-26p, 61p; c-38, 61, 94.* ***Starlin*** *a-26-29p, 36p, 37p; c-26-29, 36, 37, 93.* ***Toth*** *a-84.* ***Williamson*** *i-79, 85, 87.*

DC GRAPHIC NOVEL (Also see DC Science Fiction...)
Nov, 1983 - No. 7, 1986 ($5.95, 68 pgs.)
DC Comics

1-5,7: 1-Star Raiders. 2-Warlords; not from regular Warlord series. 3-The Medusa Chain; Ernie Colon story/a. 4-The Hunger Dogs; Kirby-c/a(p). 5-Me and Joe Priest; Chaykin-c. 7-Space Clusters; Nino-c/a 1.00 2.50 6.00
6-Metalzoic; Sienkiewicz-c ($6.95) 1.20 3.00 7.00

DC 100 PAGE SUPER SPECTACULAR
(Title is 100 Page...No. 14 on)(Square bound) (Reprints, 50 cents)
No. 4, Summer, 1971 - No. 13, 6/72; No. 14, 2/73 - No. 22, 11/73 (No #1-3)
National Periodical Publications

4,5: 4-Weird Mystery Tales; Johnny Peril & Phantom Stranger; cover & splashes by Wrightson; origin Jungle Boy of Jupiter. 5-Love Stories; Wood inks, 7pgs. 1.20 3.00
6-"World's Greatest Super-Heroes"-JLA, JSA, Spectre, Johnny Quick, Vigilante & Hawkman; contains unpublished Wildcat story; N. Adams wrap-around-c 1.40 3.50
7-13: 7-(See Superman #245). 8-(See Batman #238). 9-(See Our Army at War #242). 10-(See Adventure #416). 11-(See Flash #214).12-(See Superboy #185). 13-(See Superman #252)
14-Batman-r/Detective #31,32,156; Atom-r/Showcase #34 1.00 2.50 6.00
15-22: 15-r/2nd Boy Commandos/Det. #65. 17-JSA-r/All Star #37(38 pgs.); Sandman-r/Adv. #66. 20-Batman-r/Det. #66,68, others; origin Two-Face. 21-r/Brave & the Bold #54. 22-r/All-Flash #13 .80 2.00
NOTE: ***Anderson*** *r-11, 14, 18i, 22.* ***B. Baily*** *r-18, 20.* ***Burnley*** *r-18, 20.* ***Crandall*** *r-14p, 20.* ***Drucker*** *r-4.* ***Infantino*** *r-17, 20, 22.* ***G. Kane*** *r-18.* ***Kubert*** *r-6, 7, 16, 17; c-16, 19.* ***Meskin*** *r-4, 22.* ***Mooney*** *r-15, 21.* ***Toth*** *r-17, 20.*

DC SCIENCE FICTION GRAPHIC NOVEL
1985 - No. 7, 1987 ($5.95)
DC Comics

SF1-SF7: SF1-Hell on Earth by Robert Bloch; Giffen-p. SF2-Nightwings by Robert Silverberg; G. Colan-p. SF3-Frost & Fire by Bradbury. SF4-Merchants of Venus. SF5-Demon With A Glass Hand by Ellison; M. Rogers-a. SF6-The Magic Goes Away by Niven. SF7-Sandkings by George R.R. Martin 1.00 2.50 6.00

DC SILVER AGE CLASSICS
1992 ($1.00, color, all reprints)
DC Comics

...Action Comics #252; r/1st Supergirl...Adventure Comics #247; r/1st Legion of S.H....The Brave and the Bold #28; r/1st JLA...Detective Comics #225; r/1st Martian Manhunter...Detective Comics #327; r/1st new look Batman...Green Lantern #76; r/Green Lantern/Gr. Arrow...House of Secrets #92; r/1st Swamp Thing...Showcase #4; r/1st S.A. Flash...Showcase #22; r/1st S.A. Green Lantern ...Sugar and Spike #99; 2 unpublished stories 1.00

DC SPECIAL (Also see Super DC...)
10-12/68 - No. 15, 11-12/71; No. 16, Spr/75 - No. 29, 8-9/77
National Periodical Publications

1-All Infantino issue; Flash, Batman, Adam Strange-r; begin 68 pg., 25 cent issues, end #15 1.30 3.25 8.00
2-15: 5-All Kubert issue; Viking Prince, Sgt. Rock-r. 12-Viking Prince; Kubert-c/a(r/B&B almost entirely). 15 G.A. Plastic Man origin-r/Police #1; origin Woozy by Cole; last 68 pg. issue 1.00 2.50 6.00
16-29: 16-Super Heroes Battle Super Gorillas; r/Capt. Storm #1, 1st Johnny Cloud/All-Amer. Men of War #82. 17-Early S.A. Green Lantern-r. 22-Origin Robin Hood. 28-Earth Shattering Disaster Stories; Legion of Super-Heroes story. 27-Untold Origin of the Justice Society. 29-Secret Origin of the Justice Society 1.20 3.00
NOTE: ***N. Adams*** *c-3, 4, 6, 11, 29.* ***Grell*** *a-20; c-17.* ***Heath*** *a-12r.* ***G. Kane*** *a-6p, 13r, 17r, 19-21r.* ***Kubert*** *a-6r, 12r, 22.* ***Meskin*** *a-10.* ***Moreira*** *a-10.* ***Staton*** *a-29p.* ***Toth*** *a-13, 20r. #1-15: 25 cents; 16-27: 50 cent; 28, 29: 60 cents. #1-13, 16-21: 68 pgs.; 14, 15: 52 pgs.*

DC SPECIAL BLUE-RIBBON DIGEST
Mar-Apr, 1980 - No. 24, Aug, 1982
DC Comics

1-24: All reprints? 1.00
NOTE: ***N. Adams*** *a-16(6)r, 17r, 23r; c-16.* ***Aparo*** *a-6r, 24r; c-23.* ***Grell*** *a-8, 10; c-10.* ***Heath*** *a-14.* ***Kaluta*** *a-17r.* ***Gil Kane*** *a-22r.* ***Kirby*** *a-23r.* ***Kubert*** *a-3, 18r, 21r; c-7, 12, 14, 17, 18, 21, 24.* ***Morrow*** *a-24r.* ***Orlando*** *a-17r, 22r; c-1, 20.* ***Perez*** *c-19p.* ***Toth*** *a-21r, 24r.* ***Wood*** *a-3, 17r, 24r.* ***Wrightson*** *a-16r, 17r, 24r.*

DC SPECIAL SERIES
9/77 - No. 16, Fall, 1978; No. 17, 8/79 - No. 27, Fall, 1981
(No. 19,23,24 - digest size, 100 pgs., No. 25-27 - over-sized)
National Periodical Publications/DC Comics

1-Five-Star Super-Hero Spectacular; Atom, Flash, Green Lantern, Aquaman, Batman, Kobra app.; N. Adams-c 1.20 3.00
2(#1)-The Original Swamp Thing Saga (1977)-r/Swamp Thing #1&2 by Wrightson; Wrightson wraparound-c 1.20 0.00
3-20,22-24: 6-Jones-a. 7-Ghosts Special. 10-Origin Dr. Fate, Lightray & Black Canary. 14,17,20-Original Swamp Thing Saga; r/Swamp Thing #3-10 by Wrightson (52-68 pgs.). 15-Batman Spectacular. 16-Jonah Hex Spectacular; death of Jonah Hex; Bat Lash story. 19-Secret Origins of Super-Heroes; origins Wonder Woman (new-a), Robin, & Batman-Superman team. 22-G.I. Combat .80 2.00
21-Miller-a (1st on Batman, Spring, 1980) 1.70 5.00 12.00
V5#25-($2.95, Sum/81)-Superman II the Adventure Continues; photos from movie & photo-c (see All-New Coll. Ed. C-62) 1.20 3.00
26-($2.95, Sum/81)-Superman and His Incredible Fortress of Solitude 1.20 3.00
27-($2.50)-Batman vs. The Incredible Hulk 1.00 2.00 5.00
NOTE: ***Golden*** *a-15.* ***Heath*** *a-12i, 16.* ***Kubert*** *c-13.* ***Nasser*** *a-1.* ***Rogers*** *c/a-15.* ***Starlin*** *c-12.* ***Staton*** *a-1. #25 & 26 were advertised as All-New Collectors' Edition C-63, C-64. #26 was originally planned as All-New Coll. Ed. C-30?; has C-630 & A.N.C.E. on cover.*

DC SPOTLIGHT
1985 (50th anniversary special)
DC Comics (giveaway)

1 1.20

DC SUPER-STARS
March, 1976 - No. 18, Winter, 1978 (No.3-18: 52 pgs.)
National Periodical Publications/DC Comics

1-(68 pgs.)-Re-intro Teen Titans (predates Teen Titans #44 (11/76), tryout issue) plus Teen Titans-r 1.70 4.25
2-7,9,11-14,16,18: 2-6,8-Adam Strange; 2-(68 pgs.)-r/1st Adam Strange/Hawkman team-up from Mystery in Space #90 plus Atomic Knights origin-r. 13-Sergio Aragones Special 1.00

DC Universe: Trinity #2, © DC

Deadly Foes of Spider-Man #3, © MEG

Deadpool: The Circle Chase #3, © MEG

GD25 FN65 NM94

8-r/1st Space Ranger from Showcase #15, Adam Strange-r/Mystery in Space #89 & Star Rovers-r/M.I.S. #80 1.40 3.50
10-Strange Sports Stories; Batman/Joker-c/story 1.60 4.00
15-Batman Spectacular; Golden & Rogers-a 1.00 2.50
17-Secret Origins of Super-Heroes (origin of The Huntress); origin Green Arrow by Grell; Legion app.; Earth II Batman & Catwoman marry (1st revealed; also see B&B #197) .80 2.00

NOTE: ***M. Anderson*** *r-2, 4, 6.* ***Aparo*** *c-7, 14, 18.* ***Austin*** *a-11i.* ***Buckler*** *a-14p; c-10.* ***Grell*** *a-17.* ***G. Kane*** *a-1r, 10r.* ***Kubert*** *c-15.* ***Layton*** *c/a-16i, 17i.* ***Mooney*** *a-4r, 6r.* ***Morrow*** *c/a-11r.* ***Nasser*** *a-11.* ***Newton*** *c/a-16p.* ***Staton*** *a-17; c-17. No. 10, 12-18 contain all new material; the rest are reprints. #1 contains new and reprint material.*

DC UNIVERSE: TRINITY
Aug, 1993 - No. 2, Sept, 1993 ($2.95, color, 52 pgs.)
DC Comics

1,2-Foil-c; Green Lantern, Darkstars, Legion app. 1.20 3.00

D-DAY (Also see Special War Series)
Sum/63; No. 2, Fall/64; No. 4, 9/66; No. 5, 10/67; No. 6, 11/68
Charlton Comics (no No. 3)

1(1963)-Montes/Bache-c 3.00 7.50 15.00
2(Fall,'64)-Wood-a(3) 3.60 9.00 18.00
4-6('66-'68)-Montes/Bache-a #5 2.00 5.00 10.00

DEAD CLOWN (Malibu)(Value: cover or less)

DEAD END CRIME STORIES
April, 1949 (52 pages)
Kirby Publishing Co.

nn-(Scarce)-Powell, Roussos-a 30.00 90.00 210.00

DEAD-EYE WESTERN COMICS
Nov-Dec, 1948 - V3#1, Apr-May, 1953
Hillman Periodicals

V1#1-(52 pgs.)-Krigstein, Roussos-a 10.00 30.00 70.00
V1#2,3-(52 pgs.) 5.85 17.50 35.00
V1#4-12-(52 pgs.) 4.00 11.00 22.00
V2#1,2,5-8,10-12: 1-7-(52 pgs.) 3.60 9.00 18.00
3,4-Krigstein-a (52 pgs.) 5.35 16.00 32.00
9-One pg. Frazetta ad 3.60 9.00 18.00
V3#1 3.20 8.00 16.00

NOTE: ***Briefer*** *a-V1#8. Kinstleresque stories by* ***McCann****-12, V2#1, 2, V3#1.* ***McWilliams*** *a-V1#5.* ***Ed Moore*** *a-V1#4.*

DEADFACE: DOING THE ISLANDS WITH BACCHUS
July, 1991 - No. 3, Sept, 1991 ($2.95, B&W, mini-series, 52 pgs.)
Dark Horse Comics

1-3: By Eddie Campbell 1.20 3.00

DEADFACE: EARTH, WATER, AIR, AND FIRE
July, 1992 - No. 4, Oct, 1992 ($2.50, B&W, mini-series; British-r)
Dark Horse Comics

1-4: By Eddie Campbell 1.00 2.50

DEADLIEST HEROES OF KUNG FU
Summer, 1975 (Magazine)
Marvel Comics Group

1 .70 1.80

DEADLINE USA
Apr, 1992 - No. 8, Nov, 1992 ($3.95, B&W, 52 pgs.)
Dark Horse Comics

1-8: Johnny Nemo w/Milligan scripts in all 1.60 4.00

DEADLY FOES OF SPIDER-MAN (Marvel)(Value: cover or less)

DEADLY HANDS OF KUNG FU, THE (See Master of Kung Fu)
April, 1974 - No. 33, Feb, 1977 (75 cents) (B&W - Magazine)
Marvel Comics Group

1(V1#4 listed in error)-Origin Sons of the Tiger; Shang-Chi, Master of Kung Fu begins; Bruce Lee photo pin-up 1.20 3.00
2,3,5 .80 2.00
4-Bruce Lee painted-c by Neal Adams; 8 pg. biog of Bruce Lee 1.20 3.00
6-14 .80 2.00
15-(Annual 1, Summer '75)-Origin Iron Fist retold (predates Iron Fist #1) .80 2.00
16-19,21-27,29-33: 17-1st Giffen-a (1 pg.; 11/75). 19-1st White Tiger. 22-1st app. Jack of Hearts; 1st Giffen story-a (along with Amazing Adventures #35, 3/76) 1.50
20-Origin The White Tiger; Perez-a .80 2.00
28-Origin Jack of Hearts; Bruce Lee life story 1.20 3.00
Special Album Edition 1(Summer, '74)-Iron Fist-c/story (very early app., 3rd?); Adams-i .80 2.00

NOTE: ***N. Adams*** *a-1i(part), 27i; c-1, 2-4, 11, 12, 14, 17.* ***Giffen*** *a-22p, 24p.* ***G. Kane*** *a-23p.* ***Kirby*** *a-5r.* ***Nasser*** *a-27p, 28.* ***Perez*** *a(p)-6-14, 16, 17, 19, 21.* ***Rogers*** *a-26, 32, 33.* ***Starlin*** *a-1, 2r, 15r.* ***Staton*** *a-28p, 31, 32. Iron Fist in #10, 15, 18-24. Shang Chi, Master of Kung Fu in #1-9, 11-18, 33. Sons of the Tiger in #1, 3, 4, 6-14, 16-19 (White Tiger #20-24, 26, 27, 29-31).*

DEADMAN (See The Brave and the Bold & Phantom Stranger #39)
May, 1985 - No. 7, Nov, 1985 ($1.75, Baxter paper)
DC Comics

1-Deadman-r by Infantino, N. Adams in all .70 1.75
2-7: 5-Batman-c/story-r/Str. Advs. 7-Batman-r .70 1.75

DEADMAN
Mar, 1986 - No. 4, June, 1986 (75 cents, mini-series)
DC Comics

1-4: Lopez-c/a. 4-Byrne-c(p) 1.00

DEADMAN: EXORCISM
1992 - No. 2, 1992 ($4.95, color, mini-series, 52 pgs.)
DC Comics

1,2-Kelley Jones-c/a 1.00 2.00 5.00

DEADMAN: LOVE AFTER DEATH
1989 - No. 2, 1990 ($3.95, 2 issue series, mature readers, 52 pgs.)
DC Comics

Book One, Two: 1-Contains nudity 1.60 4.00

DEAD OF NIGHT
Dec, 1973 - No. 11, Aug, 1975
Marvel Comics Group

1-Horror reprints .70 1.75
2-11: 11-Intro Scarecrow; Kane/Wrightson-c 1.00

NOTE: ***Ditko*** *r-7, 10.* ***Everett*** *c-2.* ***Sinnott*** *r-1.*

DEADPOOL: THE CIRCLE CHASE (See New Mutants #98)
Aug, 1993 - No. 4, Nov, 1993 ($2.00, color, mini-series)
Marvel Comics

1-($2.50)-Embossed-c 1.00 2.50
2-4 .80 2.00

DEADSHOT (See Batman #59 & Detective Comics #474)
Nov, 1988 - No. 4, Feb, 1989 ($1.00, color, mini-series)
DC Comics

1-4: Deadshot is a Batman villain 1.00

DEAD WHO WALK, THE (See Strange Mysteries, Super Reprint #15, 16)
1952 (One Shot)
Realistic Comics

nn 31.00 95.00 220.00

DEADWOOD GULCH
1931 (52 pages) (B&W)
Dell Publishing Co.

nn-By Charles "Boody" Rogers 14.00 43.00 100.00

DEADWORLD (Also see The Realm)
Dec, 1986 - No. 28? ($1.50-$1.95, B&W, adults)($2.50 #15 on)
Arrow Comics/Caliber Comics

1 1.60 4.00

Dear Beatrice Fairfax #5, © KING

Deathblow #2, © Aegis Entertainment

Death's Head II #10, © MEG

	GD25	FN65	NM94
2		1.20	3.00
3,4		.80	2.00
5-11: Graphic covers		.70	1.70
5-11: Tame covers		.80	2.00
12-28: Graphic covers, 12-28: Tame covers		.80	2.00

DEAN MARTIN & JERRY LEWIS (See Adventures of...)

DEAR BEATRICE FAIRFAX
No. 5, Nov, 1950 - No. 9, Sept, 1951 (Vern Greene art)
Best/Standard Comics(King Features)

	GD25	FN65	NM94
5	5.00	15.00	30.00
6-9	3.60	9.00	18.00

NOTE: ***Schomburg** air brush c-5-9.*

DEAR HEART (Formerly Lonely Heart)
No. 15, July, 1956 - No. 16, Sept, 1956
Ajax

	GD25	FN65	NM94
15,16	3.20	8.00	16.00

DEAR LONELY HEART (...Illustrated No. 1-6)
Mar, 1951; No. 2, Oct, 1951 - No. 8, Oct, 1952
Artful Publications

	GD25	FN65	NM94
1	10.00	30.00	70.00
2	5.35	16.00	32.00
3-Matt Baker Jungle Girl story	10.00	30.00	70.00
4-8	4.70	14.00	28.00

DEAR LONELY HEARTS (Lonely Heart #9 on)
Aug, 1953 - No. 8, Oct, 1954
Harwell Publ./Mystery Publ. Co. (Comic Media)

	GD25	FN65	NM94
1	5.35	16.00	32.00
2-8	3.60	9.00	18.00

DEARLY BELOVED
Fall, 1952
Ziff-Davis Publishing Co.

	GD25	FN65	NM94
1-Photo-c	10.00	30.00	70.00

DEAR NANCY PARKER
June, 1963 - No. 2, Sept, 1963
Gold Key

	GD25	FN65	NM94
1,2-Painted-c	3.00	7.50	15.00

DEATHBLOW (Also see Darker Image)
May (April inside), 1993 - Present ($1.75, color)
Image Comics

	GD25	FN65	NM94
1-($2.50)-Red foil stamped logo on black varnish-c; Jim Lee-c/a; flip-book side has Cybernary -c/story (#2 also)		1.00	2.50
2-(8/93,$1.75)-Lee/Choi-a; with bound-in poster		.70	1.75

DEATHLOK (Also see Astonishing Tales #25)
July, 1990 - No. 4, Oct, 1990 ($3.95, limited series, 52 pgs.)
Marvel Comics

	GD25	FN65	NM94
1-Guice-a(p)	1.70	5.00	12.00
2-4: 2-Guice-a(p). 3,4-Denys Cowan-a, c-4	1.30	3.25	8.00

DEATHLOK
July, 1991 - Present ($1.75, color)
Marvel Comics

	GD25	FN65	NM94
1 Silver ink cover; Denys Cowan-c/a(p) begins		1.60	4.00
2-5: 2-Forge (X-Men) app. 3-Vs. Dr. Doom. 5-X-Men & F.F. x-over		1.20	3.00
6-10: 6,7-Punisher x-over. 9,10-Ghost Rider-c/sty		.80	2.00
11-18,20-24,26-34: 16-Infinity War x-over. 17-Jae Lee-c. 22-Black Panther app. 27-Siege app.		.70	1.75
19-($2.25)-Foil-c		.90	2.25
25-($2.95, 52 pgs.)-Holo-grafx foil-c		1.20	3.00
Annual 1 (1992, $2.25, 68 pgs.)-Guice & Cowan-p		1.00	2.50
Annual 2 (1993, $2.95, 68 pgs.)-Polybagged w/card		1.20	3.00

NOTE: ***Denys Cowan** a(p)-9-13, 15; c-9-12, 13p, 14. **Guice/Cowan** c-8.*

DEATHLOK SPECIAL
May, 1991 - No. 4, Late-June, 1991 ($2.00, bi-weekly mini-series)
Marvel Comics

	GD25	FN65	NM94
1-4: r/1-4('90) w/new Guice-c #1,2; Cowan c-3,4		1.00	2.50
1-2nd printing w/white-c		1.00	2.50

DEATHMATE
Sept, 1993 - Present ($2.95, color)
Valiant/Image Comics

	GD25	FN65	NM94
Prologue–Silver foil; Lee/Layton-c; B. Smith/Lee-a		1.20	3.00
Prologue–Special gold foil ed. of silver ed.			15.00
Prologue–Yellow foil ($4.95, 52 pgs.)		1.60	4.00
Prologue–Special gold foil ed. of yellow ed.			15.00
Prologue–Blue foil ($4.95, 52 pgs.)		1.60	4.00
Prologue–Special gold foil ed. of blue ed.			15.00
Prologue–Black ($4.95, 52 pgs.)		1.60	4.00
Prologue–Special gold foil ed. of black ed.			15.00

DEATH METAL VS. GENETIX
Dec, 1993 - No. 2, Jan, 1994 (Color, limited series)
Marvel Comics UK

	GD25	FN65	NM94
1-($2.95)-Polybagged w/2 trading cards		1.20	3.00
2-($2.50)-Polybagged w/2 trading cards		1.00	2.50

DEATH OF CAPTAIN MARVEL (See Marvel Graphic Novel #1)

DEATH OF MR. MONSTER, THE (See Mr. Monster #8)

DEATH OF SUPERMAN (See Superman, 2nd series)

DEATH RATTLE (Kitchen Sink)(Value: cover or less)

DEATH'S HEAD (See Daredevil #56, Dragon's Claws #5 & Incomplete...)
Dec, 1988 - No. 10, Sept, 1989 ($1.75, color)(Dragon's Claws spin-off)
Marvel Comics

	GD25	FN65	NM94
1-Dragon's Claws spin-off	1.65	4.00	10.00
2-Fantastic Four app.; Dragon's Claws x-over	1.00	2.50	5.50
3,4		1.00	2.50
5-10: 9-Fantastic Four x-over; Simonson-c(p)		1.10	2.75

DEATH'S HEAD II (Also see Battletide)
Mar, 1992 - No. 4, June (May inside), 1992 ($1.75, color, mini-series)
Marvel Comics UK, Ltd.

	GD25	FN65	NM94
1	1.65	4.00	10.00
1,2-Silver ink 2nd printiings		.80	2.00
2-Fantastic Four app.	1.00	2.50	5.50
3,4: 4-Punisher, Spider-Man , Daredevil, Dr. Strange, Capt. America & Wolverine in the year 2020		1.20	3.00

DEATH'S HEAD II (Also see Battletide)
Dec, 1992 - Present ($1.75/$1.95, color)
Marvel Comics UK, Ltd.

	GD25	FN65	NM94
1-5: 1-Gatefold-c. 1-4-X-Men app.		.70	1.75
6-16 ($1.95)		.80	2.00

DEATH'S HEAD II & THE ORIGIN OF DIE CUT
Aug, 1993 - No. 2, Sept, 1993 (Color, limited series)
Marvel Comics UK, Ltd.

	GD25	FN65	NM94
1-($2.95)-Embossed-c		1.20	3.00
2 ($1.75)		.70	1.75

DEATHSTROKE: THE TERMINATOR (Also see Marvel & DC Present, New Teen Titans #2, New Titans & Tales of the Teen Titans #42-44)
Aug, 1991 - Present ($1.75, color)
DC Comics

	GD25	FN65	NM94
1-New Titans spin-off	1.00	2.50	5.50
1-Gold ink 2nd printing ($1.75)		.70	1.80
2		1.40	3.50
3-5		1.00	2.50

6-35: 6,8-Batman cameo. 7,9-Batman-c/story. 9-1st new Vigilante (female) in

Death Valley #1, © Comic Media

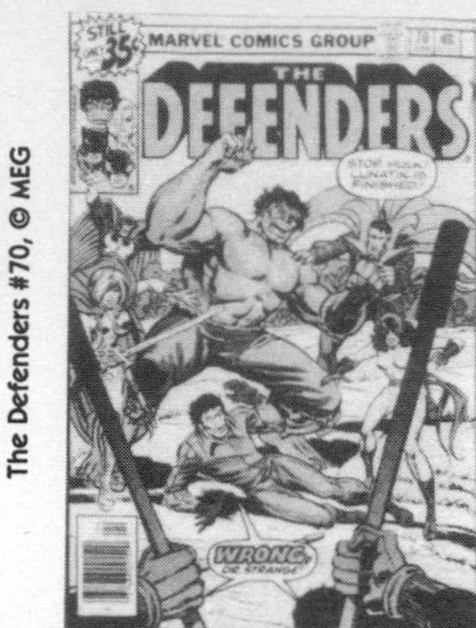

The Defenders #70, © MEG

Dell Giant #34, © DELL

cameo. 10-1st full app. new Vigilante; Perez-i. 13-Vs. Justice League; Team Titans cameo on last pg. 14-Total Chaos, part 1; Team Titans-c/story cont'd in New Titans #90. 15-Total Chaos, part 4 .70 1.75
Annual 1 (1992 $3.50, 68 pgs.)-Nightwing & Vigilante app.; minor Eclipso app. 1.40 3.50
Annual 2 (1993, $3.50, 68 pgs.) 1.40 3.50

DEATH: THE HIGH COST OF LIVING (See Books of Magic & Sandman #8)
Mar, 1993 - No. 3, May, 1993
DC Comics (Vertigo)

1-Neil Gaiman scripts in all 1.00 2.50 6.00
1-Platinum edition 35.00
2 1.60 4.00
3 1.20 3.00

DEATH 3
Sept, 1993 - No. 4, Dec, 1993 ($1.75, color, mini-series)
Marvel Comics UK

1-($2.95)-Embossed-c 1.20 3.00
2-4 .70 1.75

DEATH VALLEY
Oct, 1953 - No. 6, Aug, 1954?
Comic Media

1-Billy the Kid; Morisi-a; Andru/Esposito-c/a 6.705 20.00 40.00
2 4.00 12.00 24.00
3-6: 3,5-Morisi-a. 5-Discount-a 4.00 10.00 20.00

DEATH VALLEY (Becomes Frontier Scout, Daniel Boone No.10-13)
No. 7, 6/55 - No. 9, 10/55 (Continued from Comic Media series)
Charlton Comics

7-9: 8-Wolverton-a (half pg.) 4.00 10.00 20.00

DEBBIE DEAN, CAREER GIRL
April, 1945 - No. 2, July, 1945
Civil Service Publ.

1,2-Newspaper reprints by Bert Whitman 10.00 30.00 70.00

DEBBI'S DATES (Also see Date With Debbi)
Apr-May, 1969 - No. 11, Dec-Jan, 1970-71
National Periodical Publications

1 2.40 6.00 12.00
2-11: 4-Neal Adams text illo. 6-Superman cameo 1.20 3.00 6.00

DEEP, THE (Movie)
November, 1977
Marvel Comics Group

1-Infantino-c/a 1.50

DEFENDERS, THE (TV)
Sept-Nov, 1962 - No. 2, Feb-Apr, 1963
Dell Publishing Co.

12-176-211(#1), 12-176-304(#2) 3.60 9.00 18.00

DEFENDERS, THE (Also see Giant-Size..., Marvel Feature, Marvel Treasury Edition, Secret Defenders & Sub-Mariner #34, 35; The New...#140-on)
Aug, 1972 - No. 152, Feb, 1986
Marvel Comics Group

1-The Hulk, Doctor Strange, Sub-Mariner begin 9.00 26.00 60.00
2 4.30 13.00 30.00
3-5: 4-Valkyrie joins 3.20 8.00 20.00
6-9: 9-Avengers app. 2.15 6.50 15.00
10-Hulk vs. Thor; Avengers app. 3.20 8.00 20.00
11-14: 12-Last 20 cent issue 1.50 3.75 9.00
15,16-Magneto & Brotherhood of Evil Mutants app. from X-Men 1.70 5.00 12.00
17-20: 17-Power Man x-over (11/74) 1.20 3.00 7.00
21-25: 24,25-Son of Satan app. 1.00 2.50 6.00
26-29-Guardians of the Galaxy app. (#26 is 8/75; pre-dates Marvel Presents #3). 28-1st full app. Starhawk (cameo #27). 29-Starhawk joins Guardians 1.65 4.70 11.00
30-50: 31,32-Origin Nighthawk. 35-Intro New Red Guardian. 44-Hellcat joins. 45-Dr. Strange leaves 1.80 4.50
51-60: 53-1st app. Lunatik (cameo, Lobo lookalike). 55-Origin Red Guardian; Lunatik cameo. 56-1st full Lunatik story 1.60 4.00
61-72: 61-Lunatik & Spider-Man app. 70-73-Lunatik (origin #71) 1.40 3.50
73-75-Foolkiller II app. (Greg Salinger). 74-Nighthawk resigns 1.40 3.50
76-95,97-124,126-149,151: 77-Origin Omega. 78-Original Defenders return thru #101. 94-1st Gargoyle. 100-(52 pgs.)-Hellcat (Patsy Walker) revealed as Satan's daughter. 104-The Beast joins. 105-Son of Satan joins. 106-Death of Nighthawk. 120,121-Son of Satan-c/stories. 122-Final app. Son of Satan (2 pgs.). 129-New Mutants cameo (3/84, early x-over) .90 2.20
96-Ghost Rider app. 1.80 4.50
125-(52 pgs.)-Intro new Defenders 1.20 3.00
150-(52 pgs.)-Origin Cloud 1.20 3.00
152-(52 pgs.)-Ties in with X-Factor & Secret Wars II 1.20 3.00
Annual 1 (1976, 52 pgs.)-New book-length story 1.60 4.00

NOTE: ***Art Adams*** *c-142p.* ***Austin*** *a-53i; c-65i, 119i, 145i.* ***Frank Bolle*** *a-7i, 10i, 11i.* ***Buckler*** *c(p)-34, 38, 76, 77, 79-86, 90, 91.* ***J. Buscema*** *c-66.* ***Giffen*** *a-42-49p, 50, 51-54p.* ***Golden*** *a-53p, 54p; c-94, 96.* ***Guice*** *c-129.* ***G. Kane*** *c(p)-13, 16, 18, 19, 21-26, 31-33, 35-37, 40, 41, 52, 55.* ***Kirby*** *c-42-45.* ***Mooney*** *a-3i, 31-34i, 62i, 63i, 85i.* ***Nasser*** *c-88p.* ***Perez*** *c(p)-51, 53, 54.* ***Rogers*** *c-98.* ***Starlin*** *c-110.* ***Tuska*** *a-57p. Silver Surfer in No. 2, 3, 6, 8-11, 92, 98-101, 107, 112-115, 122-125.*

DEFENDERS OF DYNATRON CITY
Feb, 1992 - No. 6, July, 1992 ($1.25, color, limited series)
Marvel Comics

1-6-Lucasarts characters. 2-Origin 1.25

DEFENDERS OF THE EARTH (TV)
Jan, 1987 - No. 5, Sept, 1987
Star Comics (Marvel)

1-5: The Phantom, Mandrake The Magician, Flash Gordon begin 1.00

DEFINITIVE DIRECTORY OF THE DC UNIVERSE, THE (See Who's Who...)

DELECTA OF THE PLANETS (See Don Fortune & Fawcett Miniatures)

DELLA VISION (Patty Powers #4 on)
April, 1955 - No. 3, Aug, 1955
Atlas Comics

1 10.00 30.00 65.00
2,3 7.50 22.50 45.00

DELL GIANT COMICS
No. 21, Sept, 1959 - No. 55, Sept, 1961 (Most 84 pages, 25 cents)
Dell Publishing Co.

GD25 FN65 VF82 NM94

21-(#1)-M.G.M.'s Tom & Jerry Picnic Time (84pp, stapled binding) 10.00 30.00 70.00 150.00
22-Huey, Dewey & Louie Back to School(10/59, 84pp, square binding begins) 6.25 19.00 44.00 95.00
23-Marge's Little Lulu & Tubby Halloween Fun (10/59)-Tripp-a 11.00 32.00 77.00 165.00
24-Woody Woodpecker's Family Fun (11/59) 7.00 21.00 50.00 105.00
25-Tarzan's Jungle World(11/59)-Marsh-a 10.00 30.00 70.00 150.00
26-Christmas Parade-Barks-a, 16pgs.(Disney; 12/59)-Barks draws himself on wanted poster pg. 13 18.00 55.00 125.00 270.00
27-Man in Space r-/4-Color 716,866, & 954 (100 pages, 35 cents) (Disney)(TV) 9.00 27.00 63.00 135.00
28-Bugs Bunny's Winter Fun (2/60) 9.00 27.00 63.00 135.00
29-Marge's Little Lulu & Tubby in Hawaii (4/60)-Tripp-a 11.00 32.00 77.00 165.00
30-Disneyland USA(6/60)-Reprinted in Vacation in Disneyland 8.00 25.00 56.00 120.00

Dell Giant #50, © DELL

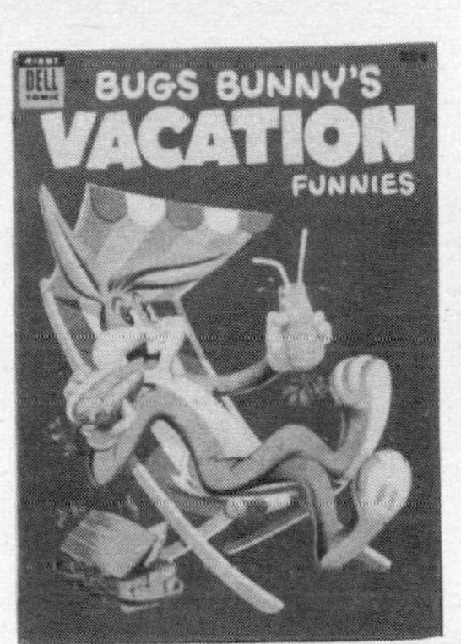

Bugs Bunny Vacation Funnies #4, © DELL

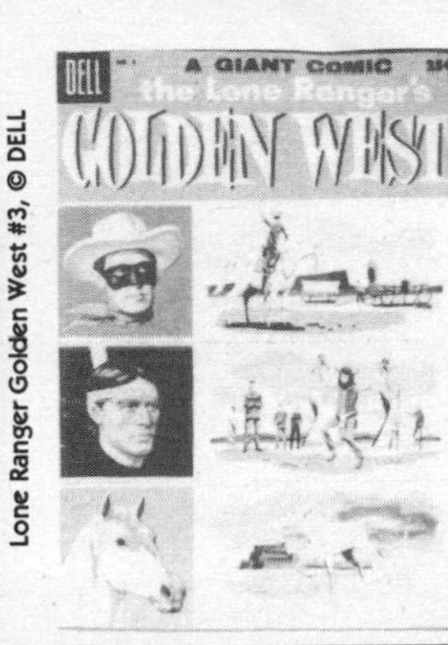

Lone Ranger Golden West #3, © DELL

GD25 FN65 NM94

31-Huckleberry Hound Summer Fun (7/60)(TV)
12.00 36.00 84.00 180.00
32-Bugs Bunny Beach Party 5.00 15.00 35.00 75.00
33-Daisy Duck & Uncle Scrooge Picnic Time (9/60)
8.00 25.00 56.00 120.00
34-Nancy & Sluggo Summer Camp (8/60)
6.00 18.00 42.00 90.00
35-Huey, Dewey & Louie Back to School (10/60)
6.25 19.00 44.00 95.00
36-Marge's Little Lulu & Witch Hazel Halloween Fun(10/60)-Tripp-a
11.00 32.00 77.00 165.00
37-Tarzan, King of the Jungle(11/60)-Marsh-a
9.00 27.00 63.00 135.00
38-Uncle Donald & His Nephews Family Fun (11/60)
5.50 16.00 39.00 83.00
39-Walt Disney's Merry Christmas(12/60)
6.25 19.00 44.00 95.00
40-Woody Woodpecker Christmas Parade(12/60)
5.00 15.00 35.00 75.00
41-Yogi Bear's Winter Sports (12/60)(TV)
12.00 36.00 84.00 180.00
42-Marge's Little Lulu & Tubby in Australia (4/61)
11.00 32.00 77.00 165.00
43-Mighty Mouse in Outer Space (5/61) 19.00 57.00 133.00 285.00
44-Around the World with Huckleberry & His Friends (7/61)(TV)
12.00 36.00 84.00 180.00
45-Nancy & Sluggo Summer Camp (8/61)
5.00 15.00 35.00 75.00
46-Bugs Bunny Beach Party (8/61) 5.00 15.00 35.00 75.00
47-Mickey & Donald in Vacationland (8/61)
6.25 19.00 44.00 95.00
48-The Flintstones (No. 1)(Bedrock Bedlam)(7/61)(TV)
15.00 45.00 105.00 225.00
49-Huey, Dewey & Louie Back to School (9/61)
4.60 14.00 32.00 70.00
50-Marge's Little Lulu & Witch Hazel Trick 'N' Treat (10/61)
11.00 32.00 77.00 165.00
51-Tarzan, King of the Jungle by Jesse Marsh (11/61)
7.00 21.00 49.00 105.00
52-Uncle Donald & His Nephews Dude Ranch (11/61)
4.60 14.00 32.00 70.00
53-Donald Duck Merry Christmas(12/61)-Not by Barks
4.60 14.00 32.00 70.00
54-Woody Woodpecker Christmas Party(12/61)-issued after No. 55
6.00 18.00 42.00 90.00
55-Daisy Duck & Uncle Scrooge Showboat (9/61)-1st app. Daisy Duck's nieces, April, May & June 14.00 41.00 98.00 210.00
NOTE: All issues printed with & without ad on back cover.

(OTHER DELL GIANT EDITIONS)

Abraham Lincoln Life Story 1(3/58, 100p) 5.50 16.00 39.00 82.00
Bugs Bunny Christmas Funnies 1(11/50, 116p)
15.00 45.00 105.00 225.00
...Christmas Funnies 2(11/51, 116p) 10.00 30.00 70.00 150.00
...Christmas Funnies 3-5(11/52-11/54, 100p)-Becomes Christmas Party #6
9.00 27.00 56.00 135.00
...Christmas Funnies 7-9(12/56-12/58, 100p)
8.00 24.00 56.00 120.00
...Christmas Party 6(11/55, 100p)-Formerly Bugs Bunny Christmas Funnies
7.00 21.00 49.00 105.00
...County Fair 1(9/57, 100p 10.00 30.00 70.00 150.00
...Halloween Parade 1(10/53, 100p) 9.00 27.00 63.00 135.00
...Halloween Parade 2(10/54, 100p)-Trick 'N' Treat Halloween Fun No. 3 on
8.00 24.00 56.00 120.00
...Trick 'N' Treat Halloween Fun 3,4(10/55-10/56, 100p)-Formerly Halloween Parade #2 8.50 25.50 60.00 128.00

GD25 FN65 NM94

...Vacation Funnies 1(7/51, 112p) 15.00 45.00 105.00 225.00
...Vacation Funnies 2('52, 100p) 12.00 36.00 84.00 180.00
...Vacation Funnies 3-5('53-'55, 100p) 9.00 27.00 63.00 135.00
...Vacation Funnies 6-9('54-6/59, 100p) 8.00 24.00 56.00 120.00
Cadet Gray of West Point 1(4/58, 100p)-Williamson-a, 10pgs.; Buscema-a; photo-c 4.60 14.00 32.00 70.00
Christmas In Disneyland 1(12/57, 100p)-Barks-a, 18pgs.
11.00 32.00 77.00 165.00
Christmas Parade 1(11/49)-Barks-a, 25pgs; r-in G.K. Christmas Parade #5
39.00 120.00 275.00 585.00
Christmas Parade 2('50)-Barks-a, 25pgs; r-in G.K. Christmas Parade #6
27.00 81.00 190.00 405.00
Christmas Parade 3-7('51-'55, 116-100p) 5.50 16.00 39.00 83.00
Christmas Parade 8(12/56, 100p)-Barks-a, 8pgs.
11.00 32.00 77.00 165.00
Christmas Parade 9(12/58, 100p)-Barks-a, 20pgs.
13.00 40.00 91.00 195.00
Christmas Treasury, A 1(11/54, 100p) 7.00 20.00 50.00 105.00
Davy Crockett, King Of The Wild Frontier 1(9/55, 100p)-Photo-c; Marsh-a 14.00 41.00 98.00 210.00
Disneyland Birthday Party 1(10/58, 100p)-Barks-a, 16pgs.
11.00 32.00 77.00 165.00
Donald and Mickey In Disneyland 1(5/58, 100p)
6.25 19.00 44.00 95.00
Donald Duck Beach Party 1(7/54, 100p) 7.00 20.00 50.00 105.00
...Beach Party 2('55, 100p) 5.00 15.00 35.00 75.00
...Beach Party 3-5('56-'58, 100p) 4.60 14.00 32.00 70.00
...Beach Party 6(8/59, 84p)-Stapled 4.60 14.00 32.00 70.00
Donald Duck Fun Book 1,2('53-10/54, 100p)-Games, puzzles, comics & cut-outs (Very rare in unused condition)(most copies commonly have defaced interior pages) 25.00 75.00 175.00 375.00
Donald Duck In Disneyland 1(9/55, 100p) 4.60 14.00 32.00 70.00
Golden West Rodeo Treasury 1(10/57, 100p)
6.25 19.00 44.00 95.00
Huey, Dewey and Louie Back To School 1(9/58, 100p)
5.50 16.00 39.00 83.00
Lady and The Tramp 1(6/55, 100p) 7.00 20.00 50.00 105.00
Life Stories of American Presidents 1(11/57, 100p)-Buscema-a
4.00 12.00 28.00 60.00
Lone Ranger Golden West 3(8/55, 100p)-Formerly Lone Ranger Western Treasury 14.00 41.00 98.00 210.00
Lone Ranger Movie Story nn(3/56, 100p)-Origin Lone Ranger in text; Clayton Moore photo-c 27.00 81.00 190.00 405.00
...Western Treasury 1(9/53, 100p)-Origin Lone Ranger, Silver, & Tonto
16.00 48.00 110.00 240.00
...Western Treasury 2(8/54, 100p)-Becomes Lone Ranger Golden West #3
9.00 27.00 63.00 135.00
Marge's Little Lulu & Alvin Story Telling Time 1(3/59)-r/#2,5,3,11,30,10, 21,17,8,14,16; Stanley-a 11.00 32.00 77.00 165.00
...& Her Friends 4(3/56, 100p)-Tripp-a 8.00 25.00 56.00 120.00
...& Her Special Friends 3(3/55, 100p)-Tripp-a
8.00 25.00 56.00 120.00
...& Tubby At Summer Camp 5(10/57, 100p)-Tripp-a
8.00 25.00 56.00 120.00
...& Tubby At Summer Camp 2(10/58, 100p)-Tripp-a
8.00 25.00 56.00 120.00
...& Tubby Halloween Fun 6(10/57, 100p)-Tripp-a
8.00 25.00 50.00 120.00
...& Tubby Halloween Fun 2(10/58, 100p)-Tripp-a
8.00 25.00 56.00 120.00
...& Tubby In Alaska 1(7/59, 100p)-Tripp-a
8.00 25.00 56.00 120.00
...On Vacation 1(7/54, 100p)-r/4C-110,14,4C-146,5,4C-97,4,4C-158,3,1; Stanley-a 14.00 41.00 98.00 210.00
...& Tubby Annual 1(3/53, 100p)-r/4C-165,4C-74,4C-146,4C-97,4C-158, 4C-139,4C-131; Stanley-a 27.00 81.00 190.00 405.00

Mickey Mouse Summer Fun #1, © Disney Co.

Silly Symphonies #7, © DELL

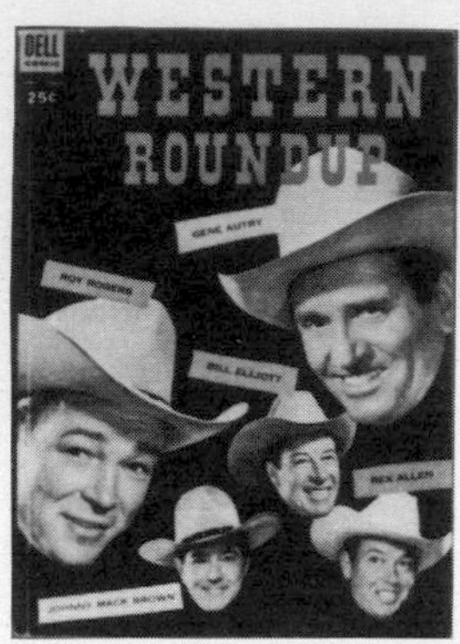

Western Roundup #6, © DELL

GD25 FN65 NM94

...& Tubby Annual 2('54, 100p)-r/4C-139,6,4C-115,4C-74,5,4C-97,3,4C-146, 18; Stanley-a 27.00 81.00 190.00 405.00

Marge's Tubby & His Clubhouse Pals 1(10/56, 100p)-1st app. Gran'pa Feeb; 1st app. Janie; written by Stanley; Tripp-a 11.00 32.00 77.00 165.00

Mickey Mouse Almanac 1(12/57, 100p)-Barks-a, 8pgs. 23.00 70.00 160.00 345.00

...Birthday Party 1(9/53, 100p)-r/entire 48pgs. of Gottfredson's "Mickey Mouse in Love Trouble" from WDC&S 36-39. Quality equal to original. Also reprints one story each from 4-Color 27, 29, & 181 plus 6 panels of highlights in the career of Mickey Mouse 21.00 62.00 147.00 315.00

...Club Parade 1(12/55, 100p)-r/4-Color 16 with some art redrawn by Paul Murry & recolored with night scenes turned into day; quality much poorer than original 18.00 55.00 125.00 270.00

...In Fantasy Land 1(5/57, 100p 8.00 25.00 56.00 120.00

...In Frontier Land 1(5/56, 100p)-Mickey Mouse Club issue 8.00 25.00 56.00 120.00

...Summer Fun 1(8/58, 100p)-Mobile cut-outs on back-c; becomes Summer Fun #2 7.50 22.50 53.00 112.00

Moses & The Ten Commandments 1(8/57, 100p)-Not based on movie; Dell's adaptation; Sekowsky-a 4.60 14.00 32.00 70.00

Nancy & Sluggo Travel Time 1(9/58, 100p) 6.25 19.00 44.00 95.00

Peter Pan Treasure Chest 1(1/53, 212p)-Disney; contains movie adaptation plus other stories 65.00 200.00 650.00 --

Picnic Party 6,7(7/55-6/56, 100p)(Formerly Vacation Parade)-UncleScrooge, Mickey & Donald 6.25 19.00 44.00 95.00

Picnic Party 8(7/57, 100p)-Barks-a, 6pgs 9.00 27.00 63.00 135.00

Pogo Parade 1(9/53, 100p)-Kelly-a(r-/Pogo from Animal Comics in this order: #11,13,21,14,27,16,23,9,18,15,17) 19.00 56.00 132.00 285.00

Raggedy Ann & Andy 1(2/55, 100p) 14.00 41.00 98.00 210.00

Santa Claus Funnies 1(11/52, 100p)-Dan Noonan -A Christmas Carol adaptation 7.00 20.00 50.00 105.00

Silly Symphonies 1(9/52, 100p)-r/Chicken Little, M. Mouse "The Brave Little Tailor," Mother Pluto, Three Little Pigs, Lady, Bucky Bug, Wise Little Hen, Little Hiawatha, Pedro, The Grasshopper & The Ants 14.00 41.00 98.00 210.00

Silly Symphonies 2(9/53, 100p)-r/M. Mouse-"The Sorcerer's Apprentice," Little Hiawatha, Peculiar Penguins, Lambert The Sheepish Lion, Pluto, Spotty Pig, The Golden Touch, Elmer Elephant, The Pelican & The Snipe 11.00 32.00 77.00 165.00

Silly Symphonies 3(2/54, 100p)-r/Mickey & The Beanstalk (4-Color #157), Little Minnehaha, Pablo, The Flying Gauchito, Pluto, & Bongo 10.50 31.00 74.00 158.00

Silly Symphonies 4(8/54, 100p)-r/Dumbo (4-Color 234), Morris The Midget Moose, The Country Cousin, Bongo, & Clara Cluck 10.00 30.00 70.00 150.00

Silly Symphonies 5(2/55, 100p)-r/Cinderella (4-Color 272), Bucky Bug, Pluto, Little Hiawatha, The 7 Dwarfs & Dumbo, Pinocchio 10.00 30.00 70.00 150.00

Silly Symphonies 6(8/55, 100p)-r/Pinocchio(WDC&S 63), The 7 Dwarfs & Thumper (WDC&S 45), M. Mouse-"Adventures With Robin Hood," Johnny Appleseed, Pluto & Peter Pan, & Bucky Bug; Cut-out on back-c 10.00 30.00 70.00 150.00

Silly Symphonies 7(2/57, 100p)-r/Reluctant Dragon (4-Color 13), Ugly Duckling, M. Mouse & Peter Pan, Jiminy Cricket, Peter & The Wolf, Brer Rabbit, Bucky Bug; Cut-out on back-c 14.00 41.00 98.00 210.00

Silly Symphonies 8(2/58, 100p)-r/Thumper Meets The 7 Dwarfs (4-Color #19), Jiminy Cricket, Niok, Brer Rabbit; Cut-out on back-c 8.00 25.00 56.00 120.00

Silly Symphonies 9(2/59, 100p)-r/Paul Bunyan, Humphrey Bear, Jiminy Cricket, The Social Lion, Goliath II; Cut-out on back-c 8.00 25.00 56.00 120.00

Sleeping Beauty 1(4/59, 100p) 17.00 50.00 120.00 255.00

Summer Fun 2(8/59, 100p)(Formerly Mickey Mouse...)-Barks-a(2), 24 pgs. 14.00 41.00 98.00 210.00

GD25 FN65 NM94

Tales From The Tomb 1(02-810-210)(10/62, 25 cent giant)-All stories written by John Stanley 10.00 30.00 70.00 150.00

Tarzan's Jungle Annual 1(8/52, 100p) 7.50 22.50 53.00 112.00

...Annual 2(8/53, 100p) 6.25 19.00 44.00 95.00

...Annual 3-7('54-9/58, 100p)(two No. 5s)-Manning-a-No. 3,5-7; Marsh-a in No. 1-7 5.50 16.00 39.00 83.00

Tom And Jerry Back To School 1(9/56, 100p) 12.00 36.00 84.00 180.00

...Picnic Time 1(7/58, 100p) 9.00 27.00 63.00 135.00

...Summer Fun 1(7/54, 100p)-Droopy written by Barks 13.00 40.00 90.00 195.00

...Summer Fun 2-4(7/55-7/57, 100p) 6.00 18.00 36.00 90.00

...Toy Fair 1(6/58, 100p) 9.00 27.00 63.00 135.00

...Winter Carnival 1(12/52, 100p)-Droopy written by Barks 22.00 65.00 154.00 330.00

...Winter Carnival 2(12/53, 100p)-Droopy written by Barks 15.00 45.00 105.00 225.00

...Winter Fun 3(12/54, 100p) 6.00 18.00 36.00 90.00

...Winter Fun 4-7(12/55-11/58, 100p) 5.00 15.00 30.00 75.00

Treasury of Dogs, A 1(10/56, 100p) 4.60 14.00 32.00 70.00

Treasury of Horses, A (9/55, 100p) 4.60 14.00 32.00 70.00

Uncle Scrooge Goes To Disneyland 1(8/57, 100p)-Barks-a, 20pgs. 14.00 41.00 98.00 210.00

Universal Presents-Dracula-The Mummy & Other Stories 02-530-311 (9-11/63, 84p)-r/Dracula 12-231-212, The Mummy 12-437-211 &part of Ghost Stories No. 1 12.00 36.00 84.00 180.00

Vacation In Disneyland 1(8/58, 100p) 5.50 16.00 39.00 83.00

Vacation Parade 1(7/50, 130p)-Donald Duck & Mickey Mouse; Barks-a, 55 pgs. 62.00 188.00 435.00 930.00

Vacation Parade 2(7/51, 100p) 11.00 32.00 77.00 165.00

Vacation Parade 3-5(7/52-7/54, 100p)-Becomes Picnic Party No. 6 on 5.50 16.00 39.00 83.00

Western Roundup 1(6/52, 100p)-Photo-c; Gene Autry, Roy Rogers, Johnny Mack Brown, Rex Allen, & Bill Elliott begin; photo back-c begin, end No. 14, 16,18 18.00 55.00 125.00 270.00

Western Roundup 2(2/53, 100p)-Photo-c 11.00 32.00 77.00 165.00

Western Roundup 3-5(7-9/53 - 1-3/54)-Photo-c 9.00 27.00 63.00 135.00

Western Roundup 6-10(4-6/54 - 4-6/55)-Photo-c 8.00 25.00 56.00 120.00

Western Roundup 11-13,16,17(100p)-Photo-c; Manning-a. 11-Flying A's Range Rider, Dale Evans begin 7.00 21.00 50.00 105.00

Western Roundup 14,15,25(1-3/59; 100p)-Photo-c 7.00 21.00 50.00 105.00

Western Roundup 18(100p)-Toth-a; last photo-c; Gene Autry ends 7.50 22.50 53.00 112.00

Western Roundup 19-24(100p)-Manning-a. 19-Buffalo Bill Jr. begins (7-9/57; early app.). 19,20,22-Toth-a. 21-Rex Allen, Johnny Mack Brown end. 22-Jace Pearson's Texas Rangers, Rin Tin Tin, Tales of Wells Fargo (2nd app., 4-6/58) & Wagon Train (2nd app.) begin 6.25 19.00 44.00 95.00

Woody Woodpecker Back To School 1(10/52, 100p) 8.00 24.00 56.00 120.00

...Back To School 2-4,6('53-10/57, 100p)-County Fair No. 5 6.00 18.00 42.00 90.00

...County Fair 5(9/56, 100p)-Formerly Back To School 6.00 18.00 42.00 90.00

...County Fair 2(11/58, 100p) 5.00 15.00 35.00 75.00

DELL JUNIOR TREASURY (15 cents)
June, 1955 - No. 10, Oct, 1957 (All painted-c)
Dell Publishing Co.

	GD25	FN65	NM94
1-Alice in Wonderland; reprints 4-Color #331 (52 pgs.)	10.00	30.00	70.00
2-Aladdin & the Wonderful Lamp	8.35	25.00	50.00

The Demon (3rd series) #13, © DC

Dennis the Menace #39, © FAW

Dennis the Menace #5 (3/82), © MEG

GD25 FN65 NM94

3-Gulliver's Travels (1/56) 6.70 20.00 40.00
4-Adventures of Mr. Frog & Miss Mouse 7.50 22.50 45.00
5-The Wizard of Oz (7/56) 8.35 25.00 50.00
6-Heidi (10/56) 6.70 20.00 40.00
7-Santa and the Angel 6.70 20.00 40.00
8-Raggedy Ann and the Camel with the Wrinkled Knees
6.70 20.00 40.00
9-Clementina the Flying Pig 6.70 20.00 40.00
10-Adventures of Tom Sawyer 6.70 20.00 40.00

DEMOLITION MAN
Nov, 1993 - No. 4, Feb, 1994 ($1.75, color, mini-series)
DC Comics
1-4-Movie adaptation .70 1.80

DEMON, THE (See Detective Comics No. 482-485)
Aug-Sept, 1972 - V3#16, Jan, 1974
National Periodical Publications
1-Origin; Kirby-c/a in 1-16 3.60 10.75 25.00
2-5 1.70 5.00 12.00
6-16 1.30 3.25 8.00

DEMON, THE (2nd series)
Jan, 1987 - No. 4, Apr, 1987 (75 cents, mini-series)(#2 has #4 of 4 on-c)
DC Comics
1-4: Matt Wagner-a(p) & scripts 1.00

DEMON, THE (3rd series)
July, 1990 - Present ($1.50, color)
DC Comics
1: 1-4-Painted-c .70 1.80
2-18,20-27: 3,8-Batman app. (cameo #4). 12-15-Lobo app. (1 pg. cameo #11). 23-Robin app. .65 1.60
19-($2.50, 44 pgs.)-Lobo poster stapled inside 1.20 3.00
28-46: 28-Superman-c/story; begin $1.75-c. 31,33-35-Lobo app.
.70 1.75
Annual 1 (1992, $3.00, 68 pgs.)-Eclipso-c/story 1.20 3.00
Annual 2 (1993, $3.50, 68 pgs.) 1.40 3.50
NOTE: *Alan Grant scripts in #1-16, 20, 21, 23-25, 30-39, Annual 1.* ***Wagner*** *a/scripts-22.*

DEMON DREAMS (Pacific)(Value: cover or less)

DEMON-HUNTER
September, 1975
Seaboard Periodicals (Atlas)
1-Origin; Buckler-c/a 1.00

DEMONIC TOYS (Eternity)(Value: cover or less)

DEMON KNIGHT: A GRIMJACK GRAPHIC NOVEL (First)(Value: cover or less)

DENNIS THE MENACE (TV with 1959 issues) (Becomes ...Fun Fest Series; See The Best of... & The Very Best of...)(... Fun Fest on-c only to #156-166)
8/53 - #14, 1/56; #15, 3/56 - #31, 11/58; #32, 1/59 - #166, 11/79
Standard Comics/Pines No.15-31/Hallden (Fawcett) No.32 on
1-1st app. Dennis, Mr. & Mrs. Wilson, Ruff & Dennis' mom & dad; Wiseman-a, written by Fred Toole-most issues 36.00 107.00 250.00
2 17.00 52.00 120.00
3-10: 8-last pre-code 10.00 30.00 70.00
11-20 8.35 25.00 50.00
21-30: 22-1st app. Margaret w/blonde hair 5.85 17.50 35.00
31-40: 31-1st app. Joey. 37-A-Bomb blast panel. 39-1st app. Gina (11/59)
4.00 11.00 22.00
41-60 3.00 7.50 15.00
61-90 1.65 4.00 10.00
91-166 1.00 2.50 6.00
...& Dirt('59,'68)-Soil Conservation giveaway; r-# 36; Wiseman-c/a
1.20 3.00 6.00
...Away We Go('70)-Caladayl giveaway 1.20 3.00 6.00
...Coping with Family Stress-giveaway .80 2.00 4.00
...Takes a Poke at Poison('61)-Food & Drug Assn. giveaway; Wiseman-c/a
1.20 3.00 6.00
...Takes a Poke at Poison-Revised 1/66, 11/70, 1972, 1974, 1977, 1981
1.60 4.00
NOTE: ***Wiseman*** *c/a-1-46, 53, 68, 60.*

DENNIS THE MENACE (Giants) (No. 1 titled Giant Vacation Special; becomes Dennis the Menace Bonus Magazine No. 76 on)
(#1-8,18,23,25,30,38: 100 pgs.; rest to #41: 84 pgs.; #42-75: 68 pgs.)
Summer, 1955 - No. 75, Dec, 1969
Standard/Pines/Hallden(Fawcett)
nn-Giant Vacation Special(Summ/55-Standard) 12.00 36.00 85.00
nn-Christmas issue (Winter '55) 11.00 32.00 75.00
2-Giant Vacation Special (Summer '56-Pines)
3-Giant Christmas issue (Winter '56-Pines)
4-Giant Vacation Special (Summer '57-Pines)
5-Giant Christmas issue (Winter '57-Pines)
6-In Hawaii (Giant Vacation Special)(Summer '58-Pines)
6-In Hawaii (Summer '59-Hallden)-2nd printing; says 3rd large printing on-c
6-In Hawaii (Summer '60)-3rd printing; says 4th large printing on-c
6-In Hawaii (Summer '62)-4th printing; says 5th large printing on-c
6-Giant Christmas issue (Winter '58)
each.... 8.35 25.00 50.00
7-In Hollywood (Winter '59-Hallden)
7-In Hollywood (Summer '61)-2nd printing
8-In Mexico (Winter '60, 100 pgs.-Hallden/Fawcett)
8-In Mexico (Summer '62, 2nd printing)
9-Goes to Camp (Summer '61, 84 pgs.)-1st CCA approved issue
9-Goes to Camp (Summer '62)-2nd printing
10-X-Mas issue (Winter '61)
11-Giant Christmas issue (Winter '62)
12-Triple Feature (Winter '62)
each.... 7.50 22.50 45.00
13-Best of Dennis the Menace (Spring '63)-Reprints
14-And His Dog Ruff (Summer '63)
15-In Washington, D.C. (Summer '63)
16-Goes to Camp (Summer '63)-Reprints No. 9
17-& His Pal Joey (Winter '63)
18-In Hawaii (Reprints No. 6)
19-Giant Christmas issue (Winter '63)
20-Spring Special (Spring '64)
each.... 4.20 12.50 25.00
21-40: 30-r/#6 2.40 6.00 12.00
41-75: 68-Partial-r/#6 1.60 4.00 8.00
NOTE: ***Wiseman*** *c/a-1-8, 12, 14, 15, 17, 20, 22, 27, 28, 31, 35, 36, 41, 49.*

DENNIS THE MENACE
Nov, 1981 - No. 13, Nov, 1982
Marvel Comics Group
1-13: 1,2-New art. 3-Part-r. 4,5-r. 5-X-Mas-c 1.00
NOTE: ***Hank Ketcham*** *c-most; a-3, 12.* ***Wiseman*** *a-4, 5.*

DENNIS THE MENACE AND HIS DOG RUFF
Summer, 1961
Hallden/Fawcett
1-Wiseman-c/a 5.35 16.00 32.00

DENNIS THE MENACE AND HIS FRIENDS
1969; No. 5, Jan, 1970 - No. 46, April, 1980 (All reprints)
Fawcett Publications
Dennis the Menace & Joey No. 2 (7/69) 2.40 6.00 12.00
Dennis the Menace & Ruff No. 2 (9/69) 2.00 5.00 10.00
Dennis the Menace & Mr. Wilson No. 1 (10/69) 2.40 6.00 12.00
Dennis & Margaret No. 1 (Winter '69) 1.20 3.00 6.00
5-20: 5-Dennis the Menace & Margaret. 6-...& Joey. 7-...& Ruff. 8-...& Mr. Wilson 1.60 4.00
21-37 1.20 3.00
38-46 (Digest size, 148 pgs., 4/78, 95 cents) 1.60 4.00

Dennis the Menace and His Pal Joey #1, © FAW

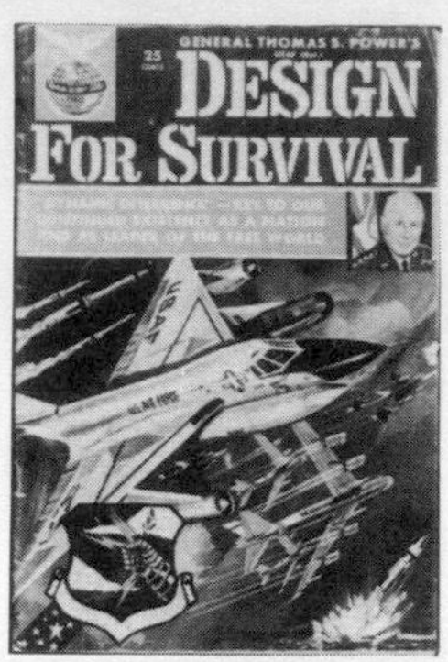

Design For Survival nn, © Amer. Security Council

The Destroyer #2 (Mag.), © Warren Murphy

NOTE: *Titles rotate every four issues, beginning with No. 5.*

DENNIS THE MENACE AND HIS PAL JOEY
Summer, 1961 (10 cents) (See Dennis the Menace Giants No. 45)
Fawcett Publications

	GD25	FN65	NM94
1-Wiseman-c/a	5.85	17.50	35.00

DENNIS THE MENACE AND THE BIBLE KIDS
1977 (36 pages)
Word Books

	GD25	FN65	NM94
1-10: 1-Jesus. 2-Joseph. 3-David. 4-The Bible Girls. 5-Moses. 6-More About Jesus. 7-The Lord's Prayer. 8-Stories Jesus told. 9-Paul, God's Traveller. 10-In the Beginning			1.00

NOTE: ***Ketcham** c/a in all.*

DENNIS THE MENACE BIG BONUS SERIES
No. 10, Feb, 1980 - No. 11, Apr, 1980
Fawcett Publications

	GD25	FN65	NM94
10,11			1.50

DENNIS THE MENACE BONUS MAGAZINE (Formerly Dennis the Menace Giants Nos. 1-75)
No. 76, 1/70 - No. 194, 10/79; (No. 76-124: 68 pgs.; No. 125-163: 52 pgs.; No. 164 on: 36 pgs.)
Fawcett Publications

	GD25	FN65	NM94
76-90		1.60	4.00
91-110		1.20	3.00
111-194: 166-Indicia printed backwards			1.20

DENNIS THE MENACE COMICS DIGEST
April, 1982 - No. 3, Aug, 1982 (Digest Size, $1.25)
Marvel Comics Group

	GD25	FN65	NM94
1-3-Reprints		.80	2.00

NOTE: ***Ketcham** c-all. **Wiseman** a-all. A few thousand #1's were published with a DC emblem on cover.*

DENNIS THE MENACE FUN BOOK
1960 (100 pages)
Fawcett Publications/Standard Comics

	GD25	FN65	NM94
1-Part Wiseman-a	6.70	20.00	40.00

DENNIS THE MENACE FUN FEST SERIES (Formerly Dennis the Menace #166)
No. 16, Jan, 1980 - No. 17, Mar, 1980 (40 cents)
Hallden (Fawcett)

	GD25	FN65	NM94
16,17-By Hank Ketcham			1.00

DENNIS THE MENACE POCKET FULL OF FUN!
Spring, 1969 - No. 50, March, 1980 (196 pages) (Digest size)
Fawcett Publications (Hallden)

	GD25	FN65	NM94
1-Reprints in all issues	2.40	6.00	12.00
2-10	1.20	3.00	6.00
11-28	.80	2.00	4.00
29-50: 35,40,46-Sunday strip-r		.80	2.00

NOTE: *No. 1-28 are 196 pgs.; No. 29-36: 164 pgs.; No. 37: 148 pgs.; No. 38 on: 132 pgs. No. 8, 11, 15, 21, 25, 29 all contain strip reprints.*

DENNIS THE MENACE TELEVISION SPECIAL
Summer, 1961 - No. 2, Spring, 1962 (Giant)
Fawcett Publications (Hallden Div.)

	GD25	FN65	NM94
1	5.85	17.50	35.00
2	4.00	10.00	20.00

DENNIS THE MENACE TRIPLE FEATURE
Winter, 1961 (Giant)
Fawcett Publications

	GD25	FN65	NM94
1-Wiseman-c/a	5.85	17.50	35.00

DEPUTY, THE (See 4-Color No. 1077, 1130, 1225)

DEPUTY DAWG (TV) (Also see New Terrytoons)
Oct-Dec, 1961 - No. 1299, 1962; No. 1, Aug, 1965
Dell Publishing Co./Gold Key

	GD25	FN65	NM94
4-Color 1238,1299	10.00	30.00	70.00
1(10164-508)(8/65)	10.00	30.00	60.00

DEPUTY DAWG PRESENTS DINKY DUCK AND HASHIMOTO-SAN
August, 1965 (TV)
Gold Key

	GD25	FN65	NM94
1(10159-508)	10.00	30.00	60.00

DESIGN FOR SURVIVAL (Gen. Thomas S. Power's...)
1968 (36 pages in color) (25 cents)
American Security Council Press

	GD25	FN65	NM94
nn-Propaganda against the Threat of Communism-Aircraft cover	4.00	10.00	20.00
Twin Circle Edition-Cover shows panels from inside	2.40	6.00	12.00

DESPERADO (Black Diamond Western No. 9 on)
June, 1948 - No. 8, Feb, 1949 (All 52 pgs.)
Lev Gleason Publications

	GD25	FN65	NM94
1-Biro-c on all; contains inside photo-c of Charles Biro, Lev Gleason & Bob Wood	10.00	30.00	60.00
2	5.00	15.00	30.00
3-Story with over 20 killings	5.00	15.00	30.00
4-8	4.00	11.00	22.00

NOTE: ***Barry** a-2. **Fuje** a-4, 8. **Guardineer** a-5-7. **Kida** a-3-7. **Ed Moore** a-4, 6.*

DESTINATION MOON (See Fawcett Movie Comics, Space Adventures #20, 23, & Strange Adventures #1)

DESTROY!! (Eclipse)(Value: cover or less)

DESTROYER, THE
Nov, 1989 - No. 9, June, 1990 ($2.25, B&W, magazine, 52 pgs.)
Marvel Comics

	GD25	FN65	NM94
1-Based on Remo Williams movie, paperbacks		.90	2.25
2-9: 2-Williamson part inks. 4-Ditko-a		.90	2.25

DESTROYER, THE
V2#1, March, 1991 ($1.95, color, 52 pgs.)
V3#1, Dec, 1991 - No. 4, Mar, 1992 ($1.95, color, mini-series)
Marvel Comics

	GD25	FN65	NM94
V2#1-Based on Remo Williams paperbacks		.80	2.00
V3#1-4: 1-4-Simonson-c. 3-Morrow-a		.80	2.00

DESTROYER DUCK
1982 (no month) - No. 7, 5/84 (#2-7: Baxter paper) ($1.50)
Eclipse Comics

	GD25	FN65	NM94
1-Origin Destroyer Duck; 1st app. Groo		1.20	3.00
2-7: 2-Starling back-up begins			1.00

NOTE: ***Neal Adams** c-1i. **Kirby** c/a-1-5p. **Miller** c-7.*

DESTRUCTOR, THE
February, 1975 - No. 4, Aug, 1975
Atlas/Seaboard

	GD25	FN65	NM94
1-Origin; Ditko/Wood-a; Wood-c(i)			1.50
2-4: 2-Ditko/Wood-a. 3,4-Ditko-a(p)			1.00

DETECTIVE COMICS (Also see Special Edition)
March, 1937 - Present
National Periodical Publications/DC Comics

	GD25	FN65	VF82
1-(Scarce)-Slam Bradley & Spy by Siegel & Shuster, Speed Saunders by Guardineer, Flat Foot Flannigan by Gustavson, Cosmo, the Phantom of Disguise, Buck Marshall, Bruce Nelson begin; Chin Lung in 'Claws of the Red Dragon' serial begins; Fu Manchu-c by Vincent Sullivan	4,800.00	12,000.00	24,000.00
(Estimated up to 30 total copies exist, 1 in NM/Mint)			
2 (Rare)-Craig Flessel-c begin; new logo	857.00	2570.00	6000.00
3 (Rare)	667.00	2000.00	4700.00

	GD25	FN65	NM94
4,5: 5-Larry Steele begins	400.00	1200.00	2800.00

Detective Comics #13, © DC

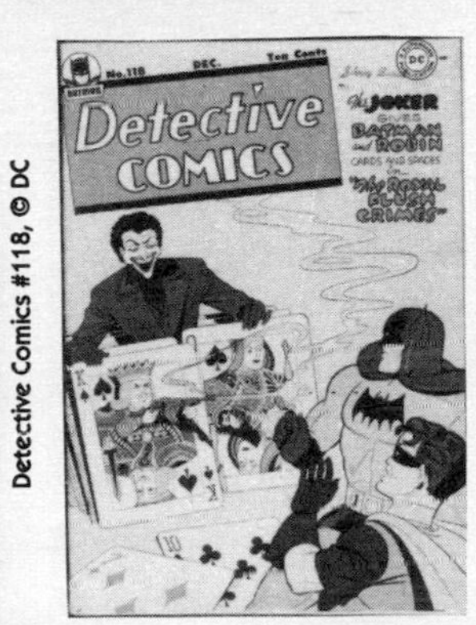

Detective Comics #118, © DC

Detective Comics #184, © DC

	GD25	FN65	NM94
6,7,9,10	257.00	770.00	1800.00
8-Mister Chang-c	315.00	945.00	2200.00
11-17,19: 17-1st app. Fu Manchu in Det.	230.00	685.00	1600.00
18-Fu Manchu-c; last Flessel-c	300.00	900.00	2100.00
20-The Crimson Avenger begins (1st app.)	357.00	1070.00	2500.00
21,23-25	170.00	515.00	1200.00
22-1st & only Crimson Avenger-c (12/38)	230.00	685.00	1600.00
26	170.00	515.00	1200.00

	GD25	FN65	NM94
27-The Batman & Commissioner Gordon begin (1st app.) by Bob Kane (5/39); Batman-c (1st)	11,500.00	34,500.00	63,250.00 92,000.00

(Estimated up to 50+ total copies exist, 3 in NM/Mint)

27-Reprint, Oversize 13-1/2"x10." WARNING: This comic is an exact duplicate reprint of the original except for its size. DC published it in 1974 with a second cover titling it as Famous First Edition. There have been many reported cases of the outer cover being removed and the interior sold as the original edition. The reprint with the new outer cover removed is practically worthless; see Famous First Edition for value.

	GD25	FN65	NM94
27(1984)-Oreo Cookies giveaway (32 pgs., paper-c, r-/Det. 27, 38 & Batman No. 1 (1st Joker)	4.35	13.00	26.00
28-2nd app. The Batman (6 pg. story)	900.00	2700.00	6300.00

	GD25	FN65	VF82	NM94
29-Batman-c; Doctor Death-c/story; Batman story now 10 pgs.	1250.00	3750.00	7875.00	12,500.00

(Estimated up to 75+ total copies exist, 6 in NM/Mint)

	GD25	FN65	NM94
30,32: 30-Dr. Death app. 32-Batman uses gun	450.00	1350.00	3000.00

	GD25	FN65	VF82	NM94
31-Classic Batman-c; 1st Julie Madison, Bat Plane (Bat-Gyro) & Batarang; 31,32-1st 2 part Batman story	1250.00	3750.00	7875.00	12,500.00

(Estimated up to 75+ total copies exist, 6 in NM/Mint)

33-Origin The Batman (1st told origin); Batman gunholster-c; Batman story now 12 pgs.	1800.00	5400.00	11,700.00	18,000.00

(Estimated up to 75+ total copies exist, 7 in NM/Mint)

	GD25	FN65	NM94
34-Steve Malone begins	350.00	1050.00	2300.00
35-Batman-c begin; hypo-c	585.00	1750.00	4000.00
36,37: 36-Origin & 1st app. Hugo Strange. 37-Cliff Crosby begins; last Batman solo story	417.00	1250.00	2800.00

	GD25	FN65	VF82	NM94
38-Origin/1st app. Robin the Boy Wonder (4/40)	1800.00	5400.00	11,700.00	18,000.00

(Estimated up to 85+ total copies exist, 9 in NM/Mint)

	GD25	FN65	NM94
39	367.00	1100.00	2400.00
40-Origin & 1st app. Clay Face (Basil Karlo); 1st Joker cover app. (6/40); Joker story intended for this issue was used in Batman #1 instead	433.00	1300.00	3000.00
41-Robin's 1st solo	233.00	700.00	1600.00
42-44: 44-Crimson Avenger-new costume	150.00	450.00	1050.00
45-1st Joker story in Det. (4th in all, 11/40)	242.00	725.00	1600.00
46-50: 48-1st time car called Batmobile; Gotham City 1st mention in Det. (1st mentioned in Wow #1). 49-Last Clay Face	135.00	405.00	900.00
51-57	108.00	325.00	700.00
58-1st Penguin app. (12/41); last Speed Saunders	267.00	800.00	1800.00
59-Last Steve Malone; 2nd Penguin; Wing becomes Crimson Avenger's aide	117.00	350.00	800.00
60-Intro. Air Wave; Joker app. (2nd in Det.)	117.00	350.00	800.00
61,63: 63-Last Cliff Crosby; 1st app. Mr. Baffle	100.00	300.00	700.00
62-Joker-c/story (2nd Joker-c, 4/42)	150.00	450.00	950.00
64-Origin & 1st app. Boy Commandos by Simon & Kirby (6/42); Joker app.	267.00	800.00	1800.00
65-1st Boy Commandos-c (S&K-a on Boy Commandos & Ray/Robinson-a on Batman & Robin on-c; 4 artists on one-c)	133.00	400.00	900.00
66-Origin & 1st app. Two-Face	200.00	600.00	1400.00
67-1st Penguin-c (9/42)	133.00	400.00	900.00
68-Two-Face-c/story; 1st Two-Face-c	100.00	300.00	700.00
69-Joker-c/story	117.00	350.00	750.00
70	87.00	260.00	580.00
71-Joker-c/story	105.00	312.00	650.00
72-75: 73-Scarecrow-c/story (1st Scarecrow-c). 74-1st Tweedledum & Tweedledee plus-c; S&K-a	80.00	240.00	520.00
76-Newsboy Legion & The Sandman x-over in Boy Commandos; S&K-a; Joker-c/story	121.00	362.00	800.00
77-79: All S&K-a	80.00	240.00	520.00
80-Two-Face app.; S&K-a	92.00	275.00	600.00
81,82,84,86-90: 81-1st Cavalier-c & app. 89-Last Crimson Avenger	71.00	212.00	460.00
83-1st "skinny" Alfred (2/44)(see Batman #21; last S&K Boy Commandos. (also #92,128), most issues #84 on signed S&K are not by them	80.00	240.00	520.00
85-Joker-c/story; Last Spy; Kirby/Klech Boy Commandos	93.00	280.00	600.00
91,102-Joker-c/story	87.00	260.00	550.00
92-98: 96-Alfred's last name 'Beagle' revealed, later changed to 'Pennyworth' in #214	64.00	192.00	410.00
99-Penguin-c	88.00	262.00	575.00
100 (6/45)	96.00	288.00	625.00
101,103-108,110-113,115-117,119: 108-1st Bat-signal-c (2/46). 114-1st small logo (8/46)	58.00	175.00	375.00
109,114,118-Joker-c/stories	80.00	240.00	520.00
120-Penguin-c (white-c, rare above fine)	92.00	275.00	600.00
121,123,125,127,129,130	56.00	168.00	375.00
122-1st Catwoman-c(4/47).	85.00	257.00	600.00
124,128-Joker-c/stories	73.00	220.00	475.00
126 Penguin-c	79.00	238.00	525.00
131-136,139: 135-Frankenstein-c/story	48.00	142.00	300.00
137-Joker-c/story; last Air Wave	64.00	192.00	400.00
138-Origin Robotman (see Star Spangled #7 for 1st app.); series ends #202	85.00	257.00	600.00
140-The Riddler-c/story (1st app., 10/48)	200.00	600.00	1400.00
141,143-148,150: 150-Last Boy Commandos	50.00	150.00	330.00
142-2nd Riddler-c/story	80.00	238.00	525.00
149-Joker-c/story	67.00	200.00	425.00
151 Origin & 1st app. Pow Wow Smith, Indian lawman (9/49) & begins series	55.00	162.00	365.00
152,154,155,157-160: 152-Last Slam Bradley	50.00	150.00	330.00
153-1st Roy Raymond app. (11/49); origin The Human Fly	55.00	162.00	350.00
156(2/50)-The new classic Batmobile	62.00	188.00	400.00
161-167,169,170,172-176: Last 52 pgs.	55.00	162.00	350.00
168-Origin the Joker	235.00	585.00	1600.00
171-Penguin-c	75.00	225.00	475.00
177-179,181-186,188,189,191,192,194-199,201,202,204,206-210,212,214-216: 185-Secret of Batman's utility belt. 187-Two-Face app. 202-Last Robotman & Pow Wow Smith. 216-Last precode (2/55)	39.00	118.00	265.00
180,193-Joker-c/story	41.00	122.00	275.00
187-Two-Face-c	41.00	122.00	275.00
190-Origin Batman retold	55.00	162.00	365.00
200	50.00	150.00	350.00
203,211-Catwoman-c	41.00	102.00	275.00
205-Origin Batcave	55.00	135.00	350.00
213-Origin Mirror Man	48.00	120.00	310.00
217-224	29.00	86.00	200.00

	GD25	FN65	VF82	NM94
225-(11/55)-1st app. Martian Manhunter-John Jones, later changed to J'onn J'onzz; origin begins; also see Batman #78	233.00	700.00	2100.00	3500.00

	GD25	FN65	NM94
226-Origin Martian Manhunter continued	107.00	321.00	750.00
227-229	43.00	129.00	300.00
230-1st app. Mad Hatter; brief recap origin of Martian Manhunter			

Detective Comics #296, © DC

Detective Comics #596, © DC

Detective Comics #665, © DC

GD25 FN65 NM94

49.00 146.00 340.00
231-Brief origin recap Martian Manhunter 29.00 86.00 200.00
232,234,237-240: 239-Early DC grey tone-c (1/57, see Showcase #3)
27.00 80.00 190.00
233-Origin & 1st app. Batwoman (7/56) 114.00 343.00 800.00
235-Origin Batman & his costume 50.00 150.00 350.00
236-J'onn J'onzz talks to parents and Mars-1st since being stranded on earth 32.00 96.00 225.00
241-260: 246-Intro. Diane Meade, John Jones' girl. 249-4th app. Batwoman. 254-Bat-Hound-c/story. 257-Intro. & 1st app. Whirly Bats
22.00 65.00 150.00
261-J. Jones tie-in to sci/fi movie "Incredible Shrinking Man"
16.00 50.00 115.00
262-264,266,269,270: 261-1st app. Dr. Double X. 262-Origin Jackal
16.00 50.00 115.00
265-Batman's origin retold with new facts 26.00 77.00 180.00
267-Origin & 1st app. Bat-Mite (5/59) 23.00 70.00 160.00
268,271-Manhunter origin recap 16.00 50.00 115.00
272,274-280: 276-2nd Bat-Mite 11.50 34.00 80.00
273-J'onn J'onzz i.d. revealed for 1st time 13.00 40.00 90.00
281-292, 294-297: 287-Origin J'onn J'onzz retold. 292-Last Roy Raymond. 297-Last 10 cent issue (11/61) 9.00 28.00 65.00
293-(7/61)-Aquaman begins (pre #1); ends #300 10.00 30.00 70.00
298-(12/61)-1st modern Clayface (Matt Hagen) 18.00 54.00 125.00
299,300(2/62) 7.00 21.00 50.00
301(3/62)-J'onn J'onzz returns to Mars (1st since stranded on earth 6 years before) 6.50 19.00 45.00
302-326,329,330: 311-Intro. Zook in John Jones; 1st app. Cat-Man. 318,325-Cat-Man-c/story (2nd & 3rd app.); also 1st & 2nd app. Batwoman as the Cat-Woman. 322-Bat-Girl's 1st/only app. in Det.; Batman cameo in J'onn J'onzz (only hero to app. in series). 326-Last J'onn J'onzz, story cont'd in H.O.M. #143; intro. Idol-Head of Diabolu 4.70 14.00 33.00
327(5/64)-Elongated Man begins, ends #383; 1st new look Batman with new costume; Infantino/Giella new look-a begins 7.00 21.00 50.00
328-Death of Alfred; Bob Kane biog, 2pg. 9.00 26.00 60.00
331,333-340,342-358,360-364,366-368,370: 334-1st app. The Outsider. 345-Intro Block Buster. 347-"What If" theme story (1/66). 351-Elongated Man new costume. 355-Zatanna x-over in Elongated Man. 356-Alfred brought back in Batman. 362,364,377-S.A. Riddler app. (early). 363-2nd app. new Batgirl. 370-1st Neal Adams-a on Batman (cover only, 12/67)
3.25 9.50 22.00
332,341,365-Joker-c/stories 4.00 12.00 28.00
359-Intro/origin new Batgirl-c/story (1/67) 4.50 14.00 32.00
369(11/67)-N. Adams-a (Elongated Man); 3rd app. S.A. Catwoman (cameo; leads into Batman #197); 3rd app. new Batgirl 5.00 16.00 37.00
371-1st new Batmobile from TV show (1/68) 3.25 9.50 22.00
372-386,389,390: 375-New Batmobile-c 1.70 5.00 12.00
387-r/1st Batman story from #27; Joker-c; last 12 cent issue
4.70 14.00 33.00
388-Joker-c/story 3.20 8.00 20.00
391-394,396,398,399,401,403,405,406,409: 392-1st app. Jason Bard. 401-2nd Batgirl/Robin team-up 1.65 4.70 11.00
395,397,402,404,407,408,410-Neal Adams-a 2.15 6.50 15.00
400-(6/70)-Origin & 1st app. Man-Bat; 1st Batgirl/Robin team-up; Neal Adams-a 4.00 12.00 28.00
411-420: 413-Last 15 cent issue. 414-25 cent, 52 pgs. begin, end #424. 418-Creeper x-over 1.50 3.75 9.00
421-436: 424-Last Batgirl; 1st She-Bat. 426,430,436-Elongated Man app. 428,434-Hawkman begins, ends #467 1.30 3.25 8.00
437-New Manhunter begins (1st app.) by Simonson, ends #443
1.70 5.00 12.00
438-445 (All 100 pgs.): 439-Origin Manhunter. 440-G.A. Manhunter, Hawkman, Dollman, Gr. Lantern; Toth-a. 441-G.A. Plastic Man, Batman, Ibis-r. 442-G.A. Newsboy Legion, Bl. Canary, Elongated Man, Dr. Fate-r. 443-Origin The Creeper-r; death of Manhunter; G.A. Green Lantern, Spectre-r; Batman-r/ Batman #18. 444-G.A. Kid Eternity-r. 445-G.A. Dr. Midnite-r

GD25 FN65 NM94

1.65 4.00 10.00
446-460: 457-Origin retold & updated 1.20 3.00 7.00
461-465,469,470,480: 480-(44 pgs.). 463,464-1st app. Black Spider
1.00 2.50 5.50
466-468,471-474,478,479-Rogers-a in all. 466-1st app. Signalman since Batman #139. 469-Intro/origin Dr. Phosphorous. 470,471-1st modern app. Hugo Strange. 474-1st app. new Deadshot. 478-1st app. 3rd Clayface (Preston Payne). 479-(44 pgs.) 1.70 5.00 12.00
475,476-Joker-c/stories; Rogers-a 3.20 8.00 20.00
477-Neal Adams-a(r); Rogers-a, 3pgs. 2.15 6.50 15.00
481-(Combined with Batman Family, 12-1/78-79, begin $1.00, 68 pg. issues, ends #495); 481-495-Batgirl, Robin solo stories 1.65 4.00 10.00
482-Starlin/Russell, Golden-a; The Demon begins (origin-r), ends #485 (by Ditko #483-485) 1.20 3.00 7.00
483-40th Anniversary issue; origin retold; Newton Batman begins
1.30 3.25 8.00
484-499: 484-Origin Robin. 485-Death of Batwoman. 487-The Odd Man by Ditko. 489-Robin/Batgirl team-up. 490-Black Lightning begins. 491-(#492 on inside) 1.60 4.00
500-($1.50)-Batman/Deadman team-up; new Hawkman story by Joe Kubert 1.50 3.75 9.00
501-503,505-523: 512-2nd app. new Dr. Death. 519-Last Batgirl. 521-Green Arrow series begins. 523-Solomon Grundy app. 1.40 3.50
504-Joker-c/story 1.10 2.70 6.50
524-2nd app. Jason Todd (cameo)(3/83) 1.80 4.50
525-3rd app. Jason Todd (See Batman #357) 1.40 3.50
526-Batman's 500th app. in Detective Comics ($1.50, 68pgs.); contains 55 pg. Joker story; Bob Kane pin-up 1.65 4.70 11.00
527-531,533,534,536-568,571,573: 542-Jason Todd quits as Robin (becomes Robin again #547). 549,550-Alan Moore scripts (Gr. Arrow). 554-1st new Black Canary. 566-Batman villains profiled. 567-Harlan Ellison scripts 1.00 2.50
532,569,570-Joker-c/stories 1.00 2.50 5.50
535-Intro new Robin (Jason Todd)-1st appeared in Batman
1.00 2.50 5.50
572 ($1.25, 60 pgs.)-50th Anniversary of Det. 1.40 3.50
574-Origin Batman & Jason Todd retold 1.00 2.00 5.00
575-Year 2 begins, ends #578 2.00 6.00 14.00
576-578: McFarlane-c/a 1.70 5.00 12.00
579-597,601-610: 579-New bat wing logo. 589-595-(52 pgs.)-Each contain free 16 pg. Batman stories. 604-607-Mudpack storyline; 604,607-Contain Batman mini-posters. 610-Faked death of Penguin; artists names app. on tombstone on-c 1.50
598-($2.95, 84 pgs.)-"Blind Justice" storyline begins by Batman movie writer Sam Hamm, ends #600 1.00 2.50 6.00
599 1.60 4.00
600-($2.95, 84 pgs.)-50th Anniversary of Batman in Det.; 1 pg. Neal Adams pin-up, among other artists 1.00 2.50 6.00
611-626,628-658: 612-1st new look Cat-Man; Catwoman app. 615-"The Penguin Affair" part 2 (See Batman #448,449). 617-Joker-c/story. 624-1st new Catwoman (w/death) & 1st new Batwoman. 642-Return of Scarface, part 2. 644-Last $1.00-c. 652,653-Huntress-c/story w/new costume plus Travis Charest-c on both 1.25
627-($2.95, 84 pgs.)-Batman's 600th app. in Det.; reprints 1st story/#27 plus 3 versions (2 new) of same story 1.40 3.50
659-Knightfall part 2; Kelley Jones-c 1.00 2.00 5.00
660-Knightfall part 4; Bane-c by Sam Kieth 2.15 6.50 15.00
661-Knightfall part 6; brief Joker & Riddler app. 1.65 4.00 10.00
662-Knightfall part 8; Riddler app.; Sam Kieth-c 1.00 2.00 5.00
663-Knightfall part 10; Kelley Jones-c 1.60 4.00
664-Knightfall part 12; Bane-c/story; Joker app.; continued in Showcase 93 #7 & 8; Jones-c 1.60 4.00
665,666-Knightfall parts 16 & 18; 666-Bane-c/story 1.60 4.00
667-Knightquest: The Crusade & new Batman begins (1st app. in Batman #500) 1.25
668-668: 668-Continues in Robin #1 1.25

Detective Comics Annual #6, © DC

Devil Dinosaur #5, © MEG

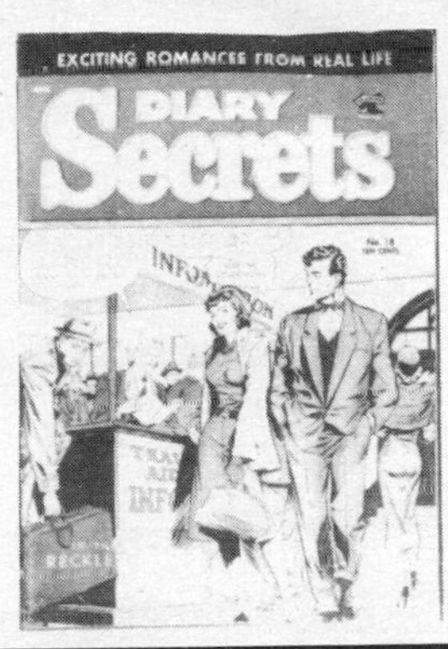

Diary Secrets #18, © STJ

	GD25	FN65	NM94
669-672: 669-Begin $1.50-c			1.50
Annual 1(1988, $1.50)	1.00	2.00	5.00
Annual 2(1989, $2.00, 68 pgs.)		1.60	4.00
Annual 3(1990, $2.00, 68 pgs.)		.80	2.00
Annual 4(1991, $2.00, 68 pgs.) Painted-c		.80	2.00
Annual 5(1992, $2.50, 68 pgs.)-Joker-c/story (54 pgs.) continued in Robin Annual #1; Sam Kieth-c; Eclipso app.		1.00	2.50
Annual 6(1993, $2.50, 68 pgs.)-Azrael as Batman in new costume; intro Geist the Twilight Man; Bloodlines storyline		1.00	2.50

NOTE: ***Neal Adams** c-370, 372, 383, 385, 389, 391, 392, 394-422, 439. **Aparo** a-437, 438, 444-446, 500, 625-632p, 638-641p; c-430, 437, 440-446, 448, 468-470, 480, 484(back), 492-502,508, 509, 515, 518-522, 641. **Austin** a(i)-450, 451, 463-468, 471-476; c(i)-474-476, 478. **Baily** a-443r. **Buckler** a-434, 446p, 479p; c(p)-467, 482, 505, 506, 511, 513-516, 518. **Burnley** a(Batman)-65, 75, 83, 100, 103, 125; c-62i, 63i, 64, 73i, 78, 83p, 96p, 103p, 105p, 108, 121p, 123p, 125p. **Colan** a(p)-510, 512, 517, 523, 528-538, 540-546, 555-567; c(p)-510, 512, 528, 530-535, 537, 538, 540, 541, 543-545, 556-558, 560-561. **J. Craig** a-488. **Ditko** a-443r, 483-405, 487. **Golden** a-482p. **Alan Grant** scripts-584-597, 601-621, 641, 642, Annual 5. **Grell** a-445, 455, 463p, 464p; c-455. **Guardineer** c-23, 24, 26, 28, 30, 32. **Gustavson** a-441r. **Infantino/Anderson** c-333, 337-340, 343, 344, 347, 351, 352, 359, 361-368, 371. **Kelley Jones** c-651, 659, 661, 663-668. **Kaluta** c-423, 424, 426-428, 431, 434, 438, 484, 486, 572. **Bob Kane** a-Most early issues #27 on, 297r, 356r, 438-440r, 442r, 443r. **Gil Kane** a(p)-368, 370-374, 384, 385, 388-407, 438r, 439r, 520. **Kane/Anderson** c-369. **Sam Kieth** c-654-656 (657, 658 w/**Kelley Jones**), 660, 662, Annual #5. **Kubert** a-438r, 439r, 500; c-348, 350. **McFarlane** c/a(p) 576-578. **Meskin** a-420r. **Moldoff** c-233-354, 259, 266, 267, 275, 287, 289, 290, 297, 300. **Moldoff/Giella** a-328, 330, 332, 334, 336, 338, 340, 342, 344, 346, 348, 350, 352, 354, 356. **Mooney** a-444r. **Moreira** a-153-300, 419r, 444r, 445r. **Newton** a(p)-480, 481, 483-499, 501-509, 511, 513-516, 518-520, 524, 526, 539; c-526p. **Irv Novick** c-375-377. **Robbins** a-426p, 429p. **Robinson** a-part: 66, 68, 71-73; all: 74-76, 79, 80; c-62, 64, 66, 68-74, 76, 79, 82, 86, 88, 442r, 443r. **Rogers** a-466-468, 471-479p, 481p; c-471p, 472p, 473, 474-479p. **Roussos** Airwave-76-105(most); c(i) 71, 72, 74-76, 79, 107. **Russell** a-481i, 482i. **Simon/Kirby** a-440r, 442r. **Simonson** a-437-443, 450, 469, 470, 500. **Dick Sprang** c-77, 82, 84, 85, 87, 89-93, 95-100, 102, 103i, 104i, 106, 108, 114, 117, 118, 122, 123, 128, 129, 131, 133, 135, 141, 148, 149, 168, 622-624. **Starlin** a-481p, 482p; c-503, 504, 567p. **Starr** a-444r. **Toth** r-414, 416, 418, 424, 440-444. **Tuska** a-486p, 490p. **Wrightson** c-425.*

DETECTIVE DAN, SECRET OP. 48
1933 (36 pgs.; 9-1/2x12") (B&W; Softcover)
Humor Publ. Co.

	GD25	FN65	NM94
nn-By Norman Marsh; forerunner of Dan Dunn	13.00	40.00	90.00

DETECTIVE EYE (See Keen Detective Funnies)
Nov, 1940 - No. 2, Dec, 1940
Centaur Publications

	GD25	FN65	NM94
1-Air Man & The Eye Sees begins; The Masked Marvel app.	125.00	375.00	825.00
2-Origin Don Rance and the Mysticape; Binder-a; Frank Thomas-c	87.00	262.00	600.00

DETECTIVE PICTURE STORIES (Keen Detective Funnies No. 8 on?)
Dec, 1936 - No. 7, 1937 (1st comic of a single theme)
Comics Magazine Company

	GD25	FN65	NM94
1	185.00	557.00	1300.00
2-The Clock app. (early app.)	79.00	235.00	550.00
3,4: 4-Eisner-a	73.00	216.00	500.00
5-7: 5-Kane-a; 6,7 (Exist)?	67.00	200.00	450.00

DETECTIVES, THE (See 4-Color No. 1168, 1219, 1240)

DETECTIVES, INC. (Eclipse)(Value: cover or less)

DEVIL DINOSAUR
April, 1978 - No. 9, Dec, 1978
Marvel Comics Group

	GD25	FN65	NM94
1-9: Kirby/Royer-a in all; all have Kirby-c			1.50

DEVIL-DOG DUGAN (Tales of the Marines No. 4 on)
July, 1956 - No. 3, Nov, 1956
Atlas Comics (OPI)

	GD25	FN65	NM94
1-Severin-c	5.85	17.50	35.00
2-Iron Mike McGraw x-over; Severin-c	4.20	12.50	25.00
3	3.60	9.00	18.00

DEVIL DOGS
1942
Street & Smith Publishers

	GD25	FN65	NM94
1-Boy Rangers, U.S. Marines	17.00	50.00	120.00

DEVILINA
Feb, 1975 - No. 2, May, 1975 (Magazine) (B&W)
Atlas/Seaboard

	GD25	FN65	NM94
1,2: 1-Reese-a		1.20	3.00

DEVIL KIDS STARRING HOT STUFF
July, 1962 - No. 107, Oct, 1981 (Giant-Size #41-55)
Harvey Publications (Illustrated Humor)

	GD25	FN65	NM94
1	11.00	32.00	75.00
2	5.85	17.50	35.00
3-10 (1/64)	4.00	10.00	20.00
11-20	2.40	6.00	12.00
21-30	1.60	4.00	8.00
31-40 ('71)	1.20	3.50	7.00
41-50: All 68 pg. Giants	1.80	4.50	9.00
51-55: All 52 pg. Giants	1.20	4.00	8.00
56-70	1.00	2.00	5.00
71-90		1.20	3.00
91-107			1.50

DEXTER COMICS
Summer, 1948 - No. 5, July, 1949
Dearfield Publ.

	GD25	FN65	NM94
1-Teen-age humor	5.00	15.00	30.00
2-Junie Prom app.	4.00	12.00	24.00
3-5	3.20	8.00	16.00

DEXTER THE DEMON (Formerly Melvin The Monster)
No. 7, Sept, 1957 (Also see Cartoon Kids & Peter the Little Pest)
Atlas Comics (HPC)

	GD25	FN65	NM94
7	3.60	9.00	18.00

DIARY CONFESSIONS (Formerly Ideal Romance)
No. 9, May, 1955 - No. 14, April, 1955
Stanmor/Key Publ.(Medal Comics)

	GD25	FN65	NM94
9	4.00	11.00	22.00
10-14	2.80	7.00	14.00

DIARY LOVES (Formerly Love Diary #1; G. I. Sweethearts #32 on)
No. 2, Nov, 1949 - No. 31, April, 1953
Quality Comics Group

	GD25	FN65	NM94
2-Ward-c/a, 9 pgs.	10.00	30.00	60.00
3 (1/50)	4.00	10.50	21.00
4-Crandall-a	5.70	17.00	34.00
5-7,10	3.00	7.50	15.00
8,9-Ward-a 6,8 pgs. plus Gustavson-#8	6.70	20.00	40.00
11,13,14,17-20	2.40	6.00	12.00
12,15,16-Ward-a 9,7,8 pgs.	5.70	17.00	34.00
21-Ward-a, 7 pgs.	4.70	14.00	28.00
22-31: 31-Whitney-a	1.80	4.50	9.00

NOTE: *Photo c-3-5, 8, 12-27.*

DIARY OF HORROR
December, 1952
Avon Periodicals

	GD25	FN65	NM94
1-Hollingsworth-c/a; bondage-c	22.00	65.00	150.00

DIARY SECRETS (Formerly Teen-Age Diary Secrets)
No. 10, Feb, 1952 - No. 30, Sept, 1955
St. John Publishing Co.

	GD25	FN65	NM94
10-Baker-c/a most issues	8.35	25.00	50.00
11-16,18,10	6.35	19.00	38.00
17,20-Kubert-a	7.00	21.00	42.00
21-30: 28-Last precode (3/55)	4.00	12.00	24.00

(See Giant Comics Edition for Annual)

Dick Cole #6 (Accepted), © STAR

Dick Tracy #52, © Tribune Media Services

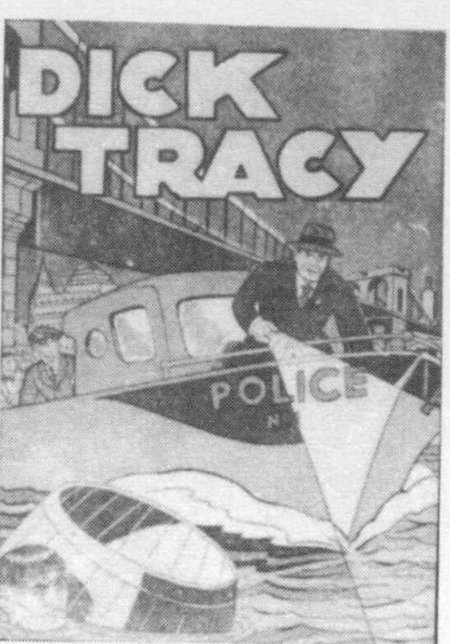

Dick Tracy Popped Wheat Giveaway, © Tribune Media Services

GD25 FN65 NM94 GD25 FN65 NM94

DICK COLE (Sport Thrills No. 11 on)(See Blue Bolt & Four Most #1)
Dec-Jan, 1948-49 - No. 10, June-July, 1950
Curtis Publ./Star Publications

	GD25	FN65	NM94
1-Sgt. Spook; L. B. Cole-c; McWilliams-a; Curt Swan's 1st work	11.00	32.00	75.00
2	7.00	21.00	42.00
3-10: 10-Joe Louis story	5.85	17.50	35.00
Accepted Reprint #7(V1#6 on-c)(1950's)-Reprints #7; L.B. Cole-c	4.00	11.00	22.00
Accepted Reprint #9(nd)-(Reprints #9 & #8-c)	4.00	11.00	22.00

*NOTE: **L. B. Cole** c-1, 3, 4, 6-10. **Al McWilliams** a-6. Dick Cole in 1-9. Baseball c-10. Basketball c-9. Football c-8.*

DICKIE DARE
1941 - No. 4, 1942 (#3 on sale 6/15/42)
Eastern Color Printing Co.

	GD25	FN65	NM94
1-Caniff-a, Everett-c	27.00	82.00	185.00
2	16.00	48.00	115.00
3,4-Half Scorchy Smith by Noel Sickles who was very influential in Milton Caniff's development	17.00	50.00	120.00

DICK POWELL (See A-1 Comics No. 22)

DICK QUICK, ACE REPORTER (See Picture News #10)

DICK'S ADVENTURES IN DREAMLAND (See 4-Color No. 245)

DICK TRACY (See Famous Feature Stories, Harvey Comics Library, Limited Collectors' Ed., Mammoth Comics, Merry Christmas, The Original..., Popular Comics, Super Book No. 1, 7, 13, 25, Super Comics & Tastee-Freez)

DICK TRACY
May, 1937 - Jan, 1938
David McKay Publications

Feature Books nn - 100 pgs., partially reprinted as 4-Color No. 1 (appeared before Large Feature Comics, 1st Dick Tracy comic book)
(Very Rare-three known copies)

	GD25	FN65	NM94
Estimated Value....	535.00	1500.00	3500.00
Feature Books 4 - Reprints nn issue but with new cover added	100.00	300.00	700.00
Feature Books 6,9	79.00	235.00	550.00

DICK TRACY (...Monthly #1-24)
1939 - No. 24, Dec, 1949
Dell Publishing Co.

	GD25	FN65	NM94
Large Feature Comic 1(1939)	115.00	345.00	800.00
Large Feature Comic 4	64.00	195.00	450.00
Large Feature Comic 8,11,13,15	57.00	170.00	400.00

	GD25	FN65	VF82	NM94
4-Color 1(1939)('35-r)	400.00	1200.00	2600.00	4000.00

(Estimated up to 75+ total copies exist, 5 in NM/Mint)

	GD25	FN65	NM94
4-Color 6(1940)('37-r)-(Scarce)	129.00	385.00	900.00
4-Color 8(1940)('38-'39-r)	75.00	225.00	525.00
Large Feature Comic 3(1941, Series II)	57.00	170.00	400.00
4-Color 21('41)('38-r)	64.00	195.00	450.00
4-Color 34('43)('39-'40-r)	43.00	130.00	300.00
4-Color 56('44)('40-r)	34.00	105.00	240.00
4-Color 96('46)('40-r)	26.00	78.00	180.00
4-Color 133('47)('40-'41-r)	22.00	65.00	150.00
4-Color 163('47)('41-r)	17.00	52.00	120.00
4-Color 215('48)-Titled "Sparkle Plenty," Tracy-r	10.00	30.00	70.00
1(1/48)('34-r)	43.00	130.00	300.00
2,3	24.00	73.00	150.00
4-10	22.00	65.00	150.00
11-18: 13-Bondage-c	14.00	43.00	100.00
19-1st app. Sparkle Plenty, B.O. Plenty & Gravel Gertie in a 3-pg. strip not by Gould	16.00	48.00	110.00
20-1st app. Sam Catchem; c/a not by Gould	12.00	36.00	85.00
21-24-Only 2 pg. Gould-a in each	12.00	36.00	85.00

*NOTE: No. 19-24 have a 2 pg. biography of a famous villain illustrated by **Gould**: 19-Little Face; 20-Flattop; 21-Breathless Mahoney; 22-Measles; 23-Itchy; 24-The Brow.*

DICK TRACY (Continued from Dell series)(...Comics Monthly #25-140)
No. 25, Mar, 1950 - No. 145, April, 1961
Harvey Publications

	GD25	FN65	NM94
25	17.00	52.00	120.00
26-28,30: 28-Bondage-c	12.00	36.00	85.00
29-1st app. Gravel Gertie in a Gould-r	16.00	48.00	110.00
31,32,34,35,37-40: 40-Intro/origin 2-way wrist radio (6/51)	11.00	32.00	75.00
33-"Measles the Teen-Age Dope Pusher"	12.00	36.00	85.00
36-1st app. B.O. Plenty in a Gould-r	12.00	36.00	85.00
41-50	9.30	28.00	65.00
51-56,58-80: 51-2pgs Powell-a	8.50	25.50	60.00
57-1st app. Sam Catchem in a Gould-r	11.00	32.00	75.00
81-99,101-140	7.50	22.50	45.00
100	8.35	25.00	50.00
141-145 (25 cents)(titled "Dick Tracy")	7.00	21.00	42.00

*NOTE: **Powell** a(1-2pgs.)-43, 44, 104, 108, 109, 145. No. 110-120, 141-145 are all reprints from earlier issues.*

DICK TRACY (Blackthorne)(Value: cover or less)

DICK TRACY (Disney)(Value: cover or less)

DICK TRACY ADVENTURES (Gladstone)(Value: cover or less)

DICK TRACY & DICK TRACY JR. CAUGHT THE RACKETEERS, HOW
1933 (88 pages) (7x8-1/2") (Hardcover)
Cupples & Leon Co.

	GD25	FN65	NM94
2-(numbered on pg. 84)-Continuation of Stooge Viller book (daily strip reprints from 8/3/33 thru 11/8/33) (Rarer than No. 1)	43.00	130.00	300.00
with dust jacket....	60.00	180.00	420.00
Book 2 (32 pgs.; soft-c; has strips 9/18/33-11/8/33)	19.00	57.00	132.00

DICK TRACY & DICK TRACY JR. AND HOW THEY CAPTURED "STOOGE" VILLER (See Treasure Box of Famous Comics)
1933 (7x8-1/2") (Hard cover; One Shot; 100 pgs.)
Reprints 1932 & 1933 Dick Tracy daily strips
Cupples & Leon Co.

	GD25	FN65	NM94
nn(No.1)-1st app. of "Stooge" Viller	34.00	105.00	240.00
with dust jacket....	46.00	140.00	325.00

DICK TRACY, EXPLOITS OF
1946 (Strip reprints) (Hardcover) ($1.00)
Rosdon Books, Inc.

	GD25	FN65	NM94
1-Reprints the near complete case of "The Brow" from 6/12/44 to 9/24/44 (story starts a few weeks late)	22.00	65.00	150.00
with dust jacket....	36.00	107.00	250.00

DICK TRACY GIVEAWAYS
1939 - 1958; 1990

	GD25	FN65	NM94
Buster Brown Shoes Giveaway (1940s?, 36 pgs. in color); 1938-39-r by Gould	25.00	75.00	175.00
Gillmore Giveaway (See Superbook)			
...Hatful of Fun (No date, 1950-52, 32pgs.; 8-1/2x10")-Dick Tracy hat promotion; Dick Tracy games, magic tricks. Miller Bros. premium	11.00	32.00	75.00
Motorola Giveaway (1953)-Reprints Harvey Comics Library #2	4.00	12.00	24.00
Original Dick Tracy by Chester Gould, The (Aug, 1990, 16 pgs., 5-1/2x8-1/2")-Gladstone Publ.; Bread Giveaway	4.00	10.00	20.00
Popped Wheat Giveaway (1947, 16 pgs. in color)-'40-r; Sig Feuchtwanger Publ.; Gould-a	2.00	5.00	10.00
...Presents the Family Fun Book; Tip Top Bread Giveaway, no date or number (1940, Fawcett Publ., 16 pgs. in color)-Spy Smasher, Ibis, Lance O'Casey app.	54.00	160.00	375.00

Die-Cut #1, © MEG

Dinky Duck #1, © STJ

Dirty Pair II #1, © Haruka Takachiho

GD25 FN65 NM94

Same as above but without app. of heroes & Dick Tracy on cover only 10.00 30.00 60.00
Service Station Giveaway (1958, 16 pgs. in color)(regular size, slick cover)-Harvey Info. Press 3.20 8.00 16.00
Shoe Store Giveaway (Weatherbird)(1939, 16 pgs.)-Gould-a 11.00 32.00 75.00

DICK TRACY MONTHLY/WEEKLY
May, 1986 - No. 99, 1989 ($2.00, B&W) (Becomes Weekly #26 on)
Blackthorne Publishing
1-99: Gould-r. 30,31-Mr. Crime app. .40 1.00 2.00
NOTE: *#1-10 reprint strips 3/10/40-7/13/41; #10(pg.8)-51 reprint strips 4/6/49-12/31/55; #52-99 reprint strips 12/26/56-4/26/64.*

DICK TRACY SHEDS LIGHT ON THE MOLE
1949 (16 pgs.) (Ray-O-Vac Flashlights giveaway)
Western Printing Co.
nn-Not by Gould 5.85 17.50 35.00

DICK TRACY SPECIAL (Blackthorne)(Value: cover or less)

DICK TRACY: THE EARLY YEARS (Blackthorne)(Value: cover or less)

DICK TRACY UNPRINTED STORIES (Blackthorne)(Value: cover or less)

DICK TURPIN (See Legend of Young...)

DICK WINGATE OF THE U.S. NAVY
1951; 1953 (no month)
Superior Publ./Toby Press
nn-U.S. Navy giveaway 2.00 5.00 10.00
1(1953, Toby) 3.20 8.00 16.00

DIE-CUT
Nov, 1993 - No. 4, Feb, 1994 ($1.75, color, mini-series)
Marvel Comics UK, Ltd
1-($2.50)-Die-cut-c; The Beast app. 1.00 2.50
2-4 .70 1.75

DIE-CUT VS. G-FORCE
Nov, 1993 - No. 2, Dec, 1993 ($2.75, color, mini-series)
Marvel Comics UK, Ltd
1,2-($2.75)-Gold foil-c on both 1.10 2.75

DIE, MONSTER, DIE (See Movie Classics)

DIG 'EM
1973 (16 pgs.) (2-3/8x6")
Kellogg's Sugar Smacks Giveaway
nn-4 different issues 1.60 4.00

DIGITEK
Dec, 1992 - No. 4, Mar, 1993 ($1.95/$2.25, color, mini-series)
Marvel Comics UK, Ltd
1-4: 1,2 ($1.95). 3,4 ($2.25): 3-Deathlock-c/story .80 2.00

DILLY (Dilly Duncan from Daredevil Comics; see Boy Comics #57)
May, 1953 - No. 3, Sept, 1953
Lev Gleason Publications
1-Biro-c 4.00 11.00 22.00
2,3-Biro-c 2.80 7.00 14.00

DILTON'S STRANGE SCIENCE (See Pep Comics #78)
May, 1989 - No. 5, May, 1990 (.75-$1.00, color)
Archie Comics
1-5 1.00

DIME COMICS
1945; 1951
Newsbook Publ. Corp.
1-Silver Streak app., L. B. Cole-c 14.00 43.00 100.00
1(1951), 5 3.00 7.50 15.00

DINGBATS (See 1st Issue Special)

GD25 FN65 NM94

DING DONG
Summer?, 1946 - No. 5, 1947 (52 pgs.)
Compix/Magazine Enterprises
1-Funny animal 10.00 30.00 70.00
2 (11/46) 5.85 17.50 35.00
3 (Wint '46-'47) - 5 4.70 14.00 28.00

DINKY DUCK (Paul Terry's...) (See Blue Ribbon & New Terrytoons)
Nov, 1951 - No. 16, Sept, 1955; No. 16, Fall, 1956; No. 17, May, 1957 - No. 19, Summer, 1958
St. John Publishing Co./Pines No. 16 on
1 6.70 20.00 40.00
2 4.00 10.00 20.00
3-10 2.40 6.00 12.00
11-16(9/55) 1.80 4.50 9.00
16(Fall,'56) - 19 1.40 3.50 7.00

DINKY DUCK & HASHIMOTO-SAN (See Deputy Dawg Presents...)

DINO (TV)(The Flintstones)
Aug, 1973 - No. 20, Jan, 1977
Charlton Publications
1 1.00 2.50 6.00
2-20 1.20 3.00

DINO ISLAND
Feb, 1994 - No. 2, Feb, 1994 ($2.75, color, limited series)
Mirage Studios
1,2 1.10 2.75

DINO RIDERS
Feb, 1989 - No. 3, 1989 ($1.00, color)
Marvel Comics
1-3: Based on toys 1.00

DINOSAUR REX (Fantagraphics)(Value: cover or less)

DINOSAURUS (See 4-Color No. 1120)

DINOSAURS ATTACK! THE GRAPHIC NOVEL
1991 - Book 3, 1992 ($3.95, color, mini-series, coated stock, stiff-c)
Eclipse Comics
Book One - Three: Based on Topps trading cards 1.60 4.00

DINOSAURS GRAPHIC NOVEL (TV)
1992 - No. 2, 1993 ($2.95, color, 52 pgs.)
Disney Comics
1,2-Staton-a; based on Dinosaurs TV show 1.20 3.00

DIPPY DUCK
October, 1957
Atlas Comics (OPI)
1-Maneely-a; code approved 4.70 14.00 28.00

DIRECTORY TO A NONEXISTENT UNIVERSE (Eclipse)(Value: cover or less)

DIRTY DOZEN (See Movie Classics)

DIRTY PAIR
Dec, 1988 - No. 4, April, 1989 ($2.00, B&W, mini-series)
Eclipse Comics
1-4: Japanese manga with original stories .80 2.00

DIRTY PAIR II
June, 1989 - No. 5, Mar, 1990 ($2.00, B&W, mini-series)
Eclipse Comics
1-5: 3-Cover is misnumbered as #1 .80 2.00

DIRTY PAIR III, THE
Aug, 1990 - No. 5, Aug, 1991 ($2.00, B&W, mini-series)
Eclipse Comics
1,2 .40 1.00 2.00
3-5: ($2.25-c) .45 1.15 2.25

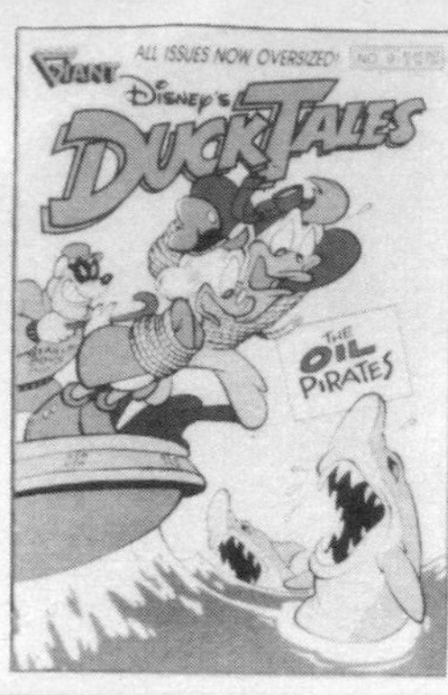

Disney's Ducktales #9, © The Disney Co.

DNAgents #15, © Mark Evanier & Will Meugniot

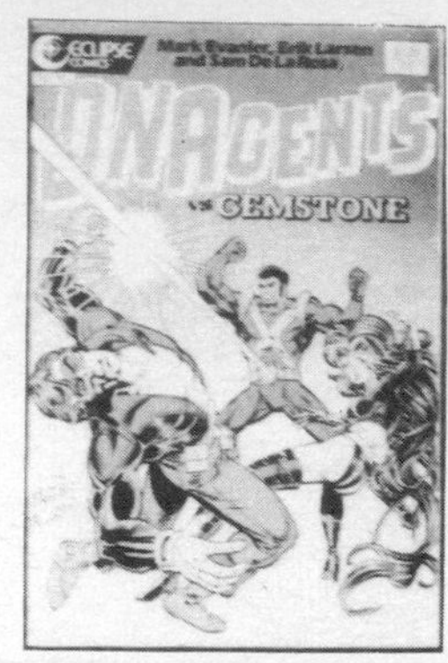

Doc Savage Comics #1, © S&S

GD25 FN65 NM94

DISHMAN (Eclipse)(Value: cover or less)

DISNEY COMIC ALBUM
1990(no month, year) - No. 8, 1991 ($6.95-$7.95, color)
Disney Comics

1,2 ($6.95): 1-Donald Duck and Gyro Gearloose by Barks(r). 2-Uncle Scrooge by Barks(r); Jr. Woodchucks app. 1.20 3.00 7.00
3-8: 3-Donald Duck-r/F.C. 308 by Barks; begin $7.95-c. 4-Mickey Mouse Meets the Phantom Blot; strip-r. 5-Chip 'n' Dale Rescue Rangers; new-a. 6-Uncle Scrooge. 7-Donald Duck in Too Many Pets; Barks-r(4). 8-Super Goof; r/S.G. #1, D.D. #102 1.30 3.25 8.00

DISNEYLAND BIRTHDAY PARTY (Also see Dell Giants)
Aug, 1985 ($2.50)
Gladstone Publishing Co.

1-Reprints Dell Giant with new-photo-c 1.00 2.00 5.00
...Comics Digest #1-(Digest) 1.00 2.50

DISNEYLAND, USA (See Dell Giant No. 30)

DISNEY'S COLOSSAL COMICS COLLECTION
1991 - No. 10, 1993 ($1.95, color, digest-size, 96-132 pgs.)
Disney Comics

1-10: Ducktales, Talespin, Chip 'n Dale's Rescue Rangers. 4-r/Darkwing Duck #1-4. 6-Goofy begins. 8-Little Mermaid .80 2.00

DISNEY'S COMICS IN 3-D
1992 ($2.95, w/glasses, polybagged)
Disney Comics

1-Infinity-c; Barks, Rosa, Gottfredson-r 1.20 3.00

DISNEY'S DUCKTALES (TV) (Also see Ducktales)
Oct, 1988 - No. 13, May, 1990 (1,2,9-11: $1.50; 3-8: 95 cents, color)
Gladstone Publishing

1-Barks-r 1.90 4.75
2-11: 2,4-6,9-11-Barks-r. 7-Barks-r(1 pg.) .80 2.00
12,13 ($1.95, 68 pgs.)-Barks-r; 12-r/F.C. #495 2.20

DISNEY'S NEW ADVENTURES OF BEAUTY AND THE BEAST (Also see Beauty and the Beast)
1992 - No. 2, 1992 ($1.50, color, mini-series)
Disney Comics

1,2-New stories based on movie 1.50

DISNEY'S TALESPIN LIMITED SERIES: "TAKE OFF" (See Talespin)
Jan, 1991 - No. 4, Apr, 1991 ($1.50, color, mini-series, 52 pgs.)
W. D. Publications (Disney Comics)

1-4: Based on animated series; 4 part origin 1.50

DISNEY'S THE LITTLE MERMAID LIMITED SERIES
Feb, 1992 - No. 4, May, 1992 ($1.50, color, limited series)
Disney Comics

1-4-All new adventures 1.50

DISNEY'S THE THREE MUSKETEERS
Jan, 1994 - No. 2, Feb, 1994 ($1.50, color, limited series)
Marvel Comics

1-4-Movie adaptation 1.50

DIVER DAN (TV)
Feb-Apr, 1962 - No. 2, June-Aug, 1962
Dell Publishing Co.

4-Color 1254(#1), 2 6.70 20.00 40.00

DIXIE DUGAN (See Big Shot, Columbia Comics & Feature Funnies)
July, 1942 - No. 13, 1949 (Strip reprints in all)
McNaught Syndicate/Columbia/Publication Ent.

1-Joe Palooka x-over by Ham Fisher 20.00 60.00 140.00
2 10.00 30.00 70.00
3 9.15 27.50 55.00
4,5(1945-46)-Bo strip-r 5.00 15.00 35.00
6-13(1/47-49): 6-Paperdoll cut-outs 4.00 12.00 28.00

GD25 FN65 NM94

DIXIE DUGAN
V3#1, Nov, 1951 - V4#4, Feb, 1954
Prize Publications (Headline)

V3#1 5.35 16.00 32.00
2-4 4.00 11.00 22.00
V4#1-4(#5-8) 3.20 8.00 16.00

DIZZY DAMES
Sept-Oct, 1952 - No. 6, July-Aug, 1953
American Comics Group (B&M Distr. Co.)

1-Whitney-c 6.70 20.00 40.00
2 4.20 12.50 25.00
3-6 3.60 9.00 18.00

DIZZY DON COMICS
1942 - No. 22, Oct, 1946; No. 3, Apr, 1947 (B&W)
F. E. Howard Publications/Dizzy Don Ent. Ltd (Canada)

1 5.85 17.50 35.00
2 3.60 9.00 18.00
4-21 3.00 7.50 15.00
22-Full color, 52 pgs. 5.85 17.50 35.00
3 (4/47)-Full color, 52 pgs. 4.70 14.00 28.00

DIZZY DUCK (Formerly Barnyard Comics)
No. 32, Nov, 1950 - No. 39, Mar, 1952
Standard Comics

32 5.85 17.50 35.00
33-39 3.60 9.00 18.00

DNAGENTS (Eclipse)(Value: cover or less)

DOBERMAN (See Sgt. Bilko's Private...)

DOBIE GILLIS (See The Many Loves of...)

DOC CARTER VD COMICS
1949 (16 pages in color) (Paper cover)
Health Publications Institute, Raleigh, N. C. (Giveaway)

nn 17.00 52.00 120.00

DOC CHAOS: THE STRANGE ATTRACTOR (Vortex)(Value: cover or less)

DOC SAVAGE
November, 1966
Gold Key

1-Adaptation of the Thousand-Headed Man; James Bama c-r/1964 Doc Savage paperback 8.00 24.00 55.00

DOC SAVAGE (Also see Giant-Size...)
Oct, 1972 - No. 8, Jan, 1974
Marvel Comics Group

1 1.20 3.00 7.00
2-8: 2,3-Steranko-c 1.60 4.00

NOTE: *Gil **Kane** c-5, 6. **Mooney** a-1i. No. 1, 2 adapts pulp story "The Man of Bronze," No. 3, 4 adapts "Death in Silver," No. 5, 6 adapts "The Monsters," No. 7, 8 adapts "The Brand of The Werewolf."*

DOC SAVAGE (Magazine)
Aug, 1975 - No. 8, Spr, 1977 ($1.00, Black & White)
Marvel Comics Group

1-Cover from movie poster; Ron Ely photo-c 1.60 4.00
2-8: 1,3-Buscema-a 1.00 2.50

DOC SAVAGE (DC, 1987 & 1988-90)(Value: cover or less)

DOC SAVAGE COMICS (Also see Shadow Comics)
May, 1940 - No. 20, Oct, 1943 (1st app. in Doc Savage pulp, 3/33)
Street & Smith Publications

1-Doc Savage, Cap Fury, Danny Garrett, Mark Mallory, The Whisperer, Captain Death, Billy the Kid, Sheriff Pete & Treasure Island begin; Norgil, the Magician app. 215.00 645.00 1500.00

Doc Savage Comics #12, © S&S

Doctor Fate #25, © DC

Doctor Solar, Man of the Atom #10, © WEST

GD25 FN65 NM94

2-Origin & 1st app. Ajax, the Sun Man; Danny Garrett, The Whisperer end 92.00 275.00 600.00
3 75.00 225.00 500.00
4-Treasure Island ends; Tuska-a 58.00 175.00 400.00
5-Origin & 1st app. Astron, the Crocodile Queen, not in #9 & 11; Norgi the Magician app. 46.00 137.00 300.00
6-10: 6-Cap Fury ends; origin & only app. Red Falcon in Astron story. 8-Mark Mallory ends; Charlie McCarthy app. on cover. 9-Supersnipe app. 10-Origin & only app. The Thunderbolt 39.00 116.00 265.00
11,12 31.00 92.00 215.00
V2#1-8(#13-20): 16-The Pulp Hero, The Avenger app. 17-Sun Man ends; Nick Carter begins. 20-Only all funny-c 31.00 92.00 215.00

DOC SAVAGE: THE DEVIL'S THOUGHTS
1992 (Says 1991) - No. 2, 1992 ($2.50, color, mini-series)
Millennium Publications
1,2 1.00 2.50

DOC SAVAGE: THE MAN OF BRONZE
1991 - No. 4, 1991 ($2.50, color, mini-series)
Millennium Publications
1-4: 1-Bronze logo 1.00 2.50
...: The Manual of Bronze 1 ($2.50, B&W, color, one-shot)-Unpublished proposed Doc Savage strip in color, B&W strip-r 1.00 2.50

DOC SAVAGE: THE MAN OF BRONZE, DOOM DYNASTY
1992 (Says 1991) - No. 2, 1992 ($2.50, color, mini-series)
Millennium Publications
1,2 1.00 2.50

DOC STEARN...MR. MONSTER (See Mr. Monster)

DR. ANTHONY KING, HOLLYWOOD LOVE DOCTOR
1952(Jan.) - No. 3, May, 1953; No. 4, May, 1954
Minoan Publishing Corp./Harvey Publications No. 4
1 7.50 22.50 45.00
2-4: 4-Powell-a 5.00 15.00 30.00

DR. ANTHONY'S LOVE CLINIC (See Mr. Anthony's...)

DR. BOBBS (See 4-Color No. 212)

DOCTOR BOOGIE (Media)(Value: cover or less)

DOCTOR CHAOS
Nov, 1993 - Present ($2.50, color)
Triumphant Comics
1-3 1.00 2.50

DR. FATE (See 1st Issue Special, The Immortal..., Justice League, More Fun #55, & Showcase)

DOCTOR FATE
July, 1987 - No. 4, Oct, 1987 ($1.50, mini-series, Baxter)
DC Comics
1-4: Giffen-c/a in all 1.50

DOCTOR FATE
Winter, 1988-'89 - No. 41, June, 1992 ($1.25-$1.50 #5 on, color)
DC Comics
1-31: 15-Justice League app. 25-1st new Dr. .75 1.50
32-41: 32-Begin $1.75-c. 36-Original Dr. returns .70 1.75
Annual 1(1989, $2.95, 68 pgs.)-Sutton-a 1.20 3.00

DR. FU MANCHU (See The Mask of...)
1964
I.W. Enterprises
1-r/Avon's "Mask of Dr. Fu Manchu;" Wood-a 5.70 17.00 40.00

DR. GIGGLES (See Dark Horse Presents #64-66)
Oct, 1992 - No. 2, Oct, 1992 ($2.50, color, mini-series)
Dark Horse Comics
1,2-Based on horror movie 1.00 2.50

GD25 FN65 NM94

DOCTOR GRAVES (Formerly The Many Ghosts of...)
No. 73, Sept, 1985 - No. 75, Jan, 1986
Charlton Comics
73-75 1.00

DR. JEKYLL AND MR. HYDE (See A Star Presentation & Supernatural Thrillers #4)

DR. KILDARE (TV)
No. 1337, 4-6/62 - No. 9, 4-6/65 (All Richard Chamberlain photo-c)
Dell Publishing Co.
4-Color 1337(#1, 1962) 6.70 20.00 40.00
2-9 5.00 15.00 30.00

DR. MASTERS (See The Adventures of Young...)

DOCTOR SOLAR, MAN OF THE ATOM (Also see The Occult Files of Dr. Spektor #14 & Solar)
10/62 - No. 27, 4/69; No. 28, 4/81 - No. 31, 3/82 (1-27 have painted-c)
Gold Key/Whitman No. 28 on
1-Origin/1st app. Dr. Solar (1st original Gold Key character) (#10000-210) 36.00 109.00 255.00
2-Prof. Harbinger begins 12.00 36.00 85.00
3-5: 5-Intro. Man of the Atom in costume 8.00 24.00 55.00
6-10 5.00 15.00 35.00
11-14,16-20 4.30 13.00 30.00
15-Origin retold 5.50 17.00 40.00
21-27 3.20 8.00 20.00
28-31: 29-Magnus Robot Fighter begins. 31-The Sentinel app. 1.30 3.25 8.00
NOTE: ***Frank Bolle** a-6-19, 29-31; c-29i, 30i. **Bob Fugitani** a-1-5. **Spiegle** a-29-31. **Al McWilliams** a-20-23.*

DOCTOR SOLAR, MAN OF THE ATOM
1990 - No. 2?, 1991 ($7.95, color, card stock-c, high quality, 96 pgs.)
Valiant Comics
1,2: Reprints Gold Key series 1.30 3.25 8.00

DOCTOR SPEKTOR (See The Occult Files of...)

DOCTOR STRANGE (Formerly Strange Tales #1-168) (Also see The Defenders, Giant Size..., Marvel Fanfare, Marvel Graphic Novel, Marvel Premiere, Marvel Treasury Ed. & Strange Tales, 2nd Series)
No. 169, 6/68 - No. 183, 11/69; 6/74 - No. 81, 2/87
Marvel Comics Group
169(#1)-Origin retold; panel swipe/M.D. #1-c 16.00 48.00 110.00
170-176 5.50 16.00 38.00
177-New costume 5.00 15.00 35.00
178-183: 178-Black Knight app. 179-Spider-Man story-r. 180-Photo montage-c. 181-Brunner-c(part-i) 4.50 14.00 32.00
1(6/74, 2nd series)-Brunner-c/a 4.30 13.00 30.00
2 2.30 6.75 16.00
3-5 1.25 3.00 7.50
6-10 1.00 2.50 5.50
11-20 1.60 4.00
21-26: 21-Origin-r/Doctor Strange #169 1.20 3.00
27-77,79-81: 56-Origin retold 1.50
78-New costume 1.00 2.50
Annual 1(1976, 52 pgs.)-New Russell-a (35 pgs.) 1.60 4.00
NOTE: ***Adkins** a-169, 170, 171i; c-169-171, 172i, 173. **Adams** a-4i. **Austin** a(i)-48-60, 66, 68, 70, 73; c(i)-38, 47-53, 55, 58-60, 70. **Brunner** a-1-5p; c-1-6, 22, 28-30, 33. **Colan** a(p)-172-178, 180-183, 6-18, 36-45, 47; c(p)-172, 174-183, 11-21, 23, 27, 35, 36, 47. **Ditko** a-179r, 3r. **Everett** c-183i. **Golden** a-46p, 55p; c-42-44, 46, 55p. **G. Kane** c(p)-8-10. **Miller** c-46p. **Nebres** a-20, 22, 23, 24i, 26i, 32i; c-32i, 34. **Rogers** a-48-53p; c-47p-53p. **Russell** a-34i, 46i, Annual 1. **B. Smith** c-179. **Paul Smith** a-54p, 56p, 65, 66p, 68p, 69, 71-73; c-56, 65, 66, 68, 71. **Starlin** a-23p, 26; c-25, 26. **Sutton** a-27-29p, 34p. Painted c-62, 63.*

DOCTOR STRANGE CLASSICS
Mar, 1984 - No. 4, June, 1984 ($1.50 cover price; Baxter paper)
Marvel Comics Group
1-4: Ditko-r; Byrne-c. 4-New Golden pin-up .80 2.00

Doctor Strange, Sorcerer Supreme #31, © MEG

Doll Man #25, © QUA

Dominion #3, © Masamune Shirow

GD25 FN65 NM94 | GD25 FN65 NM94

DOCTOR STRANGE/GHOST RIDER SPECIAL
April, 1991 ($1.50, color)
Marvel Comics
1-Same-c & contents as Dr. Strange S.S. #28 — 1.60 4.00

DOCTOR STRANGE/SILVER DAGGER (Special Edition)
Mar, 1983 ($2.50, Baxter paper)
Marvel Comics
1-r/Dr. Strange #1,2,4,5; Wrightson-c — 1.00 2.50

DOCTOR STRANGE, SORCERER SUPREME
Nov, 1988 - Present (Mando paper, $1.25-1.50, direct sales only)
Marvel Comics
1 ($1.25) — 1.60 4.00
2-10,12-14,16-27,29,30 ($1.50): 3-New Defenders app. 5-Guice-c/a begins. 26-Werewolf by Night app. — 1.50
11-Hobgoblin app. — 1.00 2.00 5.00
15-Unauthorized Amy Grant photo-c — 1.00 2.50 5.50
28-Ghost Rider story cont'd from G.R. #12; same cover & contents as Doctor Strange/Ghost Rider Special #1 — 1.60 4.00
31-36-Infinity Gauntlet x-overs 31-Silver Surfer app. 33-Thanos-c & cameo. 36-Warlock app. — 1.20 3.00
37-49,51-64: 37-Silver Surfer app. 38-Begin $1.75-c. 40-Daredevil x-over. 41-Wolverine-c/story. 42-47-Infinity War x-overs. 47-Gamora app. 52,53-Morbius-c/stories. 60-Siege of Darkness pt. 7 — .70 1.75
50-($2.95, 52 pgs.)-Holo-grafx foil-c; Hulk, Ghost Rider & Silver Surfer app.; leads into new Secret Defenders series — 1.20 3.00
Annual 2('92, $2.25, 68 pgs.)-Return of Defenders — .90 2.25
Annual 3('93, $2.95, 68 pgs.)-Polybagged w/card — 1.20 3.00
NOTE: ***Colan** c/a-19. **Guice** a-5-16, 18, 20-24; c-5-12, 20-24. See 1st series for Annual #1.*

DR. TOM BRENT, YOUNG INTERN
Feb, 1963 - No. 5, Oct, 1963
Charlton Publications
1 — 1.80 4.50 9.00
2-5 — 1.00 2.50 5.00

DR. VOLTZ (See Mighty Midget Comics)

DOCTOR WHO (Also see Marvel Premiere #57-60)
Oct, 1984 - No. 23, Aug, 1986 ($1.50, Direct sales, Baxter paper)
Marvel Comics Group
1-23-British-r — 1.00

DR. WHO & THE DALEKS (See Movie Classics)

DOCTOR ZERO
April, 1988 - No. 8, Aug, 1989 ($1.25/$1.50, color)
Epic Comics (Marvel)
1-8: 1-Sienkiewicz-c (a-3i,4i). 6,7-Spiegle-a — 1.50

DO-DO
1950 - No. 7, 1951 (5x7-1/4" Miniature) (5 cents)
Nation Wide Publishers
1 (52 pgs.); funny animal — 11.50 34.00 80.00
2-7 — 6.70 20.00 40.00

DODO & THE FROG, THE (Formerly Funny Stuff)
No. 80, 9-10/54 - No. 88, 1-2/56; No. 89, 8-9/56; No. 90, 10-11/56; No. 91, 9/57; No. 92, 11/57 (See Comic Cavalcade)
National Periodical Publications
80-1st app. Doodles Duck by Sheldon Mayer — 13.50 41.00 95.00
81-91: Doodles Duck by Mayer in #81,83-90 — 10.00 30.00 60.00
92-(Scarce)-Doodles Duck by S. Mayer — 12.00 36.00 85.00

DOGFACE DOOLEY
1951 - No. 5. 1953
Magazine Enterprises
1(A-1 40) — 4.35 13.00 26.00
2(A-1 43), 3(A-1 49), 4(A-1 53), 5(A-1 64) — 3.60 9.00 18.00

I.W. Reprint #1('64), Super Reprint #17 — 1.40 3.50 7.00

DOG OF FLANDERS, A (See 4-Color No. 1088)

DOGPATCH (See Al Capp's... & Mammy Yokum)

DOINGS OF THE DOO DADS, THE
1922 (34 pgs.; 7-3/4x7-3/4"; B&W) (50 cents)(red & white-c, square binding)
Detroit News (Universal Feat. & Specialty Co.)
nn-Reprints 1921 newspaper strip "Text & Pictures" given away as prize in the Detroit News Doo Dads contest; by Arch Dale — 13.00 40.00 90.00

DOLLFACE & HER GANG (See 4-Color No. 309)

DOLLMAN
Sept, 1991 - No. 4, Dec, 1991 ($2.50, color, mini-series)
Eternity Comics
1-4: Based on new movie — 1.00 2.50

DOLL MAN QUARTERLY, THE (Doll Man #17 on; also see Feature Comics #27 & Freedom Fighters)
Fall, 1941 - No. 7, Fall, '43; No. 8, Spring, '46 - No. 47, Oct, 1953
Quality Comics Group
1-Dollman (by Cassone), Justin Wright begin — 142.00 425.00 950.00
2-The Dragon begins; Crandall-a(5) — 72.00 215.00 475.00
3,4 — 54.00 162.00 365.00
5-Crandall-a — 42.00 125.00 275.00
6,7(1943) — 30.00 90.00 200.00
8(1946)-1st app. Torchy by Bill Ward — 33.00 100.00 225.00
9 — 25.00 75.00 170.00
10-20 — 20.00 60.00 140.00
21-30 — 17.00 50.00 120.00
31-36,38,40: 32-34-Jeb Rivers app.; 34 by Crandall(p) — 14.00 42.00 95.00
37-Origin Dollgirl; Dollgirl bondage-c — 20.00 60.00 140.00
39-"Narcotics...the Death Drug"-c-/story — 14.00 42.00 95.00
41-47 — 10.00 30.00 70.00
Super Reprint #11('64, r-#20),15(r-#23),17(r-#28): 15,17-Torchy app.; Andru/Esposito-c — 3.00 7.50 15.00
NOTE: ***Ward** Torchy in 8, 9, 11, 12, 14-24, 27; by Fox-#30, 35-47. **Crandall** a-2, 5, 10, 13 & Super #11, 17, 18. **Crandall/Cuidera** c-40-42. **Guardineer** a-3. Bondage c-27, 37, 38, 39.*

DOLLY
No. 10, July-Aug, 1951 (Funny animal)
Ziff-Davis Publ. Co.
10-Painted-c — 4.00 10.00 20.00

DOLLY DILL
1945
Marvel Comics/Newsstand Publ.
1 — 10.00 30.00 70.00

DOLLY DIMPLES & BOBBY BOONCE'
1933
Cupples & Leon Co.
nn — 11.50 34.00 80.00

DOMINION (Eclipse)(Value: cover or less)

DOMINO CHANCE (Chance)(Value: cover or less)

DONALD AND MICKEY IN DISNEYLAND (See Dell Giants)

DONALD AND MICKEY MERRY CHRISTMAS (Formerly Famous Gang Book Of Comics)
1943 - 1949 (20 pgs.)(Giveaway) Put out each Christmas; 1943 issue titled "Firestone Presents Comics" (Disney)
K. K. Publ./Firestone Tire & Rubber Co.
1943-Donald Duck reprint from WDC&S #32 by Carl Barks — 50.00 150.00 400.00
1944-Donald Duck reprint from WDC&S #35 by Barks — 48.00 145.00 385.00
1945-"Donald Duck's Best Christmas," 8 pgs. Carl Barks; intro. & 1st app.

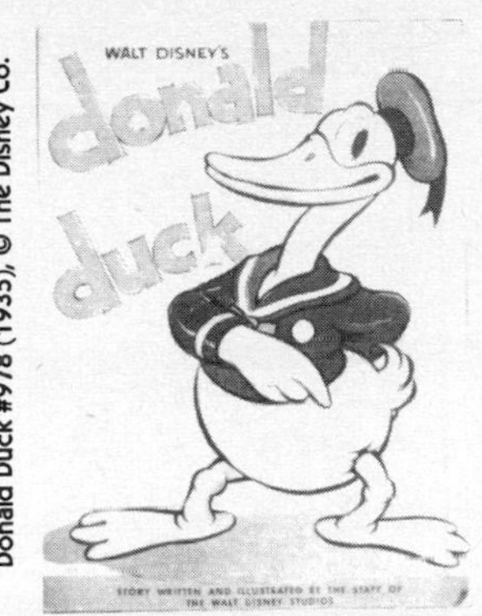

Donald Duck #978 (1935), © The Disney Co.

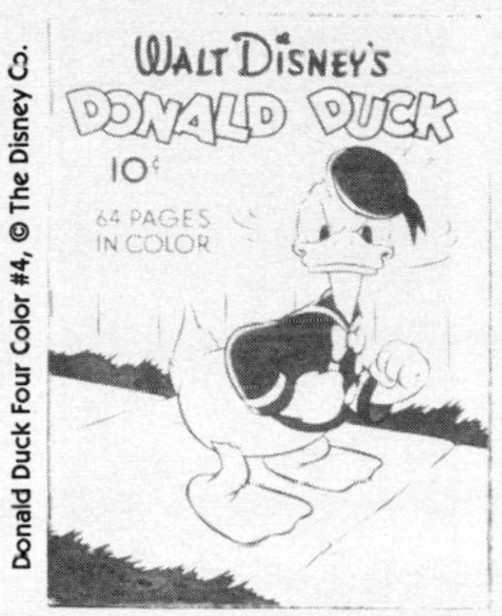

Donald Duck Four Color #4, © The Disney Co.

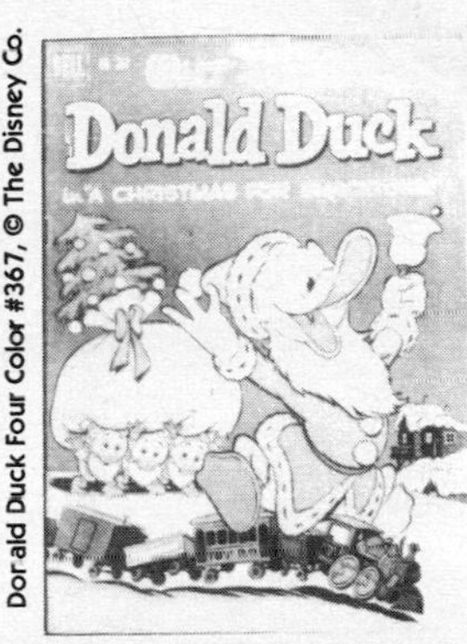

Donald Duck Four Color #367, © The Disney Co.

GD25 FN65 NM94

Grandma Duck in comic books 62.00 185.00 490.00
1946-Donald Duck in "Santa's Stormy Visit," 8 pgs. Carl Barks
47.00 140.00 370.00
1947-Donald Duck in "Three Good Little Ducks," 8 pgs. Carl Barks
38.00 115.00 305.00
1948-Donald Duck in "Toyland," 8 pgs. Carl Barks 37.00 110.00 290.00
1949-Donald Duck in "New Toys," 8 pgs. Barks 43.00 130.00 345.00

DONALD AND SCROOGE
1992 ($8.95, color, squarebound, 100 pgs.)
Disney Comics
nn-Don Rosa reprint special; r/U.S., D.D. Advs. 1.50 3.75 9.00
1-3 (1992, $1.50)-r/D.D. Advs. (Disney) #1,22,24 & U.S. #261-263,269
1.50

DONALD AND THE WHEEL (See 4-Color No. 1190)

DONALD DUCK (See Cheerios, Disney's Ducktales, Ducktales, Dynabrite Comics, Gladstone Comic Album, Mickey & Donald, Mickey Mouse Mag., Story Hour Series, Uncle Scrooge, Walt Disney's Comics & Stories, Wheaties & Whitman Comic Books)

DONALD DUCK
1935, 1936 (Linen-like text & color pictures; 1st book ever devoted to Donald Duck; see The Wise Little Hen for earlier app.) (9-1/2x13")
Whitman Publishing Co./Grosset & Dunlap/K.K.
978(1935)-16 pgs.; story book 129.00 385.00 900.00
nn(1936)-36 pgs.; reprints '35 edition with expanded ill. & text
68.00 205.00 475.00
with dust jacket.... 96.00 290.00 675.00

DONALD DUCK (Walt Disney's) (10 cents)
1938 (B&W) (8-1/2x11-1/2") (Cardboard covers)
Whitman/K.K. Publications
(Has Donald Duck with bubble pipe on front cover)
GD25 FN65 VF82
nn-The first Donald Duck & Walt Disney comic book; 1936 & 1937 Sunday strip-r(in B&W); same format as the Feature Books; 1st strips with Huey, Dewey & Louie from 10/17/37 170.00 515.00 1200.00
(Prices vary widely on this book)

DONALD DUCK (Walt Disney's...#262 on; see 4-Color listings for titles & 4-Color No. 1109 for origin story)
1940 - No. 84, Sept-Nov, 1962; No. 85, Dec, 1962 - No. 245, 1984; No. 246, Oct, 1986 - No. 279, May, 1990; No. 280, Sept, 1993 - Present
Dell Publishing Co./Gold Key No. 85-216/Whitman No. 217-245/
Gladstone Publishing No. 246 on GD25 FN65 VF82 NM94
4-Color 4(1940)-Daily 1939 strip-r by Al Taliaferro
600.00 1800.00 3900.00 6000.00
(Estimated up to 175 total copies exist, 9 in NM/Mint)
GD25 FN65 NM94
Large Feature Comic 16(1/41?)-1940 Sunday strips-r in B&W
200.00 600.00 1600.00
Large Feature Comic 20('41)-Comic Paint Book, r-single panels from Large Feature #16 at top of each page to color; daily strip-r across bottom of each page 315.00 945.00 2500.00
GD25 FN65 VF82 NM94
4-Color 9('42)-"Finds Pirate Gold;"-64 pgs. by Carl Barks & Jack Hannah (pgs. 1,2,5,12-40 are by Barks, his 1st comic book art work; © 8/17/42)
500.00 1500.00 3250.00 5000.00
(Estimated up to 270 total copies exist, 18 in NM/Mint)
4-Color 29(9/43)-"Mummy's Ring" by Barks; reprinted in Uncle Scrooge & Donald Duck #1('65), W. D. Comics Digest #44('73) & Donald Duck Advs. #14 400.00 1200.00 2600.00 4000.00
(Estimated up to 300 total copies exist, 14 in NM/Mint)
GD25 FN65 NM94
4-Color 62(1/45)-"Frozen Gold," 52 pgs. by Barks, reprinted in The Best of W.D. Comics & Donald Duck Advs. #4 120.00 360.00 1080.00
4-Color 108(1946)-"Terror of the River;" 52 pgs. by Carl Barks; reprinted in Gladstone Comic Album #2 90.00 270.00 810.00

GD25 FN65 NM94

4-Color 147(5/47)-in "Volcano Valley" by Barks 60.00 180.00 540.00
4-Color 159(8/47)-in "The Ghost of the Grotto;" 52 pgs. by Carl Barks; reprinted in Best of Uncle Scrooge & Donald Duck #1 ('66) & The Best of W.D. Comics & D.D. Advs. #9; two Barks stories 54.00 160.00 485.00
4-Color 178(12/47)-1st Uncle Scrooge by Carl Barks; reprinted in Gold Key Christmas Parade No. 3 & The Best of W.D. Comics
64.00 192.00 575.00
4-Color 189(6/48)-by Carl Barks; reprinted in Best of Donald Duck & Uncle Scrooge #1('64) & D.D. Advs. #19 54.00 160.00 485.00
4-Color 199(10/48)-by Carl Barks; mentioned in Love and Death; r/in Gladstone Comic Album #5 54.00 160.00 485.00
4-Color 203(12/48)-by Barks; reprinted as Gold Key Christmas Parade #4
36.00 108.00 325.00
4-Color 223(4/49)-by Barks; reprinted as Best of Donald Duck #1 & Donald Duck Advs. #3 50.00 150.00 450.00
4-Color 238(8/49)-in "Voodoo Hoodoo" by Barks 38.00 112.00 342.00
256(12/49)-by Barks; reprinted in Best of Donald Duck & Uncle Scrooge #2('67), Gladstone Comic Album #16 & W.D. Comics Digest #44('73)
27.00 81.00 243.00
4-Color 263(2/50)-Two Barks stories; r-in D.D. #278
27.00 81.00 243.00
4-Color 275(5/50), 282(7/50), 291(9/50), 300(11/50)-All by Carl Barks; 275, 282 reprinted in W.D. Comics Digest #44('73). #275 r/in Gladstone Comic Album #10. #291 r/in D. Duck Advs. #16 25.00 75.00 225.00
4-Color 308(1/51), 318(3/51)-by Barks; #318-reprinted in W.D. Comics Digest #34 & D.D. Advs. #2,19 21.00 63.00 190.00
4-Color 328(5/51)-by Carl Barks 23.00 70.00 205.00
4-Color 339(7-8/51), 379-not by Barks 5.35 16.00 32.00
4-Color 348(9-10/51), 356,394-Barks-c only 8.35 25.00 50.00
4-Color 367(1-2/52)-by Barks; reprinted as Gold Key Christmas Parade #2 & #8 20.00 60.00 180.00
4-Color 408(7-8/52), 422(9-10/52)-All by Carl Barks. #408-r-in Best of Donald Duck & Uncle Scrooge #1('64) & Gladstone Comic Album #13
20.00 60.00 180.00
26(11-12/52)-In "Trick or Treat" (Barks-a, 36pgs.) 1st story r-in Walt Disney Digest #16 & Gladstone C.A. #23 29.00 85.00 200.00
27-30-Barks-c only 6.70 20.00 40.00
31-40 4.20 12.50 25.00
41-44,47-50 3.60 9.00 18.00
45-Barks-a, 6 pgs. 10.00 30.00 60.00
46-"Secret of Hondorica" by Barks, 24 pgs.; reprinted in Donald Duck #98 & 154 10.00 30.00 65.00
51-Barks-a,1/2 pg. 3.20 8.00 16.00
52- "Lost Peg-Leg Mine" by Barks, 10 pgs. 9.15 27.50 55.00
53,55-59 2.80 7.00 14.00
54-"Forbidden Valley" by Barks, 26 pgs. (10¢ & 15¢ versions exist)
10.00 30.00 60.00
60-"Donald Duck & the Titanic Ants" by Barks, 20 pgs. plus 6 more pages
9.15 27.50 55.00
61-67,69,70 2.40 6.00 12.00
68-Barks-a, 5 pgs. 5.00 15.00 30.00
71-Barks-r, 1/2 pg. 2.40 6.00 12.00
72-78,80,82-97,99,100: 96-Donald Duck Album 2.40 6.00 12.00
79,81-Barks-a, 1pg. 2.40 6.00 12.00
98-Reprints #46 (Barks) 3.00 7.50 15.00
101-133: 102-Super Goof. 112-1st Moby Duck 1.60 4.00 8.00
134-Barks-r/#52 & WDC&S 194 1.60 4.00 8.00
135-Barks-r/WDC&S 198, 19 pgs. 1.00 2.50 6.00
136-153,155,156,158 1.60 4.00
154-Barks-r(#46) 1.00 2.50 6.00
157,159,160,164: 157-Barks-r(#45). 159-Reprints/WDC&S #192 (10 pgs.). 160-Barks-r(#26). 164-Barks-r(#70) 1.60 4.00
161-163,165-173,175-187,189-191 1.20 3.00
174,188: 174-r/4-Color #394. 188-Barks-r/#68 1.20 3.00
192-Barks-r(40 pgs.) from Donald Duck #60 & WDC&S #226,234 (52 pgs.)
1.20 3.00

Donald Duck #248, © The Disney Co.

Donald Duck Adventures #9, © The Disney Co.

Donald Duck's Suprise Party, © The Disney Co.

GD25 FN65 NM94

193-200,202-207,209-211,213-218: 217 has 216 on-c .80 2.00
201,208,212: 201-Barks-r/Christmas Parade #26, 16pgs. 208-Barks-r/#60 (6 pgs.). 212-Barks-r/WDC&S #130 .80 2.00
219-Barks-r/WDC&S #106,107, 10 pgs. ea. .80 2.00
220-227,231-245 1.50
228-230: 228-Barks-r/F.C. #275. 229-Barks-r/F.C. #282. 230-Barks-r/ #52 & WDC&S #194 .80 2.00
246-(1st Gladstone issue)-Barks-r/FC #422 1.65 4.00 10.00
247-249: 248,249-Barks-r/DD #54 & 26 1.60 4.00
250-($1.50, 68 pgs.)-Barks-r/4-Color #9 1.85 5.50 13.00
251-256: 251-Barks-r/1945 Firestone. 254-Barks-r/FC #328. 256-Barks-r/FC #147 1.50 3.75
257-($1.50, 52 pgs.)-Barks-r/Vac. Parade #1 1.60 4.00
258-260 1.20 3.00
261-277: 261-Barks-r/FC #300. 275-Kelly-r/FC #92 .75 1.90
278-($1.95, 68 pgs.)-Rosa-a; Barks-r/FC #263 1.00 2.50
279-($1.95, 68 pgs.)-Rosa-c; Barks-r/MOC #4 1.00 2.50
280-286: 283-Don Rosa-a .70 1.80
Mini-Comic #1(1976)-(3-1/4x6-1/2"); r/D.D. #150 .10

NOTE: ***Carl Barks** wrote all issues he illustrated, but #117, 126, 138 contain his script only. Issues 4-Color #189, 199, 203, 223, 238, 256, 263, 275, 282, 308, 348, 356, 367, 394, 408, 422, 26-30, 35, 44, 46, 52, 55, 57, 60, 65, 70-73, 77-80, 83, 101, 103, 105, 106, 111, 126, 246r, 266r, 268r, 271r, 275r, 278r(F.C. 263) all have **Barks** covers. **Barks** r-263- 267, 269-278. #96 titled "Comic Album," #99-"Christmas Album." New art issues (notreprints)-106-46, 148-63, 167, 169, 170, 172, 173, 175, 178, 179, 196, 209, 223, 225, 236.*

DONALD DUCK
1944 (16 pg. Christmas giveaway)(paper cover)(2 versions)
K. K. Publications

nn-Kelly cover reprint 41.00 125.00 290.00

DONALD DUCK ADVENTURES (Walt Disney's...#4 on)
Nov, 1987 - No. 20, Apr, 1990; No. 21, Aug, 1993 - Present
Gladstone Publishing

1 1.00 2.00 5.50
2-r/F.C. #308 .90 2.25
3,4,6,7,9-11,13,15-18: 3-r/F.C. #223. 4-r/F.C. #62. 9-r/F.C. #159. 16-r/F.C. #291; Rosa-c. 18-r/F.C. #318; Rosa-c .80 2.00
5,8-Don Rosa-a .90 2.20
12($1.50, 52pgs)-Rosa-c/a w/Barks poster 1.20 3.00
14-r/F.C. #29, "Mummy's Ring" 1.00 2.50
19 ($1.95, 68 pgs.)-Barks-r/F.C. #199 .80 2.00
20 ($1.95, 68 pgs.)-Barks-r/F.C. #189 & cover-r .80 2.00
21,22: 21-r/D.D. #46; Rosa-c. 22-r/F.C. #282 1.80
23-26 1.50

NOTE: ***Barks** a-1-19r, c-10r, 14r. **Rosa** a-5, 8, 12; c-13, 16-18.*

DONALD DUCK ADVENTURES (2nd series)(Walt Disney's... #? on)
June, 1990 - No. 38, July, 1993 ($1.50, color)
Disney Comics

1-Rosa-a & scripts 1.20 3.00
2-38: 2,3-Barks-r & new-a. 4,5-New-a? 9-r/F.C. #178 by Barks. 11-Mad #1 cover parody. 14-Barks-r. 21-r/FC #203 by Barks. 22-Rosa-a (10 pgs.) & scripts. 24-Rosa-a & scripts. 26-r/March of Comics #41 by Barks. 29-r/MOC #20 by Barks. 37-Rosa-a; Barks-r. 34-Rosa-c/a 1.50

NOTE: ***Barks** r-4, 9(F.C. #178), 14(D.D. #45), 27, 38.*

DONALD DUCK ALBUM (See Comic Album No. 1,3 & Duck Album)
5-7/59 - F.C. No. 1239, 10-12/61; 1962; 8/63 - No. 2, Oct, 1963
Dell Publishing Co./Gold Key

4-Color 995,1182, 01204-207 (1962-Dell) 4.00 10.00 20.00
4-Color 1099,1140,1239-Barks-c 4.00 11.00 22.00
1(8/63-Gold Key)-Barks-c 4.00 10.00 20.00
2(10/63) 2.40 6.00 12.00

DONALD DUCK AND THE BOYS (Also see Story Hour Series)
1948 (Hardcover book; 5-1/4x5-1/2") 100pgs., art, text
Whitman Publishing Co.

845-Partial-r/WDC&S #74 by Barks 35.00 105.00 250.00

GD25 FN65 NM94

(Prices vary widely on this book)

DONALD DUCK AND THE RED FEATHER
1948 (4 pages) (8-1/2x11") (Black & White)
Red Feather Giveaway

nn 10.00 30.00 70.00

DONALD DUCK BEACH PARTY (Also see Dell Giants)
Sept, 1965 (12 cents)
Gold Key

1(#10158-509)-Barks-r/WDC&S #45; painted-c 5.00 15.00 30.00

DONALD DUCK BOOK (See Story Hour Series)

DONALD DUCK COMIC PAINT BOOK (See Large Feature Comic No. 20)

DONALD DUCK COMICS DIGEST
Nov, 1986 - No. 5, July, 1987 ($1.25-$1.50, 96 pgs.)
Gladstone Publishing

1-5: 1-Barks-c/a-r. 4,5-$1.50-c .80 2.00

DONALD DUCK FUN BOOK (See Dell Giants)

DONALD DUCK IN DISNEYLAND (See Dell Giants)

DONALD DUCK IN "THE LITTERBUG"
1963 (16 pgs., 5x7-1/4", soft-c) (Disney giveaway)
Keep America Beautiful

nn 4.70 14.00 28.00

DONALD DUCK MARCH OF COMICS
No. 4, 1947 - No. 69, 1951; No. 263, 1964 (Giveaway) (Disney)
K. K. Publications

nn(No.4)-"Maharajah Donald;" 30 pgs. by Carl Barks-(1947) 785.00 2360.00 5500.00
20-"Darkest Africa" by Barks-(1948); 22 pgs. 380.00 1136.00 2650.00
41-"Race to South Seas" by Carl Barks-(1949); 22 pgs. 243.00 730.00 1700.00
56-(1950)-Barks-a on back-c 26.00 77.00 180.00
69-(1951)-Not by Barks; Barks-a on back-c 22.00 65.00 150.00
263-Not by Barks 7.50 22.50 45.00

DONALD DUCK MERRY CHRISTMAS (See Dell Giant No. 53)

DONALD DUCK PICNIC PARTY (See Picnic Party listed under Dell Giants)

DONALD DUCK "PLOTTING PICNICKERS" (Also see Ludwig Von Drake & Mickey Mouse)
1962 (16 pgs., 3-1/4x7", soft-c) (Disney)
Fritos Giveaway

nn 5.00 15.00 30.00

DONALD DUCK'S SURPRISE PARTY
1948 (16 pgs.) (Giveaway for Icy Frost Twins Ice Cream Bars)
Walt Disney Productions

nn-(Rare)-Kelly-c/a 245.00 730.00 1700.00

DONALD DUCK TELLS ABOUT KITES (See Kite Fun Book)

DONALD DUCK, THIS IS YOUR LIFE (See 4-Color No. 1109)

DONALD DUCK XMAS ALBUM (See regular Donald Duck No. 99)

DONALD IN MATHMAGIC LAND (See 4-Color No. 1051, 1198)

DONATELLO, TEENAGE MUTANT NINJA TURTLE
Aug, 1986 ($1.50, one-shot, B&W, 44 pgs.)
Mirage Studios

1 1.65 4.00 10.00

DONDI (See 4-Color No. 1176,1276)

DON FORTUNE MAGAZINE
Aug, 1946 - No. 6, Feb, 1947
Don Fortune Publishing Co.

1-Delecta of the Planets by C. C. Beck in all 11.50 34.00 80.00
2 9.15 27.50 55.00

Don Winslow of the Navy #53, © FAW

Doom 2099 #9, © MEG

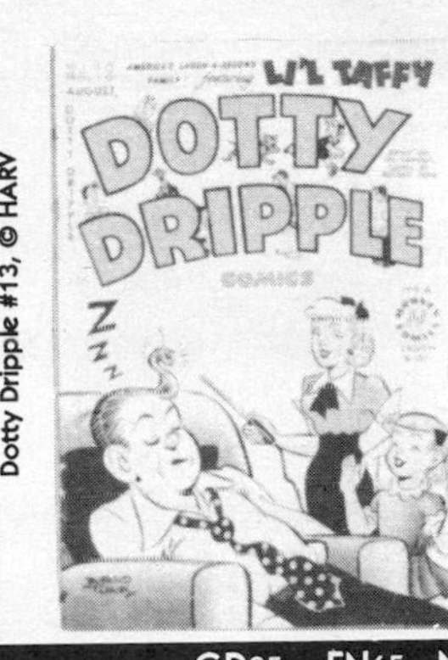

Dotty Dripple #13, © HARV

	GD25	FN65	NM94
3-6: 3-Bondage-c	5.85	17.50	35.00

DONNA MATRIX
Aug, 1993 - Present ($2.95, color, 52 pgs.)
Reactor, Inc.

	GD25	FN65	NM94
1-Computer generated-c/a by Mike Saenz		1.20	3.00

DON NEWCOMBE
1950 (Baseball)
Fawcett Publications

	GD25	FN65	NM94
nn	27.00	81.00	190.00

DON'T GIVE UP THE SHIP (See 4-Color #1049)

DON WINSLOW OF THE NAVY (See Crackajack Funnies, Famous Feature Stories, Four Color #2, 22, Popular Comics & Super Book #5,6)

DON WINSLOW OF THE NAVY (See TV Teens; Movie, Radio, TV)
(Fightin' Navy No. 74 on)
2/43 - #64, 12/48; #65, 1/51 - #69, 9/51; #70, 3/55 - #73, 9/55
Fawcett Publications/Charlton No. 70 on

	GD25	FN65	NM94
1-(68 pgs.)-Captain Marvel on cover	64.00	192.00	450.00
2	33.00	100.00	225.00
3	23.00	70.00	160.00
4-6: 6-Flag-c	17.00	52.00	120.00
7-10: 8-Last 68 pg. issue?	13.00	40.00	90.00
11-20	19.00	30.00	65.00
21-40	7.50	22.50	45.00
41-63: 51,60-Singapore Sal (villain) app.	5.85	17.50	35.00
64(12/48)-Matt Baker-a	6.70	20.00	40.00
65(1/51) -Flying Saucer attack; photo-c	7.50	22.50	45.00
66 - 69(9/51): All photo-c.	7.50	22.50	45.00
70(3/55)-73: 70-73 r-/#26,58 & 59	5.00	15.00	30.00

DOOM FORCE SPECIAL
July, 1992 ($2.95, color, mature readers, 68 pgs.)
DC Comics

	GD25	FN65	NM94
1-X-Force parody; Morrison scripts; Simonson, Steacy, others-a; Giffen/Mignola-c		1.20	3.00

DOOM PATROL, THE (Formerly My Greatest Adventure No. 1-85; see Brave and the Bold, DC Special Blue Ribbon Digest 19, Official...Index & Showcase No. 94-96)
No. 86, 3/64 - No. 121, 9-10/68; No. 122, 2/73 - No. 124, 6-7/73
National Periodical Publications

	GD25	FN65	NM94
86-1 pg. origin (#86-121 are 12 cent issues)	11.50	34.00	80.00
87-99: 88-Origin The Chief. 91-Intro. Mento. 99-Intro. Beast Boy (later became the Changeling in New Teen Titans	7.00	21.00	50.00
100-Origin Beast Boy; Robot-Maniac series begins (12/65)	9.00	26.00	60.00
101-110: 102-Challengers of the Unknown app. 105-Robot-Maniac series ends. 106-Negative Man begins (origin)	4.00	12.00	28.00
111-120	3.25	9.50	22.00
121-Death of Doom Patrol; Orlando-c	9.00	28.00	65.00
122-124: All reprints		1.00	2.50

DOOM PATROL
Oct, 1987 - Present (New format, direct sale, $1.50 #19 on)
DC Comics

	GD25	FN65	NM94
1		.80	2.00
2-18: 3-1st app. Lodestone. 4-1st app. Karma. 8,15,16-Art Adams-c(i). 18-Invasion			1.00
19-New format & Grant Morrison scripts begin	2.15	6.50	15.00
20-25	1.50	3.75	9.00
26-30: 29-Superman app.		1.60	4.00
31-40: 39-Preview of World Without End		.80	2.00
41-49,51-56,58-60: 53-Steacy-a. 60-Last $1.50-c		.70	1.80
50,57-($2.50, 52 pgs.)		1.00	2.50
61-65: 61-Photo-c. 63-Last Morrison scripts		.70	1.80
66-76 ($1.95)		.80	2.00
...And Suicide Squad Special 1(3/88, $1.50)		.65	1.60
Annual 1('88, $1.50, 52pgs.)-No Morrison scripts		.65	1.60
Annual 2 ('93, $3.95, 68 pgs.)		1.60	4.00

DOOMSDAY + 1 (Also see Charlton Bullseye)
July, 1975 - No. 6, June, 1976; No. 7, June, 1978 - No. 12, May, 1979
Charlton Comics

	GD25	FN65	NM94
1: #1-5 are 25 cent issues		1.90	4.75
2		1.20	3.00
3-6: 4-Intro Lor. 6-Begin 30 cent issues		1.10	2.75
V3#7-12 (reprints #1-6)		.65	1.60
5 (Modern Comics reprint, 1977)			1.00

NOTE: *Byrne c/a-1-12; Painted covers-2-7.*

DOOMSDAY SQUAD, THE (Fantagraphics)(Value: cover or less)

DOOM 2099 (See Marvel Comics Presents #118)
Jan, 1993 - Present ($1.25, color)
Marvel Comics

	GD25	FN65	NM94
1-($1.75)-Metallic foil stamped-c		.80	2.00
2-15			1.25

DOORWAY TO NIGHTMARE (See Cancelled Comic Cavalcade)
Jan-Feb, 1978 - No. 5, Sept-Oct, 1978
DC Comics

	GD25	FN65	NM94
1-5-Madame Xanadu in all. 4-Craig-a			1.00

NOTE: *Kaluta covers on all. Merged into The Unexpected with No. 190.*

DOPEY DUCK COMICS (Wacky Duck No. 3) (See Super Funnies)
Fall, 1945 - No. 2, April, 1946
Timely Comics (NPP)

	GD25	FN65	NM94
1,2-Casper Cat, Krazy Krow	11.00	32.00	75.00

DOROTHY LAMOUR (Formerly Jungle Lil)(Stage, screen, radio)
No. 2, June, 1950 - No. 3, Aug, 1950
Fox Features Syndicate

	GD25	FN65	NM94
2,3-Wood-a(3) each, photo-c	13.00	40.00	90.00

DOT AND DASH AND THE LUCKY JINGLE PIGGIE
1942 (12 pages)
Sears Roebuck Christmas giveaway

	GD25	FN65	NM94
nn-Contains a war stamp album and a punch out Jingle Piggie bank	6.70	20.00	40.00

DOT DOTLAND (Formerly Little Dot Dotland)
No. 62, Sept, 1974 - No. 63, November, 1974
Harvey Publications

	GD25	FN65	NM94
62,63		.80	2.00

DOTTY (...& Her Boy Friends) (Formerly Four Teeners; Glamorous Romances No. 41 on)
No. 35, June, 1948 - No. 40, May, 1949
Ace Magazines (A. A. Wyn)

	GD25	FN65	NM94
35	4.70	14.00	28.00
36,38-40	3.00	7.50	15.00
37-Transvestism story	3.60	9.00	18.00

DOTTY DRIPPLE (Horace & Dotty Dripple No. 25 on)
1946 - No. 24, June, 1952 (See A-1 No. 1-8, 10)
Magazine Ent.(Life's Romances)/Harvey No. 3 on

	GD25	FN65	NM94
nn (nd) (10 cent)	4.00	10.50	21.00
2	2.00	5.00	10.00
3-10: 3,4-Powell-a	1.40	3.50	7.00
11-24	1.00	2.50	5.00

DOTTY DRIPPLE AND TAFFY
No. 646, Sept, 1955 - No. 903, May, 1958
Dell Publishing Co.

	GD25	FN65	NM94
4-Color 646 (#1)	4.00	10.00	20.00
4-Color 691,718,746,801,903	3.00	7.50	15.00

Double Comics 1940, © Elliot Publ.

Double Dragon #1, © Technos Japan Corp.

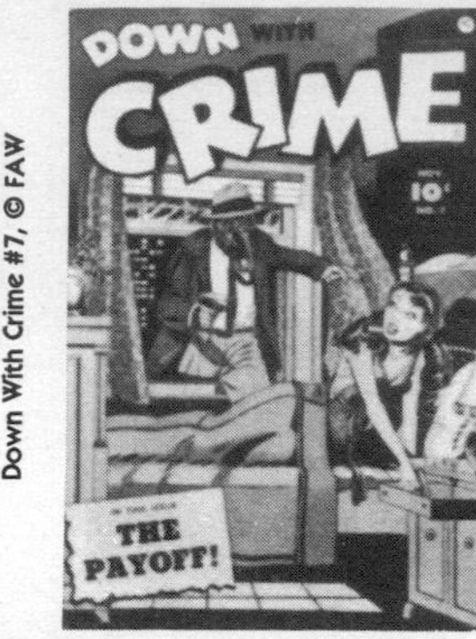
Down With Crime #7, © FAW

GD25 FN65 NM94

DOUBLE ACTION COMICS
No. 2, Jan, 1940 (Regular size; 68 pgs.; B&W, color cover)
National Periodical Publications

2-Contains original stories(?); pre-hero DC contents; same cover as Adventure No. 37. (six known copies) (not an ashcan)
Estimated value.... 7500.00

NOTE: *The cover to this book was probably reprinted from Adventure #37. #1 exists as an ash can copy with B&W cover; contains a coverless comic on inside with 1st & last page missing.*

DOUBLE COMICS
1940 - 1944 (132 pages)
Elliot Publications

	GD25	FN65	NM94
1940 issues; Masked Marvel-c & The Mad Mong vs. The White Flash covers known	150.00	450.00	950.00
1941 issues; Tornado Tim-c, Nordac-c, & Green Light covers known	108.00	325.00	700.00
1942 issues	92.00	275.00	575.00
1943,1944 issues	67.00	200.00	425.00

NOTE: *Double Comics consisted of an almost endless combination of pairs of remaindered, unsold issues of comics representing most publishers and usually mixed publishers in the same book; e.g., a Captain America with a Silver Streak, or a Feature with a Detective, etc., could appear inside the same cover. The actual contents would have to determine its price. Prices listed are for average contents. Any containing rare origin or first issues are worth much more. Covers also vary in same year. Value would be approximately 50 percent of contents.*

DOUBLE-CROSS (See The Crusaders)

DOUBLE-DARE ADVENTURES
Dec, 1966 - No. 2, March, 1967 (35-25 cents, 68 pgs.)
Harvey Publications

	GD25	FN65	NM94
1-Origin Bee-Man, Glowing Gladiator, & Magic-Master; Simon/Kirby-a (last S&K art as a team?)	4.70	14.00	33.00
2-Williamson/Crandall-a; r/Alarming Adv. #3('63)	3.40	10.00	24.00

NOTE: ***Powell** a-1. **Simon/Sparling** c-1, 2.*

DOUBLE DRAGON
July, 1991 - No. 6, Dec, 1991 (1.00, color, mini-series)
Marvel Comics

	GD25	FN65	NM94
1-6: Based on video game. 2-Arthur Adams-c			1.00

DOUBLE LIFE OF PRIVATE STRONG, THE
June, 1959 - No. 2, Aug, 1959
Archie Publications/Radio Comics

	GD25	FN65	NM94
1-Origin The Shield; Simon & Kirby-c/a; intro./1st app. The Fly	54.00	161.00	375.00
2-S&K-c/a; Tuska-a; The Fly app.	36.00	107.00	250.00

DOUBLE TALK (Also see Two-Faces)
No date (1962?) (32 pgs.; full color; slick cover)
Christian Anti-Communism Crusade (Giveaway)
Feature Publications

	GD25	FN65	NM94
nn-Sickle with blood-c	10.00	30.00	60.00

DOUBLE TROUBLE
Nov, 1957 - No. 2, Jan-Feb, 1958
St. John Publishing Co.

	GD25	FN65	NM94
1,2	4.00	10.00	20.00

DOUBLE TROUBLE WITH GOOBER
No. 417, Aug, 1952 - No. 556, May, 1954
Dell Publishing Co.

	GD25	FN65	NM94
4-Color 417	3.20	8.00	16.00
4-Color 471,516,556	2.40	6.00	12.00

DOUBLE UP
1941 (200 pages) (Pocket size)
Elliott Publications

	GD25	FN65	NM94
1-Contains rebound copies of digest sized issues of Pocket Comics, Speed Comics, & Spitfire Comics	62.00	188.00	400.00

DOVER & CLOVER (See All Funny & More Fun Comics #93)

DOVER BOYS (See Adventures of the...)

DOVER THE BIRD
Spring, 1955
Famous Funnies Publishing Co.

	GD25	FN65	NM94
1-Funny animal; code approved	4.00	10.00	20.00

DOWN WITH CRIME
Nov, 1952 - No. 7, Nov, 1953
Fawcett Publications

	GD25	FN65	NM94
1	13.00	40.00	90.00
2-5: 2,4-Powell-a in each. 3-Used in **POP**, pg. 106; "H is for Heroin" drug story. 5-Bondage-c	8.35	25.00	50.00
6,7: 6-Used in **POP**, pg. 80	5.85	17.50	35.00

DO YOU BELIEVE IN NIGHTMARES?
Nov, 1957 - No. 2, Jan, 1958
St. John Publishing Co.

	GD25	FN65	NM94
1-Mostly Ditko-c/a	22.00	65.00	150.00
2-Ayers-a	11.00	32.00	75.00

D.P. 7
Nov, 1986 - No. 32, June, 1989 (26 on: $1.50)
Marvel Comics Group

	GD25	FN65	NM94
1-32			1.25
Annual #1 (11/87)-Intro. The Witness			1.25

NOTE: ***Williamson** a-9i, 11i; c-9i.*

DRACULA (See Bram Stoker's Dracula, Giant-Size..., Little Dracula, Marvel Graphic Novel & Tomb of...; also see Movie Classics under Universal Presents as well as Dracula)

DRACULA (See Movie Classics for #1)(Also see Frankenstein & Werewolf)
No. 2, 11/66 - No. 4, 3/67; No. 6, 7/72 - No. 8, 7/73 (No #5)
Dell Publishing Co.

	GD25	FN65	NM94
2-Origin & 1st app. Dracula (11/66) (super hero)	2.40	6.00	12.00
3,4-Intro. Fleeta #4('67)	1.40	3.50	7.00
6-('72)-r/#2 w/origin		1.80	4.50
7,8: 7-r/#3, 8-r/#4		1.60	4.00

DRACULA (Magazine)
1979 (120 pages, full color)
Warren Publishing Co.

	GD25	FN65	NM94
Book 1-Maroto art; Spanish material translated into English	1.30	3.25	8.00

DRACULA LIVES! (Magazine)(Also see Tomb of Dracula)
1973(no month) - No. 13, July, 1975 (B&W) (75 cents)
Marvel Comics Group

	GD25	FN65	NM94
1	1.00	2.50	5.50
2,3: 2-Origin; Starlin-a		1.60	4.00
4-Ploog-a		1.00	2.50
5(V2#1)-13: 5-Dracula series begins		.80	2.00
Annual 1(Summer '75, $1.25)-Morrow painted-c		1.00	2.50

NOTE: ***N. Adams** a-2, 3i, 10i, Annual 1r(2, 3i). **Alcala** a-9. **Buscema** a-3p, 6p, Annual 1p. **Colan** a(p)-1, 2, 5, 6, 8. **Evans** a-7. **Heath** a-1r, 13. **Pakula** a-6r. **Weiss** r-Annual 1p.*

DRACULA 3-D (3-D Zone)(Value: cover or less)

DRACULA VERSUS ZORRO
Nov, 1993 - No. 2, Dec, 1993 ($2.95, color, limited series)
Topps Comics

	GD25	FN65	NM94
1,2: 1-Red foil-c. 2-Polybagged w/16 pg. Zorro #0		1.20	3.00

DRACULA: VLAD THE IMPALER (Also see Bram Stoker's Dracula)
Feb, 1993 - No. 3, Apr, 1993 ($2.95, color, mini-series)
Topps Comics

	GD25	FN65	NM94
1-3-Polybagged with 3 trading cards each		1.20	3.00

DRAFT, THE
1988 (One shot, $3.50, color, squarebound)
Marvel Comics

	GD25	FN65	NM94
1-Sequel to "The Pitt"		1.40	3.50

Dragon Lines #4, © Peter Quinones & Ron Lim

Dreadstar #46, © FIRST

Ducktales #1, © The Disney Co.

GD25 FN65 NM94

DRAG 'N' WHEELS (Formerly Top Eliminator)
No. 30, Sept, 1968 - No. 59, May, 1973
Charlton Comics

	GD25	FN65	NM94
30-40-Scot Jackson begins	1.60	4.00	8.00
41-50	1.20	3.00	6.00
51-59: Scot Jackson		1.60	4.00
Modern Comics Reprint 58('78)		1.20	3.00

DRAGON CHIANG (Eclipse)(Value: cover or less)

DRAGONFLIGHT (Eclipse)(Value: cover or less)

DRAGONFLY (Americomics)(Value: cover or less)(See Americomics #4)

DRAGONFORCE
1988 - No. 13, 1989 ($2.00, color)
Aircel Publishing

	GD25	FN65	NM94
1-Dale Keown-c/a/scripts in 1-12		1.80	4.50
2,3		1.60	4.00
4-6		1.20	3.00
7-12		1.00	2.50
13-No Keown-a		.80	2.00
...Chronicles Book 1-5 ($2.95, B&W, 60 pgs.): Dale Keown-r/Dragonring & Dragonforce		1.20	3.00

DRAGONLANCE (DC)(Value: cover or less)(Also see TSR Worlds)

DRAGON LINES
May, 1993 - No. 4, Aug, 1993 ($1.95, color, mini-series)
Epic Comics (Marvel)

	GD25	FN65	NM94
1-($2.50)-Embossed-c; Ron Lim-c/a in all		1.00	2.50
2-4		.80	2.00

DRAGONQUEST
Dec, 1986 - No. 3, 1987 ($1.50, B&W, 28 pgs.)
Silverwolf Comics

	GD25	FN65	NM94
1-Tim Vigil-c/a in all	1.50	3.75	9.00
2,3	1.00	2.50	5.50

DRAGONRING (Aircel)(Value: cover or less)

DRAGON'S CLAWS
July, 1988 - No. 12, June?, 1989 ($1.25-$1.75, color, British)
Marvel Comics UK, Ltd.

	GD25	FN65	NM94
1-4: 2-Begin $1.50-c. 3-Death's Head 1 pg. strip on back-c (1st app.). 4-Silhouette of Death's Head on last pg.			1.60
5-1st full app. new Death's Head; begin $1.75-c	1.40	3.50	8.50
6-12		.70	1.75

DRAGONSLAYER
October, 1981 - No. 2, Nov, 1981
Marvel Comics Group

	GD25	FN65	NM94
1,2-Paramount Disney movie adaptation			1.00

DRAGOON WELLS MASSACRE (See 4-Color No. 815)

DRAGSTRIP HOTRODDERS (World of Wheels No. 17 on)
Sum, 1963; No. 2, Jan, 1965 - No. 16, Aug, 1967
Charlton Comics

	GD25	FN65	NM94
1	3.60	9.00	18.00
2-5	2.40	6.00	12.00
6-16	1.80	4.50	9.00

DRAMA OF AMERICA, THE
1973 (224 pages) ($1.95)
Action Text

	GD25	FN65	NM94
1-"Students' Supplement to History"		1.20	3.00

DREAD (Eclipse)(Value: cover or less)(Clive Barker) (Graphic album)

DREADLANDS (Also see Epic)
1992 - No. 4, 1992 ($3.95, color, mini-series, coated stock, 52 pgs.)
Epic Comics (Marvel)

	GD25	FN65	NM94
1-4: Stiff-c		1.60	4.00

DREAD OF NIGHT (Hamilton)(Value: cover or less)

DREADSTAR (Epic/First)(Value: Cover or less)

DREADSTAR AND COMPANY (Epic)(Value: cover or less)

DREAM BOOK OF LOVE (See A-1 Comics No. 106, 114, 123)

DREAM BOOK OF ROMANCE (See A-1 No. 92, 101, 109, 110, 124)

DREAMERY, THE (Eclipse)(Value: cover or less)

DREAM OF LOVE
1958 (Reprints)
I. W. Enterprises

	GD25	FN65	NM94
1,2,8: 1-Powell-a. 8-Kinstler-c	1.20	3.00	6.00
9-Kinstler-c; 1pg. John Wayne interview & illo	1.00	2.50	5.00

DREAMS OF THE RAREBIT FIEND
1905
Doffield & Co.?

nn-By Winsor McCay (Very Rare) (Three copies known to exist)
Estimated value.... $1000.00-$2000.00

DREDD RULES (Fleetway/Quality)(Value: cover or less)

DRIFT MARLO
May-July, 1962 - No. 2, Oct-Dec, 1962
Dell Publishing Co.

	GD25	FN65	NM94
01-232-207(#1), 2(12-232-212)	3.20	8.00	16.00

DRISCOLL'S BOOK OF PIRATES
1934 (124 pgs.) (B&W; hardcover; 7x9")
David McKay Publ. (Not reprints)

	GD25	FN65	NM94
nn-By Montford Amory	14.00	43.00	100.00

DROIDS
April, 1986 - No. 8, June, 1987 (Based on Saturday morning cartoon)
Star Comics (Marvel)

	GD25	FN65	NM94
1-8: R2D2, C-3PO from Star Wars app.			1.00

NOTE: ***Romita** a-3p. **Williamson** a-2i, 5i, 7i, 8i. **Sinnott** a-3i.*

DROWNED GIRL, THE
1990 ($5.95, color, mature readers, 52 pgs.)
Piranha Press (DC)

	GD25	FN65	NM94
nn	1.00	2.50	6.00

DRUG WARS (Pioneer)(Value: cover or less)

DRUM BEAT (See 4-Color No. 610)

DRUNKEN FIST (Jademan)(Value: cover or less)

DUCK ALBUM (See Donald Duck Album)
No. 353, Oct, 1951 - No. 840, Sept, 1957
Dell Publishing Co.

	GD25	FN65	NM94
4-Color 353-Barks-c	5.00	15.00	30.00
4-Color 450-Barks-c	4.70	14.00	28.00
4-Color 492,531,560,586,611,649,686	4.00	10.00	20.00
4-Color 726,782,840	3.60	9.00	18.00

DUCKTALES (Also see Disney's Ducktales)
June, 1990 - No. 18, Nov, 1991 ($1.50, color)
Disney Comics

	GD25	FN65	NM94
1-All new stories		1.10	2.75
2-18		.65	1.60
...: The Movie nn (1990, 7.95, 68 pgs.)-Graphic novel adapting animated movie	1.30	3.25	8.00

DUDLEY (Teen-age)
Nov-Dec, 1949 - No. 3, Mar-Apr, 1950
Feature/Prize Publications

	GD25	FN65	NM94
1-By Boody Rogers	10.00	30.00	70.00
2,3	6.70	20.00	40.00

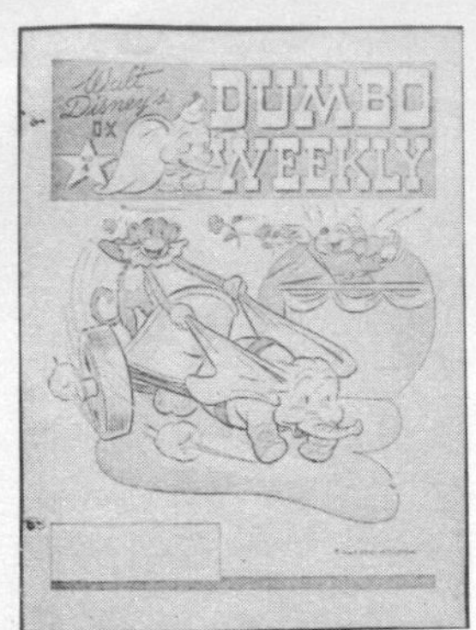

Dumbo Weekly #4, The Disney Co.

The Durango Kid #25, © ME

Dynamo #4, © TC

GD25 FN65 NM94

DUDLEY DO-RIGHT (TV)
Aug, 1970 - No. 7, Aug, 1971 (Jay Ward)
Charlton Comics

1 5.50 16.00 38.00
2-7 3.85 11.50 27.00

DUKE OF THE K-9 PATROL
April, 1963
Gold Key

1 (10052-304) 3.20 8.00 16.00

DUMBO (See 4-Color #17,234,668, Movie Comics, & Walt Disney Showcase #12)

DUMBO (Walt Disney's...)
1941 (K.K. Publ. Giveaway)
Weatherbird Shoes/Ernest Kern Co.(Detroit)

nn-16 pgs., 9x10" (Rare) 29.00 85.00 200.00
nn-52 pgs., 5-1/2x8-1/2", slick cover in color; B&W interior; half text, half reprints 4-Color No. 17 18.00 54.00 125.00

DUMBO COMIC PAINT BOOK (See Large Feature Comic No. 19)

DUMBO WEEKLY
1942 (Premium supplied by Diamond D-X Gas Stations)
Walt Disney Productions

1 23.00 70.00 160.00
2-16 11.00 32.00 75.00

NOTE: *A cover and binder came separate at gas stations. Came with membership card.*

DUNC AND LOO (1-3 titled "Around the Block with Dunc and Loo")
Oct-Dec, 1961 - No. 8, Oct-Dec, 1963
Dell Publishing Co.

1 10.00 30.00 70.00
2 6.70 20.00 40.00
3-8 5.00 15.00 30.00

NOTE: *Written by **John Stanley; Bill Williams** art.*

DUNE
April, 1985 - No. 3, June, 1985
Marvel Comics

1-3-r/Marvel Super Special; movie adaptation 1.00

DURANGO KID, THE (Also see Best of the West, Great Western & White Indian) (Charles Starrett starred in Columbia's Durango Kid movies)
Oct-Nov, 1949 - No. 41, Oct-Nov, 1955 (All 36 pgs.)
Magazine Enterprises

1-Charles Starrett photo-c; Durango Kid & his horse Raider begin; Dan Brand & Tipi (origin) begin by Frazetta & continue through #16 49.00 145.00 340.00
2(Starrett photo-c) 25.00 75.00 175.00
3-5(All-Starrett photo-c) 22.00 65.00 150.00
6-10: 7-Atomic weapon-c/story 11.00 32.00 75.00
11-16-Last Frazetta issue 9.15 27.50 55.00
17-Origin Durango Kid 11.00 32.00 75.00
18-Fred Meagher-a on Dan Brand begins 7.50 22.50 45.00
19-30: 19-Guardineer-c/a(3) begin, end #41. 23-Intro. The Red Scorpion 7.50 22.50 45.00
31-Red Scorpion returns 6.70 20.00 40.00
32-41-Bolle/Frazetta-a (Dan Brand) 8.35 25.00 50.00

NOTE: *#6, 8, 14, 15 contain **Frazetta** art not reprinted in White Indian. **Ayers** c-18. **Guardineer** a(3)-19-41; c-19-41. **Fred Meagher** a-18-29 at least.*

DURANGO KID, THE (AC)(Value: cover or less)

DWIGHT D. EISENHOWER
December, 1969
Dell Publishing Co.

01-237-912 - Life story 3.20 8.00 16.00

DYNABRITE COMICS
1978 - 1979 (69 cents; 48 pgs.)(10x7-1/8"; cardboard covers)
(Blank inside covers)
Whitman Publishing Co.

11350 - Walt Disney's Mickey Mouse & the Beanstalk (4-C 157). 11350-1 - Mickey Mouse Album (4-C 1057,1151,1246). 11351 - Mickey Mouse & His Sky Adventure (4-C 214, 343 11352 - Donald Duck (4-C 408, Donald Duck 45,52)-Barks-a. 11352-1 - Donald Duck (4-C 31 10 pg. Barks/WDC&S 125,128)-Barks-c(r). 11353 - Daisy Duck's Diary (4-C 1055,1150) Barks a. 11354 - Goofy: A Gaggle of Giggles. 11354-1 - Super Goof Meets Super Thief. 11355 - Unc Scrooge (Barks-a/U.S. 12,33). 11355-1 - Uncle Scrooge (Barks-a/U.S. 13,16) - Barks-c(r). 1135 - (?). 11357 - Star Trek (r/-Star Trek 33,41). 11358 - Star Trek (r/-Star Trek 34,36). 11359 - Bug Bunny-r. 11360 - Winnie the Pooh Fun and Fantasy (Disney-r). 11361 - Gyro Gearloose & the Disney Ducks (r/4-C 1047,1184)-Barks-c(r)
each.... 1.00

DYNAMIC ADVENTURES
No. 8, 1964 - No. 9, 1964
I. W. Enterprises

8-Kayo Kirby-r by Baker?/Fight Comics #? 2.00 5.00 10.00
9-Reprints Avon's "Escape From Devil's Island"-Kinstler-c 2.40 6.00 12.00
nn(no date)-Reprints Risks Unlimited with Rip Carson, Senorita Rio 2.00 5.00 10.00

DYNAMIC CLASSICS (See Cancelled Comic Cavalcade)
Sept-Oct, 1978 (44 pgs.)
DC Comics

1-Neal Adams Batman, Simonson Manhunter-r 1.00 2.50

DYNAMIC COMICS (No #4-7)
Oct, 1941 - No. 3, Feb, 1942; No. 8, 1944 - No. 25, May, 1948
Harry 'A' Chesler

1-Origin Major Victory by Charles Sultan (reprinted in Major Victory #1), Dynamic Man & Hale the Magician; The Black Cobra only app. 87.00 262.00 575.00
2-Origin Dynamic Boy & Lady Satan; intro. The Green Knight & sidekick Lance Cooper 45.00 135.00 300.00
3 35.00 105.00 230.00
8-Dan Hastings, The Echo, The Master Key, Yankee Boy begin; Yankee Doodle Jones app.; hypo story 35.00 105.00 230.00
9-Mr. E begins; Mac Raboy-c 37.00 110.00 240.00
10 29.00 86.00 190.00
11-15: 15-The Sky Chief app. 22.00 68.00 155.00
16-Marijuana story 24.00 72.00 165.00
17(1/46)-Illustrated in **SOTI**, "The children told me what the man was going to do with the hot poker," but Wertham saw this in Crime Reporter #2 33.00 100.00 225.00
18,19,21,22,24,25 14.00 43.00 100.00
20-Bare-breasted woman-c 21.00 63.00 145.00
23-Yankee Girl app. 14.00 43.00 100.00
I.W. Reprint #1,8('64): 1-r/#23. 8-Exist? 2.40 6.00 12.00

NOTE: ***Kinstler** c-IW #1. **Tuska** art in many issues, #3, 9, 11, 12, 16, 19. Bondage c-16.*

DYNAMITE (Becomes Johnny Dynamite No. 10 on)
May, 1953 - No. 9, Sept, 1954
Comic Media/Allen Hardy Publ.

1-Pete Morisi-a; r-as Danger #6 11.00 32.00 75.00
2 6.70 20.00 40.00
3-Marijuana story; Johnny Dynamite (1st app.) begins by Pete Morisi(c/a); Heck text-a; man shot in face at close range 8.35 25.00 50.00
4-Injury-to-eye, prostitution; Morisi-a 10.00 30.00 60.00
5-9-Morisi-a in all. 6-Morisi-c 5.85 17.50 35.00

DYNAMO (Also see Tales of Thunder & T.H.U.N.D.E.R. Agents)
Aug, 1966 - No. 4, June, 1967 (25 cents)
Tower Comics

1-Crandall/Wood, Ditko/Wood-a; Weed series begins; NoMan & Lightning cameos; Wood-c/a 4.70 14.00 33.00
2-4: Wood-c/a in all 3.25 9.50 22.00

NOTE: ***Adkins/Wood** a-2. **Ditko** a-4?. **Tuska** a-2, 3.*

DYNAMO JOE (Also see First Adventures & Mars)
May, 1986 - No. 15, Jan, 1988 (#12-15: $1.75)

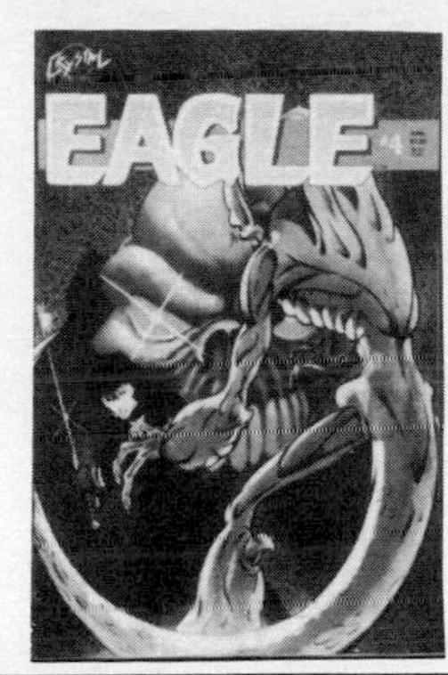

Eagle #4, © Vokes & Rankin

East Meets West #1, © Paul S. Power

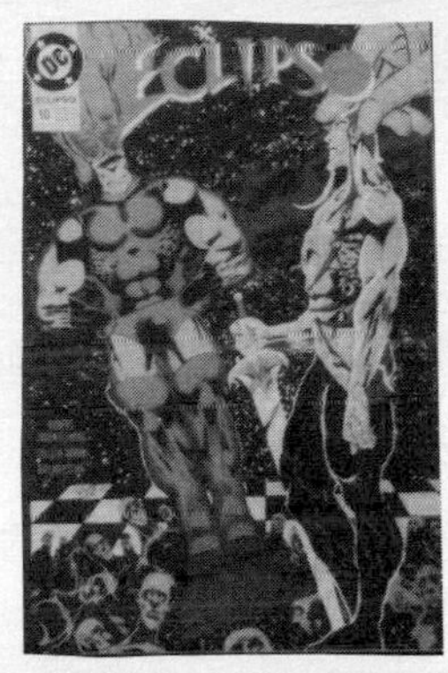

Eclipso #10, © DC

GD25 FN65 NM94

First Comics
1-15: 4-Cargonauts begin 1.50
Special 1(1/87)-Mostly-r/Mars 1.50

DYNOMUTT (TV)(See Scooby-Doo, 3rd series)
Nov, 1977 - No. 6, Sept, 1978 (Hanna-Barbera)
Marvel Comics Group
1 1.00 2.50
2-6: 3-Scooby Doo story 1.50

EAGLE, THE (1st Series) (See Science Comics & Weird Comics #8)
July, 1941 - No. 4, Jan, 1942
Fox Features Syndicate
1-The Eagle begins; Rex Dexter of Mars app. by Briefer
96.00 290.00 650.00
2-The Spider Queen begins (origin) 54.00 162.00 375.00
3,4: 3-Joe Spook begins (origin) 43.00 130.00 300.00

EAGLE (2nd Series)
Feb-Mar, 1945 - No. 2, Apr-May, 1945
Rural Home Publ.
1-Aviation stories 12.00 36.00 85.00
2-Lucky Aces 10.00 30.00 70.00
NOTE: *L. B. Cole c/a in each.*

EAGLE
Sept, 1986 - No. 26?, 1989 ($1.50/1.75/1.95, B&W)
Crystal Comics/Apple Comics #17 on
1 .80 2.00
1-Signed and limited 1.20 3.00
2-26: 12-Double size origin issue ($2.50) 1.50

EARTH MAN ON VENUS (An...) (Also see Strange Planets)
1951
Avon Periodicals
nn-Wood-a (26 pgs.); Fawcette-c 79.00 235.00 550.00

EASTER BONNET SHOP (See March of Comics No. 29)

EASTER WITH MOTHER GOOSE (See 4-Color No. 103, 140, 185, 220)

EAST MEETS WEST (Innovation)(Value: cover or less)

EAT RIGHT TO WORK AND WIN
1942 (16 pages) (Giveaway)
Swift & Company
Blondie, Henry, Flash Gordon by Alex Raymond, Toots & Casper, Thimble Theatre(Popeye), Tillie the Toiler, The Phantom, The Little King, & Bringing up Father - original strips just for this book -(in daily strip form which shows what foods we should eat and why)
20.00 60.00 140.00

E. C. CLASSIC REPRINTS
May, 1973 - No. 12, 1976 (E. C. Comics reprinted in color minus ads)
East Coast Comix Co.
1-The Crypt of Terror #1 (Tales From the Crypt #46)
1.00 2.50 6.00
2-Weird Science #15('52) 1.60 4.00
3-12: 3-Shock SuspenStories #12. 4-Haunt of Fear #12. 5-Weird Fantasy #13 ('52). 6-Crime SuspenStories #25. 7-Vault of Horror #26. 8-Shock SuspenStories #6. 9-Two-Fisted Tales #34. 10-Haunt of Fear #23. 11-Weird Science #12(#1). 12-Shock SuspenStories #2 1.20 3.00

EC CLASSICS
Aug, 1985 - No. 12, 1986? (High quality paper; each-r 8 stories in color)
Russ Cochran (#2-12 were resolicited in 1990)($4.95, 56 pgs., 8x11")
1-12: 1-Tales From the Crypt. 2-Weird Science. 3-Two-Fisted Tales. 4-Shock SuspenStories. 5-Weird Fantasy. 6-Vault of Horror. 7-Weird Science-Fantasy (r/20,24). 8-Crime SuspenStories. 9-Haunt of Fear. 10-Panic (r/1,2). 11-Tales From the Crypt (r/23,24). 12-Weird Science (r/20,22)
1.00 2.00 5.00

ECHO OF FUTUREPAST (Pacific)(Value: cover or less)

GD25 FN65 NM94

ECLIPSE GRAPHIC ALBUM SERIES
Oct, 1978 - Present (8-1/2x11") (B&W #1-5)
Eclipse Comics
1-Sabre (10/78, B&W, 1st print.); Gulacy-a; 1st direct sale graphic novel
1.30 3.25 8.00
1-Sabre (2nd printing, 1/79) 1.30 3.25 8.00
1-Sabre (3rd printing, $5.95) 1.00 2.50 6.00
2-Night Music (11/79, B&W)-Russell-a 1.00 2.00 5.00
3-Detectives, Inc. (5/80, B&W)-Rogers-a 1.20 3.00 7.00
4-Stewart The Rat ('80, B&W)-G. Colan-a 1.20 3.00 7.00
5-The Price (10/81, B&W)-Starlin-a 1.70 5.00 12.00
6-I Am Coyote (11/84, color)-Rogers-c/a 1.30 3.25 8.00
7-The Rocketeer (9/85, color)-Dave Stevens-a (r/chapters 1-5)(see Pacific Presents & Starslayer); has 7 pgs. new-a 1.30 3.25 8.00
7-The Rocketeer (2nd print, $7.95) 1.30 3.25 8.00
7-The Rocketeer (3rd print, 1991, $8.95) 1.50 3.75 9.00
7-The Rocketeer, signed & limited hardcover 9.00 26.00 60.00
7-The Rocketeer, unsigned hard-c (3rd, $32.95) 4.70 14.00 33.00
8-Zorro In Old California ('86, color) 1.30 3.25 8.00
8-Hard cover 1.70 5.00 12.00
9-Sacred And The Profane ('86)-Steacy-a 2.30 6.75 16.00
9-Hard cover ($24.95) 3.60 10.75 25.00
10-Somerset Holmes ('86, $15.95)-Adults, soft-c 2.30 6.75 16.00
10-Hard cover ($24.95) 3.60 10.75 25.00
11-Floyd Farland, Citizen of the Future ('87, $3.95, B&W) 1.60 4.00
12-Silverheels ('87, $8.95, color) 1.50 3.75 9.00
12-Hard cover ($14.95) 2.15 6.50 15.00
12-Hard cover, signed & #'d ($24.95) 3.60 10.75 25.00
13-The Sisterhood of Steel ('87, $9.95, color) 1.65 4.00 10.00
14-Samurai, Son of Death ('87, $4.95, B&W) 1.00 2.00 5.00
14-Samurai, Son of Death ($3.95, 2nd print.) 1.60 4.00
15-Twisted Tales (11/87, color)-Dave Stevens-c 1.60 4.00
16-See Airfighters Classics #1
17-Valkyrie, Prisoner of the Past ('88, $3.95, color) 1.60 4.00
18-See Airfighters Classics #2
19-Scout: The Four Monsters ('88, $14.95, color)-r/Scout #1-7; soft-c
2.15 6.50 15.00
20-See Airfighters Classics #3
21-XYR-Multiple ending comic ('88, $3.95, B&W) 1.60 4.00
22-Alien Worlds #1 (5/88, $3.95, 52 pgs.)-Nudity 1.60 4.00
23-See Airfighters Classics #4
24-Heartbreak ($4.95, B&W) 1.00 2.00 5.00
25-Alex Toth's Zorro Vol. 1 ($10.95, B&W) 1.65 4.70 11.00
26-Alex Toth's Zorro Vol. 2 ($10.95, B&W) 1.65 4.70 11.00
27-Fast Fiction (She) ($5.95, B&W) 1.00 2.50 6.00
28-Miracleman Book I ($5.95) 1.00 2.50 6.00
29-Real Love: The Best of the Simon and Kirby Romance Comics (10/88, $12.95) 1.85 5.50 13.00
30-Brought To Light; Alan Moore scripts (1989) 1.65 4.70 11.00
30-Limited hardcover ed. ($29.95) 4.30 13.00 30.00
31-Pigeons From Hell by R. E. Howard (11/88) 1.30 3.25 8.00
31-Signed & Limited Edition ($29.95) 4.30 13.00 30.00

ECLIPSE MAGAZINE (Eclipse)(Value: cover or less)

ECLIPSE MONTHLY (Eclipse)(Value: cover or less)

ECLIPSO (See Brave and the Bold #64, House of Secrets #61 & Phantom Stranger, 1987)
Nov, 1992 - Present ($1.25, color)
DC Comics
1-14: 1-Giffen plots/Breakdowns begin 1.25
15-18: 15 Begin $1.50-c 1.50
Annual 1 (1993, $2.50, 68 pgs.) 1.00 2.50

ECLIPSO: THE DARKNESS WITHIN
July, 1992 - No. 2, Oct, 1992 ($2.50, color, 68 pgs.)
DC Comics

Ectokid #1, © Clive Barker

Eerie #6, © AVON

Egbert #1, © QUA

GD25 FN65 NM94

1-With purple gem attached to-c 1.60 4.00
1-Without gem; Superman, Creeper app. 1.00 2.50
2-Concludes Eclipso storyline from annuals 1.00 2.50

E. C. 3-D CLASSICS (See Three Dimensional...)

ECTOKID (See Razorline)
Sept, 1993 - Present ($1.75, color)
Marvel Comics

1-($2.50)-Foil embossed-c; created by C. Barker 1.00 2.50
2-8: 2-Origin .70 1.75

EDDIE STANKY (Baseball Hero)
1951 (New York Giants)
Fawcett Publications

nn-Photo-c 19.00 57.00 130.00

EDGAR BERGEN PRESENTS CHARLIE McCARTHY
No. 764, 1938 (36 pgs.; 15x10-1/2"; in color)
Whitman Publishing Co. (Charlie McCarthy Co.)

764 (Scarce) 71.00 215.00 500.00

EDGE OF CHAOS (Pacific)(Value: cover or less)

EDWARD'S SHOES GIVEAWAY
1954 (Has clown on cover)
Edward's Shoe Store

Contains comic with new cover. Many combinations possible. Contents determines price, 50-60 percent of original. (Similar to Comics From Weatherbird & Free Comics to You)

ED WHEELAN'S JOKE BOOK STARRING FAT & SLAT (See Fat & Slat)

EERIE (Strange Worlds No. 18 on)
No. 1, Jan, 1947; No. 1, May-June, 1951 - No. 17, Aug-Sept, 1954
Avon Periodicals

1(1947)-1st horror comic; Kubert, Fugitani-a; bondage-c
75.00 225.00 525.00
1(1951)-Reprints story from 1947 #1 30.00 90.00 210.00
2-Wood-c/a; bondage-c 34.00 100.00 235.00
3-Wood-c; Kubert, Wood/Orlando-a 34.00 100.00 235.00
4,5-Wood-c 30.00 90.00 210.00
6,8,13,14: 8-Kinstler-a; bondage-c; Phantom Witch Doctor story
12.00 36.00 85.00
7-Wood/Orlando-c; Kubert-a 21.00 63.00 145.00
9-Kubert-a; Check-c 13.00 40.00 90.00
10,11: 10-Kinstler-a. 11-Kinstlerish-a by McCann 11.00 32.00 75.00
12-Dracula story from novel, 25 pgs. 13.50 41.00 95.00
15-Reprints No. 1('51)minus-c(bondage) 9.15 27.50 55.00
16-Wood-a r-/No. 2 10.00 30.00 65.00
17-Wood/Orlando & Kubert-a; reprints #3 minus inside & outside Wood-c
11.50 34.00 80.00

NOTE: ***Hollingsworth** a-9-11; c-10, 11.*

EERIE
1964
I. W. Enterprises

I.W. Reprint #1('64)-Wood-c(r); r-story/Spook #1 3.20 8.00 16.00
I.W. Reprint #2,6,8: 8-Dr. Drew by Grandenetti from Ghost #9
2.40 6.00 12.00
I.W. Reprint #9-r/Tales of Terror #1(Toby); Wood-c 3.20 8.00 16.00

EERIE (Magazine)(See Warren Presents)
No. 1, Sept, 1965; No. 2, Mar, 1966 - No. 139, Feb, 1983
Warren Publishing Co.

1-24 pgs., black & white, small size (5-1/4x7-1/4"), low distribution; cover from inside back cover of Creepy No. 2; stories reprinted from Creepy No. 7, 8. At least three different versions exist.

First Printing - B&W, 5-1/4" wide x 7-1/4" high, evenly trimmed. On page 18, panel 5, in the upper left-hand corner, the large rear view of a bald headed man blends into solid black and is unrecognizable. Overall printing quality is poor. 25.00 75.00 175.00

Second Printing - B&W, 5-1/4x7-1/4", with uneven, untrimmed edges (if one of these were trimmed evenly, the size would be less than as indicated). The figure of the bald headed man on page 18, panel 5 is clear and discernible. The staples have a 1/4" blue stripe.
11.00 32.00 75.00

Other unauthorized reproductions for comparison's sake would be practically worthless. One known version was probably shot off a first printing copy with some loss of detail; the finer lines tend to disappear in this version which can be determined by looking at the lower right-hand corner of page one, first story. The roof of the house is shaded with straight lines. These lines are sharp and distinct on original, but broken on this version.

NOTE: ***The Overstreet Comic Book Price Guide** recommends that, before buying a 1st issue, you consult an expert.*

GD25 FN65 NM94

2-Frazetta-c 4.30 13.00 30.00
3-Frazetta-c, 1 pg. art 3.20 8.00 20.00
4-10: 4-Frazetta-a (1/2 pg.). 9-Headlight-c 2.15 6.50 15.00
11-22,24,25: 25-Steranko-c 1.65 4.00 10.00
23-Frazetta-c 1.65 4.70 11.00
26-41,43-45 1.00 2.50 6.00
42,51-(1973 & 1974 Annuals) 1.30 3.25 8.00
46-50,52,53,56-59,61-78: 78-The Mummy-r 1.00 2.50 5.50
54,55-Color Spirit story by Eisner, reprints sections 12/21/47 & 6/16/46
1.00 2.50 6.00
60-Summer Giant (9/74, $1.25) 1.20 3.00 7.00
79,80-Origin Darklon the Mystic by Starlin (1st app.) 1.00 2.50 5.50
81-139: 82-1st app. The Rook 1.40 3.50
Year Book 1970, 1971-Reprints in both 1.65 4.70 11.00
Year Book 1972-Reprints 1.30 3.25 8.00

NOTE: *The above books contain art by many good artists: **N. Adams, Brunner, Corben, Craig (Taycee), Crandall, Ditko, Eisner, Evans, Jeff Jones, Kinstler, Krenkel, McWilliams, Morrow, Orlando, Ploog, Severin, Starlin, Torres, Toth, Williamson, Wood,** and **Wrightson**; covers by **Bode', Corben, Davis, Frazetta, Morrow,** and **Orlando**. Annuals from 1973-on are included in regular numbering. 1970-74 Annuals are complete reprints. Annuals from 1975-on are in the format of the regular issues.*

EERIE ADVENTURES (Also see Weird Adventures)
Winter, 1951
Ziff-Davis Publ. Co.

1-Powell-a(2), McCann-a; used in **SOTI;** bondage-c; Krigstein back-c
16.00 50.00 115.00

NOTE: *Title dropped due to similarity to Avon's Eerie & legal action.*

EERIE TALES (Magazine)
1959 (Black & White)
Hastings Associates

1-Williamson, Torres, Tuska-a, Powell(2), & Morrow(2)-a
6.70 20.00 40.00

EERIE TALES
1963-1964
Super Comics

Super Reprint No. 10,11,12,18: 10('63)-r/Spook #27. Purple Claw in #11,12 ('63); #12-r/Avon's Eerie #1('51)-Kida-r 1.80 4.50 9.00
15-Wolverton-a, Spacehawk-r/Blue Bolt Weird Tales #113; Disbrow-a
4.00 12.00 24.00

EGBERT
Spring, 1946 - No. 20, 1950
Arnold Publications/Quality Comics Group

1-Funny animal; intro Egbert & The Count 13.00 40.00 90.00
2 8.35 25.00 50.00
3-10 4.70 14.00 28.00
11-20 3.60 9.00 18.00

EH! (...Dig This Crazy Comic) (From Here to Insanity No. 8 on)
Dec, 1953 - No. 7, Nov-Dec, 1954 (Satire)
Charlton Comics

1-Davisish-c/a by Ayers, Woodish-a by Giordano; Atomic Mouse app.
16.00 48.00 110.00
2-Ayers-c/a 11.00 32.00 75.00
3-7: 4,6-Sexual innuendo-c. 6-Ayers-a 10.00 30.00 70.00

EIGHT IS ENOUGH KITE FUN BOOK (See Kite Fun Book)

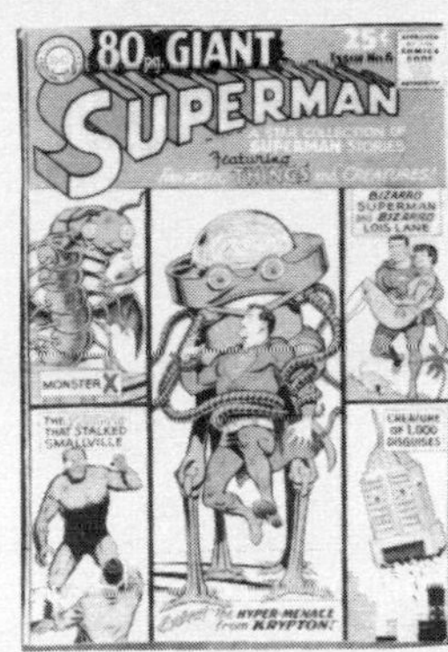

80 Page Giant #6, © DC

Electric Warrior #4, © DC

Elfquest: Blood of Ten Chiefs #1, © Warp Grafics

GD25 FN65 NM94

80 PAGE GIANT (...Magazine No. 2-15) (25 cents)
8/64 - No. 15, 10/65; No. 16, 11/65 - No. 89, 7/71 (All reprints)
National Periodical Publications (#1-56: 84 pgs.; #57-89: 68 pages)

	GD25	FN65	NM94
1-Superman Annual; originally planned as Superman Annual #9 (8/64)	21.00	63.00	250.00
2-Jimmy Olsen	10.00	31.00	125.00
3,4: 3-Lois Lane. 4-Flash-G.A.-r; Infantino-a	8.00	25.00	100.00
5-Batman; has Sunday newspaper strip; Catwoman-r; Batman's Life Story-r (25th anniversary special)	7.00	21.00	85.00
6-Superman	7.00	20.00	80.00
7-Sgt. Rock's Prize Battle Tales; Kubert-c/a	7.00	20.00	80.00
8-More Secret Origins-origins of JLA, Aquaman, Robin, Atom, & Superman; Infantino-a	18.00	54.00	215.00
9-11: 9-Flash (r/Flash #106,117,123 & Showcase #14); Infantino-a. 10-Superboy. 11 Superman; all Luthor issue	6.00	19.00	75.00
12-Batman; has Sunday newspaper strip	6.00	19.00	75.00
13,14: 13-Jimmy Olsen. 14-Lois Lane	6.00	19.00	75.00
15-Superman and Batman; Joker-c/story	7.00	20.00	80.00

Continued as part of regular series under each title in which that particular book came out, a Giant being published instead of the regular size. Issues No. 16 to No. 89 are listed for your information. See individual titles for prices.

16-JLA #39 (11/65), 17-Batman #176, 18-Superman #183, 19-Our Army at War #164, 20-Action #334, 21-Flash #160, 22-Superboy #129, 23-Superman #187, 24-Batman #182, 25-Jimmy Olsen #95, 26-Lois Lane #68, 27-Batman #185, 28-World's Finest #161, 29-JLA #48, 30-Batman #187, 31-Superman #193, 32-Our Army at War #177, 33-Action #347, 34-Flash #169, 35-Superboy #138, 36-Superman #197, 37-Batman #193, 38-Jimmy Olsen #104, 39-Lois Lane #77, 40-World's Finest #170, 41-JLA #58, 42-Superman #202, 43-Batman #198, 44-Our Army at War #190, 45-Action #360, 46-Flash #178, 47-Superboy #147, 48-Superman #207, 49-Batman #203, 50-Jimmy Olsen #113, 51-Lois Lane #86, 52-World's Finest #179, 53-JLA #67, 54-Superman #212, 55-Batman #208, 56-Our Army at War #203, 57-Action #373, 58-Flash #187, 59-Superboy #156, 60-Superman #217, 61-Batman #213, 62-Jimmy Olsen #122, 63-Lois Lane #95, 64-World's Finest #188, 65-JLA #76, 66-Superman #222, 67-Batman #218, 68-Our Army at War #216, 69-Adventure #390, 70-Flash #196, 71-Superboy #165, 72-Superman #227, 73-Batman #223, 74-Jimmy Olsen #131, 75 Lois Lane #104, 76-World's Finest #197, 77-JLA #85, 78-Superman #232, 79-Batman #228, 80-Our Army at War #229, 81-Adventure #403, 82-Flash #205, 83-Superboy #174, 84-Superman #239, 85-Batman #233, 86-Jimmy Olsen #140, 87-Lois Lane #113, 88-World's Finest #206, 89-JLA #93.

87TH PRECINCT (TV)
Apr-June, 1962 - No. 2, July-Sept, 1962
Dell Publishing Co.

	GD25	FN65	NM94
4-Color 1309(#1); Krigstein-a	10.00	30.00	60.00
2	7.50	22.50	45.00

EL BOMBO COMICS
1946
Standard Comics/Frances M. McQueeny

	GD25	FN65	NM94
nn(1946)	8.35	25.00	50.00
1(no date)	8.35	25.00	50.00

EL CID (See 4-Color No. 1259)

EL DIABLO (DC)(Value: cover or less)

EL DORADO (See Movie Classics)

ELECTRIC UNDERTOW (See Strikeforce Morituri: Electric Undertow)

ELECTRIC WARRIOR (DC)(Value: cover or less)

ELEKTRA: ASSASSIN
Aug, 1986 - No. 8, Mar, 1987 (Limited series, adults)
Epic Comics (Marvel)

	GD25	FN65	NM94
1-Miller scripts in all		1.60	4.00
2		1.20	3.00
3-7		.80	2.00
8		1.90	4.75
Signed & numbered hardcover (Graphitti Designs, $39.95, 2000 print run)-reprints 1-8			40.00

ELEKTRA SAGA, THE
Feb, 1984 - No. 4, June, 1984 ($2.00, Baxter paper)
Marvel Comics Group

	GD25	FN65	NM94
1-4-r/Daredevil 168-190; Miller-c/a		1.60	4.00

ELEMENTALS, THE (See The Justice Machine & Morningstar Spec.)
June, 1984 - No. 29, Sept, 1988; V2#1, Mar, 1989 - Present
Comico The Comic Co. ($1.50/$2.50, Baxter paper)

	GD25	FN65	NM94
1-Willingham-c/a, 1-8		1.60	4.00
2		1.00	2.50
3-10: 9-Bissette-a(p). 10-Photo-c		.80	2.00
11-29			1.50
V2#1-25: 1-3-$1.95-c. 4-Begin $2.50-c. 16-1st app. Strike Force America. 18-Prelude to Avalon mini-series. 37-Prequel to Strike Force America series		.80	2.00
Special 1 (3/86)-Willingham-a(p)		.70	1.75
Special 2 (1/89, $1.95)		.75	1.90

ELFLORD (Aircel)(Value: cover or less)

ELFQUEST (Also see Fantasy Quarterly & Warp Graphics Annual)
No. 2, Aug, 1978 - No. 21, Feb, 1985 (All magazine size)
No. 1, April, 1979
WaRP Graphics, Inc.

NOTE: *Elfquest* was originally published as one of the stories in **Fantasy Quarterly #1**. When the publisher went out of business, the creative team, Wendy and Richard Pini, formed WaRP Graphics and continued the series, beginning with **Elfquest #2. Elfquest #1**, which reprinted the story from **Fantasy Quarterly**, was published about the same time **Elfquest #4** was released. Thereafter, most issues were reprinted as demand warranted, until Marvel announced it would reprint the entire series under its Epic imprint (Aug., 1985).

	GD25	FN65	NM94
1(4/79)-Reprints Elfquest story from Fantasy Quarterly No. 1			
1st printing ($1.00-c)	5.00	15.00	35.00
2nd printing ($1.25-c)	1.65	4.70	11.00
3rd printings ($1.50-c)	1.00	2.00	5.00
4th printing; different-c ($1.50-c)			1.50
2(8/78)-5: 1st printings ($1.00-c)	3.25	9.50	22.00
2nd printings ($1.25-c)	1.00	2.00	5.00
3rd & 4th printings ($1.50-c)(all 4th prints 1989)		1.20	3.00
6-9: 1st printings ($1.25-c)	1.50	3.75	9.00
2nd printings ($1.50-c)		1.60	4.00
3rd printings ($1.50-c)		.80	2.00
10-14: ($1.50 cover); 16-8pg. preview of A Distant Soil	1.00	2.50	6.00
10-14: 2nd printings ($1.50)			1.50
15-21 (only one printing)	1.00	2.50	6.00

ELFQUEST
Aug, 1985 - No. 32, Mar, 1988
Epic Comics (Marvel)

	GD25	FN65	NM94
1-Reprints in color the Elfquest epic by WaRP Graphics		1.80	4.50
2-5		1.00	2.50
6-10		.80	2.00
11-20		.70	1.80
21-32			1.50

ELFQUEST
1989 - No. 4, 1989 ($1.50, B&W)
WaRP Graphics

	GD25	FN65	NM94
1-4: Reprints original Elfquest series			1.50

ELFQUEST: BLOOD OF THE TEN CHIEFS
July, 1993 - Present ($2.00, color)
WaRP Graphics

	GD25	FN65	NM94
1-4-By Richard & Wendy Pini		.80	2.00

ELFQUEST: HIDDEN YEARS (WaRP Graphics)(Value: cover or less)

ELFQUEST: KINGS OF THE BROKEN WHEEL
June, 1990 - No. 9, Feb, 1992 ($2.00, B&W) (3rd Elfquest saga)
WaRP Graphics

	GD25	FN65	NM94
1-9: By Richard & Wendy Pini; 1-Color insert		.80	2.00
1-2nd printing		.80	2.00

Elfquest: Siege At Blue Mountain #2, © Apple Comics

Elvira Mistress of the Dark #2, © MEG

E-Man #18, © FIRST

ELFQUEST: NEW BLOOD (...Summer Special on-c #1 only)
Aug, 1992 - Present ($2.00, color, bi-monthly)
WaRP Graphics

	GD25	FN65	NM94
1-($3.95, 68 pgs.)-Byrne-a/scripts (16 pgs.)		1.60	4.00
2-12: Barry Blair-a in all		.80	2.00

ELFQUEST: SIEGE AT BLUE MOUNTAIN
Mar, 1987 - No. 8, Dec, 1988 ($1.75/$1.95, B&W, mini-series)
WaRP Graphics/Apple Comics

	GD25	FN65	NM94
1-Staton-a(i) in all; 2nd Elfquest saga	1.00	2.50	5.50
1-2nd printing		.80	2.00
2		1.40	3.50
2,3-2nd printings		.70	1.75
3-8		.80	2.00

ELF-THING (Eclipse)(Value: cover or less)

ELIMINATOR FULL COLOR SPECIAL (Eternity)(Value: cover or less)

ELLA CINDERS (See Comics On Parade, Comics Revue #1,4, Famous Comics Cartoon Book, Giant Comics Editions, Sparkler Comics, Tip Top & Treasury of Comics)

ELLA CINDERS
1938 - 1940
United Features Syndicate

	GD25	FN65	NM94
Single Series 3(1938)	30.00	90.00	210.00
Single Series 21(#2 on-c, #21 on inside), 28('40)	26.00	78.00	180.00

ELLA CINDERS
March, 1948 - No. 5, March, 1949
United Features Syndicate

	GD25	FN65	NM94
1-(#2 on cover)	10.00	30.00	70.00
2	6.35	19.00	38.00
3-5	4.70	14.00	28.00

ELLERY QUEEN
May, 1949 - No. 4, Nov, 1949
Superior Comics Ltd.

	GD25	FN65	NM94
1-Kamen-c; L.B. Cole-a; r-in Haunted Thrills	27.00	80.00	190.00
2-4: 3-Drug use stories(2)	18.00	54.00	125.00

NOTE: *Iger shop art in all issues.*

ELLERY QUEEN (TV)
1-3/52 - No. 2, Summer/52 (Saunders painted covers)
Ziff-Davis Publishing Co.

	GD25	FN65	NM94
1-Saunders-c	27.00	80.00	190.00
2-Saunders bondage, torture-c	24.00	70.00	165.00

ELLERY QUEEN (See Crackajack Funnies #23 & 4-Color No. 1165, 1243, 1289)

ELMER FUDD (Also see Camp Comics, Daffy, Looney Tunes #1 & Super Book #10, 22)
No. 470, May, 1953 - No. 1293, Mar-May, 1962
Dell Publishing Co.

	GD25	FN65	NM94
4-Color 470,558,628,689('56)	2.80	7.00	14.00
4-Color 725,783,841,888,938,977,1032,1081,1131,1171,1222,1293('62)	2.40	6.00	12.00

ELMO COMICS
January, 1948 (Daily strip-r)
St. John Publishing Co.

	GD25	FN65	NM94
1-By Cecil Jensen	8.35	25.00	50.00

ELONGATED MAN (See Flash #112 & Justice League of America #105)
Jan, 1992 - No. 4, Apr, 1992 ($1.00, color, mini-series)
DC Comics

	GD25	FN65	NM94
1-4: 3-The Flash app.			1.00

ELRIC (Pacific/First, all titles)(Value; cover or less)

EL SALVADOR - A HOUSE DIVIDED (Eclipse)(Value: cover or less)

ELSEWHERE PRINCE, THE (Moebius' Airtight Garage)
May, 1990 - No. 6, Oct, 1990 ($1.95, color, limited series)
Epic Comics (Marvel)

	GD25	FN65	NM94
1-6: Moebius scripts & back-up-a in all		.80	2.00

ELSIE THE COW
Oct-Nov, 1949 - No. 3, July-Aug, 1950
D. S. Publishing Co.

	GD25	FN65	NM94
1-(36 pages)	16.00	50.00	115.00
2,3	13.00	40.00	90.00
Borden Milk Giveaway-(16 pgs., nn) (3 issues, 1957)	7.50	22.50	45.00
Elsie's Fun Book(1950; Borden Milk)	8.35	25.00	50.00
Everyday Birthday Fun With...(1957; 20 pgs.)(100th Anniversary); Kubert-a	7.50	22.50	45.00

ELSON'S PRESENTS
1981 (100 pgs., no cover price)
DC Comics

	GD25	FN65	NM94
Series 1-6: Repackaged 1981 DC comics; Superman, Action, Flash, DC Comics Presents & Batman known. Series I has a Batman/Joker-c. Series 3-New Teen Titans #3('81)	1.00	2.00	5.00

ELVIRA MISTRESS OF THE DARK (Claypool/Eclipse)(Value: cover or less)

ELVIRA'S HOUSE OF MYSTERY (DC)(Value: cover or less)

ELVIRA'S MISTRESS OF THE DARK (Marvel)(Value: cover or less)

ELVIS MANDIBLE, THE
1990 ($3.50, B&W, mature readers, 52 pgs.)
Piranha Press (DC)

	GD25	FN65	NM94
nn		1.40	3.50

ELVIS PRESLEY (See Career Girl Romances #32, Go-Go, Howard Chaykin's American Flagg #10, Humbug #8, I Love You #60 & Young Lovers #18)

E-MAN
Oct, 1973 - No. 10, Sept, 1975 (Painted-c No. 7-10)
Charlton Comics

	GD25	FN65	NM94
1-Origin & 1st app. E-Man; Staton c/a in all	2.15	6.50	15.00
2-4: 2,4-Ditko-a. 3-Howard-a	1.30	3.25	8.00
5-Miss Liberty Belle app. by Ditko	1.20	2.50	6.00
6,7,9,10-Early Byrne-a in all (#6 is 1/75)	1.25	3.00	7.50
8-Full-length story; Nova begins as E-Man's partner	1.50	3.75	9.00
1-4,9,10(Modern Comics reprints, '77)			1.00

NOTE: *Killjoy app.-No. 2, 4. Liberty Belle app.-No. 5. Rog 2000 app.-No. 6, 7, 9, 10. Travis app.-No. 3.* ***Tom Sutton*** *a-1.*

E-MAN (First & Comico)(Value: cover or less)

EMERALD DAWN
1991 ($4.95, color, squarebound)
DC Comics

	GD25	FN65	NM94
nn-Reprints Green Lantern: Emerald Dawn #1-6	1.00	2.00	5.00

EMERALD DAWN II (See Green Lantern...)

EMERGENCY (Magazine)
June, 1976 - No. 4, Jan, 1977 (B&W)
Charlton Comics

	GD25	FN65	NM94
1-Neal Adams-c/a; Heath, Austin-a		1.00	2.50
2,4: 2-N. Adams-c. 4-Alcala-a		.65	1.60
3-N. Adams-a		.70	1.80

EMERGENCY (TV)
June, 1976 - No. 4, Dec, 1976
Charlton Comics

	GD25	FN65	NM94
1-Staton-c; Byrne-a		1.00	2.50
2-4: 2-Staton-c			1.50

EMERGENCY DOCTOR
Summer, 1963 (One Shot)
Charlton Comics

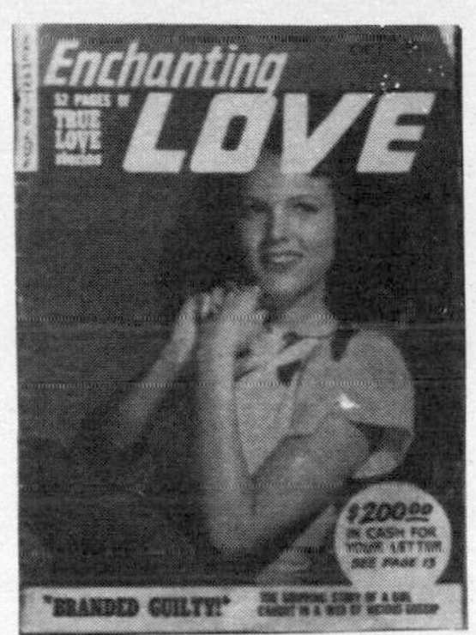

Enchanting Love #1, © Kirby Publ.

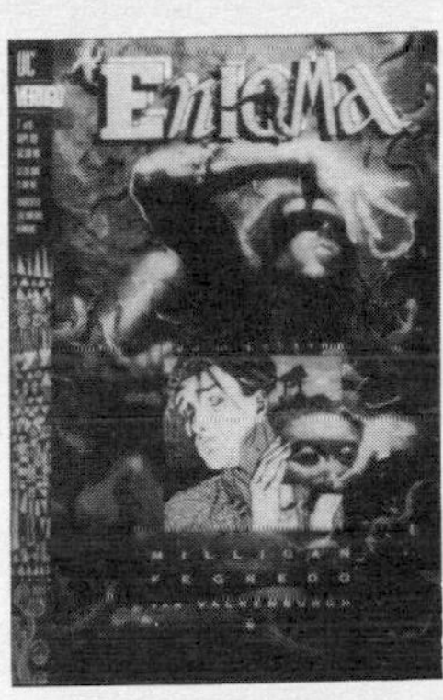

Enigma #7, © Peter Milligan & Duncan Fegredo

The Eternals #11, © MEG

	GD25	FN65	NM94
1	1.00	2.50	5.00

EMIL & THE DETECTIVES (See Movie Comics)

EMMA PEEL & JOHN STEED (See The Avengers)

EMPIRE STRIKES BACK, THE (See Marvel Comics Super Special #16 & Marvel Special Edition)

ENCHANTED APPLES OF OZ, THE (See First Comics Graphic Novel #5)

ENCHANTER (Eclipse)(Value: cover or less)

ENCHANTING LOVE
Oct, 1949 - No. 6, July, 1950 (All, 52 pgs.)
Kirby Publishing Co.

	GD25	FN65	NM94
1-Photo-c	7.00	21.00	42.00
2-Photo-c; Powell-a	4.35	13.00	26.00
3,4,6: 3-Jimmy Stewart photo-c	3.60	9.00	18.00
5-Ingels-a, 9 pgs.; photo-c	10.00	30.00	65.00

ENCHANTMENT VISUALETTES (Magazine)
Dec, 1949 - No. 5, April, 1950 (Painted c-1)
World Editions

	GD25	FN65	NM94
1-Contains two romance comic strips each	10.00	30.00	65.00
2	9.15	27.50	55.00
3-5	7.50	22.50	45.00

ENEMY ACE SPECIAL (Also see Our Army at War #151, Showcase #57, 58 & Star Spangled War Stories #138)
1990 ($1.00, color, one-shot)
DC Comics

	GD25	FN65	NM94
1-Kubert-r/Our Army #151,153; c-r/Showcase 57			1.50

ENIGMA
March, 1993 - No. 8, Oct, 1993 ($2.50, color, limited series)
DC Comics (Vertigo)

	GD25	FN65	NM94
1-8: Milligan scripts		1.00	2.50

ENSIGN O'TOOLE (TV)
Aug-Oct, 1963 - No. 2, 1964
Dell Publishing Co.

	GD25	FN65	NM94
1,2	2.80	7.00	14.00

ENSIGN PULVER (See Movie Classics)

EPIC
1992 - Book 4, 1992 ($4.95, color, mini-series, 52 pgs.)
Epic Comics (Marvel)

	GD25	FN65	NM94
Book One-Four: 2-Dorman painted-c	1.00	2.00	5.00

NOTE: *Alien Legion in #3. Cholly & Flytrap by* ***Burden****(scripts) &* ***Suydam****(art) in 3, 4. Dinosaurs in #4. Dreadlands in #1. Hellraiser in #1. Nightbreed in #2. Sleeze Brothers in #2. Stalkers in #1-4. Wild Cards in #1-4.*

EPIC ILLUSTRATED (Magazine)
Spring, 1980 - No. 36, Feb, 1986 ($2.00-$2.50, B&W/Color, adults)
Marvel Comics Group

	GD25	FN65	NM94
1-Frazetta-c		.80	2.00
2-26: 12-Wolverton Spacehawk-r edited & recolored w/article on him. 13-Bladerunner preview by Williamson. 14-Elric of Melnibone by Russell; Revenge of the Jedi preview. 15-Vallejo-c & interview; 1st Dreadstar story (cont'd in Dreadstar #1). 16-B. Smith-c/a(2). 20-The Sacred & the Profane begins by Ken Steacy. 26-Galactus series begins, ends #34; Cerebus the Aardvark story by Dave Sim			1.50
27-36: ($2.50): 27-Groo. 28-Cerebus app.		1.00	2.50

NOTE: ***N. Adams*** *a-7; c-6.* ***Austin*** *a-15-20i.* ***Bode*** *a-19, 23, 27r.* ***Bolton*** *a-7, 10-12, 15, 18, 22-25; c-10, 18, 22, 23.* ***Boris*** *c/a-15.* ***Brunner*** *c-12.* ***Buscema*** *a-1p, 9p, 11-13p.* ***Byrne/Austin*** *a-26-34.* ***Chaykin*** *a-2; c-8.* ***Conrad*** *a-2-5, 7-9, 25-34; c-17.* ***Corben*** *a-15; c-2.* ***Frazetta*** *c-1.* ***Golden*** *a-3r.* ***Gulacy*** *c/a-3.* ***Jeff Jones*** *c-25.* ***Kaluta*** *a-17r, 21, 24r, 26; c-4, 28.* ***Nebres*** *a-1.* ***Reese*** *a-12.* ***Russell*** *a-2-4, 9, 14, 33; c-14.* ***Simonson*** *a-17.* ***B. Smith*** *c/a-7, 16.* ***Starlin*** *a-1-9, 14, 15, 34.* ***Steranko*** *c-19.* ***Williamson*** *a-13, 27, 34.* ***Wrightson*** *a-13p, 22, 25, 27, 34; c-30.*

EPIC LITE
Sept, 1991 ($3.95, color, one-shot, 52 pgs.)
Epic Comics (Marvel)

	GD25	FN65	NM94
1-Bob the Alien, Normalman by Valentino		1.60	4.00

EPICURUS THE SAGE
1991 - Vol. 2, 1991 ($9.95, color, 8-1/8x10-7/8")
Piranha Press (DC Comics)

	GD25	FN65	NM94
Volume 1,2-Sam Kieth-c/a	1.65	4.00	10.00

EPSILON WAVE (Independent/Elite)(Value: cover or less)

ERNIE COMICS (Formerly Andy Comics #21; All Love Romances #26 on)
No. 22, Sept, 1948 - No. 25, Mar, 1949
Current Books/Ace Periodicals

	GD25	FN65	NM94
nn(9/48,11/48; #22,23)-Teenage humor	4.70	14.00	28.00
24,25	3.60	9.00	18.00

ESCAPADE IN FLORENCE (See Movie Comics)

ESCAPE FROM DEVIL'S ISLAND
1952
Avon Periodicals

	GD25	FN65	NM94
1-Kinstler-c; r/as Dynamic Adventures #9	22.00	65.00	150.00

ESCAPE FROM FEAR
1956, 1962, 1969 (8 pages full color) (On birth control)
Planned Parenthood of America (Giveaway)

	GD25	FN65	NM94
1956 edition	10.00	30.00	60.00
1962 edition	6.70	20.00	40.00
1969 edition	4.00	10.00	20.00

ESCAPE FROM THE PLANET OF THE APES (See Power Record Comics)

ESCAPE TO WITCH MOUNTAIN (See Walt Disney Showcase No. 29)

ESPERS (Eclipse)(Value: cover or less)

ESPIONAGE (TV)
May-July, 1964 - No. 2, Aug-Oct, 1964
Dell Publishing Co.

	GD25	FN65	NM94
1,2	3.20	8.00	16.00

ETC
1989 - No. 5, 1990 ($4.50, color, mini-series, adults, 60 pgs.)
Piranha Press (DC Comics)

	GD25	FN65	NM94
Book 1-5: Conrad scripts/layouts in all		1.80	4.50

ETERNAL BIBLE, THE
1946 (Large size) (16 pages in color)
Authentic Publications

	GD25	FN65	NM94
1	10.00	30.00	60.00

ETERNALS, THE
July, 1976 - No. 19, Jan, 1978
Marvel Comics Group

	GD25	FN65	NM94
1-Origin & 1st app. Eternals		1.60	4.00
2-19: 2-1st app. Ajak & The Celestials. 14,15-Cosmic powered Hulk-c/story		1.00	2.50
Annual 1(10/77)		1.00	2.50

NOTE: ***Kirby*** *c/a(p) in all. Price changed from 25 cents to 30 cents during run of #1.*

ETERNALS, THE
Oct, 1985 - No. 12, Sept, 1986 (Maxi-series, mando paper)
Marvel Comics Group

	GD25	FN65	NM94
1,12 ($1.25, 52 pgs.): 12-Williamson-a(i)			1.25
2-11-(75 cents)			1.00

ETERNALS: THE HEROD FACTOR
Nov, 1991 ($2.50, color, 68 pgs.)
Marvel Comics

	GD25	FN65	NM94
1		1.00	2.50

ETERNAL WARRIOR (See Solar #10 & 11)
Aug, 1992 - Present ($2.25, color)
Valiant

Eternal Warrior #15, © Voyager Comm.

Excalibur #70, © MEG

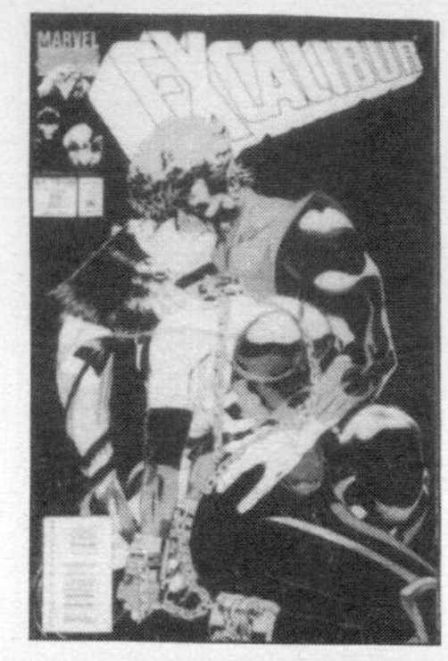

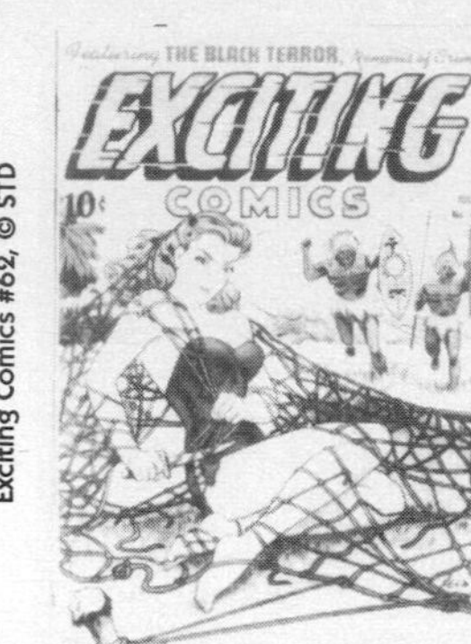

Exciting Comics #62, © STD

	GD25	FN65	NM94
1-Miller-c; B. Smith/Layton-a (Unity x-over); origin Eternal Warrior & Armstrong	1.85	5.50	13.00
1-Gold logo			26.00
1-Gold foil logo			39.00
2-Unity x-over; Simonson-c	1.20	3.00	7.00
3-Archer & Armstrong x-over	1.00	2.50	5.50
4-1st app. Bloodshot (last pg. cameo); see Rai #0 for 1st full app.; Cowan-c	1.50	3.75	9.00
5-2nd full app. Bloodshot (12/92; see Rai #0)	1.00	2.50	6.00
6,7: 6-2nd app. Master Darque		1.10	2.75
8-See Archer & Armstrong #8 for value; combined with Eternal Warrior #8		1.90	4.75
9-22: 9-1st Book of Geomancer. 14-16-Bloodshot app. 18-Doctor Mirage cameo		.90	2.25
Year Book 1 (1993, $3.95)		1.60	4.00

ETERNITY SMITH (Renegade & Hero)(Value: cover or less)

ETTA KETT
No. 11, Dec, 1948 - No. 14, Sept, 1949
King Features Syndicate/Standard

	GD25	FN65	NM94
11	7.00	21.00	42.00
12-14	4.70	14.00	28.00

EUDAEMON, THE
Aug, 1993 - No. 3, Oct, 1993
Dark Horse Comics

	GD25	FN65	NM94
1-3: Nelson-a, painted-c & scripts		1.00	2.50

EVANGELINE (Comico/First)(Value: cover or less)

EVA THE IMP
1957 - No. 2, Nov, 1957
Red Top Comic/Decker

	GD25	FN65	NM94
1,2	2.40	6.00	12.00

EVEL KNIEVEL
1974 (20 pages) (Giveaway)
Marvel Comics Group (Ideal Toy Corp.)

	GD25	FN65	NM94
nn-Contains photo on inside back-c			1.00

EVERYBODY'S COMICS (See Fox Giants)

EVERYMAN, THE
Nov, 1991 ($4.50, color, one-shot, 52 pgs.)
Epic Comics (Marvel)

	GD25	FN65	NM94
1		1.80	4.50

EVERYTHING HAPPENS TO HARVEY
Sept-Oct, 1953 - No. 7, Sept-Oct, 1954
National Periodical Publications

	GD25	FN65	NM94
1	17.00	52.00	120.00
2	10.00	30.00	70.00
3-7	9.15	27.50	55.00

EVERYTHING'S ARCHIE
May, 1969 - No. 158?, 1991 (Giant issues No. 1-20)
Archie Publications

	GD25	FN65	NM94
1	7.50	22.50	45.00
2	4.00	11.00	22.00
3-5	2.40	6.00	12.00
6-10	1.40	3.50	7.00
11-20		1.40	3.50
21-50			1.50
51-158: 142,148-Gene Colan-a			1.00

EVERYTHING'S DUCKY (See 4-Color No. 1251)

EWOKS (TV) (See Star Comics Magazine)
June, 1985 - No. 15, Sept, 1987 (75 cents; $1.00 #14 on)
Star Comics (Marvel)

	GD25	FN65	NM94
1-15 (From Star Wars): 10-Williamson-a			1.00

EXCALIBUR (Also see Marvel Comics Presents #31)
1987; Oct, 1988 - Present ($1.50, Baxter)($1.75 #24 on)
Marvel Comics

	GD25	FN65	NM94
Special Edition nn (The Sword is Drawn)(1987, $3.25)-This is the 1st Excalibur comic	1.30	3.25	8.00
Special Edition nn (2nd print, 10/88, $3.50)		1.60	4.00
Special Edition nn (3rd print, 12/89, 4.50)		1.60	4.00
...The Sword is Drawn (Apr, '92, 4.95-c)		1.80	4.50
1($1.50, 10/88)-X-Men spin-off; Nightcrawler, Shadowcat(Kitty Pryde), Capt. Britain, Phoenix & Meggan begin	1.00	2.50	6.00
2		1.40	3.50
3,4		1.00	2.50
5-10		.90	2.25
11-15: 10,11-Rogers/Austin-a		.75	1.90
16-23: 19-Austin-i. 21-Intro Crusader X. 22-Iron Man x-over			1.50
24-40,42-49,51-70,72-74,76: 32-($1.50). 24-John Byrne app. in story; begin $1.75-c. 27-B. Smith-a(p). 37-Dr. Doom & Iron Man app. 49-Neal Adams c-swipe. 52,57-X-Men (Cyclops, Wolverine) app. 53-Spider-Man-c/story. 58-X-Men(Wolverine, Gambit, Cyclops, etc.)-c/story			1.50
41-X-Men (Wolverine) app.; Cable cameo		.80	2.00
50-($2.75, 56 pgs.)-New logo		1.00	2.50
71-($3.95, 52 pgs.)-Hologram on-c; 30th anniversary		1.60	4.00
75-($3.50, 52 pgs.)-Holo-grafx foil cover edition		1.40	3.50
75-($2.25, 52 pgs.)-Regular edition		.90	2.25
Annual 1 ('93, $2.95)-1st app. Khaos		1.00	2.50
...Air Apparent nn (12/91, $4.95)-Simonson-c		1.60	4.00
...Mojo Mayhem nn (12/89, $4.50)-Art Adams/Austin-c/a		1.60	4.00
Special...The Possession nn (7/91, $2.95, 52 pgs.)		1.00	2.50
Special...XX Crossing (May, '92, 2.50-c)		.80	2.00

EXCITING COMICS
April, 1940 - No. 69, Sept, 1949
Nedor/Better Publications/Standard Comics

	GD25	FN65	NM94
1-Origin & 1st app. The Mask, Jim Hatfield, Sgt. Bill King, Dan Williams begin; early Robot-c (see Smash #1)	92.00	275.00	600.00
2-The Sphinx begins; The Masked Rider app.; Son of the Gods begins, ends #8	42.00	125.00	275.00
3-5: 3,6-Robot-c	33.00	100.00	225.00
6-8	22.00	68.00	150.00
9-Origin/1st app. of The Black Terror & sidekick Tim, begin series (5/41) (Black Terror c-9-52,54,55)	117.00	350.00	800.00
10-13	39.00	116.00	265.00
14-Last Sphinx, Dan Williams	27.00	82.00	185.00
15-The Liberator begins (origin)	32.00	85.00	210.00
16-20: 20-The Mask ends	18.00	55.00	125.00
21,23-27	17.00	50.00	115.00
22-Origin The Eaglet; The American Eagle begins	22.00	65.00	150.00
28-30: 28-Schomnburg-c begin. 28-Crime Crusader begins, ends #58	20.00	60.00	140.00
31-38: 35-Liberator ends, not in 31-33	18.00	54.00	125.00
39-Origin Kara, Jungle Princess	23.00	70.00	160.00
40-50: 42-The Scarab begins. 49-Last Kara, Jungle Princess. 50-Last American Eagle	20.00	60.00	140.00
51-Miss Masque begins (1st app.)	25.00	75.00	175.00
52-54: Miss Masque ends. 53-Miss Masque-c	20.00	60.00	140.00
55-58: 55-Judy of the Jungle begins (origin), ends #69; 1 pg. Ingels-a; Judy of the Jungle c-56-66. 56-58: All airbrush-c	25.00	75.00	175.00
59-Frazetta art in Caniff style; signed Frank Frazeta (one t), 9 pgs.	28.00	85.00	185.00
60-66: 60-Rick Howard, the Mystery Rider begins. 66-Robinson/Meskin-a	19.00	56.00	130.00
67-69-All western covers	12.00	35.00	80.00

*NOTE: **Schomburg** (Xela) c-28-68; airbrush c-57-66. Black Terror by **R. Moreira**-#65. **Roussos** a-62. Bondage-c 9, 12, 13, 20, 23, 25, 30, 59.*

EXCITING ROMANCES
1949 (nd); No. 2, Spring, 1950 - No. 5, 10/50; No. 6 (1951, nd); No. 7, 9/51 -

Exiles #1, © Malibu

The Extremist #2, © Peter Milligan & Union City

Faithful #2, © MEG

GD25 FN65 NM94

No. 14, 1/53
Fawcett Publications

1(1949) 8.35 25.00 50.00
2-5-(1950) 5.00 15.00 30.00
6-14 4.00 11.00 22.00

NOTE: ***Powell*** *a-8-10.* ***Marcus Swayze*** *a-5, 6, 9. Photo c-1-7, 10-12.*

EXCITING ROMANCE STORIES (See Fox Giants)

EXCITING WAR (Korean war)
No. 5, Sept, 1952 - No. 8, May, 1953; No. 9, Nov, 1953
Standard Comics (Better Publ.)

5 4.70 14.00 28.00
6,7,9 3.20 8.00 16.00
8-Toth-a 5.35 16.00 32.00

EXILES
Aug, 1993 - Present ($1.95, color)
Malibu Comics

1,2,4,5: 1,2-Bagged copies of each exist .80 2.00
3-($2.50, 40 pgs.)-Rune flip-c/story by B. Smith (3 pgs.) 1.00 2.50

EX-MUTANTS (Malibu)(Value: cover or less)

EXORCISTS (See The Crusaders)

EXOTIC ROMANCES (Formerly True War Romances)
No. 22, Oct, 1955 - No. 31, Nov, 1956
Quality Comics Group (Comic Magazines)

22 5.35 16.00 32.00
23-26,29 3.60 9.00 18.00
27,31-Baker-c/a 5.35 16.00 32.00
28,30-Baker-a 5.00 15.00 30.00

EXPLOITS OF DANIEL BOONE
Nov, 1955 - No. 6, Sept, 1956
Quality Comics Group

1-All have Cuidera-c(i) 14.00 43.00 100.00
2 10.00 30.00 60.00
3-6 8.35 25.00 50.00

EXPLOITS OF DICK TRACY (See Dick Tracy)

EXPLORER JOE
Winter, 1951 - No. 2, Oct-Nov, 1952
Ziff-Davis Comic Group (Approved Comics)

1-Saunders painted-c 8.35 25.00 50.00
2-Krigstein-a 8.35 25.00 50.00

EXPLORERS OF THE UNKNOWN (See Archie Giant Series #587, 599)
June, 1990 - No. 6, Apr, 1991 ($1.00, color)
Archie Comics

1-6: Featuring Archie and the gang 1.00

EXPOSED (...True Crime Cases)
Mar-Apr, 1948 - No. 9, July-Aug, 1949
D. S. Publishing Co.

1 10.00 30.00 70.00
2-Giggling killer story with excessive blood; two injury-to-eye panels; electrocution panel 11.50 34.00 80.00
3,8,9 5.85 17.50 35.00
4-Orlando-a 6.70 20.00 40.00
5-Breeze Lawson, Sky Sheriff by E. Good 6.70 20.00 40.00
6-Ingels-a; used in **SOTI**, illo.-"How to prepare an alibi" 19.00 58.00 135.00
7-Illo. in **SOTI**, "Diagram for housebreakers"; used by N.Y. Legis. Committee 19.00 58.00 135.00

EXTRA!
Mar-Apr, 1955 - No. 5, Nov-Dec, 1955
E. C. Comics

GD25 FN65 NM94

1-Not code approved 11.50 34.00 80.00
2-5 9.15 27.50 55.00

NOTE: ***Craig, Crandall, Severin*** *art in all.*

EXTRA COMICS
1948
Magazine Enterprises

1-Giant; consisting of rebound ME comics. Two versions known; (1)-Funnyman by Siegel & Shuster, Space Ace, Undercover Girl, Red Fox by L.B. Cole, Trail Colt & (2)-All Funnyman 34.00 105.00 240.00

EXTREMIST, THE
Sept, 1993 - No. 4, Dec, 1993 ($1.95, color, mini-series)
DC Comics (Vertigo)

1-4-Peter Milligan scripts; McKeever-c/a .80 2.00
1-Platinum Edition 10.00

EYEBALL KID, THE (Dark Horse)(Value; cover or less)

FACE, THE (Tony Trent, the Face No. 3 on) (See Big Shot Comics)
1941 - No. 2, 1941?
Columbia Comics Group

1-The Face; Mart Bailey-c 50.00 150.00 350.00
2-Bailey-c 33.00 95.00 220.00

FACULTY FUNNIES
June, 1989 - No. 5, May, 1990 (75 cents, color; 95 cents #2 on)
Archie Comics

1-5: 1,2-The Awesome Four app. 1.00

FAFHRD AND THE GREY MOUSER (Also see Sword of Sorcery & Wonder Woman #202)
Oct, 1990 - No. 4, 1991 ($4.50, color, 52 pgs.)
Marvel Comics

1-4: Mignola/Williamson-a; Chaykin scripts 1.80 4.50

FAIRY TALE PARADE (See Famous Fairy Tales)
June-July, 1942 - No. 121, Oct, 1946 (Most all by Walt Kelly)
Dell Publishing Co.

1-Kelly-a begins 93.00 280.00 650.00
2(8-9/42) 50.00 150.00 350.00
3-5 (10-11/42 - 2-4/43) 32.00 95.00 225.00
6-9 (5-7/43 - 11-1/43-44) 26.00 78.00 180.00
4-Color 50('44) 24.00 73.00 170.00
4-Color 69('45) 22.00 65.00 150.00
4-Color 87('45) 19.00 57.00 130.00
4-Color 104,114('46)-Last Kelly issue 16.00 50.00 115.00
4-Color 121('46)-Not by Kelly 11.00 32.00 75.00

NOTE: *#1-9, 4-Color #50, 69 have* ***Kelly*** *c/a; 4-Color #87, 104, 114-****Kelly*** *art only. #9 has a redrawn version of The Reluctant Dragon. This series contains all the classic fairy tales from Jack In The Beanstalk to Cinderella.*

FAIRY TALES
No. 10, 1951 - No. 11, June-July, 1951
Ziff-Davis Publ. Co. (Approved Comics)

10,11-Painted-c 11.00 32.00 75.00

FAITHFUL
November, 1949 - No. 2, Feb, 1950 (52 pgs.)
Marvel Comics/Lovers' Magazine

1,2-Photo-c 5.35 16.00 32.00

FALCON (Also see Avengers #181 & Captain America #117 & 133)
Nov, 1983 - No. 4, Feb, 1984 (Mini-series)(See Marvel Premiere #49)
Marvel Comics Group

1-4: 1-Paul Smith-c/a(p). 2-P. Smith-c 1.00

FALLEN ANGELS
April, 1987 - No. 8, Nov, 1987 (Mini-series)
Marvel Comics Group

1 .80 2.00

Falling in Love #1, © DC

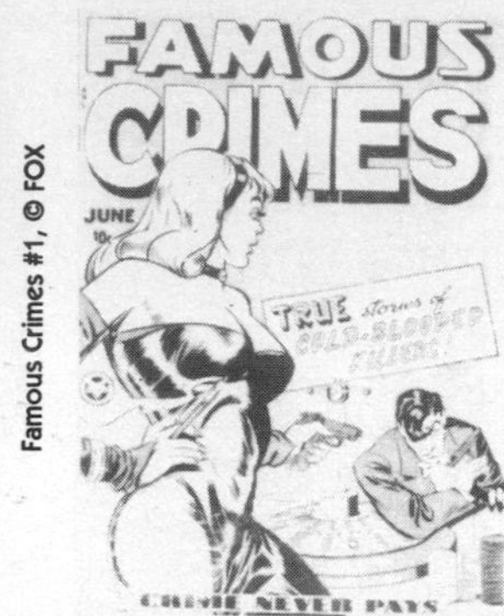

Famous Crimes #1, © FOX

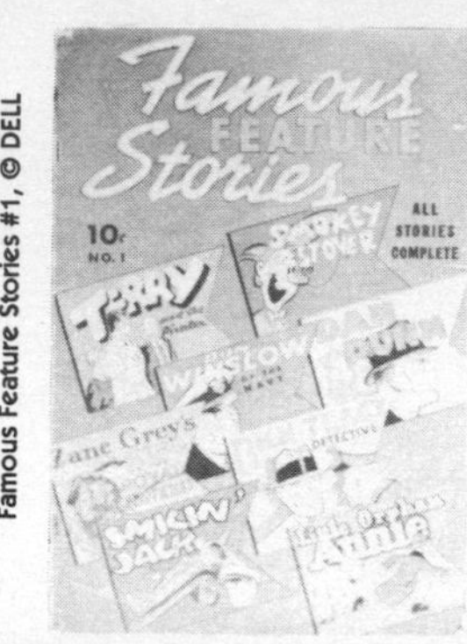

Famous Feature Stories #1, © DELL

GD25 FN65 NM94

2-8 1.40

FALLING IN LOVE
Sept-Oct, 1955 - No. 143, Oct-Nov, 1973
Arleigh Publ. Co./National Periodical Publications

	GD25	FN65	NM94
1	22.00	65.00	150.00
2	11.00	32.00	75.00
3-10	6.70	20.00	40.00
11-20	4.70	14.00	28.00
21-40	4.00	10.00	20.00
41-46: 46-Last 10 cent issue	3.20	8.00	16.00
47-100,108: 108-Wood-a (4 pgs., 7/69)	1.60	4.00	8.00
101-107,109-143	1.00	2.00	5.00

NOTE: ***Colan** c/a-75, 81. 52 pgs.-#125-133.*

FALL OF THE HOUSE OF USHER, THE (See A Corben Special & Spirit section 8/22/48)

FALL OF THE ROMAN EMPIRE (See Movie Comics)

FAMILY AFFAIR (TV)
Feb, 1970 - No. 4, Oct, 1970 (25 cents)
Gold Key

	GD25	FN65	NM94
1-With pull-out poster; photo-c	3.60	10.75	25.00
1-With poster missing	1.70	5.00	12.00
2-4: 3,4-Photo-c	2.15	6.50	15.00

FAMILY FUNNIES
No. 9, Aug-Sept, 1946
Parents' Magazine Institute

	GD25	FN65	NM94
9	3.60	9.00	18.00

FAMILY FUNNIES (Tiny Tot Funnies No. 9)
Sept, 1950 - No. 8, April, 1951
Harvey Publications

	GD25	FN65	NM94
1-Mandrake (has over 30 King Feature strips)	5.00	15.00	30.00
2-Flash Gordon, 1 pg.	4.00	10.00	20.00
3-8: 4,5,7-Flash Gordon, 1 pg.	3.60	9.00	18.00
1(Black & white)	2.00	5.00	10.00

FAMOUS AUTHORS ILLUSTRATED (See Stories by...)

FAMOUS COMICS (Also see Favorite Comics)
No date; Mid 1930's (24 pages) (paper cover)
Zain-Eppy/United Features Syndicate

	GD25	FN65	NM94
nn-Reprinted from 1933 & 1934 newspaper strips in color; Joe Palooka, Hairbreadth Harry, Napoleon, The Nebbs, etc. (Nine different versions known)	36.00	110.00	250.00

FAMOUS COMICS
1934 (100 pgs., daily newspaper reprints)
(3-1/2x8-1/2"; paper cover) (came in a box)
King Features Syndicate (Whitman Publ. Co.)

	GD25	FN65	NM94
684(#1)-Little Jimmy, Katzenjammer Kids, & Barney Google	22.00	68.00	150.00
684(#2)-Polly, Little Jimmy, Katzenjammer Kids	22.00	68.00	150.00
684(#3)-Little Annie Rooney, Polly, Katzenjammer Kids	22.00	68.00	150.00
....Box price....	15.00	45.00	100.00

FAMOUS COMICS CARTOON BOOKS
1934 (72 pgs.; 8x7-1/4"; daily strip reprints)
Whitman Publishing Co. (B&W; hardbacks)

	GD25	FN65	NM94
1200-The Captain & the Kids (1st app?); Dirks reprints credited to Bernard Dibble	20.00	60.00	130.00
1202-Captain Easy (1st app?) & Wash Tubbs by Roy Crane	25.00	75.00	165.00
1203-Ella Cinders (1st app?)	20.00	60.00	130.00
1204-Freckles & His Friends (1st app?)	17.00	50.00	110.00

NOTE: *Called Famous Funnies Cartoon Books inside.*

FAMOUS CRIMES
June, 1948 - No. 19, Sept, 1950; No. 20, Aug, 1951; No. 51, 52, 1953
Fox Features Syndicate/M.S. Dist. No. 51,52

	GD25	FN65	NM94
1-Blue Beetle app. & crime story-r/Phantom Lady #16	23.00	70.00	160.00
2-Has woman dissolved in acid; lingerie-c/panels	18.00	54.00	125.00
3-Injury-to-eye story used in **SOTI**, pg. 112; has two electrocution stories	21.00	63.00	145.00
4-6	10.00	30.00	60.00
7-"Tarzan, the Wyoming Killer" used in **SOTI**, pg. 44; drug trial/possession story	18.00	54.00	125.00
8-20: 17-Morisi-a	7.50	22.50	45.00
51(nd, 1953)	7.50	22.50	45.00
52	4.00	12.00	24.00

FAMOUS FAIRY TALES
1943 (32 pgs.); 1944 (16 pgs.) (Soft covers)
K. K. Publ. Co. (Giveaway)

	GD25	FN65	NM94
1943-Reprints from Fairy Tale Parade No. 2,3; Kelly inside art	40.00	120.00	260.00
1944-Kelly inside art	28.00	85.00	180.00

FAMOUS FEATURE STORIES
1938 (68 pgs., 7-1/2x11")
Dell Publishing Co.

	GD25	FN65	NM94
1-Tarzan, Terry & the Pirates, King of the Royal Mtd., Buck Jones (1st app.), Dick Tracy, Smilin' Jack, Dan Dunn, Don Winslow, G-Man, Tailspin Tommy, Mutt & Jeff, & Little Orphan Annie reprints - all illustrated text	62.00	188.00	425.00

FAMOUS FIRST EDITION (See Limited Collectors' Edition)
($1.00; 10x13-1/2"-Giant Size)(72pgs.; No.6-8, 68 pgs.)
1974 - No. 8, Aug-Sept, 1975; C-61, 1979
National Periodical Publications/DC Comics

	GD25	FN65	NM94
C-26-Action Comics #1; gold ink outer cover	1.00	3.00	10.00
C-28-Detective #27; silver ink outer cover	3.00	9.00	30.00
C-28-Hardbound edition	6.00	18.00	60.00
C-30-Sensation #1(1974); bronze ink outer cover	1.00	3.00	10.00
F-4-Whiz Comics #2(#1)(10-11/74)-Cover not identical to original (dropped "Gangway for Captain Marvel" from cover); gold ink on outer cover	1.00	3.00	10.00
F-5-Batman #1(F-6 inside); silver ink on outer-c	2.00	6.00	20.00
V2#F-6-Wonder Woman #1	1.00	3.00	10.00
F-7-All-Star Comics #3	1.00	3.00	10.00
F-8-Flash Comics #1(8-9/75)	1.00	3.00	10.00
V8#C-61-Superman #1(1979, $2.00)	1.00	3.00	10.00
Hardbound editions (w/dust jackets $5.00 extra) (Lyle Stuart, Inc.) C-26,C-30,F-4,F-6 known	2.00	5.00	15.00

Warning: The above books are almost **exact** reprints of the originals that they represent except for the Giant-Size format. None of the originals are Giant-Size. The first five issues and C-61 were printed with two covers. Reprint information can be found on the outside cover, but not on the inside cover which was reprinted exactly like the original (inside and out).

FAMOUS FUNNIES
1933 - No. 218, July, 1955
Eastern Color

	GD25	FN65	VF82	NM94
A Carnival of Comics (probably the second comic book), 36 pgs., no date given, no publisher, no number; contains strip reprints of The Bungle Family, Dixie Dugan, Hairbreadth Harry, Joe Palooka, Keeping Up With the Jones, Mutt & Jeff, Reg'lar Fellers, S'Matter Pop, Strange As It Seems, and others. This book was sold by M. C. Gaines to Wheatena, Milk-O-Malt, John Wanamaker, Kinney Shoe Stores, & others to be given away as premiums and radio give-aways (1933).	600.00	1800.00	3900.00	6000.00

(Estimated up to 50 total copies exist, 2 in NM/Mint)

	GD25	FN65	VF82	NM94
Series 1-(Very rare)(nd-early 1934)(68 pgs.) No publisher given (Eastern Color PrintingCo.); sold in chain stores for 10 cents. 35,000 print run. Contains Sunday strip reprints of Mutt & Jeff, Reg'lar Fellers, Nipper, Hairbreadth Harry, Strange As It Seems, Joe Palooka, Dixie Dugan, The Nebbs, Keeping Up With the Jones, and others. Inside front and back covers and pages 1-16 of Famous Funnies Series 1, #s 49-64 reprinted from **Famous Funnies**, **A Carnival of Comics**, and most of pages 17-48 reprinted from **Funnies on Parade**. This was the first comic book sold.	2000.00	6000.00	10000.00	14000.00

(Estimated up to 12 copies exist, 1 in NM/Mint)

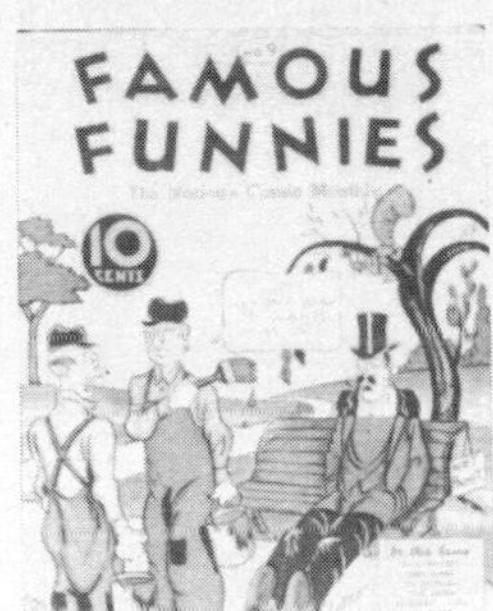

Famous Funnies #9, © EAS

Famous Gangsters #1, © AVON

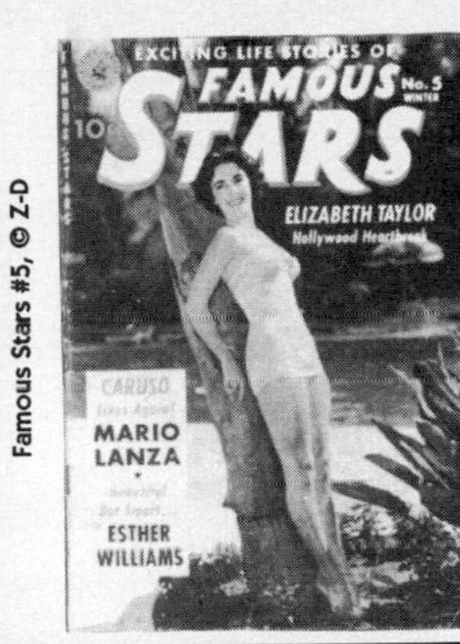

Famous Stars #5, © Z-D

GD25 FN65 NM94

No. 1 (Rare)(7/34-on stands 5/34) - Eastern Color Printing Co. First monthly newsstand comic book. Contains Sunday strip reprints of Toonerville Folks, Mutt & Jeff, Hairbreadth Harry, S'Matter Pop, Nipper, Dixie Dugan, The Bungle Family, Connie, Ben Webster, Tailspin Tommy, The Nebbs, Joe Palooka, & others.
1430.00 4290.00 7150.00 10,000.00
(Estimated up to 30 total copies exist, 2 in NM/Mint)

	GD25	FN65	VF82
2 (Rare, 9/34)	285.00	860.00	2000.00
3-Buck Rogers Sunday strip reprints by Rick Yager begins, ends #218; not in #191-208; the number of the 1st strip reprinted is pg. 190, Series No. 1	335.00	1000.00	2350.00
4	108.00	325.00	700.00
5-1st Christmas-c on a newsstand comic	92.00	275.00	600.00
6-10	71.00	212.00	500.00

	GD25	FN65	NM94
11,12,18-Four pgs. of Buck Rogers in each issue, completes stories in Buck Rogers #1 which lacks these pages; #18-Two pgs. of Buck Rogers reprinted in Daisy Comics #1	62.00	188.00	430.00
13-17,19,20: 14-Has two Buck Rogers panels missing. 17-2nd Christmas-c on a newsstand comic (12/35)	46.00	138.00	315.00
21,23-30: 27-(10/36)-War on Crime begins (4 pgs.); 1st true crime in comics (reprints); part photo-c. 29-X-Mas-c (12/36)	33.00	100.00	230.00
22-Four pgs. of Buck Rogers needed to complete stories in Buck Rogers #1	37.00	112.00	260.00
31-34,36,37,39,40: 33-Careers of Baby Face Nelson & John Dillinger traced	25.00	75.00	175.00
35-Two pgs. Buck Rogers omitted in Buck Rogers #2	27.00	80.00	190.00
38-Full color portrait of Buck Rogers	25.00	75.00	175.00
41-60: 41,53-X-Mas-c. 55-Last bottom panel, pg. 4 in Buck Rogers redrawn in Buck Rogers #3	17.00	52.00	120.00
61,63,64,66,67,69,70	14.00	43.00	100.00
62,65,68-Two pgs. Kirby-a-"Lightnin' & the Lone Rider" 65-X-Mas-c	15.00	45.00	105.00
71,73,77-80: 77-X-Mas-c. 80-(3/41)-Buck Rogers story continues from Buck Rogers #5	12.00	35.00	75.00
72-Speed Spaulding begins by Marvin Bradley (artist), ends #88. This series was written by Edwin Balmer & Phillip Wylie (later appeared as film & book "When Worlds Collide")	12.50	37.50	80.00
74-76-Two pgs. Kirby-a in all	10.00	30.00	70.00
81-Origin & 1st app. Invisible Scarlet O'Neil (4/41); strip begins #82, ends #167; 1st non-funny-c (Scarlet O'Neil)	10.00	30.00	60.00
82-Buck Rogers-c	10.00	30.00	70.00
83-87,90: 86-Connie vs. Monsters on the Moon-c (sci/fi). 87 has last Buck Rogers full page-r. 90-Bondage-c	10.005	30.00	60.00
88-Buck Rogers in "Moon's End" by Calkins, 2 pgs.(not reprints). Beginning with #88, all Buck Rogers pages have rearranged panels	10.00	30.00	65.00
89-Origin & 1st app. Fearless Flint, the Flint Man	10.00	30.00	65.00
91-93,95,96,98-99,101-110: 102-Chief Wahoo vs. Hitler, Tojo & Mussolini-c (1/43). 105-Series 2 begins (Strip Page #1)	8.35	25.00	50.00
94-Buck Rogers in "Solar Holocaust" by Calkins, 3 pgs.(not reprints)	9.15	27.50	55.00
97-War Bond promotion, Buck Rogers by Calkins, 2 pgs.(not reprints)	9.15	27.50	55.00
100	9.15	27.50	55.00
111-130: 113-X-Mas-c	6.00	18.00	36.00
131-150: 137-Strip page No. 110 omitted	4.70	14.00	28.00
151-162,164-168	4.00	12.00	24.00
163-St. Valentine's Day-c	5.00	15.00	30.00
169,170-Two text illos. by Williamson, his 1st comic book work	8.35	25.00	50.00
171-180: 171-Strip pgs. 227,229,230, Series 2 omitted. 172-Strip Pg. 232 omitted	4.00	11.00	22.00
181-190: Buck Rogers ends with start of strip pg. 302, Series 2. 190-Oaky Doaks-c/story	4.00	10.00	20.00
191-197,199,201,203,206-208: No Buck Rogers	3.60	9.00	18.00
198,202,205-One pg. Frazetta ads; no B. Rogers	4.00	11.00	22.00
200-Frazetta 1 pg. ad	4.00	11.00	22.00
204-Used in **POP**, pgs. 79,99; war-c begin, end #208	4.00	11.00	22.00
209-Buck Rogers begins (12/53) with strip pg. 480, Series 2; Frazetta-c	37.00	110.00	235.00
210-216: Frazetta-c. 211-Buck Rogers ads by Anderson begins, ends #217. #215-Contains B. Rogers strip pg. 515-518, series 2 followed by pgs. 179-181, Series 3	37.00	110.00	235.00
217,218-B. Rogers ends with pg. 199, Series 3. 218-Wee Three-c/story	4.00	12.00	24.00

NOTE: ***Rick Yager*** *did the Buck Rogers Sunday strips reprinted in Famous Funnies. The Sundays were formerly done by Russ Keaton and Lt. Dick Calkins did the dailies, but would sometimes assist Yager on a panel or two from time to time. Strip No. 169 is Yager's first full Buck Rogers page. Yager did the strip until 1958 when* ***Murphy Anderson*** *took over.* ***Tuska*** *art from 4/26/59 - 1965. Virtually every panel was rewritten for Famous Funnies. Not iden#tical to the original Sunday page. The Buck Rogers reprints run continuously through Famous Funnies issue No. 190 (Strip No. 302) with no break in story line. The story line has no continuity after No. 190. The Buck Rogers newspaper strips came out in four series: Series 1, 3/30/30 - 9/21/41 (No. 1 - 600); Series 2, 9/28/41 -10/21/51 (No. 1 -525)(Strip No. 110-1/2 (1/2 pg.) published in only a few newspapers); Series 3, 10/28/51 -2/9/58 (No. 100-428)(No No.1-99); Series 4, 2/16/58 - 6/13/65 (No numbers, dates only).* ***Everett*** *c-85, 86.* ***Moulton*** *a-100. Chief Wahoo c-93, 97, 102, 116, 136, 139, 151. Dickie Dare c-83, 88. Fearless Flint c-89. Invisible Scarlet O'Neil c-81, 87, 95, 121(part), 132. Scorchy Smith c-84, 90.*

FAMOUS FUNNIES
1964
Super Comics

Super Reprint Nos. 15-18	1.60	4.00	8.00

FAMOUS GANG BOOK OF COMICS (Becomes Donald & Mickey Merry Christmas 1943 on)
Dec, 1942 (32 pgs.; paper cover) (Christmas giveaway)
Firestone Tire & Rubber Co.

nn-(Rare)-Porky Pig, Bugs Bunny, Sniffles; r/Looney Tunes	67.00	200.00	500.00

FAMOUS GANGSTERS (Crime on the Waterfront No. 4)
April, 1951 - No. 3, Feb, 1952
Avon Periodicals/Realistic

1-Capone, Dillinger; c-/Avon paperback #329	19.00	57.00	130.00
2-Wood-c/a (1 pg.); r/Saint #7 & retitled "Mike Strong"	20.00	60.00	140.00
3-Lucky Luciano & Murder, Inc; c-/Avon paperback #66	20.00	60.00	140.00

FAMOUS INDIAN TRIBES
July-Sept, 1962; No. 2, July, 1972
Dell Publishing Co.

12-264-209(#1) (The Sioux)	1.80	4.50	9.00
2(7/72)-Reprints above	.40	1.00	2.00

FAMOUS STARS
Nov-Dec, 1950 - No. 6, Spring, 1952 (All have photo covers)
Ziff-Davis Publ. Co.

1-Shelley Winters, Susan Peters, Ava Gardner, Shirley Temple;Jimmy Stewart & Shelley Winters photo-c; Whitney-a	19.00	58.00	135.00
2-Betty Hutton, Bing Crosby, Colleen Townsend, Gloria Swanson; Betty Hutton photo-c; Everett-a(2)	13.00	40.00	90.00
3-Farley Granger, Judy Garland's ordeal, Alan Ladd; Farley Granger & Judy Garland photo-c; Whitney-a	12.00	36.00	85.00
4-Al Jolson, Bob Mitchum, Ella Raines, Richard Conte, Vic Damone; Bob Mitchum photo-c; Crandall-a, 6pgs.	11.50	34.00	80.00
5-Liz Taylor, Betty Grable, Esther Williams, George Brent; Liz Taylor photo-c; Krigstein-a	14.00	43.00	100.00
6-Gene Kelly, Hedy Lamarr, June Allyson, William Boyd, Janet Leigh, Gary Cooper	10.00	30.00	70.00

FAMOUS STORIES (...Book No. 2)
1942 - No. 2, 1942

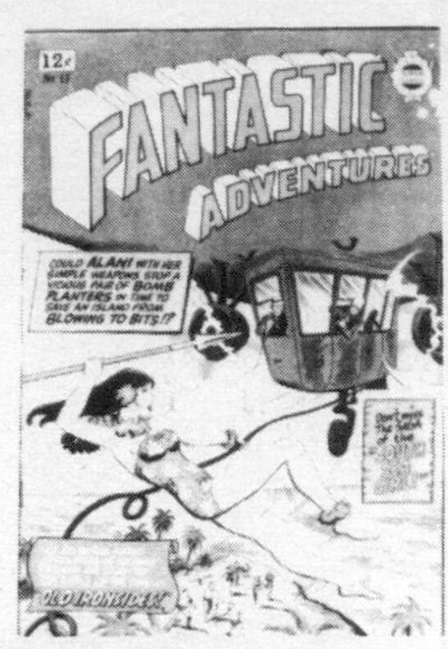

Fantastic Adventures #17, © Super Comics

Fantastic Fears #5, © AJAX

Fantastic Four #39, © MEG

GD25 FN65 NM94

Dell Publishing Co.
1,2: 1-Treasure Island. 2-Tom Sawyer 21.00 63.00 145.00

FAMOUS TV FUNDAY FUNNIES
Sept, 1961
Harvey Publications
1-Casper the Ghost 4.20 12.50 25.00

FAMOUS WESTERN BADMEN (Formerly Redskin)
No. 13, Dec, 1952 - No. 15, 1953
Youthful Magazines
13 7.50 22.50 45.00
14,15 5.35 16.00 32.00

FANTASTIC (Formerly Captain Science; Beware No. 10 on)
No. 8, Feb, 1952 - No. 9, April, 1952
Youthful Magazines
8-Capt. Science by Harrison; decapitation, shrunken head panels 18.00 54.00 125.00
9-Harrison-a 11.50 34.00 80.00

FANTASTIC ADVENTURES
1963 - 1964 (Reprints)
Super Comics
9,10,12,15,16,18: 9-r/? 10-r/He-Man #2(Toby). 12-Unpublished Chesler material? 15-r/Spook #23. 16-r/Dark Shadows #2(Steinway); Briefer-a. 18-r/Superior Stories #1 2.00 5.00 10.00
11-Wood-a; r/Blue Bolt #118 3.60 9.00 18.00
17-Baker-a(2) r/Seven Seas #6 3.20 8.00 16.00

FANTASTIC COMICS
Dec, 1939 - No. 23, Nov, 1941
Fox Features Syndicate
1-Intro/origin Samson; Stardust, The Super Wizard, Sub Saunders (by Kiefer), Space Smith, Capt. Kidd begin 200.00 600.00 1400.00
2-Powell text illos 92.00 275.00 600.00
3-5: 3-Robot-c; Powell text illos 71.00 212.00 475.00
6-9: 6,7-Simon-c 58.00 175.00 390.00
10-Intro/origin David, Samson's aide 46.00 138.00 300.00
11-17,19,20,22: 16-Stardust ends 37.00 112.00 250.00
18-1st app. Black Fury & sidekick Chuck; ends #23 42.00 125.00 275.00
21,23: 21-The Banshee begins(origin); ends #23; Hitler-c. 23-Origin The Gladiator 42.00 125.00 275.00
NOTE: *Lou Fine c-1-5. Tuska a-3-5, 8. Bondage c-6, 8, 9. Issue #11 has indicia to Mystery Men Comics #15.*

FANTASTIC COMICS (Fantastic Fears #1-9; Becomes Samson #12)
No. 10, Nov-Dec, 1954 - No. 11, Jan-Feb, 1955
Ajax/Farrell Publ.
10,11 9.15 27.50 55.00

FANTASTIC FABLES
Feb, 1987 ($1.50, B&W, 28 pgs.)
Silverwolf Comics
1-Tim Vigil-a (6 pgs.) 1.20 3.00

FANTASTIC FEARS (Formerly Captain Jet) (Fantastic Comics #10 on)
No. 7, May, 1953 - No. 9, Sept-Oct, 1954
Ajax/Farrell Publ.
7(#1, 5/53) 16.00 48.00 110.00
8(#2, 7/53) 10.00 30.00 70.00
3,4 9.15 27.50 55.00
5-(1-2/54)-Ditko story (1st in book) is written by Bruce Hamilton; r-in Weird V2#8 (Ditko's 3rd published-a) (1st pro work for Ditko but Black Magic #27 was published 1st) 41.00 122.00 285.00
6-Decapitation of girl's head with paper cutter (classic) 22.00 65.00 150.00
7(5-6/54), 9(9-10/54) 8.35 25.00 50.00

GD25 FN65 NM94

8(7-8/54)-Contains story intended for Jo-Jo; name changed to Kaza; decapitation story 10.00 30.00 70.00

FANTASTIC FOUR (See America's Best TV..., Giant- Size..., Giant Size Super- Stars, Marvel Collectors Item Classics, Marvel Milestone Edition, Marvel's Greatest,Marvel Treasury Edition, Marvel Triple Action, Official Marvel Index to... & Power Record Comics)

FANTASTIC FOUR
Nov, 1961 - Present
Marvel Comics Group

GD25 FN65 VF82 NM94

1-Origin & 1st app. The Fantastic Four (Reed Richards: Mr. Fantastic, Johnny Storm: The Human Torch, Sue Storm: The Invisible Girl, & Ben Grimm: The Thing); origin/1st app. The Mole Man (Marvel's 1st super-hero group since the G.A. 1000.00 3000.00 7,500.00 12,000.00

GD25 FN65 NM94

1-Golden Record Comic Set Reprint (1966)-cover not identical to original 14.00 43.00 100.00
with Golden Record 25.00 75.00 175.00
2-Vs. The Skrulls (last 10 cent issue) 200.00 600.00 2000.00
3-Fantastic Four don costumes & establish Headquarters; brief 1pg. origin; intro The Fantasti-Car; Human Torch drawn w/two left hands on-c 133.00 398.00 1325.00

GD25 FN65 VF82 NM94

4-1st Silver Age Sub-Mariner app. (5/62) 163.00 488.00 1056.00 1625.00
5-Origin & 1st app. Doctor Doom 175.00 525.00 1138.00 1750.00

GD25 FN65 NM94

6-Sub-Mariner, Dr. Doom team up; 1st Marvel villain team-up (2nd S.A. Sub-Mariner app. 100.00 300.00 700.00
7-10: 7-1st app. Kurrgo. 8-1st app. Puppet-Master & Alicia Masters. 9-3rd Sub-Mariner app. 10-Stan Lee (1st app. in comics?) & Jack Kirby app. in story 71.00 214.00 500.00
11-Origin/1st app. The Impossible Man (2/63) 54.00 161.00 375.00
12-Fantastic Four Vs. The Hulk (1st x-over) 69.00 208.00 485.00
13-Intro. The Watcher; 1st app. The Red Ghost 43.00 129.00 300.00
14-19: 14-Sub-Mariner x-over. 15-1st app. Mad Thinker. 16-1st Ant-Man x-over (7/63); Wasp cameo. 18-Origin/1st app. The Super Skrull. 19-Intro. Rama-Tut; Stan Lee & Jack Kirby cameo 29.00 86.00 200.00
20-Origin/1st app. The Molecule Man 32.00 96.00 225.00
21-Intro. The Hate Monger; 1st Sgt. Fury x-over (12/63) 20.00 60.00 140.00
22-24: 22-Sue Storm gains more powers 12.00 36.00 85.00
25,26-The Hulk vs. The Thing (their 1st battle). 25-2nd Avengers x-over (w/ Capt. America)(cameo, 4/64); 2nd S.A. app. Cap (takes place between Avengers #4 & 5. 26-3rd Avengers x-over 40.00 120.00 280.00
27-1st Doctor Strange x-over (6/64) 14.00 43.00 100.00
28-Early X-Men x-over (7/64) 19.00 58.00 135.00
29,30: 30-Intro. Diablo 11.00 32.00 75.00
31-40: 31-Early Avengers x-over. 33-1st app. Attuma; part photo-c. 35-Intro/1st app. Dragon Man. 36-Intro/1st app. Madam Medusa & the Frightful Four (Sandman, Wizard, Paste Pot Pete). 39-Wood inks on Daredevil (early x-over) 9.00 26.00 60.00
41-47: 41-43-Frightful Four app. 44-Intro. Gorgon. 45-Intro/1st app. The Inhumans (c/story, 12/65); also see Incredible Hulk Special #1 & Thor #146, & 147 5.50 17.00 40.00
48-Partial origin/1st app. The Silver Surfer & Galactus (3/66); Galactus cameo in last panel; 1st of 3 part story 58.00 173.00 575.00
49-2nd app. Silver Surfer & Galactus 13.00 38.00 125.00
50-Silver Surfer battles Galactus 15.00 45.00 150.00
51,54: 54-Inhumans cameo 3.00 10.00 33.00
52-1st app. The Black Panther (7/66) 6.00 17.00 58.00
53-Origin & 2nd app. The Black Panther 5.00 14.00 48.00
55-Thing battles Silver Surfer 5.00 14.00 45.00
56-60: Silver Surfer x-over. 59,60-Inhumans cameos 4.00 12.00 40.00
61-65,68-70: 61-Silver Surfer cameo 3.00 8.00 28.00
66-Begin 2 part origin of Him (Warlock); does not app. (9/67) 8.00 23.00 75.00

Fantastic Four #240, © MEG

Fantastic Four #381, © MEG

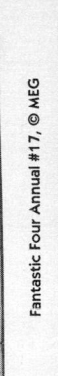

Fantastic Four Annual #17, © MEG

GD25 FN65 NM94

67-Origin/1st app. Him (Warlock); 1 pg. cameo; see Thor #165,166 for 1st full app. 9.00 26.00 85.00
71,73,78-80: 73-Spider-Man, D.D., Thor x-over; cont'd from Daredevil #38 2.00 7.00 22.00
72,74-77: Silver Surfer app. in all 2.00 7.00 24.00
81-88: 81-Crystal joins & dons costume. 82,83-Inhumans app. 84-87-Dr. Doom app. 88-Last 12 cent issue 2.00 5.00 17.00
89-99,101,102: 94-Intro. Agatha Harkness. 102,103-Fantastic Four vs. Sub-Mariner 1.00 4.00 12.00
100 (7/70) 6.00 17.00 55.00
103-111: 108-Last Kirby issue (not in #103-107) 2.00 5.00 11.00
112-Hulk Vs. Thing (7/71) 5.00 15.00 35.00
113-115: 115-Last 15 cent issue 1.65 4.00 10.00
116-120: 116-(52 pgs.) 1.30 3.25 8.00
121-123-Silver Surfer x-over. 122,123-Galactus 1.65 4.70 11.00
124,125,127,129-149: 129-Intro. Thundra. 130-Sue leaves F.F. 131-Quicksilver app. 132-Medusa joins. 133-Thundra Vs. Thing. 142-Kirbyish-a by Buckler begins. 143-Dr. Doom app. 1.20 3.00 7.00
126-Origin F.F. retold; cover swipe of F.F. #1 1.30 3.25 8.00
128-Four pg. insert of F.F. Friends & Foes 1.30 3.25 8.00
150-Crystal & Quicksilver's wedding 1.30 3.25 8.00
151-154,158-160: 151-Origin Thundra. 159-Medusa leaves; Sue rejoins 1.00 2.50 6.00
155-157: Silver Surfer in all 1.20 3.00 7.00
161-180: 164-The Crusader (old Marvel Boy) revived (origin #165). 176-Re-intro Impossible Man; Marvel artists app. 180-r/#101 by Kirby 1.20 3.00
181-199: 189-G.A. Human Torch app. & origin retold. 190,191-Fantastic Four break up .80 2.00
200-(11/78, 52 pgs.)-F.F. re-united vs. Dr. Doom 1.60 4.00
201-208,219,222-231: 211-1st Terrax 1.50
209-216,218,220,221-Byrne-a. 209-1st Herbie the Robot. 220-Brief origin .80 2.00
217-Dazzler app. by Byrne 1.20 3.00
232-Byrne-a begins 1.40 3.50
233-235,237-249,251-260: All Byrne-a. 238-Origin Frankie Raye. 244-Frankie Raye becomes Nova, Herald of Galactus. 252-Reads sideways; Annihilus app.; contains skin "Tattooz" decals 1.00 2.50
236-20th Anniversary issue(11/81, 68 pgs., $1.00)-Brief origin F.F. Byrne-c/a(p); new Kirby-a(p) 1.40 3.50
250-(52 pgs)-Spider-Man x-over; Byrne-a; Skrulls impersonate New X-Men 1.40 3.50
261-285: 261-Silver Surfer. 262-Origin Galactus; Byrne writes & draws himself into story. 264-Swipes-c of F.F. #1. 274-Spider-Man's alien costume app. (4th app., 1/85, 2 pgs.) 1.00 2.50
286-2nd app. X-Factor continued from Avengers #263; story continues in X-Factor #1 1.80 4.50
287-295: 292-Nick Fury app. 1.50
296-($1.50)-Barry Smith-c/a; Thing rejoins .85 2.10
297-305,307-318,320-330: 300-Johnny Storm & Alicia Masters wed. 312-X-Factor x-over. 327-Mr. Fantastic & Invisible Girl return 1.50
306-New team begins (9/87) .70 1.70
319-Double size 1.00 2.50
331-346,351-357,359,360: 334-Simonson-c/scripts begin. 337-Simonson-a begins. 342-Spider-Man cameo. 356-F.F. vs. The New Warriors; Paul Ryan-c/a begins. 360-Last $1.00-c 1.50
347-Ghost Rider, Wolverine, Spider-Man, Hulk-c/stories thru #349; Arthur Adams-c/a(p) in each 1.00 2.50 6.50
347-Gold 2nd printing 1.00 2.50
348,349 1.40 3.50
348-Gold 2nd printing 1.50
350 ($1.50, 52 pgs.) Dr. Doom app. 1.20 3.00
358-(11/91, $2.25, 88 pgs.)-30th anniversary issue; gives history of F.F.; die cut-c; Art Adams back-up story-a 1.20 3.00
361-368,370,372-374,376-380,382: 362-Spider-Man app. 367-Wolverine app. (brief). 370-Infinity War x-over; Thanos & Magus app. 374-Secret Defenders (Ghost Rider, Hulk, Wolverine) x-over 1.50
369-Infinity War x-over; Thanos app. 1.00 2.50
371-All white embossed-c ($2.00) 1.60 4.00
371-All red 2nd printing ($2.00) 1.00 2.50
375-($2.95, 52 pgs.)-Holo-grafx foil-c; ann. issue 1.20 3.00
381-Death of Reed Richards & Dr. Doom 1.60 4.00
Annual 1('63)-Origin F.F.; Ditko-i 40.00 120.00 400.00
Annual 2('64)-Dr. Doom origin & c/story 25.00 75.00 250.00
Annual 3('65)-Reed & Sue wed; r/#6,11 10.00 30.00 100.00
Special 4(11/66)-G.A. Torch x-over (1st S.A. app.) & origin retold; r/#25,26 (Hulk vs. Thing); Torch vs. Torch battle 6.00 17.00 55.00
Special 5(11/67)-New art; Intro. Psycho-Man; early Black Panther, Inhumans & Silver Surfer (1st solo story) app.; early Inhumans app. 6.00 18.00 60.00
Special 6(11/68)-Intro. Annihilus; birth of Franklin Richards; new 48 pg. movie length epic; last non-reprint annual 4.00 11.00 35.00
Special 7(11/69)-All reprints 2.60 7.50 18.00
Special 8(12/70). 9(12/71). 10('73)-All reprints 1.50 3.75 9.00
Annual 11-14: 11(1976)-New art begins again. 12(1978). 13(1978). 14(1979) 1.00 2.50 5.50
Annual 15-20: 15(1980). 16(1981). 17(1983)-Byrne-c/a. 18(1984). 19(1985). 20(1987) 1.40 3.50
Annual 21(1988)-Evolutionary War x-over 1.50 3.75
Annual 22-24 (1989-91, $2.00, 68 pgs.): 22-Atlantis Attacks x-over; Sub-Mariner & The Avengers app.; Buckler-a. 23-Byrne-c; Guice-p. 24-2 pg. origin recap of Fantastic Four; Guardians of the Galaxy x-over .90 2.25
Annual 25(1992, $2.25, 68 pgs.)-Moondragon story 1.00 2.50
Annual 26(1993, $2.95, 68 pgs.)-Bagged w/card 1.30 3.25
Special Edition 1(5/84)-r/Annual #1; Byrne-c/a 1.00 2.50
...: Monsters Unleashed nn(1992, $5.95)-r/F.F. #347-349 w/new Arthur Adams-c 1.00 2.50 6.00
Giveaway (nn, 1981, 32pgs., Young Model Builders Club) .65 1.60

NOTE: ***Arthur Adams*** *c/a-347-349p.* ***Austin*** *c(i)-232-236, 238, 240-242, 250i, 286i.* ***John Buscema*** *a(p)-107, 108(w/****Kirby & Romita****),109-130, 132, 134-141, 160, 173-175, 202, 296-309p, Annual 11, 13; c(p)-107-122, 124-129, 133-139, 202, Annual 12p, Special 10.* ***Byrne*** *a-209-218p, 220p, 221p, 232-265, 266i, 267-273, 274-293p, Annual 17, 19; c-211-214p, 220p, 232-236p, 237, 238p, 239, 240-242p, 243-249, 250p, 251-267, 269-277, 278-281p, 283p, 284, 285, 286p, 288-293, Annual, 17.* ***Ditko*** *a-13i, Annual 16.* ***G. Kane*** *c-150p, 160p.* ***Kirby*** *a-1-102p, 108, 180r, 189r, 236p, Special 1-10; c-1-101, 164, 167, 171-177, 180, 181, 190, 200, Annual 11, Special 1-7, 9.* ***Marcos*** *a-Annual 14i.* ***Mooney*** *a-118i, 152i.* ***Poroz*** *a-164-167, 170-172, 176-178, 184-188, 191p, 192p. Annual 14p, 15p; c(p)-183-188, 191, 192, 194-197.* ***Simonson*** *a-337-341, 343, 344p, 345p, 346, 350p, 353, 354; c-212, 334-341, 342p, 343-346, 350, 353, 354.* ***Steranko*** *c-130-132p.* ***Williamson*** *c-357i.*

FANTASTIC FOUR INDEX (See Official...)

FANTASTIC FOUR ROAST
May, 1982 (75 cents, one shot, direct sale only)
Marvel Comics Group

1-Celebrates 20th anniversary of F.F.#1; X-Men, Ghost Rider & many others cameo; Golden, Miller, Buscema, Rogers, Byme, Anderson art; Hembeck/Austin-c 1.60 4.00

FANTASTIC FOUR UNLIMITED
Mar, 1993 - Present ($3.95, color, 68 pgs.)
Marvel Comics

1-4: 1-Black Panther app. 4-Thing vs. Hulk 1.60 4.00

FANTASTIC FOUR VS. X-MEN
Feb, 1987 - No. 4, June, 1987 (Mini-series)
Marvel Comics

1 1.40 3.50
2-4: 4-Austin-a(i) 1.00 2.50

FANTASTIC GIANTS (Formerly Konga #1-23)
V2#24, September, 1966 (25 cents, 68 pgs.)
Charlton Comics

V2#24-Special Ditko issue; origin Konga & Gorgo reprinted plus two new Ditko stories 5.00 15.00 35.00

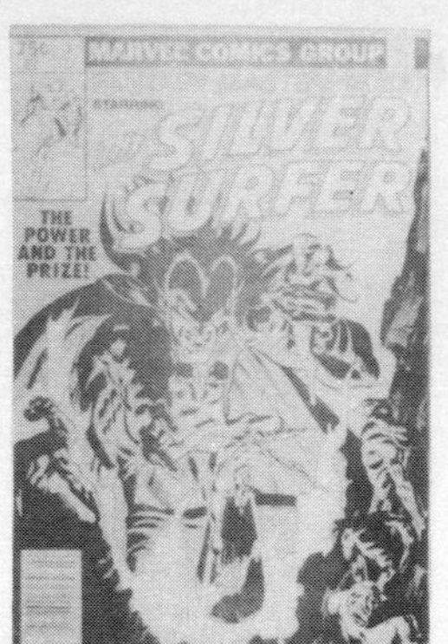
Fantasy Masterpieces V2#3, © MEG

Fashion in Action #1, © John K. Snyder III

Faust #10, © Rebel Studios

FANTASTIC TALES
1958 (no date) (Reprint)
I. W. Enterprises

	GD25	FN65	NM94
1-Reprints Avon's "City of the Living Dead"	2.80	7.00	14.00

FANTASTIC VOYAGE (See Movie Comics)
Aug, 1969 - No. 2, Dec, 1969
Gold Key

	GD25	FN65	NM94
1,2 (TV)	2.00	6.00	14.00

FANTASTIC VOYAGES OF SINDBAD, THE
Oct, 1965 - No. 2, June, 1967
Gold Key

	GD25	FN65	NM94
1,2-Painted-c	3.00	9.00	22.00

FANTASTIC WORLDS
No. 5, Sept, 1952 - No. 7, Jan, 1953
Standard Comics

	GD25	FN65	NM94
5-Toth, Anderson-a	17.00	52.00	120.00
6-Toth-c/a	16.00	48.00	110.00
7	10.00	30.00	60.00

FANTASY FEATURES (Americomics)(Value: cover or less)

FANTASY MASTERPIECES (Marvel Super Heroes No. 12 on)
Feb, 1966 - No. 11, Oct, 1967; Dec, 1979 - No. 14, Jan, 1981
Marvel Comics Group

	GD25	FN65	NM94
1-Photo of Stan Lee (12 cent-c #1,2)	4.30	13.00	30.00
2-r/1st Fin Fang Foom from Strange Tales #89	1.65	4.70	11.00
3-8: 3-G.A. Capt. America-r begin, end #11; 1st 25 cent Giant; Colan-r. 7-Begin G.A. Sub-Mariner, Torch-r/M. Mystery. 8-Torch battles the Sub-Mariner-r/Marvel Mystery #9	1.70	5.00	12.00
9-Origin Human Torch-r/Marvel Comics #1	2.15	6.50	15.00
10,11: 10-r/origin & 1st app. All Winners Squad from All Winners #19. 11-r/origin of Toro (H.T. #1) & Black Knight #1	1.65	4.70	11.00
V2#1(12/79, 75¢, 52 pgs.)-r/origin Silver Surfer from Silver Surfer #1 with editing plus reprints cover; J. Buscema-a		1.80	4.50
2-14-Reprints Silver Surfer #2-14 w/covers		1.20	3.00

NOTE: ***Buscema*** *c-V2#7-9(in part).* ***Ditko*** *r-1-3, 7, 9.* ***Everett*** *r-1,7-9.* ***Matt Fox*** *r-9i.* ***Kirby*** *r-1-11.* ***Starlin*** *r-8-13. Some direct sale V2#14's had a 50 cent cover price. #3-11 contain Capt. America-r/Capt. America #3-10. #7-11 contain G.A.Human Torch & Sub-Mariner-r.*

FANTASY QUARTERLY (Also see Elfquest)
Spring, 1978 (B&W)
Independent Publishers Syndicate

	GD25	FN65	NM94
1-1st app. Elfquest (2nd printing exist?)	5.50	17.00	40.00

FANTOMAN (Formerly Amazing Adventure Funnies)
No. 2, Aug, 1940 - No. 4, Dec, 1940
Centaur Publications

	GD25	FN65	NM94
2-The Fantom of the Fair, The Arrow, Little Dynamite-r begin; origin The Ermine by Filchock; Fantoman app. in 2-4; Burgos, J. Cole, Ernst, Gustavson-a	100.00	300.00	675.00
3,4: Gustavson-r. 4-Red Blaze app.	80.00	238.00	535.00

FARGO KID (Formerly Justice Traps the Guilty)
V11#3(#1), June-July, 1958 - V11#5, Oct-Nov, 1958
Prize Publications

	GD25	FN65	NM94
V11#3(#1)-Origin Fargo Kid, Severin-c/a; Williamson-a(2); Heath-a	11.00	32.00	75.00
V11#4,5-Severin-c/a	8.35	25.00	50.00

FARMER'S DAUGHTER, THE
Feb-Mar, 1954 - No. 3, June-July, 1954; No. 4, Oct, 1954
Stanhall Publ./Trojan Magazines

	GD25	FN65	NM94
1-Lingerie, nudity panel	11.00	32.00	75.00
2-4(Stanhall)	8.35	25.00	50.00

FASHION IN ACTION (Eclipse)(Value: cover or less)

FASTEST GUN ALIVE, THE (See 4-Color No. 741)

FAST FICTION (...Action) (Stories by Famous Authors Ill. #6 on)
Oct, 1949 - No. 5, Mar, 1950 (All have Kiefer-c)(48 pgs.)
Seaboard Publ./Famous Authors Ill.

	GD25	FN65	NM94
1-Scarlet Pimpernel; Jim Lavery-a	27.00	81.00	190.00
2-Captain Blood; H. C. Kiefer-a	24.00	71.00	170.00
3-She, by Rider Haggard; Vincent Napoli-a	32.00	95.00	225.00
4-(1/50, 52 pgs.)-The 39 Steps; Lavery-a	20.00	60.00	140.00
5-Beau Geste; Kiefer-a	20.00	60.00	140.00

NOTE: ***Kiefer*** *a-2, 5; c-2, 3,5.* ***Lavery*** *c/a-1, 4.* ***Napoli*** *a-3.*

FAST FORWARD
1992 - No. 3, 1993 ($4.95, color, 68 pgs.)
Piranha Press (DC)

	GD25	FN65	NM94
1-3: 1-Morrison script/McKean-c/a. 3-Sam Kieth-a	1.00	2.50	5.50

FAST WILLIE JACKSON
October, 1976 - No. 7, 1977
Fitzgerald Periodicals, Inc.

	GD25	FN65	NM94
1-7			1.00

FAT ALBERT (..& the Cosby Kids) (TV)
March, 1974 - No. 29, Feb, 1979
Gold Key

	GD25	FN65	NM94
1		1.20	3.00
2-29			1.00

FAT AND SLAT (Ed Wheelan) (Becomes Gunfighter No. 5 on)
Summer, 1947 - No. 4, Spring, 1948
E. C. Comics

	GD25	FN65	NM94
1-Intro/origin Voltage, Man of Lightning; "Comics" McCormick, the World's No. 1 Comic Book Fan begins, ends #4	22.00	65.00	150.00
2-4: 4-Comics McCormick-c feature	16.00	48.00	110.00

FAT AND SLAT JOKE BOOK
Summer, 1944 (One Shot, 52 pages)
All-American Comics (William H. Wise)

	GD25	FN65	NM94
nn-by Ed Wheelan	17.00	52.00	120.00

FATE (See Hand of Fate & Thrill-O-Rama)

FATHER OF CHARITY
No date (32 pgs.; paper cover)
Catechetical Guild Giveaway

	GD25	FN65	NM94
nn	2.50	5.00	10.00

FATHOM (Comico)(Value: cover or less)

FATIMA...CHALLENGE TO THE WORLD
1951, 36 pgs. (15 cent cover)
Catechetical Guild

	GD25	FN65	NM94
nn (not same as 'Challenge to the World')	2.40	6.00	12.00

FATMAN, THE HUMAN FLYING SAUCER
April, 1967 - No. 3, Aug-Sept, 1967 (68 pgs.)
Lightning Comics(Milson Publ. Co.) (Written by Otto Binder)

	GD25	FN65	NM94
1-Origin/1st app. Fatman & Tinman by Beck	5.00	15.00	36.00
2-C. C. Beck-a	3.40	10.00	24.00
3-(Scarce)-Beck-a	5.50	17.00	40.00

FAUNTLEROY COMICS (Super Duck Presents...)
1950 - No. 3, 1952
Close-Up/Archie Publications

	GD25	FN65	NM94
1-Super Duck-c/stories by Al Fagaly in all	5.85	17.50	35.00
2,3	4.00	12.00	22.00

FAUST
1989?(nd) - No. 12 (B&W; 1,2: $2.00, 3-on: $2.25; adults, violent)
Northstar Publishing/Rebel Studios #7 on

	GD25	FN65	NM94
1-Decapitation-c; Tim Vigil-c/a in all	5.00	16.00	37.00
1-2nd printing	1.70	5.00	12.00
1-3rd printing		1.20	3.00

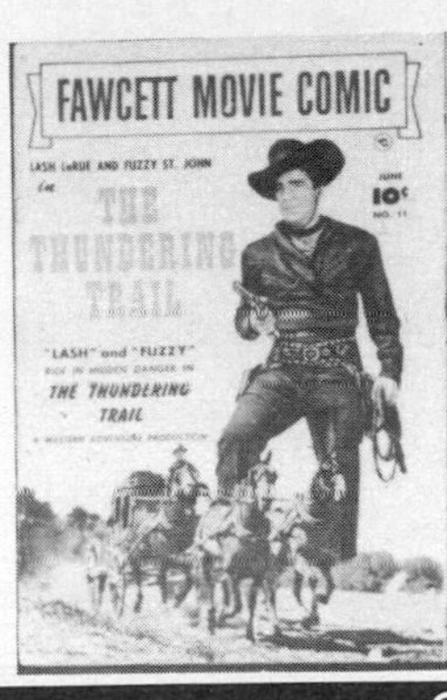
Fawcett Movie Comic #11, © FAW

Fawcett's Funny Animals #53, © FAW

Fear #17, © MEG

	GD25	FN65	NM94
2	3.85	11.50	27.00
2-2nd & 3rd printings		1.20	3.00
3-Begin $2.25-c	2.30	6.75	16.00
3-2nd printing		1.20	3.00
4	1.25	3.00	7.50
5-10		1.30	3.25

FAVORITE COMICS (Also see Famous Comics)
1934 (36 pgs.)
Grocery Store Giveaway (Diff. Corp.) (detergent)

	GD25	FN65	NM94
Book #1-The Nebbs, Strange As It Seems, Napoleon, Joe Palooka, Dixie Dugan, S'Matter Pop, Hairbreadth Harry, etc. reprints	30.00	120.00	275.00
Book #2,3	34.00	100.00	235.00

FAWCETT MINIATURES (See Mighty Midget)
1946 (12-24 pgs.; 3-3/4x5") (Wheaties giveaways)
Fawcett Publications

	GD25	FN65	NM94
Captain Marvel-"And the Horn of Plenty;" Bulletman story	7.50	22.50	45.00
Captain Marvel-"& the Raiders From Space;" Golden Arrow story	7.50	22.50	45.00
Captain Marvel Jr.-"The Case of the Poison Press!" Bulletman story	7.50	22.50	45.00
Delecta of the Planets-C. C. Beck art; B&W inside; 12 pgs.; 3 printing variations (coloring) exist	17.00	50.00	110.00

FAWCETT MOTION PICTURE COMICS (See Motion Picture Comics)

FAWCETT MOVIE COMIC
1949 - No. 20, Dec, 1952 (All photo-c)
Fawcett Publications

	GD25	FN65	NM94
nn-"Dakota Lil"-George Montgomery & Rod Cameron (1949)	24.00	73.00	170.00
nn-"Copper Canyon"-Ray Milland & Hedy Lamarr (1950)	19.00	56.00	130.00
nn-"Destination Moon"-(1950)	52.00	155.00	365.00
nn-"Montana"-Errol Flynn & Alexis Smith ('50)	19.00	57.00	130.00
nn-"Pioneer Marshal" Monte Hale (1950)	19.00	57.00	130.00
nn-"Powder River Rustlers"-Rocky Lane (1950)	22.00	65.00	150.00
nn-"Singing Guns"-Vaughn Monroe & Ella Raines (1950)	17.00	52.00	120.00
7-"Gunmen of Abilene"-Rocky Lane; Bob Powell-a (1950)	22.00	65.00	150.00
8-"King of the Bullwhip"-Lash LaRue; Bob Powell-a (1950)	34.00	100.00	235.00
9-"The Old Frontier"-Monte Hale; Bob Powell-a(2/51; mis-dated 2/50)	20.00	60.00	140.00
10-"The Missourians"-Monte Hale (4/51)	20.00	60.00	140.00
11-"The Thundering Trail"-Lash LaRue (6/51)	27.00	81.00	190.00
12-"Rustlers on Horseback"-Rocky Lane (8/51)	22.00	65.00	150.00
13-"Warpath"-Edmond O'Brien & Forrest Tucker (10/51)	14.00	43.00	100.00
14-"Last Outpost"-Ronald Reagan (12/51)	35.00	105.00	245.00
15-(Scarce)-"The Man From Planet X"-Robert Clark; Shaffenberger-a (2/52)	150.00	450.00	1050.00
16-"10 Tall Men"-Burt Lancaster	11.00	32.00	75.00
17-"Rose of Cimarron"-Jack Buetel & Mala Powers	9.15	27.50	55.00
18-"The Brigand"-Anthony Dexter; Shaffenberger-a	9.15	27.50	55.00
19-"Carbine Williams"-James Stewart; Costanza-a; James Stewart photo-c	10.00	30.00	65.00
20-"Ivanhoe"-Liz Taylor	14.00	43.00	100.00

FAWCETT'S FUNNY ANIMALS (No. 1-26, 80-on titled "Funny Animals," becomes Li'l Tomboy No. 92 on?)
12/42 - #79, 4/53; #80, 6/53 - #83, 12?/53; #84, 4/54 - #91, 2/56
Fawcett Publications/Charlton Comics No. 84 on

	GD25	FN65	NM94
1-Capt. Marvel on cover; intro. Hoppy The Captain Marvel Bunny, cloned from Capt. Marvel; Billy the Kid & Willie the Worm begin	43.00	130.00	300.00
2-Xmas-c	22.00	65.00	150.00
3-5	13.00	40.00	90.00
6,7,9,10	10.00	30.00	60.00
8-Flag-c	10.00	30.00	65.00
11-20	6.70	20.00	40.00
21-40: 25-Xmas-c. 26-St. Valentines Day-c	4.70	14.00	28.00
41-88,90,91	4.00	10.00	20.00
89-(2/55)-Merry Mailman ish (TV)-part photo-c	4.70	14.00	28.00

NOTE: *Marvel Bunny in all issues to at least No. 68 (not in 49-54).*

FAZE ONE FAZERS (Americomics)(Value: cover or less)

F.B.I., THE
April-June, 1965
Dell Publishing Co.

	GD25	FN65	NM94
1-Sinnott-a	2.80	7.00	14.00

F.B.I. STORY, THE (See 4-Color No. 1069)

FEAR (Adventure Into...)
Nov, 1970 - No. 31, Dec, 1975 (No.1-6: Giant Size)
Marvel Comics Group

	GD25	FN65	NM94
1-Fantasy & Sci-Fi reprints in early issues	1.40	3.50	8.50
2-6	1.00	2.50	5.50
7-9		1.20	3.00
10-Man-Thing begins (10/72, early app.), ends #19; see Savage Tales #1 for 1st app.; Morrow/Chaykin-c/a	1.40	3.50	8.50
11,12: 11-N. Adams-c. 12-Starlin/Buckler-a		1.60	4.00
13,14,16-18: 17 Origin/1st app. Wundarr		1.20	3.00
15-1st full-length Man-Thing story (8/73)		1.60	4.00
19-Intro. Howard the Duck; Val Mayerik-a (12/73)	2.40	7.25	17.00
20-Morbius, the Living Vampire begins, ends #31	3.20	8.00	20.00
21-25	1.65	4.70	11.00
26-31	1.40	3.50	8.50

NOTE: *Bolle a-13i. Brunner c-15-17. Buckler a-11p, 12i. Chaykin a-10i. Colan a-23r. Craig a-10p. Ditko a-6-8r. Evans a-30. Everett a-9, 10i, 21r. Gulacy a-20p. Gil Kane a-21p; c(p)-20, 21, 23-28, 31. Kirby a-8r, 9r. Maneely a-24r. Mooney a-11i, 26r. Morrow a-11i. Paul Reinman a-14r. Robbins a(p)-25-27, 31. Russell a-23p, 24p. Severin c-8. Starlin c-12p.*

FEARBOOK (Eclipse)(Value: cover or less)

FEAR IN THE NIGHT (See Complete Mystery No. 3)

FEARLESS FAGAN (See 4-Color No. 441)

FEATURE BOOK (Dell) (See Large Feature Comic)

FEATURE BOOKS (Newspaper-r, early issues)
May, 1937 - No. 57, 1948 (B&W; Full color, 68 pgs. begin #26 on)
David McKay Publications

	GD25	FN65	VF82
nn-Popeye & the Jeep (#1, 100 pgs.); reprinted as Feature Books #3 (Very Rare; only 3 known copies, 1-vf, 2-in low grade) Estimated value....	585.00	1750.00	3500.00
nn-Dick Tracy (#1)-Reprinted as Feature Book #4 (100 pgs.) & in part as 4-Color #1 (Rare, less than 10 known copies) Estimated value....	585.00	1750.00	3500.00

NOTE: *Above books were advertised together with different covers from Feat. Books #3 & 4.*

	GD25	FN65	NM94
1-King of the Royal Mtd. (#1)	64.00	195.00	450.00
2-Popeye(6/37) by Segar	64.00	195.00	450.00
3-Popeye(7/37) by Segar; same as nn issue but a new cover added	57.00	170.00	400.00
4-Dick Tracy(8/37)-Same as nn issue but a new cover added	100.00	300.00	700.00
5-Popeye(9/37) by Segar	50.00	150.00	350.00
6-Dick Tracy(10/37)	79.00	205.00	550.00
7-Little Orphan Annie (#1) (Rare)-Reprints strips from 12/31/34 to 7/17/35	82.00	245.00	575.00
8-Secret Agent X-9-Not by Raymond	33.00	100.00	230.00
9-Dick Tracy(1/38)	79.00	235.00	550.00

Feature Book #30, © KING

Feature Comics #65, © QUA

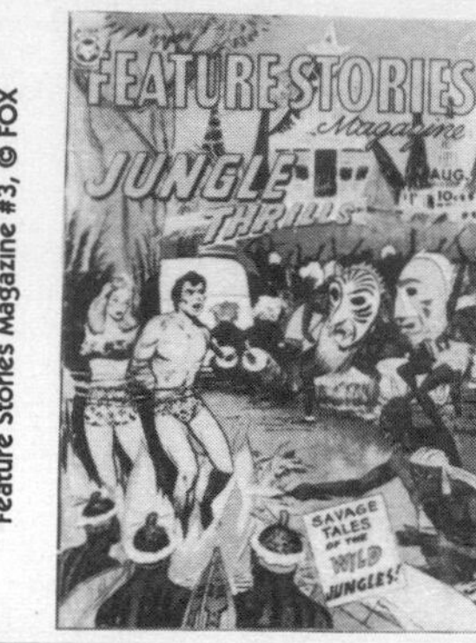

Feature Stories Magazine #3, © FOX

	GD25	FN65	NM94
10-Popeye(2/38)	50.00	150.00	350.00
11-Little Annie Rooney (#1)	26.00	80.00	185.00
12-Blondie (#1) (4/38) (Rare)	50.00	150.00	350.00
13-Inspector Wade	16.00	48.00	110.00
14-Popeye(6/38) by Segar (Scarce)	64.00	195.00	450.00
15-Barney Baxter (#1) (7/38)	24.00	72.00	165.00
16-Red Eagle	16.00	48.00	110.00
17-Gangbusters (#1) (1st app.)	38.00	115.00	265.00
18,19-Mandrake	31.00	95.00	220.00
20-Phantom (#1)	59.00	180.00	415.00
21-Lone Ranger	54.00	160.00	375.00
22-Phantom	47.00	140.00	330.00
23-Mandrake	31.00	95.00	220.00
24-Lone Ranger(1941)	54.00	160.00	375.00
25-Flash Gordon (#1)-Reprints not by Raymond	60.00	180.00	420.00
26-Prince Valian t(1941)-Harold Foster-a; newspaper strips reprinted, pgs. 1-28,30-63; color & 68 pg. issues begin	79.00	235.00	550.00
27-29,31,34-Blondie	11.50	34.00	80.00
30-Katzenjammer Kids (#1)	12.00	36.00	85.00
32,35,41,44-Katzenjammer Kids	11.00	32.00	75.00
33(nn)-Romance of Flying-World War II photos	10.00	30.00	70.00
36('43),38,40('44),42,43,45,47-Blondie	11.00	32.00	75.00
37-Katzenjammer Kids; has photo & biog. of Harold H. Knerr(1883-1949) who took over strip from Rudolph Dirks in 1914	11.50	34.00	80.00
39-Phantom	39.00	120.00	275.00
46-Mandrake in the Fire World-(58 pgs.)	26.00	80.00	185.00
48-Maltese Falcon by Dashiell Hammett('46)	55.00	165.00	385.00
49,50-Perry Mason	17.00	52.00	120.00
51,54-Rip Kirby c/a by Raymond; origin-#51	26.00	78.00	180.00
52,55-Mandrake	24.00	72.00	165.00
53,56,57-Phantom	29.00	85.00	200.00

NOTE: *All Feature Books through #25 are over-sized 8-1/2x11-3/8" comics with color covers and black and white interiors. The covers are rough, heavy stock. The page counts, including covers, are as follows: nn, #3, 4-100 pgs.; #1, 2-52 pgs.; #5-25 are all 76 pgs. #33 was found in bound set from publisher.*

FEATURE COMICS (Formerly Feature Funnies)
No. 21, June, 1939 - No. 144, May, 1950
Quality Comics Group

	GD25	FN65	NM94
21-The Clock, Jane Arden & Mickey Finn continue from Feature Funnies	37.00	110.00	250.00
22-26: 23-Charlie Chan begins (8/39, 1st app.)	27.00	82.00	185.00
26-(nn, nd)-Cover in one color, (10¢, 36 pgs.; issue No. blanked out. 2 variations exist,each contain half of the regular #26)	8.35	25.00	50.00
27-(Rare)-Origin/1st app. Doll Man by Lou Fine; Doll Man begins, ends #139	208.00	625.00	1500.00
28-Lou Fine Doll Man	90.00	270.00	600.00
29,30: 30-1st Doll Man-c	57.00	170.00	375.00
31-Last Clock & Charlie Chan issue (4/40); Charlie Chan moves to Big Shot #1 following month (5/40)	48.00	145.00	310.00
32-37: 32-Rusty Ryan & Samar begin. 34-Captain Fortune app. 37-Last Fine Doll Man	35.00	105.00	230.00
38-41: 38-Origin the Ace of Space. 39-Origin The Destroying Demon, ends #40. 40-Bruce Blackburn in costume	27.00	80.00	180.00
42,43,45-50: 42-USA, the Spirit of Old Glory begins. 46-Intro. Boyville Brigadiers in Rusty Ryan. 48-USA ends	17.00	52.00	115.00
44-Doll Man by Crandall begins, ends #63; Crandall-a(2)	26.00	78.00	175.00
51-60: 56-Marijuana story in Swing Sisson strip. 57-Spider Widow begins. 60-Raven begins, ends #71	14.00	42.00	90.00
61-68 (5/43)	13.00	40.00	85.00
69,70-Phantom Lady x-over in Spider Widow	14.00	42.00	90.00
71-80,100: 71-Phantom Lady x-over. 72-Spider Widow ends	10.00	30.00	65.00
81-99	9.15	27.50	55.00
101-144: 139-Last Doll Man & last Doll Man-c. 140-Intro. Stuntman Stetson (Stuntman Stetson c-140-144)	6.70	20.00	40.00

NOTE: ***Celardo** a-37-43. **Crandall** a-44-60, 62, 63-on(most). **Gustavson** a-(Rusty Ryan)- 32-134. **Powell** a-34, 64-73. The Clock c-25, 28, 29. Doll Man c-30, 32, 34, 36, 38, 40, 42, 44, 46, 48, 50, 52, 54, 56, 58, 60, 62, 64, 66, 68, 70, 72, 74, 77-139. Joe Palooka c-21, 24, 27.*

FEATURE FILMS
Mar-Apr, 1950 - No. 4, Sept-Oct, 1950 (All photo-c)
National Periodical Publications

	GD25	FN65	NM94
1-"Captain China" with John Payne, Gail Russell, Lon Chaney & Edgar Bergen	43.00	130.00	300.00
2-"Riding High" with Bing Crosby	50.00	150.00	350.00
3-"The Eagle & the Hawk" with John Payne, Rhonda Fleming & D. O'Keefe	43.00	130.00	300.00
4-"Fancy Pants"-Bob Hope & Lucille Ball	50.00	150.00	350.00

FEATURE FUNNIES (Feature Comics No. 21 on)
Oct, 1937 - No. 20, May, 1939
Harry 'A' Chesler

	GD25	FN65	NM94
1(V9#1-indicia)-Joe Palooka, Mickey Finn (1st app.), The Bungles, Jane Arden, Dixie Dugan (1st app.), Big Top, Ned Brant, Strange As It Seems, & Off the Record strip reprints begin	183.00	550.00	1200.00
2-The Hawk app. (11/37); Goldberg-c	87.00	262.00	550.00
3-Hawks of Seas begins by Eisner, ends #12; The Clock begins; Christmas-c	62.00	188.00	400.00
4,5	46.00	138.00	300.00
6-12: 11-Archie O'Toole by Bud Thomas begins, ends #22	37.00	112.00	250.00
13-Espionage, Starring Black X begins by Eisner, ends #20	41.00	122.00	275.00
14-20	32.00	95.00	210.00

NOTE: *Joe Palooka covers 1, 6, 9, 12, 15, 18.*

FEATURE PRESENTATION, A (Feature Presentations Magazine #6) (Formerly Women in Love) (Also see Startling Terror Tales #11)
No. 5, April, 1950
Fox Features Syndicate

	GD25	FN65	NM94
5(#1)-Black Tarantula	23.00	70.00	160.00

FEATURE PRESENTATIONS MAGAZINE (Formerly A Feature Presentation #5; becomes Feature Stories Magazine #3 on)
No. 6, July, 1950
Fox Features Syndicate

	GD25	FN65	NM94
6(#2)-Moby Dick; Wood-c	18.00	54.00	125.00

FEATURE STORIES MAGAZINE (Formerly Feature Presentations Mag. #6)
No. 3, Aug, 1950 - No. 4, Oct, 1950
Fox Features Syndicate

	GD25	FN65	NM94
3-Jungle Lil, Zegra stories; bondage-c	15.00	45.00	105.00
4	11.50	34.00	80.00

FEDERAL MEN COMICS (See Adventure Comics #32, The Comics Magazine, New Adventure Comics, New Book of Comics, New Comics & Star Spangled Comics #91)
No. 2, 1945 (DC reprints from 1930's)
Gerard Publ. Co.

	GD25	FN65	NM94
2-Siegel & Shuster-a; cover redrawn from Detective #9; spanking panel	18.00	54.00	125.00

FELIX'S NEPHEWS INKY & DINKY
Sept, 1957 - No. 7, Oct, 1958
Harvey Publications

	GD25	FN65	NM94
1-Cover shows Inky's left eye with 2 pupils	7.00	21.00	42.00
2-7	4.00	10.00	20.00

NOTE: ***Messmer** art in 1-6. **Oriolo** a-1-7.*

FELIX THE CAT
1931 (24 pgs.; 8x10-1/4")(1926, '27 color strip reprints)
McLoughlin Bros.

	GD25	FN65	NM94
260-(Rare)-by Otto Messmer	92.00	275.00	600.00

Felix the Cat #1, © KING

The Ferret #3, © Malibu

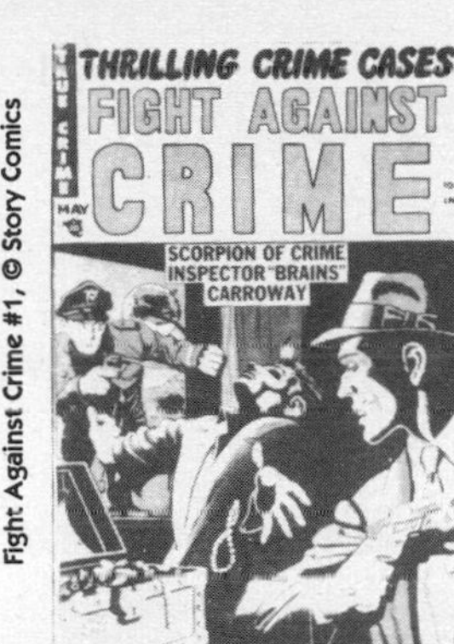

Fight Against Crime #1, © Story Comics

FELIX THE CAT (See Cat Tales 3-D, The Funnies, March of Comics #24,36, 51, New Funnies & Popular Comics)
1943 - No. 118, Nov, 1961; Sept-Nov, 1962 - No. 12, July-Sept, 1965
Dell Publ. No. 1-19/Toby No. 20-61/Harvey No. 62-118/Dell No. 1-12

	GD25	FN65	NM94
4-Color 15	61.00	185.00	425.00
4-Color 46('44)	38.00	115.00	265.00
4-Color 77('45)	36.00	110.00	250.00
4-Color 119('46)	29.00	85.00	200.00
4-Color 135('46)	22.00	65.00	150.00
4-Color 162(9/47)	16.00	48.00	110.00
1(2-3/48)(Dell)	22.00	65.00	150.00
2	11.00	32.00	75.00
3-5	10.00	30.00	60.00
6-19(2-3/51-Dell)	6.70	20.00	40.00
20-30(Toby): 28-(2/52)-Some copies have #29 on cover, #28 on inside	10.00	30.00	65.00
31,34,35-No Messmer-a	4.00	12.00	24.00
32,33,36-61(6/55-Toby)-Last Messmer issue	8.35	25.00	50.00
62(8/55)-100 (Harvey)	2.40	6.00	12.00
101-118(11/61): 101-117-Reprints. 118-All new-a	2.00	5.00	10.00
12-269-211(#1, 9-11/62)(Dell)	4.00	10.00	20.00
2-12(7-9/65)(Dell, TV)	2.40	6.00	12.00
3-D Comic Book 1(1953-One Shot)	27.00	81.00	190.00
Special nn ('52, 25¢, 100 pgs., Toby)-All new stories; X-Mas-c	25.00	75.00	175.00
Summer Annual nn ('53, 25¢, 100 pgs., Toby)-All new stories	25.00	75.00	175.00
Winter Annual 2 ('54, 25¢, 100 pgs., Toby)-1930s daily & Sunday-r	19.00	57.00	130.00
Summer Annual 3 ('55) (Exist?)	17.00	52.00	120.00

NOTE: *4-Color No. 15, 46, 77 and the Toby Annuals are all daily or Sunday newspaper reprints from the 1930's drawn by* **Otto Messmer**, *who created Felix in 1915 for the Sullivan animation studio. He drew Felix from the beginning under contract to Pat Sullivan. In 1946 he went to work for Dell and wrote and pencilled most of the stories and inked some of them through the Toby Press issues. 101-r/#64; 102-r/#65; 103-r/#67; 104-117-r/#68-81.* **Messmer**-*a in all Dell/Toby/Harvey issues except #31, 34, 35, 97, 98, 100, 118.* **Oriolo** *a-20, 31-on.*

FELIX THE CAT (Also see The Nine Lives of...)
Sept, 1991 - Present ($1.25/$1.50, color, bi-monthly)
Harvey Comics

	GD25	FN65	NM94
1-5: Reprints 1950s Toby issues by Messmer. 1-Inky and Dinky back-up story			1.25
6,7-($1.50-c)			1.50
...Big Book V2#1 (9/92, $1.95, 52 pgs.)		.80	2.00

FELIX THE CAT AND FRIENDS
1992 - Present ($1.95, color)
Felix Comics

	GD25	FN65	NM94
1-4: 1-Contains Felix trading cards		.80	2.00

FELIX THE CAT & HIS FRIENDS
Dec, 1953 - No. 3, 1954
Toby Press

	GD25	FN65	NM94
1	9.15	27.50	55.00
2-3	6.70	20.00	40.00

FELIX THE CAT DIGEST MAGAZINE
July, 1992 - Present ($1.75, color, digest-size, 98 pgs.)
Harvey Comics

	GD25	FN65	NM94
1-Felix, Richie Rich stories		.70	1.75

FEM FANTASTIQUE (AC)(Value: cover or less)

FEMFORCE (Also see Untold Origin of the Femforce)
Apr, 1985 - Present ($1.75/1.95/2.25; in color; B&W #16-56)
Americomics

	GD25	FN65	NM94
1-Black-a in most; Nightveil, Ms. Victory begin	1.00	2.50	5.50
2		1.40	3.50
3-30: 12-15-$1.95-c. 16-19-$2.25-c. 20-Begin $2.50-c, 44 pgs. 25-Origin/1st app. new Ms. Victory. 28-Colt leaves. 29,30-Camilla-r by Mayo from Jungle Comics		1.20	3.00
31-35,37-49,51-62: 31-Begin $2.75-c. 44-Contains mini-comic insert, Catman & Kitten #0. 51-Photo-c from movie. 57-Begin color issues		1.00	2.50
36-($2.95, 52 pgs.)		1.00	2.50
50-($2.95, color, 52 pgs.)-Contains flexi-disc; origin retold; most AC characters app.		1.00	2.50
63-68 ($2.95-c): 64-Re-intro Black Phantom		1.00	2.50
Special 1 (Fall, '84)(B&W, 52pgs.)-1st app. Ms. Victory, She-Cat, Blue Bulleteer, Rio Rita & Lady Luger		.80	2.00
Frightbook 1 ('92, $2.95, B&W)-Halloween special		1.20	3.00
In the House of Horror 1 ('89, $2.50, B&W)		1.00	2.50
Night of the Demon 1 ('90, $2.75, B&W)		1.10	2.75
Out of the Asylum Special 1 ('87, B&W, $1.95)		.80	2.00
Pin-Up Portfolio		.80	2.00

FEMFORCE UP CLOSE
Apr, 1992 - Present ($2.75, color, quarterly)
AC Comics

	GD25	FN65	NM94
1-4: 1-Stars Nightveil; inside f/c photo from Femforce movie. 2-Stars Stardust. 3-Stars Dragonfly. 4-Stars She-Cat		1.10	2.75

FERDINAND THE BULL (See Mickey Mouse Magazine V4#3)
1938 (10 cents)(Large size; some color, rest B&W)
Dell Publishing Co.

	GD25	FN65	NM94
nn	13.00	40.00	90.00

FERRET
Sept, 1992; May, 1993 - Present ($1.95, color)
Malibu Comics

	GD25	FN65	NM94
1-(1992, one-shot)		.80	2.00
1-($2.50)-Completely die-cut cover		1.00	2.50
2-4-($2.50)-Collector's Edition w/poster		1.00	2.50
2-4-($1.95)-Newsstand Edition w/different-c		.80	2.00
5-8-($2.25)		.90	2.25

FEUD
July, 1993 - No. 4, Oct, 1993 ($1.95, color, mini-series)
Epic Comics (Marvel)

	GD25	FN65	NM94
1-($2.50)-Embossed-c		1.00	2.50
2-4		.80	2.00

FIBBER McGEE & MOLLY (See A-1 Comics No. 25)

55 DAYS AT PEKING (See Movie Comics)

FIGHT AGAINST CRIME (Fight Against the Guilty #22, 23)
May, 1951 - No. 21, Sept, 1954
Story Comics

	GD25	FN65	NM94
1	16.00	50.00	115.00
2	8.35	25.00	50.00
3,5: 5-Frazetta-a, 1 pg.	6.70	20.00	40.00
4-Drug story-"Hopped Up Killers"	8.35	25.00	50.00
6,7: 6-Used in **POP**, pgs. 83,84	5.85	17.50	35.00
8-Last crime format issue	5.85	17.50	35.00

NOTE: *No. 9-21 contain violent, gruesome stories with blood, dismemberment, decapitation, E.C. style plot twists and several E.C. swipes. Bondage c-4, 6, 18, 19.*

	GD25	FN65	NM94
9-11,13	11.50	34.00	80.00
12-Morphine drug story-"The Big Dope"	13.00	40.00	90.00
14-Tothish art by Ross Andru; electrocution-c	11.50	34.00	80.00
15-B&W & color illos in **POP**	11.00	32.00	75.00
16-E.C. story swipe/Haunt of Fear #19; Tothish-a by Ross Andru; bondage-c	13.00	40.00	90.00
17-Wildey E.C. swipe/Shock SuspenStories #9; knife through neck-c (1/54)	13.00	40.00	90.00
18,19: 19-Bondage/torture-c	11.00	32.00	75.00
20-Decapitation cover; contains hanging, ax murder, blood & violence	20.00	60.00	140.00

Fight Comics #26, © FH

Fighting American #4, © PRIZE

Fighting Indians of the Wild West #1, © AVON

GD25 FN65 NM94

21-E.C. swipe 10.00 30.00 70.00
NOTE: *Cameron a-4, 5, 8. Hollingsworth a-3-7, 9, 10, 13. Wildey a-6, 15, 16.*

FIGHT AGAINST THE GUILTY (Formerly Fight Against Crime)
No. 22, Dec, 1954 - No. 23, Mar, 1955
Story Comics

22-Tothish-a by Ross Andru; Ditko-a; E.C. story swipe; electrocution-c 10.00 30.00 70.00
23 (Last pre-code)-Hollingsworth-a 8.350 25.00 50.00

FIGHT COMICS
Jan, 1940 - No. 83, 11/52; No. 84, Wint, 1952-53; No. 85, Spring, 1953; No. 86, Summer, 1954
Fiction House Magazines

1-Origin Spy Fighter, Starring Saber; Fine/Eisner-c; Eisner-a 133.00 400.00 900.00
2-Joe Louis life story 58.00 175.00 400.00
3-Rip Regan, the Power Man begins (3/40) 50.00 150.00 330.00
4,5: 4-Fine-c 42.00 125.00 275.00
6-10: 6,7-Powell-c 33.00 100.00 220.00
11-14: Rip Regan ends 29.00 88.00 195.00
15-1st app. Super American plus-c (10/41) 42.00 125.00 275.00
16-Captain Fight begins; Spy Fighter ends 42.00 125.00 275.00
17,18: Super American ends 33.00 100.00 220.00
19-Captain Fight ends; Senorita Rio begins (6/42, origin & 1st app.); Rip Carson, Chute Trooper begins 33.00 100.00 220.00
20 27.00 80.00 180.00
21-30 17.00 50.00 115.00
31,33-50: 31-Decapitation-c. 44-Capt. Flight returns. 48-Used in Love and Death by Legman. 49-Jungle-c begin 14.00 43.00 100.00
32-Tiger Girl begins (6/44, 1st app.?) 16.00 48.00 110.00
51-Origin Tiger Girl; Patsy Pin-Up app. 23.00 70.00 160.00
52-60,62-65-Last Baker issue 12.00 35.00 75.00
61-Origin Tiger Girl retold 14.00 43.00 100.00
66-78: 78-Used in POP, pg. 99 10.00 30.00 70.00
79-The Space Rangers app. 10.00 30.00 70.00
80-85: 81-Last jungle-c. 82-85-War-c 10.00 30.00 60.00
86-Two Tigerman stories by Evans-r/Rangers Comics #40,41; Moreira-r/Rangers Comics #45 10.00 30.00 70.00
NOTE: *Bondage covers, Lingerie, headlights panels are common. Tiger Girl by Baker- #36-60, 62-65; Kayo Kirby by Baker-#52-64, 67(not by Baker). Eisner c-1-3, 5, 10, 11. Kamen a-54?, 57? Tuska a-1, 5, 8, 10, 21, 29. Whitman c-73-84. Zolnerwich c-16, 17, 22. Power Man c-5, 6, 9. Super American c-15-17. Tiger Girl c-49-81.*

FIGHT FOR FREEDOM
1949, 1951 (16 pgs.) (Giveaway)
National Association of Mfgrs./General Comics

nn-Dan Barry-c/a; used in **POP**, pg. 102 5.00 15.00 30.00

FIGHT FOR LOVE
1952 (no month)
United Features Syndicate

nn-Abbie & Slats newspaper-r 8.75 26.00 52.00

FIGHTING AIR FORCE (See United States Fighting Air Force)

FIGHTIN' AIR FORCE (Formerly Sherlock Holmes?; Never Again? War and Attack #54 on)
No. 3, Feb, 1956 - No. 53, Feb-Mar, 1966
Charlton Comics

V1#3 4.00 11.00 22.00
4-10 2.40 6.00 12.00
11(3/58, 68 pgs.) 3.00 7.50 15.00
12 (100 pgs.) 4.00 10.00 20.00
13-30: 13,24-Glanzman-a. 24-Glanzman-c 2.00 5.00 10.00
31-50: 50-American Eagle begins 1.40 3.50 7.00
51-53 1.00 2.50 5.00

FIGHTING AMERICAN
Apr-May, 1954 - No. 7, Apr-May, 1955
Headline Publications/Prize

1-Origin & 1st app. Fighting American & Speedboy; S&K-c/a(3) 107.00 321.00 750.00
2-S&K-a(3) 52.00 156.00 365.00
3,4-S&K-a(3) 46.00 138.00 320.00
5-S&K-a(2); Kirby/?-a 46.00 138.00 320.00
6-Origin-r (4 pgs.) plus 2 pgs. by S&K 42.00 125.00 295.00
7-Kirby-a 38.00 115.00 265.00
NOTE: *Simon & Kirby covers on all. 6 is last pre-code issue.*

FIGHTING AMERICAN
October, 1966 (25 cents)
Harvey Publications

1-Origin Fighting American & Speedboy by S&K-r; S&K-c/a(3); 1 pg. Neal Adams ad 2.30 6.75 16.00

FIGHTIN' ARMY (Formerly Soldier and Marine Comics; see Captain Willy Schultz)
No. 16, 1/56 - No. 127, 12/76; No. 128, 9/77 - No. 172, 11/84
Charlton Comics

16 4.00 11.00 22.00
17-19,21-23,25-30 2.40 6.00 12.00
20-Ditko-a 4.00 10.00 20.00
24 (68 pgs., 3/58) 3.00 7.50 15.00
31-45 2.00 5.00 10.00
46-60 1.40 3.50 7.00
61-80: 75-92-The Lonely War of Willy Schultz 1.00 2.00 5.00
81-172: 89,90,92-Ditko-a; Devil Brigade in #79,82,83 1.00 2.50
108(Modern Comics-1977)-Reprint 1.50
NOTE: *Aparo c-154. Montes/Bache a-48, 49, 51, 69, 75, 76, 170r.*

FIGHTING DANIEL BOONE
1953
Avon Periodicals

nn-Kinstler-c/a, 22 pgs. 11.50 34.00 80.00
I.W. Reprint #1-Reprints #1 above; Kinstler-c/a; Lawrence/Alascia-a 1.80 4.50 9.00

FIGHTING DAVY CROCKETT (Formerly Kit Carson)
No. 9, Oct-Nov, 1955
Avon Periodicals

9-Kinstler-c 5.85 17.50 35.00

FIGHTIN' FIVE, THE (Fightin' 5 #40 on?; formerly Space War; also see The Peacemaker)
July, 1964 - No. 41, Jan, 1967; No. 42, Oct, 1981 - No. 49, Dec, 1982
Charlton Comics

V2#28-Origin & 1st app. Fightin' Five 2.70 8.00 19.00
29-39,41 1.65 4.70 11.00
40-Peacemaker begins (1st app.) 2.70 8.00 19.00
42-49: Reprints .65 1.60

FIGHTING FRONTS!
Aug, 1952 - No. 5, Jan, 1953
Harvey Publications

1 4.20 12.50 25.00
2-Extreme violence; Nostrand/Powell-a 5.00 15.00 30.00
3-5: 3-Powell-a 3.00 7.50 15.00

FIGHTING INDIAN STORIES (See Midget Comics)

FIGHTING INDIANS OF THE WILD WEST!
Mar, 1952 - No. 2, Nov, 1952
Avon Periodicals

1-Geronimo, Chief Crazy Horse, Chief Victorio, Black Hawk begin; Larsen-a; McCann-a(2) 10.00 30.00 60.00
2-Kinstler-c & inside-c only; Larsen, McCann-a 6.70 20.00 40.00
100 Pg. Annual (1952, 25¢)-Contains three comics rebound; Geronimo, Chief Crazy Horse, Chief Victorio; Kinstler-c 18.00 54.00 125.00

Fighting Leathernecks #6, © TOBY

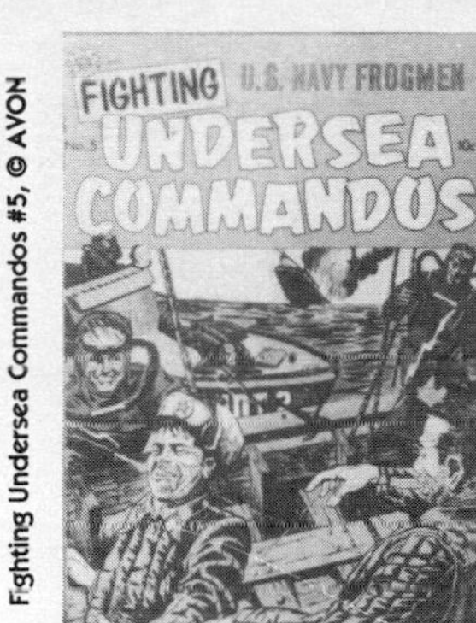

Fighting Undersea Commandos #5, © AVON

Firearm #1, © Malibu

FIGHTING LEATHERNECKS
Feb, 1952 - No. 6, Dec, 1952
Toby Press

	GD25	FN65	NM94
1-"Duke's Diary"-full pg. pin-ups by Sparling	10.00	30.00	60.00
2-"Duke's Diary"	7.00	21.00	42.00
3-5-"Gil's Gals"-full pg. pin-ups	7.00	21.00	42.00
6-(Same as No. 3-5?)	4.70	14.00	28.00

FIGHTING MAN, THE (War)
May, 1952 - No. 8, July, 1953
Ajax/Farrell Publications(Excellent Publ.)

	GD25	FN65	NM94
1	6.70	20.00	40.00
2	4.00	10.00	20.00
3-8	3.20	8.00	16.00
Annual 1 (100 pgs, 1952)	14.00	43.00	100.00

FIGHTIN' MARINES (Formerly The Texan; also see Approved Comics)
No. 15, 8/51 - No. 12, 3/53; No. 14, 5/55 - No. 132, 11/76;
No. 133, 10/77 - No. 176, 9/84 (No #13?)
St. John(Approved Comics)/Charlton Comics No. 14 on

	GD25	FN65	NM94
15(#1)-Matt Baker c/a "Leatherneck Jack;" slightly large size; Fightin' Texan No. 16 & 17?	16.00	48.00	110.00
2-1st Canteen Kate by Baker; slightly large size	18.00	54.00	125.00
3-9-Canteen Kate by Matt Baker; Baker c-#2,3,5-11	10.00	30.00	65.00
10-Baker-c	4.00	10.00	20.00
11,12-No Baker-a. 12-Last St. John issue?	2.80	7.00	14.00
14 (5/55; 1st Charlton issue; formerly?)-Canteen Kate by Baker; all stories reprinted from #2	10.00	30.00	60.00
15-Baker-c	4.00	10.00	20.00
16,18-20-Not Baker-c	2.40	6.00	12.00
17-Canteen Kate by Baker	6.70	20.00	40.00
21-24	2.40	6.00	12.00
25-(68 pgs.)(3/58)-Check-a?	4.00	10.00	20.00
26-(100 pgs.)(8/58)-Check-a(5)	5.00	15.00	30.00
27-50	1.80	4.50	9.00
51-81,83-100: 78-Shotgun Harker & the Chicken series begin		1.60	4.00
82-(100 pgs.)	1.30	3.25	8.00
101-122: 122-Pilot Issue for "War" title (Fightin' Marines Presents War)		1.20	3.00
123-176			1.50
120(Modern Comics reprint, 1977)			1.50

NOTE: *No. 14 & 16 (CC) reprint St. John issues; No. 16 reprints St. John insignia on cover.* ***Colan*** *a-3, 7.* ***Glanzman*** *c/a-92, 94.* ***Montes/Bache*** *a-48, 53, 55, 64, 65, 72-74, 77-83, 176r.*

FIGHTING MARSHAL OF THE WILD WEST (See The Hawk)

FIGHTIN' NAVY (Formerly Don Winslow)
No. 74, 1/56 - No. 125, 4-5/66; No. 126, 8/83 - No. 133, 10/84
Charlton Comics

	GD25	FN65	NM94
74	4.00	11.00	22.00
75-81	2.40	6.00	12.00
82-Sam Glanzman-a	1.80	4.50	9.00
83-99,101-105,106-125('66)	1.20	3.00	6.00
100	1.40	3.50	7.00
126-133 (1984)			1.50

NOTE: ***Montes/Bache*** *a-109.* ***Glanzman*** *a-82, 131r.*

FIGHTING PRINCE OF DONEGAL, THE (See Movie Comics)

FIGHTIN' TEXAN (Formerly The Texan & Fightin' Marines?)
No. 16, Oct, 1952 - No. 17, Dec, 1952
St. John Publishing Co.

	GD25	FN65	NM94
16,17 Tuska a each. 17 Cameron c/a	4.70	14.00	28.00

FIGHTING UNDERSEA COMMANDOS (See Undersea Fighting...)
May, 1952 - No. 5, April, 1953
Avon Periodicals

	GD25	FN65	NM94
1-Cover title is Undersea Fighting... #1 only	7.50	22.50	45.00
2	5.00	15.00	30.00
3-5: 1,3-Ravielli-c. 4-Kinstler-c	4.20	12.50	25.00

FIGHTING WAR STORIES
Aug, 1952 - No. 5, 1953
Men's Publications/Story Comics

	GD25	FN65	NM94
1	5.35	16.00	32.00
2-5	3.60	9.00	18.00

FIGHTING YANK (See America's Best Comics & Startling Comics)
Sept, 1942 - No. 29, Aug, 1949
Nedor/Better Publ./Standard

	GD25	FN65	NM94
1-The Fighting Yank begins; Mystico, the Wonder Man app; bondage-c	100.00	300.00	700.00
2	46.00	138.00	325.00
3	31.00	92.00	220.00
4	25.00	75.00	175.00
5-10: 7-The Grim Reaper app.	19.00	58.00	135.00
11-20: 11-The Oracle app. 12-Hirohito bondage-c. 10,15-Bondage/torture-c. 18-The American Eagle app.	17.00	52.00	120.00
21,23,24: 21-Kara, Jungle Princess app. 24-Miss Masque app.	20.00	60.00	140.00
22-Miss Masque-c/story	25.00	75.00	175.00
25-Robinson/Meskin-a; strangulation, lingerie panel; The Cavalier app.	25.00	75.00	175.00
26-29: All-Robinson/Meskin-a. 28-One pg. Williamson-a	19.00	57.00	130.00

NOTE: ***Schomburg (Xela)*** *c-4-29; airbrush-c 28, 29. Bondage c-4, 8, 11, 15, 17.*

FIGHT THE ENEMY
Aug, 1966 - No. 3, Mar, 1967 (25 cents, 68 pgs.)
Tower Comics

	GD25	FN65	NM94
1-Lucky 7 & Mike Manly begin	3.20	9.00	21.00
2-Boris Vallejo, McWilliams-a	2.40	7.25	17.00
3-Wood-a (1/2 pg.); McWilliams, Bolle-a	2.40	7.25	17.00

FILM FUNNIES
Nov, 1949 - No. 2, Feb, 1950 (52 pgs.)
Marvel Comics (CPC)

	GD25	FN65	NM94
1-Krazy Krow, Wacky Duck	11.50	34.00	80.00
2	10.00	30.00	60.00

FILM STARS ROMANCES
Jan-Feb, 1950 - No. 3, May-June, 1950
Star Publications

	GD25	FN65	NM94
1-Rudy Valentino & Gregory Peck stories; L. B. Cole-c; lingerie panels	19.00	58.00	135.00
2-Liz Taylor/Robert Taylor photo-c & true life story	21.00	63.00	145.00
3-Photo-c	16.00	48.00	110.00

FINAL CYCLE, THE (Dragon's Teeth)(Value: cover or less)

FIRE AND BLAST
1952 (16 pgs.; paper cover) (Giveaway)
National Fire Protection Assoc.

	GD25	FN65	NM94
nn-Mart Baily A-Bomb-c; about fire prevention	13.50	41.00	95.00

FIREARM
Sept, 1993 - Present ($1.95, color)
Malibu Comics (Ultraverse)

	GD25	FN65	NM94
1,3: 1-Chaykin-c; Hamner-a		.80	2.00
2-($2.50, 40 pgs.)-Rune flip-c/story by B. Smith (3 pgs.)		1.00	2.50

FIRE BALL XL5 (See Steve Zodiac & The ...)

FIRE CHIEF AND THE SAFE OL' FIREFLY, THE
1952 (16 pgs.) (Safety brochure given away at schools)
National Board of Fire Underwriters (produced by American Visuals Corp.) (Eisner)

Firehair Comics #1, © FH

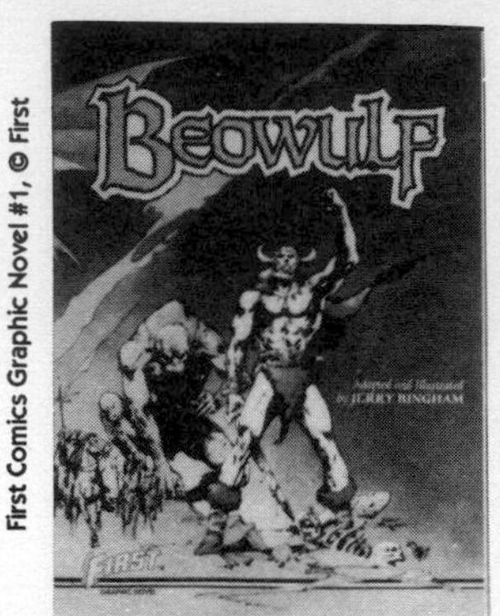

First Comics Graphic Novel #1, © First

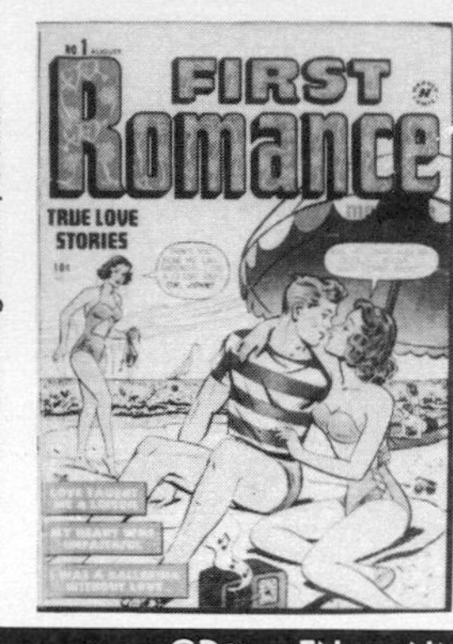

First Romance Magazine #1, © HARV

	GD25	FN65	NM94
nn-(Rare) Eisner-c/a	50.00	150.00	350.00

FIREHAIR COMICS (Formerly Pioneer West Romances #3-6; also see Rangers Comics)
Winter/48-49 - No. 2, Wint/49-50; No. 7, Spr/51 - No. 11, Spr/52
Fiction House Magazines (Flying Stories)

	GD25	FN65	NM94
1	29.00	86.00	200.00
2	14.00	43.00	100.00
7-11	11.50	34.00	80.00
I.W. Reprint 8-(nd)-Kinstler-c; reprints Rangers #57; Dr. Drew story by Grandenetti	2.40	6.00	12.00

FIRESTAR
March, 1986 - No. 4, June, 1986 (From Spider-Man TV series)
Marvel Comics Group

	GD25	FN65	NM94
1-X-Men & New Mutants app.		1.30	3.25
2-Wolverine-c; Art Adams-a(p)	1.00	2.50	6.00
3,4: 3-Art Adams-c		.90	2.25

FIRESTONE (See Donald And Mickey Merry Christmas)

FIRESTORM (See Cancelled Comic Cavalcade, DC Comics Presents, Flash #289, The Fury of... & Justice League of America #179)
March, 1978 - No. 5, Oct-Nov, 1978
DC Comics

	GD25	FN65	NM94
1-Origin & 1st app.		1.20	3.00
2-5: 2-Origin Multiplex. 3-Origin & 1st app. Killer Frost. 4-1st app. Hyena		.80	2.00

FIRESTORM, THE NUCLEAR MAN (Formerly Fury of Firestorm)
No. 65, Nov, 1987 - No. 100, Aug, 1990
DC Comics

	GD25	FN65	NM94
65-99: 66-1st app. Zuggernaut; Firestorm vs. Green Lantern. 71-Death of Capt. X. 67,68-Millennium tie-ins. 83-1st new look			1.00
100-($2.95, 68 pgs.)		1.20	3.00
Annual 5 (10/87)-1st app. new Firestorm			1.25

FIRST ADVENTURES (First)(Value: cover or less)

FIRST AMERICANS, THE (See 4-Color No. 843)

FIRST CHRISTMAS, THE (3-D)
1953 (25 cents) (Oversized - 8-1/4x10-1/4")
Fiction House Magazines (Real Adv. Publ. Co.)

	GD25	FN65	NM94
nn-(Scarce)-Kelly Freas-c; Biblical theme, birth of Christ; Nativity-c	34.00	102.00	240.00

FIRST COMICS GRAPHIC NOVEL
Jan, 1984 - No. 20? (52-176 pgs, high quality paper)
First Comics

	GD25	FN65	NM94
1-Beowulf ($5.95)	1.00	2.50	6.00
1-2nd printing ($6.95)	1.20	3.00	7.00
2-Time Beavers ($5.95)	1.00	2.50	6.00
3($11.95, 100 pgs.)-American Flagg! Hard Times. (2 printings)	1.70	5.00	12.00
4-Nexus ($6.95)-r/B&W 1-3	1.30	3.25	8.00
5-The Enchanted Apples of Oz ($7.95, 52pp)-Intro by Harlan Ellison (1986)	1.30	3.25	8.00
6-Elric of Melnibone ($14.95, 176pp)-Reprints with new color	2.15	6.50	15.00
7-The Secret Island Of Oz ($7.95)	1.30	3.25	8.00
8-Teenage Mutant Ninja Turtles Book I (132 pgs., r/TMNT #1-3 in color w/12 pgs. new-a ($9.95)-Origin	1.65	4.00	10.00
9-Time 2: The Epiphany by Chaykin, 52 pgs. ($7.95)	1.30	3.25	8.00
10-Teenage Mutant Ninja Turtles Book II ($9.95)-r/TMNT #4-6 in color	1.65	4.00	10.00
11-Sailor On The Sea of Fate ($14.95)	2.15	6.50	15.00
12-American Flagg! Southern Comfort ($11.95)	1.70	5.00	12.00
13-The Ice King Of Oz ($7.95)	1.30	3.25	8.00
14-Teenage Mutant Ninja Turtles Book III ($9.95)-r/TMNT #7,8 in color plus new 12 pg. story	1.65	4.00	10.00
15-Hex Breaker: Badger ($7.95, 64 pgs.)	1.30	3.25	8.00
16-The Forgotten Forest of Oz ($8.95)	1.50	3.75	9.00
17-Mazinger (64 pgs., $8.95)	1.50	3.75	9.00
18-Teenage Mutant Ninja Turtles Book IV ($9.95)-r/TMNT #10,11 plus 3 pg. fold-out	1.65	4.00	10.00
19-The Original Nexus Graphic Novel ($7.95, 104pgs)-Reprints First Comics Graphic Novel #4 ($7.95)	1.30	3.25	8.00
20-American Flagg!: State of the Union; r/A.F. 7-9 ($11.95, 96 pgs.)	1.70	5.00	12.00

NOTE: *Most or all issues have been reprinted.*

1ST FOLIO (The Joe Kubert School Presents...)
March, 1984 ($1.50, color)
Pacific Comics

	GD25	FN65	NM94
1-Kubert-c/a(2pgs.); Adam & Andy Kubert-a			1.50

1ST ISSUE SPECIAL
April, 1975 - No. 13, April, 1976 (Try out series)
National Periodical Publications

	GD25	FN65	NM94
1-7,9-13: 1-Intro. Atlas; Kirby-c/a. 2-Green Team (see Cancelled Comic Cavalcade). 3-Metamorpho by Ramona Fraden. 4-Lady Cop. 5-Manhunter; Kirby-c/a. 6-Dingbats; Kirby-c/a. 7-The Creeper by Ditko(c/a). 9-Dr. Fate; Kubert-c; Simonson-a. 10-The Outsiders. 11-Code Name: Assassin; Grell-c. 12-Origin/1st app. new Starman; Kubert-c		1.00	2.50
8-Origin/1st app. The Warlord; Grell-c/a (11/75)	2.30	6.75	16.00
13-Return of the New Gods; Darkseid app.; 1st new costume Orion; predates New Gods #12 by more than a year		1.60	4.00

FIRST KISS
Dec, 1957 - No. 40, Jan, 1965
Charlton Comics

	GD25	FN65	NM94
V1#1	3.00	7.50	15.00
V1#2-10	1.60	4.00	8.00
11-40	.80	2.00	4.00

FIRST LOVE ILLUSTRATED
2/49 - No. 9, 6/50; No. 10, 1/51 - No. 86, 3/58; No. 87, 9/58 - No. 88, 11/58; No. 89, 11/62, No. 90, 2/63
Harvey Publications(Home Comics)(True Love)

	GD25	FN65	NM94
1-Powell-a(2)	8.35	25.00	50.00
2-Powell-a	4.70	14.00	28.00
3-"Was I Too Fat To Be Loved" story	4.70	14.00	28.00
4-10	3.60	9.00	18.00
11-30: 30-Lingerie panel	2.40	6.00	12.00
31-34,37,39-49: 49-Last pre-code (2/55)	2.00	5.00	10.00
35-Used in **SOTI**, illo-"The title of this comic book is First Love"	10.00	30.00	60.00
36-Communism story, "Love Slaves"	3.20	8.00	16.00
38-Nostrand-a	4.00	11.00	22.00
50-90	1.60	4.00	8.00

NOTE: ***Disbrow** a-13. **Orlando** c-87. **Powell** a-1, 3-5, 7, 10, 11, 13-17, 19-24, 26-29, 33,35-41, 43, 45, 46, 50, 54, 55, 57, 58, 61-63, 65, 71-73, 76, 79r, 82, 84, 88.*

FIRST MEN IN THE MOON (See Movie Comics)

FIRST ROMANCE MAGAZINE
8/49 - #6, 6/50; #7, 6/51 - #50, 2/58; #51, 9/58 - #52, 11/58
Home Comics(Harvey Publ.)/True Love

	GD25	FN65	NM94
1	8.35	25.00	50.00
2	4.70	14.00	28.00
3-5	4.00	11.00	22.00
6-10	3.60	9.00	18.00
11-20	2.40	6.00	12.00
21-27,29-32: 32-Last pre-code issue (2/55)	2.00	5.00	10.00
28-Nostrand-a(Powell swipe)	4.00	10.00	20.00
33-52	1.60	4.00	8.00

NOTE: ***Powell** a-1-5, 8-10, 14, 18, 20-22, 24, 25, 28, 36, 46, 48, 51.*

FIRST TRIP TO THE MOON (See Space Adventures No. 20)

The Flame #2, © AJAX

Flare V2#1, © Hero Graphics

The Flash #137, © DC

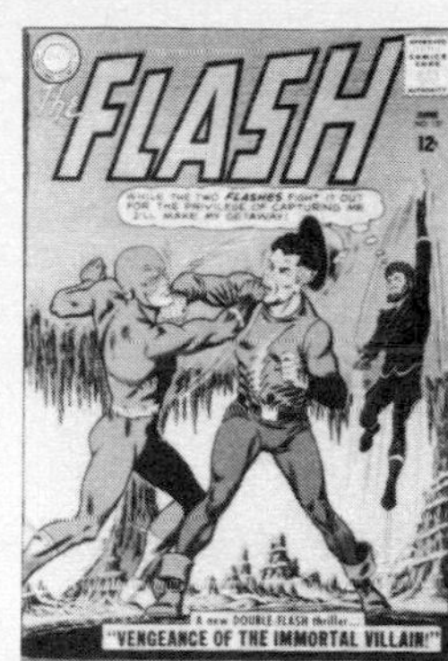

GD25 FN65 NM94

FISH POLICE (Fishwrap/Apple)(Value: cover or less)

FISH POLICE
V2#1, Oct, 1992 - Present ($1.25, color)
Marvel Comics

V2#1-8: 1-Hairballs Saga begins; r/#1 ('85) 1.25

5-STAR SUPER-HERO SPECTACULAR (See DC Special Series No. 1)

FLAME, THE (See Big 3 & Wonderworld Comics)
Summer, 1940 - No. 8, Jan, 1942 (#1,2: 68 pgs; #3-8: 44 pgs.)
Fox Features Syndicate

	GD25	FN65	NM94
1-Flame stories reprinted from Wonderworld #5-9; origin The Flame; Lou Fine-a (36 pgs.), r/Wonderworld #3,10	167.00	500.00	1100.00
2 Fine a(2). Wing Turner by Tuska	83.00	250.00	550.00
3-8: 3-Powell-a	50.00	150.00	350.00

FLAME, THE (Formerly Lone Eagle)
No. 5, Dec-Jan, 1954-55 - No. 3, April-May, 1955
Ajax/Farrell Publications (Excellent Publ.)

	GD25	FN65	NM94
5(#1)-1st app. new Flame	19.00	58.00	135.00
2,3	14.00	43.00	100.00

FLAMING CARROT (...Comics #6? on; see Anything Goes, Cerebus & Visions)
5/84 - No. 5, 1/85; No. 6, 3/85 - Present ($1.70-$2.00, B&W)
Aardvark-Vanaheim/Renegade Press #6-17/Dark Horse #18 on

	GD25	FN65	NM94
1-Bob Burden story/art	5.00	15.00	35.00
2	3.20	8.00	20.00
3	2.15	6.50	15.00
4-6	1.65	4.70	11.00
7-9	1.00	2.50	5.50
10-12		1.60	4.00
13-15		1.20	3.00
15-Variant without cover price	1.00	2.50	5.50
16-20: 18-1st Dark Horse issue		1.20	3.00
21-23,25: 25-Contains trading cards; TMNT app.		.80	2.00
24-($2.50, 52 pgs.)-10th anniversary issue		1.00	2.50
26-28: 26-Begin $2.25-c. 26,27-Teenage Mutant Ninja Turtles x-over. 27-Todd McFarlane-c		.90	2.25
29,30-($2.50-c)		1.00	2.50

FLAMING CARROT COMICS (Also see Junior Carrot Patrol)
Summer-Fall, 1981 ($1.95, One Shot) (Large size, 8-1/2x11)
Killian Barracks Press

	GD25	FN65	NM94
1-By Bob Burden	9.00	26.00	60.00

FLAMING LOVE
Dec, 1949 - No. 6, Oct, 1950 (Photo covers #2-6) (52 pgs.)
Quality Comics Group (Comic Magazines)

	GD25	FN65	NM94
1-Ward-c/a (9 pgs.)	22.00	65.00	150.00
2	10.00	30.00	65.00
3-Ward-a (9 pgs.); Crandall-a	13.50	41.00	95.00
4-6: 4-Gustavson-a	10.00	30.00	60.00

FLAMING WESTERN ROMANCES (Formerly Target Western Romances)
No. 3, Mar-Apr, 1950
Star Publications

	GD25	FN65	NM94
3-Robert Taylor, Arlene Dahl photo on-c with biographies inside; L. B. Cole-c	22.00	65.00	150.00

FLARE (Also see Champions for 1st app. & League of Champions)
Nov, 1988 - No. 3?, 1989 ($2.75, color, 52 pgs)
V2#1, Nov, 1990 - No. 7, 1991 ($2.95, color, mature readers, 52 pgs.)
Hero Comics/Hero Graphics Vol. 2 on

	GD25	FN65	NM94
1-3		1.10	2.75
V2#1-3 ($2.95)		1.20	3.00
V2#4-6,8-10: 4-Begin $3.50-c. 5-Eternity Smith returns. 6-Intro The Tigress		1.40	3.50
V2#7 ($3.95)		1.60	4.00
Annual 1(1992, $4.50, B&W, 52 pgs.)-Champions-r		1.80	4.50

FLARE ADVENTURES
Feb, 1992 (90 cents, color, 20 pgs.)
Hero Graphics

	GD25	FN65	NM94
1			1.00

FLASH, THE (See Adventure, The Brave and the Bold, Crisis On Infinite Earths, DC Comics Presents, DC Special, DC Special Series, DC Super-Stars, Green Lantern, Justice League of America, Showcase, Super Team Family, & World's Finest)

FLASH, THE (Formerly Flash Comics)
No. 105, Feb-Mar, 1959 - No. 350, Oct, 1985
National Periodical Publ./DC

	GD25	FN65	VF82	NM94
Showcase #4 (9-10/56)-Origin/1st app. The Flash (1st DC S.A. superhero) Turtle; Kubert-a	1200.00	3600.00	10,800.00	18,000.00
Showcase #8 (5-6/57)-2nd app. The Flash; origin & 1st app. Capt. Cold	500.00	1500.00	4500.00	–

	GD25	FN65	NM94
Showcase #13 (3-4/58)-Origin/1st Mr. Element	225.00	675.00	2250.00
Showcase #14 (5-6/58)-Origin & 1st app. Dr. Alchemy, formerly Mr. Element	250.00	750.00	3000.00

	GD25	FN65	VF82	NM94
105-(2-3/59)-Origin Flash(retold), & Mirror Master (1st app.)	275.00	825.00	1788.00	2750.00

	GD25	FN65	NM94
106-Origin Grodd & Pied Piper; Flash's 1st visit to Gorilla City; begin Grodd the Super Gorilla trilogy (Scarce)	78.00	233.00	700.00
107-Grodd trilogy, part 2	44.00	143.00	400.00
108-Grodd trilogy ends	39.00	117.00	350.00
109-2nd app. Mirror Master	33.00	100.00	300.00
110-Intro/origin The Weather Wizard & Kid Flash who later becomes Flash in Crisis On Infinite Earths #12; begin Kid Flash trilogy, ends #112 (also in #114,116,118)	86.00	257.00	600.00
111	29.00	86.00	200.00
112-Origin & 1st app. Elongated Man (4-5/60); also apps. in #115,119,130	31.00	94.00	220.00
113-Origin & 1st app. Trickster	31.00	94.00	220.00
114-Captain Cold app. (see Showcase #8)	24.00	73.00	170.00
115,116,118-120: 119-Elongated Man marries Sue Dearborn. 120-Flash & Kid Flash team-up for 1st time	18.00	54.00	125.00
117-Origin & 1st app. Capt. Boomerang; 1st & only S.A. app. Winky Blinky & Noddy	25.00	75.00	175.00
121,122: 122-Origin & 1st app. The Top	13.00	39.00	90.00
123-(9/61)-Re-intro. Golden Age Flash; origins of both Flashes; 1st mention of an Earth II where DC G. A. heroes live	65.00	195.00	650.00
124-Last 10 cent issue	11.50	34.00	80.00
125-128,130: 127-Return of Grodd-c/story. 128-Origin & 1st app. Abra Kadabra	11.50	34.00	80.00
129-2nd G.A. Flash x-over; J.S.A. cameo in flashback (1st S.A. app. G.A. Green Lantern, Hawkman, Atom, Black Canary & Dr. Mid-Nite)	28.00	84.00	195.00
131-136,138,140: 130-(7/62)-1st Gauntlet of Super-Villains (Mirror Master, Capt. Cold, The Top, Capt. Boomerang & Trickster). 131-Early Green Lantern x-over (9/62). 136-1st Dexter Miles. 140-Origin & 1st app. Heat Wave	11.50	34.00	80.00
137-G.A. Flash x-over; J.S.A. cameo (1st S.A. app.)(1st real app. since 2-3/51); 1st S.A. app. Vandall Savage & Johnny Thunder; JSA team decides to re-form	42.00	126.00	295.00
139-Origin & 1st app. Prof. Zoom	13.00	40.00	90.00
141-150: 142-Trickster app	7.00	21.00	50.00
151-G.A. Flash vs. The Shade	9.00	28.00	65.00
152-159	4.70	14.00	33.00
160-(80-Pg. Giant G-21); G.A. Flash & Johnny Quick-r	6.50	19.00	45.00
161-168,170: 165-Silver Age Flash weds Iris West. 167-New facts about Flash's origin. 168-Green Lantern-c/story. 170-Dr. Mid-Nite, Dr. Fate, G.A. Flash x-over	4.00	12.00	28.00
169-(80-Pg. Giant G-34)-New facts about origin	6.50	19.00	45.00

171-174,176,177,179,180: 171-JLA, Green Lantern, Atom flashbacks. 173-G.A.

The Flash #215, © DC

Flash #15 (2nd series), © DC

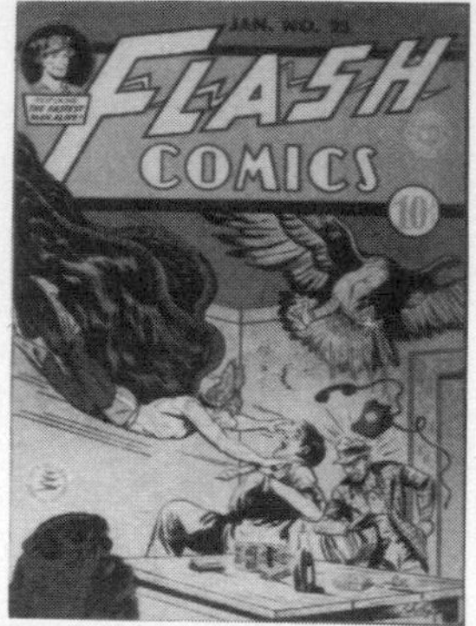

Flash Comics #25, © DC

GD25 FN65 NM94

Flash x-over. 174-Barry Allen reveals I.D. to wife 3.30 10.00 23.00
175-2nd Superman/Flash race (12/67; see Superman #199 & World's Finest #198,199); JLA cameo; gold kryptonite used (on J'onn J'onzz impersonating Superman) 12.00 36.00 85.00
178-(80-Pg. Giant G-46) 4.30 13.00 30.00
181-186,188-195,197-200: 186-Re-intro. Sargon 1.65 4.70 11.00
187,196: (68-Pg. Giants G-58, G-70) 3.20 8.00 20.00
201-204,206-210: 201-New G.A. Flash story. 208-52 pg. begin, end #213, 215,216. 206-Elongated Man begins 1.00 2.50 6.00
205-(68-Pg. Giant G-82) 1.65 4.70 11.00
211-213,216,220: 211-G.A. Flash origin-r/#104. 213-Reprints #137 1.00 2.50 6.00
214-DC 100 Page Super Spectacluar DC-11; origin Metal Men-r/Showcase #37; never before pubbed G.A. Flash story 1.30 3.25 8.00
215 (52 pgs.)-Flash-r/Showcase #4; G.A. Flash x-over, reprinted in #216 1.70 5.00 12.00
217-219: Neal Adams-a in all. 217-Green Lantern/Green Arrow series begins (9/72); 2nd G.L. & G.A. team-up series (see Green Lantern #76). 219-Last Green Arrow 1.65 4.70 11.00
221-225,227,228,230,231,233 1.00 2.50 6.00
226-Neal Adams-a 1.30 3.25 8.00
229,232-(100 pg. issues)-G.A. Flash-r & new-a 1.20 3.00 7.00
234-288,290: 243-Death of The Top. 245-Origin The Floronic Man in Green Lantern back-up, ends #246. 246-Last Green Lantern. 256-Death of The Top retold. 250-Intro Golden Glider. 265-267-(44 pgs.). 267-Origin of Flash's uniform. 270-Intro The Clown. 275,276-Iris West Allen dies. 286-Intro/origin Rainbow Raider 1.20 3.00
289-1st Perez DC art (Firestorm); new Firestorm back-up series begins (9/80), ends #304 1.00 2.50 5.50
291-299,301-305: 291-1st app. Saber-Tooth (villain). 298-Intro/origin new Shade. 301-Atomic Bomb-c. 303-The Top returns. 304-Intro/origin Colonel Computron; 305-G.A. Flash x-over 1.00 2.50
300-(52pgs.)-Origin Flash retold; 25th ann. issue 1.60 4.00
306-Dr. Fate by Giffen begins, ends #313 1.00 2.50
307-313-Giffen-a. 309-Origin Flash retold .80 2.00
314-349: 318-323-Creeper back-ups. 323,324-Two part Flash vs. Flash story. 324-Death of Reverse Flash (Prof. Zoom). 328-Iris West Allen's death retold. 344-Origin Kid Flash .80 2.00
350-Double size ($1.25) 1.00 2.50 5.50
Annual 1(10-12/63, 84pgs.)-Origin Elongated Man & Kid Flash-r; origin Grodd; G.A. Flash-r 28.00 83.00 275.00

NOTE: ***N. Adams*** *c-194, 195, 203, 204, 206-208, 211, 213, 215, 246.* ***M. Anderson*** *a-202i.* ***Austin*** *a-233i, 234i, 246i.* ***Buckler*** *a-271p, 272p; c(p)-247-250, 252, 253p, 255, 256p, 258, 262, 265-267, 269-271.* ***Giffen*** *a-306-313p; c-310p, 315.* ***Sid Greene*** *a-167-174i, 229i(r).* ***Grell*** *a-237p, 238p, 240-243p; c-236.* ***Infantino/Giella*** *c-105-112.* ***G. Kane*** *a-195p, 197-199p, 229r, 232r; c-197-199, 312p.* ***Kubert*** *a-108p, 215i(r); c-189-191.* ***Lopez*** *c-272.* ***Meskin*** *a-229r, 232r.* ***Perez*** *a-289-293p; c-293.* ***Starlin*** *a-294-296p.* ***Staton*** *c-263p, 264p. Green Lantern x-over-131, 143, 168, 171, 191.*

FLASH
June, 1987 - Present (75 cents, $1.00 #17 on)
DC Comics

1-Guice-c/a begins; New Teen Titans app. 1.00 2.00 5.00
2,3: 3-Intro. Kilgore 1.20 3.00
4-10: 5-Intro. Speed McGee. 7-1st app. Blue Trinity. 8,9-Millennium tie-ins. 9-1st app. The Chunk 1.00 2.50
11-20: 12-Free extra 16 pg. Dr. Light story. 19-Free extra 16 pg. Flash story .80 2.00
21-30: 28-Capt. Cold app. 29-New Phantom Lady app. 1.50
31-49,51-65: 40-Dr. Alchemy app. 62-Flash: Year One begins, ends #65. 65-Last $1.00-c 1.00
50-($1.75, 52 pgs.) .70 1.75
66-78,80-84: 66-Aquaman app. 69-Green Lantern app. 70-Gorilla Grodd story ends. 73-Re-intro Barry Allen & begin saga (Barry Allen revealed as Reverse Flash in #78). 80-Regular ed. 82-Nightwing & Starfire app. 84-Razer app. 1.25
79-($2.50, 68 pgs.)-Barry Allen saga ends 1.00 2.50
80-($2.50)-Foil cover edition 1.00 2.50

GD25 FN65 NM94

85-88: 85-Begin $1.50-c 1.50
Annual 1 (1987, $1.25) .80 2.00
Annual 2, 3: 2-(1988, $1.50) 3-(1989, $1.75, 68 pgs.)-Gives history of G.A., Silver Age, & new Flash in text .70 1.75
Annual 4 (1991, $2.00, 68 pgs.)-Armageddon 2001 .80 2.00
Annual 5 (1992, $2.50, 68 pgs.)-Eclipso-c/story 1.00 2.50
Annual 6 (1993, $2.50, 68 pgs.) 1.00 2.50
Special 1 (1990, $2.95, 84 pgs.)-50th anniversary issue; Kubert-c 1.20 3.00
...TV Special 1 (1991, $3.95, 76 pgs.)-Photo-c plus behind the scenes photos of TV show; Saltares-a, Byrne scripts 1.60 4.00

NOTE: ***Guice*** *a-1-9p, 11p, Annual 1p; c-1-9p, Annual 1p.* ***Perez*** *c-15-17, Annual 2i.* ***Travest Charest*** *c/a-Annual 5p.*

FLASH COMICS (Whiz Comics No. 2 on)
Jan, 1940 (12 pgs., B&W, regular size)
(Not distributed to newsstands; printed for in-house use)
Fawcett Publications

NOTE: *Whiz Comics #2 was preceded by two books,* ***Flash Comics*** *and* ***Thrill Comics****, both dated Jan, 1940, (12 pgs, B&W, regular size) and were not distributed. These two books are identical except for the title, and were sent out to major distributors as ad copies to promote sales. It is believed that the complete 68 page issue of Fawcett's* ***Flash*** *and* ***Thrill Comics #1*** *was finished and ready for publication with the January date. Since DC Comics was also about to publish a book with the same date and title, Fawcett hurriedly printed up the black and white version of* ***Flash Comics*** *to secure copyright before DC The inside covers are blank, with the covers and inside pages printed on a high quality uncoated paper stock.The eight page origin story of Captain Thunder is composed of pages 1-7 and 13 of the Captain Marvel story essentially as they appeared in the first issue of* ***Whiz Comics****. The balloon dialogue on page thirteen was relettered to tie the story into the end of page seven in* ***Flash*** *and* ***Thrill Comics*** *to produce a shorter version of the origin story for copyright purposes. Obviously, DC acquired the copyright and Fawcett dropped* ***Flash*** *as well as* ***Thrill*** *and came out with* ***Whiz Comics*** *a month later. Fawcett never used the cover to* ***Flash*** *and* ***Thrill #1****, designing a new cover for* ***Whiz Comics****. Fawcett also must have discovered that Captain Thunder had already been used by another publisher (Captain Terry Thunder by Fiction House). All references to Captain Thunder were relettered to Captain Marvel before appearing in* ***Whiz****.*

1 (nn on-c, #1 on inside)-Origin & 1st app. Captain Thunder. Eight copies of Flash and three copies of Thrill exist. All 3 copies of Thrill sold in 1986 for between $4,000-$10,000 each. A NM copy of Thrill sold in 1987 for $12,000. A vg copy of Thrill sold in 1987 for $9000 cash; another copy sold in 1987 for $2000 cash, $10,000 trade; cover by Leo O'Mealia

FLASH COMICS (The Flash No. 105 on) (Also see All-Flash)
Jan, 1940 - No. 104, Feb, 1949
National Periodical Publications/All-American

GD25 FN65 VF82 NM94

1-The Flash (origin/1st app.) by Harry Lampert, Hawkman (origin/1st app.) by Gardner Fox, The Whip, & Johnny Thunder (origin/1st app.) by Stan Asch; Cliff Cornwall by Moldoff, Flash Picture Novelets (later Minute Movies) begin; Moldoff (Shelly) cover; 1st app. Shiera Sanders who later becomes Hawkgirl, #24; reprinted in Famous First Edition (on sale 11/10/39) 2300.00 6900.00 14,950.00 23,000.00
(Estimated up to 75+ total copies exist, 7 in NM/Mint)
1-Reprint, Oversize 13-1/2"x10." **WARNING:** This comic is an exact reprint of the original except for its size. DC published it in 1974 with a second cover titling it as a Famous First Edition. There have been many reported cases of the outer cover being removed and the interior sold as the original edition. The reprint with the new outer cover removed is practically worthless. See Famouse First Edition for value.

GD25 FN65 NM94

2-Rod Rian begins, ends #11 400.00 1200.00 2700.00
3-King Standish begins, ends #41 (called The King #16-37,39-41); E.E. Hibbard-a begins on Flash 333.00 1000.00 2300.00
4-Moldoff (Shelly) Hawkman begins 275.00 825.00 1850.00
5 250.00 750.00 1700.00
6-2nd Flash-c 285.00 860.00 2000.00
7-10: 8-Male bondage-c 150.00 450.00 1100.00
11-20: 12-Les Watts begins; "Sparks" #16 on. 17-Last Cliff Cornwall 108.00 325.00 725.00
21-23 92.00 275.00 620.00
24-Shiera becomes Hawkgirl (12/41); see All-Star Comics #5 for 1st app. 125.00 375.00 850.00
25-30: 28-Last Les Sparks. 29-Ghost Patrol begins(origin, 1st app.), ends #104

Flash Comics #78, © DC

Flash Gordon #4 (DC), © KING

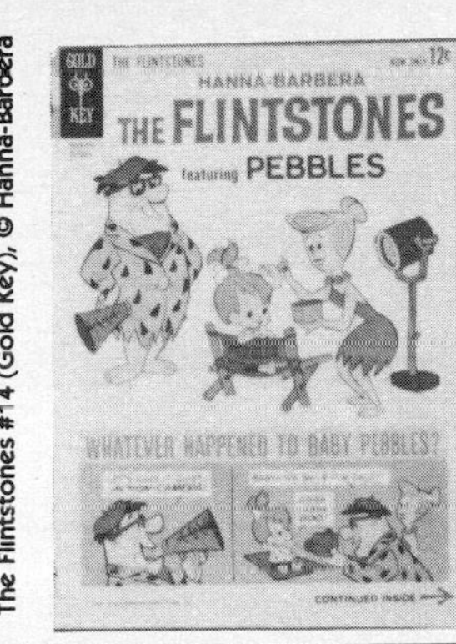

The Flintstones #14 (Gold Key), © Hanna-Barbera

GD25 FN65 NM94

75.00 225.00 500.00
31-40: 33-Origin Shade 67.00 200.00 450.00
41-50 62.00 188.00 415.00
51-61: 59-Last Minute Movies. 61-Last Moldoff Hawkman
50.00 150.00 350.00
62-Hawkman by Kubert begins 67.00 20.00 450.00
63-70: 66-68-Hop Harrigan in all. 70-Mutt & Jeff app.
50.00 150.00 350.00
71-85: 80-Atom begins, ends #104 50.00 150.00 350.00
86-Intro. The Black Canary in Johnny Thunder (8/47); see All-Star #38; rare in Mint due to black ink smearing on white-c 150.00 450.00 1000.00
87-90: 88-Origin Ghost. 89-Intro villain Thorn 71.00 212.00 475.00
91,93-99: 98-Atom dons new costume 79.00 238.00 535.00
92-1st solo Black Canary plus-c 125.00 375.00 850.00
100 (10/48),103(Scarce)-52 pgs. each 150.00 450.00 1000.00
101,102(Scarce) 117.00 350.00 800.00
104-Origin The Flash retold (Scarce) 285.00 860.00 2000.00
Wheaties Giveaway (1946, 32 pgs., 6-1/2x8-1/4")-Johnny Thunder, Ghost Patrol, The Flash & Kubert Hawkman app. NOTE: All known copies were taped to Wheaties boxes and are never found in mint condition. Copies with light tape residue bring the listed prices in all grades
185.00 550.00 –

*NOTE: **E.E. Hibbard** c-6, 12, 20, 24, 26, 28, 30, 44, 46, 48, 50, 62, 66, 68, 69, 72, 74, 76, 78, 80, 82. **Infantino** a-86p, 90, 93-95, 99-104; c-90, 92, 93, 97, 99, 101, 103. **Kinstler** a-87, 89(Hawkman); c-87. **Chet Kozlak** c-77, 79, 81. **Krigstein** a-94. **Kubert** a-62-76, 83, 85, 86, 88-104; c-63, 65, 67, 70, 71, 73, 75, 83, 85, 86, 88, 89, 91, 94, 96, 98, 100, 104. **Moldoff** a-3; c-3, 7-11, 13-17, plus odd #'s 19-61. **Martin Naydell** c-52, 54, 56, 58, 60, 64, 84.*

FLASH DIGEST, THE (See DC Special Series #24)

FLASH GORDON (See Defenders Of The Earth, Eat Right to Work..., Feature Book #25, Giant Comic Album, King Classics, King Comics, March of Comics #118, 133, 142, The Phantom #18, Street Comix & Wow Comics, 1st series)

FLASH GORDON
No. 10, 1943 - No. 512, Nov, 1953
Dell Publishing Co.

4-Color 10(1943)-by Alex Raymond; reprints "The Ice Kingdom"
52.00 156.00 365.00
4-Color 84(1945)-by Alex Raymond; reprints "The Fiery Desert"
36.00 110.00 250.00
4-Color 173,190: 190-Bondage-c 12.00 36.00 85.00
4-Color 204,247 10.00 30.00 70.00
4-Color 424 8.35 25.00 50.00
2(5-7/53-Dell)-Evans-a? 4.705 14.00 28.00
4-Color 512 4.70 14.00 28.00
Macy's Giveaway(1943)-(Rare)-20 pgs.; not by Raymond
60.00 160.00 340.00

FLASH GORDON (See Tiny Tot Funnies)
Oct, 1950 - No. 4, April, 1951
Harvey Publications

1-Alex Raymond-a; bondage-c; reprints strips from 7/14/40 to 12/8/40
17.00 51.00 120.00
2-Alex Raymond-a; r/strips 12/15/40-4/27/41 13.00 40.00 90.00
3,4-Alex Raymond-a; 3-bondage-c, r/strips 5/4/41-9/21/41. 4-r/strips 10/24/37-3/27/38 12.00 36.00 80.00
5-(Rare)-Small size-5-1/2x8-1/2"; B&W; 32 pgs.; Distributed to some mail subscribers only. Estimated value $200.00–$300.00
(Also see All-New No. 15, Boy Explorers No. 2, and Stuntman No. 3)

FLASH GORDON
1951 (Paper cover; 16 pgs. in color; regular size)
Harvey Comics (Gordon Bread giveaway)

1,2: 1-r/strips 10/24/37 - 2/6/38. 2-r/strips 7/14/40 - 10/6/40; Reprints by Raymond each.... 1.50 4.50 10.00
NOTE: Most copies have brittle edges.

FLASH GORDON
June, 1965
Gold Key

GD25 FN65 NM94

1 (1947 reprint)-Painted-c 2.70 8.00 19.00

FLASH GORDON (Also see Comics Reading Libraries)
9/66 - #11, 12/67; #12, 2/69 - #18, 1/70; #19, 10-11/78 - #37, 3/82
(Painted covers No. 19-30, 34)
King #1-11/Charlton #12-18/Gold Key #19-23/Whitman #28 on

1-Williamson c/a(2); E.C. swipe/Incredible S.F. #32. Mandrake story
3.60 9.00 19.00
1-Army giveaway(1968)("Complimentary" on cover)(Same as regular #1 minus Mandrake story & back-c) 1.70 5.00 12.00
2-Bolle, Gil Kane-c; Mandrake story 1.70 5.00 12.00
3-Williamson-c 2.00 6.00 14.00
4-Secret Agent X-9 begins, Williamson-c/a(3) 2.00 6.00 14.00
5-Williamson-c/a(2) 2.00 6.00 14.00
6,8-Crandall-a. 8-Secret Agent X-9-r 2.70 8.00 19.00
7-Raboy-a 2.00 6.00 14.00
9,10-Raymond-r. 10-Buckler's 1st pro work (11/67); Briggs-c
2.40 7.25 17.00
11-Crandall-a 1.70 5.00 12.00
12-Crandall-c/a 2.00 6.00 14.00
13-Jeff Jones-a (15 pgs.) 2.00 6.00 14.00
14-17: 17-Brick Bradford story 1.20 3.00 7.00
18-Kaluta-a (3rd pro work?)(see Teen Confess.) 1.30 3.25 8.00
19(9/78, G.K.), 20-30(10/80) 1.30 3.25
30 (7/81; re-issue) .65 1.60
31-33: Movie adaptation; Williamson-a .65 1.60
34-37: Movie adaptation 1.40

*NOTE: **Aparo** a-8. **Bolle** a-21, 22. **Boyette** a-14-18. **Buckler** a-10. **Crandall** c-6. **Estrada** a-3. **Gene Fawcette** a-29, 30, 34, 37. **McWilliams** a-31-33, 36.*

FLASH GORDON
June, 1988 - No. 9, Holiday, 1988-'89 ($1.25, color, mini-series)
DC Comics

1-9: 1,5-Painted-c 1.25

FLASH GORDON THE MOVIE
1980 ($1.95, color, 68 pgs., 8-1/4 x 11")
Western Publishing Co.

11294-Williamson-c/a; adapts movie .80 2.00
13743-Hardback edition 1.00 2.00 5.00

FLASH SPECTACULAR, THE (See DC Special Series No. 11)

FLAT-TOP
11/53 - No. 3, 5/54; No. 4, 3/55 - No. 7, 9/55
Mazie Comics/Harvey Publ.(Magazine Publ.) No. 4 on

1-Teenage 4.00 10.00 20.00
2,3 2.40 6.00 12.00
4-7 1.80 4.50 9.00

FLAXEN (Dark Horse)(Value: cover or less)

FLESH AND BONES (Fantagraphics)(Value: cover or less)

FLESH: THE LEGEND OF SHAMANA (Fleetway)(Value: cover or less)

FLINTSTONE KIDS, THE (TV; See Star Comics Digest)
Aug, 1987 - No. 11, April, 1989
Star Comics/Marvel Comics #5 on

1-11 1.00

FLINTSTONES, THE (TV)(See Dell Giant #48 for No. 1)
No. 2, Nov-Dec, 1961 - No. 60, Sept, 1970 (Hanna-Barbera)
Dell Publ. Co./Gold Key No. 7 (10/62) on

2 (TV show debuted on 9/30/60) 9.00 26.00 60.00
3-6(7-8/62): 2-5: 15¢. 6-Begin 12¢ issues 6.50 19.00 45.00
7 (10/62; 1st GK) 5.50 17.00 40.00
8-10: Mr. & Mrs. J. Evil Scientist begin? 5.00 15.00 35.00
11-1st app. Pebbles (6/63) 7.00 21.00 50.00
12-15,17-20 4.30 13.00 30.00
16-1st app. Bamm-Bamm (1/64) 5.50 17.00 40.00

Flip #2, © HARV

Flying Aces #3, © Key Publ.

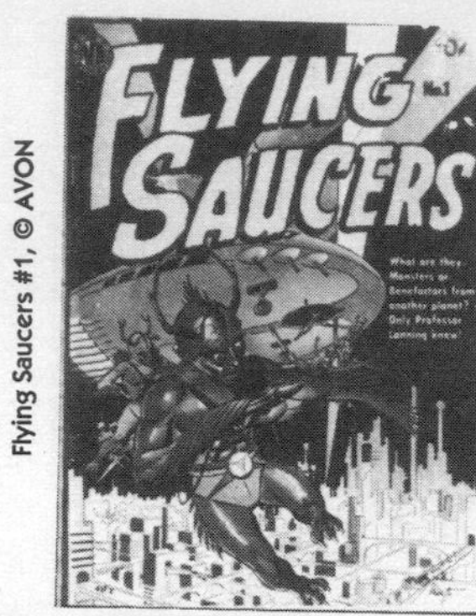

Flying Saucers #1, © AVON

GD25 FN65 NM94

21-30: 24-1st app. The Grusomes 3.40 10.00 24.00
31-33,35-40: 31-Xmas-c. 33-Meet Frankenstein & Dracula. 39-Reprints 3.25 9.50 22.00
34-1st app. The Great Gazoo 4.30 13.00 30.00
41-60: 45-Last 12 cent issue 3.20 8.00 20.00
At N. Y. World's Fair('64)-J.W. Books(25 cents)-1st printing; no date on-c (29 cent version exists, 2nd print?) 4.70 14.00 33.00
At N. Y. World's Fair (1965 on-c; re-issue). NOTE: Warehouse find in 1984 1.00 2.50 6.00
Bigger & Boulder 1(#30013-211) (Gold Key Giant, 11/62, 25 cents, 84 pgs.) 9.00 26.00 60.00
Bigger & Boulder 2-(25 cents)(1966)-reprints B&B No. 1 7.00 21.00 50.00
...With Pebbles & Bamm Bamm (100 pgs., G.K.)-30028-511 (paper-c, 25 cents)(11/65) 7.00 21.00 50.00

NOTE: *(See Comic Album #16, Bamm-Bamm & Pebbles Flintstone, Dell Giant 48, Marchof Comics #229, 243, 271, 289, 299, 317, 327, 341, Pebbles Flintstone, Top Comics #2-4, and Whitman Comic Books.)*

FLINTSTONES, THE (TV)(...& Pebbles)
Nov, 1970 - No. 50, Feb, 1977 (Hanna-Barbera)
Charlton Comics

1 5.00 15.00 35.00
2 2.60 7.50 18.00
3-7,9,10 1.70 5.00 12.00
8-"Flintstones Summer Vacation," (Summer, 1971, 52 pgs.) 2.15 6.50 15.00
11-20 1.65 4.70 11.00
21-50: 37-Byrne text illos (early work; see Nightmare #20). 36-Mike Zeck illos (early work). 42-Byrne-a (2 pgs.) 1.65 4.70 11.00
(Also see Barney & Betty Rubble, Dino, The Great Gazoo, & Pebbles & Bamm-Bamm)

FLINTSTONES, THE (TV)(See Yogi Bear, 3rd series)
October, 1977 - No. 9, Feb, 1979 (Hanna-Barbera)
Marvel Comics Group

1-9: Yogi Bear app. 4-The Jetsons app. .80 2.00

FLINTSTONES, THE
Sept, 1992 - Present ($1.25, color) (Hanna-Barbera)
Harvey Comics

V2#1-4 1.25
...Big Book 1 (11/92, $1.95, 52 pgs.), 2 .80 2.00
...Giant Size 1 (10/92, $2.25, 68 pgs.) .90 2.25

FLINTSTONES CHRISTMAS PARTY, THE (See The Funtastic World of Hanna-Barbera No. 1)

FLIP
April, 1954 - No. 2, June, 1954 (Satire)
Harvey Publications

1,2-Nostrand-a each. 2-Powell-a 14.00 43.00 100.00

FLIPPER (TV)
April, 1966 - No. 3, Nov, 1967 (All have photo-c)
Gold Key

1 5.85 17.50 35.00
2,3 4.00 11.00 22.00

FLIPPITY & FLOP
12-1/51-52 - No. 46, 8-10/59; No. 47, 9-11/60
National Periodical Publ. (Signal Publ. Co.)

1 17.00 52.00 120.00
2 10.00 30.00 70.00
3-5 8.35 25.00 50.00
6-10 7.50 22.50 45.00
11-20: 20-Last precode (3/55) 5.35 16.00 32.00
21-47 4.00 11.00 22.00

FLOATERS
Sept, 1993 - No. 5, 1994 ($2.50, B&W, limited series)
Dark Horse Comics

GD25 FN65 NM94

1-5 1.00 2.50

FLOYD FARLAND (See Eclipse Graphic Album Series #11)

FLY, THE (Also see Adventures of..., Blue Ribbon Comics & Flyman)
May, 1983 - No. 9, Oct, 1984
Archie Enterprises, Inc.

1-9: 1-Mr. Justice app; origin Shield. 2-Flygirl app. 1.00

NOTE: ***Buckler** a-1, 2. **Ditko** a-2-9; c-4-8p. **Nebres** c-3, 4, 5i, 6, 7i. **Steranko** c-1, 2.*

FLY, THE
Aug, 1991 - No. 17, Dec, 1992 ($1.00, color)
Impact Comics (DC)

1-17: 4-Vs. The Black Hood. 9-Trading card inside 1.00
Annual 1 ('92, $2.50, 68 pgs.)-Impact trading card 1.00 2.50

FLY BOY (Also see Approved Comics)
Spring, 1952 - No. 4, 1953
Ziff-Davis Publ. Co. (Approved)

1-Saunders painted-c 10.00 30.00 70.00
2-Saunders painted-c 8.35 25.00 50.00
3,4-Saunders painted-c 5.85 17.50 35.00

FLYING ACES
July, 1955 - No. 5, March, 1956
Key Publications

1 4.00 10.00 20.00
2-5: 2-Trapani-a 2.40 6.00 12.00

FLYING A'S RANGE RIDER, THE (TV) (See Western Roundup under Dell Giants)
#404, 6-7/52; #2, June-Aug, 1953 - #24, Aug, 1959 (All photo-c)
Dell Publishing Co.

4-Color 404(#1)-Titled "The Range Rider" 10.00 30.00 70.00
2 6.35 19.00 38.00
3-10 5.35 16.00 32.00
11-16,18-24 5.00 15.00 30.00
17-Toth-a 6.35 19.00 38.00

FLYING CADET (WW II Plane Photos)
Jan, 1943 - V2#8, 1947 (Half photos, half comics)
Flying Cadet Publishing Co.

V1#1 10.00 30.00 60.00
2 5.00 15.00 30.00
3-9 (Two #6's, Sept. & Oct.) 4.35 13.00 26.00
V2#1-7(#10-16) 4.00 10.00 20.00
8(#17)-Bare-breasted woman-c 10.00 30.00 65.00

FLYIN' JENNY
1946 - No. 2, 1947 (1945 strip reprints)
Pentagon Publ. Co./Leader Enterprises #2

nn-Marcus Swayze strip-r (entire insides) 8.35 25.00 50.00
2-Baker-c; Swayze strip reprints 9.15 27.50 55.00

FLYING MODELS
V61#3, May, 1954 (16 pgs.) (5 cents)
H-K Publ. (Health-Knowledge Publs.)

V61#3 (Rare) 5.35 16.00 32.00

FLYING NUN (TV)
Feb, 1968 - No. 4, Nov, 1968
Dell Publishing Co.

1-Sally Field photo-c 4.70 14.00 28.00
2-4: 2-Sally Field photo-c 2.80 7.00 14.00

FLYING NURSES (See Sue & Sally Smith...)

FLYING SAUCERS
1950; 1952; 1953
Avon Periodicals/Realistic

1(1950)-Wood-a, 21 pgs.; Fawcette-c 43.00 130.00 300.00

Fly Man #39, © AP

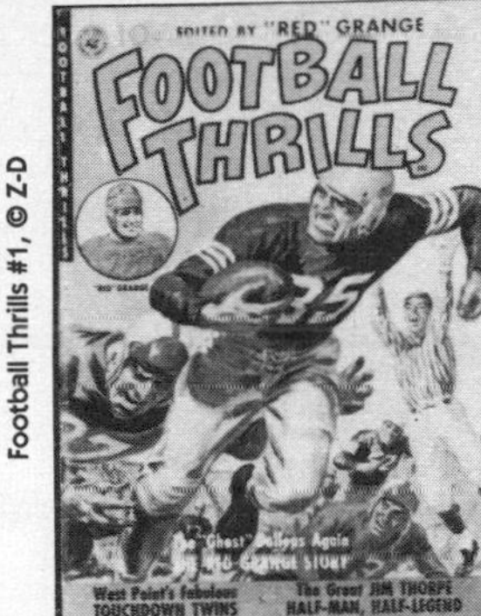

Football Thrills #1, © Z-D

Forbidden Worlds #41, © ACG

GD25 FN65 NM94

nn(1952)-Cover altered plus 2 pgs. of Wood-a not in original 41.00 122.00 285.00
nn(1953)-Reprints above 24.00 73.00 170.00

FLYING SAUCERS (Comics)
April, 1967 - No. 4, Nov, 1967; No. 5, Oct, 1969
Dell Publishing Co.

1 1.65 4.70 11.00
2-5 1.20 3.00 7.00

FLY IN MY EYE: EXPOSED (Eclipse)(Value: cover or less) (Graphic Album)

FLY MAN (Formerly Adventures of The Fly; Mighty Comics #40 on)
No. 32, July, 1965 - No. 39, Sept, 1966 (Also see Mighty Crusaders)
Mighty Comics Group (Radio Comics) (Archie)

32,33-Comet, Shield, Black Hood, The Fly & Flygirl x-over. 33-Re-intro Wizard, Hangman (1st S.A. appearances) 3.60 10.75 25.00
34-36: 34-Shield begins. 35-Origin Black Hood. 36-Hangman x-over in Shield; re-intro. & origin of Web (1st S.A. app.) 2.30 6.75 16.00
37-39: 37-Hangman, Wizard x-over in Flyman; last Shield issue. 38-Web story. 39-Steel Sterling story (1st S.A. app.) 2.30 6.75 16.00

FOES (Ram)(Value: cover or less)

FOLLOW THE SUN (TV)
May-July, 1962 - No. 2, Sept-Nov, 1962 (Photo-c)
Dell Publishing Co.

01-280-207(No.1), 12-280-211(No.2) 4.00 11.00 22.00

FOODINI (TV)(The Great...; see Jingle Dingle & Pinhead &...)
March, 1950 - No. 5, 1950
Continental Publications (Holyoke)

1 (52 pgs.) 10.00 30.00 70.00
2 6.35 19.00 38.00
3-5 5.00 15.00 30.00

FOOEY (Magazine) (Satire)
Feb, 1961 - No. 4, May, 1961
Scoff Publishing Co.

1 4.70 14.00 28.00
2-4 3.60 9.00 18.00

FOOFUR (TV)
Aug, 1987 - No. 6, June, 1988
Star Comics/Marvel Comics No. 5 on

1-6 1.00

FOOLKILLER (Also see The Amazing Spider-Man #225, The Defenders #73, Man-Thing #3 & Omega the Unknown #8)
Oct, 1990 - No. 10, Oct, 1991 ($1.75, color, limited series)
Marvel Comics

1-Origin 3rd Foolkiller; Greg Salinger app. .80 2.00
2-7,9,10: DeZuniga-a(i) in 1-4 .90 1.75
8-Spider-Man x-over 1.00 2.50

FOOTBALL THRILLS (See Tops In Adventure)
Fall-Winter, 1951-52 - No. 2, Fall, 1952
Ziff-Davis Publ. Co.

1-Powell a(2); Saunders painted-c. Red Grange, Jim Thorpe app. 17.00 52.00 120.00
2-Saunders painted-c 11.50 34.00 80.00

FOR A NIGHT OF LOVE
1951
Avon Periodicals

nn-Two stories adapted from the works of Emile Zola; Astarita, Ravielli-a; Kinstler-c 18.00 54.00 125.00

FORBIDDEN LOVE
Mar, 1950 - No. 4, Sept, 1950
Quality Comics Group

1-(Scarce)-Classic photo-c; Crandall-a 50.00 150.00 350.00
2,3-(Scarce)-Photo-c 22.00 65.00 150.00
4-(Scarce)-Ward/Cuidera-a; photo-c 24.00 72.00 170.00

FORBIDDEN LOVE (See Dark Mansion of...)

FORBIDDEN PLANET
May, 1992 - No. 4, 1992 ($2.50, color, mini-series)
Innovation Publishing

1-4: Adapts movie; painted covers 1.00 2.50

FORBIDDEN TALES OF DARK MANSION (Formerly Dark Mansion of Forbidden Love #1-4)
No. 5, May-June, 1972 - No. 15, Feb-Mar, 1974
National Periodical Publications

5-15: 13-Kane/Howard-a 1.90 4.75

NOTE: ***N. Adams** c-9. **Alcala** a-9-11, 13. **Chaykin** a-7,15. **Evans** a-14. **Kaluta** a-7, 8, 13. **G. Kane** a-13. **Kirby** a-6. **Nino** a-8, 12, 15. **Redondo** a-14.*

FORBIDDEN WORLDS
7-8/51 - No. 34, 10-11/54; No. 35, 8/55 - No. 145, 8/67
(No. 1-5: 52 pgs.; No. 6-8: 44 pgs.)
American Comics Group

1-Williamson/Frazetta-a (10 pgs.) 86.00 257.00 600.00
2 43.00 130.00 300.00
3-Williamson/Wood/Orlando-a (7 pgs.) 45.00 135.00 315.00
4 22.00 65.00 150.00
5-Krenkel/Williamson-a (8 pgs.) 36.00 110.00 250.00
6-Harrison/Williamson-a (8 pgs.) 30.00 90.00 210.00
7,8,10 15.00 45.00 105.00
9-A-Bomb explosion story 17.00 52.00 120.00
11-20 11.00 32.00 75.00
21-33: 24-E.C. swipe by Landau 8.00 24.00 55.00
34(10-11/54)(Scarce)(becomes Young Heroes #35 on)-Last pre-code issue; A-Bomb explosion story 8.00 24.00 55.00
35(8/55)-Scarce 6.50 19.00 45.00
36-62 4.30 13.00 30.00
63,69,76,78-Williamson-a in all; w/Krenkel #69 5.00 16.00 37.00
64,66-68,70-72,74,75,77,79-85,87-90 3.85 11.50 27.00
65-"There's a New Moon Tonight" listed in #114 as holding 1st record fan mail response 4.50 14.00 32.00
73-1st app. Herbie by Ogden Whitney 25.00 75.00 175.00
86-Flying saucer-c 4.70 14.00 33.00
91-93,95-100 3.20 8.00 20.00
94-Herbie app. 6.00 19.00 44.00
101-109,111-113,115,117-120 2.40 7.25 17.00
110,114,116-Herbie app. 114-1st Herbie-c; contains list of editor's top 20 ACG stories. 116-Herbie goes to Hell 3.85 11.50 27.00
121-124: 124-Magic Agent app. 2.40 7.25 17.00
125-Magic Agent app.; intro. & origin Magicman series, ends #141 2.70 8.00 19.00
126-130 2.30 6.75 16.00
131-139: 133-Origin/1st app. Dragonia in Magicman (1-2/66); returns in #138. 136-Nemesis x-over in Magicman. 2.00 6.00 14.00
140-Mark Midnight app. by Ditko 2.30 6.75 16.00
141-145 1.65 4.70 11.00

NOTE: ***Buscema** a-75, 79, 81, 82, 140r. **Cameron** a-5. **Disbrow** a-10. **Ditko** a-137p, 138, 140. **Landau** a-24, 27-29, 31-34, 48, 86r, 96, 143-45. **Lazarus** a-18, 23, 24, 57. **Moldoff** a-27, 31, 139r. **Reinman** a-93. **Whitney** a-115, 116, 137; c-40, 46, 57, 60, 68, 78, 79, 90, 93, 94, 100, 102, 103, 106-108, 114, 129.*

FORCE, THE (See The Crusaders)

FORCE OF BUDDHA'S PALM THE (Jademan)(Value: cover or less)

FORD ROTUNDA CHRISTMAS BOOK (See Christmas at the Rotunda)

FOREIGN INTRIGUES (Formerly Johnny Dynamite; becomes Battlefield Action #16 on)
No. 13, 1956 - No. 15, Aug, 1956
Charlton Comics

Forever People #2(3/88), © DC

Four Color #12 (Series I), © News Synd.

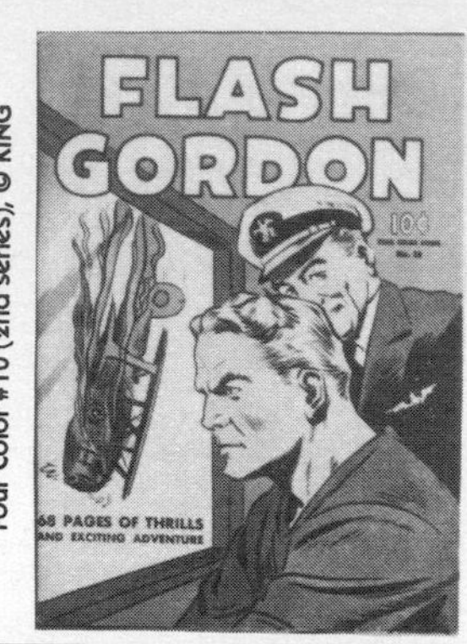

Four Color #10 (2nd series), © KING

13-15-Johnny Dynamite continues 4.00 12.00 24.00

FOREMOST BOYS (See 4Most)

FOREST FIRE (Also see Smokey The Bear)
1949 (dated-1950) (16 pgs., paper-c)
American Forestry Assn.(Commerical Comics)

nn-Intro/1st app. Smokey The Forest Fire Preventing Bear; created by Rudy Wendelein; Wendelein/Sparling-a; `Carter Oil Co.' on back-c of original 14.00 43.00 100.00

FOREVER, DARLING (See 4-Color No. 681)

FOREVER PEOPLE, THE
Feb-Mar, 1971 - No. 11, Oct-Nov, 1972
National Periodical Publications

1-1st app. Forever People; Superman x-over; Kirby-c/a begins; 1st full app. Darkseid (3rd anywhere, ties w/New Gods #1); Darkseid storyline begins, ends #8 (apps. in 1-4,6,8; cameos in #5,11) 4.50 14.00 32.00
2-5: 4-G.A. reprints begin, end #9 3.20 8.00 20.00
6-11: 9,10-Deadman app. 1.50 3.75 9.00

NOTE: ***Kirby** c/a(p)-1-11; #4-9 contain Sandman reprints from Adventure #85, 84, 75, 80, 77, 74 in that order. #1-3, 10-11 are 36pgs; #4-9 are 52pgs.*

FOREVER PEOPLE
Feb, 1988 - No. 6, July, 1988 ($1.25, mini-series)
DC Comics

1-6 1.25

FOR GIRLS ONLY
Nov, 1953 (Digest size, 100 pgs.)
Bernard Bailey Enterprises

1-Half comic book, half magazine 10.00 30.00 60.00

FORGOTTEN FOREST OF OZ, THE (See First Comics Graphic Novel #16)

FORGOTTEN REALMS (DC)(Value: cover or less)

FORGOTTEN STORY BEHIND NORTH BEACH, THE
No date (8 pgs.; paper cover)
Catechetical Guild

nn 2.40 6.00 12.00

FOR LOVERS ONLY (Formerly Hollywood Romances)
No. 60, Aug, 1971 - No. 87, Nov, 1976
Charlton Comics

60-87: 73-Spanking scene-c/story 1.20

40 BIG PAGES OF MICKEY MOUSE
No. 945, 1936 (44 pgs.; 10-1/4x12-1/2"; cardboard cover)
Whitman Publishing Co.

945-Reprints Mickey Mouse Magazine #1, but with a different cover; ads were eliminated and some illustrated stories had expanded text. The book is 3/4" shorter than Mickey Mouse Mag. #1, but the reprints are the same size (Rare) 107.00 320.00 750.00

48 FAMOUS AMERICANS
1947 (Giveaway) (Half-size in color)
J. C. Penney Co. (Cpr. Edwin H. Stroh)

nn-Simon & Kirby-a 7.50 22.50 45.00

FOR YOUR EYES ONLY (See James Bond...)

FOUR COLOR
Sept?, 1939 - No. 1354, Apr-June, 1962
Dell Publishing Co.

NOTE: *Four Color only appears on issues #19-25, 1-99,101. Dell Publishing Co. filed these as Series I, #1-25, and Series II, #1-1354. Issues beginning with #710? were printed with and without ads on back cover. Issues without ads are worth more.*

SERIES I: GD25 FN65 VF82 NM94
1(nn)-Dick Tracy 350.00 1050.00 2275.00 3500.00
(Estimated up to 115 total copies exist, 5 in NM/Mint)

GD25 FN65 NM94
2(nn)-Don Winslow of the Navy (#1) (Rare) (11/39?) 115.00 345.00 800.00
3(nn)-Myra North (1/40?) 71.00 215.00 500.00

GD25 FN65 VF82 NM94
4-Donald Duck by Al Taliaferro (1940)(Disney)(3/40?) 600.00 1500.00 3600.00 6000.00
(Prices vary widely on this book)

GD25 FN65 NM94
5-Smilin' Jack (#1) (5/40?) 57.00 170.00 400.00
6-Dick Tracy (Scarce) 129.00 385.00 900.00
7-Gang Busters 34.00 100.00 235.00
8-Dick Tracy 75.00 225.00 525.00
9-Terry and the Pirates-r/Super #9-29 57.00 170.00 400.00
10-Smilin' Jack 54.00 160.00 375.00
11-Smitty (#1) 34.00 105.00 240.00
12-Little Orphan Annie; reprints strips from 12/19/37 to 6/4/38 47.00 141.00 330.00
13-Walt Disney's Reluctant Dragon('41)-Contains 2 pages of photos from film; 2 pg. foreword to Fantasia by Leopold Stokowski; Donald Duck, Goofy, Baby Weems & Mickey Mouse (as the Sorcerer's Apprentice) app. (Disney) 115.00 345.00 800.00
14-Moon Mullins (#1) 32.00 95.00 225.00
15-Tillie the Toiler (#1) 32.00 95.00 225.00

GD25 FN65 VF82
16-Mickey Mouse (#1) (Disney) by Gottfredson 500.00 1500.00 4500.00
(Prices vary widely on this book)

GD25 FN65 NM94
17-Walt Disney's Dumbo, the Flying Elephant (#1)(1941)-Mickey Mouse, Donald Duck, & Pluto app. (Disney) 129.00 385.00 900.00
18-Jiggs and Maggie (#1)(1936-'38-r) 35.00 105.00 245.00
19-Barney Google and Snuffy Smith (#1)-(1st issue with Four Color on the cover) 35.00 105.00 245.00
20-Tiny Tim 29.00 85.00 200.00
21-Dick Tracy 64.00 195.00 450.00
22-Don Winslow 29.00 85.00 200.00
23-Gang Busters 25.00 75.00 175.00
24-Captain Easy 32.00 95.00 225.00
25-Popeye (1942) 57.00 170.00 400.00

SERIES II: 1-Little Joe (1942) 43.00 130.00 300.00
2-Harold Teen 24.00 72.00 165.00
3-Alley Oop (#1) 46.00 140.00 325.00
4-Smilin' Jack 43.00 130.00 300.00
5-Raggedy Ann and Andy (#1) 46.00 140.00 320.00
6-Smitty 19.00 58.00 135.00
7-Smokey Stover (#1) 31.00 95.00 225.00
8-Tillie the Toiler 19.00 58.00 135.00

GD25 FN65 VF82 NM94
9-Donald Duck Finds Pirate Gold, by Carl Barks & Jack Hannah (Disney) (© 8/17/42) 500.00 1250.00 3000.00 5000.00
(Prices vary widely on this book)

GD25 FN65 NM94
10-Flash Gordon by Alex Raymond; r-/from "The Ice Kingdom" 52.00 156.00 365.00
11-Wash Tubbs 29.00 85.00 200.00
12-Walt Disney's Bambi (#1); reprinted in Gladstone Comic Album #9 47.00 140.00 330.00
13-Mr. District Attorney (#1)-See The Funnies #35 for 1st app. 26.00 78.00 180.00
14-Smilin' Jack 34.00 105.00 240.00
15-Felix the Cat (#1) 61.00 185.00 425.00
16-Porky Pig (#1)(1942)-"Secret of the Haunted House" 50.00 150.00 350.00
17-Popeye 46.00 135.00 320.00
18-Little Orphan Annie's Junior Commandos; Flag-c; reprints strips from 6/14/42 to 11/21/42 38.00 115.00 265.00

Four Color #33, © Warner Bros.

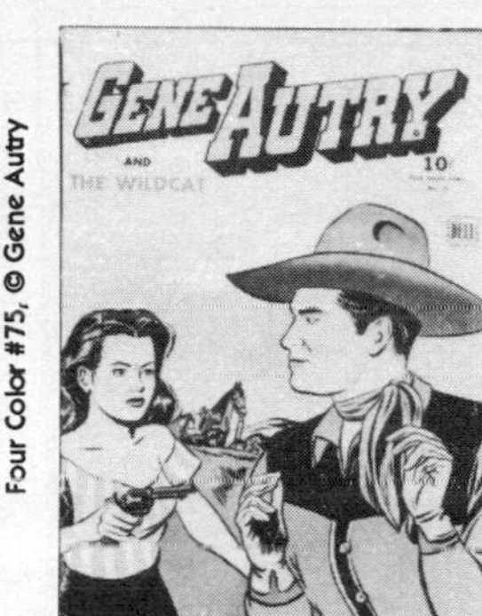

Four Color #75, © Gene Autry

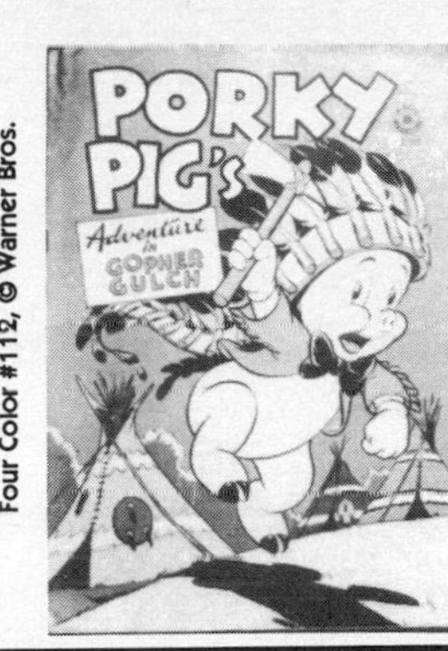

Four Color #112, © Warner Bros.

	GD25	FN65	NM94
19-Walt Disney's Thumper Meets the Seven Dwarfs (Disney); r-in Silly Symphonies	47.00	140.00	330.00
20-Barney Baxter	22.00	65.00	150.00
21-Oswald the Rabbit (#1)(1943)	34.00	100.00	235.00
22-Tillie the Toiler	16.00	48.00	110.00
23-Raggedy Ann and Andy	34.00	105.00	240.00
24-Gang Busters	25.00	75.00	175.00
25-Andy Panda (#1) (Walter Lantz)	37.00	110.00	260.00
26-Popeye	41.00	125.00	290.00
27-Walt Disney's Mickey Mouse and the Seven Colored Terror	63.00	190.00	440.00
28-Wash Tubbs	21.00	63.00	145.00

	GD25	FN65	VF82	NM94
29-Donald Duck and the Mummy's Ring, by Carl Barks (Disney) (9/43)	400.00	1000.00	2400.00	4000.00

(Prices vary widely on this book)

	GD25	FN65	NM94
30-Bambi's Children(1943)-Disney	46.00	140.00	320.00
31-Moon Mullins	17.00	52.00	120.00
32-Smitty	16.00	48.00	110.00
33-Bugs Bunny "Public Nuisance #1"	52.00	155.00	365.00
34-Dick Tracy	43.00	130.00	300.00
35-Smokey Stover	16.00	48.00	110.00
36-Smilin' Jack	22.00	65.00	150.00
37-Bringing Up Father	17.00	52.00	120.00
38-Roy Rogers (#1, © 4/44)-1st western comic with photo-c	82.00	240.00	575.00
39-Oswald the Rabbit('44)	23.00	70.00	160.00
40 Barney Google and Snuffy Smith	19.00	58.00	135.00
41-Mother Goose and Nursery Rhyme Comics (#1)-All by Walt Kelly	19.00	57.00	135.00
42-Tiny Tim (1934-r)	16.00	48.00	110.00
43-Popeye (1938-'42-r)	30.00	90.00	210.00
44-Terry and the Pirates ('38-r)	39.00	120.00	275.00
45-Raggedy Ann	29.00	85.00	200.00
46-Felix the Cat and the Haunted Castle	38.00	115.00	265.00
47-Gene Autry (copyright 6/16/44)	39.00	120.00	275.00
48-Porky Pig of the Mounties by Carl Barks (7/44)	72.00	215.00	500.00
49-Snow White and the Seven Dwarfs (Disney)	40.00	120.00	280.00
50-Fairy Tale Parade-Walt Kelly art (1944)	24.00	73.00	170.00
51-Bugs Bunny Finds the Lost Treasure	30.00	90.00	210.00
52-Little Orphan Annie; reprints strips from 6/18/38 to 11/19/38	29.00	85.00	200.00
53-Wash Tubbs	16.00	48.00	110.00
54-Andy Panda	23.00	70.00	160.00
55-Tillie the Toiler	11.50	34.00	80.00
56-Dick Tracy	34.00	105.00	240.00
57-Gene Autry	34.00	105.00	240.00
58-Smilin' Jack	22.00	65.00	150.00
59-Mother Goose and Nursery Rhyme Comics-Kelly-c/a	17.00	51.00	120.00
60-Tiny Folks Funnies	13.00	40.00	90.00
61-Santa Claus Funnies(11/44)-Kelly art	22.00	65.00	150.00
62-Donald Duck in Frozen Gold, by Carl Barks (Disney) (1/45)	120.00	360.00	1080.00
63-Roy Rogers; color photo-all 4 covers	43.00	128.00	300.00
64 Smokey Stover	11.50	34.00	80.00
65-Smitty	11.50	34.00	80.00
66-Gene Autry	34.00	105.00	240.00
67-Oswald the Rabbit	16.00	48.00	110.00
68-Mother Goose and Nursery Rhyme Comics, by Walt Kelly	17.00	51.00	120.00
69-Fairy Tale Parade, by Walt Kelly	22.00	65.00	150.00
70-Popeye and Wimpy	25.00	75.00	175.00
71-Walt Disney's Three Caballeros, by Walt Kelly (© 4/45)-(Disney)	71.00	215.00	500.00

	GD25	FN65	NM94
72-Raggedy Ann	24.00	72.00	165.00
73-The Gumps (#1)	10.00	30.00	70.00
74-Marge's Little Lulu (#1)	100.00	300.00	700.00
75-Gene Autry and the Wildcat	29.00	86.00	200.00
76-Little Orphan Annie; reprints strips from 2/28/40 to 6/24/40	24.00	72.00	165.00
77-Felix the Cat	36.00	110.00	250.00
78-Porky Pig and the Bandit Twins	22.00	65.00	150.00
79-Walt Disney's Mickey Mouse in The Riddle of the Red Hat by Carl Barks (8/45)	74.00	220.00	515.00
80-Smilin' Jack	16.00	48.00	110.00
81-Moon Mullins	10.00	30.00	65.00
82-Lone Ranger	36.00	107.00	250.00
83-Gene Autry in Outlaw Trail	29.00	86.00	200.00
84-Flash Gordon by Alex Raymond Reprints from "The Fiery Desert"	36.00	110.00	250.00
85-Andy Panda and the Mad Dog Mystery	14.00	43.00	100.00
86-Roy Rogers; photo-c	31.00	92.00	215.00
87-Fairy Tale Parade by Walt Kelly; Dan Noonan-c	19.00	57.00	130.00
88-Bugs Bunny's Great Adventure	18.00	54.00	125.00
89-Tillie the Toiler	11.50	34.00	80.00
90-Christmas with Mother Goose by Walt Kelly (11/45)	16.50	50.00	115.00
91-Santa Claus Funnies by Walt Kelly (11/45)	17.00	51.00	120.00
92-Walt Disney's The Wonderful Adventures Of Pinocchio (1945); Donald Duck by Kelly, 16 pgs. (Disney)	33.00	100.00	230.00
93-Gene Autry in The Bandit of Black Rock	23.00	70.00	160.00
94-Winnie Winkle (1945)	12.00	36.00	85.00
95-Roy Rogers Comics; photo-c	31.00	92.00	215.00
96-Dick Tracy	26.00	78.00	180.00
97-Marge's Little Lulu (1946)	47.00	140.00	330.00
98-Lone Ranger, The	27.00	81.00	190.00
99-Smitty	11.00	32.00	75.00
100-Gene Autry Comics; photo-c	23.00	70.00	160.00
101-Terry and the Pirates	26.00	80.00	180.00

NOTE: No. 101 is last issue to carry "Four Color" logo on cover; all issues beginning with No. 100 are marked "...O. S." (One Shot) which can be found in the bottom left-hand panel on the first page; the numbers following "O. S." relate to the year/month issued.

	GD25	FN65	NM94
102-Oswald the Rabbit-Walt Kelly art, 1 pg.	13.50	41.00	95.00
103-Easter with Mother Goose by Walt Kelly	16.00	48.00	110.00
104-Fairy Tale Parade by Walt Kelly	16.00	50.00	115.00
105-Albert the Alligator and Pogo Possum (#1) by Kelly (4/46)	68.00	205.00	475.00
106-Tillie the Toiler	10.00	30.00	60.00
107-Little Orphan Annie; reprints strips from 11/16/42 to 3/24/43	20.00	60.00	140.00
108-Donald Duck in The Terror of the River, by Carl Barks (Disney) (© 4/16/46)	90.00	270.00	810.00
109-Roy Rogers Comics; photo-c	24.00	71.00	165.00
110-Marge's Little Lulu	33.00	100.00	230.00
111-Captain Easy; spanking panels	11.50	34.00	80.00
112-Porky Pig's Adventure in Gopher Gulch	13.00	40.00	90.00
113-Popeye	13.00	40.00	90.00
114-Fairy Tale Parade by Walt Kelly	16.00	50.00	115.00
115-Marge's Little Lulu	33.00	100.00	230.00
116-Mickey Mouse and the House of Many Mysteries (Disney)	20.00	60.00	140.00
117-Roy Rogers Comics; photo-c	17.00	51.00	120.00
118-Lone Ranger, The	27.00	81.00	190.00
119-Felix the Cat	29.00	85.00	200.00
120-Marge's Little Lulu	30.00	90.00	210.00
121-Fairy Tale Parade-(not Kelly)	11.00	32.00	75.00
122-Henry (#1) (10/46)	10.00	30.00	70.00
123-Bugs Bunny's Dangerous Venture	12.00	36.00	85.00
124-Roy Rogers Comics; photo-c	17.00	51.00	120.00
125-Lone Ranger, The	20.00	60.00	140.00

Four Color #129, © The Disney Co.

Four Color #190, © KING

Four Color #227, © The Disney Co.

	GD25	FN65	NM94
126-Christmas with Mother Goose by Walt Kelly (1946)	13.00	40.00	90.00
127-Popeye	13.00	40.00	90.00
128-Santa Claus Funnies- "Santa & the Angel" by Gollub; "A Mouse in the House" by Kelly	13.00	40.00	90.00
129-Walt Disney's Uncle Remus and His Tales of Brer Rabbit (#1) (1946)	17.00	52.00	120.00
130-Andy Panda (Walter Lantz)	10.00	30.00	60.00
131-Marge's Little Lulu	30.00	90.00	210.00
132-Tillie the Toiler (1947)	10.00	30.00	60.00
133-Dick Tracy	22.00	65.00	150.00
134-Tarzan and the Devil Ogre; Marsh-c/a	57.00	170.00	400.00
135-Felix the Cat	22.00	65.00	150.00
136-Lone Ranger, The	20.00	60.00	140.00
137-Roy Rogers Comics; photo-c	17.00	51.00	120.00
138-Smitty	10.00	30.00	60.00
139-Marge's Little Lulu (1947)	27.00	81.00	190.00
140-Easter with Mother Goose by Walt Kelly	13.00	40.00	90.00
141-Mickey Mouse and the Submarine Pirates (Disney)	19.00	57.00	130.00
142-Bugs Bunny and the Haunted Mountain	12.00	36.00	85.00
143-Oswald the Rabbit & the Prehistoric Egg	8.35	25.00	50.00
144-Roy Rogers Comics (1947)-Photo-c	17.00	51.00	120.00
145-Popeye	13.00	40.00	90.00
146-Marge's Little Lulu	27.00	81.00	190.00
147-Donald Duck in Volcano Valley, by Carl Barks (Disney) (5/47)	60.00	180.00	540.00
148-Albert the Alligator and Pogo Possum by Walt Kelly (5/47)	56.00	170.00	395.00
149-Smilin' Jack	11.00	32.00	75.00
150-Tillie the Toiler (6/47)	8.35	25.00	50.00
151-Lone Ranger, The	17.00	51.00	120.00
152-Little Orphan Annie; reprints strips from 1/2/44 to 5/6/44	13.00	40.00	90.00
153-Roy Rogers Comics; photo-c	14.00	43.00	100.00
154-Walter Lantz Andy Panda	10.00	30.00	60.00
155-Henry (7/47)	8.35	25.00	50.00
156-Porky Pig and the Phantom	10.00	30.00	60.00
157-Mickey Mouse & the Beanstalk (Disney)	19.00	57.00	130.00
158-Marge's Little Lulu	27.00	81.00	190.00
159-Donald Duck in the Ghost of the Grotto, by Carl Barks (Disney) (8/47)	54.00	160.00	485.00
160-Roy Rogers Comics; photo-c	14.00	43.00	100.00
161-Tarzan and the Fires Of Tohr; Marsh-c/a	50.00	150.00	350.00
162-Felix the Cat (9/47)	16.00	48.00	110.00
163-Dick Tracy	17.00	52.00	120.00
164-Bugs Bunny Finds the Frozen Kingdom	12.00	36.00	85.00
165-Marge's Little Lulu	27.00	81.00	190.00
166-Roy Rogers Comics (52 pgs.)-Photo-c	14.00	43.00	100.00
167-Lone Ranger, The	17.00	51.00	120.00
168-Popeye (10/47)	13.00	40.00	90.00
169-Woody Woodpecker (#1)- "Manhunter in the North"; drug use story	14.00	43.00	100.00
170-Mickey Mouse on Spook's Island (11/47)(Disney)-reprinted in Mickey Mouse #103	16.00	48.00	110.00
171-Charlie McCarthy (#1) and the Twenty Thieves	16.00	50.00	115.00
172-Christmas with Mother Goose by Walt Kelly (11/47)	13.00	40.00	90.00
173-Flash Gordon	12.00	36.00	85.00
174-Winnie Winkle	7.50	22.50	45.00
175-Santa Claus Funnies by Walt Kelly (1947)	13.00	40.00	90.00
176-Tillie the Toiler (12/47)	8.35	25.00	50.00
177-Roy Rogers Comics-(36 pgs.); Photo-c	14.00	43.00	100.00
178-Donald Duck "Christmas on Bear Mountain" by Carl Barks; 1st app. Uncle Scrooge (Disney)(12/47)	64.00	192.00	575.00
179-Uncle Wiggily (#1)-Walt Kelly-c	14.00	43.00	100.00

	GD25	FN65	NM94
180-Ozark Ike (#1)	9.15	27.50	55.00
181-Walt Disney's Mickey Mouse in Jungle Magic	16.00	48.00	110.00
182-Porky Pig in Never-Never Land (2/48)	10.00	30.00	60.00
183-Oswald the Rabbit (Lantz)	8.35	25.00	50.00
184-Tillie the Toiler	8.35	25.00	50.00
185-Easter with Mother Goose by Walt Kelly (1948)	12.00	36.00	85.00
186-Walt Disney's Bambi (4/48)-Reprinted as Movie Classic Bambi #3 (1956)	11.00	32.00	75.00
187-Bugs Bunny and the Dreadful Dragon	10.00	30.00	70.00
188-Woody Woodpecker (Lantz, 5/48)	10.00	30.00	70.00
189-Donald Duck in The Old Castle's Secret, by Carl Barks (Disney) (6/48)	54.00	160.00	485.00
190-Flash Gordon ('48)	12.00	36.00	85.00
191-Porky Pig to the Rescue	10.00	30.00	60.00
192-The Brownies (#1)-by Walt Kelly (7/48)	12.00	36.00	85.00
193-M.G.M. Presents Tom and Jerry (#1)(1948)	12.00	36.00	85.00
194-Mickey Mouse in The World Under the Sea (Disney)-Reprinted in Mickey Mouse #101	16.00	48.00	110.00
195-Tillie the Toiler	5.85	17.50	35.00
196-Charlie McCarthy in The Haunted Hide-Out; part photo-c	14.00	43.00	100.00
197-Spirit of the Border (#1) (Zane Grey) (1948)	10.00	30.00	60.00
198-Andy Panda	10.00	30.00	60.00
199-Donald Duck in Sheriff of Bullet Valley, by Carl Barks; Barks draws himself on wanted poster, last page; used in Love & Death (Disney) (10/48)	54.00	160.00	485.00
200-Bugs Bunny, Super Sleuth (10/48)	10.00	30.00	70.00
201-Christmas with Mother Goose by W. Kelly	11.50	34.00	80.00
202-Woody Woodpecker	6.70	20.00	40.00
203-Donald Duck in the Golden Christmas Tree, by Carl Barks (Disney) (12/48)	36.00	108.00	325.00
204-Flash Gordon (12/48)	10.00	30.00	70.00
205-Santa Claus Funnies by Walt Kelly	11.50	34.00	80.00
206-Little Orphan Annie; reprints strips from 11/10/40 to 1/11/41	7.50	22.50	45.00
207-King of the Royal Mounted (#1) (12/48)	13.00	40.00	90.00
208-Brer Rabbit Does It Again (Disney) (1/49)	10.00	30.00	70.00
209-Harold Teen	4.00	12.00	24.00
210-Tippie and Cap Stubbs	4.00	12.00	24.00
211-Little Beaver (#1)	7.50	22.50	45.00
212-Dr. Bobbs	4.35	13.00	26.00
213-Tillie the Toiler	5.85	17.50	35.00
214-Mickey Mouse and His Sky Adventure (2/49)(Disney)-Reprinted in Mickey Mouse #105	12.00	36.00	85.00
215-Sparkle Plenty (Dick Tracy-r by Gould)	10.00	30.00	70.00
216-Andy Panda and the Police Pup (Lantz)	6.70	20.00	40.00
217-Bugs Bunny in Court Jester	10.00	30.00	70.00
218-3 Little Pigs and the Wonderful Magic Lamp (Disney) (3/49)	10.00	30.00	60.00
219-Swee'pea	10.00	30.00	60.00
220-Easter with Mother Goose by Walt Kelly	11.50	34.00	80.00
221-Uncle Wiggily-Walt Kelly cover in part	10.00	30.00	65.00
222-West of the Pecos (Zane Grey)	7.50	22.50	45.00
223-Donald Duck "Lost in the Andes" by Carl Barks (Disney-4/49) (square egg story)	50.00	150.00	450.00
224-Little Iodine (#1), by Hatlo (4/49)	10.00	30.00	65.00
225-Oswald the Rabbit (Lantz)	5.35	16.00	32.00
226-Porky Pig and Spoofy, the Spook	7.50	22.50	45.00
227-Seven Dwarfs (Disney)	10.00	30.00	70.00
228-Mark of Zorro, The (#1) (1949)	22.00	65.00	150.00
229-Smokey Stover	5.00	15.00	30.00
230-Sunset Pass (Zane Grey)	7.50	22.50	45.00
231-Mickey Mouse and the Rajah's Treasure (Disney)	12.00	36.00	85.00
232-Woody Woodpecker (Lantz, 6/49)	6.70	20.00	40.00
233-Bugs Bunny, Sleepwalking Sleuth	10.00	30.00	70.00

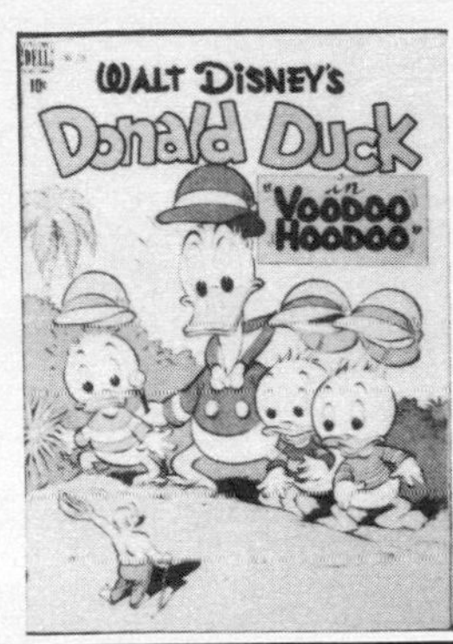

Four Color #238, © The Disney Co.

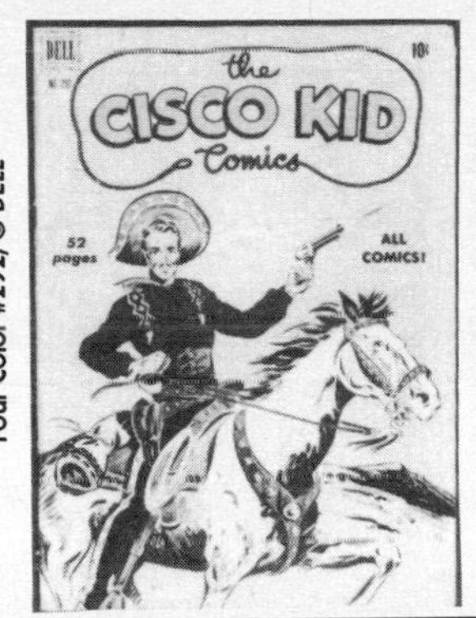

Four Color #292, © DELL

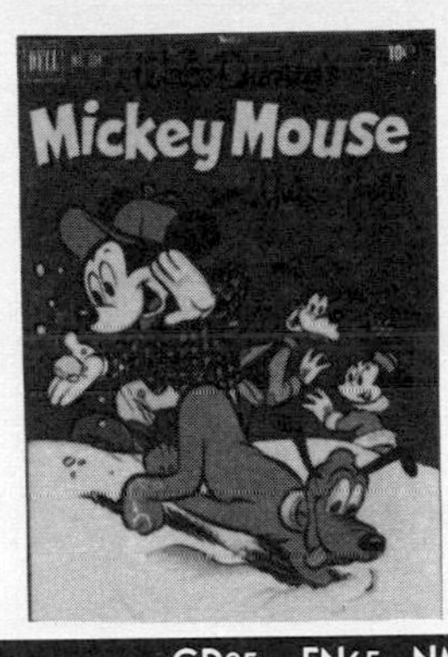

Four Color #334, © The Disney Co.

	GD25	FN65	NM94
234-Dumbo in Sky Voyage (Disney)	9.15	27.50	55.00
235-Tiny Tim	5.35	16.00	32.00
236-Heritage of the Desert (Zane Grey) (1949)	7.50	22.50	45.00
237-Tillie the Toiler	5.85	17.50	35.00
238-Donald Duck in Voodoo Hoodoo, by Carl Barks (Disney) (8/49)	38.00	112.00	342.00
239-Adventure Bound (8/49)	5.00	15.00	30.00
240-Andy Panda (Lantz)	6.70	20.00	40.00
241-Porky Pig, Mighty Hunter	7.50	22.50	45.00
242-Tipple and Cap Stubbs	4.00	12.00	24.00
243-Thumper Follows His Nose (Disney)	9.15	27.50	55.00
244-The Brownies by Walt Kelly	11.00	32.00	75.00
245-Dick's Adventures in Dreamland (9/49)	5.00	15.00	30.00
246-Thunder Mountain (Zane Grey)	5.00	15.00	30.00
247-Flash Gordon	10.00	30.00	70.00
248-Mickey Mouse and the Black Sorcerer (Disney)	12.00	36.00	85.00
249-Woody Woodpecker in the "Globetrotter" (10/49)	6.70	20.00	40.00
250-Bugs Bunny in Diamond Daze; used in **SOTI**, pg. 309	10.00	30.00	70.00
251-Hubert at Camp Moonbeam	5.00	15.00	30.00
252-Pinocchio (Disney)-not by Kelly; origin	10.00	30.00	65.00
253-Christmas with Mother Goose by W. Kelly	10.00	30.00	70.00
254-Santa Claus Funnies by Walt Kelly; Pogo & Albert story by Kelly (11/49)	11.50	34.00	80.00
255-The Ranger (Zane Grey) (1949)	5.00	15.00	30.00
256-Donald Duck in "Luck of the North" by Carl Barks (Disney) (12/49)-Shows #257 on inside	27.00	81.00	243.00
257-Little Iodine	7.50	22.50	45.00
258-Andy Panda and the Balloon Race (Lantz)	6.70	20.00	40.00
259-Santa and the Angel (Gollub art-condensed from #128) & Santa at the Zoo (12/49)-two books in one	5.35	16.00	32.00
260-Porky Pig, Hero of the Wild West (12/49)	7.50	22.50	45.00
261-Mickey Mouse and the Missing Key (Disney)	12.00	36.00	85.00
262-Raggedy Ann and Andy	6.35	19.00	38.00
263-Donald Duck in "Land of the Totem Poles" by Carl Barks (Disney) (2/50)-Has two Barks stories	27.00	81.00	243.00
264-Woody Woodpecker in the Magic Lantern (Lantz)	6.70	20.00	40.00
265-King of the Royal Mounted (Zane Grey)	10.00	30.00	60.00
266-Bugs Bunny on the "Isle of Hercules" (2/50)-Reprinted in Best of Bugs Bunny #1	10.00	30.00	60.00
267-Little Beaver-Harmon-c/a	4.00	12.00	24.00
268-Mickey Mouse's Surprise Visitor (1950) (Disney)	12.00	36.00	85.00
269-Johnny Mack Brown (#1)-Photo-c	19.00	58.00	135.00
270-Drift Fence (Zane Grey) (3/50)	5.00	15.00	30.00
271-Porky Pig in Phantom of the Plains	7.50	22.50	45.00
272-Cinderella (Disney) (4/50)	9.15	27.50	55.00
273-Oswald the Rabbit (Lantz)	5.35	16.00	32.00
274-Bugs Bunny, Hare-brained Reporter	10.00	30.00	60.00
275-Donald Duck in "Ancient Persia" by Carl Barks (Disney) (5/50)	25.00	75.00	225.00
276-Uncle Wiggily	7.50	22.50	45.00
277-Porky Pig in Desert Adventure (5/50)	7.50	22.50	45.00
278-Bill Elliott Comics (#1)-Photo-c	11.50	34.00	80.00
279-Mickey Mouse and Pluto Battle the Giant Ants (Disney); reprinted in Mickey Mouse #102 & 245	10.00	30.00	70.00
280-Andy Panda in The Isle Of Mechanical Men (Lantz)	6.70	20.00	40.00
281-Bugs Bunny in The Great Circus Mystery	10.00	30.00	60.00
282-Donald Duck and the Pixilated Parrot by Carl Barks (Disney) (© 5/23/50)	25.00	75.00	225.00
283-King of the Royal Mounted (7/50)	10.00	30.00	60.00
284-Porky Pig in The Kingdom of Nowhere	7.50	22.50	45.00
285-Bozo the Clown & His Minikin Circus (#1) (TV)	14.00	43.00	100.00

	GD25	FN65	NM94
286-Mickey Mouse in The Uninvited Guest (Disney	10.00	30.00	70.00
287-Gene Autry's Champion in The Ghost Of Black Mountain	9.15	27.50	55.00
288-Woody Woodpecker in Klondike Gold (Lantz)	6.70	20.00	40.00
289-Bugs Bunny in "Indian Trouble"	10.00	30.00	60.00
290-The Chief (#1) (8/50)	5.00	15.00	30.00
291-Donald Duck in "The Magic Hourglass" by Carl Barks (Disney) (9/50)	25.00	75.00	225.00
292-The Cisco Kid Comics (#1)	18.00	54.00	125.00
293-The Brownies-Kelly-c/a	10.00	30.00	70.00
294-Little Beaver	4.00	12.00	24.00
295-Porky Pig in President Porky (9/50)	7.50	22.50	45.00
296-Mickey Mouse in Private Eye for Hire (Disney)	10.00	30.00	70.00
297-Andy Panda in The Haunted Inn (Lantz, 10/50)	6.70	20.00	40.00
298-Bugs Bunny in Sheik for a Day	10.00	30.00	60.00
299-Buck Jones & the Iron Horse Trail (#1)	13.00	40.00	90.00
300-Donald Duck in "Big-Top Bedlam" by Carl Barks (Disney) (11/50)	25.00	75.00	225.00
301-The Mysterious Rider (Zane Grey)	5.00	15.00	30.00
302-Santa Claus Funnies (11/50)	4.00	11.00	22.00
303-Porky Pig in The Land of the Monstrous Flies	5.00	15.00	30.00
304-Mickey Mouse in Tom-Tom Island (Disney) (12/50)	8.35	25.00	50.00
305-Woody Woodpecker (Lantz)	4.70	12.50	25.00
306-Raggedy Ann	5.00	15.00	30.00
307-Bugs Bunny in Lumber Jack Rabbit	7.50	22.50	45.00
308-Donald Duck in "Dangerous Disguise" by Carl Barks (Disney) (1/51)	21.00	63.00	190.00
309-Betty Betz' Dollface and Her Gang (1951)	5.00	15.00	30.00
310-King of the Royal Mounted (1/51)	6.70	20.00	40.00
311-Porky Pig in Midget Horses of Hidden Valley	5.00	15.00	30.00
312-Tonto (#1)	11.50	34.00	80.00
313-Mickey Mouse in The Mystery of the Double-Cross Ranch (#1) (Disney) (2/51)	8.35	25.00	50.00
314-Ambush (Zane Grey)	5.00	15.00	30.00
315-Oswald the Rabbit (Lantz)	4.00	10.00	20.00
316-Rex Allen (#1)-Photo-c; Marsh-a	16.00	48.00	110.00
317-Bugs Bunny in Hair Today Gone Tomorrow (#1)	7.50	22.50	45.00
318-Donald Duck in "No Such Varmint" by Carl Barks (#1)-Indicia shows #317 (Disney, © 1/23/51)	21.00	63.00	190.00
319-Gene Autry's Champion	4.20	12.50	25.00
320-Uncle Wiggily (#1)	6.70	20.00	40.00
321-Little Scouts (#1) (3/51)	3.60	9.00	18.00
322-Porky Pig in Roaring Rockets (#1 on-c)	5.00	15.00	30.00
323-Susie Q. Smith (#1) (3/51)	4.20	12.50	25.00
324-I Met a Handsome Cowboy (3/51)	8.35	25.00	50.00
325-Mickey Mouse in The Haunted Castle (#2) (Disney) (4/51)	8.35	25.00	50.00
326-Andy Panda (#1) (Lantz)	4.00	10.00	20.00
327-Bugs Bunny and the Rajah's Treasure (#2)	7.50	22.50	45.00
328-Donald Duck in Old California (#2) by Carl Barks-Peyote drug use issue (Disney) (5/51)	23.00	70.00	205.00
329-Roy Roger's Trigger (#1)(5/51)-Photo-c	10.00	30.00	65.00
330-Porky Pig Meets the Bristled Bruiser (#2)	5.00	15.00	30.00
331-Alice in Wonderland (Disney) (1951)	10.00	30.00	70.00
332-Little Beaver	4.00	10.00	20.00
333-Wilderness Trek (Zane Grey) (5/51)	5.00	15.00	30.00
334-Mickey Mouse and Yukon Gold (Disney) (6/51)	8.35	25.00	50.00
335-Francis the Famous Talking Mule (#1, 6/51)-1st Dell non animated movie comic (all issues based on movie)	9.15	27.50	55.00
336-Woody Woodpecker (Lantz)	4.20	12.50	25.00
337-The Brownies-not by Walt Kelly	4.00	10.50	21.00
338-Bugs Bunny and the Rocking Horse Thieves	7.50	22.50	45.00
339-Donald Duck and the Magic Fountain-not by Carl Barks (Disney) (7-8/51)	5.35	16.00	32.00
340-King of the Royal Mounted (7/51)	6.70	20.00	40.00

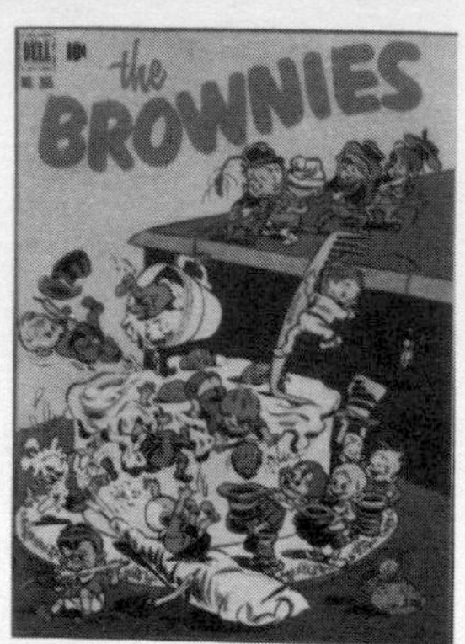

Four Color #365, © DELL

Four Color #395, © Zane Grey

Four Color #441, © DELL

	GD25	FN65	NM94
341-Unbirthday Party with Alice in Wonderland (Disney) (7/51)	11.50	34.00	80.00
342-Porky Pig the Lucky Peppermint Mine	4.00	11.00	22.00
343-Mickey Mouse in The Ruby Eye of Homar-Guy-Am (Disney)-Reprinted in Mickey Mouse #104	6.70	20.00	40.00
344-Sergeant Preston from Challenge of The Yukon (#1) (TV)	11.00	32.00	75.00
345-Andy Panda in Scotland Yard (8-10/51) (Lantz)	4.00	10.00	20.00
346-Hideout (Zane Grey)	5.00	15.00	30.00
347-Bugs Bunny the Frigid Hare (8-9/51)	7.50	22.50	45.00
348-Donald Duck "The Crocodile Collector"-Barks-c only (Disney) (9-10/51)	8.35	25.00	50.00
349-Uncle Wiggily	6.70	20.00	40.00
350-Woody Woodpecker (Lantz)	4.20	12.50	25.00
351-Porky Pig & the Grand Canyon Giant (9-10/51)	4.00	11.00	22.00
352-Mickey Mouse in The Mystery of Painted Valley (Disney)	6.70	20.00	40.00
353-Duck Album (#1)-Barks-c (Disney)	5.00	15.00	30.00
354-Raggedy Ann & Andy	5.00	15.00	30.00
355-Bugs Bunny Hot-Rod Hare	7.50	22.50	45.00
356-Donald Duck in "Rags to Riches"-Barks-c only	8.35	25.00	50.00
357-Comeback (Zane Grey)	4.35	13.00	26.00
358-Andy Panda (Lantz) (11-1/52)	4.00	10.00	20.00
359-Frosty the Snowman (#1)	7.50	22.50	45.00
360-Porky Pig in Tree of Fortune (11-12/51)	4.00	11.00	22.00
361-Santa Claus Funnies	4.00	11.00	22.00
362-Mickey Mouse and the Smuggled Diamonds (Disney)	6.70	20.00	40.00
363-King of the Royal Mounted	5.85	17.50	35.00
364-Woody Woodpecker (Lantz)	4.00	10.00	20.00
365-The Brownies-not by Kelly	4.00	10.50	21.00
366-Bugs Bunny Uncle Buckskin Comes to Town (12-1/52)	7.50	22.50	45.00
367-Donald Duck in "A Christmas for Shacktown" by Carl Barks (Disney) (1-2/52)	20.00	60.00	180.00
368-Bob Clampett's Beany and Cecil (#1)	22.00	65.00	150.00
369-The Lone Ranger's Famous Horse Hi-Yo Silver (#1); Silver's origin	8.35	25.00	50.00
370-Porky Pig in Trouble in the Big Trees	4.00	11.00	22.00
371-Mickey Mouse in The Inca Idol Case (1952) (Disney)	6.70	20.00	40.00
372-Riders of the Purple Sage (Zane Grey)	4.35	13.00	26.00
373-Sergeant Preston (TV)	7.00	21.00	42.00
374-Woody Woodpecker (Lantz)	4.00	10.00	20.00
375-John Carter of Mars (E. R. Burroughs)-Jesse Marsh-a; origin	23.00	70.00	160.00
376-Bugs Bunny, "The Magic Sneeze"	7.50	22.50	45.00
377-Susie Q. Smith	4.00	10.00	20.00
378-Tom Corbett, Space Cadet (#1) (TV)-McWilliams-a	16.00	48.00	110.00
379-Donald Duck in "Southern Hospitality" -Not by Barks (Disney)	4.50	14.00	32.00
380-Raggedy Ann & Andy	5.00	15.00	30.00
381-Marge's Tubby (#1)	14.00	43.00	100.00
382-Snow White and the Seven Dwarfs (Disney)-origin; partial reprint of 4-Color #49 (Movie)	8.35	25.00	50.00
383-Andy Panda (Lantz)	3.20	8.00	16.00
384-King of the Royal Mounted (3/52)(Zane Grey)	5.85	17.50	35.00
385-Porky Pig in The Isle of Missing Ships (3-4/52)	4.00	11.00	22.00
386-Uncle Scrooge (#1)-by Carl Barks (Disney) in "Only a Poor Old Man" (3/52)	82.00	245.00	575.00
387-Mickey Mouse in High Tibet (Disney) (4-5/52)	6.70	20.00	40.00
388-Oswald the Rabbit (Lantz)	4.00	10.00	20.00
389-Andy Hardy Comics (#1)	4.00	10.00	21.00
390-Woody Woodpecker (Lantz)	4.00	10.00	20.00
391-Uncle Wiggily	5.35	16.00	32.00

	GD25	FN65	NM94
392-Hi-Yo Silver	4.00	12.00	24.00
393-Bugs Bunny	7.50	22.50	45.00
394-Donald Duck in Malayalaya-Barks-c only (Disney)	8.35	25.00	50.00
395-Forlorn River(Zane Grey)-First Nevada (5/52)	4.35	13.00	26.00
396-Tales of the Texas Rangers(#1)(TV)-Photo-c	10.00	30.00	70.00
397-Sergeant Preston of the Yukon (TV) (5/52)	7.00	21.00	42.00
398-The Brownies-not by Kelly	4.00	10.50	21.00
399-Porky Pig in The Lost Gold Mine	4.00	11.00	22.00
400-Tom Corbett, Space Cadet (TV)-McWilliams-c/a	10.00	30.00	60.00
401-Mickey Mouse and Goofy's Mechanical Wizard (Disney) (6-7/52)	5.00	15.00	30.00
402-Mary Jane and Sniffles	10.00	30.00	60.00
403-Li'l Bad Wolf (Disney) (6/52)	4.20	12.50	25.00
404-The Range Rider (#1) (TV)-Photo-c	10.00	30.00	70.00
405-Woody Woodpecker (Lantz) (6-7/52)	4.00	10.00	20.00
406-Tweety and Sylvester (#1)	6.70	20.00	40.00
407-Bugs Bunny, Foreign-Legion Hare	5.35	16.00	32.00
408-Donald Duck and the Golden Helmet by Carl Barks (Disney) (7-8/52)	20.00	60.00	180.00
409-Andy Panda (7-9/52)	3.20	8.00	16.00
410-Porky Pig in The Water Wizard (7/52)	4.00	11.00	22.00
411-Mickey Mouse and the Old Sea Dog (Disney) (8-9/52)	5.00	15.00	30.00
412-Nevada (Zane Grey)	4.35	13.00	26.00
413-Robin Hood (Disney-Movie) (8/52)-Photo-c	5.85	17.50	35.00
414-Bob Clampett's Beany and Cecil (TV)	17.00	52.00	120.00
415-Rootie Kazootie (#1) (TV)	10.00	30.00	70.00
416-Woody Woodpecker (Lantz)	4.00	10.00	20.00
417-Double Trouble with Goober (#1) (8/52)	3.20	8.00	16.00
418-Rusty Riley, a Boy, a Horse, and a Dog (#1)-Frank Godwin-a (strip reprints) (8/52)	4.70	14.00	28.00
419-Sergeant Preston (TV)	7.00	21.00	42.00
420-Bugs Bunny in The Mysterious Buckaroo (8-9/52)	5.35	16.00	32.00
421-Tom Corbett, Space Cadet(TV)-McWilliams-a	10.00	30.00	60.00
422-Donald Duck and the Gilded Man, by Carl Barks (Disney) (9-10/52) (#423 on inside)	20.00	60.00	180.00
423-Rhubarb, Owner of the Brooklyn Ball Club (The Millionaire Cat) (#1)	4.70	14.00	28.00
424-Flash Gordon-Test Flight in Space (9/52)	8.35	25.00	50.00
425-Zorro, the Return of	13.00	40.00	90.00
426-Porky Pig in The Scalawag Leprechaun	4.00	11.00	22.00
427-Mickey Mouse and the Wonderful Whizzix (Disney) (10-11/52)-Reprinted in Mickey Mouse #100	5.00	15.00	30.00
428-Uncle Wiggily	5.00	15.00	30.00
429-Pluto in "Why Dogs Leave Home" (Disney) (10/52)	5.00	15.00	30.00
430-Marge's Tubby, the Shadow of a Man-Eater	9.15	27.50	55.00
431-Woody Woodpecker (10/52) (Lantz)	4.00	10.00	20.00
432-Bugs Bunny and the Rabbit Olympics	5.35	16.00	32.00
433-Wildfire (Zane Grey) (11-1/52-53)	4.35	13.00	26.00
434-Rin Tin Tin-"In Dark Danger" (#1) (TV) (11/52)-Photo-c	17.00	52.00	120.00
435-Frosty the Snowman (11/52)	4.00	12.00	24.00
436-The Brownies-not by Kelly (11/52)	3.60	9.00	18.00
437-John Carter of Mars (E. R. Burroughs)-Marsh-a	16.00	48.00	110.00
438-Annie Oakley (#1) (TV)	12.00	36.00	85.00
439-Little Hiawatha (Disney) (12/52)	4.70	14.00	28.00
440-Black Beauty (12/52)	3.60	9.00	18.00
441-Fearless Fagan	3.60	9.00	18.00
442-Peter Pan (Disney) (Movie)	7.50	22.50	45.00
443-Ben Bowie and His Mountain Men (#1)	7.50	22.50	45.00
444-Marge's Tubby	9.15	27.50	55.00
445-Charlie McCarthy	5.00	15.00	30.00

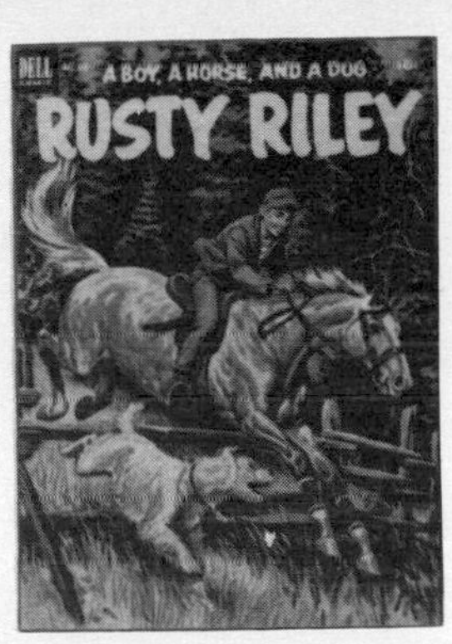

Four Color #451, © DELL

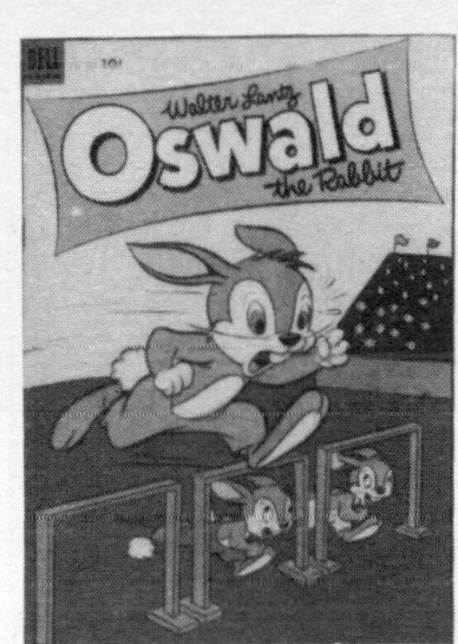

Four Color #507, © DELL

Four Color #556, © DELL

	GD25	FN65	NM94
446-Captain Hook and Peter Pan (Disney) (Movie) (1/53)	8.35	25.00	50.00
447-Andy Hardy Comics	2.80	7.00	14.00
448-Bob Clampett's Beany and Cecil (TV)	17.00	52.00	120.00
449-Tappan's Burro (Zane Grey) (2-4/53)	4.35	13.00	26.00
450-Duck Album; Barks-c (Disney)	4.70	14.00	28.00
451-Rusty Riley-Frank Godwin-a (strip-r) (2/53)	4.00	10.00	20.00
452-Raggedy Ann & Andy (1953)	5.00	15.00	30.00
453-Susie Q. Smith (2/53)	3.60	9.00	18.00
454-Krazy Kat Comics; not by Herriman	4.00	12.00	24.00
455-Johnny Mack Brown Comics(3/53)-Photo-c	5.85	17.50	35.00
456-Uncle Scrooge Back to the Klondike (#2) by Barks (3/53) (Disney)	41.00	125.00	290.00
457-Daffy (#1)	8.35	25.00	50.00
458-Oswald the Rabbit (Lantz)	3.20	8.00	16.00
459-Rootie Kazootie (TV)	7.50	22.50	45.00
460-Buck Jones (4/53)	5.00	15.00	30.00
461-Marge's Tubby	8.35	25.00	50.00
462-Little Scouts	2.00	5.00	10.00
463-Petunia (4/53)	4.00	10.00	20.00
464-Bozo (4/53)	10.00	30.00	65.00
465-Francis the Famous Talking Mule	5.00	15.00	30.00
466-Rhubarb, the Millionaire Cat	3.60	9.00	18.00
467-Desert Gold (Zane Grey) (5-7/53)	4.35	13.00	26.00
468-Goofy (#1) (Disney)	10.00	30.00	60.00
469-Beetle Bailey (#1) (5/53	9.15	27.50	55.00
470-Elmer Fudd	2.80	7.00	14.00
471-Double Trouble with Goober	2.40	6.00	12.00
472-Wild Bill Elliott (6/53)-Photo-c	5.35	16.00	32.00
473-Li'l Bad Wolf (Disney) (6/53)	4.00	10.00	20.00
474-Mary Jane and Sniffles	9.15	27.50	55.00
475-M.G.M.'s The Two Mouseketeers (#1)	6.70	20.00	40.00
476-Rin Tin Tin (TV)-Photo-c	10.00	30.00	60.00
477-Bob Clampett's Beany and Cecil (TV)	17.00	52.00	120.00
478-Charlie McCarthy	5.00	15.00	30.00
479-Queen of the West Dale Evans (#1)	13.00	40.00	90.00
480-Andy Hardy Comics	2.80	7.00	14.00
481-Annie Oakley And Tagg (TV)	8.35	25.00	50.00
482-Brownies-not by Kelly	3.60	9.00	18.00
483-Little Beaver (7/53)	4.00	10.00	20.00
484-River Feud (Zane Grey) (8-10/53)	4.35	13.00	26.00
485-The Little People-Walt Scott (#1)	6.70	20.00	40.00
486-Rusty Riley-Frank Godwin strip-r	4.00	10.00	20.00
487-Mowgli, the Jungle Book (Rudyard Kipling's)	5.00	15.00	30.00
488-John Carter of Mars (Burroughs)-Marsh-a	16.00	48.00	110.00
489-Tweety and Sylvester	4.00	10.00	20.00
490-Jungle Jim (#1)	6.70	20.00	40.00
491-Silvertip (#1) (Max Brand)-Kinstler-a (8/53)	9.15	27.50	55.00
492-Duck Album (Disney)	4.00	10.00	20.00
493-Johnny Mack Brown; photo-c	5.85	17.50	35.00
494-The Little King (#1)	10.00	30.00	60.00
495-Uncle Scrooge (#3) (Disney)-by Carl Barks (9/53)	34.00	105.00	240.00
496-The Green Hornet	25.00	75.00	175.00
497-Zorro (Sword of...)	13.00	40.00	90.00
498-Bugs Bunny's Album (9/53)	5.00	15.00	30.00
499-M.G.M.'s Spike and Tyke (#1) (9/53)	3.20	8.00	16.00
500-Buck Jones	5.00	15.00	30.00
501-Francis the Famous Talking Mule	5.00	15.00	30.00
502-Rootie Kazootie (TV)	7.50	22.50	45.00
503-Uncle Wiggily (10/53)	5.00	15.00	30.00
504-Krazy Kat; not by Herriman	4.00	12.00	24.00
505-The Sword and the Rose (Disney) (10/53) (TV)-Photo-c	5.00	15.00	30.00
506-The Little Scouts	2.00	5.00	10.00
507-Oswald the Rabbit (Lantz)	3.20	8.00	16.00

	GD25	FN65	NM94
508-Bozo (10/53)	10.00	30.00	65.00
509-Pluto (Disney) (10/53)	5.00	15.00	30.00
510-Son of Black Beauty	3.60	9.00	18.00
511-Outlaw Trail (Zane Grey)-Kinstler-a	4.70	14.00	28.00
512-Flash Gordon (11/53)	4.70	14.00	28.00
513-Ben Bowie and His Mountain Men	4.00	12.00	24.00
514-Frosty the Snowman (11/53)	4.00	10.00	20.00
515-Andy Hardy	2.80	7.00	14.00
516-Double Trouble With Goober	2.40	6.00	12.00
517-Chip 'N' Dale (#1) (Disney)	4.70	14.00	28.00
518-Rivets (11/53)	2.80	7.00	14.00
519-Steve Canyon (#1)-Not by Milton Caniff	8.35	25.00	50.00
520-Wild Bill Elliott-Photo-c	5.35	16.00	32.00
521-Beetle Bailey (12/53)	4.70	14.00	28.00
522-The Brownies	3.60	9.00	18.00
523-Rin Tin Tin (TV)-Photo-c (12/53)	10.00	30.00	60.00
524-Tweety and Sylvester	4.00	10.00	20.00
525-Santa Claus Funnies	4.00	10.00	20.00
526-Napoleon	2.40	6.00	12.00
527-Charlie McCarthy	5.00	15.00	30.00
528-Queen of the West Dale Evans; photo-c	9.15	27.50	55.00
529-Little Beaver	4.00	10.00	20.00
530-Bob Clampett's Beany and Cecil (TV) (1/54)	17.00	52.00	120.00
531-Duck Album (Disney)	4.00	10.00	20.00
532-The Rustlers (Zane Grey) (2-4/54)	4.35	13.00	26.00
533-Raggedy Ann and Andy	5.00	15.00	30.00
534-Western Marshal(Ernest Haycox's)-Kinstler-a	5.85	17.50	35.00
535-I Love Lucy (#1) (TV) (2/54)-photo-c	36.00	110.00	250.00
536-Daffy (3/54)	4.20	12.50	25.00
537-Stormy, the Thoroughbred... (Disney-Movie) on top 2/3 of each page; Pluto story on bottom 1/3 of each page (2/54)	4.20	12.50	25.00
538-The Mask of Zorro; Kinstler-a	13.50	41.00	95.00
539-Ben and Me (Disney) (3/54)	3.60	9.00	18.00
540-Knights of the Round Table (3/54) (Movie)-Photo-c	6.70	20.00	40.00
541-Johnny Mack Brown; photo-c	5.85	17.50	35.00
542-Super Circus Featuring Mary Hartline (TV) (3/54)	5.00	15.00	30.00
543-Uncle Wiggily (3/54)	5.00	15.00	30.00
544-Rob Roy (Disney-Movie)-Manning-a; photo-c	10.00	30.00	60.00
545-The Wonderful Adventures of Pinocchio-Partial reprint of 4-Color #92 (Disney-Movie)	5.00	15.00	30.00
546-Buck Jones	5.00	15.00	30.00
547-Francis the Famous Talking Mule	5.00	15.00	30.00
548-Krazy Kat; not by Herriman (4/54)	4.00	10.00	20.00
549-Oswald the Rabbit (Lantz)	3.20	8.00	16.00
550-The Little Scouts	2.00	5.00	10.00
551-Bozo (4/54)	10.00	30.00	65.00
552-Beetle Bailey	4.70	14.00	28.00
553-Susie Q. Smith	3.60	9.00	18.00
554-Rusty Riley (Frank Godwin strip-r)	4.00	10.00	20.00
555-Range War (Zane Grey)	4.35	13.00	26.00
556-Double Trouble With Goober (5/54)	2.40	6.00	12.00
557-Ben Bowie and His Mountain Men	4.00	12.00	24.00
558-Elmer Fudd (5/54)	2.80	7.00	14.00
559-I Love Lucy (#2) (TV)-Photo-c	24.00	72.00	165.00
560-Duck Album (Disney) (5/54)	4.00	10.00	20.00
561-Mr. Magoo (5/54)	10.00	30.00	60.00
562-Goofy (Disney)	5.00	15.00	30.00
563-Rhubarb, the Millionaire Cat (6/54)	3.60	9.00	18.00
564-Li'l Bad Wolf (Disney)	4.00	10.00	20.00
565-Jungle Jim	4.00	10.00	20.00
566-Son of Black Beauty	3.60	9.00	18.00
567-Prince Valiant (#1)-By Bob Fuje (Movie)-Photo-c	10.00	30.00	60.00
568-Gypsy Colt (Movie) (6/54)	5.00	15.00	30.00

Four Color #571, © Edgar Bergen

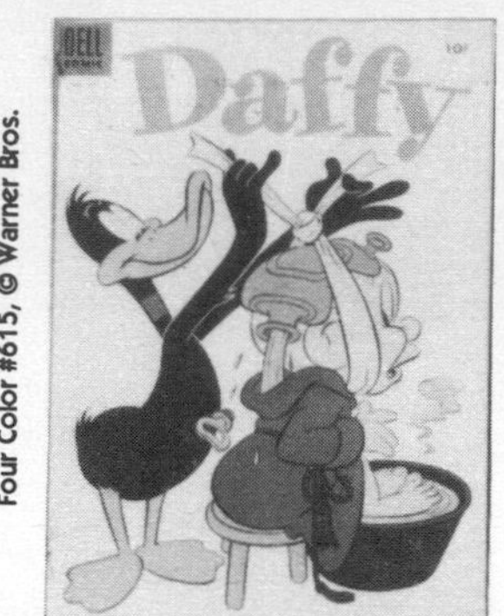

Four Color #615, © Warner Bros.

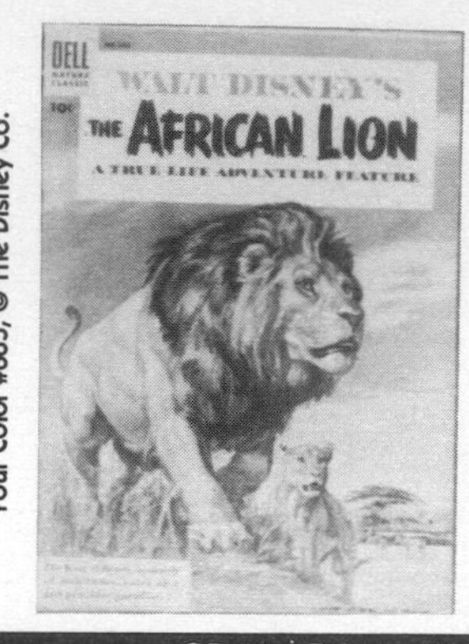

Four Color #665, © The Disney Co.

	GD25	FN65	NM94
569-Priscilla's Pop	3.60	9.00	18.00
570-Bob Clampett's Beany and Cecil (TV)	17.00	52.00	120.00
571-Charlie McCarthy	5.00	15.00	30.00
572-Silvertip (Max Brand) (7/54); Kinstler-a	5.00	15.00	30.00
573-The Little People by Walt Scott	4.00	10.00	20.00
574-The Hand of Zorro	13.50	41.00	95.00
575-Annie Oakley and Tagg (TV)-Photo-c	8.35	25.00	50.00
576-Angel (#1) (8/54)	2.80	7.00	14.00
577-M.G.M.'s Spike and Tyke	2.40	6.00	12.00
578-Steve Canyon (8/54)	5.00	15.00	30.00
579-Francis the Famous Talking Mule	5.00	15.00	30.00
580-Six Gun Ranch (Luke Short-8/54)	4.00	11.00	22.00
581-Chip 'N' Dale (#2) (Disney)	3.00	7.50	15.00
582-Mowgli Jungle Book (Kipling) (8/54)	4.00	11.00	22.00
583-The Lost Wagon Train (Zane Grey)	4.35	13.00	26.00
584-Johnny Mack Brown-Photo-c	5.85	17.50	35.00
585-Bugs Bunny's Album	4.70	14.00	28.00
586-Duck Album (Disney)	4.00	10.00	20.00
587-The Little Scouts	2.00	5.00	10.00
588-King Richard and the Crusaders (Movie) (10/54) Matt Baker-a; photo-c	10.00	30.00	65.00
589-Buck Jones	5.00	15.00	30.00
590-Hansel and Gretel; partial photo-c	5.85	17.50	35.00
591-Western Marshal(Ernest Haycox's)-Kinstler-a	5.85	17.50	35.00
592-Super Circus (TV)	5.00	15.00	30.00
593-Oswald the Rabbit (Lantz)	3.20	8.00	16.00
594-Bozo (10/54)	10.00	30.00	65.00
595-Pluto (Disney)	4.00	11.00	22.00
596-Turok, Son of Stone (#1)	71.00	214.00	500.00
597-The Little King	6.70	20.00	40.00
598-Captain Davy Jones	3.60	9.00	18.00
599-Ben Bowie and His Mountain Men	4.00	12.00	24.00
600-Daisy Duck's Diary (#1) (Disney) (11/54)	5.85	17.50	35.00
601-Frosty the Snowman	4.00	10.00	20.00
602-Mr. Magoo and Gerald McBoing-Boing	10.00	30.00	60.00
603-M.G.M.'s The Two Mouseketeers	4.00	10.00	20.00
604-Shadow on the Trail (Zane Grey)	4.35	13.00	26.00
605-The Brownies-not by Kelly (12/54)	3.60	9.00	18.00
606-Sir Lancelot (not TV)	8.35	25.00	50.00
607-Santa Claus Funnies	4.00	10.00	20.00
608-Silvertip- "Valley of Vanishing Men" (Max Brand)-Kinstler-a	5.00	15.00	30.00
609-The Littlest Outlaw (Disney-Movie) (1/55)-Photo-c	5.00	15.00	30.00
610-Drum Beat (Movie); Alan Ladd photo-c	10.00	30.00	70.00
611-Duck Album (Disney)	4.00	10.00	20.00
612-Little Beaver (1/55)	3.60	9.00	18.00
613-Western Marshal (Ernest Haycox's) (2/55)-Kinstler-a	5.85	17.50	35.00
614-20,000 Leagues Under the Sea (Disney) (Movie) (2/55)	5.85	17.50	35.00
615-Daffy	4.20	12.50	25.00
616-To the Last Man (Zane Grey)	4.35	13.00	26.00
617-The Quest of Zorro	13.00	40.00	90.00
618-Johnny Mack Brown; photo-c	5.85	17.50	35.00
619-Krazy Kat; not by Herriman	4.00	10.00	20.00
620-Mowgli Jungle Book (Kipling)	4.00	11.00	22.00
621-Francis the Famous Talking Mule (4/55)	4.20	12.50	25.00
622-Beetle Bailey	4.70	14.00	28.00
623-Oswald the Rabbit (Lantz)	2.40	6.00	12.00
624-Treasure Island(Disney-Movie)(4/55)-Photo-c	5.00	15.00	30.00
625-Beaver Valley (Disney-Movie)	4.00	12.00	24.00
626-Ben Bowie and His Mountain Men	4.00	12.00	24.00
627-Goofy (Disney) (5/55)	5.00	15.00	30.00
628-Elmer Fudd	2.80	7.00	14.00
629-Lady and the Tramp with Jock (Disney)	4.00	11.00	22.00
630-Priscilla's Pop	3.60	9.00	18.00
631-Davy Crockett, Indian Fighter (#1) (Disney) (5/55) (TV)-Fess Parker photo-c	10.00	30.00	60.00
632-Fighting Caravans (Zane Grey)	4.35	13.00	26.00
633-The Little People by Walt Scott (6/55)	4.00	10.00	20.00
634-Lady and the Tramp Album (Disney) (6/55)	4.00	10.00	20.00
635-Bob Clampett's Beany and Cecil (TV)	17.00	52.00	120.00
636-Chip 'N' Dale (Disney)	3.00	7.50	15.00
637-Silvertip (Max Brand)-Kinstler-a	5.00	15.00	30.00
638-M.G.M.'s Spike and Tyke (8/55)	2.40	6.00	12.00
639-Davy Crockett at the Alamo (Disney) (7/55) (TV)-Fess Parker photo-c	6.70	20.00	40.00
640-Western Marshal(Ernest Haycox's)-Kinstler-a	5.85	17.50	35.00
641-Steve Canyon (1955)-by Caniff	5.00	15.00	30.00
642-M.G.M.'s The Two Mouseketeers	4.00	10.00	20.00
643-Wild Bill Elliott; photo-c	4.35	13.00	26.00
644-Sir Walter Raleigh (5/55)-Based on movie "The Virgin Queen;" photo-c	7.50	22.50	45.00
645-Johnny Mack Brown; photo-c	5.85	17.50	35.00
646-Dotty Dripple and Taffy (#1)	4.00	10.00	20.00
647-Bugs Bunny's Album (9/55)	4.70	14.00	28.00
648-Jace Pearson of the Texas Rangers (TV)-Photo-c	5.85	17.50	35.00
649-Duck Album (Disney)	4.00	10.00	20.00
650-Prince Valiant; by Bob Fuje	5.85	17.50	35.00
651-King Colt (Luke Short) (9/55)-Kinstler-a	4.35	13.00	26.00
652-Buck Jones	4.00	10.00	20.00
653-Smokey the Bear (#1) (10/55)	9.15	27.50	55.00
654-Pluto (Disney)	4.00	11.00	22.00
655-Francis the Famous Talking Mule	4.20	12.50	25.00
656-Turok, Son of Stone (#2) (10/55)	43.00	129.00	300.00
657-Ben Bowie and His Mountain Men	4.00	12.00	24.00
658-Goofy (Disney)	5.00	15.00	30.00
659-Daisy Duck's Diary (Disney)	3.60	9.00	18.00
660-Little Beaver	3.60	9.00	18.00
661-Frosty the Snowman	4.00	10.00	20.00
662-Zoo Parade (TV)-Marlin Perkins (11/55)	5.35	16.00	32.00
663-Winky Dink (TV)	7.50	22.50	45.00
664-Davy Crockett in the Great Keelboat Race (TV) (Disney) (11/55)-Fess Parker photo-c	7.50	22.50	45.00
665-The African Lion (Disney-Movie) (11/55)	5.00	15.00	30.00
666-Santa Claus Funnies	4.00	10.00	20.00
667-Silvertip and the Stolen Stallion (Max Brand) (12/55)-Kinstler-a	5.00	15.00	30.00
668-Dumbo (Disney) (12/55)	5.35	16.00	32.00
668-Dumbo (Disney) (1/58) different cover, same contents as above	5.35	16.00	32.00
669-Robin Hood (Disney-Movie) (12/55)-reprint of #413; photo-c	4.00	11.00	22.00
670-M.G.M's Mouse Musketeers (#1) (1/56)-Formerly the Two Mouseketeers	3.20	8.00	16.00
671-Davy Crockett and the River Pirates (TV) (Disney) (12/55)-Jesse Marsh-a; Fess Parker photo-c	7.50	22.50	45.00
672-Quentin Durward (1/56) (Movie)-Photo-c	6.70	20.00	40.00
673-Buffalo Bill, Jr. (#1) (TV)-Photo-c	6.70	20.00	40.00
674-The Little Rascals (#1) (TV)	6.70	20.00	40.00
675-Steve Donovan, Western Marshal (#1) (TV)-Kinstler-a; photo-c	7.50	22.50	45.00
676-Will-Yum!	3.20	8.00	16.00
677-Little King	6.70	20.00	40.00
678-The Last Hunt (Movie)-Photo-c	6.70	20.00	40.00
679-Gunsmoke (#1) (TV)	11.50	34.00	80.00
680-Out Our Way with the Worry Wart (2/56)	3.20	8.00	16.00
681-Forever, Darling (Movie) with Lucille Ball & Desi Arnaz (2/56)-; photo-c	10.00	30.00	70.00
682-When Knighthood Was in Flower (Disney-Movie)-Reprint of #505;			

Four Color #691, © DELL

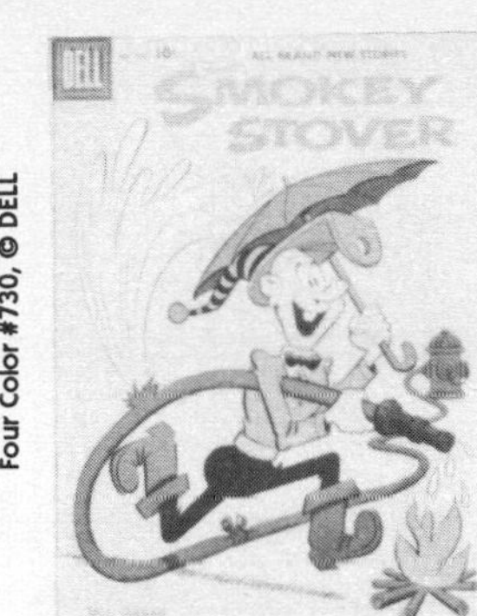

Four Color #730, © DELL

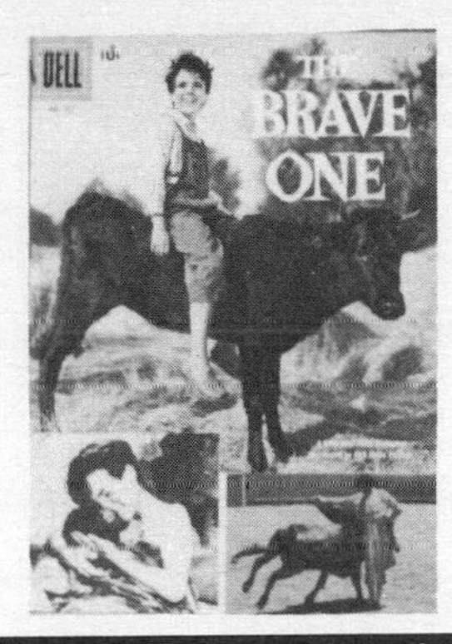

Four Color #773, © DELL

	GD25	FN65	NM94
photo-c	5.00	15.00	30.00
683-Hi and Lois (3/56)	2.80	7.00	14.00
684-Helen of Troy (Movie)-Buscema-a; photo-c	11.00	32.00	75.00
685-Johnny Mack Brown; photo-c	5.85	17.50	35.00
686-Duck Album (Disney)	4.00	10.00	20.00
687-The Indian Fighter (Movie)-Kirk Douglas photo-c	5.85	17.50	35.00
688-Alexander the Great (Movie) (5/56)-Buscema-a; photo-c	6.70	20.00	40.00
689-Elmer Fudd (3/56)	2.80	7.00	14.00
690-The Conqueror (Movie) - John Wayne photo-c	14.00	43.00	100.00
691-Dotty Dripple and Taffy	3.00	7.50	15.00
692-The Little People-Walt Scott	3.60	9.00	18.00
693-Song of the South (Disney) (1956)-Partial reprint of #129	3.60	9.00	18.00
694-Super Circus (TV)-Photo-c	5.00	15.00	30.00
695-Little Beaver	3.60	9.00	18.00
696-Krazy Kat; not by Herriman (4/56)	4.00	10.00	20.00
697-Oswald the Rabbit (Lantz)	2.40	6.00	12.00
698-Francis the Famous Talking Mule (4/56)	4.20	12.50	25.00
699-Prince Valiant-by Bob Fuje	5.85	17.50	35.00
700-Water Birds and the Olympic Elk (Disney-Movie) (4/56)	5.00	15.00	30.00
701-Jiminy Cricket (#1) (Disney) (5/56)	5.85	17.50	35.00
702-The Goofy Success Story (Disney)	5.00	15.00	30.00
703-Scamp (#1) (Disney)	5.85	17.50	35.00
704-Priscilla's Pop (5/56)	3.60	9.00	18.00
705-Brave Eagle (#1) (TV)-Photo-c	5.35	16.00	32.00
706-Bongo and Lumpjaw (Disney) (6/56)	3.60	9.00	18.00
707-Corky and White Shadow (Disney) (5/56)-Mickey Mouse Club (TV); photo-c	4.70	14.00	28.00
708-Smokey the Bear	4.70	14.00	28.00
709-The Searchers (Movie) - John Wayne photo-c	29.00	85.00	200.00
710-Francis the Famous Talking Mule	4.20	12.50	25.00
711-M.G.M's Mouse Musketeers	2.40	6.00	12.00
712-The Great Locomotive Chase (Disney-Movie) (9/56)-Photo-c	5.35	16.00	32.00
713-The Animal World (Movie) (8/56)	5.35	16.00	32.00
714-Spin and Marty (#1) (TV) (Disney)-Mickey Mouse Club (6/56); photo-c	10.00	30.00	65.00
715-Timmy (8/56)	3.60	9.00	18.00
716-Man in Space (Disney-Movie)	5.00	15.00	30.00
717-Moby Dick (Movie)-Photo-c	8.35	25.00	50.00
718-Dotty Dripple and Taffy	3.00	7.50	15.00
719-Prince Valiant; by Bob Fuje (8/56)	5.85	17.50	35.00
720-Gunsmoke (TV)-Photo-c	6.35	19.00	38.00
721-Captain Kangaroo (TV)-Photo-c	14.00	43.00	100.00
722-Johnny Mack Brown-Photo-c	5.85	17.50	35.00
723-Santiago (Movie)-Kinstler-a (9/56); Alan Ladd photo-c	11.00	32.00	75.00
724-Bugs Bunny's Album	4.70	14.00	28.00
725-Elmer Fudd (9/56)	2.40	6.00	12.00
726-Duck Album (Disney) (9/56)	3.60	9.00	18.00
727-The Nature of Things (TV) (Disney)-Jesse Marsh-a	5.35	16.00	32.00
728-M.G.M's Mouse Musketeers	2.40	6.00	12.00
729-Bob Son of Battle (11/56)	3.60	9.00	18.00
730-Smokey Stover	3.60	9.00	18.00
731-Silvertip and The Fighting Four (Max Brand)-Kinstler-a	5.00	15.00	30.00
732-Zorro, the Challenge of (10/56)	13.00	40.00	90.00
733-Buck Jones	4.00	10.00	20.00
734-Cheyenne (#1) (TV) (10/56)-Clint Walker photo-c	12.00	36.00	85.00
735-Crusader Rabbit (#1) (TV)	24.00	70.00	165.00
736-Pluto (Disney)	3.60	9.00	18.00
737-Steve Canyon-Caniff-a	5.00	15.00	30.00

	GD25	FN65	NM94
738-Westward Ho, the Wagons (Disney-Movie)-Fess Parker photo-c	5.35	16.00	32.00
739-Bounty Guns (Luke Short)-Drucker-a	4.00	11.00	22.00
740-Chilly Willy (#1) (Walter Lantz)	4.20	12.50	25.00
741-The Fastest Gun Alive (Movie)(9/56)-Photo-c	7.50	22.50	45.00
742-Buffalo Bill, Jr. (TV)-Photo-c	4.70	14.00	28.00
743-Daisy Duck's Diary (Disney) (11/56)	3.60	9.00	18.00
744-Little Beaver	3.60	9.00	18.00
745-Francis the Famous Talking Mule	4.20	12.50	25.00
746-Dotty Dripple and Taffy	3.00	7.50	15.00
747-Goofy (Disney)	5.00	15.00	30.00
748-Frosty the Snowman (11/56)	3.60	9.00	18.00
749-Secrets of Life (Disney-Movie)-Photo-c	5.35	16.00	32.00
750-The Great Cat Family (Disney-Movie)	5.35	16.00	32.00
751-Our Miss Brooks (TV)-Photo-c	7.50	22.50	45.00
752-Mandrake, the Magician	9.15	27.50	55.00
753-Walt Scott's Little People (11/56)	3.60	9.00	18.00
754-Smokey the Bear	4.70	14.00	28.00
755-The Littlest Snowman (12/56)	4.00	11.00	22.00
756-Santa Claus Funnies	4.00	10.00	20.00
757-The True Story of Jesse James (Movie)-Photo-c	10.00	30.00	60.00
758-Bear Country (Disney-Movie)	5.00	15.00	30.00
759-Circus Boy (TV)-The Monkees' Mickey Dolenz photo-c (12/56)	10.00	30.00	70.00
760-The Hardy Boys (#1) (TV) (Disney)-Mickey Mouse Club; photo-c	10.00	30.00	60.00
761-Howdy Doody (TV) (1/57)	10.00	30.00	60.00
762-The Sharkfighters (Movie) (1/57); Buscema-a; photo-c	11.00	32.00	75.00
763-Grandma Duck's Farm Friends (#1) (Disney)	6.70	20.00	40.00
764-M.G.M's Mouse Musketeers	2.40	6.00	12.00
765-Will-Yum!	3.20	8.00	16.00
766-Buffalo Bill, Jr. (TV)-Photo-c	4.70	14.00	28.00
767-Spin and Marty (TV) (Disney)-Mickey Mouse Club (2/57)	6.70	20.00	40.00
768-Steve Donovan, Western Marshal (TV)-Kinstler-a; photo-c	5.85	17.50	35.00
769-Gunsmoke (TV)	6.35	19.00	38.00
770-Brave Eagle (TV)-Photo-c	3.60	9.00	18.00
771-Brand of Empire (Luke Short)(3/57)-Drucker-a	4.00	11.00	22.00
772-Cheyenne (TV)-Clint Walker photo-c	7.50	22.50	45.00
773-The Brave One (Movie)-Photo-c	5.00	15.00	30.00
774-Hi and Lois (3/57)	2.80	7.00	14.00
775-Sir Lancelot and Brian (TV)-Buscema-a; photo-c	10.00	30.00	60.00
776-Johnny Mack Brown; photo-c	5.85	17.50	35.00
777-Scamp (Disney) (3/57)	3.60	9.00	18.00
778-The Little Rascals (TV)	4.00	10.00	20.00
779-Lee Hunter, Indian Fighter (3/57)	5.35	16.00	32.00
780-Captain Kangaroo (TV)-Photo-c	13.00	40.00	90.00
781-Fury (#1) (TV) (3/57)-Photo-c	10.00	30.00	60.00
782-Duck Album (Disney)	3.60	9.00	18.00
783-Elmer Fudd	2.40	6.00	12.00
784-Around the World in 80 Days (Movie) (2/57)-Photo-c	6.70	20.00	40.00
785-Circus Boy (TV) (4/57)-The Monkees' Mickey Dolenz photo-c	11.00	32.00	70.00
786-Cinderella (Disney) (3/57)-Partial-r of #272	4.00	10.00	20.00
787-Little Hiawatha (Disney) (4/57)	3.60	9.00	18.00
788-Prince Valiant; by Bob Fuje	5.85	17.50	35.00
789-Silvertip-Valley Thieves (Max Brand) (4/57)-Kinstler-a	5.00	15.00	30.00
790-The Wings of Eagles (Movie) (John Wayne)-Toth-a; John Wayne photo-c; 10 & 15 cent editions exist	15.00	45.00	105.00
791-The 77th Bengal Lancers (TV)-Photo-c	6.70	20.00	40.00

Four Color #798, © Tie-Ups Co.

Four Color #831, © DELL

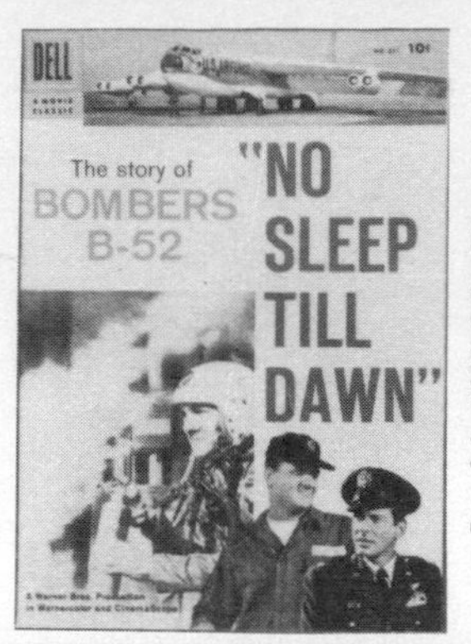

Four Color #874, © The Disney Co.

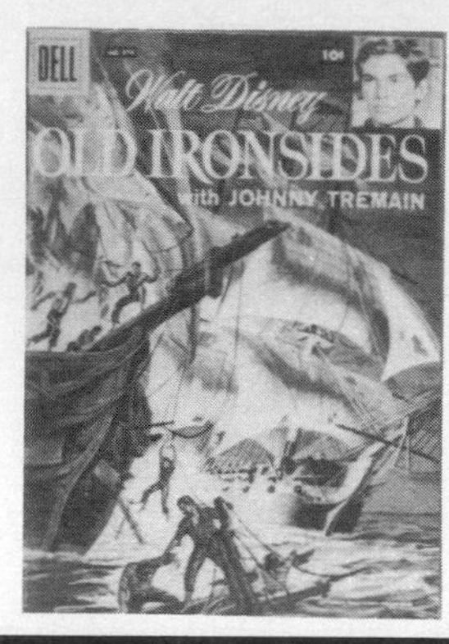

	GD25	FN65	NM94
792-Oswald the Rabbit (Lantz)	2.40	6.00	12.00
793-Morty Meekle	3.20	8.00	16.00
794-The Count of Monte Cristo (5/57) (Movie)-Buscema-a	10.00	30.00	60.00
795-Jiminy Cricket (Disney)	4.00	11.00	22.00
796-Ludwig Bemelman's Madeleine and Genevieve	4.00	11.00	22.00
797-Gunsmoke (TV)-Photo-c	6.35	19.00	38.00
798-Buffalo Bill, Jr. (TV)-Photo-c	4.70	14.00	28.00
799-Priscilla's Pop	3.60	9.00	18.00
800-The Buccaneers (TV)-Photo-c	6.35	19.00	38.00
801-Dotty Dripple and Taffy	3.00	7.50	15.00
802-Goofy (Disney) (5/57)	5.00	15.00	30.00
803-Cheyenne (TV)-Clint Walker photo-c	7.50	22.50	45.00
804-Steve Canyon-Caniff-a (1957)	5.00	15.00	30.00
805-Crusader Rabbit (TV)	20.00	60.00	140.00
806-Scamp (Disney) (6/57)	3.60	9.00	18.00
807-Savage Range (Luke Short)-Drucker-a	4.00	11.00	22.00
808-Spin and Marty (TV)(Disney)-Mickey Mouse Club; photo-c	6.70	20.00	40.00
809-The Little People (Walt Scott)	3.60	9.00	18.00
810-Francis the Famous Talking Mule	4.00	10.00	20.00
811-Howdy Doody (TV) (7/57)	10.00	30.00	60.00
812-The Big Land(Movie); Alan Ladd photo-c	10.00	30.00	65.00
813-Circus Boy (TV)-The Monkees' Mickey Dolenz photo-c	10.00	30.00	70.00
814-Covered Wagons, Ho! (Disney)-Donald Duck (TV) (6/57); Mickey Mouse app.	4.00	11.00	22.00
815-Dragoon Wells Massacre (Movie)-photo-c	8.35	25.00	50.00
816-Brave Eagle (TV)-photo-c	3.60	9.00	18.00
817-Little Beaver	3.60	9.00	18.00
818-Smokey the Bear (6/57)	4.70	14.00	28.00
819-Mickey Mouse in Magicland (Disney) (7/57)	4.00	11.00	22.00
820-The Oklahoman (Movie)-Photo-c	9.15	27.50	55.00
821-Wringle Wrangle (Disney)-Based on movie "Westward Ho, the Wagons" - Marsh-a; Fess Parker photo-c	7.50	22.50	45.00
822-Paul Revere's Ride with Johnny Tremain (TV) (Disney)-Toth-a	10.00	30.00	65.00
823-Timmy	2.80	7.00	14.00
824-The Pride and the Passion (Movie) (8/57)-Frank Sinatra & Cary Grant photo-c	9.15	27.50	55.00
825-The Little Rascals (TV)	4.00	10.00	20.00
826-Spin and Marty and Annette (TV) (Disney)-Mickey Mouse Club; Annette Funicello photo-c	12.00	36.00	85.00
827-Smokey Stover (8/57)	3.60	9.00	18.00
828-Buffalo Bill, Jr. (TV)-Photo-c	4.70	14.00	28.00
829-Tales of the Pony Express (TV) (8/57)-Painted-c	4.70	14.00	28.00
830-The Hardy Boys (TV) (Disney)-Mickey Mouse Club (8/57); photo-c	8.35	25.00	50.00
831-No Sleep 'Til Dawn (Movie)-Carl Malden photo-c	6.70	20.00	40.00
832-Lolly and Pepper (#1)	3.60	9.00	18.00
833-Scamp (Disney) (9/57)	3.60	9.00	18.00
834-Johnny Mack Brown; photo-c	5.35	17.50	35.00
835-Silvertip-The False Rider (Max Brand)	4.35	13.00	26.00
836-Man in Flight (Disney) (TV) (9/57)	5.35	16.00	32.00
837-All-American Athlete Cotton Woods	5.35	16.00	32.00
838-Bugs Bunny's Life Story Album (9/57)	5.00	15.00	30.00
839-The Vigilantes (Movie)	7.50	22.50	45.00
840-Duck Album (Disney) (9/57)	3.60	9.00	18.00
841-Elmer Fudd	2.40	6.00	12.00
842-The Nature of Things (Disney-Movie) ('57)-Jesse Marsh-a (TV series)	5.35	16.00	32.00
843-The First Americans (Disney) (TV)-Marsh-a	5.35	16.00	32.00
844-Gunsmoke (TV)-Photo-c	5.85	17.50	35.00
845-The Land Unknown (Movie)-Alex Toth-a	14.00	43.00	100.00
846-Gun Glory (Movie)-by Alex Toth; photo-c	12.00	36.00	85.00
847-Perri (squirrels) (Disney-Movie)-Two different covers published	3.60	9.00	18.00

	GD25	FN65	NM94
848-Marauder's Moon	5.35	16.00	32.00
849-Prince Valiant; by Bob Fuje	5.85	17.50	35.00
850-Buck Jones	4.00	10.00	20.00
851-The Story of Mankind (Movie) (1/58)-Hedy Lamarr & Vincent Price photo-c	6.70	20.00	40.00
852-Chilly Willy (2/58) (Lantz)	3.20	8.00	16.00
853-Pluto (Disney) (10/57)	3.60	9.00	18.00
854-The Hunchback of Notre Dame (Movie)-Photo-c	11.50	34.00	80.00
855-Broken Arrow (TV)-Photo-c	5.35	16.00	32.00
856-Buffalo Bill, Jr. (TV)-Photo-c	4.70	14.00	28.00
857-The Goofy Adventure Story (Disney) (11/57)	4.00	10.00	20.00
858-Daisy Duck's Diary (Disney) (11/57)	3.60	9.00	18.00
859-Topper and Neil (TV) (11/57)	3.60	9.00	18.00
860-Wyatt Earp (#1) (TV)-Manning-a; photo-c	11.00	32.00	75.00
861-Frosty the Snowman	3.60	9.00	18.00
862-The Truth About Mother Goose (Disney-Movie) (11/57)	5.85	17.50	35.00
863-Francis the Famous Talking Mule	4.00	10.00	20.00
864-The Littlest Snowman	4.00	11.00	22.00
865-Andy Burnett (TV) (Disney) (12/57)-Photo-c	8.35	25.00	50.00
866-Mars and Beyond (Disney-Movie)	5.35	16.00	32.00
867-Santa Claus Funnies	4.00	10.00	20.00
868-The Little People (12/57)	3.60	9.00	18.00
869-Old Yeller (Disney-Movie)-Photo-c	4.35	13.00	26.00
870-Little Beaver (1/58)	3.60	9.00	18.00
871-Curly Kayoe	4.00	10.00	20.00
872-Captain Kangaroo (TV)-Photo-c	13.00	40.00	90.00
873-Grandma Duck's Farm Friends (Disney)	4.20	12.50	25.00
874-Old Ironsides (Disney-Movie with Johnny Tremain) (1/58)	5.00	15.00	30.00
875-Trumpets West (Luke Short) (2/58)	4.00	11.00	22.00
876-Tales of Wells Fargo (#1)(TV)(2/58)-Photo-c	10.00	30.00	65.00
877-Frontier Doctor with Rex Allen (TV)-Alex Toth-a; photo-c	11.00	32.00	75.00
878-Peanuts (#1)-Schulz-c only (2/58)	13.00	40.00	90.00
879-Brave Eagle (TV) (2/58)-Photo-c	3.60	9.00	18.00
880-Steve Donovan, Western Marshal-Drucker-a (TV)-Photo-c	4.20	12.50	25.00
881-The Captain and the Kids (2/58)	3.60	9.00	18.00
882-Zorro (Disney)-1st Disney issue; by Alex Toth (TV) (2/58); photo-c	11.50	34.00	80.00
883-The Little Rascals (TV)	3.60	9.00	18.00
884-Hawkeye and the Last of the Mohicans (TV) (3/58); photo-c	6.70	20.00	40.00
885-Fury (TV) (3/58)-Photo-c	6.70	20.00	40.00
886-Bongo and Lumpjaw (Disney) (3/58)	3.60	9.00	18.00
887-The Hardy Boys (Disney) (TV)-Mickey Mouse Club (1/58)-Photo-c	8.35	25.00	50.00
888-Elmer Fudd (3/58)	2.40	6.00	12.00
889-Clint and Mac (Disney) (TV) (3/58)-Alex Toth-a; photo-c	10.00	30.00	65.00
890-Wyatt Earp (TV)-by Russ Manning; photo-c	7.50	22.50	45.00
891-Light in the Forest (Disney-Movie) (3/58)-Fess Parker photo-c	5.35	16.00	32.00
892-Maverick (#1) (TV) (4/58)-James Garner/Jack Kelly photo-c	14.00	43.00	100.00
893-Jim Bowie (TV)-Photo-c	5.85	17.50	35.00
894-Oswald the Rabbit (Lantz)	2.40	6.00	12.00
895-Wagon Train (#1) (TV) (3/58)-Photo-c	10.00	30.00	60.00
896-The Adventures of Tinker Bell (Disney)	5.35	16.00	32.00
897-Jiminy Cricket (Disney)	4.00	11.00	22.00
898-Silvertip (Max Brand)-Kinstler-a (5/58)	5.00	15.00	30.00
899-Goofy (Disney) (5/58)	4.00	10.00	20.00
900-Prince Valiant; by Bob Fuje	5.85	17.50	35.00
901-Little Hiawatha (Disney)	3.60	9.00	18.00

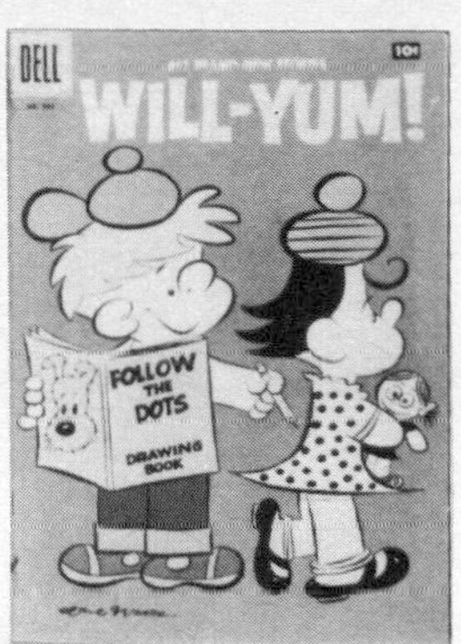

Four Color #902, © DELL

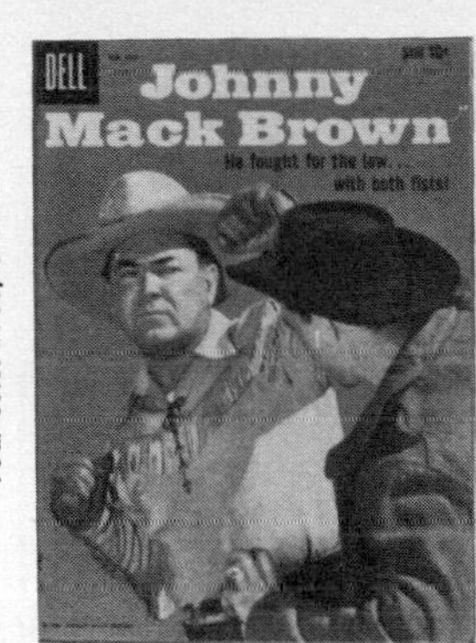

Four Color #963, © DELL

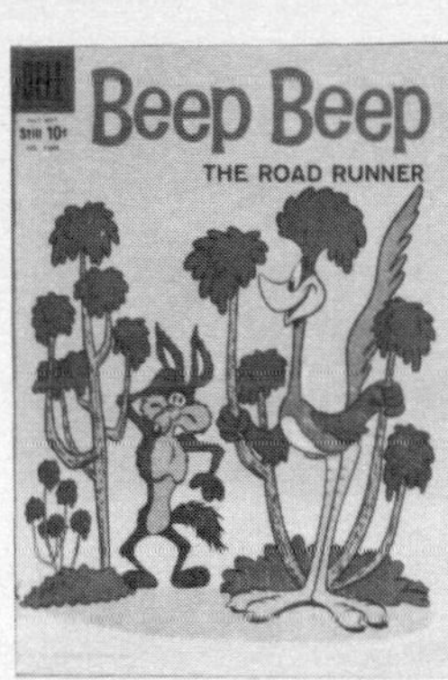

Four Color #1008, © Warner Bros.

	GD25	FN65	NM94
902-Will-Yum!	3.20	8.00	16.00
903-Dotty Dripple and Taffy	3.00	7.50	15.00
904-Lee Hunter, Indian Fighter	4.20	12.50	25.00
905-Annette (Disney) (TV) (5/58)-Mickey Mouse Club; Annette Funicello photo-c	16.00	48.00	110.00
906-Francis the Famous Talking Mule	4.00	10.00	20.00
907-Sugarfoot (#1) (TV)Toth-a; photo-c	12.00	36.00	85.00
908-The Little People and the Giant-Walt Scott (5/58)	3.60	9.00	18.00
909-Smitty	3.20	8.00	16.00
910-The Vikings (Movie)-Buscema-a; Kirk Douglas photo-c	10.00	30.00	65.00
911-The Gray Ghost (TV) (Movie)-Photo-c	8.35	25.00	50.00
912-Leave It to Beaver (#1) (TV)-Photo-c	19.00	56.00	130.00
913-The Left-Handed Gun (Movie) (7/58); Paul Newman photo-c	10.00	30.00	70.00
914-No Time for Sergeants (Movie)-Andy Griffith photo-c; Toth-a	10.00	30.00	60.00
915-Casey Jones (TV)-Alan Hale photo-c	6.70	20.00	40.00
916-Red Ryder Ranch Comics (7/58)	3.60	9.00	18.00
917-The Life of Riley (TV)-Photo-c	11.50	34.00	80.00
918-Beep Beep, the Roadrunner (#1) (7/58)-Published with two different back covers	9.15	27.50	55.00
919-Boots and Saddles (#1) (TV)-Photo-c	8.35	25.00	50.00
920-Zorro (Disney) (TV) (6/58)Toth-a; photo-c	11.50	34.00	80.00
921-Wyatt Earp (TV)-Manning-a; photo-c	7.50	22.50	45.00
922-Johnny Mack Brown by Russ Manning; photo-c	6.70	20.00	40.00
923-Timmy	2.80	7.00	14.00
924-Colt .45 (#1) (TV) (8/58)-Photo-c	10.00	30.00	60.00
925-Last of the Fast Guns (Movie) (8/58)-Photo-c	6.70	20.00	40.00
926-Peter Pan (Disney)-Reprint of #442	4.00	11.00	22.00
927-Top Gun (Luke Short) Buscema-a	4.00	11.00	22.00
928-Sea Hunt (#1) (9/58) (TV)-Lloyd Bridges photo-c	11.50	34.00	80.00
929-Brave Eagle (TV)-Photo-c	3.60	9.00	18.00
930-Maverick (TV) (7/58)-James Garner/Jack Kelly photo-c	9.15	27.50	55.00
931-Have Gun, Will Travel (#1) (TV)-Photo-c	10.00	30.00	70.00
932-Smokey the Bear (His Life Story)	4.70	14.00	28.00
933-Zorro (Disney)-by Alex Toth (TV) (9/58)	11.50	34.00	80.00
934-Restless Gun (#1) (TV)-Photo-c	10.00	30.00	70.00
935-King of the Royal Mounted	4.00	12.00	24.00
936-The Little Rascals (TV)	3.60	9.00	18.00
937-Ruff and Reddy (#1) (9/58) (TV) (1st Hanna-Barbera comic book)	11.00	32.00	75.00
938-Elmer Fudd (9/58)	2.40	6.00	12.00
939-Steve Canyon - not by Caniff	4.70	14.00	28.00
940-Lolly and Pepper (10/58)	2.80	7.00	14.00
941-Pluto (Disney) (10/58)	3.60	9.00	18.00
942-Pony Express (TV)	4.70	14.00	28.00
943-White Wilderness (Disney-Movie) (10/58)	5.35	16.00	32.00
944-The 7th Voyage of Sindbad (Movie) (9/58)-Buscema-a	13.00	40.00	90.00
945-Maverick (TV)-James Garner/Jack Kelly photo-c	9.15	27.50	55.00
946-The Big Country (Movie)-Photo-c	6.70	20.00	40.00
947-Broken Arrow (TV)-Photo-c (11/58)	5.35	16.00	32.00
948-Daisy Duck's Diary (Disney) (11/58)	3.60	9.00	18.00
949-High Adventure(Lowell Thomas')(TV)-Photo-c	5.35	16.00	32.00
950-Frosty the Snowman	3.60	9.00	18.00
951-The Lennon Sisters Life Story (TV)-Toth-a, 32 pgs.; photo-c	14.00	43.00	100.00
952-Goofy (Disney) (11/58)	4.00	10.00	20.00
953-Francis the Famous Talking Mule	4.00	10.00	20.00
954-Man in Space-Satellites (Disney-Movie)	5.35	16.00	32.00
955-Hi and Lois (11/58)	2.80	7.00	14.00
956-Ricky Nelson (#1) (TV)-Photo-c	23.00	70.00	160.00

	GD25	FN65	NM94
957-Buffalo Bee (#1) (TV)	9.15	27.50	55.00
958-Santa Claus Funnies	3.60	9.00	18.00
959-Christmas Stories-(Walt Scott's Little People) (1951-56 strip reprints)	3.60	9.00	18.00
960-Zorro (Disney) (TV) (12/58)-Toth art	11.50	34.00	80.00
961-Jace Pearson's Tales of the Texas Rangers (TV)-Spiegle-a; photo-c	5.00	15.00	30.00
962-Maverick (TV) (1/59)-James Garner/Jack Kelly photo-c	9.15	27.50	55.00
963-Johnny Mack Brown; photo-c	5.85	17.50	35.00
964-The Hardy Boys (TV) (Disney) 91/59)-Mickey Mouse Club; photo-c	8.35	25.00	50.00
965-Grandma Duck's Farm Friends (Disney)(1/59)	4.20	12.50	25.00
966-Tonka (starring Sal Mineo; Disney-Movie)-Photo-c	6.70	20.00	40.00
967-Chilly Willy (2/59) (Lantz)	3.20	8.00	16.00
968-Tales of Wells Fargo (TV)-Photo-c	8.35	25.00	50.00
969-Peanuts (2/59)	10.00	30.00	65.00
970-Lawman (#1) (TV)-Photo-c	10.00	30.00	65.00
971-Wagon Train (TV)-Photo-c	5.85	17.50	35.00
972-Tom Thumb (Movie)-George Pal (1/59)	11.00	32.00	75.00
973-Sleeping Beauty and the Prince(Disney)(5/59)	6.70	20.00	40.00
974-The Little Rascals (TV) (3/59)	3.60	9.00	18.00
975-Fury (TV)-Photo-c	6.70	20.00	40.00
976-Zorro (Disney) (TV)-Toth-a; photo-c	11.50	34.00	80.00
977-Elmer Fudd (3/59)	2.40	6.00	12.00
978-Lolly and Pepper	2.80	7.00	14.00
979-Oswald the Rabbit (Lantz)	2.40	6.00	12.00
980-Maverick (TV) (4-6/59)-James Garner/Jack Kelly photo-c	9.15	27.50	55.00
981-Ruff and Reddy (TV) (Hanna-Barbera)	8.35	25.00	50.00
982-The New Adventures of Tinker Bell (TV) (Disney)	5.35	16.00	32.00
983-Have Gun, Will Travel (TV) (4-6/59)-Photo-c	7.50	22.50	45.00
984-Sleeping Beauty's Fairy Godmothers (Disney)	6.70	20.00	40.00
985-Shaggy Dog (Disney-Movie)-Photo-c	5.35	16.00	32.00
986-Restless Gun (TV)-Photo-c	7.50	22.50	45.00
987-Goofy (Disney) (7/59)	4.00	10.00	20.00
988-Little Hiawatha (Disney)	3.60	9.00	18.00
989-Jiminy Cricket (Disney) (5-7/59)	4.00	11.00	22.00
990-Huckleberry Hound (#1)(TV)(Hanna-Barbera); 1st app. Huck, Yogi Bear, & Pixie & Dixie & Mr. Jinx	8.00	24.00	55.00
991-Francis the Famous Talking Mule	4.00	10.00	20.00
992-Sugarfoot (TV)-Toth-a; photo-c	12.00	36.00	85.00
993-Jim Bowie (TV)-Photo-c	5.85	17.50	35.00
994-Sea Hunt (TV)-Lloyd Bridges photo-c	8.35	25.00	50.00
995-Donald Duck Album (Disney) (5-7/59)	4.00	10.00	20.00
996-Nevada (Zane Grey)	4.00	10.00	20.00
997-Walt Disney Presents-Tales of Texas John Slaughter (#1) (TV) (Disney)-Photo-c	5.85	17.50	35.00
998-Ricky Nelson (TV)-Photo-c	23.00	70.00	160.00
999-Leave It to Beaver (TV)-Photo-c	17.00	50.00	115.00
1000-The Gray Ghost (Movie) (6-8/59)-Photo-c	8.35	25.00	50.00
1001-Lowell Thomas' High Adventure (TV) (8-10/59)-Photo-c	5.35	16.00	32.00
1002-Buffalo Bee (TV)	6.70	20.00	40.00
1003-Zorro (TV) (Disney)-Toth-a; photo-c	10.00	30.00	70.00
1004-Colt .45 (TV) (6-8/59)-Photo-c	7.50	22.50	45.00
1005-Maverick (TV)-James Garner/Jack Kelly photo-c	9.15	27.50	55.00
1006-Hercules (Movie)-Buscema-a	10.00	30.00	70.00
1007-John Paul Jones (Movie)-Robert Stack photo-c	5.35	16.00	32.00
1008-Beep Beep, the Road Runner (7-9/59)	5.00	15.00	30.00
1009-The Rifleman (#1) (TV)-Photo-c	16.00	48.00	110.00
1010-Grandma Duck's Farm Friends (Disney)-by Carl Barks	8.35	25.00	50.00

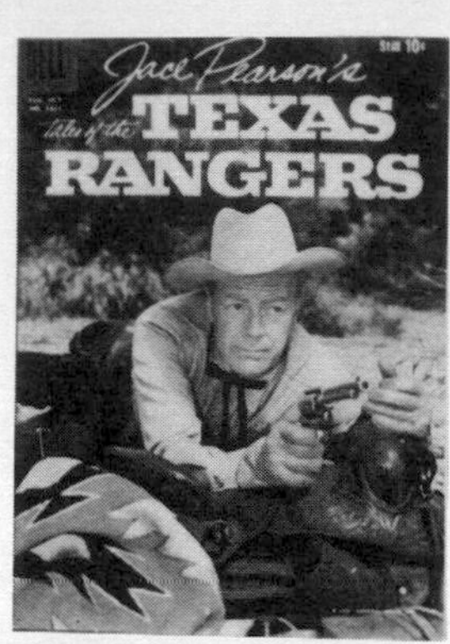

Four Color #1021, © DELL

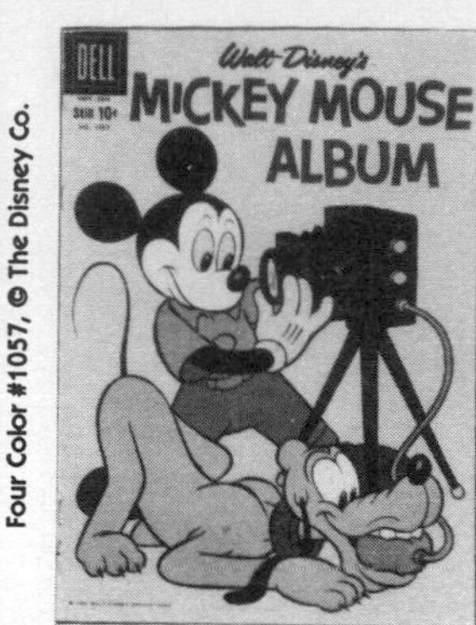

Four Color #1057, © The Disney Co.

Four Color #1108, © DELL

	GD25	FN65	NM94
1011-Buckskin (#1) (TV)-Photo-c	10.00	30.00	60.00
1012-Last Train from Gun Hill (Movie) (7/59)-Photo-c	8.35	25.00	50.00
1013-Bat Masterson (#1) (TV) (8/59)-Gene Barry photo-c	10.00	30.00	60.00
1014-The Lennon Sisters (TV)-Toth-a; photo-c	14.00	43.00	100.00
1015-Peanuts-Schulz-c	10.00	30.00	65.00
1016-Smokey the Bear Nature Stories	4.00	10.00	20.00
1017-Chilly Willy (Lantz)	3.20	8.00	16.00
1018-Rio Bravo (Movie)(6/59)-John Wayne; Toth-a; John Wayne, Dean Martin & Ricky Nelson photo-c	22.00	65.00	150.00
1019-Wagon Train (TV)-Photo-c	5.85	17.50	35.00
1020-Jungle Jim-McWilliams-a	3.20	8.00	16.00
1021-Jace Pearson's Tales of the Texas Rangers (TV)-Photo-c	4.70	14.00	28.00
1022-Timmy	2.80	7.00	14.00
1023-Tales of Wells Fargo (TV)-Photo-c	8.35	25.00	50.00
1024-Darby O'Gill and the Little People (Disney-Movie)-Toth-a; photo-c	9.15	27.50	55.00
1025-Vacation in Disneyland (8-10/59)-Carl Barks-a (Disney)	8.35	25.00	50.00
1026-Spin and Marty (TV) (Disney) (9-11/59)-Mickey Mouse Club; photo-c	6.70	20.00	40.00
1027-The Texan (#1)(TV)-Photo-c	7.50	22.50	45.00
1028-Rawhide (#1) (TV) (9-11/59)-Clint Eastwood photo-c; Tufts-a	24.00	70.00	165.00
1029-Boots and Saddles (TV) (9/59)-Photo-c	5.85	17.50	35.00
1030-Spanky and Alfalfa, the Little Rascals (TV)	3.60	9.00	18.00
1031-Fury (TV)-Photo-c	6.70	20.00	40.00
1032-Elmer Fudd	2.40	6.00	12.00
1033-Steve Canyon-not by Caniff; photo-c	4.70	14.00	28.00
1034-Nancy and Sluggo Summer Camp (9-11/59)	3.20	8.00	16.00
1035-Lawman (TV)-Photo-c	5.85	17.50	35.00
1036-The Big Circus (Movie)-Photo-c	5.35	16.00	32.00
1037-Zorro (Disney) (TV)-Tufts-a; Annette Funicello photo-c	12.00	36.00	85.00
1038-Ruff and Reddy (TV)(Hanna-Barbera)(1959)	8.35	25.00	50.00
1039-Pluto (Disney) (11-1/60)	3.60	9.00	18.00
1040-Quick Draw McGraw (#1) (TV) (Hanna-Barbera) (12-2/60)	10.00	30.00	60.00
1041-Sea Hunt (TV) (10-12/59)-Toth-a; Lloyd Bridges photo-c	10.00	30.00	60.00
1042-The Three Chipmunks (Alvin, Simon & Theodore) (#1) (TV) (10-12/59)	4.00	10.00	20.00
1043-The Three Stooges (#1)-Photo-c	17.00	52.00	120.00
1044-Have Gun, Will Travel (TV)-Photo-c	7.50	22.50	45.00
1045-Restless Gun (TV)-Photo-c	7.50	22.50	45.00
1046-Beep Beep, the Road Runner (11-1/60)	5.00	15.00	30.00
1047-Gyro Gearloose (#1) (Disney)-Barks-c/a	10.00	30.00	70.00
1048-The Horse Soldiers (Movie) (John Wayne)-Sekowsky-a	17.00	52.00	120.00
1049-Don't Give Up the Ship (Movie) (8/59)-Jerry Lewis photo-c	6.70	20.00	40.00
1050-Huckleberry Hound (TV) (Hanna-Barbera) (10-12/59)	6.70	20.00	40.00
1051-Donald in Mathmagic Land (Disney-Movie)	6.70	20.00	40.00
1052-Ben-Hur (Movie) (11/59)-Manning-a	10.00	30.00	60.00
1053-Goofy (Disney) (11-1/60)	4.00	10.00	20.00
1054-Huckleberry Hound Winter Fun (TV) (Hanna-Barbera) (12/59)	6.70	20.00	40.00
1055-Daisy Duck's Diary (Disney)-by Carl Barks (11-1/60)	6.70	20.00	40.00
1056-Yellowstone Kelly (Movie)-Clint Walker photo-c	5.35	16.00	32.00
1057-Mickey Mouse Album (Disney)	3.60	9.00	18.00
1058-Colt .45 (TV)-Photo-c	7.50	22.50	45.00
1059-Sugarfoot (TV)-Photo-c	8.35	25.00	50.00
1060-Journey to the Center of the Earth (Movie)-Pat Boone & James Mason photo-c	11.50	34.00	80.00

	GD25	FN65	NM94
1061-Buffalo Bee (TV)	6.70	20.00	40.00
1062-Christmas Stories (Walt Scott's Little People strip-r)	3.60	9.00	18.00
1063-Santa Claus Funnies	3.60	9.00	18.00
1064-Bugs Bunny's Merry Christmas (12/59)	4.70	14.00	28.00
1065-Frosty the Snowman	3.60	9.00	18.00
1066-77 Sunset Strip (#1) (TV)-Toth-a (1-3/60)-Photo-c	11.50	34.00	80.00
1067-Yogi Bear (#1) (TV) (Hanna-Barbera)	10.00	30.00	70.00
1068-Francis the Famous Talking Mule	4.00	10.00	20.00
1069-The FBI Story (Movie)-Toth-a; James Stewart photo-c	10.00	30.00	70.00
1070-Solomon and Sheba (Movie)-Sekowsky-a; photo-c	10.00	30.00	60.00
1071-The Real McCoys (#1) (TV) (1-3/60)-Toth-a; photo-c	11.50	34.00	80.00
1072-Blythe (Marge's)	4.70	14.00	28.00
1073-Grandma Duck's Farm Friends-Barks-c/a (Disney)	8.35	25.00	50.00
1074-Chilly Willy (Lantz)	3.20	8.00	16.00
1075-Tales of Wells Fargo (TV)-Photo-c	8.35	25.00	50.00
1076-The Rebel (#1) (TV)-Sekowsky-a; photo-c	10.00	30.00	70.00
1077-The Deputy (#1) (TV)-Buscema-a; Henry Fonda photo-c	11.50	34.00	80.00
1078-The Three Stooges (2-4/60)-Photo-c	10.00	30.00	60.00
1079-The Little Rascals (TV) (Spanky & Alfalfa)	3.60	9.00	18.00
1080-Fury (TV) (2-4/60)-Photo-c	6.70	20.00	40.00
1081-Elmer Fudd	2.40	6.00	12.00
1082-Spin and Marty (Disney) (TV)-Photo-c	6.70	20.00	40.00
1083-Men into Space (TV)-Anderson-a; photo-c	5.85	17.50	35.00
1084-Speedy Gonzales	3.20	8.00	16.00
1085-The Time Machine (H.G. Wells) (Movie) (3/60)-Alex Toth-a	14.00	43.00	100.00
1086-Lolly and Pepper	2.80	7.00	14.00
1087-Peter Gunn (TV)-Photo-c	10.00	30.00	60.00
1088-A Dog of Flanders (Movie)-Photo-c	5.00	15.00	30.00
1089-Restless Gun (TV)-Photo-c	7.50	22.50	45.00
1090-Francis the Famous Talking Mule	4.00	10.00	20.00
1091-Jacky's Diary (4-6/60)	5.35	16.00	32.00
1092-Toby Tyler (Disney-Movie)-Photo-c	5.00	15.00	30.00
1093-MacKenzie's Raiders (Movie)-Photo-c	6.70	20.00	40.00
1094-Goofy (Disney)	4.00	10.00	20.00
1095-Gyro Gearloose (Disney)-Barks-c/a	7.50	22.50	45.00
1096-The Texan (TV)-Rory Calhoun photo-c	7.50	22.50	45.00
1097-Rawhide (TV)-Manning-a; Clint Eastwood photo-c	16.00	48.00	110.00
1098-Sugarfoot (TV)-Photo-c	8.35	25.00	50.00
1099-Donald Duck Album (Disney) (5-7/60)-Barks-c	4.00	11.00	22.00
1100-Annette's Life Story (Disney-Movie) (5/60)-Annette Funicello photo-c	17.00	52.00	120.00
1101-Robert Louis Stevenson's Kidnapped (Disney-Movie) (5/60); photo-c	5.85	17.50	35.00
1102-Wanted: Dead or Alive (#1) (TV) (5-7/60); Steve McQueen photo-c	13.00	40.00	90.00
1103-Leave It to Beaver (TV)-Photo-c	17.00	50.00	115.00
1104-Yogi Bear Goes to College (TV) (Hanna-Barbera) (6-8/60)	7.50	22.50	45.00
1105-Gale Storm (Oh! Susanna) (TV)-Toth-a; photo-c	13.00	40.00	90.00
1106-77 Sunset Strip(TV)(6-8/60)-Toth-a; photo-c	10.00	30.00	60.00
1107-Buckskin (TV)-Photo-c	7.50	22.50	45.00
1108-The Troubleshooters (TV)-Keenan Wynn photo-c	5.85	17.50	35.00
1109-This Is Your Life, Donald Duck (Disney) (TV) (8-10/60)-Gyro flashback to WDC&S #141; origin Donald Duck(1st told)	17.00	52.00	120.00

Four Color #1118, © DELL

Four Color #1158, © DELL

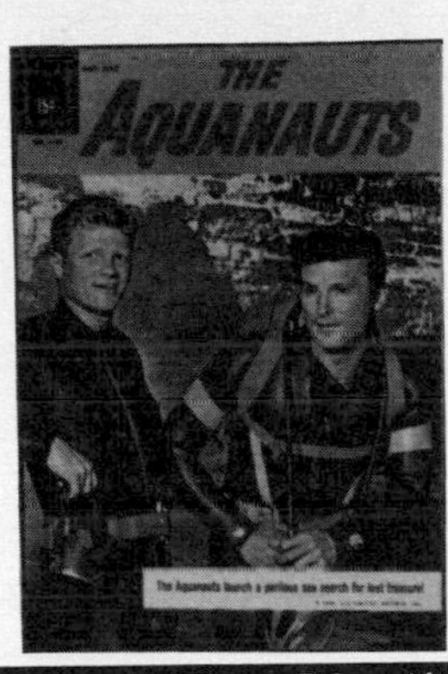

Four Color #1197, © DELL

	GD25	FN65	NM94
110-Bonanza (#1) (TV) (6-8/60)-Photo-c	31.00	95.00	220.00
111-Shotgun Slade (TV)-Photo-c	5.85	17.50	35.00
112-Pixie and Dixie and Mr. Jinks (#1) (TV) (Hanna-Barbera) (7-9/60)	6.70	20.00	40.00
113-Tales of Wells Fargo (TV)-Photo-c	8.35	25.00	50.00
114-Huckleberry Finn (Movie) (7/60)-Photo-c	5.35	16.00	32.00
115-Ricky Nelson (TV)-Manning-a; photo-c	18.00	54.00	125.00
116-Boots and Saddles (TV) (8/60)-Photo-c	5.85	17.50	35.00
117-Boy and the Pirates (Movie)-Photo-c	6.70	20.00	40.00
118-The Sword and the Dragon (Movie) (6/60)-Photo-c	8.35	25.00	50.00
119-Smokey the Bear Nature Stories	4.00	10.00	20.00
120-Dinosaurus (Movie)-Painted-c	7.50	22.50	45.00
121-Hercules Unchained (Movie) (8/60)-Crandall/Evans-a	10.00	30.00	60.00
122-Chilly Willy (Lantz)	3.20	8.00	16.00
123-Tombstone Territory (TV)-Photo-c	10.00	30.00	60.00
124-Whirlybirds (#1) (TV)-Photo-c	10.00	30.00	60.00
125-Laramie (#1) (TV)-Photo-c; G. Kane/Heath-a	9.15	27.50	55.00
126-Sundance (TV) (8-10/60)-Earl Holliman photo-c	10.00	30.00	60.00
127-The Three Stooges-Photo-c (8-10/60)	10.00	30.00	60.00
128-Rocky and His Friends (#1) (TV) (Jay Ward) (8-10/60)	26.00	78.00	180.00
129-Pollyanna (Disney-Movie)-Hayley Mills photo-c	10.00	30.00	65.00
130-The Deputy (TV)-Buscema-a; Henry Fonda photo-c	10.00	30.00	60.00
131-Elmer Fudd (9-11/60)	2.40	6.00	12.00
132-Space Mouse (Lantz) (8-10/60)	4.35	13.00	26.00
133-Fury (TV)-Photo-c	6.70	20.00	40.00
134-Real McCoys (TV)-Toth-a; photo-c	11.50	34.00	80.00
135-M.G.M.'s Mouse Musketeers (9-11/60)	2.40	6.00	12.00
136-Jungle Cat (Disney-Movie)-Photo-c	5.85	17.50	35.00
137-The Little Rascals (TV)	3.20	8.00	16.00
138-The Rebel (TV)-Photo-c	10.00	30.00	60.00
139-Spartacus (Movie) (11/60)-Buscema-a; photo-c	11.50	34.00	80.00
140-Donald Duck Album (Disney)	4.00	11.00	22.00
141-Huckleberry Hound for President (TV) (Hanna-Barbera) (10/60)	5.85	17.50	35.00
142-Johnny Ringo (TV)-Photo-c	8.35	25.00	50.00
143-Pluto (Disney) (11-1/61)	3.60	9.00	18.00
144-The Story of Ruth (Movie)-Photo-c	11.00	32.00	75.00
145-The Lost World (Movie)-Gil Kane-a; photo-c	11.50	34.00	80.00
146-Restless Gun (TV)-Photo-c; Wildey-a	7.50	22.50	45.00
147-Sugarfoot (TV)-Photo-c	8.35	25.00	50.00
148-I Aim at the Stars-the Wernher Von Braun Story (Movie) (11-1/61)-Photo-c	6.70	20.00	40.00
149-Goofy (Disney) (11-1/61)	4.00	10.00	20.00
150-Daisy Duck's Diary (Disney) (12-1/61) by Carl Barks	6.70	20.00	40.00
151-Mickey Mouse Album (Disney) (11-1/61)	3.60	9.00	18.00
152-Rocky and His Friends (TV) (Jay Ward) (12-2/61)	22.00	65.00	150.00
153-Frosty the Snowman	3.60	9.00	18.00
154-Santa Claus Funnies	3.60	9.00	18.00
155-North to Alaska (Movie) - John Wayne; photo-c	14.00	43.00	100.00
156-Walt Disney Swiss Family Robinson (Movie) (12/60)-Photo-c	5.85	17.50	35.00
157-Master of the World (Movie) (7/61)	5.85	17.50	35.00
158-Three Worlds of Gulliver (2 issues exist with different covers) (Movie)-Photo-c	5.35	16.00	32.00
159-77 Sunset Strip (TV)-Toth-a; photo-c	10.00	30.00	60.00
160-Rawhide (TV)-Clint Eastwood photo-c	16.00	48.00	110.00
161-Grandma Duck's Farm Friends (Disney) by Carl Barks (2-4/61)	8.35	25.00	50.00
1162-Yogi Bear Joins the Marines (TV) (Hanna-Barbera) (5-7/61)	7.50	22.50	45.00
1163-Daniel Boone (3-5/61); Marsh-a	5.85	17.50	35.00
1164-Wanted: Dead or Alive (TV)-Steve McQueen photo-c	11.00	32.00	75.00
1165-Ellery Queen (#1) (3-5/61)	11.00	32.00	75.00
1166-Rocky and His Friends (TV) (Jay Ward)	22.00	65.00	150.00
1167-Tales of Wells Fargo (TV)-Photo-c	7.50	22.50	45.00
1168-The Detectives (TV)-Robert Taylor photo-c	9.15	27.50	55.00
1169-New Adventures of Sherlock Holmes	16.00	48.00	110.00
1170-The Three Stooges (3-5/61)-Photo-c	10.00	30.00	60.00
1171-Elmer Fudd	2.40	6.00	12.00
1172-Fury (TV)-Photo-c	6.70	20.00	40.00
1173-The Twilight Zone (#1) (TV) (5/61)-Crandall/Evans c/a	18.00	54.00	125.00
1174-The Little Rascals (TV)	3.20	8.00	16.00
1175-M.G.M.'s Mouse Musketeers (3-5/61)	2.40	6.00	12.00
1176-Dondi (Movie)-Origin; photo-c	5.00	15.00	30.00
1177-Chilly Willy (Lantz) (4-6/61)	2.80	7.00	14.00
1178-Ten Who Dared (Disney-Movie) (12/60)-Painted-c	5.35	16.00	32.00
1179-The Swamp Fox (TV) (Disney)-Leslie Nielson photo-c	6.70	20.00	40.00
1180-The Danny Thomas Show (TV)-Toth-a; photo-c	16.00	48.00	110.00
1181-Texas John Slaughter (TV) (Disney) (4-6/61)-Photo-c	5.00	15.00	30.00
1182-Donald Duck Album (Disney) (5-7/61)	4.00	10.00	20.00
1183-101 Dalmatians (Disney-Movie) (3/61)	5.85	17.50	35.00
1184-Gyro Gearloose; Barks-c/a (Disney) (5-7/61) Two variations exist	7.50	22.50	45.00
1185-Sweetie Pie	4.00	10.00	20.00
1186-Yak Yak (#1) by Jack Davis (2 versions - one minus 3-pg. Davis-c/a)	9.15	27.50	55.00
1187-The Three Stooges (6-8/61)-Photo-c	10.00	30.00	60.00
1188-Atlantis, the Lost Continent (Movie) (5/61)-Photo-c	10.00	30.00	70.00
1189-Greyfriars Bobby (Disney-Movie) (11/61)-Photo-c	5.85	17.50	35.00
1190-Donald and the Wheel (Disney-Movie) (11/61); Barks-c	6.70	20.00	40.00
1191-Leave It to Beaver (TV)-Photo-c	17.00	50.00	115.00
1192-Ricky Nelson (TV)-Manning-a; photo-c	18.00	54.00	125.00
1193-The Real McCoys (TV) (6-8/61)-Photo-c	10.00	30.00	60.00
1194-Pepe (Movie) (4/61)-Photo-c	4.20	12.50	25.00
1195-National Velvet (#1) (TV)-Photo-c	6.70	20.00	40.00
1196-Pixie and Dixie and Mr. Jinks (TV) (Hanna-Barbera) (7-9/61)	5.00	15.00	30.00
1197-The Aquanauts (TV) (5-7/61)-Photo-c	6.70	20.00	40.00
1198-Donald in Mathmagic Land (Disney-Movie)-Reprint of #1051	6.70	20.00	40.00
1199-The Absent-Minded Professor (Disney-Movie) (4/61)-Photo-c	5.85	17.50	35.00
1200-Hennessey (TV) (8-10/61)-Gil Kane-a; photo-c	6.70	20.00	40.00
1201-Goofy (Disney) (8-10/61)	4.00	10.00	20.00
1202-Rawhide (TV)-Clint Eastwood photo-c	16.00	48.00	110.00
1203-Pinocchio (Disney) (3/62)	4.00	11.00	22.00
1204-Scamp (Disney)	2.40	6.00	12.00
1205-David and Goliath (Movie) (7/61)-Photo-c	5.85	17.50	35.00
1206-Lolly and Pepper (9-11/61)	2.80	7.00	14.00
1207-The Rebel (TV)-Sekowsky-a; photo-c	10.00	30.00	60.00
1208-Rocky and His Friends (Jay Ward) (TV)	22.00	65.00	150.00
1209-Sugarfoot (TV)-Photo-c (10-12/61)	8.35	25.00	50.00
1210-The Parent Trap (Disney-Movie) (8/61)-Hayley Mills photo-c	10.00	30.00	70.00

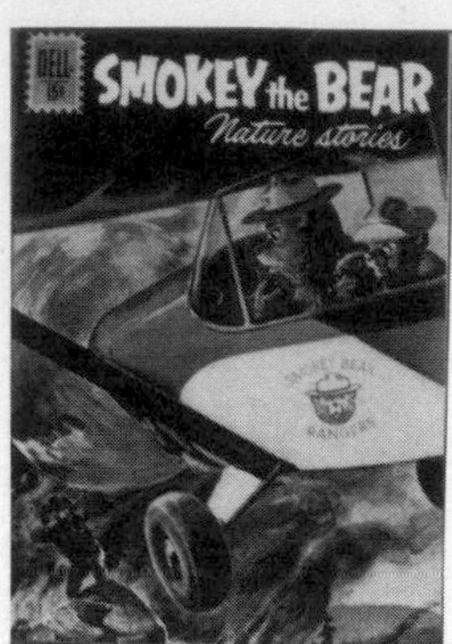

Four Color #1214, © DELL

Four Color #1264, © Hanna-Barbera

Four Color #1291, © DELL

	GD25	FN65	NM94
1211-77 Sunset Strip (TV)-Manning-a; photo-c	9.15	27.50	55.00
1212-Chilly Willy (Lantz) (7-9/61)	2.80	7.00	14.00
1213-Mysterious Island (Movie)-Photo-c	8.35	25.00	50.00
1214-Smokey the Bear	4.00	10.00	20.00
1215-Tales of Wells Fargo(TV)(10-12/61)-Photo-c	7.50	22.50	45.00
1216-Whirlybirds (TV)-Photo-c	8.35	25.00	50.00
1218-Fury (TV)-Photo-c	6.70	20.00	40.00
1219-The Detectives (TV)-Robert Taylor & Adam West photo-c	7.50	22.50	45.00
1220-Gunslinger (TV)-Photo-c	8.35	25.00	50.00
1221-Bonanza (TV) (9-11/61)-Photo-c	16.00	48.00	110.00
1222-Elmer Fudd (9-11/61)	2.40	6.00	12.00
1223-Laramie (TV)-Gil Kane-a; photo-c	5.85	17.50	35.00
1224-The Little Rascals (TV) (10-12/61)	3.20	8.00	16.00
1225-The Deputy (TV)-Henry Fonda photo-c	10.00	30.00	60.00
1226-Nikki, Wild Dog of the North (Disney-Movie) (9/61)-Photo-c	4.00	10.00	20.00
1227-Morgan the Pirate (Movie)-Photo-c	10.00	30.00	60.00
1229-Thief of Baghdad (Movie)-Evans-a; photo-c	10.00	30.00	70.00
1230-Voyage to the Bottom of the Sea (#1) (Movie)-Photo insert on-c	9.15	27.50	55.00
1231-Danger Man (TV) (9-11/61)-Patrick McGoohan photo-c	9.15	27.50	55.00
1232-On the Double (Movie)	5.00	15.00	30.00
1233-Tammy Tell Me True (Movie) (1961)	6.70	20.00	40.00
1234-The Phantom Planet (Movie) (1961)	5.85	17.50	35.00
1235-Mister Magoo (#1) (12-2/62)	8.35	25.00	50.00
1235-Mister Magoo (3-5/65) 2nd printing; reprint of 12-2/62 issue	4.70	14.00	28.00
1236-King of Kings (Movie)-Photo-c	8.35	25.00	50.00
1237-The Untouchables (#1) (TV)-Not by Toth; photo-c	14.00	43.00	100.00
1238-Deputy Dawg (TV)	10.00	30.00	70.00
1239-Donald Duck Album (Disney) (10-12/61)-Barks-c	4.00	11.00	22.00
1240-The Detectives (TV)-Tufts-a; Robert Taylor photo-c	7.50	22.50	45.00
1241-Sweetie Pie	4.00	10.00	20.00
1242-King Leonardo and His Short Subjects (#1) (TV) (11-1/62)	13.00	40.00	90.00
1243-Ellery Queen	8.35	25.00	50.00
1244-Space Mouse (Lantz) (11-1/62)	4.35	13.00	26.00
1245-New Adventures of Sherlock Holmes	16.00	48.00	110.00
1246-Mickey Mouse Album (Disney)	3.60	9.00	18.00
1247-Daisy Duck's Diary (Disney) (12-2/62)	3.60	9.00	18.00
1248-Pluto (Disney)	3.60	9.00	18.00
1249-The Danny Thomas Show (TV)-Manning-a; photo-c	16.00	48.00	110.00
1250-The Four Horsemen of the Apocalypse (Movie)-Photo-c	6.70	20.00	40.00
1251-Everything's Ducky (Movie) (1961)	5.35	16.00	32.00
1252-The Andy Griffith Show (TV)-Photo-c; 1st show aired 10/3/60	25.00	75.00	175.00
1253-Space Man (#1) (1-3/62)	7.50	22.50	45.00
1254-"Diver Dan" (#1) (TV) (2-4/62)-Photo-c	6.70	20.00	40.00
1255-The Wonders of Aladdin (Movie) (1961)	6.70	20.00	40.00
1256-Kona, Monarch of Monster Isle (#1) (2-4/62)-Glanzman-a	6.70	20.00	40.00
1257-Car 54, Where Are You? (#1) (TV) (3-5/62)-Photo-c	7.50	22.50	45.00
1258-The Frogmen (#1)-Evans-a	7.50	22.50	45.00
1259-El Cid (Movie) (1961)-Photo-c	6.70	20.00	40.00
1260-The Horsemasters (TV, Movie) (Disney) (12-2/62)-Annette Funicello photo-c	9.15	27.50	55.00
1261-Rawhide (TV)-Clint Eastwood photo-c	16.00	48.00	110.00
1262-The Rebel (TV)-Photo-c	10.00	30.00	60.00

	GD25	FN65	NM94
1263-77 Sunset Strip (TV) (12-2/62)-Manning-a; photo-c	9.15	27.50	55.00
1264-Pixie and Dixie and Mr. Jinks (TV) (Hanna-Barbera)	5.00	15.00	30.00
1265-The Real McCoys (TV)-Photo-c	10.00	30.00	60.00
1266-M.G.M.'s Spike and Tyke (12-2/62)	2.00	54.00	10.00
1267-Gyro Gearloose; Barks-c/a, 4 pgs. (Disney) (12-2/62)	5.85	17.50	35.00
1268-Oswald the Rabbit (Lantz)	2.40	6.00	12.00
1269-Rawhide (TV)-Clint Eastwood photo-c	16.00	48.00	110.00
1270-Bullwinkle and Rocky (#1) (TV) (Jay Ward) (3-5/62)	14.00	43.00	100.00
1271-Yogi Bear Birthday Party (TV) (Hanna-Barbera) (11/61)	5.35	16.00	32.00
1272-Frosty the Snowman	3.60	9.00	18.00
1273-Hans Brinker (Disney-Movie)-Photo-c	5.85	17.50	35.00
1274-Santa Claus Funnies (12/61)	3.60	9.00	18.00
1275-Rocky and His Friends (TV) (Jay Ward)	22.00	65.00	150.00
1276-Dondi	4.00	10.00	20.00
1278-King Leonardo and His Short Subjects (TV)	13.00	40.00	90.00
1279-Grandma Duck's Farm Friends (Disney)	4.00	11.00	22.00
1280-Hennessey (TV)-Photo-c	6.70	20.00	40.00
1281-Chilly Willy (Lantz) (4-6/62)	2.80	7.00	14.00
1282-Babes in Toyland (Disney-Movie) (1/62); Annette Funicello photo-c	10.00	30.00	65.00
1283-Bonanza (TV) (2-4/62)-Photo-c	16.00	48.00	110.00
1284-Laramie (TV)-Heath-a; photo-c	5.85	17.50	35.00
1285-Leave It to Beaver (TV)-Photo-c	17.00	50.00	115.00
1286-The Untouchables (TV)-Photo-c	14.00	43.00	100.00
1287-Man from Wells Fargo (TV)-Photo-c	4.70	14.00	28.00
1288-The Twilight Zone (TV) (4/62)-Crandall/Evans-c/a	11.00	32.00	75.00
1289-Ellery Queen	8.35	25.00	50.00
1290-M.G.M.'s Mouse Musketeers	2.40	6.00	12.00
1291-77 Sunset Strip (TV)-Manning-a; photo-c	9.15	27.50	55.00
1293-Elmer Fudd (3-5/62)	2.40	6.00	12.00
1294-Ripcord (TV)	6.70	20.00	40.00
1295-Mister Ed, the Talking Horse (#1) (TV) (3-5/62)-Photo-c	11.50	34.00	80.00
1296-Fury (TV) (3-5/62)-Photo-c	6.70	20.00	40.00
1297-Spanky, Alfalfa and the Little Rascals (TV)	3.20	8.00	16.00
1298-The Hathaways (TV)-Photo-c	5.35	16.00	32.00
1299-Deputy Dawg (TV)	10.00	30.00	70.00
1300-The Comancheros (Movie) (1961)-John Wayne	15.00	45.00	105.00
1301-Adventures in Paradise (TV) (2-4/62)	4.70	14.00	28.00
1302-Johnny Jason, Teen Reporter (2-4/62)	2.80	7.00	14.00
1303-Lad: A Dog (Movie)-Photo-c	4.00	12.00	24.00
1304-Nellie the Nurse (3-5/62)-Stanley-a	10.00	30.00	60.00
1305-Mister Magoo (3-5/62)	8.35	25.00	50.00
1306-Target: The Corruptors (#1) (TV) (3-5/62)-Photo-c	4.70	14.00	28.00
1307-Margie (TV) (3-5/62)	4.00	12.00	24.00
1308-Tales of the Wizard of Oz (TV) (3-5/62)	11.00	32.00	75.00
1309-87th Precinct (#1) (TV) (4-6/62)-Krigstein-a; photo-c	10.00	30.00	60.00
1310-Huck and Yogi Winter Sports (TV) (Hanna-Barbera) (3/62)	6.70	20.00	40.00
1311-Rocky and His Friends (TV) (Jay Ward)	22.00	65.00	150.00
1312-National Velvet (TV)-Photo-c	4.00	11.00	22.00
1313-Moon Pilot (Disney-Movie)-Photo-c	5.35	16.00	32.00
1328-The Underwater City (Movie) (1961)-Evans-a; photo-c	7.50	22.50	45.00
1330-Brain Boy (#1)-Gil Kane-a	8.35	25.00	50.00
1332-Bachelor Father (TV)	8.35	25.00	50.00
1333-Short Ribs (4-6/62)	5.35	16.00	32.00

Four Color #1349, © Hanna-Barbera

Four Star Spectacular #5, © DC

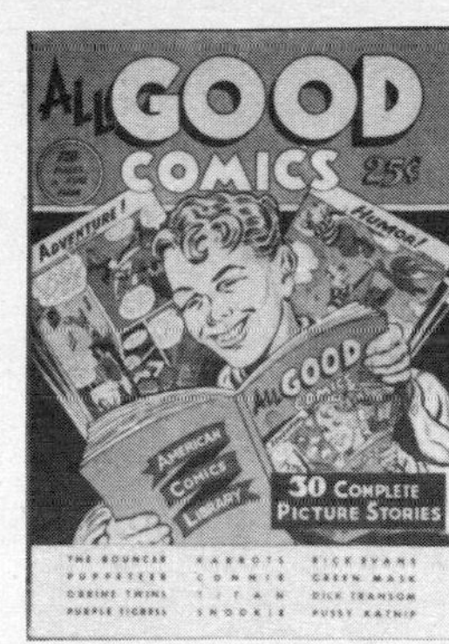

Fox Giants (All Good #1), © FOX

	GD25	FN65	NM94
335-Aggie Mack (4-6/62)	4.00	11.00	22.00
336-On Stage; not by Leonard Starr	5.00	15.00	30.00
337-Dr. Kildare (#1) (TV) (4-6/62)-Photo-c	6.70	20.00	40.00
341-The Andy Griffith Show (TV) (4-6/62)-Photo-c	25.00	75.00	175.00
348-Yak Yak (#2)-Jack Davis-c/a	8.35	25.00	50.00
349-Yogi Bear Visits the U.N. (TV) (Hanna-Barbera) (1/62)-Photo-c	10.00	30.00	65.00
350-Comanche (Disney-Movie)(1962)-Reprints 4-Color #966 (title change from "Tonka" to "Comanche") (4-6/62)-Sal Mineo photo-c	5.00	15.00	30.00
354-Calvin & the Colonel (#1) (TV) (4-6/62)	8.35	25.00	50.00

OTE: *Missing numbers probably do not exist.*

D MONKEY, THE (Leung's)(Value: cover or less)

OUR FAVORITES (Crime Must Pay the Penalty No. 33 on)
ept, 1941 - No. 32, Dec, 1947
ce Magazines

	GD25	FN65	NM94
1-Vulcan, Lash Lightning (formerly Flash Lightning in Sure-Fire), Magno the Magnetic Man & The Raven begin; flag-c	71.00	210.00	500.00
2-The Black Ace only app.	35.00	105.00	225.00
3-Last Vulcan	27.00	82.00	180.00
4,5: 4-The Raven & Vulcan end; Unknown Soldier begins (see Our Flag), ends #28. 5-Captain Courageous begins (5/42), ends #28 (moves over from Captain Courageous #6); not in #6	27.00	80.00	175.00
6-8: 6-The Flag app.; Mr. Risk begins (7/42)	22.00	68.00	150.00
9,11-Kurtzman-a; 11-Hitler, Mussolini, Hirohito-c; L.B. Cole-a	29.00	88.00	190.00
10-Classic Kurtzman-c/a	33.00	100.00	230.00
12-L.B. Cole-a	16.00	48.00	110.00
13-20: 18,20-Palais-c/a	14.00	42.00	95.00
21-No Unknown Soldier; The Unknown app.	10.00	30.00	70.00
22-26: 22-Captain Courageous drops costume. 23-Unknown Soldier drops costume. 25-29-Hap Hazard app. 26-Last Magno	10.00	30.00	70.00
27-32: 30-Funny-c begin (teen humor), end #32	9.15	27.50	55.00

OTE: ***Dave Berg** c 5. **Jim Mooney** a-6; c-1-3. **Palais** a-18-20; c-18-25. Torture chamber c-5.*

OUR HORSEMEN, THE (See The Crusaders)

OUR HORSEMEN OF THE APOCALYPSE, THE (See 4-Color No. 1250)

MOST (Foremost Boys No. 32-40; becomes Thrilling Crime Cases #41 on)
Vinter, 1941-42 - V8#5(#36), 9-10/49; #37, 11-12/49 - #40, 4-5/50
Novelty Publications/Star Publications No. 37-on

	GD25	FN65	NM94
V1#1-The Target by Sid Greene, The Cadet & Dick Cole begin with origins retold; produced by Funnies Inc.; quarterly issues begin, end V6#3	71.00	210.00	475.00
2-Last Target (Spr/42)	33.00	100.00	220.00
3-Flag-c	28.00	85.00	190.00
4-1pg. Dr. Seuss (signed) (Aut/42)	23.00	68.00	150.00
V2#1-4: 4-Hitler, Tojo & Mussolini app. as pumpkins on-c	6.70	20.00	40.00
V3#1-4	6.70	20.00	40.00
V4#1-4	5.00	15.00	30.00
V5#1-5: 1-The Target & Targeteers app.	4.35	13.00	26.00
V6#1-4,6: 1-White Rider & Super Horse begin	4.35	13.00	26.00
5-L. B. Cole-c	6.00	18.00	36.00
V7#1,3,5, V8#1	4.35	13.00	26.00
2,4,6-L. B. Cole-c. 6-Last Dick Cole	6.35	19.00	38.00
V8#2,3,5-L. B. Cole-c/a	8.35	25.00	50.00
4-L. B. Cole-a	5.00	15.00	30.00
37-40: 38-Johnny Weismuller life story & Jim Braddock (boxer) life story. 38-40-L.B. Cole-c	5.00	15.00	30.00
Accepted Reprint 38-40 (nd). 40-r/Johnny Weismuller life story; all have L.B. Cole-c	4.00	12.00	24.00

OUR-STAR BATTLE TALES
Feb-Mar, 1973 - No. 5, Nov-Dec, 1973
National Periodical Publications

	GD25	FN65	NM94
1-5: All reprints			1.00

NOTE: ***Drucker** r-1, 3-5. **Heath** r-2, 5; c-1. **Krigstein** r-5. **Kubert** r-4; c-2.*

FOUR STAR SPECTACULAR
Mar-Apr, 1976 - No. 6, Jan-Feb, 1977
National Periodical Publications

	GD25	FN65	NM94
1-6: Reprints in all. 2-Infinity cover			1.00

NOTE: *All contain DC Superhero reprints. #1 has 68 pages; #2-6, 52 pages. #1, 4-Hawkman app.; #2-Kid Flash app.; #3-Green Lantern app; #2, 4, 5-Wonder Woman, Superboy app; #5-Green Arrow, Vigilante app; #6-Blackhawk G.A.-r.*

FOUR TEENERS (Formerly Crime Must Pay The Penalty; Dotty No. 35 on)
No. 34, April, 1948 (52 pgs.)
A. A. Wyn

	GD25	FN65	NM94
34-Teen-age comic; Dotty app.; Curly & Jerry continue from Four Favorites	4.00	10.00	20.00

FOX AND THE CROW (Stanley & His Monster No. 109 on) (See Comic Cavalcade & Real Screen Comics)
Dec-Jan, 1951-52 - No. 108, Feb-Mar, 1968
National Periodical Publications

	GD25	FN65	NM94
1	79.00	235.00	550.00
2(Scarce)	38.00	115.00	265.00
3-5	24.00	72.00	165.00
6-10	16.00	50.00	115.00
11-20	11.50	34.00	80.00
21-40: 22-Last precode issue (2/55)	8.35	25.00	50.00
41-60	5.85	17.50	35.00
61-80	4.00	12.00	24.00
81-94	3.20	8.00	16.00
95-Stanley & His Monster begins(origin)(1st app?)	4.00	10.00	20.00
96-99,101-108	1.80	4.50	9.00
100 (10-11/66)	2.40	6.00	12.00

NOTE: *Many covers by **Mort Drucker**.*

FOX AND THE HOUND, THE (Disney)
Aug, 1981 - No. 3, Oct, 1981
Whitman Publishing Co.

	GD25	FN65	NM94
11292(#1),2,3-Based on animated movie			1.00

FOX GIANTS
1944 - 1950 (132 - 196 pgs.)
Fox Features Syndicate

	GD25	FN65	NM94
Album of Crime nn(1949, 132p)	31.00	95.00	220.00
Album of Love nn(1949, 132p)	28.00	85.00	195.00
All Famous Crime Stories nn('49, 132p)	31.00	95.00	220.00
All Good Comics 1(1944, 132p)(R.W. Voigt)-The Bouncer, Purple Tigress, Rick Evans, Puppeteer, Green Mask; Infinity-c	24.00	73.00	170.00
All Great nn(1944, 132p)-Capt. Jack Terry, Rick Evans, Jaguar Man	24.00	73.00	170.00
All Great nn(Chicago Nite Life News)(1945, 132p)-Green Mask, Bouncer, Puppeteer, Rick Evans, Rocket Kelly	28.00	85.00	195.00
All-Great Confessions nn(1949, 132p)	26.00	77.00	180.00
All Great Crime Stories nn('49, 132p)	30.00	90.00	210.00
All Great Jungle Adventures nn('49, 132p)	36.00	110.00	250.00
All Real Confession Magazine 3 (3/49, 132p)	26.00	77.00	180.00
All Real Confession Magazine 4 (4/49, 132p)	26.00	77.00	180.00
All Your Comics 1(1944, 132p)-The Puppeteer, Red Robbins, & Merciless the Sorcerer	27.00	81.00	190.00
Almanac Of Crime nn(1948, 148p)	31.00	95.00	220.00
Almanac Of Crime 1(1950, 132p)	30.00	90.00	210.00
Book Of Love nn(1950, 132p)	25.00	75.00	175.00
Burning Romances 1(1949, 132p)	30.00	90.00	210.00
Crimes Incorporated nn(1950, 132p)	28.00	85.00	195.00
Daring Love Stories nn(1950, 132p)	25.00	75.00	175.00
Everybody's Comics 1(1944, 196p)-The Green Mask, The Puppeteer, The Bouncer; (50 cents)	29.00	86.00	200.00
Everybody's Comics 1(1946, 196p)-Green Lama, The Puppeteer	23.00	70.00	160.00

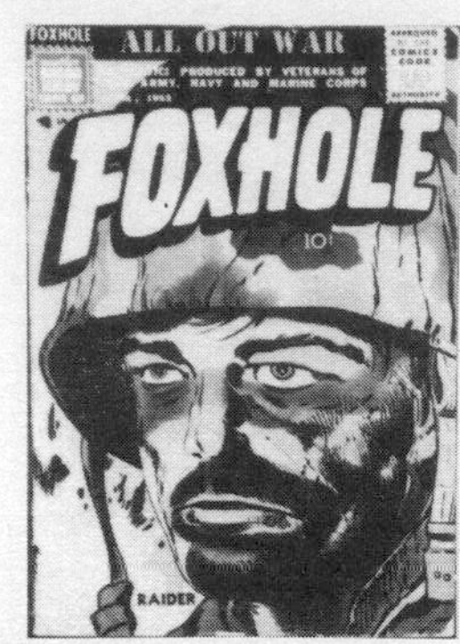

Foxhole #4, © PRIZE

Foxy Fagan #7, © Dearfield Publ.

Frank Buck #70, © FOX

	GD25	FN65	NM94
Everybody's Comics 1(1946, 196p)-Same as 1945 Ribtickler	19.00	57.00	130.00
Everybody's Comics nn(1947, 132p)-Jo-Jo, Purple Tigress, Cosmo Cat, Bronze Man	22.00	67.00	155.00
Famous Love nn(1950, 132p)	25.00	75.00	175.00
Exciting Romance Stories nn(1949, 132p)	25.00	75.00	175.00
Intimate Confessions nn(1950, 132p)	25.00	75.00	175.00
Journal Of Crime nn(1949, 132p)	30.00	90.00	210.00
Love Problems nn(1949, 132p)	26.00	80.00	185.00
Love Thrills nn(1950, 132p)	26.00	80.00	185.00
March of Crime nn('48, 132p)-Female w/rifle-c	28.00	85.00	195.00
March of Crime nn('49, 132p)-Cop w/pistol-c	28.00	85.00	195.00
March of Crime nn(1949, 132p)-Coffin & man w/machine-gun-c	28.00	85.00	195.00
Revealing Love Stories nn(1950, 132p)	25.00	75.00	175.00
Ribtickler nn(1945, 196p, 50¢)-Chicago Nite Life News; Marvel Mutt, Cosmo Cat, Flash Rabbit, The Nebbs app.	22.00	67.00	155.00
Romantic Thrills nn(1950, 132p)	25.00	75.00	175.00
Secret Love nn(1949, 132p)	25.00	75.00	175.00
Secret Love Stories nn(1949, 132p)	25.00	75.00	175.00
Strange Love nn(1950, 132p)-Photo-c	30.00	90.00	210.00
Sweetheart Scandals nn(1950, 132p)	25.00	75.00	175.00
Teen-Age Love nn(1950, 132p)	25.00	75.00	175.00
Throbbing Love nn(1950, 132p)-Photo-c; used in **POP**, pg. 107	30.00	90.00	210.00
Truth About Crime nn(1949, 132p)	30.00	90.00	210.00
Variety Comics 1(1946, 132p)-Blue Beetle, Jungle Jo	24.00	73.00	170.00
Variety Comics nn(1950, 132p)-Jungle Jo, My Secret Affair(w/Harrison/Wood-a), Crimes by Women & My Story	23.00	70.00	160.00
Western Roundup nn('50, 132p)-Hoot Gibson; Cody of the Pony Express app.	26.00	80.00	185.00

NOTE: *Each of the above usually contain four remaindered Fox books minus covers. Since these missing covers often had the first page of the first story, most Giants therefore are incomplete. Approximate values are listed. Books with appearances of Phantom Lady, Rulah, Jo-Jo, etc. could bring more.*

FOXHOLE (Becomes Never Again #8?)
9-10/54 - No. 4, 3-4/55; No. 5, 7/55 - No. 7, 3/56
Mainline/Charlton Comics No. 5 on

	GD25	FN65	NM94
1-Classic Kirby-c	13.00	40.00	90.00
2-Kirby-c/a(2)	11.00	32.00	75.00
3-5-Kirby-c only	6.70	20.00	40.00
6-Kirby-c/a(2)	10.00	30.00	7.00
7	2.80	7.00	14.00
Super Reprints #10-12,15-18: 10-r/? 11,12,18-r/Foxhole #1,2,3. 15,16-r/United States Marines #5,8. 17-r/Monty Hall #?	1.00	2.50	5.00

NOTE: ***Kirby** a(r)-Super #11, 12. **Powell** a(r)-Super #15, 16.*

FOXY FAGAN COMICS
Dec, 1946 - No. 7, Summer, 1948
Dearfield Publishing Co.

	GD25	FN65	NM94
1-Foxy Fagan & Little Buck begin	10.00	30.00	60.00
2	5.00	15.00	30.00
3-7: 6-Rocket ship-c	4.00	12.00	24.00

FOXY GRANDPA (Also see The Funnies, 1st series)
1901 - 1916 (Hardcover; strip reprints)
N. Y. Herald/Frederick A. Stokes Co./M. A. Donahue & Co./Bunny Publ.
(L. R. Hammersly Co.)

	GD25	FN65	VF82
1901-9x15" in color-N. Y. Herald	58.00	175.00	380.00
1902- "Latest Larks of...," 32 pgs. in color, 9-1/2x15-1/2"	50.00	150.00	330.00
1902- "The Many Advs. of...," 9x12", 148 pgs. in color (Hammersly)	58.00	175.00	380.00
1903- "Latest Advs.," 9x15", 24 pgs. in color, Hammersly Co.	50.00	150.00	330.00
1903- "...'s New Advs.," 10x15, 32 pgs. in color, Stokes	50.00	150.00	330.00
1904- "Up to Date," 10x15", 28 pgs. in color, Stokes	50.00	150.00	330.00
1905- "& Flip Flaps," 9-1/2x15-1/2", 52 pgs., in color	50.00	150.00	330.00
1905- "The Latest Advs. of," 9x15", 28, 52, & 66 pgs, in color, M.A. Donohue Co.; re-issue of 1902 issue	33.00	100.00	225.00
1905- "Merry Pranks of," 9-1/2x15-1/2", 52 pgs. in color, Donahue	33.00	100.00	225.00
1905- "Latest Larks of," 9-1/2x15-1/2", 52 pgs. in color, Donahue; re-issue of 1902 issue	33.00	100.00	225.00
1905- "Latest Larks of," 9-1/2x15-1/2", 24 pg. edition in color, Donahue; re-issue of 1902 issue	33.00	100.00	225.00
1906- "Frolics," 10x15", 30 pgs. in color, Stokes	33.00	100.00	225.00
1907	33.00	100.00	225.00
1908?- "Triumphs," 10x15"	33.00	100.00	225.00
1908?- "...& Little Brother," 10x15"	33.00	100.00	225.00
1911- "Latest Tricks," r-1910,1911 Sundays in color-Stokes Co.	33.00	100.00	225.00
1914-(9-1/2x15-1/2", 24 pgs.)-6 color cartoons/page, Bunny Publ.	29.00	88.00	190.00
1916- "Merry Book," 10x15", 30 pgs. in color, Stokes	29.00	88.00	190.00

FOXY GRANDPA SPARKLETS SERIES
1908 (6-1/2x7-3/4"; 24 pgs. in color)
M. A. Donahue & Co.

	GD25	FN65	VF82
"... Rides the Goat," "...& His Boys," "...Playing Ball," "...Fun on the Farm," "...Fancy Shooting," "...Show the Boys Up Sports," "Plays Santa Claus" each....	39.00	120.00	275.00
900-... "Playing Ball;" Bunny illos; 8 pgs., linen like pgs., no date	29.00	85.00	200.00

FRACTURED FAIRY TALES (TV)
October, 1962 (Jay Ward)
Gold Key

	GD25	FN65	NM94
1 (10022-210)-From Bullwinkle TV show	11.00	32.00	75.00

FRAGGLE ROCK (TV)
Apr, 1985 - No. 8, Sept, 1986; V2#1, Apr, 1988 - No. 6, Sept, 1988
Star Comics (Marvel)/Marvel V2#1 on

	GD25	FN65	NM94
1-8 (75 cents)			1.00
V2#1-6($1.00): Reprints 1st series			1.00

FRANCIS, BROTHER OF THE UNIVERSE
1980 (75 cents) (52 pgs.) (One Shot)
Marvel Comics Group

	GD25	FN65	NM94
nn-Buscema/Marie Severin-a; story of Francis Bernadone celebrating his 800th birthday in 1982			1.00

FRANCIS THE FAMOUS TALKING MULE (All based on movie) (See 4-Color #335, 465, 501, 547, 579, 621, 655, 698, 710, 745, 810, 863, 906, 953, 991, 1068, 1090)

FRANK BUCK (Formerly My True Love)
No. 70, May, 1950 - No. 3, Sept, 1950
Fox Features Syndicate

	GD25	FN65	NM94
70-Wood a(p)(3 stories)-Photo-c	13.00	40.00	90.00
71,3: 71-Wood a? (9 pgs.). 71,3-Photo/painted-c	10.00	30.00	60.00

NOTE: *Based on "Bring 'Em Back Alive" TV show.*

FRANKENSTEIN (See Dracula, Movie Classics & Werewolf)
Aug-Oct, 1964; No. 2, Sept, 1966 - No. 4, Mar, 1967
Dell Publishing Co.

	GD25	FN65	NM94
1(12-283-410)(1964)	2.15	6.50	15.00
2-Intro. & origin super-hero character (9/66)	1.50	3.75	9.00
3,4	1.20	3.00	7.00

FRANKENSTEIN (The Monster of...; also see Monsters Unleashed #2, Power Record Comics, Psycho & Silver Surfer #7)
Jan, 1973 - No. 18, Sept, 1975

Frankenstein Comics #26, © PRIZE

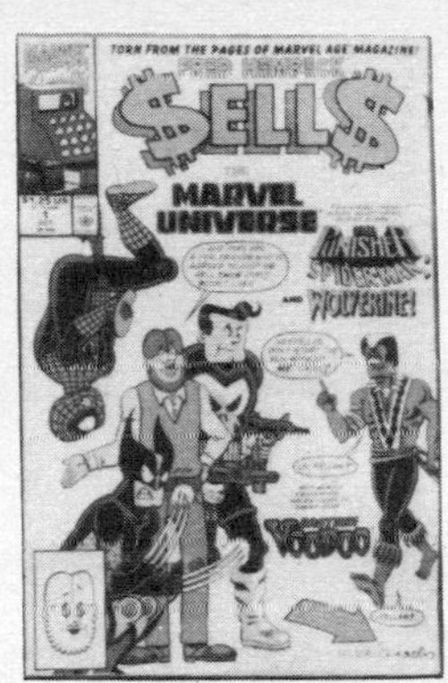

Fred Hembeck Sells the Marvel Universe #1, © MEG

Freex #2, © Malibu

	GD25	FN65	NM94

Marvel Comics Group

1-Ploog-c/a begins, ends #6	2.15	6.50	15.00
2-5,8,9: 8,9-Dracula app. 9-Death of Dracula	1.40	3.50	8.50
6,7,10	1.00	2.50	5.50
11-18		1.20	3.00

NOTE: **Adkins** c-17i. **Buscema** a-7-10p. **Ditko** a-12r. **G. Kane** c-15p. **Orlando** a-8r. **Ploog** a-1-3, 4p, 5p, 6; c-1-6. **Wrightson** c-18i.

FRANKENSTEIN COMICS (Also See Prize Comics)
Sum, 1945 - V5#5(#33), Oct-Nov, 1954
Prize Publications (Crestwood/Feature)

1-Frankenstein begins by Dick Briefer (origin); Frank Sinatra parody	57.00	170.00	400.00
2	29.00	85.00	200.00
3-5	22.00	65.00	150.00
6-10. 7-S&K a(r)/Headline Comics. 8(7-8/47)-Superman satire	18.00	54.00	125.00
11-17(1-2/49)-11-Boris Karloff parody-c/story. 17-Last humor issue	15.00	45.00	105.00
18(3/52)-New origin, horror series begins	18.00	54.00	125.00
19,20(V3#4, 8-9/52)	12.00	36.00	85.00
21(V3#5), 22(V3#6)	11.00	32.00	75.00
23(V4#1) - #28(V4#6)	11.00	32.00	75.00
29(V5#1) - #33(V5#5)	11.00	32.00	75.00

NOTE: **Briefer** c/a-all. **Meskin** a-21, 29.

FRANKENSTEIN, JR. (...& the Impossibles) (TV)
January, 1967 (Hanna-Barbera)
Gold Key

1-Super hero	2.15	6.50	15.00

FRANK FRAZETTA'S THUN'DA TALES (Fantagrahics)(Value: cover or less)

FRANK FRAZETTA'S UNTAMED LOVE (Fantagraphics)(Value: cover or less)

FRANKIE COMICS (...& Lana No. 13-15) (Formerly Movie Tunes; becomes Frankie Fuddle No. 16 on)
No. 4, Wint, 1946-47 - No. 15, June, 1949
Marvel Comics (MgPC)

4-Mitzi, Margie, Daisy app.	9.15	27.50	55.00
5-9	5.00	15.00	30.00
10-15: 13-Anti-Wertham editorial	4.00	12.00	24.00

FRANKIE DOODLE (See Single Series #7 and Sparkler, both series)

FRANKIE FUDDLE (Formerly Frankie & Lana)
No. 16, Aug, 1949 - No. 17, Nov, 1949
Marvel Comics

16,17	4.35	13.00	26.00

FRANK LUTHER'S SILLY PILLY COMICS (See Jingle Dingle...)
1950 (10 cents)
Children's Comics (Maltex Cereal)

1-Characters from radio, records, & TV	4.00	12.00	24.00

FRANK MERRIWELL AT YALE (Speed Demons No. 5 on?)
June, 1955 - No. 4, Jan, 1956 (Also see Shadow Comics)
Charlton Comics

1	4.00	10.00	20.00
2-4	2.80	7.00	14.00

FRANTIC (Magazine) (See Ratfink & Zany)
Oct, 1958 - V2#2, April, 1959 (Satire)
Pierce Publishing Co.

V1#1,2	4.00	11.00	22.00
V2#1,2: 1-Burgos-a, Severin-c/a; Powell-a?	3.00	7.50	15.00

FREAKS' ARMOUR (Dark Horse)(Value: cover or less)

FRECKLES AND HIS FRIENDS (See Crackajack Funnies, Famous Comics Cartoon Book, Honeybee Birdwhistle... & Red Ryder)

FRECKLES AND HIS FRIENDS
No. 5, 11/47 - No. 12, 8/49; 11/55 - No. 4, 6/56
Standard Comics/Argo

5-Reprints	5.00	15.00	30.00
6-12-Reprints. 7-9-Airbrush-c (by Schomburg?). 11-Lingerie panels	3.60	9.00	18.00

NOTE: *Some copies of No. 8 & 9 contain a printing oddity. The negatives were elongated in the engraving process, probably to conform to page dimensions on the filler pages. Those pages only look normal when viewed at a 45 degree angle.*

1(Argo,'55)-Reprints (NEA Service)	4.00	10.00	20.00
2-4	2.80	7.00	14.00

FREDDY (Formerly My Little Margie's Boy Friends) (Also see Blue Bird)
V2#12, June, 1958 - No. 47, Feb, 1965
Charlton Comics

V2#12	2.40	6.00	12.00
13-15	1.20	3.00	6.00
16-47	.80	2.00	4.00
Schiff's Shoes Presents... #1 (1959)-Giveaway	.80	2.00	4.00

FREDDY
May-July, 1963 - No. 3, Oct-Dec, 1964
Dell Publishing Co.

1-3	1.40	3.50	7.00

FREDDY KRUEGER'S A NIGHTMARE ON ELM STREET (Marvel)(Value: cover or less)

FREDDY'S DEAD: THE FINAL NIGHTMARE (Innovation)(Value: cover or less)

FRED HEMBECK DESTROYS THE MARVEL UNIVERSE
July, 1989 ($1.50, one-shot)
Marvel Comics

1-Punisher app.; Staton-i (5 pgs.)			1.50

FRED HEMBECK SELLS THE MARVEL UNIVERSE
Oct, 1990 ($1.25, color, one-shot)
Marvel Comics

1-Punisher, Wolverine parodies; Hembeck/Austin-c			1.25

FREE COMICS TO YOU FROM... (name of shoe store) (Has clown on cover & another with a rabbit) (Like comics from Weather Bird & Edward's Shoes)
Circa 1956, 1960-61
Shoe Store Giveaway

Contains a comic bound with new cover - several combinations possible; some Harvey titles known. Contents determines price.

FREEDOM AGENT (Also see John Steele)
April, 1963 (12¢)
Gold Key

1 (10054-304)-Painted-c	1.65	4.00	10.00

FREEDOM FIGHTERS (See Justice League of America #107,108)
Mar-Apr, 1976 - No. 15, July-Aug, 1978
National Periodical Publications/DC Comics

1-Uncle Sam, The Ray, Black Condor, Doll Man, Human Bomb, & Phantom Lady begin (all former Quality characters)	.40	1.00	2.00
2-15: 7-1st app. Crusaders. 10-Origin Doll Man; Cat-Man-c/story (4th app; 1st revival since Det. #325). 11-Origin The Ray. 12-Origin Firebrand. 13-Origin Black Condor. 14,15-Batgirl & Batwoman app. 15-Origin Phantom Lady			1.00

NOTE: **Buckler** c-5-11p, 13p, 14p.

FREEDOM TRAIN
1948 (Giveaway)
Street & Smith Publications

nn-Powell-c	3.60	9.00	18.00

FREEJACK (Now)(Value: cover or less)

FREEX
July, 1993 - Present ($1.95, color)
Malibu Comics

1-3,5,6: 1-Polybagged w/trading card		.80	2.00

The Friendly Ghost Casper #2, © Paramount

Fritzi Ritz #6, © UFS

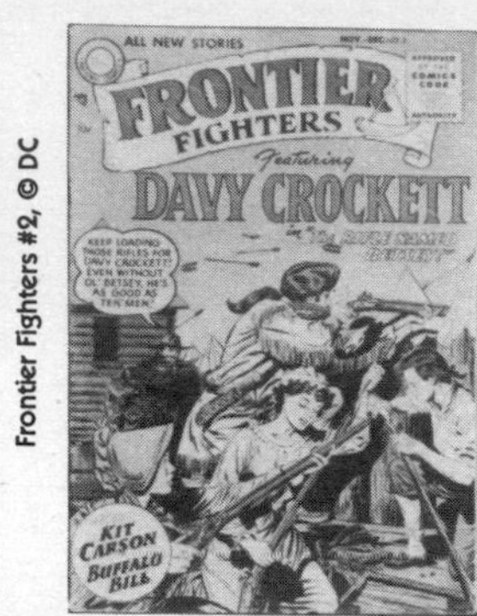

Frontier Fighters #2, © DC

GD25 FN65 NM94

1-Holographic cover edition 40.00
1-Ultra 5,000 limited silver ink-c 35.00
4-($2.50, 40 pgs.)-Rune flip-c/story by B. Smith (3 pgs.) 1.00 2.50

FRENZY (Magazine) (Satire)
April, 1958 - No. 6, March, 1959
Picture Magazine

	GD25	FN65	NM94
1	4.00	12.00	24.00
2-6	3.00	7.50	15.00

FRIDAY FOSTER
October, 1972
Dell Publishing Co.

	GD25	FN65	NM94
1	2.80	7.00	14.00

FRIENDLY GHOST, CASPER, THE (Becomes Casper... #254 on)
Aug, 1958 - No. 224, Oct, 1982; No. 225, Oct, 1986 - No. 253, 1989
Harvey Publications

	GD25	FN65	NM94
1-Infinity-c	20.00	60.00	140.00
2	10.00	30.00	65.00
3-10: 6-X-Mas-c	5.35	16.00	32.00
11-20: 18-X-Mas-c	4.00	11.00	22.00
21-30	2.40	6.00	12.00
31-50	1.60	4.00	8.00
51-100: 54-X-Mas-c	1.20	3.00	6.00
101-159	.80	2.00	4.00
160-163: All 52 pg. Giants	.90	2.25	4.50
164-237: 173,179,185-Cub Scout Specials. 230-X-mas-c. 232-Valentine's-c		.80	2.00
238-253: 238-Begin $1.00-c. 238,244-Halloween-c. 243-Last new material			1.00
American Dental Assoc. giveaway-Small size (1967, 16 pgs.)	.80	2.00	4.00

FRIGHT
June, 1975 (August on inside)
Atlas/Seaboard Periodicals

	GD25	FN65	NM94
1-Origin The Son of Dracula; Frank Thorne-c/a		.50	1.00

FRIGHT NIGHT (Now)(Value: cover or less)

FRIGHT NIGHT II (Now)(Value: cover or less)

FRISKY ANIMALS (Formerly Frisky Fables; Super Cat #56 on)
No. 44, Jan, 1951 - No. 55, Sept, 1953
Star Publications

	GD25	FN65	NM94
44-Super Cat	10.00	30.00	65.00
45-Classic L. B. Cole-c	13.00	40.00	90.00
46-51,53-55: Super Cat. 54-Super Cat-c begin	9.15	27.50	55.00
52-L. B. Cole-c/a, 3 pgs.; X-Mas-c	10.00	30.00	65.00

NOTE: *All have **L. B. Cole**-c. No. 47-No Super Cat. **Disbrow** a-49, 52. **Fago** a-51.*

FRISKY ANIMALS ON PARADE (Formerly Parade Comics; becomes Superspook)
Sept, 1957 - No. 3, Dec-Jan, 1957-1958
Ajax-Farrell Publ. (Four Star Comic Corp.)

	GD25	FN65	NM94
1-L. B. Cole-c	8.35	25.00	50.00
2-No L. B. Cole-c	4.20	12.50	25.00
3-L. B. Cole-c	5.85	17.50	35.00

FRISKY FABLES (Frisky Animals No. 44 on)
Spring, 1945 - No. 43, Oct, 1950
Premium Group/Novelty Publ./Star Publ. V5#4 on

	GD25	FN65	NM94
V1#1-Al Fago-c/a #1-38	10.00	30.00	65.00
2,3(Fall & Winter, 1945)	5.85	17.50	35.00
V2#1(#4, 4/46)-9,11,12(#15, 3/47): 4-Flag-c	3.60	9.00	18.00
10-Christmas-c	4.00	10.00	20.00
V3#1(#16, 4/47)-12(#27, 3/48): 4-Flag-c. 7,9-Infinity-c. 10-X-Mas-c	3.20	8.00	16.00
V4#1(#28, 4/48)-7(#34, 2-3/49)	3.20	8.00	16.00
V5#1(#35, 4-5/49)-4(#38, 10-11/49)	3.20	8.00	16.00
39-43-L. B. Cole-c; 40-X-mas-c	8.35	25.00	50.00
Accepted Reprint No. 43 (nd); L.B. Cole-c	4.00	12.00	24.00

FRITZI RITZ (See Comics On Parade, Single Series #5, 1(reprint), Tip Top & United Comics)

FRITZI RITZ (United Comics No. 8-26)
Fall/48 - No. 7, 1949; No. 27, 3-4/53 - No. 36, 9-10/54; No. 42, 1/55; No. 43, 6/56 - No. 55, 9-11/57; No. 56, 12-2/57-58 - No. 59, 9-11/58
United Features Synd./St. John No. 37?-55/Dell No. 56 on

	GD25	FN65	NM94
nn(1948)-Special Fall issue	10.00	30.00	60.00
2	5.00	15.00	30.00
3-7(1949): 6-Abbie & Slats app.	4.00	12.00	24.00
27-29(1953): 29-Five pg. Abbie & Slats; 1 pg. Mamie by Russell Patterson	3.20	8.00	16.00
30-59: 31-Peanuts by Schulz (1st app.?, 11-12/53). 36-1 pg. Mamie by Patterson	2.80	7.00	14.00

NOTE: *Abbie & Slats in #6,7, 27-31. Li'l Abner in #33, 35, 36. Peanuts in #31, 43, 58, 59.*

FROGMAN COMICS
Jan-Feb, 1952 - No. 11, May, 1953
Hillman Periodicals

	GD25	FN65	NM94
1	8.35	25.00	50.00
2	4.20	12.50	25.00
3,4,6-11: 4-Meskin-a	4.00	10.00	20.00
5-Krigstein-a	5.35	16.00	32.00

FROGMEN, THE
No. 1258, Feb-Apr, 1962 - No. 11, Nov-Jan, 1964-65 (Painted-c)
Dell Publishing Co.

	GD25	FN65	NM94
4-Color 1258(#1)-Evans-a	7.50	22.50	45.00
2,3-Evans-a; part Frazetta inks in #2,3	6.35	19.00	38.00
4,6-11	3.20	8.00	16.00
5-Toth-a	4.00	12.00	24.00

FROM BEYOND THE UNKNOWN
10-11/69 - No. 25, 11-12/73 (No. 7-11: 64 pgs.; No. 12-17: 52 pgs.)
National Periodical Publications

	GD25	FN65	NM94
1	1.00	2.50	6.00
2-10: 7-Intro. Col. Glenn Merrit		1.60	4.00
11-25: Star Rovers-r begin #18,19. Space Museum in #23-25		1.00	2.50

NOTE: ***N. Adams** c-3, 6, 8, 9. **Anderson** c-2, 4, 5, 10, 11i, 15-17, 22; reprints-3, 4, 6-8, 10, 11, 13-16, 24, 25. **Infantino** r-1-5, 7-19, 23-25; c-11p. **Kaluta** c-18, 19. **Kubert** c-1, 7, 12-14. **Toth** a-2r. **Wood** a-13i. Photo c-22.*

FROM HERE TO INSANITY (Satire) (Formerly Eh! #1-7)
(See Frantic & Frenzy)
No. 8, Feb, 1955 - V3#1, 1956
Charlton Comics

	GD25	FN65	NM94
8	9.15	27.50	55.00
9	7.50	22.50	45.00
10-Ditko-c/a (3 pgs.)	10.00	30.00	70.00
11,12-All Kirby except 4 pgs.	12.00	36.00	85.00
V3#1(1956)-Ward-c/a(2) (signed McCartney); 5 pgs. Wolverton-a; 3 pgs. Ditko-a; magazine format (cover says "Crazy, Man, Crazy" and becomes Crazy, Man, Crazy with V2#2)	23.00	70.00	160.00

FRONTIER DAYS
1956 (Giveaway)
Robin Hood Shoe Store (Brown Shoe)

	GD25	FN65	NM94
1	2.40	6.00	12.00

FRONTIER DOCTOR (See 4-Color No. 877)

FRONTIER FIGHTERS
Sept-Oct, 1955 - No. 8, Nov-Dec, 1956
National Periodical Publications

	GD25	FN65	NM94
1-Davy Crockett, Buffalo Bill by Kubert, Kit Carson begin (Scarce)	41.00	125.00	290.00
2	29.00	85.00	200.00

Frontier Romances #1, © AVON

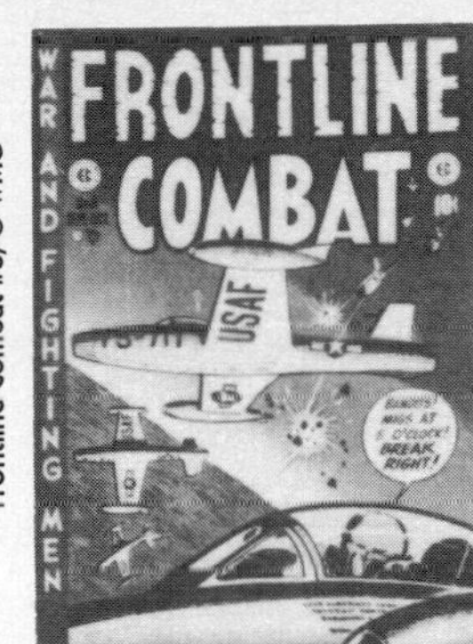

Frontline Combat #8, © WMG

Fun Comics #10, © STAR

GD25 FN65 NM94

3-8 25.00 75.00 175.00
NOTE: *Buffalo Bill by **Kubert** in all.*

FRONTIER ROMANCES
Nov-Dec, 1949 - No. 2, Feb-Mar, 1950 (Painted-c)
Avon Periodicals/I. W.

1-Used in **SOTI**, pg. 180(General reference) & illo. "Erotic spanking in a western comic book" 34.00 100.00 235.00
2 (Scarce)-Woodish-a by Stallman 20.00 60.00 140.00
I.W. Reprint #1-Reprints Avon's #1 4.00 10.50 21.00
I.W. Reprint #9-Reprints ? 2.40 6.00 12.00

FRONTIER SCOUT: DAN'L BOONE (Formerly Death Valley; The Masked Raider No. 14 on)
No. 10, Jan, 1956 - No. 13, Aug, 1956; V2#14, March, 1965
Charlton Comics

10 6.70 20.00 40.00
11-13(1956) 4.00 11.00 22.00
V2#14(3/65) 2.40 6.00 12.00

FRONTIER TRAIL (The Rider No. 1-5)
No. 6, May, 1958
Ajax/Farrell Publ.

6 3.60 9.00 18.00

FRONTIER WESTERN
Feb, 1956 - No. 10, Aug, 1957
Atlas Comics (PrPI)

1 11.00 32.00 75.00
2,3,6-Williamson-a, 4 pgs. each 9.15 27.50 55.00
4,7,9,10: 10-Check-a 5.00 15.00 30.00
5-Crandall, Baker, Davis-a; Williamson text illos 6.70 20.00 40.00
8-Crandall, Morrow, & Wildey-a 5.00 15.00 30.00
NOTE: ***Colan** a-2. **Drucker** a-3, 4. **Heath** c-5. **Maneely** c/a-2, 7. **Romita** a-7. **Severin** c-6, 8, 10. **Tuska** a-2. **Wildey** a-5, 8. Ringo Kid in No. 4.*

FRONTLINE COMBAT
July-Aug, 1951 - No. 15, Jan, 1954
E. C. Comics

1-Severin/Kurtzman-a 51.00 154.00 360.00
2 29.00 90.00 210.00
3 22.00 65.00 155.00
4-Used in **SOTI**, pg. 257; contains "Airburst" by Kurtzman which is his personal all-time favorite story 19.00 56.00 130.00
5 16.00 48.00 115.00
6-10 13.50 41.00 95.00
11-15 10.50 31.00 72.00
NOTE: ***Davis** a-in all; c-11, 12. **Evans** a-10-15. **Heath** a-1. **Kubert** a-14. **Kurtzman** a-1-5; c-1-9. **Severin** a-5-7, 9, 13, 15. **Severin/Elder** a-2-11; c-10. **Toth** a-8, 12. **Wood** a-1-4, 6-10, 12-15; c-13-15. Special issues: No. 7 (Iwo Jima), No. 9 (Civil War), No. 12 (Air Force).*
(Canadian reprints known; see Table of Contents.)

FRONT PAGE COMIC BOOK
1945
Front Page Comics (Harvey)

1-Kubert-a; intro. & 1st app. Man in Black by Powell; Fuje-c 23.00 70.00 160.00

FROST AND FIRE (See DC Science Fiction Graphic Novel)

FROSTY THE SNOWMAN
No. 359, Nov, 1951 - No. 1272, Dec-Feb?/1961-62
Dell Publishing Co.

4-Color 359 (#1) 7.50 22.50 45.00
4-Color 435 4.00 12.00 24.00
4-Color 514,601,661 4.00 10.00 20.00
4-Color 748,861,950,1065,1153,1272 3.60 9.00 18.00

FRUITMAN SPECIAL
Dec, 1969 (68 pages)
Harvey Publications

GD25 FN65 NM94

1-Funny super hero 2.80 7.00 14.00

F-TROOP (TV)
Aug, 1966 - No. 7, Aug, 1967 (All have photo-c)
Dell Publishing Co.

1 5.50 17.00 39.00
2-7 3.20 9.00 21.00

FUGITIVES FROM JUSTICE
Feb, 1952 - No. 5, Oct, 1952
St. John Publishing Co.

1 10.00 30.00 70.00
2-Matt Baker-r/Northwest Mounties #2; Vic Flint strip reprints begin 10.00 30.00 70.00
3-Reprints panel from Authentic Police Cases that was used in **SOTI** with changes; Tuska-a 10.00 30.00 70.00
4 5.35 16.00 32.00
5-Last Vic Flint-r; bondage-c 6.70 20.00 40.00

FUGITOID
1985 (One shot, B&W, magazine size)
Mirage Studios

1-Ties into Teenage Mutant Ninja Turtles #5 1.65 4.00 10.00

FULL COLOR COMICS
1946
Fox Features Syndicate

nn 9.15 27.50 55.00

FULL OF FUN
Aug, 1957 - No. 2, Nov, 1957; 1964
Red Top (Decker Publ.)(Farrell)/I. W. Enterprises

1(1957)-Dave Berg-a 4.00 12.00 24.00
2-Reprints Bingo, the Monkey Doodle Boy 3.20 8.00 16.00
8-I.W. Reprint('64) 1.00 2.50 5.00

FUN AT CHRISTMAS (See March of Comics No. 138)

FUN CLUB COMICS (See Interstate Theatres...)

FUN COMICS (Formerly Holiday Comics #1-8; Mighty Bear #13 on)
No. 9, Jan, 1953 - No. 12, Oct, 1953
Star Publications

9-(25¢ Giant)-L. B. Cole X-Mas-c; X-Mas Issue 10.00 30.00 65.00
10-12-L. B. Cole-c. 12-Mighty Bear-c/story 7.00 21.00 42.00

FUNDAY FUNNIES (See Famous TV..., and Harvey Hits No. 35,40)

FUN-IN (TV)(Hanna-Barbera)
Feb, 1970 - No. 10, Jan, 1972; No. 11, 4/74 - No. 15, 12/74
Gold Key

1-Dastardly & Muttley in Their Flying Machines; Perils of Penelope Pitstop in #1-4; It's the Wolf in all 2.30 6.75 16.00
2-4,6-Cattanooga Cats in 2-4 1.20 3.00 7.00
5,7-Motormouse & Autocat, Dastardly & Muttley in both; It's the Wolf in #7 1.50 3.75 9.00
8,10-The Harlem Globetrotters, Dastardly & Muttley in #10 1.20 3.00 7.00
9-Where's Huddles?, Dastardly & Muttley, Motormouse & Autocat app. 1.50 3.75 9.00
11-15: 11-Butch Cassidy. 12,15-Speed Buggy. 13-Hair Bear Bunch. 14-Inch High Private Eye 1.00 2.50 5.50

FUNKY PHANTOM, THE (TV)
Mar, 1972 - No. 13, Mar, 1975 (Hanna-Barbera)
Gold Key

1 1.70 5.00 12.00
2-5 1.00 2.50 6.00
6-13 1.40 3.50

FUNLAND
No date (1940s) (25 cents)

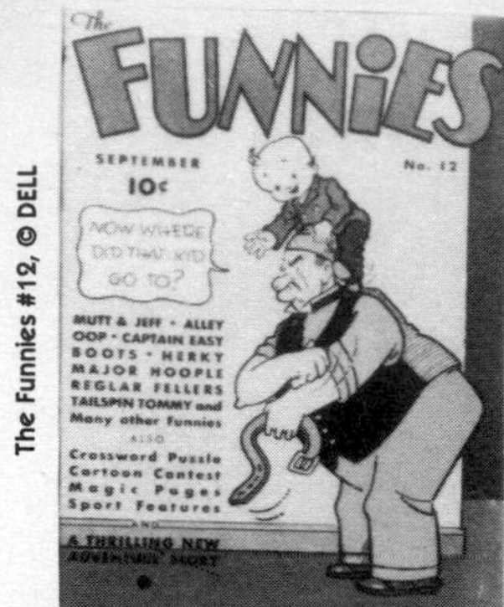

The Funnies #12, © DELL

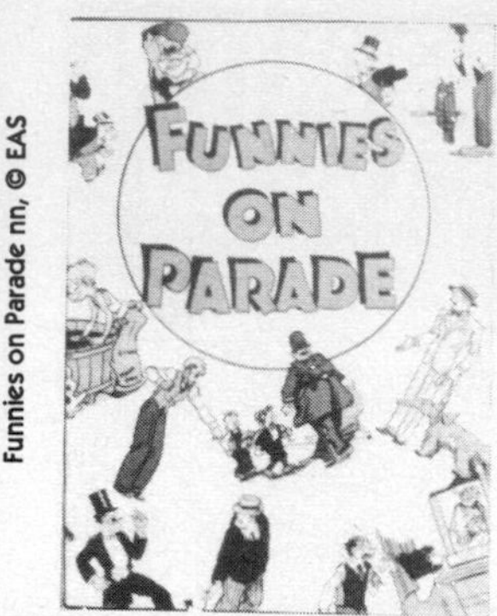

Funnies on Parade nn, © EAS

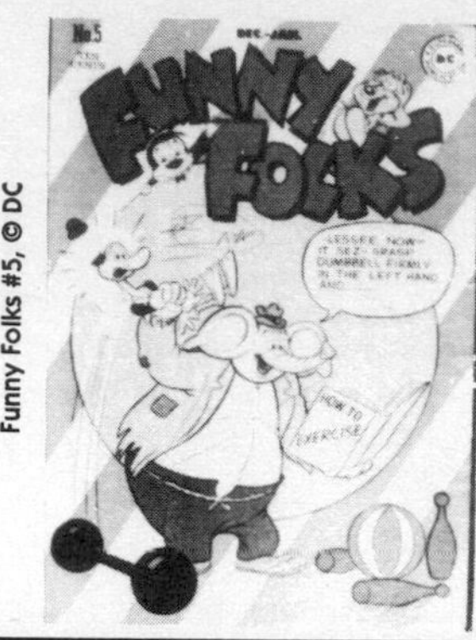

Funny Folks #5, © DC

GD25 FN65 NM94

Ziff-Davis (Approved Comics)
nn-Contains games, puzzles, etc. 10.00 30.00 70.00

FUNLAND COMICS
1945
Croyden Publishers
1-Funny animal 10.00 30.00 70.00

FUNNIES, THE (Also see Comic Cuts)
1929 - No. 36, 10/18/30 (10 cents; 5 cents No. 22 on) (16 pgs.)
Full tabloid size in color; not reprints; published every Saturday
Dell Publishing Co.
1-My Big Brudder, Johnathan, Jazzbo & Jim, Foxy Grandpa, Sniffy, Jimmy Jams & other strips begin; first four-color comic newsstand publication; also contains magic, puzzles & stories 43.00 130.00 300.00
2-21 (1930, 30 cents) 17.00 52.00 120.00
22(nn-7/12/30-5 cents) 13.00 40.00 90.00
23(nn-7/19/30-5 cents), 24(nn-7/26/30-5 cents), 25(nn-8/2/30), 26(nn-8/9/30), 27(nn-8/16/30), 28(nn-8/23/30), 29(nn-8/30/30), 30(nn-9/6/30), 31(nn-9/13/30), 32(nn-9/20/30), 33(nn-9/27/30), 34(nn-10/4/30), 35(nn-10/11/30), 36(nn, no date-10/18/30) each.... 13.00 40.00 90.00

FUNNIES, THE (New Funnies No. 65 on)
Oct, 1936 - No. 64, May, 1942
Dell Publishing Co.
1-Tailspin Tommy, Mutt & Jeff, Alley Oop (1st app?), Capt. Easy (1st app.), Don Dixon begin 143.00 430.00 1000.00
2-Scribbly by Mayer begins (1st app.) 71.00 215.00 500.00
3 57.00 171.00 400.00
4,5: 4-Christmas-c 46.00 138.00 300.00
6-10 37.00 112.00 260.00
11-20: 16-Christmas-c 32.00 95.00 220.00
21-29: 25-Crime Busters by McWilliams(4pgs.) 25.00 75.00 175.00
30-John Carter of Mars (origin/1st app.) begins by Edgar Rice Burroughs; Warner Bros.' Bosko-c 71.00 215.00 500.00
31-44: 33-John Coleman Burroughs art begins on John Carter. 34-Last funny-c. 35-(9/39)-Mr. District Attorney begins; based on radio show 46.00 138.00 310.00
45-Origin/1st app. Phantasmo, the Master of the World (Dell's 1st super-hero, 7/40) & his sidekick Whizzer McGee 36.00 110.00 250.00
46-50: 46-The Black Knight begins, ends #62 28.00 85.00 185.00
51-56-Last ERB John Carter of Mars 28.00 85.00 185.00
57-Intro. & origin Captain Midnight (7/41) 79.00 235.00 550.00
58-60: 58-Captain Midnight-c begin, end #63 29.00 88.00 200.00
61-Andy Panda begins by Walter Lantz 32.00 95.00 225.00
62,63: 63-Last Captain Midnight-c; bondage-c 29.00 88.00 200.00
64-Format change; Oswald the Rabbit, Felix the Cat, Li'l Eight Ball app.; origin & 1st app. Woody Woodpecker in Oswald; last Capt. Midnight 62.00 188.00 435.00

NOTE: ***Mayer*** *c-26, 48.* ***McWilliams*** *art in many issues on "Rex King of the Deep." Alley Oop c-17, 20. Captain Midnight c-57(i/2), 58-63. John Carter c-35-37, 40. Phantasmo c-45-56, 57(1/2), 58-61(part). Rex King c-38, 39, 42. Tailspin Tommy c-41.*

FUNNIES ANNUAL, THE
1959 ($1.00)(B&W; tabloid-size, approx. 7x10")
Avon Periodicals
1-(Rare)-Features the best newspaper comic strips of the year: Archie, Snuffy Smith, Beetle Bailey, Henry, Blondie, Steve Canyon, Buz Sawyer, The Little King, Hi & Lois, Popeye, & others. Also has a chronological history of the comics from 2000 B.C. to 1959. 34.00 100.00 235.00

FUNNIES ON PARADE (Premium)
1933 (Probably the 1st comic book) (36 pgs.; slick cover)
No date or publisher listed
Eastern Color Printing Co.

GD25 FN65 VF82 NM94

nn-Contains Sunday page reprints of Mutt & Jeff, Joe Palooka, Hairbreadth Harry, Reg'lar Fellers, Skippy, & others (10,000 print run). This book was printed for Proctor & Gamble to be given away & came out before Famous Funnies or Century of Comics. 720.00 2160.00 4680.00 7200.00

GD25 FN65 NM94

(Estimated up to 50 total copies exist, 3 in NM/Mint)

FUNNY ANIMALS (See Fawcett's Funny Animals)
Sept, 1984 - No. 2, Nov, 1984
Charlton Comics

GD25 FN65 NM94

1,2-Atomic Mouse-r 1.00

FUNNYBONE
1944 (25¢, 132 pages)
La Salle Publishing Co.
nn 20.00 60.00 140.00

FUNNY BOOK (...Magazine) (Hocus Pocus No. 9)
Dec, 1942 - No. 9, Aug-Sept, 1946
Parents' Magazine Press (Funny Book Publishing Corp.)
1-Funny animal; Alice In Wonderland app. 10.00 30.00 70.00
2 5.85 17.50 35.00
3-9: 9-Hocus-Pocus strip 4.00 12.00 24.00

FUNNY COMICS (7 cents)
1955 (36 pgs.; 5x7"; in color)
Modern Store Publ.
1-Funny animal 1.20 3.00 6.00

FUNNY COMIC TUNES (See Funny Tunes)

FUNNY FABLES
Aug, 1957 - V2#2, Nov, 1957
Decker Publications (Red Top Comics)
V1#1 3.20 8.00 16.00
V2#1,2 2.00 5.00 10.00

FUNNY FILMS
Sept-Oct, 1949 - No. 29, May-June, 1954 (No. 1-4: 52 pgs.)
American Comics Group(Michel Publ./Titan Publ.)
1-Puss An' Boots, Blunderbunny begin 12.00 36.00 85.00
2 7.00 21.00 42.00
3-10: 3-X-Mas-c 4.70 14.00 28.00
11-20 4.00 10.00 20.00
21-29 3.20 8.00 16.00

FUNNY FOLKS (Hollywood... on cover only No. 16-26; becomes Hollywood Funny Folks No. 27 on)
April-May, 1946 - No. 26, June-July, 1950 (52 pgs., #16 on)
National Periodical Publications
1-Nutsy Squirrel begins (1st app.) by Rube Grossman 32.00 96.00 225.00
2 14.00 43.00 100.00
3-5: 4-1st Nutsy Squirrel-c 10.00 30.00 70.00
6-10 8.35 25.00 50.00
11-26: 16-Begin 52 pg. issues (10-11/48) 6.70 20.00 40.00

NOTE: ***Sheldon Mayer*** *a-in some issues.* ***Post*** *a-18. Christmas c-12.*

FUNNY FROLICS
Summer, 1945 - No. 5, Dec, 1946
Timely/Marvel Comics (SPI)
1-Sharpy Fox, Puffy Pig, Krazy Krow 13.00 40.00 90.00
2 7.50 22.50 45.00
3,4 5.85 17.50 35.00
5-Kurtzman-a 7.50 22.50 45.00

FUNNY FUNNIES
April, 1943 (68 pages)
Nedor Publishing Co.
1 (Funny animals). Peter Porker app. 13.00 40.00 90.00

FUNNYMAN (Also see Cisco Kid Comics & Extra Comics)
Dec, 1947; No. 1, Jan, 1948 - No. 6, Aug, 1948
Magazine Enterprises
nn(12/47)-Prepublication B&W undistributed copy by Siegel & Shuster-

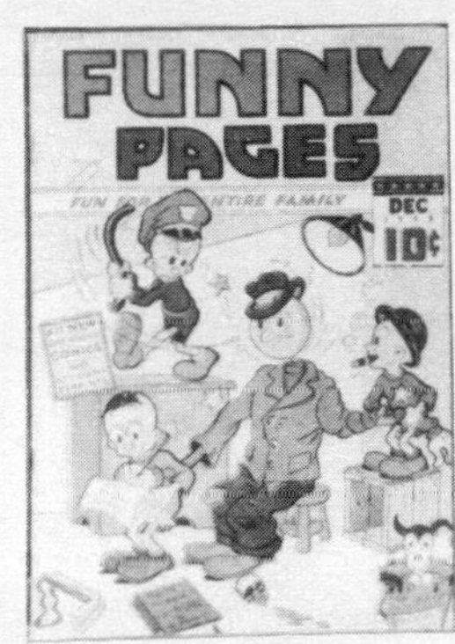

Funny Pages V2#12, © CEN

Funny Stuff #42, © DC

The Further Adventures of Indiana Jones #4, © Lucasfilm, Inc.

GD25 FN65 NM94 | GD25 FN65 NM94

(5-3/4x8"), 16 pgs.; Sold in San Francisco in 1976 for $300.00
1-Siegel & Shuster-a in all 22.00 65.00 150.00
2 15.00 45.00 110.00
3-6 13.00 40.00 90.00

FUNNY MOVIES (See 3-D Funny Movies)

FUNNY PAGES (Formerly The Comics Magazine)
No. 6, Nov, 1936 - No. 42, Oct, 1940
Comics Magazine Co./Ultem Publ.(Chesler)/Centaur Publications

V1#6 (nn, nd)-The Clock begins (2 pgs., 1st app.), ends #11; The Clock is the 1st masked comic book hero 71.00 215.00 500.00
7-11 44.00 132.00 285.00
V2#1 (9/37)(V2#2 on-c; V2#1 in indicia) 33.00 100.00 220.00
V2#2 (10/37)(V2#3 on-c; V2#2 in indicia) 33.0 100.00 220.00
3(11/37) 5 33.00 100.00 220.00
6(1st Centaur, 3/38) 58.00 175.00 375.00
7-9 40.00 120.00 265.00
10(Scarce, 9/38)-1st app. of The Arrow by Gustavson (Blue costume) 142.00 425.00 950.00
11,12 71.00 212.00 450.00
V3#1-6: 6,8-Last funny covers 71.00 212.00 450.00
7-1st Arrow-c (9/39) 88.00 262.00 565.00
8,9: 9-Tarpe Mills jungle-c 71.00 212.00 450.00
10-2nd Arrow-c 79.00 238.00 515.00
V4#1(1/40, Arrow-c)-(Rare)-The Owl & The Phantom Rider app.; origin Mantoka, Maker of Magic by Jack Cole. Mad Ming begins, ends #42; Tarpe Mills-a 83.00 250.00 540.00
35-38: 35-Arrow-c. 36-38-Mad Ming-c 61.00 182.00 420.00
39-42-Arrow-c. 42-Last Arrow 61.00 182.00 420.00

NOTE: ***Burgos*** *c-V3#10.* ***Jack Cole*** *a-V2#3, 7, 8, 10, 11, V3#2, 6, 9, 10, V4#1, 37.* ***Eisner*** *a-V1#7, 8?, 10.* ***Ken Ernst*** *a-V1#7, 8.* ***Everett*** *a-V2#11 (illos).* ***Gill Fox*** *a-V2#11.* ***Sid Greene*** *a-39.* ***Guardineer*** *a-V2#2, 3, 5.* ***Gustavson*** *a-V2#5, 11, 12, V3#1-10, 35, 38-42; c-V3#7, 35, 39-42.* ***Bob Kane*** *a-V3#1.* ***McWilliams*** *a-V2#12, V3#1, 3-6.* ***Tarpe Mills*** *a-V3#8-10, V4#1; c-V3#9.* ***Ed Moore Jr.*** *a-V2#12.* ***Bob Wood*** *a-V2#2, 3, 8, 11, V3#6, 9, 10; c- V2#6, 7. Arrow c-V3#7, 10, V4#1, 35, 40-42.*

FUNNY PICTURE STORIES (Comic Pages V3#4 on)
Nov, 1936 - V3#3, May, 1939
Comics Magazine Co./Centaur Publications

V1#1-The Clock begins (c-feature)(see Funny Pages for 1st app.) 133.00 400.00 900.00
2 62.00 188.00 425.00
3-9: 4-Eisner-a; X-Mas-c. 7-Racial humor-c 44.00 132.00 300.00
V2#1 (9/37; V1#10 on-c; V2#1 in indicia)-Jack Strand begins 33.00 100.00 225.00
2 (10/37; V1#11 on-c; V2#2 in indicia) 33.00 100.00 225.00
3-5: 4-Xmas-c 29.00 87.00 200.00
6-(1st Centaur, 3/38) 54.00 162.00 365.00
7-11 31.00 92.00 200.00
V3#1-3 27.00 82.00 185.00
Laundry giveaway (16-20 pgs., 1930s)-slick-c 18.00 55.00 120.00

NOTE: ***Biro*** *c-V2#1, 8, 9, 11.* ***Guardineer*** *a-V1#11.* ***Bob Wood*** *c/a-V1#11, V2#2; c-V2#3, 5.*

FUNNY STUFF (Becomes The Dodo & the Frog No. 80)
Summer, 1944 - No. 79, July-Aug, 1954 (#1-7 are quarterly)
All-American/National Periodical Publications No. 7 on

1-The Three Mouseketeers (ends #28) & The "Terrific Whatzit" begin; Sheldon Mayer-a 75.00 225.00 525.00
2-Sheldon Mayer-a 38.00 115.00 265.00
3-5: 3-Flash parody. 5-All Mayer-a/scripts issue 24.00 72.00 165.00
6-10 (6/46) 16.00 48.00 110.00
11-17,19,20: 20-1st Dodo & the Frog-c (4/47) 11.50 34.00 80.00
18-The Dodo & the Frog (2/47, 1st app?) begin?; X-Mas-c 20.00 60.00 140.00
21,23-30: 24-Infinity-c 8.35 25.00 50.00
22-Superman cameo 29.00 85.00 200.00
31-79: 70-1st Bo Bunny by Mayer & begins 6.35 19.00 38.00
Wheaties Giveaway(1946, 6-1/2x8-1/4") (Scarce)-Dodo & the Frog, Three Mouseketeers, etc.; came taped to Wheaties box; never found in better than fine 19.00 130.00

NOTE: ***Mayer*** *a-1-8, 55, 57, 58, 61, 62, 64, 65, 68, 70, 72, 74-79; c-2, 5, 6, 8.*

FUNNY STUFF STOCKING STUFFER
March, 1985 ($1.25, 52 pgs.)
DC Comics

1-Almost every DC funny animal featured 1.25

FUNNY 3-D
December, 1953
Harvey Publications

1 10.00 30.00 60.00

FUNNY TUNES (Animated Funny Comic Tunes No. 16-22; Funny Comic Tunes No. 23, on covers only; formerly Krazy Komics #15; Oscar No. 24 on)
No. 16, Summer, 1944 - No. 23, Fall, 1946
U.S.A. Comics Magazine Corp. (Timely)

16-Silly, Ziggy, Krazy Krow begin 9.15 27.50 55.00
17 (Fall/'44)-Becomes Gay Comics #18 on? 6.35 19.00 38.00
18-22: 21-Super Rabbit app. 5.35 16.00 32.00
23-Kurtzman-a 7.00 21.00 42.00

FUNNY TUNES (Becomes Space Comics #4 on)
July, 1953 - No. 3, Dec-Jan, 1953-54
Avon Periodicals

1-Space Mouse, Peter Rabbit, Merry Mouse, Spotty the Pup, Cicero the Cat begin; all continue in Space Comics 5.85 17.50 35.00
2,3 4.00 12.00 24.00

FUNNY WORLD
1947 - No. 3, 1948
Marbak Press

1-The Berrys, The Toodles & other strip-r begin 5.85 17.50 35.00
2,3 4.35 13.00 26.00

FUNTASTIC WORLD OF HANNA-BARBERA, THE (TV)
Dec, 1977 - No. 3, June, 1978 ($1.25) (Oversized)
Marvel Comics Group

1-3: 1-The Flintstones Christmas Party(12/77). 2-Yogi Bear's Easter Parade(3/78). 3-Laff-a-lympics(6/78) 1.00 2.00 5.00

FUN TIME
1953; No. 2, Spr, 1953; No. 3(nn), Fall, 1953; No. 4, Wint, 1953-54
Ace Periodicals

1 4.00 10.00 20.00
2-4 (25¢, 100 pgs. each) 8.35 25.00 50.00

FUN WITH SANTA CLAUS (See March of Comics No. 11, 108, 325)

FURTHER ADVENTURES OF INDIANA JONES, THE (Also see Indiana Jones and the Last Crusade & Indiana Jones and the Temple of Doom)
Jan, 1983 - No. 34, Mar, 1986
Marvel Comics Group

1-34: 1-Byrne/Austin-a. 2-Byrne/Austin-c/a 1.10

NOTE: ***Austin*** *a-6i, 9i; c-1i, 2i, 6i, 9i.* ***Chaykin*** *a-6p; c-6p, 8p-10p.* ***Ditko*** *a-21p, 25-28, 34.* ***Golden*** *c-24, 25.* ***Simonson*** *c-9. Painted c-14.*

FURTHER ADVENTURES OF NYOKA, THE JUNGLE GIRL, THE (AC)(Value: cover or less)

FURY (Straight Arrow's Horse...) (See A-1 No. 119)

FURY (TV) (See March Of Comics #200)
No. 781, Mar, 1957 - Nov, 1962 (All photo-c)
Dell Publishing Co./Gold Key

4-Color 781 10.00 30.00 60.00
4-Color 885,975,1031,1080,1133,1172,1218,1296, 01292-208(#1-'62) 6.70 20.00 40.00
10020-211(11/62-G.K.)-Crandall-a 6.70 20.00 40.00

FURY OF FIRESTORM, THE (Becomes Firestorm The Nuclear Man #65 on; also see Firestorm)

Fusion #13, © Eclipse

Gabby Hayes Western #31, © FAW

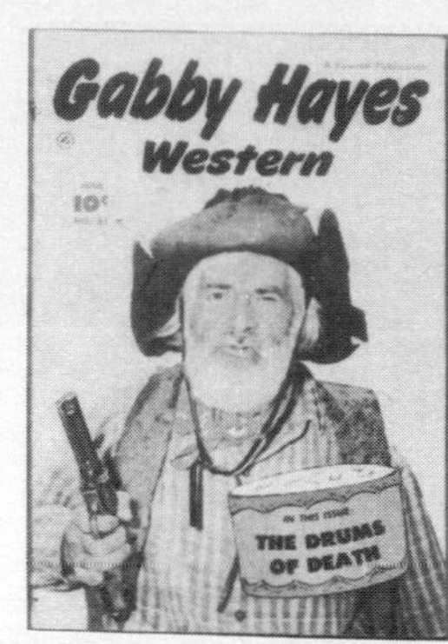

Gang Busters #12, © DC

GD25 FN65 NM94 GD25 FN65 NM94

June, 1982 - No. 64, Oct, 1987 (#19-on: 75 cents)
DC Comics

1-Intro The Black Bison; brief origin .80 2.00
2-64: 4-JLA x-over. 17-1st app. Firehawk. 21-Death of Killer Frost. 22-Origin. 23-Intro. Byte. 24-(6/84)-1st app. Blue Devil & Bug (origin); origin Byte. 34-1st app./origin Killer Frost II. 39-Weasel's i.d. revealed 41,42-Crisis x-over. 48-Intro. Moonbow. 53-Origin/1st app. Silver Shade. 55,56-Legends x-over. 58-1st app./origin Parasite 1.00
61-Test cover variant; Superman logo 5.00 15.00 35.00
Annual 1(1983) 1.25
Annual 2-4: 2(1984), 3(1985), 4(1986) 1.25
NOTE: ***Colan** a-19p, Annual 4p. **Giffen** a-Annual 4p. **Gil Kane** c-30. **Nino** a-37. **Tuska** a-(p)-17, 18, 32, 45.*

FUSION (Eclipse)(Value: cover or less)

FUTURE COMICS
June, 1940 - No. 4, Sept, 1940
David McKay Publications

1-Origin The Phantom; The Lone Ranger, & Saturn Against the Earth begin 150.00 450.00 950.00
2 83.00 250.00 550.00
3,4 67.00 200.00 450.00

FUTURE WORLD COMICS
Summer, 1946 - No. 2, Fall, 1946
George W. Dougherty

1,2-H. C. Kiefer covers 15.00 45.00 105.00

FUTURE WORLD COMIX (Warren Presents... on cover)
September, 1978
Warren Publications

1 1.50

FUTURIANS, THE (Lodestone)(Value: cover or less)

G-8 (See G-Eight)

GABBY (Formerly Ken Shannon) (Teen humor)
No. 11, July, 1953; No. 2, Sept, 1953 - No. 9, Sept, 1954
Quality Comics Group

11(#1)(7/53) 5.00 15.00 30.00
2 3.60 9.00 18.00
3-9 2.40 6.00 12.00

GABBY GOB (See Harvey Hits No. 85, 90, 94, 97, 100, 103, 106, 109)

GABBY HAYES ADVENTURE COMICS
Dec, 1953
Toby Press

1-Photo-c 10.00 30.00 70.00

GABBY HAYES WESTERN (Movie star) (See Monte Hale, Real Western Hero & Western Hero)
Nov, 1948 - No. 50, Jan, 1953; No. 51, Dec, 1954 - No. 59, Jan, 1957
Fawcett Publications/Charlton Comics No. 51 on

1-Gabby & his horse Corker begin; photo front/back-c begin 34.00 105.00 240.00
2 16.00 50.00 115.00
3-5 11.00 32.00 75.00
6-10: 9-Young Falcon begins 10.00 30.00 65.00
11-20: 19-Last photo back-c 8.00 24.00 48.00
21-49: 20,22,24,26,28,29-(52 pgs.) 5.35 16.00 32.00
50-(1/53)-Last Fawcett issue; last photo-c? 6.35 19.00 38.00
51-(12/54)-1st Charlton issue; photo-c 6.35 19.00 38.00
52-59(1955-57): 53,55-Photo-c. 58-Swayze-a 4.00 10.00 20.00
Quaker Oats Giveaway nn's(#1-5, 1951, 2-1/2x7") (Kagran Corp.)-...In Tracks of Guilt, ...In the Fence Post Mystery, ...In the "Accidental Sherlock," ... In the Frame-Up known 8.35 25.00 50.00

GAGS
July, 1937 - V3#10, Oct, 1944 (13-3/4x10-3/4")
United Features Synd./Triangle Publ. No. 9 on

1(7/37)-52 pgs.; 20 pgs. Grin & Bear It, Fellow Citizen 5.00 15.00 30.00
V1#9 (36 pgs.) (7/42) 3.60 9.00 18.00
V3#10 2.40 7.00 14.00

GALACTIC WAR COMIX (Warren Presents... on cover)
December, 1978
Warren Publications

nn-Wood, Williamson-r 1.50

GALLANT MEN, THE (TV)
October, 1963 (Photo-c)
Gold Key

1(1008-310)-Manning-a 2.40 6.00 12.00

GALLEGHER, BOY REPORTER (TV)
May, 1965 (Disney)
Gold Key

1(10149-505)-Photo-c 1.80 4.50 9.00

GAMBIT (See X-Men #266 & X-Men Annual #14)
Dec, 1993 - No. 4, Mar, 1994 ($2.00, color, mini-series)
Marvel Comics

1-($2.50)-Foil embossed-c 1.00 2.50
2-4 .80 2.00

GAMEBOY
1990 - No. 6? ($1.95, color, coated-c)
Valiant Comics

1-6: 3,4,6-Layton-c. 4-Morrow-a. 5-Layton-c(i) .80 2.00

GAMMARAUDERS (DC)(Value: cover or less)

GANDY GOOSE (See All Surprise, Paul Terry's & Terry-Toons)
Mar, 1953 - No. 5, Nov, 1953; No. 5, Fall, 1956 - No. 6, Sum/58
St. John Publ. Co./Pines No. 5,6

1-All St. John issues are pre-code 6.35 19.00 38.00
2 3.60 9.00 18.00
3-5(1953)(St. John) 3.20 8.00 16.00
5,6(1956-58)(Pines)-CBS Televison Presents... 2.40 6.00 12.00

GANG BUSTERS (See Popular Comics #38)
1938 - 1943
David McKay/Dell Publishing Co.

Feature Books 17(McKay)('38)-1st app. 38.00 115.00 265.00
Large Feature Comic 10('39)-(Scarce) 43.00 130.00 300.00
Large Feature Comic 17('41) 27.00 81.00 190.00
4-Color 7(1940) 34.00 100.00 235.00
4-Color 23,24('42-43) 25.00 75.00 175.00

GANG BUSTERS (Radio/TV)(Gangbusters #14 on)
Dec-Jan, 1947-48 - No. 67, Dec-Jan, 1958-59 (No. 1-23: 52 pgs.)
National Periodical Publications

1 54.00 160.00 375.00
2 24.00 73.00 170.00
3-10: 9,10-Photo-c 14.00 43.00 100.00
11-13-Photo-c 12.00 36.00 85.00
14,17-Frazetta-a, 8 pgs. each. 14-Photo-c 24.00 70.00 165.00
15,16,18-20 9.15 27.50 55.00
21-30: 26-Kirby-a 7.50 22.50 45.00
31-44: 44-Last Pre-code (2-3/55) 6.70 20.00 40.00
45-67 5.35 16.00 32.00
NOTE: ***Barry** a-6, 8, 10. **Drucker** a-51. **Moreira** a-48, 50, 59. **Roussos** a-8.*

GANGSTERS AND GUN MOLLS
Sept, 1951 - No. 4, June, 1952 (Painted-c)
Avon Periodical/Realistic Comics

1-Wood-a, 1 pg; c-/Avon paperback #292 27.00 81.00 190.00
2-Check-a, 8 pgs.; Kamen-a 20.00 60.00 140.00

Garrison's Gorillas #1, © Belmur Prod.

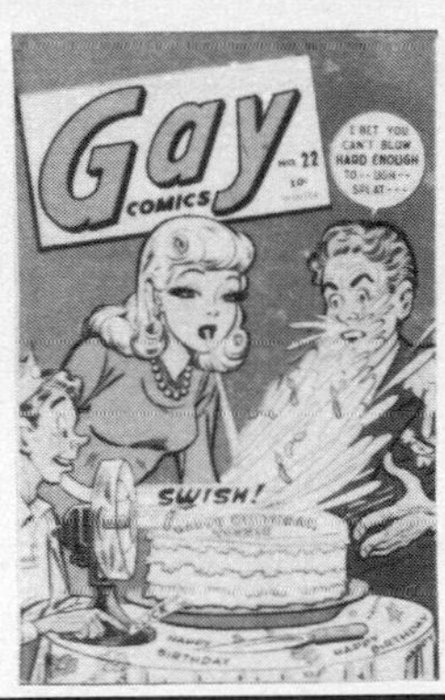

Gay Comics #22, © MEG

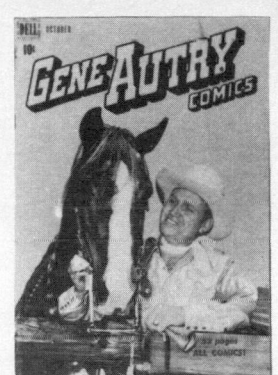

Gene Autry Comics #32, © Gene Autry

GD25 FN65 NM94

3-Marijuana mention story; used in **POP**, pg. 84-85 — 19.00 57.00 130.00
4 — 14.00 43.00 100.00

GANGSTERS CAN'T WIN
Feb-Mar, 1948 - No. 9, June-July, 1949
D. S. Publishing Co.

1 — 15.00 45.00 105.00
2 — 8.65 26.00 52.00
3-6: 4-Acid in face story — 7.00 21.00 42.00
7-9 — 5.35 16.00 32.00

NOTE: *Ingles a-5, 6.* ***McWilliams*** *a-5, 7.* ***Reinman*** *c-6.*

GANG WORLD
No. 5, Nov, 1952 - No. 6, Jan, 1953
Standard Comics

5-Bondage-c — 10.00 30.00 65.00
6 — 7.00 21.00 42.00

GARGOYLE (See The Defenders #94)
June, 1985 - No. 4, Sept, 1985 (75 cents, limited series)
Marvel Comics Group

1-4: 1-Wrightson-c; character from Defenders — 1.00

GARRISON'S GORILLAS (TV)
Jan, 1968 - No. 4, Oct, 1968; No. 5, Oct, 1969 (Photo-c)
Dell Publishing Co.

1 — 3.30 10.00 23.00
2-5: 5-Reprints #1 — 2.30 6.75 16.00

GASOLINE ALLEY (Also see Popular Comics & Super Comics)
1929 (B&W daily strip reprints)(7x8-3/4"; hardcover)
Reilly & Lee Publishers

nn-By King (96 pgs.) — 18.00 54.00 125.00

GASOLINE ALLEY (Top Love Stories No. 3 on?)
Sept-Oct, 1950 - No. 2, Dec, 1950 (Newspaper reprints)
Star Publications

1-Contains 1 pg. intro. history of the strip (The Life of Skeezix); reprints 15 scenes of highlights from 1921-1935, plus an adventure from 1935 and 1936 strips; a 2-pg. filler is included on the life of the creator Frank King, with photo of the cartoonist. — 14.00 43.00 100.00
2-(1936-37 reprints)-L. B. Cole-c — 13.00 40.00 90.00
(See Super Book No. 21)

GASP!
March, 1967 - No. 4, Aug, 1967 (12 cents)
American Comics Group

1 — 3.25 9.50 22.00
2-4 — 1.85 5.50 13.00

GAY COMICS (Honeymoon No. 41)
Mar, 1944 (no month); No. 18, Fall, 1944 - No. 40, Oct, 1949
Timely Comics/USA Comic Mag. Co. No. 18-24

1-Wolverton's Powerhouse Pepper; Tessie the Typist begins; 1st app. Millie the Model & Willie (one shot) — 30.00 90.00 210.00
18-(Formerly Funny Tunes #17?)-Wolverton-a — 15.00 45.00 105.00
19-29-Wolverton-a in all. 24,29-Kurtzman-a — 12.00 36.00 85.00
30,33,36,37-Kurtzman's "Hey Look" — 5.35 16.00 32.00
31-Kurtzman's "Hey Look"(1), Giggles 'N' Grins (1-1/2) — 5.35 16.00 32.00
32,35,38-40: 35-Nellie The Nurse begins? — 4.00 12.00 24.00
34-Three Kurtzman's "Hey Look" — 6.35 19.00 38.00

GAY COMICS (Also see Smile, Tickle, & Whee Comics)
1955 (52 pgs.; 5x7-1/4"; 7 cents)
Modern Store Publ.

1 — .80 2.00 4.00

GAY PURR-EE (See Movie Comics)

GD25 FN65 NM94

GEEK, THE (See Brother Power... & Vertigo Visions)

G-8 AND HIS BATTLE ACES
October, 1966
Gold Key

1 (10184-610)-Painted-c — 3.60 9.00 18.00

G-8 AND HIS BATTLE ACES
1991 ($1.50, color, one-shot)
Blazing Comics

1-Glanzman-a; Truman-c — 1.50

NOTE: *Flip book format with "The Spider's Web" #1 on other side w/****Glanzman****-a,* ***Truman****-c.*

GEM COMICS
April, 1945 (52 pgs.) (Bondage-c)
Spotlight Publishers

1-Little Mohee, Steve Strong app. — 16.00 48.00 110.00

GENE AUTRY (See March of Comics No. 25, 28, 39, 54, 78, 90, 104, 120, 135, 150 & Western Roundup under Dell Giants)

GENE AUTRY COMICS (Movie, Radio star; singing cowboy)
(Dell takes over with No. 11)
1941 (On sale 12/31/41) - No. 10, 1943 (68 pgs.)
Fawcett Publications

1 (Rare)-Gene Autry & his horse Champion begin — 271.00 815.00 1900.00
2 — 75.00 225.00 525.00
3-5 — 52.00 156.00 365.00
6-10 — 45.00 135.00 315.00

GENE AUTRY COMICS (...& Champion No. 102 on)
No. 11, 1943 - No. 121, Jan-Mar, 1959 (TV - later issues)
Dell Publishing Co.

11 (1943, 60 pgs.)-Continuation of Fawcett series; photo back-c — 50.00 150.00 350.00
12 (2/44, 60 pgs.) — 47.00 140.00 325.00
4-Color 47(1944, 60 pgs.) — 39.00 120.00 275.00
4-Color 57(11/44),66('45)(52 pgs. each) — 34.00 105.00 240.00
4-Color 75,83('45, 36 pgs. each) — 29.00 85.00 200.00
4-Color 93,100('45-46, 36 pgs. each) — 23.00 70.00 160.00
1(5-6/46, 52 pgs.) — 39.00 118.00 275.00
2(7-8/46)-Photo-c begin, end #111 — 20.00 60.00 140.00
3-5: 4-Intro Flapjack Hobbs — 16.00 48.00 110.00
6-10 — 11.50 34.00 80.00
11-20: 20-Panhandle Pete begins — 10.00 30.00 60.00
21-29(36pgs.) — 7.50 22.50 45.00
30-40(52pgs.) — 7.50 22.50 45.00
41-56(52pgs.) — 5.85 17.50 35.00
57-66(36pgs.): 58-X-mas-c — 4.00 11.00 22.00
67-80(52pgs.) — 4.35 13.00 26.00
81-90(52pgs.): 82-X-mas-c. 87-Blank inside-c — 4.00 10.00 20.00
91-99(36pgs. No. 91-on). 94-X-mas-c — 2.80 7.00 14.00
100 — 4.00 10.00 20.00
101-111-Last Gene Autry photo-c — 2.80 7.00 14.00
112-121-All Champion painted-c — 2.00 5.00 10.00
...Adventure Comics And Play-Fun Book ('40s)-36 pgs., 8x6-1/2"; games, comics, magic — 39.00 116.00 270.00
Pillsbury Premium('47)-36 pgs., 6-1/2x7-1/2"; games, comics, puzzles — 24.00 73.00 170.00
Quaker Oats Giveaway(1950)-2-1/2x6-3/4"; 5 different versions; "Death Card Gang," "Phantoms of the Cave," "Riddle of Laughing Mtn.," "Secret of Lost Valley," "Bond of the Broken Arrow" (came in wrapper) each... — 10.30 31.00 72.00
3-D Giveaway(1953)-Pocket-size; 5 different — 12.00 36.00 85.00

NOTE: *Photo back covers 4-18, 20-45, 48-65.* ***Manning*** *a-118.* ***Jesse Marsh*** *art: 4-Color No. 66, 75, 93, 100, No. 1-25, 27-37, 39, 40.*

GENE AUTRY'S CHAMPION (TV)
No. 287, 8/50; No. 319, 2/51; No. 3, 8-10/51 - No. 19, 8-10/55

Gene Dogs #1, © MEG

Georgie #28, © MEG

Ghost #10, © FH

Dell Publishing Co.

	GD25	FN65	NM94
4-Color 287(#1)('50, 52pgs.)-Photo-c	10.00	30.00	65.00
4-Color 319(#2, '51), 3-(Painted-c begin)	4.20	12.50	25.00
4-19: 19-Last painted-c	2.40	6.00	12.00

GENE AUTRY TIM (Formerly Tim) (Becomes Tim in Space)
1950 (Half-size) (Black & White Giveaway)
Tim Stores

	GD25	FN65	NM94
nn-Several issues (All Scarce)	8.70	26.00	52.00

GENE DOGS
Oct, 1993 - No. 4, Jan, 1994 ($1.75, color, mini-series)
Marvel Comics UK

	GD25	FN65	NM94
1-($2.75)-Polybagged w/4 trading cards		1.10	2.75
2-4		.70	1.75

GENERAL DOUGLAS MACARTHUR
1951
Fox Features Syndicate

	GD25	FN65	NM94
nn	13.00	40.00	90.00

GENERIC COMIC, THE
April, 1984 (One-shot)
Marvel Comics Group

	GD25	FN65	NM94
1			1.00

GENETIX
Oct, 1993 - No. 6, Mar, 1994 ($1.75, color, limited series)
Marvel Comics UK

	GD25	FN65	NM94
1-($2.75)-Polybagged w/4 cards; Dark Guard app.		1.10	2.75
2-6		.70	1.75

GENTLE BEN (TV)
Feb, 1968 - No. 5, Oct, 1969 (All photo-c)
Dell Publishing Co.

	GD25	FN65	NM94
1	4.00	11.00	22.00
2-5: 5-Reprints #1	2.40	6.00	12.00

GEORGE OF THE JUNGLE (TV)(See America's Best TV Comics)
Feb, 1969 - No. 2, Oct, 1969 (Jay Ward)
Gold Key

	GD25	FN65	NM94
1,2	6.50	19.00	45.00

GEORGE PAL'S PUPPETOONS
Dec, 1945 - No. 18, Dec, 1947; No. 19, 1950
Fawcett Publications

	GD25	FN65	NM94
1-Captain Marvel app. on cover	32.00	95.00	225.00
2	16.00	48.00	110.00
3-10	10.00	30.00	70.00
11-19	9.15	27.50	55.00

GEORGIE COMICS (...& Judy Comics #20-35?; see All Teen & Teen Comics)
Spring, 1945 - No. 39, Oct, 1952
Timely Comics/GPI No. 1-34

	GD25	FN65	NM94
1-Dave Berg-a	13.00	40.00	90.00
2	7.50	22.50	45.00
3-5,7,8	5.35	16.00	32.00
6-Georgie visits Timely Comics	7.00	21.00	42.00
9,10-Kurtzman's "Hey Look" (1 & ?); Margie app.	7.00	21.00	42.00
11,12: 11-Margie, Millie app.	4.00	12.00	24.00
13-Kurtzman's "Hey Look," 3 pgs.	5.85	17.50	35.00
14-Wolverton-a(1 pg.); Kurtzman's "Hey Look"	7.00	21.00	42.00
15,16,18-20	4.00	10.00	20.00
17,29-Kurtzman's "Hey Look," 1 pg.	5.00	15.00	30.00
21-24,27,28,30-39: 21-Anti-Wertham editorial	3.20	8.00	16.00
25-Painted-c by classic pin-up artist Peter Driben	5.85	17.50	35.00
26-Logo design swipe from Archie Comics	3.60	9.00	18.00

GERALD McBOING-BOING AND THE NEARSIGHTED MR. MAGOO (TV)
(Mr. Magoo No. 6 on)
Aug-Oct, 1952 - No. 5, Aug-Oct, 1953
Dell Publishing Co.

	GD25	FN65	NM94
1	8.35	25.00	50.00
2-5	7.00	21.00	42.00

GERONIMO (See Fighting Indians of the Wild West!)
1950 - No. 4, Feb, 1952
Avon Periodicals

	GD25	FN65	NM94
1-Indian Fighter; Maneely-a; Texas Rangers-r/Cowpuncher #1; Fawcette-c	11.00	32.00	75.00
2-On the Warpath; Kit West app.; Kinstler-c/a	7.00	21.00	42.00
3-And His Apache Murderers; Kinstler-c/a(2); Kit West-r/Cowpuncher #6	7.00	21.00	42.00
4-Savage Raids of; Kinstler-c & inside front-c; Kinstlerish-a by McCann(3)	5.85	17.50	35.00

GERONIMO JONES
Sept, 1971 - No. 9, Jan, 1973
Charlton Comics

	GD25	FN65	NM94
1	1.00	2.00	5.00
2-9		1.00	2.50
Modern Comics Reprint #7('78)			1.50

GETALONG GANG, THE (TV)
May, 1985 - No. 6, March, 1986
Star Comics (Marvel)

	GD25	FN65	NM94
1-6: Saturday morning TV stars			1.00

GET LOST
Feb-Mar, 1954 - No. 3, June-July, 1954 (Satire)
Mikeross Publications/New Comics

	GD25	FN65	NM94
1	14.00	43.00	100.00
2-Andru/Esposito-c; has 4 pg. E.C. parody featuring "The Sewer Keeper"	10.00	30.00	70.00
3-John Wayne 'Hondo' parody	10.00	30.00	60.00
1,2 (10,12/87-New Comics)-B&W r-original			1.00

GET SMART (TV)
June, 1966 - No. 8, Sept, 1967 (All have Don Adams photo-c)
Dell Publishing Co.

	GD25	FN65	NM94
1	9.00	26.00	60.00
2-Ditko-a	6.00	18.00	42.00
3-8: 3-Ditko-a(p)	5.50	16.00	38.00

GHOST (...Comics #9)
1951(Winter) - No. 11, Summer, 1954
Fiction House Magazines

	GD25	FN65	NM94
1-Most covers by Whitman	41.00	125.00	290.00
2-Ghost Gallery & Werewolf Hunter stories	19.00	58.00	135.00
3-9: 3,6,7,9-Bondage-c. 9-Abel, Discount-a	16.00	48.00	110.00
10,11-Dr. Drew by Grandenetti in each, reprinted from Rangers; 11-Evans-r/Rangers #39; Grandenetti-r/Rangers #49	19.00	58.00	135.00

GHOST BREAKERS (Also see Racket Squad in Action, Red Dragon & (CC) Sherlock Holmes Comics)
Sept, 1948 - No. 2, Dec, 1948 (52 pages)
Street & Smith Publications

	GD25	FN65	NM94
1-Powell-c/a(3); Dr. Neff (magician) app.	22.00	67.00	155.00
2-Powell-c/a(2); Maneely-a	18.00	54.00	125.00

GHOSTBUSTERS (TV)(First)(Value: cover or less)

GHOSTBUSTERS II (Now)(Value: cover or less)

GHOST CASTLE (See Tales of...)

GHOSTLY HAUNTS (Formerly Ghost Manor)
#20, 9/71 - #53, 12/76; #54, 9/77 - #55, 10/77; #56, 1/78 - #58, 4/78
Charlton Comics

	GD25	FN65	NM94
20-58: 27-Dr. Graves x-over. 32-New logo. 33-Back to old logo. 39-Origin & 1st app. Destiny Fox		1.20	3.00

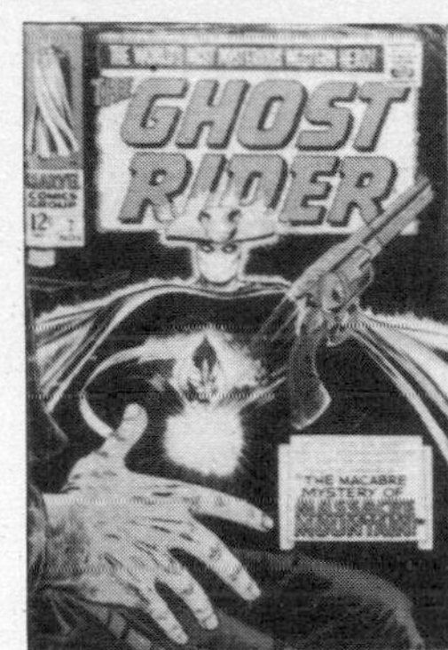

Ghost Rider #7 (11/67), © MEG

Ghost Rider #68 (5/81), © MEG

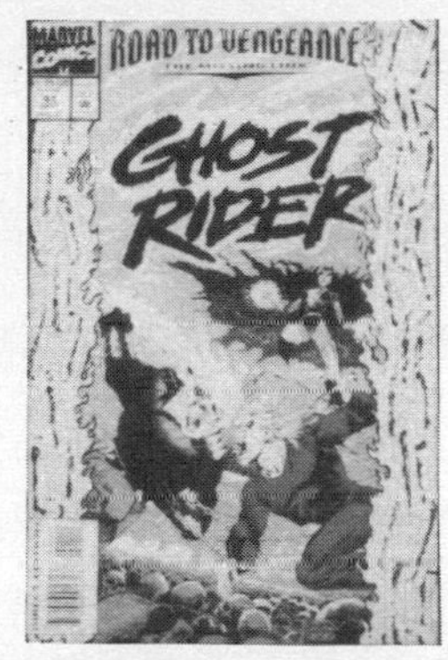

Ghost Rider V2#41, © MEG

GD25 FN65 NM94

40,41(Modern Comics-r, 1977, 1978) 1.50
NOTE: *Ditko a-22-25, 27, 28, 31-34, 36-41, 43-48, 50, 52, 54, 56r; c-22-27, 30, 33-37, 47, 54, 56. Glanzman a-20. Howard a-27, 30, 35, 42. Newton c/a-42. Staton a-35; c-20, 40. Sutton c-33, 37, 39, 41.*

GHOSTLY TALES (Formerly Blue Beetle No. 50-54)
No. 55, 4-5/66 - No. 124, 12/76; No. 125, 9/77 - No. 169, 10/84
Charlton Comics

55-Intro. & origin Dr. Graves 1.60 4.00 8.00
56-70-Dr. Graves ends .80 2.00 4.00
71-169: 107-Sutton, Wood-a. 114-Newton-a 1.20 3.00
NOTE: *Aparo a-65, 66, 68, 72, 141r, 142r; c-71, 72, 74-76, 81, 146r. Ditko a-55-58, 60, 61, 67, 69-73, 75-90, 92-95, 97, 99-118, 120-122, 125r, 126r, 131-133r, 136-141r, 143r, 144r, 152, 155, 161, 163; c-67, 69, 73, 77, 78, 83, 84, 86-90, 92-97, 99, 102, 109, 111, 118, 120-122, 125, 131-133, 163. Glanzman a-167. Howard a-95, 98, 99, 117; c-98, 107, 120, 121, 161. Morisi a-83, 84, 86. Newton a-114; c-115. Palais a-61. Staton a-161; c-117. Sutton a-107, 112-114; c-100, 106, 110, 113(painted). Wood a-107.*

GHOSTLY WEIRD STORIES (Formerly Blue Bolt Weird)
No. 120, Sept, 1953 - No. 124, Sept, 1954
Star Publications

120-Jo-Jo-r 16.00 48.00 110.00
121-Jo-Jo-r 11.50 34.00 80.00
122-The Mask-r/Capt. Flight #5; Rulah-r; has 1pg. story 'Death and the Devil Pills'-r/Western Outlaws #17 11.50 34.00 80.00
123-Jo-Jo; Disbrow-a(2) 11.50 34.00 80.00
124-Torpedo Man 11.50 34.00 80.00
NOTE: *Disbrow a-120-124. L. B. Cole covers-all issues (#122 is a sci-fi cover).*

GHOST MANOR (Ghostly Haunts No. 20 on)
July, 1968 - No. 19, July, 1971
Charlton Comics

1 1.30 3.25 8.00
2-5 1.60 4.00
6-12,17: 17-Morisi-a 1.20 3.00
13-16,18,19-Ditko-a; c-15,18,19 1.60 4.00

GHOST MANOR (2nd Series)
Oct, 1971 - No. 32, Dec, 1976; No. 33, Sept, 1977 - No. 77, 11/84
Charlton Comics

1 1.30 3.25 8.00
2-7,9,10 1.60 4.00
8-Wood-a 1.00 2.00 5.00
11-56,58-77: 18-20-Newton-a. 22-Newton-c/a. 21-E-Man, Blue Beetle, Capt. Atom cameos. 28-Nudity panels. 40-Torture & drug use. 77-Aparo-r/Space Adventures V3#60 (Paul Mann) 1.20 3.00
57-Wood, Ditko, Howard-a 1.60 4.00
19(Modern Comics reprint, 1977) 1.00
NOTE: *Ditko a-4, 8, 10, 11(2), 13, 14, 18, 20-22, 24-26, 28, 29, 31, 37r, 38r, 40r, 42-44r, 46r, 47, 51r, 52r, 54r, 57, 60, 62(4), 64r, 71; c-2-7, 9-11, 14-16, 28, 31, 37, 38, 42, 43, 46, 47, 51, 52, 60, 62, 64. Howard a-4, 8, 19-21, 57. Newton a-18-20, 22, 64. Sutton a-19;c-8, 18.*

GHOST RIDER (See A-1 Comics, Best of the West, Black Phantom, Bobby Benson, Great Western, Red Mask & Tim Holt)
1950 - No. 14, 1954
Magazine Enterprises
NOTE: *The character was inspired by Vaughn Monroe's 'Ghost Riders in the Sky,' and Disney's movie 'The Headless Horseman.'*

1(A-1 #27)-Origin Ghost Rider 47.00 141.00 330.00
2-5: 2(A-1 #29), 3(A-1 #31), 4(A-1 #34), 5(A-1 #37)-All Frazetta-c only 43.00 130.00 300.00
6,7: 6(A-1 #44)-Loco weed story, 7(A-1 #51) 17.00 52.00 120.00
8,9: 8(A-1 #57)-Drug use story, 9(A-1 #69) 15.00 45.00 105.00
10(A-1 #71)-Vs. Frankenstein 15.50 45.00 105.00
11-14: 11(A-1 #75), 12(A-1 #80)-Bondage-c; one-eyed Devil-c. 13(A-1 #84). 14(A-1 #112) 12.00 36.00 85.00
NOTE: *Dick Ayers art in all; c-1, 6-14.*

GHOST RIDER, THE (See Night Rider & Western Gunfighters)
Feb, 1967 - No. 7, Nov, 1967 (Western hero)(All 12 cent-c)
Marvel Comics Group

GD25 FN65 NM94

1-Origin & 1st app. Ghost Rider; Kid Colt-r begin 3.60 10.75 25.00
2-7: 6-Last Kid Colt-r; All Ayers-c/a(p) 1.65 4.70 11.00

GHOST RIDER (See The Champions, Marvel Spotlight #5, Marvel Team-Up #15, 58, Marvel Treasury Edition #18, Marvel Two-In-One #8, The Original Ghost Rider & The Original Ghost Rider Rides Again)
Sept, 1973 - No. 81, June, 1983 (Super-hero)
Marvel Comics Group

1-Johnny Blaze, the Ghost Rider begins; 1st app. Daimon Hellstrom (Son of Satan) in cameo 11.50 34.00 80.00
2-1st full app. Daimon Hellstrom; gives glimpse of costume (1 panel); story continues in Marvel Spotlight #12 4.85 15.00 34.00
3-5: 3-Ghost Rider gets new cycle; Son of Satan app. 3.60 10.75 25.00
6-10: 10-Reprints origin/1st app. from Marvel Spotlight #5; Ploog-a 2.30 6.75 16.00
11-19 1.85 5.50 13.00
20-Daredevil x-over; ties into D.D. #138; Byrne-a 2.40 7.25 17.00
21-30: 22-1st app. Enforcer. 29,30-Vs. Dr. Strange 1.30 3.25 8.00
31-49 1.00 2.50 6.00
50-Double size 1.20 3.00 7.00
51-67,69-76,78-80: 80-Brief origin recap 1.75 4.40
68,77-Origin retold 1.00 2.50 6.00
81-Death of Ghost Rider (Demon leaves Blaze) 1.50 3.75 9.00
NOTE: *Anderson c-64p. Infantino a(p)-43, 44, 51. G. Kane a-21p; c(p)-1, 2, 4, 5, 8, 9, 11-13, 19, 20, 24, 25. Kirby c-21-23. Mooney a-2-9p, 30i. Nebres c-26i. Newton a-23i. Perez c-26p. Shores a-2i. J. Sparling a-62p, 64p, 65p. Starlin a(p)-35. Sutton a-1p, 44i, 64i, 65i, 66, 67i. Tuska a-13p, 14p, 16p.*

GHOST RIDER (Also see Doctor Strange/Ghost Rider Special, Marvel Comics Presents & Midnight Sons Unlimited)
V2#1, May, 1990 - Present ($1.50/$1.75, color)
Marvel Comics

V2#1-($1.95, 52 pgs.)-Origin/1st app. new Ghost Rider; Kingpin app. 2.70 8.00 19.00
1-2nd printing 1.00 2.50 5.50
2 2.00 6.00 14.00
3-Kingpin app. 1.70 5.00 12.00
4-Scarcer 2.30 6.75 16.00
5-Punisher app., Jim Lee-c 2.30 6.75 16.00
5-Gold background 2nd printing 1.30 3.25 8.00
6-Punisher app. 1.30 3.25 8.00
7-10: 9-X-Factor app. 10-Reintro Johnny Blaze on last pg. 1.60 4.00
11-14: 11-Stroman-c/a(p). 12,13-Dr. Strange/cont'd in D.S. #28. 13-Painted-c. 14-Johnny Blaze vs. Ghost Rider; origin recap 1st Ghost Rider (Blaze) 1.00 2.50
15-Glow in the dark-c; begin $1.75-c 1.10 2.70 6.50
15-Gold background 2nd printing .90 2.25
16,17-Spider-Man/Hobgoblin-c/story 1.20 3.00
18-24,29,30,32-39: 18-Painted-c by Nelson. 29-Wolverine-c/story. 32-Dr. Strange x-over; Johnny Blaze app. 37-Archangel app. 44.45-Siege of Darkness part 2 & 10 .65 1.60
25-($2.75)-Contains pop-up scene .90 2.25
26,27-X-Men x-over; Lee/Williams-c on both .90 2.25
28-($2.50, 52 pgs.)-Polybagged w/poster; part 1 of Rise of the Midnight Sons storyline (see Ghost Rider/Blaze #1) 1.60 4.00
31-($2.50, 52 pgs.)-Polybagged w/poster; part 6 of Rise of the Midnight Sons .80 2.00
40-($2.25)-Outer-c is Darkhold envelope made of black parchment w/gold ink; Midnight Massacre; Demogoblin app. .75 1.90
41-48: 41-Lilith & Centurious app.; begin $1.75-c. 41-43-Neon ink-c. 43-Has free extra 16 pg. insert on Siege of Darkness .70 1.75
Annual 1 (1993, $2.95, 68 pgs.)-Bagged w/card 1.00 2.50
...And Cable 1 (9/92, $3.95, color, stiff-c, 68 pgs.)-Reprints Marvel Comics Presents #90-98 w/new Kieth-c 1.40 3.50
NOTE: *Andy & Joe Kubert c/a-28-31.*

Ghost Rider/Blaze: Spirits of Vengence #14, © MEG

Giant Comics Edition #9, © STJ

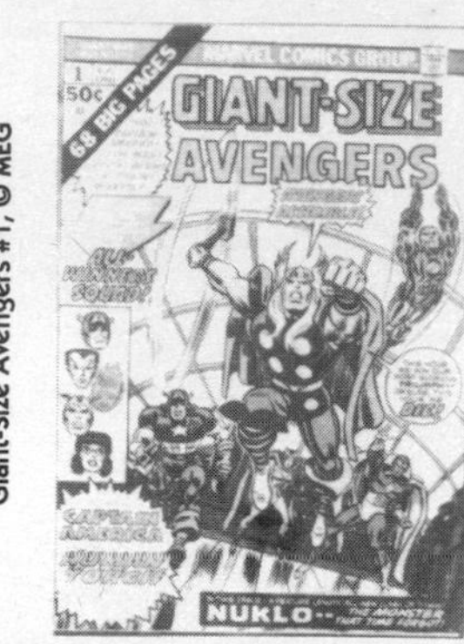

Giant-Size Avengers #1, © MEG

GD25 FN65 NM94

GHOST RIDER/BLAZE: SPIRITS OF VENGEANCE (Also see Blaze)
Aug, 1992 - Present ($1.75, color)
Marvel Comics

1-($2.75, 52 pgs.)-Polybagged w/poster; part 2 of Rise of the Midnight Sons storyline; Adam Kubert-c/a begins 1.10 2.75
2-11,14-20: 4-Art Adams & Joe Kubert-p. 5,6-Spirits of Venom parts 2 & 4 cont'd from Web of Spider-Man #95,96 w/Demogoblin. 14,15-Neon ink-c. 15-Intro Blaze's new costume & power .70 1.75
12-($2.95)-Glow-in-the-dark-c 1.20 3.00
13-($2.25)-Outer-c is Darkhold envelope made of black parchment w/gold ink; Midnight Massacre x-over .90 2.25

GHOST RIDER/CAPTAIN AMERICA: FEAR
Oct, 1992 ($5.95, color, 52 pgs.)
Marvel Comics

nn-Wraparound gatefold-c; Williamson inks 1.00 2.50 6.00

GHOST RIDER; WOLVERINE; PUNISHER: HEARTS OF DARKNESS
Dec, 1991 ($4.95, color, one-shot, 52 pgs.)
Marvel Comics

1-Double gatefold-c; John Romita, Jr.-c/a(p) 1.00 2.00 5.00

GHOSTS (Ghost No. 1)
Sept-Oct, 1971 - No. 112, May, 1982 (No. 1-5: 52 pgs.)
National Periodical Publications/DC Comics

1-Aparo-a 1.65 4.00 10.00
2-Wood-a(i) 1.60 4.00
3-5 1.20 3.00
6-20 .80 2.00
21-96 1.50
97-99-The Spectre app. 97,98-Spectre-c by Aparo .80 2.00
100-112: 100-Infinity-c 1.00
NOTE: ***B. Baily** a-77. **J. Craig** a-108. **Ditko** a-77, 111. **Giffen** a-104p, 106p, 111p. **Golden** a-88. **Kaluta** c-7, 93, 101. **Kubert** c-89, 105-108, 111. **Mayer** a-111. **McWilliams** a-99. **Win Mortimer** a-89, 91, 94. **Newton** a-92p, 94p. **Nino** a-35, 37, 57. **Orlando** a-74i; c-80. **Redondo** a-8, 13, 45. **Sparling** a(p)-90, 93, 94. **Spiegle** a-103, 105.*

GHOSTS SPECIAL (See DC Special Series No. 7)

GHOST STORIES (See Amazing Ghost Stories)

GHOST STORIES
Sept-Nov, 1962; No. 2, Apr-June, 1963 - No. 37, Oct, 1973
Dell Publishing Co.

12-295-211(#1)-Written by John Stanley 5.00 15.00 30.00
2 3.00 7.50 15.00
3-10: Two No. 6's exist with different c/a(12-295-406 & 12-295-503) #12-295-503 is actually #9 with indicia to #6 2.40 6.00 12.00
11-20 1.40 3.50 7.00
21-37 1.00 2.00 5.00
NOTE: *#21-34, 36, 37 all reprint earlier issues.*

GHOUL TALES (Magazine)
Nov, 1970 - No. 5, July, 1971 (52 pages) (B&W)
Stanley Publications

1-Aragon pre-code reprints; Mr. Mystery as host; bondage-c 3.25 9.50 22.00
2,3: 2-(1/71)Reprint/Climax #1. 3-(3/71) 1.65 4.00 10.00
4-(5/71)Reprints story "The Way to a Man's Heart" used in **SOTI** 3.25 9.50 22.00
5-ACG reprints 1.65 4.00 10.00
NOTE: *No. 1-4 contain pre-code Aragon reprints.*

GIANT BOY BOOK OF COMICS (See Boy)
1945 (Hardcover) (240 pages)
Newsbook Publications (Gleason)

1-Crimebuster & Young Robin Hood; Biro-c 67.00 200.00 470.00

GIANT COMIC ALBUM
1972 (52 pgs., 11x14", B&W, 59 cents, cardboard-c)
King Features Syndicate

Newspaper reprints: Little Iodine, Katzenjammer Kids, Henry, Mandrake the Magician ('59 Falk), Popeye, Beetle Bailey, Barney Google, Blondie, Flash Gordon ('68-69 Dan Barry), & Snuffy Smith
each... 1.65 4.00 10.00

GD25 FN65 NM94

GIANT COMICS
Summer, 1957 - No. 3, Winter, 1957 (25¢, 100 pgs.)
Charlton Comics

1-Atomic Mouse, Hoppy app. 13.00 40.00 90.00
2,3: 2-Romance. 3-Christmas Book; Atomic Mouse, Atomic Rabbit, Li'l Genius, Li'l Tomboy & Atom the Cat stories 10.00 30.00 70.00
NOTE: *The above may be rebound comics; contents could vary.*

GIANT COMICS (See Wham-O Giant Comics)

GIANT COMICS EDITION (See Terry-Toons)
1947 - No. 17, 1950 (All 100-164 pgs.) (25 cents)
St. John Publishing Co.

1-Mighty Mouse 36.00 110.00 250.00
2-Abbie & Slats 16.00 48.00 110.00
3-Terry-Toons Album; 100 pgs. 26.00 80.00 185.00
4-Crime comics; contains Red Seal No. 16, used & illo. in **SOTI** 38.00 115.00 265.00
5-Police Case Book(4/49)-Contents varies; contains remaindered St. John books - some volumes contain 5 copies rather than 4, with 160 pages; Matt Baker-c 36.00 110.00 255.00
5A-Terry-Toons Album, 132 pgs. 25.00 75.00 175.00
6-Western Picture Stories; Baker-c/a(3); Tuska-a; The Sky Chief, Blue Monk, Ventrilo app., 132 pgs. 34.00 100.00 235.00
7-Contains a teen-age romance plus 3 Mopsy comics 22.00 65.00 150.00
8-The Adventures of Mighty Mouse (10/49) 25.00 75.00 175.00
9-Romance and Confession Stories; Kubert-a(4); Baker-a; photo-c 34.00 100.00 235.00
10-Terry-Toons 25.00 75.00 175.00
11-Western Picture Stories-Baker-c/a(4); The Sky Chief, Desperado, & Blue Monk app.; another version with Son of Sinbad by Kubert 32.00 95.00 210.00
12-Diary Secrets; Baker prostitute-c; 4 St. John romance comics; Baker-a 54.00 160.00 375.00
13-Romances; Baker, Kubert-a 29.00 85.00 200.00
14-Mighty Mouse Album 25.00 75.00 175.00
15-Romances (4 love comics)-Baker-c 30.00 90.00 210.00
16-Little Audrey, Abbott & Costello, Casper 25.00 75.00 175.00
17(nn)-Mighty Mouse Album (nn, no date, but did follow No. 16); 100 pgs. on cover but has 148 pgs. 25.00 75.00 175.00
NOTE: *The above books contain remaindered comics and contents could vary with each issue. No. 11, 12 have part photo magazine insides.*

GIANT COMICS EDITIONS
1940's (132 pages)
United Features Syndicate

1-Abbie & Slats, Abbott & Costello, Jim Hardy, Ella Cinders, Iron Vic & Gordo 26.00 80.00 185.00
2-Jim Hardy, Ella Cinders, Elmo & Gordo 20.00 60.00 140.00
NOTE: *Above books contain rebound copies; contents can vary.*

GIANT GRAB BAG OF COMICS (See Archie All-Star Specials under Archie Comics)

GIANTS (See Thrilling True Story of the Baseball...)

GIANT-SIZE...
May, 1974 - Dec, 1975 (35-50 cents, 52-68 pgs.)(Some titles quarterly)
Marvel Comics Group

Avengers 1(8/74)-New-a plus G.A. H. Torch-r; 1st modern app. The Whizzer; 1st & only modern app. Miss America 1.10 2.70 6.50
Avengers 2,3: 2(11/74)-Death of the Swordsman. 3(2/75) 1.80 4.50
Avengers 4,5: 4(6/75)-Vision marries Scarlet Witch. 5(12/75)-Reprints Avengers Special #1 1.40 3.50
Captain America 1(12/75)-r/stories T.O.S. 59-63 by Kirby (#63 reprints

Giant-Size Chillers #1 (6/74), © MEG

Giant-Size Man-Thing #4, © MEG

G.I. Combat #244, © DC

GD25 FN65 NM94

origin) 1.40 3.50 8.50
Captain Marvel 1(12/75)-r/Capt. Marvel #17, 20 by Gil Kane (p) 1.25 3.00 7.50
Chillers 1(6/74, 52 pgs)-Curse of Dracula; origin/1st app. Lilith, Dracula's daughter; Heath-r, Colan-c/a(p); becomes Giant-Size Dracula #2 on 1.40 3.50
Chillers 1(2/75, 50 cents, 68 pgs.)-Alacala-a 1.20 3.00
Chillers 2(5/75)-All-r; Everett-r from Advs. into Weird Worlds 1.00 2.50
Chillers 3(8/75)-Wrightson-c(new)/a(r); Colan, Kirby, Smith-r 1.40 3.50
Conan 1(9/74)-B. Smith-r/#3; start adaptation of Howard's "Hour of the Dragon" (ends #4); 1st app. Belit; new-a begins 1.10 2.70 6.60
Conan 2(12/74)-B. Smith-r/#5, Sutton-a(i)(#1 also); Buscema-c 2.50 5.50
Conan 3-5: 3(4/75)-B. Smith-r/#6; Sutton-a(i). 4(6/75)-B. Smith-r/#7. 5(1975)-B. Smith-r/#14,15; Kirby-c 1.40 3.50
Creatures 1(5/74, 52 pgs.)-Werewolf app; 1st app. Tigra (formerly Cat); Crandall-r; becomes Giant-Size Werewolf w/#2 1.40 3.50
Daredevil 1(1975) 1.10 2.70 6.50
Defenders 1(7/74)-Silver Surfer app.; Starlin-a; Ditko, Everett & Kirby reprints 1.60 4.00 9.50
Defenders 2(10/74, 68 pgs.)-New G. Kane-c/a(p); Son of Satan app.; Sub-Mariner-r by Everett; Ditko-r/Strange Tales #119 (Dr. Strange) 2.50 5.50
Defenders 3-5: 3(1/75)-Newton, Starlin-a; Ditko, Everett-r. 4(4/75)-Ditko, Everett-r; G. Kane-c. 5-(7/75)-Guardians app. 1.80 4.50
Doc Savage 1(1975, 68 pgs.)-r/#1,2; Mooney-r 1.40 3.50
Doctor Strange 1(11/75)-Reprints stories from Strange Tales #164-168; Lawrence, Tuska-r 2.50 5.50
Dracula 2(9/74, 50 cents)-Formerly Giant-Size Chillers 1.80 4.50
Dracula 3(12/74)-Fox-r/Uncanny Tales #6 1.40 3.50
Dracula 4(3/75)-Ditko-r(2) 1.00 2.50
Dracula 5(6/75)-1st Byrne art at Marvel 1.00 2.50 5.50
Fantastic Four 2-4: 2(8/74)-Formerly Giant-Size Super-Stars; Ditko-r. 3(11/74). 4(2/75)-1st Madrox; 2-4-All have Buscema-a 1.40 3.50 8.50
Fantastic Four 5,6: 5(5/75)-All-r; Kirby, G. Kane-r. 6(10/75)-All-r; Kirby-r 1.10 2.70 6.50
Hulk 1(1975) 1.65 4.70 11.00
Invaders 1(6/75, 50 cents, 68 pgs.)-Origin; G.A. Sub-Mariner-r/Sub-Mariner #1; intro Master Man 1.00 2.50 5.50
Iron Man 1(1975)-Ditko reprint 1.40 3.50 8.50
Kid Colt 1-3: 1(1/75). 2(4/75). 3(7/75) 1.40 3.50
Man-Thing 1(8/74)-New Ploog-c/a; Ditko, Kirby-r (#1-5 all have new Man-Thing stories, pre-hero-r & are 68 pgs.) 1.00 2.50 5.50
Man-Thing 2,3: 2(11/74)-Buscema-c/a(p); Kirby, Powell-r. 3(2/75)-Alcala-a; Ditko, Kirby, Sutton-r; Gil Kane-c 1.40 3.50
Man-Thing 4,5: 4(5/75)-Howard the Duck by Brunner-c/a; Ditko-r. 5(8/75)-Howard the Duck by Brunner (p); Buscema-a(p); Sutton-a(i); G. Kane-c 1.00 2.50 5.50
Marvel Triple Action 1,2: 1(5/75). 2(7/75) 1.00 2.50
Master of Kung Fu 1(9/74)-Russell-a; Yellow Claw-r in #1-4; Gulacy-a in #1,2 1.10 2.70 6.50
Master of Kung Fu 2(12/74)-r/Yellow Claw #1 1.60 4.00
Master of Kung Fu 3(3/75)-Gulacy-a 1.40 3.50
Master of Kung Fu 4(6/75) 1.40 3.50
Power Man 1(1975) 1.00 2.50 5.50
Spider-Man 1(7/74)-Kirby/Ditko, Byrne-r plus new-a (Dracula-c/story) 3.20 9.00 21.00
Spider-Man 2,3: 2(10/74). 3(1/75)-Byrne-r 1.40 3.50 8.50
Spider-Man 4(4/75)-3rd Punisher app.; Byrne, Ditko-r 9.00 26.00 60.00
Spider-Man 5,6: 5(7/75)-Byrne-r. 6(9/75) 1.25 3.00 7.50
Super-Heroes Featuring Spider-Man 1(6/74, 35 cents, 52 pgs.)-Spider-Man vs. Man-Wolf; Morbius, the Living Vampire app.; Ditko-r; G. Kane-a(p); Spidey villains app. 5.50 17.00 40.00
Super-Stars 1(5/74, 35 cents, 52 pgs.)-Fantastic Four; Thing vs. Hulk; Kirbyish-c/a by Buckler/Sinnott; F.F. villains profiled; becomes Giant-Size Fantastic Four #2 on 1.85 5.50 13.00
Super-Villain Team-Up 1(3/75, 68 pgs.)-Craig-r(i) (Also see Fantastic Four #6 for 1st super-villain team-up) 1.10 2.70 6.50
Super-Villain Team-Up 2(6/75, 68 pgs.)-Dr. Doom, Sub-Mariner app.; Spider-Man-r/Amazing Spider-Man #8 by Ditko; Sekowsky-a(p) 1.80 4.50
Thor 1(7/75) 1.00 2.50 5.50
Werewolf 2(10/74, 68 pgs.)-Formerly Giant-Size Creatures; Ditko-r; Frankenstein app 1.40 3.50
Werewolf 3,5: 3(1/75, 68 pgs.). 5(7/75, 68 pgs.) 1.40 3.50
Werewolf 4(4/75, 68 pgs.)-Morbius the Living Vampire app. 1.80 4.50
X-Men 1(Summer, 1975, 50 cents, 68 pgs.)-1st app. new X-Men; intro Nightcrawler, Storm, Colossus & Thunderbird; 2nd full app. Wolverine after Incredible Hulk #181 33.00 100.00 230.00
X-Men 2(11/75)-N. Adams-r(51 pgs) 3.85 11.50 27.00

GIANT SPECTACULAR COMICS (See Archie All-Star Special under Archie Comics)

GIANT SUMMER FUN BOOK (See Terry-Toons...)

G. I. COMBAT
Oct, 1952 - No. 43, Dec, 1956
Quality Comics Group

	GD25	FN65	NM94
1-Crandall-c; Cuidera a-1-43i	36.00	110.00	250.00
2	15.00	45.00	105.00
3-5,10-Crandall-c/a	14.00	43.00	100.00
6-Crandall-a	13.00	40.00	90.00
7-9	11.00	32.00	75.00
11-20	10.00	30.00	60.00
21-31,33,35-43	7.50	22.50	45.00
32-Nuclear attack-c	10.00	30.00	60.00
34-Crandall-a	8.35	25.00	50.00

G. I. COMBAT (See DC Special Series #22)
No. 44, Jan, 1957 - No. 288, Mar, 1987
National Periodical Publications/DC Comics

	GD25	FN65	NM94
44-Grey tone-c	24.00	71.00	235.00
45	17.00	51.00	120.00
46-50	11.00	32.00	75.00
51-60: 51-Grey tone-c	7.00	21.00	50.00
61-66,68-80: 75-109-Grey tone-c	4.85	15.00	34.00
67-1st Tank Killer	9.00	26.00	60.00
81,82,84-86,88-90: 90-Last 10 cent issue	4.70	14.00	33.00
83-1st Big Al, Little Al, & Charlie Cigar	5.50	16.00	38.00
87-1st Haunted Tank	12.00	36.00	85.00
91-100	3.40	10.00	24.00
101-110: 108-1st Sgt. Rock x-over	2.60	7.50	18.00
111-113,115-120: 113-Grey tone-c	2.15	6.50	15.00
114-Origin Haunted Tank	6.00	19.00	44.00
121-137,139,140: 121-1st app. Sgt. Rock's father. 136-Last 12 cent issue		1.85	5.50	13.00
138-Intro. The Losers (Capt. Storm, Gunner/Sarge, Johnny Cloud) In Haunted Tank (10-11/69)	1.70	5.00	12.00
141-200: 146-148-(25 cent, 68 pgs.). 149-154-(52 pgs.). 150-Ice Cream Soldier story (tells how he got his name). 151-Capt. Storm story. 151,153-Medal of Honor series by Maurer		1.90	4.75
201-281: 201-215,217-260 are $1.00 size. 232-Origin Kana the Ninja. 244-Death of Slim Stryker; 1st app. The Mercenaries. 246-(76 pgs., $1.50)-30th Anniversary issue. 257-Intro. Stuart's Raiders. 260-Begin $1.25, 52 pg. issues, end #281. 264-Intro Sgt. Bullet; origin Kana. 269-Intro. The Bravos of Vietnam		1.20	3.00
282-288 (75 cents): 282-New advs. begin		1.20	3.00

NOTE: ***N. Adams** c-168, 201, 202. **Check** a-168, 173. **Drucker** a-48, 61, 63, 66, 71, 72, 76, 134, 140, 141, 144, 147, 148, 153. **Evans** a-135, 138, 158, 164, 166, 201, 202, 204, 205, 215, 256. Giffen a-267. **Glanzman** a-most issues. **Kubert/Heath** a-most issues; **Kubert** covers most issues. **Morrow** a-159-161(2 pgs.). **Redondo** a-189, 240i, 243i. **Sekowsky** a-162p. **Severin** a-*

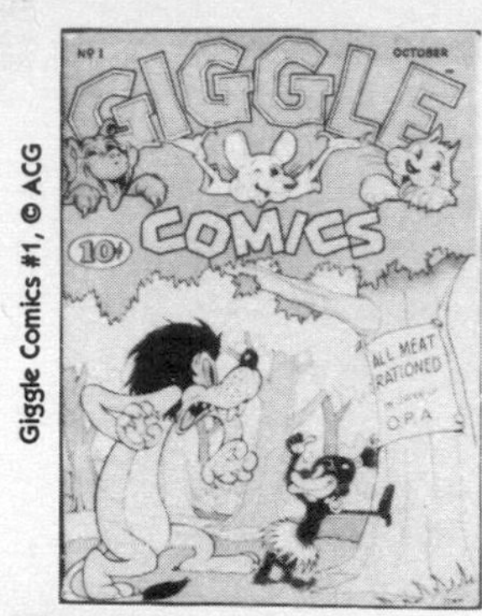

Giggle Comics #1, © ACG

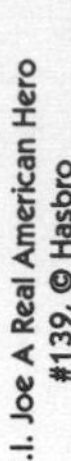
G.I. Joe A Real American Hero #139, © Hasbro

Gilgamesh II #1, © DC

GD25 FN65 NM94 GD25 FN65 NM94

147, 152, 154. ***Simonson*** *c-169.* ***Thorne*** *a-152, 156.* ***Wildey*** *a-153. Johnny Cloud app.-112, 115, 120. Mlle. Marie app.-123, 132, 200. Sgt. Rock app.-111-113, 115, 120, 125, 141, 146, 147, 149, 200. USS Stevens by* ***Glanzman****-145, 150-153, 157.* ***Grandenetti*** *c-44-48.*

G. I. COMICS (Also see Jeep & Overseas Comics)
1945 (Distributed to U. S. armed forces)
Giveaways

	GD25	FN65	NM94
1-49-Contains Prince Valiant by Foster, Blondie, Smilin' Jack, Mickey Finn, Terry & the Pirates, Donald Duck, Alley Oop, Moon Mullins & Capt. Easy strip reprints	4.00	12.00	28.00

GIDGET (TV)
April, 1966 - No. 2, Dec, 1966
Dell Publishing Co.

	GD25	FN65	NM94
1,2: 1-Sally Field photo-c	6.70	20.00	40.00

GIFT (See The Crusaders)

GIFT COMICS (50 cents)
1942 - No. 4, 1949 (No. 1-3: 50¢, 324 pgs.; No. 4: 25¢, 152 pgs.)
Fawcett Publications

	GD25	FN65	NM94
1-Captain Marvel, Bulletman, Golden Arrow, Ibis the Invincible, Mr. Scarlet, & Spy Smasher app. Not rebound, remaindered comics, printed at same time as originals	175.00	525.00	1100.00
2	123.00	370.00	800.00
3	87.00	262.00	575.00
4-The Marvel Family, Captain Marvel, etc.; each issue can vary in contents	61.00	182.00	400.00

GIFTS FROM SANTA (See March of Comics No. 137)

GIGGLE COMICS (Spencer Spook No. 100) (Also see Ha Ha Comics)
Oct, 1943 - No. 99, Jan-Feb, 1955
Creston No.1-63/American Comics Group No. 64 on

	GD25	FN65	NM94
1	22.00	65.00	150.00
2	10.00	30.00	70.00
3-5: Ken Hultgren-a begins?	7.50	22.50	45.00
6-10: 9-1st Superkatt (6/44)	6.35	19.00	38.00
11-20	4.70	14.00	28.00
21-40: 32-Patriotic-c. 39-St. Valentine's Day-c	4.00	11.00	22.00
41-54,56-59,61-99: 95-Spencer Spook app.	3.60	9.00	18.00
55,60-Milt Gross-a	4.00	12.00	24.00

G-I IN BATTLE (G-I No. 1 only)
Aug, 1952 - No. 9, July, 1953; Mar, 1957 - No. 6, May, 1958
Ajax-Farrell Publ./Four Star

	GD25	FN65	NM94
1	5.35	16.00	32.00
2	3.60	9.00	18.00
3-9	2.80	7.00	14.00
Annual 1(1952, 100 pgs.)	16.00	48.00	110.00
1(1957-Ajax)	4.00	11.00	22.00
2-6	2.40	6.00	12.00

G. I. JANE
May, 1953 - No. 11, Mar, 1955 (Misdated 3/54)
Stanhall/Merit No. 11

	GD25	FN65	NM94
1-PX Pete begins; Bill Williams-c/a	7.50	22.50	45.00
2-7(5/54)	4.00	11.00	22.00
8-10(12/54, Stanhall)	3.60	9.00	18.00
11 (3/55, Merit)	3.20	8.00	16.00

G. I. JOE (Also see Advs. of..., Showcase #53, 54 & The Yardbirds)
No. 10, 1950; No. 11, 4-5/51 - No. 51, 6/57 (52pgs.: 10-14,6-17?)
Ziff-Davis Publ. Co. (Korean War)

	GD25	FN65	NM94
10(#1, 1950)-Saunders painted-c begin	8.35	25.00	50.00
11-14(#2-5, 10/51): 11-New logo. 12-New logo	5.35	16.00	32.00
V2#6(12/51)-17-(Last 52pgs.?)	4.70	14.00	28.00
18-(100 pg. Giant-'52)	11.00	32.00	75.00
19-30: 20-22,24,28-31-The Yardbirds app.	4.00	11.00	22.00
31-47,49-51	4.00	10.00	20.00
48-Atom bomb story	4.00	11.00	22.00

NOTE: ***Powell*** *a-V2#7, 8, 11.* ***Norman Saunders*** *painted c-10-14, V2#6-14, 26, 30, 31, 35, 38, 39.* ***Tuska*** *a-7. Bondage c-29, 35, 38.*

G. I. JOE (America's Movable Fighting Man)
1967 (36 pages) (5-1/8x8-3/8")
Custom Comics

	GD25	FN65	NM94
nn-Schaffenberger-a; based on Hasbro toy			1.00

G. I. JOE AND THE TRANSFORMERS
Jan, 1987 - No. 4, Apr, 1987 (Mini-series)
Marvel Comics Group

	GD25	FN65	NM94
1-4			1.00

G. I. JOE, A REAL AMERICAN HERO
June, 1982 - Present
Marvel Comics Group

	GD25	FN65	NM94
1-Printed on Baxter paper; based on Hasbro toy	1.00	2.00	5.00
2-Printed on reg. paper		1.90	4.75
3-10		1.20	3.00
11-20: 11-Intro Airborne		.65	1.60
21,22,26,27: 26,27-Origin Snake-Eyes parts 1 & 2		.80	2.00
23-25,28-30		.70	1.80
31-134,139-146: 33-New headquarters. 60-Todd McFarlane-a. 139,140-New Transformers app.		.65	1.60
135-138-($1.75)-Polybagged w/trading card		.70	1.75
All 2nd printings			1.00
Special Treasury Edition (1982)-r/#1		1.20	3.00
...Yearbook 1 (3/85)-r/#1; Golden-c		.80	2.00
...Yearbook 2 (3/86)-Golden-c/a , 3(3/87, 68 pgs.)		.70	1.80
...Yearbook 4 (2/88)			1.50

NOTE: ***Golden*** *c-23, 29, 34, 36.* ***Heath*** *a-24.* ***Rogers*** *a(p)-75, 77-82, 84, 86; c-77.*

G. I. JOE COMICS MAGAZINE
Dec, 1986 - No. 13, 1988 ($1.50, digest-size)
Marvel Comics Group

	GD25	FN65	NM94
1-13: G.I. Joe-r			1.50

G.I. JOE EUROPEAN MISSIONS (Action Force in indicia)
June, 1988 - No. 15, Dec, 1989 ($1.50/$1.75 #12 on, color)
Marvel Comics Ltd. (British)

	GD25	FN65	NM94
1-15: Reprints Action Force			1.50

G. I. JOE ORDER OF BATTLE, THE
Dec, 1986 - No. 4, Mar, 1987 (Mini-series)
Marvel Comics Group

	GD25	FN65	NM94
1-4			1.00

G. I. JOE SPECIAL MISSIONS (Indicia title: Special Missions)
Oct, 1986 - No. 28, Dec, 1989 ($1.00, color)
Marvel Comics Group

	GD25	FN65	NM94
1-28			1.00

G. I. JUNIORS (See Harvey Hits No. 86, 91, 95, 98, 101, 104, 107, 110, 112, 114, 116, 118, 120, 122)

GILGAMESH II
1989 - No. 4, 1989 ($3.95, mini-series, prestige format)
DC Comics

	GD25	FN65	NM94
1-4: Starlin-c/a, scripts; mature readers		1.60	4.00

GIL THORP
May-July, 1963
Dell Publishing Co.

	GD25	FN65	NM94
1-Caniffish-a	2.80	7.00	14.00

GINGER (Li'l Jinx No. 11 on?)
1951 - No. 10, Summer, 1954
Archie Publications

	GD25	FN65	NM94
1	10.00	30.00	70.00
2	6.35	19.00	38.00

Ginger Fox #4, © Mike Baron & Pander Bros.

Girls in Love #49, © QUA

Girls' Romances #1, © DC

	GD25	FN65	NM94
3-6	4.35	13.00	26.00
7-10-Katy Keene app.	6.70	20.00	40.00

GINGER FOX (Also see The World of Ginger Fox)
Sept, 1988 - No. 4, Dec, 1988 ($1.75, color, mini-series)
Comico

	GD25	FN65	NM94
1-4: 1-4-part photo-c		.70	1.75

G.I. R.A.M.B.O.T.
April, 1987 - No. 2? ($1.95, color)
Wonder Color Comics/Pied Piper #2

	GD25	FN65	NM94
1,2: 2-Exist?		.80	2.00

GIRL COMICS (Becomes Girl Confessions No. 13 on)
Nov, 1949 - No. 12, Jan, 1952 (Photo-c 1-4)
Marvel/Atlas Comics(CnPC)

	GD25	FN65	NM94
1 (52 pgs.)	11.50	34.00	80.00
2-Kubert-a	7.50	22.50	45.00
3-Everett-a; Liz Taylor photo-c	10.00	30.00	60.00
4-11: 10-12-Sol Brodsky-c	4.70	16.00	32.00
12-Krigstein-a	6.70	20.00	40.00

GIRL CONFESSIONS (Formerly Girl Comics)
No. 13, Mar, 1952 - No. 35, Aug, 1954
Atlas Comics (CnPC/ZPC)

	GD25	FN65	NM94
13-Everett-a	7.00	21.00	42.00
14,15,19,20	4.70	14.00	28.00
16-18-Everett-a	5.35	16.00	32.00
21-35	3.20	8.00	16.00

GIRL FROM U.N.C.L.E., THE (TV) (Also see The Man From...)
Jan, 1967 - No. 5, Oct, 1967
Gold Key

	GD25	FN65	NM94
1-McWilliams-a; Stephanie Powers photo front/back-c & pin-ups (no ads, 12 cents)	5.50	17.00	40.00
2-5-Leonard Swift-Courier No. 5	3.85	11.50	27.00

GIRLS' FUN & FASHION MAGAZINE (Formerly Polly Pigtails)
V5#44, Jan, 1950 - V5#47, July, 1950
Parents' Magazine Institute

	GD25	FN65	NM94
V5#44	3.60	9.00	18.00
45-47	2.00	5.00	10.00

GIRLS IN LOVE
May, 1950 - No. 2, July, 1950
Fawcett Publications

	GD25	FN65	NM94
1,2-Photo-c	6.35	19.00	38.00

GIRLS IN LOVE (Formerly G. I. Sweethearts No. 45)
No. 46, Sept, 1955 - No. 57, Dec, 1956
Quality Comics Group

	GD25	FN65	NM94
46	4.20	12.50	25.00
47-56: 54-'Commie' story	3.00	7.50	15.00
57-Matt Baker-c/a	4.70	14.00	28.00

GIRLS IN WHITE (See Harvey Comics Hits No. 58)

GIRLS' LIFE
Jan, 1954 - No. 6, Nov, 1954
Atlas Comics (BFP)

	GD25	FN65	NM94
1-Patsy Walker	7.00	21.00	42.00
2	4.00	10.00	20.00
3-6	3.20	8.00	16.00

GIRLS' LOVE STORIES
Aug-Sept, 1949 - No. 180, Nov-Dec, 1973 (No. 1-13: 52 pgs.)
National Comics(Signal Publ. No. 9-65/Arleigh No. 83-117)

	GD25	FN65	NM94
1-Toth, Kinstler-a, 8 pgs. each; photo-c	36.00	110.00	250.00
2-Kinstler-a?	18.00	54.00	125.00
3-10: 1-9-Photo-c. 7-Infantino-c(p)	11.50	34.00	80.00
11-20	10.00	30.00	60.00
21-33: 21-Kinstler-a. 33-Last pre-code (1-2/55)	5.85	17.50	35.00
34-50	5.00	15.00	30.00
51-99: 83-Last 10 cent issue	3.60	9.00	18.00
100	4.00	10.00	20.00
101-146: 113-117-April O'Day app.	1.80	4.50	9.00
147-151-"Confessions" serial	1.40	3.50	7.00
152-180: 161-170, 52 pgs.	.90	2.25	4.50

GIRLS' ROMANCES
Feb-Mar, 1950 - No. 160, Oct, 1971 (No. 1-11: 52 pgs.)
National Periodical Publ.(Signal Publ. No. 7-79/Arleigh No. 84)

	GD25	FN65	NM94
1-Photo-c	36.00	110.00	250.00
2-Photo-c; Toth-a	18.00	54.00	125.00
3-10: 3-6-Photo-c	11.50	34.00	80.00
11,12,14-20	9.15	27.50	55.00
13-Toth-c	10.00	30.00	65.00
21-31: 31-Last pre-code (2-3/55)	5.35	16.00	32.00
32-50	4.70	14.00	28.00
51-99: 80-Last 10 cent issue	3.60	9.00	18.00
100	4.00	11.00	22.00
101-108,110-120	2.40	6.00	12.00
109-Beatles-c/story	6.70	20.00	40.00
121-133,135-140	1.60	4.00	8.00
134-Neal Adams-c	2.00	5.00	10.00
141-160: 159,160-52 pgs.	.90	2.25	4.50

G. I. SWEETHEARTS (Formerly Diary Loves; Girls In Love #46 on)
No. 32, June, 1953 - No. 45, May, 1955
Quality Comics Group

	GD25	FN65	NM94
32	4.00	12.00	24.00
33-45: 44-Last pre-code (3/55)	3.00	7.50	15.00

G.I. TALES (Formerly Sgt. Barney Barker No. 1-3)
No. 4, Feb, 1957 - No. 6, July, 1957
Atlas Comics (MCI)

	GD25	FN65	NM94
4-Severin-a(4)	4.70	14.00	28.00
5	3.60	9.00	18.00
6-Orlando, Powell, & Woodbridge-a	4.00	10.00	20.00

GIVE ME LIBERTY (Dark Horse)(Value: cover or less)

G. I. WAR BRIDES
April, 1954 - No. 8, June, 1955
Superior Publishers Ltd.

	GD25	FN65	NM94
1	4.00	12.00	24.00
2	2.40	6.00	12.00
3-8: 4-Kamenesque-a; lingerie panels	1.60	4.00	8.00

G. I. WAR TALES
Mar-Apr, 1973 - No. 4, Oct-Nov, 1973
National Periodical Publications

	GD25	FN65	NM94
1-4: Reprints. 2-N. Adams-a(r), 4-Krigstein-a(r)			1.00

NOTE: ***Drucker** a-3r, 4r. **Heath** a-4r. **Kubert** a-2, 3; c-4r.*

GIZMO (Also see Domino Chance)
May-June, 1985 (B&W, one shot)
Chance Ent.

	GD25	FN65	NM94
1	1.00	2.00	5.00

GIZMO
1986 - No. 6, July, 1987 ($1.50, B&W)
Mirage Studios

	GD25	FN65	NM94
1		1.60	4.00
2-6		1.00	2.50

GLADSTONE COMIC ALBUM (Also see The Original Dick Tracy Comic...)
1987 - No. 28, 1990 (8-1/2x11")($5.95)(#26-28: $9.95)
Gladstone Publishing

1-10: 1-Uncle Scrooge; Barks-r; Beck-c. 2-Donald Duck; r/F.C. #108 by Barks.

Gladstone Comic Album #17, © The Disney Co.

Godzilla #2, © MEG

The Golden Age #2, © DC

GD25 FN65 NM94

3-Mickey Mouse-r by Gottfredson. 4-Uncle Scrooge; r/F.C. #456 by Barks. 5-Donald Duck Advs.; r/F.C. #199. 6-Uncle Scrooge-r by Barks. 7-Donald Duck-r by Barks. 8-Mickey Mouse-r. 9-Bambi; r/F.C. #12. 10-Donald Duck Advs.; r/F.C. #275 1.00 2.50 6.00

11-20: 11-Uncle Scrooge; r/U.S. #4. 12-Donald And Daisy; r/F.C. #1055, WDC&S. 13-Donald Duck Advs.; r/F.C. #408. 14-Uncle Scrooge; Barks-r/U.S #21. 15-Donald And Gladstone; Barks-r. 16-Donald Duck Advs.; r/F.C. #238. 17-Mickey Mouse strip-r (The World of Tomorrow, The Pirate Ghost Ship). 18-Donald Duck and the Junior Woodchucks; Barks-r. 19-Uncle Scrooge; r/U.S. #12; Rosa-c. 20-Uncle Scrooge; r/F.C. #386; Barks-c/a(r) 1.00 2.50 6.00

21-25: 21-Donald Duck Family; Barks-c/a(r). 22-Mickey Mouse strip-r. 23-Donald Duck; Barks-r/D.D. #26. 24-Uncle Scrooge; Barks-r; Rosa-c. 25-D. Duck; Barks-c/a-r/F.C. #367 1.00 2.50 6.00

26-28: 26-Mickey and Donald; Gottfredson-c/a(r). 27-Donald Duck; r/WDC&S by Barks; Barks painted-c. 28-Uncle Scrooge & Donald Duck; Rosa-c/a (4 stories) 1.65 4.00 10.00

Special 1 (1989, $9.95)-Donald Duck Finds Pirate Gold; r/F.C. #9 1.65 4.00 10.00

Special 2 (1989, $8.95)-Uncle Scrooge and Donald Duck; Barks-r/Uncle Scrooge #5; Rosa-c 1.50 3.75 9.00

Special 3 (1989, $8.95)-Mickey Mouse strip-r 1.50 3.75 9.00

Special 4 (1989, $11.95)-Uncle Scrooge; Rosa-c/a-r/Son of the Sun from U.S. #219 plus Barks-r/U.S. 1.70 5.00 12.00

Special 5 (1990, $11.95)-Donald Duck Advs.; Barks-r/F.C. #282 & 422 plus Barks painted-c 1.70 5.00 12.00

Special 6 (1990, $12.95)-Uncle Scrooge; Barks-c/a-r/Uncle Scrooge 1.85 5.50 13.00

Special 7 (1990, $13.95)-Mickey Mouse; Gottfredson strip-r 2.00 6.00 14.00

GLAMOROUS ROMANCES (Formerly Dotty)
No. 41, July, 1949 - No. 90, Oct, 1956 (Photo-c 68-90)
Ace Magazines (A. A. Wyn)

41-Dotty app. 5.00 15.00 30.00

42-72,74-80: 44-Begin 52 pg. issues. 45,50-61-Painted-c. 80-Last pre-code (2/55) 2.80 7.00 14.00

73-L.B. Cole-r/All Love #27 3.20 8.00 16.00

81-90 2.40 6.00 12.00

GLOBAL FORCE (Silverline)(Value: cover or less)

GNOME MOBILE, THE (See Movie Comics)

GOBBLEDYGOOK
1984 - No. 2, 1984 (B&W)(1st Mirage comic, published at same time)
Mirage Studios

1,2-(24 pgs.)-1st Teenage Mutant Ninja Turtles 32.00 95.00 220.00

GOBBLEDYGOOK
Dec, 1986 (One shot, $3.50, B&W, 100 pgs.)
Mirage Studios

1-New 8 pg. TMNT story plus a Donatello/Michaelangelo 7 pg. story & a Gizmo story; Corben-i(r)/TMNT #7 1.80 4.50

GOBLIN, THE
June, 1982 - No. 4, Dec, 1982 (Magazine, $2.25)
Warren Publishing Co.

1-The Gremlin app; Golden-a(p) .90 2.25

2-4: 2-1st Hobgoblin .90 2.25

GODFATHERS, THE (See The Crusaders)

GOD IS (Spire Christian)(Value: cover or less)

GODS FOR HIRE (Hot Comics)(Value; cover or less)

GOD'S HEROES IN AMERICA
1956 (nn) (68 pgs.) (25-35 cents)
Catechetical Guild Educational Society

307 1.60 4.00 8.00

GD25 FN65 NM94

GOD'S SMUGGLER (Spire Christian)(Value: cover or less)

GODZILLA
August, 1977 - No. 24, July, 1979 (Based on movie series)
Marvel Comics Group

1-Mooney-i 1.10 2.70 6.50

2-10: 2-Tuska-i. 3-Champions app.(w/o Ghost Rider). 4,5-Sutton-a 1.80 4.50

11-24: 20-F.F. app. 21,22-Devil Dinosaur app. 1.20 3.00

GODZILLA
May, 1988 - No. 6, 1988 ($1.95, B&W, mini-series)
Dark Horse Comics

1 1.00 2.50 6.00

2-6 1.20 3.00

...Collection (1990, $10.95)-r/1-6 with new-c 1.65 4.70 11.00

...Color Special 1 (Sum, 1992, $3.50, color, 44 pgs.)-Arthur Adams wrap-around-c/a & part scripts 1.40 3.50

King Of The Monsters Special (8/87, $1.50)-Origin; Bissette-c/a 1.520 3.00

GO-GO
June, 1966 - No. 9, Oct, 1967
Charlton Comics

1-Miss Bikini Luv begins; Rolling Stones, Beatles, Elvis, Sonny & Cher, Bob Dylan, Sinatra, parody; Herman's Hermits pin-ups 3.60 10.75 25.00

2-Ringo Starr, David McCallum & Beatles photos on cover; Beatles story and photos 3.60 10.75 25.00

3,4: 3-Blooperman begins, ends #6; 1 pg. Batman & Robin satire; full pg. photo pin-ups Lovin' Spoonful & The Byrds 2.15 6.50 15.00

5-9: 5-Super Hero & TV satire by Jim Aparo & Grass Green begins. 6-8-Aparo-a. 6-Petula Clark photo-c. 7-Photo of Brian Wilson of Beach Boys on-c & Beach Boys photo inside f/b-c. 8-Monkees photo on-c & photo inside f/b-c 2.15 6.50 15.00

GO-GO AND ANIMAL (See Tippy's Friends...)

GOING STEADY (Formerly Teen-Age Temptations)
No. 10, Dec, 1954 - No. 13, June, 1955; No. 14, Oct, 1955
St. John Publishing Co.

10(1954)-Matt Baker-c/a 10.00 30.00 60.00

11(2/55, last precode), 12(4/55)-Baker-c 5.00 15.00 30.00

13(6/55)-Baker-c/a 5.85 17.50 35.00

14(10/55)-Matt Baker-c/a, 25 pgs. 6.70 20.00 40.00

GOING STEADY (Formerly Personal Love)
V3#3, Feb, 1960 - V3#6, Aug, 1960; V4#1, Sept-Oct, 1960
Prize Publications/Headline

V3#3-6, V4#1 1.80 4.50 9.00

GOING STEADY WITH BETTY (Becomes Betty & Her Steady No. 2)
Nov-Dec, 1949
Avon Periodicals

1 10.00 30.00 60.00

GOLDEN AGE, THE
1993 - No. 4, 1993 ($4.95, color, mini-series)
DC Comics

1-4-Gold foil embossed-c 1.00 2.00 5.00

GOLDEN ARROW (See Fawcett Miniatures, Mighty Midget & Whiz Comics)

GOLDEN ARROW (...Western No. 6)
Wint, 1942-43 - No. 6, Spring, 1947
Fawcett Publications

1-Golden Arrow begins 24.00 73.00 170.00

2 11.00 32.00 75.00

3-5 9.15 27.50 55.00

6-Krigstein-a 10.00 30.00 60.00

Golden Comics Digest #2, © Hanna-Barbera

Golden Lad #4, © Spark nPubl.

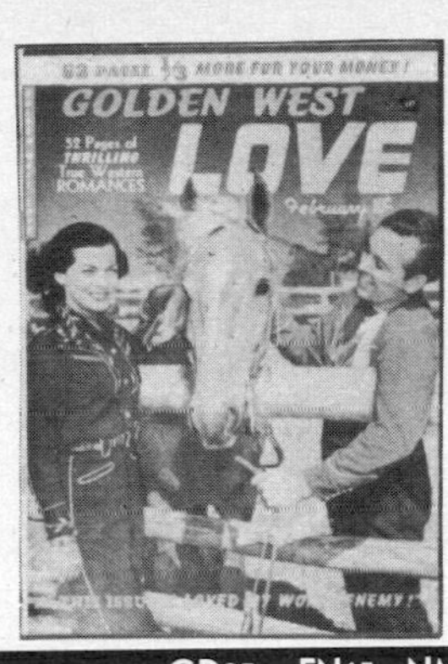

Golden West Love #3, © Kirby Publ.

GD25 FN65 NM94 GD25 FN65 NM94

...Well Known Comics (1944; 12 pgs.; 8-1/2x10-1/2"; paper-c; glued binding)-Bestmaid/Samuel Lowe giveaway; printed in green 6.00 18.00 42.00

GOLDEN COMICS DIGEST
May, 1969 - No. 48, Jan, 1976
Gold Key
NOTE: *Whitman editions exist of many titles and are generally valued less.*

1-Tom & Jerry, Woody Woodpecker, Bugs Bunny 2.40 6.00 12.00
2-Hanna-Barbera TV Fun Favorites; Space Ghost, Flintstones, Atom Ant, Jetsons, Yogi Bear, Banana Splits, others app. 1.70 5.00 12.00
3-Tom & Jerry, Woody Woodpecker 1.00 2.00 5.00
4-Tarzan; Manning & Marsh-a 2.00 6.00 14.00
5,8-Tom & Jerry, W. Woodpecker, Bugs Bunny 1.60 4.00
6-Bugs Bunny 1.60 4.00
7-Hanna-Barbera TV Fun Favorites 1.30 3.25 8.00
9-Tarzan 1.70 5.00 12.00
10-17: 10-Bugs Bunny. 11-Hanna-Barbera TV Fun Favorites. 12-Tom & Jerry, Bugs Bunny, W. Woodpecker Journey to the Sun. 13-Tom & Jerry. 14-Bugs Bunny Fun Packed Funnies. 15-Tom & Jerry, Woody Woodpecker, Bugs Bunny. 16-Woody Woodpecker Cartoon Special. 17-Bugs Bunny 1.60 4.00
18-Tom & Jerry; Barney Bear-r by Barks 1.00 2.00 5.00
19-Little Lulu 1.70 5.00 12.00
20-22: 20-Woody Woodpecker Falltime Funtime. 21-Bugs Bunny Showtime. 22-Tom & Jerry Winter Wingding 1.60 4.00
23-Little Lulu & Tubby Fun Fling 1.70 5.00 12.00
24-26,28: 24-Woody Woodpecker Fun Festival. 25-Tom & Jerry. 26-Bugs Bunny Halloween Hulla-Boo-Loo; Dr. Spektor article, also #25. 28-Tom & Jerry 1.60 4.00
27-Little Lulu & Tubby in Hawaii 1.65 4.00 10.00
29-Little Lulu & Tubby 1.65 4.00 10.00
30-Bugs Bunny Vacation Funnies 1.60 4.00
31-Turok, Son of Stone; r/4-Color #596,656 1.70 5.00 12.00
32-Woody Woodpecker Summer Fun 1.60 4.00
33,36: 33-Little Lulu & Tubby Halloween Fun; Dr. Spektor app. 36-Little Lulu & Her Friends 1.70 5.00 12.00
34,35,37-39: 34-Bugs Bunny Winter Funnies. 35-Tom & Jerry Snowtime Funtime. 37-Woody Woodpecker County Fair. 38-The Pink Panther. 39-Bugs Bunny Summer Fun 1.60 4.00
40,43: 40-Little Lulu & Tubby Trick or Treat; all by Stanley. 43-Little Lulu in Paris 1.70 5.00 12.00
41,42,44,45,47: 41-Tom & Jerry Winter Carnival. 42-Bugs Bunny. 44-Woody Woodpecker Family Fun Festival. 45-The Pink Panther. 47-Bugs Bunny 1.20 3.00
46-Little Lulu & Tubby 1.65 4.00 10.00
48-The Lone Ranger 1.00 2.00 5.00
NOTE: *#1-30, 164 pages; #31 on, 132 pages.*

GOLDEN LAD
July, 1945 - No. 5, June, 1946
Spark Publications

1-Origin & 1st app. Golden Lad & Swift Arrow 46.00 138.00 300.00
2-Mort Meskin-c/a 22.00 68.00 150.00
3,4-Mort Meskin-c/a 18.00 55.00 120.00
5-Origin Golden Girl; Shaman & Flame app. 22.00 68.00 150.00
NOTE: *All have* **Robinson, and Roussos** *art plus* **Meskin** *covers and art. #5 is 52pgs.*

GOLDEN LEGACY
1966 - 1972 (Black History) (25 cents)
Fitzgerald Publishing Co.

1-Toussaint L'Ouverture (1966), 2-Harriet Tubman (1967), 3-Crispus Attucks & the Minutemen (1967), 4-Benjamin Banneker (1968), 5-Matthew Henson (1969), 6-Alexander Dumas & Family (1969), 7-Frederick Douglass, Part 1 (1969), 8-Frederick Douglass, Part 2 (1970), 9-Robert Smalls (1970), 10-J. Cinque & the Amistad Mutiny (1970), 11-Men in Action: White, Marshall J. Wilkins (1970), 12-Black Cowboys (1972), 13-The Life of Martin Luther King, Jr. (1972), 14-The Life of Alexander Pushkin (1971), 15-Ancient African Kingdoms (1972), 16-Black Inventors (1972)
each.... 1.50
1-10,12,13,15,16(1976)-Reprints 1.00

GOLDEN LOVE STORIES (Formerly Golden West Love)
No. 4, April, 1950
Kirby Publishing Co.

4-Powell-a; Glenn Ford/Janet Leigh photo-c 10.00 30.00 65.00

GOLDEN PICTURE CLASSIC, A
1956-1957 (Text stories w/illustrations in color; 100 pgs. each)
Western Printing Co. (Simon & Shuster)

CL-401: Treasure Island 8.35 25.00 50.00
CL-402: Tom Sawyer 7.00 21.00 42.00
CL-403: Black Beauty 7.00 21.00 42.00
CL-404: Little Women 7.00 21.00 42.00
CL-405: Heidi 7.00 21.00 42.00
CL-406: Ben Hur 4.70 14.00 28.00
CL-407: Around the World in 80 Days 4.70 14.00 28.00
CL-408: Sherlock Holmes 5.85 17.50 35.00
CL-409: The Three Musketeers 4.70 14.00 28.00
CL-410: The Merry Advs. of Robin Hood 4.70 14.00 28.00
CL-411: Hans Brinker 5.85 17.50 35.00
CL-412: The Count of Monte Cristo 5.85 17.50 35.00
(Both soft & hardcover editions are valued the same)

NOTE: *Recent research has uncovered new information. Apparently #s 1-6 were issued in 1956 and #7-12 in 1957. But they can be found in five different series listings: CL-1 to CL-12 (soft-bound); CL-401 to CL-412 (also softbound); CL-101 to CL-112 (hardbound); plus two new series discoveries: A Golden Reading Adventure, publ. by Golden Press; edited down to 60 pages and reduced in size to 6x9"; only #s discovered so far are #381 (CL-4), #382 (CL-6) & #387 (CL-3). They have no reorder list and some have covers different from GPC. There have also been found British hardbound editions of GPC with dust jackets. Copies of all five listed series vary from scarce to very rare. Some editions of some series have not yet been found at all.*

GOLDEN PICTURE STORY BOOK
Dec, 1961 (52 pgs.; 50 cents; large size)(All are scarce)
Racine Press (Western)

ST-1-Huckleberry Hound (TV) 14.00 43.00 100.00
ST-2-Yogi Bear (TV) 14.00 43.00 100.00
ST-3-Babes in Toyland (Walt Disney's...)-Annette Funicello photo-c 13.00 40.00 90.00
ST-4-(...of Disney Ducks)-Walt Disney's Wonderful World of Ducks (Donald Duck, Uncle Scrooge, Donald's Nephews, Grandma Duck, Ludwig Von Drake, & Gyro Gearloose stories) 13.00 40.00 90.00

GOLDEN RECORD COMIC (See Amazing Spider-Man #1, Avengers #4, Fantastic Four #1, Journey Into Mystery #83)

GOLDEN WEST LOVE (Golden Love Stories No. 4)
Sept-Oct, 1949 - No. 3, Feb, 1950 (All 52 pgs.)
Kirby Publishing Co.

1-Powell-a in all; Roussos-a; painted-c 11.50 34.00 80.00
2,3: Photo-c 9.15 27.50 55.00

GOLDEN WEST RODEO TREASURY (See Dell Giants)

GOLDILOCKS (See March of Comics No. 1)

GOLDILOCKS & THE THREE BEARS
1943 (Giveaway)
K. K. Publications

nn 8.35 25.00 50.00

GOLD KEY CHAMPION
Mar, 1978 - No. 2, May, 1978 (52 pages) (50 cents)
Gold Key

1-Space Family Robinson; half-r 1.00
2-Mighty Samson; half-r 1.00

GOLD KEY SPOTLIGHT
May, 1976 - No. 11, Feb, 1978
Gold Key

1-Tom, Dick & Harriet 1.60 4.00

Good Girl Art Quarterly (Sum. 90), © AC

Gorgo #2, © M.G.M.

Gravestone #1, © Malibu

GD25 FN65 NM94

2-5,710,11: 2-Wacky Advs. of Cracky. 3-Wacky Witch. 4-Tom, Dick & Harriet. 5-Wacky Advs. of Cracky. 7-Wacky Witch & Greta Ghost 10-O. G. Whiz. 11-Tom, Dick & Harriet 1.20 3.00
6,8,9: 6-Dagar the Invincible; Santos-a; origin Demonomicon. 8-The Occult Files of Dr. Spektor, Simbar, Lu-sai; Santos-a. 9-Tragg 1.60 4.00

GOLD MEDAL COMICS
1945 (132 pages) (One shot)
Cambridge House

nn-Captain Truth by Fugitani, Crime Detector, The Witch of Salem, Luckyman, others app. 16.00 48.00 110.00

GOMER PYLE (TV)
July, 1966 - No. 3, Jan, 1967
Gold Key

1-Photo front/back-c 5.50 17.00 40.00
2,3 5.00 15.00 35.00

GOODBYE, MR. CHIPS (See Movie Comics)

GOOD GIRL ART QUARTERLY (AC)(Value: cover or less)

GOOD GUYS, THE
Nov, 1993 - Present ($2.50, color)
Defiant

1-($3.50, 52 pgs.)-Glory x-over from Plasm 1.40 3.50
2-4 1.00 2.50

GOOFY (Disney)(See Dynabrite Comics, Mickey Mouse Magazine V4#7, Walt Disney Showcase #35 & Wheaties)
No. 468, May, 1953 - Sept-Nov, 1962
Dell Publishing Co.

4-Color 468 (#1) 10.00 30.00 60.00
4-Color 562,627,658,747,802 5.00 15.00 30.00
4-Color 899,952,987,1053,1094,1149,1201 4.00 10.00 20.00
12-308-211(Dell, 9-11/62) 4.00 10.00 20.00

GOOFY ADVENTURES
June, 1990 - No. 17, 1991 ($1.50, color)
Disney Comics

1-17: All new stories. 2-Joshua Quagmire-a w/free poster. 7-WDC&S-r plus new-a. 9-Gottfredson-r. 14-Super Goof story. 15-All Super Goof issue. 17-Gene Colan-a(p) 1.50

GOOFY ADVENTURE STORY (See 4-Color No. 857)

GOOFY COMICS (Companion to Happy Comics)
June, 1943 - No. 48, 1953
Nedor Publ. Co. No. 1-14/Standard No. 14-48 (Animated Cartoons)

1 17.00 52.00 120.00
2 10.00 30.00 60.00
3-10 6.70 20.00 40.00
11-19 5.00 15.00 30.00
20-35-Frazetta text illos in all 6.35 19.00 38.00
36-48 4.00 11.00 22.00

GOOFY SUCCESS STORY (See 4-Color No. 702)

GOOSE (Humor magazine)
Sept, 1976 - No. 3, 1976 (52 pgs.) (75 cents)
Cousins Publ. (Fawcett)

1-3 1.00

GORDO (See Comics Revue No. 5 & Giant Comics Edition)

GORGO (Based on movie) (See Return of...)
May, 1961 - No. 23, Sept, 1965
Charlton Comics

1-Ditko-a, 22 pgs. 23.00 70.00 160.00
2,3-Ditko-c/a 11.50 34.00 80.00
4-10: 4-Ditko-c 7.00 21.00 48.00

GD25 FN65 NM94

11,13-16-Ditko-a 5.50 16.00 38.00
12,17-23: 12-Reptisaurus x-over; Montes/Bache-a-No. 17-23. 20-Giordano-c 2.70 8.00 19.00
Gorgo's Revenge('62)-Becomes Return of... 4.70 14.00 33.00

GOSPEL BLIMP, THE (Spire Christian)(Value: cover or less)

GOTHAM BY GASLIGHT (A Tale of the Batman)(See Batman: Master of...)
1989 ($3.95, one-shot, squarebound, 52 pgs.)
DC Comics

nn-Mignola/Russell-a; intro by Robert Bloch 1.60 4.00

GOTHAM NIGHTS
Mar, 1992 - No. 4, June, 1992 ($1.25, color, mini-series)
DC Comics

1-4: Featuring Batman 1.25

GOTHIC ROMANCES
January, 1975 (B&W Magazine) (75 cents)
Atlas/Seaboard Publ.

1-Neal Adams-a .70 1.80

GOVERNOR & J. J., THE (TV)
Feb, 1970 - No. 3, Aug, 1970 (Photo-c)
Gold Key

1 3.60 10.75 25.00
2,3 2.60 7.50 18.00

GRAFIK MUZIK (Caliber)(Value: cover or less)

GRANDMA DUCK'S FARM FRIENDS (See 4-Color #763, 873, 965, 1010, 1073, 1161, 1279, Walt Disney's Comics & Stories #293 & Wheaties)

GRAND PRIX (Formerly Hot Rod Racers)
No. 16, Sept, 1967 - No. 31, May, 1970
Charlton Comics

16: Features Rick Roberts 1.70 5.00 12.00
17-20 1.50 3.75 9.00
21-31 1.00 2.00 5.00

GRAVESTONE
July, 1993 - Present ($2.25, color)
Malibu Comics

1-8 .90 2.25

GRAVE TALES (Also see Maggots)
Oct, 1991 - No. 3, Feb, 1992 ($3.95, B&W, magazine, 52 pgs.)
Hamilton Comics

1-3: 1-Staton-c/a. 2-Staton-a; Morrow-c 1.60 4.00

GRAY GHOST, THE (See 4-Color No. 911, 1000)

GREAT ACTION COMICS
1958 (Reprints with new covers)
I. W. Enterprises

1-Captain Truth reprinted from Gold Medal #1 2.00 5.00 10.00
8,9-Reprints Phantom Lady #15 & 23 9.15 27.50 55.00

GREAT AMERICAN COMICS PRESENTS - THE SECRET VOICE
1945 (10 cents)
Peter George 4-Star Publ./American Features Syndicate

1-Anti-Nazi; 'What Really Happened to Hitler' 11.00 32.00 75.00

GREAT AMERICAN WESTERN, THE (AC)(Value: cover or less)

GREAT CAT FAMILY, THE (See 4-Color No. 750)

GREAT COMICS
Nov, 1941 - No. 3, Jan, 1942
Great Comics Publications

1-Origin/1st app. The Great Zarro; Madame Strange & Guy Gorham, Wizard of Science & The Great Zarro begin 71.00 210.00 475.00
2-Buck Johnson, Jungle Explorer app.; X-Mas-c 42.00 125.00 275.00
3-Futuro Takes Hitler to Hell-c/s; "The Lost City" movie story (starring William

Great Comics #1(1945), © Novack Publ.

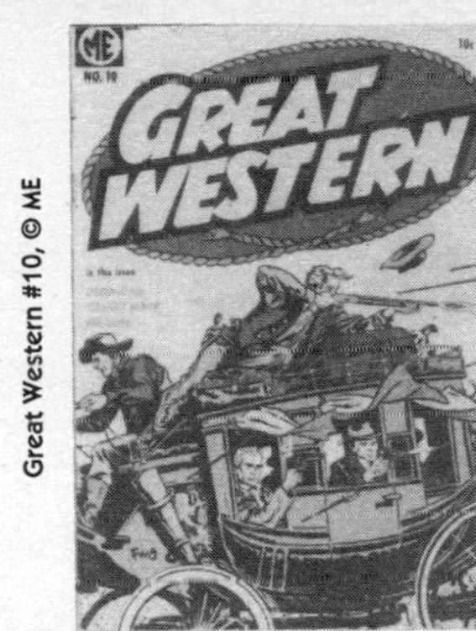

Great Western #10, © ME

Green Arrow #20, © DC

GD25 FN65 NM94

Boyd); continues in Choice Comics #3 75.00 225.00 500.00

GREAT COMICS
1945
Novack Publishing Co./Jubilee Comics/Barrel O' Fun

1-(Novack)-The Defenders, Capt. Power app.; L. B. Cole-c 13.00 40.00 80.00
1-(Jubilee)-Same cover; Boogey Man, Satanas, & The Sorcerer & His Apprentice 10.00 30.00 65.00
1-(Barrel O' Fun)-L. B. Cole-c; Barrel O' Fun overprinted in indicia; Li'l Cactus, Cuckoo Sheriff (humorous) 4.70 14.00 28.00

GREAT DOGPATCH MYSTERY (See Mammy Yokum & the...)

GREATEST BATMAN STORIES EVER TOLD, THE
1988 (Color reprints) (Greatest Stories Vol. 2)
DC Comics

Hardcover ($24.95) with dust jacket 7.00 21.00 50.00
Softcover ($15.95)-Simonson-c 2.60 7.50 18.00
Softcover (1992, $16.95, Vol. 2)-Catwoman & Penguin stories 2.40 7.25 17.00

GREATEST JOKER STORIES EVER TOLD, THE
1988 (Color reprints) (Greatest Stories Vol. 3)
DC Comics

Hardcover ($19.95) with dust jacket 5.50 17.00 40.00
Softcover ($14.95)-Brian Bolland Joker-c 2.30 6.75 16.00
Stacked Deck ...Expanded Edition (1990, $29.95)-Longmeadow Press Publ. 4.30 13.00 30.00

GREAT EXPLOITS
October, 1957
Decker Publ./Red Top

1-Krigstein-a(2) (re-issue on cover); reprints Daring Advs. #6 by Approved Comics 5.35 16.00 32.00

GREAT FOODINI, THE (See Foodini)

GREAT GAZOO, THE (The Flintstones)(TV)
Aug, 1973 - No. 20, Jan, 1977 (Hanna-Barbera)
Charlton Comics

1 1.10 2.70 6.50
2-20 1.40 3.50

GREAT GRAPE APE, THE (TV)(See TV Stars #1)
Sept, 1976 - No. 2, Nov, 1976 (Hanna-Barbera)
Charlton Comics

1,2 1.00 2.50 6.00

GREAT LOCOMOTIVE CHASE, THE (See 4-Color No. 712)

GREAT LOVER ROMANCES (Young Lover Romances #4,5)
3/51; #2, 1951(nd); #3, 1952 (nd); #6, Oct?, 1952 - No. 22, May, 1955
Toby Press (Photo-c #1-5, 10 ,13, 15, 17) (no #4, 5)

1-Jon Juan story-r/Jon Juan #1 by Schomburg; Dr. Anthony King app. 10.00 30.00 60.00
2-Jon Juan, Dr. Anthony King app. 5.00 15.00 30.00
3,7,9-14,16-22: 10-Rita Hayworth photo-c 3.20 8.00 16.00
6-Kurtzman-a (10/52) 5.35 16.00 32.00
8-Five pgs. of "Pin-Up Pete" by Sparling 5.35 16.00 32.00
15-Liz Taylor photo-c 6.35 19.00 38.00

GREAT PEOPLE OF GENESIS, THE
No date (64 pgs.) (Religious giveaway)
David C. Cook Publ. Co.

nn-Reprint/Sunday Pix Weekly 2.00 6.00 12.00

GREAT RACE, THE (See Movie Classics)

GREAT SACRAMENT, THE
1953 (36 pages, giveaway)
Catechetical Guild

nn 2.00 5.00 10.00

GREAT SCOTT SHOE STORE (See Bulls-Eye)

GREAT WEST (Magazine)
1969 (52 pages) (Black & White)
M. F. Enterprises

V1#1 .80 2.00

GREAT WESTERN
No. 8, Jan-Mar, 1954 - No. 11, Oct-Dec, 1954
Magazine Enterprises

8(A-1 93)-Trail Colt by Guardineer; Powell Red Hawk-r/Straight Arrow begins, ends #11; Durango Kid story 13.50 41.00 95.00
9(A-1 105), 11(A-1 127)-Ghost Rider, Durango Kid app. in each. 9-Red Mask-c, but no app. 8.35 25.00 50.00
10(A-1 113) The Calico Kid by Guardineer-r/Tim Holt #8; Straight Arrow, Durango Kid app. 8.35 25.00 50.00
I.W. Reprint #1,2 9: 1,2-r/Straight Arrow #36,42. 9-r/Straight Arrow #? 2.00 5.00 10.00
I.W. Reprint #8-Origin Ghost Rider(r/Tim Holt #11); Tim Holt app.; Bolle-a 2.80 7.00 14.00

NOTE: ***Guardineer** c-8. **Powell** a(r)-8-11 (from Straight Arrow).*

GREEN ARROW (See Action #440, Adventure, Brave & the Bold, DC Super Stars #17, Detective #521, Flash #217, Green Lantern #76, Justice League of America #4, Leading, More Fun #73 (1st app.) and World's Finest Comics)

GREEN ARROW
May, 1983 - No. 4, Aug, 1983 (Mini-series)
DC Comics

1-Origin; Speedy cameo 1.60 4.00
2-4 1.20 3.00

GREEN ARROW
Feb, 1988 - Present ($1.00, mature readers)(Painted-c #1-3)
DC Comics

1-Mike Grell scripts in all 1.00 2.50 5.50
2 1.00 2.50
3-49,51-74,76-84: 27,28-Warlord app. 35-38-Co-stars Black Canary; Bill Wray-i. 40-Grell-a. 47-Begin $1.50-c. 63-No longer has mature readers on-c. 63-66-Shado app. 80-Last $1.50-c .70 1.75
50,75-($2.50, 52 pgs.)-Anniversary issues 1.00 2.50
Annual 1('88, $2.00)-No Grell scripts .80 2.00
Annual 2('89, $2.50, 68pgs.)-No Grell scripts; recaps origin Green Arrow, Speedy, Black Canary & others 1.00 2.50
Annual 3('90, $2.50, 68pgs.)-Bill Wray-a 1.20 3.00
Annual 4('91, $2.95, 68pgs.)-50th anniversary issue .80 2.00
Annual 5('92, $3.00, 68pgs.)-Batman, Eclipso app. 1.20 3.00
Annual 6('93, $3.50, 68pgs.)-Bloodlines; Hook app. 1.40 3.50

NOTE: ***Denys Cowan** a(p)-39, 41-43, 47, 48; c(p)-41-43. **Mike Grell** c-1-4, 10p, 39, 40, 44, 45, 47-71, Annual 4, 5. **Springer** a-67, 68.*

GREEN ARROW: THE LONG BOW HUNTERS
Aug, 1987 - No. 3, Oct, 1987 ($2.95, color, mature readers)
DC Comics

1-Grell-c/a in all 1.25 3.00 7.50
1,2-2nd printings .80 2.00
2 1.60 4.00
3 1.20 3.00
Trade paperback (1989, $12.95) reprints #1-3 1.85 5.50 13.00

GREEN ARROW: THE WONDER YEAR
Feb, 1993 - No. 4, May, 1993 ($1.75, color, mini-series)
DC Comics

1-4: By Grell (scripts & pencils) & Morrow (inks) .70 1.75

GREEN BERET, THE (See Tales of...)

GREEN GIANT COMICS (Also see Colossus Comics)
1940 (no price on cover; distributed in New York City only)
Pelican Publ. (Funnies, Inc.)

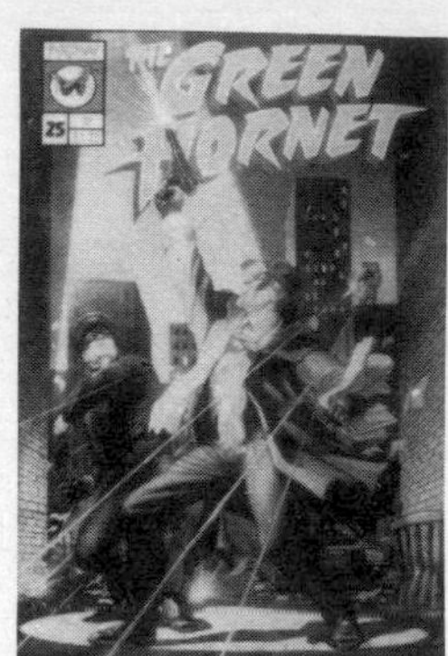

The Green Hornet #25 (Now), © The Green Hornet Inc.

Green Lantern #31 (1st series), © DC

Green Lantern #10 (2nd series), © DC

	GD25	FN65	VF82	NM94
1-Dr. Nerod, Green Giant, Black Arrow, Mundoo & Master Mystic app.; origin Colossus (Rare)	625.00	1875.00	3440.00	5000.00

(Estimated up to 17 copies exist, 3 in NM/Mint)

NOTE: *The idea for this book came from George Kapitan. Printed by Moreau Publ. of Orange, N.J. as an experiment to see if they could profitably use the idle time of their 40-page Hoe color press. The experiment failed due to the difficulty of obtaining good quality color registration and Mr. Moreau believes the book never reached the stands. The book has no price or date which lends credence to this. Contains five pages reprinted from Motion Picture Funnies Weekly.*

GREEN-GREY SPONGE-SUIT SUSHI TURTLES (Mirage)(Value: cover or less)

GREENHAVEN (Aircel)(Value: cover or less)

GREEN HORNET, THE (TV)(See Four Color #496)
Feb, 1967 - No. 3, Aug, 1967
Gold Key

	GD25	FN65	NM94
1-All have Bruce Lee photo-c	16.00	49.00	115.00
2,3	13.00	40.00	90.00

GREEN HORNET, THE (Also see Kato of the... & Tales of the...)
Nov, 1989 - No. 14, Feb, 1991 ($1.75, color)
V2#1, Sept, 1991 - Present ($1.95, color)
Now Comics

	GD25	FN65	NM94
1 ($2.95, double-size)-Steranko painted-c; G.A. Green Hornet	4.00	10.00	17.00
1-2nd printing ('90, $3.95)-New Butler-c		1.60	4.00
2	1.65	4.00	10.00
3-5: 5-Death of original (1930s) Green Hornet	1.00	2.50	6.00
6-8: 6-Dave Dorman painted-c		1.20	3.00
9-14		.80	2.00
V2#1-11,13-21,24,25: 1-Butler painted-c. 9-Mayerik-c		.80	2.00
12-Color Green Hornet button polybagged inside (2.50-c)		1.00	2.50
22,23-($2.95)-Bagged w/color hologravure card		1.20	3.00
1-($2.50)-Polybagged w/button (same as #12)		1.00	2.50
2,3-($1.95)-Same as #13 & 14		.80	2.00
Annual 1 (12/92, 2.50)		1.00	2.50

GREEN HORNET: SOLITARY SENTINEL, THE
Dec, 1992 - No. 3, 1993 ($2.50, color, mini-series)
Now Comics

	GD25	FN65	NM94
1-3		1.00	2.50

GREEN HORNET COMICS (...Racket Buster #44) (Radio, movies)
Dec, 1940 - No. 47, Sept, 1949 (See All New #13,14)
Helnit Publ. Co.(Holyoke) No. 1-6/Family Comics(Harvey) No. 7-on

	GD25	FN65	NM94
1-Green Hornet begins(1st app.); painted-c	210.00	625.00	1400.00
2-Early issues based on radio adventures	92.00	275.00	600.00
3	75.00	225.00	500.00
4-6 (8/41)	57.00	170.00	400.00
7 (6/42)-Origin The Zebra & begins; Robin Hood, Spirit of '76, Blonde Bomber & Mighty Midgets begin	54.00	162.00	350.00
8-10	46.00	138.00	300.00
11,12-Mr. Q in both	37.00	112.00	255.00
13-20: 13-1st Nazi-c; shows Hitler poster on-c	31.00	92.00	215.00
21-30: 24-Sci-Fi-c	27.00	82.00	185.00
31-The Man in Black Called Fate begins (11-12/45, early app.)	29.00	87.00	200.00
32-36	25.00	75.00	170.00
37-Shock Gibson app. by Powell; S&K Kid Adonis reprinted from Stuntman #3	27.00	80.00	175.00
38-Shock Gibson, Kid Adonis app.	25.00	75.00	170.00
39-Stuntman story by S&K	30.00	90.00	210.00
40,41	18.00	54.00	125.00
42-47-Kerry Drake in all. 45-Boy Explorers on-c only. 46-"Case of the Marijuana Racket" cover/story; Kerry Drake app.	18.00	54.00	125.00

NOTE: ***Fuje** a-23, 24, 26. **Henkle** c-7-9. **Kubert** a-20, 30. **Powell** a-7-10, 12, 14, 16-21, 30, 31(2), 32(3), 33, 34(3), 35, 36, 37(2), 38. **Robinson** a-27. **Schomburg** c-15, 17-23. Kirbyish c-7, 9, 15. Bondage c-8, 14, 18, 26, 36.*

GREEN JET COMICS, THE (See Comic Books, Series 1)

GREEN LAMA (Also see Comic Books, Series 1, Daring Adventures #17 & Prize Comics #7)
Dec, 1944 - No. 8, March, 1946
Spark Publications/Prize No. 7 on

	GD25	FN65	NM94
1-Intro. Lt. Hercules & The Boy Champions; Mac Raboy-c/a #1-8	87.00	262.00	575.00
2-Lt. Hercules borrows the Human Torch's powers for one panel	58.00	175.00	365.00
3,6-8: 7-X-mas-c; Raboy craft tint art	46.00	138.00	295.00
4-Dick Tracy take-off in Lt. Hercules story by H. L. Gold (sci-fiction writer)	46.00	138.00	295.00
5-Lt. Hercules story; Little Orphan Annie, Smilin' Jack & Snuffy Smith take-off (5/45)	46.00	138.00	295.00

NOTE: ***Robinson** a-3-5. Formerly a pulp hero who began in 1940.*

GREEN LANTERN (1st Series) (See All-American, All Flash Quarterly, All Star Comics, The Big All-American & Comic Cavalcade)
Fall, 1941 - No. 38, May-June, 1949
National Periodical Publications/All-American

	GD25	FN65	VF82	NM94
1-Origin retold	1,300.00	3,900.00	8,450.00	13,000.00

(Estimated up to 200 total copies exist, 8 in NM/Mint)

	GD25	FN65	NM94
2-1st book-length story	433.00	1300.00	3000.00
3-Classic German war-c by Mart Nodell	291.00	875.00	2000.00
4	242.00	725.00	1600.00
5	150.00	450.00	1000.00
6-8: 8-Hop Harrigan begins	125.00	375.00	850.00
9,10: 10-Origin/1st app. Vandal Savage	112.00	338.00	775.00
11-17,19,20: 12-Origin/1st app. Gambler	96.00	288.00	650.00
18-Christmas-c	108.00	325.00	750.00
21-30: 27-Origin/1st app. Sky Pirate. 30-Origin/1st app. Streak the Wonder Dog by Toth (2-3/48)	86.00	257.00	600.00
31-35: 35-Kubert-c. 35-38-New logo	71.00	210.00	475.00
36-38: 37-Sargon the Sorcerer app.	100.00	300.00	650.00

NOTE: *Book-length stories #2-7. **Mayer/Moldoff** c-9. **Mayer/Purcell** c-8. **Purcell** c-1. **Mart Nodell** c-2, 3, 7. **Paul Reinman** c-11, 12, 15-22. **Toth** a-28, 30, 31, 34-38; c-28, 30, 34p, 36-38p. Cover to #8 says Fall while the indicia says Summer Issue. Streak the Wonder Dog c-30(w/Green Lantern), 34, 36, 38.*

GREEN LANTERN (See Action Comics Weekly, Adventure Comics, Brave & the Bold, DC Special, DC Special Series, Flash, Guy Gardner, Guy Gardner Reborn, Justice League of America, Showcase & Tales of The...Corps)

GREEN LANTERN (2nd series)(Green Lantern Corps #206 on)
7-8/60 - No. 89, 4-5/72; No. 90, 8-9/76 - No. 205, 10/86
National Periodical Publ./DC Comics

	GD25	FN65	VF82	NM94
Showcase #22 (9-10/59)-Origin & 1st app. Silver Age Green Lantern by Gil Kane 1st Ferris (becomes Star Sapphire)	275.00	825.00	2060.00	3300.00
Showcase #23 (11-12/59)	122.00	367.00	733.00	1100.00
Showcase #24 (1-2/60)	128.00	383.00	767.00	1150.00
1-(7-8/60)-Origin retold; Gil Kane-c/a continues; 1st app. Guardians of the Universe	178.00	535.00	1070.00	1600.00

	GD25	FN65	NM94
2-1st Pieface	69.00	206.00	550.00
3-Contains readers poll	40.00	120.00	325.00
4,5: 5-Origin & 1st app. Hector Hammond	31.00	93.00	250.00
6-10: 6-Intro Tomar-re the alien G.L. 7-Origin/1st app. Sinestro (7-8/61) 8-1st 5700 A.D. story; painted-c. 9-1st Jordan Brothers; last 10¢ issue	21.00	63.00	170.00
11,12	16.50	50.00	115.00
13-Flash x-over	20.00	60.00	140.00
14-20: 14-Origin/1st app. Sonar. 16-Origin & 1st app. Star Sapphire. 20-Flash x-over	15.00	45.00	105.00
21-30: 21-Origin & 1st app. Dr. Polaris. 23-1st Tattooed Man. 24-Origin & 1st app. Shark. 29-JLA cameo; 1st Blackhand	12.00	36.00	85.00
31-39: 37-1st app. Evil Star (villain)	9.00	28.00	65.00

40-1st app. Crisis (10/65); 2nd solo G.A. Green Lantern in Silver Age (see Showcase #55); origin The Guardians; Doiby Dickles app.

Green Lantern #160, © DC

Green Lantern Corp Quarterly #6, © DC

Green Lantern: Mosaic #16, © DC

GD25 FN65 NM94

46.00 137.00 365.00
41-44,46-50: 42-Zatanna x-over. 43-Flash x-over 6.00 19.00 44.00
45-G.A. Green Lantern x-over 10.00 29.00 68.00
51,53-58 4.00 12.00 28.00
52-G.A. Green Lantern x-over 5.00 15.00 35.00
59-1st app. Guy Gardner (3/68) 23.00 70.00 160.00
60,62-69: 69-Wood inks; last 12 cent issue 2.60 7.50 18.00
61-G.A. Green Lantern x-over 3.85 11.50 27.00
70-75 2.15 6.50 15.00
76-(4/70)-Begin Green Lantern/Green Arrow series (by Neal Adams #76-89) ends #122 (see Flash #217 for 2nd series) 15.00 45.00 105.00
77 5.50 16.00 38.00
78-80 4.00 12.00 28.00
81-84: 82-Wrightson i(1 pg.). 83-G.L. reveals i.d. to Carol Ferris. 84-Neal Adams/Wrightson-a(22 pgs.); last 15 cent-c; partial photo-c 3.40 10.00 24.00
85,86(52 pgs.)-Drug propaganda books. 86-G.A. Green Lantern-r; Toth-a 4.85 15.00 34.00
87(52 pgs.): 2nd app. Guy Gardner (cameo); 1st app. John Stewart (12-1/71-72) (becomes Green Lantern in #182) 3.25 9.50 22.00
88(2-3/72, 52 pgs.)-Unpubbed G.A. Green Lantern story; Green Lantern-r/Showcase #23. N. Adams-a (1 pg.) 1.00 2.50 5.50
89(4-5/72, 52 pgs.)-G.A. Green Lantern-r; Green Lantern moves to Flash #217 1.65 4.00 10.00
90(8-9/76)-99: 90-Begin 3rd G.L./G.A. team-up series; Mike Grell-c/a begins 1.20 3.00
100-(1/78, Giant)-1st app. Air Wave II 1.00 2.50 5.50
101-111,113-115,117-119: 107-1st Tales of the G.L. Corps story. 108-110-(44 pgs)-G.A. Green Lantern back-ups in each. 111-Origin retold; G.A. Green Lantern app. 1.00 2.50
112-G.A. Green Lantern origin retold 1.00 2.50 6.00
116-1st app. Guy Gardner as a Gr. Lantern (5/79) 3.25 9.50 22.00
120,121,124-135,138-140,142-149: 130-132-Tales of the G.L. Corps. 132-Adam Strange series begins, ends 147. 142,143-Omega Men app.; Perez-c. 144-Omega Men cameo. 148-Tales of the G.L. Corps begins, ends #173 .65 1.60
122-Last Green Lantern/Green Arrow team-up .80 2.00
123-Green Lantern back to solo action; 2nd app. Guy Gardner as Green Lantern 1.00 2.50 5.50
136,137-1st app. Citadel; Space Ranger app. 1.00 2.50
141-1st app. Omega Men (6/81) 1.00 2.50
150-Anniversary issue, 52 pgs.; no G.L. Corps 1.00 2.50
151-170: 159-Origin Evil Star. 160,161-Omega Men app. 181-Hal Jordan resigns as G.L. 182-John Stewart becomes new G.L.; origin recap of Hal Jordan as G.L. .65 1.60
171-193,196-199,201-205: (75 cent cover). 185-Origin new G.L. (John Stewart). 188-I.D. revealed; Alan Moore back-up scripts. 191-Re-intro Star Sapphire (cameo). 192-Re-intro Star Sapphire (1st full app.). 194,198-Crisis x-over. 199-Hal Jorda returns as a member of G.L. Corps (3 G.L.s now). 201-Green Lantern Corps begins (is cover title & says premiere issue) .65 1.60
194-Hal Jordan/Guy Gardner battle; Guardians choose Guy Gardner to become new G.L. 1.00 2.50 5.50
195-Guy Gardner becomes Green Lantern; Crisis x-over 2.30 6.75 16.00
200-Double-size 1.00 2.50
Annual 1 (See Tales Of The...)
Annual 3 (See Green Lantern Corps Annual #3)
Special 1 (1988), 2 (1989)-(Both $1.50, 52 pgs.) 1.00 2.50

NOTE: ***N. Adams*** *a-76, 77-87p, 89; c-63, 76-89.* ***M. Anderson*** *a-137i.* ***Austin*** *a-93i, 94i, 171i.* ***Greene*** *a-39-49i, 58-63i; c-54-58i.* ***Grell*** *a-90-106, 108-111; c-90-106, 108-112.* ***Gil Kane*** *a-1-49p, 50-57, 58-61p, 68-75p, 85p(r), 87p(r), 88p(r), 156, 177, 184p; c-1-52, 54-61p, 67-75, 123, 154, 156, 165-171, 177, 184.* ***Newton*** *a-148p, 149p, 181.* ***Perez*** *c-132p, 141-144.* ***Sekowsky*** *a-65p, 170p.* ***Sparling*** *a-63p.* ***Starlin*** *c-129, 133.* ***Staton*** *a-117p, 123-127p, 128, 129-131p, 132-139, 140p, 141-146, 147p, 148-150, 151-155p; c-107p, 117p, 135(i), 136p, 145p, 146, 147, 148-152p, 155p.* ***Toth*** *a-86r, 171p.* ***Tuska*** *a-166-168p, 170p.*

GREEN LANTERN (3rd series)
June, 1990 - Present ($1.00/$1.25, color)
DC Comics

1-Hal Jordan, John Stewart & Guy Gardner return; Batman app. 1.20 3.00
2,3 .80 2.00
4-8 1.20
9-12-Guy Gardner solo story 1.00 2.50
13-($1.75, 52 pgs.) .80 2.00
14-18,20-24,26: 18-Guy Gardner solo story. 26-Last $1.00-c 1.00
19-($1.75, 52 pgs.)-50th anniversary issue; Mart Nodell (original G.A. artist) part-p on G.A. Gr. Lantern; G. Kane-c .70 1.75
25-($1.75, 52 pgs.)-Hal Jordan/Guy Gardner battle .40 1.00 2.00
27-45,47: 30,31-Gorilla Grodd-c/story(see Flash #69). 42-Deathstroke-c/story 1.25
46-Superman app. cont'd in Superman #82 1.20 3.00
48,49,51,52: 48-Begin $1.50-c. 51-1st app. New Green Lantern with new costume 1.50
50-($2.95, 52 pgs.)-Glow-in-the-dark-c 1.20 3.00
Annual 1 (1992, $2.50, 68 pgs.)-Eclipso app. 1.00 2.50
Annual 2 (1993, $2.50, 68 pgs.)-Intro Nightblade 1.00 2.50
...The Road Back nn (1992, $8.95)-r/1-8 w/covers 1.50 3.75 9.00

NOTE: ***Staton*** *a(p)-9-12; c-9-12.*

GREEN LANTERN CORPS, THE (Formerly Green Lantern; see Tales of...)
No. 206, Nov, 1986 - No. 224, May, 1988
DC Comics

206-223: 220,221-Millennium tie-ins 1.00
224-Double size last issue 1.50
..Corps Annual 2 (12/86)-Formerly Tales of ...Annual #1; Alan Moore scripts 1.50
..Corps Annual 3 (8/87)-Indicia says Green Lantern Annual #3; Moore scripts; Byrne-a 1.50

NOTE: ***Austin*** *a-Annual 3i.* ***Gil Kane*** *a-223, 224p; c-223, 224.* ***Russell*** *a-Annual 3i.* ***Staton*** *a-207-213p, 217p, 221p, 222p, Annual 3; c-207-213p, 217p, 221p, 222p.* ***Willingham*** *a-213p, 219p, 220p, 218p, 219p, Annual 2, 3p; c-218p, 219p.*

GREEN LANTERN CORPS QUARTERLY
Summer, 1992 - Present ($2.50, color, 68 pgs.)
DC Comics

1-0. 1-G.A. Green Lantern story, Staton-a(p). 2-G.A. G.L.-c/story; Austin-c(i); Gulacy-a(p). 3-G.A. G.L. story. 4-Austin-i 1.00 2.50

GREEN LANTERN: EMERALD DAWN (Also see Emerald Dawn)
Dec, 1989 - No. 6, May, 1990 ($1.00, color, mini-series)
DC Comics

1-Origin retold; Giffen plots in all 1.60 4.00
2 1.20 3.00
3,4 .80 2.00
5,6 1.50

GREEN LANTERN: EMERALD DAWN II (Emerald Dawn II #1 & 2)
Apr, 1991 - No. 6, Sept, 1991 ($1.00, color, mini-series)
DC Comics

1 1.50
2-6 1.00

GREEN LANTERN: GANTHET'S TALE
1992 ($5.95, color, one-shot, 68 pgs.)
DC Comics

nn-Silver foil stamped logo; Byrne-c/a 1.00 2.50 6.00

GREEN LANTERN/GREEN ARROW (Also see The Flash #217)
Oct, 1983 - No. 7, April, 1984 (52-60 pgs.)
DC Comics

1-7: Reprints Green Lantern #76-89 1.20 3.00

NOTE: ***Neal Adams*** *r-1-7; c-1-4.* ***Wrightson*** *r-4, 5.*

GREEN LANTERN: MOSAIC
June, 1992 - No. 18, Nov, 1993 ($1.25, color)

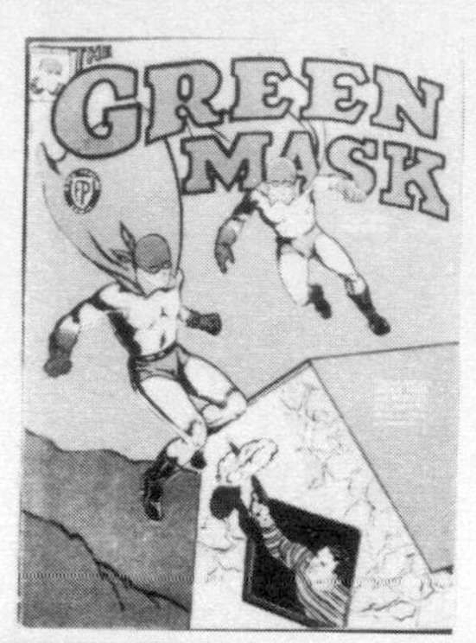

The Green Mask #5, © FOX

Grendel #4, © Matt Wagner & Comico

Grimjack #75, © First Comics

GD25 FN65 NM94

DC Comics

1-18: Featuring John Stewart. 1-Painted-c 1.25

GREEN MASK, THE (See Mystery Men)
Summer, 1940 - No. 9, 2/42; No. 10, 8/44 - No. 11, 11/44;
V2#1, Spring, 1945 - No. 6, 10-11/46
Fox Features Syndicate

	GD25	FN65	NM94
V1#1-Origin The Green Mask & Domino; reprints/Mystery Men #1-3,5-7; Lou Fine-c	133.00	400.00	900.00
2-Zanzibar The Magician by Tuska	67.00	200.00	450.00
3-Powell-a; Marijuana story	42.00	125.00	275.00
4-Navy Jones begins, ends #6	33.00	100.00	225.00
5	29.00	88.00	190.00
6-The Nightbird begins, ends #9; bondage/torture-c	25.00	75.00	165.00
7-9: 9(2/42)-Becomes The Bouncer #10(nn) on? & Green Mask #10 on	20.00	60.00	130.00
10,11: 10-Origin One Round Hogan & Rocket Kelly	17.00	50.00	110.00
V2#1	12.50	38.00	85.00
2-6	11.00	32.00	75.00

GREEN PLANET, THE
1962 (One Shot)
Charlton Comics

nn-Giordano-c 5.85 17.50 35.00

GREEN TEAM (See Cancelled Comic Cavalcade & 1st Issue Special)

GREETINGS FROM SANTA (See March of Comics No. 48)

GRENDEL (Also see Primer No. 2 and Mage)
Mar, 1983 - No. 3, Feb, 1984 ($1.50, B&W)(#1 has indicia to Skrog #1)
Comico

	GD25	FN65	NM94
1-Origin Hunter Rose	7.50	22.00	52.00
2,3: 2-Origin Argent	5.50	17.00	40.00

GRENDEL
Oct, 1986 - No. 40, Feb, 1991 ($1.50-$1.95-$2.50, color) (Mature readers)
Comico

	GD25	FN65	NM94
1		1.40	3.50
1,2-2nd printings		.65	1.60
2		1.00	2.50
3-10: 4-Dave Stevens-c(i)		.80	2.00
11-15: 13-15-Ken Steacy-c		.70	1.75
16-Re-intro Mage (series begins, ends #19)		1.40	3.50
17-32: 18-26-$1.75-c; 27-32-$1.95-c		.80	2.00
33-($2.75, 44 pgs.)		1.10	2.75
34-40: 34-Begin $2.50 cover price		1.00	2.50
Devil by the Deed (Graphic Novel, 10/86, $5.95, 52 pgs.)-r/Grendel back-ups/ Mage 6-14; Alan Moore intro.	1.20	3.00	7.00
Devil's Legacy ($14.95, 1988, Graphic Novel)	2.15	6.50	15.00
Devil's Vagary (10/87, B&W & red)-No price; included in Comico Collection	1.70	5.00	12.00

GRENDEL: DEVIL BY THE DEED
July, 1993 ($3.95, color, one-shot, spot varnish-c)
Dark Horse Comics

nn-r/Grendel back-ups from Mage #6-14 1.60 4.00

GRENDEL TALES: FOUR DEVILS, ONE HELL
Aug, 1993 - No. 6, 1994 ($2.95, color, limited series, Mature readers)
Dark Horse Comics

1-6: Wagner painted-c 1.20 3.00

GRENDEL: WAR CHILD
Aug, 1992 - No. 10, 1993 ($2.50, color, limited series, mature readers)
Dark Horse Comics

	GD25	FN65	NM94
1-9: Bisley painted-c; Wagner-i & scripts		1.00	2.50
10-($3.50, 52 pgs.)		1.40	3.50

GD25 FN65 NM94

GREYFRIARS BOBBY (See 4-Color No. 1189)

GREYLORE (Sirius)(Value: cover or less)

GRIFFIN, THE (DC)(Value: cover or less)

GRIM GHOST, THE
Jan, 1975 - No. 3, July, 1975
Atlas/Seaboard Publ.

1-3: 1-Origin. 3-Heath-c 1.00

GRIMJACK (Also see Demon Knight & Starslayer)
Aug, 1984 - No. 81, Apr, 1991
First Comics

	GD25	FN65	NM94
1		.80	2.00
2-25: 20-Sutton-c/a begins. 22-Bolland-a			1.50
26-2nd color Teenage Mutant Ninja Turtles		1.60	4.00
27-74,76-81: 30-Dynamo Joe x-over; 31-Mandrake-c/a begins (later issues $1.95, $2.25-c)			1.25
75-($5.95, 52 pgs.)-Fold-out map; coated stock	1.00	2.50	6.00

GRIMJACK CASEFILES (First)(Value: cover or less)

GRIMM'S GHOST STORIES (See Dan Curtis)
Jan, 1972 - No. 60, June, 1982 (Painted-c #1-42,44,46-56)
Gold Key/Whitman No. 55 on

	GD25	FN65	NM94
1	1.00	2.50	6.00
2-4,6,7,9,10		1.20	3.00
5,8-Williamson-a		1.60	4.00
11-16,18-35: 32,34-Reprints		.80	2.00
17-Crandall-a		1.20	3.00
36-55,57-60: 43,44-(52 pgs.). 43,45-Photo-c			1.50
56-Williamson-a(r)		.80	2.00
Mini-Comic No. 1 (3-1/4x6-1/2", 1976)			1.00

NOTE: *Reprints-#32?, 34?, 39, 43, 44, 47?, 53; 56-60(1/3).* **Bolle** *a-17, 22-25, 27, 29(2), 33, 35, 43r, 45(2), 48(2), 50, 52.* **Celardo** *a-26, 28p, 30, 31, 43(2), 45.* **Lopez** *a-24, 25.* **McWilliams** *a-33, 44r, 48, 58.* **Win Mortimer** *a-31, 33, 49, 51, 55, 56, 58(2), 59, 60.* **Roussos** *a-25, 30.* **Sparling** *a-23, 24, 28, 30, 31, 33, 43r, 44, 45, 51(2), 52, 56, 58, 59(2), 60.* **Spiegle** *a-44.*

GRIN (The American Funny Book) (Magazine)
Nov, 1972 - No. 3, April, 1973 (52 pgs.) (Satire)
APAG House Pubs

	GD25	FN65	NM94
1		.80	2.00
2,3			1.00

GRIN & BEAR IT (See Gags & Large Feature Comic No. 28)

GRIPS (Extreme violence)
Sept, 1986 - No. 4, Dec, 1986 ($1.50, B&W, adults)
Silverwolf Comics

	GD25	FN65	NM94
1-Tim Vigil-c/a in all	2.60	7.50	18.00
2	1.85	5.50	13.00
3	1.65	4.70	11.00
4	1.65	4.00	10.00

GRIT GRADY (See Holyoke One-Shot No. 1)

GROO CARNIVAL, THE
Dec, 1991 ($8.95, color, trade paperback)
Epic Comics (Marvel)

nn-Reprints Groo #9-12 by Aragones 1.50 3.75 9.00

GROO CHRONICLES, THE (Marvel)(Value: cover or less)

GROO SPECIAL
Oct, 1984 ($2.00, 52 pgs., Baxter paper)
Eclipse Comics

1-Aragones-c/a 5.00 15.00 35.00

GROO THE WANDERER (See Destroyer Duck, Marvel Graphic Novel #32 & & Starslayer)
Dec, 1982 - No. 8, Apr, 1984
Pacific Comics

1-Aragones-c/a(p) in all; Aragones biog., photo 3.85 11.50 27.00

Groo The Wanderer #103, © S. Aragones

Guardians of the Galaxy #39, © MEG

The Gunhawk #18, © MEG

	GD25	FN65	NM94
2	2.40	7.25	17.00
3-7: 5-Deluxe paper (1.00-c)	2.00	6.00	14.00
8	1.65	4.70	11.00

GROO THE WANDERER (Sergio Aragones'...)
March, 1985 - Present
Epic Comics (Marvel)

	GD25	FN65	NM94
1-Aragones-c/a in all	1.65	4.00	10.00
2	1.00	2.50	6.00
3-10		1.60	4.00
11-20		1.00	2.50
21-30		.80	2.00
31-86: 50-($1.50, double size)			1.25
87-99,101-110: 87-Begin $2.25, direct sale only, high quality paper issues		.90	2.25
100-($2.95, 52 pgs.)		1.20	3.00

GROOVY (Cartoon Comics - not CCA approved)
March, 1968 - No. 3, July, 1968
Marvel Comics Group

	GD25	FN65	NM94
1-Monkees, Ringo Starr photos	3.30	10.00	23.00
2,3	2.40	7.25	17.00

GROUP LARUE, THE (Innovation)(Value: cover or less)

GUADALCANAL DIARY (See American Library)

GUARDIANS OF JUSTICE & THE O-FORCE (Shadow)(Value: cover or less)

GUARDIANS OF THE GALAXY (Also see The Defenders #26, Marvel Presents #3, Marvel Super-Heroes #18, Marvel Two-In-One #5)
June, 1990 - Present ($1.00, color)
Marvel Comics

	GD25	FN65	NM94
1-Valentino-c/a(p) begin; painted-c	1.20	3.00	7.00
2,3: 2-Zeck-c(i)		1.80	4.50
4-6: 5-McFarlane-c(i)		1.40	3.50
7-10: 7-Intro Malevolence (Mephisto's daughter); Perez-c(i). 8-Intro Rancor (descendant of Wolverine) in cameo. 9-1st full app. Rancor; Rob Liefeld-c(i). 10-Jim Lee-c(i)		1.20	3.00
11,12,15: 15-Starlin-c(i)		.80	2.00
13,14-1st app. Spirit of Vengeance (futuristic Ghost Rider). 14-Spirit of Vengeance vs. The Guardians		1.80	4.50
16-($1.50, 52 pgs.)-Starlin-c(i)		.80	2.00
17-23,26-38,40-46: 17-20-31st century Punishers storyline. 20-Last $1.00-c. 21-Rancor app. 22-Reintro Starhawk. 26-Origin retold. 27-28-Infinity War x-over; 27-Inhumans app.			1.25
24-Silver Surfer-c/story; Ron Lim-c		1.20	3.00
25-($2.50)-Prism foil-c; Silver Surfer/Galactus-c/s		1.40	3.50
25-($2.50)-Without foil-c; newsstand edition		.80	2.00
39-($2.95, 52 pgs.)-Embossed & holo-grafx foil-c; Dr. Doom vs. Rancor		1.20	3.00
Annual 1 (1991, $2.00, 68 pgs.)-2 pg. origin		1.00	2.50
Annual 2 (1992, $2.25, 68 pgs.)-Spirit of Vengeance-c/story		.90	2.25
Annual 3 (1993, $2.95, 68 pgs.)-Bagged w/card		1.20	3.00

GUERRILLA WAR (Formerly Jungle War Stories)
No. 12, July-Sept, 1965 - No. 14, Mar, 1966
Dell Publishing Co.

	GD25	FN65	NM94
12-14	1.80	4.50	9.00

GUILTY (See Justice Traps the Guilty)

GULF FUNNY WEEKLY (Gulf Comic Weekly No. 1-4)
1933 - No. 422, 5/23/41 (in full color; 4 pgs.; tabloid size to 2/3/39; 2/10/39 on, regular comic book size)(early issues undated)
Gulf Oil Company (Giveaway)

	GD25	FN65	NM94
1	14.00	43.00	100.00
2-5	5.00	15.00	30.00
6-30	4.00	12.00	24.00
31-100	3.60	9.00	18.00
101-196	2.80	7.00	14.00
197-Wings Winfair begins(1/29/37); by Fred Meagher beginning in 1938	15.00	45.00	90.00
198-300 (Last tabloid size)	6.70	20.00	40.00
301-350 (Regular size)	4.00	10.00	20.00
351-422	2.80	7.00	14.00

GULLIVER'S TRAVELS (See Dell Jr. Treasury No. 3)
Sept-Nov, 1965 - No. 3, May, 1966
Dell Publishing Co.

	GD25	FN65	NM94
1	4.00	11.00	22.00
2,3	3.00	7.50	15.00

GUMBY'S SUMMER FUN SPECIAL
July, 1987 ($2.50, color)
Comico

	GD25	FN65	NM94
1-Art Adams-c/a, B. Burden story		1.00	2.50

GUMBY'S WINTER FUN SPECIAL
Dec, 1988 ($2.50, color, 44 pgs.)
Comico

	GD25	FN65	NM94
1-Art Adams-c/a		1.00	2.50

GUMPS, THE
No. 2, 1918; 1924 - No. 8, 1931 (10x10")(52 pgs.; black & white)
Landfield-Kupfer/Cupples & Leon No. 2

	GD25	FN65	NM94
Book No.2(1918)-(Rare); 5-1/4x13-1/3"; paper cover; 36 pgs. daily strip reprints by Sidney Smith	36.00	110.00	250.00
nn(1924)-By Sidney Smith	25.00	75.00	175.00
2,3	16.00	50.00	115.00
4-7	13.00	40.00	90.00
8-(10x14"); 36 pgs.; B&W; National Arts Co.	13.00	40.00	90.00

GUMPS, THE (See Merry Christmas..., Popular & Super Comics)
No. 73, 1945; Mar-Apr, 1947 - No. 5, Nov-Dec, 1947
Dell Publ. Co./Bridgeport Herald Corp.

	GD25	FN65	NM94
4-Color 73 (Dell)(1945)	10.00	30.00	70.00
1 (3-4/47)	10.00	30.00	70.00
2-5	6.70	20.00	40.00

GUNFIGHTER (Fat & Slat #1-4) (Becomes Haunt of Fear #15 on)
No. 5, Summer, 1948 - No. 14, Mar-Apr, 1950
E. C. Comics (Fables Publ. Co.)

	GD25	FN65	NM94
5,6-Moon Girl in each	39.00	120.00	275.00
7-14: 14-Bondage-c	26.00	80.00	185.00

NOTE: *Craig & H. C. Kiefer art in most issues. Craig c-5, 6, 13, 14. Feldstein/Craig a-10. Feldstein a-7-11. Harrison/Wood a-13, 14. Ingels a-5-14; c-7-12.*

GUNFIGHTERS, THE
1963 - 1964
Super Comics (Reprints)

	GD25	FN65	NM94
10-12,15,16,18: 10,11-r/Billy the Kid #s? 12-r/The Rider #5(Swift Arrow). 15-r/Straight Arrow #42; Powell-r. 16-r/Billy the Kid #?(Toby). 18-r/The Rider #3; Severin-c	1.20	3.00	6.00

GUNFIGHTERS, THE (Formerly Kid Montana)
No. 51, 10/66 - No. 52, 10/67; No. 53, 6/79 - No. 85, 7/84
Charlton Comics

	GD25	FN65	NM94
51,52	1.20	3.00	6.00
53-85: 53,54-Williamson/Torres-r/Six Gun Heroes #47,49. 56-Williamson/Severin-c; Severin-r/Sheriff of Tombstone #1. 85-S&K-r/1955 Bullseye		1.20	3.00

GUN GLORY (See 4-Color No. 846)

GUNHAWK, THE (Formerly Whip Wilson)(See Wild Western)
No. 12, Nov, 1950 - No. 18, Dec, 1951
Marvel Comics/Atlas (MCI)

	GD25	FN65	NM94
12	10.00	30.00	70.00
13-18: 13-Tuska-a. 16-Colan-a. 18-Maneely-c	9.15	27.50	55.00

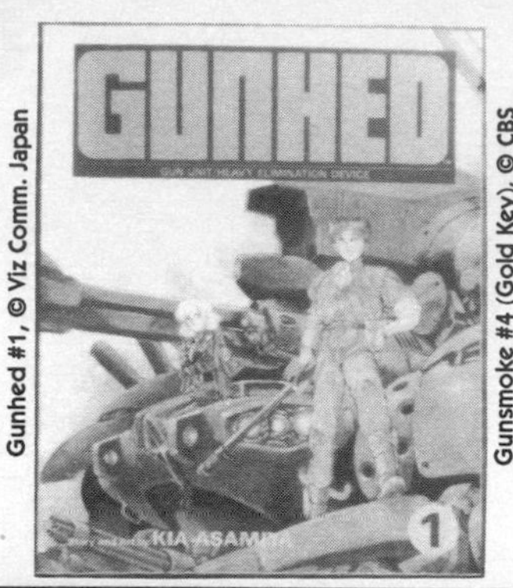

Gunhed #1, © Viz Comm. Japan

Gunsmoke #4 (Gold Key), © CBS

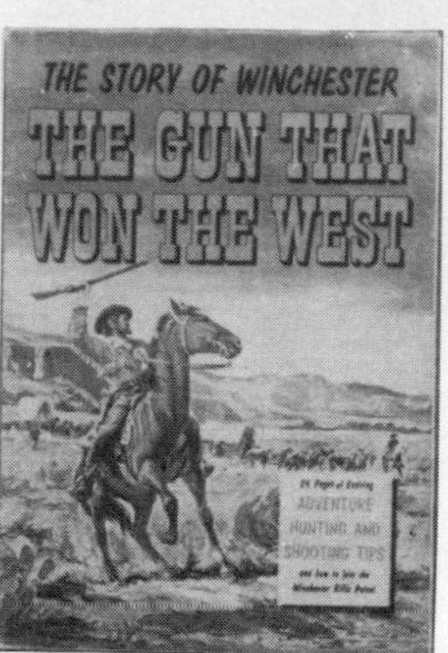

The Gun That Won the West nn, © Winchester & Olin Mathieson

GD25 FN65 NM94

GUNHAWKS (Gunhawk No. 7)
October, 1972 - No. 7, October, 1973
Marvel Comics Group
1-Reno Jones, Kid Cassidy; Shores-c/a(p) 1.60 4.00
2-7: 6-Kid Cassidy dies. 7-Reno Jones solo 1.20 3.00

GUNHED (Viz)(Value: cover or less)

GUNMASTER (Becomes Judo Master #89 on)
9/64 - No. 4, 1965; No. 84, 7/65 - No. 88, 3-4/66; No. 89, 10/67
Charlton Comics
V1#1 2.80 7.00 14.00
2-4: 4-Blank inside-c 1.60 4.00 8.00
V5#84-86: 84-Formerly Six-Gun Heroes 1.60 4.00 8.00
V5#87-89 1.20 3.00 6.00
NOTE: *Vol. 5 was originally cancelled with #88 (3-4/66). #89 on, became Judo Master, then later in 1967, Charlton issued #89 as a Gunmaster one-shot.*

GUN RUNNER
Oct, 1993 - No. 6, 1994 ($1.75, color, limited series)
Marvel Comics UK
1-($2.75)-Polybagged w/4 trading cards; Spirits of Vengeance app. 1.10 2.75
2-6: 2-Ghost Rider & Blaze app. .70 1.75

GUNS AGAINST GANGSTERS (True-To-Life Romances #8 on)
Sept-Oct, 1948 - V2#1, Sept-Oct, 1949
Curtis Publications/Novelty Press
1-Toni Gayle begins by Schomburg 13.00 40.00 100.00
2 10.00 30.00 70.00
3-6, V2#1,2: 6-Toni Gayle-c 10.00 30.00 60.00
NOTE: ***L. B. Cole** c-1-6, V2#1, 2; a-1, 2, 3(2), 4-6.*

GUNSLINGER (See 4-Color No. 1220)

GUNSLINGER (Formerly Tex Dawson...)
No. 2, April, 1973 - No. 3, June, 1973
Marvel Comics Group
2,3 1.00

GUNSMOKE
Apr-May, 1949 - No. 16, Jan, 1952
Western Comics (Youthful Magazines)
1-Gunsmoke & Masked Marvel begin by Ingels; Ingels bondage-c 26.00 77.00 180.00
2-Ingels-c/a(2) 15.00 45.00 105.00
3-Ingels bondage-c/a 12.00 36.00 85.00
4-6: Ingels-c 10.00 30.00 70.00
7-10 7.00 21.00 42.00
11-16: 15,16-Western/horror stories 5.00 15.00 30.00
NOTE: ***Stallman** a-11, 14. **Wildey** a-15, 16.*

GUNSMOKE (TV)
No. 679, 2/56 - No. 27, 6-7/61; 2/69 - No. 6, 2/70
Dell Publishing Co./Gold Key (All have James Arness photo-c)
4-Color 679(#1) 11.50 34.00 80.00
4-Color 720,769,797,844 (#2-5) 6.35 19.00 38.00
6(11-1/57-58), 7 6.35 19.00 38.00
8,9,11,12-Williamson-a in all, 4 pgs. each 7.50 22.50 45.00
10-Williamson/Crandall-a, 4 pgs. 7.50 22.50 45.00
13-27 5.85 17.50 35.00
Gunsmoke Film Story (11/62-G.K. Giant) No. 30008-211 8.35 25.00 50.00
1 (Gold Key) 4.00 12.00 24.00
2-6('69-70) 2.80 7.00 14.00

GUNSMOKE TRAIL
June, 1957 - No. 4, Dec, 1957
Ajax-Farrell Publ./Four Star Comic Corp.
1 7.00 21.00 42.00

GD25 FN65 NM94

2-4 4.00 12.00 24.00

GUNSMOKE WESTERN (Formerly Western Tales of Black Rider)
No. 32, Dec, 1955 - No. 77, July, 1963
Atlas Comics No. 32-35(CPS/NPI); Marvel No. 36 on
32-Baker & Drucker-a 10.00 30.00 65.00
33,35,36-Williamson-a in each: 5,6 & 4 pgs. plus Drucker-a #33. 33-Kinstler-a? 9.15 27.50 55.00
34-Baker-a, 4 pgs. 5.00 15.00 30.00
37-Davis-a(2); Williamson text illo 5.85 17.50 35.00
38,39: 39-Williamson text illo (unsigned) 4.20 12.50 25.00
40-Williamson/Mayo-a, 4 pgs. 5.85 17.50 35.00
41,42,45-49,51-55,57-60: 49,52-Kid from Texas story. 57-1st Two Gun Kid by Severin. 60-Sam Hawk app. in Kid Colt 3.60 9.00 18.00
43,44-Torres-a 4.00 11.00 22.00
50,61-Crandall-a 4.20 12.50 25.00
56-Matt Baker-a 4.00 11.00 22.00
62-71,73-77 2.80 7.00 14.00
72-Origin Kid Colt 4.00 10.00 20.00
NOTE: ***Colan** a-35-37, 39, 72, 76. **Davis** a-37, 52, 54, 55; c-50, 54. **Ditko** a-66. **Drucker** a-32-34. **Heath** c-33. **Jack Keller** a-35, 40, 60, 72; c-72. **Kirby** a-47, 50, 51, 59, 62(3), 63-67, 69, 71, 73, 77; c-56(w/Ditko),57, 58, 60, 61(w/Ayers), 62, 63, 66, 68, 69, 71-77. **Robinson** a-35. **Severin** a-35, 59-61; c-34, 35, 39, 42, 43. **Tuska** a-34. **Wildey** a-10, 37, 42, 56, 57. Kid Colt in all. Two-Gun Kid in No. 57, 59, 60-63. Wyatt Earp in No. 45, 48, 49, 52, 54, 55, 58.*

GUNS OF FACT & FICTION (See A-1 Comics No. 13)

GUN THAT WON THE WEST, THE
1956 (24 pgs.; regular size) (Giveaway)
Winchester-Western Division & Olin Mathieson Chemical Corp.
nn-Painted-c 4.20 12.50 25.00

GUY GARDNER (Guy Gardner: Warrior #17 on)(Also see Green Lantern #59)
Oct, 1992 - Present ($1.25, color)
DC Comics
1-14: 1-Staton-c/a(p) begins. 6-Guy vs. Hal Jordan. 8-Vs. Lobo-c/story 1.25
15-18: 15-Begin $1.50-c 1.50

GUY GARDNER REBORN
1992 - Book 3, 1992 ($4.95, color, mini-series)
DC Comics
1-3: Staton-c/a(p). 1-Lobo-c/cameo. 2,3-Lobo-c/s 1.00 2.00 5.00

GYPSY COLT (See 4-Color No. 568)

GYRO GEARLOOSE (See Dynabrite Comics, Walt Disney's C&S #140 & Walt Disney Showcase #18)
No. 1047, Nov-Jan/1959-60 - May-July, 1962 (Disney)
Dell Publishing Co.
4-Color 1047 (No. 1)-Barks-c/a 10.00 30.00 70.00
4-Color 1095,1184-All by Carl Barks 7.50 22.50 45.00
4-Color 1267-Barks c/a, 4 pgs. 5.85 17.50 35.00
No. 01-329-207 (5-7/62)-Barks-c only 4.20 12.50 25.00

HACKER FILES, THE
Aug, 1992 - No. 12, 1993 ($1.95, color)
DC Comics
1-12: 1-Sutton-a(p) begins; computer generated-c .80 2.00

HAGAR THE HORRIBLE (See Comics Reading Libraries)

HA HA COMICS (Teepee Tim No. 100 on; also see Giggle Comics)
Oct, 1943 - No. 99, Jan, 1955
Scope Mag.(Creston Publ.) No. 1-80/American Comics Group
1 22.00 65.00 150.00
2 10.00 30.00 70.00
3-5: Ken Hultgren-a begins? 7.50 22.50 45.00
6-10 6.35 19.00 38.00
11-20: 14-Infinity-c 4.70 14.00 28.00
21-40 4.00 11.00 22.00

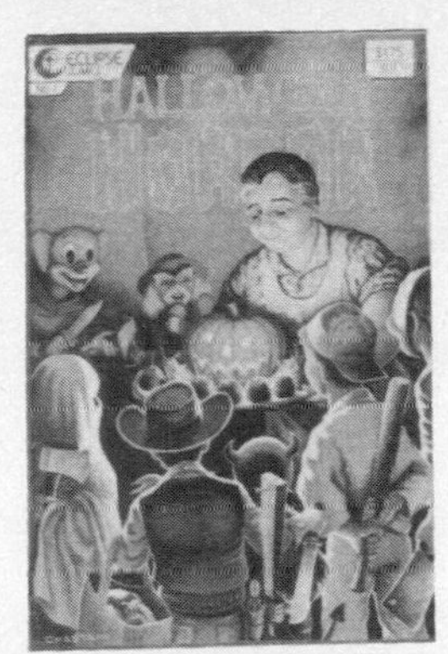
Halloween Horror #1, © Eclipse

Hand of Fate #9, © ACE

Hap Hazard Comics #2, © ACE

GD25 FN65 NM94

41-94,96-99: 49-XMas-c 3.60 9.00 18.00
95-3-D effect-c 10.00 30.00 65.00

HAIR BEAR BUNCH, THE (TV) (See Fun-In No. 13)
Feb, 1972 - No. 9, Feb, 1974 (Hanna-Barbera)
Gold Key

1 1.30 3.25 8.00
2-9 1.00 2.00 5.00

HALLELUJAH TRAIL, THE (See Movie Classics)

HALL OF FAME FEATURING THE T.H.U.N.D.E.R. AGENTS
May, 1983 - No. 3, Dec, 1983
JC Productions(Archie Comics Group)

1-3: Thunder Agents-r(Crandall, Tuska, Wood-a) .50 1.00

HALLOWEEN HORROR (Eclipse)(Value: cover or less)

HALO JONES (See The Ballad of...)

HAMMERLOCKE
Sept, 1992 - No. 9, May, 1993 ($1.75, color, mini-series)
DC Comics

1-($2.50, 52 pgs.) 1.00 2.50
2-9 .70 1.75

HAMMER OF GOD (First)(Value: cover or less)

HAMMER OF GOD: SWORD OF JUSTICE (First)(Value: cover or less)

HANDBOOK OF THE CONAN UNIVERSE, THE
June, 1985 ($1.25, color, one-shot)
Marvel Comics

1 1.25

HAND OF FATE (Formerly Men Against Crime)
No. 8, Dec, 1951 - No. 26, March, 1955
Ace Magazines

8: Surrealistic text story 17.00 52.00 120.00
9,10 10.00 30.00 65.00
11-18,20,22,23 8.35 25.00 50.00
19-Bondage, hypo needle scenes 10.00 30.00 60.00
21-Necronomicon story; drug belladonna used 10.00 30.00 65.00
24-Electric chair-c 11.50 34.00 80.00
25(11/54), 25(12/54) 7.00 21.00 42.00
26-Nostrand-a 9.15 27.50 55.00
NOTE: *Cameron a-9, 10, 19-25; c-13.* ***Sekowsky*** *a-8, 9, 13, 14.*

HAND OF FATE (Eclipse)(Value: cover or less)

HANDS OF THE DRAGON
June, 1975
Seaboard Periodicals (Atlas)

1-Origin; Mooney inks 1.00

HANGMAN COMICS (Special Comics No. 1; Black Hood No. 9 on)
(Also see Flyman, Mighty Comics, Mighty Crusaders & Pep Comics)
No. 2, Spring, 1942 - No. 8, Fall, 1943
MLJ Magazines

2-The Hangman, Boy Buddies begin 108.00 325.00 700.00
3-8: 3-Beheading splash pg.; 1st Nazi war-c. 5-1st Jap war-c. 8-2nd app. Super Duck (ties w/Jolly Jingles #11) 56.00 168.00 375.00
NOTE: ***Fuje*** *a-7(3), 8(3); c-3.* ***Reinman*** *c/a-3. Bondage c-3.* ***Sahle*** *c-6.*

HANK
1946
Pentagon Publishing Co.

nn-Coulton Waugh's newspaper reprint 5.85 17.50 35.00

HANNA-BARBERA (See Golden Comics Digest No. 2, 7, 11)

HANNA-BARBERA BAND WAGON (TV)
Oct, 1962 - No. 3, April, 1963
Gold Key

1,2-Giants, 84 pgs. 1-Augie Doggie & Lippy the Lion app. (pre-#1's) 7.00 21.00 50.00
3-Regular size; Mr. & Mrs. J. Evil Scientist app. (pre #1) & Snagglepuss app. 4.70 14.00 33.00

HANNA-BARBERA GIANT SIZE
Oct, 1992 - Present ($2.25, color, 68 pgs.)
Harvey Comics

V2#1-Flintstones, Yogi Bear, Magilla Gorilla, Huckleberry Hound, Quick Draw McGraw, Yakky Doodle & Chopper, Jetsons & other stories .90 2.25

HANNA-BARBERA HI-ADVENTURE HEROES (See Hi-Adventure...)

HANNA-BARBERA PARADE (TV)
Sept, 1971 - No. 10, Dec, 1972
Charlton Comics

1 4.30 13.00 30.00
2-10: 7-"Summer Picnic"-52 pgs. 2.40 7.25 17.00
NOTE: *No. 4 (1/72) went on sale late in 1972 with the January 1973 issues.*

HANNA-BARBERA SPOTLIGHT (See Spotlight)

HANNA-BARBERA SUPER TV HEROES (TV)
April, 1968 - No. 7, Oct, 1969 (Hanna-Barbera)
Gold Key

1-The Birdman, The Herculoids(ends #6; not in #2), Moby Dick, Young Samson & Goliath(ends #2,4), and The Mighty Mightor begin; Spiegle-a in all 11.50 34.00 80.00
2-The Galaxy Trio app.; Shazzan begins; 12 & 15 cent versions exist 9.15 27.50 75.00
3-7: 3,6,7: The Space Ghost app. in all 10.00 30.00 70.00

HANNA-BARBERA TV FUN FAVORITES (See Golden Comics Digest #2,7,11)

HANNA-BARBERA (TV STARS) (See TV Stars)

HANS BRINKER (See 4-Color No. 1273)

HANS CHRISTIAN ANDERSEN
1953 (100 pgs. - Special Issue)
Ziff-Davis Publ. Co.

nn-Danny Kaye (movie)-Photo-c 11.50 34.00 80.00

HANSEL & GRETEL (See 4-Color No. 590)

HANSI, THE GIRL WHO LOVED THE SWASTIKA (Spire Christian)(Value: cover or less)

HANS UND FRITZ
1917 (10x13-1/2"; 1916 strip-r in B&W); 1929 (28 pgs.; 10x13-1/2")
The Saalfield Publishing Co.

nn-By R. Dirks 46.00 138.00 325.00
193-(Very Rare)-By R. Dirks; contains B&W Sunday strip reprints of Katzenjammer Kids & Hawkshaw the Detective from 1916 54.00 160.00 375.00
...The Funny Larks Of 2(1929) 46.00 138.00 325.00

HAP HAZARD COMICS (Real Love No. 25 on)
1944 - No. 24, Feb, 1949
Ace Magazines (Readers' Research)

1 9.15 27.50 55.00
2 4.70 14.00 28.00
3-10 3.60 9.00 18.00
11-13,15-24 2.80 7.00 14.00
14-Feldstein-c (4/47) 5.85 17.50 35.00

HAP HOPPER (See Comics Revue No. 2)

HAPPIEST MILLIONAIRE, THE (See Movie Comics)

HAPPINESS AND HEALING FOR YOU (Also see Oral Roberts'...)
1955 (36 pgs.; slick cover) (Oral Roberts Giveaway)
Commercial Comics

nn 8.35 25.00 50.00

Harbinger #23, © Voyager Comm.

Hardcase #3, © Malibu

Hardware #6, © Milestone Media

GD25 FN65 NM94

GD25 FN65 NM94

NOTE: *The success of this book prompted Oral Roberts to go into the publishing business himself to produce his own material.*

HAPPI TIM (See March of Comics No. 182)

HAPPY COMICS (Happy Rabbit No. 41 on)
Aug, 1943 - No. 40, Dec, 1950 (Companion to Goofy Comics)
Nedor Publ./Standard Comics (Animated Cartoons)

	GD25	FN65	NM94
1	17.00	52.00	120.00
2	10.00	30.00	60.00
3-10	6.35	19.00	38.00
11-19	4.35	13.00	26.00
20-31,34-37-Frazetta text illos in all (2 in #34&35, 3 in #27,28,30). 27-Al Fago-a	5.00	15.00	30.00
32-Frazetta-a, 7 pgs. plus 2 text illos; Roussos-a	10.00	30.00	70.00
33-Frazetta-a(2), 6 pgs. each (Scarce)	16.00	48.00	110.00
38-40	3.60	9.00	18.00

HAPPY DAYS (TV)(See Kite Fun Book)
March, 1979 - No. 6, Feb, 1980
Gold Key

	GD25	FN65	NM94
1	1.00	2.00	5.00
2-6		1.20	3.00

HAPPY HOLIDAY (See March of Comics No. 181)

HAPPY HOOLIGAN (See Alphonse...)
1903 (18 pgs.) (Sunday strip reprints in color)
Hearst's New York American-Journal

	GD25	FN65	NM94
Book 1-by Fred Opper	50.00	150.00	350.00
50 Pg. Edition(1903)-10x15" in color	54.00	162.00	375.00

HAPPY HOOLIGAN (Handy...) (See The Travels of...)
1908 (32 pgs. in color) (10x15"; cardboard covers)
Frederick A. Stokes Co.

	GD25	FN65	NM94
nn	46.00	138.00	300.00

HAPPY HOOLIGAN (Story of...)
No. 281, 1932 (16 pgs.; 9-1/2x12"; softcover)
McLoughlin Bros.

	GD25	FN65	NM94
281-Three-color text, pictures on heavy paper	14.00	42.00	90.00

HAPPY HOULIHANS (Saddle Justice No. 3 on; see Blackstone, The Magician Detective)
Fall, 1947 - No. 2, Winter, 1947-48
E. C. Comics

	GD25	FN65	NM94
1-Origin Moon Girl (same date as Moon Girl #1)	34.00	100.00	235.00
2	17.00	52.00	120.00

HAPPY JACK
August, 1957 - No. 2, Nov, 1957
Red Top (Decker)

	GD25	FN65	NM94
V1#1,2	3.00	7.50	15.00

HAPPY JACK HOWARD
1957
Red Top (Farrell)/Decker

	GD25	FN65	NM94
nn-Reprints Handy Andy story from E. C. Dandy Comics #5, renamed "Happy Jack"	4.00	10.00	20.00

HAPPY RABBIT (Formerly Happy Comics)
No. 41, Feb, 1951 - No. 48, April, 1952
Standard Comics (Animated Cartoons)

	GD25	FN65	NM94
41	4.00	11.00	22.00
42-48	2.40	6.00	12.00

HARBINGER
Jan, 1992 - Present ($1.95-$2.50, color)
Valiant

	GD25	FN65	NM94
0-(Advance)	17.00	52.00	120.00
1-1st app.	14.00	43.00	100.00
2	6.50	19.00	45.00
3	4.00	12.00	28.00
4-Low print run	5.50	17.00	40.00
5,6	2.15	6.50	15.00
7-9: 8,9-Unity x-overs. 8-Miller-c. 9-Simonson-c	1.65	4.70	11.00
10-1st app. H.A.R.D Corps (10/92)	1.25	3.00	7.50
11-16: 14-1st app. Stronghold		1.40	3.50
17-24,26-28: 18-Intro Screen. 19-1st app. Stunner. 22-Archer & Armstrong app.		1.00	2.50
25-($3.50, 52 pgs.)-Harada vs. Sting		1.40	3.50
Trade paperback nn (1992, $9.95)-Reprints #1-4 & comes polybagged with a copy of Harbinger #0 w/new-c	4.30	13.00	30.00

NOTE: *Issues 1-6 have coupons with origin of Harada and are redeemable for Harbinger #0.*

HARD BOILED (Dark Horse)(Value: cover or less)

HARDCASE
June, 1993 - Present ($1.95, color)
Malibu Comics (Ultraverse)

	GD25	FN65	NM94
1-Intro Hardcase; Dave Gibbons-c		1.60	4.00
1-Platinum Edition			15.00
1-Holographic Cover Edition			45.00
2,3: 2-Polybagged w/trading card		1.30	3.25
4-8: 4-Strangers app.		.80	2.00
5-($2.50, 40 pgs.)-Rune flip-c/story by B. Smith (3 pgs.)		1.00	2.50

H.A.R.D. CORPS, THE (See Harbinger #10)
Dec, 1992 - Present ($2.25, color) (Harbinger spin-off)
Valiant

	GD25	FN65	NM94
1-(Advance)			65.00
1-($2.50)-Gatefold-c by Jim Lee & Bob Layton		1.30	3.25
1-Gold variant			25.00
2-6: 5-Bloodshot-c/story cont'd from Bloodshot #3		.90	2.25
7-18: 10-Turok app.		.90	2.25

HARD LOOKS (Dark Horse)(Value: cover or less)

HARDWARE
Apr, 1993 - Present ($1.50, color)
DC Comics (Milestone)

	GD25	FN65	NM94
1-($2.95)-Collector's Edition polybagged w/poster & trading card (direct sale only)		1.20	3.00
1-Platinum Edition			15.00
1-14			1.50

HARDY BOYS, THE (Disney)(See 4-Color No. 760, 830, 887, 964)

HARDY BOYS, THE (TV)
April, 1970 - No. 4, Jan, 1971
Gold Key

	GD25	FN65	NM94
1	1.65	4.00	10.00
2-4	1.00	2.50	6.00

HARLEM GLOBETROTTERS (TV) (See Fun-In No. 8, 10)
April, 1972 - No. 12, Jan, 1975 (Hanna-Barbera)
Gold Key

	GD25	FN65	NM94
1	1.00	2.50	6.00
2-12		1.20	3.00

NOTE: *#4, 8, and 12 contain 16 extra pages of advertising.*

HAROLD TEEN (See 4-Color #2, 209, Popular Comics, Super Comics & Treasure Box of Famous Comics)

HAROLD TEEN (Adv. of...)
1929-31 (36-52 pgs.) (Paper covers)
Cupples & Leon Co.

	GD25	FN65	NM94
nn-B&W daily strip reprints by Carl Ed	14.00	43.00	100.00

HARVEY
Oct, 1970; No. 2, 12/70; No. 3, 6/72 - No. 6, 12/72
Marvel Comics Group

	GD25	FN65	NM94
1	1.00	2.50	6.00

Harvey Comic Hits #52, © Milton Caniff

Harvey Hits #4, © HARV

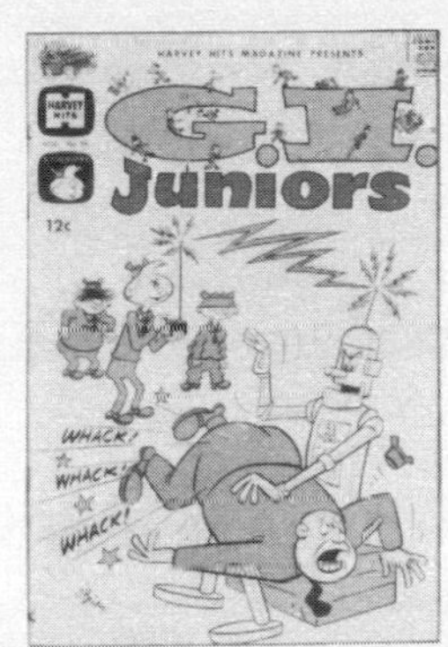

Harvey Hits #98, © HARV

	GD25	FN65	NM94
2-6		1.60	4.00

HARVEY COLLECTORS COMICS (Richie Rich Collectors Comics #10 on, cover title only)
Sept, 1975 - No. 15, Jan, 1978; No. 16, Oct, 1979 (52 pgs.)
Harvey Publications

	GD25	FN65	NM94
1-Reprints Richie Rich #1,2	1.00	2.00	5.00
2-10: 7-Splash pg. shows-c to Friendly Ghost Casper #1		1.20	3.00
11-16: 16-Sad Sack-r			1.25

NOTE: All reprints: Casper-#2, 7, Richie Rich-#1, 3, 5, 6, 8-15, Sad Sack-#16. Wendy-#4. #6 titled 'Richie Rich...'on inside.

HARVEY COMICS HITS
No. 51, Oct, 1951 - No. 62, Apr, 1953
Harvey Publications

	GD25	FN65	NM94
51-The Phantom	16.00	48.00	110.00
52-Steve Canyon's Air Power	10.00	30.00	60.00
53-Mandrake the Magician	13.00	40.00	90.00
54-Tim Tyler's Tales of Jungle Terror	8.35	25.00	50.00
55-Love Stories of Mary Worth	4.00	12.00	24.00
56-The Phantom; bondage-c	13.00	40.00	90.00
57-Rip Kirby-"Kidnap Racket;" entire book by Alex Raymond	10.00	30.00	65.00
58-Girls in White (nurses stories)	4.00	11.00	22.00
59-Tales of the Invisible featuring Scarlet O'Neil	7.50	22.50	45.00
60-Paramount Animated Comics #1 (2nd app. Baby Huey); 1st Harvey app. Baby Huey & Casper the Friendly Ghost; 1st app. Herman & Catnip (c/story) & Buzzy the Crow (9/52)	29.00	85.00	200.00
61-Casper the Friendly Ghost #6 (2nd Harvey Casper, 10/52)	26.00	80.00	185.00
62-Paramount Animated Comics; Herman & Catnip, Baby Huey & Buzzy the Crow	9.15	27.50	55.00

HARVEY COMICS LIBRARY
April, 1952 - No. 2, 1952
Harvey Publications

	GD25	FN65	NM94
1-Teen-Age Dope Slaves as exposed by Rex Morgan, M.D.; drug propaganda story; used in SOTI, pg. 27	47.00	140.00	325.00
(Prices vary widely on this book)			
2-Sparkle Plenty (Dick Tracy in "Blackmail Terror")	12.00	36.00	85.00

HARVEY COMICS SPOTLIGHT
Sept, 1987 - No. 4, Mar, 1988 (#1-3: 75 cents, #4: $1.00)
Harvey Comics

	GD25	FN65	NM94
1-4: 1,2-new material. 1-Sad Sack, 2-Baby Huey, 3-Little Dot. 4-Little Audrey. #5 was advertised but not published			1.00

HARVEY HITS
Sept, 1957 - No. 122, Nov, 1967
Harvey Publications

	GD25	FN65	NM94
1-The Phantom	18.00	54.00	125.00
2-Rags Rabbit (10/57)	2.40	6.00	12.00
3-Richie Rich (11/57)-r/Little Dot; 1st book devoted to Richie Rich; see Little Dot for 1st app.; X-mas-c	61.00	180.00	425.00
4-Little Dot's Uncles (12/57)	11.00	32.00	75.00
5-Stevie Mazie's Boy Friend	1.80	4.50	9.00
6-The Phantom (2/58); Kirby-c; 2pg. Powell-a	11.50	34.00	80.00
7-Wendy the Witch	11.00	32.00	75.00
8-Sad Sack's Army Life	4.20	12.50	25.00
9-Richie Rich's Golden Deeds-r (2nd book devoted to Richie Rich)	36.00	110.00	250.00
10-Little Lotta	9.15	27.50	55.00
11-Little Audrey Summer Fun (7/58)	5.35	16.00	32.00
12-The Phantom; Kirby-c; 2pg. Powell-a (8/58)	10.00	30.00	60.00
13-Little Dot's Uncles (9/58); Richie Rich 1pg.	7.50	22.50	45.00
14-Herman & Katnip (10/58)	2.40	6.00	12.00
15-The Phantom (12/58)-1 pg. origin	10.00	30.00	60.00
16-Wendy the Witch (1/59)	6.70	20.00	40.00
17-Sad Sack's Army Life (2/59)	4.00	10.00	20.00
18-Buzzy & the Crow	3.00	7.50	15.00
19-Little Audrey (4/59)	4.00	10.50	21.00
20-Casper & Spooky	5.00	15.00	30.00
21-Wendy the Witch	4.20	12.50	25.00
22-Sad Sack's Army Life	3.00	7.50	15.00
23-Wendy the Witch (8/59)	4.00	11.00	22.00
24-Little Dot's Uncles (9/59); Richie Rich 1pg.	5.85	17.50	35.00
25-Herman & Katnip (10/59)	2.00	5.00	10.00
26-The Phantom (11/59)	8.35	25.00	50.00
27-Wendy the Good Little Witch	4.00	11.00	22.00
28-Sad Sack's Army Life	2.00	5.00	10.00
29-Harvey-Toon (No.1)('60); Casper, Buzzy	4.00	10.00	20.00
30-Wendy the Witch (3/60)	4.00	11.00	22.00
31-Herman & Katnip (4/60)	1.00	2.50	5.00
32-Sad Sack's Army Life (5/60)	1.60	4.00	8.00
33-Wendy the Witch (6/60)	4.00	11.00	22.00
34-Harvey-Toon (7/60)	2.40	6.00	12.00
35-Funday Funnies (8/60)	1.00	2.50	5.00
36-The Phantom (1960)	6.70	20.00	40.00
37-Casper & Nightmare	4.00	10.00	20.00
38-Harvey-Toon	2.40	6.00	12.00
39-Sad Sack's Army Life (12/60)	1.60	4.00	8.00
40-Funday Funnies	.80	2.00	4.00
41-Herman & Katnip	.80	2.00	4.00
42-Harvey-Toon (3/61)	1.60	4.00	8.00
43-Sad Sack's Army Life (4/61)	1.20	3.00	6.00
44-The Phantom (5/61)	6.70	20.00	40.00
45-Casper & Nightmare	3.00	7.50	15.00
46-Harvey-Toon (7/61)	1.20	3.00	6.00
47-Sad Sack's Army Life (8/61)	1.20	3.00	6.00
48-The Phantom (9/61)	5.85	17.50	35.00
49-Stumbo the Giant (1st app. in Hot Stuff)	7.50	22.50	45.00
50-Harvey-Toon (11/61)	1.20	3.00	6.00
51-Sad Sack's Army Life (12/61)	1.20	3.00	6.00
52-Casper & Nightmare	3.00	7.50	15.00
53-Harvey-Toons (2/62)	1.00	2.50	5.00
54-Stumbo the Giant	4.00	12.00	24.00
55-Sad Sack's Army Life (4/62)	1.20	3.00	6.00
56-Casper & Nightmare	3.00	7.50	15.00
57-Stumbo the Giant	4.00	12.00	24.00
58-Sad Sack's Army Life	1.20	3.00	6.00
59-Casper & Nightmare (7/62)	3.00	7.50	15.00
60-Stumbo the Giant (9/62)	4.00	12.00	24.00
61-Sad Sack's Army Life	1.20	3.00	6.00
62-Casper & Nightmare	2.40	6.00	12.00
63-Stumbo the Giant	4.00	12.00	24.00
64-Sad Sack's Army Life (1/63)	1.20	3.00	6.00
65-Casper & Nightmare	2.40	6.00	12.00
66-Stumbo The Giant	4.00	12.00	24.00
67-Sad Sack's Army Life (4/63)	1.20	3.00	6.00
68-Casper & Nightmare	2.40	6.00	12.00
69-Stumbo the Giant (6/63)	4.00	12.00	24.00
70-Sad Sack's Army Life (7/63)	1.20	3.00	6.00
71-Casper & Nightmare (8/63)	1.80	4.50	9.00
72-Stumbo the Giant	4.00	12.00	24.00
73-Little Sad Sack (10/63)	1.20	3.00	6.00
74-Sad Sack's Muttsy... (11/63)	1.20	3.00	6.00
75-Casper & Nightmare	1.80	4.50	9.00
76-Little Sad Sack	1.20	3.00	6.00
77-Sad Sack's Muttsy...	1.20	3.00	6.00
78-Stumbo the Giant	4.00	12.00	24.00

79-87: 79-Little Sad Sack (4/64). 80-Sad Sack's Muttsy... (5/64). 81-Little Sad Sack. 82-Sad Sack's Muttsy... 83-Little Sad Sack(8/64). 84-Sad

Haunted #22, © CC

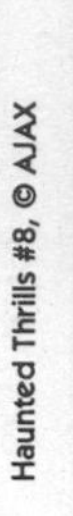
Haunted Thrills #8, © AJAX

Haunt of Fear #21, © WMG

GD25 FN65 NM94

Sack's Muttsy... 85-Gabby Gob (No.1)(10/64). 86-G. I. Juniors (No.1). 87-Sad Sack's Muttsy... (12/64) 1.20 3.00 6.00
88-Stumbo the Giant (1/65) 4.00 12.00 24.00
89-122: 89-Sad Sack's Muttsy... 90-Gabby Gob. 91-G. I. Juniors. 92-Sad Sack's Muttsy... (5/65). 93-Sadie Sack (6/65). 94-Gabby Gob. 95-G. I. Juniors. 96-Sad Sack's Muttsy... (9/65). 97-Gabby Gob. 98-G. I. Juniors (11/65). 99-Sad Sack's Muttsy... (12/65). 100-Gabby Gob. 101-G. I. Juniors (2/66). 102-Sad Sack's Muttsy... (3/66). 103-Gabby Gob. 104-G. I. Juniors. 105-Sad Sack's Muttsy... 106-Gabby Gob (7/66). 107-G. I. Juniors (8/66). 108-Sad Sack's Muttsy... 109-Gabby Gob. 110-G. I. Juniors (11/66). 111-Sad Sack's Muttsy... (12/66). 112-G. I. Juniors. 113-Sad Sack's Muttsy... 114-G. I. Juniors. 115-Sad Sack's Muttsy... 116-G. I. Juniors. 117-Sad Sack's Muttsy... 118-G. I. Juniors. 119-Sad Sack's Muttsy... (8/67). 120-G. I. Juniors (9/67). 121-Sad Sack's Muttsy... (10/67). 122-G. I. Juniors 1.00 2.50 5.00

HARVEY HITS COMICS
Nov, 1986 - No. 6, Oct, 1987
Harvey Publications

1-6: Little Lotta, Little Dot, Wendy & Baby Huey 1.00

HARVEY POP COMICS (Teen Humor)
Oct, 1968 - No. 2, Nov, 1969 (Both are 68 pg. Giants)
Harvey Publications

1,2-The Cowsills 1.70 5.00 12.00

HARVEY 3-D HITS (See Sad Sack)

HARVEY-TOON (...S) (See Harvey Hits No. 29, 34, 38, 42, 46, 50, 53)

HARVEY WISEGUYS (...Digest #? on)
Nov, 1987; #2, Nov, 1988; #3, Apr, 1989 - No. 4, Nov, 1989 (98 pgs., digest-size, $1.25-$1.75)
Harvey Comics

1,2: 1-Hot Stuff, Spooky, etc. 2 (68 pgs.) 1.25
3,4 .70 1.75

HATARI (See Movie Classics)

HATHAWAYS, THE (See 4-Color No. 1298)

HAUNTED (See This Magazine Is Haunted)

HAUNTED (Baron Weirwulf's Haunted Library #21 on)
9/71 - No. 30, 11/76; No. 31, 9/77 - No. 75, 9/84
Charlton Comics

1 1.30 3.25 8.00
2-5 1.60 4.00
6-21 1.20 3.00
22-75: 64,75-r 1.50

NOTE: ***Aparo*** *c-45.* ***Ditko*** *a-1-8, 11-16, 18, 23, 24, 28, 30, 34r, 36r, 39-42r, 47r, 49-51r, 57, 60, 74. c-1-7, 11, 13, 14, 16, 30, 41, 47, 49-51, 74.* ***Howard*** *a-18, 22, 32.* ***Morisi*** *a-13.* ***Newton*** *a-17, 21, 59r, c-21, 22(painted).* ***Staton*** *a-18, 21, 22, 30, 33; c-18, 33.* ***Sutton*** *a-21, 22, 38; c-15, 17, 18, 23(painted), 24(painted), 64r. #51 reprints #1; #49 reprints Tales of the Mysterious Traveler #4.*

HAUNTED LOVE
April, 1973 - No. 11, Sept, 1975
Charlton Comics

1-Tom Sutton-a (16 pgs.) 1.00 2.00 5.00
2,3,6-11 .80 2.00
4,5-Ditko-a 1.00 2.50
Modern Comics #1(1978) 1.00

NOTE: ***Howard*** *a-8i.* ***Newton*** *c-8, 9.* ***Staton*** *a-5.*

HAUNTED THRILLS
June, 1952 - No. 18, Nov-Dec, 1954
Ajax/Farrell Publications

1-r/Ellery Queen #1 18.00 54.00 125.00
2-L. B. Cole-a r-/Ellery Queen #1 10.00 30.00 70.00
3-5: 3-Drug use story 10.00 30.00 60.00
6-12: 7-Hitler story. 11-Nazi death camp story 8.35 25.00 50.00
13,16-18: 18-Lingerie panels 6.70 20.00 40.00
14-Jesus Christ apps. in story by Webb 6.70 20.00 40.00
15-Jo-Jo-r 7.00 21.00 42.00

NOTE: ***Kamenish*** *art in most issues.* ***Webb*** *a-12.*

HAUNT OF FEAR (Formerly Gunfighter)
No. 15, May-June, 1950 - No. 28, Nov-Dec, 1954
E. C. Comics

15(#1, 1950)(Scarce) 171.00 515.00 1200.00
16 80.00 240.00 550.00
17-Origin of Crypt of Terror, Vault of Horror, & Haunt of Fear; used in **SOTI**, pg. 43; last pg. Ingels-a used by N.Y. Legis. Comm.; story "Monster Maker" based on Frankenstein 80.00 240.00 550.00
4 57.00 170.00 400.00
5-Injury-to-eye panel, pg. 4 43.00 130.00 300.00
6-10: 8-Shrunken head cover. 10-Ingels biog. 31.00 92.00 215.00
11-13,15-18: 11-Kamen biog. 12-Feldstein biog. 16,18-Ray Bradbury adaptations. 18-Ray Bradbury biog. 22.00 65.00 150.00
14-Origin Old Witch by Ingels 34.00 100.00 235.00
19-Used in **SOTI**, ill.-"A comic book baseball game" & Senate investigation on juvenile delinq. bondage/decapitation-c 28.00 85.00 200.00
20-Feldstein-r/Vault of Horror #12 20.00 60.00 140.00
21,22,25,27: 27-Cannibalism story; Wertham cameo 13.00 40.00 90.00
23-Used in **SOTI**, pg. 241 14.00 43.00 100.00
24-Used in Senate Investigative Report, pg.8 13.00 40.00 90.00
26-Contains anti-censorship editorial, 'Are you a Red Dupe?' 13.00 40.00 90.00
28-Low distribution 14.00 43.00 100.00

NOTE: *(Canadian reprints known; see Table of Contents).* ***Craig*** *a-15-17, 5, 7, 10, 12, 13; c-15-17, 5-7.* ***Crandall*** *a-20, 21, 26, 27.* ***Davis*** *a-4-26, 28.* ***Evans*** *a-15-19, 22-25, 27.* ***Feldstein*** *a-15-17, 20; c-4, 8-10.* ***Ingels*** *a-16, 17, 4-28; c-11-28.* ***Kamen*** *a-16, 4, 6, 7, 9-11, 13-19, 21-28.* ***Krigstein*** *a-28.* ***Kurtzman*** *a-15(#1), 17(#3).* ***Orlando*** *a-9, 12.* ***Wood*** *a-15, 16, 4-6.*

HAUNT OF FEAR, THE
May, 1991 - No. 2, July, 1991 ($2.00, color, 68 pgs.)
Gladstone Publishing

1,2: 1-Ghastly Ingels-c(r); 2-Craig-c(r) 1.00 2.50

HAUNT OF FEAR
Sept, 1991 - No. 5, 1992 ($2.00, color, 68 pgs.)
Nov, 1992 - Present ($1.50, color)
Russ Cochran

1-Ingels-c(r) 1.00 2.50
2-5 .80 2.00
1-3: 1,2-r/HOF #15-17 with original-c 1.50
4,5-r/HOF #4,5 with original-c .80 2.00

HAUNT OF HORROR, THE (Magazine)
May, 1974 - No. 5, Jan, 1975 (75 cents) (B&W)
Cadence Comics Publ. (Marvel)

1 1.00 2.50 6.00
2,4: 2-Origin & 1st app. Gabriel the Devil Hunter; Satana begins. 4-Neal Adams-a 1.00 2.00 5.00
3,5: 5-Evans-a(2) 1.60 4.00

NOTE: ***Alcala*** *a-2.* ***Colan*** *a-2p.* ***Heath*** *r-1.* ***Krigstein*** *r-3.* ***Reese*** *a-1.* ***Simonson*** *a-1.*

HAVE GUN, WILL TRAVEL (TV)
No. 931, 8/58 - No. 14, 7-9/62 (All Richard Boone photo-c)
Dell Publishing Co.

4-Color 931 (#1) 10.00 30.00 70.00
4-Color 983,1044 (#2,3) 7.50 22.50 45.00
4 (1-3/60) - 14 5.85 17.50 35.00

HAVOK & WOLVERINE - MELTDOWN (See Marvel Comics Presents #24)
Mar, 1989 - No. 4, Oct, 1989 ($3.50, mini-series, squarebound)
Epic Comics (Marvel)

1-4: Mature readers, violent 1.40 3.50

HAWAIIAN EYE (TV)
July, 1963 (Troy Donahue, Connie Stevens photo-c)

The Hawk #8, © STJ

Hawkman #15 (1st series), © DC

Hawkworld #2 (7/90), © DC

GD25 FN65 NM94

Gold Key
1 (10073-307) 4.70 14.00 28.00

HAWAIIAN ILLUSTRATED LEGENDS SERIES
1975 (B&W)(Cover printed w/blue, yellow, and green)
Hogarth Press
1-Kalelealuaka, the Mysterious Warrior 1.20
2,3(Exist?) 1.00

HAWK, THE (Also see Approved Comics #1, 7 & Tops In Adventure)
Wint/51 - No. 3, 11-12/52; No. 4, 1953 - No. 12, 5/55 (Painted c-1-4)
Ziff-Davis/St. John Publ. Co. No. 4 on
1-Anderson-a 12.00 36.00 85.00
2 (Sum, '52)-Kubert, Infantino-a 8.35 25.00 50.00
3-8,11: 8-Reprints #3 with diff.-c. 11-Buckskin Belle & The Texan app. 5.85 17.50 35.00
9-Baker-c/a; Kubert-a(r)/#2 7.00 21.00 42.00
10-Baker-c/a; r/one story from #2 7.00 21.00 42.00
12-Baker-c/a; Buckskin Belle app. 7.00 21.00 42.00
3-D 1(11/53)-Baker-c 24.00 72.00 165.00
NOTE: ***Baker*** *c-8-12.* ***Larsen*** *a-10.* ***Tuska*** *a-1, 9, 12. Painted c-1, 7.*

HAWK AND DOVE (2nd series)
Oct, 1988 - No. 5, Holiday, 1988-89 ($1.00, color, mini-series)
DC Comics
1-Rob Liefeld-c/a(p) in all 1.40 3.50
2-5 .80 2.00

HAWK AND DOVE (DC, 1989-91, 3rd series)(Value: cover or less)

HAWK AND THE DOVE, THE (See Showcase #75 & Teen Titans)
Aug-Sept, 1968 - No. 6, June-July, 1969 (1st series)
National Periodical Publications
Showcase #75 (7-8/67)-Origin & 1st app. Hawk and the Dove; Ditko-c/a 6.00 19.00 64.00
1-Ditko-c/a 5.50 16.00 38.00
2-6: 5-Teen Titans cameo 4.00 12.00 28.00
NOTE: ***Ditko*** *c/a-1, 2.* ***Gil Kane*** *a-3p, 4p, 5, 6p; c-3-6.*

HAWKEYE (See The Avengers #16 & Tales Of Suspense #57)
Sept, 1983 - No. 4, Dec, 1983 (Mini-series)
Marvel Comics Group
1-4: 1-Origin Hawkeye. 3-Origin Mockingbird 1.00

HAWKEYE
Jan, 1994 - No. 4, Apr, 1994 ($1.75, color, mini-series)
Marvel Comics
1-4 .70 1.75

HAWKEYE & THE LAST OF THE MOHICANS (See 4-Color No. 884)

HAWKMAN (See Atom & Hawkman, The Brave & the Bold, DC Comics Presents, Detective, Flash Comics, Hawkworld, Justice League of America #31, Mystery in Space, Shadow War Of..., Showcase, & World's Finest)

HAWKMAN (1st series) (Also see The Atom #7)
Apr-May, 1964 - No. 27, Aug-Sept, 1968
National Periodical Publications GD25 FN65 VF82 NM94
Brave and the Bold #34 (2-3/61)-Origin & 1st app. S.A. Hawkman & Byth by Kubert; 1st S.A. Hawkman tryout 104.00 313.00 781.00 1250.00
GD25 FN65 NM94
Brave and the Bold #35 (4-5/61)-2nd app. Hawkman by Kubert. 36-Origin & 1st app. Shadow Thief 33.00 100.00 400.00
Brave and the Bold #36 (6-7/61)-3rd app. Hawkman by Kubert;origin Shadow Thief 33.00 98.00 325.00
Brave and the Bold #42 (6-7/62)-Hawkman by Kubert; #42-44 is 2nd Hawkman tryout series 23.00 68.00 225.00
Brave and the Bold #43 (8-9/62)-Gives more detaild origin Hawkman by Kubert 27.00 80.00 265.00
Brave and the Bold #44 (10-11/62)-Hawkman by Kubert 18.00 53.00 175.00
The Atom #7 (6-7/63)-1st Atom & Hawkman team-up; 7th app. Hawkman (tryout issue) 26.00 79.00 185.00
Mystery in Space #87 (11/63)-Adam Strange/Hawkman double feature; begin 3rd Hawkman tryout series 18.00 53.00 140.00
Mystery in Space #88 (12/63) 14.00 41.00 110.00
Brave and the Bold #51 (12-1/63-64)-Aquaman & Hawkman 15.00 45.00 150.00
Mystery in Space #89-Hawkman story 13.00 38.00 100.00
Mystery in Space #90 (3/64)-1st Adam Strange/Hawkman team-up; Hawkman moves to own title next month 16.00 47.00 125.00
1-(4-5/64)-Anderson-c/a begins, ends #21 31.00 94.00 375.00
2 14.00 42.00 140.00
3,5 9.00 27.00 80.00
4-Origin & 1st app. Zatanna (10-11/64) 9.00 27.00 90.00
6-10: 9-Atom cameo; Hawkman & Atom learn each other's I.D.; 2nd app. Shadow Thief 8.00 25.00 53.00
11-15 5.50 16.00 38.00
16-27: 18-Adam Strange x-over (cameo #19). 25-G.A. Hawkman-r by Moldoff. 27-Kubert-c 3.85 11.50 27.00

HAWKMAN (2nd series)
Aug, 1986 - No. 17, Dec, 1987
DC Comics
1-17: 10-Byrne-c 1.00
Special #1 (1986, $1.25) 1.50
Trade paperback (1989, $19.95)-r/Brave and the Bold #34-36,42-44 by Kubert; Kubert-c 3.20 8.00 20.00

HAWKMAN (3rd series)
Sept, 1993 - Present ($1.75, color)
DC Comics
1-($2.50)-Gold foil embossed-c; new costume & powers 1.00 2.50
2-8: 3-Airstryke app. .70 1.75
Annual 1 (1993, $2.50, 68 pgs.) 1.00 2.50

HAWKMOON: (First Comics, all titles)(Value: cover or less)

HAWKSHAW THE DETECTIVE (See Advs. of , Hans Und Fritz & Okay)
1917 (24 pgs.; B&W; 10-1/2x13-1/2") (Sunday strip reprints)
The Saalfield Publishing Co.
nn-By Gus Mager 14.00 43.00 100.00

HAWKWORLD
1989 - No. 3, 1989 ($3.95, prestige format, mini-series)
DC Comics
Book 1-Hawkman dons new costume 1.60 4.00
Book 2,3-Truman-c/a/scripts in #1-3 1.60 4.00

HAWKWORLD
June, 1990 - No. 32, Mar, 1993 ($1.50/$1.75, on-going series)
DC Comics
1-Hawkman spin-off 1.00 2.50
2-32: 15,16-War of the Gods x-over. 22-J'onn J'onzz app .70 1.75
Annual 1 (1990, $2.95, 68 pgs.)-Flash app. 1.20 3.00
Annual 2 (1991, $2.95, 68 pgs.)-2nd print exists with silver ink-c 1.20 3.00
Annual 3 (1992, $2.95, 68 pgs.)-Eclipso app. 1.20 3.00

HAWTHORN-MELODY FARMS DAIRY COMICS
No date (1950's) (Giveaway)
Everybody's Publishing Co.
nn-Cheerie Chick, Tuffy Turtle, Robin Koo Koo, Donald & Longhorn Legends 1.60 4.00 8.00

HAYWIRE (DC)(Value: cover or less)

HEADLINE COMICS (...Crime No. 32-39)
Feb, 1943 - No. 22, Nov-Dec, 1946; No. 23, 1947 - No. 77, Oct, 1956
Prize Publications

Heart Throbs #9, © DC

Heathcliff #42, © McNaught Syndicate

Hedy Devine Comics #27, © MEG

	GD25	FN65	NM94
1-Yank & Doodle x-over in Junior Rangers	27.00	81.00	190.00
2	11.50	34.00	80.00
3-Used in **POP**, pg. 84	10.00	30.00	60.00
4-7,9,10: 4,9,10-Hitler stories in each	10.00	30.00	60.00
8-Classic Hitler-c	16.00	48.00	110.00
11,12	6.70	20.00	40.00
13-15-Blue Streak in all	7.00	21.00	42.00
16-Origin Atomic Man	13.50	41.00	95.00
17,18,20,21: 21-Atomic Man ends (9-10/46)	7.50	22.50	45.00
19-S&K-a	14.00	43.00	100.00
22-Change to crime format; Kiefer-c	4.00	12.00	24.00
23,24: (All S&K-a). 24-Dope-crazy killer story	12.00	36.00	85.00
25-35-S&K-c/a. 25-Powell-a	10.00	30.00	70.00
36-S&K-a; photo-c	10.00	30.00	60.00
37-One pg. S&K, Severin-a; Jack Kirby photo-c	5.00	15.00	30.00
38,40-Meskin-a	3.60	9.00	18.00
39,41,42,46-48,50-55: 51-Kirby-c	2.40	6.00	12.00
43,49-Meskin-a	2.80	7.00	14.00
44-S&K-c; Severin/Elder, Meskin-a	5.00	15.00	30.00
45-Kirby-a	4.00	10.00	20.00
56-S&K-a	5.00	15.00	30.00
57-77: 72-Meskin-c/a(i)	2.40	6.00	12.00

NOTE: ***Hollingsworth** a-30. Photo c-36-43. Atomic Man c-17-19.*

HEADMAN (Innovation)(Value: cover or less)

HEAP, THE
Sept, 1971 (52 pages)
Skywald Publications

	GD25	FN65	NM94
1-Kinstler-r/Strange Worlds #8		1.20	3.00

HEART AND SOUL
April-May, 1954 - No. 2, June-July, 1954
Mikeross Publications

	GD25	FN65	NM94
1,2	4.70	14.00	28.00

HEARTS OF DARKNESS (See Ghost Rider; Wolverine; Punisher: Hearts of...)
Dec, 1992 ($4.95, color, double gatefold-c)
Marvel Comics

	GD25	FN65	NM94
1-Ghost Rider, Punisher, Wolverine app.	1.00	2.00	5.00

HEART THROBS (Love Stories No. 147 on)
8/49 - No. 8, 10/50; No. 9, 3/52 - No. 146, Oct, 1972
Quality Comics/National Periodical #47(4-5/57) on (Arleigh #48-101)

	GD25	FN65	NM94
1-Classic Ward-c, Gustavson-a, 9 pgs.	25.00	75.00	175.00
2-Ward-c/a (9 pgs); Gustavson-a	12.00	36.00	85.00
3-Gustavson-a	5.35	16.00	32.00
4,6,8-Ward-a, 8-9 pgs.	8.00	24.00	48.00
5,7	4.00	10.00	20.00
9-Robert Mitchum, Jane Russell photo-c	6.35	19.00	38.00
10,15-Ward-a	6.35	19.00	38.00
11-14,16-20: 12 (7/52)	3.20	8.00	16.00
21-Ward-c	5.00	15.00	30.00
22,23-Ward-a(p)	4.00	11.00	22.00
24-33: 33-Last pre-code (3/55)	2.80	7.00	14.00
34-39,41-46 (12/56; last Quality issue)	2.40	6.00	12.00
40-Ward-a; r-7 pgs./#21	4.00	10.00	20.00
47-(4-5/57; 1st DC issue)	16.00	50.00	115.00
48-60	7.50	22.50	45.00
61-70	5.00	15.00	30.00
71-100: 74-Last 10 cent issue	4.00	12.00	24.00
101-The Beatles app. on-c	9.15	27.50	55.00
102-120: 102-123-(Serial)-Three Girls, Their Lives, Their Loves. 120-Neal Adams-c	2.00	5.00	10.00
121-146: #133-142, 52 pgs.	1.00	2.50	6.00

NOTE: ***Gustavson** a-8. **Tuska** a-128. Photo c-4, 5, 8-10, 15, 17.*

HEATHCLIFF (See Star Comics Magazine)
Apr, 1985 - No. 56, Feb, 1991 (#16-on, $1.00)
Star Comics/Marvel Comics No. 23 on

	GD25	FN65	NM94
1-49,51-56: Post-a most issues. 43-X-Mas issue. 47-Batman parody (Catman vs. the Soaker)			1.00
50-($1.50, 52 pgs.)			1.50
Annual 1 ('87)			1.20

HEATHCLIFF'S FUNHOUSE
May, 1987 - No. 10, 1988
Star Comics/Marvel Comics No. 6 on

	GD25	FN65	NM94
1-10			1.00

HECKLE AND JECKLE (See Blue Ribbon, Paul Terry's & Terry-Toons Comics)
10/51 - No. 24, 10/55; No. 25, Fall/56 - No. 34, 6/59
St. John Publ. Co. No. 1-24/Pines No. 25 on

	GD25	FN65	NM94
1	22.00	65.00	150.00
2	11.00	32.00	75.00
3-5	9.15	27.50	55.00
6-10	6.35	19.00	38.00
11-20	4.70	14.00	28.00
21-34: 25-Begin CBS Television Presents on-c	4.00	10.00	20.00

HECKLE AND JECKLE (TV) (See New Terrytoons)
11/62 - No. 4, 8/63; 5/66; No. 2, 10/66; No. 3, 8/67
Gold Key/Dell Publishing Co.

	GD25	FN65	NM94
1 (11/62; Gold Key)	4.30	13.00	30.00
2-4	2.15	6.50	15.00
1 (5/66; Dell)	3.20	8.00	20.00
2,3	2.15	6.50	15.00

(See March of Comics No. 379, 472, 484)

HECKLE AND JECKLE 3-D (Spotlight)(Value: cover or less)

HECKLER, THE (DC Comics)(Value: cover or less)

HECTOR COMICS
Nov, 1953 - No. 3, 1954
Key Publications

	GD25	FN65	NM94
1-Teen humor	3.20	8.00	16.00
2,3	2.00	5.00	10.00

HECTOR HEATHCOTE (TV)
March, 1964
Gold Key

	GD25	FN65	NM94
1 (10111-403)	4.70	14.00	28.00

HECTOR THE INSPECTOR (See Top Flight Comics)

HEDY DEVINE COMICS (Formerly All Winners #21? or Teen #22?(6/47); Hedy of Hollywood #36 on; also see Annie Oakley, Comedy & Venus)
No. 22, Aug, 1947 - No. 50, Sept, 1952
Marvel Comics (RCM)/Atlas #50

	GD25	FN65	NM94
22-1st app. Hedy Devine (also see Joker #32)	9.15	27.50	55.00
23,24,27-30: 23-Wolverton-a, 1 pg; Kurtzman's "Hey Look," 2 pgs. 24,27-30-"Hey Look" by Kurtzman, 1-3 pgs.	10.00	30.00	60.00
25-Classic "Hey Look" by Kurtzman-"Optical Illusion"	10.00	30.00	65.00
26-"Giggles & Grins" by Kurtzman	7.50	22.50	45.00
31-34,36-50: 32-Anti-Wertham editorial	4.70	14.00	28.00
35-Four pgs. "Rusty" by Kurtzman	8.35	25.00	50.00

HEDY-MILLIE-TESSIE COMEDY (See Comedy Comics)

HEDY WOLFE (Also see Patsy & Hedy & Miss America Magazine V1#2)
August, 1957
Atlas Publishing Co. (Emgee)

	GD25	FN65	NM94
1-Al Hartley-c	6.70	20.00	40.00

HEE HAW (TV)
July, 1970 - No. 7, Aug, 1971
Charlton Press

Hellblazer #69, © DC

Hellstorm #7, © MEG

Herbie #4, © Sword in Stone Prod.

	GD25	FN65	NM94
1	1.70	5.00	12.00
2-7	1.30	3.25	8.00

HEIDI (See Dell Jr. Treasury No. 6)

HELEN OF TROY (See 4-Color No. 684)

HELLBLAZER (John Constantine) (See Saga of Swamp Thing #37)
Jan, 1988 - Present ($1.25-1.50, adults)
DC Comics

	GD25	FN65	NM94
1-(44 pgs.)	1.70	5.00	12.00
2-5	1.10	2.70	6.50
6-10: 9-X-over w/Swamp Thing #76. 9,10-Swamp Thing cameo		1.40	3.50
11-20		1.40	3.50
21-30: 24-Contains bound-in Shocker movie poster. 25,26-Grant Morrison scripts. 27-Neil Gaiman scripts; Dave McKean-a; fold out guide to Nightbreed		1.20	3.00
31-39,41-49: 36-Preview of World Without End. 44-Begin $1.75-c. 44,45-Sutton-a(i)		1.00	2.50
40-($2.25, 52 pgs.)-Dave McKean-a & colors; preview of Kid Eternity		1.20	3.00
50-($3.00, 52 pgs.)		1.20	3.00
51-65: 62-Special Death insert by McKean. 63-Silver metallic ink on-c		.70	1.75
66-74: 66-Begin $1.95-c		.80	2.00
75-($2.95, 52 pgs.)		1.20	3.00
Annual 1 (1989, $2.95, 68 pgs.)		1.80	4.50
Special 1 (1993, $3.95, 68 pgs.)-With pin-ups		1.60	4.00

HELLO, I'M JOHNNY CASH (Spire Christian)(Value: cover or less)

HELL ON EARTH (See DC Science Fiction Graphic Novel)

HELLO PAL COMICS (Short Story Comics)
Jan, 1943 - No. 3, May, 1943 (Photo-c)
Harvey Publications

	GD25	FN65	NM94
1-Rocketman & Rocketgirl begin; Yankee Doodle Jones app.; Mickey Rooney photo-c	50.00	150.00	300.00
2-Charlie McCarthy photo-c	35.00	95.00	210.00
3-Bob Hope photo-c	37.00	110.00	250.00

HELLRAISER NIGHTBREED – JIHAD (Epic)(Value: cover or less)

HELLRAISER III: HELL ON EARTH (Epic)(Value: cover or less)(Movie Special)

HELL-RIDER (Magazine)
Aug, 1971 - No. 2, Oct, 1971 (B&W)
Skywald Publications

	GD25	FN65	NM94
1,2: 1-Origin & 1st app.; Butterfly & Wildbunch begins	1.00	2.00	5.00

NOTE: *#3 advertised in Psycho #5 but did not come out.* ***Buckler*** *a-1, 2.* ***Morrow*** *c-3.*

HELL'S ANGEL (Becomes Dark Angel #6 on)
July, 1992 - No. 5, Nov, 1993 ($1.75, color)
Marvel Comics UK

	GD25	FN65	NM94
1-5: X-Men (Wolverine, Cyclops)-c/stories. 1-Origin. 3-Jim Lee cover swipe		.70	1.75

HELLSTORM: PRINCE OF LIES (See Ghost Rider #1 & Marvel Spotlight #12)
Apr, 1993 - Present ($2.00, color)
Marvel Comics

	GD25	FN65	NM94
1-($2.95)-Parchment-c w/red thermographic ink		1.20	3.00
2-12		.80	2.00

HE-MAN (See Masters Of The Universe)

HE-MAN (Also see Tops In Adventure)
Fall, 1952
Ziff-Davis Publ. Co. (Approved Comics)

	GD25	FN65	NM94
1-Kinstler-c; Powell-a	10.00	30.00	60.00

HE-MAN
May, 1954 - No. 2, July, 1954 (Painted-c)

Toby Press

	GD25	FN65	NM94
1	9.15	27.50	55.00
2	7.00	21.00	42.00

HENNESSEY (See 4-Color No. 1200, 1280)

HENRY
1935 (52 pages) (Daily B&W strip reprints)
David McKay Publications

	GD25	FN65	NM94
1-By Carl Anderson	11.00	32.00	75.00

HENRY (See King Comics & Magic Comics)
No. 122, Oct, 1946 - No. 65, Apr-June, 1961
Dell Publishing Co.

	GD25	FN65	NM94
4-Color 122	10.00	30.00	70.00
4-Color 155 (7/47)	8.35	25.00	50.00
1 (1-3/48)	9.15	27.50	55.00
2	4.00	11.00	22.00
3-10	3.60	9.00	18.00
11-20: 20-Infinity-c	2.40	6.00	12.00
21-30	1.80	4.50	9.00
31-40	1.40	3.50	7.00
41-65	1.20	3.00	6.00

HENRY (See Giant Comic Album and March of Comics No. 43, 58, 84, 101, 112, 129, 147, 162, 178, 189)

HENRY ALDRICH COMICS (TV)
Aug-Sept, 1950 - No. 22, Sept-Nov, 1954
Dell Publishing Co.

	GD25	FN65	NM94
1-Part series written by John Stanley; Bill Williams-a	9.15	27.50	55.00
2	4.70	14.00	28.00
3-5	4.00	12.00	24.00
6-10	4.00	10.00	20.00
11-22	3.00	7.50	15.00
Giveaway (16 pgs., soft-c, 1951)-Capehart radio	4.00	10.00	20.00

HENRY BREWSTER
Feb, 1966 - V2#7, Sept, 1967 (All Giants)
Country Wide (M.F. Ent.)

	GD25	FN65	NM94
1	1.20	3.00	6.00
2-6(12/66)-Powell-a in most	.80	2.00	4.00
V2#7	.60	1.50	3.00

HERBIE (See Forbidden Worlds & Unknown Worlds)
April-May, 1964 - No. 23, Feb, 1967 (All 12 cents)
American Comics Group

	GD25	FN65	NM94
1-Whitney-c/a in most issues	15.00	45.00	105.00
2-4	8.00	24.00	55.00
5-Beatles, Dean Martin, F. Sinatra app.	10.00	31.00	72.00
6,7,9,10	6.00	19.00	44.00
8-Origin & 1st app. The Fat Fury	8.00	24.00	55.00
11-23: 14-Nemesis & Magicman app. 17-r/2nd Herbie from Forbidden Worlds #94. 23-r/1st Herbie from F.W. #73	4.00	12.00	28.00

HERBIE
Oct, 1992 - No. 12, 1993 ($2.50, color, limited series)
Dark Horse Comics

	GD25	FN65	NM94
1-6: Whitney-r plus new-c/a. 1-Byrne-c/a/scripts. 3-Bob Burden-c/a. 4-Art Adams-c		1.00	2.50

HERBIE GOES TO MONTE CARLO, HERBIE RIDES AGAIN (See Walt Disney Showcase No. 24, 41)

HERCULES (See Hit Comics #1-21, Journey Into Mystery Annual, Marvel Graphic Novel #37, Marvel Premiere #26 & The Mighty...)

HERCULES
Oct, 1967 - No. 13, Sept, 1969; Dec, 1968
Charlton Comics

Hercules Unbound #2, © DC

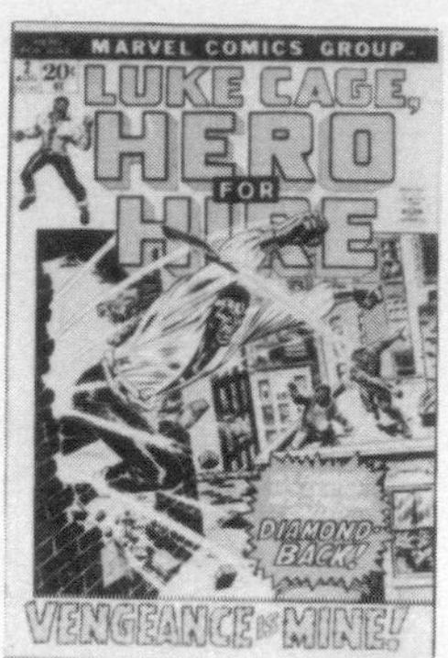

Hero For Hire #2, © MEG

Heroic Comics #20, © EAS

	GD25	FN65	NM94
1-Thane of Bagarth series begins; Glanzman	1.50	3.75	9.00
2-13: 1,3-5,7,9,10-Aparo-a	1.00	2.50	6.00
8-(Low distribution)(12/68, 35 cents, B&W); magazine format; new Hercules story plus-r story/#1; Thane-r/#1-3	2.70	8.00	19.00
Modern Comics reprint 10('77), 11('78)			1.00

HERCULES (Prince of Power) (Also see The Champions)
Sept, 1982 - No. 4, Dec, 1982; Mar, 1984 - No. 4, June, 1984
Marvel Comics Group

	GD25	FN65	NM94
1-4		.65	1.60
V2#1-4 (Mini-series)			1.00

NOTE: ***Layton** a-1, 2, 3p, 4p, V2#1-4; c-1-4, V2#1-4.*

HERCULES UNBOUND
Oct-Nov, 1975 - No. 12, Aug-Sept, 1977
National Periodical Publications

	GD25	FN65	NM94
1-Wood inks begin			1.20
2-12: 10-Atomic Knights x-over			1.00

NOTE: ***Buckler** c-7p. **Layton** inks-No. 9, 10. **Simonson** a-7-10p, 11, 12; c- 8p, 9-12. **Wood** a-1-8i; c-7i, 8i.*

HERCULES UNCHAINED (See 4-Color No. 1006, 1121)

HERE COMES SANTA (See March of Comics No. 30, 213, 340)

HERE IS SANTA CLAUS
1930s (16 pgs., 8 in color) (stiff paper covers)
Goldsmith Publishing Co. (Kann's in Washington, D.C.)

	GD25	FN65	NM94
nn	5.85	17.50	35.00

HERE'S HOW AMERICA'S CARTOONISTS HELP TO SELL U.S. SAVINGS BONDS
1950? (16 pgs.; paper cover)
Harvey Comics giveaway

	GD25	FN65	NM94
Contains: Joe Palooka, Donald Duck, Archie, Kerry Drake, Red Ryder, Blondie & Steve Canyon	12.00	36.00	85.00

HERE'S HOWIE COMICS
Jan-Feb, 1952 - No. 18, Nov-Dec, 1954
National Periodical Publications

	GD25	FN65	NM94
1	16.00	48.00	110.00
2	9.15	27.50	55.00
3-5: 5-Howie in the Army issues begin	7.00	21.00	42.00
6-10	5.00	15.00	30.00
11-18	4.00	12.00	24.00

HERMAN & KATNIP (See Harvey Comics Hits #60 & 62, Harvey Hits #14,25,31,41 & Paramount Animated Comics #1)

HERO (Marvel)(Value: cover or less)

HERO ALLIANCE, THE (Sirius)(Value: cover or less)

HERO ALLIANCE (Wonder)(Value: cover or less)

HERO ALLIANCE (Innovation, all titles)(Value: cover or less)

HEROES AGAINST HUNGER
1986 (One shot) ($1.50) (For famine relief)
DC Comics

	GD25	FN65	NM94
1-Superman, Batman app.; Neal Adams-c(p); includes many artists work; Jeff Jones assist(2pg.) on B. Smith-a			1.50

HEROES ALL CATHOLIC ACTION ILLUSTRATED
1943 - V6#5, March 10, 1948 (paper covers)
Heroes All Co.

	GD25	FN65	NM94
V1#1,2-(16 pgs., 8x11")	10.00	30.00	60.00
V2#1(1/44)-3(3/44)-(16 pgs., 8x11")	6.70	20.00	40.00
V3#1(1/45)-10(10/45)-(16 pgs., 8x11")	5.00	15.00	30.00
V4#1-35 (12/20/46)-(16 pgs.)	4.20	12.50	25.00
V5#1(1/10/47)-8(2/28/47)-(16 pgs.)	3.60	9.00	18.00
V5#9(3/7/47)-20(11/25/47)-(32 pgs.)	3.60	9.00	18.00
V6#1(1/10/48)-5(3/10/48)-(32 pgs.)	3.60	9.00	18.00

HEROES FOR HOPE STARRING THE X-MEN
Dec, 1985 ($1.50, one-shot, 52pgs., proceeds donated to famine relief)
Marvel Comics Group

	GD25	FN65	NM94
1-Stephen King scripts; Byrne, Miller, Corben-a; Wrightson/J. Jones-a (3 pgs.); Art Adams-c; Starlin back-c			1.50

HEROES, INC. PRESENTS CANNON
1969 - No. 2, 1976 (Sold at Army PX's)
Wally Wood/CPL/Gang Publ. No. 2

	GD25	FN65	NM94
nn-Ditko, Wood-a; Wood-c; Reese-a(p)	1.60	4.00	8.00
2-Wood-c; Ditko, Byrne, Wood-a; 8-1/2x10-1/2"; B&W; $2.00		1.60	4.00

NOTE: *First issue not distributed by publisher; 1,800 copies were stored and 900 copies were stolen from warehouse. Many copies have surfaced in recent years.*

HEROES OF THE WILD FRONTIER (Formerly Baffling Mysteries)
No. 27, Jan, 1956 - No. 2, Apr, 1956
Ace Periodicals

	GD25	FN65	NM94
27(#1),2	3.60	9.00	18.00

HERO FOR HIRE (Power Man No. 17 on; also see Cage)
June, 1972 - No. 16, Dec, 1973
Marvel Comics Group

	GD25	FN65	NM94
1-Origin & 1st app. Luke Cage; Tuska-a(p)	4.30	13.00	30.00
2-5: 2,3-Tuska-a(p). 3-1st app. Mace. 4-1st app. Phil Fox of the Bugle	1.70	5.00	12.00
6-10: 8,9-Dr. Doom app. 9-F.F. app.	1.00	2.50	6.00
11-16: 14-Origin retold. 15-Everett Subby-r('53). 16-Origin Stilletto; death of Rackham	1.00	2.50	5.50

HERO-GRAPHICS SUPER-SAMPLER (Hero)(Value: cover or less)

HERO HOTLINE (DC)(Value: cover or less)

HEROIC ADVENTURES (See Adventures)

HEROIC COMICS (Reg'lar Fellers...#1-15; New Heroic #41 on)
Aug, 1940 - No. 97, June, 1955
Eastern Color Printing Co./Famous Funnies(Funnies, Inc. No. 1)

	GD25	FN65	NM94
1-Hydroman (origin) by Bill Everett, The Purple Zombie (origin) & Mann of India by Tarpe Mills begins (all 1st apps.)	83.00	250.00	550.00
2	42.00	125.00	275.00
3,4	33.00	100.00	220.00
5,6	25.00	75.00	165.00
7-Origin & 1st app. Man O'Metal, 1 pg.	29.00	88.00	190.00
8-10: 10-Lingerie panels	17.00	50.00	110.00
11,13: 13-Crandall/Fine-a	15.00	45.00	100.00
12-Music Master (origin/1st app.) begins by Everett, ends No. 31; last Purple Zombie & Mann of India	17.00	50.00	110.00
14,15-Hydroman x-over in Rainbow Boy. 14-Origin & 1st app. Rainbow Boy (super hero). 15-1st app. Downbeat	17.00	50.00	110.00
16-20: 17-Rainbow Boy x-over in Hydroman. 19-Rainbow Boy x-over in Hydroman & vice versa	12.50	38.00	85.00
21-30:25-Rainbow Boy x-over in Hydroman. 28-Last Man O'Metal. 29-Last Hydroman	9.15	27.50	55.00
31,34,38	3.20	8.00	16.00
32,36,37-Toth-a, 3-4 pgs.	4.70	14.00	28.00
33,35-Toth-a, 8 & 9 pgs.	5.00	15.00	30.00
39-42-Toth, Ingels-a	5.00	15.00	30.00
43,46,47,49-Toth-a, 2-4 pgs. 47-Ingels-a	4.00	11.00	22.00
44,45,50-Toth-a, 6-9 pgs.	4.35	13.00	26.00
48,53,54	2.80	7.00	14.00
51-Williamson-a	4.70	14.00	28.00
52-Williamson-a (3 pg. story)	4.00	10.00	20.00
55-Toth-c/a	4.00	12.00	24.00
56-60-Toth-c. 60-Everett-a	4.00	10.00	20.00
61-Everett-a	2.80	7.00	14.00
62,64-Everett-c/a	3.20	8.00	16.00
63-Everett-c	2.40	6.00	12.00
65-Williamson/Frazetta-a; Evans-a, 2 pgs.	5.85	17.50	35.00
66,75,94-Frazetta-a, 2 pgs. each	3.60	9.00	18.00

Hex #13, © DC

Hillbilly Comics #1, © CC

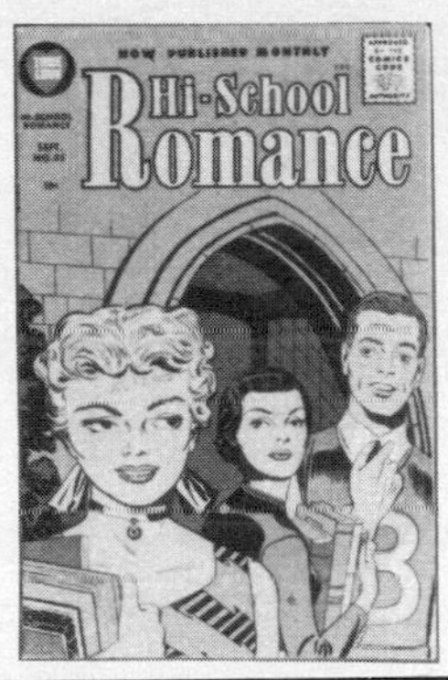

Hi-School Romance #55, © HARV

	GD25	FN65	NM94
67,73-Frazetta-a, 4 pgs. each	4.00	11.00	22.00
68,74,76-80,84,85,88-93,95-97: 95-Last pre-code	2.40	6.00	12.00
69,72-Frazetta-a (6 & 8 pgs. each)	5.05	17.50	35.00
70,71,86,87-Frazetta, 3-4 pgs. each; 1 pg. ad by Frazetta in #70	3.60	9.00	18.00
81,82-One pg. Frazetta art	2.40	6.00	12.00
83-Frazetta-a, 1/2 pg.	2.40	6.00	12.00

NOTE: ***Evans*** *a-64, 65.* ***Everett*** *a-(Hydroman-c/a-No. 1-9), 44, 60-64; c-1-9, 62-64.* ***Harvey Fuller*** *c-28-35.* ***Sid Greene*** *a-38-43, 46.* ***Guardineer*** *a-42(3), 43, 44, 45(2), 49(3), 50, 60, 61(2), 65, 67(2) 70-72.* ***Ingels*** *c-41.* ***Kiefer*** *a-46, 48; c-19-22, 24, 44, 46, 48, 51-53, 65, 67-69, 71-74, 76, 77, 79, 80, 82, 85, 88, 89, 94, 95.* ***Mort Lawrence*** *a-45.* ***Tarpe Mills*** *a-2(2), 3(2), 10.* ***Ed Moore*** *a-49, 52-54, 56-63, 65-69, 72-74, 76, 77.* ***H.G. Peter*** *a-58-74, 76, 77, 87.* ***Paul Reinman*** *a-49.* ***Rico*** *a-31. Captain Tootsie by* ***Beck****-31, 32. Painted-c #16 on. Hydroman c-1-11. Music Master c-12, 13, 15. Rainbow Boy c-14.*

HEX (Replaces Jonah Hex)
Sept, 1985 - No. 18, Feb, 1987 (Story continues from Jonah Hex 92)
DC Comics

	GD25	FN65	NM94
1-10,14-18: 1-Hex in post-atomic war world; origin. 6-Origin Stiletta			1.00
11-13: All contain future Batman storyline. 13-Intro The Dogs of War (origin #15)		.80	2.00

NOTE: ***Giffen*** *a-15-18; c-15, 17, 18.*

HEXBREAKER (See First Comics Graphic Novel #15)

HEY THERE, IT'S YOGI BEAR (See Movie Comics)

HI-ADVENTURE HEROES (TV)
May, 1969 - No. 2, Aug, 1969 (Hanna-Barbera)
Gold Key

	GD25	FN65	NM94
1-Three Musketeers, Gulliver, Arabian Knights stories	2.70	8.00	19.00
2-Three Musketeers, Micro-Venture, Arabian Knights	2.30	6.75	16.00

HI AND LOIS (See 4-Color No. 683, 774, 955)

HI AND LOIS
Nov, 1969 - No. 11, July, 1971
Charlton Comics

	GD25	FN65	NM94
1	1.70	5.00	12.00
2-11	1.00	2.50	6.00

HICKORY (See All Humor Comics)
Oct, 1949 - No. 6, Aug, 1950
Quality Comics Group

	GD25	FN65	NM94
1-Sahl-c/a in all; Feldstein?-a	10.00	30.00	65.00
2	5.00	15.00	30.00
3-6	4.00	12.00	24.00

HIDDEN CREW, THE (See The United States Air Force Presents:...)

HIDE-OUT (See 4-Color No. 346)

HIDING PLACE, THE (Spire Christian)(Value: cover or less)

HIGH ADVENTURE
October, 1957
Red Top(Decker) Comics (Farrell)

	GD25	FN65	NM94
1-Krigstein-r from Explorer Joe (re-issue on-c)	3.60	9.00	18.00

HIGH ADVENTURE (See 4-Color No. 949, 1001)

HIGH CHAPPARAL (TV)
August, 1968 (Photo-c)
Gold Key

	GD25	FN65	NM94
1 (10226-808)-Tufts-a	5.35	16.00	32.00

HIGH SCHOOL CONFIDENTIAL DIARY (Confidential Diary #12 on)
June, 1960 - No. 11, March, 1962
Charlton Comics

	GD25	FN65	NM94
1	3.20	8.00	16.00
2-11	1.60	4.00	8.00

HI-HO COMICS
nd (2/46?) - No. 3, 1946
Four Star Publications

	GD25	FN65	NM94
1-Funny Animal; L. B. Cole-c	13.00	40.00	90.00
2,3: 2-L. B. Cole-c	9.15	27.50	55.00

HI-JINX (Teen-age Animal Funnies)
July-Aug, 1947 - No. 7, July-Aug, 1948
B&I Publ. Co.(American Comics Group)/Creston/La Salle Publ. Co.

	GD25	FN65	NM94
1-Teen-age, funny animal	10.00	30.00	65.00
2,3	6.35	19.00	38.00
4-7-Milt Gross. 4-X-Mas-c	7.50	22.50	45.00
nn-(© 1945, 25 cents, 132 Pgs.)(La Salle)	11.00	32.00	75.00

HI-LITE COMICS
Fall, 1945
E. R. Ross Publishing Co.

	GD25	FN65	NM94
1-Miss Shady	10.00	30.00	60.00

HILLBILLY COMICS
Aug, 1955 - No. 4, July, 1956 (Satire)
Charlton Comics

	GD25	FN65	NM94
1	5.35	16.00	32.00
2-4	3.60	9.00	18.00

HIP-IT-TY HOP (See March of Comics No. 15)

HI-SCHOOL ROMANCE (...Romances No. 41 on)
Oct, 1949 - No. 5, June, 1950; No. 6, Dec, 1950 - No. 73, Mar, 1958; No. 74, Sept, 1958 - No. 75, Nov, 1958
Harvey Publications/True Love(Home Comics)

	GD25	FN65	NM94
1-Photo-c	7.50	22.50	45.00
2-Photo-c	4.00	11.00	22.00
3-9: 3,5-Photo-c	3.00	7.50	15.00
10-Rape story	4.00	10.50	21.00
11-20	2.00	5.00	10.00
21-31	1.80	4.50	9.00
32-"Unholy passion" story	3.20	8.00	16.00
33-36: 36-Last pre-code (2/55)	1.40	3.50	7.00
37-75	1.20	3.00	6.00

NOTE. ***Powell*** *a-1-3, 5, 8, 12-16, 18, 21-23, 25-27, 30-34, 36, 37, 39, 45-48, 50-52, 57, 58, 60, 64, 65, 67, 69.*

HI-SCHOOL ROMANCE DATE BOOK
Nov, 1962 - No. 3, Mar, 1963 (25 cent Giant)
Harvey Publications

	GD25	FN65	NM94
1-Powell, Baker-a	3.20	8.00	16.00
2,3	1.40	3.50	7.00

HIS NAME IS SAVAGE (Magazine format)
June, 1968 (35 cents, 52 pgs.)
Adventure House Press

	GD25	FN65	NM94
1-Gil Kane-a	3.20	8.00	20.00

HI-SPOT COMICS (Red Ryder No. 1 & No. 3 on)
No. 2, Nov, 1940
Hawley Publications

	GD25	FN65	NM94
2-David Innes of Pellucidar; art by J. C. Burroughs; written by Edgar Rice Burroughs	83.00	250.00	525.00

HISTORY OF THE DC UNIVERSE
Sept, 1986 - No. 2, Nov, 1986 ($2.95)
DC Comics

	GD25	FN65	NM94
1,2: 1-Perez-c/a		1.20	3.00
Limited Edition hardcover	6.50	19.00	45.00

HITCHHIKERS GUIDE TO THE GALAXY
1993 - No. 3, 1993 ($4.95, color, limited series)
DC Comics

	GD25	FN65	NM94
1-3-Adaptation of D. Adams book	1.00	2.00	5.00

Hit Comics #30, © QUA

Hokum & Hex #2, © Clive Barker

Hollywood Confessions #2, © STJ

GD25 FN65 NM94

HIT COMICS
July, 1940 - No. 65, July, 1950
Quality Comics Group

1-Origin/1st app. Neon, the Unknown & Hercules; intro. The Red Bee; Bob & Swab, Blaze Barton, the Strange Twins, X-5 Super Agent, Casey Jones & Jack & Jill (ends #7) begin 283.00 850.00 1800.00
2-The Old Witch begins, ends #14 122.00 368.00 800.00
3-Casey Jones ends; transvestism story-'Jack & Jill' 96.00 288.00 650.00
4-Super Agent (ends #17), & Betty Bates (ends #65) begin; X-5 ends 83.00 250.00 550.00
5-Classic cover 125.00 375.00 825.00
6-10: 10-Old Witch by Crandall (4 pgs.); 1st work in comics (4/41) 67.00 200.00 450.00
11-17: 13-Blaze Barton ends. 17-Last Neon; Crandall Hercules in all 61.00 182.00 410.00
18-Origin & 1st app. Stormy Foster, the Great Defender (12/41); The Ghost of Flanders begins; Crandall-c 70.00 210.00 475.00
19,20 61.00 182.00 410.00
21-24: 21-Last Hercules. 24-Last Red Bee & Strange Twins 52.00 158.00 350.00
25-Origin & 1st app. Kid Eternity and begins by Moldoff (12/42); 1st app. The Keeper (Kid Eternity's aide) 70.00 210.00 475.00
26-Blackhawk x-over in Kid Eternity 56.00 168.00 375.00
27-29 32.00 95.00 210.00
30,31-"Bill the Magnificent" by Kurtzman, 11 pgs. in each 27.00 82.00 185.00
32-40: 32-Plastic Man x-over. 34-Last Stormy Foster 14.00 43.00 100.00
41-50 10.00 30.00 70.00
51-60-Last Kid Eternity 10.00 30.00 60.00
61-63-Crandall-c/a; 61-Jeb Rivers begins 10.00 30.00 65.00
64,65-Crandall-a 10.00 30.00 60.00

NOTE: ***Crandall** a-11-17(Hercules), 23, 24(Stormy Foster); c-18-20, 23, 24. **Fine** c-1-14, 16, 17(most). **Ward** c-33. Bondage c-7, 64. Hercules c-3, 10-17. Jeb Rivers c-61-65. Kid Eternity c-25-60 (w/Keeper-28-34, 36, 39-43, 45-55). Neon the Unknown c-2, 4, 8, 9. Red Bee c-1, 5-7. Stormy Foster c-18-24.*

HI-YO SILVER (See Lone Ranger's Famous Horse... and also see The Lone Ranger and March of Comics No. 215)

HOBBIT, THE (Eclipse)(Value: cover or less)

HOCUS POCUS (Formerly Funny Book)
No. 9, Aug-Sept, 1946
Parents' Magazine Press

9 4.00 10.00 20.00

HOGAN'S HEROES (TV)
June, 1966 - No. 8, Sept, 1967; No. 9, Oct, 1969
Dell Publishing Co.

1: #1-7 photo-c 5.00 16.00 37.00
2,3-Ditko-a(p) 3.40 10.00 24.00
4-9: 9-Reprints #1 2.40 7.25 17.00

HOKUM & HEX (See Razorline)
Sept, 1993 - Present ($1.75, color)
Marvel Comics

1-($2.50)-Foil embossed-c; by Clive Barker 1.00 2.50
2-8 .70 1.75

HOLIDAY COMICS
1942 (196 pages) (25 cents)
Fawcett Publications

1-Contains three Fawcett comics; Capt. Marvel, Nyoka #1, & Whiz. Not rebound, remaindered comics printed at the same time as originals 112.00 338.00 750.00

HOLIDAY COMICS (Becomes Fun Comics #9-12)
January, 1951 - No. 8, Oct, 1952
Star Publications

GD25 FN65 NM94

1-Funny animal contents (Frisky Fables) in all; L. B. Cole-c 16.00 48.00 110.00
2-Classic L. B. Cole-c 17.00 52.00 120.00
3-8: 5,8-X-Mas-c; all L.B. Cole-c 10.00 30.00 70.00
Accepted Reprint 4 (nd)-L.B. Cole-c 5.85 17.50 35.00

HOLIDAY DIGEST
1988 ($1.25, digest-size)
Harvey Comics

1 1.25

HOLIDAY PARADE (Walt Disney's...)
Winter, 1990-91(no yr. given) - No. 2, Winter, 1990-91 ($2.95, color, 68 pgs.)
W. D. Publications (Disney)

1-Reprints 1947 Firestone by Barks plus new-a 1.20 3.00
2-Barks-r plus other stories 1.20 3.00

HOLI-DAY SURPRISE (Formerly Summer Fun)
V2#55, Mar, 1967 (25 cents)
Charlton Comics

V2#55-Giant 1.00 2.00 5.00

HOLLYWOOD COMICS
Winter, 1944 (52 pgs.)
New Age Publishers

1-Funny animals 11.50 34.00 80.00

HOLLYWOOD CONFESSIONS
Oct, 1949 - No. 2, Dec, 1949
St. John Publishing Co.

1-Kubert-c/a (entire book) 14.00 43.00 100.00
2-Kubert-c/a (entire book) (Scarce) 22.00 65.00 150.00

HOLLYWOOD DIARY
Dec, 1949 - No. 5, July-Aug, 1950
Quality Comics Group

1-No photo-c 11.00 32.00 75.00
2-Photo-c 7.50 22.50 45.00
3-5-Photo-c 6.35 19.00 38.00

HOLLYWOOD FILM STORIES
April, 1950 - No. 4, Oct, 1950 (All photo-c; "Fumetti" type movie comic)
Feature Publications/Prize

1-June Allyson photo-c 11.00 32.00 75.00
2-4: 2-Lizabeth Scott photo-c. 3-Barbara Stanwick photo-c. 4-Betty Hutton photo-c 9.15 27.50 55.00

HOLLYWOOD FUNNY FOLKS (Formerly Funny Folks; Becomes Nutsy Squirrel #61 on)
No. 27, Aug-Sept, 1950 - No. 60, July-Aug, 1954
National Periodical Publications

27 10.00 30.00 60.00
28-40 6.70 20.00 40.00
41-60 5.00 15.00 30.00

NOTE: ***Sheldon Mayer** a-27-35, 37-40, 43-46, 48-51, 53, 56, 57, 60.*

HOLLYWOOD LOVE DOCTOR (See Doctor Anthony King...)

HOLLYWOOD PICTORIAL (...Romances on cover)
No. 3, January, 1950
St. John Publishing Co.

3-Matt Baker-a; photo-c 11.00 32.00 75.00
(Becomes a movie magazine - Hollywood Pictorial Western with No. 4.)

HOLLYWOOD ROMANCES (Formerly Brides In Love; becomes For Lovers Only #60 on)
V2#46, 11/66; #47, 10/67; #48, 11/68; V3#49, 11/69 - V3#59, 6/71
Charlton Comics

V2#46-Rolling Stones-c/story 5.00 15.00 30.00

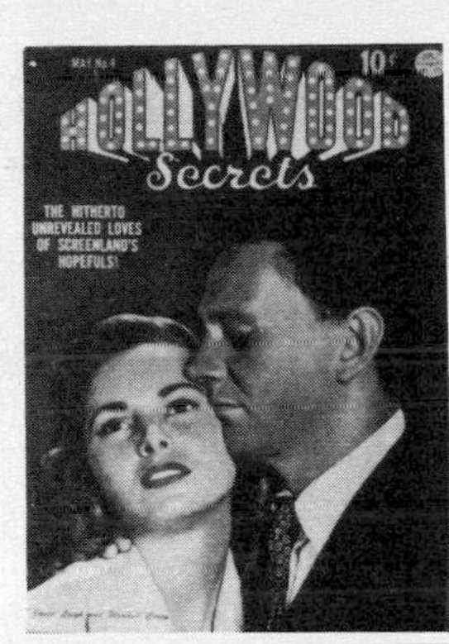

Hollywood Secrets #4, © QUA

Homicide #1, © John Arcudi & Doug Mahnke

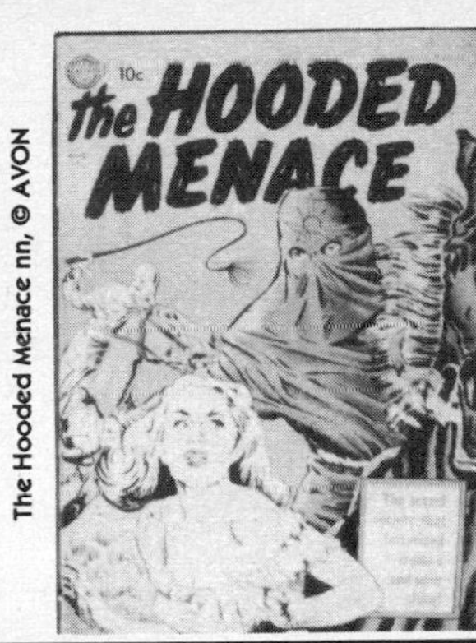

The Hooded Menace nn, © AVON

GD25 FN65 NM94 — GD25 FN65 NM94

V2#47-V3#59: 56-"Born to Heart Break" begins 1.00 2.50 5.00

HOLLYWOOD SECRETS
Nov, 1949 - No. 6, Sept, 1950
Quality Comics Group

1-Ward-c/a, 9pgs. 19.00 58.00 135.00
2-Crandall-a, Ward-c/a, 9 pgs. 11.50 34.00 80.00
3-6: All photo-c; 5-Lex Barker (Tarzan)-c 6.70 20.00 40.00
...of Romance, I.W. Reprint #9; Kinstler-c; Ward, Crandall-a
1.20 3.00 6.00

HOLLYWOOD SUPERSTARS (Epic)(Value: cover or less)

HOLO-MAN (See Power Record Comics)

HOLYOKE ONE-SHOT
1944 - No. 10, 1945 (All reprints)
Holyoke Publishing Co. (Tem Publ.)

1-Grit Grady (on cover only), Miss Victory, Alias X (origin)-All reprints from Captain Fearless 7.50 22.50 45.00
2-Rusty Dugan (Corporal); Capt. Fearless (origin), Mr. Miracle (origin) app.
7.50 22.50 45.00
3-Miss Victory-Crash #4-r; Cat Man (origin), Solar Legion by Kirby app.; Miss Victory on cover only (1945) 13.50 41.00 95.00
4-Mr. Miracle-The Blue Streak app. 6.70 20.00 40.00
5-U.S. Border Patrol Comics (Sgt. Dick Carter of the...), Miss Victory (story matches cover to #3), Citizen Smith, & Mr. Miracle app.
7.50 22.50 45.00
6-Capt. Fearless, Alias X, Capt. Stone (splash used as-c to #10); Diamond Jim & Rusty Dugan (splash from cover of #2) 6.70 20.00 40.00
7-Secret Agent Z-2, Strong Man, Blue Streak (story matches cover to #8); Reprints from Crash #2 8.00 24.00 48.00
8-Blue Streak, Strong Man (story matches cover to #7)-Crash reprints
6.70 20.00 40.00
9-Citizen Smith, The Blue Streak, Solar Legion by Kirby & Strongman, the Perfect Human app.; reprints from Crash #4 & 5; Citizen Smith on cover only-from story in #5 (1944-before #3) 10.00 30.00 65.00
10-Captain Stone (Crash reprints); Solar Legion by S&K
10.00 30.00 65.00

HOMER COBB (See Adventures of...)

HOMER HOOPER
July, 1953 - No. 4, Dec, 1953
Atlas Comics

1-Teenage humor 6.70 20.00 40.00
2-4 4.20 12.50 25.00

HOMER, THE HAPPY GHOST (See Adventures of...)
3/55 - No. 22, 11/58; V2#1, 11/69 - V2#5, 7/70
Atlas(ACI/PPI/WPI)/Marvel Comics

V1#1-Dan DeCarlo-a begins, ends #22 10.00 30.00 60.00
2-1st code approved issue 5.00 15.00 30.00
3-10 4.00 10.00 20.00
11-22 3.20 8.00 16.00
V2#1 - V2#5 (1969-70) 1.20 3.00 7.00

HOME RUN (See A-1 Comics No. 89)

HOME, SWEET HOME
1925 (10-1/4x10")
M.S. Publishing Co.

nn-By Tuthill 17.00 50.00 120.00

HOMICIDE (Dark Horse)(Value: cover or less)

HONEYBEE BIRDWHISTLE AND HER PET PEPI (Introducing...)
1969 (24 pgs.; B&W; slick cover)
Newspaper Enterprise Association (Giveaway)

nn-Contains Freckles newspaper strips with a short biography of Henry Fornhals (artist) & Fred Fox (writer) of the strip 5.35 16.00 32.00

HONEYMOON (Formerly Gay Comics)
No. 41, January, 1950
A Lover's Magazine(USA) (Marvel)

41-Photo-c; article by Betty Grable 5.85 17.50 35.00

HONEYMOONERS, THE (TV) (Lodestone)(Value: cover or less)

HONEYMOONERS, THE (TV) (Triad)(Value: cover or less)

HONEYMOON ROMANCE
April, 1950 - No. 2, July, 1950 (25 cents) (digest size)
Artful Publications(Canadian)

1,2-(Rare) 22.00 65.00 150.00

HONEY WEST (TV)
September, 1966 (Photo-c)
Gold Key

1 (10186-609) 10.00 30.00 70.00

HONG KONG PHOOEY (TV)
June, 1975 - No. 9, Nov, 1976 (Hanna-Barbera)
Charlton Comics

1 1.65 4.00 10.00
2 1.00 2.00 5.00
3-9 1.20 3.00

HOODED HORSEMAN, THE (Also see Blazing West)
No. 21, 1-2/52 - No. 27, 1-2/53; No. 18, 12-1/54-55 - No. 27, 6-7/56
American Comics Group (Michel Publ.)

21(1-2/52)-Hooded Horseman, Injun Jones continue
10.00 30.00 70.00
22 6.70 20.00 40.00
23-25,27(1-2/53) 5.35 16.00 32.00
26-Origin/1st app. Cowboy Sahib by L. Starr 8.00 24.00 48.00
18(11-12/54)(Formerly Out of the Night) 5.350 16.00 32.00
19-Last precode (1-2/55) 10.00 30.00 60.00
20-Origin Johnny Injun 5.85 17.50 35.00
21-24,26,27(6-7/56) 4.70 14.00 28.00
25-Cowboy Sahib on cover only; Hooded Horseman i.d. revealed
5.35 16.00 32.00

NOTE. *Whitney c/a-21('52), 20-22.*

HOODED MENACE, THE (Also see Daring Adventures)
1951 (One Shot)
Realistic/Avon Periodicals

nn-Based on a band of hooded outlaws in the Pacific Northwest, 1900-1906; reprinted in Daring Advs. #15 34.00 100.00 235.00

HOODS UP
1953 (16 pgs.; 15 cents) (Eisner-c/a in all)
Fram Corp. (Dist. to service station owners)

1-(Very Rare; only 2 known) 50.00 150.00 350.00
2-6-(Very Rare; only 1 known of 3-4, 2 known of #2)
50.00 150.00 350.00

NOTE: *Convertible Connie gives tips for service stations, selling Fram oil filters.*

HOOK
Early Feb, 1992 - No. 4, Late Mar, 1992 ($1.00, color, mini-series)
Marvel Comics

1-4: Adapts movie; Vess-c; 1-Morrow-a(p) 1.00
nn (1991, $5.95, 84 pgs.)-Contains #1-4; Vess-c 1.00 2.50 6.00
1 (1991, $2.95, color, magazine, 84 pgs.)-Contains #1-4; Vess-c (same cover as nn issue) 1.20 3.00

HOOT GIBSON'S WESTERN ROUNDUP (See Western Roundup under Fox Giants)

HOOT GIBSON WESTERN (Formerly My Love Story)
No. 5, May, 1950 - No. 3, Sept, 1950
Fox Features Syndicate

5,6(#1,2): 5-Photo-c. 6-Photo/painted-c 17.00 52.00 120.00
3-Wood-a; painted-c 19.00 58.00 135.00

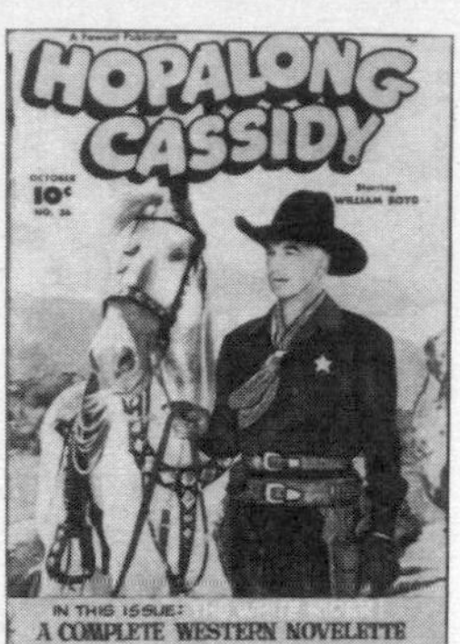

Hopalong Cassidy #36, © FAW

Horrific #13, © Comic Media

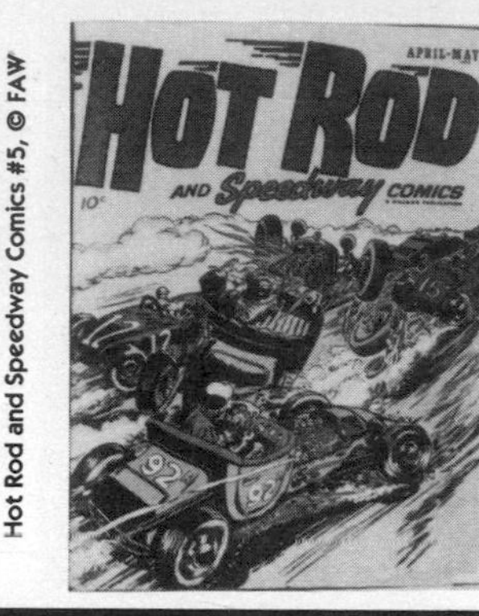

Hot Rod and Speedway Comics #5, © FAW

HOPALONG CASSIDY (Also see Bill Boyd Western, Master Comics, Real Western Hero, Six Gun Heroes & Western Hero; Bill Boyd starred as H. Cassidy in the movies; H. Cassidy in movies, radio & TV)
Feb, 1943; No. 2, Summer, 1946 - No. 85, Jan, 1954
Fawcett Publications

	GD25	FN65	NM94
1 (1943, 68 pgs.)-H. Cassidy & his horse Topper begin (on sale 1/8/43)-Captain Marvel app. on-c	257.00	770.00	1800.00
2-(Sum, '46)	50.00	150.00	350.00
3,4: 3-(Fall, '46, 52 pgs. begin)	24.00	70.00	165.00
5-"Mad Barber" story mentioned in **SOTI**, pgs. 308,309; painted-c	22.00	65.00	150.00
6-10	17.00	51.00	120.00
11-19: 11,13-19-Photo-c	12.00	36.00	85.00
20-29 (52 pgs.)-Painted/photo-c	10.00	30.00	65.00
30,31,33,34,37-39,41 (52 pgs.)-Painted-c	6.70	20.00	40.00
32,40 (36pgs.)-Painted-c	5.85	17.50	35.00
35,42,43,45 (52 pgs.)-Photo-c	7.00	21.00	42.00
36,44,48 (36 pgs.)-Photo-c	5.85	17.50	35.00
46,47,49-51,53,54,56 (52 pgs.)-Photo-c	6.35	19.00	38.00
52,55,57-70 (36 pgs.)-Photo-c	4.70	14.00	28.00
71-84-Photo-c	4.00	12.00	24.00
85-Last Fawcett issue; photo-c	5.00	15.00	30.00

NOTE: *Line-drawn c-1-10, 12.*

	GD25	FN65	NM94
Grape Nuts Flakes giveaway (1950,9x6")	10.00	30.00	70.00
...& the Mad Barber (1951 Bond Bread giveaway)-7x5"; used in **SOTI**, pgs. 308,309	17.00	51.00	120.00
...Meets the Brend Brothers Bandits (1951 Bond Bread giveaway, color, paper-c, 16pgs. 3-1/2x7")-Fawcett Publ.	8.35	25.00	50.00
...Strange Legacy ('51 Bond Bread giveaway)	8.35	25.00	50.00
White Tower Giveaway ('46, 16pgs., paper-c)	8.35	25.00	50.00

HOPALONG CASSIDY (TV)
No. 86, Feb, 1954 - No. 135, May-June, 1959 (All-36pgs.)
National Periodical Publications

	GD25	FN65	NM94
86-Photo covers continue	22.00	65.00	150.00
87	13.00	40.00	90.00
88-90	10.00	30.00	65.00
91-99 (98 has #93 on-c; last precode issue, 2/55)	8.35	25.00	50.00
100	10.00	30.00	60.00
101-108-Last photo-c	6.70	20.00	40.00
109-135: 124-Painted-c	5.85	17.50	35.00

NOTE: ***Gil Kane** art-1956 up. **Kubert** a-123.*

HOPE SHIP
June-Aug, 1963
Dell Publishing Co.

	GD25	FN65	NM94
1	1.80	4.50	9.00

HOPPY THE MARVEL BUNNY (See Fawcett's Funny Animals)
Dec, 1945 - No. 15, Sept, 1947
Fawcett Publications

	GD25	FN65	NM94
1	20.00	60.00	140.00
2	10.00	30.00	70.00
3-15: 7-Xmas-c	9.15	27.50	55.00
...Well Known Comics (1944,8-1/2x10-1/2", paper-c) Bestmaid/Samuel Lowe (printed in red or blue)	7.00	21.00	42.00

HORACE & DOTTY DRIPPLE (Dotty Dripple No. 1-24)
No. 25, Aug, 1952 - No. 43, Oct, 1955
Harvey Publications

	GD25	FN65	NM94
25-43	1.20	3.00	6.00

HORIZONTAL LIEUTENANT, THE (See Movie Classics)

HOROBI (Viz)(Value: cover or less)

HORRIFIC (Terrific No. 14 on)
Sept, 1952 - No. 13, Sept, 1954
Artful/Comic Media/Harwell/Mystery

	GD25	FN65	NM94
1	16.00	48.00	110.00
2	9.15	27.50	55.00
3-Bullet in head-c	13.00	40.00	90.00
4,5,7,9,10: 4-Shrunken head-c. 7-Guillotine-c	6.70	20.00	40.00
6-Jack The Ripper story	7.50	22.50	45.00
8-Origin & 1st app. The Teller(E.C. parody)	9.15	27.50	55.00
11-13: 11-Swipe/Witches Tales #6,27; Devil-c	5.00	15.00	30.00

NOTE: ***Don Heck** a-8; c-3-13. **Hollingsworth** a-4. **Morisi** a-8. **Palais** a-5, 7-12.*

HORROR FROM THE TOMB (Mysterious Stories No. 2 on)
Sept, 1954
Premier Magazine Co.

	GD25	FN65	NM94
1-Woodbridge/Torres, Check-a	16.00	48.00	110.00

HORRORS, THE (Formerly Startling Terror Tales #10)
No. 11, Jan, 1953 - No. 15, Apr, 1954
Star Publications

	GD25	FN65	NM94
11-Horrors of War; Disbrow-a(2)	11.00	32.00	75.00
12-Horrors of War; color illo in **POP**	10.00	30.00	70.00
13-Horrors of Mystery; crime stories	10.00	30.00	65.00
14,15-Horrors of the Underworld	10.00	30.00	70.00

NOTE: *All have **L. B. Cole** covers; a-12. **Hollingsworth** a-13. **Palais** a-13r.*

HORROR TALES (Magazine)
V1#7, 6/69 - V6#6, 12/74; V7#1, 2/75; V7#2, 5/76 - V8#5, 1977; V9#3, 8/78; (V1-V6: 52 pgs.; V7, V8#2: 112 pgs.; V8#4 on: 68 pgs.) (No V5#3, V8#1,3)
Eerie Publications

	GD25	FN65	NM94
V1#7	1.70	5.00	12.00
V1#8,9	1.30	3.25	8.00
V2#1-6('70), V3#1-6('71)	1.00	2.50	6.00
V4#1-3,5-7('72)	1.00	2.50	6.00
V4#4-LSD story reprint/Weird V3#5	1.70	5.00	12.00
V5#1,2,4,5(6/73),5(10/73),6(12/73),V6#1-6('74),V7#1,2,4('76),V7#3('76)-Giant issue,V8#2,4,5('77),V9#3(8/78, $1.50)	1.00	2.50	6.00

NOTE: *Bondage-c-V6#1, 3, V7#2.*

HORSE FEATHERS COMICS
Nov, 1945 - No. 4, July, 1948 (52 pgs.)
Lev Gleason Publications

	GD25	FN65	NM94
1-Wolverton's Scoop Scuttle, 2 pgs.	13.50	41.00	95.00
2	6.70	20.00	40.00
3,4: 3-(5/48)	5.00	15.00	30.00

HORSEMASTERS, THE (See 4-Color No. 1260)

HORSE SOLDIERS, THE (See 4-Color No. 1048)

HORSE WITHOUT A HEAD, THE (See Movie Comics)

HOT DOG
June-July, 1954 - No. 4, Dec-Jan, 1954-55
Magazine Enterprises

	GD25	FN65	NM94
1(A-1 #107)	4.70	14.00	28.00
2,3(A-1 #115),4(A-1 #136)	3.60	9.00	18.00

HOT DOG (See Jughead's Pal, Hotdog)

HOTEL DEPAREE - SUNDANCE (See 4-Color No. 1126)

HOT ROD AND SPEEDWAY COMICS
Feb-Mar, 1952 - No. 5, Apr-May, 1953
Hillman Periodicals

	GD25	FN65	NM94
1	11.50	34.00	80.00
2-Krigstein-a	10.00	30.00	65.00
3-5	4.70	14.00	28.00

HOT ROD COMICS (See XMas Comics)
Nov, 1951 (no month given) - V2#7, Feb, 1953
Fawcett Publications

	GD25	FN65	NM94
nn (V1#1)-Powell-c/a in all	16.00	48.00	110.00
2 (4/52)	10.00	30.00	65.00

Hot Rod King #1, © Z-D

Hot Rods and Racing Cars #35, © CC

The House of Mystery #75, © DC

	GD25	FN65	NM94
3-6, V2#7	6.70	20.00	40.00

HOT ROD KING (Also see Speed Smith the Hot Rod King)
Fall, 1952
Ziff-Davis Publ. Co.

	GD25	FN65	NM94
1-Giacoia-a; Saunders painted-c	14.00	43.00	100.00

HOT ROD RACERS (Grand Prix No. 16 on)
Dec, 1964 - No. 15, July, 1967
Charlton Comics

	GD25	FN65	NM94
1	5.00	15.00	30.00
2-5	3.00	7.50	15.00
6-15	2.00	5.00	10.00

HOT RODS AND RACING CARS
Nov, 1951 - No. 120, June, 1973
Charlton Comics (Motor Mag. No. 1)

	GD25	FN65	NM94
1-Speed Devils begins	12.00	36.00	85.00
2	7.50	22.50	45.00
3-10	5.00	15.00	30.00
11-20	4.00	11.00	22.00
21-34,36-40	3.00	7.50	15.00
35 (6/58, 68 pgs.)	4.00	11.00	22.00
41-60	2.40	6.00	12.00
61-80	1.60	4.00	8.00
81-100	1.00	2.50	6.00
101-120		1.60	4.00

HOT SHOT CHARLIE
1947 (Lee Elias)
Hillman Periodicals

	GD25	FN65	NM94
1	5.35	16.00	32.00

HOTSPUR (Eclipse)(Value: cover or less)

HOT STUFF (See Stumbo Tinytown)
V2#1, Sept, 1991 - No. 4? ($1.00, color)
Harvey Comics

	GD25	FN65	NM94
V2#1-4: 1-Stumbo back-up story			1.00

HOT STUFF CREEPY CAVES
Nov, 1974 - No. 7, Nov, 1975
Harvey Publications

	GD25	FN65	NM94
1	1.00	2.00	5.00
2-5		1.20	3.00
6,7			1.50

HOT STUFF DIGEST
July, 1992 - Present ($1.75, color, digest size)
Harvey Comics

	GD25	FN65	NM94
V2#1-4: Hot Stuff, Stumbo, Richie Rich stories		.70	1.75

HOT STUFF GIANT SIZE
Oct, 1992 - Present ($2.25, color, 68 pgs.)
Harvey Comics

	GD25	FN65	NM94
V2#1-Hot Stuff & Stumbo stories		.90	2.25

HOT STUFF SIZZLERS
July, 1960 - No. 59, Mar, 1974; V2#1, Aug, 1992
Harvey Publications

	GD25	FN65	NM94
1: 68 pgs. begin	10.00	30.00	60.00
2-5	4.20	12.50	25.00
6-10	3.00	7.50	15.00
11-20	2.00	5.00	10.00
21-45: Last 68 pgs.	1.00	2.50	6.00
46-52: All 52 pgs.		1.60	4.00
53-59		1.20	3.00
V2#1-($1.25)-Stumbo back-up			1.25

HOT STUFF, THE LITTLE DEVIL (Also see Devil Kids & Harvey Hits)
10/57 - No. 141, 7/77; No. 142, 2/78 - No. 164, 8/82; No. 165, 10/86 - No. 171, 11/87; No. 172, 11/88; No. 173, Sept, 1990 - No. 177, 1/91
Harvey Publications (Illustrated Humor)

	GD25	FN65	NM94
1	24.00	72.00	165.00
2-1st app. Stumbo the Giant (12/57)	13.00	40.00	90.00
3-5	10.00	30.00	70.00
6-10	6.70	20.00	40.00
11-20	4.20	12.50	25.00
21-40	3.00	7.50	15.00
41-60	1.60	4.00	8.00
61-105		1.60	4.00
106-112: All 52 pg. Giants	1.00	2.00	5.00
113-177-Later issues $1.00-c			1.00
Shoestore Giveaway('63)	1.00	2.50	6.00

HOT WHEELS (TV)
Mar-Apr, 1970 - No. 6, Jan-Feb, 1971
National Periodical Publications

	GD25	FN65	NM94
1	5.00	15.00	36.00
2,4,5	2.40	7.25	17.00
3-Neal Adams-c	3.60	10.75	25.00
6-Neal Adams-c/a	4.15	12.50	29.00

NOTE: *Toth a-1p, 2-5; c-1p, 5.*

HOURMAN (See Adventure Comics #48)

HOUSE OF MYSTERY (See Brave and the Bold #93, Elvira's House of Mystery, Limited Collectors' Edition & Super DC Giant)

HOUSE OF MYSTERY, THE
Dec-Jan, 1951-52 - No. 321, Oct, 1983 (No. 199-203: 52 pgs.)
National Periodical Publications/DC Comics

	GD25	FN65	NM94
1	85.00	255.00	850.00
2	44.00	130.00	350.00
3	34.00	103.00	275.00
4,5	28.00	85.00	225.00
6-10	22.00	66.00	175.00
11-15	18.00	53.00	140.00
16(7/53)-25	14.00	43.00	100.00
26-35(2/55)-Last pre-code issue; 30-Woodish-a	11.00	32.00	75.00
00-49	10.00	00.00	00.00
50-Text story of Orson Welles' War of the Worlds broadcast	9.00	28.00	66.00
51-60	8.00	24.00	55.00
61,63,65,66,70,72,76,84,85-Kirby-a	7.00	21.00	48.00
62,64,67-69,71,73-75,77-83,86-99	4.70	14.00	33.00
100 (7/60)	7.00	20.00	40.00
101-116: 109-Toth, Kubert-a. 116-Last 10¢ issue	3.00	9.00	30.00
117-119,121-130: 117-Swipes-c to HOS #20	2.00	6.00	20.00
120-Toth-a	2.50	7.00	24.00
131-142	2.00	5.00	17.00
143-J'onn J'onzz, Manhunter begins (6/64), ends #173; story continues from Detective #326	20.00	60.00	180.00
144	10.00	30.00	90.00
145-155,157-159: 149-Toth-a. 155-The Human Hurrican app. (12/65), Red Tornado prototype. 158-Origin/1st app. Diabolu Idol-Head in J'onn J'onzz	6.00	19.00	58.00
156-Robby Reed begins (origin/1st app.), ends #173	8.00	23.00	68.00
160-(7/66)-Robby Reed becomes Plastic Man in this issue only; 1st S.A. app. Plastic Man; intro Marco Xavier (Martian Manhunter) & Vulture Crime Organization; ends #173	9.00	28.00	85.00
161-173: 169-Origin/1st app. Gem Girl	4.00	12.00	35.00
174-177,182: 174-Mystery format begins. 176-1st app. Cain (HOM host). 182-Toth-a	1.00	4.00	11.00
178-Neal Adams-a, last 12 cent issue (2/68)	2.00	6.00	15.00
179-N. Adams/Orlando, Wrightson-a (1st pro work, 3 pgs.)	5.00	15.00	40.00
180,181,183: Wrightson-a (3, 10, & 3 pgs.). 180-Kane-Wood-a(2). 183-Wood-a	1.00	4.00	11.00

The House of Mystery #277, © DC

House of Secrets #13, © DC

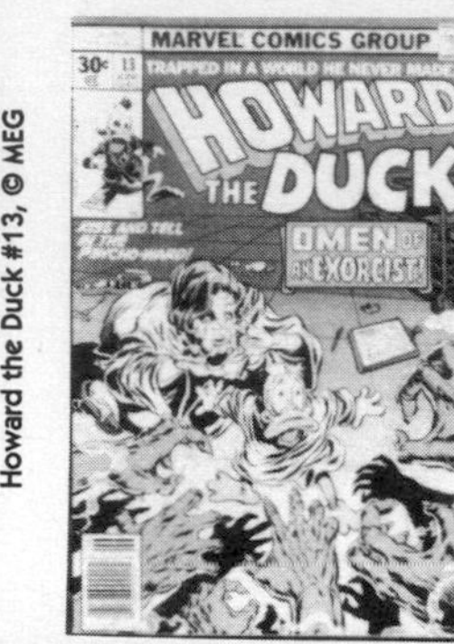

Howard the Duck #13, © MEG

GD25 FN65 NM94

184-Kane/Wood, Toth-a 1.00 4.00 10.00
185-Williamson/Kaluta-a; 3 pgs. Howard-a 1.00 4.00 10.00
186-N. Adams-a; Wrightson-a, 10 pgs. 1.00 4.00 10.00
187,190: 187-Toth-a. 190-Toth-a(r) 1.00 2.00 6.00
188,191,195-Wrightson-a (8, 3 & 10 pgs.). 195-Swamp creature story by Wrightson similar to Swamp Thing (10/71) 1.00 4.00 11.00
189,192-194,196-198: 189-Wood-a. 194-Toth, Kirby-a; 52 pgs. begin, end #198 1.00 2.00 6.00
199-Wood-a (8pg.); Kirby-a; 52pgs. begin, end 203 1.00 3.00 7.00
200-203-(25¢, 52 pgs.)-One third-r. 200-(3/72) 1.90 4.75
204-Wrightson-c/a, 9 pgs. 1.90 4.75
205-223,225-227: 207-Wrightson-a. 221-Wrightson/Kaluta-a (8 pgs.). 226-Wrightson-r; Phantom Stranger-r 1.70 4.25
224-N. Adams/Wrightson-a(r); begin 100 pg. issues; Phantom Stranger-r 1.10 2.70 6.50
228-N. Adams inks; Wrightson-r 1.90 4.75
229-235,237-321: 229-Wrightson-a(r); Toth-r; last 100 pg. issue. 230-(68 pgs.) 251-259-(84 pgs.). 251-Wood-a. 282-(68 pgs.)-Has extra story "The Computers That Saved Metropolis" Radio Shack giveaway by Jim Starlin 1.70 4.25
236-Ditko-a(p); N. Adams-i; Wrightson-c 1.90 4.75

NOTE: ***Neal Adams*** *a-236i; c-175-192, 197, 199, 251-254.* ***M. Anderson*** *c/a-37.* ***Aragones*** *a-186, 251.* ***Baily*** *a-279p.* ***Cameron*** *a-76, 79.* ***Colan*** *a-202r.* ***Craig*** *a-263, 275, 295, 300.* ***Ditko*** *a-236p, 247, 254, 258, 276; c-277.* ***Drucker*** *a-37.* ***Evans*** *c-218.* ***Fraden*** *a-251.* ***Giunta*** *a-199.* ***Golden*** *a-257, 259.* ***Heath*** *a-194r; c-203.* ***Howard*** *a-182, 185, 187, 196, 229r, 247i, 254, 279i.* ***Kaluta*** *a-195, 200, 250r; c-200-202, 210, 212, 233, 260, 261, 263, 265, 267, 268, 273, 276, 284, 287, 288, 293-295, 300, 302, 304, 305, 309-319, 321.* ***Bob Kane*** *a-84.* ***Gil Kane*** *a-196p, 253p, 300p.* ***Kirby*** *a-194r, 199r; c-65, 76, 78, 79, 85.* ***Kubert*** *c-282, 283, 285, 286, 289-292, 297-299, 301, 303, 306-308.* ***Maneely*** *a-68.* ***Mayer*** *a-317p.* ***Meskin*** *a-52-144 (most), 224r, 229r; c-63, 66, 124, 127.* ***Mooney*** *a-24, 159, 160.* ***Moreira*** *a-3, 4, 20-50, 58, 59, 62, 68, 77, 79, 90, 108, 113, 123, 201r, 228; c-4-28, 44, 47, 50, 54, 59, 62, 64, 68, 70, 73.* ***Morrow*** *a-192, 196, 255, 320i.* ***Mortimer*** *a-204(3 pgs.).* ***Nasser*** *a-276.* ***Newton*** *a-259, 272.* ***Nino*** *a-204, 212, 213, 220, 224, 225, 245, 250, 252-256, 283.* ***Orlando*** *a-175(2 pgs.), 178, 240i; c-240, 258p, 262, 264p, 270p, 271, 272, 274, 275, 278, 296i.* ***Redondo*** *a-194, 195, 197, 202, 203, 207, 211, 214, 217, 219, 226, 227, 229, 235, 241, 287(layout), 302p, 303i, 308; c-229.* ***Reese*** *a-195, 200, 205i.* ***Rogers*** *a-254, 274, 277.* ***Roussos*** *a-65, 84, 224i.* ***Sekowsky*** *a-282p.* ***Sparling*** *a-203.* ***Starlin*** *a-207(2 pgs.), 282p; c-281.* ***Leonard Starr*** *a-9.* ***Staton*** *a-300p.* ***Sutton*** *a-271, 290, 291, 293, 295, 297-299, 302, 303, 306-309, 310-313i, 314.* ***Tuska*** *a-293p, 294p, 316p.* ***Wrightson*** *c-193-195, 204, 207, 209, 211, 213, 214, 217, 221, 231, 236, 255, 256.*

HOUSE OF SECRETS (Combined with The Unexpected after #154)
11-12/56 - No. 80, 9-10/66; No. 81, 8-9/69 - No. 140, 2-3/76;
No. 141, 8-9/76 - No. 154, 10-11/78
National Periodical Publications/DC Comics

1-Drucker-a; Moreira-c 55.00 165.00 550.00
2-Moreira-a 31.00 92.00 275.00
3-Kirby-c/a 21.00 63.00 190.00
4,8-Kirby-a 13.00 38.00 115.00
5-7,9-11: 11-Lou Cameron-a(unsigned) 9.00 28.00 85.00
12-Kirby-c/a 10.00 30.00 90.00
13-15 7.00 22.00 65.00
16-20 6.00 18.00 55.00
21,22,24-30 6.00 17.00 50.00
23-1st app. Mark Merlin & begin series (8/59) 7.00 20.00 60.00
31-50: 48-Toth-a. 50-Last 10 cent issue 4.00 12.00 35.00
51-60: 58-Origin Mark Merlin 3.00 10.00 27.00
61-First Eclipso (7-8/63) and begin series 15.00 45.00 120.00
62 8.00 23.00 60.00
63-65,67-Toth-a on Eclipso (see Brave and the Bold #64) 6.00 17.00 45.00
66-1st Eclipso-c (also #67,70,78,79); Toth-a 9.00 26.00 70.00
68-80: 73-Mark Merlin becomes Prince Ra-Man (1st app.). 76-Prince Ra-Man vs. Eclipso. 80-Eclipso, Prince Ra-Man end 4.00 13.00 34.00
81-91: 81-Mystery format begins; 1st app. Abel (HOS host). 82-Neal Adams-c(i). 85-N. Adams-a(i). 87-Wrightson & Kaluta-a. 90-Buckler (early work)/N. Adams-a 1.00 3.00 8.00
92-1st app. Swamp Thing-c/story (8 pgs.)(6-7/71) by Berni Wrightson(p) w/JeffJones/Kaluta/Weiss ink assists 34.00 102.00 375.00
93-100: 94-Wrightson inks. 96-Wood-a 1.90 4.75
101-154: 140-Origin The Patchworkman 1.00 2.50

GD25 FN65 NM94

NOTE: ***Neal Adams*** *c-81, 82, 84-88, 90, 91.* ***Cameron*** *a-13, 15.* ***Colan*** *a-63.* ***Ditko*** *a-139p, 148.* ***Elias*** *a-58.* ***Evans*** *a-118.* ***Finlay*** *a-7r(Real Fact?).* ***Glanzman*** *a-91.* ***Golden*** *a-151.* ***Heath*** *a-31.* ***Kaluta*** *a-87, 98, 99; c-98, 99, 101, 102, 149, 151, 154.* ***Bob Kane*** *a-18, 21.* ***G. Kane*** *a-85p.* ***Kirby*** *c-3, 11, 12.* ***Kubert*** *a-39.* ***Meskin*** *a-2-68 (most); c-55-60.* ***Moreira*** *a-7, 8, 51, 54, 102-104, 106, 108, 113, 116, 118, 121, 123, 127; c-1, 2, 4-10, 13-20.* ***Morrow*** *a-86, 89, 90; c-89, 146-148.* ***Nino*** *a-101, 103, 106, 109, 115, 117, 126, 128, 131, 147, 153.* ***Redondo*** *a-95, 99, 102, 104p, 113, 116, 134, 139, 140.* ***Reese*** *a-85.* ***Starlin*** *c-150.* ***Sutton*** *a-154.* ***Toth*** *a-63-67, 83, 93r, 94r, 96r, 98r, 123.* ***Tuska*** *a-90, 104.* ***Wrightson*** *c-92-94, 96, 100, 103, 106, 107, 135, 139.*

HOUSE OF TERROR (3-D)
October, 1953 (1st 3-D horror comic)
St. John Publishing Co.

1-Kubert, Baker-a 22.00 65.00 150.00

HOUSE OF YANG, THE (See Yang)
July, 1975 - No. 6, June, 1976; 1978
Charlton Comics

1 1.50
2-6, Modern Comics #1,2(1978) 1.00

HOUSE II: THE SECOND STORY
Oct, 1987 (One-shot)
Marvel Comics

1-Adapts movie .80 2.00

HOWARD CHAYKIN'S AMERICAN FLAGG! (First)(Value: cover or less)

HOWARD THE DUCK (See Bizarre Adventures #34, Fear, Man-Thing & Marvel Treasury Edition)
Jan, 1976 - No. 31, May, 1979; No. 32, Jan, 1986; No. 33, Sept, 1986
Marvel Comics Group

1-Brunner-c/a; Spider-Man x-over (low distr.) 1.65 4.00 10.00
2-11: 2-Brunner-c/a (low distr.). 3-Buscema-a(p) .80 2.00
12-1st app. Kiss (cameo, 3/77) 1.60 4.00
13-Kiss app. (1st full story, 6/77); Daimon Hellstrom app. plus cameo of Howard as Son of Satan 1.80 4.50
14-33: 14-Howard as Son of Satan-c/story; Son of Satan app. 16-Album issue; 3 pgs. comics. 22,23-Man-Thing-c/stories 1.00
Annual 1(1977, 52 pgs.)-Mayerik-a 1.00

NOTE: ***Austin*** *c-29i.* ***Bolland*** *c-33.* ***Brunner*** *a-1p, 2p; c-1, 2.* ***Buckler*** *c-3p.* ***Buscema*** *a-3p.* ***Colan*** *a(p)-4-15, 17-20, 24-27, 30, 31; c(p)-4-31, Annual 1p.* ***Leialoha*** *a-1-13i; c(i)-3-5, 8-11.* ***Mayerik*** *a-22, 23, 33.* ***P. Smith*** *a-30p. Man-Thing app. in #22, 23.*

HOWARD THE DUCK (Magazine)
October, 1979 - No. 9, March, 1981 (B&W, 68 pgs.)
Marvel Comics Group

1 1.50
2,3,5-9: 3-Xmas issue. 7-Has poster by Byrne 1.00
4-Beatles, John Lennon, Elvis, Kiss & Devo cameos; Hitler app. 1.20

NOTE: ***Buscema*** *a-4p.* ***Colan*** *a-1-5p, 7-9p.* ***Jack Davis*** *c-3.* ***Golden*** *a(p)-1, 5, 6(51pgs.).* ***Rogers*** *a-7, 8.* ***Simonson*** *a-7.*

HOWARD THE DUCK: THE MOVIE
Dec, 1986 - No. 3, Feb, 1987 (Mini-series)
Marvel Comics Group

1-3: Movie adaptation; r/Marvel Super Special 1.00

HOW BOYS AND GIRLS CAN HELP WIN THE WAR
1942 (One Shot) (10 cents)
The Parents' Magazine Institute

1-All proceeds used to buy war bonds 17.00 52.00 120.00

HOWDY DOODY (TV)(See Poll Parrot)
1/50 - No. 38, 7-9/56; No. 761, 1/57; No. 811, 7/57
Dell Publishing Co.

1-(Scarce)-Photo-c; 1st TV comic 64.00 193.00 450.00
2-Photo-c 20.00 60.00 140.00
3-5: All photo-c 12.00 36.00 95.00
6-Used in **SOTI**, pg. 309; painted-c begin 13.00 40.00 90.00
7-10 11.00 32.00 75.00
11-20: 13-X-Mas-c 9.15 27.50 55.00

Huckleberry Hound #14 (Dell), © H-B

Huey, Dewey, & Louie Junior Woodchucks #2, © The Disney Co.

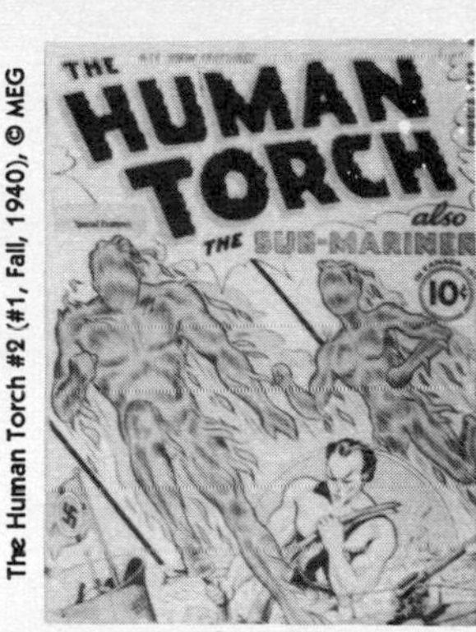

The Human Torch #2 (#1, Fall, 1940), © MEG

	GD25	FN65	NM94
21-38	8.35	25.00	50.00
4-Color 761,811	10.00	30.00	60.00

HOW IT BEGAN (See Single Series No. 15)

HOW SANTA GOT HIS RED SUIT (See March of Comics No. 2)

HOW STALIN HOPES WE WILL DESTROY AMERICA
1951 (16 pgs.) (Giveaway)
Joe Lowe Co. (Pictorial News)

	GD25	FN65	NM94
nn	39.00	118.00	275.00

(Prices vary widely on this book)

HOW THE WEST WAS WON (See Movie Comics)

HOW TO DRAW FOR THE COMICS
No date (1942?) (64 pgs.; B&W & color) (10 Cents) (No ads)
Street and Smith

	GD25	FN65	NM94
nn-Art by Winsor McCay, George Marcoux(Supersnipe artist), Vernon Greene (The Shadow artist), Jack Binder(with biog.), Thorton Fisher, Jon Small, & Jack Farr; has biographies of each artist	17.00	52.00	120.00

H. P. LOVECRAFT'S CTHULHU
Dec, 1991 - No. 3, Feb?, 1992 ($2.50, color, mini-series)
Millennium Publications

	GD25	FN65	NM94
1-3: 1-Contains trading cards on thin stock		1.00	2.50

H. R. PUFNSTUF (TV) (See March of Comics 360)
Oct, 1970 - No. 8, July, 1972
Gold Key

	GD25	FN65	NM94
1-Photo-c (all have photo-c?)	11.00	32.00	75.00
2-8	5.00	15.00	30.00

HUBERT (See 4-Color No. 251)

HUCK & YOGI JAMBOREE (TV)
March, 1961 (116 pgs.; $1.00) (B&W original material)
(6-1/4x9"; cardboard cover; high quality paper)
Dell Publishing Co.

	GD25	FN65	NM94
nn	7.50	22.50	45.00

HUCK & YOGI WINTER SPORTS (See 4-Color No. 1310)

HUCK FINN (See The New Adventures of... & Power Record Comics)

HUCKLEBERRY FINN (See 4-Color No. 1114)

HUCKLEBERRY HOUND (See Dell Giant #31,44, Golden Picture Story Book, Kite Fun Book, March of Comics #199, 214, 235, Spotlight #1 & Whitman Comic Books)

HUCKLEBERRY HOUND (TV)
No. 990, 5-7/59 - No. 43, 10/70 (Hanna-Barbera)
Dell/Gold Key No. 18 (10/62) on

	GD25	FN65	NM94
4-Color 990(#1)-1st app. Hucklebery Hound, Yogi Bear, & Pixie & Dixie & Mr. Jinx	8.00	24.00	55.00
4-Color 1050,1054 (12/59)	6.70	20.00	40.00
3(1-2/60) - 7 (9-10/60)	6.70	20.00	40.00
4-Color 1141 (10/60)	6.70	20.00	40.00
8-10	5.00	15.00	30.00
11-17 (6-8/62)	4.20	12.50	25.00
18,19 (84pgs.; 18-20 titled ...Chuckleberry Tales)	6.00	18.00	48.00
20-30: 20-Titled Chuckleberry Tales	3.60	9.00	18.00
31-43: 37-Reprints	3.00	7.50	15.00

HUCKLEBERRY HOUND (TV)
Nov, 1970 - No. 8, Jan, 1972 (Hanna-Barbera)
Charlton Comics

	GD25	FN65	NM94
1	2.30	6.75	16.00
2-8	1.65	4.70	11.00

HUEY, DEWEY, & LOUIE (See Donald Duck, 1938 for 1st app. Also see Mickey Mouse Magazine V4#2, V5#7 & Walt Disney's Junior Woodchucks Limited Series)

HUEY, DEWEY, & LOUIE BACK TO SCHOOL (See Dell Giant #22, 35, 49 & Dell Giants)

HUEY, DEWEY AND LOUIE JUNIOR WOODCHUCKS (Disney)
Aug, 1966 - No. 81, 1984 (See Walt Disney's C&S #125)
Gold Key No. 1-61/Whitman No. 62 on

	GD25	FN65	NM94
1	3.60	10.75	25.00
2,3(12/68)	2.40	7.25	17.00
4,5(4/70)-Barks-r	2.60	7.50	18.00
6-17-Written by Barks	1.70	5.00	12.00
18,27-30	1.00	2.50	6.00
19-23,25-Written by Barks. 22,23,25-Barks-r	1.25	3.00	7.50
24,26-Barks-r	1.25	3.00	7.50
31-57,60-81: 41,70,80-Reprints		1.40	3.50
58,59-Barks-r		1.80	4.50

NOTE: ***Barks** story reprints-No. 22-26, 35, 42, 45, 51.*

HUGGA BUNCH (TV) (Marvel)(Value: cover or less)

HULK (Formerly The Rampaging Hulk; also see The Incredible Hulk)
No. 10, Aug, 1978 - No. 27, June, 1981 (Magazine)($1.50, color)
Marvel Comics Group

	GD25	FN65	NM94
10			1.50
11-Moon Knight begins, ends 20		1.80	4.50
12-15: Moon Knight stories		1.20	3.00
16,19,21,22,24-27: 24-Part color. 25-27 are B&W		.75	1.90
17,18,20: Moon Knight stories		1.10	2.75
23-Last full color issue; Banner is attacked		1.00	2.50

NOTE: ***Alcala** a(i)-15, 17-20, 22, 24-27. **Buscema** a-23; c-26. **Chaykin** a-21-25. **Colan** a(p)-11, 19, 24-27. **Jusko** painted c-12. **Nebres** a-16. **Sienkiewicz** a-13, 17, 20. **Simonson** a-27; c-23. Dominic Fortune appears in #21-24.*

HULK: FUTURE IMPERFECT
Jan, 1993 - No. 2, Dec, 1992 (In error) ($5.95, color, 52 pgs.)
Marvel Comics

	GD25	FN65	NM94
1,2-Embossed-c; Perez-c/a	1.00	2.50	6.00

HUMAN FLY
1963 - 1964 (Reprints)
I.W. Enterprises/Super

	GD25	FN65	NM94
I.W. Reprint #1-Reprints Blue Beetle #44('46)	1.40	3.50	7.00
Super Reprint #10-R/Blue Beetle #46('47)	1.40	3.50	7.00

HUMAN FLY, THE
Sept, 1977 - No. 19, Mar, 1979
Marvel Comics Group

	GD25	FN65	NM94
1-Origin; Spider-Man x-over		1.60	4.00
2-Ghost Rider app.		1.90	4.75
3-19: 9-Daredevil x-over; Byrne-c(p)		.70	1.80

NOTE: ***Austin** c-4i, 9i. **Elias** a-1, 3p, 4p, 7p, 10-12p, 15p, 18p, 19p. **Layton** c-19.*

HUMAN TARGET SPECIAL (TV)
Nov, 1991 ($2.00, color, 52 pgs.)
DC Comics

	GD25	FN65	NM94
1		.80	2.00

HUMAN TORCH, THE (Red Raven #1)(See All-Select, All Winners, Marvel Mystery, Men's Adventures, Mystic Comics (2nd series), Sub-Mariner, USA & Young Men)
No. 2, Fall, 1940 - No. 15, Spring, 1944;
No. 16, Fall, 1944 - No. 35, Mar, 1949 (Becomes Love Tales);
No. 36, April, 1954 - No. 38, Aug, 1954
Timely/Marvel Comics (TP 2,3/TCI 4-9/SePI 10/SnPC 11-25/CnPC 26-35/Atlas Comics (CPC 36-38))

	GD25	FN65	VF82	NM94
2(#1)-Intro & Origin Toro, The Falcon, The Fiery Mask, Mantor the Magician, & Microman only app.; Human Torch by Burgos, Sub-Mariner by Everett begin (origin of each in text)	950.00	2850.00	6175.00	9500.00

(Estimated up to 190 total copies exist, 10 in NM/Mint)

	GD25	FN65	NM94
3(#2)-40pg. H.T. story; H.T. & S.M. battle over who is best artist in text-Everett or Burgos	300.00	900.00	2000.00
4(#3)-Origin The Patriot in text; last Everett Sub-Mariner; 1st Nazi war-c; Sid Greene-a	233.00	700.00	1600.00

The Human Torch #16, © MEG

Hyperkind #3, © Clive Barker

Icon #4, © Milestone Media

	GD25	FN65	NM94
5(#4)-The Patriot app; Angel x-over in Sub-Mariner (Summer, 1941)	171.00	515.00	1200.00
5-Human Torch battles Sub-Mariner (Fall,'41)	250.00	750.00	1700.00
6,7,9: 7-1st Japanese war-c	108.00	325.00	725.00
8-Human Torch battles Sub-Mariner; Wolverton-a, 1 pg.	171.00	515.00	1200.00
10-Human Torch battles Sub-Mariner; Wolverton-a, 1 pg.	125.00	375.00	825.00
11-15: 14-1st Atlas Globe logo (Winter, 1943-44; see All Winners #11 also)	83.00	250.00	565.00
16-20: 20-Last War issue	63.00	190.00	425.00
21-30: 23(Sum/46)-Becomes Junior Miss 24?	57.00	170.00	385.00
31-Namora x-over in Sub-Mariner (also #30); last Toro	47.00	142.00	325.00
32-Sungirl, Namora app.; Sungirl-c	47.00	142.00	325.00
33-Capt. America x-over	52.00	155.00	340.00
34-Sungirl solo	48.00	145.00	310.00
35-Captain America & Sungirl app. (1949)	52.00	155.00	340.00
36-38(1954)-Sub-Mariner in all	39.00	118.00	275.00

NOTE: ***Ayers*** *Human Torch in 36(3).* ***Brodsky*** *c-25, 31-33?, 37, 38,* ***Burgos*** *c-36.* ***Everett*** *a-1-3, 27, 28, 30, 37, 38.* ***Powell*** *a-36(Sub-Mariner).* ***Schomburg*** *c-1-3, 5-8, 10-23.* ***Sekowsky*** *c-28, 34?, 35?* ***Shores*** *c-24, 26, 27, 29, 30.* ***Mickey Spillane*** *text 4-6. Bondage c-2, 12, 19.*

HUMAN TORCH, THE (Also see Avengers West Coast, Fantastic Four, The Invaders, Saga of the Original... & Strange Tales #101)
Sept, 1974 - No. 8, Nov, 1975
Marvel Comics Group

	GD25	FN65	NM94
1: 1-8-r/stories from Strange Tales #101-108		1.80	4.50
2-8: 1st H.T. title since G.A. 7-vs. Sub-Mariner		1.20	3.00

NOTE: *Golden Age & Silver Age Human Torch-r #1-8.* ***Ayers*** *r-6, 7.* ***Kirby/Ayers*** *r-1-5, 8.*

HUMBUG (Satire by Harvey Kurtzman)
Aug, 1957 - No. 9, May, 1958; No. 10, June, 1958; No. 11, Oct, 1958
Humbug Publications

	GD25	FN65	NM94
1	14.00	43.00	100.00
2	8.35	25.00	50.00
3-9: 8-Elvis in Jailbreak Rock	5.85	17.50	35.00
10,11-Magazine format. 10-Photo-c	8.35	25.00	50.00
Bound Volume(#1-6)-Sold by publisher	26.00	77.00	180.00
Bound Volume(#1-9)	29.00	85.00	200.00

NOTE: ***Davis*** *a-1-11.* ***Elder*** *a-2-4, 6-9, 11.* ***Heath*** *a-2, 4-8, 10.* ***Jaffee*** *a-2, 4-9.* ***Kurtzman*** *a-11.* ***Wood*** *a-1.*

HUMDINGER (Becomes White Rider and Super Horse #3 on?)
May-June, 1946 - V2#2, July-Aug, 1947
Novelty Press/Premium Group

	GD25	FN65	NM94
1-Jerkwater Line, Mickey Starlight by Don Rico, Dink begin	13.00	40.00	90.00
2	6.70	20.00	40.00
3-6, V2#1,2	4.20	12.50	25.00

HUMOR (See All Humor Comics)

HUMPHREY COMICS (Also see Joe Palooka)
October, 1948 - No. 22, April, 1952
Harvey Publications

	GD25	FN65	NM94
1-Joe Palooka's pal (r); (52 pgs.)-Powell-a	10.00	30.00	60.00
2,3: Powell-a	4.70	14.00	28.00
4-Boy Heroes app.; Powell-a	5.35	16.00	32.00
5-8,10: 5,6-Powell-a. 7-Little Dot app.	4.00	10.00	20.00
9-Origin Humphrey	4.70	14.00	28.00
11-22	2.80	7.00	14.00

HUNCHBACK OF NOTRE DAME, THE (See 4-Color No. 854)

HUNK
August, 1961 - No. 11, 1963
Charlton Comics

	GD25	FN65	NM94
1	2.00	5.00	10.00
2-11	1.00	2.50	5.00

HUNTED (Formerly My Love Memoirs)
No. 13, July, 1950 - No. 2, Sept, 1950
Fox Features Syndicate

	GD25	FN65	NM94
13(#1)-Used in **SOTI**, pg. 42 & illo.-"Treating police contemptuously" (lower left); Hollingsworth bondage-c	17.00	52.00	120.00
2	8.35	25.00	50.00

HUNTRESS, THE (See All-Star Comics #69, Batman Family, Brave & the Bold #62, DC Super Stars #17, Detective #652, Infinity, Inc. #1, Sensation Comics #68 & Wonder Woman #271)
April, 1989 - No. 19, Oct, 1990 ($1.00, color, mature readers)
DC Comics

	GD25	FN65	NM94
1-19: Staton-c/a(p) in all. 17-19-Batman-c/stories			1.00

HURRICANE COMICS
1945 (52 pgs.)
Cambridge House

	GD25	FN65	NM94
1-(Humor, funny animal)	13.00	40.00	90.00

HYBRIDS (See Revengers Special)

HYDROMAN (See Heroic Comics)

HYPERKIND (See Razorline)
Sept, 1993 - Present ($1.75, color)
Marvel Comics

	GD25	FN65	NM94
1-($2.50)-Foil embossed-c; by Clive Barker		.80	2.00
2-8		.70	1.75

HYPER MYSTERY COMICS
May, 1940 - No. 2, June, 1940 (68 pgs.)
Hyper Publications

	GD25	FN65	NM94
1-Hyper, the Phenomenal begins	92.00	275.00	625.00
2	67.00	200.00	450.00

I AIM AT THE STARS (See 4-Color No. 1148)

I AM COYOTE (See Eclipse Graphic Album Series & Eclipse Magazine #2)

I AM LEGEND (Eclipse)(Value: cover or less)

IBIS, THE INVINCIBLE (See Fawcett Min., Mighty Midget & Whiz)
1943 (Feb) - #2, 1943; #3, Wint, 1945 - #5, Fall, 1946; #6, Spring, 1948
Fawcett Publications

	GD25	FN65	NM94
1-Origin Ibis; Raboy-c; on sale 1/2/43	108.00	325.00	750.00
2-Bondage-c	58.00	175.00	400.00
3-Wolverton-a #3-6 (4 pgs. each)	47.00	140.00	310.00
4-6: 5-Bondage-c	37.00	110.00	250.00

NOTE: ***Mac Raboy*** *c(p)-3-5.* ***Shaffenberger*** *c-6.*

ICE KING OF OZ, THE (See First Comics Graphic Novel #13)

ICEMAN (Also see The Champions & X-Men #94)
Dec, 1984 - No. 4, June, 1985 (Limited series)
Marvel Comics Group

	GD25	FN65	NM94
1		.80	2.00
2,4		.70	1.70
3-The Defenders, Champions (Ghost Rider) & the original X-Men x-over		1.10	2.75

ICICLE (Hero)(Value: cover or less)

I COME IN PEACE (Greater Mercury)(Value: cover or less)

ICON
May, 1993 - Present ($1.50, color)
DC Comics (Milestone)

	GD25	FN65	NM94
1-($2.95)-Collector's Edition polybagged w/poster & trading card (direct sale only)		1.20	3.00
1-12			1.50

IDAHO
June-Aug, 1963 - No. 8, July-Sept, 1965
Dell Publishing Co.

Ideal Comics #4 (Spr/46), © MEG

I Loved #29, © FOX

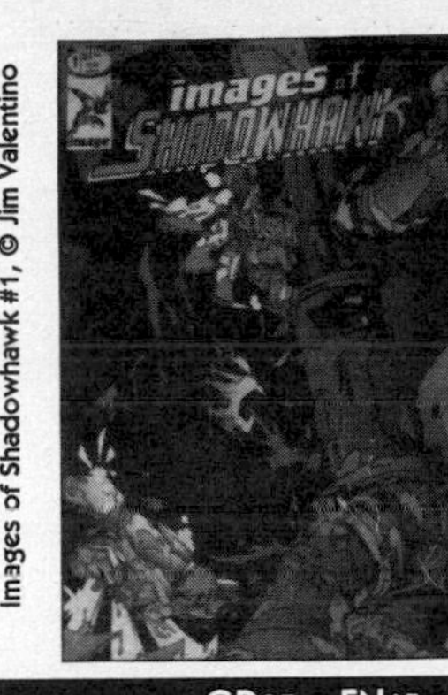

Images of Shadowhawk #1, © Jim Valentino

	GD25	FN65	NM94
1	2.00	5.00	10.00
2-8: 5-7-Painted-c	1.20	3.00	6.00

IDEAL (... a Classical Comic) (2nd Series) (Love Romances No. 6)
July, 1948 - No. 5, March, 1949 (Feature length stories)
Timely Comics

	GD25	FN65	NM94
1-Antony & Cleopatra	22.00	65.00	150.00
2-The Corpses of Dr. Sacotti	19.00	57.00	130.00
3-Joan of Arc; used in **SOTI**, pg. 308-'Boer War'	16.00	48.00	110.00
4-Richard the Lion-hearted; titled "...the World's Greatest Comics;" The Witness app.	25.00	75.00	175.00
5-Ideal Love & Romance; photo-c	10.00	30.00	65.00

IDEAL COMICS (1st Series) (Willie Comics No. 5 on)
Fall, 1944 - No. 4, Spring, 1946
Timely Comics (MgPC)

	GD25	FN65	NM94
1-Super Rabbit in all	11.50	34.00	80.00
2	9.15	27.50	55.00
3,4	8.35	25.00	50.00

IDEAL LOVE & ROMANCE (See Ideal, A Classical Comic)

IDEAL ROMANCE (Formerly Tender Romance)
No. 3, April, 1954 - No. 8, Feb, 1955 (Diary Confessions No. 9 on)
Key Publications

	GD25	FN65	NM94
3-Bernard Baily-c	4.70	14.00	28.00
4-8: 4,5-B. Baily-c	3.00	7.50	15.00

IDOL
1992 - No. 3, 1992 ($2.95, color, mini-series, 52 pgs.)
Epic Comics (Marvel)

	GD25	FN65	NM94
Book 1-3		1.20	3.00

I DREAM OF JEANNIE (TV)
April, 1965 - No. 2, Dec, 1966 (Photo-c)
Dell Publishing Co.

	GD25	FN65	NM94
1,2-Barbara Eden photo-c	9.15	27.50	55.00

IF THE DEVIL WOULD TALK
1950, 1958 (32 pgs., paper cover, in full color)
Roman Catholic Catechetical Guild/Impact Publ.

	GD25	FN65	NM94
nn-(Scarce)-About secularism (20-30 copies known to exist); very low distribution	50.00	150.00	350.00
1958 Edition-(Impact Publ.); art & script changed to meet church criticism of earlier edition; 80 plus copies known to exist	36.00	107.00	250.00
Black & White version of nn edition; small size; only 4 known copies exist	30.00	90.00	200.00

NOTE: *The original edition of this book was printed and killed by the Guild's board of directors. It is believed that a very limited number of copies were distributed. The 1958 version was a complete bomb with very limited, if any, circulation. In 1979, 11 original, 4 1958 reprints, and 4 B&W's surfaced from the Guild's old files in St. Paul, Minnesota.*

ILLUMINATOR
1993 - No. 4, 1993 ($4.99, color, 52 pgs.)
Marvel Comics/Nelson Publ.

	GD25	FN65	NM94
1-4	1.00	2.00	5.00

ILLUSTRATED GAGS (See Single Series No. 16)

ILLUSTRATED LIBRARY OF..., AN (See Classics Illustrated Giants)

ILLUSTRATED STORIES OF THE OPERAS
1943 (16 pgs.; B&W) (25 cents) (cover-B&W & red)
Baily (Bernard) Publ. Co.

	GD25	FN65	NM94
nn-(Rare)-Faust (part-r in Cisco Kid #1)	39.00	120.00	275.00
nn-(Rare)-Aida	39.00	120.00	275.00
nn-(Rare)-Carmen; Baily-a	39.00	120.00	275.00
nn-(Rare)-Rigoleito	39.00	120.00	275.00

ILLUSTRATED STORY OF ROBIN HOOD & HIS MERRY MEN, THE
(See Classics Giveaways, 12/44)

ILLUSTRATED TARZAN BOOK, THE (See Tarzan Book)

I LOVED (Formerly Rulah; Colossal Features Magazine No. 33 on)
No. 28, July, 1949 - No. 32, Mar, 1950
Fox Features Syndicate

	GD25	FN65	NM94
28	5.35	16.00	32.00
29-32	4.00	10.00	20.00

I LOVE LUCY (Eternity)(Value: cover or less)

I LOVE LUCY COMICS (TV) (Also see The Lucy Show)
No. 535, Feb, 1954 - No. 35, Apr-June, 1962 (All photo-c)
Dell Publishing Co.

	GD25	FN65	NM94
4-Color 535(#1)	36.00	110.00	250.00
4-Color 559(#2, 5/54)	24.00	70.00	165.00
3 (8-10/54) - 5	14.00	43.00	100.00
6-10	11.00	32.00	75.00
11-20	9.00	28.00	65.00
21-35	8.00	24.00	55.00

I LOVE YOU
June, 1950 (One shot)
Fawcett Publications

	GD25	FN65	NM94
1-Photo-c	10.00	30.00	60.00

I LOVE YOU (Formerly In Love)
No. 7, 9/55 - No. 121, 12/76; No. 122, 3/79 - No. 130, 5/80
Charlton Comics

	GD25	FN65	NM94
7-Kirby-c, Powell-a	6.70	20.00	40.00
8-10	3.00	7.50	15.00
11-16,18-20	1.80	4.50	9.00
17-68 pg. Giant	2.40	6.00	12.00
21-25,27-50	1.00	2.50	6.00
26-Torres-a	1.20	3.00	7.00
51-59		1.60	4.00
60(1/66)-Elvis Presley line drawn c/story	10.00	30.00	70.00
61-85		1.20	3.00
86-130			1.00

I'M A COP
1954 - No. 3, 1954?
Magazine Enterprises

	GD25	FN65	NM94
1(A-1 #111)-Powell-c/a in all	9.15	27.50	55.00
2(A-1 #126), 3(A-1 #128)	5.00	15.00	30.00

IMAGE GRAPHIC NOVEL (Image International)(Value: cover or less)

IMAGES OF SHADOWHAWK (Also see Shadowhawk)
Sept, 1993 - Present ($1.95, color, limited series)
Image Comics

	GD25	FN65	NM94
1,2		.80	2.00

I'M DICKENS - HE'S FENSTER (TV)
May-July, 1963 - No. 2, Aug-Oct, 1963 (Photo-c)
Dell Publishing Co.

	GD25	FN65	NM94
1,2	4.00	11.00	22.00

I MET A HANDSOME COWBOY (See 4-Color No. 324)

IMMORTAL DOCTOR FATE, THE (DC)(Value: cover or less)

IMPACT
Mar-Apr, 1955 - No. 5, Nov-Dec, 1955
E. C. Comics

	GD25	FN65	NM94
1-Not code approved	11.50	34.00	80.00
2	9.15	27.50	55.00
3-5: 4-Crandall-a	7.50	22.50	45.00

NOTE: ***Crandall** a-1-4. **Davis** a-2-4; c-1-5. **Evans** a-1, 4, 5. **Ingels** a-in all. **Kamen** a-3. **Krigstein** a-1, 5. **Orlando** a-2, 5.*

IMPACT CHRISTMAS SPECIAL
1991 ($2.50, color, 68 pgs.)
Impact Comics (DC Comics)

Incomplete Death's Head #10, © MEG

The Incredible Hulk #113, © MEG

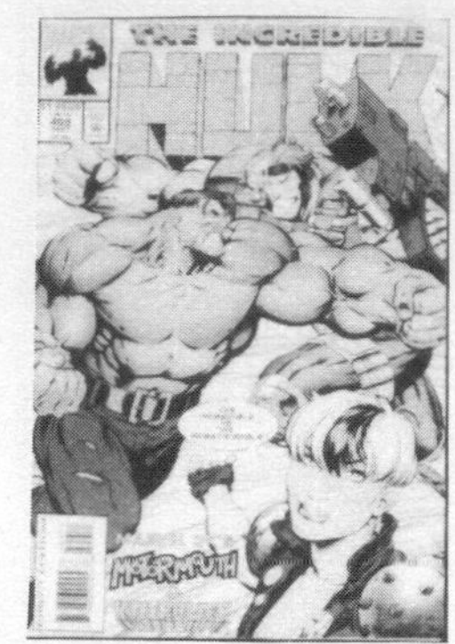

The Incredible Hulk #409, © MEG

GD25 FN65 NM94

1-Gift of the Magi by Infantino/Rogers; The Black Hood, The Fly, The Jaguar, & The Shield stories 1.00 2.50

IMPOSSIBLE MAN SUMMER VACATION SPECTACULAR, THE (Marvel)
(Value: cover or less)

INCAL, THE
Nov, 1988 - No. 3, Jan, 1989 ($10.95/$12.95, adults)
Epic Comics (Marvel)

1,3: Moebius-c/a in all; sexual content 1.65 4.70 11.00
2-($12.95) 1.85 5.50 13.00

INCOMPLETE DEATH'S HEAD (Also see Death's Head)
Jan, 1993 - No. 12, Dec, 1993 ($1.75, color, limited series)
Marvel Comics UK

1-($2.95, 56 pgs.)-Die-cut cover 1.20 3.00
2-11: 2-Re-intro original Death's Head. 3-Original Death's Head vs. Dragon's Claws .70 1.75
12-($2.50, 52 pgs.) 1.00 2.50

INCREDIBLE HULK, THE (See Aurora, The Avengers #1, The Defenders #1, Giant-Size..., Hulk, Marvel Collectors Item Classics, Marvel Comics Presents #26, Marvel Fanfare, Marvel Treasury Edition, Power Record Comics, Rampaging Hulk, She-Hulk & 2099 Unlimited)

INCREDIBLE HULK, THE
May, 1962 - No. 6, Mar, 1963; No. 102, Apr, 1968 - Present
Marvel Comics Group

GD25 FN65 VF82 NM94

1-Origin & 1st app. (skin is grey colored) 592.00 1775.00 4438.00 7100.00
2-1st green skinned Hulk; Ditko-a(i) 160.00 480.00 1040.00 1600.00

GD25 FN65 NM94

3-Origin retold; 1st app. Ringmaster & Hercules (9/62) 108.00 325.00 975.00
4,5: 4-Brief origin retold 87.00 260.00 780.00
6-Intro. Teen Brigade; all Ditko-a 144.00 433.00 1300.00
102-(Formerly Tales to Astonish)-Origin retold; story continued from Tales to Astonish #101 23.00 69.00 160.00
103 9.00 26.00 60.00
104-Rhino app. 8.00 24.00 55.00
105-108: 105-1st Missing Link 6.00 19.00 44.00
109,110: 109-Ka-Zar app. 4.30 13.00 30.00
111-117: 117-Last 12 cent issue 3.25 9.50 22.00
118-Hulk vs. Sub-Mariner 2.40 7.25 17.00
119-121,123-125 1.70 5.00 12.00
122-Hulk battles Thing (12/69) 2.70 8.00 19.00
126-140: 126-1st Barbara Norriss (Valkyrie). 131-Hulk vs. Iron Man; 1st Jim Wilson, Hulk's new sidekick. 136-1st Xeron, The Star-Slayer. 140-Written by Harlan Ellison; 1st Jarella, Hulk's love 1.30 3.20 7.70
141-1st app. Doc Samson (7/71) 1.30 3.25 8.00
142-144,146-157,159-161: 149-1st app. The Inheritor. 155-1st app. Shaper. 161-The Mimic dies; Beast app. 1.00 2.50 5.50
145-(52 pgs.)-Origin retold 1.30 3.20 7.70
158-Warlock cameo(12/72) 1.00 2.50 6.00
162-1st app. The Wendigo (4/73); Beast app. 1.25 3.00 7.50
163-171,173-175: 163-1st app. The Gremlin. 164-1st Capt. Omen & Colonel John D. Armbruster. 166-1st Zzzax. 168-1st The Harpy; nudity panels of Betty Brant. 169-1st app. Bi-Beast 1.00 2.50 5.50
165-Variant w/4 extra pgs. of ads on slick paper (7/73) 1.00 2.50 6.00
172-X-Men cameo; origin Juggernaut retold 1.10 2.75 6.60
176-Warlock cameo (2 panels only); same date as Strange Tales #178 (6/74) 1.00 2.50 6.00
177-1st actual death of Warlock (last panel only) 1.40 3.50 8.50
178-Rebirth of Warlock 2.15 6.50 15.00
179-No Warlock 1.80 4.50
180-(10/74)-1st app. Wolverine (cameo last pg.) 7.00 21.00 50.00
181-(11/74)-1st full Wolverine story 36.00 110.00 255.00
182-Wolverine cameo; see Giant-Size X-Men #1 for next app.; 1st Crackajack Jackson 6.00 18.00 42.00
183-199: 185-Death of Col. Armbruster 1.40 3.50
200-Silver Surfer app.; anniversary issue 3.20 8.00 20.00
201-240: 212-1st app. The Constrictor. 227-Original Avengers app. 232-Capt. America x-over from C.A. #230. 233-Marvel Man app. 234-(4/79)-1st app. Quasar (formerly Marvel Man & changes name to Quasar) 1.20 3.00
241-249,251-299: 271-Rocket Raccoon app. 272-Sasquatch & Wendigo app.; Wolverine & Alpha Flight cameo in flashback. 278,279-Most Marvel characters app. (Wolverine in both). 279-X-Men & Alpha Flight cameos. 282-284-She-Hulk app. 293-F.F. app. .80 2.00
250-Giant size; Silver Surfer app. 1.40 3.50 8.50
300-(10/84, 52 pgs.)-Spider-Man app in new black costume on-c & 2 pg. cameo 1.60 4.00
301-313: 312-Origin Hulk retold 1.00 2.50
314-Byrne-c/a begins, ends #319 1.90 4.75
315-319: 319-Bruce Banner & Betty Talbot wed 1.00 2.50
320-323,325,327-329 .80 2.00
324-1st app. Grey Hulk since #1 (c-swipe of #1) 1.65 4.70 11.00
326-Grey vs. Green Hulk 1.90 4.75
330-1st McFarlane issue (4/87) 3.20 8.00 20.00
331-Grey Hulk series begins 2.15 6.50 15.00
332-334,336-339: 336,337-X-Factor app. 1.65 4.70 11.00
335-No McFarlane-a 1.20 3.00
340-Hulk battles Wolverine by McFarlane 5.50 17.00 40.00
341-344 1.20 3.00 7.00
345-($1.50, 52 pgs.) 1.30 3.25 8.00
346-Last McFarlane issue 1.00 2.50 6.00
347-349,351-358,360-366 1.20 3.00
350-Double size; Hulk/Thing battle 1.60 4.00
359-Wolverine app. (illusion only) 1.80 4.50
367-1st Dale Keown-a on Hulk (3/90) 3.25 9.50 22.00
368-Sam Kieth-c/a 2.30 6.75 16.00
369,370-Dale Keown-c/a. 370,371-Original Defenders app. 1.65 4.70 11.00
371,373-376: Keown-c/a. 376-Green vs. Grey Hulk 1.10 2.70 6.50
372-Green Hulk app.; Keown-c/a 2.70 8.00 19.00
377-1st all new Hulk; fluorescent-c; Keown-c/a 3.20 9.00 21.00
377-Gold logo 2nd printing 1.40 3.50 5.50
378,380,389: No Keown-a. 380-Doc Samson app. 1.20 3.00
379-Keown-a 1.25 3.00 7.50
381-388,390-392-Keown-a. 385-Infinity Gauntlet x-over. 389-Last $1.00-c. 392-X-Factor app. 1.60 4.00
393-($2.50, 72 pgs.)-30th anniversary issue; green foil stamped-c; swipes-c to #1; has pin-ups of classic battles 1.25 3.00 7.50
393-2nd printing 1.20 3.00
394-No Keown-c/a; intro Trauma .65 1.60
395,396-Punisher-c/stories; Keown-c/a .80 2.00
397-Begin "Ghost of the Past" 4-part sty; Keown c/a .80 2.00
398,399: 398-Last Keown-c/a .65 1.60
400-($2.50, 68 pgs.)-Holo-grafx foil-c & r/TTA #63 1.00 2.50
401-416: 402-Return of Doc Samson .65 1.60
Special 1 (10/68, 25 cents, 68 pg.)-New 51 pg. story, Hulk battles The Inhumans (early app.; Steranko-c 8.00 24.00 55.00
Special 2 (10/69, 25 cents, 68 pg.)-Origin retold 4.70 14.00 33.00
Special 3 (1/71, 25 cents, 68 pg.) 1.25 3.00 7.50
Special 4 (1/72) 1.00 2.50 5.50
Annual 5 (1976) 1.60 4.00
Annual 6 (1977) .80 2.00
Annual 7 (1978)-Byrne/Layton-c/a; Iceman & Angel app. in book-length story 1.30 3.00
Annual 8-17: 8('79)-Book-length Sasquatch-c/story. 9('80). 10('81). 11('82)-Doc Samson back-up by Miller(p)(5 pgs.); Spider-Man & Avengers app. Buckler-a(p). 12('83). 13('84). 14('85). 15('86). 16('90, $2.00, 68 pgs.)-She-Hulk app. 17(1991, $2.00)-Origin retold .80 2.00
Annual 18 (1992 ($2.25, 68 pgs.)-Return of the Defenders, part I; no Keown-c/a .90 2.25

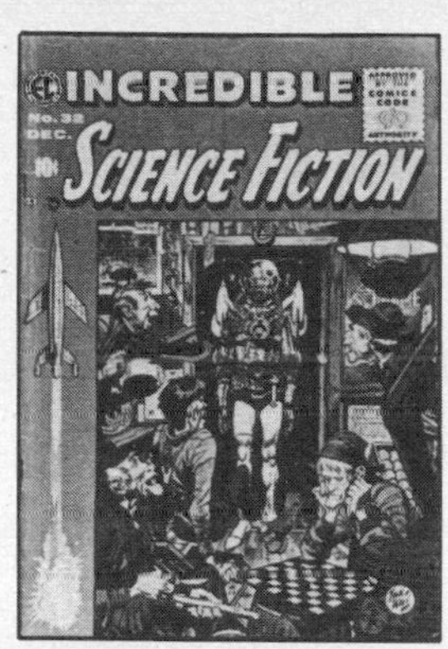

Incredible Science Fiction #32, © WMG

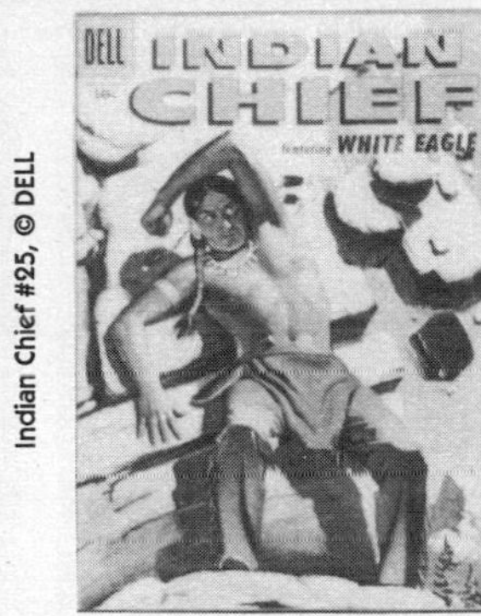

Indian Chief #25, © DELL

The Inferior Five #4, © DC

	GD25	FN65	NM94
Annual 19 (1993, $2.95, 68 pgs.)-Bagged w/card		1.20	3.00
...Versus Quasimodo 1 (3/83, one-shot)-Based on Saturday morning cartoon		.65	1.60

NOTE: **Adkins** *a-111-116i.* **Austin** *a(i)-350, 351, 353, 354; c-302i, 350i.* **Ayers** *a-3-5i.* **John Buscema** *c-202p.* **Byrne** *a-314-319p; c-314-316, 318, 319, 359.* **Colan** *c-363.* **Ditko** *a-2i, 6, 249, Annual 2r(5), 3r, 9p; c-2i, 6, 235, 249.* **Everett** *c-133i.* **Golden** *c-248, 251.* **Kane** *c(p)-193, 194, 196, 198.* **Dale Keown** *a(p)-367, 369-377, 379, 381-388, 390-393, 395-398; c-369-377p, 381, 382p, 384, 385, 386, 387p, 388, 390p, 391-393, 395p, 396, 397p, 398.* **Kirby** *a-1-5p, Special 2, 3p, Annual 5p; c-1-5, Annual 5.* **McFarlane** *a-330-334p, 336-339p, 340-343, 344-346p; c-330p, 340p, 341-343, 344p, 345, 346p.* **Miller** *c-258p, 261, 264, 268.* **Mooney** *a-230p, 287i, 288i.* **Powell** *a-Special 3r(2).* **Romita** *a-Annual 17p.* **Severin** *a(i)-108-110, 131-133, 141-151, 153-155; c(i)-109, 110, 132, 142, 144-155.* **Simonson** *c-283, 364-367.* **Starlin** *a-222p; c-217.* **Staton** *a(i)-187-189, 191-209.* **Tuska** *a-102i, 105i, 106i, 218p.* **Williamson** *a-310i; c-310i, 311i.* **Wrightson** *c-197.*

INCREDIBLE HULK AND WOLVERINE, THE
Oct, 1986 (One shot, $2.50, color)
Marvel Comics Group

	GD25	FN65	NM94
1-r-/1st app. Wolverine from Incred. Hulk #180,181; Wolverine back-up by Austin(i); Byrne-c	1.70	5.00	12.00

INCREDIBLE MR. LIMPET, THE (See Movie Classics)

INCREDIBLE SCIENCE FICTION (Formerly Weird Science-Fantasy)
No. 30, July-Aug, 1955 - No. 33, Jan-Feb, 1956
E. C. Comics

	GD25	FN65	NM94
30,33: 33-Story-r/Weird Fantasy #18	27.00	81.00	190.00
31-Williamson/Krenkel-a, Wood-a(2)	30.00	90.00	210.00
32-Williamson/Krenkel-a	30.00	90.00	210.00

NOTE: **Davis** *a-30, 32, 33; c-30-32.* **Krigstein** *a-in all.* **Orlando** *a-30, 32, 33('Judgement Day' reprint).* **Wood** *a-30, 31, 33; c-33.*

INDIANA JONES (See Dark Horse Comics & Further Adventures of...)

INDIANA JONES AND THE FATE OF ATLANTIS
March, 1991 - No. 4, Sept, 1991 ($2.50, color, mini-series)
Dark Horse Comics

	GD25	FN65	NM94
1-4: Dorman painted-c on all; 1,2-Contain trading cards (#1 has a 2nd printing, 10/91)		1.00	2.50

INDIANA JONES AND THE LAST CRUSADE
1989 - No. 4, 1989 ($1.00, color, limited series, movie adaptation)
Marvel Comics

	GD25	FN65	NM94
1-4: Dan Barry-a(p); Williamson-i assist			1.00
1 (1989, $2.95, B&W mag., 80 pgs.)		1.20	3.00

INDIANA JONES AND THE TEMPLE OF DOOM
Sept, 1984 - No. 3, Nov, 1984 (Movie adaptation)
Marvel Comics Group

	GD25	FN65	NM94
1-3-r/Marvel Super Special; Guice-a			1.00

INDIANA JONES: THUNDER IN THE ORIENT
Sept, 1993 - No. 6, 1994 ($2.50, color, limited series)
Dark Horse Comics

	GD25	FN65	NM94
1-6: 1-Dorman painted-c; Dan Barry story & art		1.00	2.50

INDIAN BRAVES (Baffling Mysteries No. 5 on)
March, 1951 - No. 4, Sept, 1951
Ace Magazines

	GD25	FN65	NM94
1-Green Arrowhead begins, ends #3	6.70	20.00	40.00
2	4.00	10.00	20.00
3,4	3.20	8.00	16.00
I.W. Reprint #1 (nd)-r/Indian Braves #4	1.20	3.00	6.00

INDIAN CHIEF (White Eagle...) (Formerly The Chief)
No. 3, July-Sept, 1951 - No. 33, Jan-Mar, 1959 (All painted-c)
Dell Publishing Co.

	GD25	FN65	NM94
3	4.00	11.00	22.00
4-11: 6-White Eagle app.	2.80	7.00	14.00
12-1st White Eagle(10-12/53)-Not same as earlier character	4.00	10.00	20.00
13-29	2.00	5.00	10.00
30-33-Buscema-a	2.40	6.00	12.00

INDIAN CHIEF (See March of Comics No. 94, 110, 127, 140, 159, 170, 187)

INDIAN FIGHTER, THE (See 4-Color No. 687)

INDIAN FIGHTER
May, 1950 - No. 11, Jan, 1952
Youthful Magazines

	GD25	FN65	NM94
1	7.50	22.50	45.00
2-Wildey-a/c(bondage)	4.20	12.50	25.00
3-11: 3,4-Wildey-a	3.20	8.00	16.00

NOTE: **Walter Johnson** *c-1, 3, 4, 6.* **Palais** *a-10.* **Stallman** *a-7.* **Wildey** *a-2-4; c-2, 5.*

INDIAN LEGENDS OF THE NIAGARA (See American Graphics)

INDIANS
Spring, 1950 - No. 17, Spring, 1953 (1-8: 52 pgs.)
Fiction House Magazines (Wings Publ. Co.)

	GD25	FN65	NM94
1-Manzar The White Indian, Long Bow & Orphan of the Storm begin	16.00	48.00	110.00
2-Starlight begins	9.15	27.50	55.00
3-5: 5-17-Most-c by Whitman	7.50	22.50	45.00
6-10	5.85	17.50	35.00
11-17	4.70	14.00	28.00

INDIANS OF THE WILD WEST
Circa 1958? (no date) (Reprints)
I. W. Enterprises

	GD25	FN65	NM94
9-Kinstler-c; Whitman-a; r/Indians #?	1.60	4.00	8.00

INDIANS ON THE WARPATH
No date (Late 40s, early 50s) (132 pages)
St. John Publishing Co.

	GD25	FN65	NM94
nn-Matt Baker-c; contains St. John comics rebound. Many combinations possible	19.00	58.00	135.00

INDIAN TRIBES (See Famous Indian Tribes)

INDIAN WARRIORS (Formerly White Rider and Super Horse; becomes Western Crime Cases #9)
No. 7, June, 1951 - No. 8, Sept, 1951
Star Publications

	GD25	FN65	NM94
7-White Rider & Superhorse continue; L.B. Cole-c	7.00	21.00	42.00
8-L. B. Cole-c	5.35	16.00	32.00
3-D 1(12/53)-L. B. Cole-c	25.00	75.00	175.00
Accepted Reprint(nn)(inside cover shows White Rider & Superhorse #11)-r/cover/#7; origin White Rider &...; L. B. Cole-c	3.60	9.00	18.00
Accepted Reprint #8 (nd); L.B. Cole-c	3.60	9.00	18.00

INDOORS-OUTDOORS (See Wisco)

INDOOR SPORTS
nd (64 pgs.; 6x9"; B&W reprints; hardcover)
National Specials Co.

	GD25	FN65	NM94
nn-By Tad	4.35	13.00	26.00

INFERIOR FIVE, THE (Inferior 5 #11, 12) (See Showcase #62, 63, 65)
3-4/67 - No. 10, 9-10/68; No. 11, 8-9/72 - No. 12, 10-11/72
National Periodical Publications (#1-10: 12 cents)

	GD25	FN65	NM94
Showcase #62 (5-6/66)-Origin & 1st app.	5.00	15.00	46.00
Showcase #63,65 (7-8/66, 11-12/66)-2nd & 3rd app.	3.00	8.00	23.00
1-(3-4/67)-Sekowsky-a(p)	4.50	14.00	32.00
2-Plastic Man, F.F. app.; Sekowsky-a(p)	2.30	6.75	16.00
3-10: 4-Thor app. 6-Stars DC staff. 10-Superman x-over; F.F., Spider-Man & Sub-Mariner app.	1.65	4.70	11.00
11,12-Orlando-c/a; both r/Showcase #62,63	1.65	4.70	11.00

INFINITY CRUSADE
June, 1993 - No. 6, Nov, 1993 ($2.50, color, limited series)
Marvel Comics

Infinity, Inc. #15, © DC

Interface #9, © James Hudnall & Paul Johnson

Intimate Confessions #4, © REAL

GD25 FN65 NM94

1-6: By Jim Starlin & Ron Lim 1.00 2.50

INFINITY GAUNTLET (The... #2 on; see Infinity Crusade, The Infinity War & Warlock & the Infinity Watch)
July, 1991 - No. 6, Dec, 1991 ($2.50, color, limited series)
Marvel Comics

1-Thanos-c/stories in all; Starlin scripts in all 1.00 2.50 5.50
2 1.40 3.50
3-6: 5,6-Ron Lim-c/a 1.00 2.50
NOTE: *Lim a-3p(part), 5p, 6p; c-5i, 6i.* ***Perez*** *a-1-3p, 4p(part); c-1(painted), 2-4, 5i, 6i.*

INFINITY, INC. (See All-Star Squadron #25)
Mar, 1984 - No. 53, Aug, 1988 ($1.25, Baxter paper, 36 pgs.)
DC Comics

1-Brainwave, Jr., Fury, The Huntress, Jade, Northwind, Nuklon, Obsidian, Power Girl, Silver Scarab & Star Spangled Kid begin 1.50
2-5: 2-Dr. Midnite, G.A. Flash, W. Woman, Dr. Fate, Hourman, Green Lantern, Wildcat app. 5-Nudity panels 1.20
6-13,38-49,51-53: 46,47-Millennium tie-ins 1.20
14-Todd McFarlane-a (5/85, 2nd full story) 1.00 2.50
15-37-McFarlane-a (20,23,24: 5 pgs. only; 33: 2 pgs.); 18-24-Crisis x-over. 21-Intro new Hourman & Dr. Midnight. 26-New Wildcat app. 31-Star Spangled Kid becomes Skyman. 32-Green Fury becomes Green Flame. 33-Origin Obsidian .70 1.80
50 ($2.50, 52 pgs.) 1.00 2.50
Annual 1,2: 1(12/85)-Crisis x-over. 2('88, $2.00) .80 2.00
Special 1 (1987, $1.50) 1.50
NOTE: ***Kubert*** *r-4.* ***McFarlane*** *a-14-37p, Annual 1p; c(p)-14-19, 22, 25, 26, 31-33, 37, Annual 1.* ***Newton*** *a-12p, 13p(last work 4/85).* ***Tuska*** *a-11p. JSA app. 3-10.*

INFINITY WAR, THE (Also see Infinity Gauntlet & Warlock and the Infinity...)
June, 1992 - No. 6, Nov, 1992 ($2.50, color, mini-series)
Marvel Comics

1-Starlin scripts, Lim-c/a(p), Thanos app. in all 1.80 4.50
2-6: All have wraparound gatefold covers 1.00 2.50

INFORMER, THE
April, 1954 - No. 5, Dec, 1954
Feature Television Productions

1-Sekowsky-a begins 6.70 20.00 40.00
2 4.35 13.00 26.00
3-5 4.00 11.00 22.00

IN HIS STEPS (Spire Christiain)(Value: cover or less)

INHUMANOIDS, THE (TV) (Marvel)(Value: cover or less)

INHUMANS, THE (See Amazing Adventures, Fantastic Four #54 & Special #5, Incredible Hulk Special #1, Marvel Graphic Novel & Thor #146)
Oct, 1975 - No. 12, Aug, 1977
Marvel Comics Group

1: #1-4 are 25 cent issues 1.20 3.00
2-12: 9-Reprints Amazing Adventures #1,2('70) .65 1.60
Special 1(4/90, $1.50, 52 pgs.)-F.F. cameo .65 1.60
NOTE: ***Buckler*** *c-2-4p, 5.* ***Gil Kane*** *a-5-7p; c-1p, 7p, 8p.* ***Kirby*** *a-9r.* ***Mooney*** *a-11i.* ***Perez*** *a-1-4p, 8p.*

INKY & DINKY (See Felix's Nephews...)

IN LOVE (I Love You No. 7 on)
Aug-Sept, 1954 - No. 6, July, 1955 ('Adult Reading' on-c)
Mainline/Charlton No. 5 (5/55)-on

1-Simon & Kirby-a 14.00 43.00 100.00
2-S&K-a; book-length novel 10.00 30.00 60.00
3,4-S&K-a. 3-Last pre-code (12-1/54-55) 7.50 22.50 45.00
5-S&K-c only 4.35 13.00 26.00
6-No S&K-a 2.80 7.00 14.00

IN LOVE WITH JESUS
1952 (36 pages) (Giveaway)
Catechetical Educational Society

GD25 FN65 NM94

nn 2.80 7.00 14.00

INNOVATION SPECTACULAR (Innovation)(Value: cover or less)

INNOVATION SUMMER FUN SPECIAL (Innovation)(Value: cover or less)

INSANE (Dark Horse)(Value: cover or less)

IN SEARCH OF THE CASTAWAYS (See Movie Comics)

INSIDE CRIME (Formerly My Intimate Affair)
No. 3, July, 1950 - No. 2, Sept, 1950
Fox Features Syndicate (Hero Books)

3-Wood-a, 10 pgs.; L. B. Cole-c 13.00 40.00 90.00
2-Used in **SOTI**, pg. 182,183; r/Spook #24 10.00 30.00 70.00
nn(no publ. listed, nd) 5.00 15.00 30.00

INSPECTOR, THE (TV) (Also see The Pink Panther)
July, 1974 - No. 19, Feb, 1978
Gold Key

1 1.20 3.00 7.00
2-5 1.40 3.50
6-19: 11-Reprints .70 1.75

INSPECTOR GILL OF THE FISH POLICE (See Fish Police)

INSPECTOR WADE (See Feature Books #13)

INTERFACE (Epic)(Value: cover or less)

INTERNATIONAL COMICS (...Crime Patrol No. 6)
Spring, 1947 - No. 5, Nov-Dec, 1947
E. C. Comics

1-Schaffenberger-a begins, ends #4 50.00 150.00 350.00
2 36.00 107.00 250.00
3-5 30.00 90.00 210.00

INTERNATIONAL CRIME PATROL (Formerly International Comics #1-5; becomes Crime Patrol No. 7 on)
No. 6, Spring, 1948
E. C. Comics

6-Moon Girl app. 50.00 150.00 350.00

INTERSTATE THEATRES' FUN CLUB COMICS
Mid 1940's (10 cents on cover) (B&W cover) (Premium)
Interstate Theatres

Cover features MLJ characters looking at a copy of Top-Notch Comics, but contains an early Detective Comic on inside; many combinations possible 5.00 15.00 30.00

IN THE DAYS OF THE MOB (Magazine)
Fall, 1971 (Black & White)
Hampshire Dist. Ltd. (National)

1-Kirby-a; John Dillinger wanted poster inside 1.00 2.50 6.00

IN THE PRESENCE OF MINE ENEMIES (Spire Christian)(Value: cover or less)

INTIMATE (Teen-Age Love No. 4 on)
December, 1957 - No. 3, May, 1958
Charlton Comics

1-3 1.60 4.00 8.00

INTIMATE CONFESSIONS (See Fox Giants)

INTIMATE CONFESSIONS
July-Aug, 1951 - No. 7, Aug, 1952; No. 8, Mar, 1953 (All painted-c)
Realistic Comics

1-Kinstler-c/a; c/Avon paperback #222 50.00 150.00 350.00
2 10.00 30.00 60.00
3-c/Avon paperback #250; Kinstler-c/a 12.00 36.00 80.00
4-6,8: 4-c/Avon paperback #304; Kinstler-c. 6-c/Avon paperback #120. 8-c/Avon paperback #375; Kinstler-a 10.00 30.00 60.00
7-Spanking panel 10.00 30.00 70.00

INTIMATE CONFESSIONS
1964
I. W. Enterprises/Super Comics

Intimate Love #27, © STD

The Invaders #4 (mini Series), © MEG

Iron Man #38, © MEG

	GD25	FN65	NM94
I.W. Reprint #9,10	1.00	2.50	5.00
Super Reprint #12,18	1.00	2.50	5.00

INTIMATE LOVE
No. 5, 1950 - No. 28, Aug, 1954
Standard Comics

	GD25	FN65	NM94
5	4.00	12.00	24.00
6-8-Severin/Elder-a	4.70	14.00	28.00
9	2.40	6.00	12.00
10-Jane Russell, Robert Mitchum photo-c	4.70	14.00	28.00
11-18,20,23,25,27,28	1.80	4.50	9.00
19,21,22,24,26-Toth-a	5.00	15.00	30.00

NOTE: ***Celardo** a-8, 10. **Colletta** a-23. **Moreira** a-13(2). Photo-c-6, 7, 10, 12, 14, 15, 18-20, 24, 26, 27.*

INTIMATE SECRETS OF ROMANCE
Sept, 1953 - No. 2, April, 1954
Star Publications

	GD25	FN65	NM94
1,2-L. B. Cole-c	7.00	21.00	42.00

INTRIGUE
January, 1955
Quality Comics Group

	GD25	FN65	NM94
1-Horror; Jack Cole reprint/Web of Evil	14.00	43.00	100.00

INTRUDER (TSR)(Value; cover or less)

INVADERS, THE (TV)
Oct, 1967 - No. 4, Oct, 1968 (All have photo-c)
Gold Key

	GD25	FN65	NM94
1-Spiegle-a in all	5.00	15.00	35.00
2-4	3.60	10.75	25.00

INVADERS, THE (Also see The Avengers #71 & Giant-Size Invaders)
August, 1975 - No. 40, May, 1979; No. 41, Sept, 1979
Marvel Comics Group

	GD25	FN65	NM94
1-Captain America & Bucky, Human Torch & Toro, & Sub-Mariner begin; #1-7 are 25 cent issues	1.30	3.25	8.00
2-10: 2-1st app. Mailbag & Brain-Drain. 3-Battle issue; intro U-Man. 6-Liberty Legion app; two cover prices, 25 & 30 cents. 7-Intro Baron Blood & intro/1st app. Union Jack; Human Torch origin retold. 8-Union Jack-c/story. 9-Origin Baron Blood. 10-G.A. Capt. America-r/C.A #22	1.00	2.50	5.50
11-19: 11-Origin Spitfire; intro The Blue Bullet. 14-1st app. The Crusaders. 16-Re-intro The Destroyer. 17-Intro Warrior Woman. 18-Re-intro The Destroyer w/new origin. 19-Hitler-c/story		1.60	4.00
20-Reprints origin/1st app. Sub-Mariner from Motion Picture Funnies Weekly with color added & brief write-up about MPFW; 1st app. new Union Jack II	1.00	2.50	5.50
21-Reprints Marvel Mystery #10 (battle issue)		1.40	3.50
22,23,25-40: 22-New origin Toro. 25-All new-a begins. 28-Intro new Human Top & Golden Girl. 29-Intro Teutonic Knight. 31-Frankenstein-c/story. 32,33-Thor app. 34-Mighty Destroyer joins. 35-The Whizzer app.		1.00	2.50
24-r/Marvel Mystery #17 (team-up issue; all-r)		1.20	3.00
41-Double size last issue		1.20	3.00
Annual 1(9/77)-Schomburg, Rico stories (new); Schomburg-c/a (1st for Marvel in 30 years); Avengers app.; re-intro The Shark & The Hyena		1.20	3.00

NOTE: ***Buckler** a-5. **Everett** r-20('39), 21(1940), 24, Annual 1. **Gil Kane** c(p)-13, 17, 18, 20-27. **Kirby** c(p)-3-12, 14-16, 32, 33. **Mooney** a-5i, 16, 22. **Robbins** a-1-4, 6-9, 10(3 pg.), 11-15, 17-21, 23, 25-28; c-28.*

INVADERS (See Namor, the Sub-Mariner #12)
May, 1993 - No. 4, Aug, 1993 ($1.75, color, mini-series)
Marvel Comics Group

	GD25	FN65	NM94
1-4		.70	1.75

INVADERS FROM HOME (DC)(Value: cover or less)

INVASION
Holiday, 1988-'89 - No. 3, Jan, 1989 ($2.95, mini-series, 84 pgs.)
DC Comics

	GD25	FN65	NM94
1-McFarlane/Russell-a		1.20	3.00
2,3: 2-McFarlane/Russell-a		1.20	3.00

INVINCIBLE FOUR OF KUNGFU & NINJA (Leung)(Value: cover or less)

INVISIBLE BOY (See Approved Comics)

INVISIBLE MAN, THE (See Superior Stories #1 & Supernatural Thrillers #2)

INVISIBLE SCARLET O'NEIL (Also see Famous Funnies #81 & Harvey Comics Hits #59)
Dec, 1950 - No. 3, April, 1951
Famous Funnies (Harvey)

	GD25	FN65	NM94
1	10.00	30.00	65.00
2,3	7.50	22.50	45.00

IRON CORPORAL, THE (See Army War Heroes #22)
No. 23, Oct, 1985 - No. 25, Feb, 1986
Charlton Comics

	GD25	FN65	NM94
23-25: Glanzman-a(r)			1.00

IRON FIST (See Deadly Hands of Kung Fu, Marvel Premiere & Power Man)
Nov, 1975 - No. 15, Sept, 1977
Marvel Comics Group

	GD25	FN65	NM94
1-Iron Fist battles Iron Man (#1-6: 25 cent-c)	3.70	11.00	26.00
2	2.30	6.75	16.00
3-5	1.65	4.70	11.00
6-10: 8-Origin retold	1.30	3.25	8.00
11-13: 12-Capt. America app.	1.20	3.00	7.00
14-1st app. Sabretooth (8/77)(see Power Man)	14.00	43.00	100.00
15-X-Men app., Byrne-a (30 & 35 cents)	3.70	11.00	26.00

NOTE: ***Adkins** a-8p, 10i, 13i; c-8i. **Byrne** a-1-15p; c-8p, 15p. **G. Kane** c-4-6p. **McWilliams** a-1i.*

IRONHAND OF ALMURIC (Dark Horse)(Value: cover or less)

IRON HORSE (TV)
March, 1967 - No. 2, June, 1967
Dell Publishing Co.

	GD25	FN65	NM94
1,2	2.40	6.00	12.00

IRONJAW (Also see The Barbarians)
Jan, 1975 - No. 4, July, 1975
Atlas/Seaboard Publ.

	GD25	FN65	NM94
1-Neal Adams-c; Sekowsky-a(p)			1.50
2-4: 2-Neal Adams-c. 4-Origin			1.00

IRON MAN (Also see The Avengers #1, Giant-Size..., Marvel Collectors Item Classics, Marvel Double Feature, Marvel Fanfare & Tales of Suspense #39)
May, 1968 - Present
Marvel Comics Group

	GD25	FN65	NM94
1-Origin; Colan-c/a(p); story continued from Iron Man & Sub-Mariner #1	51.00	155.00	360.00
2	16.00	50.00	115.00
3	10.00	29.00	76.00
4,5	7.00	21.00	56.00
6-10: 9-Iron Man battles green Hulk-like android	5.00	16.00	42.00
11-15: 15-Last 12 cent issue	3.00	10.00	26.00
16-20	3.00	8.00	22.00
21-24,26-42: 22-Death of Janice Cord. 27-Intro Fire Brand. 33-1st app. Spymaster. 35-Nick Fury & Daredevil x-over. 42-Last 15 cent issue	2.00	6.00	16.00
25-Iron Man battles Sub-Mariner	3.00	8.00	21.00
43-Intro The Guardsman; 25 cent giant	2.00	6.00	16.00
44-46,48-50: 46-The Guardsman dies. 50-Princess Python app.	1.00	4.00	11.00
47-Origin retold; Barry Smith-a(p)	2.00	6.00	17.00
51-53: 53-Starlin part pencils	1.30	3.25	8.00

54-Iron Man battles Sub-Mariner; 1st app. Moondragon (1/73) as Madame

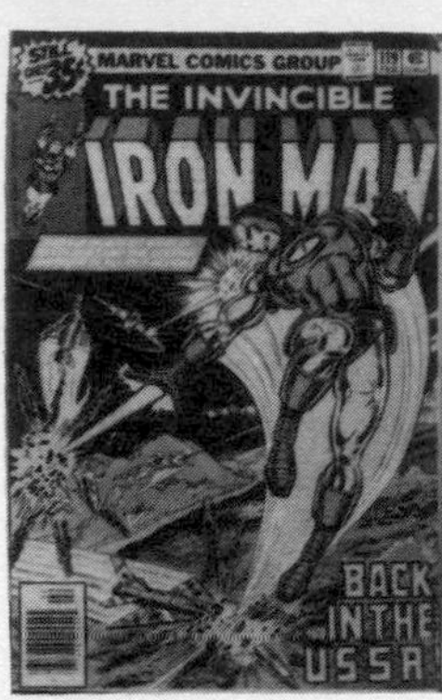

Iron Man #119, © MEG

Iron Man #296, © MEG

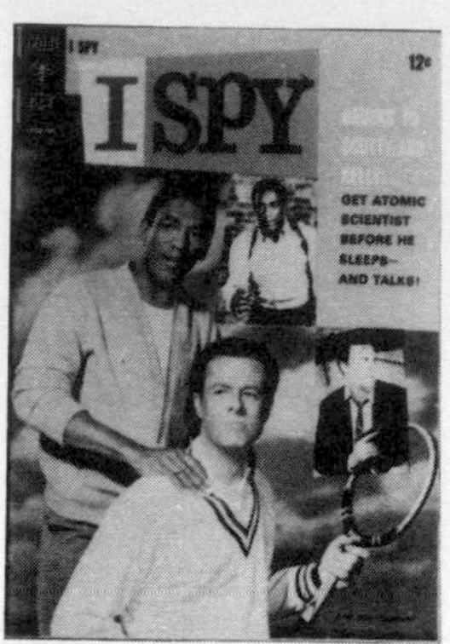

I Spy #2, © Three F Prod.

MacEvil; Everett part-c 2.00 5.00 14.00
55-1st app. Thanos, Drax the Destroyer, Mentor, Starfox & Kronos (2/73); Starlin-c/a 13.00 38.00 100.00
56-Starlin-a 3.00 8.00 20.00
57-67,69,70: 59-Firebrand returns. 65-Origin Dr. Spectrum. 66-Iron Man vs. Thor. 67-Last 20 cent issue 1.30 3.25 8.00
68-Starlin-c; origin retold 1.65 4.00 10.00
71-99: 72-Cameo portraits of N. Adams, Brunner. 76-r/#9. 86-1st app. Blizzard. 87-Origin Blizzard. 89-Last 25 cent issue. 96-1st app. new Guardsman 1.00 2.50 5.50
100-(7/77)-Starlin-c 1.65 4.00 10.00
101-117: 101-Intro DreadKnight. 109-1st app. new Crimson Dynamo; 1st app. Vanguard. 110-Origin Jack of Hearts retold 1.00 2.50 5.50
118-Byrne-a(p) 1.10 2.70 6.50
119,120,123-128-Tony Stark recovers from alcohol problem. 120,121-Sub-Mariner x-over. 125-Ant-Man app. 1.90 4.75
121,122,129-149: 122-Origin. 131,132-Hulk x-over 1.10 2.75
150-Double size 1.60 4.00
151-168: 152-New armor. 161-Moon Knight app. 167-Tony Stark alcohol problem starts again .80 2.50
169-New Iron Man (Jim Rhodes replaces Tony Stark) 1.50 3.75 9.00
170 1.80 4.50
171 1.30 3.25
172-199: 172-Captain America x-over. 186-Intro Vibro. 190-Scarlet Witch app. 191-198-Tony Stark returns as original Iron Man. 192-Both Iron Men battle .90 2.25
200-(11/85, $1.25, 52 pgs.)-Tony Stark returns as new Iron Man (red & white armor) thru #230 1.90 4.75
201-224: 213-Intro new Dominic Fortune. 214-Spider-Woman apps. in new black costume (1/87) .70 1.80
225-Double size ($1.25) 1.90 4.75
226-243,245-249: 228-Vs. Capt. America. 231-Intro new Iron Man. 233-Antman app. 234-Spider-Man x-over. 243-Tony Stark looses use of legs. 247-Hulk x-over .70 1.80
244-($1.50, 52 pgs.)-New Armor makes him walk 1.80 4.50
250-($1.50, 52 pgs.)-Dr. Doom-c/story .70 1.80
251-274,276-283,285-287,289,291-299,301,302: 258-277-Byrne scripts. 271-Fin Fang Foom app. 276-Black Widow-c/story; last $1.00-c 1.25
275-($1.50, 52 pgs.) 1.50
284-Death of Iron Man 1.00 2.00 5.00
288-($2.50, 52pg.)-Silver foil stamped-c; Iron Man's 350th app. in comics 1.00 2.50
290-($2.95, 52pg.)-Gold foil stamped-c; 30th ann. 1.20 3.00
300-($3.95, 68 pgs.)-Collector's Edition w/embossed foil-c; anniversary issue 1.60 4.00
300-($2.50, 68 pgs.)-Newsstand Edition .80 2.50
Special 1(8/70)-Sub-Mariner x-over; Everett-c 2.60 7.50 18.00
Special 2(11/71)-r/TOS #81,82,91 (all-r) 1.30 3.25 8.00
Annual 3(1976)-Man-Thing app. 1.60 4.00
King Size 4(8/77)-The Champions (w/Ghost Rider) app.; Newton-a(i) 1.20 3.00
Annual 5-9: 5(1982)-New-a. 6(1983)-New Iron Man(J. Rhodes) app. 7(1984). 8(1986)-X-Factor app. 9(1987) .80 2.00
Annual 10(1989, $2.00, 68 pgs.)-Atlantis Attacks x-over; P. Smith-a; Layton/Guice-a; Sub-Mariner app. 1.00 2.50
Annual 11,12 ($2.00, 68 pgs.): 11-(1990)-Origin of Mrs. Arbogast by Ditko (p&i). 12-(1991)-1 pg. origin recap; Ant-Man back-up story .80 2.00
Annual 13 (1992, $2.25, 68 pgs.)-Darkhawk & Avengers West Coast app.; Colan/Williamson-a 1.00 2.50
Annual 14 (1993, $2.95, 68 pgs.)-Bagged w/card 1.20 3.00
Manual 1 (1993, $1.75)-Operations handbook .70 1.75
Graphic Novel: Crash (1988, $12.95, Adults, 72 pgs?)-Computer generated art & color; violence & nudity 1.85 5.50 13.00

NOTE: ***Austin*** *c-105i, 109-111i, 151i.* ***Byrne*** *a-118p; c-109p, 253.* ***Colan*** *a-1p, 253, Special 1p(3); c-1p.* ***Craig*** *a-1i, 2-4, 5-13i, 14, 15-19i, 24p, 25p, 26-28i; c-2-4.* ***Ditko*** *a-160p.* ***Everett*** *c-29.* ***Guice*** *a-233-241p.* ***G. Kane*** *c(p)-52-54, 63, 67, 72-75, 77, 78, 88, 98.* ***Kirby*** *a-Special 1p; c-13, 80p, 90, 92-95.* ***Mooney*** *a-40i, 43i, 47i.* ***Perez*** *c-103p.* ***Simonson*** *c-Annual 8.* ***B. Smith*** *a-229, 232p, 243i; c-229, 232.* ***P. Smith*** *a-159p, 245p, Annual 10p; c-159.* ***Starlin*** *a-53p(part), 55p, 56p; c-55p, 160, 163.* ***Tuska*** *a-5-13p, 15-23p, 24i, 32p, 38-46p, 48-54p, 57-61p, 63-69p, 70-72p, 78p, 86-92p, 95-106p, Annual 4p.* ***Wood*** *a-Special 1i.*

IRON MAN & SUB-MARINER
April, 1968 (One Shot, 12¢) (Pre-dates Iron Man #1 & Sub-Mariner #1)
Marvel Comics Group

1-Iron Man story by Colan/Craig continued from Tales of suspense #99 & continued in Iron Man #1; Sub-Mariner story by Colan continued from Tales to Astonish #101 & continued in Sub-Mariner #1; Colan/Everett-c 22.00 66.00 155.00

IRON MARSHALL (Jademan)(Value: cover or less)

IRON VIC (See Comics Revue No. 3 & Giant Comics Editions)
1940; Aug, 1947 - No. 3, 1947
United Features Syndicate/St. John Publ. Co.

Single Series 22 21.00 63.00 145.00
2,3(St. John) 4.70 14.00 28.00

IRONWOLF (DC)(Value: cover or less)

ISIS (TV) (Also see Shazam)
Oct-Nov, 1976 - No. 8, Dec-Jan, 1977-78
National Periodical Publications/DC Comics

1-Wood inks 1.50
2-8: 5-Isis new look. 7-Origin 1.00

ISLAND AT THE TOP OF THE WORLD (See Walt Disney Showcase #27)

ISLAND OF DR. MOREAU, THE (Movie)
October, 1977 (52 pgs.)
Marvel Comics Group

1-Gil Kane-c 1.00

I SPY (TV)
Aug, 1966 - No. 6, Sept, 1968 (All have photo-c)
Gold Key

1-Bill Cosby, Robert Culp photo covers 16.00 50.00 115.00
2-6: 3,4-McWilliams-a 10.00 30.00 70.00

IS THIS TOMORROW?
1947 (One Shot) (3 editions) (52 pages)
Catechetical Guild

1-Theme of communists taking over the USA; (no price on cover) Used in **POP**, pg. 102 10.00 30.00 70.00
1-(10 cents on cover) 14.00 42.00 100.00
1-Has blank circle with no price on cover 14.00 42.00 100.00
Black & White advance copy titled "Confidential"-(52 pgs.)-Contains script and art edited out of the color edition, including one page of extreme violence showing mob nailing a Cardinal to a door; (only two known copies) 43.00 130.00 300.00

NOTE: *The original color version first sold for 10 cents. Since sales were good, it was later printed as a giveaway. Approximately four million in total were printed. The two black and white copies listed plus two other versions as well as a full color untrimmed version surfaced in 1979 from the Guild's old files in St. Paul, Minnesota.*

IT! (See Astonishing Tales No. 21-24 & Supernatural Thrillers No. 1)

ITCHY & SCRATCHY COMICS (Simpson's TV show)
1993 - Present ($1.95, color)
Bongo Comics

1-($2.25)-Bound-in jumbo poster .90 2.25
2 .80 2.00

IT HAPPENS IN THE BEST FAMILIES
1920 (52 pages) (B&W Sundays)
Powers Photo Engraving Co.

nn-By Briggs 13.00 40.00 90.00
Special Railroad Edition(30 cents)-r/strips from 1914-1920 11.00 32.00 75.00

IT REALLY HAPPENED

It's A Duck's Life #4, © MEG

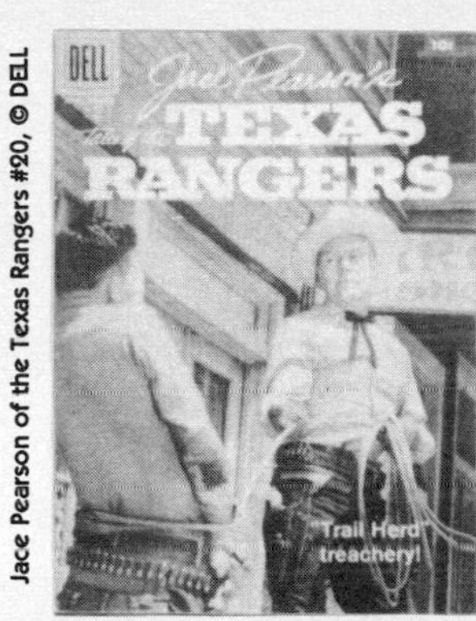

Jace Pearson of the Texas Rangers #20, © DELL

Jack Kirby's TeenAgents #1, © Jack Kirby

1944 - No. 11, Oct, 1947
William H. Wise No. 1,2/Standard (Visual Editions)

	GD25	FN65	NM94
1-Kit Carson & Ben Franklin stories	11.50	34.00	80.00
2	6.70	20.00	40.00
3,4,6,9	4.70	14.00	28.00
5-Lou Gehrig & Lewis Carroll stories	10.00	30.00	60.00
7-Teddy Roosevelt story	5.00	15.00	30.00
8-Story of Roy Rogers	11.00	32.00	75.00
10-Honus Wagner story	8.35	25.00	50.00
11-Baker-a	7.00	21.00	42.00

NOTE: ***Guardineer** a-7(2), 8(2), 11. **Schomburg** c-1-7, 9-11.*

IT RHYMES WITH LUST (Also see Bold Stories & Candid Tales)
1950 (Digest size) (128 pages)
St. John Publishing Co.

	GD25	FN65	NM94
nn (Rare)-Matt Baker & Ray Osrin-a	28.00	85.00	200.00

IT'S ABOUT TIME (TV)
January, 1967
Gold Key

	GD25	FN65	NM94
1 (10195-701)-Photo-c	3.30	10.00	23.00

IT'S A DUCK'S LIFE
Feb, 1950 - No. 11, Feb, 1952
Marvel Comics/Atlas(MMC)

	GD25	FN65	NM94
1-Buck Duck, Super Rabbit begin	10.00	30.00	60.00
2	5.00	15.00	30.00
3-11	4.00	10.00	20.00

IT'S FUN TO STAY ALIVE (Giveaway)
1948 (16 pgs.) (heavy stock paper)
National Automobile Dealers Association

	GD25	FN65	NM94
Featuring: Bugs Bunny, The Berrys, Dixie Dugan, Elmer, Henry, Tim Tyler, Bruce Gentry, Abbie & Slats, Joe Jinks, The Toodles, & Cokey; all art copyright 1946-48 drawn especially for this book.	14.00	43.00	100.00

IT'S GAMETIME
Sept-Oct, 1955 - No. 4, Mar-Apr, 1956
National Periodical Publications

	GD25	FN65	NM94
1-(Scarce)-Infinity-c; Davy Crockett app. in puzzle	54.00	160.00	375.00
2-4(Scarce): 2-Dodo & The Frog	45.00	135.00	315.00

IT'S LOVE, LOVE, LOVE
November, 1957 - No. 2, Jan, 1958 (10 cents)
St. John Publishing Co.

	GD25	FN65	NM94
1,2	3.00	7.50	15.00

IVANHOE (See Fawcett Movie Comics No. 20)

IVANHOE
July-Sept, 1963
Dell Publishing Co.

	GD25	FN65	NM94
1 (12-373-309)	4.00	10.00	20.00

IWO JIMA (See Spectacular Features Magazine)

JACE PEARSON OF THE TEXAS RANGERS (4-Color #396 is titled Tales of the Texas Rangers; ...'s Tales of ... #11-on)(See Western Roundup under Dell Giants)(Radio/TV)
No. 396, 5/52 - No. 1021, 8-10/59 (No #10) (All-Photo-c)
Dell Publishing Co.

	GD25	FN65	NM94
4-Color 396 (#1)	10.00	30.00	70.00
2(5-7/53) - 9(2-4/55)	5.85	17.50	35.00
4-Color 648(#10, 9/55)	5.85	17.50	35.00
11(11-2/55-56) - 14,17-20(6-8/58)	4.70	14.00	28.00
15,16-Toth-a	5.85	17.50	35.00
4-Color 961-Spiegle-a	5.00	15.00	30.00
4-Color 1021	4.70	14.00	28.00

NOTE: *Joel McCrea photo c-1-9, F.C. 648 (starred on radio show only); Willard Parker photo c-11-on (starred on TV series).*

JACK & JILL VISIT TOYTOWN WITH ELMER THE ELF
1949 (16 pgs.) (paper cover)
Butler Brothers (Toytown Stores Giveaway)

	GD25	FN65	NM94
nn	2.40	6.00	12.00

JACK ARMSTRONG (Radio)(See True Comics)
Nov, 1947 - No. 9, Sept, 1948; No. 10, Mar, 1949 - No. 13, Sept, 1949
Parents' Institute

	GD25	FN65	NM94
1	16.00	48.00	110.00
2	10.00	30.00	65.00
3-5	9.15	27.50	55.00
6-13	7.50	22.50	45.00
12-Premium version(distr. in Chicago only); Free printed on upper right-c; no price (Rare)	12.00	36.00	85.00

JACK HUNTER (Blackthorne)(Value: cover or less)

JACKIE GLEASON (TV) (Also see The Honeymooners)
1948 - No. 2, 1948; Sept, 1955 - No. 4, Dec, 1955?
St. John Publishing Co.

	GD25	FN65	NM94
1(1948)	57.00	171.00	400.00
2(1948)	46.00	140.00	325.00
1(1955)(TV)-Photo-c	47.00	141.00	330.00
2-4	32.00	95.00	225.00

JACKIE GLEASON AND THE HONEYMOONERS (TV)
June-July, 1956 - No. 12, Apr-May, 1958
National Periodical Publications

	GD25	FN65	NM94
1-1st app. Ralph Kramden	66.00	197.00	460.00
2	50.00	150.00	350.00
3-11	36.00	107.00	250.00
12 (Scarce)	55.00	165.00	385.00

JACKIE JOKERS (Became Richie Rich &...)
March, 1973 - No. 4, Sept, 1973 (#5 was advertised, but not published)
Harvey Publications

	GD25	FN65	NM94
1-4: 2-President Nixon app.			1.00

JACKIE ROBINSON (Famous Plays of...) (Also see Negro Heroes #2 & Picture News #4)
May, 1950 - No. 6, 1952 (Baseball hero) (All photo-c)
Fawcett Publications

	GD25	FN65	NM94
nn	57.00	171.00	400.00
2	37.00	110.00	260.00
3-6	29.00	85.00	220.00

JACK IN THE BOX (Formerly Yellowjacket Comics #1-10; becomes Cowboy Western Comics #17 on)
Feb, 1946; No. 11, Oct, 1946 - No. 16, Nov-Dec, 1947
Frank Comunale/Charlton Comics No. 11 on

	GD25	FN65	NM94
1-Stitches, Marty Mouse & Nutsy McKrow	9.15	27.50	55.00
11-Yellowjacket	10.00	30.00	60.00
12,14,15	4.00	12.00	24.00
13-Wolverton-a	12.00	36.00	85.00
16-12pg. adapt. of Silas Marner; Kiefer-a	6.70	20.00	40.00

JACK KIRBY'S SECRET CITY SAGA
No. 0, Apr, 1993; No. 1, 1993 - No. 4, 1993 ($2.95, color, mini-series)
Topps Comics

	GD25	FN65	NM94
0-(No cover price, 20 pgs.)-Simonson-c/a		1.80	2.00
1-4-Bagged w/3 trading cards. 1-Ditko/Art. Adams-c. #1-4 contain coupons redeemable for Kirbychrome version of #1		1.20	3.00

JACK KIRBY'S TEENAGENTS (See Satan's Six)
Aug, 1993 - No. 4, 1993 ($2.95, color, mini-series)
Topps Comics

	GD25	FN65	NM94
1-Polybagged with/3 trading cards; Austin-c(i)		1.20	3.00

JACK OF HEARTS (Also see The Deadly Hands of Kung Fu #22 & Marvel Premiere #44)

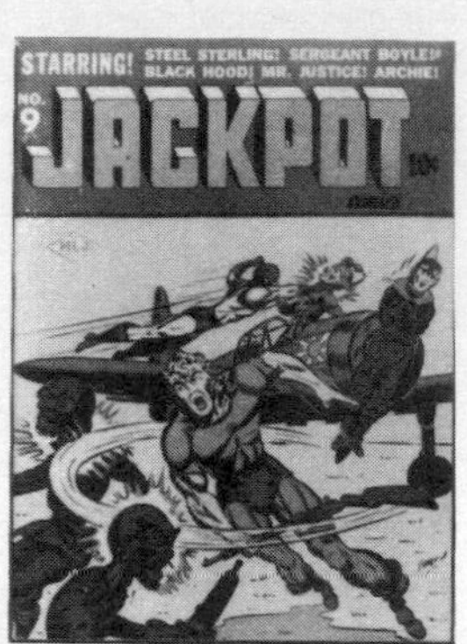

Jackpot Comics #9, © AP

Jann of the Jungle #10, © MEG

Jemm, Son of Saturn #3, © DC

	GD25	FN65	NM94

Jan, 1984 - No. 4, April, 1984 (60 cents, mini-series)
Marvel Comics Group

1-4			1.00

JACKPOT COMICS (Jolly Jingles #10 on)
Spring, 1941 - No. 9, Spring, 1943
MLJ Magazines

1-The Black Hood, Mr. Justice, Steel Sterling & Sgt. Boyle begin; Biro-c	150.00	450.00	1000.00
2-S. Cooper-c	73.00	218.00	500.00
3-Hubbell-c	58.00	175.00	400.00
4-Archie begins (Win/41; on sale 12/41)-(also see Pep Comics #22); 1st app. Mrs. Grundy, the principal; Novick-c	150.00	450.00	1000.00
5-Hitler-c by Montana; 1st definitive Mr. Weatherbee; 1st app. Reggie in 1 panel cameo	73.00	218.00	500.00
6-9: 6,7-Bondage-c by Novick. 8,9-Sahle-c	63.00	128.00	425.00

JACK Q FROST (See Unearthly Spectaculars)

JACK THE GIANT KILLER (See Movie Classics)

JACK THE GIANT KILLER (New Adventures of...)
Aug-Sept, 1953
Bimfort & Co.

V1#1-H. C. Kiefer-c/a	13.00	40.00	90.00

JACKY'S DIARY (See 4-Color No. 1091)

JADEMAN COLLECTION (Jademan)(Value: cover or less)

JADEMAN KUNG FU SPECIAL (Jademan)(Value: cover or less)

JAGUAR, THE (Also see The Adventures of...)
Aug, 1991 - No. 14, Oct, 1992 ($1.00, color)
Impact Comics (DC)

1-14: 4-The Black Hood x-over; 7-Sienkiewicz-c. 9-Contains Crusaders trading card			1.00
Annual 1 (1992, $2.50, 68 pgs.)-W/trading card		1.00	2.50

JAKE THRASH (Aircel)(Value: cover or less)

JAMBOREE
Feb, 1946(no mo. given) - No. 3, April, 1946
Round Publishing Co.

1-Funny animal	11.00	32.00	75.00
2,3	8.35	25.00	50.00

JAMES BOND: A SILENT ARMAGEDDON
Mar, 1993 - No. 4, 1993
Dark Horse Comics/Acme Comics

1-4		1.250	3.00

JAMES BOND FOR YOUR EYES ONLY
Oct, 1981 - No. 2, Nov, 1981
Marvel Comics Group

1,2-Movie adapt.; r-/Marvel Super Spec. #19			1.00

JAMES BOND JR. (TV)
Jan, 1992 - No. 12, Dec, 1992 (#1: $1.00, #2-on: $1.25, color)
Marvel Comics

1-12: Based on animated TV show			1.25

JAMES BOND: LICENCE TO KILL (See Licence To Kill)

JAMES BOND 007: SERPENT'S TOOTH
July, 1992 - No. 3, Sept, 1992 ($4.95, color, mini-series)
Acme Comics/Dark Horse Comics

1-3: Paul Gulacy-c/a	1.00	2.00	5.00

JAMES BOND: PERMISSION TO DIE
1989 - No. 3, 1991 ($3.95, color, mini-series, squarebound, 52 pgs.)
Eclipse Comics/ACME Press

1-3: Mike Grell-c/a/scripts in all. 3-($4.95)	1.00	2.00	5.00

	GD25	FN65	NM94

JAM: SUPER COOL COLOR INJECTED TURBO ADVENTURE #1 FROM HELL!, THE (Comico)(Value: cover or less)

JANE ARDEN (See Feature Funnies & Pageant of Comics)
March, 1948 - No. 2, June, 1948
St. John (United Features Syndicate)

1-Newspaper reprints	12.00	36.00	85.00
2	9.15	27.50	55.00

JANN OF THE JUNGLE (Jungle Tales No. 1-7)
No. 8, Nov, 1955 - No. 17, June, 1957
Atlas Comics (CSI)

8(#1)	14.00	43.00	100.00
9,11-15	8.35	25.00	50.00
10-Williamson/Colletta-c	9.15	27.50	55.00
16,17-Williamson/Mayo-a(3), 5 pgs. each	10.00	30.00	70.00

NOTE: ***Everett*** *c-15-17.* ***Heck*** *a-8, 15, 17.* ***Maneely*** *c-11.* ***Shores*** *a-8.*

JASON & THE ARGONAUTS (See Movie Classics)

JASON'S QUEST (See Showcase #88-90)

JAWS 2 (See Marvel Comics Super Special, A)

JCP FEATURES
Feb, 1982-c; Dec, 1981-indicia ($2.00, one-shot, B&W)
J.C. Productions (Archie)

1-T.H.U.N.D.E.R. Agents; Black Hood by Morrow & Neal Adams		.80	2.00

JEANIE COMICS (Formerly All Surprise; Cowgirl Romances #28)
No. 13, April, 1947 - No. 27, Oct, 1949
Marvel Comics/Atlas(CPC)

13-Mitzi, Willie begin	10.00	30.00	65.00
14,15	7.50	22.50	45.00
16-Used in Love and Death by Legman; Kurtzman's "Hey Look"	10.00	30.00	60.00
17-19,22-Kurtzman's "Hey Look," 1-3 pgs. each	6.70	20.00	40.00
20,21,23-27	5.00	15.00	30.00

JEEP COMICS (Also see G.I. Comics and Overseas Comics)
Winter, 1944 - No. 3, Mar-Apr, 1948
R. B. Leffingwell & Co.

1-Capt. Power, Criss Cross & Jeep & Peep (costumed) begin	14.00	43.00	100.00
2	10.00	30.00	65.00
3-L. B. Cole dinosaur-c	10.00	30.00	70.00
1-29(Giveaways)-Strip reprints in all; Tarzan, Flash Gordon, Blondie, The Nebbs, Little Iodine, Red Ryder, Don Winslow, The Phantom, Johnny Hazard, Katzenjammer Kids; distr. to U.S. Armed Forces in mid 1940's	4.00	10.00	20.00

JEFF JORDAN, U.S. AGENT
Dec, 1947 - Jan, 1948
D. S. Publishing Co.

1	8.35	25.00	50.00

JEMM, SON OF SATURN
Sept, 1984 - No. 12, Aug, 1985 (12 part maxi-series; mando paper)
DC Comics

1-12: Colan p-all; c-1-5p, 7-12p. 3-Origin			1.00

JERRY DRUMMER (Formerly Soldier & Marine V2#9)
V2#10, Apr, 1957 - V3#12, Oct, 1957
Charlton Comics

V2#10, V3#11,12: 11-Whitman-c/a	3.60	9.00	18.00

JERRY IGER'S... (All titles, Blackthorne/First)(Value: cover or less)

JERRY LEWIS (See The Adventures of...)

JESSE JAMES (See 4-Color No. 757 & The Legend of...)

JESSE JAMES (See Badmen of the West & Blazing Sixguns)

Jesse James #25, © AVON

Jet Aces #1, © FH

Jezebel Jade #1, © Hanna-Barbera

8/50 - No. 9, 11/52; No. 15, 10/53 - No. 29, 8-9/56
Avon Periodicals

	GD25	FN65	NM94
1-Kubert Alabam-r/Cowpuncher #1	12.00	36.00	85.00
2-Kubert-a(3)	10.00	30.00	70.00
3-Kubert Alabam-r/Cowpuncher #2	10.00	30.00	60.00
4,9-No Kubert	4.00	12.00	24.00
5,6-Kubert Jesse James-a(3); 5-Wood-a(1pg.)	10.00	30.00	60.00
7-Kubert Jesse James-a(2)	8.00	24.00	48.00
8-Kinstler-a(3)	5.35	16.00	32.00
15-Kinstler-r/#3	4.00	10.00	20.00
16-Kinstler-r/#3 & story-r/Butch Cassidy #1	4.00	11.00	22.00
17-19,21: 17-Jesse James-r/#4; Kinstler-c idea from Kubert splash in #6. 18-Kubert Jesse James-r/#5. 19-Kubert Jesse James-r/#6. 21-Two Jesse James-r/#4, Kinstler-r/#4	3.20	8.00	16.00
20-Williamson/Frazetta-a; r/Chief Vic. Apache Massacre; Kubert Jesse James-r/#6; Kit West story by Larsen	10.00	30.00	65.00
22,23-No Kubert	3.20	8.00	16.00
24-New McCarty strip by Kinstler; Kinstler-r	3.20	8.00	16.00
25-New McCarty Jesse James strip by Kinstler; Jesse James-r/#7,9	3.20	8.00	16.00
26,27-New McCarty Jesse James strip plus a Kinstler/McCann Jesse James-r	3.20	8.00	16.00
28,29: 28-Reprints most of Red Mountain, Featuring Quantrells Raiders	3.20	8.00	16.00
Annual nn (1952; 25¢, 100 pgs.)-"...Brings Six-Gun Justice to the West"-3 earlier issues rebound; Kubert, Kinstler-a(3)	19.00	58.00	135.00

NOTE: *Mostly reprints #10 on.* ***Fawcette*** *c-1, 2.* ***Kida*** *a-5.* ***Kinstler*** *a-3, 4, 7-9, 15r, 16r(2), 21-27; c-3, 4, 9, 17-27. Painted c-5, 6. 22 has 2 stories r/Sheriff Bob Dixon's Chuck Wagon #1 with name changed to Sheriff Bob Trent.*

JESSE JAMES
July, 1953
Realistic Publications

	GD25	FN65	NM94
nn-Reprints Avon's #1; same-c, colors different	6.70	20.00	40.00

JEST (Formerly Snap; becomes Kayo #12)
No. 10, 1944; No. 11, 1944
Harry 'A' Chesler

	GD25	FN65	NM94
10-Johnny Rebel & Yankee Boy app. in text	9.15	27.50	55.00
11-Little Nemo in Adventure Land	10.00	30.00	60.00

JESTER
No. 10, 1945
Harry 'A' Chesler

	GD25	FN65	NM94
10	8.35	25.00	50.00

JESUS (Spire Christian)(Value: cover or less)

JET (See Jet Powers)

JET ACES
1952 - No. 4, 1953
Fiction House Magazines

	GD25	FN65	NM94
1	9.15	27.50	55.00
2-4	5.00	15.00	30.00

JET DREAM (...& Her Stuntgirl Counterspies)(See The Man from Uncle #7)
June, 1968
Gold Key

	GD25	FN65	NM94
1	2.40	7.25	17.00

JET FIGHTERS (Korean War)
No. 5, Nov, 1952 - No. 7, Mar, 1953
Standard Magazines

	GD25	FN65	NM94
5,7-Toth-a. 5-Toth-c	8.35	25.00	50.00
6-Celardo-a	4.00	10.00	20.00

JET POWER
1963
I.W. Enterprises

	GD25	FN65	NM94
I.W. Reprint 1,2-r/Jet Powers #1,2	3.20	8.00	16.00

JET POWERS (American Air Forces No. 5 on)
1950 - No. 4, 1951
Magazine Enterprises

	GD25	FN65	NM94
1(A-1 #30)-Powell-c/a begins	22.00	67.00	155.00
2(A-1 #32)	16.00	48.00	110.00
3(A-1 #35)-Williamson/Evans-a	25.00	75.00	175.00
4(A-1 #38)-Williamson/Wood-a; "The Rain of Sleep" drug story	25.00	75.00	175.00

JET PUP (See 3-D Features)

JETSONS, THE (TV)(See March of Comics #276, 330, 348 & Spotlight #3)
Jan, 1963 - No. 36, Oct, 1970 (Hanna-Barbera)
Gold Key

	GD25	FN65	NM94
1	18.00	53.00	160.00
2	9.00	28.00	85.00
3-10	7.00	22.00	65.00
11-20	5.00	15.00	44.00
21-36	4.00	11.00	33.00

JETSONS, THE (TV)
Nov, 1970 - No. 20, Dec, 1973 (Hanna-Barbera)
Charlton Comics

	GD25	FN65	NM94
1	7.50	22.00	52.00
2	3.70	11.00	26.00
3-10	3.20	9.00	21.00
11-20	1.85	5.50	13.00

JETSONS, THE (TV)
V2#1, Sept, 1992 - Present ($1.25, color) (Hanna-Barbera)
Harvey Comics

	GD25	FN65	NM94
V2#1,2			1.25
...Big Book V2#1,2 ($1.95, 52 pgs.): 1-(11/92)		.80	2.00
...Giant Size 1,2 ($2.25, 68 pgs): 1-(10/92)		.90	2.25

JETTA OF THE 21ST CENTURY
No. 5, Dec, 1952 - No. 7, Apr, 1953 (Teen-age Archie type)
Standard Comics

	GD25	FN65	NM94
5	13.00	40.00	90.00
6,7	8.35	25.00	50.00

JEZEBEL JADE (Comico)(Value: cover or less)

JIGGS & MAGGIE (See 4-Color No. 18)

JIGGS & MAGGIE
No. 11, 1949(June) - No. 21, 2/53; No. 22, 4/53 - No. 27, 2-3/54
Standard Comics/Harvey Publications No. 22 on

	GD25	FN65	NM94
11	8.35	25.00	50.00
12-15,17-21	4.35	13.00	26.00
16-Wood text illos.	5.85	17.50	35.00
22-25,27: 22-24-Little Dot app.	4.00	10.00	20.00
26-Four pgs. partially in 3-D	11.00	32.00	75.00

NOTE: *Sunday page reprints by McManus loosely blended into story continuity. Based on Bringing Up Father strip. Advertised on covers as "All New."*

JIGSAW (Big Hero Adventures)
Sept, 1966 - No. 2, Dec, 1966 (36 pgs.)
Harvey Publications (Funday Funnies)

	GD25	FN65	NM94
1-Origin & 1st app.; Crandall-a, 5pgs.	1.25	3.00	7.50
2-Man From S.R.A.M.	1.00	2.50	5.50

JIGSAW OF DOOM (See Complete Mystery No. 2)

JIM BOWIE (Formerly Danger; Black Jack No. 20 on)
No. 15, 1955? - No. 19, April, 1957
Charlton Comics

	GD25	FN65	NM94
15	5.00	15.00	30.00
16-19	3.60	9.00	18.00

JIM BOWIE (See 4-Color No. 893, 993, & Western Tales)

Jimmy Wakely #11, © DC

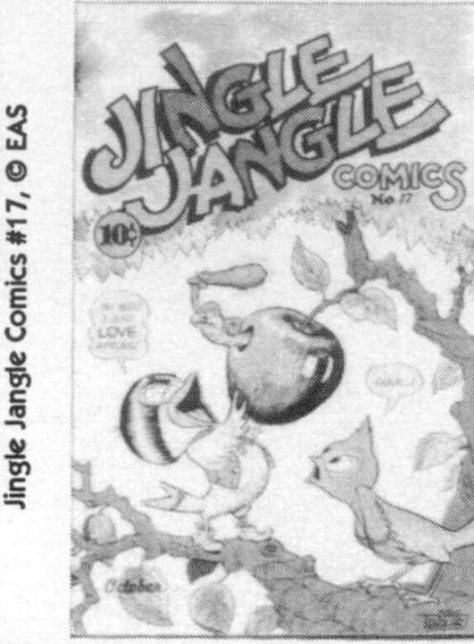

Jingle Jangle Comics #17, © EAS

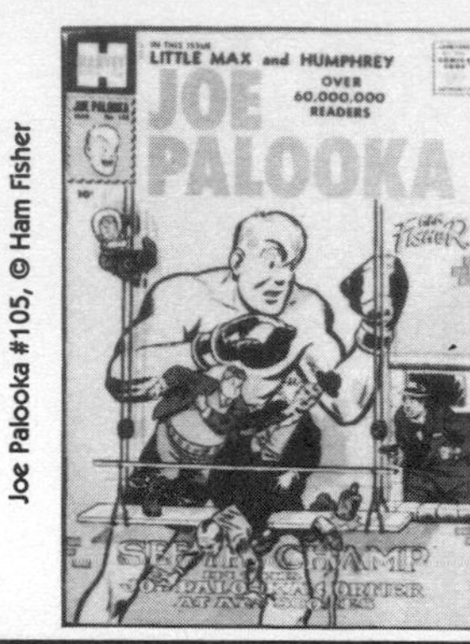

Joe Palooka #105, © Ham Fisher

JIM DANDY
May, 1956 - No. 3, Sept, 1956 (Charles Biro)
Dandy Magazine (Lev Gleason)

	GD25	FN65	NM94
1-Biro-c	4.70	14.00	28.00
2,3	3.20	8.00	16.00

JIM HARDY (See Giant Comics Eds., Sparkler & Treasury of Comics #2 & 5)
1939; 1942; 1947 - No. 2, 1947
United Features Syndicate/Spotlight Publ.

	GD25	FN65	NM94
Single Series 6 ('39)	29.00	85.00	200.00
Single Series 27('42)	22.00	67.00	155.00
1('47)-Spotlight Publ.	9.15	27.50	55.00
2	5.00	15.00	30.00

JIM HARDY
1944 (132 pages, 25 cents) (Tip Top, Sparkler-r)
Spotlight/United Features Syndicate

	GD25	FN65	NM94
(1944)-Origin Mirror Man; Triple Terror app.	33.00	100.00	215.00

JIMINY CRICKET (See 4-Color No. 701, 795, 897, 989, Mickey Mouse Mag. V5#3 & Walt Disney Showcase #37)

JIMMY (James Swinnerton)
1905 (10x15") (40 pages in color)
N. Y. American & Journal

	GD25	FN65	NM94
nn	36.00	110.00	250.00

JIMMY DURANTE (See A-1 Comics No. 18, 20)

JIMMY OLSEN (See Superman's Pal...)

JIMMY WAKELY (Cowboy movie star)
Sept-Oct, 1949 - No. 18, July-Aug, 1952 (1-13: 52pgs.)
National Periodical Publications

	GD25	FN65	NM94
1-Photo-c, 52 pgs. begin; Alex Toth-a; Kit Colby Girl Sheriff begins	57.00	170.00	400.00
2-Toth-a	36.00	110.00	250.00
3,6,7-Frazetta-a in all, 3 pgs. each; Toth-a in all. 7-Last photo-c	39.00	120.00	275.00
4-Frazetta-a, 3 pgs.; Kurtzman "Pot-Shot Pete," 1 pg; Toth-a	39.00	120.00	275.00
5,8-15,18-Toth-a; 12,14-Kubert-a, 3 & 2 pgs.	29.00	85.00	200.00
16,17	23.00	70.00	160.00

NOTE: *Gil Kane c-10-19p.*

JIM RAY'S AVIATION SKETCH BOOK
Mar-Apr, 1946 - No. 2, May-June, 1946
Vital Publishers

	GD25	FN65	NM94
1,2-Picture stories about planes and pilots	18.00	55.00	120.00

JIM SOLAR (See Wisco/Klarer)

JINGLE BELLS (See March of Comics No. 65)

JINGLE BELLS CHRISTMAS BOOK
1971 (20 pgs.; B&W inside; slick cover)
Montgomery Ward (Giveaway)

	GD25	FN65	NM94
nn		.80	2.00

JINGLE DINGLE CHRISTMAS STOCKING COMICS
V2#1, 1951 (no date listed) (100 pgs.; giant-size)(25 cents)
Stanhall Publications (Publ.-annually)

	GD25	FN65	NM94
V2#1-Foodini & Pinhead, Silly Pilly plus games & puzzles	11.00	32.00	75.00

JINGLE JANGLE COMICS (Also see Puzzle Fun Comics)
Feb, 1942 - No. 42, Dec, 1949
Eastern Color Printing Co.

	GD25	FN65	NM94
1-Pie-Face Prince of Old Pretzleburg, Jingle Jangle Tales by George Carlson, Hortense, & Benny Bear begin	29.00	85.00	200.00
2,3-No Pie-Face Prince	13.00	40.00	90.00
4-Pie-Face Prince cover	13.00	40.00	90.00
5	11.50	34.00	80.00
6-10: 8-No Pie-Face Prince	10.00	30.00	70.00
11-15	7.50	22.50	45.00
16-30: 17,18-No Pie-Face Prince. 30-XMas-c	5.85	17.50	35.00
31-42: 36,42-Xmas-c	4.35	13.00	26.00

NOTE: *George Carlson a-(2) in all except No. 2, 3, 8; c-1-6. Carlson 1 pg. puzzles in 9, 10, 12-15, 18, 20. Carlson illustrated a series of Uncle Wiggily books in 1930's.*

JING PALS
Feb, 1946 - No. 4, Aug?, 1946 (Funny animal)
Victory Publishing Corporation

	GD25	FN65	NM94
1-Wishing Willie, Puggy Panda & Johnny Rabbit begin	9.15	27.50	55.00
2-4	5.00	15.00	30.00

JINKS, PIXIE, AND DIXIE (See Kite Fun Book & Whitman Comic Books)

JOAN OF ARC (See A-1 Comics No. 21 & Ideal a Classical Comic)

JOAN OF ARC
No date (28 pages)
Catechetical Guild (Topix) (Giveaway)

	GD25	FN65	NM94
nn	9.15	27.50	55.00

NOTE: *Unpublished version exists which came from the Guild's files.*

JOE COLLEGE
Fall, 1949 - No. 2, Winter, 1950 (Teen-age humor, 52 pgs.)
Hillman Periodicals

	GD25	FN65	NM94
1,2-Powell-a; 1-Briefer-a	6.70	20.00	40.00

JOE JINKS (See Single Series No. 12)

JOE LOUIS (See Fight Comics #2, Picture News #6 & True Comics #5)
Sept, 1950 - No. 2, Nov, 1950 (Photo-c) (Boxing champ)(See Dick Cole #10)
Fawcett Publications

	GD25	FN65	NM94
1-Photo-c; life story	43.00	130.00	300.00
2-Photo-c	29.00	85.00	200.00

JOE PALOOKA
1933 (B&W daily strip reprints) (52 pages)
Cupples & Leon Co.

	GD25	FN65	NM94
nn-(Scarce)-by Fisher	71.00	215.00	500.00

JOE PALOOKA (1st Series)(Also see Big Shot Comics, Columbia Comics & Feature Funnies)
1942 - No. 4, 1944
Columbia Comic Corp. (Publication Enterprises)

	GD25	FN65	NM94
1-1st to portray American president; gov't permission required	50.00	150.00	350.00
2 (1943)-Hitler-c	31.00	92.00	215.00
3,4: 3-Nazi Sub-c	22.00	65.00	150.00

JOE PALOOKA (2nd Series) (Battle Adv. #68-74; ...Advs. #75, 77-81, 83-85, 87; Champ of the Comics #76, 82, 86, 89-93) (See All-New)
Nov, 1945 - No. 118, Mar, 1961
Harvey Publications

	GD25	FN65	NM94
1	39.00	120.00	275.00
2	17.00	52.00	120.00
3,4,6,7-1st Flyin' Fool, ends #25	10.00	30.00	70.00
5-Boy Explorers by S&K (7-8/46)	14.00	43.00	100.00
8-10	9.15	27.50	55.00
11-14,16-20: 19-Freedom Train-c	7.00	21.00	42.00
15-Origin & 1st app. Humphrey (12/47); Super heroine Atoma app. by Powell	10.00	30.00	70.00
21-30: 27-1st app. Little Max? (12/48). 30-Nude female painting	5.35	16.00	32.00
31-61: 35-Little Max-c/story. 36-Humphrey story. 39-Humphrey & Little Max begin (12/49). 41-Bing Crosby photo on-c. 44-Joe Palooka marries Ann Howe	4.00	12.00	24.00
62-S&K Boy Explorers-r	5.00	15.00	30.00
63-80: 66,67-'Commie' torture story	4.00	10.00	20.00

John Byrne's Next Men #16, © John Byrne

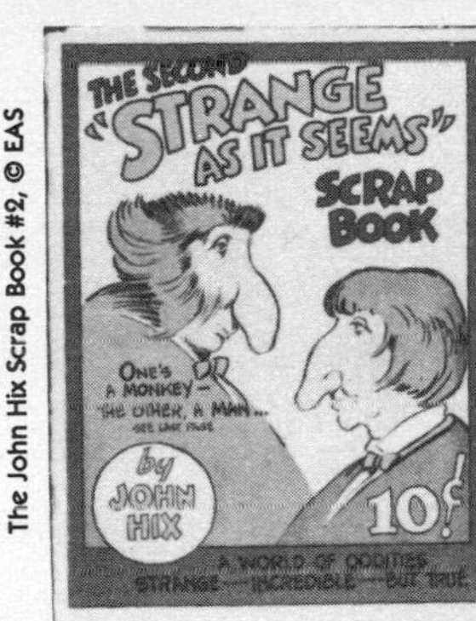

The John Hix Scrap Book #2, © EAS

Johnny Law, Sky Ranger #1, © LEV

	GD25	FN65	NM94
81-99,101-115	3.20	8.00	16.00
100	4.00	10.00	20.00
116-S&K Boy Explorers-r (Giant, '60)	5.00	15.00	30.00
117,118 Giants	4.00	12.50	25.00
...Body Building Instruction Book (1958 B&M Sports Toy giveaway, 16pgs., 5-1/4x7")-Origin	9.15	27.50	55.00
...Fights His Way Back (1945 Giveaway, 24 pgs.) Family Comics	16.00	48.00	110.00
...in Hi There! (1949 Red Cross giveaway, 12 pgs., 4-3/4x6")	8.35	25.00	50.00
...in It's All in the Family (1945 Red Cross giveaway, 16 pgs., regular size)	10.00	30.00	60.00
...**Visits the Lost City** nn (1945)(One Shot)(50 cents)-164 page continuous story strip reprint. Has biography & photo of Ham Fisher; possibly the single longest comic book story published (159 pgs.?)	93.00	280.00	650.00

NOTE: ***Nostrand/Powell** a-73. **Powell** a-7, 8, 10, 12, 14, 17, 19, 26-45, 47-53, 70, 73 at least. Black Cat text stories #8, 12, 13, 19.*

JOE YANK
No. 5, March, 1952 - No. 16, 1954
Standard Comics (Visual Editions)

	GD25	FN65	NM94
5-Celardo, Tuska-a	4.00	12.00	24.00
6-Toth, Severin/Elder-a	5.85	17.50	35.00
7	3.20	8.00	16.00
8-Toth-c	4.20	12.50	25.00
9-16: 9-Andru-c. 12-Andru-a	2.80	7.00	14.00

JOHN BOLTON'S HALLS OF HORROR (Eclipse)(Value: cover or less)

JOHN BYRNE'S NEXT MEN (See Dark Horse Presents #54)
Jan, 1992 - Present ($2.50, color)
Dark Horse Comics

	GD25	FN65	NM94
1-Silver foil embossed-c; Byrne-c/a/scripts in all	1.20	3.00	7.00
1-2nd printing with gold ink logo		1.40	3.50
0-(2/92)-r/chapters 1-4 from DHP w/new Byrne-c	1.00	2.00	5.00
2		1.40	3.50
3,4		1.20	3.00
5-22: 7-10-MA #1-4 mini-series on flip side. 16-Origin of Mark IV. 17-Miller-c. 19-Faith storyline begins, ends #22		1.00	2.50

NOTE: *Issues 1 through 6 contain certificates redeemable for an exclusive Next Men trading card set by Byrne. Prices are for complete books.*

JOHN CARTER OF MARS (See 4-Color #375, 437, 488, The Funnies & Tarzan #207)

JOHN CARTER OF MARS
April, 1964 - No. 3, Oct, 1964
Gold Key

	GD25	FN65	NM94
1(10104-404)-r/4-Color #375; Jesse Marsh-a	3.00	8.00	22.00
2(407), 3(410)-r/4-Color #437 & 488; Marsh-a	2.00	7.00	18.00

JOHN CARTER OF MARS
1970 (72 pgs.; paper cover; 10-1/2x16-1/2"; B&W)
House of Greystroke

	GD25	FN65	NM94
1941-42 Sunday strip reprints; John Coleman Burroughs-a	3.20	8.00	20.00

JOHN CARTER, WARLORD OF MARS (Also see Weird Worlds)
June, 1977 - No. 28, Oct, 1979
Marvel Comics Group

	GD25	FN65	NM94
1-17,19-28: 1-Origin. 11-Origin Dejah Thoris			1.00
18-Miller a(p)			1.50
Annuals 1-3: 1(1977). 2(1978). 3(1979)-All 52 pgs. with new book-length stories			1.00

NOTE: ***Austin** c-24i. **Gil Kane** a-1-10p; c-1p, 2p, 3, 4-9p, 10, 15p, Annual 1p. **Layton** a-17i. **Miller** c-25, 26p. **Nebres** a-2-4i, 8-16i; c(i)-6-9, 11-22, 25, Annual 1. **Perez** c-24p. **Simonson** a-15p. **Sutton** a-7i.*

JOHN F. KENNEDY, CHAMPION OF FREEDOM
1964 (no month) (25 cents)
Worden & Childs

	GD25	FN65	NM94
nn-Photo-c	7.00	21.00	42.00

JOHN F. KENNEDY LIFE STORY
Aug-Oct, 1964; Nov, 1965; June, 1966 (12 cents)
Dell Publishing Co.

	GD25	FN65	NM94
12-378-410-Photo-c	5.00	15.00	30.00
12-378-511 (reprint, 11/65)	4.00	10.00	20.00
12-378-606 (reprint, 6/66)	3.60	9.00	18.00

JOHN FORCE (See Magic Agent)

JOHN HIX SCRAP BOOK, THE
Late 1930's (no date) (68 pgs.; reg. size; 10 cents)
Eastern Color Printing Co. (McNaught Synd.)

	GD25	FN65	NM94
1-Strange As It Seems (resembles Single Series books)	22.00	65.00	150.00
2-Strange As It Seems	17.00	52.00	120.00

JOHN LAW DETECTIVE (Eclipse)(Value: cover or less)(See Smash Comics #3)

JOHNNY APPLESEED (See Story Hour Series)

JOHNNY CASH (See Hello, I'm...)

JOHNNY DANGER (See Movie Comics, 1946)
1950 (Based on movie serial)
Toby Press

	GD25	FN65	NM94
1-Photo-c; Sparling-a	10.00	30.00	70.00

JOHNNY DANGER PRIVATE DETECTIVE
1954 (Reprinted in Danger #11 by Super)
Toby Press

	GD25	FN65	NM94
1-Opium den story	9.15	27.50	55.00

JOHNNY DYNAMITE (Formerly Dynamite #1-9; Foreign Intrigues #13 on)
No. 10, June, 1955 - No. 12, Oct, 1955
Charlton Comics

	GD25	FN65	NM94
10-12	4.70	14.00	28.00

JOHNNY HAZARD
No. 5, Aug, 1948 - No. 8, May, 1949; No. 35, date?
Best Books (Standard Comics) (King Features)

	GD25	FN65	NM94
5-Strip reprints by Frank Robbins (c/a)	10.00	30.00	65.00
6,8-Strip reprints by Frank Robbins	7.50	22.50	45.00
7-New art, not Robbins	5.85	17.50	35.00
35	5.85	17.50	35.00

JOHNNY JASON (...Teen Reporter)
Feb-Apr, 1962 - No. 2, June-Aug, 1962
Dell Publishing Co.

	GD25	FN65	NM94
4-Color 1302, 2(01380-208)	2.80	7.00	14.00

JOHNNY JINGLE'S LUCKY DAY
1956 (16 pgs.; 7-1/4x5-1/8") (Giveaway) (Disney)
American Dairy Association

	GD25	FN65	NM94
nn	3.60	9.00	18.00

JOHNNY LAW, SKY RANGER
Apr, 1955 - No. 3, Aug, 1955; No. 4, Nov, 1955
Good Comics (Lev Gleason)

	GD25	FN65	NM94
1-Edmond Good-c/a	5.00	15.00	30.00
2-4	3.60	9.00	18.00

JOHNNY MACK BROWN (TV western star; see Western Roundup under Dell Giants)
No. 269, Mar, 1950 - No. 963, Feb, 1959 (All Photo-c)
Dell Publishing Co.

	GD25	FN65	NM94
4-Color 269(#1)(3/50, 52pgs.)-Johnny Mack Brown & his horse Rebel begin; photo front/back-c begin; Marsh-a begins, ends #9	19.00	58.00	135.00
2(10-12/50, 52pgs.)	10.00	30.00	70.00
3(1-3/51, 52pgs.)	9.15	27.50	55.00

Johnny Thunder #2, © DC

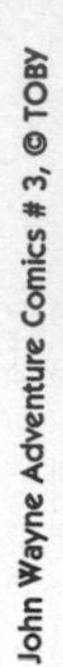
John Wayne Adventure Comics # 3, © TOBY

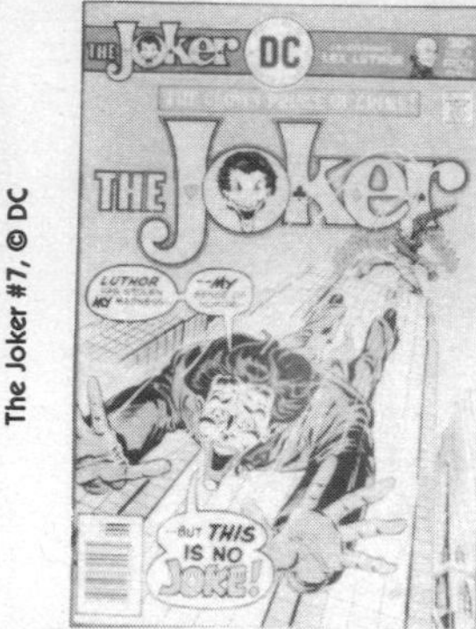

The Joker #7, © DC

GD25 FN65 NM94

4-10 (9-11/52)(36pgs.) 5.85 17.50 35.00
4-Color 455,493,541,584,618 5.85 17.50 35.00
4-Color 645,685,722,776,834,963 5.85 17.50 35.00
4-Color 922-Manning-a 6.70 20.00 40.00

JOHNNY NEMO
Sept, 1985 - No. 3, Feb, 1986 (Mini-series)
Eclipse Comics
1,2 ($1.75 cover) .70 1.80
3 ($2.00 cover) .80 2.00

JOHNNY PERIL (See Comic Cavalcade #15, Sensation #107 & Sensation Mystery)

JOHNNY RINGO (See 4-Color No. 1142)

JOHNNY STARBOARD (See Wisco)

JOHNNY THUNDER
Feb-Mar, 1973 - No. 3, July-Aug, 1973
National Periodical Publications
1-3: Johnny Thunder & Nighthawk-r. 2-Trigger Twins app. 1.00
NOTE: *All contain 1950s DC reprints from All-American Western.* ***Drucker*** *r-2, 3.* ***G. Kane*** *r-2, 3.* ***Moriera*** *r-1.* ***Toth*** *r-1, 3; c-1r, 3r. Also see All-American, All-Star Western, Flash Comics, Western Comics, World's Best & World's Finest.*

JOHN PAUL JONES (See Four Color No. 1007)

JOHN STEED & EMMA PEEL (See The Avengers, Gold Key series)

JOHN STEELE SECRET AGENT (Also see Freedom Agent)
December, 1964 (Freedom Agent)
Gold Key
1 9.00 26.00 62.00

JOHN WAYNE ADVENTURE COMICS (Movie star; See Big Tex, Oxydol-Dreft, Tim McCoy & With The Marines...#1)
Winter, 1949-50 - No. 31, May, 1955 (Photo-c: 1-12,17,25-on)
Toby Press
1 (36pgs.)-Photo-c begin 62.00 185.00 435.00
2 (36pgs.)-Williamson/Frazetta-a(2) 6 & 2 pgs. (one story-r/Billy the Kid #1); photo back-c 45.00 135.00 315.00
3 (36pgs.)-Williamson/Frazetta-a(2), 16 pgs. total; photo back-c 45.00 135.00 315.00
4 (52pgs.)-Williamson/Frazetta-a(2), 16 pgs. total 45.00 135.00 315.00
5 (52pgs.)-Kurtzman-a-(Alfred "L" Newman in Potshot Pete) 32.00 95.00 225.00
6 (52pgs.)-Williamson/Frazetta-a, 10 pgs; Kurtzman a-'Pot-Shot Pete,' 5pgs.; & "Genius Jones," 1 pg. 44.00 133.00 310.00
7 (52pgs.)-Williamson/Frazetta-a, 10 pgs. 36.00 107.00 250.00
8 (36pgs.)-Williamson/Frazetta-a(2), 12 & 9 pgs. 44.00 133.00 310.00
9-11: Photo western-c 24.00 72.00 165.00
12,14-Photo war-c. 12-Kurtzman-a, 2 pgs. "Genius" 24.00 72.00 165.00
13,15: 13,15-Line-drawn-c begin, end #24 21.00 63.00 145.00
16-Williamson/Frazetta-r/Billy the Kid #1 22.00 67.00 155.00
17-Photo-c 24.00 72.00 165.00
18-Williamson/Frazetta-a (r/#4 & 8, 19 pgs.) 26.00 77.00 180.00
19-24: 23-Evans-a? 18.00 55.00 128.00
25-Photo-c resume; end #31; Williamson/Frazetta-r/Billy the Kid #3 26.00 77.00 180.00
26-28,30-Photo-c 22.00 67.00 155.00
29,31-Williamson/Frazetta-a in each (r/#4, 2) 24.00 72.00 165.00
NOTE: *Williamsonish art in later issues by* ***Gerald McCann.***

JO-JO COMICS (...Congo King #7-29; My Desire #30 on)
(Also see Fantastic Fears and Jungle Jo)
1945 - No. 29, July, 1949 (two No.7's; no No. 13)
Fox Feature Syndicate
nn(1945)-Funny animal, humor 10.00 30.00 60.00
2(Sum,'46)-6(4-5/47): Funny animal. 2-Ten pg. Electro story (Fall/46) 5.00 15.00 30.00
7(7/47)-Jo-Jo, Congo King begins (1st app.); Bronze Man & Purlpe Tigress app. 39.00 120.00 275.00
7(#8) (9/47) 29.00 85.00 200.00
8-10(#9-11): 8-Tanee begins 24.00 72.00 165.00
11,12(#12,13),14,16: 11,16-Kamen bondage-c 20.00 60.00 140.00
15-Cited by Dr. Wertham in 5/47 Saturday Review of Literature 22.00 65.00 150.00
17-Kamen bondage-c 22.00 65.00 150.00
18-20 20.00 60.00 140.00
21-29: 21-Hollingsworth-a(4 pgs.; 23-1 pg.) 19.00 57.00 130.00
NOTE: *Many bondage-c/a by* ***Baker/Kamen/Feldstein/Good.*** *No. 7's have Princesses Gwenna, Geesa, Yolda, & Safra before settling down on Tanee.*

JO-JOY (The Adventures of...)
1945 - 1953 (Christmas gift comic, 16 pgs., 7-1/16x10-1/4")
W. T. Grant Dept. Stores
1945-53 issues 4.00 10.00 20.00

JOKEBOOK COMICS DIGEST ANNUAL (...Magazine No. 5 on)
Oct, 1977 - No. 13, Oct, 1983 (Digest Size)
Archie Publications
1(10/77)-Reprints; Neal Adams-a 1.20 3.00
2(4/78)-13 1.20 3.00

JOKER, THE (See Batman #1, Batman: The Killing Joke, Brave & the Bold, Detective, Greatest Joker Stories & Justice League Annual #2)
May, 1975 - No. 9, Sept-Oct, 1976
National Periodical Publications
1-Two-Face app. 1.65 4.70 11.00
2,3: 3-The Creeper app. 1.25 3.00 7.50
4-6: 4-Green Arrow-c/s. 6-Sherlock Holmes-c/s 1.00 2.50 5.50
7-9: 7-Lex Luthor-c/story. 8-Scarecrow-c/story. 9-Catwoman-c/story 1.00 2.00 5.00

JOKER COMICS (Adventures Into Terror No. 43 on)
April, 1942 - No. 42, August, 1950
Timely/Marvel Comics No. 36 on (TCI/CDS)
1-(Rare)-Powerhouse Pepper (1st app.) begins by Wolverton; Stuporman app. from Daring 121.00 365.00 850.00
2-Wolverton-a; 1st app. Tessie the Typist & begin series 50.00 150.00 350.00
3-5-Wolverton-a 34.00 100.00 235.00
6-10-Wolverton-a. 6-Tessie-c begin 24.00 72.00 165.00
11-20-Wolverton-a 19.00 58.00 135.00
21,22,24-27,29,30-Wolverton cont'd. & Kurtzman's "Hey Look" in #24-27 16.00 48.00 110.00
23-1st "Hey Look" by Kurtzman; Wolverton-a 17.00 52.00 120.00
28,32,34,37-41: 28-Millie the Model begins. 32-Hedy begins. 41-Nellie the Nurse app. 4.70 14.00 28.00
31-Last Powerhouse Pepper; not in #28 11.00 32.00 75.00
33,35,36-Kurtzman's "Hey Look" 6.70 20.00 40.00
42-Only app. 'Patty Pinup,' a clone of Millie the Model 5.85 17.50 35.00

JOLLY CHRISTMAS, A (See March of Comics No. 269)

JOLLY CHRISTMAS BOOK (See Christmas Journey Through Space)
1951; 1954; 1955 (36 pgs.; 24 pgs.)
Promotional Publ. Co.
1951-(Woolworth giveaway)-slightly oversized; no slick cover; Marv Levy-c/a 5.00 15.00 30.00
1954-(Hot Shoppes giveaway)-regular size-reprints 1951 issue; slick cover added; 24 pgs.; no ads 5.00 15.00 30.00
1955-(J. M. McDonald Co. giveaway)-reg. size 4.00 10.00 20.00

JOLLY COMICS
1947
Four Star Publishing Co.
1 5.35 16.00 32.00

JOLLY JINGLES (Formerly Jackpot Comics)
No. 10, Sum, 1943 - No. 16, Wint, 1944/45

Jonah Hex: Two-Gun Mojo #2, © DC

Jonny Quest #8 (Comico), © Hanna-Barbera

Journey Into Mystery #22, © MEG

	GD25	FN65	NM94
MLJ Magazines			
10-Super Duck begins (origin & 1st app.); Woody The Woodpecker begins (not same as Lantz character)	25.00	75.00	175.00
11 (Fall, '43)-2nd Super Duck(see Hangman #8)	12.00	36.00	85.00
12-Hitler-c	10.00	30.00	65.00
13-16	8.35	25.00	50.00

JONAH HEX (See All-Star Western, Hex and Weird Western Tales)
Mar-Apr, 1977 - No. 92, Aug, 1985
National Periodical Publications/DC Comics

	GD25	FN65	NM94
1	4.30	13.00	30.00
2-6,9,10: 9-Wrightson-c	1.40	3.50	8.50
7,8-Explains Hex's face disfigurement	1.40	3.50	8.50
11-20: 12-Starlin-c		1.90	4.75
21-50: 31,32-Origin retold		1.50	3.75
51-92: 92-Story continued in Hex #1		1.10	2.75

NOTE: ***Ayers** a(p)-35-37, 40, 41, 44-53, 56, 58-82. **Kubert** c-43-46. **Morrow** a-90-92; c-10. **Spiegle(Tothish)** a-34, 38, 40, 49, 52. Batlash back-ups in 49, 52. El Diablo back-ups in 48, 56-60, 73-75. Scalphunter back-ups in 40, 41, 45-47.*

JONAH HEX AND OTHER WESTERN TALES (Blue Ribbon Digest)
Sept-Oct, 1979 - No. 3, Jan-Feb, 1980 (100 pgs.)
DC Comics

	GD25	FN65	NM94
1-3: 1-Origin Scalphunter-r; painted-c. 2-Weird Western Tales-r; Neal Adams, Toth, Aragones, Gil Kane-a			1.00

JONAH HEX SPECTACULAR (See DC Special Series No. 16)

JONAH HEX: TWO-GUN MOJO
Aug, 1993 - No. 5, Dec, 1993 ($2.95, color, mini-series)
DC Comics (Vertigo)

	GD25	FN65	NM94
1-Truman/Glanzman-a in all w/Truman-c	1.10	2.70	6.50
1-Silver ink edition with no price on cover	1.65	4.70	11.00
2-5		1.60	4.00

JONESY (Formerly Crack Western)
No. 85, Aug, 1953; No. 2, Oct, 1953 - No. 8, Oct, 1954
Comic Favorite/Quality Comics Group

	GD25	FN65	NM94
85(#1)-Teen-age humor	4.20	12.50	25.00
2	3.20	8.00	16.00
3-8	2.00	5.00	10.00

JON JUAN (Also see Great Lover Romances)
Spring, 1950
Toby Press

	GD25	FN65	NM94
1-All Schomburg-a (signed Al Reid on-c); written by Siegel; used in **SOTI**, pg. 38	14.00	43.00	100.00

JONNI THUNDER (...A.K.A. Thunderbolt)
Feb, 1985 - No. 4, Aug, 1985 (75 cents, mini-series)
DC Comics

	GD25	FN65	NM94
1-4: 1-Origin & 1st app.			1.00

JONNY QUEST (TV)
December, 1964 (Hanna-Barbera)
Gold Key

	GD25	FN65	NM94
1 (10139-412)	23.00	68.00	225.00

JONNY QUEST (TV) (Comico)(Value: cover or less)

JONNY QUEST CLASSICS (TV) (First)(Value: cover or less)

JON SABLE, FREELANCE (First)(Value: cover or less)

JOSEPH & HIS BRETHREN (See The Living Bible)

JOSIE (She's... #1-16) (...& the Pussycats #45 on) (See Archie Giant Series Magazine #528, 540, 551, 562, 571, 584, 597, 610, 622)
Feb, 1963 - No. 106, Oct, 1982
Archie Publications/Radio Comics

	GD25	FN65	NM94
1	13.00	40.00	90.00
2	7.50	22.50	45.00
3-5	4.20	12.50	25.00
6-10	3.60	9.00	18.00
11-20	2.80	7.00	14.00
21-30: 22-Mighty Man & Mighty (Josie Girl) app.	1.60	4.00	8.00
31-54	1.00	2.00	5.00
55-74(52pg. issues)		.80	2.00
75-106			1.50

JOURNAL OF CRIME (See Fox Giants)

JOURNEY (Also see Journey: Wardrums)
1983 - No. 14, 9/84; No. 15, 4/85 - No. 27, 7/86 (B&W)
Aardvark-Vanaheim #1-14/Fantagraphics Books #15-on

	GD25	FN65	NM94
1	1.00	2.00	5.00
2		1.20	3.00
3-27: 20-Sam Kieth-a			1.50

JOURNEY INTO FEAR
May, 1951 - No. 21, Sept, 1954
Superior-Dynamic Publications

	GD25	FN65	NM94
1-Baker-r(2)	25.00	75.00	175.00
2	15.00	45.00	105.00
3,4	12.00	36.00	85.00
5-10,15: 15-Used in **SOTI**, pg. 389	10.00	30.00	65.00
11-14,16-21	9.15	27.50	55.00

NOTE: *Kamenish 'headlight'-a most issues. **Robinson** a-10.*

JOURNEY INTO MYSTERY (1st Series) (Thor No. 126 on)
6/52 - No. 48, 8/57; No. 49, 11/58 - No. 125, 2/66
Atlas(CPS No. 1-48/AMI No. 49-68/Marvel No. 69 (6/61) on)

	GD25	FN65	NM94
1	100.00	300.00	1200.00
2	63.00	190.00	500.00
3,4	47.00	140.00	375.00
5-11	28.00	84.00	225.00
12-20,22: 22-Davisesque-a; last pre-code issue (2/55)	23.00	69.00	180.00
21-Kubert-a; Tothish-a by Andru	24.00	71.00	190.00
23-32,35-38,40. 24-Torres?-a	14.00	41.00	110.00
33-Williamson-a	16.00	48.00	125.00
34,39: 34-Krigstein-a. 39-Wood-a	14.00	43.00	115.00
41-Crandall-a; Frazettaesque-a by Morrow	11.00	34.00	90.00
42,48-Torres-a	11.00	34.00	90.00
43,44-Williamson/Mayo-a in both	13.00	38.00	100.00
45,47,52,53	10.00	30.00	80.00
46-Torres & Krigstein-a	12.00	36.00	95.00
49-Matt Fox, Check-a	13.00	38.00	100.00
50,54: 50-Davis-a. 54-Williamson-a	8.00	24.00	80.00
51-Kirby/Wood-a	9.50	29.00	95.00
55-61,63-65,67-69,71,72,74,75: 58-Ad for Fantastic Four #1-c. 74-Contents change to Fantasy. 75-Last 10 cent issue	8.50	26.00	85.00
62-Prototype ish. (The Hulk)-1st app. Xemnu (Titan) called "The Hulk"	13.00	40.00	130.00
66-Prototype ish. (The Hulk)-Return of Xemnu "The Hulk"	11.00	33.00	110.00
70-Prototype ish. (The Sandman)(7/61); similar to Spidey villain	10.00	30.00	100.00
73-Prototype ish. (Spider-Man)	13.00	40.,00	130.00
76,77,80-82: 80-Anti-communist propaganda story	7.50	23.00	75.00
78-The Sorceror (Dr. Strange prototype) app. (3/62)	12.00	36.00	120.00
79-Prototype ish. (Mr. Hyde)	10.00	30.00	100.00

	GD25	FN65	VF82	NM94
83-Origin & 1st app. The Mighty Thor by Kirby (8/62) and begin series; Thor-c also begin	273.00	820.00	1640.00	2730.00

	GD25	FN65	NM94
83-Reprint from the Golden Record Comic Set	8.00	24.00	65.00
with the record (1966)	16.00	49.00	130.00
84-2nd app. Thor	78.00	234.00	625.00

Journey Into Mystery #101, © MEG

Journey Into Unknown Worlds #49, © MEG

Judgement Day #2, © Joseph A. Zyskowski

GD25 FN65 NM94

85-1st app. Loki & Heimdall; Odin cameo (1 panel) 43.00 128.00 340.00
86-1st full app. Odin 30.00 90.00 240.00
87-89: 89-Reprints origin Thor from #83 20.00 60.00 160.00
90-No Kirby-a 13.00 38.00 100.00
91,92,94-96-Sinnott-a 11.00 34.00 90.00
93,97-Kirby-a; Tales of Asgard series begins #97 (origin which concludes in #99) 14.00 43.00 115.00
98-100-Kirby/Heck-a. 98-Origin/1st app. The Human Cobra. 99-1st app. Surtur & Mr. Hyde 10.00 30.00 80.00
101-108,110: 102-Intro Sif. 103-1st app. Enchantress. 105-109-Ten extra pgs. Kirby-a in each. 107-1st app. Grey Gargoyle. 108-(9/64)-Early Dr. Strange & Avengers x-over. 7.00 20.00 52.00
109-Magneto-c & app. (10/64) 9.00 28.00 75.00
111,113,114,116-125: 118-1st app. Destroyer. 119-Intro Hogun, Fandrall, Volstagg. 124-Hercules-c/story 6.00 18.00 48.00
112-Thor Vs. Hulk (1/65). 112,113-Origin Loki 14.00 43.00 115.00
115-Detailed origin Loki 7.00 21.00 55.00
Annual 1('65, 25 cents, 72 pgs.)-New Thor vs. Hercules-c/story (see The Incredible Hulk #3); Kirby-c/a; r/#85,93,95,97 13.00 38.00 100.00

NOTE: ***Ayers*** *a-14, 39, 64i, 71i, 74i, 80i.* ***Bailey*** *a-43.* ***Briefer*** *a-5, 12.* ***Cameron*** *a-35.* ***Check*** *a-17.* ***Colan*** *a-23, 81; c-14.* ***Ditko*** *a-33, 38, 50-96; c-71, 88i.* ***Ditko/Kirby*** *a-50-83.* ***Everett*** *a-20, 48; c-4-7, 9, 36, 37, 39-42, 44, 45, 47.* ***Forte*** *a-19, 35, 40, 53.* ***Heath*** *a-4-6, 11, 14; c-1, 8, 11, 15, 51.* ***Heck*** *a-53, 73.* ***Kirby*** *a(p)-51, 52, 56, 57, 60, 62, 64, 66, 69, 71-74, 76, 79, 80-89, 93, 97, 98, 100(w/****Heck****), 101-125; c-50-82(w/****Ditko****), 83 & 84(w/****Sinnott****), 85-96(w/****Ayers****), 97-152p.* ***Leiber/Fox*** *a-93, 98-102.* ***Maneely*** *c-20-22.* ***Morisi*** *a-42.* ***Morrow*** *a-41, 42.* ***Orlando*** *a-30, 45, 57.* ***Mac Pakula*** *(Tothish) a-9, 35, 41.* ***Powell*** *a-20, 27, 34.* ***Reinman*** *a-39, 87, 92, 96i.* ***Robinson*** *a-9.* ***Roussos*** *a-39.* ***Robert Sale*** *a-14.* ***Severin*** *a-27; c-30.* ***Sinnott*** *a-41; c-50.* ***Tuska*** *a-11.* ***Wildey*** *a-16.*

JOURNEY INTO MYSTERY (2nd Series)
Oct, 1972 - No. 19, Oct, 1975
Marvel Comics Group

1-Robert Howard adaptation; Starlin/Ploog-a 1.00 2.50 6.00
2,3,5-Bloch adaptation; 5-Last new story 1.20 3.00
4,6-19: 4-H. P. Lovecraft adaptation .80 2.00

NOTE: ***N. Adams*** *a-2i.* ***Ditko*** *r-7, 10, 12, 14, 15, 19; c-10.* ***Everett*** *r-9, 14.* ***G. Kane*** *a-1p, 2p; c-1-3p.* ***Kirby*** *r-7, 13, 18, 19; c-7.* ***Mort Lawrence*** *r-2.* ***Maneely*** *r-3.* ***Orlando*** *r-16.* ***Reese*** *a-1, 2i.* ***Starlin*** *a-1p, 3p.* ***Torres*** *r-16.* ***Wildey*** *r-9, 14.*

JOURNEY INTO UNKNOWN WORLDS (Formerly Teen)
No. 36, 9/50 - No. 38, 2/51; No. 4, 4/51 - No. 59, 8/57
Atlas Comics (WFP)

36(#1)-Science fiction/weird; "End Of The Earth" c/story 103.00 310.00 725.00
37(#2)-Science fiction; "When Worlds Collide" c/story; Everett-c/a; Hitler story 52.00 156.00 365.00
38(#3)-Science fiction 44.00 133.00 310.00
4-6,8,10-Science fiction/weird 27.00 81.00 190.00
7-Wolverton-a-"Planet of Terror," 6 pgs; electric chair c-inset/story 46.00 140.00 325.00
9-Giant eyeball story 33.00 100.00 230.00
11,12-Krigstein-a 22.00 65.00 150.00
13,16,17,20 14.00 43.00 100.00
14-Wolverton-a-"One of Our Graveyards Is Missing," 4 pgs; Tuska-a 36.00 110.00 250.00
15-Wolverton-a-"They Crawl by Night," 5 pgs.; 2 pg. Maneely s/f story 36.00 110.00 250.00
18,19-Matt Fox-a 16.00 50.00 115.00
21-33: 21-Decapitation-c. 24-Sci/fic story. 26-Atom bomb panel. 27-Sid Check-a. 33-Last pre-code (2/55) 11.00 32.00 75.00
34-Kubert, Torres-a 10.00 30.00 60.00
35-Torres-a 9.15 27.50 55.00
36-42 8.35 25.00 50.00
43,44: 43-Krigstein-a. 44-Davis-a 9.15 27.50 55.00
45,55,59-Williamson-a in all; with Mayo #55,59. 55-Crandall-a 9.15 27.50 55.00
46,47,49,52,56-58 7.50 22.50 45.00
48,53-Crandall-a; Check-a, #48 9.15 27.50 55.00
50-Davis, Crandall-a 9.15 27.50 55.00
51-Ditko, Wood-a 10.00 30.00 60.00
54-Torres-a 7.50 22.50 45.00

NOTE: ***Ayers*** *a-24, 43,* ***Berg*** *a-38(#3), 43.* ***Lou Cameron*** *a-33.* ***Colan*** *a-37(#2), 6, 17, 19, 20, 23, 39.* ***Ditko*** *a-45, 51.* ***Drucker*** *a-35, 58.* ***Everett*** *a-37(#2), 11, 14, 41, 55, 56; c-37(#2), 11, 13, 14, 17, 22, 47, 48, 50, 53-55, 59.* ***Forte*** *a-49.* ***Fox*** *a-21i.* ***Heath*** *a-36(#1), 4, 6-8, 17, 20, 22, 36i; c-18.* ***Keller*** *a-15.* ***Mort Lawrence*** *a-38, 39.* ***Maneely*** *a-7, 8, 15, 16, 22, 49, 58; c-25, 52.* ***Morrow*** *a-48.* ***Orlando*** *a-44, 57.* ***Pakula*** *a-36.* ***Powell*** *a-42, 53, 54.* ***Reinman*** *a-8.* ***Rico*** *a-21.* ***Robert Sale*** *a-24, 49.* ***Sekowsky*** *a-4, 5, 9.* ***Severin*** *a-38, 51; c-38, 48i, 56.* ***Sinnott*** *a-9, 21, 24.* ***Tuska*** *a-38(#3), 14.* ***Wildey*** *a-25, 43, 44.*

JOURNEY OF DISCOVERY WITH MARK STEEL (See Mark Steel)

JOURNEY TO THE CENTER OF THE EARTH (See 4-Color No. 1060)

JUDE, THE FORGOTTEN SAINT
1954 (16 pgs.; 8x11"; full color; paper cover)
Catechetical Guild Education Society

nn 2.00 5.00 10.00

JUDGE COLT
Oct, 1969 - No. 4, Sept, 1970
Gold Key

1 1.30 3.25 8.00
2-4 1.00 2.00 5.00

JUDGE DREDD (...Classics #62 on; also see Batman - Judge Dredd, Dredd Rules, The Law of Dredd & 2000 A.D. Monthly)
Nov, 1983 - No. 35, 1986; V2#1, Oct, 1986 - No. 77, 1993
Eagle Comics/IPC Magazines Ltd./Quality Comics #34-35, V2#1-37/ Fleetway #38 on

1-Bolland-c/a in #1-10,15 1.50 3.75 9.00
2-35 1.20 3.00
V2#1-('86)-New look begins .80 2.00
V2#2-6 1.50
V2#7-21/22: 14-Bolland-a. 20-Begin $1.50-c 1.30
V2#23/24-Two issue numbers in one 1.50
25-38: 28-1st app. Megaman (super-hero) 1.50
39-50: 39-Begin $1.75-c .70 1.75
51-77: 51-Begin $1.95-c. 53-Bolland-a. 57-Reprints 1st published Judge Dredd story .80 2.00
Special 1 1.40

NOTE: ***Guice*** *c-V2#23/24, 26, 27.*

JUDGE DREDD (Definitive Editions) (Fleetway/Quality)(Value: cover or less)

JUDGE DREDD'S CRIME FILE (Eagle & Quality)(Value: cover or less)

JUDGE DREDD'S HARDCASE PAPERS (Fleetway/Quality)(Value: cover or less)

JUDGE DREDD: THE EARLY CASES (Eagle)(Value: cover or less)

JUDGE DREDD: THE JUDGE CHILD QUEST (Eagle)(Value: cover or less)

JUDGE DREDD: THE MEGAZINE (Fleetway/Quality)(Value: cover or less)

JUDGEMENT DAY
Sept, 1993 - Present ($2.95, color)
Lightning Comics

1-($3.50)-Red foil-c 1.40 3.50
1-Gold Prism Edition 15.00
2-5: 2-Polybagged with trading card 1.20 3.00

JUDGE PARKER
Feb, 1956 - No. 2, 1956
Argo

1-Newspaper strip reprints 4.35 13.00 26.00
2 3.00 7.50 15.00

JUDO JOE
Aug, 1953 - No. 3, Dec, 1953 (Judo lessons in each issue)
Jay-Jay Corp.

1-Drug ring story 5.35 16.00 32.00
2,3: 3-Hypo needle story 4.00 11.00 22.00

JUDOMASTER (Gun Master #84-89) (Also see Crisis on Infinite Earths, Sarge Steel #6 & Special War Series)

Jughead's Diner #1, © AP

Jughead's Time Police #2, © AP

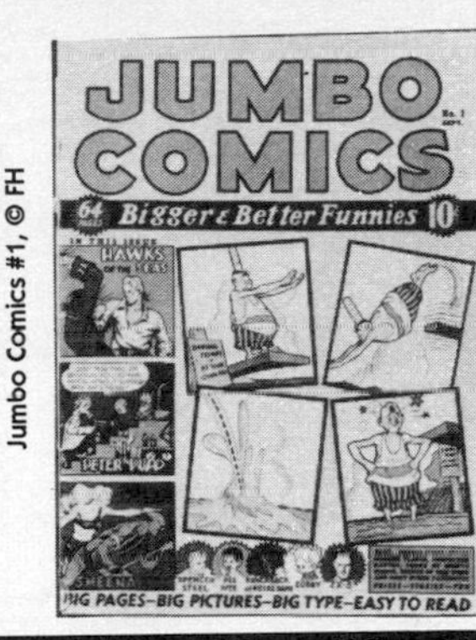

Jumbo Comics #1, © FH

GD25 FN65 NM94

No. 89, May-June, 1966 - No. 98, Dec, 1967 (Two No. 89's)
Charlton Comics

	GD25	FN65	NM94
89-3rd app. Judomaster	2.30	6.75	16.00
90-98: 91-Sarge Steel begins. 93-Intro. Tiger	1.70	5.00	12.00
93,94,96,98(Modern Comics reprint, 1977)			1.00

NOTE: *Morisi Thunderbolt #90. #91 has 1 pg. biography on writer/artist Frank McLoughlin.*

JUDY CANOVA (Formerly My Experience) (Stage, screen, radio)
No. 23, May, 1950 - No. 3, Sept, 1950
Fox Features Syndicate

	GD25	FN65	NM94
23(#1)-Wood-c,a(p)?	11.50	34.00	80.00
24-Wood-a(p)	11.50	34.00	80.00
3-Wood-c; Wood/Orlando-a	13.50	41.00	95.00

JUDY GARLAND (See Famous Stars)

JUDY JOINS THE WAVES
1951 (For U.S. Navy)
Toby Press

	GD25	FN65	NM94
nn	4.00	12.00	24.00

JUGHEAD (Formerly Archie's Pal...)
No. 127, Dec, 1965 - No. 352, June, 1987
Archie Publications

	GD25	FN65	NM94
127-130	1.70	5.00	12.00
131,133,135-160	1.50	3.75	9.00
132,134: 132-Shield-c; The Fly & Black Hood app.; Shield cameo. 134-Shield-c	1.65	4.00	10.00
161-200		1.60	4.00
201-240		.80	2.00
241-352: 300-Anniversary issue; infinity-c			1.50

JUGHEAD (2nd series)(Becomes Archie's Pal Jughead Comics #46 on)
Aug, 1987 - No. 45, May, 1993 (.75/$1.00/$1.25)
Archie Enterprises

	GD25	FN65	NM94
1-45: 4-X-Mas issue. 17-Colan-c/a			1.25

JUGHEAD AS CAPTAIN HERO (See Archie as Purehear the Powerful, Archie Giant Series Magazine #142 & Life With Archie)
Oct, 1966 - No. 7, Nov, 1967
Archie Publications

	GD25	FN65	NM94
1-Super hero parody	3.85	11.50	27.00
2	2.40	7.25	17.00
3-7	1.65	4.70	11.00

JUGHEAD JONES COMICS DIGEST, THE (...Magazine No. 10-64; Jughead Jones Digest Magazine #65)
June, 1977 - Present ($1.35-$1.50, digest-size, 128 pgs.)
Archie Publications

	GD25	FN65	NM94
1-Neal Adams-a; Capt. Hero-r	1.00	2.50	6.00
2(9/77)-Neal Adams-a		1.60	4.00
3-50: 7-Origin Jaguar-r; N. Adams-a. 13-r/1957 Jughead's Folly		.80	2.00
51-85			1.50

JUGHEAD'S DINER
Apr, 1990 - No. 7, Apr, 1991 ($1.00, color)
Archie Comics

	GD25	FN65	NM94
1-7			1.00

JUGHEAD'S DOUBLE DIGEST (...Magazine #5)
Oct, 1989 - Present ($2.25/$2.50, quarterly, 256 pgs.)
Archie Comics

	GD25	FN65	NM94
1-18: 2,5-Capt. Hero stories		1.00	2.50

JUGHEAD'S EAT-OUT COMIC BOOK MAGAZINE (See Archie Giant Series Magazine No. 170)

JUGHEAD'S FANTASY
Aug, 1960 - No. 3, Dec, 1960
Archie Publications

	GD25	FN65	NM94
1	16.00	48.00	110.00
2	10.00	30.00	75.00
3	10.00	30.00	65.00

JUGHEAD'S FOLLY
1957 (36 pgs.)(One Shot)
Archie Publications (Close-Up)

	GD25	FN65	NM94
1-Jughead a la Elvis (Rare) (1st reference to Elvis in comics?)	36.00	110.00	250.00

JUGHEAD'S JOKES
Aug, 1967 - No. 78, Sept, 1982
(No. 1-8, 38 on: reg. size; No. 9-23: 68 pgs.; No. 24-37: 52 pgs.)
Archie Publications

	GD25	FN65	NM94
1	5.50	17.00	40.00
2	3.20	8.00	20.00
3-5	1.65	4.00	10.00
6-10	1.00	2.00	5.00
11-30		1.20	3.00
31-50		.80	2.00
51-78			1.50

JUGHEAD'S PAL HOT DOG (See Laugh #14 for 1st app.)
Jan, 1990 - No. 5, Oct, 1990 ($1.00, color)
Archie Comics

	GD25	FN65	NM94
1-5			1.00

JUGHEAD'S SOUL FOOD (Spire Christian)(Value: cover or less)

JUGHEAD'S TIME POLICE
July, 1990 - No. 6, May, 1991 ($1.00, color, bi-monthly)
Archie Comics

	GD25	FN65	NM94
1-6: Colan a-3-6p; c-3-6			1.00

JUGHEAD WITH ARCHIE DIGEST (...Plus Betty & Veronica & Reggie Too No. 1,2; ...Magazine #33-?, 101-on; ...Comics Digest Mag.)
March, 1974 - Present (Digest Size; $1.00-$1.25-$1.35-$1.50)
Archie Publications

	GD25	FN65	NM94
1	2.15	6.50	15.00
2	1.20	3.00	7.00
3-10		1.60	4.00
11-20: Capt. Hero-r in #14-16; Pureheart the Powerful #18,21,22; Capt. Pureheart #17,19		1.20	3.00
21-50: 29-The Shield-r. 30-The Fly-r		.80	2.00
51-118			1.50

JUKE BOX COMICS
March, 1948 - No. 6, Jan, 1949
Famous Funnies

	GD25	FN65	NM94
1-Toth-c/a; Hollingsworth-a	32.00	95.00	225.00
2-Transvestism story	18.00	54.00	125.00
3-6: 3-Peggy Lee story. 4-Jimmy Durante line drawn-c. 6-Features Desi Arnaz plus Arnaz line drawn-c	13.00	40.00	90.00

JUMBO COMICS (Created by S.M. Iger)
Sept, 1938 - No. 167, Mar, 1953 (No. 1-3: 68 pgs.; No. 4-8: 52 pgs.)
(No. 1-8 oversized-10-1/2x14-1/2"; black & white)
Fiction House Magazines (Real Adv. Publ. Co.)

	GD25	FN65	VF82
1-(Rare)-Sheena Queen of the Jungle (1st app.) by Meskin, Hawks of the Seas (The Hawk #10 on; see Feature Funnies #3) by Eisner, The Hunchback by Dick Briefer (ends #8) begin; 1st comic art by Jack Kirby (Count of Monte Cristo & Wilton of the West); Mickey Mouse appears (1 panel) with brief biography of Walt Disney; 1st app. Peter Pupp by Bob Kane. Note: Sheena was created by Iger for publication in England as a newspaper strip. The early issues of Jumbo contain Sheena strip-r; mutiple panel-c 1,2,7	850.00	2550.00	8500.00

(Estimated up to 45 total copies exist, 1 in NM/Mint)

2-(Rare)-Origin Sheena. Diary of Dr. Hayward by Kirby (also #3) plus 2 other stories; contains strip from Universal Film featuring Edgar Bergen & Charlie

Jumbo Comics #96, © FH

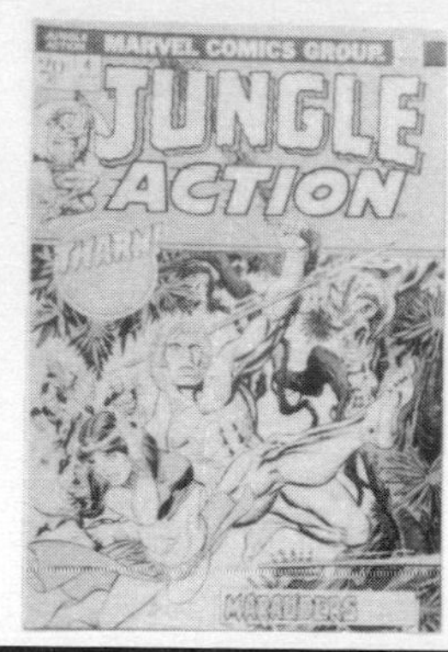

Jungle Action #4 (4/73), © MEG

Jungle Comics #74, © FH

GD25 FN65 NM94

McCarthy plus-c (preview of film) 400.00 1200.00 2700.00
3-Last Kirby issue 300.00 900.00 2000.00
4-(Scarce)-Origin The Hawk by Eisner; Wilton of the West by Fine (ends #14)(1st comic work); Count of Monte Cristo by Fine (ends #15); The Diary of Dr. Hayward by Fine (cont'd #8,9) 285.00 855.00 1900.00
5-Christmas-c 200.00 600.00 1400.00
6-8-Last B&W issue. #8 was a 1939 N. Y. World's Fair Special Edition; Frank Buck's Jungleland story 158.00 475.00 1100.00
9-Stuart Taylor begins by Fine; Fine-c; 1st color issue (8-9/39)-1st Sheena (jungle) cover; 8-1/4x10-1/4"(oversized in width only)
171.00 515.00 1200.00

GD25 FN65 NM94

10-13: 10-Regular size 68 pg. issues begin; Sheena dons new costume w/ origin costume; Stuart Taylor sci/fi-c. 12-The Hawk-c
83.00 250.00 550.00
14-Intro. Lightning (super-hero) on-c only 95.00 290.00 625.00
15,17-20: 15-1st Lightning story. 17-Lightning part-c
54.00 162.00 365.00
16-Lightning-c 67.00 200.00 450.00
21-30: 22-1st Tom, Dick & Harry; origin The Hawk retold
42.00 125.00 275.00
31-40: 31-(9/41)-1st app. Mars God of War in Stuart Taylor story (see Planet Comics #15. 35-Shows V2#11 (correct number does not appear)
37.00 112.00 245.00
41-50 29.00 88.00 185.00
51-60: 52-Last Tom, Dick & Harry 26.00 78.00 165.00
61-70: 68-Sky Girl begins, ends #130; not in #79 18.00 55.00 120.00
71-99: 89-ZX5 becomes a private eye. 94-Used in Love and Death by Legman 15.00 45.00 95.00
100 18.00 55.00 120.00
101-110 13.00 40.00 85.00
111-140,150-158: 155-Used in **POP**, pg. 98 12.00 35.00 75.00
141-149-Two Sheena stories. 141-Long Bow, Indian Boy begins, ends #160
14.00 42.00 90.00
159-163: Space Scouts serial in all. 160-Last jungle-c (6/52). 161-Ghost Gallery-c begin, end #167. 163-Suicide Smith app.
11.00 32.00 70.00
164-The Star Pirate begins, ends #165 11.00 32.00 70.00
165-167: 165,167-Space Rangers app. 11.00 32.00 70.00

NOTE: *Bondage covers, negligee panels, torture, etc. are common in this series. Hawks of the Seas, Inspector Dayton, Spies in Action, Sports Shorts, & Uncle Otto by Eisner, #1-7. Hawk by* ***Eisner**-#10-15.* ***Eisner** c-1-7, 11-13, 15. 1pg. Patsy pin-ups in 92-97, 99-101. Sheena by* ***Meskin**-#1, 4; by* ***Powell**-#2, 3, 5-28;* ***Powell** c-14, 16, 17, 19. Sky Girl by* ***Matt Baker**-#69-78, 80-124.* ***Bailey** a-3-8.* ***Briefer** a-1-8, 10.* ***Fine** a-14; c-8-10.* ***Kamen** a-101, 105, 123, 132; c-105, 121-145.* ***Bob Kane** a-1-8.* ***Whitman** c-146-167(most). Jungle c-9, 13, 15, 17 on.*

JUMPING JACKS PRESENTS THE WHIZ KIDS

1978 (In 3-D) with glasses (4 pages)
Jumping Jacks Stores giveaway

nn 1.00

JUNGLE ACTION

Oct, 1954 - No. 6, Aug, 1955
Atlas Comics (IPC)

1-Leopard Girl begins by Al Hartley (#1,3); Jungle Boy by Forte; Maneely-a in all 17.00 52.00 120.00
2-(3-D effect cover) 22.00 65.00 150.00
3-6: 3-Last precode (2/55) 11.50 34.00 80.00

NOTE: ***Maneely** c-1, 2, 5, 6.* ***Romita** a-3, 6.* ***Shores** a-3, 6; c-3, 4?.*

JUNGLE ACTION (...& Black Panther #18-21?)

Oct, 1972 - No. 24, Nov, 1976
Marvel Comics Group

1-Lorna, Jann-r (All reprints in 1-4) 1.00 2.50 6.00
2-4 1.20 3.00
5-Black Panther begins; new stories begin 1.00 2.50 6.00
6-18: 8-Origin Black Panther. 9-Contains pull-out centerfold ad by Mark Jewelers 1.20 3.00

GD25 FN65 NM94

19-24: 19-23-KKK x-over. 23-r/#22. 24-1st Wind Eagle .80 2.00

NOTE: ***Buckler** a-6-9p, 22; c-8p, 12p.* ***Buscema** a-5p; c-22.* ***Byrne** c-23.* ***Gil Kane** a-8p; c-2, 4, 10p, 11p, 13-17, 19, 24.* ***Kirby** c-18.* ***Maneely** r-1.* ***Russell** a-13i.* ***Starlin** c-3p.*

JUNGLE ADVENTURES

1963 - 1964 (Reprints)
Super Comics

10,12,15: 10-r/Terrors of the Jungle #10(Rulah). 12-r/Zoot #14(Rulah).15-r/Jungle Comics #152(Kaanga/Jungle #152) 3.60 9.00 18.00
17-All Jo-Jo reprints 3.60 9.00 18.00
18-Reprints/White Princess of the Jungle #1; no Kinstler-a; origin of both White Princess & Cap'n Courage 4.00 11.00 22.00

JUNGLE ADVENTURES

March, 1971 - No. 3, June, 1971 (25 cents, 52 pgs.)
Skywald Comics

1-Zangar origin; reprints of Jo-Jo, Blue Gorilla(origin)/White Princess #3, Kinstler-r/White Princess #2 1.30 3.25 8.00
2-Zangar, Sheena-r/Sheena #17 & Jumbo #162, Jo-Jo, origin Slave Girl Princess-r 1.30 3.25 8.00
3-Zangar, Jo-Jo, White Princess-r 1.30 3.25 8.00

JUNGLE BOOK (See King Louie and Mowgli, Movie Comics, Walt Disney Showcase #45 & Walt Disney's The Jungle Book)

JUNGLE CAT (See 4-Color No. 1136)

JUNGLE COMICS

1/40 - No. 157, 3/53; No. 158, Spr, 1953 - No. 163, Summer, 1954
Fiction House Magazines

1-Origin The White Panther, Kaanga, Lord of the Jungle, Tabu, Wizard of the Jungle; Wambi, the Jungle Boy, Camilla & Capt. Terry Thunder begin (all 1st app.) 200.00 600.00 1400.00
2-Fantomah, Mystery Woman of the Jungle begins, ends #51; The Red Panther begins, ends #26 92.00 275.00 600.00
3,4 79.00 238.00 525.00
5 62.00 188.00 415.00
6-10: 7,8-Powell-c 50.00 150.00 325.00
11-20: 13-Tuska-c 37.00 112.00 250.00
21-30: 25-Shows V2#1 (correct number does not appear). #27-New origin Fantomah, Daughter of the Pharoahs; Camilla dons new costume
31.00 92.00 200.00
31-40 25.00 75.00 160.00
41,43-50 20.00 60.00 130.00
42-Kaanga by Crandall, 12 pgs. 23.00 70.00 150.00
51-60 18.00 55.00 120.00
61-70 15.00 45.00 100.00
71-80: 79-New origin Tabu 13.00 40.00 85.00
81-97,99,101-110 12.50 37.50 80.00
98-Used in **SOTI**, pg. 185 & illo-"In ordinary comic books, there are pictures within pictures for children who know how to look"; used by N.Y. Legis. Comm. 21.00 62.00 135.00
100 15.00 45.00 100.00
111-163: 104-In Camilla story villain is Dr. Wertham. 118-Clyde Beatty app. 135-Desert Panther begins in Terry Thunder (origin), not in #137; ends (dies) #138. 143,145-Used in **POP**, pg. 99. 152-Tiger Girl begins. 158-Sheena app. 12.50 37.50 80.00
I.W. Reprint #1,9: 1-r/? 9-r/#151 2.80 7.00 14.00

NOTE: *Bondage covers, negligee panels, torture, etc. are common to this series. Camilla by* ***Fran Hopper**-#70-91; by* ***Baker**-#100-113, 115, 116; by* ***Lubbers**-#98, 99 by* ***Tuska**-#63. Kaanga by* ***John Celardo**-#80-113; by* ***Larsen**-#71, 75, 76, 79; by* ***Moreira**-#68-70, 72-74; by* ***Maurice Whitman**-#114, 115, 117, 118, 124-163. Kaanga by* ***Moriera**-#58, 63, 64, 66, 67; by* ***Tuska**-#37. Tabu by* ***Larsen**-#63, 64, 67-75, 84, 85, 90, 91; by* ***Whitman**-#93-110, 114. Terry Thunder by* ***Celardo**-#79; by* ***Lubbers**-#80, 85. Tiger Girl-r by* ***Baker**-#152, 156, 157, 159.* ***Astarita** c-46.* ***Baker** c-114-131(most).* ***Celardo** a-78; c-59-113(most).* ***Eisner** c-2, 5, 6.* ***Fine** c-1.* ***Larsen** a-65, 66, 71, 72, 74, 75, 79, 83, 84, 87-90.* ***Lubbers** a-84(Terry Thunder).* ***Moriera** c-43, 44.* ***Morisi** a-51.* ***Powell** c-7, 8.* ***Sultan** c-3, 4.* ***Tuska** c-13.* ***Whitman** c-132-163(most).* ***Zolnerwich** c-11, 12, 18-41.*

JUNGLE COMICS (Blackthorne)(Value: cover or less)

JUNGLE GIRL (See Lorna,...)

Jungle Jim #14 (Standard), © KING

Jungle Tales of Tarzan #2, © ERB

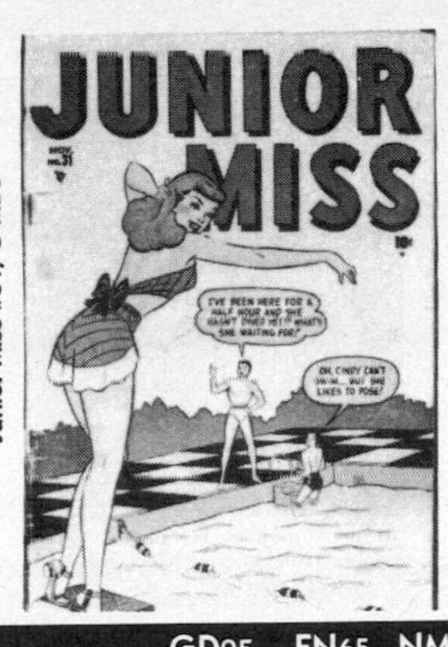

Junior Miss #31, © MEG

	GD25	FN65	NM94

JUNGLE GIRL (Nyoka, Jungle Girl No. 2 on)
Fall, 1942 (One shot)(No month listed)
Fawcett Publications

	GD25	FN65	NM94
1-Bondage-c; photo of Kay Aldridge who played Nyoka in movie serial app. on-c. Adaptation of the classic Republic movie serial Perils of Nyoka. 1st comic to devote entire contents to a movie serial adaptation	70.00	210.00	450.00

JUNGLE JIM (Also see Ace Comics)
No. 11, Jan, 1949 - No. 20, Apr, 1951
Standard Comics (Best Books)

	GD25	FN65	NM94
11	5.00	15.00	30.00
12-20	3.60	9.00	18.00

JUNGLE JIM
No. 490, 8/53 - No. 1020, 8-10/59 (Painted-c)
Dell Publishing Co.

	GD25	FN65	NM94
4-Color 490(#1)	6.70	20.00	40.00
4-Color 565(#2, 6/54)	4.00	10.00	20.00
3(10-12/54)-5	3.60	9.00	18.00
6-19(1-3/59)	3.20	8.00	16.00
4-Color 1020(#20)	3.20	8.00	16.00

JUNGLE JIM
No. 5, December, 1967
King Features Syndicate

	GD25	FN65	NM94
5-Reprints Dell #5; Wood-c	1.70	5.00	12.00

JUNGLE JIM (Continued from Dell series)
No. 22, Feb, 1969 - No. 28, Feb, 1970 (#21 was an overseas edition only)
Charlton Comics

	GD25	FN65	NM94
22-Dan Flagg begins; Ditko/Wood-a	3.25	9.50	22.00
23-26: 23-Last Dan Flagg; Howard-c. 24-Jungle People begin	2.00	6.00	14.00
27,28: 27-Ditko/Howard-a. 28-Ditko-a	2.60	7.50	18.00

JUNGLE JO
Mar, 1950 - No. 6, Mar, 1951
Fox Feature Syndicate (Hero Books)

	GD25	FN65	NM94
nn-Jo-Jo blanked out, leaving Congo King; came out after Jo-Jo #29 (Intended as Jo-Jo #30?)	19.00	57.00	130.00
1-Tangi begins; part Wood-a	22.00	65.00	150.00
2	16.00	48.00	110.00
3-6	14.00	43.00	100.00

JUNGLE LIL (Dorothy Lamour #2 on; also see Feature Stories Magazine)
April, 1950
Fox Feature Syndicate (Hero Books)

	GD25	FN65	NM94
1	17.00	52.00	120.00

JUNGLE TALES (Jann of the Jungle No. 8 on)
Sept, 1954 - No. 7, Sept, 1955
Atlas Comics (CSI)

	GD25	FN65	NM94
1-Jann of the Jungle	17.00	52.00	120.00
2-7: 3-Last precode (1/55)	12.00	36.00	85.00

NOTE: *Heath c-5. Heck a-6, 7. Maneely a-2; c-1, 3. Shores a-5-7; c-4, 6. Tuska a-2.*

JUNGLE TALES OF TARZAN
Dec, 1964 - No. 4, July, 1965
Charlton Comics

	GD25	FN65	NM94
1	3.20	9.00	21.00
2-4	2.40	7.25	17.00

NOTE: *Giordano c-3p. Glanzman a-1-3. Montes/Bache a-4.*

JUNGLE TERROR (See Harvey Comics Hits No. 54)

JUNGLE THRILLS (Formerly Sports Thrills; Terrors of the Jungle #17 on)
No. 16, Feb, 1952; Dec, 1953; No. 7, 1954
Star Publications

	GD25	FN65	NM94
16-Phantom Lady & Rulah story-reprint/All Top No. 15; used in **POP**, pg. 98,99; L. B. Cole-c	22.00	65.00	155.00
3-D 1(12/53)-Jungle Lil & Jungle Jo appear; L. B. Cole-c	26.00	80.00	185.00
7-Titled 'Picture Scope Jungle Adventures;' (1954, 36 pgs, 15 cents)-3-D effect c/stories; story & coloring book; Disbrow-a/script; L.B. Cole-c	24.00	73.00	170.00

JUNGLE TWINS, THE (Tono & Kono)
Apr, 1972 - No. 17, Nov, 1975; No. 18, May, 1982
Gold Key/Whitman No. 18

	GD25	FN65	NM94
1	1.00	2.50	6.00
2-5		1.40	3.50
6-18: 18-Reprints		.80	2.00

NOTE: *UFO c/story No. 13. Painted-c No. 1-17. Spiegle c-18.*

JUNGLE WAR STORIES (Guerrilla War No. 12 on)
July-Sept, 1962 - No. 11, Apr-June, 1965 (Painted-c)
Dell Publishing Co.

	GD25	FN65	NM94
01-384-209 (#1)	2.80	7.00	14.00
2-11	1.80	4.50	9.00

JUNIE PROM (Also see Dexter Comics)
Winter, 1947-48 - No. 7, Aug, 1949
Dearfield Publishing Co.

	GD25	FN65	NM94
1-Teen-age	8.35	25.00	50.00
2	4.70	14.00	28.00
3-7	3.60	9.00	18.00

JUNIOR CARROT PATROL (Dark Horse)(Value: cover or less)

JUNIOR COMICS (Formerly Li'l Pan; becomes Western Outlaws with #17)
No. 9, Sept, 1947 - No. 16, July, 1948
Fox Feature Syndicate

	GD25	FN65	NM94
9-Feldstein-c/a; headlights-c	41.00	122.00	285.00
10-16-Feldstein-c/a; headlights-c on all	37.00	112.00	260.00

JUNIOR FUNNIES (Formerly Tiny Tot Funnies No. 9)
No. 10, Aug, 1951 - No. 13, Feb, 1952
Harvey Publications (King Features Synd.)

	GD25	FN65	NM94
10-Partial reprints in all; Blondie, Dagwood, Daisy, Henry, Popeye, Felix, Katzenjammer Kids	2.80	7.00	14.00
11-13	2.40	6.00	12.00

JUNIOR HOPP COMICS
Feb, 1952 - No. 3, July, 1952
Stanmor Publ.

	GD25	FN65	NM94
1-Teenage humor	6.35	19.00	38.00
2,3: 3-Dave Berg-a	4.00	10.00	20.00

JUNIOR MEDICS OF AMERICA, THE
No. 1359, 1957 (15 cents)
E. R. Squire & Sons

	GD25	FN65	NM94
1359	2.40	6.00	12.00

JUNIOR MISS
Winter, 1944; No. 24, April, 1947 - No. 39, Aug, 1950
Timely/Marvel Comics (CnPC)

	GD25	FN65	NM94
1-Frank Sinatra & June Allyson life story	16.00	48.00	110.00
24-Formerly The Human Torch #23?	6.70	20.00	40.00
25-38: 29,31,34-Cindy-c/stories (others?)	4.00	12.00	24.00
39-Kurtzman-a	5.00	15.00	30.00

NOTE: *Painted-c 35-37. 35, 37-all romance. 36, 38-mostly teen humor.*

JUNIOR PARTNERS (Formerly Oral Roberts' True Stories)
No. 120, Aug, 1959 - V3#12, Dec, 1961
Oral Roberts Evangelistic Assn.

	GD25	FN65	NM94
120(#1)	4.20	12.50	25.00
2(9/59)	3.20	8.00	16.00
3-12(7/60)	2.00	5.00	10.00
V2#1(8/60)-5(12/60)	1.40	3.50	7.00

Jurassic Park #1, © Universal City Studios & Amblin Entertainment

Justice League International #54 (9/93), © DC

Justice League of America #6 (6-7/61), © DC

GD25 FN65 NM94

V3#1(1/61)-12 1.20 3.00 6.00

JUNIOR TREASURY (See Dell Junior...)

JUNIOR WOODCHUCKS LIMITED SERIES (Walt Disney's...)
July, 1991 - No. 4, Oct, 1991 ($1.50, color, limited series; new & reprint-a)
W. D. Publications (Disney)

1-4: 1-The Beagle Boys app.; Barks-r 1.50

JUNIOR WOODCHUCKS (See Huey, Dewey & Louie...)

JUNKER (Fleetway)(Value: cover or less)

JURASSIC PARK
June, 1993 - No. 4, Aug, 1993 (Color, mini-series, movie adaptation)
Topps Comics

1-($2.50)-Newsstand Edition; Kane/Perez-a in all 1.60 4.00
1-($2.95)-Collector's Ed.; polybagged w/3 cards 1.10 2.70 6.50
1-Amberchrome Edition w/no price or ads 20.00
2-4-($2.50)-Newsstand Edition 1.00 2.50
2,3-($2.95)-Collector's Ed.; polybagged w/3 cards 1.20 3.00
4-($2.95)-Collector's Ed.; polybagged w/action hologram trading card 1.20 3.00

JUSTICE
Nov, 1986 - No. 32, June, 1989
Marvel Comics Group

1-32: 26-32-$1.50-c 1.00

JUSTICE COMICS (Formerly Wacky Duck; Tales of Justice #53 on)
No. 7, Fall/47 - No. 9, 6/48; No. 4, 8/48 - No. 52, 3/55
Marvel/Atlas Comics (NPP 7-9,4-19/CnPC 20-23/MjMC 24-38/Male 39-52

7(#1, 1947) 13.00 40.00 90.00
8(#2)-Kurtzman-a-"Giggles 'N' Grins" (3) 10.00 30.00 60.00
9(#3, 6/48) 9.15 27.50 55.00
4 8.35 25.00 50.00
5-9: 8-Anti-Wertham editorial 6.70 20.00 40.00
10-15-Photo-c 5.85 17.50 35.00
16-30 4.70 14.00 28.00
31-40,42-47,49-52-Last precode 4.00 12.00 24.00
41-Electrocution-c 8.65 26.00 52.00
48-Pakula & Tuska-a 4.00 12.00 24.00

NOTE: ***Heath** a-24. **Maneely** c-44, 52. **Pakula** a-43, 45, 48. **Louis Ravielli** a-39. **Robinson** a-22, 25, 41. **Shores** c-7(#1), 8(#2)? **Tuska** a-48. **Wildey** a-52.*

JUSTICE, INC. (The Avenger)
May-June, 1975 - No. 4, Nov-Dec, 1975
National Periodical Publications

1-McWilliams-a, Kubert-c; origin 1.25
2-4: 2-4-Kirby-a(p), c-2,3p. 4-Kubert-c 1.00

NOTE: *Adapted from Kenneth Robeson novel, creator of Doc Savage.*

JUSTICE, INC. (DC)(Value: cover or less)

JUSTICE LEAGUE (...International #7-25; ...America #26 on)
May, 1987 - Present (Also see Legends #6)
DC Comics

1-Batman, Green Lantern(Guy Gardner), Blue Beetle, Mr. Miracle, Capt. Marvel & Martian Manhunter begin 1.25 3.00 7.50
2 1.70 4.25
3-Regular cover (white background) 1.30 3.25
3-Limited cover (yellow background, Superman logo) 14.00 41.00 95.00
4-6: 4-Booster Gold joins. 5-Origin Gray Man; Batman vs. Guy Gardner; Creeper app. 1.00 2.50
7-($1.25, 52 pgs.)-Capt. Marvel & Dr. Fate resign; Capt. Atom, Rocket Red join 1.20 3.00
8-10: 9,10-Millennium x-over 1.50
11-23: 16-Bruce Wayne-c/story. 18-21-Lobo app. 1.20
24-($1.50)-1st app. Justice League Europe 1.50
25-49,51-62: 31,32-Justice League Europe x-over. 58-Lobo app. 61-New team begins; swipes-c to JLA #1(10-11/60). 62-Last $1.00-c 1.00
50-($1.75, 52 pgs.) .70 1.75
63-68,72-82 1.25
69-Doomsday tie-in; takes place between Superman: The Man of Steel #18 & Superman #74 2.30 6.75 16.00
69,70-2nd printings 1.25
70-Funeral for a Friend part 1; red outer-c 1.65 4.00 10.00
70-Newsstand version w/o outer-c 1.80 4.50
71-Direct sale version w/black outer-c .80 2.00
71-Newsstand version w/o outer-c .65 1.25
83-86: 83-Begin $1.50-c 1.50
Annual 1 (1987) .80 2.00
Annual 2 (1988)-Joker-c/story; Batman cameo .80 2.00
Annual 3 (1989, $1.75, 68 pgs.) .80 2.00
Annual 4 (1990, $2.00, 68 pgs.) .80 2.00
Annual 5 (1991, $2.00, 68 pgs.)-Armageddon 2001 x-over; 2nd printing exists with silver ink-c .80 2.00
Annual 6 (1992, $2.50, 68 pgs.) 1.00 2.50
Annual 7 (1993, $2.50, 68 pgs.)-Bloodlines x-over 1.00 2.50
Special 1 (1990, $1.50, 52 pgs.)-Giffen plots 1.50
Special 2 (1991, $2.95, 52 pgs.)-Staton-a(p) 1.20 3.00
Spectacular 1 (1992, $1.50, 52 pgs.)-Intro new JLI & JLE teams; ties into JLI #61 & JLE #37 1.50
A New Beginning Trade Paperback ($12.95, 1989)-r/1-7 1.85 5.50 13.00

NOTE: ***Austin** a-1i, 60i; c-1i. **Giffen** a-8-10; c-21p. **Guice** a-62i. **Russell** c-54i. **Willingham** a-30p, Annual 2.*

JUSTICE LEAGUE EUROPE (Justice League International #51 on)
April, 1989 - Present (75 cents; $1.00 #5 on)
DC Comics

1-Giffen plots in all; breakdowns in 1-8,13-30 .80 2.00
2-49,51-57: 7-9-Batman app. 7,8-JLA x-over. 8,9-Superman app. 12-Metal Men app. 20,21-Rogers-c/a(p). 33,34-Lobo vs. Despero. 37-New team begins; swipes-c to JLA #9; see JLA Spectacular. 38-Last $1.00-c 1.25
50-($2.50, 68 pgs.)-Battles Sonar 1.00 2.50
58-62: 58-Begin $1.50-c 1.50
Annual 1 (1990, $2.00, 68 pgs.)-Return of the Global Guardians; Giffen plots/breakdowns .80 2.00
Annual 2 (1991, $2.00, 68pgs.)-Armageddon 2001; Giffen-p; Golden-i; Rogers-p .80 2.00
Annual 3 (1992, $2.50, 68 pgs.)-Eclipso app. 1.00 2.50
Annual 4 (1993, $2.50, 68 pgs.)-Intro Lionheart 1.00 2.50

JUSTICE LEAGUE OF AMERICA (See Brave & the Bold #28-30, Mystery In Space #75 & Official...Index)
Oct-Nov, 1960 - No. 261, Apr, 1987 (91-99,139-157: 52 pgs.)
National Per. Publ./DC

GD25 FN65 VF82 NM94

Brave and the Bold #28 (2-3/60)-Intro/1st app. Justice League of America; origin & 1st app. Snapper Carr 256.00 768.00 1920.00 3070.00
Brave and the Bold #29 (4-5/60) 175.00 525.00 1138.00 1750.00
Brave and the Bold #30 (6-7/60) 145.00 435.00 943.00 1450.00
1-(10-11/60)-Origin & 1st app. Despero; Aquaman, Batman, Flash, Green Lantern, J'onn J'onzz, Superman & Wonder Woman continue from Brave and the Bold 220.00 660.00 1430.00 2200.00

GD25 FN65 NM94

2 74.00 221.00 590.00
3-Origin/1st app. Kanjar Ro (see Mystery in Space #75) 50.00 150.00 450.00
4-Green Arrow joins JLA 32.00 95.00 285.00
5-Origin & 1st app. Dr. Destiny 28.00 84.00 225.00
6-8,10: 6-Origin/1st app. Prof. Amos Fortune. 7-Last 10 cent issue. 10-Origin & 1st app. Felix Faust; 1st app. Time Lord 22.00 66.00 175.00
9-Origin J.L.A. (1st origin) 33.00 100.00 300.00
11-15: 12-Origin & 1st app. Dr. Light. 13-Speedy app. 14-Atom joins JLA 17.00 51.00 120.00

Justice League of America #261, © DC

Justice League Task Force #3, © DC

Justice Society of America #5 (8/91), © DC

GD25 FN65 NM94 — GD25 FN65 NM94

16-20: 17-Adam Strange flashback 14.00 41.00 95.00
21-"Crisis on Earth-One;" re-intro. of JSA in this title (8/63)(see Flash #129)(1st S.A. app. Hourman & Dr. Fate) 32.00 96.00 225.00
22-"Crisis on Earth-Two;" JSA x-over (story continued from #21) 29.00 86.00 200.00
23-28: 24-Adam Strange app. 28-Robin app. 7.00 21.00 50.00
29,30-JSA x-over. 29-1st Silver Age app. Starman; "Crisis on Earth-Three" 9.00 26.00 60.00
31-Hawkman joins JLA, Hawkgirl cameo 5.50 17.00 40.00
32-Intro & Origin Brain Storm 3.50 11.00 28.00
33,35,36,40,41: 41-Intro & origin The Key 3.00 9.00 25.00
34-Joker-c/story 4.00 12.00 32.00
37,38-JSA x-over (1st S.A. app. Mr. Terrific #37). 37-Batman cameo. 38-"Crisis on Earth-A" 6.00 17.00 44.00
39-Giant G-16; r/B&B #28,30 & JLA #5 7.00 20.00 65.00
42-45: 42-Metamorpho app. 43-Intro. Royal Flush Gang 2.00 6.00 15.00
46-JSA x-over; 1st S.A. app. Sandman; 1st S.A. app. of G.A. Spectre & Wildcat 6.00 19.00 50.00
47-JSA x-over 3.00 8.00 22.00
48-Giant G-29; r/JLA #2,3 & B&B #29 3.00 8.00 22.00
49-54,57,59,60 2.00 5.00 14.00
55-Intro. Earth 2 Robin (1st G.A. Robin in S.A.) 4.00 11.00 30.00
56-JLA vs. JSA 2.00 6.00 16.00
58-Giant G-41; r/JLA #6,8,1 2.00 5.00 14.00
61-63,66,68-72: 69-Wonder Woman quits. 71-Manhunter leaves. 72-Last 12 cent issue 1.60 4.00 8.50
64,65-JSA story. 64-Origin/1st app. S.A. Red Tornado (8/68) 1.00 3.00 9.50
67-Giant G-53; r/JLA #4,14,31 1.00 3.00 9.50
73-1st S.A. app. of G.A. Superman 1.00 3.00 9.50
74,77-80: 74-Black Canary joins (1st S.A. app.). 78-Re-intro Vigilante (1st S.A. app?) 1.00 2.00 5.50
75-2nd app. Green Arrow in new costume (see Brave & the Bold #85) 1.00 2.00 6.50
76-Giant G-65 1.00 2.00 6.50
81-84,86-92: 83-Death of Spectre 1.80 4.50
85,93-(Giant G-77,G-89; 68 pgs.) 1.00 2.00 6.50
94-Reprints 1st Sandman story (Adv. #40) & origin/1st app. Starman (Adv. #61); Deadman x-over; N. Adams-a(4 pgs.); begin 25 cent, 52 pg. issues, ends #99 2.00 6.00 19.00
95-Origin Dr. Fate & Dr. Midnight reprint (from More Fun #67, All-American #25) 1.00 3.00 7.50
96-Origin Hourman (Adv. #48); Wildcat-r 1.00 3.00 7.50
97-Origin JLA retold; Sargon, Starman-r 1.00 2.00 5.50
98,99: 98-G.A. Sargon, Starman-r. 99-G.A. Sandman, Starman, Atom-r; last 52 pg. issue 1.00 2.00 5.50
100-(8/72) 1.00 2.00 6.50
101,102: JSA x-overs. 102-Red Tornado dies 1.00 2.00 6.00
103-106,109: 103-Phantom Stranger joins. 105-Elongated Man joins. 106-New Red Tornado joins. 109-Hawkman resigns 1.40 3.50
107,108-G.A. Uncle Sam, Black Condor, The Ray, Dollman, Phantom Lady & The Human Bomb (JSA) x-over 1.10 2.70 6.50
110-116: All 100 pgs. 111-Shining Knight, Green Arrow-r. 112-Crimson Avenger, Vigilante-r; origin Starman-r/Adv. #81 1.80 4.50
117-190: 117-Hawkman rejoins. 120,121,138-Adam Strange app. 128-Wonder Woman rejoins. 129-Death of Red Tornado. 135-137-G.A. Bulletman, Bulletgirl, Spy Smasher, Mr. Scarlet, Pinky & Ibis x-over. 137 Superman battles G.A. Capt. Marvel. 138-Adam Strange-c by Neal Adams. 139-157-(52 pgs.). 144-Origin retold; origin J'onn J'onnz. 145-Red Tornado resurrected. 158-160-(44 pgs.). 161-Zatanna joins & new costume. 171-Mr. Terrific murdered. 178-Cover similar to #1; J'onn J'onzz app. 179-Firestorm joins. 181-Green Arrow leaves 1.00 2.50
191-199: 192,193-Real origin Red Tornado. 193-1st app. All-Star Squadron as free 16 pg. insert .70 1.80
200-Anniversary issue (76pgs., $1.50); origin retold; Green Arrow rejoins 1.30 3.25
201-250: 203-Intro/origin new Royal Flush Gang. 207,208-JSA, JLA, & All-Star Squadron team-up. 219,220-True origin Black Canary. 228 Re-intro Martian Manhunter. 233-New JLA begins. 243-Aquaman leaves. 244,245-Crisis x-over. 250-Batman rejoins .70 1.80
251-260: 253-Origin Despero. 258-Death of Vibe. 258-261-Legends x-over. 260-Death of Steel 1.25
261-Last issue 1.10 2.75
Annual 1(1983) 1.10 2.75
Annual 2(1984)-Intro new J.L.A. .70 1.80
Annual 3(1985)-Crisis x-over .70 1.80

NOTE: ***Neal Adams** c-63, 66, 67, 70, 74, 79, 81, 82, 86-89, 91, 92, 94, 96-98, 138, 139. **M. Anderson** c-1-4, 6, 7, 10, 12-14. **Aparo** a-200. **Austin** a-200i. **Baily** a-96r. **Burnley** r-94, 98, 99. **Greene** a-46-61i, 64-73i, 110i(r). **Grell** c-117, 122. **Kaluta** c-154p. **Gil Kane** a-200. **Krigstein** a-96(r/Sensation #84). **Kubert** a-200; c-72, 73. **Nino** a-228i, 230i. **Orlando** c-151i. **Perez** a-184-186p, 192-197p, 200p; c-184p, 186, 192-195, 196p, 197p, 199, 200, 201p, 202, 203-205p, 207-209, 212-215, 217, 219, 220. **Reinman** r-97. **Roussos** a-62i. **Sekowsky** a-37, 38, 44-63p, 110-112p(r); c-46-48p, 51p. **Sekowsky/Anderson** c-5, 8, 9, 11, 15. **B. Smith** c-185i. **Starlin** c-178-180, 183, 185p. **Staton** a-244p; c-157p, 244p. **Toth** r-110. **Tuska** a-153, 228p, 241-243p. JSA x-overs-21, 22, 29, 30, 37, 38, 46, 47, 55, 56, 64, 65, 73, 74, 82, 83, 91, 92, 100, 101, 102, 107, 108, 110, 113, 115, 123, 124, 135-137, 147, 148, 159, 160, 171, 172, 183-185, 195-197, 207-209, 219, 220, 231, 232, 244.*

JUSTICE LEAGUE QUARTERLY (DC)(Value: cover or less)

JUSTICE LEAGUE TASK FORCE
June, 1993 - Present ($1.25, color)
DC Comics

1-7: Aquaman, Nightwing, Flash, J'onn J'onzz, & Gypsy begin. 5,6-Knightquest tie-ins (new Batman cameo #5, 1 pg.) 1.25
8-10: 8-Begin $1.50-c 1.50

JUSTICE MACHINE, THE
June, 1981 - No. 5, Nov, 1983 ($2.00, No. 1-3, Magazine size)
Noble Comics

1-Byrne-c(p) 1.10 2.70 6.50
2-Austin-c(i) 1.80 4.50
3 1.20 3.00
4,5 1.00 2.50
Annual 1 (1/84, 68 pgs.)(published by Texas Comics); 1st app. The Elementals; Golden-c(p) 1.60 4.00

JUSTICE MACHINE (Comico)(Value: cover or less)

JUSTICE MACHINE, THE (Innovation)(Value: cover or less)

JUSTICE MACHINE FEATURING THE ELEMENTALS (Comico)(Value: cover or less)

JUSTICE SOCIETY OF AMERICA (See Adventure #461 & All-Star #3)
April, 1991 - No. 8, Nov, 1991 ($1.00, color, limited series)
DC Comics

1-8: 1-Flash. 2-Black Canary. 3-Green Lantern. 4-Hawkman. 5-Flash/Hawkman. 6-Gr. Lantern/Black Canary. 7-JSA 1.00

JUSTICE SOCIETY OF AMERICA (Also see Last Days of the... Special)
Aug, 1992 - No. 10, May, 1993 ($1.25, color)
DC Comics

1-10 1.25

JUSTICE TRAPS THE GUILTY (Fargo Kid V11#3 on)
Oct-Nov, 1947 - V11#2(#92), Apr-May, 1958
Prize/Headline Publications

V2#1-S&K-c/a; electrocution-c 29.00 85.00 200.00
2-S&K-c/a 14.00 43.00 100.00
3-5-S&K-c/a 13.00 40.00 90.00
6-S&K-c/a; Feldstein-a 14.00 43.00 100.00
7,9-S&K-c/a. 7-9-V2#1-3 in indicia; #7-9 on-c 11.50 34.00 80.00
8,10-Krigstein-a; S&K-c. 10-S&K-a 13.00 40.00 90.00
11,19-S&K-c 7.50 22.50 45.00
12,14-17,20-No S&K. 14-Severin/Elder-a(8pg.) 4.00 10.00 20.00
13-Used in **SOTI**, pg. 110-111 5.00 15.00 30.00
18-S&K-c, Elder-a 4.70 14.00 28.00

Ka'a'nga Comics #9, © FH

Kamandi: At Earth's End #5, © DC

Katy Keene #56, © AP

	GD25	FN65	NM94
21,30-S&K-c/a	5.35	16.00	32.00
22,23,27-S&K-c	4.00	12.00	24.00
24-26,28,29,31-50	2.80	7.00	14.00
51-57,59-70: 56-Ben Oda, Joe Simon, Joe Genola, Mort Meskin, & Jack Kirby app. in police line-up on-c	2.40	6.00	12.00
58-Illo. in **SOTI**, "Treating police contemptuously" (top left); text on heroin	13.00	40.00	90.00
71-92: 76-Orlando-a	2.40	6.00	12.00

NOTE: ***Bailey*** *a-12, 13.* ***Elder*** *a-8.* ***Kirby*** *a-19p.* ***Meskin*** *a-22, 27, 63, 64; c-45, 46.* ***Robinson/Meskin*** *a-5, 19.* ***Severin*** *a-8, 11p. Photo c-12, 15-17.*

JUST KIDS
No. 283, 1932 (16 pages; 9-1/2x12"; paper cover)
McLoughlin Bros.

	GD25	FN65	NM94
283-Three-color text, pictures on heavy paper	10.00	30.00	70.00

JUST MARRIED
January, 1958 - No. 114, Dec, 1976
Charlton Comics

	GD25	FN65	NM94
1	4.00	11.00	22.00
2	2.40	6.00	12.00
3-10	1.60	4.00	8.00
11-30	.90	2.25	4.50
31-50	.40	1.00	2.00
51-114		.50	1.00

JUSTY (Viz)(Value: cover or less)

KA'A'NGA COMICS (...Jungle King)(See Jungle Comics)
Spring, 1949 - No. 20, Summer, 1954
Fiction House Magazines (Glen-Kel Publ. Co.)

	GD25	FN65	NM94
1-Ka'a'nga, Lord of the Jungle begins	36.00	110.00	250.00
2 (Wint., '49-'50)	17.00	52.00	120.00
3,4	13.50	41.00	95.00
5-Camilla app.	10.00	30.00	65.00
6-10: 7-Tuska-a. 9-Tabu, Wizard of the Jungle app. 10-Used in **POP**, pg. 99	9.15	27.50	55.00
11-15: 15-Camilla-r by Baker/Jungle #106	7.50	22.50	45.00
16-Sheena app.	8.35	25.00	50.00
17-20	6.70	20.00	40.00
I.W. Reprint #1,8: 1-r/#18; Kinstler-c. 8-r/#10	1.80	4.50	9.00

NOTE: ***Celardo*** *c-1.* ***Whitman*** *c-8-20(most).*

KAMANDI: AT EARTH'S END
June, 1993 - No. 6, Nov, 1993 ($1.75, color, limited series)
DC Comics

	GD25	FN65	NM94
1-6: Elseworlds storyline		.70	1.75

KAMANDI, THE LAST BOY ON EARTH (Also see Alarming Tales #1, Brave and the Bold #120 & 157 & Cancelled Comic Cavalcade)
Oct-Nov, 1972 - V7#59, Sept-Oct, 1978
National Periodical Publications/DC Comics

	GD25	FN65	NM94
1-Origin & 1st app. Kamandi	4.00	12.00	28.00
2	2.40	7.25	17.00
3-5: 4-Intro. Prince Tuftan of the Tigers	1.65	4.70	11.00
6-10	1.20	3.00	7.00
11-20		1.90	4.75
21-40: 24-Last 20 cent issue. 29-Superman x-over. 31-Intro Pyra. 32-(68 pgs.)-r/origin from #1 plus one new story; 4 pg. biog. of Jack Kirby with B&W photos		1.40	3.50
41-59: 58-Karate Kid x-over from LSH. 59-(44 pgs.)-Cont'd in B&B #157; The Return of Omac back-up by Starlin-c/a(p)		1.10	2.75

NOTE: ***Ayers*** *a(p)-48-59 (most).* ***Giffen*** *a-44p, 45p.* ***Kirby*** *a-1-40p; c-1-33.* ***Kubert*** *c-34-41.* ***Nasser*** *a-45p, 46p.* ***Starlin*** *a-59p; c-57, 59p.*

KAMUI (Eclipse)(Value: cover or less)

KARATE KID (See Action, Adventure, Legion of Super-Heroes, & Superboy)
Mar-Apr, 1976 - No. 15, July-Aug, 1978 (Legion spin-off)
National Periodical Publications/DC Comics

	GD25	FN65	NM94
1-Meets Iris Jacobs; Estrada/Staton-a		.80	2.00
2-15: 2-Major Disaster app. 15-Continued into Kamandi #58		.70	1.80

NOTE: ***Grell*** *c-1-4, 5p, 6p, 7, 8.* ***Staton*** *a-1-9i. Legion x-over-No. 1, 2, 4, 6, 10, 12, 13. Princess Projectra x-over-#8, 9.*

KASCO KOMICS
1945; No. 2, 1949 (regular size; paper cover)
Kasko Grainfeed (Giveaway)

	GD25	FN65	NM94
1(1945)-Similar to Katy Keene; Bill Woggon-a; 28 pgs.; 6-7/8x9-7/8"	11.50	34.00	80.00
2(1949)-Woggon-a	10.00	30.00	70.00

KATHY
September, 1949 - No. 17, Sept, 1955
Standard Comics

	GD25	FN65	NM94
1-Teen-age	6.70	20.00	40.00
2-Schomburg-c	4.00	10.00	20.00
3-5	2.80	7.00	14.00
6-17: 17-Code approved	2.00	5.00	10.00

KATHY
Oct, 1959 - No. 27, Feb, 1964
Atlas Comics/Marvel (ZPC)

	GD25	FN65	NM94
1-Teen-age	5.35	16.00	32.00
2	3.20	8.00	16.00
3-15	1.80	4.50	9.00
16-27	1.20	3.00	6.00

KAT KARSON
No date (Reprint)
I. W. Enterprises

	GD25	FN65	NM94
1-Funny animals	1.20	3.00	6.00

KATO OF THE GREEN HORNET (Now)(Value: cover or less)

KATY AND KEN VISIT SANTA WITH MISTER WISH
1948 (16 pgs.; paper cover)
S. S. Kresge Co. (Giveaway)

	GD25	FN65	NM94
nn	4.00	10.00	20.00

KATY KEENE (Also see Kasco Komics, Laugh, Pep, Suzie, & Wilbur)
1949 - No. 4, 1951; No. 5, 3/52 - No. 62, Oct, 1961
Archie Publ./Close-Up/Radio Comics

	GD25	FN65	NM94
1-Bill Woggon-a begins	79.00	235.00	550.00
2	39.00	120.00	275.00
3-5	33.00	100.00	230.00
6-10	27.00	80.00	190.00
11,13-20	24.00	72.00	165.00
12-(Scarce)	26.00	78.00	180.00
21-40	17.00	52.00	120.00
41-62	13.00	40.00	90.00
Annual 1('54)	43.00	130.00	300.00
Annual 2-6('55-59)	24.00	72.00	165.00
3-D 1(1953-Large size)	36.00	107.00	250.00
Charm 1(9/58)	22.00	65.00	150.00
Glamour 1(1957)	22.00	65.00	150.00
Spectacular 1('56)	22.00	65.00	150.00

KATY KEENE COMICS DIGEST MAGAZINE
1987 - No. 10, July, 1990 ($1.25-$1.35-$1.50, digest size)
Close-Up, Inc. (Archie Ent.)

	GD25	FN65	NM94
1-10			1.50

KATY KEENE FASHION BOOK MAGAZINE
1955 - No. 13, Sum, '56 - N. 23, Wint, '58-59 (nn 3-10)
Radio Comics/Archie Publications

	GD25	FN65	NM94
1	39.00	120.00	275.00
2	24.00	72.00	165.00
11-18: 18-Photo Bill Woggon	17.00	52.00	120.00

Katy Keene Special #2, © AP

Ka-Zar #9 (12/81), © MEG

Keen Detective Funnies #18, © CEN

GD25 FN65 NM94

9-23 13.00 40.00 90.00

ATY KEENE HOLIDAY FUN (See Archie Giant Series Magazine No. 7, 12)

ATY KEENE PINUP PARADE
955 - No. 15, Summer, 1961 (25 cents)
adio Comics/Archie Publications

	GD25	FN65	NM94
1	39.00	120.00	275.00
2	24.00	72.00	165.00
3-5	19.00	58.00	135.00
6-10,12-14: 8-Mad parody. 10-Photo of Bill Woggon	16.00	48.00	110.00
11-Story of how comics get CCA approved, narrated by Katy	20.00	60.00	140.00
15(Rare)-Photo artist & family	39.00	116.00	270.00

ATY KEENE SPECIAL (Katy Keene #7 on; see Laugh Comics Digest)
ept, 1983 - No. 33, 1990 (Later issues published quarterly)
rchie Enterprises

1-33: 1-Woggon-r; new Woggon-c. 3-Woggon-r 1.00

ATZENJAMMER KIDS, THE (Also see Hans Und Fritz)
903 (50 pgs.; 10x15-1/4"; in color)
ew York American & Journal
By Rudolph Dirks; strip 1st appeared in 1898)

	GD25	FN65	NM94
903 (Rare)	67.00	200.00	450.00
905-Tricks of...(10x15)	46.00	138.00	300.00
906-Stokes-10x16", 32 pgs. in color	46.00	138.00	300.00
910-The Komical...(10x15)	42.00	125.00	275.00
921-Embee Dist. Co., 10x16", 20 pgs. in color	33.00	100.00	225.00

ATZENJAMMER KIDS, THE (See Giant Comic Album)
945-1946; Summer, 1947 - No. 27, Feb-Mar, 1954
avid McKay Publ./Standard No. 12-21(Spring/'50 - 53)/Harvey
o. 22, 4/53 on

	GD25	FN65	NM94
eature Books 30	12.00	36.00	85.00
eature Books 32,35('45),41,44('46)	11.00	32.00	75.00
eature Book 37-Has photos & biography of Harold Knerr	11.50	34.00	80.00
1(1947)	11.50	34.00	80.00
2	6.70	20.00	40.00
3-11	4.70	14.00	28.00
12-14(Standard)	4.00	11.00	22.00
15-21(Standard)	3.60	9.00	18.00
22-25,27(Harvey): 22-24-Henry app.	2.80	7.00	14.00
26-Half in 3-D	16.00	48.00	110.00

AYO (Formerly Bullseye & Jest; becomes Carnival Comics)
o. 12, March, 1945
arry 'A' Chesler

12-Green Knight, Capt. Glory, Little Nemo (not by McCay) 10.00 30.00 60.00

A-ZAR (Also see Marvel Comics #1, Savage Tales #6 & X-Men #10)
ug, 1970 - No. 3, Mar, 1971 (Giant-Size, 68 pgs.)
arvel Comics Group

	GD25	FN65	NM94
1-Reprints earlier Ka-Zar stories; Avengers x-over in Hercules; Daredevil, X-Men app.; hidden profanity-c	1.70	5.00	12.00
2,3-Daredevil-r. 2-Ka-Zar origin, X-Men-r	1.30	3.25	8.00

OTE: *Kirby c/a-all. Colan a-1p(r). #1-Reprints X-Men #10? & Daredevil #13?*

A-ZAR
an, 1974 - No. 20, Feb, 1977 (Regular Size)
arvel Comics Group

	GD25	FN65	NM94
1		1.00	2.50
2-20		.70	1.00

OTE: ***Alcala** a-6i, 8i. **Brunner** c-4. **J. Buscema** a-6-10p; c-1, 5, 7. **Heath** a-12. **G. Kane** (p)-3, 5, 8-11, 15, 20. **Kirby** c-12p. **Reinman** a-1p.*

A-ZAR THE SAVAGE (See Marvel Fanfare)
Apr, 1981 - No. 34, Oct, 1984 (Regular size) (Mando paper #10 on)
Marvel Comics Group

1-34: 11-Origin Zabu. 12-Two versions: With & without panel missing (1600 printed with panel). 20-Kraven the Hunter-c/story (also apps. in #21). 21-23,25,26-Spider-Man app. 26-Photo-c. 29-Double size; Ka-Zar & Shanna wed 1.00

NOTE: ***B. Anderson** a-1-15p, 18, 19; c-1-17, 18p, 20(back). **G. Kane** a(back-up)-11, 12, 14.*

KEEN DETECTIVE FUNNIES (Formerly Detective Picture Stories?)
No. 8, July, 1938 - No. 24, Sept, 1940
Centaur Publications

	GD25	FN65	NM94
V1#8-The Clock continues-r/Funny Picture Stories #1; Roy Crane-a (1st?)	107.00	321.00	750.00
9-Tex Martin by Eisner	58.00	175.00	370.00
10,11: 11-Dean Denton story (begins?)	50.00	150.00	330.00
V2#1,2-The Eye Sees by Frank Thomas begins; ends #23(Not in V2#3&5). 2-Jack Cole-a	44.00	132.00	290.00
3-6,9-11: 3-TNT Todd begins. 4-Gabby Flynn begins. 5,6-Dean Denton story	44.00	132.00	290.00
7-The Masked Marvel by Ben Thompson begins (7/39, 1st app.)	83.00	250.00	530.00
8-Nudist ranch panel w/four girls	50.00	150.00	320.00
12(12/39)-Origin The Eye Sees by Frank Thomas; death of Masked Marvel's sidekick ZL	58.00	175.00	370.00
V3#1,2	50.00	150.00	320.00
18,19,21,22: 18-Bondage/torture-c	50.00	150.00	320.00
20-Classic Eye Sees-c by Thomas	62.00	188.00	400.00
23,24: 23-Air Man begins (intro). 23, 24-Air Man-c	58.00	175.00	370.00

NOTE: ***Burgos** a-V2#2. **Jack Cole** a-V2#2. **Eisner** a-10, V2#6r. **Ken Ernst** a-V2#4, 7, 9, 10, 21. **Everett** a-V2#6, 7, 9, 11, 12, 20. **Guardineer** a-V2#5, 66. **Gustavson** a-V2#4-6. **Simon** c-V3#1.*

KEEN KOMICS
V2#1, May, 1939 - V2#3, Nov, 1939
Centaur Publications

	GD25	FN65	NM94
V2#1(Large size)-Dan Hastings (s/f), The Big Top, Bob Phantom the Magician, The Mad Goddess app.	66.00	200.00	430.00
V2#2(Reg. size)-The Forbidden Idol of Machu Picchu; Cut Carson by Burgos begins	42.00	125.00	270.00
V2#3-Saddle Sniff by Jack Cole, Circus Pays, Kings Revenge app.	42.00	125.00	270.00

NOTE: ***Binder** a-V2#2. **Burgos** a-V2#2, 3. **Ken Ernst** a-V2#3. **Gustavson** a-V2#2. **Jack Cole** a-V2#3.*

KEEN TEENS (Girls magazine)
1945 - No. 6, Aug-Sept, 1947
Life's Romances Publ./Leader/Magazine Enterprises

	GD25	FN65	NM94
nn (#1)-14 pgs. Claire Voyant (cont'd. in other nn issue) movie photos, Dotty Dripple, Gertie O'Grady & Sissy; Van Johnson, Frank Sinatra photo-c	16.00	48.00	110.00
nn (#2, 1946)-16 pgs. Claire Voyant & 16 pgs. movie photos	16.00	48.00	110.00
3-6: 4-Glenn Ford photo-c. 5-Perry Como-c	5.35	16.00	32.00

KEEPING UP WITH THE JONESES
1920 - No. 2, 1921 (52 pgs.; 9-1/4x9-1/4"; B&W daily strip reprints)
Cupples & Leon Co.

1,2-By Pop Momand 17.00 52.00 120.00

KELLYS, THE (Formerly Rusty Comics; Spy Cases No. 26 on)
No. 23, Jan, 1950 - No. 25, June, 1950
Marvel Comics (HPC)

	GD25	FN65	NM94
23	9.15	27.50	55.00
24,25: 24-Margie app.	5.35	16.00	32.00

KELVIN MACE (Vortex)(Value: cover or less)

KEN MAYNARD WESTERN (Movie star)(See Wow Comics, 1936)
Sept, 1950 - No. 8, Feb, 1952 (All 36 pgs; photo front/back-c)

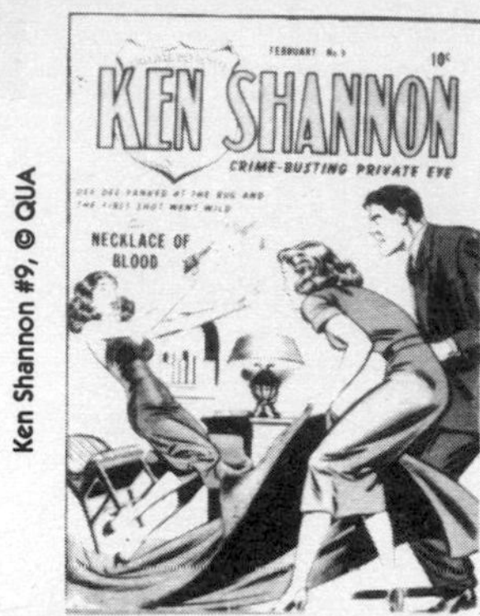

Ken Shannon #9, © QUA

Key Ring Comics #1, © DELL

Kid Colt Outlaw #46, © MEG

GD25 FN65 NM94

Fawcett Publications

1-Ken Maynard & his horse Tarzan begin 43.00 130.00 300.00
2 27.00 81.00 190.00
3-8: 6-Atomic bomb explosion panel 22.00 65.00 150.00

KEN SHANNON (Becomes Gabby #11 on) (Also see Police Comics #103)
Oct, 1951 - No. 10, Apr, 1953 (A private eye)
Quality Comics Group

1-Crandall-a 18.00 54.00 125.00
2-Crandall c/a(2) 14.00 43.00 100.00
3-5-Crandall-a. 3-Horror-c 10.00 30.00 70.00
6-Crandall-c/a; "The Weird Vampire Mob"-c/s 11.00 32.00 75.00
7,9-Crandall-a 10.00 30.00 60.00
8-Opium den drug use story 8.35 25.00 50.00
10-Crandall-c 10.00 30.00 60.00

NOTE: ***Crandall/Cuidera** c-1-10. **Jack Cole** a-1-9. No. 11-15 published after title change to Gabby.*

KEN STUART
Jan, 1949 (Sea Adventures)
Publication Enterprises

1-Frank Borth-c/a 5.85 17.50 35.00

KENT BLAKE OF THE SECRET SERVICE (Spy)
May, 1951 - No. 14, July, 1953
Marvel/Atlas Comics(20CC)

1-Injury to eye, bondage, torture; Brodsky-c 10.00 30.00 70.00
2-Drug use w/hypo scenes; Brodsky-c 7.50 22.50 45.00
3-14: 8-R.Q. Sale-a (2 pgs.) 4.70 14.00 28.00

NOTE: ***Heath** c-5, 7, 8. **Infantino** c-12. **Maneely** c-3. **Sinnott** a-2(3). **Tuska** a-8(3pg.)*

KERRY DRAKE
Jan, 1956 - No. 2, March, 1956
Argo

1,2-Newspaper-r 4.70 14.00 28.00

KERRY DRAKE DETECTIVE CASES (...Racket Buster No. 32,33)
(Also see Chamber of Clues & Green Hornet Comics #42-47)
1944 - No. 5, 1944; No. 6, Jan, 1948 - No. 33, Aug, 1952
Life's Romances/Com/Magazine Ent. No.1-5/Harvey No.6 on

nn(1944)(A-1 Comics)(slightly over-size) 16.00 48.00 110.00
2 10.00 30.00 70.00
3-5(1944) 9.15 27.50 55.00
6,8(1948): Lady Crime by Powell. 8-Bondage-c 5.35 16.00 32.00
7-Kubert-a; biog of Andriola (artist) 6.35 19.00 38.00
9,10-Two-part marijuana story; Kerry smokes marijuana in #10
9.65 29.00 58.00
11-15 4.70 14.00 28.00
16-33 4.00 10.00 22.00
...in the Case of the Sleeping City-(1951-Publishers Synd.)-16 pg. giveaway for armed forces; paper cover 4.00 10.00 20.00

NOTE: ***Andiola** c-6-9. **Berg** a-5. **Powell** a-10-23, 28, 29.*

KEWPIES
Spring, 1949
Will Eisner Publications

1-Feiffer-a; Kewpie Doll ad on back cover 34.00 100.00 235.00

KEY COMICS
Jan, 1944 - No. 5, Aug, 1946
Consolidated Magazines

1-The Key, Will-O-The-Wisp begin 21.00 62.00 140.00
2 (3/44) 10.00 30.00 70.00
3,4: 4-(5/46)-Origin John Quincy The Atom (begins)
9.15 27.50 55.00
5-4pg. Faust Opera adapt; Kiefer-a; back-c advertises "Masterpieces Illustrated" by Lloyd Jacquet after he left Classic Comics (no copies of Masterpieces Illustrated known) 11.00 32.00 75.00

KEY COMICS
1951 - 1956 (32 pages) (Giveaway)
Key Clothing Co./Peterson Clothing

Contains a comic from different publishers bound with new cover. Cover changed each year. Many combinations possible. Distributed in Nebraska, Iowa, & Kansas. Contents would determine price, 40-60 percent of original.

KEY RING COMICS
1941 (16 pgs.; two colors) (sold 5 for 10 cents)
Dell Publishing Co.

1-Sky Hawk 3.00 7.50 15.0
1-Viking Carter 3.00 7.50 15.0
1-Features Sleepy Samson 3.20 8.00 16.0
1-Origin Greg Gilday-r/War Comics #2 3.20 8.00 16.0
1-Radior(Super hero) 2.80 7.00 14.0

NOTE: *Each book has two holes in spine to put in binder.*

KICKERS, INC. (Marvel)(Value: cover or less)

KID CARROTS
September, 1953
St. John Publishing Co.

1-Funny animal 4.00 11.00 22.0

KID COLT OUTLAW (Kid Colt #1-4; ...Outlaw #5-on)(Also see All Western Winners, Best Western, Black Rider, Giant-Size..., Two-Gun Kid, Two-Gun Western, Western Winners, Wild Western, Wisco)
8/48 - No. 139, 3/68; No. 140, 11/69 - No. 229, 4/79
Marvel Comics(LCC) 1-16; Atlas(LMC) 17-102; Marvel 103-on

1-Kid Colt & his horse Steel begin; Two-Gun Kid app.
57.00 170.00 400.0
2 29.00 85.00 200.0
3-5: 4-Anti-Wertham editorial; Tex Taylor app. 5-Blaze Carson app.
22.00 65.00 150.0
6-8: 6-Tex Taylor app; 7-Nimo the Lion begins, ends #10
14.00 43.00 100.0
9,10 (52 pgs.) 15.00 45.00 105.0
11-Origin 17.00 52.00 120.0
12-20 11.00 32.00 75.0
21-32 9.15 27.50 55.0
33-45: Black Rider in all 7.50 22.50 45.0
46,47,49,50 6.70 20.00 40.0
48-Kubert-a 7.50 22.50 45.0
51-53,55,56 5.35 16.00 32.0
54-Williamson/Maneely-c 6.70 20.00 40.0
57-60,66: 4-pg. Williamson-a in all. 59-Reprints Rawhide Kid #79; Colan text illo 7.50 22.50 45.0
61-63,67-78,80-86: 86-Kirby-a(r) 4.00 11.00 22.0
64,65-Crandall-a 5.00 15.00 30.0
79,87: 79-Origin retold. 87-Davis-a(r) 4.70 14.00 28.0
88,89-Williamson-a in both (4 pgs.). 89-Redrawn Matt Slade #2
5.00 15.00 30.0
90-99,101-Last 10 cent issues 2.40 6.00 14.0
100 3.60 9.00 20.0
101-120 2.40 6.00 12.0
121-140: 121-Rawhide Kid x-over. 125-Two-Gun Kid x-over. 130-132-68 pg. issues with one new story each. 130-Origin. 140-Reprints begin
1.30 3.25 8.0
141-160: 156-Giant; reprints (later issues all-r) 1.60 4.0
161-229: 170-Origin retold. 229-Rawhide Kid-r .80 2.0
...Album (no date; 1950's; Atlas Comics)-132 pgs.; random binding, cardboard cover, B&W stories; contents can vary (Rare) 61.00 182.00 425.0

NOTE: ***Ayers** a-many. **Colan** a-52, 53; c(p)-223, 228, 229. **Crandall** a-140r, 167r. **Everett** a-90, 137i, 225i(r). **Heath** a-8(2); c-34, 35, 39, 44, 46, 48, 49, 57, 64. **Jack Keller** a-25(2), 26-68(3-4), 78, 94p, 98, 99, 108, 110, 132. **Kirby** a-86r, 93, 96, 119, 176(part); c-87, 92-95, 97, 99-112, 114, 117, 121-123, 197r. **Maneely** a-12, 68, 81; c-17, 19, 40-43, 47, 52, 53, 62, 65, 68, 78, 81. **Morrow** a-173r, 216r. **Rico** a-13, 18. **Severin** c-58, 59. **Shores** a-39, 41-43; c-1-10(most), 24. **Sutton** a-137p, 225p(r). **Wildey** a-47, 54, 82. **Williamson** r-147, 170, 172, 216. **Woodbridge** a-64, 81. Black Rider in #33-45, 74, 86. Iron Mask in #110, 114, 121, 127. Sam Hawk in #84, 101, 111, 121, 146, 174, 181, 188.*

Kid Komics #6, © MEG

Killpower: The Early Years #1, © MEG

	GD25	FN65	NM94

COWBOY (Also see Approved Comics #4 & Boy Cowboy)
0 - No. 14, 1954 (painted covers)
Davis Publ./St. John (Approved Comics)

Lucy Belle & Red Feather begin	9.15	27.50	55.00
Maneely-c	5.00	15.00	30.00
14: 5-Berg-a	4.00	12.00	24.00

DIE KAPERS
5?(nd); Oct, 1957; 1963 - 1964
die Kapers Co., 1945/Decker Publ. (Red Top-Farrell)

nd, 1945-46?, 36 pgs.)-Infinity-c; funny animal	5.35	16.00	32.00
10/57)(Decker)-Little Bit reprints from Kiddie Karnival	3.00	7.50	15.00
per Reprint #7, 10('63), 12, 14('63), 15,17('64), 18('64)	.80	2.00	4.00

DIE KARNIVAL
52 (100 pgs., 25 cents) (One Shot)
Davis Publ. Co. (Approved Comics)

Robound Little Bit #1,2	24.00	72.00	165.00

ETERNITY (Becomes Buccaneers) (See Hit Comics)
ring, 1946 - No. 18, Nov, 1949
ality Comics Group

	47.00	140.00	300.00
	24.00	72.00	155.00
Mac Raboy-a	26.00	78.00	165.00
10	13.00	40.00	85.00
-18	10.00	30.00	60.00

ETERNITY
91 - No. 3, Nov, 1991 ($4.95, color, mini-series)
Comics

3: Grant Morrison scripts	1.00	2.00	5.00

ETERNITY
y, 1993 - Present ($1.95, color, mature readers)
Comics (Vertigo)

12: 1-Gold ink-c. 6-Photo-c		.80	2.00

FROM DODGE CITY, THE
y, 1957 - No. 2, Sept, 1957
as Comics (MMC)

Don Heck-c	5.85	17.50	35.00
Everett-c	4.00	10.00	20.00

FROM TEXAS, THE (A Texas Ranger)
ne, 1957 - No. 2, Aug, 1957
as Comics (CSI)

Powell-a; Severin-c	6.70	20.00	40.00
	4.00	11.00	22.00

KOKO
58
V. Enterprises

eprint #1,2-(r/M.E.'s Koko & Kola #4, 1947)	1.00	2.50	5.00

KOMICS (Kid Movie Komics No. 11)
b, 1943 - No. 10, Spring, 1946
mely Comics (USA 1,2/FCI 3-10)

-Origin Captain Wonder & sidekick Tim Mulrooney, & Subbie; intro the Sea-Going Lad, Pinto Pete, & Trixie Trouble; Knuckles & Whitewash Jones only app.; Wolverton art, 7 pgs.	200.00	600.00	1400.00
-The Young Allies, Red Hawk, & Tommy Tyme begin; last Captain Wonder & Subbie	92.00	275.00	600.00
-The Vision, Daredevils & Red Hawk app.	62.00	188.00	410.00
-The Destroyer begins; Sub-Mariner app.; Red Hawk & Tommy Tyme end	58.00	175.00	375.00
,6: 5-Tommy Tyme begins, ends #10	45.00	135.00	300.00
7-10: 7,10-The Whizzer app. Destroyer not in #7,8; 10-Last Destroyer, Young Allies & Whizzer	42.00	125.00	275.00

NOTE: *Brodsky c-5. Schomburg c-2-4, 6-10. Shores c-1.*

KID MONTANA (Formerly Davy Crockett Frontier Fighter; The Gunfighters No. 51 on)
V2#9, Nov, 1957 - No. 50, Mar, 1965
Charlton Comics

V2#9	5.35	16.00	32.00
10	3.20	8.00	16.00
11,12,14-20	2.40	6.00	12.00
13-Williamson-a	3.60	9.00	18.00
21-35	1.20	3.00	6.00
36-50	.80	2.00	4.00

NOTE: *Title change to Montana Kid on cover only on #44; remained Kid Montana on inside.*

KID MOVIE KOMICS (Formerly Kid Komics; Rusty Comics #12 on)
No. 11, Summer, 1946
Timely Comics

11-Silly Seal & Ziggy Pig; 2 pgs. Kurtzman "Hey Look" plus 6 pg. "Pigtales" story	17.00	52.00	120.00

KIDNAPPED (See 4-Color No. 1101 & Movie Comics)

KIDNAP RACKET (See Harvey Comics Hits No. 57)

KID 'N PLAY (Marvel)(Value: cover or less)

KID SLADE GUNFIGHTER (Formerly Matt Slade...)
No. 5, Jan, 1957 - No. 8, July, 1957
Atlas Comics (SPI)

5-Maneely, Roth, Severin-a in all; Maneely-c	7.50	22.50	45.00
6,8-Severin-c	4.00	11.00	22.00
7-Williamson/Mayo-a, 4 pgs.	6.35	19.00	38.00

KID ZOO COMICS
July, 1948 (52 pgs.)
Street & Smith Publications

1-Funny Animal	17.00	52.00	120.00

KILLER (...Tales By Timothy Truman)
March, 1985 ($1.75, one-shot, color, Baxter paper)
Eclipse Comics

1-Timothy Truman-c/a		.70	1.75

KILLERS, THE
1947 - No. 2, 1948 (No month)
Magazine Enterprises

1-Mr. Zin, the Hatchet Killer; mentioned in **SOTI**, pgs. 179,180; used by N.Y. Legis. Comm.; L. B. Cole-c	47.00	141.00	330.00
2-(Scarce)-Hashish smoking story; "Dying, Dying, Dead" drug story; Whitney, Ingels-a; Whitney hanging-c	46.00	139.00	325.00

KILLING JOKE, THE (See Batman: The Killing Joke)

KILLPOWER: THE EARLY YEARS
Sept, 1993 - No. 4, Dec, 1993 ($1.75, color, mini-series)
Marvel Comics UK

1-($2.95)-Foil embossed-c		1.20	3.00
2-4: 2-Genetix app. 3-Punisher app.		.70	1.75

KILROYS, THE
June-July, 1947 - No. 54, June-July, 1955
D&I Publ. Co. No. 1-19/American Comics Group

1	16.00	48.00	110.00
2	9.15	27.50	55.00
3-5: 5-Gross-a	6.70	20.00	40.00
6-10: 8-Milt Gross's Moronica	5.00	15.00	30.00
11-20: 14-Gross-a	4.20	12.50	25.00
21-30	3.60	9.00	18.00
31-47,50-54	3.20	8.00	16.00
48,49-(3-D effect)	13.00	40.00	90.00

King Comics #61, © KING

King of the Royal Mounted #19, © Stephen Slesinger

Kit Carson #7, © AVON

KING ARTHUR AND THE KNIGHTS OF JUSTICE
Dec, 1993 - No. 3, Feb, 1994 ($1.25, color, mini-series)
Marvel Comics UK

	GD25	FN65	NM94
1-3: TV adaptation			1.25

KING CLASSICS
1977 (85 cents each) (36 pages, cardboard covers)
King Features (Printed in Spain for U.S. distr.)

1-Connecticut Yankee, 2-Last of the Mohicans, 3-Moby Dick, 4-Robin Hood, 5-Swiss Family Robinson, 6-Robinson Crusoe, 7-Treasure Island, 8-20,000 Leagues, 9-Christmas Carol, 10-Huck Finn, 11-Around the World in 80 Days, 12-Davy Crockett, 13-Don Quixote, 14-Gold Bug, 15-Ivanhoe, 16-Three Musketeers, 17-Baron Munchausen, 18-Alice in Wonderland, 19-Black Arrow, 20-Five Weeks in a Balloon, 21-Great Expectations, 22-Gulliver's Travels, 23-Prince & Pauper, 24-Lawrence of Arabia (Originals, 1977-78)

	GD25	FN65	NM94
each....	1.30	3.25	8.00
Reprints, 1979; HRN-24)	1.00	2.50	6.00

NOTE: *The first eight issues were not numbered. Issues No. 25-32 were advertised but not published. The 1977 originals have HRN 32a; the 1978 originals have HRN 32b.*

KING COLT (See 4-Color No. 651)

KING COMICS (Strip reprints)
Apr, 1936 - No. 159, Feb, 1952 (Winter on cover)
David McKay Publications/Standard #156-on

	GD25	FN65	VF82
1-1st app. Flash Gordon by Alex Raymond; Brick Bradford (1st app.), Popeye, Henry (1st app.) & Mandrake the Magician (1st app.) begin	600.00	1800.00	4000.00

(Estimated up to 25 total copies exist, none in NM/Mint)

	GD25	FN65	NM94
2	192.00	575.00	1250.00
3	133.00	400.00	900.00
4	96.00	288.00	640.00
5	75.00	225.00	500.00
6-10: 9-X-Mas-c	50.00	150.00	330.00
11-20	40.00	120.00	265.00
21-30: 21-X-Mas-c	32.00	95.00	210.00
31-40: 33-Last Segar Popeye	27.00	80.00	175.00
41-50: 46-Little Lulu, Alvin & Tubby app. as text illos by Marge Buell. 50-The Lone Ranger begins	24.00	72.00	160.00
51-60: 52-Barney Baxter begins?	17.00	52.00	115.00
61-The Phantom begins	15.00	45.00	100.00
62-80: 76-Flag-c	12.50	37.50	85.00
81-99: 82-Blondie begins?	10.00	30.00	70.00
100	13.00	40.00	90.00
101-114: 114-Last Raymond issue (1 pg.); Flash Gordon by Austin Briggs begins, ends #155	10.00	30.00	65.00
115-145: 117-Phantom origin retold	8.35	25.00	50.00
146,147-Prince Valiant in both	5.85	17.50	35.00
148-155-Flash Gordon ends	5.85	17.50	35.00
156-159	5.00	15.00	30.00

NOTE: *Marge Buell text illos in No. 24-46 at least.*

KING CONAN (Conan The King No. 20 on)
March, 1980 - No. 19, Nov, 1983 (52 pgs.)
Marvel Comics Group

	GD25	FN65	NM94
1		1.00	2.50
2-19: 4-Death of Thoth Amon. 7-1st Paul Smith-a, 1 pg. pin-up (9/81)		.70	1.75

NOTE: ***J. Buscema** a-1-9p, 17p; c(p)-1-5, 7-9, 14, 17. **Kaluta** c-19. **Nebres** a-17i, 18, 19i. **Severin** c-18. **Simonson** c-6.*

KING KONG (See Movie Comics)

KING LEONARDO & HIS SHORT SUBJECTS (TV)
Nov-Jan, 1961-62 - No. 4, Sept, 1963
Dell Publishing Co./Gold Key

	GD25	FN65	NM94
4-Color 1242,1278	13.00	40.00	90.00
01390-207(5-7/62)(Dell)	10.00	30.00	70.00
1 (10/62)	10.00	30.00	70.00
2-4	8.35	25.00	50.00

KING LOUIE & MOWGLI
May, 1968 (Disney)
Gold Key

	GD25	FN65	NM94
1 (#10223-805)-Characters from Jungle Book	2.15	6.50	15.

KING OF DIAMONDS (TV)
July-Sept, 1962
Dell Publishing Co.

	GD25	FN65	NM94
01-391-209-Photo-c	4.20	12.50	25.

KING OF KINGS (See 4-Color No. 1236)

KING OF THE BAD MEN OF DEADWOOD
1950 (See Wild Bill Hickok #16)
Avon Periodicals

	GD25	FN65	NM94
nn-Kinstler-c; Kamen/Feldstein-r/Cowpuncher #2	11.00	32.00	75.

KING OF THE ROYAL MOUNTED (See Famous Feature Stories, Feature Books #1, Large Feature Comic #9, King Comics, Red Ryder #3 & Super Book #2, 6)

KING OF THE ROYAL MOUNTED (Zane Grey's)
No. 207, Dec, 1948 - No. 935, Sept-Nov, 1958
Dell Publishing Co.

	GD25	FN65	NM94
4-Color 207(#1, 12/48)	13.00	40.00	90.
4-Color 265,283	10.00	30.00	60.
4-Color 310,340	6.70	20.00	40.
4-Color 363,384	5.85	17.50	35.
8(6-8/52)-10	5.85	17.50	35.0
11-20	4.70	14.00	28.0
21-28(3-5/58)	4.00	12.00	24.0
4-Color 935(9-11/58)	4.00	12.00	24.0

NOTE: *4-Color No. 207, 265, 283, 310, 340, 363, 384 are all newspaper reprints with **Jim Gary** art. No. 8 on are all Dell originals. Painted c-No. 9-on.*

KING RICHARD & THE CRUSADERS (See 4-Color No. 588)

KINGS OF THE NIGHT (Dark Horse)(Value: cover or less)

KING SOLOMON'S MINES
1951 (Movie)
Avon Periodicals

	GD25	FN65	NM94
nn(#1 on 1st page)	24.00	72.00	165.0

KISS (See Crazy Magazine, Howard the Duck #12, 13, Marvel Comics Super Special #1, 5, Rock Fantasy Comics #10 & Rock N' Roll Comics #9)

KISSYFUR (TV) (DC)(Value: cover or less)

KIT CARSON (Formerly All True Detective Cases No. 4; Fighting Davy Crockett No. 9; see Blazing Sixguns & Frontier Fighters)
1950; No. 2, 8/51 - No. 3, 12/51; No. 5, 11-12/54 - No. 8, 9/55 (No #4)
Avon Periodicals

	GD25	FN65	NM94
nn(#1) (1950)	10.00	30.00	60.0
2(8/51)	5.85	17.50	35.0
3(12/51)	5.00	15.00	30.0
5-6,8(11-12/54-9/55): 5-Formerly All True Detective Cases (last pre-code)	4.70	14.00	28.0
7-McCann-a?	5.00	15.00	30.0
I.W. Reprint #10('63)-r/Kit Carson #1; Severin-c	1.40	4.00	8.0

NOTE: ***Kinstler** c-1-3, 5-8.*

KIT CARSON & THE BLACKFEET WARRIORS
1953
Realistic

	GD25	FN65	NM94
nn-Reprint; Kinstler-c	7.50	22.50	45.0

KITE FUN BOOK
1954 - 1981 (16pgs, 5x7-1/4", soft-c)
Pacific, Gas & Electric/Sou. California Edison/Florida Power & Light

	GD25	FN65	NM94
1954-Donald Duck Tells About Kites-Fla. Power, S.C.E. & version with label issues-Barks pencils-8 pgs.; inks-7 pgs. (Rare)	285.00	850.00	1800.0

1954-Donald Duck Tells About Kites-P.G.&E. issue -7th page redrawn

ity Pryde and Wolverine #5, © MEG

Kobra #6, © DC

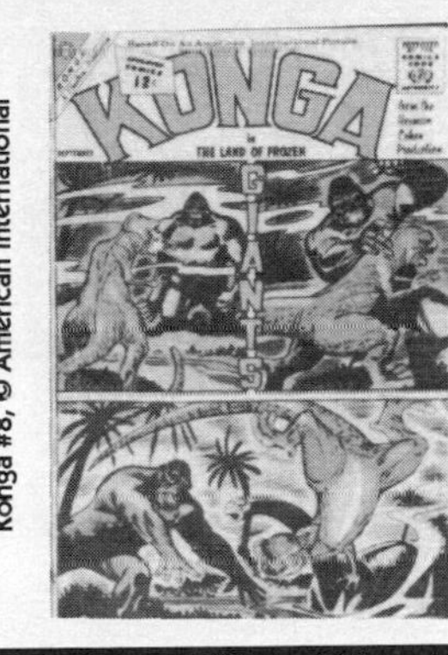

Konga #8, © American International

GD25 FN65 NM94

changing middle 3 panels to show P.G.&E. in story line; (All barks; last page Barks pencils only) Scarce 250.00 750.00 1600.00
i4-Pinocchio Learns About Kites 29.00 85.00 200.00
i5-Brer Rabbit in "A Kite Tail" (Disney) 25.00 75.00 175.00
i6-Woody Woodpecker 10.00 30.00 70.00
i7-?
i8-Tom And Jerry 6.70 20.00 40.00
i0-Porky Pig 5.00 15.00 30.00
i0-Bugs Bunny 5.00 15.00 30.00
i1-Huckleberry Hound (Hanna-Barbera) 5.85 17.50 35.00
i2-Yogi Bear (Hanna-Barbera) 4.20 12.50 25.00
63-Rocky and Bullwinkle (Jay Ward) 12.00 35.00 70.00
63-Top Cat (Hanna-Barbera) 4.20 12.50 25.00
i4-Magilla Gorilla (Hanna-Barbera) 4.00 10.00 20.00
i5-Jinks, Pixie and Dixie (Hanna-Barbera) 2.80 7.00 14.00
i5-Tweety and Sylvester (Warner); S.C.E. version with Reddy Kilowatt app. 1.30 3.25 8.00
66-Secret Squirrel (Hanna-Barbera); S.C.E. version with Reddy Kilowatt app. 7.00 21.00 50.00
67-Beep! Beep! The Road Runner (TV) 2.15 6.50 15.00
68-Bugs Bunny 2.15 6.50 15.00
69-Dastardly and Muttley (Hanna-Barbera) 3.20 8.00 20.00
70-Rocky and Bullwinkle (Jay Ward) 8.00 24.00 55.00
71-Beep! Beep! The Road Runner (TV) 1.65 4.00 10.00
72-The Pink Panther (TV) 1.20 3.00 7.00
73-Lassie (TV) 3.20 8.00 20.00
74-Underdog (TV) 1.70 5.00 12.00
75-Ben Franklin 1.60 4.00
76-The Brady Bunch (TV) 1.65 4.00 10.00
77-Ben Franklin 1.60 4.00
77-Popeye 1.70 5.00 12.00
78-Happy Days (TV) 1.20 3.00 7.00
79-Eight is Enough (TV) 1.30 3.25 8.00
80-The Waltons (TV, released in 1981) 1.65 4.00 10.00

T KARTER
ay-July, 1962
ell Publishing Co.

2.00 7.00 14.00

TTY
ctober, 1948
. John Publishing Co.
-Lily Renee-a 5.00 15.00 30.00

TTY PRYDE AND WOLVERINE
ov, 1984 - No. 6, April, 1985 (Mini-series)
arvel Comics Group
(From X-Men) 1.40 3.50
-6 .80 2.00

LARER GIVEAWAYS (See Wisco)

NIGHTS OF PENDRAGON, THE (Also see Pendragon)
ly, 1990 - No. 18, Dec, 1991 ($1.95, color)
arvel Comics Ltd.
-18: 1-Capt. Britain app. 2,8-Free poster inside. 9,10-Bolton-c. 11,18-Iron Man app. .80 2.00

NIGHTS OF THE ROUND TABLE (See 4-Color No. 540)

NIGHTS OF THE ROUND TABLE
). 10, April, 1957
nes Comics
) 3.20 8.00 16.00

NIGHTS OF THE ROUND TABLE
ov-Jan, 1963-64
ell Publishing Co.
(12-397-401)-Painted-c 4.00 10.00 20.00

GD25 FN65 NM94

KNOCK KNOCK (...Who's There?)
No. 801, 1936 (52 pages) (8x9", B&W)
Whitman Publ./Gerona Publications
801-Joke book; Bob Dunn-a 5.00 15.00 30.00

KNOCKOUT ADVENTURES
Winter, 1953-54
Fiction House Magazines
1-Reprints Fight Comics #53 10.00 30.00 65.00

KNOW YOUR MASS
No. 303, 1958 (100 Pg. Giant) (35 cents) (square binding)
Catechetical Guild
303-In color 3.20 8.00 16.00

KOBRA (See DC Special Series No. 1)
Feb-Mar, 1976 - No. 7, Mar-Apr, 1977
National Periodical Publications
1-1st app.; art plotted by Kirby; only 25 cent issue .70 1.80
2-7: (30 cent-c) 3-Giffen-a 1.50
NOTE: ***Austin** a-3i. **Buckler** a-5p; c-5p. **Kubert** c-4. **Nasser** a-6p, 7; c-7.*

KOKEY KOALA
May, 1952
Toby Press
1 6.70 20.00 40.00

KOKO AND KOLA (Also see A-1 Comics #16 & Tick Tock Tales)
Fall, 1946 - No. 5, May, 1947; No. 6, 1950
Com/Magazine Enterprises
1-Funny animal 7.50 22.50 45.00
2 4.00 11.00 22.00
3-6: 6(A-1 28) 4.00 10.00 20.00

KO KOMICS
October, 1945
Gerona Publications
1-The Duke of Darkness & The Menace (hero); Kirby-c 34.00 105.00 240.00

KOMIC KARTOONS
Fall, 1945 - No. 2, Winter, 1945
Timely Comics (EPC)
1,2-Andy Wolf, Bertie Mouse 13.00 40.00 90.00

KOMIK PAGES (Formerly Snap; becomes Bullseye #11)
April, 1945 (All reprints)
Harry 'A' Chesler, Jr. (Our Army, Inc.)
10(#1 on inside)-Land O' Nod by Rick Yager (2 pgs.), Animal Crackers, Foxy GrandPa, Tom, Dick & Mary, Cheerio Minstrels, Red Starr plus other 1-2 pg. strips; Cole-a 11.00 32.00 75.00

KONA (...Monarch of Monster Isle)
Feb-Apr, 1962 - No. 21, Jan-Mar, 1967 (Painted-c)
Dell Publishing Co.
4-Color 1256 (#1) 5.50 17.00 40.00
2-10: 4-Anak begins 2.60 7.50 18.00
11-21 1.85 5.50 13.00
NOTE: ***Glanzman** a-all issues.*

KONGA (Fantastic Giants No. 24) (See Return of...)
1960; No. 2, Aug, 1961 - No. 23, Nov, 1965
Charlton Comics
1(1960)-Based on movie; Giordano-c 26.00 77.00 180.00
2-Giordano-c 12.00 36.00 85.00
3-5 10.00 30.00 70.00
6-15 6.50 19.00 45.00
16-23 4.50 14.00 32.00
NOTE: ***Ditko** a-1, 3-15; c-4, 6-9. **Glanzman** a-12. **Montes & Bache** a-16-23.*

Korak, Son of Tarzan #3, © ERB

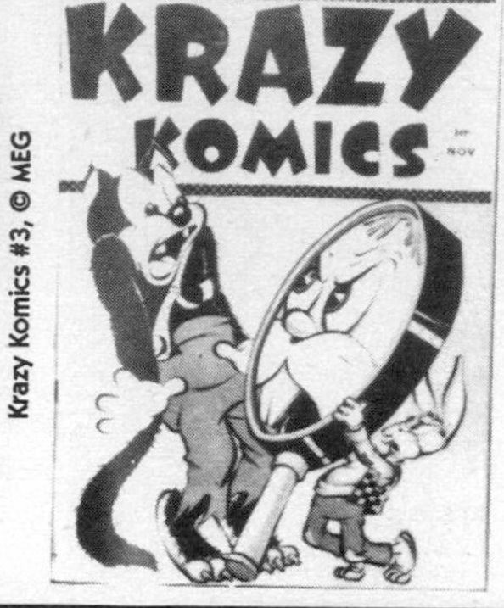

Krazy Komics #3, © MEG

Krofft Supershow #1, © Krofft TV Prod.

GD25 FN65 NM94

KONGA'S REVENGE (Formerly Return of...)
No. 2, Summer, 1963 - No. 3, Fall, 1964; Dec, 1968
Charlton Comics

2,3: 2-Ditko-c/a 4.70 14.00 33.00
1(12/68)-Reprints Konga's Revenge #3 2.40 7.25 17.00

KONG THE UNTAMED
June-July, 1975 - V2#5, Feb-Mar, 1976
National Periodical Publications

1-1st app. Kong; Wrightson-c; Alcala-a 1.50
2-5: 2-Wrightson-c. 2,3-Alcala-a 1.00

KOOKIE
Feb-Apr, 1962 - No. 2, May-July, 1962 (15 cents)
Dell Publishing Co.

1,2-Written by John Stanley; Bill Williams-a 8.35 25.00 50.00

KOOSH KINS
Oct, 1991 - No. 4, Apr, 1992 ($1.00, color, bi-monthly, mini-series)
Archie Comics

1-4 1.00

K. O. PUNCH, THE (Also see Lucky Fights It Through)
1948 (Educational giveaway)
E. C. Comics

nn-Feldstein-splash; Kamen-a 125.00 375.00 750.00

KORAK, SON OF TARZAN (Edgar Rice Burroughs)(See Tarzan #139)
Jan, 1964 - No. 45, Jan, 1972 (Painted-c No. 1-?)
Gold Key

1-Russ Manning-a 5.50 16.00 38.00
2-11-Russ Manning-a 3.20 8.00 20.00
12-21: 12,13-Warren Tufts-a. 14-Jon of the Kalahari ends. 15-Mabu, Jungle Boy begins. 21-Manning-a 2.15 6.50 15.00
22-30 1.50 3.75 9.00
31-45 1.20 3.00 7.00

KORAK, SON OF TARZAN (Tarzan Family #60 on; see Tarzan #230)
V9#46, May-June, 1972 - V12#56, Feb-Mar, 1974; No. 57, May-June, 1975 - No. 59, Sept-Oct, 1975 (Edgar Rice Burroughs)
National Periodical Publications

46-(52 pgs.)-Carson of Venus begins (origin), ends #56; Pellucidar feature; Weiss-a 1.40 3.50
47-59: 49-Origin Korak retold .80 2.00
NOTE: ***Kaluta** a-46-56. All have covers by **Joe Kubert**. **Manning** strip reprints-No. 57-59. **Frank Thorn** a-46-51.*

KOREA MY HOME (Also see Yalta to Korea)
nd (1950s)
Johnstone and Cushing

nn-Anti-communist; Korean War 22.00 65.00 150.00

KORG: 70,000 B. C. (TV)
May, 1975 - No. 9, Nov, 1976 (Hanna-Barbera)
Charlton Publications

1 1.80 4.50
2-9: 2-Painted-c; Byrne text illos 1.00 2.50

KORNER KID COMICS
1947
Four Star Publications

1 5.00 15.00 30.00

KRAZY KAT
1946 (Hardcover)
Holt

Reprints daily & Sunday strips by Herriman 26.00 78.00 180.00
with dust jacket (Rare).... 64.00 192.00 450.00

KRAZY KAT (See Ace Comics & March of Comics No. 72, 87)

KRAZY KAT COMICS (...& Ignatz the Mouse early issues)
May-June, 1951 - F.C. #696, Apr, 1956; Jan, 1964 (None by Herriman)
Dell Publishing Co./Gold Key

1(1951) 7.50 22.50 45.
2-5 (#5, 8-10/52) 5.00 15.00 30.
4-Color 454,504 4.00 12.00 24.
4-Color 548,619,696 (4/56) 4.00 10.00 20.
1(10098-401)(1/64-Gold Key)(TV) 4.00 10.00 20.

KRAZY KOMICS (1st Series) (Cindy Comics No. 27 on)
July, 1942 - No. 26, Spr, 1947 (Also see Ziggy Pig)
Timely Comics (USA No. 1-21/JPC No. 22-26)

1-Ziggy Pig & Silly Seal begins 30.00 90.00 210.
2 14.00 43.00 100.
3-10: 9-Hitler parody 10.00 30.00 70.
11,13,14 8.35 25.00 50.
12-Timely's entire art staff drew themselves into a Creeper story 13.00 40.00 90.
15-(8-9/44)-Becomes Funny Tunes #16; has "Super Soldier" by Pfc. Stan Lee 8.35 25.00 50.
16-24,26: 16-(10-11/44) 5.85 17.50 35.
25-Kurtzman-a, 6 pgs. 8.35 25.00 50.

KRAZY KOMICS (2nd Series)
Aug, 1948 - No. 2, Nov, 1948
Timely/Marvel Comics

1-Wolverton (10 pgs.) & Kurtzman (8 pgs.)-a; Eustice Hayseed begins (Li'l Abner swipe) 27.00 81.00 190.
2-Wolverton-a, 10 pgs.; Powerhouse Pepper cameo 19.00 58.00 135.

KRAZY KROW (Also see Dopey Duck, Film Funnies, Funny Frolics & Movie Tunes)
Summer, 1945 - No. 3, Wint, 1945/46
Marvel Comics (ZPC)

1 11.50 34.00 80.0
2,3 8.35 25.00 50.0
I.W. Reprint #1('57), 2('58), 7 1.60 4.00 8.0

KRAZYLIFE (Becomes Nutty Life #2)
1945 (no month)
Fox Feature Syndicate

1-Funny animal 10.00 30.00 60.0

KREE/SKRULL WAR STARRING THE AVENGERS, THE
Sept, 1983 - No. 2, Oct, 1983 ($2.50, 68 pgs.; Baxter paper)
Marvel Comics Group

1,2 1.00 2.5
NOTE: ***Neal Adams** p-1r, 2. **Buscema** a-1r, 2r. **Simonson** a-1p; c-1p.*

KRIM-KO KOMICS
5/18/35 - No. 6, 6/22/35; 1936 - 1939 (Giveaway) (weekly)
Krim-ko Chocolate Drink

1-(16 pgs., soft-c, Dairy giveaways)-Tom, Mary & Sparky Advs. by Russell Keaton, Jim Hawkins by Dick Moores, Mystery Island! by Rick Yager begin 10.00 30.00 70.0
2-6 (6/22/35) 8.35 25.00 50.0
Lola, Secret Agent; 184 issues, 4 pg. giveaways - all original stories each.... 5.85 17.50 35.0

KROFFT SUPERSHOW (TV)
April, 1978 - No. 6, Jan, 1979
Gold Key

1-Photo-c 1.20 3.0
2-6: 6-Photo-c 1.5

KRULL
Nov, 1983 - No. 2, Dec, 1983 (Movie adaptation)
Marvel Comics Group

Krypton Chronicles #1, © DC

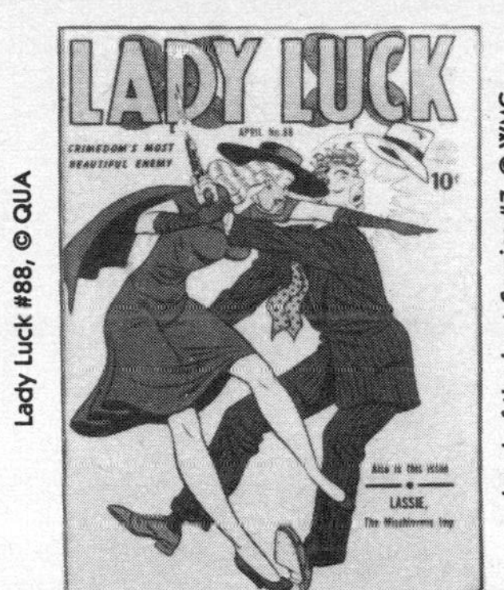

Lady Luck #88, © QUA

Land of the Lost Comics #7, © WMG

	GD25	FN65	NM94
1,2-r/Marvel Super Special. 1-Photo-c from movie			1.00

KRYPTON CHRONICLES
Sept, 1981 - No. 3, Nov, 1981
DC Comics

1-Buckler-c(p)			1.50
2,3			1.00

KULL AND THE BARBARIANS (Magazine)
May, 1975 - No. 3, Sept, 1975 ($1.00, B&W, 84 pgs.)
Marvel Comics Group

1-Andru/Wood-r/Kull #1; 2 pgs. Neal Adams; Gil Kane(p), Marie & John Severin-a(r); Krenkel text illo			1.00
2,3: 2-Red Sonja by Chaykin begins; Soloman Kane by Weiss/N. Adams; Gil Kane-a. 3-Origin Red Sonja by Chaykin; N. Adams-a; Solomon Kane app.			1.00

KULL THE CONQUEROR (...the Destroyer #11 on; see Creatures on the Loose #10 and Marvel Preview)
June, 1971 - No. 2, Sept, 1971; No. 3, July, 1972 - No. 15, Aug, 1974; No. 16, Aug, 1976 - No. 29, Oct, 1978
Marvel Comics Group

1-Andru/Wood-a; origin Kull; 15 cent-c	1.50	3.75	9.00
2-5: 2-Last 15 cent issue. 3-13: 20 cent-c		1.70	4.25
6-10		1.30	3.25
11-29: 11-15-Ploog-a. 14-16: 25 cent-c		.90	2.25

NOTE: *No. 1, 2, 7-9, 11 are based on Robert E. Howard stories.* ***Alcala*** *a-17p, 18-20i; c-24.* ***Ditko*** *a-12r, 15r.* ***Gil Kane*** *c-15p, 21.* ***Nebres*** *a-22i-27i; c-25i, 27i.* ***Ploog*** *c-11, 12p, 13.* ***Severin*** *a-2-9i; c-2-10i, 19.* ***Starlin*** *c-14.*

KULL THE CONQUEROR (Marvel, 1982)(Value: cover or less)

KULL THE CONQUEROR (Marvel, 1983)(Value: cover or less)

KUNG FU (See Deadly Hands of..., & Master of...)

KUNG FU FIGHTER (See Richard Dragon...)

LABOR IS A PARTNER
1949 (32 pgs. in color; paper cover)
Catechetical Guild Educational Society

nn-Anti-communism	17.00	51.00	120.00
Confidential Preview-(B&W, 8-1/2x11", saddle stitched)-only one known copy, text varies from color version, advertises next book on secularism (If the Devil Would Talk)	35.00	100.00	200.00

LABYRINTH (Marvel)(Value: cover or less)

LAD: A DOG
1961 - No. 2, July-Sept, 1962
Dell Publishing Co.

4-Color 1303 (movie), 2	4.00	12.00	24.00

LADY AND THE TRAMP (See Dell Giants, 4-Color No. 629, 634, & Movie Comics)

LADY AND THE TRAMP IN "BUTTER LATE THAN NEVER"
1955 (16 pgs., 5x7-1/4", soft-c) (Walt Disney)
American Dairy Association (Premium)

nn	5.35	16.00	32.00

LADY ARCANE (Hero)(Value: cover or less)

LADY BOUNTIFUL
1917 (10-1/4x13-1/2"; 24 pgs.; B&W; cardboard cover)
Saalfield Publ. Co./Press Publ. Co.

nn-By Gene Carr; 2 panels per page	13.00	40.00	90.00

LADY COP (See 1st Issue Special)

LADY FOR A NIGHT (See Cinema Comics Herald)

LADY LUCK (Formerly Smash #1-85) (Also see Spirit Sections #1)
No. 86, Dec, 1949 - No. 90, Aug, 1950
Quality Comics Group

	GD25	FN65	NM94
86(#1)	45.00	135.00	315.00
87-90	34.00	100.00	235.00

LAFF-A-LYMPICS (TV)(See The Funtastic World of Hanna-Barbera)
Mar, 1978 - No. 13, Mar, 1979 (Hanna Barbera)
Marvel Comics Group

1-13: Yogi Bear, Scooby Doo, Pixie & Dixie, etc.			1.00

LAFFY-DAFFY COMICS
Feb, 1945 - No. 2, March, 1945
Rural Home Publ. Co.

1,2-Funny animal	5.00	15.00	30.00

LANA (Little Lana No. 8 on)
Aug, 1948 - No. 7, Aug, 1949 (Also see Annie Oakley)
Marvel Comics (MjMC)

1-Rusty, Millie begin	10.00	30.00	70.00
2-Kurtzman's "Hey Look" (1); last Rusty	7.50	22.50	45.00
3-7: 3-Nellie begins	4.70	14.00	28.00

LANCELOT & GUINEVERE (See Movie Classics)

LANCELOT LINK, SECRET CHIMP (TV)
April, 1971 - No. 8, Feb, 1973
Gold Key

1-Photo-c	2.00	6.00	14.00
2-8: 2-Photo-c	1.30	3.25	8.00

LANCELOT STRONG (See The Shield)

LANCE O'CASEY (See Mighty Midget & Whiz Comics)
Spring, 1946 - No. 3, Fall, 1946; No. 4, Summer, 1948
Fawcett Publications

1-Captain Marvel app. on-c	14.00	43.00	100.00
2	10.00	30.00	60.00
3,4	7.50	22.50	45.00

NOTE: *The cover for the 1st issue was done in 1942 but was not published until 1946. The cover shows 68 pages but actually has only 36 pages.*

LANCER (TV)(Western)
Feb, 1969 - No. 3, Sept, 1969 (All photo-c)
Gold Key

1	3.20	8.00	20.00
2,3	2.15	6.50	15.00

LAND OF THE GIANTS (TV)
Nov, 1968 - No. 5, Sept, 1969 (All have photo-c)
Gold Key

1	5.00	15.00	35.00
2-5	3.20	8.00	20.00

LAND OF THE LOST COMICS (Radio)
July-Aug, 1946 - No. 9, Spring, 1948
E. C. Comics

1	23.00	70.00	160.00
2	15.00	45.00	105.00
3-9	12.00	36.00	85.00

LAND UNKNOWN, THE (See 4-Color No. 845)

LARAMIE (TV)
Aug, 1960 - July, 1962 (All photo-c)
Dell Publishing Co.

4-Color 1125-Gil Kane/Heath-a	9.15	27.50	55.00
4-Color 1223,1284	5.85	17.50	35.00
01-418-207 (7/62)	5.85	17.50	35.00

LAREDO (TV)
June, 1966
Gold Key

1 (10179-606)-Photo-c	3.20	8.00	16.00

LARGE FEATURE COMIC (Formerly called Black & White)
1939 - No. 13, 1943

Large Feature Comics #19(SeriesI), © WDC

Large Feature Comics #8(SeriesII), © WDC

Lassie #18, © M.G.M.

Dell Publishing Co.

	GD25	FN65	NM94
1 (**Series I**)-Dick Tracy Meets the Blank	115.00	345.00	800.00
2-Terry & the Pirates (#1)	57.00	170.00	400.00
3-Heigh-Yo Silver! The Lone Ranger (text & ill.)(76 pgs.); also exists as a Whitman #710	57.00	170.00	400.00
4-Dick Tracy Gets His Man	64.00	195.00	450.00
5-Tarzan (#1) by Harold Foster (origin); reprints 1st dailies from 1929	100.00	300.00	700.00
6-Terry & the Pirates & The Dragon Lady; reprints dailies from 1936	54.00	160.00	375.00
7-(Scarce)-52 pgs.; The Lone Ranger-Hi-Yo Silver the Lone Ranger to the Rescue; also exists as a Whitman #715	64.00	195.00	450.00
8-Dick Tracy Racket Buster	57.00	170.00	400.00
9-King of the Royal Mounted	29.00	85.00	200.00
10-(Scarce)-Gang Busters (No. appears on inside front cover); first slick cover (based on radio program)	43.00	130.00	300.00
11-Dick Tracy Foils the Mad Doc Hump	57.00	170.00	400.00
12-Smilin' Jack	40.00	120.00	280.00
13-Dick Tracy & Scotty	57.00	170.00	400.00
14-Smilin' Jack	40.00	120.00	280.00
15-Dick Tracy & the Kidnapped Princes	57.00	170.00	400.00
16-Donald Duck-1st app. Daisy Duck on back cover (6/41-Disney)	200.00	600.00	1600.00
(Prices vary widely on this book)			
17-Gang Busters (1941)	27.00	81.00	190.00
18-Phantasmo (see The Funnies #45)	23.00	70.00	160.00
19-Dumbo Comic Paint Book (Disney); partial-r from 4-Color #17	175.00	525.00	1400.00
20-Donald Duck Comic Paint Book (rarer than #16) (Disney)	315.00	945.00	2500.00
(Prices vary widely on this book)			
21,22: 21-Private Buck. 22-Nuts & Jolts	10.00	30.00	70.00
23-The Nebbs	13.50	41.00	95.00
24-Popeye in Thimble Theatre by Segar	50.00	150.00	350.00
25-Smilin' Jack-1st issue to show title on-c	40.00	120.00	280.00
26-Smitty	24.00	72.00	165.00
27-Terry & the Pirates; Caniff-c/a	43.00	130.00	300.00
28-Grin & Bear It	10.00	30.00	65.00
29-Moon Mullins	22.00	65.00	150.00
30-Tillie the Toiler	19.00	58.00	135.00
1 (**Series II**)-Peter Rabbit by Harrison Cady; arrival date-3/27/42	41.00	125.00	290.00
2-Winnie Winkle (#1)	14.00	43.00	100.00
3-Dick Tracy	57.00	170.00	400.00
4-Tiny Tim (#1)	29.00	85.00	200.00
5-Toots & Casper	10.00	30.00	65.00
6-Terry & the Pirates; Caniff-a	43.00	130.00	300.00
7-Pluto Saves the Ship (#1)(Disney) written by Carl Barks, Jack Hannah, & Nick George (Barks' 1st comic book work)	65.00	195.00	455.00
8-Bugs Bunny (#1)('42)	80.00	240.00	565.00
9-Bringing Up Father	14.00	43.00	100.00
10-Popeye (Thimble Theatre)	42.00	125.00	290.00
11-Barney Google & Snuffy Smith	19.00	58.00	135.00
12-Private Buck	10.00	30.00	65.00
13-(nn)-1001 Hours Of Fun; puzzles & games; by A. W. Nugent. This book was bound as #13 with Large Feature Comics in publisher's files	10.00	30.00	65.00

NOTE: *The Black & White Feature Books are oversized 8-1/2x11-3/8" comics with color covers and black and white interiors. The first nine issues all have rough, heavy stock covers and, except for #7, all have 76 pages, including covers. #7 and #10-on all have 52 pages. Beginning with #10 the covers are slick and thin and, because of their size, are difficult to handle without damaging. For this reason, they are seldom found in fine to mint condition. The paper stock, unlike Wow #1 and Capt. Marvel #1, is itself not unstable ...just thin.*

LARRY DOBY, BASEBALL HERO
1950 (Cleveland Indians)
Fawcett Publications

	GD25	FN65	NM94
nn-Bill Ward-a; photo-c	50.00	150.00	350.00

LARRY HARMON'S LAUREL AND HARDY (...Comics)
July-Aug, 1972 (Regular size)
National Periodical Publications

	GD25	FN65	NM94
1		1.60	4.00

LARS OF MARS
No. 10, Apr-May, 1951 - No. 11, July-Aug, 1951 (Painted-c)
Ziff-Davis Publishing Co.

	GD25	FN65	NM94
10-Origin; Anderson-a(3) in each	40.00	122.00	285.00
11-Gene Colan-a	34.00	105.00	240.00

LARS OF MARS 3-D (Eclipse)(Value: cover or less)

LASER ERASER & PRESSBUTTON (Eclipse)(Value: cover or less)

LASH LARUE WESTERN (Movie star; king of the bullwhip)(See Fawcett Movie Comic, Motion Picture Comics & Six-Gun Heroes)
Sum, 1949 - No. 46, Jan, 1954 (36pgs., 1-7,9,13,16-on)
Fawcett Publications

	GD25	FN65	NM94
1-Lash & his horse Black Diamond begin; photo front/back-c begin	82.00	245.00	575.00
2(11/49)	36.00	110.00	250.00
3-5	30.00	90.00	210.00
6,7,9: 6-Last photo back-c; intro. Frontier Phantom (Lash's twin brother)	23.00	70.00	160.00
8,10 (52pgs.)	24.00	73.00	170.00
11,12,14,15 (52pgs.)	15.00	45.00	105.00
13,16-20 (36pgs.)	13.50	41.00	95.00
21-30: 21-The Frontier Phantom app.	11.50	34.00	80.00
31-45	10.00	30.00	70.00
46-Last Fawcett issue & photo-c	11.00	32.00	75.00

LASH LARUE WESTERN (Continues from Fawcett series)
No. 47, Mar-Apr, 1954 - No. 84, June, 1961
Charlton Comics

	GD25	FN65	NM94
47-Photo-c	12.00	36.00	85.00
48	10.00	30.00	60.00
49-60	7.50	22.50	45.00
61-66,69,70: 52-r/#8; 53-r/#22	6.70	20.00	40.00
67,68-(68 pgs.). 68-Check-a	6.70	20.00	40.00
71-83	4.20	12.50	25.00
84-Last issue	5.00	15.00	30.00

LASH LARUE WESTERN (AC)(Value: cover or less)

LASSIE (TV)(M-G-M's... #1-36; see Kite Fun Book)
June, 1950 - No. 70, July, 1969
Dell Publishing Co./Gold Key No. 59 (10/62) on

	GD25	FN65	NM94
1 (52 pgs.)-Photo-c; inside lists One Shot #282 in error	12.00	36.00	85.00
2-Painted-c begin	6.70	20.00	40.00
3-10	4.35	13.00	26.00
11-19: 12-Rocky Langford (Lassie's master) marries Gerry Lawrence. 15-1st app. Timbu	3.60	9.00	18.00
20-22-Matt Baker-a	4.00	11.00	22.00
23-40: 33-Robinson-a. 39-1st app. Timmy as Lassie picks up her TV family	2.80	7.00	14.00
41-70: 63-Last Timmy (10/63). 64-r/#19. 65-Forest Ranger Corey Stuart begins, ends #69. 70-Forest Rangers Bob Ericson & Scott Turner app. (Lassie's new masters)	1.80	4.50	9.00
11193(1978, $1.95, 224 pgs., Golden Press)-Baker-r (92 pgs.)	1.00	2.50	5.00
The Adventures of...(Red Heart Dog Food giveaway, 1949)-16 pgs, soft-c; 1st app. Lassie in comics	13.00	40.00	90.00

NOTE: *Photo c-57, 63. (See March of Comics #210, 217, 230, 254, 266, 278, 296, 308, 324, 334, 346, 358, 370, 381, 394, 411, 432)*

LAST AMERICAN, THE
Dec, 1990 - No. 4, March, 1991 ($2.25, color, mini-series)
Epic Comics (Marvel)

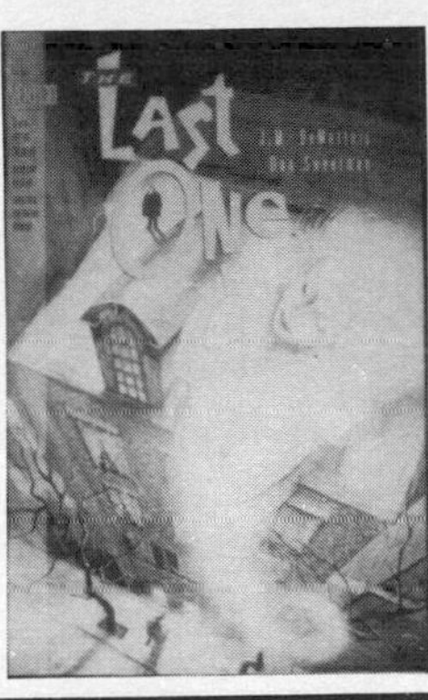

The Last One #3, © J. M. DeMatteis & Dan Sweetman

Laugh Comics #21, © AP

Law Against Crime #1, © Essenkay Publ.

	GD25	FN65	NM94
1-4: Alan Grant scripts		.90	2.25

LAST DAYS OF THE JUSTICE SOCIETY SPECIAL
1986 ($2.50, one shot, 68 pgs.)
DC Comics

	GD25	FN65	NM94
1-62 pg. JSA story plus unpubbed G.A. pg.		1.00	2.50

LAST GENERATION, THE (Black Tie)(Value: cover or less)

LAST HUNT, THE (See 4-Color No. 678)

LAST KISS (Acme)(Value: cover or less)

LAST OF THE COMANCHES (See Wild Bill Hickok #28)
1953 (Movie)
Avon Periodicals

	GD25	FN65	NM94
nn-Kinstler-c/a, 21pgs.; Ravielli-a	11.00	32.00	75.00

LAST OF THE ERIES, THE (See American Graphics)

LAST OF THE FAST GUNS, THE (See 4-Color No. 925)

LAST OF THE MOHICANS (See King Classics & White Rider and...)

LAST OF THE VIKING HEROES, THE (Also see Silver Star #1)
Mar, 1987 - Present ($1.50-$1.95, color)
Genesis West Comics

	GD25	FN65	NM94
1-4: 4-Intro The Phantom Force		1.00	2.50
1-Signed edition ($1.50)			1.50
5A-Kirby/Stevens-c		1.20	3.00
5B,6 ($1.95)		.80	2.00
7-Art Adams-c		1.20	3.00
8-12: 8-Kirby back-c. 9,10,12-($2.50)		1.00	2.50
Summer Special 1-3: 1-(1988)-Frazetta-c & illos. 2(1990, $2.50)-A TMNT app. 3 (1991, $2.50)-Teenage Mutant Ninja Turtles		1.20	3.00
Summer Special 1-Signed edition (sold for $1.95)		.80	2.00

NOTE: *Art Adams c-7. Byrne c-3. Kirby c-1p, 5p. Perez c-2i. Stevens c-5Ai.*

LAST ONE, THE
July, 1993 - No. 6, Dec, 1993 ($2.50, color, limited series, mature readers)
DC Comics (Vertigo)

	GD25	FN65	NM94
1-6		1.00	2.50

LAST STARFIGHTER, THE
Oct, 1984 - No. 3, Dec, 1984 (75 cents, movie adaptation)
Marvel Comics Group

	GD25	FN65	NM94
1-3: r/Marvel Super Special; Guice-c			1.00

LAST TRAIN FROM GUN HILL (See 4-Color No. 1012)

LATEST ADVENTURES OF FOXY GRANDPA (See Foxy Grandpa)

LATEST COMICS (Super Duper No. 3?)
March, 1945 - No. 2, 1945?
Spotlight Publ./Palace Promotions (Jubilee)

	GD25	FN65	NM94
1-Super Duper	10.00	30.00	60.00
2-Bee-29 (nd)	7.50	22.50	45.00

LAUGH
June, 1987 - No. 30, 1991 (.75-$1.00, color)
Archie Enterprises

	GD25	FN65	NM94
V2#1-30: 5,19-X-Mas issues. 14-1st app. Hot Dog. 24-Re-intro Super Duck			1.00

LAUGH COMICS (Formerly Black Hood #1-19) (Laugh #226 on)
No. 20, Fall, 1946 - No. 400, Apr, 1987
Archie Publications (Close-Up)

	GD25	FN65	NM94
20-Archie begins; Katy Keene & Taffy begin by Woggon; Suzie & Wilbur also begin	47.00	141.00	330.00
21-25: 24-"Pipsy" by Kirby, 6 pgs.	23.00	70.00	160.00
26-30	12.00	36.00	85.00
31-40	10.00	30.00	65.00
41-60: 41,54-Debbi by Woggon	6.35	19.00	38.00
61-80: 67-Debbi by Woggon	4.20	12.50	25.00
81-99	4.00	10.00	20.00
100	4.70	14.00	28.00
101-126: 125-Debbi app.	2.80	7.00	14.00
127-144: Super-hero app. in all (see note)	3.20	8.00	16.00
145-160: 157-Josie app.	1.30	3.25	8.00
161-165,167-200	1.00	2.00	5.00
166-Beatles-c	2.30	6.75	16.00
201-240		1.00	2.50
241-280			1.50
281-400: 381-384-Katy Keene app.; by Woggon-381,382			1.00

NOTE: *The Fly app. in 128, 129, 132, 134, 138, 139. Flygirl app. in 136, 137, 143. Flyman app. in 137. The Jaguar app. in 127, 130, 131, 133, 135, 140-142, 144. Josie app. in 145, 160, 164. Katy Keene app. in 20-125, 129, 130, 133. Many issues contain paper dolls.*

LAUGH COMICS DIGEST (...Magazine #23-89; Laugh Digest Mag. #90 on)
8/74; No. 2, 9/75; No. 3, 3/76 - Present (Digest-size)
Archie Publications (Close-Up No. 1, 3 on)

	GD25	FN65	NM94
1-Neal Adams-a	1.20	3.00	7.00
2,7,8,19-Neal Adams-a		1.60	4.00
3-6,9-18,20-50		1.00	2.50
51-108: Later issues $1.35,$1.50-c			1.50

NOTE: *Katy Keene in 23, 25, 27, 32-38, 40, 45-48, 50. The Fly-r in 19, 20. The Jaguar-r in 25, 27. Mr. Justice-r in 21. The Web-r in 23.*

LAUGH COMIX (Formerly Top Notch Laugh; Suzie Comics No. 49 on)
No. 46, Summer, 1944 - No. 48, Winter, 1944-45
MLJ Magazines

	GD25	FN65	NM94
46-Wilbur & Suzie in all; Harry Sahle-c	13.00	40.00	90.00
47,48: 47-Sahle-c	10.00	30.00	70.00

LAUGH-IN MAGAZINE (TV)(Magazine)
Oct, 1968 - No. 12, Oct, 1969 (50 cents) (Satire)
Laufer Publ. Co.

	GD25	FN65	NM94
V1#1	2.15	6.50	15.00
2-12	1.20	3.00	7.00

LAUREL & HARDY (See Larry Harmon's... & March of Comics No. 302, 314)

LAUREL AND HARDY (...Comics)
3/49 - No. 3, 9/49; No. 26, 11/55 - No. 28, 3/56 (No #4-25)
St. John Publishing Co.

	GD25	FN65	NM94
1	46.00	140.00	325.00
2	27.00	81.00	190.00
3	20.00	60.00	140.00
26-28 (Reprints)	11.50	34.00	80.00

LAUREL AND HARDY (TV)
Oct, 1962 - No. 4, Sept-Nov, 1963
Dell Publishing Co.

	GD25	FN65	NM94
12-423-210 (8-10/62)	5.85	17.50	35.00
2-4 (Dell)	4.35	13.00	26.00

LAUREL AND HARDY (Larry Harmon's...)
Jan, 1967 - No. 2, Oct, 1967
Gold Key

	GD25	FN65	NM94
1,2: 1-Photo back-c	4.00	12.00	24.00

LAW AGAINST CRIME (Law-Crime on cover)
April, 1948 - No. 3, Aug, 1948
Essenkay Publishing Co.

	GD25	FN65	NM94
1-(#1-3: Half funny animal, half crime stories)-L. B. Cole electrocution-c/a	35.00	105.00	245.00
2-L. B. Cole-c/a	25.00	75.00	175.00
3-L. B. Cole-c/a; used in **SOTI**, pg. 180,181 & illo-"The wish to hurt or kill couples in lovers' lanes;" reprinted in All-Famous Crime #9	32.00	95.00	225.00

LAWBREAKERS (...Suspense Stories No. 10 on)
Mar, 1951 - No. 9, Oct-Nov, 1952
Law and Order Magazines (Charlton Comics)

Lawdog #6, © Chuck Dixon & Flint Henry

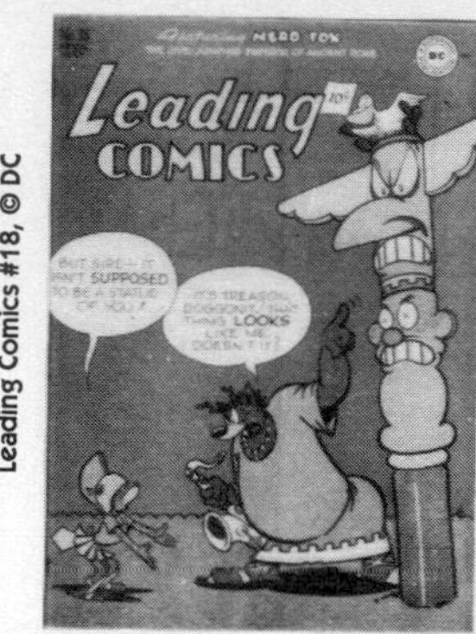

Leading Comics #18, © DC

Leave It To Binky #2, © DC

	GD25	FN65	NM94
1	16.00	48.00	110.00
2	8.35	25.00	50.00
3,5,6,8,9	6.35	19.00	38.00
4-"White Death" junkie story	8.35	25.00	50.00
7-"The Deadly Dopesters" drug story	8.35	25.00	50.00

LAWBREAKERS ALWAYS LOSE!
Spring, 1948 - No. 10, Oct, 1949
Marvel Comics (CBS)

	GD25	FN65	NM94
1-2pg. Kurtzman-a, 'Giggles 'n Grins'	16.00	48.00	110.00
2	9.15	27.50	55.00
3-5: 4-Vampire story	7.50	22.50	45.00
6(2/49)-Has editorial defense against charges of Dr. Wertham	8.35	25.00	50.00
7-Used in **SOTI**, illo-"Comic-book philosophy"	16.00	48.00	110.00
8-10: 9,10-Photo-c	5.85	17.50	35.00

NOTE: ***Brodsky** c-4, 5. **Shores** c-1-3, 6-8.*

LAWBREAKERS SUSPENSE STORIES (Formerly Lawbreakers; Strange Suspense Stories No. 16 on)
No. 10, Jan, 1953 - No. 15, Nov, 1953
Capitol Stories/Charlton Comics

	GD25	FN65	NM94
10	11.00	32.00	75.00
11 (3/53)-Severed tongues-c/story & woman negligee scene	33.00	100.00	230.00
12-14	6.70	20.00	40.00
15-Acid-in-face-c/story; hands dissolved in acid sty	17.00	51.00	120.00

LAW-CRIME (See Law Against Crime)

LAWDOG (Epic Comics)(Value: cover or less)

LAWDOG/GRIMROD: TERROR AT THE CROSSROADS (Epic Comics)(Value: cover or less)

LAWMAN (TV)
No. 970, Feb, 1959 - No. 11, Apr-June, 1962 (All photo-c)
Dell Publishing Co.

	GD25	FN65	NM94
4-Color 970(#1)	10.00	30.00	65.00
4-Color 1035('60)	5.85	17.50	35.00
3(2-4/60)-Toth-a	6.35	19.00	38.00
4-11	4.70	14.00	28.00

LAW OF DREDD, THE (Quality)(Value: cover or less)

LAWRENCE (See Movie Classics)

LAZARUS CHURCHYARD
June, 1992 - No. 3, 1992 ($3.95, color, coated stock, 44 pgs.)
Tundra Publishing

	GD25	FN65	NM94
1-3		1.60	4.00

LEADING COMICS (...Screen Comics No. 42 on)
Winter, 1941-42 - No. 41, Feb-Mar, 1950
National Periodical Publications

	GD25	FN65	NM94
1-Origin The Seven Soldiers of Victory; Crimson Avenger, Green Arrow & Speedy, Shining Knight, The Vigilante, Star Spangled Kid & Stripesy begin; The Dummy (Vigilante villain) app.	250.00	750.00	1700.00
2-Meskin-a	85.00	260.00	600.00
3	71.00	215.00	500.00
4,5	59.00	178.00	415.00
6-10	52.00	160.00	365.00
11-14(Spring, 1945)	39.00	116.00	270.00
15-(Sum,'45)-Contents change to funny animal	17.00	52.00	120.00
16-22,24-30: 16-Nero Fox-c begin, end #22	9.15	27.50	55.00
23-1st app. Peter Porkchops by Otto Feur	19.00	57.00	130.00
31,32,34-41: 34-41-Leading Screen... on-c only	7.50	22.50	45.00
33-(Scarce)	10.00	30.00	65.00

NOTE: ***Rube Grossman**-a(Peter Porkchops)-most #15-on; c-15-41. **Post** a-23-37, 39, 41.*

LEADING SCREEN COMICS (Formerly Leading Comics)
No. 42, Apr-May, 1950 - No. 77, Aug-Sept, 1955
National Periodical Publications

	GD25	FN65	NM94
42-Peter Porkchops-c/stories continue	8.35	25.00	50.00
43-77	6.70	20.00	40.00

NOTE: ***Grossman** a-most. **Mayer** a-45-48, 50, 54-57, 60, 62-74, 75(3), 76, 77.*

LEAGUE OF CHAMPIONS, THE (Hero)(Value: cover or less)

LEATHERFACE (Arpad)(Value: cover or less)

LEATHERNECK THE MARINE (See Mighty Midget Comics)

LEAVE IT TO BEAVER (TV)
No. 912, June, 1958 - May-July, 1962 (All photo-c)
Dell Publishing Co.

	GD25	FN65	NM94
4-Color 912	19.00	56.00	130.00
4-Color 999,1103,1191,1285, 01-428-207	17.00	50.00	115.00

LEAVE IT TO BINKY (Binky No. 72 on) (Super DCGiant) (No. 1-22: 52 pgs.)
2-3/48 - #60, 10/58; #61, 6-7/68 - #71, 2-3/70 (Teen-age humor)
National Periodical Publications

	GD25	FN65	NM94
1-Lucy wears Superman costume	24.00	72.00	165.00
2	11.50	34.00	80.00
3,4	7.00	21.00	42.00
5-Superman cameo	11.00	32.00	75.00
6-10	6.35	19.00	38.00
11-14,16-20	5.00	15.00	30.00
15-Scribbly story by Mayer	8.35	25.00	50.00
21-28,30-45: 45-Last pre-code (2/55)	4.00	10.00	20.00
29-Used in **POP**, pg. 78	4.00	10.00	20.00
46-60: 60-(10/58)	2.80	7.00	14.00
Showcase #70 (9-10/67)-Tryout issue	1.65	4.70	11.00
61-71: 61-(6-7/68)	1.30	3.25	8.00

NOTE: ***Drucker** a-28. **Mayer** a-1, 2, 15. Created by **Mayer**.*

LEE HUNTER, INDIAN FIGHTER (See 4-Color No. 779, 904)

LEFT-HANDED GUN, THE (See 4-Color No. 913)

LEGACY
Oct, 1993 - Present ($2.25, color)
Majestic Entertainment

	GD25	FN65	NM94
1-3: 1-Glow-in-the-dark-c		.90	2.25

LEGEND OF CUSTER, THE (TV)
January, 1968
Dell Publishing Co.

	GD25	FN65	NM94
1-Wayne Maunder photo-c	1.65	4.00	10.00

LEGEND OF JESSE JAMES, THE (TV)
February, 1966
Gold Key

	GD25	FN65	NM94
10172-602-Photo-c	3.00	7.50	15.00

LEGEND OF KAMUI, THE (See Kamui)

LEGEND OF LOBO, THE (See Movie Comics)

LEGEND OF THE SHIELD, THE
July, 1991 - No. 16, Oct, 1992 ($1.00, color)
Impact Comics (DC)

	GD25	FN65	NM94
1-16: 6,7-The Fly x-over. 12-Contains trading card			1.00
Annual 1 (1992, $2.50, 68 pgs.)-With trading card		1.00	2.50

LEGEND OF WONDER WOMAN, THE (DC)(Value: cover or less)

LEGEND OF YOUNG DICK TURPIN, THE (TV)
May, 1966 (Disney TV episode)
Gold Key

	GD25	FN65	NM94
1 (10176-605)-Photo/painted-c	1.50	3.75	9.00

LEGEND OF ZELDA, THE (Link: The Legend... in indicia)
1990 - No. 4, 1990 ($1.95, color, coated stiff-c)
V2#1, 1991 - No. 5, 1991 ($1.50, color)
Valiant Comics

Legends of the Dark Knight #10, © DC

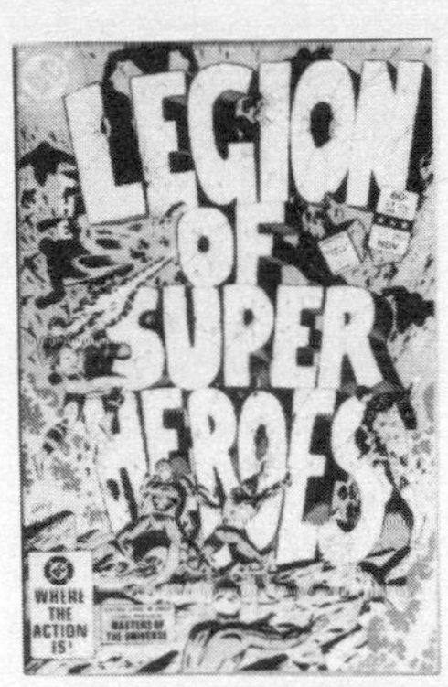

Legion of Super-Heroes #293, © DC

Legion of Super-Heroes #14 (9/85), © DC

GD25 FN65 NM94

1-4: 4-Layton-c(i) .80 2.00
V2#1-5 1.50

LEGENDS
Nov, 1986 - No. 6, Apr, 1987 (75 cents, mini-series)
DC Comics
1-Byrne-c/a(p) in all; 1st app. new Capt. Marvel .90 2.25
2-5: 3-1st app. new Suicide Squad; death of Blockbuster .70 1.80
6-1st app. new Justice League 1.90 4.75

LEGENDS OF DANIEL BOONE, THE
Oct-Nov, 1955 - No. 8, Dec-Jan, 1956-57
National Periodical Publications
1 (Scarce)-Nick Cardy c-1-8 43.00 130.00 300.00
2 (Scarce) 32.00 95.00 225.00
3-8 (Scarce) 29.00 85.00 200.00

LEGENDS OF NASCAR, THE
1990 - No. 14? (Color)(#1 3rd printing (1/91) says 2nd printing inside)
Vortex Comics
1-Bill Elliott biog.; Trimpe-a ($1.50-c) 1.65 4.00 10.00
1-2nd printing (11/90, $2.00-c) 1.60 4.00
1-3rd print; contains Maxx racecards ($3.00-c) 1.90 4.75
2-Richard Petty 1.20 3.00
3-14: 3-Ken Schrader (7/91). 4-Bobby Allison; Spiegle-a(p); Adkins part-i. 5-Sterling Marlin. 6-Bill Elliott .80 2.00
1-13-Hologram cover versions. 2-Hologram shows Bill Elliott's car by mistake (all are numbered & limited) 1.90 4.75
2-Hologram corrected version 1.90 4.75

LEGENDS OF THE DARK KNIGHT (Batman: ... #37 on)
Nov, 1989 - Present ($1.50/$1.75, color)
DC Comics
1-"Shaman" begins, ends #5; outer cover has four different color variations, all worth same 1.00 2.00 5.00
2 1.20 3.00
3-5 .80 2.00
6-10 "Gothic" by Grant Morrison (scripts) 1.20 3.00
11-18: 11-15-Gulacy/Austin-a. 14-Catwoman app. 16-20-Venom story introduces drug that Bane uses. 18-Last $1.50-c .80 2.00
19-49,51-58: 38-Bat-Mite-c/story; Alan Grant scripts. 46-49-Catwoman app. 51-Ragman app.; Joe Kubert-c .80 2.00
50-($3.95, 68 pgs.)-Embossed gold foil-c; Joker-c/s 1.60 4.00
Annual 1 (1991, $3.95, 68 pgs.)-Joker app. 1.60 4.00
Annual 2 (1992, $3.50, 68 pgs.)-Netzer-c/a 1.40 3.50
Annual 3 (1993, $3.50, 68 pgs.)-New Batman app. 1.40 3.50
Halloween Special 1 (12/93, $6.95, 84 pgs.)-Embossed & foil stamped-c 1.20 3.00 7.00
NOTE: ***Chaykin** scripts-24-26. **Gil Kane** c/a-24-26. **Russell** c/a-42, 43.*

LEGENDS OF THE STARGRAZERS (Innovation)(Value: cover or less)

L.E.G.I.O.N. (The # to right of title represents year of print; also see Lobo)
Feb, 1989 - Present ($1.50, color)
DC Comics
1-Giffen plots/breakdowns in #1-12 .80 2.00
2-22,24-47: 3-Lobo app. #3 on. 4-1st Lobo-c this title. 5-Lobo joins Legion. 28-Giffen-c(p). 31-Capt. Marvel app. 1.50
23-($2.50, 52 pgs.) 1.00 2.50
48,49,51-64: 48-Begin $1.75-c .70 1.75
50-($3.50, 68 pgs.) 1.40 3.50
Annual 1-3 (1990-1992, $2.95, 68 pgs.): 1-Lobo, Superman app. 2-Alan Grant scripts 1.20 3.00
Annual 4 (1993, $3.50, 68 pgs.) 1.40 3.50
NOTE: ***Alan Grant** scripts in #1-39, Annual 1, 2.*

LEGIONNAIRES (See Legion of Super-Heroes #40, 41)
Apr, 1992 - Present ($1.25-$1.50, color)
DC comics
1-8: 1-Polybagged w/SkyBox trading card 1.25
9-12: 9-Begin $1.50-c 1.50

LEGIONNAIRES THREE
Jan, 1986 - No. 4, May, 1986 (75 cents, mini-series)
DC comics
1-4 1.00

LEGION OF MONSTERS (Magazine)(Also see Marvel Premiere #28 & Marvel Preview #8)
September, 1975 ($1.00, B&W, 76 pgs.)
Marvel Comics Group
1-Origin & 1st app. Legion of Monsters; Neal Adams-c; Morrow-a; origin & only app. The Manphiblan; Frankenstein by Mayerik, Bram Stoker's Dracula adaptation; Reese-a; painted-c (#2 was advertised with /Morbius & Satana, but was never published) 1.20 3.00

LEGION OF NIGHT, THE
Oct, 1991 - No. 2, Oct, 1991 ($4.95, color, 52 pgs.)
Marvel Comics
1,2-Whilce Portacio-c/a(p) 1.00 2.00 5.00

LEGION OF SUBSTITUTE HEROES SPECIAL (DC)(Value: cover or less)

LEGION OF SUPER-HEROES (See Action, Adventure, All New Collectors Edition, Limited Collectors Ed., Secrets of the..., Superboy & Superman)
Feb, 1973 - No. 4, July-Aug, 1973
National Periodical Publications
1-Legion & Tommy Tomorrow reprints begin 1.30 3.25 8.00
2-4: 2-Forte-r. 3-r/Adv. #340. Action #240. 4-r/Adv. #341, Action #233; Mooney-r 1.00 2.50 5.50

LEGION OF SUPER-HEROES, THE (Formerly Superboy and...; Tales of The Legion No. 314 on)
No. 259, Jan, 1980 - No. 313, July, 1984
DC Comics
259(#1)-Superboy leaves Legion 1.20 3.00
260-270: 265-Contains 28pg. insert 'Superman & the TRS-80 Computer;' origin Tyroc; Tyroc leaves Legion .80 2.00
271-284: 272-Blok joins; origin; 20pg. insert-Dial 'H' For Hero. 277-Intro Reflecto. 280-Superboy re-joins legion. 282-Origin Reflecto. 283-Origin Wildfire .65 1.60
285,286-Giffen back up story .80 2.00
287-Giffen-a on Legion begins 1.10 2.80
288-290: 290-294-Great Darkness saga .80 2.00
291-293 .65 1.60
294-Double size (52 pgs.); Giffen-a(p) .70 1.80
295-299,301-305: 297-Origin retold. 298-Free 16pg. Amethyst preview .65 1.60
300-Double size, 64 pgs., Mando paper; c/a by almost everyone at DC .80 2.00
306-313 (75 cent-c): 306-Brief origin Star Boy 1.00
Annual 1(1982, 52 pgs.)-Giffen-c/a; 1st app./origin new Invisible Kid who joins Legion .80 2.00
Annual 2,3: 2(1983, 52 pgs.)-Giffen-c; Karate Kid & Princess Projectra wed & resign. 3(1984, 52 pgs.) .65 1.60
...The Great Darkness Saga (1989, $17.95, 196 pgs.)-r/LSH #287,290-294 & Annual #3; Giffen-c/a 2.60 7.50 18.00
NOTE: ***Aparo** c-282, 283, 300(part). **Austin** c-268i. **Buckler** c-273p, 274p, 276p. **Colan** a-311p. **Ditko** a(p)-267, 268, 272, 274, 276, 281. **Giffen** a-285-313p, Annual 1p; c-287p, 288p, 289, 290p, 291p, 292, 293, 294-299p, 300, 301-313p, Annual 1p, 2p. **Perez** c-268p, 277-280, 281p. **Starlin** a-265. **Staton** a-259p, 260p, 280. **Tuska** a-308p.*

LEGION OF SUPER-HEROES (Reprinted in Tales of the Legion)
Aug, 1984 - No. 63, Aug, 1989 ($1.25-$1.75, deluxe format)
DC Comics
1-Silver ink logo .80 2.00
2-10: 4-Death of Karate Kid. 5-Death of Nemesis Kid 1.60
11-14: 12-Cosmic Boy, Lightning Lad, & Saturn Girl resign. 14-Intro new members: Tellus, Sensor Girl, Quislet 1.20

The Lemonade Kid #1, © AC

The Lethal Foes of Spider-Man #1, © MEG

The Liberty Project #6, © Busiek/Fry/Hazelwood

GD25 FN65 NM94

15-18: 15-17-Crisis tie-ins. 18-Crisis x-over .65 1.60
19-25: 25-Sensor Girl i.d. revealed as Princess Projectra 1.20
26-36,39-44: 35-Saturn Girl rejoins. 40-$1.75 cover price begins. 42,43-Millennium tie-ins. 44-Origin Quislet 1.10
37,38-Death of Superboy 1.65 4.70 11.00
45 ($2.95, 68 pgs.) 1.20 3.00
46-49,51-62 1.10
50-Double size, $2.50 1.00 2.50
63-Final issue 1.40
Annual 1 (10/85, 52 pgs.)-Crisis tie-in .70 1.80
Annual 2 (1986, 52 pgs.). 3 (1987, 52 pgs.) .65 1.60
Annual 4 (1988, $2.50, 52 pgs.) .80 2.00

NOTE: ***Byrne** c-36p. **Giffen** a(p)-1, 2, 50-55, 57-63, Annual 1p, 2; c-1-5p, 54p, Annual 1. **Orlando** a-6p. **Steacy** c-45-50, Annual 3.*

LEGION OF SUPER-HEROES
Nov, 1989 - Present ($1.75, color)
DC Comics

1-Giffen-c/a(p) & scripts begin (4 pg.-a only #18) .70 1.75
2-49,51-55: 8-Origin. 13-Free poster by Giffen showing new costumes. 21-24-Lobo & Darkseid storyline. 26-New map of headquarters. 34-Six pg. preview of Timber Wolf mini-series. 40-Minor Legionnaires app. 41-Intro Legionnaires (3/93) .70 1.75
50-($3.50, 68 pgs.) 1.40 3.50
Annual 1,2 (1990, 1991, $3.50, 68 pgs.) 1.40 3.50
Annual 3,4 (1992-93, $3.50, 68 pgs.): 4-Bloodlines 1.40 3.50

NOTE: ***Giffen** a-1-24; breakdowns-26-32, 34-36; c-1-7, 8(part), 9-24. **Brandon Peterson** a(p)-15(1st for DC), 16, 18, Annual 2(54 pgs.); c-Annual 2p. **Swan/Anderson** c-8(part).*

LEMONADE KID, THE (See Bobby Benson's B-Bar-B Riders)
1990 ($2.50, color, 28 pgs.)
AC Comics

1-Powell-c(r); Red Hawk-r by Powell; Lemonade Kid-r/Bobby Benson by Powell (2 stories) 1.00 2.50

LENNON SISTERS LIFE STORY, THE (See 4-Color No. 951, 1014)

LEONARDO (Also see Teenage Mutant Ninja Turtles)
Dec, 1986 ($1.50, B&W, One shot)
Mirage Studios

1 1.30 3.25 8.00

LEO THE LION
No date (10 cents)
I. W. Enterprises

1-Reprint 1.00 2.00 5.00

LEROY (Teen-age)
Nov, 1949 - No. 6, Nov, 1950
Standard Comics

1 5.00 15.00 30.00
2-Frazetta text illo. 4.00 11.00 22.00
3-6: 3-Lubbers-a 3.60 9.00 18.00

LETHAL FOES OF SPIDER-MAN (Sequel to Deadly Foes of Spider-Man)
Sept, 1993 - No. 4, Dec, 1993 ($1.75, color, mini-series)
Marvel Comics

1-4 1.00

LET'S PRETEND (CBS radio)
May-June, 1950 - No. 3, Sept-Oct, 1950
D. S. Publishing Co.

1 10.00 30.00 65.00
2,3 8.35 25.00 50.00

LET'S READ THE NEWSPAPER
1974
Charlton Press

nn-Features Quincy by Ted Sheares 1.00

LET'S TAKE A TRIP (TV) (CBS TV Presents)
Spring, 1958
Pines Comics

1-Marv Levy-c/a 2.80 7.00 14.00

LETTERS TO SANTA (See March of Comics No. 228)

LEX LUTHOR: THE UNAUTHORIZED BIOGRAPHY (DC)(Value: cover or less)

LIBERTY COMICS (Miss Liberty No. 1)
No. 4, 1945 - No. 15, July, 1946 (MLJ & other reprints)
Green Publishing Co.

4 10.00 30.00 75.00
5 (5/46)-The Prankster app; Starr-a 10.00 30.00 60.00
10-Hangman & Boy Buddies app.; Suzie & Wilbur begin; reprints Hangman story from Hangman #8 12.00 36.00 85.00
11(V2#2, 1/46)-Wilbur in women's clothes 10.00 30.00 70.00
12-Black Hood & Suzie app. 10.00 30.00 70.00
14,15-Patty of Airliner; Starr-a in both 6.70 20.00 40.00

LIBERTY GUARDS
No date (1946?)
Chicago Mail Order

nn-Reprints Man of War #1 with cover of Liberty Scouts #1; Gustavson-c 23.00 70.00 160.00

LIBERTY PROJECT, THE (Eclipse)(Value: cover or less)

LIBERTY SCOUTS (See Liberty Guards & Man of War)
No. 2, June, 1941 - No. 3, Aug, 1941
Centaur Publications

2(#1)-Origin The Fire-Man, Man of War; Vapo-Man & Liberty Scouts begin; Gustavson-c/a in both 100.00 300.00 650.00
3(#2)-Origin & 1st app. The Sentinel 75.00 225.00 500.00

LICENCE TO KILL (Eclipse)(Value: cover or less)

LIDSVILLE (TV)
Oct, 1972 - No. 5, Oct, 1973
Gold Key

1 1.70 5.00 12.00
2-5 1.00 2.50 6.00

LIEUTENANT, THE (TV)
April-June, 1964
Dell Publishing Co.

1-Photo-c 2.00 5.00 10.00

LIEUTENANT BLUEBERRY (Also see Blueberry)
1991 - No. 3, 1991 (Color, graphic novel)
Epic Comics (Marvel)

1,2 ($8.95)-Moebius-a in all 1.50 3.75 9.00
3 ($14.95) 2.15 6.50 15.00

LT. ROBIN CRUSOE, U.S.N. (See Movie Comics & Walt Disney Showcase #26)

LIFE OF CAPTAIN MARVEL, THE
Aug, 1985 - No. 5, Dec, 1985 ($2.00 cover; Baxter paper)
Marvel Comics Group

1-All reprint Starlin issues of Iron Man #55, Capt. Marvel #25-34 plus Marvel Feature #12 (all with Thanos) .80 2.00
2-5: 4-New Thanos back-c by Starlin .80 2.00

LIFE OF CHRIST, THE
No. 301, 1949 (100 pages) (35 cents)
Catechetical Guild Educational Society

301-Reprints from Topix(1949)-V5#11,12 3.60 9.00 18.00

LIFE OF CHRIST VISUALIZED
1942 - No. 3, 1943
Standard Publishers

1-3: All came in cardboard case 3.60 9.00 18.00
With case..... 6.70 20.00 40.00

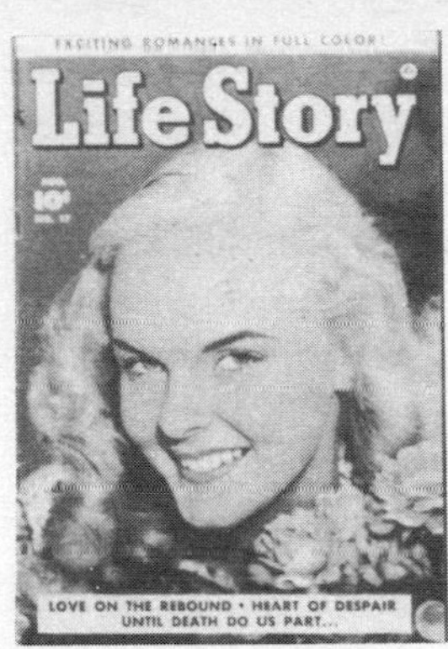

Life Story #17, © FAW

Lightning Comics V2#2, © ACE

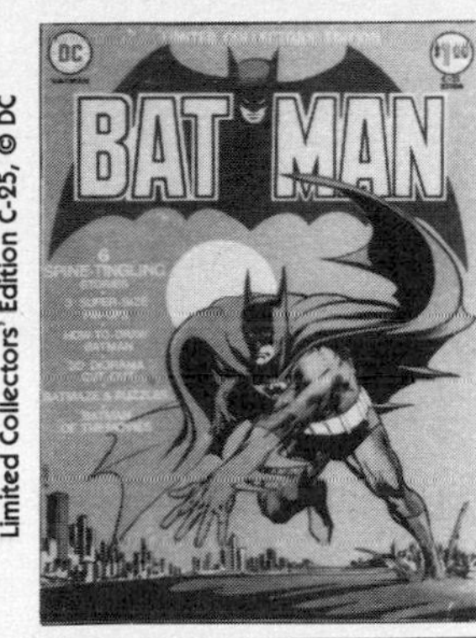

Limited Collectors' Edition C-25, © DC

GD25 FN65 NM94

LIFE OF CHRIST VISUALIZED
1946? (48 pgs. in color)
The Standard Publ. Co.

nn 1.60 4.00 8.00

LIFE OF ESTHER VISUALIZED
No. 2062, 1947 (48 pgs. in color)
The Standard Publ. Co.

2062 1.60 4.00 8.00

LIFE OF JOSEPH VISUALIZED
No. 1054, 1946 (48 pgs. in color)
The Standard Publ. Co.

1054 1.60 4.00 8.00

LIFE OF PAUL (See The Living Bible)

LIFE OF POPE JOHN PAUL II, THE
Jan, 1983
Marvel Comics Group

1 1.50

LIFE OF RILEY, THE (See 4-Color No. 917)

LIFE OF THE BLESSED VIRGIN
1950 (68 pages) (square binding)
Catechetical Guild (Giveaway)

nn-Contains "The Woman of the Promise" & "Mother of Us All" rebound 3.60 9.00 18.00

LIFE'S LIKE THAT
1945 (68 pgs.; B&W; 25 cents)
Croyden Publ. Co.

nn-Newspaper Sunday strip-r by Neher 4.70 14.00 28.00

LIFE'S LITTLE JOKES
No date (1924) (52 pgs.; B&W)
M.S. Publ. Co.

nn-By Rube Goldberg 32.00 95.00 225.00

LIFE STORIES OF AMERICAN PRESIDENTS (See Dell Giants)

LIFE STORY
Apr, 1949 - V8#46, Jan, 1953; V8#47, Apr, 1953 (All have photo-c?)
Fawcett Publications

V1#1 8.35 25.00 50.00
2 4.00 10.00 20.00
3-6 3.60 9.00 18.00
V2#7-12 3.20 8.00 16.00
V3#13-Wood-a 10.00 30.00 60.00
V3#14-18, V4#19-21,23,24 3.20 8.00 16.00
V4#22-Drug use story 3.60 9.00 18.00
V5#25-30, V6#31-35 3.20 8.00 16.00
V6#36-"I sold drugs" on-c 3.60 9.00 18.00
V7#37,40-42, V8#44,45 2.00 5.00 10.00
V7#38, V8#43-Evans-a 4.00 10.00 20.00
V7#39-Drug Smuggling & Junkie story 3.20 8.00 16.00
V8#46,47 (Scarce) 3.20 8.00 16.00

NOTE: ***Powell** a-13, 23, 24, 26, 28, 30, 32, 39. **Marcus Swayze** a-1-3, 10-12, 15, 16, 20, 21, 23-25, 31, 35, 37, 40, 44, 46.*

LIFE WITH ARCHIE
Sept, 1958 - No. 290?, 1991
Archie Publications

1 20.00 60.00 200.00
2-(9/59) 13.00 40.00 90.00
3-5: 3-(7/60) 9.00 28.00 65.00
6-10 4.50 14.00 32.00
11-20 3.20 8.00 20.00
21-30 2.15 6.50 15.00
31-41 1.60 4.00 9.50
42-45: 42-Pureheart begins (1st app.?, 1965?) 1.25 3.00 7.50
46-Origin Pureheart 1.65 4.70 11.00
47-59: 50-United Three begin: Pureheart (Archie), Superteen (Betty), Capt. Hero (Jughead). 59-Pureheart ends 1.00 2.50 5.50
60-100: 60-Archie band begins 1.20 3.00
101-290: 279-Intro Mustang Sally ($1.00) 1.25

NOTE: ***Gene Colan** a-272-279, 285, 286.*

LIFE WITH MILLIE (Formerly A Date With Millie) (Modeling With Millie No. 21 on)
No. 8, Dec, 1960 - No. 20, Dec, 1962
Atlas/Marvel Comics Group

8 5.85 17.50 35.00
9-11 4.20 12.50 25.00
12-20 3.60 9.00 18.00

LIFE WITH SNARKY PARKER (TV)
August, 1950
Fox Feature Syndicate

1-Early TV comic; photo-c from TV puppet show 17.00 52.00 120.00

LIGHT AND DARKNESS WAR, THE
Oct, 1988 - No. 6, Dec, 1989 ($1.95, color, limited series)
Epic Comics (Marvel)

1-6 .80 2.00

LIGHT FANTASTIC, THE (Terry Pratchett's)
June, 1992 - No. 4, Sept, 1992 ($2.50, color, mini-series)
Innovation Publishing

1-4: Adapts 2nd novel in Discworld series 1.00 2.50

LIGHT IN THE FOREST (See 4-Color No. 891)

LIGHTNING COMICS (Formerly Sure-Fire No. 1-3)
No. 4, Dec, 1940 - No. 13(V3#1), June, 1942
Ace Magazines

4-Characters continue from Sure-Fire 54.00 162.00 350.00
5,6: 6-Dr. Nemesis begins 37.00 110.00 250.00
V2#1-6: 2-"Flash Lightning" becomes "Lash..." 32.00 95.00 210.00
V3#1-Intro. Lightning Girl & The Sword 32.00 95.00 210.00

NOTE: ***Anderson** a-V2#6. **Mooney** c-V1#5, 6, V2#1-6, V3#1. Bondage c-V2#6. Lightning-c on all.*

LI'L (See Little)

LILY OF THE ALLEY IN THE FUNNIES
No date (1920's?) (10-1/4x15-1/2"; 28 pgs. in color)
Whitman Publishers

W936 - By T. Burke 13.00 40.00 90.00

LIMITED COLLECTORS' EDITION (See Famous First Edition & Rudolph the Red Nosed Reindeer; becomes All-New Collectors' Edition)
(#21-34,51-59: 84 pgs.; #35-41: 68 pgs.; #42-50: 60 pgs.)
C-21, Summer, 1973 - No. C-59, 1978 ($1.00) (10x13-1/2")
National Periodical Publications/DC Comics

nn(C-20)-Rudolph (date?) 1.30 3.25 8.00
C-21: Shazam (TV); r/Captain Marvel Jr. #11 by Raboy; C.C. Beck-c, biog. & photo 1.00 2.50 6.00
C-22: Tarzan; complete origin reprinted from #207-210; all Kubert-c/a; Joe Kubert biography & photo inside 1.00 2.50 6.00
C-23: House of Mystery; Wrightson, N. Adams/Orlando, G. Kane/Wood, Toth, Aragones, Sparling reprints 1.60 4.00
C-24: Rudolph The Red-nosed Reindeer 1.60 4.00
C-25: Batman; Neal Adams-c/a(r); G.A. Joker-r; Batman/Enemy Ace-r; has photos from TV show 1.30 3.25 8.00
C-26: See Famous First Edition C-26 (same contents)
C-27: Shazam (TV); G.A. Capt. Marvel & Mary Marvel-r; Beck-r 1.60 4.00
C-29: Tarzan; reprints "Return of Tarzan" from #219-223 by Kubert; Kubert-c 1.00 2.50 6.00

Limited Collectors' Edition C-48, © DC

Linda Carter, Student Nurse #5, © MEG

Little Al of the F.B.I. #10, © Z-D

	GD25	FN65	NM94
C-31: Superman; origin-r; N. Adams-a; photos of George Reeves from 1950s TV show on inside b/c; Burnley, Boring-r	1.00	2.50	6.00
C-32: Ghosts (new-a)		1.60	4.00
C-33: Rudolph The Red-nosed Reindeer(new-a)		1.60	4.00
C-34: Christmas with the Super-Heroes; unpublished Angel & Ape story by Oksner & Wood; Batman & Teen Titans-r	1.00	2.50	6.00
C-35: Shazam (TV); photo cover features TV's Captain Marvel, Jackson Bostwick; Beck-r; TV photos inside b/c		1.60	4.00
C-36: The Bible; all new adaptation beginning with Genesis by Kubert, Redondo & Mayer; Kubert-c	1.00	2.50	6.00
C-37: Batman; r-1946 Sundays; inside b/c photos of Batman TV show villains (all villain issue; r/G.A. Joker, Catwoman, Penguin, Two-Face, & Scarecrow stories plus 1946 Sundays-r)	1.30	3.25	8.00
C-38: Superman; 1 pg. N. Adams; part photo-c; photos from TV show on inside back-c		1.60	4.00
C-39: Secret Origins of Super-Villains; N. Adams-i(r); G.A. Batman-r; Beck-r		1.60	4.00
C-40: Dick Tracy by Gould featuring Flattop; newspaper-r from 12/21/43 - 5/17/44; biog. of Chester Gould	1.00	2.50	6.00
C-41: Super Friends (TV); JLA-r(1965); Toth-c/a		1.60	4.00
C-42: Rudolph		1.60	4.00
C-43: Christmas with the Super-Heroes; Wrightson, S&K, Neal Adams-a	1.00	2.50	6.00
C-44: Batman; N. Adams-p(r) & G.A.-r; painted-c	1.30	3.25	8.00
C-45: More Secret Origins of Super-Villains; Flash-r/#105; G.A. Wonder Woman & Batman/Catwoman-r		1.60	4.00
C-46: Justice League of America(1963-r); 3 pgs. Toth-a	1.00	2.50	6.00
C-47: Superman Salutes the Bicentennial (Tomahawk interior); 2 pgs. new-a		1.20	3.00
C-48: Superman Vs. The Flash (Superman/Flash race); swipes-c to Superman #199; r/Superman #199 & Flash #175; 6 pgs. Neal Adams-a	1.00	2.50	6.00
C-49: Superboy & the Legion of Super-Heroes		1.60	4.00
C-50: Rudolph The Red-nosed Reindeer		1.20	3.00
C-51: Batman; Neal Adams-c/a	1.30	3.25	8.00
C-52: The Best of DC; Neal Adams-c/a; Toth, Kubert-a	1.00	2.50	6.00
C-57: Welcome Back, Kotter-r(TV)(5/78)		1.20	3.00
C-59: Batman's Strangest Cases; N. Adams-r; Wrightson-r/Swamp Thing #7; N. Adams/Wrightson-c	1.30	3.25	8.00

NOTE: *All-r with exception of some special features and covers.* ***Aparo*** *a-52r, c-37.* ***Grell*** *c-49.* ***Infantino*** *a-25, 39, 44, 45, 52.* ***Bob Kane*** *r-25.* ***Robinson*** *r-25, 44.* ***Sprang*** *r-44. Issues #21-31, 35-39, 45, 48 have back cover cut-outs.*

LINDA (Everybody Loves...) (Phantom Lady No. 5 on)
Apr-May, 1954 - No. 4, Oct-Nov, 1954
Ajax-Farrell Publ. Co.

	GD25	FN65	NM94
1-Kamenish-a	10.00	30.00	65.00
2-Lingerie panel	8.35	25.00	50.00
3,4	6.70	20.00	40.00

LINDA CARTER, STUDENT NURSE
Sept, 1961 - No. 9, Jan, 1963
Atlas Comics (AMI)

	GD25	FN65	NM94
1-Al Hartley-c	4.20	12.50	25.00
2-9	3.60	9.00	18.00

LINDA LARK
Oct-Dec, 1961 - No. 8, Aug-Oct, 1963
Dell Publishing Co.

	GD25	FN65	NM94
1	2.80	7.00	14.00
2-8	1.40	3.50	7.00

LINUS, THE LIONHEARTED (TV)
September, 1965
Gold Key

	GD25	FN65	NM94
1 (10155-509)	7.50	22.50	45.00

LION, THE (See Movie Comics)

LION OF SPARTA (See Movie Classics)

LIPPY THE LION AND HARDY HAR HAR (TV)
March, 1963 (Hanna-Barbera) (12¢) (See Hanna-Barbera Band Wagon #1)
Gold Key

	GD25	FN65	NM94
1 (10049-303)	7.50	22.50	45.00

LI'L ABNER (See Comics on Parade, Sparkle, Sparkler Comics, Tip Top Comics & Tip Topper)
1939 - 1940
United Features Syndicate

	GD25	FN65	NM94
Single Series 4 ('39)	47.00	140.00	330.00
Single Series 18 ('40) (#18 on inside, #2 on-c)	39.00	120.00	275.00

LI'L ABNER (Al Capp's) (See Oxydol-Dreft)
No. 61, Dec, 1947 - No. 97, Jan, 1955
Harvey Publ. No. 61-69 (2/49)/Toby Press No. 70 on

	GD25	FN65	NM94
61(#1)-Wolverton & Powell-a	23.00	70.00	160.00
62-65: 65-Powell-a	14.00	43.00	100.00
66,67,69,70	11.50	34.00	80.00
68-Full length Fearless Fosdick story plus-c	13.00	40.00	90.00
71-74,76,80	10.00	30.00	65.00
75,77-79,86,91-All with Kurtzman art; 91-r/#77	11.50	34.00	80.00
81-85,87-90,92-94,96,97: 93-reprints #71	9.15	27.50	55.00
95-Full length Fearless Fosdick story	11.00	32.00	75.00
...& the Creatures from Drop-Outer Space-nn (Job Corps giveaway; 36 pgs., in color)	11.00	32.00	75.00
...Joins the Navy (1950) (Toby Press Premium)	9.15	27.50	55.00
...by Al Capp Giveaway (Circa 1955, nd)	9.15	27.50	55.00

LI'L ABNER
1951
Toby Press

	GD25	FN65	NM94
1	13.00	40.00	90.00

LI'L ABNER'S DOGPATCH (See Al Capp's...)

LITTLE AL OF THE F.B.I.
No. 10, 1950 (no month) - No. 11, Apr-May, 1951
Ziff-Davis Publications (Saunders painted-c)

	GD25	FN65	NM94
10(1950)	10.00	30.00	60.00
11(1951)	7.00	21.00	42.00

LITTLE AL OF THE SECRET SERVICE
No. 10, 7-8/51; No, 2, 9-10/51; No. 3, Winter, 1951
Ziff-Davis Publications (Saunders painted-c)

	GD25	FN65	NM94
10(#1)-Spanking panels (2)	10.00	30.00	70.00
2,3	7.00	21.00	42.00

LITTLE ALONZO
1938 (B&W, 5-1/2x8-1/2")(Christmas giveaway)
Macy's Dept. Store

	GD25	FN65	NM94
nn-By Ferdinand the Bull's Munro Leaf	6.70	20.00	40.00

LITTLE AMBROSE
September, 1958
Archie Publications

	GD25	FN65	NM94
1-Bob Bolling-c	10.00	30.00	65.00

LITTLE ANGEL
No. 5, Sept, 1954; No. 6, Sept, 1955 - No. 16, Sept, 1959
Standard (Visual Editions)/Pines

	GD25	FN65	NM94
5-Last pre-code issue	4.20	12.50	25.00
6-16	2.80	7.00	14.00

LITTLE ANNIE ROONEY
1935 (48 pgs.; B&W dailies) (25 cents)
David McKay Publications

	GD25	FN65	NM94
Book 1-Daily strip-r by Darrell McClure	12.00	36.00	85.00

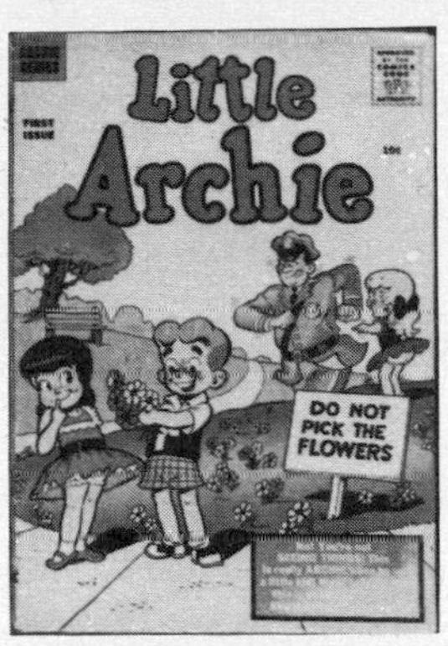

Little Archie #1, © AP

Little Audrey #18, © HARV

Little Beaver #8, © DELL

	GD25	FN65	NM94

LITTLE ANNIE ROONEY (See King Comics & Treasury of Comics)
1938; Aug, 1948 - No. 3, Oct, 1948
David McKay/St. John/Standard

	GD25	FN65	NM94
Feature Books 11 (McKay, 1938)	26.00	80.00	185.00
1 (St. John)	10.00	30.00	65.00
2,3	5.85	17.50	35.00

LITTLE ARCHIE (The Adventures of... #13-on) (See Archie Giant Series Mag. #527, 534, 538, 545, 549, 556, 560, 566, 570, 583, 594, 596, 607, 609, 619)
1956 - No. 180, Feb, 1983 (Giants No. 3-84)
Archie Publications

	GD25	FN65	NM94
1-(Scarce)	39.00	120.00	275.00
2 (1957)	19.00	58.00	135.00
3-5	13.00	40.00	90.00
6-10	10.00	30.00	60.00
11-20	6.00	18.00	36.00
21-30	4.00	11.00	22.00
31-40: Little Pureheart apps. #40-42,44	2.40	6.00	12.00
41-60: 42-Intro. The Little Archies. 59-Little Sabrina begins	1.40	3.50	7.00
61-84: 84-Last Giant-Size	1.00	2.00	5.00
85-100		1.20	3.00
101-180			1.50
...In Animal Land 1(1957)	11.50	34.00	80.00
...In Animal Land 17(Winter, 1957-58)-19(Summer,1958)-Formerly Li'l Jinx	6.70	20.00	40.00

LITTLE ARCHIE
Apr, 1991 ($1.00, color)
Archie Comics

	GD25	FN65	NM94
1			1.00

LITTLE ARCHIE CHRISTMAS SPECIAL (See Archie Giant Series #581)

LITTLE ARCHIE COMICS DIGEST ANNUAL (...Magazine #5 on)
10/77 - No. 48, 5/91 (Digest-size, 128 pgs., later issues $1.35-$1.50)
Archie Publications

	GD25	FN65	NM94
1(10/77)-Reprints		.80	2.00
2(4/78)-Neal Adams-a			1.40
3(11/78)-The Fly-r by S&K; Neal Adams-a			1.40
4(4/79) - 48: 28,40,46-Christmas-c			1.40

NOTE: *Little Archie, Little Jinx, Little Jughead & Little Sabrina in most issues.*

LITTLE ARCHIE DIGEST MAGAZINE
July, 1991 - Present ($1.50, digest size)
Archie Comics

	GD25	FN65	NM94
V2#1-7			1.50

LITTLE ARCHIE MYSTERY
Aug, 1963 - No. 2, Oct, 1963 (12¢ issues)
Archie Publications

	GD25	FN65	NM94
1	10.00	30.00	70.00
2	5.85	17.50	35.00

LITTLE ASPIRIN (See Little Lenny & Wisco)
July, 1949 - No. 3, Dec, 1949 (52 pages)
Marvel Comics (CnPC)

	GD25	FN65	NM94
1-Oscar app.; Kurtzman-a, 4 pgs.	10.00	30.00	70.00
2-Kurtzman-a, 4 pgs.	6.35	19.00	38.00
3-No Kurtzman-a	4.00	10.00	20.00

LITTLE AUDREY (Also see Playful...)
April, 1948 - No. 24, May, 1952
St. John Publ.

	GD25	FN65	NM94
1-1st app. Little Audrey	25.00	75.00	175.00
2	11.50	34.00	80.00
3-5	9.15	27.50	55.00
6-10	5.35	16.00	32.00
11-20: 16-X-Mas-c	4.00	10.00	20.00
21-24	3.00	7.50	15.00

	GD25	FN65	NM94

LITTLE AUDREY (See Harvey Hits #11, 19)
No. 25, Aug, 1952 - No. 53, April, 1957
Harvey Publications

	GD25	FN65	NM94
25 (Paramount Pictures Famous Star on-c)	7.50	22.50	45.00
26-30: 26-28-Casper app.	4.00	12.00	24.00
31-40: 32-35-Casper app.	3.60	9.00	18.00
41-53	2.40	6.00	12.00
...Clubhouse 1 (9/61, 68 pg. Giant) w/reprints	5.85	17.50	35.00

LITTLE AUDREY
Aug, 1992 - Present ($1.25, color)
Harvey Comics

	GD25	FN65	NM94
V2#1-3			1.25

LITTLE AUDREY (...Yearbook)
1950 (50 cents, 260 pages)
St. John Publishing Co.

	GD25	FN65	NM94
Contains 8 complete 1949 comics rebound; Casper, Alice in Wonderland, Little Audrey, Abbott & Costello, Pinocchio, Moon Mullins, Three Stooges (from Jubilee), Little Annie Rooney app. (Rare)	57.00	171.00	400.00

(Also see All Good & Treasury of Comics)

NOTE: *This book contains remaindered St. John comics; many variations possible.*

LITTLE AUDREY & MELVIN (Audrey & Melvin No. 62)
May, 1962 - No. 61, Dec, 1973
Harvey Publications

	GD25	FN65	NM94
1	7.50	22.50	45.00
2-5	4.00	10.00	21.00
6-10	2.80	7.00	14.00
11-20	1.80	4.50	9.00
21-40	1.00	2.50	6.00
41-50,54-61	1.00	2.00	5.00
51-53: All 52 pg. Giants	1.00	2.50	6.00

LITTLE AUDREY TV FUNTIME
Sept, 1962 - No. 33, Oct, 1971 (#1-31: 68 pgs.; #32,33: 52 pgs.)
Harvey Publications

	GD25	FN65	NM94
1-Richie Rich app.	5.35	16.00	32.00
2,3: Richie Rich app.	3.60	9.00	18.00
4,5: 5-25 & 35 cent issues exist	2.80	7.00	14.00
6-10	1.40	3.50	7.00
11-20	1.00	2.50	6.00
21-33	1.00	2.00	5.00

LITTLE BAD WOLF (See 4-Color #403, 473, 564, Walt Disney's C&S #52, Walt Disney Showcase #21 & Wheaties)

LITTLE BEAVER
No. 211, Jan, 1949 - No. 870, Jan, 1958 (All painted-c)
Dell Publishing Co.

	GD25	FN65	NM94
4-Color 211('49)-All Harman-a	7.50	22.50	45.00
4-Color 267,294,332(5/51)	4.00	12.00	24.00
3(10-12/51)-8(1-3/53)	4.00	10.00	20.00
4-Color 483(8-10/53),529	4.00	10.00	20.00
4-Color 612,660,695,744,817,870	3.60	9.00	18.00

LITTLE BIT
March, 1949 - No. 2, June, 1949
Jubilee/St. John Publishing Co.

	GD25	FN65	NM94
1,2	4.00	10.00	20.00

LITTLE DOT (See Humphrey, Li'l Max, Sad Sack, and Tastee-Freez Comics)
Sept, 1953 - No. 164, April, 1976
Harvey Publications

	GD25	FN65	NM94
1-Intro./1st app. Richie Rich & Little Lotta	60.00	180.00	425.00
2-1st app. Freckles & Pee Wee (Richie Rich's poor friends)	30.00	90.00	210.00
3	19.00	57.00	130.00

Little Dot #12, © HARV

Little Groucho #1, © Reston Publ.

Little Iodine #32, © DELL

	GD25	FN65	NM94
4	14.00	43.00	100.00
5-Origin dots on Little Dot's dress	22.00	65.00	150.00
6-Richie Rich, Little Lotta, & Little Dot all on cover; 1st Richie Rich cover featured	17.00	52.00	120.00
7-10: 8-Last pre-code issue? (11/54)	10.00	30.00	60.00
11-20	7.50	22.50	45.00
21-40	4.00	10.00	20.00
41-60	2.40	6.00	12.00
61-80	1.60	4.00	8.00
81-100	1.00	2.00	5.00
101-141		1.40	3.50
142-145: All 52 pg. Giants	1.00	2.00	5.00
146-164			1.50
Shoe store giveaway 2	5.00	15.00	30.00

NOTE: *Richie Rich & Little Lotta in all.*

LITTLE DOT
Sept, 1992 - Present ($1.25, color)
Harvey Comics

	GD25	FN65	NM94
V2#1-4: Little Dot, Little Lotta, Richie Rich in all			1.25

LITTLE DOT DOTLAND (Dot Dotland No. 62, 63)
July, 1962 - No. 61, Dec, 1973
Harvey Publications

	GD25	FN65	NM94
1-Richie Rich begins	7.50	22.50	45.00
2,3	4.00	11.00	22.00
4,5	3.20	8.00	16.00
6-10	2.40	6.00	12.00
11-20	1.80	4.50	9.00
21-30	1.00	2.00	5.00
31-50,55-61		1.40	3.50
51-54: All 52 pg. Giants	1.00	2.50	6.00

LITTLE DOT'S UNCLES & AUNTS (See Harvey Hits No. 4, 13, 24)
Oct, 1961; No. 2, Aug, 1962 - No. 52, April, 1974
Harvey Enterprises

	GD25	FN65	NM94
1-Richie Rich begins; 68 pgs. begin	8.35	25.00	50.00
2,3	4.20	12.50	25.00
4,5	3.00	7.50	15.00
6-10	2.00	5.00	10.00
11-20	1.60	4.00	8.00
21-37: Last 68 pg. issue	1.00	2.50	6.00
38-52: All 52 pg. Giants	1.00	2.00	5.00

LITTLE DRACULA
Jan, 1992 - No. 3, July?, 1992 ($1.25, color, quarterly, mini-series)
Harvey Comics

	GD25	FN65	NM94
1-3			1.25

LITTLE EVA
May, 1952 - No. 31, Nov, 1956
St. John Publishing Co.

	GD25	FN65	NM94
1	9.15	27.50	55.00
2	4.70	14.00	28.00
3-5	3.60	9.00	18.00
6-10	2.40	6.00	12.00
11-31	2.00	5.00	10.00
3-D 1,2(10/53-11/53); 1-Infinity-c	13.00	40.00	90.00
I.W. Reprint #1-3,6-8	.60	1.50	3.00
Super Reprint #10,12('63),14,16,18('64)	.60	1.50	3.00

LITTLE FIR TREE, THE
nd (1942) (8-1/2x11") (12 pgs. with cover, color & B&W, heavy paper)
W. T. Grant Co. (Christmas giveaway)

nn-Story by Hans Christian Anderson; 8 pg. Kelly-r/Santa Claus Funnies; not signed.
(One copy in Mint sold for $1750.00 in 1986 & another copy in VF sold for $1000.00 in 1991)

LI'L GENIUS (Summer Fun No. 54) (See Blue Bird & Giant Comics #3)
1954 - No. 52, 1/65; No. 53, 10/65; No. 54, 10/85 - No. 55, 1/86
Charlton Comics

	GD25	FN65	NM94
1	6.70	20.00	40.00
2	4.00	10.00	20.00
3-15,19,20	2.80	7.00	14.00
16,17-(68 pgs.)	4.00	10.00	20.00
18-(100 pgs., 10/58)	5.00	15.00	30.00
21-35	2.40	6.00	12.00
36-53	1.00	2.50	6.00
54,55			1.50

LI'L GHOST
Feb, 1958; Nov?, 1958 - No. 3, Mar, 1959
St. John Publishing Co./Fago No. 1 on

	GD25	FN65	NM94
1(St. John)	5.85	17.50	35.00
1(Fago)-Al Fago-c/a begins	4.00	11.00	22.00
2,3: 2-(1/59)	3.20	8.00	16.00

LITTLE GIANT COMICS
7/38 - No. 3, 10/38; No. 4, 2/39 (132 pgs.) (6-3/4x4-1/2")
Centaur Publications

	GD25	FN65	NM94
1-B&W with color-c; stories, puzzles, magic	37.00	110.00	250.00
2,3-B&W with color-c	30.00	90.00	210.00
4 (6-5/8x9-3/8")(68 pgs., B&W inside)	32.00	95.00	220.00

NOTE: ***Filchock** c-2, 4. **Gustavson** a-1. **Pinajian** a-4. **Bob Wood** a-1.*

LITTLE GIANT DETECTIVE FUNNIES
Oct, 1938 - No. 4, Jan, 1939 (132 pgs., B&W) (6-3/4x4-1/2")
Centaur Publications

	GD25	FN65	NM94
1-B&W with color-c	37.00	110.00	250.00
2,3	30.00	90.00	210.00
4(1/39, B&W; color-c; 68 pgs., 6-1/2x9-1/2")-Eisner-r	32.00	95.00	220.00

LITTLE GIANT MOVIE FUNNIES
Aug, 1938 - No. 2, Oct, 1938 (132 pgs., B&W) (6-3/4x4-1/2")
Centaur Publications

	GD25	FN65	NM94
1-Ed Wheelan's "Minute Movies"-r	37.00	110.00	250.00
2-Ed Wheelan's "Minute Movies"-r	27.00	82.00	190.00

LITTLE GROUCHO (...Grouchy No. 2) (See Tippy Terry)
No. 16; Feb-Mar, 1955 - No. 2, June-July, 1955
Reston Publ. Co.

	GD25	FN65	NM94
16, 1 (2-3/55)	5.35	16.00	32.00
2(6-7/55)	4.00	10.00	20.00

LITTLE HIAWATHA (See 4-Color #439, 787, 901, 988 & Walt Disney's C&S #143)

LITTLE IKE
April, 1953 - No. 4, Oct, 1953
St. John Publishing Co.

	GD25	FN65	NM94
1	6.70	20.00	40.00
2	4.00	10.00	20.00
3,4	3.20	8.00	16.00

LITTLE IODINE (See Giant Comic Album)
No. 224, 4/49 - No. 257, 1949: 3-5/50 - No. 56, 4-6/62 (1-4: 52pgs.)
Dell Publishing Co.

	GD25	FN65	NM94
4-Color 224-By Jimmy Hatlo	10.00	30.00	65.00
4-Color 257	7.50	22.50	45.00
1(3-5/50)	9.15	27.50	55.00
2-5	4.00	11.00	22.00
6-10	2.80	7.00	14.00
11-20	2.40	6.00	12.00
21-30: 27-Xmas-c	2.00	5.00	10.00
31-40	1.60	4.00	8.00
41-56	1.20	3.00	6.00

LITTLE JACK FROST

Little Joe #1, © STJ

Little Lotta #22, © HARV

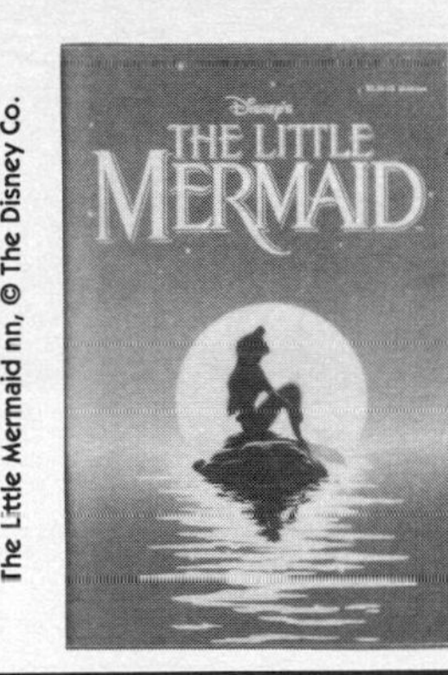

The Little Mermaid nn, © The Disney Co.

1951
Avon Periodicals

	GD25	FN65	NM94
1	5.00	15.00	30.00

LI'L JINX (Formerly Ginger?) (Little Archie in Animal Land #17) (Also see Pep Comics #62)
No. 11, Nov, 1956 - No. 16, Sept, 1957
Archie Publications

	GD25	FN65	NM94
11 (#1)	7.50	22.50	45.00
12-16	5.00	15.00	30.00

LI'L JINX (See Archie Giant Series Magazine No. 223)

LI'L JINX CHRISTMAS BAG (See Archie Giant Series Mag. No. 195, 206, 219)

LI'L JINX GIANT LAUGH-OUT (See Archie Giant Series Mag. No. 176, 185)
No. 33, Sept, 1971 - No. 43, Nov, 1973 (52 pgs.)
Archie Publications

	GD25	FN65	NM94
33-43		1.20	3.00

LITTLE JOE (See 4-Color #1, Popular Comics & Super Comics)

LITTLE JOE
April, 1953
St. John Publishing Co.

	GD25	FN65	NM94
1	3.00	7.50	15.00

LITTLE JOHNNY & THE TEDDY BEARS
1907 (10x14") (32 pgs. in color)
Reilly & Britton Co.

	GD25	FN65	NM94
nn-By J. R. Bray	23.00	70.00	160.00

LI'L KIDS (Also see Li'l Pals)
8/70 - No. 2, 10/70; No. 3, 11/71 - No. 12, 6/73
Marvel Comics Group

	GD25	FN65	NM94
1	1.50	3.75	9.00
2-12: 10,11-Calvin app.		1.80	4.50

LITTLE KING (See 4-Color No. 494, 597, 677)

LITTLE KLINKER
Nov, 1960 (20 pgs.) (slick cover)
Little Klinker Ventures (Montgomery Ward Giveaway)

	GD25	FN65	NM94
nn	2.00	5.00	10.00

LITTLE LANA (Formerly Lana)
No. 8, Nov, 1949; No. 9, Mar, 1950
Marvel Comics (MjMC)

	GD25	FN65	NM94
8,9	4.35	13.00	26.00

LITTLE LENNY
June, 1949 - No. 3, Nov, 1949
Marvel Comics (CDS)

	GD25	FN65	NM94
1-Little Aspirin app.	7.00	21.00	42.00
2,3	4.00	10.00	20.00

LITTLE LIZZIE
6/49 - No. 5, 4/50; 9/53 - No. 3, Jan, 1954
Marvel Comics (PrPI)/Atlas (OMC)

	GD25	FN65	NM94
1	8.35	25.00	50.00
2-5	4.00	12.50	25.00
1 (9/53, 2nd series by Atlas)-Howie Post-c	5.00	15.00	30.00
2,3	4.00	10.00	20.00

LITTLE LOTTA (See Harvey Hits No. 10)
11/55 - No. 110, 11/73; No. 111, 9/74 - No. 121, 5/76
V2#1, Oct, 1992 - Present ($1.25, color)
Harvey Publications

	GD25	FN65	NM94
1-Richie Rich (r) & Little Dot begin	29.00	85.00	200.00
2,3	13.00	40.00	90.00
4,5	8.35	25.00	50.00
6-10	6.70	20.00	40.00
11-20	4.20	12.50	25.00
21-40	3.00	7.50	15.00
41-60	2.40	6.00	12.00
61-80	1.00	2.50	6.00
81-99		1.60	4.00
100-103: All 52 pg. Giants	1.00	2.00	5.00
104-121: 121-Exist?		.85	2.10
V2#1-3 (1992)			1.25

LITTLE LOTTA FOODLAND
9/63 - No. 14, 10/67; No. 15, 10/68 - No. 29, Oct, 1972
Harvey Publications

	GD25	FN65	NM94
1: 68 pgs. begin, end #26	10.00	30.00	65.00
2,3	5.85	17.50	35.00
4,5	4.00	11.00	22.00
6-10	3.00	7.50	15.00
11-20	2.00	6.00	12.00
21-26	1.80	4.50	9.00
27,28: Both 52 pgs.	1.00	2.50	6.00
29: 36 pgs.		1.80	4.50

LITTLE LULU (Formerly Marge's...)
No. 207, Sept, 1972 - No. 268, April, 1984
Gold Key 207-257/Whitman 258 on

	GD25	FN65	NM94
207,209,220-Stanley-r. 207-1st app. Henrietta	1.00	2.50	6.00
208,210-219: 208-1st app. Snobbly, Wilbur's brother	1.00	2.00	5.00
221-240,242-249, 250(r/#166), 251-254(r/#206)		1.60	4.00
241,263,268-Stanley-r		1.60	4.00
255-262,264-267: 256-r/#212		.80	2.00

LITTLE MARY MIXUP (See Comics On Parade & Single Series #10, 26)

LITTLE MAX COMICS (Joe Palooka's Pal; see Joe Palooka)
Oct, 1949 - No. 73, Nov, 1961
Harvey Publications

	GD25	FN65	NM94
1-Infinity-c; Little Dot begins; Joe Palooka on-c	11.00	32.00	75.00
2-Little Dot app.; Joe Palooka on-c	6.35	19.00	38.00
3-Little Dot app.; Joe Palooka on-c	4.70	14.00	28.00
4-10: 5-Little Dot app., 1pg.	3.20	8.00	10.00
11-20	2.40	6.00	12.00
21-73: 23-Little Dot app. 38-r/#20. 70-73-Little Lotta, Richie Rich app.	1.60	4.00	8.00

LI'L MENACE
Dec, 1958 - No. 3, May, 1959
Fago Magazine Co.

	GD25	FN65	NM94
1-Peter Rabbit app.	4.70	14.00	28.00
2-Peter Rabbit (Vincent Fago's)	4.00	10.00	20.00
3	3.20	8.00	16.00

LITTLE MERMAID, THE (Walt Disney's...; also see Disney's...)
1990 (no date given)($5.95, color, no ads, 52 pgs.)
W. D. Publications (Disney)

	GD25	FN65	NM94
nn-Adapts animated movie	1.00	2.50	6.00
nn-Comic version ($2.50)		1.00	2.50

LITTLE MERMAID, THE
1992 - No. 4, 1992 ($1.50, color, mini-series)
Disney Comics

	GD25	FN65	NM94
1-4: Based on movie			1.50
1-4: 2nd printings sold at Wal-Mart w/different-c			1.50

LITTLE MISS MUFFET
No. 11, Dec, 1948 - No. 13, March, 1949
Best Books (Standard Comics)/King Features Synd.

	GD25	FN65	NM94
11-Strip reprints; Fanny Cory-c/a	6.35	19.00	38.00
12,13-Strip reprints; Fanny Cory-c/a	4.20	12.50	25.00

LITTLE MISS SUNBEAM COMICS

Little Orphan Annie #4 (1929), © News Synd.

Little Orphan Annie #1, (3-5/48), © News Synd.

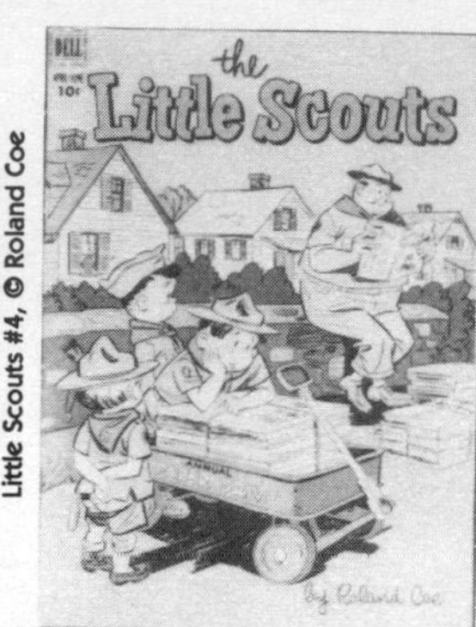

Little Scouts #4, © Roland Coe

GD25 FN65 NM94

June-July, 1950 - No. 4, Dec-Jan, 1950-51
Magazine Enterprises/Quality Bakers of America

	GD25	FN65	NM94
1	9.15	27.50	55.00
2-4	4.70	14.00	28.00
...Advs. In Space ('55)	4.00	10.00	20.00
Bread Giveaway 1-4(Quality Bakers, 1949-50)-14 pgs. each	3.60	9.00	18.00
Bread Giveaway (1957,61; 16pgs, reg. size)	3.20	8.00	16.00

LITTLE MONSTERS, THE (See March of Comics #423, Three Stooges #17)
Nov, 1964 - No. 44, Feb, 1978
Gold Key

	GD25	FN65	NM94
1	3.00	7.50	15.00
2	1.60	4.00	8.00
3-10	1.00	2.50	6.00
11-20		1.20	3.00
21-44: 20,34-39,43-reprints			1.50

LITTLE MONSTERS (Now)(Value: cover or less)

LITTLE NEMO (See Cocomalt, Future Comics, Help, Jest, Kayo, Punch, Red Seal, & Superworld; most by Winsor McCay Jr., son of famous artist) (Other McCay books: see Little Sammy Sneeze & Dreams of the Rarebit Fiend)

LITTLE NEMO (...in Slumberland)
1906, 1909 (Sunday strip reprints in color) (cardboard covers)
Doffield & Co.(1906)/Cupples & Leon Co.(1909)

	GD25	FN65	NM94
1906-11x16-1/2" in color by Winsor McCay; 30 pgs. (Very Rare)	285.00	860.00	2000.00
1909-10x14" in color by Winsor McCay (Very Rare)	257.00	770.00	1800.00

LITTLE NEMO (...in Slumberland)
1945 (28 pgs.; 11x7-1/4"; B&W)
McCay Features/Nostalgia Press('69)

	GD25	FN65	NM94
1905 & 1911 reprints by Winsor McCay	5.00	15.00	35.00
1969-70 (Exact reprint)	1.30	4.00	8.00

LITTLE ORPHAN ANNIE (See Annie, Famous Feature Stories, Feature Books #7, Marvel Super Special, Merry Christmas..., Popular Comics, Super Book #7, 11, 23 & Super Comics)

LITTLE ORPHAN ANNIE (See Treasure Box of Famous Comics)
1926 - 1934 (Daily strip reprints) (7x8-3/4") (B&W)
Cupples & Leon Co.
(Hardcover Editions, 100 pages)

	GD25	FN65	NM94
1(1926)-Little Orphan Annie	23.00	70.00	160.00
2('27)-In the Circus	17.00	50.00	110.00
3('28)-The Haunted House	17.00	50.00	110.00
4('29)-Bucking the World	17.00	50.00	110.00
5('30)-Never Say Die	17.00	50.00	110.00
6('31)-Shipwrecked	17.00	50.00	110.00
7('32)-A Willing Helper	12.50	37.50	80.00
8('33)-In Cosmic City	12.50	37.50	80.00
9('34)-Uncle Dan	17.00	50.00	110.00

NOTE: *Hardcovers with dust jackets are worth 20-50 percent more; the earlier the book, the higher the percentage. Each book reprints dailies from the previous year.*

LITTLE ORPHAN ANNIE
No. 7, 1937 - No. 3, Sept-Nov, 1948; No. 206, Dec, 1948
David McKay Publ./Dell Publishing Co.

	GD25	FN65	NM94
Feature Books(McKay) 7-(1937) (Rare)	82.00	245.00	575.00
4-Color 12(1941)	47.00	141.00	330.00
4-Color 18(1943)-Flag-c	38.00	115.00	265.00
4-Color 52(1944)	29.00	85.00	200.00
4-Color 76(1945)	24.00	72.00	165.00
4-Color 107(1946)	20.00	60.00	140.00
4-Color 152(1947)	13.00	40.00	90.00
1(3-5/48)-r/strips from 5/7/44 to 7/30/44	13.50	41.00	95.00
2-r/strips from 7/21/40 to 9/9/40	9.15	27.50	55.00
3-r/strips from 9/10/40 to 11/9/40	9.15	27.50	55.00
4-Color 206(12/48)	7.50	22.50	45.00
Junior Commandos Giveaway(same-c as 4-Color #18, K.K. Publ.)(Big Shoe Store); same back cover as '47 Popped Wheat giveaway; 16 pgs; flag-c; r/strips 9/7/42-10/10/42	22.00	65.00	150.00
Popped Wheat Giveaway('47)-16 pgs. full color; reprints strips from 5/3/40 to 6/20/40	1.60	4.00	8.00
Quaker Sparkies Giveaway(1940)	11.50	34.00	80.00
Quaker Sparkies Giveaway(1941, Full color, 20 pgs.); :LOA and the Rescue;" r/strips 4/13/39-6/21/39 & 7/6/39-7/17/39. "LOA and the Kidnappers;" r/strips 11/28/38-1/28/39	10.00	30.00	70.00
Quaker Sparkies Giveaway(1942, Full color, 20 pgs.); "LOA and Mr. Gudge;" r/strips 2/13/38-3/21/38 & 4/18/37-5/30/37. "LOA and the Great Am"	10.00	30.00	60.00

LI'L PALS (Also see Li'l Kids)
Sept, 1972 - No. 5, May, 1973
Marvel Comics Group

	GD25	FN65	NM94
1-5		1.40	3.50

LI'L PAN (Formerly Rocket Kelly; becomes Junior Comics with #9)
No. 6, Dec-Jan, 1946-47 - No. 8, Apr-May, 1947
Fox Features Syndicate

	GD25	FN65	NM94
6	5.85	17.50	35.00
7,8: 7-Atomic bomb story	4.00	11.00	22.00

LITTLE PEOPLE (See 4-Color #485, 573, 633, 692, 753, 809, 868, 908, 959, 1024, 1062)

LITTLE RASCALS (See 4-Color #674, 778, 825, 883, 936, 974, 1030, 1079, 1137, 1174, 1224, 1297)

LI'L RASCAL TWINS (Formerly Nature Boy)
No. 6, 1957 - No. 18, Jan, 1960
Charlton Comics

	GD25	FN65	NM94
6-Li'l Genius & Tomboy in all	4.20	12.50	25.00
7-18	2.40	6.00	12.00

LITTLE ROQUEFORT COMICS
June, 1952 - No. 9, Oct, 1953; No. 10, Summer, 1958
St. John Publishing Co./Pines No. 10

	GD25	FN65	NM94
1-By Paul Terry	7.00	21.00	42.00
2	4.00	10.00	20.00
3-10: 10-CBS Television Presents on-c	3.00	7.50	15.00

LITTLE SAD SACK (See Harvey Hits No. 73, 76, 79, 81, 83)
Oct, 1964 - No. 19, Nov, 1967
Harvey Publications

	GD25	FN65	NM94
1-Richie Rich app. on cover only	3.00	7.50	15.00
2-19	1.00	2.50	5.00

LITTLE SAMMY SNEEZE
1905 (28 pgs. in color; 11x16-1/2")
New York Herald Co.

	GD25	FN65	NM94
nn-By Winsor McCay (Rare)	285.00	860.00	2000.00

NOTE: *Rarely found in fine to mint condition.*

LITTLE SCOUTS
No. 321, Mar, 1951 - No. 587, Oct, 1954
Dell Publishing Co.

	GD25	FN65	NM94
4-Color #321 (#1, 3/51)	3.60	9.00	18.00
2(10-12/51) - 6(10-12/52)	2.00	5.00	10.00
4-Color #462,506,550,587	2.00	5.00	10.00

LITTLE SHOP OF HORRORS SPECIAL (DC)(Value: cover or less)

LITTLE SPUNKY
No date (1963?) (10 cents)
I. W. Enterprises

	GD25	FN65	NM94
1-Reprint	.80	2.00	4.00

LITTLE STOOGES, THE (The Three Stooges' Sons)
Sept, 1972 - No. 7, Mar, 1974

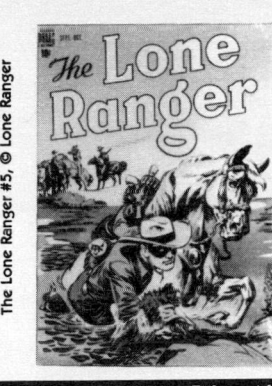

Li'l Willie #20, © MEG

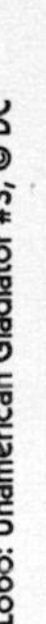
Lobo: Unamerican Gladiator #3, © DC

The Lone Ranger #5, © Lone Ranger

GD25 FN65 NM94

Gold Key

	GD25	FN65	NM94
1-Norman Maurer cover/stories in all	1.30	3.25	8.00
2-7		1.60	4.00

LITTLEST OUTLAW (See 4 Color #609)

LITTLEST SNOWMAN, THE
No. 755, 12/56; No. 864, 12/57; 12-2/1963-64
Dell Publishing Co.

	GD25	FN65	NM94
4-Color #755,864, 1(1964)	4.00	11.00	22.00

LI'L TOMBOY (Formerly Fawcett's Funny Animals; see Giant Comics #3)
V14#92, Oct, 1956; No. 93, Mar, 1957 - No. 107, Feb, 1960
Charlton Comics

	GD25	FN65	NM94
V14#92	4.00	10.00	20.00
93-107: 97-Atomic Bunny app.	3.00	7.50	15.00

LITTLE TREE THAT WASN'T WANTED, THE
1960, (Color, 28 pgs.)
W. T. Grant Co. (Giveaway)

	GD25	FN65	NM94
nn-Christmas giveaway	1.00	4.00	8.00

LI'L WILLIE COMICS (Formerly & becomes Willie Comics #22 on)
No. 20, July, 1949 - No. 21, Sept, 1949
Marvel Comics (MgPC)

	GD25	FN65	NM94
20,21: 20-Little Aspirin app.	4.70	14.00	28.00

LITTLE WOMEN (See Power Record Comics)

LIVE IT UP (Spire Christian)(Value: cover or less)

LIVING BIBLE, THE
Fall, 1945 - No. 3, Spring, 1946
Living Bible Corp.

	GD25	FN65	NM94
1-The Life of Paul	16.00	48.00	110.00
2-Joseph & His Brethren; Jonah & the Whale	10.00	30.00	70.00
3-Chaplains At War (classic-c)	17.00	52.00	120.00

NOTE: *All have **L. B. Cole** -c.*

LOBO
Dec, 1965; No. 2, Oct, 1966
Dell Publishing Co.

	GD25	FN65	NM94
1,2	1.60	4.00	8.00

LOBO (Also see Action #650, Adventures of Superman, Justice League, L.E.G.I.O.N., Mister Miracle, Omega Men #3 & Superman #41)
Nov, 1990 - No. 4, Feb, 1991 ($1.50, color, mini-series)

	GD25	FN65	NM94
1-(99 cents)-Giffen plots/Breakdowns in all		1.90	4.75
2-Legion '89 spin-off		1.00	2.50
3,4: 1-4 have Bisley painted covers & art		.80	2.00
Annual 1 (1993, $3.50, 68 pgs.)-Bloodlines x-over		1.40	3.50
...: Blazing Chain of Love 1 (9/92, $1.50)-Denys Cowan-c/a; Alan Grant scripts			1.50
...Convention Special 1 (1993, $1.75)		.70	1.75
...Paramilitary Christmas Special 1 (1991, $2.39, 52 pgs.)-Bisley-c/a		1.00	2.50
...: Portrait of a Victim 1 (1993, $1.75)		.70	1.75

LOBO: INFANTICIDE
Oct, 1992 - No. 4, Jan, 1993 ($1.50, color, mini-series, mature readers)
DC Comics

	GD25	FN65	NM94
1-4: Giffen-c/a; Alan Grant scripts			1.50

LOBO'S BACK
May, 1992 - No. 4, Nov, 1992 ($1.50, color, mini-series, mature readers)
DC Comics

	GD25	FN65	NM94
1-4: 1 Has 3 outer covers. Bisley painted-c 1,2; a-1-3. 3-Sam Kieth-c; all have Giffen plots/breakdown & Grant scripts			1.50

LOBO: UNAMERICAN GLADIATORS
June, 1993 - No. 4, Sept, 1993 ($1.75, color, mini-series, mature readers)
DC Comics

	GD25	FN65	NM94
1-4: Mignola-c; Grant/Wagner scripts		.70	1.75

LOCKE! (Blackthorne)(Value: cover or less)

LOCO (Magazine) (Satire)
Aug, 1958 - V1#3, Jan, 1959
Satire Publications

	GD25	FN65	NM94
V1#1-Chic Stone-a	4.00	11.00	22.00
V1#2,3-Severin-a, 2 pgs. Davis; 3-Heath-a	3.20	8.00	16.00

LOGAN'S RUN
Jan, 1977 - No. 7, July, 1977
Marvel Comics Group

	GD25	FN65	NM94
1: 1-5-Based on novel & movie		1.40	3.50
2-5,7: 6,7-New stories adapted from novel		.80	2.00
6-1st Thanos solo story (back-up) by Zeck (6/77)	2.15	6.50	15.00

NOTE: ***Austin** a-6i. **Gulacy** c-6. **Kane** c-7p. **Perez** a-1-5p; c-1-5p. **Sutton** a-6p, 7p.*

LOIS LANE (DC)(Value: cover or less)(Also see Daring New Adventures of Supergirl, Showcase & Superman's Girlfriend Lois Lane)

LOLLY AND PEPPER
No. 832, Sept, 1957 - July, 1962
Dell Publishing Co.

	GD25	FN65	NM94
4-Color 832(#1)	3.60	9.00	18.00
4-Color 940,978,1086,1206	2.80	7.00	14.00
01-459-207 (7/62)	2.80	7.00	14.00

LOMAX (See Police Action)

LONE EAGLE (The Flame No. 5 on)
Apr-May, 1954 - No. 4, Oct-Nov, 1954
Ajax/Farrell Publications

	GD25	FN65	NM94
1	8.35	25.00	50.00
2-4: 3-Bondage-c	5.00	15.00	30.00

LONELY HEART (Formerly Dear Lonely Hearts; Dear Heart #15 on)
No. 9, March, 1955 - No. 14, Feb, 1956
Ajax/Farrell Publ. (Excellent Publ.)

	GD25	FN65	NM94
9-Kamenesque-a; (Last precode)	5.35	16.00	32.00
10-14	3.60	9.00	18.00

LONE RANGER, THE (See Ace Comics, Aurora, Dell Giants, Feature Books #21, 24, Future Comics, Golden Comics Digest #48, King Comics, Magic Comics & March of Comics #165, 174, 193, 208, 225, 238, 310, 322, 338, 350)

LONE RANGER, THE
No. 3, 1939 - No. 167, Feb, 1947
Dell Publishing Co.

	GD25	FN65	NM94
Large Feature Comic 3(1939)-Heigh-Yo Silver; text with illus. by Robert Weisman; also exists as a Whitman #710	57.00	170.00	400.00
Large Feature Comic 7(1939)-Ill. by Henry Vallely; Hi-Yo Silver the Lone Ranger to the Rescue; also exists as a Whitman #715	64.00	195.00	450.00
Feature Book 21('40), 24('41)	54.00	160.00	375.00
4-Color 82('45)	36.00	107.00	250.00
4-Color 98('45),118('46)	27.00	81.00	190.00
4-Color 125('46),136('47)	20.00	60.00	140.00
4-Color 151,167('47)	17.00	51.00	120.00

LONE RANGER, THE (Movie, radio & TV; Clayton Moore starred as Lone Ranger in the movies; No. 1-37: strip reprints)(See Dell Giants)
Jan-Feb, 1948 - No. 145, May-July, 1962
Dell Publishing Co.

	GD25	FN65	NM94
1 (36pgs.)-The Lone Ranger, his horse Silver, companion Tonto & his horse Scout begin	57.00	170.00	400.00
2 (52pgs. begin, end #41)	27.00	80.00	190.00
3-5	22.00	65.00	150.00
6,7,9,10	17.00	51.00	120.00
8-Origin retold; Indian back-c begin, end #35	22.00	65.00	155.00
11-20: 11-"Young Hawk" Indian boy serial begins, ends #145	11.50	34.00	80.00

The Lone Ranger #114, © Lone Ranger

The Lone Rider #23, © AJAX

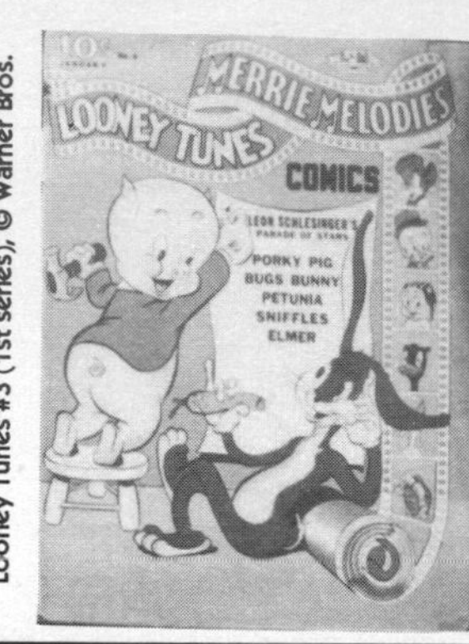

Looney Tunes #3 (1st series), © Warner Bros.

	GD25	FN65	NM94
21,22,24-31: 51-Reprint. 31-1st Mask logo	10.00	30.00	65.00
23-Origin retold	13.00	40.00	90.00
32-37: 32-Painted-c begin. 36-Animal photo back-c begin, end #49. 37-Last newspaper-r issue; new outfit	8.35	25.00	50.00
38-41 (All 52pgs.)	7.00	21.00	42.00
42-50 (36pgs.)	5.85	17.50	35.00
51-74 (52pgs.): 56-One pg. origin story of Lone Ranger & Tonto. 71-Blank inside-c	5.85	17.50	35.00
75-99: 76-Flag-c. 79-X-mas-c	4.70	14.00	28.00
100	6.70	20.00	40.00
101-111: Last painted-c	5.00	15.00	30.00
112-Clayton Moore photo-c begin, end #145	16.00	48.00	110.00
113-117	9.15	27.50	55.00
118-Origin Lone Ranger, Tonto, & Silver retold; Special anniversary issue	14.00	43.00	100.00
119-145: 139-Last issue by Fran Striker	8.35	25.00	50.00
Cheerios Giveaways (1954, 16 pgs., 2-1/2x7", soft-c) #1-"The Lone Ranger, His Mask & How He Met Tonto." #2-"The Lone Ranger & the Story of Silver" each....	13.00	40.00	90.00
Doll Giveaways (Gabriel Ind.)(1973, 3-1/4x5")-"The Story of The L.R." & The Carson City Bank Robbery"	1.60	4.00	8.00
How the Lone Ranger Captured Silver Book(1936)-Silvercup Bread giveaway	47.00	140.00	320.00
...In Milk for Big Mike (1955, Dairy Association giveaway), soft-c; 5x7-1/4", 16 pgs.	11.00	32.00	75.00
Merita Bread giveaway (1954, 16 pgs., 5x7-1/4")-"How to Be a Lone Ranger Health & Safety Scout"	11.00	32.00	75.00

NOTE: ***Hank Hartman*** *painted c(signed)-65, 66, 70, 75, 82; unsigned-64?, 67-69?, 71, 72, 73?, 74?, 76-78, 80, 81, 83-91, 92?, 93-111.* ***Ernest Nordli*** *painted c(signed)-42, 50, 52, 53, 56, 59, 60; unsigned-39-41, 44-49, 51, 54, 55, 57, 58, 61-63?*

LONE RANGER, THE
9/64 - No. 16, 12/69; No. 17, 11/72; No. 18, 9/74 - No. 28, 3/77
Gold Key (Reprints in #13-20)

	GD25	FN65	NM94
1-Retells origin	4.00	10.00	20.00
2	2.00	5.00	10.00
3-10: Small Bear-r in #6-12	1.40	3.50	7.00
11-17	1.20	3.00	6.00
18-28	1.00	2.50	5.00
Golden West 1(30029-610, 10/66)-Giant-r/most Golden West #3-including Clayton Moore photo front/back-c	6.50	19.00	45.00

LONE RANGER COMICS, THE
1939(inside) (shows 1938 on-c) (52 pgs. in color; regular size)
Lone Ranger, Inc. (Ice cream mail order)

	GD25	FN65	VF82
nn-(Scarce)-The first western comic devoted to a single character; not by Vallely	285.00	860.00	2000.00

(Estimated up to 20 total copies exist, none in NM/Mint)

LONE RANGER'S COMPANION TONTO, THE (TV)
No. 312, Jan, 1951 - No. 33, Nov-Jan/58-59 (All painted-c)
Dell Publishing Co.

	GD25	FN65	NM94
4-Color 312(#1, 1951)	11.50	34.00	80.00
2(8-10/51),3: (#2 titled 'Tonto')	6.70	20.00	40.00
4-10	4.00	11.00	22.00
11-20	3.60	9.00	18.00
21-33	2.40	6.00	12.00

NOTE: ***Ernest Nordli*** *painted c(signed)-2, 7; unsigned-3-6, 8-11, 12?, 13, 14, 18?, 22-24? See Aurora Comic Booklets.*

LONE RANGER'S FAMOUS HORSE HI-YO SILVER, THE (TV)
No. 369, Jan, 1952 - No. 36, Oct-Dec, 1960 (All painted-c)
Dell Publishing Co.

	GD25	FN65	NM94
4-Color 369(#1)-Silver's origin as told by The Lone Ranger	8.35	25.00	50.00
4-Color 392(#2, 4/52)	4.00	12.00	24.00
3(7-9/52)-10(4-6/52)	2.40	7.00	14.00
11-36	2.00	5.00	10.00

LONE RIDER (Also see The Rider)
April, 1951 - No. 26, July, 1955 (36pgs., 3-on)
Superior Comics(Farrell Publications)

	GD25	FN65	NM94
1 (52pgs.)-The Lone Rider & his horse Lightnin' begin; Kamenish-a begins	11.00	32.00	75.00
2 (52pgs.)-The Golden Arrow begins (origin)	6.70	20.00	40.00
3-6: 6-Last Golden Arrow	5.35	16.00	32.00
7-Golden Arrow becomes Swift Arrow; origin of his shield	6.70	20.00	40.00
8-Origin Swift Arrow	8.35	25.00	50.00
9,10	4.70	14.00	28.00
11-14	4.00	11.00	22.00
15-Golden Arrow origin-r from #2, changing name to Swift Arrow	4.70	14.00	28.00
16-20,22-26: 23-Apache Kid app.	4.00	10.00	20.00
21-3-D effect-c	10.00	30.00	60.00

LONE WOLF AND CUB (First)(Value: cover or less)

LONG BOW (...Indian Boy)(See Indians & Jumbo Comics #141)
1951 - No. 9, Wint, 1952/53
Fiction House Magazines (Real Adventures Publ.)

	GD25	FN65	NM94
1-Most covers by Maurice Whitman	10.00	30.00	65.00
2	7.00	21.00	42.00
3-9	5.35	16.00	32.00

LONG JOHN SILVER & THE PIRATES (Formerly Terry & the Pirates)
No. 30, Aug, 1956 - No. 32, March, 1957 (TV)
Charlton Comics

	GD25	FN65	NM94
30-32: Whitman-c	5.85	17.50	35.00

LONGSHOT (Also see X-Men #10, 1992)
Sept, 1985 - No. 6, Feb, 1986 (Limited series)
Marvel Comics Group

	GD25	FN65	NM94
1-Arthur Adams/Whilce Portacio-c/a in all	1.70	5.00	12.00
2	1.65	4.00	10.00
3-5: 4-Spider-Man app.	1.30	3.25	8.00
6-Double size	1.50	3.75	9.00
Trade Paperback (1989, $16.95)-r/1-6	2.40	7.25	17.00

LOONEY TUNES (2nd Series)
April, 1975 - No. 47, July, 1984
Gold Key/Whitman

	GD25	FN65	NM94
1		.80	2.00
2-47: Reprints: #1-4,16; 38-46(1/3-r)			1.00

LOONEY TUNES AND MERRIE MELODIES COMICS ("Looney Tunes" #166 (8/55) on)
1941 - No. 246, July-Sept, 1962
Dell Publishing Co.

	GD25	FN65	VF82	NM94
1-Porky Pig, Bugs Bunny, Daffy Duck, Elmer Fudd, Mary Jane & Sniffles, Pat, Patsy and Pete begin (1st comic book app. of each). Bugs Bunny story by Win Smith (early Mickey Mouse artist)	300.00	900.00	1950.00	3000.00

(Estimated up to 170 total copies exist, 8 in NM/Mint)

	GD25	FN65	NM94
2 (11/41)	93.00	280.00	650.00
3-Kandi the Cave Kid begins by Walt Kelly; also in #4-6,8,11,15	79.00	235.00	550.00
4-Kelly-a	70.00	210.00	485.00
5-Bugs Bunny The Super-Duper Rabbit story (1st funny animal super hero, 3/42; also see Coo Coo); Kelly-a	57.00	171.00	400.00
6,8-Kelly-a	43.00	130.00	300.00
7,9,10: 9-Painted-c. 10-Flag-c	34.00	105.00	240.00
11,15-Kelly-a; 15-X-Mas-c	34.00	105.00	240.00
12-14,16-19	31.00	92.00	215.00
20-25: Pat, Patsy & Pete by Walt Kelly in all	31.00	92.00	215.00
26-30	22.00	65.00	150.00

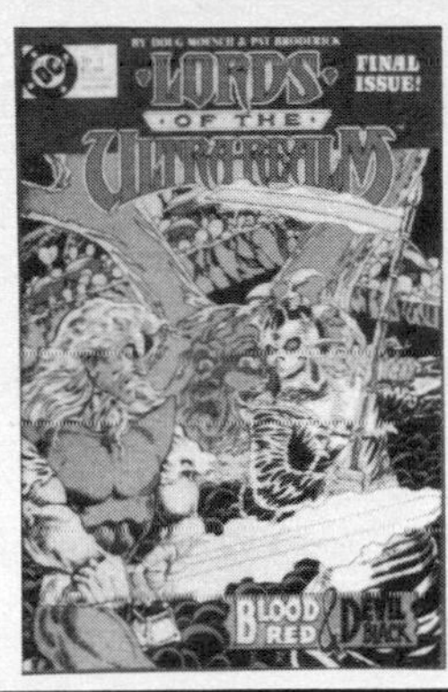

Lords of the Ultra-Realm #6, © DC

Lost In Space #1 (8/91), © Space Productions

Love At First Sight #1, © ACE

	GD25	FN65	NM94
31-40: 33-War bond-c. 39-X-Mas-c	16.00	48.00	110.00
41-50	12.00	36.00	85.00
51-60	8.35	25.00	50.00
61-80	5.85	17.50	35.00
81-99: 87-X-Mas-c	4.20	12.50	25.00
100	5.00	15.00	30.00
101-120	4.00	10.00	20.00
121-150	3.00	7.50	15.00
151-200: 159-X-Mas-c	2.00	5.00	10.00
201-246	1.40	3.50	7.00

LOONY SPORTS (Magazine)
Spring, 1975 (68 pages)
3 Strikes Publishing Co.

	GD25	FN65	NM94
1-Sports satire		.80	2.00

LOOY DOT DOPE (See Single Series No. 13)

LORD JIM (See Movie Comics)

LORDS OF THE ULTRA-REALM (DC)(Value: cover or less)

LORNA THE JUNGLE GIRL (...Jungle Queen #1-5)
July, 1953 - No. 26, Aug, 1957
Atlas Comics (NPI 1/OMC 2-11/NPI 12-26)

	GD25	FN65	NM94
1-Origin	18.00	54.00	125.00
2-Intro. & 1st app. Greg Knight	10.00	30.00	60.00
3-5	8.35	25.00	50.00
6-11: 11-Last pre-code (1/55)	6.70	20.00	40.00
12-17,19-26: 14-Colletta & Maneely-c	5.00	15.00	30.00
18-Williamson/Colleta-c	5.85	17.50	35.00

NOTE: ***Brodsky*** *c-1-3, 5, 9.* ***Everett*** *c-21, 23-26.* ***Heath*** *c-6, 7.* ***Maneely*** *c-12, 15.* ***Romita*** *a-20, 22, 24, 26.* ***Shores*** *a-14-16, 24, 26; c-11, 13, 16.* ***Tuska*** *a-6.*

LOSERS SPECIAL (DC)(Value: cover or less)(See G.I. Combat & Our Fighting Forces)

LOST CONTINENT (Eclipse)(Value: cover or less)

LOST IN SPACE (TV) (Space Family Robinson..., on Space Station One)
(Formerly Space Family Robinson; see Gold Key Champion)
No. 37, 10/73 - No. 54, 11/78; No. 55, 3/81 - No. 59, 5/82
Gold Key

	GD25	FN65	NM94
37-48		1.40	3.50
49-59: Reprints-#49,50,55-59		.80	2.00

NOTE: ***Spiegle*** *a-37-59. All have painted-c.*

LOST IN SPACE
Aug, 1991 - No. 12, Jan, 1993 ($2.50, color, limited series)
Innovation Publishing

	GD25	FN65	NM94
1-12: Bill Mumy (Will Robinson) scripts in #1-9. 9-Perez-c		1.00	2.50
1,2-Special Ed.; r/#1,2 plus new art & new-c		1.00	2.50
Annual 1,2 (1991, 1992, $2.95, 48 pgs.)		1.20	3.00

LOST IN SPACE: VOYAGE TO THE BOTTOM OF THE SOUL
No. 13, Aug, 1993 - No. 24, 1994 ($2.50, color, limited series)
Innovation Publishing

	GD25	FN65	NM94
13(V1#1, $2.95)-Embossed silver logo edition; Bill Mumy scripts begin; painted-c		1.00	2.50
13(V1#1)-Embossed gold logo edition	1.00	2.00	5.00
14-18: Painted-c		1.00	2.50

LOST PLANET (Eclipse)(Value: cover or less)

LOST WORLD, THE (See 4-Color #1145)

LOST WORLDS
No. 5, Oct, 1952 - No. 6, Dec, 1952
Standard Comics

	GD25	FN65	NM94
5-"Alice in Terrorland" by Toth; J. Katz-a	20.00	60.00	140.00
6-Toth-a	17.00	52.00	120.00

LOTS 'O' FUN COMICS
1940's? (5 cents) (Heavy stock; blue covers)
Robert Allen Co.
nn-Contents can vary; Felix, Planet Comics known; contents would determine value. Similar to Up-To-Date Comics. Remainders - re-packaged.

LOU GEHRIG (See The Pride of the Yankees)

LOVE ADVENTURES (Actual Confessions #13)
Oct, 1949; No. 2, Jan, 1950; No. 3, Feb, 1951 - No. 12, Aug, 1952
Marvel (IPS)/Atlas Comics (MPI)

	GD25	FN65	NM94
1-Photo-c	9.15	27.50	55.00
2-Powell-a; Tyrone Power, Gene Tierney photo-c	9.15	27.50	55.00
3-8,10-12. 8-Robinson-a	4.00	12.00	24.00
9-Everett-a	4.70	14.00	28.00

LOVE AND MARRIAGE
March, 1952 - No. 16, Sept, 1954
Superior Comics Ltd.

	GD25	FN65	NM94
1	7.50	22.50	45.00
2	4.00	11.00	22.00
3-10	3.20	8.00	16.00
11-16	2.40	6.00	12.00
I.W. Reprint #1,2,8,11,14	.80	2.00	4.00
Super Reprint #10('63),15,17('64)	.80	2.00	4.00

NOTE: *All issues have* ***Kamenish*** *art.*

LOVE AND ROCKETS
July, 1982 - Present (B&W, adults only)
Fantagraphics Books

	GD25	FN65	NM94
1-B&W-c ($2.95; small size, publ. by Hernandez Bros.)(800 printed)	6.50	20.00	46.00
1 (Fall, '82; color-c)	3.25	9.50	22.00
1-2nd & 3rd printing		1.10	2.75
2	1.65	4.70	11.00
2-11,29-31: 2nd printings ($2.50)		1.10	2.75
3-5	1.25	3.00	7.50
6-10		1.70	4.25
11-40: 30($2.95, 52 pgs.). 31-on: $2.50-c		1.10	2.75

LOVE AND ROMANCE
Sept, 1971 - No. 24, Sept, 1975
Charlton Comics

	GD25	FN65	NM94
1		1.20	3.00
2-24			1.00

LOVE AT FIRST SIGHT
Oct, 1949 - No. 42, Aug, 1956 (Photo-c: 21-42)
Ace Magazines (RAR Publ. Co./Periodical House)

	GD25	FN65	NM94
1-Painted-c	8.35	25.00	50.00
2-Painted-c	4.00	11.00	22.00
3-10: 4-Painted-c	3.20	8.00	16.00
11-20	2.40	6.00	12.00
21-33: 33-Last pre-code	1.80	4.50	9.00
34-42	1.40	3.50	7.00

LOVE BUG, THE (See Movie Comics)

LOVE CLASSICS
Nov, 1949 - No. 2, Feb, 1950 (Photo-c, 52 pgs.)
A Lover's Magazine/Marvel Comics

	GD25	FN65	NM94
1,2: 2-Virginia Mayo photo-c; 30 pg. story "I Was a Small Town Flirt"	8.35	25.00	50.00

LOVE CONFESSIONS
Oct, 1949 - No. 54, Dec, 1956 (Photo-c: 3,4,6,7,9,11-18,21)
Quality Comics Group

	GD25	FN65	NM94
1-Ward-c/a, 9 pgs; Gustavson-a	16.00	48.00	110.00
2-Gustavson-a	6.35	19.00	38.00
3	4.35	13.00	26.00
4-Crandall-a	5.85	17.50	35.00
5-Ward-a, 7 pgs.	6.70	20.00	40.00
6,7,9,11-13,15,16,18	2.80	7.00	14.00

Love Diary #11, © Our Publ.

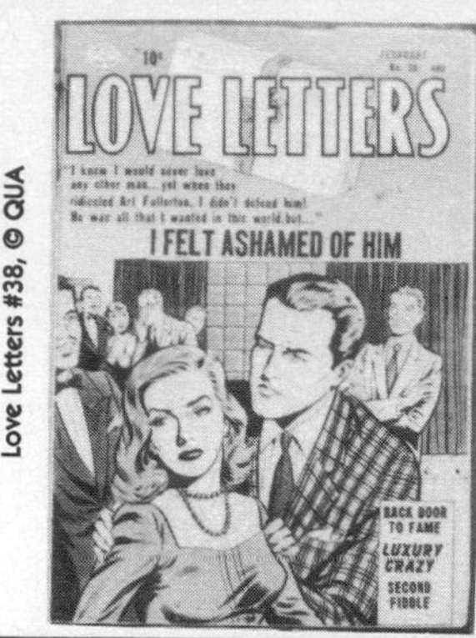

Love Letters #38, © QUA

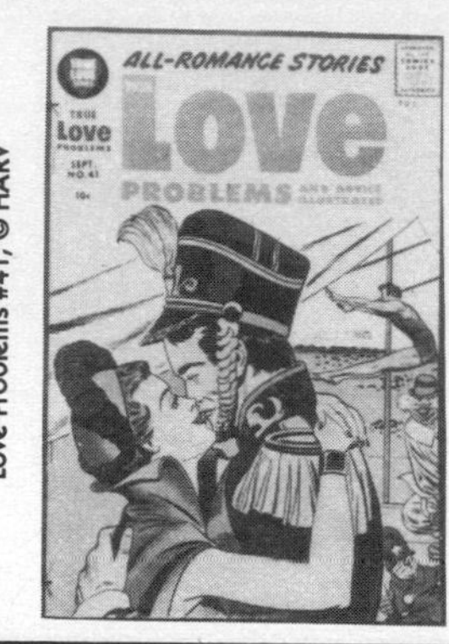

Love Problems #41, © HARV

	GD25	FN65	NM94
8,10-Ward-a(2 stories in #10)	5.85	17.50	35.00
14,17,19,22-Ward-a; 17-Faith Domerque photo-c	5.00	15.00	30.00
20-Baker-a?, Ward-a(2)	5.85	17.50	35.00
21,23-28,30-38,40-42: Last precode, 4/55	1.80	4.50	9.00
29-Ward-a	4.70	14.00	28.00
39-Matt Baker-a	2.80	7.00	14.00
43,44,46-48,50-54: 47-Ward-c?	1.60	4.00	8.00
45-Ward-a	3.20	8.00	16.00
49-Baker-c/a	4.00	10.00	20.00

LOVE DIARY
July, 1949 - No. 48, Oct, 1955 (Photo-c: 1-24,27,29) (52 pgs. #1-11?)
Our Publishing Co./Toytown/Patches

	GD25	FN65	NM94
1-Krigstein-a	10.00	30.00	65.00
2,3-Krigstein & Mort Leav-a in each	7.50	22.50	45.00
4-8	3.60	9.00	18.00
9,10-Everett-a	4.00	11.00	22.00
11-20: 16,20-Mort Leav-a	2.80	7.00	14.00
21-30,32-48: 45-Leav-a. 47-Last precode(12/54)	2.00	5.00	10.00
31-John Buscema headlights-c	2.80	7.00	14.00

LOVE DIARY (Diary Loves #2 on)
September, 1949
Quality Comics Group

	GD25	FN65	NM94
1-Ward-c/a, 9 pgs.	13.00	40.00	90.00

LOVE DIARY
July, 1958 - No. 102, Dec, 1976
Charlton Comics

	GD25	FN65	NM94
1	5.00	15.00	30.00
2	3.00	7.50	15.00
3-5,7-10: 10-Photo-c	2.00	5.00	10.00
6-Torres-a	2.80	7.00	14.00
11-20: 20-Photo-c	1.40	3.50	7.00
21-40	1.00	2.00	5.00
41-60		1.20	3.00
61-102			1.00

LOVE DOCTOR (See Dr. Anthony King...)

LOVE DRAMAS (True Secrets No. 3 on?)
Oct, 1949 - No. 2, Jan, 1950
Marvel Comics (IPS)

	GD25	FN65	NM94
1-Jack Kamen-a; photo-c	10.00	30.00	70.00
2	7.50	22.50	45.00

LOVE EXPERIENCES (Challenge of the Unknown No. 6)
Oct, 1949 - No. 5, June, 1950; No. 6, Apr, 1951 - No. 38, June, 1956
Ace Periodicals (A.A. Wyn/Periodical House)

	GD25	FN65	NM94
1-Painted-c	6.70	20.00	40.00
2	4.00	10.00	20.00
3-5: 5-Painted-c	2.80	7.00	14.00
6-10	2.40	6.00	12.00
11-30: 30-Last pre-code (2/55)	1.80	4.50	9.00
31-38: 38-Indicia date-6/56; c-date-8/56	1.60	4.00	8.00

NOTE: ***Anne Brewster** a-15. Photo c-4, 15-35, 38.*

LOVE JOURNAL
No. 10, Oct, 1951 - No. 25, July, 1954
Our Publishing Co.

	GD25	FN65	NM94
10	5.00	15.00	35.00
11-25: 19-Mort Leav-a	3.60	9.00	18.00

LOVELAND
Nov, 1949 - No. 2, Feb, 1950 (52 pgs.)
Mutual Mag./Eye Publ. (Marvel)

	GD25	FN65	NM94
1,2-Photo-c	5.85	17.50	35.00

LOVE LESSONS
Oct, 1949 - No. 5, June, 1950
Harvey Comics/Key Publ. No. 5

	GD25	FN65	NM94
1-Metallic silver-c printed over the cancelled covers of Love Letters #1; indicia title is "Love Letters"	7.50	22.50	45.00
2-Powell-a; photo-c	4.00	10.00	20.00
3-5: 3-Photo-c	3.20	8.00	16.00

LOVE LETTERS (10/49, Harvey; advertised but never published; covers were printed before cancellation and were used as the cover to Love Lessons #1)

LOVE LETTERS (Love Secrets No. 32 on)
11/49 - #6, 9/50; #7, 3/51 - #31, 6/53; #32, 2/54 - #51, 12/56
Quality Comics Group

	GD25	FN65	NM94
1-Ward-c, Gustavson-a	11.50	34.00	80.00
2-Ward-c, Gustavson-a	10.00	30.00	65.00
3-Gustavson-a	7.50	22.50	45.00
4-Ward-a, 9 pgs.	10.00	30.00	65.00
5-8,10	3.20	8.00	16.00
9-One pg. Ward "Be Popular with the Opposite Sex"; Robert Mitchum photo-c	4.35	13.00	26.00
11-Ward-r/Broadway Romances #2 & retitled	4.35	13.00	26.00
12-15,18-20	2.40	6.00	12.00
16,17-Ward-a; 16-Anthony Quinn photo-c. 17-Jane Russell photo-c	6.35	19.00	38.00
21-29	2.00	5.00	10.00
30,31(6/53)-Ward-a	4.00	11.00	22.00
32(2/54) - 39: 39-Last precode (4/55)	1.80	4.50	9.00
40-48	1.40	3.50	7.00
49,50-Baker-a	4.00	10.00	20.00
51-Baker-c	3.20	8.00	16.00

NOTE: *Photo-c on most 3-28.*

LOVE LIFE
Nov, 1951
P. L. Publishing Co.

	GD25	FN65	NM94
1	5.00	15.00	30.00

LOVELORN (Confessions of the Lovelorn #52 on)
Aug-Sept, 1949 - No. 51, July, 1954 (No. 1-26, 52 pgs.)
American Comics Group (Michel Publ./Regis Publ.)

	GD25	FN65	NM94
1	9.15	27.50	55.00
2	4.70	14.00	28.00
3-10	4.00	10.00	20.00
11-20,22-48: 18-Drucker-a(2pgs.). 46-Lazarus-a	2.80	7.00	14.00
21-Prostitution story	4.00	12.00	24.00
49-51-Has 3-D effect-c/stories	10.00	30.00	70.00

LOVE MEMORIES
1949 (no month) - No. 4, July, 1950 (All photo-c)
Fawcett Publications

	GD25	FN65	NM94
1	7.00	21.00	42.00
2-4: 2-(Win/49-50)	4.00	12.00	24.00

LOVE MYSTERY
June, 1950 - No. 3, Oct, 1950 (All photo-c)
Fawcett Publications

	GD25	FN65	NM94
1-George Evans-a	13.00	40.00	90.00
2,3-Evans-a. 3-Powell-a	10.00	30.00	70.00

LOVE PROBLEMS (See Fox Giants)

LOVE PROBLEMS AND ADVICE ILLUSTRATED (Becomes Romance Stories of True Love No. 45 on)
June, 1949 - No. 6, Apr, 1950; No. 7, Jan, 1951 - No. 44, Mar, 1957
McCombs/Harvey Publ./Home Comics

	GD25	FN65	NM94
V1#1	8.35	25.00	50.00
2	4.20	12.50	25.00
3-10: 7-9-Elias-c	3.60	9.00	18.00
11-13,15-23,25-31: 31-Last pre-code (1/55)	2.40	6.00	12.00
14,24-Rape scene	2.80	7.00	14.00
32-37,39-44	1.80	4.50	9.00

Love Romances #14, © MEG

Love Secrets #36, © QUA

Lucifer's Hammer #1, © Larry Niven & Jerry Pournelle

	GD25	FN65	NM94
38-S&K-c	4.00	11.00	22.00

NOTE: ***Powell** a-1, 2, 7-14, 17-25, 28, 29, 33, 40, 41. #3 has True Love... on inside.*

LOVE ROMANCES (Formerly Ideal #5)
No. 6, May, 1949 - No. 106, July, 1963
Timely/Marvel/Atlas(TCI No. 7-71/Male No. 72-106)

	GD25	FN65	NM94
6-Photo-c	7.50	22.50	45.00
7-Photo-c; Kamen-a	5.00	15.00	30.00
8-Kubert-a; photo-c	5.35	16.00	32.00
9-20: 9-12-Photo-c	4.00	10.00	20.00
21,24-Krigstein-a	5.35	16.00	32.00
22,23,25-35,37,39,40	3.20	8.00	16.00
36,38-Krigstein-a	4.70	14.00	28.00
41-44,46,47: Last precode (2/55)	3.20	8.00	16.00
45,57-Matt Baker-a	3.60	9.00	18.00
48,50-52,54-56,58-74	2.40	6.00	12.00
49,53-Toth-a, 6 & ? pgs.	5.00	15.00	30.00
75,77,82-Matt Baker-a	3.20	8.00	16.00
76,78-81,84,86-95: Last 10 cent issue?	2.40	6.00	12.00
83-Kirby-c, Severin-a	4.00	10.00	20.00
85,96-Kirby-c/a	4.00	11.00	22.00
97,100-104	2.00	5.00	10.00
98-Kirby-a(4)	5.85	17.50	35.00
99,105,106-Kirby-a	4.00	10.00	20.00

NOTE: ***Anne Brewster** a-67, 72. **Colletta** a-37, 40, 42, 44, 67(2); c-42, 44, 49, 80. **Everett** c-70. **Heath** a-87. **Kirby** c-80, 85, 88. **Robinson** a-29.*

LOVERS (Formerly Blonde Phantom)
No. 23, May, 1949 - No. 86, Aug?, 1957
Marvel Comics No. 23,24/Atlas No. 25 on (ANC)

	GD25	FN65	NM94
23-Photo-c begin, end #28	7.50	22.50	45.00
24-Tothish plus Robinson-a	4.00	11.00	22.00
25,30-Kubert-a; 7, 10 pgs.	4.70	14.00	28.00
26-29,31-36,39,40	3.20	8.00	16.00
37,38-Krigstein-a	5.35	16.00	32.00
41-Everett-a(2)	4.00	11.00	22.00
42,44-65: 65-Last pre-code (1/55)	2.80	7.00	14.00
43-Frazetta 1 pg. ad	2.80	7.00	14.00
66,68-86	2.40	6.00	12.00
67-Toth-a	4.70	14.00	20.00

NOTE: ***Anne Brewster** a-86. **Colletta** a-54, 59, 62, 64, 65, 69, 85; c-61, 64, 65, 75. **Heath** a-61. **Powell** a-27, 30. **Robinson** a-54, 56.*

LOVERS' LANE
Oct, 1949 - No. 41, June, 1954 (No. 1-18: 52 pgs.)
Lev Gleason Publications

	GD25	FN65	NM94
1-Biro-c	6.70	20.00	40.00
2-Biro-c	4.00	10.00	20.00
3-20: 20-Frazetta 1 pg. ad	2.80	7.00	14.00
21-38,40,41	1.60	4.00	8.00
39-Story narrated by Frank Sinatra	4.00	10.00	20.00

NOTE: ***Briefer** a-6, 21. **Fuje** a-4, 16; c-many. **Guardineer** a-1. **Kinstler** c-41. **Tuska** a-6. Painted c-3-18. Photo c-19-22, 26-28.*

LOVE SCANDALS
Feb, 1950 - No. 5, Oct, 1950 (Photo-c #2-5) (All 52 pgs.)
Quality Comics Group

	GD25	FN65	NM94
1-Ward-c/a, 9 pgs.	13.00	40.00	90.00
2,3: 2-Gustavson-a	5.35	16.00	32.00
4-Ward-a, 18 pgs; Gil Fox-a	11.00	32.00	75.00
5-C. Cuidera-a; tomboy story 'I Hated Being a Woman'	5.00	15.00	30.00

LOVE SECRETS (Formerly Love Letters #31)
No. 32, Aug, 1953 - No. 56, Dec, 1956
Quality Comics Group

	GD25	FN65	NM94
32	5.00	15.00	30.00
33,35-39	3.00	7.50	15.00
34-Ward-a	5.00	15.00	30.00
40-Matt Baker-c	4.00	11.00	22.00
41-43: 43-Last precode (3/55)	2.40	6.00	12.00
44,47-50,53,54	1.80	4.50	9.00
45,46-Ward-a. 46-Baker-a	4.00	12.00	24.00
51,52-Ward(r). 52-r/Love Confessions #17	3.20	8.00	16.00
55,56-Baker-a. 56-Baker-c	3.20	8.00	16.00

LOVE SECRETS
Oct, 1949 - No. 2, Jan, 1950 (52 pgs., photo-c)
Marvel Comics(IPC)

	GD25	FN65	NM94
1	7.50	22.50	45.00
2	5.35	16.00	32.00

LOVE STORIES (Formerly My Love Affair #5)
No. 6, 1950 - No. 12, 1951
Fox Feature Syndicate

	GD25	FN65	NM94
6,8-Wood-a	11.00	32.00	75.00
7,9-12	5.00	15.00	30.00

LOVE STORIES (Formerly Heart Throbs)
No. 147, Nov, 1972 - No. 152, Oct-Nov, 1973
National Periodical Publications

	GD25	FN65	NM94
147-152		1.60	4.00

LOVE STORIES OF MARY WORTH (See Harvey Comics Hits #55 & Mary Worth)
Sept, 1949 - No. 5, May, 1950
Harvey Publications

	GD25	FN65	NM94
1-1940's newspaper reprints-#1-4	4.35	13.00	26.00
2	4.00	10.00	20.00
3-5: 3-Kamen/Baker-a?	3.60	9.00	18.00

LOVE TALES (Formerly The Human Torch #35)
No. 36, 5/49 - No. 58, 8/52; No. 59, date? - No. 75, Sept, 1957
Marvel/Atlas Comics (ZPC No. 36-50/MMC No. 67-75)

	GD25	FN65	NM94
36-Photo-c	7.50	22.50	45.00
37	4.70	14.00	28.00
38-44,46-50: 39-41-Photo-c	3.60	9.00	18.00
45-Powell-a	4.00	10.00	20.00
51,69-Everett-a	4.00	11.00	22.00
52-Krigstein-a	4.00	12.00	24.00
53-60: 60-Last pre-code (2/55)	2.00	5.00	10.00
61-68,70-75: 75-Brewster, Cameron, Colletta-a	1.60	4.00	8.00

LOVE THRILLS (See Fox Giants)

LOVE TRAILS (Western romance)
Dec, 1949 - No. 2, Mar, 1950 (52 pgs.)
A Lover's Magazine (CDS)(Marvel)

	GD25	FN65	NM94
1,2: 1-Photo-c	6.70	20.00	40.00

LOWELL THOMAS' HIGH ADVENTURE (See 4-Color #949, 1001)

LT. (See Lieutenant)

LUCIFER'S HAMMER (Larry Niven & Jerry Pournelle's...)
Nov, 1993 - No. 6, 1994 ($2.50, color, limited series)
Innovation Publishing

	GD25	FN65	NM94
1-6-Painted-c & art; adapts novel		1.00	2.50

LUCKY COMICS
Jan, 1944; No. 2, Summer, 1945 - No. 5, Summer, 1946
Consolidated Magazines

	GD25	FN65	NM94
1-Lucky Starr, Bobbie	10.00	30.00	70.00
2-5: 5-Devil-c by Walter Johnson	6.35	19.00	38.00

LUCKY DUCK
No. 5, Jan, 1953 - No. 8, Sept, 1953
Standard Comics (Literary Ent.)

	GD25	FN65	NM94
5-Irving Spector-a	6.70	20.00	40.00
6-8-Irving Spector-a	4.70	14.00	28.00

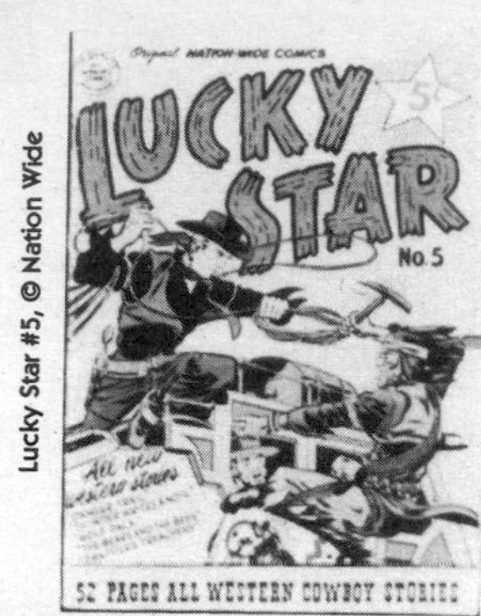

Lucky Star #5, © Nation Wide

Mack Bolan: The Executioner #1 (gold), © Don & Linda Pendleton

Mad #21, © EC

GD25 FN65 NM94

LUCKY FIGHTS IT THROUGH (Also see The K. O. Punch)
1949 (16 pgs. in color; paper cover) (Giveaway)
Educational Comics

	GD25	FN65	NM94
nn-(Very Rare)-1st Kurtzman work for E. C.; V.D. prevention	142.00	425.00	1000.00

(Prices vary widely on this book)
NOTE: *Subtitled "The Story of That Ignorant, Ignorant Cowboy." Prepared for Communications Materials Center, Columbia University.*

LUCKY "7" COMICS
1944 (No date listed)
Howard Publishers Ltd.

	GD25	FN65	NM94
1-Congo Raider, Punch Powers; bondage-c	18.00	55.00	120.00

LUCKY STAR (Western)
1950 - No. 7, 1951; No. 8, 1953 - No. 14, 1955 (5x7-1/4"; full color, 5 cents)
Nation Wide Publ. Co.

	GD25	FN65	NM94
nn (#1)-(52 pgs.)-Davis-a	9.15	27.50	55.00
2,3-(52 pgs.)-Davis-a	6.35	19.00	38.00
4-7-(52 pgs.)-Davis-a	5.00	15.00	30.00
8-14-(36 pgs.)	4.00	10.00	20.00
Given away with Lucky Star Western Wear by the Juvenile Mfg. Co.	4.00	10.00	20.00

LUCY SHOW, THE (TV) (Also see I Love Lucy)
June, 1963 - No. 5, June, 1964 (Photo-c: 1,2)
Gold Key

	GD25	FN65	NM94
1	10.00	30.00	68.00
2	6.50	20.00	46.00
3-5: Photo back c-1,2,4,5	6.00	18.00	42.00

LUCY, THE REAL GONE GAL (Meet Miss Pepper #5 on)
June, 1953 - No. 4, Dec, 1953
St. John Publishing Co.

	GD25	FN65	NM94
1-Negligee panels	8.35	25.00	50.00
2	4.70	14.00	28.00
3,4: 3-Drucker-a	4.00	11.00	22.00

LUDWIG BEMELMAN'S MADELEINE & GENEVIEVE (See 4-Color #796)

LUDWIG VON DRAKE (TV)(Disney)(See Walt Disney's C&S #256)
Nov-Dec, 1961 - No. 4, June-Aug, 1962
Dell Publishing Co.

	GD25	FN65	NM94
1	4.20	12.50	25.00
2-4	2.80	7.00	14.00
...Fish Stampede (1962, Fritos giveaway)-16 pgs., 3-1/4x7", soft-c; also see Donald Duck & Mickey Mouse	4.00	11.00	22.00

LUGER (Eclipse)(Value: cover or less)

LUKE CAGE (See Cage & Hero for Hire)

LUKE SHORT'S WESTERN STORIES
No. 580, Aug, 1954 - No. 927, Aug, 1958
Dell Publishing Co.

	GD25	FN65	NM94
4-Color 580(8/54)	4.00	11.00	22.00
4-Color 651(9/55)-Kinstler-a	4.35	13.00	26.00
4-Color 739,771,807,875,927	4.00	11.00	22.00
4-Color 848	5.35	16.00	32.00

LUNATIC FRINGE, THE (Innovation)(Value: cover or less)

LUNATICKLE (Magazine) (Satire)
Feb, 1956 - No. 2, Apr, 1956
Whitstone Publ.

	GD25	FN65	NM94
1,2-Kubert-a	2.40	6.00	12.00

LYNDON B. JOHNSON
March, 1965
Dell Publishing Co.

	GD25	FN65	NM94
12-445-503-Photo-c	2.40	6.00	12.00

M (Eclipse)(Value: cover or less)

MACHINE MAN (Also see 2001, A Space Odyssey)
Apr, 1978 - No. 9, Dec, 1978; No. 10, Aug, 1979 - No. 19, Feb, 1981
Marvel Comics Group

	GD25	FN65	NM94
1		1.20	3.00
2-17			1.50
18-Wendigo, Alpha Flight-ties into X-Men #140	1.00	2.50	5.50
19-1st app. Jack O'Lantern (Macendale, who later becomes 2nd Hobgoblin)	2.15	6.50	15.00

NOTE: ***Austin** c-7i, 19i. **Buckler** c-17p, 18p. **Byrne** c-14p. **Ditko** a-10-19; c-10-13, 14i, 15, 16. **Kirby** a-1-9p; c-1-5, 7-9p. **Layton** c-7i. **Miller** c-19p. **Simonson** c-6.*

MACHINE MAN
Oct, 1984 - No. 4, Jan, 1985 (Limited-series)
Marvel Comics Group

	GD25	FN65	NM94
1-Barry Smith-c/a(p) & colors in all			1.50
2-4			1.20

MACK BOLAN: THE EXECUTIONER (Don Pendleton's...)
July, 1993 - Present ($2.50, color)
Innovation Publishing

	GD25	FN65	NM94
1-($3.95)-Indestructible Cover Edition		1.60	4.00
1-($2.95)-Collector's Gold Edition; foil stamped		1.20	3.00
1-($3.50)-Double Cover Edition; red foil outer-c		1.40	3.50
2-7		1.00	2.50

MACKENZIE'S RAIDERS (See 4-Color #1093)

MACO TOYS COMIC
1959 (36 pages; full color) (Giveaway)
Maco Toys/Charlton Comics

	GD25	FN65	NM94
1-All military stories featuring Maco Toys	1.20	3.00	6.00

MACROSS (Becomes Robotech: The Macross Saga #2 on)
Dec, 1984 ($1.50)
Comico

	GD25	FN65	NM94
1	1.25	3.00	7.50

MACROSS II
1992 - No. 10, 1993 ($2.75, B&W, limited series)
Viz Select Comics

	GD25	FN65	NM94
1-10: Based on video series		1.10	2.75

MAD
Oct-Nov, 1952 - Present (No. 24 on are magazine format)
(Kurtzman editor No. 1-28, Feldstein No. 29 - No. ?)
E. C. Comics

	GD25	FN65	NM94
1-Wood, Davis, Elder start as regulars	315.00	940.00	2500.00
2-Dick Tracy cameo	90.00	270.00	625.00
3,4: 3-Stan Lee mentioned. 4-Reefer mention story "Flob Was a Slob" by Davis; Superman parody	57.00	170.00	400.00
5-Low distr.; W.M. Gaines biog.	85.00	255.00	675.00
6-11: 6-Popeye cameo. 11-Wolverton-a	43.00	130.00	300.00
12-15	34.00	105.00	240.00
16-23(5/55): 18-Alice in Wonderland by Jack Davis. 21-1st app. Alfred E. Neuman on-c in fake ad. 22-All by Elder. 23-Special cancel announcement	26.00	78.00	180.00
24(7/55)-1st magazine issue (25 cents); Kurtzman logo & border on-c; 1st "What? Me Worry?" on-c; 2nd printing exists	79.00	235.00	550.00
25-Jaffee starts as regular writer	29.00	85.00	200.00
26,27: 27-Jaffee starts as story artist; new logo	23.00	70.00	160.00
28-Last issue edited by Kurtzman; (three cover variations exist with different wording on contents banner on lower right of cover; value of each the same)	20.00	60.00	140.00
29-Kamen-a; Don Martin starts as regular; Feldstein editing begins	20.00	60.00	140.00
30-1st A. E. Neuman cover by Mingo; last Elder-a; Bob Clarke starts as regular; Disneyland & Elvis Presley spoof	30.00	90.00	210.00
31-Freas starts as regular; last Davis-a until #99	16.00	50.00	115.00

Mad #37, © EC

Mad-Dog #5, © Paramount Pictures

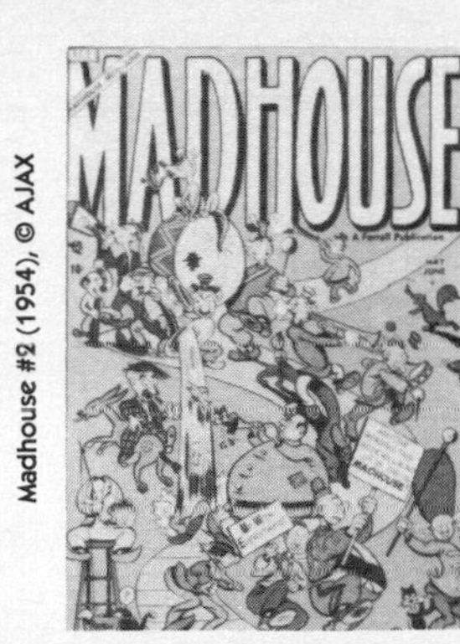

Madhouse #2 (1954), © AJAX

GD25 FN65 NM94

32,33: 32-Orlando, Drucker, Woodbridge start as regulars; Wood back-c. 33-Orlando back-c 14.00 43.00 100.00
34-Borg starts as regular 13.00 40.00 90.00
35-Mingo wraparound-c; Crandall-a 13.00 40.00 90.00
36-40 10.00 30.00 60.00
41-50 7.50 22.50 45.00
51-60: 60-Two Clarke-c; Prohias starts as reg. 6.70 20.00 40.00
61-70: 64-Rickard starts as regular. 68-Martin-c 4.70 14.00 28.00
71-80: 76-Aragones starts as regular 4.20 12.50 25.00
81-90: 86-1st Fold-in. 89-One strip by Walt Kelly. 90-Frazetta back-c; Beatles app. 4.00 10.00 20.00
91-100: 91-Jaffee starts as story artist. 99-Davis-a resumes 3.60 9.00 18.00
101-104,106-120: 101-Infinity-c. 106-Frazetta back-c 3.00 7.50 15.00
105-Batman TV show take-off 4.00 10.00 20.00
121-140: 121-Beatles app. 122-Ronald Reagan photo inside; Drucker & Mingo-c. 128-Last Orlando. 130-Torres begins as reg. 131-Reagan photo back-c. 135,139-Davis-c 1.65 4.00 10.00
141-170: 165-Martin-c. 169-Drucker-c 1.30 3.25 8.00
171-200: 182-Bob Jones starts as regular. 186-Star Trek take-off. 187-Harry North starts as regular. 196-Star Wars take-off 1.20 3.00 7.00
201-330: 203-Star Wars take-off. 204-Hulk TV show take-off. 208-Superman movie take-off. 245- Last Rikard-a. 274-Last Martin-a. 284-Roger Rabbit-c/story. 289-Batman movie parody. 291-TMNT-c only. 299-Simpson's-c/story. 306-TMNT III movie parody. 308-Terminator parody. 311-Addams Family-c/story. 314-Batman Returns-c/story .80 2.00
300-303 (1/91-6/91)-Special Hussein Asylum Editions; only distributed to the troops in the Middle East(see Mad Super Spec.) 1.60 4.00

NOTE: ***Aragones*** *c-210, 293.* ***Davis*** *c-2, 27, 135, 139, 173, 178, 212, 213, 219, 246, 260, 296, 308.* ***Drucker*** *c-122, 169, 176, 225, 234, 264, 266, 274, 280, 285, 297, 299, 303, 314, 315.* ***Elder*** *c-5, 259, 261, 268.* ***Jules Feiffer*** *a(r)-42.* ***Freas*** *c-39-59, 62-67, 69-70, 72, 74.* ***Heath*** *a-14, 27.* ***Jaffee*** *c-199, 217, 224, 258.* ***Kamen*** *a-29.* ***Krigstein*** *a-12, 17, 24, 26.* ***Kurtzman*** *c-1, 3, 4, 6-10, 13, 16, 18.* ***Martin*** *c-68, 165, 229.* ***Mingo*** *c-30-37, 61, 71, 75-80, 82-114, 117-124, 126, 129, 131, 133, 134, 136, 140, 143-148, 150-162, 164, 166-168, 171, 172, 174, 175, 177, 179, 181, 183, 185, 198, 206, 209, 211, 214, 218, 221, 222, 300.* ***John Severin*** *a-1-6, 9, 10.* ***Wolverton*** *c-11; a-11, 17, 29, 31, 36, 40, 82, 137.* ***Wood*** *a-24-45, 59; c-26, 28, 29.* ***Woodbridge*** *a-43.*

MAD (See ...Follies, ...Special, More Trash from..., and The Worst from...)

MAD ABOUT MILLIE (Also see Millie the Model)
April, 1969 - No. 17, Dec, 1970
Marvel Comics Group

1-Giant issue 4.30 13.00 30.00
2-17: 10,17-r 2.15 6.50 15.00
Annual 1(11/71) 1.65 4.00 10.00

MADAME XANADU (DC)(Value: cover or less)

MADBALLS
Sept, 1986 - No. 3, Nov, 1986; No. 4, June, 1987 - No. 10, June, 1988
Star Comics/Marvel Comics #9 on

1-10: Based on toys. 9-Post-a 1.00

MAD DISCO
1980 (One shot)(36 pgs.)
E.C. Comics

1-Includes 30 minute flexi-disc of Mad disco music .80 2.00

MAD-DOG (Marvel)(Value: cover or less)

MAD DOGS
Feb, 1992 - No. 3, July, 1992 ($2.50, B&W, mini-series)
Eclipse Comics

1-3 1.00 2.50

MAD 84 (Mad Extra)
1984 (84 pgs.)
E.C. Comics

1 .80 2.00

MAD FOLLIES (Special)
1963 - No. 7, 1969
E. C. Comics

nn(1963)-Paperback book covers 19.00 58.00 135.00
2(1964)-Calendar 13.00 40.00 90.00
3(1965)-Mischief Stickers 10.00 30.00 65.00
4(1966)-Mobile; Frazetta-r/back-c Mad #90 11.00 32.00 75.00
5(1967)-Stencils 8.35 25.00 50.00
6(1968)-Mischief Stickers 6.70 20.00 40.00
7(1969)-Nasty Cards 6.70 20.00 40.00

NOTE: ***Clarke*** *c-4.* ***Frazetta*** *r-4, 6 (1 pg. ea.).* ***Mingo*** *c-1-3.* ***Orlando*** *a-5.*

MAD HATTER, THE (Costumed Hero)
Jan-Feb, 1946; No. 2, Sept-Oct, 1946
O. W. Comics Corp.

1-Freddy the Firefly begins; Giunta-c/a 39.00 115.00 270.00
2-Has ad for E.C.'s Animal Fables #1 25.00 75.00 175.00

MADHOUSE
3-4/54 - No. 4, 9-10/54; 6/57 - No. 4, Dec?, 1957
Ajax/Farrell Publ. (Excellent Publ./4-Star)

1(1954) 16.00 50.00 115.00
2,3 10.00 30.00 60.00
4-Surrealistic-c 14.00 43.00 100.00
1(1957, 2nd series) 6.70 20.00 40.00
2-4 5.35 16.00 32.00

MAD HOUSE (Formerly Madhouse Glads; ...Comics #104? on)
No. 95, 9/74 - No. 97, 1/75; No. 98, 8/75 - No. 130, 10/82
Red Circle Productions/Archie Publications

95,96-Horror stories through #97 1.20 3.00
97-Intro. Henry Hobson; Morrow, Thorne-a 1.50
98-130-Satire/humor stories 1.50
Annual 8(1970-71)- 12(1974-75)-Formerly Madhouse Ma-ad Annual. 11-Wood-a(r) .80 2.00
...Comics Digest 1('75-76)- 8(8/82)(...Mag. #5 on) 1.00 2.50

NOTE: ***B. Jones*** *a-96.* ***McWilliams*** *a-97.* ***Morrow*** *a-96; c-95-97.* ***Wildey*** *a-95, 96. See Archie Comics Digest #1, 13.*

MADHOUSE GLADS (Formerly ...Ma-ad; Madhouse #95 on)
No. 73, May, 1970 - No. 94, Aug, 1974 (No. 78-92: 52 pgs.)
Archie Publications

73 1.00 2.00 5.00
74-94 1.60 4.00

MADHOUSE MA-AD(...Jokes #67-70; ...Freak-Out #71-74)
(Formerly Archie's Madhouse) (Becomes Madhouse Glads #75 on)
No. 67, April, 1969 - No. 72, Jan, 1970
Archie Publications

67-72 1.00 2.00 5.00
...Annual 7(1969-70)-Formerly Archie's Madhouse Annual; becomes Madhouse Annual 1.00 2.00 5.00

MADMAN
Mar, 1992 - No. 3, 1992 ($3.95, duotone, high quality, 52 pgs.)
Tundra Publishing

1-3 1.00 2.00 5.00

MAD MONSTER PARTY (See Movie Classics)

MAD SPECIAL (...Super Special)
Fall, 1970 - Present (84 - 116 pages)
E. C. Publications, Inc.

Fall 1970(#1)-Bonus-Voodoo Doll; contains 17 pgs. new material 8.35 25.00 50.00
Spring 1971(#2)-Wall Nuts; 17 pgs. new material 5.00 15.00 30.00
3-Protest Stickers 5.00 15.00 30.00
4-8: 4-Mini Posters. 5-Mad Flag. 6-Mad Mischief Stickers. 7-Presidential

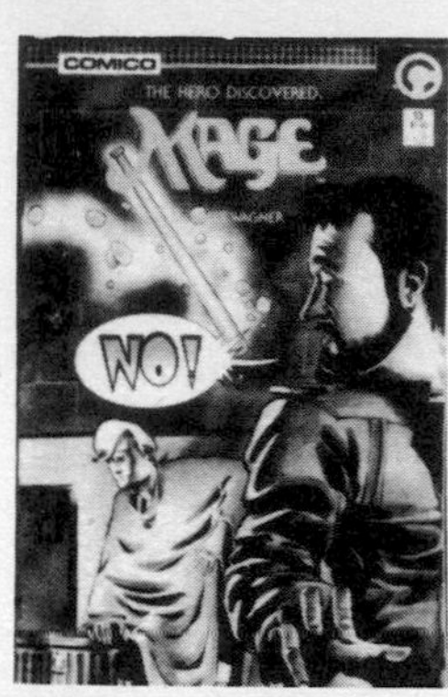

Mage #13, © Matt Wagner

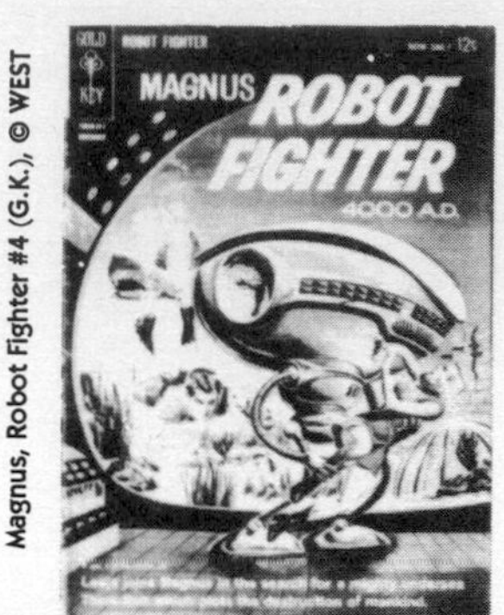

Magnus, Robot Fighter #4 (G.K.), © WEST

Magnus, Robot Fighter #30 (Valiant), © WEST

candidate posters, Wild Shocking Message posters. 8-TV Guise 3.60 10.75 25.00
9(1972)-Contains Nostalgic Mad #1 (28pp) 2.60 7.50 18.00
10,11,13: 10-Nonsense Stickers (Don Martin). 11-33-1/3 RPM record. 13-Sickie Stickers; 3 pgs. new Wolverton 2.60 7.50 18.00
12-Contains Nostalgic Mad #2 (36 pgs.); Davis, Wolverton-a 2.60 7.50 18.00
14-Vital Message posters & Art Depreciation paintings 1.70 5.00 12.00
15-Contains Nostalgic Mad #3 (28 pgs.) 2.15 6.50 15.00
16,17,19,20: 16-Mad-hesive Stickers. 17-Don Martin posters. 20-Martin Stickers 1.70 5.00 12.00
18-Contains Nostalgic Mad #4 (36 pgs.) 1.70 5.00 12.00
21,24-Contains Nostalgic Mad #5 (28 pgs.) & #6 (28 pgs.) 1.70 5.00 12.00
22,23,25-27,29,30: 22-Diplomas. 23-Martin Stickers. 25-Martin Posters. 26-33-1/3 RPM record. 27-Mad Shock-Sticks. 29-Mad Collectable-Correctables Posters. 30-The Movies 1.00 2.50 6.00
28-Contains Nostalgic Mad #7 (36 pgs.) 1.20 3.00 7.00
31,33-60: 36-Has 96 pgs. of comic book & comic strip spoofs: titles "The Comics" on-c 1.00 2.50 6.00
32-Contains Nostalgic Mad #8 1.30 3.25 8.00
61-88,90-96: 71-Batman parodies-r by Wood, Drucker. 83-All Star Trek spoof issue 1.40 3.50
76-(Fall, 1991)-Special Hussein Asylum Edition; distributed only to the troops in the Middle East (see Mad #300-303) 1.00 2.00 5.00
89-($3.95)-Polybaged w/1st of 3 Spy vs. Spy hologram trading cards (direct sale only issue)(other cards came w/card set) 1.60 4.00
NOTE: *#28-30 have no number on cover.* ***Freas*** *c-76.* ***Mingo*** *c-9, 11, 15, 19, 23.*

MAGE (The Hero Discovered...; also see Grendel #16)
Feb, 1984 (no month) - #15, Dec, 1986 ($1.50, Mando paper)
Comico

1-Violence; Comico's 1st color comic 1.20 3.00 7.00
2 1.00 2.00 5.00
3-5: 3-Intro Edsel 1.20 3.00
6-Grendel begins (1st in color) 2.15 6.50 15.00
7-1st new Grendel story 1.30 3.25 8.00
8-14: 13-Grendel dies. 14-Grendel story ends 1.00 2.50
15-$2.95, Double size w/pullout poster 1.20 3.00

MAGGOTS (Hamilton)(Value: cover or less)

MAGIC AGENT (See Forbidden Worlds & Unknown Worlds)
Jan-Feb, 1962 - No. 3, May-June, 1962
American Comics Group

1-Origin & 1st app. John Force 2.40 7.25 17.00
2,3 1.65 4.70 11.00

MAGIC COMICS
Aug, 1939 - No. 123, Nov-Dec, 1949
David McKay Publications

1-Mandrake the Magician, Henry, Popeye (not by Segar), Blondie, Barney Baxter, Secret Agent X-9 (not by Raymond), Bunky by Billy DeBeck & Thornton Burgess text stories illustrated by Harrison Cady begin; Henry covers begin 133.00 400.00 900.00
2 63.00 188.00 415.00
3 47.00 140.00 300.00
4 40.00 120.00 260.00
5 33.00 100.00 220.00
6-10: 8-11,21-Mandrake/Henry-c 27.00 80.00 175.00
11-16,18-20: 12-Mandrake-c begin. 19-Robot-c 22.00 65.00 140.00
17-The Lone Ranger begins 23.00 70.00 150.00
21-30: 25-Only Blondie-c. 26-Dagwood-c begin 15.00 45.00 100.00
31-40: 36-Flag-c 12.00 35.00 75.00
41-50 10.00 30.00 60.00
51-60 8.35 25.00 50.00
61-70 5.85 17.50 35.00
71-99 4.70 14.00 28.00
100 5.85 17.50 35.00
101-106,109-123: 123-Last Dagwood-c 4.00 12.00 24.00
107,108-Flash Gordon app; not by Raymond 4.70 14.00 28.00

MAGICA DE SPELL (See Walt Disney Showcase #30)

MAGIC FLUTE, THE (See Night Music #9-11)

MAGIC OF CHRISTMAS AT NEWBERRYS, THE
1967 (20 pgs.; slick cover; B&W inside)
E. S. London (Giveaway)

nn 1.20 3.00

MAGIC SWORD, THE (See Movie Classics)

MAGIK (Illyana and Storm Limited Series)
Dec, 1983 - No. 4, Mar, 1984 (60 cents, mini-series)
Marvel Comics Group

1-Characters from X-Men; Inferno begins; X-Men cameo (Buscema pencils 1,2; c-1p 1.20 3.00
2-4: 2-Nightcrawler app. & X-Men cameo 1.20 3.00

MAGILLA GORILLA (TV)(See Kite Fun Book)
May, 1964 - No. 10, Dec, 1968 (Hanna-Barbera)
Gold Key

1 5.50 17.00 40.00
2-10: 3-Vs. Yogi Bear for President 3.25 9.50 22.00

MAGILLA GORILLA (TV)(See Spotlight #4)
Nov, 1970 - No. 5, July, 1971 (Hanna-Barbera)
Charlton Comics

1 2.70 8.00 19.00
2-5 1.85 5.50 13.00

MAGNETO (See X-Men #1)
Sept, 1993 (no date given) (Giveaway, color, one-shot)
Marvel Comics

0-Embossed foil-c by Sienkiewicz; r/Classic X-Men #19 & 12 by John Bolton 1.00 2.00 5.00

MAGNUS, ROBOT FIGHTER (...4000 A.D.)(See Doctor Solar)
Feb, 1963 - No. 46, Jan, 1977 (Painted covers)
Gold Key

1-Origin & 1st app. Magnus; Aliens (1st app.) series begins 31.00 95.00 220.00
2,3 16.00 49.00 115.00
4-10: 10-Simonson fan club illo (5/65, 1st-a?) 9.00 28.00 65.00
11-20 6.00 18.00 42.00
21,24-28: 22-Origin-r/#1. 28-Aliens ends 3.85 11.50 27.00
22,23-12 cent and 15 cent editions exist 3.70 11.00 26.00
29-46-Reprints 1.65 4.70 11.00
NOTE: ***Manning*** *a-1-22, 29-43(r).* ***Spiegle*** *a-23, 44r.*

MAGNUS ROBOT FIGHTER (Also see Vintage Magnus)
May, 1991 - Present ($1.75/$1.95/$2.25, color, high quality paper)
Valiant Comics

1-Nichols/Layton-c/a; 1-8 have trading cards 3.20 8.00 20.00
2 1.70 5.00 12.00
3,4: 4-Rai cameo 2.00 6.00 14.00
5-Origin & 1st full app. Rai (10/91); 5-8 are in flip book format and back-c & half of book are Rai #1-4 mini-series 2.60 7.50 18.00
6-8: 6-1st Solar x-over. 7-Magnus vs. Rai-c/story; 1st X-O Armor. 8-Begin $1.95-c 1.50 3.75 9.00
0-Origin issue; Layton-a; ordered through mail w/coupons from 1st 8 issues plus 50 cents; B. Smith trading card 9.00 26.00 60.00
0-Sold thru comic shops without trading card 4.30 13.00 30.00
9-11: 11-Last $1.95-c 1.10 2.70 6.50
12-($3.25, 44pgs.)-Turok-c/story (1st app. in Valiant universe, 5/92); has 8 pg. Magnus story insert 6.50 19.00 45.00
13-20,22-24,26-35: 14-1st app. Isak. 15,16-Unity x-overs. 15-Miller-c. 16-Birth

Mai: The Psychic Girl #9, © Kazuya Kudo, Ryoichi Ikehami/Shogakukan

Man Comics #6, © MEG

Manhunter #4, © DC

GD25 FN65 NM94

of Magnus. 24-Story cont'd in Rai & the Future Force #9 .90 2.25
21-New direction & new logo; Rocco inks 1.20 3.00
21-(Gold) 10.00
25-($2.95)-Embossed silver foil-c; new costume 1.20 3.00
NOTE: ***Ditko/Reese** a-18. **Layton** a(i)-5; c(i)-6-9; back(i)-5-8. **Simonson** c-16. Issues 1-8 must have trading cards and coupons intact.*

MAGNUS ROBOT FIGHTER 4000 A.D.
1990 - No. 2, 1991 ($7.95, color, high quality paper, card stock-c, 96 pgs.)
Valiant Comics
1,2-Russ Manning-r. 1-Origin 1.30 3.25 8.00

MAID OF THE MIST (See American Graphics)

MAI, THE PSYCHIC GIRL (Eclipse)(Value: cover or less)

MAJOR HOOPLE COMICS (See Crackajack Funnies)
nd (Jan, 1943)
Nedor Publications
1-Mary Worth, Phantom Soldier app. by Moldoff 25.00 75.00 160.00

MAJOR INAPAK THE SPACE ACE
1951 (20 pages) (Giveaway)
Magazine Enterprises (Inapac Foods)
1-Bob Powell-c/a 1.00
NOTE: *Many warehouse copies surfaced in 1973.*

MAJOR VICTORY COMICS (Also see Dynamic Comics)
1944 - No. 3, Summer, 1945
H. Clay Glover/Service Publ./Harry 'A' Chesler
1-Origin Major Victory by C. Sultan (reprint from Dynamic #1); 1st app. Spider Woman 38.00 115.00 250.00
2-Dynamic Boy app. 25.00 75.00 165.00
3-Rocket Boy app. 19.00 58.00 125.00

MALTESE FALCON (See Feature Books No. 48)

MALU IN THE LAND OF ADVENTURE
1964 (See White Princess of Jungle #2)
I. W. Enterprises
1-r/Avon's Slave Girl Comics #1; Severin-c 4.70 14.00 28.00

MAMMOTH COMICS
1938 (84 pages) (Black & White, 8-1/2x11-1/2")
Whitman Publishing Co.(K. K. Publications)
1-Alley Oop, Terry & the Pirates, Dick Tracy, Little Orphan Annie, Wash Tubbs, Moon Mullins, Smilin' Jack, Tailspin Tommy, Don Winslow, Dan Dunn, Smokey Stover & other reprints 96.00 288.00 600.00

MAMMY YOKUM & THE GREAT DOGPATCH MYSTERY
1951 (Giveaway)
Toby Press
nn-Li'l Abner 17.00 52.00 120.00

MAN-BAT (See Batman Family, Brave & the Bold, & Detective #400)
Dec-Jan, 1975-76 - No. 2, Feb-Mar, 1976; Dec, 1984
National Periodical Publications/DC Comics
1-Ditko-a(p); Aparo-c; Batman, She-Bat app. 1.80 4.50
2-Aparo-c 1.20 3.00
1 (12/84)-N. Adams-r(3)/Det.(Vs. Batman on-c) 1.60 4.00

MAN COMICS
Dec, 1949 - No. 28, Sept, 1953 (#1-6: 52 pgs.)
Marvel/Atlas Comics (NPI)
1-Tuska-a 11.00 32.00 75.00
2-Tuska-a 5.85 17.50 38.00
3-5 5.00 15.00 30.00
6-8 4.00 12.00 24.00
9-13,15: 9-Format changes to war 4.00 10.00 20.00
14-Henkel (3 pgs.); Pakula-a 4.70 14.00 28.00
16-21,23-28: 28-Crime issue 3.60 9.00 18.00

GD25 FN65 NM94

22-Krigstein-a, 5 pgs. 5.85 17.50 35.00
NOTE: ***Berg** a-14, 15, 19. **Colan** a-9, 21. **Everett** a-8, 22; c-22, 25. **Heath** a-11, 17, 21. Kubertish a-by **Bob Brown**-3. **Maneely** a-11; c-10, 11. **Reinman** a-11. **Robinson** a-7, 10, 14. **Robert Sale** a-9, 11. **Sinnott** a-22, 23. **Tuska** a-14, 23.*

MANDRAKE THE MAGICIAN (See Defenders Of The Earth, Feature Books #18, 19, 123, 46, 52, 55, Giant Comic Album, King Comics, Magic Comics, The Phantom #21, Tiny Tot Funnies & Wow Comics, '36)

MANDRAKE THE MAGICIAN (See Harvey Comics Hits #53)
Sept, 1966 - No. 10, Nov, 1967 (Also see Four Color #752)
King Comics (All 12 cents)
1-Begin S.O.S. Phantom, ends #3 3.40 10.00 24.00
2-7,9: 4-Girl Phantom app. 5-Flying Saucer-c/story. 5,6-Brick Bradford app. 7-Origin Lothar. 9-Brick Bradford app. 1.85 5.50 13.00
8-Jeff Jones-a (4 pgs.) 2.70 8.00 19.00
10-Rip Kirby app., Raymond-a (14 pgs.) 3.40 10.00 24.00

MAN FROM ATLANTIS (TV)
Feb, 1978 - No. 7, Aug, 1978
Marvel Comics Group
1-($1.00, 84 pgs.)-Sutton-a(p), Buscema-c; origin 1.20
2-7 (#1: cast photos & origin Mark Harris inside) 1.00

MAN FROM PLANET X, THE (Planet X Productions)(Value: cover or less)

MAN FROM U.N.C.L.E., THE (TV) (Also see The Girl From...)
Feb, 1965 - No. 22, April, 1969 (All photo covers)
Gold Key
1 12.00 36.00 85.00
2-Photo back c-2-8 8.50 25.00 58.00
3-10: 7-Jet Dream begins (1st app., also see Jet Dream) (all new stories) 5.00 15.00 36.00
11-22: 21,22-Reprint #10 & 7 4.15 12.50 29.00

MAN FROM U.N.C.L.E., THE (Entertainment)(Value: cover or less)

MAN FROM WELLS FARGO (TV)
No. 1287, Feb-Apr, 1962 - May-July, 1962 (Photo-c)
Dell Publishing Co.
4-Color 1287, #01-495-207 4.70 14.00 28.00

MANGLE TANGLE TALES (Innovation)(Value: cover or less)

MANHUNT! (Becomes Red Fox #15 on)
Oct, 1947 - No. 14, 1953
Magazine Enterprises
1-Red Fox by L. B. Cole, Undercover Girl by Whitney, Space Ace begin (1st app.); negligee panels 25.00 75.00 175.00
2-Electrocution-c 20.00 60.00 140.00
3-6 16.00 50.00 115.00
7-10: 7-Space Ace ends. 8-Trail Colt begins (intro/1st app., 5/48) by Guardineer; Trail Colt-c. 10-G. Ingels-a 13.50 41.00 95.00
11(8/48)-Frazetta-a, 7 pgs.; The Duke, Scotland Yard begin 21.00 63.00 145.00
12 11.00 32.00 75.00
13(A-1 #63)-Frazetta, r-/Trail Colt #1, 7 pgs. 19.00 58.00 135.00
14(A-1 #77)-Bondage/hypo-c; last L. B. Cole Red Fox; Ingels-a 13.50 41.00 95.00
NOTE: ***Guardineer** a-1-5; c-8. **Whitney** a-2-14; c-1-6, 10. Red Fox by **L. B. Cole**-#1-14. #15 was advertised but came out as Red Fox #15. Bondage c-6.*

MANHUNTER (See Adventure #58, 73, Brave & the Bold, Detective Comics, 1st Issue Special, House of Mystery #143 and Justice League of America)
1984 ($2.50, 76 pgs; high quality paper)
DC Comics
1-Simonson-c/a(r)/Detective; Batman app. 1.00 2.50

MANHUNTER (DC Comics, 1988-90)(Value: cover or less)

MAN IN BLACK (See Thrill-O-Rama) (Also see All New Comics, Front Page, Green Hornet #31, Strange Story & Tally-Ho Comics)
Sept, 1957 - No. 4, Mar, 1958

The Man of Steel #4, © DC

Mantra #2, © Malibu

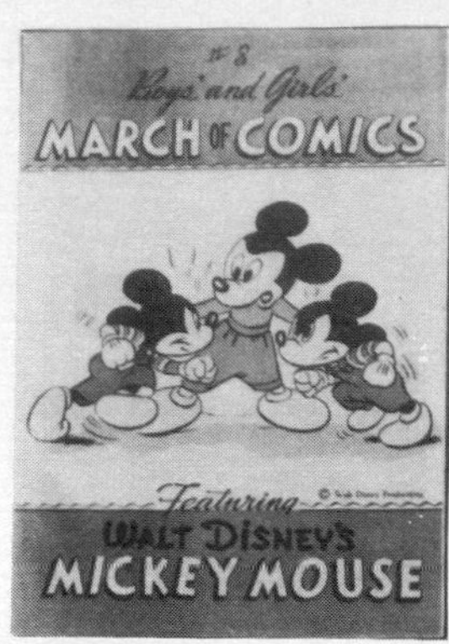

March of Comics #8, © The Disney Co.

GD25 FN65 NM94

Harvey Publications
1-Bob Powell-c/a 9.00 26.00 62.00
2-4: Powell-c/a 6.00 18.00 42.00

MAN IN FLIGHT (See 4-Color #836)

MAN IN SPACE (See Dell Giant #27 & 4-Color #716, 954)

MAN OF PEACE, POPE PIUS XII
1950 (See Pope Pius XII... & To V2#8)
Catechetical Guild
nn-All Powell-a 4.00 10.50 21.00

MAN OF STEEL, THE (Also see Superman: The Man of Steel)
1986 (June release) - No. 6, 1986 (75 cents, mini-series)
DC Comics
1-Silver logo; Byrne-c/a/scripts in all; origin 1.00
1-Alternate-c for newsstand sales 1.00
1-Distr. to toy stores by So Much Fun 1.00
2-6: 2-Intro. Lois Lane, Jimmy Olsen. 3-Intro/origin Magpie; Batman-c/story. 4-Intro. new Lex Luthor 1.00
1-6-Silver Editions (1993, $1.95)-r/1-6 .80 2.00
...The Complete Saga nn-Contains #1-6, given away in contest .80 2.00
Limited Edition, softcover 4.30 13.00 30.00
NOTE: *Issues 1-6 were released between Action #583 (9/86) & Action #584 (1/87) plus Superman #423 (9/86) & Superman #424 (1/87).*

MAN OF WAR (See Liberty Guards & Liberty Scouts)
Nov, 1941 - No. 2, Jan, 1942
Centaur Publications
1-The Fire-Man, Man of War, The Sentinel, Liberty Guards, & Vapo-Man begin; Gustavson-c/a; Flag-c 108.00 325.00 700.00
2-Intro The Ferret; Gustavson-c/a 92.00 275.00 600.00

MAN OF WAR (Eclipse Comics)(Value: cover or less)

MAN OF WAR (See The Protectors)
1993 - Present ($2.50/$2.25/$1.95, color)
Malibu Comics
1-5 ($1.95)-Newsstand Editions w/different-c .80 2.00
1-5 ($2.50)-Collector's Editions w/poster 1.00 2.50
6,7 ($2.25) .90 2.25

MAN O' MARS
1953; 1964
Fiction House Magazines
1-Space Rangers; Whitman-c 25.00 75.00 175.00
I.W. Reprint #1-r/Man O'Mars #1 & Star Pirate; Murphy Anderson-a 5.00 15.00 30.00

MANTECH ROBOT WARRIORS (Archie)(Value: cover or less)

MAN-THING (See Fear, Giant-Size..., Marvel Comics Presents, Marvel Fanfare, Monsters Unleashed, Power Record Comics & Savage Tales)
Jan, 1974 - No. 22, Oct, 1975; V2#1, Nov, 1979 - V2#11, July, 1981
Marvel Comics Group
1-Howard the Duck(2nd app.) cont'd/Fear #19 2.40 7.25 17.00
2 1.30 3.25 8.00
3-1st app. original Foolkiller 1.20 3.00 7.00
4-Origin Foolkiller; last app. 1st Foolkiller 1.60 4.00
5-11-Ploog-a. 11-Foolkiller cameo (flashback) 1.20 3.00
12-22: 19-1st app. Scavenger. 20-Spidey cameo. 21-Origin Scavenger, Man-Thing. 22-Howard the Duck cameo .90 2.25
V2#1(1979) - 11 1.30
NOTE: ***Alcala** a-14. **Brunner** c-1. J. **Buscema** a-12p, 13p, 16p. **Gil Kane** c-4p, 10p, 12-20p, 21. **Mooney** a-17, 18, 19p, 20-22, V2#1-3p. **Ploog** Man-Thing-5p, 6p, 7, 8, 9-11p; c-5, 6, 8, 9, 11. **Sutton** a-13i. No. 19 says #10 in indicia.*

MANTRA
July, 1993 - Present ($1.95, color)
Malibu Comics (Ultraverse)
1-Polybagged w/trading card & coupon 1.00 2.00 5.00
1-Newsstand edition w/o trading card or coupon 1.40 3.50
1-Holographic cover edition 40.00
2,3,5-8: 3-Intro Warstrike & Kismet .90 2.25
4-($2.50, 40 pgs.)-Rune flip-c/story by B. Smith (3 pgs.) 1.00 2.50

MAN WITH THE X-RAY EYES, THE (See X,... under Movie Comics)

MANY GHOSTS OF DR. GRAVES, THE (Doctor Graves #73 on)
5/67 - No. 60, 12/76; No. 61, 9/77 - No. 62, 10/77; No. 63, 2/78 - No. 65, 4/78; No. 66, 6/81 - No. 72, 5/82
Charlton Comics
1-Palais-a; early issues 12 cent-c 1.50 3.75 9.00
2-10 1.80 4.50
11-20 1.20 3.00
21-44,46-72: 47,49-Newton-a .80 2.00
45-1st Newton comic work (8 pgs.); new logo 1.20 3.00
Modern Comics Reprint 12,25 ('78) 1.00
NOTE: ***Aparo** a-4, 5, 7, 8, 66r, 69r; c-8, 14, 19, 66r, 67r. **Byrne** c-54. **Ditko** a-1, 7, 9, 11-13, 15-18, 20-22, 24, 26, 27, 35, 37, 38, 40-44, 47, 48, 51-54, 58, 60r-65r, 70, 72; c-11-13, 16-18, 22, 24, 26-35, 38, 40, 55, 58, 62-65. **Howard** a-45i; c-48. **Morisi** a-13, 14, 23, 26. **Newton** a-45, 47p, 49p; c-49, 52. **Sutton** a-42, 49; c-42, 44, 45; painted c-53.*

MANY LOVES OF DOBIE GILLIS (TV)
May-June, 1960 - No. 26, Oct, 1964
National Periodical Publications
1-Most covers by Bob Oskner 19.00 56.00 150.00
2-5 9.00 28.00 75.00
6-10 8.00 23.00 60.00
11-26: 20-Drucker-a 6.00 19.00 50.00

MARAUDER'S MOON (See 4-Color #848)

MARCH OF COMICS (Boys' and Girls'...#3-353)
1946 - No. 488, April, 1982 (#1-4 are not numbered)
(K.K. Giveaway) (Founded by Sig Feuchtwanger)
K. K. Publications/Western Publishing Co.
Early issues were full size, 32 pages, and were printed with and without an extra cover of slick stock, just for the advertiser. The binding was stapled if the slick cover was added; otherwise, the pages were glued together at the spine. Most 1948 - 1951 issues were full size,24 pages, pulp covers. Starting in 1952 they were half-size and 32 pages with slick covers.1959 and later issues had only 16 pages plus covers. 1952 -1959 issues read oblong; 1960 and later issues read upright.
nn (#1, 1946)-Goldilocks; Kelly back-c; 16pgs., stapled 31.00 95.00 220.00
nn (#2, 1946)-How Santa Got His Red Suit; Kelly-a (11 pgs., r/4-Color #61) ('44); 16pgs., stapled 31.00 95.00 220.00
nn (#3, 1947)-Our Gang (Walt Kelly) 43.00 130.00 300.00
nn (#4)-Donald Duck by Carl Barks, "Maharajah Donald," 28 pgs.; Kelly-c? (Disney) 785.00 2360.00 5500.00
5-Andy Panda 17.00 52.00 120.00
6-Popular Fairy Tales; Kelly-c; Noonan-a(2) 21.00 63.00 145.00
7-Oswald the Rabbit 21.00 63.00 145.00
8-Mickey Mouse, 32 pgs. (Disney) 54.00 160.00 375.00
9(nn)-The Story of the Gloomy Bunny 10.00 30.00 65.00
10-Out of Santa's Bag 9.15 27.50 55.00
11-Fun With Santa Claus 7.50 22.50 45.00
12-Santa's Toys 7.50 22.50 45.00
13-Santa's Surprise 7.50 22.50 45.00
14-Santa's Candy Kitchen 7.50 22.50 45.00
15-Hip-It-Ty Hop & the Big Bass Viol 7.50 22.50 45.00
16-Woody Woodpecker (1947) 12.00 36.00 85.00
17-Roy Rogers (1948) 22.00 65.00 150.00
18-Popular Fairy Tales 11.50 34.00 80.00
19-Uncle Wiggily 10.00 30.00 65.00
20-Donald Duck by Carl Barks, "Darkest Africa," 22 pgs.; Kelly-c (Disney) 380.00 1136.00 2650.00
21-Tom and Jerry 11.00 32.00 75.00
22-Andy Panda 10.00 30.00 65.00
23-Raggedy Ann; Kerr-a 14.00 43.00 100.00
24-Felix the Cat, 1932 daily strip reprints by Otto Messmer

March of Comics #20, © The Disney Co.

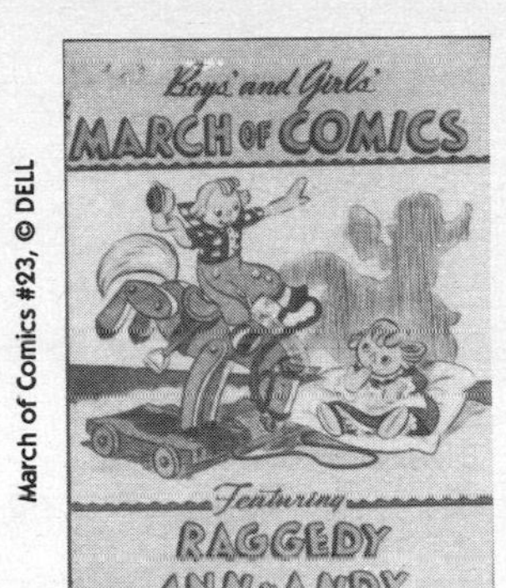

March of Comics #23, © DELL

March of Comics #52, © KING

	GD25	FN65	NM94
	24.00	72.00	165.00
25-Gene Autry	24.00	72.00	150.00
26-Our Gang; Walt Kelly	24.00	72.00	105.00
27-Mickey Mouse; r/in M. M. #240 (Disney)	39.00	120.00	275.00
28-Gene Autry	22.00	65.00	150.00
29-Easter Bonnet Shop	5.35	16.00	32.00
30-Here Comes Santa	4.35	13.00	26.00
31-Santa's Busy Corner	4.35	13.00	26.00
32-No book produced			
33-A Christmas Carol (12/48)	4.35	13.00	26.00
34-Woody Woodpecker	10.00	30.00	65.00
35-Roy Rogers (1948)	22.00	65.00	150.00
36-Felix the Cat(1949); by Messmer; 1934 daily strip r	19.00	58.00	135.00
37-Popeye	16.00	48.00	110.00
38-Oswald the Rabbit	8.35	25.00	50.00
39-Gene Autry	22.00	65.00	150.00
40-Andy and Woody	8.35	25.00	50.00
41-Donald Duck by Carl Barks, "Race to the South Seas," 22 pgs.; Kelly-c	243.00	730.00	1700.00
42-Porky Pig	8.35	25.00	50.00
43-Henry	6.70	20.00	40.00
44-Bugs Bunny	10.00	30.00	65.00
45-Mickey Mouse (Disney)	34.00	100.00	235.00
46-Tom and Jerry	10.00	30.00	65.00
47-Roy Rogers	19.00	57.00	130.00
48-Greetings from Santa	4.00	11.00	22.00
49-Santa Is Here	4.00	11.00	22.00
50-Santa Claus' Workshop (1949)	4.00	11.00	22.00
51-Felix the Cat (1950) by Messmer	16.00	48.00	110.00
52-Popeye	13.00	40.00	90.00
53-Oswald the Rabbit	8.35	25.00	50.00
54-Gene Autry	17.00	52.00	120.00
55-Andy and Woody	7.50	22.50	45.00
56-Donald Duck-not by Barks; Barks art on back-c (Disney)	26.00	78.00	180.00
57-Porky Pig	7.50	22.50	45.00
58-Henry	5.00	15.00	30.00
59-Bugs Bunny	9.15	27.50	55.00
60-Mickey Mouse (Disney)	21.00	63.00	145.00
61-Tom and Jerry	7.50	22.50	45.00
62-Roy Rogers	17.00	52.00	120.00
63-Welcome Santa; 1/2-size, oblong	4.00	11.00	22.00
64(nn)-Santa's Helpers; 1/2-size, oblong	4.00	11.00	21.00
65(nn)-Jingle Bells (1950)–1/2-size, oblong	4.00	11.00	22.00
66-Popeye (1951)	11.50	34.00	80.00
67-Oswald the Rabbit	6.705	20.00	40.00
68-Roy Rogers	16.00	48.00	110.00
69-Donald Duck; Barks-a on back-c (Disney)	22.00	65.00	150.00
70-Tom and Jerry	6.70	20.00	40.00
71-Porky Pig	6.70	20.00	40.00
72-Krazy Kat	9.15	27.50	55.00
73-Roy Rogers	13.00	40.00	90.00
74-Mickey Mouse (1951)(Disney)	17.00	52.00	120.00
75-Bugs Bunny	7.50	22.50	45.00
76-Andy and Woody	6.70	20.00	40.00
77-Roy Rogers	14.00	42.00	85.00
78-Gene Autry (1951); last regular size issue	14.00	42.00	85.00
79-Andy Panda (1952, 5x7" size)	4.00	12.00	24.00
80-Popeye	10.00	30.00	70.00
81-Oswald the Rabbit	4.35	13.00	26.00
82-Tarzan; Lex Barker photo-c	10.00	40.00	110.00
83-Bugs Bunny	5.85	17.50	35.00
84-Henry	4.00	10.00	20.00
85-Woody Woodpecker	4.00	10.00	20.00
86-Roy Rogers	11.00	32.00	75.00

	GD25	FN65	NM94
87-Krazy Kat	7.50	22.50	45.00
88-Tom and Jerry	5.00	15.00	30.00
89-Porky Pig	4.00	10.00	20.00
90-Gene Autry	11.00	32.00	75.00
91-Roy Rogers & Santa	11.00	32.00	75.00
92-Christmas with Santa	3.60	9.00	18.00
93-Woody Woodpecker (1953)	4.00	10.00	20.00
94-Indian Chief	9.15	27.50	55.00
95-Oswald the Rabbit	4.00	10.00	20.00
96-Popeye	10.00	30.00	60.00
97-Bugs Bunny	5.00	15.00	30.00
98-Tarzan; Lex Barker photo-c	17.00	52.00	120.00
99-Porky Pig	4.00	10.00	20.00
100-Roy Rogers	10.00	30.00	60.00
101-Henry	3.60	9.00	18.00
102-Tom Corbett (TV)('53, early app).; painted-c	14.00	43.00	100.00
103-Tom and Jerry	4.00	10.00	20.00
104-Gene Autry	10.00	30.00	60.00
105-Roy Rogers	10.00	30.00	60.00
106-Santa's Helpers	3.60	9.00	18.00
107-Santa's Christmas Book - not published			
108-Fun with Santa (1953)	3.60	9.00	18.00
109-Woody Woodpecker (1954)	3.60	9.00	18.00
110-Indian Chief	5.00	15.00	30.00
111-Oswald the Rabbit	3.60	9.00	18.00
112-Henry	3.20	8.00	16.00
113-Porky Pig	3.60	9.00	18.00
114-Tarzan; Russ Manning-a	17.00	52.00	120.00
115-Bugs Bunny	4.00	12.00	24.00
116-Roy Rogers	10.00	30.00	60.00
117-Popeye	10.00	30.00	60.00
118-Flash Gordon; painted-c	12.00	36.00	85.00
119-Tom and Jerry	3.60	9.00	18.00
120-Gene Autry	10.00	30.00	60.00
121-Roy Rogers	10.00	30.00	60.00
122-Santa's Surprise (1954)	2.80	7.00	14.00
123-Santa's Christmas Book	2.80	7.00	14.00
124-Woody Woodpecker (1955)	3.20	8.00	16.00
125-Tarzan; Lex Barker photo-c	16.00	48.00	110.00
126-Oswald the Rabbit	3.20	8.00	16.00
127-Indian Chief	4.35	13.00	26.00
128-Tom and Jerry	3.20	8.00	16.00
129-Henry	2.80	7.00	14.00
130-Porky Pig	3.20	8.00	16.00
131-Roy Rogers	10.00	30.00	60.00
132-Bugs Bunny	4.00	10.00	20.00
133-Flash Gordon; painted-c	11.00	32.00	75.00
134-Popeye	6.70	20.00	40.00
135-Gene Autry	9.15	27.50	55.00
136-Roy Rogers	9.15	27.50	55.00
137-Gifts from Santa	2.40	6.00	12.00
138-Fun at Christmas (1955)	2.40	6.00	12.00
139-Woody Woodpecker (1956)	3.20	8.00	16.00
140-Indian Chief	4.35	13.00	26.00
141-Oswald the Rabbit	3.20	8.00	16.00
142-Flash Gordon	11.00	32.00	75.00
143-Porky Pig	3.20	8.00	16.00
144-Tarzan; Russ Manning-a, painted-c	14.00	40.00	100.00
145-Tom and Jerry	3.20	8.00	16.00
146-Roy Rogers; photo-c	10.00	30.00	60.00
147-Henry	2.40	6.00	12.00
148-Popeye	6.70	20.00	40.00
149-Bugs Bunny	3.60	9.00	18.00
150-Gene Autry	9.15	27.50	55.00
151-Roy Rogers	9.15	27.50	55.00
152-The Night Before Christmas	2.40	6.00	12.00

March of Comics #142, © KING

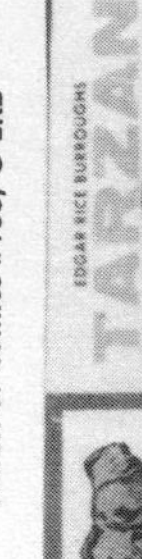

March of Comics #155, © ERB

March of Comics #205, © Viacom

	GD25	FN65	NM94
153-Merry Christmas (1956)	2.40	6.00	12.00
154-Tom and Jerry (1957)	3.20	8.00	16.00
155-Tarzan; photo-c	14.00	43.00	100.00
156-Oswald the Rabbit	3.20	8.00	16.00
157-Popeye	5.85	17.50	35.00
158-Woody Woodpecker	3.20	8.00	16.00
159-Indian Chief	4.35	13.00	26.00
160-Bugs Bunny	3.60	9.00	18.00
161-Roy Rogers	7.50	22.50	45.00
162-Henry	2.40	6.00	12.00
163-Rin Tin Tin (TV)	5.85	17.50	35.00
164-Porky Pig	3.20	8.00	16.00
165-The Lone Ranger	8.35	25.00	50.00
166-Santa and His Reindeer	2.40	6.00	12.00
167-Roy Rogers and Santa	7.50	22.50	45.00
168-Santa Claus' Workshop (1957)	2.40	6.00	12.00
169-Popeye (1958)	5.85	17.50	35.00
170-Indian Chief	4.35	13.00	26.00
171-Oswald the Rabbit	2.80	7.00	14.00
172-Tarzan	11.50	34.00	80.00
173-Tom and Jerry	2.80	7.00	14.00
174-The Lone Ranger	8.35	25.00	50.00
175-Porky Pig	2.80	7.00	14.00
176-Roy Rogers	7.00	21.00	42.00
177-Woody Woodpecker	2.80	7.00	14.00
178-Henry	2.40	6.00	12.00
179-Bugs Bunny	3.00	7.50	15.00
180-Rin Tin Tin (TV)	5.00	15.00	30.00
181-Happy Holiday	2.00	5.00	10.00
182-Happi Tim	2.80	7.00	14.00
183-Welcome Santa (1958)	2.00	5.00	10.00
184-Woody Woodpecker (1959)	2.80	7.00	14.00
185-Tarzan; photo-c	11.50	34.00	80.00
186-Oswald the Rabbit	2.80	7.00	14.00
187-Indian Chief	4.35	13.00	26.00
188-Bugs Bunny	3.00	7.50	15.00
189-Henry	2.40	6.00	12.00
190-Tom and Jerry	2.80	7.00	14.00
191-Roy Rogers	7.00	21.00	42.00
192-Porky Pig	2.80	7.00	14.00
193-The Lone Ranger	8.35	25.00	50.00
194-Popeye	5.35	16.00	32.00
195-Rin Tin Tin (TV)	5.00	15.00	30.00
196-Sears Special - not published			
197-Santa Is Coming	2.00	5.00	10.00
198-Santa's Helpers (1959)	2.00	5.00	10.00
199-Huckleberry Hound (TV)(1960, early app.)	5.85	17.50	35.00
200-Fury (TV)	5.00	15.00	30.00
201-Bugs Bunny	3.00	7.50	15.00
202-Space Explorer	7.50	22.50	45.00
203-Woody Woodpecker	2.40	6.00	12.00
204-Tarzan	10.00	30.00	60.00
205-Mighty Mouse	5.85	17.50	35.00
206-Roy Rogers; photo-c	7.00	21.00	42.00
207-Tom and Jerry	2.40	6.00	12.00
208-The Lone Ranger; Clayton Moore photo-c	11.00	32.00	75.00
209-Porky Pig	2.40	6.00	12.00
210-Lassie (TV)	5.00	15.00	30.00
211-Sears Special - not published			
212-Christmas Eve	2.00	5.00	10.00
213-Here Comes Santa (1960)	2.00	5.00	10.00
214-Huckleberry Hound (TV)(1961)	5.35	16.00	32.00
215-Hi Yo Silver	5.00	15.00	30.00
216-Rocky & His Friends (TV)(1961); predates Rocky and His Fiendish Friends #1 (see Four Color #1128)	10.00	30.00	65.00
217-Lassie (TV)	4.00	12.00	24.00

	GD25	FN65	NM94
218-Porky Pig	2.40	6.00	12.00
219-Journey to the Sun	5.00	15.00	30.00
220-Bugs Bunny	3.00	7.50	15.00
221-Roy and Dale; photo-c	6.35	19.00	38.00
222-Woody Woodpecker	2.40	6.00	12.00
223-Tarzan	10.00	30.00	60.00
224-Tom and Jerry	2.40	6.00	12.00
225-The Lone Ranger	6.35	19.00	38.00
226-Christmas Treasury (1961)	2.00	5.00	10.00
227-Sears Special - not published?			
228-Letters to Santa (1961)	2.00	5.00	10.00
229-The Flintstones (TV)(1962); early app.; predates 1st Flintstones Gold Key issue (#7)	9.15	27.50	55.00
230-Lassie (TV)	4.00	12.00	24.00
231-Bugs Bunny	3.00	7.50	15.00
232-The Three Stooges	9.15	27.50	55.00
233-Bullwinkle (TV) (1962, very early app.)	10.00	30.00	70.00
234-Smokey the Bear	3.60	9.00	18.00
235-Huckleberry Hound (TV)	5.35	16.00	32.00
236-Roy and Dale	5.00	15.00	30.00
237-Mighty Mouse	4.35	13.00	26.00
238-The Lone Ranger	6.35	19.00	38.00
239-Woody Woodpecker	2.40	6.00	12.00
240-Tarzan	7.50	22.50	45.00
241-Santa Claus Around the World	2.00	5.00	10.00
242-Santa's Toyland (1962)	2.00	5.00	10.00
243-The Flintstones (TV)(1963)	8.35	25.00	50.00
244-Mister Ed (TV); early app.; photo-c	5.35	16.00	32.00
245-Bugs Bunny	3.00	7.50	15.00
246-Popeye	4.00	12.00	24.00
247-Mighty Mouse	4.35	13.00	26.00
248-The Three Stooges	9.15	27.50	55.00
249-Woody Woodpecker	2.40	6.00	12.00
250-Roy and Dale	5.00	15.00	30.00
251-Little Lulu & Witch Hazel	13.50	41.00	95.00
252-Tarzan; painted-c	7.50	22.50	45.00
253-Yogi Bear (TV)	5.85	17.50	35.00
254-Lassie (TV)	4.00	12.00	24.00
255-Santa's Christmas List	2.00	5.00	10.00
256-Christmas Party (1963)	2.00	5.00	10.00
257-Mighty Mouse	4.35	13.00	26.00
258-The Sword in the Stone (Disney)	8.35	25.00	50.00
259-Bugs Bunny	3.00	7.50	15.00
260-Mister Ed (TV)	4.35	13.00	26.00
261-Woody Woodpecker	2.40	6.00	12.00
262-Tarzan	7.50	22.50	45.00
263-Donald Duck; not by Barks (Disney)	7.50	22.50	45.00
264-Popeye	4.00	12.00	24.00
265-Yogi Bear (TV)	4.35	13.00	26.00
266-Lassie (TV)	4.00	10.00	20.00
267-Little Lulu; Irving Tripp-a	11.00	32.00	75.00
268-The Three Stooges	8.35	25.00	50.00
269-A Jolly Christmas	2.00	5.00	10.00
270-Santa's Little Helpers	2.00	5.00	10.00
271-The Flintstones (TV)(1965)	8.35	25.00	50.00
272-Tarzan	7.50	22.50	45.00
273-Bugs Bunny	3.00	7.50	15.00
274-Popeye	4.00	12.00	24.00
275-Little Lulu; Irving Tripp-a	10.00	30.00	62.00
276-The Jetsons (TV)	13.00	40.00	90.00
277-Daffy Duck	2.80	7.00	14.00
278-Lassie (TV)	4.00	10.00	20.00
279-Yogi Bear (TV)	4.35	13.00	26.00
280-The Three Stooges; photo-c	8.35	25.00	50.00
281-Tom and Jerry	2.00	5.00	10.00
282-Mister Ed (TV)	4.35	13.00	26.00

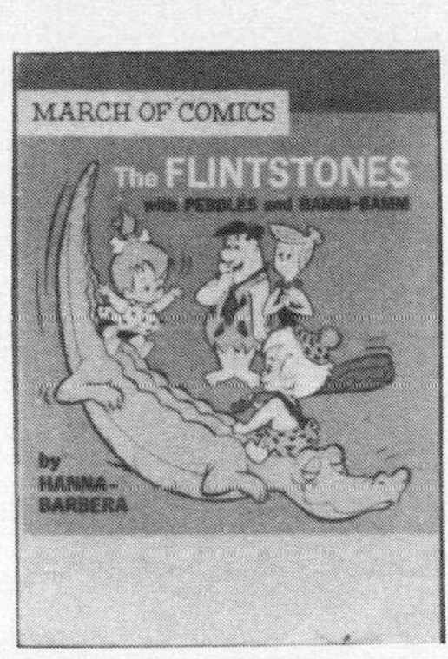

March of Comics #289, © Hanna-Barbera

March of Comics #302, © DELL

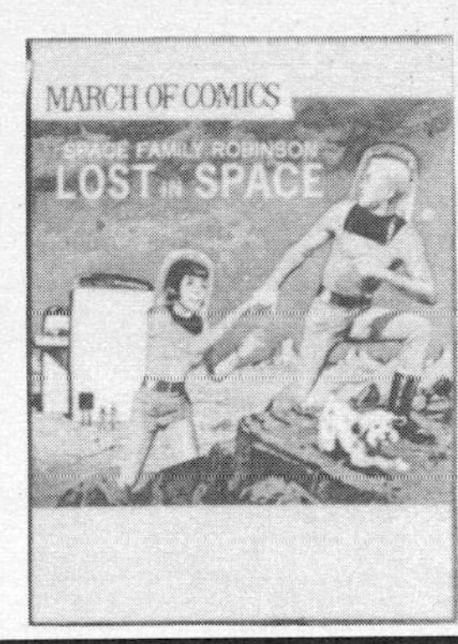

March of Comics #352, © WEST

	GD25	FN65	NM94
283-Santa's Visit	2.00	5.00	10.00
284-Christmas Parade (1965)	2.00	5.00	10.00
285-Astro Boy (TV); 2nd app. Astro Boy	29.00	85.00	200.00
286-Tarzan	6.70	20.00	40.00
287-Bugs Bunny	3.00	7.50	15.00
288-Daffy Duck	2.40	6.00	12.00
289-The Flintstones (TV)	7.50	22.50	45.00
290-Mister Ed (TV); photo-c	4.00	10.00	22.00
291-Yogi Bear (TV)	4.00	10.00	22.00
292-The Three Stooges; photo-c	8.35	25.00	50.00
293-Little Lulu; Irving Tripp-a	8.35	25.00	50.00
294-Popeye	4.00	12.00	24.00
295-Tom and Jerry	2.00	5.00	10.00
296-Lassie (TV); photo-c	3.60	9.00	18.00
297-Christmas Bells	2.00	5.00	10.00
298-Santa's Sleigh (1966)	2.00	5.00	10.00
299-The Flintstones (TV)(1967)	7.50	22.50	45.00
300-Tarzan	6.70	20.00	40.00
301-Bugs Bunny	2.40	6.00	12.00
302-Laurel and Hardy (TV); photo-c	4.70	14.00	28.00
303-Daffy Duck	1.60	4.00	8.00
304-The Three Stooges; photo-c	7.50	22.50	45.00
305-Tom and Jerry	1.60	4.00	8.00
306-Daniel Boone (TV); Fess Parker photo-c	4.70	14.00	28.00
307-Little Lulu; Irving Tripp-a	6.70	20.00	40.00
308-Lassie (TV); photo-c	3.20	8.00	16.00
309-Yogi Bear (TV)	4.00	10.00	20.00
310-The Lone Ranger; Clayton Moore photo-c	11.00	32.00	75.00
311-Santa's Show	2.00	5.00	10.00
312-Christmas Album (1967)	2.00	5.00	10.00
313-Daffy Duck (1968)	1.60	4.00	8.00
314-Laurel and Hardy (TV)	4.35	13.00	26.00
315-Bugs Bunny	2.40	6.00	12.00
316-The Three Stooges	6.35	19.00	38.00
317-The Flintstones (TV)	6.35	19.00	38.00
318-Tarzan	6.35	19.00	38.00
319-Yogi Bear (TV)	4.00	10.00	20.00
320-Space Family Robinson (TV); Spiegle-a	11.50	34.00	80.00
321-Tom and Jerry	1.60	4.00	8.00
322-The Lone Ranger	5.35	16.00	32.00
323-Little Lulu; not by Stanley	4.00	12.00	24.00
324-Lassie (TV); photo-c	3.20	8.00	16.00
325-Fun with Santa	2.00	5.00	10.00
326-Christmas Story (1968)	2.00	5.00	10.00
327-The Flintstones (TV)(1969)	6.35	19.00	38.00
328-Space Family Robinson (TV); Spiegle-a	11.50	34.00	80.00
329-Bugs Bunny	2.40	6.00	12.00
330-The Jetsons (TV)	10.00	30.00	65.00
331-Daffy Duck	1.60	4.00	8.00
332-Tarzan	5.00	15.00	30.00
333-Tom and Jerry	1.60	4.00	8.00
334-Lassie (TV)	2.80	7.00	14.00
335-Little Lulu	4.00	12.00	24.00
336-The Three Stooges	6.35	19.00	38.00
337-Yogi Bear (TV)	4.00	10.00	20.00
338-The Lone Ranger	5.35	16.00	32.00
339-(Was not published)			
340-Here Comes Santa (1969)	2.00	5.00	10.00
341-The Flintstones (TV)	6.35	19.00	38.00
342-Tarzan	5.00	15.00	30.00
343-Bugs Bunny	2.00	5.00	10.00
344-Yogi Bear (TV)	3.60	9.00	18.00
345-Tom and Jerry	1.60	4.00	8.00
346-Lassie (TV)	2.80	7.00	14.00
347-Daffy Duck	1.60	4.00	8.00
348-The Jetsons (TV)	9.15	27.50	55.00

	GD25	FN65	NM94
349-Little Lulu; not by Stanley	4.00	10.00	21.00
350-The Lone Ranger	4.70	14.00	28.00
351-Beep-Beep, the Road Runner (TV)	2.40	6.00	12.00
352-Space Family Robinson (TV); Spiegle-a	11.50	34.00	80.00
353-Beep-Beep, the Road Runner (1971) (TV)	2.40	6.00	12.00
354-Tarzan (1971)	4.35	13.00	26.00
355-Little Lulu; not by Stanley	4.00	10.00	21.00
356-Scooby Doo, Where Are You? (TV)	4.00	10.00	20.00
357-Daffy Duck & Porky Pig	1.60	4.00	8.00
358-Lassie (TV)	2.80	7.00	14.00
359-Baby Snoots	2.40	6.00	12.00
360-H. R. Pufnstuf (TV); photo-c	2.40	6.00	12.00
361-Tom and Jerry	1.60	4.00	8.00
362-Smokey the Bear (TV)	1.60	4.00	8.00
363-Bugs Bunny & Yosemite Sam	2.00	5.00	10.00
364-The Banana Splits (TV); photo-c	2.00	5.00	10.00
365-Tom and Jerry (1972)	1.60	4.00	8.00
366-Tarzan	4.00	12.00	24.00
367-Bugs Bunny & Porky Pig	2.00	5.00	10.00
368-Scooby Doo (TV)(4/72)	3.60	9.00	18.00
369-Little Lulu; not by Stanley	3.20	8.00	16.00
370-Lassie (TV); photo-c	2.80	7.00	14.00
371-Baby Snoots	2.00	5.00	10.00
372-Smokey the Bear (TV)	1.60	4.00	8.00
373-The Three Stooges	5.35	16.00	32.00
374-Wacky Witch	1.60	4.00	8.00
375-Beep-Beep & Daffy Duck (TV)	1.60	4.00	8.00
376-The Pink Panther (1972) (TV)	2.40	6.00	12.00
377-Baby Snoots (1973)	2.00	5.00	10.00
378-Turok, Son of Stone	13.00	40.00	90.00
379-Heckle & Jeckle New Terrytoons (TV)	1.60	4.00	8.00
380-Bugs Bunny & Yosemite Sam	1.60	4.00	8.00
381-Lassie (TV)	2.40	6.00	12.00
382-Scooby Doo, Where Are You? (TV)	2.80	7.00	16.00
383-Smokey the Bear (TV)	1.20	3.00	6.00
384-Pink Panther (TV)	1.60	4.00	8.00
385-Little Lulu	2.80	7.00	14.00
386-Wacky Witch	1.20	3.00	6.00
387-Beep-Beep & Daffy Duck (TV)	1.20	3.00	6.00
388-Tom and Jerry (1973)	1.20	3.00	6.00
389-Little Lulu; not by Stanley	2.80	7.00	14.00
390-Pink Panther (TV)	1.40	3.50	7.00
391-Scooby Doo (TV)	2.80	7.00	14.00
392-Bugs Bunny & Yosemite Sam	1.00	2.50	5.00
393-New Terrytoons (Heckle & Jeckle) (TV)	1.00	2.50	5.00
394-Lassie (TV)	1.60	4.00	8.00
395-Woodsy Owl	1.00	2.50	5.00
396-Baby Snoots	1.20	3.00	6.00
397-Beep-Beep & Daffy Duck (TV)	1.00	2.50	5.00
398-Wacky Witch	1.00	2.50	5.00
399-Turok, Son of Stone	10.00	30.00	70.00
400-Tom and Jerry	1.00	2.50	5.00
401-Baby Snoots (1975) (r/#371)	1.20	3.00	6.00
402-Daffy Duck (r/#313)	.80	2.00	4.00
403-Bugs Bunny (r/#343)	1.00	2.50	5.00
404-Space Family Robinson (TV)(r/#328)	10.00	30.00	60.00
405-Cracky	.80	2.00	4.00
406-Little Lulu (r/#355)	2.40	6.00	12.00
407-Smokey the Bear (TV)(r/#362)	1.00	2.50	5.00
408-Turok, Son of Stone	8.35	25.00	50.00
409-Pink Panther (TV)	.80	2.00	4.00
410-Wacky Witch	.60	1.50	3.00
411-Lassie (TV)(r/#324)	1.60	4.00	8.00
412-New Terrytoons (1975) (TV)	.60	1.50	3.00
413-Daffy Duck (1976)(r/#331)	.60	1.50	3.00
414-Space Family Robinson (r/#328)	8.35	25.00	50.00

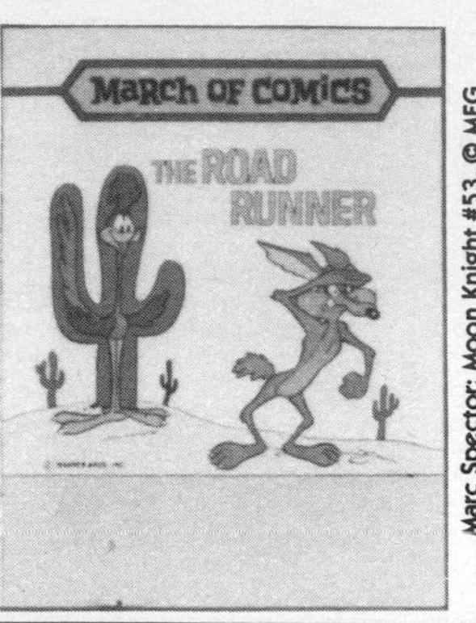

March of Comics #416, © Warner Bros.

Marc Spector: Moon Knight #53, © MEG

Marge's Little Lulu #58, © WEST

	GD25	FN65	NM94
415-Bugs Bunny (r/#329)	.60	1.50	3.00
416-Beep-Beep, the Road Runner (r/#353)(TV)	.60	1.50	3.00
417-Little Lulu (r/#323)	2.40	6.00	12.00
418-Pink Panther (r/#384) (TV)	.60	1.50	3.00
419-Baby Snoots (r/#377)	.80	2.00	4.00
420-Woody Woodpecker	.60	1.50	3.00
421-Tweety & Sylvester	.60	1.50	3.00
422-Wacky Witch (r/#386)	.60	1.50	3.00
423-Little Monsters	.80	2.00	4.00
424-Cracky (12/76)	.60	1.50	3.00
425-Daffy Duck	.60	1.50	3.00
426-Underdog (TV)	3.00	7.50	15.00
427-Little Lulu (r/#335)	1.60	4.00	8.00
428-Bugs Bunny	.60	1.50	3.00
429-The Pink Panther (TV)	.60	1.50	3.00
430-Beep-Beep, the Road Runner (TV)	.60	1.50	3.00
431-Baby Snoots	.80	2.00	4.00
432-Lassie (TV)	1.00	2.50	5.00
433-437: 433-Tweety & Sylvester. 434-Wacky Witch. 435-New Terrytoons (TV). 436-Wacky Advs. of Cracky. 437-Daffy Duck	.60	1.50	3.00
438-Underdog (TV)	3.00	7.50	15.00
439-Little Lulu (r/#349)	1.60	4.00	8.00
440-442,444-446: 440-Bugs Bunny. 441-The Pink Panther (TV). 442-Beep-Beep, the Road Runner (TV). 444-Tom and Jerry. 445-Tweety and Sylvester. 446-Wacky Witch	.60	1.50	3.00
443-Baby Snoots	.80	2.00	4.00
447-Mighty Mouse	1.20	3.00	6.00
448-455,457,458: 448-Cracky. 449-Pink Panther (TV). 450-Baby Snoots 451-Tom and Jerry. 452-Bugs Bunny. 453-Popeye. 454-Woody Woodpecker. 455-Beep-Beep, the Road Runner (TV). 457-Tweety & Sylvester. 458-Wacky Witch	.60	1.50	3.00
456-Little Lulu (r/#369)	1.20	3.00	6.00
459-Mighty Mouse	1.20	3.00	6.00
460-466: 460-Daffy Duck. 461-The Pink Panther (TV). 462-Baby Snoots. 463-Tom and Jerry. 464-Bugs Bunny. 465-Popeye. 466-Woody Woodpecker	.60	1.50	3.00
467-Underdog (TV)	2.40	6.00	12.00
468-Little Lulu (r/#385)	.80	2.00	4.00
469-Tweety & Sylvester	.60	1.50	3.00
470-Wacky Witch	.60	1.50	3.00
471-Mighty Mouse	.80	2.50	5.00
472-474,476-478: 472-Heckle & Jeckle(12/80). 473-Pink Panther(1/81)(TV). 474-Baby Snoots. 476-Bugs Bunny. 477-Popeye. 478-Woody Woodpecker	.60	1.50	3.00
475-Little Lulu (r/#323)	.80	2.00	4.00
479-Underdog (TV)	2.00	5.00	10.00
480-482: 480-Tom and Jerry. 481-Tweety and Sylvester. 482-Wacky Witch	.60	1.50	3.00
483-Mighty Mouse	.80	2.00	5.00
484-487: 484-Heckle & Jeckle. 485-Baby Snoots. 486-The Pink Panther (TV). 487-Bugs Bunny	.60	1.50	3.00
488-Little Lulu (4/82) (r/#335)	.80	2.00	4.00

MARCH OF CRIME (Formerly My Love Affair #1-6) (See Fox Giants)
No. 7, July, 1950 - No. 2, Sept, 1950; No. 3, Sept, 1951
Fox Features Syndicate

	GD25	FN65	NM94
7(#1)(7/50)-Wood-a	20.00	60.00	140.00
2(9/50)-Wood-a (exceptional)	20.00	60.00	140.00
3(9/51)	10.00	30.00	60.00

MARCO POLO
1962 (Movie classic)
Charlton Comics Group

	GD25	FN65	NM94
nn (Scarce)-Glanzman-c/a, 25pgs.	11.00	32.00	75.00

MARC SPECTOR: MOON KNIGHT (Also see Moon Knight)
June, 1989 - No. 60, Mar, 1994 ($1.50/$1.75, color, direct sale only)
Marvel Comics

	GD25	FN65	NM94
1		1.30	3.25
2-7: 4-Intro new Midnight		.90	2.25
8,9-Punisher app.	1.20	3.00	7.00
10-18: 20-Guice-c. 21-23-Cowan-c(p)		.90	2.25
19-21-Spider-Man & Punisher app.	1.10	2.70	6.50
22-24,26-31,34: 34-Last $1.50-c		.70	1.80
25-($2.50, 52 pgs.)-Ghost Rider app.		1.30	3.25
32,33-Hobgoblin II (Macendale) & Spider-Man (in black costume) app.		1.30	3.25
35-38-Punisher story		.90	2.25
39-49,51-54,58-60: 42-44-Infinity War x-over. 46-Demogoblin app. 51,53-Gambit app.		.70	1.75
50-($2.95)-Special die-cut cover		1.30	3.25
55-New look & Stephen Platt-c/a begin	1.00	2.00	5.00
56,57-Platt-c/a		1.20	3.00

MARGARET O'BRIEN (See The Adventures of...)

MARGE'S LITTLE LULU (Little Lulu #207 on)
No. 74, 6/45 - No. 164, 7-9/62; No. 165, 10/62 - No. 206, 8/72
Dell Publishing Co./Gold Key #165-206

Marjorie Henderson Buell, born in Philadelphia, Pa., in 1904, created Little Lulu, a cartoon character that appeared weekly in the Saturday Evening Post from Feb. 23, 1935 through Dec. 30, 1944. She was not responsible for any of the comic books. **John Stanley** did pen- cils only on all Little Lulu comics through at least #135 (1959). He did pencils and inks on Four Color #74 & 97. **Irving Tripp** began inking stories from #1 on, and remained the comic's illustrator throughout its entire run. **Stanley** did storyboards (layouts), pencils, and scripts in all cases and inking only on covers. His word balloons were written in cursive. **Tripp** and occasionally other artists at Western Publ. in Poughkeepsie, N.Y. blew up the pencilled pages, inked the blowups, and lettered them. **Arnold Drake** did storyboards, pencils and scripts starting with #197 (1970) on, amidst reprinted issues. **Buell** sold her rights exclusively to Western Publ. in Dec., 1971. The earlier issues had to be approved by **Buell** prior to publication.

	GD25	FN65	NM94
4-Color 74('45)-Intro Lulu, Tubby & Alvin	100.00	300.00	700.00
4-Color 97(2/46)	47.00	140.00	330.00
(Above two books are all John Stanley - cover, pencils, and inks.)			
4-Color 110('46)-1st Alvin Story Telling Time; 1st app. Willy	33.00	100.00	230.00
4-Color 115-1st app. Boys' Clubhouse	33.00	100.00	230.00
4-Color 120, 131: 120-1st app. Eddie	30.00	90.00	210.00
4-Color 139('47),146,158	27.00	81.00	190.00
4-Color 165 (10/47)-Smokes doll hair & has wild hallucinations. 1st Tubby detective story	27.00	81.00	190.00
1(1-2/48)-Lulu's Diary feature begins	56.00	168.00	390.00
2-1st app. Gloria; 1st Tubby story in a L.L. comic; 1st app. Miss Feeny	29.00	87.00	200.00
3-5	25.00	75.00	175.00
6-10: 7-1st app. Annie; Xmas-c	18.00	54.00	125.00
11-20: 19-1st app. Wilbur. 20-1st app. Mr. McNabbem	16.00	48.00	110.00
21-30: 26-r/F.C. 110. 30-Xmas-c	12.00	36.00	85.00
31-38,40: 35-1st Mumday story	10.00	30.00	65.00
39-Intro. Witch Hazel in "That Awful Witch Hazel"	11.00	32.00	75.00
41-60: 42-Xmas-c. 45-2nd Witch Hazel app. 49-Gives Stanley & others credit	10.00	30.00	60.00
61-80: 63-1st app. Chubby (Tubby's cousin). 68-1st app. Prof. Cleff. 78-Xmas-c. 80-Intro. Little Itch (2/55)	7.50	22.50	45.00
81-99: 90-Xmas-c	5.35	16.00	32.00
100	6.35	19.00	38.00
101-130: 123-1st app. Fifi	4.70	14.00	28.00
131-164: 135-Last Stanley-p	4.00	12.00	24.00
165-Giant; ...In Paris ('62)	6.35	19.00	38.00
166-Giant; ...Christmas Diary ('62-'63)	6.35	19.00	38.00
167-169	3.60	9.00	18.00
170,172,175,176,178-196,198-200-Stanley-r. 182-1st app. Little Scarecrow Boy	2.80	7.00	14.00
171,173,174,177,197	1.60	4.00	8.00
201,203,206-Last issue to carry Marge's name	1.20	3.00	6.00
202,204,205-Stanley-r	1.80	4.50	9.00

Marge's Tubby #32, © WEST

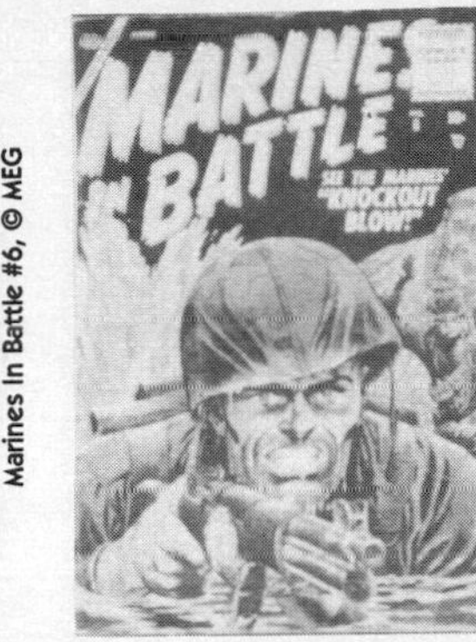

Marines In Battle #6, © MEG

Marmaduke Mouse #10, © QUA

GD25 FN65 NM94

...& Tubby in Japan (12¢)(5-7/62) 01476-207 9.15 27.50 55.00
...Summer Camp 1(8/67-G.K.-Giant) '57-58-r 6.35 19.00 38.00
...Trick 'N' Treat 1(12¢)(12/62-Gold Key) 7.50 22.50 45.00
NOTE: *See Dell Giant Comics #23, 29, 36, 42, 50, & Dell Giants for annuals. All Giants not by Stanley from L.L. on Vacation (7/54) on. Irving Tripp a-#1-on. Christmas c-7, 18, 30, 42, 78, 90, 126, 166, 250. Summer Camp issues #173, 177, 181, 189, 197, 201, 206.*

MARGE'S LITTLE LULU (See Golden Comics Digest #19, 23, 27, 29, 33, 36, 40, 43, 46, & March of Comics #251, 267, 275, 293, 307, 323, 335, 349, 355, 369, 385, 406, 417, 427, 439, 456, 468, 475, 488)

MARGE'S TUBBY (Little Lulu)(See Dell Giants)
No. 381, Aug, 1952 - No. 49, Dec-Feb, 1961-62
Dell Publishing Co./Gold Key

4-Color 381(#1)-Stanley script; Irving Tripp-a 14.00 43.00 100.00
4-Color 430,444-Stanley-a 9.15 27.50 55.00
4-Color 461 (4/53)-1st Tubby & Men From Mars story; Stanley-a 8.35 25.00 50.00
5 (7-9/53)-Stanley-a 6.70 20.00 40.00
6-10 4.00 12.00 26.00
11-20 4.00 10.50 22.00
21-30 3.60 9.00 20.00
31-49 3.20 8.00 18.00
...& the Little Men From Mars No. 30020-410(10/64-G.K.)-25 cents, 68 pgs. 8.35 25.00 50.00
NOTE: ***John Stanley** did all storyboards & scripts through at least #35 (1959). **Lloyd White** did all art except F.C. 381, 430, 444, 461 & #5.*

MARGIE (See My Little...)

MARGIE (TV)
No. 1307, Mar-May, 1962 - No. 2, July-Sept, 1962 (Photo-c)
Dell Publishing Co.

4-Color 1307(#1), 2 4.00 12.00 24.00

MARGIE COMICS (Formerly Comedy Comics; Reno Browne #50 on)
(Also see Cindy Comics & Teen Comics)
No. 35, Winter, 1946-47 - No. 49, Dec, 1949
Marvel Comics (ACI)

35 8.35 25.00 50.00
36-38,42,45,47-49 4.70 14.00 28.00
39,41,43(2),44,46-Kurtzman's "Hey Look" 6.35 19.00 38.00
40-Three "Hey Looks," three "Giggles & Grins" by Kurtzman 7.50 22.50 45.00

MARINES (See Tell It to the...)

MARINES ATTACK
Aug, 1964 - No. 9, Feb-Mar, 1966
Charlton Comics

1 2.40 6.00 12.00
2-9 1.20 3.00 6.00

MARINES AT WAR (Formerly Tales of the Marines #4)
No. 5, April, 1957 - No. 7, Aug, 1957
Atlas Comics (OPI)

5-7 3.60 9.00 18.00
NOTE: ***Colan** a-5. **Drucker** a-5. **Everett** a-5. **Maneely** a-5. **Orlando** a-7. **Severin** c-5.*

MARINES IN ACTION
June, 1955 - No. 14, Sept, 1957
Atlas News Co.

1-Rock Murdock, Boot Camp Brady begin 5.35 16.00 32.00
2-14 3.20 8.00 16.00
NOTE: ***Berg** a-2, 8, 9, 11, 14. **Heath** c-2, 9. **Maneely** c-1. **Severin** a-4; c-7-11, 14.*

MARINES IN BATTLE
Aug, 1954 - No. 25, Sept, 1958
Atlas Comics (ACI No. 1-12/WPI No. 13-25)

1-Heath-c; Iron Mike McGraw by Heath; history of U.S. Marine Corps. begins 9.15 27.50 55.00
2-Heath-c 4.70 14.00 28.00
3-6,8-10: 4-Last precode (2/55) 4.00 11.00 22.00
7-Kubert/Moskowitz-a (6 pgs.) 5.00 15.00 30.00
11-16,18-21,24 3.60 9.00 18.00
17-Williamson-a (3 pgs.) 6.35 19.00 38.00
22,25-Torres-a 4.00 11.00 22.00
23-Crandall-a; Mark Murdock app. 4.70 14.00 28.00
NOTE: ***Berg** a-22. **G. Colan** a-22, 23. **Drucker** a-6. **Everett** a-4, 15; c-21. **Heath** c-1, 2, 4. **Maneely** c-23, 24. **Orlando** a-14. **Pakula** a-6, 23. **Powell** a-16. **Severin** a-22; c-12. **Sinnott** a-23. **Tuska** a-15.*

MARINE WAR HEROES (Charlton Premiere #19 on)
Jan, 1964 - No. 18, Mar, 1967
Charlton Comics

1-Montes/Bache-c/a 2.40 6.00 12.00
2-18: 14,18-Montes/Bache-a 1.20 3.00 6.00

MARK, THE (Dark Horse)(Value: cover or less)(Also see Mayhem)

MARK HAZZARD: MERC (Marvel)(Value: cover or less)

MARK OF ZORRO (See 4-Color #228)

MARKSMAN, THE (Hero Comics)(Value: cover or less)(Also see Champions)

MARK STEEL
1967, 1968, 1972 (24 pgs.) (Color)
American Iron & Steel Institute (Giveaway)

1967,1968-"Journey of Discovery with..."; Neal Adams art 3.60 9.00 18.00
1972-"...Fights Pollution"; N. Adams-a 1.50 3.75 9.00

MARK TRAIL
Oct, 1955; No. 5, Summer, 1959
Standard Magazines (Hall Syndicate)/Fawcett Publ. No. 5

1(1955)-Sunday strip-r 5.00 15.00 30.00
5(1959) 3.60 9.00 18.00
...Adventure Book of Nature 1(Summer, 1958; Pines)-100 pg. Giant; contains 78 Sunday strip-r 7.50 22.50 45.00

MARMADUKE MONK
No date; 1963 (10 cents)
I. W. Enterprises/Super Comics

1-I.W. Reprint(nd), 14-(Super Reprint)(1963) .80 2.00 4.00

MARMADUKE MOUSE
Spring, 1946 - No. 65, Dec, 1956 (Early issues: 52 pgs.)
Quality Comics Group (Arnold Publ.)

1-Funny animal 10.00 30.00 70.00
2 5.85 17.50 35.00
3-10 4.70 14.00 28.00
11-30 4.00 10.00 20.00
31-65: Later issues are 36 pgs. 2.80 7.00 14.00
Super Reprint #14(1963) 1.40 3.50 7.00

MARRIED ... WITH CHILDREN (TV)
June, 1990 - No. 7, Feb, 1991(12/90 inside) ($1.75, color)
V2#1, Sept, 1991 - No. 12, 1992 ($1.95, color)
Now Comics

1-Based on Fox TV show 1.00 2.50 6.00
1-2nd printing ($1.75) 1.00 2.50
2-Photo-c 1.90 4.75
2-2nd printing ($1.75) .65 1.60
3 .80 2.00
4-7 .65 1.60
V2#1-12: 1,4,5,9-Photo-c .80 2.00
Special 1 (7/92, $1.95)-Kelly Bundy photo-c/poster .80 2.00

MARRIED ... WITH CHILDREN: KELLY BUNDY
Aug, 1992 - No. 3, Oct, 1992 ($1.95, color, mini-series)
Now Comics

1-3: Kelly Bundy photo-c & poster in each .80 2.00

Married ... With Children 2099 #3, © ELP Comm.

Marvel Chillers #3, © MEG

Marvel Comics Presents #61, © MEG

GD25 FN65 NM94 | GD25 FN65 NM94

MARRIED ... WITH CHILDREN: 2099
June, 1993 - No. 3, Aug, 1993 ($1.95, color, mini-series)
Now Comics
1-3 .80 2.00

MARS (First Comics)(Value: cover or less)

MARS & BEYOND (See 4-Color #866)

MARSHAL BLUEBERRY (See Blueberry)
1991 ($14.95, color, graphic novel)
Epic Comics (Marvel)
1-Moebius-a 2.15 6.50 15.00

MARSHAL LAW (Also see Crime And Punishment: Marshall Law...)
Oct, 1987 - No. 6, May, 1989 ($1.95, color, adults)
Epic Comics (Marvel)
1-6 .80 2.00

MARSHALL LAW - KINGDOM OF THE BLIND (Apocalypse Publishing) (Value: cover or less)

MARSHALL LAW: SUPER BABYLON (Dark Horse)(Value: cover or less)

M.A.R.S. PATROL TOTAL WAR (Formerly Total War #1,2)
No. 3, Sept, 1966 - No. 10, Aug, 1969 (All-Painted-c)
Gold Key
3-Wood-a 4.30 13.00 30.00
4-10 2.15 6.50 15.00

MARTHA WAYNE (See The Story of...)

MARTIAN MANHUNTER (DC, 1988)(Value: cover or less)(See Detective Comics)

MARTIAN MANHUNTER: AMERICAN SECRETS (DC Comics)(Value: cover or less)

MARTIN KANE (Formerly My Secret Affair) (Radio-TV)(Private Eye)
No. 4, June, 1950 - No. 2, Aug, 1950
Fox Features Syndicate (Hero Books)
4(#1)-Wood-c/a(2); used in **SOTI**, pg. 160; photo back cover
20.00 60.00 130.00
2-Orlando-a, 5pgs; Wood-a(2) 13.50 41.00 95.00

MARTY MOUSE
No date (1958?) (10 cents)
I. W. Enterprises
1-Reprint .80 2.00 4.00

MARVEL ACTION UNIVERSE (TV)
Jan, 1989 ($1.00, color, one-shot)
Marvel Comics
1-r/Spider-Man And His Amazing Friends 1.00

MARVEL ADVENTURES STARRING DAREDEVIL (Marvel)(Value: cover or less)

MARVEL AND DC PRESENT FEATURING THE UNCANNY X-MEN AND THE NEW TEEN TITANS
1982 ($2.00, one shot, 68 pgs., printed on Baxter paper)
Marvel Comics Group/DC Comics
1-3rd app. Deathstroke the Terminator; Darkseid app.; Simonson/Austin-c/a
1.65 4.00 10.00

MARVEL BOY (Astonishing #3 on; see Marvel Super Action #4)
Dec, 1950 - No. 2, Feb, 1951
Marvel Comics (MPC)
1-Origin Marvel Boy by Russ Heath 50.00 150.00 350.00
2-Everett-a 43.00 130.00 300.00

MARVEL CHILLERS (Also see Giant-Size Chillers)
Oct, 1975 - No. 7, Oct, 1976 (All 25 cent issues)
Marvel Comics Group
1-Intro. Modred the Mystic, ends #2; Kane-c(p) 1.30 3.25
2-7: 3-Tigra, the Were-Woman begins (origin), ends #7 (see Giant-Size Creatures #1). Chaykin/Wrightson-c. 4-Kraven app. 5,6-Red Wolf app. 6-Byrne-a(p); Buckler-c(p). 7-Kirby-c; Tuska-p .70 1.70

MARVEL CLASSICS COMICS SERIES FEATURING... (Also see Pendulum Illustrated Classics)
1976 - No. 36, Dec, 1978 (52 pgs., no ads)
Marvel Comics Group
1-Dr. Jekyll and Mr. Hyde 1.50 3.75
2-27,29-36 1.10 2.75
28-1st Golden-c/a; The Pit and the Pendulum 1.10 2.70 6.50
NOTE: ***Adkins** c-1i, 4i, 12i. **Alcala** a-34i; c-34. **Bolle** a-35. **Buscema** c-17p, 19p, 26p. **Golden** c/a-28. **Gil Kane** c-1-16p, 21p, 22p, 24p, 32p. **Nebres** a-5; c-24i. **Nino** a-2, 8, 12. **Redondo** a-1, 9. No. 1-12 were reprinted from Pendulum Illustrated Classics.*

MARVEL COLLECTOR'S EDITION
1992 (Ordered thru mail with Charleston Chew candy wrapper)
Marvel Comics
1-Flip-book format; Spider-Man, Silver Surfer, Wolverine (by Sam Kieth), & Ghost Rider stories; Wolverine back-c by Kieth .80 2.00

MARVEL COLLECTORS ITEM CLASSICS (Marvel's Greatest #23 on)
Feb, 1965 - No. 22, Aug, 1969 (68 pgs.)
Marvel Comics Group(ATF)
1-Fantastic Four, Spider-Man, Thor, Hulk, Iron Man-r begin; all are 25 cent cover price 6.50 19.00 45.00
2 (4/66) - 4 3.40 10.00 24.00
5-22: 22-r/The Man in the Ant Hill/TTA #27 1.65 4.00 10.00
NOTE: *All reprints; **Ditko, Kirby** art in all.*

MARVEL COMICS (Marvel Mystery Comics #2 on)
October, November, 1939
Timely Comics (Funnies, Inc.)
NOTE: The first issue was originally dated October 1939. Most copies have a black circle stamped over the date (on cover and inside) with "November" printed over it. However, some copies do not have the November overprint and could have a higher value. Most No. 1's have printing defects, i.e., tilted pages which caused trimming into the panels usually on right side and bottom. Covers exist with and without gloss finish.

GD25 FN65 VF82 NM94

1-Origin Sub-Mariner by Bill Everett(1st newsstand app.); 1st 8 pgs. were produced for Motion Picture Funnies Weekly #1 which was probably not distributed outside of advance copies; intro Human Torch by Carl Burgos, Kazar the Great (1st Tarzan clone), & Jungle Terror(only app.); intro. The Angel by Gustavson, The Masked Raider & his horse Lightning(ends #12); cover by sci/fi pulp illustrator Frank R. Paul
8,335.00 25,000.00 50,000.00 75,000.00
(Estimated up to 50 total copies exist, 4 in NM/Mint)

MARVEL COMICS PRESENTS
Early Sept, 1988 - Present ($1.25/$1.50, color, bi-weekly)
Marvel Comics

GD25 FN65 NM94

1-Wolverine by Buscema in #1-10 1.65 4.70 11.00
2-5 1.00 2.00 5.00
6-10: 6-Sub-Mariner app. 10-Colossus begins 1.40 3.50
11-32,34-37: 17-Cyclops begins. 19-1st app. Damage Control. 24-Havok begins. 25-Origin/1st app. Nth Man. 26-Hulk begins by Rogers. 29-Quasar app. 31-Excalibur begins by Austin (i). 37-Devil-Slayer app.
.80 2.00
33-Capt. America; Jim Lee-a 1.10 2.75
38-Wolverine begins by Buscema; Hulk app. 1.00 2.00 5.00
39-47,51-53: 39-Spider-Man app. 46-Liefeld Wolverine-c. 51-53-Wolverine by Rob Liefeld 1.10 2.75
48-50-Wolverine & Spider-Man team-up by Erik Larsen. 48-Wasp app. 49, 50-Savage Dragon prototype app. by Larsen. 50-Silver Surfer. 50-53-Comet Man; Bill Mumy scripts 1.00 2.50 5.50
54-61-Wolverine/Hulk; 54-Werewolf by Night begins; The Shroud by Ditko. 58-Iron Man by Ditko. 59-Punisher 1.00 2.50 6.00
62-Deathlok & Wolverine stories 1.25 3.00 7.50
63-Wolverine 1.50 3.75
64-71-Wolverine/Ghost Rider 8 part story. 70-Liefeld Ghost Rider/

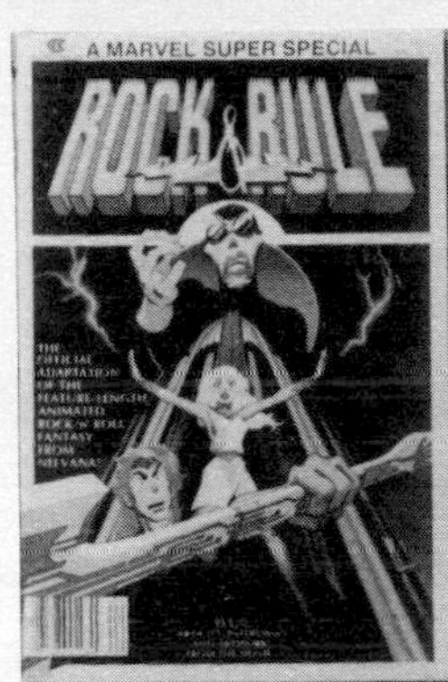

Marvel Comics Super Special #25, © Canada Trust Co.

Marvel Double Feature #18, © MEG

The Marvel Family #75, © DC

GD25 FN65 NM94

Wolverine-c 1.60 4.00
72-Begin 13 part Weapon-X story(Wolverine origin) by B. Windsor-Smith (prologue) 1.25 3.00 7.50
73-Weapon-X part 1; Black Knight, Sub-Mariner 1.00 2.00 5.00
74-Weapon-X part 2; Black Knight, Sub-Mariner 1.50 3.75
75-80: 77-Mr. Fantastic story. 78-Iron Man by Steacy. 80,81-Capt. America by Ditko/Austin 1.10 2.75
81-84: 81-Daredevil by Rogers/Williamson. 82-Power Man. 83-Human Torch by Ditko(a&scripts); $1.00-c direct, $1.25 newsstand. 84-Last Weapon-X (24 pg. conclusion) .90 2.25
85-Begin 8 part Wolverine story by Sam Keith (c/a); 1st Kieth-a on Wolverine; begin 8 part Beast story by Jae Lee(p) with Liefeld part pencils #85,86; 1st Jae Lee-a (assisted w/Liefeld, 1991) 1.25 3.00 7.50
86-89 1.50 3.75
90-Begin 8 part Ghost Rider & Cable story, ends #97; begin flip book format with two covers 1.90 4.75
91-94: 93-Begin 6 part Wolverine story, ends #98 1.10 2.75
95-98: 95-Begin $1.50-c. 98-Begin 2 part Ghost Rider story .70 1.80
99,101-107,112-116: 99-Spider-Man story. 101-Begin 6 part Ghost Rider/Dr. Strange story & begin 8 part Wolverine/Nightcrawler story by Colan/ Williamson; Punisher story. 107-Begin 6 part Ghost Rider/Werewolf by Night story. 112-Demogoblin story by Colan/Williamson; Pip the Troll story w/Starlin scripts & Gamora cameo. 113-Begin 6 part Giant-Man & begin 6 part Ghost Rider/Iron Fist stories .65 1.60
100-Full-length Ghost Rider/Wolverine story by Sam Keith w/Tim Vigil assists; anniversary issue, non flip-book 1.00 2.50
108-111: 108-Begin 4 part Thanos story; Starlin scripts. 109-Begin 8 part Wolverine/Typhoid Mary story. 111-Iron Fist .80 2.00
117-Preview of Ravage 2099 (1st app.); begin 6 part Wolverine/Venom story w/Kieth-a 1.00 2.50
118-Preview of Doom 2099 (1st app.) 1.00 2.50
119-142,147-150: 119-Begin Ghost Rider/Cloak & Dagger story by Colan. 120,136-Spider-Man. 123-Begin 8 part Ghost Rider/Typhoid Mary story; begin 4 part She Hulk story; begin 8 partWolverine/Lynx story. 125-Begin 6 part Iron Fist story. 131-Begin 6 part Ghost Rider/Cage story. 132-Begin 5 part Wolverine story. 133-136-Iron Fist vs. Sabretooth. 137-Begin 6 part Wolverine story & 6 part Ghost Rider story .70 1.80
143-146-($1.75)-Siege of Darkness parts 3,6,11,14; all have spot-varnished covers .70 1.75

NOTE: ***Austin*** *a-31-37i; c-48i, 50i, 99i.* ***Buscema*** *a-1-10, 38-47; c-6.* ***Byrne*** *a-79; c-71.* ***Colan*** *a(p)-36, 37.* ***Colan/Williamson*** *a-101-108.* ***Ditko*** *a-7p, 10, 56p, 58, 80, 81, 83.* ***Guice*** *a-62.* ***Sam Kieth*** *a-85-92, 117-122; c-85-98, 99p, 100-108, 118; back c-109-113, 117.* ***Liefeld*** *a-51, 52, 53p(2), 85p; c-46, 70.* ***McFarlane*** *c-32.* ***Mooney*** *a-73.* ***Rogers*** *a-26, 38, 46i, 81p.* ***Russell*** *c-4i* ***Saltares*** *a-8p(early), 38-45p.* ***Simonson*** *c-1.* ***B. Smith*** *a-72-84; c-72-84.* ***P. Smith*** *c-34.* ***Sparling*** *a-33.* ***Starlin*** *a-89i.* ***Staton*** *a-74.* ***Steacy*** *a-78.* ***Sutton*** *a-101-105.* ***Williamson*** *c-62i. Two Gun Kid by* ***Gil Kane*** *in #116, 122.*

MARVEL COMICS SUPER SPECIAL, A (Marvel Super Special #5 on)
1977 - No. 41(?), Nov, 1986 (nn 7) (Magazine; $1.50)
Marvel Comics Group

1-Kiss, 40 pgs. comics plus photos & features; Simonson-a(p); also see Howard the Duck #12 9.00 26.00 62.00
2-Conan (1978) 1.50
3-Close Encounters of the Third Kind (1978); Simonson-a 1.50
4-The Beatles Story (1978)-Perez/Janson-a; has photos & articles 1.65 4.70 11.00
5-Kiss (1978)-Includes poster 5.00 15.00 36.00
6-Jaws II (1978) 1.50
7-Sgt. Pepper; Beatles movie adaptation; withdrawn from U.S. distribution
8-Battlestar Galactica; tabloid size ($1.50, 1978); adapts TV show 1.50
8-Battlestar Galactica; publ. in reg. magazine format; low distribution ($1.50, 8-1/2x11") 1.50
9,10: 9-Conan. 10-Star-Lord 1.50
11-13-Weirdworld begins #11; 25 copy special press run of each with gold seal and signed by artists (Proof quality), Spring-June, 1979 9.00 26.00 62.00
11-13-Weirdworld (regular issues): 11-Fold-out centerfold 1.50

GD25 FN65 NM94

14-Miller-c(p); adapts movie "Meteor" 1.20
15-Star Trek with photos & pin-ups($1.50) 1.20
15-With $2.00 price (scarce); the price was changed at tail end of a 200,000 press run 80 2.00
16-20 (Movie adaptations): 16-Empire Strikes Back; Williamson-a. 17-Xanadu. 18-Raiders of the Lost Ark. 19-For Your Eyes Only (James Bond). 20-Dragonslayer .70 1.75
21-41 (Movie adaptations): 21-Conan. 22-Bladerunner; Williamson-a; Steranko-c. 23-Annie. 24-The Dark Crystal. 25-Rock and Rule-w/photos; artwork is from movie. 26-Octopussy (James Bond). 27-Return of the Jedi. 28-Krull; photo-c. 29-Tarzan of the Apes (Greystoke movie). 30-Indiana Jones and the Temple of Doom. 31-The Last Star Fighter. 32-The Muppets Take Manhattan. 33-Buckaroo Bonzai. 34-Sheena. 35-Conan The Destroyer. 36-Dune. 37-2010. 38-Red Sonja. 39-Santa Claus: The Movie. 40-Labyrinth. 41-Howard The Duck .70 1.75

NOTE: ***J. Buscema*** *a-1, 2, 9, 11-13, 18p, 21, 35, 40; c-11(part), 12.* ***Chaykin*** *a-9, 19p; c-18, 19.* ***Colan*** *a(p)-6, 10, 14.* ***Morrow*** *a-34; c-1i, 34.* ***Nebres*** *a-11.* ***Spiegle*** *a-29.* ***Stevens*** *a-27.* ***Williamson*** *a-27. #22-28 contain photos from movies.*

MARVEL DOUBLE FEATURE
Dec, 1973 - No. 21, Mar, 1977
Marvel Comics Group

1-Capt. America, Iron Man-r/T.O.S. begin 1.60 4.00
2-16,20,21 .80 2.00
17-Reprints story/Iron Man & Sub-Mariner #1 1.20 3.00
18,19-Colan/Craig-r from Iron Man #1 in both 1.60 4.00

NOTE: ***Colan*** *r-1-19p.* ***Craig*** *r-17-19i.* ***G. Kane*** *r-15p; c-15p.* ***Kirby*** *r-1-16p, 20, 21; c-17-20.*

MARVEL FAMILY (Also see Captain Marvel Adventures No. 18)
Dec, 1945 - No. 89, Jan, 1954
Fawcett Publications

1-Origin Captain Marvel, Captain Marvel Jr., Mary Marvel, & Uncle Marvel retold; origin/1st app. Black Adam 100.00 300.00 700.00
2-The 3 Lt. Marvels & Uncle Marvel app. 50.00 150.00 350.00
3 37.00 110.00 250.00
4,5 32.00 95.00 210.00
6-10: 7-Shazam app. 25.00 75.00 165.00
11-20 18.00 55.00 120.00
21-30 13.00 40.00 90.00
31-40 12.00 35.00 75.00
41-46,48-50 10.00 30.00 60.00
47-Flying Saucer-c/story 12.50 37.50 85.00
51-76,78-89: 78,81-Used in **POP**, pg. 92,93 10.00 30.00 60.00
77-Communist Threat-c 12.50 37.50 85.00

MARVEL FANFARE
March, 1982 - No. 60, Jan, 1992 ($1.25-$2.25, slick paper, direct sale)
Marvel Comics Group

1-Spider-Man/Angel team-up; 1st Paul Smith-a (1st full story; see King Conan #7); Daredevil app. 1.65 4.00 10.00
2-Spider-Man, Ka-Zar, The Angel. F.F. origin retold 1.00 2.50 5.50
3,4-X-Men & Ka-Zar. 4-Deathlok, Spidey app. 1.90 4.75
5-Dr. Strange, Capt. America 1.20 3.00
6-15: 6-Spider-Man, Scarlet Witch. 7-Incredible Hulk; D.D. back-up(also 15). 8-Dr. Strange; Wolf Boy begins. 9-Man-Thing. 10-13-Black Widow. 14-The Vision. 15-The Thing by Barry Smith, c/a 1.00 2.50
16-32,34-50: 16,17-Skywolf. 16-Sub-Mariner back-up. 17-Hulk back-up. 18-Capt. America by Miller. 19-Cloak and Dagger. 20-Thing/Dr. Strange. 21-Thing/Dr. Strange/Hulk. 22,23-Iron Man vs. Dr. Octopus. 24-26-Weird-world. 24-Wolverine back-up. 27-Daredevil/Spider-Man. 28-Alpha Flight. 29-Hulk. 30-Moon Knight. 31,32-Captain America. 34-37-Warriors Three. 38-Moon Knight/Dazzler. 39-Moon Knight/Hawkeye. 40-Angel/Rogue & Storm. 41-Dr. Strange. 42-Spider-Man. 43-Sub-Mariner/Human Torch. 44-Iron Man vs. Dr. Doom by Ken Steacy. 45-All pin-up issue by Steacy, Art Adams & others. 46-Fantastic Four. 47-Hulk. 48-She-Hulk/Vision. 49-Dr. Strange/Nick Fury. 50-X-Factor; begin $2.25-c 1.00 2.50
33-X-Men, Wolverine app.; Punisher pin-up 1.00 2.50 5.50
51-($2.95, 52 pgs.)-Silver Surfer; Fantastic Four & Capt. Marvel app.;

Marvel Feature #7 (11/76), © MEG

Marvel Masterpieces #4, © MEG

Marvel Milestone Edition Avengers #16, © MEG

GD25 FN65 NM94

51,52-Colan/Williamson back-up (Dr. Strange) 1.20 3.00
52,53: 52-54-Black Knight; 53-Iron Man back up 1.00 2.50
54,55-Wolverine back-ups. 55-Power Pack 1.20 3.00
56-60: 56-59-Shanna the She-Devil. 58-Vision & Scarlet Witch back-up. 60-Black Panther/Rogue/Daredevil stories 1.00 2.50

NOTE: ***Art Adams** c-13. **Austin** a-1i, 4i, 33i, 38i; c-8i, 33i. **Buscema** a-51p. **Byrne** a-1p, 29, 48; c-29. **Chiodo** painted c-56-59. **Colan** a-51p. **Cowan/Simonson** c/a-60. **Golden** a-1, 2, 4p, 47; c-1, 2, 47. **Infantino** c/a(p)-8. **Gil Kane** a-8-11p. **Miller** a-18; c-1(Back-c), 18. **Perez** a-10, 11p, 12, 13p; c-10-13p. **Rogers** a-5p; c-5p. **Russell** a-5i, 6i, 8-11i, 43i; c-5i, 6. **Paul Smith** a-1p, 4p, 32, 60; c-4p. Staton c/a-50(p). **Williamson** a-30i, 51i.*

MARVEL FEATURE (See Marvel Two-In-One)
Dec, 1971 - No. 12, Nov, 1973 (1,2: 25 cent giants)(1-3: Quarterly)
Marvel Comics Group

1-Origin/1st app. The Defenders (Sub-Mariner, Hulk & Dr. Strange); see Sub-Mariner #34,35 for prequel; Dr. Strange solo story (predates D.S. #1) plus 1950s Sub-Mariner-r; Neal Adams-c 10.00 30.00 68.00
2-2nd app. Defenders; 1950s Sub-Mariner-r 4.30 13.00 30.00
3-Defenders ends 4.30 13.00 30.00
4-Re-intro Antman(1st app. since 1960s), begin series; brief origin; Spider-Man app. 1.85 5.50 13.00
5-10: 6-Wasp app. & begins team-ups. 8-Origin Antman & Wasp-r/TTA #44. 9-Iron Man app. 10-Last Antman 1.00 2.50 5.50
10-(7/73)-Variant w/4 extra pgs. ads on slick paper 1.00 2.50 6.00
11-Thing vs. Hulk; 1st Thing solo book (9/73); origin Fantastic Four retold 1.25 3.00 7.50
12-Thing/Iron Man; early Thanos app.; occurs after Capt. Marvel #33; Starlin-a(p) 1.65 4.00 10.00

NOTE: ***Bolle** a-9i. **Everett** a-1i, 3i. **Hartley** r-10. **Kane** c-3p, 7p. **Russell** a-7-10p. **Starlin** a-8, 11, 12; c-8.*

MARVEL FEATURE (Also see Red Sonja)
Nov, 1975 - No. 7, Nov, 1976 (Story continues in Conan #68)
Marvel Comics Group

1-Red Sonja begins (pre-dates Red Sonja #1); adapts Howard short story; Adams-r/Savage Sword of Conan #1 1.50 3.75
2-7: Thorne-c/a in #2-7. 7-Battles Conan .90 2.25

MARVEL FUMETTI BOOK
April, 1984 (One shot) ($1.00 cover price)
Marvel Comics Group

1-All photos; Stan Lee photo-c; A. Adams touch-ups 1.00

MARVEL GRAPHIC NOVEL
1982 - Present ($5.95-$6.95)
Marvel Comics Group (Epic Comics)

1-Death of Captain Marvel (1st Marvel graphic novel); Capt. Marvel battles Thanos by Jim Starlin (c/a/scripts) 4.20 12.50 25.00
1 (2nd & 3rd printings) 1.20 3.00 5.50
2-Elric: The Dreaming City 1.60 4.00 8.50
3-Dreadstar; Starlin-c/a, 52 pgs. 1.40 3.50 7.50
4-Origin/1st app. The New Mutants (1982) 3.00 6.50 16.00
4,5-2nd printings 1.20 3.00 5.50
5-X-Men; book-length story (1982) 2.40 6.00 13.00
6-18: 6-The Star Slammers. 7-Killraven. 8-Super Boxers; Byrne scripts. 9-The Futurians. 10-Heartburst. 11-Void Indigo. 12-The Dazzler. 13-Starstruck. 14-The Swords Of The Swashbucklers. 15-The Raven Banner (Asgard). 16-The Aladdin Effect. 17-Revenge Of The Living Monolith. 18-She Hulk 1.20 3.00 5.50
19-32: 19-The Witch Queen of Acheron (Conan). 20-Greenberg the Vampire. 21-Marada the She-Wolf. 22-Amaz. Spider-Man in Hooky by Wrightson. 23-Dr. Strange. 24-Love and War (Daredevil); Miller scripts. 25-Alien Legion. 26-Dracula. 27-Avengers (Emperor Doom). 28-Conan the Reaver. 29-The Big Chance (Thing vs. Hulk). 30-A Sailor's Story. 31-Wolfpack. 32-Death of Groo 1.40 3.50 7.50
32-2nd printing ($5.95) 1.20 3.00 6.00
33,34,36,37: 33-Thor. 34-Predator & Prey (Cloak & Dagger). 36-Willow (movie adapt.). 37-Hercules 1.40 3.50 7.00
35-Hitler's Astrologer (Shadow, $12.95, hard-c) 1.85 5.50 13.00
35-Soft cover reprint (1990, $10.95) 1.65 4.70 11.00
38-Silver Surfer (Judgement Day)($14.95) 2.15 6.50 15.00
nn-Inhumans (1988, $7.95)-Williamson-i 1.30 3.25 8.00
nn-Last of the Dragons (1988, $6.95) 1.20 3.00 7.00
nn-Who Framed Roger Rabbit (1989, $6.95) 1.20 3.00 7.00
nn-Roger Rabbit In The Resurrection Of Doom (1989, $8.95) 1.50 3.75 9.00
nn-Arena by Bruce Jones ($5.95) 1.00 2.50 6.00

NOTE: ***Aragones** a-27, 32. **Byrne** c/a-18. **Kaluta** a-13, 35p; c-13. **Miller** a-24p. **Simonson** a-6; c-6. **Starlin** c/a-1,3. **Williamson** a-34. **Wrightson** c-29i.*

MARVEL HOLIDAY SPECIAL
1991 ($2.25, color, 84 pgs.); Jan, 1993 ($2.95, color, 68 pgs.)
Marvel Comics

1-X-Men, Fantastic Four, Punisher, Thor, Capt. America, Ghost Rider, Capt. Ultra, Spidey stories; Art Adams-c/a .90 2.25
nn-Wolverine, Thanos (by Starlin/Lim/Austin) 1.20 3.00

MARVEL ILLUSTRATED: SWIMSUIT ISSUE (See Marvel Swimsuit Spec.)
1991 ($3.95, color, magazine, 52 pgs.)
Marvel Comics

V1#1-Parody of Sports Illustrated swimsuit issue; Mary Jane Parker centerfold pin-up by Jusko; 2nd print exists 1.60 4.00

MARVEL MASTERPIECES COLLECTION, THE
May, 1993 - No. 4, Aug, 1993 ($2.95, color, coated paper, mini-series)
Marvel Comics

1-4-Reprints Marvel Masterpieces trading cards w/ new Jusko paintings in each; Jusko painted-c/a 1.20 3.00

MARVEL MILESTONE EDITION
1991 - Present ($2.95, coated stock)(r/originals with original ads w/silver ink-c)
Marvel Comics

...: X-Men #1-Reprints X-Men #1 (1991) 1.20 3.00
...: Giant Size X-Men #1-(1991, $3.95, 68 pgs.) 1.60 4.00
...: Fantastic Four #1 (11/91) 1.20 3.00
...: Incredible Hulk #1 (3/92, says 3/91 by error) 1.20 3.00
...: Amazing Fantasy #15 (3/92) 1.20 3.00
...: Fantastic Four #5 (11/92) 1.20 3.00
...: Amazing Spider-Man #129 (11/92) 1.20 3.00
...: Iron Man #55 (11/92) 1.20 3.00
...: Iron Fist #14 (11/92) 1.20 3.00
...: Amazing Spider-Man #1 (1/93) 1.20 3.00
...: Tales of Suspense #39 (3/93) 1.20 3.00
...: Avengers #1 (10/93) 1.20 3.00
...: X-Men #9 (10/93) 1.20 3.00
...: Avengers #16 (10/93) 1.20 3.00

MARVEL MINI-BOOKS
1966 (50 pgs., B&W; 5/8"x7/8") (6 different issues)
Marvel Comics Group (Smallest comics ever published)

Captain America, Spider-Man, Sgt. Fury, Hulk, Thor 1.70 5.00 12.00
Millie the Model 1.70 5.00 12.00

NOTE: *Each came in six different color covers, usually one color: Pink, yellow, green, etc.*

MARVEL MOVIE PREMIERE (Magazine)
Sept, 1975 (One Shot) (Black & White)
Marvel Comics Group

1-Burroughs' "The Land That Time Forgot" adaptation .80 2.00

MARVEL MOVIE SHOWCASE FEATURING STAR WARS
Nov, 1982 - No. 2, Dec, 1982 ($1.25, 68 pgs.)
Marvel Comics Group

1,2-Star Wars movie adaptation; reprints Star Wars #1-6 by Chaykin; 1-Reprints-c to Star Wars #1. 2-Stevens-r 1.25

MARVEL MOVIE SPOTLIGHT FEATURING RAIDERS OF THE LOST ARK
Nov, 1982 ($1.25, 68 pgs.)

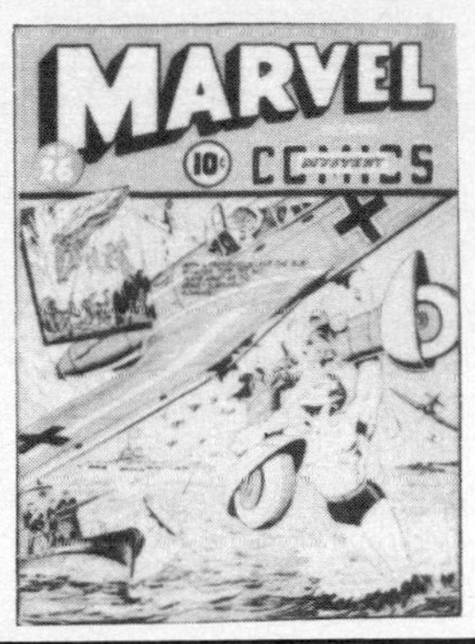
Marvel Mystery Comics #26, © MEG

Marvel Mystery Comics #90, © MEG

Marvel Premiere #49, © MEG

GD25 FN65 NM94 GD25 FN65 NM94

arvel Comics Group
1-Edited-r/Raiders of the Lost Ark #1-3; Buscema-c/a(p); movie adaptation 1.25

ARVEL MYSTERY COMICS (Formerly Marvel Comics) (Becomes Marvel ales No. 93 on)
o. 2, Dec, 1939 - No. 92, June, 1949
imely /Marvel Comics (TP #2-17/TCI #18-54/MCI #55-92)

GD25 FN65 VF82 NM94
2-American Ace begins, ends #3; Human Torch (blue costume) by Burgos, Sub-Mariner by Everett continue; 2 pg. origin recap of Human Torch 1190.00 3560.00 6550.00 9500.00
(Estimated up to 50 total copies exist, 5 in NM/Mint)
GD25 FN65 NM94
3-New logo from Marvel pulp begins 542.00 1630.00 3800.00
4-Intro. Electro, the Marvel of the Age (ends #19), The Ferret, Mystery Detective (ends #9); 1st Nazi war-c on a comic book & 1st German flag (Swastika) on-c of a comic (2/40) 433.00 1300.00 3000.00
GD25 FN65 VF82 NM94
5 (Scarce) 875.00 2625.00 4800.00 7000.00
(Estimated up to 75 total copies exist, 3 in NM/Mint)
GD25 FN65 NM94
6,7: 6-Gustavson Angel story 285.00 850.00 1900.00
8-1st Human Torch & Sub-Mariner battle(6/40) 350.00 1050.00 2300.00
GD25 FN65 VF82 NM94
9-(Scarce)-Human Torch & Sub-Mariner battle (cover/story) 815.00 2450.00 4475.00 6500.00
(Estimated up to 75 total copies exist, 6 in NM/Mint)
GD25 FN65 NM94
10-Human Torch & Sub-Mariner battle, conclusion; Torry Vance, the Schoolboy Sleuth begins, ends #57 267.00 800.00 1800.00
11 200.00 600.00 1400.00
12-Classic Kirby-c 185.00 560.00 1300.00
13-Intro. & 1st app. The Vision by S&K (11/40); Sub-Mariner dons new costume, ends #15 225.00 675.00 1500.00
14-16: 14-Shows-c to Human Torch #1 on-c (12/40). 15-S&K Vision, Gustavson Angel story 125.00 375.00 850.00
17-Human Torch/Sub-Mariner team-up by Burgos/Everett; pin-up on back-c; shows-c to Human Torch #2 on-c 142.00 425.00 950.00
18 117.00 350.00 800.00
19-Origin Toro in text; shows-c to Sub-Mariner #1 on-c 125.00 375.00 850.00
20-Origin The Angel in text 125.00 375.00 850.00
21-Intro. & 1st app. The Patriot (7/41); not in #46-48; pin-up on back-c 108.00 325.00 750.00
22-25: 23-Last Gustavson Angel; origin The Vision in text. 24-Injury-to-eye story 92.00 275.00 600.00
26-30: 27-Ka-Zar ends; last S&K Vision who battles Satan. 28-Jimmy Jupiter in the Land of Nowhere begins, ends #48; Sub-Mariner vs. The Flying Dutchman. 30-1st Japanese war-c 87.00 262.00 575.00
31-Sub-Mariner by Everett ends, begins again #84 83.00 250.00 550.00
32-1st app. The Boboes 83.00 250.00 550.00
33,35-40: 40-Zeppelin-c 83.00 250.00 550.00
34-Everett, Burgos, Martin Goodman, Funnies, Inc. office appear in story & battles Hitler; last Burgos Human Torch 96.00 288.00 625.00
41-43,45-48: 46-Hitler-c. 48-Last Vision; flag-c 75.00 225.00 500.00
44-Classic Super Plane-c 75.00 225.00 500.00
49-Origin Miss America 96.00 288.00 625.00
50-Mary becomes Miss Patriot (origin) 75.00 225.00 500.00
51-60: 53-Bondage-c. 60-Last Japanese war-c 67.00 200.00 450.00
61,62,64-Last German war-c 62.00 188.00 425.00
63-Classic Hitler War-c; The Villainess Cat-Woman only app. 67.00 200.00 450.00
65,66-Last Japanese War-c 62.00 188.00 425.00
67-75: 74-Last Patriot. 75-Young Allies begin 58.00 175.00 390.00
76-78: 76-Ten Chapter Miss America serial begins, ends #85 58.00 175.00 390.00
79-New cover format; Super Villains begin on cover; last Angel 58.00 175.00 390.00
80-1st app. Capt. America in Marvel Comics 72.00 218.00 475.00
81-Captain America app. 62.00 188.00 415.00
82-Origin & 1st app. Namora (5/47); 1st Sub-Mariner/Namora team-up; Captain America app. 108.00 325.00 720.00
83,85: 83-Last Young Allies. 85-Last Miss America; Blonde Phantom app. 54.00 162.00 375.00
84-Blonde Phantom begins (on-c of #84,88,89); Sub-Mariner by Everett begins; Captain America app. 75.00 225.00 500.00
86-Blonde Phantom i.d. revealed; Captain America app.; last Bucky app. 62.00 188.00 415.00
87-1st Capt. America/Golden Girl team-up 67.00 200.00 450.00
88-Golden Girl, Namora, & Sun Girl (1st in Marvel Comics) x-over; Captain America, Blonde Phantom app.; last Toro 62.00 188.00 415.00
89-1st Human Torch/Sun Girl team-up; 1st Captain America solo; Blonde Phantom app. 64.00 192.00 425.00
90-Blonde Phantom un-masked; Captain America app. 67.00 200.00 450.00
91-Capt. America app.; Blonde Phantom & Sub-Mariner end, early Venus app. (4/49) 67.00 200.00 450.00
92-Feature story on the birth of the Human Torch and the death of Professor Horton (his creator); 1st app. The Witness in Marvel Comics; Captain America app. 105.00 310.00 725.00
132 Pg. issue, B&W, 25 cents (1943-44)-printed in N. Y.; square binding, blank inside covers; has Marvel No. 33-c in color; contains Capt. America #18 & Marvel Mystery Comics #33; same contents as Captain America Annual (only three copies known to exist) 567.00 1700.00 3600.00

NOTE: ***Brodsky** c-49, 72, 86, 88-92. **Crandall** a-26i. **Everett** c-7-9, 27, 84. **Gabrielle** c-30-32. **Schomburg** c-3-11, 13-29, 33-36, 39-48, 50-59, 63-69, 74, 76, 132 pg. issue. **Shores** c-37, 38, 75p, 77, 78p, 79p, 80, 81p, 82-84, 85p, 87p. **Sekowsky** c-73. Bondage covers-3, 4, 7, 12, 28, 29, 49, 50, 52, 56, 57, 58, 59, 65. Angel c-2, 3, 8, 12. Remember Pearl Harbor issues-#30-32.*

MARVEL NO-PRIZE BOOK, THE (The Official... on-c)
Jan, 1983 (One Shot, Direct Sale only)
Marvel Comics Group
1-Golden-c 1.00

MARVEL PREMIERE
April, 1972 - No. 61, Aug, 1981 (A tryout book for new characters)
Marvel Comics Group
1-Origin Warlock (pre #1) by Gil Kane/Adkins; origin Counter-Earth; Hulk & Thor cameo (#1-14 are 25 cent-c) 6.50 19.00 45.00
2-Warlock ends; Kirby Yellow Claw-r 3.60 10.75 25.00
3-Dr. Strange series begins (pre #1, 7/72), B. Smith-a(p); Smith-c? 3.85 11.50 27.00
4-Smith/Brunner-a 1.65 4.70 11.00
5-9: 8-Starlin-c/a(p) 1.10 2.70 6.50
10-Death of the Ancient One 1.50 3.75 9.00
11-14: 11-Dr. Strange origin-r by Ditko. 14-Last Dr. Strange (3/74), gets own title 3 months later 1.80 4.50
15-Origin/1st app. Iron Fist (5/74), ends #25 6.50 19.00 45.00
16-24: Iron Fist in all. 16-Hama's 1st Marvel-a 1.85 5.50 13.00
25-1st Byrne Iron Fist (moves to own title next) 2.30 6.75 16.00
26,27: 26-Hercules. 27-Satana 1.80 4.50
28-Legion of Monsters (Ghost Rider, Man-Thing, Morbius, Werewolf) 1.70 5.00 12.00
29-49,51-56,61: 29,30-The Liberty Legion. 29-1st modern app. Patriot. 31-1st app. Woodgod; last 25 cent issue. 32-1st app. Monark Starstalker. 33,34-1st color app. Solomon Kane (Robert E. Howard adaptation "Red Shadows." 35-Origin/1st app. 3-D Man. 36,37-3-D Man. 38-1st Weirdworld. 39,40-Torpedo. 41-1st Seeker 3001! 42-Tigra. 43-Paladin. 44-Jack of Hearts (1st solo book, 10/78). 45,46-Man-Wolf. 47-Origin/1st app. new Ant-Man. 48-Ant-Man. 49-The Falcon (1st solo book, 8/79). 51-53-Black Panther. 54-1st Caleb Hammer. 55-Wonder Man. 56-1st color app. Dominic Fortune. 61-Star Lord .65 1.60
50-1st app. Alice Cooper; co-plotted by Alice 1.00 2.50 5.50
57-Dr. Who (1st U.S. app.) 1.40 3.50

Marvel Preview #18, © MEG

Marvel's Greatest Comics #77, © MEG

Marvel Spotlight #13, © MEG

GD25 FN65 NM94

58-60-Dr. Who .90 2.25

NOTE: ***N. Adams*** *(Crusty Bunkers) part inks-10, 12, 13.* ***Austin*** *a-50i, 56i; c-46i, 50i, 56i, 58.* ***Brunner*** *a-4i, 6p, 9-14p; c-9-14.* ***Byrne*** *a-47p, 48p.* ***Chaykin*** *a-32-34; c-32, 33, 56.* ***Giffen*** *a-31p, 44p; c-44.* ***Gil Kane*** *a(p)-1, 2, 15; c(p)-1, 2, 15, 16, 22-24, 27, 36, 37.* ***Kirby*** *c-26, 29-31, 35.* ***Layton*** *a-47i, 48i; c-47.* ***McWilliams*** *a-25i.* ***Miller*** *c-49p, 53p, 58p.* ***Nebres*** *a-44i; c-38i.* ***Nino*** *a-38i.* ***Perez*** *c/a-38p, 45p, 46p.* ***Ploog*** *a-38; c-5-7.* ***Russell*** *a-7p.* ***Simonson*** *a-60(2pgs.); c-57.* ***Starlin*** *a-8p; c-8.* ***Sutton*** *a-41, 43, 50p, 61; c-50p, 61. #57-60 published w/two different prices on-c.*

MARVEL PRESENTS
October, 1975 - No. 12, Aug, 1977 (#1-5 are 25 cent-c)
Marvel Comics Group

1-Origin & 1st app. Bloodstone 1.90 4.75
2-Origin Bloodstone continued; Kirby-c 1.70 4.25
3-Guardians of the Galaxy (1st solo book, 2/76) begins, ends #12 3.20 8.00 20.00
4-7,9-12: 9,10-Origin Starhawk 1.85 5.50 13.00
8-r/story from Silver Surfer #2 plus 4 pgs. new-a 2.15 6.50 15.00

NOTE: ***Austin*** *a-6i.* ***Buscema*** *r-8p.* ***Chaykin*** *a-5p.* ***Kane*** *c-1p.* ***Starlin*** *layouts-10.*

MARVEL PREVIEW (Magazine) (Bizarre Adventures #25 on)
Feb (no month), 1975 - No. 24, Winter, 1980 (B&W) ($1.00)
Marvel Comics Group

1-Man-Gods From Beyond the Stars; Crusty Bunkers (Neal Adams)-a(i) & cover; Nino-a .80 2.00
2-1st origin The Punisher (see Amaz. Spider-Man #129 & Classic Punisher); 1st app. Dominic Fortune; Morrow-c 22.00 65.00 150.00
3-7,9,10: 3-Blade the Vampire Slayer. 4-Star-Lord & Sword in the Star (origins & 1st app.). 5,6-Sherlock Holmes. 6-N. Adams frontispiece. 7-Satana, Sword in the Star app. 9-Man-God; origin Star Hawk, ends #20. 10-Thor the Mighty. 10,11-Starlin frontispiece in each .80 2.00
8-Legion of Monsters; Morbius app. 1.40 3.50 8.50
11-20,22-24: 11-Star-Lord; Byrne-a. 12-Haunt of Horror. 14,15-Star-Lord; 14-Starlin painted-c. 16-Masters of Terror. 17-Blackmark by G. Kane (see SSOC #1-3). 18-Star-Lord. 19-Kull. 20-Bizarre Advs. 22-King Arthur. 23-Bizarre Advs.; Miller-a. 24-Debut Paradox .80 2.00
21-Moon Knight (Spr/80)-Predates Moon Knight #1; The Shroud by Ditko 1.90 4.75

NOTE: ***N. Adams*** *(C. Bunkers) r-20i.* ***Buscema*** *a-22, 23.* ***Byrne*** *a-11.* ***Chaykin*** *a-20r; c-20 (new).* ***Colan*** *a-8, 16p(3), 18p, 23p; c-16p.* ***Elias*** *a-18.* ***Giffen*** *a-7.* ***Infantino*** *a-14p.* ***Kaluta*** *a-12; c-15.* ***Miller*** *a-23.* ***Morrow*** *a-8i; c-2-4.* ***Perez*** *a-20p.* ***Ploog*** *a-8.* ***Starlin*** *c-13, 14. Nudity in some issues*

MARVELS
Jan, 1994 - No. 4, Apr, 1994 ($5.95, color, mini-series, 52 pgs.)
Marvel Comics

1-4: Painted-c. 1-Double-c w/acetate overlay 1.00 2.50 6.00

MARVEL SAGA, THE
Dec, 1985 - No. 25, Dec, 1987
Marvel Comics Group

1 1.50
2-25 1.00

NOTE: ***Williamson*** *a(i)-9, 10; c(i)-7, 10-12, 14, 16.*

MARVEL'S GREATEST COMICS (Marvel Collectors Item Classics #1-22)
No. 23, Oct, 1969 - No. 96, Jan, 1981
Marvel Comics Group

23-30: Begin Fantastic Four-r/#30s?-116 1.20 3.00
31-34,38-96: 42-Silver Surfer-r/F.F.(others?) .80 2.00
35-37-Silver Surfer-r/Fantastic Four #48-50 .80 2.00

NOTE: *Dr. Strange, Fantastic Four, Iron Man, Watcher-#23, 24. Capt. America, Dr. Strange, Iron Man, Fantastic Four-#25-28. Fantastic Four-#38-96.* ***Buscema*** *r-85-92; c-87-92r.* ***Ditko*** *r-23-28.* ***Kirby*** *r-23-82; c-75, 77p, 80p. #81 reprints Fantastic Four #100.*

MARVELS OF SCIENCE
March, 1946 - No. 4, June, 1946
Charlton Comics

1-A-Bomb story 13.00 40.00 90.00
2-4 10.00 30.00 60.00

MARVEL SPECIAL EDITION FEATURING... (Also see Special Collectors' Ed.)
1975 - 1978 (84 pgs.) (Oversized)
Marvel Comics Group

1-The Spectacular Spider-Man ($1.50); r/Amazing Spider-Man #6,35, Annual 1; Ditko-a(r) .80 2.0
1-Star Wars (1977, $1.00); r/Star Wars #1-3 .80 2.0
2-Star Wars (1978, $1.00); r/Star Wars #4-6 1.5
3-Star Wars ('78, $2.50, 116pgs.); r/S. Wars #1-6 1.00 2.5
3-Close Encounters of the Third Kind (1978, $1.50, 56 pgs.)-Movie adaptation; Simonson-a(p) 1.5
V2#2(Spring, 1980, $2.00, oversized)-"Star Wars: The Empire Strikes Back;" r/Marvel Comics Super Special #16 1.5

NOTE: ***Chaykin*** *c/a(r)-1(1977), 2, 3.* ***Stevens*** *a(r)-2i, 3i.* ***Williamson*** *a(r)-V2#2.*

MARVEL SPECTACULAR
Aug, 1973 - No. 19, Nov, 1975
Marvel Comics Group

1-Thor-r from mid-sixties begin by Kirby .80 2.0
2-19 1.5

MARVEL SPOTLIGHT (...& Son of Satan #19, 20, 23, 24)
Nov, 1971 - No. 33, Apr, 1977; V2#1, July, 1979 - V2#11, Mar, 1981
Marvel Comics Group (A try-out book for new characters)

1-Origin Red Wolf (western hero)(1st solo book, pre #1); Wood inks, Neal Adams-c; only 15 cent issue 3.20 8.00 20.0
2-(25 cents, 52 pgs.)-Venus-r by Everett; origin/1st app. Werewolf By Night (begins) by Ploog; N. Adams-c 5.00 15.00 35.0
3,4: 4-Werewolf By Night ends (6/72); gets own title 9/72 1.70 5.00 12.0
5-Origin/1st app. Ghost Rider (8/72) & begins 16.00 50.00 115.0
6-8: 6-Origin G.R. retold. 8-Last Ploog issue 7.00 21.00 50.0
9-11-Last Ghost Rider (gets own title next mo.) 5.50 17.00 40.0
12-Origin & 2nd full app. The Son of Satan (10/73); story cont'd from Ghost Rider #2 & into #3; series begins, ends #24 1.50 3.75 9.0
12-Variant w/4 extra pgs. of ads on slick paper plus a Mark Jeweler pull-out centerfold ad 1.65 4.00 10.00
13-21,23,24: 13-Partial origin Son of Satan. 14-Last 20 cent issue. 24-Last Son of Satan (10/75); gets own title 12/75 1.60 4.00
22-Ghost Rider-c & cameo (5 panels) 1.50 3.75 9.00
25-27,30,31: 25-Sinbad; contains pull-out Mark Jewelers ad. 26-Scarecrow. 27-Sub-Mariner. 30-The Warriors Three. 31-Nick Fury 1.20 3.0
28,29: Moon Knight. 28-1st solo Moon Knight app., 6/76). 29-Last 25 cent issue 1.65 4.00 10.00
32-1st app./partial origin Spider-Woman (2/77); Nick Fury app. 1.25 3.00 7.50
33-Deathlok; 1st app. Devil-Slayer 1.25 3.00 7.50
V2#1-11: 1-4,8-Capt. Marvel. 5-Dragon Lord. 6,7-StarLord; origin #6. 9-11-Capt. Universe (see Micronauts #8) 1.00

NOTE: ***Austin*** *c-V2#2i, 8.* ***J. Buscema*** *c/a-30p.* ***Chaykin*** *a-31; c-26, 31.* ***Colan*** *a-18p, 19p.* ***Ditko*** *a-V2#4, 5, 9-11; c-V2#4, 9-11.* ***Kane*** *c-21p, 32p.* ***Kirby*** *c-29p.* ***McWilliams*** *a-20i.* ***Miller*** *a V2#8p; c(p)-V2#2, 5, 7, 8.* ***Mooney*** *a-8i, 10i, 14p, 15, 16p, 17p, 24p, 27, 32i.* ***Nasser*** *a-33p.* ***Ploog*** *a-2-5, 6-8p; c-3-9.* ***Romita*** *c-13.* ***Sutton*** *a-9-11p, V2#6, 7. #29-25 cent & 30 cent issues exist.*

MARVEL SUPER ACTION (Magazine)
January, 1976 (One Shot) (76 pgs.; black & white)
Marvel Comics Group

1-Origin/2nd app. Dominic Fortune(see Marv. Preview); early Punisher app.; Weird World & The Huntress; Evans, Ploog-a 11.50 34.00 80.00

MARVEL SUPER ACTION
May, 1977 - No. 37, Nov, 1981
Marvel Comics Group

1-Reprints Capt. America #100 by Kirby 1.00 2.50
2,3,5-13: r/Capt. America #101,102,103-111. 11-Origin-r. 12,13-Classic Steranko-c/a(r) 1.50
4-Marvel Boy-r(origin)/M. Boy #1 1.50
14-37: r/Avengers #55,56, Annual 2, others. 30-r/Hulk #6 from U.K. 1.00

Marvel Super-Heroes #1 (10/66), © MEG

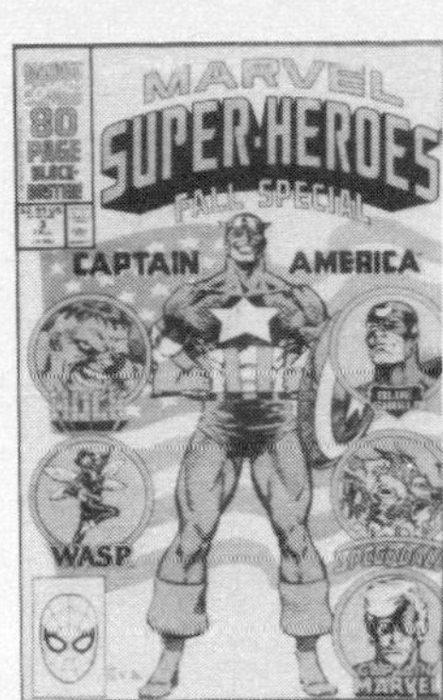

Marvel Super-Heroes V2#3, © MEG

Marvel Tales #135, © MEG

GD25 FN65 NM94

NOTE: ***Buscema*** *a(r)-14p, 15p; c-18-20, 22, 35r-37.* ***Everett*** *a-4.* ***Heath*** *a-4r.* ***Kirby*** *r-1-3, 5-11.* ***B. Smith*** *a-27r, 28r.* ***Steranko*** *a(r)-12p, 13p; c-12r, 13r.*

MARVEL SUPER HERO CONTEST OF CHAMPIONS
June, 1982 - No. 3, Aug, 1982 (Mini-Series)
Marvel Comics Group

1-3: Features nearly all Marvel characters currently appearing in their comics; 1st Marvel limited series 1.60 4.00

MARVEL SUPER HEROES
October, 1966 (25 cents, 68 pgs.) (1st Marvel One-shot)
Marvel Comics Group

1-r/origin Daredevil from D.D. #1; r/Avengers #2; G.A. Sub-Mariner-r/ Marvel Mystery #8 (Human Torch app.) 9.00 28.00 65.00

MARVEL SUPER-HEROES (Formerly Fantasy Masterpieces #1-11)
(Also see Giant-Size Super Heroes) (#12-20: 25 cents, 68 pgs.)
No. 12, 12/67 - No. 31, 11/71; No. 32, 9/72 - No. 105, 1/82
Marvel Comics Group

12-Origin & 1st app. Capt. Marvel of the Kree; G.A. Human Torch, Destroyer, Capt. America, Black Knight, Sub-Mariner-r (#12-20 all contain new stories and reprints) 15.00 45.00 105.00
13-2nd app. Capt. Marvel; G.A. Black Knight, Torch, Vision, Capt. America, Sub-Mariner-r 7.00 21.00 50.00
14-Amazing Spider-Man (5/68, new-a by Andru/Everett); G.A. Sub-Mariner, Torch, Mercury (1st Kirby-a at Marvel), Black Knight, Capt. America reprints 14.00 41.00 95.00
15-Black Bolt cameo in Medusa (new-a); Black Knight, Sub-Mariner, Black Marvel, Capt. America-r 2.15 6.50 15.00
16-Origin & 1st app. S. A. Phantom Eagle; G.A. Torch, Capt. America, Black Knight, Patriot, Sub-Mariner-r 2.15 6.50 15.00
17-Origin Black Knight (new-a); G.A. Torch, Sub-Mariner-r; reprint from All-Winners Squad #21 (cover & story) 2.15 6.50 15.00
18-Origin/1st app. Guardians of the Galaxy (1/69); G.A. Sub-Mariner, All-Winners Squad-r 9.00 26.00 60.00
19-Ka-Zar (new-a); G.A. Torch, Marvel Boy, Black Knight, Sub-Mariner reprints; Smith-c(p); Tuska-a(r) 1.70 5.00 12.00
20-Doctor Doom (5/69); r/Young Men #24 w/-c 1.70 5.00 12.00
21-31: All-r issues. 21-X-Men-r begin? 31-Last Giant issue 1.00 2.50 5.50
32-105: 32-Hulk/Sub-Mariner-r begin from TTA. 56-r/origin Hulk/Inc. Hulk #102; Hulk-r begin 1.00

NOTE: ***Austin*** *a-104.* ***Colan*** *a(p)-12, 13, 15, 18; c-12, 13, 15, 18.* ***Everett*** *a-14i(new); r-14, 15i, 18, 19, 33; c-85(r). New* ***Kirby*** *c-22, 27.* ***Maneely*** *r-14, 15, 19.* ***Severin*** *r-83-85i, 100-102; c-100-102r.* ***Starlin*** *c-47.* ***Tuska*** *a-19p. Black Knight-r by* ***Maneely*** *in 12-16, 19. Sub-Mariner-r by* ***Everett*** *in 12-20.*

MARVEL SUPER-HEROES
May, 1990 - Present ($2.95-$2.25/$2.50, quarterly, 68-84 pgs.)
Marvel Comics

1-Moon Knight, Hercules, Black Panther, Magik, Brother Voodoo, Speedball (by Ditko) & Hellcat; Hembeck-a 1.20 3.00
2,4,5: 2-Rogue, Speedball (by Ditko), Iron Man, Falcon, Tigra & Daredevil. 4-Spider-Man/Nick Fury, Daredevil, Speedball, Wonder Man, Spitfire & Black Knight; Byrne-c. 5-Thor, Dr. Strange, Thing & She-Hulk; Speedball by Ditko(p) 1.20 3.00
V2#3-Retells origin Capt. America w/new facts; Blue Shield, Capt. Marvel, Speedball, Wasp; Hulk by Ditko/Rogers 1.20 3.00
V2#6-9: 6-8-$2.25-c. 6,7-X-Men, Cloak & Dagger, The Shroud (by Ditko) & Marvel Boy in each. 8-X-Men, Namor & Iron Man (by Ditko). 9-W.C. Avengers, Iron Man app.; Kieth-c(p); begin $2.50-c 1.00 2.50
V2#10-Ms. Marvel/Sabretooth-c/story (intended for Ms. Marvel #24; shows-c to #24); Namor, Vision, Scarlet Witch stories 1.00 2.50
V2#11,12: 11-Ghost Rider-c/story (origin); Giant-Man, Ms. Marvel stories. 12-Dr. Strange, Falcon, Iron Man 1.00 2.50
V2#13-15 ($2.75, 84 pgs.): 13-All Iron Man issue; 30th anniversary. 15-Iron Man/Thor/Volstagg/Dr. Druid 1.10 2.75

MARVEL SUPER HEROES SECRET WARS (See Secret Wars II)

May, 1984 - No. 12, Apr, 1985 (Limited series)
Marvel Comics Group

1 1.40 3.50
1-3-2nd printings (sold in multi-packs) 1.00
2-7,9-12: 6-The Wasp dies. 7-Intro. new Spider-Woman. 12-($1.00, 52 pgs.) .80 2.00
8-Spider-Man's new black costume explained as Alien costume (later becomes Venom) 2.60 7.50 18.00

MARVEL SUPER SPECIAL A (See Marvel Comics Super...)

MARVEL SWIMSUIT SPECIAL (Also see Marvel Illustrated...)
1992 ($3.95, color, magazine, 52 pgs.)
Marvel Comics

1-Silvestri-c; pin-ups by many good artists 1.60 4.00

MARVEL TAILS STARRING PETER PORKER THE SPECTACULAR SPIDER-HAM
Nov, 1983 (One Shot)
Marvel Comics Group

1-Peter Porker, the Spectacular Spider-Ham, Captain Americat, Goose Rider, Hulk Bunny app. 1.50

MARVEL TALES (Formerly Marvel Mystery Comics #1-92)
No. 93, Aug, 1949 - No. 159, Aug, 1957
Marvel/Atlas Comics (MCI)

93-Horror/weird stories begin 64.00 193.00 450.00
94-Everett-a 46.00 140.00 325.00
95,96,99,101,103,105: 95-New logo 33.00 100.00 230.00
97-Sun Girl, 2 pgs; Kirbyish-a; one story used in N.Y. State Legislative document 38.00 115.00 265.00
98-Krigstein-a 33.00 100.00 230.00
100 33.00 100.00 230.00
102-Wolverton-a "The End of the World," 6 pgs. 44.00 135.00 310.00
104-Wolverton-a "Gateway to Horror," 6 pgs. 41.00 122.00 285.00
106,107-Krigstein-a. 106-Decapitation story 27.00 81.00 190.00
108-120: 118-Hypo-c/panels in End of World story. 120-Jack Katz-a 18.00 54.00 125.00
121,123-131: 128-Flying Saucer-c. 131-Last precode (2/55) 13.50 41.00 95.00
122-Kubert-a 14.00 43.00 100.00
132,133,135-141,143,145 10.00 30.00 60.00
134-Krigstein, Kubert-a; flying saucer-c 11.00 32.00 75.00
142-Krigstein-a 10.00 30.00 60.00
144-Williamson/Krenkel-a, 3 pgs. 10.00 30.00 60.00
146,148-151,154,155,158 7.50 22.50 45.00
147-Ditko-a 10.00 30.00 60.00
152-Wood, Morrow-a 10.00 30.00 60.00
153-Everett End of World c/story 10.00 30.00 65.00
156-Torres-a 7.50 22.50 45.00
157,159-Krigstein-a 9.15 27.50 55.00

NOTE: ***Andru*** *a-103.* ***Briefer*** *a-118.* ***Check*** *a-147.* ***Colan*** *a-105, 107, 118, 120, 121, 127, 131.* ***Drucker*** *a-127, 135, 141, 146, 150.* ***Everett*** *a-98, 104, 106(2), 108(2), 131, 148, 151, 153, 155; c-107, 109, 111, 112, 114, 117, 127, 143, 147-151, 153, 155, 156.* ***Forte*** *a-119, 125, 130.* ***Heath*** *a-110, 113, 118, 119, c-104-106, 110, 130.* ***Gil Kane*** *a-117.* ***Lawrence*** *a-130.* ***Maneely*** *a-111, 126, 129; c-108, 116, 120, 129, 152.* ***Mooney*** *a-114.* ***Morisi*** *a-153.* ***Morrow*** *a-150, 152, 156.* ***Orlando*** *a-149, 151, 157.* ***Pakula*** *a-119, 121, 135, 144, 150, 152, 156.* ***Powell*** *a-136, 137, 150, 154.* ***Ravielli*** *a-117.* ***Rico*** *a-97, 99.* ***Romita*** *a-108.* ***Sekowsky*** *a-96-98.* ***Shores*** *a-110; c-96.* ***Sinnott*** *a-105, 116.* ***Tuska*** *a-114.* ***Whitney*** *a-107.* ***Wildey*** *a-126, 138.*

MARVEL TALES (...Annual #1,2; ...Starring Spider-Man #123 on)
1964 - Present (No. 1-32: 72 pgs.)
Marvel Comics Group (NPP earlier issues)

1-Reprints origins of Spider-Man/Amazing Fantasy #15, Hulk/Inc. Hulk#1, Ant-Man/T.T.A. #35, Giant Man/T.T.A. #49, Iron Man/T.O.S. #39,48, Thor/ J.I.M. #83 & r/Sgt. Fury #1 28.00 83.00 220.00
2 ('65)-r/X-Men #1(origin), Avengers #1(origin), origin Dr. Strange-r/Strange Tales #115 & origin Hulk(Hulk #3) 10.00 30.00 70.00
3 (7/66)-Spider-Man, Strange Tales, Journey into Mystery, Tales to

Marvel Tales #192, © MEG

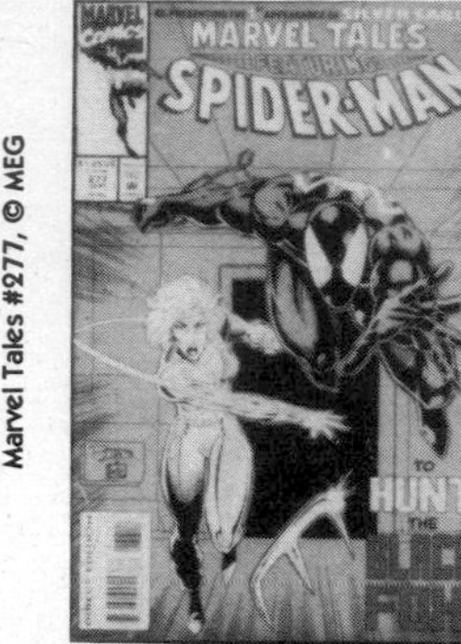

Marvel Tales #277, © MEG

Marvel Team-Up #128, © MEG

GD25 FN65 NM94

Astonish-r begin (r/Strange Tales #101) 4.30 13.00 30.00
4,5 2.00 6.00 14.00
6-8,10: 10-Reprints 1st Kraven/Amaz. S-M #15 1.50 3.75 9.00
9-r/Amazing Spider-Man #14 w/cover 1.65 4.70 11.00
11-32: 11-Spider-Man battles Daredevil-r/Amaz. Spider-Man #16. 13-Origin Marvel Boy-r/M. Boy #1. 22-Green Goblin-c/story-r/Amaz. Spider-Man #27. 30-New Angel story. 32-Last 72 pg. issue 1.00 2.50 5.50
33-105: 33-Kraven-r; 52 pgs. 34-Begin reg. size issues. 75-Origin Spider-Man-r. 77-79-Drug issues-r/A. Spider-Man #96-98. 98-Death of Gwen Stacy-r/A. Spider-Man #121 (Green Goblin). 99-Death Green Goblin-r/A. Spider-Man #122. 100-(52 pgs.)-New Hawkeye/Two Gun Kid story. 101-105-All Spider-Man-r 1.50
106-1st Punisher-r/Amazing Spider-Man #129 1.50 3.75 9.00
107-133-All Spider-Man-r. 111,112-r/Spider-Man #134,135 (Punisher). 113, 114-r/Spider-Man #136,137(Green Goblin) 1.00
134-136-Dr. Strange-r begin; SpM stories continue. 134-Dr. Strange-r/ Strange Tales #110 1.00
137-Origin-r Dr. Strange; shows original unprinted-c & origin Spider-Man/ Amazing Fantasy #15 1.80 4.50
137-Nabisco giveaway 1.00
138-Reprints all Amazing Spider-Man #1; begin reprints of Spider-Man with covers similar to originals 1.80 4.50
139-144: r/Amazing Spider-Man #2-7 .80 2.00
145-191,193-199: Spider-Man-r continue w/#8 on. 149-Contains skin "Tattooz." 150-($1.00, 52pgs.)-r/Spider-Man Annual 1(Kraven app.). 153-r/1st Kraven/Spider-Man #15. 155-r/2nd Gr. Goblin/Spider-Man #17. 161,164,165-Gr. Goblin-c/stories-r/Spider-Man #23,26,27. 178,179-Green Goblin-c/story-r/Spider-Man #39,40. 187,189-Kraven-r. 191-($1.50, 68pgs.)-r/Spider-Man #96-98. 193-Byrne-r/Marvel Team-Up begin w/scripts 1.20
192-($1.25, 52 pgs.)-r/Spider-Man #121,122 .80 2.00
200-Double size ($1.25)-Miller-c & r/Annual #14 1.50
201-208,210-222: 208-Last Byrne-r. 210,211-r/Spidey 134,135. 212,213-r/ Gnt. Size Spidey 4. 213-r/1st solo Silver Surfer story/F.F. Annual #5. 214, 215-r/Spidey 161,162. 222-Reprints origin Punisher/Spectacular Spider-Man #83; last Punisher reprint 1.00
209-Reprints 1st app. The Punisher/Amazing Spider-Man #129; Punisher reprints begin, end #222 1.00 2.50
223-McFarlane-c begin, end #239 1.50
224-249,251,252,254-257: 233-Spider-Man/X-Men team-ups begin; r/X-Men #35. 234-r/Marvel Team-Up #4. 235,236-r/M. Team-Up Annual #1. 237, 238-r/M. Team-Up #150. 239,240-r/M. Team-Up #38,90(Beast). 242-r/M. Team-Up #89. 243-r/M. Team-Up #117(Wolverine). 251-r/Spider-Man #100(Gr. Goblin-c/story). 252-r/1st app. Morbius/Amaz. Spider-Man #101. 254-r/M. Team-Up #15(Ghost Rider); new painted-c. 255,256-Spider-Man & Ghost Rider-r/Marvel Team-Up #58,91. 257-Hobgoblin-r begin(r/A. Spider-Man #238); last $1.00-c 1.00
250-($1.50, 52pgs.)-r/1st Karma/M. Team-Up #100 1.50
253-($1.50, 52 pgs.)-r/Amaz. S-M #102 1.50
258-284: 258-261-r/A. Spider-Man #239,249-251(Hobgoblin). 262,263-r/Marv. Team-Up #53,54. 262-New X-Men vs. Sunstroke story. 263-New Wood-god origin story. 264,265-r/A. Spider-Man Annual 5. 266-273-Reprints alien costume stories/A. S-M 252-259. 277-r/1st Silver Sable/A. S-M #265 1.25

NOTE: *All contain reprints; some have new art. #89-97-r/Amazing Spider-Man #110-118; #98-136-r/#121-159; #137-150-r/Amazing Fantasy #15, #1-12 & Annual 1; #151-167-r/#13-28 & Annual 2; #168-186-r/#29-46.* **Austin** *a-100i; c-272i, 273i.* **Byrne** *a(r)-193-198p, 201-208p.* **Ditko** *a-1-30, 83, 100, 137-155.* **G. Kane** *a-71, 81, 98-101p, 249r; c-125-127p, 130p, 137-155.* **Sam Kieth** *c-255, 262, 263.* **Ron Lim** *c-266p-278p.* **McFarlane** *c-223-239.* **Mooney** *a-63, 95-97i, 103(i).* **Nasser** *a-100p.* **Nebres** *a-242i.* **Perez** *c-259-261.* **Rogers** *c-240, 241, 243-251.*

MARVEL TEAM-UP (See Marvel Treasury Edition #18 & Official Marvel Index To...)
March, 1972 - No. 150, Feb, 1985
Marvel Comics Group
NOTE: *Spider-Man team-ups in all but Nos. 18, 23, 26, 29, 32, 35, 97, 104, 105, 137.*

1-Human Torch 10.00 30.00 70.00
2-Human Torch 3.60 10.75 25.00

GD25 FN65 NM94

3-Spider-Man/Human Torch vs. Morbius (part 1) 5.50 16.00 38.00
4-Spider-Man/X-Men vs. Morbius (part 2 of story) 7.00 21.00 48.00
5-10: 5-Vision. 6-Thing. 7-Thor. 8-The Cat (4/73, came out between The Cat #3 & 4). 9-Iron Man. 10-H-T 1.85 5.50 13.00
11-14,16-20: 11-Inhumans. 12-Werewolf. 13-Capt. America. 14-Sub-Mariner. 16-Capt. Marvel. 17-Mr. Fantastic. 18-H-T/Hulk. 19-Ka-Zar. 20-Black Panther; last 20 cent issue 1.50 3.75 9.00
15-1st Spider-Man/Ghost Rider team-up (11/73) 2.15 6.50 15.00
21-30: 21-Dr. Strange. 22-Hawkeye. 23-H-T/Iceman (X-Men cameo). 24-Brother Voodoo. 25-Daredevil. 26-H-T/Thor. 27-Hulk. 28-Hercules. 29-H-T/Iron Man. 30-Falcon 1.00 2.50 6.00
31-45,47-50: 31-Iron Fist. 32-H-T/Son of Satan. 33-Nighthawk. 34-Valkyrie. 35-H-T/Dr. Strange. 36-Frankenstein. 37-Man-Wolf. 38-Beast. 39-H-T. 40-Sons of the Tiger/H-T. 41-Scarlet Witch. 42-The Vision. 43-Dr. Doom; retells origin. 44-Moondragon. 45-Killraven. 47-Thing. 48-Iron Man; last 25 cent issue. 49-Dr. Strange; Iron Man app. 50-Iron Man; Dr. Strange app. 1.00 2.00 5.00
46-Spider-Man/Deathlok team-up 1.70 5.00 12.00
51,52,56,57: 51-Iron Man; Dr. Strange app. 52-Capt. America. 56-Daredevil. 57-Black Widow 1.60 4.00
53-Hulk; Woodgod & X-Men app., 1st Byrne-a on X-Men (1/77) 1.85 5.50 13.00
54,59,60: 54-Hulk; Woodgod app. 59-Yellowjacket/The Wasp. 60-The Wasp (Byrne-a in all) 1.20 3.00 6.00
55-Warlock-c/story; Byrne-a 1.60 4.00 8.00
58-Ghost Rider 1.00 2.50 6.00
61-70: All Byrne-a; 61-H-T. 62-Ms. Marvel; last 30 cent issue. . 63-Iron Fist. 64-Daughters of the Dragon. 65-Capt. Britain (1st U.S. app.). 66-Capt. Britain; 1st app. Arcade. 67-Tigra; Kraven the Hunter app. 68-Man-Thing. 69-Havok (from X-Men). 70-Thor 1.20 3.00
71-74,76-78,80: 71-Falcon. 72-Iron Man. 73-Daredevil. 74-Not Ready for Prime Time Players (Belushi). 76-Dr. Strange. 77-Ms. Marvel. 78-Wonder Man. 80-Dr. Strange/Clea; last 35 cent issue 1.20 3.00
75,79: Byrne-a(p). 75-Power Man. 79-Mary Jane Watson as Red Sonja; Clark Kent cameo (1 panel, 3/79) 1.20 3.00
81-85,87,88,90,92-99: 81-Satana. 82-Black Widow. 83-Nick Fury. 84-Shang-Chi. 92-Hawkeye. 93-Werewolf by Night. 94-SpM vs. The Shroud. 95-Mockingbird (intro.); Nick Fury app. 96-Howard the Duck; last 40 cent issue. 97-Spider-Woman/Hulk. 98-Black Widow. 99-Machine Man. 85-Shang-Chi/Black Widow/Nick Fury. 87-Black Panther. 88-Invisible Girl. 90-Beast .80 2.00
86-Guardians of the Galaxy 1.60 4.00
89-Nightcrawler (from X-Men) 1.20 3.00
91-Ghost Rider 1.00 2.00 5.00
100-(Double-size)-Fantastic Four/Storm/Black Panther; origin/1st app. Karma, one of the New Mutants; origin Storm; X-Men x-over; Miller-c/a(p); Byrne-a (on X-Men app. only) 1.30 3.25 8.00
101-116: 101-Nighthawk(Ditko-a). 102-Doc Samson. 103-Ant-Man. 104-Hulk/ Ka-Zar. 105-Hulk/Powerman/Iron Fist. 106-Capt. America. 107-She-Hulk. 108-Paladin; Dazzler cameo. 109-Dazzler; Paladin app. 110-Iron Man. 111-Devil-Slayer. 112-King Kull; last 50 cent issue. 113-Quasar. 114-Falcon. 115-Thor. 116-Valkyrie 1.50
117-Wolverine-c/story 1.70 5.00 12.00
118-140,142-149: 118-Professor X; Wolverine app. (4 pgs.); X-Men cameo. 119-Gargoyle. 120-Dominic Fortune. 121-Human Torch. 122-Man-Thing. 123-Daredevil. 124-The Beast. 125-Tigra. 126-Hulk & Powerman/Son of Satan. 127-The Watcher. 128-Capt. America; Spider-Man/Capt. America photo-c. 129-The Vision. 130-Scarlet Witch. 131-Frogman. 132-Mr. Fantastic. 133-Fantastic Four. 134-Jack of Hearts. 135-Kitty Pryde; X-Men cameo. 136-Wonder Man. 137-Aunt May/Franklin Richards. 138-Sandman. 139-Nick Fury. 140-Black Widow. 142-Capt. Marvel. 143-Starfox. 144-Moon Knight. 145-Iron Man. 146-Nomad. 147-Human Torch; SpM back to old costume. 148-Thor. 149-Cannonball 1.50
141-Daredevil; SpM/Black Widow app. (Spidey in new black costume; ties w/ Amaz. S-M #252 for 1st black costume) 1.20 3.00
150-X-Men ($1.00, double-size); B. Smith-c 1.40 3.50

Marvel Treasury Special (1976), © MEG

Marvel Two-In-One Annual #7, © MEG

Mary Marvel Comics #3, © DC

GD25 FN65 NM94

Annual 1(1976)-SpM/X-Men (early app.) 2.00 6.00 14.00
Annuals 2-7: 2(1979)-SpM/Hulk. 3(1980)-Hulk/Power Man/Machine Man/Iron Fist; Miller-c(p). 4(1981)-SpM/Daredevil/Moon Knight/Power Man/Iron Fist; brief origins of each; Miller-c; Miller scripts on Daredevil. 5(1982)-SpM/The Thing/Scarlet Witch/Dr. Strange/Quasar. 6(1983)-SpM/New Mutants (early app.), Cloak & Dagger. 7(1984)-Alpha Flight; Byrne-c(i) .80 2.00

NOTE: ***Art Adams*** *c-141p.* ***Austin*** *a-79i; c-76i, 79i, 96i, 101i, 112i, 130i.* ***Bolle*** *a-9i.* ***Byrne*** *a(p)-53-55, 59-70, 75, 79, 100; c-68p, 70p, 72p, 75, 76p, 79p, 129i, 133i.* ***Colan*** *a-87p.* ***Ditko*** *a-101.* ***Kane*** *a(p)-4-6, 13, 14, 16-19, 23; c(p)-4, 13, 14, 17-19, 23, 25, 26, 32-35, 37, 41, 44, 45, 47, 53, 54.* ***Miller*** *a-100p; c-95p, 99p, 100p, 102p, 106.* ***Mooney*** *a-2i, 7i, 8, 10p, 11p, 16i, 24-31p, 72, 93i, Annual 5i.* ***Nasser*** *a-89p; c-101p.* ***Simonson*** *c-99i, 148.* ***Paul Smith*** *c-131, 132.* ***Starlin*** *c-27.* ***Sutton*** *a-93p. "H-T" means Human Torch; "SpM" means Spider-Man; "S-M" means Sub-Mariner.*

MARVEL TREASURY EDITION ($1.50-$2.50)
1974; No 2, Dec, 1974 - No. 28, 1981 (100 pgs.; oversized, new-a &-r)
Marvel Comics Group

1-Spectacular Spider-Man; story-r/Marvel Super-Heroes #14; Romita-c/a(r); G. Kane, Ditko-r; Green Goblin/Hulk-r 1.00 2.00 5.00
1-1,000 numbered copies signed by Stan Lee & John Romita on front-c & sold thru mail for $5.00; 1st 1,000 copies off the press 1.70 5.00 12.00
2-4: 2-Fantastic Four-r/F.F. 6,11,48-50(Silver Surfer). 3-The Mighty Thor-r/Thor #125-130. 4-Conan the Barbarian; Barry Smith-c/a(r)/Conan #11 1.00 2.50
5-14,16,17: 5-The Hulk (origin-r/Hulk #3). 6-Dr. Strange. 7-Mighty Avengers. 8-Giant Superhero Holidy Grab-Bag; Spider-Man, Hulk, Nick Fury. 9-Giant; Super-hero Team-up. 10-Thor; r/Thor #154-157. 11-Fantastic Four. 12-Howard the Duck(r/#H. the Duck #1 & G.S. Man-Thing #4,5) plus new Defenders story. 13-Giant Super-Hero Holiday Grab-Bag. 14-The Sensational Spider-Man; r/1st Morbius from Amazing S-M #101,102 plus #100 & r/Not Brand Echh #6. 16-The Defenders (origin) & Valkyrie; r/Defenders #1,4,13,14. 17-The Hulk .80 2.00
15-Conan; B. Smith, Neal Adams-i; r/Conan #24 1.00 2.50
18-The Astonishing Spider-Man; r/Spider-Man's 1st team-ups with Iron Fist, The X-Men, Ghost Rider & Werewolf by Night; inside back-c has photos from 1978 Spider-Man TV show .80 2.00
19-20: 19-Conan the Barbarian. 20-Hulk. 21-Fantastic Four. 22-Spider-Man. 23-Conan. 24-Rampaging Hulk. 25-Spider-Man vs. The Hulk. 26-The Hulk; Wolverine app. 27-Spider-Man. 28-Spider-Man/Superman; (origin of each) 1.60 4.00

NOTE: *Reprints-2, 3, 5, 7-9, 13, 14, 16, 17.* ***Neal Adams*** *a(i)-6, 15.* ***Brunner*** *a-6, 12; c-6.* ***Buscema*** *a-15, 19, 28; c-28.* ***Colan*** *a-6r; c-12p.* ***Ditko*** *a-1, 6.* ***Gil Kane*** *c-16p.* ***Kirby*** *a-2, 10, 11; c-7.* ***Romita*** *c-1, 5.* ***B. Smith*** *a-4, 15, 19; c-4, 19.*

MARVEL TREASURY OF OZ FEATURING THE MARVELOUS LAND OF OZ
1975 ($1.50, oversized) (See MGM's Marvelous...)
Marvel Comics Group

1-Buscema-a; Romita-c .80 2.00

MARVEL TREASURY SPECIAL (Also see 2001: A Space Odyssey)
1974; 1976 ($1.50, oversized, 84 pgs.)
Marvel Comics Group

Vol. 1-Spider-Man, Torch, Sub-Mariner, Avengers "Giant Superhero Holiday Grab-Bag;" Wood, Colan/Everett, plus 2 Kirby-r; reprints Hulk vs. Thing from Fantastic Four #25,26 1.50
Vol. 1-... Featuring Captain America's Bicentennial Battles (6/76)-Kirby-a; B. Smith inks, 11 pgs. 1.50

MARVEL TRIPLE ACTION (See Giant-Size...)
Feb, 1972 - No. 24, Mar, 1975; No. 25, Aug, 1975 - No. 47, Apr, 1979
Marvel Comics Group

1-(25 cent giant, 52pgs.)-Dr. Doom, Silver Surfer, The Thing begin, end #4 ('66 reprints from Fantastic Four) 1.20 3.00
2-47: 45-r/X-Men #45. 46-r/Avengers #53(X-Men) 1.00

NOTE: *#5-44, 46, 47 reprint Avengers #11 thru ?. #40-r/Avengers #48(1st Black Knight).* ***Buscema*** *a(r)-35p, 36p, 38p, 39p, 41, 42, 43p, 44p, 46p, 47p.* ***Ditko*** *a-2r; c-47.* ***Kirby*** *a(r)-1-4p.* ***Starlin*** *c-7.* ***Tuska*** *a(r)-40p, 43i, 46i, 47i. #2 through at least #17 are 20 cent-c.*

GD25 FN65 NM94

MARVEL TWO-IN-ONE (...Featuring ... #82? on; see The Thing)
January, 1974 - No. 100, June, 1983
Marvel Comics Group

1-Thing team-ups begin; Man-Thing 3.60 10.75 25.00
2-4: 2-Sub-Mariner; last 20 cent issue. 3-Daredevil. 4-Capt. America 1.65 4.00 10.00
5-Guardians of the Galaxy (9/74, 2nd app.?) 2.40 7.25 17.00
6-Dr. Strange (11/74) 2.15 6.50 15.00
7,9,10 1.10 2.70 6.50
8-Early Ghost Rider app. (3/75) 1.65 4.70 11.00
11-20: 13-Power Man. 14-Son of Satan (early app.). 17-Spider-Man. 18-Last 25 cent issue 1.70 4.25
21-26,28,29,31-40: 29-Master of Kung Fu; Spider-Woman cameo. 39-Vision 1.30 3.25
27-Deathlok 1.10 2.70 6.50
30-2nd full app. Spider-Woman (see Marvel Spotlight #32 for 1st app.) 1.00 2.50 5.50
41,42,44-49: 42-Capt. America. 45 Capt. Marvel. 46-Thing battles Hulk-c/story 1.50
43,50,53,55-Byrne-a(p). 53-Quasar(7/79, 2nd app.) 1.00 2.50
51-The Beast, Nick Fury, Ms. Marvel; Miller-p 1.20 3.00
52-Moon Knight app. 1.20 3.00
54-Death of Deathlok; Byrne-a 2.15 6.50 15.00
56-60,64-68,70-79,81,82: 60-Intro. Impossible Woman. 68-Angel. 71-1st app. Maelstrom. 75-Avengers (52 pgs.). 76-Iceman 1.00
61-63: 61-Starhawk (from Guardians); "The Coming of Her" storyline begins, ends #63; cover similar to F.F. #67 (Him-c). 62-Moondragon; Thanos & Warlock cameo in flashback; Starhawk app. 63-Warlock?; Warlock revived shortly; Starhawk & Moondragon app. .80 2.00
69-Guardians of the Galaxy 1.60 4.00
80-Ghost Rider 1.00 2.50 6.00
83,84: 83-Sasquatch. 84-Alpha Flight app. .80 2.00
85-99: 90-Spider-Man. 93-Jocasta dies. 96-X-Men-c & cameo 1.00
100-Double size, Byrne scripts 1.50
Annual 1 (1976, 52 pgs.)-Thing/Liberty Legion .80 2.00
Annual 2(1977, 52 pgs.)-Thing/Spider-Man; 2nd death of Thanos; end of Thanos saga; Warlock app.; Starlin-c/a 3.60 10.75 25.00
Annual 3,4 ('78-79, 52 pgs.): 3-Nova. 4-Black Bolt 1.50
Annual 5-7: 5(1980, 52 pgs.)-Hulk. 6(1981, 52 pgs.)-1st app. American Eagle. 7(1982, 52 pgs.)-The Thing/Champion; Sasquatch, Colossus app. 1.00

NOTE: ***Austin*** *c(i)-42, 54, 56, 58, 61, 63, 66.* ***John Buscema*** *a-30p, 45; c-30p.* ***Byrne*** *(p)-43, 50, 53-55; c-43, 53p, 56p, 98i, 99i.* ***Gil Kane*** *a-1p, 2p; c(p)-1-3, 9, 11, 14, 28.* ***Kirby*** *c-10, 12, 19p, 20, 25, 27.* ***Mooney*** *a-18i, 38i, 90i.* ***Nasser*** *a-70p.* ***Perez*** *a(p)-56-58, 60, 64, 65; c(p)-32, 33, 42, 50-52, 54, 55, 57, 58, 61-66, 70.* ***Roussos*** *a-Annual 1i.* ***Simonson*** *c-43i, 97p, Annual 6i.* ***Starlin*** *c-6, Annual 1.* ***Tuska*** *a-6p.*

MARVEL UNIVERSE (See Official Handbook Of The...)

MARVIN MOUSE
September, 1957
Atlas Comics (BPC)

1-Everett-c/a; Maneely-a 6.70 20.00 40.00

MARY JANE & SNIFFLES (See 4-Color #402, 474 & Looney Tunes)

MARY MARVEL COMICS (Monte Hale #29 on) (Also see Captain Marvel #18, Marvel Family, Shazam, & Wow Comics)
Dec, 1945 - No. 28, Sept, 1948
Fawcett Publications

1-Captain Marvel introduces Mary on-c; intro/origin Georgia Sivana 83.00 250.00 550.00
2 42.00 125.00 275.00
3,4: 3-New logo 30.00 90.00 200.00
5-8: 8-Bulletgirl x-over in Mary Marvel; X-Mas-c 20.00 60.00 135.00
9,10 17.00 50.00 110.00
11-20 11.50 34.00 80.00
21-28: 28-Western-c 10.00 30.00 70.00

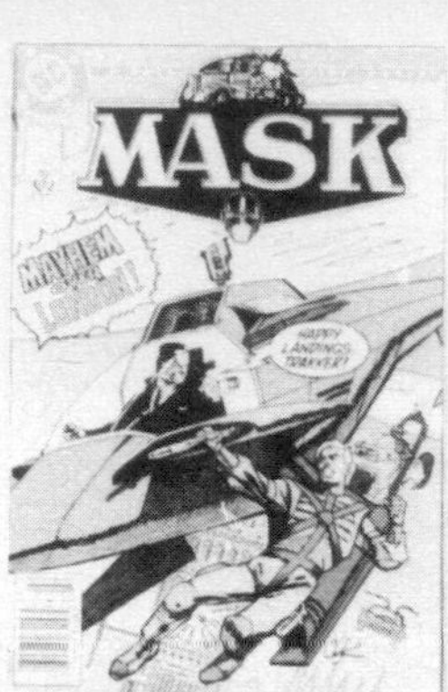

Mask #3 (DC)(2/86), © CPG Products, Corp.

Masked Ranger #6, © PG

Master Comics #92, © FAW

GD25 FN65 NM94

MARY POPPINS (See Movie Comics & Walt Disney Showcase No. 17)

MARY'S GREATEST APOSTLE (St. Louis Grignion de Montfort)
No date (16 pages; paper cover)
Catechetical Guild (Topix) (Giveaway)

	GD25	FN65	NM94
nn	2.40	6.00	12.00

MARY WORTH (See Harvey Comics Hits #55 & Love Stories of...)
March, 1956 (Also see Romantic Picture Novelettes)
Argo

	GD25	FN65	NM94
1	5.00	15.00	30.00

MASK (TV)(DC Comics, 1985 & 1987)(Value: cover or less)

MASK, THE (Dark Horse)Value: cover or less)

MASK RETURNS, THE (Dark Horse)(Value: cover or less)

MASK COMICS
Feb-Mar, 1945 - No. 2, Apr-May, 1945; No. 2, Fall, 1945
Rural Home Publications

	GD25	FN65	NM94
1-Classic L. B. Cole Satan-c/a; Palais-a	93.00	280.00	650.00
2-(Scarce)-Classic L. B. Cole Satan-c; Black Rider, The Boy Magician, & The Collector app.	54.00	160.00	375.00
2-(Fall, 1945)-No publ.-same as regular #2; L. B. Cole-c	38.00	115.00	265.00

MASKED BANDIT, THE
1952
Avon Periodicals

	GD25	FN65	NM94
nn-Kinstler-a	10.00	30.00	70.00

MASKED MAN, THE (Eclipse)(Value: cover or less)

MASKED MARVEL (See Keen Detective Funnies)
Sept, 1940 - No. 3, Dec, 1940
Centaur Publications

	GD25	FN65	NM94
1-The Masked Marvel begins	117.00	350.00	750.00
2,3: 2-Gustavson, Tarpe Mills-a	83.00	250.00	550.00

MASKED RAIDER, THE (Billy The Kid #9 on; Frontier Scout, Daniel Boone #10-13; also see Blue Bird)
June, 1955 - No. 8, July, 1957; No. 14, Aug, 1958 - No. 30, June, 1961
Charlton Comics

	GD25	FN65	NM94
1-Painted-c	8.35	25.00	50.00
2	4.20	12.50	25.00
3-8: 8-Billy The Kid app.	4.00	10.00	20.00
14,16-30: 22-Rocky Lane app.	2.80	7.00	14.00
15-Williamson-a, 7 pgs.	4.00	10.00	20.00

MASKED RANGER
April, 1954 - No. 9, Aug, 1955
Premier Magazines

	GD25	FN65	NM94
1-The M. Ranger, his horse Streak, & The Crimson Avenger (origin) begin, end #9; Woodbridge/Frazetta-a	23.00	70.00	160.00
2,3	7.50	22.50	45.00
4-8-All Woodbridge-a. 5-Jesse James by Woodbridge. 6-Billy The Kid by Woodbridge. 7-Wild Bill Hickok by Woodbridge. 8-Jim Bowie's Life Story	9.15	27.50	55.00
9-Torres-a; Wyatt Earp by Woodbridge	10.00	30.00	60.00

NOTE: *Check a-1. Woodbridge c/a-1, 4-9.*

MASK OF DR. FU MANCHU, THE (See Dr. Fu Manchu)
1951
Avon Periodicals

	GD25	FN65	NM94
1-Sax Rohmer adapt.; Wood-c/a (26 pgs.); Hollingsworth-a	60.00	180.00	420.00

MASQUE OF THE RED DEATH (See Movie Classics)

MASQUES (J. N. Williamson's...)(Innovation)(Value: cover or less)

MASTER COMICS (Combined with Slam Bang Comics #7 on)
Mar, 1940 - No. 133, Apr, 1953 (No. 1-6: oversized issues)
(#1-3: 15 cents, 52pgs.; #4-6: 10 cents, 36pgs.)
Fawcett Publications

	GD25	FN65	VF82	NM94
1-Origin & 1st app. Master Man; The Devil's Dagger, El Carim, Master of Magic, Rick O'Say, Morton Murch, White Rajah, Shipwreck Roberts, Frontier Marshal, Streak Sloan, Mr. Clue begin (all features end #6)	320.00	960.00	2080.00	3200.00

(Estimated up to 100 total copies exist, 4 in NM/Mint)

	GD25	FN65	NM94
2	142.00	425.00	900.00
3-5	100.00	300.00	700.00
6-Last Master Man	100.00	300.00	700.00

NOTE: *#1-6 rarely found in near mint to mint condition due to large-size format.*

	GD25	FN65	NM94
7-(10/40)-Bulletman, Zoro, the Mystery Man (ends #22), Lee Granger, Jungle King, & Buck Jones begin; only app. The War Bird & Mark Swift & the Time Retarder; Zoro, Lee Granger, Jungle King & Mark Swift all continue from Slam Bang; Bulletman moves from Nickel	167.00	500.00	1150.00
8-The Red Gaucho (ends #13), Captain Venture (ends #22) & The Planet Princess begin	92.00	275.00	600.00
9,10: 10-Lee Granger ends	75.00	225.00	500.00
11-Origin & 1st app. Minute-Man (2/41)	167.00	500.00	1150.00
12	92.00	275.00	600.00
13-Origin & 1st app. Bulletgirl; Hitler-c	129.00	388.00	825.00
14-16: 14-Companions Three begins, ends #31	75.00	225.00	500.00
17-20: 17-Raboy-a on Bulletman begins. 20-Captain Marvel cameo app. in Bulletman	72.00	218.00	475.00

	GD25	FN65	VF82	NM94
21-(12/41; Scarce)-Captain Marvel & Bulletman team up against Capt. Nazi; origin & 1st app. Capt. Marvel Jr's most famous nemesis Captain Nazi who will cause creation of Capt. Marvel Jr. in Whiz #25. Part I of trilogy origin of Capt. Marvel Jr.; 1st Mac Raboy-c for Fawcett; Capt. Nazi-c	240.00	720.00	1560.00	2400.00

(Estimated up to 110 total copies exist, 6 in NM/Mint)

	GD25	FN65	VF82	NM94
22-(1/42)-Captain Marvel Jr. moves over from Whiz #25 & teams up with Bulletman against Captain Nazi; part III of trilogy origin of Capt. Marvel Jr. & his 1st cover and adventure	220.00	660.00	1430.00	2200.00

(Estimated up to 135 total copies exist, 7 in NM/Mint)

	GD25	FN65	NM94
23-Capt. Marvel Jr. c/stories begin (1st solo story); fights Capt. Nazi by himself	167.00	500.00	1150.00
24,25,29: 29-Hitler & Hirohito-c	67.00	200.00	440.00
26-28,30-Captain Marvel Jr. vs. Capt. Nazi. 30-Flag-c	67.00	200.00	440.00
31,32: 32-Last El Carim & Buck Jones; intro Balbo, the Boy Magician in El Carim story	48.00	145.00	320.00
33-Balbo, the Boy Magician (ends #47), Hopalong Cassidy (ends #49) begins	48.00	145.00	320.00
34-Capt. Marvel Jr. vs. Capt. Nazi-c/story	49.00	146.00	340.00
35	47.00	140.00	310.00
36-40: 40-Flag-c	42.00	125.00	275.00
41-Bulletman, Capt. Marvel Jr. & Bulletgirl x-over in Minute-Man; only app. Crime Crusaders Club (Capt. Marvel Jr., Minute-Man, Bulletman & Bulletgirl); only team in Fawcett Comics	46.00	138.00	315.00
42-47,49: 47-Hitler becomes Corpl. Hitler Jr. 49-Last Minute-Man	27.00	80.00	175.00
48-Intro. Bulletboy; Capt. Marvel cameo in Minute-Man	32.00	95.00	210.00
50-Radar, Nyoka the Jungle Girl begin (1st app. of each, 5/44); Capt. Marvel x-over in Radar; origin Radar; Capt. Marvel & Capt. Marvel, Jr. introduce Radar on-c	20.00	60.00	130.00
51-58	13.50	41.00	95.00
59-62: Nyoka serial "Terrible Tiara" in all; 61-Capt. Marvel Jr. 1st meets Uncle Marvel	15.00	45.00	105.00
63-80	11.00	32.00	75.00
81,83-87,89-91,95-99: 88-Hopalong Cassidy begins (ends #94). 95-Tom Mix begins (ends #133)	10.00	30.00	65.00

Master of Kung Fu #125, © MEG

Maverick #12, © Warner Bros.

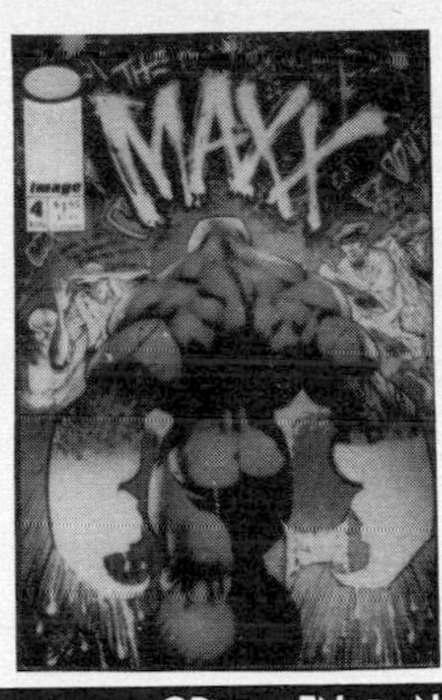

Maxx #4, © Sam Kieth

	GD25	FN65	NM94
82,88,92-94-Krigstein-a	10.00	30.00	65.00
100	10.00	30.00	65.00
101-106-Last Bulletman	8.35	25.00	50.00
107-132: 132-B&W and color illos in POP	7.50	22.50	45.00
133-Bill Battle app.	9.15	27.50	55.00

NOTE: ***Mac Raboy*** *a-15-39, 40 in part, 42, 58; c-21-49, 51, 52, 54, 56, 58, 59. Bulletman c-7-11, 13(half), 15, 18(part), 19, 20, 21(w/Capt. Marvel & Capt. Nazi), 22(w/Capt. Marvel, Jr.). Capt. Marvel, Jr. c-23-133. Master Man c-1-6. Minute Man c-12, 13(half), 14, 16, 17, 18(part).*

MASTER DETECTIVE
1964 (Reprints)
Super Comics

	GD25	FN65	NM94
10,17,18: 10,18-Exist? 17-r/Young King Cole #?; McWilliams-r	1.00	2.50	5.00

MASTER OF KUNG FU (Formerly Special Marvel Edition; see Deadly Hands of Kung Fu & Giant-Size...)
No. 17, April, 1974 - No. 125, June, 1983
Marvel Comics Group

	GD25	FN65	NM94
17-Starlin a; intro Black Jack Tarr	2.30	6.75	16.00
18-20: 19-Man-Thing-c/story	1.50	3.75	9.00
21-23,25-30	1.00	2.50	5.50
24-Starlin, Simonson-a	1.10	2.70	6.50
31-99: 33-1st Leiko Wu. 43-Last 25 cent issue		1.20	3.00
100-Double size		1.40	3.50
101-117,119-124		1.00	2.50
118,125-Double size issues		1.20	3.00
Annual 1(4/76)-Iron Fist app.		1.80	4.50

NOTE: ***Austin*** *c-63i, 74i.* ***Buscema*** *c-44p.* ***Gulacy*** *a(p)-18-20, 22, 25, 29-31, 33-35, 38, 39, 40(p&i), 42-50, 53r(#20); c-51, 55, 64, 67.* ***Gil Kane*** *c(p)-20, 38, 39, 42, 45, 59, 63.* ***Nebres*** *c-73i.* ***Starlin*** *a-17p, 24; c-54.* ***Sutton*** *a-42i. #53 reprints #20.*

MASTER OF KUNG-FU: BLEEDING BLACK (Marvel)(Value: cover or less)

MASTER OF RAMPLING GATE (Anne Rice's...)(Innovation)(Value: cover or less)

MASTER OF THE WORLD (See 4-Color #1157)

MASTERS OF TERROR (Magazine)
July, 1975 - No. 2, Sept, 1975 (Black & White) (All reprints)
Marvel Comics Group

	GD25	FN65	NM94
1-Brunner, Barry Smith-a; Morrow-c; Neal Adams-r(i); Starlin a(p); Gil Kane-a		.70	1.80
2-Reese, Kane, Mayerik-a; Steranko-c			1.20

MASTERS OF THE UNIVERSE (DC, 1982 & 1986-88)(Value: cover or less)

MASTERS OF THE UNIVERSE (Comic Album)
1984 (8-1/2x11"; $2.95; 64 pgs.)
Western Publishing Co.

	GD25	FN65	NM94
11362-Based on Mattel toy & cartoon		1.20	3.00

MASTERWORKS SERIES OF GREAT COMIC BOOK ARTISTS, THE (Sea Gate/DC)(Value: cover or less)

MATT SLADE GUNFIGHTER (Kid Slade Gunfighter #5 on; See Western Gunfighters)
May, 1956 - No. 4, Nov, 1956
Atlas Comics (SPI)

	GD25	FN65	NM94
1-Matt & his horse Eagle; Williamson/Torres-a	11.00	32.00	75.00
2-Williamson-a	7.00	21.00	42.00
3,4	5.35	16.00	32.00

NOTE: ***Maneely*** *a-1, 3, 4; c-1, 2, 4.* ***Roth*** *a-2-4.* ***Severin*** *a-1, 3, 4.* ***Maneely*** *c/a-1.*

MAUD
1906 (32 pgs. in color; 10x15-1/2") (Cardboard covers)
Frederick A. Stokes Co.

	GD25	FN65	NM94
nn-By Fred Opper	26.00	80.00	185.00

MAVERICK (TV)
No. 892, 4/58 - No. 19, 4-6/62 (All have photo-c)
Dell Publishing Co.

	GD25	FN65	NM94
4-Color 892 (#1): James Garner/Jack Kelly photo-c begin	14.00	43.00	100.00
4-Color 930,945,962,980,1005 (6-8/59)	9.15	27.50	55.00
7 (10-12/59) - 14: Last Garner/Kelly-c	7.50	22.50	45.00
15-18: Jack Kelly/Roger Moore photo-c	7.50	22.50	45.00
19-Jack Kelly photo-c	7.50	22.50	45.00

MAVERICK MARSHAL
Nov, 1958 - No. 7, May, 1960
Charlton Comics

	GD25	FN65	NM94
1	4.00	10.00	20.00
2-7	2.00	5.00	10.00

MAX BRAND (See Silvertip)

MAXIMORTAL, THE (King Hell/Tundra)(Value: cover or less)

MAXX (Also see Darker Image)
Mar, 1993 - Present ($1.95, color)
Image Comics

	GD25	FN65	NM94
1-6-Sam Kieth-c/a & scripts		.80	2.00
1-Glow-in-the-dark variant			15.00

MAYA (See Movie Classics)
March, 1968
Gold Key

	GD25	FN65	NM94
1 (10218-803)(TV)	1.70	5.00	12.00

MAYHEM (Dark Horse)(Value: cover or less)

MAZE AGENCY, THE (Comico/Innovation)(Value: cover or less)

MAZIE (...& Her Friends) (See Mortie, Stevie & Tastee-Freez)
1953 - #12, 1954; #13, 12/54 - #22, 9/56; #23, 9/57 - #28, 8/58
Mazie Comics(Magazine Publ.)/Harvey Publ. No. 13-on

	GD25	FN65	NM94
1-(Teen-age)-Stevie's girl friend	5.00	15.00	30.00
2	3.00	7.50	15.00
3-10	2.00	5.00	10.00
11-28	1.40	3.50	7.00

MAZIE
1950 - No. 7, 1951 (5 cents) (5x7-1/4"-miniature)(52 pgs.)
Nation Wide Publishers

	GD25	FN65	NM94
1-Teen-age	10.00	30.00	65.00
2-7	5.00	15.00	00.00

MAZINGER (See First Comics Graphic Novel #17)

'MAZING MAN (DC)(Value: cover or less)

McCRORY'S CHRISTMAS BOOK
1955 (36 pgs.; slick cover)
Western Printing Co. (McCrory Stores Corp. giveaway)

	GD25	FN65	NM94
nn-Painted-c	3.20	8.00	16.00

McCRORY'S TOYLAND BRINGS YOU SANTA'S PRIVATE EYES
1956 (16 pgs.)
Promotional Publ. Co. (Giveaway)

	GD25	FN65	NM94
nn-Has 9 pg. story plus 7 pgs. toy ads	2.40	6.00	12.00

McCRORY'S WONDERFUL CHRISTMAS
1954 (20 pgs.; slick cover)
Promotional Publ. Co. (Giveaway)

	GD25	FN65	NM94
nn	3.20	8.00	16.00

McHALE'S NAVY (TV) (See Movie Classics)
May-July, 1963 - No. 3, Nov-Jan, 1963-64 (All have photo-c)
Dell Publishing Co.

	GD25	FN65	NM94
1	3.70	11.00	26.00
2,3	4.00	11.00	22.00

McKEEVER & THE COLONEL (TV)
Feb-Apr, 1963 - No. 3, Aug-Oct, 1963
Dell Publishing Co.

	GD25	FN65	NM94
1-Photo-c	5.35	16.00	32.00
2,3	4.20	12.50	25.00

MD #1, © WMG

Megalith #1, © Continuity

Menace #3, © MEG

GD25 FN65 NM94

McLINTOCK (See Movie Comics)

MD
Apr-May, 1955 - No. 5, Dec-Jan, 1955-56
E. C. Comics

	GD25	FN65	NM94
1-Not approved by code	10.00	30.00	65.00
2-5	8.00	24.00	48.00

NOTE: ***Crandall, Evans, Ingels, Orlando** art in all issues; **Craig** c-1-5.*

MECHA (Dark Horse)(Value: cover or less)

MEDAL FOR BOWZER, A
No date (1948-50?)
Will Eisner Giveaway

	GD25	FN65	NM94
nn-Eisner-c/script	26.00	78.00	180.00

MEDAL OF HONOR COMICS
Spring, 1946
A. S. Curtis

	GD25	FN65	NM94
1-War stories	7.50	22.50	45.00

MEDIA STARR (Innovation)(Value: cover or less)

MEET ANGEL (Formerly Angel & the Ape)
No. 7, Nov-Dec, 1969
National Periodical Publications

	GD25	FN65	NM94
7-Wood-a(i)	1.50	3.75	9.00

MEET CORLISS ARCHER (Radio/Movie)(My Life #4 on)
March, 1948 - No. 3, July, 1948
Fox Features Syndicate

	GD25	FN65	NM94
1-(Teen-age)-Feldstein-c/a; headlight-c	34.00	103.00	240.00
2-Feldstein-c only	26.00	77.00	180.00
3-Part Feldstein-c only	20.00	60.00	140.00

NOTE: *No. 1-3 used in Seduction of the Innocent, pg. 39.*

MEET HERCULES (See Three Stooges)

MEET HIYA A FRIEND OF SANTA CLAUS
1949 (18 pgs.?) (paper cover)
Julian J. Proskauer/Sundial Shoe Stores, etc. (Giveaway)

	GD25	FN65	NM94
nn	5.00	15.00	30.00

MEET MERTON
Dec, 1953 - No. 4, June, 1954
Toby Press

	GD25	FN65	NM94
1-(Teen-age)-Dave Berg-a	5.35	16.00	32.00
2-Dave Berg-c/a	3.60	9.00	18.00
3,4-Dave Berg-a. 3-Berg-c	3.20	8.00	16.00
I.W. Reprint #9	.60	1.50	3.00
Super Reprint #11('63), 18	.60	1.50	3.00

MEET MISS BLISS (Becomes Stories Of Romance #5 on)
May, 1955 - No. 4, Nov, 1955
Atlas Comics (LMC)

	GD25	FN65	NM94
1-Al Hartley-c/a	7.50	22.50	45.00
2-4	5.00	15.00	30.00

MEET MISS PEPPER (Formerly Lucy, The Real Gone Gal)
No. 5, April, 1954 - No. 6, June, 1954
St. John Publishing Co.

	GD25	FN65	NM94
5-Kubert/Maurer-a	13.00	40.00	90.00
6-Kubert/Maurer-a; Kubert-c	11.00	32.00	75.00

MEET THE NEW POST GAZETTE SUNDAY FUNNIES
3/12/49 (16 pgs.; paper covers) (7-1/4x10-1/4")
Commercial Comics (insert in newspaper)
Pittsburgh Post Gazette

Dick Tracy by Gould, Gasoline Alley, Terry & the Pirates, Brenda Starr, Buck Rogers by Yager, The Gumps, Peter Rabbit by Fago, Superman, Funnyman by Siegel & Shuster, The Saint, Archie, & others done especially for this book. A fine copy sold at auction in 1985 for $276.00.
Estimated value.... $150 – $300

MEGALITH (Continuity)(Value: cover or less)

MEGATON (A super hero)
Nov, 1983; No. 2, Oct, 1985 - No. 8, Aug, 1987 (B&W)
Megaton Publ. (#3: 44 pgs.; #4: 52 pgs.)

	GD25	FN65	NM94
1-($2.00, 68 pgs.)-Erik Larsen's 1st pro work; Vanguard by Larsen begins (1st app.), ends #4; 1st app. Megaton, Berzerker, & Ethrian; Guice-c/a(p); Gustovich-a(p) in #1,2	1.85	5.50	13.00
2 ($2.00, 68 pgs.)-The Dragon cameo (1 pg.) by Larsen (later The Savage Dragon in Image Comics); Guice-c/a(p)	1.50	3.75	9.00
3-1st full app. Savage Dragon-c/story by Larsen; 1st comic book work by Angel Medina (pin-up)	2.60	7.50	18.00
4-2nd app. Savage Dragon by Larsen; 4,5-Wildman by Grass Green	1.70	5.00	12.00
5-1st Liefeld published-a (inside f/c, 6/86)	1.00	2.50	5.50
6,7: 6-Larsen-c		1.20	3.00
8-1st Liefeld story-a (7 pg. super hero story) plus 1 pg. Youngblood ad		1.20	3.00
...Explosion (6/87, 16 pg. color giveaway)-1st app. Youngblood by Rob Liefeld (2 pg. spread); shows Megaton heroes	3.25	9.50	22.00

NOTE: *Copies of Megaton Explosion were also released in early 1992 all signed by Rob Liefeld and were made available to retailers.*

MEGATON MAN (Kitchen Sink)(Value: cover or less)

MEL ALLEN SPORTS COMICS
No. 5, Nov, 1949; No. 6, June, 1950
Standard Comics

	GD25	FN65	NM94
5(#1 on inside)-Tuska-a	13.00	40.00	90.00
6(#2)-Lou Gehrig story	10.00	30.00	60.00

MELTING POT
Dec, 1993 - Present ($2.95, color)
Kitchen Sink Press

	GD25	FN65	NM94
1,2-By Eastman/Talbot/Bisley		1.20	3.00

MELVIN MONSTER (See Peter, the Little Pest)
Apr-June, 1965 - No. 10, Oct, 1969
Dell Publishing Co.

	GD25	FN65	NM94
1-By John Stanley	13.00	40.00	90.00
2-10-All by Stanley. #10-r/#1	10.00	30.00	65.00

MELVIN THE MONSTER (Dexter The Demon #7)
July, 1956 - No. 6, July, 1957
Atlas Comics (HPC)

	GD25	FN65	NM94
1-Maneely-c/a	8.35	25.00	50.00
2-6: 4-Maneely-c/a	5.85	17.50	35.00

MEMORIES (Epic Comics)(Value: cover or less)

MENACE
March, 1953 - No. 11, May, 1954
Atlas Comics (HPC)

	GD25	FN65	NM94
1-Everett-c/a	29.00	85.00	200.00
2-Post-atom bomb disaster by Everett; anti-Communist propaganda/torture scenes; Sinnott s/f story	18.00	54.00	125.00
3,4,6-Everett-a. 6-Romita s/f story	13.50	41.00	95.00
5-Origin & 1st app. The Zombie by Everett (reprinted in Tales of the Zombie #1)(7/53)	22.00	65.00	150.00
7,8,10,11: 7-Frankenstein story. 8-End of world story; Heath 3-D art(3 pgs.). 10-H-Bomb panels	11.00	32.00	75.00
9-Everett-a r-in Vampire Tales #1	12.00	36.00	85.00

NOTE: ***Brodsky** c-7, 8, 11. **Colan** a-6; c-9. **Everett** a-1-6, 9; c-1-6. **Heath** a-1-8; c-10. **Katz** a-11. **Maneely** a-3, 5, 7-9. **Powell** a-11. **Romita** a-3, 6, 8, 11. **Shelly** a-10. **Shores** a-7. **Sinnott** a-2, 7. **Tuska** a-1, 2, 5.*

MEN AGAINST CRIME (Formerly Mr. Risk; Hand of Fate #8 on)
No. 3, Feb, 1951 - No. 7, Oct, 1951
Ace Magazines

	GD25	FN65	NM94
3-Mr. Risk app.	5.85	17.50	35.00
4-7: 4-Colan-a; entire book reprinted as Trapped! #4			

Men's Adventures #12, © MEG

Merry-Go-Round #1 ('47), © Rotary Litho.

Meta-4 #1, © First

GD25 FN65 NM94

4.00 10.00 20.00

MEN, GUNS, & CATTLE (See Classics Illustrated Special Issue)

MEN IN ACTION (Battle Brady #10 on)
April, 1952 - No. 9, Dec, 1952
Atlas Comics (IPS)

1-Berg, Reinman-a 8.35 25.00 50.00
2 4.20 12.50 25.00
3-6,8,9: 3-Heath-c/a 3.60 9.00 18.00
7-Krigstein-a; Heath-c 5.85 17.50 35.00
NOTE: ***Brodsky** c-1,4-6. **Maneely** c-5. **Pakula** a-1, 6. **Robinson** c-8. **Shores** c-9.*

MEN IN ACTION
April, 1957 - No. 9, 1958
Ajax/Farrell Publications

1 5.35 16.00 32.00
2 3.60 9.00 18.00
3-9 2.80 7.00 14.00

MEN INTO SPACE (See 4-Color No. 1083)

MEN OF BATTLE (Also see New Men of Battle)
V1#5, March, 1943 (Hardcover)
Catechetical Guild

V1#5-Topix reprints 3.00 7.50 15.00

MEN OF COURAGE
1949
Catechetical Guild

Bound Topix comics-V7#2,4,6,8,10,16,18,20 3.00 7.50 15.00

MEN OF WAR
August, 1977 - No. 26, March, 1980 (#9,10: 44 pgs.)
DC Comics, Inc.

1-Enemy Ace, Gravedigger (origin #1,2) begin .80 2.00
2-26: 9-Unknown Soldier app. 1.00
NOTE: ***Chaykin** a-9, 10, 12-14, 19, 20. **Evans** c-25. **Kubert** c-2-23, 24p, 26.*

MEN'S ADVENTURES (Formerly True Adventures)
No. 4, Aug, 1950 - No. 28, July, 1954
Marvel/Atlas Comics (CCC)

4(#1)(52 pgs.) 14.00 43.00 100.00
5-Flying Saucer story 9.15 27.50 55.00
6-8: 8-Sci/fic story 6.70 20.00 40.00
9-20: All war format 4.35 13.00 26.00
21,22,24-26: All horror format. 25-Shrunken head-c 6.00 18.00 36.00
23-Crandall-a; Fox-a(i); horror format 7.50 22.50 45.00
27,28-Captain America, Human Torch, & Sub-Mariner app. in each (also see Young Men #24-28) 43.00 130.00 300.00
NOTE: ***Ayers** a-27(H. Torch). **Berg** a-15, 16. **Brodsky** c-4-9, 11, 12, 16-18, 24. **Burgos** c-27, 28(H. Torch). **Colan** a-14, 19. **Everett** a-10, 14, 22, 25, 28; c-14, 21-23. **Heath** a-8, 11, 24; c-13, 20, 26. **Lawrence** a-23; 27(C. America). **Maneely** a-24; c-10, 15. **Mac Pakula** a-15, 25. **Post** a-23. **Powell** a-27(Sub-Mariner). **Reinman** a-11, 12. **Robinson** c-19. **Romita** a-22. **Shores** c-25. **Sinnott** a-21. **Tuska** a-24. Adventure-#4-8; War-#9-20; Horror-#21-26.*

MEN WHO MOVE THE NATION
(Giveaway) (Black & White)
Publisher unknown

nn-Neal Adams-a 4.00 10.00 20.00

MEPHISTO VS... (See Silver Surfer #3)
Apr, 1987 - No. 4, July, 1987 ($1.50, mini-series)
Marvel Comics Group

1-Fantastic Four; Austin-i .80 2.00
2-4: 2-X Factor. 3-X-Men. 4-Avengers .65 1.60

MERC (See Mark Hazzard: Merc)

MERCHANTS OF DEATH (Acme Press (Eclipse))(Value: cover or less)

MERCY
1993 ($5.95, color, mature readers, 68 pgs.)

GD25 FN65 NM94

DC Comics (Vertigo)

nn 1.00 2.50 6.00

MERLIN JONES AS THE MONKEY'S UNCLE (See Movie Comics and The Misadventures of... under Movie Comics)

MERRILL'S MARAUDERS (See Movie Classics)

MERRY CHRISTMAS (See A Christmas Adv., Donald Duck..., Dell Giant #39, & March of Comics #153)

MERRY CHRISTMAS, A
1948 (nn) (Giveaway)
K. K. Publications (Child Life Shoes)

nn 4.00 12.00 24.00

MERRY CHRISTMAS
1956 (7-1/4x5-1/4")
K. K. Publications (Blue Bird Shoes Giveaway)

nn 1.80 4.50 9.00

MERRY CHRISTMAS FROM MICKEY MOUSE
1939 (16 pgs.) (Color & B&W)
K. K. Publications (Shoe store giveaway)

nn-Donald Duck & Pluto app.; text with art (Rare); c-reprint/Mickey Mouse Mag. V3#3 (12/37) 83.00 210.00 550.00

MERRY CHRISTMAS FROM SEARS TOYLAND
1939 (16 pgs.) (In color)
Sears Roebuck Giveaway

nn-Dick Tracy, Little Orphan Annie, The Gumps, Terry & the Pirates 20.00 60.00 140.00

MERRY COMICS
December, 1945 (No cover price)
Carlton Publishing Co.

nn-Boogeyman app. 11.50 34.00 80.00

MERRY COMICS
1947
Four Star Publications

1 8.35 25.00 50.00

MERRY-GO-ROUND COMICS
1944 (25 cents, 132 pgs.); 1946; 9-10/47 - No. 2, 1948
LaSalle Publ. Co./Croyden Publ./Rotary Litho.

nn(1944)(LaSalle)-Funny animal 11.50 34.00 80.00
21 4.35 13.00 26.00
1(1946)(Croyden)-Al Fago-c; funny animal 6.70 20.00 40.00
V1#1,2(1947-48; 52 pgs.)(Rotary Litho. Co. Ltd., Canada);Ken Hultgren-a 4.70 14.00 28.00

MERRY MAILMAN (See Fawcett's Funny Animals #89)

MERRY MOUSE (Also see Funny Tunes & Space Comics)
June, 1953 - No. 4, Jan-Feb, 1954
Avon Periodicals

1-1st app. 5.35 16.00 32.00
2-4 3.60 9.00 18.00

META-4 (First)(Value: cover or less)

METAL MEN (See Brave & the Bold, DC Comics Presents, and Showcase)
4-5/63 - No. 41, 12-1/69-70; No. 42, 2-3/73 - No. 44, 7-8/73;
No. 45, 4-5/76 - No. 56, 2-3/78
National Periodical Publications/DC Comics

Showcase #37 (3-4/62)-1st app. Metal Men 50.00 150.00 400.00
Showcase #38 (5-6/62)-2nd app. Metal Men 38.00 113.00 300.00
Showcase #39 (7-8/62)-3rd app. Metal Men 28.00 84.00 225.00
Showcase #40 (9-10/62)-4th app.Metal Men 27.00 81.00 215.00
1-(4-5/63)-5th app. Metal Men 50.00 150.00 350.00
2 16.00 48.00 110.00
3-5 11.00 32.00 75.00

Metamorpho #3 (10/93), © DC

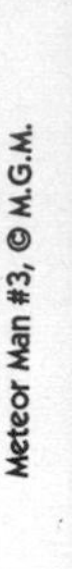
Meteor Man #3, © M.G.M.

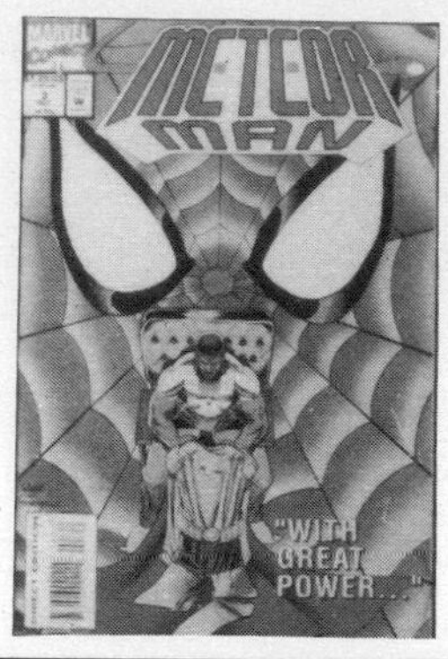

Mickey and Donald #5, © The Disney Co.

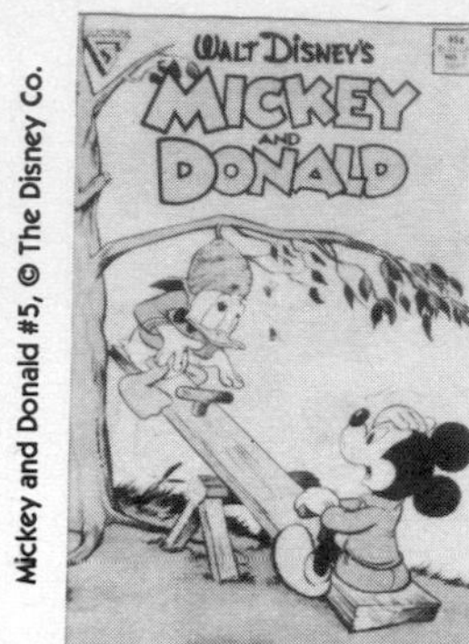

	GD25	FN65	NM94
6-10	6.50	19.00	45.00
11-20	5.00	15.00	35.00
21-26,28-30	3.30	10.00	23.00
27-Origin Metal Men	6.50	19.00	45.00
31-41(1968-70): 38-Last 12 cent issue. 41-Last 15 cent issue	2.60	7.50	18.00
42-44(1973)-Reprints	1.65	4.70	11.00
45('76)-49-Simonson-a in all	1.65	4.70	11.00
50-56: 50-Part-r. 54,55-Green Lantern x-over	1.65	4.70	11.00

NOTE: ***Andru/Esposito** c-1-29. **Aparo** c-53-56. **Giordano** c-45, 46. **Kane** a-30, 31p; c-31. **Simonson** a-45-49; c-47-52. **Staton** a-50-56.*

METAL MEN
Oct, 1993 - No. 4, Jan, 1994 ($1.25, color, mini-series)
Avon Periodicals

	GD25	FN65	NM94
1-($2.50)-Multi-colored foil-c		1.00	2.50
2-4: 2-Origin			1.25

METAMORPHO (See Action Comics, Brave & the Bold, 1st Issue Special, & World's Finest)
July-Aug, 1965 - No. 17, Mar-Apr, 1968 (All 12 cent issues)
National Periodical Publications

	GD25	FN65	NM94
Brave and the Bold #57 (12-1/64-65)-Origin & 1st app. Metamorpho by Ramona Fraden	14.00	41.00	95.00
Brave and the Bold #58 (2-3/65)-2nd app.	6.00	19.00	44.00
1-(7-8/65)-3rd app. Metamorpho	10.00	30.00	68.00
2,3	5.50	16.00	38.00
4-6	3.25	9.50	22.00
7-9	2.60	7.50	18.00
10-Origin & 1st app. Element Girl (1-2/67)	3.30	10.00	23.00
11-17	1.85	5.50	13.00

NOTE: ***Ramona Fraden** a-B&B 57, 58, 1-4. **Orlando** a-5, 6; c-5-9, 11. **Sal Trapani** a-7-16.*

METAMORPHO
Aug, 1993 - No. 4, Nov, 1993 ($1.50, color, mini-series)
DC Comics

	GD25	FN65	NM94
1-4			1.50

METAPHYSIQUE (Norm Breyfogle's...)(Eclipse)(Value: cover or less)

METEOR COMICS
November, 1945
L. L. Baird (Croyden)

	GD25	FN65	NM94
1-Captain Wizard, Impossible Man, Race Wilkins app.; origin Baldy Bean, Capt. Wizard's sidekick; bare-breasted mermaids story	20.00	60.00	140.00

METEOR MAN
Aug, 1993 - No. 6, Jan, 1994 ($1.25, color, limited series)
Marvel Comics

	GD25	FN65	NM94
1-6: 1-Polybagged w/button & rap newspaper			1.25

METROPOL (See Ted McKeever's...)

MGM'S MARVELOUS WIZARD OF OZ (See Marvel Treasury of Oz)
1975 ($1.50, 84 pgs.; oversize)
Marvel Comics Group/National Periodical Publications

	GD25	FN65	NM94
1-Adaptation of MGM's movie; J. Buscema-a		1.60	4.00

M.G.M'S MOUSE MUSKETEERS (Formerly M.G.M.'s The Two Mouseketeers)
No. 670, Jan, 1956 - No. 1290, Mar-May, 1962
Dell Publishing Co.

	GD25	FN65	NM94
4-Color 670 (#4)	3.20	8.00	16.00
4-Color 711,728,764	2.40	6.00	12.00
8 (4-6/57) - 21 (3-5/60)	2.00	5.00	10.00
4-Color 1135,1175,1290	2.40	6.00	12.00

M.G.M.'S SPIKE AND TYKE
No. 499, Sept, 1953 - No. 1266, Dec-Feb, 1961-62
Dell Publishing Co.

	GD25	FN65	NM94
4-Color 499 (#1)	3.20	8.00	16.00
4-Color 577,638	2.40	6.00	12.00
4(12-2/55-56)-10	2.00	5.00	10.00
11-24(12-2/60-61)	1.60	4.00	8.00
4-Color 1266	2.00	5.00	10.00

M.G.M.'S THE TWO MOUSKETEERS (See 4-Color 475, 603, 642)

MICHAELANGELO CHRISTMAS SPECIAL (See Teenage Mutant Ninja Turtles Christmas Special)

MICHAELANGELO, TEENAGE MUTANT NINJA TURTLE
1986 (One shot) ($1.50, B&W)
Mirage Studios

	GD25	FN65	NM94
1	1.70	5.00	12.00
1-2nd printing ('89, $1.75)-Reprint plus new-a		1.20	3.00

MICKEY AND DONALD (Walt Disney's...#3 on)(Becomes Walt Disney's Donald & Mickey #19 on)
Mar, 1988 - No. 18, May, 1990 (95 cents, color)
Gladstone Publishing

	GD25	FN65	NM94
1-Don Rosa-a; r/1949 Firestone giveaway		1.60	4.00
2		1.00	2.50
3-Infinity-c		.80	2.00
4-8: Barks-r			1.20
9-15: 9-r/1948 Firestone giveaway; X-Mas-c			1.00
16 ($1.50, 52 pgs.)-r/FC #157			1.50
17,18 ($1.95, 68 pgs.): 17-Barks M.M.-r/FC #79 plus Barks D.D.-r; Rosa-a; X-Mas-c. 18-Kelly-c(r); Barks-r		.80	2.00

NOTE: ***Barks** reprints in 1-15, 17, 18. **Kelly** c-13r, 14 (r/Walt Disney's C&S #58), 18r.*

MICKEY AND DONALD IN VACATIONLAND (See Dell Giant No. 47)

MICKEY & THE BEANSTALK (See Story Hour Series)

MICKEY & THE SLEUTH (See Walt Disney Showcase #38, 39, 42)

MICKEY FINN (Also see Big Shot Comics #74 & Feature Funnies)
Nov?, 1942 - V3#2, May, 1952
Eastern Color 1-4/McNaught Synd. #5 on (Columbia)/Headline V3#2

	GD25	FN65	NM94
1	22.00	65.00	150.00
2	11.00	32.00	75.00
3-Charlie Chan app.	9.15	27.50	55.00
4	6.35	19.00	38.00
5-10	4.70	14.00	28.00
11-15(1949): 12-Sparky Watts app.	4.00	10.00	20.00
V3#1,2(1952)	2.80	7.00	14.00

MICKEY MANTLE (See Baseball's Greatest Heroes #1)

MICKEY MOUSE
1931 - No. 4, 1934 (52 pgs.; 10x9-3/4"; cardboard covers)
David McKay Publications

	GD25	FN65	NM94
1(1931)	115.00	345.00	800.00
2(1932)	82.00	245.00	575.00
3(1933)-All color Sunday reprints; page #'s 5-17, 32-48 reissued in Whitman #948	129.00	385.00	900.00
4(1934)	71.00	215.00	500.00

NOTE: *Each book reprints strips from previous year - dailies in black and white in #1, 2, 4; Sundays in color in No. 3. Later reprints exist; i.e., #2 (1934).*

MICKEY MOUSE
1933 (Copyright date, printing date unknown)
(30 pages; 10x8-3/4"; cardboard covers)
Whitman Publishing Co.

	GD25	FN65	NM94
948-(1932 Sunday strips in color)	107.00	320.00	750.00

NOTE: *Some copies were bound with a second front cover upside-down instead of the regular back cover; both covers have the same art, but different right and left margins. The above book is an exact, but abbreviated reissue of David McKay No. 3 but with 1/2-inch of border trimmed from the top and bottom.*

MICKEY MOUSE (See The Best of Walt Disney Comics, Cheerios giveaways, Donald Donald and ..., Dynabrite Comics, 40 Big Pages..., Gladstone Comic Album, Merry Christmas From..., Mickey and Donald, Walt Disney's Comics & Stories & Wheaties)

Mickey Mouse #240, © The Disney Co.

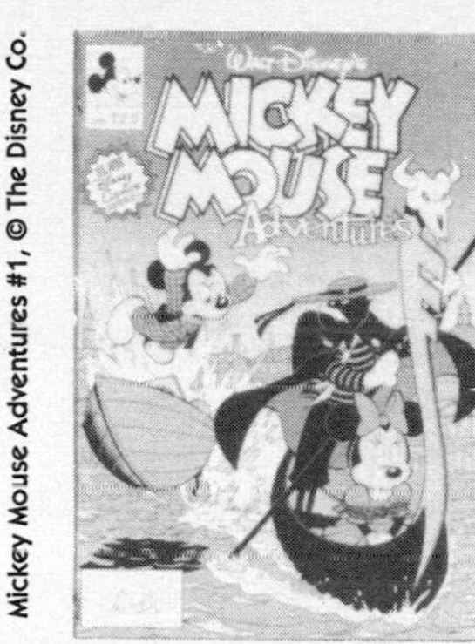

Mickey Mouse Adventures #1, © The Disney Co.

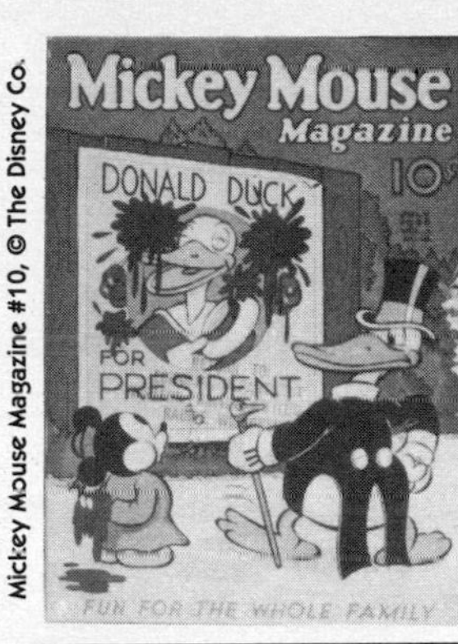

Mickey Mouse Magazine #10, © The Disney Co.

MICKEY MOUSE (...Secret Agent #107-109; Walt Disney's... #148-205?)
(See Dell Giants for annuals)
#16, 1941 - #84, 7-9/62; #85, 11/62 - #218, 7/84; #219, 10/86 - #256, 4/90
Dell Publ. Co./Gold Key #85-204/Whitman #205-218/Gladstone #219 on

	GD25	FN65	VF82
4-Color 16(1941)-1st M.M. comic book-"vs. the Phantom Blot" by Gottfredson	510.00	1535.00	4600.00

(Estimated up to 200 total copies exist, 5 in VF-NM)

	GD25	FN65	NM94
4-Color 27(1943)-"7 Colored Terror"	63.00	190.00	440.00
4-Color 79(1945)-By Carl Barks (1 story)	74.00	220.00	515.00
4-Color 116(1946)	20.00	60.00	140.00
4-Color 141,157(1947)	19.00	57.00	130.00
4-Color 170,181,194('48)	16.00	48.00	110.00
4-Color 214('49),231,248,261	12.00	36.00	85.00
4-Color 268-Reprints/WDC&S #22-24 by Gottfredson ("Surprise Visitor")	12.00	36.00	85.00
4-Color 279,286,296	10.00	30.00	70.00
4-Color 304,313(#1),325(#2),334	8.35	25.00	50.00
4-Color 343,352,362,371,387	6.70	20.00	40.00
4-Color 401,411,427(10-11/52)	5.00	15.00	30.00
4-Color 819-Mickey Mouse in Magicland	4.00	11.00	22.00
4-Color 1057,1151,1246(1959-61)-Album	3.60	9.00	18.00
28(12-1/52-53)-32,34	3.20	8.00	16.00
33-(Exists with 2 dates, 10-11/53 & 12-1/54)	3.20	8.00	16.00
35-50	1.70	5.00	12.00
51-73,75-80	1.50	3.75	9.00
74-Story swipe-"The Rare Stamp Search" from 4-Color #422-"The Gilded Man"	1.70	5.00	12.00
81-99: 93,95-titled "Mickey Mouse Club Album"	1.50	3.75	9.00
100-105: Reprints 4-Color #427,194,279,170,343,214 in that order	1.65	4.00	10.00
106-120	1.50	3.75	9.00
121-130	1.00	2.50	6.00
131-146	1.00	2.00	5.00
147,148: 147-Reprints "The Phantom Fires" from WDC&S #200-202. 148-Reprints "The Mystery of Lonely Valley" from WDC&S #208-210	1.00	2.50	6.00
149-158		1.60	4.00
159-Reprints "The Sunken City" from WDC&S #205-207	1.00	2.00	5.00
160-170: 162-170-r		1.40	3.50
171-178,180-218: 200-r/Four Color #371			1.50
179-(52 pgs.)			1.50
219-1st Gladstone issue; The Seven Ghosts serial-r begins by Gottfredson		1.90	4.75
220,221		1.20	3.00
222-225: 222-Editor-in Grief strip-r		1.00	2.50
226-230			1.50
231-243,245-254: 240-r/March of Comics #27. 245-r/F.C. #279. 250-r/F.C. #248			1.00
244 (1/89, $2.95, 100 pgs.)-Squarebound 60th anniversary issue; gives history of Mickey		1.20	3.00
255,256 ($1.95, 68 pgs.)		.80	2.00

NOTE: *Reprints #195-197, 198(2/3), 199(1/3), 200-208, 211(1/2), 212, 213, 215(1/3), 216-on.*

	GD25	FN65	NM94
Album 01-518-210(Dell), 1(10082-309)(9/63-Gold Key)	2.00	5.00	10.00
...& Goofy "Bicep Bungle"(1952, 16 pgs., 3-1/4x7") Fritos giveaway, soft-c (also see Donald Duck & Ludwig Von Drake)	4.35	13.00	26.00
...& Goofy Explore Business(1978)			1.50
...& Goofy Explore Energy(1976-1978, 36 pgs.); Exxon giveaway in color; regular size			1.50
...& Goofy Explore Energy Conservation(1976-1978)-Exxon			1.50
...& Goofy Explore The Universe of Energy(1985, 20 pgs.); Exxon giveaway in color; regular size			1.50
...Club 1(1/64-Gold Key)(TV)	3.60	9.00	18.00
Mini Comic 1(1976)(3-1/4x6-1/2")-Reprints 158			1.50
New Mickey Mouse Club Fun Book 11190 (Golden Press, 1977, $1.95, 224 pgs.)		1.20	3.00
The Perils of Mickey nn (1993, 5-1/4x7-1/4", 16 pgs.)-Nabisco giveaway w/ games, Nabisco coupons & 6 pgs. of stories; Phantom Blot app.			1.00
Surprise Party 1(30037-901, G.K.)(1/69)-40th Anniversary (see Walt Disney Showcase #47)	4.00	10.00	20.00
Surprise Party 1(1979)-r/1969 issue		1.00	2.50

MICKEY MOUSE ADVENTURES
June, 1990 - No. 18, Nov, 1991 ($1.50, color)
Disney Comics

	NM94
1-18: 1-Bradbury, Murry-r/M.M. #45,73 plus new-a. 2-Begin all new stories. 8-Byrne-c. 9-Fantasia 50th ann. issue w/new adapt. of movie. 10-r/F.C. #214	1.50

MICKEY MOUSE BOOK
1930 (4 printings, 20pgs., magazine size, paperbound)
Bibo & Lang

nn-Very first Disney book with games, cartoons & songs; only Disney book to offer the origin of Mickey (based on a story originated by 11 yr. old Bobette Bibo). First app. Mickey & Minnie Mouse. Clarabelle Cow & Horace Horsecollar app. on back cover. Walt Disney, so the story goes, named him 'Mickey Mouse' after the green color of Ireland because he ate old green cheese. The book was printed in black & green to reinforce the Irish theme.

NOTE: One of the printings has a daily Win Smith M. Mouse strip at bottom of back cover; another printing is blank in this area. It has not been definitely proven how to identify each printing. Most copies are missing pages 9 & 10 which contain a puzzle to be cut out. Ublwerks-c

	GD25	FN65	VF82	NM94
1st-4th Prints (complete)	785.00	2350.00	3925.00	5500.00

(Estimated up to 75 total copies exist, 4 in NM/Mint)

	GD25	FN65	VF82
1st-4th Printings (pgs. 9&10 cut out, but not missing)	400.00	900.00	2000.00
1st-4th Printings (pgs. 9&10 missing)	350.00	800.00	1800.00

MICKEY MOUSE CLUB MAGAZINE (See Walt Disney...)

MICKEY MOUSE CLUB SPECIAL (See The New Mickey Mouse...)

MICKEY MOUSE COMICS DIGEST
1986 - No. 5, 1987 (96 pgs.)
Gladstone Publishing

	GD25	FN65	NM94
1-3 ($1.25)			1.25
4,5 ($1.50)			1.50

MICKEY MOUSE MAGAZINE
V1#1, Jan, 1933 - V1#9, Sept, 1933 (5-1/4x7-1/4")
No. 1-3 published by Kamen-Blair (Kay Kamen, Inc.)
Walt Disney Productions

(Scarce)-Distributed by dairies and leading stores through their local theatres. First few issues had 5 cents listed on cover, later ones had no price.

	GD25	FN65	VF82
V1#1	400.00	800.00	2300.00
2-9	117.00	350.00	700.00

MICKEY MOUSE MAGAZINE
V1#1, Nov, 1933 - V2#12, Oct, 1935
Mills giveaways issued by different dairies
Walt Disney Productions

	GD25	FN65	NM94
V1#1	79.00	235.00	550.00
2-12: 2-X-Mas issue	30.00	90.00	210.00
V2#1-12: 2-X-Mas issue. 4-St. Valentine-c	19.00	58.00	135.00

MICKEY MOUSE MAGAZINE (Becomes Walt Disney's Comics & Stories)
(No V3#1, V4#6)
Summer, 1935 (June-Aug, indicia) - V5#12, Sept, 1940

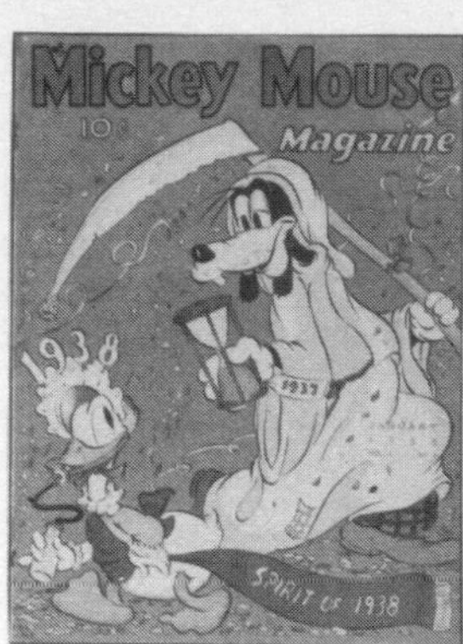

Mickey Mouse Magazine V3#4, © The Disney Co.

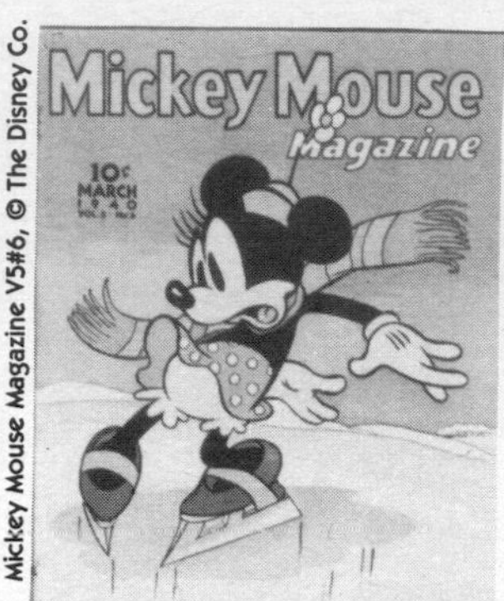

Mickey Mouse Magazine V5#6, © The Disney Co.

Micronauts #54, © MEG

V1#1-5, V3#11,12, V4#1-3 are 44 pgs; V2#3-100 pgs; V5#12-68 pgs; rest are 36 pgs.
K. K. Publ./Western Publishing Co. GD25 FN65 VF82 NM94

V1#1 (Large size, 13-1/4x10-1/4"; 25 cents)-Contains puzzles, games, cels, stories and comics of Disney characters. Promotional magazine for Disney cartoon movies and paraphernalia 900.00 3000.00 5850.00 9000.00
(Estimated up to 100 total copies exist, 3 in NM/Mint)

Note: *Some copies were autographed by the editors & given away with all early one year subscriptions.*

GD25 FN65 VF82

2 (Size change, 11-1/2x8-1/2"; 10/35; 10 cents)-High quality paper begins; Messmer-a 121.00 365.00 850.00
3,4: 3-Messmer-a 68.00 205.00 475.00
5-1st Donald Duck solo-c; last 44pg. & high quality paper issue 72.00 215.00 500.00
6-9: 6-36 pg. issues begin; Donald becomes editor. 8-2nd Donald solo-c. 9-1st Mickey/Minnie-c 64.00 193.00 450.00
10-12, V2#1,2: 11-1st Pluto/Mickey-c; Donald fires himself and appoints Mickey as editor 61.00 182.00 425.00
V2#3-Special 100 pg. Christmas issue (25 cents); Messmer-a; Donald becomes editor of Wise Quacks 200.00 600.00 1400.00
4-Mickey Mouse Comics & Roy Ranger (adventure strip) begin; both end V2#9; Messmer-a 54.00 160.00 375.00

GD25 FN65 NM94

5-Ted True (adventure strip, ends V2#9) & Silly Symphony Comics (ends V3#3) begin 43.00 130.00 300.00
6-9: 6-1st solo Minnie-c. 6-9-Mickey Mouse Movies cut-out in each 43.00 130.00 300.00
10-1st full color issue; Mickey Mouse (by Gottfredson; ends V3#12) & Silly Symphony (ends V3#3) full color Sunday-r, Peter The Farm Detective (ends V5#8) & Ole Of The North (ends V3#3) begins 57.00 170.00 400.00
11-13: 12-Hiawatha-c & feature story 43.00 130.00 300.00
V3#2-Big Bad Wolf Halloween-c 43.00 130.00 300.00
3 (12/37)-1st app. Snow White & The Seven Dwarfs (before release of movie)(possibly 1st in print); Mickey Christmas-c 86.00 260.00 600.00
4 (1/38)-Snow White & The Seven Dwarfs serial begins (on stands before release of movie); Ducky Symphony (ends V3#11) begins 72.00 215.00 500.00
5-1st Snow White & Seven Dwarfs-c (St. Valentine's Day) 86.00 260.00 600.00
6-Snow White serial ends; Lonesome Ghosts app. (2 pp.) 50.00 150.00 350.00
7-Seven Dwarfs Easter-c 43.00 130.00 300.00
8-10: 9-Dopey-c. 10-1st solo Goofy-c 40.00 120.00 280.00
11,12 (44 pgs; 8 more pgs. color added). 11-Mickey the Sheriff serial (ends V4#3) & Donald Duck strip-r (ends V3#12) begin. Color feature on Snow White's Forest Friends 43.00 130.00 300.00
V4#1 (10/38; 44 pgs.)-Brave Little Tailor-c/feature story, nominated for Academy Award; Bobby & Chip by Otto Messmer (ends V4#2) & The Practical Pig (ends V4#2) begin 43.00 130.00 300.00
2 (44 pgs.)-1st Huey, Dewey & Louie-c 40.00 120.00 280.00
3 (12/38, 44 pgs.)-Ferdinand The Bull-c/feature story, Academy Award winner; Mickey Mouse & The Whalers serial begins, ends V4#12 43.00 130.00 300.00
4-Spotty, Mother Pluto strip-r begin, end V4#8 40.00 120.00 280.00
5-St. Valentine's day-c. 1st Pluto solo-c 43.00 130.00 300.00
7 (3/39)-The Ugly Duckling-c/feature story, Academy Award winner 43.00 130.00 300.00
7 (4/39)-Goofy & Wilbur The Grasshopper classic-c/feature story from 1st Goofy solo cartoon movie; Timid Elmer begins, ends V5#5 43.00 130.00 300.00
8-Big Bad Wolf-c from Practical Pig movie poster; Practical Pig feature story 43.00 130.00 300.00
9-Donald Duck & Mickey Mouse Sunday-r begin; The Pointer feature story, nominated for Academy Award 43.00 130.00 300.00
10-Classic July 4th drum & fife-c; last Donald Sunday-r 50.00 150.00 350.00
11-1st slick-c; last over-sized issue 40.00 120.00 280.00
12 (9/39; format change, 10-1/4x8-1/4")-1st full color, cover to cover issue; Donald's Penguin-c/feature story 48.00 145.00 335.00
V5#1-Black Pete-c; Officer Duck-c/feature story; Autograph Hound feature story; Robinson Crusoe serial begins 48.00 145.00 335.00
2-Goofy-c; 1st app. Pinocchio (cameo) 64.00 195.00 450.00
3 (12/39)-Pinocchio Christmas-c (Before movie release). 1st app. Jiminy Cricket; Pinocchio serial begins 72.00 215.00 500.00
4,5: 5-Jiminy Cricket-c; Pinocchio serial ends; Donald's Dog Laundry feature story 48.00 145.00 335.00
6-Tugboat Mickey feature story; Rip Van Winkle feature begins, ends V5#8 47.00 140.00 325.00
7-2nd Huey, Dewey & Louie-c 47.00 140.00 325.00
8-Last magazine size issue; 2nd solo Pluto-c; Figaro & Cleo feature story 47.00 140.00 325.00
9 (6/40; change to comic book size)-Jiminy Cricket feature story; Donald-c & Sunday-r begin 52.00 155.00 360.00
10-Special Independence Day issue 52.00 155.00 360.00
11-Hawaiian Holiday & Mickey's Trailor feature stories; last 36 pg. issue 52.00 155.00 360.00
12 (Format change)-The transition issue (68 pgs.) becoming a comic book. With only a title change to follow, becomes Walt Disney's Comics & Stories #1 with the next issue 350.00 1070.00 2800.00
V4#1 (Giveaway) 36.00 107.00 250.00

NOTE: *Otto Messmer-a is in many issues of the first two-three years. The following story titles and issues have gags created by* **Carl Barks:** *V4#3(12/38)-'Donald's Better Self' & 'Donald's Golf Game;' V4#4(1/39)-'Donald's Lucky Day;' V4#7(3/39)-'Hockey Champ;' V4#7(4/39)-'Donald's Cousin Gus;' V4#9(6/39)-'Sea Scouts;' V4#12(9/39)-'Donald's Penguin;' V5#9 (6/40)-'Donald's Vacation;' V5#10(7/40)-'Bone Trouble;' V5#12(9/40)-'Window Cleaners.'*

MICKEY MOUSE MARCH OF COMICS
1947 - 1951 (Giveaway)
K. K. Publications

8(1947)-32 pgs. 54.00 160.00 375.00
27(1948) 39.00 120.00 275.00
45(1949) 34.00 100.00 235.00
60(1950) 21.00 63.00 145.00
74(1951) 17.00 52.00 120.00

MICKEY MOUSE SUMMER FUN (See Dell Giants)

MICKEY MOUSE'S SUMMER VACATION (See Story Hour Series)

MICROBOTS, THE
December, 1971 (One Shot)
Gold Key

1 (10271-112) 1.20 3.00 7.00

MICRONAUTS
Jan, 1979 - No. 59, Aug, 1984 (Mando paper #53 on)
Marvel Comics Group

1-Intro/1st app. Baron Karza .90 2.20
2-5 1.20
6-36,39-59: 7-Man-Thing app. 8-1st app. Capt. Universe (8/79). 9-1st app. Cilicia. 13-1st app. Jasmine. 15-Death of Microtron. 15-17-Fantastic Four app. 17-Death of Jasmine. 20-Ant-Man app. 21-Microverse series begins. 25-Origin Baron Karza. 25-29-Nick Fury app. 27-Death of Biotron. 34,35-Dr. Strange app. 35-Double size; origin Microverse; intro Death Squad. 40-Fantastic Four app. 57-Double size. 59-Golden painted-c 1.00
37-Nightcrawler app.; X-Men cameo (2 pgs.) .80 2.00
38-First direct sale .65 1.60
nn-Reprints #1-3; blank UPC; diamond on top .40
Annual 1(12/79)-Ditko-c/a 1.00 2.50
Annual 2(10/80)-Ditko-c/a .80 2.00

NOTE: *#38-on distributed only through comic shops.* **N. Adams** *c-7i.* **Chaykin** *a-13-18p.* **Ditko** *a-39p.* **Giffen** *a-36p, 37p(part).* **Golden** *a-1-12p; c-2-7p, 8-23, 24p, 38, 39, 59.* **Guice** *a-48-58p;*

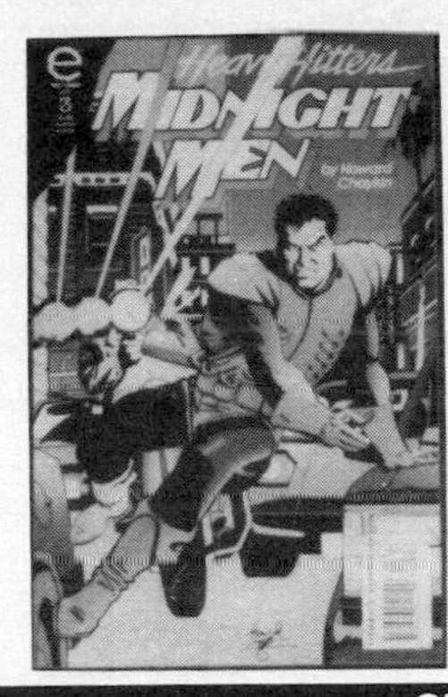

Midnight Men #3, © Howard Chaykin

Midnight Sons Unlimited #3, © MEG

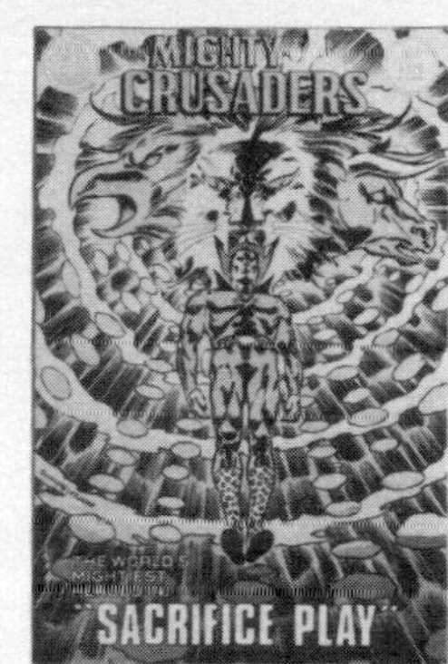

Mighty Crusaders #5 (1/84), © AP

GD25 FN65 NM94

c-49-58. ***Gil Kane*** *a-38, 40-45p; c-40-45.* ***Layton*** *c-33-37.* ***Miller*** *c-31.*

MICRONAUTS (Marvel, 1984-86)(Value: cover or less)

MICRONAUTS SPECIAL EDITION (Marvel)(Value: cover or less)

MIDGET COMICS (Fighting Indian Stories)
Feb, 1950 - No. 2, Apr, 1950 (5-3/8"x7-3/8," 68 pgs.)
St. John Publishng Co.

	GD25	FN65	NM94
1-Fighting Indian Stories; Matt Baker-c	10.00	30.00	60.00
2-Tex West, Cowboy Marshal (also in #1)	5.85	17.50	35.00

MIDNIGHT (See Smash Comics #18)

MIDNIGHT
April, 1957 - No. 6, June, 1958
Ajax/Farrell Publ. (Four Star Comic Corp.)

	GD25	FN65	NM94
1-Reprints from Voodoo & Strange Fantasy with some changes	8.35	25.00	50.00
2-6	4.70	14.00	28.00

MIDNIGHT EYE
1991 - No. 6, 1992 ($4.95, color, adults, 44 pgs.)
Viz Premiere Comics

	GD25	FN65	NM94
1-6: Japenese stories translated into English	1.00	2.00	5.00

MIDNIGHT MEN
June, 1993 - No. 4, Sept, 1993 ($1.95, color, mini-series)
Epic Comics (Marvel)

	GD25	FN65	NM94
1-($2.50)-Embossed-c; Chaykin-c/a & scripts in all		1.00	2.50
2-4		.80	2.00

MIDNIGHT MYSTERY
Jan-Feb, 1961 - No. 7, Oct, 1961
American Comics Group

	GD25	FN65	NM94
1-Sci/Fi story	8.35	25.00	50.00
2-7: 7-Gustavson-a	4.20	12.50	25.00

NOTE: ***Reinman*** *a-1, 3.* ***Whitney*** *a-1, 4-6; c-1-3, 5, 7.*

MIDNIGHT SONS UMLIMITED
Apr, 1993 - Present ($3.95, color, 68 pgs.)
Marvel Comics

	GD25	FN65	NM94
1-4: Blaze, Darkhold (by Quesada #1), Ghost Rider, Morbius & Nightstalkers in all. 3-Spider-Man app. 4-Siege of Darkness		1.60	4.00

MIDNIGHT TALES
Dec, 1972 - No. 18, May, 1976
Charlton Press

	GD25	FN65	NM94
V1#1		1.60	4.00
2-18: 11-14-Newton-a(p)		1.20	3.00
12,17(Modern Comics reprint, 1977)			1.00

NOTE: ***Adkins*** *a-12i, 13i.* ***Ditko*** *a-12.* ***Howard*** *(Wood imitator) a-1-15, 17, 18; c-1-18.* ***Don Newton*** *a-11-14p.* ***Staton*** *a-1, 3-11, 13.* ***Sutton*** *a-3-5, 7-10.*

MIGHTY ATOM, THE (...& the Pixies #6) (Formerly The Pixies #1-5)
No. 6, 1949; Nov, 1957 - No. 6, Aug-Sept, 1958
Magazine Enterprises

	GD25	FN65	NM94
6(1949-M.E.)-no month (1st Series)	4.00	12.00	24.00
1-6(2nd Series)-Pixies-r	2.40	6.00	12.00
I.W. Reprint #1(nd)	.40	1.00	2.00
Giveaway(1959, '63, Whitman)-Evans-a	1.60	4.00	8.00
Giveaway ('64r, '65r, '67r, '68r, '73r, '76r)		.50	1.00

MIGHTY BEAR (Formerly Fun Comics; becomes Unsane #15)
No. 13, Jan, 1954 - No. 14, Mar, 1954; 9/57 - No. 3, 2/58
Star Publ. No. 13,14/Ajax-Farrell (Four Star)

	GD25	FN65	NM94
13,14-L. B. Cole-c	6.70	20.00	40.00
1-3('57-58)Four Star; becomes Mighty Ghost #4	3.60	9.00	18.00

MIGHTY COMICS (...Presents) (Formerly Flyman)
No. 40, Nov, 1966 - No. 50, Oct, 1967 (All 12 cent issues)
Radio Comics (Archie)

	GD25	FN65	NM94
40-Web	1.70	5.00	12.00
41-50: 41-Shield, Black Hood. 42-Black Hood. 43-Shield, Web & Black Hood. 44-Black Hood, Steel Sterling & The Shield. 45-Shield & Hangman; origin Web retold. 46-Steel Sterling, Web & Black Hood. 47-Black Hood & Mr. Justice. 48-Shield & Hangman; Wizard x-over in Shield. 49-Steel Sterling & Fox; Black Hood x-over in Steel Sterling. 50-Black Hood & Web; Inferno x-over in Web	1.65	4.00	10.00

NOTE: ***Paul Reinman*** *a-40-50.*

MIGHTY CRUSADERS, THE (Also see Adventures of the Fly, The Crusaders & Fly Man)
Nov, 1965 - No. 7, Oct, 1966 (All 12 cent issues)
Mighty Comics Group (Radio Comics)

	GD25	FN65	NM94
1-Origin The Shield	3.70	11.00	26.00
2-Origin Comet	2.15	6.50	15.00
3-Origin Fly-Man	1.85	5.50	13.00
4-1st S.A. app. Fireball, Inferno & Fox, Firefly, Web, Bob Phantom, Blackjack, Hangman, Zambini, Kardak, Steel Sterling, Mr. Justice, Wizard, Capt. Flag, Jaguar x-over	2.40	7.25	17.00
5-Intro. Ultra-Men (Fox, Web, Capt. Flag) & Terrific Three (Jaguar, Mr. Justice, Steel Sterling)	1.85	5.50	13.00
6,7: 7-Steel Sterling feature; origin Fly-Girl	1.85	5.50	13.00

NOTE: ***Reinman*** *a-6.*

MIGHTY CRUSADERS, THE (All New Advs. of...#2)
Mar, 1983 - No. 13, Sept, 1985 ($1.00, 36 pgs, Mando paper)
Red Circle Prod./Archie Ent. No. 6 on

	GD25	FN65	NM94
1-13: 1-Origin Black Hood, The Fly, Fly Girl, The Shield, The Wizard, The Jaguar, Pvt. Strong & The Web. 2-Mister Midnight begins. 4-Darkling replaces Shield. 5-Origin Jaguar, Shield begins. 7-Untold origin Jaguar			1.00

NOTE: ***Buckler*** *a-1-3, 4i, 5p, 7p, 8i, 9i; c-1-10p.*

MIGHTY GHOST (Formerly Mighty Bear #1-3)
No. 4, June, 1958
Ajax/Farrell Publ.

	GD25	FN65	NM94
4	2.80	7.00	14.00

MIGHTY HERCULES, THE (TV)
July, 1963 - No. 2, Nov, 1963
Gold Key

	GD25	FN65	NM94
1,2(10072-307, 10072-311)	11.00	34.00	80.00

MIGHTY HEROES, THE (TV) (Funny)
Mar, 1967 - No. 4, July, 1967
Dell Publishing Co.

	GD25	FN65	NM94
1-Also has a 1957 Heckle & Jeckle-r	11.00	32.00	75.00
2-4: 4-Has two 1958 Mighty Mouse-r	8.35	25.00	50.00

MIGHTY MARVEL WESTERN, THE
Oct, 1968 - No. 46, Sept, 1976 (#1-14: 68 pgs.; #15,16: 52 pgs.)
Marvel Comics Group (LMC earlier issues)

	GD25	FN65	NM94
1-Begin Kid Colt, Rawhide Kid, Two-Gun Kid-r	1.00	2.50	6.00
2-10		1.20	3.00
11-20		.80	2.00
21-46: 24-Kid Colt-r end. 25-Matt Slade-r begin. 31-Baker-r. 32-Origin-r/Rawhide Kid #23; Williamson-r/Kid Slade #7. 37-Williamson, Kirby-r/Two-Gun Kid 51			1.20

NOTE: ***Jack Davis*** *a(r)-21-24.* ***Keller*** *r-1, 22.* ***Kirby*** *a(r)-1-3, 6, 9, 12, 14, 16, 26, 29, 32, 36, 41, 43, 44; c-29.* ***Maneely*** *a(r)-22. No Matt Slade-#43.*

MIGHTY MIDGET COMICS, THE (Miniature)
No date; circa 1942-1943 (36 pages) (Approx. 5x4")
(Black & White & Red) (Sold 2 for 5 cents)
Samuel E. Lowe & Co.

	GD25	FN65	NM94
Bulletman #11(1943)-r/cover/Bulletman #3	8.35	25.00	50.00
Captain Marvel #11	8.35	25.00	50.00

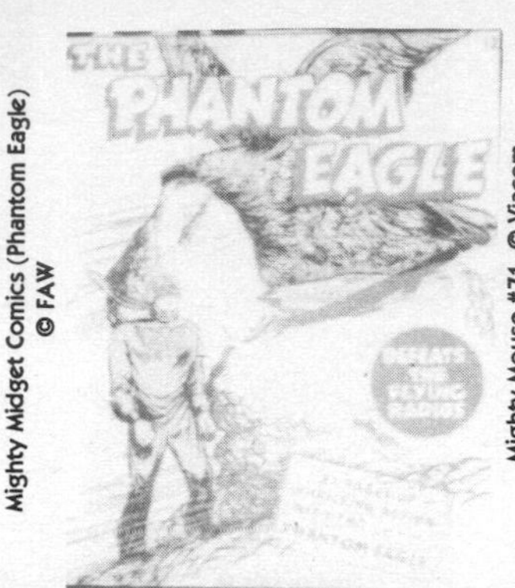

Mighty Midget Comics (Phantom Eagle) © FAW

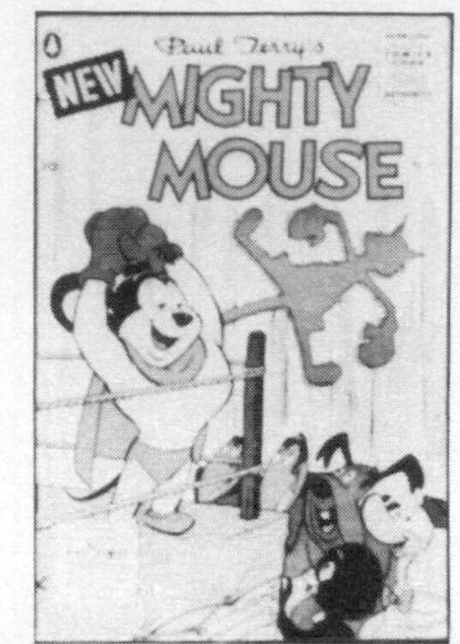

Mighty Mouse #71, © Viacom

Mike Grell's Sable #3, © First

GD25 FN65 NM94 — GD25 FN65 NM94

Captain Marvel #11 (Same as above except for full color ad on back cover; this issue was glued to cover of Captain Marvel #20 and is not found in fine-mint condition) 200.00 625.00 -

GD25 FN65 NM94

Captain Marvel Jr. #11 8.35 25.00 50.00

GD25 FN65 -

Captain Marvel Jr. #11 (Same as above except for full color ad on back-c; this issue was glued to cover of Captain Marvel #21 and is not found in fine-mint condition) 200.00 625.00 -

GD25 FN65 NM94

Golden Arrow #11 6.70 20.00 40.00
Ibis the Invincible #11(1942)-Origin; reprints cover to Ibis #1 8.35 25.00 50.00
Spy Smasher #11(1942) 8.35 25.00 50.00

NOTE: *The above books came in a box called "box full of books" and was distributed with other Samuel Lowe puzzles, paper dolls, coloring books, etc. They are not titled Mighty Midget Comics. All have a war bond seal on back cover which is otherwise blank. These books came in a "Mighty Midget" flat cardboard counter display rack.*

	GD25	FN65	NM94
Balbo, the Boy Magician #12	4.00	10.00	20.00
Bulletman #12	7.50	22.50	45.00
Commando Yank #12	5.00	15.00	30.00
Dr. Voltz the Human Generator	4.00	10.00	20.00
Lance O'Casey #12	4.00	10.00	20.00
Leatherneck the Marine	4.00	10.00	20.00
Minute Man #12	7.50	22.50	45.00
Mister Q	4.00	10.00	20.00
Mr. Scarlet & Pinky #12	5.85	17.50	35.00
Pat Wilton & His Flying Fortress	4.00	10.00	20.00
The Phantom Eagle #12	4.35	13.00	26.00
State Trooper Stops Crime	4.00	10.00	20.00
Tornado Tom; r-/from Cyclone #1-3; origin	4.00	11.00	22.00

MIGHTY MOUSE (See Adventures of..., Dell Giant #43, Giant Comics Edition, March of Comics #205, 237, 247, 257, 447, 459, 471, 483, Oxydol-Dreft, Paul Terry's, & Terry-Toons Comics)

MIGHTY MOUSE (1st Series)
Fall, 1946 - No. 4, Summer, 1947
Timely/Marvel Comics (20th Century Fox)

	GD25	FN65	NM94
1	82.00	245.00	575.00
2	40.00	120.00	280.00
3,4	27.00	81.00	190.00

MIGHTY MOUSE (2nd Series) (Paul Terry's... #62-71)
Aug, 1947 - No. 67, 11/55; No. 68, 3/56 - No. 83, 6/59
St. John Publishing Co./Pines No. 68 (3/56) on (TV issues #72 on)

	GD25	FN65	NM94
5(#1)	26.00	77.00	180.00
6-10	13.50	41.00	95.00
11-19	9.15	27.50	55.00
20 (11/50) - 25-(52 pg. editions)	7.00	21.00	42.00
20-25-(36 pg. editions)	6.35	19.00	38.00
26-37: 35-Flying saucer-c	5.35	16.00	32.00
38-45-(100 pgs.)	12.00	36.00	85.00
46-83: 62-64,67-Painted-c. 82-Infinity-c	5.00	15.00	30.00
Album 1(10/52, 25¢, 100 pgs.)-St. John	20.00	60.00	140.00
Album 2(11/52-St. John) - 3(12/52) (100 pgs.)	16.00	48.00	110.00
Fun Club Magazine 1(Fall, 1957-Pines, 25¢, 100 pgs.) (CBS TV)-Tom Terrific, Heckle & Jeckle, Dinky Duck, Gandy Goose	11.50	34.00	80.00
Fun Club Magazine 2-6(Winter, 1958-Pines)	7.50	22.50	45.00
3-D 1-(1st printing-9/53)(St. John)-stiff covers	23.00	70.00	160.00
3-D 1-(2nd printing-10/53)-slick, glossy covers, slightly smaller	20.00	60.00	140.00
3-D 2(11/53), 3(12/53)-(St. John)	19.00	57.00	130.00

MIGHTY MOUSE (TV)(3rd Series)(Formerly Adventures of Mighty Mouse)
No. 161, Oct, 1964 - No. 172, Oct, 1968
Gold Key/Dell Publishing Co. No. 166-on

	GD25	FN65	NM94
161(10/64)-165(9/65)-(Becomes Advs. of... No. 166 on)	3.60	10.75	25.00
166(3/66), 167(6/66)-172	2.60	7.50	18.00

MIGHTY MOUSE (TV)(Spotlight, 1987)(Value: cover or less)

MIGHTY MOUSE (TV)
Oct, 1990 - No. 10, July, 1991 ($1.00, color)(Based on Sat. cartoon)
Marvel Comics

1-10: 1-Dark Knight-c parody. 2-10: 3-Intro Bat-Bat; Byrne-c. 4,5-Crisis-c/story parodies w/Perez-c. 6-Spider-Man-c parody. 7-Origin Bat-Bat 1.00

MIGHTY MOUSE ADVENTURES (Adventures of... #2 on)
November, 1951
St. John Publishing Co.

	GD25	FN65	NM94
1	25.00	75.00	175.00

MIGHTY MOUSE ADVENTURE STORIES (Paul Terry's... on-c only)
1953 (50 cents, 384 pgs.)
St. John Publishing Co.

	GD25	FN65	NM94
nn-Rebound issues	38.00	115.00	265.00

MIGHTY MUTANIMALS (See Teenage Mutant Ninja Turtles Advs. #19)
May, 1991 - No. 3, July, 1991 ($1.00, color, mini-series)
Apr, 1992 - Present ($1.25, color)
Archie Comics

	GD25	FN65	NM94
1-3: 1-Story cont'd from TMNT Advs. #19			1.00
1-8 (1992): 7-1st app. Merdude			1.25

MIGHTY SAMSON (Also see Gold Key Champion)
7/64 - #20, 11/69; #21, 8/72; #22, 12/73 - #31, 3/76; #32, 8/82
Gold Key (Painted c-1-31)

	GD25	FN65	NM94
1-Origin/1st app.; Thorne-a begins	4.30	13.00	30.00
2-5	2.00	6.00	14.00
6-10: 7-Tom Morrow begins, ends #20	1.65	4.70	11.00
11-20	1.50	3.75	9.00
21-32: 21,22,32-r		1.90	4.75

MIGHTY THOR (See Thor)

MIKE BARNETT, MAN AGAINST CRIME (TV)
Dec, 1951 - No. 6, Oct, 1952
Fawcett Publications

	GD25	FN65	NM94
1	10.00	30.00	65.00
2	6.35	19.00	38.00
3,4,6	5.00	15.00	30.00
5-"Market for Morphine" cover/story	7.00	21.00	42.00

MIKE GRELL'S SABLE (First)(Value: cover or less)

MIKE MIST MINUTE MIST-ERIES (See Ms. Tree/Mike Mist in 3-D)
April, 1981 ($1.25, B&W, one-shot)
Eclipse Comics

	GD25	FN65	NM94
1			1.25

MIKE SHAYNE PRIVATE EYE
Nov-Jan, 1962 - No. 3, Sept-Nov, 1962
Dell Publishing Co.

	GD25	FN65	NM94
1	2.80	7.00	14.00
2,3	1.80	4.50	9.00

MILITARY COMICS (Becomes Modern Comics #44 on)
Aug, 1941 - No. 43, Oct, 1945
Quality Comics Group

	GD25	FN65	VF82	NM94
1-Origin/1st app. Blackhawk by C. Cuidera (Eisner scripts); Miss America, The Death Patrol by Jack Cole (also #2-7,27-30), & The Blue Tracer by Guardineer; X of the Underground, The Yankee Eagle, Q-Boat & Shot & Shell, Archie Atkins, Loops & Banks by Bud Ernest (Bob Powell)(ends #13) begin	390.00	1170.00	2535.00	3900.00

(Estimated up to 160 total copies exist, 9 in NM/Mint)

GD25 FN65 NM94

2-Secret War News begins (by McWilliams #2-16); Cole-a; new uniform with

Military Comics #43, © QUA

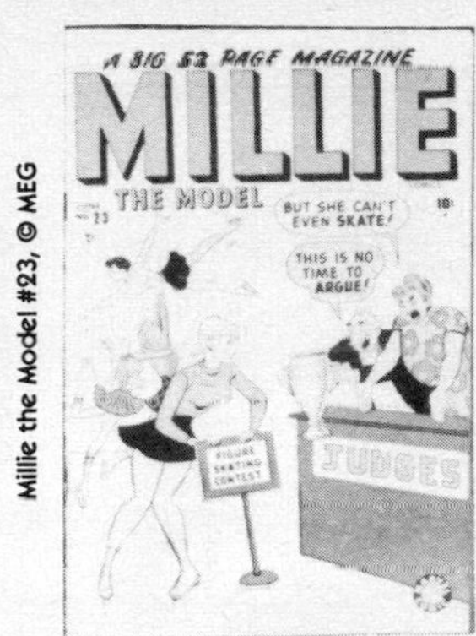

Millie the Model #23, © MEG

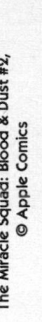

The Miracle Squad: Blood & Dust #2, © Apple Comics

	GD25	FN65	NM94
yellow circle & hawk's head for Blackhawk	183.00	550.00	1250.00
3-Origin/1st app. Chop Chop	150.00	450.00	1000.00
4	125.00	375.00	825.00
5-The Sniper begins; Miss America in costume #4-7	100.00	300.00	650.00
6-9: 8-X of the Underground begins (ends #13). 9-The Phantom Clipper begins (ends #16)	83.00	250.00	550.00
10-Classic Eisner-c	92.00	275.00	600.00
11-Flag-c	67.00	200.00	450.00
12-Blackhawk by Crandall begins, ends #22	92.00	275.00	600.00
13-15: 14-Private Dogtag begins (ends #83)	62.00	188.00	425.00
16-20: 16-Blue Tracer ends. 17-P.T. Boat begins	54.00	162.00	365.00
21-31: 22-Last Crandall Blackhawk. 23-Shrunken head-c. 27 Death Patrol revived	48.00	145.00	320.00
32-43	42.00	125.00	270.00

NOTE: ***Berg** a-6. **Al Bryant** c-31-34, 38, 40-43. **J. Cole** a-1-3, 27-32. **Crandall** a-12-22; c-13-20. **Cuidera** c-2-9. **Eisner** c-1, 2(part), 9, 10. **Kotsky** c-21-29, 35, 37, 39. **McWilliams** a-2-16. **Powell** a-1-13. **Ward** Blackhawk-30, 31(15 pgs. each); c-30.*

MILITARY WILLY
1907 (14 pgs.; half in color (every other page))
(regular comic book format)(7x9-1/2")(stapled)
J. I. Austen Co.

	GD25	FN65	NM94
nn-By F. R. Morgan	21.00	62.00	145.00

MILLENNIUM (DC)(Value: cover or less)

MILLENNIUM INDEX (Independent)(Value: cover or less)

MILLIE, THE LOVABLE MONSTER
Sept-Nov, 1962 - No. 6, Jan, 1973
Dell Publishing Co.

	GD25	FN65	NM94
12-523-211, 2(8-10/63)	4.20	12.50	25.00
3(8-10/64)	3.60	9.00	18.00
4(7/72), 5(10/72), 6(1/73)	1.65	4.00	10.00

NOTE: ***Woggon** a-3-6; c-3-6. 4 reprints 1; 5 reprints 2; 6 reprints 3.*

MILLIE THE MODEL (See Comedy Comics, A Date With..., Gay Comics, Joker Comics #28, Life With..., Mad About... & Modeling With...)
1945 - No. 207, December, 1973
Marvel/Atlas/Marvel Comics (CnPC #1)(SPI/Male/VPI)

	GD25	FN65	NM94
1-Origin	43.00	130.00	300.00
2 (10/46)-Millie becomes The Blonde Phantom to sell Blonde Phantom perfume; a pre-Blonde Phantom app. (see All-Select #11, Fall, '46)	25.00	75.00	175.00
3-7: 4,5- Willie app. 7-Willie smokes extra strong tobacco	14.00	43.00	100.00
8,10-Kurtzman's "Hey Look." 8-Willie & Rusty app.	14.00	43.00	100.00
9-Powerhouse Pepper by Wolverton, 4 pgs.	18.00	54.00	125.00
11-Kurtzman-a, "Giggles 'n Grins"	10.00	30.00	70.00
12,15,17-20: 12-Rusty & Hedy Devine app.	8.35	25.00	50.00
13,14,16-Kurtzman's "Hey Look." 13-Hedy Devine app.	10.00	30.00	65.00
21-30	5.85	17.50	35.00
31-60	4.20	12.50	25.00
61-99	3.60	9.00	18.00
100	4.20	12.50	25.00
101-153,155-190: 107-Jack Kirby app. in story	2.40	6.00	12.00
154-New Millie begins (10/67)	3.60	9.00	18.00
191-207: 192-(52 pgs.)	1.40	3.50	7.00
Annual 1(1962)-Early Marvel annual (2nd?)	14.00	43.00	100.00
Annual 2(1963)	11.00	32.00	75.00
Annual 3-5)1964-1966)	8.35	25.00	50.00
Annual 6-10(1967-11/71)	5.85	17.50	35.00
Queen-Size 11(9/74), 12(1975)	4.20	12.50	25.00

NOTE: ***Dan DeCarlo** a-18-93.*

MILLION DOLLAR DIGEST (Richie Rich... #23 on; also see Richie Rich...)
11/86 - No. 7, 11/87; No. 8, 4/88 - Present ($1.25-$1.75, digest size)
Harvey Publications

	GD25	FN65	NM94
1-8			1.25
9-32 (1994)		.70	1.75

MILT GROSS FUNNIES (Also see Picture News #1)
Aug, 1947 - No. 2, Sept, 1947
Milt Gross, Inc. (ACG?)

	GD25	FN65	NM94
1,2	8.35	25.00	50.00

MILTON THE MONSTER & FEARLESS FLY (TV)
May, 1966
Gold Key

	GD25	FN65	NM94
1 (10175-605)	7.50	22.50	45.00

MINUTE MAN (See Master Comics & Mighty Midget Comics)
Summer, 1941 - No. 3, Spring, 1942 (68 pgs.)
Fawcett Publications

	GD25	FN65	NM94
1	100.00	300.00	650.00
2,3	79.00	238.00	500.00

MINUTE MAN
No date (B&W; 16 pgs.; paper cover blue & red)
Sovereign Service Station giveaway

	GD25	FN65	NM94
nn-American history	1.20	3.00	6.00

MINUTE MAN ANSWERS THE CALL, THE
1942 (4 pages)
By M. C. Gaines (War Bonds giveaway)

	GD25	FN65	NM94
nn-Sheldon Moldoff-a	8.35	25.00	50.00

MIRACLE COMICS
Feb, 1940 - No. 4, March, 1941
Hillman Periodicals

	GD25	FN65	NM94
1-Sky Wizard Master of Space, Dash Dixon, Man of Might, Pinkie Parker, Dusty Doyle, The Kid Cop, K-7, Secret Agent, The Scorpion, & Blandu, Jungle Queen begin; Masked Angel only app. (all 1st app.)	108.00	325.00	700.00
2	57.00	170.00	360.00
3,4: 3-Bill Colt, the Ghost Rider begins. 4-The Veiled Prophet & Bullet Bob app.	50.00	150.00	325.00

MIRACLEMAN (Eclipse)(Value: cover or less)

MIRACLEMAN: APOCRYPHA (Eclipse)(Value: cover or less)

MIRACLEMAN FAMILY (Eclipse)(Value: cover or less)

MIRACLE OF THE WHITE STALLIONS, THE (See Movie Comics)

MIRACLE SQUAD, THE (Fantagraphics)(Value: cover or less)

MIRACLE SQUAD: BLOOD AND DUST, THE (Apple)(Value: cover or less)

MIRRORWALKER (Now)(Value: cover or less)

MISADVENTURES OF MERLIN JONES, THE (See Movie Comics & Merlin Jones as the Monkey's Uncle under Movie Comics)

MISCHIEVOUS MONKS OF CROCODILE ISLE, THE
1908 (8-1/2x11-1/2"; 4 pgs. in color; 12 pgs.)
J. I. Austen Co., Chicago

	GD25	FN65	NM94
nn-By F. R. Morgan; reads longwise	17.00	51.00	120.00

MISS AMERICA COMICS (Miss America Magazine #2 on; also see Blonde Phantom & Marvel Mystery Comics)
1944 (One Shot)
Marvel Comics (20CC)

	GD25	FN65	NM94
1-2 pgs. pin-ups	76.00	230.00	535.00

MISS AMERICA MAGAZINE (Formerly Miss America; Miss America #51 on)
V1#2, Nov, 1944 - No. 93, Nov, 1958
Miss America Publ. Corp./Marvel/Atlas (MAP)

	GD25	FN65	NM94
V1#2-Photo-c of teenage girl in Miss America costume; Miss America, Patsy Walker (intro.) comic stories plus movie reviews & stories; intro. Buzz Baxter & Hedy Wolfe; 1 pg. origin Miss America	75.00	225.00	525.00

Miss America Magazine V7#36, © MEG

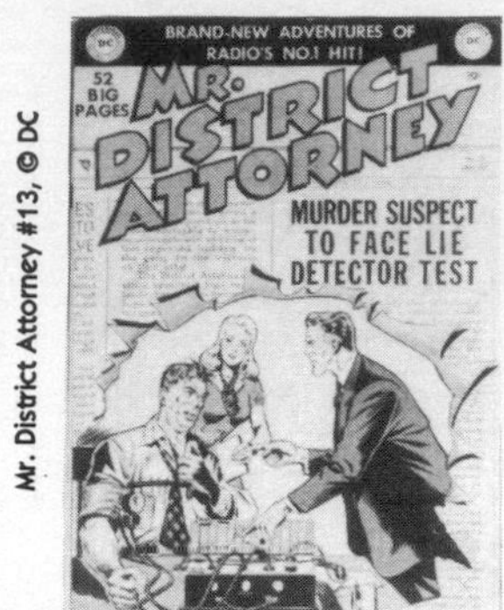

Mr. District Attorney #13, © DC

Mister Ed, The Talking Horse #4, © The Mister Ed. Co.

	GD25	FN65	NM94
3-5-Miss America & Patsy Walker stories	32.00	95.00	225.00
6-Patsy Walker only	7.50	22.50	45.00
V2#1(4/45)-6(9/45)-Patsy Walker continues	4.00	12.00	24.00
V3#1(10/45)-6(4/46)	4.00	12.00	24.00
V4#1(5/46),2,5(9/46)	4.00	11.00	22.00
V4#3(7/46)-Liz Taylor photo-c	6.70	20.00	40.00
V4#4 (8/46; 68pgs.)	4.00	10.00	20.00
V4#6 (10/46; 92pgs.)	4.00	10.00	20.00
V5#1(11/46)-6(4/47), V6#1(5/47)-3(7/47)	4.00	10.00	20.00
V7#1(8/47)-14,16-23(#56, 6/49)	3.20	8.00	16.00
V7#15-All comics	4.00	10.00	20.00
V7#24(#57, 7/49)-Kamen-a (becomes Best Western #58 on?)	3.20	8.00	16.00
V7#25(8/49), 27-44(3/52), VII,nn(5/52)	2.80	7.00	14.00
V7#26(9/49)-All comics	4.00	10.00	20.00
V1,nn(7/52)-V1,nn(1/53)(#46-49)	2.80	7.00	14.00
V7#50(Spring '53), V1#51-V7?#54(7/53)	2.80	7.00	14.00
55-93	2.80	7.00	14.00

NOTE: *Photo-c #1, 4, V2#4, 5, V3#5, V4#3, 4, 6, V7#15, 16, 24, 26, 34, 37, 38. Painted c-3. **Powell** a-V7#31.*

MISS BEVERLY HILLS OF HOLLYWOOD (See Adventures of Bob Hope)
Mar-Apr, 1949 - No. 9, July-Aug, 1950 (52 pgs.)
National Periodical Publications

	GD25	FN65	NM94
1 (Meets Alan Ladd)	39.00	120.00	275.00
2-William Holden photo on-c	29.00	85.00	200.00
3-5: 2-9-Part photo-c. 5-Bob Hope photo on-c	24.00	73.00	170.00
6,7,9	22.00	65.00	150.00
8-Reagan photo on-c	29.00	85.00	200.00

NOTE: *Beverly meets Alan Ladd in #1, Eve Arden #2, Betty Hutton #4, Bob Hope #5.*

MISS CAIRO JONES
1945
Croyden Publishers

	GD25	FN65	NM94
1-Bob Oksner daily newspaper-r (1st strip story); lingerie panels	14.00	43.00	100.00

MISS FURY COMICS (Newspaper strip reprints)
Winter, 1942-43 - No. 8, Winter, 1946 (Published quarterly)
Timely Comics (NPI 1/CmPI 2/MPC 3-8)

	GD25	FN65	NM94
1-Origin Miss Fury by Tarpe' Mills (68 pgs.) in costume w/pin-ups	207.00	620.00	1450.00
2-(60 pgs.)-In costume w/pin-ups	96.00	288.00	650.00
3-(60 pgs.)-In costume w/pin-ups; Hitler-c	79.00	238.00	525.00
4-(52 pgs.)-In costume, 2 pgs. w/pin-ups	63.00	188.00	415.00
5-(52 pgs.)-In costume w/pin-ups	58.00	175.00	400.00
6-(52 pgs.)-Not in costume in inside stories, w/pin-ups	54.00	162.00	350.00
7,8-(36 pgs.)-In costume 1 pg. each; no pin-ups	54.00	162.00	350.00

NOTE: ***Schomburg** c-1, 5, 6.*

MISS FURY
1991 - No. 4, 1991 ($2.50, color, mini-series)
Adventure Comics

	GD25	FN65	NM94
1-4: 1-Origin; granddaughter of original Miss Fury		1.00	2.50
1-Limited ed. ($4.95)	1.00	2.00	5.00

MISSION IMPOSSIBLE (TV)
May, 1967 - No. 4, Oct, 1968; No. 5, Oct, 1969 (All have photo-c)
Dell Publishing Co.

	GD25	FN65	NM94
1	6.00	19.00	44.00
2-5: 5-Reprints #1	4.70	14.00	33.00

MISS LIBERTY (Becomes Liberty Comics)
1945 (MLJ reprints)
Burten Publishing Co.

	GD25	FN65	NM94
1-The Shield & Dusty, The Wizard, & Roy, the Super Boy app.; r/Shield-Wizard #13	23.00	68.00	150.00

MISS MELODY LANE OF BROADWAY (See The Adventures of Bob Hope)
Feb-Mar, 1950 - No. 3, June-July, 1950 (52 pgs.)
National Periodical Publications

	GD25	FN65	NM94
1-Movie stars photos app. on all-c	39.00	120.00	275.00
2,3: 3-Ed Sullivan photo on-c	27.00	81.00	190.00

MISS PEACH
Oct-Dec, 1963; 1969
Dell Publishing Co.

	GD25	FN65	NM94
1-Jack Mendelsohn-a/script	9.15	27.50	55.00
...Tells You How to Grow(1969; 25 cents)-Mel Lazarus-a; also given away (36 pgs.)	5.35	16.00	32.00

MISS PEPPER (See Meet Miss Pepper)

MISS SUNBEAM (See Little Miss...)

MISS VICTORY (See Captain Fearless #1,2, Holyoke One-Shot #3, Veri Best Sure Fire & Veri Best Sure Shot Comics)

MISS VICTORY GOLDEN ANNIVERSARY SPECIA (AC)(Value: cover or less)

MR. & MRS.
1922 (52 & 28 pgs.) (9x9-1/2", cardboard-c)
Whitman Publishing Co.

	GD25	FN65	NM94
nn-By Briggs (B&W, 52pgs.)	15.00	45.00	105.00
nn-28 pgs.-(9x9-1/2")-Sunday strips-r in color	18.00	55.00	125.00

MR. & MRS. BEANS (See Single Series #11)

MR. & MRS. J. EVIL SCIENTIST (TV)(See The Flintstones & Hanna-Barbera Band Wagon #3)
Nov, 1963 - No. 4, Sept, 1966 (Hanna-Barbera, all 12¢)
Gold Key

	GD25	FN65	NM94
1-From The Flintstones	5.00	15.00	35.00
2-4	3.20	8.00	20.00

MR. ANTHONY'S LOVE CLINIC (Based on radio show)
Nov, 1949 - No. 5, Apr-May, 1950 (52 pgs.)
Hillman Periodicals

	GD25	FN65	NM94
1-Photo-c	8.35	25.00	50.00
2	5.00	15.00	30.00
3-5: 5-Photo-c	4.35	13.00	26.00

MR. BUG GOES TO TOWN (See Cinema Comics Herald)
1941 (52 pgs.)(Giveaway)
K.K. Publications

	GD25	FN65	NM94
nn-Cartoon movie	37.00	110.00	260.00

MR. DISTRICT ATTORNEY (Radio/TV)
Jan-Feb, 1948 - No. 67, Jan-Feb, 1959 (1-23: 52 pgs.)
National Periodical Publications

	GD25	FN65	NM94
1-Howard Purcell c-5-23 (most)	68.00	205.00	475.00
2	27.00	81.00	190.00
3-5	20.00	60.00	140.00
6-10	16.00	48.00	110.00
11-20	13.00	40.00	90.00
21-43: 43-Last pre-code (1-2/55)	10.00	30.00	65.00
44-67	8.35	25.00	50.00

MR. DISTRICT ATTORNEY (See 4-Color #13 & The Funnies #35)

MISTER E (DC)(Value: cover or less)

MISTER ED, THE TALKING HORSE (TV)
Mar-May, 1962 - No. 6, Feb, 1964 (All photo-c; photo back-c: 1-6)
Dell Publishing Co./Gold Key

	GD25	FN65	NM94
4-Color 1295	11.50	34.00	80.00
1(11/62) (Gold Key)-Photo-c	8.35	25.00	50.00
2-6-Photo-c	5.00	15.00	30.00

(See March of Comics #244, 260, 282, 290)

MR. MAGOO (TV) (The Nearsighted..., ...& Gerald McBoing Boing 1954 issues; formerly Gerald McBoing-Boing And ...)

Mister Miracle #2 ('89), © DC

Mister Mystery #19, © Stanmore

Mister X V2#4, © Vortex

GD25 FN65 NM94

No. 6, Nov-Jan, 1953-54; 5/54 - 3-5/62; 9-11/63 - 3-5/65
Doll Publishing Co
6 10.00 30.00 60.00
4-Color 561(5/54),602(11/54) 10.00 30.00 60.00
4-Color 1235(#1, 12-2/62),1305(#2, 3-5/62) 8.35 25.00 50.00
3(9-11/63) - 5 7.50 22.50 45.00
4-Color 1235(12-536-505)(3-5/65)-2nd Printing 4.70 14.00 28.00

MISTER MIRACLE (See Cancelled Comic Cavalcade)
3-4/71 - V4#18, 2-3/74; V5#19, 9/77 - V6#25, 8-9/78; 1987
National Periodical Publications/DC Comics
1-1st app. Mr. Miracle (#1-3 are 15 cents) 2.40 7.25 17.00
2,3 1.65 4.70 11.00
4-8: 4-Boy Commandos-r begin; all 52 pgs. 1.65 4.00 10.00
9,10: 9-Origin Mr. Miracle; Darkseid cameo 1.30 3.25 8.00
11-18: 15-Intro/1st app. Shilo Norman. 18-Barda & Scott Free wed; New Gods app. & Darkseid cameo 1.20 3.00 7.00
19-25 (1977-1978) 1.50 3.75
Special 1(1987, $1.25, 52 pgs.) 1.10 2.75
NOTE: ***Austin** a-19i. **Ditko** a-6r. **Golden** a-23-25p; c-25p. **Heath** a-24i, 25i; c-25i. **Kirby** a(p)/c-1-18. **Nasser** a-19i. **Rogers** a-19-22p; c-19, 20p, 21p, 22-24. 4-8 contain **Simon & Kirby** Boy Commandos reprints from Detective 82,76, Boy Commandos 1, 3 & Detective 64 in that order.*

MISTER MIRACLE (DC, 1989-91)(Value: cover or less)

MR. MIRACLE (See Capt. Fearless #1 & Holyoke One-Shot #4)

MR. MONSTER (Doc Steam... #7 on; See Airboy-Mr. Monster Special, Dark Horse Presents, Super Duper Comics & Vanguard Illustrated #7)
Jan, 1985 - No. 10, June, 1987 ($1.75, color, Baxter paper)
Eclipse Comics
1-1st story-r from Vanguard Ill. #7(1st app.) 1.00 2.50 5.50
2-Dave Stevens-c 1.20 3.00
3-10: 3-Alan Moore scripts; Wolverton-r/Weird Mysteries #5. 6-Ditko-r/Fantastic Fears #5 plus new Giffen-a 10 6-D issue .80 2.00

MR. MONSTER (Dark Horse, 1988)(Value: cover or less)

MR. MONSTER ATTACKS! (Tundra)(Value: cover or less)

MR. MONSTER'S SUPER-DUPER SPECIAL (Eclipse)(Value: cover or less)

MR. MUSCLES (Formerly Blue Beetle #18-21)
No. 22, Mar, 1956; No. 23, Aug, 1956
Charlton Comics
22,23 4.00 11.00 22.00

MISTER MYSTERY (Tales of Horror and Suspense)
Sept, 1951 - No. 19, Oct, 1954
Mr. Publ. (Media Publ.) No. 1-3/SPM Publ./Stanmore (Aragon)
1-Kurtzmanesque horror story 30.00 90.00 210.00
2,3-Kurtzmanesque story. 3-Anti-Wertham edit. 22.00 65.00 150.00
4,6: Bondage-c; 6-Torture 22.00 65.00 150.00
5,8,10 17.00 52.00 120.00
7-"The Brain Bats of Venus" by Wolverton; partially re-used in Weird Tales of the Future #7 54.00 160.00 375.00
9-Nostrand-a 17.00 52.00 120.00
11-Wolverton "Robot Woman" story/Weird Mysteries #2, cut up, rewritten & partially redrawn 30.00 90.00 210.00
12-Classic injury to eye-c 49.00 145.00 340.00
13,14,17,19: 17-Severed heads-c 13.50 41.00 95.00
15-"Living Dead" junkie story 13.50 41.00 95.00
16-Bondage-c 13.50 41.00 95.00
18-"Robot Woman" by Wolverton reprinted from Weird Mysteries #2; decapitation, bondage-c 26.00 80.00 185.00
NOTE: ***Andru** a-1, 2p, 3p. **Andru/Esposito** c-1-3. **Baily** c-10-18(most). **Mortellaro** c-5-7. Bondage c-7. Some issues have graphic dismemberment scenes.*

MR. MYSTIC (See Will Eisner Presents)

MISTER Q (See Mighty Midget Comics & Our Flag Comics #5)

MR. RISK (Formerly All Romances; Men Against Crime #3 on)(Also see Our Flag Comics & Super-Mystery Comics)
No. 7, Oct, 1950 - No. 2, Dec, 1950
Ace Magazines
7,2 4.70 14.00 28.00

MR. SCARLET & PINKY (See Mighty Midget Comics)

MR. T AND THE T-FORCE
June, 1993 - Present ($1.95, color)
Now Comics
1-6-Newsstand editions polybagged with photo trading card in each; 1,2-Neal Adams-c/a(p). 3-Dave Dorman painted-c .80 2.00
1-6-Direct Sale editions polybagged w/line drawn trading cards. 1-Contains gold foil trading card by Neal Adams .80 2.00

MISTER UNIVERSE (Professional wrestler)
July, 1951; No. 2, Oct, 1951 - No. 5, April, 1952
Mr. Publications Media Publ. (Stanmor, Aragon)
1 11.50 34.00 80.00
2-"Jungle That Time Forgot," (24 pg. story); Andru/Esposito-c 9.15 27.50 55.00
3-Marijuana story 9.15 27.50 55.00
4,5-"Goes to War" cover/stories 5.35 16.00 32.00

MISTER X (See Vortex)
6/84 - No. 14, 8/88 ($1.50-$2.25, direct sales, color, coated paper)
V2#1, Apr, 1989 - V2#12, Mar, 1990 ($2.00-$2.50, B&W, newsprint)
Mr. Publications/Vortex Comics
1 1.00 2.50 5.50
2 1.20 3.00
3-14: 11-Dave McKean story & art (6 pgs.) .80 2.00
V2#1-11 (Second Coming, $2.00, B&W): 1-Four different covers. 10-Photo-c .80 2.00
V2#12 ($2.50) 1.00 2.50
Special (no date, 1990? .80 2.00
Graphic Novel, Return of... ($11.95)-r/1-4 1.70 5.00 12.00
Hardcover Limited Edition ($34.95) 5.00 15.00 35.00

MISTY (Marvel)(Value: cover or less)

MITZI COMICS (...Boy Friend #2 on)(See All Teen)
Spring, 1948 (One Shot)
Timely Comics
1-Kurtzman's "Hey Look" plus 3 pgs. "Giggles 'n' Grins" 11.50 34.00 80.00

MITZI'S BOY FRIEND (Formerly Mitzi; becomes Mitzi's Romances)
No. 2, June, 1948 - No. 7, April, 1949
Marvel Comics (TCI)
2 5.85 17.50 35.00
3-7 4.70 14.00 28.00

MITZI'S ROMANCES (Formerly Mitzi's Boy Friend)
No. 8, June, 1949 - No. 10, Dec, 1949
Timely/Marvel Comics (TCI)
8-Becomes True Life Tales #8 (10/49) on? 5.85 17.50 35.00
9,10: 10-Painted-c 4.70 14.00 28.00

MOBY DICK (See Feature Presentations #6, Four Color #717, and King Classics)

MOBY DUCK (See Donald Duck #112 & Walt Disney Showcase #2,11)
Oct, 1967 - No. 11, Oct, 1970; No. 12, Jan, 1974 - No. 30, Feb, 1978
Gold Key (Disney)
1 1.65 4.00 10.00
2-5 1.00 2.50 6.00
6-11 1.40 3.50
12-30: 21,30-r .80 2.00

MODEL FUN (With Bobby Benson)
No. 3, Winter, 1954-55 - No. 5, July, 1955
Harle Publications

Modern Comics #92, © QUA

Molly O'Day #1, © AVON

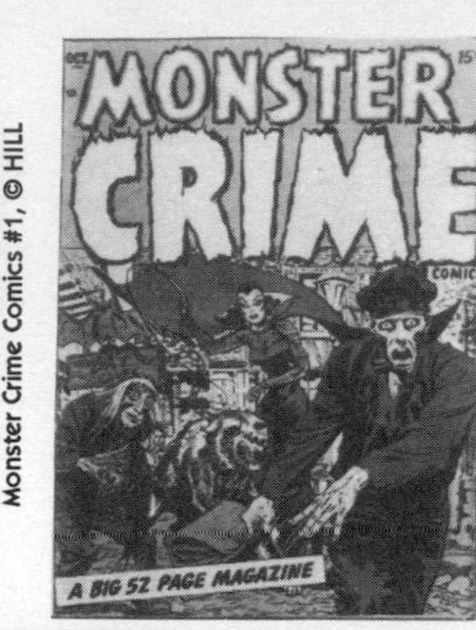

Monster Crime Comics #1, © HILL

	GD25	FN65	NM94
3-Bobby Benson	5.00	15.00	30.00
4,5-Bobby Benson	3.60	9.00	18.00

MODELING WITH MILLIE (Formerly Life With Millie)
No. 21, Feb, 1963 - No. 54, June, 1967
Atlas/Marvel Comics Group (Male Publ.)

21	6.70	20.00	40.00
22-30	4.20	12.50	25.00
31-54	4.00	10.00	20.00

MODERN COMICS (Formerly Military Comics #1-43)
No. 44, Nov, 1945 - No. 102, Oct, 1950
Quality Comics Group

44-Blackhawk continues	42.00	125.00	275.00
45-52: 49-1st app. Fear, Lady Adventuress	25.00	75.00	175.00
53-Torchy by Ward begins (9/46)	32.00	95.00	210.00
54-60: 55-J. Cole-a	22.00	65.00	150.00
61-77,79,80: 73-J. Cole-a	20.00	60.00	140.00
78-1st app. Madame Butterfly	22.00	65.00	150.00
81-99,101: 82,83-One pg. J. Cole-a. 83-The Spirit app.; last 52 pg. issue? 99-Blackhawk on the moon-c/story	20.00	60.00	140.00
100	20.00	60.00	140.00
102-(Scarce)-J. Cole-a; Spirit by Eisner app.	23.00	70.00	160.00

NOTE: ***Al Bryant** c-44-51, 54, 55, 66, 69. **Jack Cole** a-55, 73. **Crandall** Blackhawk-#46-51, 54, 56, 58-60, 64, 67-70, 73, 76-78, 80-83; c-60-65, 67, 68, 70-95. **Crandall/Cuidera** c-56-59, 96-102. **Gustavson** a-47. **Ward** Blackhawk-#52, 53, 55 (15 pgs. each). Torchy in #53-102; by **Ward** only in #53-89(9/49); by **Gil Fox** #93, 102.*

MODERN LOVE
June-July, 1949 - No. 8, Aug-Sept, 1950
E. C. Comics

1	44.00	133.00	310.00
2-Craig/Feldstein-c	36.00	107.00	250.00
3-Spanking panel	30.00	90.00	210.00
4-6 (Scarce): 4-Bra/panties panels	42.00	126.00	295.00
7,8	32.00	95.00	225.00

NOTE: ***Craig** a-3. **Feldstein** a-in most issues; c-1, 2i, 3-8. **Harrison** a-4. **Iger** a-6-8. **Ingels** a-1, 2, 4-7. **Palais** a-5. **Wood** a-7. **Wood/Harrison** a-5-7. (Canadian reprints known; see Table of Contents.)*

MOD LOVE
1967 (36 pages) (50 cents)
Western Publishing Co.

1	4.00	10.00	20.00

MODNIKS, THE
Aug, 1967 - No. 2, Aug, 1970
Gold Key

10206-708(#1), 2	1.30	3.25	8.00

MOD SQUAD (TV)
Jan, 1969 - No. 3, Oct, 1969 - No. 8, April, 1971
Dell Publishing Co.

1-Photo-c	3.25	9.50	22.00
2-8: 2-4-Photo-c. 8-Reprints #2	1.85	5.50	13.00

MOD WHEELS
March, 1971 - No. 19, Jan, 1976
Gold Key

1	1.65	4.00	10.00
2-19: 11,15-Extra 16pgs. ads	1.00	2.00	5.00

MOE & SHMOE COMICS
Spring, 1948 - No. 2, Summer, 1948
O. S. Publ. Co.

1	5.85	17.50	35.00
2	4.20	12.50	25.00

MOEBIUS (Graphic novel)
Oct, 1987 - No. 6, 1988; No. 7, 1990; No. 8, 1991 ($9.95, adults, 8x11")
Epic Comics (Marvel)

	GD25	FN65	NM94
1,2,4-6,8: (#2, 2nd printing, $9.95)	1.65	4.00	10.00
3,7: 3-(1st & 2nd printings, $12.95)	1.85	5.50	13.00
0 (1990, $12.95)	1.85	5.50	13.00
Moebius I-Signed & numbered hard-c ($45.95, Graphitti Designs, 1,500 copies printed)-r/#1-3	6.50	20.00	46.00

MOLLY MANTON'S ROMANCES (Romantic Affairs #3)
Sept, 1949 - No. 2, Dec, 1949 (52 pgs.)
Marvel Comics (SePI)

1-Photo-c (becomes Blaze the Wonder Collie #2 (10/49) on? & Molly Manton's Romances #2	8.35	25.00	50.00
2-Titled "Romances of...;" photo-c	5.35	16.00	32.00

MOLLY O'DAY (Super Sleuth)
February, 1945 (1st Avon comic)
Avon Periodicals

1-Molly O'Day, The Enchanted Dagger by Tuska (r/Yankee #1), Capt'n Courage, Corporal Grant app.	32.00	95.00	220.00

MONKEES, THE (TV)(Also see Circus Boy, Groovy, Not Brand Echh #3, Teen-Age Talk, Teen Beam & Teen Beat)
March, 1967 - No. 17, Oct, 1969 (#1-4,6,7,10 have photo-c)
Dell Publishing Co.

1	10.00	30.00	70.00
2-4,6,7,10: All photo-c	5.00	15.00	35.00
5,8,9,11-17: 17 reprints #1	3.60	10.75	25.00

MONKEY AND THE BEAR, THE
Sept, 1953 - No. 3, Jan, 1954
Atlas Comics (ZPC)

1-Howie Post-c/a in all; funny animal	4.70	14.00	28.00
2,3	3.20	8.00	16.00

MONKEYSHINES COMICS
Summer, 1944 - No. 27, July, 1949
Ace Periodicals/Publishers Specialists/Current Books/Unity Publ.

1-Funny animal	7.50	22.50	45.00
2-(Aut/44)	4.00	11.00	22.00
3-10: 3-(Win/44)	3.60	9.00	18.00
11-27: 23,24-Fago-c/a	3.20	8.00	16.00

MONKEY SHINES OF MARSELEEN
1909 (11-1/2x17") (28 pages in two colors)
Cupples & Leon Co.

nn-By Norman E. Jennett	20.00	60.00	140.00

MONKEY'S UNCLE, THE (See Merlin Jones As... under Movie Comics)

MONOLITH (Comico)(Value: cover or less)

MONROES, THE (TV)
April, 1967
Dell Publishing Co.

1-Photo-c	3.00	7.50	15.00

MONSTER
1953 - No. 2, 1953
Fiction House Magazines

1-Dr. Drew by Grandenetti; reprint from Rangers Comics #48; Whitman-c	25.00	75.00	175.00
2 -Whitman-c	20.00	60.00	140.00

MONSTER CRIME COMICS (Also see Crime Must Stop)
October, 1952 (15 cents, 52 pgs.)
Hillman Periodicals

1 (Scarce)	55.00	165.00	350.00

MONSTER HOWLS (Magazine)
December, 1966 (Satire) (35 cents) (68 pgs.)
Humor-Vision

1	4.00	11.00	22.00

Monte Hale Western #68, © FAW

Moon Girl and the Prince #7, © WMG

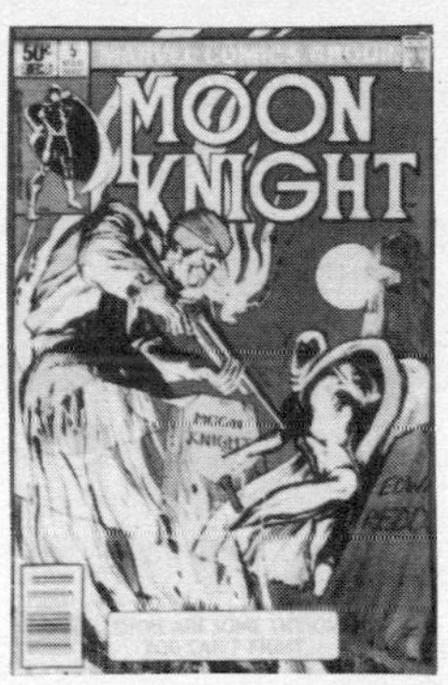

Moon Knight #5 (3/81), © MEG

GD25 FN65 NM94

MONSTER HUNTERS
Aug, 1975 - No. 9, Jan, 1977; No. 10, Oct, 1977 - No. 18, Feb, 1979
Charlton Comics

	GD25	FN65	NM94
1,2: 1-Howard-a; Newton-c. 2-Ditko-a	1.00	2.00	5.00
3-13,15-18		.80	2.00
14-Special all-Ditko issue		1.40	3.50
1,2(Modern Comics reprints, 1977)			1.00

NOTE: *Ditko a-2, 6, 8, 10, 13-15r, 18r; c-13-15, 18. **Howard** r-13. **Morisi** a-1. **Staton** a-1, 13. **Sutton** a-2, 4; c-2, 4. Reprints in #12-18.*

MONSTER IN MY POCKET (Harvey)(Value: cover or less)

MONSTER MENACE
Dec, 1993 - No. 4, Mar, 1994 ($1.25, color, mini-series)
Marvel Comics

	GD25	FN65	NM94
1-4-Kirby/Ditko pre-code Atlas horror reprints			1.25

MONSTER OF FRANKENSTEIN (See Frankenstein)

MONSTERS ON THE PROWL (Chamber of Darkness #1-8)
No. 9, 2/71 - No. 27, 11/73; No. 28, 6/74 - No. 30, 10/74
Marvel Comics Group (No. 13,14: 52 pgs.)

	GD25	FN65	NM94
9-Barry Smith inks		1.70	4.25
10-30: 16-King Kull app.; Severin-c		.90	2.25

NOTE: ***Ditko** r-5, 9, 14, 16. **Kirby** r-10-17, 21, 23, 25, 27, 28, 30; c-9, 25. **Kirby/Ditko** r-14, 17-20, 22, 24, 26, 29. **Reinman** r-5. **Marie/John Severin** a-16(Kull). 9-13, 15 contain one new story. Woodish art by **Reese**-11. King Kull created by Robert E. Howard.*

MONSTERS UNLEASHED (Magazine)
July, 1973 - No. 11, April, 1975; Summer, 1975 (B&W)
Marvel Comics Group

	GD25	FN65	NM94
1	1.00	2.50	5.50
2-11: 2-The Frankenstein Monster begins. 3-Neal Adams-c/a; The Man-Thing begins (origin-r). 4-Intro. Satana, the Devil's daughter; Krigstein-r. 7-Williamson-a(r). 8-N. Adams-r. 9-Wendigo app. 10-Origin Tigra		1.30	3.25
Annual 1(Summer,1975)-Kane-a		.90	2.25

NOTE: ***Boris** c-2, 6. **Brunner** a-2; c-11. **J. Buscema** a-2p, 4p, 5p. **Colan** a-1, 4r. **Davis** a-3r. **Everett** a-2r. **G. Kane** a-3. **Morrow** a-3; c-1. **Perez** a-8. **Ploog** a-6. **Reese** a-1, 2. **Tuska** a-3p. **Wildey** a-1r.*

MONTANA KID, THE (See Kid Montana)

MONTE HALE WESTERN (Movie star; Formerly Mary Marvel #1-28; also see Fawcett Movie Comic, Motion Picture Comics, Picture News #8, Real Western Hero, Six-Gun Heroes, Western Hero & XMas Comics)
No. 29, Oct, 1948 - No. 88, Jan, 1956
Fawcett Publications/Charlton No. 83 on

	GD25	FN65	NM94
29-(#1, 52pgs.)-Photo-c begin, end #82; Monte Hale & his horse Pardner begin	36.00	107.00	250.00
30-(52 pgs.)-Big Bow and Little Arrow begin, end #34; Captain Tootsie by Beck	17.00	52.00	120.00
31-36,38-40-(52 pgs.): 34-Gabby Hayes begins, ends #80. 39-Captain Tootsie by Beck	13.50	41.00	95.00
37,41,45,49-(36 pgs.)	10.00	30.00	60.00
42-44,46-48,50-(52 pgs.): 47-Big Bow & Little Arrow app.	10.00	30.00	65.00
51,52,54-56,58,59-(52 pgs.)	8.35	25.00	50.00
53,57-(36 pgs.): 53-Slim Pickens app.	6.70	20.00	40.00
60-81: 36pgs. #60-on. 80-Gabby Hayes ends	6.70	20.00	40.00
82-Last Fawcett issue (6/53)	8.65	25.00	52.00
83-1st Charlton issue (2/55); B&W photo back-c begin. Gabby Hayes returns, ends #86	8.35	26.00	52.00
84 (4/55)	6.70	20.00	40.00
85-86	6.35	19.00	38.00
87-Wolverton-r, pg.	6.70	20.00	40.00
88-Last issue	6.70	20.00	40.00

NOTE: ***Gil Kane** a-33?, 34? Rocky Lane -1 pg. (Carnation ad)-38, 40, 41, 43, 44, 46, 55.*

MONTY HALL OF THE U.S. MARINES (See With the Marines...)
Aug, 1951 - No. 11, Apr, 1953
Toby Press

	GD25	FN65	NM94
1	6.70	20.00	40.00
2	4.35	13.00	26.00
3-5	4.00	11.00	22.00
6-11	3.60	9.00	18.00

NOTE: *Full page pin-ups (Pin-Up Pete) by **Jack Sparling** in #1-9.*

MOON, A GIRL...ROMANCE, A (Becomes Weird Fantasy #13 on; formerly Moon Girl #1-8)
No. 9, Sept-Oct, 1949 - No. 12, Mar-Apr, 1950
E. C. Comics

	GD25	FN65	NM94
9-Moon Girl cameo; spanking panel	57.00	171.00	400.00
10,11	43.00	130.00	300.00
12-(Scarce)	60.00	180.00	420.00

NOTE: ***Feldstein, Ingels** art in all. **Feldstein** c-9-12. **Wood/Harrison** a-10-12. Canadian reprints known; see Table of Contents.*

MOON GIRL AND THE PRINCE (#1) (Moon Girl #2-6; Moon Girl Fights Crime #7, 8; becomes A Moon, A Girl, Romance #9 on)(Also see Animal Fables #7 and Happy Houlihans)
Fall, 1947 - No. 8, Summer, 1949
E. C. Comics

	GD25	FN65	NM94
1-Origin Moon Girl (see Happy Houlihans #1)	72.00	215.00	500.00
2	39.00	115.00	270.00
3,4: 4-Moon Girl vs. a vampire	33.00	100.00	230.00
5-E.C.'s 1st horror story, "Zombie Terror"	72.00	215.00	500.00
6-8 (Scarce): 7-Origin Star (Moongirl's sidekick)	39.00	120.00	275.00

NOTE: ***Craig** a-2, 5. **Moldoff** a-1-8; c-2-6. **Wheelan's** Fat and Slat app. in #3, 4, 6. #2 & #3 are 52 pgs., #4 on, 36 pgs. Canadian reprints known; (see Table of Contents.)*

MOON KNIGHT (Also see The Hulk, Marc Spector..., Marvel Preview #21, Marvel Spotlight & Werewolf by Night #32)
November, 1980 - No. 38, July, 1984 (Mando paper No. 33 on)
Marvel Comics Group

	GD25	FN65	NM94
1-Origin resumed in #4; begin Sienkiewicz-c/a		1.60	4.00
2-34,36-38: 4-Intro Midnight Man. 16-The Thing app. 25-Double size			1.50
35-($1.00, 52 pgs.)-X-men app.; F.F. cameo		.80	2.00

NOTE: ***Austin** c-27i, 31i. **Kaluta** c-36-38; back c-35. **Miller** c-9, 12p, 13p, 15?, 27p. **Ploog** back c-35. **Sienkiewicz** a-1-15, 17-20, 22-26, 28-30, 37; c-1-5, 7, 8, 10, 11, 14-26, 28-30, 31p, 33, 34.*

MOON KNIGHT
June, 1985 - No. 6, Dec, 1985
Marvel Comics Group

	GD25	FN65	NM94
V2#1-6: 1-Double size; new costume. 6-Painted-c			1.00

MOON KNIGHT: DIVIDED WE FALL
1992 ($4.95, color, 52 pgs.)
Marvel Comics

	GD25	FN65	NM94
nn-Denys Cowan-c/a(p)	1.00	2.00	5.00

MOON KNIGHT SPECIAL
Oct, 1992 ($2.50, color, 52 pgs.)
Marvel Comics

	GD25	FN65	NM94
1-Shang Chi, Master of Kung Fu-c/story		1.00	2.50

MOON KNIGHT SPECIAL EDITION
Nov, 1983 - No. 3, Jan, 1984 ($2.00, mini-series, Baxter paper)
Marvel Comics Group

	GD25	FN65	NM94
1-3: Reprints from Hulk mag. by Sienkiewicz			1.50

MOON MULLINS
1927 - 1933 (52 pgs.) (daily B&W strip reprints)
Cupples & Leon Co.

	GD25	FN65	NM94
Series 1('27)-By Willard	29.00	85.00	200.00
Series 2('28), Series 3('29), Series 4('30)	17.00	52.00	120.00
Series 5('31), 6('32), 7('33)	14.00	43.00	100.00
Big Book 1('30)-B&W	24.00	73.00	170.00

MOON MULLINS (See Popular Comics, Super Book #3 & Super Comics)

Moon Mullins #2, © N.Y. News Synd.

Morbius: The Living Vampire #13, © MEG

More Fun Comics #18, © DC

	GD25	FN65	NM94
1941 - 1945			
Dell Publishing Co.			
4-Color 14(1941)	32.00	95.00	225.00
Large Feature Comic 29(1941)	22.00	65.00	150.00
4-Color 31(1943)	17.00	52.00	120.00
4-Color 81(1945)	10.00	30.00	65.00

MOON MULLINS
Dec-Jan, 1947-48 - No. 8, 1949 (52 pgs.)
Michel Publ. (American Comics Group)

	GD25	FN65	NM94
1-Alternating Sunday & daily strip-r	13.50	41.00	95.00
2	8.35	25.00	50.00
3-8: 8-Featuring Kayo on-c	6.35	19.00	38.00

NOTE: ***Milt Gross** a-2-6, 8. **Frank Willard** r-all.*

MOON PILOT (See 4-Color #1313)

MOONSHADOW
May, 1985 - No. 12, Feb, 1987 ($1.50-$1.75)(Adults only)
Epic Comics (Marvel)

	GD25	FN65	NM94
1-Origin		1.60	4.00
2-12: 11-Origin		1.00	2.50
Trade paperback (1987?)-reprints	2.00	6.00	14.00
Signed & #'d hard-c ($39.95, 1,200 copies)-r/1-12	5.50	17.00	40.00

MOON-SPINNERS, THE (See Movie Comics)

MOPSY (See Pageant of Comics & TV Teens)
Feb, 1948 - No. 19, Sept, 1953
St. John Publ. Co.

	GD25	FN65	NM94
1-Part-r; r-/"Some Punkins" by Neher	13.00	40.00	90.00
2	8.35	25.00	50.00
3-10(1953): 8-Lingerie panels	6.35	19.00	38.00
11-19: 19-Lingerie-c	5.00	15.00	30.00

NOTE: *#1, 3-6, 13, 18, 19 have paper dolls.*

MORBIUS REVISITED
Aug, 1993 - No. 5, Dec, 1993 ($1.95, color, mini-series)
Marvel Comic

	GD25	FN65	NM94
1-5-Reprints Fear #27-31		.80	2.00

MORBIUS: THE LIVING VAMPIRE (Also see Amazing Spider-Man #101, 102, Fear #20, Marvel Team-Up #3, 4, Midnight Sons Unl. & Vampire Tales)
Sept, 1992 - Present ($1.75, color)
Marvel Comics

	GD25	FN65	NM94
1-($2.75, 52 pgs.)-Polybagged w/poster; Ghost Rider & Johnny Blaze x-over (part 3 of Rise of the Midnight Sons)	1.00	2.50	5.50
2		1.00	2.50
3-5: 3,4-Vs. Spider-Man-c/story		.80	2.00
6-11,13-20: 16-Siege of Darkness part 5		.70	1.75
12-($2.25)-Outer-c is a Darkhold envelope made of black parchment w/gold ink; Midnight Massacre x-over		.90	2.25

MORE FUN COMICS (Formerly New Fun Comics #1-6)
No. 7, Jan, 1936 - No. 127, Nov-Dec, 1947 (No. 7,9-11: paper-c)
National Periodical Publications

	GD25	FN65	VF82
7(1/36)-Oversized, paper-c; 1 pg. Kelly-a	550.00	1375.00	2500.00
(Estimated up to 15 total copies exist, none in NM/Mint)			
8(2/36)-Oversized (10x12"), slick-c; 1 pg. Kelly-a	415.00	1250.00	2500.00
9(3-4/36)(Very rare, 1st comic-sized issue)-Last Henri Duval by Siegel & Shuster; last multiple panel-c	415.00	1250.00	2500.00
10,11(7/36): 11-1st 'Calling All Cars' by Siegel & Shuster; new classic logo begins	267.00	800.00	1600.00
12(8/36)-Slick-c begin	233.00	700.00	1400.00
V2#1(9/36, #13)	225.00	675.00	1350.00
2(10/36, #14)-Dr. Occult in costume (1st in color)(Superman proto-type-1st DC appearance) continues from The Comics Magazine, ends #17	1000.00	3000.00	6000.00
(Estimated up to 10 total copies exist, none in NM/Mint)			
V2#3(11/36, #15), 16(V2#4), 17(V2#5): 16-Cover numbering begins; Xmas-c; last Superman tryout issue	433.00	1300.00	2600.00
18-20(V2#8, 5/37)	142.00	425.00	850.00

	GD25	FN65	NM94
21(V2#9)-24(V2#12, 9/37)	108.00	325.00	650.00
25(V3#1, 10/37)-27(V3#3, 12/37): 27-Xmas-c	108.00	325.00	650.00
28-30: 30-1st non-funny cover	108.00	325.00	650.00
31-35: 32-Last Dr. Occult	100.00	300.00	600.00
36-40: 36-(10/38)-The Masked Ranger & sidekick Pedro begins; Ginger Snap by Bob Kane (2 pgs.). 39-Xmas-c	92.00	275.00	550.00
41-50: 41-Last Masked Ranger	79.00	240.00	475.00
51-The Spectre app. (in costume) in one panel ad at end of Buccaneer story	333.00	1000.00	2000.00

	GD25	FN65	VF82	NM94
52-(2/40)-Origin/1st app. The Spectre (in costume splash panel only), part 1 by Bernard Baily (parts 1 & 2 written by Jerry Siegel; Spectre's costume changes color from purple & blue to green & grey; last Wing Brady	2800.00	8400.00	18,200.00	28,000.00
(Estimated up to 60 total copies exist, 3 in NM/Mint)				
53-Origin The Spectre (in costume at end of story), part 2; Capt. Desmo begins	1750.00	5250.00	11,375.00	17,500.00
(Estimated up to 60 total copies exist, 3 in NM/Mint)				
54-The Spectre in costume; last King Carter	600.00	1800.00	3300.00	4800.00
55-(Scarce, 5/40)-Dr. Fate begins (Intro & 1st app.); last Bulldog Martin	875.00	2625.00	4800.00	7000.00
(Estimated up to 100 total copies exist, 6 in NM/Mint)				

	GD25	FN65	NM94
56-60: 56-Congo Bill begins (6/40); 1st Dr. Fate-c (classic). 58-Classic Spectre-c	240.00	725.00	1675.00
61-66: 61-Classic Dr. Fate-c. 63-Last St. Bob Neal. 64-Lance Larkin begins. 65-Classic Spectre-c	185.00	550.00	1300.00

	GD25	FN65	VF82	NM94
67-(5/41)-Origin (1st) Dr. Fate; last Congo Bill & Biff Bronson	440.00	1300.00	2400.00	3500.00
(Estimated up to 105 total copies exist, 6 in NM/Mint)				

	GD25	FN65	NM94
68-70: 68-Clip Carson begins. 70-Last Lance Larkin	150.00	450.00	1000.00

	GD25	FN65	VF82	NM94
71-Origin & 1st app. Johnny Quick by Mort Wysinger (9/41); sci/fi-c	375.00	1125.00	2060.00	3000.00
(Estimated up to 90 total copies exist, 6 in NM/Mint)				

	GD25	FN65	NM94
72-Dr. Fate's new helmet; last Sgt. Carey, Sgt. O'Malley & Captain Desmo; German submarine-c (only German war-c)	125.00	375.00	850.00

	GD25	FN65	VF82	NM94
73-Origin & 1st app. Aquaman (11/41) & begins; intro. Green Arrow & Speedy	625.00	1875.00	3440.00	5000.00
(Estimated up to 85 total copies exist, 5 in NM/Mint)				

	GD25	FN65	NM94
74-2nd Aquaman	150.00	450.00	1000.00
75-80: 76-Last Clip Carson; Johnny Quick (by Meskin #76-97) begins, ends #107. 80-Last large logo	133.00	400.00	900.00
81-88: 81-1st small logo. 84-Only Japanese war-c. 87-Last Radio Squad	92.00	275.00	625.00
89-Origin Green Arrow & Speedy Team-up	108.00	325.00	725.00
90-99: 91-1st bi-monthly issue. 93-Dover & Clover begin (1st app., 9-10/43). 97-Kubert-a. 98-Last Dr. Fate	62.00	188.00	425.00
100	92.00	275.00	600.00

	GD25	FN65	VF82	NM94
101-Origin & 1st app. Superboy (1-2/45)(not by Siegel & Shuster); last Spectre issue	450.00	1350.00	2925.00	4500.00
(Estimated up to 200 total copies exist, 9 in NM/Mint)				

	GD25	FN65	NM94
102-2nd Superboy	108.00	325.00	725.00
103-3rd Superboy	75.00	225.00	500.00
104-107: 107-Last Johnny Quick & Superboy	62.00	188.00	415.00

Morningstar Special #1, © Bill Willingham

Motion Picture Comics #102, © Republic Pictures

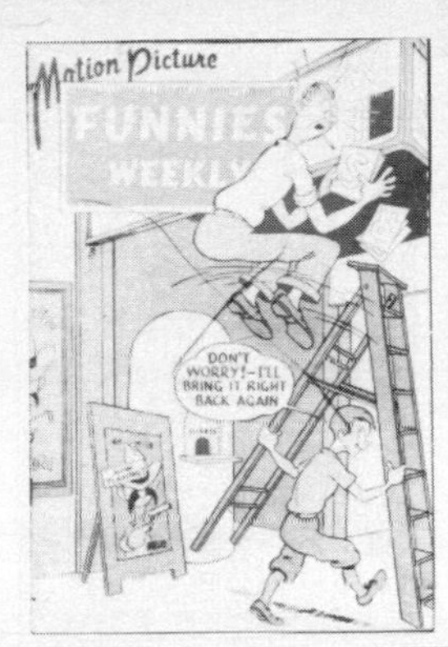

Motion Picture Funnies Weekly #1, © MEG

GD25 FN65 NM94

108-120: 108-Genius Jones begins (3-4/46; cont'd from Adventure Comics #102) 13.00 40.00 90.00
121-124,126: 121-123,126-Post-c (Jimminy-c) 10.00 30.00 70.00
125-Superman on cover 58.00 175.00 400.00
127-(Scarce)-Post-c/a 22.00 65.00 150.00
NOTE: *All issues are scarce to rare. Cover features: The Spectre-#52-55, 57-60, 62-67. Dr. Fate-#56, 61, 68-76. The Green Arrow & Speedy-#77-85, 88-97, 99, 101 (w/Dover & Clover-#98, 103). Johnny Quick-#86, 87, 100. Dover & Clover-#102, (104, 106 w/Superboy), 107, 108(w/Genius Jones), 110, 112, 114, 117, 119. Genius Jones-#109, 111, 113, 115, 118, 120.* **Baily** *a-45, 52-on; c-52-55, 57-60, 62-67.* **Al Capp** *a-45(signed Koppy).* **Ellsworth** *c-7.* **Craig Flessel** *c-30, 31, 35-48(most).* **Guardineer** *c-47, 49, 50.* **Kiefer** *a-20.* **Meskin** *c-86, 87, 100?* **Moldoff** *c-51.* **George Papp** *c-77-85.* **Post** *c-121-127.* **Vincent Sullivan** *c-8-28, 32-34.*

MORE SEYMOUR (See Seymour My Son)
October, 1963
Archie Publications
1 2.40 6.00 12.00

MORE TRASH FROM MAD (Annual)
1958 - No. 12, 1969
E. C. Comics
nn(1958)-8 pgs. color Mad reprint from #20 19.00 57.00 130.00
2(1959)-Market Product Labels 13.00 40.00 90.00
3(1960)-Text book covers 11.50 34.00 80.00
4(1961)-Sing Along with Mad booklet 11.50 34.00 80.00
5(1962)-Window Stickers; r/from Mad #39 9.15 27.50 55.00
6(1963)-TV Guise booklet 10.00 30.00 65.00
7(1964)-Alfred E. Neuman commemorative stamps 6.70 20.00 40.00
8(1965)-Life size poster-Alfred E. Neuman 5.00 15.00 30.00
9,10(1966-67)-Mischief Sticker 4.20 12.50 25.00
11(1968)-Campaign poster & bumper sticker 4.20 12.50 25.00
12(1969)-Pocket medals 4.20 12.50 25.00
NOTE: **Kelly Freas** *c-1, 2, 4.* **Mingo** *c-3, 5-9, 12.*

MORGAN THE PIRATE (See 4-Color #1227)

MORLOCK 2001
Feb, 1975 - No. 3, July, 1975
Atlas/Seaboard Publ.
1,2: 1-(Super-hero)-Origin & 1st app. 1.00
3-Ditko/Wrightson-a; origin The Midnight Man & The Midnight Men 1.20

MORNINGSTAR SPECIAL (Comico)(Value: cover or less)

MORTIE (Mazie's Friend)
Dec, 1952 - No. 4, June, 1953?
Magazine Publishers
1 4.70 14.00 28.00
2-4 3.00 7.50 15.00

MORTIGAN GOTH: IMMORTALIS
Sept, 1993 - No. 4, Dec, 1993 ($1.95, color, mini-series)
Marvel Comics
1-($2.95)-Foil-c 1.20 3.00
2-4 .80 2.00

MORT THE DEAD TEENAGER
Nov, 1993 - No. 4, Feb, 1994 ($1.75, color, mini-series)
Marvel Comics
1-4 .70 1.75

MORTY MEEKLE (See 4-Color #793)

MOSES & THE TEN COMMANDMENTS (See Dell Giants)

MOTHER GOOSE (See Christmas With Mother Goose & 4-Color #41, 59, 68, 862)

MOTHER OF US ALL
1950? (32 pgs.)
Catechetical Guild Giveaway
nn 1.60 4.00 8.00

MOTHER TERESA OF CALCUTTA
1984
Marvel Comics Group
1 1.25

MOTION PICTURE COMICS (See Fawcett Movie Comics)
No. 101, 1950 - No. 114, Jan, 1953 (All-photo-c)
Fawcett Publications
101-"Vanishing Westerner"-Monte Hale (1950) 25.00 75.00 175.00
102-"Code of the Silver Sage"-Rocky Lane (1/51) 24.00 72.00 165.00
103-"Covered Wagon Raid"-Rocky Lane (3/51) 24.00 72.00 165.00
104-"Vigilante Hideout"-Rocky Lane (5/51)-Book length Powell-a 24.00 72.00 165.00
105-"Red Badge of Courage"-Audie Murphy; Bob Powell-a (7/51) 29.00 85.00 200.00
106-"The Texas Rangers"-George Montgomery (9/51) 24.00 72.00 165.00
107-"Frisco Tornado"-Rocky Lane (11/51) 22.00 65.00 150.00
108-"Mask of the Avenger"-John Derek 14.00 43.00 100.00
109-"Rough Rider of Durango"-Rocky Lane 22.00 65.00 150.00
110-"When Worlds Collide"-George Evans-a (1951); Williamson & Evans drew themselves in story; (also see Famous Funnies No. 72-88) 69.00 208.00 485.00
111-"The Vanishing Outpost"-Lash LaRue 26.00 78.00 180.00
112-"Brave Warrior"-Jon Hall & Jay Silverheels 13.00 40.00 90.00
113-"Walk East on Beacon"-George Murphy; Shaffenberger-a 10.00 30.00 65.00
114-"Cripple Creek"-George Montgomery (1/53) 11.00 32.00 75.00

MOTION PICTURE FUNNIES WEEKLY (Amazing Man #5 on?)
1939 (36 pgs.)(Giveaway)(Black & White)
No month given; last panel in Sub-Mariner story dated 4/39
(Also see Colossus, Green Giant & Invaders No. 20)
First Funnies, Inc.
1-Origin & 1st printed app. Sub-Mariner by Bill Everett (8 pgs.); Fred Schwab-c; reprinted in Marvel Mystery #1 with color added over the craft tint which was used to shade the black & white version; Spy Ring, American Ace (reprinted in Marvel Mystery #3) app. (Rare)-only eight (8) known copies,one near mint with white pages, the rest with brown pages. 2600.00 5500.00 -----
Covers only to #2-4 (set) 600.00
NOTE: The only eight known copies (with a ninth suspected) were discovered in 1974 in the estate of the deceased publisher. Covers only to issues No. 2-4 were also found which evidently were printed in advance along with #1. #1 was to be distributed only through motion picture movie houses. However, it is believed that only advanced copies were sent out and the motion picture houses not going for the idea. Possible distribution at local theaters in Boston suspected. The last panel of Sub-Mariner contains a rectangular box with "Continued Next Week" printed in it. When reprinted in Marvel Mystery, the box was left in with lettering omitted.

MOTORBIKE PUPPIES, THE (Dark Zulu Lies)(Value: cover or less)

MOTORMOUTH (... & Killpower #7? on)
June, 1992 - No. 13, June, 1993 ($1.75, color)
Marvel Comics UK
1-13: 1,2-Nick Fury app. 3-Punisher-c/story. 5,6-Nick Fury & Punisher app. 6-Cable cameo. 7-9-Cable app. .70 1.80

MOUNTAIN MEN (See Ben Bowie)

MOUSE MUSKETEERS (See M.G.M.'s...)

MOUSE ON THE MOON, THE (See Movie Classics)

MOVIE CLASSICS
Jan, 1963 - Dec, 1969
Dell Publishing Co.
(Before 1963, most movie adaptations were part of the 4-Color series)
(Disney movie adaptations after 1970 are in Walt Disney Showcase)
Around the World Under the Sea 12-030-612 (12/66) 3.20 8.00 16.00
Bambi 3(4/56)-Disney; r/4-Color #186 3.20 8.00 16.00
Battle of the Bulge 12-056-606 (6/66) 4.00 10.00 20.00
Beach Blanket Bingo 12-058-509 7.50 22.50 45.00
Bon Voyage 01-068-212 (12/62)-Disney; photo-c 3.20 8.00 16.00

Movie Classics (Incredible Mr. Limpet), © Warner Bros.

Movie Classics (The Raven), © Alta Vista Prod.

Movie Comics #1 (4/39), © DC

	GD25	FN65	NM94
Castilian, The 12-110-401	4.00	11.00	22.00
Cat, The 12-109-612 (12/66)	2.80	7.00	14.00
Cheyenne Autumn 12-112-506 (4-6/65)	6.70	20.00	40.00
Circus World, Samuel Bronston's 12-115-411; John Wayne app.; John Wayne photo-c	11.00	32.00	75.00
Countdown 12-150-710 (10/67)-James Caan photo-c	3.60	9.00	18.00
Creature, The 1 (12-142-302) (12-2/62-63)	5.00	15.00	30.00
Creature, The 12-142-410 (10/64)	3.60	9.00	18.00
David Ladd's Life Story 12-173-212 (10-12/62)-Photo-c	9.15	27.50	55.00
Die, Monster, Die 12-175-603 (3/66)-Photo-c	5.35	16.00	32.00
Dirty Dozen 12-180-710 (10/67)	5.00	15.00	30.00
Dr. Who & the Daleks 12-190-612 (12/66)-Peter Cushing photo-c	12.00	36.00	85.00
Dracula 12-231-212 (10-12/62)	4.20	12.50	25.00
El Dorado 12-240-710 (10/67)-John Wayne; photo-c	12.00	36.00	85.00
Ensign Pulver 12-257-410 (8-10/64)	3.60	9.00	18.00
Frankenstein 12-283-305 (3-5/63)	4.20	12.50	25.00
Great Race, The 12-299-603 (3/66)-Natallie Wood, Tony Curtis photo-c	4.70	14.00	28.00
Hallelujah Trail, The 12-307-602 (2/66) (Shows 1/66 inside); Burt Lancaster, Lee Remick photo-c	5.35	16.00	32.00
Hatari 12-340-301 (1/63)-John Wayne	9.15	27.50	55.00
Horizontal Lieutenant, The 01-348-210 (10/62)	3.60	9.00	18.00
Incredible Mr. Limpet, The 12-370-408; Don Knotts photo-c	4.00	11.00	25.00
Jack the Giant Killer 12-374-301 (1/63)	9.15	27.50	55.00
Jason & the Argonauts 12-376-310 (8-10/63)-Photo-c	10.00	30.00	65.00
Lancelot & Guinevere 12-416-310 (10/63)	7.50	22.50	45.00
Lawrence 12-426-308 (8/63)-Story of Lawrence of Arabia; movie ad on back-c; not exactly like movie	6.35	19.00	38.00
Lion of Sparta 12-439-301 (1/63)	3.60	9.00	18.00
Mad Monster Party 12-460-801 (9/67)	7.00	21.00	42.00
Magic Sword, The 01-496-209 (9/62)	6.35	19.00	38.00
Masque of the Red Death 12-490-410 (8-10/64)-Vincent Price photo-c	5.35	16.00	32.00
Maya 12-495-612 (12/66)-Clint Walker & Jay North part photo-c	5.00	15.00	30.00
McHale's Navy 12-500-412 (10-12/64)	4.00	10.00	20.00
Merrill's Marauders 12-510-301 (1/63)-Photo-c	3.60	9.00	18.00
Mouse on the Moon, The 12-530-312 (10/12/63)-Photo-c	4.00	10.00	20.00
Mummy, The 12-537-211 (9-11/62) 2 versions with different back-c	5.00	15.00	30.00
Music Man, The 12-538-301 (1/63)	3.60	9.00	18.00
Naked Prey, The 12-545-612 (12/66)-Photo-c	7.50	22.50	45.00
Night of the Grizzly, The 12-558-612 (12/66)-Photo-c	4.70	14.00	28.00
None But the Brave 12-565-506 (4-6/65)	7.50	22.50	45.00
Operation Bikini 12-597-310 (10/63)-Photo-c	4.00	11.00	22.00
Operation Crossbow 12-590-512 (10-12/65)	4.00	11.00	22.00
Prince & the Pauper, The 01-654-207 (5-7/62)-Disney	4.00	11.00	22.00
Raven, The 12-680-309 (9/63)-Vincent Price photo-c	5.35	16.00	32.00
Ring of Bright Water 01-701-910 (10/69) (inside shows #12-701-909)	4.70	14.00	28.00
Runaway, The 12-707-412 (10-12/64)	3.20	8.00	16.00
Santa Claus Conquers the Martians #? (1964)-Photo-c	9.15	27.50	55.00
Santa Claus Conquers the Martians 12-725-603 (3/66, 12 cents)-Reprints 1964 issue; photo-c	7.50	22.50	45.00
Another version given away with a Golden Record, SLP 170, nn, no price (3/66)-Complete with record	14.00	43.00	120.00
Six Black Horses 12-750-301 (1/63)-Photo-c	4.00	11.00	22.00
Ski Party 12-743-511 (9-11/65)-Frankie Avalon photo-c	5.35	16.00	32.00
Smoky 12-746-702 (2/67)	3.20	8.00	16.00
Sons of Katie Elder 12-748-511 (9-11/65); John Wayne app.; photo-c	14.00	43.00	100.00
Tales of Terror 12-793-302 (2/63)-Evans-a	4.00	10.00	20.00
Three Stooges Meet Hercules 01-828-208 (8/62)-Photo-c	10.00	30.00	60.00
Tomb of Ligeia 12-830-506 (4-6/65)	3.60	9.00	18.00
Treasure Island 01-845-211 (7-9/62)-Disney; r/4-Color #624	2.80	7.00	14.00
Twice Told Tales (Nathaniel Hawthorne) 12-840-401 (11-1/63-64); Vincent Price photo-c	4.20	12.50	25.00
Two on a Guillotine 12-850-506 (4-6/65)	3.60	9.00	18.00
Valley of Gwangi 01-880-912 (12/69)	10.00	30.00	60.00
War Gods of the Deep 12-900-509 (7-9/65)	4.00	10.00	20.00
War Wagon, The 12-533-709 (9/67); John Wayne app.	10.00	30.00	70.00
Who's Minding the Mint? 12-924-708 (8/67)	3.60	9.00	18.00
Wolfman, The 12-922-308 (6-8/63)	4.00	10.00	20.00
Wolfman, The 1(12-922-410)(8-10/64)-2nd printing; r/#12-922-308	4.00	10.00	20.00
Zulu 12-950-410 (8-10/64)-Photo-c	10.00	30.00	65.00

MOVIE COMICS (See Cinema Comics Herald & Fawcett Movie Comics)

MOVIE COMICS
April, 1939 - No. 6, Sept-Oct, 1939 (Most all photo-c)
National Periodical Publications/Picture Comics

	GD25	FN65	NM94
1-"Gunga Din," "Son of Frankenstein," "The Great Man Votes," "Fisherman's Wharf," & "Scouts to the Rescue" part 1; Wheelan "Minute Movies" begin	233.00	700.00	1600.00
2-"Stagecoach," "The Saint Strikes Back," "King of the Turf," "Scouts to the Rescue" part 2, "Arizona Legion"	150.00	450.00	1000.00
3-"East Side of Heaven," "Mystery in the White Room," "Four Feathers," "Mexican Rose" with Gene Autry, "Spirit of Culver," "Many Secrets," "The Mikado"	123.00	370.00	825.00
4-"Captain Fury," Gene Autry in "Blue Montana Skies," "Streets of N.Y." with Jackie Cooper, "Oregon Trail" part 1 with Johnny Mack Brown, "Big Town Czar" with Barton MacLane, & "Star Reporter" with Warren Hull	105.00	315.00	675.00
5-"The Man in the Iron Mask," "Five Came Back," "Wolf Call," "The Girl & the Gambler," "The House of Fear," "The Family Next Door," "Oregon Trail" part 2	105.00	315.00	675.00
6-"The Phantom Creeps," "Chumps at Oxford," & "The Oregon Trail" part 3; 2nd Robot-c	130.00	390.00	850.00

NOTE: *Above books contain many original movie stills with dialogue from movie scripts. All issues are scarce. 2-Andy Devine photo-c.*

MOVIE COMICS
Dec, 1946 - No. 4, 1947
Fiction House Magazines

	GD25	FN65	NM94
1-Big Town & Johnny Danger begin; Celardo-a	37.00	110.00	250.00
2-(2/47)-"White Tie & Tails" with William Bendix; Mitzi of the Movies begins by Matt Baker, ends #4	27.00	80.00	180.00
3-(6/47)-Andy Hardy starring Mickey Rooney	27.00	80.00	180.00
4-Mitzi In Hollywood by Matt Baker; Merton of the Movies with Red Skelton	32.00	95.00	210.00

MOVIE COMICS
Oct, 1962 - March, 1972
Gold Key/Whitman

	GD25	FN65	NM94
Alice in Wonderland 10144-503 (3/65)-Disney; partial reprint of 4-Color #331	3.20	8.00	16.00
Aristocats, The 1 (30045-103)(3/71)-Disney; with pull-out poster (25 cents)	6.35	19.00	38.00
Bambi 1 (10087-309)(9/63)-Disney; r/4-C #186	3.60	9.00	18.00
Bambi 2 (10087-607)(7/66)-Disney; r/4-C #186	3.20	8.00	16.00
Beneath the Planet of the Apes 30044-012 (12/70)-with pull-out poster; photo-c	5.00	15.00	30.00

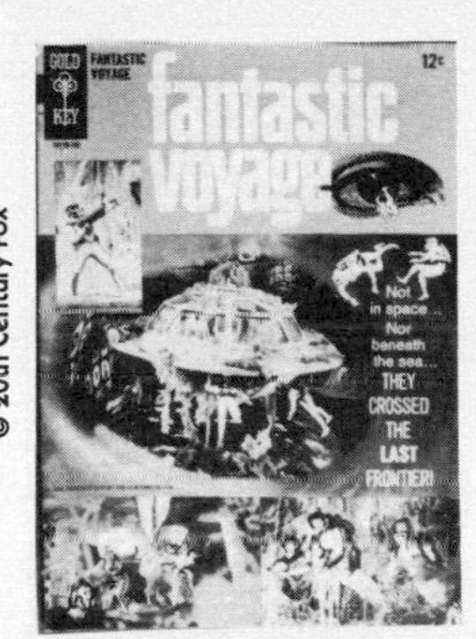

Movie Comics (Fantastic Voyage) © 20th Century Fox

Movie Comics (Moon-Spinners), © The Disney Co.

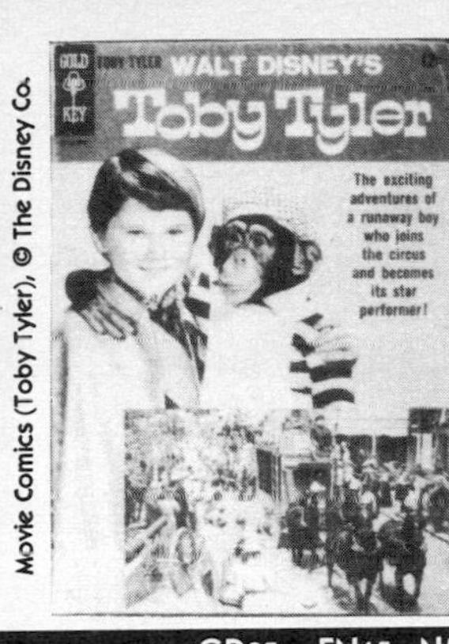

Movie Comics (Toby Tyler), © The Disney Co.

	GD25	FN65	NM94
Big Red 10026-211 (11/62)-Disney; photo-c	2.40	6.00	12.00
Big Red 10026-503 (3/65)-Disney; reprints 10026-211; photo-c	2.40	6.00	12.00
Blackbeard's Ghost 10222-806 (6/68)-Disney	2.80	7.00	14.00
Bullwhip Griffin 10181-706 (6/67)-Disney; Manning-a; photo-c	4.00	11.00	22.00
Captain Sindbad 10077-309 (9/63)-Manning-a; photo-c	6.70	20.00	40.00
Chitty Chitty Bang Bang 1 (30038-902)(2/69)-with pull-out poster; Disney; photo-c	4.70	14.00	28.00
Cinderella 10152-508 (8/65)-Disney; r/4-C #786	2.80	7.00	14.00
Darby O'Gill & the Little People 10251-001(1/70)-Disney; reprints 4-Color #1024 (Toth-a); photo-c	4.70	14.00	28.00
Dumbo 1 (10090-310)(10/63)-Disney; r/4-C #668	2.80	7.00	14.00
Emil & the Detectives 10120-502 (2/65)-Disney; photo-c	4.00	10.00	20.00
Escapade in Florence 1 (10043-301)(1/63)-Disney; starring Annette Funicello	7.50	22.50	45.00
Fall of the Roman Empire 10118-407 (7/64); Sophia Loren photo-c	4.00	11.00	22.00
Fantastic Voyage 10178-702 (2/67)-Wood/Adkins-a; photo-c	5.35	16.00	32.00
55 Days at Peking 10081-309 (9/63)-Photo-c	4.00	11.00	22.00
Fighting Prince of Donegal, The 10193-701 (1/67)-Disney	3.20	8.00	16.00
First Men in the Moon 10132-503 (3/65)-Fred Fredericks-a; photo-c	4.00	10.00	20.00
Gay Purr-ee 30017-301(1/63, 84pgs.)	4.70	14.00	28.00
Gnome Mobile, The 10207-710 (10/67)-Disney	4.00	10.00	20.00
Goodbye, Mr. Chips 10246-006 (6/70)-Peter O'Toole photo-c	3.60	9.00	18.00
Happiest Millionaire, The 10221-804 (4/68)-Disney	2.40	6.00	12.00
Hey There, It's Yogi Bear 10122-409 (9/64)-Hanna-Barbera	5.00	15.00	30.00
Horse Without a Head, The 10109-401 (1/64)-Disney	2.80	7.00	14.00
How the West Was Won 10074-307 (7/63)-Tufts-a	4.70	14.00	28.00
In Search of the Castaways 10048-303 (3/63)-Disney; Hayley Mills photo-c	6.35	19.00	38.00
Jungle Book, The 1 (6022-801)(1/68-Whitman)-Disney; large size (10x13-1/2"); 59 cents	4.00	10.00	20.00
Jungle Book, The 1 (30033-803)(3/68, 68 pgs.)-Disney; same contents as Whitman #1	2.40	6.00	12.00
Jungle Book, The 1 (6/78, $1.00 tabloid)			1.20
Jungle Book (1984)-r/Giant			1.00
Kidnapped 10080-306 (6/63)-Disney; reprints 4-Color #1101; photo-c	2.40	6.00	12.00
King Kong 30036-809(9/68-68 pgs.)-painted-c	3.60	9.00	18.00
King Kong nn-Whitman Treasury($1.00, 68pgs.,1968), same cover as Gold Key issue	1.00	2.50	5.00
King Kong 11299(#1-786, 10x13-1/4", 68pgs., $1.00, 1978)			1.00
Lady and the Tramp 10042-301 (1/63)-Disney; r/4-Color #629	3.00	7.50	15.00
Lady and the Tramp 1 (1967-Giant; 25 cents)-Disney; reprints part of Dell #1	4.70	14.00	28.00
Lady and the Tramp 2 (10042-203)(3/72)-Disney; r/4-Color #629	2.00	5.00	10.00
Legend of Lobo, The 1 (10059-303)(3/63)-Disney; photo-c	2.40	6.00	12.00
Lt. Robin Crusoe, U.S.N. 10191-610 (10/66)-Disney; Dick Van Dyke photo-c	2.80	7.00	14.00
Lion, The 10035-301 (1/63)-Photo-c	2.40	6.00	12.00
Lord Jim 10156-509 (9/65)-Photo-c	3.20	8.00	16.00
Love Bug, The 10237-906 (6/69)-Disney; Buddy Hackett photo-c	2.80	7.00	14.00
Mary Poppins 10136-501 (1/65)-Disney; photo-c	4.70	14.00	28.00
Mary Poppins 30023-501 (1/65-68 pgs.)-Disney; photo-c	7.50	22.50	45.00
McLintock 10110-403 (3/64); John Wayne app.; John Wayne & Maureen O'Hara photo-c	13.00	40.00	90.00
Merlin Jones as the Monkey's Uncle 10115-510 (10/65)-Disney; Annette Funicello front/back photo-c	4.70	14.00	28.00
Miracle of the White Stallions, The 10065-306 (6/63)-Disney	3.20	8.00	16.00
Misadventures of Merlin Jones, The 10115-405 (5/64)-Disney; Annette Funicello photo front/back-c	4.70	14.00	28.00
Moon-Spinners, The 10124-410 (10/64)-Disney; Haley Mills photo-c	6.35	19.00	38.00
Mutiny on the Bounty 1 (10040-302)(2/63)-Marlon Brando photo-c	4.00	11.00	22.00
Nikki, Wild Dog of the North 10141-412 (12/64)-Disney; reprints 4-Color #1226	2.00	5.00	10.00
Old Yeller 10168-601 (1/66)-Disney; reprints 4-Color #869; photo-c	2.40	6.00	12.00
One Hundred & One Dalmations 1 (10247-002) (2/70)-Disney; reprints 4-Color #1183	3.00	7.50	15.00
Peter Pan 1 (10086-309)(9/63)-Disney; reprints 4-Color #442	3.60	9.00	18.00
Peter Pan 2 (10086-909)(9/69)-Disney; reprints 4-Color #442	2.40	6.00	12.00
Peter Pan 1 ('83)-r/4-Color #442			1.00
P.T. 109 10123-409 (9/64)-John F. Kennedy	5.35	16.00	32.00
Rio Conchos 10143-503(3/65)	5.00	15.00	30.00
Robin Hood 10163-506 (6/65)-Disney; reprints 4-Color #413	2.80	7.00	14.00
Shaggy Dog & the Absent-Minded Professor 30032-708 (8/67-Giant, 68 pgs.) Disney; reprints 4-Color #985,1199	5.00	15.00	30.00
Sleeping Beauty 1 (30042-009)(9/70)-Disney; reprints 4-Color #973; with pull-out poster	5.35	16.00	32.00
Snow White & the Seven Dwarfs 1 (10091-310)(10/63)-Disney; reprints 4-Color #382	3.20	8.00	16.00
Snow White & the Seven Dwarfs 10091-709 (9/67)-Disney; reprints 4-Color #382	2.80	7.00	14.00
Snow White & the Seven Dwarfs 90091-204 (2/84)-Reprints 4-Color #382			1.00
Son of Flubber 1 (10057-304)(4/63)-Disney; sequel to "The Absent-Minded Professor"	3.20	8.00	16.00
Summer Magic 10076-309 (9/63)-Disney; Hayley Mills photo-c; Manning-a	6.70	20.00	40.00
Swiss Family Robinson 10236-904 (4/69)-Disney; reprints 4-Color #1156; photo-c	3.20	8.00	16.00
Sword in the Stone, The 30019-402 (2/64-Giant, 84 pgs.)-Disney (see March of Comics #258 & Wart and the Wizard	5.35	16.00	32.00
That Darn Cat 10171-602 (2/66)-Disney; Hayley Mills photo-c	6.35	19.00	38.00
Those Magnificent Men in Their Flying Machines 10162-510 (10/65); photo-c	3.60	9.00	18.00
Three Stooges in Orbit 30016-211 (11/62-Giant, 32 pgs.)-All photos from movie; stiff-photo-c	11.00	32.00	75.00
Tiger Walks, A 10117-406 (6/64)-Disney; Torres?, Tufts-a; photo-c	5.00	15.00	30.00
Toby Tyler 10142-502 (2/65)-Disney; reprints 4-Color #1092; photo-c	3.00	7.50	15.00
Treasure Island 1 (10200-703)(3/67)-Disney; reprints 4-Color #624; photo-c	2.40	6.00	12.00
20,000 Leagues Under the Sea 1 (10095-312)(12/63)-Disney; reprints 4-Color #614	2.40	6.00	12.00
Wonderful Adventures of Pinocchio, The 1 (10089-310)(10/63)-Disney; reprints 4-Color #545 (see Wonderful Advs. of...)	2.40	6.00	12.00
Wonderful Adventures of Pinocchio, The 10089-109 (9/71)-Disney; reprints 4-Color #545	2.40	6.00	12.00
Wonderful World of the Brothers Grimm 1 (10008-210)(10/62)	4.20	12.50	25.00

Movie Love #1, © FF

Ms. Marvel #23, © MEG

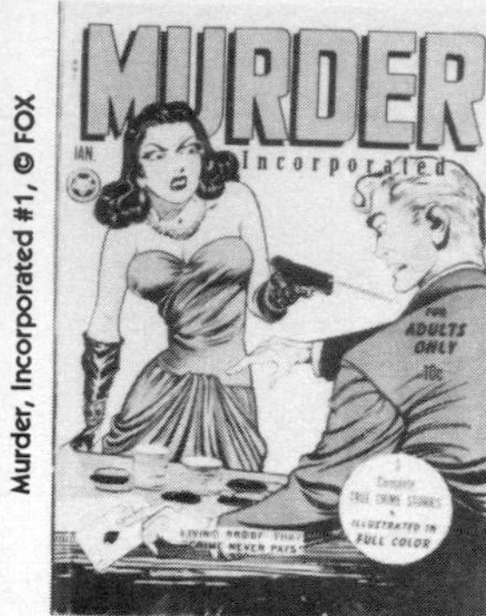

Murder, Incorporated #1, © FOX

GD25 FN65 NM94

X, the Man with the X-Ray Eyes 10083-309 (9/63)-Ray Milland photo on-c 7.50 22.50 45.00
Yellow Submarine 35000-902 (2/69-Giant, 68 pgs.)-With pull-out poster; The Beatles cartoon movie 21.00 64.00 150.00
Without poster 7.00 21.00 50.00

MOVIE LOVE (Also see Personal Love)
Feb, 1950 - No. 22, Aug, 1953
Famous Funnies

1-Dick Powell photo-c; Mickey Rooney on-c 9.15 27.50 55.00
2-Myrna Loy photo-c 4.70 14.00 28.00
3-7,9: 6-Ricardo Montalban photo-c 4.00 11.00 22.00
8-Williamson/Frazetta-a, 6 pgs. 23.00 70.00 160.00
10-Frazetta-a, 6 pgs. 28.00 85.00 200.00
11,14-16: 14-Janet Leigh photo-c 3.60 9.00 18.00
12-Dean Martin & Jerry Lewis photo-c (12/51, pre-dates Advs. of Dean Martin & Jerry Lewis comic) 4.20 12.50 25.00
13-Ronald Reagan photo-c with 1 pg. biog. 15.00 45.00 105.00
17-One pg. Frazetta ad 4.00 10.00 20.00
18-22: 19-John Derek photo-c 3.60 9.00 18.00
NOTE: *Each issue has a full-length movie adaptation with photo covers.*

MOVIE THRILLERS
1949 (Movie adaptation; Burt Lancaster photo-c)
Magazine Enterprises

1-"Rope of Sand" with Burt Lancaster 23.00 70.00 160.00

MOVIE TOWN ANIMAL ANTICS (Formerly Animal Antics; becomes Raccoon Kids #52 on)
No. 24, Jan-Feb, 1950 - No. 51, July-Aug, 1954
National Periodical Publications

24-Raccoon Kids continue 9.15 27.50 55.00
25-51 7.50 22.50 45.00
NOTE: ***Sheldon Mayer** a-28-33, 35, 37-41, 43, 44, 47, 49-51.*

MOVIE TUNES COMICS (Formerly Animated...; Frankie No. 4 on)
No. 3, Fall, 1946
Marvel Comics (MgPC)

3-Super Rabbit, Krazy Krow, Silly Seal & Ziggy Pig 8.35 25.00 50.00

MOWGLI JUNGLE BOOK (See 4-Color #487, 582, 620)

MR. (See Mister)

MS. MARVEL (Also see The Avengers #183)
Jan, 1977 - No. 23, Apr, 1979
Marvel Comics Group

1-1st app. Ms. Marvel; Scorpion app. in #1,2 1.40 3.50
2-Origin 1.00 2.50
3-10: 5-Vision app. 10-Last 30 cent issue .70 1.80
11-23: 18-Avengers x-over. 19-Capt. Marvel app. 20-New costume. 23-Vance Astro (leader of the Guardians) app. 1.50
NOTE: ***Austin** c-14i, 16i, 17i, 22i. **Buscema** a-1-3p; c(p)-2, 4, 6, 7, 15. **Infantino** a-14p, 19p. **Gil Kane** c-8. **Mooney** a-4-8p, 13p, 15-18p. **Starlin** c-12.*

MS. MYSTIC (Pacific & Continuity)(Value; cover or less)

MS. TREE QUARTERLY (DC)(Value: cover or less)

MS. TREE'S THRILLING DETECTIVE ADVS (Eclipse)(Value: cover or less)

MS. VICTORY SPECIAL(Americomics)(Value: cover or less)

MUGGSY MOUSE (Also see Tick Tock Tales)
1951 - No. 3, 1951; No. 4, 1954 - No. 5, 1954; 1963
Magazine Enterprises

1(A-1 #33) 4.70 14.00 28.00
2(A-1 #36)-Racist-c 5.85 17.50 35.00
3(A-1 #39), 4(A-1 #95), 5(A-1 #99) 2.80 7.00 14.00
Super Reprint #14(1963) .80 2.00 4.00
I.W. Reprint #1,2 (nd) .80 2.00 4.00

MUGGY-DOO, BOY CAT
July, 1953 - No. 4, Jan, 1954
Stanhall Publ.

1-Funny animal; Irving Spector-a 5.35 16.00 32.00
2-4 4.00 11.00 22.00
Super Reprint #12('63), 16('64) .80 2.00 4.00

MUMMY, THE (See Universal Presents... under Dell Giants & Movie Classics)

MUMMY ARCHIVES, THE (Millennium)(Value: cover or less)

MUNDEN'S BAR ANNUAL (First)(Value: cover or less)

MUNSTERS, THE (TV)
Jan, 1965 - No. 16, Jan, 1968 (All photo-c)
Gold Key

1 (10134-501) 18.00 54.00 125.00
2 9.00 26.00 62.00
3-5 7.50 22.00 52.00
6-16 6.50 20.00 46.00

MUPPET BABIES, THE (TV)(Marvel & Harvey)(Value: cover or less)

MUPPETS TAKE MANHATTAN, THE (Marvel)(Value: cover or less)

MURDER, INCORPORATED (My Private Life #16 on)
1/48 - No. 15, 12/49; (2 No.9's); 6/50 - No. 3, 8/51
Fox Feature Syndicate

1 (1st Series); 1,2 have 'For Adults Only' on-c 24.00 72.00 165.00
2-Electrocution story 17.00 52.00 120.00
3-7,9(4/49),10(5/49),11-15 10.00 30.00 60.00
8-Used in **SOTI**, pg. 160 11.50 34.00 80.00
9(3/49)-Possible use in **SOTI**, pg. 145; r/Blue Beetle #56('48) 10.00 30.00 65.00
5(#1, 6/50)(2nd Series)-Formerly My Desire #4 8.35 25.00 50.00
2(8/50)-Morisi-a 6.70 20.00 40.00
3(8/51)-Used in **POP**, pg. 81; Rico-a; lingerie-c/panels 8.35 25.00 50.00

MURDEROUS GANGSTERS
July, 1951; No. 2, Dec, 1951 - No. 4, June, 1952
Avon Periodicals/Realistic No. 3 on

1-Pretty Boy Floyd, Leggs Diamond; 1 pg. Wood-a 24.00 73.00 170.00
2-Baby-Face Nelson; 1 pg. Wood-a; painted-c 15.00 45.00 105.00
3-Painted-c 11.50 34.00 80.00
4-"Murder by Needle" drug story; Mort Lawrence-a; Kinstler-c 15.00 45.00 105.00

MURDER TALES (Magazine)
V1#10, Nov, 1970 - V1#11, Jan, 1971 (52 pages)
World Famous Publications

V1#10-One pg. Frazetta ad 1.70 5.00 12.00
11-Guardineer-r; bondage-c 1.00 2.50 6.00

MUSHMOUSE AND PUNKIN PUSS (TV)
September, 1965 (Hanna-Barbera)
Gold Key

1 (10153-509) 7.50 22.50 45.00

MUSIC MAN, THE (See Movie Classics)

MUTANT MISADVENTURES OF CLOAK AND DAGGER, THE (Becomes Cloak and Dagger #14 on)
Oct, 1988 - No. 19, Aug, 1991 (#1: $1.25; #2-on: $1.50, color)
Marvel Comics

1-8,10-18: 1-X-Factor app. 9,10-Painted-c. 12-Dr. Doom app. 14-Begin new direction. 16-18-Spider-Man x-over. 18-Infinity Gauntlet x-over; Thanos cameo; Ghost Rider app. 1.50
9-($2.50, 52 pgs.)-The Avengers x-over 1.00 2.50
19-($2.50, 52 pgs.)-Origin Cloak & Dagger 1.00 2.50
NOTE: ***Austin** a-12i; c(i)-4, 12, 13; scripts-all. **Russell** a-2i. **Williamson** a-14i-16i; c-15i.*

MUTANTS & MISFITS (Silverline)(Value: cover or less)

MUTATIS

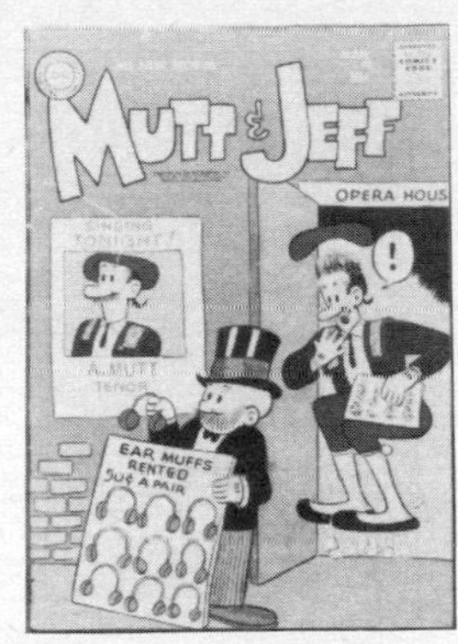

Mutt & Jeff #93, © DC

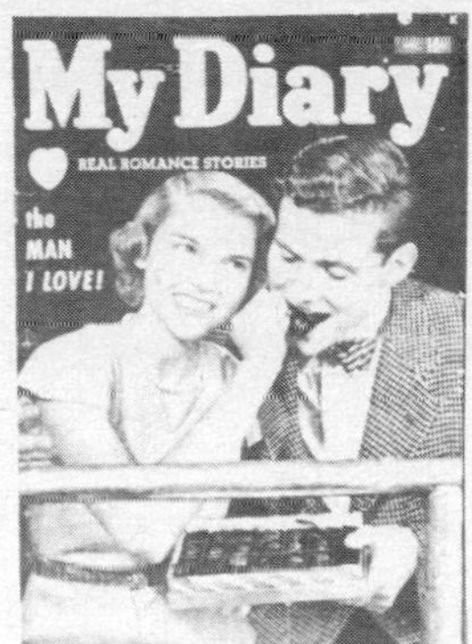

My Diary #1, © MEG

My Girl Pearl #1, © MEG

GD25 FN65 NM94

1992 - No. 3, 1992 ($2.25, color, mini-series)
Epic Comics (Marvol)
1-3: Painted-c .90 2.25

MUTINY (Stormy Tales of the Seven Seas)
Oct, 1954 - No. 3, Feb, 1955
Aragon Magazines
1 10.00 30.00 65.00
2,3: 2-Capt. Mutiny. 3-Bondage-c 7.50 22.50 45.00

MUTINY ON THE BOUNTY (See Classics Illustrated #100 & Movie Comics)

MUTT & JEFF (...Cartoon, The)
1910 - No. 5, 1916 (5-3/4x15-1/2") (Hardcover B&W)
Ball Publications GD25 FN65 VF82
1(1910)(68 pgs., 50 cents) 64.00 195.00 450.00
2,3: 2(1911, 68 pgs.)-Opium den panels; Jeff smokes opium (pipe dreams). 3(1912, 68 pgs.) 57.00 170.00 400.00
4(1915)(68 pgs., 50 cents)(Rare) 64.00 195.00 450.00
5(1916)(68 pgs.)(Rare)-Photos of Fisher, 1st pg. 71.00 215.00 500.00
NOTE: *Mutt & Jeff first appeared in newspapers in 1908. Cover variations exist showing Mutt & Jeff reading various newspapers; i.e., The Oregon Journal, The American, and The Detroit News. Reprinting of each issue began soon after publication. No. 5 may not have been reprinted. Values listed include the reprints.*

MUTT & JEFF
No. 6, 1916 - No. 22, 1933? (B&W dailies) (9-1/2x9-1/2"; stiff-c; 52 pgs.)
Cupples & Leon Co.
6-22-By Bud Fisher 39.00 120.00 275.00
NOTE: *Later issues are somewhat rarer.*
nn(1920)-(Advs. of...) 16x11"; 20 pgs.; reprints 1919 Sunday strips 57.00 170.00 400.00
Big Book nn(1926, 144pgs., hardcovers) 43.00 130.00 300.00
w/dust jacket.... 64.00 195.00 450.00
Big Book 1(1928)-Thick book (hardcovers) 43.00 130.00 300.00
w/dust jacket.... 64.00 195.00 450.00
Big Book 2(1929)-Thick book (hardcovers) 43.00 130.00 300.00
w/dust jacket.... 64.00 195.00 450.00
NOTE: *The Big Books contain three previous issues rebound.*

MUTT & JEFF
1921 (9x15")
Embee Publ. Co.
nn-Sunday strips in color (Rare) 86.00 260.00 600.00

MUTT AND JEFF (See All-American, All-Flash #18, Cicero's Cat, Comic Cavalcade, Famous Feature Stories, The Funnies, Popular & Xmas Comics)
Summer, 1939 (nd) - No. 148, Nov, 1965
All American/National 1-103(6/58)/Dell 104(10/58)-115 (10-12/59)/
Harvey 116(2/60)-148 GD25 FN65 NM94
1(nn)-Lost Wheels 108.00 325.00 750.00
2(nn)-Charging Bull (Summer, 1940, nd; on sale 6/20/40) 58.00 175.00 375.00
3(nn)-Bucking Broncos (Summer, 1941, nd) 42.00 125.00 265.00
4(Winter, '41), 5(Summer, '42) 31.00 92.00 200.00
6-10 18.00 55.00 120.00
11-20: 20-X-Mas-c 12.50 37.50 85.00
21-30 9.15 27.50 55.00
31-50: 32-X-Mas-c 5.85 17.50 35.00
51-75-Last Fisher issue. 53-Last 52pgs. 4.70 14.00 28.00
76-99,101-103: 76-Last precode issue(1/55) 4.00 10.00 20.00
100 4.00 11.00 22.00
104-148: 117,118,120-131-Richie Rich app. 3.00 7.50 15.00
...Jokes 1-3(8/60-61, Harvey)-84 pgs.; Richie Rich in all; Little Dot in #2,3 4.00 10.00 20.00
...New Jokes 1-4(10/63-11/65, Harvey)-68 pgs.; Richie Rich in #1-3; Stumbo in #1 2.00 5.00 10.00
NOTE: *Issues 1-74 by **Bud Fisher.** 86 on by **Al Smith.** Issues from 1963 on have **Fisher** reprints. Clarification: early issues signed by Fisher are mostly drawn by Smith.*

MY BROTHERS' KEEPER (Spire Christian)(Value: cover or less)

MY CONFESSIONS (My Confession #7&8; formerly Western True Crime; A Spectacular Feature Magazine #11)
No. 7, Aug, 1949 - No. 10, Jan-Feb, 1950
Fox Feature Syndicate
7-Wood-a (10 pgs.) 12.00 36.00 85.00
8-Wood-a (19 pgs.) 11.00 32.00 75.00
9,10 5.35 16.00 32.00

MY DATE COMICS
July, 1947 - V1No.4, Jan, 1948 (2nd Romance comic; see Rom. Pic. Nov.)
Hillman Periodicals
1-S&K-c/a 19.00 58.00 135.00
2-4-S&K, Dan Barry-a 13.00 40.00 90.00

MY DESIRE (Formerly Jo-Jo Comics; becomes Murder, Inc. #5 on)
No. 30, Aug, 1949 - No. 4, April, 1950
Fox Feature Syndicate
30(#1) 8.35 25.00 50.00
31 (#2, 10/49),3(2/50),4 5.35 16.00 32.00
31 (Canadian edition) 4.00 11.00 22.00
32(12/49)-Wood-a 11.00 32.00 75.00

MY DIARY (Becomes My Friend Irma #3 on?)
Dec, 1949 - No. 2, Mar, 1950
Marvel Comics (A Lovers Mag.)
1,2-Photo-c 8.35 25.00 50.00

MY DOG TIGE (Buster Brown's Dog)
1957 (Giveaway)
Buster Brown Shoes
nn 4.00 10.00 20.00

MY EXPERIENCE (Formerly All Top; becomes Judy Canova #23 on)
No. 19, Sept, 1949 - No. 22, Mar, 1950
Fox Feature Syndicate
19-Wood-a 13.00 40.00 90.00
20 5.35 16.00 32.00
21-Wood-a(2) 13.50 41.00 95.00
22-Wood-a, 9 pgs. 11.00 32.00 75.00

MY FAVORITE MARTIAN (TV)
1/64; No. 2, 7/64 - No. 9, 10/66 (No. 1,3-9 have photo-c)
Gold Key
1-Russ Manning-a 10.00 30.00 68.00
2 4.70 14.00 33.00
3-9 5.00 16.00 37.00

MY FRIEND IRMA (Radio/TV) (Formerly My Diary? and/or Western Life Romances?)
No. 3, June, 1950 - No. 47, Dec, 1954; No. 48, Feb, 1955
Marvel/Atlas Comics (BFP)
3-Dan DeCarlo-a in all; 52 pgs. begin, end ? 9.15 27.50 55.00
4-Kurtzman-a, 10 pgs. 10.00 30.00 65.00
5-"Egghead Doodle" by Kurtzman, 4 pgs. 8.35 25.00 50.00
6,8-10: 9-paper dolls, 1pg; Millie app. (5 pgs.) 5.00 15.00 30.00
7-One pg. Kurtzman-a 5.35 16.00 32.00
11-23: 23-One pg. Frazetta-a 4.00 10.00 20.00
24-48 2.80 7.00 14.00

MY GIRL PEARL
4/55 - #4, 10/55; #5, 7/57 - #6, 9/57; #7, 8/60 - #11, ?/61
Atlas Comics
1-Dan DeCarlo-a in #1-6 8.35 25.00 50.00
2 4.70 14.00 28.00
3-6 2.80 7.00 14.00
7-11 2.40 6.00 12.00

MY GREATEST ADVENTURE (Doom Patrol #86 on)
Jan-Feb, 1955 - No. 85, Feb, 1964
National Periodical Publications

My Greatest Adventure #24, © DC

My Little Margie #18, © CC

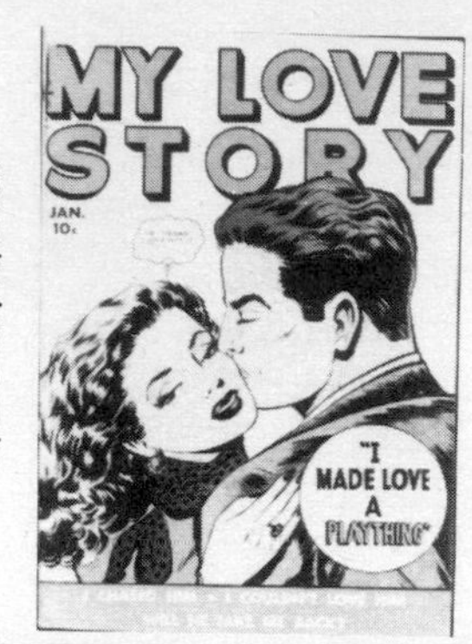

My Love Story #3, © FOX

	GD25	FN65	NM94
1-Before CCA	82.00	247.00	740.00
2	39.00	118.00	355.00
3-5	25.00	75.00	225.00
6-10: 6-Science fiction format begins	18.00	55.00	165.00
11-15,19	13.00	38.00	115.00
16-18,20,21,28-Kirby-a. 18-Kirby-c	15.00	45.00	135.00
22-27,29,30	9.00	27.00	80.00
31-40	7.00	20.00	60.00
41-57,59	4.00	12.00	35.00
58,60,61-Toth-a; Last 10 cent issue	5.00	15.00	45.00
62-79: 77-Toth-a	2.00	7.00	20.00
80-(6/63)-Intro/origin Doom Patrol and begin series; origin & 1st app. Negative Man, Elasti-Girl & S.A. Robotman	32.00	95.00	290.00
81-85: 81,85-Toth-a	12.00	36.00	110.00

NOTE: ***Anderson** a-42. **Cameron** a-24. **Colan** a-77. **Meskin** a-25, 26, 32, 39, 45, 50, 56, 57, 61, 64, 70, 73, 74, 76, 79; c-76. **Moreira** a-11, 12, 15, 17, 20, 23, 25, 27, 37, 40-43, 46, 48, 55-57, 59, 60, 62-65, 67, 69, 70; c-1-4, 7-10. **Roussos** c/a-71-73. **Wildey** a-32.*

MY GREATEST THRILLS IN BASEBALL
Date? (16 pg. Giveaway)
Mission of California

	GD25	FN65	NM94
nn-By Mickey Mantle	43.00	130.00	300.00

MY GREAT LOVE (Becomes Will Rogers Western #5)
Oct, 1949 - No. 4, Apr, 1950
Fox Feature Syndicate

	GD25	FN65	NM94
1	8.35	25.00	50.00
2-4	4.70	14.00	28.00

MY INTIMATE AFFAIR (Inside Crime #3)
Mar, 1950 - No. 2, May, 1950
Fox Feature Syndicate

	GD25	FN65	NM94
1	8.35	25.00	50.00
2	4.70	14.00	28.00

MY LIFE (Formerly Meet Corliss Archer)
No. 4, Sept, 1948 - No. 15, July, 1950
Fox Feature Syndicate

	GD25	FN65	NM94
4-Used in **SOTI**, pg. 39; Kamen/Feldstein-a	22.00	65.00	150.00
5-Kamen-a	10.00	30.00	65.00
6-Kamen/Feldstein-a	10.00	30.00	70.00
7-Wash cover	7.50	22.50	45.00
8,9,11-15	4.70	14.00	28.00
10-Wood-a	10.00	30.00	70.00

MY LITTLE MARGIE (TV)
July, 1954 - No. 54, Nov, 1964
Charlton Comics

	GD25	FN65	NM94
1-Photo front/back-c	19.00	57.00	130.00
2-Photo front/back-c	10.00	30.00	60.00
3-7,10	5.35	16.00	32.00
8,9-Infinity-c	5.85	17.50	35.00
11-14: Part-photo-c (#13, 8/56)	4.70	14.00	28.00
15-19	4.00	10.00	20.00
20-(25¢, 100 pg. issue)	8.35	25.00	50.00
21-38-Last 10 cent issue?	3.00	7.50	15.00
39-53	2.00	5.00	10.00
54-Beatles on cover; lead story spoofs the Beatle haircut craze of the 1960's	12.00	36.00	85.00

NOTE: *Doll cut-outs in 32, 33, 40, 45, 50.*

MY LITTLE MARGIE'S BOY FRIENDS (TV) (Freddy V2#12 on)
Aug, 1955 - No. 11, Apr?, 1958
Charlton Comics

	GD25	FN65	NM94
1-Has several Archie swipes	8.35	25.00	50.00
2	5.35	16.00	32.00
3-11	4.00	10.00	20.00

MY LITTLE MARGIE'S FASHIONS (TV)
Feb, 1959 - No. 5, Nov, 1959
Charlton Comics

	GD25	FN65	NM94
1	8.35	25.00	50.00
2-5	5.35	16.00	32.00

MY LOVE (Becomes Two Gun Western #5 (11/50) on?)
July, 1949 - No. 4, Apr, 1950 (All photo-c)
Marvel Comics (CLDS)

	GD25	FN65	NM94
1	7.50	22.50	45.00
2,3	5.00	15.00	30.00
4-Betty Page photo-c (see Cupid #2)	19.00	57.00	130.00

MY LOVE
Sept, 1969 - No. 39, Mar, 1976
Marvel Comics Group

	GD25	FN65	NM94
1	2.00	5.00	10.00
2-9: 4-6-Colan-a	1.00	2.50	5.00
10-Williamson-r/My Own Romance #71; Kirby-a	1.20	3.00	6.00
11-20: 14-Morrow-c/a; Kirby/Colletta-r	.60	1.50	3.00
21,22,24-39: 38,39-Reprints	.60	1.50	3.00
23-Steranko-r/Our Love Story #5	.80	2.00	4.00
Special(12/71)	.60	1.50	3.00

NOTE: ***John Buscema** a-2-7, 10; c-13, 15, 25, 27. **Colan/Everett** a-13, 15, 27(r/#13).*

MY LOVE AFFAIR (March of Crime #7 on)
July, 1949 - No. 6, May, 1950
Fox Feature Syndicate

	GD25	FN65	NM94
1	8.35	25.00	50.00
2	5.00	15.00	30.00
3-6-Wood-a. 5-(3/50)-Becomes Love Stories #6	10.00	30.00	70.00

MY LOVE LIFE (Formerly Zegra)
No. 6, June, 1949 - No. 13, Aug, 1950; No. 13, Sept, 1951
Fox Feature Syndicate

	GD25	FN65	NM94
6-Kamenish-a	10.00	30.00	60.00
7-13	5.00	15.00	30.00
13 (9/51)	4.20	12.50	25.00

MY LOVE MEMOIRS (Formerly Women Outlaws; Hunted #13 on)
No. 9, Nov, 1949 - No. 12, May, 1950
Fox Feature Syndicate

	GD25	FN65	NM94
9,11,12-Wood-a	10.00	30.00	70.00
10	5.00	15.00	30.00

MY LOVE SECRET (Formerly Phantom Lady; Animal Crackers #31)
No. 24, June, 1949 - No. 30, June, 1950; No. 53, 1954
Fox Feature Syndicate/M. S. Distr.

	GD25	FN65	NM94
24-Kamen/Feldstein-a	10.00	30.00	65.00
25-Possible caricature of Wood on-c?	5.85	17.50	35.00
26,28-Wood-a	10.00	30.00	70.00
27,29,30: 30-Photo-c	4.70	14.00	28.00
53-(Reprint, M.S. Distr.) 1954? nd given; formerly Western Thrillers; becomes Crimes by Women #54; photo-c	3.60	9.00	18.00

MY LOVE STORY (Hoot Gibson Western #5 on)
Sept, 1949 - No. 4, Mar, 1950
Fox Feature Syndicate

	GD25	FN65	NM94
1	8.35	25.00	50.00
2	4.70	14.00	28.00
3,4-Wood-a	10.00	30.00	70.00

MY LOVE STORY
April, 1956 - No. 9, Aug, 1957
Atlas Comics (GPS)

	GD25	FN65	NM94
1	6.70	20.00	40.00
2	4.00	10.00	20.00
3-Matt Baker-a	4.35	13.00	26.00
4-6,8,9	3.60	9.00	18.00
7-Matt Baker, Toth-a	4.70	14.00	28.00

NOTE: ***Brewster** a-3. **Colletta** a-1(2), 3, 4(2), 5; c-3.*

My Own Romance #16, © MEG

My Secret Life #26, © FOX

Mysteries #6, © SUPR

	GD25	FN65	NM94

MY NAME IS CHAOS
1992 - No. 4, 1992 ($4.95, color, mini-series, 52 pgs.)
DC Comics

Book 1-4: Tom Veitch scripts; painted-c	1.00	2.00	5.00

MY ONLY LOVE
July, 1975 - No. 9, Nov, 1976
Charlton Comics

1,2,4-9		1.20	3.00
3-Toth-a		1.60	4.00

MY OWN ROMANCE (Formerly My Romance; Teen-Age Romance #77 on)
No. 4, Mar, 1949 - No. 76, July, 1960
Marvel/Atlas (MjPC/RCM No. 4-59/ZPC No. 60-76)

4-Photo-c	8.35	25.00	50.00
5-10: 5,6,8-10-Photo-c	4.00	11.00	22.00
11-20: 14-Powell-a	3.60	9.00	18.00
21-42: 42-Last precode (2/55)	3.20	8.00	16.00
43-54,56-60	2.40	6.00	12.00
55-Toth-a	4.00	12.00	24.00
61-70,72-76	2.00	5.00	10.00
71-Williamson-a	4.35	13.00	26.00

NOTE: ***Brewster** a-59. **Colletta** a-45(2), 48, 50, 55, 57(2), 59; c-58i, 59, 61. **Everett** a-25; c-58p. **Morisi** a-18. **Orlando** a-61. **Romita** a-36. **Tuska** a 10.*

MY PAL DIZZY (See Comic Books, Series I)

MY PAST (...Confessions) (Formerly Western Thrillers)
No. 7, Aug, 1949 - No. 11, April, 1950 (Crimes Inc. #12)
Fox Feature Syndicate

7	8.35	25.00	50.00
8-10	5.00	15.00	30.00
11-Wood-a	10.00	30.00	70.00

MY PERSONAL PROBLEM
11/55; No. 2, 2/56; No. 3, 9/56 - No. 4, 11/56; 10/57 - No. 3, 5/58
Ajax/Farrell/Steinway Comic

1	5.35	16.00	32.00
2-4	4.00	10.00	20.00
1-3('57-'58)-Steinway	3.20	8.00	16.00

MY PRIVATE LIFE (Formerly Murder, Inc.; becomes Pedro #18)
No. 16, Feb, 1950 - No. 17, April, 1950
Fox Feature Syndicate

16,17	7.00	21.00	42.00

MYRA NORTH (See The Comics, Crackajack Funnies, 4-Color #3 & Red Ryder)

MY REAL LOVE
No. 5, June, 1952
Standard Comics

5-Toth-a, 3 pgs.; Tuska, Cardy, Vern Greene-a; photo-c	7.50	22.50	45.00

MY ROMANCE (Becomes My Own Romance #4 on)
Sept, 1948 - No. 3, Jan, 1949
Marvel Comics (RCM)

1	8.35	25.00	50.00
2,3: 2-Anti-Wertham editorial (11/48)	4.70	14.00	28.00

MY ROMANTIC ADVENTURES (Formerly Romantic Adventures)
No. 68, 8/56 - No. 115, 12/60; No. 116, 7/61 - No. 138, 3/64
American Comics Group

68	5.00	15.00	30.00
69-85	3.20	8.00	16.00
86-Three pg. Williamson-a (2/58)	4.70	14.00	28.00
87-100	2.40	6.00	12.00
101-138	1.40	3.50	7.00

NOTE: ***Whitney** art in most issues.*

MY SECRET (Becomes Our Secret #4 on)
Aug, 1949 - No. 3, Oct, 1949
Superior Comics, Ltd.

1	8.35	25.00	50.00
2,3	5.35	16.00	32.00

MY SECRET AFFAIR (Becomes Martin Kane #4)
Dec, 1949 - No. 3, April, 1950
Hero Book (Fox Feature Syndicate)

1-Harrison/Wood-a, 10 pgs.	11.50	34.00	80.00
2-Wood-a (poor)	8.35	25.00	50.00
3-Wood-a	10.00	30.00	70.00

MY SECRET CONFESSION
September, 1955
Sterling Comics

1-Sekowsky-a	4.70	14.00	28.00

MY SECRET LIFE (Formerly Western Outlaws; Romeo Tubbs #26 on)
No. 22, July, 1949 - No. 27, May, 1950
Fox Feature Syndicate

22	6.70	20.00	40.00
23,26-Wood-a, 6 pgs.	10.00	30.00	70.00
24,25,27	4.35	13.00	26.00

NOTE: *The title was changed to Romeo Tubbs after #25 even though #26 & 27 did come out.*

MY SECRET LIFE (Formerly Young Lovers; Sue & Sally Smith #48)
No. 19, Aug, 1957 - No. 47, Sept, 1962
Charlton Comics

19	2.80	7.00	14.00
20-35	1.40	3.50	7.00
36-47: 44-Last 10 cent issue	1.00	2.50	5.00

MY SECRET MARRIAGE
May, 1953 - No. 24, July, 1956
Superior Comics, Ltd.

1	6.70	20.00	40.00
2	4.00	10.00	20.00
3-24	2.80	7.00	14.00
I.W. Reprint #9	.60	1.50	3.00

NOTE: *Many issues contain **Kamenish** art.*

MY SECRET ROMANCE (Becomes A Star Presentation #3)
Jan, 1950 - No. 2, March, 1950
Hero Book (Fox Feature Syndicate)

1-Wood-a	11.00	32.00	75.00
2-Wood-a	10.00	30.00	70.00

MY SECRET STORY (Formerly Captain Kidd #25; Sabu #30 on)
No. 26, Oct, 1949 - No. 29, April, 1950
Fox Feature Syndicate

26	8.35	25.00	50.00
27-29	5.35	16.00	32.00

MYS-TECH WARS
Mar, 1993 - No. 4, June, 1993 ($1.75, color, mini-series)
Marvel Comics UK

1-4: 1-Gatefold-c		.70	1.75

MYSTERIES (...Weird & Strange)
May, 1953 - No. 11, Jan, 1955
Superior/Dynamic Publ. (Randall Publ. Ltd.)

1	16.00	48.00	110.00
2-A-Bomb blast story	9.15	27.50	55.00
3-9,11	6.35	19.00	38.00
10-Kamenish-c/a reprinted from Strange Mysteries #2, cover is from a panel in Strange Mysteries #2	7.50	22.50	45.00

MYSTERIES OF SCOTLAND YARD (See A-1 Comics #121)

MYSTERIES OF UNEXPLORED WORLDS (See Blue Bird) (Becomes Son of Vulcan V2#49 on)

Mysterious Adventures #10, © Story Comics

Mystery Comics #1, © WHW

Mystery In Space #45, © DC

GD25 FN65 NM94 GD25 FN65 NM94

Aug, 1956; No. 2, Jan, 1957 - No. 48, Sept, 1965
Charlton Comics

	GD25	FN65	NM94
1	21.00	62.00	145.00
2-No Ditko	7.00	21.00	50.00
3,4,8,9-Ditko-a	12.00	36.00	85.00
5,6-Ditko-c/a (all)	14.00	43.00	100.00
7-(2/58, 68 pgs.); Ditko-a(4)	14.00	43.00	100.00
10-Ditko-c/a(4)	14.00	43.00	100.00
11-Ditko-c/a(3); signed J. Kotdi	14.00	43.00	100.00
12,19,21-24,26-Ditko-a	10.00	30.00	70.00
13-18,20	3.20	8.00	20.00
25,27-30	2.30	6.75	16.00
31-45	1.65	4.00	10.00
46(5/65)-Son of Vulcan begins (origin/1st app.)	2.40	7.25	17.00
47,48	1.65	4.00	10.00

NOTE: ***Ditko** c-3-6, 10, 11, 19, 21-24. Covers to #23 & 24 reprint story panels.*

MYSTERIOUS ADVENTURES
March, 1951 - No. 24, Mar, 1955; No. 25, Aug, 1955
Story Comics

	GD25	FN65	NM94
1-All horror stories	23.00	70.00	160.00
2	11.50	34.00	80.00
3,4,6,10	10.00	30.00	65.00
5-Bondage-c	12.00	36.00	85.00
7-Daggar in eye panel	17.00	52.00	120.00
8-Eyeball story	16.00	48.00	110.00
9-Extreme violence	13.00	40.00	90.00
11-13: 11(12/52)-Used in **SOTI**, pg. 84	13.00	40.00	90.00
14-E.C. Old Witch swipe	10.00	30.00	65.00
15-21: 18-Used in Senate Investigative report, pgs. 5,6; E.C. swipe/TFTC #35; The Coffin-Keeper & Corpse (hosts). 20-Used by Wertham in the Senate hearings. 21-Bondage/beheading-c	16.00	50.00	115.00
22-'Cinderella' parody	11.00	32.00	75.00
23-Disbrow-a (6 pgs.); E.C. swipe "The Mystery Keeper's Tale" (host) and "Mother Ghoul's Nursery Tale"	10.00	30.00	70.00
24,25	9.15	27.50	55.00

NOTE: *Tothish art by **Ross Andru**-#22, 23. **Bache** a-8. **Cameron** a-5-7. **Harrison** a-12. **Hollingsworth** a-3-8, 12. **Schaffenberger** a-24, 25. **Wildey** a-15, 17.*

MYSTERIOUS ISLAND (See 4-Color #1213)

MYSTERIOUS ISLE
Nov-Jan, 1963/64 (Jules Verne)
Dell Publishing Co.

	GD25	FN65	NM94
1	2.40	6.00	12.00

MYSTERIOUS STORIES (Formerly Horror From the Tomb #1)
No. 2, Dec-Jan, 1954-1955 - No. 7, Dec, 1955
Premier Magazines

	GD25	FN65	NM94
2-Woodbridge-c; last pre-code issue	14.00	43.00	100.00
3-Woodbridge-c/a	10.00	30.00	70.00
4-7: 5-Cinderella parody. 6-Woodbridge-c	10.00	30.00	65.00

NOTE: ***Hollingsworth** a-2, 4.*

MYSTERIOUS SUSPENSE
October, 1968 (12 cents)
Charlton Comics

	GD25	FN65	NM94
1-Return of the Question by Ditko (c/a)	3.60	10.75	25.00

MYSTERIOUS TRAVELER (See Tales of the...)

MYSTERIOUS TRAVELER COMICS (Radio)
Nov, 1948
Trans-World Publications

	GD25	FN65	NM94
1-Powell-c/a(2); Poe adaptation, "Tell Tale Heart"	33.00	100.00	225.00

MYSTERY COMICS
1944 - No. 4, 1944 (No months given)
William H. Wise & Co.

	GD25	FN65	NM94
1-The Magnet, The Silver Knight, Brad Spencer, Wonderman, Dick Devins, King of Futuria, & Zudo the Jungle Boy begin (all 1st app.); Schomburg-c on all	50.00	150.00	350.00
2-Bondage-c	32.00	95.00	225.00
3-Lance Lewis, Space Detective begins (1st app.); Robot-c	27.00	82.00	190.00
4(V2#1 inside)	27.00	82.00	190.00

MYSTERY COMICS DIGEST
March, 1972 - No. 26, Oct, 1975
Gold Key

	GD25	FN65	NM94
1-Ripley's Believe It or Not; reprint of Ripley's #1 origin Ra-Ka-Tep the Mummy; Wood-a	1.00	2.00	5.00
2-Boris Karloff Tales of Mystery; Wood-a; 1st app. Werewolf Count Wulfstein		1.00	2.50
3-Twilight Zone (TV); Crandall, Toth & George Evans-a; 1st app. Tragg & Simbar the Lion Lord; 2 Crandall/Frazetta-r/Twilight Zone #1		1.00	2.50
4-Ripley's Believe It or Not; 1st app. Baron Tibor, the Vampire		.80	2.00
5-Boris Karloff Tales of Mystery; 1st app. Dr. Spektor		.80	2.00
6-Twilight Zone (TV); 1st app. U.S. Marshal Reid & Sir Duane; Evans-r		.80	2.00
7-Ripley's Believe It or Not; origin The Lurker in the Swamp; 1st app. Duroc			1.20
8-Boris Karloff Tales of Mystery; McWilliams-r			1.20
9-Twilight Zone (TV); Williamson, Crandall, McWilliams-a; 2nd Tragg app.		1.00	2.50
10,13-Ripley's Believe It or Not			1.00
11,14-Boris Karloff Tales of Mystery. 14-1st app. Xorkon			1.00
12,15-Twilight Zone (TV)			1.00
16,19,22,25-Ripley's Believe It or Not			1.00
17-Boris Karloff Tales of Mystery; Williamson-r			1.50
18,21,24-Twilight Zone (TV)			1.00
20,23,26-Boris Karloff Tales of Mystery			1.00

NOTE: *Dr. Spektor app.-#5, 10-12, 21. Durak app.-#15. Duroc app.-#14 (later called Durak). King George 1st app.-#8.*

MYSTERY IN SPACE
4-5/51 - No. 110, 9/66; No. 111, 9/80 - No. 117, 3/81 (#1-3: 52 pgs.)
National Periodical Publications

	GD25	FN65	NM94
1-Frazetta-a, 8 pgs.; Knights of the Galaxy begins, ends #8	230.00	685.00	1600.00
2	86.00	260.00	600.00
3	71.00	215.00	500.00
4,5	57.00	170.00	400.00
6-10: 7-Toth-a	49.00	145.00	340.00
11-15: 13-Toth-a	32.00	95.00	225.00
16-18,20-25: Interplanetary Insurance feature by Infantino in all. 21-1st app. Space Cabbie. 24-Last pre-code issue	29.00	85.00	200.00
19-Virgil Finlay-a	32.00	95.00	225.00
26-40: 26-Space Cabbie feature begins	23.00	70.00	160.00
41-52: 47-Space Cabbie feature ends	17.00	52.00	120.00

	GD25	FN65	VF82	NM94
Showcase #17 (11-12/58)-Origin & 1st app. Adam Strange	100.00	300.00	750.00	1200.00

	GD25	FN65	NM94
Showcase #18 (1-2/59)-2nd app. Adam Strange	90.00	270.00	720.00
Showcase #19 (3-4/59)-3rd app. Adam Strange	85.00	255.00	850.00

	GD25	FN65	VF82	NM94
53-Adam Strange begins (8/59, 10 pg. story)	80.00	241.00	603.00	965.00

	GD25	FN65	NM94
54	33.00	98.00	260.00
55-Grey tone-c	20.00	60.00	160.00
56-60: 59-Kane/Anderson-a	14.00	43.00	115.00

Mystery Men Comics #25, © FOX

Mystery Tales #25, © MEG

Mystic #23, © MEG

GD25 FN65 NM94

61-71: 61-1st app. Adam Strange foe Ulthoon. 62-1st app. A.S. foe Mortan. 63-Origin Vandor. 66-Star Rovers begin (1st app.). 68-Dust Devils app. 71-Last 10 cent issue 9.00 20.00 75.00
72-74,76-80 7.00 21.00 55.00
75-JLA x-over in Adam Strange (5/62)(sequel to JLA #3) 20.00 60.00 160.00
81-86 4.00 13.00 35.00
87-(11/63)-Adam Strange/Hawkman double feat begins; 3rd Hawkman tryout series 18.00 53.00 140.00
88-Adam Strange & Hawkman stories 14.00 41.00 110.00
89-Adam Strange & Hawkman stories 13.00 38.00 100.00
90-Adam Strange & Hawkman team-up for 1st time (3/64); Hawkman moves to own title next month 16.00 47.00 125.00
91-103. 91-End Infantino art on Adam Strange; double-length Adam Strange story. 92-Space Ranger begins (6/64), ends #103. 92-94,96,98-Space Ranger-c. 94,98-Adam Strange/Space Ranger team-up. 102-Adam Strange ends (no Space Ranger). 103-Origin Ultra, the Multi-Alien; last Space Ranger 2.15 6.50 15.00
104-110: 110-(9/66)-Last 12 cent issue 1.00 2.00 5.00
V17#111(9/80)-117: 117-Newton-a(3 pgs.) 1.20 3.00

NOTE: ***Anderson** a-2, 4, 8-10, 12-17, 19, 45-48, 51, 57, 59i, 61-64, 70, 76, 87-91; c-9, 10, 15-25, 87, 89, 105-108, 110. **Aparo** a-111. **Austin** a-112i. **Bolland** a-115. **Craig** a-114, 116. **Ditko** a-111, 114-116. **Drucker** a-13, 14. **Elias** a-98, 102, 103. **Golden** a-113p. **Sid Greene** a-78, 91. **Infantino** a-1-8, 11, 14-25, 27-46, 48, 49, 51, 53-91, 103, 117; c-60-86, 88, 90, 91, 105, 107. **Gil Kane** a-14p, 15p, 18p, 19p, 26p, 29-59p(most), 100-102; c-52, 101. **Kubert** a-113; c-111-115. **Moriera** c-27, 28. **Rogers** a-111. **Sekowsky** a-52. **Simon & Kirby** a-4(2 pgs.). **Spiegle** a-111, 114. **Starlin** c-116. **Sutton** a-112. **Tuska** a-115p, 117p.*

MYSTERY MEN COMICS
Aug, 1939 - No. 31, Feb, 1942
Fox Features Syndicate

1-Intro. & 1st app. The Blue Beetle, The Green Mask, Rex Dexter of Mars by Briefer, Zanzibar by Tuska, Lt. Drake, D-13-Secret Agent by Powell, Chen Chang, Wing Turner, & Captain Denny Scott 214.00 645.00 1500.00
2-Robot & sci/fi-c (2nd Robot-c w/Movie #6) 100.00 300.00 650.00
3 (10/39) 88.00 262.00 575.00
4-Capt. Savage begins (11/39) 75.00 225.00 500.00
5 58.00 175.00 400.00
6-8 50.00 160.00 350.00
9-The Moth begins 44.00 132.00 300.00
10-Wing Turner by Kirby 44.00 132.00 300.00
11-Intro. Domino 33.00 100.00 225.00
12,14-18 30.00 90.00 200.00
13-Intro. Lynx & sidekick Blackie (8/40) 35.00 105.00 230.00
19-Intro. & 1st app. Miss X (ends #21) 35.00 105.00 230.00
20-31: 26-The Wraith begins 28.00 85.00 190.00

NOTE: ***Briefer** a-1-15, 20, 24; c-9. **Cuidera** a-22. **Lou Fine** c-1-8. **Powell** a-1-15, 24. **Simon** c-10-12. **Tuska** a-1-16, 22, 24, 27. Bondage-c 1, 3, 7, 8, 25, 27-29, 31. Blue Beetle c-7, 8, 10-31. D-13 Secret Agent c-6. Green Mask c-1, 3-5. Rex Dexter of Mars c-2, 9.*

MYSTERY TALES
March, 1952 - No. 54, Aug, 1957
Atlas Comics (20CC)

1-Horror/weird stories in all 38.00 115.00 265.00
2-Krigstein-a 20.00 60.00 140.00
3-10: 6-A-Bomb panel. 10-Story similar to 'The Assassin' from Shock SuspenStories 14.00 43.00 100.00
11,13-21: 14-Maneely s/f story. 20-Electric chair issue. 21-Matt Fox-a; decapitation story 11.00 32.00 75.00
12-Matt Fox-a 11.50 34.00 80.00
22-Forte/Matt Fox-c; a(i) 11.50 34.00 80.00
23-26 (2/55)-Last precode issue 10.00 30.00 60.00
27,29-35,37,38,41-43,48,49: 43-Morisi story contains Frazetta art swipes from Untamed Love 8.35 25.00 50.00
28-Jack Katz-a 9.15 27.50 55.00
36,39-Krigstein-a 9.15 27.50 55.00
40,45-Ditko-a (#45 is 3 pgs. only) 9.15 27.50 55.00
44,51-Williamson/Krenkel-a 10.00 30.00 60.00
46-Williamson/Krenkel-a; Crandall text illos 10.00 30.00 60.00
47-Crandall, Ditko, Powell-a 10.00 30.00 60.00
50-Torres, Morrow-a 9.15 27.50 55.00
52,53 6.70 20.00 40.00
54-Crandall, Check-a 8.35 25.00 50.00

NOTE: ***Ayers** a-18, 49, 52. **Berg** a-17, 51. **Colan** a-1, 3, 18, 35, 43. **Colletta** a-10. **Drucker** a-41. **Everett** a-2, 29, 33, 35, 41; c-8-11, 14, 38, 39, 41, 43, 44, 46, 48-51, 53. **Fass** a-16. **Forte** a-21, 22, 45, 46. **Matt Fox** a-12?, 21, 22; c-22. **Heath** a-3; c-3, 15, 17, 26. **Heck** a-25. **Kinstler** a-15. **Mort Lawrence** a-26, 32, 34. **Maneely** a-1, 9, 14, 22; c-12, 23, 24, 27. **Mooney** a-3, 40. **Morisi** a-43, 49, 52. **Morrow** a-50. **Orlando** a-51. **Pakula** a-16. **Powell** a-21, 29, 37, 38, 47. **Reinman** a-1, 14, 17. **Robinson** a-7p, 42. **Romita** a-37. **Roussos** a-4, 44. **R.Q. Sale** a-45, 46, 49. **Severin** c-52. **Shores** a-17, 45. **Tuska** a-10, 12, 14. **Whitney** a-2. **Wildey** a-37.*

MYSTERY TALES
1964
Super Comics

Super Reprint #16,17('64): 16-r/Tales of Horror #2. 17-r/Eerie #14(Avon) 1.20 3.00 6.00
Super Reprint #18-Kubert-r/Strange Terrors #4 1.20 3.00 6.00

MYSTIC (3rd Series)
March, 1951 - No. 61, Aug, 1957
Marvel/Atlas Comics (CLDS 1/CSI 2-21/OMC 22-35/CSI 35-61)

1-Atom bomb panels; horror/weird stories in all 36.00 110.00 250.00
2 20.00 60.00 140.00
3-Eyes torn out 17.00 52.00 120.00
4-"The Devil Birds" by Wolverton, 6 pgs. 34.00 105.00 240.00
5,7-10 12.00 36.00 85.00
6-"The Eye of Doom" by Wolverton, 7 pgs. 34.00 105.00 240.00
11-20: 16-Bondage/torture c/story 11.00 32.00 75.00
21-25,27-36-Last precode (3/55). 25-E.C. swipe 10.00 30.00 60.00
26-Atomic War, severed head stories 10.00 30.00 70.00
37-51,53-57,61: 57-Story "Trapped in the Ant-Hill" (1957) is very similar to "The Man in the Ant Hill" in TTA #27 8.35 25.00 50.00
52-Wood-a; Crandall-a? 10.00 30.00 65.00
58,59-Krigstein-a 9.15 27.50 55.00
60-Williamson/Mayo-a, 4 pgs. 9.15 27.50 55.00

NOTE: ***Andru** a-23, 25. **Ayers** a-35, 53; c-8. **Berg** a-49. **Cameron** a-49, 51. **Check** a-31, 60. **Colan** a-3, 7, 12, 21, 37, 60. **Colletta** a-29. **Drucker** a-46, 52, 56. **Everett** a-8, 9, 17, 40, 44, 57; c-13, 18, 21, 42, 47, 49, 51-55, 57-59, 61. **Forte** a-35, 52, 58. **Fox** a-24i. **Al Hartley** a-35. **Heath** a-10; c-10, 20, 22, 23, 25, 30. **Infantino** a-12. **Kane** a-8, 24p. **Jack Katz** a-31, 33. **Mort Lawrence** a-19, 37. **Maneely** a-22, 24, 58; c-7, 15, 28, 29, 31. **Moldoff** a-29. **Morisi** a-40, 49, 52. **Morrow** a-51. **Orlando** a-57, 61. **Pakula** a-52, 57, 59. **Powell** a-52, 54-56. **Robinson** a-5. **Romita** a-11, 15. **R.Q. Sale** a-35, 53, 58. **Sekowsky** a-1, 2, 4, 5. **Severin** c-56, 60. **Tuska** a-15. **Whitney** a-33. **Wildey** a-28, 30. **Ed Win** a-17, 20. Canadian reprints known-title 'Startling.'*

MYSTICAL TALES
June, 1956 - No. 8, Aug, 1957
Atlas Comics (CCC 1/EPI 2-8)

1-Everett-c/a 20.00 60.00 140.00
2,4: 2-Berg-a 10.00 30.00 70.00
3,5: 3-Crandall-a. 5-Williamson-a, 4 pgs. 11.00 32.00 75.00
6-Torres, Krigstein-a 10.00 30.00 65.00
7-Bolle, Forte, Torres, Orlando-a 10.00 30.00 60.00
8-Krigstein, Check-a 10.00 30.00 65.00

NOTE: ***Everett** a-1; c-1-4, 6, 7. **Orlando** a-1, 2, 7. **Pakula** a-3. **Powell** a-1, 4.*

MYSTIC COMICS (1st Series)
March, 1940 - No. 10, Aug, 1942
Timely Comics (TPI 1-5/TCI 8-10)

GD25 FN65 VF82 NM94

1-Origin The Blue Blaze, The Dynamic Man, & Flexo the Rubber Robot; Zephyr Jones, 3X's & Deep Sea Demon app.; The Magician begins (all 1st app.); c-from Spider pulp V18#1, 6/39 812.00 2440.00 4470.00 6500.00
(Estimated up to 110 total copies exist, 4 in NM/Mint)

GD25 FN65 NM94

2-The Invisible Man & Master Mind Excello begin; Space Rangers, Zara of the Jungle, Taxi Taylor app. 233.00 700.00 1600.00
3-Origin Hercules, who last appears in #4 185.00 557.00 1300.00
4-Origin The Thin Man & The Black Widow; Merzak the Mystic app.; last Flexo, Dynamic Man, Invisible Man & Blue Blaze (some issues have date sticker on cover; others have July w/August overprint in silver color);

The 'Nam #83, © MEG

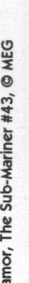

Namor, The Sub-Mariner #43, © MEG

Nancy and Sluggo #185, © DELL

	GD25	FN65	NM94
Roosevelt assassination-c	208.00	625.00	1450.00
5-(3/41)-Origin The Black Marvel, The Blazing Skull, The Sub-Earth Man, Super Slave & The Terror; The Moon Man & Black Widow app.; 5-German war-c begin, end #10	200.00	600.00	1400.00
6-(10/41)-Origin The Challenger & The Destroyer (1st app.?; also see All-Winners #2, Fall, 1941)	185.00	557.00	1300.00
7-The Witness begins (12/41, origin & 1st app.); origin Davey & the Demon; last Black Widow; Hitler opens his trunk of terror-c by Simon & Kirby	158.00	475.00	1100.00
8,9: 9-Gary Gaunt app.; last Black Marvel, Mystic & Blazing Skull; Hitler-c	117.00	350.00	800.00
10-Father Time, World of Wonder, & Red Skeleton app.; last Challenger & Terror	117.00	350.00	800.00

NOTE: ***Gabrielle*** *c-8-10.* ***Kirby/Schomburg*** *c-6.* ***Rico*** *a-9(2).* ***Schomburg*** *a-1-4; c-1-5.* ***Sekowsky*** *a-9.* ***Sekowsky/Klein*** *a-8(Challenger). Bondage c-1, 2, 9.*

MYSTIC COMICS (2nd Series)
Oct, 1944 - No. 3, Win, 1944-45; No. 4, Mar, 1945
Timely Comics (ANC)

	GD25	FN65	NM94
1-The Angel, The Destroyer, The Human Torch, Terry Vance the Schoolboy Sleuth, & Tommy Tyme begin	107.00	320.00	750.00
2-(Fall/44)-Last Human Torch & Terry Vance; bondage/hypo-c	63.00	188.00	425.00
3-Last Angel (two stories) & Tommy Tyme	58.00	175.00	400.00
4-The Young Allies-c & app.; Schomburg-c	53.00	160.00	365.00

MY STORY (...True Romances in Pictures #5,6) (Formerly Zago)
No. 5, May, 1949 - No. 12, Aug, 1950
Hero Books (Fox Features Syndicate)

	GD25	FN65	NM94
5-Kamen/Feldstein-a	10.00	30.00	70.00
6-8,11,12: 12-Photo-c	5.00	15.00	30.00
9,10-Wood-a	11.00	32.00	75.00

MY TRUE LOVE (Formerly Western Killers #64; Frank Buck #70 on)
No. 65, July, 1949 - No. 69, March, 1950
Fox Features Syndicate

	GD25	FN65	NM94
65	7.50	22.50	45.00
66-69: 69-Morisi-a	5.35	16.00	32.00

NAIVE INTER-DIMENSIONAL COMMANDO KOALAS (Eclipse)(Value: cover or less)

NAKED PREY, THE (See Movie Classics)

'NAM, THE (See Savage Tales #1, 2nd series)
Dec, 1986 - No. 84, Sept, 1993
Marvel Comics Group

	GD25	FN65	NM94
1-Golden a(p)/c begins, ends #13		1.40	3.50
1 (2nd printing)			1.00
2		1.00	2.50
3-7: 7 Golden-a, 2 pgs.		.80	2.00
8-51,54-64: 32-Death R. Kennedy. 58-Silver logo			1.50
52-Frank Castle (The Punisher) app.		1.20	3.00
53-Frank Castle (The Punisher) app.		.80	2.00
52,53-Gold 2nd printings			1.25
65-74,76-84: 65-Heath-c/a; begin $1.75-c. 67-69-Punisher 3 part story. 70-Lomax scripts begin		.70	1.75
75-($2.25, 52 pgs.)		.90	2.25
Trade Paperback 1-r/#1-4		1.80	4.50
Trade Paperback 2-r/#5-8	1.10	2.70	6.50

'NAM MAGAZINE, THE (Marvel)(Value: value: cover or less)

NAMORA (See Marvel Mystery Comics #82 & Sub-Mariner Comics)
Fall, 1948 - No. 3, Dec, 1948
Marvel Comics (PrPI)

	GD25	FN65	NM94
1-Sub-Mariner x-over in Namora; Namora by Everett(2), Sub-Mariner by Rico (10 pgs.)	100.00	300.00	700.00
2-The Blonde Phantom & Sub-Mariner story; Everett-a	83.00	250.00	550.00
3-(Scarce)-Sub-Mariner app.; Everett-a	75.00	225.00	500.00

NAMOR, THE SUB-MARINER (See Prince Namor & Sub-Mariner)
Apr, 1990 - Present ($1.00/$1.25, color)
Marvel Comics

	GD25	FN65	NM94
1-Byrne-c/a/scripts in 1-25 (scripts only #26-32)		1.40	3.50
2-5: 5-Iron Man app.		.80	2.00
6-11: 8,10,16-Re-intro Iron Fist (8-cameo only)			1.50
12-($1.50, 52 pgs.)-Re-intro. The Invaders		.80	2.00
13-22: 18-Punisher cameo (1 panel); 21-23,25-Wolverine cameos. 22-Last $1.00-c. 22,23-Iron Fist app.			1.00
23-25: 24-Namor vs. Wolverine			1.25
26-New look for Namor w/new costume; 1st Jae Lee-c/a this title (5/92) & begins	1.30	3.25	8.00
27		1.80	4.50
28-Iron Fist-c/story		1.60	4.00
29,30		1.00	2.50
31-36,38-48: 31-Dr. Doom-c/story. 33,34-Iron Fist cameo. 35-New Tiger Shark-c/story		.60	1.25
37-($2.00)-Aqua holo-grafx foil-c		.80	2.00
Annual 1 (1991, $2.00, 68 pgs.)-3 pg. origin recap		.80	2.00
Annual 2 (1992, $2.25, 68 pgs.)-Return/Defenders		.90	2.25
Annual 3 (1993, $2.95, 68 pgs.)-Bagged w/card		1.20	3.00

NOTE: ***Jae Lee*** *a-26-30p, 31-37, 38p, 39, 40; c-26-40.*

NANCY AND SLUGGO (See Comics On Parade & Sparkle Comics)
No. 16, 1949 - No. 23, 1954
United Features Syndicate

	GD25	FN65	NM94
16(#1)	5.85	17.50	35.00
17-23	4.00	10.00	20.00

NANCY & SLUGGO (Nancy #146-173; formerly Sparkler Comics)
No. 121, Apr, 1955 - No. 192, Oct, 1963
St. John/Dell #146-187/Gold Key #188 on

	GD25	FN65	NM94
121(4/55)(St. John)	4.20	12.50	25.00
122-145(7/57)(St. John)	3.60	9.00	18.00
146(9/57)-Peanuts begins, ends #192 (Dell)	4.00	11.00	22.00
147-161 (Dell)	3.20	8.00	16.00
162-165,177-180-John Stanley-a	6.35	19.00	38.00
166-176-Oona & Her Haunted House series; Stanley-a	7.50	22.50	45.00
181-187(3-5/62)(Dell)	2.80	7.00	14.00
188(10/62)-192 (Gold Key)	2.80	7.00	14.00
4-Color 1034(9-11/59)-Summer Camp	3.20	8.00	16.00

(See Dell Giant #34, 45 & Dell Giants)

NANNY AND THE PROFESSOR (TV)
Aug, 1970 - No. 2, Oct, 1970 (Photo-c)
Dell Publishing Co.

	GD25	FN65	NM94
1(01-546-008), 2	5.00	15.00	30.00

NAPOLEON (See 4-Color No. 526)

NAPOLEON & SAMANTHA (See Walt Disney Showcase No. 10)

NAPOLEON & UNCLE ELBY (See Clifford McBride's...)
July, 1942 (68 pages) (One Shot)
Eastern Color Printing Co.

	GD25	FN65	NM94
1	23.00	70.00	160.00
1945-American Book-Strafford Press (128 pgs.) (8x10-1/2"-B&W reprints; hardcover)	12.00	35.00	70.00

NASCUB ADVENTURES, THE (New Image)(Value: cover or less)

NATHANIEL DUSK (DC)(Value: cover or less)

NATHANIEL DUSK II (DC)(Value: cover or less)

NATIONAL COMICS
July, 1940 - No. 75, Nov, 1949
Quality Comics Group

1-Uncle Sam begins (1st app.); origin sidekick Buddy by Eisner; origin

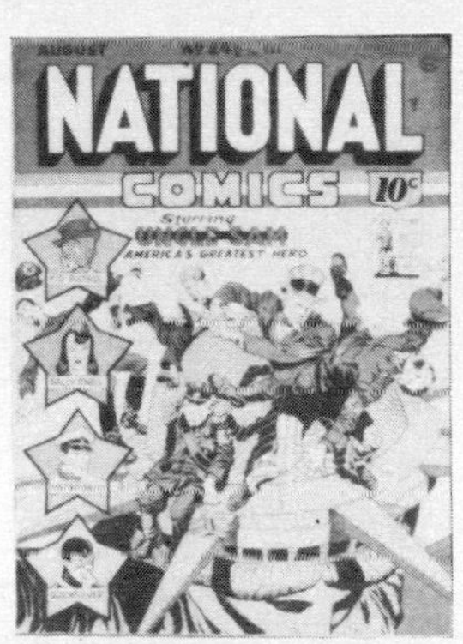

National Comics #24, © QUA

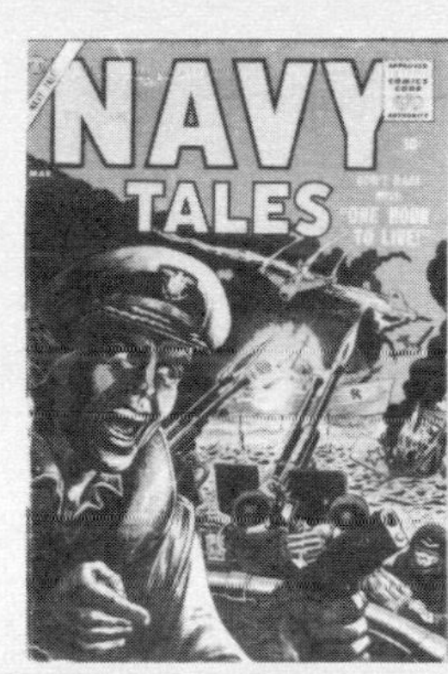

Navy Tales #2, © MEG

The Nazz #1, © Tom Veitch & Bryan Talbot

GD25 FN65 NM94 | GD25 FN65 NM94

Wonder Boy & Kid Dixon; Merlin the Magician (ends #45); Cyclone, Kid Patrol, Sally O'Neil Policewoman, Pen Miller (ends #22), Prop Powers (ends #26), & Paul Bunyan (ends #22) begin 250.00 750.00 1700.00
2 117.00 350.00 800.00
3-Last Eisner Uncle Sam 92.00 275.00 600.00
4-Last Cyclone 67.00 200.00 450.00
5-(11/40)-Quicksilver begins (1st app.)(3rd w/lightning speed?); origin Uncle Sam; bondage-c 83.00 250.00 550.00
6-11: 8-Jack & Jill begins (ends #22). 9-Flag-c 63.00 188.00 425.00
12 46.00 138.00 315.00
13-16-Lou Fine-a 54.00 162.00 365.00
17,19-22 43.00 130.00 290.00
18-(12/41)-Shows orientals attacking Pearl Harbor; on stands one month before actual event 54.00 162.00 350.00
23-The Unknown & Destroyer 171 begin 40.00 130.00 [illegible]
24-26,28,30: 26-Wonder Boy ends 32.00 95.00 220.00
27-G-2 the Unknown begins (ends #46) 32.00 95.00 220.00
29-Origin The Unknown 32.00 95.00 220.00
31-33: 33-Chic Carter begins (ends #47) 30.00 90.00 210.00
34-40: 35-Last Kid Patrol. 39-Hitler-c 18.00 55.00 125.00
41-50: 42-The Barker begins (1st app?, 5/44); The Barker covers begin. 48-Origin The Whistler 13.00 40.00 90.00
51-Sally O'Neil by Ward, 8 pgs. (12/45) 18.00 55.00 120.00
52-60 10.00 30.00 70.00
61-67: 67-Format change; Quicksilver app. 8.35 25.00 50.00
68-75: The Barker ends 5.85 17.50 35.00

NOTE: ***Cole*** *Quicksilver-13; Barker-43; c-43, 46, 47, 49-51.* ***Crandall*** *Uncle Sam-11-13 (with* ***Fine****), 25, 26; c-24-26, 30-33, 43.* ***Crandall*** *Paul Bunyan-10-13.* ***Fine*** *Uncle Sam-13 (w/****Crandall****), 17, 18; c-1-14, 16, 18, 21.* ***Gill Fox*** *c-69-74.* ***Guardineer*** *Quicksilver-27, 35.* ***Gustavson*** *Quicksilver-14-26.* ***McWilliams*** *a-23-28, 55, 57. Uncle Sam c-1-41. Barker c-42-75.*

NATIONAL CRUMB, THE (Magazine-Size)
August, 1975 (52 pages) (Satire)
Mayfair Publications
1 1.30 3.25 8.00

NATIONAL VELVET (TV)
May-July, 1961 - No. 2, March, 1963 (All photo-c)
Dell Publishing Co./Gold Key
4-Color 1195 (#1) 6.70 20.00 40.00
4-Color 1312 4.00 11.00 22.00
01-556-207, 12-556-210 (Dell) 4.00 10.00 20.00
1(12/62), 2(3/63) (Gold Key) 4.00 10.00 20.00

NATION OF SNITCHES
1990 ($4.95, color, 52 pgs.)
Piranha Press (DC)
nn 1.00 2.00 5.00

NATURE BOY (Formerly Danny Blaze; Li'l Rascal Twins #6 on)
No. 3, March, 1956 - No. 5, Feb, 1957
Charlton Comics
3-Origin; Blue Beetle story; Buscema-c/a 16.00 48.00 112.00
4,5 12.00 37.00 87.00

NOTE: ***John Buscema*** *a-3, 4p, 5; c-3.* ***Powell*** *a-4.*

NATURE OF THINGS (See 4-Color No. 727, 842)

NAUSICAA OF THE VALLEY OF WIND (Viz)(Value: cover or less)

NAVY ACTION (Sailor Sweeney #12-14)
Aug, 1954 - No. 11, Apr, 1956; No. 15, 1/57 - No. 18, 8/57
Atlas Comics (CDS)
1-Powell-a 9.15 27.50 55.00
2-Lawrence-a 4.70 14.00 28.00
3-11: 4-Last precode (2/55) 3.60 9.00 18.00
15-18 3.00 7.50 15.00

NOTE: ***Berg*** *a-7, 9.* ***Colan*** *a-8.* ***Drucker*** *a-7, 17.* ***Everett*** *a-3, 7, 16; c-16, 17.* ***Heath*** *c-1, 2, 6.* ***Maneely*** *a-7, 8, 18; c-9, 11.* ***Pakula*** *a-2, 3, 9.* ***Reinman*** *a-17.*

NAVY COMBAT
June, 1955 - No. 20, Oct, 1958
Atlas Comics (MPI)
1-Torpedo Taylor begins by Don Heck 9.15 27.50 55.00
2 4.70 14.00 28.00
3-10 4.00 10.00 20.00
11,13,15,16,18-20 3.60 9.00 18.00
12-Crandall-a 5.35 16.00 32.00
14-Torres-a 4.00 12.00 24.00
17-Williamson-a, 4 pgs.; Torres-a 4.35 13.00 26.00

NOTE: ***Berg*** *a-10, 11.* ***Colan*** *a-11.* ***Drucker*** *a-7.* ***Everett*** *a-3, 20; c-8 & 9 w/****Tuska****, 10, 13-16.* ***Heck*** *a-11(2).* ***Maneely*** *c-1, 6, 11, 17.* ***Morisi*** *a-8.* ***Pakula*** *a-7.* ***Powell*** *a-20.*

NAVY HEROES
1945
Almanac Publishing Co.
1-Heavy in propaganda 7.50 22.50 45.00

NAVY: HISTORY & TRADITION
1958 - 1961 (nn) (Giveaway)
Stokes Walesby Co./Dept. of Navy
1772-1778, 1778-1782, 1782-1817, 1817-1865, 1865-1936, 1940-1945 4.00 12.00 24.00
1861: Naval Actions of the Civil War: 1865 4.00 12.00 24.00

NAVY PATROL
May, 1955 - No. 4, Nov, 1955
Key Publications
1 4.20 12.50 25.00
2-4 2.40 6.00 12.00

NAVY TALES
Jan, 1957 - No. 4, July, 1957
Atlas Comics (CDS)
1-Everett-c; Berg, Powell-a 7.50 22.50 45.00
2-Williamson/Mayo-a(5 pgs); Crandall-a 7.50 22.50 45.00
3,4-Reinman-a; Severin-c. 4-Crandall-a 6.00 18.00 36.00

NOTE: ***Colan*** *a-4.* ***Maneely*** *c-2.* ***Sinnott*** *a-4.*

NAVY TASK FORCE
Feb, 1954 - No. 8, April, 1956
Stanmor Publications/Aragon Mag. No. 4-8
1 5.00 15.00 30.00
2 3.00 7.50 15.00
3-8: #8-r/Navy Patrol #1 2.00 5.00 10.00

NAVY WAR HEROES
Jan, 1964 - No. 7, Mar-Apr, 1965
Charlton Comics
1 1.60 4.00 8.00
2-7 .60 1.50 3.00

NAZA (Stone Age Warrior)
Nov-Jan, 1963-64 - No. 9, March, 1966
Dell Publishing Co.
12-555-401 (#1)-Painted-c 1.85 5.50 13.00
2-9: 2-4-Painted-c 1.50 3.75 9.00

NAZZ, THE (DC)(Value: cover or less)

NEBBS, THE
1928 (Daily B&W strip reprints; 52 pages)
Cupples & Leon Co.
nn-By Sol Hess; Carlson-a 13.00 40.00 90.00

NEBBS, THE (Also see Crackajack Funnies)
1941; 1945
Dell Publishing Co./Croydon Publishing Co.
Large Feature Comic 23(1941) 13.50 41.00 95.00
1(1945, 36 pgs.)-Reprints 9.15 27.50 55.00

NECROMANCER: THE GRAPHIC NOVEL

Nemesis the Warlock #1, © Fleetway

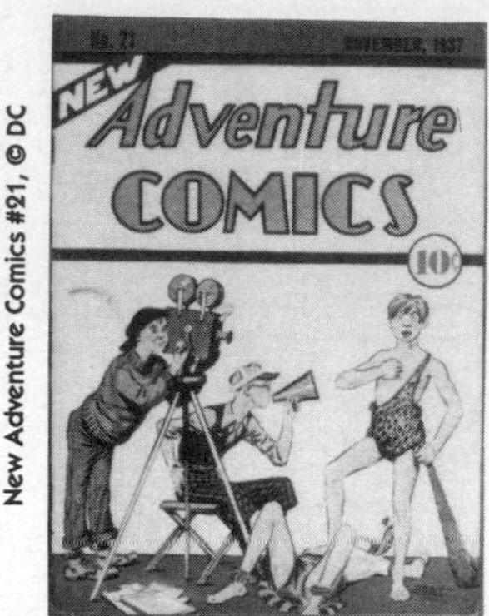

No. 21
NOVEMBER, 1937
NEW Adventure COMICS
10¢

New Adventure Comics #21, © DC

New Adventures of Superboy #10, © DC

GD25 FN65 NM94

1989 ($8.95, color)
Epic Comics (Marvel)

	GD25	FN65	NM94
nn	1.50	3.75	9.00

NECROPOLIS (Fleetway/Quality)(Value: cover or less)

NECROSCOPE (Malibu)(Value: cover or less)

NEGRO (See All-Negro)

NEGRO HEROES (Calling All Girls, Real Heroes, & True Comics reprints)
Spring, 1947 - No. 2, Summer, 1948
Parents' Magazine Institute

	GD25	FN65	NM94
1	43.00	130.00	300.00
2-Jackie Robinson-c/story	50.00	150.00	350.00

NEGRO ROMANCE (Negro Romances #4)
June, 1950 - No. 3, Oct, 1950 (All photo-c)
Fawcett Publications

	GD25	FN65	NM94
1-Evans-a	79.00	235.00	550.00
2,3	64.00	195.00	450.00

NEGRO ROMANCES (Formerly Negro Romance; Romantic Secrets #5 on)
No. 4, May, 1955
Charlton Comics

	GD25	FN65	NM94
4-Reprints Fawcett #2	50.00	150.00	350.00

NEIL THE HORSE (Aardvark-Vanaheim/Renegade)(Value: cover or less)

NELLIE THE NURSE (Also see Gay Comics & Joker Comics)
1945 - No. 36, Oct, 1952; 1957
Marvel/Atlas Comics (SPI/LMC)

	GD25	FN65	NM94
1-(1945)	22.00	65.00	150.00
2-(Spring/46)	11.00	32.00	75.00
3,4: 3-New logo (9/46)	8.35	25.00	50.00
5-Kurtzman's "Hey Look"(3); Georgie app.	10.00	30.00	65.00
6-8,10: 7,8-Georgie app. 10-Millie app.	6.70	20.00	40.00
9-Wolverton-a (1 pg.); Mille the Model app.	8.35	25.00	50.00
11,14-16,18-Kurtzman's "Hey Look"	9.15	27.50	55.00
12-"Giggles 'n' Grins" by Kurtzman	7.50	22.50	45.00
13,17,19,20: 17-Annie Oakley app.	5.85	17.50	35.00
21-27,29,30	4.70	14.00	28.00
28-Kurtzman's Rusty reprint	5.35	16.00	32.00
31-36: 36-Post-c	4.00	11.00	22.00
1('57)-Leading Mag. (Atlas)-Everett-a, 20 pgs	5.85	17.50	35.00

NELLIE THE NURSE (See 4-Color No. 1304)

NEMESIS THE WARLOCK (Eagle)(Value: cover or less)

NEMESIS THE WARLOCK (Fleetway/Quality)(Value: cover or less)

NEUTRO
January, 1967
Dell Publishing Co.

	GD25	FN65	NM94
1-Jack Sparling-c/a (super hero)	2.30	6.75	16.00

NEVADA (See Zane Grey's Stories of the West #1)

NEVER AGAIN (War stories; becomes Soldier & Marine V2#9)
Aug, 1955 - No. 2, Oct?, 1955; No. 8, July, 1956 (No #3-7)
Charlton Comics

	GD25	FN65	NM94
1	5.85	17.50	35.00
2-(Becomes Fightin' Air Force #3), 8-(Formerly Foxhole?)	4.00	10.00	20.00

NEW ADVENTURE COMICS (Formerly New Comics; becomes Adventure Comics #32 on)
V1#12, Jan, 1937 - No. 31, Oct, 1938
National Periodical Publications

	GD25	FN65	VF82	NM94
V1#12-Federal Men by Siegel & Shuster continues; Jor-L mentioned; Whitney Ellsworth-c begin, end #14	250.00	750.00	1500.00	-
V2#1(2/37, #13), V2#2 (#14)	183.00	550.00	1100.00	-

	GD25	FN65	NM94
15(V2#3)-20(V2#8): 15-1st Adventure logo; Craig Flessel-c begin, end #31. 16-1st Shuster-c; 1st non-funny cover. 17-Nadir, Master of Magic begins, ends #30	183.00	550.00	1100.00
21(V2#9),22(V2#10, 2/37): 22-X-Mas-c	150.00	450.00	900.00
23-31	125.00	375.00	750.00

NEW ADVENTURE OF WALT DISNEY'S SNOW WHITE AND THE SEVEN DWARFS, A (See Snow White Bendix Giveaway)

NEW ADVENTURES OF CHARLIE CHAN, THE (TV)
May-June, 1958 - No. 6, Mar-Apr, 1959
National Periodical Publications

	GD25	FN65	NM94
1 (Scarce)-Gil Kane/Sid Greene-a in all	45.00	135.00	360.00
2 (Scarce)	29.00	88.00	235.00
3-6 (Scarce)-Greene/Giella-a	23.00	69.00	185.00

NEW ADVENTURES OF CHOLLY AND FLYTRAP: TILL DEATH DO US PART, THE (Epic)(Value: cover or less)

NEW ADVENTURES OF HUCK FINN, THE (TV)
December, 1968 (Hanna-Barbera)
Gold Key

	GD25	FN65	NM94
1-"The Curse of Thut;" part photo-c	3.20	8.00	16.00

NEW ADVENTURES OF PETER PAN (Disney)
1953 (36 pgs.; 5x7-1/4") (Admiral giveaway)
Western Publishing Co.

	GD25	FN65	NM94
nn	7.50	22.50	45.00

NEW ADVENTURES OF PINOCCHIO (TV)
Oct-Dec, 1962 - No. 3, Sept-Nov, 1963
Dell Publishing Co.

	GD25	FN65	NM94
12-562-212(#1)	9.15	27.50	55.00
2,3	7.50	22.50	45.00

NEW ADVENTURES OF ROBIN HOOD (See Robin Hood)

NEW ADVENTURES OF SHERLOCK HOLMES (See 4-Color #1169, 1245)

NEW ADVENTURES OF SUPERBOY, THE (Also see Superboy)
Jan, 1980 - No. 54, June, 1984
DC Comics

	GD25	FN65	NM94
1-54: 7-Has extra story "The Computers That Saved Metropolis" by Starlin (Radio Shack giveaway w/indicia). 11-Superboy gets new power. 14-Lex Luthor app. 15-Superboy gets new parents. 28-Dial "H" For Hero begins, ends #49. 45-47-1st app. Sunburst. 48-Begin 75 cent-c. 50-Legion app.			1.00

NOTE: ***Buckler*** *a-9p; c-36p.* ***Giffen*** *a-50; c-50. 40i.* ***Gil Kane*** *c-32p, 33p, 35, 39, 41-49.* ***Miller*** *c-51.* ***Starlin*** *a-7. Krypto back-ups in 17, 22. Superbaby in 11, 14, 19, 24.*

NEW ADVENTURES OF THE PHANTOM BLOT, THE (See The Phantom Blot)

NEW AMERICA (Eclipse)(Value: cover or less)

NEW ARCHIES, THE (TV)
Oct, 1987 - No. 22, May, 1990 (75 cents)
Archie Comic Publications

	GD25	FN65	NM94
1-16: 3-Xmas issue			1.00
17-22 (.95-$1.00): 21-Xmas issue			1.00

NEW ARCHIES DIGEST (TV)(...Comics Digest Magazine #4?-10; ... Digest Magazine #11 on)
1988 - No. 14, July, 1991 ($1.35-$1.50, digest size, quarterly)
Archie Comics

	GD25	FN65	NM94
1-14: 6-Begin $1.50-c			1.50

NEW BOOK OF COMICS (Also see Big Book Of Fun)
1937; No. 2, Spring, 1938 (100 pgs. each) (Reprints)
National Periodical Publ.

	GD25	FN65	VF82	NM94
1(Rare)-1st regular size comic annual; 2nd DC annual; contains r/New Comics #1-4 & More Fun #9; r/Federal Men (8 pgs.), Henri Duval (1 pg.), & Dr. Occult in costume (1pg.) by Siegel & Shuster; Moldoff, Sheldon Mayer (15 pgs.)-a	1200.00	3600.00	6500.00	-

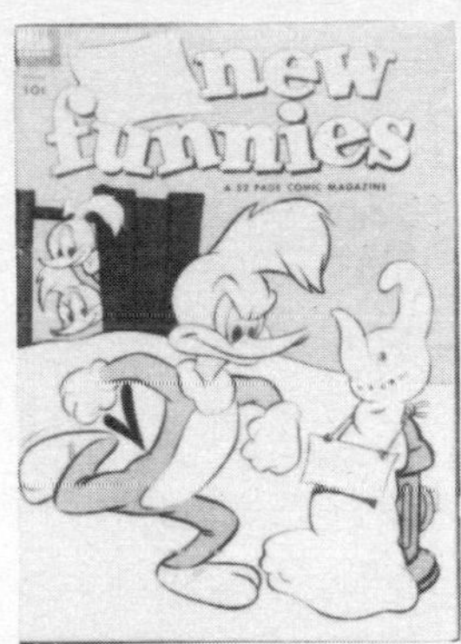
New Funnies #193, © DELL

New Gods (6/90) #17, © DC

The New Mutants #85, © MEG

	GD25	FN65	NM94

(Estimated up to 50 total copies exist, none in NM/Mint)

	GD25	FN65	VF82	NM94
2 Contains-r/More Fun #15 & 16; r/Dr. Occult in costume (a Superman proto-type), & Calling All Cars (4 pgs.) by Siegel & Shuster	540.00	1620.00	3500.00	-

NEW COMICS (New Adventure #12 on)
12/35 - No. 11, 12/36 (No. 1-6: paper cover) (No. 1-5: 84 pgs.)
National Periodical Publ.

	GD25	FN65	VF82	NM94
V1#1-Billy the Kid, Sagebrush 'n' Cactus, Jibby Jones, Needles, The Vikings, Sir Loin of Beef, Now-When I Was a Boy, & other 1-2 pg. strips; 2 pgs. Kelly art(1st)-(Gulliver's Travels); Sheldon Mayer-a(1st)(2 2pg. strips); Vincent Sullivan-c(1st)	1085.00	3250.00	7000.00	-
(Estimated up to 50 total copies exist, none in NM/Mint)				
2-1st app. Federal Men by Siegel & Shuster & begins (also see The Comics Magazine #2); Mayer, Kelly-a (Rare)(1/36)	467.00	1400.00	2800.00	-
3-6: 3,4-Sheldon Mayer-a which continues in The Comics Magazine #1. 3-Vincent Sullivan-c. 4-Dickens' "A Tale of Two Cities" adaptation begins. 5-Junior Federal Men Club; Kiefer-a. 6-"She" adaptation begins	283.00	850.00	1700.00	-
7-11: 11-Christmas-c	233.00	700.00	1400.00	-

NOTE: *#1-6 rarely occur in mint condition.* ***Whitney Ellsworth*** *c-4-11.*

NEW DEFENDERS (See Defenders)

NEW DNAGENTS, THE (Eclipse)(Value: cover or less)(Formerly DNAgents)

NEW FUN COMICS (More Fun #7 on; see Big Book of Fun Comics)
Feb, 1935 - No. 6, Oct, 1935 (10x15", No. 1-4,: slick covers)
(No. 1-5: 36 pgs; 40 pgs. No. 6)
National Periodical Publications

	GD25	FN65	VF82	NM94
V1#1 (1st DC comic); 1st app. Oswald The Rabbit; Jack Woods (cowboy) begins	3600.00	10,800.00	20,000.00	-
(Estimated up to 10 total copies exist, 1 in VF/NM)				
2(3/35)-(Very Rare)	1500.00	4500.00	8500.00	-
(Estimated up to 5 total copies exist)				
3-5(8/35): 3-Don Drake on the Planet Soro-c/story (sci/fi, 4/35). 5-Soft-c	750.00	2250.00	4500.00	-
6(10/35)-1st Dr. Occult by Siegel & Shuster (Leger & Reuths); last "New Fun" title. "New Comics" #1 begins in Dec. which is reason for title change to More Fun; Henri Duval (ends #9) by Siegel & Shuster begins; paper-c	1360.00	4100.00	7500.00	-
(Estimated up to 10 total copies exist of #3-6)				

NEW FUNNIES (The Funnies #1-64; Walter Lantz...#109 on; New TV... #259, 260, 272, 273; TV Funnies #261-271)
No. 65, July, 1942 - No. 288, Mar-Apr, 1962
Dell Publishing Co.

	GD25	FN65	NM94
65(#1)-Andy Panda in a world of real people, Raggedy Ann & Andy, Oswald the Rabbit (with Woody Woodpecker x-overs), Li'l Eight Ball & Peter Rabbit begin	54.00	160.00	375.00
66-70: 66-Felix the Cat begins. 67-Billy & Bonnie Bee by Frank Thomas begins. 69-Kelly-a (2 pgs.); The Brownies begin (not by Kelly)	27.00	80.00	190.00
71-75: 72-Kelly illos. 75-Brownies by Kelly?	16.00	50.00	115.00
76-Andy Panda (Carl Barks & Pabian-a); Woody Woodpecker x-over in Oswald ends	57.00	171.00	400.00
77,78: 78-Andy Panda in a world with real people ends	16.00	50.00	115.00
79-81	11.50	34.00	80.00
82-Brownies by Kelly begins; Homer Pigeon begins	13.00	40.00	90.00
83-85-Brownies by Kelly in ea. 83-X-mas-c. 85-Woody Woodpecker, 1pg. strip begins	13.00	40.00	90.00
86-90: 87-Woody Woodpecker stories begin	9.15	27.50	55.00
91-99	5.85	17.50	35.00
100 (6/45)	6.70	20.00	40.00
101-110	4.00	11.00	22.00
111-120: 119-X-mas-c	3.60	9.00	18.00
121-150: 131,143-X-mas-c	2.80	7.00	14.00
151-200: 155-X-mas-c. 168-X-mas-c. 182-Origin & 1st app. Knothead & Splintor. 191-X-mas-c	1.80	4.50	9.00
201-240	1.40	3.50	7.00
241-288: 270,271-Walter Lantz c-app. 281-1st story swipes/WDC&S #100	1.00	2.50	5.00

NOTE: *Early issues written by* ***John Stanley.***

NEW GODS, THE (New Gods #12 on)(See Adventure #459, 1st Issue Special #13 & Super-Team Family)
2-3/71 - V2#11, 10-11/72; V3#12, 7/77 - V3#19, 7-8/78
National Periodical Publications/DC Comics

	GD25	FN65	NM94
1-Intro/1st app. Orion; 3rd app. Darkseid (cameo; ties w/Forever People #1 as 3rd app.) (#1-3 are 15 cent issues)	4.50	14.00	32.00
2-Darkseid-c/story (2nd full app., 4-5/71)	2.30	6.75	16.00
3-1st app. Black Racer	2.00	6.00	14.00
4-9: (25 cent, 52 pg. giants): 4-Darkseid cameo; origin Manhunter-r. 5,7,8-Young Gods feature. 7-Darkseid app. (2-3/72); origin Orion. 9-1st app. Bug	1.65	4.70	11.00
10,11	1.50	3.75	9.00
12-19: Darkseid storyline w/minor apps. 12-New costume Orion (see 1st Issue Special #13 for 1st new costume). 19-Story continued in Adventure Comics #459,460		1.40	3.50

NOTE: *#4-9(25 cents, 52 pgs.) contain Manhunter-r by* ***Simon*** *&* ***Kirby*** *from Adventure #73, 74, 75, 76, 77, 78 with covers in that order.* ***Adkins*** *i-12-14, 17-19.* ***Kirby*** *c/a-1-11p.* ***Newton*** *a(p)-12-14, 16-19.* ***Starlin*** *c-17.* ***Staton*** *c-19p.*

NEW GODS, THE (DC, 1984 & 1989 series)(Value: cover or less)

NEW GUARDIANS, THE (DC)(Value: cover or less)

NEW HEROIC (See Heroic)

NEW JUSTICE MACHINE, THE (Innovation)(Value: cover or less)

NEW KIDS ON THE BLOCK, THE (Harvey)(Value: cover or less)

NEWLYWEDS
1907; 1917 (cardboard covers)
Saalfield Publ. Co.

	GD25	FN65	NM94
...& Their Baby' by McManus; Saalfield, (1907, 13x10", 52 pgs.); daily strips in full color	46.00	140.00	325.00
...& Their Baby's Comic Pictures, The, by McManus, Saalfield, (1917, 14x10", 22 pgs, oblong, cardboard-c); reprints 'Newlyweds' (Baby Snookums stips) mainly from 1916; blue cover; says for painting & crayoning, but some pages in color. (Scarce)	39.00	120.00	275.00

NEW MEN OF BATTLE, THE
1949 (nn) (Carboard covers)
Catechetical Guild

	GD25	FN65	NM94
nn(V8#1-3,5,6)-192 pgs.; contains 5 issues of Topix rebound	4.20	12.50	25.00
nn(V8#7-V8#11)-160 pgs.; contains 5 iss. of Topix	4.20	12.50	25.00

NEW MUTANTS, THE (See Marvel Graphic Novel #4 for 1st app.)
March, 1983 - No. 100, April, 1991
Marvel Comics Group

	GD25	FN65	NM94
1	1.10	2.70	6.50
2,3: 3,4-Ties into X-Men #167		1.50	3.75
4-10: 10-1st app. Magma		1.20	3.00
11-17,19,20: 13-Kitty Pryde app. 16-1st app. Warpath (w/out costume); see X-Men #193		1.00	2.50
18 Intro. new Warlock	1.25	3.00	7.50
21-Double size; origin new Warlock; newsstand version has cover price written in by Sienkiewicz	1.00	2.50	5.50
22-30: 23-25-Cloak & Dagger app.		1.00	2.50
31-58: 35-Magneto introduced as new headmaster. 50-Double size. 58-Contains pull-out mutant registration form		.80	2.00
59-Fall of The Mutants begins, ends #61		1.40	3.50
60-($1.25, 52 pgs.)		1.00	2.50
61-Fall of The Mutants ends		.80	2.00

62,64-72,74-85: 68-Intro Spyder. 76-X-Factor & X-Terminator app. 85-

The New Mutants #97, © MEG

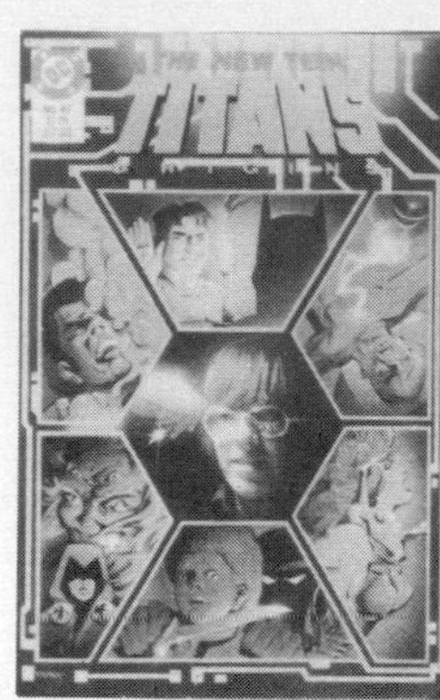

The New Teen Titans #47 (9/88), © DC

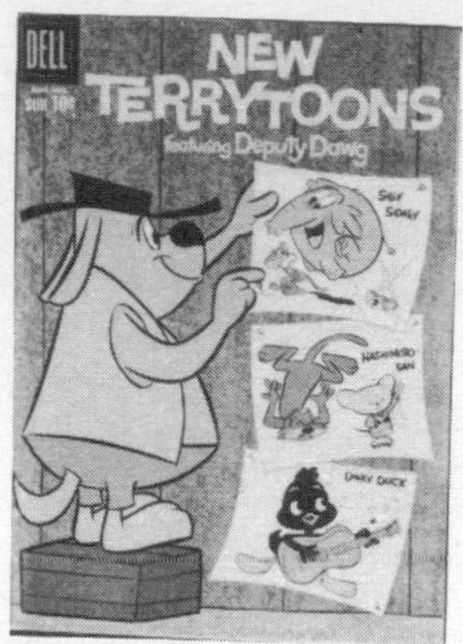

New Terrytoons #1 (1960), © Paul Terry

GD25 FN65 NM94

Liefeld-c begin 1.25
63-X-Men & Wolverine clones app.; begin $1.00-c 1.40 3.50
73-($1.50, 52 pgs.) .80 2.00
86-Rob Liefeld-a begins; McFarlane-c(i) swiped from Ditko splash pg.; Cable cameo (last page teaser) 1.70 5.00 12.00
87-1st full app. Cable (3/90) 5.00 15.00 36.00
87-2nd printing; gold metallic ink-c ($1.00) 1.50
88-2nd app. Cable 2.15 6.50 15.00
89-3rd app. Cable 1.70 5.00 12.00
90,91: 90-New costumes. 90,91-Sabretooth app. 1.65 4.70 11.00
92-No Liefeld-a; Liefeld-c 1.80 4.50
93,94-Cable vs. Wolverine 1.70 5.00 12.00
95-97-X-Tinction Agenda x-over. 95-Death of new Warlock. 97-Wolverine & Cable-c, but no app. 1.65 4.70 11.00
95-Gold 2nd printing 1.00 2.50
98-1st app. Deadpool, Gideon & Domino (2/91); 2nd Shatterstar (cameo) 1.65 4.70 11.00
99-1st app. of Feral (of X-Force) 1.20 3.00 7.00
100-($1.50, 52 pgs.)-1st app. X-Force (cameo) 1.10 2.70 6.50
100-Gold 2nd printing 1.20 3.00
100-Silver ink 3rd printing 1.50
Annual 1 (1984) 1.20 3.00
Annual 2 (1986, $1.25) .90 2.25
Annual 3 (1987, $1.25) .70 1.80
Annual 4 (1988, $1.75)-Evolutionary War x-over .80 2.00
Annual 5 (1989, $2.00, 68 pgs.)-Atlantis Attacks; 1st Liefeld-a on New Mutants 2.00 6.00 14.00
Annual 6 (1990, $2.00, 68 pgs.)-1st new costumes by Liefeld (3 pgs.); 1st app. (cameo) Shatterstar (of X-Force) .40 1.00 2.00
Annual 7 (1991, $2.00, 68 pgs.)-Liefeld pin-up only; X-Terminators back-up story; 2nd app. X-Force (continued in New Warriors Annual #1) .40 1.00 2.00
Special 1-Special Edition ('85, 68 pgs.)-ties in with X-Men Alpha Flight mini-series; cont'd in X-Men Annual #9; Art Adams/Austin-a 1.00 2.00 5.00
Summer Special 1(Sum/90, $2.95, 84 pgs.) 1.20 3.00

NOTE: ***Art Adams** c-38, 39. **Austin** c-57i. **Byrne** c/a-75p. **Liefeld** a-86-91p, 93-96p, 98-100, Annual 5p, 6(3 pgs.); c-85-91p, 92, 93p, 94, 95, 96p, 97-100, Annual 5, 6p. **McFarlane** c-85-89i, 93i. **Russell** a-48i. **Sienkiewicz** a-18-31, 35-38i; c-18-31, 35, 37. **Simonson** c-11p. **B. Smith** c-36, 40-48. **Williamson** a(i)-69, 71-73, 78-80, 82, 83; c(i)-69, 72, 73, 78i.*

NEW PEOPLE, THE (TV)
Jan, 1970 - No. 2, May, 1970
Dell Publishing Co.

1,2 1.70 5.00 12.00

NEW ROMANCES
No. 5, May, 1951 - No. 21, Apr?, 1954
Standard Comics

5-Photo-c 7.50 22.50 45.00
6-9: 6-Barbara Bel Geddes, Richard Basehart "Fourteen Hours." 7-Ray Milland photo-c. 9-Photo-c from '50s movie 4.00 11.00 22.00
10,14,16,17-Toth-a 8.00 24.00 48.00
11-Toth-a; Liz Taylor, Montgomery Cliff photo-c 10.00 30.00 60.00
12,13,15,18-21 3.20 8.00 16.00

NOTE: ***Celardo** a-9. **Moreira** a-6. **Tuska** a-7, 20. Photo c-5-16.*

NEW STATESMEN, THE (Fleetway/Quality)(Value: cover or less)

NEWSTRALIA (Innovation)(Value: cover or less)

NEW TALENT SHOWCASE (DC)(Value: cover or less)

NEW TEEN TITANS, THE (See DC Comics Presents 26, Marvel and DC Present & Teen Titans; Tales of the Teen Titans #41 on)
November, 1980 - No. 40, March, 1984
DC Comics

1-Robin, Kid Flash, Wonder Girl, The Changeling (1st app.), Starfire, The Raven, Cyborg begin; partial origin 1.65 4.00 10.00
2-1st app. Deathstroke the Terminator 2.00 6.00 14.00

GD25 FN65 NM94

3-9: 3-Origin Starfire; Intro The Fearsome Five. 4-Origin continues; J.L.A. app. 6-Origin Raven. 7-Cyborg origin. 8-Origin Kid Flash retold. 9-Minor cameo Deathstroke on last pg. 1.70 4.25
10-2nd app. Deathstroke the Terminator (see Marvel & DC Present for 3rd app.); origin Changeling retold 1.50 3.75 9.00
11-20: 13-Return of Madame Rouge & Capt. Zahl; Robotman revived. 14-Return of Mento; origin Doom Patrol. 15-Death of Madame Rouge & Capt. Zahl; intro. new Brotherhood of Evil. 16-1st app. Capt. Carrot (free 16 pg. preview). 18-Return of Starfire. 19-Hawkman teams-up 1.50
21-30: 21-Intro Night Force in free 16 pg. insert; intro Brother Blood. 23-1st app. Vigilante (not in costume), & Blackfire. 24-Omega Men app. 25-Omega Men cameo; free 16 pg. preview Masters of the Universe. 26-1st Terra. 27-Free 16 pg. preview Atari Force. 29-The New Brotherhood of Evil & Speedy app. 30-Terra joins the Titans 1.20
31-33,35-38,40: 38-Origin Wonder Girl 1.00
34-4th app. Deathstroke the Terminator 1.60 4.00
39-Last Dick Grayson as Robin; Kid Flash quits .80 2.00
Annual 1(11/82)-Omega Men app. 1.40
Annual V2#2(9/83)-1st app. Vigilante in costume .70 1.75
Annual 3 (See Tales of the Teen Titans Annual #3)
nn(11/83-Keebler Co. Giveaway)-In cooperation with "The President's Drug Awareness Campaign" .60 1.20
nn-(re-issue of above on Mando paper for direct sales market); American Soft Drink Ind. version; I.B.M. Corp. version .50 1.00

NOTE: ***Perez** a-1-4p, 6-34p, 37-40p, Annual 1p, 2p; c-1-12, 13-17p, 18-21, 22p, 23p, 24-37, 38, 39(painted), 40, Annual 1, 2.*

NEW TEEN TITANS, THE (Becomes The New Titans #50 on)
Aug, 1984 - No. 49, Nov, 1988 ($1.25-$1.75; deluxe format)
DC Comics

1-New storyline; Perez-c/a begins 1.60 4.00
2,3: 2-Re-intro Lilith 1.00 2.50
4-10: 5-Death of Trigon. 7-9-Origin Lilith. 8-Intro Kole. 10-Kole joins .70 1.80
11-19: 13,14-Crisis x-over 1.20
20-Robin (Jason Todd) joins; original Teen Titans return .80 2.00
21-49: 37-Begin $1.75-c. 38-Infinity, Inc. x-over. 47-Origin all Titans 1.40
Annual 1 (9/85)-Intro. Vanguard .80 2.00
Annual 2 (8/86; $2.50): Byrne c/a(p); origin Brother Blood; intro new Dr. Light 1.00 2.50
Annual 3 (11/87)-Intro. Danny Chase .80 2.00
Annual 4 ('88, $2.50)-Perez-c .90 2.25

NOTE: ***Orlando** c-33p. **Perez** a-1-5; c-1-6, 19-23, 43. **Steacy** c-47.*

NEW TERRYTOONS (TV)
6-8/60 - No. 8, 3-5/62; 10/62 - No. 54, 1/79
Dell Publishing Co./Gold Key

1(1960-Dell)-Deputy Dawg, Dinky Duck & Hashimoto San begin (1st app. of each) 5.00 15.00 30.00
2-8(1962) 3.60 9.00 18.00
1(30010-210)(10/62-Gold Key, 84 pgs.)-Heckle & Jeckle begins 6.70 20.00 45.00
2(30010-301)-84 pgs. 5.85 17.50 40.00
3-10 2.40 6.00 12.00
11-20 1.20 3.00 6.00
21-30 .60 1.50 3.00
31-54 .40 1.00 2.00

NOTE: *Reprints: #4-12, 38, 40, 47. (See March of Comics #379, 393, 412, 435)*

NEW TESTAMENT STORIES VISUALIZED
1946 - 1947
Standard Publishing Co.

"New Testament Heroes–Acts of Apostles Visualized, Book I"
"New Testament Heroes–Acts of Apostles Visualized, Book II"
"Parables Jesus Told" Set.... 10.00 30.00 65.00

NOTE: *All three are contained in a cardboard case, illustrated on front and info about the set.*

The New Titans #101, © DC

The New Warriors #39, © MEG

Nickel Comics #1, © FAW

GD25 FN65 NM94

NEW TITANS, THE (Formerly The New Teen Titans)
No. 50, Dec, 1988 - Present ($1.75, color)
DC Comics

50-Perez-c/a begins; new origin Wonder Girl 1.60 4.00
51-59: 50-55-Painted-c. 55-Nightwing (Dick Grayson) forces Danny Chase to resign; Batman app. in flashback .90 2.25
60-A Lonely Place of Dying Part 2 continues from Batman #440; new Robin tie-in; Timothy Drake app. 1.00 2.50 5.50
61-A Lonely Place of Dying Part 4 1.50 3.75
62-65: Deathstroke the Terminator app. 65-Timothy Drake (Robin) app. 1.90 4.75
66-69,71: 71-(44 pgs.)-10th anniversary issue; Deathstroke cameo 1.10 2.75
70-1st Deathstroke solo cover/story 1.20 3.00
72-79: Deathstroke in all. 74-Intro. Pantha. 79-Terra brought back to life; 1 panel cameo Team Titans (1st app.) 1.20 3.00
80-99,101-110: Deathstroke in #80-84,86. 80-2nd full app. Team Titans. 83,84-Deathstroke kills his son, Jericho. 85-Team Titans app. 86-Deathstroke vs. Nightwing-c/story; last Deathstroke app. 87-New costume Nightwing. 90-92-Parts 2,5,8 Total Chaos (Team Titans) .70 1.75
100-($3.50, 52 pgs.)-Holo-grafx foil-c 1.40 3.50
Annual 5,6 (1989, 1990, $3.50, 68 pgs.) 1.40 3.50
Annual 7 (1991, $3.50, 68 pgs.)-Armaggedon 2001 x-over; 1st full app. Teen (Team) Titans (new group) 1.40 3.50
Annual 8,9 (1992, '93, $3.50, 68 pgs.): 8-Deathstroke app.; Eclipso app. (minor) 1.40 3.50

NOTE: ***Perez** a-50-55p, 57-60p, 61(layouts); c-50-61, 62-67i, Annual 5i; co-plots-66.*

NEW TV FUNNIES (See New Funnies)

NEW TWO-FISTED TALES (Dark Horse Comics)(Value: cover or less)

NEW WARRIORS, THE (See Thor #411,412)
July, 1990 - Present ($1.00/$1.25, color)
Marvel Comics

1-Williamson-i; Bagley-c/a(p) in 1-13, Annual 1 2.60 7.50 18.00
1-Gold 2nd printing (7/91) 1.10 2.75
2-Williamson-c/a(i) 1.65 4.70 11.00
3: 1,3-Guice-c(i) 1.20 3.00 7.00
4,5 1.00 2.50 6.00
6,7,10: 7-Punisher cameo (last pg.) 1.50 3.75
8,9-Punisher app. 1.00 2.50 5.50
11-14: 14-Darkhawk & Namor x-over .90 2.25
15-19: 17-Fantastic Four & Silver Surfer x-over. 19-Gideon (of X-Force) app.; last $1.00-c 1.25
20-24,26-46: 28-Intro Turbo & Cardinal 1.25
25-($2.50, 52 pgs.)-Die-cut cover 1.00 2.50
40-($2.25)-Gold foil collector's edition .90 2.25
Annual 1 (1991, $2.00, 68 pgs.)-Origins all members; 3rd app. X-Force (cont'd from New Mutants Annual #7 & cont'd in X-Men Annual #15); x-over before X-Force #1 1.80 4.50
Annual 2 (1992, $2.25, 68 pgs.) .90 2.25
Annual 3 (1993, $2.95, 68 pgs.)-Bagged w/card 1.20 3.00

NEW WAVE, THE (Eclipse)(Value: cover or less)

NEW WORLD (See Comic Books, series I)

NEW YORK GIANTS (See Thrilling True Story of the Baseball Giants)

NEW YORK STATE JOINT LEGISLATIVE COMMITTEE TO STUDY THE PUBLICATION OF COMICS, THE
1951, 1955
N.Y. State Legislative Document

This document was referenced by Wertham for **Seduction of the Innocent.** Contains numerous repros from comics showing violence, sadism, torture, and sex.
1955 version (196p, No. 37, 2/23/55)-Sold for $180 in 1986.

NEW YORK WORLD'S FAIR (Also see Big Book of Fun & New Book of Fun)
1939, 1940 (100pgs.; cardboard covers) (DC's 4th & 5th annuals)
National Periodical Publ.

GD25 FN65 VF82 NM94

1939-Scoop Scanlon, Superman (blonde haired Superman on-c), Sandman, Zatara, Slam Bradley, Ginger Snap by Bob Kane begin; 1st published app. The Sandman (see Adventure #40 for his 1st drawn story); Vincent Sullivan-c 1375.00 4125.00 7565.00 11,000.00
(Estimated up to 110 total copies exist, 4 in NM/Mint)
1940-Batman, Hourman, Johnny Thunderbolt, Red, White & Blue & Hanko (by Craig Flessel) app.; Superman, Batman & Robin-c (1st time they all appear together); early Robin app.; 1st Burnley-c/a (per Burnley) 750.00 2250.00 4125.00 6000.00

NOTE: *The 1939 edition was published 4/30/39, the day the fair opened, at 25 cents, and was first sold only at the fair. Since all other comics were 10 cents, it didn't sell. Remaining copies were advertised beginning in the August issues of most DC comics for 25 cents, but soon the price was dropped to 15 cents. Everyone that sent a quarter through the mail for it received a free Superman #1 or a #2 to make up the dime difference. 15 cent stickers were placed over the 25 cent price. Four variations on the 15 cent stickers are known. The 1940 edition was priced at 15 cents.*

NEW YORK: YEAR ZERO (Eclipse)(Value: cover or less)

NEXT MAN (Comico)(Value: cover or less)

NEXT MEN (See John Byrne's...)

NEXT NEXUS, THE (First)(Value: cover or less)

NEXUS (See First Comics Graphic Novel #4, 19 & The Next Nexus)
June, 1981 - No. 6, Mar, 1984; No. 7, Apr, 1985 - No. 80?, May, 1991
(Direct sale only, 36 pgs.; V2#1('83)-printed on Baxter paper
Capital Comics/First Comics No. 7 on

1-B&W version; mag. size; w/double size poster 1.70 5.00 12.00
1-B&W 1981 limited edition; 500 copies printed and signed; same as above except this version has a 2-pg. poster & a pencil sketch on paperboard by Rude 2.60 7.50 18.00
2-B&W, magazine size 1.20 3.00 7.00
3-B&W, magazine size; contains 33-1/3 rpm record ($2.95 price) 1.60 4.00
V2#1-Color version 1.20 3.00
2-80: 2-Nexus' origin begins. 50-($3.50, 52 pgs.). 73-Begin $2.25-c .80 2.00

NOTE: ***Bissette** c-29. **Rude** c-3(B&W), V2#1-22, 24-27, 33-36, 39-42, 45-48, 50, 58-60; a-1-3, V2#1-7, 8-16p, 18-22p, 24-27p, 33-36p, 39-42p, 45-48p, 50, 58, 59p, 60. **Paul Smith** a-37, 38, 43, 44, 51-55p; c-37, 38, 43, 44, 51-55*

NEXUS: ALIEN JUSTICE (Dark Horse)(Value: cover or less)

NEXUS FILES (First)(Value: cover or less)

NEXUS LEGENDS (First)(Value: cover or less)

NEXUS THE LIBERATOR (Dark Horse)(Value: cover or less)

NEXUS: THE ORIGIN (Dark Horse)(Value: cover or less)

NFL SUPERPRO (Marvel)(Value: cover or less)

NICKEL COMICS
1938 (Pocket size - 7-1/2x5-1/2")(132 pgs.)
Dell Publishing Co.

1-"Bobby & Chip" by Otto Messmer, Felix the Cat artist. Contains some English reprints 47.00 140.00 325.00

NICKEL COMICS
May, 1940 - No. 8, Aug, 1940 (36 pgs.; Bi-Weekly; 5 cents)
Fawcett Publications

1-Origin/1st app. Bulletman 150.00 450.00 1000.00
2 70.00 210.00 475.00
3 58.00 175.00 400.00
4-The Red Gaucho begins 54.00 162.00 350.00
5-8: 8-World's Fair-c; Bulletman moved to Master Comics #7 in Oct. 50.00 150.00 335.00

NOTE: ***Beck** c-5-8. **Jack Binder** c-1-4. Bondage c-5.*

NICK FURY, AGENT OF SHIELD (See Marvel Spotlight #31 & Shield)
6/68 - No. 15, 11/69; No. 16, 11/70 - No. 18, 3/71
Marvel Comics Group

Nick Fury, Agent of Shield V2#1, © MEG

Nightmare #13, © STJ

Nightmares on Elm Street #1, © New Line-Heron

GD25 FN65 NM94

1 6.00 18.00 42.00
2-4: 4-Origin retold 3.25 9.50 22.00
5-Classic-c 3.70 11.00 26.00
6,7: 7-Salvador Dali painting swipe 1.85 5.50 13.00
8-11,13: 9-Hate Monger begins (ends #11). 11-Smith-c. 13-1st app. Super-Patriot; last 12 cent issue 1.10 2.70 6.50
12-Smith-c/a 1.40 3.50 8.50
14-Begin 15 cent-c 1.60 4.00
15-1st app. & death of Bullseye-c/story(11/69) 3.70 11.00 26.00
16-18-(25 cents, 52 pgs.)-r/Str. Tales #135-143 .90 2.25

NOTE: ***Adkins** a-3i. **Craig** a-10i. **Sid Greene** a-12i. **Kirby** a-16-18r. **Springer** a-4, 6, 7, 8p, 9, 10p, 11; c-8, 9. **Steranko** a(p)-1-3, 5; c-1-7.*

NICK FURY AGENT OF SHIELD (Also see Strange Tales #135)
Dec, 1983 - No. 2, Jan, 1984 ($2.00, Baxter paper, 52 pgs.)
Marvel Comics Group

1,2-r/Nick Fury #1-4; new Steranko-c .80 2.00

NICK FURY, AGENT OF S.H.I.E.L.D.
Sept, 1989 - No. 47, May, 1993 ($1.50/$1.75, color)
Marvel Comics

V2#1-26: 10-Capt. America app. 13-Return of The Yellow Claw. 15-Fantastic Four app. 1.50
27-29-Wolverine-c/stories .80 2.00
30-47: 30,31-Deathlok app. 32-Begin $1.75-c. 36-Cage app. 37-Woodgod c/story. 38-41-Flashes back to pre-Shield days after WWII .70 1.75

NOTE: ***Alan Grant** scripts-11. **Guice** a(p)-20-23, 25, 26; c-20-28.*

NICK FURY VS. S.H.I.E.L.D.
June, 1988 - No. 6, Nov, 1988 ($3.50, 52pgs, color, deluxe format)
Marvel Comics

1-Steranko-c 1.10 2.70 6.50
2-(Low print run) Sienkiewicz-c 1.25 3.00 7.50
3-6 1.30 3.25

NICK HALIDAY (Thrill of the Sea)
May, 1956
Argo

1-Daily & Sunday strip-r by Petree 5.85 17.50 35.00

NIGHT AND THE ENEMY (Graphic Novel)
1988 (8-1/2x11") ($11.95, color, 80pgs.)
Comico

1-Harlan Ellison scripts/Ken Steacy-c/a; r/Epic Illustrated & new-a (1st and 2nd printings) 1.70 5.00 12.00
1-Limited edition ($39.95) 5.50 17.00 40.00

NIGHT BEFORE CHRISTMAS, THE (See March of Comics No. 152)

NIGHTBREED (See Clive Barker's Nightbreed)

NIGHTCAT (Marvel)(Value: cover or less)

NIGHTCRAWLER
Nov, 1985 - No. 4, Feb, 1986 (Mini-series from X-Men)
Marvel Comics Group

1-Cockrum-c/a 1.00 2.50
2-4 .70 1.75

NIGHT FORCE, THE (See New Teen Titans #21)
Aug, 1982, No. 14, Sept, 1983 (60 cents)
DC Comics

1-14: 13-Origin The Baron. 14-Nudity panels 1.00

NOTE: ***Colan** c/a-1-14p. **Giordano** c-1i, 2i, 4i, 5i, 7i, 12i.*

NIGHT GLIDER
April, 1993 ($2.95, color, one-shot)
Topps Comics

1-Polybagged w/Kirbychrome trading card 1.20 3.00

NIGHTINGALE, THE
1948 (14 pgs., 7-1/4x10-1/4", B&W) (10 cents)
Henry H. Stansbury Once-Upon-A-Time Press, Inc.

(Very Rare)-Low distribution; distributed to Westchester County & Bronx, N.Y. only; used i[illegible] **Seduction of the Innocent**, pg. 312,313 as the 1st and only "good" comic book ever published Ill. by Dong Kingman; 1,500 words of text, printed on high quality paper & no word balloons Copyright registered 10/22/48, distributed week of 12/5/48. (By Hans Christian Andersen Estimated value. $200

NIGHT MAN, THE (See Sludge #1)
Oct, 1993 - Present ($1.95, color)
Malibu Comics (Ultraverse)

1-($2.50, 40 pgs.)-Rune flip-c/story by B. Smith (3 pgs.) 1.00 2.50
2-4 .80 2.00

NIGHTMARE
Summer, 1952 - No. 2, Fall, 1952; No. 3,4, 1953 (Painted-c)
Ziff-Davis (Approved Comics)/St. John No. 3,4

1-1pg. Kinstler-a; Tuska-a(2) 26.00 77.00 180.00
2-Kinstler-a-Poe's "Pit & the Pendulum" 19.00 58.00 135.00
3-Kinstler-a 16.00 48.00 110.00
4-Exist? 12.00 36.00 85.00

NIGHTMARE (Weird Horrors #1-9) (Amazing Ghost Stories #14 on)
No. 10, Dec, 1953 - No. 13, Aug, 1954
St. John Publishing Co.

10-Reprints Ziff-Davis Weird Thrillers #2 w/new Kubert-c plus 2 pgs. Kinstler-a; Anderson, Colan & Toth-a 27.00 81.00 190.00
11-Krigstein-a; Poe adapt., "Hop Frog" 19.00 57.00 130.00
12-Kubert bondage-c; adaptation of Poe's "The Black Cat;" Cannibalism story 16.00 48.00 110.00
13-Reprints Z-D Weird Thrillers #3 with new cover; Powell-a(2), Tuska-a; Baker-c 10.00 30.00 70.00

NIGHTMARE (Magazine)
Dec, 1970 - No. 23, Feb, 1975 (B&W, 68 pages)
Skywald Publishing Corp.

1-Everett-a 2.60 7.50 18.00
2-5: 4-Decapitation story 1.30 3.25 8.00
6-Kaluta-a; Jeff Jones photo & interview 1.65 4.00 10.00
7,9,10: 9-Wrightson-a 1.20 3.00 7.00
8-Features E. C. movie "Tales From the Crypt;" reprints some E.C. comics panels 1.65 4.00 10.00
11-23: 12-Excessive gore, severed heads. 20-Byrne's 1st artwork (8/74); severed head-c. 21-(1974 Summer Special)-Kaluta-a. 22-Tomb of Horror issue. 23-(1975 Winter Special) 1.00 2.00 5.00
Annual 1(1972)-B. Jones-a 1.20 3.00 7.00
Winter Special 1(1973) 1.20 3.00 7.00
Yearbook nn(1974) 1.00 2.50 6.00

NOTE: ***Adkins** a-5. **Boris** c-2, 3, 5 (#4 is not by Boris). **Byrne** a-20p. **Everett** a-4, 5. **Jeff Jones** a-6, 21r(Psycho #6); c-6. **Katz** a-5. **Reese** a-4, 5. **Wildey** a-5, 6, 21, '74 Yearbook.*

NIGHTMARE (Alex Nino's...)(Innovation)(Value: cover or less)

NIGHTMARE & CASPER (See Harvey Hits #71) (Casper & Nightmare #6 on)
(See Casper The Friendly Ghost #19)
Aug, 1963 - No. 5, Aug, 1964 (25 cents)
Harvey Publications

1-All reprints? 6.00 18.00 36.00
2-5: All reprints? 3.60 9.00 18.00

NIGHTMARE ON ELM STREET, A (See Freddy Krueger's...)

NIGHTMARE ON ELM STREET: THE BEGINNING, A (Innovation)(Value: cover or less)

NIGHTMARES (See Do You Believe in Nightmares)

NIGHTMARES (Eclipse)(Value: cover or less)

NIGHTMARES ON ELM STREET (Innovation)(Value: cover or less)

NIGHTMASK (Marvel)(Value: cover or less)

NIGHT MASTER (Silverwolf)(Value: cover or less)

Nightstalkers #11, © MEG

1963 #3, © Moore/Veitch/Bissette

Nomad V2#17, © MEG

GD25 FN65 NM94 | GD25 FN65 NM94

NIGHT MUSIC (Eclipse)(Value: cover or less)

NIGHT NURSE
Nov, 1972 - No. 4, May, 1973
Marvel Comics Group
1-4 1.20 3.00

NIGHT OF MYSTERY
1953 (no month) (One Shot)
Avon Periodicals
nn-1pg. Kinstler-a, Hollingsworth-c 20.00 60.00 140.00

NIGHT OF THE GRIZZLY, THE (See Movie Classics)

NIGHTRAVEN: THE COLLECTED STORIES
1990 ($9.95, color, graphic novel)
Marvel Comics UK, Ltd.
nn-Bolton-r/British Hulk mag.; David Lloyd-c/a 1.65 4.00 10.00

NIGHT RIDER
Oct, 1974 - No. 6, Aug, 1975 (Western)
Marvel Comics Group
1: 1-6 reprint Ghost Rider #1-6 (#1-origin) .80 2.00
2-6 1.25

NIGHTSTALKERS (See Midnight Sons Unlimited)
Nov, 1992 - Present ($1.75, color)
Marvel Comics
1-($2.75, 52 pgs.)-Polybagged w/poster; part 5 of Rise of the Midnight Sons storyline; Garney/Palmer-c/a begins 1.10 2.75
2-9,11-18: 5-Punisher app. 7-Ghost Rider app. 8,9-Morbius app. 14-Siege of Darkness part 1 .70 1.75
10-($2.25)-Outer-c is a Darkhold envelope made of black parchment w/gold ink; Midnight Massacre part 1 .90 2.25

NIGHT THRASHER (See The New Warriors)
Aug, 1993 - Present ($1.75, color)
Marvel Comics
1-($2.95, 52 pgs.)-Red holo-grafx foil-c; origin 1.20 3.00
2-8: 2-Intro Tantrum. 3-Gideon (of X-Force) app. .70 1.75

NIGHT THRASHER: FOUR CONTROL
Oct, 1992 - No. 4, Jan, 1993 ($2.00, color, mini-series)
Marvel Comics
1-Hero from New Warriors 1.00 2.50
2-4: 2-Intro Tantrum. 3-Gideon (of X-Force) app. .80 2.00

NIGHTVEIL (Americomics)(Value: cover or less)

NIGHTWALKER (Fleetway)(Value: cover or less)

NIGHTWINGS (See DC Science Fiction Graphic Novel)

NIKKI, WILD DOG OF THE NORTH (See 4-Color 1226 & Movie Comics)

NINE LIVES OF FELIX THE CAT, THE (Harvey)(Value: cover or less)

1963
Apr, 1993 - No. 6, 1993 ($1.95, color, mini-series)
Image Comics
1-6-Alan Moore scripts; Veitch-a(p) .80 2.00

1984 (Magazine) (1994 #11 on)
June, 1978 - No. 10, Jan, 1980 ($1.50)
Warren Publishing Co.
1-Nino-a in all 1.20 3.00
2-10 .70 1.80
NOTE: ***Alacla*** *a-1-3, 5i.* ***Corben*** *a-1-8; c-1, 2.* ***Thorne*** *a-7-10.* ***Wood*** *a-1, 2, 5i.*

1994 (Formerly 1984) (Magazine)
No. 11, Feb, 1980 - No. 29, Feb, 1983
Warren Publishing Co.
11-29: 27-The Warhawks return .80 2.00
NOTE: ***Corben*** *c-26.* ***Nino*** *a-11-19, 20(2), 21, 25, 26, 28; c-21.* ***Redondo*** *c-20.* ***Thorne*** *a-11-14, 17-21, 25, 26, 28, 29.*

NINJA HIGH SCHOOL IN COLOR (Eternity)(Value: cover or less)

NINJA HIGH SCHOOL: THE PROM FORMULA (Eternity)(Value: cover or less)

NINJAK (See Bloodshot #6, 7)
Feb, 1994 - Present ($2.25, color)
Valiant
1-($3.50)-Chromium-c; Quesada-c/a(p) in all 1.40 3.50
2-4 .90 2.25

NINTENDO COMICS SYSTEM (Valiant)(Value: cover or less)

NIPPY'S POP
1917 (Sunday strip reprints-B&W) (10-1/2x13-1/2")
The Saalfield Publishing Co.
nn-32 pages 13.00 40.00 90.00

NOAH'S ARK (Spire Christian)(Value: cover or less)

NOMAD (See Captain America #180)
Nov, 1990 - No. 4, Feb, 1991 ($1.50, color)
Marvel Comics
1-4: 1,4-Captain America app. 1.50

NOMAD
V2#1, May, 1992 - Present ($1.75, color)
Marvel Comics
V2#1-($2.00)-Has gatefold-c w/map/wanted poster 1.40 3.50
2-5: 5-Punisher vs. Nomad-c/story. .80 2.00
6-24: 6-Punisher & Daredevil-c/story cont'd in Punisher War Journal #48. 7-Gambit-c/story. 10-Red Wolf app. .70 1.75

NOMAN (See Thunder Agents)
Nov, 1966 - No. 2, March, 1967 (25 cents, 68 pgs.)
Tower Comics
1-Wood/Williamson-c; Lightning begins; Dynamo cameo; Kane-a(p) & Whitney-a 5.00 15.00 36.00
2-Wood-c only; Dynamo x-over; Whitney-a 3.60 10.75 25.00

NONE BUT THE BRAVE (See Movie Classics)

NOODNIK COMICS (See Pinky the Egghead)
1953; No. 2, Feb, 1954 - No. 5, Aug, 1954
Comic Media/Mystery/Biltmore
3-D(1953-Comic Media)(#1) 27.00 80.00 185.00
2-5 4.70 14.00 28.00

NORMALMAN (Renegade)(Value: cover or less)

NORTH AVENUE IRREGULARS (See Walt Disney Showcase #49)

NORTH TO ALASKA (See 4-Color No. 1155)

NORTHWEST MOUNTIES (Also see Approved Comics #12)
Oct, 1948 - No. 4, July, 1949
Jubilee Publications/St. John
1-Rose of the Yukon by Matt Baker; Walter Johnson-a; Lubbers-c 22.00 65.00 150.00
2-Baker-a; Lubbers-c. Ventrilo app. 15.00 45.00 105.00
3-Bondage-c, Baker-a; Sky Chief, K-9 app. 16.00 48.00 110.00
4-Baker-c, 2 pgs.; Blue Monk & The Desperado app. 16.00 48.00 110.00

NOSFERATU (Dark Horse)(Value: cover or less)

NOSFERATU, PLAGUE OF TERROR (Millennium)(Value: cover or less)

NO SLEEP 'TIL DAWN (See 4-Color #831)

NOT BRAND ECHH (Brand Echh #1-4; See Crazy, 1973)
Aug, 1967 - No. 13, May, 1969 (No. 9-13: 25 cents, 68 pages)
Marvel Comics Group (LMC)
1: 1-8 are 12 cent issues 3.70 11.00 26.00
2-4: 3-Origin Thor, Hulk & Capt. America; Monkees, Alfred E. Neuman

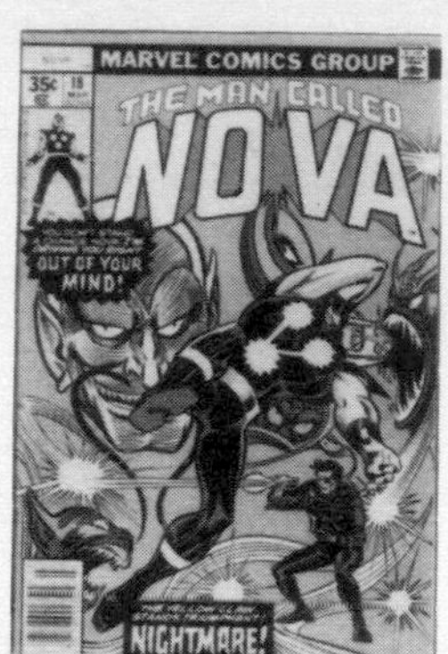

Nova #18, © MEG

Nutty Comics #8, © HARV

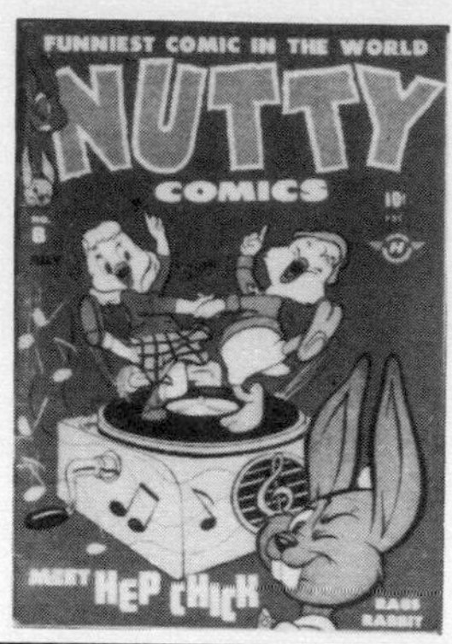

Nyoka, the Jungle Girl #66, © FAW

GD25 FN65 NM94

cameo. 4-X-Men app. 1.85 5.50 13.00
5-8: 5-Origin/intro. Forbush Man. 7-Origin Fantastical-4 & Stuporman. 8-Beatles cameo; X-Men satire 1.85 5.50 13.00
9-13-All Giants. 9-Beatles cameo. 10-All-r; The Old Witch, Crypt Keeper & Vault Keeper cameos. 12,13-Beatles cameo 2.00 6.00 14.00

NOTE: *Colan a-4p, 5p, 8p. Everett a-1i. Kirby a(p)-1, 3, 5-7, 10; c-1. Severin a-1; c-3, 7, 8. Sutton a-4, 5i, 7i, 8; c-5. Archie satire in #9. Avengers satire in #8, 12.*

NOTHING CAN STOP THE JUGGERNAUT (Marvel)(Value: cover or less)

NO TIME FOR SERGEANTS (TV)
No. 914, July, 1958; Feb-Apr, 1965 - No. 3, Aug-Oct, 1965
Dell Publishing Co.

4-Color 914 (Movie)-Toth-a; Andy Griffith photo-c 10.00 30.00 60.00
1(2-4/65)-3 (TV): Photo-c 4.35 13.00 26.00

NOVA (The Man Called... No. 22-25)
Sept, 1976 - No. 25, May, 1979
Marvel Comics Group

1-Origin/1st app. Nova 1.00 2.50 6.00
2-11: 4-Thor x-over 1.20 3.00
12-Spider-Man x-over 1.90 4.75
13-25: 13-Intro Crime-Buster. 14-Last 30 cent issue. 18-Yellow Claw app. .65 1.60

NOTE: *Austin c-21i, 23i. John Buscema a(p)-1-3, 8, 21; c-1p, 2, 15. Infantino a(p)-15-20, 22-25; c-17-20, 21p, 23p, 24p. Kirby c-4p, 5, 7. Nebres c-25i. Simonson a-23i.*

NOVA
Jan, 1994 - No. 4, Apr, 1994 ($1.75, color, mini-series)
Marvel Comics

1-($2.95, 52 pgs.)-Collector's Edition w/gold foil-c; new costume for Nova 1.20 3.00
1-($2.25, 52 pgs.)-Newsstand Edition w/o foil-c .90 2.25
2-4 .70 1.75

NOW AGE ILLUSTRATED (See Pendulum Illustrated Classics)

NTH MAN THE ULTIMATE NINJA (See Marvel Comics Presents 25)
Aug, 1989 - No. 16, Sept, 1990 ($1.00, color)
Marvel Comics

1-7,9-16-Ninja mercenary 1.00
8-Dale Keown's 1st Marvel work (1/90, pencils) 1.80 4.50

NUCLEUS (Also see Cerebus)
May, 1979 ($1.50, B&W, adult fanzine)
Heiro-Graphic Publications

1-Contains "Demonhorn" by Dave Sim; early app. of Cerebus The Aardvark (4 pg. story) 3.60 10.75 25.00

NUKLA
Oct-Dec, 1965 - No. 4, Sept, 1966
Dell Publishing Co.

1-Origin & 1st app. Nukla (super hero) 3.20 8.00 20.00
2,3 1.65 4.70 11.00
4-Ditko-a, c(p) 3.20 9.00 21.00

NURSE BETSY CRANE (Formerly Teen Secret Diary)
V2#12, Aug, 1961 - V2#27, Mar, 1964 (See Soap Opera Romances)
Charlton Comics

V2#12-27 .80 2.00 4.00

NURSE HELEN GRANT (See The Romances of...)

NURSE LINDA LARK (See Linda Lark)

NURSERY RHYMES
No. 10, July-Aug, 1951 - No. 2, Winter, 1951 (Painted-c)
Ziff-Davis Publ. Co. (Approved Comics)

10 (#1), 2: 10-Howie Post-a 10.00 30.00 60.00

NURSES, THE (TV)
April, 1963 - No. 3, Oct, 1963 (Photo-c: #1,2)
Gold Key

GD25 FN65 NM94

1 3.60 9.00 18.00
2,3 2.40 6.00 12.00

NUTS! (Satire)
March, 1954 - No. 5, Nov, 1954
Premiere Comics Group

1-Hollingsworth-a 17.00 52.00 120.00
2,4,5: 5-Capt. Marvel parody 11.50 34.00 80.00
3-Drug "reefers" mentioned 12.00 36.00 85.00

NUTS (Magazine) (Satire)
Feb, 1958 - No. 2, April, 1958
Health Knowledge

1 5.85 17.50 35.00
2 4.20 12.50 25.00

NUTS & JOLTS (See Large Feature Comic #22)

NUTSY SQUIRREL (Formerly Hollywood Funny Folks)(Also see Comic Cavalcade)
#61, 9-10/54 - #69, 1-2/56; #70, 8-9/56 - #71, 10-11/56; #72, 11/57
National Periodical Publications

61-Mayer-a; Grossman-a in all 10.00 30.00 65.00
62-72: Mayer a-62,65,67-72 7.00 21.00 42.00

NUTTY COMICS
Winter, 1946 (Funny animal)
Fawcett Publications

1-Capt. Kidd story; 1 pg. Wolverton-a 10.00 30.00 65.00

NUTTY COMICS
1945 - No. 8, June-July, 1947
Home Comics (Harvey Publications)

nn-Helpful Hank, Bozo Bear & others 5.00 15.00 30.00
2-4 4.00 10.00 20.00
5-8: 5-Rags Rabbit begins(1st app.); infinity-c 3.20 8.00 16.00

NUTTY LIFE (Formerly Krazy Life #1; becomes Wotalife Comics #3 on)
No. 2, Summer, 1946
Fox Features Syndicate

2 6.70 20.00 40.00

NYOKA, THE JUNGLE GIRL (Formerly Jungle Girl; see The Further Adventures of..., Master Comics #50 & XMas Comics)
No. 2, Winter, 1945 - No. 77, June, 1953 (Movie serial)
Fawcett Publications

2 40.00 120.00 280.00
3 23.00 70.00 160.00
4,5 19.00 57.00 130.00
6-10 13.00 40.00 90.00
11,13,14,16-18-Krigstein-a 13.00 40.00 90.00
12,15,19,20 11.00 32.00 75.00
21-30: 25-Clayton Moore photo-c? 7.50 22.50 45.00
31-40 5.85 17.50 35.00
41-50 4.70 14.00 28.00
51-60 4.00 11.00 22.00
61-77 3.60 9.00 18.00

NOTE: *Photo-c from movies 25, 30-70, 72, 75-77. Bondage c-4, 5, 7, 8, 14, 24.*

NYOKA, THE JUNGLE GIRL (Formerly Zoo Funnies; Space Adventures #23 on)
No. 14, Nov, 1955 - No. 22, Nov, 1957
Charlton Comics

14 5.85 17.50 35.00
15-22 4.20 12.50 25.00

OAKLAND PRESS FUNNYBOOK, THE
9/17/78 - 4/13/80 (16 pgs.) (Weekly)
Full color in comic book form; changes to tabloid size 4/20/80-on
The Oakland Press

The Occult Files Of Dr. Spektor #23, © GK

Official Handbook of the Marvel Universe V3#8, © MEG

OK Comics #1, © UFS

GD25 FN65 NM94 GD25 FN65 NM94

Contains Tarzan by Manning, Marmaduke, Bugs Bunny, etc. (low distribution); 9/23/79 - 4/13/80 contain Buck Rogers by Gray Morrow & Jim Lawrence .65 1.60

OAKY DOAKS (See Famous Funnies #190)
July, 1942 (One Shot)
Eastern Color Printing Co.
1 23.00 68.00 150.00

OBIE
1953 (6 cents)
Store Comics
1 .80 2.00 4.00

OBNOXIO THE CLOWN
April, 1983 (One Shot) (Character from Crazy Magazine)
Marvel Comics Group
1-Vs. the X-Men 1.00

OCCULT FILES OF DR. SPEKTOR, THE
Apr, 1973 - No. 24, Feb, 1977; No. 25, May, 1982 (Painted-c #1-24)
Gold Key/Whitman No. 25
1-1st app. Lakota; Baron Tibor begins 1.40 3.50 8.50
2-5 1.70 4.25
6-10: 8-Dracula app. 1.20 3.00
11-13,15-25: 11-1st app. Spektor as Werewolf. 25-Reprints .40 1.00 2.00
14-Dr. Solar app. 1.00 2.50 6.00
9(Modern Comics reprint, 1977) 1.50
NOTE: *Also see Dan Curtis, Golden Comics Digest 33, Gold Key Spotlight, Mystery Comics Digest 5, & Spine Tingling Tales.*

ODELL'S ADVENTURES IN 3-D (See Adventures in 3-D)

OFFCASTES (Epic Comics)(Value: cover or less)

OFFICIAL CRISIS ON INFINITE EARTHS INDEX, THE (Eclipse)(Value: cover or less)

OFFICIAL CRISIS ON INFINITE EARTHS CROSSOVER INDEX, THE (Eclipse)(Value: cover or less)

OFFICIAL DOOM PATROL INDEX, THE (Eclipse)(Value: cover or less)

OFFICIAL HANDBOOK OF THE CONAN UNIVERSE (See Handbook of...)

OFFICIAL HANDBOOK OF THE MARVEL UNIVERSE, THE
Jan, 1983 - No. 15, May, 1984
Marvel Comics Group
1-Lists Marvel heroes & villains (letter A) 1.90 4.75
2 (B-C) 1.60 4.00
3-5: 3-(C-D). 4-(D-G). 5-(H-J) 1.20 3.00
6-9: 6-(K-L). 7-(M). 8-(N-P); Punisher-c. 9-(Q-S) 1.00 2.50
10-15: 10-(S). 11-(S-U). 12-(V-Z); Wolverine-c. 13,14-Book of the Dead. 15-Weaponry catalogue .90 2.25
NOTE: ***Byrne** c/a(p)-1-14; c-15p. **Grell** a-9. **Layton** a-2, 5, 7. **Miller** a-2, 3. **Nebres** a-3, 4, 8. **Simonson** a-11. **Paul Smith** a-1-3, 6, 7, 9, 10, 12. **Starlin** a-7. **Steranko** a-8p.*

OFFICIAL HANDBOOK OF THE MARVEL UNIVERSE, THE
Dec, 1985 - No. 20, Feb, 1988 ($1.50 cover; maxi-series)
Marvel Comics Group
V2#1-Byrne-c 1.40 3.50
2-5: 2,3-Byrne-c 1.10 2.75
6-10 .90 2.25
11-20 .70 1.70
Trade paperback Vol. 1-10 1.20 3.00 7.00

OFFICIAL HANDBOOK OF THE MARVEL UNIVERSE, THE
July, 1989 - No. 8, Mid-Dec, 1990 ($1.50, color, mini-series, 52 pgs.)
Marvel Comics
V3#1-8: 1-McFarlane-a(2 pgs.) 1.50

OFFICIAL HAWKMAN INDEX, THE (Independent)(Value: cover or less)

OFFICIAL JUSTICE LEAGUE OF AMERICA INDEX, THE (Independent)(Value: cover or less)

OFFICIAL LEGION OF SUPER-HEROES INDEX, THE (Independent)(Value: cover or less)

OFFICIAL MARVEL INDEX TO MARVEL TEAM-UP (Marvel)(Value: cover or less)

OFFICIAL MARVEL INDEX TO THE AMAZING SPIDER-MAN (Marvel)(Value: cover or less)

OFFICIAL MARVEL INDEX TO THE AVENGERS, THE (Marvel)(Value: cover or less)

OFFICIAL MARVEL INDEX TO THE FANTASTIC FOUR (Marvel)(Value: cover or less)

OFFICIAL MARVEL INDEX TO THE X-MEN, THE (Marvel)(Value: cover or less)

OFFICIAL SOUPY SALES COMIC (See Soupy Sales)

OFFICIAL TEEN TITANS INDEX, THE (Eclipse)(Value: cover or less)

OFFICIAL TRUE CRIME CASES (Formerly Sub-Mariner #23; All-True Crime Cases #26 on)
No. 24, Fall, 1947 - No. 25, Winter, 1947-48
Marvel Comics (OCI)
24(#1)-Burgos-a; Syd Shores-c 12.00 36.00 85.00
25-Syd Shores-c; Kurtzman's "Hey Look" 10.00 30.00 70.00

OF SUCH IS THE KINGDOM
1955 (36 pgs., 15 cents)
George A. Pflaum
nn-Reprints from 1951 Treasure Chest 2.00 5.00 10.00

O.G. WHIZ (See Gold Key Spotlight #10)
2/71 - No. 6, 5/72; No. 7, 5/78 - No. 11, 1/79 (No. 7: 52 pgs.)
Gold Key
1,2-John Stanley scripts 7.00 21.00 50.00
3-6(1972) 3.60 10.75 25.00
7-11(1978-79)-Part-r: 9-Tubby app. 1.20 3.00 7.00

OH, BROTHER! (Teen Comedy)
Jan, 1953 - No. 5, Oct, 1953
Stanhall Publ.
1-By Bill Williams 4.70 14.00 28.00
2-5 0.20 0.00 10.00

OH SKIN-NAY!
1913 (8-1/2x13")
P.F. Volland & Co.
nn-The Days Of Real Sport by Briggs 17.00 50.00 120.00

OH SUSANNA (See 4-Color #1105)

OKAY COMICS
July, 1940
United Features Syndicate
1-Captain & the Kids & Hawkshaw the Detective reprints 30.00 90.00 200.00

OK COMICS
July, 1940 - No. 2, Oct, 1940
United Features Syndicate
1-Little Giant, Phantom Knight, Sunset Smith, & The Teller Twins begin 47.00 140.00 300.00
2 (Rare)-Origin Mister Mist 45.00 135.00 310.00

OKLAHOMA KID
June, 1957 - No. 4, 1958
Ajax/Farrell Publ.
1 6.70 20.00 40.00
2-4 4.00 11.00 22.00

OKLAHOMAN, THE (See 4-Color #820)

OLD GLORY COMICS
1944 (Giveaway)

The Omega Men #9, © DC

One Million Years Ago #1, © STJ

Operation Peril #5, © ACG

GD25 FN65 NM94

Chesapeake & Ohio Railway
nn-Capt. Fearless reprint 4.20 12.50 25.00

OLD IRONSIDES (See 4-Color #874)

OLD YELLER (See 4-Color #869, Movie Comics, and Walt Disney Showcase #25)

OLYMPIANS, THE (Epic)(Value: cover or less)

OMAC (One Man Army, ...Corps. #4 on; also see Kamandi #59 & Warlord)
Sept-Oct, 1974 - No. 8, Nov-Dec, 1975
National Periodical Publications

1-Origin 1.00 2.50 6.00
2-8: 8-2pg. Neal Adams ad 1.40 3.50
NOTE: *Kirby a-1-8p; c-1-7p. Kubert c-8. See Cancelled Comic Cavalcade.*

OMAC: ONE MAN ARMY CORPS
1991 - No. 4, 1991 ($3.95, B&W, mini-series, mature readers, 52 pgs.)
DC Comics

Book One - Four: John Byrne-c/a & scripts 1.60 4.00

O'MALLEY AND THE ALLEY CATS
April, 1971 - No. 9, Jan, 1974 (Disney)
Gold Key

1 1.70 5.00 12.00
2-9 1.30 3.25 8.00

OMEGA ELITE (Blackthorne)(Value: cover or less)

OMEGA MEN, THE (See Green Lantern #141)
Dec, 1982 - No. 38, May, 1986 ($1.00-$1.50; Baxter paper)
DC Comics

1 1.50
2,4,6-8,11-18,21-36,38: 2-Origin Broot. 7-Origin The Citadel. 26,27-Alan Moore scripts. 30-Intro new Primus. 31-Crisis x-over. 34,35-Teen Titans x-over 1.00
3-1st app. Lobo (5 pgs.)(6/83); Lobo-c 1.30 3.25 8.00
5,9-2nd & 3rd app. Lobo (cameo, 2 pgs. each) 1.20 3.00
10-1st full Lobo story 1.30 3.25 8.00
19-Lobo cameo 1.50
20-2nd full Lobo story 1.90 4.75
37-1st solo Lobo story (8 pg. back-up by Giffen) 1.10 2.75
Annual 1(11/84, 52 pgs.), 2(11/85) 1.50
NOTE: *Giffen c/a-1-6p. Morrow a-24r. Nino c/a-16, 21.*

OMEGA THE UNKNOWN
March, 1976 - No. 10, Oct, 1977
Marvel Comics Group

1-1st app. Omega 1.20 3.00
2-7,10: 2-Hulk-c/story. 3-Electro-c/story .70 1.80
8-1st app. 2nd Foolkiller (Greg Salinger), 1 panel only (cameo) 1.20 3.00
9-1st full app. Foolkiller 1.60 4.00
NOTE: *Kane c(p)-3, 5, 8, 9. Mooney a-1-3, 4p, 5, 6p, 7, 8i, 9, 10.*

OMEN
1989 - No. 3? ($2.00, B&W, adults)
Northstar Publishing

1-Tim Vigil-c/a in all 1.25 3.00 7.50
1-2nd printing .90 2.25
2,3 1.10 2.75

OMNI MEN (Blackthorne)(Value: cover or less)

ONE (Pacific)(Value: cover or less)

ONE, THE (Epic)(Value: cover or less)

ONE-ARM SWORDSMAN, THE (Victory)(Value: cover or less)

ONE HUNDRED AND ONE DALMATIANS (See 4-Color #1183, Cartoon Tales, Movie Comics, and Walt Disney Showcase #9, 51)

101 DALMATIONS
1991 (Color, graphic novel, 52 pgs.)

GD25 FN65 NM94

Disney Comics
nn-($4.95, direct sale)-r/movie adaptation & more 1.00 2.00 5.00
1-($2.95, newsstand edition) 1.20 3.00

100 PAGES OF COMICS
1937 (Stiff covers; square binding)
Dell Publishing Co.

101(Found on back cover)-Alley Oop, Wash Tubbs, Capt. Easy, Og Son of Fire, Apple Mary, Tom Mix, Dan Dunn, Tailspin Tommy, Doctor Doom 100.00 300.00 600.00

100 PAGE SUPER SPECTACULAR (See DC 100 Page ...)

ONE MILE UP (Eclipse)(Value: cover or less)

$1,000,000 DUCK (See Walt Disney Showcase #5)

ONE MILLION YEARS AGO (Tor #2 on)
September, 1953
St. John Publishing Co.

1-Origin & 1st app. Tor; Kubert-c/a 14.00 43.00 100.00

ONE SHOT (See 4-Color...)

1001 HOURS OF FUN (See Large Feature Comic #13)

ON STAGE (See 4-Color #1336)

ON THE AIR
1947 (Giveaway) (paper cover)
NBC Network Comic

nn-(Rare) 17.00 52.00 120.00

ON THE DOUBLE (See 4-Color #1232)

ON THE LINKS
December, 1926 (48 pages) (9x10")
Associated Feature Service

nn-Daily strip-r 13.00 40.00 90.00

ON THE ROAD WITH ANDRAE CROUCH (Spire Christian)(Value: cover or less)

ON THE SPOT (Pretty Boy Floyd...)
Fall, 1948
Fawcett Publications

nn-Pretty Boy Floyd photo on-c; bondage-c 20.00 60.00 140.00

ONYX OVERLORD (Marvel)(Value: cover or less)

OPEN SPACE (Marvel)(Value: cover or less)

OPERATION BIKINI (See Movie Classics)

OPERATION BUCHAREST (See The Crusaders)

OPERATION CROSSBOW (See Movie Classics)

OPERATION PERIL
Oct-Nov, 1950 - No. 16, Apr-May, 1953 (#1-5: 52 pgs.)
American Comics Group (Michel Publ.)

1-Time Travelers, Danny Danger (by Leonard Starr) & Typhoon Tyler (by Ogden Whitney) begin 22.00 65.00 150.00
2 12.00 36.00 85.00
3-5: 3-Horror story. 5-Sci/fi-c/story 11.00 32.00 75.00
6-12-Last Time Travelers. 6,8,9-Sci/fi-c 10.00 30.00 65.00
13-16: All war format 5.00 15.00 30.00
NOTE: *Starr a-2, 5. Whitney a-1, 2, 5-10, 12; c-1, 3, 5, 8, 9.*

ORAL ROBERTS' TRUE STORIES (Junior Partners #120 on)
1956 (no month) - No. 119, 7/59 (15 cents)(No #102: 25 cents)
TelePix Publ. (Oral Roberts' Evangelistic Assoc./Healing Waters)

V1#1(1956)-(Not code approved)-"The Miracle Touch" 14.00 43.00 100.00
102-(Only issue approved by code, 10/56) 9.15 27.50 55.00
103-119: 115-(114 on inside) 5.85 17.50 35.00
NOTE: *Also see Happiness & Healing For You.*

ORANGE BIRD, THE

The Original Ghost Rider Rides Again #4, © MEG

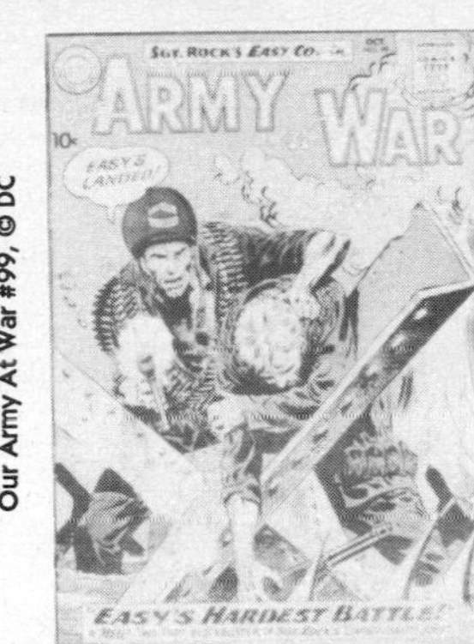

Our Army At War #99, © DC

Our Fighting Forces #1, © DC

GD25 FN65 NM94 | GD25 FN65 NM94

No date (1980) (36 pgs.; in color; slick cover)
Walt Disney Educational Media Co.

nn-Included with educational kit on foods 1.00
...in Nutrition Adventures nn (1980) .60
...and the Nutrition Know-How Revue nn (1983) .60

ORBIT (Eclipse)(Value: cover or less)

ORIENTAL HEROES (Jademan)(Value: cover or less)

ORIGINAL ASTRO BOY, THE (Now)(Value: cover or less)(Also see Astro Boy)

ORIGINAL BLACK CAT, THE (Recollections)(Value: cover or less)

ORIGINAL DICK TRACY, THE (Gladstone)(Value: cover or less)

ORIGINAL E-MAN AND MICHAEL MAUSER, THE (First)(Value: cover or less)

ORIGINAL GHOST RIDER, THE
July, 1992 - Present ($1.75, color)
Marvel Comics

1-20: 1-7-r/Marvel Spotlight #5-11 by Ploog w/new-c. 3-New Phantom Rider (former Night Rider) back-ups begin by Ayers. 4-Quesada-c(p). 8-Ploog-c. 8,9-r/Ghost Rider #1,2. 10-r/Marvel Spotlight #12. 11-20-r/Ghost Rider #3-12 .70 1.75

ORIGINAL GHOST RIDER RIDES AGAIN, THE
July, 1991 - No. 7, Jan, 1992, ($1.50, color, mini-series, 52 pgs.)
Marvel Comics

1-Reprints Ghost Rider #68(origin),69 w/covers 1.50
2-7: Reprints G.R. #70-81 w/covers 1.50

ORIGINAL NEXUS GRAPHIC NOVEL (See First Comics Graphic Novel #19)

ORIGINAL SHIELD, THE
April, 1984 - No. 4, Oct, 1984
Archie Enterprises, Inc.

1-4: 1,2-Origin Shield; Ayers p-1-4, Nebres c-1,2 1.00

ORIGINAL SWAMP THING SAGA, THE (See DC Special Series #2, 14, 17, 20)

OSCAR COMICS (Formerly Funny Tunes; Awful...#11 & 12)
(Also see Cindy Comics)
No. 24, Spring, 1947 - No. 10, Apr, 1949; No. 13, Oct, 1949
Marvel Comics

	GD25	FN65	NM94
24(#1, Spring, 1947)	9.15	27.50	55.00
25(#2, Sum, 1947)-Wolverton-a plus Kurtzman's "Hey Look"	10.00	30.00	70.00
26(#3)-Same as regular #3 except #26 was printed over in black ink with #3 appearing on-c below the over print	5.85	17.50	35.00
3-9,13: 8-Margie app.	5.85	17.50	35.00
10-Kurtzman's "Hey Look"	8.35	25.00	50.00

OSWALD THE RABBIT (Also see New Fun Comics #1)
No. 21, 1943 - No. 1268, 12-2/61-62 (Walter Lantz)
Dell Publishing Co.

	GD25	FN65	NM94
4-Color 21(1943)	34.00	100.00	235.00
4-Color 39(1943)	23.00	70.00	160.00
4-Color 67(1944)	16.00	48.00	110.00
4-Color 102(1946)-Kelly-a, 1 pg.	13.50	41.00	95.00
4-Color 143,183	8.35	25.00	50.00
4-Color 225,273	5.35	16.00	32.00
4-Color 315,388	4.00	10.00	20.00
4-Color 458,507,549,593	3.20	8.00	16.00
4-Color 623,697,792,894,979,1268	2.40	6.00	12.00

OSWALD THE RABBIT (See The Funnies, March of Comics #7, 38, 53, 67, 81, 95, 111, 126, 141, 156, 171, 186, New Funnies & Super Book #8, 20)

OUR ARMY AT WAR (Becomes Sgt. Rock #302 on; also see Army At War)
Aug, 1952 - No. 301, Feb, 1977
National Periodical Publications

	GD25	FN65	NM94
1	100.00	300.00	700.00
2	50.00	150.00	350.00
3,4: 4-Krigstein-a	39.00	120.00	275.00
5-7	29.00	85.00	200.00
8-11,14-Krigstein-a	29.00	85.00	200.00
12,15-20	22.00	65.00	150.00
13-Krigstein-c/a; flag-c	25.00	75.00	175.00
21-31: Last precode (2/55)	15.00	45.00	105.00
32-40	13.00	40.00	90.00
41-60	11.00	32.00	75.00
61-70	10.00	30.00	65.00
71-80	9.15	27.50	55.00
81-1st Sgt. Rock app. (4/59) by Andru & Esposito in Easy Co. story	100.00	300.00	1000.00
82-Sgt. Rock cameo in Easy Co. story (6 panels)	34.00	103.00	275.00
83-1st Kubert Sgt. Rock (6/59)	35.00	105.00	350.00
84,86-90	16.00	47.00	125.00
85-Origin & 1st app. Ice Cream Soldier	17.00	52.00	140.00
91-All Sgt. Rock issue	36.00	109.00	325.00
92-100: 95-1st app. Bulldozer; 1st app. Zack	9.00	28.00	75.00
101-120: 101-1st app. Buster. 111-1st app. Wee Willie & Sunny. 113-1st app. Wildman & Jackie Johnson. 118-Sunny dies	5.00	15.00	40.00
121-127,129-150: 126-1st app. Canary. 139-1st app. Little Sure Shot. 140-All Sgt. Rock issue	3.00	8.00	22.00
128-Training & origin Sgt. Rock	14.00	41.00	110.00
151-Intro. Enemy Ace by Kubert (2/65)	15.00	43.00	115.00
152,154,156,157,159-163,165-170: 157-2 pg. pin-up. 162,163-Viking Prince x-over in Sgt. Rock	3.00	8.00	20.00
153-2nd app. Enemy Ace (4/65)	7.00	21.00	55.00
155-3rd app. Enemy Ace (6/65)(see Showcase)	3.00	9.00	23.00
158-Origin & 1st app. Iron Major(9/65), formerly Iron Captain	2.00	7.00	19.00
164-Giant G-19	3.00	8.00	22.00
171-176,178-181	1.65	4.70	11.00
177-(80 pg. Giant G-32)	1.70	5.00	12.00
182,183,186-Neal Adams-a. 186-Origin retold	1.70	5.00	12.00
184,185,187-189,191-199: 184-Wee Willie dies. 189-Intro. The Teen-age Underground Fighters of Unit 3	1.50	3.75	9.00
190-(80 pg. Giant G-44)	1.65	4.00	10.00
200-12 pg. Rock story told in verse; Evans-a	1.70	5.00	12.00
201-Krigstein-r/#14	1.25	3.00	7.50
202,204-215: 204,205-All reprints; no Sgt. Rock	1.00	2.50	5.50
203-(80 pg. Giant G-56)-All-r, Sgt. Rock story	1.20	3.00	7.00
216,229-(80 pg. Giants G-68, G-80): 216-Has G-58 on-c by mistake	1.00	2.50	6.00
217-228,230-239,241		1.90	4.75
240-Neal Adams-a	1.00	2.50	6.00
242-(50 cent issue DC-9)-Kubert-c	1.00	2.50	6.00
243-301: 244-N. Adams-a? 280-200th app. Sgt. Rock; reprints Our Army at War #81,83		1.80	4.50

NOTE ***Alcala** a-251. **Drucker** a-27, 67, 68, 79, 82, 83, 96, 164, 177, 203, 212, 243r, 244, 269r, 275r, 280r. **Evans** a-165-175, 200, 266, 269, 270, 274, 276, 278, 280. **Glanzman** a-218, 220, 222, 223, 225, 227, 230-232, 238, 240, 241, 244, 247, 248, 256-259, 261, 265-267, 271, 282, 283, 298. **Grell** a-287. **Heath** a-50, 164, & most 176-281. **Kubert** a-38, 59, 67, 68 & most issues from 83-165, 233, 267, 275, 300. **Maurer** a-233, 237, 239, 240, 45, 280, 284, 288, 290, 291, 295. **Severin** a-236, 252, 265, 267, 269r, 272. **Toth** a-235, 241, 254. **Wildey** a-283-285, 287p. **Wood** a-249.*

OUR FIGHTING FORCES
Oct-Nov, 1954 - No. 181, Sept-Oct, 1978
National Periodical Publications/DC Comics

	GD25	FN65	NM94
1-Grandenetti-c/a	45.00	135.00	450.00
2	24.00	73.00	220.00
3-Kubert-c; last precode issue (3/55)	21.00	62.00	185.00
4,5	15.00	45.00	135.00
6-9	12.00	37.00	110.00
10-Wood-a	13.00	40.00	120.00
11-20: 20-Grey tone-c (4/57)	10.00	30.00	90.00
21-30	7.00	21.00	55.00
31-40	7.00	21.00	50.00

Our Flag Comics #2, © ACE

The Outer Limits #1, © United Artists TV

The Outlaw Kid #13, © MEG

GD25 FN65 NM94 GD25 FN65 NM94

41-Unknown Soldier tryout 9.00 28.00 65.00
42-44 6.00 18.00 42.00
45-Gunner & Sarge begin (1st app., ends #94) 23.00 68.00 158.00
46 10.00 31.00 72.00
47 7.00 21.00 48.00
48-50 4.70 14.00 33.00
51-64: 51-Grey tone-c. 64-Last 10 cent issue 3.25 9.50 22.00
65-70 2.40 7.25 17.00
71-80: 71-Grey tone-c 1.65 4.70 11.00
81-90 1.40 3.50 8.00
91-100: 95-Devil-Dog begins, ends 98. 99-Capt. Hunter begins, ends #106 1.00 2.50 6.00
101-181: 106-Hunters Hellcats begin. 116-Mlle. Marie app. 121-Intro. Heller. 123-Losers (Capt. Storm, Gunner & Sarge, Johnny Cloud) begin. 134,146-Toth-a 1.60 4.00

NOTE: ***N. Adams*** *c-147.* ***Drucker*** *a-28, 37, 39, 42-44, 49, 53, 133r.* ***Evans*** *a-149, 164-174, 177-181.* ***Glanzman*** *a-125-128, 132, 134, 138-141, 143, 144.* ***Heath*** *a-2, 16, 18, 28, 41, 44, 49, 114, 135-138r; c-51.* ***Kirby*** *a-151-162p; c-152-159.* ***Kubert*** *c/a in many issues.* ***Maurer*** *a-135.* ***Redondo*** *a-166.* ***Severin*** *a-123-130, 131i, 132-150.*

OUR FIGHTING MEN IN ACTION (See Men In Action)

OUR FLAG COMICS
Aug, 1941 - No. 5, April, 1942
Ace Magazines

1-Captain Victory, The Unknown Soldier (intro.) & The Three Cheers begin 133.00 400.00 900.00
2-Origin The Flag (patriotic hero); 1st app? 72.00 215.00 490.00
3-5: 5-Intro & 1st app. Mr. Risk 63.00 188.00 425.00

NOTE: ***Anderson*** *a-1, 4.* ***Mooney*** *a-1, 2; c-2.*

OUR GANG COMICS (With Tom & Jerry #39-59; becomes Tom & Jerry #60 on; based on film characters)
Sept-Oct, 1942 - No. 59, June, 1949
Dell Publishing Co.

1-Our Gang & Barney Bear by Kelly, Tom & Jerry, Pete Smith, Flip & Dip, The Milky Way begin (all 1st app.) 71.00 215.00 500.00
2 34.00 100.00 235.00
3-5: 2-Benny Burro begins (#2 by Kelly) 22.00 65.00 150.00
6-Bumbazine & Albert only app. by Kelly 36.00 107.00 250.00
7-No Kelly story 17.00 52.00 120.00
8-Benny Burro begins by Barks 36.00 107.00 250.00
9-Barks-a(2): Benny Burro & Happy Hound; no Kelly story 29.00 85.00 200.00
10-Benny Burro by Barks 23.00 70.00 160.00
11-1st Barney Bear & Benny Burro by Barks (5-6/44); Happy Hound by Barks 23.00 70.00 160.00
12-20 14.00 43.00 100.00
21-30: 30-X-Mas-c 11.00 32.00 75.00
31-36-Last Barks issue 9.15 27.50 55.00
37-40 4.20 12.50 25.00
41-50 3.60 9.00 18.00
51-57 3.00 7.50 15.00
58,59-No Kelly art or Our Gang stories 2.40 6.00 12.00

NOTE: ***Barks*** *art in part only.* ***Barks*** *did not write Barney Bear stories #30-34. (See March of Comics #3, 26). Early issues have photo back-c.*

OUR LADY OF FATIMA
3/11/55 (15 cents) (36 pages)
Catechetical Guild Educational Society

395 3.00 7.50 15.00

OUR LOVE (True Secrets #3 on?)
Sept, 1949 - No. 2, Jan, 1950
Marvel Comics (SPC)

1-Photo-c 8.35 25.00 50.00
2-Photo-c 5.00 15.00 30.00

OUR LOVE STORY
Oct, 1969 - No. 38, Feb, 1976
Marvel Comics Group

1 1.60 4.00 8.00
2-4,6-13 .80 2.00 4.00
5-Steranko-a 2.40 6.00 12.00
14-New story by Gary Fredrich & Tarpe' Mills 1.00 2.50 5.00
15-38: 27-Colan/Everett-a(r?); Kirby/Colletta-r .40 1.00 2.00

NOTE: ***J. Buscema*** *a-1-3, 5-7, 9, 35r; c-11, 23, 24, 27, 35.* ***Colan*** *a-3-6, 21r(#6), 23r(#3), 24r(#4), 27; c-19.* ***Katz*** *a-17.* ***Weiss*** *a-17.*

OUR MISS BROOKS (See 4-Color #751)

OUR SECRET (Formerly My Secret)
No. 4, Nov, 1949 - No. 8, Jun, 1950
Superior Comics Ltd.

4-Kamen-a; spanking scene 9.15 27.50 55.00
5,6,8 5.85 17.50 35.00
7-Contains 9 pg. story intended for unpublished Ellery Queen #5 6.70 20.00 40.00

OUTBURSTS OF EVERETT TRUE
1921 (32 pages) (B&W)
Saalfield Publ. Co.

1907 (2-panel strips reprint) 14.00 43.00 100.00

OUTCASTS (DC)(Value: cover or less)

OUTER LIMITS, THE (TV)
Jan-Mar, 1964 - No. 18, Oct, 1969 (All painted-c)
Dell Publishing Co.

1 6.00 18.00 42.00
2 3.25 9.50 22.00
3-10 2.30 6.75 16.00
11-18: 17-Reprints #1. 18-r/#2 1.85 5.50 13.00

OUTER SPACE (Formerly This Magazine Is Haunted, 2nd Series)
No. 17, May, 1958 - No. 25, Dec, 1959; Nov, 1968
Charlton Comics

17-Williamson/Wood style art; not by them (Sid Check?) 9.15 27.50 55.00
18-20-Ditko-a 11.00 32.00 75.00
21-25: 21-Ditko-c 7.50 22.50 45.00
V2#1(11/68)-Ditko-a, Boyette-c 4.00 10.00 20.00

OUTLANDERS (Dark Horse)(Value: cover or less)

OUTLAW (See Return of the...)

OUTLAW FIGHTERS
Aug, 1954 - No. 5, April, 1955
Atlas Comics (IPC)

1-Tuska-a 8.35 25.00 50.00
2-5: 5-Heath-c/a, 7pgs. 5.35 16.00 32.00

NOTE: ***Heath*** *c/a-5.* ***Maneely*** *c-2.* ***Pakula*** *a-2.* ***Reinman*** *a-2.* ***Tuska*** *a-1, 2.*

OUTLAW KID, THE (1st Series; see Wild Western)
Sept, 1954 - No. 19, Sept, 1957
Atlas Comics (CCC No. 1-11/EPI No. 12-29)

1-Origin; The Outlaw Kid & his horse Thunder begin; Black Rider app. 14.00 43.00 100.00
2-Black Rider app. 8.35 25.00 50.00
3-7,9: 3-Wildey-a(3) 7.50 22.50 45.00
8-Williamson/Woodbridge-a, 4 pgs. 5.85 17.50 35.00
10-Williamson-a 6.35 19.00 38.00
11-17,19: 13-Baker text illo. 15-Williamson text illo (unsigned) 4.20 12.50 25.00
18-Williamson/Mayo-a 5.35 16.00 32.00

NOTE: ***Berg*** *a-4, 7, 13.* ***Maneely*** *c-1-3, 5-8, 11-13, 15, 16, 18.* ***Pakula*** *a-3.* ***Severin*** *c-10, 17, 19.* ***Shores*** *a-1.* ***Wildey*** *a-1(3), 2-8, 10, 11, 12(4), 13(4), 15-19(4 each); c-4.*

OUTLAW KID, THE (2nd Series)
Aug, 1970 - No. 30, Oct, 1975
Marvel Comics Group

Outlaws #6, © DS

Out of the Shadows #6, © STD

The Owl #1, © WEST

	GD25	FN65	NM94
1,2-Reprints; 1-Orlando-r, Wildey-r(3)		1.90	4.75
3,9-Williamson-a(r)		1.10	2.75
4-8: 8-Double size; Crandall-r		.80	2.00
10-30: 10-Origin; new-a in #10-16. 27-Origin-r/#10		.70	1.80

NOTE: *Ayers a-10, 27r.* ***Berg*** *a-7, 25r.* ***Everett*** *a-2(2 pgs.).* ***Gil Kane*** *c-10, 11, 15, 27r, 28.* ***Roussos*** *a-10i, 27i(r).* ***Severin*** *c-1, 9, 20, 25.* ***Wildey*** *r-1-4, 6-9, 19-22, 25, 26.* ***Williamson*** *a-28r.* ***Woodbridge/Williamson*** *a-9r.*

OUTLAWS
Feb-Mar, 1948 - No. 9, June-July, 1949
D. S. Publishing Co.

	GD25	FN65	NM94
1-Violent & suggestive stories	16.00	48.00	110.00
2-Ingels-a	16.00	48.00	110.00
3,5,6: 3-Not Frazetta. 5-Sky Sheriff by Good app. 6-McWilliams-a	7.50	22.50	45.00
4-Orlando-a	9.15	27.50	55.00
7,8-Ingels-a in each	12.00	36.00	85.00
9-(Scarce)-Frazetta-a, 7 pgs.	30.00	90.00	210.00

NOTE: *Another #3 was printed in Canada with* ***Frazetta*** *art "Prairie Jinx," 7 pgs.*

OUTLAWS, THE (Formerly Western Crime Cases)
No. 10, May, 1952 - No. 13, Sept, 1953; No. 14, April, 1954
Star Publishing Co.

	GD25	FN65	NM94
10-L. B. Cole-c	5.85	17.50	35.00
11-14-L. B. Cole-c. 14-Reprints Western Thrillers #4 (Fox) w/new L.B. Cole-c; Kamen, Feldstein-r	4.70	14.00	28.00

OUTLAWS, THE (DC)(Value: cover or less)

OUTLAWS OF THE WEST (Formerly Cody of the Pony Express #10)
No. 11, 7/57 - No. 81, 5/70; No. 82, 7/79 - No. 88, 4/80
Charlton Comics

	GD25	FN65	NM94
11	5.85	17.50	35.00
12,13,15-17,19,20	3.60	9.00	18.00
14-(68 pgs., 2/58)	4.00	11.00	22.00
18-Ditko-a	7.50	22.50	45.00
21-30	2.40	6.00	12.00
31-50	1.40	3.50	7.00
51-70: 54-Kid Montana app. 64-Captain Doom begins (1st app.)	1.00	2.00	5.00
71-81: 79-Origin & 1st app. The Sharp Shooter, last app. #74. 75-Last Capt. Doom. 80,81-Ditko-a		1.20	3.00
82-88			1.50
64,79(Modern Comics-r, 1977, '78)			1.00

OUTLAWS OF THE WILD WEST
1952 (132 pages) (25 cents)
Avon Periodicals

	GD25	FN65	NM94
1-Wood back-c; Kubert-a (3 Jesse James-r)	20.00	60.00	140.00

OUT OF SANTA'S BAG (See March of Comics #10)

OUT OF THE NIGHT (The Hooded Horseman #18 on)
Feb-Mar, 1952 - No. 17, Oct-Nov, 1954
American Comics Group (Creston/Scope)

	GD25	FN65	NM94
1-Williamson/LeDoux-a, 9 pgs.	34.00	105.00	240.00
2-Williamson-a, 5 pgs.	29.00	85.00	200.00
3,5-10: 9-Sci/Fic story	11.50	34.00	80.00
4-Williamson-a, 7 pgs.	25.00	75.00	175.00
11-17: 13-Nostrand-a? 17-E.C. Wood swipe	10.00	30.00	65.00

NOTE: ***Landau*** *a-14, 16, 17.* ***Shelly*** *a-12.*

OUT OF THE PAST A CLUE TO THE FUTURE
1946? (16 pages) (paper cover)
E. C. Comics (Public Affairs Comm.)

	GD25	FN65	NM94
nn-Based on public affairs pamphlet-"What Foreign Trade Means to You"	19.00	57.00	130.00

OUT OF THE SHADOWS
No. 5, July, 1952 - No. 14, Aug, 1954
Standard Comics/Visual Editions

	GD25	FN65	NM94
5-Toth-p; Moreira, Tuska-a; Roussos-c	20.00	60.00	140.00
6-Toth/Celardo-a; Katz-a(2)	14.00	43.00	100.00
7-Jack Katz-c/a(2)	10.00	30.00	70.00
8,10: 8-Katz shrunken head-c. 10-Sekowsky-a	8.35	25.00	50.00
9-Crandall-a(2)	10.00	30.00	70.00
11-Toth-a, 2 pgs.; Katz-a; Andru-c	10.00	30.00	70.00
12-Toth/Peppe-a(2); Katz-a	14.00	43.00	100.00
13-Cannabalism story; Sekowsky-a; Roussos-c	11.50	34.00	80.00
14-Toth-a	11.50	34.00	80.00

OUT OF THIS WORLD
June, 1950 (One Shot)
Avon Periodicals

	GD25	FN65	NM94
1-Kubert-a(2) (one reprinted/Eerie #1, 1947) plus Crom the Barbarian by Giunta (origin); Fawcette-c	43.00	130.00	300.00

OUT OF THIS WORLD
Aug, 1956 - No. 16, Dec, 1959
Charlton Comics

	GD25	FN65	NM94
1	12.00	36.00	85.00
2	7.50	22.50	45.00
3-6-Ditko-a(4) each	15.00	45.00	105.00
7-(2/58, 15 cents, 68 pgs.)-Ditko-c/a(4)	15.00	45.00	105.00
8-(5/58, 15 cents, 68 pgs.)-Ditko-a(2)	12.00	36.00	85.00
9-12,16-Ditko-a	11.00	32.00	75.00
13-15	4.70	14.00	28.00

NOTE: ***Ditko*** *c-3-7, 11, 12, 16.* ***Reinman*** *a-10.*

OUT OUR WAY WITH WORRY WART (See 4-Color No. 680)

OUTPOSTS (Blackthorne)(Value: cover or less)

OUTSIDERS, THE (DC)(Value: cover or less)

OUTSIDERS
Nov, 1993 - Present ($1.75, color)
DC Comics

	GD25	FN65	NM94
1-Alpha; Travis Charest-c		.70	1.75
1-Omega; Travis Charest-c		.70	1.75
2-6		.70	1.75

OUTSTANDING AMERICAN WAR HEROES
1944 (16 pgs.) (paper cover)
The Parents' Institute

	GD25	FN65	NM94
nn-Reprints from True Comics	4.00	10.00	20.00

OVERSEAS COMICS (Also see G.I. Comics & Jeep Comics)
1944 (7-1/4x10-1/4"; 16 pgs. in color)
Giveaway (Distributed to U.S. armed forces)

	GD25	FN65	NM94
23-65-Bringing Up Father, Popeye, Joe Palooka, Dick Tracy, Superman, Gasoline Alley, Buz Sawyer, Li'l Abner, Blondie, Terry & the Pirates, Out Our Way	4.00	10.50	21.00

OWL, THE (See Crackajack Funnies #25 & Popular Comics #72)
April, 1967; No. 2, April, 1968
Gold Key

	GD25	FN65	NM94
1,2-Written by Jerry Siegel; '40s super hero	3.20	8.00	20.00

OXYDOL-DREFT
1950 (Set of 6 pocket-size giveaways; distributed through the mail as a set)
Oxydol-Dreft (Scarce)

	GD25	FN65	NM94
1-3: 1-Li'l Abner. 2-Daisy Mae. 3-Shmoo	10.00	30.00	60.00
4-John Wayne; Williamson/Frazetta-c from John Wayne #3	13.00	40.00	90.00
5-Archie	10.00	30.00	60.00
6-Terrytoons Mighty Mouse	10.00	30.00	60.00

NOTE: *Set is worth more with original envelope.*

OZ (See First Comics Graphic Novel, Marvel Treaury Of Oz & MGM's Marvelous...)

OZARK IKE
Feb, 1948; Nov, 1948 - No. 24, Dec, 1951; No. 25, Sept, 1952

Pancho Villa, © AVON

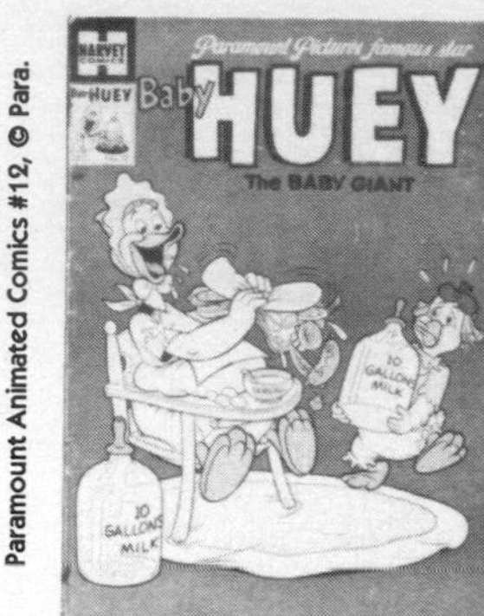

Paramount Animated Comics #12, © Para.

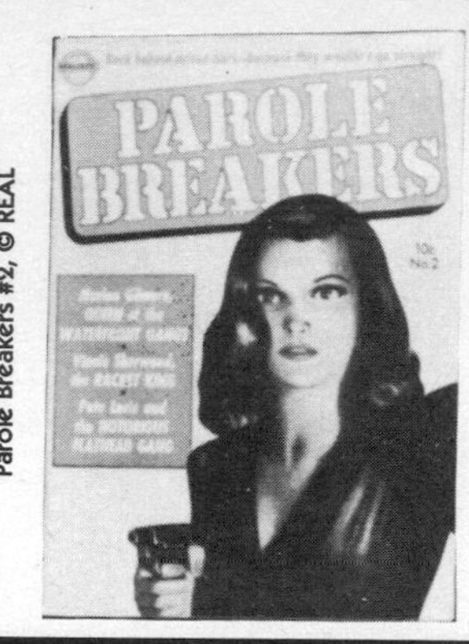

Parole Breakers #2, © REAL

GD25 FN65 NM94

Dell Publishing Co./Standard Comics B11 on
4-Color 180(1948-Dell) 9.15 27.50 55.00
B11, B12, 13-15 6.70 20.00 40.00
16-25 5.00 15.00 30.00

OZ-WONDERLAND WARS, THE
Jan, 1986 - No. 3, March, 1986 (Mini-series)
DC Comics
1-3 .40 1.00 2.00

OZZIE & BABS (TV Teens #14 on)
Dec, 1947 - No. 13, Fall, 1949
Fawcett Publications
1-Teen-age 6.70 20.00 40.00
2 4.00 10.00 20.00
3-13 3.00 7.50 15.00

OZZIE & HARRIET (See The Adventures of...)

PACIFIC COMICS GRAPHIC NOVEL (See Image Graphic Novel)

PACIFIC PRESENTS (Also see Starslayer #2, 3)
Oct, 1982 - No. 2, Apr, 1983; No. 3, Mar, 1984 - No. 4, June, 1984
Pacific Comics
1-Chapter 3 of The Rocketeer; Stevens-c/a 1.00 2.50 6.00
2-Chapter 4 of The Rocketeer (4th app.); nudity; Stevens-c/a 1.60 4.00
3,4: 3-1st app. Vanity .80 2.00
NOTE: *Conrad a-3, 4; c-3. Ditko a-1-3; c-1(1/2). Dave Stevens a-1, 2; c-1(1/2), 2.*

PADRE OF THE POOR
nd (Giveaway) (16 pgs.; paper cover)
Catechetical Guild
nn 2.00 5.00 10.00

PAGEANT OF COMICS (See Jane Arden & Mopsy)
Sept, 1947 - No. 2, Oct, 1947
Archer St. John
1-Mopsy strip-r 6.35 19.00 38.00
2-Jane Arden strip-r 6.35 19.00 38.00

PANCHO VILLA
1950
Avon Periodicals
nn-Kinstler-c 14.00 43.00 100.00

PANHANDLE PETE AND JENNIFER (TV) (See Gene Autry #20)
July, 1951 - No. 3, Nov, 1951
J. Charles Laue Publishing Co.
1 6.70 20.00 40.00
2,3 4.70 14.00 28.00

PANIC (Companion to Mad)
Feb-Mar, 1954 - No. 12, Dec-Jan, 1955-56
E. C. Comics (Tiny Tot Comics)
1-Used in Senate Investigation hearings; Elder draws entire E. C. staff 17.00 52.00 120.00
2 10.00 30.00 60.00
3,4: 3-Senate Subcommittee parody; Davis draws Gaines, Feldstein & Kelly, 1 pg.; Old King Cole smokes marijuana. 4-Infinity-c 8.35 25.00 50.00
5-11: 8-Last pre-code issue 7.00 21.00 42.00
12 (Low distribution; thousands were destroyed) 10.00 30.00 60.00
NOTE: *Davis a-1-12; c-12. Elder a-1-12. Feldstein c-1-3, 5. Kamen a-1. Orlando a-1-9. Wolverton c-4, panel-3. Wood a-2-9, 11, 12.*

PANIC (Magazine) (Satire)
July, 1958 - No. 6, July, 1959; V2#10, Dec, 1965 - V2#12, 1966
Panic Publications
1 7.50 22.50 45.00
2-6 4.00 11.00 22.00

GD25 FN65 NM94

V2#10-12: Reprints earlier issues 3.00 7.50 15.00
NOTE: *Davis a-3(2 pgs.), 4, 5, 10; c-10. Elder a-5. Powell a-V2#10, 11. Torres a-1-5. Tuska a-V2#11.*

PARADAX (Eclipse & Vortex)(Value: cover or less)

PARADE (See Hanna-Barbera...)

PARADE COMICS (Frisky Animals on Parade #2 on)
Sept, 1957
Ajax/Farrell Publ. (World Famous Publ.)
1 4.00 11.00 22.00
NOTE: *Cover title: Frisky Animals on Parade.*

PARADE OF PLEASURE
1954 (192 pgs.) (Hardback book)
Derric Verschoyle Ltd., London, England
By Geoffrey Wagner. Contains section devoted to the censorship of American comic books with illustrations in color and black and white. (Also see **Seduction of the Innocent**). Distributed in USA by Library Publishers, N. Y. 33.00 100.00 230.00
with dust jacket.... 55.00 165.00 385.00

PARAMOUNT ANIMATED COMICS (See Harvey Comics Hits #60, 62)
Feb, 1953 - No. 22, July, 1956
Harvey Publications
1-Baby Huey, Herman & Katnip, Buzzy the Crow begin 13.00 40.00 90.00
2 8.35 25.00 50.00
3-6 6.35 19.00 38.00
7-Baby Huey becomes permanent cover feature; cover title becomes Baby Huey with #9 13.00 40.00 90.00
8-10: 9-Infinity-c 5.85 17.50 35.00
11-22 4.20 12.50 25.00

PARANOIA (Adventure)(Value: cover or less)

PARENT TRAP, THE (See 4-Color #1210)

PARODY
Mar, 1977 - No. 3, Aug, 1977 (B&W humor magazine)
Armour Publishing
1-3 .80 2.00

PAROLE BREAKERS
Dec, 1951 - No. 3, July, 1952
Avon Periodicals/Realistic #2 on
1(#2 on inside)-r-c/Avon paperback #283 23.00 70.00 160.00
2-Kubert-a; r-c/Avon paperback #114 16.00 48.00 110.00
3-Kinstler-c 15.00 45.00 105.00

PARTRIDGE FAMILY, THE (TV)
March, 1971 - No. 21, Dec, 1973
Charlton Comics
1 2.00 6.00 14.00
2-4,6-21 1.20 3.00 7.00
5-Partridge Family Summer Special (52 pgs.); The Shadow, Lone Ranger, Charlie McCarthy, Flash Gordon, Hopalong Cassidy, Gene Autry & others app. 2.40 7.25 17.00

PARTS UNKNOWN
July, 1992 - No. 4, Oct, 1992 ($2.50, B&W, mini-series, mature readers)
Eclipse Comics/FX
1-4: All contain FX gaming cards 1.00 2.50

PASSION, THE
No. 394, 1955
Catechetical Guild
394 2.80 7.00 14.00

PAT BOONE (TV)(Also see Superman's Girlfriend Lois Lane #9)
Sept-Oct, 1959 - No. 5, May-Jun, 1960 (All have photo-c)
National Periodical Publications

Patsy Walker #31, © MEG

Pay-Off #1, © DS

Peacemaker #2 (DC), © DC

	GD25	FN65	NM94
1	32.00	95.00	225.00
2-5: 3-Fabian photo on-c. 4-Previews "Journey To The Center Of The Earth". 5-Dick Clark photo on-c	24.00	70.00	165.00

PATCHES
Mar-Apr, 1945 - No. 11, Nov, 1947
Rural Home/Patches Publ. (Orbit)

	GD25	FN65	NM94
1-L. B. Cole-c	14.00	43.00	100.00
2	8.35	25.00	50.00
3-11: 5-Danny Kaye-c/story; L.B. Cole-c. 6-Henry Aldrich story. 7-Hopalong Cassidy-c/story. 8-Smiley Burnette-c/story (6/47); pre-dates Smiley Burnette #1. 9-Mr. District Attorney story (radio). Leav/Keigstein-a (16 pgs.). 9-11-Leav-c. 10-Jack Carson (radio) c/story; Leav-c. 11-Red Skelton story	7.50	22.50	45.00

PATHWAYS TO FANTASY
July, 1984
Pacific Comics

	GD25	FN65	NM94
1-Barry Smith-c/a; Jeff Jones-a (4 pgs.)			1.50

PATORUZU (See Adventures of...)

PATSY & HEDY (Also see Hedy Wolfe)
Feb, 1952 - No. 110, Feb, 1967
Atlas Comics/Marvel (GPI/Male)

	GD25	FN65	NM94
1-Patsy Walker & Hedy Wolfe; Al Jaffee-c	11.50	34.00	80.00
2	6.70	20.00	40.00
3-10: 3,8-Al Jaffee-c	5.35	16.00	32.00
11-20	4.00	11.00	22.00
21-40	3.20	8.00	16.00
41-60	2.00	5.00	10.00
61-110: 88-Lingerie panel	1.40	3.50	7.00
Annual 1(1963)-Early Marvel annual	5.85	17.50	35.00

PATSY & HER PALS
May, 1953 - No. 29, Aug, 1957
Atlas Comics (PPI)

	GD25	FN65	NM94
1-Patsy Walker	10.00	30.00	65.00
2	5.85	17.50	35.00
3-10	4.20	12.50	25.00
11-29: 24-Everett-c	3.60	9.00	18.00

PATSY WALKER (See All Teen, A Date With Patsy, Girls' Life, Miss America Magazine, Patsy & Hedy, Patsy & Her Pals & Teen Comics)
1945 (no month) - No. 124, Dec, 1965
Marvel/Atlas Comics (BPC)

	GD25	FN65	NM94
1	34.00	105.00	240.00
2	16.00	48.00	110.00
3-10: 5-Injury-to-eye-c	10.00	30.00	70.00
11,12,15,16,18	8.35	25.00	50.00
13,14,17,19-22-Kurtzman's "Hey Look"	10.00	30.00	60.00
23,24	5.85	17.50	35.00
25-Rusty by Kurtzman; painted-c	10.00	30.00	60.00
26-29,31: 26-31: 52 pgs.	4.70	14.00	28.00
30(52 pgs.)-Egghead Doodle by Kurtzman, 1pg.	6.70	20.00	40.00
32-57: Last precode (3/55)	3.60	9.00	18.00
58-80	2.80	7.00	14.00
81-99: 92,98-Millie x-over	2.00	5.00	10.00
100	2.40	6.00	12.00
101-124	1.40	3.50	7.00
Fashion Parade 1(1966)-68 pgs.	5.85	17.50	35.00

NOTE: *Painted c-25-28. Anti-Wertham editorial in #21. Georgie app. in #8, 11. Millie app. in #10, 92, 98. Mitzi app. in #11. Rusty app. in #12, 25. Willie app. in #12.* ***Al Jaffee*** *c-57, 58.*

PAT THE BRAT (Adventures of Pipsqueak #34 on)
June, 1953; Summer, 1955 - No. 4, 5/56; No. 15, 7/56 - No. 33, 7/59
Archie Publications (Radio)

	GD25	FN65	NM94
nn(6/53)	10.00	30.00	60.00
1(Summer, 1955)	6.35	19.00	38.00
2-4-(5/56) (#5-14 not published)	4.00	11.00	22.00
15-(7/56)-33	2.40	6.00	12.00

PAT THE BRAT COMICS DIGEST MAGAZINE
October, 1980
Archie Publications

	GD25	FN65	NM94
1			1.50

PATTY POWERS (Formerly Della Vision #3)
No. 4, Oct, 1955 - No. 7, Oct, 1956
Atlas Comics

	GD25	FN65	NM94
4	5.35	16.00	32.00
5-7	3.60	9.00	18.00

PAT WILTON (See Mighty Midget Comics)

PAUL (Spire Christian)(Value: cover or less)

PAULINE PERIL (See The Close Shaves of...)

PAUL REVERE'S RIDE (See 4-Color #822 & Walt Disney Showcase #34)

PAUL TERRY'S ADVENTURES OF MIGHTY MOUSE (See Adventures of...)

PAUL TERRY'S COMICS (Formerly Terry-Toons Comics; becomes Adventures of Mighty Mouse No. 126 on)
No. 85, Mar, 1951 - No. 125, May, 1955
St. John Publishing Co.

	GD25	FN65	NM94
85,86-Same as Terry-Toons #85, & 86 with only a title change; published at same time?	8.35	25.00	50.00
87-99: 89-Mighty Mouse begins, ends #125	5.00	15.00	30.00
100	6.35	19.00	38.00
101-104,107-125: 121,122,125-Painted-c	4.70	14.00	28.00
105,106 Giant Comics Edition, 100pgs. (9/53 & ?)	11.50	34.00	80.00

PAUL TERRY'S HOW TO DRAW FUNNY CARTOONS
1940's (14 pages) (Black & White)
Terrytoons, Inc. (Giveaway)

	GD25	FN65	NM94
nn-Heckle & Jeckle, Mighty Mouse, etc.	10.00	30.00	65.00

PAUL TERRY'S MIGHTY MOUSE (See Mighty Mouse)

PAUL TERRY'S MIGHTY MOUSE ADVENTURE STORIES (See Mighty Mouse Adventure Stories)

PAWNEE BILL
Feb, 1951 - No. 3, July, 1951
Story Comics (Youthful Magazines?)

	GD25	FN65	NM94
1-Bat Masterson, Wyatt Earp app.	8.35	25.00	50.00
2,3: 3-Origin Golden Warrior; Cameron-a	5.00	15.00	30.00

PAY-OFF (This Is the..., ...Crime, ...Detective Stories)
July-Aug, 1948 - No. 5, Mar-Apr, 1949 (52 pages)
D. S. Publishing Co.

	GD25	FN65	NM94
1	12.00	36.00	85.00
2	8.35	25.00	50.00
3-5	6.70	20.00	40.00

PEACEMAKER, THE (Also see Fightin' Five)
V3#1, Mar, 1967 - No. 5, Nov, 1967 (All 12 cent cover price)
Charlton Comics

	GD25	FN65	NM94
1-Fightin' Five begins	2.15	6.50	15.00
2,3,5	1.30	3.25	8.00
4-Origin The Peacemaker	2.15	6.50	15.00
1,2(Modern Comics reprint, 1978)			1.00

PEACEMAKER (DC)(Value: cover or less)(Also see Crisis On Infinite Earths)

PEANUTS (Charlie Brown) (See Fritzi Ritz, Nancy & Sluggo, Tip Top, Tip Topper & United Comics)
No. 878, 2/58 No. 13, 5 7/62; 5/63 No. 4, 2/64
Dell Publishing Co./Gold Key

	GD25	FN65	NM94
4-Color 878(#1)	13.00	40.00	90.00
4-Color 969,1015('59)	10.00	30.00	65.00

Pebbles Flintstone #1, © Hanna-Barbera

Pendragon #14, © MEG

Pep Comics #2, © AP

GD25 FN65 NM94

4(2-4/60) 7.50 22.50 45.00
5-13 5.00 15.00 30.00
1(Gold Key, 5/63) 8.35 25.00 50.00
2-4 5.85 17.50 35.00
1(1953-54)-Reprints United Features' Strange As It Seems, Willie, Ferdnand 10.00 30.00 70.00

PEBBLES & BAMM BAMM (TV) (See Cave Kids #7, 12)
Jan, 1972 - No. 36, Dec, 1976 (Hanna-Barbera)
Charlton Comics

1-From the Flintstones 3.85 11.50 27.00
2-10 2.00 6.00 14.00
11-36 1.40 3.50 8.50

PEBBLES & BAMM BAMM (TV)
Oct, 1993 ($2.25, color, 68 pgs.) (Hanna-Barbera)
Harvey Comics

V2#1 1.00 2.50

PEBBLES FLINTSTONE (TV)
Sept, 1963 (Hanna-Barbera)
Gold Key

1 (10088-309) 7.00 21.00 50.00

PECKS BAD BOY
1906 - 1908 (Strip reprints) (11-1/4x15-3/4")
Thompson of Chicago (by Walt McDougal)

...& Cousin Cynthia(1907)-In color 32.00 95.00 225.00
...& His Chums(1908)-Hardcover; in full color; 16 pgs. 32.00 95.00 225.00
Advs. of...And His Country Cousins (1906)-In color, 18 pgs., oblong 32.00 95.00 225.00
Advs. of...in Pictures(1908)-In color; Stanton & Van V. Liet Co. 32.00 95.00 225.00

PEDRO (Formerly My Private Life #17; also see Romeo Tubbs)
No. 18, June, 1950 - No. 2, Aug, 1950?
Fox Features Syndicate

18(#1)-Wood-c/a(p) 16.00 48.00 110.00
2-Wood-a? 11.50 34.00 80.00

PEE-WEE PIXIES (See The Pixies)

PELLEAS AND MELISANDE (See Night Music #4, 5)

PENALTY (See Crime Must Pay the...)

PENDRAGON (Knights of... #5 on; also see Knights of...)
July, 1992 - No. 15, Sept, 1993 ($1.75, color)
Marvel Comics UK, Ltd.

1-15: 1-4-Iron Man app. 6-8-Spider-Man app. .70 1.75

PENDULUM ILLUSTRATED BIOGRAPHIES
1979 (B&W)
Pendulum Press

19-355x-George Washington/Thomas Jefferson, 19-3495-Charles Lindbergh/Amelia Earhart, 19-3509-Harry Houdini/Walt Disney, 19-3517-Davy Crockett/Daniel Boone-Redondo-a, 19-3525-Elvis Presley/Beatles, 19-3533-Benjamin Franklin/Martin Luther King Jr, 19-3541-Abraham Lincoln/Franklin D. Roosevelt, 19-3568-Marie Curie/Albert Einstein-Redondo-a, 19-3576-Thomas Edison/Alexander Graham Bell-Redondo-a, 19-3584-Vince Lombardi/Pele, 19-3592-Babe Ruth/Jackie Robinson, 19-3606-Jim Thorpe/Althea Gibson
Softback 1.50
Hardback 4.50

NOTE: *Above books still available from publisher.*

PENDULUM ILLUSTRATED CLASSICS (Now Age Illustrated)
1973 - 1978 (75 cents, 62pp, B&W, 5-3/8x8") (Also see Marvel Classics)
Pendulum Press

64-100x(1973)-Dracula-Redondo art, 64-131x-The Invisible Man-Nino art, 64-0968-Dr. Jekyll and Mr. Hyde-Redondo art, 64-1005-Black Beauty, 64-1010-Call of the Wild, 64-1020-Frankenstein, 64-1025-Hucklebury Finn, 64-1030-Moby Dick-Nino-a, 64-1040-Red Badge of Courage, 64-1045-The Time Machine-Nino-a, 64-1050-Tom Sawyer, 64-1055-Twenty Thousand Leagues Under the Sea, 64-1069-Treasure Island, 64-1328(1974)-Kidnapped, 64-1336-Three Musketeers-Nino art, 64-1344-A Tale of Two Cities, 64-1352-Journey to the Center of the Earth, 64-1360-The War of the Worlds-Nino-a, 64-1379-The Greatest Advs. of Sherlock Holmes-Redondo art, 64-1387-Mysterious Island, 64-1395-Hunchback of Notre Dame, 64-1409-Helen Keller-story of my life, 64-1417-Scarlet Letter, 64-1425-Gulliver's Travels, 64-2618(1977)-Around the World in Eighty Days, 64-2626-Captains Courageous, 64-2634-Connecticut Yankee, 64-2642-The Hound of the Baskervilles, 64-2650-The House of Seven Gables, 64-2669-Jane Eyre, 64-2677-The Last of the Mohicans, 64-2685-The Best of O'Henry, 64-2693-The Best of Poe-Redondo-a, 64-2707-Two Years Before the Mast, 64-2715-White Fang, 64-2723-Wuthering Heights, 64-3126(1978)-Ben Hur-Redondo art, 64-3134-A Christmas Carol, 64-3142-The Food of the Gods, 64-3150-Ivanhoe, 64-3169-The Man in the Iron Mask, 64-3177-The Prince and the Pauper, 64-3185-The Prisoner of Zenda, 64-3193-The Return of the Native, 64-3207-Robinson Crusoe, 64-3215-The Scarlet Pimpernel, 64-3223-The Sea Wolf, 64-3231-The Swiss Family Robinson, 64-3851-Billy Budd, 64-386x-Crime and Punishment, 64-3878-Don Quixote, 64-3886-Great Expectations, 64-3894-Heidi, 64-3908-The Iliad, 64-3916-Lord Jim, 64-3924-The Mutiny on Board H.M.S. Bounty, 64-3932-The Odyssey, 64-3940-Oliver Twist, 64-3959-Pride and Prejudice, 64-3967-The Turn of the Screw
Softback 1.45
Hardback 4.50

NOTE: *All of the above books can be ordered from the publisher; some were reprinted as Marvel Classic Comics #1-12. In 1972 there was another brief series of 12 titles which contained Classics Ill. artwork. They were entitled* ***Now Age Books*** *Illustrated, but can be easily distinguished from later series by the small Classics Illustrated logo at the top of the front cover. The format is the same as the later series. The 48 pg. C.I. art was stretched out to make 62 pgs. After Twin Circle Publ. terminated the Classics Ill. series in 1971, they made a one year contract with Pendulum Press to print these twelve titles of C.I. art. Pendulum was unhappy with the contract, and at the end of 1972 began their own art series, utilizing the talents of the Filipino artist group. One detail which makes this rather confusing is that when they redid the art in 1973, they gave it the same identifying no. as the 1972 series. All 12 of the 1972 C.I. editions have new covers, taken from internal art panels. In spite of their recent age, all of the 1972 C.I. series are very rare. Mint copies would fetch at least $50. Here is a list of the 1972 series, with C.I. title no. counterpart:*

64-1005 (CI#60-A2) 64-1010 (CI#91) 64-1015 (CI-Jr #503) 64-1020 (CI#26)
64-1025 (CI#19-A2) 64-1030 (CI#5-A2) 64-1035 (CI#169) 64-1040 (CI#98)
64-1045 (CI#133) 64-1050 (CI#50-A2) 64-1055 (CI#47) 64-1060 (CI-Jr#535)

PENDULUM ILLUSTRATED ORIGINALS
1979 (In color)
Pendulum Press

94-4254-Solarman: The Beginning .65 1.60

PENDULUM'S ILLUSTRATED STORIES
1990 - No. 72, 1990? (No cover price ($4.95), color, squarebound, 68 pgs.)
Pendulum Press

1-72: Reprints Pendulum Ill. Classics series 1.00 2.00 5.00

PENNY
1947 - No. 6, Sept-Oct, 1949 (Newspaper reprints)
Avon Comics

1-Photo & biography of creator 8.35 25.00 50.00
2-5 4.70 14.00 28.00
6-Perry Como photo on-c 5.35 16.00 32.00

PEP COMICS (See Archie Giant Series #576, 589, 601, 614, 624)
Jan, 1940 - No. 411?, 1987
MLJ Magazines/Archie Publications No. 56 (3/46) on

GD25 FN65 VF82 NM94

1-Intro. The Shield by Irving Novick (1st patriotic hero); origin & 1st app. The Comet by Jack Cole, The Queen of Diamonds & Kayo Ward; The Rocket, The Press Guardian (The Falcon #1 only), Sergeant Boyle, Fu Chang, & Bentley of of Scotland Yard; Robot-c 438.00 1310.00 2410.00 3500.00
(Estimated up to 150 total copies exist, 7 in NM/Mint)

GD25 FN65 NM94

2-Origin The Rocket 117.00 350.00 800.00
3 93.00 280.00 650.00
4-Wizard cameo 73.00 220.00 500.00
5-Wizard cameo in Shield story 73.00 220.00 500.00
6-10: 8-Last Cole Comet; no Cole-a in #6,7 55.00 165.00 375.00
11-Dusty, Shield's sidekick begins (1st app.); last Press Guardian, Fu Chang 62.00 188.00 425.00
12-Origin & 1st app. Fireball (2/41); last Rocket & Queen of Diamonds; Danny in Wonderland begins 75.00 225.00 525.00

Pep Comics #89, © AP

Perg #1, © Joseph A. Zyskowski

Perry Mason Mystery Magazine #2, © DELL

	GD25	FN65	NM94
13-15	50.00	150.00	340.00
16-Origin Madam Satan; blood drainage-c	75.00	225.00	525.00
17-Origin/1st app. The Hangman (7/41); death of The Comet; Comet is revealed as Hangman's brother	158.00	475.00	1050.00
18-21: 20-Last Fireball. 21-Last Madam Satan	48.00	145.00	325.00

	GD25	FN65	VF82	NM94
22-Intro. & 1st app. Archie, Betty, & Jughead(12/41); (also see Jackpot)	500.00	1500.00	2750.00	4000.00

(Estimated up to 150 total copies exist, 7 in NM/Mint)

	GD25	FN65	NM94
23	80.00	240.00	550.00
24,25: 24-Coach Kleets app. (unnamed until Archie #94). 25-1st app. Archie's jalopy; 1st skinny Mr. Weatherbee prptotype	70.00	210.00	475.00
26-1st app. Veronica Lodge (4/42)	93.00	280.00	650.00
27-30: 30-Capt. Commando begins; 1st Ms. Grundy (definitive version); see Jackpot #4	57.00	170.00	375.00
31-35: 31-MLJ offices & artists are visited in Sgt. Boyle story; 1st app. Mr. Lodge. 34-Bondage/Hypo-c. 33-Pre-Moose tryout (see Jughead #1)	47.00	140.00	300.00
36-1st Archie-c (2/43)	79.00	238.00	525.00
37-40	35.00	105.00	230.00
41-50: 41-Archie-c begin. 47-Last Hangman issue; infinity-c. 48-Black Hood begins (5/44); ends #51,59,60	25.00	75.00	165.00
51-60: 52-Suzie begins. 56-Last Capt. Commando. 59-Black Hood not in costume; spanking & lingerie panels; Archie dresses as his aunt; Suzie ends. 60-Katy Keene begins(3/47), ends #154	17.00	52.00	115.00
61-65-Last Shield. 62-1st app. Li'l Jinx (7/47)	13.00	40.00	90.00
66-80: 66-G-Man Club becomes Archie Club (2/48); Nevada Jones by Bill Woggon. 78-1st app. Dilton	10.00	30.00	60.00
81-99	7.00	21.00	42.00
100	10.00	30.00	60.00
101-130	4.00	11.00	22.00
131-149	2.40	6.00	12.00
150-160-Super-heroes app. in each (see note). 150 (10/61?)-2nd or 3rd app. The Jaguar? 157-Li'l Jinx story	2.80	7.00	14.00
161-167,169-200	1.00	2.50	6.00
168-Jaguar app.	1.20	3.00	7.00
201-260		1.20	3.00
261-411: 383-Marvelous Maureen begins (Sci/fi). 393-Thunderbunny begins			1.00

NOTE: **Biro** a-2, 4, 5. **Jack Cole** a-1-5, 8. **Al Fagaly** c-55-72(most). **Fuje** a-39, 45, 47; c-34. **Meskin** a-2, 4, 5, 11(2). **Montana** c-30, 32, 33, 36, 73-87(most). **Novick** c-1-28, 29(w/ Schomburg), 31i. **Harry Sahle** c-35, 39-50. **Schomburg** c-38. **Bob Wood** a-2, 4-6, 11. The Fly app. in 151, 154, 160. Flygirl app. in 153, 155, 156, 158. Jaguar app. in 150, 152, 157, 159, 168. Katy Keene by **Bill Woggon** in many later issues. Bondage c-7, 12, 13, 15, 18, 21, 31, 32.

PEPE (See 4-Color #1194)

PERCY & FERDIE
1921 (52 pages) (B&W dailies, 10x10", cardboard-c)
Cupples & Leon Co.

	GD25	FN65	NM94
nn-By H. A. MacGill	12.00	36.00	85.00

PERFECT CRIME, THE
Oct, 1949 - No. 33, May, 1953 (#2-12, 52 pgs.)
Cross Publications

	GD25	FN65	NM94
1-Powell-a(2)	13.00	40.00	90.00
2 (4/50)	9.15	27.50	55.00
3-10: 7-Steve Duncan begins, ends #30	7.50	22.50	45.00
11-Used in SOTI, pg. 159	9.15	27.50	55.00
12-14	5.85	17.50	35.00
15-"The Most Terrible Menace"-2 pg. drug editorial	6.70	20.00	40.00
16,17,19-25,27-29,31-33	4.35	13.00	26.00
18-Drug cover, heroin drug propaganda story, plus 2 pg. drug editorial	11.00	32.00	75.00
26-Drug-c with hypodermic; drug propaganda story	11.50	34.00	80.00
30-Strangulation cover	11.00	32.00	75.00

NOTE: **Powell** a-No. 1, 2, 4. **Wildey** a-1, 5. Bondage c-11.

PERFECT LOVE
#10, 8-9/51 (cover date; 5-6/51 indicia date); #2, 10-11/51 - #10, 12/53
Ziff-Davis(Approved Comics)/St. John No. 9 on

	GD25	FN65	NM94
10(#1)(8-9/51)-Painted-c	10.00	30.00	65.00
2(10-11/51)	7.50	22.50	45.00
3,5-7: 3-Painted-c. 5-Photo-c	5.00	15.00	30.00
4,8 (Fall, 1952)-Kinstler-a; last Z-D issue	5.35	16.00	32.00
9,10 (10/53, 12/53, St. John): 9-Painted-c. 10-Photo-c	4.70	14.00	28.00

PERG
Oct, 1993 - Present ($2.95, color)
Lightning Comics

	GD25	FN65	NM94
1-($3.50)-Flip-c is glow-in-the-dark by Saltares		1.40	3.50
1-Platinum Edition			10.00
2-4: 4-Origin Perg		1.20	3.00
2-Platinum Edition			5.00

PERRI (See 4-Color #847)

PERRY MASON (See Feature Books #49, 50)

PERRY MASON MYSTERY MAGAZINE (TV)
June-Aug, 1964 - No. 2, Oct-Dec, 1964
Dell Publishing Co.

	GD25	FN65	NM94
1,2: 2-Raymond Burr photo-c	4.00	10.00	20.00

PERSONAL LOVE (Also see Movie Love)
Jan, 1950 - No. 33, June, 1955
Famous Funnies

	GD25	FN65	NM94
1	10.00	30.00	70.00
2	5.85	17.50	35.00
3-7,10	4.35	13.00	26.00
8,9-Kinstler-a. 8-Esther Williams photo-c	5.00	15.00	30.00
11-Toth-a; Glenn Ford photo-c	7.50	22.50	45.00
12,16,17-One pg. Frazetta each. 17-Rock Hudson/Yvonne DeCarlo photo-c	4.35	13.00	26.00
13-15,18-23: 14-Kirk Douglas photo-c. 18-Gregory Peck/Susan Hayworth photo-c. 19-Anthony Quinn photo-c	4.00	11.00	22.00
24,27,28-Frazetta-a in all-8,8&6 pgs.	23.00	70.00	160.00
25-Frazetta-a (tribute to Betty Page, 7 pg. story); Tyrone Power/Terry Moore photo-c from "King of the Khyber Rifles"	23.00	70.00	160.00
26,29-31,33: 29-Charlton Heston photo-c. 31-Marlon Brando photo-c; last pre-code (2/55)	3.60	9.00	18.00
32-Classic Frazetta-a, 8 pgs.; Kirk Douglas/Bella Darvi photo-c	39.00	116.00	270.00

NOTE: *All have photo-c. Many feature movie stars.* **Everett** a-5, 9, 10, 24.

PERSONAL LOVE (Going Steady V3#3 on)
V1#1, Sept, 1957 - V3#2, Nov-Dec, 1959
Prize Publ. (Headline)

	GD25	FN65	NM94
V1#1	5.00	15.00	30.00
2	3.20	8.00	16.00
3-6(7-8/58)	2.80	7.00	14.00
V2#1(9-10/58)-V2#6(7-8/59)	2.40	6.00	12.00
V3#1-Wood/Orlando-a	3.60	9.00	18.00
2	2.00	5.00	10.00

PETER CANNON - THUNDERBOLT (Also see Thunderbolt)
Sept, 1992 - No. 12, Aug, 1993 ($1.25, color)(See Crisis on Infinite Earths)
DC Comics

	GD25	FN65	NM94
1-12			1.25

PETER COTTONTAIL
Jan, 1954; Feb, 1954 - No. 2, Mar, 1954 (Says 3/53 in error)
Key Publications

	GD25	FN65	NM94
1(1/54)-Not 3-D	5.35	16.00	32.00
1(2/54)-(3-D); Written by Bruce Hamilton	17.00	52.00	120.00
2-Reprints 3-D #1 but not in 3-D	4.35	13.00	26.00

Peter Penny and his Magic Dollar nn, © American Bankers Association N.Y.

Peter Rabbit 3-D #1, © Malibu Graphics

Petticoat Junction #2, © DELL

GD25 FN65 NM94

PETER GUNN (See 4-Color #1087)

PETER PAN (See 4-Color #442, 446, 926, Hook, Movie Classics & Comics, New Adventures of... & Walt Disney Showcase #36)

PETER PAN
1991 ($5.95, color, graphic novel, 68 pgs.)(Celebrates release of video)
Disney Comics

nn-r/Peter Pan Treasure Chest from 1953 1.00 2.50 6.00

PETER PANDA
Aug-Sept, 1953 - No. 31, Aug-Sept, 1958
National Periodical Publications

1-Grossman-c/a in all 29.00 85.00 200.00
2 13.00 40.00 90.00
3-10 10.00 30.00 65.00
11-31 7.00 21.00 42.00

PETER PAN: THE RETURN TO NEVER-NEVER LAND (Adventure)(Value: cover or less)

PETER PAN TREASURE CHEST (See Dell Giants)

PETER PARKER (See The Spectacular Spider-Man)

PETER PAT (See Single Series #8)

PETER PAUL'S 4 IN 1 JUMBO COMIC BOOK
No date (1953)
Capitol Stories (Charlton)

1-Contains 4 comics bound; Space Adventures, Space Western, Crime & Justice, Racket Squad in Action 29.00 88.00 175.00

PETER PENNY AND HIS MAGIC DOLLAR
1947 (16 pgs.; paper cover; regular size)
American Bankers Association, N. Y. (Giveaway)

nn-(Scarce)-Used in **SOTI**, pg. 310, 311 11.50 34.00 80.00
Diff. version (7-1/4x11")-redrawn, 16 pgs., paper-c 7.50 22.50 45.00

PETER PIG
No. 5, May, 1953 - No. 6, Aug, 1953
Standard Comics

5,6 3.60 9.00 18.00

PETER PORKCHOPS (See Leading Comics #23)
11-12/49 - No. 61, 9-11/59; No. 62, 10-12/60 (1-5: 52 pgs.)
National Periodical Publications

1 29.00 85.00 200.00
2 14.00 43.00 100.00
3-10 10.00 30.00 70.00
11-30 8.35 25.00 50.00
31-62 6.70 20.00 40.00
NOTE: ***Otto Feur** a-all. **Sheldon Mayer** a-30-38, 40-44, 46-52, 61.*

PETER PORKER, THE SPECTACULAR SPIDER-HAM
May, 1985 - No. 17, Sept, 1987 (Also see Marvel Tails)
Star Comics (Marvel)

1-Michael Golden-c .80 2.00
2-17: 13-Halloween issue 1.00
NOTE: *Back-up features: 2-X-Bugs. 3-Iron Mouse. 4-Croctor Strange. 5-Thrr, Dog of Thunder.*

PETER POTAMUS (TV)
January, 1965 (Hanna-Barbera)
Gold Key

1 6.70 20.00 40.00

PETER RABBIT (See Large Feature Comic #1, New Funnies #65 & Space Comics)

PETER RABBIT
1922 - 1923 (9-1/4x6-1/4") (paper cover)
John H. Eggers Co. The House of Little Books Publishers

B1-B4-(Rare)-(Set of 4 books which came in a cardboard box)-Each book reprints half of a Sunday page per page and contains 8 B&W and 2 color pages; by Harrison Cady
each.... 29.00 85.00 200.00

GD25 FN65 NM94

PETER RABBIT (Adventures of...; New Advs. of... later issues)(Also see Funny Tunes & Space Comics)
1947 - No. 34, Aug-Sept, 1956
Avon Periodicals

1(1947)-Reprints 1943-44 Sunday strips; contains a biography & drawing of Cady 26.00 80.00 185.00
2 (4/48) 20.00 60.00 140.00
3 ('48) - 6(7/49)-Last Cady issue 18.00 54.00 125.00
7-10(1950-8/51) 4.00 12.00 24.00
11(11/51)-34('56)-Avon's character 3.00 7.50 15.00
...Easter Parade (1952, 25¢, 132 pgs.) 11.00 32.00 75.00
...Jumbo Book (1954-Giant Size, 25 cents)-6 pgs. Jesse James by Kinstler 16.00 50.00 115.00

PETER RABBIT
1958
Fago Magazine Co.

1 5.00 15.00 30.00

PETER RABBIT 3-D (Eternity)(Value: cover or less)

PETER, THE LITTLE PEST (#4 titled Petey)
Nov, 1969 - No. 4, May, 1970
Marvel Comics Group

1 1.40 3.50 7.00
2-4-R-Dexter the Demon & Melvin the Monster .80 2.00 4.00

PETER WHEAT (The Adventures of...)
1948 - 1956? (16 pgs. in color) (paper covers)
Bakers Associates Giveaway

nn(No.1)-States on last page, end of 1st Adventure of...; Kelly-a 24.00 72.00 165.00
nn(4 issues)-Kelly-a 16.00 48.00 110.00
6-10-All Kelly-a 11.50 34.00 80.00
11-20-All Kelly-a 10.00 30.00 65.00
21-35-All Kelly-a 8.35 25.00 50.00
36-66 5.85 17.50 35.00
...Artist's Workbook ('54, digest size) 5.35 16.00 32.00
...Four-In-One Fun Pack (Vol. 2, '54), oblong, comics w/puzzles 6.70 20.00 40.00
...Fun Book ('52, 32pgs., paper-c, B&W & color, 8-1/2x10-3/4"), contains cut-outs, puzzles, games, magic & pages to color 10.00 30.00 60.00
NOTE: ***Al Hubbard** art #36 on; written by **Del Connell**.*

PETER WHEAT NEWS
1948 - No. 30, 1950 (4 pgs. in color)
Bakers Associates

Vol. 1-All have 2 pgs. Peter Wheat by Kelly 24.00 72.00 165.00
2-10 14.00 43.00 100.00
11-20 8.35 25.00 50.00
21-30 5.35 16.00 32.00
NOTE: *Early issues have no date & **Kelly** art.*

PETE'S DRAGON (See Walt Disney Showcase #43)

PETE THE PANIC
November, 1955
Stanmor Publications

nn-Code approved 3.00 7.50 15.00

PETEY (See Peter, the Little Pest)

PETTICOAT JUNCTION (TV)
Oct-Dec, 1964 - No. 5, Oct-Dec, 1965 (#1-3, 5 have photo-c)
Dell Publishing Co.

1 7.50 22.50 45.00
2-5 5.00 15.00 30.00

PETUNIA (See 4-Color #463)

The Phantom #5 (Gold Key), © KING

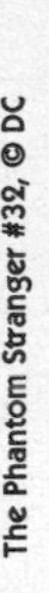
The Phantom Stranger #32, © DC

Phoenix #3, © Atlas/Seaboard Publ.

GD25 FN65 NM94

PHANTASMO (See The Funnies #45 and Large Feature Comic #18)

PHANTOM, THE
1939 - 1949
David McKay Publishing Co.

	GD25	FN65	NM94
Feature Books 20	59.00	180.00	415.00
Feature Books 22	47.00	140.00	330.00
Feature Books 39	39.00	120.00	275.00
Feature Books 53,56,57	29.00	85.00	200.00

PHANTOM, THE (See Ace Comics, Defenders Of The Earth, Eat Right to Work and Win, Future Comics, Harvey Comics Hits #51,56, Harvey Hits #1, 6, 12, 15, 26, 36, 44, 48, & King Comics)

PHANTOM, THE (nn 29-Published overseas only) (Also see Comics Reading Library)
Nov, 1962 - No. 17, July, 1966; No. 18, Sept, 1966 - No. 28, Dec, 1967; No. 30, Feb, 1969 - No. 74, Jan, 1977
Gold Key (#1-17)/King (#18-28)/Charlton (#30 on)

	GD25	FN65	NM94
1-Manning-a	9.00	26.00	62.00
2-King, Queen & Jack begins, ends #11	4.50	14.00	32.00
3-10	3.70	11.00	26.00
11-17: 12-Track Hunter begins	3.20	9.00	21.00
18-Flash Gordon begins; Wood-a	3.30	10.00	23.00
19,20-Flash Gordon ends (both by Gil Kane)	2.30	6.75	16.00
21-24,26,27: 21-Mandrake begins. 20,24-Girl Phantom app. 26-Brick Bradford app.	2.30	6.75	16.00
25-Jeff Jones-a(4 pgs.); 1 pg. Williamson ad	2.30	6.75	16.00
28(nn)-Brick Bradford app.	1.85	5.50	13.00
30-40: 36,39-Ditko-a	1.65	4.70	11.00
41-66: 46-Intro. The Piranha. 62-Bolle-c	1.40	3.50	8.50
67-71,73-Newton-c/a; 67-Origin retold	1.00	2.50	5.50
72,74: 74-Newton Flag-c; Newton-a	1.00	2.50	5.50

NOTE: *Aparo a-31-34, 36-38; c-31-38, 60, 61. Painted c-1-17.*

PHANTOM, THE
May, 1988 - No. 4, Aug, 1988 ($1.25, color, mini-series)
DC Comics

1-4: Orlando-c/a in all — 1.25

PHANTOM, THE
Mar, 1989 - No. 13, Mar, 1990 ($1.50, color)
DC Comics

1-13: 1-Brief origin — 1.50

PHANTOM, THE
1992 - Present? ($2.25, color)
Wolf Publishing

1-8 — .90 — 2.25

PHANTOM BLOT, THE (#1 titled New Adventures of...)
Oct, 1964 - No. 7, Nov, 1966 (Disney)
Gold Key

	GD25	FN65	NM94
1 (Meets The Beagle Boys)	3.30	10.00	23.00
2-1st Super Goof	2.30	6.75	16.00
3-7	1.85	5.50	13.00

PHANTOM EAGLE (See Mighty Midget, Marvel Super Heroes #16 & Wow #6)

PHANTOM LADY (1st Series) (My Love Secret #24 on) (Also see All Top, Daring Adventures, Freedom Fighters, Jungle Thrills, & Wonder Boy)
No. 13, Aug, 1947 - No. 23 April, 1949
Fox Features Syndicate

	GD25	FN65	NM94
13(#1)-Phantom Lady by Matt Baker begins (1st app.); The Blue Beetle app.	135.00	407.00	1050.00
14(#2)	93.00	280.00	725.00
15-P.L. injected with experimental drug	72.00	215.00	550.00
16-Negligee-c, panels	72.00	215.00	550.00
17-Classic bondage cover; used in **SOTI**, illo-"Sexual stimulation by combining 'headlights' with the sadist's dream of tying up a woman"	165.00	495.00	1250.00
18,19	71.00	215.00	500.00
20-23: 23-Bondage-c	63.00	190.00	440.00

NOTE: *Matt Baker a-in all; c-13, 16-21. Kamen a-22, 23.*

PHANTOM LADY (2nd Series) (See Terrific Comics) (Formerly Linda)
V1#5, Dec-Jan, 1954/1955 - No. 4, June, 1955
Ajax/Farrell Publ.

	GD25	FN65	NM94
V1#5(#1)-By Matt Baker	43.00	130.00	300.00
V1#2-Last pre-code	36.00	107.00	250.00
3,4-Red Rocket	29.00	85.00	200.00

PHANTOM PLANET, THE (See 4-Color No. 1234)

PHANTOM STRANGER, THE (1st Series)(See Saga of Swamp Thing)
Aug-Sept, 1952 - No. 6, June-July, 1953
National Periodical Publications

	GD25	FN65	NM94
1(Scarce)	115.00	345.00	800.00
2 (Scarce)	79.00	235.00	550.00
3-6 (Scarce)	63.00	190.00	440.00

PHANTOM STRANGER, THE (2nd Series) (See Showcase #80)
May-June, 1969 - No. 41, Feb-Mar, 1976
National Periodical Publications

	GD25	FN65	NM94
1-1st S.A. app. P. Stranger; only 12¢ issue	6.00	18.00	42.00
2,3	2.15	6.50	15.00
4-1st new look Phantom Stranger; N. Adams-a	2.40	7.25	17.00
5-7	1.65	4.70	11.00
8-14: 14-Last 15¢ issue	1.30	3.25	8.00
15-19: All 25¢ giants (52 pgs.)		1.90	4.75
20-41: 22-Dark Circle begins. 23-Spawn of Frankenstein begins by Kaluta; series ends #30. 31-The Black Orchid begins (6-7/74). 34-Last 20¢ issue (#35 on are 25¢). 39-41-Deadman app.		1.60	4.00

NOTE: ***N. Adams** a-4; c-3-19. **Aparo** a-7-26; c-20-24, 33-41. **B. Bailey** a-27-30. **DeZuniga** a-14-16, 19-22, 31, 34. **Grell** a-33. **Kaluta** a-23-25; c-26. **Meskin** r-15, 16, 18. **Redondo** a-32, 35, 36. **Sparling** a-20. **Starr** a-17r. **Toth** a-15r. Black Orchid by **Carrilo**-38-41. Dr. 13 solo in-13, 18, 20. Frankenstein by **Kaluta**-23-25; by **Baily**-27-30. No Black Orchid-33, 34, 37.*

PHANTOM STRANGER (See Justice League of America #103)
Oct, 1987 - No. 4, Jan, 1988 (75 cents, color, mini-series)
DC Comics

1-Mignola/Russell c/a & Eclipso app. in all — 1.50
2-4: 3,4-Eclipso-c — 1.00

PHANTOM WITCH DOCTOR (Also see Durango Kid #8 & Eerie #8)
1952
Avon Periodicals

1-Kinstler-c/a (7 pgs.) — 26.00 — 77.00 — 180.00

PHANTOM ZONE, THE (See Adventure #283 & Superboy #100, 104)
January, 1982 - No. 4, April, 1982
DC Comics

1-Superman app. in all — 1.00
2-4: Batman, Green Lantern app. — 1.25

NOTE: ***Colan** a-1-4p; c-1-4p. **Giordano** c-1-4i.*

PHAZE (Eclipse)(Value: cover or less)

PHIL RIZZUTO (Baseball Hero)(See Sport Thrills, Accepted reprint)
1951 (New York Yankees)
Fawcett Publications

nn-Photo-c — 43.00 — 130.00 — 300.00

PHOENIX
Jan, 1975 - No. 4, Oct, 1975
Atlas/Seaboard Publ.

1-Origin — 1.20
2-4: 3-Origin & only app. The Dark Avenger. 4-New origin/costume The Protector (formerly Phoenix) — 1.00

NOTE: ***Infantino** appears in #1, 2. **Austin** a-3i. **Thorne** c-3.*

PHOENIX (...The Untold Story)

Pictorial Confessions #1, © STJ

Picture Stories From Science #1, © WMG

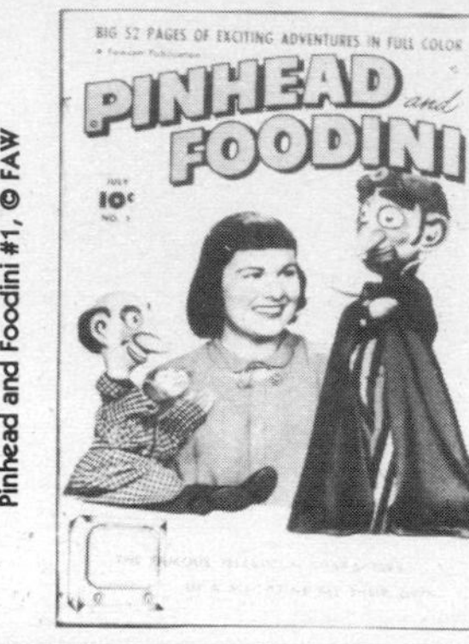

Pinhead and Foodini #1, © FAW

GD25 FN65 NM94

April, 1984 ($2.00, One shot)
Marvel Comics Group

1-Byrne/Austin-r/X-Men #137 with original unpublished ending 1.90 4.75

PICNIC PARTY (See Dell Giants)

PICTORIAL CONFESSIONS (Pictorial Romances #4 on)
Sept, 1949 - No. 3, Dec, 1949
St. John Publishing Co.

1-Baker-c/a(3) 13.00 40.00 90.00
2-Baker-a; photo-c 7.50 22.50 45.00
3-Kubert, Baker-a; part Kubert-c 10.00 30.00 60.00

PICTORIAL LOVE STORIES (Formerly Tim McCoy)
No. 22, Oct, 1949 - No. 26, July, 1950
Charlton Comics

22-26-"Me-Dan Cupid" in all 10.00 30.00 65.00

PICTORIAL LOVE STORIES
October, 1952
St. John Publishing Co.

1-Baker-c/a 11.50 34.00 80.00

PICTORIAL ROMANCES (Formerly Pictorial Confessions)
No. 4, Jan, 1950; No. 5, Jan, 1951 - No. 24, Mar, 1954
St. John Publishing Co.

4-All Baker; photo-c 11.50 34.00 80.00
5,10-All Matt Baker issues 10.00 30.00 60.00
6-9,12,13,15,16-Baker-c, 2-3 stories 6.70 20.00 40.00
11-Baker-c/a(3); Kubert-a 7.50 22.50 45.00
14,21-24-Baker-c/a each 5.35 16.00 32.00
17-20(7/53)-100 pgs. each; Baker-c/a 12.00 36.00 85.00
NOTE: ***Matt Baker** art in most issues. **Estrada** a-19(2).*

PICTURE NEWS
Jan, 1946 - No. 10, Jan-Feb, 1947
Lafayette Street Corp.

1-Milt Gross begins, ends No. 6; 4 pg. Kirby-a; A-Bomb-c/story 23.00 68.00 160.00
2-Atomic explosion panels; Frank Sinatra, Perry Como stories 10.00 30.00 70.00
3-Atomic explosion panels; Frank Sinatra, June Allyson, Benny Goodman stories 10.00 30.00 65.00
4-Atomic explosion panels; "Caesar and Cleopatra" movie adaptation; Jackie Robinson story 10.00 30.00 70.00
5-7: 5-Hank Greenberg story. 6-Joe Louis-c/story 7.50 22.50 45.00
8-Monte Hale story (9-10/46; 1st?) 10.00 30.00 60.00
9-A-Bomb story; "Crooked Mile" movie adaptation; Joe DiMaggio story 10.00 30.00 60.00
10-Dick Quick; A-Bomb story; Krigstein, Gross-a 10.00 30.00 60.00

PICTURE PARADE (Picture Progress #5 on)
Sept, 1953 - V1#4, Dec, 1953 (28 pages)
Gilberton Company (Also see A Christmas Adventure)

V1#1-Andy's Atomic Adventures-A-bomb blast-c; (Teachers version distributed to schools exists) 11.00 32.00 75.00
2-Around the World with the United Nations 8.35 25.00 50.00
3-Adventures of the Lost One(The American Indian), 4-A Christmas Adventure (r-under same title in '69) 8.35 25.00 50.00

PICTURE PROGRESS (Formerly Picture Parade)
V1#5, Jan, 1954 - V3#2, Oct, 1955 (28-36 pgs.)
Gilberton Corp.

V1#5-9,V2#1-9: 5-News in Review 1953, 6-The Birth of America, 7-The Four Seasons, 8-Paul Revere's Ride, 9-The Hawaiian Islands(5/54), V2#1-The Story of Flight(9/54), 2-Vote for Crazy River(The Meaning of Elections), 3-Louis Pasteur, 4-The Star Spangled Banner, 5-News in Review 1954, 6-Alaska: The Great Land, 7-Life in the Circus, 8-The Time of the Cave Man, 9-Summer Fun(5/55) 3.60 9.00 18.00
V3#1,2: 1-The Man Who Discovered America, 2-The Lewis & Clark Expedition 3.60 9.00 18.00

PICTURE SCOPE JUNGLE ADVENTURES (See Jungle Thrills)

PICTURE STORIES FROM AMERICAN HISTORY
1945 - No. 4, Sum, 1947 (#1,2: 10 cents, 56pgs.; #3,4: 15 cents, 52pgs.)
National/All-American/E. C. Comics

1 16.00 48.00 110.00
2-4 10.00 30.00 70.00

PICTURE STORIES FROM SCIENCE
Spring, 1947 - No. 2, Fall, 1947
E.C. Comics

1,2: 1-(15¢). 2-(10¢) 16.00 48.00 110.00

PICTURE STORIES FROM THE BIBLE
Fall, 1942-3 & 1944-46
National/All-American/E.C. Comics

1-4('42-Fall,'43)-Old Testament (DC) 16.00 48.00 110.00
Complete Old Testament Edition, 232pgs.(12/43-DC);-1st printing; contains #1-4; 2nd - 8th (1/47) printings exist; later printings by E.C. 19.00 58.00 135.00
Complete Old Testament Edition (1945-publ. by Bible Pictures Ltd.)-232 pgs., hardbound, in color with dust jacket 19.00 58.00 135.00
NOTE: *Both Old and New Testaments published in England by Bible Pictures Ltd. in hardback, 1943, in color, 376 pages, and were also published by Scarf Press in 1979 (Old Test., $9.95) and in 1980 (New Test., $7.95)*

1-3(New Test.; 1944-46, DC)-52pgs. ea. 11.50 34.00 80.00
The Complete Life of Christ Edition (1945)-96pgs.; contains #1&2 of the New Testament Edition 16.00 48.00 110.00
1,2(Old Testament-r in comic book form)(E.C., 1946; 52pgs.) 11.50 34.00 80.00
1-3(New Testament-r in comic book form)(E.C., 1946; 52pgs.) 11.50 34.00 80.00
Complete New Testament Edition (1946-E.C.)-144 pgs.; contains #1-3 16.00 48.00 110.00
NOTE: *Another British series entitled **The Bible Illustrated** from 1947 has recently been discovered, with the same internal artwork. This eight edition series (5-OT, 3-NT) is of particular interest to Classics Ill. collectors because it exactly copied the C.I. logo format. The British publisher was Thorpe & Porter, who in 1951 began publishing the British Classics Ill. series. All editions of The Bible Ill. have new British painted covers. While this market is still new, and not all editions have as yet been found, current market value is about the same as the first U.S. editions of Picture Stories From The Bible.*

PICTURE STORIES FROM WORLD HISTORY
Spring, 1947 - No. 2, Summer, 1947 (52,48 pgs.)
E.C. Comics

1,2: 1-(15¢). 2-(10¢) 16.00 48.00 110.00

PINHEAD
Dec, 1993 - Present ($2.50, color)
Epic Comics (Marvel)

1-($2.95)-Embossed foil-c; Intro Pinhead & Disciples (Snakeoil, Hangman, Fan Dancer & Dixie) 1.20 3.00
2-4 1.00 2.50

PINHEAD & FOODINI (TV)(Also see Foodini & Jingle Dingle Christmas...)
July, 1951 - No. 4, Jan, 1952 (Early TV comic)
Fawcett Publications

1-(52 pgs.)-Photo-c; based on TV puppet show 22.00 65.00 150.00
2-Photo-c 10.00 30.00 70.00
3,4: 3-Photo-c 8.35 25.00 50.00

PINHEAD/MARSHALL LAW: LAW IN HELL
Nov, 1993 - No. 2, 1993 ($2.95, color, mini-series)
Epic Comics (Marvel)

1,2: 1-Embossed red foil-c. 2-Embossed silver foil-c 1.20 3.00

PINK LAFFIN

Pink Panther Super Special #1, © United Artists

Pin-Up Pete #1, © TOBY

Planet Comics #30, © FH

	GD25	FN65	NM94

1922 (9x12")(Strip-r)
Whitman Publishing Co.

	GD25	FN65	NM94
...the Lighter Side of Life, ...He Tells 'Em, ...and His Family, ...Knockouts; Ray Gleason-a (All rare) each...	13.00	40.00	90.00

PINK PANTHER, THE (TV)(See The Inspector & Kite Fun Book)
April, 1971 - No. 87, 1984
Gold Key

	GD25	FN65	NM94
1-The Inspector begins	2.30	6.75	16.00
2-10	1.30	3.25	8.00
11-30: Warren Tufts-a #16-on	1.00	2.50	6.00
31-60		1.40	3.50
61-87		1.10	2.75
Mini-comic No. 1(1976)(3-1/4x6-1/2")		.80	2.00

NOTE: *Pink Panther began as a movie cartoon. (See Golden Comics Digest #38, 45 and March of Comics #370, 384, 390, 409, 418, 429, 441, 449, 461, 473, 486); #37, 72, 80-85 contain reprints.*

PINK PANTHER SUPER SPECIAL (TV)
Oct, 1993 ($2.25, color, 68 pgs.)
Harvey Comics

	GD25	FN65	NM94
V2#1-The Inspector & Wendy Witch stories also		.90	2.25

PINKY LEE (See Adventures of...)

PINKY THE EGGHEAD
1963 (Reprints from Noodnik)
I.W./Super Comics

	GD25	FN65	NM94
I.W. Reprint #1,2(nd)	.80	2.00	4.00
Super Reprint #14	.80	2.00	4.00

PINOCCHIO (See 4-Color #92, 252, 545, 1203, Mickey Mouse Mag. V5#3, Movie Comics under Wonderful Advs. of..., New Advs. of..., Thrilling Comics #2, Walt Disney Showcase, Walt Disney's..., Wonderful Advs. of..., & World's Greatest Stories #2)

PINOCCHIO
1940 (10 pages; linen-like paper)
Montgomery Ward Co. (Giveaway)

	GD25	FN65	NM94
nn	14.00	43.00	100.00

PINOCCHIO AND THE EMPEROR OF THE NIGHT (Marvel)(Value: cover or less)

PINOCCHIO LEARNS ABOUT KITES (See Kite Fun Book)

PIN-UP PETE (Also see Great Lover Romances & Monty Hall...)
1952
Toby Press

	GD25	FN65	NM94
1-Jack Sparling pin-ups	11.50	34.00	80.00

PIONEER MARSHAL (See Fawcett Movie Comics)

PIONEER PICTURE STORIES
Dec, 1941 - No. 9, Dec, 1943
Street & Smith Publications

	GD25	FN65	NM94
1-The Legless Air Ace begins	18.00	54.00	125.00
2 -True life story of Errol Flynn	10.00	30.00	65.00
3-9	8.35	25.00	50.00

PIONEER WEST ROMANCES (Firehair #1,2,7-11)
No. 3, Spring, 1950 - No. 6, Winter, 1950-51
Fiction House Magazines

	GD25	FN65	NM94
3-(52 pgs.)-Firehair continues	11.50	34.00	80.00
4-6	10.00	30.00	65.00

PIPSQUEAK (See The Adventures of...)

PIRACY
Oct-Nov, 1954 - No. 7, Oct-Nov, 1955
E. C. Comics

	GD25	FN65	NM94
1-Williamson/Torres-a	20.00	60.00	140.00
2-Williamson/Torres-a	13.00	40.00	90.00
3-7	11.00	32.00	75.00

NOTE: *Crandall a-in all; c-2-4.* ***Davis*** *a-1, 2, 6.* ***Evans*** *a-3-7; c-7.* ***Ingels*** *a-3-7.* ***Krigstein*** *a-3-5, 7; c-5, 6.* ***Wood*** *a-1, 2; c-1.*

PIRANA (See The Phantom #46 & Thrill-O-Rama #2, 3)

PIRATE CORPS, THE (Eternity)(Value: cover or less)

PIRATE OF THE GULF, THE (See Superior Stories #2)

PIRATES COMICS
Feb-Mar, 1950 - No. 4, Aug-Sept, 1950 (All 52 pgs.)
Hillman Periodicals

	GD25	FN65	NM94
1	14.00	43.00	100.00
2-Dave Berg-a	10.00	30.00	70.00
3,4-Berg-a	10.00	30.00	65.00

PIRATES OF DARK WATER, THE (TV)(Marvel)(Value: cover or less)

P.I.'S: MICHAEL MAUSER AND MS. TREE, THE (First)(Value: cover or less)

PITT, THE (Marvel)(Value: cover or less)(Also see The Draft & The War)

PITT (See Youngblood #4)
Jan, 1993 - Present ($1.95, color)
Image Comics

	GD25	FN65	NM94
1,2-Dale Keown-c/a		.80	2.00

PIUS XII MAN OF PEACE
No date (12 pgs.; 5-1/2x8-1/2") (B&W)
Catechetical Guild Giveaway

	GD25	FN65	NM94
nn	4.00	10.50	21.00

PIXIE & DIXIE & MR. JINKS (TV)(See Jinks, Pixie, and Dixie & Whitman Comic Books)
July-Sept, 1960 - Feb, 1963 (Hanna-Barbera)
Dell Publishing Co./Gold Key

	GD25	FN65	NM94
4-Color 1112	6.70	20.00	40.00
4-Color 1196,1264	5.00	15.00	30.00
01-631-207 (Dell, 7/62), 1(2/63-Gold Key)	5.00	15.00	30.00

PIXIE PUZZLE ROCKET TO ADVENTURELAND
November, 1952
Avon Periodicals

	GD25	FN65	NM94
1	10.00	30.00	60.00

PIXIES, THE (Advs. of...)(The Mighty Atom and ...#6 on)(See A-1 Comics #16)
Winter, 1946 - No. 4, Fall?, 1947; No. 5, 1948
Magazine Enterprises

	GD25	FN65	NM94
1-Mighty Atom	5.00	15.00	30.00
2-5-Mighty Atom	3.20	8.00	16.00
I.W. Reprint #1(1958), 8-(Pee-Wee Pixies), 10-I.W. on cover, Super on inside	1.20	3.00	6.00

PLANET COMICS
1/40 - No. 62, 9/49; No. 63, Wint, 1949-50; No. 64, Spring, 1950; No. 65, 1951(nd); No. 66-68, 1952(nd); No. 69, Wint, 1952-53; No. 70-72, 1953(nd); No. 73, Winter, 1953-54
Fiction House Magazines

	GD25	FN65	VF82	NM94
1-Origin Auro, Lord of Jupiter by Briefer; Flint Baker & The Red Comet begin; Eisner/Fine-c	690.00	2060.00	3800.00	5500.00

(Estimated up to 160 total copies exist, 10 in NM/Mint)

	GD25	FN65	NM94
2-Lou Fine-c (Scarce)	283.00	850.00	1900.00
3-Eisner-c	217.00	650.00	1450.00
4-Gale Allen and the Girl Squadron begins	192.00	575.00	1250.00
5,6-(Scarce): 5-Eisner/Fine-c	175.00	525.00	1150.00
7-12: 8-Robot-c. 12-The Star Pirate begins	140.00	420.00	925.00
13-14: 13-Reff Ryan begins	112.00	338.00	725.00
15-(Scarce)-Mars, God of War begins (11/42); see Jumbo Comics #31 for 1st app.	217.00	650.00	1400.00
16-20,22	104.00	310.00	685.00
21-The Lost World & Hunt Bowman begin	107.00	320.00	700.00
23-26: 26-The Space Rangers begin (9/43)	96.00	288.00	625.00
27-30	77.00	230.00	500.00

Planet of Vampires #2, © Atlas/Seaboard

Plastic Man #21 (1/50), © QUA

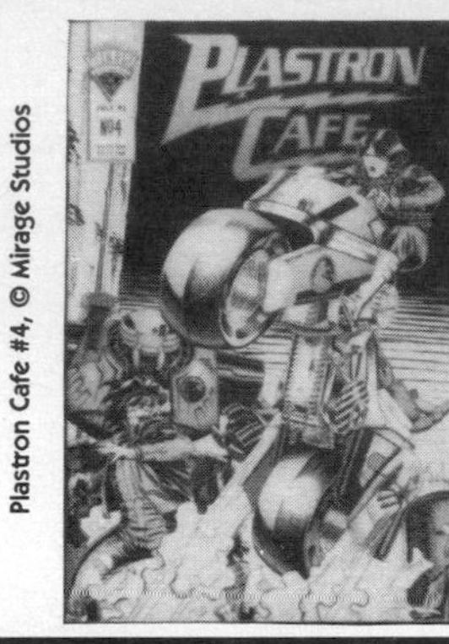

Plastron Cafe #4, © Mirage Studios

GD25 FN65 NM94

31-35: 33-Origin Star Pirates Wonder Boots, reprinted in #52. 35-Mysta of the Moon begins 64.00 192.00 425.00
36-45: 41-New origin of "Auro, Lord of Jupiter." 42-Last Gale Allen. 43-Futura begins 58.00 175.00 375.00
46-60: 48-Robot-c. 53-Used in **SOTI**, pg. 32 44.00 132.00 300.00
61-68,70: 64,70-Robot-c. 65-70-All partial-r of earlier issues 32.00 95.00 210.00
69-Used in **POP**, pgs. 101,102 32.00 95.00 210.00
71-73-No series stories 23.00 70.00 155.00
I.W. Reprint #1(nd)-r/#70; cover-r from Attack on Planet Mars 5.35 16.00 32.00
I.W. Reprint #8 (r/#72), 9-r/#73 5.35 16.00 32.00

NOTE: ***Anderson*** *a-33-38, 40-51 (Star Pirate).* ***Matt Baker*** *a-53-59 (Mysta of the Moon).* ***Celardo*** *c-12.* ***Elias*** *c-70.* ***Evans*** *a-46-49 (Auro, Lord of Jupiter), 50-64 (Lost World).* ***Fine*** *c-2, 5.* ***Hopper*** *a-31, 35 (Gale Allen), 48, 49 (Mysta of the Moon).* ***Ingels*** *a-24-31 (Lost World), 56-61 (Auro, Lord of Jupiter).* ***Lubbers*** *a-44, 46 (Space Rangers); c-40, 41.* ***Renee*** *a-40 (Lost World); c-33, 35, 39.* ***Tuska*** *a-30 (Star Pirate).* ***M. Whitman*** *a-50-52 (Mysta of the Moon), 53-56 (Star Pirate); c-71-73.* ***Starr*** *a-59.* ***Zolnerwich*** *c-10. 13-25. Bondage c-53.*

PLANET COMICS
Apr, 1988 - No. 3? (2.00, color; B&W #3)
Blackthorne Publishing

1-3: New stories. 1-Dave Stevens-c .80 2.00

PLANET OF THE APES (Magazine) (Also see Adventures on the... & Power Record Comics)
Aug, 1974 - No. 29, Feb, 1977 (B&W) (Based on movies)
Marvel Comics Group

1-Ploog-a 1.00 2.50 5.50
2-Ploog-a 1.10 2.75
3-10 .70 1.80
11-20 1.50
21-29 1.00

NOTE: ***Alcala*** *a-7-11, 17-22, 24.* ***Ploog*** *a-1-4, 6, 8, 11, 13, 14, 19.* ***Sutton*** *a-11, 12, 15, 17, 19, 20, 23, 24, 29.* ***Tuska*** *a-1-6.*

PLANET OF THE APES
Apr, 1990 - No. 24, 1992 ($2.50, B&W)
Adventure Comics

1-New movie tie-in; comes w/outer-c(3 colors) 1.00 2.50 5.50
1-Limited serial numbered edition ($5.00) 1.00 2.00 5.00
1-2nd printing (no outer-c) 1.00 2.50
2-24 1.00 2.50
Annual 1 ($3.50) 1.40 3.50

PLANET OF VAMPIRES
Feb, 1975 - No. 3, July, 1975
Seaboard Publications (Atlas)

1-Neal Adams-c(i); 1st Broderick c/a(p) 1.50
2,3: 2-Neal Adams-c. 3-Heath-c/a 1.00

PLANET TERRY (Marvel)(Value: cover or less)

PLASM (See Warriors of Plasm)
June, 1993 (Color)
Defiant Comics

0-Came bound into Diamond Previews V3#6 (6/93); price is for complete Previews with comic still attached 1.00 2.50 5.50
0-Comic only removed from Previews 1.60 4.00

PLASMER
Nov, 1993 - No. 4, Feb, 1994 ($1.95, color, mini-series)
Marvel Comics UK

1-($2.50)-Polybagged w/4 trading cards 1.00 2.50
2-4 .80 2.00

PLASTIC FORKS (Marvel)(Value: cover or less)

PLASTIC MAN (Also see Police Comics & Smash Comics #17)
Sum, 1943 - No. 64, Nov, 1956
Vital Publ. No. 1,2/Quality Comics No. 3 on

GD25 FN65 NM94

nn(#1)-'In The Game of Death;' Jack Cole-c/a begins; ends-#64? 215.00 645.00 1500.00
nn(#2, 2/44)-'The Gay Nineties Nightmare' 117.00 350.00 800.00
3 (Spr, '46) 75.00 225.00 500.00
4 (Sum, '46) 62.00 188.00 425.00
5 (Aut, '46) 54.00 162.00 365.00
6-10 42.00 125.00 275.00
11-20 37.00 110.00 250.00
21-30: 26-Last non-r issue? 30.00 90.00 200.00
31-40: 40-Used in POP, pg. 91 23.00 70.00 155.00
41-64: 53-Last precode issue. 54-Robot-c 18.00 55.00 125.00
Super Reprint 11,16,18: 11('63)-r/#16. 16-r/#18; Cole-a. 18('64)-Spirit-r by Eisner from Police #95 5.00 15.00 30.00

NOTE: ***Cole*** *r-44, 49, 56, 58, 59 at least.* ***Cuidera*** *c-32-64i.*

PLASTIC MAN (See DC Special #15 & House of Mystery #160)
11-12/66 - No. 10, 5-6/68; V4#11, 2-3/76 - No. 20, 10-11/77
National Periodical Publications/DC Comics

1-Real 1st app. Silver Age Plastic Man (House of Mystery #160 is actually tryout); Gil Kane-c/a; 12 cent issues begin 6.50 20.00 46.00
2-5: 4-Infantino-c; Mortimer-a 3.20 9.00 21.00
6-10('68): 7-G.A. Plastic Man & Woozy Winks (1st S.A. app.) app.; origin retold. 10-Sparling-a; last 12 cent issue 1.65 4.70 11.00
V4#11('76)-20: 11-20-Fraden-p. 17-Origin retold 1.20 3.00

PLASTIC MAN (DC, 1988-89)(Value: cover or less)

PLASTRON CAFE
Dec, 1992 - Present ($2.25, B&W)
Mirage Studios

1-4: 1-Teenage Mutant Ninja Turtles app.; Kelly Freas-c. 2-Hildebrandt painted-c. 4-Spaced & Alien Fire stories .90 2.25

PLAYFUL LITTLE AUDREY (TV)(Also see Little Audrey #25)
6/57 - No. 110, 11/73; No. 111, 8/74 - No. 121, 4/76
Harvey Publications

1 16.00 48.00 110.00
2 9.15 27.50 55.00
3-5 7.00 21.00 42.00
6-10 4.70 14.00 28.00
11-20 2.80 7.00 14.00
21-40 2.00 5.00 10.00
41-60 1.60 4.00 8.00
61-80 1.00 2.50 6.00
81-99 1.60 4.00
100: 52 pg. Giant 1.20 3.00 7.00
101-103: 52 pg. Giants 1.00 2.50 6.00
104-121 1.20 3.00

PLAYFUL LITTLE AUDREY IN 3-D (See Blackthorne 3-D Series #66)

PLOP! (Also see The Best of DC #60)
Sept-Oct, 1973 - No. 24, Nov-Dec, 1976
National Periodical Publications

1-20: Sergio Aragones-a. 1,5-Wrightson-a 1.80 4.50
21,22,24 (52 pgs.) 1.60 4.00
23-No Aragones-a (52 pgs.) 1.50

NOTE: ***Alcala*** *a-1-3.* ***Anderson*** *a-5.* ***Aragones*** *a-1-22, 24.* ***Ditko*** *a-16p.* ***Evans*** *a-1.* ***Mayer*** *a-1.* ***Orlando*** *a-21, 22; c-21.* ***Sekowsky*** *a-5, 6p.* ***Toth*** *a-11.* ***Wolverton*** *r-4, 22, 23(1 pg.); c(r)-1-12, 14, 17, 18.* ***Wood*** *a-14, 16i, 18-24; c-13, 15, 16, 19.*

PLUTO (See Cheerios Premiums, Four Color #537, Mickey Mouse Magazine, Walt Disney Showcase #4, 7, 13, 20, 23, 33 & Wheaties)
No. 7, 1942; No. 429, 10/52 - No. 1248, 11-1/61-62 (Walt Disney)
Dell Publishing Co.

Large Feature Comic 7(1942) 65.00 195.00 455.00
4-Color 429,509 5.00 15.00 30.00
4-Color 595,654 4.00 11.00 22.00
4-Color 736,853,941,1039,1143,1248 3.60 9.00 18.00

POCAHONTAS

Police Academy #6, © Warner Bros.

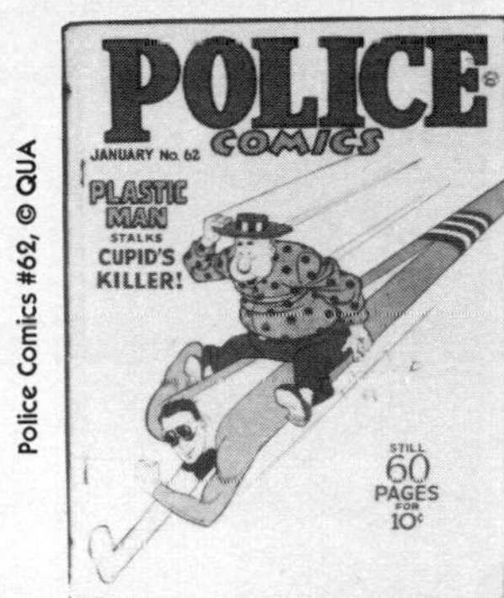

Police Comics #62, © QUA

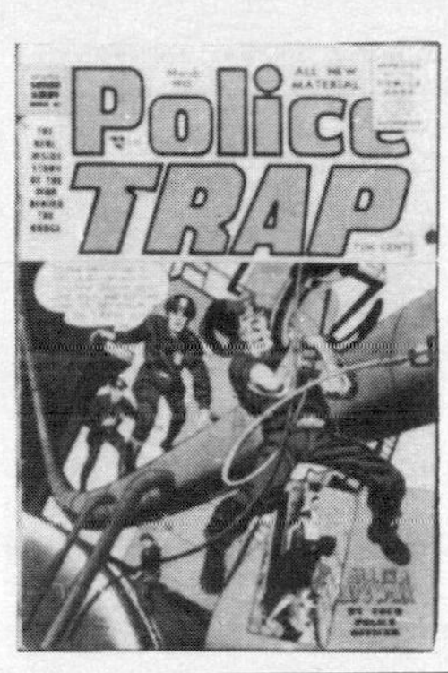

Police Trap #4, © PRIZE

GD25 FN65 NM94

1941 - No. 2, 1942
Pocahontas Fuel Company

	GD25	FN65	NM94
nn(#1), 2	10.00	30.00	60.00

POCKET COMICS (Also see Double Up)
Aug, 1941 - No. 4, Jan, 1942 (Pocket size; 100 pgs.)
Harvey Publications (1st Harvey comic)

	GD25	FN65	NM94
1-Origin & 1st app. The Black Cat, Cadet Blakey the Spirit of '76, The Red Blazer, The Phantom, Sphinx, & The Zebra; Phantom Ranger, British Agent #99, Spin Hawkins, Satan, Lord of Evil begin (1st app. of each)	61.00	182.00	400.00
2: Simon-c/a in #1-3; Black Cat on-c #2-4	40.00	120.00	265.00
3,4	30.00	90.00	200.00

POGO PARADE (See Dell Giants)

POGO POSSUM (Also see Animal Comics & Special Delivery)
No. 105, 4/46 - No. 148, 5/47; 10-12/49 - No. 16, 4-6/54
Dell Publishing Co.

	GD25	FN65	NM94
4-Color 105(1946)-Kelly-c/a	68.00	205.00	475.00
4-Color 148-Kelly-c/a	56.00	170.00	395.00
1-(10-12/49)-Kelly-c/a in all	52.00	155.00	365.00
2	28.00	85.00	195.00
3-5	21.00	63.00	145.00
6-10: 10-Infinity-c	17.00	52.00	120.00
11-16: 11-X-mas-c	14.00	43.00	100.00

NOTE: *#1-4, 9-13: 52 pgs.; #5-8, 14-16: 36 pgs.*

POINT BLANK (Eclipse)(Value: cover or less)

POLICE ACADEMY (TV)(Marvel)(Value: cover or less)

POLICE ACTION
Jan, 1954 - No. 7, Nov, 1954
Atlas News Co.

	GD25	FN65	NM94
1-Violent-a by Robert Q. Sale	10.00	30.00	70.00
2	5.85	17.50	35.00
3-7: 7-Powell-a	5.00	15.00	30.00

NOTE: ***Ayers** a-4, 5. **Colan** a-1. **Forte** a-1, 2. **Mort Lawrence** a-5. **Maneely** a-3; c-1, 5. **Reinman** a-6, 7.*

POLICE ACTION
Feb, 1975 - No. 3, June, 1975
Atlas/Seaboard Publ.

	GD25	FN65	NM94
1-3: 1-Lomax, N.Y.P.D., Luke Malone begin; McWilliams-a. 2-Origin Luke Malone, Manhunter			1.00

NOTE: ***Ploog** art in all. **Sekowsky/McWilliams** a-1-3. **Thorne** c-3.*

POLICE AGAINST CRIME
April, 1954 - No. 9, Aug, 1955
Premiere Magazines

	GD25	FN65	NM94
1-Disbrow-a; extreme violence (man's face slashed with knife); Hollingsworth-a	11.50	34.00	80.00
2-Hollingsworth-a	7.50	22.50	45.00
3-9	5.00	15.00	35.00

POLICE BADGE #479 (Formerly Spy Thrillers #1-4)
No. 5, Sept, 1955
Atlas Comics (PrPI)

	GD25	FN65	NM94
5-Maneely-c	5.85	17.50	35.00

POLICE CASE BOOK (See Giant Comics Editions)

POLICE CASES (See Authentic... & Record Book of...)

POLICE COMICS
Aug, 1941 - No. 127, Oct, 1953
Quality Comics Group (Comic Magazines)

	GD25	FN65	NM94
1-Origin/1st app. Plastic Man by Jack Cole (r-in DC Special #15), The Human Bomb by Gustavson, & No. 711; intro. Chic Carter by Eisner, The Firebrand by Reed Crandall, The Mouthpiece by Guardineer, Phantom Lady, & The Sword; Firebrand-c 1-4	417.00	1250.00	2800.00
2-Plastic Man smuggles opium	200.00	600.00	1400.00
3	142.00	425.00	950.00
4	133.00	400.00	900.00
5-Plastic Man-c begin; Plastic Man forced to smoke marijuana; Plastic Man covers begin, end #102	125.00	375.00	850.00
6,7	115.00	345.00	800.00
8-Manhunter begins (origin/1st app.) (3/42)	142.00	425.00	950.00
9,10	108.00	325.00	700.00
11-The Spirit strip reprints begin by Eisner (origin-strip #1); 1st comic book app. The Spirit & 1st cover app. (9/42)	167.00	500.00	1100.00
12-Intro. Ebony	104.00	312.00	700.00
13-Intro. Woozy Winks; last Firebrand	104.00	312.00	700.00
14-19: 15-Last No. 711; Destiny begins	69.00	208.00	450.00
20-The Raven x-over in Phantom Lady; features Jack Cole himself	69.00	208.00	450.00
21,22: 21-Raven & Spider Widow x-over in Phantom Lady (cameo in #22)	54.00	162.00	365.00
23-30: 23-Last Phantom Lady. 24-26-Flatfoot Burns by Kurtzman in all	47.00	140.00	300.00
31-41: 37-1st app. Candy by Sahle & begins (12/44). 41-Last Spirit-r by Eisner	33.00	100.00	225.00
42,43-Spirit-r by Eisner/Fine	29.00	88.00	200.00
44-Fine Spirit-r begin, end #88,90,92	25.00	75.00	175.00
45-50: 50-(#50 on-c, #49 on inside, 1/46)	25.00	75.00	175.00
51-60: 58-Last Human Bomb	20.00	60.00	140.00
61-88: 63-(Some issues have #65 printed on cover, but #63 on inside) Kurtzman-a, 6pgs.	17.00	50.00	110.00
89,91,93-No Spirit stories	15.00	45.00	100.00
90,92-Spirit by Fine	18.00	55.00	120.00
94-99,101,102: Spirit by Eisner in all; 101-Last Manhunter. 102-Last Spirit & Plastic Man by Jack Cole	23.00	70.00	165.00
100	27.00	80.00	180.00
103-Content change to crime; Ken Shannon & T-Man begin (1st app. of each, 12/50)	13.00	40.00	90.00
104-111,114-127: Crandall-a most issues (not in 104,122,125-127). 109-Atomic bomb story	10.00	30.00	65.00
112-Crandall-a	10.00	30.00	65.00
113-Crandall-c/a(2), 9 pgs. each	10.00	30.00	70.00

NOTE: *Most Spirit stories signed by Eisner are not by him; all are reprints. **Cole** c-17, 19-21, 24-26, 28-31, 36-38, 40-42, 45-48, 65-68, 69, 73, 75. **Crandall** Firebrand-1-8. Spirit by **Eisner** 1-41, 94-102; by **Eisner/Fine**-42, 43; by **Fine**-44-88, 90, 92, 103, 109. **Al Bryant** c-33, 34. **Cole** c-17-32, 35-102(most). **Crandall** c-13, 14. **Crandall/Cuidera** c-105-127. **Eisner** c-4i. **Gill Fox** c-1-3, 4p, 5-12, 15. Bondage c-103, 109, 125.*

POLICE LINE-UP
Aug, 1951 - No. 4, July, 1952 (Painted-c #1-3)
Avon Periodicals/Realistic Comics #3,4

	GD25	FN65	NM94
1-Wood-a, 1 pg. plus part-c; spanking panel-r/Saint #5	22.00	65.00	150.00
2-Classic story "The Religious Murder Cult," drugs, perversion; r/Saint #5; c-r/Avon paperback #329	16.00	50.00	115.00
3-Kubert-a(r)/part-c, Kinstler-a	11.00	32.00	75.00
4-Kinstler-a	11.00	32.00	75.00

POLICE THRILLS
1954
Ajax/Farrell Publications

	GD25	FN65	NM94
1-Exist?	5.85	17.50	35.00

POLICE TRAP (Public Defender In Action #7 on)
8-9/54 - No. 4, 2-3/55; No. 5, 7/55 - No. 6, 9/55
Mainline (Prize) No. 1-4/Charlton No. 5,6

	GD25	FN65	NM94
1-S&K covers-all issues	12.00	36.00	85.00
2-4	8.35	25.00	50.00
5,6-S&K-c/a	11.50	34.00	80.00

POLICE TRAP
No. 11, 1963; No. 16-18, 1964
Super Comics

Polly Pigtales #30, © PMI

Popeye #78, © KING

Popeye Summer Special #1, © KING

GD25 FN65 NM94

Reprint #11,16-18: 11-r/Police Trap #3. 16-r/Justice Traps the Guilty #? 17-r/Inside Crime #3 — 1.20 3.00 6.00

POLL PARROT
Poll Parrot Shoe Store/International Shoe
1950 - No. 4, 1951; No. 2, 1959 - No. 16, 1962
K. K. Publications (Giveaway)

1 ('50)-Howdy Doody; small size — 11.50 34.00 80.00
2-4('51)-Howdy Doody — 10.00 30.00 60.00
2('59)-16('62): 2-The Secret of Crumbley Castle. 5-Bandit Busters. 7-The Make-Believe Mummy. 8-Mixed Up Mission('60). 10-The Frightful Flight. 11-Showdown at Sunup. 12-Maniac at Mubu Island. 13-...and the Runaway Genie. 14-Bully for You. 15-Trapped In Tall Timber. 16-...& the Rajah's Ruby('62) — 3.00 7.50 15.00

POLLY & HER PALS (See Comic Monthly #1)

POLLYANNA (See 4-Color #1129)

POLLY PIGTAILS (Girls' Fun & Fashion Magazine #44 on)
Jan, 1946 - V4#43, Oct-Nov, 1949
Parents' Magazine Institute/Polly Pigtails

1-Infinity-c; photo-c — 8.35 25.00 50.00
2-Photo-c — 4.20 12.50 25.00
3-5: 3,4-Photo-c — 3.60 9.00 18.00
6-10: 7-Photo-c — 2.80 7.00 14.00
11-30: 22-Photo-c — 2.00 5.00 10.00
31-43 — 1.60 4.00 8.00

PONY EXPRESS (See Four Color #942)

PONYTAIL
7-9/62 - No. 12, 10-12/65; No. 13, 11/69 - No. 20, 1/71
Dell Publishing Co./Charlton No. 13 on

12-641-209(#1) — 2.00 5.00 10.00
2-12 — 1.20 3.00 6.00
13-20 — .80 2.00 4.00

POP COMICS (7 cents)
1955 (36 pgs.; 5x7"; in color)
Modern Store Publ.

1-Funny animal — .80 2.00 4.00

POPEYE (See Comic Album #7, 11, 15, Comics Reading Libraries, Eat Right to Work and Win, Giant Comic Album, King Comics, Kite Fun Book, Magic Comics, March of Comics #37, 52, 66, 80, 96, 117, 134, 148, 157, 169, 194, 246, 264, 274, 294, 453, 465, 477 & Wow Comics, 1st series)

POPEYE (See Thimble Theatre)
1935 (25 cents; 52 pgs.; B&W) (By Segar)
David McKay Publications

1-Daily strip serial reprints-"The Gold Mine Thieves" — 57.00 170.00 400.00
2-Daily strip-r — 50.00 150.00 350.00
NOTE: *Popeye first entered Thimble Theatre in 1929.*

POPEYE
1937 - 1939 (All by Segar)
David McKay Publications

Feature Books nn (100 pgs.) (Very Rare) — 585.00 1750.00 3500.00
Feature Books 2 (52 pgs.) — 64.00 195.00 450.00
Feature Books 3 (100 pgs.)-r/nn issue with a new-c — 57.00 170.00 400.00
Feature Books 5,10 (76 pgs.) — 50.00 150.00 350.00
Feature Books 14 (76 pgs.) (Scarce) — 64.00 195.00 450.00

POPEYE (Strip reprints through 4-Color #70)
1941 - 1947; #1, 2-4/48 - #65, 7-9/62; #66, 10/62 - #80, 5/66; #81, 8/66 - #92, 12/67; #94, 2/69 - #138, 1/77; #139, 5/78 - #171, 7/84 (no #93,160,161)
Dell #1-65/Gold Key #66-80/King #81-92/Charlton #94-138/Gold Key #139-155/Whitman #156 on

Large Feature Comic 24('41)-Half by Segar — 50.00 150.00 350.00
4-Color 25('41)-by Segar — 57.00 170.00 400.00

GD25 FN65 NM94

Large Feature Comic 10('43) — 42.00 125.00 290.00
4-Color 17('43)-by Segar — 46.00 135.00 320.00
4-Color 26('43)-by Segar — 41.00 125.00 290.00
4-Color 43('44) — 30.00 90.00 210.00
4-Color 70('45)-Title: ...& Wimpy — 25.00 75.00 175.00
4-Color 113('46-original strips begin),127,145('47),168 — 13.00 40.00 90.00
1(2-4/48)(Dell) — 30.00 90.00 210.00
2 — 16.00 48.00 110.00
3-10: 5-Popeye on moon w/rocket-c — 13.00 40.00 90.00
11-20 — 11.50 34.00 80.00
21-40 — 10.00 30.00 60.00
41-45,47-50 — 6.70 20.00 40.00
46-Origin Swee' Pee — 10.00 30.00 60.00
51-60 — 5.85 17.50 35.00
61-65 (Last Dell issue) — 4.70 14.00 28.00
66,67-Both 84 pgs. (Gold Key) — 7.50 22.50 45.00
68-80 — 3.60 9.00 18.00
81-92,94-100 — 2.40 6.00 12.00
101-130 — 1.30 3.25 8.00
131-159,162-171: 144-50th Anniversary issue — 1.00 2.50 6.00
Bold Detergent giveaway (Same as regular issue #94) — 1.60 4.00
NOTE: *Reprints-#145, 147, 149, 151, 153, 155, 157, 163-68(1/3), 170.*

POPEYE
1972 - 1974 (36 pgs. in color)
Charlton (King Features) (Giveaway)

E-1 to E-15 (Educational comics) — .80 2.00
nn-Popeye Gettin' Better Grades-4 pgs. used as intro. to above giveaways (in color) — .80 2.00

POPEYE CARTOON BOOK
1934 (40 pgs. with cover)(8-1/2x13")(cardboard covers)
The Saalfield Publ. Co.

2095-(Rare)-1933 strip reprints in color by Segar; each page contains a vertical half of a Sunday strip, so the continuity reads row by row completely across each double page spread. If each page is read by itself, the continuity makes no sense. Each double page spread reprints one complete Sunday page (from 1933) — 108.00 325.00 650.00
12 Page Version — 63.00 188.00 375.00

POPEYE SPECIAL (Ocean)(Value: cover or less)

POPEYE SUMMER SPECIAL
Oct, 1993 ($2.25, color, 68 pgs.)
Harvey Comics

V2#1-Sagendorf-r & others — .90 2.25

POPPLES (TV, movie)(Marvel)(Value: cover or less)

POPPO OF THE POPCORN THEATRE
10/29/55 - No. 13, 1956 (Published weekly)
Fuller Publishing Co. (Publishers Weekly)

1 — 5.85 17.50 35.00
2-5 — 4.00 11.00 22.00
6-13 — 3.20 8.00 16.00
NOTE: *By **Charles Biro**. 10 cent cover, given away by supermarkets such as IGA.*

POP-POP COMICS
No date (Circa 1945) (52 pgs.)
R. B. Leffingwell Co.

1-Funny animal — 6.70 20.00 40.00

POPSICLE PETE FUN BOOK (See All-American Comics #6)
1947, 1948
Joe Lowe Corp.

nn-36 pgs. in color; Sammy 'n' Claras, The King Who Couldn't Sleep & Popsicle Pete stories, games, cut-outs — 9.15 27.50 55.00
Adventure Book ('48)-Has Classics ad with checklist to HRN #343 (Great Expectations #43) — 7.50 22.50 45.00

Popular Comics #33, © DELL

Popular Teen-Agers #6, © STAR

Power Comics #2, © Eclipse

GD25 FN65 NM94 GD25 FN65 NM94

POPULAR COMICS
Feb, 1936 - No. 145, July-Sept, 1948
Dell Publishing Co.

	GD25	FN65	VF82
1-Dick Tracy (1st comic book app.), Little Orphan Annie, Terry & the Pirates, Gasoline Alley, Don Winslow (1st app.), Harold Teen, Little Joe, Skippy, Moon Mullins, Mutt & Jeff, Tailspin Tommy, Smitty, Smokey Stover, Winnie Winkle & The Gumps begin (all strip-r)	380.00	1140.00	1900.00
(Estimated up to 90 total copies exist, 4 in NM/Mint)			
2	105.00	315.00	700.00
3	88.00	262.00	575.00
4,5: 5-Tom Mix begins	67.00	200.00	450.00
6-10: 8,9-Scribbly, Reglar Fellers app.	54.00	162.00	350.00
	GD25	FN65	NM94
11-20: 12-Xmas-c	44.00	132.00	300.00
21-27: 27-Last Terry & the Pirates, Little Orphan Annie, & Dick Tracy	32.00	95.00	220.00
28-37: 28-Gene Autry app. 31,32-Tim McCoy app. 35-Christmas-c; Tex Ritter app.	27.00	80.00	185.00
38-43-Tarzan in text only. 38-(4/39)-Gang Busters (radio, 2nd app.) & Zane Grey's Tex Thorne begins? 43-1st non-funny-c?	30.00	90.00	210.00
44,45: 45-Hurricane Kid-c	22.00	65.00	145.00
46-Origin/1st app. Martan, the Marvel Man(12/39)	30.00	90.00	210.00
47-50	20.00	60.00	135.00
51-Origin The Voice (The Invisible Detective) strip begins (5/40)	22.00	65.00	150.00
52-59: 55-End of World story	17.00	50.00	110.00
60-Origin/1st app. Professor Supermind and Son (2/41)	17.50	52.00	115.00
61-71: 63-Smilin' Jack begins	14.00	42.00	90.00
72-The Owl & Terry & the Pirates begin (2/42); Smokey Stover reprints begin	25.00	75.00	175.00
73-75	17.50	52.00	115.00
76-78-Capt. Midnight in all	22.00	65.00	150.00
79-85-Last Owl	15.00	45.00	100.00
86-99: 98-Felix the Cat, Smokey Stover-r begin	12.00	35.00	80.00
100	13.00	40.00	90.00
101-130	8.35	25.00	50.00
131-145: 142-Last Terry & the Pirates	7.50	22.50	45.00

NOTE: *Martan, the Marvel Man c-47-49, 52, 57-59. Professor Supermind c-60-63, 64(1/2), 65, 66. The Voice c-53.*

POPULAR FAIRY TALES (See March of Comics #6, 18)

POPULAR ROMANCE
No. 5, Dec, 1949 - No. 29, July, 1954
Better-Standard Publications

	GD25	FN65	NM94
5	5.35	16.00	32.00
6-9: 7-Palais-a; lingerie panels	4.00	10.00	20.00
10-Wood-a, 2 pgs.	5.35	16.00	32.00
11,12,14-16,18-21,28,29	3.20	8.00	16.00
13,17-Severin/Elder-a, 3&8 pgs.	4.00	10.00	20.00
22-27-Toth-a	6.70	20.00	40.00

NOTE: *All have photo-c.* ***Tuska*** *art in most issues.*

POPULAR TEEN-AGERS (Secrets of Love) (School Day Romances #1-4)
No. 5, Sept, 1950 - No. 23, Nov, 1954
Star Publications

	GD25	FN65	NM94
5-Toni Gay, Honey Bunn, etc.; L. B. Cole-c	14.00	43.00	100.00
6-8 (7/51)-Toni Gay, Honey Bunn, etc.; all have L. B. Cole-c; 6-Negligee panels	11.50	34.00	80.00
9-(...Romances; 1st romance issue, 10/51)	6.70	20.00	40.00
10-(...Secrets of Love)	6.70	20.00	40.00
11,16,18,19,22,23	5.35	16.00	32.00
12,13,17,20,21-Disbrow-a	5.85	17.50	35.00
14-Harrison/Wood-a; 2 spanking scenes	12.00	36.00	85.00
15-Wood?, Disbrow-a	10.00	30.00	65.00
Accepted Reprint 5,6 (nd); L.B. Cole-c	3.60	9.00	18.00

NOTE: *All have* ***L. B. Cole*** *covers.*

PORE LI'L MOSE
1902 (30 pgs.; 10-1/2x15"; in full color)
New York Herald Publ. by Grand Union Tea
Cupples & Leon Co.

	GD25	FN65	NM94
nn-By R. F. Outcault; 1 pg. strips about early Negroes	64.00	195.00	450.00

PORKY PIG (See Bugs Bunny &..., Kite Fun Book, March of Comics #42, 57, 71, 89, 99, 113, 130, 143, 164, 175, 192, 209, 218, 367, and Super Book #6, 18, 30)

PORKY PIG (...& Bugs Bunny #40-69)
No. 16, 1942 - No. 81, Mar-Apr, 1962; Jan, 1965 - No. 109, July, 1984
Dell Publishing Co./Gold Key No. 1-93/Whitman No. 94 on

	GD25	FN65	NM94
4-Color 16(#1, 1942)	50.00	150.00	350.00
4-Color 48(1944)-Carl Barks-a	72.00	215.00	500.00
4-Color 78(1945)	22.00	65.00	150.00
4-Color 112(7/46)	13.00	40.00	90.00
4-Color 156,182,191('49)	10.00	30.00	60.00
4-Color 226,241('49),260,271,277,284,295	7.50	22.50	45.00
4-Color 303,311,322,330	5.00	15.00	30.00
4-Color 342,351,360,370,385,399,410,426	4.00	11.00	22.00
25 (11-12/52)-30	2.80	7.00	14.00
31-50	1.60	4.00	8.00
51-81(3-4/62)	1.00	2.00	5.00
1(1/65-Gold Key)(2nd Series)	2.00	5.00	10.00
2,4,5-r/4-Color 226,284 & 271 in that order	1.00	2.00	5.00
3,6-10		1.20	3.00
11-50			1.50
51-109			1.00

NOTE: *Reprints-#1-8, 9-35(2/3); 36-46, 58, 67, 69-74, 76, 78, 102-109(1/3-1/2).*

PORKY'S BOOK OF TRICKS
1942 (48 pages) (8-1/2x5-1/2")
K. K. Publications (Giveaway)

	GD25	FN65	NM94
nn-7 pg. comic story, text stories, plus games & puzzles	30.00	90.00	210.00

PORTIA PRINZ OF THE GLAMAZONS (Eclipse)(Value: cover or less)

POST GAZETTE (See Meet the New...)

POWDER RIVER RUSTLERS (See Fawcett Movie Comics)

POWER COMICS
1944 - No. 4, 1945
Holyoke Publ. Co./Narrative Publ.

	GD25	FN65	NM94
1-L. B. Cole-c	50.00	150.00	340.00
2-Hitler, Hirohito-c	50.00	150.00	340.00
3-Classic L.B. Cole-c; Dr. Mephisto begins?	50.00	150.00	340.00
4-L.B. Cole-c; Miss Espionage app. #3,4; Leav-a	42.00	125.00	275.00

POWER COMICS
1977 - No. 5, Dec, 1977 (B&W)
Power Comics Co.

	GD25	FN65	NM94
1- "A Boy And His Aardvark" by Dave Sim; first Dave Sim aardvark (not Cerebus)	1.20	3.00	7.50
1-Reprint (3/77, black-c)		1.70	4.25
2-Cobalt Blue by Gustovich		.90	2.25
3-5: 3-Nightwitch. 4-Northern Light. 5-Bluebird		.90	2.25

POWER COMICS (Eclipse)(Value: cover or less)

POWER FACTOR (Wonder & Innovation)(Value: cover or less)

POWER GIRL (DC)(Value: cover or less)(See All-Star 58, Infinity, Inc., Showcase #97-99)

POWERHOUSE PEPPER COMICS (See Gay Comics, Joker Comics & Tessie the Typist)
No. 1, 1943; No. 2, May, 1948 - No. 5, Nov, 1948
Marvel Comics (20CC)

	GD25	FN65	NM94
1-(60 pgs.)-Wolverton-a in all; c-2,3	86.00	260.00	600.00
2	50.00	150.00	350.00
3,4	46.00	140.00	325.00

Power of the Atom #2, © DC

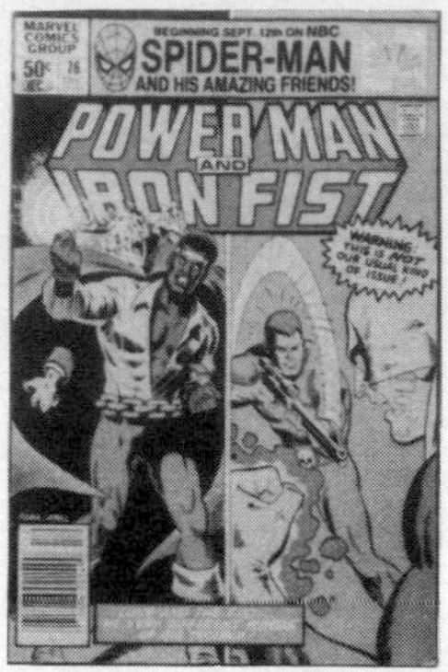

Power Man #76, © MEG

Predator vs Magnus: Robot Fighter #1, © 20th Century Fox/Western Publ.

GD25 FN65 NM94

5-(Scarce) 54.00 160.00 375.00

POWER LINE (Marvel)(Value: cover or less)

POWER LORDS (DC)(Value: cover or less)

POWER MAN (Formerly Hero for Hire; ...& Iron Fist #68 on; see Cage & Giant-Size...)
No. 17, Feb, 1974 - No. 125, Sept, 1986
Marvel Comics Group

17-Luke Cage continues; Iron Man app. 1.65 4.70 11.00
18-20: 18-Last 20 cent issue 1.00 2.50 5.50
21-31: 31-Part Neal Adams-i. 34-Last 25 cents 1.50 3.75
32-48: 36-r/Hero For Hire #12. 41-1st app. Thunderbolt. 45-Starlin-c. 48-Byrne-a; Power Man/Iron Fist 1st meet 1.00 2.50
49,50-Byrne-a(p); 50-Iron Fist joins Cage 1.00 2.50
51-56,58-60: 58-Intro El Aguila 1.50
57-New X-Men app. (6/79) 1.50 3.75
61-65,67-77,79-83,85-124: 75-Double size. 77-Daredevil app. 87-Moon Knight app. 90-Unus app. 109-The Reaper app. 100-Double size; origin K'un L'un 1.00
66-2nd app. Sabretooth (see Iron Fist #14) 3.20 8.00 20.00
78-3rd app. Sabretooth (cameo under cloak) 1.50 3.75 9.00
84-4th app. Sabretooth 1.50 3.75 9.00
125-Double size; death of Iron Fist .75 1.90
Annual 1(1976)-Punisher cameo in flashback 1.20 3.00
NOTE: ***Austin*** *c-102i.* ***Byrne*** *a-48-50; c-102, 104, 106, 107, 112-116.* ***Kane*** *c(p)-24, 25, 28, 48.* ***Miller*** *a-68, 76(2pgs.); c-66-68, 70-74, 80i.* ***Mooney*** *a-38i, 53i, 55i.* ***Nebres*** *a-76p.* ***Nino*** *a-42i, 43i.* ***Perez*** *a-27.* ***B. Smith*** *a-47i.* ***Tuska*** *a(p)-17, 20, 24, 26, 28, 29, 36, 47. Painted c-75, 100.*

POWER OF STRONGMAN, THE (AC)(Value: cover or less)

POWER OF THE ATOM (DC)(Value: cover or less)(See Secret Origins #29)

POWER PACHYDERMS (Marvel)(Value: cover or less)

POWER PACK
Aug, 1984 - No. 62, Feb, 1991
Marvel Comics Group

1-($1.00, 52 pgs.)-Origin & 1st app. Power Pack .80 2.00
2-18,20-26,28,30-45,47-62 1.00
19-Dbl. size; Cloak & Dagger, Wolverine app. 1.00 2.50 5.50
27-Mutant massacre; Wolverine & Sabretooth app. 1.00 2.50 6.00
29-Spider-Man & Hobgoblin app. .75 1.90
46-Punisher app. 1.20 3.00
...Holiday Special 1 (2/92, $2.25, 68 pgs.) 1.00
NOTE: ***Austin*** *scripts-53.* ***Morrow*** *a-51.* ***Spiegle*** *a-55i.* ***Williamson*** *a(i)-43, 50, 52.*

POWER RECORD COMICS
1974 - 1978 ($1.49, 7x10" comics, 20 pgs. with 45 R.P.M. record)
Marvel Comics/Power Records

PR10-Spider-Man-r/from #124,125; Man-Wolf app. PR11-Hulk-r. PR12-Captain America-r/#168. PR13-Fantastic Four-r/#126. PR14-Frankenstein-Ploog-r/#1. PR15-Tomb of Dracula-Colan-r/#2. PR16-Man-Thing-Ploog-r/#5. PR17-Werewolf By Night-Ploog-r/Marvel Spotlight #2. PR18-Planet of the Apes-r. PR19-Escape From the Planet of the Apes-r. PR20-Beneath the Planet of the Apes-r. PR21-Battle for the Planet of the Apes-r. PR24-Spider-Man II-New-a begins. PR25-Star Trek "Passage to Moauv." PR26-Star Trek "Crier in Emptiness." PR27-Batman "Stacked Cards;" N. Adams-a(p). PR28-Superman "Alien Creatures." PR29-Space: 1999 "Breakaway." PR30-Batman; N. Adams-r/Det.(7 pgs.). PR31-Conan-N. Adams-a; reprinted in Conan #116. PR32-Space: 1999 "Return to the Beginning." PR33-Superman-G.A. origin, Buckler-a(p). PR34-Superman. PR35-Wonder Woman-Buckler-a(p). PR36-Holo-Man. PR37-Robin Hood. PR39-Huckleberry Finn. PR40-Davy Crockett. PR41-Robinson Crusoe. PR42-20,000 Leagues Under the Sea. PR47-Little Women
With record; each... 1.65 4.00 10.00

POW MAGAZINE (Bob Sproul's) (Satire Magazine)
Aug, 1966 - No. 3, Feb, 1967 (30 cents)
Humor-Vision

1-3: 2-Jones-a. 3-Wrightson-a 4.00 10.00 20.00

PRAIRIE MOON AND OTHER STORIES (Dark Horse)(Value: cover or less)

PREDATOR (Also see Aliens Vs. Predator, Batman vs. ... & Dark Horse Presents)
June, 1989 - No. 4, Mar, 1990 ($2.25, color, mini-series)
Dark Horse Comics

GD25 FN65 NM94

1-Based on movie; 1st app. Predator 3.60 10.75 25.00
1-2nd printing 1.00 2.50 6.00
2 1.70 5.00 12.00
3 1.50 3.75 9.00
4 1.00 2.50 6.00
Trade paperback (1990, $12.95)-r/#1-4 1.85 5.50 13.00

PREDATOR: BIG GAME
Mar, 1991 - No. 4, June, 1991 ($2.50, color, mini-series)
Dark Horse Comics

1: 1-3-Contain 2 Dark Horse trading cards 1.60 4.00
2-4 1.20 3.00

PREDATOR BLOODY SANDS OF TIME
Feb, 1992 - No. 2, Feb, 1992 ($2.50, color, mini-series)
Dark Horse Comics

1,2-Dan Barry-c/a(p)/scripts 1.00 2.50

PREDATOR COLD WAR
Sept, 1991 - No. 4, Dec, 1991 ($2.50, color, mini-series)
Dark Horse Comics

1-4: All have painted-c 1.00 2.50

PREDATOR: RACE WAR
Feb, 1993 - No. 4, Oct, 1993 ($2.50, color, mini-series)
Dark Horse Comics

1-4-Dorman painted-c #1-4 1.00 2.50
0-(4/93) 1.00 2.50

PREDATOR 2
Feb, 1991 - No. 2, June, 1991 ($2.50, color, mini-series)
Dark Horse Comics

1-Adapts movie; trading cards inside; photo-c 1.00 2.50
2-Trading cards inside; photo-c 1.00 2.50

PREDATOR VS. MAGNUS ROBOT FIGHTER
Oct, 1992 - No. 2, 1993 ($2.95, color)
Dark Horse/Valiant

1 (Regular)-Barry Smith-c; Lee Weeks-a in both 1.30 3.25 8.00
1 (Platinum edition, 11/92)-Barry Smith-c 35.00
2-Barry Smith-c 1.00 2.50 6.00

PREHISTORIC WORLD (See Classics Illustrated Special Issue)

PREMIERE (See Charlton Premiere)

PRESTO KID, THE (See Red Mask)

PRETTY BOY FLOYD (See On the Spot)

PREZ (See Cancelled Comic Cavalcade & Supergirl #10)
Aug-Sept, 1973 - No. 4, Feb-Mar, 1974
National Periodical Publications

1-4: 1-Origin; Joe Simon scripts 1.00

PRICE, THE (See Eclipse Graphic Album Series)

PRIDE AND THE PASSION, THE (See 4-Color #824)

PRIDE OF THE YANKEES, THE (See Real Heroes & Sport Comics)
1949 (The Life of Lou Gehrig)
Magazine Enterprises

nn-Photo-c; Ogden Whitney-a 54.00 160.00 375.00

PRIMAL (Dark Horse)(Value: cover or less)

PRIMAL MAN (See The Crusaders)

PRIME
June, 1993 - Present ($1.95, color)
Malibu Comics (Ultraverse)

1-1st app. Prime 1.00 2.50 6.00
1-Holographic-c edition 5.50 17.00 40.00

Primer #2, © Comico

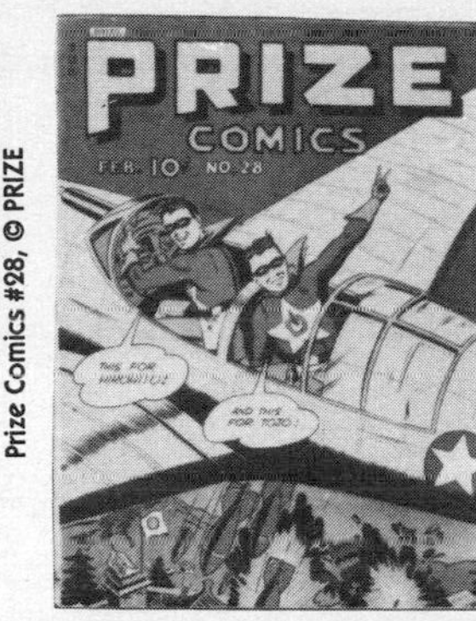

Prize Comics #28, © PRIZE

Prize Comics Western #108, © PRIZE

	GD25	FN65	NM94
2-Polybagged with trading card	1.00	2.50	5.50
3,4-Prototype app. 4-Has 2 cover variations		1.10	2.75
5-($2.50, 40 pgs.)-Rune flip-c/story part B by Barry Smith; see Sludgo #1 for 1st Rune story		1.00	2.50
6-8		.80	2.00

PRIMER (Comico...)
Oct (no month), 1982 - No. 6, Feb, 1984 (B&W)
Comico

	GD25	FN65	NM94
1 (52 pgs.)		1.60	4.00
2-1st app. Grendel & Argent by Wagner	3.25	9.50	22.00
3,4		.90	2.25
5-1st Sam Kieth art in comics (1983)	1.00	2.50	5.50
6-Intro & 1st app. Evangeline		1.60	4.00

PRIMUS (TV)
Feb, 1972 - No. 7, Oct, 1972
Charlton Comics

	GD25	FN65	NM94
1-Staton-a in all	1.30	3.25	8.00
2-7: 6-Drug propaganda story	1.00	2.00	5.00

PRINCE: ALTER EGO (Piranha)(Value: cover or less)

PRINCE AND THE PAUPER, THE (Disney)(Value: cover or less)

PRINCE NAMOR, THE SUB-MARINER (Marvel)(Value: cover or less)(Also see Namor...)

PRINCE NIGHTMARE (Aaaargh)(Value: cover or less)

PRINCE VALIANT (See Ace Comics, Comics Reading Libraries, Feature Books #26, Four Color #567, 650, 699, 719, 788, 849, 900 & King Comics #146, 147)

PRINCE VANDAL
Nov, 1993 - Present ($2.50, color)
Triumphant Comics

	GD25	FN65	NM94
1-Triumphant Unleashed x-over		1.00	2.50

PRIORITY: WHITE HEAT (AC)(Value: cover or less)

PRISCILLA'S POP (See 4-Color #569, 630, 704, 799)

PRISON BARS (See Behind...)

PRISON BREAK!
1951 (Sept) - No. 5, Sept, 1952
Avon Periodicals/Realistic No. 3 on

	GD25	FN65	NM94
1-Wood-c & 1 pg.; has-r/Saint #7 retitled Michael Strong Private Eye	24.00	72.00	165.00
2-Wood-c; Kubert-a; Kinstler inside front-c	16.00	50.00	115.00
3-Orlando, Check-a; c-/Avon paperback 179	13.50	41.00	95.00
4,5: 4-Kinstler-c & inside f/c; Lawrence, Lazarus-a. 5-Kinstler-c; Infantino-a	12.00	36.00	85.00

PRISONER, THE (TV)
1988 - No. 4, 1989 ($3.50, color, squarebound, mini-series)
DC Comics

	GD25	FN65	NM94
Book One - Four		1.40	3.50

PRISON RIOT
1952
Avon Periodicals

	GD25	FN65	NM94
1-Marijuana Murders-1 pg. text; Kinstler-c	16.00	48.00	110.00

PRISON TO PRAISE
1974 (35 cents)
Logos International

	GD25	FN65	NM94
nn-True Story of Merlin R. Carothers			1.00

PRIVATE BUCK (See Large Feature Comic #12 & 21)

PRIVATEERS (Vanguard)(Value: cover or less)

PRIVATE EYE (Cover title: Rocky Jordan...#6-8)
Jan, 1951 - No. 8, March, 1952
Atlas Comics (MCI)

	GD25	FN65	NM94
1-Cover title: Crime Cases... #1-5	11.00	32.00	75.00
2,3-Tuska c/a(3)	7.50	22.50	45.00
4-8	5.85	17.50	35.00

NOTE: *Henkel a-6(3), 7; c-7. Sinnott a-6.*

PRIVATE EYE (See Mike Shayne...)

PRIVATE SECRETARY
Dec-Feb, 1962-63 - No. 2, Mar-May, 1963
Dell Publishing Co.

	GD25	FN65	NM94
1,2	2.00	5.00	10.00

PRIVATE STRONG (See The Double Life of...)

PRIZE COMICS (...Western #69 on) (Also see Treasure Comics)
March, 1940 - No. 68, Feb-Mar, 1948
Prize Publications

	GD25	FN65	NM94
1-Origin Power Nelson, The Futureman & Jupiter, Master Magician; Ted O'Neil, Secret Agent M-11, Jaxon of the Jungle, Bucky Brady & Storm Curtis begin (1st app. of each)	133.00	400.00	900.00
2-The Black Owl begins (1st app.)	58.00	175.00	400.00
3,4: 4-Robot-c	40.00	145.00	325.00
5,6: Dr. Dekkar, Master of Monsters app. in each	46.00	138.00	300.00
7-(Scarce)-Black Owl by S&K; origin/1st app. Dr. Frost & Frankenstein; The Green Lama, Capt. Gallant, The Great Voodini & Twist Turner begin; 1st app. The Green Lama (12/40)	105.00	315.00	735.00
8,9-Black Owl & Ted O'Neil by S&K	54.00	162.00	375.00
10-12,14-20: 11-Origin Bulldog Denny. 16-Spike Mason begins	46.00	138.00	300.00
13-Yank & Doodle begin (8/41, origin/1st app.)	50.00	150.00	350.00
21-24	32.00	95.00	225.00
25-30	18.00	55.00	125.00
31-33	14.00	43.00	100.00
34-Origin Airmale, Yank & Doodle; The Black Owl joins army, Yank & Doodle's father assumes Black Owl's role	18.00	54.00	125.00
35-36,38-40: 35-Flying Fist & Bingo begin	12.50	37.50	85.00
37-Intro. Stampy, Airmale's sidekick; Hitler-c	13.00	40.00	90.00
41-50: 45-Yank & Doodle learn Black Owl's I.D. (their father). 48-Prince Ra begins	10.00	30.00	60.00
51-62,64,67,68: 53-Transvestism story. 55-No Frankenstein. 57-X-Mas-c. 64-Black Owl retires	8.35	25.00	50.00
63-Simon & Kirby c/a	10.00	30.00	65.00
65,66-Frankenstein-c by Briefer	9.15	27.50	55.00

NOTE: ***Briefer** a 7-on; c-65, 66. **J. Binder** a-16; c-21-29. **Guardineer** a-62. **Kiefer** c-62. **Palais** c-68. **Simon & Kirby** c-63, 75, 83.*

PRIZE COMICS WESTERN (Formerly Prize Comics #1-68)
No. 69(V7#2), Apr-May, 1948 - No. 119, Nov-Dec, 1956
Prize Publications (Feature) (No. 69-84: 52 pgs.)

	GD25	FN65	NM94
69(V7#2)	11.00	32.00	75.00
70-75	9.15	27.50	55.00
76-Randolph Scott photo-c; "Canadian Pacific" movie adaptation	10.00	30.00	70.00
77-Photo-c; Severin/Elder, Mart Bailey-a; "Streets of Laredo" movie adapt.	10.00	30.00	60.00
78-Photo-c; Kurtzman-a, 10 pgs.; Severin, Mart Bailey-a; "Bullet Code," & "Roughshod" movie adapt.	12.00	36.00	85.00
79-Photo-c; Kurtzman-a, 8 pgs.; Severin/Elder, Severin, Mart Bailey-a; "Stage To Chino" movie adapt.	12.00	36.00	85.00
80,81-Photo-c; Severin/Elder-a(2)	10.00	30.00	65.00
82-Photo-c; 1st app. The Preacher by Mart Bailey, Severin/Elder-a(3)	10.00	30.00	65.00
83,84	8.35	25.00	50.00
85-1st app. American Eagle by John Severin & begins (V9#6, 1-2/51)	17.00	52.00	120.00
86,92,101-105	9.15	27.50	55.00
87-91,93-99,110,111-Severin/Elder a(2-3) each	10.00	30.00	60.00
100	10.00	30.00	70.00
106-108,112	6.70	20.00	40.00

Protectors #11, © Malibu

Prototype #2, © Malibu

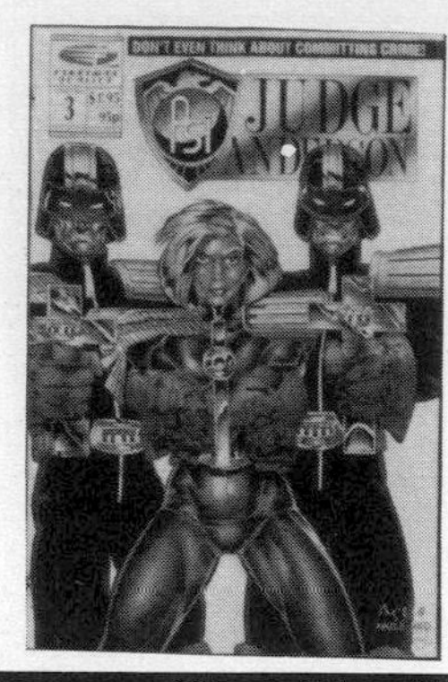

PSI-Judge Anderson #3, © Fleetway/Quality

	GD25	FN65	NM94
109-Severin/Williamson-a	10.00	30.00	60.00
113-Williamson/Severin-a(2)/Frazetta?	10.00	30.00	65.00
114-119: Drifter series in all; by Mort Meskin #114-118	5.35	16.00	32.00

NOTE: ***Fass** a-81. **Severin & Elder** c-84-99. **Severin** a-72, 75, 77-79, 83-86, 96, 97, 100-105; c-100-109(most), 110-119. **Simon & Kirby** c-75, 83.*

PRIZE MYSTERY
May, 1955 - No. 3, Sept, 1955
Key Publications

	GD25	FN65	NM94
1	5.35	16.00	32.00
2,3	4.00	11.00	22.00

PROFESSIONAL FOOTBALL (See Charlton Sport Library)

PROFESSOR COFFIN
No. 19, Oct, 1985 - No. 21, Feb, 1986
Charlton Comics

	GD25	FN65	NM94
19-21: Wayne Howard-a(r)			1.00

PROFESSOR OM (Innovation)(Value: cover or less)

PROJECT: HERO (Vanguard)(Value: cover or less)

PROPELLERMAN
Jan, 1993 - No. 8, 1993 ($2.95, color, limited series)
Dark Horse Comics

	GD25	FN65	NM94
1-6: 2,4-Contain 2 trading cards		1.20	3.00

PROPHET
Oct, 1993 - Present ($1.95, color)
Image Comics

	GD25	FN65	NM94
1-($2.50)-By Liefeld/Panosian; #1-4 contain coupons for Prophet #0		1.10	2.75
1-Gold Foil Edition			5.00
2-4		.80	2.00

PROTECTORS (Also see The Ferret)
Sept, 1992 - Present ($1.95/$2.50, color)
Malibu Comics

	GD25	FN65	NM94
1-12 ($2.50, direct sale)-With poster. 1-Origin; has half outer-c		1.00	2.50
1-12 ($1.95, newsstand)-Without poster		.80	2.00
13-16 ($2.25)		.90	2.25

PROTOTYPE
Aug, 1993 - Present ($1.95, color)
Malibu Comics (Ultraverse)

	GD25	FN65	NM94
1,2,4		.90	2.25
3-($2.50, 40 pgs.)-Rune flip-c/story by B. Smith (3pgs.)		1.00	2.50

PROWLER (Eclipse)(Value: cover or less)(Also see Revenge of the...)

PROWLER IN "WHITE ZOMBIE", THE (Eclipse)(Value: cover or less)

PSI-FORCE (Marvel)(Value: cover or less)

PSI-JUDGE ANDERSON (Fleetway/Quality)(Value: cover or less)

PSYCHO (Magazine)
Jan, 1971 - No. 24, Mar, 1975 (68 pgs.; B&W) (No #22?)
Skywald Publishing Corp.

	GD25	FN65	NM94
1-All reprints	1.65	4.00	10.00
2-Origin & 1st app. The Heap, & Frankenstein series by Adkins	1.20	3.00	7.00
3-24: 13-Cannabalism. 18-Injury to eye-c. 20-Severed Head-c. 24-1975 Winter Special		1.60	4.00
Annual 1(1972)	1.00	2.50	6.00
Fall Special(1974)-Reese, Wildey-a(r)		1.60	4.00
Yearbook(1974-nn)		1.60	4.00

NOTE: ***Boris** c-3, 5. **Buckler** a-4, 5. **Everett** a-3-6. **Jeff Jones** a-6, 7, 9; c-12. **Kaluta** a-13. **Katz/Buckler** a-3. **Morrow** a-1. **Reese** a-5. **Sutton** a-3. **Wildey** a-5.*

PSYCHO, THE (DC)(Value: cover or less)

PSYCHO (Alfred Hitchcock's...)(Innovation)(Value: cover or less)(Adapts movie)

PSYCHOANALYSIS
Mar-Apr, 1955 - No. 4, Sept-Oct, 1955
E. C. Comics

	GD25	FN65	NM94
1-All Kamen-c/a; not approved by code	11.50	34.00	80.00
2-4-Kamen-c/a in all	10.00	30.00	65.00

PSYCHOBLAST (First)(Value: cover or less)

PSYCHONAUTS (Epic Comics)(Value: cover or less)

P.T. 109 (See Movie Comics)

PUBLIC DEFENDER IN ACTION (Formerly Police Trap)
No. 7, Mar, 1956 - No. 12, Oct, 1957
Charlton Comics

	GD25	FN65	NM94
7	6.35	19.00	38.00
8-12	4.00	11.00	22.00

PUBLIC ENEMIES
1948 - No. 9, June-July, 1949
D. S. Publishing Co.

	GD25	FN65	NM94
1	11.00	32.00	75.00
2-Used in **SOTI**, pg. 95	11.50	34.00	80.00
3-5: 5-Arrival date of 10/1/48	8.35	25.00	50.00
6,8,9	6.70	20.00	40.00
7-McWilliams-a; injury to eye panel	8.35	25.00	50.00

PUDGY PIG
Sept, 1958 - No. 2, Nov, 1958
Charlton Comics

	GD25	FN65	NM94
1,2	3.00	7.50	15.00

PUMA BLUES (Aardvark-Vanaheim)(Value: cover or less)

PUMPKINHEAD: THE RITES OF EXORCISM (Dark Horse)(Value: cover or less)

PUNCH & JUDY COMICS
1944; No. 2, Fall, 1944 - V3#2, 12/47; V3#3, 6/51 - V3#9, 12/51
Hillman Periodicals

	GD25	FN65	NM94
V1#1-(60 pgs.)	12.00	36.00	85.00
2	7.00	21.00	42.00
3-12(7/46)	5.35	16.00	32.00
V2#1,3-9	4.00	10.00	20.00
V2#2,10-12, V3#1-Kirby-a(2) each	12.00	36.00	85.00
V3#2-Kirby-a	11.00	32.00	75.00
3-9	3.60	9.00	18.00

PUNCH COMICS
12/41; #2, 2/42; #9, 7/44 - #19, 10/46; #20, 7/47 - #23, 1/48
Harry 'A' Chesler

	GD25	FN65	NM94
1-Mr. E, The Sky Chief, Hale the Magician, Kitty Kelly begin	67.00	200.00	450.00
2-Captain Glory app.	37.00	110.00	250.00
9-Rocketman & Rocket Girl & The Master Key begin	25.00	75.00	175.00
10-Sky Chief app.; J. Cole-a; Master Key-r/Scoop #3	18.00	54.00	125.00
11-Origin Master Key-r/Scoop #1; Sky Chief, Little Nemo app.; Jack Cole-a; Fineish art by Sultan	18.00	54.00	125.00
12-Rocket Boy & Capt. Glory app; Skull-c	18.00	54.00	125.00
13-17,19: 13-Cover has list of 4 Chesler artists' names on tombstone	16.00	50.00	115.00
18-Bondage-c; hypodermic panels	18.00	55.00	125.00
20-Unique cover with bare-breasted women	33.00	100.00	225.00
21-Hypo needle story	17.00	50.00	115.00
22,23-Little Nemo-not by McCay. 22-Intro Baxter (teenage)	14.00	43.00	100.00

PUNCHY AND THE BLACK CROW
No. 10, Oct, 1985 - No. 12, Feb, 1986

Punisher #82, © MEG

Punisher 2099 #7, © MEG

Punisher War Journal #59, © MEG

GD25 FN65 NM94

Charlton Comics
10-12: Al Fago funny animal-r 1.00

PUNISHER (See Amazing Spider-Man #129, Blood and Glory, Captain America #241, Classic Punisher, Daredevil #182-184, 257, Daredevil and the..., Ghost Rider V2#5, 6, Marc Spector #8 & 9, Marvel Preview #2, Marvel Super Action, Marvel Tales, Power Pack #46, Spectacular Spider-Man #81-83, 140, 141, 143 & new Strange Tales #13 & 14)

PUNISHER
Jan, 1986 - No. 5, May, 1986 (Mini-series)
Marvel Comics Group
1-Double size 5.50 17.00 40.00
2 3.20 8.00 20.00
3-Has 2 cover prices, 75 & 95(w/UPC) cents 1.70 5.00 12.00
4,5 1.65 4.00 10.00
Trade Paperback-r/#1-5 (1988) 1.65 4.70 11.00

PUNISHER
July, 1987 - Present
Marvel Comics Group
V2#1 3.20 8.00 20.00
2 1.70 5.00 12.00
3-5 1.20 3.00 7.00
6,7: 7-Last 75 cent issue 1.00 2.50 6.00
8-Portacio/Williams-c/a begins, ends #18 1.30 3.25 8.00
9-Scarcer, low distribution 1.50 3.75 9.00
10-Daredevil app.; ties in w/Daredevil #257 3.20 9.00 21.00
11-15: 13-18-Kingpin app. 1.00 2.50 5.50
16-20: 19-Stroman-c/a. 20-Portacio-c(p) 1.60 4.00
21-24,26-30: 24-1st app. Shadowmasters .80 2.00
25-Double size ($1.50)-Shadowmasters app. 1.20 3.00
31-40 .65 1.60
41-49 1.00
50-($1.50, 52 pgs.) 1.50
51-59: 57-Photo-c; came with outer-c. 59-Punisher is severely cut & has skin grafts (has black skin); last $1.00-c 1.00
60-74,76-84: 60-Begin $1.25-c. 60,61-Luke Cage app. 62-Punisher back to white skin. 68-Tarantula-c/story 1.00
75-($2.75, 52 pgs.)-Embossed silver foil-c 1.10 2.75
85,87,88: 85-Prequel to Suicide Run 1.25
86-($2.95, 52 pgs.) Suicide Run part 3 1.20 3.00
Annual 1 (1988)-Evolutionary War x-over 1.65 4.00 10.00
Annual 2 (1989, $2.00, 68 pgs.)-Atlantis Attacks x-over; Jim Lee-a(p) (back-up story, 6 pgs.); Moon Knight app. 1.00 2.50 5.50
Annual 3,4 ('90-'91, $2.00, 68 pgs.): 4-Golden-c(p) .80 2.00
Annual 5 (1992, $2.25, 68 pgs.) .90 2.25
Annual 6 (1993, $2.95, 68 pgs.)-Bagged w/card 1.20 3.00
Back to School Special 1 (11/92, $2.95, 68 pgs.) 1.20 3.00
Back to School Special 2 (10/93, $2.95, 68 pgs.) 1.20 3.00
...Holiday Special 1 (1/93, $2.95, 52 pgs.)-Foil-c 1.20 3.00
...Holiday Special 2 (1/94, $2.95, 68 pgs.) 1.20 3.00
Summer Special 1 (8/91, $2.95, 52 pgs.)-No ads 1.20 3.00
Summer Special 2 (8/92, $2.50, 52 pgs.)-Bisley painted-c; Austin-a(i) 1.00 2.50
Summer Special 3 (8/93, $2.50, 52 pgs.)-No ads 1.00 2.50
...and Wolverine in African Saga nn (1989, $5.95, 52 pgs.)-Reprints Punisher War Journal #6 & 7; Jim Lee-c/a(r) 1.00 2.50 6.00
...Bloodlines nn (1991, $5.95, 68 pgs.) 1.00 2.50 6.00
...: Die Hard in the Big Easy nn (1992, $4.95, 52 pgs.) 1.00 2.00 5.00
...G-Force nn (1992, $4.95, 52 pgs.)-Painted-c 1.00 2.00 5.00
...Movie Special 1 (6/90, $5.95, 68 pgs.) 1.00 2.50 6.00
...: No Escape nn (1990, $4.95, 52pgs.)-New-a 1.00 2.50 6.00
...The Prize nn (1990, $4.95, 68 pgs.)-New-a 1.00 2.00 5.00
NOTE: *Austin c(i)-47, 48.* ***Cowan*** *c-39.* ***Heath*** *a-26, 27; c-26, 27.* ***Quesada*** *c-56p.* ***Sienkiewicz*** *c-Back to School 1.* ***Williamson*** *a(i)-25, 61, 62, 64-70, 74, Annual 5; c(i)-62, 65-68.*

PUNISHER ARMORY, THE
7/90 ($1.50); No. 2, 6/91; No. 3, 4/92 - Present ($1.75/$2.00)
Marvel Comics
1-r/weapons pgs. from War Journal; Jim Lee-c 1.60 4.00
2-Jim Lee-c .90 2.25
3-8 ($2.00-c): All new material. 3-Jusko painted-c .80 2.00

PUNISHER MAGAZINE, THE
Oct, 1989 - No. 16, Nov, 1990 ($2.25, B&W, Magazine, 52 pgs.)
Marvel Comics
1-3: 1-r/Punisher #1('86). 2,3-r/Punisher 2-5 .90 2.25
4-16: 4-7-r/Punisher V2#1-8. 4-Chiodo-c. 8-r/Punisher #10 & Daredevil #257; Portacio & Lee-r. 14-r/Punisher War Journal #1,2 w/new Lee-c. 16-r/Punisher W. J. #3,8 .90 2.25
NOTE: ***Chiodo*** *painted c-4, 7, 16.* ***Jusko*** *painted c-6, 8.* ***Jim Lee*** *r-8, 14-16; c-14.* ***Portacio/Williams*** *r-7-12.*

PUNISHER MOVIE COMIC
Nov, 1989 - No. 3, Dec, 1989 ($1.00, color, mini-series)
Marvel Comics
1-3: Movie adaptation 1.50
1 (1989, $4.95, squarebound)-contains #1-3 1.00 2.00 5.00

PUNISHER: ORIGIN OF MICRO CHIP, THE
July, 1993 - No. 2, Aug, 1993 ($1.75, color, mini-series)
Marvel Comics
1,2 .70 1.75

PUNISHER: P.O.V.
1991 - No. 4, 1991 ($4.95, color, mini-series, 52 pgs.)
Marvel Comics
1-4: Starlin scripts & Wrightson painted-c/a in all. 2-Nick Fury app. 1.00 2.00 5.00

PUNISHER: THE GHOSTS OF INNOCENTS
Jan, 1993 - No. 2, Jan, 1993 ($5.95, color, 52 pgs.)
Marvel Comics
1,2-Starlin scripts 1.00 2.50 6.00

PUNISHER 2099 (See Punisher War Journal #50)
Feb, 1993 - Present ($1.25, color)
Marvel Comics
1-($1.75)-Foil stamped-c 1.00 2.50
2-14 1.25

PUNISHER WAR JOURNAL, THE
Nov, 1988 - Present ($1.50/$1.75, color)
Marvel Comics
1-Origin The Punisher; Jim Lee-c/a begins; Matt Murdock cameo; 1st Lee-a on Punisher 2.60 7.50 18.00
2-Daredevil x-over 1.65 4.70 11.00
3-5: 3-Daredevil x-over 1.30 3.25 8.00
6-Two part Wolverine story begins 2.30 6.75 16.00
7-Wolverine story ends 1.30 3.25 8.00
8-10 1.00 2.50 5.50
11-13,17-19: 19-Last Jim Lee-c/a 1.60 4.00
14-16,20-22: No Jim Lee-a. 13-15-Heath-i. 14,15-Spider-Man x-over .80 2.00
23-28,31-49,51-60,62,63: 23-Begin $1.75-c. 31-Andy & Joe Kubert art. 36-Photo-c. 47,48-Nomad/Daredevil-c/stories; see Nomad. 57,58-Daredevil & Ghost Rider-c/stories 1.50
29,30-Ghost Rider app. .80 2.00
50-($2.95, 52 pgs.)-Preview of Punisher 2099 (1st app.); embossed-c 1.20 3.00
61-($2.95, 52 pgs.)-Embossed foil-c; Suicide Run part 1 1.20 3.00
64-($2.95, 52 pgs.)-Die-cut-c; Suicide Run part 10 1.20 3.00
64-($2.25, 52 pgs.)-Regular cover edition .90 2.25
NOTE: ***Jusko*** *painted c-31, 32.* ***Jim Lee*** *a(p)-1-13, 17-19; c-1-15, 17, 18, 19p. Painted c-40.*

PUNISHER: WAR ZONE, THE
Mar, 1992 - Present ($1.75, color)
Marvel Comics

The Purple Claw # 2, © TOBY

Quantum Leap: Time and Space © Universal City Studios

The Question Annual #2, © DC

GD25 FN65 NM94

1-($2.25, 40 pgs.)-Die-cut-c; Romita, Jr.-c/a begins .90 2.25
2 .80 2.00
3-22,24: 8-Last Romita, Jr.-c/a. 19-Wolverine app. .70 1.75
23-($2.95, 52 pgs.)-Enbossed foil-c; Suicide Run part 2 1.20 3.00
25-($2.25, 52 pgs.)-Suicide Run part 8 .90 2.25
Annual 1 (1993, $2.95, 68 pgs.)-Bagged w/card; John Buscema-a 1.20 3.00

PUPPET COMICS
Spring, 1946 - No. 2, Summer, 1946
George W. Dougherty Co.

1,2-Funny animal 6.70 20.00 40.00

PUPPET MASTER 2: CHILDREN OF THE PUPPET MASTER (Eternity)(Value: cover or less)

PUPPETOONS (See George Pal's...)

PURE OIL COMICS (Also see Salerno Carnival of Comics, 24 Pages of Comics, & Vicks Comics)
Late 1930's (24 pgs.; regular size) (Paper cover)
Pure Oil Giveaway

nn-Contains 1-2 pg. strips; i.e., Hairbreadth Harry, Skyroads, Buck Rogers by Calkins & Yager, Olly of the Movies, Napoleon, S'Matter Pop, etc. 32.00 95.00 225.00
Also a 16 pg. 1938 giveaway w/Buck Rogers 29.00 85.00 200.00

PURGE
Aug, 1993 - Present ($1.95, color, limited series)
ANIA/U.P. Comics

1 .80 2.00

PURPLE CLAW, THE (Also see Tales of Horror)
Jan, 1953 - No. 3, May, 1953
Minoan Publishing Co./Toby Press

1-Origin; horror/weird stories in all 14.00 43.00 110.00
2,3: 1-3 r-in Tales of Horror #9-11 11.00 32.00 75.00
I.W. Reprint #8-Reprints #1 2.00 5.00 10.00

PUSSYCAT (Magazine)
Oct, 1968 (B&W reprints from Men's magazines)
Marvel Comics Group

1-(Scarce)-Ward, Everett, Wood-a; Everett-c 17.00 52.00 120.00

PUZZLE FUN COMICS (Also see Jingle Jangle)
Spring, 1946 - No. 2, Summer, 1946 (52 pgs.)
George W. Dougherty Co.

1-Gustavson-a 14.00 43.00 100.00
2 11.00 32.00 75.00

NOTE: *#1 & 2('46) each contain a* ***George Carlson*** *cover plus a 6 pg. story "Alec in Fumbleland;" also many puzzles in each.*

QUACK!
July, 1976 - No. 6, 1977? ($1.25, B&W)
Star Reach Productions

1-Brunner-c/a on Duckaneer (Howard the Duck clone); Stevens, Gilbert, Shaw-a 1.80 4.50
1-2nd printing (10/76) 1.50
2,4-6: 2-Newton the Rabbit Wonder by Aragones/Leialoha; Gilbert, Shaw-a; Leialoha-c. 6-Brunner-a (Duckeneer); Gilbert-a .80 2.00
3-The Beavers by Dave Sim; Gilbert, Shaw-a; Sim/Leialoha-c 1.60 4.00

QUADRANT
1983 - No. 7, 1986 (B&W, nudity, adults)
Quadrant Publications

1-Peter Hsu-c/a in all 1.65 4.00 10.00
2 1.40 3.50
3-7 .75 1.90

QUAKER OATS (Also see Cap'n Crunch)
1965 (Giveaway) (2-1/2x5-1/2") (16 pages)
Quaker Oats Co.

"Plenty of Glutton," starring Quake & Quisp; "Lava Come-Back," "Kite Tale," "A Witch in Time" .60 1.50 3.00

QUANTUM LEAP (TV) (See A Nightmare on Elm Street)
Sept, 1991 - No. 12, June?, 1993 ($2.50, color, painted-c)
Innovation Publishing

1-12: Based on TV show; all have painted-c. 8-Has photo gallery 1.00 2.50
Special Edition 1 (10/92)-r/#1 w/8 extra pgs. of photos & articles 1.00 2.50
Time and Space Special 1 (#13) ($2.95)-Foil logo 1.20 3.00

QUASAR (See Avengers #302, Captain America #217, Incredible Hulk #234, Marvel Team-Up #113 & Marvel Two-in-One #53)
Oct, 1989 - Present ($1.00/$1.25, color) (Direct sale #17 on)
Marvel Comics

1-Origin; formerly Marvel Boy/Marvel Man .80 2.00
2-5: 3-Human Torch app. 1.50
6-Venom cameo (2 pgs.) .80 2.00
7-Cosmic Spidey app. 1.00 2.50
8-15,18-24: 11-Excalibur x-over. 14-McFarlane-c. 20-Fantastic Four app. 23-Ghost Rider x-over 1.20
16-($1.50, 52 pgs.) 1.50
17-Flash parody (Buried Alien) .80 2.00
25-($1.50, 52 pgs.)-New costume Quasar 1.50
26-Infinity Guantlet x-over; Thanos-c/story .80 2.00
27-Infinity Guantlet x-over 1.50
28-30: 30-Thanos cameo in flashback; last $1.00-c 1.00
31-49,51-56: 31-D.P. 7 guest stars. 38-40-Infinity War x-overs. 38-Battles Warlock. 39-Thanos-c & cameo. 40-Thanos app. .60 1.25
50-($2.95, 52 pgs.)-Holo-grafx foil-c; Silver Surfer, Man-Thing, Ren & Stimpy app. 1.20 3.00
Special #1-3 ($1.25, newsstand)-Same as #32-34 1.25

QUEEN OF THE DAMNED, THE (Anne Rice's...)(Innovation)(Value: cover or less)

QUEEN OF THE WEST, DALE EVANS (TV)(See Dale Evans Comics & Western Roundup under Dell Giants)
No. 479, 7/53 - No. 22, 1-3/59 (All photo-c; photo back c-4-8, 15)
Dell Publishing Co.

4-Color 479(#1, '53) 13.00 40.00 90.00
4-Color 528(#2, '54) 9.15 27.50 55.00
3(4-6/54)-Toth-a 10.00 30.00 60.00
4-Toth, Manning-a 10.00 30.00 60.00
5-10-Manning-a. 5-Marsh-a 7.00 21.00 42.00
11,19,21-No Manning 21-Tufts-a 5.00 15.00 30.00
12-18,20,22-Manning-a 6.35 19.00 38.00

QUENTIN DURWARD (See 4-Color #672)

QUESTAR ILLUSTRATED SCIENCE FICTION CLASSICS
1977 (224 pgs.) ($1.95)
Golden Press

11197-Stories by Asimov, Sturgeon, Silverberg & Niven; Starstream-r 1.20 3.00

QUEST FOR DREAMS LOST
1987 ($2.00, B&W, 52 pgs.)(Proceeds donated to help illiteracy)
Literacy Volunteers of Chicago

1-Teenage Mutant Ninja Turtles, Trollords, Silent Invasion, The Realm, Wordsmith, Reacto Man, Eb'nn, the Aniverse 1.00 2.50

QUESTION, THE (See Americomics, Blue Beetle (1967), Charlton Bullseye & Mysterious Suspense)

QUESTION, THE (DC)(Value: cover or less)

QUESTION QUARTERLY, THE (DC)(Value: cover or less)

QUESTPROBE

Quick-Trigger Western #12, © MEG

Race of Scorpions #1, © Leo Duranona

Ragman #5 (6-7/77), © DC

8/84; No. 2, 1/85; No. 3, 11/85 - No. 4, 12/85 (Limited series)
Marvel Comics Group

	GD25	FN65	NM94
1-4: 1-The Hulk app. by Romita. 2-Spider-Man; Mooney-a(i). 3-Human Torch & Thing			1.00

QUICK-DRAW McGRAW (TV) (Hanna-Barbera)
No. 1040, 12-2/59-60 - No. 11, 7-9/62; No. 12, 11/62; No. 13, 2/63; No. 14, 4/63; No. 15, 6/69 (1st show aired 9/29/59)
Dell Publishing Co./Gold Key No. 12 on

	GD25	FN65	NM94
4-Color 1040(#1)	10.00	30.00	60.00
2(4-6/60)-6: 2-Augie Doggie & Snooper & Blabber stories (8 pgs. each); pre-dates both of their #1 issues. 4-Augie Doggie & Snooper & Blabber stories. 5-Early Snagglepuss app.; last 10¢ issue	6.70	20.00	40.00
7-11	5.00	15.00	30.00
12,13-Title change to ..Fun Typo Roundup (84 pgs.)	7.00	20.00	55.00
14,15	4.20	12.50	25.00

(See Whitman Comic Books)

QUICK-DRAW McGRAW (TV)(See Spotlight #2)
Nov, 1970 - No. 8, Jan, 1972 (Hanna-Barbera)
Charlton Comics

	GD25	FN65	NM94
1	4.30	13.00	30.00
2-8	2.15	6.50	15.00

QUICK-TRIGGER WESTERN (...Action #12; Cowboy Action #5-11)
No. 12, May, 1956 - No. 19, Sept, 1957
Atlas Comics (ACI No. 12/WPI No. 13-19)

	GD25	FN65	NM94
12-Baker-a	8.35	25.00	50.00
13-Williamson-a, 5 pgs.	9.15	27.50	55.00
14-Everett, Crandall, Torres-a; Heath-c	7.50	22.50	45.00
15-Torres, Crandall-a	6.35	19.00	38.00
16-Orlando, Kirby-a	5.35	16.00	32.00
17,18: 18-Baker-a	5.35	16.00	32.00
19	4.20	12.50	25.00

NOTE: ***Ayers** a-17. **Colan** a-16. **Maneely** a-15, 17; c-15, 18. **Morrow** a-18. **Powell** a-14. **Severin** a-19; c-12, 13, 16, 17, 19. **Shores** a-16. **Tuska** a-17.*

QUINCY (See Comics Reading Libraries)

RACCOON KIDS, THE (Formerly Movietown Animal Antics)
No. 52, Sept-Oct, 1954 - No. 64, Nov, 1957
National Periodical Publications (Arleigh No. 63,64)

	GD25	FN65	NM94
52-Doodles Duck by Mayer	10.00	30.00	70.00
53-64: 53-62-Doodles Duck by Mayer	8.35	25.00	50.00

RACE FOR THE MOON
March, 1958 - No. 3, Nov, 1958
Harvey Publications

	GD25	FN65	NM94
1-Powell-a(5); -pg. S&K-a; cover redrawn from Galaxy Science Fiction pulp (5/53)	10.00	30.00	60.00
2-Kirby/Williamson-c(r)/a(3)	17.00	52.00	120.00
3-Kirby/Williamson-c/a(4)	18.00	54.00	125.00

RACE OF SCORPIONS (Dark Horse)(Value: cover or less)

RACER-X (Now)(Value: cover or less)

RACKET SQUAD IN ACTION
May-June, 1952 - No. 29, March, 1958
Capitol Stories/Charlton Comics

	GD25	FN65	NM94
1	16.00	48.00	110.00
2-4	8.35	25.00	50.00
5-Dr. Neff, Ghost Breaker app; headlights-c	9.15	27.50	70.00
6-Dr. Neff, Ghost Breaker app.	8.35	25.00	50.00
7-10: 10-Explosion-c	6.70	20.00	40.00
11 Ditko c/a	14.00	43.00	100.00
12-Ditko explosion-c (classic); Shuster-a(2)	26.00	80.00	185.00
13-Shuster-c(p)/a; acid in woman's face	9.15	27.50	55.00
14-"Shakedown" marijuana story	8.35	25.00	50.00
15-28	5.00	15.00	30.00
29-(68 pgs.)(15 cents)	5.85	17.50	35.00

RADIANT LOVE (Formerly Daring Love #1)
No. 2, Dec, 1953 - No. 6, Aug, 1954
Gilmor Magazines

	GD25	FN65	NM94
2	4.20	12.50	25.00
3-6	3.00	7.50	15.00

RADIOACTIVE MAN (Simpson's TV show)
1993 - No. 6, 1994 ($1.95, color, limited series)
Bongo Comics

	GD25	FN65	NM94
1-($2.95)-Glow-in-the-dark-c; bound-in jumbo poster; origin Radioactive Man		1.20	3.00
2		.80	2.00

RAGAMUFFINS (Eclipse)(Value: cover or less)

RAGGEDY ANN AND ANDY (See Dell Giants, March of Comics #23 & New Funnies)
No. 5, 1942 - No. 533, 2/54; 10-12/64 - No. 4, 3/66
Dell Publishing Co.

	GD25	FN65	NM94
4-Color 5(1942)	46.00	140.00	320.00
4-Color 23(1943)	34.00	105.00	240.00
4-Color 45(1943)	29.00	85.00	200.00
4-Color 72(1945)	24.00	72.00	165.00
1(6/46)-Billy & Bonnie Bee by Frank Thomas	24.00	72.00	165.00
2,3: 3-Egbert Elephant by Dan Noonan begins	11.50	34.00	80.00
4-Kelly-a, 16 pgs.	12.00	36.00	85.00
5-10: 7-Little Black Sambo, Black Mumbo & Black Jumbo only app; Christmas-c	10.00	30.00	65.00
11-21: 21-Alice In Wonderland cover/story	9.15	27.50	55.00
22-27,29-39(8/49), 4-Color 262(1/50)	6.35	19.00	38.00
28-Kelly-c	7.00	21.00	42.00
4-Color 306,354,380,452,533	5.00	15.00	30.00
1(10-12/64-Dell)	3.60	9.00	18.00
2,3(10-12/65), 4(3/66)	1.80	4.50	9.00

NOTE: ***Kelly** art ("Animal Mother Goose")-#1-34, 36, 37; c-28. Peterkin Pottle by **John Stanley** in 32-38.*

RAGGEDY ANN AND ANDY
Dec, 1971 - No. 6, Sept, 1973
Gold Key

	GD25	FN65	NM94
1	1.30	3.25	8.00
2-6		1.60	4.00

RAGGEDY ANN & THE CAMEL WITH THE WRINKLED KNEES (See Dell Jr. Treasury #8)

RAGMAN (See Batman Family #20, The Brave & The Bold #196 & Cancelled Comic Cavalcade)
Aug-Sept, 1976 - No. 5, June-July, 1977
National Periodical Publications/DC Comics No. 5

	GD25	FN65	NM94
1-Origin & 1st app.		1.20	3.00
2-5: 2-Origin ends; Kubert-c. 4-Drug use story			1.50

NOTE: ***Kubert** a-4, 5; c-1-5. **Redondo** studios a-1-4.*

RAGMAN (2nd series)
Oct, 1991 - No. 8, May, 1992 ($1.50, color, mini-series)
DC Comics

	GD25	FN65	NM94
1-Giffen plots/breakdowns		1.00	2.50
2-8: 3-Origin. 8-Batman-c/story			1.50

RAGMAN: CRY OF THE DEAD
Aug, 1993 - No. 6, Jan, 1994 ($1.75, color, mini-series)
DC Comics

	GD25	FN65	NM94
1-6: Joe Kubert-c		.70	1.75

RAGS RABBIT (See Harvey Hits #2, Harvey Wiseguys & Tastee Freez)
No. 11, June, 1951 - No. 18, March, 1954 (Written & drawn for little folks)
Harvey Publications

	GD25	FN65	NM94
11-(See Nutty Comics #5 for 1st app.)	2.80	7.00	14.00

Rai and the Future Force #11, © Voyager

Ranger Comics #23, © FH

Raphael #1 (2nd printing), © Mirage Studios

RAPHAEL
TEENAGE MUTANT NINJA TURTLE

	GD25	FN65	NM94
12-18	2.40	6.00	12.00

RAI (Rai and the Future Force #9 on; see Magnus #5-8)
Mar, 1992 - No. 0, Nov, 1992; No. 9, May, 1993 - Present ($1.95/$2.25, color)
Valiant

	GD25	FN65	NM94
1-Valiant's 1st original character	3.20	8.00	20.00
2	2.40	7.25	17.00
3	4.70	14.00	33.00
4-Low printing; last $1.95-c	5.50	16.00	38.00
5-8: 6,7-Unity x-overs. 7-Death of Rai	1.85	5.50	13.00
0-(11/92)-Origin/1st app. new Rai (Rising Spirit) & 1st full app. & partial origin Bloodshot; also see Eternal Warrior #4; tells future of all characters	1.65	4.00	10.00
9-($2.50)-Gatefold-c; story cont'd from Magnus #24; Magnus, Eternal Warrior & X-O app.		.90	2.25
10-20: 15-Manowar Armor app.		.90	2.25

NOTE: ***Layton** c-2i. **Miller** c-6. **Simonson** c-7.*

RAIDERS OF THE LOST ARK
Sept, 1981 - No. 3, Nov, 1981 (Movie adaptation)
Marvel Comics Group

	GD25	FN65	NM94
1-r/Marvel Comics Super Special #18			1.50
2,3			1.00

NOTE: ***Buscema** a(p)-1-3; c(p)-1. **Simonson** a-3i; scripts-1-3.*

RAINBOW BRITE AND THE STAR STEALER (DC)(Value: cover or less)

RALPH KINER, HOME RUN KING
1950 (Pittsburgh Pirates)
Fawcett Publications

	GD25	FN65	NM94
nn-Photo-c	37.00	110.00	260.00

RALPH SNART ADVENTURES (Now)(Value: cover or less)

RAMAR OF THE JUNGLE (TV)
1954 (no month); No. 2, Sept, 1955 - No. 5, Sept, 1956
Toby Press No. 1/Charlton No. 2 on

	GD25	FN65	NM94
1-Jon Hall photo-c; last pre-code issue	10.00	30.00	70.00
2-5: 2-Jon Hall photo-c	8.35	25.00	50.00

RAMM
May, 1987 - No. 2, Sept, 1987 ($1.50, B&W)
Megaton Comics

	GD25	FN65	NM94
1,2-Both have 1 pg. Youngblood ad by Liefeld			1.50

RAMPAGING HULK (The Hulk #10 on; see Marvel Treasury Edition)
Jan, 1977 - No. 9, June, 1978 ($1.00, B&W magazine)
Marvel Comics Group

	GD25	FN65	NM94
1-Bloodstone featured		1.70	4.25
2-Old X-Men app; origin old & new X-Men in text w/Cockrum illos	1.30	3.25	8.00
3-9: 9-Thor vs. Hulk battle; Shanna the She-Devil story		.90	2.25

NOTE: ***Alcala** a-1-3i, 5i, 8i. **Buscema** a-1. **Giffen** a-4. **Nino** a-4i. **Simonson** a-1-3p. **Starlin** a-4(w/Nino), 7; c-4, 5, 7.*

RANDOLPH SCOTT (Movie star)(See Crack Western #67, Prize Comics Western #76, Western Hearts #8, Western Love #1 & Western Winners #7)

RANGE BUSTERS
Sept, 1950 - No. 8, 1951
Fox Features Syndicate

	GD25	FN65	NM94
1	10.00	30.00	65.00
2	7.00	21.00	42.00
3-8	5.85	17.50	35.00

RANGE BUSTERS (Formerly Cowboy Love?; Wyatt Earp, Frontier Marshall #11 on)
No. 8, May, 1955 - No. 10, Sept, 1955
Charlton Comics

	GD25	FN65	NM94
8	5.00	15.00	30.00
9,10	3.60	9.00	18.00

RANGELAND LOVE
Dec, 1949 - No. 2, Mar, 1950 (52 pgs.)
Atlas Comics (CDS)

	GD25	FN65	NM94
1-Robert Taylor & Arlene Dahl photo-c	10.00	30.00	60.00
2-Photo-c	9.15	27.50	55.00

RANGER, THE (See 4-Color #255)

RANGE RIDER (See The Flying A's...)

RANGE RIDER, THE (See 4-Color #404)

RANGE ROMANCES
Dec, 1949 - No. 5, Aug, 1950 (#5: 52 pgs.)
Comic Magazines (Quality Comics)

	GD25	FN65	NM94
1-Gustavson-c/a	15.00	45.00	105.00
2-Crandall-c/a; "spanking" scene	19.00	57.00	130.00
3-Crandall, Gustavson-a; photo-c	12.00	36.00	85.00
4-Crandall-a; photo-c	10.00	30.00	70.00
5-Gustavson-a; Crandall-a(p); photo-c	11.00	32.00	75.00

RANGERS COMICS (...of Freedom #1-7)
10/41 - No. 67, 10/52; No. 68, Fall, 1952; No. 69, Winter, 1952-53
Fiction House Magazines (Flying stories)

	GD25	FN65	NM94
1-Intro. Ranger Girl & The Rangers of Freedom; ends #7, cover app. only-#5	117.00	350.00	800.00
2	54.00	162.00	350.00
3	46.00	138.00	300.00
4,5	42.00	125.00	275.00
6-10: 8-U.S. Rangers begin	33.00	100.00	220.00
11,12-Commando Rangers app.	30.00	90.00	200.00
13-Commando Ranger begins-not same as Commando Rangers	30.00	90.00	200.00
14-20	22.00	65.00	150.00
21-Intro/origin Firehair (begins, 2/45)	27.00	80.00	175.00
22-30: 23-Kazanda begins, ends #28. 28-Tiger Man begins (origin/1st app., 4/46). 30-Crusoe Island begins, ends #40	18.00	55.00	120.00
31-40: 33-Hypodermic panels	15.00	45.00	100.00
41-46	12.00	35.00	75.00
47-56-"Eisnerish" Dr. Drew by Grandenetti	12.50	37.50	80.00
57-60-Straight Dr. Drew by Grandenetti	10.00	30.00	65.00
61,62,64-66: 64-Suicide Smith begins	9.15	27.50	55.00
63-Used in **POP**, pgs. 85, 99	9.15	27.50	55.00
67-69: 67-Space Rangers begin, end #69	9.15	27.50	55.00

NOTE: *Bondage, discipline covers, lingerie panels are common. **M. Anderson** a-30? **Baker** a-36-38, 42, 44. **John Celardo** a-34, 36-39. **Lee Elias** a-21-28. **Evans** a-19, 38-46, 48-52. **Hopper** a-25, 26. **Ingels** a-13-16. **Larsen** a-34. **Bob Lubbers** a-30-38, 40-44; c-40-45. **Moreira** a-41-47. **Tuska** a-16, 17, 19, 22. **M. Whitman** c-61-66. **Zolnerwich** c-1-17.*

RANGO (TV)
August, 1967
Dell Publishing Co.

	GD25	FN65	NM94
1-Tim Conway photo-c	3.20	8.00	16.00

RANMA 1/2 (Viz)(Value: cover or less)

RAPHAEL (See Teenage Mutant Ninja Turtles)
1985 (One shot, $1.50, B&W w/2 color cover, 7-1/2x11")
Mirage Studios

	GD25	FN65	NM94
1-1st Turtles one-shot spin-off; contains 1st drawing of the Turtles as a group from 1983	1.65	4.00	10.00
1-2nd printing (11/87); new-c & 8 pgs. art		1.60	4.00

RATFINK (See Frantic & Zany)
October, 1964
Canrom, Inc.

	GD25	FN65	NM94
1-Woodbridge-a	4.00	11.00	22.00

RAT PATROL, THE (TV)
March, 1967 - No. 5, Nov, 1967; No. 6, Oct, 1969
Dell Publishing Co.

Rawhide Kid #10, © MEG

Real Clue Crime Stories V8#1, © HILL

Real Fact Comics #5, © DC

GD25 FN65 NM94

1-Christopher George photo-c 5.85 17.50 35.00
2 4.20 12.50 25.00
3-6: 3-6-Photo-c 3.60 9.00 18.00

RAVAGE 2099 (See Marvel Comics Presents #117)
Dec, 1992 - Present ($1.25, color)
Marvel Comics
1-($1.75)-Gold foil stamped-c; Stan Lee scripts 1.00 2.50
2,3 .80 2.00
4-16 1.25

RAVEN, THE (See Movie Classics)

RAVENS AND RAINBOWS (Pacific)(Value: cover or less)

RAWHIDE (TV)
Sept-Nov, 1959 - June-Aug, 1962; July, 1963 - No. 2, Jan, 1964
Dell Publishing Co./Gold Key
4-Color 1028 (#1) 24.00 70.00 165.00
4-Color 1097,1160,1202,1261,1269 16.00 48.00 110.00
01-684-208(8/62-Dell) 14.00 43.00 100.00
1(10071-307, G.K.), 2-(12 cents) 12.00 36.00 85.00
NOTE: *All have Clint Eastwood photo-c.* ***Tufts*** *a-1028.*

RAWHIDE KID
3/55 - No. 16, 9/57; No. 17, 8/60 - No. 151, 5/79
Atlas/Marvel Comics (CnPC No. 1-16/AMI No. 17-30)
1-Rawhide Kid, his horse Apache & sidekick Randy begin; Wyatt Earp app.; #1 was not code approved 50.00 150.00 350.00
2 20.00 60.00 140.00
3-5 13.00 40.00 90.00
6-10: 7-Williamson-a (4 pgs.) 10.00 30.00 70.00
11-16: 16-Torres-a 9.15 27.50 55.00
17-Origin by Jack Kirby 12.00 36.00 85.00
18-22,24-30: 22-Monster-c/story by Kirby/Ayers 6.70 20.00 40.00
23-Origin retold by Jack Kirby 11.00 32.00 75.00
31,32,36-44,46: 38-Red Raven-c/story; Kirby-c (2/64). 40-Two-Gun Kid x-over. 42-1st Larry Lieber issue. 46-Toth-a 5.85 17.50 35.00
33-35-Davis-a. 35-Intro & death of The Raven 6.70 20.00 40.00
45-Origin retold 6.70 20.00 40.00
47-70: 50-Kid Colt x-over. 64-Kid Colt story. 66-Two-Gun Kid story. 67-Kid Colt story 3.60 9.00 18.00
71-86: 79-Williamson-a(r). 86-Origin-r; Williamson-r/Ringo Kid #13 (4 pgs.) 1.65 4.00 10.00
87-99,101-151: 115-Last new story 1.00 2.50 6.00
100-Origin retold & expanded 1.70 5.00 12.00
Special 1(9/71, 25 cents, 68pgs.)-All Kirby/Ayers-r 1.30 3.25 8.00
NOTE: ***Ayers*** *a-13, 14, 16.* ***Colan*** *a-5, 35, 37; c-145p, 148p, 149p.* ***Davis*** *a-125r.* ***Everett*** *a-54i, 65, 66, 88, 96i, 148i(r).* ***Gulacy*** *c-147.* ***Heath*** *c-4.* ***G. Kane*** *c-101, 144.* ***Keller*** *a-5, 144r.* ***Kirby*** *a-17-32, 34, 42, 43, 84, 86, 92, 109r, 112r, 137r, Spec. 1; c-17-35, 37, 38, 40, 41, 43-47, 137r.* ***Maneely*** *c-1, 2, 5, 6, 14.* ***Morisi*** *a-13.* ***Morrow/Williamson*** *r-111.* ***Roussos*** *r-146i, 147i, 149-151i.* ***Severin*** *a-16; c-8, 13.* ***Torres*** *a-99r.* ***Tuska*** *a-14.* ***Wildey*** *r-146-151(Outlaw Kid).* ***Williamson*** *r-79, 86, 95.*

RAWHIDE KID (Marvel)(Value: cover or less)

RAY, THE (See Freedom Fighters & Smash Comics #14)
Feb, 1992 - No. 6, July, 1992 ($1.00, color, mini-series)
DC Comics
1-Sienkiewicz-c; Joe Quesada-a(p) in 1-5 1.00 2.50 6.00
2 1.30 3.25
3: 3-6-Quesada-c(p) 1.10 2.75
4-6: 6-Quesada layouts only .70 1.80

RAY BRADBURY COMICS
Feb, 1993 - Present ($2.95, color)
Topps Comics
1-5-Polybagged w/3 trading cards each. 1-Corben-a; Williamson/Torres/Krenkel-r/Weird Science-Fantasy #25 1.20 3.00

RAZORLINE
Sept, 1993 (75¢, color)
Marvel Comics
1-Clive Barker super-heroes: Ectokid, Hokum & Hex, Hyperkind & Saint Sinner (all 1st app.) 1.00

REAL ADVENTURE COMICS (Action Adventure #2 on)
April, 1955
Gillmor Magazines
1 3.60 9.00 18.00

REAL CLUE CRIME STORIES (Formerly Clue Comics)
V2#4, June, 1947 - V8#3, May, 1953
Hillman Periodicals
V2#4(#1)-S&K c/a(3); Dan Barry-a 24.00 72.00 165.00
5-7-S&K c/a(3-4). 7-Iron Lady app. 18.00 54.00 125.00
8-12 5.35 16.00 32.00
V3#1-8,10-12, V4#1-3,5-8,11,12 4.00 11.00 22.00
V3#9-Used in **SOTI**, pg. 102 7.50 22.50 45.00
V4#4-S&K-a 6.70 20.00 40.00
V4#9,10-Krigstein-a 6.70 20.00 40.00
V5#1-5,7,8,10,12 4.00 10.00 20.00
6,9,11-Krigstein-a 6.35 19.00 38.00
V6#1-5,8,9,11 3.20 8.00 16.00
6,7,10,12-Krigstein-a. 10-Bondage-c 6.35 19.00 38.00
V7#1-3,5-11, V8#1-3: V7#6-1 pg. Frazetta ad 3.20 8.00 16.00
4,12-Krigstein-a 6.35 19.00 38.00
NOTE: ***Barry*** *a-9, 10; c-V2#8.* ***Briefer*** *a-V6#6.* ***Fuje*** *a- V2#7(2), 8, 11.* ***Infantino*** *a-V2#8; c-V2#11.* ***Lawrence*** *a-V3#8, V5#7.* ***Powell*** *a-V4#11, 12. V5#4, 5, 7 are 68 pgs.*

REAL EXPERIENCES (Formerly Tiny Tessie)
No. 25, January, 1950
Atlas Comics (20CC)
25 4.00 11.00 22.00

REAL FACT COMICS
Mar-Apr, 1946 - No. 21, July-Aug, 1949
National Periodical Publications
1-S&K-c/a; Harry Houdini story; Just Imagine begins (not by Finlay); Fred Ray-a 37.00 110.00 250.00
2-S&K-a; Rin-Tin-Tin story 24.00 72.00 165.00
3-H.G. Wells, Lon Chaney story; 1st DC letter column 14.00 43.00 100.00
4-Virgil Finlay-a on 'Just Imagine' begins, ends #12 (2 pgs. each); Jimmy Stewart story 22.00 65.00 150.00
5-Batman/Robin-c taken from cover of Batman #9; 5 pg. story about creation of Batman & Robin; Tom Mix story 125.00 375.00 825.00
6-Origin & 1st app. Tommy Tomorrow by Finlay (1-2/47); Flag-c; 1st writing by Harlan Ellison (letter column, non-professional); "First Man to Reach Mars" epic-c/story 83.00 250.00 565.00
7-(No. 6 on inside)-Roussos-a 11.00 32.00 75.00
8-2nd app. Tommy Tomorrow by Finlay (5-6/47) 42.00 125.00 285.00
9-S&K-a; Glenn Miller story 19.00 57.00 130.00
10-Vigilante by Meskin (based on movie serial); 4 pg. Finlay s/f story 17.00 52.00 120.00
11,12: 11-Annie Oakley story, Kinstler-a 11.00 32.00 75.00
13-Dale Evans and Tommy Tomorrow-c/stories 39.00 118.00 275.00
14,17,18: 14-Will Rogers story 10.00 30.00 65.00
15-Nuclear explosion part-c ("Last War on Earth" story); Clyde Beatty story 11.00 32.00 75.00
16-Tommy Tomorrow app.; 1st Planeteers? 34.00 105.00 240.00
19-Sir Arthur Conan Doyle story 10.00 30.00 65.00
20-Kubert-a, 4 pgs; Daniel Boone story 13.00 40.00 90.00
21-Kubert-a, 2 pgs; Kit Carson story 10.00 30.00 65.00
NOTE: ***Barry*** *c-16.* ***Virgil Finlay*** *c-6, 8.* ***Meskin*** *c-10.* ***Roussos*** *a-1-4, 6.*

REAL FUN OF DRIVING!!, THE
1965, 1967 (Regular size)
Chrysler Corp.
nn-Shaffenberger-a, 12pgs. 1.00 2.50 5.00

The Real Ghostbusters #1 © NOW

The Realm #4, © Arrow Comics

Real Screen Comics #21, © DC

REAL FUNNIES
Jan, 1943 - No. 3, June, 1943
Nedor Publishing Co.

	GD25	FN65	NM94
1-Funny animal, humor; Black Terrier app. (clone of The Black Terror)	20.00	60.00	140.00
2,3	10.00	30.00	70.00

REAL GHOSTBUSTERS, THE (Now)(Value: cover or less)(Also see Slimer)

REAL HEROES COMICS
Sept, 1941 - No. 16, Oct, 1946
Parents' Magazine Institute

	GD25	FN65	NM94
1-Roosevelt-c/story	20.00	60.00	140.00
2-J. Edgar Hoover-c/story	9.15	27.50	55.00
3-5,7-10: 4-Churchill, Roosevelt stories	7.50	22.50	45.00
6-Lou Gehrig-c/story	12.00	35.00	75.00
11-16: 13-Kiefer-a	4.70	14.00	28.00

REAL HIT
1944 (Savings Bond premium)
Fox Features Publications

	GD25	FN65	NM94
1-Blue Beetle-r	12.00	35.00	75.00

NOTE: *Two versions exist, with and without covers. The coverless version has the title, No. 1 and price printed at top of splash page.*

REALISTIC ROMANCES
July-Aug, 1951 - No. 17, Aug-Sept, 1954 (No #9-14)
Realistic Comics/Avon Periodicals

	GD25	FN65	NM94
1-Kinstler-a; c-/Avon paperback #211	11.50	34.00	80.00
2	6.70	20.00	40.00
3,4	5.00	15.00	30.00
5,8-Kinstler-a	5.35	16.00	32.00
6-c-/Diversey Prize Novels #6; Kinstler-a	6.35	19.00	38.00
7-Evans-a?; c-/Avon paperback #360	6.35	19.00	38.00
15,17	4.70	14.00	28.00
16-Kinstler marijuana story-r/Romantic Love #6	6.35	19.00	38.00
I.W. Reprint #1,8,9	.40	1.00	2.00

NOTE: ***Astarita** a-2-4, 7, 8. Photo c-1, 2. Painted c-3, 4.*

REAL LIFE COMICS
Sept, 1941 - No. 59, Sept, 1952
Nedor/Better/Standard Publ./Pictorial Magazine No. 13

	GD25	FN65	NM94
1-Uncle Sam-c/story; Daniel Boone story	25.00	75.00	175.00
2	11.50	34.00	80.00
3-Hitler cover	17.00	52.00	120.00
4,5: 4-Story of American flag "Old Glory"	9.15	27.50	55.00
6-10: 6-Wild Bill Hickok story	8.35	25.00	50.00
11-20: 17-Albert Einstein story	5.85	17.50	35.00
21-23,25,26,28-30: 29-A-Bomb story	4.70	14.00	28.00
24-Story of Baseball (Babe Ruth)	9.15	27.50	55.00
27-Schomburg A-Bomb-c; story of A-Bomb	9.15	27.50	55.00
31-33,35,36,42-44,48,49: 49-Baseball issue	4.00	11.00	22.00
34,37-41,45-47: 34-Jimmy Stewart story. 37-Story of motion pictures; Bing Crosby story. 38-Jane Froman story. 39-"1,000,000 A.D." story. 40-Bob Feller story. 41-Jimmie Foxx story; "Home Run" Baker story. 45-Story of Olympic games; Burl Ives & Kit Carson story. 46-Douglas Fairbanks Jr. & Sr. story. 47-George Gershwin story	4.70	14.00	28.00
50-Frazetta-a (5 pgs.)	15.00	45.00	105.00
51-Jules Verne "Journey to the Moon" by Evans	10.00	30.00	65.00
52-Frazetta-a (4 pgs.); Severin/Elder-a(2); Evans-a	15.00	45.00	105.00
53-57-Severin/Elder-a. 54-Bat Masterson-c/story	7.50	22.50	45.00
58-Severin/Elder-a(2)	8.35	25.00	50.00
59-1pg. Frazetta; Severin/Elder-a	7.50	22.50	45.00

NOTE: *Some issues had two titles. **Guardineer** a-40(2), 44. **Meskin** a-52. **Roussos** a-50. **Schomburg** c-1, 2, 4, 5, 7, 11, 13-21, 23, 24, 26, 28, 30-32, 34-40, 42, 44-47, 55. **Tuska** a-53. Photo-c 5, 6.*

REAL LIFE SECRETS (Real Secrets #2 on)
Sept, 1949 (One shot)
Ace Periodicals

	GD25	FN65	NM94
1-Painted-c	5.85	17.50	35.00

REAL LIFE STORY OF FESS PARKER (Magazine)
1955
Dell Publishing Co.

	GD25	FN65	NM94
1	10.00	30.00	70.00

REAL LIFE TALES OF SUSPENSE (See Suspense)

REAL LOVE (Formerly Hap Hazard)
No. 25, April, 1949 - No. 76, Nov, 1956
Ace Periodicals (A. A. Wyn)

	GD25	FN65	NM94
25	6.70	20.00	40.00
26	4.00	10.00	20.00
27-L. B. Cole-a	5.00	15.00	30.00
28-35	2.80	7.00	14.00
36-66: 66-Last pre-code (2/55)	2.40	6.00	12.00
67-76	1.60	4.00	8.00

NOTE: *Photo c-50-76. Painted c-46.*

REALM, THE
Feb, 1986 - No. 20? ($1.50-$1.95, B&W)
Arrow Comics/WeeBee Comics #13/Caliber Press #14 on

	GD25	FN65	NM94
1		1.60	4.00
2		.80	2.00
3,5-16: 13-Begin $1.95-c			1.25
4-1st app. Deadworld (9/86)	2.15	6.50	15.00
17-20: 17-Begin $2.50-c		1.00	2.50
Book 1 ($4.95, B&W)	1.00	2.00	5.00

REAL McCOYS, THE (TV)
No. 1071, 1-3/60 - 5-7/1962 (Photo-c)
Dell Publishing Co.

	GD25	FN65	NM94
4-Color 1071,1134-Toth-a in both	11.50	34.00	80.00
4-Color 1193,1265	10.00	30.00	60.00
01-689-207 (5-7/62)	9.15	27.50	55.00

REAL SCREEN COMICS (#1 titled Real Screen Funnies; TV Screen Cartoons #129-138)
Spring, 1945 - No. 128, May-June, 1959 (#1-40: 52 pgs.)
National Periodical Publications

	GD25	FN65	NM94
1-The Fox & the Crow, Flippity & Flop, Tito & His Burrito begin	86.00	260.00	600.00
2	43.00	130.00	300.00
3-5	26.00	80.00	185.00
6-10 (2-3/47)	17.00	52.00	120.00
11-20 (10-11/48): 13-The Crow x-over in Flippity & Flop	13.00	40.00	90.00
21-30 (6-7/50)	10.00	30.00	65.00
31-50	9.15	27.50	55.00
51-99	6.70	20.00	40.00
100	7.50	22.50	45.00
101-128	4.70	14.00	28.00

REAL SECRETS (Formerly Real Life Secrets)
No. 2, Nov, 1950 - No. 5, May, 1950
Ace Periodicals

	GD25	FN65	NM94
2-Painted-c	5.85	17.50	35.00
3-5: 3-Photo-c	3.60	9.00	18.00

REAL SPORTS COMICS (All Sports Comics #2 on)
Oct-Nov, 1948 (52 pgs.)
Hillman Periodicals

	GD25	FN65	NM94
1-Powell-a (12 pgs.)	25.00	75.00	160.00

REAL WAR STORIES
July, 1987; No. 2, Jan, 1991 ($2.00, color, 52 pgs.)
Eclipse Comics

Real West Romances #2, © PRIZE

Record Book Of Famous Police Cases nn, © STJ

Red Circle Sorcery #7, © AP

GD25 FN65 NM94

1-Bolland-a(p), Bissette-a, Totleben-a(i); Alan Moore scripts (2nd printing exists, 2/88) .80 2.00
2-($4.95) 1.00 2.00 5.00

REAL WESTERN HERO (Formerly Wow #1-69; Western Hero #76 on)
No. 70, Sept, 1948 - No. 75, Feb, 1949 (All 52 pgs.)
Fawcett Publications

70(#1)-Tom Mix, Monte Hale, Hopalong Cassidy, Young Falcon begin 25.00 75.00 175.00
71-75: 71 Gabby Hayes begins. 71,72-Captain Tootsie by Beck. 75-Big Bow and Little Arrow app. 16.00 48.00 110.00
NOTE: *Painted/photo c-70-73; painted c-74, 75.*

REAL WEST ROMANCES
4-5/49 - V1#6, 3/50; V2#1, Apr-May, 1950 (All 52 pgs. & photo-c)
Crestwood Publishing Co./Prize Publ.

V1#1-S&K-a(p) 13.00 40.00 90.00
2-Spanking panel 11.00 32.00 75.00
3-Kirby-a(p) only 7.50 22.50 45.00
4-S&K-a; Whip Wilson, Reno Browne photo-c 11.50 34.00 80.00
5-Audie Murphy, Gale Storm photo-c; S&K-a 10.00 30.00 70.00
6-Produced by S&K, no S&K-a 9.15 27.50 55.00
V2#1-Kirby-a(p) 6.70 20.00 40.00
NOTE: ***Meskin** a-V1#5, 6. **Severin/Elder** a-V1#3-6, V2#1. **Meskin** a-V1#6. **Leonard Starr** a-1-3. Photo-c V1#1-5, V2#1.*

RE-ANIMATOR IN FULL COLOR
Oct, 1991 - No. 3, 1992 ($2.95, color, mini-series)
Adventure Comics

1-3: Adapts horror movie. 1-Dorman painted-c 1.20 3.00

REAP THE WILD WIND (See Cinema Comics Herald)

REBEL, THE (See 4-Color #1076, 1138, 1207, 1262)

RECORD BOOK OF FAMOUS POLICE CASES
1949 (25 cents, 132 pgs.)
St. John Publishing Co.

nn-Kubert-a(3); r/Son of Sinbad; Baker-c 25.00 75.00 175.00

RED ARROW
May-June, 1951 - No. 3, Oct, 1951
P. L. Publishing Co.

1 7.00 21.00 42.00
2,3 5.35 16.00 32.00

RED BALL COMIC BOOK
1947 (Red Ball Shoes giveaway)
Parents' Magazine Institute

nn-Reprints from True Comics 2.40 6.00 12.00

RED BAND COMICS
Feb, 1945 - No. 4, May, 1945
Enwil Associates

1 17.00 50.00 120.00
2-Origin Bogeyman & Santanas 14.00 43.00 100.00
3,4-Captain Wizard app. in both (1st app.); each has identical contents/cover 12.50 37.50 85.00

REDBLADE
Apr, 1993 - No. 3, July, 1993 ($2.50, color, mini-series)
Dark Horse Comics

1-3: 1-Double gatefold-c 1.00 2.50

RED CIRCLE COMICS
Jan, 1945 - No. 4, April, 1945
Rural Home Publications (Enwil)

1-The Prankster & Red Riot begin 17.00 50.00 120.00
2-Starr-a; The Judge (costumed hero) app. 13.00 40.00 90.00
3,4-Starr-c/a. 3-The Prankster not in costume 10.00 30.00 70.00
4-(Dated 4/45)-Leftover covers to #4 were later restapled over early 1950s coverless comics; variations in the coverless comics used are endless; Woman Outlaws, Dorothy Lamour, Crime Does Not Pay, Sabu, Diary Loves, Love Confessions & Young Love V3#3 known 8.35 25.00 50.00

GD25 FN65 NM94

RED CIRCLE SORCERY (Chilling Adventures in Sorcery #1-5)
No. 6, Apr, 1974 - No. 11, Feb, 1975
Red Circle Productions (Archie)

6-11: 8-Only app. The Cobra. 10-Wood-a(i) 1.50
NOTE: ***Chaykin** a-6, 10. **B. Jones** a-7(w/**Wrightson, Kaluta, J. Jones**). **McWilliams** a-10(2 & 3 pgs.). **Mooney** a-11p. **Morrow** a-6-8, 9(text illos), 10, 11i; c-6-11. **Thorne** a-8, 10. **Toth** a-8, 9.*

REDDEVIL (AC)(Value: cover or less)

RED DOG (See Night Music #7)

RED DRAGON COMICS (1st Series) (Formerly Trail Blazers; see Super Magician V5#7, 8)
No. 5, Jan, 1943 - No. 9, Jan, 1944
Street & Smith Publications

5-Origin Red Rover, the Crimson Crimebuster; Rex King, Man of Adventure, Captain Jack Commando, & The Minute Man begin; text origin Red Dragon; Binder-c 54.00 162.00 350.00
6-Origin The Black Crusader & Red Dragon (3/43); 1st story app. Red Dragon & 1st cover 47.00 142.00 315.00
7,8: 8-The Red Knight app. 32.00 95.00 210.00
9-Origin Chuck Magnon, Immortal Man 32.00 95.00 210.00

RED DRAGON COMICS (2nd Series)(See Super Magician V2#8)
Nov, 1947 - No. 6, Jan, 1949; No. 7, July, 1949
Street & Smith Publications

1-Red Dragon begins; Elliman, Nigel app.; Edd Cartier-c/a 58.00 175.00 400.00
2-Cartier-c 47.00 142.00 315.00
3-1st app. Dr. Neff Ghost Breaker by Powell; Elliman, Nigel app. 38.00 115.00 265.00
4-Cartier c/a 52.00 162.00 350.00
5-7 29.00 88.00 200.00
NOTE: ***Maneely** a-5, 7. **Powell** a-2-7; c-3, 5, 7.*

REDDY GOOSE
No #, 1958?; No. 2, Jan, 1959 - No. 16, July, 1962 (Giveaway)
International Shoe Co. (Western Printing)

nn (#1) 6.70 20.00 40.00
2-16 4.00 10.50 21.00

REDDY KILOWATT (5 cents) (Also see Story of Edison)
1946 - No. 2, 1947; 1956 - 1960 (no month) (16 pgs.; paper cover)
Educational Comics (E. C.)

nn-Reddy Made Magic (1946, 5 cents) 12.00 35.00 70.00
nn-Reddy Made Magic (1958) 5.35 16.00 32.00
2-Edison, the Man Who Changed the World (3/4" smaller than #1) (1947, 5 cents) 12.00 35.00 70.00
...Comic Book 2 (1954)-"Light's Diamond Jubilee" 6.70 20.00 40.00
...Comic Book 2 (1958)-"Wizard of Light," 16 pgs. 5.35 16.00 32.00
...Comic Book 3 (1956)-"The Space Kite," 8 pgs.; Orlando story; regular size 5.35 16.00 32.00
...Comic Book 3 (1960)-"The Space Kite," 8 pgs.; Orlando story; regular size 4.70 14.00 28.00
NOTE: *Several copies surfaced in 1979.*

REDDY MADE MAGIC
1956, 1958 (16 pages) (paper cover)
Educational Comics (E. C.)

1-Reddy Kilowatt-r (splash panel changed) 8.00 24.00 48.00
1 (1958 edition) 5.00 15.00 30.00

RED EAGLE (See Feature Books #16)

REDEYE (See Comics Reading Libraries)

RED FOX (Formerly Manhunt! #1-14; also see Extra Comics)

Red Mask of the Rio Grande #1, © AC

Red Raven Comics #1, © MEG

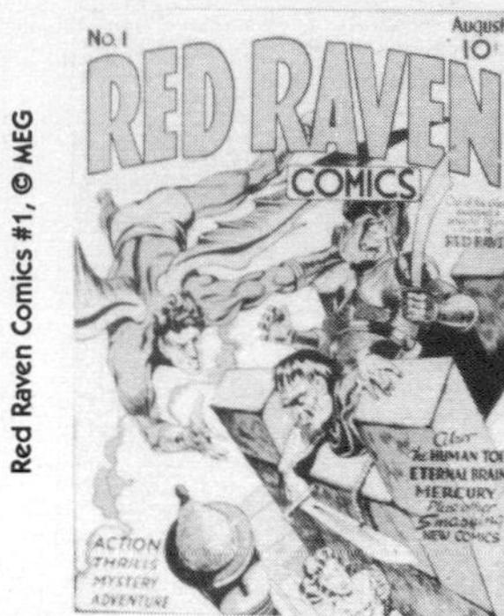

Red Ryder Comics #5, © DELL

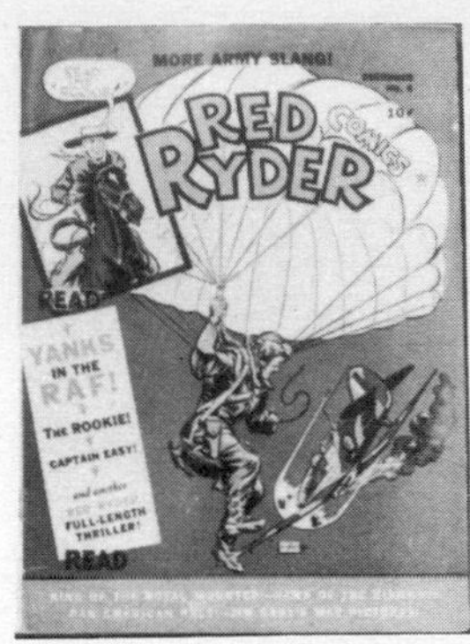

GD25 FN65 NM94

No. 15, 1954
Magazine Enterprises

15(A-1 #108)-Undercover Girl story; L.B. Cole-c/a (Red Fox); r-from Manhunt; Powell-a 10.00 30.00 70.00

RED GOOSE COMIC SELECTIONS (See Comic Selections)

RED HAWK (See A-1 Comics #90, Bobby Benson's... #14-16 & Straight Arrow #2)

RED ICEBERG, THE
1960 (10 cents) (16 pgs.) (Communist propaganda)
Impact Publ. (Catechetical Guild)

nn-(Rare)-'We The People'-back-c 37.00 110.00 240.00
2nd version-'Impact Press'-back-c 43.00 130.00 280.00
NOTE: *This book was the Guild's last anti-communist propaganda book and had very limited circulation. 3 - 4 copies surfaced in 1979 from the defunct publisher's files. Other copies do turn up.*

RED MASK (Formerly Tim Holt; see Best Comics, Blazing Six-Guns)
No. 42, 6-7/1954 - No. 53, 5/56; No. 54, 9/57
Magazine Enterprises No. 42-53/Sussex No. 54 (M.E. on-c)

42-Ghost Rider by Ayers continues, ends #50; Black Phantom continues; 3-D effect c/stories begin 14.00 43.00 100.00
43-3-D effect-c/stories 13.00 40.00 90.00
44-50: 3-D effect stories only. 47-Last pre-code issue. 50-Last Ghost Rider 12.00 36.00 85.00
51-The Presto Kid begins by Ayers (1st app.); Presto Kid-c begins, ends #54; last 3-D effect story 12.00 36.00 85.00
52-Origin The Presto Kid 12.00 36.00 85.00
53,54-Last Black Phantom 10.00 30.00 60.00
I.W. Reprint #1 (r-/#52). 2 (nd, r/#51 w/diff.-c). 3, 8 (nd; Kinstler-c); 8-r/Red Mask #52 2.00 5.00 10.00
NOTE: ***Ayers** art on Ghost Rider & Presto Kid. **Bolle** art in all (Red Mask); c-43, 44, 49. **Guardineer** a-52. Black Phantom in #42-44, 47-50, 53, 54.*

REDMASK OF THE RIO GRANDE (AC)(Value: cover or less)

RED MOUNTAIN FEATURING QUANTRELL'S RAIDERS
1952 (Movie) (Also see Jesse James #28)
Avon Periodicals

nn-Alan Ladd; Kinstler-c/a 17.00 52.00 120.00

"RED" RABBIT COMICS
Jan, 1947 - No. 22, Aug-Sept, 1951
Dearfield Comic/J. Charles Laue Publ. Co.

1 8.35 25.00 50.00
2 4.70 14.00 28.00
3-10 4.00 10.00 20.00
11-17,19-22 3.20 8.00 16.00
18-Flying Saucer-c (1/51) 4.20 12.50 25.00

RED RAVEN COMICS (Human Torch #2 on; also see X-Men #44)
August, 1940 (Also see Sub-Mariner #26, 2nd series)
Timely Comics

GD25 FN65 VF82 NM94

1-Origin & 1st app. Red Raven; Comet Pierce & Mercury by Kirby, The Human Top & The Eternal Brain; intro. Magar, the Mystic & only app.; Kirby-c (his 1st signed work) 812.00 2440.00 4470.00 6500.00
(Estimated up to 135 total copies exist, 6 in NM/Mint)

RED RYDER COMICS (Hi Spot #2)(Movies, radio)(See Crackajack Funnies)
9/40; No. 3, 8/41 - No. 5, 12/41; No. 6, 4/42 - No. 151, 4-6/57
Hawley Publ. No. 1-5/Dell Publishing Co.(K.K.) No. 6 on

GD25 FN65 NM94

1-Red Ryder, his horse Thunder, Little Beaver & his horse Papoose strip reprints begin by Fred Harman; 1st meeting of Red & Little Beaver; Harman line-drawn-c #1-85 115.00 345.00 800.00
3-(Scarce)-Alley Oop, King of the Royal Mtd., Capt. Easy, Freckles & His Friends, Myra North, Dan Dunn strip-r begin 71.00 215.00 500.00
4,5 39.00 120.00 275.00
6-1st Dell issue 39.00 120.00 275.00
7-10 32.00 95.00 225.00

GD25 FN65 NM94

11-20 24.00 73.00 170.00
21-32-Last Alley Oop, Dan Dunn, Capt. Easy, Freckles 16.00 48.00 110.00
33-40 (52 pgs.) 10.00 30.00 65.00
41 (52 pgs.)-Rocky Lane photo back-c; photo back-c begin, end #57 10.00 30.00 70.00
42-46 (52 pgs.): 46-Last Red Ryder strip-r 9.15 27.50 55.00
47-53 (52 pgs.): 47-New stories on Red Ryder begin 7.50 22.50 45.00
54-57 (36 pgs.) 6.00 18.00 36.00
58-73 (36 pgs.): 73-Last King of the Royal Mtd; strip-r by Jim Gary 6.00 18.00 36.00
74-85,93 (52 pgs.)-Harman line-drawn-c 6.00 18.00 36.00
86-92 (52 pgs.)-Harman painted-c 6.00 18.00 36.00
94-96 (36 pgs.)-Harman painted-c 4.70 14.00 28.00
97,98,107,108 (36 pgs.)-Harman line-drawn-c 4.70 14.00 28.00
99,101-106 (36 pgs.)-Jim Bannon Photo-c 4.70 14.00 28.00
100 (36 pgs.)-Bannon photo-c 5.35 16.00 32.00
109-118 (52 pgs.)-Harman line-drawn-c 4.00 11.00 22.00
119-129 (52 pgs.): 119-Painted-c begin, not by Harman, end #151 4.00 10.00 20.00
130-144 (#130 on have 36 pgs.) 3.60 9.00 18.00
145-148: 145-Title change to Red Ryder Ranch Magazine with photos 2.80 7.00 14.00
149-151: 149-Title changed to Red Ryder Ranch Comics 2.80 7.00 14.00
4-Color 916 (7/58) 3.60 9.00 18.00
Buster Brown Shoes Giveaway (1941, 32pgs., color, soft-c) 24.00 72.00 165.00
Red Ryder Super Book Of Comics 10 (1944; paper-c; 32 pgs.; blank back-c)-Magic Morro app. 24.00 72.00 165.00
Red Ryder Victory Patrol-nn(1944, 32 pgs.)-r-/#43,44; comic has a paper-c & is stapled inside a triple cardboard fold-out-c; contains membership card, decoder, map of R.R. home range, etc. Herky app. (Langendorf Bread giveaway; sub-titled 'Super Book of Comics')(Rare) 315.00 945.00 2200.00
Wells Lamont Corp. giveaway (1950)-16 pgs. in color; regular size; paper-c; 1941-r 20.00 60.00 140.00
NOTE: ***Fred Harman** a-1-99; c-1-98, 107-118. Don Red Barry, Allan Rocky Lane, Wild Bill Elliott & Jim Bannon starred as Red Ryder in the movies. Robert Blake starred as Little Beaver.*

RED RYDER PAINT BOOK
1941 (148 pages) (8-1/2x11-1/2")
Whitman Publishing Co.

nn-Reprints 1940 daily strips 22.00 65.00 150.00

RED SEAL COMICS (Formerly Carnival Comics, and/or Spotlight Comics?)
No. 14, 10/45 - No. 18, 10/46; No. 19, 6/47 - No. 22, 12/47
Harry 'A' Chesler/Superior Publ. No. 19 on

14-The Black Dwarf begins (continued from Spotlight?); Little Nemo app; bondage/hypo-c; Tuska-a 32.00 95.00 225.00
15-Torture story; funny-c 25.00 75.00 175.00
16-Used in **SOTI**, pg. 181, illo-"Outside the forbidden pages of de Sade, you find draining a girl's blood only in children's comics;" drug club story r-later in Crime Reporter #1; Veiled Avenger & Barry Kuda app; Tuska-a; funny-c 34.00 100.00 235.00
17-Lady Satan, Yankee Girl & Sky Chief app; Tuska-a 22.00 65.00 150.00
18,20-Lady Satan & Sky Chief app. 22.00 65.00 150.00
19-No Black Dwarf (on cover only); Zor, El Tigre app. 17.00 50.00 115.00
21-Lady Satan & Black Dwarf app. 17.00 50.00 115.00
22-Zor, Rocketman app. (68 pgs.) 17.00 50.00 115.00

REDSKIN (Thrilling Indian Stories)(Famous Western Badmen #13 on)
Sept, 1950 - No. 12, Oct, 1952
Youthful Magazines

1-Walter Johnson-a (7 pgs.) 9.15 27.50 55.00
2 6.35 19.00 38.00

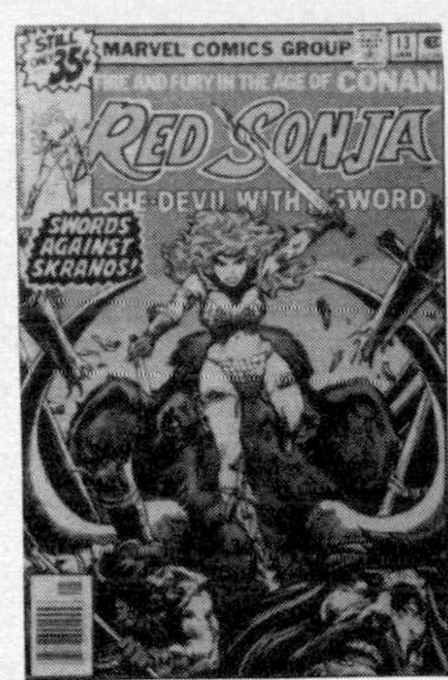

Red Sonja #13, © MEG

Reid Fleming, Worlds Toughest Milkman V2#1, © David Boswell

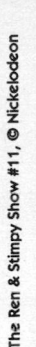

The Ren & Stimpy Show #11, © Nickelodeon

GD25 FN65 NM94

3-12: 3-Daniel Boone app. 6,12-Bondage-c 4.70 14.00 28.00
IOTE: *Palais a-11. Wildey a-5, 11.*

RED SONJA (Also see Conan #23, Kull & The Barbarians, Marvel Feature & Savage Sword Of Conan #1)
/77 - No. 15, 5/79; V1#1, 2/83 - V2#2, 3/83; V3#1, 8/83 - V3#4, 2/84; V3#5, 1/85 - V3#13, 1986
Marvel Comics Group
1-Created by Robert E. Howard 1.20 3.00
2-5: 5-Last 30 cent issue .80 2.00
6-15, V1#1,V2#2: 14-Last 35 cent issue 1.00
V3#1-4 ($1.00, 52 pgs.) 1.20
5-13 (65-75 cents) 1.00
NOTE: *Brunner c-12-14. J. Buscema a(p)-12, 13, 15; c-V#1. Nebres a-V3#3i(part). N. Redondo a-8i, V3#2i, 3i. Simonson a-V3#1. Thorne c/a-1-11.*

RED SONJA: THE MOVIE (Marvel)(Value: cover or less)

RED TORNADO (DC)(Value: cover or less)(See All-American #20 & Justice League of America #64)

RED WARRIOR
Jan, 1951 - No. 6, Dec, 1951
Marvel/Atlas Comics (TCI)
1-Red Warrior & his horse White Wing; Tuska-a 10.00 30.00 70.00
2-Tuska-c 7.50 22.50 45.00
3-6: 4-Origin White Wing. 6-Maneely-c 5.85 17.50 35.00

RED WOLF (See Avengers #80 & Marvel Spotlight #1)
May, 1972 - No. 9, Sept, 1973
Marvel Comics Group
1-(Western hero); Gil Kane/Severin-c; Shores-a 1.40 3.50
2-9: 2-Kane-c; Shores-a. 6-Tuska-r in back-up. 7-Red Wolf as super hero begins. 9-Origin sidekick, Lobo (wolf) .70 1.80

REESE'S PIECES (Eclipse)(Value: cover or less)

REFORM SCHOOL GIRL!
1951
Realistic Comics
nn-Used in SOTI, pg. 358, & cover ill. with caption "Comic books are supposed to be like fairy tales" 79.00 235.00 550.00
(Prices vary widely on this book)
NOTE: *The cover and title originated from a digest-sized book published by Diversey Publishing Co. of Chicago in 1948. The original book "House of Fury," Doubleday, came out in 1941. The girl's real name which appears on the cover of the digest and comic is Marty Collins, Canadian model and ice skating star who posed for this special color photograph for the Diversey novel.*

REGENTS ILLUSTRATED CLASSICS
1981 (Plus more recent reprintings)
(48 pgs., b&w-a with 14 pages of teaching helps)
Prentice Hall Regents, Englewood Cliffs, NJ 07632
NOTE: *This series contains Classics Ill. art, and was produced from the same illegal source as* **Cassette Books.** *But when Twin Circle sued to stop the sale of the Cassette Books, they decided to permit this series to continue. This series was produced as a teaching aid. The 20 title series is divided into four levels based upon number of basic words used therein. There is also a teacher's manual for each level. All of the titles are still available from the publisher for about $5 each retail. The number to call for mail order purchases is (201)767-5937. Almost all of the issues have new covers taken from some interior art panel. Here is a list of the series by Regents ident. no. and the Classics Ill. counterpart.*
16770(Cl#24-A2)18333(Cl#3-A2)21668(Cl#13-A2)32224(Cl#21)33051(Cl#26)
35788(Cl#84)37153(Cl#16)44460(Cl#19-A2)44808(Cl#18-A2)52395(Cl#4-A2)
58627(Cl#5-A2)60067(Cl#30)68405(Cl#23-A1)70302(Cl#29)78192(Cl#7-A2)
78193(Cl#10-A2)79679(Cl#85)92046(Cl#1-A2)93062(Cl#64)93512(Cl#25)

REGGIE (Formerly Archie's Rival...; Reggie & Me #19 on)
No. 15, Sept, 1963 - No. 18, Nov, 1965
Archie Publications
15(9/63), 16(10/64) 5.85 17.50 35.00
17(8/65), 18(11/65) 5.85 17.50 35.00
NOTE: *Cover title No. 15 & 16 is Archie's Rival Reggie.*

REGGIE AND ME (Formerly Reggie)
No. 19, Aug, 1966 - No. 126, Sept, 1980 (No. 50-68: 52 pgs.)
Archie Publications
19-Evilheart app. 3.20 8.00 16.00
20-23-Evilheart app.; with Pureheart #22 1.60 4.00 8.00
24-40 1.00 2.50
41-60 1.50
61-126 1.00

REGGIE'S JOKES (See Reggie's Wise Guy Jokes)

REGGIE'S WISE GUY JOKES
Aug, 1968 - No. 60, Jan, 1982 (#5 on are Giants)
Archie Publications
1 2.00 6.00 14.00
2-4 1.00 2.50 6.00
5-10 1.20 3.00
11-28 1.50
29-60 1.00

REGISTERED NURSE
Summer, 1963
Charlton Comics
1-r/Nurse Betsy Crane & Cynthia Doyle 1.00 2.50 5.00

REG'LAR FELLERS (See All-American Comics, Popular Comics & Treasure Box of Famous Comics)
1921 - 1929
Cupples & Leon Co./MS Publishng Co.
1(1921)-52 pgs. B&W dailies (Cupples & Leon, 10x10") 15.00 45.00 100.00
1925, 48 pgs. B&W dailies (MS Publ.) 15.00 45.00 100.00
Softcover (1929, nn, 36 pgs.) 15.00 45.00 100.00
Hardcover (1929)-B&W reprints, 96 pgs. 17.00 50.00 110.00

REG'LAR FELLERS
No. 5, Nov, 1947 - No. 6, Mar, 1948
Visual Editions (Standard)
5,6 6.35 19.00 38.00

REG'LAR FELLERS HEROIC (See Heroic Comics)

REID FLEMING, WORLD'S TOUGHEST MILKMAN (Eclipse)(Value: cover or less)

RELUCTANT DRAGON, THE (See 4-Color #13)

REMEMBER PEARL HARBOR
1942 (68 pages) (Illustrated story of the battle)
Street & Smith Publications
nn-Uncle Sam-c; Jack Binder-a 32.00 95.00 225.00

REN & STIMPY SHOW, THE (TV)
Dec, 1992 - Present ($1.75, color)
Marvel Comics
1-($2.25)-Polybagged w/scratch & sniff Ren or Stimpy air fowler (equal amounts of each were made) 2.60 7.50 18.00
1-2nd printing .90 2.25
2 2.15 6.50 15.00
3 1.00 2.50 5.50
4-6: 6-Spider-Man x-over 1.90 4.75
7-16: 12-1st solo back-up story w/Tank & Brenner .70 1.75

RENO BROWNE, HOLLYWOOD'S GREATEST COWGIRL (Formerly Margie Comics; Apache Kid #53 on; also see Western Hearts, Western Life Romances & Western Love)
No. 50, April, 1950 - No. 52, Sept, 1950 (52 pgs.)
Marvel Comics (MPC)
50-Reno Browne photo-c on all 20.00 60.00 140.00
51,52 18.00 54.00 125.00

REPTILICUS (Becomes Reptisaurus #3 on)
Aug, 1961 - No. 2, Oct, 1961
Charlton Comics

The Return of Gorgo #3, © M.G.M.

Rex Allen Comics #12, © DELL

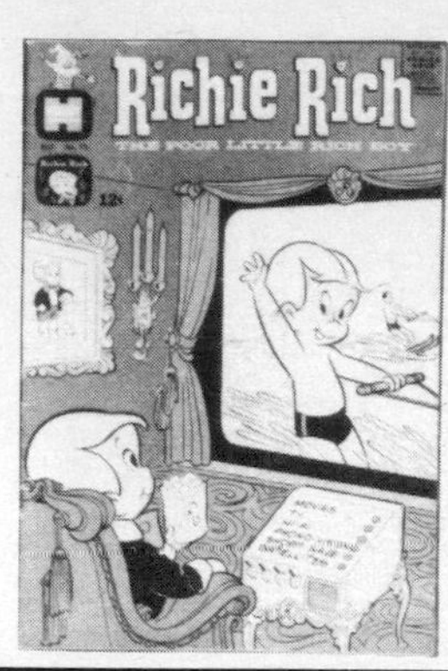

Richie Rich #13, © HARV

	GD25	FN65	NM94
1 (Movie)	11.00	32.00	75.00
2	7.00	21.00	50.00

REPTISAURUS (Reptilicus #1,2)
V2#3, Jan, 1962 - No. 8, Dec, 1962; Summer, 1963
Charlton Comics

	GD25	FN65	NM94
V2#3-8: 8-Montes/Bache-c/a	4.00	12.00	28.00
Special Edition 1 (Summer, 1963)	3.60	10.75	25.00

REQUIEM FOR DRACULA
Feb, 1993 ($2.00, color, 52 pgs.)
Marvel Comics

	GD25	FN65	NM94
nn-r/Tomb of Dracula #69,70 by Gene Colan		.80	2.00

RESCUERS, THE (See Walt Disney Showcase #40)

RESCUERS DOWN UNDER (Disney)(Value: cover or less)

RESTLESS GUN (See 4-Color #934, 986, 1045, 1089, 1146)

RETURN FROM WITCH MOUNTAIN (See Walt Disney Showcase #44)

RETURN OF GORGO, THE (Formerly Gorgo's Revenge)
No. 2, Aug, 1963; No. 3, Fall, 1964 (#2 is last 10 cent issue; #3 is 12 cents)
Charlton Comics

	GD25	FN65	NM94
2,3-Ditko-c/a; based on M.G.M. movie	6.00	18.00	42.00

RETURN OF KONGA, THE (Konga's Revenge #2 on)
1962
Charlton Comics

	GD25	FN65	NM94
nn	6.00	18.00	42.00

RETURN OF MEGATON MAN (Kitchen Sink)(Value: cover or less)

RETURN OF THE OUTLAW
Feb, 1953 - No. 11, 1955
Toby Press (Minoan)

	GD25	FN65	NM94
1-Billy the Kid	6.70	20.00	40.00
2	4.00	11.00	22.00
3-11	3.60	9.00	18.00

REVEALING LOVE STORIES (See Fox Giants)

REVEALING ROMANCES
Sept, 1949 - No. 6, Aug, 1950
Ace Magazines

	GD25	FN65	NM94
1	5.35	16.00	32.00
2	3.60	9.00	18.00
3-6	2.80	7.00	14.00

REVELATIONS (Eclipse)(Value: cover or less)

REVENGE OF THE PROWLER (Eclipse)(Value: cover or less)

REVENGERS FEATURING ARMOR AND SILVER STREAK, THE (Continuity)(Value: cover or less)(Becomes Armor #4 on)

REVENGERS FEATURING MEGALITH (Continuity)(Value: cover or less)

REVENGERS SPECIAL (Continuity)(Value: cover or less)

REX ALLEN COMICS (Movie star)(Also see 4-Color #877 & Western Roundup under Dell Giants)
No. 316, Feb, 1951 - No. 31, Dec-Feb, 1958-59 (All-photo-c)
Dell Publishing Co.

	GD25	FN65	NM94
4-Color 316(#1)(52 pgs.)-Rex Allen & his horse Koko begin; Marsh-a	16.00	48.00	110.00
2 (9-11/51, 36 pgs.)	9.15	27.50	55.00
3-10	6.70	20.00	40.00
11-20	5.35	16.00	32.00
21-23,25-31	5.00	15.00	30.00
24-Toth-a	6.35	19.00	38.00

NOTE: ***Manning*** *a-20, 27-30. Photo back-c F.C. #316, 2-12, 20, 21.*

REX DEXTER OF MARS (See Mystery Men Comics)
Fall, 1940 (68 pgs.)
Fox Features Syndicate

	GD25	FN65	NM94
1-Rex Dexter, Patty O'Day, & Zanzibar (Tuska-a) app.; Briefer-c/a	125.00	375.00	825.0

REX HART (Formerly Blaze Carson; Whip Wilson #9 on)
No. 6, Aug, 1949 - No. 8, Feb, 1950 (All photo-c)
Timely/Marvel Comics (USA)

	GD25	FN65	NM94
6-Rex Hart & his horse Warrior begin; Black Rider app; Captain Tootsie by Beck	18.00	54.00	125.0
7,8: 18pg. Thriller in each. 8-Blaze the Wonder Collie app. in text	13.00	40.00	90.0

REX MORGAN, M.D. (Also see Harvey Comics Library)
Dec, 1955 - No. 3, Apr?, 1956
Argo Publ.

	GD25	FN65	NM94
1-r/Rex Morgan daily newspaper strips & daily panel-r of "These Women" by D'Alessio & "Timeout" by Jeff Keate	8.35	25.00	50.0
2,3	5.85	17.50	35.0

REX THE WONDER DOG (See The Adventures of...)

RHUBARB, THE MILLIONAIRE CAT (See 4-Color #423, 466, 563)

RIBIT! (Comico)(Value: cover or less)

RIBTICKLER (Also see Fox Giants)
1945 - No. 9, Aug, 1947; 1957; 1959
Fox Feature Synd./Green Publ. (1957)/Norlen (1959)

	GD25	FN65	NM94
1-Funny animal	10.00	30.00	60.00
2-(1946)	5.00	15.00	30.00
3-9: 3,7-Cosmo Cat app.	4.00	10.00	20.00
3,7,8 (Green Publ.-1957)	2.40	6.00	12.00
3,7,8 (Norlen Mag.-1959)	2.40	6.00	12.00

RICHARD DRAGON, KUNG-FU FIGHTER (See Brave & the Bold)
Apr-May, 1975 - No. 18, Nov-Dec, 1977 (1-4 are based on novel)
National Periodical Publications/DC Comics

	GD25	FN65	NM94
1,2: 1-Based on novel. 2-Starlin/Weiss-a			1.50
3-18: 3-Kirby-a(p). 4-8-Wood inks			1.00

RICHARD THE LION-HEARTED (See Ideal a Classical Comic)

RICHIE RICH (See Harvey Collectors Comics, Harvey Hits, Little Dot, Little Lotta, Little Sad Sack, Million Dollar Digest, Mutt & Jeff, Super Richie, and 3-D Dolly)

RICHIE RICH (...the Poor Little Rich Boy) (See Harvey Hits #3, 9)
Nov, 1960 - #218, Oct, 1982; #219, Oct, 1986 - #254, Jan, 1991
Harvey Publications

	GD25	FN65	NM94
1-(See Little Dot for 1st app.)	86.00	260.00	600.00
2	43.00	130.00	300.00
3-5	25.00	75.00	175.00
6-10: 8-Christmas-c	15.00	45.00	105.00
11-20	8.35	25.00	50.00
21-40	5.85	17.50	35.00
41-60	4.00	10.00	20.00
61-80: 65-1st app. Dollar the Dog	2.40	6.00	12.00
81-99	1.20	3.00	8.00
100(12/70)-1st app. Irona the robot maid	2.40	6.00	12.00
101-111,117-120	1.00	2.50	6.00
112-116: All 52 pg. Giants	1.20	3.00	7.00
121-140		1.60	4.00
141-160: 145-Infinity-c		1.30	3.25
161-180		.85	2.10
181-254: 237-Last original material		.65	1.60

RICHIE RICH (2nd series)(Harvey)(Value: cover or less)

RICHIE RICH ADVENTURE DIGEST MAGAZINE (Harvey)(Value: cover or less)

RICHIE RICH AND... (Harvey)(Value: cover or less)

RICHIE RICH AND BILLY BELLHOPS
October, 1977 (One Shot) (52pgs.)
Harvey Publications

	GD25	FN65	NM94
1		1.20	3.00

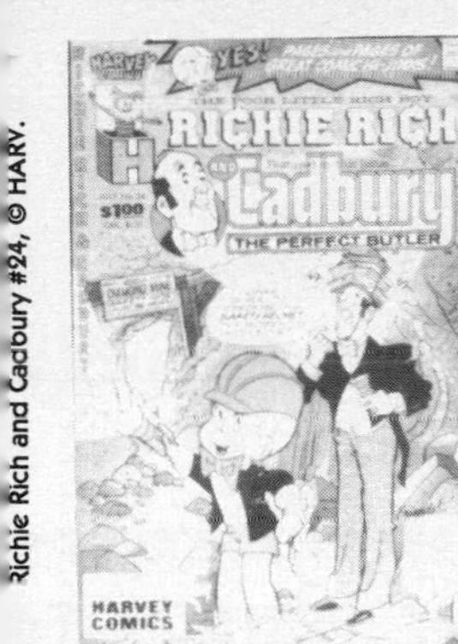
ichie Rich and Cadbury #24, © HARV.

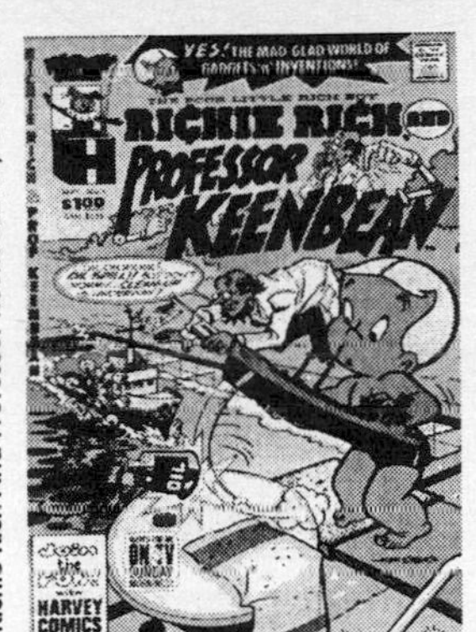
Richie Rich And Professor Keenbean #1, © HARV

Richie Rich Big Bucks #1, © HARV

ICHIE RICH AND CADBURY
0/77; #2, 9/78 - #23, 7/82; #24, 7/90 - #29, 1/91 (1-10: 52pgs.)
arvey Publications

	GD25	FN65	NM94
1	1.00	2.00	5.00
2-5		.80	2.00
6-29: 24-Begin $1.00-c			1.00

ICHIE RICH AND CASPER
ug, 1974 - No. 45, Sept, 1982
arvey Publications

	GD25	FN65	NM94
1	1.30	3.25	8.00
2-5		1.60	4.00
0-10: 10-Xmas-c		.80	2.00
1-20			1.50
1-40: 22-Xmas-c			1.20
1-45			1.00

ICHIE RICH AND DOLLAR THE DOG (See Richie Rich #65)
ept, 1977 - No. 24, Aug, 1982 (#1-10: 52pgs.)
arvey Publications

	GD25	FN65	NM94
1		1.60	4.00
2-10		.80	2.00
1-24			1.00

ICHIE RICH AND DOT
ctober, 1974 (One Shot)
arvey Publications

	GD25	FN65	NM94
1	1.00	2.50	6.00

ICHIE RICH AND GLORIA
ept, 1977 - No. 25, Sept, 1982 (#1-11: 52pgs.)
arvey Publications

	GD25	FN65	NM94
1		1.60	4.00
2-5		.80	2.00
6-25			1.00

ICHIE RICH AND HIS GIRLFRIENDS
pril, 1979 - No. 16, Dec, 1982
arvey Publications

	GD25	FN65	NM94
1: 52 pg. Giant		1.20	3.00
2: 52 pg. Giant		1.00	2.40
3-10		.80	2.00
11-16			1.00

ICHIE RICH AND HIS MEAN COUSIN REGGIE
pril, 1979 - No. 3, 1980 (50 cents) (#1,2: 52pgs.)
arvey Publications

	GD25	FN65	NM94
1		1.80	2.00
2-3: (#4 was advertised, but never released)			1.50

RICHIE RICH AND JACKIE JOKERS (Also see Jackie Jokers)
ov, 1973 - No. 48, Dec, 1982
arvey Publications

	GD25	FN65	NM94
1: 52 pg. Giant; contains material from unpublished Jackie Jokers #5	2.60	7.50	18.00
2,3-(52 pg. Giants). 2-R.R. & Jackie 1st meet	1.50	3.75	9.00
4,5	1.00	2.50	6.00
6-10		1.60	4.00
11-20; 11-1st app. Kool Katz		1.20	3.00
21-40: 26-Star Wars parody			1.50
41-48			1.00

RICHIE RICH AND PROFESSOR KEENBEAN
Sept, 1990 - No. 2, Nov, 1990 ($1.00, color)
Harvey Comics

	GD25	FN65	NM94
1,2			1.00

RICHIE RICH AND THE NEW KIDS ON THE BLOCK (Harvey)(Value: cover or less)

RICHIE RICH AND TIMMY TIME
Sept, 1977 (50 Cents) (One Shot) (52 pages)
Harvey Publications

	GD25	FN65	NM94
1		1.20	3.00

RICHIE RICH BANK BOOKS
Oct, 1972 - No. 59, Sept, 1982
Harvey Publications

	GD25	FN65	NM94
1	3.20	8.00	20.00
2-5	1.65	4.00	10.00
6-10	1.00	2.50	6.00
11-20		1.60	4.00
21-30		1.20	3.00
31-40		.80	2.00
41-59			1.00

RICHIE RICH BEST OF THE YEARS
Oct, 1977 - No. 6, June, 1980 (Digest) (128 pages)
Harvey Publications

	GD25	FN65	NM94
1(10/77)-Reprints, #2(10/78)-Reprints, #3(6/79-75 cents)		.80	2.00
4-6(11/79-6/80-95 cents)			1.00

RICHIE RICH BIG BUCKS (Harvey)(Value: cover or less)

RICHIE RICH BILLIONS
Oct, 1974 - No. 48, Oct, 1982 (#1-33: 52pgs.)
Harvey Publications

	GD25	FN65	NM94
1	2.00	6.00	14.00
2-5	1.20	3.00	7.00
6-10	1.00	2.00	5.00
11-20		1.20	3.00
21-33 (Last 52 pgs.)		.80	2.00
34-48			1.00

RICHIE RICH CASH
Sept, 1974 - No. 47, Aug, 1982
Harvey Publications

	GD25	FN65	NM94
1-1st app. Dr. N-R-Gee	2.00	6.00	14.00
2-5	1.20	3.00	7.00
6-10		1.60	4.00
11-20		1.20	3.00
21-30		.80	2.00
31-47			1.00

RICHIE RICH CASH MONEY
May, 1992 - No. 2?, 1992 ($1.25, color)
Harvey Comics

	GD25	FN65	NM94
1,2			1.25

RICHIE RICH, CASPER & WENDY NATIONAL LEAGUE
June, 1976 (52 pages)
Harvey Publications

	GD25	FN65	NM94
1 (Released-3/76 with 6/76 date)		1.20	3.00
1 (6/76)-2nd version w/San Francisco Giants & KTVU 2 logos; has "Compliments of Giants and Straw Hat Pizza" on-c		1.20	3.00

RICHIE RICH COLLECTORS COMICS (See Harvey Collectors Comics)

RICHIE RICH DIAMONDS
Aug, 1972 - No. 59, Aug, 1982 (#1, 23-45: 52pgs.)
Harvey Publications

	GD25	FN65	NM94
1-(52 pg. Giant)	3.60	10.75	25.00
2-5	1.65	4.00	10.00
6-10	1.00	2.50	6.00
11-22		1.60	4.00
23-30		1.20	3.00
31-45: 39-Origin Little Dot			1.50
46-50			1.20
51-59			1.00

THE POOR LITTLE RICH BOY
Richie Rich
DOLLAR$..CENTS

Richie Rich Dollars & Cents #11, © HARV

Richie Rich Giant Size V2#1, © HARV

Richie Rich Millions #45, © HARV

RICHIE RICH DIGEST (Harvey)(Value: cover or less)

RICHIE RICH DIGEST STORIES (Harvey)(Value: cover or less)

RICHIE RICH DIGEST WINNERS (Harvey)(Value: cover or less)

RICHIE RICH DOLLARS & CENTS
Aug, 1963 - No. 109, Aug, 1982 (#1-43: 68 pgs.; 44-60, 71-94: 52pgs.)
Harvey Publications

	GD25	FN65	NM94
1: (#1-64 are all reprint issues)	13.00	40.00	90.00
2	6.70	20.00	40.00
3-5: 5-r/1st app. of R.R. from Little Dot #1	4.20	12.50	25.00
6-10	3.20	8.00	16.00
11-20	2.80	7.00	14.00
21-30	1.60	4.00	8.00
31-43: Last 68 pg. issue	1.00	2.00	5.00
44-60: All 52 pgs.		1.20	3.00
61-70		1.00	2.50
71-94: All 52 pgs.			1.50
95-109: 100-Anniversary issue			1.00

RICHIE RICH FORTUNES
Sept, 1971 - No. 63, July, 1982 (#1-15: 52pgs.)
Harvey Publications

	GD25	FN65	NM94
1	3.60	10.75	25.00
2-5	1.65	4.00	10.00
6-10	1.20	3.00	6.00
11-15: Last 52 pg. Giant	1.00	2.00	5.00
16-30		1.20	3.00
31-40			1.50
41-63			1.00

RICHIE RICH GEMS
Sept, 1974 - No. 43, Sept, 1982
Harvey Publications

	GD25	FN65	NM94
1	2.00	6.00	14.00
2-5	1.20	3.00	7.00
6-10		1.60	4.00
11-20		1.00	2.50
21-30			1.50
31-43: 38-1st app. Stone-Age Riches			1.00

RICHIE RICH GIANT SIZE
Oct, 1992 - No. 2? ($2.25, color, 68 pgs.)
Harvey Comics

	GD25	FN65	NM94
V2#1,2-Richie Rich, Little Audrey & Melvin, Little Dot & Little Lotta stories		.90	2.25

RICHIE RICH GOLD AND SILVER
Sept, 1975 - No. 42, Oct, 1982 (#1-27: 52pgs.)
Harvey Publications

	GD25	FN65	NM94
1	1.65	4.00	10.00
2-5	1.00	2.00	5.00
6-10		.80	2.00
11-27			1.50
28-42			1.00

RICHIE RICH GOLD NUGGETS DIGEST (Harvey)(Value: cover or less)

RICHIE RICH HOLIDAY DIGEST MAGAZINE (...Digest #4)
Jan, 1980 - #3, Jan, 1982; #4, 3/88; #5, 2/89 (Published annually)
Harvey Publications

	GD25	FN65	NM94
1-3: All X-Mas-c			1.00
4-(3/88, $1.25), 5-(2/89, $1.75)			1.25

RICHIE RICH INVENTIONS
Oct, 1977 - No. 26, Oct, 1982 (#1-11: 52pgs.)
Harvey Publications

	GD25	FN65	NM94
1	1.00	2.00	5.00
2-5		1.00	2.50
6-11			1.50
12-26			1.0

RICHIE RICH JACKPOTS
Oct, 1972 - No. 58, Aug, 1982 (#41-43: 52pgs.)
Harvey Publications

	GD25	FN65	NM94
1	3.60	10.75	25.0
2-5	1.70	5.00	12.0
6-10	1.20	3.00	7.0
11-20		1.60	4.0
21-30		1.20	3.0
31-40,44-50		.80	2.0
41-43 (52 pgs.)		1.20	3.0
51-58			1.5

RICHIE RICH MILLION DOLLAR DIGEST (...Magazine #?-on)(Also see Million Dollar Digest)
October, 1980 - No. 9, Oct, 1982 ($1.50)
Harvey Publications

	GD25	FN65	NM94
1-9			1.50

RICHIE RICH MILLIONS
9/61; #2, 9/62 - #113, 10/82 (#1-48: 68 pgs.; 49-64, 85-97: 52 pgs.)
Harvey Publications

	GD25	FN65	NM94
1: (#1-5 are all reprint issues)	14.00	43.00	100.00
2	8.35	25.00	50.00
3-10: (All other giants are new & reprints)	6.70	20.00	40.00
11-20	4.00	11.00	22.00
21-30	2.40	6.00	12.00
31-48: Last 68 pg. Giant	1.60	4.00	8.00
49-64: 52 pg. Giants	1.00	2.00	5.00
65-74: 68-1st app. Super Richie (11/74)		1.20	3.00
75-94: 52 pg. Giants		1.40	3.50
95-100			1.50
101-113			1.00

RICHIE RICH MONEY WORLD
Sept, 1972 - No. 59, Sept, 1982
Harvey Publications

	GD25	FN65	NM94
1: 52 pg. Giant	3.60	10.75	25.00
2-5	1.65	4.00	10.00
6-10: 9,10-Richie Rich mistakenly named Little Lotta on covers	1.00	2.00	5.00
11-20		1.20	3.00
21-30		.80	2.00
31-50			1.50
51-59			1.00
...Digest 1 (2/91, $1.75) - 6 (1993)		.70	1.75

RICHIE RICH PROFITS
Oct, 1974 - No. 47, Sept, 1982
Harvey Publications

	GD25	FN65	NM94
1	2.30	6.75	16.00
2-5	1.30	3.25	8.00
6-10		1.60	4.00
11-20: 15-Christmas-c		1.20	3.00
21-30			1.50
31-47			1.00

RICHIE RICH RELICS (Harvey)(Value: cover or less)

RICHIE RICH RICHES
July, 1972 - No. 59, Aug, 1982 (#1, 2, 41-45: 52pgs.)
Harvey Publications

	GD25	FN65	NM94
1-(52 pg. Giant)	2.60	7.50	18.00
2-(52 pg. Giant)	1.50	3.75	9.00
3-5	1.20	3.00	7.00
6-10		1.60	4.00
11-20: 17-Super Richie app. (3/75)		1.20	3.00
21-40			1.50

Richie Rich Success Stories #17, © HARV

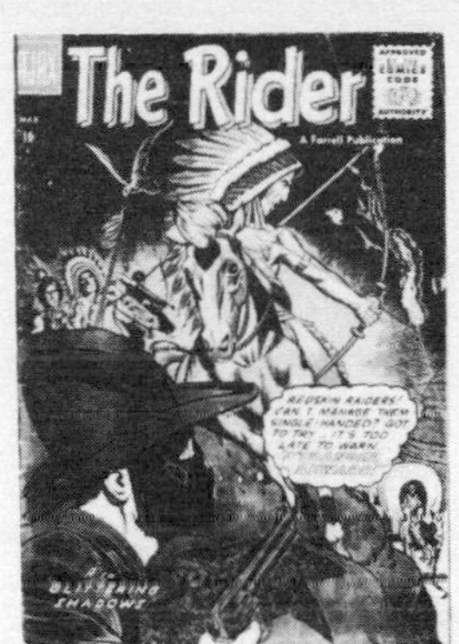

The Rider #1, © AJAX

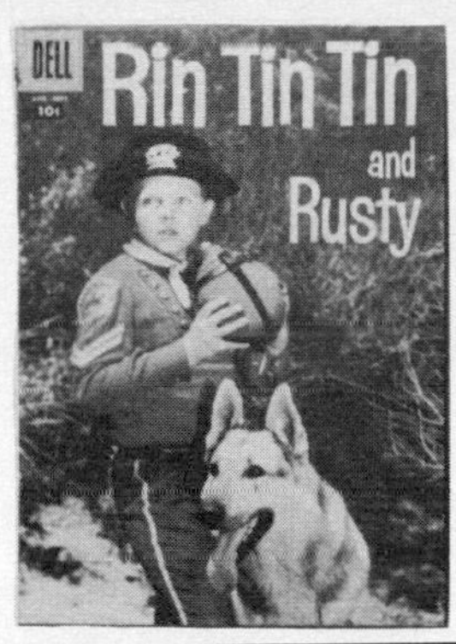

Rin Tin Tin #20, © Screen Gems

GD25 FN65 NM94

1-45: 52 pg. Giants .80 2.00
6-59 1.00

CHIE RICH SUCCESS STORIES
ov, 1964 - No. 105, Sept, 1982 (#1-38: 68pgs., 39-55, 67-90: 52pgs.)
arvey Publications

	13.00	40.00	90.00
!-5	6.70	20.00	40.00
-10	4.00	11.00	22.00
1-30: 27-1st Penny Van Dough (8/69)	2.40	6.00	12.00
1-38: Last 68 pg. Giant	1.60	4.00	8.00
9-55: 52 pgs.	1.00	2.50	6.00
6-66		1.60	4.00
7-90: 52 pgs. (Early issues are reprints)		.80	2.00
1-105			1.50

CHIE RICH TREASURE CHEST DIGEST (...Magazine #3)
pr, 1982 - No. 3, Aug, 1982 (95 Cents, Digest Magazine)
arvey Publications

1-3 1.50

CHIE RICH VACATION DIGEST
ct, 1992 - Present ($1.75, color, digest size)
arvey Comics

		.70	1.75

CHIE RICH VACATIONS DIGEST
/77; No. 2, 10/78 - No. 7, 10/81; No. 8, 8/82 (Digest, 132 pgs.)
arvey Publications

1-Reprints		.80	2.00
2-8			1.50

ICHIE RICH VAULT OF MYSTERY
ov, 1974 - No. 47, Sept, 1982
arvey Publications

1	1.65	4.00	10.00
2-10	1.00	2.00	5.00
1-20		1.20	3.00
1-30		.80	2.00
31-47			1.00

ICHIE RICH ZILLIONZ
ct, 1976 - No. 33, Sept, 1982 (#1-4: 68pgs.; #5-18: 52pgs.)
arvey Publications

1	1.65	4.00	10.00
2-4: Last 68 pg. Giant	1.00	2.00	5.00
5-10		1.20	3.00
11-18: Last 52 pg. Giant			1.50
19-33			1.00

ICK GEARY'S WONDERS AND ODDITIES (Dark Horse)(Value: cover or less)

ICKY
lo. 5, September, 1953
tandard Comics (Visual Editions)

5-Teenage humor	3.60	9.00	18.00

ICKY NELSON (TV)(See Sweethearts V2#42)
lo. 956, Dec, 1958 - No. 1192, June, 1961 (All photo-c)
ell Publishing Co.

-Color 956,998	20.00	70.00	160.00
-Color 1115,1192-Manning-a	18.00	54.00	125.00

IDER, THE (Frontier Trail #6; also see Blazing Sixguns I.W. #10, 11)
larch, 1957 - No. 5, 1958
jax/Farrell Publ. (Four Star Comic Corp.)

1-Swift Arrow, Lone Rider begin	7.00	21.00	42.00
2-5	4.20	12.50	25.00

IFLEMAN, THE (TV)
lo. 1009, 7-9/59 - No. 12, 7-9/62; No. 13, 11/62 - No. 20, 10/64
Dell Publ. Co./Gold Key No. 13 on

	GD25	FN65	NM94
4-Color 1009 (#1)	16.00	48.00	110.00
2 (1-3/60)	10.00	30.00	65.00
3-Toth-a, 4 pgs.	11.00	32.00	75.00
4,5,7-10	9.15	27.50	55.00
6-Toth-a, 4pgs.	10.00	30.00	65.00
11-20	7.50	22.50	45.00

NOTE: ***Warren Tufts** a-2-9. All have Chuck Connors photo-c. Photo back c-13-15.*

RIMA, THE JUNGLE GIRL
Apr-May, 1974 - No. 7, Apr-May, 1975
National Periodical Publications

1-Origin, part 1 (#1-5: 20 cent-c, 6,7: 25 cents)		.80	2.00
2-4-Origin, parts 2-4			1.00
5-7: 7-Origin & only app. Space Marshal			1.00

NOTE: ***Kubert** c-1-7. **Nino** a-1-5. **Redondo** a-1-6.*

RING OF BRIGHT WATER (See Movie Classics)

RING OF THE NIBELUNG, THE (DC)(Value: cover or less)

RINGO KID, THE (2nd Series)
Jan, 1970 - No. 23, Nov, 1973; No. 24, Nov, 1975 - No. 30, Nov, 1976
Marvel Comics Group

1-Williamson-a r-from #10, 1956		1.60	4.00
2-30: 13-Wildey-r. 20-Williamson-r/#1		.80	2.00

RINGO KID WESTERN, THE (See Wild Western & Western Trails)
Aug, 1954 - No. 21, Sept, 1957 (1st series)
Atlas Comics (HPC)/Marvel Comics

1-Origin; The Ringo Kid begins	17.00	52.00	120.00
2-Black Rider app.; origin/1st app. Ringo's Horse Arab	10.00	30.00	60.00
3-5	6.70	20.00	40.00
6-8-Severin-a(3) each	7.50	22.50	45.00
9,11,12,14-21: 12-Orlando-a, 4pgs.	4.70	14.00	28.00
10,13-Williamson-a, 4 pgs.	6.35	19.00	38.00

NOTE: ***Berg** a-8. **Maneely** a-1-5, 15, 16(text illos only), 17(4), 18, 20, 21; c-1-6, 8, 13, 15-18, 20. **J. Severin** c-10, 11. **Sinnott** a-1. **Wildey** a-16-18.*

RIN TIN TIN (See March of Comics #163,180,195)

RIN TIN TIN (TV) (...& Rusty #21 on; see Western Roundup under Dell Giants)
Nov, 1952 - No. 38, May-July, 1961; Nov, 1963 (All Photo-c)
Dell Publishing Co./Gold Key

4-Color 434 (#1)	17.00	52.00	120.00
4-Color 476,523	10.00	30.00	60.00
4(3-5/54)-10	7.50	22.50	45.00
11-20	6.35	19.00	38.00
21-38	5.35	16.00	32.00
... & Rusty 1 (11/63-Gold Key)	7.00	21.00	42.00

RIO (Comico)(Value: cover or less)(Also see Eclipse Monthly)

RIO AT BAY (Dark Horse)(Value: cover or less)

RIO BRAVO (See 4-Color #1018)

RIO CONCHOS (See Movie Comics)

RIOT (Satire)
Apr, 1954 - No. 3, Aug, 1954; No. 4, Feb, 1956 - No. 6, June, 1956
Atlas Comics (ACI No. 1-5/WPI No. 6)

1-Russ Heath-a	16.00	48.00	110.00
2-Li'l Abner satire by Post	12.00	36.00	85.00
3-Last precode (8/54)	10.00	30.00	70.00
4-Infinity-c; Marilyn Monroe "7 Year Itch" movie satire; Mad Rip-off ads	15.00	45.00	105.00
5-Marilyn Monroe, John Wayne parody; part photo-c	16.00	48.00	110.00
6-Lorna of the Jungle satire by Everett; Dennis the Menace satire-c/story; part photo-c	10.00	30.00	70.00

NOTE: ***Berg** a-3. **Burgos** c-1, 2. **Colan** a-1. **Everett** a-1, 4, 6. **Heath** a-1. **Maneely** a-1, 2,*

R.I.P. #2, © TSR

Rip Hunter Time Master #6, © DC

Robin: A Hero Reborn, © DC

	GD25	FN65	NM94

4-6; c-3, 4, 6. ***Post*** *a-1-4.* ***Reinman*** *a-2.* ***Severin*** *a-4-6.*

RIOT GEAR
Sept, 1993 - Present ($2.50, color, serially numbered comics)
Triumphant Comics

	GD25	FN65	NM94
1-5: 3-Triumphant Unleashed x-over		1.00	2.50

R.I.P. (TSR)(Value: cover or less)

RIPCORD (See 4-Color #1294)

RIP HUNTER TIME MASTER (See Showcase #20, 21, 25, 26)
Mar-Apr, 1961 - No. 29, Nov-Dec, 1965 (Also see Time Masters)
National Periodical Publications

	GD25	FN65	NM94
Showcase #20 (5-6/59)-Origin & 1st app. Rip Hunter; Moriera-a	56.00	170.00	500.00
Showcase #21 (7-8/59)-2nd app. Rip Hunter; Sekowsky-c/a	31.00	92.00	275.00
Showcase #25,26 (3-4/60, 5-6/60)-3rd & 4th app. Rip Hunter by Kubert	22.00	66.00	175.00
1-(3-4/61)	45.00	135.00	315.00
2	22.00	66.00	155.00
3-5: 5-Last 10 cent issue	13.00	40.00	90.00
6,7-Toth-a in each	10.00	30.00	70.00
8-15	7.00	21.00	50.00
16-20	5.50	17.00	40.00
21-29: 29-Gil Kane-c	4.70	14.00	33.00

RIP IN TIME (Fantagor)(Value: cover or less)

RIP KIRBY (See Feature Books #51, 54, Harvey Comics Hits #57, & Street Comix)

RIPLEY'S BELIEVE IT OR NOT! (See Ace Comics, All-American Comics, Mystery Comics Digest #1, 4, 7, 10, 13, 16, 19, 22, 25)

RIPLEY'S BELIEVE IT OR NOT!
Sept, 1953 - No. 4, March, 1954
Harvey Publications

	GD25	FN65	NM94
1-Powell-a	9.15	27.50	55.00
2-4	5.85	17.50	35.00
J. C. Penney giveaway (1948)	6.70	20.00	40.00

RIPLEY'S BELIEVE IT OR NOT! (Formerly ...True War Stories)
No. 4, April, 1967 - No. 94, Feb, 1980
Gold Key

	GD25	FN65	NM94
4-Photo-c; McWilliams-a	4.00	10.00	20.00
5-Subtitled "True War Stories;" Evans-a; 1st Jeff Jones-a in comics? (2 pgs.)	2.40	6.00	12.00
6-10: 6-McWilliams-a. 10-Evans-a(2)	2.40	6.00	12.00
11-20: 15-Evans-a	1.80	4.50	9.00
21-30	1.00	2.50	6.00
31-38,40-60		1.60	4.00
39-Crandall-a	1.00	2.00	5.00
61-94: 74,77-83 (52 pgs.)		1.20	3.00
Story Digest Mag. 1(6/70)-4-3/4x6-1/2"	1.20	3.00	7.00

NOTE: ***Evanish*** *art by* ***Luiz Dominguez*** *#22-25, 27, 30, 31, 40.* ***Jeff Jones*** *a-5(2 pgs.).* ***McWilliams*** *a-65, 66, 70, 89.* ***Orlando*** *a-8.* ***Sparling*** *c-68. Reprints-74, 77-84, 87 (part); 91, 93 (all).* ***Williamson, Wood*** *a-80r/#1.*

RIPLEY'S BELIEVE IT OR NOT TRUE GHOST STORIES (Becomes ...True War Stories) (See Dan Curtis)
June, 1965 - No. 2, Oct, 1966
Gold Key

	GD25	FN65	NM94
1-Williamson, Wood & Evans-a; photo-c	5.00	15.00	30.00
2-Orlando, McWilliams-a; photo-c	3.60	9.00	18.00
Mini-Comic 1(1976-3-1/4x6-1/2")			1.50
11186(1977)-Golden Press; ($1.95, 224 pgs.)-All-r		1.20	3.00
11401(3/79)-Golden Press; ($1.00, 96 pgs.)-All-r			1.50

RIPLEY'S BELIEVE IT OR NOT TRUE WAR STORIES (Formerly ...True Ghost Stories; becomes Ripley's Believe It or Not #4 on)
Nov, 1966
Gold Key

	GD25	FN65	NM94
1(#3)-Williamson-a	4.00	10.00	20.0

RIPLEY'S BELIEVE IT OR NOT! TRUE WEIRD
June, 1966 - No. 2, Aug, 1966 (B&W Magazine)
Ripley Enterprises

	GD25	FN65	NM94
1,2-Comic stories & text	1.20	3.00	6.0

RIVERDALE HIGH
Aug, 1990 - No. 5, Apr, 1991 ($1.00, color, bi-monthly)
Archie Comics

	GD25	FN65	NM94
1-5			1.0

RIVETS (See 4-Color #518)

RIVETS (A dog)
Jan, 1956 - No. 3, May, 1956
Argo Publ.

	GD25	FN65	NM94
1-Reprints Sunday & daily newspaper strips	4.00	11.00	22.0
2,3	2.80	7.00	14.0

ROACHMILL (Blackthorne & Dark Horse, 1986 & '88)(Value: cover or less)

ROAD RUNNER (See Beep Beep, the...)

ROBERT E. HOWARD'S CONAN THE BARBARIAN (Marvel)(Value: cover or less)

ROBIN (See Aurora, Detective Comics #38, New Teen Titans, Robin II, Robin III, Robin 3000 Star Spangled Comics #65 & Teen Titans)

ROBIN (See Batman #457)
Jan, 1991 - No. 5, May, 1991 ($1.00, color, mini-series)
DC Comics

	GD25	FN65	NM94
1-Free poster by N. Adams; Bolland-c on all	1.00	2.50	5.5
1-2nd & 3rd printings (without poster)			1.5
2			1.2
2-2nd printing			1.0
3-5			1.5
Annual 1,2 (1992-93, $2.50, 68 pgs.): 1-Grant/Wagner scripts; Sam Kieth-c. 2-Intro Razorsharp		1.00	2.5

ROBIN (See Detective #668)
Nov, 1993 - Present ($1.50, color)
DC Comics

	GD25	FN65	NM94
1-($2.95)-Collector's edition w/foil embossed-c; 1st app. Robin's car, The Redbird; Azrael as Batman app.		1.20	3.0
1-6: Regular editions			1.5

ROBIN: A HERO REBORN
1991 ($4.95, squarebound, trade paperback)
DC Comics

	GD25	FN65	NM94
nn-r/Batman #455-457 & Robin #1-5; Bolland-c	1.00	2.00	5.0

ROBIN HOOD (See The Advs. of..., Brave and the Bold, Four Color #413, 669, King Classics, Movie Comics & Power Record Comics)

ROBIN HOOD (...& His Merry Men, The Illustrated Story of...) (See Classic Comics #7 & Classics Giveaways, 12/44)

ROBIN HOOD (New Adventures of...)
1952 (36 pages) (5x7-1/4")
Walt Disney Productions (Flour giveaways)

	GD25	FN65	NM94
"New Adventures of Robin Hood," "Ghosts of Waylea Castle," & "The Miller's Ransom" each....	4.00	10.00	20.0

ROBIN HOOD (Adventures of... #7, 8)
No. 52, Nov, 1955 - No. 6, June, 1957
Magazine Enterprises (Sussex Publ. Co.)

	GD25	FN65	NM94
52 (#1)-Origin Robin Hood & Sir Gallant of the Round Table	10.00	30.00	65.0
53 (#2), 3-6: 6-Richard Greene photo-c (TV)	8.35	25.00	50.0
I.W. Reprint #1,2,9: 1-r/#3. 2-r/#4. 9-r/#52 (1963)	1.60	4.00	8.0
Super Reprint #10,15: 10-r/#53. 15-r/#5	1.60	4.00	8.0
Super Reprint #11,17(1964)-Both exist?	1.60	4.00	8.0

NOTE: ***Bolle*** *a-in all; c-52.* ***Powell*** *a-6.*

Robocop #1, © Orion Pictures

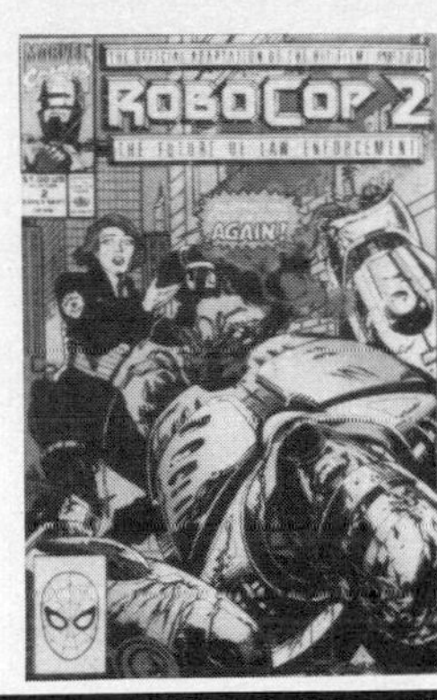

Robocop II #2, © Orion Pictures

GD25 FN65 NM94

)BIN HOOD (Not Disney)
ıy-July, 1963 (One shot)
ll Publishing Co.
 2.80 7.00 14.00

)BIN HOOD
73 (Disney) (8-1/2x11"; cardboard covers) ($1.50, 52 pages)
estern Publishing Co.
151-"Robin Hood," based on movie, 96152-"The Mystery of Sherwood Forest," 96153-"In King Richard's Service," 96154-"The Wizard's Ring" each.... 1.60 4.00

)BIN HOOD
ly, 1991 - No. 3, 1991 ($2.50, color, mini-series)
lipse Comics
-3: Timothy Truman layouts 1.00 2.50

)BIN HOOD AND HIS MERRY MEN (Formerly Danger & Adventure)
. 28, April, 1956 - No. 38, Aug, 1958
ıarlton Comics
8 5.85 17.50 35.00
9-37 4.20 12.50 25.00
8-Ditko-a (5 pgs.) 10.00 30.00 60.00

)BIN HOOD'S FRONTIER DAYS (...Western Tales)
› date (Circa 1955) 20 pages, slick-c (Seven issues?)
ıoe Store Giveaway (Robin Hood Stores)
 4.20 12.50 25.00
-Issues with Crandall-a 7.50 22.50 45.00

)BIN HOOD TALES (Published by National Periodical #7 on)
ıb, 1956 - No. 6, Nov-Dec, 1956
uality Comics Group (Comic Magazines)
-All have Baker/Culdera-c 15.00 45.00 105.00
2-5-Matt Baker-a 15.00 45.00 105.00
 11.00 32.00 75.00
rontier Days giveaway (1956) 5.35 16.00 32.00

)BIN HOOD TALES (Continued from Quality series)
). 7, Jan-Feb, 1957 - No. 14, Mar-Apr, 1958
ational Periodical Publications
7-All have Andru/Esposito-c 25.00 75.00 175.00
3-14 20.00 60.00 140.00

)BINSON CRUSOE (See King Classics & Power Record Comics)
ov-Jan, 1963-64
ell Publishing Co.
1 1.60 4.00 8.00

)BIN II (The Joker's Wild)
ct, 1991 - No. 4, Dec, 1991 ($1.50, color, mini-series)
C Comics
1-(Direct sale, $1.50)-With 4 different-c; same hologram on each 1.50
1-(Newsstand, $1.00)-No hologram; 1 version 1.00
1-Collector's set ($10.00)-Contains all 5 versions bagged with hologram trading card inside 1.65 4.00 10.00
2-(Direct sale, $1.50)-With 3 different-c 1.50
2-4-(Newsstand, $1.00)-1 version of each 1.00
2-Collector's set ($8.00)-Contains all 4 versions bagged with hologram trading card inside 1.30 3.25 8.00
3-(Direct sale, $1.50)-With 2 different-c 1.50
3-Collector's set ($6.00)-Contains all 3 versions bagged with hologram trading card inside 1.00 2.50 6.00
4-(Direct sale, $1.50)-Only one version 1.50
4-Collector's set ($4.00)-Contains both versions bagged with Bat-Signal hologram trading card 1.60 4.00
Iulti-pack (All four issues w/hologram sticker) 1.60 4.00
eluxe Complete Set ($30.00)-Contains all 14 versions of #1-4 plus a new hologram trading card; numbered & limited to 25,000; comes with slipcase & 2 acid free backing boards 4.30 13.00 30.00

GD25 FN65 NM94

ROBIN III: CRY OF THE HUNTRESS
Dec, 1992 - No. 6, Mar, 1993 (Color, mini-series)
DC Comics
1-6 ($2.50, collector's ed.)-Polybagged w/movement enhanced-c plus mini-poster of newsstand-c by Zeck 1.00 2.50
1-6 ($1.25, newsstand ed.): All have Zeck-c 1.25

ROBIN 3000
1992 - No. 2, 1992 ($4.95, color, mini-series, 52 pgs.)
DC Comics
1,2-Foil logo; Elseworlds storyline; Russell-c/a 1.00 2.00 5.00

ROBOCOP
Oct, 1987 ($2.00, B&W, magazine, one-shot)
Marvel Comics
1-Movie adaptation .80 2.00

ROBOCOP
March, 1990 - No. 23, Jan, 1992 ($1.50, color)
Marvel Comics
1-Based on movie 1.00 2.50 5.50
2 1.60 4.00
3-6 1.20 3.00
7-23 1.50
nn (7/90, $4.95, color, 52 pgs.)-r/B&W magazine in color; adapts 1st movie 1.80 4.50

ROBOCOP: PRIME SUSPECT
Oct, 1992 - No. 4, Jan, 1993 ($2.50, color, mini-series)
Dark Horse Comics
1-4: Nelson painted-c 1.00 2.50

ROBOCOP 2
Aug, 1990 ($2.25, B&W, magazine, 68 pgs.)
Marvel Comics
1-Adapts movie sequel .90 2.25

ROBOCOP 2
Aug, 1990; Late Aug, 1990 - #3, Late Sept, 1990 ($1.00, mini-series)
Marvel Comics
nn-(8/90, $4.95, color, 68 pgs.)-Same contents as B&W magazine 1.00 2.00 5.00
1: #1-3 reprint no number issue 1.20 3.00
2,3: 2-Guice-c(i) 1.50

ROBOCOP 3
Aug, 1992 - No. 3, 1992 ($2.50, color, mini-series)
Dark Horse Comics
1-3 1.00 2.50

ROBOCOP 3
July, 1993 - No. 3, Nov, 1993 ($2.50, color, mini-series)
Dark Horse Comics
1-3: Nelson painted-c; Nguyen-a 1.00 2.50

ROBOCOP VERSUS THE TERMINATOR
Sept, 1992 - No. 4, 1992 (Dec.) ($2.50, color, mini-series)
Dark Horse Comics
1-4: Miller scripts & Simonson-c/a in all 1.00 2.50
1-Platinum Edition 15.00
NOTE: *All contain a different Robocop cardboard cut-out stand-up.*

ROBO-HUNTER (Eagle)(Value: cover or less)(Also see Sam Slade...)

R.O.B.O.T. BATTALION 2050 (Eclipse)(Value: cover or less)

ROBOT COMICS (Renegade)(Value: cover or less)

ROBOTECH DEFENDERS

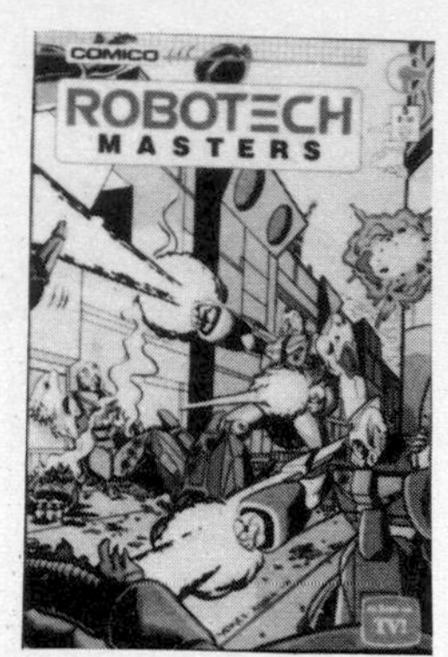

Robotech Masters #5, © Harmony Gold/Tatsunoko

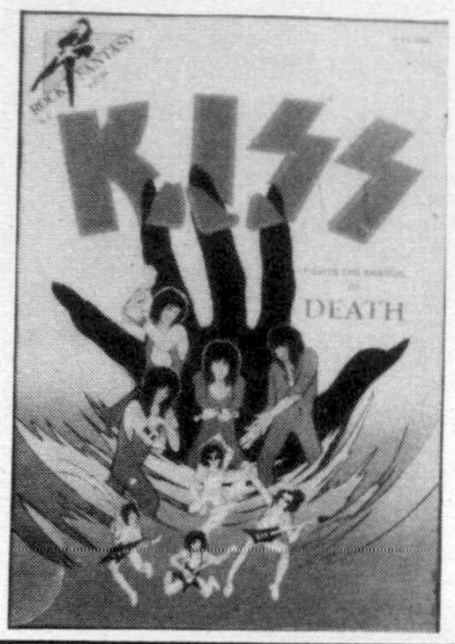

Rock Fantasy #10, © Rock Fantasy Comics

Rock & Roll Comics #1, © Revolutionary

GD25 FN65 NM94

Mar, 1985 - No. 2, Apr, 1985 (Mini-series)
DC Comics

1,2 — 1.00

ROBOTECH IN 3-D (Comico)(Value: cover or less)

ROBOTECH MASTERS (TV)
July, 1985 - No. 23, Apr, 1988 ($1.50, color)
Comico

1 — 1.00 — 2.50
2-23 — .65 — 1.60

ROBOTECH SPECIAL (Comico)(Value: cover or less)

ROBOTECH THE GRAPHIC NOVEL (Comico)(Value: cover or less)

ROBOTECH: THE MACROSS SAGA (TV)(Formerly Macross)
No. 2, Feb, 1985 - No. 36, Feb, 1989 ($1.50, color)
Comico

2 — 1.20 — 3.00
3-10 — .80 — 2.00
11-36: 12,17-Ken Steacy painted-c — .70 — 1.75

ROBOTECH: THE NEW GENERATION (TV)(Comico)(Value: cover or less)

ROBOTECH II: THE SENTINELS SWIMSUIT SPECTACULAR (Eternity)(Value: cover or less)

ROBOTIX (Marvel)(Value: cover or less)

ROBOTMEN OF THE LOST PLANET (Also see Space Thrillers)
1952 (Also see Strange Worlds #19)
Avon Periodicals

1-Kinstler-a (3 pgs.); Fawcette-a — 66.00 — 200.00 — 465.00

ROB ROY (See 4-Color #544)

ROCK AND ROLLO (Formerly TV Teens)
V2#14, Oct, 1957 - No. 19, Sept, 1958
Charlton Comics

V2#14-19 — 3.60 — 9.00 — 18.00

ROCKET COMICS
Mar, 1940 - No. 3, May, 1940
Hillman Periodicals

1-Rocket Riley, Red Roberts the Electro Man (origin), The Phantom Ranger, The Steel Shark, The Defender, Buzzard Barnes, Lefty Larson, & The Defender, the Man with a Thousand Faces begin (1st app. of each) — 142.00 — 425.00 — 950.00
2,3 — 75.00 — 225.00 — 500.00

ROCKETEER, THE (See Eclipse Graphic Album Series, Pacific Presents & Starslayer)

ROCKETEER ADVENTURE MAGAZINE, THE
July, 1988 ($2.00, color); No. 2, July, 1989 ($2.75, color)
Comico

1-Dave Stevens-c/a in all; Kaluta back-up-a — 1.00 — 2.50 — 5.50
2 (7/89, $2.75)-Stevens/Dorman painted-c — 1.50 — 3.75

ROCKETEER SPECIAL EDITION, THE
Nov, 1984 ($1.50, color, Baxter paper)(Chapter 5 of Rocketeer serial)
Eclipse Comics

1-Stevens-c/a; Kaluta back-c; pin-ups inside — 1.65 — 4.00 — 10.00

ROCKETEER THE OFFICIAL MOVIE ADAPT. THE (Disney)(Value: cover or less)

ROCKET KELLY (See The Bouncer, Green Mask #10); becomes Li'l Pan #6)
1944; Fall, 1945 - No. 5, Oct-Nov, 1946
Fox Feature Syndicate

nn (1944) — 17.00 — 50.00 — 110.00
1 — 17.00 — 50.00 — 110.00
2-The Puppeteer app. (costumed hero) — 12.00 — 35.00 — 80.00
3-5: 5-(#5 on cover, #4 inside) — 10.00 — 30.00 — 70.00

ROCKETMAN (Strange Fantasy #2 on) (See Hello Pal & Scoop Comics)
June, 1952
Ajax/Farrell Publications

1-Rocketman & Cosmo — 24.00 — 72.00 — 165.

ROCKET MAN: KING OF THE ROCKET MEN (Innovation)(Value: cover or less)

ROCKET RACCOON (Marvel)(Value: cover or less)

ROCKET RANGER (Adventure)(Value: cover or less)

ROCKETS AND RANGE RIDERS
May, 1957 (16 pages, soft-c) (Giveaway)
Richfield Oil Corp.

nn-Toth-a — 14.00 — 43.00 — 100.

ROCKET SHIP X
September, 1951; 1952
Fox Features Syndicate

1 — 40.00 — 120.00 — 280.
1952 (nn, nd, no publ.)-Edited 1951-c — 27.00 — 81.00 — 190.C

ROCKET TO ADVENTURE LAND (See Pixie Puzzle...)

ROCKET TO THE MOON
1951
Avon Periodicals

nn-Orlando-c/a; adapts Otis Aldebert Kline's "Maza of the Moon" — 69.00 — 205.00 — 480.C

ROCK FANTASY COMICS
Dec, 1989 - No. 16?, 1991 ($2.25-$3.00, B&W)(No cover price)
Rock Fantasy Comics

1-Pink Floyd part I — 1.60 — 4.0
1-2nd printing ($3.00-c) — 1.20 — 3.0
2,3: 2-Rolling Stones #1. 3-Led Zeppelin #1 — 1.20 — 3.C
2,3: 2nd printings ($3.00-c, 1/90 & 2/90) — 1.20 — 3.0
4-Stevie Nicks Not published
5-Monstrosities of Rock #1; photo back-c — 1.00 — 2.5
5-2nd printing ($3.00, 3/90 indicia, 2/90-c) — 1.20 — 3.0
6-15: 6-Guns n' Roses #1 (1st & 2nd prints, 3/90)-Begin $3.00-c. 7-Sex Pistols #1. 8-Alice Cooper Not published. 9-Van Halen #1; photo back-c. 10-Kiss #1; photo back-c. 11-Jimi Hendrix #1; wraparound-c — 1.20 — 3.0
16-($5.00, 68 pgs.)-The Great Gig in the Sky — 1.00 — 2.00 — 5.0

ROCK HAPPENING (Harvey Pop Comics:...)(See Bunny)
Sept, 1969 - No. 2, Nov, 1969
Harvey Publications

1,2: Featuring Bunny — 3.00 — 7.50 — 15.0

ROCK N' ROLL COMICS
June, 1989 - Present ($1.50-$1.95, B&W; color #15 on)
Revolutionary Comics

1-Guns N' Roses — 1.65 — 4.00 — 10.0
1-2nd thru 6th printings — 1.5
1-7th printing (full color w/new-c/a; $1.95) — .80 — 2.0
2-Metallica — 1.00 — 2.00 — 5.0
2-2nd thru 6th printings (6th in color) — 1.5
3-Bon Jovi (no reprints) — 1.00 — 2.5
4-8,10-68: 4-Motley Crue(2nd printing only, 1st destroyed). 5-Def Leppard (2 printings). 6-Rolling Stones(4 printings). 7-The Who(3 printings). 8-Skid Row; not published. 10-Warrant/Whitesnake(2 printings; 1st has 2 diff.-c) 11-Aerosmith (2 printings?). 12-New Kids on the Block(2 printings). 12-3rd printing; rewritten & titled NKOTB Hate Book. 13-Led Zeppelin. 14-Sex Pistols. 15-Poison; 1st color issue. 16-Van Halen. 17-Madonna. 18-Alice Cooper. 19-Public Enemy/2 Live Crew. 20-Queensryche/Tesla. 21-Prince? 22-AC/DC; begin $2.50-c. 23-Living Colour. 24-Anthrax — 1.00 — 2.5
9-Kiss — 1.60 — 4.0
9-2nd & 3rd printings — .80 — 2.0

NOTE: *Most issues were reprinted except #3. Later reprints are in color. #8 was not released.*

Rocky Lane Western #18, © FAW

Rod Cameron Western # 20, © FAW

Rogue Trooper #1, © Quality Comics

	GD25	FN65	NM94

ROCKY AND HIS FIENDISH FRIENDS (TV)(Bullwinkle)
Oct, 1962 - No. 5, Sept, 1963 (Jay Ward)
Gold Key

	GD25	FN65	NM94
1 (84 pgs., 25 cents)	20.00	69.00	160.00
2,3 (84 pgs., 25 cents)	12.00	41.00	95.00
4,5 (Regular size, 12 cents)	8.00	28.00	65.00

ROCKY AND HIS FRIENDS (See 4-Color #1128, 1152, 1166, 1208, 1275, 1311, Kite Fun Book and March of Comics #216)

ROCKY HORROR PICTURE SHOW THE COMIC BOOK, THE
July, 1990 - No. 3, 1990 ($2.95, color, mini-series, 52 pgs.)(Photo-c #1)
Caliber Press

	GD25	FN65	NM94
1-Adapts cult film plus photos, etc.	1.00	2.00	5.00
1-2nd printing		1.20	3.00
2,3		1.40	3.50
...Collection ($4.95)	1.00	2.00	5.00

ROCKY JONES SPACE RANGER (See Space Adventures #15-18)

ROCKY JORDAN PRIVATE EYE (See Private Eye)

ROCKY LANE WESTERN (Allan Rocky Lane starred in Republic movies & TV (for a short time as Allan Lane, Red Ryder & Rocky Lane) (See Black Jack Fawcett Movie Comics, Motion Picture Comics & Six Gun Heroes)
May, 1949 - No. 87, Nov, 1959
Fawcett Publications/Charlton No. 56 on

	GD25	FN65	NM94
1 (36 pgs.)-Rocky, his stallion Black Jack, & Slim Pickens begin; photo-c begin, end #57; photo back-c	71.00	215.00	500.00
2 (36 pgs.)-Last photo back-c	29.00	85.00	200.00
3-5 (52 pgs.): 4-Captain Tootsie by Beck	20.00	60.00	140.00
6,10 (36 pgs.)	16.00	48.00	110.00
7-9 (52 pgs.)	17.00	52.00	120.00
11-13,15-17 (52 pgs.): 15-Black Jack's Hitching Post begins, ends #25	12.00	36.00	85.00
14,18 (36 pgs.)	10.00	30.00	70.00
19-21,23,24 (52 pgs.): 20-Last Slim Pickens. 21-Dee Dickens begins, ends #55,57,65-68	10.00	30.00	70.00
22,25-28,30 (36 pgs. begin)	10.00	30.00	65.00
29-Classic complete novel "The Land of Missing Men," hidden land of ancient temple ruins (r-in #65)	12.00	36.00	85.00
31-40	10.00	30.00	60.00
41-54	8.35	25.00	50.00
55-Last Fawcett issue (1/54)	9.15	27.50	55.00
56-1st Charlton issue (2/54)-Photo-c	11.00	32.00	75.00
57,60-Photo-c	8.35	25.00	50.00
58,59,61-64: 59-61-Young Falcon app. 64-Slim Pickens app.	5.85	17.50	35.00
65-r/#29, "The Land of Missing Men"	6.70	20.00	40.00
66-68: Reprints #30,31,32	5.85	17.50	35.00
69-78,80-86	5.85	17.50	35.00
79-Giant Edition, 68 pgs.	7.00	21.00	42.00
87-Last issue	6.70	20.00	40.00

NOTE: *Complete novels in #10, 14, 18, 22, 25, 30-32, 36, 38, 39, 49. Captain Tootsie in #4, 12, 20. Big Bow and Little Arrow in #11, 28, 63. Black Jack's Hitching Post in #15-25, 64, 73.*

ROCKY LANE WESTERN (AC)(Value: cover or less)

ROD CAMERON WESTERN (Movie star)
Feb, 1950 - No. 20, April, 1953
Fawcett Publications

	GD25	FN65	NM94
1-Rod Cameron, his horse War Paint, & Sam The Sheriff begin; photo front/back-c begin	46.00	140.00	325.00
2	20.00	60.00	140.00
3-Novel length story "The Mystery of the Seven Cities of Cibola"	17.00	52.00	120.00
4-10: 9-Last photo back-c	14.00	43.00	100.00
11-19	11.50	34.00	80.00
20-Last issue & photo-c	12.00	36.00	85.00

NOTE: *Novel length stories in No. 1-8, 12-14.*

[illegible]

ROGER BEAN, R. G. (Regular Guy)
1915 - No. 5, 1917 (34 pgs.; B&W; 4-3/4x16"; cardboard covers)
(No. 1 & 4 bound on side, No. 3 bound at top)
The Indiana News Co.

	GD25	FN65	NM94
1-By Chic Jackson (48 pgs.)	13.00	40.00	90.00
2-5	10.00	30.00	65.00

ROGER DODGER (Also in Exciting Comics #57 on)
No. 5, Aug, 1952
Standard Comics

	GD25	FN65	NM94
5-Teen-age	3.60	9.00	18.00

ROGER RABBIT (Also see Marvel Graphic Novel)
June, 1990 - No. 18, Nov, 1991 ($1.50, color)
Disney Comics

	GD25	FN65	NM94
1-All new stories		1.20	3.50
2,3		.80	2.00
4-18			1.50
In 3-D 1 ('92, $2.50)-Sold at Wal-Mart?; w/glasses		1.00	2.50

ROGER RABBIT'S TOONTOWN
Aug, 1991 - No. 5, Dec, 1991 ($1.50, color)
Disney Comics

	GD25	FN65	NM94
1-5			1.50

ROG 2000 (Pacific & Fantagraphics)(Value: cover or less)

ROGUE TROOPER (Fleetway/Quality)(Value: cover or less)

ROGUE TROOPER: THE FINAL WARRIOR (Quality)(Value: cover or less)

ROLY POLY COMIC BOOK
1945 - No. 15, 1946 (MLJ reprints)
Green Publishing Co.

	GD25	FN65	NM94
1-Red Rube & Steel Sterling begin; Sahle-c	20.00	60.00	140.00
6-The Blue Circle & The Steel Fist app.	10.00	30.00	70.00
10-Origin Red Rube retold; Steel Sterling story (Zip #41)	10.00	30.00	65.00
11,12,14: The Black Hood app. in each. 14-Decapitation-c	10.00	30.00	70.00
15-The Blue Circle & The Steel Fist app.; cover exact swipe from Fox Blue Beetle #1	23.00	70.00	160.00

ROM
December, 1979 - No. 75, Feb, 1986
Marvel Comics Group

	GD25	FN65	NM94
1-Based on a Parker Bros. toy; origin/1st app.		1.00	2.50
2-5			1.20
6-16: 13-Saga of the Space Knights begins			1.00
17,18-X-Men app.		1.00	2.50
19-24,26-30: 19-X-Men cameo. 24-F.F. cameo; Skrulls, Nova & The New Champions app. 26,27-Galactus app.			1.00
25-Double size			1.20
31-75: 31,32-Brother of Evil Mutants app. 32-X-Men cameo. 34,35-Sub-Mariner app. 41,42-Dr. Strange app. 50-Skrulls app. (52 pgs.). 56,57-Alpha Flight app. 58,59-Ant-Man app. 65-West Coast Avengers & Beta Ray Bill app. 65,66-X-Men app.			1.00
Annual 1,4: 1(1982, 52 pgs.). 4(1985, 52 pgs.)			1.20
Annual 2,3: 2(1983, 52 pgs.). 3(1984, 52 pgs.)			1.00

NOTE: ***Austin** c-3i, 18i, 61i. **Byrne** a-74i; c-56, 57, 74. **Ditko** a-59-75p. **Golden** c-7-12, 19. **Guice** a-61i; c-55, 58, 60p, 70p. **Layton** a-59i, 72i; c-15, 59i, 69. **Miller** c-2p?, 3p, 17p, 18p. **Russell** a(i)-64, 65, 67, 69, 71, 75; c-64, 65i, 66, 71i, 75. **Severin** c-41p. **Sienkiewicz** a-53i; c-46, 47, 52-54, 68, 71p, Annual 2. **P. Smith** c-59p. **Starlin** c-67.*

ROMANCE (See True Stories of...)

ROMANCE AND CONFESSION STORIES (See Giant Comics Edition)
No date (1949) (25¢, 100pgs.)
St. John Publishing Co.

	GD25	FN65	NM94
1-Baker-c/a; remaindered St. John love comics	25.00	75.00	175.00

Romances Of The West #1, © MEG

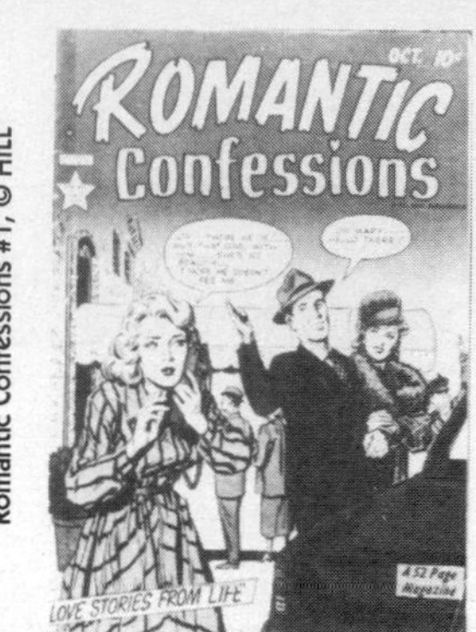

Romantic Confessions #1, © HILL

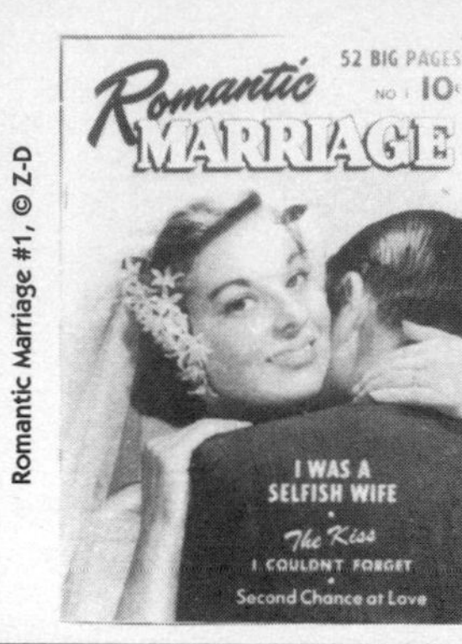

Romantic Marriage #1, © Z-D

ROMANCE DIARY
December, 1949 - No. 2, March, 1950
Marvel Comics (CDS)(CLDS)

	GD25	FN65	NM94
1,2	8.35	25.00	50.00

ROMANCE OF FLYING, THE (See Feature Books #33)

ROMANCES OF MOLLY MANTON (See Molly Manton)

ROMANCES OF NURSE HELEN GRANT, THE
August, 1957
Atlas Comics (VPI)

	GD25	FN65	NM94
1	4.00	11.00	22.00

ROMANCES OF THE WEST (Becomes Romantic Affairs #3?)
Nov, 1949 - No. 2, Mar, 1950 (52 pgs.)
Marvel Comics (SPC)

	GD25	FN65	NM94
1-Movie photo-c of Yvonne DeCarlo & Howard Duff (Calamity Jane & Sam Bass)	13.00	40.00	90.00
2-Photo-c	10.00	30.00	60.00

ROMANCE STORIES OF TRUE LOVE (Formerly Love Problems & Advice)
No. 45, 5/57 - No. 50, 3/58; No. 51, 9/58 - No. 52, 11/58
Harvey Publications

	GD25	FN65	NM94
45-51: 45,46,48-50-Powell-a	2.40	6.00	12.00
52-Matt Baker-a	4.00	10.50	21.00

ROMANCE TALES (Formerly Western Winners #6?)
No. 7, Oct, 1949 - No. 9, March, 1950 (7,8: photo-c)
Marvel Comics (CDS)

	GD25	FN65	NM94
7	7.50	22.50	45.00
8,9: 8-Everett-a	5.35	16.00	32.00

ROMANCE TRAIL
July-Aug, 1949 - No. 6, May-June, 1950 (All photo-c)
National Periodical Publications

	GD25	FN65	NM94
1-Kinstler, Toth-a; Jimmy Wakely photo-c	39.00	120.00	275.00
2-Kinstler-a; Jim Bannon photo-c	19.00	58.00	135.00
3-Photo-c; Kinstler, Toth-a	22.00	65.00	150.00
4-Photo-c; Toth-a	16.00	48.00	110.00
5,6-Photo-c	13.00	40.00	90.00

ROMAN HOLIDAYS, THE (TV)
Feb, 1973 - No. 4, Nov, 1973 (Hanna-Barbera)
Gold Key

	GD25	FN65	NM94
1	1.70	5.00	12.00
2-4	1.50	3.75	9.00

ROMANTIC ADVENTURES (My... #49-67, covers only)
Mar-Apr, 1949 - No. 67, July, 1956 (Becomes My... No. 68 on)
American Comics Group (B&I Publ. Co.)

	GD25	FN65	NM94
1	10.00	30.00	60.00
2	5.35	16.00	32.00
3-10	4.00	10.00	20.00
11-20 (4/52)	3.20	8.00	16.00
21-45,49,51,52: 52-Last Pre-code (2/55)	2.40	6.00	12.00
46-48-3-D effect (TrueVision)	6.70	20.00	40.00
50-Classic cover/story "Love of A Lunatic"	5.35	16.00	32.00
53-67	1.80	4.50	9.00

NOTE: *#1-23, 52 pgs.* ***Shelly*** *a-40. Whitney c/art in many issues.*

ROMANTIC AFFAIRS (Formerly Molly Manton's Romances #2 and/or Romances of the West #2?)
No. 3, March, 1950
Marvel Comics (SPC)

	GD25	FN65	NM94
3-Photo-c from Molly Manton's Romances #2	5.00	15.00	30.00

ROMANTIC CONFESSIONS
Oct, 1949 - V3#1, April-May, 1953
Hillman Periodicals

	GD25	FN65	NM94
V1#1-McWilliams-a	9.15	27.50	55.00
2-Briefer-a; negligee panels	5.35	16.00	32.00
3-12	4.00	10.00	20.00
V2#1,2,4-8,10-12: 2-McWilliams-a	3.20	8.00	16.00
3-Krigstein-a	5.85	17.50	35.00
9-One pg. Frazetta ad	3.20	8.00	16.00
V3#1	3.20	8.00	16.00

ROMANTIC HEARTS
Mar, 1951 - No. 10, Oct, 1952; July, 1953 - No. 12, July, 1955
Story Comics/Master/Merit Pubs.

	GD25	FN65	NM94
1(3/51) (1st Series)	8.35	25.00	50.00
2	4.20	12.50	25.00
3-10	4.00	10.00	20.00
1(7/53) (2nd Series)	5.00	15.00	30.00
2	3.60	9.00	18.00
3-12	2.80	7.00	14.00

ROMANTIC LOVE
9-10/49 - #3, 1-2/50; #4, 2-3/51 - #13, 10/52; #20, 3-4/54 - #23, 9-10/54
Avon Periodicals/Realistic (No #14-19)

	GD25	FN65	NM94
1-c-/Avon paperback #252	13.50	41.00	95.00
2-5: 3-c-/paperback Novel Library #12. 4-c-/paperback Diversey Prize Novel #5. 5-c-/paperback Novel Library #34	9.15	27.50	55.00
6-"Thrill Crazy"-marijuana story; c-/Avon paperback #207; Kinstler-a	10.00	30.00	70.00
7,8: 8-Astarita-a(2)	8.35	25.00	50.00
9-12: 9-c-/paperback Novel Library #41; Kinstler-a. 10-c-/Avon paperback #212. 11-c-/paperback Novel Library #17; Kinstler-a. 12-c-/paperback Novel Library #13	9.15	27.50	55.00
13,21,22: 22-Kinstler-c	8.35	25.00	50.00
20-Kinstler-c/a	8.35	25.00	50.00
23-Kinstler-c	6.35	19.00	38.00
nn(1-3/53)(Realistic-r)	5.35	16.00	32.00

NOTE: ***Astarita*** *a-7, 10, 11, 21. Painted c-7, 9, 10, 11. Photo c-4, 6.*

ROMANTIC LOVE
No. 4, June, 1950
Quality Comics Group

	GD25	FN65	NM94
4 (6/50)(Exist?)	4.20	12.50	25.00
I.W. Reprint #2,3,8	.40	1.00	2.00

ROMANTIC MARRIAGE (Cinderella Love #25 on)
#1-3 (1950, no months); #4, 5-6/51 - #17, 9/52; #18, 9/53 - #24, 9/54
Ziff-Davis/St. John No. 18 on (#1-8: 52 pgs.)

	GD25	FN65	NM94
1-Photo-c	11.00	32.00	75.00
2-Painted-c; Anderson-a (also #15)	7.00	21.00	42.00
3-9: 3,4,8,9-Painted-c; 5-7-Photo-c	5.35	16.00	32.00
10-Unusual format; front-c is a painted-c; back-c is a photo-c complete with logo, price, etc.	10.00	30.00	65.00
11-17 13-Photo-c. 17-(9/52)-Last Z-D issue	4.70	14.00	28.00
18-22,24: 20-Photo-c	4.70	14.00	28.00
23-Baker-c	5.00	15.00	30.00

ROMANTIC PICTURE NOVELETTES
1946
Magazine Enterprises

	GD25	FN65	NM94
1-Mary Worth-r; Craig Flessel-c	10.00	30.00	65.00

ROMANTIC SECRETS (Becomes Time For Love)
Sept, 1949 - No. 39, 4/53; No. 5, 10/55 - No. 52, 11/64 (#1-5: photo-c)
Fawcett/Charlton Comics No. 5 (10/55) on

	GD25	FN65	NM94
1	10.00	30.00	60.00
2,3	5.35	16.00	32.00
4,9-Evans-a	6.35	19.00	38.00
5-8,10	4.00	10.00	20.00
11-23	3.60	9.00	18.00
24-Evans-a	4.70	14.00	28.00

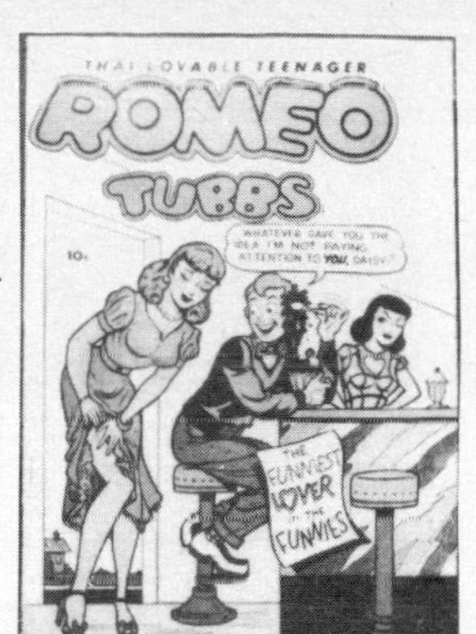

Romeo Tubbs #27, © FOX

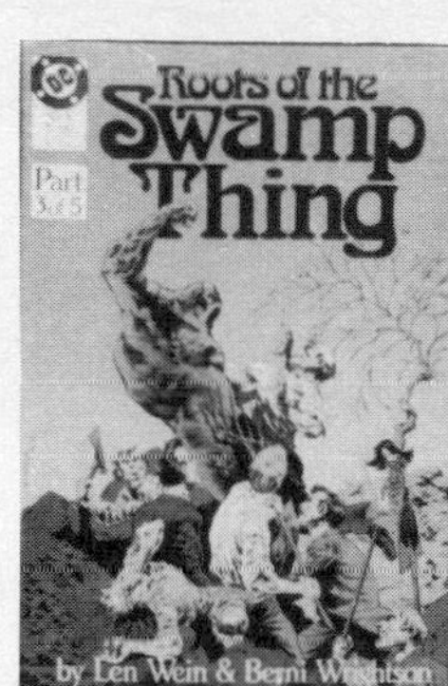

Roots of the Swampthing #3, © DC

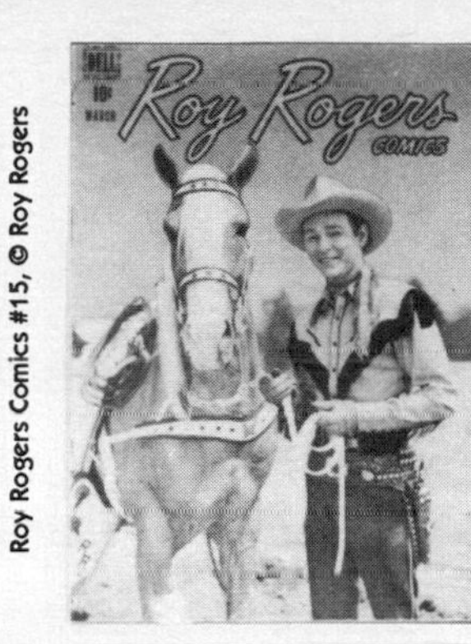

Roy Rogers Comics #15, © Roy Rogers

	GD25	FN65	NM94
25-39	2.80	7.00	14.00
5 (Charlton, 2nd series)(10/55, formerly Negro Romances #4)	5.00	15.00	30.00
6-10	3.00	7.50	15.00
11-20	1.40	3.50	7.00
21-35: Last 10 cent issue?	1.00	2.50	5.00
36-52('64)	.60	1.50	3.00

NOTE: ***Bailey** a-20. **Powell** a(1st series)-5, 7, 10, 12, 16, 17, 20, 26, 29, 33, 34, 36, 37. **Sekowsky** a-26. Photo c(1st series)-1-5, 16, 25, 27, 33. **Swayze** a(1st series)-16, 18, 19, 23, 26-28, 31, 32, 39.*

ROMANTIC STORY (Cowboy Love #28 on)
11/49 - #22, Sum, 1953; #23, 5/54 - #27, 12/54; #28, 8/55 - #130, 11/73
Fawcett/Charlton Comics No. 23 on

	GD25	FN65	NM94
1-Photo-c begin, end #24	10.00	30.00	65.00
2	5.35	16.00	32.00
3-5	4.70	14.00	28.00
6-14	4.00	10.00	20.00
15-Evans-a	4.70	14.00	28.00
16-22(Sum, '53; last Fawcett issue). 21-Toth-a?	3.00	7.50	15.00
23-39: 26,29-Wood swipes	3.00	7.50	15.00
40-(100 pgs.)	4.70	14.00	28.00
41-50	2.40	6.00	12.00
51-80: 57-Hypo needle story	1.00	2.50	6.00
81-100		1.20	3.00
101-130		.80	2.00

NOTE: ***Jim Aparo** a-94. **Powell** a-7, 8, 16, 20, 30. **Marcus Swayze** a-2, 12, 20, 32.*

ROMANTIC THRILLS (See Fox Giants)

ROMANTIC WESTERN
Winter, 1949 - No. 3, June, 1950 (All Photo-c)
Fawcett Publications

	GD25	FN65	NM94
1	11.50	34.00	80.00
2-(Spr/50)-Williamson, McWilliams-a	13.00	40.00	90.00
3	10.00	30.00	60.00

ROMEO TUBBS (Formerly My Secret Life)
No. 26, 5/50 - No. 28, 7/50; No. 1, 1950; No. 27, 12/52
Fox Feature Syndicate/Green Publ. Co. No. 27

	GD25	FN65	NM94
26-Teen-age	8.35	25.00	50.00
27-Contains Pedro on inside; Wood-a	11.00	32.00	75.00
28, 1	6.70	20.00	40.00

RONALD McDONALD (TV)
Sept, 1970 - No. 4, March, 1971
Charlton Press (King Features Synd.)

	GD25	FN65	NM94
1	1.00	2.00	5.00
2-4		1.20	3.00

RONIN
July, 1983 - No. 6, Aug, 1984 ($2.50, mini-series, 52 pgs.)
DC Comics

	GD25	FN65	NM94
1-Miller script, c/a in all		1.60	4.00
2-5		1.20	3.00
6-Scarcer; has fold-out poster		2.50	6.00
Trade paperback (1987, $12.95)-Reprints #1-6	1.85	5.50	13.00

ROOK (See Eerie Magazine & Warren Presents: The Rook)
November, 1979 - No. 14, April, 1982
Warren Publications

	GD25	FN65	NM94
1-Nino-a			1.50
2-14: 3,4-Toth-a			1.00

ROOKIE COP (Formerly Crime and Justice?)
No. 27, Nov, 1955 - No. 33, Aug, 1957
Charlton Comics

	GD25	FN65	NM94
27	5.85	17.50	35.00
28-33	4.00	10.00	20.00

ROOM 222 (TV)
Jan, 1970; No. 2, May, 1970 - No. 4, Jan, 1971
Dell Publishing Co.

	GD25	FN65	NM94
1	5.00	15.00	35.00
2-4: 2,4-Photo-c. 3-Marijuana story. 4 r/#1	3.00	9.00	20.00

ROOTIE KAZOOTIE (TV)(See 3-D-ell)
No. 415, Aug, 1952 - No. 6, Oct-Dec, 1954
Dell Publishing Co.

	GD25	FN65	NM94
4-Color 415 (#1)	10.00	30.00	70.00
4-Color 459,502(#2,3)	7.50	22.50	45.00
4(4-6/54)-6	7.50	22.50	45.00

ROOTS OF THE SWAMPTHING (DC)(Value: cover or less)

ROUND THE WORLD GIFT
No date (mid 1940's) (4 pages)
National War Fund (Giveaway)

	GD25	FN65	NM94
nn	11.50	34.00	80.00

ROUNDUP (Western Crime)
July-Aug, 1948 - No. 5, Mar-Apr, 1949 (All 52 pgs.)
D. S. Publishing Co.

	GD25	FN65	NM94
1-Kiefer-a	11.50	34.00	80.00
2-Marijuana drug mention story	10.00	30.00	60.00
3-5	7.50	22.50	45.00

ROYAL ROY (Marvel)(Value: cover or less)

ROY CAMPANELLA, BASEBALL HERO
1950 (Brooklyn Dodgers)
Fawcett Publications

	GD25	FN65	NM94
nn-Photo-c	46.00	138.00	300.00

ROY ROGERS (See March of Comics #17, 35, 47, 62, 68, 73, 77, 86, 91, 100, 105, 116, 121, 131, 136, 146, 151, 161, 167, 176, 191, 206, 221, 236, 250)

ROY ROGERS AND TRIGGER
April, 1967
Gold Key

	GD25	FN65	NM94
1-Photo-c; reprints	4.70	14.00	28.00

ROY ROGERS COMICS (See Western Roundup under Dell Giants)
No. 38, 4/44 - No. 177, 12/47 (#38-166: 52 pgs.)
Dell Publishing Co.

	GD25	FN65	NM94
4-Color 38 (1944)-49pg. story; photo front/back-c on all 4-Color issues (1st western comic with photo-c)	82.00	245.00	575.00
4-Color 63 (1945)-Color photos on all four-c	43.00	128.00	300.00
4-Color 86,95 (1945)	31.00	92.00	215.00
4-Color 109 (1946)	24.00	71.00	165.00
4-Color 117,124,137,144	17.00	51.00	120.00
4-Color 153,160,166: 166-48pg. story	14.00	43.00	100.00
4-Color 177 (36 pgs.)-32pg. story	14.00	43.00	100.00

ROY ROGERS COMICS (...& Trigger #92(8/55)-on)(Roy starred in Republic movies, radio & TV) (Singing cowboy) (Also see Dale Evans, It Really Happened #8, Queen of the West..., & Roy Rogers' Trigger)
Jan, 1948 - No. 145, Sept-Oct, 1961 (#1-19: 36 pgs.)
Dell Publishing Co.

	GD25	FN65	NM94
1-Roy, his horse Trigger, & Chuck Wagon Charley's Tales begin; photo-c begin, end #145	50.00	150.00	350.00
2	23.00	70.00	160.00
3-5	18.00	54.00	125.00
6-10	13.00	40.00	90.00
11-19: 19-...Charley's Tales ends	10.00	30.00	65.00
20 (52 pgs.)-Trigger feature begins, ends #46	10.00	30.00	65.00
21-30 (52 pgs.)	9.15	27.50	55.00
31-46 (52 pgs.): 37-X-mas-c	7.00	21.00	42.00
47-56 (36 pgs.): 47-Chuck Wagon Charley's Tales returns, ends #133. 49-X-mas-c. 55-Last photo back-c	5.35	16.00	32.00
57 (52 pgs.)-Heroin drug propaganda story	6.35	19.00	38.00

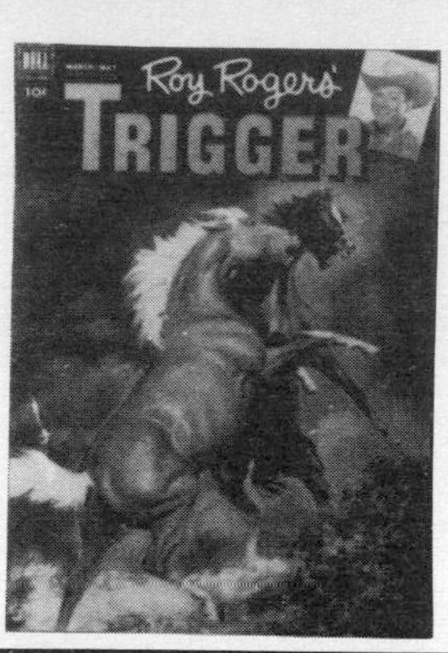
Roy Rogers Trigger #4, © Roy Rogers

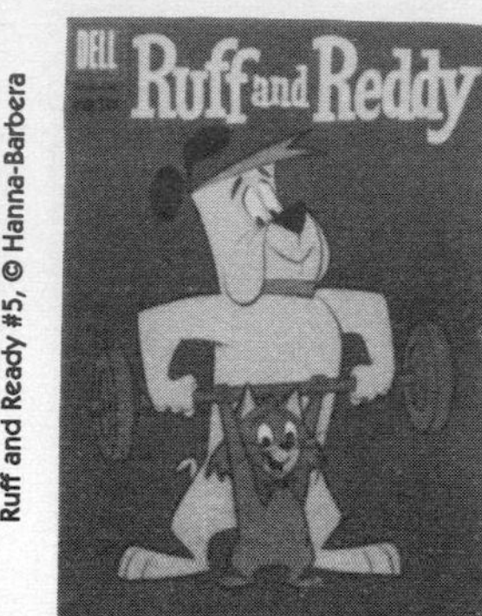

Ruff and Ready #5, © Hanna-Barbera

Sable #25, © First

GD25 FN65 NM94

58-70 (52 pgs.): 61-X-mas-c 5.00 15.00 30.00
71-80 (52 pgs.): 73-X-mas-c 4.20 12.50 25.00
81-91 (36 pgs. #81-on): 85-X-mas-c 4.00 10.00 20.00
92-99,101-110,112-118: 92-Title changed to Roy Rogers and Trigger (8/55)
4.00 10.00 20.00
100-Trigger feature returns, ends #133? 5.35 16.00 32.00
111,119-124-Toth-a 5.85 17.50 35.00
125-131: 125-Toth-a (1 pg.) 4.20 12.50 25.00
132-144-Manning-a. 144-Dale Evans featured 4.70 14.00 28.00
145-Last issue 5.85 17.50 35.00
...& the Man From Dodge City (Dodge giveaway, 16 pgs., 1954)-Frontier, Inc. (5x7-1/4") 11.00 32.00 75.00
Official Roy Rogers Riders Club Comics (1952; 16 pgs., reg. size, paper-c)
12.00 36.00 85.00

NOTE: ***Buscema*** *a-74-108(2 stories each).* ***Manning*** *a-123, 124, 132-144.* ***Marsh*** *a-110. Photo back-c No. 1-9, 11-35, 38-55.*

ROY ROGERS' TRIGGER (TV)
No. 329, May, 1951 - No. 17, June-Aug, 1955
Dell Publishing Co.

4-Color 329 (#1)-Painted-c 10.00 30.00 65.00
2 (9-11/51)-Photo-c 10.00 30.00 60.00
3-5: 3-Painted-c begin, end #17 2.80 7.00 14.00
6-17: Title merges with Roy Rogers after #17 1.50 4.50 9.00

ROY ROGERS WESTERN CLASSICS (AC)(Value: cover or less)

RUDOLPH, THE RED NOSED REINDEER (See Limited Collectors' Edition #20, 24, 33, 42, 50)

RUDOLPH, THE RED NOSED REINDEER
1939 (2,400,000 copies printed); Dec, 1951
Montgomery Ward (Giveaway)

Paper cover - 1st app. in print; written by Robert May; ill. by Denver Gillen
10.00 30.00 70.00
Hardcover version 14.00 43.00 100.00
1951 version (Has 1939 date)-36 pgs., illos in three colors; red-c
4.70 14.00 28.00

RUDOLPH, THE RED-NOSED REINDEER
1950 - No. 13?, Winter, 1962-63 (Issues are not numbered)
National Periodical Publications

1950 issue; Grossman-c/a begins 11.00 32.00 75.00
1951-54 issues (4 total) 7.50 22.50 45.00
1955-62 issues (8 total) 4.70 14.00 28.00

NOTE: *The 1962-63 issue is 84 pages. 13 total issues published.*

RUFF AND REDDY (TV)
No. 937, 9/58 - No. 12, 1-3/62 (Hanna-Barbera)(#9 on: 15 cents)
Dell Publishing Co.

4-Color 937(#1)(1st Hanna-Barbera comic book) 11.00 32.00 75.00
4-Color 981,1038 8.35 25.00 50.00
4(1-3/60)-12: 8-Last 10 cent issue 5.00 15.00 35.00

RUGGED ACTION (Strange Stories of Suspense #5 on)
Dec, 1954 - No. 4, June, 1955
Atlas Comics (CSI)

1-Brodsky-c 7.50 22.50 45.00
2-4: 2-Last precode (2/55) 4.70 14.00 28.00

NOTE: ***Ayers*** *a-2, 3.* ***Maneely*** *c-2, 3.* ***Severin*** *a-2.*

RULAH JUNGLE GODDESS (Formerly Zoot; I Loved #28 on) (Also see All Top Comics & Terrors of the Jungle)
No. 17, Aug, 1948 - No. 27, June, 1949
Fox Features Syndicate

17 47.00 140.00 330.00
18-Classic girl-fight interior splash 36.00 110.00 250.00
19,20 34.00 100.00 235.00
21-Used in **SOTI**, pg. 388,389 36.00 110.00 250.00
22-Used in **SOTI**, pg. 22,23 34.00 100.00 235.00

GD25 FN65 NM94

23-27 24.00 73.00 170.00

NOTE: ***Kamen*** *c-17-19, 21, 22.*

RUNAWAY, THE (See Movie Classics)

RUN BABY RUN
1974 (39 cents)
Logos International

nn-By Tony Tallarico from Nicky Cruz's book 1.00

RUN, BUDDY, RUN (TV)
June, 1967 (Photo-c)
Gold Key

1 (10204-706) 3.00 7.50 15.00

RUNE (See Sludge, & all other Ultraverse titles for previews)
1994 - Present ($1.95, color)
Malibu Comics (Ultraverse)

1,2-By Barry Windsor-Smith .80 2.00

RUST
7/87 - No. 15, 11/88; V2#1, 2/89 - No. 7, 1989 ($1.50-$1.75, color)
Now Comics

1-3 ($1.50) 1.50
4-11,13-15, V2#1-7 ($1.75) .70 1.75
12-(8/88, $1.75)-5 pg. preview of The Terminator (1st app.)
1.30 3.25 8.00

RUST (Adventure, '92)(Value: cover or less)

RUSTY, BOY DETECTIVE
Mar-April, 1955 - No. 5, Nov, 1955
Good Comics/Lev Gleason

1-Bob Wood, Carl Hubbell-a begins 5.85 17.50 35.00
2-5 4.00 11.00 22.00

RUSTY COMICS (Formerly Kid Movie Comics; Rusty and Her Family #21, 22; The Kelleys #23 on; see Millie The Model)
No. 12, Apr, 1947 - No. 22, Sept, 1949
Marvel Comics (HPC)

12-Mitzi app. 10.00 30.00 70.00
13 7.00 21.00 42.00
14-Wolverton's Powerhouse Pepper (4 pgs.) plus Kurtzman's "Hey Look"
11.00 32.00 75.00
15-17-Kurtzman's "Hey Look" 10.00 30.00 60.00
18,19 5.00 15.00 30.00
20-Kurtzman, 5 pgs. 10.00 30.00 60.00
21,22-Kurtzman, 17 & 22 pgs. 12.00 36.00 85.00

RUSTY DUGAN (See Holyoke One-Shot #2)

RUSTY RILEY (See 4-Color #418, 451, 486, 554)

SAARI (The Jungle Goddess)
November, 1951
P. L. Publishing Co.

1 25.00 75.00 175.00

SABLE (First)(Value: cover or less)(Formerly Jon Sable, Freelance; also see Mike Grell's...)

SABRE (Eclipse)(Value: cover or less)(Also see Eclipse Graphic Album Series)

SABRETOOTH (See Iron Fist, Power Man & X-Men)
Aug, 1993 - No. 4, Nov, 1993 ($2.95, color, mini-series, coated paper)
Marvel Comics

1-4: 1-Die-cut-c 1.20 3.00

SABRINA'S CHRISTMAS MAGIC (See Archie Giant Series Magazine #196, 207, 220, 231, 243, 455, 467, 479, 491, 503, 515)

SABRINA'S HALLOWEEN SPOOOKTACULAR
1993 ($2.00, color, 52 pgs.)
Archie Publications

1-Neon orange ink-c; bound-in poster .80 2.00

Sachs And Violens # 1, © Epic

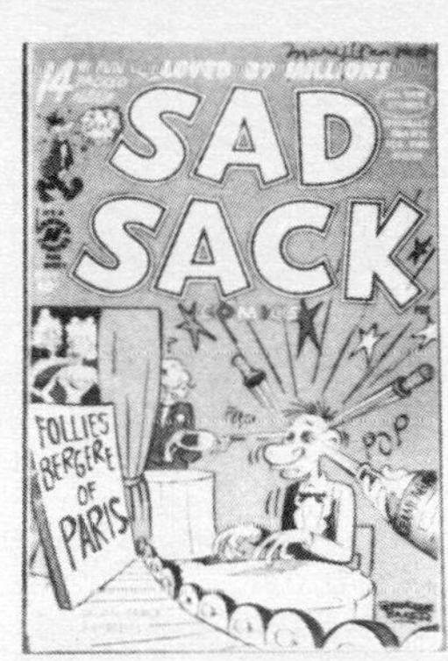

Sad Sack Comics #14, © HARV

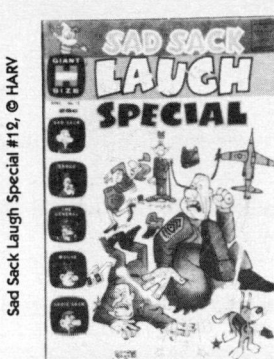

Sad Sack Laugh Special #12, © HARV

SABRINA, THE TEEN-AGE WITCH (TV)(See Archie Giant Series 544, Archie's Madhouse 22, Archie's TV..., Chilling Advs. In Sorcery)
April, 1971 - No. 77, Jan, 1983 (Giants No. 1-17)
Archie Publications

	GD25	FN65	NM94
1	5.00	15.00	35.00
2	2.30	6.75	16.00
3-5: 3,4-Archie's Group x-over	1.30	3.25	8.00
6-10	1.00	2.00	5.00
11-20		1.20	3.00
21-77		.80	2.00

SABU, "ELEPHANT BOY" (Movie; formerly My Secret Story)
No. 30, June, 1950 - No. 2, Aug, 1950
Fox Features Syndicate

	GD25	FN65	NM94
30(#1)-Wood-a; photo-c	14.00	43.00	100.00
2-Photo-c; Kamen-a	10.00	30.00	65.00

SACHS & VIOLENS
Nov, 1993 - No. 4, Feb, 1994 ($2.25, color, mini-series)
Epic Comics (Marvel)

	GD25	FN65	NM94
1-($2.75)-Embossed-c		1.10	2.75
2-4: Perez-a in all		.90	2.25

SACRAMENTS, THE
October, 1955 (25 cents)
Catechetical Guild Educational Society

	GD25	FN65	NM94
304	2.40	6.00	12.00

SACRED AND THE PROFANE, THE (See Eclipse Graphic Album Series #9 & Epic Illustrated #20)

SAD CASE OF WAITING ROOM WILLIE, THE
1950? (nd) (14 pgs. in color; paper covers; regular size)
American Visuals Corp. (For Baltimore Medical Society)

	GD25	FN65	NM94
nn-By Will Eisner (Rare)	43.00	130.00	300.00

SADDLE JUSTICE (Happy Houlihans #1,2; Saddle Romances #9 on)
No. 3, Spring, 1948 - No. 8, Sept-Oct, 1949
E. C. Comics

	GD25	FN65	NM94
3-The 1st E.C. by Bill Gaines to break away from M. C. Gaines' old Educational Comics format. Craig, Feldstein, H. C. Kiefer, & Stan Asch-a. Mentioned in Love and Death	34.00	100.00	235.00
4-1st Graham Ingels-a for E.C.	34.00	100.00	235.00
5-8-Ingels-a in all	30.00	90.00	210.00

NOTE: *Craig and **Feldstein** art in most issues. Canadian reprints known; see Table of Contents. **Craig** c-3, 4. **Ingels** c-5-8. #4 contains a biography of **Craig**.*

SADDLE ROMANCES (Saddle Justice #3-8; Weird Science #12 on)
No. 9, Nov-Dec, 1949 - No. 11, Mar-Apr, 1950
E. C. Comics

	GD25	FN65	NM94
9-Ingels-c/a	36.00	107.00	250.00
10-Wood's 1st work at E. C.; Ingels-a	38.00	115.00	265.00
11-Ingels-a	36.00	107.00	250.00

NOTE: *Canadian reprints known; see Table of Contents. **Feldstein** c-10. **Wood/Harrison** a-10, 11.*

SADIE SACK (See Harvey Hits #93)

SAD SACK AND THE SARGE
Sept, 1957 - No. 155, June, 1982
Harvey Publications

	GD25	FN65	NM94
1	11.00	32.00	75.00
2	5.00	15.00	30.00
3-10	4.00	12.00	24.00
11-20	3.00	7.50	15.00
21-30	1.80	4.50	9.00
31-50	1.40	3.50	7.00
51-90,97-100		1.40	3.50
91-96: All 52 pg. Giants		1.80	4.50
101-155		.90	2.25

SAD SACK COMICS (See Harvey Collector's Comics #16, Little Sad Sack, Tastee Freez Comics #4 & True Comics #55)
Sept, 1949 - No. 287, Oct, 1982; No. 288, 1992 - Present
Harvey Publications

	GD25	FN65	NM94
1-Infinity-c; Little Dot begins (1st app.); civilian issues begin, end #21	36.00	110.00	250.00
2-Flying Fool by Powell	17.00	52.00	120.00
3	10.00	30.00	70.00
4-10	8.35	25.00	50.00
11-21	5.85	17.50	35.00
22-("Back In The Army Again" on covers #22-36). : "The Specialist" story about Sad Sack's return to Army	4.00	10.00	20.00
23-50	2.40	6.00	12.00
51-100	1.60	4.00	8.00
101-150		1.60	4.00
151-222		1.00	2.50
223-228 (25 cent Giants, 52 pgs.)		1.40	3.50
229-287: 286,287 had limited distribution		.90	2.25
288,289 ($2.75, 1992): 289-50th anniversary issue		1.10	2.75
290-293 ($1.00, 1993, B&W)			1.00
3-D 1 (1/54-titled "Harvey 3-D Hits")	18.00	54.00	125.00
Armed Forces Complimentary copies, HD #1-40 ('57-'62)	1.20	3.00	6.00

NOTE: *The Sad Sack Comics comic book was a spin-off from a Sunday Newspaper strip launched through John Wheeler's Bell Syndicate. The previous Sunday page and the first 21 comics depicted the Sad Sack in civvies. Unpopularity caused the Sunday page to be discontinued in the early '50s. Meanwhile Sad Sack returned to the Army, by popular demand, in issue No. 22, remaining there ever since. Incidentally, relatively few of the first 21 issues were ever collected and remain scarce due to this.*

SAD SACK FUN AROUND THE WORLD
1974 (no month)
Harvey Publications

	GD25	FN65	NM94
1-About Great Britain		1.60	4.00

SAD SACK GOES HOME
1951 (16 pgs. in color, no cover price)
Harvey Publications

	GD25	FN65	NM94
nn By George Baker	5.85	17.50	35.00

SAD SACK LAUGH SPECIAL
Winter, 1958-59 - No. 93, Feb, 1977 (#1-60: 68 pgs.; #61-76: 52 pgs.)
Harvey Publications

	GD25	FN65	NM94
1	8.35	25.00	50.00
2	4.20	12.50	25.00
3-10	3.60	9.00	18.00
11-30	2.00	5.00	10.00
31-60: Last 68 pg. Giant	1.00	2.50	6.00
61-76: 52 pg. issues	1.00	2.00	5.00
77-93		1.20	3.00

SAD SACK NAVY, GOBS 'N' GALS
Aug, 1972 - No. 8, Oct, 1973
Harvey Publications

	GD25	FN65	NM94
1: 52 pg. Giant	1.00	2.50	6.00
2-8		1.40	3.50

SAD SACK'S ARMY LIFE (See Harvey Hits #8, 17, 22, 28, 32, 39, 43, 47, 51, 55, 58, 61, 64, 67, 70)

SAD SACK'S ARMY LIFE (...Parade #1-57, ...Today #58 on)
Oct, 1963 - No. 60, Nov, 1975; No. 61, May, 1976
Harvey Publications

	GD25	FN65	NM94
1: 68 pg. issues begin	5.00	15.00	30.00
2-10	3.00	7.50	15.00
11-20	1.60	4.00	8.00
21-34: Last 68 pg. issue	1.00	2.00	5.00
35-51: All 52 pgs.		1.20	3.00
52-61		.80	2.00

The Saga Of Ra's Al Ghul #2, © DC

The Saga of Swamp Thing #44, © DC

Saint Sinner #4 (MEG), © Clive Barker

	GD25	FN65	NM94

SAD SACK'S FUNNY FRIENDS (See Harvey Hits #75)
Dec, 1955 - No. 75, Oct, 1969
Harvey Publications

	GD25	FN65	NM94
1	8.35	25.00	50.00
2-10	4.20	12.50	25.00
11-20	2.40	6.00	12.00
21-30	1.20	3.00	6.00
31-75		1.60	4.00

SAD SACK'S MUTTSY (See Harvey Hits #74, 77, 80, 82, 84, 87, 89, 92, 96, 99, 102, 105, 108, 111, 113, 115, 117, 119, 121)

SAD SACK USA (...Vacation #8)
Nov, 1972 - No. 7, Nov, 1973; No. 8, Oct, 1974
Harvey Publications

	GD25	FN65	NM94
1	1.00	2.00	5.00
2-8		1.00	2.50

SAD SACK WITH SARGE & SADIE
Sept, 1972 - No. 8, Nov, 1973
Harvey Publications

	GD25	FN65	NM94
1-(52 pg. Giant)	1.00	2.00	5.00
2-8		1.00	2.50

SAD SAD SACK WORLD
Oct, 1964 - No. 46, Dec, 1973 (#1-31: 68 pgs.; #32-38: 52 pgs.)
Harvey Publications

	GD25	FN65	NM94
1	3.20	8.00	16.00
2-10	1.60	4.00	8.00
11-31: Last 68 pg. issue	1.00	2.50	6.00
32-38: All 52 pgs.		1.60	4.00
39-46		1.00	2.50

SAFEST PLACE IN THE WORLD, THE
1993 ($2.50, color, one-shot)
Dark Horse Comics

	GD25	FN65	NM94
1-By Steve Ditko (c/a/scripts)		1.00	2.50

SAGA OF BIG RED, THE
Sept, 1976 ($1.25) (In color)
Omaha World-Herald

	GD25	FN65	NM94
nn-by Win Mumma; story of the Nebraska Cornhuskers (sports)		.80	2.00

SAGA OF CRYSTAR, CRYSTAL WARRIOR, THE (Marvel)(Value: cover or less)

SAGA OF RA'S AL GHUL, THE (DC)(Value: cover or less)

SAGA OF SWAMP THING, THE (Swamp Thing #39-41, 46 on)
May, 1982 - Present (Later issues for mature readers; #86 on: $1.50)
DC Comics

	GD25	FN65	NM94
1-Origin retold; Phantom Stranger series begins; ends #13; Yeates-c/a begins		.70	1.80
2-15: 2-Photo-c from movie			1.25
16-19: Bissette-a. 13-Last Yeates-a		.90	2.25
20-1st Alan Moore issue	2.70	8.00	19.00
21-New origin	2.30	6.75	16.00
22-25: 24-JLA x-over; Last Yeates-c	1.10	2.70	6.50
26-30		1.70	4.25
31-33: 33-r/1st app. from House of Secrets #92		1.10	2.75
34	1.50	3.75	9.00
35,36		.90	2.25
37-1st app. John Constantine (Hellblazer)(6/85)	1.65	4.00	10.00
38-40: John Constantine app.		1.60	4.00
41-45: 44-Batman cameo. 44-51-John Constantine app		.70	1.75
46-51: 46-Crisis x-over; Batman cameo. 50-($1.25, 52 pgs.)-Deadman, Dr. Fate, Demon			1.50
52-Arkham Asylum-c/story; Joker-c/cameo		1.40	3.50
53-($1.25, 52 pgs.)-Arkham Asylum; Batman-c/story		1.80	4.50
54-64: 58-Spectre preview. 64-Last Moore issue			1.50
65-99,101-124,126-130: 65-Direct only begins. 66-Batman & Arkham Asylum story. 70,76-John Constantine x-over; 76-X-over w/Hellblazer #9. 79-Superman-c/story. 84-Sandman cameo. 85-Jonah Hex app. 102-Preview of World Without End. 129-Metallic ink on-c		.70	1.75
100 ($2.50, 52 pgs.)		1.00	2.50
125-($2.95, 52 pgs.)-20th anniversary issue		1.20	3.00
131-140: 131-Begin $1.95-c		.80	2.00
Annual 1(1982, $1.00)-Movie Adapt.; painted-c			1.00
Annual 2(1985)-Alan Moore scripts, Bissette-a(p)		1.20	3.00
Annual 3(1987, $2.00)-New format; Bolland-c		.80	2.00
Annual 4(1988, $2.00)-Batman-c/story		1.20	3.00
Annual 5(1989, $2.95, 68 pgs.)-Batman cameo; re-intro Brother Power (Geek), 1st app. since 1968		1.20	3.00
Annual 6(1991, $2.95, 68 pgs.)		1.20	3.00
Saga of the Swamp Thing ('87, $10.95)-r/#21-27	1.65	4.70	11.00
2nd printing (1989, $12.95)	1.85	5.50	13.00
...Love and Death (1990, $17.95)-r/#28-34 & Annual #2; Totleben painted-c	2.60	7.50	18.00

NOTE: ***Bissette*** *a(p)-16-19, 21-27, 29, 30, 34-36, 39-42, 44, 46, 50, 64; c-17i, 24-32p, 35-37p, 40p, 44p, 46-50p, 51-58, 61, 62, 63p.* ***Kaluta*** *c/a-74.* ***Spiegle*** *a-1-3, 6.* ***Sutton*** *a-98p.* ***Totleben*** *a(i)-10, 16-27, 29, 31, 34-40, 42, 44, 46, 48, 50, 53, 55i; c-25-32i, 33, 35-40i, 42i, 44i, 46-50i, 53, 55i, 59p, 64, 65, 68, 73, 76, 80, 82, 84, 89, 91-100, Annual 4, 5.* ***Vess*** *c-121.* ***Williamson*** *86i.* ***Wrightson*** *a-18i(r), 33r. John Constantine appears in #44-51, 65-67, 70-74, 76, 77, 114, 115.*

SAGA OF THE ORIGINAL HUMAN TORCH (Marvel)(Value: cover or less)

SAGA OF THE SUB-MARINER, THE (Marvel)(Value: cover or less)

SAILOR ON THE SEA OF FATE (See First Comics Graphic Novel #11)

SAILOR SWEENEY (Navy Action #1-11, 15 on)
No. 12, July, 1956 - No. 14, Nov, 1956
Atlas Comics (CDS)

	GD25	FN65	NM94
12-14: 12-Shores-a. 13-Severin-c	5.85	17.50	35.00

SAINT, THE (Also see Movie Comics(DC) #2 & Silver Streak #18)
Aug, 1947 - No. 12, Mar, 1952
Avon Periodicals

	GD25	FN65	NM94
1-Kamen bondage-c/a	45.00	135.00	315.00
2	22.00	65.00	165.00
3,4: 4-Lingerie panels	18.00	54.00	125.00
5-Spanking panel	26.00	77.00	180.00
6-Miss Fury app., 14 pgs.	29.00	85.00	200.00
7-c-/Avon paperback #118	16.00	50.00	115.00
8,9(12/50): Saint strip-r in #8-12; 9-Kinstler-c	13.00	40.00	90.00
10-Wood-a, 1 pg; c-/Avon paperback #289	13.00	40.00	90.00
11	10.00	30.00	65.00
12-c-/Avon paperback #123	11.50	34.00	80.00

NOTE: *Lucky Dale, Girl Detective in #1,2,4,6.* ***Hollingsworth*** *a-4, 6. Painted-c 8,10,11.*

ST. GEORGE (Marvel)(Value: cover or less)

SAINT SINNER (See Razorline)
Oct, 1993 - Present ($1.75, color)
Marvel Comics

	GD25	FN65	NM94
1-($2.50)-Foil embossed-c; by Clive Barker		1.00	2.50
2-6		.70	1.75

ST. SWITHIN'S DAY (Trident)(Value: cover or less)

SALERNO CARNIVAL OF COMICS (Also see Pure Oil Comics, 24 Pages of Comics, & Vicks Comics)
Late 1930s (16 pgs.) (paper cover) (Giveaway)
Salerno Cookie Co.

	GD25	FN65	NM94
nn-Color reprints of Calkins' Buck Rogers & Skyroads, plus other strips from Famous Funnies	42.00	125.00	275.00

SALOME' (See Night Music #6)

SAM & MAX FREELANCE POLICE (Marvel)(Value: cover or less)

SAM AND MAX, FREELANCE POLICE SPECIAL (Comico)(Value: cover or less)

SAM & MAX FREELANCE POLICE SPECIAL COLOR COLLECTION (Marvel)(Value: cover or less)

Sam Slade Robohunter #29, © QC

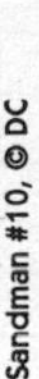

Sandman #10, © DC

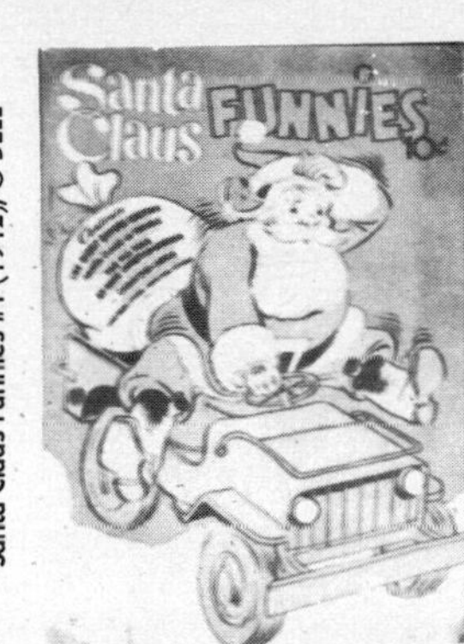

Santa Claus Funnies #1 (1942), © DELL

SAM HILL PRIVATE EYE
1950 - No. 7, 1951
Close Up (Archie)

	GD25	FN65	NM94
1	10.00	30.00	65.00
2	6.35	19.00	38.00
3-7	5.00	15.00	30.00

SAM SLADE ROBOHUNTER (Quality)(Value: cover or less)

SAMSON (1st Series) (Capt. Aero #7 on; see Big 3 Comics)
Fall, 1940 - No. 6, Sept, 1941 (See Fantastic Comics)
Fox Features Syndicate

	GD25	FN65	NM94
1-Samson begins, ends #6; Powell-a, signed 'Rensie;' Wing Turner by Tuska app; Fine-c?	87.00	262.00	600.00
2-Dr. Fung by Powell; Fine-c?	44.00	132.00	300.00
3-Navy Jones app.; Simon-c	35.00	105.00	250.00
4-Yarko the Great, Master Magician begins	30.00	90.00	200.00
5,6: 6-Origin The Topper	27.00	82.00	180.00

SAMSON (2nd Series) (Formerly Fantastic Comics #10, 11)
No. 12, April, 1955 - No. 14, Aug, 1955
Ajax/Farrell Publications (Four Star)

	GD25	FN65	NM94
12-Wonder Boy	16.00	48.00	110.00
13,14: 13-Wonder Boy, Rocket Man	11.50	34.00	80.00

SAMSON (See Mighty Samson)

SAMSON & DELILAH (See A Spectacular Feature Magazine)

SAMUEL BRONSTON'S CIRCUS WORLD (See Circus World under Movie Comics)

SAMURAI (Also see Eclipse Graphic Album Series #14)
1985 - No. 22 ($1.70, B&W)
Aircel Publications

	GD25	FN65	NM94
1		1.60	4.00
1-2nd & 3rd printings		.70	1.70
2-12,17-22		.70	1.70
2-2nd printing		.70	1.70
13-Dale Keown's 1st published artwork	1.10	2.70	6.50
14-16-Dale Keown-a		1.80	4.50

SAMURAI CAT (Marvel)(Value: cover or less)

SAMUREE (Continuity, Vol. 1 & 2)(Value: cover or less)

SANCTUARY (Viz)(Value: cover or less)

SANDMAN, THE (See Adventure Comics #40 & World's Finest #3)
Winter, 1974; No. 2, Apr-May, 1975 - No. 6, Dec-Jan, 1975-76
National Periodical Publications

	GD25	FN65	NM94
1-1st app. Sandman; Kirby-a; Joe Simon scripts (last S&K collaboration)	1.30	3.25	8.00
2-6: 6-Kirby/Wood-c/a		1.70	4.25

NOTE: ***Kirby** a-1p, 4-6p; c-1-5, 6p.*

SANDMAN (See Books of Magic, Vertigo Jam & Vertigo Preview)
Jan, 1989 - Present ($1.50/$1.75, color, mature readers)
DC Comics

	GD25	FN65	NM94
1 ($2.00, 52 pgs.)-1st app. new Sandman; Neil Gaiman scripts begin; Sam Kieth-a(p) in #1-5	8.00	24.00	55.00
2-Cain & Abel app. (from HOM & HOS)	5.00	15.00	35.00
3-5: 3-John Constantine app.	4.30	13.00	30.00
6,7	3.20	8.00	20.00
8-Regular ed. has Jeanette Kahn publishorial & American Cancer Society ad w/no indicia on inside front-c; Death-c/story (1st app.)	5.00	15.00	35.00
8-Limited ed. (600+ copies?); has Karen Berger editorial and next issue teaser (has indicia)	22.00	70.00	160.00
9-13: 10-Has explaination about #8 mixup; has bound-in Shocker movie poster	1.65	4.00	10.00
14-($2.50, 52 pgs.)	1.70	5.00	12.00
15-20: 16-Photo-c. 19-Vess-a	1.00	2.50	6.00
[illegible] storyline. [illegible] World Without End preview. 24-Russell-i	1.00	2.50	5.50
28-30		1.50	3.75
31-35,37-48: 38-40-Photo-c. 44-50-Metallic ink on-c		.90	2.25
36-($2.50, 52 pgs.)		1.60	4.00
49,51-53,55: 49-Begin $1.95-c		.90	2.25
50-($2.95, 52 pgs.)-McKean-c		1.40	3.50
50-($2.95)-Signed & limited (5,000) Treasury Edition with sketch of Neil Gaiman	1.65	4.00	10.00
54-Re-intro Prez; Death app.		1.40	3.50
56-58		.80	2.00
Special 1(1991, $3.50, 68 pgs.)-Glow-in-the-dark-c	1.10	2.70	6.50
Trade paperback (1990, $12.95, 296 pgs.)-r/#8-16	1.85	5.50	13.00

SANDMAN MYSTERY THEATRE
Mar, 1993 - Present ($1.95, color)
DC Comics

	GD25	FN65	NM94
1-12		.80	2.00

SANDS OF THE SOUTH PACIFIC
January, 1953
Toby Press

	GD25	FN65	NM94
1	11.50	34.00	80.00

SANTA AND HIS REINDEER (See March of Comics #166)

SANTA AND POLLYANNA PLAY THE GLAD GAME
Aug, 1960 (16 pages) (Disney giveaway)
Sales Promotion

	GD25	FN65	NM94
nn	2.40	6.00	12.00

SANTA AND THE ANGEL (See Dell Junior Treasury #7 & Four Color #260)

SANTA & THE BUCCANEERS
1959
Promotional Publ. Co. (Giveaway)

	GD25	FN65	NM94
nn-Reprints 1952 Santa & the Pirates	1.80	4.50	9.00

SANTA & THE CHRISTMAS CHICKADEE
1974 (20 pgs.)
Murphy's (Giveaway)

	GD25	FN65	NM94
nn	1.00	2.00	5.00

SANTA & THE PIRATES
1952
Promotional Publ. Co. (Giveaway)

	GD25	FN65	NM94
nn-Marv Levy-c/a	1.80	4.50	9.00

SANTA AT THE ZOO (See 4-Color #259)

SANTA CLAUS AROUND THE WORLD (See March of Comics #241)

SANTA CLAUS CONQUERS THE MARTIANS (See Movie Classics)

SANTA CLAUS FUNNIES (Also see The Little Fir Tree)
nd; 1940 (Color & B&W; 8x10"; 12pgs., heavy paper)
W. T. Grant Co./Whitman Publishing (Giveaway)

	GD25	FN65	NM94
nn-(2 versions)	10.00	30.00	60.00

SANTA CLAUS FUNNIES (Also see Dell Giants)
Dec?, 1942 - No. 1274, Dec, 1961
Dell Publishing Co.

	GD25	FN65	NM94
nn(#1)(1942)-Kelly-a	36.00	107.00	250.00
2(12/43)-Kelly-a	23.00	70.00	160.00
4-Color 61(1944)-Kelly-a	22.00	65.00	150.00
4-Color 91(1945)-Kelly-a	17.00	51.00	120.00
4-Color 128('46),175('47)-Kelly-a	13.00	40.00	90.00
4-Color 205,254-Kelly-a	11.50	34.00	80.00
4-Color 302,361	4.00	11.00	22.00
4-Color 525,607,666,756,867	4.00	10.00	20.00
4-Color 958,1063,1154,1274	3.60	9.00	18.00

NOTE: *Most issues contain only one Kelly story.*

Santa's Christ. Time Stories, © Prem. Sales

Santa's Surprise, © WEST

Sarge Steel #7, © CC

GD25 FN65 NM94

SANTA CLAUS PARADE
1951; No. 2, Dec, 1952; No. 3, Jan, 1955 (25 cents)
Ziff-Davis (Approved Comics)/St. John Publishing Co.

	GD25	FN65	NM94
nn(1951-Ziff-Davis)-116 pgs. (Xmas Special 1,2)	17.00	52.00	120.00
2(12/52-Ziff-Davis)-100 pgs.; Dave Berg-a	13.00	40.00	90.00
V1#3(1/55-St. John)-100 pgs.; reprints-c/#1	11.50	34.00	80.00

SANTA CLAUS' WORKSHOP (See March of Comics #50, 168)

SANTA IS COMING (See March of Comics #197)

SANTA IS HERE (See March of Comics #49)

SANTA ON THE JOLLY ROGER
1965
Promotional Publ. Co. (Giveaway)

	GD25	FN65	NM94
nn-Marv Levy-c/a	.80	2.00	4.00

SANTA! SANTA!
1974 (20 pgs.)
R. Jackson (Montgomery Ward giveaway)

	GD25	FN65	NM94
nn		1.20	3.00

SANTA'S BUSY CORNER (See March of Comics #31)

SANTA'S CANDY KITCHEN (See March of Comics #14)

SANTA'S CHRISTMAS BOOK (See March of Comics #123)

SANTA'S CHRISTMAS COMICS
December, 1952 (100 pages)
Standard Comics (Best Books)

	GD25	FN65	NM94
nn-Supermouse, Dizzy Duck, Happy Rabbit, etc.	11.50	34.00	80.00

SANTA'S CHRISTMAS COMIC VARIETY SHOW
1943 (24 pages)
Sears Roebuck & Co.

	GD25	FN65	NM94
Contains puzzles & new comics of Dick Tracy, Little Orphan Annie, Moon Mullins, Terry & the Pirates, etc.	14.00	43.00	100.00

SANTA'S CHRISTMAS LIST (See March of Comics #255)

SANTA'S CHRISTMAS TIME STORIES
nd (Late 1940s) (16 pgs.; paper cover)
Premium Sales, Inc. (Giveaway)

	GD25	FN65	NM94
nn	4.00	10.00	20.00

SANTA'S CIRCUS
1964 (Half-size)
Promotional Publ. Co. (Giveaway)

	GD25	FN65	NM94
nn-Marv Levy-c/a	1.20	3.00	6.00

SANTA'S FUN BOOK
1951, 1952 (Regular size, 16 pages, paper-c)
Promotional Publ. Co. (Murphy's giveaway)

	GD25	FN65	NM94
nn	2.40	6.00	12.00

SANTA'S GIFT BOOK
No date (16 pgs.)
No Publisher

	GD25	FN65	NM94
nn-Puzzles, games only	1.80	4.50	9.00

SANTA'S HELPERS (See March of Comics #64, 106, 198)

SANTA'S LITTLE HELPERS (See March of Comics #270)

SANTA'S NEW STORY BOOK
1949 (16 pgs.; paper cover)
Wallace Hamilton Campbell (Giveaway)

	GD25	FN65	NM94
nn	4.20	12.50	25.00

SANTA'S REAL STORY BOOK
1948, 1952 (16 pgs.)
Wallace Hamilton Campbell/W. W. Orris (Giveaway)

	GD25	FN65	NM94
nn	4.00	11.00	22.00

SANTA'S RIDE
1959
W. T. Grant Co. (Giveaway)

	GD25	FN65	NM94
nn	2.40	6.00	12.00

SANTA'S RODEO
1964 (Half-size)
Promotional Publ. Co. (Giveaway)

	GD25	FN65	NM94
nn-Marv Levy-a	1.00	2.00	5.00

SANTA'S SECRETS
1951, 1952? (16 pgs.; paper cover)
Sam B. Anson Christmas giveaway

	GD25	FN65	NM94
nn	2.80	7.00	14.00

SANTA'S SHOW (See March of Comics #311)

SANTA'S SLEIGH (See March of Comics #298)

SANTA'S STORIES
1953 (Regular size; paper cover)
K. K. Publications (Klines Dept. Store)

	GD25	FN65	NM94
nn-Kelly-a	14.00	43.00	100.00
nn-Another version (1953, glossy-c, half-size, 7-1/4x5-1/4")-Kelly-a	10.00	30.00	70.00

SANTA'S SURPRISE (See March of Comics #13)

SANTA'S SURPRISE
1947 (36 pgs.; slick cover)
K. K. Publications (Giveaway)

	GD25	FN65	NM94
nn	4.20	12.50	25.00

SANTA'S TINKER TOTS
1958
Charlton Comics

	GD25	FN65	NM94
1-Based on "The Tinker Tots Keep Christmas"	2.40	6.00	12.00

SANTA'S TOYLAND (See March of Comics #242)

SANTA'S TOYS (See March of Comics #12)

SANTA'S TOYTOWN FUN BOOK
1952, 1953?
Promotional Publ. Co. (Giveaway)

	GD25	FN65	NM94
nn-Marv Levy-c	1.40	3.50	7.00

SANTA'S VISIT (See March of Comics #283)

SANTIAGO (See 4-Color #723)

SARGE SNORKEL (Beetle Bailey)
Oct, 1973 - No. 17, Dec, 1976
Charlton Comics

	GD25	FN65	NM94
1	1.00	2.00	5.00
2-17		.80	2.00

SARGE STEEL (Becomes Secret Agent #9 on; also see Judomaster)
Dec, 1964 - No. 8, Mar-Apr, 1966 (All 12¢ issues)
Charlton Comics

	GD25	FN65	NM94
1-Origin & 1st app.	1.65	4.70	11.00
2-5,7,8:	1.00	2.50	5.50
6-2nd app. Judomaster	1.30	3.25	8.00

SATAN'S SIX
Apr, 1993 - No. 4, 1993 ($2.95, color, mini-series)
Topps Comics

	GD25	FN65	NM94
1-Polybagged w/Kirbychrome trading card; Kirby/McFarlane-c plus 8 pgs. Kirby-a(p)		1.20	3.00
2-4-Polybagged w/3 cards. 4-Teenagents preview		1.20	3.00

SAVAGE COMBAT TALES
Feb, 1975 - No. 3, July, 1975
Atlas/Seaboard Publ.

The Savage Sword of Conan # 7, © MEG

Savage Henry #2, © Vortex

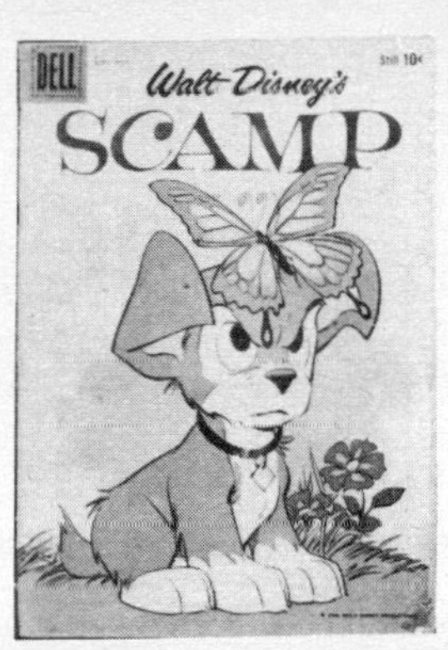

Scamp #11 (Dell), © WDC

GD25 FN65 NM94

1-3: 1-Sgt. Stryker's Death Squad begins (origin). 2-Only app. Warhawk 1.00

NOTE: ***McWilliams** a-1-3; c-1. **Sparling** a-1, 3. **Toth** a-2.*

SAVAGE DRAGON, THE (See Megaton #3 & 4)
July, 1992 - No. 3, Dec, 1992 ($1.95, color, mini-series)
Image Comics

1-Erik Larsen-c/a/scripts & bound-in poster in all 1.10 2.70 6.50
2 1.60 4.00
3-Contains coupon for Image Comics #0 1.30 3.25
3-With coupon missing .80 2.00
...Vs. Savage Megaton Man 1 (3/93, $1.95)-Larsen & Simpson-c/a .80 2.00

SAVAGE DRAGON, THE
June, 1993 - Present ($1.95, color)
Image Comics

1,3-7-Erik Larsen-c/a/scripts. 3-Mighty Man back-up story w/Austin-i. 4-Flip book w/Ricochet. 5-Mighty Man flip-c & back-up .90 2.25
2-($2.95, 52 pgs.)-Teenage Mutant Ninja Turtles-c/story; flip book features Vanguard #0 (see Megaton for 1st app.) 1.30 3.25

SAVAGE DRAGON/TEENAGE MUTANT NINJA TURTLES CROSSOVER
Sept, 1993 ($2.75, color)
Mirage Studios

1 1.10 2.75

SAVAGE HENRY (Vortex)(Value: cover or less)

SAVAGE RAIDS OF GERONIMO (See Geronimo #4)

SAVAGE RANGE (See 4-Color #807)

SAVAGE RETURN OF DRACULA
1992 ($2.00, color, 52 pgs.)
Marvel Comics

1-r/Tomb of Dracula #1,2 by Gene Colan .80 2.00

SAVAGE SHE-HULK, THE (See The Avengers, Marvel Graphic Novel #18 & The Sensational She-Hulk)
Feb, 1980 - No. 25, Feb, 1982
Marvel Comics Group

1-Origin & 1st app. She-Hulk 1.00 2.50 6.00
2-10 1.10 2.75
11-25: 25-(52 pgs.) .90 2.25

NOTE: ***Austin** a-25i; c-23i-25i. **J. Buscema** a-1p; c-1, 2p. **Golden** c-8-11.*

SAVAGE SWORD OF CONAN (The... #41 on; ...The Barbarian #175 on)
Aug, 1974 - Present ($1.00, B&W magazine)(Mature readers)
Marvel Comics Group

1-Smith-r; J. Buscema/N. Adams/Krenkel-a; origin Blackmark by Gil Kane (part 1, ends #3); Blackmark's 1st app. in magazine form-r/from paperback) & Red Sonja (3rd app.) 11.00 32.00 75.00
2-Neal Adams-c; Chaykin/N. Adams-a 4.70 14.00 33.00
3-Severin/B. Smith-a; N. Adams-a 2.40 7.25 17.00
4-Neal Adams/Kane-a(r) 1.85 5.50 13.00
5-10: 5-Jeff Jones frontispiece (r) 1.65 4.70 11.00
11-20 1.40 3.50 8.50
21-50: 34-3 pg. preview of Conan newspaper strip. 35-Cover similar to Savage Tales #1. 45-Red Sonja returns; begin $1.25-c 1.25 3.00 7.50
51-100: 63-Toth frontispiece. 65-Kane-a w/Chaykin/Miller/Simonson/Sherman finishes. 70-Article on movie. 83-Red Sonja-r by Neal Adams from #1 1.80 4.50
101-176: 163-Begin $2.25-c. 169-King Kull story. 171-Soloman Kane by Williamson (i). 172-Red Sonja story 1.20 3.00
177-220: 179,187,192-Red Sonja app. 190-193-4 part King Kull story. 196, 202-King Kull story. 200-New Buscema-a; Robert E. Howard app. with Conan in story. 204-60th anniversary (1932-92). 214-Sequel to Red Nails by Robert E. Howard .90 2.25
Special 1(1975, B&W)-B. Smith-r/Conan #10,13 1.30 3.25 8.00

NOTE: ***N. Adams** a-14p, 60, 83p(r). **Alcala** a-2 ,4, 7, 12, 15-20, 23, 24, 28, 59, 67, 69, 75, 76i, 80i, 82i, 83i, 89, 180i, 184i, 187i, 189i. **Austin** a-78i. **Boris** painted c-1, 4, 5, 7, 9, 10, 12, 15. **Brunner** a-30; c-8, 30. **Buscema** a-1-5, 7, 10-12, 15-24, 26-28, 31, 32, 36-43, 45, 47-58p, 60-67p, 70, 71-74p, 76-81p, 87-96p, 98, 99-101p, 190-203p; painted c-40. **Chaykin** c-31. **Chiodo** painted c-71, 76, 79, 81, 84, 85, 178. **Conrad** c-212. **Corben** a-4, 16, 29. **Finlay** a-16. **Golden** a-98, 101; c-98, 101, 105, 106, 117, 124, 150. **Kaluta** a-11, 18; c-3, 91, 93. **Gil Kane** a-2, 3, 8, 13r, 29, 47, 64, 65, 67, 85p, 86p. **Krenkel** a-9, 11, 14, 16, 24. **Morrow** a-7. **Nebres** a-93i, 101i, 107, 114. **Newton** a-6. **Nino** c/a-6. **Redondo** painted c-48-50, 52, 56, 57, 85i, 90, 96i. **Marie & John Severin** a-Special 1. **Simonson** a-7, 8, 12, 15-17. **Barry Smith** a-7, 16, 24, 82r, Special 1r. **Starlin** c-26. **Toth** a-64. **Williamson** a(i)-162, 171, 186. No. 8 & 10 contain a Robert E. Howard Conan adaptation.*

SAVAGE TALES (...Featuring Conan #4 on)(Magazine)
May, 1971; No. 2, 10/73; No. 3, 2/74 - No. 12, Summer, 1975 (B&W)
Marvel Comics Group

1-Origin/1st app. The Man-Thing by Morrow; Conan the Barbarian by Barry Smith (1st Conan x-over outside his own title); Femizons by Romita begin; Ka-Zar story by Buscema 18.00 54.00 125.00
2-B. Smith, Brunner, Morrow, Williamson-a; Wrightson King Kull reprint/Creatures on the Loose #10 6.00 19.00 44.00
3-B. Smith, Brunner, Steranko, Williamson-a 3.85 11.50 27.00
4,5-N. Adams-c; last Conan (Smith-r/#4) plus Kane/N. Adams-a. 5-Brak the Barbarian begins, ends #8 2.40 7.25 17.00
6-Ka-Zar begins; Williamson-r; N. Adams-c 1.00 2.00 6.00
7-N. Adams-i 1.80 4.50
8-Shanna, the She-Devil app. thru #10; Williamson-r 1.60 4.00
9,11 1.20 3.00
10-Neal Adams-a(i), Williamson-r 1.60 4.00
...Featuring Ka-Zar Annual 1 (Summer '75, B&W)(#12 on inside)-Ka-Zar origin by G. Kane; B. Smith-r/Astonish. Tales 1.00 2.00 5.00

NOTE: ***Boris** c-7, 10. **Buscema** a-5r, 6p, 8p; c-2. **Colan** a-1p. **Fabian** c-8. **Golden** a-1, 4; c-1. **Heath** a-10p, 11p. **Kaluta** c-9. **Maneely** r-2, 4(The Crusader in both). **Morrow** a-1, 2, Annual 1. **Reese** a-2. **Severin** a-1-7. **Starlin** a-5. Robert E. Howard adaptations-1-4.*

SAVAGE TALES (Magazine size)
Nov, 1985 - No. 9, Mar, 1987 ($1.50, B&W, mature readers)
Marvel Comics Group

1-1st app. The Nam; Golden, Morrow-a 1.00 2.00 5.00
2-9: 2,7-Morrow-a. 4-2nd Nam story; Golden-a 1.50

SAVED BY THE BELL (Harvey)(Value: cover or less)

SCAMP (Walt Disney)(See Walt Disney's Comics & Stories #204)
No. 703, 5/56 - No. 1204, 8-10/61; 11/67 - No. 45, 1/79
Dell Publishing Co./Gold Key

4-Color 703(#1) 5.85 17.50 35.00
4-Color 777,806('57),833 3.60 9.00 18.00
5(3-5/58)-10(6-8/59) 3.00 7.50 15.00
11-16(12-2/60-61) 2.40 6.00 12.00
4-Color 1204(1961) 2.40 6.00 12.00
1(12/67-Gold Key)-Reprints begin 2.00 5.00 10.00
2(3/69)-10 1.00 2.50 5.00
11-20 .60 1.50 3.00
21-45 .30 .75 1.50

NOTE: *New stories-#20(in part), 22-25, 27, 29-31, 34, 36-40, 42-45. New covers-#11, 12, 14, 15, 17-25, 27, 29-31, 34, 36-38.*

SCARAB
Nov, 1993 - No. 8, June, 1994 ($1.95, color, limited series)
DC Comics (Vertigo)

1-8 .80 2.00

SCAR FACE (See The Crusaders)

SCARECROW OF ROMNEY MARSH, THE (See W. Disney Showcase #53)
April, 1964 - No. 3, Oct, 1965 (Disney TV Show)
Gold Key

10112-404 (#1) 4.00 10.00 20.00
2,3 3.00 7.50 15.00

SCARLET O'NEIL (See Harvey Comics Hits #59 & Invisible...)

SCARLETT
Jan, 1993 - No. 14, Feb, 1994 ($1.75, color)

Scavengers #13, © Quality Comics

Scooby-Doo #4 (Marvel), © Hanna-Barbera

Scooter Comics #1, © Rucker Publ.

GD25 FN65 NM94

DC Comics

1-($2.95) 1.20 3.00
2-14 .70 1.75

SCARLET WITCH (See Avengers #16, Vision & ...& X-Men #4)
Jan, 1994 - No. 4, Apr, 1994 ($1.75, color)
Marvel Comics

1-4 .70 1.75

SCARY TALES
8/75 - #9, 1/77; #10, 9/77 - #20, 6/79; #21, 8/80 - #46, 10/84
Charlton Comics

1-Origin/1st app. Countess Von Bludd, not in #2 1.20 3.00
2-11: 3-Sutton painted-c 1.50
12-36,39,46-All reprints 1.50
37,38,40-45-New-a. 38-Mr. Jigsaw app. 1.50
1(Modern Comics reprint, 1977) 1.00

NOTE: ***Adkins** a-31i; c-31i. **Ditko** a-3, 5, 7, 8(2), 11, 12, 14-16r, 18(3)r, 19r, 21r, 30r, 32, 39r; c-5, 11, 14, 18, 30, 32. **Newton** a-31p; c-31p. **Powell** a-18r. **Staton** a-1(2 pgs.), 4, 20r; c-1, 20. **Sutton** a-9; c-4, 9.*

SCAVENGERS (Quality)(Value: cover or less)

SCAVENGERS
1993 - Present ($2.50, color)
Triumphant Comics

1-6-Serially numbered comics 1.00 2.50

SCHOOL DAY ROMANCES (...of Teen-Agers #4; Popular Teen-Agers #5 on)
Nov-Dec, 1949 - No. 4, May-June, 1950
Star Publications

1-Tony Gayle (later Gay), Gingersnapp 11.50 34.00 80.00
2,3: 3-Jane Powell photo on-c 8.00 24.00 48.00
4-Ronald Reagan photo on-c/L.B. Cole-c 14.00 43.00 100.00

NOTE: *All have **L. B. Cole** covers.*

SCHWINN BICYCLE BOOK (...Bike Thrills, 1959)
1949; 1952; 1959 (10 cents)
Schwinn Bicycle Co.

1949 4.00 10.50 21.00
1952-Believe It or Not type facts; comic format; 36 pgs.
2.00 5.00 10.00
1959 1.60 4.00 8.00

SCIENCE COMICS (1st Series)
Feb, 1940 - No. 8, Sept, 1940
Fox Features Syndicate

1-Origin Dynamo (1st app., called Electro in #1), The Eagle (1st app.), & Navy Jones; Marga, The Panther Woman (1st app.), Cosmic Carson & Perisphere Payne, Dr. Doom begin; bondage/hypo-c; Electro-c
200.00 600.00 1400.00
2: 2,3-Dynamo-c 100.00 300.00 650.00
3,4: 4-Kirby-a; Cosmic Carson-c 83.00 250.00 550.00
5-8: 5,8-Eagle-c. 6,7-Dynamo-c 58.00 175.00 400.00

NOTE: *Cosmic Carson by **Tuska-#1-3**; by **Kirby-#4**. **Lou Fine** c-1-3 only.*

SCIENCE COMICS (2nd Series)
January, 1946 - No. 5, 1946
Humor Publications (Ace Magazines?)

1-Palais-c/a in #1-3; A-Bomb-c 8.35 25.00 50.00
2 4.20 12.50 25.00
3-Feldstein-a, 6 pgs. 10.00 30.00 60.00
4,5: 4-Palais-c 4.00 11.00 22.00

SCIENCE COMICS
May, 1947 (8 pgs. in color)
Ziff-Davis Publ. Co.

nn-Could be ordered by mail for 10 cents; like the nn Amazing Advs. & Boy Cowboy; (1950)-used to test the market 29.00 85.00 200.00

SCIENCE COMICS (True Science Illustrated)
March, 1951
Export Publication Ent., Toronto, Canada
Distr. in U.S. by Kable News Co.

1-Science Adventure stories plus some true science features; man on moon story 5.85 17.50 35.00

SCIENCE FICTION SPACE ADVENTURES (See Space Adventures)

SCOOBY DOO (TV)(...Where are you? #1-16,26; ...Mystery Comics #17-25, 27 on)(See March Of Comics #356, 368, 382, 391)
March, 1970 - No. 30, Feb, 1975 (Hanna-Barbera)
Gold Key

1 4.00 12.00 28.00
2-5 2.30 6.75 16.00
6-10 1.70 5.00 12.00
11-20: 11-Tufts-a 1.30 3.25 8.00
21-30 1.00 2.00 5.00

SCOOBY DOO (TV)
April, 1975 - No. 11, Dec, 1976 (Hanna-Barbera)
Charlton Comics

1 2.15 6.50 15.00
2-5 1.00 2.50 6.00
6-11 1.00 2.00 5.00

SCOOBY-DOO (TV)
Oct, 1977 - No. 9, Feb, 1979 (Hanna-Barbera)
Marvel Comics Group

1-Dyno-Mutt begins 1.20 3.00
2-9 1.50

SCOOBY-DOO (TV)
Sept, 1992 - No. 2? ($1.25, color)
Harvey Comics

V2#1,2 1.25
...Giant Size 1 (10/92, $2.25, 68 pgs.) - 2 .90 2.25

SCOOP COMICS (Becomes Yankee Comics #4-7, a digest sized cartoon book not listed in this guide; becomes Snap #9)
November, 1941 - No. 3, Mar, 1943; No. 8, 1944
Harry 'A' Chesler (Holyoke)

1-Intro. Rocketman & Rocketgirl; origin The Master Key; Dan Hastings begins; Charles Sultan-c/a 58.00 175.00 400.00
2-Rocket Boy app; Injury to eye story (reprinted in Spotlight #3)
35.00 105.00 235.00
3-Injury to eye story-r from #2; Rocket Boy 29.00 88.00 200.00
8-Formerly Yankee Comics; becomes Snap 20.00 60.00 140.00

SCOOTER (See Swing With...)

SCOOTER COMICS
April, 1946
Rucker Publ. Ltd. (Canadian)

1-Teen-age/funny animal 6.70 20.00 40.00

SCORCHED EARTH (Tundra)(Value: cover or less)

SCORE, THE (Piranha)(Value: cover or less)

SCORPION
Feb, 1975 - No. 3, July, 1975
Atlas/Seaboard Publ.

1-Intro.; bondage-c by Chaykin 1.20
2,3: 2-Wrightson-a; Kaluta, Simonson assists(p) 1.00

NOTE: ***Chaykin** a-1, 2; c-1. **Mooney** a-3i.*

SCORPIO ROSE (Eclipse)(Value: cover or less)

SCOTLAND YARD (Inspector Farnsworth of...) (Texas Rangers in Action #5 on?)
June, 1955 - No. 4, March, 1956
Charlton Comics Group

Scout #11, © Timothy Truman

Sea Hunt #9, © United Artists

The Second Life of Doctor Mirage #2, © Voyager

	GD25	FN65	NM94
1-Tothish-a	10.00	30.00	60.00
2-4: 2-Tothish-a	6.70	20.00	40.00

SCOUT (Eclipse)(Value: cover or less)

SCOUT: WAR SHAMAN (Eclipse)(Value: cover or less)(Formerly Scout)

SCREAM (...Comics) (Andy Comics #20 on)
Autumn, 1944 - No. 19, April, 1948
Humor Publications/Current Books(Ace Magazines)

	GD25	FN65	NM94
1-Teenage humor	11.00	32.00	75.00
2	6.35	19.00	38.00
3-15: 11-Racist humor (Indians)	5.00	15.00	30.00
16-Intro. Lily-Belle	5.00	15.00	30.00
17,19	4.00	11.00	22.00
18-Hypo needle story	5.00	15.00	30.00

SCREAM (Magazine)
Aug, 1973 - No. 11, Feb, 1975 (68 pgs.) (B&W)
Skywald Publishing Corp.

	GD25	FN65	NM94
1	1.30	3.25	8.00
2-5: 2-Origin Lady Satan. 3 (12/73)-#3 found on pg. 22		1.60	4.00
6-11: 6-Origin The Victims. 9-Severed head-c. 11-"Mr. Poe and the Raven" story		1.20	3.00

SCRIBBLY (See All-American Comics, Buzzy, The Funnies, Leave It To Binky & Popular Comics)
8-9/48 - No. 13, 8-9/50; No. 14, 10-11/51 - No. 15, 12-1/51-52
National Periodical Publications

	GD25	FN65	NM94
1-Sheldon Mayer-c/a in all; 52pgs. begin	82.00	245.00	575.00
2	54.00	160.00	375.00
3-5	43.00	130.00	300.00
6-10	32.00	95.00	225.00
11-15: 13-Last 52 pgs.	26.00	80.00	185.00

SEA DEVILS (See Limited Collectors' Edition #39,45, & Showcase #27-29)
Sept-Oct, 1961 - No. 35, May-June, 1967
National Periodical Publications

	GD25	FN65	NM94
Showcase #27 (7-8/60)-1st app. Sea Devils; Russ Heath-c/a begins, ends #10; grey tone-c begin, end #5	63.00	188.00	500.00
Showcase #28 (9-10/60)-2nd app. Sea Devils	31.00	94.00	250.00
Showcase #29 (11-12/60)-3rd app. Sea Devils	33.00	99.00	265.00
1-(9-10/61)	40.00	120.00	320.00
2-Last 10 cent issue	17.00	51.00	135.00
3-Begin 12 cent issues thru #35	13.00	40.00	90.00
4,5	12.00	36.00	85.00
6-10	6.00	19.00	44.00
11,12,14-20	4.70	14.00	33.00
13-Kubert, Colan-a; Joe Kubert app. in story	5.00	15.00	35.00
21-35: 22-Intro. International Sea Devils; origin & 1st app. Capt. X & Man Fish	3.30	10.00	23.00

NOTE: *Heath a-B&B 27-29, 1-10; c-B&B 27-29, 1-10, 14-16. Moldoff a-16i.*

SEADRAGON (Elite)(Value: cover or less)

SEA HOUND, THE (Capt. Silver's Log Of The...)
1945 (no month) - No. 4, Jan-Feb, 1946
Avon Periodicals

	GD25	FN65	NM94
nn (#1)	10.00	30.00	60.00
2-4 (#2, 9-10/45)	7.50	22.50	45.00

SEA HOUND, THE (Radio)
No. 3, July, 1949 - No. 4, Sept, 1949
Capt. Silver Syndicate

	GD25	FN65	NM94
3,4	6.35	19.00	38.00

SEA HUNT (TV)
No. 928, 8/58 - No. 1041, 10-12/59; No. 4, 1-3/60 - No. 13, 4-6/62
Dell Publishing Co. (All have Lloyd Bridges photo-c)

	GD25	FN65	NM94
4-Color 928(#1)	11.50	34.00	80.00
4-Color 994(#2), 4-13: Manning-a #4-6,8-11,13	8.35	25.00	50.00
4-Color 1041(#3)-Toth-a	10.00	30.00	60.00

SEARCH FOR LOVE
Feb-Mar, 1950 - No. 2, Apr-May, 1950 (52 pgs.)
American Comics Group

	GD25	FN65	NM94
1	7.50	22.50	45.00
2,3(6-7/50): 3-Exist?	4.20	12.50	25.00

SEARCHERS (See 4-Color #709)

SEARS (See Merry Christmas From...)

SEASON'S GREETINGS
1935 (6-1/4x5-1/4") (32 pgs. in color)
Hallmark (King Features)

nn-Cover features Mickey Mouse, Popeye, Jiggs & Skippy. "The Night Before Christmas" told one panel per page, each panel by a famous artist featuring their character. Art by Alex Raymond, Gottfredson, Swinnerton, Segar, Chic Young, Milt Gross, Sullivan (Messmer), Herriman, McManus, Percy Crosby & others (22 artists in all)
Estimated value.... $300.00– $500.00

SEBASTION (Disney Comics)(Value: cover or less)

SEBASTION O
May, 1993 - No. 3, July, 1993 ($1.95, color, mini-series)
DC Comics (Vertigo)

	GD25	FN65	NM94
1-3-Grant Morrison scripts		.80	2.00

SECOND LIFE OF DOCTOR MIRAGE, THE (See Shadowman #16)
Nov, 1993 - Present ($2.50, color)
Valiant

	GD25	FN65	NM94
1-6: 1-With bound-in poster		1.00	2.50
1-Gold ink logo edition; no price on-c			7.50

SECRET AGENT (Formerly Sarge Steel)
V2#9, Oct, 1966; V2#10, Oct, 1967
Charlton Comics

	GD25	FN65	NM94
V2#9-Sarge Steel part-r begins	1.30	3.25	8.00
10-Tiffany Sinn, CIA app. (from Career Girl Romances #39); Aparo-a		1.60	4.00

SECRET AGENT (TV)
Nov, 1966; No. 2, Jan, 1968
Gold Key

	GD25	FN65	NM94
1-Photo-c	9.00	28.00	65.00
2-Photo-c	6.00	19.00	44.00

SECRET AGENT X-9 (See Flash Gordon #4 by King)
1934 (Book 1: 84 pgs.; Book 2: 124 pgs.) (8x7-1/2")
David McKay Publications

	GD25	FN65	NM94
Book 1-Contains reprints of the first 13 weeks of the strip by Alex Raymond; complete except for 2 dailies	38.00	115.00	265.00
Book 2-Contains reprints immediately following contents of Book 1, for 20 weeks by Alex Raymond; complete except for two dailies. Note: Raymond mis-dated the last five strips from 6/34, and while the dating sequence is confusing, the continuity is correct	32.00	95.00	225.00

SECRET AGENT X-9 (See Feature Books #8 & Magic Comics)

SECRET AGENT Z-2 (See Holyoke One-Shot No. 7)

SECRET CITY SAGA (See Jack Kirby's Secret City Saga)

SECRET DEFENDERS (Also see The Defenders & Fantastic Four #374)
Mar, 1993 - Present ($1.75, color)
Marvel Comics

	GD25	FN65	NM94
1-($2.50)-Red foil stamped-c; Dr. Strange, Nomad, Wolverine, Spider Woman & Darkhawk begin		1.10	2.75
2-11,13,14		.70	1.75
12-($2.50)-Prismatic foil-c		1.00	2.50

SECRET DIARY OF EERIE ADVENTURES
1953 (One Shot) (25 cent giant; 100 pgs.)

Secret Hearts #8, © DC

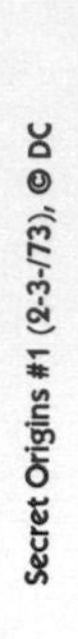

Secret Origins #1 (2-3-/73), © DC

Secret Origins #47, © DC

GD25 FN65 NM94

GD25 FN65 NM94

Avon Periodicals
nn-(Rare) Kubert-a; Hollingsworth-c; Sid Check back-c 93.00 280.00 650.00

SECRET HEARTS
9-10/49 - No. 6, 7-8/50; No. 7, 12-1/51-52 - No. 153, 7/71 (All 52 pgs.)
National Periodical Publications (Beverly)(Arleigh No. 50-113)

1-Kinstler-a; photo-c begin, end #6 32.00 95.00 225.00
2-Toth-a 16.00 48.00 110.00
3,6 (1950) 14.00 43.00 100.00
4,5-Toth-a 15.00 45.00 105.00
7(12-1/51-52) (Rare) 15.00 45.00 105.00
8-10 (1952) 10.00 30.00 65.00
11-20 9.15 27.50 55.00
21-26: 26-Last precode (2-3/55) 7.50 22.50 45.00
27-40 5.35 16.00 32.00
41-50 4.00 11.00 22.00
51-60 3.60 9.00 18.00
61-75: 75-Last 10 cent issue 2.80 7.00 14.00
76-109 2.00 5.00 10.00
110-"Reach for Happiness" serial begins, ends #138 1.60 4.00 8.00
111-119,121-126,128-133,135-138-140 1.00 2.50 5.00
120,134-Neal Adams-c 1.20 3.00 6.00
127 (4/68)-Beatles cameo 1.40 3.50 7.00
141,142-"20 Miles to Heartbreak," Chapter 2 & 3 (see Young Love for Chapters 1 & 4); Toth, Colletta-a .80 2.00 4.00
143-148,150-153: 144-Morrow-a. 153-Kirby-i .80 2.00 4.00
149-Toth-a 1.00 2.50 5.00

SECRET ISLAND OF OZ, THE (See First Comics Graphic Novel)

SECRET LOVE (See Fox Giants & Sinister House of...)

SECRET LOVE
12/55 - No. 3, 8/56; 4/57 - No. 5, 2/58; No. 6, 6/58
Ajax-Farrell/Four Star Comic Corp. No. 2 on

1(12/55-Ajax, 1st series) 5.35 16.00 32.00
2,3 4.00 10.00 20.00
1(4/57-Ajax, 2nd series) 4.20 12.50 25.00
2-6: 5-Bakerish-a 3.00 7.50 15.00

SECRET LOVES
Nov, 1949 - No. 6, Sept, 1950 (#5: photo-c)
Comic Magazines/Quality Comics Group

1-Ward-c 12.00 36.00 85.00
2-Ward-c 11.00 32.00 75.00
3-Crandall-a 8.65 26.00 52.00
4,6 5.35 16.00 32.00
5-Suggestive art "Boom Town Babe" 7.50 22.50 45.00

SECRET LOVE STORIES (See Fox Giants)

SECRET MISSIONS
February, 1950
St. John Publishing Co.

1-Kubert-c 11.50 34.00 80.00

SECRET MYSTERIES (Formerly Crime Mysteries & Crime Smashers)
No. 16, Nov, 1954 - No. 19, July, 1955
Ribage/Merit Publications No. 17 on

16-Horror, Palais-a 11.00 32.00 75.00
17-19-Horror; #17-mis-dated 3/54? 7.50 22.50 45.00

SECRET ORIGINS (See 80 Page Giant #8)
Aug-Oct, 1961 (Annual) (Reprints)
National Periodical Publications

1-Origin Adam Strange (Showcase #17), Green Lantern (Gr. Lantern #1), Challengers (partial-r/Showcase #6, 6 pgs. Kirby-a). J'onn J'onzz (Det. #225), The Flash (Showcase #4). Green Arrow (1pg. text). Superman-Batman team (W. Finest #94). Wonder Woman (Wonder Woman #105) 23.00 69.00 275.00

SECRET ORIGINS
Feb-Mar, 1973 - No. 6, Jan-Feb, 1974; No. 7, Oct-Nov, 1974
National Periodical Publications (All origin reprints)

1-Superman(r/1 pg. origin/Action #1, 1st time since G.A.), Batman(Det. #33), Ghost(Flash #88), The Flash(Showcase #4) 1.65 4.00 10.00
2-4: 2-Green Lantern & The Atom(Showcase #22 & 34), Supergirl(Action #252). 3-Wonder Woman(W.W. #1), Wildcat(Sensation #1). 4-Vigilante (Action #42) by Meskin, Kid Eternity(Hit #25) 1.00 2.00 5.00
5-7: 5-The Spectre by Baily(More Fun #52,53). 6-Blackhawk(Military #1) & Legion of Super-Heroes(Superboy #147). 7-Robin(Detective #38), Aquaman (More Fun #73) 1.60 4.00
NOTE: ***Infantino** a-1. **Kane** a-2. **Kubert** a-1.*

SECRET ORIGINS
4/86 - No. 50, 8/90 (All origins)(52 pgs. #6 on)(#27 on: $1.50)
DC Comics

1-Origin Superman 1.50 3.75
2-Blue Beetle 1.10 2.75
3-5: 3-Shazam. 4-Firestorm. 5-Crimson Avenger .90 2.25
6-Halo/G.A. Batman 1.70 4.25
7-12,14-26: 7-Green Lantern(Guy Gardner)/G.A. Sandman. 8-Shadow Lass/ Doll Man. 9-G.A. Flash/Skyman. 10-Phantom Stranger w/Alan Moore scripts; Legends spin-off. 11-G.A. Hawkman/Power Girl. 12-Challengers of Unknown/G.A. Fury. 14-Suicide Squad; Legends spin-off. 15-Spectre/ Deadman. 16-G.A. Hourman/Warlord. 17-Adam Strange/Dr. Occult. 18-G.A. Gr. Lantern/The Creeper. 19-Uncle Sam/The Guardian. 20-Batgirl/ G.A. Dr. Mid-Nite. 21-Jonah Hex/Black Condor. 22-Manhunters. 23-Floronic Man/Guardians of the Universe. 24-Blue Devil/Dr. Fate. 25-LSH/ Atom. 26-Black Lightning/Miss America .90 2.25
13-Origin Nightwing; Johnny Thunder app. 1.70 4.25
27-38,40-44: 27-Zatara/Zatanna. 28-Midnight/Nightshade. 29-Power of the Atom/Mr. America; new 3 pg. Red Tornado story by Mayer (last app. of Scribbly, 8/88). 30-Plastic Man/Elongated Man. 31-JSA. 32-JLA. 33-35-JLI. 36-Green Lantern/Poison Ivy. 37-Legion Of Substitute Heroes/Doctor Light. 38-Green Arrow/Speedy; Grell scripts. 40-All Ape issue. 41-Rogues Gallery of Flash. 42-Phantom Girl/Grim Ghost. 43-Original Hawk & Dove/ Cave Carson/Chris KL-99. 44-Batman app.; story based on Det. #40 .75 1.90
39-Animal Man-c/story continued in Animal Man #10; Grant Morrison scripts; Batman app. 1.70 4.25
45-49: 45-Blackhawk/El Diablo. 46-JLA/LSH/New Titans. 47-LSH. 48-Ambush Bug/Stanley & His Monster/Rex the Wonder Dog/Trigger Twins. 49-Newsboy Legion/Silent Knight/brief origin Bouncing Boy 1.50
50-($3.95, 100 pgs.)-Batman & Robin in text, Flash of Two Worlds, Johnny Thunder, Dolphin, Black Canary & Space Museum 1.60 4.00
Annual 1 (8/87)-Capt. Comet/Doom Patrol .80 2.00
Annual 2 ('88, $2.00)-Origin Flash II & Flash III .80 2.00
Annual 3 ('89, $2.95, 84 pgs.)-Teen Titans; 1st app. new Flamebird who replaces original Bat-Girl 1.20 3.00
Special 1 (10/89, $2.00)-Batman villains: Penguin, Riddler, & Two-Face; Bolland-c; Sam Kieth-a; Neil Gaiman scripts(2) 1.10 2.75
NOTE: ***Art Adams** a-33i(part). **M. Anderson** 8, 19, 21; c-19(part). **Bolland** c-7. **Byrne** c/a-Annual 1. **Colan** c/a-5p. **Forte** a-37. **Giffen** a-18p, 44p, 48. **Kaluta** c-39. **Gil Kane** a-2, 28; c-2p. **Kirby** c-19(part). **Mayer** a-29. **Morrow** a-21. **Orlando** a-10. **Perez** a-50i; c- Annual 3. **Rogers** a-6p. **Russell** a-27i. **Staton** a-36, 50p. **Steacy** a-35. **Tuska** a-4p, 9p.*

SECRET ORIGINS OF SUPER-HEROES (See DC Special Series #10, 19)

SECRET ORIGINS OF THE WORLD'S GREATEST SUPER-HEROES
(DC)(Value: cover or less)

SECRET ROMANCE
Oct, 1968 - No. 41, Nov, 1976; No. 42, Mar, 1979 - No. 48, Feb, 1980
Charlton Comics

1-Begin 12 cent issues, ends ? 1.60 4.00 8.00
2-10: 9-Reese-a .80 2.00 4.00
11-48 .40 1.00 2.00

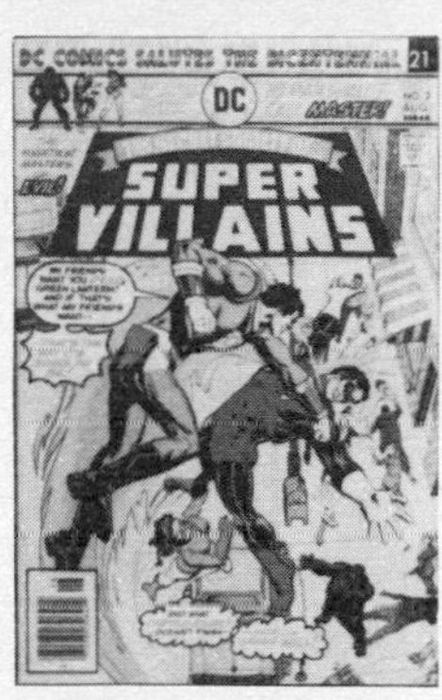

Secret Society of Super-Villains #2, © DC

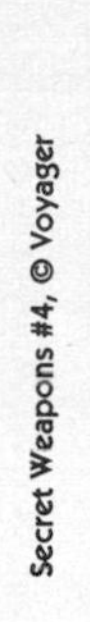
Secret Weapons #4, © Voyager

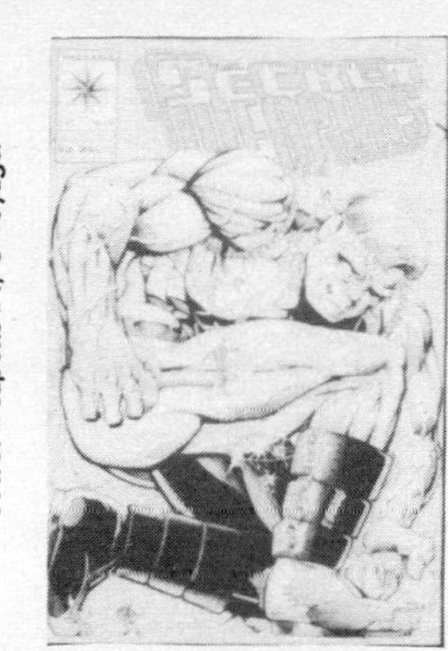

Seduction Of The Innocent #1, © Eclipse

	GD25	FN65	NM94

NOTE: *Beyond the Stars app.-No. 9, 11, 12, 14.*

SECRET ROMANCES
April 1951 - No. 27, July, 1955
Superior Publications Ltd.

	GD25	FN65	NM94
1	8.35	25.00	50.00
2	4.70	14.00	28.00
3-10	4.00	11.00	22.00
11-13,15-18,20-27	3.20	8.00	16.00
14,19-Lingerie panels	4.00	11.00	22.00

SECRET SERVICE (See Kent Blake of the...)

SECRET SIX (See Action Comics Weekly)
Apr-May, 1968 - No. 7, Apr-May, 1969 (12 cents)
National Periodical Publications

	GD25	FN65	NM94
1-Origin/1st app.	4.50	14.00	32.00
2-7	2.70	8.00	19.00

SECRET SOCIETY OF SUPER-VILLAINS
May-June, 1976 - No. 15, June-July, 1978
National Periodical Publications/DC Comics

	GD25	FN65	NM94
1-Origin; JLA cameo & Capt. Cold app.		.90	2.25
2-5: 2-Re-intro/origin Capt. Comet; Green Lantern x-over. 5-Green Lantern, Hawkman x-over; Darkseid app.		.70	1.80
6-15: 9,10-Creeper x-over. 11-Capt. Comet; Orlando-i. 15-G.A. Atom, Dr. Midnite, & JSA app.			1.35

SECRET SOCIETY OF SUPER-VILLAINS SPECIAL (See DC Special Series #6)

SECRETS OF HAUNTED HOUSE
4-5/75 - #5, 12-1/75-76; #6, 6-7/77 - #14, 10-11/78; #15, 8/79 - #46, 3/82
National Periodical Publications/DC Comics

	GD25	FN65	NM94
1		1.20	3.00
2-10		.80	2.00
11-46: 31-Mr. E series begins, ends #41			1.25

NOTE: ***Bissette** a-46. **Buckler** c-32-40p. **Ditko** a-9, 12, 41, 45. **Golden** a-10. **Howard** a-13i. **Kaluta** c-8, 10, 11, 14, 16, 29. **Kubert** c-41, 42. **Sheldon Mayer** a-43p. **McWilliams** a-35. **Nasser** a-24. **Newton** a-30p. **Nino** a-1, 13, 19. **Orlando** c-13, 30, 43, 45i. **N. Redondo** a-4, 5, 29. **Rogers** c-26. **Spiegle** a-31-41. **Wrightson** c-5, 44.*

SECRETS OF HAUNTED HOUSE SPECIAL (See DC Special Series #12)

SECRETS OF LIFE (See 4-Color #749)

SECRETS OF LOVE (See Popular Teen-Agers...)

SECRETS OF LOVE AND MARRIAGE
V2#1, Aug, 1956 - V2#25, June, 1961
Charlton Comics

	GD25	FN65	NM94
V2#1	3.60	9.00	18.00
V2#2-6	2.00	5.00	10.00
V2#7-9(All 68 pgs.)	1.60	4.00	8.00
10-25	1.20	3.00	6.00

SECRETS OF MAGIC (See Wisco)

SECRETS OF SINISTER HOUSE (Sinister House of Secret Love #1-4)
No. 5, June-July, 1972 - No. 18, June-July, 1974
National Periodical Publications

	GD25	FN65	NM94
5-9: 7-Redondo-a		.90	2.25
10-Neal Adams-a(i)	1.00	2.50	5.50
11-18: 17-Barry-a; early Chaykin 1 pg. strip		.65	1.60

NOTE: ***Alcala** a-6, 13, 14. **Kaluta** c-6, 7. **Nino** a-8, 11-13. Ambrose Bierce adapt.-#14.*

SECRETS OF THE LEGION OF SUPER-HEROES
Jan, 1981 - No. 3, March, 1981 (Mini-series)
DC Comics

	GD25	FN65	NM94
1-3: 1-Origin of the Legion. 2-Retells origins of Brainiac 5, Shrinking Violet, Sun-Boy, Bouncing Boy, Ultra-Boy, Matter-Eater Lad, Mon-El, Karate Kid, & Dream Girl			1.00

SECRETS OF TRUE LOVE
February, 1958
St. John Publishing Co.

	GD25	FN65	NM94
1	3.60	9.00	18.00

SECRETS OF YOUNG BRIDES
No. 5, Sept, 1957 - No. 44, Oct, 1964; July, 1975 - No. 9, Nov, 1976
Charlton Comics

	GD25	FN65	NM94
5	4.00	10.00	20.00
6-10: 8-Negligee panel	2.00	5.00	10.00
11-20	1.60	4.00	8.00
21-30: Last 10 cent issue?	1.00	2.50	6.00
31-44		1.20	3.00
1-9 (2nd series)			1.50

SECRET SQUIRREL (TV)(See Kite Fun Book)
October, 1966 (Hanna-Barbera, 12¢)
Gold Key

	GD25	FN65	NM94
1	8.00	23.00	60.00

SECRET STORY ROMANCES (Becomes True Tales of Love)
Nov, 1953 - No. 21, Mar, 1956
Atlas Comics (TCI)

	GD25	FN65	NM94
1-Everett-a	8.35	25.00	50.00
2	4.20	12.50	25.00
3-11: 11-Last pre-code (2/55)	4.00	10.00	20.00
12-21	3.20	8.00	16.00

NOTE: ***Colletta** a-10, 14, 15, 17, 21; c-10, 14, 17.*

SECRET VOICE, THE (See Great American Comics Presents...)

SECRET WARS II (Also see Marvel Super Heroes...)
July, 1985 - No. 9, Mar, 1986 (Maxi-series)
Marvel Comics Group

	GD25	FN65	NM94
1-9: 2,8,9-X-Men app. 5,8,9-Spider-Man app. 9-Double sized (75 cents)			1.00

SECRET WEAPONS
Sept, 1993 - Present ($2.25, color)
Valiant

	GD25	FN65	NM94
1-8: 3-Reese-a(i). 5-Ninjak app.		.90	2.25

SECTAURS (Marvel)(Value: cover or less)

SEDUCTION OF THE INNOCENT (Also see N. Y. State Joint Legis. Committee to Study...)
1953, 1954 (399 pages) (Hardback)
Rinehart & Co., Inc., N. Y. (Also printed in Canada by Clarke, Irwin & Co. Ltd., Toronto)
Written by Dr. Fredric Wertham

	GD25	FN65	NM94
(1st Version)-with bibliographical note intact (several copies got out before the comic publishers forced the removal of this page)		70.00	175.00
with dust jacket....		175.00	350.00
(2nd Version)-without bibliographical note		42.00	90.00
with dust jacket....		80.00	160.00
(3rd Version)-Published in England by Kennikat Press, 1954, 399 pgs. has bibliographical page		30.00	60.00
1972 r-/of 3rd version; 400 pgs. w/bibliography page; Kennikat Press		12.00	24.00

NOTE: *Material from this book appeared in the November, 1953(Vol.70, pp50-53,214) issue of the **Ladies' Home Journal** under the title "What Parents Don't Know About Comic Books." With the release of this book, Dr. Wertham reveals seven years of research attempting to link juvenile delinquency to comic books. Many illustrations showing excessive violence, sex, sadism, and torture are shown. This book was used at the Kefauver Senate hearings which led to the Comics Code Authority. Because of the influence this book had on the comic in dustry and the collector's interest in it, we feel this listing is justified. Also see **Parade of Pleasure.***

SEDUCTION OF THE INNOCENT! (Eclipse)(Value: cover or less)

SELECT DETECTIVE
Aug-Sept, 1948 - No. 3, Dec-Jan, 1948-49
D. S. Publishing Co.

	GD25	FN65	NM94
1-Matt Baker-a	11.50	34.00	80.00
2-Baker, McWilliams-a	10.00	30.00	60.00

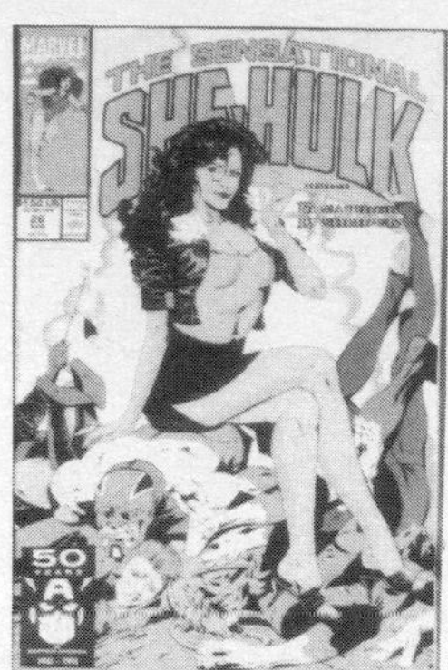

The Sensational She-Hulk #26, © MEG

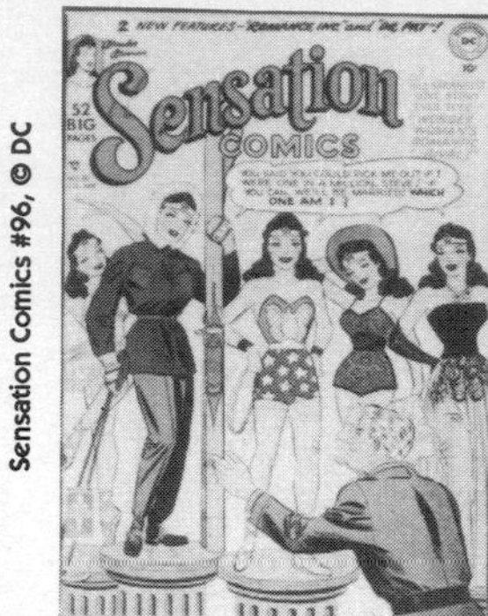

Sensation Comics #96, © DC

Sgt. Bilko's Pvt. Doberman #9, © CBS

GD25 FN65 NM94 | GD25 FN65 NM94

3 — 8.35 — 25.00 — 50.00

SEMPER FI (Marvel)(Value: cover or less)

SENSATIONAL POLICE CASES (Becomes Captain Steve Savage, 2nd series)
1952; 1954 - No. 4, July-Aug, 1954
Avon Periodicals

nn-(1952, 25¢, 100 pgs.)-Kubert-a?; Check, Larsen, Lawrence & McCann-a; Kinstler-c — 25.00 — 75.00 — 175.00
1 (1954) — 10.00 — 30.00 — 60.00
2-4: 2-Kirbyish-a (3-4/54). 4-Reprint/Saint #5 — 7.50 — 22.50 — 45.00
I.W. Reprint #5-(1963?, nd)-Reprints Prison Break #5(1952-Realistic); Infantino-a — 2.40 — 6.00 — 12.00

SENSATIONAL SHE-HULK, THE (She-Hulk #21-23; see Savage She-Hulk)
V2#1, 5/89 - No. 60, Feb, 1994 ($1.50/$1.75, color, deluxe format)
Marvel Comics

V2#1-Byrne-c/a(p)/scripts begin, end #8 — 1.30 — 3.25
2-8: 3-Spidey. 4-Reintro G.A. Blonde Phantom — .85 — 2.20
9-49,51-58: 14-17-Howard the Duck app. 21-23-Return of the Blonde Phantom. 22-All Winners Squad app. 25-Thor app. 26-Excalibur app.; Guice-c. 29-Wolverine app. (3 pgs.). 30-Hobgoblin-c & cameo. 31-Byrne-c/a/scripts begin again. 35-Last $1.50-c. 37-Wolverine/Punisher/Spidey-c, but no app. 39-Thing app. 56-Hulk — .70 — 1.75
50-($2.95, 52 pgs.)-Embossed green foil-c; Byrne app.; last Byrne-c/a; Austin, Chaykin, Simonson-a; Miller-a(2 pgs.) — 1.20 — 3.00

SENSATIONAL SHE-HULK IN CEREMONY, THE (Marvel)(Value: cover or less)

SENSATIONAL SPIDER-MAN (Marvel)(Value: cover or less)

SENSATION COMICS (Sensation Mystery #110 on)
Jan, 1942 - No. 109, May-June, 1952
National Per. Publ./All-American

GD25 — FN65 — VF82 — NM94

1-Origin Mr. Terrific(1st app.), Wildcat(1st app.), The Gay Ghost, & Little Boy Blue; Wonder Woman(cont'd from All Star #8), The Black Pirate begin; intro. Justice & Fair Play Club — 600.00 — 1800.00 — 3900.00 — 6000.00
(Estimated up to 150 total copies exist, 7 in NM/Mint)

1-Reprint, Oversize 13-1/2x10." WARNING: This comic is an exact duplicate reprint of the original except for its size. DC published it in 1974 with a second cover titling it as a Famous First Edition. There have been many reported cases of the outer cover being removed and the interior sold as the original edition. The reprint with the new outer cover removed is practically worthless. See Famous First Edition for value.

GD25 — FN65 — NM94

2-Etta Candy begins — 233.00 — 700.00 — 1600.00
3-W. Woman gets secretary's job — 125.00 — 375.00 — 850.00
4-1st app. Stretch Skinner in Wildcat — 108.00 — 325.00 — 725.00
5-Intro. Justin, Black Pirate's son — 83.00 — 250.00 — 550.00
6-Origin/1st app. Wonder Woman's magic lasso — 83.00 — 250.00 — 550.00
7-10 — 68.00 — 205.00 — 465.00
11,12,14-20 — 58.00 — 175.00 — 400.00
13-Hitler, Tojo, Mussolini-c (as bowling pins) — 67.00 — 200.00 — 450.00
21-30 — 44.00 — 132.00 — 300.00
31-33 — 35.00 — 105.00 — 235.00
34-Sargon, the Sorcerer begins (10/44), ends #36; begins again #52 — 35.00 — 105.00 — 235.00
35-40: 38-Xmas-c — 28.00 — 85.00 — 190.00
41-50: 43-The Whip app. — 24.00 — 72.00 — 165.00
51-60: 51-Last Black Pirate. 56,57-Sargon by Kubert — 21.00 — 63.00 — 145.00
61-67,69-80: 63-Last Mr. Terrific. 66-Wildcat by Kubert — 21.00 — 63.00 — 145.00
68-Origin & 1st app.Huntress (8/47) — 23.00 — 68.00 — 155.00
81-Used in **SOTI**, pg. 33,34; Krigstein-a — 23.00 — 68.00 — 155.00
82-90: 83-Last Sargon. 86-The Atom app. 90-Last Wildcat — 17.00 — 50.00 — 115.00
91-Streak begins by Alex Toth — 17.00 — 50.00 — 115.00
92,93: 92-Toth-a, 2 pgs. — 17.00 — 52.00 — 120.00
94-1st all girl issue — 22.00 — 65.00 — 150.00
95-99,101-106: 95-Unmasking of W.W.-c/story. 99-1st app. Astra, Girl of the Future, ends #106. 103-Robot-c. 105-Last 52 pgs. 106-Wonder Woman ends — 22.00 — 65.00 — 150.00
100-(11-12/50) — 31.00 — 92.00 — 215.00
107-(Scarce)-1st mystery issue; Johnny Peril by Toth(p), 8 pgs. & begins (see Comic Cavalcade #15 for 1st app.) — 33.00 — 100.00 — 250.00
108-(Scarce)-Johnny Peril by Toth(p) — 31.00 — 92.00 — 215.00
109-(Scarce)-Johnny Peril by Toth(p) — 33.00 — 100.00 — 250.00

NOTE: ***Krigstein** a-(Wildcat)-81, 83, 84. **Moldoff** Black Pirate-1-25; Black Pirate not in 34-36, 43-48. **Oskner** c(i)-89-91, 94-106. Wonder Woman by **H. G. Peter**, all issues except #8, 17-19, 21; c-4-7, 9-18, 20-88, 92, 93. **Toth** a-91, 98; c-107. Wonder Woman c-1-106.*

SENSATION MYSTERY (Formerly Sensation Comics #1-109)
No. 110, July-Aug, 1952 - No. 116, July-Aug, 1953
National Periodical Publications

110-Johnny Peril continues — 22.00 — 65.00 — 150.00
111-116-Johnny Peril in all. 116-M. Anderson-a — 22.00 — 65.00 — 150.00

NOTE: ***M. Anderson** c-110. **Colan** a-114p. **Giunta** a-112. **G. Kane** c(p)-108, 109, 111-115.*

SENTINELS OF JUSTICE, THE (See Americomics & Captain Paragon &...)

SENTRY SPECIAL
1991 ($2.75, color)(Hero Alliance spin-off)
Innovation Publishing

1-Lost in Space preview (3 pgs.) — 1.10 — 2.75

SERAPHIM (Innovation)(Value: cover or less)

SERGEANT BARNEY BARKER (Becomes G. I. Tales #4 on)
Aug, 1956 - No. 3, Dec, 1956
Atlas Comics (MCI)

1-Severin-c/a(4) — 11.50 — 34.00 — 80.00
2,3: 2-Severin-c/a(4). 3-Severin-c/a(5) — 10.00 — 30.00 — 60.00

SERGEANT BILKO (Phil Silvers) (TV)
May-June, 1957 - No. 18, Mar-Apr, 1960
National Periodical Publications

1-All have Bob Oskner-c — 52.00 — 155.00 — 365.00
2 — 29.00 — 85.00 — 200.00
3-5 — 23.00 — 70.00 — 160.00
6-18: 11,12,15,17-Photo-c — 19.00 — 57.00 — 130.00

SGT. BILKO'S PVT. DOBERMAN (TV)
June-July, 1958 - No. 11, Feb-Mar, 1960
National Periodical Publications

1-Bob Oskner c-1-4,7,11 — 31.00 — 92.00 — 215.00
2 — 19.00 — 57.00 — 130.00
3-5: 5-Photo-c — 14.00 — 43.00 — 100.00
6-11: 6,9-Photo-c — 10.00 — 30.00 — 70.00

SGT. DICK CARTER OF THE U.S. BORDER PATROL (See Holyoke One-Shot)

SGT. FURY (& His Howling Commandos)(See Special Marvel Edition)
May, 1963 - No. 167, Dec, 1981
Marvel Comics Group (BPC earlier issues)

1-1st app. Sgt. Nick Fury (becomes agent of Shield in Strange Tales #135); Kirby/Ayers-c/a; 1st Dum-Dum Dugan & the Howlers — 60.00 — 180.00 — 600.00
2-Kirby-a — 25.00 — 75.00 — 200.00
3-5: 3-Reed Richards x-over. 4-Death of Junior Juniper. 5-1st Baron Strucker app.; Kirby-a — 13.00 — 38.00 — 100.00
6-10: 8-Baron Zemo, 1st Percival Pinkerton app. 9-Hitler-c & app. 10-1st app. Capt. Savage (the Skipper)(9/64) — 9.00 — 26.00 — 70.00
11,12,14-20: 14-1st Blitz Squad. 18-Death of Pamela Hawley — 5.50 — 17.00 — 40.00
13-Captain America & Bucky app.(12/64); 1st solo Capt. America x-over outside The Avengers; Kirby-a — 19.00 — 56.00 — 150.00
21-30: 25-Red Skull app. 27-1st app. Eric Koenig; origin Fury's eye patch — 4.00 — 12.00 — 28.00
31-50: 34-Origin Howling Commandos. 35-Eric Koenig joins Howlers. 43-Bob Hope, Glen Miller app. 44-Flashback-Howlers 1st mission — 2.40 — 7.25 — 17.00

Sgt. Fury #147, © MEG

Sgt. Rock #15, © DC

Shade the Changing Man #2 (8/90), © DC

	GD25	FN65	NM94
51-60	2.00	6.00	14.00
61-80: 64-Capt. Savage & Raiders x-over. 76-Fury's Father app. in WWI story	1.70	5.00	12.00
81-100: 98-Deadly Dozen x-over. 100-Capt. America, Fantastic 4 cameos; Stan Lee, Martin Goodman & others app.	1.50	3.75	9.00
101-120: 101-Origin retold	1.00	2.50	5.50
121-130		1.90	4.75
131-150		1.30	3.25
151-167: 167-Reprints		1.20	3.00
Annual 1(1965, 25 cents, 72pgs.)-r/#4,5 & new-a	11.00	32.00	75.00
Special 2(1966)	5.00	15.00	35.00
Special 3(1967)	3.20	8.00	20.00
Special 4(1968)	1.70	5.00	12.00
Special 5-7(1969-11/71)	1.20	3.00	7.00

NOTE: ***Ayers** a-8. **Ditko** a-15i. **Gil Kane** c-37, 96. **Kirby** a-1-7, 13p, 167p(r), Special 5; c-1-20, 25, 167p. **Severin** a-44-46, 48, 162, 164; inks-49-79, Special 4, 6; c-4i, 5, 6, 44, 46, 110, 149i, 155i, 162-166. **Sutton** a-57p. Reprints in #80, 82, 85, 87, 89, 91, 93, 95, 99, 101, 103, 105, 107, 109, 111, 145.*

SGT. FURY AND HIS HOWLING DEFENDERS (See The Defenders #147)

SERGEANT PRESTON OF THE YUKON (TV)
No. 344, Aug, 1951 - No. 29, Nov-Jan, 1958-59
Dell Publishing Co.

	GD25	FN65	NM94
4-Color 344(#1)-Sergeant Preston & his dog Yukon King begin; painted-c begin, end #18	11.00	32.00	75.00
4-Color 373,397,419('52)	7.00	21.00	42.00
5(11-1/52-53)-10(2-4/54)	5.00	15.00	30.00
11,12,14-17	4.20	12.50	25.00
13-Origin Sgt. Preston	5.00	15.00	30.00
18-Origin Yukon King; last painted-c	5.00	15.00	30.00
19-29: All photo-c	5.85	17.50	35.00

SERGEANT PRESTON OF THE YUKON
1956 (4 comic booklets) (Soft-c, 16pgs., 7x2-1/2" & 5x2-1/2")
Giveaways with Quaker Cereals

	GD25	FN65	NM94
"How He Found Yukon King," "The Case That Made Him A Sergeant," "How Yukon King Saved Him From The Wolves," "How He Became A Mountie" each...	5.35	16.00	32.00

SGT. ROCK (Formerly Our Army at War, see Brave & the Bold #52)
No. 302, March, 1977 - No. 422, July, 1988 (See G.I. Combat #108)
National Periodical Publications/DC Comics

	GD25	FN65	NM94
302	1.40	3.50	8.50
303-310	1.10	2.70	6.50
311-320: 318-Reprints		1.80	4.50
321-350		1.30	3.25
351-422: 422-1st Joe, Adam, Andy Kubert-a team		.70	1.80
Annual 2-4: 2(1982)-Formerly Sgt. Rock's Prize Battle Tales #1. 3(1983). 4(1984)		1.10	2.75

NOTE: ***Estrada** a-322, 327, 331, 336, 337, 341, 342i. **Glanzman** a-384, 421. **Kubert** a-302, 303, 305r, 306, 328, 351, 356, 368, 373, 422; c-317, 318r, 319-323, 325-333-on, Annual 2, 3. **Severin** a-347. **Spiegle** a-382, Annual 2, 3. **Thorne** a-384. **Toth** a-385r. **Wildey** a-307, 311, 313, 314.*

SGT. ROCK SPECIAL (Sgt. Rock #14 on; see DC Special Series #3)
Oct, 1988 - No. 21, Feb, 1992; No. 1, 1992 ($2.00, color, quarterly, 52 pgs.)
DC Comics

	GD25	FN65	NM94
1		1.00	2.50
2-8,10-21: All-r; 5-r/1st Sgt. Rock/Our Army at War #81. 7-Tomahawk-r by Thorne. 10 All Rock issue. 11-r/1st Haunted Tank story. 12-All Kubert issue; begins monthly. 13-Dinosaur story by Heath(r). 14-Enemy Ace-r (22 pgs.) by Adams/Kubert. 15-Enemy Ace (22 pgs.) by Kubert. 16-Iron Major-c/story. 16,17-Enemy Ace-r. 19-r/Batman/Sgt. Rock team-up/B&B #108 by Aparo		.80	2.00
9-Enemy Ace-r by Kubert		1.00	2.50
1 (1992, $2.95, 68 pgs.)-Simonson-c; unpubbed Kubert-a; Glanzman, Russell, Pratt, & Wagner-a		1.20	3.00

NOTE: ***Neal Adams** r-1, 8, 14p. **Chaykin** r-3, 9(2pg.); c-3. **Drucker** r-6. **Glanzman** r-20. **Heath** r-5, 9-13, 16, 19, 21. **Krigstein** r-4, 8. **Kubert** r-1-17, 20, 21; c-1p, 2, 8, 14-21. **Miller** r-6p. **Severin** r-3, 6, 10. **Simonson** r-2, 4; c-4. **Thorne** r-7. **Toth** r-2, 8, 11. **Wood** r-4.*

SGT. ROCK SPECTACULAR (See DC Special Series #13)

SGT. ROCK'S PRIZE BATTLE TALES (Becomes Sgt. Rock Annual #2 on; see DC Special Series #18 & 80 Page Giant #7)
Winter, 1964 (One Shot) (Giant - 80 pgs.)
National Periodical Publications

	GD25	FN65	NM94
1-Kubert, Heath-r; new Kubert-c	14.00	43.00	100.00

SGT. STRYKER'S DEATH SQUAD (See Savage Combat Tales)

SERGIO ARAGONES' GROO THE WANDERER (See Groo...)

SEVEN BLOCK (Marvel)(Value: cover or less)

SEVEN DEAD MEN (See Complete Mystery #1)

SEVEN DWARFS (See 4-Color #227, 382)

SEVEN SAMUROID, THE (See Image Graphic Novel)

SEVEN SEAS COMICS
Apr, 1946 - No. 6, 1947 (no month)
Universal Phoenix Features/Leader No. 6

	GD25	FN65	NM94
1-South Sea Girl by Matt Baker, Capt. Cutlass begin; Tugboat Tessie by Baker app.	40.00	120.00	280.00
2	36.00	110.00	250.00
3-6: 3-Six pg. Feldstein-a	31.00	95.00	220.00

NOTE: ***Baker** a-1-6; c-3-6.*

1776 (See Charlton Classic Library)

7TH VOYAGE OF SINBAD, THE (See 4-Color #944)

77 SUNSET STRIP (TV)
No. 1066, Jan-Mar, 1960 - No. 2, Feb, 1963 (All photo-c)
Dell Publ. Co./Gold Key

	GD25	FN65	NM94
4-Color 1066-Toth-a	11.50	34.00	80.00
4-Color 1106,1159-Toth-a	10.00	30.00	60.00
4-Color 1211,1263,1291, 01-742-209(7-9/62)-Manning-a in all	9.15	27.50	55.00
1(11/62-G.K.), 2-Manning-a in each	9.15	27.50	55.00

77TH BENGAL LANCERS, THE (See 4-Color #791)

SEX, LIES AND MUTUAL FUNDS OF THE YUPPIES FROM HELL (Marvel)(Value: cover or less)(Also see Yuppies From Hell)

SEYMOUR, MY SON (See More Seymour)
September, 1963
Archie Publications (Radio Comics)

	GD25	FN65	NM94
1	4.00	11.00	22.00

SHADE, THE CHANGING MAN (See Cancelled Comic Cavalcade)
June-July, 1977 - No. 8, Aug-Sept, 1978
National Periodical Publications/DC Comics

	GD25	FN65	NM94
1-1st app. Shade; Ditko-c/a in all		1.70	4.25
2-8		1.10	2.75

SHADE, THE CHANGING MAN (2nd series) (Also see Suicide Squad #16)
July, 1990 - Present ($1.50/$1.75, color, mature readers)
DC Comics

	GD25	FN65	NM94
1-($2.50, 52 pgs.)		1.00	2.50
2-16: 6-Preview of World Without End		.70	1.75
17-46: 17-Begin $1.75-c. 33-Metallic ink on-c		.70	1.75

SHADO: SONG OF THE DRAGON (See Green Arrow #63-66)
1992 - No. 4, 1992 ($4.95, color, mini-series, 52 pgs.)
DC Comics

	GD25	FN65	NM94
Book One - Four: Grell scripts; Morrow-a(i)	1.00	2.00	5.00

SHADOW, THE
Aug, 1964 - No. 8, Sept, 1965 (All 12 cents)
Archie Comics (Radio Comics)

	GD25	FN65	NM94
1	3.70	11.00	26.00
2-8: 3,4,6,7-The Fly 1 pg. strips. 7-Shield app.	2.40	7.25	17.00

Shadow Comics V2#6, © Conde Nast

Shadowman #11, © Voyager

Shanna the She-Devil #5, © MEG

GD25 FN65 NM94

SHADOW, THE
Oct-Nov, 1973 - No. 12, Aug-Sept, 1975
National Periodical Publications

	GD25	FN65	NM94
1-Kaluta-a begins	3.20	9.00	21.00
2	1.70	5.00	12.00
3-Kaluta/Wrightson-a	2.15	6.50	15.00
4,6-Kaluta-a ends. 4-Chaykin, Wrightson part-i	1.65	4.00	10.00
5,7-12: 11-The Avenger (pulp character) x-over	1.00	2.50	6.00

NOTE: ***Craig** a-10. **Cruz** a-10-12. **Kaluta** a-1, 2, 3p, 4, 6; c-1-4, 6, 10-12. **Kubert** c-9. **Robbins** a-5, 7-9; c-5, 7, 8.*

SHADOW, THE (DC, 1986 & 1987 editions)(Value: cover or less)

SHADOW COMICS (Pulp, radio)
March, 1940 - V9#5, Aug-Sept, 1949
Street & Smith Publications
NOTE: *The Shadow first appeared on radio in 1929 and was featured in pulps beginning in 1931. The early covers of this series were reprinted from the pulp covers.*

	GD25	FN65	NM94
V1#1-Shadow, Doc Savage, Bill Barnes, Nick Carter (radio), Frank Merriwell, Iron Munro, the Astonishing Man begin	285.00	860.00	2000.00
2-The Avenger begins, ends #6; Capt. Fury only app.	100.00	300.00	700.00
3(nn-5/40)-Norgil the Magician app.; cover is exact swipe of Shadow pulp from 1/33	83.00	250.00	550.00
4,5: 4-The Three Musketeers begins, ends #8. 5-Doc Savage ends	67.00	200.00	450.00
6,8,9: 9-Norgil the Magician app.	55.00	165.00	375.00
7-Origin/1st app. The Hooded Wasp & Wasplet (11/40); series ends V3#8; Hooded Wasp/Wasplet app. on-c thru #9	62.00	188.00	415.00
10-Origin The Iron Ghost, ends #11; The Dead End Kids begins, ends #14	55.00	165.00	375.00
11-Origin Hooded Wasp & Wasplet retold	55.00	165.00	375.00
12-Dead End Kids app.	47.00	140.00	300.00
V2#1,2(11/41): 2-Dead End Kids story	39.00	120.00	275.00
3-Origin & 1st app. Supersnipe (3/42); series begins; Little Nemo story	55.00	165.00	375.00
4,5: 4,8-Little Nemo story	40.00	120.00	265.00
6-9: 6-Blackstone the Magician story	37.00	110.00	240.00
10-12: 10-Supersnipe app.	37.00	110.00	240.00
V3#1-12: 10-Doc Savage begins, not in V5#5, V6#10-12, V8#4	33.00	100.00	220.00
V4#1-12	29.00	88.00	200.00
V5#1-12	27.00	82.00	185.00
V6#1-11: 9-Intro. Shadow, Jr. (12/46)	25.00	75.00	165.00
12-Powell-c/a; atom bomb panels	27.00	82.00	185.00
V7#1,2,5,7-9,12: 2,5-Shadow, Jr. app.; Powell-a	27.00	82.00	185.00
3,6,11-Powell-c/a	29.00	88.00	200.00
4-Powell-c/a; Atom bomb panels	33.00	100.00	220.00
10(1/48)-Flying Saucer-c/story (2nd of this theme; see The Spirit 9/28/47); Powell-c/a	37.00	110.00	250.00
V8#1-12-Powell-a. 8-Powell Spider-c/a	29.00	88.00	200.00
V9#1,5-Powell-a	27.00	82.00	185.00
2-4-Powell-c/a	29.00	88.00	200.00

NOTE: ***Binder** c-V3#1. **Powell** art in most issues beginning V6#12. Painted c-1-6.*

SHADOWHAWK (See Images of Shadowhawk & Youngblood #2)
Aug, 1992 - No. 4, Mar, 1993 ($1.95, color, mini-series)
Image Comics

	GD25	FN65	NM94
1-($2.50)-Embossed silver foil stamped-c; Valentino/Liefeld-c; Valentino-c/a/scripts in all; has coupon for Image #0	1.65	4.00	10.00
1-With coupon missing		1.40	3.50
1-($1.95)-Newsstand version w/o foil stamp		1.00	2.50
2-Shadowhawk poster w/McFarlane-i; brief Spawn app.; wraparound-c w/silver ink highlights		1.20	3.00
3-($2.50)-Glow-in-the-dark-c		1.00	2.50
4-($1.95)-Savage Dragon-c/story		.80	2.00

SHADOWHAWK II
May, 1993 - No. 3, Aug, 1993 (Color, mini-series)
Image Comics

	GD25	FN65	NM94
1-($3.50)-Die-cut mirricard-c		1.40	3.50
2-($1.95)-Foil embossed logo; reveals identity		.80	2.00
3-($2.95)-Pop-up-c w/Pact ashcan insert		1.20	3.00

SHADOWHAWK III
Nov, 1993 - No. 4, 1994 ($2.50, color, mini-series)
Image Comics

	GD25	FN65	NM94
1,2: 1-Foil stamped-c		1.00	2.50

SHADOWLINE SAGA: CRITICAL MASS, A (Marvel)(Value: cover or less)

SHADOWMAN (See X-O Manowar #4)
May, 1992 - Present ($2.50, color)
Valiant

	GD25	FN65	NM94
1-Partial origin	2.15	6.50	15.00
2,3: 3-1st app. Sousa the Soul Eater	1.25	3.00	7.50
4,5	1.25	3.00	7.50
6,7		1.00	2.50
8-1st app. Master Darque	1.00	2.50	6.00
9,10		1.00	2.50
11-15,17-24: 15-Minor Turok app. 17,18-Archer & Armstrong x-over. 19-Aerosmith-c/story		1.00	2.50
16-1st app. Dr. Mirage		1.90	4.75
0-($3.50)-Wraparound chromium-c edition		1.40	3.50
0-($2.50)-Regular edition		1.00	2.50

SHADOWMASTERS (Marvel)(Value: cover or less)

SHADOW OF THE BATMAN
Dec, 1985 - No. 5, Apr, 1986 ($1.75, mini-series)
DC Comics

	GD25	FN65	NM94
1-Detective-r (all have wraparound-c)	1.00	2.50	5.50
2,3,5: 3-Penguin-c & cameo. 5-Clayface app.		1.40	3.50
4-Joker-c/story		1.90	4.75

NOTE: ***Austin** a(new)-2i, 3i; r-2-4i. **Rogers** a(new)-1, 2p, 3p, 4, 5; r-1-5p; c-1-5.*

SHADOW OF THE TORTURER, THE (Innovation)(Value: cover or less)

SHADOW PLAY (Whitman)(Value: cover or less)

SHADOW RIDERS
June, 1993 - No. 4, Sept, 1993 ($1.75, color, mini-series)
Marvel Comics UK, Ltd.

	GD25	FN65	NM94
1-($2.50)-Embossed-c; Cable-c/story		1.00	2.50
2-4-Cable app. 2-Ghost Rider app.		.70	1.75

SHADOWS FROM BEYOND (Formerly Unusual Tales)
V2#50, October, 1966
Charlton Comics

	GD25	FN65	NM94
V2#50-Ditko-c	1.00	2.50	6.00

SHADOW STRIKES!, THE (DC)(Value: cover or less)

SHADOW WAR OF HAWKMAN (DC)(Value: cover or less)

SHAGGY DOG & THE ABSENT-MINDED PROFESSOR (See 4-Color #985, Movie Comics & Walt Disney Showcase #46)

SHAMAN'S TEARS
May, 1993 - No. 2, 1993 ($2.50, color)
Image Comics

	GD25	FN65	NM94
1,2: 1-Embossed red foil stamped-c; Mike Grell-c/a & scripts in all. 2-Cover unfolds into poster (8/93-c, 7/93 inside)		1.00	2.50

SHANNA, THE SHE-DEVIL (See Savage Tales #8)
Dec, 1972 - No. 5, Aug, 1973 (All are 20 cent issues)
Marvel Comics Group

	GD25	FN65	NM94
1-1st app. Shanna; Steranko-c; Tuska-a(p)		1.90	4.75
2-Steranko-c; heroin drug story		1.00	2.50
3-5		.70	1.80

SHARK FIGHTERS, THE (See 4-Color No. 762)

SHARP COMICS (Slightly large size)

Shazam #5, © DC

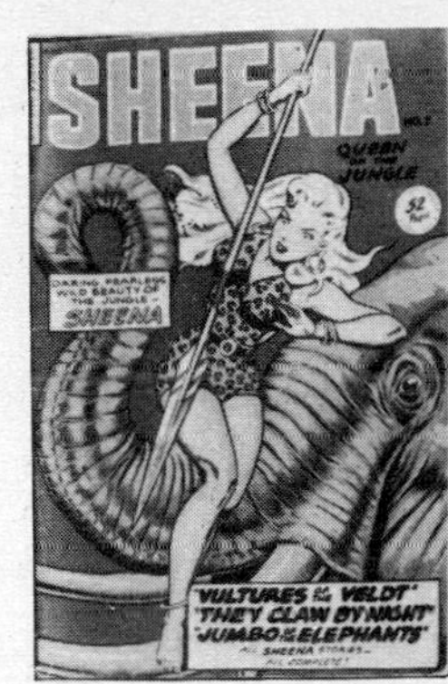

Sheena, Queen of the Jungle #7, © FH

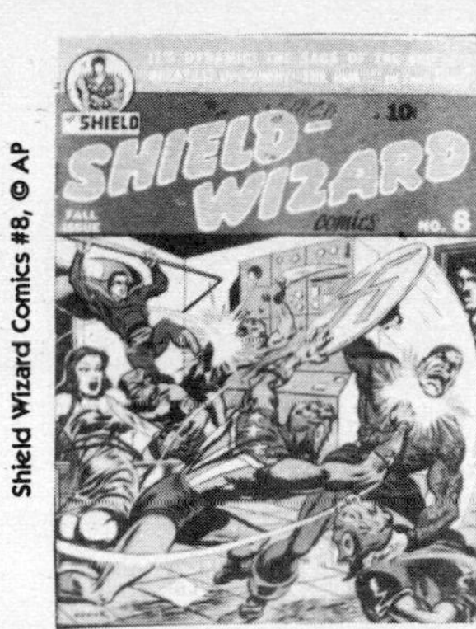

Shield Wizard Comics #8, © AP

GD25 FN65 NM94

Winter, 1945-46 - V1#2, Spring, 1946 (52 pgs.)
H. C. Blackerby

V1#1-Origin Dick Royce Planetarian 26.00 78.00 175.00
2-Origin The Pioneer; Michael Morgan, Dick Royce, Sir Gallagher, Planetarian, Steve Hagen, Weeny and Pop app. 25.00 75.00 175.00

SHARPY FOX (See Comic Capers & Funny Frolics)
1958; 1963
I. W. Enterprises/Super Comics

1,2-I.W. Reprint (1958) 1.00 2.50 5.00
14-Super Reprint (1963) 1.00 2.50 5.00

SHATTER (First Comics, all issues)(Value: cover or less)

SHAZAM (See Giant Comics to Color & Limited Collectors' Edition)

SHAZAM! (TV)(See World's Finest #253)
Feb, 1973 - No. 35, May-June, 1978
National Periodical Publications/DC Comics

1-1st revival of original Captain Marvel since G.A. (origin retold), by Beck; Capt. Marvel Jr. & Mary Marvel x-over 1.60 4.00
2-35: 2,6-Infinity photo-c. 2-Re-intro Mr. Mind & Tawney. 4-Origin retold. 5-Capt. Marvel Jr. origin retold. 8-(100 pgs.)-r/Capt. Marvel Jr. by Raboy; origin/C.M. #80; origin Mary Marvel/C.M. #18; origin Mr. Tawny/C.M. #79. 10-Last C.C. Beck issue. 11-Shaffenberger-a begins. 12-17-(All 100 pgs.). 15-Lex Luthor x-over. 25-1st app. Isis. 30-1st DC app. 3 Lt. Marvels. 31-1st DC app. Minuteman. 34-Origin Capt. Nazi & Capt. Marvel Jr. retold .80 2.00

NOTE: *Reprints in #1-8, 10, 12-17, 21-24.* ***Beck*** *a-1-10, 12-17r, 21-24r, c-1, 3-9.* ***Nasser*** *c-35p.* ***Newton*** *a-35p.* ***Raboy*** *a-5r, 8r, 17r.* ***Shaffenberger*** *a-11, 14-20, 25, 26, 27p, 28, 29-31p, 33i, 35i; c-20, 22, 23, 25, 26i, 27i, 28-33.*

SHAZAM: THE NEW BEGINNING
Apr, 1987 - No. 4, July, 1987 (Mini-series; Legends spin-off)
DC Comics

1-New origin & 1st modern app. Captain Marvel; Marvel Family cameo.
2-4: Sivana & Black Adam app. 1.00

SHEA THEATRE COMICS (Also see Theatre Comics)
No date (1940's) (32 pgs.)
Shea Theatre

nn-Contains Rocket Comics; MLJ cover in one color 7.50 22.50 45.00

SHE-BAT (See Valeria the She-Bat)

SHEENA (Marvel)(Value: cover or less)

SHEENA, QUEEN OF THE JUNGLE (See Jerry Iger's Classic..., Jumbo Comics, & 3-D Sheena)
Spring, 1942; No. 2, Wint, 1942-43; No. 3, Spring, 1943; No. 4, Fall, 1948; No. 5, Sum, 1949; No. 6, Spring, 1950; No. 7-10, 1950(nd); No. 11, Spring, 1951 - No. 18, Winter, 1952-53 (#1,2: 68 pgs.)
Fiction House Magazines

1-Sheena begins 150.00 450.00 950.00
2 (Winter, 1942/43) 79.00 238.00 500.00
3 (Spring, 1943) 54.00 162.00 350.00
4,5 (Fall, 1948, Sum, '49): 4-New logo 33.00 100.00 225.00
6,7 (Spring, 1950 - 1950, 52 pgs.) 29.00 88.00 190.00
8-10('50, 36 pgs.) 25.00 75.00 160.00
11-18: 18-Used in **POP**, pg. 98 20.00 70.00 140.00
I.W. Reprint #9-r/#18; c-r/White Princess #3 4.70 14.00 28.00

NOTE: ***Baker*** *c-5-10?* ***Whitman*** *c-11-18(most).*

SHEENA 3-D SPECIAL (Blackthorne)(Value: cover or less)

SHE-HULK (See The Savage She-Hulk & The Sensational She-Hulk)

SHERIFF BOB DIXON'S CHUCK WAGON (TV)
November, 1950 (See Wild Bill Hickok #22)
Avon Periodicals

1-Kinstler-c/a(3) 10.00 30.00 60.00

SHERIFF OF COCHISE, THE
1957 (16 pages) (TV Show)
Mobil Giveaway

nn-Shaffenberger-a 2.40 6.00 12.00

SHERIFF OF TOMBSTONE
Nov, 1958 - No. 17, Sept, 1961
Charlton Comics

V1#1-Williamson/Severin-c; Severin-a 7.50 22.50 45.00
2 4.20 12.50 25.00
3-17 3.20 8.00 16.00

SHERLOCK HOLMES (See 4-Color #1169,1245, Marvel Preview & Spectacular Stories)

SHERLOCK HOLMES (All New Baffling Adventures of...)
Oct, 1955 - No. 2, Mar, 1956 (Young Eagle #3 on?)
Charlton Comics

1-Dr. Neff, Ghost Breaker app. 30.00 90.00 210.00
2 26.00 80.00 185.00

SHERLOCK HOLMES (Also see The Joker)
Sept-Oct, 1975
National Periodical Publications

1-Cruz-a; Simonson-c 1.50

SHERRY THE SHOWGIRL (Showgirls #4)
July, 1956 - No. 3, Dec, 1956; No. 5, Apr, 1957 - No. 7, Aug, 1957
Atlas Comics

1-Dan DeCarlo-a in all 8.35 25.00 50.00
2 5.35 16.00 32.00
3,5-7 4.20 12.50 25.00

SHE'S JOSIE (See Josie)

SHIELD (Nick Fury & His Agents of...) (Also see Nick Fury)
Feb, 1973 - No. 5, Oct, 1973 (All 20 cents)
Marvel Comics Group

1-Steranko-c 1.90 4.75
2-5: 2-Steranko flag-c. 1-5 all contain-r from Str. Tales #146-155. 3-5-are cover-r; 3-Kirby/Steranko-c(r). 4-Steranko-c(r) .90 2.25

NOTE: ***Buscema*** *a-3p(r).* ***Kirby*** *layouts 1-5; c-3 (w/****Steranko****).* ***Steranko*** *a-3r, 4r(2).*

SHIELD, THE (Becomes Shield-Steel Sterling #3; #1 titled Lancelot Strong; also see Advs. of the Fly, Double Life of Private Strong, Fly Man, Mighty Comics, The Mighty Crusaders, The Original... & Pep Comics #1)
June, 1983 - No. 2, Aug, 1983
Archie Enterprises, Inc.

1,2: Steel Sterling app. 1.00

SHIELD-STEEL STERLING (Formerly The Shield)
No. 3, Dec, 1983 (Becomes Steel Sterling No. 4)
Archie Enterprises, Inc.

3-Nino-a 1.00

SHIELD WIZARD COMICS (Also see Pep Comics & Top-Notch Comics)
Summer, 1940 - No. 13, Spring, 1944
MLJ Magazines

1-(V1#5 on inside)-Origin The Shield by Irving Novick & The Wizard by Ed Ashe, Jr; Flag-c 200.00 600.00 1400.00
2-(Winter/40)-Origin The Shield retold; Wizard's sidekick, Roy the Super Boy begins (see Top-Notch #8 for 1st app.) 87.00 262.00 575.00
3,4 62.00 188.00 400.00
5-Dusty, the Boy Detective begins 58.00 175.00 375.00
6-8: 6-Roy the Super Boy begins 50.00 150.00 325.00
9-13: 13-Bondage-c 46.00 138.00 300.00

NOTE: ***Bob Montana*** *c-13.* ***Novick*** *c-1-11.* ***Harry Sahle*** *c-12.*

SHINING KNIGHT (See Adventure Comics #66)

SHIP AHOY
November, 1944 (52 pgs.)
Spotlight Publishers

Shock Illustrated #3, © WMG

Shogun Warriors #11, © Mattel

Showcase #13, © DC

GD25 FN65 NM94

1-L. B. Cole-c 9.15 27.50 55.00

SHIPWRECKED! (Disney)(Value: cover or less)

SHMOO (See Al Capp's... & Washable Jones &...)

SHOCK (Magazine)
May, 1969 - V3#4, Sept, 1971 (B&W)(Reprints from horror comics)
Stanley Publications

	GD25	FN65	NM94
V1#1-Cover-r/Weird Tales of the Future #7 by Bernard Baily	3.20	8.00	20.00
2-Wolverton-r/Weird Mysteries 5; r-Weird Mysteries #7 used in **SOTI**; cover reprints cover to Weird Chills #1	2.15	6.50	15.00
3,5,6	1.65	4.00	10.00
4-Harrison/Williamson-r/Forbid. Worlds #6	1.70	5.00	12.00
V2#2, V1#8, V2#4-6, V3#1-4	1.65	4.00	10.00

NOTE: ***Disbrow** r-V2#4; Bondage c-V1#4, V2#6, V3#1.*

SHOCK DETECTIVE CASES (Formerly Crime Fighting Detective)
(Becomes Spook Detective Cases No. 22)
No. 20, Sept, 1952 - No. 21, Nov, 1952
Star Publications

	GD25	FN65	NM94
20,21-L.B. Cole-c	8.35	25.00	50.00

NOTE: ***Palais** a-20. No. 21-Fox-r.*

SHOCK ILLUSTRATED (Magazine format)
Sept-Oct, 1955 - No. 3, Spring, 1956 (Adult Entertainment on-c #1,2)
E. C. Comics

	GD25	FN65	NM94
1-All by Kamen; drugs, prostitution, wife swapping	4.70	14.00	28.00
2-Williamson-a redrawn from Crime SuspenStories #13 plus Ingels, Crandall, & Evans; painted-c	5.85	17.50	35.00
3-Only 100 known copies bound & given away at E.C. office; Crandall, Evans-a; painted-c	100.00	300.00	700.00

(Prices vary widely on this book)

SHOCKING MYSTERY CASES (Formerly Thrilling Crime Cases)
No. 50, Sept, 1952 - No. 60, Oct, 1954
Star Publications

	GD25	FN65	NM94
50-Disbrow "Frankenstein" story	17.00	52.00	120.00
51-Disbrow-a	10.00	30.00	60.00
52-55,57-60	8.35	25.00	50.00
56-Drug use story	9.15	27.50	55.00

NOTE: ***L. B. Cole** covers on all; a-60(2 pgs.). **Hollingsworth** a-52. **Morisi** a-55.*

SHOCKING TALES DIGEST MAGAZINE
Oct, 1981 (95 cents)
Harvey Publications

	GD25	FN65	NM94
1-1957-58-r; Powell, Kirby, Nostrand-a		.80	2.00

SHOCK SUSPENSTORIES
Feb-Mar, 1952 - No. 18, Dec-Jan, 1954-55
E. C. Comics

	GD25	FN65	NM94
1-Classic Feldstein electrocution-c; Ray Bradbury adaptation	57.00	170.00	400.00
2	34.00	100.00	235.00
3	23.00	70.00	160.00
4-Used in **SOTI**, pg. 387,388	23.00	70.00	160.00
5-Hanging-c	22.00	65.00	150.00
6,7: 6-Classic bondage-c. 7-Classic face melting-c	27.00	81.00	190.00
8-Williamson-a	23.00	70.00	160.00
9-11: 9-Injury to eye panel. 10-Junkie story	19.00	57.00	130.00
12- "The Monkey" classic junkie cover/story; anti-drug propaganda issue	22.00	65.00	155.00
13-Frazetta's only solo story for E.C., 7 pgs.	27.00	81.00	190.00
14-Used in Senate Investigation hearings	14.00	43.00	100.00
15-Used in 1954 Reader's Digest article, "For the Kiddies to Read;" Bill Gaines stars in prose story "The EC Caper"	14.00	43.00	100.00
16- "Red Dupe" editorial; rape story	13.00	40.00	90.00
17,18	13.00	40.00	90.00

NOTE: ***Ray Bradbury** adaptations-1, 7, 9. **Craig** a-11; c-11. **Crandall** a-9-13, 15-18. **Davis** a-1-5. **Evans** a-7, 8, 14-18; c-16-18. **Feldstein** c-1, 7-9, 12. **Ingels** a-1, 2, 6. **Kamen** a-in all; c-10. **Krigstein** a-14, 18. **Orlando** a-1, 3-7, 9, 10, 12, 16, 17. **Wood** a-2-15; c-2-6, 14.*

SHOCK SUSPENSTORIES
Sept, 1992 - Present ($1.50-$2.00, color, quarterly)
Russ Cochran

	GD25	FN65	NM94
1,2-r/#1,2 above. 1-Feldstein-c. 2-Wood-c			1.50
3-5-($2.00)-r/#3-5 above. 5-Wood-c		.80	2.00

SHOGUN WARRIORS
Feb, 1979 - No. 20, Sept, 1980 (Based on Mattel toys)
Marvel Comics Group

	GD25	FN65	NM94
1-Raydeen, Combatra, & Dangard Ace begin		.80	2.00
2-20: 11-Austin-c. 12-Simonson-c			1.50

SHOOK UP (Magazine) (Satire)
November, 1958
Dodsworth Publ. Co.

	GD25	FN65	NM94
V1#1	3.20	8.00	16.00

SHORT RIBS (See 4-Color #1333)

SHORT STORY COMICS (See Hello Pal,...)

SHORTY SHINER
June, 1956 - No. 3, Oct, 1956
Dandy Magazine (Charles Biro)

	GD25	FN65	NM94
1	4.20	12.50	25.00
2,3	3.20	8.00	16.00

SHOTGUN SLADE (See 4-Color #1111)

SHOWCASE (See Cancelled Comic Cavalcade & New Talent...)
3-4/56 - No. 93, 9/70; No. 94, 8-9/77 - No. 104, 9/78
National Per. Publ./DC Comics

	GD25	FN65	VF82	NM94
1-Fire Fighters	180.00	540.00	1170.00	1800.00

	GD25	FN65	NM94
2-King of the Wild; Kubert-a (animal stories)	66.00	199.00	530.00
3-The Frogmen by Russ Heath; 1st DC grey tone-c (7-8/56); Heath grey tone-c	63.00	188.00	500.00

	GD25	FN65	VF82	NM94
4-Origin/1st app. The Flash (1st DC Silver Age hero, Sept-Oct, 1956) & The Turtle; Kubert-a; r/in Secret Origins #1 ('61 & '73); Flash shown reading G.A. Flash #13	1200.00	3600.00	10,800.00	18,000.00

	GD25	FN65	NM94
5-Manhunters	79.00	236.00	630.00

	GD25	FN65	VF82	NM94
6-Origin/1st app. Challengers of the Unknown by Kirby, partly r/in Secret Origins #1 & Challengers #64,65 (1st Silver Age super-hero team & 1st original concept S.A. series)	143.00	430.00	1290.00	2150.00

	GD25	FN65	NM94
7-Challengers of the Unknown by Kirby (2nd app.) reprinted in Challengers of the Unknown #75	94.00	281.00	1125.00

	GD25	FN65	VF82	NM94
8-The Flash (2nd app.); origin & 1st app. Capt. Cold	500.00	1500.00	4500.00	-
9-Lois Lane (Pre-#1, 7-8/57) (1st Showcase character to win own series)	216.00	650.00	1875.00	-

	GD25	FN65	NM94
10-Lois Lane; Jor-el cameo	121.00	362.00	1450.00
11-Challengers of the Unknown by Kirby (3rd)	100.00	300.00	1000.00
12-Challengers of the Unknown by Kirby (4th)	90.00	269.00	1075.00
13-The Flash (3rd app.); origin Mr. Element	225.00	675.00	2250.00
14-The Flash (4th app.); origin Dr. Alchemy, former Mr. Element	250.00	750.00	3000.00

	GD25	FN65	VF82	NM94
15-Space Ranger (1st app., 7-8/58)	62.00	185.00	555.00	925.00

	GD25	FN65	NM94
16-Space Ranger (2nd app., 9-10/58)	58.00	173.00	575.00

Showcase #21, © DC

Showcase #97, © DC

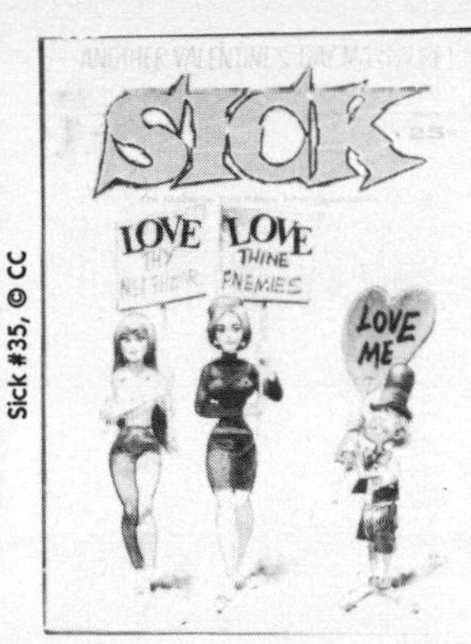

Sick #35, © CC

GD25 FN65 NM94 GD25 FN65 NM94

	GD25	FN65	VF82	NM94
17-Adventures on Other Worlds; origin/1st app. Adam Strange (11-12/58)	100.00	300.00	750.00	1200.00
18-Adventures on Other Worlds (2nd A. Strange)	90.00	270.00	720.00	
19-Adam Strange; 1st Adam Strange logo	85.00	255.00	850.00	
20-Origin & 1st app. Rip Hunter (5-6/59); Moriera-a	56.00	170.00	500.00	
21-Rip Hunter (2nd app.); Sekowsky-c/a	31.00	92.00	275.00	

	GD25	FN65	VF82	NM94
22-Origin & 1st app. Silver Age Green Lantern by Gil Kane (9-10/59); reprinted in Secret Origins #2	275.00	825.00	2060.00	3300.00
23-Green Lantern (2nd); nuclear explosion-c	122.00	367.00	733.00	1100.00
24-Green Lantern (3rd app., 1-2/60)	128.00	383.00	767.00	1150.00

	GD25	FN65	NM94
25,26-Rip Hunter by Kubert. 25-Grey tone-c	22.00	66.00	175.00
27-1st app. Sea Devils (7-8/60); Heath-c/a	63.00	188.00	500.00
28-Sea Devils (2nd app., 9-10/60); Heath-c/a	31.00	94.00	250.00
29-Sea Devils; Heath-c/a; grey tone c-27-29	33.00	99.00	265.00
30-Origin Silver Age Aquaman (1-2/61) (see Adventure #260 for 1st S.A. origin)	45.00	135.00	450.00
31,32-Aquaman	25.00	75.00	250.00
33-Aquaman	30.00	90.00	300.00

	GD25	FN65	VF82	NM94
34-Origin & 1st app. Silver Age Atom by Kane & Anderson (9-10/61); reprinted in Secret Origins #2	108.00	325.00	650.00	975.00

	GD25	FN65	NM94
35-The Atom by Gil Kane (2nd); last 10¢ issue	86.00	257.00	600.00
36-The Atom by Gil Kane (3rd app., 1-2/62)	61.00	182.00	425.00
37-1st app. Metal Men (3-4/62)	50.00	150.00	400.00
38-Metal Men (2nd app., 5-6/62)	38.00	113.00	300.00
39-Metal Men (3rd app., 7-8/62)	28.00	84.00	225.00
40-Metal Men (4th app., 9-10/62)	27.00	81.00	215.00
41,42-Tommy Tomorrow (parts 1&2). 42-Origin	13.00	38.00	100.00
43-Dr. No (James Bond); Nodel-a; originally published as British Classics Illustrated #158A & as #6 in a European Detective series, all with diff. painted-c. This Showcase #43 version is actually censored, deleting all racial skin color and dialogue thought to be racially demeaning (1st DC S.A. movie adaptation)(based on Ian Fleming novel & movie)	39.00	118.00	315.00
44-Tommy Tomorrow	8.00	24.00	65.00
45-Sgt. Rock; origin retold; Heath-c	16.00	47.00	125.00
46,47-Tommy Tomorrow	6.00	19.00	50.00
48,49-Cave Carson (3rd tryout series; see B&B)	3.00	9.00	28.00
50,51-I Spy (Danger Trail-r by Infantino), King Farady story (#50 has new 4 pg. story)	4.00	11.00	33.00
52-Cave Carson	3.00	9.00	28.00
53,54-G.I. Joe; Heath-a	4.00	12.00	37.00
55-Dr. Fate & Hourman (3-4/65); origin of each in text; 1st solo app. G.A. Green Lantern in Silver Age (pre-dates Gr. Lantern #40); 1st S.A. app. Solomon Grundy	17.00	50.00	150.00
56-Dr. Fate & Hourman	5.00	15.00	45.00
57-Enemy Ace by Kubert (4th app. after Our Army at War #155)	10.00	30.00	68.00
58-Enemy Ace by Kubert (5th app.)	8.35	25.00	65.00
59-Teen Titans (3rd app., 11-12/65)	7.00	22.00	65.00
60-1st Silver Age app. The Spectre; Anderson-a (1-2/66); origin in text	20.00	60.00	140.00
61-The Spectre by Anderson (2nd app.)	11.00	34.00	80.00
62-Origin & 1st app. Inferior Five (5-6/66)	5.00	15.00	46.00
63,65-Inferior Five. 65-X-Men parody (11-12/66)	3.00	8.00	23.00
64-The Spectre by Anderson (3rd app.)	11.00	32.00	75.00
66,67-B'wana Beast	1.65	4.70	11.00
68,69,71-Maniaks	1.65	4.70	11.00
70-Binky (9-10/67)-Tryout issue	1.65	4.70	11.00
72-Top Gun (Johnny Thunder-r)-Toth-a	1.65	4.70	11.00
73-Origin/1st app. Creeper; Ditko-c/a (3-4/68)	8.00	25.00	75.00
74-Intro/1st app. Anthro; Post-c/a (5/68)	5.00	14.00	45.00
75-Origin/1st app. Hawk & the Dove; Ditko-c/a	6.00	19.00	64.00
76-1st app. Bat Lash (8/68)	3.00	9.00	30.00
77-1st app. Angel & The Ape (9/68)	3.00	10.00	32.00
78-1st app. Jonny Double (11/68)	2.00	6.00	14.00
79-1st app. Dolphin (12/68); Aqualad origin-r	2.00	7.00	24.00
80-Phantom Stranger-r; Neal Adams-c	1.70	5.00	12.00
81-Windy & Willy	1.70	5.00	12.00
82-1st app. Nightmaster (5/69) by Grandenetti & Giordano; Kubert-c	4.00	11.00	37.00
83,84-Nightmaster by Wrightson w/Jones/Kaluta ink assist in each; Kubert-c. 84-Origin retold; last 12 cent-c?	4.00	11.00	35.00
85-87-Firehair; Kubert-a	1.65	4.00	10.00
88-90-Jason's Quest: 90-Manhunter 2070 app.	1.00	2.50	5.50
91-93-Manhunter 2070, origin-92	1.00	2.50	5.50
94-Intro/origin new Doom Patrol & Robotman	1.20	3.00	7.00
95,96-The Doom Patrol. 95-Origin Celsius		1.60	4.00
97-99-Power Girl; origin-97,98; JSA cameos		1.60	4.00
100-(52 pgs.)-Most Showcase characters featured		1.60	4.00
101-103-Hawkman; Adam Strange x-over		1.60	4.00
104-(52 pgs.)-O.S.S. Spies at War		1.60	4.00

NOTE: ***Anderson*** *a-22-24i, 34-36i, 55, 56, 60, 61, 64, 101-103i; c-50i, 51i, 55, 56, 60, 61, 64.* ***Aparo*** *c-94-96.* ***Boring*** *c-10.* ***Estrada*** *a-104.* ***Fraden*** *c(p)-30, 31, 33.* ***Heath*** *c-3, 27-29.* ***Infantino*** *c/a(p)-4, 8, 13, 14; c-50p, 51p.* ***Gil Kane*** *a-22-24p, 34-36p; c-17-19, 22-24p(w/* ***Giella****), 31.* ***Kane/Anderson*** *c-34-36.* ***Kirby*** *c-11, 12.* ***Kirby/Stein*** *c-6, 7.* ***Kubert*** *a-2, 4i, 25, 26, 45, 53, 54, 72; c-25, 26, 53, 54, 57, 58, 82-87, 101-104; c-2, 4i.* ***Moriera*** *c-5.* ***Orlando*** *a-62p, 63p, 97i; c-62, 63, 97i.* ***Sekowsky*** *a-65p.* ***Sparling*** *a-78.* ***Staton*** *a-94, 95-99p, 100, c-97-100p.*

SHOWCASE 93

Jan, 1993 - No. 12, Dec, 1993 ($1.95, color, limited series, 52 pgs.)
DC Comics

1-12: 1-Begin 4 part Catwoman story & 6 part Blue Devil story; begin Cyborg story; Art Adams/Austin-c. 2-Maguire/Austin-c; Flash by Travis Charest (p) begins; Bolland-c. 6-Azrael in Bat-costume (2 pgs.). 7,8-Knightfall parts 13 & 14. 6-10-Deathstroke app. (6,10-cameo). 9,10-Austin-i. 10-Azrael as Batman in new costume app.; Gulacy-c — .80 — 2.00

SHOWCASE 94

Jan, 1994 - No. 12, Dec, 1994 ($1.95, color, limited series, 52 pgs.)
DC Comics

1-4: 1,2-Joker & Gunfire 2 part stories — .80 — 2.00

SHOWGIRLS (Formerly Sherry the Showgirl #3)

No. 4, 2/57; June, 1957 - No. 2, Aug, 1957
Atlas Comics (MPC No. 2)

	GD25	FN65	NM94
4-Dan DeCarlo-a	5.85	17.50	35.00
1-Millie, Sherry, Chili, Pearl & Hazel begin	7.50	22.50	45.00
2	5.35	16.00	32.00

SHROUD OF MYSTERY (Whitman)(Value: cover or less)

SICK (Sick Special #131) (Magazine) (Satire)

Aug, 1960 - No. 131, Feb, 1980
Feature Publ./Headline Publ./Crestwood Publ. Co./Hewfred Publ./
Pyramid Comm./Charlton Publ. No. 109 (4/76) on

	GD25	FN65	NM94
V1#1-Jack Paar photo on-c; Torres-a	12.00	36.00	85.00
2-5-Torres-a in all	7.50	22.50	45.00
6	5.00	15.00	30.00
V2#1-8(#7-14)	4.20	12.50	25.00
V3#1-8(#15-22)	3.60	9.00	18.00
V4#1-5(#23-27)	3.00	7.50	15.00
28-32,34-40	2.00	5.00	10.00
33-Ringo Starr photo-c & spoof on "A Hard Day's Night;" inside-c has Beatles photos	4.00	11.00	22.00
41-131: 45 has #44 on-c & #45 on inside. 70-John & Yoko-c. 128-Superman-c/movie parody. 131-Superman parody	1.00	2.50	6.00
Annual 1969, 1970, 1971	2.15	6.50	15.00
Annual 2-4(1980)	1.20	3.00	7.00
Big Sick Laff-in (1968)-w/psychedelic posters	3.60	9.00	18.00
Birthday Annual (1967)-3pg. Huckleberry Fink fold out			

Silverblade #3, © DC

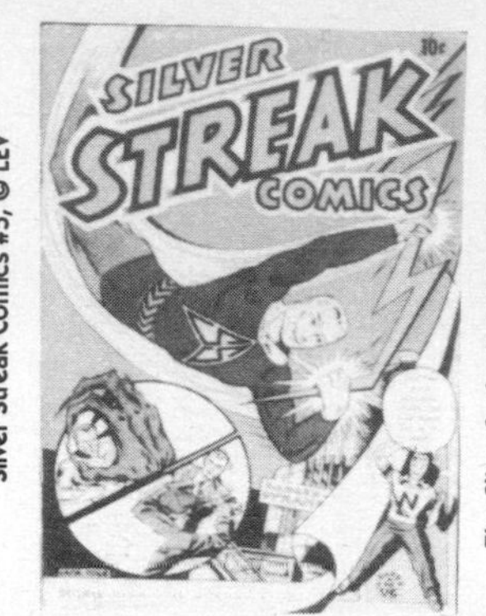

Silver Streak Comics #5, © LEV

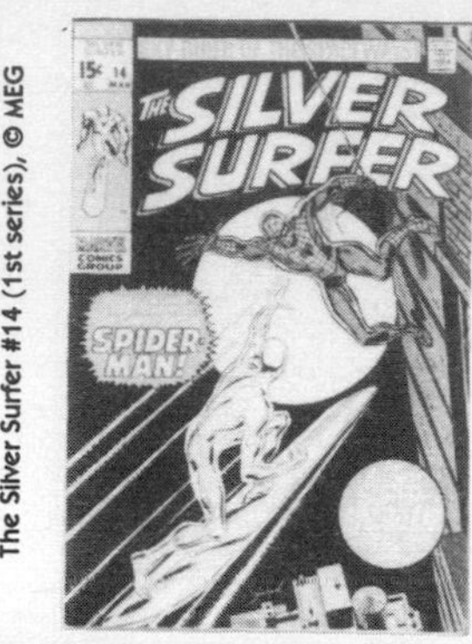

The Silver Surfer #14 (1st series), © MEG

GD25 FN65 NM94

3.60 9.00 18.00
7th Annual Yearbook (1967)-Davis-c, 2pg. glossy poster insert
3.60 9.00 18.00
Special 2 (1978) 1.00 2.00 5.00
Yearbook 14(1974), 15(1975)-84pgs. 1.00 2.50 6.00
NOTE: ***Davis*** *a-42, 87; c-31, 32.* ***Powell*** *a-7, 31, 57.* ***Simon*** *a-1-3, 10, 41, 42, 87, 99; c-1, 47, 57, 59, 69, 91, 95-97, 99, 100, 102, 107, 112.* ***Torres*** *a-1-3, 31, 47, 49.* ***Tuska*** *a-14, 41-43. Civil War Blackouts-23, 24. #42 has biography of Bob Powell.*

SIDESHOW
1949 (One Shot)
Avon Periodicals
1-(Rare)-Similar to Bachelor's Diary 18.00 54.00 125.00

SIEGEL AND SHUSTER: DATELINE 1930s (Eclipse)(Value: cover or less)

SILENT INVASION, THE (Renegade)(Value: cover or less)

SILENT MOBIUS (Viz)(Value: cover or less)

SILK HAT HARRY'S DIVORCE SUIT
1912 (5-3/4x15-1/2") (B&W)
M. A. Donoghue & Co.
Newspaper reprints by Tad (Thomas Dorgan) 12.00 36.00 85.00

SILLY PILLY (See Frank Luther's...)

SILLY SYMPHONIES (See Dell Giants)

SILLY TUNES
Fall, 1945 - No. 7, June, 1947
Timely Comics
1-Silly Seal, Ziggy Pig begin 12.00 36.00 85.00
2-(2/46) 7.50 22.50 45.00
3-7: 6-New logo 5.85 17.50 35.00

SILVER (See Lone Ranger's Famous Horse...)

SILVERBACK (Comico)(Value: cover or less)

SILVERBLADE (DC)(Value: cover or less)

SILVERHAWKS (Marvel)(Value: cover or less)

SILVERHEELS (Pacific)(Value: cover or less)

SILVER KID WESTERN
Oct, 1954 - No. 5, July?, 1955
Key/Stanmor Publications
1 6.70 20.00 40.00
2 4.00 10.00 20.00
3-5 3.60 9.00 18.00
I.W. Reprint #1,2-Severin-c: 1-r/#? 2-r/#1 1.00 2.50 5.00

SILVER SABLE AND THE WILD PACK (See Amazing Spider-Man #265)
June, 1992 - Present ($1.25, color)
Marvel Comics
1-($2.00)-Silver embossed & foil stamped-c; Spider-Man app.
1.20 3.00
2-4: 4,5-Dr. Doom c/story .70 1.75
5-22: 6,7-Deathlok-c/story. 9-Origin Silver Sable. 15-Capt. America app. 16,17-Intruders app. 18-Venom app. 19-Siege of Darkness x-over; Venom app. 1.25

SILVER STAR (Pacific)(Value: cover or less)

SILVER STREAK COMICS (Crime Does Not Pay #22 on)
Dec, 1939 - No. 21, May, 1942; No. 22-24, 1946 (Silver logo-#1-5)
Your Guide Publs. No. 1-7/New Friday Publs. No. 8-17/Comic House Publ./Newsbook Publ.
GD25 FN65 VF82 NM94
1-(Scarce)-Intro The Claw by Cole (r-/in Daredevil #21), Red Reeves, Boy Magician, & Captain Fearless; The Wasp, Mister Midnight begin; Spirit Man app. Silver metallic-c begin, end #5; Claw c-1,2,6-8
600.00 1800.00 3300.00 4800.00
(Estimated up to 100 total copies exist, 6 in NM/Mint)
GD25 FN65 NM94
2-The Claw by Cole; Simon-c/a 217.00 650.00 1500.00
3-1st app. & origin Silver Streak (2nd with lightning speed); Dickie Dean the Boy Inventor, Lance Hale, Ace Powers, Bill Wayne, & The Planet Patrol begin 183.00 550.00 1250.00
4-Sky Wolf begins; Silver Streak by Jack Cole (new costume); 1st app. Jackie, Lance Hale's sidekick 96.00 285.00 650.00
5-Jack Cole c/a(2) 117.00 350.00 750.00
GD25 FN65 VF82 NM94
6-(Scarce, 9/40)-Origin & 1st app. Daredevil (blue & yellow costume) by Jack Binder; The Claw returns; classic Cole Claw-c
525.00 1575.00 2890.00 4200.00
7-Claw vs. Daredevil (new costume-blue & red) by Jack Cole & 3 other Cole stories (38 pgs.) 429.00 1285.00 2145.00 3000.00
(#6, 7-Estimated up to 120 total copies of each exist, 7-10 in NM/Mint)
GD25 FN65 NM94
8-Claw vs. Daredevil by Cole; last Cole Silver Streak
146.00 438.00 1000.00
9-Claw vs. Daredevil by Cole 118.00 355.00 825.00
10-Origin & 1st app. Captain Battle (5/41); Claw vs. Daredevil by Cole; Robot-c 100.00 300.00 675.00
11-Intro. Mercury by Bob Wood, Silver Streak's sidekick; conclusion Claw vs. Daredevil by Rico; in 'Presto Martin,' 2nd pg., newspaper says 'Roussos does it again' 71.00 210.00 450.00
12-14: 13-Origin Thun-Dohr 58.00 175.00 375.00
15-17-Last Daredevil issue. 16-Hitler-c 54.00 162.00 350.00
18-The Saint begins (2/42, 1st app.) by Leslie Charteris (see Movie Comics #2 by DC); The Saint-c 44.00 132.00 290.00
19-21(1942): 20,21 have Wolverton's Scoop Scuttle. 21-Hitler app. in strip on cover 30.00 90.00 200.00
22,24(1946)-Reprints 18.00 55.00 125.00
23-Reprints?; bondage-c 18.00 55.00 125.00
nn(11/46)(Newsbook Publ.)-R-/S.S. story from #4-7 plus 2 Captain Fearless stories, all in color; bondage/torture-c 29.00 88.00 205.00
NOTE: ***Binder*** *c-3, 4, 13-15, 17.* ***Jack Cole*** *a-(Daredevil)-#6-10, (Dickie Dean)-#3-10, (Pirate Prince)-#7, (Silver Streak)-#4-8, nn; c-5 (Silver Streak), 6 (Claw), 7, 8 (Daredevil).* ***Everett*** *Red Reed begins #20.* ***Guardineer*** *a-#8-13.* ***Don Rico*** *a-11-17 (Daredevil); c-11, 12, 16.* ***Simon*** *a-3 (Silver Streak).* ***Bob Wood*** *a-9 (Silver Streak); c-9, 10. Captain Battle c-11, 13-15, 17. Claw c-#1, 2, 6-8. Daredevil c-7, 8, 12. Dickie Dean c-19. Ned of the Navy c-20 (war). The Saint c-18. Silver Streak c-5, 9, 10, 16, 23.*

SILVER SURFER (See Fantastic Four, Fantasy Masterpieces V2#1, Marvel Graphic Novel, Marvel Presents #8, Marvel's Greatest Comics & Tales To Astonish #92)

SILVER SURFER, THE
Aug, 1968 - No. 18, Sept, 1970; June, 1982 (No. 1-7: 25 cents, 68 pgs.)
Marvel Comics Group
1-More detailed origin by John Buscema (p); The Watcher back-up stories begin (origin), end #7 45.00 135.00 360.00
2 16.00 47.00 135.00
3-1st app. Mephisto 14.00 41.00 110.00
4-Low distribution; Thor & Loki app. 43.00 129.00 345.00
5-7-Last giant size. 5-The Stranger app. 6-Brunner inks. 7-(8/69)-1st app. Frankenstein's monster (cameo); Brunner-c 9.00 26.00 70.00
8-10: 8-18-(15 cent issues) 6.00 19.00 50.00
11-13,15-18: 15-Silver Surfer vs. Human Torch; Fantastic Four app. 17-Nick Fury app. 18-Vs. The Inhumans; Kirby-c/a 5.00 14.00 38.00
14-Spider-Man x-over 7.00 22.00 58.00
V2#1 (6/82, 52 pgs.)-Byrne-c/a 1.50 3.75 9.00
NOTE: ***Adkins*** *a-8-15i.* ***Brunner*** *a-6i; c-7.* ***J. Buscema*** *a-1-17p.* ***Colan*** *a-1-3p.* ***Reinman*** *a-1-4i. #1-14 were reprinted in Fantasy Masterpieces V2#1-14.*

SILVER SURFER (See Marvel Graphic Novel #38)
V3#1, July, 1987 - Present
Marvel Comics Group
V3#1-Double size ($1.25) 1.30 3.25 8.00
2 1.40 3.50
3-10 .90 2.25
11-14 .80 2.00
15-Ron Lim-c/a begins (9/88) 1.30 3.25 8.00

The Silver Surfer V3#56, © MEG

Single Series #26, © UFS

Six From Sirius #1, © MEG

GD25 FN65 NM94

16,17 1.90 4.75
18-20 1.40 3.50
21-24,26-30,33 .75 1.90
25,31 ($1.50, 52 pgs.). 25-Skrulls app. 1.00 2.00
32,39-No Ron Lim-c/a. 39-Alan Grant scripts 1.50
34-Thanos returns (cameo); Starlin scripts begin 1.65 4.70 11.00
35-1st full Thanos app. in Silver Surfer (3/90); reintro Drax the Destroyer on last pg. (cameo) 1.85 5.50 13.00
36-Recaps history of Thanos; Capt. Marvel & Warlock app. in recap 1.10 2.70 6.50
37-1st full app. Drax the Destroyer; Drax-c 1.90 4.75
38-Silver Surfer battles Thanos 1.25 3.00 7.50
40-43,48: 48,50-Last Starlin scripts .75 1.90
44,45,49-Thanos stories (c-44,45) 1.10 2.75
46,47: 46-Return of Adam Warlock (2/91); re-intro Gamora & Pip the Troll. 47-Warlock battles Drax 1.00 2.50 6.00
50-($1.50, 52 pgs.)-Embossed & silver foil-c; Silver Surfer has brief battle w/Thanos; story cont'd in Infinity Gauntlet #1 1.25 3.00 7.50
50-2nd & 3rd printings 1.00 2.50
51-53: Infinity Gauntlet x-over 1.10 2.75
54-57: Infinity Gauntlet x-overs. 54-Rhino app. 55,56-Thanos-c & app. 57-Thanos-c & cameo .90 2.25
58,59-Infinity Guantlet x-overs; 58-Ron Lim-c only. 59-Thanos battles Silver Surfer-c/story; Thanos joins 1.50 3.75
60-66: 61-Last $1.00-c. 63-Capt. Marvel app. 1.50
67-69-Infinity War x-overs .80 2.00
70-74,76-81,83-90: 83-85-Infinity Crusade x-over; 83,84-Thanos cameo. 85-Storm, Wonder Man x-over .60 1.25
75-($2.50, 52 pgs.)-Embossed foil-c; Lim-c/a .70 1.75 3.50
82-($1.75, 52 pgs.) .35 .90 1.75
Annual 1 (1988, $1.75)-Evolutionary War app.; 1st Ron Lim-a on Silver Surfer (20 pg. back-up story & pin-ups) 1.00 2.50 6.00
Annual 2-4 (1989-91, $2.00, 68 pgs.): 2-Atlantis Attacks. 4-3 pg. origin story; Silver Surfer battles Guardians of the Galaxy 1.00 2.50
Annual 5 (1992, $2.25, 68 pgs.)-Return of the Defenders, part 3; Lim-c/a (3 pgs. of pin-ups only) 1.00 2.50
Annual 6 (1993, $2.95, 68 pgs.)-Polybagged w/trading card; 1st app. Legacy; card is by Lim/Austin 1.20 3.00
...: The First Coming of Galactus nn (11/92, $5.95, 68 pgs.)-Reprints Fantastic Four #48-50 with new Lim-c 1.00 2.50 6.00
NOTE: ***Austin*** *c(i)-71, 73, 74.* ***Ron Lim*** *a(p)-15-31, 33-38, 40-55, (56, 57-part-p), 60-65, 73-75, 83; c(p)-15-31, 32-38, 40-75, 83, 85, Annual 5, 6.* ***M. Rogers*** *a-1-10, 12, 19, 21; c-1-12, 21.*

SILVER SURFER, THE
Dec, 1988 - No. 2, Jan, 1989 ($1.00, limited series)
Epic Comics (Marvel)
1,2: By Stan Lee (scripts) & Moebius (art) 1.00 2.50

SILVER SURFER/WARLOCK: RESURRECTION
Mar, 1993 - No. 4, June, 1993 ($2.50, color, mini-series)
Marvel Comics
1-4: Starlin-c/a & scripts 1.00 2.50

SILVERTIP (Max Brand)
No. 491, Aug, 1953 - No. 898, May, 1958
Dell Publishing Co.
4-Color 491 (#1) 9.15 27.50 55.00
4-Color 572,608,637,667,731,789,898-Kinstler-a; all painted-c 5.00 15.00 30.00
4-Color 835 4.35 13.00 26.00

SIMPSON'S COMICS (See Bartman, Itchy & Scratchy & Radioactive Man)
1993 - Present ($1.95, color)
Bongo Comics
1-($2.25)-Bound-in jumbo poster; flip book format .90 2.25
2-Flip-book format featuring Patty & Selma .80 2.00

SIMPSON'S COMICS AND STORIES
1993 ($2.95, color, one-shot)
Welsh Publishing Group
1-(Direct Sale)-Polybagged w/Bartman poster 1.20 3.00
1-(Newsstand Edition)-Without poster 1.20 3.00

SIMULATORS, THE (Neatly Chiseled Features)(Value: cover or less)

SINBAD, JR (TV Cartoon)
Sept-Nov, 1965 - No. 3, May, 1966
Dell Publishing Co.
1 3.00 7.50 15.00
2,3 2.00 5.00 10.00

SINDBAD (See Capt. Sindbad under Movie Comics, and Fantastic Voyages of Sindbad)

SINGING GUNS (See Fawcett Movie Comics)

SINGLE SERIES (Comics on Parade #30 on)(Also see John Hix...)
1938 - No. 28, 1942 (All 68 pgs.)
United Features Syndicate
1-Captain and the Kids (#1) 59.00 180.00 415.00
2-Broncho Bill (1939) (#1) 34.00 105.00 240.00
3-Ella Cinders (1939) 30.00 90.00 210.00
4-Li'l Abner (1939) (#1) 47.00 140.00 330.00
5-Fritzi Ritz (#1) 22.00 65.00 150.00
6-Jim Hardy by Dick Moores (#1) 29.00 85.00 200.00
7-Frankie Doodle 22.00 65.00 150.00
8-Peter Pat (On sale 7/14/39) 22.00 65.00 150.00
9-Strange As It Seems 22.00 65.00 150.00
10-Little Mary Mixup 22.00 65.00 150.00
11-Mr. and Mrs. Beans 22.00 65.00 150.00
12-Joe Jinks 19.00 58.00 135.00
13-Looy Dot Dope 19.00 58.00 135.00
14-Billy Make Believe 19.00 58.00 135.00
15-How It Began (1939) 22.00 65.00 150.00
16-Illustrated Gags (1940)-Has ad for Captain and the Kids #1 reprint listed below 11.50 34.00 80.00
17-Danny Dingle 16.00 48.00 110.00
18-Li'l Abner (#2 on-c) 39.00 120.00 275.00
19-Broncho Bill (#2 on-c) 29.00 85.00 200.00
20-Tarzan by Hal Foster 93.00 280.00 650.00
21-Ella Cinders (#2 on-c, on sale 3/19/40) 20.00 70.00 160.00
22-Iron Vic 21.00 63.00 145.00
23-Tailspin Tommy by Hal Forrest (#1) 24.00 72.00 165.00
24-Alice in Wonderland (#1) 31.00 95.00 220.00
25-Abbie and Slats 24.00 73.00 170.00
26-Little Mary Mixup (#2 on-c, 1940) 22.00 65.00 150.00
27-Jim Hardy by Dick Moores (1942) 22.00 67.00 155.00
28-Ella Cinders and Abbie and Slats (1942) 22.00 65.00 150.00
1-Captain and the Kids (1939 reprint)-2nd Edition 36.00 110.00 250.00
1-Fritzi Ritz (1939 reprint)-2nd edition 17.00 52.00 120.00
NOTE: *Some issues given away at the 1939-40 New York World's Fair (#6).*

SINISTER HOUSE OF SECRET LOVE, THE (Becomes Secrets of Sinister House No. 5 on)
Oct-Nov, 1971 - No. 4, Apr-May, 1972
National Periodical Publications
1 1.20 3.00
2-4: 2-Jeff Jones-c. 3-Toth-a, 36 pgs. 1.00 2.50

SIR LANCELOT (See 4-Color #606, 775)

SIR WALTER RALEIGH (See 4-Color #644)

SISTERHOOD OF STEEL (Marvel)(Value: cover or less)

6 BLACK HORSES (See Movie Classics)

SIX FROM SIRIUS (Marvel, series I & II)(Value: cover or less)

SIX-GUN HEROES
March, 1950 - No. 23, Nov, 1953 (Photo-c #1-23)
Fawcett Publications
1-Rocky Lane, Hopalong Cassidy, Smiley Burnette begin (same date as

Six-Gun Heroes #33, © CC

Skull the Slayer #8, © MEG

Skyrocket nn, © CHES

	GD25	FN65	NM94
Smiley Burnette #1)	39.00	120.00	275.00
2	22.00	65.00	150.00
3-5	13.50	41.00	95.00
6-15: 6-Lash LaRue begins	10.00	30.00	75.00
16-22: 17-Last Smiley Burnette. 18-Monte Hale begins	10.00	30.00	65.00
23-Last Fawcett issue	10.00	30.00	70.00

NOTE: *Hopalong Cassidy photo c-1-3. Monte Hale photo c-18. Rocky Lane photo c-4, 5, 7, 9, 11, 13, 15, 17, 20, 21, 23. Lash LaRue photo c-6, 8, 10, 12, 14, 16, 19, 22.*

SIX-GUN HEROES (Continued from Fawcett; Gunmasters #84 on)
No. 24, Jan, 1954 - No. 83, Mar-Apr, 1965 (All Vol. 4)(See Blue Bird)
Charlton Comics

	GD25	FN65	NM94
24-Lash LaRue, Hopalong Cassidy, Rocky Lane & Tex Ritter begin; photo-c	12.00	36.00	85.00
25	7.50	22.50	45.00
26-30: 26-Rod Cameron story. 28-Tom Mix begins?	6.35	19.00	38.00
31-40: 38-Jingles & Wild Bill Hickok (TV)	5.00	15.00	30.00
41-46,48,50	4.70	14.00	28.00
47-Williamson-a, 2 pgs; Torres-a	5.35	16.00	32.00
49-Williamson-a, 5 pgs	5.35	16.00	32.00
51-56,58-60: 58-Gunmaster app.	3.60	9.00	18.00
57-Origin & 1st app. Gunmaster	4.20	12.50	25.00
61-70: 62-Origin Gunmaster	2.80	7.00	14.00
71-83: 76-Gunmaster begins	2.40	6.00	12.00

SIXGUN RANCH (See 4-Color #580)

SIX-GUN WESTERN
Jan, 1957 - No. 4, July, 1957
Atlas Comics (CDS)

	GD25	FN65	NM94
1-Crandall-a; two Williamson text illos	11.00	32.00	75.00
2,3-Williamson-a in both	10.00	30.00	60.00
4-Woodbridge-a	5.85	17.50	35.00

NOTE: ***Ayers** a-2, 3. **Maneely** a-1; c-2, 3. **Orlando** a-2. **Pakula** a-2. **Powell** a-3. **Romita** a-1, 4. **Severin** c-1, 4. **Shores** a-2.*

SIX MILLION DOLLAR MAN, THE (TV)
6/76 - No. 4, 12/76; No. 5, 10/77; No. 6, 2/78 - No. 9, 6/78
Charlton Comics

	GD25	FN65	NM94
1-Staton-c/a; Lee Majors photo on-c			1.20
2-9: 2-Neal Adams-c; Staton-a			1.00

SIX MILLION DOLLAR MAN, THE (TV)(Magazine)
July, 1976 - No. 7, Nov, 1977 (B&W)
Charlton Comics

	GD25	FN65	NM94
1-Neal Adams-c/a			1.20
2-Neal Adams-c			1.20
3-7: 3-N. Adams part inks; Chaykin-a			1.20

666 THE MARK OF THE BEAST (Fleetway/Quality)(Value: cover or less)

SKATEMAN (Pacific)(Value: cover or less)

SKATING SKILLS
1957 (36 & 12 pages; 5x7", two versions) (10 cents)
Custom Comics, Inc./Chicago Roller Skates

	GD25	FN65	NM94
nn-Resembles old ACG cover plus interior art	1.00	2.50	5.00

SKEEZIX (Also see Gasoline Alley)
1925 - 1928 (Strip reprints) (soft covers) (pictures & text)
Reilly & Lee Co.

	GD25	FN65	NM94
...and Uncle Walt (1924)-Origin	16.00	48.00	110.00
...and Pal (1925)	12.00	36.00	85.00
...at the Circus (1926)	12.00	36.00	85.00
...& Uncle Walt (1927)	12.00	36.00	85.00
...Out West (1928)	12.00	36.00	85.00
Hardback Editions...	16.00	48.00	110.00

SKELETON HAND (...In Secrets of the Supernatural)
Sept-Oct, 1952 - No. 6, July-Aug, 1953
American Comics Group (B&M Dist. Co.)

	GD25	FN65	NM94
1	23.00	70.00	160.00
2	14.00	43.00	100.00
3-6	12.00	36.00	85.00

SKIN GRAFT: THE ADVENTURES OF A TATTOOED MAN
July, 1993 - No. 4, Oct, 1993 ($2.50, color, mini-series, mature readers)
DC Comics (Vertigo)

	GD25	FN65	NM94
1-4		1.00	2.50

SKI PARTY (See Movie Classics)

SKIPPY
Circa 1920s (10x8", 16 pgs., color/B&W cartoons)
No publisher listed

	GD25	FN65	NM94
nn-By Percy Crosby	67.00	200.00	465.00

SKIPPY'S OWN BOOK OF COMICS (See Popular Comics)
1934 (52 pages) (Giveaway)(Strip reprints)
No publisher listed

	GD25	FN65	VF82	NM94
nn-(Rare)-By Percy Crosby	450.00	1350.00	2925.00	4500.00

(Estimated up to 40 total copies exist, 2 in NM/Mint)

Published by Max C. Gaines for Phillip's Dental Magnesia to be advertised on the Skippy Radio Show and given away with the purchase of a tube of Phillip's Tooth Paste. This is the first four-color comic book of reprints about one character.

SKREEMER (DC)(Value: cover or less)

SKULL & BONES
1992 - No. 3, 1992 ($4.95, color, mini-series, 52 pgs.)
DC Comics

	GD25	FN65	NM94
Book 1-3: 1-1st app.	1.00	2.00	5.00

SKULL, THE SLAYER
August, 1975 - No. 8, Nov, 1976
Marvel Comics Group

	GD25	FN65	NM94
1-Origin & 1st app.; Gil Kane-c			1.50
2-8: 2-Gil Kane-c. 8-Kirby-c			1.00

SKY BLAZERS (CBS Radio)
Sept, 1940 - No. 2, Nov, 1940
Hawley Publications

	GD25	FN65	NM94
1-Sky Pirates, Ace Archer, Flying Aces begin	30.00	90.00	200.00
2	25.00	75.00	175.00

SKY KING "RUNAWAY TRAIN" (TV)
1964 (16 pages) (regular size)
National Biscuit Co.

	GD25	FN65	NM94
nn	3.60	9.00	18.00

SKYMAN (See Big Shot Comics & Sparky Watts)
Fall?, 1941 - No. 2, 1941; No. 3, 1948 - No. 4, 1948
Columbia Comics Group

	GD25	FN65	NM94
1-Origin Skyman, The Face, Sparky Watts app.; Whitney-c/a; 3rd story-r from Big Shot #1; Whitney c-1-4	57.00	170.00	375.00
2 (1941)-Yankee Doodle	31.00	92.00	200.00
3,4 (1948)	20.00	60.00	140.00

SKY PILOT
No. 10, 1950(nd) - No. 11, Apr-May, 1951 (Saunders painted-c)
Ziff-Davis Publ. Co.

	GD25	FN65	NM94
10,11-Frank Borth-a	8.35	25.00	50.00

SKY RANGER (See Johnny Law...)

SKYROCKET
1944
Harry 'A' Chesler

	GD25	FN65	NM94
nn-Alias the Dragon, Dr. Vampire, Skyrocket & The Desperado app.	17.00	50.00	110.00

SKY SHERIFF (Breeze Lawson...) (Also see Exposed & Outlaws)
Summer, 1948
D. S. Publishing Co.

Sky Wolf #3, © Eclipse

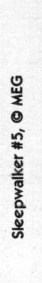

Sleepwalker #5, © MEG

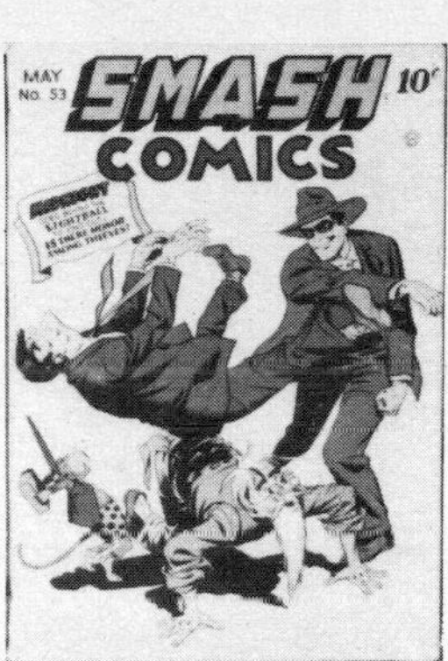

Smash Comics #53, © QUA

GD25 FN65 NM94

1-Edmond Good-c/a 8.35 25.00 50.00

SKY WOLF (Eclipse Comics)(Value: cover or less)(Also see Airboy)

SLAINE, THE BERSERKER (Quality)(Value: cover or less)

SLAM BANG COMICS (Western Desperado #8)
March, 1940 - No. 7, Sept, 1940 (Combined with Master Comics #7)
Fawcett Publications

1-Diamond Jack, Mark Swift & The Time Retarder, Lee Granger, Jungle King begin & continue in Master 92.00 275.00 600.00
2 43.00 1305.00 300.00
3-Classic-c 57.00 170.00 400.00
4-7: 6-Intro Zoro, the Mystery Man (also in #7). 7-Bondage-c 39.00 120.00 275.00

SLAM BANG COMICS
No. 9, No date
Post Cereal Giveaway

9-Dynamic Man, Echo, Mr. E, Yankee Boy app. 3.60 9.00 18.00

SLAPSTICK
Nov, 1992 - No. 4, Feb, 1993 ($1.25, color, mini-series)
Marvel Comics

1-4: Fry/Austin-c/a. 4-Ghost Rider, D.D., F.F. app. 1.25

SLAPSTICK COMICS
nd (1946?) (36 pages)
Comic Magazines Distributors

nn-Firetop feature; Post-a(2) 12.00 36.00 85.00

SLASH-D DOUBLECROSS
1950 (132 pgs.) (pocket size)
St. John Publishing Co.

nn-Western comics 13.00 40.00 90.00

SLASH MARAUD (DC)(Value: cover or less)

SLAUGHTERMAN (Comico)(Value: cover or less)

SLAVE GIRL COMICS (See Malu... & White Princess of the Jungle #2)
Feb, 1949 - No. 2, Apr, 1949 (52 pgs.)
Avon Periodicals/Eternity Comics

1-Larsen-c/a 50.00 150.00 350.00
2-Larsen-a 39.00 120.00 275.00
1 (3/89, $2.25, B&W, 44 pgs., Eternity)-r/#1 .90 2.25

SLEDGE HAMMER (TV)(Marvel)(Value: cover or less)

SLEEPING BEAUTY (See Dell Giants, 4-Color #973, 984 & Movie Comics)

SLEEPWALKER
June, 1991 - Present ($1.00/$1.25, color)
Marvel Comics

1-1st app. 1.50
2-5: 4-Williamson-i. 5-Spider-Man-c/story 1.50
6-10: 7-Infinity Gauntlet x-over. 8-Vs. Deathlok-c/story 1.50
11-18,20-24,26-34: 11-Ghost Rider-c/story. 12-Quesada-c/a(p) 14-Intro Spectra. 15-F.F.-c/story. 17-Darkhawk & Spider-Man x-over. 18-Infinity War x-over; Quesada/Williamson-c. 20,21-Sam Kieth-c. 21,22-Hobgoblin app. 1.25
19-($2.00)-Die-cut Sleepwalker mask cover .80 2.00
25-($2.95, 52 pgs.)-Holo-grafx foil-c; origin 1.20 3.00
Holiday Special 1 (1/93, $2.00, 52 pgs.)-Quesada-c .80 2.00

SLEEZE BROTHERS, THE (Marvel)(Value: cover or less)

SLICK CHICK COMICS
1947(nd) - No. 3, 1947(nd)
Leader Enterprises

1-Teenage humor 8.35 25.00 50.00
2,3 6.35 19.00 38.00

SLIMER! (TV) (Now)(Value: cover or less)

GD25 FN65 NM94

SLIM MORGAN (See Wisco)

SLUDGE
Oct, 1993 - Present ($1.95, color)
Malibu Comics (Ultraverse)

1-($2.50)-Intro Sludge; flip-side has Rune-c/story (1st app., 3 pgs.) by Barry Windsor-Smith; 1st app. The Night Man (3 pg. preview) 1.00 2.50
2-4 .80 2.00

SLUGGER (Of the Little Wise Guys)
April, 1956
Lev Gleason Publications

1-Biro-c 4.00 11.00 22.00

SMASH COMICS (Becomes Lady Luck #86 on)
Aug, 1939 - No. 85, Oct, 1949
Quality Comics Group

1-Origin Hugh Hazard & His Iron Man, Bozo the Robot, Espionage, Starring Black X by Eisner, & Hooded Justice (Invisible Justice #2 on); Chic Carter & Wings Wendall begin; 1st Robot on the cover of a comic book (Bozo) 117.00 350.00 780.00
2-The Lone Star Rider app; Invisible Hood gains power of invisibility 48.00 145.00 325.00
3-Captain Cook & Eisner's John Law begin 33.00 100.00 225.00
4,5: 4-Flash Fulton begins 30.00 90.00 200.00
6-12: 12-One pg. Fine-a 25.00 75.00 175.00
13-Magno begins (8/40); last Eisner issue; The Ray app. in full page ad; The Purple Trio begins 25.00 75.00 175.00
14-Intro. The Ray (9/40) by Lou Fine & others 145.00 438.00 925.00
15,16: 16-The Scarlet Seal begins 70.00 210.00 465.00
17-Wun Cloo becomes plastic super-hero by Jack Cole (9-months before Plastic Man) 70.00 210.00 465.00
18-Midnight by Jack Cole begins (origin & 1st app., 1/41) 83.00 250.00 540.00
19-22: Last Fine Ray; The Jester begins-#22 50.00 150.00 320.00
23,24: 24-The Sword app.; last Chic Carter; Wings Wendall dons new costume #24,25 43.00 130.00 280.00
25-Origin/1st app. Wildfire; Rookie Rankin begins 50.00 150.00 325.00
26-30: 28-Midnight-c begin, end #85 40.00 120.00 260.00
31,32,34: Ray by Rudy Palais; also #33 29.00 88.00 190.00
33-Origin The Marksman 37.00 110.00 250.00
35-37 29.00 88.00 190.00
38-The Yankee Eagle begins; last Midnight by Jack Cole 29.00 88.00 190.00
39,40-Last Ray issue 24.00 72.00 160.00
41,43-50 12.00 35.00 75.00
42-Lady Luck begins by Klaus Nordling 13.00 40.00 85.00
51-60 10.00 30.00 65.00
61-70 9.15 27.50 55.00
71-85 8.35 25.00 50.00

NOTE: ***Al Bryant*** *c-54, 63-68.* ***Cole*** *a-17-38, 68, 69, 72, 73, 78, 80, 83, 85; c-38, 60-62, 69-84.* ***Crandall*** *a-(Ray)-23-29, 35-38; c-36, 39, 40, 42-44, 46.* ***Fine*** *a(Ray)-14, 15, 16(w/****Tuska****), 17-22.* ***Fox*** *c-24-35.* ***Fuje*** *Ray-30.* ***Gil Fox*** *a-6-7, 9, 11-13.* ***Guardineer*** *a-(The Marksman)-39-?, 49, 52.* ***Gustavson*** *a-4-7, 9, 11-13 (The Jester)-22-46; (Magno)-13-21; (Midnight)-39(Cole inks), 49, 52, 63-65.* ***Kotzky*** *a-(Espionage)-33-38; c-45, 47-53.* ***Nordling*** *a-49, 52, 63-65.* ***Powell*** *a-11, 12, (Abdul the Arab)-13-24.Black X c-2, 6, 9, 11, 13, 16. Bozo the Robot c-1, 3, 5, 8, 10, 12, 14, 18, 20, 22, 24, 26. Midnight c-28-85. The Ray c-15, 17, 19, 21, 23, 25, 27. Wings Wendall c-4, 7.*

SMASH HIT SPORTS COMICS
V2#1, Jan, 1949
Essankay Publications

V2#1-L.B. Cole-c/a 13.00 40.00 90.00

S'MATTER POP?
1917 (44 pgs.; B&W; 10x14"; cardboard covers)
Saalfield Publ. Co.

nn-By Charlie Payne; in full color; pages printed on one side 25.00 75.00 175.00

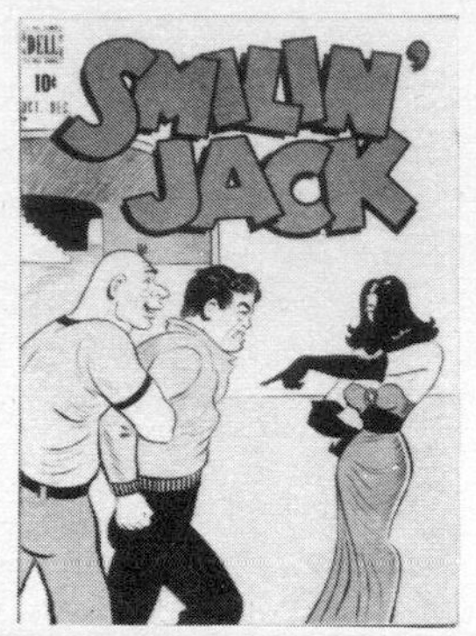

Smilin Jack #8, © N.Y. News Synd.

Smitty #7, © N.Y. News Synd.

Snagglepuss #4, © Hanna-Barbera

SMILE COMICS (Also see Gay Comics, Tickle, & Whee)
1955 (52 pages; 5x7-1/4") (7 cents)
Modern Store Publ.

	GD25	FN65	NM94
1	.60	1.50	3.00

SMILEY BURNETTE WESTERN (Also see Patches #8 & Six-Gun Heroes)
March, 1950 - No. 4, Oct, 1950 (All photo front & back-c)
Fawcett Publications

	GD25	FN65	NM94
1-Red Eagle begins	36.00	110.00	250.00
2-4	24.00	73.00	170.00

SMILIN' JACK (See Famous Feature Stories, Popular Comics, Super Book #1, 2, 7, 19 & Super Comics)
No. 5, 1940 - No. 8, Oct-Dec, 1949
Dell Publishing Co.

	GD25	FN65	NM94
4-Color 5	57.00	170.00	400.00
4-Color 10 (1940)	54.00	160.00	375.00
Large Feature Comic 12,14,25 (1941)	40.00	120.00	280.00
4-Color 4 (1942)	43.00	130.00	300.00
4-Color 14 (1943)	34.00	105.00	240.00
4-Color 36,58 (1943-44)	22.00	65.00	150.00
4-Color 80 (1945)	16.00	48.00	110.00
4-Color 149 (1947)	11.00	32.00	75.00
1 (1-3/48)	11.00	32.00	75.00
2	6.35	19.00	38.00
3-8 (10-12/49)	4.70	14.00	28.00
Popped Wheat Giveaway (1947)-1938 strip reprints; 16 pgs. in full color	.95	2.40	4.80
Shoe Store Giveaway-1938 strip reprints; 16 pgs.	4.00	11.00	22.00
Sparked Wheat Giveaway (1942)-16 pgs. in full color	4.00	11.00	22.00

SMILING SPOOK SPUNKY (See Spunky)

SMITTY (See Treasure Box of Famous Comics)
1928 - 1933 (B&W newspaper strip reprints)
(cardboard covers; 9-1/2x9-1/2", 52 pgs.; 7x8-1/4", 36 pgs.)
Cupples & Leon Co.

	GD25	FN65	NM94
1928-(96pgs. 7x8-3/4")	17.00	50.00	100.00
1928-(Softcover, 36pgs., nn)	17.50	52.00	105.00
1929-At the Ball Game, 1930-The Flying Office Boy, 1931-The Jockey, 1932-In the North Woods....each....	12.50	37.50	75.00
1933-At Military School	12.50	37.50	75.00
Mid-1930s issue (reprint of 1928 Treasure Box issue)-36 pgs.; 7x8-3/4"	10.00	30.00	65.00
Hardback Editions (100 pgs., 7x8-1/4") with dust jacket each....	23.00	70.00	160.00

SMITTY (See Popular Comics, Super Book #2, 4 & Super Comics)
No. 11, 1940 - No. 7, Aug-Oct, 1949; No. 909, Apr, 1958
Dell Publishing Co.

	GD25	FN65	NM94
4-Color 11 (1940)	34.00	105.00	240.00
Large Feature Comic 26 (1941)	24.00	72.00	165.00
4-Color 6 (1942)	19.00	58.00	135.00
4-Color 32 (1943)	16.00	48.00	110.00
4-Color 65 (1945)	11.50	34.00	80.00
4-Color 99 (1946)	11.00	32.00	75.00
4-Color 138 (1947)	10.00	30.00	60.00
1 (11-1/47-48)	10.00	30.00	60.00
2	5.00	15.00	30.00
3 (8-10/48), 4 (1949)	4.00	10.00	20.00
5-7, 4-Color 909 (4/58)	3.20	8.00	16.00

SMOKEY BEAR (TV) (See March Of Comics #234, 362, 372, 383, 407)
Feb, 1970 - No. 13, Mar, 1973
Gold Key

	GD25	FN65	NM94
1	1.00	2.50	6.00
2-13		1.20	3.00

SMOKEY STOVER (See Popular Comics, Super Book #5, 17, 29 & Super Comics)
No. 7, 1942 - No. 827, Aug, 1957
Dell Publishing Co.

	GD25	FN65	NM94
4-Color 7 (1942)-Reprints	31.00	95.00	220.00
4-Color 35 (1943)	16.00	48.00	110.00
4-Color 64 (1944)	11.50	34.00	80.00
4-Color 229 (1949)	5.00	15.00	30.00
4-Color 730,827	3.60	9.00	18.00
General Motors giveaway (1953)	4.35	13.00	26.00
National Fire Protection giveaway(1953 & 1954)-16 pgs., paper-c	4.35	13.00	26.00

SMOKEY THE BEAR (See Forest Fire for 1st app.)
No. 653, 10/55 - No. 1214, 8/61 (See March of Comics #234)
Dell Publishing Co.

	GD25	FN65	NM94
4-Color 653 (#1)	9.15	27.50	55.00
4-Color 708,754,818,932	4.70	14.00	28.00
4-Color 1016,1119,1214	4.00	10.00	20.00
True Story of..., The('59)-U.S. Forest Service giveaway-Publ. by Western Printing Co. (reprinted in 1964 & 1969)-Reprints 1st 16 pgs. of 4-Color 932	2.80	7.00	14.00

SMOKY (See Movie Classics)

SMURFS (TV)(Marvel)(Value: cover or less)

SNAFU (Magazine)
Nov, 1955 - V2#2, Mar, 1956 (B&W)
Atlas Comics (RCM)

	GD25	FN65	NM94
V1#1-Heath/Severin-a; Everett, Maneely-a	9.15	27.50	55.00
V2#1,2-Severin-a	7.50	22.50	45.00

SNAGGLEPUSS (TV)(See Hanna-Barbera Band Wagon #3, Quick-Draw McGraw & Spotlight #4)
Oct, 1962 - No. 4, Sept, 1963 (Hanna-Barbera)
Gold Key

	GD25	FN65	NM94
1	8.35	25.00	50.00
2-4	5.00	15.00	30.00

SNAP (Formerly Scoop #8; becomes Jest #10,11 & Komik Pages #10)
No. 9, 1944
Harry 'A' Chesler

	GD25	FN65	NM94
9-Manhunter, The Voice	10.00	30.00	70.00

SNAPPY COMICS
1945
Cima Publ. Co. (Prize Publ.)

	GD25	FN65	NM94
1-Airmale app; 9 pg. Sorcerer's Apprentice adapt; Kiefer-a	14.00	43.00	100.00

SNARKY PARKER (See Life With...)

SNIFFY THE PUP
No. 5, Nov, 1949 - No. 18, Sept, 1953
Standard Publications (Animated Cartoons)

	GD25	FN65	NM94
5-Two Frazetta text illos	7.50	22.50	45.00
6-10	3.20	8.00	16.00
11-18	2.40	6.00	12.00

SNOOPER AND BLABBER DETECTIVES (TV) (See Whitman Comic Books)
Nov, 1962 - No. 3, May, 1963 (Hanna-Barbera)
Gold Key

	GD25	FN65	NM94
1	8.35	25.00	50.00
2,3	5.85	17.50	35.00

SNOW FOR CHRISTMAS
1957 (16 pages) (Giveaway)
W. T. Grant Co.

	GD25	FN65	NM94
nn	3.00	7.50	15.00

SNOW WHITE (See Christmas With..., 4-Color #49,227,382, Mickey Mouse Magazine,

Solar #23, © WEST/Voyager

Soldier Comics #7, © FAW

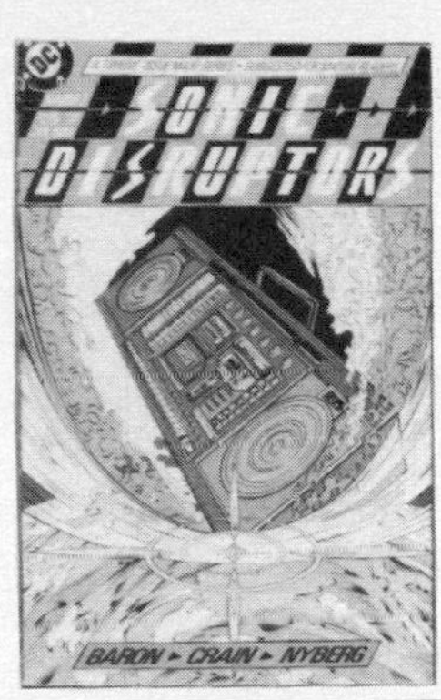

Sonic Disruptors #2, © DC

GD25 FN65 NM94

& Movie Comics)

SNOW WHITE AND THE SEVEN DWARFS
1952 (32 pgs.; 5x7-1/4", soft-c) (Disney)
Bendix Washing Machines
nn 6.70 20.00 40.00

SNOW WHITE AND THE SEVEN DWARFS
1957 (small size)
Promotional Publ. Co.
nn 4.00 10.50 21.00

SNOW WHITE AND THE SEVEN DWARFS
1958 (16 pgs, 5x7-1/4", soft-c) (Disney premium)
Western Printing Co.
nn-"Mystery of the Missing Magic" 4.35 13.00 26.00

SNOW WHITE AND THE SEVEN DWARFS
April, 1982 (60 cent cover price)
Whitman Publications
nn-r/Four Color #49 1.00

SNOW WHITE AND THE SEVEN DWARFS GOLDEN ANNIVERSARY
Fall, 1987 ($2.95, color, magazine size, 52 pgs.)
Gladstone Publishing
1-Contains poster 1.20 3.00

SNOW WHITE AND THE 7 DWARFS IN "MILKY WAY"
1955 (16 pgs., soft-c, 5x7-1/4") (Disney premium)
American Dairy Association
nn 6.70 20.00 40.00

SOAP OPERA LOVE
Feb, 1983 - No. 3, June, 1983
Charlton Comics
1-3 1.00

SOAP OPERA ROMANCES
July, 1982 - No. 5, March, 1983
Charlton Comics
1-5-Nurse Betsy Crane-r 1.00

SOJOURN ($1.50)
Sept, 1977 - No. 2, 1978 (Full tabloid size) (Color & B&W)
White Cliffs Publ. Co.
1-Tor by Kubert, Eagle by Severin, E. V. Race, Private Investigator by Doug Wildey, T. C. Mars by S. Aragones begin plus other strips .65 1.60
2 .65 1.60

SOLAR (...Man of the Atom; also see Doctor Solar)
Sept, 1991 - Present ($1.75/$1.95, color, 44 pgs.)
Valiant
1-Layton-i on Solar; Barry Windsor-Smith-c/a 2.40 7.25 17.00
2-Layton-i on Solar, Smith-a 1.70 5.00 12.00
3-1st app. Harada (11/91) 3.20 8.00 20.00
4 2.30 6.75 16.00
5-7: 7-vs. X-O Armor; last $1.95-c 1.85 5.50 13.00
8,9: 8-Begin $2.25-c 1.85 5.50 13.00
10-(6/92, $3.95)-1st app. Eternal Warrior (6 pgs.); black embossed-c; origin & 1st app. Geoff McHenry (Geomancer) 5.50 17.00 40.00
10-2nd printing ($3.95) 1.60 4.00
11-1st full app. Eternal Warrior 1.00 2.50 6.00
12,13,15: 12,13-Unity x-overs. 15-2nd Dr. Eclipse 1.90 4.75
14-1st app. Fred Bender (becomes Dr. Eclipse) 1.70 5.00 12.00
16-32: 17-X-O Manowar app. 23-Solar splits .90 2.25
NOTE: *#1-10 all have free 8 pg. insert "Alpha and Omega" which is a 10 chapter Solar origin story. All 10 centerfolds can pieced together to show climax of story.* ***Ditko*** *a-11p, 14p.* ***Layton*** *a-1-3i; c-2i, 11i, 17i, 25i.* ***Miller*** *c-12.* ***Quesada*** *c-17p, 20-23p.* ***Simonson*** *c-13.* ***B. Smith*** *a-1-10; c-1, 3, 5, 7, 19i.* ***Thibert*** *c-22i, 23i.*

GD25 FN65 NM94

SOLARMAN (Marvel)(Value: cover or less)

SOLDIER & MARINE COMICS (Fightin' Army #16 on)
No. 11, Dec, 1954 - No. 15, Aug, 1955; V2#9, Dec, 1956
Charlton Comics (Toby Press of Conn. V1#11)
V1#11 (12/54)-Bob Powell-a 4.00 10.00 20.00
V1#12(2/55)-15: 12-Photo-c 2.40 6.00 12.00
V2#9(Formerly Never Again; Jerry Drummer V2#10 on) 2.40 6.00 12.00

SOLDIER COMICS
Jan, 1952 - No. 11, Sept, 1953
Fawcett Publications
1 7.50 22.50 45.00
2 4.00 11.00 22.00
3-5 3.60 9.00 18.00
6-11: 8-Illo. in POP 2.80 7.00 14.00

SOLDIERS OF FORTUNE
Mar-Apr, 1951 - No. 13, Feb-Mar, 1953
American Comics Group (Creston Publ. Corp.)
1-Capt. Crossbones by Shelly, Ace Carter, Lance Larson begin 13.00 40.00 100.00
2 10.00 30.00 60.00
3-10: 6-Bondage-c 8.35 25.00 50.00
11-13 (War format) 4.00 10.00 20.00
NOTE: ***Shelly*** *a-1-3, 5.* ***Whitney*** *a-6, 8-11, 13; c-1-3, 5, 6.*

SOLDIERS OF FREEDOM (Americomics)(Value: cover or less)

SOLITAIRE
Nov, 1993 - Present ($1.95, color)
Malibu Comics (Ultraverse)
1-($2.50)-Collector's edition bagged w/playing card 1.00 2.50
1-3: 1-Regular edition w/o playing card .80 2.00

SOLO AVENGERS (Marvel)(Value: cover or less)

SOLOMON AND SHEBA (See 4-Color #1070)

SOLOMON KANE (Marvel)(Value: cover or less)

SOLUTION, THE
Sept, 1993 - Present ($1.95, color)
Malibu Comics
1,3,4: 1-Intro Meathook, Deathdance, Black Tiger, Tech .80 2.00
2-($2.50, 40 pgs.)-Rune flip-c/story by B. Smith 1.00 2.50

SOMERSET HOLMES (Pacific/Eclipse)(Value: cover or less)

SONG OF THE SOUTH (See Brer Rabbit & 4-Color #693)

SONIC DISRUPTORS (DC)(Value: cover or less)

SONIC HEDGEHOG
Feb, 1993 - No. 3, May, 1993 ($1.25, color, mini-series)
Archie Comics
0(2/93),1-3: Shaw-a(p) & covers 1.25

SON OF AMBUSH BUG (DC)(Value: cover or less)

SON OF BLACK BEAUTY (See 4-Color #510, 566)

SON OF CELLULOID (Eclipse)(Value: cover or less)

SON OF FLUBBER (See Movie Comics)

SON OF MUTANT WORLD (Fantagor)(Value: cover or less)

SON OF SATAN (Also see Ghost Rider #1 & Marvel Spotlight #12)
Dec, 1975 - No. 8, Feb, 1977
Marvel Comics Group
1-Mooney-a; Kane-c(p), Starlin splash(p) 1.40 3.50 8.50
2-8: 2-Origin The Possessor. 8-Heath-a 1.80 4.50

SON OF SINBAD (Also see Abbott & Costello & Daring Adventures)
February, 1950

Space Adventures V3#30, © CC

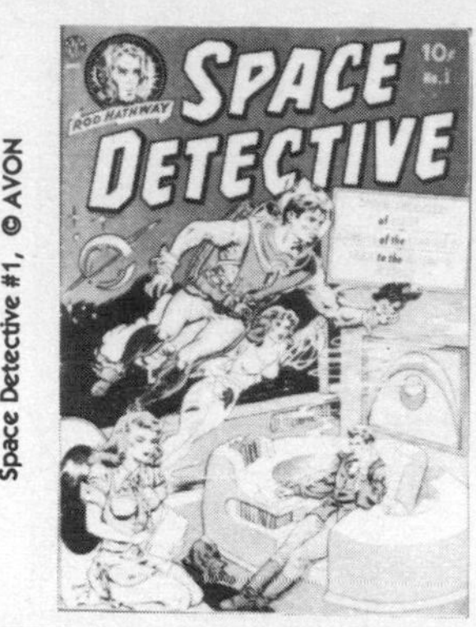

Space Detective #1, © AVON

Space Family Robinson #15, © WEST

GD25 FN65 NM94

St. John Publishing Co.
1-Kubert-c/a 28.00 85.00 195.00

SON OF TOMAHAWK (See Tomahawk)

SON OF VULCAN (Formerly Mysteries of Unexplored Worlds #1-48; Thunderbolt V3#51 on)
V2#49, Nov, 1965 - V2#50, Jan, 1966
Charlton Comics
V2#49,50: 50-Roy Thomas scripts (1st pro work) 2.00 5.00 10.00

SON OF YUPPIES FROM HELL (Marvel)(Value: cover or less)(See Yuppies From Hell)

SONS OF KATIE ELDER (See Movie Classics)

SORCERY (See Chilling Adventures in... & Red Circle...)

SORORITY SECRETS
July, 1954
Toby Press
1 5.00 15.00 30.00

SOULQUEST (Innovation)(Value: cover or less)

SOUPY SALES COMIC BOOK (TV)(The Official...)
1965
Archie Publications
1 10.00 30.00 65.00

SOUTHERN KNIGHTS, THE (Guild Publ./Fictioneer Books)(Formerly Crusaders #1) (Value: cover or less)

SOVIET SUPER SOLDIERS (Marvel)(Value: cover or less)

SPACE ACE (Also see Manhunt!)
No. 5, 1952
Magazine Enterprises
5(A-1 #61)-Guardineer-a 30.00 90.00 210.00

SPACE ACTION
June, 1952 - No. 3, Oct, 1952
Ace Magazines (Junior Books)
1 43.00 130.00 300.00
2,3 34.00 105.00 240.00

SPACE ADVENTURES (War At Sea #22 on)
7/52 - No. 21, 8/56; No. 23, 5/58 - No. 59, 11/64; V3#60, 10/67; V1#2, 7/68 - V1#8, 7/69; No. 9, 5/78 - No. 13, 3/79
Capitol Stories/Charlton Comics
1 29.00 85.00 200.00
2 13.00 40.00 90.00
3-5: 4,6-Flying saucer-c/stories 10.00 30.00 70.00
6-9: 7-Sex change story 10.00 30.00 65.00
10,11-Ditko-c/a; 11-Two Ditko stories 25.00 75.00 175.00
12-Ditko-c (classic) 29.00 88.00 205.00
13-(Fox-r, 10-11/54); Blue Beetle story 10.00 30.00 70.00
14-Blue Beetle story; Fox-r (12-1/54-55, last pre-code) 10.00 30.00 65.00
15,17,18-Rocky Jones app.(TV); 15-Part photo-c 10.00 30.00 70.00
16-Krigstein-a; Rocky Jones app. (TV) 13.00 40.00 90.00
19 9.15 27.50 55.00
20-Reprints Fawcett's "Destination Moon" 17.00 52.00 120.00
21-(8/56) (no #22)(Becomes War At Sea) 9.15 27.50 55.00
23-(5/58; formerly Nyoka, The Jungle Girl)-Reprints Fawcett's "Destination Moon" 14.00 43.00 100.00
24,25,31,32-Ditko-a 11.00 32.00 75.00
26,27-Ditko-a(4) each. 26,28-Flying saucer-c 12.00 36.00 85.00
28-30 5.00 15.00 30.00
33-Origin/1st app. Capt. Atom by Ditko (3/60) 25.00 75.00 200.00
34-40,42-All Captain Atom by Ditko 10.00 30.00 80.00
41,43-59: 44-1st app. Mercury Man; also in #45 2.00 6.00 15.00
V3#60(#1, 10/67)-Origin & 1st app. Paul Mann & The Saucers From the Future 3.00 8.00 20.00

GD25 FN65 NM94

2-8('68-'69)-2,5,6,8-Ditko-a; 2,4-Aparo-c/a 1.40 3.50 8.5
9-13('78-'79)-Capt. Atom-r/Space Adventures by Ditko; 9-Reprints origin/1st app. Capt. Atom from #33 1.5
NOTE: *Aparo* a-V3#60. c-V3#8. *Ditko* c-12, 31-42. *Giordano* c-3, 4, 7-9. *Krigstein* c-15. *Shuster* a-11.

SPACE ARK (AC)(Value: cover or less)

SPACE BUSTERS
Spring, 1952 - No. 2, Fall, 1952 (Painted covers by Norman Saunders)
Ziff-Davis Publ. Co.
1-Krigstein-a(3) 46.00 140.00 325.00
2-Kinstler-a(2pgs.); Krigstein-a(3) 39.00 115.00 270.00
NOTE: *Anderson* a-2. Bondage c-2.

SPACE CADET (See Tom Corbett,...)

SPACE COMICS (Formerly Funny Tunes)
No. 4, Mar-Apr, 1954 - No. 5, May-June, 1954
Avon Periodicals
4,5-Space Mouse, Peter Rabbit, Super Pup (formerly Spotty the Pup), & Merry Mouse continue from Funny Tunes 4.20 12.50 25.00
I.W. Reprint #8 (nd)-Space Mouse-r 1.00 2.50 5.00

SPACED
1982 - No. 13, 1988 ($1.25/$1.50, B&W, quarterly)
Anthony Smith Publ. #1,2/Unbridled Ambition/Eclipse Comics #10 on
1-($1.25-c) 3.60 10.75 25.00
2 -($1.25-c) 2.15 6.50 15.00
3,4: 3-Begin $1.50-c 1.20 3.00 7.00
5,6 1.20 3.00
7-13 1.50
Special Edition (1983, Mimeo) 1.00 2.50 6.00

SPACE DETECTIVE
July, 1951 - No. 4, July, 1952
Avon Periodicals
1-Rod Hathway, Space Det. begins, ends #4; Wood-c/a(3)-23 pgs.; "Opium Smugglers of Venus" drug story; Lucky Dale-r/Saint #4 71.00 215.00 500.00
2-Tales from the Shadow Squad story; Wood/Orlando-c; Wood inside layouts 39.00 120.00 275.00
3-Kinstler-c 24.00 72.00 165.00
4-Kinstlerish-a by McCann 24.00 72.00 165.00
I.W. Reprint #1(Reprints #2), 8(Reprints cover #1 & part Famous Funnies #191) 3.60 9.00 18.00
I.W. Reprint #9-Exist? 3.60 9.00 18.00

SPACE EXPLORER (See March of Comics #202)

SPACE FAMILY ROBINSON (TV)(...Lost in Space #15-36)(Becomes Lost in Space #37 on)
Dec, 1962 - No. 36, Oct, 1969 (All painted covers)
Gold Key
1-(Low distribution); Spiegle-a in all 22.00 66.00 175.00
2(3/63)-Family becomes lost in space 9.00 28.00 75.00
3-10: 6-Captain Venture begins 5.00 14.00 38.00
11-20 3.00 9.00 25.00
21-36 2.00 6.00 16.00

SPACE FAMILY ROBINSON (See March of Comics #320, 328, 352, 404, 414)

SPACE GHOST (TV) (Also see Golden Comics Digest #2 & Hanna-Barbera Super TV Heroes #3-7)
March, 1967 (Hanna-Barbera) (TV debut was 9/10/66)
Gold Key
1 (10199-703)-Spiegle-a 25.00 75.00 225.00

SPACE GHOST (TV)(Comico)(Value: cover or less)

SPACE GIANTS, THE
1979 (One shot, $1.00, B&W, TV)
FBN Publications

Space Man #8, © DELL

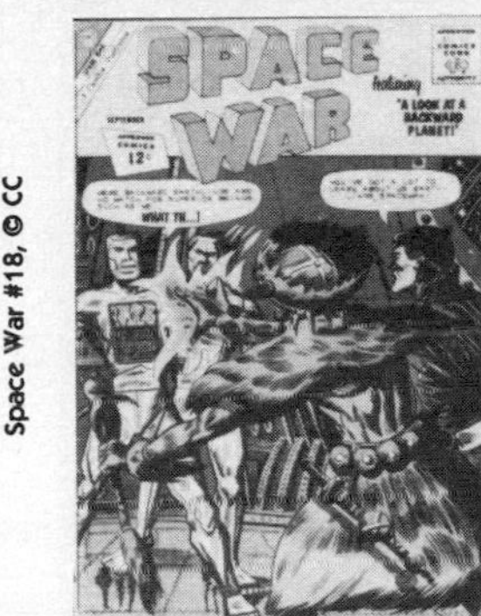

Space War #18, © CC

Space Western Comics #42, © CC

	GD25	FN65	NM94
1-Based on Japanese TV series	1.00	2.00	5.00

SPACEHAWK (Dark Horse)(Value: cover or less)

SPACE KAT-ETS (in 3-D)
Dec, 1953 (25 cents)
Power Publishing Co.

	GD25	FN65	NM94
1	25.00	75.00	175.00

SPACEMAN (Speed Carter...)
Sept, 1953 - No. 6, July, 1954
Atlas Comics (CnPC)

	GD25	FN65	NM94
1	39.00	120.00	275.00
2	25.00	75.00	175.00
3-6: 4-A-Bomb-c	22.00	65.00	150.00

NOTE: *Everett c-1, 3. Heath a-1. Maneely a-1(3), 2(4), 3(3), 4-6; c-5, 6. Romita a-1. Sekowsky c-4. Sekowsky/Abel a-4(3). Tuska a-5(3).*

SPACE MAN
No. 1253, 1-3/62 - No. 8, 3-5/64; No. 9, 7/72 - No. 10, 10/72
Dell Publishing Co.

	GD25	FN65	NM94
4-Color 1253 (#1)(1-3/62)	7.50	22.50	45.00
2,3	4.00	11.00	22.00
4-8	3.20	8.00	16.00
9,10: 9-Reprints #1253. 10-Reprints #2	1.20	3.00	6.00

SPACE MOUSE (Also see Funny Tunes & Space Comics)
April, 1953 - No. 5, Apr-May, 1954
Avon Periodicals

	GD25	FN65	NM94
1	6.70	20.00	40.00
2	4.70	14.00	28.00
3-5	3.60	9.00	18.00

SPACE MOUSE (Walter Lantz...#1; see Comic Album #17)
No. 1132, Aug-Oct, 1960 - No. 5, Nov, 1963 (Walter Lantz)
Dell Publishing Co./Gold Key

	GD25	FN65	NM94
4-Color 1132,1244	4.35	13.00	26.00
1(11/62)(G.K.)	4.00	11.00	22.00
2-5	3.20	8.00	16.00

SPACE MYSTERIES
1964 (Reprints)
I.W. Enterprises

	GD25	FN65	NM94
1-r/Journey Into Unknown Worlds #4 w/new-c	1.40	3.50	7.00
8,9: 9-r/Planet Comics #73	1.60	4.00	8.00

SPACE: 1999 (TV) (Also see Power Record Comics)
Nov, 1975 - No. 7, Nov, 1976
Charlton Comics

	GD25	FN65	NM94
1-Origin Moonbase Alpha; Staton-c/a		1.30	3.25
2,7: 2-Staton-a		.90	2.25
3-6: All Byrne-a; c-3,5,6		1.70	4.25

SPACE: 1999 (TV)(Magazine)
Nov, 1975 - No. 8, Nov, 1976 (B&W) (#7 shows #6 on inside)
Charlton Comics

	GD25	FN65	NM94
1-Origin Moonbase Alpha; Morrow-c/a		1.30	3.25
2,3-Morrow-c/a		.90	2.25
4-8: 4-6-Morrow-c. 5,8-Morrow-a		1.70	4.25

SPACE PATROL (TV)
Summer, 1952 - No. 2, Oct-Nov, 1952 (Painted-c by Norman Saunders)
Ziff-Davis Publishing Co. (Approved Comics)

	GD25	FN65	NM94
1-Krigstein-a	54.00	160.00	375.00
2-Krigstein-a(3)	43.00	130.00	300.00
...'s Special Mission (8 pgs., B&W, Giveaway)	53.00	160.00	370.00

SPACE PIRATES (See Archie Giant Series #533)

SPACE RANGER (See Mystery in Space #92, Showcase #15 & Tales of the Unexpected)

SPACE SQUADRON (Becomes Space Worlds #6)
June, 1951 - No. 5, Feb, 1952
Marvel/Atlas Comics (ACI)

	GD25	FN65	NM94
1: Brodsky c-1,5	40.00	122.00	285.00
2: Tuska c-2-4	35.00	105.00	245.00
3-5: 3-Capt. Jet Dixon by Tuska(3)	27.00	81.00	190.00

SPACE THRILLERS
1954 (Giant) (25 cents)
Avon Periodicals

	GD25	FN65	NM94
nn-(Scarce)-Robotmen of the Lost Planet; contains 3 rebound comics of The Saint & Strange Worlds. Contents could vary	71.00	215.00	500.00

SPACE TRIP TO THE MOON (See Space Adventures #23)

SPACE USAGI
June, 1992 - No. 3, 1992 ($2.00, B&W, mini-series)
Mirage Studios

	GD25	FN65	NM94
1-3: Usagi Yojimbo by Stan Sakai		.80	2.00

SPACE WAR (Fightin' Five #28 on)
Oct, 1959 - No. 27, Mar, 1964; No. 28, Mar, 1978 - No. 34, 3/79
Charlton Comics

	GD25	FN65	NM94
V1#1-Giordano-c begin, end #3	11.00	34.00	80.00
2,3	5.50	17.00	40.00
4-6,8,10-Ditko-c/a	11.00	34.00	80.00
7,9,11-15: Last 10 cent issue?	3.20	8.00	20.00
16-27	2.40	7.25	17.00
28,29,33,34-Ditko-c/a(r)	4.50	14.00	32.00
30-Ditko-c/a(r); Staton, Sutton/Wood-a	4.85	15.00	34.00
31-Ditko-c/a; atom-blast-c	4.85	15.00	34.00
32-r/Charlton Premiere V2#2; Sutton-a		1.00	2.50

SPACE WESTERN (Formerly Cowboy Western Comics; becomes Cowboy Western Comics #46 on)
No. 40, Oct, 1952 - No. 45, Aug, 1953
Charlton Comics (Capitol Stories)

	GD25	FN65	NM94
40-Intro Spurs Jackson & His Space Vigilantes; flying saucer story	35.00	105.00	245.00
41,43-45: 41-Flying saucer-c	26.00	77.00	180.00
42-Atom bomb explosion-c	30.00	85.00	200.00

SPACE WORLDS (Formerly Space Squadron #1-5)
No. 6, April, 1952
Atlas Comics (Male)

	GD25	FN65	NM94
6-Sol Brodsky-c	24.00	70.00	165.00

SPANKY & ALFALFA & THE LITTLE RASCALS (See The Little Rascals)

SPANNER'S GALAXY (DC)(Value: cover or less)

SPARKIE, RADIO PIXIE (Radio)(Becomes Big Jon & Sparkie #4)
Winter, 1951 - No. 3, July-Aug, 1952 (Painted-c)(Sparkie #2,3; #1?)
Ziff-Davis Publ. Co.

	GD25	FN65	NM94
1-Based on children's radio program	14.00	43.00	100.00
2,3: 3-Big Jon and Sparkie on-c only	11.00	32.00	75.00

SPARKLE COMICS
Oct-Nov, 1948 - No. 33, Dec-Jan, 1953-54 (#1-3: 52 pgs.)
United Features Syndicate

	GD25	FN65	NM94
1-Li'l Abner, Nancy, Captain & the Kids, Ella Cinders	10.00	30.00	65.00
2	5.35	16.00	32.00
3-10	4.00	11.00	22.00
11-20	4.00	10.00	20.00
21-33	3.00	7.50	15.00

SPARKLE PLENTY (See 4-Color #215 & Harvey Comics Library #2)

SPARKLER COMICS (1st Series)
July, 1940 - No. 2, 1940
United Feature Comic Group

Sparkler Comics #64, © UFS

Spawn #4 (Image), © Todd McFarlane

Special Edition #4, © DC

	GD25	FN65	NM94
1-Jim Hardy	27.00	82.00	175.00
2-Frankie Doodle	18.00	55.00	120.00

SPARKLER COMICS (2nd Series)(Nancy & Sluggo #121 on)(Cover title becomes Nancy and Sluggo #101? on)
July, 1941 - No. 120, Jan, 1955
United Features Syndicate

	GD25	FN65	NM94
1-Origin 1st app. Sparkman; Tarzan (by Hogarth in all issues), Captain & the Kids, Ella Cinders, Danny Dingle, Dynamite Dunn, Nancy, Abbie & Slats, Broncho Bill, Frankie Doodle, begin; Sparkman c-1-9,11,12; Hap Hopper c-10,13	117.00	350.00	780.00
2	50.00	150.00	330.00
3,4	42.00	125.00	275.00
5-10: 9-Sparkman's new costume	37.00	110.00	240.00
11-13,15-20: 12-Sparkman's new costume (color change). 19-1st Race Riley and the Commandos plus-c	28.00	85.00	190.00
14-Tarzan-c by Hogarth	32.00	95.00	210.00
21,25,28,31,34,37,39-Tarzan-c by Hogarth	27.00	82.00	185.00
22-24,26,27,29,30: 22-Race Riley & the Commandos strips begin, ends #44	22.00	68.00	150.00
32,33,35,36,38,40	12.50	37.50	85.00
41,43,45,46,48,49	10.00	30.00	60.00
42,44,47,50-Tarzan-c (42,47,50 by Hogarth)	17.00	50.00	110.00
51,52,54-70: 57-Li'l Abner begins (not in #58); Fearless Fosdick app. in #58	8.35	25.00	50.00
53-Tarzan-c by Hogarth	14.00	42.50	95.00
71-80	5.35	16.00	32.00
81,82,84-90: 85-Li'l Abner ends. 86-Lingerie panels	4.70	14.00	28.00
83-Tarzan-c	8.35	25.00	50.00
91-96,98-99	4.70	14.00	28.00
97-Origin Casey Ruggles by Warren Tufts	10.00	30.00	60.00
100	5.85	17.50	35.00
101-107,109-112,114-120	4.00	10.00	20.00
108,113-Toth-a	7.50	22.50	45.00

SPARKLING LOVE
June, 1950; 1953
Avon Periodicals/Realistic (1953)

	GD25	FN65	NM94
1(Avon)-Kubert-a; photo-c	13.00	40.00	90.00
nn(1953)-Reprint; Kubert-a	5.85	17.50	35.00

SPARKLING STARS
June, 1944 - No. 33, March, 1948
Holyoke Publishing Co.

	GD25	FN65	NM94
1-Hell's Angels, FBI, Boxie Weaver, Petey & Pop, & Ali Baba begin	10.00	30.00	70.00
2-Speed Spaulding story	7.00	21.00	42.00
3-Actual FBI case photos & war photos	5.00	15.00	30.00
4-10: 7-X-mas-c	4.35	13.00	26.00
11-19: 13-Origin/1st app. Jungo the Man-Beast	4.00	11.00	22.00
20-Intro Fangs the Wolf Boy	4.35	13.00	26.00
21-29,32,33: 29-Bondage-c	4.00	11.00	22.00
31-Sid Greene-a	4.35	13.00	26.00

SPARK MAN (See Sparkler Comics)
1945 (One Shot) (36 pages)
Frances M. McQueeny

	GD25	FN65	NM94
1-Origin Spark Man; female torture story; cover redrawn from Sparkler #1	20.00	60.00	140.00

SPARKY WATTS (Also see Big Shot Comics & Columbia Comics)
Nov?, 1942 - No. 10, 1949
Columbia Comic Corp.

	GD25	FN65	NM94
1(1942)-Skyman & The Face app; Hitler-c	25.00	75.00	170.00
2(1943)	12.00	35.00	80.00
3(1944)	10.00	30.00	65.00
4(1944)-Origin	10.00	30.00	60.00
5(1947)-Skyman app.; Boody Rogers-c/a	7.50	22.50	45.00
6,7,9,10: 6(1947),10(1949)	5.00	15.00	30.00
8(1948)-Surrealistic-c	6.70	20.00	40.00

NOTE: ***Boody Rogers** c-1-8.*

SPARTACUS (See 4-Color #1139)

SPAWN
May, 1992 - Present ($1.95, color, mature readers)
Image Comics

	GD25	FN65	NM94
1-1st app. Spawn; McFarlane-c/a begins; McFarlane/Steacy-c	1.25	3.00	7.50
2-McFarlane/Steacy-c	1.20	3.00	7.00
3	1.10	2.70	6.50
4-Has coupon for Image Comics #0-Alan Moore scripts w/Miller poster	1.00	2.50	6.00
4-With coupon missing		.80	2.00
5-18: 5-Cerebus cameo (1 pg.) as stuffed animal. 7-Spawn Mobile poster. 8-Miller poster. 9-Neil Gaiman scripts; Jim Lee poster. 10-Cerebus app.; Bloodwulf poster by Liefeld. 11-Miller scripts		.80	2.00

SPECIAL AGENT (Steve Saunders...)(Also see True Comics #68)
Dec, 1947 - No. 8, Sept, 1949
Parents' Magazine Institute (Commended Comics No. 2)

	GD25	FN65	NM94
1-J. Edgar Hoover photo on-c	8.35	25.00	50.00
2	4.20	12.50	25.00
3-8	4.00	10.00	20.00

SPECIAL COLLECTORS' EDITION
Dec, 1975 (No month given) (10-1/4x13-1/2")
Marvel Comics Group

	GD25	FN65	NM94
1-Kung Fu, Iron Fist (early), Sons of the Tiger		1.30	3.25

SPECIAL COMICS (Becomes Hangman #2 on)
Winter, 1941-42
MLJ Magazines

	GD25	FN65	NM94
1-Origin The Boy Buddies (Shield & Wizard x-over); death of The Comet; origin The Hangman retold; Hangman-c	135.00	410.00	950.00

SPECIAL DELIVERY
1951 (32 pgs.; B&W)
Post Hall Synd. (Giveaway)

nn-Origin of Pogo, Swamp, etc.; 2 pg. biog. on Walt Kelly
(One copy sold in 1980 for $150.00)

SPECIAL EDITION (See Gorgo and Reptisaurus)

SPECIAL EDITION (U. S. Navy Giveaways)
1944 - 1945 (Regular comic format with wording simplified, 52 pgs.)
National Periodical Publications

	GD25	FN65	NM94
1-Action (1944)-reprints Action #80	82.00	245.00	490.00
2-Action (1944)-reprints Action #81	82.00	245.00	490.00
3-Superman (1944)-reprints Superman #33	82.00	245.00	490.00
4-Detective (1944)-reprints Detective #97	87.00	262.00	525.00
5-Superman (1945)-reprints Superman #34	82.00	245.00	490.00
6-Action (1945)-reprints Action #84	82.00	245.00	490.00

NOTE: ***Wayne Boring** c-1, 2, 6. **Dick Sprang** c-4.*

SPECIAL EDITION COMICS
1940 (August) (One Shot, 68 pgs.)
Fawcett Publications

	GD25	FN65	VF82	NM94
1-1st book devoted entirely to Captain Marvel; C.C. Beck-c/a; only app. of Capt. Marvel with belt buckle; Capt. Marvel appears with button-down flap; 1st story (came out before Captain Marvel #1)	550.00	1650.00	3575.00	5500.00

(Estimated up to 150 total copies exist, 7 in NM/Mint)

NOTE: *Prices vary widely on this book. Since this book is all Captain Marvel stories, it is actually a pre-Captain Marvel #1. There is speculation that this book almost became **Captain Marvel** #1. After **Special Edition** was published, there was an editor change at Fawcett. The new editor commissioned Kirby to do a nn **Captain Marvel** book early in 1941. This book was followed by a 2nd book several months later. This 2nd book was advertised as a #3 (making Special Edition*

Special War Series V4#4, © CC

The Spectacular Spider-Man #65, © MEG

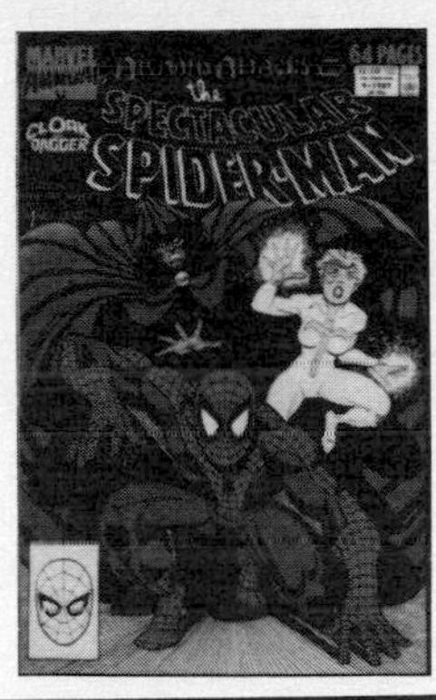

The Spectacular Spider-Man Annual #9, © MEG

GD25 FN65 NM94

the #1, & the nn issue the #2). However, the 2nd book did come out as a #2.

SPECIAL EDITION: SPIDER-MAN VS. THE HULK (See listing under The Amazing Spider-Man)

SPECIAL EDITION X-MEN
Feb, 1983 (One Shot) ($2.00, Baxter paper)
Marvel Comics Group

	GD25	FN65	NM94
1-r/Giant-Size X-Men #1 plus one new story	1.85	5.50	13.00

SPECIAL MARVEL EDITION (Master of Kung Fu #17 on)
Jan, 1971 - No. 16, Feb, 1974
Marvel Comics Group

	GD25	FN65	NM94
1-Thor-r by Kirby; 68 pgs.	1.00	2.50	6.00
2-4: Thor-r by Kirby; 68 pg. Giant		1.80	4.50
5-14: Sgt. Fury-r; 11-Reprints Sgt. Fury #13 (Captain America app.)		1.50	3.75
15-Master of Kung Fu (Shang-Chi) begins (1st app., 12/73); Starlin-a; origin/1st app. Nayland Smith & Dr. Petric	5.00	16.00	37.00
16-1st app. Midnight; Starlin-a (2nd Shang-Chi)	3.60	10.75	25.00

SPECIAL MISSIONS (See G.I. Joe...)

SPECIAL WAR SERIES (Attack V4#3 on?)
Aug, 1965 - No. 4, Nov, 1965
Charlton Comics

	GD25	FN65	NM94
V4#1-D-Day (also see D-Day listing)	1.40	3.50	8.50
2-Attack!	1.00	2.50	6.00
3-War & Attack (also see War & Attack)	1.00	2.50	6.00
4-Judomaster (intro/1st app.; see Sarge Steel)	3.25	9.50	22.00

SPECTACULAR ADVENTURES (See Adventures)

SPECTACULAR FEATURE MAGAZINE, A (Formerly My Confessions) (Spectacular Features Magazine #12)
No. 11, April, 1950
Fox Feature Syndicate

	GD25	FN65	NM94
11 (#1)-Samson & Delilah	16.00	48.00	110.00

SPECTACULAR FEATURES MAGAZINE (Formerly A Spectacular Feature Magazine)
No. 12, June, 1950 - No. 3, Aug, 1950
Fox Feature Syndicate

	GD25	FN65	NM94
12 (#2)-Iwo Jima; photo flag-c	16.00	48.00	110.00
3-True Crime Cases From Police Files	11.00	32.00	75.00

SPECTACULAR SPIDER-MAN, THE (See Marvel Special Edition and Marvel Treasury Edition)

SPECTACULAR SPIDER-MAN, THE (Magazine)
July, 1968 - No. 2, Nov, 1968 (35 cents)
Marvel Comics Group

	GD25	FN65	NM94
1-(B&W)-Romita/Mooney 52 pg. story plus updated origin story with Everett-a(i)	8.50	25.00	58.00
2-(Color)-Green Goblin-c & 58 pg. story; Romita painted-c (story reprinted in King Size Spider-Man #9); Romita/Mooney-a	11.00	33.00	78.00

SPECTACULAR SPIDER-MAN, THE (Peter Parker...#54-132,134)
Dec, 1976 - Present
Marvel Comics Group

	GD25	FN65	NM94
1-Origin recap in text; return of Tarantula	6.00	19.00	44.00
2-Kraven the Hunter app.	2.60	7.50	18.00
3-5: 3-Intro Lightmaster. 4-Vulture app.	1.70	5.00	12.00
6-8-Morbius app.; 6-r/Marvel Team-Up #3 w/Morbius	2.60	7.50	18.00
9-20: 9,10-White Tiger app. 17,18-Champions cameo (Ghost Rider)	1.00	2.50	6.00
21,24-26: 21-Scorpion app. 26-Daredevil app.	1.00	2.00	5.00
22,23-Moon Knight app.	1.50	3.75	9.00
27-Miller's 1st art on Daredevil (2/79); also see Captain America #235	1.85	5.50	13.00
28-Miller Daredevil (p)	1.65	4.00	10.00
29-55,57,59: 33-Origin Iguana. 38-Morbius app.		1.70	4.25
56-2nd app. Jack O'Lantern (Macendale) & 1st Spidey/Jack O'Lantern battle (7/81)	1.40	3.50	8.50
58-Byrne-a(p)	1.00	2.00	5.00
60-Double size; origin retold with new facts revealed		1.80	4.50
61-63,65-68,71-74: 65-Kraven the Hunter app.		1.30	3.25
64-1st app. Cloak & Dagger (3/82)	1.85	5.50	13.00
69,70-Cloak & Dagger app.	1.65	4.00	10.00
75-Double size		1.80	4.50
76-80: 79-Punisher cameo		1.20	3.00
81,82-Punisher, Cloak & Dagger app.	1.70	5.00	12.00
83-Origin Punisher retold (10/83)	2.15	6.50	15.00
84,86-99: 90-Spider-man's new black costume, last panel(ties w/Amazing Spider-Man #252 & Marvel Team-Up #141 for 1st app.). 94-96-Cloak & Dagger app. 98-Intro The Spot		1.40	3.50
85-Hobgoblin (Ned Leeds) app. (12/83); gains powers of original Green Goblin (see Amazing Spider-Man #238)	3.85	11.50	27.00
100-(3/85)-Double size		1.80	4.50
101-115,117,118,120-129: 107-110-Death of Jean DeWolff. 111-Secret Wars II tie-in. 128-Black Cat new costume		1.20	3.00
116,119-Sabretooth-c/story	1.00	2.50	6.00
130-Hobgoblin app.		1.80	4.50
131-Six part Kraven tie-in	1.10	2.70	6.50
132-Kraven tie-in	1.00	2.50	5.50
133-139: 138-1st full app. Tombstone (origin #139)		.80	2.00
140-Punisher cameo app.		1.20	3.00
141-Punisher app.	1.10	2.70	6.50
142,143-Punisher app.		1.60	4.00
144-146,148-157: 151-Tombstone returns		.80	2.00
147-1st app. new Hobgoblin (Macendale) in 1 pg. cameo; continued in Web of Spider-Man #48	3.25	9.50	22.00
158-Spider-Man gets new powers (1st Cosmic Spidey, continued in Web of Spider-Man #59)	1.85	5.50	13.00
159-Cosmic Spider-Man app.	1.40	3.50	8.50
160-170: 161-163-Hobgoblin app. 168-170-Avengers x-over. 169-1st app. The Outlaws		.70	1.80
171-184: 180,181,183,184-Green Goblin app.			1.25
185-188,190-199: 197-199-Original X-Men-c/story			1.25
189-($2.95, 52 pgs.)-Hologram-c; battles Green Goblin; origin Spidey retold; Vess poster w/Spidey & Hobgoblin	1.40	3.50	8.50
189 (2nd printing)		1.00	2.50
195-(Deluxe ed.)-Polybagged w/audio cassette	.50	1.25	2.50
200-($2.95)-Holo-grafx foil-c; Green Goblin-c/story		1.20	3.00
201-210: 203-Maximum Carnage x-over. 208-Siege of Darkness x-over (#207 is a tie-in)			1.25
Annual 1 (1979)-Doc Octopus-c/46 pg. story	1.00	2.50	5.50
Annual 2 (1980)-Origin/1st app. Rapier		1.70	4.25
Annual 3-7: 3(1981)-Last Man-Wolf. 4(1984). 5(1985). 6(10/86). 7(1987)		1.30	3.25
Annual 8 (1988, $1.75)-Evolutionary War x-over		1.60	4.00
Annual 9 (1989, $2.00, 68 pgs.)-Atlantis Attacks		1.20	3.00
Annual 10 (1990, $2.00, 68 pgs.)-McFarlane-a		1.00	2.50
Annual 11 (1991, $2.00, 68 pgs.)-Iron Man app.		.80	2.00
Annual 12 (1992, $2.25, 68 pgs.)-Venom solo story cont'd from Amazing Spider-Man Annual #26		.90	2.25
Annual 13 (1993, $2.95, 68 pgs.)-Polybagged w/trading card; John Romita, Sr. back-up-a		1.20	3.00

NOTE: ***Austin** c-21i, Annual 11i. **Byrne** c(p)-17, 43, 58, 101, 102. **Giffen** a-120p. **Hembeck** c/a-86p. **Miller** c-46p, 48p, 50, 51p, 52p, 54p, 55, 56p, 57, 60. **Mooney** a-7i, 11i, 21p, 23p, 25p, 26p, 29-34p, 36p, 37p, 39i, 41, 42i, 49p, 50i, 51i, 53p, 54-57i, 59-66i, 68i, 71i, 73-79i, 81-83i, 85i, 87-99i, 102i, 125p, Annual 1i, 2p. **Nasser** c-37p. **Perez** c-10. **Simonson** c-54i.*

SPECTACULAR STORIES MAGAZINE (Formerly A Star Presentation)
No. 4, July, 1950 - No. 3, Sept, 1950
Fox Feature Sydicate (Hero Books)

	GD25	FN65	NM94
4-Sherlock Holmes	23.00	70.00	160.00
3-The St. Valentine's Day Massacre	14.00	43.00	100.00

Spectre #11, © DC

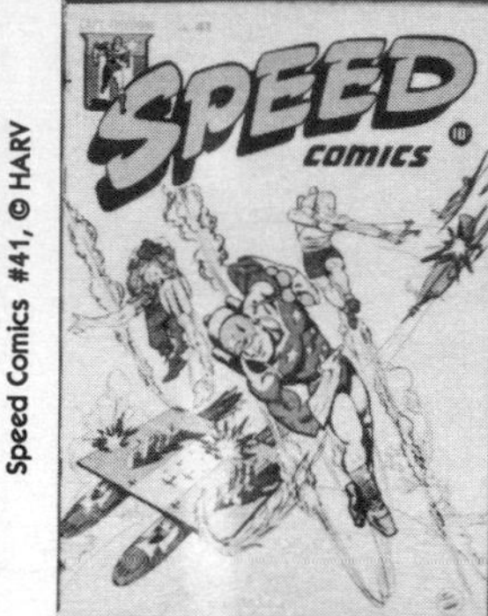
Speed Comics #41, © HARV

Spelljammer #3 (DC), © TSR

SPECTRE, THE (See Adventure Comics 431, More Fun & Showcase)
Nov-Dec, 1967 - No. 10, May-June, 1969 (All 12 cents)
National Periodical Publications

	GD25	FN65	NM94
Showcase #60 (1-2/66)-1st Silver Age app. The Spectre; Murphy Anderson-a; origin in text	20.00	60.00	140.00
Showcase #61 (3-4/66,)-2nd app. The Spectre by Murphy Anderson	11.00	34.00	80.00
Showcase #64 (9010/66)-3rd app. by Anderson	11.00	32.00	75.00
Brave and the Bold #72 (6-7/67)-4th app. Spectre	2.40	7.25	17.00
1-(11-12/67)-Anderson-c/a	9.00	28.00	65.00
2-5-Neal Adams-c/a; 3-Wildcat x-over	6.00	18.00	42.00
6-8,10: 6-8-Anderson inks. 7-Hourman app.	2.40	7.25	17.00
9-Wrightson-a	3.20	8.00	20.00

SPECTRE, THE (DC 1987-'89)(Value: cover or less)

SPECTRE, THE (Also see Brave and the Bold #72, 75, 116, 180, 199)
Dec, 1992 - Present ($1.75, color)
DC Comics

	GD25	FN65	NM94
1-($1.95)-Glow-in-the-dark-c; Mandrake-a begins		1.20	3.00
2-7,9-12,14-16: 10-Kaluta-c. 11-Hildebrandt painted-c		.70	1.75
8,13-($2.50)-Glow-in-the-dark-c		1.00	2.50

SPEEDBALL (See Amazing Spider-Man Annual #12, Marvel Super-Heroes & The New Warriors)
Sept, 1988(10/88-inside) - No. 11, July, 1989 (75 cents, color)
Marvel Comics

	GD25	FN65	NM94
1-11: Ditko/Guice a-1-4, c-1; Ditko a-1-10; c-1-11p			1.00

SPEED BUGGY (TV)(Also see Fun-In #12, 15)
July, 1975 - No. 9, Nov, 1976 (Hanna-Barbera)
Charlton Comics

	GD25	FN65	NM94
1		1.20	3.00
2-9			1.50

SPEED CARTER SPACEMAN (See Spaceman)

SPEED COMICS (New Speed)(Also see Double Up)
10/39 - #11, 8/40; #12, 3/41 - #44, 1-2/47 (#14-16: pocket size, 100 pgs.)
Brookwood Publ./Speed Publ./Harvey Publications No. 14 on

	GD25	FN65	NM94
1-Origin & 1st app. Shock Gibson; Ted Parrish, the Man with 1000 Faces begins; Powell-a	117.00	350.00	780.00
2-Powell-a	58.00	175.00	380.00
3	37.00	110.00	240.00
4,5: 4-Powell-a?	31.00	92.00	200.00
6-11: 7-Mars Mason begins, ends #11	26.00	78.00	175.00
12 (3/41; shows #11 in indicia)-The Wasp begins; Major Colt app. (Capt. Colt #12)	31.00	92.00	200.00
13-Intro. Captain Freedom & Young Defenders; Girl Commandos, Pat Parker (costumed heroine), War Nurse begins; Major Colt app.	37.00	110.00	250.00
14-16 (100 pg. pocket size, 1941): 14-2nd Harvey comic (See Pocket); Shock Gibson dons new costume. 15-Pat Parker dons costume, last in costume #23; no Girl Commandos	29.00	88.00	200.00
17-Black Cat begins (4/42, early app.; see Pocket #1); origin Black Cat-r/ Pocket #1; not in #40,41	46.00	138.00	310.00
18-20	25.00	75.00	170.00
21,22,25-30: 26-Flag-c	22.00	65.00	150.00
23-Origin Girl Commandos	31.00	92.00	210.00
24-Pat Parker team-up with Girl Commandos	22.00	65.00	150.00
31-44: 31-Hitler & Hirohito-c. 38-Flag-c	18.00	55.00	125.00

NOTE: ***Al Avison*** *c-14-16, 30, 43.* ***Briefer*** *a-6, 7.* ***Jon Henri*** *(Kirbyesque) c-17-20.* ***Kubert*** *a-7-11(Mars Mason), 37, 38, 42-44.* ***Kirby/Caseneuve*** *c-21-23.* ***Palais*** *c-37, 39-42.* ***Powell*** *a-1, 2, 4-7, 28, 31, 44.* ***Schomburg*** *c-31-36.* ***Tuska*** *a-3, 6, 7. Bondage c-18, 35. Captain Freedom c-16-24, 25(part), 26-44(w/Black Cat #27, 29, 31, 32-40). Shock Gibson c-1-15.*

SPEED DEMONS (Formerly Frank Merriwell at Yale #1-4?; Submarine Attack #11 on)
No. 5, Feb, 1957 - No. 10, 1958
Charlton Comics

	GD25	FN65	NM94
5-10	2.40	6.00	12.00

SPEED RACER (Now)(Value: cover or less)

SPEED RACER FEATURING NINJA HIGH SCHOOL (Now)(Value: cover or less)

SPEED SMITH THE HOT ROD KING (Also see Hot Rod King)
Spring, 1952
Ziff-Davis Publishing Co.

	GD25	FN65	NM94
1-Saunders painted-c	13.00	40.00	90.00

SPEEDY GONZALES (See 4-Color #1084)

SPEEDY RABBIT (See Television Puppet Show)
nd (1953); 1963
Realistic/I. W. Enterprises/Super Comics

	GD25	FN65	NM94
nn (1953)-Realistic Reprint?	1.60	4.00	8.00
I.W. Reprint #1 (2 versions w/diff. c/stories exist)	.60	1.50	3.00
Super Reprint #14(1963)	.60	1.50	3.00

SPELLBINDERS (Quality)(Value: cover or less)

SPELLBOUND (See The Crusaders)

SPELLBOUND (Tales to Hold You... #1, Stories to Hold You...)
Mar, 1952 - #23, June, 1954; #24, Oct, 1955 - #34, June, 1957
Atlas Comics (ACI 1-15/Male 16-23/BPC 24-34)

	GD25	FN65	NM94
1-Horror/weird stories in all	34.00	105.00	240.00
2-Edgar A. Poe app.	16.00	50.00	115.00
3-5: 3-Whitney-a; cannibalism story	14.00	43.00	100.00
6-Krigstein-a	14.00	43.00	100.00
7-10: 8-Ayers-a	11.00	32.00	75.00
11-16,18-20: 14-Ed Win-a	10.00	30.00	60.00
17-Krigstein-a	10.00	30.00	70.00
21-23: 23-Last precode (6/54)	9.15	27.50	55.00
24-28,30,31,34: 25-Orlando-a	7.50	22.50	45.00
29-Ditko-a (4 pgs.)	9.15	27.50	55.00
32,33-Torres-a	8.35	25.00	50.00

NOTE: ***Brodsky*** *a-5; c-1, 5-7, 10, 11, 13, 15, 25-27, 32.* ***Colan*** *a-17.* ***Everett*** *a-2, 5, 7, 10, 16, 28, 31; c-2, 8, 9, 14, 17-19, 28, 30.* ***Forgione/Abel*** *a-29.* ***Forte/Fox*** *a-16.* ***Al Hartley*** *a-2.* ***Heath*** *a-2, 4, 8, 9, 12, 14, 16; c-3, 4, 12, 16, 20, 21.* ***Infantino*** *a-15.* ***Keller*** *a-5.* ***Kida*** *a-2, 14.* ***Maneely*** *a-7, 14, 27; c-24, 29, 31.* ***Mooney*** *a-5, 13, 18.* ***Mac Pakula*** *a-22, 32.* ***Post*** *a-8.* ***Powell*** *a-19, 20, 32.* ***Robinson*** *a-1.* ***Romita*** *a-24, 26, 27.* ***R.Q. Sale*** *a-29.* ***Sekowsky*** *a-5.* ***Severin*** *c-29.* ***Sinnott*** *a-8, 16, 17.*

SPELLBOUND (Marvel, 1988)(Value: cover or less)

SPELLJAMMER (DC)(Value: cover or less)

SPENCER SPOOK (Formerly Giggle Comics; see Advs. of...)
No. 100, Mar-Apr, 1955 - No. 101, May-June, 1955
American Comics Group

	GD25	FN65	NM94
100,101	4.20	12.50	25.00

SPIDER, THE (Eclipse)(Value: cover or less)

SPIDER-MAN (See Amazing..., Giant-Size..., Marvel Tales, Marvel Team-Up, Spectacular..., Spidey Super Stories, Venom, & Web Of...)

SPIDER-MAN
Aug, 1990 - Present ($1.75, color)
Marvel Comics

	GD25	FN65	NM94
1-Silver edition, direct sale only (unbagged)	1.00	2.50	6.00
1-Silver bagged edition; direct sale, no price on comic, but $2.00 on plastic bag (125,000 print run)	3.20	8.00	20.00
1-Regular edition w/Spidey face in UPC area (unbagged); green-c		1.80	4.50
1-Regular bagged edition w/Spidey face in UPC area; green cover (125,000)	1.65	4.00	10.00
1-Newsstand bagged w/UPC code		1.90	4.75
1-Gold edition, 2nd printing (unbagged) with Spider-Man in box (400,000-450,000)		1.80	4.50
1-Gold 2nd printing w/UPC code; sold in Wal-Mart; not scarce		1.40	3.50

1-Platinum ed. mailed to retailers only (10,000 print run); has new McFarlane-a

Spider-Man #37, © MEG

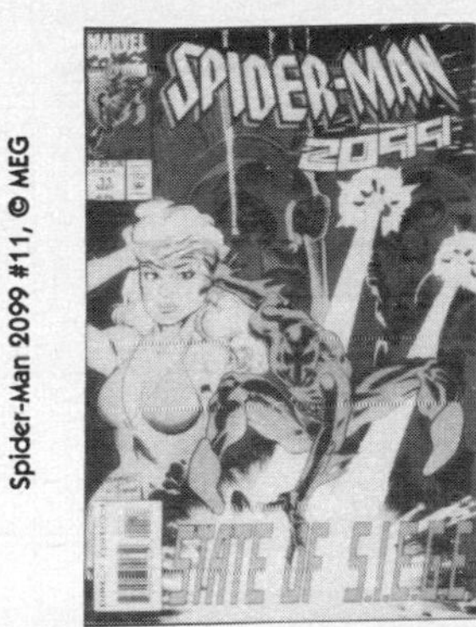

Spider-Man 2099 #11, © MEG

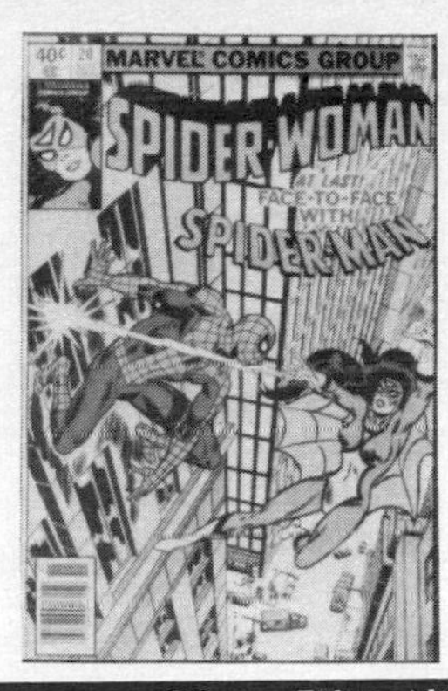

Spider-Woman #20, © MEG

GD25 FN65 NM94

& editorial material instead of ads; stiff-c, no cover price 250.00
2-McFarlane-c/a/scripts continue 1.80 4.50
3-5 1.10 2.75
6,7-Ghost Rider & Hobgoblin app. 1.90 4.75
8-Wolverine cameo; Wolverine storyline begins 1.10 2.75
9-12: 12-Wolverine storyline ends 1.10 2.75
13-Spidey's black costume returns 1.00 2.00 5.00
14,15: 15-Erik Larsen c/a; Beast c/story .80 2.00
16-X-Force-c/story w/Liefeld assists; continues in X-Force #4; reads sideways; last McFarlane issue 1.00 2.50
17-Thanos-c/story; Leonardi/Williamson-c/a 1.00 2.50
18-23,25: 13,14-Spidey in black costume. 18-Ghost Rider-c/story. 18-23-Sinister Six storyline w/Erik Larsen-c/a/scripts. 19-Hulk & Hobgoblin-c & app. 20-22-Deathlok app. 22-Ghost Rider, Hulk, Hobgoblin app. 23-Wraparound gatefold-c. 24-Infinity War x-over w/Demogoblin & Hobgoblin-c/story .70 1.75
24-Demogoblin dons new costume & battles Hobgoblin-c/story .40 1.00 2.00
26-($3.50, 52 pgs.)-Hologram-c w/gatefold poster by Ron Lim; Spidey retells his origin .70 1.75 3.50
27-44: 32-34-Punisher-c/story. 37-Maximum Carnage x-over. 41,42-Iron Fist app.; Jae Lee-c/a in #41-43 .65 1.60
Special Edition 1 (12/92-c, 11/92 inside)-The Trial of Venom; ordered thru mail with $5.00 donation or more to UNICEF; contains bound-in poster 1.65 4.00 10.00

NOTE: *Erik Larsen c/a-15, 18-23.* ***M. Rogers/Keith Williams*** *c/a-27, 28.*

SPIDER-MAN AND DAREDEVIL
March, 1984 ($2.00, one-shot, deluxe paper)
Marvel Comics Group
1-r/Spectacular Spider-Man #26-28 by Miller 1.20 3.00

SPIDER-MAN AND HIS AMAZING FRIENDS
Dec, 1981 (One shot) (See Marvel Action Universe)
Marvel Comics Group
1-Adapted from NBC TV cartoon show; Green Goblin-c/story; 1st Spidey, Firestar, Iceman team-up; Spiegle-p 1.20 3.00

SPIDER-MAN AND THE INCREDIBLE HULK (See listing under Amazing...)

SPIDER-MAN: CARNAGE
June, 1993 ($6.95, color, spot varnish-c)
Marvel Comics
nn-r/Amazing Spider-Man #344,345,359-363 1.20 3.00 7.00

SPIDER-MAN CLASSICS
Apr, 1993 - Present ($1.25, color)
Marvel Comics
1-12: 1-r/Amaz. Fantasy #15. 2-12-r/Amaz. Spider-Man #1-11. 6-Austin-c(i) 1.25

SPIDER-MAN COMICS MAGAZINE
Jan, 1987 - No. 13, 1988 ($1.50, Digest-size)
Marvel Comics Group
1-13-Reprints 1.50

SPIDER-MAN/DR. STRANGE: THE WAY TO DUSTY DEATH
1992 ($6.95, 68 pgs.)
Marvel Comics
nn 1.20 3.00 7.00

SPIDER-MAN MAGAZINE
1994 - Present ($1.95, color, magazine)
Marvel Comics
1-Bound with trading card sheet; Romita, Sr.-a .80 2.00

SPIDER-MAN: MUTANT AGENDA
Mar, 1994 - No. 3, May, 1994 ($1.75, color, mini-series)
Marvel Comics
0-($1.25)-Crosses over w/newspaper strip 1.25

GD25 FN65 NM94

1-3 .70 1.75

SPIDER-MAN SAGA (Marvel)(Value: cover or less)

SPIDER-MAN 2099 (See Amazing Spider-Man #365)
Nov, 1992 - Present ($1.25, color)
Marvel Comics
1-($1.75, stiff-c)-Red foil stamped-c; begins origin of Miguel O'Hara (Spider-Man 2099); Leonardi/Williamson-c/a begins 1.10 2.75
2-Origin continued, ends #3 1.00 2.50
3,4: 4-Doom 2099 app. .80 2.00
5-18: 13-Extra 16 pg. insert on Midnight Sons 1.25

SPIDER-MAN UNLIMITED
May, 1993 - Present ($3.95, color, quarterly, 68 pgs.)
Marvel Comics
1-4: 1-Begin Maximum Carnage storyline, ends #2, Ron Lim-c/a(p) in #1. 2-Lim-c(p) 1.60 4.00

SPIDER-MAN VS. DRACULA
Jan, 1994 ($1.75, color, 52 pgs.)
Marvel Comics
1-r/Giant-Size Spider-Man #1 plus new Matt Fox-a .70 1.75

SPIDER-MAN VS. VENOM
1990 ($8.95, trade paperback)
Marvel Comics
nn-r/Amazing Spider-Man #300,315-317 w/new McFarlane-c 1.50 3.75 9.00

SPIDER-MAN VS. WOLVERINE
Feb, 1987 (One-shot); V2#1, 1990 (Both have 68 pgs.)
Marvel Comics Group
1-Williamson-c/a(i); intro Charlemagne; death of Ned Leeds (old Hobgoblin) 3.20 8.00 20.00
V2#1 (1990, $4.95)-Reprints #1 (2/87) 1.00 2.00 5.00

SPIDER REIGN OF THE VAMPIRE KING, THE (Also see The Spider)
1992 - No. 3, 1992 ($4.95, color, coated stock, mini-series, 52 pgs.)
Eclipse Books
Book One - Three: Truman scripts & painted-c 1.00 2.00 5.00

SPIDER'S WEB, THE (See G-8 and His Battle Aces)

SPIDER-WOMAN (Also see The Avengers #240, Marvel Spotlight #32, Marvel Super Heroes Secret Wars #7 & Marvel Two-In-One #29)
April, 1978 - No. 50, June, 1983 (New logo #47 on)
Marvel Comics Group
1-New complete origin & mask added 1.60 4.00
2-36,39-49: 6,19-Werewolf by Night app. 20,28,29-Spider-Man app. 46-Kingpin app. 49-Tigra app. 1.50
37,38-X-Men x-over; 37-1st app. Siryn of X-Force; origin retold 1.20 3.00
50-(52 pgs.)-Death of Spider-Woman; photo-c 1.20 3.00
NOTE: ***Austin*** *a-37i.* ***Byrne*** *c-26p.* ***Layton*** *c-19.* ***Miller*** *c-32p.*

SPIDER-WOMAN
Nov, 1993 - No. 4, Feb, 1994 ($1.75, color, mini-series)
Marvel Comics
V2#1-4: 1,2-Origin; U.S. Agent app. .70 1.75

SPIDEY SUPER STORIES (Spider-Man)
Oct, 1974 - No. 57, Mar, 1982 (35 cents) (no ads)
Marvel/Children's TV Workshop
1-Origin (stories simplified) 1.10 2.75
2-12: 2-Kraven. 6-Iceman .75 1.90
13-38,40-44,46-57: 31-Moondragon-c/story; Dr. Doom app. 33-Hulk. 34-Sub-Mariner. 38-F.F. 44-Vision. 56-Battles Jack O'Lantern-c/story (exactly one year after 1st app. in Machine Man #19) .70 1.75
39-Thanos-c/story 1.00 2.50
45-Silver Surfer & Dr. Doom app. 1.00 2.50

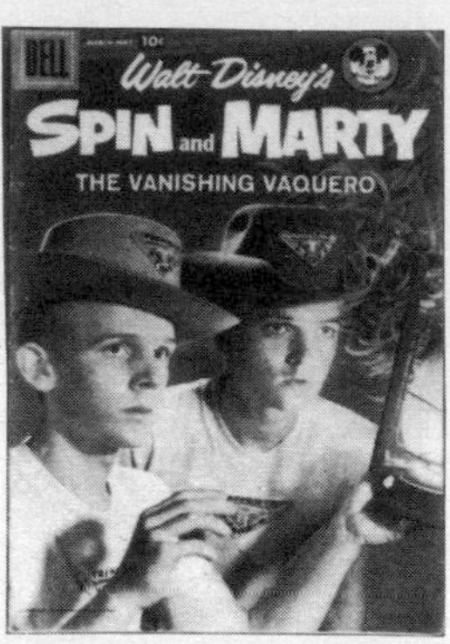

Spin & Marty #5, © WDC

The Spirit, 8/11/40, © Will Eisner

The Spirit, 8/1/48, © Will Eisner

SPIKE AND TYKE (See M.G.M.'s...)

SPIN & MARTY (TV) (Walt Disney's)(See Walt Disney Showcase #32)
No. 714, June, 1956 - No. 1082, Mar-May, 1960 (All photo-c)
Dell Publishing Co. (Mickey Mouse Club)

	GD25	FN65	NM94
4-Color 714 (#1)	10.00	30.00	65.00
4-Color 767,808 (#2,3)	6.70	20.00	40.00
4-Color 826 (#4)-Annette Funicello photo-c	12.00	36.00	85.00
5(3-5/58) - 9(6-8/59)	6.70	20.00	40.00
4-Color 1026,1082	6.70	20.00	40.00

SPINE-TINGLING TALES (Doctor Spektor Presents...)
May, 1975 - No. 4, Jan, 1976 (All 25 cent issues)
Gold Key

	GD25	FN65	NM94
1-4: 1-1st Tragg-r/Mystery Comics Digest #3. 2-Origin Ra-Ka-Tep-r/Mystery Comics Digest #1; Dr. Spektor #12. 3-All Durak-r issue; 4-Baron Tibor's 1st app.-r/Mystery Comics Digest #4			1.00

SPIRAL PATH, THE (Eclipse)(Value: cover or less)

SPIRAL ZONE
Feb, 1988 - No. 4, May, 1988 ($1.00, mini-series)
DC Comics

	GD25	FN65	NM94
1-4-Based on Tonka toys			1.00

SPIRIT, THE (Weekly Comic Book)
6/2/40 - 10/5/52 (16 pgs.; 8 pgs.) (no cover) (in color)
(Distributed through various newspapers and other sources)
Will Eisner
NOTE: **Eisner** script, pencils/inks for the most part from 6/2/40-4/26/42; a few stories assisted by Jack Cole, Fine, Powell and Kotsky.

	GD25	FN65	NM94
6/2/40(#1)-Origin/1st app. The Spirit; reprinted in Police #11; Lady Luck (Brenda Banks)(1st app.) by Chuck Mazoujian & Mr. Mystic (1st. app.) by S. R. (Bob) Powell begin	60.00	180.00	420.00
6/9/40(#2)	26.00	78.00	180.00
6/16/40(#3)-Black Queen app. in Spirit	17.00	51.00	110.00
6/23/40(#4)-Mr. Mystic receives magical necklace	13.00	40.00	90.00
6/30/40(#5)	13.00	40.00	90.00
7/7/40(#6)-Black Queen app. in Spirit	13.00	40.00	90.00
7/14/40(#7)-8/4/40(#10)	10.00	30.50	70.00
8/11/40-9/22/40	9.00	27.00	62.00
9/29/40-Ellen drops engagement with Homer Creep	8.00	24.00	56.00
10/6/40-11/3/40	8.00	24.00	56.00
11/10/40-The Black Queen app.	8.00	24.00	56.00
11/17/40, 11/24/40	8.00	24.00	56.00
12/1/40-Ellen spanking by Spirit on cover & inside; Eisner-1st 3 pgs., J. Cole rest	11.50	34.00	80.00
12/8/40-3/9/41	5.70	17.00	40.00
3/16/41-Intro. & 1st app. Silk Satin	10.00	30.00	70.00
3/23/41-6/1/41: 5/11/41-Last Lady Luck by Mazoujian; 5/18/41-Lady Luck by Nick Viscardi begins, ends 2/22/42	5.70	17.00	40.00
6/8/41-2nd app. Satin; Spirit learns Satin is also a British agent	8.50	25.50	60.00
6/15/41-1st app. Twilight	7.00	21.00	50.00
6/22/41-Hitler app. in Spirit	5.00	15.00	35.00
6/29/41-1/25/42,2/8/42	5.00	15.00	35.00
2/1/42-1st app. Duchess	7.00	21.00	50.00
2/15/42-4/26/42-Lady Luck by Klaus Nordling begins 3/1/42	5.00	15.00	35.00
5/3/42-8/16/42-Eisner/Fine/Quality staff assists on Spirit	4.00	12.00	24.00
8/23/42-Satin cover splash; Spirit by Eisner/Fine although signed by Fine	8.00	24.00	56.00
8/30/42,9/27/42-10/11/42,10/25/42-11/8/42-Eisner/Fine/Quality staff assists on Spirit	4.00	12.00	24.00
9/6/42-9/20/42,10/18/42-Fine/Belfi art on Spirit; scripts by Manly Wade Wellman	2.75	8.00	16.00
11/15/42-12/6/42,12/20/42,12/27/42,1/17/43-4/18/43,5/9/43-8/8/43-Wellman/Woolfolk scripts, Fine pencils, Quality staff inks	2.75	8.00	16.00
12/13/42,1/3/43,1/10/43,4/25/43,5/2/43-Eisner scripts/layouts; Fine pencils, Quality staff inks	3.35	10.00	20.00
8/15/43-Eisner script/layout; pencils/inks by Quality staff; Jack Cole-a	2.00	6.00	12.00
8/22/43-12/12/43-Wellman/Woolfolk scripts, Fine pencils, Quality staff inks; Mr. Mystic by Guardineer-10/10/43-10/24/43	2.00	6.00	12.00
12/19/43-8/13/44-Wellman/Woolfolk/Jack Cole scripts; Cole, Fine & Robin King-a; Last Mr. Mystic-5/14/44	1.70	5.00	10.00
8/20/44-12/16/45-Wellman/Woolfolk scripts; Fine art with unknown staff assists	1.70	5.00	10.00

NOTE: *Scripts/layouts by Eisner, or Eisner/Nordling, Eisner/Mercer or Spranger/Eisner; inks by Eisner or Eisner/Spranger in issues 12/23/45-2/2/47.*

	GD25	FN65	NM94
12/23/45-1/6/46: 12/23/45-Christmas-c	3.50	10.50	24.00
1/13/46-Origin Spirit retold	5.00	15.00	35.00
1/20/46-1st postwar Satin app.	4.50	14.00	32.00
1/27/46-3/10/46: 3/3/46-Last Lady Luck by Nordling	3.50	10.50	24.00
3/17/46-Intro. & 1st app. Nylon	4.50	14.00	32.00
3/24/46,3/31/46,4/14/46	3.50	10.50	24.00
4/7/46-2nd app. Nylon	4.00	12.00	28.00
4/21/46-Intro. & 1st app. Mr. Carrion & His Pet Buzzard Julia	5.00	15.00	35.00
4/28/46-5/12/46,5/26/46-6/30/46: Lady Luck by Fred Schwab in issues 5/5/46-11/3/46	3.50	10.50	24.00
5/19/46-2nd app. Mr. Carrion	4.00	12.00	28.00
7/7/46-Intro. & 1st app. Dulcet Tone & Skinny	5.00	15.00	35.00
7/14/46-9/29/46	3.50	10.50	24.00
10/6/46-Intro. & 1st app. P'Gell	5.70	17.00	40.00
10/13/46-11/3/46,11/16/46-11/24/46	3.50	10.50	24.00
11/10/46-2nd app. P'Gell	4.00	12.00	28.00
12/1/46-3rd app. P'Gell	3.70	11.00	26.00
12/8/46-2/2/47	3.00	9.00	21.00

NOTE: *Scripts, pencils/inks by Eisner except where noted in issues 2/9/47-12/19/48.*

	GD25	FN65	NM94
2/9/47-7/6/47: 6/8/47-Eisner self satire	3.00	9.00	21.00
7/13/47-"Hansel & Gretel" fairy tales	4.50	14.00	32.00
7/20/47-Li'L Abner, Daddy Warbucks, Dick Tracy, Fearless Fosdick parody; A-Bomb blast-c	4.50	14.00	32.00
7/27/47-9/14/47	3.00	9.00	21.00
9/21/47-Pearl Harbor flashback	3.00	9.00	21.00
9/28/47-1st mention of Flying Saucers in comics-3 months after 1st sighting in Idaho on 6/25/47	6.50	19.00	45.00
10/5/47-"Cinderella" fairy tales	4.50	14.00	32.00
10/12/47-11/30/47	3.00	9.00	21.00
12/7/47-Intro. & 1st app. Powder Pouf	5.00	15.00	35.00
12/14/47-12/28/47	3.00	9.00	21.00
1/4/48-2nd app. Powder Pouf	4.00	12.00	28.00
1/11/48-1st app. Sparrow Fallon; Powder Pouf app.	4.00	12.00	28.00
1/18/48-He-Man ad cover; satire issue	4.00	12.00	28.00
1/25/48-Intro. & 1st app. Castanet	4.50	14.00	32.00
2/1/48-2nd app. Castanet	3.50	10.50	24.00
2/8/48-3/7/48	3.00	9.00	21.00
3/14/48-Only app. Kretchma	3.50	10.50	24.00
3/21/48,3/28/48,4/11/48-4/25/48	3.00	9.00	21.00
4/4/48-Only app. Wild Rice	3.50	10.50	24.00
5/2/48-2nd app. Sparrow	3.00	9.00	21.00
5/9/48-6/27/48,7/11/48,7/18/48: 6/13/48-Television issue	3.00	9.00	21.00
7/4/48-Spirit by Andre Le Blanc	2.00	6.00	14.00
7/25/48-Ambrose Bierce's "The Thing" adaptation classic by Eisner/Grandenetti	6.50	19.00	45.00
8/1/48-8/15/48,8/29/48-9/12/48	3.00	9.00	21.00
8/22/48-Poe's "Fall of the House of Usher" classic by Eisner/Grandenetti	6.50	19.00	45.00
9/19/48-Only app. Lorelei	3.70	11.00	26.00
9/26/48-10/31/48	3.00	9.00	21.00
11/7/48-Only app. Plaster of Paris	4.00	12.00	28.00
11/14/48-12/19/48	3.00	9.00	21.00

NOTE: *Scripts by Eisner or Feiffer or Eisner/Feiffer or Nordling. Art by Eisner with*

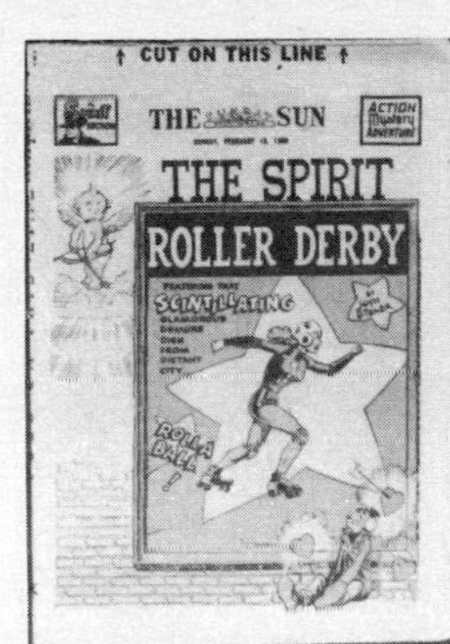

The Spirit, 2/12/50, © Will Eisner

The Spirit, #18 (Qualty), © Will Eisner

The Spirit, #12 (Kitchen Sink), © Will Eisner

	GD25	FN65	NM94
backgrounds by Eisner, Grandenetti, Le Blanc, Stallman, Nordling, Dixon and/or others in issues 12/26/48-4/1/51 except where noted.			
12/26/48-Reprints some covers of 1948 with flashbacks	3.00	9.00	21.00
1/2/49-1/10/49	3.00	9.00	21.00
1/23/49,1/30/49-1st & 2nd app. Thorne	4.00	12.00	28.00
2/6/49-8/14/49	3.00	9.00	21.00
8/21/49,8/28/49-1st & 2nd app. Monica Veto	4.00	12.00	28.00
9/4/49,9/11/49	3.00	9.00	21.00
9/18/49-Love comic cover; has gag love comic ads on inside	4.30	13.00	30.00
9/25/49-Only app. Ice	3.70	11.00	26.00
10/2/49,10/9/49-Autumn News appears & dies in 10/9 issue	3.70	11.00	26.00
10/16/49-11/27/49,12/18/49,12/25/49	3.00	9.00	21.00
12/4/49,12/11/49-1st & 2nd app. Flaxen	4.00	12.00	24.00
1/1/50-Flashbacks to all of the Spirit girls-Thorne, Ellen, Satin, & Monica	5.00	15.00	35.00
1/8/50-Intro. & 1st app. Sand Saref	7.00	21.00	50.00
1/15/50-2nd app. Saref	5.00	15.00	35.00
1/22/50-2/5/50	3.00	9.00	21.00
2/12/50-Roller Derby issue	3.50	10.50	24.00
2/19/50-Half Dead Mr. Lox - Classic horror	3.70	11.00	26.00
2/26/50-4/23/50,5/14/50,5/28/50,7/23/50-9/3/50	3.00	9.00	21.00
4/30/50-Script/art by Le Blanc with Eisner framing	1.70	5.00	10.00
5/7/50,6/4/50-7/16/50-Abe Kanegson-a	1.70	5.00	10.00
5/21/50-Script by Feiffer/Eisner, art by Blaisdell, Eisner framing	1.70	5.00	10.00
9/10/50-P'Gell returns	4.00	12.00	28.00
9/17/50-1/7/51	3.00	9.00	21.00
1/14/51-Life Magazine cover; brief biography of Comm. Dolan, Sand Saref, Silk Satin, P'Gell, Sammy & Willum, Darling O'Shea, & Mr. Carrion & His Pet Buzzard Julia, with pin-ups by Eisner	3.70	11.00	26.00
1/21/51,2/4/51-4/1/51	3.00	9.00	21.00
1/28/51-"The Meanest Man in the World" classic by Eisner	3.70	11.00	26.00
4/8/51-7/29/51,8/12/51-Last Eisner issue	3.00	9.00	21.00
8/5/51,8/19/51-7/20/52-Not Eisner	1.70	5.00	10.00
7/27/52-(Rare)-Denny Colt in Outer Space by Wally Wood; 7 pg. S/F story of E.C. vintage	32.00	95.00	225.00
8/3/52-(Rare)-"Mission...The Moon" by Wood	32.00	95.00	225.00
8/10/52-(Rare)-"A DP On The Moon" by Wood	32.00	95.00	225.00
8/17/52-(Rare)-"Heart" by Wood/Eisner	27.00	81.00	190.00
8/24/52-(Rare)-"Rescue" by Wood	32.00	95.00	225.00
8/31/52-(Rare)-"The Last Man" by Wood	32.00	95.00	225.00
9/7/52-(Rare)-"The Man in The Moon" by Wood	32.00	95.00	225.00
9/14/52-(Rare)-Eisner/Wenzel-a	6.50	19.00	45.00
9/21/52-(Rare)-"Denny Colt, Alias The Spirit/Space Report" by Eisner/Wenzel	11.50	34.00	80.00
9/28/52-(Rare)-"Return From The Moon" by Wood	32.00	95.00	225.00
10/5/52-(Rare)-"The Last Story" by Eisner	11.50	34.00	80.00

Large Tabloid pages from 1946 on (Eisner) - Price 30 percent over listed prices.

NOTE: *Spirit sections came out in both large and small format. Some newspapers went to the 8-pg. format months before others. Some printed the pages so they cannot be folded into a small comic book section; these are worth less. (Also see Three Comics & Spiritman).*

SPIRIT, THE (1st Series)(Also see Police Comics #11)
1944 - No. 22, Aug, 1950
Quality Comics Group (Vital)

	GD25	FN65	NM94
nn(#1)-"Wanted Dead or Alive"	54.00	160.00	375.00
nn(#2)-"Crime Doesn't Pay"	32.00	95.00	220.00
nn(#3)-"Murder Runs Wild"	24.00	73.00	170.00
4,5: 4-Flatfoot Burns begins, ends #22	18.00	54.00	125.00
6-10	16.00	48.00	110.00
11	14.00	43.00	100.00
12-17-Eisner-c. 19-Honeybun app.	24.00	73.00	170.00
18-21-Strip-r by Eisner; Eisner-c	33.00	100.00	230.00
22-Used by N.Y. Legis. Comm; classic Eisner-c	46.00	137.00	320.00
Super Reprint #11-r/Quality Spirit #19 by Eisner	2.80	7.00	14.00
Super Reprint #12-r/Spirit #17 by Fine; Simon-c	2.40	6.00	12.00

SPIRIT, THE (2nd Series)
Spring, 1952 - No. 5, 1954
Fiction House Magazines

	GD25	FN65	NM94
1-Not Eisner	26.00	80.00	180.00
2-Eisner-c/a(2)	27.00	80.00	185.00
3-Eisner/Grandenetti-c	17.00	52.00	120.00
4-Eisner/Grandenetti-c; Eisner-a	20.00	60.00	140.00
5-Eisner-c/a(4)	26.00	77.00	180.00

SPIRIT, THE
Oct, 1966 - No. 2, Mar, 1967 (Giant Size, 25 cents, 68 pgs.)
Harvey Publications

	GD25	FN65	NM94
1-Eisner-r plus 9 new pgs (origin Denny Colt, Take 3, plus 2 filler pages) (#3 was advertised, but never published)	4.30	13.00	30.00
2-Eisner-r plus 9 new pgs.(origin of the Octopus)	4.30	13.00	30.00

SPIRIT, THE (Underground)
Jan, 1973 - No. 2, Sept, 1973 (Black & White)
Kitchen Sink Enterprises (Krupp Comics)

	GD25	FN65	NM94
1-New Eisner-c, 4 pgs. new Eisner-a plus-r (titled Crime Convention)	1.30	3.25	8.00
2-New Eisner-c, 4 pgs. new Eisner-a plus-r (titled Meets P'Gell)	1.65	4.00	10.00

SPIRIT, THE (Magazine)
4/74 - No. 16, 10/76; No. 17, Winter, 1977 - No. 41, 6/83 (B&W w/color)
Warren Publ. Co./Krupp Comic Works No. 17 on

	GD25	FN65	NM94
1-Eisner-r begin	1.00	2.00	5.00
2-5		1.20	3.00
6-9,11-16: 7-All Ebony issue. 8-Female Foes issue. 12-X-Mas issue. 16-Giant Summer Special ($1.50)		.90	2.40
10-Giant Summer Special ($1.50)-Origin		1.10	2.80
17,18(8/78): 17-Lady Luck-r. 20-Outer Space-r			1.20
19-21-New Eisner-a. 20,21-Wood-r (#21-r/A DP on the Moon by Wood)			1.20
22,23-Wood-r (#22-r/Mission the Moon by Wood)			1.20
24-29,31-35: 28-r/last story (10/5/52)			1.20
30 (7/81)-Special Spirit Jam issue w/Caniff, Corben, Bolland, Byrne, Miller, Kurtzman, Rogers, Sienkiewicz-a & 40 others			1.50
36-Begin Spirit Section-r; r/1st story (6/2/40) in color; new Eisner-c/a (18 pgs.)($2.95)		1.20	3.00
37-41: 37-r/2nd story in color plus 18 pgs. new Eisner-a. 38-41: r/3rd - 6th stories in color. 41-Lady Luck Mr. Mystic in color		1.20	3.00
Special 1(1975)-All Eisner-a		.70	1.80

NOTE: *Covers pencilled/inked by* ***Eisner*** *only #1-9,12-16; painted by Eisner & Ken Kelly #10 & 11; painted by Eisner #17-up; one color story reprinted in #1-10.* ***Austin*** *a-30i.* ***Byrne*** *a-30p.* ***Miller*** *a-30p.*

SPIRIT, THE (See Will Eisner's 3-D Classics Featuring...)
Oct, 1983 - No. 87, Jan, 1992 (Baxter paper) ($2.00)
Kitchen Sink Enterprises

	GD25	FN65	NM94
1-4: 1-Origin-r/12/23/45 Spirit Section. 2-r/sections 1/20/46-2/10/46. 3-r/2/17/46-3/10/46. 4-r/3/17/46-4/7/46		.80	2.00
5-11 ($2.95 cover): 11-Last color issue		.80	2.00
12-87 ($1.95-$2.00, B&W): 54-r/section 2/19/50. 85-87-Reprint the Outer Space Spirit stories by Wood. 86-r/A DP on the Moon by Wood from 1952		.80	2.00

SPIRIT: THE ORIGIN YEARS
May, 1992 - Present ($2.95, B&W, high quality paper)
Kitchen Sink Press

	GD25	FN65	NM94
1-4: 1-r/sections 6/2/40(origin)-6/23/40 (all 1940s)		1.20	3.00

SPIRITMAN (Also see Three Comics)

Splitting Image #1, © Image

Spooky #31, © HARV

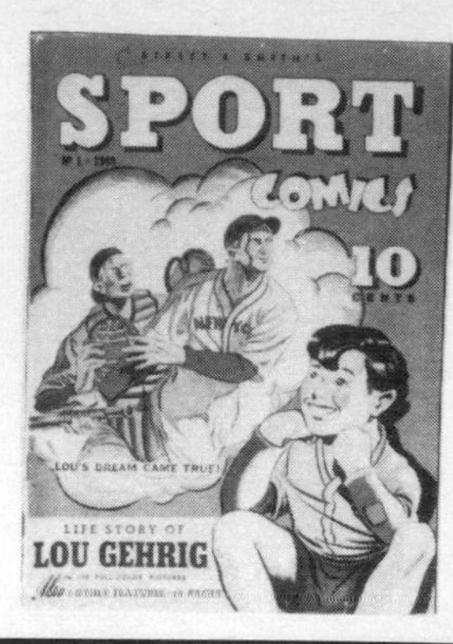

Sport Comics #1, © S & S

GD25 FN65 NM94

No date (1944) (10 cents)
(Triangle Sales Co. ad on back cover)
No publisher listed

1-Three 16pg. Spirit sections bound together, (1944, 10 cents, 52 pgs.) 15.00 45.00 105.00
2-Two Spirit sections (3/26/44, 4/2/44) bound together; by Lou Fine 12.00 36.00 85.00

SPIRIT WORLD (Magazine)
Fall, 1971 (Black & White)
National Periodical Publications

1-Kirby-a; Neal Adams-c 1.00 2.50 6.00

SPITFIRE
No. 132, 1944 (Aug) - No. 133, 1945 (Female undercover agent)
Malverne Herald (Elliot)(J. R. Mahon)

132,133: Both have Classics Gift Box ads on b/c with checklist to #20 13.00 40.00 90.00

SPITFIRE AND THE TROUBLESHOOTERS (Marvel)(Value: cover or less)

SPITFIRE COMICS (Also see Double Up)
Aug, 1941 - No. 2, Oct, 1941 (Pocket size; 100 pgs.)
Harvey Publications

1-Origin The Clown, The Fly-Man, The Spitfire & The Magician From Bagdad 40.00 120.00 265.00
2 35.00 105.00 230.00

SPLITTING IMAGE
Mar, 1993 - No. 2, 1993 ($1.95, color)
Image Comics

1,2-Simpson-c/a; parody comic .80 2.00

SPOOF
Oct, 1970; No. 2, Nov, 1972 - No. 5, May, 1973
Marvel Comics Group

1-Infinity-c; Dark Shadows-c & parody 1.70 4.25
2-5: 3-Beatles, Osmond's, Jackson 5, David Cassidy, Nixon & Agnew-c. 5-Rod Serling, Woody Allen, Ted Kennedy-c .90 2.25

SPOOK (Formerly Shock Detective Cases)
No. 22, Jan, 1953 - No. 30, Oct, 1954
Star Publications

22-Sgt. Spook-r; acid in face story; hanging-c 14.00 43.00 100.00
23,25,27: 27-Two Sgt. Spook-r 10.00 30.00 60.00
24-Used in **SOTI**, pg. 182,183-r/Inside Crime #2; Transvestism story 11.00 32.00 75.00
26-Disbrow-a 10.00 30.00 65.00
28,29-Rulah app. 29-Jo-Jo app. 10.00 30.00 65.00
30-Disbrow-c/a(2); only Star-c 10.00 30.00 65.00

NOTE: ***L. B. Cole** covers-all issues; a-28(1pg.). **Disbrow** a-26(2), 28, 29(2), 30(2); No. 30 r/Blue Bolt Weird Tales #114.*

SPOOK COMICS
1946
Baily Publications/Star

1-Mr. Lucifer story 16.00 48.00 110.00

SPOOKY (The Tuff Little Ghost; see Casper The Friendly Ghost)
11/55 - 139, 11/73; No. 140, 7/74 - No. 155, 3/77; No. 156, 12/77 - No. 158, 4/78; No. 159, 9/78; No. 160, 10/79; No. 161, 9/80
Harvey Publications

1-Nightmare begins (see Casper #19) 24.00 72.00 165.00
2 11.50 34.00 80.00
3-10(1956-57) 6.70 20.00 40.00
11-20(1957-58) 4.00 10.00 20.00
21-40(1958-59) 2.40 6.00 12.00
41-60 1.60 4.00 8.00
61-80 1.10 2.70 6.50
81-120 1.40 3.50
121-126,133-140 .90 2.25
127-132: All 52 pg. Giants 1.40 3.50
141-161 .65 1.60

SPOOKY
1991 - No. 4, 1992 ($1.00/$1.25, color)
Harvey Comics

1-4: 3-Begin $1.25-c 1.25
...Digest 1 (10/92, $1.75)-Casper, Wendy, etc. .70 1.75

SPOOKY HAUNTED HOUSE
Oct, 1972 - No. 15, Feb, 1975
Harvey Publications

1 1.70 5.00 12.00
2-5 1.00 2.50 6.00
6-10 1.20 3.00
11-15 1.50

SPOOKY MYSTERIES
No date (1946) (10 cents)
Your Guide Publ. Co.

1-Mr. Spooky, Super Snooper, Pinky, Girl Detective app. 10.00 30.00 70.00

SPOOKY SPOOKTOWN
9/61; No. 2, 9/62 - No. 52, 12/73; No. 53, 10/74 - No. 66, Dec, 1976
Harvey Publications

1-Casper, Spooky; 68 pgs. begin 10.00 30.00 70.00
2 5.85 17.50 35.00
3-5 4.20 12.50 25.00
6-10 3.00 7.50 15.00
11-20 2.00 5.00 10.00
21-39: Last 68 pg. issue 1.00 2.00 5.00
40-45: All 52 pgs. 1.20 3.00
46-66 .80 2.00

SPORT COMICS (Becomes True Sport Picture Stories #5 on)
Oct, 1940(No mo.) - No. 4, Nov, 1941
Street & Smith Publications

1-Life story of Lou Gehrig 37.00 110.00 250.00
2 18.00 55.00 120.00
3,4 17.00 50.00 110.00

SPORT LIBRARY (See Charlton Sport Library)

SPORTS ACTION (Formerly Sport Stars)
No. 2, Feb, 1950 - No. 14, Sept, 1952
Marvel/Atlas Comics (ACI No. 2,3/SAI No. 4-14)

2-Powell painted-c; George Gipp life story 20.00 60.00 140.00
3-Everett-a 13.00 40.00 90.00
4-11,14: Weiss-a 12.00 35.00 80.00
12,13: 12-Everett-c. 13-Krigstein-a 13.00 40.00 90.00

NOTE: *Title may have changed after No. 3, to Crime Must Lose No. 4 on, due to publisher change. **Sol Brodsky** c-4-7, 13, 14. **Maneely** c-3, 8-11.*

SPORT STARS
Feb-Mar, 1946 - No. 4, Aug-Sept, 1946 (Half comic, half photo magazine)
Parents' Magazine Institute (Sport Stars)

1-"How Tarzan Got That Way" story of Johnny Weissmuller 25.00 75.00 175.00
2-Baseball greats 17.00 50.00 110.00
3,4 13.00 40.00 90.00

SPORT STARS (Becomes Sports Action #2 on)
Nov, 1949 (52 pgs.)
Marvel Comics (ACI)

1-Knute Rockne; painted-c 25.00 75.00 165.00

SPORT THRILLS (Formerly Dick Cole; becomes Jungle thrills #16)
No. 11, Nov, 1950 - No. 15, Nov, 1951
Star Publications

Spotlight Comics #1, © CHES

Spy-Hunters #15, © ACG

Stalkers #1, © MEG

	GD25	FN65	NM94
11-Dick Cole app.; Ted Williams & Ty Cobb life stories	12.00	35.00	75.00
12-L. B. Cole c/a	9.15	27.50	55.00
13-15-All L. B. Cole-c; 13-Dick Cole app. 14-Johnny Weissmuler life story	9.15	27.50	55.00
Accepted Reprint #11 (#15 on-c, nd); L.B. Cole-c	4.00	10.00	20.00
Accepted Reprint #12 (nd); L.B. Cole-c; Joe DiMaggio & Phil Rizzuto life stories	4.00	10.00	20.00

SPOTLIGHT (TV)
Sept, 1978 - No. 4, Mar, 1979 (Hanna-Barbera)
Marvel Comics Group

	GD25	FN65	NM94
1-4: 1-Huckleberry Hound, Yogi Bear; Shaw-a. 2-Quick Draw McGraw. Augie Doggie, Snooper & Blabber. 3-The Jetsons, Yakky Doodle. 4-Magilla Gorilla, Snagglepuss		.80	2.00

SPOTLIGHT COMICS (Becomes Red Seal Comics #14 on?)
Nov, 1944 - No. 3, 1945
Harry 'A' Chesler (Our Army, Inc.)

	GD25	FN65	NM94
1-The Black Dwarf (cont'd in Red Seal?), The Veiled Avenger, & Barry Kuda begin; Tuska-c	35.00	105.00	240.00
2	29.00	85.00	200.00
3-Injury to eye story (reprinted from Scoop #3)	31.00	92.00	215.00

SPOTTY THE PUP (Becomes Super Pup #4, see Television Puppet Show)
No. 2, Oct-Nov, 1953 - No. 3, Dec-Jan, 1953-54 (Also see Funny Tunes)
Avon Periodicals/Realistic Comics

	GD25	FN65	NM94
2,3	4.00	10.00	20.00
nn (1953, Realistic-r)	2.00	5.00	10.00

SPUNKY (...Junior Cowboy)(...Comics #2 on)
April, 1949 - No. 7, Nov, 1951
Standard Comics

	GD25	FN65	NM94
1,2-Text illos by Frazetta	5.85	17.50	35.00
3-7	3.60	9.00	18.00

SPUNKY THE SMILING SPOOK
Aug, 1957 - No. 4, May, 1958
Ajax/Farrell (World Famous Comics/Four Star Comic Corp.)

	GD25	FN65	NM94
1-Reprints from Frisky Fables	5.00	15.00	30.00
2-4	3.60	9.00	18.00

SPY AND COUNTERSPY (Becomes Spy Hunters #3 on)
Aug-Sept, 1949 - No. 2, Oct-Nov, 1949 (52 pgs.)
American Comics Group

	GD25	FN65	NM94
1-Origin, 1st app. Jonathan Kent, Counterspy	12.00	36.00	85.00
2	10.00	30.00	60.00

SPY CASES (Formerly The Kellys)
No. 26, Sept, 1950 - No. 19, Oct, 1953
Marvel/Atlas Comics (Hercules Publ.)

	GD25	FN65	NM94
26 (#1)	11.50	34.00	80.00
27(#2),28(#3, 2/51): 27-Everett-a; bondage-c	8.35	25.00	50.00
4(4/51) - 7,9,10	5.85	17.50	35.00
8-A-Bomb-c/story	7.50	22.50	45.00
11-19: 11-14-War format	4.70	14.00	28.00

NOTE: ***Sol Brodsky** c-1-5, 8, 9, 11-14, 17, 18. **Maneely** a-8; c-7, 10. **Tuska** a-7.*

SPY FIGHTERS
March, 1951 - No. 15, July, 1953
Marvel/Atlas Comics (CSI)

	GD25	FN65	NM94
1-Clark Mason begins; Tuska-a; Brodsky-c	12.00	36.00	85.00
2-Tuska-a	7.00	21.00	42.00
3-13: 3-5-Brodsky-c. 7-Heath-c	5.85	17.50	35.00
14,15-Pakula-a(3), Ed Win-a. 15-Brodsky-c	6.35	19.00	38.00

SPY-HUNTERS (Formerly Spy & Counterspy)
No. 3, Dec-Jan, 1949-50 - No. 24, June-July, 1953 (#3-14: 52 pgs.)
American Comics Group

	GD25	FN65	NM94
3-Jonathan Kent continues, ends #10	12.00	36.00	85.00
4-10: 4,8,10-Starr-a	8.35	25.00	50.00
11-15,17-22,24: 18-War-c begin. 21-War-c/stories begin	5.85	17.50	35.00
16-Williamson-a (9 pgs.)	10.00	30.00	65.00
23-Graphic torture, injury to eye panel	11.00	32.00	75.00

NOTE: ***Drucker** a-12. **Whitney** a-many issues; c-7, 8, 10-12, 15, 16.*

SPYKE (Epic Comics)(Value: cover or less)

SPYMAN (Top Secret Adventures on cover)
Sept, 1966 - No. 3, Feb, 1967 (12 cents)
Harvey Publications (Illustrated Humor)

	GD25	FN65	NM94
1-Steranko-a(p)-1st pro work; 1pg. Neal Adams ad; Tuska-c/a, Crandall-a(i)	3.60	11.75	25.00
2,3: Simon-c. 2-Steranko-a(p)	2.60	7.50	18.00

SPY SMASHER (See Mighty Midget, Whiz & XMas Comics)
Fall, 1941 - No. 11, Feb, 1943 (Also see Crime Smasher)
Fawcett Publications

	GD25	FN65	NM94
1-Spy Smasher begins; silver metallic-c	200.00	600.00	1400.00
2-Raboy-c	93.00	280.00	650.00
3,4: 3-Bondage-c	75.00	225.00	500.00
5-7: Raboy-a; 6-Raboy-c/a. 7-Part photo-c	67.00	200.00	450.00
8-11: 9-Hitler, Tojo, Mussolini-c. 10-Hitler-c	58.00	175.00	375.00
Well Known Comics (1944, 12 pgs., 8-1/2x10-1/2"), paper-c, glued binding, printed in green; Bestmaid/Samuel Lowe giveaway	17.00	50.00	100.00

SPY THRILLERS (Police Badge No. 479 #5)
Nov, 1954 - No. 4, May, 1955
Atlas Comics (PrPI)

	GD25	FN65	NM94
1-Brodsky c-1,2	10.00	30.00	70.00
2-Last precode (1/55)	6.35	19.00	38.00
3,4	4.70	14.00	28.00

SQUADRON SUPREME (Marvel)(Value: cover or less)

SQUALOR (First)(Value: cover or less)

SQUEEKS
Oct, 1953 - No. 5, June, 1954
Lev Gleason Publications

	GD25	FN65	NM94
1-Funny animal; Biro-c	5.00	15.00	30.00
2-Biro-c	3.20	8.00	16.00
3-5: 3-Biro-c	2.80	7.00	14.00

STAINLESS STEEL RAT (Eagle)(Value: cover or less)

STALKER
June-July, 1975 - No. 4, Dec-Jan, 1975-76
National Periodical Publications

	GD25	FN65	NM94
1-Origin & 1st app; Ditko/Wood-c/a		1.30	3.25
2-4-Ditko/Wood-c/a		.90	2.25

STALKERS (Marvel)(Value: cover or less)(Also see Epic)

STAMP COMICS (Stamps... on-c; Thrilling Advs. In...#8)
Oct, 1951 - No. 7, Oct, 1952 (No. 1: 15 cents)
Youthful Magazines/Stamp Comics, Inc.

	GD25	FN65	NM94
1('Stamps' on indicia No. 1)	22.00	65.00	150.00
2	11.50	34.00	80.00
3-6: 3,4-Kiefer, Wildey-a	10.00	30.00	70.00
7-Roy Krenkel, 4 pgs.	13.00	40.00	90.00

NOTE: *Promotes stamp collecting; gives stories behind various commemorative stamps. No. 2, 10 cents printed over 15 cents c-price. **Kiefer** a-1-7. **Kirkel** a-1-6. **Napoli** a-2-7. **Palais** a-2-4, 7.*

STANLEY & HIS MONSTER (Formerly The Fox & the Crow)
No. 109, Apr-May, 1968 - No. 112, Oct-Nov, 1968
National Periodical Publications

	GD25	FN65	NM94
109-112	1.75	5.00	10.50

STANLEY & HIS MONSTER

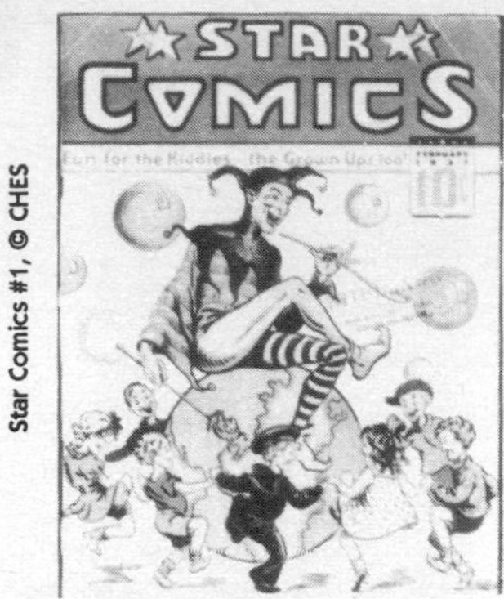

Star Comics #1, © CHES

Starman #14, © DC

Star Ranger Funnies #1, © CEN

GD25 FN65 NM94

Feb, 1993 - No. 4, May, 1993 ($1.50, color, mini-series)
DC Comics

1-4 — 1.50

STARBLAST
Jan, 1994 - Present ($1.75, color)
Marvel Comics

1-($2.00, 52 pgs.)-Nova, Quasar, Black Bolt — .80 — 2.00
2-4 — .70 — 1.75

STAR BLAZERS (Comico, 1987 & 1989)(Value: cover or less)

STAR BRAND (Marvel)(Value: cover or less)

STAR COMICS
Feb, 1937 - V2#7 (No. 23), Aug, 1939 (#1-6: large size)
Ultem Publ. (Harry 'A' Chesler)/Centaur Publications

V1#1-Dan Hastings (s/f) begins — 100.00 — 300.00 — 650.00
2 — 50.00 — 150.00 — 325.00
3-6 (#6, 9/37): 4,5-Little Nemo-c/stories — 46.00 — 138.00 — 300.00
7-9: 8-Severed head centerspread; Impy & Little Nemo by Winsor McCay Jr, Popeye app. by Bob Wood; Mickey Mouse & Popeye app. as toys in Santa's bag on-c; X-Mas-c — 38.00 — 115.00 — 265.00
10 (1st Centaur; 3/38)-Impy by Winsor McCay Jr; Don Marlow by Guardineer begins — 58.00 — 175.00 — 375.00
11-1st Jack Cole comic-a, 1 pg. (4/38) — 38.00 — 115.00 — 265.00
12-15: 12-Riders of the Golden West begins; Little Nemo app. 15-Speed Silvers by Gustavson & The Last Pirate by Burgos begins — 37.00 — 110.00 — 250.00
16 (12/38)-The Phantom Rider & his horse Thunder begins, ends V2#6 — 37.00 — 110.00 — 250.00
V2#1(#17, 2/39)-Phantom Rider-c (only non-funny-c) — 37.00 — 110.00 — 250.00
2-7(#18-23): 2-Diana Deane by Tarpe Mills app. 3-Drama of Hollywood by Mills begins. 7-Jungle Queen app. — 35.00 — 105.00 — 210.00

NOTE: ***Biro** c-6, 9, 10. **Burgos** a-15, 16, V2#1-7. **Ken Ernst** a-10, 12, 14. **Filchock** c-15, 18, 22. **Gill Fox** c-14, 19. **Guardineer** a-6, 8-14. **Gustavson** a-13-16, V2#1-7. **Winsor McCay** c-4, 5. **Tarpe Mills** a-15, V2#1-7. **Schwab** c-20, 23. **Bob Wood** a-10, 12, 13; c-7, 8.*

STAR COMICS MAGAZINE (Marvel)(Value: cover or less)

S.T.A.R. CORPS
Nov, 1993 - No. 6, Apr, 1994 ($1.50, color, limited series)
DC Comics

1-6: 1,2-Austin-c(i); Superman app. — 1.50

STAR FEATURE COMICS
1963
I. W. Enterprises

Reprint #9-Stunt-Man Stetson-r/Feat. Comics #141 — .80 — 2.00 — 4.00

STARFIRE (See New Teen Titans & Teen Titans #18)
Aug-Sept, 1976 - No. 8, Oct-Nov, 1977
National Periodical Publications/DC Comics

1-Origin (CCA stamp fell off cover art; so it was approved by code) — .65 — 1.60
2-8 — 1.20

STAR HUNTERS (See DC Super Stars #16)
Oct-Nov, 1977 - No. 7, Oct-Nov, 1978
National Periodical Publications/DC Comics

1-7: 1-Newton-a(p). 7-Giant — 1.00

NOTE: ***Buckler** a-4-7p; c-1-7p. **Layton** a-1-5i; c-1-6i. **Nasser** a-3p. **Sutton** a-6i.*

STARJAMMERS (See X-Men Spotlight on Starjammers)

STARK TERROR (Magazine)
Dec, 1970 - No. 5, Aug, 1971 (52 pages) (B&W)
Stanley Publications

1-Bondage, torture-c — 3.00 — 7.50 — 15.00
2-4 (Gillmor/Aragon-r) — 1.60 — 4.00 — 8.00
5 (ACG-r) — 1.40 — 3.50 — 7.00

GD25 FN65 NM94

STARLET O'HARA IN HOLLYWOOD (Teen-age) (Also see Cookie)
Dec, 1948 - No. 4, Sept, 1949
Standard Comics

1-Owen Fitzgerald-a in all — 12.00 — 36.00 — 85.00
2 — 10.00 — 30.00 — 60.00
3,4 — 8.35 — 25.00 — 50.00

STAR-LORD THE SPECIAL EDITION (Also see Marvel Comics Super Special #10, Marvel Premiere & Preview & Marvel Spotlight V2#6,7)
Feb, 1982 (One Shot) (Direct sale, 1st Baxter paper comic)
Marvel Comics Group

1-Byrne/Austin-a; Austin-c, Golden-a(p); 8 pgs. of new-a; Dr. Who story — 1.00 — 2.00 — 5.00

STARMAN (See Adventure #467, Brave & the Bold, 1st Issue Special, Justice League & Showcase)
Oct, 1988 - No. 45, Apr, 1992 ($1.00, color)
DC Comics

1-27,29-45: 1-Origin. 4-Intro The Power Elite. 9,10,34-Batman app. 14-Superman app. 17-Power Girl app. 26,27-G.A. Starman app. 38-War of the Gods x-over. 42-Lobo cameo. 42-45-Eclipso-c/stories (#43,44 with Lobo) — 1.00
28-Starman disguised as Superman; leads into Superman #50 — .80 — 2.00

STARMASTERS (Americomics)(Value: cover or less)

STAR PRESENTATION, A (Formerly My Secret Romance #1,2; Spectacular Stories #4 on) (Also see This Is Suspense)
No. 3, May, 1950
Fox Features Syndicate (Hero Books)

3-Dr. Jekyll & Mr. Hyde by Wood & Harrison (reprinted in Startling Terror Tales #10); "The Repulsing Dwarf" by Wood; Wood-c — 36.00 — 107.00 — 250.00

STAR QUEST COMIX (Warren Presents... on cover)
October, 1978
Warren Publications

1 — 1.00

STAR RAIDERS (See DC Graphic Novel #1)

STAR RANGER (Cowboy Comics #13 on)
Feb, 1937 - No. 12, May, 1938 (Large size: No. 1-6)
Ultem Publ./Centaur Publications

1-(1st Western comic)-Ace & Deuce, Air Plunder; Flessel-a — 108.00 — 325.00 — 700.00
2 — 50.00 — 150.00 — 325.00
3-6 — 47.00 — 130.00 — 280.00
7-9: 8-Christmas-c — 37.00 — 110.00 — 250.00
V2#10 (1st Centaur; 3/38) — 58.00 — 175.00 — 375.00
11,12 — 46.00 — 138.00 — 300.00

NOTE: ***J. Cole** a-10, 12; c-12. **Ken Ernst** a-11. **Gill Fox** a-8(illo), 9, 10. **Guardineer** a-1, 3, 6, 7, 8(illos), 9, 10, 12. **Gustavson** a-8-10, 12. **Fred Schwab** c-2-11. **Bob Wood** a-8-10.*

STAR RANGER FUNNIES (Formerly Cowboy Comics)
V1#15, Oct, 1938 - V2#5, Oct, 1939
Centaur Publications

V1#15-Eisner, Gustavson-a — 70.00 — 200.00 — 450.00
V2#1 (1/39) — 50.00 — 150.00 — 325.00
2-5: 2-Night Hawk by Gustavson. 4-Kit Carson app. — 42.00 — 125.00 — 275.00

NOTE: ***Jack Cole** a-V2#1, 3; c-V2#1. **Filchock** c-V2#2, 3. **Guardineer** a-V2#3. **Gustavson** a-V2#2. **Pinajian** c/a-V2#5.*

STAR REACH CLASSICS (Eclipse)(Value: cover or less)

STARR FLAGG, UNDERCOVER GIRL (See Undercover...)

STARRIORS (Marvel)(Value: cover or less)

STARS AND STRIPES COMICS
No. 2, May, 1941 - No. 6, Dec, 1941

Starslayer #18, © First Comics

Star Spangled Comics #50, © DC

Star Spangled War Stories #72, © DC

Centaur Publications

2(#1)-The Shark, The Iron Skull, A-Man, The Amazing Man, Mighty Man, Minimidget begin; The Voice & Dash Dartwell, the Human Meteor, Reef Kinkaid app.; Gustavson Flag-c 136.00 410.00 950.00
3-Origin Dr. Synthe, The Black Panther app. 92.00 275.00 600.00
4-Origin/1st app. The Stars and Stripes; injury to eye-c 77.00 230.00 525.00
5(#5 on cover & inside) 58.00 175.00 390.00
5(#6)-(#5 on cover, #6 on inside) 58.00 175.00 390.00

NOTE: ***Gustavson** c/a-3. **Myron Strauss** c-4, 5(#5), 5(#6).*

STARSLAYER
Feb, 1982 - No. 6, Apr, 1983; No. 7, Aug, 1983 - No. 34, Nov, 1985
Pacific Comics/First Comics No. 7 on

1-Origin & 1st app.; excessive blood & gore; 1 pg. Rocketeer cameo which continues in #2 1.20 3.00
2-Origin/1st full app. the Rocketeer (4/82) by Dave Stevens (Chapter 1 of Rocketeer saga; see Pacific Presents #1,2) 1.70 5.00 12.00
3-Chapter 2 of Rocketeer saga by Stevens 1.20 3.00 7.00
4 .80 2.00
5-2nd app. Groo the Wanderer by Aragones 2.50 6.00
6,7: 7-Grell-a ends .80 2.00
8-34: 10-1st app. Grimjack (11/83, ends #17). 18-Starslayer meets Grimjack. 20-The Black Flame begins (9/84, 1st app.), ends #33. 27-Book length Black Flame story 1.00

NOTE: ***Grell** a-1-7; c-1-8. **Stevens** back c-2, 3. **Sutton** a-17p, 20-22p, 24-27p, 29-33p.*

STAR SPANGLED COMICS (...War Stories #131 on)
Oct, 1941 - No. 130, July, 1952
National Periodical Publications

1-Origin Tarantula; Captain X of the R.A.F., Star Spangled Kid (see Action #40), Armstrong of the Army begin; Robot-c 257.00 770.00 1800.00
2 96.00 288.00 650.00
3-5 63.00 188.00 415.00
6-Last Armstrong of the Army 42.00 125.00 275.00

GD25 FN65 VF82 NM94

7-(4/42)-Origin/1st app. The Guardian by S&K, & Robotman by Paul Cassidy; The Newsboy Legion (1st app.), Robotman & TNT begin; last Captain X 412.00 1240.00 2270.00 3300.00
(Estimated up to 100 total copies exist, 5 in NM/Mint)

GD25 FN65 NM94

8-Origin TNT & Dan the Dyna-Mite 142.00 425.00 950.00
9,10 117.00 350.00 800.00
11-17 96.00 288.00 650.00
18-Origin Star Spangled Kid 121.00 362.00 825.00
19-Last Tarantula 96.00 288.00 635.00
20-Liberty Belle begins (5/43) 96.00 288.00 635.00
21-29-Last S&K issue; 23-Last TNT. 25-Robotman by Jimmy Thompson begins 75.00 225.00 510.00
30-40: 31-S&K-c 34.00 105.00 240.00
41-50 30.00 90.00 205.00
51-64: Last Newsboy Legion & The Guardian; last Liberty Belle? #53 by S&K 30.00 90.00 205.00
65-Robin begins with cover app. (2/47); Batman cameo in 1 panel; Robin-c begin, end #95 100.00 300.00 700.00
66-Batman cameo in Robin story 63.00 190.00 440.00
67,68,70-80: 72-Burnley Robin-c 50.00 150.00 365.00
69-Origin/1st app. Tomahawk by F. Ray (6/47) 75.00 225.00 550.00
81-Origin Merry, Girl of 1000 Gimmicks in Star Spangled Kid story 40.00 120.00 275.00
82,85: 82-Last Robotman? 40.00 120.00 275.00
83-Tomahawk enters the lost valley, a land of dinosaurs; Capt. Compass begins, ends #130 40.00 120.00 275.00
84,87 (Rare): 87-Batman cameo in Robin 58.00 175.00 400.00
86-Batman cameo in Robin story; last Star Spangled Kid 44.00 132.00 300.00
88(1/49)-94: Batman-c/stories in all. 91-Federal Men begin, end #93. 94-Manhunters Around the World begin, end #121 50.00 150.00 330.00
95-Batman story; last Robin-c 44.00 132.00 300.00
96,98-Batman cameo in Robin stories. 96-1st Tomahawk-c (also #97-121) 32.00 95.00 210.00
97,99 25.00 75.00 165.00
100 32.00 95.00 210.00
101-109,118,119,121: 121-Last Tomahawk-c 23.00 70.00 150.00
110,111,120-Batman cameo in Robin stories. 120-Last 52 pg. issue 25.00 75.00 160.00
112-Batman & Robin story 27.00 82.00 185.00
113-Frazetta-a (10 pgs.) 37.00 110.00 235.00
114-Retells Robin's origin (3/51); Batman & Robin story 33.00 100.00 225.00
115,117-Batman app. in Robin stories 25.00 75.00 165.00
116-Flag-c 23.00 70.00 150.00
122-(11/51)-Ghost Breaker-c/stories begin (origin/1st app.), ends #130 (Ghost Breaker covers #122-130) 23.00 70.00 150.00
123-126,128,129 17.00 50.00 110.00
127-Batman cameo 18.00 55.00 120.00
130-Batman cameo in Robin story 20.00 60.00 140.00

NOTE: *Most all issues after #29 signed by Simon & Kirby are not by them. **Bill Ely** c-122-130. **Mortimer** c-65-74(most), 76-95(most). **Fred Ray** c-96-121. **S&K** c-7-31, 33, 34, 36, 37, 39, 40, 48, 49, 50-54, 56-58. **Hal Sherman** c-1-6. **Dick Sprang** c-75.*

STAR SPANGLED KID (See Action #40, Leading Comics & Star Spangled Comics)

STAR SPANGLED WAR STORIES (Formerly Star Spangled Comics #1-130; The Unknown Soldier #205 on) (See Showcase)
No. 131, 8/52 - No. 133, 10/52; No. 3, 11/52 - No. 204, 2-3/77
National Periodical Publications

131(#1) 63.00 188.00 500.00
132 44.00 131.00 350.00
133-Used in **POP**, Pg. 94 38.00 113.00 300.00
3-6: 4-Devil Dog Dugan app. 6-Evans-a 23.00 69.00 185.00
7-10 18.00 53.00 140.00
11-20 15.00 45.00 120.00
21-30: Last precode (2/55) 13.00 38.00 100.00
31-33,35-40 9.00 26.00 60.00
34-Krigstein-a 9.00 27.00 64.00
41-50: 45-Grey tone-c 7.00 21.00 48.00
51-83: 67-Easy Co. story without Sgt. Rock 6.00 17.00 39.00
84-Origin Mlle. Marie 12.00 36.00 84.00
85-89-Mlle. Marie in all 6.50 20.00 46.00
90-1st dinosaur issue-c/story (4-5/60) 22.00 67.00 200.00
91,93-No dinosaur stories 4.30 13.00 31.00
92,94-99: All dinosaur-c/stories 12.00 36.00 85.00
100-Dinosaur-c/story 15.00 45.00 105.00
101-115: All dinosaur issues 9.00 26.00 60.00
116-125,127-133,135-137-Last dinosaur story; Heath Birdman-#129,131 7.00 21.00 50.00
126-No dinosaur story 4.00 11.00 26.00
134-Dinosaur story; Neal Adams-a 9.00 28.00 65.00
138-New Enemy Ace-c/stories begin by Joe Kubert (4-5/68), end #150 (also see Our Army at War #151 & Showcase #57) 6.00 19.00 44.00
139-Origin Enemy Ace (7/68) 4.30 13.00 30.00
140-143,145: 145-Last 12 cent issue (6-7/69) 3.20 8.00 20.00
144-Neal Adams/Kubert-a 3.25 9.50 22.00
146-Enemy Ace-c only 1.65 4.70 11.00
147,148-New Enemy Ace sty 2.15 6.50 15.00
149,150-Last new Enemy Ace by Kubert. Viking Prince by Kubert 1.85 5.50 13.00
151-1st Unknown Soldier (6-7/70); Enemy Ace-r begin (from Our Army at War, Showcase & SSWS); end #161 3.85 11.50 27.00
152,153,155-Enemy Ace reprints 1.65 4.70 11.00
154-Origin Unknown Soldier 3.20 9.00 21.00
156-1st Battle Album 1.30 3.25 8.00
157-161: 157-Sgt. Rock x-over in Unknown Soldier story. 161-Last Enemy

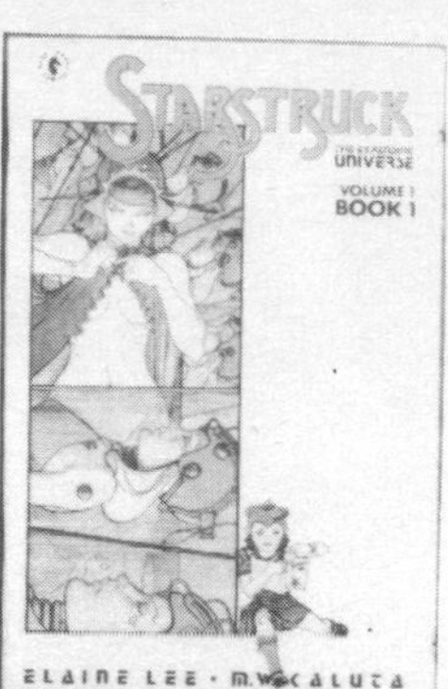

Starstruck #1 (Dark Horse), © Elaine Lee & Michael Kaluta

Startling Comics #41, © BP

Star Trek #18 (Marvel), © Paramount

GD25 FN65 NM94

Ace reprint 1.00 2.50 6.00
162-204: 181-183-Enemy Ace vs. Balloon Buster serial app. .40 1.00 2.00
NOTE: ***Chaykin*** *a-167.* ***Drucker*** *a-59, 61, 64, 66, 67, 73-84.* ***Estrada*** *a-149.* ***John Giunta*** *a-72.* ***Glanzman*** *a-167, 171, 172, 174.* ***Heath*** *a-122, 132, 133; c-67, 122, 132-134.* ***Kaluta*** *a-197i; c-167.* ***G. Kane*** *a-169.* ***Kubert*** *a-6-163(most later issues), 200.* ***Maurer*** *a-160, 165.* ***Severin*** *a-65, 162.* ***S&K*** *c-7-31, 33, 34, 37, 40.* ***Simonson*** *a-170, 172, 174, 180.* ***Sutton*** *a-168.* ***Thorne*** *a-183.* ***Toth*** *a-164.* ***Wildey*** *a-161. Suicide Squad in 110, 116-118, 120, 121, 127.*

STARSTREAM (Whitman)(Value: cover or less)

STARSTRUCK (Marvel & Dark Horse)(Value: cover or less)

STAR STUDDED
1945 (25 cents; 132 pgs.); 1945 (196 pgs.)
Cambridge House/Superior Publishers

nn-Captain Combat by Giunta, Ghost Woman, Commandette, & Red Rogue app.; Infantino-a 17.00 52.00 120.00
nn-The Cadet, Edison Bell, Hoot Gibson, Jungle Lil (196 pgs.); copies vary - Blue Beetle in some 13.00 40.00 90.00

STAR TEAM
1977 (20 pgs.) (6-1/2x5")
Marvel Comics Group (Ideal Toy Giveaway)

nn 1.00

STARTLING COMICS
June, 1940 - No. 53, May, 1948
Better Publications (Nedor)

1-Origin Captain Future-Man Of Tomorrow, Mystico (By Eisner/Fine), The Wonder Man; The Masked Rider & his horse Pinto begins; Masked Rider formerly in pulps; drug use story 105.00 315.00 735.00
2 -Don Davis, Espionage Ace begins 46.00 138.00 300.00
3 35.00 105.00 240.00
4 27.00 82.00 185.00
5-9 20.00 60.00 140.00
10-The Fighting Yank begins (9/41, origin/1st app.) 115.00 345.00 800.00
11-15: 12-Hitler, Hirohito, Mussolini-c 26.00 78.00 175.00
16-Origin The Four Comrades; not in #32,35 30.00 90.00 210.00
17-Last Masked Rider & Mystico 20.00 60.00 140.00
18-Pyroman begins (12/42, origin)(also see America's Best Comics #3 for 1st app., 11/42) 50.00 150.00 340.00
19 20.00 60.00 140.00
20-The Oracle begins (3/43); not in #26,28,33,34 20.00 60.00 140.00
21-Origin The Ape, Oracle's enemy 19.00 57.00 130.00
22-33 17.00 52.00 120.00
34-Origin The Scarab & only app. 19.00 57.00 130.00
35-Hypodermic syringe attacks Fighting Yank in drug story 19.00 57.00 130.00
36-43: 36-Last Four Comrades. 38-Bondage/torture-c. 40-Last Capt. Future & Oracle. 41-Front Page Peggy begins; A-Bomb-c. 43-Last Pyroman 17.00 52.00 120.00
44-Lance Lewis, Space Detective begins; Ingels-c; sci/fi-c begin 27.00 82.00 185.00
45-Tygra begins (intro/origin, 5/47); Ingels-c/a 27.00 82.00 185.00
46-Ingels-c/a 27.00 82.00 185.00
47,48,50-53: 50,51-Sea-Eagle app. 20.00 60.00 140.00
49-Classic Schomburg Robot-c; last Fighting Yank 39.00 120.00 275.00
NOTE: ***Ingels*** *a-45; c-44, 45, 46(wash).* ***Schomburg (Xela)*** *c-21-43; 47-53 (airbrush).* ***Tuska*** *c-45? Bondage c-16, 21, 37, 46-49. Captain Future c-1-9, 13, 14. Fighting Yank c-10-12, 15-17, 21, 22, 24, 26, 28, 30, 32, 34, 36, 38, 40, 42. Pyroman c-18-20, 23, 25, 27, 29, 31, 33, 35, 37, 39, 41, 43.*

STARTLING TERROR TALES
No. 10, May, 1952 - No. 14, Feb, 1953; No. 4, Apr, 1953 - No. 11, 1954
Star Publications

10-(1st Series)-Wood/Harrison-a (r/A Star Presentation #3) Disbrow/Cole-c; becomes 4 different titles after #10; becomes Confessions of Love #11 on, The Horrors #11 on, Terrifying Tales #11 on, Terrors of the Jungle #11 on & continues w/Startling Terror #11 30.00 90.00 210.00
11-(#1a, 8/52)-L. B. Cole Spider-c; r-Fox's "A Feature Presentation" #5 17.00 52.00 120.00
12(#1b),14(#3) 8.35 25.00 50.00
13(#2)-Jo-Jo-r; Disbrow-a 9.15 27.50 55.00
4-7,9,11(1953-54) (2nd Series): 11-New logo 7.50 22.50 45.00
8-Spanking scene-r/Crimes By Women #14 8.35 25.00 50.00
10-Disbrow-a 8.35 25.00 50.00
NOTE: ***L. B. Cole*** *covers-all issues.* ***Palais*** *a-V2#8r, V2#11r.*

STAR TREK (TV) (See Dan Curtis Giveaways, Dynabrite Comics & Power Record Comics)
7/67; No. 2, 6/68; No. 3, 12/68; No. 4, 6/69 - No. 61, 3/79
Gold Key

1-Photo-c begin, end #9 51.00 154.00 360.00
2 26.00 77.00 180.00
3-5 21.00 64.00 150.00
6-9 16.00 49.00 115.00
10-20 9.00 27.00 64.00
21-30 6.50 20.00 46.00
31-40 4.15 12.50 29.00
41-61: 52-Drug propaganda story 2.70 8.00 19.00
...the Enterprise Logs nn(8/76)-Golden Press, ($1.95, 224 pgs.)-r/#1-8 plus 7 pgs. by McWilliams (#11185)-Photo-c 1.50 3.75 9.00
...the Enterprise Logs Vol.2('76)-r/#9-17 (#11187)-Photo-c 1.30 3.25 8.00
...the Enterprise Logs Vol.3('77)-r/#18-26 (#11188); McWilliams-a (4 pgs.)-Photo-c 1.20 3.00 7.00
Star Trek Vol.4(Winter'77)-Reprints #27,28,30-34,36,38 (#11189) plus 3 pgs. new art 1.20 3.00 7.00
NOTE: ***McWilliams*** *a-38, 40-44, 46-61. #29 reprints #1; #35 reprints #4; #37 reprints #5; #45 reprints #7. The tabloids all have photo covers and blank inside covers. Painted covers #10-44, 46-59.*

STAR TREK
April, 1980 - No. 18, Feb, 1982
Marvel Comics Group

1-r/Marvel Super Special; movie adapt. 1.90 4.75
2-18: 5-Miller-c 1.30 3.25
NOTE: ***Austin*** *c-18i.* ***Buscema*** *a-13.* ***Gil Kane*** *a-15.* ***Nasser*** *c/a-7.* ***Simonson*** *c-17.*

STAR TREK (Also see Who's Who In Star Trek)
Feb, 1984 - No. 56, Nov, 1988 (Mando paper, 75 cents)
DC Comics

1-Sutton-a(p) begins 1.65 4.00 10.00
2-5 1.00 2.50 6.00
6-10: 7-Origin Saavik 1.90 4.75
11-20 1.30 3.25
21-32 1.00 2.50
33-($1.25, 52 pgs.)-20th anniversary issue 1.50 3.75
34-49: 37-Painted-c. 49-Begin $1.00-c .70 1.80
50-($1.50, 52 pgs.) 1.10 2.75
51-56 1.25
Annual 1-3: 1(1985). 2(1986). 3(1988, $1.50) 1.10 2.75
NOTE: ***Morrow*** *a-28, 35, 36, 56.* ***Orlando*** *c-8i.* ***Perez*** *c-1-3.* ***Spiegle*** *a-19.* ***Starlin*** *c-24, 25.* ***Sutton*** *a-1-6p, 8-18p, 20-27p, 29p, 31-34p, 39-52p, 55p; c-4-6p, 8-22p, 46p.*

STAR TREK
Oct, 1989 - Present ($1.50/$1.75, color)
DC Comics

1-Capt. Kirk and crew 1.20 3.00 7.00
2,3 1.30 3.25
4-23,25-30: 10-12-The Trial of James T. Kirk. 21-Begin $1.75-c .90 2.25
24-($2.95, 68 pgs.)-40 pg. epic w/pin-ups 1.20 3.00
31-49,51-58 .70 1.75
50-($3.50, 68 pgs.) 1.40 3.50
Annual 1,2('90, '91, $2.95, 68pgs.): 1-Morrow-a 1.20 3.00
Annual 3 (1992, $3.50, 68 pgs.)-Painted-c 1.40 3.50

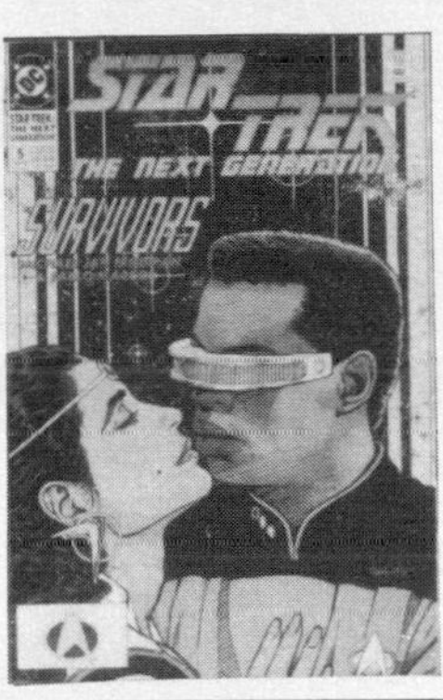

Star Trek: The Next Generation #5 (2/90), © Paramount

Star Wars #81, © Lucasfilms

Star Wars: Dark Empire #6 (Dark Horse), © Lucas Films

GD25 FN65 NM94

Annual 4 (1993, $3.50, 68 pgs.) 1.40 3.50

STAR TREK: DEEP SPACE NINE (TV)
Aug, 1993 - Present ($2.50, color)
Malibu Comics
1-Direct Sale Edition w/line drawn-c 1.00 2.50
1-Newsstand Edition with photo-c 1.00 2.50
2-6: 2-Polybagged w/trading card 1.00 2.50

STAR TREK VI: THE UNDISCOVERED COUNTRY
1992 (Movie adaptation)
DC Comics
1-($2.95, regular edition, 68 pgs.) 1.20 3.00
nn-($5.95, prestige edition)-Has photos of movie not included in regular edition; painted-c by Palmer; photo back-c 1.00 2.50 6.00

STAR TREK MOVIE SPECIAL
June, 1984 - No. 2, 1987 ($1.50, 68pgs); 1989 ($2.00, 52 pgs.)
DC Comics
1-Adapts Star Trek III; Sutton-p (64 pgs.) 1.50
2-Adapts Star Trek IV; Sutton-a (64 pgs.) 1.50
1 (1989)-Adapts Star Trek V; painted-c .80 2.00

STAR TREK - THE MODALA IMPERATIVE
Late July, 1991 - No. 4, Late Sept, 1991 ($1.75, color, mini-series)
DC Comics
1 1.00 2.50
2-4 .80 2.00

STAR TREK: THE NEXT GENERATION (TV)
Feb, 1988 - No. 6, July, 1988 (Mini series, based on TV show)
DC Comics
1 (52 pgs.)-Sienkiewicz painted-c 1.65 4.70 11.00
2-6 ($1.00) 1.10 2.70 6.50

STAR TREK: THE NEXT GENERATION (TV)
Oct, 1989 - Present ($1.50/$1.75, color)
DC Comics
1-Capt. Picard and crew from TV show 1.80 4.50 10.00
2,3 1.20 3.00 7.00
4,5 1.90 4.75
6-10 1.30 3.25
11-23,25-30: 21-Begin $1.75-c .90 2.25
24-($2.50, 52 pgs.) 1.00 2.50
31-49,51-58 .70 1.75
50-($3.50, 68 pgs.)-Painted-c 1.40 3.50
Annual 1 (1990, $2.95, 68 pgs.) 1.40 3.50
Annual 2-4 (1991-93, $3.50, 68 pgs.) 1.60 4.00
Special 1 (1993, $3.50, 68 pgs.)-Contains 3 stories 1.40 3.50

STAR TREK: THE NEXT GENERATION - THE MODALA IMPERATIVE
Early Sept, 1991 - No. 4, 1991 ($1.75, color, mini-series)
DC Comics
1 1.00 2.50
2-4 .80 2.00

STAR WARS (Movie) (See Classic..., Contemporary Motivators, Dark Horse Comics, The Droids, The Ewoks, Marvel Movie Showcase & Marvel Special Edition)
July, 1977 - No. 107, Sept, 1986
Marvel Comics Group
1-(Regular 30 cent edition)-Price in square w/UPC code; #1-6 adapt first movie 3.20 8.00 20.00
1-(35 cent cover; limited distribution - 1500 copies?)- Price in square w/UPC code (see note below) 51.00 154.00 360.00
2-6: 4-Battle with Darth Vader 6-Dave Stevens-i 1.10 2.70 6.50
7-10 1.40 3.50
11-20 .90 2.25
21-38 .75 1.90
39-44-The Empire Strikes Back-r by Al Williamson in all .90 2.25
45-107: 92,100-($1.00, 52 pgs.) 1.00
1-9-Reprints; has "reprint" in upper lefthand corner of cover or on inside or price and number inside a diamond with no date or UPC on cover; 30 cent and 35 cent issues published 1.00
Annual 1 (12/79) .80 2.00
Annual 2 (11/82), 3(12/83) 1.20

NOTE: *The rare 35 cent edition has the cover price in a square box, and the UPC box in the lower left hand corner has the UPC code lines running through it.* ***Austin*** *c-11-15i, 21i, 38; c-12-15i, 21i.* ***Byrne*** *c-13p.* ***Chaykin*** *a-1-10p; c-1.* ***Golden*** *c/a-38.* ***Miller*** *c-47p.* ***Nebres*** *c/a-Annual 2i.* ***Portacio*** *a-107i.* ***Sienkiewicz*** *c-92i, 98.* ***Simonson*** *a-16p, 49p, 51-63p, 65p, 66p; c-16, 49-51, 52p, 53-62, Annual 1.* ***Steacy*** *painted a-105i, 106i; c-105.* ***Williamson*** *a-39-44p, 50p, 98; c-39, 40, 41-44p. Painted c-81, 87, 92, 95, 98, 100, 105.*

STAR WARS: DARK EMPIRE
Dec, 1991 - No. 6, Oct, 1992 ($2.95, color, limited series)
Dark Horse Comics
1-All have Dorman painted-c 3.25 9.50 22.00
1-2nd printing 1.20 3.00
2-Low print run 3.70 11.00 26.00
2,3-2nd printings 1.20 3.00
3 1.10 2.70 6.50
4 1.80 4.50
5,6 1.20 3.00
Gold Embossed Set (#1-6)-With gold embossed foil logo (price is for set) 65.00

STAR WARS: RETURN OF THE JEDI
Oct, 1983 - No. 4, 1984 (Mini-series, movie adaptation)
Marvel Comics Group
1-4-Williamson-p in all; r/Marvel Super Special #27 1.00
Oversized issue (1983, $2.95, 10-3/4x8-1/4", 68 pgs., cardboard-c)-Reprints above 4 issues 1.20 3.00

STAR WARS: TALES OF THE JEDI (See Dark Horse Comics #7)
Oct, 1993 - No. 5, 1994 ($2.50, color, limited series)
Dark Horse Comics
1-5: All have Dave Dorman painted-c 1.00 2.50

STATIC (Charlton)(Value: cover or less)

STATIC
June, 1993 - Present ($1.50, color)
DC Comics (Milestone)
1-($2.95)-Collector's Edition; polybagged w/poster & trading card & backing board (direct sale only 1.20 3.00
1-10: 2-Origin 1.50

STEALTH SQUAD
Sept, 1993 - No. 4, 1994 ($2.50, color, mini-series)
Petra Comics
1-Super hero team 1.00 2.50

STEED AND MRS. PEEL (TV)(Eclipse)(Value: cover or less)

STEEL
Feb, 1994 - Present ($1.50, color,)
DC Comics
1,2 1.50

STEELGRIP STARKEY (Epic)(Value: cover or less)

STEEL STERLING (Formerly Shield-Steel Sterling; see Blue Ribbon, Jackpot, Mighty Comics, Mighty Crusaders, Roly Poly & Zip Comics)
No. 4, Jan, 1984 - No. 7, July, 1984
Archie Enterprises, Inc.
4-7: 6-McWilliams-a 1.00

STEEL, THE INDESTRUCTIBLE MAN (See All-Star Squadron #8)
March, 1978 - No. 5, Oct-Nov, 1978
DC Comics
1 1.20

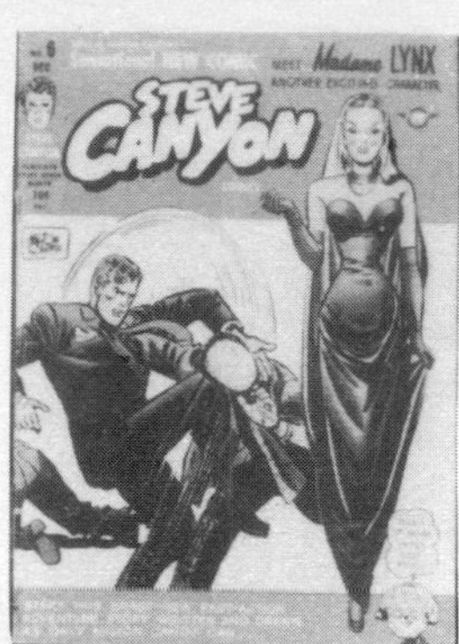

Steve Canyon #6, © Milton Caniff

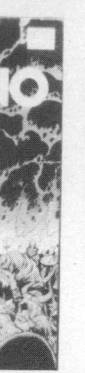

Stigg's Inferno #7, © Ty Templeton

Stories by Famous Authors #1, © Seaboard

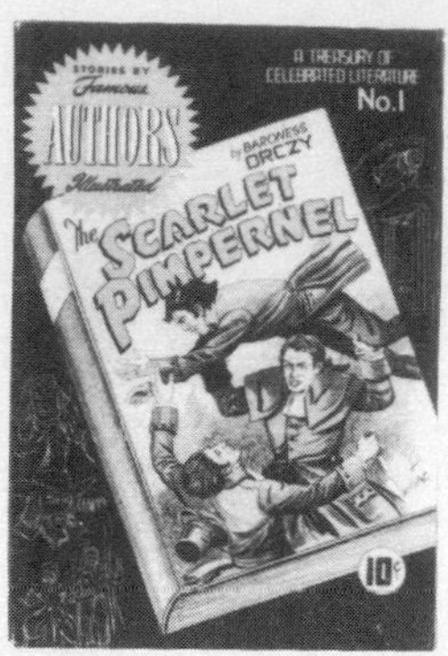

	GD25	FN65	NM94
2-5: 5-Giant			1.00

STEELTOWN ROCKERS (Marvel)(Value: cover or less)

STEVE CANYON (See 4-Color #519, 578, 641, 737, 804, 939, 1033, and Harvey Comics Hits #52)

STEVE CANYON
1959 (96 pgs.; no text; 6-3/4x9"; hardcover)(B&W inside)
Grosset & Dunlap

	GD25	FN65	NM94
100100-Reprints 2 stories from strip (1953, 1957)	4.20	12.50	25.00
100100 (softcover edition)	4.00	10.00	20.00

STEVE CANYON COMICS
Feb, 1948 - No. 6, Dec, 1948 (Strip reprints) (No. 4,5: 52pgs.)
Harvey Publications

	GD25	FN65	NM94
1-Origin; has biog of Milton Caniff; Powell-a, 2 pgs.; Caniff-a	17.00	52.00	120.00
2-Caniff, Powell-a in #2-6	11.50	34.00	80.00
3-6: 6-Intro Madame Lynx-c/story	10.00	30.00	70.00
Dept. Store giveaway #3(6/48, 36pp)	10.00	30.00	65.00
...'s Secret Mission (1951, 16 pgs., Armed Forces giveaway); Caniff-a	10.00	30.00	60.00
Strictly for the Smart Birds-16 pgs., 1951; Information Comics Div. (Harvey) Premium	9.35	28.00	56.00

STEVE CANYON IN 3-D
June, 1986 ($2.25, one-shot)
Kitchen Sink Press

	GD25	FN65	NM94
1-Contains unpublished story from 1954		.90	2.25

STEVE DONOVAN, WESTERN MARSHAL (TV)
No. 675, Feb, 1956 - No. 880, Feb, 1958 (All photo-c)
Dell Publishing Co.

	GD25	FN65	NM94
4-Color 675-Kinstler-a	7.50	22.50	45.00
4-Color 768-Kinstler-a	5.85	17.50	35.00
4-Color 880	4.20	12.50	25.00

STEVE ROPER
April, 1948 - No. 5, Dec, 1948
Famous Funnies

	GD25	FN65	NM94
1-Contains 1944 daily newspaper-r	9.15	27.50	55.00
2	5.00	15.00	30.00
3-5	4.00	12.00	24.00

STEVE SAUNDERS SPECIAL AGENT (See Special Agent)

STEVE SAVAGE (See Captain...)

STEVE ZODIAC & THE FIRE BALL XL-5 (TV)
January, 1964
Gold Key

	GD25	FN65	NM94
10108-401 (#1)	6.50	20.00	46.00

STEVIE (Mazie's boy friend)(Also see Mazie & Mortie)
Nov, 1952 - No. 6, April, 1954
Mazie (Magazine Publ.)

	GD25	FN65	NM94
1-Teenage humor; Stevie, Mortie & Mazie begin	4.70	14.00	28.00
2-6	3.20	8.00	16.00

STEVIE MAZIE'S BOY FRIEND (See Harvey Hits #5)

STEWART THE RAT (See Eclipse Graphic Album Series)

ST. GEORGE (See listing under Saint...)

STIGG'S INFERNO (Vortex/Eclipse)(Value: cover or less)

STING OF THE GREEN HORNET (See The Green Hornet)
June, 1992 - No. 4, 1992 ($2.50, color, mini-series)
Now Comics

	GD25	FN65	NM94
1-4: Butler-c/a		1.00	2.50
1-4 ($2.75)-Collectors Ed.; polybagged w/poster		1.10	2.75

STONEY BURKE (TV)
June-Aug, 1963 - No. 2, Sept-Nov, 1963
Dell Publishing Co.

	GD25	FN65	NM94
1,2	2.00	5.00	10.00

STONY CRAIG
1946 (No #)
Pentagon Publishing Co.

	GD25	FN65	NM94
nn-Reprints Bell Syndicate's "Sgt. Stony Craig" newspaper strips	5.00	15.00	30.00

STORIES BY FAMOUS AUTHORS ILLUSTRATED (Fast Fiction #1-5)
No. 6, Aug, 1950 - No. 13, March, 1951
Seaboard Publ./Famous Authors Ill.

	GD25	FN65	NM94
1-Scarlet Pimpernel-Baroness Orczy	24.00	73.00	170.00
2-Capt. Blood-Raphael Sabatini	24.00	73.00	170.00
3-She, by Haggard	30.00	90.00	210.00
4-The 39 Steps-John Buchan	16.00	48.00	110.00
5-Beau Geste-P. C. Wren	16.00	50.00	115.00

NOTE: *The above five issues are exact reprints of Fast Fiction #1-5 except for the title change and new Kiefer covers on #1 and 2. Kiefer c(r)-3-5. The above 5 issues were released before Famous Authors #6.*

	GD25	FN65	NM94
6-Macbeth, by Shakespeare; Kiefer art (8/50); used in **SOTI**, pg. 22,143; Kiefer-c; 36 pgs.	19.00	58.00	135.00
7-The Window; Kiefer-c/a; 52 pgs.	15.00	45.00	105.00
8-Hamlet, by Shakespeare; Kiefer-c/a; 36pgs.	19.00	58.00	135.00
9-Nicholas Nickleby, by Dickens; G. Schrotter-a; 52 pgs.	16.00	48.00	110.00
10-Romeo & Juliet, by Shakespeare; Kiefer-c/a; 36 pgs.	16.00	48.00	110.00
11-Ben-Hur; Schrotter-a; 52 pgs.	16.00	50.00	115.00
12-La Svengali; Schrotter-a; 36 pgs.	16.00	50.00	115.00
13-Scaramouche; Kiefer-c/a; 36 pgs.	16.00	50.00	115.00

NOTE: *Artwork was prepared/advertised for #14, The Red Badge Of Courage. Gilberton bought out Famous Authors, Ltd. and used that story as C.I. #98. Famous Authors, Ltd. then published the Classics Junior series. The Famous Authors titles were published as part of the regular Classics Ill. Series in Brazil starting in 1952.*

STORIES OF CHRISTMAS
1942 (32 pages; paper cover) (Giveaway)
K. K. Publications

	GD25	FN65	NM94
nn-Adaptation of "A Christmas Carol;" Kelly story-"The Fir Tree;" Infinity-c	32.00	95.00	220.00

STORIES OF ROMANCE (Formerly Meet Miss Bliss)
No. 5, Mar, 1956 - No. 13, Aug, 1957
Atlas Comics (LMC)

	GD25	FN65	NM94
5-Baker-a?	5.00	15.00	30.00
6-13	3.20	8.00	16.00

NOTE: ***Ann Brewster** a-13. **Colletta** a-9(2); c-5.*

STORMWATCH
May, 1993 - Present ($1.95, color)
Image Comics

	GD25	FN65	NM94
1-5-Jim Lee-c & part scripts in all. 1-3 contain coupon for limited edition Stormwatch trading card #00 by Lee		.80	2.00

STORMWATCHER (Eclipse)(Value: cover or less)

STORMY (See 4-Color #537)

STORY HOUR SERIES (Disney)
1948, 1949; 1951-1953 (36 pgs., paper-c) (4-1/2x6-1/4")
Given away with subscription to Walt Disney's Comics & Stories
Whitman Publishing Co.

	GD25	FN65	NM94
nn(1948)-Mickey Mouse and Boy Thursday	10.00	30.00	60.00
nn(1948)-Mickey Mouse Miracle Maker	10.00	30.00	60.00
nn(1948)-Minnie Mouse and Antique Chair	10.00	30.00	60.00
nn(1949)-The Three Orphan Kittens(B&W & color)	5.00	15.00	30.00
nn(1949)-Danny-The Little Black Lamb	5.00	15.00	30.00
800(1948)-Donald Duck in "Bringing Up the Boys"	10.00	30.00	70.00
1953 edition	6.70	20.00	40.00

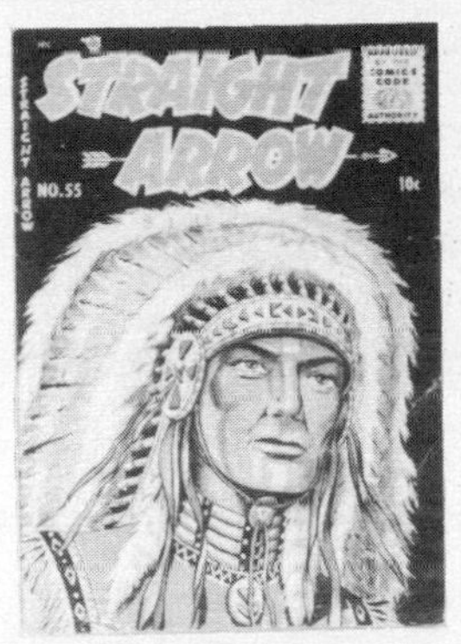

Straight Arrow #55, © ME

Strange Adventures #50, © DC

Strange Adventures #201, © DC

	GD25	FN65	NM94
401(1948)-Mickey Mouse's Summer Vacation	7.50	22.50	45.00
1951, 1952 edition	4.00	10.00	20.00
402(1948)-Bugs Bunny's Adventures	5.85	17.50	35.00
403(1948)-Bongo	4.20	12.50	25.00
404(1948)-Mickey and the Beanstalk	5.85	17.50	35.00
405-15(1949)-Andy Panda and His Friends	4.70	14.00	28.00
406-15(1949)-Tom and Jerry	5.00	15.00	30.00
408-15(1949)-Johnny Appleseed	4.20	12.50	25.00
1948, 1949 Hard Cover Edition of each....	$2.00 - $3.00 more.		

STORY OF EDISON, THE
1956 (16 pgs.) (Reddy Killowatt)
Educational Comics

nn-Reprint of Reddy Kilowatt #2(1947) 5.00 15.00 30.00

STORY OF HARRY S. TRUMAN, THE
1948 (16 pgs.) (In color, regular size)(Soft-c)
Democratic National Committee (Giveaway)

nn-Gives biography on career of Truman; used in **SOTI**, pg. 311 10.00 30.00 70.00

STORY OF JESUS (See Classics Illustrated Special Issue)

STORY OF MANKIND, THE (See 4-Color #851)

STORY OF MARTHA WAYNE, THE
April, 1956
Argo Publ.

1-Newspaper-r 4.00 10.00 20.00

STORY OF RUTH, THE (See 4-Color #1144)

STORY OF THE COMMANDOS, THE (Combined Operations)
1943 (68 pgs.; B&W) (15 cents)
Long Island Independent (Distr. by Gilberton)

nn-All text (no comics); photos & illustrations; ad for Classic Comics on back cover (Rare) 22.00 65.00 150.00

STORY OF THE GLOOMY BUNNY, THE (See March of Comics #9)

STRAIGHT ARROW (Radio)(See Best of the West & Great Western)
Feb-Mar, 1950 - No. 55, Mar, 1956 (All 36 pgs.)
Magazine Enterprises

	GD25	FN65	NM94
1-Straight Arrow (alias Steve Adams) & his palomino Fury begin; 1st mention of Sundown Valley & the Secret Cave; Whitney-a	29.00	85.00	200.00
2-Red Hawk begins (1st app?) by Powell (Origin), ends #55	14.00	43.00	100.00
3-Frazetta-c	19.00	58.00	135.00
4,5: 4-Secret Cave-c	10.00	30.00	60.00
6-10	8.35	25.00	50.00
11-Classic story "The Valley of Time," with an ancient civilization made of gold	9.15	27.50	55.00
12-19	6.70	20.00	40.00
20-Origin Straight Arrow's Shield	10.00	30.00	60.00
21-Origin Fury	10.00	30.00	65.00
22-Frazetta-c	13.00	40.00	90.00
23,25-30: 25-Secret Cave-c. 28-Red Hawk meets The Vikings	5.85	17.50	35.00
24-Classic story "The Dragons of Doom!" with prehistoric pteradactyls	7.50	22.50	45.00
31-38: 36-Red Hawk drug story by Powell	5.00	15.00	30.00
39-Classic story "The Canyon Beast," with a dinosaur egg hatching a Tyranosaurus Rex	6.70	20.00	40.00
40-Classic story "Secret of The Spanish Specters," with Conquistadors' lost treasure	6.70	20.00	40.00
41,42,44-54: 45-Secret Cave-c	4.00	12.00	24.00
43-Intro & 1st app. Blaze, Straight Arrow's Warrior dog	5.85	17.50	35.00
55-Last issue	6.70	20.00	40.00

NOTE: ***Fred Meagher** a 1-55; c-1, 2, 4-21, 23-55. **Powell** a 2-55. Many issues advertise the radio premiums associated with Straight Arrow.*

STRAIGHT ARROW'S FURY (See A-1 Comics #119)

STRANGE
March, 1957 - No. 6, May, 1958
Ajax-Farrell Publ. (Four Star Comic Corp.)

	GD25	FN65	NM94
1	10.00	30.00	60.00
2	5.35	16.00	32.00
3-6	4.20	12.50	25.00

STRANGE ADVENTURES
Aug-Sept, 1950 - No. 244, Oct-Nov, 1973 (No. 1-12: 52 pgs.)
National Periodical Publications

	GD25	FN65	NM94
1-Adaptation of "Destination Moon;" preview of movie w/photo-c from movie (also see Fawcett Movie Comic #2); adapt. of Edmond Hamilton's "Chris KL-99" in #1-3; Darwin Jones begins	215.00	645.00	1500.00
2	100.00	300.00	700.00
3,4	64.00	195.00	450.00
5-8,10: 7-Origin Kris KL-99	57.00	170.00	400.00
9-Captain Comet begins (6/51, intro/origin)	121.00	365.00	850.00
11-20: 12,13,17,18-Toth-a	40.00	120.00	280.00
21-30: 28-Atomic explosion panel. 30-Robot-c	31.00	92.00	215.00
31,34-38	26.00	80.00	185.00
32,33-Krigstein-a	27.00	81.00	190.00
39-Ill. in SOTI-"Treating police contemptuously" (top right)	34.00	105.00	240.00
40-49-Last Capt. Comet; not in 45,47,48	25.00	75.00	175.00
50-53-Last precode issue (2/55)	19.00	58.00	135.00
54-70	9.00	28.00	75.00
71-99	7.00	21.00	55.00
100	10.00	30.00	70.00
101-110: 104-Space Museum begins by Sekowsky	6.00	17.00	40.00
111-116,118,119: 114-Star Hawkins begins, ends #185; Heath-a in Wood E.C. style	5.00	15.00	35.00
117-Origin/1st app. Atomic Knights (6/60)	33.00	99.00	330.00
120-2nd app. Atomic Knights	15.00	44.00	145.00
121,122,124,125,127,128,130,131,133,134: 124-Origin Faceless Creature. 134-Last 10 cent issue	3.85	11.50	27.00
126,128-3rd & 4th app. Atomic Knights	8.00	24.00	80.00
129,132,135,138,141,144,147-Atomic Knights app. 144-Only Atomic Knights cover (by Murphy Anderson)	4.00	13.00	40.00
136,137,139,140,142,143,145,146,148,149,151,152,154,155,157-159	3.25	9.50	22.00
150,153,156,160: Atomic Knights in each. 153-2nd app. Faceless Creature; atomic explosion-c (6/63). 159-Star Rovers app.; Gil Kane/Anderson-a. 160-Last Atomic Knights	3.85	11.50	27.00
161-179: 161-Last Space Museum. 163-Star Rovers app. 170-Infinity-c. 177-Origin Immortal Man	1.70	5.00	12.00
180-Origin/1st app. Animal Man	27.00	81.00	190.00
181-183,185-189: 187-Origin The Enchantress	1.30	3.25	8.00
184-2nd app. Animal Man by Gil Kane	16.00	48.00	110.00
190-1st app. Animal Man in costume	19.00	58.00	135.00
191-194,196-200,202-204	1.00	2.50	6.00
195-1st full app. Animal Man	11.00	32.00	75.00
201-Last Animal Man; 2nd full app.	5.50	17.00	40.00
205-Intro/origin Deadman by Infantino (10/67) & begin series, ends #216	6.50	19.00	45.00
206-Neal Adams-a begins	4.70	14.00	33.00
207-210	3.25	9.50	22.00
211-216: 211-Space Museum-r. 216-Secret message panel by Neal Adams (pg. 13)	2.40	7.25	17.00
217-221,223-231: 217-Adam Strange & Atomic Knights-r begin. 218-Last 12 cent issue. 225-Last 15 cent issue. 226-New Adam Strange text story w/illos by Anderson (8 pgs.). 226-236-(68-52 pgs.). 231-Last Atomic Knights reprint		1.80	4.50
222-New Adam Strange story; Kane/Anderson-a	1.40	3.50	8.50
232-244		1.00	2.50

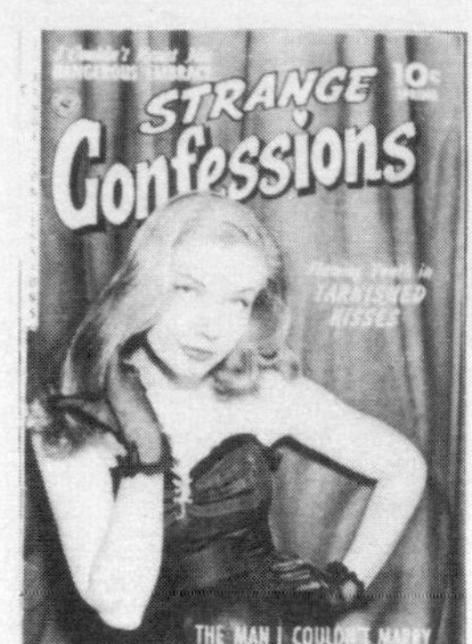

Strange Confessions #1, © Z-D

Strange Planets #16, © Super

The Strangers #1, © Malibu

GD25 FN65 NM94

NOTE: ***Neal Adams*** *a-206-216; c-207-216, 228, 235.* ***Anderson*** *a-8-52, 94, 96, 99, 115, 117, 119-163, 217r, 218r, 222, 223-225r, 226, 242i(r); c-18, 19, 21, 23, 24, 27, 30, 32-44(most); c/r-157i, 190i, 217-224, 228-231, 233, 235-239, 241-243.* ***Ditko*** *a-188, 189.* ***Drucker*** *a-42, 43, 45.* ***Elias*** *a-212.* ***Finlay*** *a-2, 3, 6, 7, 210r, 229r.* ***Giunta*** *a-237r.* ***Heath*** *a-116.* ***Infantino*** *a-10-101, 106-151, 154, 157-163, 180, 190, 218-221r, 223-244p(r); c-50; c(r)-190p, 197, 199-211, 218-221, 223-244.* ***Kaluta*** *c-238, 240.* ***Gil Kane*** *a-8-116, 124, 125, 130, 138, 146-157, 173-186, 204r, 222r, 227-231r; c(p)-11-17, 25, 154, 157.* ***Kubert*** *a-55(2 pgs.), 226; c-219, 220, 225-227, 232, 234.* ***Moriera*** *c-26, 28, 29, 71.* ***Morrow*** *c-230.* ***Mortimer*** *c-8.* ***Powell*** *a-4.* ***Sekowsky*** *a-71p, 97-162p, 217p(r), 218p(r); c-206, 217-219r.* ***Simon & Kirby*** *a-2r (2 pg.)* ***Sparling*** *a-201.* ***Toth*** *a-8, 12, 13, 17-19.* ***Wood*** *a-154i. Atomic Knights in #117, 120, 123, 126, 129, 132, 135, 138, 141, 144, 147, 150, 153, 156, 160. Atomic Knights reprints by* ***Anderson*** *in 119-221. Chris KL99 in 1-3, 5, 7, 9, 11, 15. Capt. Comet covers-9-14, 17-19, 24, 26, 27, 32-44.*

STRANGE AS IT SEEMS (See Famous Funnies-A Carnival of Comics, Feature Funnies #1, The John Hix Scrap Book & Peanuts)

STRANGE AS IT SEEMS
1932 (64 pgs.; B&W; square binding)
Blue-Star Publishing Co.

1-Newspaper-r 17.00 52.00 120.00
NOTE: *Published with and without No. 1 and price on cover.*
Ex-Lax giveaway(1936, B&W, 24pgs., 5x7")-McNaught Synd.
3.60 9.00 18.00

STRANGE AS IT SEEMS
1939
United Features Syndicate

Single Series 9, 1, 2 22.00 65.00 150.00

STRANGE COMBAT TALES
Oct, 1993 - No. 4, Jan, 1994 ($2.50, color, mini-series)
Epic Comics (Marvel)

1-4 1.00 2.50

STRANGE CONFESSIONS
Jan-Mar (Spring on-c), 1952 - No. 4, Fall, 1952 (All have photo-c)
Ziff-Davis Publ. Co. (Approved)

1(Scarce)-Kinstler-a 27.00 80.00 185.00
2(Scarce, 7-8/52) 19.00 57.00 130.00
3(Scarce, 9-10/52)-#3 on-c, #2 on inside; Reformatory girl story; photo-c
19.00 57.00 130.00
4(Scarce)-Reformatory girl story 19.00 57.00 130.00

STRANGE DAYS (Eclipse)(Value: cover or less)

STRANGE FANTASY (Eerie Tales of Suspense)(Formerly Rocketman)
Aug, 1952 - No. 14, Oct-Nov, 1954
Ajax-Farrell

2(#1, 8/52)-Jungle Princess story; Kamenish-a; reprinted from Ellery Queen #1 17.00 52.00 120.00
2(10/52)-No Black Cat or Rulah; Bakerish, Kamenish-a; hypo/meathook-c
13.50 41.00 95.00
3-Rulah story, called Pulah 13.00 40.00 90.00
4-Rocket Man app. 11.50 34.00 80.00
5,6,8,10,12,14 9.15 27.50 55.00
7-Madam Satan/Slave story 11.50 34.00 80.00
9(w/Black Cat), 9(w/Boy's Ranch; S&K-a)(A rebinding of Harvey interiors; not publ. by Ajax) 10.00 30.00 70.00
9-Regular issue 9.15 27.50 55.00
11-Jungle story 10.00 30.00 60.00
13-Bondage-c; Rulah (Kolah) story 11.50 34.00 80.00

STRANGE GALAXY (Magazine)
V1#8, Feb, 1971 - No. 11, Aug, 1971 (B&W)
Eerie Publications

V1#8-Reprints-c/Fantastic V19#3 (2/70) (a pulp) 1.70 5.00 12.00
9-11 1.30 3.25 8.00

STRANGE JOURNEY
Sept, 1957 - No. 4, June, 1958 (Farrell reprints)
America's Best (Steinway Publ.) (Ajax/Farrell)

1 10.00 30.00 70.00

GD25 FN65 NM94

2-4: 2-Flying saucer-c 6.70 20.00 40.00

STRANGE LOVE (See Fox Giants)

STRANGE MYSTERIES
Sept, 1951 - No. 21, Jan, 1955
Superior/Dynamic Publications

1-Kamenish-a begins 26.00 80.00 185.00
2 14.00 43.00 100.00
3-5 11.00 32.00 75.00
6-8 10.00 30.00 70.00
9-Bondage 3-D effect-c 13.00 40.00 90.00
10-Used in **SOTI**, pg. 181 10.00 30.00 65.00
11-18 9.15 25.00 55.00
19-r/Journey Into Fear #1; cover is a splash from one story; Baker-r(2)
10.00 30.00 65.00
20,21-Reprints; 20-r/#1 with new-c 6.70 20.00 40.00

STRANGE MYSTERIES
1963 - 1964
I. W. Enterprises/Super Comics

I.W. Reprint #9; Rulah-r/Spook #28 2.00 5.00 10.00
Super Reprint #10-12,15-17('63-'64): 10,11-r/Strange #2,1. 12-r/Tales of Horror #5 (3/53) less-c. 15-r/Dark Mysteries #23. 16-r/The Dead Who Walk. 17-r/Dark Mysteries #22 2.00 5.00 10.00
Super Reprint #18-r/Witchcraft #1; Kubert-a 2.00 5.00 10.00

STRANGE PLANETS
1958; 1963-64
I. W. Enterprises/Super Comics

I.W. Reprint #1(nd)-Reprints E. C. Incredible S/F #30 plus-c/Strange Worlds #3 5.85 17.50 35.00
I.W. Reprint #8-r/? Exist? 3.20 8.00 16.00
I.W. Reprint #9-Orlando/Wood-r/Strange Worlds #4; cover-r from Flying Saucers #1 9.15 27.50 55.00
Super Reprint #10-Wood-r (22 pg.) from Space Detective #1; cover-r/Attack on Planet Mars 8.35 25.00 50.00
Super Reprint #11-Wood-r (25 pg.) from An Earthman on Venus
10.00 30.00 70.00
Super Reprint #12-Orlando-r/Rocket to the Moon 8.35 25.00 50.00
Super Reprint #15-Reprints Journey Into Unknown Worlds #8; Heath, Colan-r
3.00 7.50 15.00
Super Reprint #16-Reprints Avon's Strange Worlds #6; Kinstler, Check-a
4.00 10.00 20.00
Super Reprint #17-r/? 1.80 4.50 9.00
Super Reprint #18-Reprints Great Exploits #1 (Daring Adventures #6); Space Busters, Explorer Joe, The Son of Robin Hood; Krigstein-a
3.20 8.00 16.00

STRANGERS, THE
June, 1993 - Present ($1.95, color)
Malibu Comics (Ultraverse)

1-4,6-8: 1-1st app. The Strangers. 2-Polybagged w/trading card
.80 2.00
1-Holographic-c Edition 35.00
5-($2.50, 40 pgs.)-Rune flip-c/story by B. Smith (3 pgs.) 1.00 2.50

STRANGE SPORTS STORIES (See Brave & the Bold, DC Special, and DC Super Stars #10)
Sept-Oct, 1973 - No. 6, July-Aug, 1974
National Periodical Publications

Brave and the Bold #45-49 (12-1/62-63 - 8-9/63)-Strange Sports Stories by Infantino 4.30 13.00 30.00
1 1.20 3.00 7.00
2-6: 3-Swan/Anderson-a 1.60 4.00

STRANGE STORIES FROM ANOTHER WORLD (Unknown World #1)
No. 2, Aug, 1952 - No. 5, Feb, 1953
Fawcett Publications

Strange Suspense Stories #62, © CC

Strange Tales #21, © MEG

Strange Tales #105, © MEG

GD25 FN65 NM94

2-Saunders painted-c 25.00 75.00 175.00
3-5-Saunders painted-c 19.00 57.00 130.00

TRANGE STORIES OF SUSPENSE (Rugged Action #1 4)
lo. 5, Oct, 1955 - No. 16, Aug, 1957
tlas Comics (CSI)

5(#1) 17.00 52.00 120.00
6,9 10.00 30.00 70.00
7-E. C. swipe cover/Vault of Horror #32 11.00 32.00 75.00
8-Morrow/Williamson-a; Pakula-a 11.00 32.00 75.00
10-Crandall, Torres, Meskin-a 11.00 32.00 75.00
11-13: 12-Torres, Pakula-a. 13-E.C. art swipes 8.35 25.00 50.00
14-16: 14-Williamson/Mayo-a. 15-Krigstein-a. 16-Fox, Powell-a 9.15 27.50 55.00

OTE: ***Everett** a-6, 7, 13; c-8, 9, 11-14. **Heath** a-5. **Maneely** c-5. **Morisi** a-11. **Morrow** a-13. owell a-8. **Severin** c-7. **Wildey** a-14.*

TRANGE STORY (Also see Front Page)
une-July, 1946 (52 pages)
arvey Publications

1-The Man In Black Called Fate by Powell 14.00 43.00 100.00

TRANGE SUSPENSE STORIES (Lawbreakers Suspense Stories #10-15; his Is Suspense #23-26; Captain Atom V1#78 on)
/52 - No. 5, 2/53; No. 16, 1/54 - No. 22, 11/54; No. 27, 10/55 - No. 77, 0/65; V3#1, 10/67 - V1#9, 9/69
awcett Publications/Charlton Comics No. 16 on

1-(Fawcett)-Powell, Sekowsky-a 38.00 115.00 265.00
2-George Evans horror story 24.00 73.00 170.00
3-5 (2/53)-George Evans horror stories 21.00 63.00 145.00
16(1-2/54) 11.50 34.00 80.00
17,21 10.00 30.00 60.00
18-E.C. swipe/HOF 7; Ditko-c/a(2) 17.00 52.00 120.00
19-Ditko electric chair-c; Ditko-a 22.00 67.00 155.00
20-Ditko-c/a(2) 16.00 50.00 115.00
22(11/54)-Ditko-c, Shuster-a; last pre-code issue; becomes This Is Suspense 13.50 41.00 95.00
27(10/55)-(Formerly This Is Suspense #26) 5.85 17.50 35.00
28-30,38 4.20 12.50 25.00
31-33,35,37,40-Ditko-c/a(2-3 each) 11.00 32.00 70.00
34-Story of ruthless business man, Wm. B. Gaines; Ditko-c/a 20.00 60.00 140.00
36-(15¢, 68 pgs.); Ditko-a(4) 11.00 32.00 75.00
39,41,52,53-Ditko-a 10.00 30.00 60.00
42-44,46,49,54-60 4.00 10.00 20.00
45,47,48,50,51-Ditko-c/a 8.35 25.00 50.00
61-74 1.60 4.00 8.00
75(6/65)-Reprints origin/1st app. Captain Atom by Ditko from Space Adventures #33 (75-77: 12 cent issues) 10.00 30.00 68.00
76,77-Captain Atom-r by Ditko/Space Advs. 3.60 10.75 25.00
V3#1(10/67)-4: All 12 cent issues 1.30 3.25 8.00
V1#2-9: 2-Ditko-a, atom bomb-c (all 12¢ issues) 1.00 2.00 5.00

NOTE: ***Alascia** a-19. **Aparo** a-60, V3#1, 2, 4; c-V1#4, 8. **Baily** a-1-3; c-2, 5. **Evans** c-3, 4. **Montes/Bache** c-66. **Powell** a-4. **Shuster** a-19, 21. **Marcus Swayze** a-27.*

STRANGE TALES (... Featuring Warlock #178-181; becomes Doctor Strange #169 on)
June, 1951 - #168, May, 1968; #169, Sept, 1973 - #188, Nov, 1976
Atlas (CCPC #1-67/ZPC #68-79/VPI #80-85)/Marvel #86(7/61) on

1-Horror/weird stories begin 145.00 435.00 1450.00
2 62.00 190.00 500.00
3,5: 3-Atom bomb panels 46.00 136.00 365.00
4-"The Evil Eye," cosmic eyeball story 50.00 150.00 400.00
6-9: 6-Heath-c/a 33.00 100.00 265.00
10-Krigstein-a 36.00 107.00 285.00
11-14,16-20 19.00 56.00 150.00
15-Krigstein-a 20.00 60.00 160.00
21,23-27,29-34: 27-Atom bomb panels. 33-Davis-a. 34-Last pre-code issue (2/55) 16.00 47.00 125.00
22-Krigstein, Forte/Fox-a 16.00 48.00 130.00
28-Jack Katz story used in Senate Investigation report, pgs. 7 & 169 16.00 48.00 130.00
35-41,43,44: 37-Vampire story by Colan 12.00 36.00 95.00
42,45,59,61-Krigstein-a; #61 (2/58) 13.00 38.00 100.00
46-57,60: 53,56-Crandall-a. 60-(8/57) 9.00 28.00 75.00
58,64-Williamson-a in each, with Mayo-#58 10.00 30.00 80.00
62,63,65,66: 62-Torres-a. 66-Crandall-a 8.00 23.00 70.00
67-Prototype ish. (Quicksilver) 12.00 37.00 110.00
68,71,72,74,77,80: Ditko/Kirby-a in #67-80 10.00 30.00 90.00
69-Prototype ish. (Prof. X) 15.00 45.00 135.00
70-Prototype ish. (Giant Man) 15.00 45.00 135.00
73-Prototype ish. (Ant-Man) 15.00 45.00 135.00
75-Prototype ish. (Iron Man) 15.00 45.00 135.00
76-Prototype ish. (Human Torch) 15.00 45.00 135.00
78-Prototype ish. (Ant-Man) 15.00 45.00 135.00
79-Prototype ish. (Dr. Strange) (12/60) 15.00 45.00 135.00
81-83,85-88,90,91: Ditko/Kirby-a in all. 92-Last 10 cent issue 8.00 26.00 76.00
84-Prototype ish. (Magneto)(5/61); has powers like Magneto of X-Men over two years later; Ditko/Kirby-a 13.00 40.00 115.00
89-1st app. Fin Fang Foom (10/61) by Kirby 25.00 75.00 225.00
92-Prototype ish. (Ancient One) 10.00 30.00 90.00
93-96,98-100: Kirby-a 8.00 23.00 70.00
97-Prototype ish. (Aunt May & Uncle Ben) by Ditko (6/62), before Amazing Fantasy #15; Kirby-a 22.00 65.00 200.00

GD25 FN65 VF82 NM94

101-Human Torch begins by Kirby (10/62); origin recap Fantastic Four & Human Torch 64.00 192.00 383.00 575.00

GD25 FN65 NM94

102-1st app. Wizard 28.00 84.00 225.00
103-105: 104-1st app. Trapster. 105-2nd Wizard 21.00 64.00 170.00
106,108,109: 106-Fantastic Four guests (3/63) 14.00 43.00 115.00
107-Human Torch/Sub-Mariner battle; 4th S.A. Sub-Mariner app. & 1st app. outside of Fantastic Four 17.00 51.00 135.00

GD25 FN65 VF82 NM94

110-(7/63)-Intro Doctor Strange, Ancient One & Wong by Ditko 75.00 225.00 450.00 675.00

GD25 FN65 NM94

111-2nd Dr. Strange 28.00 84.00 225.00
112,113 9.00 28.00 75.00
114-Acrobat disguised as Captain America, 1st app. since the G.A.; intro. & 1st app. Victoria Bentley; 3rd Dr. Strange app. & begin series (11/63) 27.00 80.00 240.00
115-Origin Dr. Strange; Human Torch vs. Sandman (Spidey villain; 2nd app. & brief origin); early Spider-Man x-over, 12/63 36.00 108.00 325.00
116-Human Torch battles The Thing; 1st Thing x-over 9.00 26.00 70.00
117,118,120: 120-1st Iceman x-over (from X-Men) 6.00 19.00 50.00
119-Spider-Man x-over (2 pg. cameo) 9.00 28.00 75.00
121,122,124,126-134: Thing/Torch team-up in 121-134. 126-Intro Clea. 128-Quicksilver & Scarlet Witch app. (1/65). 130-The Beatles cameo. 134-Last Human Torch; The Watcher-c/story; Wood-a(i) 5.50 17.00 40.00
123-1st app. The Beetle (see Amazing Spider-Man #21 for next app.); 1st Thor x-over (8/64); Loki app. 6.00 19.00 45.00
125-Torch & Thing battle Sub-Mariner (10/64) 5.50 17.00 40.00
135-Col. (formerly Sgt.) Nick Fury becomes Nick Fury Agent of Shield (origin/1st app.) by Kirby (8/65); series begins 8.00 25.00 75.00
136-147,149: 138-Intro Eternity. 146-Last Ditko Dr. Strange who is in consecutive stories since #113. 147-Dr. Strange (by Everett #147-152) continues thru #168, then Dr. Strange #169 3.60 10.75 25.00
148-Origin Ancient One 6.00 17.00 50.00
150(11/66)-John Buscema's 1st work at Marvel 3.60 10.75 25.00
151-Kirby/Steranko-c/a; 1st Marvel work by Steranko 4.70 14.00 33.00
152,153-Kirby/Steranko-a 3.60 10.75 25.00

Strange Tales V2#18, © MEG

Strange Worlds #4, © AVON

Strike #1, © Chuck Dixon & Tom Lyle

	GD25	FN65	NM94
154-158-Steranko-a/script	3.60	10.75	25.00
159-Origin Nick Fury retold; Intro Val; Captain America-c/story; Steranko-a	4.00	12.00	28.00
160-162-Steranko-a/scripts; Capt. America app.	3.30	10.00	23.00
163-166,168-Steranko-a(p). 168-Last Nick Fury (gets own book next month) & last Dr. Strange who also gets own book	3.30	10.00	23.00
167-Steranko pen/script; classic flag-c	4.85	15.00	34.00
169-177: 169-1st app. Brother Voodoo(origin in 169,170) & begin series, ends 173. 174-Origin Golem. 177-Brunner-c		1.00	2.50
178-(2/75)-Warlock by Starlin begins; origin Warlock & Him retold; 1st app. Magus; Starlin-c/a & scripts in 178-181 (all before Warlock #9)	2.60	7.50	18.00
179-181-All Warlock. 179-Intro/1st app. Pip the Troll. 180-Intro Gamora. 181-(8/75)-Warlock story continued in Warlock #9	1.50	3.75	9.00
182-188		1.00	2.50
Annual 1(1962)-Reprints from Strange Tales #73,76,78, Tales of Suspense #7,9, Tales to Astonish #1,6,7, & Journey Into Mystery #53,55,59	36.00	108.00	325.00
Annual 2(7/63)-Reprints from Strange Tales #67, Strange Worlds (Atlas) #1-3, World of Fantasy #16; new Human Torch vs. Spider-Man story by Kirby/Ditko (1st Spidey x-over; tied for 6th app. with Amazing Spider-Man #5); Kirby-c	43.00	128.00	385.00

NOTE: ***Briefer** a-17. **Burgos** a-123p. **J. Buscema** a-174p. **Colan** a-11, 20, 37, 53, 169-173p, 188p. **Davis** c-71. **Ditko** a-46, 50, 67-122, 123-125p, 126-146, 175r, 182-188r; c-51, 93, 115, 121, 146. **Everett** a-4, 21, 40-42, 73, 147-152, 164i; c-8, 10, 11, 13, 15, 24, 45, 49-54, 56, 58, 60, 61, 63, 148, 150, 152, 158i. **Forte** a-27, 43, 50, 53, 54, 60. **Heath** a-6; c-6, 18-20. **Kamen** a-45. **G. Kane** c-170-173, 182p. **Kirby** Human Torch-101-105, 108, 109, 114, 120; Nick Fury-135p, 141-143p; (Layouts)-135-153; other **Kirby** a-67-100p; c-68-70, 72-92, 94, 95, 101-114, 116-123, 125-130, 132-135, 136p, 138-145, 147, 149, 151p. **Kirby/Ayers** c-101-106, 108-110. **Lawrence** a-29. **Leiber/ Fox** a-110, 111, 113. **Maneely** a-3, 37, 42; c-33, 40. **Moldoff** a-20. **Mooney** a-174i. **Morisi** a-53, 56. **Morrow** a-54. **Orlando** a-41, 44, 46, 49, 52. **Powell** a-42, 44, 49, 54, 130-134p; c-131p. **Reinman** a-11, 50, 74, 88, 91, 95, 104, 106, 112i, 124-127i. **Robinson** a-17. **Roussos** c-201i. **R.Q. Sale** a-56; c-16. **Sekowski** a-3, 11. **Severin** a(i)-136-138; c-137. **Starlin** a-178, 179, 180p, 181p; c-178-180, 181p. **Steranko** a-151-161, 162-168p; c-151i, 153, 155, 157, 159, 161, 163, 165, 167. **Torres** a-53, 62. **Tuska** a-14, 166p. **Whitney** a-149. **Wildey** a-42, 56. **Woodbridge** a-59. Fantastic Four cameos #101-134. Jack Katz app.-26.*

STRANGE TALES (Marvel, 1987-'88)(Value: cover or less)

STRANGE TALES OF THE UNUSUAL
Dec, 1955 - No. 11, Aug, 1957
Atlas Comics (ACI No. 1-4/WPI No. 5-11)

	GD25	FN65	NM94
1-Powell-a	22.00	65.00	150.00
2	11.00	32.00	75.00
3-Williamson-a, 4 pgs.	11.50	34.00	80.00
4,6,8,11	8.35	25.00	50.00
5-Crandall, Ditko-a	11.00	32.00	75.00
7,9: 7-Kirby, Orlando-a. 9-Krigstein-a	10.00	30.00	60.00
10-Torres, Morrow-a	8.35	25.00	50.00

NOTE: ***Baily** a-6. **Brodsky** c-2-4. **Everett** a-2, 6; c-6, 9, 11. **Heck** a-1. **Maneely** c-1. **Orlando** a-7. **Pakula** a-10. **Romita** a-1. **R.Q. Sale** a-3. **Wildey** a-3.*

STRANGE TERRORS
June, 1952 - No. 7, Mar, 1953
St. John Publishing Co.

	GD25	FN65	NM94
1-Bondage-c; Zombies spelled Zoombies on-c; Fineesque-a	22.00	65.00	150.00
2	12.00	36.00	85.00
3-Kubert-a; painted-c	16.00	50.00	115.00
4-Kubert-a (reprinted in Mystery Tales #18); Ekgren-c; Fineesque-a; Jerry Iger caricature	22.00	65.00	150.00
5-Kubert-a; painted-c	16.00	48.00	110.00
6-Giant (25¢, 100 pgs.)(1/53); bondage-c	22.00	65.00	150.00
7-Giant (25¢, 100 pgs.); Kubert-c/a	25.00	75.00	175.00

NOTE: ***Cameron** a-6, 7. **Morisi** a-6.*

STRANGE WORLD OF YOUR DREAMS
Aug, 1952 - No. 4, Jan-Feb, 1953
Prize Publications

	GD25	FN65	NM94
1-Simon & Kirby-a	36.00	110.00	250.00
2,3-Simon & Kirby-a. 2-Meskin-a	29.00	85.00	200.00
4-S&K-c; Meskin-a	24.00	70.00	165.00

STRANGE WORLDS (#18 continued from Avon's Eerie #1-17)
11/50 - No. 9, 11/52; No. 18, 10-11/54 - No. 22, 9-10/55 (No #11-17)
Avon Periodicals

	GD25	FN65	NM94
1-Kenton of the Star Patrol by Kubert (r/Eerie #1-'47); Crom the Barbarian by John Giunta	49.00	146.00	340.00
2-Wood-a; Crom the Barbarian by Giunta; Dara of the Vikings app.; used in **SOTI**, pg. 112; injury to eye panel	43.00	130.00	300.00
3-Wood/Orlando-a (Kenton), Wood/Williamson/Frazetta/Krenkel/Orlando-a (7 pgs.); Malu Slave Girl Princess app.; Kinstler-c	80.00	240.00	560.00
4-Wood-c/a (Kenton); Orlando-a; origin The Enchanted Daggar; Sultan-a	41.00	125.00	290.00
5-Orlando/Wood-a (Kenton); Wood-c	34.00	105.00	240.00
6-Kinstler-a(2); Orlando/Wood-c; Check-a	24.00	72.00	165.00
7-Fawcette & Becker/Alascia-a	17.00	52.00	120.00
8-Kubert, Kinstler, Hollingsworth & Lazarus-a; Lazarus Robot-c	19.00	58.00	135.00
9-Kinstler, Fawcette, Alascia-a	17.00	52.00	120.00
18-(Formerly Eerie #17)-r/"Attack on Planet Mars" by Kubert	17.00	52.00	120.00
19-r/Avon's "Robotmen of the Lost Planet;" last pre-code issue; Robot-c	17.00	52.00	120.00
20-War-c/stories; Wood-c(r)/U.S. Paratroops #1	5.35	16.00	32.00
21,22-War-c/stories	4.20	12.50	25.00
I.W. Reprint #5-Kinstler-a(r)/Avon's #9	2.00	5.00	10.00

STRANGE WORLDS
Dec, 1958 - No. 5, Aug, 1959
Marvel Comics (MPI No. 1,2/Male No. 3,5)

	GD25	FN65	NM94
1-Kirby & Ditko-a; flying saucer issue	30.00	90.00	300.00
2-Ditko-c/a	18.00	53.00	175.00
3-Kirby-a(2)	15.00	44.00	145.00
4-Williamson-a	14.00	42.00	140.00
5-Ditko-a	12.00	36.00	120.00

NOTE: ***Buscema** a-3, 4. **Ditko** a-1-5; c-2. **Kirby** a-1, 3. **Kirby/Brodsky** c-1, 3-5.*

STRAWBERRY SHORTCAKE (Marvel)(Value: cover or less)

STRAY TOASTERS (Marvel)(Value: cover or less)

STREET COMIX (50 cents)
1973 (36 pgs.; B&W) (20,000 print run)
Street Enterprises/King Features

	GD25	FN65	NM94
1-Rip Kirby			1.00
2-Flash Gordon			1.20

STREETFIGHTER (Ocean)(Value: cover or less)

STREET POET RAY (Blackthorne)(Value: cover or less)

STREETS (DC)(Value: cover or less)

STRICTLY PRIVATE
July, 1942 (#1 on sale 6/15/42)
Eastern Color Printing Co.

	GD25	FN65	NM94
1,2	17.00	50.00	110.00

STRIKE! (Eclipse)(Value: cover or less)

STRIKE FORCE AMERICA (Comico)(Value: cover or less)(See The Elementals V2#16)

STRIKEFORCE: MORITURI (Marvel, 1986 & 1989 titles)(Value: cover or less)

STRIKER (Viz)(Value: cover or less)

STRONG MAN (Also see Complimentary Comics & Power of...)
Mar-Apr, 1955 - No. 4, Sept-Oct, 1955
Magazine Enterprises

	GD25	FN65	NM94
1(A-1 #130)-Powell-c/a	14.00	43.00	100.00
2-4: (A-1 #132,134,139)-Powell-a. 2-Powell-c	11.50	34.00	80.00

STRONTIUM DOG (Eagle & Quality)(Value: cover or less)

The Sub-Mariner #14, © MEG

Sub-Mariner Comics #16, © MEG

Sub-Mariner Comics #28, © MEG

GD25 FN65 NM94 | GD25 FN65 NM94

STRYFE'S STRIKE FILE
Jan, 1993 ($1.75, color, no ads)
Marvel Comics
1-Stroman, Capullo, Andy Kubert, Brandon Peterson-a; silver metallic ink-c; X-Men tie-in to X-Cutioner's Song .70 1.75
1-Gold metallic ink 2nd printing .70 1.75

STUMBO THE GIANT (See Harvey Hits #49, 54, 57, 60, 63, 66, 69, 72, 78, 88 & Hot Stuff #2)

STUMBO TINYTOWN
Oct, 1963 - No. 13, Nov, 1966 (All 25¢ giants)
Harvey Publications
1-Stumbo, Hot Stuff & others begin 11.50 34.00 80.00
2 6.70 20.00 40.00
3-5 4.70 14.00 28.00
6-13 4.00 12.00 24.00

STUNTMAN COMICS (Also see Thrills Of Tomorrow)
Apr-May, 1946 - No. 2, June-July, 1946; No. 3, Oct-Nov, 1946
Harvey Publications
1-Origin Stuntman by S&K reprinted in Black Cat #9; S&K-c 75.00 225.00 475.00
2-S&K-c/a; The Duke of Broadway story 50.00 150.00 330.00
3-Small size (5-1/2x8-1/2"; B&W; 32 pgs.); distributed to mail subscribers only; S&K-a; Kid Adonis by S&K reprinted in Green Hornet #37
Estimated value... $250.00-$400.00
(Also see All-New #15, Boy Explorers #2, Flash Gordon #5 & Thrills of Tomorrow)

STUPID HEROES
Sept, 1993 - Present ($2.75, color)
Mirage Studios
1-Laird-c/a & scripts; 2 trading cards bound in 1.10 2.75

SUBMARINE ATTACK (Formerly Speed Demons)
No. 11, May, 1958 - No. 54, Feb-Mar, 1966
Charlton Comics
11 3.20 8.00 16.00
12-20 2.00 5.00 10.00
21-54 1.60 4.00 8.00
NOTE: *Glanzman c/a-25. Montes/Bache a-38, 40, 41.*

SUB-MARINER (See All-Select, All-Winners, Blonde Phantom, Daring, The Defenders, Fantastic Four #4, Human Torch, The Invaders, Iron Man &..., Marvel Mystery, Marvel Spotlight #27, Men's Adventures, Motion Picture Funnies Weekly, Namora, Namor, The..., Prince Namor, The Sub-Mariner, Saga Of The..., Tales to Astonish #70 & 2nd series, USA & Young Men)

SUB-MARINER, THE (2nd Series)(Sub-Mariner #31 on)
May, 1968 - No. 72, Sept, 1974 (No. 43: 52 pgs.)
Marvel Comics Group
1-Origin Sub-Mariner; story continued from Iron Man & Sub-Mariner #1 19.00 56.00 130.00
2-Triton app. 7.00 21.00 50.00
3-10: 5-1st Tiger Shark (9/68). 7-Photo-c. 8-Sub-Mariner vs. Thing. 9-1st app. Serpent Crown (origin in #10 & 12) 4.00 12.00 28.00
11-13,15: 15-Last 12 cent issue 3.20 8.00 20.00
14-Sub-Mariner vs. G.A. Human Torch; death of Toro (1st modern app. & only app. Toro, 6/69) 4.70 14.00 33.00
16-20: 19-1st Sting Ray (11/69); Stan Lee, Romita, Heck, Thomas, Everett & Kirby cameos. 20-Dr. Doom app. 1.70 5.00 12.00
21-33,36-40: 22-Dr. Strange x-over. 25-Origin Atlantis. 30-Capt. Marvel x-over. 37-Death of Lady Dorma. 38-Origin. 40-Spider-Man x-over 1.25 3.00 7.50
34,35-Prelude to 1st Defenders story. 34-Hulk & Silver Surfer x-over. 35-Namor/Hulk/Silver Surfer team up to battle The Avengers-c/story (3/71); hints at teaming up again 2.30 6.75 16.00
41-49,51-72: 42-Last 15 cent issue. 44,45-Sub-Mariner vs. H. Torch. 47,48-Dr. Doom app. 49-Cosmic Cube story. 59-1st battle with Thor. 61-Last artwork by Everett; 1st 4 pgs. completed by Mortimer; pgs. 5-20 by Mooney. 62-1st Tales of Atlantis, ends 66. 64-Hitler cameo. 67-New costume; F.F. x-over. 69-Spider-Man x-over (6 panels) 1.80 4.50
50-1st app. Nita, Namor's niece (later Namorita in New Warriors) 1.10 2.70 6.50
Special 1,2: 1(1/71)-r/Tales to Astonish #70-73. 2(1/72)-r/T.T.A. #74-76; Everett-a 1.10 2.70 6.50
NOTE: ***Bolle** a-67i. **Buscema** a(p)-1-8, 20, 24. **Colan** a(p)-10, 11, 40, 43, 46-49, Special 1, 2; c(p)-10, 11, 40. **Craig** a-17, 19-23i. **Everett** a-45r, 50-55, 57, 58, 59-61(plot), 63(plot); c-47, 48i, 55, 57-59i, 61, Spec. 2. **G. Kane** c(p)-42-52, 58, 66, 70, 71. **Mooney** a-24i, 25i, 32-35i, 39i, 42i, 44i, 45i, 60i, 61i, 65p, 66p, 68i. Severin c/a-38i. **Starlin** c-59p. **Tuska** a-41p, 42p, 69-71p. **Wrightson** a-36i. #53, 54-r/stories Sub-Mariner Comics #41 & 39.*

SUB-MARINER COMICS (1st Series) (The Sub-Mariner #1, 2, 33-42)(Official True Crime Cases #24 on; Amazing Mysteries #32 on; Best Love #33 on)
Spring, 1941 - No. 23, Sum, 1947; No. 24, Wint, 1947 - No. 31, 4/49; No. 32, 7/49; No. 33, 4/54 - No. 42, 10/55
Timely/Marvel Comics (TCI 1-7/SePI 8/MPI 9-32/Atlas Comics (CCC 33-42))

	GD25	FN65	VF82	NM94
1-The Sub-Mariner by Everett & The Angel begin	720.00	2160.00	4680.00	7200.00

(Estimated up to 190 total copies exist, 8 in NM/Mint)

	GD25	FN65	NM94
2-Everett-a	283.00	850.00	1900.00
3-Churchill assassination-c; 40 pg. Sub-Mariner story	217.00	650.00	1450.00
4-Everett-a, 40 pgs.; 1 pg. Wolverton-a	183.00	550.00	1200.00
5: 5,8-Gabrielle/Klein-c	133.00	400.00	875.00
6-10: 9-Wolverton-a, 3 pgs.; flag-c	100.00	300.00	650.00
11-15	68.00	205.00	460.00
16-20	63.00	190.00	420.00
21-Last Angel; Everett-a	54.00	162.00	365.00
22-Young Allies app.	54.00	162.00	365.00
23-The Human Torch, Namora x-over (Sum/47); 2nd app. Namora after Marvel Mystery #82	54.00	162.00	365.00
24-Namora x-over (3rd app.)	54.00	162.00	365.00
25-The Blonde Phantom begins (Spr/48), ends No. 31; Kurtzman-a; Namora x-over; last quarterly issue	63.00	190.00	435.00
26-28: 28-Namora cover; Everett-a	54.00	162.00	365.00
29-31 (4/49): 29-The Human Torch app. 31-Capt. America app.	54.00	162.00	365.00
32 (7/49, Scarce)-Origin Sub-Mariner	104.00	312.00	700.00
33 (4/54)-Origin Sub-Mariner; The Human Torch app.; Namora x-over in Sub-Mariner #33-42	51.00	154.00	360.00
34,35-Human Torch in each	43.00	130.00	300.00
36,37,39-41: 36,39-41-Namora app.	43.00	130.00	300.00
38-Origin Sub-Mariner's wings; Namora app.; last pre-code (2/55)	51.00	154.00	360.00
42-Last issue	51.00	154.00	360.00

NOTE: *Angel by **Gustavson**-#1, 8. **Brodsky** c-34-36, 42. **Everett** a-1-4, 22-24, 26-42; c-32, 33, 40. **Maneely** a-38; c-37, 39-41. **Rico** c-27-31. **Schomburg** c-1-4, 6, 8-18, 20. **Sekowsky** c-24. 25, 26(w/Rico). **Shores** c-21-23, 38. Bondage c-13, 22, 24, 25, 34.*

SUBSPECIES
May, 1991 - No. 4, Aug, 1991 ($2.50, color, mini-series)
Eternity Comics
1-4: New stories based on horror movie 1.00 2.50

SUBURBAN SHE-DEVILS (Marvel)(Value: cover or less)

SUE & SALLY SMITH (Formerly My Secret Life)
V2#48, Nov, 1962 - No. 54, Nov, 1963 (Flying Nurses)
Charlton Comics
V2#48 1.20 3.00 6.00
49-54 .80 2.00 4.00

SUGAR & SPIKE (Also see The Best of DC)
Apr-May, 1956 - No. 98, Oct-Nov, 1971
National Periodical Publications
1 (Scarce) 70.00 210.00 700.00
2 39.00 118.00 355.00

Sugar Bowl Comics #1, © FF

Suicide Squad #40, © DC

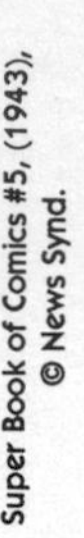

Super Book of Comics #5, (1943), © News Synd.

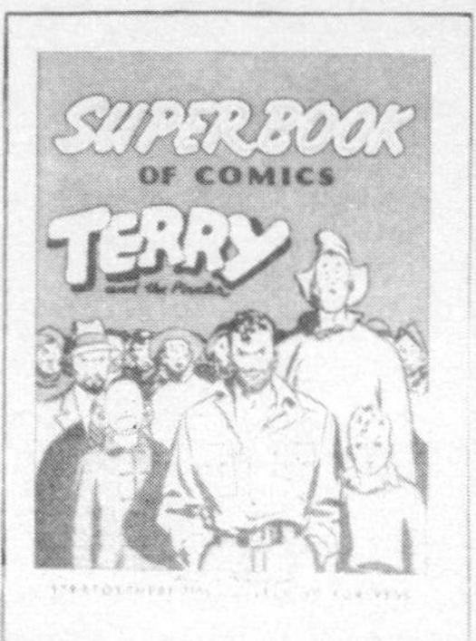

	GD25	FN65	NM94
3-5	33.00	100.00	300.00
6-10	19.00	58.00	175.00
11-20	18.00	53.00	160.00
21-29,31-40: 26-X-Mas-c	11.00	34.00	80.00
30-Scribbly & Scribbly, Jr. x-over	13.00	40.00	90.00
41-60	7.00	21.00	50.00
61-80: 69-1st app. Tornado-Tot-c/story. 72-Origin & 1st app. Bernie the Brain	4.30	13.00	30.00
81-98: 84-Bernie the Brain apps. as Superman in 1 panel (9/69). 85-(68 pgs.); r-#72. #96-(68 pgs.). #97,98-(52 pgs.)	3.25	9.50	22.00

NOTE: *All written and drawn by* ***Sheldon Mayer.***

SUGAR BEAR
No date, circa 1975? (16 pages) (2-1/2x4-1/2")
Post Cereal Giveaway

	GD25	FN65	NM94
"The Almost Take Over of the Post Office," "The Race Across the Atlantic," "The Zoo Goes Wild" each...			1.00

SUGAR BOWL COMICS (Teen-age)
May, 1948 - No. 5, Jan, 1949
Famous Funnies

	GD25	FN65	NM94
1-Toth-c/a	10.00	30.00	70.00
2,4,5	4.20	12.50	25.00
3-Toth-a	8.35	25.00	50.00

SUGARFOOT (See 4-Color #907, 992, 1059, 1098, 1147, 1209)

SUICIDE SQUAD (DC)(Value: cover or less)(See Brave & the Bold and Doom Patrol & Suicide Squad)

SUMMER FUN (See Dell Giants)

SUMMER FUN (Formerly Li'l Genius; Holiday Surprise #55)
No. 54, Oct, 1966 (Giant)
Charlton Comics

	GD25	FN65	NM94
54	1.60	4.00	8.00

SUMMER FUN (Disney, 1991)(Value: cover or less)

SUMMER LOVE (Formerly Brides in Love?)
V2#46, Oct, 1965; V2#47, Oct, 1966; V2#48, Nov, 1968
Charlton Comics

	GD25	FN65	NM94
V2#46-Beatles-c/story	7.50	22.50	45.00
47-Beatles story	7.50	22.50	45.00
48	.80	2.00	4.00

SUMMER MAGIC (See Movie Comics)

SUNDANCE (See 4-Color #1126)

SUNDANCE KID (Also see Blazing Six-Guns)
June, 1971 - No. 3, Sept, 1971 (52 pages)
Skywald Publications

	GD25	FN65	NM94
1-Durango Kid; Two Kirby Bullseye-r		1.20	3.00
2-Swift Arrow, Durango Kid, Bullseye by S&K; Meskin plus 1 pg. origin		.80	2.00
3-Durango Kid, Billy the Kid, Red Hawk-r			1.50

SUNDAY FUNNIES
1950
Harvey Publications

	GD25	FN65	NM94
1	2.80	7.00	14.00

SUN DEVILS (DC)(Value: cover or less)

SUN FUN KOMIKS
1939 (15 cents; black, white & red)
Sun Publications

	GD25	FN65	NM94
1-Satire on comics	19.00	58.00	135.00

SUN GIRL (See The Human Torch & Marvel Mystery Comics #88)
Aug, 1948 - No. 3, Dec, 1948
Marvel Comics (CCC)

	GD25	FN65	NM94
1-Sun Girl begins; Miss America app.	79.00	238.00	550.00
2,3: 2-The Blonde Phantom begins	62.00	188.00	425.00

SUNNY, AMERICA'S SWEETHEART (Formerly Cosmo Cat #1-10)
No. 11, Dec, 1947 - No. 14, June, 1948
Fox Features Syndicate

	GD25	FN65	NM94
11-Feldstein-c/a	39.00	120.00	275.00
12-14-Feldstein-c/a; 14-Lingerie panels	32.00	95.00	225.00
I.W. Reprint #8-Feldstein-a; r/Fox issue	10.00	30.00	60.00

SUN-RUNNERS (Pacific/Eclipse/Amazing)(Value: cover or less)

SUNSET CARSON (Also see Cowboy Western)
Feb, 1951 - No. 4, 1951 (No month)
Charlton Comics

	GD25	FN65	NM94
1-Photo/retouched-c (Scarce, all issues)	64.00	195.00	450.00
2	50.00	150.00	350.00
3,4	39.00	118.00	275.00

SUPER ANIMALS PRESENTS PIDGY & THE MAGIC GLASSES
Dec, 1953
Star Publications

	GD25	FN65	NM94
3-D 1-L. B. Cole-c	32.00	95.00	225.00

SUPER BOOK OF COMICS
nd (1943?) (32 pgs., soft-c) (Pan-Am/Gilmore Oil/Kelloggs premiums)
Western Publishing Co.

	GD25	FN65	NM94
nn-Dick Tracy (Gilmore)-Magic Morro app.	39.00	118.00	275.00
1-Dick Tracy & The Smuggling Ring; Stratosphere Jim app. (Rare) (Pan-Am)	32.00	96.00	225.00
1-Smilin' Jack, Magic Morro (Pan-Am)	10.00	30.00	60.00
2-Smilin' Jack, Stratosphere Jim (Pan-Am)	10.00	30.00	60.00
2-Smitty, Magic Morro (Pan-Am)	10.00	30.00	60.00
3-Captain Midnight, Magic Morro (Pan-Am)	13.00	40.00	90.00
3-Moon Mullins?	8.35	25.00	50.00
4-Red Ryder, Magic Morro (Pan-Am)	8.35	25.00	50.00
4-Smitty, Stratosphere Jim (Pan-Am)	8.35	25.00	50.00
5-Don Winslow, Magic Morro (Gilmore)	8.35	25.00	50.00
5-Don Winslow, Stratosphere Jim (Pan-Am)	8.35	25.00	50.00
5-Terry & the Pirates	13.00	40.00	90.00
6-Don Winslow, Stratosphere Jim (Pan-Am)-McWilliams-a	10.00	30.00	60.00
6-King of the Royal Mounted, Magic Morro (Pan-Am)	10.00	30.00	60.00
7-Dick Tracy, Magic Morro (Pan-Am)	14.00	43.00	100.00
7-Little Orphan Annie	10.00	30.00	60.00
8-Dick Tracy, Stratosphere Jim (Pan-Am)	14.00	43.00	100.00
8-Dan Dunn, Magic Morro (Pan-Am)	10.00	30.00	60.00
9-Terry & the Pirates, Magic Morro (Pan-Am)	11.50	34.00	80.00
10-Red Ryder, Magic Morro (Pan-Am)	8.35	25.00	50.00

SUPER-BOOK OF COMICS
(Omar Bread & Hancock Oil Co. giveaways)
1944 - No. 30, 1947 (Omar); 1947 - 1948 (Hancock) (16 pgs.)
Western Publishing Co.

Note: The Hancock issues are all exact reprints of the earlier Omar issues. The issue numbers were removed in some of the reprints.

	GD25	FN65	NM94
1-Dick Tracy (Omar, 1944)	17.00	51.00	120.00
1-Dick Tracy (Hancock, 1947)	13.00	40.00	90.00
2-Bugs Bunny (Omar, 1944)	5.85	17.50	35.00
2-Bugs Bunny (Hancock, 1947)	4.70	14.00	28.00
3-Terry & the Pirates (Omar, 1944)	10.00	30.00	70.00
3-Terry & the Pirates (Hancock, 1947)	10.00	30.00	60.00
4-Andy Panda (Omar, 1944)	6.35	19.00	38.00
4-Andy Panda (Hancock, 1947)	4.70	14.00	28.00
5-Smokey Stover (Omar, 1945)	4.70	14.00	28.00
5-Smokey Stover (Hancock, 1947)	3.60	9.00	18.00
6-Porky Pig (Omar, 1945)	5.85	17.50	35.00
6-Porky Pig (Hancock, 1947)	4.70	14.00	28.00

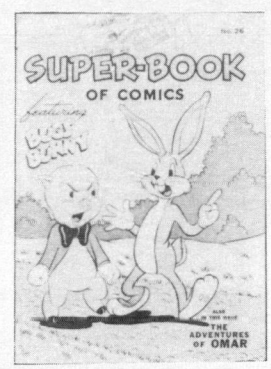

Super Book of Comics #26, © Warner Bros.

Superboy #143, © DC

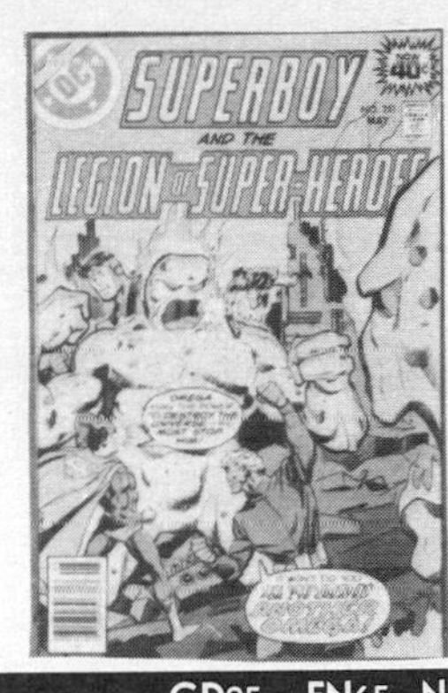

Superboy #251, © DC

	GD25	FN65	NM94
7-Smilin' Jack (Omar, 1945)	5.85	17.50	35.00
7-Smilin' Jack (Hancock, 1947)	4.70	14.00	28.00
8-Oswald the Rabbit (Omar, 1945)	4.70	14.00	28.00
8-Oswald the Rabbit (Hancock, 1947)	3.60	9.00	18.00
9-Alley Oop (Omar, 1945)	11.00	32.00	75.00
9-Alley Oop (Hancock, 1947)	10.00	30.00	65.00
10-Elmer Fudd (Omar, 1945)	4.70	14.00	28.00
10-Elmer Fudd (Hancock, 1947)	3.60	9.00	18.00
11-Little Orphan Annie (Omar, 1945)	6.70	20.00	40.00
11-Little Orphan Annie (Hancock, 1947)	5.00	15.00	30.00
12-Woody Woodpecker (Omar, 1945)	4.70	14.00	28.00
12-Woody Woodpecker (Hancock, 1947)	3.60	9.00	18.00
13-Dick Tracy (Omar, 1945)	11.00	32.00	75.00
13-Dick Tracy (Hancock, 1947)	10.00	30.00	65.00
14-Bugs Bunny (Omar, 1945)	4.70	14.00	28.00
14-Bugs Bunny (Hancock, 1947)	3.60	9.00	18.00
15-Andy Panda (Omar, 1945)	4.00	12.00	24.00
15-Andy Panda (Hancock, 1947)	3.60	9.00	18.00
16-Terry & the Pirates (Omar, 1945)	10.00	30.00	65.00
16-Terry & the Pirates (Hancock, 1947)	8.35	25.00	50.00
17-Smokey Stover (Omar, 1946)	4.70	14.00	28.00
17-Smokey Stover (Hancock, 1948?)	3.60	9.00	18.00
18-Porky Pig (Omar, 1946)	4.00	12.00	24.00
18-Porky Pig (Hancock, 1948?)	3.60	9.00	18.00
19-Smilin' Jack (Omar, 1946)	4.70	14.00	28.00
nn-Smilin' Jack (Hancock, 1948)	3.60	9.00	18.00
20-Oswald the Rabbit (Omar, 1946)	4.00	12.00	24.00
nn-Oswald the Rabbit (Hancock, 1948)	3.60	9.00	18.00
21-Gasoline Alley (Omar, 1946)	6.70	20.00	40.00
nn-Gasoline Alley (Hancock, 1948)	5.00	15.00	30.00
22-Elmer Fudd (Omar, 1946)	4.00	12.00	24.00
nn-Elmer Fudd (Hancock, 1948)	3.60	9.00	18.00
23-Little Orphan Annie (Omar, 1946)	5.85	17.50	35.00
nn-Little Orphan Annie (Hancock, 1948)	4.70	14.00	28.00
24-Woody Woodpecker (Omar, 1946)	4.00	12.00	24.00
nn-Woody Woodpecker (Hancock, 1948)	3.60	9.00	18.00
25-Dick Tracy (Omar, 1946)	10.00	30.00	65.00
nn-Dick Tracy (Hancock, 1948)	8.35	25.00	50.00
26-Bugs Bunny (Omar, 1946))	4.00	12.00	24.00
nn-Bugs Bunny (Hancock, 1948)	3.60	9.00	18.00
27-Andy Panda (Omar, 1946)	4.00	12.00	24.00
27-Andy Panda (Hancock, 1948)	3.60	9.00	18.00
28-Terry & the Pirates (Omar, 1946)	10.00	30.00	65.00
28-Terry & the Pirates (Hancock, 1948)	8.35	25.00	50.00
29-Smokey Stover (Omar, 1947)	4.00	12.00	24.00
29-Smokey Stover (Hancock, 1948)	3.60	9.00	18.00
30-Porky Pig (Omar, 1947)	4.00	12.00	24.00
30-Porky Pig (Hancock, 1948)	3.60	9.00	18.00
nn-Bugs Bunny (Hancock, 1948)-Does not match any Omar book	3.60	9.00	18.00

SUPERBOY (See Adventure, Aurora, DC Comics Presents, DC 100 Page Super Spectacular #15, DC Super Stars, 80 Page Giant #10, More Fun, The New Advs. of... & Superman Family #191)

SUPERBOY (...& the Legion of Super-Heroes with #231)(Becomes The Legion of Super-Heroes No. 259 on)
Mar-Apr, 1949 - No. 258, Dec, 1979 (#1-16: 52 pgs.)
National Periodical Publications/DC Comics

	GD25	FN65	VF82	NM94
1-Superman cover	380.00	1140.00	2470.00	3800.00

(Estimated up to 275 total copies exist, 15 in NM/Mint)

	GD25	FN65	NM94
2-Used in **SOTI**, pg. 35-36,226	135.00	410.00	950.00
3	100.00	300.00	700.00
4,5: 5-1st pre-Supergirl tryout (c/story, 11-12/49)	64.00	195.00	450.00
6-10: 8-1st Superbaby. 10-1st app. Lana Lang	59.00	180.00	415.00
11-15	43.00	130.00	300.00
16-20	31.00	95.00	220.00
21-26,28-30: 21-Lana Lang app.	24.00	72.00	165.00
27-Low distribution	27.00	80.00	185.00
31-38. 38-Last pre-code issue (1/55)	17.00	52.00	120.00
39-48,50 (7/56)	11.00	32.00	95.00
49 (6/56)-1st app. Metallo (Jor-El's robot)	14.00	42.00	125.00
51-60	8.00	25.00	75.00
61-67	7.00	20.00	60.00
68-Origin/1st app. original Bizarro (10-11/58)	39.00	117.00	350.00
69-77,79: 75-Spanking-c. 76-1st Supermonkey. 77-Pre-Pete Ross tryout	6.00	17.00	50.00
78-Origin Mr. Mxyzptlk & Superboy's costume	10.00	29.00	88.00
80-1st meeting Superboy/Supergirl (4/60)	9.00	27.00	80.00
81,83-85,87,88: 83-Origin/1st app. Kryptonite Kid	4.00	13.00	40.00
82-1st Bizarro Krypto	5.00	14.00	42.00
86(1/61)-4th Legion app; Intro Pete Ross	10.00	29.00	86.00
89(6/61)-1st app. Mon-el; 2nd Phantom Zone	17.00	52.00	155.00
90-92: 90-Pete Ross learns Superboy's I.D. 92-Last 10 cent issue	4.00	13.00	40.00
93-10th Legion app.(12/61); Chameleon Boy app.	4.50	14.00	32.00
94-97,99	3.20	8.00	20.00
98(7/62)-18th Legion app; origin & 1st app. Ultra Boy; Pete Ross joins Legion	4.30	13.00	30.00
100(10/62)-Ultra Boy app; 1st app. Phantom Zone villains, Dr. Xadu & Erndine. 2 pg. map of Krypton; origin Superboy retold; r-cover of Superman #1; Pete Ross joins Legion	18.00	54.00	125.00
101-120: 104-Origin Phantom Zone. 115-Atomic bomb-c. 117-Legion app.	1.65	4.70	11.00
121-128: 124(10/65)-1st app. Insect Queen (Lana Lang). 125-Legion cameo. 126-Origin Krypto the Super Dog retold with new facts	1.25	3.00	7.50
129 (80-pg. Giant G-22)-Reprints origin Mon-el	1.50	3.75	9.00
130-137,139,140: 131-Legion statues cameo in Dog Legionnaires story. 132-1st app. Supremo. 133-Superboy meets Robin		1.60	4.00
138 (80-pg. Giant G-35)	1.50	3.75	9.00
141-146,148-155,157-164,166-173,175,176: 145-Superboy's parents regain their youth. 171-1st app. Aquaboy? 172,173,176-Legion app.; 172-Origin Yango (Super Ape)		1.20	3.00
147(6/68)-Giant G-47; origin Saturn Girl, Lightning Lad, Cosmic Boy; origin Legion of Super-Pets-r/Adv. #293?	1.30	3.25	8.00
156,165,174 (Giants G-59,71,83)	1.00	2.50	6.00
177-184,186,187 (All 52 pgs.): 184-Origin Dial H for Hero-r		1.10	2.75
185-DC 100 Pg. Super Spectacular #12; Legion-c/story; Teen Titans, Kid Eternity(r/Hit #46), Star Spangled Kid-r(S.S. 55)		1.20	3.00
188-196: 188-Origin Karkan. 191-Origin Sunboy retold; Legion app. 193-Chameleon Boy & Shrinking Violet get new costumes. 195-1st app. Erg/Wildfire; Phantom Girl gets new costume. 196-Last Superboy solo story		.70	1.80
197-Legion series begins; Lightning Lad's new costume	1.00	2.50	5.50
198,199: 198-Element Lad & Princess Projectra get new costumes		.90	2.25
200-Bouncing Boy & Duo Damsel marry; J'onn J'onzz cameo		1.90	4.75
201,204,206,207,209: 201-Re-intro Erg as Wildfire. 204-Supergirl resigns from Legion. 206-Ferro Lad & Invisible Kid app. 209-Karate Kid gets new costume		1.00	2.50
202,205-(100 pgs.): 202-Light Lass gets new costume		1.20	3.00
203-Invisible Kid dies		1.40	3.50
208,210: 208-(68 pgs.). 210-Origin Karate Kid		1.20	3.00
211-220: 212-Matter-Eater Lad resigns. 216-1st app. Tyroc who joins Legion in #218		.90	2.25
221-249: 226-Intro. Dawnstar. 228-Death of Chemical King. 240-Origin Dawnstar. 242-(52 pgs.). 243-Legion of Substitute Heroes app. 243-245-(44 pgs.)		.65	1.60
250-258: 253-Intro Blok. 257-Return of Bouncing Boy & Duo Damsel by Ditko			

Supercar #1, © GK

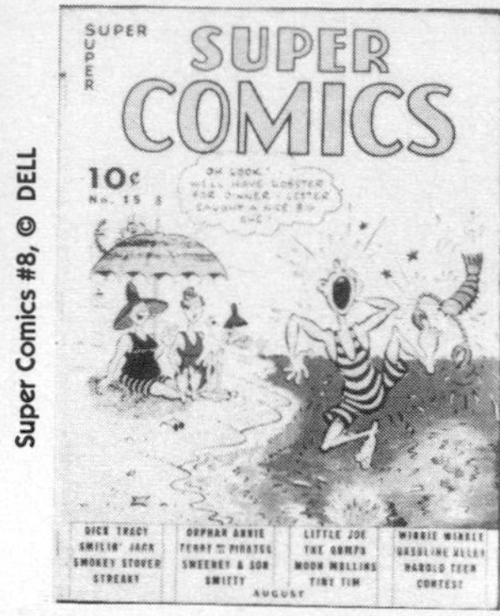

Super Comics #8, © DELL

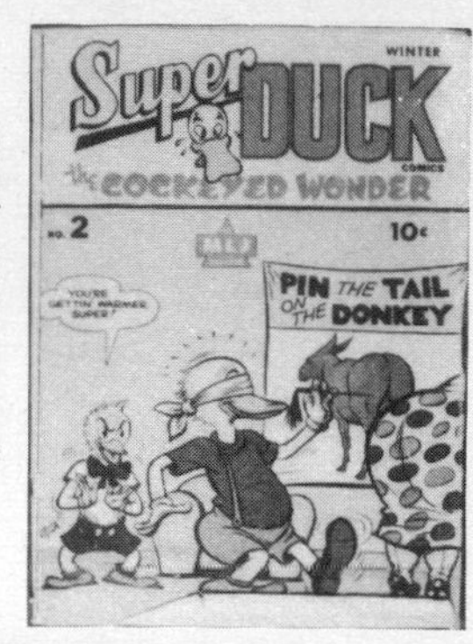

Super Duck Comics #2, © AP

GD25 FN65 NM94

.65 1.60
Annual 1(Sum/64, 84 pgs.)-Origin Krypto-r 10.00 30.00 90.00
Spectacular 1(1980, Giant)-Distr. through comic stores; mostly-r
.70 1.70

NOTE: ***Neal Adams*** *c-143, 145, 146, 148-155, 157-161, 163, 164, 166-168, 172, 173, 175, 176, 178.* ***M. Anderson*** *a-245i.* ***Ditko*** *a-257p.* ***Grell*** *a-202i, 203-219, 220-224p, 235p; c-207-232, 235, 236p, 237, 239p, 240p, 243p, 246, 258.* ***Nasser*** *a(p)-222, 225, 226, 230, 231, 233, 236.* ***Simonson*** *a-237p.* ***Starlin*** *a(p)-239, 250, 251; c-238.* ***Staton*** *a-227p, 243-249p, 252-258p; c-247-251p.* ***Swan/Moldoff*** *c-109.* ***Tuska*** *a-172, 173, 176, 183, 235p.* ***Wood*** *inks-152-155, 157-161. Legion app.-172, 173, 176, 177, 183, 184, 188, 190, 191, 193, 195.*

SUPERBOY (TV)(DC, 1990-'91)(Value: cover or less)

SUPEROY (3rd series)
Feb, 1994 - Present ($1.50, color)
DC Comics

1-3: Metropolis Kid from Reign of the Supermen 1.50

SUPER BRAT
January, 1954 - No. 4, July, 1954
Toby Press

1 (1954) 4.00 10.00 20.00
2-4: 4-Li'l Teevy by Mel Lazarus 2.40 6.00 12.00
I.W. Reprint #1,2,3,7,8('58) .40 1.00 2.00
I.W. (Super) Reprint #10('63) .40 1.00 2.00

SUPERCAR (TV)
Nov, 1962 - No. 4, Aug, 1963 (All painted covers)
Gold Key

1 22.00 66.00 155.00
2,3 11.00 34.00 80.00
4 16.00 49.00 115.00

SUPER CAT (Formerly Frisky Animals; also see Animal Crackers)
No. 56, Nov, 1953 - No. 58, May, 1954; Sept, 1957 - No. 4, May, 1958
Star Publications #56-58/Ajax/Farrell Publ. (Four Star Comic Corp.)

56-58-L.B. Cole-c on all 9.15 27.50 55.00
1(1957-Ajax) 4.70 14.00 28.00
2-4 3.60 9.00 18.00

SUPER CIRCUS (TV)
January, 1951 - No. 5, Sept, 1951 (Mary Hartline)
Cross Publishing Co.

1-Cast photos on-c 8.35 25.00 50.00
2-Cast photos on-c 6.35 19.00 38.00
3-5 4.70 14.00 28.00

SUPER CIRCUS (TV)
No. 542, March, 1954 - No. 694, Mar, 1956 (Feat. Mary Hartline)
Dell Publishing Co.

4-Color 542,592,694: Mary Hartline photo-c 5.00 15.00 30.00

SUPER COMICS
May, 1938 - No. 121, Feb-Mar, 1949
Dell Publishing Co.

1-Terry & The Pirates, The Gumps, Dick Tracy, Little Orphan Annie, Little Joe, Gasoline Alley, Smilin' Jack, Smokey Stover, Smitty, Tiny Tim, Moon Mullins, Harold Teen, Winnie Winkle begin 129.00 385.00 900.00
2 61.00 182.00 400.00
3 53.00 160.00 350.00
4,5: 4-Dick Tracy-c; also #8-10,17,26(part),31 44.00 132.00 300.00
6-10 35.00 105.00 230.00
11-20: 20-Smilin' Jack-c (also #29,32) 28.00 85.00 190.00
21-29: 21-Magic Morro begins (origin & 1st app., 2/40). 22,27-Ken Ernst-c (also #25?); Magic Morro c-22,25,27,34 24.00 72.00 165.00
30-"Sea Hawk" movie adaptation-c/story with Errol Flynn
24.00 72.00 165.00
31-40: 34-Ken Ernst-c. 35-Dick Tracy-c begin 20.00 60.00 135.00
41-50: 41-Intro Lightning Jim. 43-Terry & The Pirates ends
16.00 47.00 105.00
51-60 12.00 35.00 80.00
61-70: 62-Flag-c. 65-Brenda Starr-r begin? 67-X-Mas-c
10.00 30.00 70.00
71-80 10.00 30.00 60.00
81-99 7.50 22.50 45.00
100 10.00 30.00 60.00
101-115-Last Dick Tracy (moves to own title) 5.85 17.50 35.00
116,118-All Smokey Stover 5.00 15.00 30.00
117-All Gasoline Alley 5.00 15.00 30.00
119-121-Terry & The Pirates app. in all 5.00 15.00 30.00

SUPER COPS, THE (Red Circle)(Value: cover or less)

SUPER COPS (Now)(Value: cover or less)

SUPER CRACKED (See Cracked)

SUPER DC GIANT (25-50 cents, all 68-52 pg. Giants)
No. 13, 9-10/70 - No. 26, 7-8/71; V3#27, Summer, 1976 (No #1-12)
National Periodical Publications

S-13-Binky 1.40 3.50
S-14-Top Guns of the West; Kubert-c; Trigger Twins, Johnny Thunder, Wyoming Kid-r; Moreira-r (9-10/70) 1.40 3.50
S-15-Western Comics; Kubert-c; Pow Wow Smith, Vigilante, Buffalo Bill-r; new Gil Kane-a (9-10/70) 1.80 4.50
S-16-Best of the Brave & the Bold; Batman-r & Metamorpho origin-r from Brave & the Bold 1.80 4.50
S-17-Love 1970 1.20 3.00
S-18-Three Mouseketeers; Dizzy Dog, Doodles Duck, Bo Bunny-r; Sheldon Mayer-a 1.40 3.50
S-19-Jerry Lewis; no Neal Adams-a 1.40 3.50
S-20-House of Mystery; N. Adams-c; Kirby-r(3) 1.40 3.50
S-21-Love 1971 1.00 2.50
S-22-Top Guns of the West 1.20 3.00
S-23-The Unexpected 1.00 2.50
S-24-Supergirl 1.00 2.50
S-25-Challengers of the Unknown; all Kirby/Wood-r 1.40 3.50
S-26-Aquaman (1971) 1.40 3.50
27-Strange Flying Saucers Advs. (Sum, 1976) 1.00 2.50

NOTE: ***Sid Greene*** *r-27p(2),* ***Heath*** *r-27.* ***G. Kane*** *a-14r(2), 15, 27r(p).* ***Kubert*** *r-16.*

SUPER-DOOPER COMICS
1946 - No. 8, 1946 (10 cents)(32 pages)(paper cover)
Able Manufacturing Co.

1-The Clock, Gangbuster app. 11.00 32.00 75.00
2 7.00 21.00 42.00
3,4,6 5.35 16.00 32.00
5,7-Capt. Freedom & Shock Gibson 7.00 21.00 42.00
8-Shock Gibson, Sam Hill 7.00 21.00 42.00

SUPER DUCK COMICS (The Cockeyed Wonder) (See Jolly Jingles)
Fall, 1944 - No. 94, Dec, 1960 (Also see Laugh #24)
MLJ Mag. No. 1-4(9/45)/Close-Up No. 5 on (Archie)

1-Origin 32.00 95.00 225.00
2-Bill Vigoda-c 16.00 48.00 110.00
3-5: 4-20-Al Fagaly-c (most) 11.00 32.00 75.00
6-10 10.00 30.00 60.00
11-20 6.35 19.00 38.00
21,23-40 4.70 14.00 28.00
22-Used in **SOTI**, pg. 35,307,308 5.85 17.50 35.00
41-60 4.00 10.00 20.00
61-94 3.00 7.50 15.00

SUPER DUPER
No. 5, 1941 - No. 11, 1941
Harvey Publications

5-Captain Freedom & Shock Gibson app. 19.00 57.00 130.00
8,11 10.00 30.00 70.00

SUPER DUPER COMICS (Formerly Latest Comics?)

Supergirl #17, © DC

Super Green Beret #2, © Lightning

Super Heroes #1, © DELL

GD25 FN65 NM94 GD25 FN65 NM94

No. 3, May-June, 1947
F. E. Howard Publ.

3-1st app. Mr. Monster 6.35 19.00 38.00

SUPER FRIENDS (TV) (Also see Best of DC & Limited Collectors' Edition)
Nov, 1976 - No. 47, Aug, 1981 (#14 is 44 pgs.)
National Periodical Publications/DC Comics

1-Superman, Batman, Robin, Wonder Woman, Aquaman, Atom, Wendy, Marvin & Wonder Dog begin (1st Super Friends) .90 2.25
2-47: 7-1st app. Wonder Twins, & The Seraph. 8-1st app. Jack O'Lantern. 9-1st app. Icemaiden. 13-1st app. Dr. Mist. 14-Origin Wonder Twins. 25-1st app. Fire & Green Fury. 31-Black Orchid app. 36,43-Plastic Man app. 47-Origin Fire & Green Fury .75 1.90
...Special 1 (1981, giveaway, no ads, no code or price)-r/Super Friends #19 & 36 .65 1.60

NOTE: ***Estrada** a-1p, 2p. **Orlando** a-1p. **Staton** a-43, 45.*

SUPER FUN
January, 1956 (By A.W. Nugent)
Gillmor Magazines

1-Comics, puzzles, cut-outs by A.W. Nugent 2.40 6.00 12.00

SUPER FUNNIES (...Western Funnies #3,4)
Dec, 1953 - No. 4, Sept, 1954
Superior Comics Publishers Ltd. (Canada)

1-(3-D)-Dopey Duck; make your own 3-D glasses cut-out inside front-c; did not come w/glasses 31.00 95.00 220.00
2-Horror & crime satire 6.70 20.00 40.00
3-Phantom Ranger, Geronimo, Billy The Kid app. 4.00 11.00 22.00
4-Phantom Ranger-c/story 4.00 11.00 22.00

SUPERGEAR COMICS
1976 (4 pages in color) (slick paper)
Jacobs Corp. (Giveaway)

nn-(Rare)-Superman, Lois Lane; Steve Lombard app. (500 copies printed, over half destroyed?) 1.00 2.50 6.00

SUPERGIRL (See Action, Adventure #281, Brave & the Bold, Crisis on Infinite Earths #7, Daring New Advs. of..., Super DC Giant, Superman Family, & Super-Team Family)

SUPERGIRL
Nov, 1972 - No. 9, Dec-Jan, 1973-74; No. 10, Sept-Oct, 1974
National Periodical Publications

1-1st solo title; Zatanna begins, ends #5 1.00 2.50
2-10: 5-Zatanna origin-r. 8-JLA x-over; Batman cameo .65 1.60

NOTE: *Zatanna in #1-5, 7(Guest); Prez app. in #10. #1-8 are 20 cent issues.*

SUPERGIRL (Formerly Daring New Adventures of...)
No. 14, Dec, 1983 - No. 23, Sept, 1984
DC Comics

14-23: 16-Ambush Bug app. 20-JLA & New Teen Titans app. 1.00
... Movie Special (1985)-Adapts movie; Morrow-a; photo back-c 1.20
Giveaway ('84, '86 Baxter, nn)(American Honda/U.S. Dept. Transportation)-Torres-c/a 1.20

SUPERGIRL
Feb, 1993 - No. 4, May, 1994 ($1.50, color, mini-series)
DC Comics

1-4: Guice-i 1.50

SUPERGIRL/LEX LUTHOR SPECIAL (Supergirl and Team Luthor on-c)
1993 ($2.50, color, 68 pgs.)
DC Comics

1-Pin-ups by Byrne & Thibert also 1.00 2.50

SUPER GOOF (Walt Disney) (See Dynabrite & The Phantom Blot)
Oct, 1965 - No. 74, 1982
Gold Key No. 1-57/Whitman No. 58 on

1 3.60 9.00 18.00
2-10 1.80 4.50 9.00
11-20 1.00 2.00 5.00
21-30 1.20 3.00
31-50 .80 2.00
51-74 1.00

NOTE: *Reprints in #16, 24, 28, 29, 37, 38, 43, 45, 46, 54(1/2), 56-58, 65(1/2), 72(r-#2).*

SUPER GREEN BERET (Tod Holton...)
April, 1967 - No. 2, June, 1967 (25 cents, 68 pgs.)
Lightning Comics (Milson Publ. Co.)

1,2 3.60 9.00 18.00

SUPER HEROES (See Giant-Size... & Marvel...)

SUPER HEROES
Jan, 1967 - No. 4, June, 1967
Dell Publishing Co.

1-Origin & 1st app. Fab 4 2.70 8.00 19.00
2-4 1.65 4.70 11.00

SUPER-HEROES BATTLE SUPER-GORILLAS (See DC Special #16)
Winter, 1976 (One Shot, 52 pgs.; all reprints)
National Periodical Publications

1-Superman, Batman, Flash stories; Infantino-a(p) 1.00

SUPER HEROES PUZZLES AND GAMES
1979 (32 pgs.) (regular size)
General Mills Giveaway (Marvel Comics Group)

nn-Four 2-pg. origin stories of Spider-Man, Captain America, The Hulk, & Spider-Woman 1.60 4.00

SUPER HEROES VERSUS SUPER VILLAINS
July, 1966 (no month given)(68 pgs.)
Archie Publications (Radio Comics)

1-Flyman, Black Hood, The Web, Shield-r; Reinman-a 4.50 14.00 32.00

SUPERICHIE (Formerly Super Richie)
No. 5, Oct, 1976 - No. 18, Jan, 1979 (52 pgs. giants)
Harvey Publications

5-18: 5-Origin/1st app. new costumes for Rippy & Crashman 1.00

SUPERIOR STORIES
May-June, 1955 - No. 4, Nov-Dec, 1955
Nesbit Publishing Co.

1-H.G. Well's The Invisible Man 11.00 32.00 75.00
2-The Pirate of the Gulf by J.H. Ingrahams 6.70 20.00 40.00
3-Wreck of the Grosvenor 6.70 20.00 40.00
4-O'Henry's "The Texas Rangers" 6.70 20.00 40.00

NOTE: ***Morisi** c/a in all.*

SUPER MAGIC (Super Magician Comics #2 on)
May, 1941
Street & Smith Publications

V1#1-Blackstone the Magician-c/story; origin/1st app. Rex King (Black Fury); Charles Sultan-c; Blackstone-c begin 57.00 170.00 400.00

SUPER MAGICIAN COMICS (Super Magic #1)
No. 2, Sept, 1941 - V5#8, Feb-Mar, 1947
Street & Smith Publications

V1#2-Blackstone the Magician continues; Rex King, Man of Adventure app. 23.00 70.00 160.00
3-Tao-Anwar, Boy Magician begins 14.00 43.00 100.00
4-Origin Transo 13.00 40.00 90.00
5-7,9-12: 11-Supersnipe app. 13.00 40.00 90.00
8-Abbott & Costello story (1st app?, 11/42) 15.00 45.00 105.00
V2#1-The Shadow app. 21.00 63.00 145.00
2-12: 5-Origin Tigerman. 8-Red Dragon begins 9.15 27.50 55.00
V3#1-12: 5-Origin Mr. Twilight 9.15 27.50 55.00
V4#1-12: 11-Nigel Elliman begins 7.50 22.50 45.00
V5#1-6 7.50 22.50 45.00

Superman #12, © DC

Superman #83, © DC

Superman #204, © DC

GD25 FN65 NM94

7,8-Red Dragon by Edd Cartier-c/a 19.00 58.00 135.00

NOTE: ***Jack Binder** c-1-14(most). Red Dragon c-V5#7, 8.*

SUPERMAN (See Action Comics, Advs. of..., All-New Coll. Ed., All-Star Comics, Best of DC DC, Brave & the Bold, Cosmic Odyssey, DC Comics Presents, Heroes Against Hunger, Krypton Chronicles, Limited Coll. Ed., Man of Steel, Phantom Zone, Power Record Comics, Special Edition, Super Friends, Superman: The Man of Steel, Taylor's Christmas Tabloid, Three-Dimension Advs., World Of Krypton, World Of Metropolis, World Of Smallville & World's Finest)

SUPERMAN (Becomes Adventures Of...#424 on)
Summer, 1939 - No. 423, Sept, 1986 (#1-5 are quarterly)
National Periodical Publications/DC Comics

GD25 FN65 VF82 NM94

1(nn)-1st four Action stories reprinted; origin Superman by Siegel & Shuster; has a new 2 pg. origin plus 4 pgs. omitted in Action story; see The Comics Magazine #1 & More Fun #14-17 for Superman proto-type app.; 1st pin-up Superman on back-c 7,000.00 21,000.00 45,500.00 70,000.00
(Estimated up to 190 total copies exist, 3 in NM/Mint)

1-Reprint, Oversize 13-1/2x10". **WARNING**: This comic is an exact duplicate reprint of the original except for its size. DC published it in 1978 with a second cover titling it as a Famous First Edition. There have been many reported cases of the outer cover being removed and the interior sold as the original edition. The reprint with the new outer cover removed is practically worthless. See Famous First Edition for value.

GD25 FN65 NM94

2-All daily strip-r 750.00 2250.00 5000.00
3-2nd story-r from Action #5; 3rd story-r from Action #6 500.00 1500.00 3500.00
4-2nd mention of Daily Planet (Spr/40); also see Action #23; 2nd & 3rd app. Luthor (red-headed; also see Action #23) 392.00 1175.00 2700.00
5-4th Luthor app. (red hair) 283.00 850.00 1900.00
6,7: 7-1st Perry White? (11-12/40) 225.00 675.00 1550.00
8-10: 10-5th app. Luthor (1st bald Luthor, 5-6/41) 186.00 560.00 1300.00
11-13,15: 13-Jimmy Olsen & Luthor app. 133.00 400.00 900.00
14-Patriotic Shield-c by Fred Ray 200.00 600.00 1350.00
16-20: 16-1st Lois Lane-c this title (5-6/42); 2nd Lois-c after Action #29. 17-Hitler, Hirohito-c 117.00 350.00 800.00
21-23,25: 25-Clark Kent's only military service 92.00 275.00 600.00
24-Jack Burnley flag-c 108.00 325.00 725.00
26-29: 27,29-31-Lois Lane-c. 28-Lois Lane Girl Reporter series begins, ends #40,42 85.00 255.00 565.00
28-Overseas edition for Armed Forces; same as reg. #28 85.00 255.00 565.00
30-Origin & 1st app. Mr. Mxyztplk (9-10/44)(pronounced "Mix-it-plk") in comic books; name later became Mxyzptlk ("Mix-yez-pit-l-ick"); the character was inspired by a combination of the name of Al Capp's Joe Blyfstyk (the little man with the black cloud over his head) & the devilish antics of Bugs Bunny; he 1st app. in newspaper 3/7/44 133.00 400.00 875.00
31-40: 33-(3-4/45)-3rd app. Mxyztplk. 35,36-Lois Lane-c. 38-Atomic bomb story (1-2/46); delayed because of gov't cencorship; Superman shown reading Batman #32 on cover 72.00 218.00 485.00
41-50: 42-Lois Lane-c. 45-Lois Lane as Superwoman (see Action #60 for 1st app.) 54.00 162.00 365.00
51,52: 51-Lois Lane-c 44.00 132.00 290.00
53-Origin Superman retold; 10th anniversary 157.00 470.00 1100.00
54,56-60 47.00 140.00 310.00
55-Used in **SOTI**, pg. 33 48.00 145.00 320.00
61-Origin Superman retold; origin Green Kryptonite (1st Kryptonite story); Superman returns to Krypton for 1st time & sees his parents for 1st time since infancy, discovers he's not earth man 83.00 250.00 565.00
62-65,67-70: 62-Orson Welles app. 65-1st Krypton Foes: Mala, K120, & U-Ban. 68-1st Luthor-c this title (see Action Comics) 46.00 138.00 300.00
66-2nd Superbaby story 46.00 138.00 300.00
71-75: 74-2nd Luthor-c this title. 75-Some have #74 on-c 42.00 125.00 275.00
72-Giveaway(9-10/51)-(Rare)-Price blackened out; came with banner wrapped around book; without banner 53.00 160.00 350.00
72-Giveaway with banner 67.00 200.00 450.00
76-Batman x-over; Superman & Batman learn each other's I.D. 117.00 350.00 800.00
77-81: 78-Last 52 pg. issue. 81-Used in **POP**, pg. 88 38.00 115.00 265.00

GD25 FN65 NM94

82-87,89,90 34.00 105.00 240.00
88-Prankster, Toyman & Luthor app. 36.00 110.00 250.00
91-95: 95-Last precode issue 32.00 95.00 225.00
96-99 22.00 67.00 200.00

GD25 FN65 VF82 NM94

100 (9-10/55) 95.00 285.00 618.00 950.00

GD25 FN65 NM94

101-110 22.00 66.00 175.00
111-120 19.00 56.00 150.00
121-130: 123-Pre-Supergirl tryout-c/story (8/58). 127-Origin/1st app. Titano. 128-Red Kryptonite used (4/59). 129-Intro/origin Lori Lemaris, The Mermaid 16.00 47.00 125.00
131-139: 139-Lori Lemaris app.; "Untold Story of Red Kryptonite" back-up story 12.00 36.00 95.00
140-1st Blue Kryptonite & Bizarro Supergirl; origin Bizarro Jr. #1 13.00 39.00 105.00
141-145,148: 142-2nd Batman x-over 9.00 26.00 70.00
146-Superman's life story 11.00 34.00 90.00
147(8/61)-7th Legion app; 1st app. Legion of Super-Villains; 1st app. Adult Legion; swipes-c to Adv. #247 10.00 30.00 80.00
149(11/61)-9th Legion app. (cameo); last 10 cent issue 9.00 26.00 70.00
150-162: 152(4/62)-15th Legion app. 155-(8/62)-19th Legion app; Lightning Man & Cosmic Man, & Adult Legion app. 156,162-Legion app. 157-Gold Kryptonite used (see Adv. 299); Mon-el app.; Lightning Lad cameo (11/62). 158-1st app. Flamebird & Nightwing & Nor-Kan of Kandor (12/62). 161-1st told death of Ma and Pa Kent 4.00 13.00 30.00
161-2nd printing (1987, $1.25-c)-New DC logo; sold thru So Much Fun Toy Stores (cover title: Superman Classic) .70 1.80
163-166,168-180: 166-XMas-c. 168-All Luthor issue. 169-Last Sally Selwyn. 170-Pres. Kennedy story is finally published after delay from #169 due to assassination. 172,173-Legion cameos. 174-Super-Mxyzptlk; Bizarro app. 3.40 10.00 24.00
167-New origin Brainiac & Brainiac 5; intro Tixarla (later Luthor's wife) 7.00 21.00 50.00
181,182,184-186,188-192,194-196,198,200: 181-1st 2965 story/series. 189-Origin/destruction of Krypton II 2.30 6.75 16.00
183,187,193,197 (Giants G-18,G-23,G-31,G-36) 2.60 7.50 18.00
199-1st Superman/Flash race (8/67): also see Flash #175 & World's Finest #198,199 (r-in Limited Coll. Ed. #48) 19.00 58.00 135.00
201,203-206,208-211,213-216,218-221,223-226,228-231: 213-Brainiac-5 app. 1.65 4.00 10.00
202 (80-pg. Giant G-42)-All Bizarro issue 1.85 5.50 13.00
207,212,217,222,239 (Giants G-48,G-54,G-60,G-66,G-84): 207-Legion app.; 30th anniversary Superman (6/68) 1.85 5.50 13.00
227,232(Giants, G-78,G-72)-All Krypton issues 1.85 5.50 13.00
233-238: 233-2nd app. Morgan Edge, Clark Kent switch from newspaper reporter to TV newscaster 1.65 4.00 10.00
240-Kaluta-a 1.00 2.50 5.50
241-244 (All 52 pgs.): 243-G.A.-r/#38 1.80 4.50
245-DC 100 Pg. Super Spectacular #7; Air Wave, Kid Eternity, Hawkman-r; Atom-r/Atom #3 1.00 2.50 5.50
246-248,250,251,253 (All 52 pgs.): 246-G.A.-r/#40. 248-World of Krypton story. 251-G.A.-r/#45. 253-Finlay-a, 2 pgs., G.A.-r/#1 1.40 3.50
249,254-Neal Adams-a. 249-(52 pgs.); origin & 1st app. Terra-Man by Neal Adams (inks) 1.25 3.00 7.50
252-DC 100 Pg. Super Spectacular #13; Ray(r/Smash #17), Black Condor, (r/Crack #18), Hawkman(r/Flash #24); Starman-r/Adv. #67; Dr. Fate & Spectre-r/More Fun #57; N. Adams-c 1.10 2.70 6.50
255-271,273-277,279-283: 263-Photo-c. 264-1st app. Steve Lombard. 276-Intro Capt. Thunder. 279-Batman, Batgirl app. .90 2.25
272,278,284-All 100 pgs. G.A.-r in all. 272-r/2nd app. Mr. Mxyztplk from Action #80 1.30 3.25
285-299: 292-Origin Lex Luthor retold .70 1.80
300-Retells origin (6/76) 1.00 2.50 5.50

Superman #423, © DC

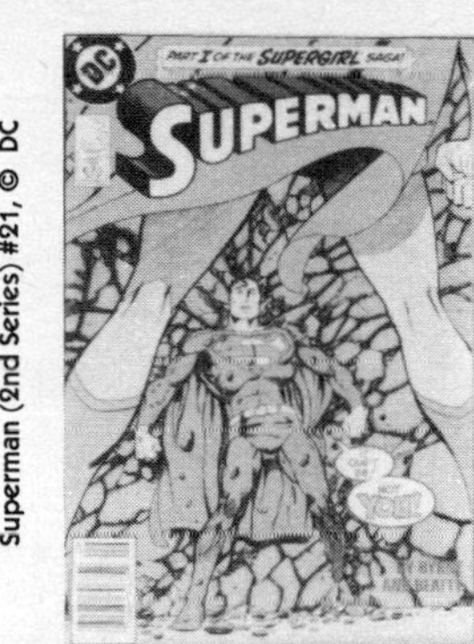

Superman (2nd Series) #21, © DC

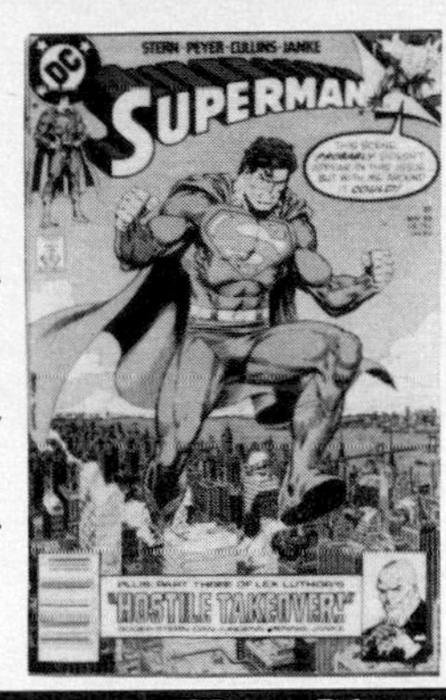

Superman (2nd Series) #31, © DC

GD25 FN65 NM94

301-399: 301,320-Solomon Grundy app. 323-Intro. Atomic Skull. 327-329-(44 pgs.). 330-More facts revealed about I. D. 338-The bottled city of Kandor enlarged. 344-Frankenstein & Dracula app. 353-Brief origin. 354,355,357-Superman 2020 stories (354-Debut of Superman III). 356-World of Krypton story (also #360,367,375). 366-Fan letter by Todd McFarlane. 372-Superman 2021 story. 376-Free 16 pg. preview Daring New Advs. of Supergirl. 377-Free 16 pg. preview Masters of the Universe .70 1.80
400 (10/84, $1.50, 68 pgs.)-Many top artists featured; Chaykin painted cover, Miller back-c 1.40 3.50
401-410,412-422: 405-Super-Batman story. 408-Nuclear Holocaust-c/story. 414,415-Crisis x-over. 422-Horror-c .70 1.80
411-Special Julius Schwartz tribute issue .70 1.80
423-Alan Moore scripts; Perez-a(i) 1.25 3.00 7.50
Annual 1(10/60, 84 pgs.)-Reprints 1st Supergirl story/Action #252, r/Lois Lane #1; Krypto-r (1st Silver Age DC annual) 50.00 150.00 500.00
Annual 2(Wint, 1960-61)-Super-villain issue; Brainiac, Titano, Metallo, Bizarro origin-r 28.00 83.00 250.00
Annual 3(Sum, 1961)-Strange Lives of Superman 23.00 68.00 180.00
Annual 4(Wint, 1961-62)-11th Legion app; 1st Legion origins (text & pictures) 19.00 56.00 150.00
Annual 5(Sum, 1962)-All Krypton issue 17.00 51.00 120.00
Annual 6(Wint, 1962-63)-Legion-r/Adv. #247 14.00 43.00 100.00
Annual 7(Sum, 1963)-Origin-r/Superman-Batman team/Adv. 275; r/1955 Superman dailies 11.00 32.00 75.00
Annual 8(Wint, 1963-64)-All origins issue 9.00 26.00 60.00
Annual 9(8/64)-Was advertised but came out as 80 Page Giant #1 instead
Annual 9(1983)-Toth/Austin-a 1.00 2.00 5.00
Annuals 10-12: 10(1984, $1.25)-M. Anderson inks. 11(1985)-Moore scripts. 12(1986) 1.60 4.00
...IV Movie Special (1987, $2.00, one-shot)-Movie adaptation; Heck-a .80 2.00
Special 1(1983)-G. Kane-c/a; contains German-r 1.60 4.00
Special 2,3(1984, 1985, $1.25, 52 pgs.) 1.60 4.00
The Amazing World of Superman "Official Metropolis Edition" (1973, $2.00, 14x10-1/2")-Origin retold; Wood-r(i) from Superboy #153,161 1.60 4.00 8.00
Kelloggs Giveaway-(2/3 normal size, 1954)-r-two stories/Superman #55 30.00 90.00 200.00
...Meets the Quik Bunny (1987, Nestles Quik premium, 36 pgs.) 1.00
...Movie Special-(9/83)-Adaptation of Superman III; other versions exist with store logos on bottom 1/3 of-c 1.00
Pizza Hut Premium(12/77)-Exact-r of #97,113 1.50
Radio Shack Giveaway-36pgs. (7/80) "The Computers That Saved Metropolis;" Starlin/Giordano-a; advertising insert in Action 509, New Advs. of Superboy 7, Legion of Super-Heroes 265, & House of Mystery 282. (All comics were 68 pgs.) Cover of inserts printed on newsprint. Giveaway contains 4 extra pgs. of Radio Shack advertising that inserts do not 1.50
Radio Shack Giveaway-(7/81) "Victory by Computer" 1.50
Radio Shack Giveaway-(7/82) "Computer Masters of Metropolis" 1.00
11195(2/79,224pp,$1.95)-Golden Press 1.00 2.40

NOTE: ***N. Adams*** *a-249i, 254p; c-204-208, 210, 212-215, 219, 231, 233-237, 240-243, 249-252, 254, 263, 307, 308, 313, 314, 317.* ***Adkins*** *a-323i.* ***Austin*** *c-368i.* ***Wayne Boring*** *art-late 1940's to early 1960's.* ***Buckler*** *a(p)-352, 363, 364, 369; c(p)-324-327, 356, 363, 368, 369, 373, 376, 378.* ***Burnley*** *a-252r; c-19-25, 30, 33, 34, 35p, 38p, 39p, 45p.* ***Fine*** *a-252r.* ***Gil Kane*** *a-272r, 367, 372, 375, Special 2; c-374p, 375p, 377, 381, 382, 384-390, 392, Annual 9.* ***Kubert*** *c-216.* ***Morrow*** *a-238.* ***Perez*** *c-364p.* ***Starlin*** *c-355.* ***Staton*** *a-354i, 355i.* ***Swan/Moldoff*** *c-149.* ***Williamson*** *a(i)-408-410, 412-416; c-408i, 409i.* ***Wrightson*** *a-400, 416.*

SUPERMAN (2nd series)
Jan, 1987 - Present (.75/$1.00/$1.25)
DC Comics

1-Byrne-c/a begins; intro new Metallo .80 2.25
2-8,10: 3-Legends x-over; Darkseid-c & app. 7-Origin/1st app. Rampage. 8-Legion app. .65 1.60
9-Joker-c 1.30 3.25
11-49,51,52,54-56,58-67: 11-1st new Mr. Mxyzptlk. 12-Lori Lemaris revived. 13-1st app. Toyman. 13,14-Millennium x-over. 20-Doom Patrol app.; Supergirl revived in cameo. 21-Supergirl-c/story; 1st app. Matrix who becomes new Supergirl. 31-Mr. Mxyzptlk app. 37-Newsboy Legion app. 41-Lobo app. 44-Batman storyline, part 1. 45-Free extra 8 pgs. 54-Newsboy Legion story. 63-Aquaman x-over. 67-Last $1.00-c .65 1.60
50-($1.50, 52 pgs.)-Clark Kent proposes to Lois 1.70 4.25
50-2nd printing .65 1.60
53-Clark reveals i.d. to Lois cont'd from Action #662 1.10 2.75
53-2nd printing 1.50
57-($1.75, 52 pgs.) .70 1.75
68-72: 65,66,68-Deathstroke-c/stories. 70-Superman & Robin team-up 1.50
73-Doomsday cameo 1.70 4.25
74-Doomsday battle issue, part 2, cont'd from Justice League #69. 1.00 2.50 6.00
73,74-2nd printings .70 1.80
75-($2.50)-Collector's Ed.; Doomsday, part 6, death of Superman; polybagged w/poster of funeral, obituary from Daily Planet, postage stamp & armband premiums (direct sale only) 1.65 4.00 10.00
75-Direct sale copy (no upc code, 1st print) 1.50 3.75
75-Direct sale copy (no upc code, 2nd print) 1.25
75-Direct sale copy (no upc code, 3rd, 4th prints) 1.25
75-Newsstand copy w/upc code 1.40 3.50
75-Platinum Edition; given away to retailers 100.00
76,77-Funeral for a friend parts 4 & 8 .90 2.25
78-($1.95)-Collector's Edition with die-cut outer-c & bound-in mini poster; Doomsday cameo .90 2.25
78-($1.50)-Newsstand Edition w/poster and different-c; Doomsday-c & cameo .70 1.80
79-81,83-88: 83-Funeral for a friend epilogue .70 1.80
82-($3.50)-Collector's Edition w/all chromium-c; real Superman revealed; Green Lantern x-over from G.L. #46; no ads 1.40 3.50
82-($2.00, 44 pgs.)-Regular Edition w/different-c .80 2.00
Annual 1,2: 1 (1987)-No Byrne-a. 2 (1988)-Byrne-a; Newsboy Legion; return of the Guardian 1.50
Annual 3 (1991, $2.00, 68 pgs.)-Armageddon 2001 x-over; Batman app.; Austin-c(i) & part inks .80 2.00
Annual 3-2nd & 3rd printings; 3rd has silver ink .80 2.00
Annual 4 (1992, $2.50, 68 pgs.)-Eclipso app. 1.00 2.50
Annual 5 (1993, $2.50, 68 pgs.) 1.00 2.50
Special 1 (1992, $3.50, 68 pgs.)-Simonson-c/a 1.40 3.50
Superman Gallery, The 1 (1993, $2.95)-Poster-a 1.20 3.00
The Death of Superman trade paperback nn (1993, $4.95)-Reprints Man of Steel #17-19, Superman #73-75, Advs. of Superman #496,497, Action #683,684 & Justice League #69 2.00 5.00
The Death of Superman, 2nd & 3rd printings 2.00 5.00
The Death of Superman Platinum Edition 15.00
...: The Legacy of Superman #1 (3/93, $2.50, one-shot, 68 pgs.)-Art Adams-c; Simonson-a 1.00 2.50
Daily News Magazine Presents DC Comics' Superman (1987, giveaway)-Supplement to New York Daily News; Perez-c/a 1.00

NOTE: ***Austin*** *a(i)-1-3.* ***Byrne*** *a-1-16p, 17, 19-21p, 22; c-1-17, 20-22; scripts-1-22.* ***Guice*** *c/a-64.* ***Kirby*** *c-37p.* ***Joe Quesada*** *c-Annual 4.* ***Russell*** *c/a-23i.* ***Simonson*** *c-69i. #19-21 2nd printings sold in multi-packs.*

SUPERMAN & THE GREAT CLEVELAND FIRE (Giveaway)
1948 (4 pages, no cover)(Hospital Fund)
National Periodical Publications

nn-In full color 50.00 150.00 350.00

SUPERMAN FAMILY, THE (Formerly Superman's Pal Jimmy Olsen)
No. 164, Apr-May, 1974 - No. 222, Sept, 1982
National Periodical Publications/DC Comics

164-Jimmy Olsen, Supergirl, Lois Lane begin .65 1.60
165-176 (100-68 pgs.) 1.35
177-181 (52 pgs.) 1.25
182,194: Marshall Rogers-a in each. 182-$1.00 issues begin; Krypto begins, ends #192 .90 2.25

Superman For Earth nn, © DC

Superman's Girlfriend Lois Lane #38, © DC

Superman's Pal Jimmy Olsen #144, © DC

GD25 FN65 NM94

183-193,195-222: 183-Nightwing-Flamebird begins, ends #194. 189-Brainiac 5, Mon-el app. 191-Superboy begins, ends #198. 200-Book length story. 211-Earth II Batman & Catwoman marry 1.25

NOTE: ***N. Adams** c-182-185. **Anderson** a-186i. **Buckler** c(p)-190, 191, 209, 210, 215, 217, 220. **Jones** a-191-193. **Gil Kane** c(p)-221, 222. **Mortimer** a(p)-191-193, 199, 201-222. **Orlando** a(i)-186, 187. **Rogers** a-182, 194. **Staton** a-191-194, 196p. **Tuska** a(p)-203, 207-209.*

SUPERMAN FOR EARTH
1991 ($4.95, color, 52 pgs.)(Printed on recycled paper)
DC Comics

nn-Ordway wraparound-c 1.00 2.00 5.00

SUPERMAN (Miniature)
1942; 1955 - 1956 (3 issues; no #'s; 32 pgs.)
The pages are numbered in the 1st issue: 1-32; 2nd: 1A-32A, and 3rd: 1B-32B
National Periodical Publications

No date-Py-Co-Pay Tooth Powder giveaway (8 pgs.; circa 1942) 79.00 235.00 550.00
1-The Superman Time Capsule (Kellogg's Sugar Smacks)(1955) 47.00 140.00 330.00
1A-Duel in Space (1955) 36.00 110.00 250.00
1B-The Super Show of Metropolis (also #1-32, no B)(1955) 36.00 110.00 250.00

NOTE: *Numbering variations exist. Each title could have any combination-#1, 1A, or 1B.*

SUPERMAN RECORD COMIC
1966 (Golden Records)
National Periodical Publications

(with record)-Record reads origin of Superman from comic; came with iron-on patch, decoder, membership card & button; comic-r/Superman #125,146 11.00 34.00 80.00
Comic only 4.30 13.00 30.00

SUPERMAN'S BUDDY (Costume Comic)
1954 (4 pgs.) (One Shot) (Came in box w/costume; slick-paper/c)
National Periodical Publications

1-(Rare)-w/box & costume 130.00 385.00 900.00
Comic only 57.00 171.00 400.00
1-(1958 edition)-Printed in 2 colors 14.00 43.00 100.00

SUPERMAN'S CHRISTMAS ADVENTURE
1940, 1944 (16 pgs.) (Giveaway)
Distr. by Nehi drinks, Bailey Store, Ivey-Keith Co., Kennedy's Boys Shop, Macy's Store, Boston Store
National Periodical Publications

1(1940)-Burnley-a; Fred Ray-c 285.00 860.00 2000.00
nn(1944) w/Santa Claus & X-mas tree-c 86.00 260.00 600.00
nn(1944) w/Candy cane & Superman-c 75.00 225.00 525.00

SUPERMAN SCRAPBOOK (Has blank pages; contains no comics)

SUPERMAN'S GIRLFRIEND LOIS LANE (See Action Comics #1, 80 Page Giant #3, 14, Lois Lane, Showcase #9, 10, Superman #28 & Superman Family)

SUPERMAN'S GIRLFRIEND LOIS LANE
Mar-Apr, 1958 - No. 136, Jan-Feb, 1974; No. 137, Sept-Oct, 1974
National Periodical Publ.

GD25 FN65 VF82 NM94
Showcase #9 (7-8/57)-Lois Lane (pre #1); 1st Showcase character to win own series 216.00 650.00 1875.00 –
GD25 FN65 NM94
Showcase #10 (9-10/57)-Jor-el cameo 121.00 362.00 1450.00
GD25 FN65 VF82 NM94
1-(3-4/58) 120.00 360.00 780.00 1200.00
GD25 FN65 NM94
2 55.00 165.00 440.00
3 38.00 113.00 300.00
4,5 25.00 75.00 200.00
6-10: 9-Pat Boone app. 18.00 53.00 140.00
11-20: 14-Supergirl x-over; Batman app? 10.00 30.00 70.00

GD25 FN65 NM94

21-29: 23-1st app. Lena Thorul, Lex Luthor's sister. 27-Bizarro-c/story. 29-Aquaman, Batman, Green Arrow cameo; last 10 cent issue 7.00 21.00 50.00
30-32,34-49: 47-Legion app. 3.60 10.75 25.00
33(5/62)-Mon-el app. 4.00 12.00 28.00
50(7/64)-Triplicate Girl, Phantom Girl & Shrinking Violet app. 3.20 8.00 20.00
51-55,57-67,69: 59-Jor-el app.; Batman back-up sty 2.00 6.00 14.00
56-Saturn Girl app. 2.15 6.50 15.00
68-(Giant G-26) 3.20 8.00 20.00
70-Penguin & Catwoman app. (1st S.A. Catwoman, 11/66; also see Det. #369 for 3rd app.); Batman & Robin cameo 16.00 48.00 110.00
71-Catwoman story cont'd from #70 (2nd app.) 11.00 34.00 80.00
72,73,75,76,78 1.40 3.50 8.50
74-1st Bizarro Flash (5/67); JLA cameo 2.30 6.75 16.00
77-(Giant G-39) 1.65 4.00 10.00
79-Neal Adams-c begin, end #95,108 1.00 2.50 5.50
80-85,87-94: 89-Batman x-over; all N. Adams-c 1.80 4.50
86,95: (Giants G-51,G-63)-Both have Neal Adams-c. 95-Wonder Woman x-over 1.10 2.70 6.50
96-103,105-111: 105-Origin/1st app. The Rose & the Thorn. 108-Neal Adams-c. 111-Morrow-a 1.60 4.00
104,113-(Giants G-75,87) 1.10 2.70 6.50
112,114-123 (52 pgs.): 122-G.A. Lois Lane-r/Superman #30. 123-G.A. Batman-r/Batman #35 (w/Catwoman) 1.40 3.50
124-137: 130-Last Rose & the Thorn. 132-New Zatanna story. 136-Wonder Woman x-over 1.00 2.50
Annual 1(Sum, 1962)-Aquaman app. 10.00 30.00 100.00
Annual 2(Sum, 1963) 6.00 17.00 55.00

NOTE: ***Buckler** a-117-121p. **Curt Swan** a-1-50(most); c(p)-1-15.*

SUPERMAN'S PAL JIMMY OLSEN (Superman Family #164 on)
(See Action Comics #6 for 1st app. & 80 Page Giant)
Sept-Oct, 1954 - No. 163, Feb-Mar, 1974
National Periodical Publ.

GD25 FN65 VF82 NM94
1 170.00 510.00 1105.00 1700.00
GD25 FN65 NM94
2 75.00 225.00 675.00
3-Last pre-code issue 47.00 142.00 425.00
4,5 31.00 92.00 275.00
6-10 22.00 67.00 200.00
11-20 14.00 43.00 130.00
21-30: 29-1st app. Krypto in Jimmy Olsen 10.00 30.00 70.00
31-40: 31-Origin & 1st app.Elastic Lad (Jimmy Olsen). 33-One pg. biography of Jack Larson (TV Jimmy Olsen). 36-Intro Lucy Lane. 37-2nd app. Elastic Lad; 1st cover app. 7.00 21.00 50.00
41-50: 41-1st J.O. Robot. 48-Intro/origin Superman Emergency Squad 4.00 13.00 35.00
51-56: 56-Last 10 cent issue 3.00 9.00 25.00
57-62,64-70: 57-Olsen marries Supergirl. 62-Mon-el & Elastic Lad app. but not as Legionnaires. 70-Element Lad app. 1.65 4.70 11.00
63(9/62)-Legion of Super-Villains app. 1.70 5.00 12.00
71,74,75,78,80-84,86,89,90: 86-Jimmy Olsen Robot becomes Congorilla 1.40 3.50 8.50
72(10/63)-Legion app; Elastic Lad (Olsen) joins 1.65 4.00 10.00
73-Ultra Boy app. 1.65 4.00 10.00
76,85-Legion app. 1.65 4.00 10.00
77,79: 77-Olsen with Colossal Boy's powers & costume; origin Titano retold. 79-(9/64)-Titled The Red-headed Beatle of 1000 B.C. 1.30 3.25 8.00
87-Legion of Super-Villains app. 1.65 4.00 10.00
88-Star Boy app. 1.30 3.25 8.00
91-94,96-99: 99-Olsen w/powers & costumes of Lightning Lad, Sun Boy & Star Boy 1.00 2.50 6.00
95,104 (Giants G-25,G-38) 1.70 5.00 12.00
100-Legion cameo 1.25 3.00 7.50
101-103,105-112,114-121,123-130,132: 106-Legion app. 110-Infinity-c.

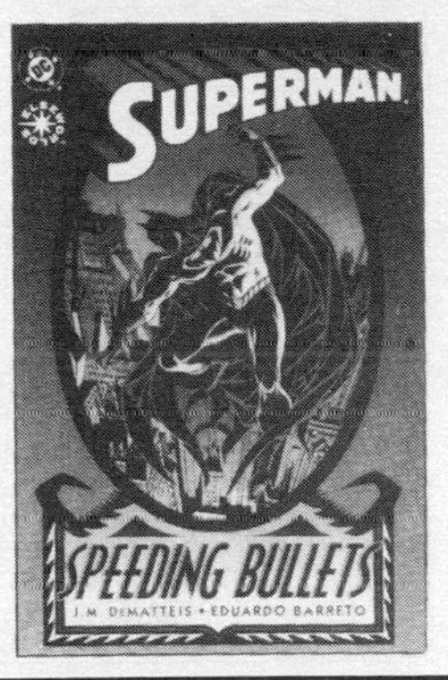

Superman: Speeding Bullets #1, © DC

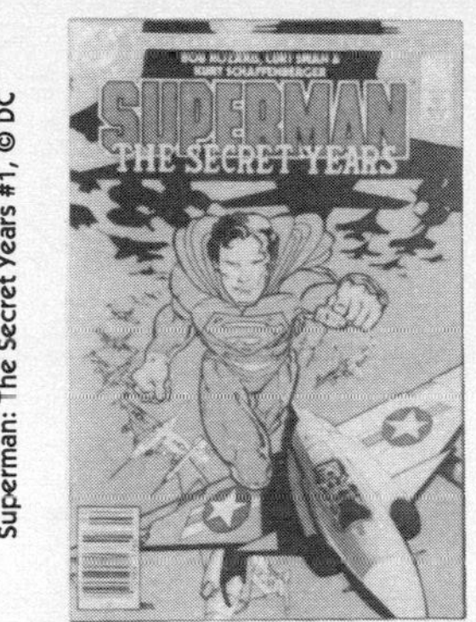

Superman: The Secret Years #1, © DC

Super Mario Bros. #1, © Nintendo/Voyager

GD25 FN65 NM94

117-Batman & Legion cameo 1.40 3.50
13,122,131,140 (Giants G-50,G-62,G-74,G-86): 113-Unpublished G.A. Kubert-a (2 pgs.) 1.60 4.00
33-Re-intro Newsboy Legion & begins by Kirby; 1st app. Morgan Edge in 1 panel cameo 1.00 2.50 5.50
34-1st app. Darkseid (1 panel, 12/70) 1.00 2.50 6.00
35-139,141-163: 135-2nd app. Darkseid (1 pg. cameo; see New Gods & Forever People); G.A. Guardian app. 136-Origin new Guardian. 139-Last 15 cent issue. 141-Newsboy Legion-r by S&K begin (52 pgs. begin); full pg. self-portrait Kirby. 149,150-G.A. Plastic Man-r in both; last 52 pg. issue. 150-Newsboy Legion app. 1.40 3.50

OTE: *Issues #141-148 contain* ***Simon & Kirby*** *Newsboy Legion reprints from Star Spangled 7, 8, 9, 10, 11, 12, 13, 14 in that order.* ***N. Adams*** *c-109-112, 115, 117, 118, 120, 121, 132, 34-136, 147, 148.* ***Kirby*** *a-133-139p, 141-140p; c-133, 139, 145p.* ***Kirby/N. Adams*** *c 137, 138, 41-144, 146.* ***Curt Swan*** *c-1-14(most).*

SUPERMAN SPECTACULAR (Also see DC Special Series #5)
982 (Magazine size)(Square binding)
DC Comics

1 .80 2.00

SUPERMAN: SPEEDING BULLETS
993 ($4.95, color, one-shot, 52 pgs.)
DC Comics

1-Elseworlds storyline 1.00 2.00 5.00

SUPERMAN: THE EARTH STEALERS
988 ($2.95, one-shot, 52pgs, prestige format)
DC Comics

1-Byrne scripts; painted-c 1.40 3.50
1-2nd printing 1.20 3.00

SUPERMAN: THE MAN OF STEEL (Also see The Man of Steel)
uly, 1991 - Present ($1.00/$1.25, color)
DC Comics

1-($1.75, 52 pgs.) .70 1.75
2-10: 3-War of the Gods x-over. 5-Reads sideways. 10-Last $1.00-c 1.00
11-16: 14-Superman & Robin team-up 1.25
17-1st app. Doomsday (cameo) 1.40 3.50
17-2nd printing 1.25
18-1st full app. Doomsday 1.65 4.00 10.00
18-2nd & 3rd printings 1.25
19-Doomsday battle issue (c/story) 1.00 2.50
20,21-Funeral for a Friend .80 2.00
22-($1.95)-Collector's Edition w/die-cut outer-c & bound-in poster .40 1.00 2.00
22-($1.50)-Newsstand Ed. w/poster & different-c 1.50
23-32: 30-Regular edition 1.50
30-($2.50)-Collector's Edition; polybagged with Superman & Lobo vinyl clings that stick to wraparound-c 1.00 2.50
Annual 1,2 (1992-93, $2.50, 68 pgs.): 1-Eclipso app.; Joe Quesada-c(p). 2-Intro Edge 1.00 2.50

SUPERMAN: THE SECRET YEARS
Feb, 1985 - No. 4, May, 1985 (Mini-series)
DC Comics

1-Miller-c on all 1.50
2-4 1.00

SUPERMAN 3-D (See Three-Dimension Adventures)

SUPERMAN-TIM (Becomes Tim)
Aug, 1942 - May, 1950 (Half size) (B&W Giveaway w/2 color covers)
Superman-Tim Stores/National Periodical Publications

3/42 67.00 200.00 450.00
2/43, 3/43, 6/43, 8/43, 9/43, 3/44, 2/45, 11/49 issues-Two pg. Superman illos in each 15.00 45.00 100.00
10/43, 12/43, 2/44, 4/44-1/45, 3/45, 4/45, 4/46, 5/46, 6/46, 7/46, 8/46 issues-no Superman 12.00 35.00 80.00
9/46-1st stamp album issue (worth more if complete with Superman stamps) 33.00 100.00 220.00
10/46-1st Superman story 22.00 68.00 150.00
11/46, 12/46, 1/47, 2/47, 3/47, 4/47, 5/47-8/47 issues-Superman story in each; 2/47-Infinity-c 22.00 68.00 150.00
9/47-Stamp album issue & Superman story 30.00 90.00 200.00
10/47, 11/47, 12/47-Superman stories 22.00 68.00 150.00
1/48, 2/48, 6/48, 8/48, 10/48, 11/48, 2/49-10/49 issues-no Superman 17.00 50.00 110.00
9/48-Stamp album issue 18.00 55.00 120.00
12/49-5/50 Superman stories 20.00 60.00 135.00

NOTE: *16 pgs. through 9/47; 8 pgs. 10/47 on? The stamp album issues (3) may contain Superman stamps that were made to glue in these books. Books with the stamps in cluded would be worth more, and the value would depend upon completeness of the album. There is no stamp album in the 9/49 issue.*

SUPERMAN VS. THE AMAZING SPIDER-MAN (Also see Marvel Treasury Edition No. 28)
1976 (100 pgs.) ($2.00) (Over-sized)
National Periodical Publications/Marvel Comics Group

1-Andru/Giordano-a .80 2.00
1-2nd printing; 5000 numbered copies signed by Stan Lee & Carmine Infantino on front cover & sold through mail 2.15 6.50 15.00

SUPERMAN WORKBOOK
1945 (One Shot) (68 pgs; reprints) (B&W)
National Periodical Publ./Juvenile Group Foundation

nn-Cover-r/Superman #14 108.00 325.00 700.00

SUPER MARIO BROS. (Also see Adventures of the...)
1990 - No. 5?, 1991 ($1.95, color, slick-c)
V2#1, 1991 - No. 5, 1991 ($1.50, color)
Valiant Comics

1-5: 1-Wildman-a .80 2.00
V2#1-5 1.50
Special Edition 1 (1990, $1.95)-Wildman-a .80 2.00

SUPERMOUSE (...the Big Cheese; see Coo Coo Comics)
Dec, 1948 - No. 34, Sept, 1955; No. 35, Apr, 1956 - No. 45, Fall, 1958
Standard Comics/Pines No. 35 on (Literary Ent.)

1-Frazetta text illos (3) 20.00 60.00 140.00
2-Frazetta text illos 10.00 30.00 70.00
3,5,6-Text illos by Frazetta in all 9.15 27.50 55.00
4-Two pg. text illos by Frazetta 10.00 30.00 60.00
7-10 4.00 11.00 22.00
11-20: 13-Racist humor (Indians) 3.60 9.00 18.00
21-45 2.40 6.00 12.00
1-Summer Holiday issue (Summer, 1957, 25¢, 100 pgs.)-Pines 9.15 27.50 55.00
2-Giant Summer issue (Summer, 1958, 25¢, 100 pgs.)-Pines 6.70 20.00 40.00

SUPER-MYSTERY COMICS
July, 1940 - V8#6, July, 1949
Ace Magazines (Periodical House)

V1#1-Magno, the Magnetic Man & Vulcan begins (1st app.) 108.00 325.00 700.00
2 50.00 150.00 330.00
3-The Black Spider begins (1st app.) 43.00 130.00 300.00
4-Origin Davy 37.00 110.00 240.00
5-Intro. The Clown & begin series (12/40) 37.00 110.00 240.00
6(2/41) 31.00 92.00 205.00
V2#1(4/41)-Origin Buckskin 31.00 92.00 205.00
2-6(2/42): 6-Vulcan begins again 28.00 85.00 190.00
V3#1(4/42),2: 1-Black Ace begins 25.00 75.00 175.00
3-Intro. The Lancer; Dr. Nemesis & The Sword begin; Kurtzman-c/a(2) (Mr. Risk & Paul Revere Jr.) 35.00 105.00 230.00
4-Kurtzman-c/a 28.00 85.00 190.00
5-Kurtzman-a(2); L.B. Cole-a; Mr. Risk app. 29.00 88.00 200.00

Superpatriot #2 (Image), © Erik Larsen

Super Spy #1, © CEN

Super Western Comics #1, © YM

GD25 FN65 NM94

6(10/43)-Mr. Risk app.; Kurtzman's Paul Revere Jr.; L.B. Cole-a 29.00 88.00 200.00
V4#1(1/44)-L.B. Cole-a 22.00 68.00 150.00
2-6(4/45): 2,5,6-Mr. Risk app. 17.00 52.00 120.00
V5#1(7/45)-6 14.00 43.00 100.00
V6#1-6: 3-Torture story. 4-Last Magno. Mr. Risk app. in #2,4-6 12.00 35.00 80.00
V7#1-6, V8#1-4,6 12.00 35.00 80.00
V8#5-Meskin, Tuska, Sid Greene-a 13.00 40.00 90.00

NOTE: ***Sid Greene** a-V7#4. **Mooney** c-V1#5, 6, V2#1-6. **Palais** a-V5#3, 4; c-V4#6-V5#4, V6#2, V8#4. Bondage c-V2#5, 6, V3#2, 5. Magno c-1-V3#6, V4#2-V5#5, V6#2. The Sword c-V4#1.*

SUPERNATURAL THRILLERS
Dec, 1972 - No. 6, Nov, 1973; No. 7, July, 1974 - No. 15, Oct, 1975
Marvel Comics Group

1-3: 1-It!-Sturgeon adaptation. 2-The Invisible Man. 3-The Valley of the Worm 1.20
4-15: 4-Dr. Jekyll & Mr. Hyde. 5-1st app. The Living Mummy. 6-The Headless Horseman. 7-The Living Mummy begins 1.00

NOTE: ***Brunner** c-11. **Buckler** a-5p. **Ditko** a-8r, 9r. **G. Kane** a-3p; c-3, 9p, 15p. **Mayerik** a-2p, 7, 8, 9p, 10p, 11. **McWilliams** a-14i. **Mortimer** a-4. **Steranko** c-1, 2. **Sutton** a-15. **Tuska** a-6p. Robert E. Howard story-#3.*

SUPERPATRIOT
July, 1993 - Present ($1.95, color)
Image Comics

1-3: D. Johnson-c/a; Larsen scripts; Giffen plots .80 2.00

SUPER POWERS
7/84 - No. 5, 11/84; 9/85 - No. 6, 2/86; 9/86 - No. 4, 12/86
DC Comics

1 (7/84, 1st series)-Joker/Penguin-c/story; Batman app.; Kirby-c 1.30
2-5: 5-Kirby-c/a 1.20
1 (9/85, 2nd series)-Kirby-c/a in all; Capt. Marvel & Firestorm join; Batman cameo 1.20
2-6: 4-Batman cameo. 5,6-Batman app. 1.20
1-4 (1986, 3rd series): 1-Cyborg joins; 1st app. Samurai from Super Friends TV show. 1-4-Batman cameos 1.20

SUPER PUP (Formerly Spotty The Pup) (See Space Comics)
No. 4, Mar-Apr, 1954 - No. 5, 1954
Avon Periodicals

4,5: 5-Robot-c 3.60 9.00 18.00

SUPER RABBIT (See All Surprise, Animated Movie Tunes, Comedy Comics, Comic Capers, Ideal Comics, It's A Duck's Life, Movie Tunes & Wisco)
Fall, 1944 - No. 14, Nov, 1948
Timely Comics (CmPI)

1-Hitler & Hirohito-c; Ziggy Pig & Silly begin? 47.00 140.00 330.00
2 25.00 75.00 175.00
3-5 15.00 45.00 105.00
6-Origin 17.00 52.00 120.00
7-10: 9-Infinity-c 10.00 30.00 65.00
11-Kurtzman's "Hey Look" 11.00 32.00 75.00
12-14 10.00 30.00 60.00
I.W. Reprint #1,2('58),7,10('63) 1.60 4.00 8.00

SUPER RICHIE (Superichie #5 on) (See Richie Rich Millions #68)
Sept, 1975 - No. 4, Mar, 1976 (All 52 pg. Giants)
Harvey Publications

1 1.20 3.00
2-4 .80 2.00

SUPERSNIPE COMICS (Formerly Army & Navy #1-5)
V1#6, Oct, 1942 - V5#1, Aug-Sept, 1949 (See Shadow Comics V2#3)
Street & Smith Publications

V1#6-Rex King - Man of Adventure (costumed hero, see Super Magic/ Magician) by Jack Binder begins; Supersnipe by George Marcoux continues from Army & Navy #5; Bill Ward-a 58.00 175.00 375.00

GD25 FN65 NM94

7,8,10-12: 8-Hitler, Tojo, Mussoliniin Hell with Devil-c. 11-Little Nemo app. 35.00 105.00 230.00
9-Doc Savage x-over in Supersnipe; Hitler-c 46.00 138.00 300.00
V2#1-12: 1-Huck Finn by Clare Dwiggins begins, ends V3#5 23.00 70.00 160.00
V3#1-12: 8-Bobby Crusoe by Dwiggins begins, ends V3#12. 9-Xmas-c 20.00 60.00 135.00
V4#1-12, V5#1: V4#10-Xmas-c 14.00 42.00 95.00

NOTE: ***George Marcoux** c-V1#6-V3#4. Doc Savage app. in some issues.*

SUPER SOLDIERS
Apr, 1993 - Present ($1.75, color)
Marvel Comics UK

1-($2.50)-Embossed silver foil logo 1.00 2.50
2-8: 5-Capt. America app. 6-Origin; Nick Fury app. .70 1.75

SUPERSPOOK (Formerly Frisky Animals on Parade)
No. 4, June, 1958
Ajax/Farrell Publications

4 4.00 10.00 20.00

SUPER SPY (See Wham Comics)
Oct, 1940 - No. 2, Nov, 1940 (Reprints)
Centaur Publications

1-Origin The Sparkler 100.00 300.00 700.00
2-The Inner Circle, Dean Denton, Tim Blain, The Drew Ghost, The Night Hawk by Gustavson, & S.S. Swanson by Glanz app. 70.00 210.00 450.00

SUPER STAR HOLIDAY SPECIAL (See DC Special Series #21)

SUPER-TEAM FAMILY
10-11/75 - No. 15, 3-4/78 (#1-4: 68 pgs.; #5 on: 52 pgs.)
National Periodical Publications/DC Comics

1-Reprints by Neal Adams & Kane/Wood .80 2.00
2,3-New stories 1.50
4-7-Reprints; 4-G.A. JSA-r & Superman/Batman/Robin-r from World's Finest 1.00
8-10-New Challengers of the Unknown stories .80 2.00
11-15-New stories 1.20

NOTE: ***Neal Adams** r-1-3. **Brunner** c-3. **Buckler** c-8p. **Tuska** a-7r. **Wood** a-1i(r), 3.*

SUPER TV HEROES (See Hanna-Barbera...)

SUPER-VILLAIN CLASSICS (Marvel)(Value: cover or less)

SUPER-VILLAIN TEAM-UP (See Fantastic Four #6 & Giant-Size...)
8/75 - No. 14, 10/77; No. 15, 11/78; No. 16, 5/79; No. 17, 6/80
Marvel Comics Group

1-Sub-Mariner & Dr. Doom begin, end #10 1.90 4.75
2-17: 5-1st Shroud. 6-F.F., Shroud app. 7-Origin Shroud. 9-Avengers app. 11-15-Dr. Doom & Red Skull app. .90 2.25

NOTE: ***Buckler** c-4p, 5p, 7p. **Buscema** c-1. **Byrne/Austin** c-14. **Evans** a-1p, 3p. **Everett** a-1p. **Giffen** a-8p, 13p; c-13p. **Kane** c-2p, 9p. **Mooney** a-4i. **Starlin** c-6. **Tuska** r-1p, 15p. **Wood** r-15p.*

SUPER WESTERN COMICS (Also see Buffalo Bill)
Aug, 1950 - No. 4, Mar, 1951
Youthful Magazines

1-Buffalo Bill begins; Wyatt Earp, Calamity Jane & Sam Slade app; Powell-c/a 8.35 25.00 50.00
2-4 5.00 15.00 30.00

SUPER WESTERN FUNNIES (See Super Funnies)

SUPERWORLD COMICS
April, 1940 - No. 3, Aug, 1940 (All have 68 pgs.)
Hugo Gernsback (Komos Publ.)

1-Origin & 1st app. Hip Knox, Super Hypnotist; Mitey Powers & Buzz Allen, the Invisible Avenger, Little Nemo begin; cover by Frank R. Paul (all have sci/fi-c) 230.00 685.00 1600.00
2-Marvo 1-2 Go+, the Super Boy of the Year 2680 (1st app.) 125.00 375.00 850.00
3 100.00 300.00 700.00

Supreme #5 (Image), © Rob Liefeld

Suspense #21, © MEG

Swamp Thing #20, © DC

GD25 FN65 NM94 | GD25 FN65 NM94

:UPREME (See Youngblood #3)
lov, 1992 - Present ($1.95, color, created by Rob Liefeld)
mage Comics
'2#1-Embossed foil logo; Liefeld a(i) & scripts 1.40 3.50
1-Gold Edition 25.00
2-(3/93)-Liefeld co-plots & inks .80 2.00
3-7: (6/93-8/93): Liefeld co-plots. 7-Intro Starguard .80 2.00

:URE-FIRE COMICS (Lightning Comics #4 on)
lune, 1940 - No. 4, Oct, 1940 (Two No. 3's)
\ce Magazines
'1#1-Origin Flash Lightning; X-The Phantom Fed, Ace McCoy, Buck Steele, Marvo the Magician, The Raven, Whiz Wilson (Time Traveler) begin (all 1st app.); Flash Lightning c-1-4 92.00 275.00 550.00
2 55.00 165.00 330.00
3(9/40) 46.00 138.00 275.00
3(#4)(10/40)-nn on-c, #3 on inside 46.00 138.00 275.00

:URF 'N' WHEELS
Nov, 1969 - No. 6, Sept, 1970
Charlton Comics
1 1.30 3.25 8.00
2-6 1.00 2.50 6.00

:URGE (Eclipse)(Value: cover or less)

:URPRISE ADVENTURES (Formerly Tormented)
No. 3, Mar, 1955 - No. 5, July, 1955
Sterling Comic Group
3-5: 3,5-Sekowsky-a 4.00 11.00 22.00

:USIE Q. SMITH (See Four Color #323, 377, 453, 553)

SUSPENSE (Radio/TV issues #1-11; Real Life Tales of... #1-4) (Amazing Detective Cases #3 on?)
Dec, 1949 - No. 29, Apr, 1953 (#1-8,17-23: 52 pgs.)
Marvel/Atlas Comics (CnPC No. 1-10/BFP No. 11-29)
1-Powell-a; Peter Lorre, Sidney Greenstreet photo-c from Hammett's "The Verdict" 34.00 105.00 240.00
2-Crime stories; Gale Storm & Dennis O'Keefe photo-c from Universal movie "Abandoned" 16.00 50.00 115.00
3-Change to horror 17.00 52.00 120.00
4,7-10 11.50 34.00 80.00
5-Krigstein, Tuska, Everett-a 13.00 40.00 90.00
6-Tuska, Everett, Morisi-a 11.50 34.00 80.00
11-17,19,20: 14-Hypo-c; A-Bomb panels 10.00 30.00 70.00
18,22-Krigstein-a 11.50 34.00 80.00
21,23,26-29 9.15 27.50 55.00
24-Tuska-a 10.00 30.00 60.00
25-Electric chair-c/story 11.50 34.00 80.00
NOTE: ***Ayers** a-20. **Briefer** a-5, 7, 27. **Brodsky** c-4, 6-9, 11, 16, 17, 25. **Colan** a-8(2), 9. **Everett** a-5, 6(2), 19, 23, 28; c-21-23, 26. **Fuje** a-29. **Heath** a-5, 6, 8, 10, 12, 14; c-14, 19, 24. **Maneely** a-12, 23, 24, 28, 29; c-5, 6p, 10, 13, 15, 18. **Mooney** a-24, 28. **Morisi** a-6, 12. **Palais** a-10. **Rico** a-7-9. **Robinson** a-29. **Romita** a-20(2), 25. **Sekowsky** a-11, 13, 14. **Sinnott** a-23, 25. **Tuska** a-5, 6(2), 12; c-12. **Whitney** a-15, 16, 22. **Ed Win** a-27.*

SUSPENSE COMICS
Dec, 1943 - No. 12, Sept, 1946
Continental Magazines
1-The Grey Mask begins; bondage/torture-c; L. B. Cole-a (7 pgs.) 75.00 225.00 525.00
2-Intro. The Mask; Rico, Giunta, L. B. Cole-a (7 pgs.) 43.00 130.00 300.00
3-L.B. Cole-a; classic Schomburg-c 100.00 300.00 700.00
4-6: 5-L. B. Cole-c begin 39.00 118.00 265.00
7,9,10,12: 9-L.B. Cole eyeball-c 36.00 110.00 250.00
8-Classic L. B. Cole spider-c 86.00 260.00 600.00
11-Classic Devil-c 71.00 215.00 500.00
NOTE: ***L. B. Cole** c-5-12. **Larsen** a-11. **Palais** a-10, 11. Bondage c-1, 3, 4.*

SUSPENSE DETECTIVE
June, 1952 - No. 5, Mar, 1953
Fawcett Publications
1-Evans-a (11 pgs); Baily-c/a 22.00 65.00 150.00
2-Evans-a (10 pgs.) 13.00 40.00 90.00
3-5 10.00 30.00 65.00
NOTE: ***Baily** a-4, 5; c-1-3. **Sekowsky** a-2, 4, 5; c-5.*

SUSPENSE STORIES (See Strange Suspense Stories)

SUZIE COMICS (Formerly Laugh Comix; see Laugh Comics, Liberty Comics #10, Pep Comics & Top-Notch Comics #28)
No. 49, Spring, 1945 - No. 100, Aug, 1954
Close-Up No. 49,50/MLJ Mag./Archie No. 51 on
49-Ginger begins 17.00 52.00 120.00
50-55: 54-Transvestism story 11.00 32.00 75.00
56-Katy Keene begins by Woggon 10.00 30.00 70.00
57-65 8.35 25.00 50.00
66-80 7.50 22.50 45.00
81-100: 88-Used in **POP**, pgs. 76,77; Bill Woggon draws himself in story. 100-Last Katy Keene 6.35 19.00 38.00
NOTE: ***Al Fagaly** c-49-67. Katy Keene app. in 53-82, 85-100.*

SWAMP FOX, THE (See 4-Color #1179 & Walt Disney Presents #2)

SWAMP FOX, THE
1960 (14 pgs, small size) (Canada Dry Premiums)
Walt Disney Productions
Titles: (A)-Tory Masquerade, (B)-Rindau Rampage, (C)-Turnabout Tactics; each came in paper sleeve, books 1,2 & 3;
Set with sleeves 4.70 14.00 28.00
Comic only 1.60 4.00 8.00

SWAMP THING (See Brave & the Bold, Challengers of the Unknown #82, DC Comics Presents #8 & 85, DC Special Series #2, 14, 17, 20, House of Secrets #92, Limited Collectors' Edition C-59, Roots of the..., & The Saga of...)

SWAMP THING
Oct-Nov, 1972 - No. 24, Aug-Sept, 1976
National Periodical Publications/DC Comics
1-Wrightson-c/a begins 8.00 24.00 55.00
2-1st app. Patchwork Man (1 panel cameo) 4.30 13.00 30.00
3-1st full app. Patchwork Man 2.30 6.75 16.00
4-6,8-10: 10-Last Wrightson issue 2.00 6.00 14.00
7-Batman-c/story 2.30 6.75 16.00
11-24-Redondo-a. 13-Origin retold (1 pg.). 23-Swamp Thing reverts back to Dr. Holland. 23,24-New logo 1.40 3.50
NOTE: ***J. Jones** a-9(assist). **Kaluta** a-9i. **Redondo** c-12-19, 21. **Wrightson** issues (#1-10) reprinted in DC Special Series #2, 14, 17, 20 & Roots of the Swampthing.*

SWAT MALONE (America's Home Run King)
Sept, 1955
Swat Malone Enterprises
V1#1-Hy Fleishman-a 7.00 21.00 42.00

SWEENEY (Formerly Buz Sawyer)
No. 4, June, 1949 - No. 5, Sept, 1949
Standard Comics
4,5: 5-Crane-a 6.35 19.00 38.00

SWEE'PEA (See 4-Color #219)

SWEETHEART DIARY (Cynthia Doyle #66-on)
Wint, 1949; #2, Spr, 1950; #3, 6/50 - #5, 10/50; #6, 1951(nd); #7, 9/51 - #14, 1/53; #32, 10/55; #33, 4/56 - #65, 8/62 (#1-14: photo-c)
Fawcett Publications/Charlton Comics No. 32 on
1 10.00 30.00 65.00
2 5.35 16.00 32.00
3,4-Wood-a 10.00 30.00 70.00
5-10: 8-Bailey-a 4.70 14.00 28.00
11-14: 13-Swayze-a. 14-Last Fawcett issue 3.00 7.50 15.00
32 (10/55; 1st Charlton issue)(Formerly Cowboy Love #31) 4.00 10.00 20.00

Sweethearts #112, © FAW

Swords of Texas #2, © Timothy Truman

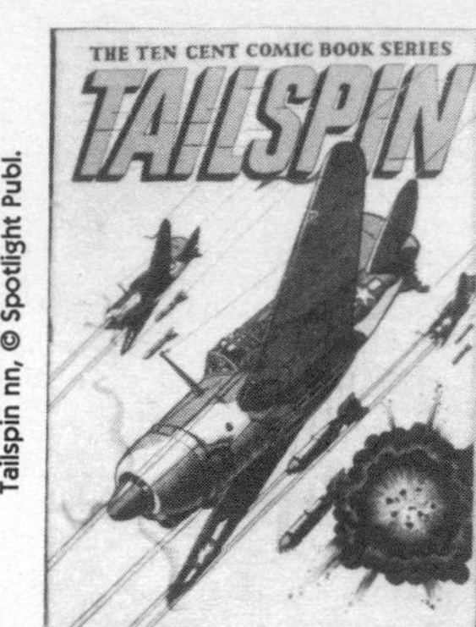

Tailspin nn, © Spotlight Publ.

	GD25	FN65	NM94
33-40: 34-Swayze-a	2.00	5.00	10.00
41-60	1.20	3.00	6.00
61-65	.60	1.50	3.00

SWEETHEARTS (Formerly Captain Midnight)
#68, 10/48 - #121, 5/53; #122, 3/54; V2#23, 5/54 - #137, 12/73
Fawcett Publications/Charlton No. 122 on

	GD25	FN65	NM94
68-Robert Mitchum photo-c	10.00	30.00	70.00
69-80	4.00	11.00	22.00
81-84,86-93,95-99	3.20	8.00	16.00
85,94,103,105,110,117-George Evans-a	4.70	14.00	28.00
100	4.00	10.00	20.00
101,107-Powell-a	3.60	9.00	18.00
102,104,106,108,109,112-116,118,121	2.40	6.00	12.00
111-1 pg. Ronald Reagan biography	4.70	14.00	28.00
119-Marilyn Monroe photo-c; also appears in story; part Wood-a	26.00	80.00	180.00
120-Atom Bomb story	6.70	20.00	40.00
122-(1st Charlton? 3/54)-Marijuana story	5.35	16.00	32.00
V2#23 (5/54)-28: 28-Last precode issue (2/55)	2.40	6.00	12.00
29-39,41,43-45,47-50	1.60	4.00	8.00
40-Photo-c; Tommy Sands story	3.20	8.00	16.00
42-Ricky Nelson photo-c/story	6.70	20.00	40.00
46-Jimmy Rodgers photo-c/story	3.20	8.00	16.00
51-60	1.60	4.00	8.00
61-80	1.00	2.00	5.00
81-100		1.20	3.00
101-110		.80	2.00
111-137			1.50

NOTE: *Photo c-68-121(Fawcett), 40, 42, 46(Charlton).* ***Swayze*** *a(Fawcett)-70-118(most).*

SWEETHEART SCANDALS (See Fox Giants)

SWEETIE PIE (See 4-Color #1185, 1241)

SWEETIE PIE
Dec, 1955 - No. 15, Fall, 1957
Ajax-Farrell/Pines (Literary Ent.)

	GD25	FN65	NM94
1-By Nadine Seltzer	4.20	12.50	25.00
2 (5/56; last Ajax?)	2.80	7.00	14.00
3-15 (#3-10, exist?)	1.80	4.50	9.00

SWEET LOVE
Sept, 1949 - No. 5, May, 1950
Home Comics (Harvey)

	GD25	FN65	NM94
1-Photo-c	5.00	15.00	30.00
2-Photo-c	3.60	9.00	18.00
3,4: 3-Powell-a; 4-Photo-c	2.80	7.00	14.00
5-Kamen, Powell-a; photo-c	4.20	12.50	25.00

SWEET ROMANCE
October, 1968
Charlton Comics

	GD25	FN65	NM94
1		1.20	3.00

SWEET SIXTEEN
Aug-Sept, 1946 - No. 13, Jan, 1948 (All have movie stars photos on covers)
Parents' Magazine Institute

	GD25	FN65	NM94
1-Van Johnson's life story; Dorothy Dare, Queen of Hollywood Stunt Artists begins (in all issues); part photo-c	11.50	34.00	80.00
2-Jane Powell, Roddy McDowall "Holiday in Mexico" photo on-c; Alan Ladd story	9.15	27.50	55.00
3-6,8-11: 4-Elizabeth Taylor photo on-c. 5-Ann Francis photo on-c; Gregory Peck story. 6-Dick Haymes story. 8-Shirley Jones photo on-c. 10-Jean Simmons photo on-c; James Stewart story	7.00	21.00	42.00
7-Ronald Reagan's life story	13.50	41.00	95.00
12-Bob Cummings, Vic Damone story	7.00	21.00	42.00
13-Robert Mitchum's life story	8.35	25.00	50.00

SWEET XVI (Marvel)(Value: cover or less)

SWIFT ARROW (Also see Lone Rider & The Rider)
Feb-Mar, 1954 - No. 5, Oct-Nov, 1954; Apr, 1957 - No. 3, Sept, 1957
Ajax/Farrell Publications

	GD25	FN65	NM94
1(1954) (1st Series)	9.15	27.50	55.00
2	5.35	16.00	32.00
3-5: 5-Lone Rider story	4.00	12.00	24.00
1 (2nd Series) (Swift Arrow's Gunfighters #4)	4.20	12.50	25.00
2,3: 2-Lone Rider begins	3.60	9.00	18.00

SWIFT ARROW'S GUNFIGHTERS (Formerly Swift Arrow)
No. 4, Nov, 1957
Ajax/Farrell Publ. (Four Star Comic Corp.)

	GD25	FN65	NM94
4	4.20	12.50	25.00

SWIFTSURE (Harrier)(Value: cover or less)

SWING WITH SCOOTER
June-July, 1966 - No. 35, Aug-Sept, 1971; No. 36, Oct-Nov, 1972
National Periodical Publications

	GD25	FN65	NM94
1	3.60	9.00	18.00
2-10: 9-Alfred E. Newman swipe in last panel	2.00	5.00	10.00
11-20	1.60	4.00	8.00
21-36: 33-Interview with David Cassidy. 34-Interview with Ron Ely (Doc Savage)	1.00	2.50	6.00

NOTE: ***Orlando*** *a-1-11; c-1-11, 13. #20, 33, 34: 68 pgs.; #35: 52 pgs.*

SWISS FAMILY ROBINSON (See 4-Color #1156, King Classics & Movie Comics)

SWORD & THE DRAGON, THE (See 4-Color #1118)

SWORD & THE ROSE, THE (See 4-Color #505, 682)

SWORD IN THE STONE, THE (See March of Comics #258 & Movie Comics & Wart and the Wizard)

SWORD OF SORCERY
Feb-Mar, 1973 - No. 5, Nov-Dec, 1973
National Periodical Publications

	GD25	FN65	NM94
1-Leiber Fafhrd & The Grey Mouser; Chaykin/Neal Adams (Crusty Bunkers) art; Kaluta-c		1.20	3.00
2-Wrightson-c(i); Neal Adams-a(i)		.80	2.00
3-5: 3-Wrightson-i(5pg.). 5-Starlin-a(p); Conan cameo			1.50

NOTE: ***Chaykin*** *a-1-4p; c-2p, 3-5.* ***Kaluta*** *a-3i.* ***Simonson*** *a-3i, 4i, 5p; c-5.*

SWORD OF THE ATOM (DC)(Value: cover or less)

SWORDS OF TEXAS (Eclipse)(Value: cover or less)

SWORDS OF THE SWASHBUCKLERS (Marvel)(Value: cover or less)

SYPHONS (Now)(Value: cover or less)

TAFFY COMICS
Mar-Apr, 1945 - No. 12, 1948
Rural Home/Orbit Publ.

	GD25	FN65	NM94
1-L.B. Cole-c; origin & 1st app. of Wiggles The Wonderworm plus 7 chapter WWII funny animal adventures	11.50	34.00	80.00
2-L.B. Cole-c; Wiggles-c/stories in #1-4	8.35	25.00	50.00
3,4,6-12: 6-Perry Como-c/story. 7-Duke Ellington, 2 pgs. 8-Glenn Ford-c/story. 9-Lon McCallister part photo-c & story. 10-Mort Leav-c. 11-Mickey Rooney-c/story	5.85	17.50	35.00
5-L.B. Cole-c; Van Johnson-c/story	6.70	20.00	40.00

TAILGUNNER JO (DC)(Value: cover or less)

TAILSPIN
November, 1944
Spotlight Publishers

	GD25	FN65	NM94
nn-Firebird app.; L.B. Cole-c	10.00	30.00	70.00

TAILSPIN TOMMY STORY & PICTURE BOOK
No. 266, 1931? (nd) (Color strip reprints; 10-1/2x10")
McLoughlin Bros.

	GD25	FN65	NM94
266-By Forrest	20.00	60.00	120.00

TAILSPIN TOMMY (Also see Famous Feature Stories & The Funnies)

Tales From The Crypt #32, © WMG

Tales of Asgard #1(10/68), © MEG

Tales of Horror #6, © TOBY

	GD25	FN65	NM94
932 (100 pages, hardcover)			
Cupples & Leon Co.			
n-(Rare)-B&W strip reprints from 1930 by Hal Forrest & Glenn Claffin	25.00	75.00	175.00

TAILSPIN TOMMY (Also see Popular Comics)
1940; 1946
United Features Syndicate/Service Publ. Co.

	GD25	FN65	NM94
Single Series 23(1940)	24.00	72.00	165.00
Best Seller (nd, 1946)-Service Publ. Co.	10.00	30.00	70.00

TALENT SHOWCASE (See New Talent Showcase)

TALES CALCULATED TO DRIVE YOU BATS
Nov, 1961 - No. 7, Nov, 1962; 1966 (Satire)
Archie Publications

	GD25	FN65	NM94
1-Only 10 cent issue; has cut-out Werewolf mask (price includes mask)	7.00	21.00	50.00
2-Begin 12 cent issues	4.00	12.00	28.00
3-6	3.20	8.00	20.00
7-Storyline change	2.40	7.25	17.00
1(1966)-25 cents	3.25	9.50	22.00

TALES FROM THE ANIVERSE (Arrow)(Value: cover or less)

TALES FROM THE CRYPT (Formerly The Crypt Of Terror; see Three Dimensional...)
No. 20, Oct-Nov, 1950 - No. 46, Feb-Mar, 1955
E.C. Comics

	GD25	FN65	NM94
20-See Crime Patrol #15 for 1st Crypt Keeper	93.00	280.00	650.00
21-Kurtzman-r/Haunt of Fear #15(#1)	75.00	225.00	525.00
22-Moon Girl costume at costume party, one panel	60.00	180.00	420.00
23-25: 24-E. A. Poe adaptation	45.00	135.00	315.00
26-30	38.00	115.00	265.00
31-Williamson-a(1st at E.C.); B&W and color illos. in **POP**; Kamen draws himself, Gaines & Feldstein; Ingels, Craig & Davis draw themselves in his story	41.00	125.00	290.00
32,35-39	30.00	90.00	210.00
33-Origin The Crypt Keeper	50.00	150.00	350.00
34-Used in **POP**, pg. 83; lingerie panels	30.00	90.00	210.00
40-Used in Senate hearings & in Hartford Courant anti-comics editorials-1954	30.00	90.00	210.00
41-45: 45-2pgs. showing E.C. staff	29.00	85.00	200.00
46-Low distribution; pre-advertised cover for unpublished 4th horror title 'Crypt of Terror' used on this book	34.00	105.00	240.00

NOTE: ***Ray Bradbury** adaptations-34, 36. **Craig** a-20, 22-24; c-20. **Crandall** a-38, 44. **Davis** a-24-46; c-29-46. **Elder** a-37, 38. **Evans** a-32-34, 36, 40, 41, 43, 46. **Feldstein** a-20-23; c-21-25, 28. Ingels a-in all. **Kamen** a-20, 22, 25, 27-31, 33-36, 39, 41-45. **Krigstein** a-40, 42, 45. **Kurtzman** a-21. **Orlando** a-27-30, 35, 37, 39, 41-45. **Wood** a-21, 24, 25; c-26, 27. Canadian reprints known; see Table of Contents.*

TALES FROM THE CRYPT (Magazine)
No. 10, July, 1968 (35 cents)(B&W)
Eerie Publications

	GD25	FN65	NM94
10-Contains Farrell reprints from 1950s	2.00	6.00	14.00

TALES FROM THE CRYPT
July, 1990 - No. 6, May, 1991 ($1.95, color, 68 pgs.)(#4 on: $2.00)
Gladstone Publishing

	GD25	FN65	NM94
1-r/TFTC #33 & Crime S.S. #17; Davis-c(r)		.80	2.00
2-6: 2,3,5,6-Davis-c(r). 4-Craig-c(r)		.80	2.00

TALES FROM THE CRYPT (Cochran, large size)(Value: cover or less)

TALES FROM THE CRYPT
Sept, 1992 - Present ($1.50, color)
Russ Cochran

	GD25	FN65	NM94
1-4: 1-r/Crypt of Terror #17; Craig-c(r)			1.50
5,6 ($2.00)		.80	2.00

TALES FROM THE GREAT BOOK
Feb, 1955 - No. 4, Jan, 1956
Famous Funnies

	GD25	FN65	NM94
1-Story of Samson; John Lehti-a in all	5.35	16.00	32.00
2-4: 2-Joshua	3.60	9.00	18.00

TALES FROM THE HEART OF AFRICA (Marvel)(Value: cover or less)

TALES FROM THE TOMB (See Dell Giants)

TALES FROM THE TOMB (Magazine)
V1#6, July, 1969 - V7#1, Feb, 1975 (52 pgs.)
Eerie Publications

	GD25	FN65	NM94
V1#6-8	2.60	7.50	18.00
V2#1-3,5,6: 6-Rulah-r	1.65	4.00	10.00
4-LSD story-r/Weird V3#5	1.65	4.00	10.00
V3#1-Rulah-r	1.65	4.00	10.00
2-6('70),V4#1-5('72),V5#1-6('73),V6#1-6('74),V7#1('75)	1.30	3.25	8.00

TALES OF ASGARD
Oct, 1968 (25 cents, 68 pages); Feb, 1984 ($1.25, 52 pgs.)
Marvel Comics Group

	GD25	FN65	NM94
1-Reprints Tales of Asgard (Thor) back-up stories from Journey into Mystery #97-106; new Kirby-c	3.60	10.75	25.00
V2#1 (2/84)-Thor-r; Simonson-c			1.00

TALES OF DEMON DICK & BUNKER BILL
1934 (78 pgs; 5x10-1/2"; B&W)(hardcover)
Whitman Publishing Co.

	GD25	FN65	NM94
793-By Dick Spencer	14.00	43.00	100.00

TALES OF EVIL
Feb, 1975 - No. 3, July, 1975
Atlas/Seaboard Publ.

	GD25	FN65	NM94
1-3: 2-Intro. The Bog Beast; Sparling-a. 3-Origin The Man-Monster; Buckler-a(p)			1.00

NOTE: ***Grandenetti** a-1, 2. **Lieber** c-1. **Sekowsky** a-1. **Sutton** a-2. **Thorne** c-2.*

TALES OF GHOST CASTLE
May-June, 1975 - No. 3, Sept-Oct, 1975 (All 25¢ issues)
National Periodical Publications

	GD25	FN65	NM94
1-3: 1,3-Redondo-a. 2-Nino-a			1.00

TALES OF G.I. JOE (Marvel)(Value: cover or less)

TALES OF HORROR
June, 1952 - No. 13, Oct, 1954
Toby Press/Minoan Publ. Corp.

	GD25	FN65	NM94
1	18.00	54.00	125.00
2-Torture scenes	13.50	41.00	95.00
3-8,13	9.15	27.50	55.00
9-11-Reprints Purple Claw #1-3	10.00	30.00	60.00
12-Myron Fass-c/a; torture scenes	10.00	30.00	65.00

NOTE: ***Andru** a-5. **Baily** a-5. **Myron Fass** a-2, 3, 12; c-1-3, 12. **Hollingsworth** a-2. **Sparling** a-6, 9; c-9.*

TALES OF JUSTICE
No. 53, May, 1955 - No. 67, Aug, 1957
Atlas Comics(MjMC No. 53-66/Male No. 67)

	GD25	FN65	NM94
53	10.00	30.00	60.00
54-57: 54-Powell-a	6.70	20.00	40.00
58,59-Krigstein-a	8.35	25.00	50.00
60-63,65: 60-Powell-a	5.00	15.00	30.00
64,67-Crandall-a	6.70	20.00	40.00
66-Torres, Orlando-a	6.70	20.00	40.00

NOTE: ***Everett** a-53, 60. **Orlando** a-65, 66. **Severin** a-64; c-58, 60, 65. **Wildey** a-64, 67.*

TALES OF ORDINARY MADNESS (Dark Horse)(Value: cover or less)

TALES OF SUSPENSE (Becomes Captain America #100 on)
Jan, 1959 - No. 99, March, 1968
Atlas (WPI No. 1,2/Male No. 3-12/VPI No. 13-18)/Marvel No. 19 on

Tales of Suspense #19, © MEG

Tales of Terror #12, © Eclipse

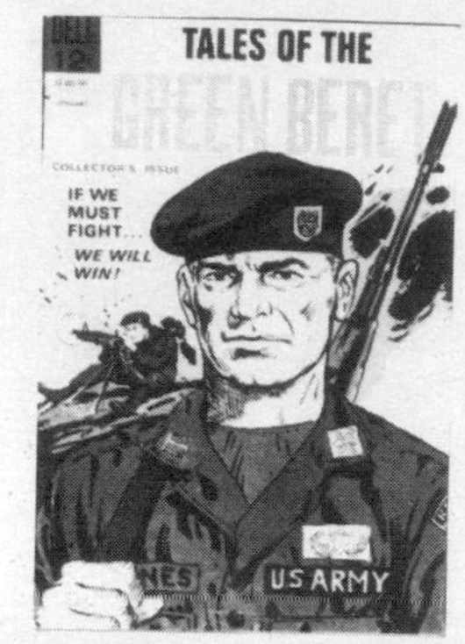

Tales of the Green Beret #1, © DELL

	GD25	FN65	NM94
1-Williamson-a, 5 pgs.; #1-4 have sci/fi-c	95.00	285.00	950.00
2,3: 3-Flying saucer-c/story	39.00	117.00	350.00
4-Williamson-a, 4 pgs; Kirby/Everett-c/a	36.00	108.00	325.00
5,6,8,10: 5-Kirby monster-c begin	23.00	70.00	210.00
7-Prototype ish. (Lava Man)	30.00	90.00	240.00
9-Prototype ish. (Iron Man)	33.00	98.00	260.00
11-15,17-20: 12-Crandall-a. 13-Elektro-c/story. 14-Intro. Colossus-c/story. 20-Colossus-c/story	19.00	56.00	150.00
16-1st Metallo-c/story (4/61, Iron Man prototype)	25.00	75.00	200.00
21-25: 25-Last 10 cent issue	14.00	41.00	110.00
26,27,29,30,33,34,36-38	13.00	38.00	100.00
28-Prototype ish. (Stone Men)	14.00	42.00	110.00
31-Prototype ish. (Dr. Doom)	15.00	45.00	120.00
32-Prototype ish. (Dr. Strange)(8/62)-Sazzik The Sorcerer app.; "The Man and the Beehive," story, 1 month before TTA #35 (2nd Antman), came out after "The Man in the Ant Hill" in TTA #27 (1/62) (1st Antman)-Characters from both stories were tested to see which got best fan response	15.00	45.00	120.00
35-Prototype ish. (The Watcher)	14.00	42.00	110.00

	GD25	FN65	VF82	NM94
39 (3/63)-Origin/1st app. Iron Man & begin series; 1st Iron Man story has Kirby layouts	283.00	850.00	1700.00	2550.00

	GD25	FN65	NM94
40-2nd app. Iron Man (in new armor)	111.00	333.00	1000.00
41-3rd app. Iron Man; Dr. Strange (villain) app.	71.00	212.00	495.00
42-45: 45-Intro. & 1st app. Happy & Pepper	32.00	96.00	225.00
46,47: 46-1st app. Crimson Dynamo	19.00	58.00	135.00
48-New Iron Man armor by Ditko	24.00	71.00	165.00
49-1st X-Men x-over (same date as X-Men #3, 1/64); also 1st Avengers x-over (w/o Captain America); 1st Tales of the Watcher back-up story & begins (2nd app. Watcher; see F.F. #13)	16.00	48.00	110.00
50-1st app. Mandarin	11.00	34.00	80.00
51-1st Scarecrow	10.00	30.00	70.00
52-1st app. The Black Widow (4/64)	14.00	41.00	95.00
53-Origin The Watcher; 2nd Black Widow app.	11.00	34.00	80.00
54-56: 56-1st app. Unicorn; Avengers x-over	7.00	21.00	50.00
57-Origin/1st app. Hawkeye (9/64)	16.00	49.00	115.00
58-Captain America battles Iron Man (10/64)-Classic-c; 2nd Kraven app. (Cap's 1st app. in this title)	29.00	86.00	200.00
59-Iron Man plus Captain America double feature begins (11/64); 1st S.A. Captain America solo story; intro Jarvis, Avenger's butler; classic-c	29.00	86.00	200.00
60-2nd app. Hawkeye (#64 is 3rd app.)	13.00	40.00	90.00
61,62,64: 62-Origin Mandarin (2/65)	7.00	21.00	50.00
63-1st Silver Age origin Captain America (3/65)	20.00	60.00	140.00
65-1st Silver-Age Red Skull (5/65)	13.00	40.00	90.00
66-Origin Red Skull	13.00	40.00	90.00
67-78,81-98: 69-1st app. Titanium Man. 75-1st app. Agent 13 later named Sharon Carter. 76-Intro Batroc & Sharon Carter, Agent 13 of Shield. 78-Col. Nick Fury app. 92-1st Nick Fury x-over (cameo, as Agent of Shield, 8/67). 94-Intro Modok. 95-Capt. America's i.d. revealed. 98-1st app. Zemo in cameo (#99 is 1st full app.)	5.50	17.00	40.00
79-Begin 3 part Iron Man Sub-Mariner battle story; Sub-mariner-c & cameo; 1st app. Cosmic Cube	6.50	19.00	45.00
80-Iron Man battles Sub-Mariner story cont'd in Tales to Astonish #82	7.00	21.00	48.00
99-Captain America story cont'd in Captain America #100; Iron Man story cont'd in Iron Man & Sub-Mariner #1	8.00	24.00	55.00

NOTE: ***J. Buscema** a-1. **Colan** a-39, 73-99p; c(p)-73, 75, 77, 79, 81, 83, 85-87, 89, 91, 93, 95, 97, 99. **Craig** a-99i. **Crandall** a-12. **Davis** a-38. **Ditko** c(i)-2, 10, 13. **Ditko/Kirby** art in most issues #2-15, 17-49. **Everett** a-8. **Forte** a-5, 9. **Heath** a-10. **Gil Kane** a-88p, 89-91; c-88, 89-91p. **Kirby** a(p)-40, 41, 43, 59-75, 77-86, 92-99; layouts-69-75, 77; c(p)4-28(most), 29-56, 58-72, 74, 76, 78, 80, 82, 84, 86, 92, 94, 96, 98. **Leiber/Fox** a-42, 43, 45, 51. **Reinman** a-26, 44i, 49i, 52i, 53i. **Tuska** a-58, 70-74. **Wood** c/a-71i.*

TALES OF SWORD & SORCERY (See Dagar)

TALES OF TERROR
1952 (no month)
Toby Press Publications

	GD25	FN65	NM94
1-Fawcette-c; Ravielli-a	10.00	30.00	70.00

NOTE: *This title was cancelled due to similarity to the E.C. title.*

TALES OF TERROR (See Movie Classics)

TALES OF TERROR (Magazine)
Summer, 1964
Eerie Publications

	GD25	FN65	NM94
1	3.60	9.00	18.00

TALES OF TERROR (Eclipse)(Value: cover or less)

TALES OF TERROR ANNUAL
1951 - No. 3, 1953 (25 cents, 132 pgs., 16 stories each)
E.C. Comics

	GD25	FN65	VF82
nn(1951)(Scarce)-Feldstein infinity-c	367.00	1100.00	2400.00

(Estimated up to 35 total copies exist, 3 in NM/Mint)

	GD25	FN65	NM94
2(1952)-Feldstein-c	158.00	475.00	1000.00
3(1953)-Feldstein bondage/torture-c	117.00	350.00	750.00

NOTE: *No. 1 contains three horror and one science fiction comic which came out in 1950. No. 2 contains a horror, crime, and science fiction book which generally had cover dates in 1951, and No. 3 had horror, crime, and shock books that generally appeared in 1952. All E.C. annuals contain four complete books that did not sell on the stands which were rebound in the annual format, minus the covers, and sold from the E.C. office and on the stands in key cities. The contents of each annual may vary in the same year.*

TALES OF TERROR ILLUSTRATED (See Terror Illustrated)

TALES OF TEXAS JOHN SLAUGHTER (See 4-Color #997)

TALES OF THE BEANWORLD
Feb, 1985 - No. 19, 1991; No. 20, 1993 - Present ($1.50/$2.00, B&W)
Beanworld Press/Eclipse Comics

	GD25	FN65	NM94
1		1.60	4.00
2-19		.80	2.00
20 ($2.50)		1.00	2.50

TALES OF THE GREEN BERET
Jan, 1967 - No. 5, Oct, 1969
Dell Publishing Co.

	GD25	FN65	NM94
1-Glanzman-a in 1-4 & 5r	3.00	7.50	15.00
2-5: 5-Reprints #1	1.80	4.50	9.00

TALES OF THE GREEN HORNET (Now)(Value: cover or less)

TALES OF THE GREEN LANTERN CORPS (DC)(Value: cover or less)(See Green Lantern #107)

TALES OF THE INVISIBLE SCARLET O'NEIL (See Harvey Comics Hits #59)

TALES OF THE KILLERS (Magazine)
V1#10, Dec, 1970 - V1#11, Feb, 1971 (B&W, 52pgs.)
World Famous Periodicals

	GD25	FN65	NM94
V1#10-One pg. Frazetta	2.15	6.50	15.00
11	1.65	4.00	10.00

TALES OF THE LEGION (DC)(Value: cover or less)(Formerly The Legion of Super-Heroes)

TALES OF THE MARINES (Formerly Devil-Dog Dugan #1-3)
No. 4, Feb, 1957 (Marines At War #5 on)
Atlas Comics (OPI)

	GD25	FN65	NM94
4-Powell-a; Severin-c	4.00	10.00	20.00

TALES OF THE MYSTERIOUS TRAVELER (See Mysterious...)
Aug, 1956 - No. 13, June, 1959; V2#14, Oct, 1985 - No. 15, Dec, 1985
Charlton Comics

	GD25	FN65	NM94
1-No Ditko-a; Giordano/Alascia-c	26.00	78.00	180.00
2-Ditko-a(1)	23.00	70.00	160.00
3-Ditko-c/a(1)	22.00	65.00	150.00
4-6-Ditko-c/a(3-4 stories each)	27.00	80.00	190.00
7-9-Ditko-a(1-2 each). 8-Rocko-c	22.00	65.00	150.00
10,11-Ditko-c/a(3-4 each)	24.00	72.00	170.00

Tales of the Teen Titans #60, © DC

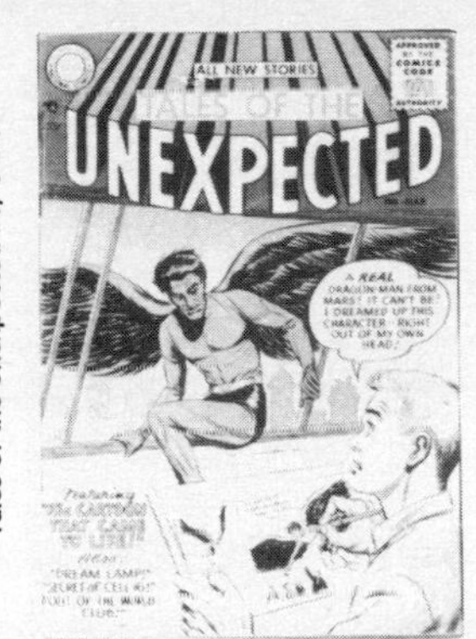

Tales of the Unexpected #1, © DC

Tales to Astonish #52, © MEG

GD25 FN65 NM94 | GD25 FN65 NM94

12,13 8.00 24.00 55.00
V2#14,15 (1985)-Ditko-c/a 1.00

TALES OF THE NEW TEEN TITANS (DC)(Value: cover or less)

TALES OF THE PONY EXPRESS (See 4-Color #829, 942)

TALES OF THE SUN RUNNERS (Sirius)(Value: cover or less)

TALES OF THE TEENAGE MUTANT NINJA TURTLES
May, 1987 - No. 7, Aug (Apr-c), 1989 (B&W, $1.50)(See Teenage Mutant...)
Mirage Studios

1 1.90 4.75
2-7: Title merges w/Teenage Mutant Ninja... 1.10 2.75

TALES OF THE TEEN TITANS (Formerly The New Teen Titans)
No. 41, April, 1984 - No. 91, July, 1988 (75 cents)
DC Comics

41,45-59: 46 Aqualad & Aquagirl join. 50-Double size. 52-1st app. Azrael in cameo. 53-1st full app. Azrael; Deathstroke cameo (1 panel). 54,55-Deathstroke-c/stories. 56-Intro Jinx. 57-Neutron app. 59-r/DC Comics Presents #26 1.00
42-44: The Judas Contract part 1-3 with Deathstroke the Terminator in all; concludes in Annual #3. 44-Dick Grayson becomes Nightwing (3rd to be Nightwing) & joins Titans; Jericho (Deathstroke's son) joins; origin Deathstroke 1.30 3.25 8.00
60-91-r/New Teen Titans Baxter series. 68-B. Smith-c. 70-Origin Kole. 83-91 are $1.00 cover 1.00
Annual 3(1984, $1.25)-Part 4 of The Judas Contract; Deathstroke-c/story; Death of Terra; indicia says Teen Titans Annual; formerly New Teen Titans Annual #1,2 1.20 3.00
Annual 4,5: 4-(1986, $1.25)-Reprints. 5(1987) 1.25

TALES OF THE TEXAS RANGERS (See Jace Pearson...)

TALES OF THE UNEXPECTED (The Unexpected #105 on)(See Super DC Giant)
Feb-Mar, 1956 - No. 104, Dec-Jan, 1967-68
National Periodical Publications

1 70.00 210.00 700.00
2 41.00 122.00 325.00
3-5 28.00 84.00 225.00
6-10 21.00 62.00 165.00
11,14,19,20 12.00 36.00 95.00
12,13,15-18,21-24: All have Kirby-a. 16-Character named 'Thor' with a magic hammer (8/57, not like later Thor) 16.00 47.00 125.00
25-30 11.00 32.00 85.00
31-39 9.00 27.00 70.00

GD25 FN65 VF82 NM94
Showcase #15 (7-8/58)-1st app. Space Ranger 62.00 185.00 555.00 925.00

GD25 FN65 NM94
Showcase #16 (9-10/58)-2nd Space Ranger 58.00 173.00 575.00

GD25 FN65 VF82 NM94
40-Space Ranger begins (8/59), ends #82 60.00 180.00 390.00 600.00

GD25 FN65 NM94
41,42-Space Ranger stories 25.00 75.00 200.00
43-1st Space Ranger-c this title; grey tone-c 45.00 135.00 450.00
44-46 19.00 58.00 135.00
47-50 14.00 41.00 95.00
51-60: 54-Dinosaur-c/story 11.00 34.00 80.00
61-67: 67-Last 10 cent issue 9.00 26.00 60.00
68-82: 82-Last Space Ranger 4.00 13.00 30.00
83-100: 91-1st Automan (also in #94,97) 3.20 8.00 20.00
101-104 2.30 6.75 16.00

NOTE: ***Neal Adams** c-104. **Anderson** a-50. **Brown** a-50-82(Space Ranger); c-19, 40, & many Space Ranger-c. **Cameron** a-24, 27, 29; c-24. **Heath** a-49. **Bob Kane** a-24, 48. **Kirby** a-12, 13, 15-18, 21-24; c-13, 18, 22. **Meskin** a-15, 18, 26, 27, 35, 66. **Moreira** a-16, 20, 29, 38, 44, 62, 71; c-38. **Roussos** c-10. **Wildey** a-31.*

TALES OF THE WEST (See 3-D...)

TALES OF THE WIZARD OF OZ (See 4-Color #1308)

TALES OF THE ZOMBIE (Magazine)
Aug, 1973 - No. 10, Mar, 1975 (75 cents)(B&W)
Marvel Comics Group

V1#1-Reprint/Menace #5; origin 2.15 6.50 15.00
2,3: 2-Everett biography & memorial 1.30 3.25 8.00
V2#1(#4)-Photos & text of James Bond movie "Live & Let Die" 1.30 3.25 8.00
5-10: 8-Kaluta-a 1.30 3.25 8.00
Annual 1(Summer,'75)(#11)-B&W; Everett, Buscema-a 1.00 2.00 5.00

NOTE: ***Alcala** a-7-9. **Boris** c-1-4. **Colan** a-2r, 6. **Heath** a-5r. **Reese** a-2. **Tuska** a-2r.*

TALES OF THUNDER (Deluxe)(Value: cover or less)

TALES OF VOODOO (Magazine)
V1#11, Nov, 1968 - V7#6, Nov, 1974
Eerie Publications

V1#11 3.20 8.00 20.00
V2#1(3/69)-V2#4(9/69) 1.70 5.00 12.00
V3#1-6('70): 4-'Claws of the Cat' redrawn from Climax #1 1.65 4.00 10.00
V4#1-6('71), V5#1-6('72), V6#1-6('73), V7#1-6('74) 1.65 4.00 10.00
Annual 1 1.65 4.00 10.00

NOTE: *Bondage-c-V1#10, V2#4, V3#4.*

TALES OF WELLS FARGO (See 4-Color #876, 968, 1023,1075, 1113, 1167, 1215, & Western Roundup under Dell Giants)

TALESPIN (Also see Cartoon Tales & Disney's Talespin Limited Series)
June, 1991 - No. 7, Dec, 1991 ($1.50, color)
Disney Comics

1-7 1.50

TALES TO ASTONISH (Becomes The Incredible Hulk #102 on)
Jan, 1959 - No. 101, March, 1968
Atlas (MAP No. 1/ZPC No. 2-14/VPI No. 15-21/Marvel No. 22 on

1-Jack Davis-a; #1-4 have sci/fi-c 90.00 270.00 900.00
2-Ditko flying saucer-c 44.00 133.00 400.00
3-4 31.00 92.00 275.00
5-Prototype ish. (Stone Men); Williamson-a (4 pgs.); Kirby monster-c begin 33.00 100.00 300.00
6,8-10 24.00 72.00 215.00
7-Prototype ish. (Toad Men) 26.00 77.00 230.00
11-14,17-20: 13-Swipes story from Menace #8 19.00 56.00 150.00
15-Prototype ish. (Electro) 22.00 65.00 175.00
16-Prototype ish. (Stone Men) 22.00 65.00 175.00
21-26,28-34 14.00 41.00 110.00

GD25 FN65 VF82 NM94
27-1st Ant-Man app. (1/62); last 10 cent issue (see Strange Tales #73,78 & Tales of Suspense #32) 191.00 575.00 1440.00 2300.00
35-(9/62)-2nd app. Ant-Man, 1st in costume; begin series & Ant-Man-c 110.00 330.00 715.00 1100.00

GD25 FN65 NM94
36-3rd app. Ant-Man 46.00 138.00 415.00
37-40: 38-1st app. Egghead 29.00 88.00 205.00
41-43 19.00 58.00 135.00
44-Origin & 1st app. The Wasp (6/63) 24.00 71.00 165.00
45-48 14.00 43.00 100.00
49-Ant-Man becomes Giant Man (11/63) 18.00 54.00 125.00
50-56,58: 50-Origin/1st app. Human Top (alias Whirlwind). 52-Origin/1st app. Black Knight (2/64) 10.00 30.00 70.00
57-Early Spider-Man app. (7/64) 13.00 40.00 90.00
59-Giant Man vs. Hulk feature story (9/64) 15.00 45.00 105.00
60-Giant Man & Hulk double feature begins 18.00 54.00 125.00
61-69: 62-1st app./origin The Leader; new Wasp costume. 65-New Giant Man costume. 68-New Human Top costume. 69-Last Giant Man

Tapping The Vein #2, © Clive Barker

Target Comics V3#7, © NOVP

Tarzan #29, © ERB

7.00 21.00 50.00
70-Sub-Mariner & Incredible Hulk begins (8/65) 10.00 30.00 70.00
71-81,83-91,94-99: 79-Hulk vs. Hercules-c/story. 81-1st app. Boomerang. 90-1st app. The Abomination. 97-X-Men cameo (brief)
5.00 15.00 35.00
82-Iron Man battles Sub-Mariner (1st Iron Man x-over outside The Avengers); story cont'd from Tales of Suspense #80 7.00 21.00 48.00
92-1st Silver Surfer x-over (outside of Fantastic Four, 6/67); 1 panel cameo only 6.00 18.00 42.00
93-Hulk battles Silver Surfer-c/s (1st full x-over) 7.00 21.00 48.00
100-Hulk battles Sub-Mariner full-length story 6.00 18.00 42.00
101-Hulk story cont'd in Incredible Hulk #102; Sub-Mariner story continued in Iron Man & Sub-Mariner #1 9.00 26.00 60.00

NOTE: ***Ayers*** *c(i)-9-12, 16, 18, 19.* ***Berg*** *a-1.* ***Burgos*** *a-62-64p.* ***Buscema*** *a-85-87p.* ***Colan*** *a(p)-70-76, 78-82, 84, 85, 101; c(p)-71-76, 78, 80, 82, 84, 86, 88, 90.* ***Ditko*** *a-most issues-1-48, 50i, 60-67; c-2, 7i, 8i, 14i, 17i.* ***Everett*** *a-78, 79i, 80-84, 85-90i, 94i, 95, 96; c(i)-79-81, 83, 86, 88.* ***Forte*** *a-6.* ***Kane*** *a-76, 88-91; c-89, 91.* ***Kirby*** *a(p)-1-34(most), 35-40, 44, 49-51, 68-70, 82, 83; layouts-71-84; c(p)-1, 3-48, 50-70, 72, 73, 75, 77, 78, 79, 81, 85, 90.* ***Leiber/Fox*** *a-47, 48, 50, 51.* ***Powell*** *a-65-69p, 73, 74.* ***Reinman*** *a-6, 36, 45, 46, 54i, 56-60i.*

TALES TO ASTONISH (2nd Series)
Dec, 1979 - No. 14, Jan, 1981
Marvel Comics Group

V1#1-Reprints Sub-Mariner #1 by Buscema 1.40
2-14: Reprints Sub-Mariner #2-14 1.20

TALES TO HOLD YOU SPELLBOUND (See Spellbound)

TALKING KOMICS
1947 (20 pages) (Slick covers)
Belda Record & Publ. Co.

Each comic contained a record that followed the story - much like the Golden Record sets. Known titles: Chirpy Cricket, Lonesome Octopus, Sleepy Santa, Grumpy Shark, Flying Turtle, Happy Grasshopper with records... 1.60 4.00 8.00

TALLY-HO COMICS
December, 1944
Swappers Quarterly (Baily Publ. Co.)

nn-Frazetta's 1st work as Giunta's assistant; Man in Black horror story; violence; Giunta-c 23.00 70.00 160.00

TALOS OF THE WILDERNESS SEA (DC)(Value: cover or less)

TALULLAH (See Comic Books Series I)

TAMMY, TELL ME TRUE (See 4-Color #1233)

TANK GIRL (Dark Horse)(Value: cover or less)

TAPPING THE VEIN (Eclipse)(Value: cover or less)

TARANTULA (See Weird Suspense)

TARGET: AIRBOY (Eclipse)(Value: cover or less)

TARGET COMICS (...Western Romances #106 on)
Feb, 1940 - V10#3 (#105), Aug-Sept, 1949
Funnies, Inc./Novelty Publications/Star Publications

V1#1-Origin & 1st app. Manowar, The White Streak by Burgos, & Bulls-Eye Bill by Everett; City Editor (ends #5), High Grass Twins by Jack Cole (ends #4), T-Men by Joe Simon(ends #9), Rip Rory (ends #4), Fantastic Feature Films by Tarpe Mills (ends #39), & Calling 2-R(ends #14) begin; marijuana use story 233.00 700.00 1500.00
2 117.00 350.00 750.00
3,4 83.00 250.00 550.00
5-Origin The White Streak in text; Space Hawk by Wolverton begins (6/40) (see Blue Bolt & Circus) 191.00 575.00 1200.00
6-The Chameleon by Everett begins (7/40, 1st app.); White Streak origin cont'd. in text; early mention of comic collecting in letter column; 1st letter column in comics? (7/40) 108.00 325.00 675.00
7-Wolverton Spacehawk-c (Scarce) 250.00 750.00 1600.00
8,9,12: 12-(1/41) 83.00 250.00 550.00
10-Intro. & 1st app. The Target (11/40); Kirby-c 117.00 350.00 750.00
11-Origin The Target & The Targeteers 108.00 325.00 700.00
V2#1-Target by Bob Wood; flag-c 58.00 175.00 350.00
2-Ten part Treasure Island serial begins; Harold Delay-a; reprinted in Catholic Comics V3#1-10 (see Key Comics #5) 55.00 165.00 330.00
3-5: 4-Kit Carter, The Cadet begins 42.00 125.00 250.00
6-9: Red Seal with White Streak in 6-10 42.00 125.00 250.00
10-Classic-c 50.00 150.00 300.00
11,12: 12-10-part Last of the Mohicans serial begins; Delay-a
42.00 125.00 250.00
V3#1-10: 8-Flag-c; 6-part Gulliver Travels serial begins; Delay-a. 10-Last Wolverton issue 42.00 125.00 250.00
11,12 9.15 27.50 55.00
V4#1-12: 6-Targetoons by Wolverton, 1 pg. 8-X-Mas-c
6.70 20.00 40.00
V5#1-8 5.85 17.50 35.00
V6#1-10, V7#1-12 5.00 15.00 30.00
V8#1,3-5,8,9,11,12 4.70 14.00 28.00
2,6,7-Krigstein-a 5.85 17.50 35.00
10-L.B. Cole-c 10.00 30.00 60.00
V9#1,4,6,8,10,12, V10#2,3-L.B. Cole-c 10.00 30.00 60.00
V9#2,3,5,7,9,11, V10#1 4.70 14.00 28.00

NOTE: ***Jack Cole*** *a-1-8.* ***Everett*** *a-1-9; c(signed Blake)-1, 2.* ***Al Fago*** *c-V6#8.* ***Sid Greene*** *c-V2#9, 12, V3#3.* ***Walter Johnson*** *c-V5#6, V6#4.* ***Tarpe Mills*** *a-1-4, 6, 8, 11, V3#1.* ***Rico*** *a-V7#4, 10, V8#5, 6, V9#3; c-V7#6, 8, 10, V8#2, 4, 6, 7.* ***Simon*** *a-1, 2.* ***Bob Wood*** *c-V2#2, 3, 5, 6.*

TARGET: THE CORRUPTORS (TV)
No. 1306, Mar-May, 1962 - No. 3, Oct-Dec, 1962 (All have photo-c)
Dell Publishing Co.

4-Color 1306(#1), #2,3 4.70 14.00 28.00

TARGET WESTERN ROMANCES (Formerly Target Comics; becomes Flaming Western Romances #3)
No. 106, Oct-Nov, 1949 - No. 107, Dec-Jan, 1949-50
Star Publications

106(#1)-Silhouette nudity panel; L.B. Cole-c 17.00 52.00 120.00
107(#2)-L.B. Cole-c; lingerie panels 14.00 43.00 100.00

TARGITT
March, 1975 - No. 3, July, 1975
Atlas/Seaboard Publ.

1-3: 1-Origin; Nostrand-a in all. 2-1st in costume 1.00

TARZAN (See Aurora, Comics on Parade, Crackajack, DC 100-Page Super Spec., Famous Feature Stories #1, Golden Comics Digest #4, 9, Jeep Comics #1-29, Jungle Tales of..., Limited Collectors' Edition, Popular, Sparkler, Sport Stars #1, Tip Top & Top Comics)

TARZAN
No. 5, 1939 - No. 161, Aug, 1947
Dell Publishing Co./United Features Syndicate

Large Feature Comic 5('39)-(Scarce)-By Hal Foster; reprints 1st dailies from 1929 100.00 300.00 700.00
Single Series 20(:40)-By Hal Foster 93.00 280.00 650.00
4-Color 134(2/47)-Marsh-c/a 57.00 170.00 400.00
4-Color 161(8/47)-Marsh-c/a 50.00 150.00 350.00

TARZAN (...of the Apes #138 on)
1-2/48 - No. 131, 7-8/62; No. 132, 11/62 - No. 206, 2/72
Dell Publishing Co./Gold Key No. 132 on

1-Jesse Marsh-a begins 86.00 260.00 600.00
2 50.00 150.00 350.00
3-5 38.00 115.00 265.00
6-10: 6-1st Tantor the Elephant. 7-1st Valley of the Monsters
30.00 90.00 210.00
11-15: 11-Two Against the Jungle begins, ends #24. 13-Lex Barker photo-c begin 25.00 75.00 175.00
16-20 19.00 58.00 135.00
21-24,26-30 14.00 43.00 100.00
25-1st "Brothers of the Spear" episode; series ends #156,160,161,196-206
17.00 52.00 120.00

Tarzan (Dell) #131, © ERB

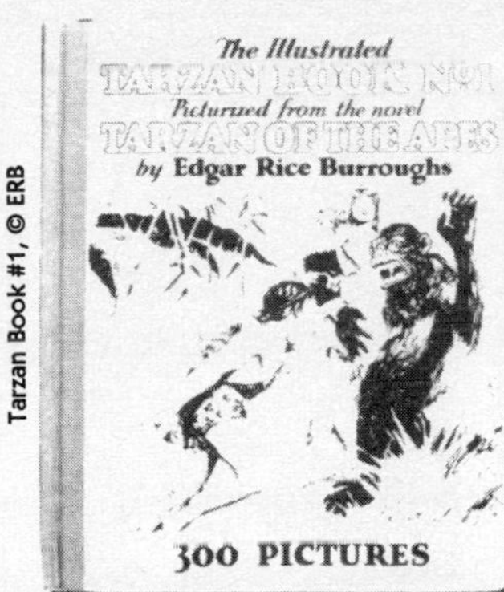

Tarzan Book #1, © ERB

Tarzan, Lord of the Jungle #1, © ERB

GD25 FN65 NM94 GD25 FN65 NM94

31-40 10.00 30.00 60.00
41-54: Last Barker photo-c 6.50 19.00 45.00
55-60: 56-Eight pg. Boy story 5.00 15.00 35.00
61,62,64-70 4.00 12.00 28.00
33-Two Tarzan stories, 1 by Manning 4.30 13.00 30.00
71-79 3.15 9.50 22.00
30-99: 80-Gordon Scott photo-c begin 3.50 10.50 24.00
00 4.30 13.00 30.00
01-109 2.85 8.50 20.00
10 (Scarce)-Last photo-c 4.20 12.50 25.00
11-120 2.30 7.00 16.00
21-131: Last Dell issue 1.70 5.00 12.00
32-154: 132-1st Gold Key issue. 139-(12/63)-1st app. Korak (Boy); leaves
Tarzan & gets own book 1/64 1.50 4.50 10.00
55-Origin Tarzan 3.00 7.50 15.00
56-161: 157-Banlu, Dog of the Arande begins, ends #159, 195. 160
Leopard Girl app. 1.20 3.00 7.00
62,165,168,171 (TV)-Ron Ely photo covers 1.70 5.00 12.00
63,164,166,167,169,170: 169-Leopard Girl app. 1.00 2.50 6.00
72-199,201-206: 178-Tarzan origin-r/#155; Leopard Girl app., also in
#179,190-193 1.00 2.00 5.00
00 (Scarce) 1.00 2.50 6.00
Story Digest 1(6/70)-G.K. 1.00 2.50 6.00

NOTE: *#162, 165, 168, 171 are TV issues. #1-153 all have* ***Marsh*** *art on Tarzan. #154-161, 163, 164, 166, 167, 172-177 all have* ***Manning*** *art on Tarzan. #178, 202 have* ***Manning*** *Tarzan reprints. No "Brothers of the Spear" in #1-24, 157-159, 162-195. #39-126, 128-156 all have* ***Russ Manning*** *art on "Brothers of the Spear." #196-201, 203-205 all have* ***Manning*** *B.O.T.S. reprints; #25-38, 127 all have Jesse* ***Marsh*** *art on B.O.T.S. #206 has a Marsh B.O.T.S. reprint.* ***Gollub*** *c-8-12.* ***Marsh*** *c-1-7.* ***Doug Wildey*** *a-162, 179-187. Many issues have front and back photo covers.*

TARZAN (Continuation of Gold Key series)
No. 207, April, 1972 - No. 258, Feb, 1977
National Periodical Publications

207-Origin Tarzan by Joe Kubert, part 1; John Carter begins (origin);
52 pg. issues thru #209 1.30 3.25 8.00
208,209: 208-210-Parts 2-4 of origin. 209-Last John Carter
1.00 2.00 5.00
210,211: 210-Kubert-a. 211-Hogarth, Kubert-a .40 1.40 3.50
212-214: Adaptations from "Jungle Tales of Tarzan." 213-Beyond the
Farthest Star begins, ends #218 .40 1.40 3.50
215-218,224,225-All by Kubert. 215-part Foster-r .40 1.40 3.50
219-223: Adapts "The Return of Tarzan" by Kubert .40 1.40 3.50
226-229: 226-Manning-a .40 1.40 3.50
230-100 pgs.; Kubert, Kaluta-a(p); Korak begins, ends #234; Carson of
Venus app. 1.70 4.25
231-234: Adapts "Tarzan and the Lion Man;" all 100 pgs.; Rex, the Wonder
Dog r-#232, 233 .40 1.40 3.50
235-Last Kubert issue; 100 pgs. .40 1.40 3.50
236-258: 238-(68 pgs.). 240-243 adapts "Tarzan & the Castaways." 250-256-
Adapts "Tarzan the Untamed." 252,253-r/#213 .40 1.40 3.50
Comic Digest 1(Fall, 1972)(DC)-50 cents; 160 pgs.; digest size; Kubert-c,
Manning-a 1.70 4.25

NOTE: ***Anderson*** *a-207, 209, 217, 218.* ***Chaykin*** *a-216.* ***Finlay*** *a(r)-212.* ***Foster*** *strip-r #207-209, 211, 212, 221.* ***Heath*** *a-230i.* ***G. Kane*** *a-232p, 233p.* ***Kubert*** *a-207-225, 227-235, 257r, 258r; c-207-249, 253. Lopez a-250-555p; c-250p, 251, 252, 254.* ***Manning*** *strip-r 230-235, 238.* ***Morrow*** *a-208.* ***Nino*** *a-231-234.* ***Sparling*** *a-230.* ***Starr*** *a-233r.*

TARZAN
June, 1977 - No. 29, Oct, 1979
Marvel Comics Group

1 .80 2.00
2-29: 2-Origin by John Buscema 1.50
Annual 1-3: 1-(1977). 2-(1978). 3-(1979) 1.50

NOTE: ***N. Adams*** *c-11i, 12i.* ***Alcala*** *a-9i, 10i; c-8i, 9i.* ***Buckler*** *c-25-27p, Annual 3p.* ***John Buscema*** *a-1-3, 4-18p, Annual 1; c-1-7, 8p, 9p, 10, 11p, 12p, 13, 14-19p, 21p, 22, 23p, 24p, 28p, Annual 1.* ***Mooney*** *a-22i.* ***Nebres*** *a-22i.* ***Russell*** *a-29i.*

TARZAN BOOK (The Illustrated...)
1929 (80 pages)(7x9")
Grosset & Dunlap

1(Rare)-Contains 1st B&W Tarzan newspaper comics from 1929.
Cloth reinforced spine & dust jacket (50 cents); Foster-c
with dust jacket... 57.00 170.00 400.00
without dust jacket... 25.00 75.00 175.00
2nd Printing(1934)-76 pgs.; 25 cents; 4 Foster pages dropped; paper spine, circle in lower right cover with 25 cents price. The 25 cents is barely visible on some copies 15.00 45.00 105.00
1967-House of Greystoke reprint-7x10", using the complete 300 illustrations/ text from the 1929 edition minus the original indicia, foreword, etc. Initial version bound in gold paper & sold for $5. Officially titled **Burroughs Biblophile #2.** A very few additional copies were bound in heavier blue paper.
Gold binding... 3.60 9.00 18.00
Blue binding... 4.00 12.00 24.00

TARZAN FAMILY, THE (Formerly Korak, Son of Tarzan)
No. 60, Nov-Dec, 1975 - No. 66, Nov-Dec, 1976
(No. 60-62: 68 pgs.; No. 63 on: 52 pgs.)
National Periodical Publications

60-66: 60-Korak begins; Kaluta-r 1.00

NOTE: *Carson of Venus-r 60-65. New John Carter-62-64, 65r, 66r. New Korak-60-66. Pellucidar feature-66. Foster strip r-60(9/4/32-10/16/32), 62(6/29/32-7/31/32), 63(10/11/31-12/13/31).* ***Kaluta*** *Carson of Venus-60-65.* ***Kubert*** *a-61, 64; c-60-64.* ***Manning*** *strip-r 60-62, 64.* ***Morrow*** *a-66r.*

TARZAN KING OF THE JUNGLE (See Dell Giant #37, 51)

TARZAN, LORD OF THE JUNGLE
Sept, 1965 (Giant)(soft paper cover)(25 cents)
Gold Key

1-Marsh-r 5.00 15.00 35.00

TARZAN: LOVE, LIES AND THE LOST CITY (See Tarzan the Warrior)
Aug. 10, 1992 - No. 3, Sept, 1992 ($2.50, color, mini-series)
Malibu Comics

1-($3.95, 68 pgs.)-Flip book format; Simonson & Wagner scripts
1.60 4.00
2,3-No Simonson or Wagner scripts 1.00 2.50

TARZAN MARCH OF COMICS (See March of Comics #82, 98, 114, 125, 144, 155, 172, 185, 204, 223, 240, 252, 262, 272, 286, 300, 332, 342, 354, 366)

TARZAN OF THE APES
1934? (Hardcover, 68 pgs., 4x12")
Metropolitan Newspaper Service

1-Strip reprints 16.00 48.00 110.00

TARZAN OF THE APES (Marvel)(Value: cover or less)

TARZAN OF THE APES TO COLOR
No. 988, 1933 (24 pages)(10-3/4x15-1/4")(Coloring book)
Saalfield Publishing Co.

988-(Very Rare)-Contains 1929 daily reprints with some new art by Hal Foster. Two panels blown up large on each page; 25 percent in color; believed to be the only time these panels ever appeared in color
100.00 300.00 700.00

TARZAN'S JUNGLE ANNUAL (See Dell Giants)

TARZAN'S JUNGLE WORLD (See Dell Giant #25)

TARZAN THE WARRIOR (Also see Tarzan: Love, Lies and the Lost City)
March 19, 1992 - No. 5, 1992 ($2.50, color, mini-series)
Malibu Comics

1-5: 1-Bisley painted pack-c (flip book format-c) 1.00 2.50
1-2nd printing w/o flip-c by Bisley 1.00 2.50

TASMANIAN DEVIL & HIS TASTY FRIENDS
November, 1962 (12¢)
Gold Key

1-Bugs Bunny & Elmer Fudd x-over 6.00 18.00 60.00

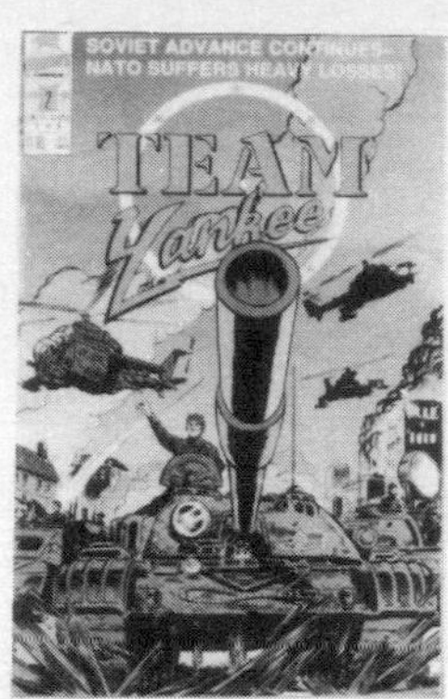

Team Yankee #2, © First

Team Youngblood #1, © Rob Liefeld

Teena #22, © STD

TASTEE-FREEZ COMICS
1957 (36 pages)(10¢ value on-c)(6 different issues given away)
Harvey Comics

	GD25	FN65	NM94
1,3: 1-Little Dot. 3-Casper	5.00	15.00	30.00
2,4,5: 2-Rags Rabbit. 4-Sad Sack. 5-Mazie	3.60	9.00	18.00
6-Dick Tracy	5.00	15.00	30.00

TAYLOR'S CHRISTMAS TABLOID
Mid 1930s, Cleveland, Ohio
Dept. Store Giveaway (Tabloid size; in color)

	GD25	FN65	NM94
nn-(Very Rare)-Among the earliest pro work of Siegel & Shuster; one full color page called "The Battle in the Stratosphere," with a pre-Superman look; Shuster art thoughout. (Only 1 known copy) Estimated value...			$1600.00

TEAM AMERICA (See Captain America #269)
June, 1982 - No. 12, May, 1983
Marvel Comics Group

	GD25	FN65	NM94
1-Origin; Ideal Toy motorcycle characters			1.20
2-10: 9-Iron man app.			1.00
11-Ghost Rider app.	1.00	2.00	5.00
12-Double size		.80	2.00

TEAM ANARCHY
Oct, 1993 - Present ($2.75, color)
Dagger Comics

	GD25	FN65	NM94
1-4: 1-Intro Team Anarchy		1.10	2.75

TEAM HELIX
Jan, 1993 - No. 4, Apr, 1993 ($1.75, color, mini-series)
Marvel Comics

	GD25	FN65	NM94
1-4: Teen Super Group. 1,2-Wolverine app.		.70	1.75

TEAM TITANS (See Deathstroke & New Titans Annual #7)
Sept, 1992 - Present ($1.75, color)
DC Comics

	GD25	FN65	NM94
1-Five different #1s exist w/origins in 1st half & the same 2nd story in each: Kilowat, Mirage, Nightrider w/Netzer/Perez-a, Redwing, & Terra w/part Perez-p; part 3 of Total Chaos		.90	2.25
2-Total Chaos, part 6		.80	2.00
3-18: 11-Metallik app.		.70	1.75
Annual 1 (1993, $3.50, 68 pgs.)		1.40	3.50

TEAM YANKEE (First)(Value: cover or less)

TEAM YOUNGBLOOD (Also see Youngblood)
Sept, 1993 - Present ($1.95, color, on-going series)
Image Comics

	GD25	FN65	NM94
1-3: 1-Liefeld story; Thibert-c(i)		.80	2.00

TEDDY ROOSEVELT & HIS ROUGH RIDERS (See Real Heroes #1)
1950
Avon Periodicals

	GD25	FN65	NM94
1-Kinstler-c; Palais-a; Flag-c	12.00	36.00	85.00

TEDDY ROOSEVELT ROUGH RIDER (See Battlefield #22 & Classics Illustrated Special Issue)

TED MCKEEVER'S METROPOL (Epic, 1991 & 1992)(Value: cover or less)

TEE AND VEE CROSLEY IN TELEVISION LAND COMICS
(Also see Crosley's House of Fun)
1951 (52 pgs.; 8x11"; paper cover; in color)
Crosley Division, Avco Mfg. Corp. (Giveaway)

	GD25	FN65	NM94
Many stories, puzzles, cut-outs, games, etc.	4.70	14.00	28.00

TEENA
No. 11, 1948 - No. 15, 1948; No. 20, Aug, 1949 - No. 22, Oct, 1950
Magazine Enterprises/Standard Comics No. 20 on

	GD25	FN65	NM94
A-1 #11-Teen-age	5.85	17.50	35.00
A-1 #12, 15	5.00	15.00	30.00
20-22 (Standard)	3.20	8.00	16.0

TEEN-AGE BRIDES (True Bride's Experiences #8 on)
Aug, 1953 - No. 7, Aug, 1954
Harvey/Home Comics

	GD25	FN65	NM94
1-Powell-a	5.85	17.50	35.0
2-Powell-a	4.00	11.00	22.0
3-7: 3,6-Powell-a	3.60	9.00	18.0

TEEN-AGE CONFESSIONS (See Teen Confessions)

TEEN-AGE CONFIDENTIAL CONFESSIONS
July, 1960 - No. 22, 1964
Charlton Comics

	GD25	FN65	NM94
1	4.00	10.00	20.0
2-10	2.00	5.00	10.0
11-22	1.20	3.00	6.0

TEEN-AGE DIARY SECRETS (Formerly Blue Ribbon Comics; becomes Diary Secrets #10 on)
No. 4, 9/49; nn (#5), 9/49 - No. 7, 11/49; No. 8, 2/50; No. 9, 8/50
St. John Publishing Co.

	GD25	FN65	NM94
4(9/49)-Oversized; part mag., part comic	14.00	43.00	100.0
nn(#5),6,8: 6,8-Photo-c; Baker-a(2-3) in each	10.00	30.00	70.0
7,9-Digest size	11.50	34.00	80.0

TEEN-AGE DOPE SLAVES (See Harvey Comics Library #1)

TEENAGE HOTRODDERS (Top Eliminator #25 on; see Blue Bird)
April, 1963 - No. 24, July, 1967
Charlton Comics

	GD25	FN65	NM94
1	4.00	10.00	20.00
2-10	2.00	5.00	10.00
11-24	1.60	4.00	8.00

TEEN-AGE LOVE (See Fox Giants)

TEEN-AGE LOVE (Formerly Intimate)
V2#4, July, 1958 - No. 96, Dec, 1973
Charlton Comics

	GD25	FN65	NM94
V2#4	3.60	9.00	18.00
5-9	2.00	5.00	10.00
10(9/59)-20	1.60	4.00	8.00
21-35	1.00	2.50	6.00
36-70		1.20	3.00
71-96: 61&62-Jonnie Love begins (origin)			1.20

TEENAGE MUTANT NINJA TURTLES (Also see Anything Goes, Donatello, First Comics Graphic Novel, Gobbledygook, Grimjack #26, Leonardo, Michaelangelo, Raphael & Tales Of The...)
1984 - No. 62, Aug?, 1993 ($1.50-$1.75, B&W; all 44-52 pgs.)
Mirage Studios

	GD25	FN65	NM94
1-1st printing (3000 copies)-Only printing to have ad for Gobbledygook #1 & 2; Shredder app. (#1-4: 7-1/2x11")	34.00	103.00	240.00
1-2nd printing (6/84)(15,000 copies)	4.30	13.00	30.00
1-3rd printing (2/85)(36,000 copies)	1.65	4.00	10.00
1-4th printing, new-c (50,000 copies)	1.25	3.00	7.50
1-5th printing, new-c (8/88-c, 11/88 inside)		.80	2.00
1-Counterfeit. **Note**: Most counterfeit copies have a half inch wide white streak or scratch marks across the center of back cover. Black part of cover is a bluish black instead of a deep black. Inside paper is very white & inside cover is bright white. These counterfeit the 1st printings (no value).			
2-1st printing (1984; 15,000 copies)	10.00	30.00	70.00
2-2nd printing	1.50	3.75	9.00
2-3rd printing; new Corben-c/a (2/85)		1.10	2.75
2-Counterfeit with glossy cover stock (no value).			
3-1st printing (1985, 44 pgs.)	3.85	11.50	27.00
3-Variant, 500 copies, given away in NYC. Has 'Laird's Photo' in white rather than light blue	11.00	34.00	80.00
3-2nd printing; contains new back-up story		1.10	2.75

Teenage Mutant Ninja Turtles V2#3 (3/93), © MS

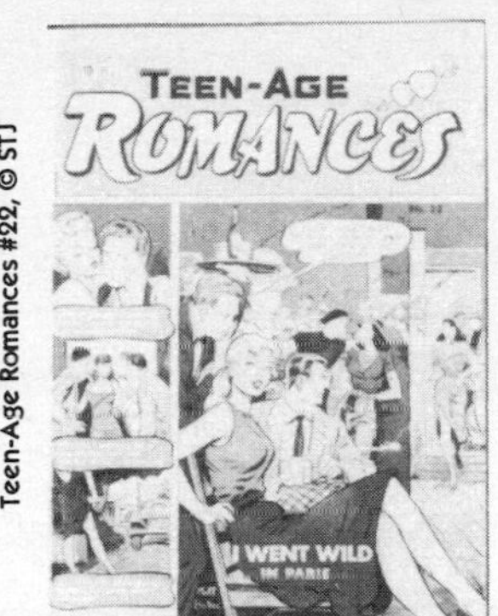

Teen-Age Romances #22, © STJ

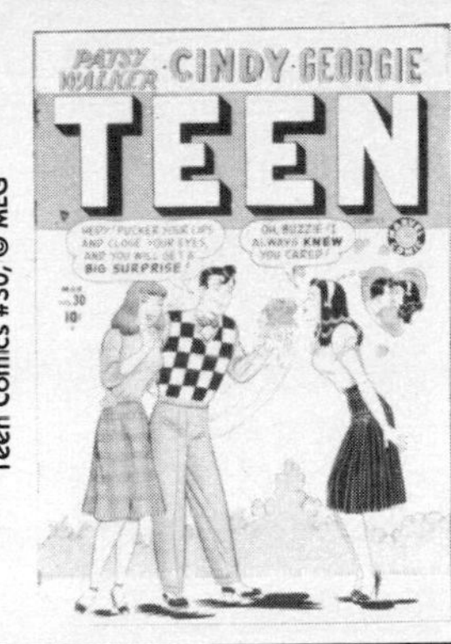

Teen Comics #30, © MEG

GD25 FN65 NM94

-1st printing (1985, 44 pgs.)- 1.85 5.50 13.00
-2nd printing (5/87) .70 1.75
-Fugitoid begins, ends #7; 1st full color-c ('85) 1.65 4.00 10.00
-2nd printing (11/87) .70 1.75
-1st printing (1986) 1.25 3.00 7.50
-2nd printing (4/88-c, 5/88 inside) .70 1.75
-4 pg. Eastman/Corben color insert; 1st color TMNT (1986, $1.75-c);
Bade Biker back-up story 1.25 3.00 7.50
-2nd printing (1/89) w/o color insert .70 1.75
-Cerebus-c/story with Dave Sim-a (1986) 1.00 2.50 5.50
,10: 9 (9/86)-Rip In Time by Corben 1.90 4.75
1-15 1.30 3.25
6-18: 18-Mark Bode'-a 1.10 2.75
8-2nd printing ($2.25, color, 44 pgs.)-New-c .70 1.80
9-51: 19-Begin $1.75-c. 24-26-Veitch-c/a. 35-Begin $2.00-c. 50-Features
pin-ups by Larsen, McFarlane, Simonson, etc. .70 1.80
2-2nd printing ($2.75, 52 pgs., full color) 1.00 2.50
2-62: 52-Begin $2.25-c .90 2.25
ook 1,2($1.50, B&W): 2-Corben-c 1.50
Christmas Special 1 (12/90, $1.75, B&W, 52 pgs.)-Cover title:
Michaelangelo Christmas Special; r/Michaelangelo one-shot plus new
Raphael story .70 1.75
pecial: "Times" Pipeline nn (9/92, $2.95, color, 44 pgs.)-Mark Bode-c/a
1.20 3.00

EENAGE MUTANT NINJA TURTLES
2#1, 1993 - Present ($2.75, color)
irage Studios
1,2: 1-Wraparound-c 1.10 2.75

EENAGE MUTANT NINJA TURTLES (Archie)(Value: cover or less)(The Movie)

EENAGE MUTANT NINJA TURTLES ADVENTURES (TV)
'88 - No. 3, 12/88; 3/89 - Present ($1.00, color)
rchie Comics
1-Adapts TV cartoon; not by Eastman/Laird 1.20 3.00
2,3 (Mini-series) .80 2.00
1 (2nd on going series) 1.00 2.50
2-5: 5-Begins original stories not based on TV .80 2.00
6-49,51-56: 14-Simpson-a(p). 19-1st Mighty Mutanimals (also in #20). 20-
Begin $1.25-c. 22-Gene Colan-c/a 1.25
0-($1.50)-Poster by Eastman/Laird 1.50
1-11: 2nd printings 1.00
n (Spring, 1991, $2.50, 68 pgs.)-(Meet Archie) 1.00 2.50
n (Sum, 1991, $2.50, 68 pgs.)-(Movie II)-Adapts movie sequel
1.00 2.50
.Meet the Conservation Corps 1 (1992, $2.50, 68 pgs.) 1.00 2.50
.III The Movie: The Turtles are Back...In Time (1993, $2.50, 68 pgs.)
1.00 2.50
.Special 1 (Sum/92, $2.50, 68 pgs.)-Bill Wray-c 1.00 2.50
.Special 4 (Spr/93, $2.50, 68 pgs.) 1.00 2.50
.Special 5 (Sum/93, $2.50, 68 pgs.) 1.00 2.50
.Giant Size Special 6 (Fall/93, $1.95, 52 pgs.) .80 2.00
.Special 7,8 (Win/93, Spr/94, $1.95, 52 pgs.) .80 2.00
OTE: *There are 2nd printings of #1-11 w/B&W inside covers. Originals are color.*

EENAGE MUTANT NINJA TURTLES CLASSICS DIGEST (TV)
ug, 1993 - Present ($1.75, color)
rchie Comics
1-4-Reprints TMNT Advs. .70 1.75

EENAGE MUTANT NINJA TURTLES PRESENTS: APRIL O'NEIL
lar, 1993 - No. 3, June, 1993 ($1.25, color, mini-series)
rchie Comics
1-3 .60 1.25

EENAGE MUTANT NINJA TURTLES PRESENTS: DONATELLO AND EATHERHEAD
uly, 1993 - No. 3, Sept, 1993 ($1.25, color, mini-series)
Archie Comics
1-3 .60 1.25

TEENAGE MUTANT NINJA TURTLES PRESENTS: MERDUDE
Oct, 1993 - No. 3, Dec, 1993 ($1.25, color, mini-series)
Archie Comics
1-3-See Mighty Mutanimals #7 for 1st app. Merdude .60 1.25

TEEN-AGE ROMANCE (Formerly My Own Romance)
No. 77, Sept, 1960 - No. 86, March, 1962
Marvel Comics (ZPC)
77-86 2.40 6.00 12.00

TEEN-AGE ROMANCES
Jan, 1949 - No. 45, Dec, 1955
St. John Publ. co. (Approved Comics)
1-Baker-c/a(1) 19.00 57.00 130.00
2-Baker-c/a 10.00 30.00 70.00
3-Baker-c/a(3); spanking panel 11.00 32.00 75.00
4,5,7,8-Photo-c; Baker-a(2-3) each 9.15 27.50 55.00
6-Slightly large size; photo-c; part magazine; Baker-a (10/49)
10.00 30.00 60.00
9-Baker-c/a; Kubert-a 11.00 32.00 75.00
10-12,20-Baker-c/a(2-3) each 8.35 25.00 50.00
13-19,21,22-Complete issues by Baker 11.00 32.00 75.00
23-25-Baker-c/a(2-3) each 7.00 21.00 42.00
26,27,33,34,36-42-Last pre-code, 3/55; Baker-a. 38-Suggestive-c
4.35 13.00 26.00
28-30-No Baker-a 3.20 8.00 16.00
31-Baker-c 3.60 9.00 18.00
32-Baker-c/a, 1pg. 3.60 9.00 18.00
35-Baker-c/a, 16pgs. 4.20 12.50 25.00
43-45-Baker-a 4.00 10.00 20.00

TEEN-AGE TALK
1964
I.W. Enterprises
Reprint #1-Monkees photo-c 1.80 4.50 9.00
Reprint #5,8,9 .60 1.50 3.00

TEEN-AGE TEMPTATIONS (Going Steady #10 on)(See True Love Pictorial)
Oct, 1952 - No. 9, Aug, 1954
St. John Publishing co.
1-Baker-c/a; has story "Reform School Girl" by Estrada
20.00 60.00 140.00
2-Baker-c 8.35 25.00 50.00
3-7,9-Baker-c/a 10.00 30.00 70.00
8-Teenagers smoke reefers; Baker-c/a 11.00 32.00 75.00
NOTE: ***Estrada** a-1, 3-5.*

TEEN BEAM (Formerly Teen Beat #1)
No. 2, Jan-Feb, 1968
National Periodical Publications
2-Orlando, Drucker-a(r); Monkees photo-c 1.85 5.50 13.00

TEEN BEAT (Becomes Teen Beam #2)
Nov-Dec, 1967
National Periodical Publications
1-Photos & text only; Monkees photo-c 3.20 8.00 20.00

TEEN COMICS (Formerly All Teen; Journey Into Unknown Worlds #36 on)
No. 21, April, 1947 - No. 35, May, 1950
Marvel comics (WFP)
21-Kurtzman's "Hey Look;" Patsy Walker, Cindy (1st app.?), Georgie, Margie
app.; Syd Shores-a begins, end #23 8.35 25.00 50.00
22,23,25,27,29,31-35: 22-(6/47)-Becomes Hedy Devine #22 (8/47) on?
5.00 15.00 30.00
24,26,28,30-Kurtzman's "Hey Look" 8.35 25.00 50.00

Teen Titans #9, © DC

Tekworld #13, © William Shatner

Tell It to the Marines #14, © TOBY

GD25 FN65 NM94

TEEN CONFESSIONS
Aug, 1959 - No. 97, Nov, 1976
Charlton Comics

	GD25	FN65	NM94
1	7.00	21.00	42.00
2	4.00	10.00	21.00
3-10	3.00	7.50	15.00
11-30	1.80	4.50	9.00
31-Beatles-c	7.50	22.50	45.00
32-36,38-55	1.00	2.50	5.00
37 (1/66)-Beatles Fan Club story; Beatles-c	7.50	22.50	45.00
56-58,60-97: 89,90-Newton-c		.50	1.00
59-Kaluta's 1st pro work? (12/69)	1.00	2.50	5.00

TEENIE WEENIES, THE
No. 10, 1950 - No. 11, Apr-May, 1951 (Newspaper reprints)
Ziff-Davis Publishing Co.

	GD25	FN65	NM94
10,11-Painted-c	11.50	34.00	80.00

TEEN-IN (Tippy Teen)
Summer, 1968 - No. 4, Fall, 1969
Tower Comics

	GD25	FN65	NM94
nn(#1, Summer, 1968), nn(#2, Spring, 1969),3,4	3.00	7.50	15.00

TEEN LIFE (Formerly Young Life)
No. 3, Winter, 1945 - No. 5, Fall, 1945 (Teenage magazine)
New Age/Quality Comics Group

	GD25	FN65	NM94
3-June Allyson photo on-c & story	6.70	20.00	40.00
4-Duke Ellington photo on-c & story	5.85	17.50	35.00
5-Van Johnson, Woody Herman & Jackie Robinson articles; Van Johnson & Woody Herman photos on-c	7.50	22.50	45.00

TEEN ROMANCES
1964
Super Comics

	GD25	FN65	NM94
10,11,15-17-Reprints	.60	1.50	3.00

TEEN SECRET DIARY (Nurse Betsy Crane #12 on)
Oct, 1959 - No. 11, June, 1961; No. 1, 1972
Charlton Comics

	GD25	FN65	NM94
1	4.00	10.00	20.00
2	2.00	5.00	10.00
3-11	1.20	3.00	6.00
1 (1972)	.40	1.00	2.00

TEEN TALK (See Teen)

TEEN TITANS (See Brave & the Bold, DC Super-Stars #1, Marvel & DC Present, New Teen Titans, New Titans, Official...Index and Showcase)
1-2/66 - No. 43, 1-2/73; No. 44, 11/76 - No. 53, 2/78
National Periodical Publications/DC Comics

	GD25	FN65	NM94
Brave and the Bold #54 (6-7/64)-Origin & 1st app. Teen Titans; Kid Flash, Robin & Aqualad begin	26.00	77.00	180.00
Brave and the Bold #60 (6-7/65)-2nd app. Teen Titans; 1st app. new Wonder Girl (Donna Troy), who joins Titans	9.00	27.00	63.00
Showcase #59 (11-12/65)-3rd app. Teen Titans	7.00	22.00	65.00
1-(1-2/66)-Titans join Peace Corps; Batman, Flash, Aquaman, Wonder Woman cameos	21.00	62.00	145.00
2	10.00	29.00	68.00
3-5: 4-Speedy app.	5.00	15.00	35.00
6-10: 6-Doom Patrol app.; Beast Boy x-over; readers polled on him joining Titans	3.85	11.50	27.00
11-19: 11-Speedy app. 13-X-Mas-c. 18-1st app. Starfire (11-12/68). 19-Wood-i; Speedy begins as regular	2.40	7.25	17.00
20-22: All Neal Adams-a. 21-Hawk & Dove app.; last 12 cent issue. 22-Origin Wonder Girl	3.20	9.00	21.00
23-30: 23-Wonder Girl dons new costume. 25-Flash, Aquaman, Batman, Green Arrow, Green Lantern, Superman, & Hawk & Dove guests; 1st app. Lilith who joins T.T. West in #50. 29-Hawk & Dove & Ocean Master app. 30-Aquagirl app.	1.65	4.70	11.00
31-43: 31-Hawk & Dove app. 36,37-Superboy-r. 38-Green Arrow/Speedy-r; Aquaman/Aqualad story. 39-Hawk & Dove-r. (36-39: 52 pgs.)	1.25	3.00	7.5
44,45,47,49,51,52: 44-Mal becomes the Guardian		1.70	4.2
46-Joker's daughter begins(see Batman Family)	1.50	3.75	9.0
48-Intro Bumblebee; Joker's daughter becomes Harlequin	1.50	3.75	9.0
50-1st revival original Bat-Girl; intro. Teen Titans West	1.40	3.50	8.5
53-Origin retold		1.90	4.7

NOTE: ***Aparo** a-36. **Buckler** c-46-53. **Cardy** c-1-16. **Kane** a(p)-19, 22-24, 39r. **Tuska** a(p)-31, 36, 38, 39. DC Super-Stars #1 (3/76) was released before #44.*

TEEN TITANS SPOTLIGHT (DC)(Value: cover or less)

TEEPEE TIM (Formerly Ha Ha Comics)
No. 100, Feb-Mar, 1955 - No. 102, June-July, 1955
American Comics Group

	GD25	FN65	NM94
100-102	2.80	7.00	14.0

TEGRA JUNGLE EMPRESS (Zegra Jungle Empress #2 on)
August, 1948
Fox Features Syndicate

	GD25	FN65	NM94
1-Blue Beetle, Rocket Kelly app.; used in **SOTI**, pg. 31	25.00	75.00	175.0

TEKWORLD (William Shatner's... on-c only)
Sept, 1992 - Present ($1.75, color)
Epic comics (Marvel)

	GD25	FN65	NM94
1-Based on Shatner's novel, TekWar, set in L.A. in the year 2120		1.00	2.5
2-20		.70	1.7

TELEVISION (See TV)

TELEVISION COMICS
No. 5, Feb, 1950 - No. 8, Nov, 1950
Standard Comics (Animated Cartoons)

	GD25	FN65	NM94
5-1st app. Willy Nilly	6.70	20.00	40.0
6-8: 6 has #2 on inside	4.70	14.00	28.0

TELEVISION PUPPET SHOW (See Spotty the Pup)
1950 - No. 2, Nov, 1950
Avon Periodicals

	GD25	FN65	NM94
1,2: 1st app. Speedy Rabbit, Spotty The Pup	11.00	32.00	75.0

TELEVISION TEENS MOPSY (See TV Teens)

TELL IT TO THE MARINES
Mar, 1952 - No. 15, July, 1955
Toby Press Publications

	GD25	FN65	NM94
1-Lover O'Leary and His Liberty Belles (with Pin-ups), ends #6	10.00	30.00	70.00
2-Madame Cobra-c/story	6.70	20.00	40.00
3-5	4.70	14.00	28.00
6-12,14,15: 7-9,14,15-Photo-c	3.60	9.00	18.00
13-John Wayne photo-c	7.50	22.50	45.00
I.W. Reprint #1,9: 1-Exist? 9-r/#1 above	.60	1.50	3.00
Super Reprint #16('64)-r/#4 above	.60	1.50	3.00

TEMPUS FUGITIVE (DC)(Value: cover or less)

TEN COMMANDMENTS (See Moses & the... and Classics Illustrated Special)

TENDER LOVE STORIES
Feb, 1971 - No. 4, July, 1971 (All 52pgs.)(25 cents)
Skywald Publ. Corp.

	GD25	FN65	NM94
1-4	.60	1.50	3.00

TENDER ROMANCE (Ideal Romance #3 on)
Dec, 1953 - No. 2, Feb, 1954
Key Publications (Gilmour Magazines)

	GD25	FN65	NM94
1-Headlight & lingerie panels; B. Baily-c	10.00	30.00	60.00

Ten Story Love V29#5, © ACE

Terminator 2: Judgement Day, © Cinema '84

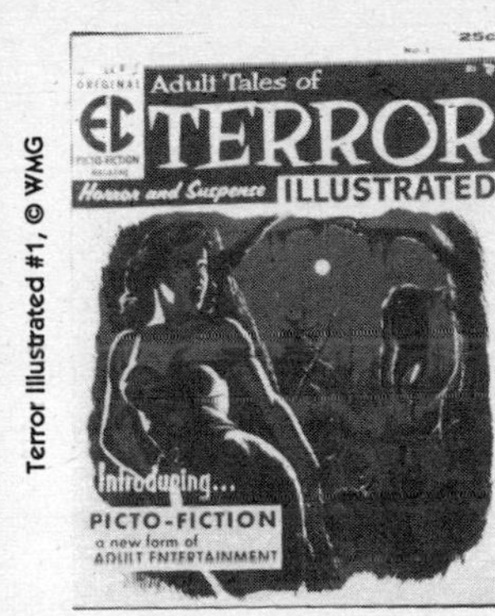

Terror Illustrated #1, © WMG

	GD25	FN65	NM94
2-Bernard Baily-c	5.35	16.00	32.00

TENNESSEE JED (Radio)
nd (1945) (16 pgs.; paper cover; regular size; giveaway)
Fox Syndicate? (Wm. C. Popper & Co.)

	GD25	FN65	NM94
nn	11.50	34.00	80.00

TENNIS (...For Speed, Stamina, Strength, Skill)
1956 (16 pgs.; soft cover; 10 cents)
Tennis Educational Foundation

	GD25	FN65	NM94
Book 1-Endorsed by Gene Tunney, Ralph Kiner, etc. showing how tennis has helped them	4.00	12.00	24.00

TENSE SUSPENSE
Dec, 1958 - No. 2, Feb, 1959
Fago Publications

	GD25	FN65	NM94
1,2	4.70	14.00	28.00

TEN STORY LOVE (Formerly a pulp magazine with same title)
V29#3, June-July, 1951 - V36#5(#209), Sept, 1956 (#3-6: 52 pgs.)
Ace Periodicals

	GD25	FN65	NM94
V29#3(#177)-Part comic, part text; painted-c	6.70	20.00	40.00
4-6(1/52)	4.00	10.00	20.00
V30#1(3/52)-6(1/53)	3.20	8.00	16.00
V31#1(2/53),V32#2(4/53)-6(12/53)	2.40	6.00	12.00
V33#1(1/54)-3(5#54, #195), V34#4(7/54, #196)-6(10/54, #198)	2.40	6.00	12.00
V35#1(12/54, #199)-3(4/55, #201)-Last precode	1.80	4.50	9.00
V35#4-6(9/55, #201-204), V36#1(11/55, #205)-3, 5(9/56, #209)	1.60	4.00	8.00
V36#4-L.B. Cole-a	3.20	8.00	16.00

TEN WHO DARED (See 4-Color #1178)

TERMINATOR, THE (See Robocop vs. ... & Rust #12 for 1st app.)
Sept, 1988 - No. 17, 1989 ($1.75, color, Baxter paper)
Now Comics

	GD25	FN65	NM94
1-Based on movie	3.20	8.00	20.00
2	1.65	4.00	10.00
3-5	1.00	2.50	6.00
6-10		1.90	4.75
11,13-17		.90	2.25
12 ($2.95, 52 pgs.)-Intro. John Connor		1.20	3.00
Trade paperback (1989, $9.95)	1.65	4.00	10.00

TERMINATOR, THE
Aug, 1990 - No. 4, Nov, 1990 ($2.50, color, mini-series)
Dark Horse Comics

	GD25	FN65	NM94
1-Set 39 years later than the movie		1.90	4.75
2-4		1.00	2.50

TERMINATOR: ALL MY FUTURES PAST, THE
V3#1, Aug, 1990 - V3#2, Sept, 1990 ($1.75, color, mini-series)
Now Comics

	GD25	FN65	NM94
V3#1,2		.70	1.75

TERMINATOR: ENDGAME, THE
Sept, 1992 - No. 3, Nov, 1992 ($2.50, color, mini-series)
Dark Horse Comics

	GD25	FN65	NM94
1-3: Guice-a(p); painted-c		1.00	2.50

TERMINATOR: HUNTERS AND KILLERS, THE
Mar, 1992 - No. 3, May, 1992 ($2.50, color, mini-series)
Dark Horse Comics

	GD25	FN65	NM94
1-3		1.00	2.50

TERMINATOR: ONE SHOT, THE
July, 1991 ($5.95, color, 56 pgs.)
Dark Horse Comics

	GD25	FN65	NM94
nn-Matt Wagner-a; contains stiff pop-up inside		2.50	6.00

TERMINATOR: SECONDARY OBJECTIVES, THE
July, 1991 - No. 4, Oct, 1991 ($2.50, color, mini-series)
Dark Horse Comics

	GD25	FN65	NM94
1-Gulacy-c/a(p) in all		1.00	2.50
2-4		1.00	2.50

TERMINATOR: THE BURNING EARTH, THE
V2#1, Mar, 1990 - V2#5, July, 1990 ($1.75, color, mini-series)
Now Comics

	GD25	FN65	NM94
V2#1-5		.70	1.75
Trade paperback (1990, $9.95)-Reprints V2#1-5	1.65	4.00	10.00

TERMINATOR: THE ENEMY WITHIN, THE
Nov, 1991 - No. 4, Feb, 1992 ($2.50, color, mini-series)
Dark Horse Comics

	GD25	FN65	NM94
1-4: All have Simon Bisley painted-c		1.00	2.50

TERMINATOR 2: JUDGEMENT DAY
Early Sept, 1991 - No. 3, Early Oct, 1991 ($1.00, color, mini-series)
Marvel Comics

	GD25	FN65	NM94
1-3: Based on movie sequel; 1-3-Same as nn issues			1.00
nn (1991, $4.95, squarebound, 68 pgs.)-Photo-c	1.00	2.00	5.00
nn (1991, $2.25, B&W, magazine, 68 pgs.)		.90	2.25

TERRAFORMERS (Wonder)(Value: cover or less)

TERRANAUTS (Epic)(Value: cover or less)

TERRARISTS (Fantasy General)(Value: cover or less)

TERRIFIC COMICS
Jan, 1944 - No. 6, Nov, 1944
Continental Magazines

	GD25	FN65	NM94
1-Kid Terrific; opium story	75.00	225.00	500.00
2-1st app. The Boomerang by L.B. Cole & Ed Wheelan's "Comics" McCormick, called the world's #1 comic book fan begins	62.00	188.00	400.00
3-Diana becomes Boomerang's costumed aide	50.00	150.00	325.00
4-Classic war-c	62.00	188.00	400.00
5-The Reckoner begins; Boomerang & Diana by L.B. Cole; Schomburg bondage-c	54.00	162.00	350.00
6-L.B. Cole-c/a	54.00	162.00	350.00

NOTE: ***L.B. Cole** a-1, 2(?), 3-6. **Fuje** a-5, 6. **Rico** a-3; c-1. **Schomburg** c-2, 5.*

TERRIFIC COMICS (Formerly Horrific; Wonder Boy #17 on)
No. 14, Dec, 1954; No. 16, Mar, 1955 (No #15)
Mystery Publ.(Comic Media)/(Ajax/Farrell)

	GD25	FN65	NM94
14-Art swipe/Advs. into the Unknown #37; injury-to-eye-c; page-2, panel 5 swiped from Phantom Stranger #4; surrealistic Palais-a; Human Cross story	11.50	34.00	80.00
16-Wonder Boy-c/story (last pre-code)	10.00	30.00	60.00

TERRIFYING TALES (Formerly Startling Terror Tales #10)
No. 11, Jan, 1953 - No. 15, Apr, 1954
Star Publications

	GD25	FN65	NM94
11-Used in **POP**, pgs. 99,100; all Jo-Jo-r	24.00	72.00	165.00
12-All Jo-Jo-r; L.B. Cole splash	19.00	58.00	135.00
13-All Rulah-r; classic devil-c	25.00	75.00	175.00
14-All Rulah reprints	20.00	60.00	140.00
15-Rulah, Zago-r; used in **SOTI**-r/Rulah #22	20.00	60.00	140.00

NOTE: *All issues have **L.B. Cole** covers; bondage covers-No. 12-14.*

TERROR ILLUSTRATED (Adult Tales of...)
Nov-Dec, 1955 - No. 2, Spring (April on-c), 1956 (Magazine, 25 cents)
E.C. Comics

	GD25	FN65	NM94
1-Adult Entertainment on-c	10.00	30.00	60.00
2-Charles Sultan-a	8.35	25.00	50.00

NOTE: ***Craig, Evans, Ingels, Orlando** art in each. **Crandall** c-1, 2.*

TERROR INC. (See A Shadowline Saga #3)
July, 1992 - No. 13, July, 1993 ($1.75, color)
Marvel Comics

Terrors of the Jungle #4, © STAR

Terry and the Pirates #8, © News Synd.

Tessie the Typist #17, © MEG

GD25 FN65 NM94

1-13: 6,7-Punisher-c/story. 9,10-Wolverine-c/story. 13-Ghost Rider app.
.70 1.75

TERRORS OF THE JUNGLE (Formerly Jungle Thrills)
No. 17, 5/52 - No. 21, 2/53; No. 4, 4/53 - No. 10, 9/54
Star Publications

17-Reprints Rulah #21, used in **SOTI**; L.B. Cole bondage-c
23.00 70.00 160.00
18-Jo-Jo-r 14.00 43.00 100.00
19,20(1952)-Jo-Jo-r; Disbrow-a 13.00 40.00 90.00
21-Jungle Jo, Tangi-r; used in **POP**, pg. 100 & color illos.; shrunken heads on-c 16.00 48.00 110.00
4-10: All Disbrow-a. 5-Jo-Jo-r. 8-Rulah, Jo-Jo-r. 9-Jo-Jo-r; Disbrow-a; Tangi by Orlando10-Rulah-r 13.00 40.00 90.00
NOTE: ***L.B. Cole** c-all; bondage c-17, 19, 21, 5, 7.*

TERROR TALES (See Beware Terror Tales)

TERROR TALES (Magazine)
V1#7, 1969 - V6#6, Dec, 1974; V7#1, Apr, 1976 - V10, 1979?
(V1-V6: 52 pgs.; V7 on: 68 pgs.)
Eerie Publications

V1#7 2.60 7.50 18.00
V1#8-11('69): 9-Bondage-c 1.65 4.00 10.00
V2#1-6('70), V3#1-6('71), V4#1-7('72), V5#1-6('73), V6#1-6('74)
1.30 3.25 8.00
V7#1,4(no V7#2), V8#1-3('77), V9, V10 1.30 3.25 8.00
V7#3-LSD story-r/Weird V3#5 1.30 3.25 8.00

TERRY AND THE PIRATES (See Famous Feature Stories, Merry Christmas From Sears Toyland, Popular Comics, Super Book #3,5,9,16,28, & Super Comics)

TERRY AND THE PIRATES
1939 - 1953 (By Milton Caniff)
Dell Publishing Co.

Large Feature Comic 2(1939) 57.00 170.00 400.00
Large Feature Comic 6(1939)-r/1936 dailies 54.00 160.00 375.00
4-Color 9(1940) 57.00 170.00 400.00
Large Feature Comic 27('41), 6('42) 43.00 130.00 300.00
4-Color 44('43) 39.00 120.00 275.00
4-Color 101('45) 26.00 80.00 180.00
Buster Brown Shoes giveaway(1938)-32 pgs.; in color
24.00 73.00 170.00
Canada Dry Premiums-Books #1-3(1953-Harvey)-36 pgs.; 2x5"
11.50 34.00 80.00
Family Album(1942) 14.00 43.00 100.00
Gambles Giveaway (1938)-16 pgs. 6.70 20.00 40.00
Gillmore Giveaway(1938)-24 pgs. 7.50 22.50 45.00
Popped Wheat Giveaway(1938)-Strip reprints in full color; Caniff-a
1.00 2.50 5.00
Shoe Store giveaway (Weatherbird)(1938, 16 pgs., soft-c)(2-diff.)
6.70 20.00 40.00
Sparked Wheat Giveaway(1942)-16 pgs. in color 6.70 20.00 40.00

TERRY AND THE PIRATES
1941 (16 pgs.; regular size)
Libby's Radio Premium

"Adventure of the Ruby of Genghis Khan" - Each pg. is a puzzle that must be completed to read the story 57.00 171.00 400.00

TERRY AND THE PIRATES (Formerly Boy Explorers; Long John Silver & the Pirates #30 on) (Daily strip-r) (Two #26's)
No. 3, 4/47 - No. 26, 4/51; No. 26, 6/55 - No. 28, 10/55
Harvey Publications/Charlton No. 26-28

3(#1)-Boy Explorers by S&K; Terry & the Pirates begin by Caniff; 1st app. The Dragon Lady 22.00 65.00 150.00
4-S&K Boy Explorers 14.00 43.00 100.00
5-10 8.35 25.00 50.00
11-Man in Black app. by Powell 8.35 25.00 50.00
12-20: 16-Girl threatened with red hot poker 6.70 20.00 40.00

GD25 FN65 NM94

21-26(4/51)-Last Caniff issue 5.85 17.50 35.00
26-28('55)(Formerly This Is Suspense)-No Caniff-a 5.00 15.00 28.00
NOTE: ***Powell** a (Tommy Tween)-5-10, 12, 14; 15-17(1/2 to 2 pgs. each).*

TERRY BEARS COMICS (TerryToons, The... #4)
June, 1952 - No. 3, Mar, 1953
St. John Publishing Co.

1 4.20 12.50 25.00
2,3 4.00 10.00 20.00

TERRY-TOONS COMICS (1st Series) (Becomes Paul Terry's Comics #85 on; later issues titled "Paul Terry's...") (See Giant Comics Edition)
Oct, 1942 - No. 86, May, 1951
Timely/Marvel No. 1-59 (8/47)(Becomes Best Western No. 58 on?, Marvel)/
St. John No. 60 (9/47) on

1 (Scarce)-Features characters that 1st app. on movie screen; Gandy Goose begins; war-c; Gandy Goose c-1-37 89.00 270.00 625.00
2 43.00 130.00 300.00
3-5 29.00 85.00 200.00
6-10: 7-Hitler, Hirohito, Mussolini-c 20.00 60.00 140.00
11-20 13.00 40.00 90.00
21-37 10.00 30.00 60.00
38-Mighty Mouse begins (1st app., 11/45); Mighty Mouse-c begin, end #86
86.00 260.00 600.00
39-2nd app. Mighty Mouse 23.00 70.00 160.00
40-49: 43-Infinity-c 11.00 32.00 75.00
50-1st app. Heckle & Jeckle (11/46) 26.00 77.00 180.00
51-60: 55-Infinity-c. 60(9/47)-Atomic explosion panel; 1st St. John issue
9.15 27,.50 55.00
61-84 6.70 20.00 40.00
85,86-Same book as Paul Terry's Comics #85,86 with only a title change; published at same time? 6.70 20.00 40.00

TERRY-TOONS COMICS (2nd Series)
June, 1952 - No. 9, Nov, 1953; 1957; 1958
St. John Publishing Co./Pines

1 11.00 32.00 75.00
2 6.35 19.00 38.00
3-9 5.35 16.00 32.00
Giant Summer Fun Book 101,102(Summer, 1957, Summer, 1958, Pines)(TV; Tom Terrific app.); CBS Television Presents... 9.15 27.50 55.00

TERRYTOONS, THE TERRY BEARS (Formerly Terry Bears)
No. 4, Summer, 1958 (CBS Television Presents...)
Pines Comics

4 3.60 9.00 18.00

TESSIE THE TYPIST (Tiny Tessie #24; see Comedy Comics, Gay Comics & Joker Comics)
Summer, 1944 - No. 23, Aug, 1949
Timely/Marvel Comics (20CC)

1-Doc Rockblock & others by Wolverton 36.00 110.00 250.00
2-Wolverton's Powerhouse Pepper 22.00 65.00 150.00
3-No Wolverton 7.50 22.50 45.00
4,5,7,8-Wolverton-a 13.00 40.00 90.00
6-Kurtzman's "Hey Look," 2 pgs. Wolverton 13.50 41.00 95.00
9-Wolverton's Powerhouse Pepper (8 pgs.) & 1 pg. Kurtzman's "Hey Look
16.00 50.00 115.00
10-Wolverton's Powerhouse Pepper (4 pgs.) 15.00 45.00 105.00
11-Wolverton's Powerhouse Pepper (8 pgs.) 16.00 50.00 115.00
12-Wolverton's Powerhouse Pepper (4 pgs.) & 1 pg. Kurtzman's "Hey Look"
15.00 45.00 105.00
13-Wolverton's Powerhouse Pepper (4 pgs.) 14.00 43.00 100.00
14-Wolverton's Dr. Whackyhack (1 pg.); 1-1/2 pgs. Kurtzman's "Hey Look"
11.00 32.00 75.00
15-Kurtzman's "Hey Look" (3 pgs.) & 3 pgs. Giggles 'n' Grins
11.50 34.00 80.00
16-18-Kurtzman's "Hey Look" (?, 2 & 1 pg.) 8.35 25.00 50.00

Texas Kid #6, © MEG

Tex Ritter Western #24, © FAW

Tex Taylor #9, © MEG

GD25 FN65 NM94

19-Annie Oakley story (8 pgs.) 6.70 20.00 40.00
20-23: 20-Anti-Wertham editorial (2/49) 5.85 17.50 35.00

NOTE: *Lana app.-21. Millie The Model app.-13, 15, 17, 21. Rusty app.-10, 11, 13, 15, 17.*

TEXAN, THE (Fightin' Marines #15 on; Fightin' Texan #16 on)
Aug, 1948 - No. 15, Oct, 1951
St. John Publishing Co.

1-Buckskin Belle 10.00 30.00 70.00
2 5.85 17.50 35.00
3,10: 10-Oversized issue 5.00 15.00 30.00
4,5,7,15-Baker-c/a 9.15 27.50 55.00
6,9-Baker-c 5.85 17.50 35.00
8,11,13,14-Baker-c/a(2-3) each 9.15 27.50 55.00
12-All Matt Baker; Peyote story 10.00 30.00 70.00

NOTE: ***Matt Baker** c-4-15. **Larsen** a-4-6, 8-10, 15. **Tuska** a-1, 2, 7-9.*

TEXAN, THE (See 4-Color #1027, 1096)

TEXAS JOHN SLAUGHTER (See 4-Color #997, 1181 & Walt Disney Presents #2)

TEXAS KID (See Two-Gun Western, Wild Western)
Jan, 1951 - No. 10, July, 1952
Marvel/Atlas Comics (LMC)

1-Origin; Texas Kid (alias Lance Temple) & his horse Thunder begin; Tuska-a 12.00 36.00 85.00
2 7.50 22.50 45.00
3-10 5.85 17.50 35.00

NOTE: ***Maneely** a-1-4; c-1, 3, 5-10.*

TEXAS RANGERS, THE (See Jace Pearson of... and Superior Stories #4)

TEXAS RANGERS IN ACTION (Formerly Captain Gallant or Scotland Yard?)
No. 5, July, 1956 - No. 79, Aug, 1970 (See Blue Bird Comics)
Charlton Comics

5 5.35 16.00 32.00
6-10 3.60 9.00 18.00
11-Williamson-a(5&8 pgs.); Torres/Williamson-a (5 pgs.) 5.85 17.50 35.00
12,14-20 2.40 6.00 12.00
13-Williamson-a (5 pgs); Torres, Morisi-a 4.70 14.00 28.00
21-30: 31-Last 10 cent issue? 2.00 5.00 10.00
31-59 1.60 4.00 8.00
60-Riley's Rangers begin 1.00 2.00 5.00
61-70: 65-1st app. The Man Called Loco, origin in #67 1.60 4.00
71-79 .80 2.00
76(Modern Comics-r, 1977) 1.00

TEXAS SLIM (See A-1 Comics #2-8,10)

TEX DAWSON, GUN-SLINGER (Gunslinger #2 on)
January, 1973 (20 cents)(Also see Western Kid, 1st series)
Marvel Comics Group

1-Steranko-c; Williamson-r(4 pgs.); Tex Dawson-r by Romita(3) from 1955; Tuska-r 1.50

TEX FARNUM (See Wisco)

TEX FARRELL
Mar-Apr, 1948
D. S. Publishing Co.

1-Tex Farrell & his horse Lightning; Shelly-c 10.00 30.00 60.00

TEX GRANGER (Formerly Calling All Boys; see True Comics)
No. 18, June, 1948 - No. 24, Sept, 1949
Parents' Magazine Institute/Commended

18-Tex Granger & his horse Bullet begin 8.35 25.00 50.00
19 6.70 20.00 40.00
20-24: 22-Wild Bill Hickok story. 23-Vs. Billy the Kid 5.00 15.00 30.00

TEX MORGAN (See Blaze Carson and Wild Western)
Aug, 1948 - No. 9, Feb, 1950
Marvel Comics (CCC)

GD25 FN65 NM94

1-Tex Morgan, his horse Lightning & sidekick Lobo begin 17.00 52.00 120.00
2 11.00 32.00 75.00
3-6: 3,4-Arizona Annie app. 9.15 27.50 55.00
7-9: All photo-c. 7-Captain Tootsie by Beck. 8-18pg. story "The Terror of Rimrock Valley," Diablo app. 11.50 34.00 80.00

NOTE: *Tex Taylor app.-6, 7, 9. **Brodsky** c-6. **Syd Shores** c-2, 5.*

TEX RITTER WESTERN (Movie star; singing cowboy; see Six-Gun Heroes and Western Hero)
Oct, 1950 - No. 46, May, 1959 (Photo-c: 1-21)
Fawcett No. 1-20 (1/54)/Charlton No. 21 on

1-Tex Ritter, his stallion White Flash & dog Fury begin; photo front/back-c begin 50.00 150.00 350.00
2 22.00 65.00 150.00
3-5: 5-Last photo back-c 18.00 54.00 125.00
6-10 14.00 43.00 100.00
11-19 8.50 25.50 65.00
20-Last Fawcett issue (1/54) 11.00 32.00 75.00
21-1st Charlton issue; photo-c (3/54) 12.00 36.00 85.00
22-B&W photo back-c begin, end #32 8.35 25.00 50.00
23-30: 23-25-Young Falcon app. 6.70 20.00 40.00
31-38,40-45 5.85 17.50 35.00
39-Williamson-a; Whitman-c (1/58) 7.50 22.50 45.00
46-Last issue 6.70 20.00 40.00

TEX TAYLOR (See Blaze Carson, Kid Colt, Tex Morgan, Wild West, Wild Western, & Wisco)
Sept, 1948 - No. 9, March, 1950
Marvel Comics (HPC)

1-Tex Taylor & his horse Fury begin 17.00 52.00 120.00
2 10.00 30.00 70.00
3 10.00 30.00 65.00
4-6: All photo-c. 4-Anti-Wertham editorial. 5,6-Blaze Carson app. 11.00 32.00 75.00
7-Photo-c; 18 pg. Movie-Length Thriller "Trapped in Time's Lost Land!" with sabre toothed tigers, dinosaurs; Diablo app. 12.00 36.00 85.00
8-Photo-c; 18 pg. Movie-Length Thriller "The Mystery of Devil-Tree Plateau!" with dwarf horses, dwarf people & a lost miniature Inca type village; Diablo app. 12.00 36.00 85.00
9-Photo-c; 18 pg. Movie-Length Thriller "Guns Along the Border!" Captain Tootsie by Schreiber; Nimo The Mountain Lion app. 12.00 36.00 85.00

NOTE: ***Syd Shores** c-1-3.*

THANE OF BAGARTH (Also see Hercules, 1967 series)
No. 24, Oct, 1985 - No. 25, Dec, 1985
Charlton Comics

24,25 1.00

THANOS QUEST, THE (See Capt. Marvel #25, Infinity Gauntlet, Iron Man #55, Logan's Run, Marvel Feature #12, Silver Surfer #34 & Warlock #9)
1990 - No. 2, 1990 ($4.95, color, squarebound, 52 pgs.)
Marvel Comics

1-Both have Starlin scripts & covers 1.65 4.00 10.00
2 1.25 3.00 7.50
1,2-2nd printings ($4.95) 1.00 2.00 5.00

THAT DARN CAT (See Movie Comics & Walt Disney Showcase #19)

THAT'S MY POP! GOES NUTS FOR FAIR
1939 (76 pages) (B&W)
Bystander Press

nn-by Milt Gross 19.00 57.00 130.00

THAT THE WORLD MAY BELIEVE
No date (16 pgs.) (Graymoor Friars distr.)
Catechetical Guild Giveaway

nn 1.60 4.00 8.00

The Thing #3, © CC

Third World War #2, © Fleetway

This Magazine Is Haunted #8, © FAW

GD25 FN65 NM94

THAT WILKIN BOY (Meet Bingo...)
Jan, 1969 - No. 52, Oct, 1982
Archie Publications

	GD25	FN65	NM94
1	3.00	7.50	15.00
2-10	1.60	4.00	8.00
11-26: 26-Last Giant issue	1.00	2.00	5.00
27-52		.80	2.00

T.H.E. CAT (TV)
Mar, 1967 - No. 4, Oct, 1967 (All have photo-c)
Dell Publishing Co.

	GD25	FN65	NM94
1	2.70	8.00	19.00
2-4	1.85	5.50	13.00

THERE'S A NEW WORLD COMING (Spire Christian)(Value: cover or less)

THEY ALL KISSED THE BRIDE (See Cinema Comics Herald)

THEY RING THE BELL
1946
Fox Feature Syndicate

	GD25	FN65	NM94
1	10.00	30.00	60.00

THIEF OF BAGHDAD (See 4-Color #1229)

THIMBLE THEATRE STARRING POPEYE
1931 - No. 2, 1932 (52 pgs.; 25 cents; B&W)
Sonnet Publishing Co.

	GD25	FN65	NM94
1-Daily strip serial-r in both by Segar	86.00	260.00	600.00
2	71.00	215.00	500.00

NOTE: *Probably the first Popeye reprint book. Popeye first entered Thimble Theatre in 1929.*

THIMK (Magazine) (Satire)
May, 1958 - No. 6, May, 1959
Counterpoint

	GD25	FN65	NM94
1	5.00	15.00	30.00
2-6	3.60	9.00	18.00

THING!, THE (Blue Beetle #18 on)
Feb, 1952 - No. 17, Nov, 1954
Song Hits No. 1,2/Capitol Stories/Charlton

	GD25	FN65	NM94
1-Weird/horror stories in all; shrunken head-c	43.00	130.00	300.00
2,3	31.00	95.00	220.00
4-6,8,10: 5-Severed head-c; headlights	23.00	70.00	160.00
7-Injury to eye-c & inside panel; E.C. swipes from Vault of Horror #28	39.00	120.00	275.00
9-Used in **SOTI**, pg. 388 & illo-"Stomping on the face is a form of brutality which modern children learn early"	43.00	130.00	300.00
11-Necronomicon story; Hansel & Gretel parody; Injury-to-eye panel; Check-a	36.00	110.00	250.00
12-"Cinderella" parody; Ditko-c/a; lingerie panels	47.00	140.00	330.00
13,15-Ditko c/a(3 & 5); 13-Ditko E.C. swipe/Haunt of Fear #15(#1)-"House of Horror"	47.00	140.00	330.00
14-Extreme violence/torture; Rumpelstiltskin story; Ditko-c/a(4)	47.00	140.00	330.00
16-Injury to eye panel	29.00	85.00	200.00
17-Ditko-c; classic parody-"Through the Looking Glass;" Powell-a(r)	39.00	120.00	275.00

NOTE: *Excessive violence, severed heads, injury to eye are common No. 5 on.* ***Al Fago*** *c-4.* ***Forgione*** *c-1i, 2, 6, 8, 9.* ***Palais*** *c-16.*

THING, THE (See Fantastic Four, Marvel Fanfare, Marvel Feature #11, 12 & Marvel Two-In-One)
July, 1983 - No. 36, June, 1986
Marvel Comics Group

	GD25	FN65	NM94
1-Life story of Ben Grimm; Byrne scripts begin		.80	2.00
2-36: 5-Spider-Man, She-Hulk app.			1.20

NOTE: ***Byrne*** *a-2i, 7; c-1, 7, 36i; scripts-1-13, 19-22.* ***Sienkiewicz*** *c-13i.*

THING, THE (From Another World)
1991 - No. 2, 1992 ($2.95, color, mini-series, stiff-c)
Dark Horse Comics

	GD25	FN65	NM94
1,2-Based on Universal movie; painted-c/a		1.20	3.00

THING FROM ANOTHER WORLD: CLIMATE OF FEAR, THE
July, 1992 - No. 4, Dec, 1992 ($2.50, color, mini-series)
Dark Horse Comics

	GD25	FN65	NM94
1-4: Painted-c		1.00	2.50

THIRD WORLD WAR (Fleetway)(Value: cover or less)

THIRTEEN (...Going on 18)
11-1/61-62 - No. 25, 12/67; No. 26, 7/69 - No. 29, 1/71
Dell Publishing Co.

	GD25	FN65	NM94
1	5.85	17.50	35.00
2-10	4.70	14.00	28.00
11-29: 26-29-r	3.20	8.00	20.00

NOTE: ***John Stanley*** *script-No. 3-29; art?*

13: ASSASSIN (TSR)(Value: cover or less)

THIRTY SECONDS OVER TOKYO (See American Library)

THIS IS SUSPENSE! (Formerly Strange Suspense Stories; Strange Suspense Stories #27 on)
No. 23, Feb, 1955 - No. 26, Aug, 1955
Charlton Comics

	GD25	FN65	NM94
23-Wood-a(r)/A Star Presentation #3-"Dr. Jekyll & Mr. Hyde;" last pre-code issue	14.00	43.00	100.00
24-Evans-a	9.15	27.50	55.00
25,26: 26-Marcus Swayze-a	5.85	17.50	35.00

THIS IS THE PAYOFF (See Pay-Off)

THIS IS WAR
No. 5, July, 1952 - No. 9, May, 1953
Standard Comics

	GD25	FN65	NM94
5-Toth-a	10.00	30.00	60.00
6,9-Toth-a	8.35	25.00	50.00
7,8: 8-Ross Andru-c	3.60	9.00	18.00

THIS IS YOUR LIFE, DONALD DUCK (See 4-Color #1109)

THIS MAGAZINE IS CRAZY (Crazy #? on)
V3#2, July, 1957 - V4#8, Feb, 1959 (25 cents, magazine, 68 pgs.)
Charlton Publ. (Humor Magazines)

	GD25	FN65	NM94
V3#2-V4#7: V4#5-Russian Sputnik-c parody	4.00	10.00	20.00
V4#8-Davis-a (8 pgs.)	4.70	14.00	28.00

THIS MAGAZINE IS HAUNTED (Danger and Adventure #22 on)
Oct, 1951 - No. 14, 12/53; No. 15, 2/54 - V3#21, Nov, 1954
Fawcett Publications/Charlton No. 15(2/54) on

	GD25	FN65	NM94
1-Evans-a(i?)	31.00	95.00	220.00
2,5-Evans-a	22.00	65.00	150.00
3,4: 3-Vampire-c/story	11.00	32.00	75.00
6-9,11,12,14	10.00	30.00	60.00
10-Severed head-c	14.00	43.00	100.00
13-Severed head-c/story	13.00	40.00	90.00
15,20	8.35	25.00	50.00
16,19-Ditko-c. 19-Injury-to-eye panel; story-r/#1	16.00	48.00	110.00
17-Ditko-c/a(4); blood drainage story	21.00	63.00	145.00
18-Ditko-c/a(1 story); E.C. swipe/Haunt of Fear #5; injury-to-eye panel	18.00	54.00	125.00
21-Ditko-c, Evans-a	14.00	43.00	100.00

NOTE: ***Baily*** *a-1, 3, 4, 21r/#1.* ***Moldoff*** *c/a-1-13.* ***Powell*** *a-3-5, 11, 12, 17.* ***Shuster*** *a-18-20.*

THIS MAGAZINE IS HAUNTED (2nd Series) (Formerly Zaza the Mystic; Outer Space #17 on)
V2#12, July, 1957 - V2#16, April, 1958
Charlton Comics

	GD25	FN65	NM94
V2#12-14-Ditko-c/a in all	18.00	54.00	125.00
15-No Ditko-c/a	4.00	11.00	22.00
16-Ditko-a	12.00	36.00	85.00

Thor #373, © MEG

Thor Annual #16, © MEG

3-D Action #1 © MEG

GD25 FN65 NM94 | GD25 FN65 NM94

THIS MAGAZINE IS WILD (See Wild)

THIS WAS YOUR LIFE (Chick)(Value: cover or less)

THOR (See Avengers #1, Giant-Size..., Marvel Collectors Item Classics, Marvel Graphic Novel 33, Marvel Preview, Marvel Spectacular, Marvel Treasury Edition, Special Marvel Edition & Tales of Asgard)

THOR (Formerly Journey Into Mystery)(The Mighty Thor #413 on)
March, 1966 - Present
Marvel Comics Group

126-Thor continues (125-130 Thor vs. Hercules) 11.00 34.00 90.00
127-133,135-140: 127-1st app. Pluto 5.00 15.00 40.00
134-Intro High Evolutionary 7.00 20.00 52.00
141-157,159,160: 146-Inhumans begin (11,67, 1st full app., tied w/F.F. Special #5; see F.F. #54), end #151. 146,147-Origin The Inhumans. 148,149-Origin Black Bolt in each. 149-Origin Medusa, Crystal, Maximus, Gorgon, Kornak 3.00 10.00 27.00
158-Origin-r/#83; 158,159-Origin Dr. Blake (Thor) 7.00 21.00 56.00
161,167,170-179: 179-Last Kirby issue 2.00 6.00 17.00
162,168,169-Origin Galactus; Kirby-a 4.00 11.00 29.00
163,164-Brief cameo Warlock (Him); Kirby-a 2.00 7.00 19.00
165-1st full app. Warlock (Him) (6/69, see Fantastic Four #67); last 12 cent issue; Kirby-a 5.00 16.00 42.00
166-2nd full app. Warlock (Him); battles Thor 5.00 14.00 37.00
180,181-Neal Adams-a 1.00 4.00 11.00
182-192,194-200 1.00 2.50 5.50
193-(25 cents, 52 pgs.); Silver Surfer x-over 4.00 11.00 30.00
201-250: 225-Intro. Firelord 1.50 3.75
251-280: 271-Iron Man x-over. 274-Death of Balder the Brave 1.10 2.75
281-299: 294-Origin Asgard & Odin .90 2.25
300-(12/80)-End of Asgard; origin of Odin & The Destroyer 1.00 2.50 5.50
301-336: 316-Iron Man x-over .70 1.70
337-Simonson-c/a begins, ends #382, Beta Ray Bill becomes new Thor 1.00 2.50 5.50
338-Two variants exist, 60 & 75 cents 1.30 3.25
339,340: 340-Donald Blake returns as Thor .70 1.70
341-373,375-381,383: 341-Clark Kent & Lois Lane cameo. 373-X-Factor tie-in 1.25
374-Mutant Massacre; X-Factor app. 1.40 3.50 8.50
382-($1.25)-Anniversary issue; last Simonson-a .90 2.25
384-Intro. new Thor .90 2.25
385-399,401-410,413-428: 385-Hulk x-over. 391-Spider-Man x-over. 395-Intro Earth Force. 408-Eric Masterson becomes Thor. 427,428-Excalibur x-over 1.25
400-($1.75, 68 pgs.)-Origin Loki 1.00 2.50
411-Intro New Warriors (apps. in costume in last panel); Juggernaut-c/story 1.30 3.25
412-1st full app. New Warriors (Marvel Boy, Kid Nova, Namorita, Night Thrasher, Firestar & Speedball) 2.70 8.00 19.00
429,430-Ghost Rider x-over 1.30 3.25
431,434-443: 434-Capt. America x-over. 437-Thor vs. Quasar; Hercules app.; Tales of Asgard back-up stories begin. 443-Dr. Strange & Silver Surfer x-over; last $1.00-c 1.50
432-($1.50, 52 pgs.)-Thor's 300th app. (vs. Loki); reprints origin & 1st app. from Journey into Mystery #83 1.30 3.25
433-Intro new Thor 1.00 2.50 5.50
444-449,451-472: 448-Spider-Man-c/story. 455-Dr. Strange back-up. 457-Old Thor returns (3 pgs.). 459-Intro Thunderstrike. 460-Starlin scripts begin. 465-Super Skrull app. 466-Drax app. 1.50
450-($2.50, 68 pgs.)-Flip-book format; r/story JIM #87 (1st Loki) plus-c plus a gallery of past-c; gatefold-c 1.20 3.00
Special 2(9/66)-See Journey Into Mystery for 1st annual 5.00 15.00 40.00
King Size Special 3(1/71) 1.40 3.50 8.50
Special 4(12/71)-r/Thor #131,132 & JIM #113 1.40 3.50 8.50
Annual 5-8: 5(11/76). 6(10/77)-Guardians of the Galaxy app. 7(1978). 8(1979)-Thor vs. Zeus-c/story 1.10 2.70 6.50
Annual 9-12: 9('81). 10('82). 11('83). 12('84) 1.30 3.25
Annual 13-16: 13(1985). 14('89, $2.00, 68 pgs.)-Atlantis Attacks. 15('90, $2.00, 68 pgs.). 16('91, $2.00, 68 pgs.)-3 pg. origin; Guardians of the Galaxy x-over .80 2.00
Annual 17 (1992, $2.25, 68 pgs.) .90 2.25
Annual 18 (1993, $2.95, 68 pgs.)-Bagged w/card 1.20 3.00
...Alone Against the Celestials nn (6/92, $5.95)-r/Thor #387-389 1.00 2.50 6.00

NOTE: ***Neal Adams*** *a-180,181; c-179-181.* ***Austin*** *a-342i, 346i; c-312i.* ***Buscema*** *a(p)-178, 182-213, 215-226, 231-238, 241-253, 254r, 256-259, 272-278, 283-285, 370, Annual 6, 8, 11i; c(p)-175, 182-196, 198-200, 202-204, 206, 211, 212, 215, 219, 221, 226, 256, 259, 261, 262, 272-278, 283, 289, 370, Annual 6.* ***Everett*** *a(i)-143, 170-175; c(i)-171, 172, 174, 176, 241.* ***Gil Kane*** *a-318p, c(p)-201, 205, 207-210, 216, 220, 222, 223, 231, 233-240, 242, 243, 318.* ***Kirby*** *a(p)-126-177, 179, 194r, 254r; c(p)-126-169, 171-174, 176-178, 249-253, 255, 257, 258, Annual 5, Special 1-4.* ***Mooney*** *a(i)-201, 204, 214-216, 218, 322i, 324i, 326i, 327i.* ***Sienkiewicz*** *c-332, 333, 335.* ***Simonson*** *a-260-271p, 337-354, 357-367, 380, Annual 7p; c-260, 263-271, 337-355, 357-369, 371, 373-382, Annual 7.* ***Starlin*** *c-213.*

THOR CORPS
Sept, 1993 - No. 4, Dec, 1993 ($1.75, color, mini-series)
Marvel Comics

1-4: 1-Invaders cameo. 2-Invaders app. .70 1.75

THOSE MAGNIFICENT MEN IN THEIR FLYING MACHINES (See Movie Comics)

THREE CABALLEROS (See 4-Color #71)

THREE CHIPMUNKS, THE (See 4-Color #1042)

THREE COMICS (Also see Spiritman)
1944 (10 cents, 52 pgs.) (2 different covers exist)
The Penny King Co.

1,3,4-Lady Luck, Mr. Mystic, The Spirit app. (3 Spirit sections bound together)-Lou Fine-a 17.00 52.00 120.00

NOTE: *No. 1 contains Spirit Sections 4/9/44 - 4/23/44, and No. 4 is also from 4/44.*

3-D (NOTE: The prices of all the 3-D comics listed include glasses. Deduct 40-50 percent if glasses are missing, and reduce slightly if glasses are loose.)

3-D ACTION
Jan, 1954 (Oversized) (15 cents)(2 pairs of glasses included)
Atlas Comics (ACI)

1-Battle Brady; Sol Brodsky-c 34.00 100.00 235.00

3-D ADVENTURE COMICS (Stats)(Value: cover or less)

3-D ALIEN TERROR (Eclipse)(Value: cover or less)

3-D ANIMAL FUN (See Animal Fun)

3-D BATMAN (Also see Batman 3-D)
1953 (Reprinted in 1966)
National Periodical Publications

1953-Reprints Batman #42 & 48 (Penguin-c/story); Tommy Tomorrow app. (25 cents) 93.00 280.00 650.00
1966-Tommy Tomorrow app.; Penguin-c/story(r); has inside-c photos of Batman & Robin from TV show (50 cents) 32.00 95.00 225.00

3-D CIRCUS
1953 (25 cents)
Fiction House Magazines (Real Adventures Publ.)

1 34.00 100.00 235.00

3-D COMICS (See Mighty Mouse, Tor and Western Fighters)

3-D DOLLY
December, 1953 (2 pairs glasses included)
Harvey Publications

1-Richie Rich story redrawn from his 1st app. in Little Dot #1 20.00 60.00 140.00

3-D-ELL
1953 - No. 3, 1953 (3-D comics) (25 cents)
Dell Publishing Co.

3-D Funny Movies #1, © Comic Media

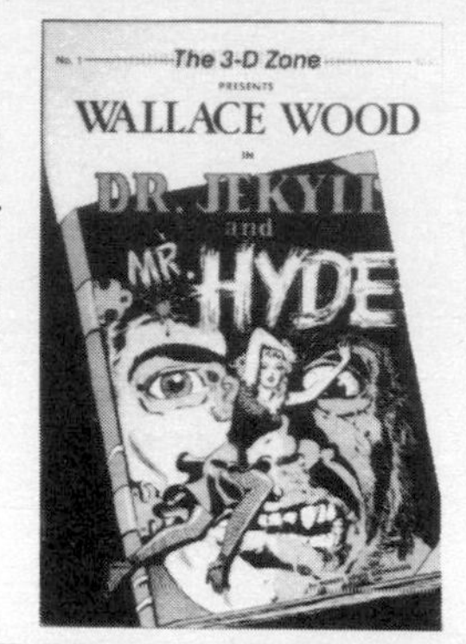

The 3-D Zone #1, © Ray Zone

The Three Stooges #7 (Dell), © Norman Maurer Prod.

GD25 FN65 NM94

1,2-Rootie Kazootie 34.00 105.00 240.00
3-Flukey Luke 32.00 95.00 225.00

3-D EXOTIC BEAUTIES (3-D Zone)(Value: cover or less)

3-D FEATURES PRESENT JET PUP
Oct-Dec, 1953
Dimensions Public

1-Irving Spector-a(2) 34.00 100.00 235.00

3-D FUNNY MOVIES
1953 (25 cents)
Comic Media

1-Bugsey Bear & Paddy Pelican 34.00 100.00 235.00

THREE-DIMENSION ADVENTURES (Superman)
1953 (Large size)
National Periodical Publications

nn-Origin Superman (new art) 93.00 280.00 650.00

THREE DIMENSIONAL ALIEN WORLDS (Pacific)(Value: cover or less)

THREE DIMENSIONAL DNAGENTS (See New DNAgents)

THREE DIMENSIONAL E. C. CLASSICS (Three Dimensional Tales From the Crypt No. 2)
Spring, 1954 (Prices include glasses; came with 2 pairs)
E. C. Comics

1-Stories by Wood (Mad #3), Krigstein (W.S. #7), Evans (F.C. #13), & Ingels (CSS #5); Kurtzman-c (rare in high grade due to unstable paper) 60.00 180.00 465.00

NOTE: *Stories redrawn to 3-D format. Original stories not necessarily by artists listed. CSS: Crime SuspenStories; F.C.: Frontline Combat; W.S.: Weird Science.*

THREE DIMENSIONAL TALES FROM THE CRYPT (Formerly Three Dimensional E. C. Classics)(Cover title: ...From the Crypt of Terror)
No. 2, Spring, 1954 (Prices include glasses; came with 2 pair)
E. C. Comics

2-Davis (TFTC #25), Elder (VOH #14), Craig (TFTC #24), & Orlando (TFTC #22) stories; Feldstein-c (rare in high grade due to unstable paper 60.00 180.00 465.00

NOTE: *Stories redrawn to 3-D format. Original stories not necessarily by artists listed. TFTC: Tales From the Crypt; VOH: Vault of Horror.*

3-D LOVE
December, 1953 (25 cents)
Steriographic Publ. (Mikeross Publ.)

1 34.00 100.00 235.00

3-D NOODNICK (See Noodnick)

3-D ROMANCE
January, 1954 (25 cents)
Steriographic Publ. (Mikeross Publ.)

1 34.00 100.00 235.00

3-D SHEENA, JUNGLE QUEEN (Also see Sheena 3-D)
1953 (25 cents)
Fiction House Magazines

1-Maurice Whitman-c 57.00 170.00 400.00

3-D SUBSTANCE (3-D Zone)(Value: cover or less)

3-D TALES OF THE WEST
Jan, 1954 (Oversized) (15 cents)(2 pair glasses included)
Atlas Comics (CPS)

1 (3-D)-Sol Brodsky-c 35.00 105.00 245.00

3-D THREE STOOGES (Eclipse)(Value: cover or less)

3-D WHACK (See Whack)

3-D ZONE, THE (3-D Zone)(Value: cover or less)

3 FUNMAKERS, THE
1908 (64 pgs.) (10x15")
Stokes and Company

nn-Maude, Katzenjammer Kids, Happy Hooligan (1904-06 Sunday strip reprints in color) 40.00 120.00 280.00

3 LITTLE PIGS (See 4-Color #218)

3 LITTLE PIGS, THE (See Walt Disney Showcase #15 & 21)
May, 1964; No. 2, Sept, 1968 (Walt Disney)
Gold Key

1-Reprints 4-Color #218 3.20 8.00 16.00
2 2.00 5.00 10.00

THREE MOUSEKETEERS, THE (1st Series)(See Funny Stuff #1)
3-4/56 - No. 24, 9-10/59; No. 25, 8-9/60 - No. 26, 10-12/60
National Periodical Publications

1 18.00 54.00 125.00
2 10.00 30.00 60.00
3-10 8.35 25.00 50.00
11-26: 24-Cover says 11/59, inside says 9-10/59 6.70 20.00 40.00

NOTE: ***Rube Grossman** a-1-26. **Sheldon Mayer** a-1-8; c-1, 3, 4, 6, 7.*

THREE MOUSEKETEERS, THE (2nd Series) (See Super DC Giant)
May-June, 1970 - No. 7, May-June, 1971 (#5-7: 68 pgs.)
National Periodical Publications

1-Mayer-r in all 1.65 4.00 10.00
2-7: 5-Dodo & the Frog, Bo Bunny & Doodles Duck begin 1.00 2.00 5.00

THREE MUSKETEERS, THE (See Disney's The Three Musketeers)

THREE NURSES (Confidential Diary #12-17; Career Girl Romances #24 on)
V3#18, May, 1963 - V3#23, Mar, 1964
Charlton Comics

V3#18-23 1.00 2.00 5.00

THREE RASCALS
1958; 1963
I. W. Enterprises

I.W. Reprint #1,2,10: 1-(Says Super Comics on inside)-(M.E.'s Clubhouse Rascals). #2-(1958). 10-(1963)-r/#1 .60 1.50 3.00

THREE RING COMICS
March, 1945
Spotlight Publishers

1-Funny animal 10.00 30.00 60.00

THREE ROCKETEERS (See Blast-Off)

THREE STOOGES (See Comic Album #18, The Little Stooges, March of Comics #232, 248, 268, 280, 292, 304, 316, 336, 373, Movie Classics & Comics & 3-D Three Stooges)

THREE STOOGES
Feb, 1949 - No. 2, May, 1949; Sept, 1953 - No. 7, Oct, 1954
Jubilee No. 1,2/St. John No. 1 (9/53) on

1-(Scarce, 1949)-Kubert-a; infinity-c 75.00 225.00 525.00
2-(Scarce)-Kubert, Maurer-a 59.00 180.00 415.00
1(9/53)-Hollywood Stunt Girl by Kubert, 7 pgs. 50.00 150.00 350.00
2(3-D, 10/53)-Stunt Girl story by Kubert 36.00 110.00 250.00
3(3-D, 11/53) 36.00 110.00 250.00
4(3/54)-7(10/54): 4-1st app. Li'l Stooge? 27.00 81.00 190.00

NOTE: *All issues have **Kubert-Maurer** art & **Maurer** covers. 6, 7-Partial photo-c.*

THREE STOOGES
No. 1043, Oct-Dec, 1959 - No. 55, June, 1972
Dell Publishing Co./Gold Key No. 10 (10/62) on

4-Color 1043 (#1) 17.00 52.00 120.00
4-Color 1078,1127,1170,1187 10.00 30.00 60.00
6(9-11/61) - 10: 6-Professor Putter begins; ends #16 8.35 25.00 50.00
11-14,16-20: 17-The Little Monsters begin (5/64)(1st app.?) 6.70 20.00 40.00
15-Go Around the World in a Daze (movie scenes) 8.35 25.00 50.00

Thriller #5, © DC

Thrilling Comics #61, © STD

Thun'da #2, © ME

GD25 FN65 NM94 — GD25 FN65 NM94

21,23-30 5.85 17.50 35.00
22-Movie scenes/"The Outlaws Is Coming" 6.70 20.00 40.00
31-55 5.00 15.00 30.00
NOTE: *All Four Colors, 6-50, 52-55 have photo-c.*

THREE STOOGES IN 3-D, THE (Eternity)(Value: cover or less)

3 WORLDS OF GULLIVER (See 4-Color #1158)

THRILL COMICS (See Flash Comics, Fawcett)

THRILLER (DC)(Value: cover or less)

THRILLING ADVENTURES IN STAMPS COMICS
V1#8, Jan, 1953 (25 cents) (100 pages) (Formerly Stamp Comics)
Stamp Comics, Inc. (Very Rare)
V1#8-Harrison, Wildey, Kiefer, Napoli-a 54.00 160.00 375.00

THRILLING ADVENTURE STORIES (See Tigerman)
Feb, 1975 - No. 2, Aug, 1975 (B&W, 68 pgs.)
Atlas/Seaboard Publ.
1,2: 1-Tigerman, Kromag the Killer begin; Heath, Thorne-a. 2-Heath, Toth, Severin, Simonson-a; Neal Adams-c 1.00 2.40

THRILLING COMICS
Feb, 1940 - No. 80, April, 1951
Better Publ./Nedor/Standard Comics
1-Origin & 1st app. Dr. Strange (37 pgs.), ends #?; Nickie Norton of the Secret Service begins 100.00 300.00 700.00
2-The Rio Kid, The Woman in Red, Pinocchio begins 43.00 130.00 300.00
3-The Ghost & Lone Eagle begin 37.00 110.00 250.00
4-10: 5-Dr. Strange changed to Doc Strange 26.00 80.00 185.00
11-18,20 22.00 65.00 150.00
19-Origin & 1st app. The American Crusader (8/41), ends #39,41 29.00 85.00 200.00
21-30: 24-Intro. Mike, Doc Strange's sidekick (1/42). 29-Last Rio Kid 19.00 58.00 135.00
31-40: 36-Commando Cubs begin (7/43, 1st app.) 14.00 43.00 100.00
41,44-Hitler-c 14.00 43.00 100.00
42,43,45-52: 52-The Ghost ends 11.50 34.00 80.00
53-The Phantom Detective begins; The Cavalier app.; no Commando Cubs 11.50 34.00 80.00
54-The Cavalier app.; no Commando Cubs 11.50 34.00 80.00
55-Lone Eagle ends 11.50 34.00 80.00
56-Princess Pantha begins (10/46, 1st app.) 22.00 65.00 150.00
57-66: 61-Ingels-a; The Lone Eagle app. 65-Last Phantom Detective & Commando Cubs. 66-Frazetta text illo 18.00 54.00 125.00
67,70-73: Frazetta-a(5-7 pgs.) in each. 72-Sea Eagle app.; Buck Ranger, Cowboy Detective begins 22.00 65.00 150.00
68,69-Frazetta-a(2), 8 & 6 pgs.; 9 & 7 pgs. 22.00 67.00 155.00
74-Last Princess Pantha; Tara app. 11.00 32.00 75.00
75-78: 75-All western format begins 6.70 20.00 40.00
79-Krigstein-a 8.35 25.00 50.00
80-Severin & Elder, Celardo, Moreira-a 8.35 25.00 50.00
NOTE: *Bondage c-5, 9, 13, 20, 22, 27-30, 38, 41, 52, 54, 70.* ***Kinstler*** *a-45, 48.* ***Leo Morey*** *a-7.* ***Schomburg (Xela)*** *c-7, 9-19, 36-80 (airbrush 62-71).* ***Tuska*** *a-63. Woman in Red not in #19, 23, 31-33, 39-45. No. 72 exists as a Canadian reprint with no* ***Frazetta*** *story. American Crusader c-20-24. Buck Ranger c-72-80. Commando Cubs c-37, 39, 41, 43, 45, 47, 49, 51. Doc Strange c-1-19, 25-36, 38, 40, 42, 44, 46, 48, 50, 52-57, 59. Princess Pantha c-58, 60-71.*

THRILLING CRIME CASES (Formerly 4Most; becomes Shocking Mystery Cases #50 on)
No. 41, June-July, 1950 - No. 49, 1952
Star Publications
41 10.00 30.00 60.00
42-45-Chameleon story (Fox-r) 8.35 25.00 50.00
46-48: 47-Used in POP, pg. 84 7.50 22.50 45.00
49-Classic L. B. Cole-c 16.00 50.00 115.00
NOTE: ***L. B. Cole*** *c-all; a-43p, 45p, 46p, 49(2pgs.).* ***Disbrow*** *a-48.* ***Hollingsworth*** *a-48.*

THRILLING ROMANCES
No. 5, Dec, 1949 - No. 26, June, 1954
Standard Comics
5 7.50 22.50 45.00
6,8 4.00 10.00 20.00
7-Severin/Elder-a, 7 pgs. 5.00 15.00 30.00
9,10-Severin/Elder-a; photo-c 4.70 14.00 28.00
11,14-21,26: 14-Danny Kaye photo-c. 15-Tony Martin/Janet Leigh photo-c 3.20 8.00 16.00
12-Wood-a, 2 pgs. 7.00 21.00 42.00
13-Severin-a 4.00 12.00 24.00
22-25-Toth-a 5.35 16.00 32.00
NOTE: *All photo-c.* ***Celardo*** *a-9, 16.* ***Colletta*** *a-23, 24(2).* ***Tuska*** *a-9.*

THRILLING SCIENCE TALES (AC)(Value: cover or less)

THRILLING TRUE STORY OF THE BASEBALL....
1952 (Photo-c, each)
Fawcett Publications
...Giants-photo-c; has Willie Mays rookie photo-biography 50.00 150.00 350.00
...Yankees-photo-c 44.00 135.00 310.00

THRILLOGY (Pacific)(Value: cover or less)

THRILL-O-RAMA
Oct, 1965 - No. 3, Dec, 1966
Harvey Publications (Fun Films)
1-Fate (Man in Black) by Powell app.; Doug Wildey-a(2); Simon-c 1.50 3.75 9.00
2-Pirana begins (see Phantom #46); Williamson 2 pgs.; Fate (Man in Black) app.; Tuska/Simon-c 1.50 3.75 9.00
3-Fate (Man in Black) app.; Sparling-c 1.00 2.50 6.00

THRILLS OF TOMORROW (Formerly Tomb of Terror)
No. 17, Oct, 1954 - No. 20, April, 1955
Harvey Publications
17-Powell-a (horror); r/Witches Tales #7 5.85 17.50 35.00
18-Powell-a (horror); r/Tomb of Terror #1 4.20 12.50 25.00
19,20-Stuntman-c/stories by S&K (r/from Stuntman #1 & 2); 19 has origin & is last pre-code (2/55) 17.00 52.00 120.00
NOTE: ***Kirby*** *c-19, 20.* ***Palais*** *a-17.* ***Simon*** *c-18?*

THROBBING LOVE (See Fox Giants)

THROUGH GATES OF SPLENDOR (Spire Christian)(Value: cover or less)

THUMPER (See 4-Color #19 & 243)

THUN'DA (...King of the Congo)
1952 - No. 6, 1953
Magazine Enterprises
1(A-1 #47)-Origin; Frazetta c/a; only comic done entirely by Frazetta; all Thun'da stories, no Cave Girl 86.00 260.00 600.00
2(A-1 #56)-Powell-c/a begins, ends #6; Intro/1st app. Cave Girl in filler strip (also app. in 3-6) 13.00 40.00 90.00
3(A-1 #73), 4(A-1 #78) 10.00 30.00 65.00
5(A-1 #83), 6(A-1 #86) 10.00 30.00 60.00

THUN'DA TALES (See Frank Frazetta's...)

THUNDER AGENTS (See Dynamo, Noman & Tales Of Thunder)
11/65 - No. 17, 12/67; No. 18, 9/68, No. 19, 11/68, No. 20, 11/69
(No. 1-16: 68 pgs.; No. 17 on: 52 pgs.)(All are 25 cents)
Tower Comics
1-Origin & 1st app. Dynamo, Noman, Menthor, & The Thunder Squad; 1st app. The Iron Maiden 11.00 32.00 75.00
2-Death of Egghead; A-bomb blast panel 5.50 17.00 40.00
3-5: 4-Guy Gilbert becomes Lightning who joins Thunder Squad; Iron Maiden app. 4.00 12.00 28.00
6-10: 7-Death of Menthor. 8-Origin & 1st app. The Raven 2.60 7.50 18.00
11-15: 13-Undersea Agent app.; no Raven story 1.70 5.00 12.00

Thunderstrike #1, © MEG

Thunder Agents #6, © TC

Tiger Girl #1, © WEST

GD25 FN65 NM94

16-19 1.50 3.75 9.00
20-Special Collectors Edition; all reprints 1.90 4.75
NOTE: ***Crandall** a-1, 4p, 5p, 18, 20r; c-18. **Ditko** a-6, 7p, 12p, 13?, 14p, 16, 18. **Giunta** a-6. **Kane** a-1, 5p, 6p?, 14, 16p; c-14, 15. **Reinman** a-13. **Sekowsky** a-6. **Tuska** a-1p, 7, 8, 10, 13-17, 19. **Whitney** a-9p, 10, 13, 15, 17, 18; c-17. **Wood** a-1-11, 15(w/**Ditko**-12, 18), (inks-#9, 13, 14, 16, 17), 19i, 20r; c-1-8, 9i, 10-13(#10 w/**Williamson**(p)), 16.*

T.H.U.N.D.E.R. AGENTS (See Blue Ribbon Comics, Hall of Fame Featuring the..., JCP Features & Wally Wood's...)
May, 1983 - No. 2, Jan, 1984
JC Comics (Archie Publications)

1,2-New material .80 2.00

THUNDER BIRDS (See Cinema Comics Herald)

THUNDERBOLT (See The Atomic...)

THUNDERBOLT (Peter Cannon...; see Crisis on Infinite Earths & Peter...)
Jan, 1966; No. 51, Mar-Apr, 1966 - No. 60, Nov, 1967
Charlton Comics

1-Origin & 1st app. Thunderbolt 1.30 3.25 8.00
51-(Formerly Son of Vulcan #50) 1.90 4.75
52-59: 54-Sentinels begin. 59-Last Thunderbolt & Sentinels (back-up story) 1.20 3.00
60-Prankster app. 1.90 4.75
57,58 ('77)-Modern Comics-r 1.00
NOTE: ***Aparo** a-60. **Morisi** a-1, 51-56, 58; c-1, 51-56, 58, 59.*

THUNDERBUNNY (Red Circle)(Value: cover or less)(Also see Blue Ribbon Comics #13, Charlton Bullseye & Pep Comics #393)

THUNDER MOUNTAIN (See 4-Color #246)

THUNDERSTRIKE (See Thor #459)
June, 1993 - Present ($1.25, color)
Marvel Comics

1-($2.95, 52 pgs.)-Holo-grafx lightning patterned foil-c; Bloodaxe returns 1.20 3.00
2-6 1.25

TICK, THE (Also see The Chroma-Tick)
June, 1988 - No. 12, May, 1993 ($1.75-$1.95-$2.25; B&W, over-sized)
New England Comics Press

Special Edition 1-1st comic book app. serially numbered & limited to 5,000 copies 5.00 15.00 35.00
Special Edition 2-Serially numbered and limited to 3000 copies 4.00 12.00 28.00
1-Reprints Special Ed. 1 w/minor changes 4.00 12.00 28.00
1-2nd printing 1.40 3.50
1-3rd printing ($1.95, 6/89) .80 2.00
1-4th printing ($2.25) .90 2.25
1-5th printing ($2.75) 1.10 2.75
2-Reprints Special Ed. 2 w/minor changes 2.30 6.75 16.00
2-2nd printing ($1.95) 1.20 3.00
2-3rd & 4th printings ($2.25) .90 2.25
2-5th printing ($2.75) 1.10 2.75
3-5 ($1.95): 4-1st app. Paul the Samurai 1.70 4.25
3-2nd & 3rd printings ($2.25) .90 2.25
3-4th printing ($2.75) 1.10 2.75
4-2nd printing ($2.25) .90 2.25
4-3rd - 5th printings ($2.75) .10 2.75
6-8 ($2.25) .90 2.25
5-8-2nd printings ($2.75) 1.10 2.75
6-3rd printing ($2.75) 1.10 2.75
8-Variant with no logo, price, issue number or company logos 1.65 4.00 10.00
9-12 ($2.75) .10 2.75
The Tick's Giant Circus of the Mighty 1,2: 1-(Summer, 1992, $2.75, B&W, magazine size) .10 2.75

TICK KARMA TORNADO, THE
Oct, 1993 ($3.25, color)
New England Comics Press

1 1.30 3.25

TICKLE COMICS (Also see Gay, Smile, & Whee Comics)
1955 (52 pages) (5x7-1/4") (7 cents)
Modern Store Publ.

1 .50 1.25 2.50

TICK TOCK TALES
Jan, 1946 - V3#33, Jan-Feb, 1951
Magazine Enterprises

1-Koko & Kola begin 9.15 27.50 55.00
2 4.70 14.00 28.00
3-10 4.00 11.00 22.00
11-33: 19-Flag-c. 23-Muggsy Mouse, The Pixies & Tom-Tom The Jungle Boy app. 25-The Pixies & Tom-Tom app. 3.00 7.50 15.00

TIGER (Also see Comics Reading Libraries)
March, 1970 - No. 6, Jan, 1971 (15 cents)
Charlton Press (King Features)

1 1.00 2.00 5.00
2-6 1.20 3.00

TIGER BOY (See Unearthly Spectaculars)

TIGER GIRL
September, 1968 (15¢)
Gold Key

1(10227-809)-Sparling-c/a; Jerry Siegel scripts 3.20 8.00 20.00

TIGERMAN (Also see Thrilling Adventure Stories)
April, 1975 - No. 3, Sept, 1975 (All 25 cent issues)
Seaboard Periodicals (Atlas)

1-3: 2,3-Ditko-p in each 1.00

TIGER WALKS, A (See Movie Comics)

TILLIE THE TOILER
1925 - No. 8, 1933 (52 pgs.) (B&W daily strip reprints)
Cupples & Leon Co.

nn (#1) 18.00 55.00 125.00
2-8 11.00 32.00 75.00
NOTE: *First strip appearance was January, 1921.*

TILLIE THE TOILER (See Comic Monthly)
No. 15, 1941 - No. 237, July, 1949
Dell Publishing Co.

4-Color 15(1941) 32.00 95.00 225.00
Large Feature Comic 30(1941) 19.00 58.00 135.00
4-Color 8(1942) 19.00 58.00 135.00
4-Color 22(1943) 16.00 48.00 110.00
4-Color 55(1944) 11.50 34.00 80.00
4-Color 89(1945) 11.50 34.00 80.00
4-Color 106('45),132('46) 10.00 30.00 60.00
4-Color 150,176,184 8.35 25.00 50.00
4-Color 195,213,237 5.85 17.50 35.00

TILLY AND TED-TINKERTOTLAND
1945 (Giveaway) (20 pgs.)
W. T. Grant Co.

nn-Christmas comic 5.00 15.00 30.00

TIM (Formerly Superman-Tim; becomes Gene Autry-Tim)
June, 1950 - Oct, 1950 (Half-size, B&W)
Tim Stores

4 issues; 6/50, 9/50, 10/50 known 5.85 17.50 35.00

TIMBER WOLF (See Action Comics #372, & Legion of Super-Heroes)
Nov, 1992 - No. 5, Mar, 1993 ($1.25, color, mini-series)
DC Comics

1-5 1.25

Time Masters #2, © DC

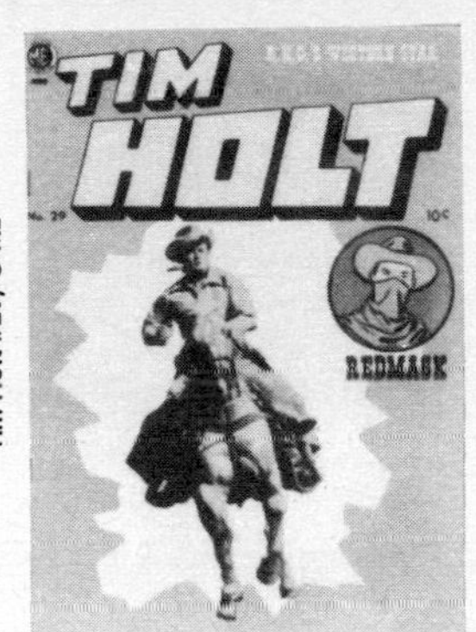

Tim Holt #29, © ME

Timmy the Timid Ghost #2 (12/67), © CC

GD25 FN65 NM94 | GD25 FN65 NM94

TIME BANDITS (Marvel)(Value: cover or less)

TIME BEAVERS (See First Comics Graphic Novel #2)

TIME FOR LOVE (Formerly Romantic Secrets)
V2#53, Oct, 1966; Oct, 1967 - No. 47, May, 1976
Charlton Comics
V2#53(10/66), 1(10/67), 2(12/67)-20 — 1.60 4.00
21-47 — .80 2.00

TIME KILLERS (Fleetway/Quality)(Value: cover or less)

TIMELESS TOPIX (See Topix)

TIME MACHINE, THE (See 4-Color #1085)

TIME MASTERS (DC)(Value: cover or less)

TIMESPIRITS (Marvel)(Value: cover or less)

TIME TUNNEL, THE (TV)
Feb, 1967 - No. 2, July, 1967 (12¢ issues)
Gold Key
1,2-Photo back-c — 4.00 12.00 28.00

TIME TWISTERS (Quality)(Value: cover or less)

TIME 2: THE EPIPHANY (See First Comics Graphic Novel #9)

TIME WARP (DC)(Value: cover or less)(See The Unexpected #210)

TIME WARRIORS THE BEGINNING (Fantasy General)(Value: cover or less)

TIM HOLT (Movie star) (Becomes Red Mask #42 on; also see Crack Western #72, & Great Western)
1948 - No. 41, April-May, 1954 (All 36 pgs.)
Magazine Enterprises
1-(A-1 #14)-Line drawn-c w/Tim Holt photo on-c; Tim Holt, His horse Lightning & sidekick Chito begin — 43.00 130.00 300.00
2-(A-1 #17)(9-10/48)-Photo-c begin, end #18 — 25.00 75.00 175.00
3-(A-1 #19)-Photo back-c — 18.00 55.00 125.00
4(1-2/49),5: 5-Photo front/back-c — 14.00 43.00 100.00
6-(5/49)-1st app. The Calico Kid (alias Rex Fury), his horse Ebony & Sidekick Sing-Song (begin series); photo back-c — 20.00 60.00 140.00
7-10: 7-Calico Kid by Ayers. 8-Calico Kid by Guardineer (r-in/Great Western #10). 9-Map of Tim's Home Range — 11.50 34.00 80.00
11-The Calico Kid becomes The Ghost Rider (origin & 1st app.) by Dick Ayers (r-in/Great Western I.W. #8); his horse Spectre & sidekick Sing-Song begin series — 30.00 90.00 210.00
12-16,18-Last photo-c — 10.00 30.00 60.00
17-Frazetta Ghost Rider-c — 25.00 75.00 175.00
19,22,24: 19-Last Tim Holt-c; Bolle line-drawn-c begin; Tim Holt photo on covers #19-28,30-41 — 8.35 25.00 50.00
20-Tim Holt becomes Redmask (origin); begin series; Redmask-c #20-on — 11.00 32.00 75.00
21-Frazetta Ghost Rider/Redmask-c — 21.50 65.00 150.00
23-Frazetta Redmask-c — 17.00 51.00 120.00
25-1st app. Black Phantom — 13.00 40.00 90.00
26-30: 28-Wild Bill Hickok, Bat Masterson team up with Redmask. 29-B&W photo-c — 6.70 20.00 40.00
31-33-Ghost Rider ends — 5.85 17.50 35.00
34-Tales of the Ghost Rider begins (horror)-Classic "The Flower Women" & "Hard Boiled Harry!" — 7.50 22.50 45.00
35-Last Tales of the Ghost Rider — 6.70 20.00 40.00
36-The Ghost Rider returns, ends #41; liquid hallucinogenic drug story — 7.50 22.50 45.00
37-Ghost Rider classic "To Touch Is to Die!," about Inca treasure — 7.50 22.50 45.00
38-The Black Phantom begins (not in #39); classic Ghost Rider "The Phantom Guns of Feather Gap!" — 7.50 22.50 45.00
39-41: All 3-D effect c/stories — 10.00 30.00 65.00

NOTE: *Dick Ayers a-7, 9-41. Bolle a-1-41; c-19, 20, 22, 24-28, 30-41.*

TIM IN SPACE (Formerly Gene Autry Tim; becomes Tim Tomorrow)
1950 (1/2 size giveaway) (B&W)
Tim Stores
nn — 3.60 9.00 18.00

TIM McCOY (Formerly Zoo Funnies; Pictorial Love Stories #22 on)
No. 16, Oct, 1948 - No. 21, Aug, 1949 (Western Movie Stories)
Charlton Comics
16-John Wayne, Montgomery Clift app. in "Red River;" photo back-c — 34.00 100.00 235.00
17-21: 17-Allan "Rocky" Lane guest stars. 18-Rod Cameron guest stars. 20-Jimmy Wakely guest stars. 21-Johnny Mack Brown guest stars — 29.00 85.00 200.00

TIM McCOY, POLICE CAR 17
No. 674, 1934 (32 pgs.) (11x14-3/4") (B&W) (Like Feature Books)
Whitman Publishing Co.
674-1933 movie ill. — 18.00 54.00 125.00

TIMMY (See 4-Color #715, 823, 923, 1022)

TIMMY THE TIMID GHOST (Formerly Win-A-Prize?; see Blue Bird)
No. 3, 2/56 - No. 44, 10/64; No. 45, 9/66; 10/67 - No. 23, 7/71; V4#24, 9/85 - No. 26, 1/86
Charlton Comics
3(1956) (1st Series) — 5.85 17.50 35.00
4,5 — 3.60 9.00 18.00
6-10 — 2.00 5.00 10.00
11,12(4/58,10/58)(100pgs.) — 4.00 12.00 24.00
13-20 — 1.80 4.50 9.00
21-45(1966) — 1.00 2.00 5.00
1(10/67, 2nd series) — 1.00 2.50 6.00
2-23 — 1.00 2.50
24-26 (1985-86): Fago-r — 1.10

TIM TOMORROW (Formerly Tim In Space)
8/51, 9/51, 10/51, Christmas, 1951 (5x7-3/4")
Tim Stores
nn-Prof. Fumble & Captain Kit Comet in all — 4.00 10.00 20.00

TIM TYLER (See Harvey Comics Hits #54)

TIM TYLER (Also see Comics Reading Libraries)
1942
Better Publications
1 — 10.00 30.00 60.00

TIM TYLER COWBOY
No. 11, Nov, 1948 - No. 18, 1950
Standard Comics (King Features Synd.)
11-By Lyman Young — 5.85 17.50 35.00
12-18 — 4.00 12.00 24.00

TINKER BELL (See 4-Color #896, 982, & Walt Disney Showcase #37)

TINY FOLKS FUNNIES (See 4-Color #60)

TINY TESSIE (Tessie #1-23; Real Experiences #25)
No. 24, Oct, 1949
Marvel Comics (20CC)
24 — 5.35 16.00 32.00

TINY TIM (Also see Super Comics)
No. 4, 1941 - No. 235, July, 1949
Dell Publishing Co.
Large Feature Comic 4('41) — 29.00 85.00 200.00
4-Color 20(1941) — 29.00 85.00 200.00
4-Color 42(1943) — 16.00 48.00 110.00
4-Color 235 — 5.35 16.00 32.00

TINY TOT COMICS
Mar, 1946 - No. 10, Nov-Dec, 1947 (For younger readers)
E. C. Comics
1(nn)-52 pg. issues begin, end #4 — 22.00 65.00 150.00

Tip Top Comics #110, © UFS

T-Man #20, © QUA

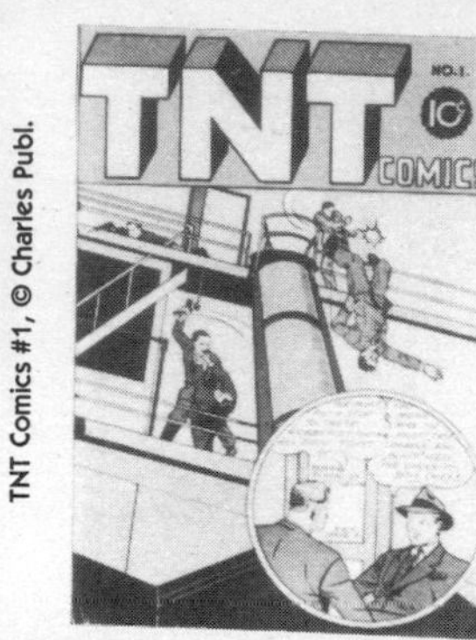

TNT Comics #1, © Charles Publ.

GD25 FN65 NM94

2 (5/46) 14.00 43.00 100.00
3-10: 10-Christmas-c 12.00 36.00 85.00

TINY TOT FUNNIES (Formerly Family Funnies; becomes Junior Funnies)
No. 9, June, 1951
Harvey Publ. (King Features Synd.)

9-Flash Gordon, Mandrake 4.20 12.50 25.00

TINY TOTS COMICS
1943 (Not reprints)
Dell Publishing Co.

1-Kelly-a(2); fairy tales 32.00 95.00 25.00

TIPPY & CAP STUBBS (See 4-Color #210, 242 & Popular Comics)

TIPPY'S FRIENDS GO-GO & ANIMAL
July, 1966 - No. 15, Oct, 1969 (25 cents)
Tower Comics

1 3.60 9.00 18.00
2-5,7,9-15: 12-15 titled "Tippy's Friend Go-Go" 2.40 6.00 12.00
6-The Monkees photo-c 5.00 15.00 30.00
8-Beatles app. on front/back-c 7.50 22.50 45.00

TIPPY TEEN (See Vicki)
Nov, 1965 - No. 27, Feb, 1970 (25 cents)
Tower Comics

1 2.15 6.50 15.00
2-27: 5-1pg. Beatles pin-up. 16-Twiggy photo-c 1.30 3.25 8.00
Special Collectors' Editions nn-(1969, 25 cents) 1.30 3.25 8.00

TIPPY TERRY
1963
Super/I. W. Enterprises

Super Reprint #14('63)-Little Grouchy reprints .60 1.50 3.00
I.W. Reprint #1 (nd) .60 1.50 3.00

TIP TOP COMICS
4/36 - No. 210, 1957; No. 211, 11-1/57-58 - No. 225, 5-7/61
United Features #1-187/St. John #188-210/Dell Publishing Co. #211 on

GD25 FN65 VF82 NM94

1-Tarzan by Hal Foster, Li'l Abner, Broncho Bill, Fritzi Ritz, Ella Cinders, Capt. & The Kids begin; strip-r (1st comic book app. of each)
500.00 1500.00 2500.00 3500.00
(Estimated up to 80 total copies exist, 4 in NM/Mint)

GD25 FN65 VF82

2 108.00 325.00 750.00
3 85.00 260.00 600.00
4 62.00 188.00 425.00
5-10: 7-Photo & biography of Edgar Rice Burroughs. 8-Christmas-c
50.00 150.00 350.00

GD25 FN65 NM94

11-20: 20-Christmas-c 42.00 125.00 275.00
21-31,33-35,37-40 32.00 95.00 210.00
32,36: 32-1st published Jack Davis-a (cartoon). 36-Kurtzman panel (1st published comic work) 32.00 95.00 225.00
41-Reprints 1st Tarzan Sunday 32.00 95.00 210.00
42-50: 43-Mort Walker panel 28.00 85.00 190.00
51-53 25.00 75.00 165.00
54-Origin Mirror Man & Triple Terror, also featured on cover
32.00 95.00 210.00
55,56,58,60: Last Tarzan by Foster 19.00 57.00 125.00
57,59,61,62-Tarzan by Hogarth 25.00 75.00 165.00
63-80: 65,67-70,72-74,77,78-No Tarzan 11.50 34.00 80.00
81-90 10.00 30.00 70.00
91-99 9.15 27.50 55.00
100 10.00 30.00 65.00
101-140: 110-Gordo story. 111-Li'l Abner app. 118, 132-No Tarzan. 137-Sadie Hawkins Day story 5.85 17.50 35.00
141-170: 145,151-Gordo stories. 157-Last Li'l Abner; lingerie panels
4.00 12.50 25.00
171-188-Tarzan reprints by B. Lubbers in all. 177-Peanuts by Schulz begins?; no Peanuts in #178,179,181-183 4.70 14.00 28.00
189-225 3.60 9.00 18.00
Bound Volumes (Very Rare) sold at 1939 World's Fair; bound by publisher in pictorial comic boards (also see Comics on Parade)
Bound issues 1-12 200.00 600.00 1400.00
Bound issues 13-24 133.00 400.00 900.00
Bound issues 25-36 108.00 325.00 750.00
NOTE: *Tarzan covers-#1(part), 2(part), 3, 9, 11, 13, 16, 18, 21, 24, 27, 30, 32-34, 36, 37, 39, 41, 43, 45, 47, 50, 52 (all worth 10-20 percent more). Tarzan by **Foster**-#1-40, 44-50; by **Rex Maxon**-#41-43; by **Burne Hogarth**-#57, 59, 62.*

TIP TOPPER COMICS
Oct-Nov, 1949 - No. 28, 1954
United Features Syndicate

1-Li'l Abner, Abbie & Slats 8.35 25.00 50.00
2 5.00 15.00 30.00
3-5: 5-Fearless Fosdick app. 4.20 12.50 25.00
6-10: 6-Fearless Fosdick app. 4.00 11.00 22.00
11-25: 17-22,24,26-Peanuts app. (2 pgs.) 3.20 8.00 16.00
26-28-Twin Earths 4.35 13.00 26.00
NOTE: *Many lingerie panels in Fritzi Ritz stories.*

TITANS SELL-OUT SPECIAL
Nov, 1992 ($3.50, color, 52 pgs.)
DC Comics

1-Fold-out Nightwing poster; 1st Teeny Titans 1.40 3.50

T-MAN (Also see Police Comics #103)
Sept, 1951 - No. 38, Dec, 1956
Quality Comics Group

1-Jack Cole-a 22.00 65.00 150.00
2-Crandall-c 11.50 34.00 80.00
3,6-8: All Crandall-c 10.00 30.00 70.00
4,5-Crandall-c/a each 11.00 32.00 75.00
9,10-Crandall-c 10.00 30.00 60.00
11-Used in **POP**, pg. 95 & color illo. 7.50 22.50 45.00
12-19,21,22,24,26: 24-Last pre-code (4/55) 5.85 17.50 35.00
20,23-H-Bomb explosion-c/stories 9.15 27.50 55.00
25-All Crandall-a 8.35 25.00 50.00
27-38 5.00 15.00 30.00
NOTE: *Anti-communist stories common. **Crandall** c-2-10p. **Cuidera** c(i)-1-38. Bondage c-15.*

TMNT MUTANT UNIVERSE SOURCEBOOK
1992 - Present ($1.95, color, 52 pgs.)(Lists characters from A-Z)
Archie Comics

1-3: 3-New characters; fold-out poster .80 2.00

TNT COMICS
Feb, 1946 (36 pgs.)
Charles Publishing Co.

1-Yellowjacket app. 15.00 45.00 100.00

TOBY TYLER (See 4-Color #1092 and Movie Comics)

TODAY'S BRIDES
Nov, 1955; No. 2, Feb, 1956; No. 3, Sept, 1956; No. 4, Nov, 1956
Ajax/Farrell Publishing Co.

1 4.70 14.00 28.00
2-4 3.20 8.00 16.00

TODAY'S ROMANCE
No. 5, March, 1952 - No. 8, Sept, 1952 (All photo-c?)
Standard Comics

5-Photo-c 4.70 14.00 28.00
6-Photo-c; Toth-a 5.35 16.00 32.00
7,8 2.80 7.00 14.00

TOKA (Jungle King)
Aug-Oct, 1964 - No. 10, Jan, 1967 (Painted-c #1,2)

Tomahawk #2, © DC

Tomb of Dracula #50, © MEG

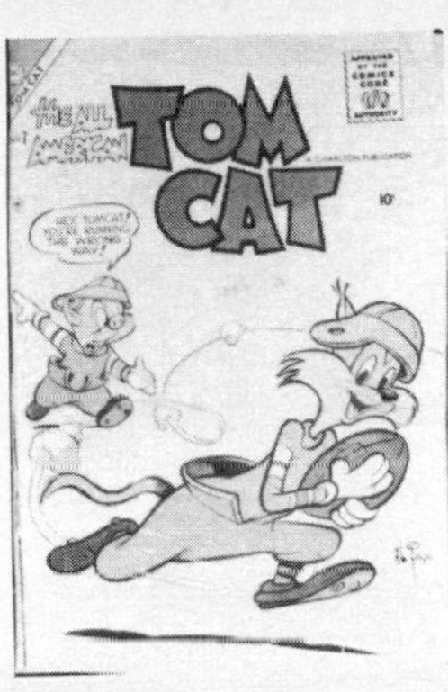

Tom Cat #7, © CC

	GD25	FN65	NM94
Dell Publishing Co.			
1	2.00	6.00	14.00
2	1.20	3.00	7.00
3-10	1.00	2.50	6.00

TOMAHAWK (Son of... on-c of #131-140; see Star Spangled Comics #69 & World's Finest Comics #65)
Sept-Oct, 1950 - No. 140, May-June, 1972
National Periodical Publications

	GD25	FN65	NM94
1-Tomahawk & boy sidekick Dan Hunter begin by Fred Ray	93.00	280.00	650.00
2-Frazetta/Williamson-a (4 pgs.)	45.00	135.00	315.00
3-5	30.00	90.00	210.00
6-10: 7-Last 52 pg. issue	22.00	65.00	150.00
11-20	14.00	43.00	100.00
21-27,30: 30-Last precode (2/55)	11.00	32.00	75.00
28-1st app. Lord Shilling (arch-foe)	12.00	36.00	85.00
29-Frazetta-r/Jimmy Wakely #3 (3 pgs.)	16.00	50.00	115.00
31-40	10.00	30.00	70.00
41-50	9.15	27.50	55.00
51-56,58-60	6.70	20.00	40.00
57-Frazetta-r/Jimmy Wakely #6 (3 pgs.)	10.00	30.00	70.00
61-77: 77-Last 10 cent issue	5.00	15.00	30.00
78-85: 81-1st app. Miss Liberty. 83-Origin Tomahawk's Rangers	4.00	10.00	20.00
86-100: 96-Origin/1st app. The Hood, alias Lady Shilling	2.40	6.00	12.00
101-110: 107-Origin/1st app. Thunder-Man	1.80	4.50	9.00
111-130,132-138,140	1.00	2.00	5.00
131-Frazetta-r/Jimmy Wakely #7 (3 pgs.); origin Firehair retold	1.00	2.50	6.00
139-Frazetta-r/Star Spangled #113		1.60	4.00

NOTE: ***Neal Adams** c-116-119, 121, 123-130. **Fred Ray** c-1-4, 7-19, 21-25, 28. Firehair by **Kubert**-131-134, 136. **Maurer** a-138. **Severin** a-135. **Starr** a-5. **Thorne** a-137, 140.*

TOM AND JERRY (See Comic Album #4, 8, 12, Dell Giant #21, Dell Giants, Four Color #193, Golden Comics Digest #1, 5, 8, 13, 15, 18, 22, 25, 28, 35, Kite fun Book & March of Comics #21, 46, 61, 70, 88, 103, 119, 128, 145, 154, 173, 190, 207, 224, 281, 295, 305, 321, 333, 345, 361, 365, 388, 400, 444, 451, 463, 480)

TOM AND JERRY (...Comics, early issues) (M.G.M.)
(Formerly Our Gang No. 1-59) (See Dell Giants for annuals)
No. 193, 6/48; No. 60, 7/49 - No. 212, 7-9/62; No. 213, 11/62 - No. 291, 2/75; No. 292, 3/77 - No. 342, 5/82 - No. 344, 1982?
Dell Publishing Co./Gold Key No. 213-327/Whitman No. 328 on

	GD25	FN65	NM94
4-Color 193 (#1)-Titled "M.G.M. Presents..."	12.00	36.00	85.00
60	7.50	22.50	45.00
61	6.70	20.00	40.00
62-70: 66-X-mas-c	5.00	15.00	30.00
71-80: 77-X-mas-c	4.00	12.00	24.00
81-99: 90-X-mas-c	4.00	10.00	20.00
100	4.00	11.00	22.00
101-120	3.20	8.00	16.00
121-140: 126-X-mas-c	2.80	7.00	14.00
141-160	2.00	5.00	10.00
161-200	1.60	4.00	8.00
201-212(7-9/62)(Last Dell issue)	1.40	3.50	7.00
213,214-(84 pgs.)-Titled "...Funhouse"	4.00	12.00	24.00
215-240: 215-Titled "...Funhouse"	1.00	2.50	6.00
241-270	1.00	2.00	5.00
271-300: 286 "Tom & Jerry"		1.20	3.00
301-344			1.50
Mouse From T.R.A.P. 1(7/66)-Giant, G. K.	4.00	11.00	22.00
Summer Fun 1(7/67, 68pgs.)(Gold Key)-Reprints Barks' Droopy from Summer Fun #1	4.00	11.00	22.00

NOTE: *#60-87, 98-121, 268, 277, 289, 302 are 52 pages. Reprints-#225, 241, 245, 247, 252, 254, 266, 268, 270, 292-327, 329-342, 344.*

TOM & JERRY (Harvey)(Value: cover or less)

TOM & JERRY AND FRIENDS (Harvey)(Value: cover or less)

TOMB OF DARKNESS (Formerly Beware)
No. 9, July, 1974 - No. 23, Nov, 1976
Marvel Comics Group

	GD25	FN65	NM94
9-23: 15,19-Ditko-r. 17-Woodbridge-r/Astonishing #62; Powell-r. 20-Everett Venus-r/Venus #19. 22-r/Venus #19. 23-Everett-r		.60	1.25

TOMB OF DRACULA (See Giant-Size Dracula, Dracula Lives, Power Record Comics & Requiem for Dracula)
April, 1972 - No. 70, Aug, 1979
Marvel Comics Group

	GD25	FN65	NM94
1-1st app. Dracula; Colan-p in all	8.00	24.00	55.00
2	5.00	15.00	35.00
3-5: 3-Intro. Dr. Rachel Van Helsing & Inspector Chelm	3.30	10.00	23.00
6-10: 10-1st app. Blade the Vampire Slayer	2.40	7.25	17.00
11-20: 12-Brunner-c(p). 13-Origin Blade	1.65	4.70	11.00
21-40	1.40	3.50	8.50
41-49,51-60	1.00	2.50	5.50
50-Silver Surfer app.	1.40	3.50	8.50
61-70: 70-Double size		1.80	4.50

NOTE: ***N. Adams** c-1, 6. **Colan** a-1-70p; c(p)-8, 38-42, 44-56, 58-70. **Wrightson** c-43.*

TOMB OF DRACULA, THE (Magazine)
Oct, 1979 - No. 6, Aug, 1980 (B&W)
Marvel Comics Group

	GD25	FN65	NM94
1,4-6		1.40	3.50
2,3: 2-Ditko-a (36 pgs.). 3-Miller-a(2 pg. sketch)		1.80	4.50

NOTE: ***Buscema** a-4p, 5p. **Chaykin** c-5, 6. **Colan** a(p)-1, 3-6. **Miller** a-3. **Romita** a-2p.*

TOMB OF DRACULA
1991 - No. 4, 1992 ($4.95, color, squarebound, mini-series, 52 pgs.)
Epic Comics (Marvel)

	GD25	FN65	NM94
Book 1-4: Colan/Williamson-a; Colan painted-c	1.00	2.00	5.00

TOMB OF LEGEIA (See Movie Classics)

TOMB OF TERROR (Thrills of Tomorrow #17 on)
June, 1952 - No. 16, July, 1954
Harvey Publications

	GD25	FN65	NM94
1	14.00	43.00	100.00
2	9.15	27.50	55.00
3-Bondage-c; atomic disaster story	10.00	30.00	65.00
4-12: 4-Heart ripped out. 8-12-Nostrand-a	9.15	27.50	55.00
13,14-Special S/F issues. 14-Check-a	11.00	32.00	75.00
15-S/F issue; c-shows head exploding	13.00	40.00	90.00
16-Special S/F issue; Nostrand-a	11.00	32.00	75.00

NOTE: ***Edd Cartier** a-13? **Elias** c-2, 5-16. **Kremer** a-1, 7; c-1. **Nostrand** a-8-12, 15r 16. **Palais** a-2, 3, 5-7. **Powell** a-1, 3, 5, 9-16. **Sparling** a-12, 13, 15.*

TOMBSTONE TERRITORY (See 4-Color #1123)

TOM CAT (Formerly Bo; Atom The Cat #9 on)
No. 4, Apr, 1956 - No. 8, July, 1957
Charlton Comics

	GD25	FN65	NM94
4-Al Fago-c/a	4.20	12.50	25.00
5-8	3.20	8.00	16.00

TOM CORBETT, SPACE CADET (TV)
No. 378, Jan-Feb, 1952 - No. 11, Sept-Nov, 1954 (All painted covers)
Dell Publishing Co.

	GD25	FN65	NM94
4-Color 378 (#1)-McWilliams-a	16.00	48.00	110.00
4-Color 400,421-McWilliams-a	10.00	30.00	60.00
4(11-1/53) - 11	6.70	20.00	40.00

TOM CORBETT SPACE CADET (See March of Comics #102)

TOM CORBETT SPACE CADET (TV)
V2#1, May-June, 1955 - V2#3, Sept-Oct, 1955
Prize Publications

	GD25	FN65	NM94
V2#1	16.00	50.00	115.00

Tom Mix Western #26, © FAW

Tomorrow Knights #3, © MEG

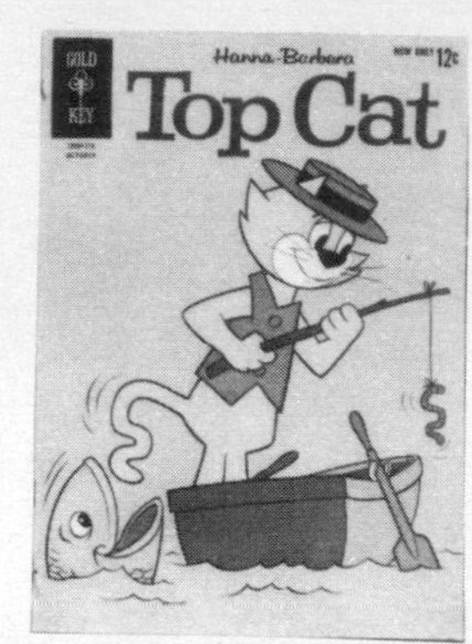

Top Cat #4 (Gold Key), © Hanna-Barbera

GD25 FN65 NM94

2,3-Meskin-c 15.00 45.00 105.00

TOM, DICK & HARRIET (See Gold Key Spotlight)

TOM LANDRY AND THE DALLAS COWBOYS (Spire Christiain)(Value: cover or less)

TOM MIX (...Commandos Comics #10-12)
Sept, 1940 - No. 12, Nov, 1942 (36 pages); 1983 (One-shot)
Given away for two Ralston box-tops; in cereal box, 1983
Ralston-Purina Co.

1-Origin (life) Tom Mix; Fred Meagher-a 171.00 515.00 1200.00
2 64.00 195.00 450.00
3-9 46.00 140.00 325.00
10-12: 10-Origin Tom Mix Commando Unit; Speed O'Dare begins; Japanese sub-c. 12-Sci/fi-c 38.00 115.00 265.00
1983-"Taking of Grizzly Grebb," Toth-a; 16 pg. miniature 1.20 3.00 6.00

TOM MIX WESTERN (Movie, radio star) (Also see The Comics, Crackajack Funnies, Master Comics, 100 Pages Of Comics, Popular Comics, Real Western Hero, Six Gun Heroes, Western Hero & XMas Comics)
Jan, 1948 - No. 61, May, 1953 (1-17: 52 pgs.)
Fawcett Publications

1 (Photo-c, 52 pgs.)-Tom Mix & his horse Tony begin; Tumbleweed Jr. begins, ends #52,54,55 71.00 215.00 500.00
2 (Photo-c) 32.00 95.00 225.00
3-5 (Painted/photo-c): 5-Billy the Kid & Oscar app. 25.00 75.00 175.00
6,7 (Painted/photo-c) 20.00 60.00 140.00
8-Kinstler tempera-c 20.00 60.00 140.00
9,10 (Painted/photo-c)-Used in **SOTI**, pgs. 323-25 18.00 54.00 125.00
11-Kinstler oil-c 17.00 52.00 120.00
12 (Painted/photo-c) 14.00 43.00 100.00
13-17 (Painted-c, 52 pgs.) 14.00 43.00 100.00
18,22 (Painted-c, 36 pgs.) 12.00 36.00 85.00
19 (Photo-c, 52 pgs.) 13.00 40.00 90.00
20,21,23 (Painted-c, 52 pgs.) 11.00 32.00 75.00
24,25,27-29 (52 pgs.): 24-Photo-c begin, end #61. 29-Slim Pickens app. 11.00 32.00 75.00
26,30 (36 pgs.) 10.00 30.00 70.00
31-33,35-37,39,40,42 (52 pgs.): 39-Red Eagle app. 10.00 30.00 65.00
34,38 (36 pgs. begin) 9.15 27.50 55.00
41,43-60 6.70 20.00 40.00
61-Last issue 8.35 25.00 50.00

NOTE: *Photo-c from 1930s Tom Mix movies (he died in 1940). Many issues contain ads for Tom Mix, Rocky Lane, Space Patrol and other premiums. Captain Tootsie by* ***C.C. Beck*** *in #6-11, 20.*

TOM MIX WESTERN
1988 - No. 2, 1989? ($2.95, B&W w/16 pgs. color, 44 pgs.)
AC Comics

1-Tom Mix-r/Master #124,128,131,102 plus Billy the Kid-r by Severin; photo front/back/inside-c 1.20 3.00
2-($2.50, B&W)-Gabby Hayes-r; photo covers 1.00 2.50
...Holiday Album 1 (1990, $3.50, B&W, one-shot, 44 pgs.)-Contains photos & 1950s Tom Mix-r; photo inside-c 1.40 3.50

TOMMY OF THE BIG TOP
No. 10, Sept, 1948 - No. 12, Mar, 1949
King Features Syndicate/Standard Comics

10-By John Lehti 4.20 12.50 25.00
11,12 3.00 7.50 15.00

TOMMY TOMORROW (See Action Comics #127, Real Fact #6 & World's Finest #102)

TOMORROW KNIGHTS (Marvel)(Value: cover or less)

TOM SAWYER (See Adventures of... & Famous Stories)

TOM SAWYER & HUCK FINN
1925 (52 pgs.) (10-3/4x10") (stiff covers)
Stoll & Edwards Co.

nn-By Dwiggins; reprints 1923, 1924 Sunday strips in color 17.00 52.00 120.00

GD25 FN65 NM94

TOM SAWYER COMICS
1951? (paper cover)
Giveaway

nn-Contains a coverless Hopalong Cassidy from 1951; other combinations possible 1.60 4.00 8.00

TOM SKINNER-UP FROM HARLEM (See Up From Harlem)

TOM TERRIFIC! (TV)(See Mighty Mouse Fun Club Magazine #1)
Summer, 1957 - No. 6, Fall, 1958 (See Terry Toons Giant Summer Fun Book)
Pines Comics (Paul Terry)

1-1st app.?; see Terry Toons G.S. Fun Book 14.00 43.00 100.00
2-6 11.00 32.00 75.00

TOM THUMB (See 4-Color #972)

TOM-TOM, THE JUNGLE BOY (See A-1 Comics & Tick Tock Tales)
1947 - No. 3, 1947; Nov, 1957 - No. 3, Mar, 1958
Magazine Enterprises

1-Funny animal 5.85 17.50 35.00
2,3(1947): 3-Christmas issue 4.20 12.50 25.00
Tom-Tom & Itchi the Monk 1(11/57) - 3(3/58) 2.40 6.00 12.00
I.W. Reprint No. 1,2,8,10 .60 1.50 3.00

TONKA (See 4-Color #966)

TONTO (See The Lone Ranger's Companion...)

TONY TRENT (The Face #1,2)
No. 3, 1948 - No. 4, 1949
Big Shot/Columbia Comics Group

3,4: 3-The Face app. by Mart Bailey 10.00 30.00 60.00

TOODLES, THE (The Toodle Twins with #1)
No. 10, July-Aug, 1951; Mar, 1956 (Newspaper-r)
Ziff-Davis (Approved Comics)/Argo

10-Painted-c, some newspaper-r by The Baers 5.00 15.00 30.00
...Twins 1(Argo, 3/56)-Reprints by The Baers 4.00 12.00 24.00

TOONERVILLE TROLLEY
1921 (Daily strip reprints) (B&W) (52 pgs.)
Cupples & Leon Co.

1-By Fontaine Fox 25.00 75.00 175.00

TOOTS & CASPER (See Large Feature Comic #5)

TOP ADVENTURE COMICS
1964 (Reprints)
I. W. Enterprises

1-r/High Adv. (Explorer Joe #2); Krigstein-r 2.00 5.00 10.00
2-Black Dwarf-r/Red Seal #22; Kinstler-c 2.00 5.00 10.00

TOP CAT (TV) (Hanna-Barbera)(See Kite Fun Book)
12-2/61-62 - No. 3, 6-8/62; No. 4, 10/62 - No. 31, 9/70
Dell Publishing Co./Gold Key No. 4 on

1 (TV show debuted 9/27/61) 13.00 40.00 90.00
2 7.50 22.50 45.00
3-5: 3-Last 15¢ issue. 4-Begin 12¢ issues; 1st app. Yakky Doodle in 1 pg. strip. 5-1st app. Touche' Turtle 5.00 15.00 30.00
6-10 4.00 10.00 20.00
11-20 3.00 7.50 15.00
21-31: 21,24,25,29-Reprints 1.65 4.00 10.00

NOTE: *Augie Doggie back up stories in #1-4.*

TOP CAT (TV) (Hanna-Barbera)(See TV Stars #4)
Nov, 1970 - No. 20, Nov, 1973
Charlton Comics

1 3.60 10.75 25.00
2-10 2.15 6.50 15.00
11-20 1.65 4.00 10.00

NOTE: *#8 (1/72) went on sale late in 1972 between #14 and #15 with the 1/73 issues.*

TOP COMICS

Topix V9#29, © CG

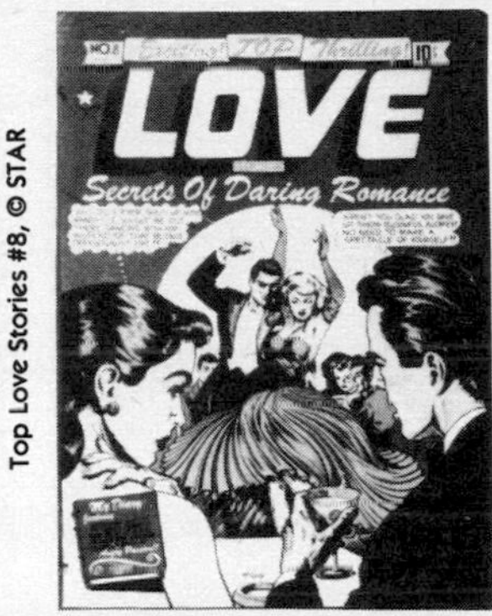

Top Love Stories #8, © STAR

Top-Notch Comics #21, © AP

GD25 FN65 NM94

July, 1967 (All reprints)
K. K. Publications/Gold Key

nn-The Gnome-Mobile (Disney-movie) 1.60 4.00 8.00
1-Beagle Boys (#7), Beep Beep the Road Runner (#5), Bugs Bunny, Chip 'n' Dale, Daffy Duck (#50), Flipper, Huckleberry Hound, Huey, Dewey & Louie, Junior Woodchucks, Lassie, The Little Monsters (#71), Moby Duck, Porky Pig (has Gold Key label - says Top Comics on inside), Scamp, Super Goof, Tarzan of the Apes (#169), Three Stooges (#35), Tom & Jerry Top Cat (#21), Tweety & Sylvester (#7), Walt Disney C&S (#322), Woody Woodpecker, Yogi Bear, Zorro (r/G.K. Zorro #7 w/Toth-a; says 2nd printing) known; each character given own book 1.60 4.00 8.00
1-Uncle Scrooge (#70) 2.40 6.00 12.00
1-Donald Duck (not Barks), Mickey Mouse 2.00 5.00 10.00
1-Flintstones 4.20 12.50 25.00
1-The Jetsons 5.85 17.50 35.00
2 Bugs Bunny, Daffy Duck, Donald Duck (not Barks), Mickey Mouse (#114), Porky Pig, Super Goof, Three Stooges, Tom & Jerry, Tweety & Sylvester, Uncle Scrooge (#71)-Barks-c, Walt Disney's C&S (r/#325), Woody Woodpecker, Yogi Bear (#30), Zorro (r/#8; Toth-a) 1.60 4.00 8.00
2-Snow White & 7 Dwarfs(6/67)(1944-r) 2.00 5.00 10.00
3-Donald Duck 1.80 4.50 9.00
3-Uncle Scrooge (#72) 2.00 6.00 12.00
3,4-The Flintstones 4.20 12.50 25.00
3-Mickey Mouse (r/#115), Tom & Jerry, Woody Woodpecker, Yogi Bear 1.60 4.00 8.00
4-Mickey Mouse, Woody Woodpecker 1.60 4.00 8.00

NOTE: *Each book in this series is identical to its counterpart except for cover, and came out at same time. The number in parentheses is the original issue it contains.*

TOP DETECTIVE COMICS
1964 (Reprints)
I. W. Enterprises

9-r/Young King Cole #14; Dr. Drew (not Grandenetti) 1.20 3.00 6.00

TOP DOG (See Star Comics Magazine, 75 cents)
Apr, 1985 - No. 14, June, 1987 (Children's book)
Star Comics (Marvel)

1-14: 10-Peter Parker & J. Jonah Jameson cameo 1.00

TOP ELIMINATOR (Teenage Hotrodders #1-24; Drag 'n' Wheels #30 on)
No. 25, Sept, 1967 - No. 29, July, 1968
Charlton Comics

25-29 1.00 2.50 6.00

TOP FLIGHT COMICS
1947; July, 1949
Four Star Publications/St. John Publishing Co.

1(1947) 6.70 20.00 40.00
1(7/49, St. John)-Hector the Inspector 5.00 15.00 30.00

TOP GUN (See 4-Color #927 & Showcase #72)

TOP GUNS OF THE WEST (See Super DC Giant)

TOPIX (...Comics) (Timeless Topix-early issues) (Also see Men of Battle, Men of Courage & Treasure Chest)(V1-V5#1,V7#1-20-paper c)
11/42 - V10#15, 1/28/52 (Weekly - later issues)
Catechetical Guild Educational Society

V1#1(8pgs.,8x11") 11.50 34.00 80.00
2,3(8pgs.,8x11") 8.35 25.00 50.00
4-8(16pgs.,8x11") 5.85 17.50 35.00
V2#1-10(16pgs.,8x11"): V2#8-Pope Pius XII 4.20 12.50 25.00
V3#1-10(16pgs.,8x11") 4.20 12.50 25.00
V4#1-10 4.00 11.00 22.00
V5#1(10/46,52pgs.)-9,12-15(12/47)-#13 shows V5#4 3.00 7.50 15.00
10,11-Life of Christ editions 4.70 14.00 28.00
V6#1-14 2.00 5.00 10.00
V7#1(9/1/48)-20(6/15/49), 32pgs. 2.00 5.00 10.00
V8#1(9/19/49)-3,5-11,13-30(5/15/50) 2.00 5.00 10.00
4-Dagwood Splits the Atom(10/10/49)-Magazine format 3.00 7.50 15.00
12-Ingels-a 5.00 15.00 30.00
V9#1(9/25/50)-11,13-30(5/14/51) 1.60 4.00 8.00
12-Special 36pg. Xmas issue, text illos format 2.00 5.00 10.00
V10#1(10/1/51)-15: 14-Hollingsworth-a 1.60 4.00 8.00

TOP JUNGLE COMICS
1964 (Reprint)
I. W. Enterprises

1(nd)-Reprints White Princess of the Jungle #3, minus cover 2.00 5.00 10.00

TOP LOVE STORIES (Formerly Gasoline Alley #2)
No. 3, 5/51 - No. 19, 3/54
Star Publications

3(#1) 8.35 25.00 50.00
4,5,7-9 6.70 20.00 40.00
6-Wood-a 10.00 30.00 70.00
10-16,18,19-Disbrow-a 6.70 20.00 40.00
17-Wood art (Fox-r) 8.35 25.00 50.00

NOTE: *All have* ***L. B. Cole*** *covers.*

TOP-NOTCH COMICS (...Laugh #28-45; Laugh Comix #46 on)
Dec, 1939 - No. 45, June, 1944
MLJ Magazines

1-Origin/1st app. The Wizard; Kardak the Mystic Magician, Swift of the Secret Service (ends #3), Air Patrol, The Westpointer, Manhunters (by J. Cole), Mystic (ends #2) & Scott Rand (ends #3) begin; Wizard covers begin, end #8 270.00 815.00 1900.00
2-Dick Storm (ends #8), Stacy Knight M.D. (ends #4) begin; Jack Cole-a 107.00 320.00 750.00
3-Bob Phantom, Scott Rand on Mars begin; J. Cole-a 86.00 260.00 600.00
4-Origin/1st app. Streak Chandler on Mars; Moore of the Mounted only app.; J. Cole-a 64.00 195.00 450.00
5-Flag-c; origin/1st app. Galahad, Shanghai Sheridan begins (ends #8); Shield cameo; Novick-a 64.00 195.00 450.00
6-Meskin-a 54.00 160.00 375.00
7-The Shield x-over in Wizard; The Wizard dons new costume 64.00 195.00 450.00
8-Origin/1st app. The Firefly & Roy, the Super Boy (9/40, 2nd costumed boy hero after Robin?; also see Toro in Human Torch #1 (Fall/40) 71.00 215.00 500.00
9-Origin & 1st app. The Black Hood; 1st Black Hood-c & logo (10/40); Fran Frazier begins 217.00 650.00 1500.00
10 88.00 265.00 600.00
11-20 48.00 145.00 335.00
21-30: 23-26-Roy app. 24-No Wizard. 25-Last Bob Phantom. 27-Last Firefly. 28-Suzie begins. 29-Last Kardak 39.00 120.00 275.00
31-44: 33-Dotty & Ditto by Woggon begins (2/43, 1st app.). 44-Black Hood series ends 23.00 70.00 160.00
45-Last issue 25.00 75.00 175.00

NOTE: ***J. Binder*** *a-1-3.* ***Meskin*** *a-2, 3, 6, 15.* ***Bob Montana*** *a-30, c-28-31.* ***Harry Sahle*** *c-42-45.* ***Woggon*** *a-33-40, 42. Bondage c-17, 19. Black Hood also appeared on radio in 1944. Black Hood app. on c-9-34, 41-44. Roy the Super Boy app. on c-8, 9, 11-27. The Wizard app. on c-1-8, 11-13, 15-22, 24, 25, 27.*

TOPPER & NEIL (See 4-Color #859)

TOPPS COMICS
1947
Four Star Publications

1-L. B. Cole-c 10.00 30.00 60.00

TOPS
July, 1949 - No. 2, Sept, 1949 (25 cents, 68 pgs.) (10-1/4x13-1/4")
(Large size-magazine format; for the adult reader)
Tops Magazine, Inc. (Lev Gleason)

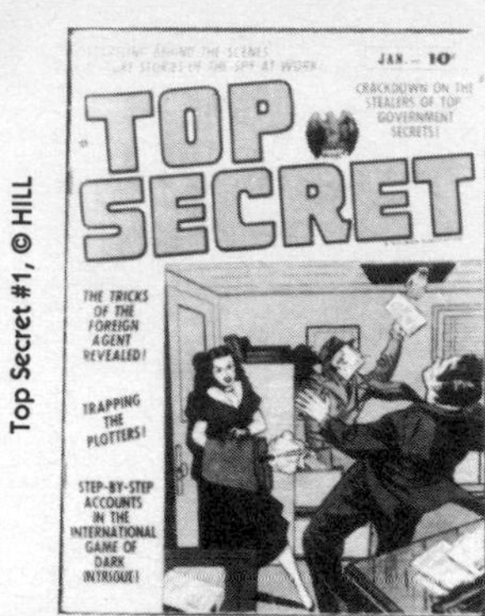

Top Secret #1, © HILL

Tor 3-D #2 (Eclipse), © Joe Kubert

The Tormented #1, © Sterling Comics

GD25 FN65 NM94

1 (Rare)-Story by Dashiell Hammett; Crandall/Lubbers, Tuska, Dan Barry, Fuje-a; Biro painted-c 83.00 250.00 550.00
2 (Rare)-Crandall/Lubbers, Biro, Kida, Fuje, Guardineer-a 75.00 225.00 500.00

TOPS COMICS
1944 (132 pages) (10 cents)
Consolidated Book Publishers

2000-(Color-c, inside in red shade & some in full color)-Ace Kelly by Rick Yager, Black Orchid, Don on the Farm, Dinky Dinkerton (Rare) 22.00 65.00 140.00
NOTE: *This book is printed in such a way that when the staple is removed, the strips on the left side of the book correspond with the same strips on the right side. Therefore, if strips are removed from the book, each strip can be folded into a complete comic section of its own.*

TOPS COMICS (See Tops in Humor)
1944 (Small size, 32 pgs.) (7-1/4x5")
Consolidated Book (Lev Gleason)

2001-The Jack of Spades (costumed hero) 11.00 32.00 75.00
2002-Rip Raider 6.70 20.00 40.00
2003-Red Birch (gag cartoons) 1.60 4.00 8.00

TOP SECRET
January, 1952
Hillman Publ.

1 11.50 34.00 80.00

TOP SECRET ADVENTURES (See Spyman)

TOP SECRETS (...of the F.B.I.)
Nov, 1947 - No. 10, July-Aug, 1949
Street & Smith Publications

1-Powell-c/a 20.00 60.00 140.00
2-Powell-c/a 14.00 43.00 100.00
3-6,8-10-Powell-a 12.00 36.00 85.00
7-Used in **SOTI**, pg. 90 & illo.-"How to hurt people;" used by N.Y. Legis. Comm.; Powell-c/a 18.00 54.00 125.00
NOTE: ***Powell** c-1-3, 5-10.*

TOPS IN ADVENTURE
Fall, 1952 (25 cents, 132 pages)
Ziff-Davis Publishing Co.

1-Crusader from Mars, The Hawk, Football Thrills, He-Man; Powell-a; painted-c 30.00 90.00 210.00

TOPS IN HUMOR (See Tops Comics?)
1944 (Small size) (7-1/4x5")
Consolidated Book Publ. (Lev Gleason)

2001(#1)-Origin The Jack of Spades, Ace Kelly by Rick Yager, Black Orchid (female crime fighter) app. 12.00 36.00 85.00
2 7.50 22.50 45.00

TOP SPOT COMICS
1945
Top Spot Publ. Co.

1-The Menace, Duke of Darkness app. 16.00 48.00 110.00

TOPSY-TURVY
April, 1945
R. B. Leffingwell Publ.

1-1st app. Cookie 6.35 19.00 38.00

TOR (Prehistoric Life on Earth) (Formerly One Million Years Ago)
No. 2, Oct, 1953; No. 3, May, 1954 - No. 5, Oct, 1954
St. John Publishing Co.

3-D 2(10/53)-Kubert-c/a 10.00 30.00 65.00
3-D 2(10/53)-Oversized, otherwise same contents 9.15 27.50 55.00
3-D 2(11/53)-Kubert-c/a 9.15 27.50 55.00
3-5-Kubert-c/a; 3-Danny Dreams by Toth 10.00 30.00 65.00
NOTE: *The two October 3-D's have same contents and **Powell** art; the October & November issues are titled 3-D Comics.*

GD25 FN65 NM94

TOR (See Sojourn)
May-June, 1975 - No. 6, Mar-Apr, 1976
National Periodical Publications

1-6: 1-New origin by Kubert. 2-Origin-r/St. John #1 1.00
NOTE: ***Kubert** a-1, 2-6r; c-1-6. **Toth** a(p)-3r.*

TOR (3-D)(Eclipse)(Value: cover or less)

TOR
June, 1993 - No. 4, 1993 ($5.95, color, mini-series)
Epic Comics (Marvel)

1-4: Joe Kubert-a & story 1.00 2.50 6.00

TORCHY (...Blonde Bombshell) (See Dollman, Military, & Modern)
Nov, 1949 - No. 6, Sept, 1950
Quality Comics Group

1-Bill Ward-c, Gil Fox-a 79.00 235.00 550.00
2,3-Fox-c/a 36.00 107.00 250.00
4-Fox-c/a(3), Ward-a, 9pgs. 47.00 140.00 325.00
5,6-Ward-c/a, 9 pgs; Fox-a(3) each 57.00 170.00 390.00
Super Reprint #16(1964)-r/#4 with new-c 6.70 20.00 40.00

TO RIVERDALE AND BACK AGAIN (Archie Comics Presents...)
1990 ($2.50, 68 pgs.)
Archie Comics

nn-Byrne-c, Colan-a(p); adapts NBC TV movie 1.00 2.50

TORMENTED, THE (Becomes Surprise Adventures #3 on)
July, 1954 - No. 2, Sept, 1954
Sterling Comics

1,2-Weird/horror stories 10.00 30.00 70.00

TORNADO TOM (See Mighty Midget Comics)

TOTAL ECLIPSE (Eclipse)(Value: cover or less)

TOTAL ECLIPSE: THE SERAPHIM OBJECTIVE (Eclipse)(Value: cover or less)

TOTAL RECALL (DC)(Value: cover or less)

TOTAL WAR (M.A.R.S. Patrol #3 on)
July, 1965 - No. 2, Oct, 1965 (Painted covers)
Gold Key

1,2-Wood-a in each 3.85 11.50 27.00

TOUGH KID SQUAD COMICS
March, 1942
Timely Comics (TCI)

GD25 FN65 VF82 NM94
1-(Scarce)-Origin & 1st app.The Human Top & The Tough Kid Squad; The Flying Flame app. 525.00 1575.00 2890.00 4200.00
(Estimated up to 100 total copies exist, 6 in NM/Mint)

TOWER OF SHADOWS (Creatures on the Loose #10 on)
Sept, 1969 - No. 9, Jan, 1971
Marvel Comics Group

GD25 FN65 NM94
1-Steranko, Craig-a 3.20 8.00 20.00
2-Neal Adams-a 1.65 4.00 10.00
3-Barry Smith, Tuska-a 1.65 4.00 10.00
4-Marie Severin-c 1.20 3.00 7.00
5,7-B. Smith(p), Wood-a. 5-Wood draws himself (1st pg., 1st panel) 1.50 3.75 9.00
6,8: Wood-a; 8-Wrightson-c 1.20 3.00 7.00
9-Wrightson-c; Roy Thomas app. 1.00 2.50 6.00
Special 1(12/71)-Neal Adams-a 1.00 2.50 6.00
NOTE: ***J. Buscema** a-1p, 2p, Special 1. **Colan** a-3p, 6p, Special 1. **J. Craig** a-1. **Ditko** a-6, 8, 9r, Special 1. **Everett** a-9(i)r; c-5i. **Kirby** a-9(p)r. **Severin** c-5p, 6. **Steranko** a-1. **Tuska** a-3. **Wood** a-5-8. Issues 1-9 contain new stories with some pre-Marvel age reprints in 6-9. **H. P. Lovecraft** adaptation-9.*

TOWN & COUNTRY
May, 1940
Publisher?

nn-Origin The Falcon 30.00 90.00 210.00

Toyboy #1, © Continuity Comics

Trapped #1, © ACE

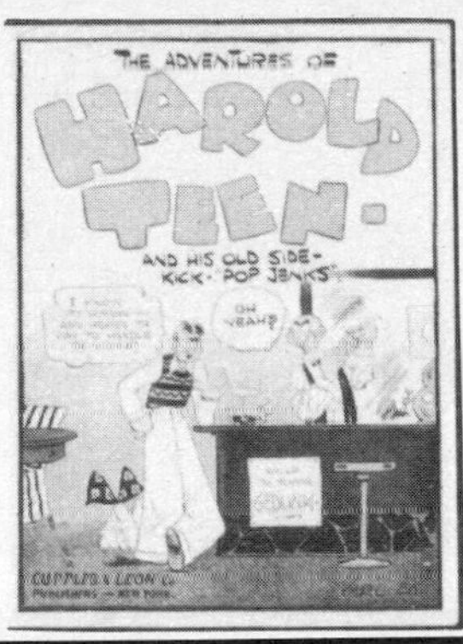

Treasure Box of Famous Comics, © C&L

GD25 FN65 NM94

'OWN THAT FORGOT SANTA, THE
961 (24 pages) (Giveaway)
V. T. Grant Co.

	GD25	FN65	NM94
nn	2.80	7.00	14.00

TOXIC AVENGER (Marvel)(Value: cover or less)

TOXIC CRUSADERS (TV)
May, 1992 - No. 8, Dec, 1992 ($1.25, color)
Marvel Comics

	GD25	FN65	NM94
1-3-Sam Kieth-c; based on USA network cartoon			1.50
4-8: 8-Kieth-c(i)			1.25

TOYBOY (Continuity)(Value: cover or less)

TOYLAND COMICS
Jan, 1947 - No. 2, Mar, 1947; No. 3, July, 1947 - No. 4, 1947
Fiction House Magazines

	GD25	FN65	NM94
1	16.00	48.00	110.00
2-4: 2,3-Bob Lubbers-c. 3-Tuska-a	10.00	30.00	65.00
148 pg. issue	17.00	52.00	120.00

NOTE: *All above contain strips by* ***Al Walker.***

TOY TOWN COMICS
1945 - No. 7, May, 1947
Toytown/Orbit Publ./B. Antin/Swapper Quarterly

	GD25	FN65	NM94
1-Mertie Mouse; L. B. Cole-c/a; funny animal	13.00	40.00	90.00
2-L. B. Cole-a	10.00	30.00	60.00
3-7-L. B. Cole-a. 5-Wiggles the Wonderworm-c	8.35	25.00	50.00

TRAGG AND THE SKY GODS (See Gold Key Spotlight, Mystery Comics Digest #3,9 & Spine Tingling Tales)
June, 1975 - No. 8, Feb, 1977; No. 9, May, 1982 (Painted-c #3-8)
Gold Key/Whitman No. 9

	GD25	FN65	NM94
1-Origin		.80	2.00
2-9: 4-Sabre-Fang app. 8-Ostellon app.; 9-r/#1			1.00

NOTE: ***Santos*** *a-1, 2, 9r; c-3-7.* ***Spiegel*** *a-3-8.*

TRAIL BLAZERS (Red Dragon #5 on)
1941; No. 2, Apr, 1942 - No. 4, Oct, 1942 (True stories of American heroes)
Street & Smith Publications

	GD25	FN65	NM94
1-Life story of Jack Dempsey	22.00	65.00	150.00
2-Brooklyn Dodgers-c/story; Ben Franklin story	13.00	40.00	90.00
3,4: 3-Fred Allen, Red Barber, Yankees stories	12.00	35.00	80.00

TRAIL COLT (Also see Extra Comics & Manhunt!)
1949 - No. 2, 1949
Magazine Enterprises

	GD25	FN65	NM94
nn(A-1 #24)-7 pg. Frazetta-a r-in Manhunt #13; Undercover Girl app.; The Red Fox by L. B. Cole; Ingels-c; Whitney-a (Scarce)	29.00	85.00	200.00
2(A-1 #26)-Undercover Girl; Ingels-c; L. B. Cole-a, 6 pgs.	23.00	70.00	160.00

TRANCERS (Eternity)(Value: cover or less)

TRANSFORMERS, THE (TV)(Marvel, all titles)(Value: cover or less)(See G.I. Joe and...)

TRANSFORMERS: GENERATION 2
Nov, 1993 - Present ($1.75, color)
Marvel Comics

	GD25	FN65	NM94
1-($2.95)-Collector's edition w/bi-fold metallic-c		1.20	3.00
1-6: 1-Newsstand edition		.70	1.75

TRANSMUTATION OF IKE GARUDA, THE (Marvel)(Value: cover or less)

TRAPPED
1951 (Giveaway) (16 pages) (soft cover)
Harvey Publications (Columbia University Press)

	GD25	FN65	NM94
nn-Drug education comic (30,000 printed?) distributed to schools.; mentioned in **SOTI**, pgs. 256,350	2.40	6.00	12.00

NOTE: *Many copies surfaced in 1979 causing a setback in price; beware of trimmed edges, because many copies have a brittle edge.*

TRAPPED!
Oct, 1954 - No. 5, June?, 1955
Periodical House Magazines (Ace)

	GD25	FN65	NM94
1 (All reprints)	6.35	19.00	38.00
2-5: 4-r/Men Against Crime #4 in its entirety	4.20	12.50	25.00

NOTE: ***Colan*** *a-1, 4.* ***Sekowsky*** *a-1.*

TRASH (Trash)(Value: cover or less)

TRAVELS OF HAPPY HOOLIGAN, THE
1906 (10-1/4x15-3/4", 32 pgs., cardboard covers)
Frederick A. Stokes Co.

	GD25	FN65	NM94
nn-Contains reprints from 1905	37.00	110.00	260.00

TRAVELS OF JAIMIE McPHEETERS, THE (TV)
December, 1963
Gold Key

	GD25	FN65	NM94
1-Kurt Russell	4.00	10.00	20.00

TREASURE BOX OF FAMOUS COMICS
Mid 1930's (36 pgs.) (6-7/8x8-1/2") (paper covers)
Cupples & Leon Co.

Box plus 5 titles: Reg'lar Fellers(1928), Little Orphan Annie(1926), Smitty (1928), Harold Teen(1931), How D. Tracy & D. Tracy Jr. Caught The Racketeers (1933) (These are abbreviated versions of hardcover editions)

	GD25	FN65	NM94
Softcovers (Set)....	100.00	300.00	700.00
Hardcovers (Set)...	115.00	345.00	800.00

NOTE: *Dates shown are copyright dates; all books actually came out in 1934 or later.*

TREASURE CHEST (Catholic Guild; also see Topix)
3/12/46 - V27#8, July, 1972 (Educational comics)
George A. Pflaum (not publ. during Summer)

	GD25	FN65	NM94
V1#1	13.00	40.00	90.00
2-6 (5/21/46): 5-Dr. Styx app. by Baily	6.70	20.00	40.00
V2#1-20 (9/3/46-5/27/47)	4.20	12.50	25.00
V3#1-5,7-20 (1st slick cover)	4.00	10.00	20.00
V3#6-Jules Verne's "Voyage to the Moon"	5.35	16.00	32.00
V4#1-20 (9/9/48-5/31/49)	3.00	7.50	15.00
V5#1-20 (9/6/49-5/31/50)	2.40	6.00	12.00
V6#1-20 (9/14/50-5/31/51)	2.40	6.00	12.00
V7#1-20 (9/13/51-6/5/52)	1.60	4.00	8.00
V8#1-20 (9/11/52-6/4/53)	1.60	4.00	8.00
V9#1-20 ('53-'54)	1.40	3.50	7.00
V10#1-20 ('54-'55)	1.40	3.50	7.00
V11('55-'56), V12('56-'57)	1.20	3.00	6.00
V13#1,3-5,7,9-V17#1 ('57-'63)	1.00	2.50	5.00
V13#2,6,8-Ingels-a	5.00	15.00	30.00
V17#2-'This Godless Communism' series begins(not in odd #'d issues); cover shows hammer & sickle over Statue of Liberty; 8pg. Crandall-a of family life under communism	11.50	34.00	80.00
V17#3,5,7,9,11,13,15,17,19	.80	2.00	4.00
V17#4,6,14-'This Godless Communism' stories	9.15	27.50	55.00
V17#8-Shows red octopus encompassing Earth, firing squad; 8pg. Crandall-a	10.00	30.00	65.00
V17#10-'This Godless Communism' - how Stalin came to power, part I; Crandall-a	10.00	30.00	60.00
V17#12-Stalin in WWII, forced labor, death by exhaustion; Crandall-a	10.00	30.00	60.00
V17#16-Kruschev takes over; de-Stalinization	10.00	30.00	60.00
V17#18-Kruschev's control; murder of revolters, brainwash, space race by Crandall	10.00	30.00	60.00
V17#20-End of series; Kruschev-people are puppets, firing squads hammer & sickle over Statue of Liberty, snake around communist manifesto by Crandall	10.00	30.00	60.00
V18#1-20, V19#11-20, V20#1-20('64-'65): V19#11-Crandall draws himself & 13 other artists on cover	.80	2.00	4.00
V18#5-'What About Red China?' - describes how communists took over China	4.20	12.50	25.00

Treasure Comics #1, © PRIZE

Trigger Twins #1, © DC

Trollords: Death and Kisses #2, © Beaderstadt & Fricke

GD25 FN65 NM94

V19#1-10-'Red Victim' anti-communist series in all 4.20 12.50 25.00
V21-V25('65-'70)-(two V24#5's 11/7/68 & 11/21/68) (no V24#6)
.60 1.50 3.00
V26, V27#1-8 (V26,27-68 pgs.) .40 1.00 2.00
Summer Edition V1#1-6('66), V2#1-6('67) .40 1.00 2.00

NOTE: ***Anderson** a-V18#13. **Borth** a-V7#10-19 (serial), V8#8-17 (serial), V9#1-10 (serial), V13#2, 6, 11, V14-V25 (except V22#1-3, 11-13), Summer Ed. V1#3-6. **Crandall** a-V16#7, 9, 12, 14, 16-18, 20; V17#1, 2, 4-6, 10, 12, 14, 16-18, 20; V18#1, 2, 3(2pg.), 7, 9-20; V19#4, 11, 13, 16, 19, 20; V20#1, 2, 4, 6, 8-10, 12, 14-16, 18, 20; V21#1-5, 8-11, 13, 16-18; V22#3, 7, 9-11, 14; V23#3, 6, 9, 16, 18; V24#7, 8, 10, 13, 16; V25#8, 16; V27#1-7r, 8r(2 pg.), Summer Ed. V1#3-5, V2#3; c-V16#7, V18#2(part), 7, 11, V19#4, 19, 20, V20#15, V21#5, 9, V22#3, 7, 9, 11, V23#9, 16, V24#13, 16, V25#8, Summer Ed. V1#2 (back c-V1#2-5). **Powell** a-V10#11. V19#11, 15, V10#13, V13#6, 8 all have wraparound covers. All the above Crandall issues should be priced by condition from $4-8.00 in mint unless already priced.*

TREASURE CHEST OF THE WORLD'S BEST COMICS
1945 (500 pgs.) (hardcover)
Superior, Toronto, Canada

Contains Blue Beetle, Captain Combat, John Wayne, Dynamic Man, Nemo, Li'l Abner; contents can vary - represents random binding of extra books; Capt. America on-c 67.00 200.00 450.00

TREASURE COMICS
No date (1943) (324 pgs.; cardboard covers) (50 cents)
Prize Publications? (no publisher listed)

1-(Rare)-Contains rebound Prize Comics #7-11 from 1942 (blank inside-c)
167.00 500.00 1100.00

TREASURE COMICS
June-July, 1945 - No. 12, Fall, 1947
Prize Publications (American Boys' Comics)

1-Paul Bunyan & Marco Polo begin; Highwayman & Carrot Topp only app.; Kiefer-a 17.00 52.00 120.00
2-Arabian Knight, Gorilla King, Dr. Styx begin 10.00 30.00 60.00
3,4,9,12: 9-Kiefer-a 7.50 22.50 45.00
5-Marco Polo-c; Krigstein-a 11.50 34.00 80.00
6,11-Krigstein-a; 11-Krigstein-c 10.00 30.00 70.00
7,8-Frazetta-a, 5 pgs. each 24.00 72.00 165.00
10-Simon & Kirby-c/a 15.00 45.00 105.00
NOTE: ***Barry** a-9-11. **Kiefer** a-3, 5, 7; c-7. **Roussos** a-11.*

TREASURE ISLAND (See Classics Illustrated #64, Doc Savage Comics #1, 4-Color #624, King Classics, Movie Classics & Movie Comics)

TREASURY OF COMICS
1947; No. 2, July, 1947 - No. 4, Sept, 1947; No. 5, Jan, 1948
St. John Publishing Co.

nn(#1)-Abbie an' Slats (nn on-c, #1 on inside) 12.00 36.00 85.00
2-Jim Hardy Comics 10.00 30.00 60.00
3-Bill Bumlin 6.70 20.00 40.00
4-Abbie an' Slats 10.00 30.00 60.00
5-Jim Hardy Comics #1 10.00 30.00 60.00

TREASURY OF COMICS
Mar, 1948 - No. 5, 1948 (Reg. size); 1948-1950 (Over 500 pgs., $1.00)
St. John Publishing Co.

1 15.00 45.00 105.00
2(#2 on-c, #1 on inside) 10.00 30.00 60.00
3-5 8.35 25.00 50.00
1-(1948, 500 pgs., hard-c)-Abbie & Slats, Abbott & Costello, Casper, Little Annie Rooney, Little Audrey, Jim Hardy, Ella Cinders (16 books bound together) (Rare) 100.00 300.00 700.00
1(1949, 500 pgs.)-Same format as above 100.00 300.00 700.00
1(1950, 500 pgs.)-Same format as above; different-c; (also see Little Audrey Yearbook) (Rare) 100.00 300.00 700.00

TREASURY OF DOGS, A (See Dell Giants)

TREASURY OF HORSES, A (See Dell Giants)

TREKKER (Dark Horse)(Value: cover or less)

TRENCHER
May, 1993 - No. 4?, 1993 ($1.95, color)
Image Comics

1-4: By Keith Giffen. 3-Supreme-c/story .80 2.00

TRIALS OF LULU AND LEANDER, THE
1906 (32 pgs. in color) (10x16")
William A. Stokes Co.

nn-By F. M. Howarth 22.00 65.00 150.00

TRIBE (See Wildcats #4)
April, 1993 ($2.50, color)
Image Comics

1-By Johnson & Stroman 1.00 2.50
1-Ivory Edition; gold foil & embossed-c; available only through the creators
4.75

TRIBE
V1#2, Sept, 1993 - Present ($1.95, color)
Axis Comics

V1#2-By Johnson & Stroman .80 2.00

TRIGGER (See Roy Rogers'...)

TRIGGER TWINS
Mar-Apr, 1973 (One Shot, 20 cent issue)
National Periodical Publications

1-Trigger Twins & Pow Wow Smith-r/All-Star Western #94,103 & Western Comics #81; Infantino-r(p) 1.20 3.00

TRINITY (See DC Universe: Trinity)

TRIPLE GIANT COMICS (See Archie All-Star Specials under Archie Comics)

TRIPLE THREAT
Winter, 1945
Special Action/Holyoke/Gerona Publ.

1-Duke of Darkness, King O'Leary 10.00 30.00 60.00

TRIP WITH SANTA ON CHRISTMAS EVE, A
No date (Early 1950s) (16 pgs.; full color; paper cover)
Rockford Dry Goods Co. (Giveaway)

nn 3.20 8.00 16.00

TRIUMPHANT UNLEASHED
Nov, 1993 - No. 1, 1994 ($2.50, color)
Triumphant Comics

0 1.00 2.50
0-Red logo 1.00 2.50
0-White logo (no cover price; giveaway) 1.00 2.50
1 1.00 2.50

TROLLORDS (Comico & Apple)(Value: cover or less)

TROUBLE SHOOTERS, THE (See 4-Color #1108)

TROUBLE WITH GIRLS, THE (Malibu/Eternity/Epic)(Value: cover or less)

TRUE ADVENTURES (Formerly True Western)(Men's Adventures #4 on)
No. 3, May, 1950 (52 pgs.)
Marvel Comics (CCC)

3-Powell, Sekowsky-a; Brodsky-c 10.00 30.00 70.00

TRUE ANIMAL PICTURE STORIES
Winter, 1947 - No. 2, Spr-Summer, 1947
True Comics Press

1,2 6.35 19.00 38.00

TRUE AVIATION PICTURE STORIES (Becomes Aviation Adventures & Model Building #16 on)
1942; No. 2, Jan-Feb, 1943 - No. 15, Sept-Oct, 1946
Parents' Magazine Institute

1-(#1 & 2 titled ...Aviation Comics Digest)(not digest size)
10.00 30.00 70.00

True Comics #76, © PMI

True Crime Comics #5, © Magazine Village

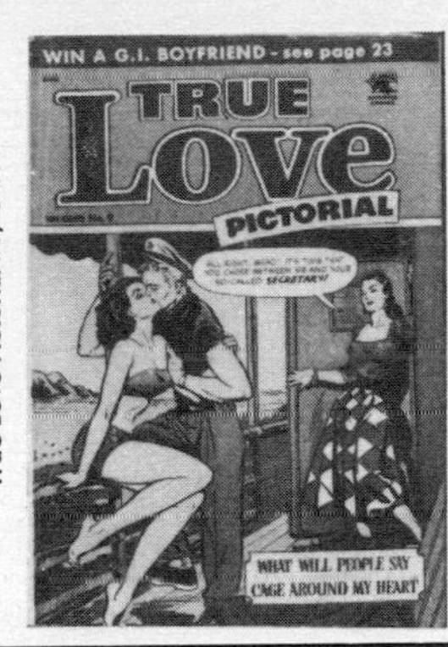

True Love Pictorial #9, © STJ

GD25 FN65 NM94

2 6.35 19.00 38.00
3-14: 3-10-Photos on-c. 11,13-Photo-c 5.35 16.00 32.00
15-(Titled "True Aviation Adventures & Model Building")
4.70 14.00 28.00

TRUE BRIDE'S EXPERIENCES (Formerly Teen-Age Brides)
(True Bride-To-Be Romances No. 17 on)
No. 8, Oct, 1954 - No. 16, Feb, 1956
True Love (Harvey Publications)

8 4.00 11.00 22.00
9,10: 10-Last pre-code (2/55) 2.80 7.00 14.00
11-15 2.00 5.00 10.00
16-Spanking panels (3) 4.00 12.00 24.00
NOTE: *Powell a-8-10, 12, 13.*

TRUE BRIDE-TO-BE ROMANCES (Formerly True Bride's Experiences)
No. 17, Apr, 1956 - No. 30, Nov, 1958
Home Comics/True Love (Harvey)

17-S&K-c, Powell-a 5.00 15.00 30.00
18,20,22,25-28,30 2.40 6.00 12.00
21,23,24,29-Powell-a. 29-Baker-a (1 pg.) 3.20 8.00 16.00

TRUE COMICS (Also see Outstanding American War Heroes)
April, 1941 - No. 84, Aug, 1950
True Comics/Parents' Magazine Press

1-Marathon run story; life story Winston Churchill 23.00 70.00 160.00
2-Red Cross story; Everett-a 11.50 34.00 80.00
3-Basebasll Hall of Fame story 13.00 40.00 90.00
4,5: 4-Story of American flag "Old Glory." 5-Life story of Joe Louis
10.00 30.00 70.00
6-Baseball World Series story 12.00 36.00 85.00
7-10: 7-Buffalo Bill story. 10,11-Teddy Roosevelt 7.50 22.50 45.00
11-17,18-20: 13-Harry Houdini story. 14-Charlie McCarthy story. 15-Flag-c; Bob Feller story. 18-Story of America begins, ends #26
6.70 20.00 40.00
17-Brooklyn Dodgers story 8.35 25.00 50.00
21-30 5.85 17.50 35.00
31-Red Grange story 4.20 12.50 25.00
32-46: 39-FDR story. 46-George Gershwin story 4.00 11.00 22.00
47-Atomic bomb issue (3/46) 7.50 22.50 45.00
48-66: 55(12/46)-1st app. Sad Sack by Baker, pg. 58-Jim Jeffries (boxer) story; Harry Houdini story. 59-Bob Hope story. 66-Will Rogers-c/story
4.00 10.00 20.00
67-1st oversized issue (12/47); Steve Saunders, Special Agent begins
5.00 15.00 30.00
68-72,74-79: 69-Jack Benny story. 71-Joe DiMaggio-c/story. 72-Jackie Robinson story. 78-Stan Musial-c/story 4.00 10.00 20.00
73-Walt Disney's life story 5.00 15.00 30.00
80-84 (Scarce)-All distr. to subscribers through mail only; paper-c. 80-Rocket trip to the moon story. 81-Red Grange story 16.00 48.00 110.00
(Prices vary widely on issues 80-84)
NOTE: *Bob Kane a-7. Palais a-80. Powell c/a-80. #80-84 have soft covers and combined with Tex Granger, Jack Armstrong, and Calling All Kids. #68-78 featured true FBI adventures.*

TRUE COMICS AND ADVENTURE STORIES
1965 (Giant) (25 cents)
Parents' Magazine Institute

1,2-Fighting Hero of Viet Nam; LBJ on-c 1.40 3.50 7.00

TRUE COMPLETE MYSTERY (Formerly Complete Mystery)
No. 5, April, 1949 - No. 8, Oct, 1949
Marvel Comics (PrPI)

5 14.00 43.00 100.00
6-8: 6-8-Photo-c 11.50 34.00 80.00

TRUE CONFIDENCES
1949 (Fall) - No. 4, June, 1950 (All photo-c)
Fawcett Publications

1-Has ad for Fawcett Love Adventures #1, but publ. as Love Memoirs #1 as Marvel published the title first; Swayze-a 10.00 30.00 70.00
2-4: 3-Swayze-a. 4-Powell-a 6.70 20.00 40.00

TRUE CRIME CASES
1944 (25¢, 100 pgs.)
St. John Publishing Co.

nn-Matt Baker-c 25.00 75.00 175.00

TRUE CRIME COMICS (Also see Complete Book of...)
No. 2, May, 1947; No. 3, July-Aug, 1948 - No. 6, June-July, 1949; V2#1, Aug-Sept, 1949 (52 pgs.)
Magazine Village

2-Jack Cole-c/a; used in **SOTI**, pg. 81,82 plus illo.-"A sample of the injury-to-eye motif" & illo.-"Dragging living people to death;" used in **POP**, pg. 105; "Murder, Morphine and Me" classic drug propaganda story used by N.Y. Legis. Comm. 86.00 260.00 600.00
3-Classic Cole-c/a; drug story with hypo, opium den & withdrawing addict
60.00 180.00 420.00
4-Jack Cole-c/a; c-taken from a story panel in #3; r-(2) **SOTI** & **POP** stories/#2 54.00 160.00 375.00
5-Jack Cole-c; Marijuana racket story 31.00 95.00 220.00
6 16.00 48.00 110.00
V2#1-Used in **SOTI**, pgs. 81,82 & illo.-"Dragging living people to death;" Toth, Wood (3 pgs.), Roussos-a; Cole-r from #2 46.00 140.00 320.00
NOTE: *V2#1 was reprinted in Canada as V2#9 (12/49); same-c & contents minus Wood-a.*

TRUE GHOST STORIES (See Ripley's...)

TRUE LIFE ROMANCES (...Romance on cover)
Dec, 1955 - No. 3, Aug, 1956
Ajax/Farrell Publications

1 6.70 20.00 40.00
2 4.00 10.00 20.00
3-Disbrow-a 4.20 12.50 25.00

TRUE LIFE SECRETS
Mar-April, 1951 - No. 28, Sept, 1955; No. 29, Jan, 1956
Romantic Love Stories/Charlton

1-Photo-c begin, end #3? 8.35 25.00 50.00
2 4.20 12.50 25.00
3-19 4.00 10.00 20.00
20-29: 25-Last precode(3/55) 3.00 7.50 15.00

TRUE LIFE TALES Formerly Mitzi's Romances #8?)
No. 8, Oct, 1949 - No. 2, Jan, 1950 (52 pgs.)
Marvel Comics (CCC)

8(#1, 10/49), 2-Photo-c 6.35 19.00 38.00

TRUE LOVE (Eclipse)(Value: cover or less)

TRUE LOVE CONFESSIONS
May, 1954 - No. 11, Jan, 1956
Premier Magazines

1-Marijuana story 6.70 20.00 40.00
2 4.00 10.00 20.00
3-11 3.00 7.50 15.00

TRUE LOVE PICTORIAL
1952 - No. 11, Aug, 1954
St. John Publishing Co.

1-Only photo-c 10.00 30.00 65.00
2-Baker-c 5.35 16.00 32.00
3-5(All 25¢, 100 pgs.): 5-(4/53)-Formerly Teen-Age Temptations; Kubert-a in #3,5; Baker-a in #3-5 19.00 57.00 130.00
6,7-Baker-c/a 9.15 27.50 55.00
8,10,11-Baker-c/a 8.35 25.00 50.00
9-Baker-c 6.70 20.00 40.00

TRUE MOVIE AND TELEVISION (Part teenage magazine)
Aug, 1950 - No. 3, Nov, 1950; No. 4, Mar, 1951 (52 pgs.) (1-3: 10 cents)
Toby Press

True Sport Picture Stories V4#7, © S&S

True-To-Life Romances #22, © STAR

TSR Worlds Annual #1, © TSR

GD25 FN65 NM94

1-Liz Taylor photo-c; Gene Autry, Shirley Temple, Li'l Abner app. 27.00 80.00 185.00
2-Janet Leigh/Liz Taylor/others photo-c; Frazetta John Wayne illo 20.00 60.00 140.00
3-June Allyson photo-c; Montgomery Cliff, Esther Williams, Andrews Sisters app; Li'l Abner featured; Sadie Hawkins' Day 18.00 54.00 125.00
4-Jane Powell photo-c (15¢) 8.35 25.00 50.00
NOTE: *16 pages in color, rest movie material in black & white.*

TRUE SECRETS (Formerly Our Love?)
No. 3, Mar, 1950; No. 4, Feb, 1951 - No. 40, Sept, 1956
Marvel (IPS)/Atlas Comics (MPI) #4 on

3 (52 pgs.)(IPS one-shot) 8.35 25.00 50.00
4,5,7-10 4.20 12.50 25.00
6,22-Everett-a 5.35 16.00 32.00
11-20 4.00 10.00 20.00
21,23-28: 28-Last pre-code (2/55) 2.80 7.00 14.00
29-40: 24-Colletta-c. 34,36-Colletta-a 2.40 6.00 12.00

TRUE SPORT PICTURE STORIES (Formerly Sport Comics)
V1#5, Feb, 1942 - V5#2, July-Aug, 1949
Street & Smith Publications

V1#5-Joe DiMaggio story 19.00 58.00 135.00
6-12 (1942-43): 12-Jack Dempsey story 10.00 30.00 70.00
V2#1-12 (1944-45): 7-Stan Musial-c/story 10.00 30.00 60.00
V3#1-12 (1946-47): 7-Joe DiMaggio, Stan Musial back from the armed service story 8.35 25.00 50.00
V4#1-12 (1948-49), V5#1,2 7.50 22.50 45.00
NOTE: ***Powell** a-V3#10, V4#1-4, 6-8, 10-12; V5#1, 2; c-V4#5-7, 9-12. **Ravielli** c-V5#2.*

TRUE STORIES OF ROMANCE
Jan, 1950 - No. 3, May, 1950 (All photo-c)
Fawcett Publications

1 8.35 25.00 50.00
2,3: 3-Marcus Swayze-a 5.85 17.50 35.00

TRUE STORY OF JESSE JAMES, THE (See 4-Color #757)

TRUE SWEETHEART SECRETS
5/50; No. 2, 7/50; No. 3, 1951(nd); No. 4, 9/51 - No. 11, 1/53
Fawcett Publications (All photo-c)

1-Photo-c; Debbie Reynolds? 9.15 27.50 55.00
2-Wood-a, 11 pgs. 11.50 34.00 80.00
3-11: 4,5-Powell-a. 8-Marcus Swayze-a 5.35 16.00 32.00

TRUE TALES OF LOVE (Formerly Secret Story Romances)
No. 22, April, 1956 - No. 31, Sept, 1957
Atlas Comics (TCI)

22 4.70 14.00 28.00
23-31-Colletta-a in most 2.80 7.00 14.00

TRUE TALES OF ROMANCE
No. 4, June, 1950
Fawcett Publications

4-Photo-c 5.00 15.00 30.00

TRUE 3-D
Dec, 1953 - No. 2, Feb, 1954
Harvey Publications

1-Nostrand, Powell-a 6.70 20.00 40.00
2-Powell-a 10.00 30.00 70.00
NOTE: *Many copies of #1 surfaced in 1984.*

TRUE-TO-LIFE ROMANCES (Formerly Guns Against Gangsters)
#8, 11-12/49; #9, 1-2/50; #3, 4/50 - #5, 9/50; #6, 1/51 - #23, 10/54
Star Publications

8(#1, 1949) 10.00 30.00 65.00
9(#2),4-10 7.50 22.50 45.00
3-Janet Leigh/Glenn Ford photo on-c plus true life story of each 9.15 27.50 55.00

GD25 FN65 NM94

11,22,23 6.35 19.00 38.00
12-14,17-21-Disbrow-a 8.35 25.00 50.00
15,16-Wood & Disbrow-a in each 11.00 32.00 75.00
NOTE: ***Kamen** a-13. **Kamen/Feldstein** a-14. All have **L.B. Cole** covers.*

TRUE WAR EXPERIENCES
Aug, 1952 - No. 4, Dec, 1952
Harvey Publications

1 5.85 17.50 35.00
2-4 3.60 9.00 18.00

TRUE WAR ROMANCES
Sept, 1952 - No. 21, June, 1955
Quality Comics Group

1-Photo-c 8.35 25.00 50.00
2 4.20 12.50 25.00
3-10: 9-Whitney-a 3.60 9.00 18.00
11-21: 20-Last precode (4/55). 14-Whitney-a 2.80 7.00 14.00

TRUE WAR STORIES (See Ripley's...)

TRUE WESTERN (True Adventures #3)
Dec, 1949 - No. 2, March, 1950
Marvel Comics (MMC)

1-Photo-c; Billy The Kid story 11.00 32.00 75.00
2: Alan Ladd photo-c 14.00 43.00 100.00

TRUE WEST ROMANCE
No. 21, 1952
Quality Comics Group

21 (Exist?) 3.60 9.00 18.00

TRUMP (Magazine format)
Jan, 1957 - No. 2, Mar, 1957 (50 cents)
HMH Publishing Co.

1-Harvey Kurtzman satire 14.00 43.00 100.00
2-Harvey Kurtzman satire 12.00 36.00 85.00
NOTE: ***Davis, Elder, Heath, Jaffee** art-#1,2; **Wood** a-1. Article by Mel Brooks in #2.*

TRUMPETS WEST (See 4-Color #875)

TRUTH ABOUT CRIME (See Fox Giants)

TRUTH ABOUT MOTHER GOOSE (See 4-Color #862)

TRUTH BEHIND THE TRIAL OF CARDINAL MINDSZENTY, THE (See Cardinal Mindszenty)

TRUTHFUL LOVE (Formerly Youthful Love)
No. 2, July, 1950
Youthful Magazines

2-Ingrid Bergman's true life story 5.35 16.00 32.00

TRY-OUT WINNER BOOK (Marvel)(Value: cover or less)

TSR WORLDS (DC)(Value: cover or less)

TUBBY (See Marge's...)

TUFF GHOSTS STARRING SPOOKY
July, 1962 - No. 39, Nov, 1970; No. 40, Sept, 1971 - No. 43, Oct, 1972
Harvey Publications

1 7.50 22.50 45.00
2-5 4.20 12.50 25.00
6-10 3.00 7.50 15.00
11-20 1.60 4.00 8.00
21-30 1.00 2.50 6.00
31-39,43 1.20 3.00
40-42: 52 pg. Giants 1.60 4.00

TUFFY
No. 5, July, 1949 - No. 9, Oct, 1950
Standard Comics

5-All by Sid Hoff 4.00 11.00 22.00
6-9 2.40 6.00 12.00

Turok, Dinosaur Hunter #1, © WEST/Voyager

Turok, Son of Stone #38, © WEST

Tweety and Sylvester #7 (DELL), © Warner Bros.

GD25 FN65 NM94

TUFFY TURTLE
No date
I. W. Enterprises
1-Reprint .60 1.50 3.00

TUROK, DINOSAUR HUNTER (See Magnus Robot Fighter #12)
June, 1993 - Present ($2.50, color)
Valiant
1-($3.50)-Chromium & foil-c 1.40 3.50
1-Gold variant 15.00
2-8: 4-Andar app. 5-Death of Andar 1.00 2.50

TUROK, SON OF STONE (See Dan Curtis, Golden Comics Digest #31 & March of Comics #378, 399, 408)
No. 596, 12/54 - No. 29, 9/62; No. 30, 12/62 - No. 91, 7/74; No. 92, 9/74 - No. 125, 1/80; No. 126, 3/81 - No. 130, 4/82
Dell Publ. Co. #1-29(9/62)/Gold Key #30(12/62)-85(7/73)/Gold Key or Whitman #86(9/73)-125(1/80)/Whitman #126(3/81) on
4-Color 596 (12/54)(#1)-1st app./origin Turok & Andar
71.00 214.00 500.00
4-Color 656 (10/55)(#2)-1st mention of Lanok 43.00 129.00 300.00
3(3-5/56)-5: 3-Cave men 29.00 86.00 200.00
6-10: 8-Dinosaur of the deep 18.00 54.00 125.00
11-20: 17-Prehistoric Pygmies 11.00 32.00 75.00
21-30: 30-33-Painted back-c pin-ups 7.00 21.00 50.00
31-40 5.50 17.00 40.00
41-50 4.30 13.00 30.00
51-60: 58-Flying Saucer c/story 3.60 10.75 25.00
61-70: 62-12 & 15 cent-c. 63-Only line drawn-c 3.20 8.00 20.00
71-84: 84-Origin & 1st app. Hutec 1.85 5.50 13.00
85-130: 98-r/#58 w/o spaceship & spacemen on-c. 114,115-(52 pgs.)
1.30 3.25 8.00
Giant 1(30031-611) (11/66)-Slick-c 11.00 32.00 75.00
Giant 1-Same as above but with paper-c 12.00 36.00 85.00
NOTE: *Most painted-c; line-drawn #63 & 130.* **Alberto Gioletti** *a-24-27, 30-119, 123; painted-c No. 30-129.* **Sparling** *a-117, 120-130. Reprints-#36, 54, 57, 75, 112, 114(1/3), 115(1/3), 118, 121, 125, 127(1/3), 128, 129(1/3), 130(1/3), Giant 1. Cover r-93, 94, 97-99, 126(all different from original covers.*

TURTLE SOUP
Sept, 1987 ($2.00, B&W, one shot, 76 pgs.)
Mirage Studios
1-Featuring Teenage Mutant Ninja Turtles 1.40 3.50

TURTLE SOUP (Mirage, 1991-92)(Value: cover or less)

TV CASPER & COMPANY
Aug, 1963 - No. 46, April, 1974 (25 cent Giants)
Harvey Publications
1: 68 pg. Giants begin; Casper, Little Audrey, Baby Huey, Herman & Catnip, Buzzy the Crow begin 8.35 25.00 50.00
2-5 4.20 12.50 25.00
6-10 3.00 7.50 15.00
11-20 1.60 4.00 8.00
21-31: 31-Last 68 pg. issue 1.00 2.50 6.00
32-46: All 52 pgs. 1.60 4.00
NOTE: *Many issues contain reprints.*

TV FUNDAY FUNNIES (See Famous TV...)

TV FUNNIES (See New Funnies)

TV FUNTIME (See Little Audrey)

TV LAUGHOUT (See Archie's...)

TV SCREEN CARTOONS (Formerly Real Screen)
No. 129, July-Aug, 1959 - No. 138, Jan-Feb, 1961
National Periodical Publications
129-138 (Scarce) 7.50 22.50 45.00

TV STARS (TV)
Aug, 1978 - No. 4, Feb, 1979 (Hanna-Barbera)
Marvel Comics Group
1-Great Grape Ape app. 1.00 2.50 5.50
2,4: 4-Top Cat app. 1.00 2.50
3-Toth-c/a; Dave Stevens inks 1.80 4.50

TV TEENS (Formerly Ozzie & Babs; Rock and Rollo #14 on)
V1#14, Feb, 1954 - V2#13, July, 1956
Charlton Comics
V1#14 (#1)-Ozzie & Babs 6.00 18.00 36.00
15 (#2) 3.60 9.00 18.00
V2#3(6/54) - 6-Don Winslow 4.00 10.00 20.00
7-13-Mopsy. 8(7/55) 3.60 9.00 18.00

TWEETY AND SYLVESTER (1st Series)
No. 406, June, 1952 - No. 37, June-Aug, 1962
Dell Publishing Co.
4-Color 406 (#1)-1st app.? 6.70 20.00 40.00
4-Color 489,524 4.00 10.00 20.00
4 (3-5/54) - 20 2.40 6.00 12.00
21-37 1.20 3.00 6.00
(See March of Comics #421, 433, 445, 457, 469, 481)

TWEETY AND SYLVESTER (2nd Series)(See Kite Fun Book)
Nov, 1963; No. 2, Nov, 1965 - No. 121, July, 1984
Gold Key No. 1-102/Whitman No. 103 on
1 3.00 7.50 15.00
2-10 1.40 3.50 7.00
11-30 1.60 4.00
31-70 .80 2.00
71-121: 99,119-r(1/3) 1.00
Mini Comic No. 1(1976, 3-1/4x6-1/2") 1.00

12 O'CLOCK HIGH (TV)
Jan-Mar, 1965 - No. 2, Apr-June, 1965 (Photo-c)
Dell Publishing Co.
1,2 4.30 13.00 30.00

24 PAGES OF COMICS (No title) (Also see Pure Oil Comics, Salerno Carnival of Comics, & Vicks Comics)
Late 1930s
Giveaway by various outlets including Sears
nn-Contains strip reprints-Buck Rogers, Napoleon, Sky Roads, War on Crime
26.00 80.00 180.00

2099 UNLIMITED
Sept, 1993 - Present ($3.95, color)
Marvel Comics
1,2: 1-1st app. Hulk 2099 & begins. 1,2-Spider-Man 2099 app.
1.60 4.00

20,000 LEAGUES UNDER THE SEA (See 4-Color #614, King Classics, Movie Comics & Power Record Comics)

TWICE TOLD TALES (See Movie Classics)

TWILIGHT (DC)(Value: cover or less)

TWILIGHT AVENGER, THE (Elite)(Value: cover or less)

TWILIGHT MAN (First)(Value: cover or less)

TWILIGHT ZONE, THE (TV) (See Dan Curtis)
No. 1173, 3-5/61 - No. 91, 4/79; No. 92, 5/82
Dell Publishing Co./Gold Key/Whitman No. 92
4-Color 1173 (#1)-Crandall/Evans-c/a 18.00 54.00 125.00
4-Color 1288-Crandall/Evans-c/a 11.00 32.00 75.00
01-860-207 (5-7/62-Dell, 15 cents) 7.00 21.00 50.00
12-860-210 on-c; 01-860-210 on inside(8-10/62-Dell)-Evans-c/a (3 stories)
7.00 21.00 50.00
1(11/62-Gold Key)-Crandall-a(10 & 11 pgs.) 8.50 25.00 58.00
2 5.50 16.00 38.00

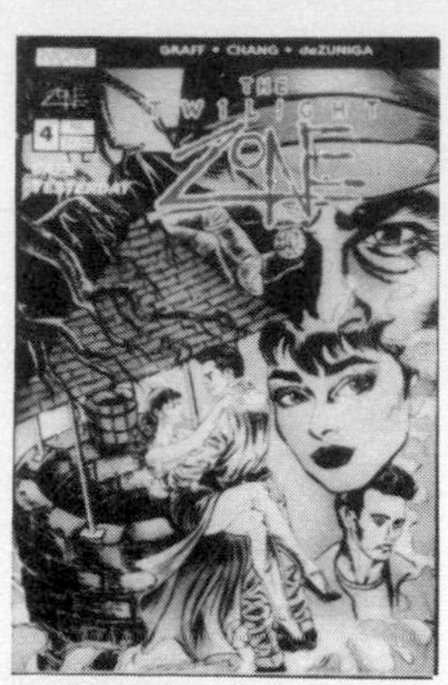

The Twilight Zone V3#4 (Now), © CBS Ent.

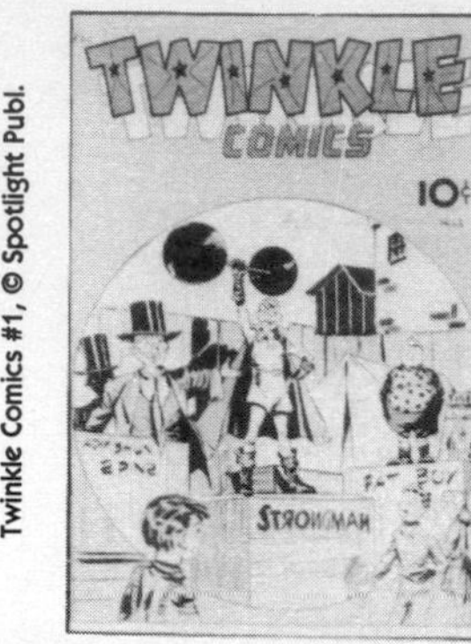

Twinkle Comics #1, © Spotlight Publ.

Two-Gun Kid #21, © MEG

GD25 FN65 NM94

3-11: 3,4-Toth-a, 11 & 10 pgs. 3.30 10.00 23.00
12-15: 12-Williamson-a. 13-Williamson/Crandall-a. 15-Crandall-a. 14-Williamson/Orlando/Crandall/Torres-a 3.20 8.00 20.00
16-20 2.00 6.00 14.00
21-27: 21-Crandall-a(r). 25-Evans/Crandall-a(r); Toth-r/#4. 26-Flying Saucer-c/story; Crandall, Evans-a(r). 27-Evans-r(2) 1.65 4.00 10.00
28-32: 32-Evans-a(r) 1.90 4.75
33-51: 43-Celardo-a. 51-Williamson-a 1.60 4.00
52-70 .80 2.00
71-92: 71-Reprint. 83,84-(52 pgs.) 1.50
Mini Comic #1(1976-3-1/4x6-1/2") 1.50
NOTE: **Bolle** *a-13(w/***McWilliams***), 50, 55, 57, 59, 77, 78, 80, 83, 84.* **McWilliams** *a-59, 78, 80, 82, 84.* **Miller** *a-84, 85.* **Orlando** *a-15, 19, 20, 22, 23.* **Sekowsky** *a-3.* **Simonson** *a-50, 54, 55, 83r.* **Weiss** *a-39, 79r(#39). (See Mystery Comics Digest 3, 6, 9, 12, 15, 18, 21, 24). Reprints-26(1/3), 71, 73, 79, 83, 84, 86, 92. Painted c-1-91.*

TWILIGHT ZONE, THE (TV)
Nov, 1990 ($2.95, color)
Oct, 1991; V2#1, Nov, 1991 - No. 14? 1992 ($1.95, color)
V3#1, 1993 - Present ($2.50, color)
Now Comics

1-(11/90, $2.95, 52 pgs.)-Direct sale edition; Neal Adams-a, Sienkiewicz-c; Harlan Ellison scripts 1.00 2.50 6.00
1-(11/90, $1.75)-Newsstand ed. w/N. Adams-c .80 2.00
1-Prestige Format (10/91, $4.95)-Reprints above with extra Harlan Ellison short story 1.00 2.00 5.00
1-Collector's Edition (10/91, $2.50)-None-code approved and polybagged; reprints 11/90 issue; gold logo 1.50 3.75 9.00
1-Reprint ($2.50)-r/direct sale 11/90 version 1.00 2.50
1-Reprint ($2.50)-r/newsstand 11/90 version 1.00 2.50
V2#1-Direct sale & newsstand ed. w/different-c .80 2.00
V2#2-8,10-14 .80 2.00
V2#9-($2.95)-3-D Special; polybagged w/glasses & hologram on-c 1.20 3.00
V2#9-($4.95)-Prestige Edition; contains 2 extra stories & a different hologram on-c; polybagged w/glasses 1.00 2.00 5.00
V3#1-4 1.00 2.50
Anniversary Special 1 (1992, $2.50) 1.00 2.50
Annual 1 (4/93, $2.50)-No ads 1.00 2.50

TWINKLE COMICS
May, 1945
Spotlight Publishers

1 13.00 40.00 90.00

TWIST, THE
July-September, 1962
Dell Publishing Co.

01-864-209-Painted-c 4.20 12.50 25.00

TWISTED TALES (Pacific)(Value: cover or less)

TWO BIT THE WACKY WOODPECKER (See Wacky...)
1951 - No. 3, May, 1953
Toby Press

1 5.00 15.00 30.00
2,3 3.00 7.50 15.00

TWO FACES OF COMMUNISM (Also see Double Talk)
1961 (36 pgs.; paper cover) (Giveaway)
Christian Anti-Communism Crusade, Houston, Texas

nn 11.00 32.00 75.00

TWO-FISTED TALES (Formerly Haunt of Fear #15-17)
No. 18, Nov-Dec, 1950 - No. 41, Feb-Mar, 1955
E. C. Comics

18(#1)-Kurtzman-c 75.00 225.00 525.00
19-Kurtzman-c 55.00 165.00 385.00
20-Kurtzman-c 34.00 100.00 235.00
21,22-Kurtzman-c 25.00 75.00 175.00

GD25 FN65 NM94

23-25-Kurtzman-c 19.00 58.00 135.00
26-35: 33-"Atom Bomb" by Wood 13.50 41.00 95.00
36-41 10.00 30.00 65.00
Two-Fisted Annual (1952, 25¢, 132 pgs.) 68.00 205.00 475.00
Two-Fisted Annual (1953, 25¢, 132 pgs.) 50.00 150.00 350.00
NOTE: **Berg** *a-29.* **Colan** *a-39p.* **Craig** *a-18, 19, 32.* **Crandall** *a-35, 36.* **Davis** *a-20-36, 40; c-30, 34, 35, 41, Annual 2.* **Evans** *a-34, 40, 41; c-40.* **Feldstein** *a-18.* **Krigstein** *a-41.* **Kubert** *a-32, 33.* **Kurtzman** *a-18-25; c-18-29, 31, Annual 1.* **Severin** *a-26, 28, 29, 31, 34-41 (No. 37-39 are all-***Severin** *issues); c-36-39.* **Severin/Elder** *a-19-29, 31, 33, 36.* **Wood** *a-18-28, 30-35, 41; c-32, 33. Special issues: #26 (ChanJin Reservoir), 31 (Civil War), 35 (Civil War). Canadian reprints known; see Table of Contents. #25-Davis biog. #27-Wood biog. #28-Kurtzman biog.*

TWO-FISTED TALES
Oct, 1992 - Present ($1.50, color)
Russ Cochran

1-4: 1-r/Two-Fisted #18(#1); Kurtzman-c 1.50

TWO-GUN KID (Also see All Western Winners, Best Western, Black Rider, Blaze Carson, Kid Colt, Western Winners, Wild West, & Wild Western)
3/48(No mo.) - No. 10, 11/49; No. 11, 12/53 - No. 59, 4/61; No. 60, 11/62 - No. 92, 3/68; No. 93, 7/70 - No. 136, 4/77
Marvel/Atlas (MCI No. 1-10/HPC No. 11-59/Marvel No. 60 on)

1-Two-Gun Kid & his horse Cyclone begin; The Sheriff begins 61.00 182.00 425.00
2 26.00 80.00 185.00
3,4: 3-Annie Oakley app. 20.00 60.00 140.00
5-Pre-Black Rider app. (Wint. 48/49); Spanking panel. Anti-Wertham editorial (1st?) 26.00 78.00 180.00
6-10(11/49): 8-Blaze Carson app. 9-Black Rider app. 17.00 52.00 120.00
11(12/53)-Black Rider app.; explains how Kid Colt became an outlaw 12.00 36.00 85.00
12-Black Rider app. 12.00 36.00 85.00
13-20: 13-1st to have Atlas globe on-c 10.00 30.00 65.00
21-24,26-29 9.15 27.50 55.00
25,30: 25-Williamson-a(5 pgs.). 30-Williamson/Torres-a(4 pgs.) 10.00 30.00 60.00
31-33,35,37-40 6.70 20.00 40.00
34-Crandall-a 7.50 22.50 45.00
36,41,42,48-Origin in all 7.50 22.50 45.00
43,44,47 5.00 15.00 30.00
45,46-Davis-a 5.85 15.00 35.00
49,50,52,55,57-Severin-a(2) in each 4.70 14.00 28.00
51-Williamson-a, 5 pgs. 5.85 17.50 35.00
53,54-Severin-a(3) in each 5.00 15.00 30.00
56,59: 59-Last 10 cent issue (4/61) 3.20 8.00 16.00
58,60-New origin. 58-Kirby/Ayers-c/a "The Monster of Hidden Valley" cover/story (Kirby monster-c) 3.20 8.00 16.00
61-80: 64-Intro. Boom-Boom 1.60 4.00 8.00
81-92: 92-Last new story; last 12 cent issue .70 1.75 3.50
93-100,102-136 .30 .75 1.50
101-Origin retold/#58 .60 1.50 3.00
NOTE: **Ayers** *a-26, 27.* **Davis** *c-45-47.* **Drucker** *a-23.* **Everett** *a-82, 91.* **Fuje** *a-13.* **Heath** *a-3(2), 4(3), 5(2), 7; c-13, 21, 23, 53.* **Keller** *a-16, 19, 28.* **Kirby** *a-54, 55, 57-62, 75-77, 90, 95, 101, 119, 120, 129; c-10, 52, 54-65, 67-72, 74-76, 116.* **Maneely** *a-20; c-11, 12, 16, 19, 20, 25-28, 35, 49.* **Powell** *a-38, 102, 104.* **Severin** *a-9, 29, 51, 55, 57, 99r(3); c-9, 51, 99.* **Shores** *c-1-8, 11.* **Tuska** *a-11, 12.* **Whitney** *a-87, 89-91, 98-113, 124, 129; c-87, 89, 91, 113.* **Wildey** *a-21.* **Williamson** *a-110r. Kid Colt in #13, 14, 16-21.*

TWO GUN WESTERN (1st Series) (Formerly Casey Crime Photographer #1-4? or My Love #1-4?)
No. 5, Nov, 1950 - No. 14, June, 1952
Marvel/Atlas Comics (MPC)

5-The Apache Kid (Intro & origin) & his horse Nightwind begin by Buscema 14.00 43.00 100.00
6-10: 8-Kid Colt, The Texas Kid & his horse Thunder begin? 10.00 30.00 70.00
11-14: 13-Black Rider app. 8.35 25.00 50.00
NOTE: **Maneely** *a-6, 7, 9; c-6, 11-13.* **Morrow** *a-9.* **Romita** *a-8.* **Wildey** *a-8.*

2000 AD Presents #16, © Quality Comics

Uncanny Tales #12, © MEG

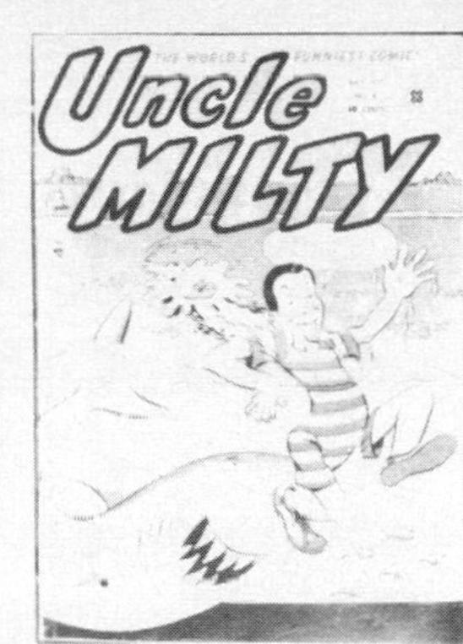

Uncle Milty #4, © Victoria Publ.

GD25 FN65 NM94

-GUN WESTERN (2nd Series) (Formerly Billy Buckskin #1-3; Two-Gun
Vestern #5 on)
lo. 4, May, 1956
.tlas Comics (MgPC)
4-Apache Kid; Colan, Ditko, Severin, Sinnott-a; Maneely-c 10.00 30.00 65.00

'WO-GUN WESTERN (Formerly 2-Gun Western)
lo. 5, July, 1956 - No. 12, Sept, 1957
.tlas Comics (MgPC)
5-Black Rider app. 9.15 27.50 55.00
6,7 5.85 17.50 35.00
8,10,12-Crandall-a 7.50 22.50 45.00
9,11-Williamson-a in both, 5 pgs. each 7.50 22.50 45.00
lOTE: ***Ayers*** *a-9.* ***Colan*** *a-5.* ***Everett*** *c-12.* ***Forgione*** *a-5, 6.* ***Kirby*** *a-12.* ***Maneely*** *a-6, 8, 12; c-, 6, 8, 11.* ***Morrow*** *a-9, 10.* ***Powell*** *a-7, 11.* ***Severin*** *c-10.* ***Sinnott*** *a-5.* ***Wildey*** *a-9.*

'WO MOUSEKETEERS, THE (See 4-Color #475, 603, 642 under M.G.M.'s...; ecomes M.G.M.'s Mouse Musketeers)

'WO ON A GUILLOTINE (See Movie Classics)

'000 A.D. MONTHLY/PRESENTS (Eagle/Quality)(Value: cover or less)

'000AD SHOWCASE (Quality)(Value: cover or less)

'001,A SPACE ODYSSEY (Marvel, Treasury Special & '76 series)(Value: cover or less)

'001 NIGHTS (Viz)(Value: cover or less)

'010 (Marvel)(Value: cover or less)

JFO & ALIEN COMIX
lan, 1978 (One Shot)
Varren Publishing Co.
ın-Toth, Severin-a(r) .65 1.60

JFO & OUTER SPACE (Formerly UFO Flying Saucers)
No. 14, June, 1978 - No. 25, Feb, 1980 (All painted covers)
Gold Key
14-Reprints UFO Flying Saucers #3 .80 2.00
15,16-Reprints 1.20
17-20-New material 1.50
21-25: 23-McWilliams-a. 24-(3 pg.-r). 25-Reprints UFO Flying Saucers #2 w/cover 1.00

JFO ENCOUNTERS
May, 1978 (228 pages) ($1.95)
Western Publishing Co.
11192-Reprints UFO Flying Saucers 1.60 4.00
11404-Vol.1 (128 pgs.)-See UFO Mysteries for Vol.2 .80 2.00

JFO FLYING SAUCERS (UFO & Outer Space #14 on)
Oct, 1968 - No. 13, Jan, 1977 (No. 2 on, 36 pgs.)
Gold Key
1(30035-810) (68 pgs.) 2.15 6.50 15.00
2(11/70), 3(11/72), 4(11/74) 1.30 3.25 8.00
5(2/75)-13: Bolle-a #4 on 1.00 2.00 5.00

UFO MYSTERIES
1978 (96 pages) ($1.00) (Reprints)
Western Publishing Co.
11400($1.00, 96 pgs.) .80 2.00
11404(Vol.2)-Cont'd from UFO Encounters, pgs. 129-224 .80 2.00

ULTRA KLUTZ (Onward)(Value: cover or less)

UNBIRTHDAY PARTY WITH ALICE IN WONDERLAND (See 4-Color #341)

UNCANNY TALES
June, 1952 - No. 56, Sept, 1957
Atlas Comics (PrPI/PPI)
1-Heath-a; horror/weird stories begin 39.00 120.00 275.00
2 20.00 60.00 140.00
3-5 17.00 52.00 120.00
6-Wolvertonish-a by Matt Fox 17.00 52.00 120.00
7-10: 8-Tothish-a. 9-Crandall-a 15.00 45.00 105.00
11-20: 17-Atom bomb panels; anti-communist story; Hitler story. 19-Krenkel-a 12.00 36.00 85.00
21-27: 25-Nostrand-a? 10.00 30.00 70.00
28-Last precode issue (1/55); Kubert-a; #1-28 contain 2-3 sci/fi stories each 11.00 32.00 75.00
29-41,43-49-52 7.50 22.50 45.00
42,54,56-Krigstein-a 9.15 27.50 55.00
50,53,55-Torres-a 7.50 22.50 45.00
NOTE: ***Andru*** *a-15, 27.* ***Ayers*** *a-22.* ***Bailey*** *a-51.* ***Briefer*** *a-19, 20.* ***Brodsky*** *c-1, 3, 4, 6, 8, 12-16, 19.* ***Brodsky/Everett*** *c-9.* ***Cameron*** *a-47.* ***Colan*** *a-11, 16, 17, 52.* ***Drucker*** *a-37, 42, 45.* ***Everett*** *a-2, 12, 32, 36, 39, 48; c-7, 11, 17, 39, 41, 50, 52, 53.* ***Fass*** *a-9, 10, 15, 24.* Forte *a-18, 27, 34, 52, 53.* ***Heath*** *a-13, 14; c-5, 10, 18.* ***Keller*** *a-3.* ***Lawrence*** *a-14, 17, 19, 23, 27, 28, 35.* ***Maneely*** *a-4, 8, 10, 16, 29, 35; c-2, 22, 26, 33, 38.* ***Moldoff*** *a-23.* ***Morisi*** *a-48, 52.* ***Morrow*** *a-46, 51.* ***Orlando*** *a-49, 50, 53.* ***Powell*** *a-12, 18, 34, 36, 38, 43, 50, 56.* ***Robinson*** *a-3, 13.* ***Reinman*** *a-12.* ***Romita*** *a-10.* ***Roussos*** *a-8.* ***Sale*** *a-47, 53; c-20.* ***Sekowsky*** *a-25.* ***Sinnott*** *a-15, 52.* ***Torres*** *a-53.* ***Tothish****-a by* ***Andru****-27.* ***Wildey*** *a-22, 48.*

UNCANNY TALES
Dec, 1973 - No. 12, Oct, 1975
Marvel Comics Group
1-12: 1-Crandall-r/Uncanny Tales #9('50s) 1.00 2.50
NOTE: ***Ditko*** *reprints-#4, 6-8, 10-12.*

UNCANNY X-MEN, THE (See X-Men)

UNCANNY X-MEN AND THE NEW TEEN TITANS (See Marvel and DC Present...)

UNCANNY X-MEN AT THE STATE FAIR OF TEXAS, THE
1983 (36 pgs.)(One-Shot)
Marvel Comics Group
nn Supplement to the Dallas Times Herald 3.20 8.00 20.00

UNCANNY X-MEN IN DAYS OF FUTURE PAST, THE
1989 ($3.95, color, squarebound, 52 pgs.)
Marvel Comics
nn-Byrne/Austin-r (2 stories); Guice-c(p) 1.60 4.00

UNCENSORED MOUSE, THE
Apr, 1989 - No. 2, Apr, 1989 ($1.95, B&W)(Came sealed in plastic bag)
Eternity Comics
1-Early Gottfredson strip-r in each 1.00 4.00
2-Both contain racial stereotyping & violence 1.00 2.50 6.00
NOTE: *Both issues contain unauthorized reprints. Series was cancelled.* ***Win Smith*** *r-1, 2.*

UNCLE CHARLIE'S FABLES
Jan, 1952 - No. 5, Sept, 1952 (All have Biro painted-c)
Lev Gleason Publications
1-Norman Maurer-a; has Biro's picture 8.35 25.00 50.00
2-Fuje-a; Biro photo 5.85 17.50 35.00
3-5 4.70 14.00 28.00

UNCLE DONALD & HIS NEPHEWS DUDE RANCH (See Dell Giant #52)

UNCLE DONALD & HIS NEPHEWS FAMILY FUN (See Dell Giant #38)

UNCLE JOE'S FUNNIES
1938 (B&W)
Centaur Publications
1-Games, puzzles & magic tricks, some interior art; Bill Everett-c 29.00 85.00 200.00

UNCLE MILTY (TV)
Dec, 1950 - No. 4, July, 1951 (52 pgs.)(Early TV comic)
Victoria Publications/True Cross
1-Milton Berle photo on-c of #1,2 32.00 95.00 225.00
2 18.00 54.00 125.00
3,4 14.00 43.00 100.00

UNCLE REMUS & HIS TALES OF BRER RABBIT (See 4-Color #129, 208, 693)

UNCLE SAM QUARTERLY (Blackhawk #9 on)(See Freedom Fighters)
Autumn, 1941 - No. 8, Fall, 1943 (Also see National Comics)

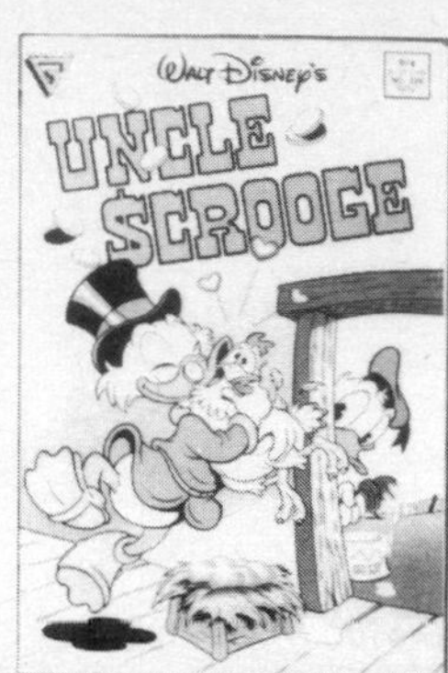

Uncle Scrooge #239, © Walt Disney Co.

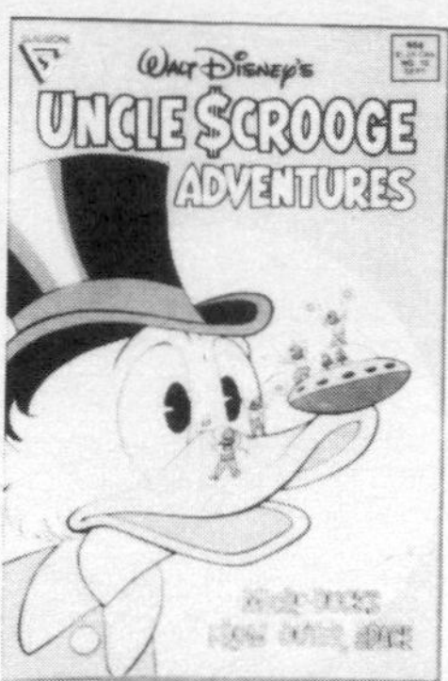

Uncle Scrooge Adventures #15, © Walt Disney Co.

Undercover Girl #6, © ME

GD25 FN65 NM94

Quality Comics Group

1-Origin Uncle Sam; Fine/Eisner-c, chapter headings, 2 pgs. by Eisner. (2 versions: dark cover, no price; light cover with price sticker); Jack Cole-a 158.00 475.00 1100.00
2-Cameos by The Ray, Black Condor, Quicksilver, The Red Bee, Alias the Spider, Hercules & Neon the Unknown; Eisner, Fine-c/a 79.00 238.00 525.00
3-Tuska-c/a 58.00 175.00 375.00
4 50.00 150.00 325.00
5-8 42.00 125.00 275.00
NOTE: ***Kotzky** (or **Tuska**) a-3-8.*

UNCLE SAM'S CHRISTMAS STORY
1958
Promotional Publ. Co. (Giveaway)

nn-Reprints 1956 Christmas USA 2.40 6.00 12.00

UNCLE SCROOGE (Disney)(See Cartoon Tales, Dell Giants #33, 55, Disney Comic Album, Donald and Scrooge, Dynabrite, Four Color #178, Gladstone Comic Album, Walt Disney's Comics & Stories #98)
No. 386, 3/52 - No. 39, 8-10/62; No. 40, 12/62 - No. 209, 1984; No. 210, 10/86 - No. 242, 4/90; No. 243, 6/90 - Present
Dell #1-39/Gold Key #40-173/Whitman #174-209/Gladstone #210-242/ Disney Comics #243-280/Gladstone #281 on

4-Color 386(#1)-in "Only a Poor Old Man" by Carl Barks; r-in Uncle Scrooge & Donald Duck #1('65) & The Best of Walt Disney Comics (1974) 82.00 245.00 575.00
1-(1986)-Reprints F.C. #386; given away with lithograph "Dam Disaster at Money Lake" & as a subscription offer giveaway to Gladstone subscribers .80 2.00
4-Color 456(#2)-in "Back to the Klondike" by Carl Barks; r-in Best of U.S. & D.D. #1('66) & Gladstone C.A. #4 41.00 125.00 290.00
4-Color 495(#3)-r-in #105 34.00 105.00 240.00
4(12-2/53-54)-r-in Gladstone Comic Album #11 27.00 81.00 190.00
5-r-in Gladstone Spec. #2 & W.D. Digest #1 22.00 67.00 155.00
6-r-in U.S. #106,165,233 & Best of U.S. & D.D. #1('66) 20.00 60.00 140.00
7-The Seven Cities of Cibola by Barks; r-in #217 & Best of D.D. & U.S. #2 ('67) 16.00 48.00 110.00
8-10: 8-r-in #111,222. 9-r-in #104,214. 10-r-in #67 13.00 40.00 90.00
11-20: 11-r-in #237. 17-r-in #215. 19-r-in Gladstone C.A. #1. 20-r-in #213 11.50 34.00 80.00
21-30: 24-X-Mas-c. 26-r-in #211 10.00 30.00 65.00
31-40: 34-r-in #228. 40-X-Mas-c 9.15 27.50 55.00
41-50: 49-Sci/fi-c 7.50 22.50 45.00
51-60 6.70 20.00 40.00
61-66,68-70: 64-On Disney's reprint banned list; Barks Vietnam war story "Treasure of Marco Polo" banned since 1970s. 70-Last Barks issue w/ original story 5.00 15.00 30.00
67,72,73-Barks-r 4.20 12.50 25.00
71-Written by Barks only 4.20 12.50 25.00
74-One pg. Barks-r 3.00 7.50 15.00
75-81,83-Not by Barks 3.00 7.50 15.00
82,84-Barks-r begin 3.00 7.50 15.00
85-100 2.40 6.00 12.00
101-110 2.00 5.00 10.00
111-120 1.80 4.50 9.00
121-141,143-152,154-157 1.20 3.00 7.00
142-Reprints 4-Color #456 with-c 1.30 3.25 8.00
153,158,162-164,166,168-170,178,180: No Barks 1.00 2.00 5.00
159-160,165,167,172-176-Barks-a 1.00 2.50 5.00
161(r/#14), 171(r/#11), 177(r/#16), 179(r/#9), 183(r/#6)-Barks-r 1.00 2.00 5.00
181(r/4-Color #495), 195(r/4-Color #386) 1.20 3.00
182,186,191-194,197-202,204-206: No Barks 1.50
184,185,187,188-Barks-a 1.50
189(r/#5), 190(r/#4), 196(r/#13), 203(r/#12), 207(r/#93,92), 208(r/U.S. #18), 209(r/U.S. #21)-Barks-r 1.50
210-1st Gladstone issue; r/WDC&S #134 (1st Beagle Boys) 1.00 2.50 6.00
211-218: 217-r/U.S. #7(Seven Cities of Cibola) 1.00 2.50
219-Son Of The Sun by Rosa 1.70 5.00 12.00
220-Don Rosa story/a 1.50 3.75
221-230: 224-Rosa-c/a. 226,227-Rosa-a .75 1.90
231-240: 235-Rosa story/art 1.50
241-($1.95, 68 pgs.)-Rosa finishes over Barks-r .90 2.25
242-($1.95, 68 pgs.)-Barks-r; Rosa-a(1 pg.) .90 2.25
243-249,251-286($1.50): 243-1st by Disney Comics; new-a begins. 261-263-Don Rosa-c/a. 274-All Barks issue. 275-Contains poster by Rosa. 283-r/WDC&S #98 .70 1.80
250-($2.25, 52 pgs.)-Barks-r; wraparound-c 1.00 2.50
Uncle Scrooge & Money(G.K.)-Barks-r/from WDC&S #130 (3/67) 4.00 12.00 28.00
Mini Comic #1(1976)(3-1/4x6-1/2")-r/U.S. #115; Barks-c 1.00
NOTE: ***Barks** c-4-Color 386, 456, 495, #4-37, 39, 40, 43-71. **Barks** r-210-218, 220-223, 224 (2pg.), 225-234, 236-242, 245, 246, 250-253, 255, 256, 258, 261(2 pg.), 265, 267, 268, 272-282, 284; c(r)-210, 212, 221, 228, 229, 232, 233, 284. **Rosa** a-219, 220, 224, 226, 227, 235, 261-263, 268, 275-277; c-219, 224, 231, 261-263, 276, 278-281; scripts-219, 220, 224, 235, 261-263, 268, 276.*

UNCLE SCROOGE ADVENTURES (Walt Disney's...#4 on)
Nov, 1987 - No. 21, May, 1990; No. 22, Sept, 1993 - Present
Gladstone Publishing

1-Barks-r begin 1.00 2.50 6.00
2-5: 5-Rosa-c/a .70 1.80
6-19: 9,14-Rosa-a. 10-r/U.S. #18(all Barks) 1.30
20,21 ($1.95, 68 pgs.) 20-Rosa-c/a. 21-Rosa-a .90 2.25
22,24-26 ($1.50): 22-Reprints U.S. #26 .75 1.90
23-($2.95, 68 pgs.)-Vs. The Phantom Blot-r/P.B. #3; Barks-r; painted-c 1.40 3.50
NOTE: ***Barks** r-1-4, 6-8, 10-13, 15-21, 23; c(r)-15, 16, 17, 21. **Rosa** a-5, 9, 14, 20, 21; c-5, 13, 14, 17(finishes), 20, 22; scripts-5, 9, 14.*

UNCLE SCROOGE & DONALD DUCK
June, 1965 (25 cents, paper cover)
Gold Key

1-Reprint of 4-Color #386(#1) & lead story from 4-Color #29 8.35 25.00 50.00

UNCLE SCROOGE COMICS DIGEST
Dec, 1986 - No. 5, Aug, 1987 ($1.25, Digest-size)
Gladstone Publishing

1-5 1.25

UNCLE SCROOGE GOES TO DISNEYLAND (See Dell Giants)
Aug, 1985 ($2.50)
Gladstone Publishing Ltd.

1-Reprints Dell Giant w/new-c by Mel Crawford, based on old cover 1.00 2.50
...Comics Digest 1 ($1.50, digest size) 1.50

UNCLE WIGGILY (See 4-Color #179, 221, 276, 320, 349, 391, 428, 503, 543, & March of Comics #19)

UNDERCOVER GIRL (Starr Flagg) (See Extra Comics & Manhunt!)
No. 5, 1952 - No. 7, 1954
Magazine Enterprises

5(#1)(A-1 #62)-Fallon of the F.B.I. in all 26.00 77.00 180.00
6(A-1 #98), 7(A-1 #118)-All have Starr Flagg 24.00 70.00 165.00
NOTE: ***Powell** c-6, 7. **Whitney** a-5-7.*

UNDERDOG (TV)(See Kite Fun Book, March of Comics #426, 438, 467, 479)
July, 1970 - No. 10, Jan, 1972; Mar, 1975 - No. 23, Feb, 1979
Charlton Comics/Gold Key

1 (1st series, Charlton)-1st app. Underdog 5.00 15.00 35.00
2-10 2.60 7.50 18.00
1 (2nd series, Gold Key) 3.25 9.50 22.00

#1, © FAW

Union #1 (Image), © Aegis Ent.

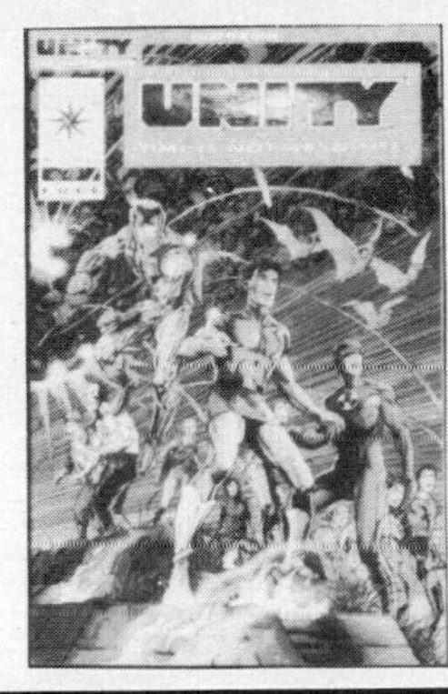
Unity #0, © Voyager Comm.

	GD25	FN65	NM94
2-10	1.65	4.00	10.00
1-23: 13-1st app. Shack of Solitude	1.20	3.00	7.00

NDERDOG (Spotlight)(Value: cover or less)

NDERDOG SUMMER SPECIAL (TV)
ct, 1993 ($2.25, color, 68 pgs.)
arvey Comics

	GD25	FN65	NM94
1		.90	2.25

NDERSEA AGENT
an, 1966 - No. 6, Mar, 1967 (25 cents, 68 pages)
ower Comics

	GD25	FN65	NM94
1-Davy Jones, Undersea Agent begins	5.50	17.00	40.00
2-6: 2-Jones gains magnetic powers. 5-Origin & 1st app. of Merman. 6-Kane?/Wood-c(r)	3.70	11.00	26.00

OTE: *Gil Kane a-3-6; c-4, 5. Moldoff a-2i.*

NDERSEA FIGHTING COMMANDOS (See Fighting Undersea...)
964
W. Enterprises

	GD25	FN65	NM94
W. Reprint #1,2('64): 1-r/#? 2-r/#1; Severin-c	1.40	3.50	7.00

NDERWATER CITY, THE (See 4-Color #1328)

NDERWORLD (True Crime Stories)
eb-Mar, 1948 - No. 9, June-July, 1949 (52 pgs.)
. S. Publishing Co.

	GD25	FN65	NM94
1-Moldoff-c; excessive violence	23.00	70.00	160.00
2-Moldoff-c; Ma Barker story used in SOTI, pg. 95; female electrocution panel; lingerie art	24.00	73.00	170.00
3-McWilliams c/a; extreme violence, mutilation	19.00	58.00	135.00
4-Used in Love and Death by Legman; Ingels-a	14.00	43.00	100.00
5-Ingels-a	11.00	32.00	75.00
6-9: 8-Ravielli-a	10.00	30.00	60.00

NDERWORLD (DC)(Value: cover or less)

NDERWORLD CRIME
une, 1952 - No. 9, Oct, 1953
awcett Publications

	GD25	FN65	NM94
1	17.00	52.00	120.00
2	10.00	30.00	70.00
3-6,8,9 (8,9-exist?)	10.00	30.00	60.00
7-(6/53)-Bondage/torture-c	14.00	43.00	100.00

NDERWORLD STORY, THE
950 (Movie)
von Periodicals

	GD25	FN65	NM94
n-(Scarce)-Ravielli-c	17.00	52.00	120.00

NEARTHLY SPECTACULARS
ct, 1965 - No. 3, Mar, 1967 (#1: 12 cents; #2,3: 25 cent giants)
arvey Publications

	GD25	FN65	NM94
1-Tiger Boy; Simon-c	1.65	4.70	11.00
2-Jack Q. Frost, Tiger Boy & Three Rocketeers app.; Williamson, Wood, Kane-a; r-1 story/Thrill-O-Rama #2	3.20	8.00	20.00
3-Jack Q. Frost app.; Williamson/Crandall-a; r-from Alarming Advs. #1, 1962	3.20	8.00	20.00

NOTE: *Crandall a-3r. G. Kane a-2. Orlando a-3. Simon, Sparling, Wood c-2. Simon/Kirby a-3r. Torres a-1?. Wildey a-1(3). Williamson a-2, 3r. Wood a-2(2).*

NEXPECTED, THE (Formerly Tales of the...)
No. 105, Feb-Mar, 1968 - No. 222, May, 1982
National Periodical Publications/DC Comics

	GD25	FN65	NM94
105-Begin 12 cent cover price	1.85	5.50	13.00
106-113: 113-Last 12 cent issue (6-7/69)	1.50	3.75	9.00
114,115,117,118,120,122-127	1.00	2.50	5.50
116,119,121,128-Wrightson-a	1.25	3.00	7.50
129-162: 132-136-(52 pgs.). 157-162-(100 pgs.)		1.10	2.75
163-188: 187,188-(44 pgs.)			1.40
189,190,192-195 ($1.00, 68 pgs.): 189 on are combined with House of Secrets & The Witching Hour			1.50
191-Rogers-a(p) ($1.00, 68 pgs.)		1.10	2.75
196-221: 200-Return of Johnny Peril by Tuska. 205-213-Johnny Peril app. 210-Time Warp story			1.20

NOTE: *Neal Adams c-110, 112-118, 121, 124. J. Craig a-195. Ditko a-189, 221p, 222p; c-222. Drucker a-107r, 132r. Giffen a-219, 222. Kaluta c-203, 212. Kirby a-127r, 162. Kubert c-204, 214-216, 219-221. Mayer a-217p, 220, 221p. Moldoff a-136r. Moreira a-133. Mortimer a-212p. Newton a-204p. Orlando a-202; c-191. Perez a-217p. Redondo a-155, 166, 195. Reese a-145. Sparling a-107, 205-209p, 212p. Spiegle a-217. Starlin c-198. Toth a-126r, 127r. Tuska a-127, 132, 134, 136, 139, 152, 180, 200p. Wildey a-128r, 193. Wood a-122i, 133i, 137i, 138i. Wrightson a-161r(2 pgs.). Johnny Peril in #106-117, 200, 205-213.*

UNEXPECTED ANNUAL, THE (See DC Special Series #4)

UNIDENTIFIED FLYING ODDBALL (See Walt Disney Showcase #52)

UNION
June, 1993 - Present ($1.95, color)
Image Comics

	GD25	FN65	NM94
1-($2.50)-Embossed foil-c; Texeira-c/a		1.00	2.50
2		.80	2.00

UNITED COMICS (Formerly Fritzi Ritz #7)
Aug, 1940; No. 8, 1950 - No. 26, Jan-Feb, 1953
United Features Syndicate

	GD25	FN65	NM94
1(68 pgs.)-Fritzi Ritz & Phil Fumble	16.00	48.00	110.00
8-Fritzi Ritz, Abbie & Slats	4.00	10.00	20.00
9-26: 20-Strange As It Seems; Russell Patterson Cheesecake-a. 22,25-Peanuts app.	3.20	8.00	16.00

NOTE: *Abbie & Slats reprinted from Tip Top.*

UNITED NATIONS, THE (See Classics Illustrated Special Issue)

UNITED STATES AIR FORCE PRESENTS: THE HIDDEN CREW
1964 (36 pages) (Full color)
U.S. Air Force

	GD25	FN65	NM94
nn-Shaffenberger-a	.60	1.50	3.00

UNITED STATES FIGHTING AIR FORCE (Also see U.S. Fighting Air Force)
Sept, 1952 - No. 29, Oct, 1956
Superior Comics Ltd.

	GD25	FN65	NM94
1	5.85	17.50	35.00
2	3.60	9.00	18.00
3-10	2.00	5.00	10.00
11-29	1.60	4.00	8.00

UNITED STATES MARINES
1943 - No. 4, 1944; No. 5, 1952 - No. 8, 1952; No. 7 - No. 11, 1953
William H. Wise/Life's Romances Publ. Co./Magazine Enterprises #5-8/Toby Press #7-11

	GD25	FN65	NM94
nn-Mart Bailey-a	6.70	20.00	40.00
2-Bailey-a	5.00	15.00	30.00
3,4	4.20	12.50	25.00
5(A-1 #55), 6(A-1 #60), 7(A-1 #68), 8(A-1 #72)	4.00	11.00	22.00
7-11 (Toby)	2.00	5.00	10.00

NOTE: *Powell a-5-7.*

UNITY
Aug, 1992 - No. 1, 1992 (Color, free, both limited, 20 pgs.)
Valiant

	GD25	FN65	NM94
0-(8/92)-Prequel to Unity x-overs in all Valiant titles; free to everone that bought all 8 titles that month; B. Smith-c/a	1.25	3.00	7.50
0-Red logo; sames above, but w/red logo (5,000)			60.00
0-Gold variant			35.00
1-(?/92)-Epilogue to unity x-overs; B. Smith-c/a	1.25	3.00	7.50
1(Gold)			65.00
1 (Platinum)			75.00

UNIVERSAL MONSTERS: FRANKENSTEIN
1993 - Present ($4.95, color, 52 pgs.)
Dark Horse Comics

Universal Soldier #1, © Fleetway

Unknown Worlds of Science Fiction #1, © MEG

Unusual Tales #21, © CC

GD25 FN65 NM94

nn-Adapts movie; painted-c/a 1.00 2.00 5.00
...: The Mummy nn-Adapts movie; painted-c 1.00 2.00 5.00
...: Dracula nn-Adapts movie 1.00 2.00 5.00

UNIVERSAL PRESENTS DRACULA (See Dell Giants)

UNIVERSAL SOLDIER
Sept, 1992 - No. 3, Nov, 1992 (Color, mini-series, based on movie)
Now Comics

1-3 ($2.50, direct sale ed.)-Polybagged, mature readers. 1-Hologram on-c; all direct sale editions have painted-c 1.00 2.50
1-3 ($1.95, newsstand ed.)-Rewritten & redrawn code approved version; all newsstand editions have photo-c .80 2.00

UNIVERSAL SOLDIER (Fleetway Editions, Ltd.)(Value: cover or less)

UNKEPT PROMISE
1949 (24 pages)
Legion of Truth (Giveaway)

nn-Anti-alcohol 6.70 20.00 40.00

UNKNOWN MAN, THE
1951 (Movie)
Avon Periodicals

nn-Kinstler-c 18.00 54.00 125.00

UNKNOWN SOLDIER (Formerly Star-Spangled War Stories)
No. 205, Apr-May, 1977 - No. 268, Oct, 1982
National Periodical Publications/DC Comics

205-268: 219-221-(44 pgs.). 248,249-Origin. 251-Enemy Ace begins. 268-Death of Unknown Soldier 1.50
NOTE: ***Chaykin*** *a-234.* ***Evans*** *a-265-267; c-235.* ***Kubert*** *c-Most.* ***Miller*** *a-219p.* ***Severin*** *a-251-253, 260, 261, 265-267.* ***Simonson*** *a-254-256.* ***Spiegle*** *a-258, 259, 262-264.*

UNKNOWN SOLDIER, THE (DC)(Value: cover or less)(See Brave & the Bold #146)

UNKNOWN WORLD (Strange Stories From Another World #2 on)
June, 1952
Fawcett Publications

1-Norman Saunders painted-c 22.00 65.00 150.00

UNKNOWN WORLDS (See Journey Into...)

UNKNOWN WORLDS
Aug, 1960 - No. 57, Aug, 1967
American Comics Group/Best Synd. Features

1 11.00 33.00 100.00
2-5: 2-Dinosaur-c/story 6.00 18.00 55.00
6-11: 9-Dinosaur-c/story. 11-Last 10 cent issue 4.00 13.00 40.00
12-19: 12-Begin 12 cent issues?; ends #57 3.00 10.00 30.00
20-Herbie cameo (12-1/62-63) 4.00 12.00 35.00
21-35 2.00 7.00 20.00
36-"The People vs. Hendricks" by Craig; most popular ACG story ever 3.00 8.00 25.00
37-46 2.00 6.00 18.00
47-Williamson-a r-from Adventures Into the Unknown #96, 3 pgs.; Craig-a 2.00 7.00 20.00
48-57: 53-Frankenstein app. 2.00 5.00 15.00
NOTE: ***Ditko*** *a-49, 50p, 54.* ***Forte*** *a-3, 6, 11.* ***Landau*** *a-56(2).* ***Reinman*** *a-3, 9, 13, 20, 22, 23, 36, 38, 54.* ***Whitney*** *c/a-most issues. John Force, Magic Agent app.-35, 36, 48, 50, 52, 54, 56.*

UNKNOWN WORLDS OF FRANK BRUNNER (Eclipse)(Value: cover or less)

UNKNOWN WORLDS OF SCIENCE FICTION
Jan, 1975 - No. 6, Nov, 1975; 1976 (B&W Magazine) ($1.00)
Marvel Comics Group

1-Williamson/Krenkel/Torres/Frazetta-r/Witzend #1, Neal Adams-r/Phase 1; Brunner & Kaluta-r; Freas/Romita-c 1.40 3.50
2-6: 5-Kaluta text illos 1.10 2.75
Special 1(1976,100 pgs.)-Newton painted-c 1.10 2.75
NOTE: ***Brunner*** *a-2; c-4, 6.* ***Buscema*** *a Special 1p.* ***Chaykin*** *a-5.* ***Colan*** *a(p)-1, 3, 5, 6.* ***Corben*** *a-4.* ***Kaluta*** *a-2, Special 1(ext illos); c-2.* ***Morrow*** *a-3, 5.* ***Nino*** *a-3, 6, Special 1.* ***Perez*** *a-2, 3. Ray Bradbury interview in #1.*

GD25 FN65 NM94

UNSANE (Formerly Mighty Bear #13, 14? or The Outlaws #10-14?)
No. 15, June, 1954
Star Publications

15-Disbrow-a(2); L. B. Cole-c 17.00 52.00 120.0

UNSEEN, THE
No. 5, 1952 - No. 15, July, 1954
Visual Editions/Standard Comics

5-Horror stories in all; Toth-a 16.00 48.00 110.0
6,7,9,10-Jack Katz-a 11.00 32.00 75.0
8,11,13,14 8.35 25.00 50.0
12,15-Toth-a. 12-Tuska-a 11.00 32.00 75.0
NOTE: ***Nick Cardy*** *c-12.* ***Fawcette*** *a-13, 14.* ***Sekowsky*** *a-7, 8(2), 10, 13, 15.*

UNTAMED
June, 1993 - No. 3, Aug, 1993 ($1.95, color, mini-series)
Epic Comics (Marvel)

1-($2.50)-Embossed-c 1.00 2.50
2,3 .80 2.00

UNTAMED LOVE (Also see Frank Frazetta's Untamed Love)
Jan, 1950 - No. 5, Sept, 1950
Quality Comics Group (Comic Magazines)

1-Ward-c, Gustavson-a 14.00 43.00 100.00
2,4: 2-5-Photo-c 10.00 30.00 60.00
3,5-Gustavson-a 10.00 30.00 65.00

UNTOLD LEGEND OF THE BATMAN, THE
July, 1980 - No. 3, Sept, 1980 (Mini-series)
DC Comics

1-Origin; Joker-c; Byrne's 1st work at DC 1.60 4.00
2,3 1.20 3.00
1-3: Batman cereal premiums (1989, 28 pgs., 6X9"); 1st & 2nd printings known .80 2.00
NOTE: ***Aparo*** *a-1i, 2, 3.* ***Byrne*** *a-1p.*

UNTOLD ORIGIN OF THE FEMFORCE, THE (AC)(Value: cover or less)

UNTOUCHABLES, THE (TV)
No. 1237, 10-12/61 - No. 4, 8-10/62 (All have Robert Stack photo-c)
Dell Publishing Co.

4-Color 1237,1286 14.00 43.00 100.00
01-879-207, 12-879-210(01879-210 on inside) 10.00 30.00 60.00
Topps Bubblegum premiums-2-1/2x4-1/2", 8 pgs. (3 diff. issues) "The Organization, Jamaica Ginger, The Otto Frick Story (drug), 3000 Suspects, The Antidote, Mexican Stakeout, Little Egypt, Purple Gang, Bugs Moran Story, & Lily Dallas Story" 2.80 7.00 14.00

UNUSUAL TALES (Blue Beetle & Shadows From Beyond #50 on)
Nov, 1955 - No. 49, Mar-Apr, 1965
Charlton Comics

1 13.00 40.00 105.00
2 6.00 19.00 50.00
3-5 4.00 11.00 30.00
6-Ditko-c only 5.00 14.00 38.00
7,8-Ditko-c/a 11.00 34.00 90.00
9-Ditko-c/a (20 pgs.) 12.00 36.00 95.00
10-Ditko-c/a(4) 14.00 43.00 110.00
11-(3/58, 68 pgs.)-Ditko-a(4) 13.00 38.00 100.00
12,14-Ditko-a 9.00 26.00 70.00
13,16-20 3.00 9.00 24.00
15-Ditko-c/a 9.00 25.00 68.00
21,24,28 2.00 6.00 16.00
22,23,25-27,29-Ditko-a 5.50 17.00 44.00
30-49 2.00 5.00 14.00
NOTE: ***Colan*** *a-11.* ***Ditko*** *c-22, 23, 25-27, 31(part).*

UP FROM HARLEM (Spire Christian)(Value: cover or less)

UP-TO-DATE COMICS

USA Comics #16, © MEG

USA Is Ready #1, © DELL

U.S. Tank Commandos #8, © AVON

No date (1938) (36 pgs.; B&W cover) (10 cents)
King Features Syndicate

	GD25	FN65	NM94
nn-Popeye & Henry cover; The Phantom, Jungle Jim & Flash Gordon by Raymond, The Katzenjammer Kids, Curley Harper & others	20.00	60.00	140.00

(Variations to above contents exist.)

UP YOUR NOSE AND OUT YOUR EAR (Magazine)
April, 1972 - No. 2, June, 1972 (52 pgs.) (Satire)
Klevart Enterprises

	GD25	FN65	NM94
V1#1,2		1.20	3.00

URTH 4 (Continuity)(Value: cover or less)

USA COMICS
Aug, 1941 - No. 17, Fall, 1945
Timely Comics (USA)

	GD25	FN65	VF82	NM94
1-Origin Major Liberty (called Mr. Liberty #1), Rockman by Wolverton, & The Whizzer by Avison; The Defender with sidekick Rusty & Jack Frost begin; The Young Avenger only app.; S&K-c plus 1 pg. art	575.00	1725.00	3160.00	4600.00

(Estimated up to 145 total copies exist, 7 in NM/Mint)

	GD25	FN65	NM94
2-Origin Captain Terror & The Vagabond; last Wolverton Rockman	225.00	675.00	1500.00
3-No Whizzer	175.00	525.00	1200.00
4-Last Rockman, Major Liberty, Defender, Jack Frost, & Capt. Terror; Corporal Dix app.	140.00	420.00	930.00
5-Origin American Avenger & Roko the Amazing; The Blue Blade, The Black Widow & Victory Boys, Gypo the Gypsy Giant & Hills of Horror only app.; Sergeant Dix begins; no Whizzer; Hitler-c	117.00	350.00	750.00
6-Captain America, The Destroyer, Jap Buster Johnson, Jeep Jones begin; Terror Squad only app.	140.00	420.00	930.00
7-Captain Daring, Disk-Eyes the Detective by Wolverton app.; origin & only app. Marvel Boy (3/43); Secret Stamp begins; no Whizzer, Sergeant Dix	122.00	365.00	800.00
8-10: 9-Last Secret Stamp. 10-The Thunderbird only app.	88.00	262.00	575.00
11,12: 11-No Jeep Jones	75.00	225.00	500.00
13-17: 13-No Whizzer; Jeep Jones ends. 15-No Destroyer; Jap Buster Johnson ends	55.00	165.00	375.00

NOTE: ***Brodsky** c-14. **Gabrielle** c-4, 8. **Schomburg** c-6-8, 10, 12, 13, 15-17. **Shores** a-1, 4; c-3, 9, 11. **Ed Win** a-4.*

U.S. AGENT (See Jeff Jordan...)

U.S. AGENT (See Captain America #354)
June, 1993 - No. 4, Sept, 1993 ($1.75, color, mini-series)
Marvel Comics

	GD25	FN65	NM94
1-4		.70	1.75

USAGI YOJIMBO (See Albedo, Doomsday Squad #3 & Space Usagi)
July, 1987 - No. 36? ($2.00, B&W)
Fantagraphics Books

	GD25	FN65	NM94
1		1.60	4.00
1,8,10-2nd printings		.80	2.00
2-9,11-28: 11-Aragones-a		.80	2.00
10-Leonardo app. (TMNT)		1.60	4.00
29-36: 29-Begin $2.25-c		.90	2.25
Color Special 1 (11/89, $2.95, 68 pgs.)-new & r		1.20	3.00
Summer Special 1 (1986, B&W, $2.75)-r/early Albedo issues	1.30	3.25	8.00

USAGI YOJIMBO
Mar, 1993 - Present ($2.75, Color)
Mirage Studios

	GD25	FN65	NM94
V2#1-4: 1-Teenage Mutant Ninja Turtles app.		1.10	2.75

U.S. AIR FORCE COMICS (Army Attack #38 on)
Oct, 1958 - No. 37, Mar-Apr, 1965
Charlton Comics

	GD25	FN65	NM94
1	4.20	12.50	25.00
2	2.40	6.00	12.00
3-10	1.60	4.00	8.00
11-20	1.20	3.00	6.00
21-37	.80	2.00	4.00

NOTE: ***Glanzman** c/a-9, 10, 12. **Montes/Bache** a-33.*

USA IS READY
1941 (68 pgs.) (One Shot)
Dell Publishing Co.

	GD25	FN65	NM94
1-War propaganda	29.00	90.00	185.00

U.S. BORDER PATROL COMICS (Sgt. Dick Carter of the...) (See Holyoke One Shot)

U.S. FIGHTING AIR FORCE (Also see United States Fighting Air Force)
No date (1960s?)
I. W. Enterprises

	GD25	FN65	NM94
1,9(nd): 1-r/United States Fighting...#?. 9-r/#1		.90	2.25

U.S. FIGHTING MEN
1963 - 1964 (Reprints)
Super Comics

	GD25	FN65	NM94
10-r/With the U.S. Paratroops #4(Avon)	1.00	2.50	5.00
11,12,15-18: 11-r/Monty Hall #10. 12,16,17,18-r/U.S. Fighting Air Force #10,3,?&? 15-r/Man Comics #11	.60	1.50	3.00

U.S. JONES (Also see Wonderworld Comics #28)
Nov, 1941 - No. 2, Jan, 1942
Fox Features Syndicate

	GD25	FN65	NM94
1-U.S. Jones & The Topper begin	78.00	232.00	500.00
2	60.00	182.00	395.00

U.S. MARINES
Fall, 1964 (One shot, 12 cents)
Charlton Comics

	GD25	FN65	NM94
1	1.00	2.50	5.00

U.S. MARINES IN ACTION!
Aug, 1952 - No. 3, Dec, 1952
Avon Periodicals

	GD25	FN65	NM94
1-Louis Ravielli-c/a	5.00	15.00	30.00
2,3: 3-Kinstler-c	3.60	9.00	18.00

U.S. 1 (Marvel)(Value: cover or less)

U.S. PARATROOPS (See With the...)

U.S. PARATROOPS
1964?
I. W. Enterprises

	GD25	FN65	NM94
1,8: 1-r/With the U.S. Paratroops #1; Wood-c. 8-r/With the U.S. Paratroops #6; Kinstler-c	1.00	2.50	5.00

U.S. TANK COMMANDOS
June, 1952 - No. 4, March, 1953
Avon Periodicals

	GD25	FN65	NM94
1-Kinstler-c	5.85	17.50	35.00
2-4: Kinstler-c	4.00	11.00	22.00
I.W. Reprint #1,8: 1-r/#1. 8-r/#3	1.00	2.50	5.00

NOTE: ***Kinstler** a-I.W. #1; c-1-4, I.W. #1, 8.*

"V" (TV)(DC)(Value: cover or less)

VACATION COMICS (See A-1 Comics #16)

VACATION DIGEST (Harvey)(Value: cover or less)

VACATION IN DISNEYLAND (Also see Dell Giants)
Aug-Oct, 1959; May, 1965 (Walt Disney)
Dell Publishing Co./Gold Key (1965)

	GD25	FN65	NM94
4-Color 1025-Barks-a	8.35	25.00	50.00

1(30024-508)(G.K., 5/65, 25 cents)-r/Dell Giant #30 & cover to #1 ('58);

Valor #3, © WMG

Vampirella #19, © WP

Vanity #2, © PC

	GD25	FN65	NM94
celebrates Disneyland's 10th anniversary	3.00	7.50	15.00

VACATION PARADE (See Dell Giants)

VALERIA THE SHE BAT
May, 1993 - Present (Color)
Continuity Comics

	GD25	FN65	NM94
1-Premium; glow-in-the-dark-c; N. Adams-a	6.50	19.00	45.00

VALKYRIE (Eclipse, 1987 & 1988)(Value: cover or less)

VALLEY OF THE DINOSAURS (TV)
April, 1975 - No. 11, Dec, 1976 (Hanna-Barbara)
Charlton Comics

	GD25	FN65	NM94
1		1.20	3.00
2-11: 3-Byrne text illos (early work, 7/75)			1.50

VALLEY OF GWANGI (See Movie Classics)

VALOR
Mar-Apr, 1955 - No. 5, Nov-Dec, 1955
E. C. Comics

	GD25	FN65	NM94
1-Williamson/Torres-a; Wood-c/a	22.00	65.00	150.00
2-Williamson-c/a; Wood-a	19.00	57.00	130.00
3,4: 3-Williamson, Crandall-a. 4-Wood-c	13.00	40.00	90.00
5-Wood-c/a; Williamson/Evans-a	11.50	34.00	80.00

NOTE: ***Crandall** a-3, 4. **Ingels** a-1, 2, 4, 5. **Krigstein** a-1-5. **Orlando** a-3, 4; c-3. **Wood** a-1, 2, 5; c-1, 4, 5.*

VALOR
Nov, 1992 - Present ($1.25, color)
DC Comics

	GD25	FN65	NM94
1-18: 1-Eclipso the Darkness Within aftermath. 2-Vs. Supergirl. 4-Vs. Lobo. 12-Lobo cameo			1.25

VALOR THUNDERSTAR AND HIS FIREFLIES (Now)(Value: cover or less)

VAMPIRE LESTAT, THE
Jan, 1990 - No. 12, 1991 ($2.50, painted color, mini-series)
Innovation Publishing

	GD25	FN65	NM94
1-Adapts novel; Bolton painted-c on all	3.85	11.50	27.00
1-2nd printing (has UPC code, 1st prints don't)		1.20	3.00
1-3rd & 4th printings		1.00	2.50
2-1st printing	1.65	4.70	11.00
2-2nd & 3rd printings		1.00	2.50
3-5	1.00	2.50	6.00
3-6,9-2nd printings		1.00	2.50
6-12		1.60	4.00

VAMPIRELLA (Magazine)(See Warren Presents)
Sept, 1969 - No. 112, Feb, 1983; No. 113, Jan, 1988? (B&W)
Warren Publishing Co./Harris Publications #113

	GD25	FN65	NM94
1-Intro. Vampirella	25.00	75.00	175.00
2-Amazonia series begins, ends #12	10.00	30.00	70.00
3 (Low distribution)	29.00	86.00	200.00
4-7	5.00	15.00	36.00
8-Vampi begins by Tom Sutton as serious strip (early issues-gag line)	4.85	15.00	34.00
9-Barry Smith-a; Boris-c	5.00	16.00	37.00
10-No Vampi story	2.70	8.00	19.00
11-15: 11-Origin, 1st app. Pendragon. 12-Vampi by Gonzales begins	3.60	10.75	25.00
16-18,20-25: 17-Tomb of the Gods begins, ends #22. 25-Begin partial color issues	2.15	6.50	15.00
19 (1973 Annual)	3.20	8.00	20.00
26,28-36,38-40: 30-Intro. Pantha. 31-Origin Luana, the Beast Girl. 33-Pantha ends	1.30	3.25	8.00
27 (1974 Annual)	1.65	4.00	10.00
37 (1975 Annual)	1.50	3.75	9.00
41-45,47-50: 50-Spirit cameo by Eisner	.80	1.90	4.75
46-Origin retold (10/75)	.90	1.90	4.75
51-99: 93-Cassandra St. Knight begins, ends #103; new Pantha series begins, ends 108		1.40	3.50
100 (96 pg. r-special)-Origin reprinted		1.50	3.75
101-110,112: 108-Torpedo series by Toth begins		.90	2.25
111-Giant Collector's Edition ($2.50)		1.00	2.50
113 (1988)		.80	2.00
Annual 1(1972)-New origin Vampirella by Gonzales; reprints by Neal Adams (from #1), Wood (from #9)	14.00	43.00	100.00
Special 1 (1977; large-square bound)	1.50	3.75	9.00

NOTE: ***Neal Adams** a-1, 10p, 19p(r/#10). **Alcala** a-90, 93i. **Bode'/Todd** c-3. **Bode'/Jones** c-4. **Boris** c-9. **Brunner** a-10. **Corben** a-30, 31, 33, 54. **Crandall** a-1, 19(r/#1). **Frazetta** c-1, 5, 7, 11, 31. **Heath** a-76-78, 83. **Jones** a-5, 9, 12, 27, 32, 33(2pg.), 34, 50i, 83r. **Nino** a-59i, 61i, 67, 76, 85, 90. **Ploog** a-14. **Barry Smith** a-9. **Starlin** a-78. **Sutton** a-11. **Toth** a-90i, 108, 110. **Wood** a-9, 10, 12, 19(r/#12), 27; c-9. **Wrightson** a-33(w/Jones), 63. All reprint issues-37, 74, 83, 87, 91, 105, 107, 109, 111. Annuals from 1973 on are included in regular numbering. Later annuals are same format as regular issues.*

VAMPIRELLA
Nov, 1992 - No. 6, 1993t ($2.95, color)
Harris Publications

	GD25	FN65	NM94
1-Jim Balent inks	2.60	7.50	18.00
1-2nd printing		1.20	3.00
2-6		1.20	3.00

NOTE: *Issues 1-6 contain certificates for free **Dave Stevens** Vampirella poster.*

VAMPIRELLA: MORNING IN AMERICA
1991 - No. 4, 1992 ($3.95, B&W, mini-series, 52 pgs.)
Harris Publications/Dark Horse Comics

	GD25	FN65	NM94
1: All have Kaluta painted covers		1.80	4.5
2-4		1.60	4.0

VAMPIRE TALES (Magazine)
Aug, 1973 - No. 11, June, 1975 (B&W) (75 cents)
Marvel Comics Group

	GD25	FN65	NM94
1-Morbius, the Living Vampire begins by Pablo Marcos (1st solo Morbius series)	3.20	8.00	20.00
2-Intro. Satana; Steranko-r	1.25	3.00	7.50
3,4,6-11: 3-Satana app. 6-1st Lilith app. 8-Blade app. (see Tomb of Dracula)		1.40	3.50
5-Origin Morbius	1.20	3.00	7.00
Annual 1(10/75)-Heath-r/#9		.80	2.00

NOTE: ***Alcala** a-6, 8, 9i. **Boris** c-4, 6. **Chaykin** a-7. **Everett** a-1r. **Gulacy** a-7p. **Heath** a-9. **Infantino** a-3r. **Gil Kane** a-4, 5r.*

VANGUARD (...Outpost: Earth) (See Megaton & Savage Dragon #2)
1987 ($1.50, color)
Megaton Comics

	GD25	FN65	NM94
1-Erik Larsen-c(p)		1.40	3.50

VANGUARD
Oct, 1993 - Present ($1.95, color)
Image Comics

	GD25	FN65	NM94
1-3-Erik Larsen-a		.80	2.00

VANGUARD ILLUSTRATED
Nov, 1983 - No. 7, May, 1984 (Color, Baxter paper)
Pacific Comics

	GD25	FN65	NM94
1-6: 1,7-Nudity scenes. 2-1st app. Stargrazers (see Legends of the Stargrazers; Dave Stevens-c			1.50
7-1st app. Mr. Monster (r-in Mr. Monster #1)	1.00	2.00	5.00

NOTE: ***Evans** a-7. **Kaluta** c-5, 7p. **Perez** a-6; c-6. **Rude** a-1-4; c-4. **Williamson** c-3.*

VANITY (Pacific)(Value: cover or less)

VARIETY COMICS
1944 - No. 2, 1945; No. 3, 1946 - No. 5, 1946?
Rural Home Publications/Croyden Publ. Co.

	GD25	FN65	NM94
1-Origin Captain Valiant	11.50	34.00	80.00
2-Captain Valiant	6.70	20.00	40.00
3(1946-Croyden)-Captain Valiant	5.85	17.50	35.00
4,5-Exist?	5.00	15.00	30.00

Vault of Horror #6, © WMG

Venom: Funeral Pyre #3, © MEG

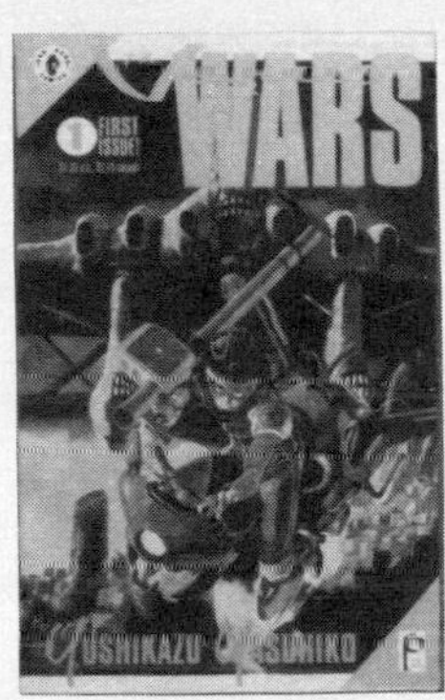

Venus Wars #1, © Yoshikazu Yasuhiko & Gakken

GD25 FN65 NM94 GD25 FN65 NM94

VARIETY COMICS (See Fox Giants)

VARSITY
1945
Parents' Magazine Institute

1 5.00 15.00 30.00

VAUDEVILLE AND OTHER THINGS
1900 (10-1/2x13") (in color) (18+ pgs.)
Isaac H. Blandiard Co.

nn-By Bunny 43.00 130.00 300.00

VAULT OF EVIL
Feb, 1973 - No. 23, Nov, 1975
Marvel Comics Group

1 (1950s reprints begin) .80 2.00
2-23: 3,4-Brunner-c 1.50

NOTE: ***Ditko*** *a-14r, 15r, 20-22r.* ***Drucker*** *a-10r(Mystic #52), 13r(Uncanny Tales #42).* ***Everett*** *a-11r(Menace #2), 13r(Menace #4); c-10.* ***Heath*** *a-5r.* ***Krigstein*** *a-20r(Uncanny Tales #54).* ***Reinman*** *r-1.* ***Tuska*** *a-6r.*

VAULT OF HORROR (Formerly War Against Crime #1-11)
No. 12, Apr-May, 1950 - No. 40, Dec-Jan, 1954-55
E. C. Comics

12 (Scarce) 315.00 945.00 2500.00
13-Morphine story 82.00 245.00 575.00
14 75.00 225.00 525.00
15 60.00 180.00 425.00
16 43.00 130.00 300.00
17-19 33.00 100.00 230.00
20-25: 22-Frankenstein-c & adaptation. 23-Used in **POP**, pg. 84. 24-Craig biography 26.00 80.00 180.00
26-B&W & color illos in **POP** 26.00 80.00 180.00
27-35: 30-Dismemberment-c. 31-Ray Bradbury biog. 32-Censored-c. 35-X-Mas-c 19.00 58.00 135.00
36-"Pipe Dream"-classic opium addict story by Krigstein; "Twin Bill" cited in articles by T.E. Murphy, Wertham 19.00 58.00 135.00
37-1st app. Drusilla, a Vampirella look alike; Williamson-a 18.00 58.00 135.00
38-39: 39-Bondage-c 16.00 48.00 110.00
40-Low distribution 19.00 58.00 135.00

NOTE: ***Craig*** *art in all but No. 13 & 33; c-12-40.* ***Crandall*** *a-33, 34, 39.* ***Davis*** *a-17-38.* ***Evans*** *a-27, 28, 30, 32, 33.* ***Feldstein*** *a-12-16.* ***Ingels*** *a-13-20, 22-40.* ***Kamen*** *a-15-22, 25, 29, 35.* ***Krigstein*** *a-36, 38-40.* ***Kurtzman*** *a-12, 13.* ***Orlando*** *a-24, 31, 40.* ***Wood*** *a-12-14. #22, 29 & 31 have Ray Bradbury adaptations. #16 & 17 have H. P. Lovecraft adaptations.*

VAULT OF HORROR, THE
Aug, 1990 - No. 6, June, 1991 ($1.95, color, 68 pgs.)(#4 on: $2.00)
Gladstone Publishing

1-Craig-c(r); all contain EC reprints 1.60 4.00
2-6: 2,4-6-Craig-c(r). 3-Ingels-c(r) .80 2.00

VAULT OF HORROR
Sept, 1991 - No. 5, May, 1992? ($2.00, color)
Oct, 1992 - Present ($1.50, color)
Russ Cochran

1-5: E.C reprints .80 2.00
1-4: 1-r/VOH #12 (#1); Craig-c 1.50

V...-COMICS (Morse code for "V" - 3 dots, 1 dash)
Jan, 1942 - No. 2, Mar-Apr, 1942
Fox Features Syndicate

1-Origin V-Man & the Boys; The Banshee & The Black Fury, The Queen of Evil, & V-Agents begin 79.00 238.00 525.00
2-Bondage/torture-c 65.00 195.00 450.00

VECTOR (Now)(Value: cover or less)

VEGAS KNIGHTS
1989 ($1.95, color)
Pioneer Comics

1 .80 2.00

VENGEANCE SQUAD
July, 1975 - No. 6, May, 1976 (#1-3 are 25 cent issues)
Charlton Comics

1-Mike Mauser, Private Eye begins by Staton .70 1.80
2-6: Morisi-a in all 1.50
5,6(Modern Comics-r, 1977) 1.25

VENOM: FUNERAL PYRE
Aug, 1993 - No. 3, Oct, 1993 ($2.95, color, limited series)
Marvel Comics

1-3: 1-Holo-grafx foil-c; Punisher app. in all 1.20 3.00

VENOM: LETHAL PROTECTOR (Also see Amazing Spider-Man #298 & Marvel Comics Presents)
Feb, 1993 - No. 6, July, 1993 ($2.95, color, limited series)
Marvel Comics

1-Red holo-grafx foil-c; Bagley-c/a in all 1.00 2.00 5.00
1-Gold variant sold to retailers 25.00
2-6: Spider-Man app. in all 1.20 3.00

VENOM: THE ENEMY WITHIN
Feb, 1994 - No. 3, Apr, 1994 ($2.95, color, limited series)
Marvel Comics

1-3: 1-Glow-in-the-dark-c 1.20 3.00

VENOM: THE MADNESS
Nov, 1993 - No. 3, Jan, 1994 ($2.95, color, limited series)
Marvel Comics

1-3: 1-Embossed-c; Juggernaut app. 1.20 3.00

VENTURE (AC)(Value: cover or less)

VENUS (See Marvel Spotlight #2 & Weird Wonder Tales)
August, 1948 - No. 19, April, 1952 (Also see Marvel Mystery #91)
Marvel/Atlas Comics (CMC 1-9/LCC 10-19)

1-Venus & Hedy Devine begin; 1st app. Venus; Kurtzman's "Hey Look" 68.00 205.00 475.00
2 39.00 120.00 275.00
3,5 34.00 105.00 240.00
4-Kurtzman's "Hey Look" 36.00 110.00 250.00
6-9: 6-Loki app. 7,8-Painted-c 33.00 100.00 230.00
10-S/F-horror issues begin (7/50) 36.00 110.00 250.00
11-S/F end of the world(11/50) 40.00 120.00 280.00
12-Colan-a 29.00 85.00 200.00
13-19-Venus by Everett, 2-3 stories each; covers-#13,15-19; 14-Everett part cover (Venus). 17-Bondage-c 45.00 135.00 315.00

NOTE: ***Berg*** *s/f story-13.* ***Everett*** *c-13, 14(part; Venus only), 15-19.* ***Heath*** *s/f story-11.* ***Maneely*** *s/f story-10(3pg.), 16.* ***Morisi*** *a-19.* ***Syd Shores*** *c-6.*

VENUS WARS, THE (Dark Horse)(Value: cover or less)

VENUS WARS II, THE (Dark Horse)(Value: cover or less)

VERI BEST SURE FIRE COMICS
No date (circa 1945) (Reprints Holyoke One-Shots)
Holyoke Publishing Co.

1-Captain Aero, Alias X, Miss Victory, Commandos of the Devil Dogs, Red Cross, Hammerhead Hawley, Capt. Aero's Sky Scouts, Flagman app. 20.00 60.00 140.00

VERI BEST SURE SHOT COMICS
No date (circa 1945) (Reprints Holyoke One-Shots)Holyoke Publishing Co.

1-Capt. Aero, Miss Victory by Quinlan, Alias X, The Red Cross, Flagman, Commandos of the Devil Dogs, Hammerhead Hawley, Capt. Aero's Sky Scouts 20.00 60.00 140.00

VERONICA (Also see Archie's Girls, Betty &...)
April, 1989 - Present (75 & 95 cents, color)
Archie Comics

1-30: 1,2-(75 cents). 3-30 (95¢-$1.00) 1.00

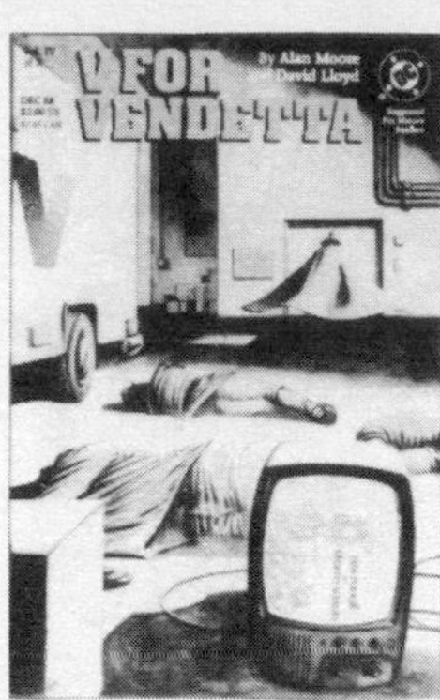

V For Vendetta #4, © DC

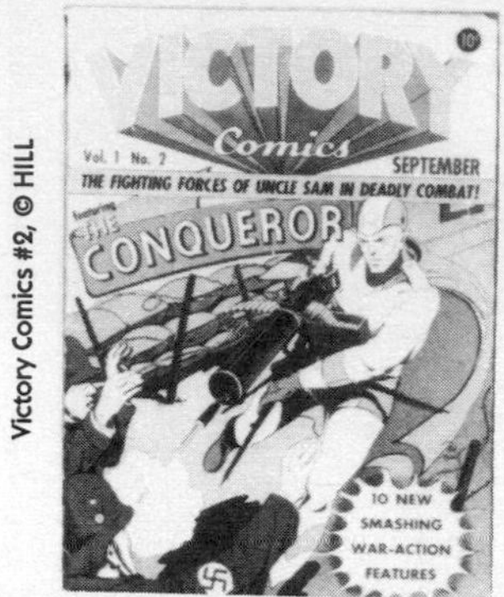

Victory Comics #2, © HILL

Vietnam Journal #7, © Apple Press/Don Lomax

GD25 FN65 NM94

21-34: 21-Begin $1.25-c 1.25

VERONICA'S PASSPORT DIGEST MAGAZINE
Nov, 1992 - Present ($1.50, color, digest size)
Harvey Comics

1,2 1.50

VERONICA'S SUMMER SPECIAL (See Archie Giant Series Magazine #615, 625)

VERTIGO JAM
Aug, 1993 ($3.95, color, 68 pgs.)(Painted-c by Fabry)
DC Comics (Vertigo)

1-Sandman by Neil Gaiman, Hellblazer, Animal Man, Doom Patrol, Swamp Thing, Kid Eternity & Shade the Changing Man 1.60 4.00

VERTIGO PREVIEW
1992 (75¢, color, 36 pgs.)
DC Comics (Vertigo)

1-Vertigo previews; Sandman by Neil Gaiman 1.00

VERTIGO VISIONS
June, 1993 - Present (Color, 68 pgs.)
DC Comics (Vertigo)

The Geek 1 (6/93, $3.95) 1.60 4.00
The Phantom Stranger 1 (10/93, $3.50) 1.40 3.50

VERY BEST OF DENNIS THE MENACE, THE
July, 1979 - No. 2, Apr, 1980 (132 pgs., Digest, 95 cents, $1.00)
Fawcett Publications

1,2-Reprints .80 2.00

VERY BEST OF DENNIS THE MENACE, THE
April, 1982 - No. 3, Aug, 1982 ($1.25, digest size)
Marvel Comics Group

1-3-Reprints 1.25
NOTE: ***Hank Ketcham** c-all. A few thousand of #1 & 2 were printed with DC emblem.*

V FOR VENDETTA (DC)(Value: cover or less)

VIC BRIDGES FAZERS SKETCHBOOK AND FACT FILE (AC)(Value: cover or less)

VIC FLINT (Crime Buster...)(See Authentic Police Cases #10-14 & Fugitives From Justice #2)
August, 1948 - No. 5, April, 1949 (Newspaper reprints; NEA Service)
St. John Publishing Co.

1 8.35 25.00 50.00
2 5.00 15.00 30.00
3-5 4.20 12.50 25.00

VIC FLINT
Feb, 1956 - No. 2, May, 1956 (Newspaper reprints)
Argo Publ.

1,2 5.00 15.00 30.00

VIC JORDAN (Also see Big Shot Comics #32)
April, 1945
Civil Service Publ.

1-1944 daily newspaper-r 10.00 30.00 60.00

VICKI (Humor)
Feb, 1975 - No. 4, July, 1975 (No. 1,2: 68 pgs.)
Atlas/Seaboard Publ.

1-Reprints Tippy Teen 1.20 3.00
2-4 .65 1.60

VICKI VALENTINE (Renegade)(Value: cover or less)

VICKS COMICS (Also see Pure Oil Comics, Salerno Carnival of Comics & 24 Pages of Comics)
nd (circa 1938) (68 pgs. in color) (Giveaway)
Eastern Color Printing Co. (Vicks Chemical Co.)

nn-Famous Funnies-r (before #40); contains 5 pgs. Buck Rogers (4 pgs. from F.F. #15, & 1 pg. from #16) Joe Palooka, Napoleon, etc. app. 60.00 180.00 425.00
nn-16 loose, untrimmed page giveaway; paper-c; r/Famous Funnies #14; Buck Rogers, Joe Palooka app. 23.00 70.00 160.00

VICKY
Oct, 1948 - No. 5, June, 1949
Ace Magazine

nn(10/48)-Teenage humor 4.20 12.50 25.00
4(12/48), nn(2/49), 4(4/49), 5(6/49) 4.00 10.00 20.00

VIC TORRY & HIS FLYING SAUCER (Also see Mr. Monster's...#5)
1950 (One Shot)
Fawcett Publications

nn-Book-length saucer story by Powell; photo/painted-c 38.00 115.00 265.00

VICTORY COMICS
Aug, 1941 - No. 4, Dec, 1941 (#1 by Funnies, Inc.)
Hillman Periodicals

1-The Conqueror by Bill Everett, The Crusader, & Bomber Burns begin; Conqueror's origin in text; Everett-c 150.00 450.00 1000.00
2-Everett-c/a 75.00 225.00 500.00
3,4 50.00 150.00 330.00

VIC VERITY MAGAZINE
1945; No. 2, Jan?, 1947 - No. 7, Sept, 1946 (A comic book)
Vic Verity Publications

1-C. C. Beck-c/a 11.00 32.00 75.00
2-Beck-c 6.35 19.00 38.00
3-7: 6-Beck-a. 7-Beck-c 5.35 16.00 32.00

VIDEO JACK (Marvel)(Value: cover or less)

VIETNAM JOURNAL
Nov, 1987 - No. 11, July, 1989 ($1.75/$1.95, B&W)
Apple Comics

1-Don Lomax-c/a/scripts in all .80 2.00
1-2nd print .80 2.00
2-11: 10,11-$2.00/$2.25-c .80 2.00
...: Indian Country Vol. 1 (1990, $12.95)-r/#1-4 plus one new story 1.85 5.50 13.00

VIGILANTE, THE (DC)(Value: cover or less)(Also see Action Comics #42, Justice League of America #78, Leading Comics, New Teen Titans #23 & World's Finest #244)

VIGILANTES, THE (See 4-Color #839)

VIKINGS, THE (See 4-Color #910)

VILLAINS AND VIGILANTES (Eclipse)(Value: cover or less)

VINTAGE MAGNUS (...Robot Fighter)
Jan, 1992 - No. 4, Apr, 1992 ($1.95, color, mini-series)
Valiant

1-Layton-c; r/origin from Magnus R.F. #22 1.00 2.00 5.00
2-4 1.20 3.00

VIRGINIAN, THE (TV)
June, 1963
Gold Key

1(10060-306)-Part photo-c 4.20 12.50 25.00

VIRUS
1993 - No. 4, 1993 ($2.50, color, mini-series)
Dark Horse Comics

1-4: Ploog-c 1.00 2.50

VISION AND THE SCARLET WITCH, THE (Marvel, 1982 & 1985)(Value: cover or less)

VISIONARIES (Marvel)(Value: cover or less)

VISIONS
1979 - No. 5, 1983 (B&W, fanzine)

Voodoo #16, © AJAX

Voyage to the Bottom of the Sea #11, © 20th Century Fox

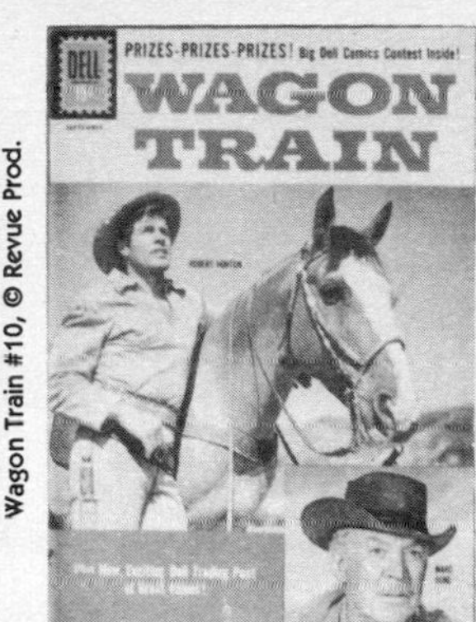

Wagon Train #10, © Revue Prod.

GD25 FN65 NM94

Vision Publications
1-Flaming Carrot begins(1st app?); N. Adams-c 8.00 23.00 54.00
2-N. Adams, Rogers-a; Gulacy back-c; signed & numbered to 2000
4.00 12.00 28.00
3-Williamson-c(p); Steranko back-c 1.70 5.00 12.00
4-Flaming Carrot-c & info. 2.30 6.75 16.00
5-1 pg. Flaming Carrot 1.30 3.25 8.00
NOTE: *After #4, Visions became an annual publication of The Atlanta Fantasy Fair.*

VOID INDIGO (Marvel)(Value: cover or less)

VOLTRON (TV)(Modern)(Value: cover or less)

VOODA (Jungle Princess) (Formerly Voodoo)
No. 20, April, 1955 - No. 22, Aug, 1955
Ajax-Farrell (Four Star Publications)
20-Baker-c/a (r/Seven Seas #6) 14.00 43.00 100.00
21,22-Baker-a plus Kamen/Baker story, Kimbo Boy of Jungle, & Baker-c (p) in all. 22-Censored Jo-Jo-r (name Powaa) 13.00 40.00 90.00
NOTE: *#20-22 each contain one heavily censored r of South Sea Girl by* **Baker** *from Seven Seas Comics with name changed to Vooda. #20-r/Seven Seas #6; #21-r/#4; #22-4/#3.*

VOODOO (Weird Fantastic Tales) (Vooda #20 on)
May, 1952 - No. 19, Jan-Feb, 1955
Ajax-Farrell (Four Star Publ.)
1-South Sea Girl-r by Baker 25.00 75.00 175.00
2-Rulah story-r plus South Sea Girl from Seven Seas #2 by Baker (name changed from Alani to El'nee) 20.00 60.00 140.00
3-Bakerish-a; man stabbed in face 14.00 43.00 100.00
4,8-Baker-r. 8-Severed head panels 14.00 43.00 100.00
5-7,9,10: 5-Nazi death camp story (flaying alive). 6-Severed head panels
11.00 32.00 75.00
11-14,16-18: 14-Zombies take over America. 16-Post nuclear world story. 17-Electric chair panels 10.00 30.00 65.00
15-Opium drug story-r/Ellery Queen #3 10.00 30.00 70.00
19-Bondage-c; Baker-a(2)(r); last pre-code; contents & covers chane to jungle theme 12.00 36.00 85.00
Annual 1(1952, 25¢, 100 pgs.); Baker-a 33.00 100.00 230.00

VOODOO (See Tales of...)

VORTEX
Nov, 1982 - No. 15, 1988(No month) ($1.50-$1.75, B&W)
Vortex Publs.
1 ($1.95)-Peter Hsu-a; Ken Steacy-c; nudity 1.65 4.00 10.00
2-1st app. Mister X (on-c only) 1.60 4.00
3 1.20 3.00
4-15: 12-Sam Kieth-a .70 1.80

VORTEX
1991 - No. 2? ($2.50, color, limited series)
Comico
1,2: Heroes from The Elementals 1.00 2.50

VOYAGE TO THE BOTTOM OF THE SEA (TV)
No. 1230, Sept-Nov, 1961; Dec, 1964 - #16, Apr, 1970 (Painted covers)
Dell Publishing Co./Gold Key
4-Color 1230(Movie-1961) 9.15 27.50 55.00
10133-412(#1, 12/64)(Gold Key) 5.85 17.50 35.00
2(7/65) - 5: Photo back-c, 1-5 4.20 12.50 25.00
6-14 3.60 9.00 18.00
15,16-Reprints 2.40 6.00 12.00

VOYAGE TO THE DEEP
Sept-Nov, 1962 - No. 4, Nov-Jan, 1964 (Painted-c)
Dell Publishing Co
1 5.00 15.00 30.00
2-4 3.60 9.00 18.00

WACKO
Sept, 1980 - No. 3, Oct, 1981 (B&W magazine, 84 pgs.)
Ideal Publ. Corp.
1-3 .80 2.00

WACKY ADVENTURES OF CRACKY (Also see Gold Key Spotlight)
Dec, 1972 - No. 12, Sept, 1975
Gold Key
1 1.50 3.75 9.00
2 1.60 4.00
3-12 .80 2.00
(See March of Comics #405, 424, 436, 448)

WACKY DUCK (Formerly Dopey Duck?; Justice Comics #7 on)(See Film Funnies)
No. 3, Fall, 1946 - No. 6, Summer, 1947; 8/48 - No. 2, 10/48
Marvel Comics (NPP)
3 10.00 30.00 70.00
4-Infinity-c 13.00 40.00 90.00
5,6(1947) 10.00 30.00 60.00
1,2(1948) 6.70 20.00 40.00
I.W. Reprint #1,2,7('58) .80 2.00 4.00
Super Reprint #10(I.W. on-c, Super-inside) .80 2.00 4.00

WACKY QUACKY (See Wisco)

WACKY RACES (TV)
Aug, 1969 - No. 7, Apr, 1972 (Hanna-Barbera)
Gold Key
1 2.15 6.50 15.00
2-7 1.30 3.25 8.00

WACKY SQUIRREL (Also see Dark Horse Presents)
Oct, 1987 - No. 4, 1988 ($1.75, B&W)
Dark Horse Comics
1-4: 4-Superman parody .70 1.75
Halloween Adventure Special 1 (1987, $2.00) .80 2.00
Summer Fun Special 1 (1988, $2.00) .80 2.00

WACKY WITCH (Also see Gold Key Spotlight)
March, 1971 - No. 21, Dec, 1975
Gold Key
1 2.15 6.50 15.00
2 1.30 3.25 8.00
3-10 1.00 2.00 5.00
11-21 1.20 3.00
(See March of Comics #374, 398, 410, 422, 434, 446, 458, 470, 482)

WACKY WOODPECKER (See Two Bit...)
1958; 1963
I. W. Enterprises/Super Comics
I.W. Reprint #1,2,7(nd-r-/Two Bit...) .60 1.50 3.00
Super Reprint #10('63) .60 1.50 3.00

WAGON TRAIN (1st Series) (TV) (See Western Roundup under Dell Giants)
No. 895, Mar, 1958 - No. 13, Apr-June, 1962 (All photo-c)
Dell Publishing Co.
4 Color 895 (#1) 10.00 30.00 60.00
4-Color 971(#2),1019(#3) 5.85 17.50 35.00
4(1-3/60),6-13 4.70 14.00 28.00
5-Toth-a 5.35 16.00 32.00

WAGON TRAIN (2nd Series)(TV)
Jan, 1964 - No. 4, Oct, 1964 (All photo-c)
Gold Key
1-Tufts-a in all 4.20 12.50 25.00
2-4 3.60 9.00 18.00

WAITING ROOM WILLIE (See Sad Case of...)

WALLY (Teen-age)
Dec, 1962 - No. 4, Sept, 1963
Gold Key

Wally Wood's Thunder Agents #2, © Deluxe

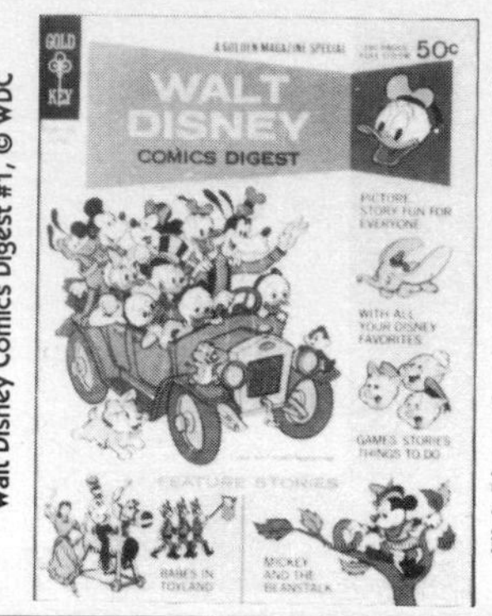

Walt Disney Comics Digest #1, © WDC

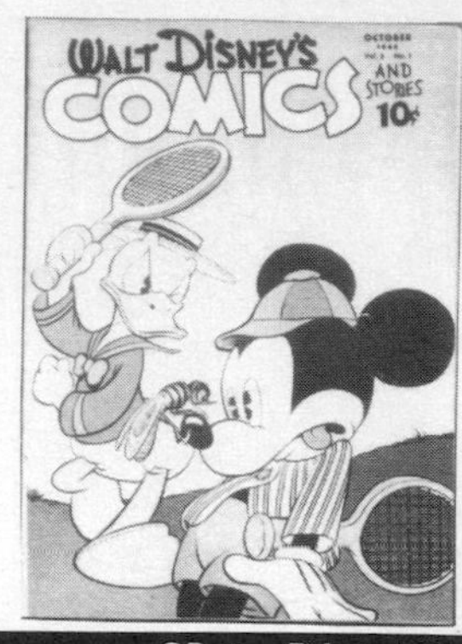

Walt Disney Comics and Stories #49, © WDC

GD25 FN65 NM94

1 3.00 7.50 15.00
2-4 1.60 4.00 8.00

WALLY THE WIZARD (Marvel)(Value: cover or less)

WALLY WOOD'S T.H.U.N.D.E.R. AGENTS (Deluxe)(Value: cover or less)

WALT DISNEY CHRISTMAS PARADE (Also see Christmas Parade)
Winter, 1977 (224 pgs.) (cardboard covers, $1.95)
Whitman Publishing Co. (Golden Press)

11191-Barks-r/Christmas in Disneyland #1, Dell Christmas Parade #9 & Dell Giant #53 1.00 2.40

WALT DISNEY COMICS DIGEST
June, 1968 - No. 57, Feb, 1976 (50 cents) (Digest size)
Gold Key

1-Reprints Uncle Scrooge #5; 192 pgs. 3.20 9.00 21.00
2-4-Barks-r 1.70 5.00 12.00
5-Daisy Duck by Barks (8 pgs.); last published story by Barks (art only) plus 21 pg. Scrooge-r by Barks 2.00 6.00 14.00
6-13-All Barks-r 1.00 2.50 6.00
14,15 1.60 4.00
16-Reprints Donald Duck #26 by Barks 1.30 3.25 8.00
17-20-Barks-r 1.00 2.50 6.00
21-31,33,35-37-Barks-r; 24-Toth Zorro 1.60 4.00
32 1.20 3.00
34-Reprints 4-Color #318 1.30 3.25 8.00
38-Reprints Christmas in Disneyland #1 1.00 2.50 6.00
39-Two Barks-r/WDC&S #272, 4-Color #1073 plus Toth Zorro-r 1.00 2.50 6.00
40-Mickey Mouse-r by Gottfredson 1.20 3.00
41,45,47-49 1.20 3.00
42,43-Barks-r 1.20 3.00
44-(Has Gold Key emblem, 50 cents)-Reprints 1st story of 4-Color #29,256, 275,282 2.00 6.00 14.00
44-Republished in 1976 by Whitman; not identical to original; a bit smaller, blank back-c, 69 cent-c 1.00 2.50 6.00
46,50,52-Barks-r. 52-Barks-r/WDC&S #161,132 1.20 3.00
51-Reprints 4-Color #71 1.00 2.50 6.00
53-55: 53-Reprints Dell Giant #30. 54-Reprints Donald Duck Beach Party #2. 55-Reprints Dell Giant #49 1.20 3.00
56-Reprint/Uncle Scrooge #32 (Barks) plus another Barks story 1.20 3.00
57-Reprint/Mickey Mouse Almanac('57) & two Barks stories 1.20 3.00

NOTE: *#1-10, 196 pgs.; #11-41, 164 pgs.; #42 on, 132 pgs. Old issues were being reprinted & distributed by Whitman in 1976.*

WALT DISNEY PRESENTS (TV)
No. 997, June-Aug, 1959 - No. 6, Dec-Feb, 1960-61 (All photo-c)
Dell Publishing Co.

4-Color 997 (#1) 5.85 17.50 35.00
2(12-2/60)-The Swamp Fox(origin), Elfego Baca, Texas John Slaughter (Disney TV show) begin 4.00 11.00 22.00
3-6: 5-Swamp Fox by Warren Tufts 4.00 11.00 22.00

WALT DISNEY'S CHRISTMAS PARADE (Also see Christmas Parade)
Winter, 1988; No. 2, Winter, 1989 ($2.95, 100 pgs.)
Gladstone Publishing

1,2: 1-Barks-r/painted-c. 2-Barks-r 1.20 3.00

WALT DISNEY'S COMICS AND STORIES (Cont. of Mickey Mouse Magazine) (#1-30 contain Donald Duck newspaper reprints)
(Titled 'Comics And Stories' #264 on)
10/40 - #263, 8/62; #264, 10/62 - #510, 1984; #511, 10/86 - Present
Dell Publishing Co./Gold Key #264-473/Whitman #474-510/Gladstone #511-547(4/90)/Disney Comics #548(6/90)-#585/Gladstone #586(8/93) on

NOTE: The whole number can always be found at the bottom of the title page in the lower left-hand or right hand panel.

GD25 FN65 VF82 NM94

1(V1#1-c; V2#1-indicia)-Donald Duck strip-r by Al Taliaferro & Gottfredson's Mickey Mouse begin 700.00 2100.00 4550.00 7000.00
(Estimated up to 245 total copies exist, 12 in NM/Mint)

GD25 FN65 NM94

2 360.00 1070.00 2800.00
3 115.00 345.00 850.00
4-X-mas-c 86.00 257.00 650.00
4-Special promotional, complimentary issue; cover same except one corner was blanked out & boxed in to identify the giveaway (not a paste-over). This special pressing was probably sent out to former subscribers to Mickey Mouse Mag. whose subscriptions had expired. (Very rare-5 known copies) 129.00 385.00 1000.00
5 71.00 215.00 550.00
6-10 57.00 170.00 450.00
11-14 50.00 150.00 375.00
15-17: 15-The 3 Little Kittens (17 pgs.). 16-The 3 Little Pigs (29 pgs.); X-mas-c. 17-The Ugly Duckling (4 pgs.) 45.00 135.00 335.00
18-21 38.00 115.00 285.00
22-30: 22-Flag-c 32.00 95.00 250.00
31-New Donald Duck stories by Carl Barks begin; see Four Color #9 for first Barks Donald Duck 215.00 645.00 1600.00
32-Barks-a 100.00 300.00 750.00
33-Barks-a (infinity-c) 71.00 215.00 550.00
34-Gremlins by Walt Kelly begin, end #41; Barks-a 59.00 178.00 450.00
35,36-Barks-a 52.00 155.00 400.00
37-Donald Duck by Jack Hannah 26.00 77.00 200.00
38-40-Barks-a. 39-Christmas-c. 40-Gremlins by Kelly; no Barks-a 36.00 107.00 275.00
41-50-Barks-a; 41-Gremlins by Kelly 29.00 85.00 225.00
51-60-Barks-a; 51-Christmas-c. 52-Li'l Bad Wolf begins, ends #203 (not in #55). 58-Kelly flag-c 22.00 65.00 160.00
61-70: Barks-a. 61-Dumbo story. 63,64-Pinocchio stories. 63-Cover swipe from New Funnies #94. 64-X-mas-c. 65-Pluto story. 66-Infinity-c. 67,68-Mickey Mouse Sunday-r by Bill Wright 16.00 48.00 130.00
71-80: Barks-a. 75-77-Brer Rabbit stories, no Mickey Mouse. 76-X-Mas-c 12.00 35.00 95.00
81-87,89,90: Barks-a. 82-84-Bongo stories. 86-90-Goofy & Agnes app. 89-Chip 'n' Dale story 10.00 30.00 80.00
88-1st app. Gladstone Gander by Barks 12.00 35.00 95.00
91-97,99: Barks-a. 95-1st WDC&S Barks-c. 96-No Mickey Mouse; Little Toot begins, ends #97. 99-X-Mas-c 8.00 24.00 65.00
98-1st Uncle Scrooge app. in WDC&S 18.00 50.00 135.00
100-Barks-a 9.50 28.00 75.00
101-110-Barks-a. 107-Taliaferro-c; Donald acquires super powers 7.00 20.50 55.00
111,114,117-All Barks 5.65 17.00 45.00
112-Drug (ether) issue (Donald Duck) 5.65 17.00 45.00
113,115,116,118-123: No Barks. 116-Dumbo x-over. 121-Grandma Duck begins, ends #168; not in #135,142,146,155 2.50 7.50 20.00
124,126-130-All Barks. 124-X-Mas-c 5.00 15.00 40.00
125-1st app. Junior Woodchucks (2/51); Barks-a 7.50 22.50 60.00
131,133,135-139-All Barks 5.00 15.00 40.00
132-Barks-a(2) (D. Duck & Grandma Duck) 5.65 17.00 45.00
134-Intro. & 1st app. The Beagle Boys (11/51) 8.75 26.00 70.00
140-1st app. Gyro Gearloose by Barks (5/52) 8.75 26.00 70.00
141-150-All Barks. 143-Little Hiawatha begins, ends #151,159 3.50 11.00 25.00
151-170-All Barks 2.50 7.50 20.00
171-200-All Barks 2.25 6.75 18.00
201-240: All Barks. 204-Chip 'n' Dale & Scamp begin 2.00 6.00 16.00
241-283: Barks-a. 241-Dumbo x-over. 247-Gyro Gearloose begins, ends #274. 256-Ludwig Von Drake begins, ends #274 1.70 5.00 12.00
284,285,287,290,295,296,309-311-Not by Barks 1.00 3.00 7.00
286,288,289,291-294,297,298,308-All Barks stories; 293-Grandma Duck's Farm Friends. 297-Gyro Gearloose. 298-Daisy Duck's Diary-r 1.45 4.25 10.00

Walt Disney Comics and Stories #511, © WDC

Walt Disney Comics and Stories #546, © WDC

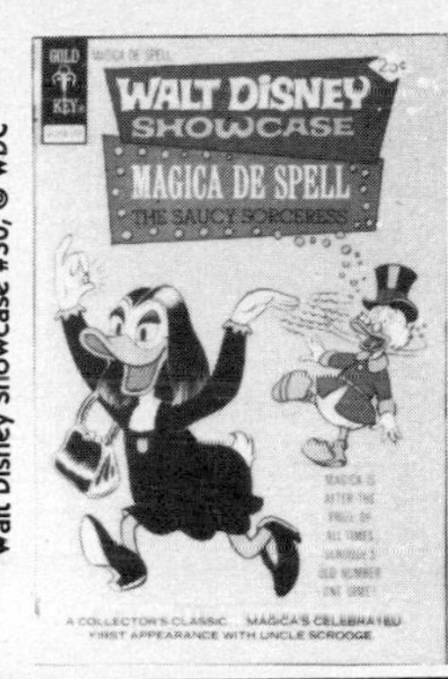

Walt Disney Showcase #30, © WDC

GD25 FN65 NM94

99-307-All contain early Barks-r (#43-117). 305-Gyro Gearloose 1.50 4.50 12.00
12-Last Barks issue with original story 1.35 4.00 10.00
13-315,317-327,329-334,336-341 .85 2.50 6.00
16-Last issue published during life of Walt Disney .85 2.50 6.00
28,335,342-350-Barks-r 1.00 3.00 7.00
51-360-With posters inside; Barks reprints (2 versions of each with & without posters)-without posters... .85 2.50 6.00
51-360-With posters 1.50 4.50 12.00
61-400-Barks-r .85 2.50 6.00
01-429-Barks-r .70 2.00 5.00
30,433,437,438,441,444,445,466,506-No Barks 1.00 2.50
31,432,434-436,439,440,442,443 Barks-r 1.00 2.50
46-465,467-505,507-510: All Barks-r. 494-r/WDC&S #98 .80 2.00
11-Wuzzles by Disney studio (1st by Gladstone) 1.00 2.50 5.50
12 1.20 3.00
13-520: 518-Infinity-c .70 1.80
21-545: 522-r/1st app. Huey, Dewey & Louie from D. Duck Sunday page. 535-546 Barks-r. 541-545-($1.50, 52 pgs.) .65 1.60
46,547-($1.95, 68 pgs.): 546-Kelly-r. 547-Rosa-a .90 2.25
48-($1.50, 6/90)-1st Disney issue; New-a; no M. Mouse .70 1.75
49,551-570,572,573,577-579,581,584 ($1.50): 549-Barks-r begin. 551-r/1 story from F.C. #29. 556,578-r/Mickey Mouse Cheerios Premium by Dick Moores. 570-Valentine issue; has Mickey/Minnie centerfold .65 1.60
50 ($2.25, 52 pgs.)-Donald Duck by Barks; previously only printed in The Netherlands (1st time in U.S.); also r/Chip 'n Dale & Scamp from #204 1.00 2.50
71-r/Donald Duck's Atomic Bomb by Barks/Cheerios 1.50 3.75
74-576,580,582,583 ($2.95, 68 pgs.): 574-r/1st Pinocchio Sunday strip(1939-40). 580-r/Donald Duck's 1st app./Little Red Hen. 582,583-r/Mickey Mouse on Skylsland from WDC&S #1,2 1.30 3.25
85-($2.50, 52 pgs.)-r/#140; Barks-r 1.30 3.25
86-587: 586-Gladstone issues begin .70 1.75
88-590 1.50

NOTE: (#1-38, 68 pgs.; #39-42, 60 pgs.; #43-57, 61-134, 143-168, 446, 447, 52 pgs.; #58-60, 135-142, 169-540, 36 pgs.)

*NOTE: **Barks** art in all issues #31 on, except where noted: c-95, 96, 104, 108, 109, 130-172, 174-170, 100, 108 200, 204, 206-209, 212-216, 218, 220, 226, 228-233, 235-238, 240-243, 247, 250, 253, 256, 260, 261, 276-283, 288-292, 295-298, 301, 303, 304, 306, 307, 309, 310, 313-316, 319, 321, 322, 324, 326, 328, 329, 331, 332, 334, 341, 342, 350, 351, 540(never before published), 546r, 557-582r(most). **Kelly** r-546, 547, 582, 583; covers(most)-34-94, 97-103, 105, 106, 110-123, 537r, 538r, 541r, 543r, 544r. Walt Disney's Comics & Stories featured Mickey Mouse serials which were in practically every issue from #1 through #394. The titles of the serials, along with the issues they are in, are listed in previous editions of this price guide. **Floyd Gottfredson** Mickey Mouse serials in issues #1-12, 18-61, 63-74, 78-92, 568-572, 582, 583, 586 plus "Mickey Mouse in a Warplant" (3 pgs.), and "Pluto Catches a Nazi Spy" (4 pgs.) in #62; "Mystery Next Door," #93; "Sunken Treasure," #94; "Aunt Marissa," #95; "Gangland," #98; "Thanksgiving Dinner," #99; and "The Talking Dog," #100. Mickey Mouse by **Paul Murry** #152 on except 155-57 (**Dick Moore**), 327-29 (**Tony Strobl**), 348-50 (**Jack Manning**). **Don Rosa** story/a-523, 524, 526, 528, 531, 547. **Al Taliaferro** Silly Symphonies in #5-"Three Little Pigs;" #13-"Birds of a Feather;" #14-"The Boarding School Mystery;" #15-"Cookieland" and "Three Little Kittens;" #16-"The Practical Pig;" #17-"The Ugly Duckling;" "The Wise Little Hen" in #580; and "Ambrose the Robber Kitten;" #19-"Penguin Isle;" and "Bucky Bug" in #20-23, 25, 26, 28 (one continuous story from 1932-34; first 2 pgs. not Taliaferro). **Gottfredson** strip r-562, 563, 568-572, 581, 585, 586. **Taliaferro** strip r-584, 580.*

WALT DISNEY'S COMICS & STORIES
1943 (36 pgs.) (Dept. store Xmas giveaway)
Walt Disney Productions

nn 45.00 135.00 300.00

WALT DISNEY'S COMICS & STORIES
Mid 1940's ('45-48), 1952 (4 pgs. in color) (slick paper)
Dell Publishing Co.(Special Xmas offer)

1940's version - subscription form for WDC&S - (Reprints two different WDC&S covers with subscription forms printed on inside covers) 10.00 30.00 70.00
1952 version 6.70 20.00 40.00

WALT DISNEY'S COMICS DIGEST
Dec, 1986 - No. 7, Sept, 1987
Gladstone Publishing

1-7 1.25

WALT DISNEY'S DONALD AND MICKEY (Formerly Mickey and Donald)
No. 19, Sept, 1993 - Present ($1.50, color)
Gladstone Publishing (Bruce Hamilton Company)

19-25-New & reprints 1.50

WALT DISNEY SHOWCASE
Oct, 1970 - No. 54, Jan, 1980 (No. 44-48: 68pgs., 49-54: 52pgs.)
Gold Key

1-Boatniks (Movie)-Photo-c 2.15 6.50 15.00
2-Moby Duck 1.30 3.25 8.00
3,4,7: 3-Bongo & Lumpjaw-r. 4,7-Pluto-r 1.20 3.00 7.00
5-$1,000,000 Duck (Movie)-Photo-c 1.65 4.00 10.00
6-Bedknobs & Broomsticks (Movie) 1.65 4.00 10.00
8-Daisy & Donald 1.20 3.00 7.00
9-101 Dalmatians (cartoon feat.); r/F.C. #1183 1.30 3.25 8.00
10-Napoleon & Samantha (Movie)-Photo-c 1.65 4.00 10.00
11-Moby Duck-r 1.00 2.50 6.00
12-Dumbo-r/Four Color #668 1.20 3.00 7.00
13-Pluto-r 1.00 2.50 6.00
14-World's Greatest Athlete (Movie)-Photo-c 1.65 4.00 10.00
15-3 Little Pigs-r 1.20 3.00 7.00
16-Aristocats (cartoon feature); r/Aristocats #1 1.65 4.00 10.00
17-Mary Poppins; r/M.P. #10136-501-Photo-c 1.65 4.00 10.00
18-Gyro Gearloose; Barks-r/F.C. #1047,1184 1.65 4.00 10.00
19-That Darn Cat; r/That Darn Cat #10171-602-Hayley Mills photo-c 1.65 4.00 10.00
20,23-Pluto-r 1.20 3.00 7.00
21-Li'l Bad Wolf & The Three Little Pigs 1.00 2.50 6.00
22-Unbirthday Party with Alice in Wonderland; r/Four Color #341 1.30 3.25 8.00
24-26: 24-Herbie Rides Again (Movie); sequel to "The Love Bug;" photo-c. 25-Old Yeller (Movie); r/F.C. #869; Photo-c. 26-Lt. Robin Crusoe USN (Movie); r/Lt. Robin Crusoe USN #10191-601; photo-c 1.20 3.00 7.00
27-Island at the Top of the World (Movie)-Photo-c 1.30 3.25 8.00
28-Brer Rabbit, Bucky Bug-r/WDC&S #58 1.20 3.00 7.00
29-Escape to Witch Mountain (Movie)-Photo-c 1.30 3.25 8.00
30-Magica De Spell; Barks-r/Uncle Scrooge #36 & WDC&S #258 2.00 6.00 14.00
31-Bambi (cartoon feature); r/Four Color #186 1.30 3.25 8.00
32-Spin & Marty-r/F.C. #1026; Mickey Mouse Club (TV)-Photo-c 1.65 4.00 10.00
33-39: 33-Pluto-r/F.C. #1143. 34-Paul Revere's Ride with Johnny Tremain (TV); r/F.C. #822. 35-Goofy-r/F.C. #952. 36-Peter Pan-r/F.C. #442. 37-Tinker Bell & Jiminy Cricket-r/F.C. #982,989. 38,39-Mickey & the Sleuth, Parts 1 & 2 1.00 2.00 5.00
40-The Rescuers (cartoon feature) 1.00 2.50 6.00
41-Herbie Goes to Monte Carlo (Movie); sequel to "Herbie Rides Again;" photo-c 1.20 3.00 7.00
42-Mickey & the Sleuth 1.00 2.00 5.00
43-Pete's Dragon (Movie)-Photo-c 1.30 3.25 8.00
44-Return From Witch Mountain (new) & In Search of the Castaways-r (Movies)-Photo-c; 68 pg. giants begin 1.30 3.25 8.00
45-The Jungle Book (Movie); r/#30033-803 1.30 3.25 8.00
46-The Cat From Outer Space (Movie)(new), & The Shaggy Dog (Movie)-r/F.C. #985; photo-c 1.00 2.50 6.00
47-Mickey Mouse Surprise Party-r 1.00 2.50 6.00
48-The Wonderful Advs. of Pinocchio-r/F.C. #1203; last 68 pg. issue 1.00 2.50 6.00
49-54: 49-North Avenue Irregulars (Movie); Zorro-r/Zorro #11; 52 pgs. begin; photo-c. 50-Bedknobs & Broomsticks-r/#6; Mooncussers-r/World of Adv. #1; photo-c. 51-101 Dalmatians-r. 52-Unidentified Flying Oddball (Movie); r/Picnic Party #8; photo-c. 53-The Scarecrow-r (TV). 54-The Black Hole (Movie)-Photo-c (predates Black Hole #1) 1.60 4.00

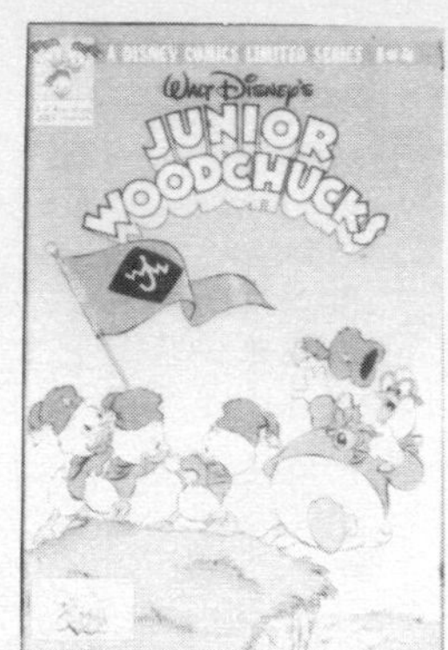

Walt Disney's Junior Woodchucks #1, © WDC

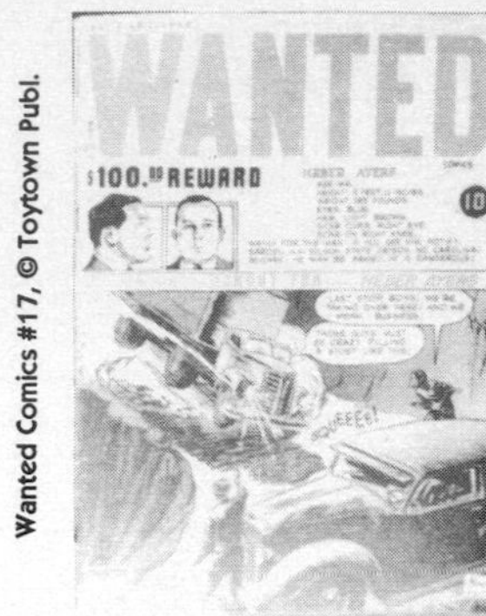

Wanted Comics #17, © Toytown Publ.

War Adventures #6, © MEG

WALT DISNEY'S JUNIOR WOODCHUCKS LIMITED SERIES
July, 1991 - No. 4, Oct, 1991 ($1.50, color, limited series; new & reprint-a)
W. D. Publications (Disney)

	GD25	FN65	NM94
1-4: 1-The Beagle Boys app.; Barks-r			1.50

WALT DISNEY'S MAGAZINE (TV)(Formerly Walt Disney's Mickey Mouse Club Magazine) (50 cents) (Bi-monthly)
V2#4, June, 1957 - V4#6, Oct, 1959
Western Publishing Co.

	GD25	FN65	NM94
V2#4-Stories & articles on the Mouseketeers, Zorro, & Goofy and other Disney characters & people	5.85	17.50	35.00
V2#5, V2#6(10/57)	4.70	14.00	28.00
V3#1(12/57), V3#3-6(10/58)	4.00	10.50	21.00
V3#2-Annette Funicello photo-c	7.50	22.50	45.00
V4#1(12/58) - V4#2-4,6(10/59)	4.00	10.50	21.00
V4#5-Annette Funicello photo-c	6.70	20.00	40.00

NOTE: *V2#4-V3#6 were 11-1/2x8-1/2", 48 pgs.; V4#1 on were 10x8", 52 pgs. (Peak circulation of 400,000).*

WALT DISNEY'S MERRY CHRISTMAS (See Dell Giant #39)

WALT DISNEY'S MICKEY MOUSE CLUB MAGAZINE (TV)(Becomes Walt Disney's Magazine) (Quarterly)
Winter, 1956 - V2#3, April, 1957 (11-1/2x8-1/2") (48 pgs.)
Western Publishing Co.

	GD25	FN65	NM94
V1#1	13.00	40.00	90.00
2-4	7.50	22.50	45.00
V2#1-3	5.85	17.50	35.00
Annual(1956)-Two different issues; ($1.50-Whitman); 120 pgs., cardboard covers, 11-3/4x8-3/4"; reprints	14.00	43.00	100.00
Annual(1957)-Same as above	12.00	36.00	85.00

WALT DISNEY'S PINOCCHIO SPECIAL (Gladstone)(Value: cover or less)

WALT DISNEY'S SEBASTIAN (See Sebastian)

WALT DISNEY'S SPRING FEVER (Disney)(Value: cover or less)

WALT DISNEY'S THE JUNGLE BOOK (Disney)(Value: cover or less)

WALT DISNEY'S WHEATIES PREMIUMS (See Wheaties)

WALTER LANTZ ANDY PANDA (Also see Andy Panda)
Aug, 1973 - No. 23, Jan, 1978 (Walter Lantz)
Gold Key

	GD25	FN65	NM94
1-Reprints	1.00	2.00	5.00
2-10-All reprints		.80	2.00
11-23: 15,17-19,22-Reprints			1.50

WALT KELLY'S...
Dec, 1987; April, 1988 ($1.75-$2.50, color, Baxter)
Eclipse Comics

	GD25	FN65	NM94
...Christmas Classics 1 (1987, $1.75)-Kelly-r/Peter Wheat & Santa Claus Funnies		.70	1.75
...Springtime Tales 1 (4/88, $2.50)-Kelly-r		1.00	2.50

WALTONS, THE (See Kite Fun Book)

WALT SCOTT'S CHRISTMAS STORIES (See 4-Color #959, 1062)

WAMBI, JUNGLE BOY (See Jungle Comics)
Spring, 1942; No. 2, Wint, 1942-43; No. 3, Spring, 1943; No. 4, Fall, 1948; No. 5, Sum, 1949; No. 6, Spring, 1950; No. 7-10, 1950(nd); No. 11, Spring, 1951 - No. 18, Winter, 1952-53 (#1-3: 68 pgs.)
Fiction House Magazines

	GD25	FN65	NM94
1-Wambi, the Jungle Boy begins	46.00	138.00	300.00
2 (1942)-Kiefer-c	25.00	75.00	165.00
3 (1943)-Kiefer-c/a	17.50	52.50	115.00
4 (1948)-Origin in text	11.50	34.00	80.00
5 (Fall, 1949, 36 pgs.)-Kiefer-c/a	10.00	30.00	65.00
6-10: 7-(52 pgs.)-New logo	9.15	27.50	55.00
11-18	6.35	19.00	38.00
I.W. Reprint #8('64)-r/#12 with new-c	2.00	5.00	10.00

NOTE: ***Alex Blum** c-8. **Kiefer** c-1-5. **Whitman** c-11-18.*

WANDERERS (DC)(Value: cover or less)(See Adventure Comics #375, 376)

WANTED COMICS
No. 9, Sept-Oct, 1947 - No. 53, April, 1953 (#9-33: 52 pgs.)
Toytown Publications/Patches/Orbit Publ.

	GD25	FN65	NM94
9-True crime cases	10.00	30.00	65.00
10,11: 10-Giunta-a; radio's Mr. D. A. app.	6.35	19.00	38.00
12-Used in **SOTI**, pg. 277	7.00	21.00	42.00
13-Heroin drug propaganda story	6.35	19.00	38.00
14-Marijuana drug mention story, 2 pgs.	4.70	14.00	28.00
15-17,19,20	4.00	12.00	24.00
18-Marijuana story, "Satan's Cigarettes"; r-in #45 & retitled	11.50	34.00	80.00
21,22: 21-Krigstein-a. 22-Extreme violence	5.35	16.00	32.00
23,25-34,36-38,40-44,46-48,53	3.20	8.00	16.00
24-Krigstein-a; "The Dope King," marijuana mention story	5.85	17.50	35.00
35-Used in **SOTI**, pg. 160	5.00	15.00	30.00
39-Drug propaganda sty "The Horror Weed"	8.35	25.00	50.00
45-Marijuana story from #18	4.70	14.00	28.00
49-Has unstable pink-c that fades easily; rare in mint condition	3.60	9.00	18.00
50-Has unstable pink-c like #49; surrealist-c by Buscema; horror stories	7.50	22.50	45.00
51-"Holiday of Horror"-junkie story; drug-c	5.00	15.00	30.00
52-Classic "Cult of Killers" opium use story	5.00	15.00	30.00

NOTE: ***Buscema** c-50, 51. **Lawrence** and **Leav** c/a most issues. **Syd Shores** c/a-48; c-37.*

WANTED: DEAD OR ALIVE (See 4-Color #1102,1164)

WANTED, THE WORLD'S MOST DANGEROUS VILLAINS
July-Aug, 1972 - No. 9, Aug-Sept, 1973 (All reprints)
National Periodical Publications (See DC Special)

	GD25	FN65	NM94
1-Batman, Green Lantern (story r-from G.L. #1), & Green Arrow		1.60	4.00
2-Batman/Joker/Penguin-c/story r-from Batman #25; plus Flash story (r-from Flash #121)	1.00	2.50	6.00
3-9: 3-Dr. Fate(r/More Fun #65), Hawkman(r/Flash #100), & Vigilante(r/Action #69). 4-Gr. Lantern(r/All-American #61) & Kid Eternity(r/Kid Eternity #15). 5-Dollman/Green Lantern. 6-Burnley Starman; Wildcat/Sargon. 7-Johnny Quick(r/More fun #76), Hawkman(r/Flash #90), Hourman by Baily(r/Adv. #72). 8-Dr. Fate/Flash(r/Flash #114). 9-S&K Sandman/Superman		.80	2.00

NOTE: ***Kane** r-1, 5. **Kubert** r-3i, 6, 7. **Meskin** r-3, 7. **Reinman** r-4, 6.*

WAR
July, 1975 - No. 9, Nov, 1976; No. 10, Sept, 1978 - No. 49?, 1984
Charlton Comics

	GD25	FN65	NM94
1-49: 47-Reprints			1.00
7,9(Modern Comics-r, 1977)			1.00

WAR, THE (Marvel)(Value: cover or less)

WAR ACTION
April, 1952 - No. 14, June, 1953
Atlas Comics (CPS)

	GD25	FN65	NM94
1	10.00	30.00	70.00
2	5.85	17.50	35.00
3-10,14: 7-Pakula-a	4.20	12.50	25.00
11-13-Krigstein-a	6.35	19.00	38.00

NOTE: ***Brodsky** c-1-4. **Heath** a-1; c-7, 14. **Keller** a-6. **Maneely** a-1. **Tuska** a-2, 8.*

WAR ADVENTURES
Jan, 1952 - No. 13, Feb, 1953
Atlas Comics (HPC)

	GD25	FN65	NM94
1-Tuska-a	10.00	30.00	60.00
2	5.00	15.00	30.00
3-7,9-13: 3-Pakula-a. 7-Maneely-c	4.00	10.00	20.00

War Against Crime #11, © WMG

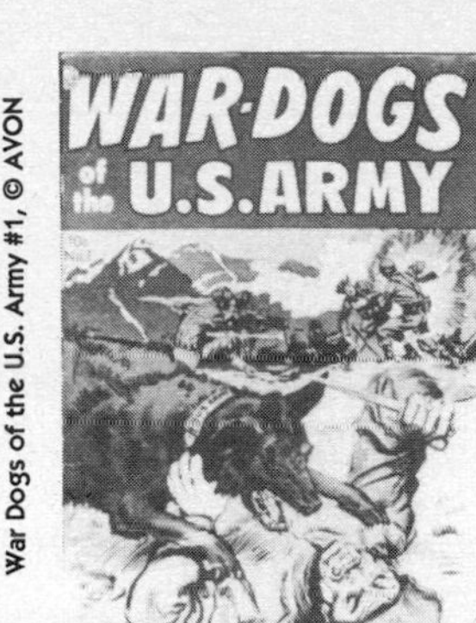
War Dogs of the U.S. Army #1, © AVON

Warhawks #2, © TSR

	GD25	FN65	NM94
8-Krigstein-a	6.35	19.00	38.00

NOTE: ***Brodsky** c-1-3, 6, 8, 11, 12. **Heath** a-5, 7, 10; c-4, 5, 9, 13. **Robinson** a-3; c-10.*

WAR ADVENTURES ON THE BATTLEFIELD (See Battlefield)

WAR AGAINST CRIME! (Becomes Vault of Horror #12 on)
Spring, 1948 - No. 11, Feb-Mar, 1950
E. C. Comics

	GD25	FN65	NM94
1	50.00	150.00	350.00
2,3	27.00	81.00	190.00
4-9	26.00	77.00	180.00
10-1st Vault Keeper app. & 1st Vault of Horror	143.00	430.00	1000.00
11-2nd Vault Keeper app.; 1st horror-c	85.00	260.00	600.00

NOTE: *All have **Johnny Craig** covers. **Feldstein** a-4, 7-9. **Harrison/Wood** a-11. **Ingels** a-1, 2, 8. **Palais** a-8.*

WAR AND ATTACK (Also see Special War Series #3)
Fall, 1964; V2#54, June, 1966 - V2#63, Dec, 1967
Charlton Comics

	GD25	FN65	NM94
1-Wood-a	3.00	7.50	15.00
V2#54(6/66)-#63 (Formerly Fightin' Air Force)	1.40	3.50	7.00

NOTE: ***Montes/Bache** a-55, 56, 60, 63.*

WAR AT SEA (Formerly Space Adventures)
No. 22, Nov, 1957 - No. 42, June, 1961
Charlton Comics

	GD25	FN65	NM94
22	3.60	9.00	18.00
23-30	1.80	4.50	9.00
31-42	1.20	3.00	6.00

WAR BATTLES
Feb, 1952 - No. 9, Dec, 1953
Harvey Publications

	GD25	FN65	NM94
1-Powell-a	6.70	20.00	40.00
2-Powell-a	4.20	12.50	25.00
3-5,7-9: 3,7-Powell-a	3.60	9.00	18.00
6-Nostrand-a	5.00	15.00	30.00

WAR BIRDS
1952(nd) - No. 3, Winter, 1952-53
Fiction House Magazines

	GD25	FN65	NM94
1	10.00	30.00	65.00
2,3	6.35	19.00	38.00

WAR COMBAT (Combat Casey #6 on)
March, 1952 - No. 5, Nov, 1952
Atlas Comics (LBI No. 1/SAI No. 2-5)

	GD25	FN65	NM94
1	8.35	25.00	50.00
2	4.70	14.00	28.00
3-5	4.00	10.00	20.00

NOTE: ***Berg** a-2, 4, 5. **Brodsky** c-1, 2, 4, 5. **Henkel** a-5. **Maneely** a-1, 4; c-3.*

WAR COMICS (War Stories #5 on)(See Key Ring Comics)
May, 1940 (No mo. given) - No. 4, 1941(nd)
Dell Publishing Co.

	GD25	FN65	NM94
1-Sikandur the Robot Master, Sky Hawk, Scoop Mason, War Correspondent begin; McWilliams-c	34.00	105.00	240.00
2-Origin Greg Gilday	17.00	52.00	120.00
3-Joan becomes Greg Gilday's aide	12.00	36.00	85.00
4-Origin Night Devils	14.00	43.00	100.00

WAR COMICS
Dec, 1950 - No. 49, Sept, 1957
Marvel/Atlas (USA No. 1-41/JPI No. 42-49)

	GD25	FN65	NM94
1	12.00	36.00	85.00
2	7.50	22.50	45.00
3-10	5.35	16.00	32.00
11-20	4.00	10.00	20.00
21,23-32: 26-Valley Forge story. 32-Last precode (2/55)	3.60	9.00	18.00
22-Krigstein-a	6.70	20.00	40.00
33-37,39-42,44,45,47,48	3.60	9.00	18.00
38-Kubert/Moskowitz-a	5.35	16.00	32.00
43,49-Torres-a. 43-Davis E.C. swipe	4.70	14.00	28.00
46-Crandall-a	5.35	16.00	32.00

NOTE: ***Colan** a-4, 36, 48, 49. **Drucker** a-37, 43, 48. **Everett** a-17. **Heath** a-7-9, 16, 19, 25, 36; c-11, 16, 19, 25, 26, 29-31, 36. **G. Kane** a-19. **Lawrence** a-36. **Maneely** a-7, 9; c-6, 27, 37. **Orlando** a-42, 48. **Pakula** a-26. **Ravielli** a-27. **Reinman** a-26. **Robinson** a-15; c-13. **Severin** a-26, 27; c-48.*

WAR DOGS OF THE U.S. ARMY
1952
Avon Periodicals

	GD25	FN65	NM94
1-Kinstler-c/a	10.00	30.00	60.00

WARFRONT
9/51 - #35, 11/58; #36, 10/65; #37, 9/66 - #38, 12/66; #39, 2/67
Harvey Publications

	GD25	FN65	NM94
1	7.50	22.50	45.00
2	4.00	11.00	22.00
3-10	3.20	8.00	16.00
11,12,14,16-20	2.40	6.00	12.00
13,15,22-Nostrand-a	5.35	16.00	32.00
21,23-27,29,31-33,35	2.00	5.00	10.00
28,30,34-Kirby-c	4.00	12.00	24.00
36-Dynamite Joe begins, ends #39; Williamson-a	2.80	7.00	14.00
37-Wood-a, 17pgs.	3.60	9.00	18.00
38,39-Wood-a, 2-3 pgs.; Lone Tiger app.	2.00	5.00	10.00

NOTE: ***Powell** a-1-6, 9-11, 14, 17, 20, 23, 25-28, 30, 31, 34, 36. **Powell/Nostrand** a-12, 13, 15. **Simon** c-36?, 38.*

WAR FURY
Sept, 1952 - No. 4, March, 1953
Comic Media/Harwell (Allen Hardy Associates)

	GD25	FN65	NM94
1-Heck-c/a in all; Palais-a; bullet hole in forehead-c; all issues are very violent	5.85	17.50	35.00
2-4: 4-Morisi-a	4.00	11.00	22.00

WAR GODS OF THE DEEP (See Movie Classics)

WARHAWKS (TSR)(Value: cover or less)

WARHEADS
June, 1992 - No. 14, Aug, 1993 ($1.75, color)
Marvel Comics UK

	GD25	FN65	NM94
1-Wolverine-c/story; indicia says #2 by mistake		1.20	3.00
2-14: 2-Nick Fury app. 3-Iron Man-c/story. 4,5-X-Force. 5-Liger vs. Cable. 6,7-Death's Head II app. (#6 is cameo)		.70	1.75

WARHEADS: BLACK DAWN (Epic)(Value: cover or less)

WAR HEROES (See Marine War Heroes)

WAR HEROES
7-9/42 (no month); No. 2, 10-12/42 - No. 10, 10-12/44; No. 11, 3/45
Dell Publishing Co.

	GD25	FN65	NM94
1-General Douglas MacArthur-c	16.00	48.00	110.00
2	9.15	27.50	55.00
3,5: 3-Pro-Russian back-c	6.70	20.00	40.00
4-Disney's Gremlins app.	12.00	36.00	85.00
6-11: 6-Tothish-a by Discount	5.85	17.50	35.00

NOTE: *No. 1 was to be released in July, but was delayed.*

WAR HEROES
May, 1952 - No. 8, April, 1953
Ace Magazines

	GD25	FN65	NM94
1	6.70	20.00	40.00
2-Lou Cameron-a	4.20	12.50	25.00
3-8: 6,7-Cameron-a	3.60	9.00	18.00

WAR HEROES (Also see Blue Bird Comics)
Feb, 1963 - No. 27, Nov, 1967
Charlton Comics

Warlock #4 (2/73), © MEG

The Warlord #55, © DC

Warriors of Plasm #2, © Enlightened Entertainment

GD25 FN65 NM94

1 2.40 6.00 12.00
2-10: 2-John F. Kennedy story 1.20 3.00 6.00
11-27: 27-1st Devils Brigade by Glanzman .80 2.00 4.00
NOTE: ***Montes/Bache*** *a-3-7, 21, 25, 27; c-3-7.*

WAR IS HELL
Jan, 1973 - No. 15, Oct, 1975
Marvel Comics Group

1-Williamson-a(r), 5 pgs.; Ayers-a 1.50
2-15: 2-9-All reprints 1.00
NOTE: ***Bolle*** *a-3r.* ***Powell*** *a-1.* ***Woodbridge*** *a-1. Sgt. Fury reprints-7, 8.*

WARLOCK (The Power of...)(Also see Fantastic Four #66, 67, Incredible Hulk #178, Infinity Crusade, Infinity Gauntlet, Infinity War, Marvel Premiere #1, Silver Surfer V3#46, Strange Tales #178-181 & Thor #165)
Aug, 1972 - No. 8, Oct, 1973; No. 9, Oct, 1975 - No. 15, Nov, 1976
Marvel Comics Group

1-Origin by Kane 3.60 10.75 25.00
2,3 1.70 5.00 12.00
4-8: 4-Death of Eddie Roberts 1.30 3.25 8.00
9-Starlin's 2nd Thanos saga begins, ends #15; new costume Warlock; Thanos cameo only; story cont'd from Strange Tales #178-181; Starlin-c/a in #9-15 1.65 4.00 10.00
10-Origin Thanos & Gamora; recaps events from Capt. Marvel #25-34. Thanos vs.The Magus-c/story 4.50 14.00 32.00
11-Thanos app. 3.70 11.00 26.00
12-14: 14-Origin Star Thief; last 25 cent issue 1.65 4.70 11.00
15-Thanos-c/story 3.30 10.00 23.00
NOTE: ***Buscema*** *a-2p; c-8p.* ***G. Kane*** *a-1p, 3-5p; c-1p, 2, 3, 4p, 5p, 7p.* ***Starlin*** *a-9-14p, 15; c-9, 10, 11p, 12p, 13-15.* ***Sutton*** *a-1-8i.*

WARLOCK (...Special Edition on-c)
Dec, 1982 - No. 6, May, 1983 ($2.00, 52 pgs.) (slick paper)
Marvel Comics Group

1-6: 1-Warlock-r/Strange Tales #178-180. 2-r/Str. Tales #180,181 & Warlock #9. 3-r/Warlock #10-12(Thanos origin recap). 4-r/Warlock #12-15. 5-r/Warlock #15, Marvel Team-Up #55 & Avengers Ann. #7. 6-r/2nd half Avengers Annual #7 & Marvel Two-in-One Annual #2 1.20 3.00 7.00
Special Edition #1(12/83) 1.00 2.50
NOTE: ***Byrne*** *a-5r.* ***Starlin*** *a-1-6r; c-1-6(new). Direct sale only.*

WARLOCK
V2#1, May, 1992 - No. 6, Oct, 1992 ($2.50, color, limited series)
Marvel Comics

V2#1-6: 1-Reprints 1982 reprint series w/Thanos 1.00 2.50

WARLOCK AND THE INFINITY WATCH
Feb, 1992 - Present ($1.75, color)(Sequel to Infinity Gauntlet)
Marvel Comics

1-Starlin scripts begin; brief origin recap Warlock 1.60 4.00
2-Reintro Moondragon 1.40 3.50
3 1.00 2.50
4-24,26: 7-Reintro The Magus; Moondragon app.; Thanos cameo on last 2 pgs. 8,9-Thanos battles Gamora-c/story. 8-Magus & Moondragon app. 10-Thanos-c/story; Magus app. 21-Drax vs. Thor .70 1.75
25-($2.95)-Embossed die-cut-c 1.20 3.00
NOTE: ***Austin*** *a-1-4i; c-1-4i.*

WARLOCK CHRONICLES
June, 1993 - No. 8, Feb, 1994 ($2.00, color, limited series)
Marvel Comics

1-($2.95)-Holo-grafx foil & embossed-c; origin retold; Starlin scripts begin; Keith Williams-a(i) in all 1.20 3.00
2-8: 3-Thanos & Mephisto-c/story. 4-Vs. Magus-c/s .80 2.00

WARLOCK 5 (Aircel)(Value: cover or less)

WARLORD (See 1st Issue Special)
1-2/76; No.2, 3-4/76; No.3, 10-11/76 - No. 133, Wint, 1988-89
National Periodical Publications/DC Comics #123 on

GD25 FN65 NM94

1-Story cont'd. from 1st Issue Special #8 2.15 6.50 15.00
2-Intro. Machiste 1.30 3.25 8.00
3-5 1.00 2.50 5.50
6-10: 6-Intro Mariah. 7-Origin Machiste. 9-Dons new costume 1.70 4.25
11-20: 11-Origin-r. 12-Intro Aton. 15-Tara returns; Warlord has son 1.30 3.25
21-40: 27-New facts about origin. 28-1st app. Wizard World. 32-Intro Shakira. 37,38-Origin Omac by Starlin. 38-Intro Jennifer Morgan, Warlord's daughter. 39-Omac ends. 40-Warlord gets new costume .90 2.25
41-47,49-52: 42-47-Omac back-up series. 49-Claw The Unconquered app. 50-Death of Aton. 51-Reprints #1 1.40
48-(52 pgs.)-1st app. Arak; contains free 14 pg. Arak Son of Thunder; Claw The Unconquered app. .90 2.25
53-130,132: 55-Arion Lord of Atlantis begins, ends #62. 63-The Barren Earth begins; free 16pg. Masters of the Universe preview. 91-Origin w/new facts. 114,115-Legends x-over. 100-($1.25, 52 pgs.). 125-Death of Tara 1.40
131-1st DC work by Rob Liefeld (9/88) 1.20 3.00
133-($1.50, 52 pgs.) 1.50
Remco Toy Giveaway (2-3/4x4") 1.00
Annual 1(1982)-Grell-c, a(p) .80 2.00
Annual 2-6: 2('83). 3('84). 4('85). 5('86). 6('87) 1.00
NOTE: ***Grell*** *a-1-15, 16-50p, 51r, 52p, 59p, Annual 1p; c-1-70, 100-104, 112, 116, 117, Annual 1, 5.* ***Wayne Howard*** *a-64i.* ***Starlin*** *a-37-39p.*

WARLORD (DC, 1992 mini-series)(Value: cover or less)

WARLORDS (See DC Graphic Novel #2)

WAR OF THE GODS (DC)(Value: cover or less)

WARP (First)(Value: cover or less)

WARPED (Empire/Solson)(Value: cover or less)

WARPATH
Nov, 1954 - No. 3, April, 1955
Key Publications/Stanmor

1 7.50 22.50 45.00
2,3 4.20 12.50 25.00

WARP GRAPHICS ANNUAL (WaRP)(Value: cover or less)

WARREN PRESENTS
Jan, 1979 - No. 14, Nov, 1981
Warren Publications

1-14-Eerie, Creepy, & Vampirella-r .80 2.00
...The Rook 1 (5/79)-r/Eerie #82-85 .80 2.00

WAR REPORT
Sept, 1952 - No. 5, May, 1953
Ajax/Farrell Publications (Excellent Publ.)

1 6.70 20.00 40.00
2 4.00 10.00 20.00
3-5: 4-Used in **POP**, pg. 94 3.60 9.00 18.00

WARRIOR COMICS
1945 (1930s DC reprints)
H.C. Blackerby

1-Wing Brady, The Iron Man, Mark Markon 11.00 32.00 75.00

WARRIORS OF PLASM (Also see Plasm)
Aug, 1993 - Present ($2.95, color)
Defiant Comics

1-6: Lapham-c/a 1.20 3.00

WAR ROMANCES (See True...)

WAR SHIPS
1942 (36 pgs.)(Similar to Large Feature Comics)
Dell Publishing Co.

nn-Cover by McWilliams; contains photos & drawings of U.S. war ships

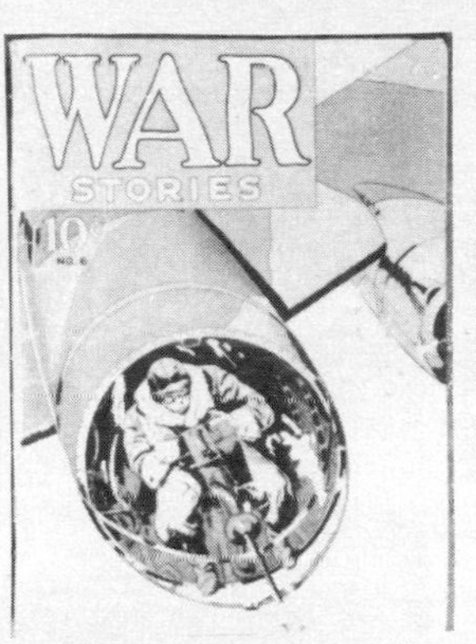

War Stories #6, © DELL

The Web #1, © AP

Web of Mystery #28, © ACE

	GD25	FN65	NM94
	10.00	30.00	70.00

WAR STORIES (Formerly War Comics)
No. 5, 1942(nd) - No. 8, Feb-Apr, 1943
Dell Publishing Co.

	GD25	FN65	NM94
5-Origin The Whistler	16.00	48.00	110.00
6-8: 6-8-Night Devils app. 8-Painted-c	11.50	34.00	80.00

WAR STORIES (Korea)
Sept, 1952 - No. 5, May, 1953
Ajax/Farrell Publications (Excellent Publ.)

	GD25	FN65	NM94
1	5.85	17.50	35.00
2	3.60	9.00	18.00
3-5	3.20	8.00	16.00

WAR STORIES (See Star Spangled...)

WART AND THE WIZARD (See The Sword & the Stone under Movie Comics)
Feb, 1964 (Walt Disney)(Characters from Sword in the Stone movie)
Gold Key

	GD25	FN65	NM94
1 (10102-402)	3.00	7.50	15.00

WARTIME ROMANCES
July, 1951 - No. 18, Nov, 1953
St. John Publishing co.

	GD25	FN65	NM94
1-All Baker-a	13.00	40.00	90.00
2-All Baker-a	9.15	27.50	55.00
3,4-All Baker-a	8.00	24.00	48.00
5-8-Baker-c/a(2-3) each	7.00	21.00	42.00
9-12,16,18-Baker-c/a each	5.35	16.00	32.00
13-15,17-Baker-c only	4.00	12.00	24.00

WAR VICTORY ADVENTURES (#1 titled War Victory Comics)
Summer, 1942 - No. 3, Winter, 1943-44 (5 cents)
U.S. Treasury Dept./War Victory/Harvey Publ.

	GD25	FN65	NM94
1-(Promotion of Savings Bonds)-Featuring America's greatest comic art by top syndicated cartoonists; Blondie, Joe Palooka, Green Hornet, Dick Tracy, Superman, Gumps, etc.; (36 pgs.); All profits contributed to U.S.O. & Army/Navy relief funds	25.00	75.00	175.00
2-Battle of Stalingrad story; Powell-a (8/43)	12.00	36.00	85.00
3-Capt. Red Cross-c & text only; Powell-a	11.00	32.00	75.00

WAR WAGON, THE (See Movie Classics)

WAR WINGS
October, 1968
Charlton Comics

	GD25	FN65	NM94
1		1.60	4.00

WARWORLD! (Dark Horse)(Value: cover or less)

WASHABLE JONES & SHMOO
June, 1953
Harvey Publications

	GD25	FN65	NM94
1	13.00	40.00	90.00

WASH TUBBS (See The Comics, Crackajack Funnies & 4-Color #11, 28, 53)

WASTELAND (DC)(Value: cover or less)

WATCHMEN
Sept, 1986 - No. 12, Oct, 1987 (12 issue maxi-series)
DC Comics

	GD25	FN65	NM94
1-Alan Moore scripts in all		1.50	3.75
2-12		1.10	2.75

WATCH OUT FOR BIG TALK
1950
Giveaway

	GD25	FN65	NM94
nn-Dan Barry-a (about crooked politicians)	4.00	11.00	22.00

WATER BIRDS AND THE OLYMPIC ELK (See 4-Color #700)

WCW WORLD CHAMPIONSHIP WRESTLING (Marvel)(Value: cover or less)

WEASEL PATROL SPECIAL, THE (Eclipse)(Value: cover or less)

WEATHER-BIRD (See Comics From..., Dick Tracy, Free Comics to You... & Terry and the Pirates)
1958 - No. 16, July, 1962 (Shoe store giveaway)
International Shoe Co./Western Printing Co.

	GD25	FN65	NM94
1	3.60	9.00	18.00
2-16	1.80	4.50	9.00

NOTE: *The numbers are located in the lower bottom panel, pg. 1. All feature a character called Weather-Bird.*

WEATHER BIRD COMICS (See Comics From Weather Bird)
1957 (Giveaway)
Weather Bird Shoes

nn-Contains a comic bound with new cover. Several combinations possible; contents determines price (40 - 60 percent of contents).

WEAVEWORLD (Epic)(Value: cover or less)

WEB, THE (Also see Mighty Comics & Mighty Crusaders)
Sept, 1991 - No. 14, Oct, 1992 ($1.00, color)
Impact Comics (DC)

	GD25	FN65	NM94
1-14: 5-The Fly x-over 9-Trading card inside			1.00
Annual 1 (1992, $2.50, 68 pgs.)-W/Trading card		1.00	2.50

NOTE: ***Gil Kane** c-5, 9, 10, 12-14. **Bill Wray** a(i)-1-9, 10(part).*

WEB OF EVIL
Nov, 1952 - No. 21, Dec, 1954
Comic Magazines/Quality Comics Group

	GD25	FN65	NM94
1-Used in **SOTI**, pg. 388. Jack Cole-a; morphine use story	29.00	85.00	200.00
2,3-Jack Cole-a	18.00	54.00	125.00
4,6,7-Jack Cole-c/a	18.00	45.00	125.00
5-Electrocution-c; Jack Cole-c/a	22.00	67.00	155.00
8-11-Jack Cole-a	14.00	43.00	100.00
12,13,15,16,19-21	8.35	25.00	50.00
14-Part Crandall-c; Old Witch swipe	9.15	27.50	55.00
17-Opium drug propaganda story	8.35	25.00	50.00
18-Acid-in-face story	10.00	30.00	65.00

NOTE: ***Jack Cole** a(2 each)-2, 6, 8, 9. **Cuidera** c-1-21i. **Ravielli** a-13.*

WEB OF HORROR (Magazine)
Dec, 1969 - No. 3, Apr, 1970
Major Magazines

	GD25	FN65	NM94
1-Jeff Jones painted-c; Wrightson-a	5.00	15.00	30.00
2-Jones painted-c; Wrightson-a(2), Kaluta-a	4.00	10.00	20.00
3-Wrightson-c/a (1st published-c); Brunner, Kaluta, Bruce Jones-a	4.00	10.00	20.00

WEB OF MYSTERY
Feb, 1951 - No. 29, Sept, 1955
Ace Magazines (A. A. Wyn)

	GD25	FN65	NM94
1	22.00	65.00	150.00
2-Bakerish-a	13.00	40.00	90.00
3-10: 4-Colan-a	11.50	34.00	80.00
11-18,20-26: 12-John Chilly's 1st cover art. 13-Surrealistic-c. 20-r/The Beyond #1	10.00	30.00	70.00
19-Reprints Challenge of the Unknown #6 used in N.Y. Legislative Committee	10.00	30.00	70.00
27-Bakerish-a(r/The Beyond #2); last pre-code ish	10.00	30.00	65.00
28,29: 28-All-r	7.50	22.50	45.00

NOTE: *This series was to appear as "Creepy Stories," but title was changed before publication. **Cameron** a-6, 8, 11-13, 17-20, 22, 24, 25, 27; c-8, 13, 17. **Palais** a-28r. **Sekowsky** a-1-3, 7, 8, 11, 14, 21, 29. **Tothish** a-by **Bill Discount** #16. 29-all-r, 19-28-partial-r.*

WEB OF SPIDER-MAN
Apr, 1985 - Present
Marvel Comics Group

	GD25	FN65	NM94
1-Painted-c (5th app. black costume?)	4.00	12.00	28.00
2,3	1.30	3.25	8.00

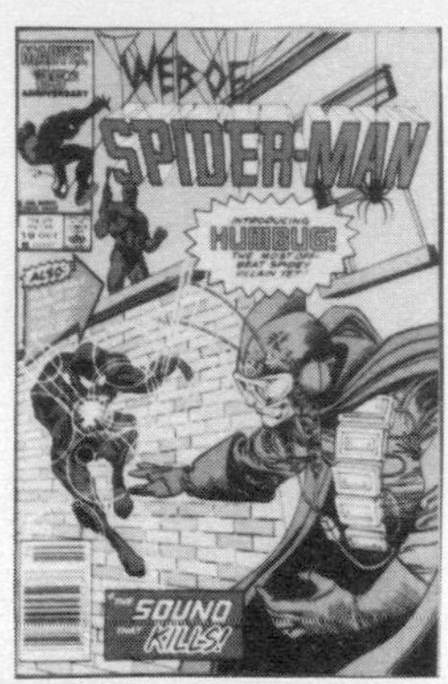

Web of Spider-Man #19, © MEG

The Weird #3, © DC

Weird Comics #16, © FOX

GD25 FN65 NM94

4-8: 7-Hulk x-over; Wolverine splash 1.00 2.50 6.00
9-13: 10-Dominic Fortune guest stars; painted-c 1.00 2.00 5.00
14-28: 19-Intro Humbug & Solo 1.80 4.50
29-Wolverine, new Hobgoblin (Macendale) app. 2.15 6.50 15.00
30-Origin recap The Rose & Hobgoblin I (entire book is flashback story); Punisher & Wolverine cameo 2.00 6.00 14.00
31,32-Six part Kraven storyline begins 1.50 3.75 9.00
33-37,39-47,49: 36-1st app. Tombstone (cameo) 1.00 2.50
38-Hobgoblin app.; begin $1.00-c 1.20 3.00 7.00
48-Origin Hobgoblin II(Demogoblin) cont'd from Spectacular Spider-Man #147; Kingpin app. 3.40 10.00 24.00
50-($1.50, 52 pgs.) .90 2.25
51-58 .80 2.00
59-Cosmic Spidey cont'd from Spect. Spider-Man 1.65 4.00 10.00
60-65,68-85,87-89,91-94: 69,70-Hulk x-over. 74-76-Austin-c(i). 76-Fantastic Four x-over. 78-Cloak & Dagger app. 84-Begin 6 part Rose & Hobgoblin II storyline; last $1.00-c. 93-Gives brief history of Hobgoblin. 93,94-Hobgoblin (Macendale) Reborn-c/story, parts 1,2; Moon Knight app. 94-Venom cameo .70 1.80
66,67-Green Goblin (Norman Osborn) app. as a super-hero 1.10 2.75
86-Demon leaves Hobgoblin; 1st Demogoblin 1.00 2.50
90-($2.95, 52 pgs.)-Polybagged w/hologram-c, gatefold poster showing Spider-Man & Spider-Man 2099 (Williamson-i) 1.90 4.75
90 (2nd printing) 1.20 3.00
95-Begin 4 part x-over w/Spirits of Venom w/Ghost Rider/Blaze/Spidey vs. Venom & Demogoblin (cont'd in Ghost Rider/Blaze #5,6) 1.30 3.25
96-99,101-106: 96-Spirits of Venom part 3. 103-Maximum Carnage w/Venom & Carnage .70 1.80
100-($2.95, 52 pgs.)-Holo-grafx foil-c; intro new Spider-Armor 1.30 3.25
107-110: 107-Intro Sandstorm; Sand & Quicksand app. 1.25
Annual 1 (1985) 1.10 2.75
Annual 2 (1986)-New Mutants; Art Adams-a 1.25 3.00 7.50
Annual 3 (1987) 1.10 2.75
Annual 4 (1988, $1.75)-Evolutionary War x-over 1.30 3.25
Annual 5 (1989, $2.00, 68 pgs.)-Atlantis Attacks; Captain Universe by Ditko (p) & Silver Sable stories; F.F. app. 1.10 2.75
Annual 6 ('90, $2.00, 68 pgs.)-Punisher back-up plus Capt. Universe by Ditko; G. Kane-a 1.10 2.75
Annual 7 (1991, $2.00, 68 pgs.)-Origins of Hobgoblin I, Hobgoblin II, Green Goblin I & II & Venom; Austin-c(i) 1.10 2.75
Annual 8 (1992, $2.25, 68 pgs.)-Part 3 of Venom story; New Warriors x-over; Black Cat back-up story 1.10 2.75
Annual 9 (1993, $2.95, 68 pgs.)-Bagged w/card 1.30 3.25

WEDDING BELLS
Feb, 1954 - No. 19, Nov, 1956
Quality Comics Group

1-Whitney-a 10.00 30.00 60.00
2 5.35 16.00 32.00
3-9: 8-Last precode (4/55) 4.00 10.00 20.00
10-Ward-a, 9 pgs. 8.00 24.00 48.00
11-14,17 2.80 7.00 14.00
15-Baker-c 3.20 8.00 16.00
16-Baker-c/a 4.00 12.00 24.00
18,19-Baker-a each 4.00 10.00 20.00

WEDDING OF DRACULA
Jan, 1993 ($2.00, color, 52 pgs.)
Marvel Comics

1-Reprints Tomb of Dracula #30,45,46 .80 2.00

WEEKENDER, THE (Illustrated...)
V1#3, Sept, 1945 - V1#4, 1945 - V2#1, Jan, 1946 (52 pages)
Rucker Publ. Co.

V1#3,4(1945): 3-Super hero-c 11.00 32.00 75.00
V2#1-36 pgs. comics, 16 in newspaper format with photos; partial Dynamic Comics reprints; 4 pgs. of cels from the Disney film Pinocchio; Little Nemo story by Winsor McCay, Jr.; Jack Cole-a 13.00 40.00 90.00

WEEKLY COMIC MAGAZINE
May 12, 1940 (16 pgs.) (Full Color) (Others exist without super-heroes)
Fox Publications

(1st Version)-8 pg. Blue Beetle story, 7 pg. Patty O'Day story; two copies known to exist. Estimated value.... $500.00
(2nd Version)-7 two-pg. adventures of Blue Beetle, Patty O'Day, Yarko, Dr. Fung, Green Mask, Spark Stevens, & Rex Dexter; one copy known to exist. Estimated value.... $400.00
Discovered with business papers, letters and exploitation material promoting **Weekly Comic Magazine** for use by newspapers in the same manner of **The Spirit** weeklies. Interesting note: these are dated three weeks before the first Spirit comic. Letters indicate that samples may have been sent to a few newspapers. These sections were actually 15-1/2x22" pages which will fold down to an approximate 8x10" comic booklet. Other various comic sections were found with the above, but were more like the Sunday comic sections in format.

WEIRD (Magazine)
V1#10, 1/66 - V8#6, 12/74; V9#1, 1/75 - V11#4, Dec, 1978
(V1-V8: 52 pgs.; V9 on: 68 pgs.)
Eerie Publications

V1#10(#1)-Intro. Morris the Caretaker of Weird (ends V2#10); Burgos-a 3.25 9.50 22.00
11,12 1.65 4.00 10.00
V2#1-4(10/67), V3#1(1/68), V2#6(4/68)-V2#7,9,10(12/68), V3#1(2/69)-V3#4 1.65 4.00 10.00
V2#8-r/Ditko's 1st story/Fantastic Fears #5 2.15 6.50 15.00
5(12/69)-Rulah reprint; "Rulah" changed to "Pulah;" LSD story reprinted in Horror Tales V4#4, Tales From the Tomb V2#4, & Terror Tales V7#3 1.65 4.00 10.00
V4#1-6('70), V5#1-6('71), V6#1-7('72), V7#1-7('73), V8#1-6('74), V9#1-4 (1/75-'76)(no V9#1), V10#1-3('77), V11#1-4 1.65 4.00 10.00

WEIRD, THE (DC)(Value: cover or less)

WEIRD ADVENTURES
May-June, 1951 - No. 3, Sept-Oct, 1951
P. L. Publishing Co. (Canada)

1-"The She-Wolf Killer" by Matt Baker, 6 pgs. 22.00 65.00 150.00
2-Bondage/hypodermic panel 17.00 52.00 120.00
3-Male bondage/torture-c; severed head story 16.00 48.00 110.00

WEIRD ADVENTURES
No. 10, July-Aug, 1951
Ziff-Davis Publishing Co.

10-Painted-c 17.00 52.00 120.00

WEIRD CHILLS
July, 1954 - No. 3, Nov, 1954
Key Publications

1-Wolverton-r/Weird Mysteries No. 4; blood transfusion-c by Baily 33.00 100.00 230.00
2-Extremely violent injury to eye-c by Baily 32.00 95.00 225.00
3-Bondage E.C. swipe-c by Baily 18.00 54.00 125.00

WEIRD COMICS
April, 1940 - No. 20, Jan, 1942
Fox Features Syndicate

1-The Birdman, Thor, God of Thunder (ends #5), The Sorceress of Zoom, Blast Bennett, Typhon, Voodoo Man, & Dr. Mortal begin; Lou Fine bondage-c 171.00 515.00 1200.00
2-Lou Fine-c 82.00 245.00 575.00
3,4: 3-Simon-c. 4-Torture-c 54.00 162.00 375.00
5-Intro. Dart & sidekick Ace (8/40) (ends #20); bondage/hypo-c 58.00 175.00 400.00
6,7-Dynamite Thor app. in each. 6-Super hero covers begin; Dart & Ace c-6-13,15; Eagle c-14,16-20 54.00 162.00 375.00
8-Dynamo, the Eagle (11/40, early app.; see Science #1) & sidekick Buddy & Marga, the Panther Woman begin 54.00 162.00 375.00

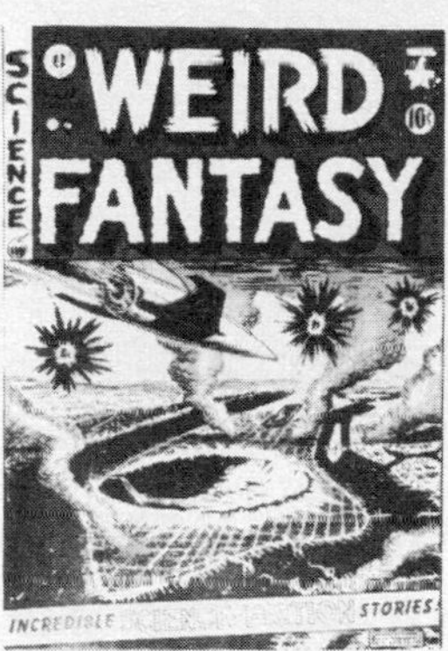

Weird Fantasy #11, © WMG

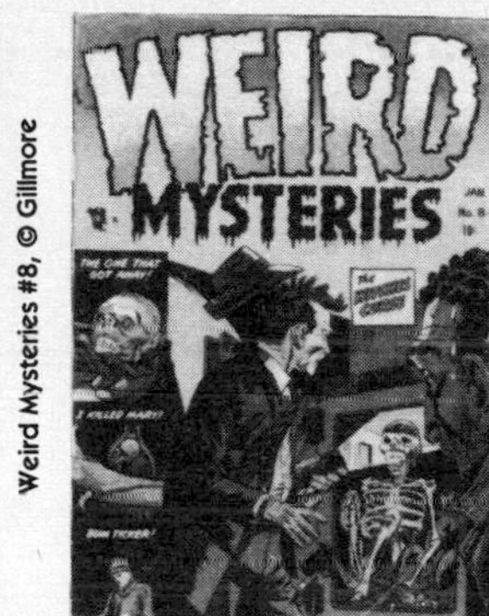

Weird Mysteries #8, © Gillmore

Weird Science-Fantasy #24, © WMG

GD25 FN65 NM94

9,10: 10-Navy Jones app. 46.00 138.00 315.00
11-20: 16-Flag-c. 17-Origin The Black Rider. 20-Origin The Rapier; Swoop Curtic app; Churchill & Hitler-c 37.00 110.00 250.00

WEIRD FANTASY (Formerly A Moon, A Girl, Romance; becomes Weird Science-Fantasy #23 on)
No. 13, May-June, 1950 - No. 22, Nov-Dec, 1953
E. C. Comics

13(#1) (1950) 100.00 300.00 700.00
14-Necronomicon story; atomic explosion-c 55.00 165.00 385.00
15,16: 16-Used in **SOTI**, pg. 144 46.00 140.00 325.00
17 (1951) 39.00 118.00 275.00
6-10: 6-Robot-c 29.00 86.00 200.00
11-13 (1952): 12-E.C. artists cameo. 13-Anti-Wertham "Cosmic Correspondence" 22.00 65.00 150.00
14-Frazetta/Williamson(1st team-up at E.C.)/Krenkel-a, 7 pgs.; Orlando draws E.C. staff; "Cosmic Ray Bomb Explosion" by Feldstein stars Gaines & Feldstein 36.00 107.00 250.00
15-Williamson/Evans-a(3), 4,3,&7 pgs. 24.00 71.00 165.00
16-19-Williamson/Krenkel-a in all. 18-Williamson/Feldstein-c 22.00 65.00 150.00
20-Frazetta/Williamson-a, 7 pgs. 24.00 71.00 165.00
21-Frazetta/Williamson-c & Williamson/Krenkel-a 36.00 107.00 250.00
22-Bradbury adaptation 16.00 48.00 110.00

NOTE: *Ray Bradbury adaptations-13, 17-20, 22. **Crandall** a-22. **Elder** a-17. **Feldstein** a-13(#1)-8; c-13(#1)-18 (#18 w/Williamson), 20. **Harrison/Wood** a-13. **Kamen** a-13(#1)-16, 18-22. **Krigstein** a-22. **Kurtzman** a-13(#1)-17(#5), 6. **Orlando** a-9-22 (2 stories in #16); c-19, 22. **Severin/Elder** a-18-21. **Wood** a-13(#1)-14, 17(2 stories ea. in #10-13). Ray Bradbury adaptations in #17-19, 22. Canadian reprints exist; see Table of Contents.*

WEIRD FANTASY
Oct, 1992 - Present ($1.50, color)
Russ Cochran

1,2-r/Weird Fantasy #13,14(#1,2); Feldstein-c 1.50
3-5-r/Weird Fantasy #15-17(#3-5) .80 2.00

WEIRD HORRORS (Nightmare #10 on)
June, 1952 - No. 9, Oct, 1953
St. John Publishing Co.

1-Tuska-a 22.00 65.00 150.00
2,3: 3-Hashish story 11.00 32.00 75.00
4,5 10.00 30.00 70.00
6-Ekgren-c; atomic bomb story 19.00 58.00 135.00
7-Ekgren-c; Kubert, Cameron-a 22.00 65.00 150.00
8,9-Kubert-c/a 14.00 43.00 100.00

NOTE: ***Cameron** a-7, 9. **Finesque** a-1-5. **Forgione** a-6. **Morisi** a-3. Bondage c-8.*

WEIRD MYSTERIES
Oct, 1952 - No. 12, Sept, 1954
Gillmore Publications

1-Partial Wolverton-c swiped from splash page "Flight to the Future" in Weird Tales of the Future #2; "Eternity" has an Ingels swipe 32.00 95.00 225.00
2-"Robot Woman" by Wolverton; Bernard Baily-c-reprinted in Mister Mystery #18; acid in face panel 50.00 150.00 350.00
3,6: Both have decapitation-c 22.00 67.00 155.00
4-"The Man Who Never Smiled" (3 pgs.) by Wolverton; B. Baily skull-c 42.00 125.00 295.00
5-Wolverton story "Swamp Monster," 6 pgs. 42.00 125.00 295.00
7-Used in **SOTI**, illo "Indoor" & illo-"Sex and blood" 36.00 110.00 250.00
8-Wolverton-c panel reprint/#5; used in a 1954 Readers Digest anti-comics article by T. E. Murphy entitled "For the Kiddies to Read" 22.00 65.00 150.00
9-Excessive violence, gore & torture 20.00 60.00 140.00
10-Silhouetted nudity panel 18.00 54.00 125.00
11,12 14.00 43.00 100.00

NOTE: ***Baily** c-2-12.*

WEIRD MYSTERIES (Magazine)
Mar-Apr, 1959 (68 pages) (35 cents) (B&W)
Pastime Publications

1-Torres-a; E. C. swipe from Tales From the Crypt #46 by Tuska "The Ragman" 4.70 14.00 28.00

WEIRD MYSTERY TALES (See DC 100 Page Super Spectacular)

WEIRD MYSTERY TALES (See Cancelled Comic Cavalcade)
July-Aug, 1972 - No. 24, Nov, 1975
National Periodical Publications

1-Kirby-a; Wrightson splash pg. 1.00 2.00 5.00
2-24: 21-Wrightson-c 1.00 2.50

NOTE: ***Alcala** a-5, 10, 13, 14. **Aparo** c-4. **Bolle** a-8. **Howard** a-4. **Kaluta** a-24; c-1. **G. Kane** a-10. **Kirby** a-1, 2p, 3p. **Nino** a-5, 6, 9, 13, 16, 21. **Redondo** a-9. **Starlin** a-3?, 4. **Wood** a-23.*

WEIRD ROMANCE (Eclipse)(Value: cover or less)

WEIRD SCIENCE (Formerly Saddle Romances) (Becomes Weird Science-Fantasy #23 on)
No. 12, May-June, 1950 - No. 22, Nov-Dec, 1953
E. C. Comics

12(#1) (1950) 105.00 310.00 725.00
13 59.00 175.00 410.00
14,15 (1950): 14-Robot-c 52.00 154.00 360.00
5-10: 5-Atomic explosion-c 33.00 100.00 230.00
11-14 (1952): 12-"Dream of Doom" star Gaines & E.C. artists 22.00 65.00 150.00
15-18-Williamson/Krenkel-a in each; 15-Williamson-a. 17-Used in **POP**, pgs. 81,82. 18-Bill Gaines doll app. in story 24.00 73.00 170.00
19,20-Williamson/Frazetta-a, 7 pgs each. 19-Used in **SOTI**, illo-"A young girl on her wedding night stabs her sleeping husband to death with a hatpin..." 33.00 100.00 230.00
21-Williamson/Frazetta-a, 6 pgs.; Wood draws E.C. staff; Gaines & Feldstein app. in story 33.00 100.00 230.00
22-Williamson/Frazetta/Krenkel/Krigstein-a, 8 pgs.; Wood draws himself in his story (last pg. & panel) 33.00 100.00 230.00

NOTE: ***Elder** a-14, 19. **Evans** a-22. **Feldstein** a-12(#1)-8; c-12(#1)-8, 11. **Ingels** a-15. **Kamen** a-12(#1)-13, 15-18, 20, 21. **Kurtzman** a-12(#1)-7. **Orlando** a-10-22. **Wood** a-12(#1), 13(#2), 5-22 (#9, 10, 12, 13 all have 2 **Wood** stories); c-9, 10, 12-22. Canadian reprints exist; see Table of Contents.*

WEIRD SCIENCE
Sept, 1990 - No. 4, Mar, 1991 ($1.95, color, 68 pgs.)(#3 on: $2.00)
Gladstone Publishing

1-Wood-c(r); all reprints in each .80 2.00
2-4: 2-4-Wood-c(r) .80 2.00

WEIRD SCIENCE
Sept, 1992 - Present ($1.50-$2.00, color)
Russ Cochran

1,2-r/Weird Science #12,13(#1,2); Feldstein-c 1.50
3-5 ($2.00): r/#14,15(#3,4),5 .80 2.00

WEIRD SCIENCE-FANTASY (Formerly Weird Science & Weird Fantasy) (Becomes Incredible Science Fiction #30)
No. 23 Mar, 1954 - No. 29, May-June, 1955 (#23,24: 15 cent-c)
E. C. Comics

23-Williamson, Wood-a; Bradbury adaptation 24.00 71.00 165.00
24-Williamson & Wood-a; Harlan Ellison's 1st professional story, 'Upheaval!,' later adapted into a short story as 'Mealtime,' and then into a TV episode of Voyage to the Bottom of the Sea as 'The Price of Doom' 24.00 71.00 165.00
25-Williamson-c; Williamson/Torres/Krenkel-a plus Wood-a; Bradbury adaptation; cover price back to 10 cents 27.00 81.00 190.00
26-Flying Saucer Report; Wood, Crandall, Orlando-a 22.00 65.00 155.00
27 24.00 71.00 165.00
28-Williamson/Krenkel/Torres-a; Wood-a 26.00 77.00 180.00
29-Frazetta-c; Williamson/Krenkel & Wood-a; last pre-code issue; new logo 45.00 135.00 315.00

Weird Suspense #1, © Atlas/Seaboard

Weird War Tales #73, © DC

Weird Wonder Tales #17, © MEG

GD25 FN65 NM94

NOTE: ***Crandall** a-26, 27, 29. **Evans** a-26. **Feldstein** c-24, 26, 28. **Kamen** a-27, 28. **Krigstein** a-23-25. **Orlando** a-in all. **Wood** a-in all; c-23, 27. The cover to #29 was originally intended for Famous Funnies #217, but was rejected.*

WEIRD SCIENCE-FANTASY
Nov, 1992 - Present ($1.50-$2.00, color)
Russ Cochran

1,2-r/Weird Science-Fantasy #23,24 — 1.50
3-5: r/#25-27 — .80 2.00

WEIRD SCIENCE-FANTASY ANNUAL
1952, 1953 (Sold thru the E. C. office & on the stands in some major cities) (25 cents, 132 pgs.)
E. C. Comics

1952-Feldstein-c — 129.00 385.00 1000.00
1953-Feldstein-c — 82.00 245.00 575.00
NOTE: *The 1952 annual contains books cover-dated in 1951 & 1952, and the 1953 annual from 1952 & 1953. Contents of each annual may vary in same year.*

WEIRD SUSPENSE
Feb, 1975 - No. 3, July, 1975
Atlas/Seaboard Publ.

1-3: 1-Tarantula begins. 3-Buckler-c — 1.00

WEIRD SUSPENSE STORIES (Canadian reprint of Crime SuspenStories #1-3; see Table of Contents)

WEIRD TALES ILLUSTRATED
1992 - No. 2, 1992 ($2.95, color, high quality paper)
Millennium Publications

1,2-Bolton painted-c. 1-Adapts E.A. Poe & Harlan Ellison stories. 2-E.A. Poe & H.P. Lovecraft adaptations — 1.20 3.00
1-($4.95, 52 pgs.)-Deluxe edition w/Tim Vigil-a not in regular #1; stiff-c; Bolton painted-c — 1.00 2.00 5.00

WEIRD TALES OF THE FUTURE
March, 1952 - No. 8, July-Aug, 1953
S.P.M. Publ. No. 1-4/Aragon Publ. No. 5-8

1-Andru-a(2); Wolverton partial-c — 39.00 118.00 275.00
2,3-Wolverton-c/a(3) each. 2-"Jumpin Jupiter" satire by Wolverton begins, ends #5 — 64.00 195.00 450.00
4-"Jumpin Jupiter" satire by Wolverton; partial Wolverton-c — 36.00 110.00 250.00
5-Wolverton-c/a(2) — 64.00 195.00 450.00
6-Bernard Baily-c — 23.00 70.00 160.00
7-"The Mind Movers" from the art to Wolverton's "Brain Bats of Venus" from Mr. Mystery #7 which was cut apart, pasted up, partially redrawn, and rewritten by Harry Kantor, the editor; Baily-c — 36.00 110.00 250.00
8-Reprints Weird Mysteries #1(10/52) minus cover; gory cover showing heart ripped out by B. Baily — 23.00 70.00 160.00

WEIRD TALES OF THE MACABRE (Magazine)
Jan, 1975 - No. 2, Mar, 1975 (B&W) (75 cents)
Atlas/Seaboard Publ.

1-Jeff Jones painted-c — .80 2.00
2-Boris Vallejo painted-c, Severin-a — .65 1.60

WEIRD TERROR (Also see Horrific)
Sept, 1952 - No. 13, Sept, 1954
Allen Hardy Associates (Comic Media)

1-"Portrait of Death," adapted from Lovecraft's "Pickman's Model;" lingerie panels, Hitler story — 20.00 60.00 140.00
2-Text on Marquis DeSade, Torture, Demonology, & St. Elmo's Fire — 13.00 40.00 90.00
3-Extreme violence, whipping, torture; article on sin eating, dowsing — 12.00 36.00 85.00
4-Dismemberment, decapitation, article on human flesh for sale, Devil, whipping — 16.00 50.00 115.00
5-Article on body snatching, mutilation; cannibalism story — 12.00 36.00 85.00
6-Dismemberment, decapitation, man hit by lightning — 16.00 48.00 110.00
7,9,10 — 11.00 32.00 75.00
8-Decapitation story; Ambrose Bierce adapt. — 14.00 43.00 100.00
11-End of the world story with atomic blast panels; Tothish-a by Bill Discount — 14.00 43.00 100.00
12-Discount-a — 10.00 30.00 65.00
13-Severed head panels — 11.00 32.00 75.00
NOTE: ***Don Heck** a-most issues; 1-13. **Landau** a-6. **Morisi** a-2-5, 7, 9, 12. **Palais** a-1, 5, 6, 8(2), 10, 12. **Powell** a-10. **Ravielli** a-11, 20.*

WEIRD THRILLERS
Sept-Oct, 1951 - No. 5, Oct-Nov, 1952 (#2-5: painted-c)
Ziff-Davis Publ. Co. (Approved Comics)

1-Rondo Hatton photo-c — 29.00 85.00 200.00
2-Toth, Anderson, Colan-a — 22.00 65.00 150.00
3-Two Powell, Tuska-a; classic-c — 20.00 60.00 140.00
4-Kubert, Tuska-a — 18.00 54.00 125.00
5-Powell-a — 16.00 50.00 115.00
NOTE: ***M. Anderson** a-2, 3. **Roussos** a-4. #2, 3 reprinted in Nightmare #10 & 13; #4, 5 r-/in Amazing Ghost Stories #16 & #15.*

WEIRD WAR TALES
Sept-Oct, 1971 - No. 124, June, 1983
National Periodical Publications/DC Comics

1-Kubert-a in #1-4,7; c-1-7 — 1.40 3.50
2,3-Drucker-a. 3,5-Heath-a — 1.00 2.50
4-7,9,10: 5,6,10-Toth-a — .80 2.00
8-Neal Adams-c/a(i) — 1.40 3.50
11-50: 36-Crandall & Kubert-r/#2 — 1.50
51-124: 64,68-Frank Miller-a. 93-Intro/origin Creature Commandos. 101-Intro/origin G.I. Robot — 1.50

WEIRD WESTERN TALES (Formerly All-Star Western)
No. 12, June-July, 1972 - No. 70, Aug, 1980
National Periodical Publications/DC Comics

12-(52 pgs.)-Bat Lash, Pow Wow Smith reprints; El Diablo by Neal Adams/Wrightson — 1.20 3.00 7.00
13,15-Neal Adams-a. 15-N. Adams-c — 1.20 3.00 7.00
14,29: 14-Toth-a. 29-Origin Jonah Hex — 1.80 4.50
16-28,30-70: 39-Origin/1st app. Scalphunter. 64-Bat Lash-c/story — .80 2.00
NOTE: ***Evans** inks-39-48; c-39i, 40, 47. **G. Kane** a-15. **Kubert** c-12, 33. **Starlin** c-44, 45. **Wildey** a-26. 48 & 49 are 44 pages.*

WEIRD WONDER TALES
Dec, 1973 - No. 22, May, 1977
Marvel Comics Group

1-Wolverton-r/Mystic #6 (Eye of Doom) — .90 2.25
2-22: 16-18-Venus-r by Everett from Venus #19,18 & 17. 19-22-Dr. Druid (Droom)-r — .70 1.80
NOTE: ***All 1950s & early 1960s reprints. **Check** r-1. **Colan** r-17. **Ditko** r-4, 5, 10-13, 19-21. **Drucker** r-12, 20. **Everett** r-3(Spellbound #16), 6(Astonishing #10), 9(Adv. Into Mystery #5). **Kirby** r-6, 11, 13, 16-22; c-17, 19, 20. **Krigstein** r-19. **Kubert** r-22. **Maneely** r-8. **Mooney** r-7p. **Powell** r-3, 7. **Torres** r-7. **Wildey** r-2, 7.*

WEIRD WORLDS (See Adventures Into...)

WEIRD WORLDS (Magazine)
V1#10(12/70), V2#1(2/71) - No. 4, Aug, 1971 (52 pgs.)
Eerie Publications

V1#10 — 2.00 5.00 10.00
V2#1-4 — 1.60 4.00 8.00

WEIRD WORLDS
Aug-Sept, 1972 - No. 9, Jan-Feb, 1974; No. 10, Oct-Nov, 1974
National Periodical Publications

1-Edgar Rice Burrough's John Carter Warlord of Mars & David Innes begin (1st DC app.); Kubert-c — 1.60 4.00
2-7: 7-Last John Carter — .80 2.00
8-10: 8-Iron Wolf begins by Chaykin (1st app.) — 1.50

Welcome Back Kotter #1, © Wolper Organization

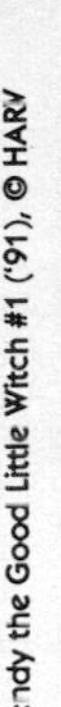
Wendy the Good Little Witch #1 ('91), © HARV

Western Adventures Comics #1, © ACE

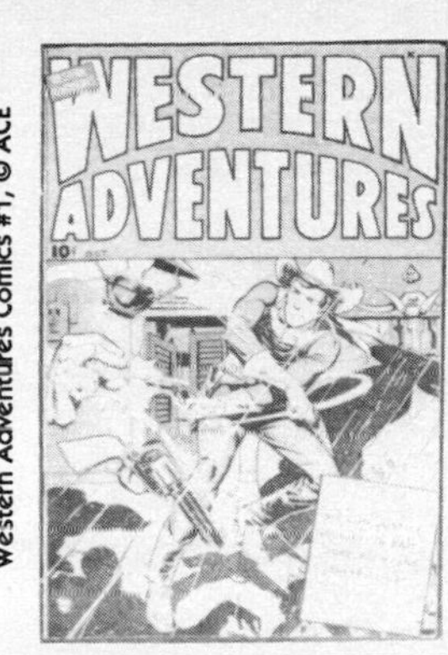

	GD25	FN65	NM94

NOTE: ***Neal Adams** a-2i, 3i. John Carter by **Andersonin** #1-3. **Chaykin** c-7, 8. **Kaluta** a-4; c-4-6, 10. **Orlando** a-4i; c-2, 3. **Wrightson** a-2i.*

WELCOME BACK, KOTTER (TV) (See Limited Collectors' Edition #57)
Nov, 1976 - No. 10, Mar-Apr, 1978
National Periodical Publications/DC Comics

	GD25	FN65	NM94
1-Sparling-a(p)		.80	2.00
2-10: 3-Estrada-a			1.00

WELCOME SANTA (See March of Comics #63,183)

WELLS FARGO (See Tales of...)

WENDY AND THE NEW KIDS ON THE BLOCK (Harvey)(Value: cover or less)

WENDY DIGEST (Harvey)(Value: cover or less)

WENDY PARKER COMICS
July, 1953 - No. 8, July, 1954
Atlas Comics (OMC)

	GD25	FN65	NM94
1	7.50	22.50	45.00
2	4.20	12.50	25.00
3-8	4.00	10.00	20.00

WENDY, THE GOOD LITTLE WITCH (TV)
8/60 - #82, 11/73; #83, 8/74 - #93, 4/76; #94, 9/90 - #97, 12/90
Harvey Publications

	GD25	FN65	NM94
1-Casper the Friendly Ghost begins	13.00	40.00	90.00
2	6.70	20.00	40.00
3-5	5.00	15.00	30.00
6-10	4.00	11.00	22.00
11-20	2.40	6.00	12.00
21-30	1.60	4.00	8.00
31-50	1.00	2.00	5.00
51-69		1.60	4.00
70-74: All 52 pg. Giants	1.00	2.00	5.00
75-93		.80	2.00
94-97 (1990, $1.00-c)			1.00

(See Casper the Friendly Ghost #20 & Harvey Hits #7, 16, 21, 23, 27, 30, 33)

WENDY THE GOOD LITTLE WITCH (2nd series)
Apr, 1991 - Present ($1.00/$1.25, color)
Harvey Comics

	GD25	FN65	NM94
1-10-Reprints Wendy & Casper stories. 6-Last $1.00-c			1.00

WENDY WITCH WORLD
10/61; No. 2, 9/62 - No. 52, 12/73; No. 53, 9/74
Harvey Publications

	GD25	FN65	NM94
1: 68 pg. Giants begin	9.15	27.50	55.00
2-5	4.20	12.50	25.00
6-10	3.00	7.50	15.00
11-20	1.80	4.50	9.00
21-30	1.00	2.00	5.00
31-39: Last 68 pg. issue		1.60	4.00
40-45: 52 pg. issues		1.20	3.00
46-53		.90	2.25

WEREWOLF (Super Hero) (Also see Dracula & Frankenstein)
Dec, 1966 - No. 3, April, 1967
Dell Publishing Co.

	GD25	FN65	NM94
1-1st app.	1.00	2.00	5.00
2,3		1.20	3.00

WEREWOLF BY NIGHT (See Giant-Size..., Marvel Spotlight #2-4 & Power Record Comics)
Sept, 1972 - No. 43, Mar, 1977
Marvel Comics Group

	GD25	FN65	NM94
1-Ploog-a cont'd. from Marvel Spotlight #4	5.00	15.00	35.00
2	2.60	7.50	18.00
3-5	1.70	5.00	12.00
6-10	1.50	3.75	9.00
11-20: 15-New origin Werewolf; Dracula app.	1.30	3.25	8.00
21-31	1.00	2.50	5.50
32-Origin & 1st app. Moon Knight (8/75)	7.00	21.00	50.00
33-2nd app. Moon Knight	4.30	13.00	30.00
34-36,38-43: 35-Starlin/Wrightson-c		1.40	3.50
37-Moon Knight app; part Wrightson-c	1.25	3.00	7.50

NOTE: ***Bolle** a-6i. **G. Kane** a-11p, 12p; c-21, 22, 24-30, 34p. **Mooney** a-7i. **Ploog** 1-4p, 5, 6p, 7p, 13-16p; c-5-8, 13-16. **Reinman** a-8i. **Sutton** a(i)-9, 11, 16, 35.*

WEREWOLVES & VAMPIRES (Magazine)
1962 (One Shot)
Charlton Comics

	GD25	FN65	NM94
1	5.85	17.50	35.00

WEST COAST AVENGERS
Sept, 1984 - No. 4, Dec, 1984 (Mini-series; Mando paper)
Marvel Comics Group

	GD25	FN65	NM94
1-Origin & 1st app. W.C. Avengers; Hawkeye, Iron Man, Mockingbird & Tigra		1.20	3.00
2-4			1.50

WEST COAST AVENGERS (Becomes Avengers West Coast #48 on)
Oct, 1985 - No. 47, Aug, 1989 (On-going series)
Marvel Comics Group

	GD25	FN65	NM94
V2#1		1.20	3.00
2-10		.80	2.00
11-20			1.50
21-41			1.00
42-Byrne-a(p)/scripts begin		.90	2.20
43-47: 46,46-Byrne-c. 46-1st app. Great Lakes Avengers			1.10
Annual 1 (1986)		.90	2.20
Annual 2 (1987)		.80	2.00
Annual 3 (1988, $1.75)-Evolutionary War app.		1.10	2.75
Annual V2#4 (1989, $2.00, 68 pgs.)-Atlantis Attacks; Byrne/Austin-a		.90	2.20
Annual V2#5 (1990, $2.00, 68 pgs.)		.80	2.00
Annual V2#6 (1991, $2.00, 68 pgs.)		.80	2.00
Annual V2#7 (1992, $2.25, 68 pgs.)-Darkhawk app.		.90	2.25

WESTERN ACTION
No. 7, 1964
I. W. Enterprises

	GD25	FN65	NM94
7-Reprints Cow Puncher #? by Avon	.60	1.50	3.00

WESTERN ACTION
February, 1975
Atlas/Seaboard Publ.

	GD25	FN65	NM94
1-Kid Cody by Wildey & The Comanche Kid stories; intro. The Renegade			1.00

WESTERN ACTION THRILLERS
April, 1937 (100 pages)(Square binding)
Dell Publishers

	GD25	FN65	NM94
1-Buffalo Bill, The Texas Kid, Laramie Joe, Two-Gun Thompson, & Wild West Bill app.	58.00	175.00	400.00

WESTERN ADVENTURES COMICS (Western Love Trails #7 on)
Oct, 1948 - No. 6, Aug, 1949
Ace Magazines

	GD25	FN65	NM94
nn(#1)-Sheriff Sal, The Cross-Draw Kid, Sam Bass begin	13.50	41.00	95.00
nn(#2)(12/48)	8.35	25.00	50.00
nn(#3)(2/49)-Used in **SOTI**, pgs. 30,31	9.15	27.50	55.00
4-6	6.35	19.00	38.00

WESTERN BANDITS
1952 (Painted-c)
Avon Periodicals

	GD25	FN65	NM94
1-Butch Cassidy, The Daltons by Larsen; Kinstler-a; c-part-r/paperback Avon Western Novel #1	10.00	30.00	70.00

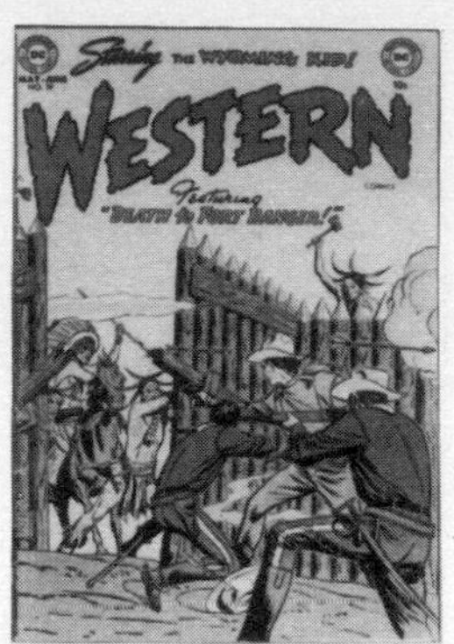

Western Comics #39, © DC

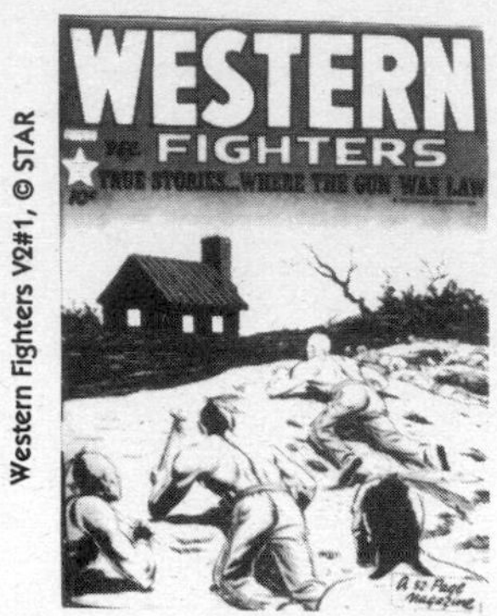

Western Fighters V2#1, © STAR

Western Gunfighters (2nd series) #4, © MEG

GD25 FN65 NM94

WESTERN BANDIT TRAILS (See Approved Comics)
Jan, 1949 - No. 3, July, 1949
St. John Publishing Co.

1-Tuska-a; Baker-c; Blue Monk, Ventrilo app. 13.00 40.00 90.00
2-Baker-c 10.00 30.00 65.00
3-Baker-c/a; Tuska-a 11.00 32.00 75.00

WESTERN COMICS (See Super DC Giant #15)
Jan-Feb, 1948 - No. 85, Jan-Feb, 1961 (1-27: 52pgs.)
National Periodical Publications

1-The Wyoming Kid & his horse Racer, The Vigilante (Meskin-a), The Cowboy Marshal, Rodeo Rick begin 59.00 180.00 415.00
2 29.00 85.00 200.00
3,4-Last Vigilante 24.00 72.00 165.00
5-Nighthawk & his horse Nightwind begin (not in #6); Captain Tootsie by Beck 20.00 60.00 140.00
6,7,9,10 16.00 48.00 110.00
8-Origin Wyoming Kid; 2 pg. pin-ups of rodeo queens 22.00 65.00 150.00
11-20 13.00 40.00 90.00
21-40: 24-Starr-a. 27-Last 52 pgs. 10.00 30.00 65.00
41-49: Last precode (2/55). 43-Pow Wow Smith begins, ends #85 10.00 30.00 60.00
50-60 9.15 27.50 55.00
61-85-Last Wyoming Kid. 77-Origin Matt Savage Trail Boss. 82-1st app. Fleetfoot, Pow Wow's girlfriend 6.70 20.00 40.00

NOTE: ***G. Kane, Infantino*** *art in most.* ***Meskin*** *a-1-4.* ***Moreira*** *a-28-39.* ***Post*** *a-3-5.*

WESTERN CRIME BUSTERS
Sept, 1950 - No. 10, Mar-Apr, 1952
Trojan Magazines

1-Six-Gun Smith, Wilma West, K-Bar-Kate, & Fighting Bob Dale begin; headlight-a 20.00 60.00 140.00
2 11.00 32.00 75.00
3-5: 3-Myron Fass-c 10.00 30.00 65.00
6-Wood-a 23.00 70.00 160.00
7-Six-Gun Smith by Wood 23.00 70.00 160.00
8 10.00 30.00 65.00
9-Tex Gordon & Wilma West by Wood; Lariat Lucy app. 23.00 70.00 160.00
10-Wood-a 22.00 65.00 150.00

WESTERN CRIME CASES (Formerly Indian Warriors #7,8; becomes The Outlaws #10 on)
No. 9, Dec, 1951
Star Publications

9-White Rider & Super Horse; L. B. Cole-c 6.70 20.00 40.00

WESTERN DESPERADO COMICS (Formerly Slam Bang Comics)
No. 8, 1940 (Oct.?)
Fawcett Publications

8-(Rare) 54.00 160.00 375.00

WESTERNER, THE (Wild Bill Pecos)
No. 14, June, 1948 - No. 41, Dec, 1951 (#14-31: 52 pgs.)
"Wanted" Comic Group/Toytown/Patches

14 9.15 27.50 55.00
15-17,19-21: 19-Meskin-a 4.20 12.50 25.00
18,22-25-Krigstein-a 7.50 22.50 45.00
26(4/50)-Origin & 1st app. Calamity Kate, series ends #32; Krigstein-a 9.15 27.50 55.00
27-Krigstein-a(2) 10.00 30.00 65.00
28-41: 33-Quest app. 37-Lobo, the Wolf Boy begins 3.60 9.00 18.00

NOTE: ***Mort Lawrence*** *a-20-27, 29, 37, 39; c-19, 22-24, 26, 27.* ***Leav*** *c-14, 31.* ***Syd Shores*** *a-39; c-34, 35, 37-41.*

WESTERNER, THE
1964
Super Comics

Super Reprint 15-17: 15-r/Oklahoma Kid #? 16-r/Crack West. #65; Severin-c; Crandall-r. 17-r/Blazing Western #2; Severin-c .60 1.50 3.00

WESTERN FIGHTERS
Apr-May, 1948 - V4#7, Mar-Apr, 1953 (#1-V3#2: 52 pgs.)
Hillman Periodicals/Star Publ.

V1#1-Simon & Kirby-c 22.00 65.00 150.00
2-Kirby-a(p)? 8.35 25.00 50.00
3-Fuje-c 6.70 20.00 40.00
4-Krigstein, Ingels, Fuje-a 8.35 25.00 50.00
5,6,8,9,12 5.00 15.00 30.00
7,10-Krigstein-a 8.35 25.00 50.00
11-Williamson/Frazetta-a 19.00 57.00 130.00
V2#1-Krigstein-a 8.35 25.00 50.00
2-12: 4-Berg-a 4.00 10.00 20.00
V3#1-11 3.60 9.00 18.00
12-Krigstein-a 7.50 22.50 45.00
V4#1,4-7 3.60 9.00 18.00
2,3-Krigstein-a 7.50 22.50 45.00
3-D 1(12/53, Star Publ.)- L. B. Cole -c 25.00 75.00 175.00

NOTE: ***Kinstlerish*** *a-V2#6, 8, 9, 12; V3#2, 5-7, 11, 12; V4#1(plus cover).* ***McWilliams*** *a-11.* ***Powell*** *a-V2#2.* ***Reinman*** *a-1-12, V4#3.* ***Rowich*** *c-5, 6i.* ***Starr*** *a-5.*

WESTERN FRONTIER
Apr-May, 1951 - No. 7, 1952
P. L. Publishers

1 8.35 25.00 50.00
2 5.00 15.00 30.00
3-7 4.00 10.00 20.00

WESTERN GUNFIGHTERS (1st Series) (Apache Kid #11-19)
No. 20, June, 1956 - No. 27, Aug, 1957
Atlas Comics (CPS)

20 8.35 25.00 50.00
21-Crandall-a 8.35 25.00 50.00
22-Wood & Powell-a 11.50 34.00 80.00
23,24: 23-Williamson-a. 24-Toth-a 8.35 25.00 50.00
25-27 5.85 17.50 35.00

NOTE: ***Berg*** *a-20.* ***Colan*** *a-20, 27.* ***Crandall*** *a-21.* ***Heath*** *a-25.* ***Maneely*** *a-24, 25; c-22, 23, 25.* ***Morisi*** *a-24.* ***Pakula*** *a-23.* ***Severin*** *c-20, 27.* ***Woodbridge*** *a-27.*

WESTERN GUNFIGHTERS (2nd Series)
Aug, 1970 - No. 33, Nov, 1975 (#1-6: 25 cents, 68 pgs.; #7: 52 pgs.)
Marvel Comics Group

1-Ghost Rider begins; Fort Rango, Renegades & Gunhawk app. 1.90 4.75
2-33: 2-Origin Nightwind (Apache Kid's horse). 7-Origin Ghost Rider retold. 10-Origin Black Rider. 12-Origin Matt Slade 1.10 2.75

NOTE: ***Baker*** *r-2, 3.* ***Colan*** *r-2.* ***Drucker*** *r-3.* ***Everett*** *a-6i.* ***G. Kane*** *c-29, 31.* ***Kirby*** *a-1p(r), 10, 11.* ***Kubert*** *r-2.* ***Maneely*** *r-2, 10.* ***Morrow*** *r-29.* ***Severin*** *c-10.* ***Barry Smith*** *a-4.* ***Steranko*** *c-14.* ***Sutton*** *a-1, 2i, 3, 4.* ***Torres*** *r-26('57).* ***Wildey*** *r-8, 9.* ***Williamson*** *r-2, 18.* ***Woodbridge*** *r-27('57). Renegades in #4, 5; Ghost Rider in #1-7.*

WESTERN HEARTS
Dec, 1949 - No. 10, Mar, 1952 (All photo-c)
Standard Comics

1-Severin-a; Whip Wilson & Reno Browne photo-c 12.00 36.00 85.00
2-Beverly Tyler & Jerome Courtland photo-c from movie "Palomino;" Williamson/Frazetta-a (2 pgs.) 13.00 40.00 90.00
3-Rex Allen photo-c 6.70 20.00 40.00
4-7,10-Severin & Elder, Al Carreno-a. 5-Ray Milland & Hedy Lamarr photo-c. 6-Fred MacMurray photo-c. 7-Jock Mahoney photo-c. 10-Bill Williams & Jane Nigh photo-c 6.70 20.00 40.00
8-Randolph Scott/Janis Carter photo-c from "Santa Fe;" Severin & Elder-a 7.50 22.50 45.00
9-Whip Wilson & Reno Browne photo-c; Severin & Elder-a 9.15 27.50 55.00

WESTERN HERO (Wow Comics #1-69; Real Western Hero #70-75)
No. 76, Mar, 1949 - No. 112, Mar, 1952

Western Hero #90, © FAW

Western Outlaws #17, © MEG

Western Tales of Black Rider #31, © MEG

GD25 FN65 NM94

Fawcett Publications

	GD25	FN65	NM94
76(#1, 52 pgs.)-Tom Mix, Hopalong Cassidy, Monte Hale, Gabby Hayes, Young Falcon (ends #78,80), & Big Bow and Little Arrow (ends #102,105) begin; painted-c begin	22.00	65.00	150.00
77 (52 pgs.)	11.50	34.00	80.00
78,80-82 (52 pgs.): 81-Capt. Tootsie by Beck	11.50	34.00	80.00
79,83 (36 pgs.): 83-Last painted-c	10.00	30.00	65.00
84-86,88-90 (52 pgs.): 84-Photo-c begin, end #112. 86-Last Hopalong Cassidy	10.00	30.00	70.00
87,91,95,99 (36 pgs.): 87-Bill Boyd begins, ends #95	10.00	30.00	60.00
92-94,96-98,101 (52 pgs.): 96-Tex Ritter begins. 101-Red Eagle app.	10.00	30.00	65.00
100 (52 pgs.)	10.00	30.00	70.00
102-111: 102-Begin 36 pg. issues	10.00	30.00	60.00
112-Last issue	10.00	30.00	65.00

NOTE: *1/2 to 1 pg. Rocky Lane (Carnation) in 80-83, 86, 88, 97.*

WESTERN KID (1st Series)
Dec, 1954 - No. 17, Aug, 1957
Atlas Comics (CPC)

	GD25	FN65	NM94
1-Origin; The Western Kid (Tex Dawson), his stallion Whirlwind & dog Lightning begin	11.50	34.00	80.00
2 (2/55)-Last pre-code	6.70	20.00	40.00
3-8	5.85	17.50	35.00
9,10-Williamson-a in both, 4 pgs. each	6.70	20.00	40.00
11-17	4.20	12.50	25.00

NOTE: *Ayers a-6, 7. **Maneely** c-2-7, 10, 14. **Romita** a-1-17; c-1, 12. **Severin** c-17.*

WESTERN KID, THE (2nd Series)
Dec, 1971 - No. 5, Aug, 1972 (All 20 cent issues)
Marvel Comics Group

	GD25	FN65	NM94
1-Reprints; Romita-c/a(3)		1.20	3.00
2-5: 2-Romita-a; Severin-c. 3-Williamson-r. 4-Everett-r		.80	2.00

WESTERN KILLERS
nn, Aug?, 1948; No. 60, Sept, 1948 - No. 64, May, 1949; No. 6, July, 1949
Fox Features Syndicate

	GD25	FN65	NM94
nn(#59?)(nd, F&J Trading Co.)-Range Busters; formerly Blue Beetle #57?	11.00	32.00	75.00
60 (#1, 9/48)-Extreme violence; lingerie panel	14.00	43.00	100.00
61-64, 6: 61-Jack Cole, Starr-a	10.00	30.00	70.00

WESTERN LIFE ROMANCES (My Friend Irma #3 on?)
Dec, 1949 - No. 2, Mar, 1950 (52 pgs.)
Marvel Comics (IPP)

	GD25	FN65	NM94
1-Whip Wilson & Reno Browne photo-c	12.00	36.00	85.00
2-Audie Murphy photo-c; spanking scene	10.00	30.00	65.00

WESTERN LOVE
July-Aug, 1949 - No. 5, Mar-Apr, 1950 (All photo-c & 52 pgs.)
Prize Publications

	GD25	FN65	NM94
1-S&K-a; Randolph Scott "Canadian Pacific" photo-c (see Prize Comics #76)	16.00	48.00	110.00
2,5-S&K-a: 2-Whip Wilson & Reno Browne photo-c. 5-Dale Robertson photo-c	13.00	40.00	90.00
3,4: 3-Reno Browne? photo-c	10.00	30.00	60.00

NOTE: ***Meskin & Severin/Elder** a-2-5.*

WESTERN LOVE TRAILS (Formerly Western Adventures)
No. 7, Nov, 1949 - No. 9, Mar, 1950
Ace Magazines (A. A. Wyn)

	GD25	FN65	NM94
7	9.15	27.50	55.00
8,9	6.70	20.00	40.00

WESTERN MARSHAL (See Steve Donovan... & Ernest Haycox's 4-Color 534, 591, 613, 640 & [based on Haycox's "Trailtown"])

WESTERN OUTLAWS (Junior Comics #9-16; My Secret Life #22 on)
No. 17, Sept, 1948 - No. 21, May, 1949
Fox Features Syndicate

	GD25	FN65	NM94
17-Kamen-a; Iger shop-a in all; 1 pg. 'Death and the Devil Pills' r-in Ghostly Weird #122	16.00	48.00	110.00
18-21	10.00	30.00	70.00

WESTERN OUTLAWS
Feb, 1954 - No. 21, Aug, 1957
Atlas Comics (ACI No. 1-14/WPI No. 15-21)

	GD25	FN65	NM94
1-Heath, Powell-a; Maneely hanging-c	12.00	36.00	85.00
2	7.50	22.50	45.00
3-10: 7-Violent-a by R.Q. Sale	5.85	17.50	35.00
11,14-Williamson-a in both, 6 pgs. each	7.00	21.00	42.00
12,18,20,21: Severin covers	5.00	15.00	30.00
13-Baker-a	5.35	16.00	32.00
15-Torres-a	5.85	17.50	35.00
16-Williamson text illo	4.20	12.50	25.00
17,19-Crandall-a. 17-Williamson text illo	5.85	17.50	35.00

NOTE: ***Ayers** a-7, 10, 18, 20. **Bolle** a-21. **Colan** a-5, 10, 11, 17. **Drucker** a-11. **Everett** a-9, 10. **Heath** a-1; c-3, 4, 8, 16. **Kubert** a-9p. **Maneely** a-13, 16, 17, 19; c-5, 7, 9, 10, 12, 13. **Morisi** a-18. **Powell** a-3, 16. **Romita** a-7, 13. **Severin** a-8, 16, 19; c-17, 18, 20, 21. **Tuska** a-6, 15.*

WESTERN OUTLAWS & SHERIFFS (Formerly Best Western)
No. 60, Dec, 1949 - No. 73, June, 1952
Marvel/Atlas Comics (IPC)

	GD25	FN65	NM94
60 (52 pgs.)	14.00	43.00	100.00
61-65: 61-Photo-c	11.50	34.00	80.00
66,68-72: 66-Story contains 5 hangings	9.15	27.50	55.00
67-Cannibalism story	11.00	32.00	75.00
73-Black Rider story; Everett-c	10.00	30.00	60.00

NOTE: ***Maneely** a-62, 67; c-62, 69-73. **Robinson** a-68. **Sinnott** a-70. **Tuska** a-69-71.*

WESTERN PICTURE STORIES (1st Western comic)
Feb, 1937 - No. 4, June, 1937
Comics Magazine Company

	GD25	FN65	NM94
1-Will Eisner-a	117.00	350.00	750.00
2-Will Eisner-a	75.00	225.00	500.00
3,4: 3-Eisner-a	62.00	188.00	400.00

WESTERN PICTURE STORIES (See Giant Comics Edition #6, 11)

WESTERN ROMANCES (See Target...)

WESTERN ROUGH RIDERS
Nov, 1954 - No. 4, May, 1955
Gillmor Magazines No. 1,4 (Stanmor Publications)

	GD25	FN65	NM94
1	5.35	16.00	32.00
2-4	4.00	10.00	20.00

WESTERN ROUNDUP (See Dell Giants & Fox Giants)

WESTERN TALES (Formerly Witches...)
No. 31, Oct, 1955 - No. 33, July-Sept, 1956
Harvey Publications

	GD25	FN65	NM94
31,32-All S&K-a; Davy Crockett app. in each	10.00	30.00	70.00
33-S&K-a; Jim Bowie app.	10.00	30.00	70.00

NOTE: *#32 & 33 contain Boy's Ranch reprints. **Kirby** c-31.*

WESTERN TALES OF BLACK RIDER (Formerly Black Rider; Gunsmoke Western #32 on)
No. 28, May, 1955 - No. 31, Nov, 1955
Atlas Comics (CPS)

	GD25	FN65	NM94
28 (#1): The Spider (a villain) dies	11.00	32.00	75.00
29-31	8.35	25.00	50.00

NOTE: ***Lawrence** a-30. **Maneely** c-28-30. **Severin** a-28. **Shores** c-31.*

WESTERN TEAM-UP
November, 1973 (20 cents)
Marvel Comics Group

	GD25	FN65	NM94
1-Origin & 1st app. The Dakota Kid; Rawhide Kid-r; Gunsmoke Kid-r by Jack Davis		.70	1.80

WESTERN THRILLERS (My Past Confessions #7 on)

Western Trails #1, © MEG

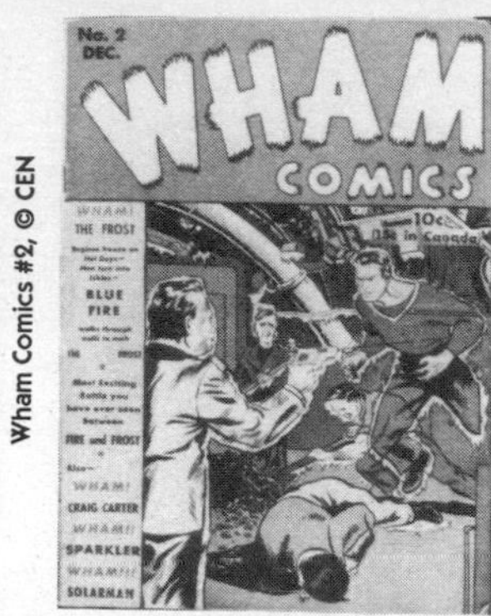

Wham Comics #2, © CEN

What If...? (2nd series) #24, © MEG

GD25 FN65 NM94

Aug, 1948 - No. 6, June, 1949; No. 52, 1954?
Fox Features Syndicate/M.S. Distr. No. 52

1-"Velvet Rose"-Kamenish-a; "Two-Gun Sal," "Striker Sisters" (all women outlaws issue); Brodsky-c 29.00 85.00 200.00
2 10.00 30.00 70.00
3,6 10.00 30.00 60.00
4,5-Bakerish-a; 5-Butch Cassidy app. 11.00 32.00 75.00
52-(Reprint, M.S. Dist.)-1954? No date given (becomes My Love Secret #53) 4.70 14.00 28.00

WESTERN THRILLERS (Cowboy Action #5 on)
Nov, 1954 - No. 4, Feb, 1955 (All-r/Western Outlaws & Sheriffs)
Atlas Comics (ACI)

1 10.00 30.00 65.00
2-4 5.85 17.50 35.00
NOTE: ***Heath** c-3. **Maneely** a-1; c-2. **Powell** a-4. **Robinson** a-4. **Romita** c-4. **Tuska** a-2.*

WESTERN TRAILS
May, 1957 - No. 2, July, 1957
Atlas Comics (SAI)

1-Ringo Kid app.; Severin-c 7.50 22.50 45.00
2-Severin-c 5.35 16.00 32.00
NOTE: ***Bolle** a-1, 2. **Maneely** a-1, 2. **Severin** c-1, 2.*

WESTERN TRUE CRIME (Becomes My Confessions)
No. 15, Aug, 1948 - No. 6, June, 1949
Fox Features Syndicate

15(#1)-Kamenish-a; formerly Zoot #14 (5/48)? 14.00 43.00 100.00
16(#2)-Kamenish-a; headlight panels, violence 11.00 32.00 75.00
3,5,6 7.50 22.50 45.00
4-Johnny Craig-a 11.50 34.00 80.00

WESTERN WINNERS (Formerly All-Western Winners; becomes Black Rider #8 on & Romance Tales #7 on?)
No. 5, June, 1949 - No. 7, Dec, 1949
Marvel Comics (CDS)

5-Two-Gun Kid, Kid Colt, Black Rider; Shores-c 22.00 65.00 150.00
6-Two-Gun Kid, Black Rider, Heath Kid Colt story; Captain Tootsie by C.C. Beck 18.00 54.00 125.00
7-Randolph Scott Photo-c w/true stories about the West 18.00 54.00 125.00

WEST OF THE PECOS (See 4-Color #222)

WESTWARD HO, THE WAGONS (See 4-Color #738)

WETWORKS (See WILDC.A.T.S: Covert Action Teams #2)

WHACK (Satire)
Oct, 1953 - No. 3, May, 1954
St. John Publishing Co. (Jubilee Publ.)

1-(3-D)-Kubert-a; Maurer-c 22.00 65.00 150.00
2,3-Kubert-a in each. 2-Bing Crosby on-c; Mighty Mouse & Steve Canyon parodies. 3-Maurer-c 11.00 32.00 75.00

WHACKY (See Wacky)

WHAM COMICS (See Super Spy)
Nov, 1940 - No. 2, Dec, 1940
Centaur Publications

1-The Sparkler, The Phantom Rider, Craig Carter and the Magic Ring Detector, Copper Slug, Speed Silvers by Gustavson, Speed Centaur & Jon Linton (s/f) begin 96.00 288.00 650.00
2-Origin Blue Fire & Solarman; The Buzzard app. 71.00 210.00 475.00

WHAM-O GIANT COMICS (98 cents)
April, 1967 (Newspaper size) (One Shot) (Full Color)
Wham-O Mfg. Co. (Six issue subscription was advertised)

1-Radian & Goody Bumpkin by Wood; 1 pg. Stanley-a; Fine, Tufts-a; flying saucer reports; wraparound c 4.30 13.00 30.00

WHAT DO YOU KNOW ABOUT THIS COMICS SEAL OF APPROVAL?
nd (1955) (4pgs.; color; slick paper-c)
No publisher listed (DC Comics Giveaway)

nn-(Rare) 54.00 160.00 375.0

WHAT IF? (What If? Featuring... #13 & #?-33)(1st series)
Feb, 1977 - No. 47, Oct, 1984; June, 1988 (All 52 pgs.)
Marvel Comics Group

1-Brief origin Spider-Man, Fantastic Four 2.30 6.75 16.0
2-Origin The Hulk retold 1.65 4.00 10.0
3-5: 3-Avengers. 4-Invaders. 5-Capt. America 1.10 2.70 6.5
6-10: 8-Daredevil; Spidey parody. 9-Origins Venus, Marvel Boy, Human Robot, 3-D Man. 11-Marvel Bullpen as F. F. 1.00 2.50 5.5
11,12 1.80 4.5
13-Conan app.; John Buscema-c/a(p) 1.10 2.70 6.5
14-16,18-26,29,30: 18-Dr. Strange. 19,30-Spider-Man. 22-Origin Dr. Doom retold 1.70 4.25
17-Ghost Rider & Son of Satan app. 1.25 3.00 7.50
27-X-Men app.; Miller-c 1.65 4.70 11.00
28-Daredevil by Miller; Ghost Rider app. 1.65 4.70 11.00
31-Featuring Wolverine & the Hulk; X-Men app.; death of Hulk, Wolverine & Magneto 2.15 6.50 15.00
32-47: 32,36-Byrne-a. 34-Marvel crew each draw themselves. 35-What if Elektra had lived?; Miller/Austin-a. 37-Old X-Men & Silver Surfer app. 39-Thor battles Conan 1.00 2.50
Special 1 ($1.50, 6/88)-Iron Man, F.F., Thor app. .80 2.00
NOTE: ***Austin** a-27p, 32i, 34, 35i; c-35i, 36i. **J. Buscema** a-13p, 15p; c-10, 13p, 23p. **Byrne** a-32i, 36; c-36p. **Colan** a-21p; c-17p, 18p, 21p. **Ditko** a-35, Special 1. **Golden** c-29, 40-42. **Guice** a-40p. **Gil Kane** a-3p, 24p; c(p)-2-4, 7, 8. **Kirby** a-11p; c-9p, 11p. **Layton** a-32i, 33i; c-30, 32p, 33i, 34. **Miller** a-28p, 32i, 35p; c-27, 28p. **Mooney** a-8i, 30i. **Perez** a-15p. **Robbins** a-4p. **Simonson** a-15p, 32i. **Starlin** a-32i. **Stevens** a-16i(part). **Sutton** a-2i, 18p, 28. **Tuska** a-5p. **Weiss** a-37p.*

WHAT IF...? (2nd series)
V2#1, July, 1989 - Present ($1.25 color)
Marvel Comics

V2#1-...The Avengers Had Lost the Evol. War 1.90 4.75
2-5: 2-Daredevil, Punisher app. 1.10 2.75
6-X-Men app. 1.60 4.00
7-Wolverine app.; Liefeld-c/a(1st on Wolvie?) 1.00 2.50 5.50
8,11: 11-Fantastic Four app.; McFarlane-c(i) .90 2.25
9,12-X-Men 1.20 3.00
10-Punisher 1.20 3.00
13-15,17-21,23,27-29: 13-Prof. X; Jim Lee-c. 14-Capt. Marvel; Lim/Austin-c. 15-F.F.; Capullo-c/a(p). 17-Spider-Man/Kraven. 18-F.F. 19-Vision. 20,21-Spider-Man. 23-X-Men. 27-Namor/F.F. 28,29-Capt. America. 29-Swipes cover to Avengers #4 1.50
16-Wolverine battles Conan; Red Sonja app.; X-Men cameo 1.80 4.50
22-Silver Surfer by Lim/Austin-c/a 1.20 3.00
24-Wolverine; Punisher app. 1.10 2.75
25-($1.50, 52 pgs.)-Wolverine app. 1.20 3.00
26-Punisher app. .80 2.00
30-($1.75, 52 pgs.)-Sue Richards/F.F. .70 1.75
31-40: 31-Cosmic Spider-Man & Venom app.; Hobgoblin cameo. 32,33-Phoenix; X-Men app. 35-Fantastic Five (w/Spidey). 36-Avengers vs. Guardians of the Galaxy. 37-Wolverine. 38-Thor; Rogers-p(part). 40-Storm; X-Men app. 1.50
41-($1.75, 52 pgs.)-Avengers vs. Galactus .70 1.75
42-49,51-60: 42-Spider-Man. 43-Wolverine. 44-Venom/Punisher. 45-Ghost Rider. 46,47-Cable 2 part story 1.25
50-($2.95, 52 pgs.)-Foil embossed-c; "What If Hulk Had Killed Wolverine" 1.20 3.00

WHAT'S BEHIND THESE HEADLINES
1948 (16 pgs.)
William C. Popper Co.

nn-Comic insert-"The Plot to Steal the World" 3.60 9.00 18.00

'WHAT'S NEW? - THE COLLECTED ADVENTURES OF PHIL & DIXIE'

What The-?! #8, © MEG

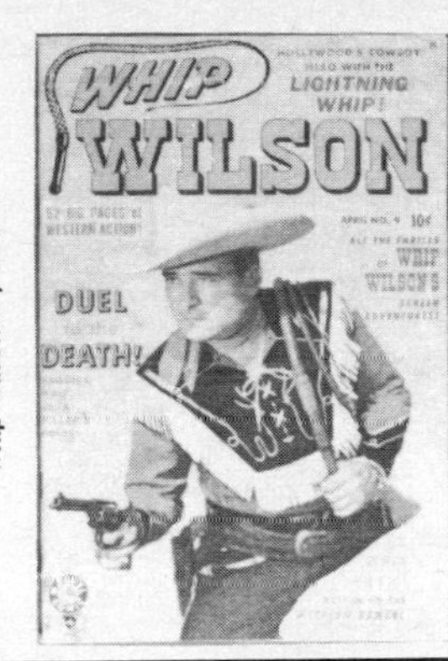

Whip Wilson #9, © MEG

White Princess of the Jungle #4, © AVON

GD25 FN65 NM94 | GD25 FN65 NM94

Oct, 1991 - No. 2, 1991? ($5.95, mostly color, squarebound, 52 pgs.)
Palliard Press

1,2-By Phil Foglio 1.00 2.50 6.00

WHAT THE--?!
Aug, 1988 - Present ($1.25-$1.50, semi-annually #5 on)
Marvel Comics

1-All contain parodies 1.00 2.50
2,4,5: 5-Punisher/Wolverine parody; Jim Lee-a 1.50
3-X-Men parody; Todd McFarlane-a 1.20 3.00
6-25: 6-($1.00)-Punisher, Wolverine, Alpha Flight. 9-Wolverine. 16-EC back-c parody. 17-Wolverine/Punisher parody. 18-Star Trek parody w/ Wolverine. 19-Punisher, Wolverine, Ghost Rider. 21-Weapon X parody. 22-Punisher/Wolverine parody 1.25
26-Fall Special ($2.50, 68 pgs.)-Spider Ham 2099-c/story; origin Silver Surfer; Hulk & Doomsday parody .90 2.50
Summer Special 1 (1993, $2.50)-X-Men parody .90 2.50
NOTE: ***Austin** a-6i. **Byrne** a-2, 6, 10; c-2, 6-8, 10, 12, 13. **Golden** a-22. **Dale Keown** a-8p(8 pgs.). **McFarlane** a-3. **Rogers** c-15i, 16p. **Severin** a-2. **Staton** a-21p. **Williamson** a-2i.*

WHEATIES (Premiums) (32 titles)
1950 & 1951 (32 pages) (Pocket size)
Walt Disney Productions

(Set A-1 to A-8, 1950)
A-1-Mickey Mouse & the Disappearing Island, A-2-Grandma Duck, Homespun Detective, A-3-Donald Duck & the Haunted Jewels, A-4-Donald Duck & the Giant Ape, A-5-Mickey Mouse, Roving Reporter, A-6-Li'l Bad Wolf, Forest Ranger, A-7-Goofy, Tightrope Acrobat, A-8-Pluto & the Bogus Money each.... 4.00 10.00 20.00

(Set B-1 to B-8, 1950)
B-1-Mickey Mouse & the Pharoah's Curse, B-2-Pluto, Canine Cowpoke, B-3-Donald Duck & the Buccaneers, B-4-Mickey Mouse & the Mystery Sea Monster, B-5-Li'l Bad Wolf in the Hollow Tree Hideout, B-6-Donald Duck, Trail Blazer, B-7-Goofy & the Gangsters, B-8 Donald Duck, Klondike Kid each.... 3.60 9.00 18.00

(Set C-1 to C-8, 1951)
C-1-Donald Duck & the Inca Idol, C-2-Mickey Mouse & the Magic Mountain, C-3-Li'l Bad Wolf, Fire Fighter, C-4-Gus & Jaq Save the Ship, C-5-Donald Duck in the Lost Lakes, C-6-Mickey Mouse & the Stagecoach Bandits, C-7-Goofy, Big Game Hunter, C-8-Donald Duck Deep-Sea Diver each.... 3.60 9.00 18.00

(Set D-1 to D-8, 1951)
D-1-Donald Duck in Indian Country, D-2-Mickey Mouse and the Abandoned Mine, D-3-Pluto & the Mysterious Package, D-4-Bre'r Rabbit's Sunken Treasure, D-5-Donald Duck, Mighty Mystic, D-6-Mickey Mouse & the Medicine Man, D-7-Li'l Bad Wolf and the Secret of the Woods, D-8-Minnie Mouse, Girl Explorer each.... 3.60 9.00 18.00
NOTE: *Some copies lack the Wheaties ad.*

WHEE COMICS (Also see Gay, Smile & Tickle Comics)
1955 (52 pgs.) (5x7-1/4") (7 cents)
Modern Store Publications

1-Funny animal .80 2.00 4.00

WHEELIE AND THE CHOPPER BUNCH (TV)
July, 1975 - No. 7, July, 1976 (Hanna-Barbera)
Charlton Comics

1,2: 1-Byrne text illo (see Nightmare for 1st art); Staton-a. 2-Byrne-c/a.
2,3-Mike Zeck text illos 1.25 3.00 7.50
3-7-Staton-a. 3-Byrne-c/a 1.60 4.00

WHEN KNIGHTHOOD WAS IN FLOWER (See 4-Color #505, 682)

WHEN SCHOOL IS OUT (See Wisco)

WHERE CREATURES ROAM
July, 1970 - No. 8, Sept, 1971
Marvel Comics Group

1-Kirby/Ayers-r 1.60 4.00
2-8-Kirby-r .80 2.00
NOTE: ***Ditko** r-1, 2, 4, 6, 7. All contain pre super-hero reprints.*

WHERE MONSTERS DWELL
Jan, 1970 - No. 38, Oct, 1975
Marvel Comics Group

1-Kirby/Ditko-r; all contain pre super-hero-r 1.60 4.00
2-10,12: 4-Crandall-a(r). 12-Giant issue .80 2.00
11,13-37: 18,20-Starlin-c 1.50
38-Williamson-r/World of Suspense #3 .80 2.00
NOTE: ***Ditko** a(r)-4, 8, 10, 12, 17-19, 23-25, 37. **Reinman** a-4r. **Severin** c-15.*

WHERE'S HUDDLES? (TV) (See Fun-In #9)
Jan, 1971 - No. 3, Dec, 1971 (Hanna-Barbera)
Gold Key

1 1.30 3.25 8.00
2,3: 3-r-most #1 1.00 2.00 5.00

WHIP WILSON (Movie star) (Formerly Rex Hart; Gunhawk #12 on; see Western Hearts, Western Life Romances, Western Love)
No. 9, April, 1950 - No. 11, Sept, 1950 (#9,10: 52pgs.; #11: 36pgs.)
Marvel Comics

9-Photo-c; Whip Wilson & his horse Bullet begin; origin Bullet; issue #23 listed on splash page; cover changed to #9 39.00 118.00 275.00
10,11-Photo-c 25.00 75.00 175.00
I.W. Reprint #1(1964)-Kinstler-c; r-Marvel #11 2.40 6.00 12.00

WHIRLWIND COMICS (Also see Cyclone Comics)
June, 1940 - No. 3, Sept, 1940
Nita Publication

1-Cyclone begins (origin/1st app.) 60.00 180.00 425.00
2,3 43.00 130.00 300.00

WHIRLYBIRDS (See 4-Color #1124, 1216)

WHISPER (Capital & First)(Value: cover or less)

WHITE CHIEF OF THE PAWNEE INDIANS
1951
Avon Periodicals

nn-Kit West app.; Kinstler-c 10.00 30.00 70.00

WHITE EAGLE INDIAN CHIEF (See Indian Chief)

WHITE FANG (Disney, movie adapt.)(Value: cover or less)

WHITE INDIAN
No. 11, July, 1953 - No. 15, 1954
Magazine Enterprises

11(A-1 94), 12(A-1 101), 13(A-1 104)-Frazetta-r(Dan Brand) in all from Durango Kid. 11-Powell-c 16.00 48.00 110.00
14(A-1 117), 15(A-1 135)-Check-a; Torres-a-#15 8.35 25.00 50.00
NOTE: *#11 contains reprints from Durango Kid #1-4; #12 from #5, 9, 10, 11; #13 from #7, 12, 13, 16. #14 & 15 contain all new stories.*

WHITE PRINCESS OF THE JUNGLE (Also see Jungle Adventures & Top Jungle Comics)
July, 1951 - No. 5, Nov, 1952
Avon Periodicals

1-Origin of White Princess (Taanda) & Capt'n Courage (r); Kinstler-c 26.00 80.00 185.00
2-Reprints origin of Malu, Slave Girl Princess from Avon's Slave Girl Comics #1 w/Malu changed to Zora; Kinstler-c/a(2) 22.00 65.00 150.00
3-Origin Blue Gorilla; Kinstler-c/a 16.00 48.00 110.00
4-Jack Barnum, White Hunter app.; r/Sheena #9 14.00 43.00 100.00
5-Blue Gorilla by McCann?; Kinstler inside-c; Fawcette/Alascia-a(3) 14.00 43.00 100.00

WHITE RIDER AND SUPER HORSE (Formerly Humdinger V2#2; Indian Warriors #7 on; also see Blue Bolt #1, 4Most & Western Crime Cases)
1950 - No. 6, Mar, 1951
Novelty-Star Publications/Accepted Publ.

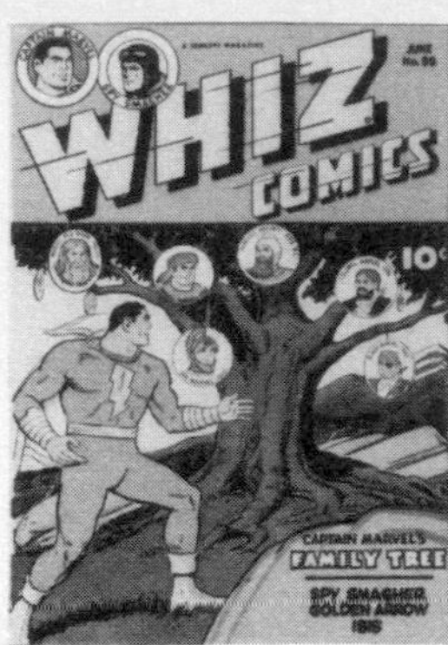

Whiz Comics #55, © FAW

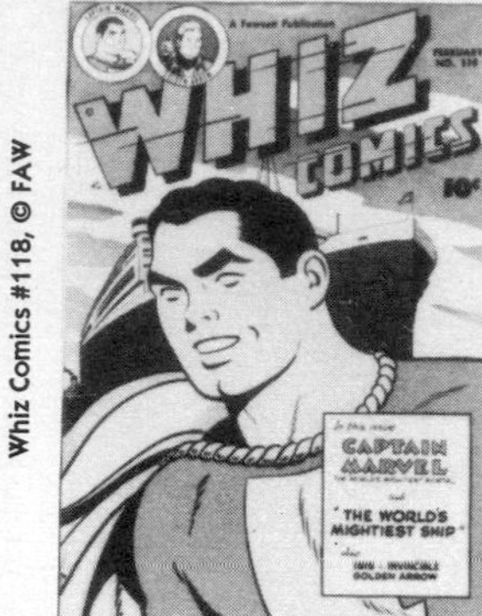

Whiz Comics #118, © FAW

Wilbur #39, © AP

GD25 FN65 NM94

1: 1-3-Exist? 9.15 27.50 55.00
2,3 6.70 20.00 40.00
4-6-Adapts "The Last of the Mohicans." 4-(9/50)-Says #11 on inside
6.70 20.00 40.00
Accepted Reprint #5(r/#5),6 (nd); L.B. Cole-c 4.20 12.50 25.00
NOTE: *All have **L. B. Cole** covers.*

WHITE WILDERNESS (See 4-Color #943)

WHITMAN COMIC BOOKS
1962 (136 pgs.; 7-3/4x5-3/4; hardcover) (B&W)
Whitman Publishing Co.

1-7: 1-Yogi Bear. 2-Huckleberry Hound. 3-Mr. Jinks and Pixie & Dixie. 4-The Flintstones. 5-Augie Doggie & Loopy de Loop. 6-Snooper & Blabber Fearless Detectives/Quick Draw McGraw of the Wild West. 7-Bugs Bunny-r from #47,51,53,54 & 55 .80 2.00 4.00
8-Donald Duck-reprints most of WDC&S #209-213. Includes 5 Barks stories, 1 complete Mickey Mouse serial & 1 Mickey Mouse serial missing the 1st episode 7.75 22.00 44.00
NOTE: *Hanna-Barbera #1-6(TV), original stories. Dell reprints-#7, 8.*

WHIZ COMICS (Formerly Flash Comics & Thrill Comics #1)
No. 2, Feb, 1940 - No. 155, June, 1953
Fawcett Publications

GD25 FN65 VF82 NM94

1-(nn on cover, #2 inside)-Origin & 1st newsstand app. Captain Marvel (formerly Captain Thunder) by C. C. Beck (created by Bill Parker), Spy Smasher, Golden Arrow, Ibis the Invincible, Dan Dare, Scoop Smith, Sivana, & Lance O'Casey begin 4,200.00 12,600.00 25,200.00 42,000.00
(Estimated up to 100 total copies exist, 3 in NM/Mint)
(The only Mint copy sold in 1990 for $74,000 cash/trade)

1-Reprint, oversize 13-1/2"x10". **WARNING**: This comic is an exact duplicate reprint (except for dropping "Gangway for Captain Marvel" from-c) of the original except for its size. DC published it in 1974 with a second cover titling it as a Famous First Edition. There have been many reported cases of the outer cover being removed and the interior sold as the original edition. The reprint with the new outer cover removed is practically worthless. See Famous First Edition for value.

GD25 FN65 NM94

2-(3/40, nn on cover, #3 inside); cover to Flash #1 redrawn, pg. 12, panel 4; Spy Smasher reveals I.D. to Eve 370.00 1115.00 2600.00
3-(4/40, #3 on-c, #4 inside)-1st app. Beautia 250.00 750.00 1600.00
4-(5/40, #4 on cover, #5 inside)-Brief origin Capt. Marvel retold
208.00 625.00 1350.00
5-Captain Marvel wears button-down flap on splash page only
158.00 475.00 1050.00
6-10: 7-Dr. Voodoo begins (by Raboy-#9-22) 122.00 368.00 800.00
11-14: 12-Capt. Marvel does not wear cape 87.00 262.00 550.00
15-Origin Sivana; Dr. Voodoo by Raboy 105.00 315.00 675.00
16-18-Spy Smasher battles Captain Marvel 105.00 315.00 675.00
19,20 62.00 188.00 400.00
21-Origin & 1st app. Lt. Marvels 67.00 200.00 425.00
22-24: 23-Only Dr. Voodoo by Tuska 50.00 150.00 325.00
25-(12/41)-Captain Nazi jumps from Master Comics #21 to take on Capt. Marvel solo after being beaten by Capt. Marvel/Bulletman team, causing the creation of Capt. Marvel Jr.; 1st app./origin of Capt. Marvel Jr. (part II of trilogy origin); Captain Marvel sends Jr. back to Master #22 to aid Bulletman against Capt. Nazi; origin Old Shazam in text 215.00 645.00 1500.00
26-30 44.00 132.00 285.00
31,32: 32-1st app. The Trolls; Hitler/Mussolini satire by Beck
37.00 110.00 240.00
33-Spy Smasher, Captain Marvel x-over on cover and inside
42.00 125.00 275.00
34,36-40: 37-The Trolls app. by Swayze 29.00 88.00 190.00
35-Captain Marvel & Spy Smasher-c 33.00 100.00 220.00
41-50: 43-Spy Smasher, Ibis, Golden Arrow x-over in Capt. Marvel. 44-Flag-c. 47-Origin recap (1 pg.) 20.00 60.00 135.00
51-60: 52-Capt. Marvel x-over in Ibis. 57-Spy Smasher, Golden Arrow, Ibis cameo 17.00 50.00 115.00
61-70 15.00 45.00 105.00
71,77-80 12.00 35.00 80.00

GD25 FN65 NM94

72-76-Two Captain Marvel stories in each; 76-Spy Smasher becomes Crime Smasher 12.50 37.50 85.00
81-99: 86-Captain Marvel battles Sivana Family. 91-Infinity-c
12.50 37.50 85.00
100 15.00 45.00 105.00
101-106: 102-Commando Yank app. 106-Bulletman app.
10.00 30.00 70.00
107-152: 107-White House photo-c. 108-Brooklyn Bridge photo-c. 112-Photo-c 139-Infinity-c. 142-Used in **POP**, pg. 89 10.00 30.00 70.00
153-155-(Scarce): 155-Dr. Death story 14.00 43.00 100.00
Wheaties Giveaway(1946, Miniature, 6-1/2x8-1/4", 32 pgs.); all copies were taped at each corner to a box of Wheaties and are never found in fine or mint condition; "Capt. Marvel & the Water Thieves," plus Golden Arrow, Ibis stories 60.00 225.00 -
NOTE: ***Krigstein** Golden Arrow-No. 75, 78, 91, 95, 96, 98-100. **M.Swayze** a-37, 38, 59; c-38. **Schaffenberger** c-138-158(most). **Wolverton** 1/2 pg. "Culture Corner"-No. 65-68, 70-85, 87-96, 98-100, 102-109, 112-121, 123, 125, 126, 128-131, 133, 134, 136, 142, 143, 146.*

WHODUNIT
Aug-Sept, 1948 - No. 3, Dec-Jan, 1948-49 (#1: 52 pgs.)
D.S. Publishing Co.

1-Baker-a, 7pgs. 10.00 30.00 70.00
2,3 7.50 22.50 45.00

WHODUNNIT? (Eclipse)(Value: cover or less)

WHO FRAMED ROGER RABBIT (See Marvel Graphic Novel)

WHO IS NEXT?
No. 5, January, 1953
Standard Comics

5-Toth, Sekowsky, Andru-a 12.00 36.00 85.00

WHO'S MINDING THE MINT? (See Movie Classics)

WHO'S WHO IN STAR TREK
Mar, 1987 - #2, Apr, 1987 ($1.50, color)
DC Comics

1,2 1.90 4.75

WHO'S WHO IN THE LEGION OF SUPER-HEROES (DC)(Value: cover or less)

WHO'S WHO: THE DEFINITIVE DIRECTORY OF THE DC UNIVERSE (DC)(Value: cover or less)

WHO'S WHO UPDATE '87 (DC)(Value: cover or less)

WHO'S WHO UPDATE '88 (DC)Value: cover or less)

WILBUR COMICS (Teen-age) (Also see Laugh Comics, Laugh Comix, Liberty Comics #10 & Zip Comics)
Sum', 1944 - No. 87, 11/59; No. 88, 9/63; No. 89, 10/64; No. 90, 10/65 (No. 1-46: 52 pgs.)
MLJ Magazines/Archie Publ. No. 8, Spring, 1946 on

1 36.00 110.00 250.00
2(Fall, 1944) 18.00 54.00 125.00
3,4(Wint, '44-45; Spr, '45) 13.00 40.00 90.00
5-1st app. Katy Keene (Sum, 1945) & begin series; Wilbur story same as Archie story in Archie #1 except that Wilbur replaces Archie
46.00 140.00 325.00
6-10(Fall, 1946) 13.00 40.00 90.00
11-20 9.15 27.50 55.00
21-30(1949) 5.85 17.50 35.00
31-50 4.00 11.00 22.00
51-70 3.00 7.50 15.00
71-90: 88-Last 10 cent issue (9/63) 1.60 4.00 8.00
NOTE: *Katy Keene in No. 5-56, 58-69.*

WILD
Feb, 1954 - No. 5, Aug, 1954
Atlas Comics (IPC)

1 13.00 40.00 90.00
2 10.00 30.00 60.00

Wild Bill Elliott #16, © DELL

WildC.A.T.S. #4, © Jim Lee

Wild Dog #3, © DC

GD25 FN65 NM94

3-5 7.50 22.50 45.00

NOTE: *Berg a-5; c-4. Burgos c-3. Colan a-4. Everett a-1-3. Heath a-2, 3, 5. Maneely a-1-3, 5; c-1, 5. Post a-2, 5. Ed Win a-1, 3.*

WILD (This Magazine Is...) (Magazine)
Jan, 1968 - No. 3, 1968 (52 pgs.) (Satire)
Dell Publishing Co.

1-3 1.00 2.50 6.00

WILD ANIMALS (Pacific)(Value: cover or less)

WILD BILL ELLIOTT (Also see Western Roundup under Dell Giants)
No. 278, 5/50 - No. 643, 7/55 (No #11,12) (All photo-c)
Dell Publishing Co.

4-Color 278(#1, 52pgs.)-Titled "Bill Elliott;" Bill & his horse Stormy begin; photo front/back-c begin 11.50 34.00 80.00
2 (11/50), 3 (52 pgs.) 6.70 20.00 40.00
4-10(10-12/52) 5.35 16.00 32.00
4-Color 472(6/53),520(12/53)-Last photo back-c 5.35 16.00 32.00
13(4-6/54) - 17(4-6/55) 4.35 13.00 26.00
4-Color 643 (7/55) 4.35 13.00 26.00

WILD BILL HICKOK (Also see Blazing Sixguns)
Sept-Oct, 1949 - No. 28, May-June, 1956
Avon Periodicals

1-Ingels-c 12.00 36.00 85.00
2-Painted-c; Kit West app. 6.70 20.00 40.00
3-5-Painted-c (4-Cover by Howard Winfield) 4.00 11.00 22.00
6-10,12: 8-10-Painted-c 4.00 11.00 22.00
11,14-Kinstler-c/a 4.20 12.50 25.00
13,15,17,18,20: 20-Kit West by Larsen 3.00 7.50 15.00
16-Kamen-a; r-3 stories/King of the Badmen of Deadwood 4.00 10.50 21.00
19-Meskin-a 3.00 7.50 15.00
21-Reprints 2 stories/Chief Crazy Horse 3.00 7.50 15.00
22-McCann-a?; r-/Sheriff Bob Dixon's... 3.00 7.50 15.00
23-27-Kinstler-c/a(r) 4.00 10.00 20.00
28-Kinstler-c/a (new); r-/Last of the Comanches 4.00 10.00 20.00
I.W. Reprint #1-r/#2; Kinstler-c .80 2.00 4.00
Super Reprint #10-12: 10-r/#18, 11-r/#?, 12-r/#8 .80 2.00 4.00

NOTE: *#23, 25 contain numerous editing deletions in both art and script due to code. Kinstler c-6, 7, 11-14, 17, 18, 20-22, 24-28. Howard Larsen a-1, 2, 4, 5, 6(3), 7-9, 11, 12, 17, 18, 20-24, 26. Meskin a-7. Reinman a-6, 17.*

WILD BILL HICKOK AND JINGLES (TV)(Formerly Cowboy Western)
No. 68, March, 1958 - No. 75, Dec, 1959 (Also see Blue Bird)
Charlton Comics

68,69-Williamson-a (all are 10 cent issues) 7.50 22.50 45.00
70-Two pgs. Williamson-a 5.00 15.00 30.00
71-75 (#76, exist?) 3.60 9.00 18.00

WILD BILL PECOS WESTERN (AC)(Value: cover or less)

WILD BOY OF THE CONGO (Also see Approved Comics)
No. 10, 2-3/51 - No. 12, 8-9/51; No. 4, 10-11/51 - No. 15, 6/55
Ziff-Davis No. 10-12,4-6/St. John No. 7? on

10(#1)(2-3/51)-Origin; bondage-c by Saunders; used in **SOTI**, pg. 189 11.50 34.00 80.00
11(4-5/51),12(8-9/51)-Norman Saunders-c 7.50 22.50 45.00
4(10-11/51)-Saunders bondage-c 7.50 22.50 45.00
5(Winter,'51)-Saunders-c 6.35 19.00 38.00
6,8,9(10/53),10: 6-Saunders-c 6.35 19.00 38.00
7(8-9/52)-Baker-c; Kinstler-a 7.00 21.00 42.00
11-13-Baker-c. 11-Kinstler-a (2 pgs.) 7.00 21.00 42.00
14(4/55)-Baker-c; r-#12('51) 7.00 21.00 42.00
15(6/55) 5.00 15.00 30.00

WILD CARDS (Marvel)(Value: cover or less)

WILDCAT (See Sensation Comics #1)

WILDC.A.T.S: COVERT ACTION TEAMS
Aug, 1992 - No. 4, Mar, 1993; No. 5, 1993 - Present ($1.95, color)
Image Comics

1-1st app.; Jim Lee/Williams-c/a & Lee scripts begin; contains 2 trading cards 1.30 3.25 8.00
1-All gold foil signed edition 60.00
1-All gold foil unsigned edition 20.00
2-($2.50)-Prism foil stamped-c; contains coupon for Image Comics #0 & 4 pg. preview to Portacio's Wetworks (back-up) 1.90 4.75
2-Direct sale misprint w/o foil-c .80 2.00
2-Newsstand ed., no prism or coupon .80 2.00
3-Lee/Liefeld-c (1/93-c, 12/92 inside) .80 2.00
4-($2.50)-Polybagged w/Topps trading card; 1st app. Tribe by Johnson & Stroman 1.00 2.50
5,6 .80 2.00
...Sourcebook 1 ($2.50)-Foil embossed-c 1.00 2.50

WILDC.A.T.S TRILOGY
June, 1993 - No. 2, 1993 ($1.95, color, mini-series)
Image Comics

1-($2.50)-Multi-color foil-c; Jae Lee-c/a 1.00 2.50
2-($1.95)-Jae Lee-c/a .80 2.00

WILD DOG (DC)(Value: cover or less)

WILD FRONTIER (Cheyenne Kid #8 on)
Oct, 1955 - No. 7, April, 1957
Charlton Comics

1-Davy Crockett 5.85 17.50 35.00
2-6-Davy Crockett in all 4.00 10.00 20.00
7-Origin & 1st app. Cheyenne Kid 4.00 10.00 20.00

WILD KINGDOM (TV)
1965 (Giveaway) (regular size) (16 pgs., slick-c)
Western Printing Co.

nn-Mutual of Omaha's... 2.40 6.00 12.00

WILDSTAR: SKY ZERO
Mar, 1993 - No. 4, 1993 ($1.95, color, mini-series)
Image Comics

1-($2.50)-Embossed-c w/silver ink 1.00 2.50
1-Gold variant 20.00
2,3 .80 2.00

WILDTHING
Apr, 1993 - Present ($1.75, color)
Marvel Comics UK

1-($2.50)-Embossed-c; Venom & Carnage cameo 1.00 2.50
2-10: 2-Spider-Man & Venom. 6-Mysterio app. .70 1.75

WILD WEST (Wild Western #3 on)
Spring, 1948 - No. 2, July, 1948
Marvel Comics (WFP)

1-Two-Gun Kid, Arizona Annie, & Tex Taylor begin; Shores-c 16.00 48.00 110.00
2-Captain Tootsie by Beck; Shores-c 14.00 43.00 100.00

WILD WEST (Black Fury #1-57)
V2#58, November, 1966
Charlton Comics

V2#58 .80 2.00

WILD WEST C.O.W.-BOYS OF MOO MESA (TV)
Dec, 1992 - No. 3, Feb, 1993; Mar, 1993 - No. 3, July, 1993 ($1.25, color)
Archie Comics

1-3 (Mini-series) 1.25
1-3 1.25

WILD WESTERN (Formerly Wild West #1,2)
No. 3, 9/48 - No. 57, 9/57 (3-11: 52 pgs; 12-on: 36 pgs)
Marvel/Atlas Comics (WFP)

Wild Western #34, © MEG

Wings Comics #54, © FH

Wings Comics #61, © FH

GD25 FN65 NM94

3(#1)-Tex Morgan begins; Two-Gun Kid, Tex Taylor, & Arizona Annie continue from Wild West 18.00 54.00 125.00
4-Last Arizona Annie; Captain Tootsie by Beck; Kid Colt app. 12.00 36.00 85.00
5-2nd app. Black Rider (1/49); Blaze Carson, Captain Tootsie (by Beck) app. 14.00 43.00 100.00
6-8: 6-Blaze Carson app; anti-Wertham editorial 10.00 30.00 65.00
9-Photo-c; Black Rider begins, ends #19 12.00 36.00 85.00
10-Charles Starrett photo-c 14.00 43.00 100.00
11-(Last 52 pg. issue) 10.00 30.00 60.00
12-14,16-19: All Black Rider-c/stories. 12-14-The Prairie Kid & his horse Fury app. 8.35 25.00 50.00
15-Red Larabee, Gunhawk (origin), his horse Blaze, & Apache Kid begin, end #22; Black Rider-c/story 9.15 27.50 55.00
20-29: 20-Kid Colt-c begin. 24-Has 2 Kid Colt stories. 26-1st app. The Ringo Kid? (2/53); 4 pg. story 7.00 21.00 42.00
30-Katz-a 7.50 22.50 45.00
31-40 5.35 16.00 32.00
41-47,49-51,53,57 4.00 12.00 24.00
48-Williamson/Torres-a (4 pgs); Drucker-a 6.70 20.00 40.00
52-Crandall-a 6.70 20.00 40.00
54,55-Williamson-a in both (5 & 4 pgs.), #54 with Mayo plus 2 text illos 6.35 19.00 38.00
56-Baker-a? 4.00 12.00 24.00

NOTE: *Annie Oakley in #46, 47. Apache Kid in #15-22, 39. Arizona Kid in #21, 23. Arrowhead in #34-39. Black Rider in #5, 9-19, 33-44. Fighting Texan in #17. Kid Colt in #4-6, 9-11, 20-47, 52, 54-56. Outlaw Kid in #43. Red Hawkins in #13, 14. Ringo Kid in #26, 39, 41, 43, 44, 46, 47, 50, 52-56. Tex Morgan in #3, 4, 6, 9, 11. Tex Taylor in #3-6, 9, 11. Texas Kid in #23-25. Two-Gun Kid in #3-6, 9, 11, 12, 33-39, 41. Wyatt Earp in #47.* **Ayers** *a-41, 42.* **Berg** *a-26; c-24.* **Colan** *a-49.* **Forte** *a-28, 30.* **Al Hartley** *a-16.* **Heath** *a-4, 5, 8; c-34, 44.* **Keller** *a-24, 26(2), 29-40, 44-46, 48, 52.* **Maneely** *a-10, 12, 15, 16, 28, 35, 38, 40-45; c-18-22, 33, 35, 36, 38, 39, 41, 42, 45.* **Morisi** *a-23, 52.* **Pakula** *a-42, 52.* **Powell** *a-51.* **Romita** *a-24(2).* **Severin** *a-46, 47; c-48.* **Shores** *a-3, 5, 30, 31, 33, 35, 36, 38, 41; c-3-5.* **Sinnott** *a-34-39.* **Wildey** *a-43. Bondage c-19.*

WILD WESTERN ACTION (Also see The Bravados)
March, 1971 - No. 3, June, 1971 (Reprints, 25 cents, 52 pgs.)
Skywald Publishing Corp.

1-Durango Kid, Straight Arrow; with all references to "Straight" in story relettered to "Swift;" Bravados begin; Shores-r .80 2.00
2-Billy Nevada, Durango Kid 1.50
3-Red Mask, Durango Kid 1.50

WILD WESTERN ROUNDUP
Oct, 1957; 1960-'61
Red Top/Decker Publications/I. W. Enterprises

1(1957)-Kid Cowboy-r 2.40 6.00 12.00
I.W. Reprint #1('60-61)-r/#1 by Red Top .80 2.00 4.00

WILD WEST RODEO
1953 (15 cents)
Star Publications

1-A comic book coloring book with regular full color cover & B&W inside 3.60 9.00 18.00

WILD WILD WEST, THE (TV)
June, 1966 - No. 7, Oct, 1969
Gold Key

1,2-McWilliams-a 7.00 21.00 50.00
3-7 5.00 15.00 35.00

WILD, WILD WEST, THE (TV)(Millennium)(Value: cover or less)

WILKIN BOY (See That...)

WILL EISNER PRESENTS (Eclipse)(Value: cover or less)

WILL EISNER'S 3-D CLASSICS FEATURING THE SPIRIT (Kitchen Sink)(Value: cover or less)

WILLIE COMICS (Formerly Ideal #1-4; Crime Cases #24 on; Li'l Willie #20 & 21) (See Gay Comics, Laugh, Millie The Model & Wisco)
#5, Fall, 1946 - #19, 4/49; #22, 1/50 - #23, 5/50 (No #20 & 21)
Marvel Comics (MgPC)

GD25 FN65 NM94

5(#1)-George, Margie, Nellie The Nurse & Willie begin 10.00 30.00 70.00
6,8,9 5.85 17.50 35.00
7(1),10,11-Kurtzman's "Hey Look" 7.50 22.50 45.00
12,14-18,22,23 4.70 14.00 28.00
13,19-Kurtzman's "Hey Look" 6.70 20.00 40.00
NOTE: *Cindy app. in #17. Jeanie app. in #17. Little Lizzie app. in #22.*

WILLIE MAYS (See The Amazing...)

WILLIE THE PENGUIN
April, 1951 - No. 6, April, 1952
Standard Comics

1 4.70 14.00 28.00
2-6 3.20 8.00 16.00

WILLIE THE WISE-GUY (Also see Cartoon Kids)
Sept, 1957
Atlas Comics (NPP)

1-Kida, Maneely-a 5.00 15.00 30.00

WILLIE WESTINGHOUSE EDISON SMITH THE BOY INVENTOR
1906 (36 pgs. in color) (10x16")
William A. Stokes Co.

nn-By Frank Crane 29.00 85.00 200.00

WILLOW (Marvel)(Value: cover or less)

WILL ROGERS WESTERN (Formerly My Great Love #1-4; see Blazing & True Comics #66)
No. 5, June, 1950 - No. 2, Aug, 1950
Fox Features Syndicate

5(#1),2: Photo-c 22.00 65.00 150.00

WILL-YUM (See 4-Color #676, 765, 902)

WIN A PRIZE COMICS (Timmy The Timid Ghost #3 on?)
Feb, 1955 - No. 2, Apr, 1955
Charlton Comics

V1#1-S&K-a; Poe adapt; E.C. War swipe 46.00 140.00 325.00
2-S&K-a 31.00 92.00 215.00

WINDY & WILLY
May-June, 1969 - No. 4, Nov-Dec, 1969
National Periodical Publications

1-4: r/Dobie Gillis with some art changes 1.60 4.00

WINGS COMICS
9/40 - No. 109, 9/49; No. 110, Wint, 1949-50; No. 111, Spring, 1950; No. 112, 1950(nd); No. 113 - No. 115, 1950(nd); No. 116, 1952(nd); No. 117, Fall, 1952 - No. 122, Wint, 1953-54; No. 123 - No. 124, 1954(nd)
Fiction House Magazines

1-Skull Squad, Clipper Kirk, Suicide Smith, Jane Martin, War Nurse, Phantom Falcons, Greasemonkey Griffin, Parachute Patrol & Powder Burns begin 117.00 350.00 750.00
2 54.00 162.00 350.00
3-5 41.00 122.00 265.00
6-10 35.00 105.00 230.00
11-15 30.00 90.00 200.00
16-Origin Captain Wings 33.00 100.00 220.00
17-20 22.00 68.00 150.00
21-30 20.00 60.00 135.00
31-40 15.00 45.00 100.00
41-50 12.50 37.50 85.00
51-60: 60-Last Skull Squad 10.00 30.00 70.00
61-67: 66-Ghost Patrol begins (becomes Ghost Squadron #71 on), ends #112? 10.00 30.00 70.00
68,69: 68-Clipper Kirk becomes The Phantom Falcon-origin, Part 1; part 2 in #69 10.00 30.00 70.00
70-72: 70-1st app. The Phantom Falcon in costume, origin-Part 3; Capt. Wings battles Col. Kamikaze in all 10.00 30.00 60.00

Winnie Winkle #7, © DELL

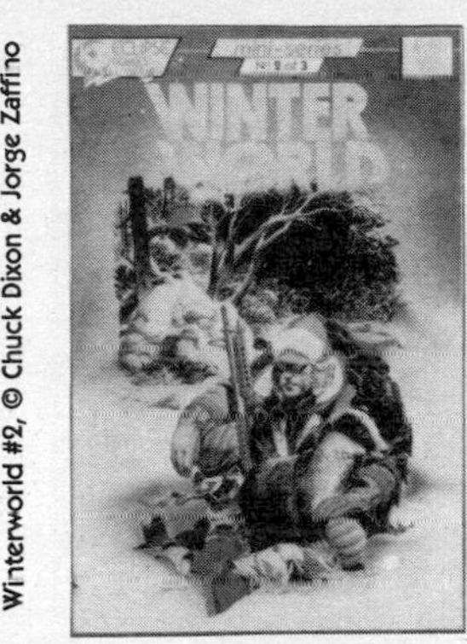

Winterworld #2, © Chuck Dixon & Jorge Zaffino

Witches Tales #19, © HARV

GD25 FN65 NM94

73-99: 80-Phantom Falcon by Larsen 10.00 30.00 60.00
00 10.00 30.00 65.00
01-124: 111-Last Jane Martin 112-Flying Saucer-c/story (1950). 115-Used in **POP**, pg. 89 8.35 25.00 50.00

NOTE: *Bondage covers are common. Captain Wings battles Sky Hag-#75, 76; ...Mr. Atlantis-#85-92; ...Mr. Pupin(Red Agent)-#98-103. Capt. Wings by* ***Elias****-#52-64, 68; by* ***Lubbers****-#29-32, 70-103, 110; by* ***Renee****-#33-46.* ***Evans*** *a-85-103, 105, 106, 108-111(Jane Martin).* ***Larsen*** *a-52, 59, 64, 73-77. Jane Martin by* ***Fran Hopper****-#68-84; Suicide Smith by* ***John Celardo****-#76, 79-103; by* ***Hollingsworth****-#68, 105-109, 111; Ghost Squadron by* ***Maurice Whitman****-#68, 72-78, 80, 82-110; Skull Squad by* ***M. Baker****-#52-60; Clipper Kirk by* ***Baker****-#60, 61; by* ***Colan****-#53; by* ***Ingels****-(some issues?). Phantom Falcon by* ***Larsen****-#78, 80-83.* ***Elias*** *c-58-72.* ***Fawcette*** *c-3-12, 16, 17, 19, 22-33.* ***Lubbers*** *c-74-109.* ***Tuska*** *a-5.* ***Whitman*** *c-110-124.* ***Zolnerwich*** *c-15, 21.*

WINGS OF THE EAGLES, THE (See 4-Color #790)

WINKY DINK (Adventures of...)
No. 75, March, 1957 (One Shot)
Pines Comics

75-Marv Levy-c/a 4.00 10.00 20.00

WINKY DINK (See 4-Color #663)

WINNIE-THE-POOH (Also see Dynabrite Comics)
January, 1977 - No. 33, 1984 (Walt Disney)
(Winnie-The-Pooh began as Edward Bear in 1926 by Milne)
Gold Key No. 1-17/Whitman No. 18 on

1-New art 1.50
2-33: 5,12-33-New material 1.00

WINNIE WINKLE
1930 - No. 4, 1933 (52 pgs.) (B&W daily strip reprints)
Cupples & Leon Co.

1 16.00 48.00 110.00
2-4 10.00 30.00 70.00

WINNIE WINKLE (See Popular Comics & Super Comics)
1941 - No. 7, Sept-Nov, 1949
Dell Publishing Co.

Large Feature Comic 2('41) 14.00 43.00 100.00
4-Color 94('45) 12.00 36.00 85.00
4-Color 174 7.50 22.50 45.00
1(3-5/48)-Contains daily & Sunday newspaper-r from 1939-1941 6.70 20.00 40.00
2 (6-8/48) 4.20 12.50 25.00
3-7 3.20 8.00 16.00

WINTERWORLD (Eclipse)(Value: cover or less)

WISCO/KLARER COMIC BOOK (Miniature)
1948 - 1964 (24 pgs.) (3-1/2x6-3/4")
Marvel Comics/Vital Publications/Fawcett Publications

Given away by Wisco "99" Service Stations, Carnation Malted Milk, Klarer Health Wieners, Fleers Dubble Bubble Gum, Rodeo All-Meat Wieners, Perfect Potato Chips, & others; see ad in Tom Mix #21

Blackstone & the Gold Medal Mystery(1948) 4.35 13.00 26.00
Blackstone "Solves the Sealed Vault Mystery"(1950) 4.35 13.00 26.00
Blaze Carson in "The Sheriff Shoots It Out"(1950) 4.35 13.00 26.00
Captain Marvel & Billy's Big Game (r/Capt. Marvel Adv. #76) 29.00 85.00 200.00
(Prices vary widely on this book)
China Boy in "A Trip to the Zoo" #10(1948) 1.60 4.00 8.00
Indoors-Outdoors Game Book 1.60 4.00 8.00
Jim Solar Space Sheriff in "Battle for Mars," "Between Two Worlds," "Conquers Outer Space," "The Creatures on the Comet," "Defeats the Moon Missile Men," "Encounter Creatures on Comet," "Meet the Jupiter Jumpers," "Meets the Man From Mars," "On Traffic Duty," "Outlaws of the Spaceways," "Pirates of the Planet X," "Protects Space Lanes," "Raiders From the Sun," "Ring Around Saturn," "Robots of Rhea," "The Sky Ruby," "Spacetts of the Sky," "Spidermen of Venus," "Trouble on Mercury" 3.60 9.00 18.00
Johnny Starboard & the Underseas Pirates('48) 3.00 7.50 15.00
Kid Colt in "He Lived by His Guns"(1950) 5.85 17.50 35.00
Little Aspirin as "Crook Catcher" #2(1950) 1.60 4.00 8.00
Little Aspirin in "Naughty But Nice" #6(1950) 1.60 4.00 8.00
Return of the Black Phantom (not M.E. character)(Roy Dare)(1948) 2.40 6.00 12.00
Secrets of Magic 2.00 5.00 10.00
Slim Morgan "Brings Justice to Mesa City" #3 2.00 5.00 10.00
Super Rabbit(1950)-Cuts Red Tape, Stops Crime Wave! 5.00 15.00 30.00
Tex Farnum, Frontiersman(1948) 2.40 6.00 12.00
Tex Taylor in "Draw or Die, Cowpoke!" (1950) 4.20 12.50 25.00
Tex Taylor in "An Exciting Adventure at the Gold Mine" (1950) 4.20 12.50 25.00
Wacky Quacky in "All-Aboard" 1.20 3.00 6.00
When School Is Out 1.20 3.00 6.00
Willie in a "Comic-Comic Book Fall" #1 1.60 4.00 8.00
Wonder Duck "An Adventure at the Rodeo of the Fearless Quacker!" (1950) 3.00 7.50 15.00
Rare uncut version of three; includes Capt. Marvel, Tex Farnum, Black Phantom Estimated value.... $300.00

WISE GUYS (See Harvey...)

WISE LITTLE HEN, THE
1934 (48 pgs.); 1935; 1937 (Story book)
David McKay Publ./Whitman

nn-2nd book app. Donald Duck; Donald app. on cover with Wise Little Hen & Practical Pig; painted cover; same artist as the B&W's from Silly Symphony Cartoon, The Wise Little Hen (1934) (McKay) 64.00 195.00 450.00
1935 Edition with dust jacket; 44 pgs. with color, 8-3/4x9-3/4" (Whitman) 43.00 130.00 300.00
888(1937)-9-1/2x13", 12 pgs. (Whitman) Donald Duck app. 20.00 60.00 140.00

WITCHCRAFT (See Strange Mysteries, Super Reprint #18)
Mar-Apr, 1952 - No. 6, Mar, 1953
Avon Periodicals

1-Kubert-a; 1 pg. Check-a 36.00 110.00 250.00
2-Kubert & Check-a 25.00 75.00 175.00
3,6: 3-Lawrence-a; Kinstler inside-c 16.00 50.00 115.00
4-People cooked alive c/story 20.00 60.00 140.00
5-Kelly Freas-c 24.00 70.00 170.00

NOTE: ***Hollingsworth*** *a-4-6; c-4, 6.* ***McCann*** *a-3?*

WITCHES TALES (Witches Western Tales #29,30)
Jan, 1951 - No. 28, Dec, 1954 (date misprinted as 4/55)
Witches Tales/Harvey Publications

1-Powell-a (1 pg.) 20.00 60.00 140.00
2-Eye injury panel 10.00 30.00 65.00
3-7,9,10 7.50 22.50 45.00
8-Eye injury panels 9.15 27.50 55.00
11-13,15,16: 12-Acid in face story 6.35 19.00 38.00
14,17-Powell/Nostrand-a. 17-Atomic disaster story 9.15 27.50 55.00
18-Nostrand-a; E.C. swipe/Shock S.S. 9.15 27.50 55.00
19-Nostrand-a; E.C. swipe/"Glutton;" Devil-c 9.15 27.50 55.00
20-24-Nostrand-a. 21-E.C. swipe; rape story. 23-Wood E.C. swipes/Two-Fisted Tales #34 9.15 27.50 55.00
25-Nostrand-a; E.C. swipe/Mad Barber 9.15 27.50 55.00
26-28: 27-r/#6 with diff.-c. 28-r/#8 with diff.-c 5.85 17.50 35.00

NOTE: ***Check*** *a-24.* ***Elias*** *c-8, 10, 16-27.* ***Kremer*** *a-18; c-25.* ***Nostrand*** *a-17-25; 14, 17(w/****Powell****).* ***Palais*** *a-1, 2, 4(2), 5(2), 7-9, 12, 14, 15, 17.* ***Powell*** *a-3-7, 10, 11, 19-27. Bondage-c 1, 3, 5, 6, 8, 9.*

WITCHES TALES (Magazine)
V1#7, July, 1969 - V7#1, Feb, 1975 (52 pgs.) (B&W)
Eerie Publications

V1#7(7/69) - 9(11/69) 2.00 6.00 14.00
V2#1-6('70), V3#1-6('71) 1.65 4.00 10.00
V4#1-6('72), V5#1-6('73), V6#1-6('74), V7#1 1.50 3.75 9.00

NOTE: *Ajax/Farrell reprints in early issues.*

With the U.S. Paratroops... #1, © AVON

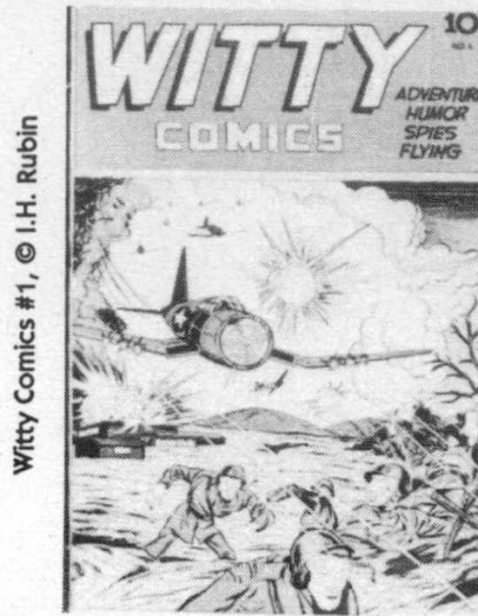

Witty Comics #1, © I.H. Rubin

Wolverine Annual #2, © MEG

GD25 FN65 NM94

WITCHES' WESTERN TALES (Formerly Witches Tales) (Western Tales#31on)
No. 29, Feb, 1955 - No. 30, April, 1955
Harvey Publications

29,30-S&K-r/from Boys' Ranch including-c. 29-Last pre-code 11.00 32.00 75.00

WITCHING HOUR (The ... later issues)
Feb-Mar, 1969 - No. 85, Oct, 1978
National Periodical Publications/DC Comics

1-Toth-a, plus Neal Adams-a (2 pgs.) 2.40 7.25 17.00
2,6 1.50 3.75 9.00
3,5-Wrightson-a; Toth-p. 3-Last 12 cent issue 1.20 3.00 7.00
4,7,9-12: Toth-a in all 1.00 2.50 5.50
8-Toth, Neal Adams-a 1.10 2.70 6.50
13-Neal Adams-c/a, 2pgs. 1.60 4.00
14-Williamson/Garzon, Jones-a; N. Adams-c 1.60 4.00
15-20 .80 2.00
21-85: 38-(100 pgs.). 84-(44 pgs.) 1.00

NOTE: *Combined with The Unexpected with #189.* ***Neal Adams*** *c-7-11, 13, 14.* ***Alcala*** *a-24, 27, 33, 41, 43.* ***Anderson*** *a-9, 38.* ***Cardy*** *c-4, 5.* ***Kaluta*** *a-7.* ***Kane*** *a-12p.* ***Morrow*** *a-10, 13, 15, 16.* ***Nino*** *a-31, 40, 45, 47.* ***Redondo*** *a-20, 23, 24, 34, 65; c-53.* ***Reese*** *a-23.* ***Sparling*** *a-1.* ***Toth*** *a-1, 3-5, 7-12, 38r.* ***Tuska*** *a-11, 12.* ***Wood*** *a-15.*

WITHIN OUR REACH (Star Reach)(Value: cover or less)

WITH THE MARINES ON THE BATTLEFRONTS OF THE WORLD
1953 (no month) - No. 2, March, 1954 (Photo covers)
Toby Press

1-John Wayne story 19.00 58.00 135.00
2-Monty Hall in #1,2 4.70 14.00 28.00

WITH THE U.S. PARATROOPS BEHIND ENEMY LINES (Also see U.S. Paratroops...; #2-5 titled U.S. Paratroops...)
1951 - No. 6, Dec, 1952
Avon Periodicals

1-Wood-c & inside f/c 11.00 32.00 75.00
2-Kinstler-c & inside f/c only 6.35 19.00 38.00
3-6: 6-Kinstler-c & inside f/c only 5.00 15.00 30.00

NOTE: ***Kinstler*** *c-2, 4-6.*

WITNESS, THE (Also see Amazing Mysteries, Captain America #71, Ideal #4, Marvel Mystery #92 & Mystic #7)
Sept, 1948
Marvel Comics (MjMe)

1(Scarce)-Rico-c? 71.00 215.00 500.00

WITTY COMICS
1945 - No. 7, 1945
Irwin H. Rubin Publ./Chicago Nite Life News No. 2

1-The Pioneer, Junior Patrol 10.00 30.00 65.00
2-The Pioneer, Junior Patrol 6.35 19.00 38.00
3-7-Skyhawk 5.35 16.00 32.00

WIZARD OF FOURTH STREET, THE (Dark Horse)(Value: cover or less)

WIZARD OF OZ (See Classics Illustrated Jr. 535, Dell Jr. Treasury No. 5, First Comics Graphic Novel, 4-Color No. 1308, Marvelous..., & Marvel Treasury of Oz)

WOLF GAL (See Al Capp's...)

WOLFMAN, THE (See Movie Classics)

WOLFPACK (Marvel)(Value: cover or less)

WOLVERINE (See Alpha Flight, Daredevil #196, 249, Ghost Rider; Wolverine; Punisher, Havok & ..., Incredible Hulk #180, Incredible Hulk &..., Kitty Pryde And..., Marvel Comics Presents, Power Pack, Punisher and..., Spider-Man vs... & X-Men #94)

WOLVERINE
Sept, 1982 - No. 4, Dec, 1982 (Mini-series)
Marvel Comics Group

1-Frank Miller-c/a(p) in all 4.50 14.00 32.00
2,3 3.25 9.50 22.00
4 3.60 10.75 25.00

GD25 FN65 NM94

Trade Paperback #1 (7/87, $4.95)-Reprints #1-4 with new Miller-c 1.30 3.25 8.00
Trade Paperback nn-2nd printing ($9.95)-r/#1-4 1.65 4.00 10.00

WOLVERINE
Nov, 1988 - Present ($1.50-$1.75, color, Baxter paper)
Marvel Comics

1-Buscema a-1-16, c-1-10; Williamson i-1,4-8 4.30 13.00 30.00
2 2.00 6.00 14.00
3-5: 4-Barry Smith back-c 1.65 4.00 10.00
6-9: 6-McFarlane back-c. 7,8-Hulk app. 1.30 3.25 8.00
10-1st battle with Sabretooth (before Wolverine had his claws) 3.60 10.75 25.00
11-16: 11-New costume 1.00 2.50 6.00
17-20: 17-Byrne-c/a(p) begins, ends #23 1.60 4.00
21-30 1.20 3.00
31-40,44,47: 26-Begin $1.75-c .80 2.00
41-Sabretooth claims to be Wolverine's father; Cable cameo 1.25 3.00 7.50
41-Gold 2nd printing ($1.75) .65 1.60
42-Sabretooth, Cable & Nick Fury app.; Sabretooth proven not to be Wolverine's father 1.00 2.00 5.00
42-Gold ink 2nd printing ($1.75) .70 1.75
43-Sabretooth cameo (2 panels); saga ends 1.60 4.00
45,46-Sabretooth-c/stories 1.40 3.50
48,49-Sabretooth app. 48-Begin 3 part Weapon X sequel 1.00 2.50
50-($2.50, 64 pgs.)-Die-cut-c; Wolverine back to old yellow costume; Forge, Cyclops, Jubilee, Jean Grey & Nick Fury app. 1.00 2.00 5.00
51-74,76-80: 51-Sabretooth-c & app. 54-Shatterstar(from X-Force) app. 55-Gambit, Jubilee, Sunfire-c/story. 58,59-Terror, Inc. x-over. 60-64-Sabretooth storyline (60,62,64-c also). 73-Gambit .70 1.75
75-($3.95, 52 pgs.)-Hologram on-c 1.60 4.00
Annual nn (1990, $4.50, squarebound, 52 pgs.)-The Jungle Adventure; Simonson scripts; Mignola-c/a 1.80 4.50
Annual 2 (12/90, $4.95, squarebound, 52 pgs.)-Bloodlust 1.00 2.00 5.00
Annual nn (#3, 8/91, $5.95, 68 pgs.)-Rahne of Terror; Cable & The New Mutants app.; Andy Kubert-c/a (2nd print exists) 1.00 2.50 6.00
...Battles the Incredible Hulk nn (1989, $4.95, squarebound, 52 pg.)-r/Incredible Hulk #180,181 1.00 2.00 5.00
...: Blood Hungry nn (1993, $6.95, 68 pgs.)-Kieth-a 1.20 3.00 7.00
...: Bloody Choices nn (1993, $7.95, 68 pgs.)-r/Graphic Novel; Nick Fury app. 1.30 3.25 8.00
...: Inner Fury nn (1992, $5.95, 52 pgs.)-Sienkiewicz-c/a 1.00 2.50 6.00
...: Save the Tiger 1 (7/92, $2.95, 84 pgs.)-Reprints Wolverine stories from Marvel Comics Presents #1-10 w/new Kieth-c 1.20 3.00

NOTE: ***Austin*** *c-3i.* ***Bolton*** *c(back)-5.* ***Buscema*** *25, 27p.* ***Byrne*** *a-17-22p, 23; c-1(back), 17-22, 23p.* ***Colan*** *a-24.* ***Andy Kubert*** *c/a-51.* ***Stroman*** *a-44p.* ***Williamson*** *a-3i; c(i)-1, 3-6.*

WOLVERINE AND THE PUNISHER: DAMAGING EVIDENCE
Oct, 1993 - No. 3, 1993 ($2.00, color, mini-series)
Marvel Comics

1-3 .80 2.00

WOLVERINE: GLOBAL JEOPARY
Dec, 1993 ($2.95, color, one-shot)
Marvel Comics

1-Sub-Mariner, Zabu, Ka-Zar, Shanna & Wolverine app.; produced in cooperation with World Wildlife Fund 1.20 3.00

WOLVERINE SAGA
Sept, 1989 - No. 4, Mid-Dec, 1989 ($3.95, color, mini-series, 52 pgs.)
Marvel Comics

1-Gives history; Liefeld/Austin-c (front & back) 1.00 2.00 5.00
2-4: 2-Romita, Jr./Austin-c. 4-Kaluta-c 1.60 4.00

WOMAN OF THE PROMISE, THE
1950 (General Distr.) (32 pgs.) (paper cover)

Women Outlaws #7, © FOX

Wonder Comics #15, © BP

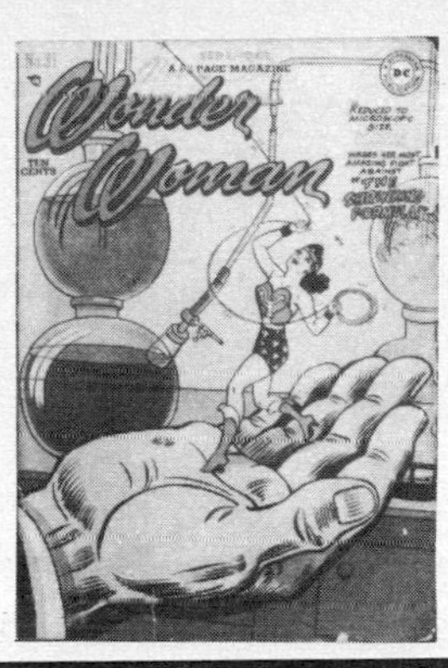

Wonder Woman #31, © DC

GD25 FN65 NM94

Catechetical Guild
nn 3.00 7.50 15.00

WOMEN IN LOVE (A Feature Presentation #5)
Aug, 1949 - No. 4, Feb, 1950
Fox Features Synd./Hero Books
1 13.50 41.00 95.00
2-Kamen/Feldstein-c 11.00 32.00 75.00
3 8.35 25.00 50.00
4-Wood-a 11.00 32.00 75.00

WOMEN IN LOVE
Winter, 1952 (100 pgs.)
Ziff-Davis Publishing Co.
nn-Kinstler-a (Scarce) 32.00 95.00 225.00

WOMEN OUTLAWS (My Love Memories #9 on)(Also see Red Circle)
July, 1948 - No. 8, Sept, 1949
Fox Features Syndicate
1-Used in **SOTI**, illo "Giving children an image of American womanhood"; negligee panels 36.00 110.00 250.00
2-Spanking panel 30.00 90.00 210.00
3-Kamenish-a 27.00 81.00 190.00
4-8 20.00 60.00 140.00
nn(nd)-Contains Cody of the Pony Express; same cover as #7 15.00 45.00 105.00

WOMEN TO LOVE
No date (1953)
Realistic
nn-(Scarce)-Reprints Complete Romance #1; c-/Avon paperback #165 24.00 73.00 170.00

WONDER BOY (Formerly Terrific Comics) (See Blue Bolt, Bomber Comics & Samson)
No. 17, May, 1955 - No. 18, July, 1955 (Code approved)
Ajax/Farrell Publ.
17-Phantom Lady app. Bakerish-c/a 17.00 52.00 120.00
18-Phantom Lady app. 16.00 48.00 110.00
NOTE: *Phantom Lady not by Matt Baker.*

WONDER COMICS (Wonderworld #3 on)
May, 1939 - No. 2, June, 1939
Fox Features Syndicate

GD25 FN65 VF82 NM94

1-(Scarce)-Wonder Man only app. by Will Eisner; Dr. Fung (by Powell), K-51 begins; Bob Kane-a; Eisner-c 600.00 1800.00 3300.00 4800.00
(Estimated up to 70 total copies exist, 3 in NM/Mint)

GD25 FN65 NM94

2-(Scarce)-Yarko the Great, Master Magician (see Samson) by Eisner begins; 'Spark' Stevens by Bob Kane, Patty O'Day, Tex Mason app. Lou Fine's 1st-c; Fine-a (2 pgs.) 257.00 770.00 1800.00

WONDER COMICS
May, 1944 - No. 20, Oct, 1948
Great/Nedor/Better Publications
1-The Grim Reaper & Spectro, the Mind Reader begin; Hitler/Hirohito bondage-c 50.00 150.00 350.00
2-Origin The Grim Reaper; Super Sleuths begin, end #8,17 29.00 85.00 200.00
3-5 25.00 75.00 175.00
6-10: 6-Flag-c. 8-Last Spectro. 9-Wonderman begins 22.00 65.00 150.00
11-14-Dick Devens, King of Futuria begins #11, ends #14 25.00 75.00 175.00
15-Tara begins (origin), ends #20 29.00 85.00 200.00
16,18: 16-Spectro app.; last Grim Reaper. 18-The Silver Knight begins 25.00 75.00 175.00
17-Wonderman with Frazetta panels; Jill Trent with all Frazetta inks 27.00 80.00 190.00
19-Frazetta panels 25.00 75.00 175.00
20-Most of Silver Knight by Frazetta 30.00 90.00 210.00
NOTE: *Ingels c-11, 12. Schomburg (Xela) c-1-10; (airbrush)-13-20. Bondage c-12, 13, 15.*

WONDER DUCK (See Wisco)
Sept, 1949 - No. 3, Mar, 1950
Marvel Comics (CDS)
1 10.00 30.00 60.00
2,3 7.50 22.50 45.00

WONDERFUL ADVENTURES OF PINOCCHIO, THE (See Movie Comics & Walt Disney Showcase #48)
No. 3, April, 1982 (Walt Disney)
Whitman Publishing Co.
3-(Continuation of Movie Comics?); r/FC #92 1.00

WONDERFUL WORLD OF DUCKS (See Golden Picture Story Book)
1975
Colgate Palmolive Co.
1-Mostly-r 1.00

WONDERFUL WORLD OF THE BROTHERS GRIMM (See Movie Comics)

WONDERLAND COMICS
Summer, 1945 - No. 9, Feb-Mar, 1947
Feature Publications/Prize
1 6.70 20.00 40.00
2-Howard Post-c/a(2) 4.20 12.50 25.00
3-9: 4-Post-c 3.20 8.00 16.00

WONDER MAN (Marvel, 1986 & 1991)(Value: cover or less)(See The Avengers #9, 151)

WONDERS OF ALADDIN, THE (See 4-Color #1255)

WONDER WOMAN (See Adventure Comics #459, All-Star Comics, Brave & the Bold, DC Comics Presents, Justice League of America, Legend of..., Power Record Comics, Sensation Comics, Super Friends and World's Finest Comics #244)

WONDER WOMAN
Summer, 1942 - No. 329, Feb, 1986
National Periodical Publications/All-American Publ./DC Comics

GD25 FN65 VF82 NM94

1-Origin Wonder Woman retold (more detailed than All-Star #8); H. G. Peter-c/a begins 812.00 2440.00 4470.00 6500.00
(Estimated up to 150 total copies exist, 8 in NM/Mint)
1-Reprint, Oversize 13-1/2"x10." **WARNING:** This comic is an exact reprint of the original except for its size. DC published it in 1974 with a second cover titling it as a Famous First Edition. There have been many reported cases of the outer cover being removed and the interior sold as the original edition. The reprint with the new outer cover removed is practically worthless. See Famous First Edition for value.

GD25 FN65 NM94

2-Origin/1st app. Mars; Duke of Deception app. 171.00 515.00 1200.00
3 118.00 355.00 825.00
4,5: 5-1st Dr. Psycho app. 86.00 260.00 600.00
6-10: 6-1st Cheetah app. 68.00 205.00 475.00
11-20 50.00 150.00 350.00
21-30 43.00 130.00 300.00
31-40: 38-Last H.G. Peter-c 33.00 100.00 230.00
41-44,46-49: 49-Used in **SOTI**, pgs. 234,236; last 52 pg. issue 23.00 70.00 160.00
45-Origin retold 46.00 138.00 315.00
50-(44 pgs.)-Used in **POP**, pg. 97 22.00 65.00 150.00
51-60 16.00 48.00 110.00
61-72: 62-Origin of W.W. i.d. 64-Story about 3-D movies. 70-1st Angle Man app. 72-Last pre-code (2/55) 14.00 43.00 100.00
73-90: 80-Origin The Invisible Plane. 89-Flying saucer-c/story 10.00 30.00 80.00
91-94,96-99: 97-Last H. G. Peter-a. 98-Origin W.W. i.d. with new facts 6.00 19.00 50.00
95-A-Bomb-c 7.00 21.00 55.00
100-(8/58) 9.00 26.00 70.00
101-104,106-110: 107-1st advs. of Wonder Girl; 1st Merboy; tells how

Wonder Woman #308, © DC

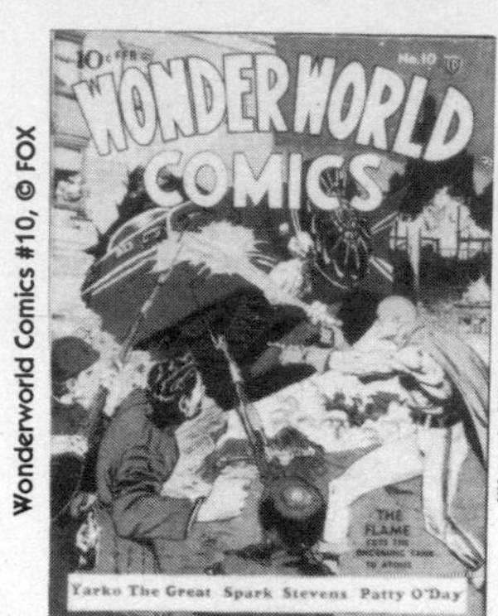

Wonderworld Comics #10, © FOX

Woody Woodpecker #1(9/91), Walter Lantz Prod.

GD25 FN65 NM94

Wonder Woman won her costume 6.00 17.00 44.00
105-(Scarce, 4/59)-Wonder Woman's secret origin; W. Woman appears as a girl (not Wonder Girl) 22.00 67.00 200.00
111-120 4.00 12.00 33.00
121-126: 122-1st app. Wonder Tot. 124-1st app. Wonder Woman Family. 126-Last 10 cent issue 2.00 7.00 18.00
127-130: 128-Origin The Invisible Plane retold. 129-2nd app. Wonder Woman Family (#133 is 3rd app.) 1.00 4.00 11.00
131-150: 132-Flying saucer-c 1.00 3.00 7.50
151-155,157,158,160-170 (1967) 1.00 2.70 6.50
156-(8/65)-Early mention of a comic book shop & comic collecting; mentions DCs selling for $100 a copy 1.00 2.70 6.50
159-Origin retold (1/66); 1st S.A. origin? 1.00 3.00 7.50
171-178 1.80 4.50
179-195: 179-Wears no costume to issue #203. 180-Death of Steve Trevor. 195-Wood inks? 1.40 3.50
196 (52 pgs.)-Origin-r/All-Star #8(6 out of 9 pgs.) 1.60 4.00
197,198 (52 pgs.)-Reprints 1.60 4.00
199,200 (5-6/72)-Jeff Jones-c; 52 pgs. 1.00 2.00 5.00
201-210: 201,202-Catwoman app. 204-Return to old costume; death of I Ching. 202-Fafhrd & The Grey Mouser debut 1.50
211-230,233-240: 211,214-(100 pgs.), 217-(68 pgs.). 220-N. Adams assist. 223-Steve Trevor revived as Steve Howard & learns W.W.'s I.D. 228-Both Wonder Women team up & new World War II stories begin, end #243. 237-Origin retold. 243-Both W. Women team-up again 1.00
231,232-JSA guest star 1.50
241-266,269-280,284-286: 241-Intro Bouncer. 247-249-(44 pgs.). 248-Steve Trevor Howard dies. 249-Hawkgirl app. 250-Origin/1st app. Orana, the new W. Woman. 251-Orana dies. 269-Last Wood a(i) for DC? (7/80). 271-Huntress & 3rd Life of Steve Trevor begin 1.00
267,268-Re-intro Animal Man (5/80 & 6/80) 2.30 6.75 16.00
281-283: Joker covers & stories 1.20 3.00
287-New Teen Titans x-over 1.50
288-299,301-328: 288-New costume & logo. 291-293-Three part epic with Super-Heroines 1.00
300-($1.50, 76 pgs.)-Anniversary issue; Giffen-a; New Teen Titans, JLA & G.A. Wonder Woman app. 1.50
329-Double size 1.50
Pizza Hut Giveaways (12/77)-Reprints #60,62 1.00

NOTE: *Andru/Esposito c-66-160(most). Colan a-288-305p; c-288-290p. Giffen a-300p. Grell c-217. Kaluta c-297. Gil Kane c-294p, 303-305, 307, 312, 314. Miller c-298p. Morrow c-233. Nasser a-232p; c-231p, 232p. Bob Oskner c(i)-39-65(most). Perez c-283p, 284p. Spiegle a-312. Staton a(p)-241, 271-287, 289, 290, 294-299; c(p)-241, 245, 246. Huntress app. 271-290, 294-299, 301-321.*

WONDER WOMAN
Feb, 1987 - Present (.75/$1.00/$1.25)
DC Comics

1-New origin; Perez-c/a begins 1.20 3.00
2-20: 8-Origin Cheetah. 12,13-Millennium x-over. 18,26-Free 16 pg. story 1.25
21-49,51-62: 24-Last Perez-a; scripts continue thru #62. 60-Vs. Lobo; last Perez-c. 62-Last $1.00-c 1.00
50-($1.50, 52 pgs.)-New Titans, Justice League 1.50
63-84: 63-New direction & Bolland-c begin; Deathstroke story continued from Wonder Woman Special #1 1.25
Annual 1,2: 1 ('88, $1.50)-Art Adams-a(p&i). 2 ('89, $2.00, 68 pgs.)-All women artists issue; Perez-c(i) .80 2.00
Annual 3 (1992, $2.50, 68 pgs.)-Quesada-c(p) 1.00 2.50
Special 1 (1992, $1.75, 52 pgs.)-Deathstroke-c/story continued in Wonder Woman #63 .80 2.00

WONDER WOMAN SPECTACULAR (See DC Special Series #9)

WONDER WORKER OF PERU
No date (16 pgs.) (B&W) (5x7")
Catechetical Guild (Giveaway)

nn 3.60 9.00 18.00

GD25 FN65 NM94

WONDERWORLD COMICS (Formerly Wonder Comics)
No. 3, July, 1939 - No. 33, Jan, 1942
Fox Features Syndicate

3-Intro The Flame by Fine; Dr. Fung (Powell-a), K-51 (Powell-a?), & Yarko the Great, Master Magician (Eisner-a) continues; Eisner/Fine-c 230.00 685.00 1600.00
4 86.00 260.00 600.00
5-10 75.00 225.00 525.00
11-Origin The Flame 93.00 280.00 650.00
12-20: 13-Dr. Fung ends 47.00 140.00 325.00
21-Origin The Black Lion & Cub 43.00 130.00 300.00
22-27: 22,25-Dr. Fung app. 32.00 95.00 225.00
28-1st app/origin U.S. Jones (8/41); Lu-Nar, the Moon Man begins 47.00 140.00 325.00
29,31-33: 32-Hitler-c 26.00 80.00 185.00
30-Origin Flame Girl 52.00 155.00 350.00

NOTE: *Spies at War by Eisner in #13, 17. Yarko by Eisner in #3-11. Eisner text illos-3. Lou Fine a-3-11; c-3-13, 15; text illos-4. Nordling a-4-14. Powell a-3-12. Tuska a-5-9. Bondage-c 14, 15, 28, 31, 32. The Flame c-3, 5-31. U.S. Jones c-32, 33.*

WONDERWORLDS
1992 ($3.50, color, squarebound, 100 pgs.)
Innovation Publishing

1-Rebound super-hero comics, contents may vary; Hero Alliance, Terraformers, etc. 1.40 3.50

WOODSY OWL (See March of Comics #395)
Nov, 1973 - No. 10, Feb, 1976
Gold Key

1 1.60 4.00
2-10 .80 2.00

WOODY WOODPECKER (Walter Lantz... #73 on?)(See Dell Giants for annuals) (Also see The Funnies, Jolly Jingles, Kite Fun Book, New Funnies)
No. 169, 10/47 - No. 72, 5-7/62; No. 73, 10/62 - No. 201, 4/84 (nn 192)
Dell Publishing Co./Gold Key No. 73-187/Whitman No. 188 on

4-Color 169-Drug turns Woody into a Mr. Hyde 14.00 43.00 100.00
4-Color 188 10.00 30.00 70.00
4-Color 202,232,249,264,288 6.70 20.00 40.00
4-Color 305,336,350 4.20 12.50 25.00
4-Color 364,374,390,405,416,431('52) 4.00 10.00 20.00
16 (12-1/52-53) - 30('55) 2.40 6.00 12.00
31-50 2.00 5.00 10.00
51-72 (Last Dell) 1.60 4.00 8.00
73-75 (Giants, 84 pgs., Gold Key) 3.50 10.50 28.00
76-80 1.60 4.00 8.00
81-100 1.00 2.00 5.00
101-120 1.60 4.00
121-191,193-201 (No #192) .80 2.00
Christmas Parade 1(11/68-Giant)(G.K.) 3.60 9.00 18.00
Clover Stamp-Newspaper Boy Contest('56)-9 pg. story-(Giveaway) 3.00 7.50 15.00
In Chevrolet Wonderland(1954-Giveaway)(Western Publ.)-20 pgs., full story line; Chilly Willy app. 7.50 22.50 45.00
...Meets Scotty McTape(1953-Scotch Tape giveaway)-16 pgs., full size 6.70 20.00 40.00
Summer Fun 1(6/66-G.K.)(84 pgs.) 3.50 10.50 28.00

NOTE: *15 cent editions exist. Reprints-No. 92, 102, 103, 105, 106, 124, 125, 152, 153, 157, 162, 165, 194(1/3)-200(1/3).*

WOODY WOODPECKER (See Comic Album #5,9,13, Dell Giant #24, 40, 54, Dell Giants, The Funnies, Golden Comics Digest #1, 3, 5, 8, 15, 16, 20, 24, 32, 37, 44, March of Comics #16, 34, 85, 93, 109, 124, 139, 158, 177, 184, 203, 222, 239, 249, 261, 420, 454, 466, 478, New Funnies & Super Book #12, 24)

WOODY WOODPECKER (Harvey)(Value: cover or less)

WOODY WOODPECKER AND FRIENDS (Harvey)(Value: cover or less)

WOOLWORTH'S CHRISTMAS STORY BOOK
1952 - 1954 (16 pgs., paper-c) (See Jolly Christmas Book)

The World Around Us #5, © GIL

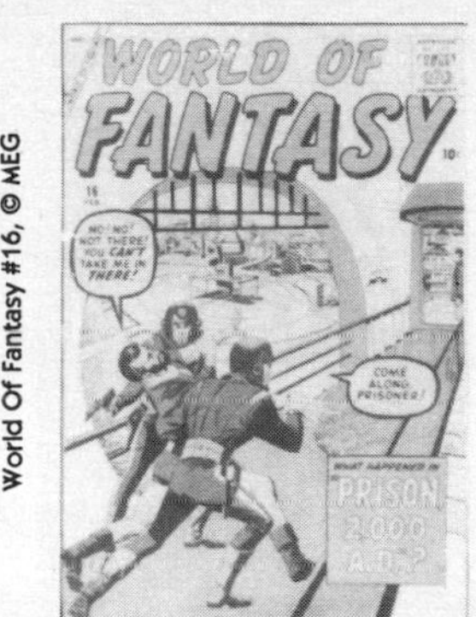

World Of Fantasy #16, © MEG

The World Of Smallville #2, © DC

GD25 FN65 NM94

omotional Publ. Co.(Western Printing Co.)
1 4.00 11.00 22.00
OTE: *1952 issue-Marv Levy c/a.*

OOLWORTH'S HAPPY TIME CHRISTMAS BOOK
952 (Christmas giveaway, 36 pgs.)
W. Woolworth Co.(Whitman Publ. Co.)
1 4.00 11.00 22.00

ORLD AROUND US, THE (Illustrated Story of...)
ept, 1958 - No. 36, Oct, 1961 (25 cents)
ilberton Publishers (Classics Illustrated)
1-Dogs; Evans-a 4.20 12.50 25.00
2-4: 2-Indians, Check-a. 3-Horses; L. B. Cole-c. 4-Railroads; L. B. Cole-a (5 pgs.) 4.20 12.50 25.00
5-Space; Ingels-a 5.85 17.50 35.00
6-The F.B.I.; Disbrow, Evans, Ingels-a 4.70 14.00 28.00
7-Pirates; Disbrow, Ingels-a 5.35 16.00 32.00
8-Flight; Evans, Ingels, Crandall-a 4.70 14.00 28.00
0 Army; Disbrow, Ingels, Orlando-a 4.35 13.00 26.00
0-13: 10-Navy; Disbrow, Kinstler-a. 11-Marine Corps. 12-Coast Guard; Ingels-a(9 pgs.). 13-Air Force; L.B. Cole-c 4.00 11.00 22.00
4-French Revolution; Crandall, Evans, Kinstler-a 6.00 18.00 36.00
5-Prehistoric Animals; Al Williamson-a, 6 & 10 pgs. plus Morrow-a 6.35 19.00 38.00
6-18: 16-Crusades; Kinstler-a. 17-Festivals; Evans, Crandall-a. 18-Great Scientists; Crandall, Evans, Torres, Williamson, Morrow-a 5.00 15.00 30.00
9-Jungle; Crandall, Williamson, Morrow-a 6.35 19.00 38.00
20-Communications; Crandall, Evans, Torres-a 6.70 20.00 40.00
21-American Presidents; Crandall/Evans, Morrow-a 5.35 16.00 32.00
22-Boating; Morrow-a 4.00 10.00 20.00
23-Great Explorers; Crandall, Evans-a 4.20 12.50 25.00
24-Ghosts; Morrow, Evans-a 5.35 16.00 32.00
25-Magic; Evans, Morrow-a 5.35 16.00 32.00
26-The Civil War 6.35 19.00 38.00
27-Mountains (High Advs.); Crandall/Evans, Morrow, Torres-a 5.35 16.00 32.00
28-Whaling; Crandall, Evans, Morrow, Torres, Wildey-a; L.B. Cole-c 4.70 14.00 28.00
29-Vikings; Crandall, Evans, Torres, Morrow-a 5.85 17.50 35.00
30-Undersea Adventure; Crandall/Evans, Kirby, Morrow, Torres-a 6.35 19.00 38.00
31-Hunting; Crandall/Evans, Ingels, Kinstler, Kirby-a 4.70 14.00 28.00
32,33: 32-For Gold & Glory; Morrow, Kirby, Crandall, Evans-a. 33-Famous Teens; Torres, Crandall, Evans-a 5.00 15.00 30.00
34-36: 34-Fishing; Crandall/Evans-a. 35-Spies; Kirby, Morrow?, Evans-a. 36-Fight for Life (Medicine); Kirby-a 4.20 12.50 25.00
OTE: See Classics Illustrated Special Edition. Another *World Around Us* issue entitled *The Sea* ad been prepared in 1962 but was never published in the U.S. It was published in the British/European *World Around Us* series. Those series then continued with seven additional WAU titles not in the U.S. series.

ORLD FAMOUS HEROES MAGAZINE
Oct, 1941 - No. 4, Apr, 1942 (a comic book)
Comic Corp. of America (Centaur)
1-Gustavson-c; Lubbers, Glanzman-a; Davy Crockett story; Flag-c 68.00 205.00 475.00
2-Lou Gehrig life story; Lubbers-a 36.00 110.00 250.00
3,4-Lubbers-a; 4-Wild Bill Hickok app. 30.00 90.00 210.00

ORLD FAMOUS STORIES
1945
Croyden Publishers
1-Ali Baba, Hansel & Gretel, Rip Van Winkle, Mid-Summer Night's Dream 9.15 27.50 55.00

ORLD IS HIS PARISH, THE
1953 (15 cents)
George A. Pflaum
nn-The story of Pope Pius XII 4.00 11.00 22.00

WORLD OF ADVENTURE (Walt Disney's...)(TV)
April, 1963 - No. 3, Oct, 1963 (All 12 cents)
Gold Key
1-3-Disney TV characters; Savage Sam, Johnny Shiloh, Capt. Nemo, The Mooncussers 1.20 3.00 6.00

WORLD OF ARCHIE, THE (See Archie Giant Series Mag. #148, 151, 156, 160, 165, 171, 177, 182, 188, 193, 200, 208, 213, 225, 232, 237, 244, 249, 456, 461, 468, 473, 480, 485, 492, 497, 504, 509, 516, 521, 532, 543, 554, 565, 574, 587, 599, 612, 627)

WORLD OF ARCHIE
Aug, 1992 - Present ($1.25, color)
Archie Comics
1-8 1.25

WORLD OF FANTASY
May, 1956 - No. 19, Aug, 1959
Atlas Comics (CPC No. 1-15/ZPC No. 16-19)
1 20.00 60.00 140.00
2-Williamson-a, 4 pgs. 13.00 40.00 90.00
3-Sid Check, Roussos-a 10.00 30.00 65.00
4-7 9.15 27.50 55.00
8-Matt Fox, Orlando, Berg-a 10.00 30.00 65.00
9-Krigstein-a 9.15 27.50 55.00
10,12-15 7.50 22.50 45.00
11-Torres-a 8.35 25.00 50.00
16-Williamson-a, 4 pgs.; Ditko, Kirby-a 10.00 30.00 70.00
17-19-Ditko, Kirby-a 10.00 30.00 65.00
NOTE: **Ayers** a-3. **B. Baily** a-4. **Berg** a-5, 6, 8. **Brodsky** c-3. **Check** a-3. **Ditko** a-17, 19. **Everett** a-2; c-4-7, 9, 12, 13. **Forte** a-4. **Infantino** a-14. **Kirby** c-15, 17-19. **Krigstein** a-9. **Maneely** c-2, 14. **Mooney** a-14. **Morrow** a-7. **Orlando** a-8, 13, 14. **Pakula** a-9. **Powell** a-4, 6. **R.Q. Sale** a-3, 9. **Severin** c-1.

WORLD OF GIANT COMICS, THE (See Archie All-Star Specials under Archie Comics)

WORLD OF GINGER FOX, THE (Comico)(Value: cover or less)

WORLD OF JUGHEAD, THE (See Archie Giant Series Mag. #9, 14, 19, 24, 30, 136, 143, 149, 152, 157, 161, 166, 172, 178, 183, 189, 194, 202, 209, 215, 227, 233, 239, 245, 251, 457, 463, 469, 475, 481, 487, 493, 499, 505, 511, 517, 523, 531, 542, 553, 564, 577, 590, 602)

WORLD OF KRYPTON, THE (World of...#3; see Superman #248)
7/79 - No. 3, 9/79; 12/87 - No. 4, 3/88 (Both are mini-series)
DC Comics, Inc.
1-3 (1979, 40 cents): 1-Jor-El marries Lara. 3-Baby Superman sent to Earth; Krypton explodes; Mon-el app. 1.00
1-4 (75 cents)-Byrne scripts; Byrne/Simonson-c 1.00

WORLD OF METROPOLIS (DC)(Value: cover or less)

WORLD OF MYSTERY
June, 1956 - No. 7, July, 1957
Atlas Comics (GPI)
1-Torres, Orlando-a; Powell-a? 20.00 60.00 140.00
2-Woodish-a 8.35 25.00 50.00
3-Torres, Davis, Ditko-a 10.00 30.00 65.00
4-Pakula, Powell-a 10.00 30.00 70.00
5,7: 5-Orlando-a 8.35 25.00 50.00
6-Williamson/Mayo-a, 4 pgs.; Ditko-a; Crandall text illo 11.00 32.00 75.00
NOTE: **Brodsky** c-2. **Colan** a-7. **Everett** c-1, 3. **Pakula** a-4, 6. **Romita** a-2. **Severin** c-7.

WORLD OF SMALLVILLE (DC)(Value: cover or less)

WORLD OF SUSPENSE
April, 1956 - No. 8, July, 1957
Atlas News Co.
1 19.00 57.00 130.00
2-Ditko-a (4 pgs.) 10.00 30.00 65.00
3,7-Williamson-a in both, 4 pgs. each; #7-with Mayo

Worlds Beyond #1, © FAW

World's Finest Comics #20, © DC

World's Finest Comics #277, © DC

	GD25	FN65	NM94
	10.00	30.00	70.00
4-6,8	8.35	25.00	50.00

NOTE: ***Berg*** *a-6.* ***Cameron*** *a-2.* ***Ditko*** *a-2.* ***Drucker*** *a-1.* ***Everett*** *a-1, 5; c-6.* ***Heck*** *a-5.* ***Maneely*** *a-1; c-1-3.* ***Orlando*** *a-5.* ***Powell*** *a-6.* ***Reinman*** *a-4.* ***Roussos*** *a-6.* ***Shores*** *a-1.*

WORLD OF WHEELS (Formerly Dragstrip Hotrodders)
No. 17, Oct, 1967 - No. 32, June, 1970
Charlton Comics

	GD25	FN65	NM94
17-20-Features Ken King	1.00	2.50	6.00
21-32-Features Ken King		1.60	4.00
Modern Comics Reprint 23(1978)		.80	2.00

WORLD OF WOOD (Eclipse)(Value: cover or less)

WORLD'S BEST COMICS (World's Finest Comics #2 on)
Spring, 1941 (Cardboard-c)(DC's 6th annual format comic)
National Per. Publications (100 pgs.)

	GD25	FN65	VF82	NM94
1-The Batman, Superman, Crimson Avenger, Johnny Thunder, The King, Young Dr. Davis, Zatara, Lando, Man of Magic, & Red, White & Blue begin; Superman, Batman & Robin covers begin (inside-c is blank); Fred Ray-c	875.00	2625.00	4800.00	7000.00

(Estimated up to 185 total copies exist, 6 in NM/Mint)

WORLDS BEYOND (Worlds of Fear #2 on)
Nov, 1951
Fawcett Publications

	GD25	FN65	NM94
1-Powell, Bailey-a; Moldoff-c	19.00	58.00	135.00

WORLD'S FAIR COMICS (See New York....)

WORLD'S FINEST (DC, 1990)(Value: cover or less)

WORLD'S FINEST COMICS (Formerly World's Best Comics #1)
No. 2, Sum, 1941 - No. 323, Jan, 1986 (early issues have 100 pgs.)
National Periodical Publ./DC Comics (#1-17 have cardboard covers)

	GD25	FN65	NM94
2 (100 pgs.)-Superman, Batman & Robin covers continue from World's Best	300.00	900.00	2000.00
3-The Sandman begins; last Johnny Thunder; origin & 1st app. The Scarecrow	233.00	700.00	1600.00
4-Hop Harrigan app.; last Young Dr. Davis	167.00	500.00	1150.00
5-Intro. TNT & Dan the Dyna-Mite; last King & Crimson Avenger	167.00	500.00	1150.00
6-Star Spangled Kid begins (Sum/42); Aquaman app.; S&K Sandman with Sandy in new costume begins, ends #7	125.00	375.00	825.00
7-Green Arrow begins (Fall/42); last Lando, King, & Red, White & Blue; S&K art	125.00	375.00	825.00
8-Boy Commandos begin (by Simon(p) #12)	117.00	350.00	750.00
9-Batman cameo in Star Spangled Kid; S&K-a; last 100 pg. issue; Hitler, Mussolini, Tojo-c	121.00	362.00	775.00
10-S&K-a	104.00	310.00	675.00
11-17-Last cardboard cover issue	96.00	288.00	625.00
18-20: 18-Paper covers begin; last Star Spangled Kid	83.00	250.00	550.00
21-30: 30-Johnny Peril app.	58.00	175.00	400.00
31-40: 33-35-Tomahawk app.	50.00	150.00	340.00
41-50: 41-Boy Commandos end. 42-Wyoming Kid begins, ends #63. 43-Full Steam Foley begins, ends #48. 48-Last square binding. 49-Tom Sparks, Boy Inventor begins	40.00	120.00	265.00
51-60: 51-Zatara ends. 59-Manhunters Around the World begins, ends #62	40.00	120.00	265.00
61-64: 61-Joker story. 63-Capt. Compass app.	18.00	54.00	125.00
65-Origin Superman; Tomahawk begins (7-8/53), ends #101	48.00	145.00	320.00
66-70-(15 cent issues, scarce)-Last 68pg. issue	37.00	110.00	250.00
71-(10 cent issue, scarce)-Superman & Batman begin as team	50.00	150.00	500.00
72-(10 cent issue, scarce)	39.00	117.00	350.00
73-(10 cent issue, scarce)	42.00	127.00	380.00
74-Last pre-code issue	33.00	100.00	300.00
75-(1st code approved, 3-4/55)	31.00	93.00	280.00
76-80: 77-Superman loses powers & Batman obtains them this issue only	25.00	75.00	200.
81-90: 88-1st Joker/Luthor team-up. 90-Batwoman's 1st app. in World's Finest (3rd app. anywhere) plus-c app.	19.00	56.00	150.
91-93,95-99: 96-99-Kirby Green Arrow	13.00	38.00	100.
94-Origin Superman/Batman team retold	42.00	126.00	335.
100 (3/59)	25.00	75.00	200.
101-110: 102-Tommy Tomorrow begins, ends #124	9.00	28.00	75.
111-121: 111-1st app. The Clock King. 113-Intro. Miss Arrowette in Green Arrow; 1st Bat-Mite/Mr. Mxyzptlk team-up. 121-Last 10 cent issue	7.00	21.00	55.
122-128,130-142: 123-2nd Bat-Mite/Mr. Mxyzptlk team-up. 125-Aquaman begins (1962), ends #139. 135-Last Dick Sprang story. 140-Last Green Arrow. 142-Origin The Composite Superman (villain); Legion app.	3.30	10.00	23.
129-Joker/Luthor team-up-c/story	5.00	15.00	34.
143-150: 143-1st Mailbag	2.15	6.50	15.
151-155,157-160: 154-Last Batwoman in costume until Batman Family #10. 157-Last Batwoman	1.70	5.00	12.
156-1st Bizarro Batman; Joker-c/story	8.00	24.00	55.
161,170 (80-Pg. Giants G-28,G-40)	2.00	6.00	14.
162-165,167-169,171-174: 168,172-Adult Legion app.	1.40	3.50	8.5
166-Joker-c/story	1.85	5.50	13.
175,176-Neal Adams-a; both r-J'onn J'onzz origin/Detective #225,226	1.65	4.70	11.
177-Joker/Luthor team-up-c/story	1.65	4.70	11.
178,180-187: 182-Silent Knight-r/Brave & Bold #6. 186-Johnny Quick-r. 187-Green Arrow origin-r/Adv. #256		1.90	4.7
179,188 (80-Pg. Giants G-52,G-64): 179-r/#94	1.00	2.50	6.0
189-196: 190-193-Robin-r		1.40	3.5
197-(80 Pg. Giant G-76)		1.80	4.5
198,199-3rd Surperman/Flash race (see Flash #175 & Superman #199)	7.00	21.00	50.0
200-205: 205-(52 pgs.)-6 pgs. Shining Knight-r by Frazetta/Adv. #153; Teen Titans x-over		1.10	2.7
206 (80-Pg. Giant G-88)		1.10	2.7
207-248: 207-212-(52 pgs.). 208-Origin Robotman-r/Det. #138. 215-Intro. Batman Jr. & Superman Jr. 217-Metamorpho begins, ends #220; Batman/Superman team-ups begin. 223-228-(100 pgs.). 223-N. Adams-r. 223-Deadman origin. 226-N. Adams, S&K, Toth-r; Manhunter part origin-r/Det. #225,226. 229-r/origin Superman-Batman team. 244-Green Arrow, Black Canary, Wonder Woman, Vigilante begin; $1.00, 84 pg. issues begin. 246-Death of Stuff in Vigilante; origin Vigilante retold. 248-Last Vigilante		1.00	2.5
249-The Creeper begins by Ditko, ends #255		1.80	4.5
250-270,272-299: 250-The Creeper origin retold by Ditko. 252-Last 84 pg. issue. 253-Capt. Marvel begins; 68 pgs. begin, end #265. 255-Last Creeper. 256-Hawkman begins. 257-Black Lightning begins. 266-282-(52 pgs.). 267-Challengers of the Unknown app. 268-Capt. Marvel Jr. origin retold. 274-Zatanna begins. 279,280-Capt. Marvel Jr. & Kid Eternity learn they are brothers. 284-Legion app.		.80	2.0
271-Origin Superman/Batman team retold		.90	2.2
300-($1.25, 52pgs.)-Justice League of America, New Teen Titans & The Outsiders app.; Perez-a(3 pgs.)		.90	2.2
301-323: 304-Origin Null and Void. 309,319-Free 16 pg. story in each (309-Flash Force 2000, 319-Mask preview)		.80	2.0
Giveaway (c. 1944-45, 8 pgs., in color, paper-c)-Johnny Everyman-r/World's Finest	13.00	40.00	90.0
Giveaway (c. 1949, 8 pgs., in color, paper-c)-"Make Way For Youth"-r/World's Finest; based on film of same name	10.00	30.00	70.0

NOTE: ***Neal Adams*** *a-230r; c-174-176, 178-180, 182, 183, 185, 186, 199-205, 208-211, 244-246, 258.* ***Austin*** *a-244-246i.* ***Burnley*** *a-8, 10; c-7-9, 11-14, 15p?, 16-18p, 20-31p.* ***Colan*** *a-274p, 297, 299.* ***Ditko*** *a-249-255.* ***Giffen*** *a-322; c-284p, 322.* ***G. Kane*** *a-38, 174r, 282, 283; c-281, 282, 289.* ***Kirby*** *a-187.* ***Kubert*** *Zatara-40-44.* ***Miller*** *c-285p.* ***Mooney*** *c-134.* ***Morrow*** *a-24 248.* ***Mortimer*** *c-16-21, 26-71.* ***Nasser*** *a(p)-244-246, 259, 260.* ***Newton*** *a-253-281p.* ***Orlando*** *a 224r.* ***Perez*** *a-300i; c-271, 276, 277p, 278p.* ***Fred Ray/Robinson*** *c-2-6, 13-16.* ***Robinson*** *a-2, 13-15.* ***Rogers*** *a-259p.* ***Roussos*** *a-212r.* ***Simonson*** *c-291.* ***Spiegle*** *a-275-278, 284.* ***Staton*** *a-262p, 273p.* ***Swan/Moldoff*** *c-126.* ***Swan/Mortimer*** *c-79-82.* ***Toth*** *a-228r.* ***Tuska*** *a-230r, 250p,*

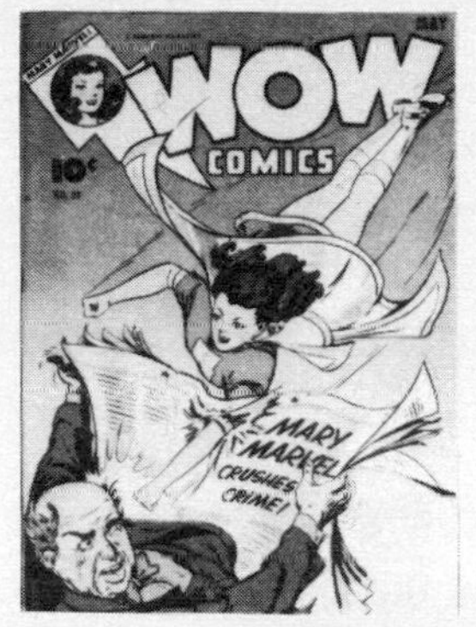

Wow Comics #25, © FAW

Wow Comics #62, © FAW

GD25 FN65 NM94

[illegible] Infantino #30-41
(Also see 80 Page Giant #15)

ORLD'S FINEST COMICS DIGEST (See DC Special Series #23)

ORLD'S GREATEST ATHLETE (See Walt Disney Showcase #14)

ORLD'S GREATEST SONGS
ot, 1954
as Comics (Male)

(Scarce) Heath & Harry Anderson-a; Eddie Fisher life story — 24.00 72.00 165.00

ORLD'S GREATEST STORIES
, 1949 - No. 2, May, 1949
bilee Publications

Alice in Wonderland — 14.00 43.00 100.00
Pinocchio — 13.00 40.00 90.00

ORLD'S GREATEST SUPER HEROES
77 (3-3/4x3-3/4") (24 pgs. in color) (Giveaway)
: Comics (Nutra Comics) (Child Vitamins, Inc.)

Batman & Robin app.; health tips — .80 2.00

ORLDS OF FEAR (Formerly Worlds Beyond #1)
#2, Jan, 1952 - V2#10, June, 1953
wcett Publications

#2 — 20.00 60.00 140.00
3-Evans-a — 15.00 45.00 105.00
4-6(9/52) — 13.00 40.00 90.00
#7-9 — 11.50 34.00 80.00
10-Saunders Painted-c; man with no eyes surrounded by eyeballs-c — 22.00 67.00 155.00

TE: *Moldoff c-2-8. Powell a-2, 4, 5. Sekowsky a-4, 5.*

ORLDS UNKNOWN
y, 1973 - No. 8, Aug, 1974
arvel Comics Group

-r/from Astonishing #54; Torres, Reese-a — 1.30 3.25
8 — .90 2.25

TE: *Adkins/Mooney a-5. Buscema c/a-4p. W. Howard c/a-3i. Kane a(p)-1,2; c(p)-5, 6, 8. tton a-2. Tuska a(p)-7, 8; c-7p. No. 7, 8 has Golden Voyage of Sinbad movie adaptation.*

ORLD WAR STORIES
r-June, 1965 - No. 3, Dec, 1965
ll Publishing Co.

-Glanzman-a in all — 4.00 11.00 22.00
,3 — 2.40 6.00 12.00

ORLD WAR II (See Classics Illustrated Special Issue)

ORLD WAR III
ar, 1953 - No. 2, May, 1953
e Periodicals

-(Scarce)-Atomic bomb-c — 41.00 125.00 285.00
-Used in **POP**, pg. 78 & B&W & color illos; Cameron-a — 36.00 110.00 250.00

ORLD WITHOUT END (DC)(Value: cover or less)

ORLD WRESTLING FEDERATION BATTLEMANIA
91 - No. 5?, 1991 ($2.50, color, magazine size, 68 pgs.)
liant

-5: 5-Includes 2 free pull-out posters — 1.00 2.50

ORST FROM MAD, THE (Annual)
58 - No. 12, 1969 (Each annual cover is reprinted from the cover of the ad issues being reprinted)
C. Comics

(1958)-Bonus; record labels & travel stickers; 1st Mad annual; r/Mad #29-34 — 24.00 70.00 165.00
(1959)-Bonus is small 33¹/3 rpm record entitled "Meet the Staff of Mad;" r/Mad #35-40 — 31.00 92.00 215.00
3(1960)-20x30" campaign poster "Alfred E. Neuman for President;" r/Mad #41-46 — 17.00 [illegible] [illegible]
4(1961)-Sunday comics section; r/Mad #47-54 — 17.00 52.00 120.00
5(1962)-Has 33-1/3 record; r/Mad #55 62 — 25.00 75.00 175.00
6(1963)-Has 33-1/3 record; r/Mad #63-70 — 27.00 80.00 185.00
7(1964)-Mad protest signs; r/Mad #71-76 — 10.00 30.00 70.00
8(1965)-Build a Mad Zeppelin — 11.50 34.00 80.00
9(1966)-33-1/3 rpm record — 17.00 52.00 120.00
10(1967)-Mad bumper sticker — 6.70 20.00 40.00
11(1968)-Mad cover window stickers — 6.70 20.00 40.00
12(1969)-Mad picture postcards; Orlando-a — 6.70 20.00 40.00

NOTE: *Covers: Bob Clarke-#8. Mingo-#7, 9-12.*

WOTALIFE COMICS (Formerly Nutty Life #2; Phantom Lady #13 on)
No. 3, Aug-Sept, 1946 - No. 12, July, 1947; 1959
Fox Features Syndicate/Norlen Mag.

3-Cosmo Cat — 7.50 22.50 45.00
4-12-Cosmo Cat — 4.70 14.00 28.00
1(1959-Norlen)-Atomic Rabbit, Atomic Mouse — 4.20 12.50 25.00

WOTALIFE COMICS
1957 - No. 5, 1957
Green Publications

1 — 3.60 9.00 18.00
2-5 — 2.80 7.00 14.00

WOW COMICS
July, 1936 - No. 4, Nov, 1936 (52 pgs., magazine size)
Henle Publishing Co.

1-Fu Manchu; Eisner-a; Briefer-c — 200.00 500.00 1300.00
2-Ken Maynard, Fu Manchu, Popeye by Segar plus article on Popeye; Eisner-a — 125.00 315.00 800.00
3-Eisner-c/a(3); Popeye by Segar, Fu Manchu, Hiram Hick by Bob Kane, Space Limited app.; Jimmy Dempsey talks about Popeye's punch; Briefer-a — 125.00 315.00 800.00
4-Flash Gordon by Raymond, Mandrake, Popeye by Segar, Tillie The Toiler, Fu Manchu, Hiram Hick by Bob Kane; Eisner-a(3); Briefer-c/a — 158.00 395.00 1000.00

WOW COMICS (Real Western Hero #70 on)(See XMas Comics)
Winter, 1940-41; No. 2, Summer, 1941 - No. 69, Fall, 1948
Fawcett Publications

GD25 FN65 VF82 NM94

nn(#1)-Origin Mr. Scarlet by S&K; Atom Blake, Boy Wizard, Jim Dolan, & Rick O'Shay begin; Diamond Jack, The White Rajah, & Shipwreck Roberts, only app.; 1st mention of Gotham City in comics; the cover was printed on unstable paper stock and is rarely found in fine or mint condition; blank inside-c; bondage-c by Beck — 900.00 2700.00 5850.00 9000.00
(Estimated up to 100 total copies exist, 3 in NM/Mint)

GD25 FN65 NM94

2 (Scarce)-The Hunchback begins — 108.00 325.00 750.00
3 (Fall, 1941) — 67.00 200.00 430.00
4-Origin Pinky — 75.00 225.00 465.00
5 — 50.00 150.00 325.00
6-Origin & 1st app. The Phantom Eagle (7/15/42); Commando Yank begins — 42.00 125.00 265.00
7,8,10: 10-Swayze-c/a on Mary Marvel — 38.00 115.00 245.00
9 (1/6/43)-Capt. Marvel, Capt. Marvel Jr., Shazam app.; Scarlet & Pinky x-over; Mary Marvel-c/stories begin (cameo #9) — 75.00 225.00 475.00
11-17,19,20: 15-Flag-c — 25.00 75.00 165.00
18-1st app. Uncle Marvel (10/43); infinity-c — 30.00 90.00 200.00
21-30: 28-Pinky x-over in Mary Marvel — 14.00 42.00 95.00
31-40: 32-68-Phantom Eagle by Swayze — 10.00 30.00 65.00
41-50 — 9.15 27.50 55.00
51-58: Last Mary Marvel — 8.35 25.00 50.00
59-69: 59-Ozzie begins. 62-Flying Saucer gag-c (1/48). 65-69-Tom Mix stories — 7.50 22.50 45.00

WRATH OF THE SPECTRE, THE

Wyatt Earp #4, © MEG

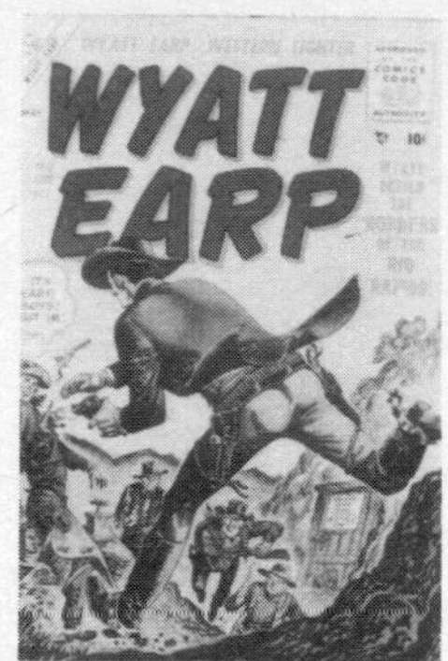

X-Factor #67, © MEG

X-Factor Annual #6, © MEG

GD25 FN65 NM94

May, 1988 - No. 4, Aug, 1988 ($2.50, color, mini-series)
DC Comics

1-4: Aparo-r/Adventure #431-440 1.00 2.50

WRECK OF GROSVENOR (See Superior Stories #3)

WRINGLE WRANGLE (See 4-Color #821)

WULF THE BARBARIAN
Feb, 1975 - No. 4, Sept, 1975
Atlas/Seaboard Publ.

1-4: 1-Origin. 2-Intro. Berithe the Swordswoman; Neal Adams, Wood, Reese-a assists 1.00

WYATT EARP
Nov, 1955 - #29, June, 1960; #30, Oct, 1972 - #34, June, 1973
Atlas Comics/Marvel No. 23 on (IPC)

1 12.00 36.00 85.00
2-Williamson-a, 4 pgs. 8.35 25.00 50.00
3-6,8-11: 3-Black Bart app. 8-Wild Bill Hickok app. 6.70 20.00 40.00
7,12-Williamson-a, 4 pgs. ea.; #12 with Mayo 7.00 21.00 42.00
13-20: 17-1st app. Wyatt's deputy, Grizzly Grant 5.35 16.00 32.00
21-Davis-c 4.20 12.50 25.00
22-24,26-29: 22-Ringo Kid app. 23-Kid From Texas app. 29-Last 10 cent issue 3.60 9.00 18.00
25-Davis-a 4.00 10.00 20.00
30-Williamson-r (1972) .80 2.00
31-34-Reprints. 32-Torres-a(r) 1.00

NOTE: ***Ayers*** *a-8, 10(2), 17, 20(4).* ***Berg*** *a-9.* ***Everett*** *c-6.* ***Kirby*** *c-25, 29.* ***Maneely*** *a-1; c-1-4, 8, 12, 17, 20.* ***Maurer*** *a-2(2), 3(4), 4(4), 8(4).* ***Severin*** *a-4, 9(4), 10; c-2, 9, 10, 14.* ***Wildey*** *a-5, 17, 24, 28.*

WYATT EARP (TV) (Hugh O'Brian Famous Marshal)
No. 860, Nov, 1957 - No. 13, Dec-Feb, 1960-61 (Photo-c)
Dell Publishing Co.

4-Color 860 (#1)-Manning-a 11.00 32.00 75.00
4-Color 890,921(6/58)-All Manning-a 7.50 22.50 45.00
4 (9-11/58) - 12-Manning-a 5.35 16.00 32.00
13-Toth-a 6.35 19.00 38.00

WYATT EARP FRONTIER MARSHAL (Formerly Range Busters)
No. 12, Jan, 1956 - No. 72, Dec, 1967 (Also see Blue Bird)
Charlton Comics

12 5.00 15.00 30.00
13-19 3.00 7.50 15.00
20-(68 pgs.)-Williamson-a(4), 8,5,5,& 7 pgs. 6.70 20.00 40.00
21-30 2.00 5.00 10.00
31-50: 31-Crandall-r 1.40 3.50 7.00
51-72 .80 2.00 4.00

XANADU COLOR SPECIAL (Eclipse)(Value: cover or less)

XENON (Eclipse)(Value: cover or less)

XENOTECH
Sept, 1993 - Present ($2.75, color)
Mirage Studios

1-3-Bound with 2 trading cards 1.10 2.75

XENOZOIC TALES (Kitchen Sink)(Value: cover or less)

X-FACTOR (Also see The Avengers #263 & Fantastic Four #286)
Feb, 1986 - Present
Marvel Comics Group

1-($1.25, 52 pgs)-Story recaps 1st app. from Avengers #263; story cont'd from F.F. #286; return of original X-Men (now X-Factor); Guice/Layton-a; Baby Nathan app. (2nd after X-Men #201) 1.70 5.00 12.00
2,3 1.00 2.50 6.00
4,5: 5-1st app. Apocalypse (cameo) 1.00 2.00 5.00
6-10: 6-1st full app. Apocalypse 1.60 4.00
11-20: 13-Baby Nathan app. in flashback. 15-Intro wingless Angel 1.20 3.00

GD25 FN65 NM9

21-23: 23-1st app. Archangel (cameo) 1.00 2.
24-1st full app. Archangel (now in Uncanny X-Men); Fall Of The Mutants begins; origin Apocalypse 2.15 6.50 15.
25,26: Fall Of The Mutants; 26-New outfits 1.60 4.
27-30 .80 2.
31-37,39,41-49: 35-Origin Cyclops 1.
38,50-($1.50, 52 pgs.): 50-Liefeld/McFarlane-c .80 2.
40-Rob Liefeld-c/a (4/89, 1st at Marvel?) 1.00 2.50 6.
51-53-Sabretooth app. 52-Liefeld-c(p) 1.00 2.00 5.
54-59: 54-Intro Crimson 1.
60-X-Tinction Agenda x-over; New Mutants (w/Cable) x-over in #60-62; Wolverine in #62 1.30 3.25 8.
60-Gold 2nd printing 1.00 2.
61,62-X-Tinction Agenda. 62-Jim Lee-c 1.00 2.50 6.
63-Whilce Portacio-c/a(p) begins, ends #69 1.00 2.50 6.
64-67,69,70: 65-68-Lee co-plots. 67-Inhumans app. 69,70-X-Men (w/ Wolverine) x-over .80 2.
68-Baby Nathan is sent into future to save his life 1.00 2.00 5.
71-New team begins (Havok, Polaris, Wolfsbane & Madrox); Stroman-c/a begins 1.00 2.50 6.
71-2nd printing ($1.25) 1.
72-74: 74-Last $1.00-c 1.
75-($1.75, 52 pgs.) .70 1.
76-83,87-91,93-99: 77-Cannonball (of X-Force) app. 87-Quesada-c/a(p) begins 1.
84-86 ($1.50)-X-Cutioner's Song x-overs; polybagged with trading card in each. 84-Jae Lee-a(p). 85-Jae Lee-c/a(p) .80 2.
92-($3.50, 68 pgs.)-Wraparound-c w/Havok hologram on-c; begin X-Men 30th anniversary issues; Quesada-c/a .70 1.75 3.
92-2nd printing .70 1.75 3.
100-($2.95, 52 pgs.)-Embossed foil-c 1.20 3.
100-($1.75, 52 pgs.)-Regular edition .70 1.
Annual 1-6: 1-(10/86). 2-(10/87). 3-(1988, $1.75)-Evolutionary War x-over. 4-(1989, $2.00, 68 pgs.)-Atlantis Attacks; Byrne/Simonson-a; Byrne-c, 5-(1990, $2.00, 68 pgs.)-Fantastic Four, New Mutants x-over. 6 (1991, $2.00, 68 pgs.)-New Warriors app.; 5th app. X-Force cont'd from X-Men Annual #15 1.00 2.
Annual 7 (1992, $2.25, 68 pgs.)-1st Quesada-a(p) on X-Factor plus-c(p) .90 2.
...Prisoner of Love nn (1990, $4.95, 52 pgs.)-Starlin scripts; Guice-a 1.00 2.00 5.

NOTE: ***Art Adams*** *a-41p, 42p.* ***Buckler*** *a-50p.* ***Liefeld*** *a-40; c-40, 50i, 52p.* ***McFarlane*** *c-50i.* ***Brandon Peterson*** *a-78p(part).* ***Whilce Portacio*** *c/a(p)-63-69.* ***Quesada*** *c(p)-78, 79, 82.* ***Simonson*** *c/a-10, 11, 13-15, 17-19, 21, 23-31, 33, 34, 36-39; c-16.* ***Paul Smith*** *a-44-48; c-43.* ***Stroman*** *a(p)-71-75, 77, 78(part), 80, 81; c(p)-71-77, 80, 81, 84.*

X-FORCE (Also see The New Mutants #100 & 1992 X-Men Annuals)
Aug, 1991 - Present ($1.00/$1.25, color)
Marvel Comics

1-($1.50, 52 pgs.)-Polybagged with 1 of 5 diff. Marvel Universe trading cards inside(1 each); 6th app. of X-Force; Liefeld-c/a begins, ends #9 1.60 4.0
1-1st printing with Cable trading card inside 1.00 2.50 6.0
1-2nd printing; metallic ink-c (no bag or card) 1.5
2,3: 2-Deadpool-c/story. 3-New Brotherhood of Evil Mutants app. .80 2.0
4-Spider-Man x-over; cont'd from Spider-Man #16; reads sideways 1.20 3.0
5-10: 6-Last $1.00-c. 7,9-Weapon X back-ups. 10-Weapon X full-length story (part 3). 11-1st Weapon Prime (cameo) 1.5
11-15,19-24,26-32: 15-Cable leaves X-Force 1.2
16-18-($1.50)-Polybagged w/trading card in each .80 2.0
25-($3.50, 52 pgs.)-Wraparound-c w/Cable hologram on-c; Cable returns 1.40 3.5
Annual 1 (1992, $2.25, 68 pgs.)-1st Greg Capullo-a(p) on X-Force .90 2.2
Annual 2 (1993, $2.95, 68 pgs.)-Polybagged w/trading card; intro X-Treme

The X-Men #87, © MEG

The X-Men #138, © MEG

GD25 FN65 NM94

& Neurtap 1.20 3.00
...nd Spider-Man: Sabotage nn (11/92, $6.95)-Reprints X-Force #3,4 & Spider-Man #16 1.20 3.00 7.00
...TE: *Capullo a(p)-15-19, Annual 1; c(p)-14-17. **Rob Liefeld** a-1-7, 9p; c-1-9, 11i; plots-1-12. ...gnola a-8p.*

...IAS COMICS
...?/1941 - No. 2, 12?/1942 (324 pgs.) (50 cents)
... 3, 12?/1943 - No. 7, 12?/1947 (132 pgs.)
...wcett Publications

	GD25	FN65	VF82	NM94
-Contains Whiz #21, Capt. Marvel #3, Bulletman #2, Wow #3, & Master #18; Raboy back-c. Not rebound, remaindered comics; printed at same time as originals	185.00	555.00	1200.00	1850.00

(Estimated up to 110 total copies exist, 5 in NM/Mint)

	GD25	FN65	NM94
-Capt. Marvel, Bulletman, Spy Smasher	83.00	250.00	550.00
-7-Funny animals	30.00	90.00	200.00

...IAS COMICS
... 4, Dec, 1949 - No. 7, Dec, 1952 (50 cents, 196 pgs.)
...wcett Publications
-Contains Whiz, Master, Tom Mix, Captain Marvel, Nyoka, Capt. Video, Bob Colt, Monte Hale, Hot Rod Comics, & Battle Stories. Not rebound, remaindered comics; printed at the same time as originals 37.00 110.00 240.00
-7-Same as above. 7-Bill Boyd app.; stocking on cover is made of green felt (novelty cover) 32.00 95.00 210.00

...IAS FUNNIES
... date (Paper cover) (36 pgs.?)
...nney Shoes (Giveaway)
...ntains 1933 color strip-r; Mutt & Jeff, etc. 29.00 85.00 200.00

...MEN, THE (See Amazing Adventures, Capt. America #172, Classic X-Men, Giant-...ze..., Heroes For Hope..., Kitty Pryde &..., Marvel & DC Present, Marvel Fanfare, Marvel ...aphic Novel, Marvel Super Heroes, Marvel Team-up, Marvel Triple Action, Nightcrawler, ...ficial Marvel Index To..., Special Edition..., The Uncanny..., X-Factor & X-Terminators)

...MEN, THE (X-Men #94-141; The Uncanny X-Men on-c only #114-141; The ...ncanny X-Men #142 on)
...ept, 1963 - No. 66, Mar, 1970; No. 67, Dec, 1970 - Present
...arvel Comics Group

	GD25	FN65	VF82	NM94
-Origin/1st app. X-Men (Angel, Beast, Cyclops, Iceman & Marvel Girl); 1st app. Magneto & Professor X	330.00	1000.00	2000.00	3000.00

	GD25	FN65	NM94
...-1st app. The Vanisher	114.00	342.00	1025.00
...-1st app. The Blob	50.00	150.00	450.00
...-1st Quick Silver & Scarlet Witch & Brotherhood of the Evil Mutants; 1st app. Toad; Magneto app.	39.00	117.00	350.00
...-Magneto & Evil Mutants-c/story	28.00	83.00	250.00
...-10: 6-Sub-Mariner app. 8-1st Unus the Untouchable. 9-Early Avengers app.; 1st Lucifer. 10-1st S.A. app. Ka-Zar	19.00	58.00	175.00
...1,13-15: 11-1st app. The Stranger. 14-1st app. Sentinels. 15-Origin Beast	19.00	56.00	150.00
...2-Origin Prof. X; Origin/1st app. Juggernaut	20.00	60.00	160.00
...6-20: 19-1st app. The Mimic	8.00	24.00	65.00
...1-27,29,30: 27-Re-enter The Mimic (r-in #75)	8.00	24.00	55.00
...8-1st app. The Banshee (r-in #76)	11.00	32.00	75.00
...1-34,36,37,39,40: 39-New costumes	5.50	16.00	38.00
...5-Spider-Man x-over (8/67)(r-in #83); 1st app. Changeling	0.00	28.00	65.00
...8-Origins of the X-Men series begins, ends #57	9.00	26.00	60.00
...1-49: 42-Death of Prof. X (Changeling disguised as). 44-1st S.A. app. G.A. Red Raven. 49-Steranko-c; 1st Polaris	4.85	15.00	34.00
...0,51 Steranko c/a	5.50	17.00	39.00
...2	3.60	10.75	25.00
...3-Barry Smith-c/a (1st comic book work)	5.50	17.00	39.00
...4,55-B. Smith-c. 54-1st app. Alex Summers who later becomes Havok. 55-Summers discovers he has mutant powers	4.85	15.00	34.00
56,57,59-63,65-Neal Adams-a(p). 56-Intro Havok without costume. 65-Return of Professor X	5.00	15.00	35.00
58-1st app. Havok in costume; N. Adams-a(p)	8.00	24.00	55.00
64-1st app. Sunfire	5.50	17.00	39.00
66-Last new story w/original X-Men; battles Hulk	3.30	10.00	23.00
67-70,72: (52 pgs.). 67-Reprints begin, end #93	2.40	7.25	17.00
71,73-93: 71-Last 15 cent issue. 73-86-r/#25-38 w/new-c. 83-Spider-Man-c/story. 87-93-r/#39-45 with covers	2.00	6.00	14.00
94(8/75)-New X-Men begin (see Giant-Size X-Men for 1st app.); Colossus, Nightcrawler, Thunderbird, Storm, Wolverine, & Banshee join; Angel, Marvel Girl, & Iceman resign	25.00	75.00	250.00
95-Death of Thunderbird	7.00	21.00	50.00
96-99: 98,99-25 cent & 30 cent-c exist	5.50	17.00	40.00
100-Old vs. New X-Men; part origin Phoenix; last 25 cent issue (8/76)	6.00	19.00	44.00
101-Phoenix origin concludes	4.70	14.00	33.00
102-107: 102-Origin Storm. 104-1st app. Starjammers (brief cameo); Magneto-c/story. 106-Old vs. New X-Men; 30 & 35 cent issues exist. 107-1st full app. Starjammers; last 30 cent issue	2.40	7.25	17.00
108-Byrne-a begins (see Marvel Team-Up #53)	4.70	14.00	33.00
109-1st app. Weapon Alpha (becomes Vindicator)	4.00	12.00	28.00
110,111: 110-Phoenix joins	2.40	7.25	17.00
112-119: 117-Origin Professor X	2.00	6.00	14.00
120-1st app. Alpha Flight (cameo), story line begins; 1st app. Vindicator (formerly Weapon Alpha); last 35 cent issue	4.50	14.00	32.00
121-1st full Alpha Flight story	4.70	14.00	33.00
122-128: 123-Spider-Man x-over. 124-Colossus becomes Proletarian	1.85	5.50	13.00
129-Intro Kitty Pryde; last Banshee	2.00	6.00	14.00
130-1st app. The Dazzler by Byrne	2.15	6.50	15.00
131-135: 131-Dazzler app. 132-1st White Queen. 133-Wolverine app. 134-Phoenix becomes Dark Phoenix	1.65	4.70	11.00
136,138: 138-Dazzler app.; Cyclops leaves	1.50	3.75	9.00
137-Giant; death of Phoenix	1.70	5.00	12.00
139-Alpha Flight app.; Kitty Pryde joins; new costume for Wolverine	3.25	9.50	22.00
140-Alpha Flight app.	3.20	8.00	20.00
141-Intro Future X-Men & The New Brotherhood of Evil Mutants; 1st app. Rachel (Phoenix II); death of Frank Richards	3.25	9.50	22.00
142-Rachel app.; deaths of Wolverine, Storm & Colossus	2.40	7.25	17.00
143-Last Byrne issue	1.30	3.25	8.00
144-150: 144-Man-Thing app. 145-Old X-Men app. 148-Spider-Woman, Dazzler app. 150-Double size	1.20	3.00	7.00
151-157,159-161,163,164: 161-Origin Magneto. 163-Origin Binary. 164-1st app. Binary as Carol Danvers		1.90	4.75
158-1st app. Rogue in X-Men (see Avengers Annual #10)	1.00	2.50	5.50
162-Wolverine solo story	1.50	3.75	9.00
165-Paul Smith-c/a begins, ends #175	1.20	3.00	7.00
166-Double size; Paul Smith-a	1.00	2.50	6.00
167-170: 167-New Mutants app. (3/83); same date as New Mutants #1; 1st meeting w/X-Men; ties into N.M. #3,4; Starjammers app.; contains skin "Tattooz" decals. 168-1st app. Madelyne Pryor (last pg. cameo) in X-Men (see Avengers Annual #10)	1.00	2.00	5.00
171-Rogue joins X-Men; Simonson-c/a	1.30	3.25	8.00
172-174: 172,173-Two part Wolverine solo story. 173-Two cover variations, blue & black. 174-Phoenix cameo		1.90	4.75
175-(52 pgs.)-Anniversary issue; Phoenix returns	1.00	2.50	5.50
176-185: 181-Sunfire app. 182-Rogue solo story. 184-1st app. Forge		1.50	3.75
186-Double-size; Barry Smith/Austin-a		1.90	4.75
187-192,194-199: 190,191-Spider-Man & Avengers x-over. 195-Power Pack x-over		1.50	3.75
193-Double size; 100th app. New X-Men; 1st app. Warpath in costume (see New Mutants #16)	1.00	2.50	5.50

The Uncanny X-Men #204, © MEG

The Uncanny X-Men #261, © MEG

The Uncanny X-Men #276, © MEG

GD25 FN65 NM94

200-(12/85, $1.25, 52 pgs.) 1.50 3.75 9.00
201-(1/86)-1st app. Cable? (as baby Nathan; see X-Factor #1); 1st Whilce Portacio-c/a(i) on X-Men (guest artist) 3.25 9.50 22.00
202-204,206-209: 204-Nightcrawler solo story; Portacio-a(i). 207-Wolverine/ Phoenix story 1.00 2.50 5.50
205-Wolverine solo story by Barry Smith 2.30 6.75 16.00
210,211-Mutant Massacre begins 2.70 8.00 19.00
212,213-Wolverine vs. Sabretooth (Mutant Mass.) 4.70 14.00 33.00
214-221,223,224: 219-Havok joins (7/87); brief app. Sabretooth 1.90 4.75
222-Wolverine battles Sabretooth 2.30 6.75 16.00
225-227: Fall Of The Mutants. 226-Double size 1.40 3.50 8.50
228-239,241: 229-$1.00 begin 1.80 4.50
240-Sabretooth app. 1.00 2.50 5.50
242-Double size, X-Factor app., Inferno tie-in 1.80 4.50
243,245-247: 245-Rob Liefeld-a(p) 1.40 3.50
244-1st app. Jubilee 1.40 3.50 8.50
248-1st Jim Lee art on X-Men (1989) 4.30 13.00 30.00
248-2nd printing (1992, $1.25) 1.25
249-252: 252-Lee-c .90 2.25
253-255: 253-All new X-Men begin. 254-Lee-c 1.70 4.25
256,257-Jim Lee-c/a begins 1.65 4.70 11.00
258-Wolverine solo story; Lee-c/a 1.85 5.50 13.00
259-Sylvestri-a; no Lee-a 1.00 2.50 5.50
260-265-No Lee-a. 260,261,264-Lee-c .90 2.25
266-1st full app. Gambit (see Ann. #14)-No Lee-a 3.85 11.50 27.00
267-Jim Lee-c/a resumes 1.85 5.50 13.00
268-Capt. America, Black Widow & Wolverine team-up; Lee-a 3.25 9.50 22.00
269-Lee-a 1.10 2.70 6.50
270-X-Tinction Agenda begins 1.65 4.70 11.00
270-Gold 2nd printing 1.40 3.50
271,272-X-Tinction Agenda 1.25 3.00 7.50
273-New Mutants (Cable) & X-Factor x-over; Golden, Byrne & Lee part pencils 1.10 2.70 6.50
274 1.00 2.50 5.50
275-($1.50, 52 pgs.)-Tri-fold-c by Jim Lee (p) 1.10 2.70 6.50
275-Gold 2nd printing .90 2.25
276-280: 277-Last Lee-c/a. 280-X-Factor x-over 1.50
281-New team begins (Storm, Archangel, Colossus, Iceman & Marvel Girl); Whilce Portacio-c/a begins; Byrne scripts begin; wraparound-c (white logo) 1.00 2.50 6.00
281-2nd printing with red metallic ink logo w/o UPC box ($1.00-c); does not say 2nd printing inside 1.00
282-1st app. Bishop (cover & 1 pg. cameo) 1.00 2.50 6.00
282-Gold 2nd printing ($1.00-c) 1.00
283-1st full app. Bishop 1.50 3.75 9.00
284-293,297-299: 284-Last $1.00-c. 286,287-Lee plots. 287-Bishop joins team. 288-Lee/Portacio plots. 290-Last Portacio-c/a. 294-Brandon Peterson-a(p) begins (#292 is 1st Peterson-c) 1.25
294-296 ($1.50)-X-Cutioner's Song x-overs; polybagged w/trading card in each; all have Peterson/Austin-c/a .80 2.00
300-($3.95, 68 pgs.)-Holo-grafx foil-c; Magneto app. 1.60 4.00
301-303,305-309 1.25
304-($3.95, 68 pgs.)-Wraparound-c with Magneto hologram on-c; 30th anniversary issue 1.60 4.00
310-($1.95)-Bound-in trading cards (3) .80 2.00
Special 1(12/70)-Kirby-c/a; origin The Stranger 5.50 17.00 40.00
Special 2(11/71) 5.00 15.00 35.00
Annual 3(1979, 52pgs.)-New story; Miller/Austin-c 2.15 6.50 15.00
Annual 4(1980, 52 pgs.)-Dr. Strange guest stars 1.20 3.00 7.00
Annual 5(1981, 52 pgs.) 1.00 2.50 5.50
Annual 6(1982, 52 pgs.) 1.80 4.50
Annual 7,8: 7-(1983, 52 pgs.). 8-(1984, 52 pgs.) 1.80 4.50
Annual 9(1985)-New Mutants x-over cont'd from New Mutants Special Ed. #1; Art Adams-a 1.85 5.50 13.00

GD25 FN65 NM9

Annual 10(1986)-Art Adams-a 1.65 4.70 11.
Annual 11(1987) 1.20 3.
Annual 12(1988, $1.75)-Evolutionary War app. 1.60 4.
Annual 13(1989, $2.00, 68 pgs.)-Atlantis Attacks 1.20 3.
Annual 14(1990, $2.00, 68 pgs.)-1st app. Gambit (minor app., 5 pgs.); Fantastic Four, New Mutants (Cable) & X-Factor x-over; Arthur Adams-c/a(p) 1.30 3.25 8.
Annual 15 (1991, $2.00, 68 pgs.)-4 pg. origin; New Mutants x-over; 4 pg. Wolverine solo back-up story; 4th app. X-Force cont'd from New Warriors Annual #1 1.60 4.
Annual 16 (1992, $2.25, 68 pgs.) .90 2.
Annual 17 (1993, $2.95, 68 pgs.)-Bagged w/card 1.20 3.

NOTE: **Art Adams** *a-Annual 9, 10p, 12p, 14p; c-218p.* **Neal Adams** *a-56-63p, 65p; c-56-63.* **Adkins** *c-34.* **Austin** *a-108i, 109i, 111-117i, 119-143i, 186i, 204i, 228i, 294-297i, Annual 3i, 7, 9i, 13; c-109-111i, 114-122i, 123, 124-141i, 142, 143, 196i, 204i, 228i, 294-297i, Annual 3i.* **J. Buscema** *c-42, 43p, 45p.* **Byrne** *a(p)-108, 109, 111-143, 273; c(p)-113-116, 127, 129, 131-14* **Ditko** *r-86, 90.* **Everett** *c-73.* **Golden** *a-273, Annual 7p.* **Guice** *a-216p, 217p.* **G. Kane** *c(p)-33 74-76, 79, 80, 94, 95.* **Kirby** *a(p)-1-17 (#12-17, 24, 27-29, 32, 67r-layouts); c(p)-1-22, 25, 26, 31, 35.* **Layton** *a-105i; c-112i, 113i.* **Jim Lee** *a(p)-248, 256-258, 267-277; c(p)-252, 254, 256-261, 264, 267, 270, 275-277, 286.* **Perez** *a-Annual 3p; c(p)-112, 128, Annual 3.* **Peterson** *c/a(294-299; a-300p.* **Whilce Portacio** *a(p)-281-286, 289, 290; c-281-285p, 289p, 290.* **Roussos** *84i.* **Simonson** *a-171p; c-171, 217.* **B. Smith** *a-53, 186p, 198p, 205, 214; c-53-55, 186p, 198, 205, 212, 214, 216.* **Paul Smith** *a(p)-165-170, 172-175, 278; c-165-170, 172-175, 278.* **Sparli** *a-78p.* **Steranko** *a-50p, 51p; c-49-51.* **Sutton** *a-106i.* **Toth** *a-12p, 67p(r).* **Tuska** *a-40-42i, 44-46p, 88i(r); c-39-41, 77p, 78p.* **Williamson** *a-202i, 203i, 211i; c-202i, 203i, 206i.* **Wood** *c-14i.*

X-MEN (2nd series)
Oct, 1991 - Present ($1.00-$1.25, color)
Marvel Comics

1-($1.50, 52 pgs.)-Jim Lee-c/a begins; new team begins (Cyclops, Beast, Wolverine, Gambit, Psylocke & Rogue); new Uncanny X-Men & Magneto app.; cover 1a-Beast & Storm-c .80 2.(
1-b-Colossus & Gambit-c .80 2.(
1-c-Wolverine & Cyclops-c .80 2.(
1-d-Magneto-c .80 2.(
1-e-($3.95)-Double gate-fold-c consisting of all four covers from 1a-d by Jim Lee; contains all pin-ups from #1a-d plus inside-c foldout poster; no ads; printed on coated stock 1.00 2.50 5.5
2,3,5,7: 5-Byrne scripts 1.60 4.0
4-Wolverine back to old yellow costume (same date as Wolverine #50); last $1.00-c 1.60 4.0
6-Sabretooth-c/story 1.60 4.0
8-Gambit vs. Bishop-c/story; last Lee-a; Ghost Rider cameo cont'd in Ghost Rider #26 1.60 4.0
9-Wolverine vs. Ghost Rider; cont'd/G.R. #26 1.60 4.0
10-Return of Longshot 1.60 4.0
11-13,17-24,26-29: 12,13-Art Thibert-c/a .60 1.2
11-Silver ink 2nd printing; came with X-Men board game 3.20 8.00 20.0
14-16-($1.50)-X-Cutioner's Song x-overs; polybagged with trading card in each. 14-Andy Kubert-c/a begins .80 2.0
25-($3.50, 52 pgs.)-Wraparound-c with Gambit hologram on-c; Magneto storyline 1.40 3.5
25-30th anniversary issue w/B&W-c with Magneto in color & Magneto hologram & no price on-c 25.0
30-($1.95)-Bound-in trading cards (3) .80 2.0
Annual 1 (1992, $2.25, 68 pgs.)-Lee-c & layouts .90 2.2
Annual 2 (1993, $2.95, 68 pgs.)-Bagged w/card 1.20 3.0

NOTE: **Jim Lee** *a-1-11p; c-1-6p, 7, 8, 9p, 10, 11p.* **Art Thibert** *a-6-9i, 12, 13; c-6i, 12, 13.*

X-MEN ADVENTURES (TV)
Nov, 1992 - No. 15, Jan, 1994 ($1.25, color)
Marvel Comics

1-Wolverine, Cyclops, Jubilee, Rogue, Gambit 1.80 4.5
2-5: 3-Magneto-c/story 1.40 3.5
6-10: 6-Sabretooth-c/s. 7-Cable-c/s. 10-Archangel guest star .80 2.0
11-14: 11-Cable-c/s 1.2
15-($1.75, 52 pgs.) .70 1.7

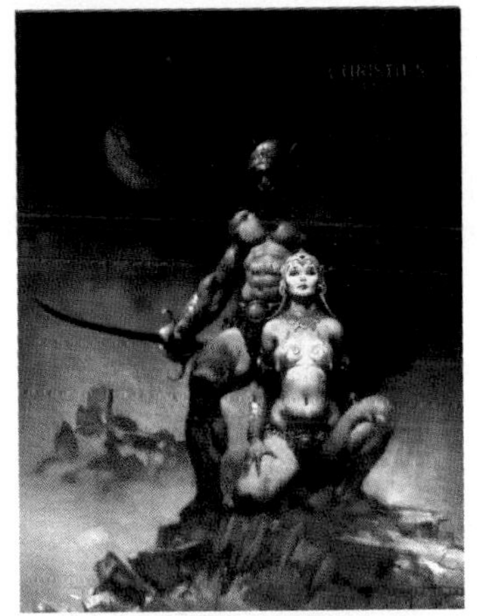

CHRISTIE'S SETS RECORDS

for comic books, comic art and fantasy

COMICS AND STORIES, the greatest "name" in comics, has been a leader in comic collectibles for over 15 years. We are also the exclusive Comic Collectibles Consultants for Christie's, the world renowned auction house. We are able to secure our clients record prices for prime COMIC BOOKS, ORIGINAL COMIC ART, AND COMIC STRIP ART.

KEY WANTS

- **Comic Books - 1933-1965**
- **Comic Art - Shuster to Lee**
- **Strip Art - Foster to Schulz**

Over 1,000 prime comic collectibles valued over 2 million dollars are featured in the first 2 Christie's catalogues. A $70 value, they are available from Comics & Stories for $21 each ppd. Simply call or write.

122 West End Avenue
Ridgewood, NJ 07450
(201) 652-1305

DO YOU

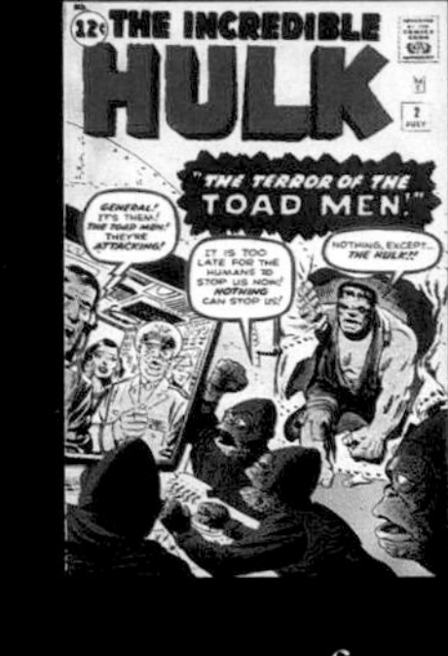

REMEMBER

There are some things you never forget. Your first pet.

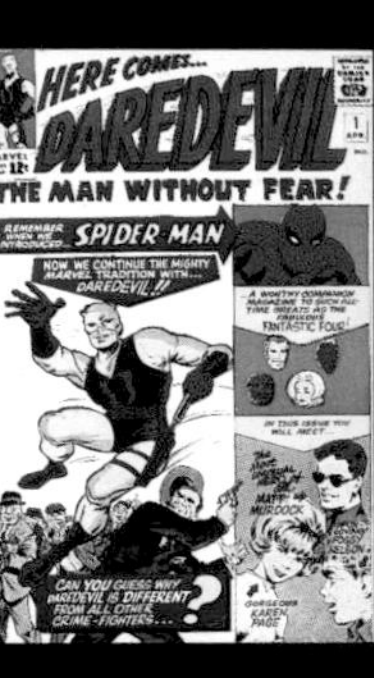

YOUR

FIRST

appearance of Spider-Man in Amazing Fantasy #15

MARVEL

your first Marvel Comic will always be something special

COMIC?

Who said "You can never go back?"

Ghost Rider #2, 1973, © MEG

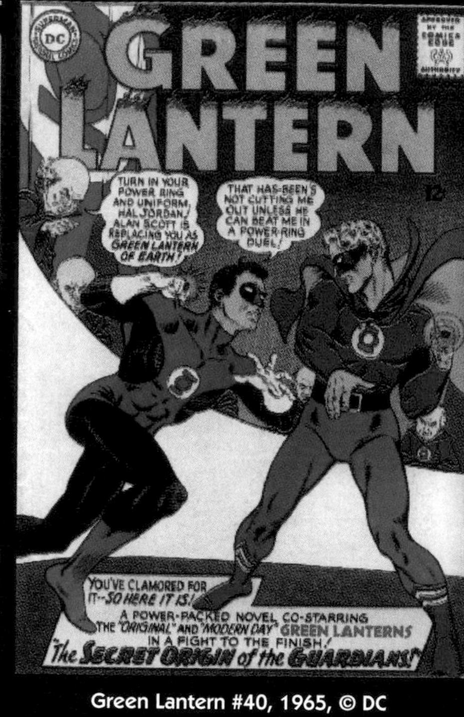

Green Lantern #40, 1965, © DC

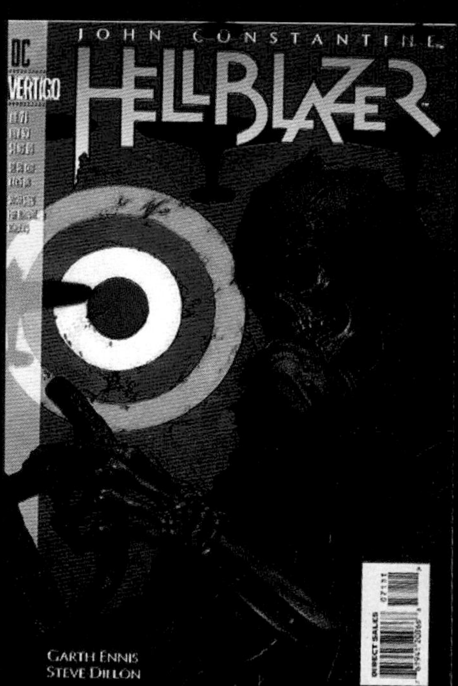

Hellblazer #71, 1993, © DC

Hong Kong Phooey #1, 1975, © Hanna-Barbera

House of Secrets #14, 1958, © DC

Human Torch #36, 1954, © MEG

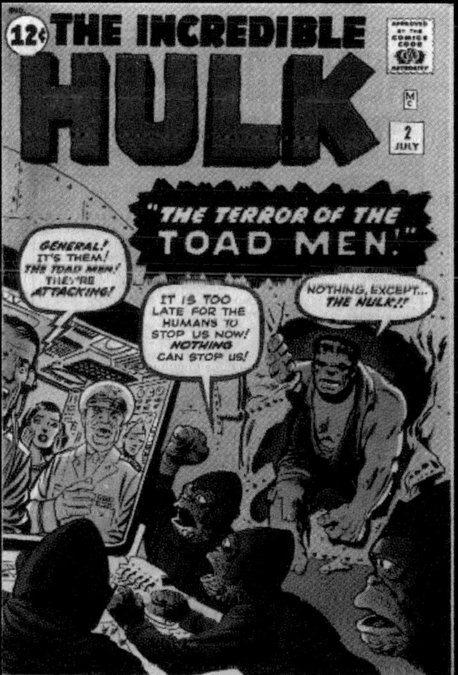

The Incredible Hulk #2, 1962, © MEG

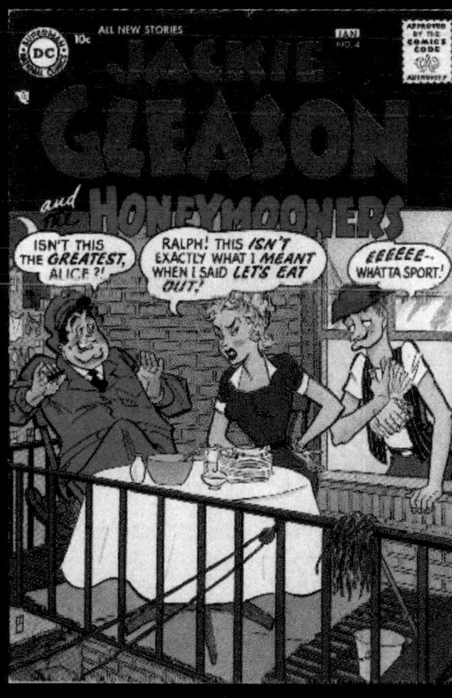

Jackie Gleason & the Honeymooners #4, 1956, © DC

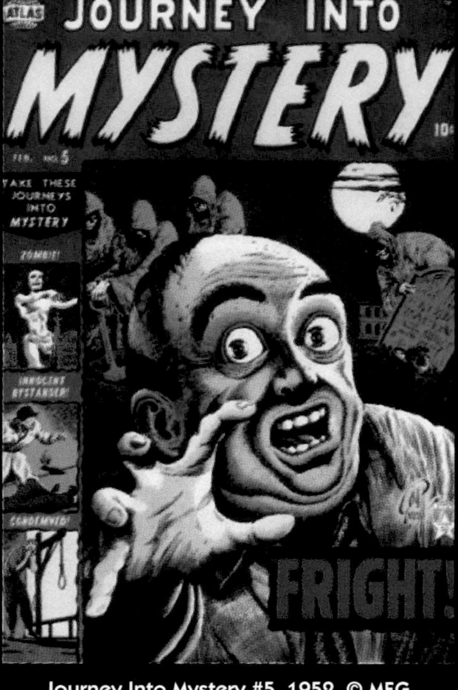

Journey Into Mystery #5, 1952, © MEG

Journey Into Unknown Worlds #37, 1950, © Western

Jungle Comics #17, 1941, © Fiction House

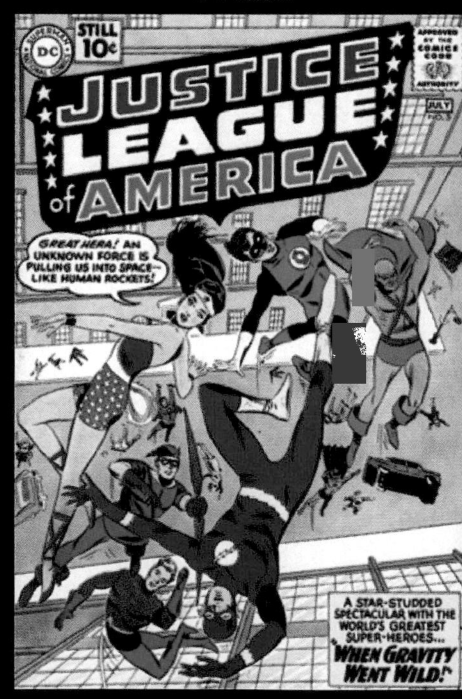

Justice League of America #5, 1961, © DC

Keen Detective Funnies V1/#8, 1938, © Centaur

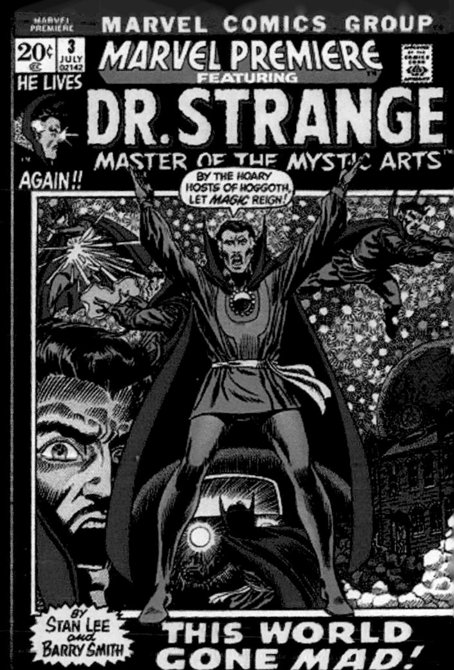

Marvel Premiere #3, 1972, © MEG

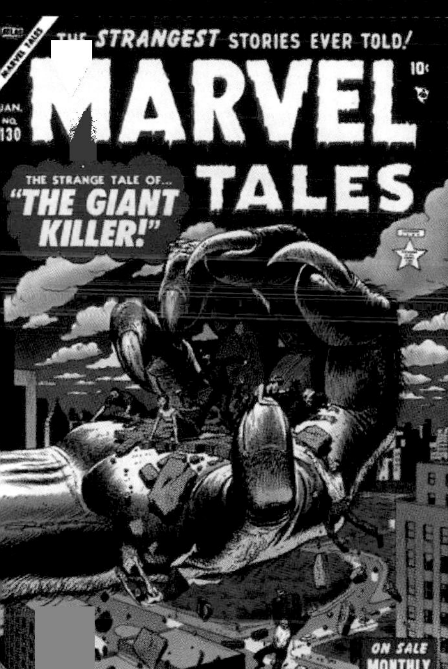

Marvel Tales #130, 1955, © MEG

My Greatest Adventure #17, 1957, © DC

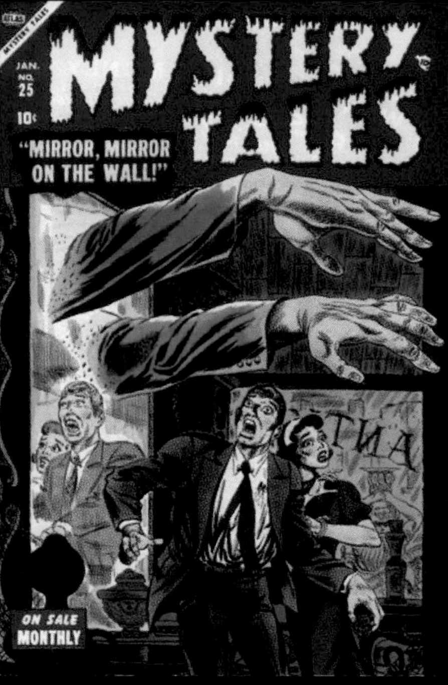

Mystery Tales #25, 1954, © MEG

New Book of Comics #1, 1936, © DC

Prime #1, 1993, © Malibu

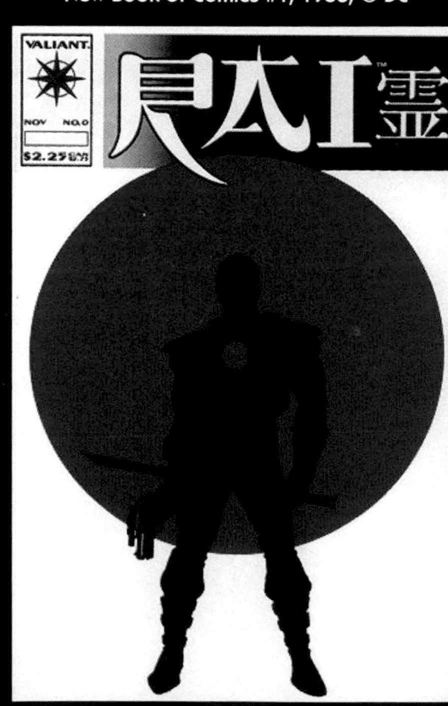

Rai #0, 1992, © Voyager Comm.

Showcase #9, 1957, © DC

Showcase #45, 1963, © DC

Space Western Comics #43, 1953, © Charlton

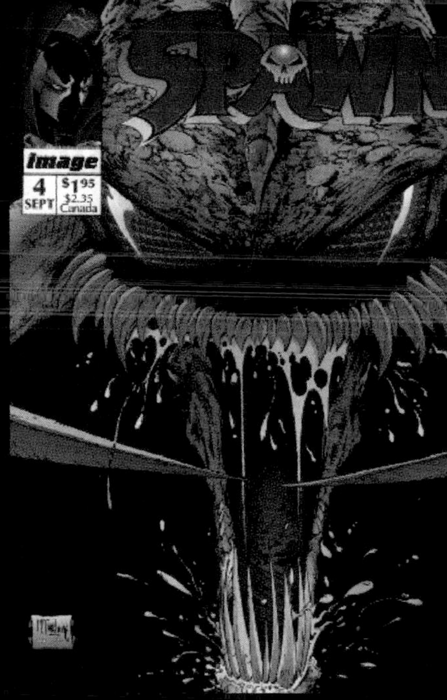

Spawn #4, 1992, © Todd McFarlane

Spectacular Spider-Man #27, 1978, © MEG

Spectre #5, 1968, © DC

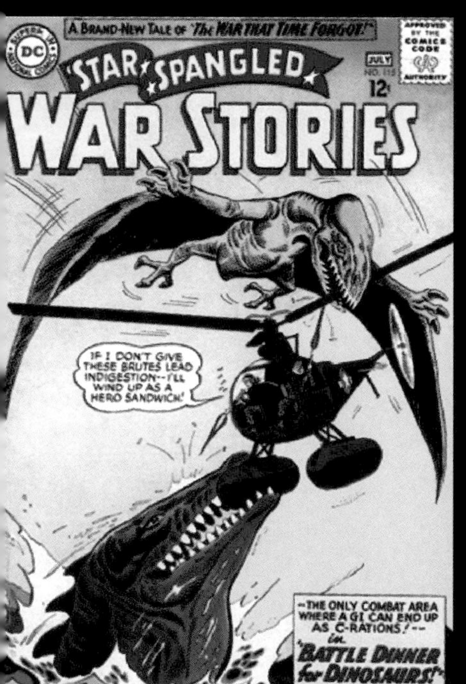

Star Spangled War Stories #115, 1964, © DC

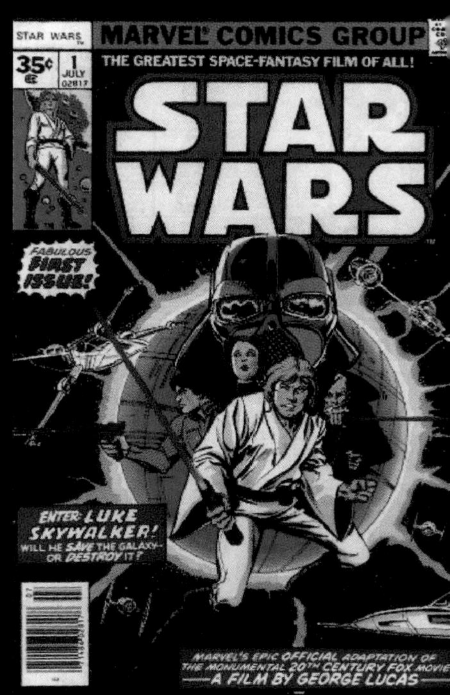

Star Wars #1, 1977, © Lucasfilms

Strange Adventures #151, 1963, © DC

Strange Stories from Another World #3, 1952, © Fawcett

Strange Suspense Stories #75, 1965, © Charlton

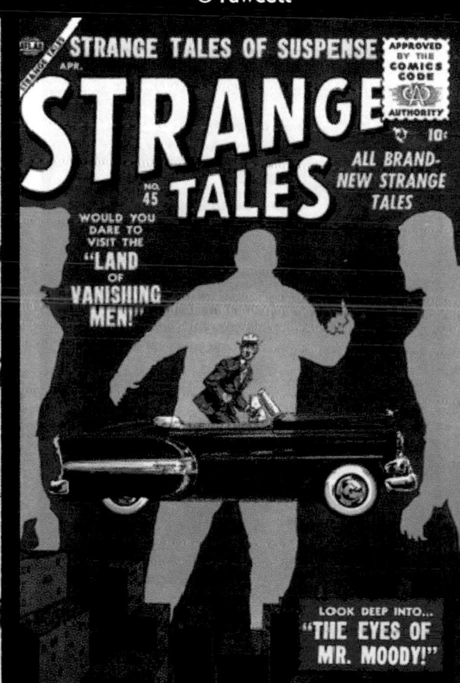

Strange Tales #45, 1956, © MEG

Sub-Mariner Comics #24, 1947, © MEG

Supersnipe Comics #7, 1948, © Street & Smith

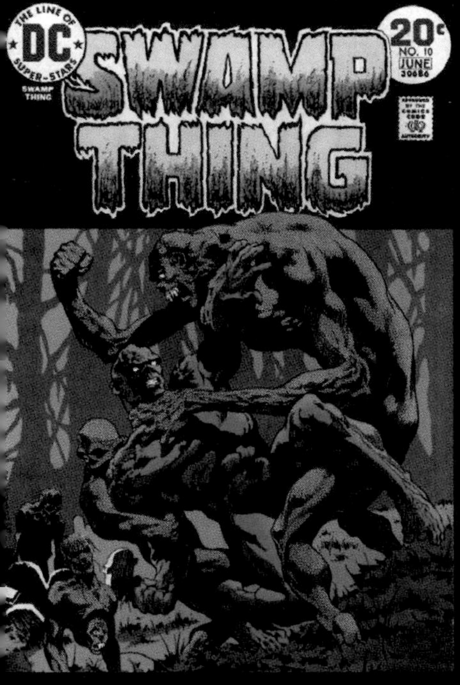

Swamp Thing #10, 1974, © DC

Tales of Suspense #1, 1959, © MEG

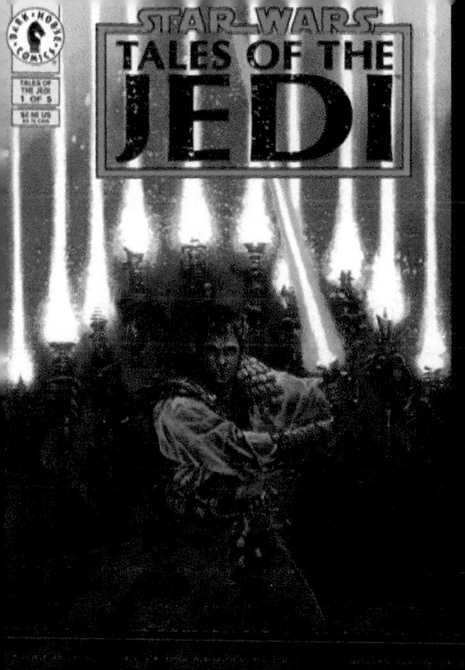

Tales of the Jedi #1, 1993, © Lucasfilms

Tales of the Unexpected #31, 1958, © DC

True Western #2, 1993, © MEG

Turok #596, 1954, © Western Pub.

So you think you know Golden Age & Silver Age comics!

Subscribe to the serious collector's magazine! Gold & Silver Overstreet's Comic Book Quarterly. The magazine for the advanced collector...

LIKE YOU!

3 Giant Issues mailed priority only $23.95!

Overstreet Publications, PO Box 2610, Cleveland, TN 37320-2610

or call our subscription hotline:

(615) 472-4135.

X-Men Classic #50, © MEG

X-O Manowar #5, © Voyager Comm.

X-Venture #1, © Victory Mag.

GD25 FN65 NM94

X-MEN ADVENTURES II (TV)
Feb, 1994 - Present ($1.25, color)
Marvel Comics
1,2-Based on second season of TV show 1.25

X-MEN/ALPHA FLIGHT
Dec, 1985 - No. 2, Dec, 1985 ($1.50, mini-series)
Marvel Comics Group
1,2: 1-Intro The Berserkers; Paul Smith-a 1.40 3.50

X-MEN AND THE MICRONAUTS, THE
Jan, 1984 - No. 4, April, 1984 (Mini-series)
Marvel Comics Group
1-4: Guice-c/a(p) in all 1.50

X-MEN CLASSIC (Formerly Classic X-Men)
No. 46, Apr, 1990 - Present ($1.25, color)
Marvel Comics
46-69,71-78,80-89,91-94: Reprints from X-Men. 54-($1.25, 52 pgs.). 57,60-63, 65-Russell-c(i); 62-r/X-Men #158(Rogue). 66-r/#162(Wolverine). 69-Begins-r of Paul Smith issues (#165 on) 1.25
70,79,90-($1.75, 52 pgs.): 70-r/X-Men #166 .70 1.75

X-MEN CLASSICS
Dec, 1983 - No. 3, Feb, 1984 ($2.00; Baxter paper)
Marvel Comics Group
1-3; X-Men-r by Neal Adams 1.20 3.00

X-MEN SPOTLIGHT ON... STARJAMMERS (Marvel)(Value: cover or less)(See X-Men #104)

X-MEN SURVIVAL GUIDE TO THE MANSION
Aug, 1993 ($6.95, color)
Marvel Comics
1-Spiral bound 1.20 3.00 7.00

X-MEN 2099
Oct, 1993 - Present ($1.25, color)
Marvel Comics
1-($1.75)-Foil-c; Ron Lim/Andy Kubert-a .70 1.75
2-6: 3-Death of Tina 1.25

X-MEN UNLIMITED
1993 - Present ($3.95, color, 68 pgs.)
Marvel Comics
1-4: 2-More detailed origin Magneto. 3-Sabretooth 1.60 4.00

X-MEN VS. DRACULA
Dec, 1993 ($1.75, color)
Marvel Comics
1-r/X-Men Annual #6 .70 1.75

X-MEN VS. THE AVENGERS, THE
Apr, 1987 - No. 4, July, 1987 ($1.50, mini-series, Baxter paper)
Marvel Comics Group
1 1.40 3.50
2-4 1.00 2.50

X-O MANOWAR
Feb, 1992 - Present ($1.95/$2.25, color, high quality)
Valiant
1-Barry Windsor-Smith/Layton-a; Layton-c; partial origin
5.00 15.00 35.00
2-B. Smith/Layton-c; Layton part inks 3.60 10.75 25.00
3-Layton-c(i) 3.20 8.00 20.00
4-1st app. Shadowman (cameo) 4.30 13.00 30.00
5,6: 5-B. Smith-c; last $1.95-c. 6-Ditko-a(p) 1.00 2.50 6.00
7,8-Unity x-overs. 7-Miller-c. 8-Simonson-c 1.25 3.00 7.50
9-13: 12-1st app. Randy Calder 1.60 4.00
14,15-Turok-c/stories 1.00 2.00 5.00
15-Hot pink logo variant; came with Ultra Pro Rigid Comic Sleeves box; no price on cover 1.65 4.00 10.00
16-24,26-28: 20-Serial number contest insert .90 2.25
25-($3.50)-Has 16 pg. Armorines insert w/origin 1.40 3.50
0-(8/93, $3.50)-Wraparound foil embossed plastic coated-c by Quesada; origin X-O Manowar 1.40 3.50
Retribution trade paperback nn (1993, $9.95)-Polybagged with copy of X-O Database #1 inside 1.65 4.00 10.00
NOTE: *Layton a-1i, 2i(part); c-1, 2i, 3i, 6i. Reese a-4i(part).*

X-TERMINATORS
Oct, 1988 - No. 4, Jan, 1989 ($1.00, color, mini-series)
Marvel Comics
1-1st app.; X-Men/X-Factor tie-in; Williamson-i 1.20 3.00
2 .70 1.75
3,4 1.25

X, THE MAN WITH THE X-RAY EYES (See Movie Comics)

X-VENTURE
July, 1947 - No. 2, Nov, 1947 (Super heroes)
Victory Magazines Corp.
1-Atom Wizard, Mystery Shadow, Lester Trumble begin
50.00 150.00 350.00
2 30.00 90.00 210.00

XYR (See Eclipse Graphic Album Series #21)

YAK YAK (See 4-Color #1186, 1348)

YAKKY DOODLE & CHOPPER (TV) (Also see Spotlight #3 & Top Cat #4)
Dec, 1962 (Hanna-Barbera)
Gold Key
1 5.00 15.00 30.00

YALTA TO KOREA (Also see Korea My Home)
1952 (8 pgs.) (Giveaway) (Paper cover)
M. Phillip Corp. (Republican National Committee)
nn-Anti-communist propaganda book 16.00 48.00 110.00

YANG (See House of Yang)
Nov, 1973 - No. 13, May, 1976; V14#14, Sept, 1985 - No. 17, Jan, 1986
Charlton Comics
1-Origin 1.60 4.00
2-13(1976) .80 2.00
14-17(1986) 1.00
3,10,11(Modern Comics-r, 1977) 1.00

YANKEE COMICS
Sept, 1941 - No. 4, Mar, 1942
Harry 'A' Chesler
1-Origin The Echo, The Enchanted Dagger, Yankee Doodle Jones, The Firebrand, & The Scarlet Sentry; Black Satan app.
62.00 188.00 425.00
2-Origin Johnny Rebel; Major Victory app.; Barry Kuda begins
38.00 115.00 265.00
3,4 32.00 95.00 215.00
4 (nd, 1940s; 7-1/4x5", 68 pgs, distr. to the service)-Foxy Grandpa, Tom, Dick & Harry, Impy, Ace & Deuce, Dot & Dash, Ima Slooth by Jack Cole (Remington Morse publ.) 1.70 5.00 12.00

YANKS IN BATTLE
Sept, 1956 - No. 4, Dec, 1956; 1963
Quality Comics Group
1-Cuidera-c(i) 5.85 17.50 35.00
2-4: Cuidera-c(i) 3.60 9.00 18.00
I.W. Reprint #3(1963)-r/#?; exist? .80 2.00 4.00

YARDBIRDS, THE (G. I. Joe's Sidekicks)
Summer, 1952
Ziff-Davis Publishing Co.

Yogi Bear #8 (Dell), © Hanna Barbera

Young Allies Comics #9, © MEG

Youngblood Strikefile #3, © Rob Liefeld

	GD25	FN65	NM94
1-By Bob Oskner	6.70	20.00	40.00

YARNS OF YELLOWSTONE
1972 (36 pages) (50 cents)
World Color Press

nn-Illustrated by Bill Chapman	1.00	2.00	5.00

YELLOW CLAW (Also see Giant Size Master of Kung Fu)
Oct, 1956 - No. 4, April, 1957
Atlas Comics (MjMC)

1-Origin by Joe Maneely	38.00	115.00	375.00
2-Kirby-a	28.00	83.00	275.00
3,4-Kirby-a; 4-Kirby/Severin-a	25.00	75.00	250.00

NOTE: ***Everett** c-3. **Maneely** c-1. **Reinman** a-2i, 3. **Severin** c-2, 4.*

YELLOWJACKET COMICS (Jack in the Box #11 on)(See TNT Comics)
Sept, 1944 - No. 10, June, 1946
E. Levy/Frank Comunale/Charlton

1-Origin Yellowjacket; Diana, the Huntress begins; E.A. Poe's "The Black Cat" adaptation	32.00	95.00	225.00
2	17.00	52.00	120.00
3,5	17.00	50.00	110.00
4-E.A. Poe's "Fall Of The House Of Usher" adaptation; Palais-a	17.00	52.00	120.00
6-10: 1,3,4,6-10-Have stories narrated by old witch in "Tales of Terror"	14.00	43.00	100.00

YELLOWSTONE KELLY (See 4-Color #1056)

YELLOW SUBMARINE (See Movie Comics)

YIN FEI THE CHINESE NINJA (Leung)(Value: cover dor less)

YOGI BEAR (See Dell Giant #41, Kite Fun Book, March of Comics #253, 265, 279, 291, 309, 319, 337, 344, Movie Comics under "Hey There It's..." & Whitman Comic Books)

YOGI BEAR (TV) (Hanna-Barbera) (See Four Color #990)
No. 1067, 12-2/59-60 - No. 9, 7-9/62; No. 10, 10/62 - No. 42, 10/70
Dell Publishing Co./Gold Key No. 10 on

4-Color 1067 (#1)-TV show debuted 1/30/61	10.00	30.00	70.00
4-Color 1104,1162 (5-7/61)	7.50	22.50	45.00
4(8-9/61) - 6(12-1/61-62)	5.35	16.00	32.00
4-Color 1271(11/61)	5.35	16.00	32.00
4-Color 1349(1/62)-Photo-c	10.00	30.00	65.00
7(2-3/62) - 9(7-9/62)-Last Dell	5.35	16.00	32.00
10(10/62-G.K.), 11(1/63)-titled "Yogi Bear Jellystone Jollies"-80 pgs.; 11-Xmas-c	4.50	13.50	36.00
12(4/63), 14-20	4.00	11.00	22.00
13(7/63)-Surprise Party, 68 pgs.	5.35	16.00	32.00
21-30	2.80	7.00	14.00
31-42	1.80	4.50	9.00
Giveaway ('84, '86)-City of Los Angeles, "Creative First Aid" & "Earthquake Preparedness for Children"		.80	2.00

YOGI BEAR (TV)
Nov, 1970 - No. 35, Jan, 1976 (Hanna-Barbera)
Charlton Comics

1	3.25	9.50	22.00
2-6,8-10	1.70	5.00	12.00
7-Summer Fun (Giant, 52 pgs.)	2.30	6.75	16.00
11-35: 28-31-partial-r	1.30	3.25	8.00

YOGI BEAR (TV)(See The Flintstones, 3rd series & Spotlight #1)
Nov, 1977 - No. 9, Mar, 1979 (Hanna-Barbera)
Marvel Comics Group

1-Flintstones begin		.80	2.00
2-9			1.00

YOGI BEAR (TV)
Sept, 1992 - Present ($1.25, color)
Harvey Comics

V2#1,2			1.25
...Big Book V2#1,2: 1-(11/92, $1.95, 52 pgs)		.80	2.0
...Giant Size V2#1,2: 1-(10/92, $2.25, 68 pgs.)		.90	2.2

YOGI BEAR'S EASTER PARADE (See The Funtastic World of Hanna-Barbera #2)

YOGI BERRA (Baseball hero)
1951 (Yankee catcher)
Fawcett Publications

nn-Photo-c	46.00	140.00	325.0

YOSEMITE SAM (...& Bugs Bunny)
Dec, 1970 - No. 81, Feb, 1984
Gold Key/Whitman

1	1.70	5.00	12.00
2-10	1.00	2.00	5.00
11-30		1.20	3.00
31-81: 81-r(1/3)		.80	2.00

(See March of Comics #363, 380, 392)

YOUNG ALLIES COMICS (All-Winners #21; see Kid Komics #2)
Summer, 1941 - No. 20, Oct, 1946
Timely Comics (USA 1-7/NPI 8,9/YAI 10-20)

	GD25	FN65	VF82	NM94
1-Origin/1st app. The Young Allies; 1st meeting of Captain America & Human Torch; Red Skull app.; S&K-c/splash; Hitler-c	500.00	1500.00	2750.00	4000.00

(Estimated up to 165 total copies exist, 9 in NM/Mint)

	GD25	FN65	NM94
2-Captain America & Human Torch app.; Simon & Kirby-c	150.00	450.00	1000.00
3-Fathertime, Captain America & Human Torch app.	121.00	362.00	800.00
4-The Vagabond & Red Skull, Capt. America, Human Torch app.	125.00	375.00	815.00
5-Captain America & Human Torch app.	67.00	200.00	450.00
6-10: 9-Hitler, Tojo, Mussolini-c. 10-Origin Tommy Tyme & Clock of Ages; ends #19	54.00	162.00	365.00
11-20: 12-Classic decapitation story	42.00	125.00	275.00

NOTE: ***Brodsky** c-15. **Gabrielle** c-3, 4. **S&K** c-1, 2. **Schomburg** c-5-14, 16-19. **Shores** c-20.*

YOUNG ALL-STARS (DC)(Value: cover or less)

YOUNGBLOOD (See Megaton Explosion & Team Youngblood)
Apr, 1992 - No. 4, Feb, 1993 ($2.50, color, mini-series)
Image Comics

1-Liefeld-c/a/scripts in all; flip book format with 2 trading cards; 1st Image comic book published	1.30	3.25	8.00
1-2nd printing		1.00	2.50
2-1st app. Shadowhawk in solo back-up story; 2 trading cards inside; flip book format		1.90	4.75
2-2nd printing (1.95)		.80	2.00
3-Contains 2 trading cards inside (flip book); 1st app. Supreme in back-up story		1.00	2.50
0-(12/92)-Contains 2 trading cards		.80	2.00
4-Glow-in-the-dark-c w/2 trading cards; Dale Keown's The Pitt app.		1.00	2.50
...Battlezone 1 (5/93-c, 4/93 inside, $1.95)-Arsenal book; Liefeld-c(p)		.80	2.00
...Yearbook 1 (7/93, $2.50)-Fold out panel		1.00	2.50

YOUNGBLOOD: STRIKEFILE
Apr, 1993 - No. 4, 1993 ($1.95-$2.50, color, mini-series)
Image Comics

1-Flip book w/Jae Lee-c/a & Liefeld-c/a in all		.80	2.00
2-4-($2.50)		1.00	2.50

YOUNG BRIDES
Sept-Oct, 1952 - No. 30, Nov-Dec, 1956 (Photo-c: 1-4)
Feature/Prize Publications

V1#1-Simon & Kirby-a	13.00	40.00	90.00

Young Eagle #4, © FAW

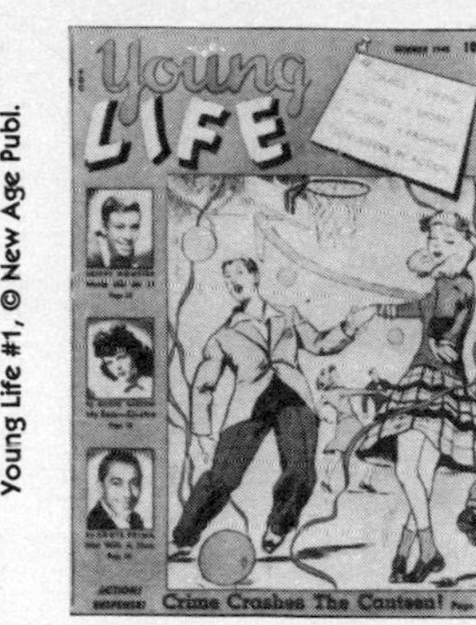

Young Life #1, © New Age Publ.

Young Love #27, © PRIZE

	GD25	FN65	NM94
2-S&K-a	7.50	22.50	45.00
3-6-S&K-a	6.70	20.00	40.00
V2#1,3-7,10-12 (#7-18)-S&K-a	5.85	17.50	35.00
2,8,9-No S&K-a	2.80	7.00	14.00
V3#1-3(#19-21)-Last precode (3-4/55)	2.40	6.00	12.00
4,6(#22,24), V4#1,3(#25,27)	1.80	4.50	9.00
V3#5(#23)-Meskin-c	2.80	7.00	14.00
V4#2(#26)-All S&K issue	5.85	17.50	35.00
V4#4(#28)-S&K-a	4.70	14.00	28.00
V4#5,6(#29,30)	3.60	9.00	18.00

YOUNG DEATH (Fleetway/Quality)(Value: cover or less)

YOUNG DR. MASTERS (See The Adventures of Young Dr. Masters)

YOUNG DOCTORS, THE
January, 1963 - No. 6, Nov, 1963
Charlton Comics

	GD25	FN65	NM94
V1#1	1.20	3.00	6.00
2-6	.60	1.50	3.00

YOUNG EAGLE
12/50 - No. 10, 6/52; No. 3, 7/56 - No. 5, 4/57 (Photo-c: 1-10)
Fawcett Publications/Charlton

	GD25	FN65	NM94
1	11.00	32.00	75.00
2	6.35	19.00	38.00
3-9	5.00	15.00	30.00
10-Origin Thunder, Young Eagle's Horse	4.00	12.00	24.00
3-5(Charlton)-Formerly Sherlock Holmes?	3.00	7.50	15.00

YOUNG HEARTS
Nov, 1949 - No. 2, Feb, 1950
Marvel Comics (SPC)

	GD25	FN65	NM94
1-Photo-c	7.50	22.50	45.00
2-Photo-c from movie	4.70	14.00	28.00

YOUNG HEARTS IN LOVE
1964
Super Comics

	GD25	FN65	NM94
17,18: 17-r/Young Love V5#6 (4-5/62)	.80	2.00	4.00

YOUNG HEROES (Formerly Forbidden Worlds #34)
No. 35, Feb-Mar, 1955 - No. 37, June-July, 1955
American Comics Group (Titan)

	GD25	FN65	NM94
35-37-Frontier Scout	6.00	18.00	36.00

YOUNG INDIANA JONES CHRONICLES, THE
Feb, 1992 - Present ($2.50, color)
Dark Horse Comics

	GD25	FN65	NM94
1-12: Dan Barry scripts in all		1.00	2.50

NOTE: ***Dan Barry*** *a(p)-1, 2, 5, 6, 10; c-1-10.* ***Morrow*** *a-3, 4, 5p, 6p.* ***Springer*** *a-1i, 2i.*

YOUNG INDIANA JONES CHRONICLES, THE
1992 - Present ($3.95, color, squarebound, 68 pgs.)
Hollywood Comics (Disney)

	GD25	FN65	NM94
1-3: 1-r/YIJC #1,2 by D. Horse. 2-r/#3,4. 3-r/#5,6		1.60	4.00

YOUNG KING COLE (Becomes Criminals on the Run)
Fall, 1945 - V3#12, July, 1948
Premium Group/Novelty Press

	GD25	FN65	NM94
V1#1-Toni Gayle begins	13.50	41.00	95.00
2	8.35	25.00	50.00
3-4	6.35	19.00	38.00
V2#1-7(8-9/46-7/47)	5.00	15.00	30.00
V3#1,3-6,12: 5-McWilliams-c/a	4.00	12.00	24.00
2-L.B. Cole-a	5.35	16.00	32.00
7-L.B. Cole-c/a	7.00	21.00	42.00
8-11-L.B. Cole-c	6.35	19.00	38.00

YOUNG LAWYERS, THE (TV)
Jan, 1971 - No. 2, April, 1971
Dell Publishing co.

	GD25	FN65	NM94
1,2	1.70	5.00	12.00

YOUNG LIFE (Teen Life #3 on)
Spring, 1945 - No. 2, Summer, 1945
New Age Publ./Quality Comics Group

	GD25	FN65	NM94
1-Skip Homeier, Louis Prima stories	8.35	25.00	50.00
2-Frank Sinatra photo on-c plus story	8.35	25.00	50.00

YOUNG LOVE
2-3/49 - No. 73, 12-1/56-57; V3#5, 2-3/60 - V7#1, 6-7/63
Prize(Feature)Publ.(Crestwood)

	GD25	FN65	NM94
V1#1-S&K-c/a(2)	22.00	67.00	155.00
2-Photo-c begin; S&K-a	10.00	30.00	70.00
3-S&K-a	9.15	27.50	55.00
4-5-Minor S&K-a	5.85	17.50	35.00
V2#1(#7)-S&K-a(2)	9.15	27.50	55.00
2-5(#8-11)-Minor S&K-a	4.35	13.00	26.00
6,8(#12,14)-S&K-c only. 14-S&K 1 pg. art	5.85	17.50	35.00
7,9-12(#13,15-18)-S&K-c/a	9.15	27.50	55.00
V3#1-4(#19-22)-S&K-c/a	6.70	20.00	40.00
5-7,9-12(#23-25,27-30)-Photo-c resume; S&K-a	5.35	16.00	32.00
8(#26)-No S&K-a	3.20	8.00	16.00
V4#1,6(#31,36)-S&K-a	5.35	16.00	32.00
2-5,7-12(#32-35,37-42) Minor S&K-a	4.20	12.50	25.00
V5#1-12(#43-54), V6#1-9(#55-63)-Last precode; S&K-a in some	3.20	8.00	16.00
V6#10-12(#64-66)	2.40	6.00	12.00
V7#1-7(#67-73)	1.80	4.50	9.00
V3#5(2-3/60),6(4-5/60)(Formerly All For Love)	1.40	3.50	7.00
V4#1(6-7/60)-6(4-5/61)	1.20	3.00	6.00
V5#1(6-7/61)-6(4-5/62)	1.20	3.00	6.00
V6#1(6-7/62)-6(4-5/63), V7#1	1.00	2.50	5.00

NOTE: ***Meskin*** *a-14(2), 27, 42.* ***Powell*** *a-V4#6.* ***Severin/Elder*** *a-V1#3. S&K art not in #53, 57, 58, 61, 63-65. Photo c-V3#5-V5#11.*

YOUNG LOVE
#39, 9-10/63 - #120, Wint./75-76; #121, 10/76 - #126, 7/77
National Periodical Publ.(Arleigh Publ. Corp #49-60)/DC Comics

	GD25	FN65	NM94
39	3.20	8.00	16.00
40-50	2.00	5.00	10.00
51-70: 64-Simon & Kirby-a	1.40	3.50	7.00
71,72,74-77,80	1.00	2.00	5.00
73,78,79-Toth-a		1.20	3.00
81-126: 107-114-(100 pgs.)			1.50

NOTE: ***Bolle*** *a-117.* ***Colan*** *a-107r.* ***Nasser*** *a-123, 124.* ***Orlando*** *a-122.* ***Simonson*** *c-125.* ***Toth*** *a-73, 78, 79, 122-125r.* ***Wood*** *a-109r(4 pgs.).*

YOUNG LOVER ROMANCES (Formerly & becomes Great Lover...)
No. 4, June, 1952 - No. 5, Aug, 1952
Toby Press

	GD25	FN65	NM94
4,5-Photo-c	4.00	10.00	20.00

YOUNG LOVERS (My Secret Life #19 on)(Formerly Brenda Starr?)
No. 16, July, 1956 - No. 18, May, 1957
Charlton Comics

	GD25	FN65	NM94
16,17('56): 16-Marcus Swayze-a	3.20	8.00	16.00
18-Elvis Presley picture-c, text story (biography)(Scarce)	38.00	115.00	265.00

YOUNG MARRIAGE
June, 1950
Fawcett Publications

	GD25	FN65	NM94
1-Powell-a; photo-c	8.35	25.00	50.00

YOUNG MEN (Formerly Cowboy Romances)(...on the Battlefield #12-20 (4/53); ...In Action #21)
No. 4, 6/50 - No. 11, 10/51; No. 12, 12/51 - No. 28, 6/54
Marvel/Atlas Comics (IPC)

Young Men #28, © MEG

Young Romance #54, © PRIZE

Zane Grey's Stories of the West #29, © DELL

GD25 FN65 NM94

4-(52 pgs.) 10.00 30.00 70.00
5-11 6.70 20.00 40.00
12-23: 15-Colan, Pakula-a. 21-23-Hot Rod issues starring Flash Foster 5.85 17.50 35.00
24-(12/53)-Origin Captain America, Human Torch, & Sub-Mariner which are revived thru #28; Red Skull app. 40.00 120.00 400.00
25-28: 25-Romita-c/a (see Men's Advs.) 31.00 92.00 315.00
NOTE: ***Berg** a-7, 14, 17, 18, 20; c-17? **Brodsky** c-4-9, 13, 14, 16, 17, 21-25. **Burgos** c-26-28. **Colan** a-14, 15. **Everett** a-18-20. **Heath** a-13, 14. **Maneely** c-10, 12, 15. **Pakula** a-14. **Robinson** c-18. Captain America by **Romita**-#24?, 25, 26?, 27, 28. Human Torch by **Burgos**-#25, 27, 28. Sub-Mariner by **Everett**-#24-28.*

YOUNG REBELS, THE (TV)
January, 1971
Dell Publishing Co.
1-Photo-c 1.65 4.00 10.00

YOUNG ROMANCE COMICS (The 1st romance comic)
Sept-Oct, 1947 - V16#4, June-July, 1963 (#1-33: 52 pgs.)
Prize/Headline (Feature Publ.)
V1#1-S&K-c/a(2) 24.00 72.00 165.00
2-S&K-c/a(2-3) 13.00 40.00 90.00
3-6-S&K-c/a(2-3) each 11.00 32.00 75.00
V2#1-6(#7-12)-S&K-c/a(2-3) each 10.00 30.00 65.00
V3#1-3(#13-15): V3#1-Photo-c begin; S&K-a 7.50 22.50 45.00
4-12(#16-24)-Photo-c; S&K-a 7.50 22.50 45.00
V4#1-11(#25-35)-S&K-a 6.70 20.00 40.00
12(#36)-S&K, Toth-a 9.15 27.50 55.00
V5#1-12(#37-48), V6#4-12(#52-60)-S&K-a 6.70 20.00 40.00
V6#1-3(#49-51)-No S&K-a 4.00 10.00 20.00
V7#1-11(#61-71)-S&K-a in most 5.85 17.50 35.00
V7#12(#72), V8#1-3(#73-75)-Last precode (12-1/54-55)-No S&K-a 2.40 6.00 12.00
V8#4(#76, 4-5/55), 5(#77)-No S&K-a 2.00 5.00 10.00
V8#6-8(#78-80, 12-1/55-56)-S&K-a 4.00 11.00 22.00
V9#3,5,6(#81, 2-3/56, 83,84)-S&K-a 4.00 11.00 22.00
4, V10#1(#82,85)-All S&K-a 4.70 14.00 28.00
V10#2-6(#86-90, 10-11/57)-S&K-a 4.00 11.00 22.00
V11#1,2,5,6(#91,92,95,96)-S&K-a 4.00 11.00 22.00
3,4(#93,94), V12#2,4,5(#98,100,101)-No S&K 1.80 4.50 9.00
V12#1,3,6(#97,99,102)-S&K-a 4.00 11.00 22.00
V13#1(#103)-S&K, Powell-a 4.00 11.00 22.00
2-6(#104-108) 1.20 3.00 6.00
V14#1-6, V15#1-6, V16#1-4(#109-124) 1.00 2.50 5.00
NOTE: ***Meskin** a-16, 24(2), 33, 47, 50. **Robinson/Meskin** a-6. **Leonard Starr** a-11. Photo c-13-32, 34-65.*

YOUNG ROMANCE COMICS (Continued from Prize series)
No. 125, Aug-Sept, 1963 - No. 208, Nov-Dec, 1975
National Periodical Publ.(Arleigh Publ. Corp. No. 127)
125 4.00 10.00 20.00
126-162: 154-Neal Adams-c 2.00 5.00 10.00
163,164-Toth-a 1.40 3.50 7.00
165-196: 170-Michell from Young Love ends; Lily Martin, the Swinger begins 1.20 3.00
197 (100 pgs.)-208 1.20 3.00

YOUR DREAMS (See Strange World of...)

YOUR TRIP TO NEWSPAPERLAND
June, 1955 (12 pgs.; 14x11-1/2")
Philadelphia Evening Bulletin (Printed by Harvey Press)
nn-Joe Palooka takes kids on tour through newspaper 4.00 11.00 22.00

YOUR UNITED STATES
1946
Lloyd Jacquet Studios
nn-Used in **SOTI**, pg. 309,310; Sid Greene-a 17.00 52.00 120.00

GD25 FN65 NM94

YOUTHFUL HEARTS (Daring Confessions #4 on)
May, 1952 - No. 3, Sept, 1952
Youthful Magazines
1-"Monkey on Her Back" swipes E.C. drug story from Shock SuspenStories #12; Frankie Laine photo on-c; Doug Wildey-a in all 13.00 40.00 90.00
2,3: 2-Vic Damone photo on-c. 3-Johnny Raye photo on-c 10.00 30.00 65.00

YOUTHFUL LOVE (Truthful Love #2)
May, 1950
Youthful Magazines
1 6.35 19.00 38.00

YOUTHFUL ROMANCES
8-9/49 - No. 5, 4/50; No. 6, 2/51; No. 7, 5/51 - #14, 10/52; #15, 1/53 - #18, 7/53; #5, 9/53 - #8, 5/54
Pix-Parade #1-14/Ribage #15 on
1-(1st series)-Titled Youthful Love-Romances 13.00 40.00 90.00
2 8.35 25.00 50.00
3-5 6.70 20.00 40.00
6,7,9-14(10/52, Pix-Parade; becomes Daring Love #15); 7-Tony Martin photo on-c 5.35 16.00 32.00
8-Wood-c 11.50 34.00 80.00
15-18 (Ribage) 4.20 12.50 25.00
5(9/53, Ribage) 3.60 9.00 18.00
6,7(#7, 2/54), 8(5/54) 3.20 8.00 16.00

YUPPIES FROM HELL (Marvel)(Value: cover or less)(See Sex, Lies, &..., Son of...)

ZAGO, JUNGLE PRINCE (My Story #5 on)
Sept, 1948 - No. 4, March, 1949
Fox Features Syndicate
1-Blue Beetle app.; partial-r/Atomic #4 (Toni Luck) 27.00 80.00 190.00
2,3-Kamen-a 19.00 58.00 135.00
4-Baker-c 17.00 52.00 120.00

ZANE GREY'S STORIES OF THE WEST
No. 197, 9/48 - No. 996, 5-7/59; 11/64 (All painted-c)
Dell Publishing Co./Gold Key 11/64
4-Color 197(#1)(9/48) 10.00 30.00 60.00
4-Color 222,230,236('49) 7.50 22.50 45.00
4-Color 246,255,270,301,314,333,346 5.00 15.00 30.00
4-Color 357,372,395,412,433,449,467,484 4.35 13.00 26.00
4-Color 511-Kinstler-a 4.70 14.00 28.00
4-Color 532,555,583,604,616,632(5/55) 4.35 13.00 26.00
27(9-11/55) - 39(9-11/58) 4.00 10.00 20.00
4-Color 996(5-7/59) 4.00 10.00 20.00
10131-411-(11/64-G.K.)-Nevada; r/4-Color #996 2.40 6.00 12.00

ZANY (Magazine)(Satire)(See Frantic & Ratfink)
Sept, 1958 - No. 4, May, 1959
Candor Publ. Co.
1-Bill Everett-c 6.35 19.00 38.00
2-4: 4-Everett-c 4.20 12.50 25.00

ZATANNA (DC)(Value: cover or less)(See Adventure Comics #413, Justice League of America #161, Supergirl #1, & World's Finest Comics #274)

ZATANNA SPECIAL (DC)(Value: cover or less)

ZAZA, THE MYSTIC (Formerly Charlie Chan; This Magazine Is Haunted V2#12 on)
No. 10, April, 1956 - No. 11, Sept, 1956
Charlton Comics
10,11 7.50 22.50 45.00

ZEGRA JUNGLE EMPRESS (Formerly Tegra)(My Love Life #6 on)
No. 2, Oct, 1948 - No. 5, April, 1949
Fox Features Syndicate

Zen: Intergalactic Ninja #2 (Entity), © Zen Comics

Zip Comics #44, © AP

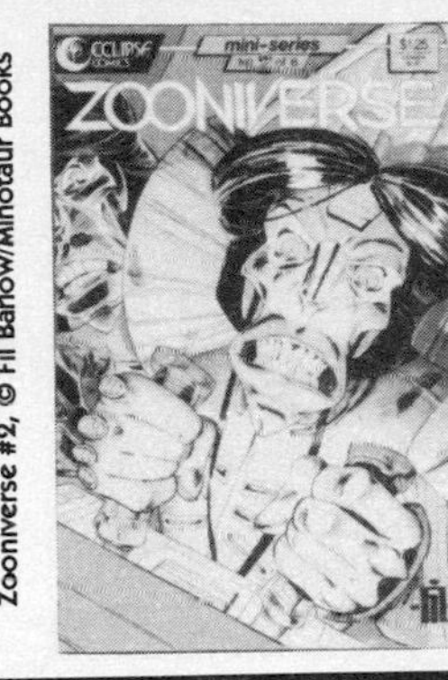

Zooniverse #2, © Fil Barlow/Minotaur Books

	GD25	FN65	NM94
2	29.00	85.00	200.00
3-5	22.00	65.00	150.00

ZEN, INTERGALACTIC NINJA
Sept, 1992 - Present ($1.25, color)(Formerly a B&W comic by Zen Comics)
Zen Comics/Archie Comics

	GD25	FN65	NM94
1-4: 1-Origin Zen; contains mini-poster			1.25

ZEN, INTERGALACTIC NINJA
No. 0, June-July, 1993 - No. 3, 1994 ($2.95, B&W, mini-series)
Eternity Comics

	GD25	FN65	NM94
0-Gold foil stamped-c; photo-c of Zen model		1.20	3.00
1-3-Gold foil stamped-c; Bill Maus-c/a		1.20	3.00
0-($3.50, color)-Chromium-c by Jae Lee		1.40	3.50

ZEN, INTERGALACTIC NINJA: THE HUNTED
1993 - No. 3, 1994 ($2.95, B&W, mini-series)
Eternity Comics

	GD25	FN65	NM94
1-3-($2.95)-Newsstand Edition; foil logo		1.20	3.00
1-($3.50)-Polybagged w/chromium card by Kieth; foil logo		1.20	3.00

ZERO PATROL, THE (Continuity)(Value: cover or less)

ZERO TOLERANCE
Oct, 1990 - No. 4, Jan, 1991 ($2.25, color, limited series)
First Comics

	GD25	FN65	NM94
1-4: Tim Vigil-c/a(p) (his 1st color mini-series)		.90	2.25

ZIGGY PIG-SILLY SEAL COMICS (See Animal Fun, Animated Movie-Tunes, Comic Capers, Krazy Komics, Silly Tunes & Super Rabbit)
Fall, 1944 - No. 6, Fall, 1946
Timely Comics (CmPL)

	GD25	FN65	NM94
1-Vs. the Japs	14.00	43.00	100.00
2	8.35	25.00	50.00
3-5	7.00	21.00	42.00
6-Infinity-c	10.00	30.00	60.00
I.W. Reprint #1('58)-r/Krazy Komics	1.00	2.50	5.00
I.W. Reprint #2,7,8	.80	2.00	4.00

ZIP COMICS
Feb, 1940 - No. 47, Summer, 1944
MLJ Magazines

	GD25	FN65	NM94
1-Origin Kalathar the Giant Man, The Scarlet Avenger, & Steel Sterling; Mr. Satan, Nevada Jones (masked hero) & Zambini, the Miracle Man, War Eagle, Captain Valor begins	207.00	620.00	1450.00
2-Nevada Jones adds mask & horse Blaze	100.00	300.00	700.00
3	75.00	225.00	500.00
4,5	60.00	180.00	400.00
6-9: 9-Last Kalathar & Mr. Satan	50.00	150.00	340.00
10-Inferno, the Flame Breather begins, ends #13	56.00	167.00	375.00
11,12: 11-Inferno without costume	44.00	132.00	300.00
13-17,19: 17-Last Scarlet Avenger	44.00	132.00	300.00
18-Wilbur begins (1st app.)	47.00	142.00	325.00
20-Origin Black Jack (1st app.); Hitler-c	62.00	188.00	435.00
21-26: 25-Last Nevada Jones. 26-Black Witch begins; last Captain Valor	42.00	125.00	275.00
27-Intro. Web	62.00	188.00	435.00
28-Origin Web	62.00	188.00	435.00
29,30: 29-The Hyena app.	33.00	100.00	220.00
31-38: 34-1st Applejack app. 35-Last Zambini, Black Jack. 38-Last Web issue	25.00	75.00	175.00
39-Red Rube begins (origin, 8/43)	25.00	75.00	175.00
40-47: 45-Wilbur ends	18.00	55.00	125.00

NOTE: *Biro a-5, 9, 17; c-3-17. **Meskin** a-1-3, 5-7, 9, 10, 12, 13, 15, 16 at least. **Montana** c-29, 30, 32-35. **Novick** c-18-28, 31. **Sahle** c-37, 38, 40-46. Bondage c-8, 9, 33, 34. Steel Sterling c-1-19 (w/Blackjack-20-27), 28-39. Red Rube c-40-47.*

ZIP-JET (Hero)
Feb, 1953 - No. 2, Apr-May, 1953
St. John Publishing Co.

	GD25	FN65	NM94
1,2-Rocketman-r from Punch Comics; #1-c from splash in Punch #10	29.00	85.00	200.00

ZIPPY THE CHIMP (CBS TV Presents...)
No. 50, March, 1957; No. 51, Aug, 1957
Pines (Literary Ent.)

	GD25	FN65	NM94
50,51	4.20	12.50	25.00

ZODY, THE MOD ROB
July, 1970
Gold Key

	GD25	FN65	NM94
1	1.20	3.00	7.00

ZOMBIE 3-D (3-D Zone)(Value: cover or less)

ZONE (Dark Horse)(Value: cover or less)

ZOO ANIMALS
No. 8, 1954 (36 pages; 15 cents)
Star Publications

	GD25	FN65	NM94
8-(B&W for coloring)	3.60	9.00	18.00

ZOO FUNNIES (Tim McCoy #16 on)
Nov, 1945 - No. 15, 1947
Charlton Comics/Children Comics Publ.

	GD25	FN65	NM94
101(#1)(1945; 1st Charlton comic book?)-Funny animal; Al Fago-c	10.00	30.00	70.00
2(12/45, 52 pgs.)	5.85	17.50	35.00
3-5	4.70	14.00	28.00
6-15: 8-Diana the Huntress app.	4.00	10.00	20.00

ZOO FUNNIES (Becomes Nyoka, The Jungle Girl #14 on?)
July, 1953 - No. 13, Sept, 1955; Dec, 1984
Capitol Stories/Charlton Comics

	GD25	FN65	NM94
1-1st app.? Timothy The Ghost; Fago-c/a	6.70	20.00	40.00
2	4.00	11.00	22.00
3-7 (8/46)	3.60	9.00	18.00
8-13-Nyoka app.	5.35	16.00	32.00
1(1984)			1.00

ZOONIVERSE (Eclipse)(Value: cover or less)

ZOO PARADE (See 4-Color #662)

ZOOM COMICS
December, 1945 (One Shot)
Carlton Publishing Co.

	GD25	FN65	NM94
nn-Dr. Mercy, Satannas, from Red Band Comics; Capt. Milksop origin retold	27.00	82.00	185.00

ZOOT (Rulah Jungle Goddess #17 on)
nd (1946) - No. 16, July, 1948 (Two #13s & 14s)
Fox Features Syndicate

	GD25	FN65	NM94
nn-Funny animal only	11.50	34.00	80.00
2-The Jaguar app.	10.00	30.00	70.00
3(Fall, 1946) - 6-Funny animals & teen-age	6.35	19.00	38.00
7-(6/47)-Rulah, Jungle Goddess begins (origin & 1st app.)	46.00	140.00	320.00
8-10	34.00	105.00	240.00
11-Kamen bondage-c	37.00	112.00	260.00
12-Injury-to-eye panels, torture scene	22.00	65.00	150.00
13(2/48)	22.00	65.00	150.00
14(3/48)-Used in **SOTI**, pg. 104, "One picture showing a girl nailed by her wrists to trees with blood flowing from the wounds, might be taken straight from an ill. ed. of the Marquis deSade"	26.00	78.00	180.00
13(4/48),14(5/48)-Becomes Western True Crime #15 on?	22.00	65.00	150.00
15,16	22.00	65.00	150.00

ZORRO (Walt Disney with #882)(TV)(See Eclipse Graphic Album)
May, 1949 - No. 15, Sept-Nov, 1961 (Photo-c 882 on)
Dell Publishing Co.

Zorro #8 (DELL), © The Disney Co.

Zorro #3 (MEG), © Zorro Productions

Zot! #11, © Scott McCloud

	GD25	FN65	NM94
4-Color 228	22.00	65.00	150.00
4-Color 425,497,617,732	13.00	40.00	90.00
4-Color 538,574-Kinstler-a	13.50	41.00	95.00
4-Color 882-Photo-c begin; Toth-a	11.50	34.00	80.00
4-Color 920,933,960,976-Toth-a in all	11.50	34.00	80.00
4-Color 1003('59)-Toth-a	10.00	30.00	70.00
4-Color 1037-Annette Funicello photo-c	12.00	36.00	85.00
8(12-2/59-60)	10.00	30.00	60.00
9,12-Toth-a. 12-Last 10 cent issue	10.00	30.00	65.00
10,11,13-15-Last photo-c	8.35	25.00	50.00

NOTE: ***Warren Tufts** a-4-Color 1037, 8, 9, 10, 13.*

ZORRO (Walt Disney)(TV)
Jan, 1966 - No. 9, March, 1968 (All photo-c)
Gold Key

	GD25	FN65	NM94
1-Toth-a	7.50	22.50	45.00
2,4,5,7-9-Toth-a. 5-r/F.C. #1003 by Toth	4.70	14.00	28.00
3,6-Tufts-a	4.00	11.00	22.00

NOTE: *#1-9 are reprinted from Dell issues.* ***Tufts** a-3, 4. #1-r/F.C. #882. #2-r/F.C. #960. #3-r/#12-c & #8 inside. #4-r/#9-c & insides. #6-r/#11(all); #7-r/#14-c. #8-r/F.C. #933 inside & back-c & #976-c. #9-r/F.C. #920.*

ZORRO (TV)
Dec, 1990 - No. 12, Nov, 1991 ($1.00, color)
Marvel Comics

	GD25	FN65	NM94
1-12: Based on new TV show. 12-Toth-c			1.00

ZOT! (Eclipse)(Value: cover or less)

Z-2 COMICS (Secret Agent...)(See Holyoke One-Shot #7)

ZULU (See Movie Classics)

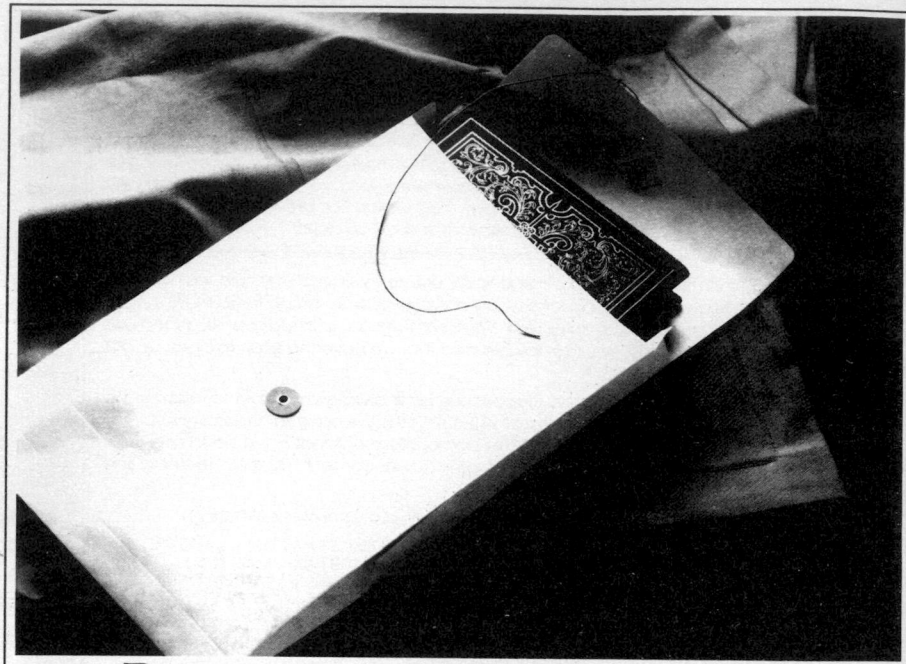

BEDROCK CITY

COMIC COMPANY

6521 WESTHEIMER
HOUSTON, TX 77057
PH: (713) 780-0675
FAX: (713) 780-2366

★ *Quality Service*
★ *Accurate Grading*
★ *Fantastic Selection*

STONE AGE COMICS ☆ FOR ☆ MODERN DAY COLLECTORS

(Our Back Issue Department is always buying Silver and Golden Age Comics!)

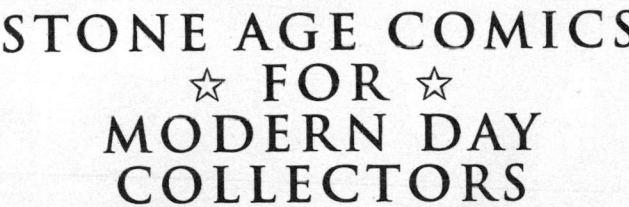

WHEN YOU'RE IN NEW YORK CITY–
COME VISIT OUR BRAND NEW SHOWROOM!
OPEN WEEKDAYS, 10 AM TO 5 PM: BY APPOINTMENT ONLY
SILVER
THE INCREDIBLE HULK
THE STRANGEST MAN OF ALL TIME!!
IS HE MAN OR MONSTER OR... IS HE BOTH?
the AMAZING SPIDER-MAN
2 GREAT FEATURE-LENGTH SPIDER MAN THRILLERS!
the CHAMELEON STRIKES!
AMAZING FANTASY
SPIDER MAN
Fantastic Four
THE FLASH
MASTER OF MIRRORS!
JUSTICE LEAGUE of AMERICA
STARRO THE CONQUEROR!
LIST OF DC CONTEST WINNERS
SHOWCASE
Presenting THE FLASH!
WHIRLWIND ADVENTURES OF THE FASTEST MAN ALIVE!
DESIGN: ARNIE SAWYER All artwork © DC COMICS, © MARVEL ENTERTAINMENT GROUP, INC.

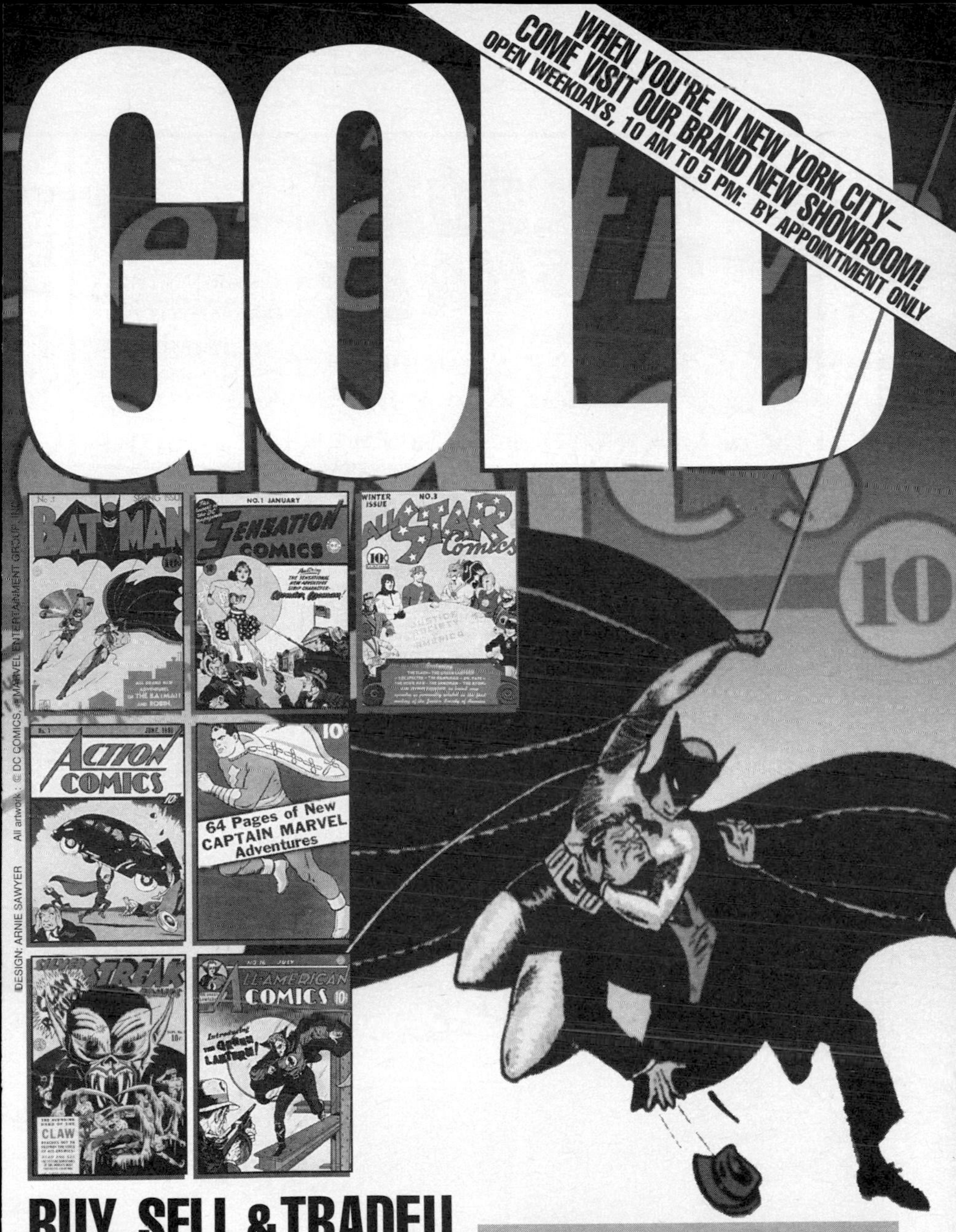

BUY, SELL & TRADE!!

WHY YOU SHOULD BUY FROM US:
We always have a great selection of high-grade Silver and Golden age books on hand! Plus artwork and memorabilia, too! We work hard, everyday, to give you the service, quality and attention to detail that you deserve. Our grading is strictly by Overstreet, and your satisfaction is guaranteed–or we'll give you your money back! Mail in your want list or CALL US TODAY!

FOUR COLOR COMICS

NEW YORK SHOWROOM:
115 West 27th Street, New York, NY 10001
TEL: (212) 675-6990

BUYING
NO. 21
TOMORROWS' TREASURES
Send Inquires To:
Richard Muchin
P.O. Box 925
Commack, NY 11725
Phone: (516) 543-7574
Fax:(516) 543-5737
SELLING
Specializing in
Golden Age • Silver Age (1933-1975)
DC • MARVEL • EC • DISNEY • DELL
WANTED
GOLDEN AGE
SILVER AGE
INDIVIDUAL BOOKS
OR
WHOLE COLLECTIONS
I WILL ALSO BUY COVERLESS
AND
INCOMPLETE COMICS,
POOR AND FAIR
CONDITION BOOKS TOO
SEND $1.00
FOR
COMIC
CATALOGUE
WE TRAVEL
ANYWHERE
Steve Lowenthal

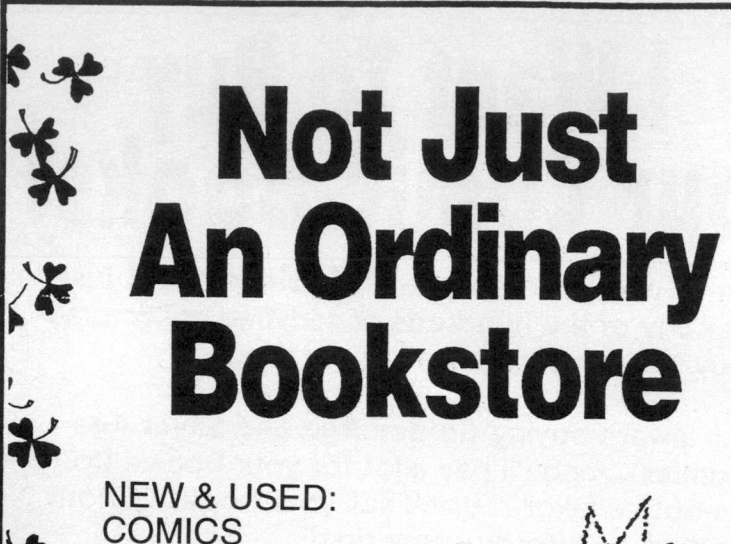

ENTER STRANGE NEW WORLDS! INTRODUCING A NEW COMIC MAIL-ORDER SERVICE!
THE
KOMIC KRYPT
WE LOVE COMICS SO WILL YOU...
YOU COULD WIN $1000.00 WORTH OF COMIC BOOKS EVERY YEAR!
WE ALSO CREATE OUR OWN COMICS! ONLY OUR CUSTOMERS GET THEM!
25% OFF ALL COMICS! (BIGGER ORDER? BIGGER DISCOUNT!) ALL COMICS INDIVIDUALLY BAGGED & BOARDED, FREE! BI-WEEKLY POSTAGE AND SHIPPING IS PAID BY US!! THOUSANDS OF BACK ISSUES!
THE KOMIC KRYPT CRITIQUE! THIS MONTHLY NEWSPAPER CONTAINS ARTICLES, LETTERS, INVESTOR'S TIPS, COMICS, GAMES AND MUCH MORE! BE A PART OF IT! ALL CUSTOMER LETTERS & DRAWINGS WILL BE PRINTED! IT'S YOURS, FREE!

CBG
Customer Service
Award - 1991
PHILIP M. LEVINE AND SONS
RARE AND ESOTERIC BOOKS
Toy Shop
Customer Service Award
1991
P. O. Box 246
Three Bridges, NJ 08887
Phone (908) 788-0532
FAX (908) 788-1028
ON
SEND US ALL OF YOUR PRE-1975 COMIC BOOKS TODAY!
We will make you an immediate cash offer. If we don't buy your books, we will pay the "book rate postage" both ways. We are always buying and selling comics, giveaway comics, Big Little books, old paperbacks, MAD memorabilia, Seduction of the Innocent and related censorship material, radio premiums, early crime magazines, "Cardboard Age" comics, antediluvian comics and related material, pulps, Catechetical Guild comics and related material, Golden Age comics, Silver Age comics, old toys and Gum Cards. We have the largest inventory of old "TV Guides" in North America. Send us your name & address today to get on our mailing list.
You can come and see us at all the Atlantique City shows, all New York area collectible shows and all Wex-Rex shows, Chicago Comic Con, Motor City Comic Cons, Allentown Pennsylvania Paper Fairs and the San Diego Comic Con.
Don't forget to send us your books. We have been buying and selling comic books for 39 years.
SEND US YOUR WANT LIST TODAY!

©DC

©MCG

Buying
Golden Age
Silver Age

©MCG

©DC

I offer the following to all customers:

BUYING:

- Top Prices Paid
- Immediate Cash
- Will travel to view large collections
- Experience

©DC

©FH

SELLING:

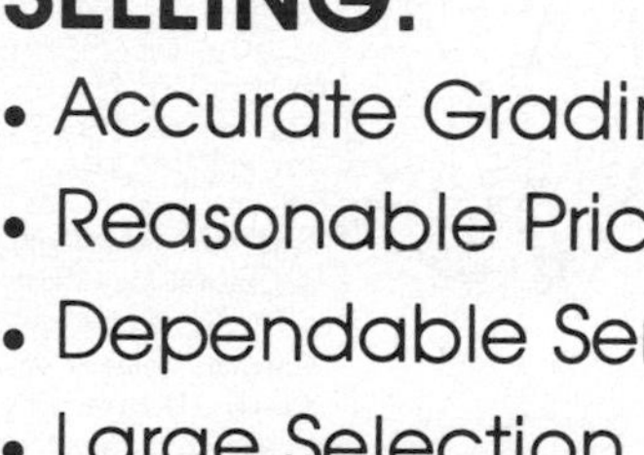

- Accurate Grading
- Reasonable Prices
- Dependable Service
- Large Selection
- Experience

©CEN

©DC

Send For Latest List

CBG Customer Service Award — 1989

HARLEY YEE

CBG Customer Service Award — 1989

P.O. Box 19578
Detroit, MI 48219-0578

(313) 533-2731

©MCG

©DC

John Hauser
P.O. Box 51673
New Berlin, WI 53151-0673
(414) 789-8227
ALGEBRA
USA
EXHIBIT A
I've been collecting for twenty years, but I'm not done *yet!* That's why I'm always buying large & small collections and travelling anywhere to get books that I still need. I'm especially looking for pre-code horror & sci-fi, superhero DC & Marvels—any 10¢ & 12¢ comics—and I will of course pay top dollar.
I also send out a catalogue nine times a year listing all the Golden & Silver Age comics which I have for sale in all grades to accommodate all tastes and budgets. All my books are always strictly graded and fairly priced, and friendly, reliable service is guaranteed. Since I'm not just another dealer, maybe we can trade and fill those gaps in each other's collections! If you'd like my catalogue, just send $1 and let's get acquainted!
Alan Dulfon

X

MARKS THE SPOT !!
YOU HAVE FOUND...

COMIC TREASURES

Marvel ♦ DC ♦ Independents
Golden Age to Modern Age

Strict Grading ♦ Great Service

⇨⇨ Send for latest **FREE** catalog!! ⇦⇦

ALSO BUYING COLLECTIONS, LARGE OR SMALL!

Comic Treasures ♦ Dept A ♦ PO Box 17036 ♦ Irvine, CA 92713-7036

J-A-V COMICS
PRESENTS
QUALITY COMICS
AND
COMPETITIVE PRICING

- OVER 200,000 COMICS IN STOCK
- AN EVER EXPANDING SILVER AGE SELECTION
- A LARGE SELECTION OF RECENT BACK ISSUES
- BUYING *** SELLING *** TRADING
- ALL BOOKS STRICTLY GRADED
- SEND WANT LIST W/S.A.S.E. FOR REPLY
- SEND $1.00 FOR OUR NEW CATALOG ... AND A YEAR OF QUARTERLY SALE ITEM UPDATES

WRITE OR CALL:

J-A-V COMICS
1028 W. EL NORTE PKWY.
SUITE #141
ESCONDIDO, CA 92026
(619)471-1827

Vampirella #2, 1993, © Harris Pub.

Venus #18, 1952, © Leading

Warriors of Plasm #1, 1993, © EEP LP

Web of Spider-Man #95, 1992, © MEG

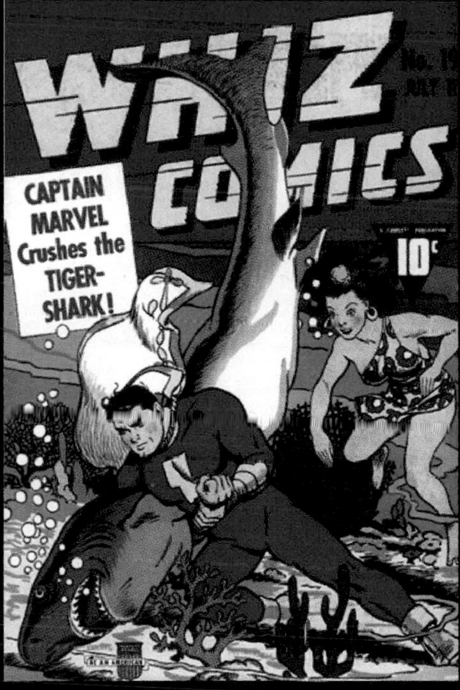

Whiz Comics #19, 1941, © Fawcett

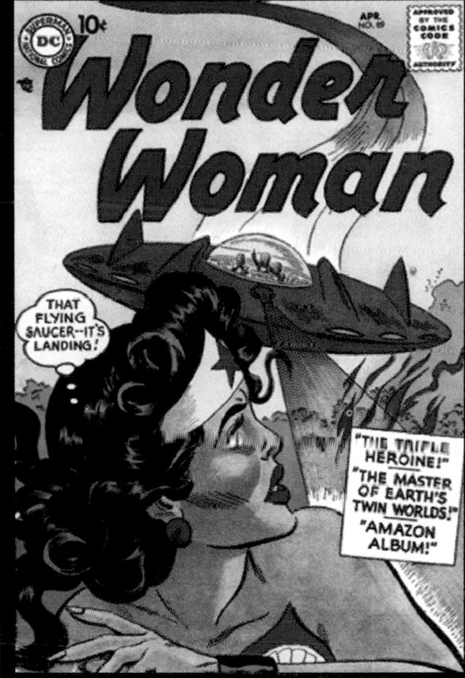

Wonder Woman #89, 1957, © DC

Young Romances #1, 1947, © Feature Pub.

Zip Comics #30, 1942, © MLJ

L.B.Cole
JOIN THE PARADE TO. . .

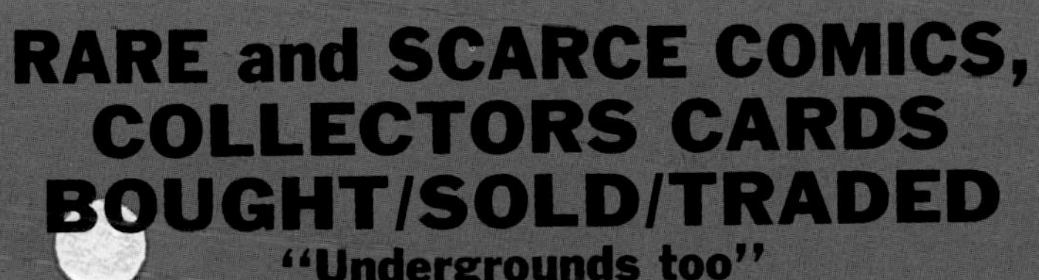
RARE and SCARCE COMICS,
COLLECTORS CARDS
BOUGHT/SOLD/TRADED
"Undergrounds too"

BILLY "FATBAG" VOGEL AND TROPIC COMICS NOW SPAN SOUTH FLORIDA FROM NORTH MIAMI TO VERO BEACH!!*
*AND GOD HELP ANYONE UNDER BILLY WHO LOOKS UP!

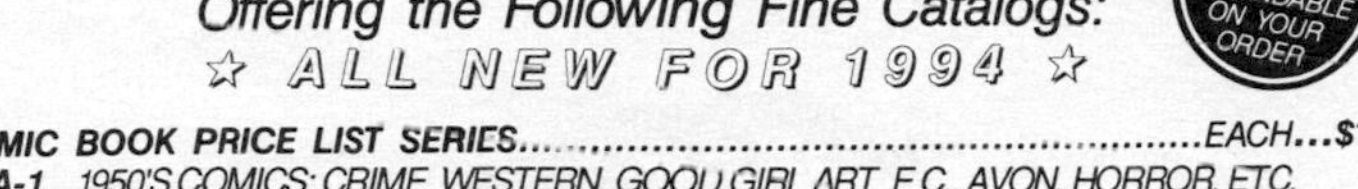

P.O. BOX 273086 • TAMPA, FLORIDA 33618 • (813) 968-1805
FAX (813) 264-6226
"CONTACT US FIRST"

ALL CATALOG COSTS ARE REFUNDABLE ON YOUR ORDER

Offering the Following Fine Catalogs:

☆ ALL NEW FOR 1994 ☆

A COMIC BOOK PRICE LIST SERIES..........EACH...$1.00
- **A-1** 1950'S COMICS: CRIME, WESTERN, GOOD GIRL ART, E.C., AVON, HORROR, ETC.
- **A-2** GOLDEN AGE COMICS, CLASSICS, ETC.
- **A-3** UNDERGROUNDS, MISC. OLD COMICS, MOVIE & TV COMICS
- **A-4** FUNNY COMICS, DISNEY, ARCHIE, HARVEY, DELL, GOLD KEY, ETC.
- **A-5** INDEPENDENT PUBLISHERS 1960'S TO 1993

B MARVEL AND D.C. LIST..........$1.00
ALSO INCLUDES INDEPENDENT TITLES, GOLD KEY, AND THE SMALLER PUBLISHERS FROM THE 60'S TO DATE.

C THE SPECIAL BLEND..........$1.00
WE NEVER KNOW WHAT'S ON THIS LIST — CONSISTS OF NEW ARRIVALS MIXED IN WITH SOME OLD FAVORITES — GOLDEN AGE, EARLY MARVELS, PULPS, ART, COMIC BOOK-RELATED COLLECTABLES, WHO KNOWS WHAT WE WILL GET, COULD BE ANYTHING, BUT WE GUARANTEE YOU'LL LIKE THIS SELECTION AND THE PRICES.

D PULP MAGAZINE LIST #16..........$1.00
HOT OFF THE PRESS: SHADOW, WEIRD TALES, SPICY DETECTIVE, AMAZING, BLACK MASK, G-8, DOC SAVAGE, WESTERNS, ARGOSY, ETC.

E THE CATALOG OF GLAMOUR..........$2.00
THIS PHOTO ILLUSTRATED LARGE CATALOG FEATURES THE WORLDS LARGEST COLLECTION OF PIN-UP MAGAZINES, MOVIE AND TV MAGAZINES, MEN'S ADVENTURE, TRUE DETECTIVE, MARILYN MONROE, BETTY PAGE, JAYNE MANSFIELD, ETC. - MANY RARE AND OBSCURE TITLES FROM -1900 TO THE 90'S.

F MAGAZINE LIST..........$1.00
ALL VARIETIES INCLUDING MAD, FAMOUS MONSTERS, SAVAGE TALES, MARVELS, HEAVY METAL, FANZINES, WARREN TITLES, D.C., COMIC BOOK AND HUMOR — HUGE SELECTION.

G PAPERBACK BOOK LIST..........$1.00
NOW AVAILABLE..........AVON, MAPBACKS, DUST JACKETS, POPULAR LIBRARY, ACE, DELL, ETC.— OVER 20,000 VINTAGE PAPERBACKS AVAILABLE.

H EDGAR RICE BURROUGHS LIST..........$1.00
TARZAN 1ST EDITION, HARDBACKS, PULPS, COMICS, BIG LITTLE BOOKS, VINTAGE MOVIE POSTERS, ORIGINAL ART, PAPERBACKS AND OTHER SCARCE ITEMS.

I THE ART CATALOG..........$1.00
ORIGINAL COMIC BOOK AND NEWSPAPER ART, COLOR MAGAZINE AND PULP COVERS, PORTFOLIOS, PRINTS, POSTERS, LIMITED EDITIONS.

J BIG LITTLE BOOKS..........$1.00
MICKEY MOUSE, FLASH GORDON, POPEYE, SHADOW, DICK TRACY, GENE AUTRY, SERIES BOOKS, WHITMAN BOOKS, ETC.

K MOVIE POSTERS..........$1.00
HORROR, WESTERN, FIILM NOIR, SCIENCE FICTION, EXPLOITATION, CLASSICS — 1930's to 1990's — ONE SHEETS, LOBBY CARDS, PRESS BOOKS, MAGAZINES, MOVIE/TV COMICS, BOOKS, ETC.

L SPORTS COLLECTORS ITEMS..........$2.00
PROGRAMS, YEARBOOKS, SPORT MAGAZINE, SPORTS ILLUSTRATED, BASEBALL, FOOTBALL, BOXING, YANKEES, DODGERS, METS, RAMS, AUTOGRAPHS, OLYMPICS, SPORTING NEWS, MEDIA GUIDES— WE SPECIALIZE IN HISTORICALLY IMPORTANT MATERIAL.

M BASEBALL CARDS..........$1.00
THE HOT TICKET TO THE NINETIES — TOPS, FLEER, DONRUSS, UPPER DECK, OLD JUDGE, T-CARDS, ETC. — SINGLES, SETS, UNOPENED MATERIAL PLUS FOOTBALL, BASKETBALL, ETC.

N AUTO RACING MEMORABILIA..........$1.00
A NEW RAGE IN COLLECTING, THIS CATALOG FEATURES: INDY 500, DAYTONA 500, FORMULA ONE, DRAG RACING, SPRINT CARS, DIRT TRACKS, SUPER-SPEEDWAYS, PROGRAMS, YEAR-BOOKS, POST CARDS, DRIVER AUTOGRAPHS, MAGAZINES AND MUCH MORE—MUCH MORE—THE ONLY CATALOG OF ITS KIND IN THE WORLD INCLUDES ITEMS FROM 1906 TO 1993.

WANT ALL CATALOGS? SEND $15.00

CATALOGING IS A CONTINUAL PROCESS FOR US SINCE WE HAVE A CONSTANT INFLUX OF COLLECTORS ITEMS INTO OUR INVENTORY. AS WE GET NEW MATERIAL, OUR CATALOGS ARE CONSTANTLY BEING UPDATED. IF YOU DO NOT RECEIVE A CATALOG SHORTLY AFTER SENDING FOR IT, THAT MEANS WE ARE UPDATING THAT PARTICULAR CATALOG AND WE WILL RUSH YOU THE LATEST EDITION WHEN IT IS PRINTED.

THE RADICAL WANT LIST SYSTEM

Have wants you just can't seem to find? Plug into *The Radical Want List System!* We always accept want lists and will check our inventory, but to have your want list kept on file and checked against the inventory of stores around the country or the huge selection at the largest conventions all without having to pay admission or high travel expenses, just follow these simple steps:

1. Make a list of the items, plus condition, you want to obtain.
2. Send the list, along with your address, phone number and $5.00 (to cover handling) to us.
3. Sit back and let our workers do the rest!

Your $5.00 service charge is refundable with your first order, so act now!

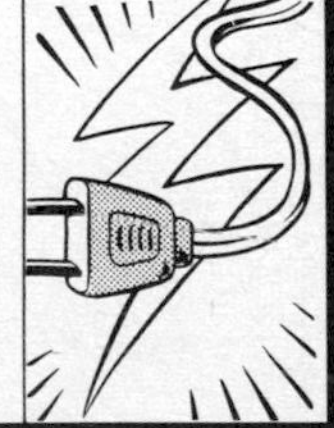

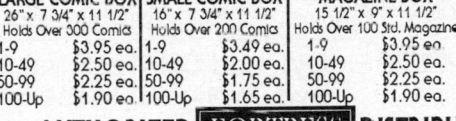

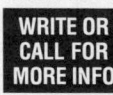

ORIGINAL ART

BUY - SELL - TRADE

Specializing in ORIGINAL COMIC BOOK & COMIC STRIP ART I have a selection of THOUSANDS of ORIGINALS in stock. Possibly the LARGEST SELECTION of classic, quality comic art IN THE WORLD!

From ALEX RAYMOND's "Flash Gordon" & HAL FOSTER's "Prince Valiant" & "Tarzan", to JACK KIRBY's "Fantastic Four" or DITKO's "Spider-man". SEGAR's "Popeye", WAYNE BORING or CURT SWAN's "Superman", SCHULZ's "Peanuts", GEORGE HERRIMAN's "Krazy Kat", CANIFF's "Terry" or "Steve Canyon". WILL EISNER, LOU FINE, BERNI WRIGHTSON, JOE KUBERT, CARMINE INFANTINO, WALLY WOOD, FRANK FRAZETTA , AL WILLIAMSON, R. CRUMB, STERRETT, SPRANG, FINLAY, BOK and on and on....

If original comic art & other graphic media are your hobby, then you should call or write me. If you are interested in buying, trading or selling fine quality originals, I HAVE MORE THAN ANYONE ELSE!! Contact me today....

My interests are: SILVER AGE DC & MARVEL; CLASSIC COMIC STRIPS; PIN-UP, PULP & PAPERBACK ART; MOVIE POSTER ART and UNDERGROUND COMIC ART.

Send $2. in stamps for my current catalog, $4. Foreign & Canada.

above: JACK KIRBY DC splash. One of 2 known, inked by WALLY WOOD. below: HERRIMAN's Krazy Kat

RICHARD HALEGUA

P.O.BOX 46454 LasVegas,NV.89114

phone 702-796-3299

RARE COMIC ART IS MY BAG
. . .and I love to trade bags of money, or other art for items of special interest to me. I'll pay top dollar for original artwork by Carl Barks, E.C. Segar, and other classic cartoonists, as well as paintings, cartoon movie posters from the '30s and '40s, and other rare comic oriented esoterica.
If you have rare material for sale **contact me first**. If you don't, you may be selling your collection short.
Bruce Hamilton
P.O. Box 4235
Prescott, AZ 86302
(602)776-1300

SHOWCASE
COLLECTIBLES

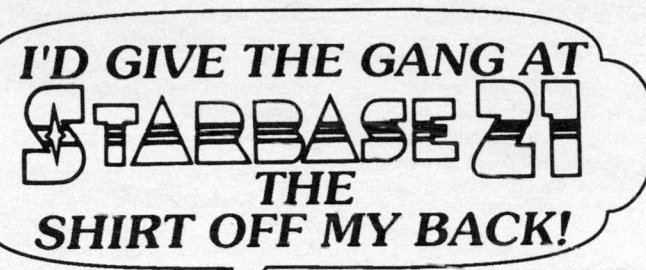

CLASSIFIED ADVERTISING

(Write in Sept. for our reasonable rates)

Classified Advertising (Continued)

Dungeon & Dragon modules liquidation sale $2 each brand new! Write for list of over 2000 for sale: Modules, Box 93214, Milwaukee, WI 53203, Please include self-addressed stamped envelope.

Newer comics at 50% O.P.G. (G.A. 75% & up). Send a SASE plus 25 cents per list. Request lists desired. Comic Book • BLB • N.P. Comic Strip • Pulp • Paperbacks • Movie TV Items • Old Life, Look, Post, Misc. Magazines. Above also bought. Glenn's Books, 3500 Manila Dr., Westerville, OH 43081.

Wanted old gum cards - G-Men, Mars Attacks, Civil War News, Outer Limits, 007, Lost In Space, Munsters, Bev. Hillbillies, Combat, Get Smart, Brady Bunch, Batman, etc. D. Wilson. 14 Berryman St. N. Ryde NSW Australia.

WANTED! Anything by or about HOWARD CHAYKIN, especially obscure and unusual material and not just comic book. Also wanted: syndicated work by FRAZETTA, and live tapes and printed collectibles relating to RANDY CALIFORNIA/SPIRIT. Write me: TIM BARNES, 103 Tredworth Road, Gloucester, Glos. GL1 4QU ENGLAND. Sixth Glorious Year!

Adult Magazines for sale 1950's to present. Please send SASE for a list to: Magazines, Box 93214, Milwaukee, WI 53203

BUYING * OLD PAPER COLLECTIBLES * SELLING COMIC BOOK, SUNDAY COMIC PAGES, FULL SECTIONS; "BIG LITTLE BOOKS" and all types of nostalgic & comic-related paper (magazines, pulps, sports, Oz, books on comics, music, etc.). Send Want Lists. NOBODY, ANYWHERE, PAYS MORE FOR OLD COMIC BOOKS!!! KEN MITCHELL, 710 CONACHER DRIVE, WILLOWDALE, ONTARIO. M2M 3N6 (Telephone 416-222-5808)
"SERVING COMIC FANDOM SUCCESSFULLY SINCE 1964"

E. K. WONG, 4282 10th Ave., Port Alberni, BC

Robert J. La Tremouille
Attorney At Law
875 Massachusetts Avenue, Suite 31
Cambridge, Massachusetts 02139
Telephone 617-864-8055 / 617-491-7181
FAX 617-868-3175

FREE Comic Catalogue. LOW PRICES. Golden-Silver Age, Marvels, DCs, Disneys. All Kinds. I like to TRADE too. Money Back Guarantee. SPECIAL BONUS WITH PURCHASE. Send an EXTRA 1st Class Stamp to: DAVE YARUSS, 7916 BLUE LAKE DR., SAN DIEGO, CALIF. 92119. WANTED: Disney Animation Art.

We specialize in selling affordable Silver and Golden Age comics. Send a SASE to: Comic Book Hotline, Inc., P O Box 8230, North Bergen, NJ 07047 (201) 656-3228.

BUYING COMICS

Highest prices paid for comics from 1930-1970, call 908-495-0184 leave msg. D. F., 6 Annette Ct. Hazlet, NJ 07730

Buying Classics Illustrated and Classic Comics - Call or write Phil Gaudino, 84 - 19 106 St., Richmond Hill, NY 11418 - 718-847-6850.

COMIC BOOKS WANTED 1933-1968

DC, TIMELY, FAWCETTS, QUALITY, MLJ, MARVELS, FICTION HOUSE, EC, DISNEY, HORROR, WESTERNS, AND TV/MOVIE. PAYING 50% to 150%. (313) 533-2731, HARLEY YEE, PO BOX 19578, DETROIT, MI 48219-0578.

SILVER AGE COMIC COLLECTION. LOW PRICES. SASE FOR LIST. RICK DUPIUS, P O BOX 1325, BUNNELL, FL 32110 PH: 904-439-9207.

MAIL ORDER!! New Issue Comics Subscription Service. Write or call: MOUNTAIN EMPIRE COLLECTIBLES #4, 509 State St., 2nd Floor, Bristol, VA 24201 703-466-6337.

WANTED- Star Wars toys, dolls, plates, bed items, watches, etc. Also G.I. Joe, Raiders, 007, Uncle, Thunderbirds, Fireball XL5, 1999, Supercar, Capt. Action, Superman, Munsters, Shogun W., Add. Family & all TV, Movie etc. D. Wilson, 14 Berryman St, North Ryde NSW Åustralia

---

MONKEY HOUSE COMICS

is always buying pre-1970 comic books, especially Marvel and Atlas. Write for my offer before you sell. Send your want-list today. All books guaranteed. Monkey House Comics, c/o David Cummings, 28 Hawthorne Cir., Peabody, MA 01960 PH: (508) 532-2448 4-9PM EST

"AMERICA'S FAVORITE COMIC BOOK DEALER"
GARY DOLGOFF COMICS
Brooklyn Navy Yard / Building 280 / Suite 608/609
Brooklyn, NY 11205
PH: 718-596-5719
M-F 10 a.m. - 5 p.m.

Tight grading satisfaction guaranteed!

Strictly Graded

ALL TREASURY ORDERS PLEASE MULTIPLY POSTAGE RATES BY 6.

ALL MAGAZINE MULTIPLY RATES BY 3.

POSTAGE:
East U.S. - add 3¢/Bk (Insured)
West U.S. - add 6¢/Bk (Insured)
Outside U.S. - add 8¢/Bk (Insured)
Outside U.S. - add 25¢/Bk (Insured)

Orders shipped within 7 days of receipt, however cks must clear our banks.

In The "Biz" For

WELCOME TO THE WORLD OF GARY DOLGOFF COMICS!
"A World of Honesty, Tough Grading & Satisfaction Guaranteedeed"

800,000 Comics, Mags & Art in Stock! (1940's - 1990's)

New, or Expanding Store-Owners: Call Me and I'll Advise You "Right!!"

"Chock-Full" of bargains galore; make 2x - 3x your money, easy...

Please note my "across the board" deals...stock it right (in one shot)!

All Prices Do Not Include Postage (Unless o/w Stated)

Good Deals For Collectors &Dealers

Note! P.G. = Latest Overstreet Publication

DEAL #1

1940's (Early) 1960's Priced & Graded Books

• Hero, Western, Funny, Dell, Gold-Key, WDS&S, Movie & TV-Comics, etc., etc. • 80% "GVG" or better • Value Per Book: $4-$30 Range • Strictly Graded!

PRICE:
$200.00 Worth of Bks..............$150.00 (25% Off P.G.)
$750.00 Worth of Bks...........$500.00 (33 1/3% off P.G.)
$2,000.00 Worth of Bks...........$1,200.00 (40% off P.G.)
Postage on Deal #1 $6.00 (U.S.), $15.00 • (Outside U.S. Insured)

DEAL #1 1/2

80's & 90's "Decent" Superhero Marvel & DC/cs

• 1982-1990 • 80-90% Marvel & DC Hero Stuff • No "Junk" ie No N. Talent, Showcase, No "New Universe" etc. • 90% VFNM, Unread, etc. • TITLE EXAMPLES Action, Alpha-Fight, Batman, Dazzler, Moon-Knights, Superman, T, Titans, Vis & Sc. Witch, Vigilante, Flash, JLA, Conan, Demon, Robin, Detective, Warnor, etc.

PRICE:
400 Books (3 each).............$140.00 (comes to 35¢/Bk)
800 Books (3-5 each)............$240.00 (comes to 30¢/Bk)
1,600 Books (5-6 each)..........$400.00 (comes to 25¢/Bk)
3,000 Books (5-10 each).........$750.00 (comes to 25¢/Bk)

DEAL #2

60's "Warehouse-Sharp" Marvels (80-90% 12c Cover, o/w 15c Cover)

• Strictly Graded! • 1-3 Of An Issue # (mostly 1-2 of an ish#!) • 90% Superhero Titles (ie, Avergers, D.D., F. Four, Hulk, S. Tales, T.O.S., T.T.A., Thor, Sub-Mariner, Capt. Marvel, X-Men, Shield, etc.) • 1965-1971 (mostly '65-'70)

PRICE VFNM Shape
$200.00 in NM "PG".....$120.00 $1,500.00 in NM "PG"....$900.00
$500.00 in NM "PG".....$300.00 $2,500.00 in NM "PG"...$1,500.00

FVF Shape: (VFNM w/slight ding on corner, or some other "minor imperfection)
$250.00 in NM "PG".....$100.00 $1,500.00 in NM "PG".....$600.00
$500.00 in NM "PG".....$200.00 $2,500.00 in NM "PG....$1,000.00

VG-F Shape: (still nice, slightly larger dings, many call many of these FN+, but what I guarantee is a nice VG/F)
$400.00 in NM "PG".....$100.00 $2,000.00 in "PG".........$500.00
$800.00 in NM "PG".....$200.00

Postage on Deal #2: U.S. $6.00, Outside U.S. $15.00 Insured

DEAL #3

70's Marvels

• 1974-1982 (90% Superhero) • All Books Strictly Graded! • TITLES - SAMPLES: Cap. Amer., D. Devil, F. Four, Hulk, Thor, M Team Up, Defender, Jung-Fu, Invaders, Bl. Panther, Iron-Fist, M. Spotlight, Hero-for-Hire, Werewolf, M's Greatest, M Tales, etc., etc.

PRICE: VFNM
$200.00 in NM "PG"..$100.00 (2-3 ea) $1,000 in NM "PG"....$500.00 (3-4 ea)
$500.00 in NM "PG"..$250.00 (3-4 ea)

FVF
$300.00 in NM "PG"..$120.00 (2-3 ea) $1,500 in NM "PG"....$600.00 (3-6 ea)
$600.00 in NM "PG"..$240.00 (3-4 ea)

VGF
$400.00 in NM "PG"..$100.00 (2-3 ea) $2,000 in NM "PG"....$500.00 (3-6 ea)
$800.00 in NM "PG"..$200.00 (3-5 ea)

Postage on Deal #3: Assume Value of each "Deal #3" bk in NM PG to be $2.50/bk, then use postage rate on top of this pg.

DEAL #4

80's & 90's Mainline Marvels (Good, Solid, "Long-Running", Titles Only - no "Dogs")

• 90% VFNM, Clean & "unread" • TITLE - SAMPLES: Avengers, D.D., F. Four (#233-Up) Hulk, Iron-Man, New Mutants, Cap. Hulk, Thor, P. Parker, Batman, Detective, Silver Surfer, X Factor, Mar. Presents w/ Wolverine etc.

PRICE:
400 Comics..............$180.00 (3 Each Max) (comes to 45¢/Bk)
1,000 Comics..........$400.00 (3-5 Each Max) (comes to 40¢/Bk)
2,000 Comics.......$750.00 (5-8 Each Max) (comes to 37 1/2¢/Bk)
4,000 Comics.......$1,400.00 (10-15 Each Max) (comes to 35¢/Bk)

DEAL #5

80's & 90's Mainline & "Sideline" Marvel & DC! (A Combo of deal #1 1/2 & 4)

A nice, well-balanced combo of "Superhero Stuff" for the new (or "Expanding) store, owner of "Convention" Dealer.

• 90% VFNM, "Unread" • 1982-1990 Books • SAMPLES - TITLES: Avengers, D.D., Action, Alpha Fi., F.F., Cab, Hulk, Batman, Dazzler, Superman, Iron-Man, Thor, T. Titans, Vis & Sc. Witch, Vigilante, P. Parker, etc., etc.

400 Bks (3 Each)............................$160.00 (comes to 40¢/Bk)
1,000 Bks (3-5 Each)................$350.00 (comes to 35¢/Bk)
2,000 Bks (4-6 Each)................$650.00 (comes to 32¢/Bk)
4,000 Bks (5-8 Each)...............$1,200.00 (comes to 30¢/Bk)